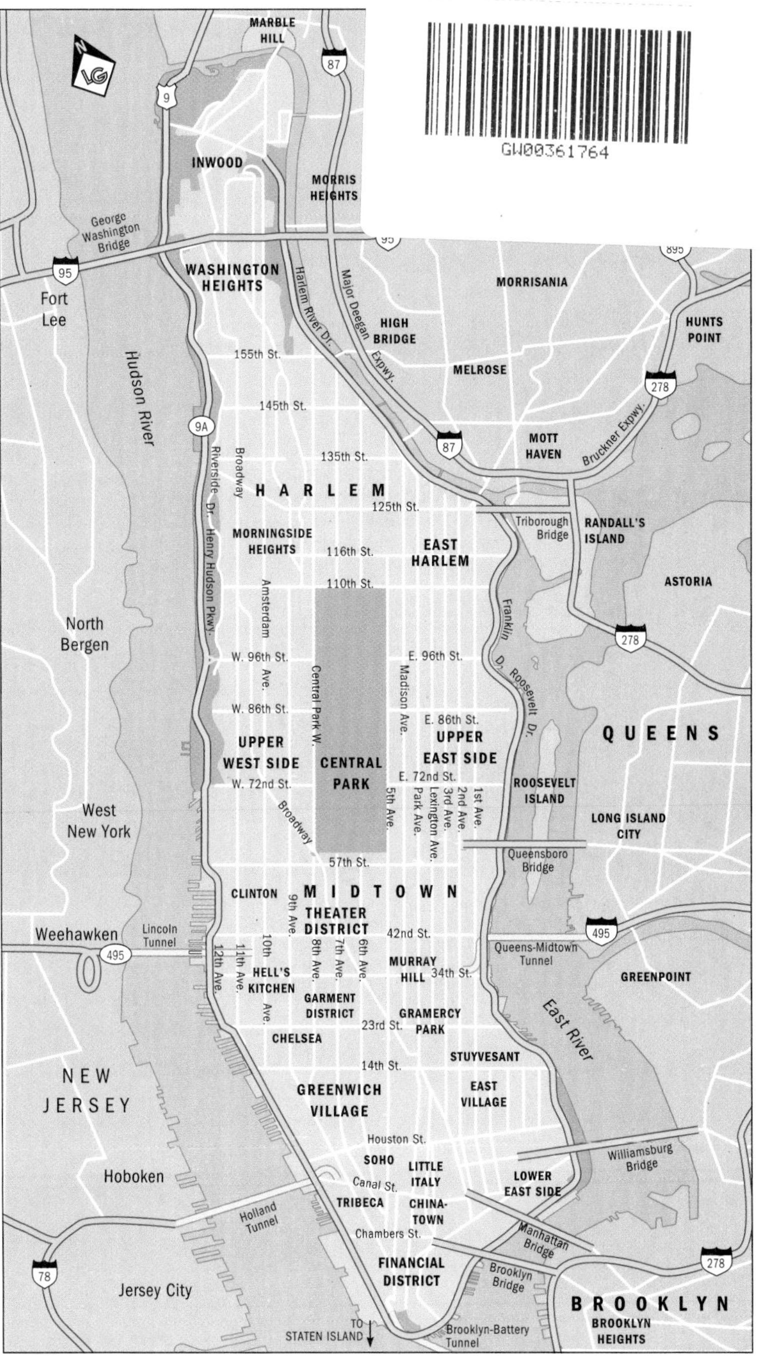
MARBLE HILL
INWOOD
MORRIS HEIGHTS
George Washington Bridge
WASHINGTON HEIGHTS
Fort Lee
Harlem River Dr.
Major Deegan Expwy.
MORRISANIA
HIGH BRIDGE
HUNTS POINT
MELROSE
Hudson River
155th St.
145th St.
135th St.
125th St.
116th St.
110th St.
MOTT HAVEN
Bruckner Expwy.
Riverside Dr.
Broadway
HARLEM
Henry Hudson Pkwy.
MORNINGSIDE HEIGHTS
EAST HARLEM
Triborough Bridge
RANDALL'S ISLAND
ASTORIA
Amsterdam Ave.
Franklin D. Roosevelt Dr.
North Bergen
W. 96th St.
E. 96th St.
Central Park W.
Madison Ave.
W. 86th St.
E. 86th St.
UPPER WEST SIDE
CENTRAL PARK
UPPER EAST SIDE
QUEENS
W. 72nd St.
E. 72nd St.
ROOSEVELT ISLAND
West New York
Broadway
5th Ave.
Park Ave.
Lexington Ave.
3rd Ave.
2nd Ave.
1st Ave.
LONG ISLAND CITY
Queensboro Bridge
57th St.
CLINTON
MIDTOWN
9th Ave.
THEATER DISTRICT
Weehawken
Lincoln Tunnel
42nd St.
Queens-Midtown Tunnel
10th Ave.
8th Ave.
7th Ave.
6th Ave.
MURRAY HILL
34th St.
12th Ave.
11th Ave.
HELL'S KITCHEN
GREENPOINT
GARMENT DISTRICT
GRAMERCY PARK
23rd St.
CHELSEA
East River
STUYVESANT
14th St.
NEW JERSEY
GREENWICH VILLAGE
EAST VILLAGE
Houston St.
Williamsburg Bridge
SOHO
LITTLE ITALY
Hoboken
Canal St.
LOWER EAST SIDE
TRIBECA
CHINA-TOWN
Holland Tunnel
Chambers St.
Manhattan Bridge
FINANCIAL DISTRICT
Brooklyn Bridge
Jersey City
BROOKLYN
BROOKLYN HEIGHTS
TO STATEN ISLAND
Brooklyn-Battery Tunnel
9
87
95
895
278
9A
495
78

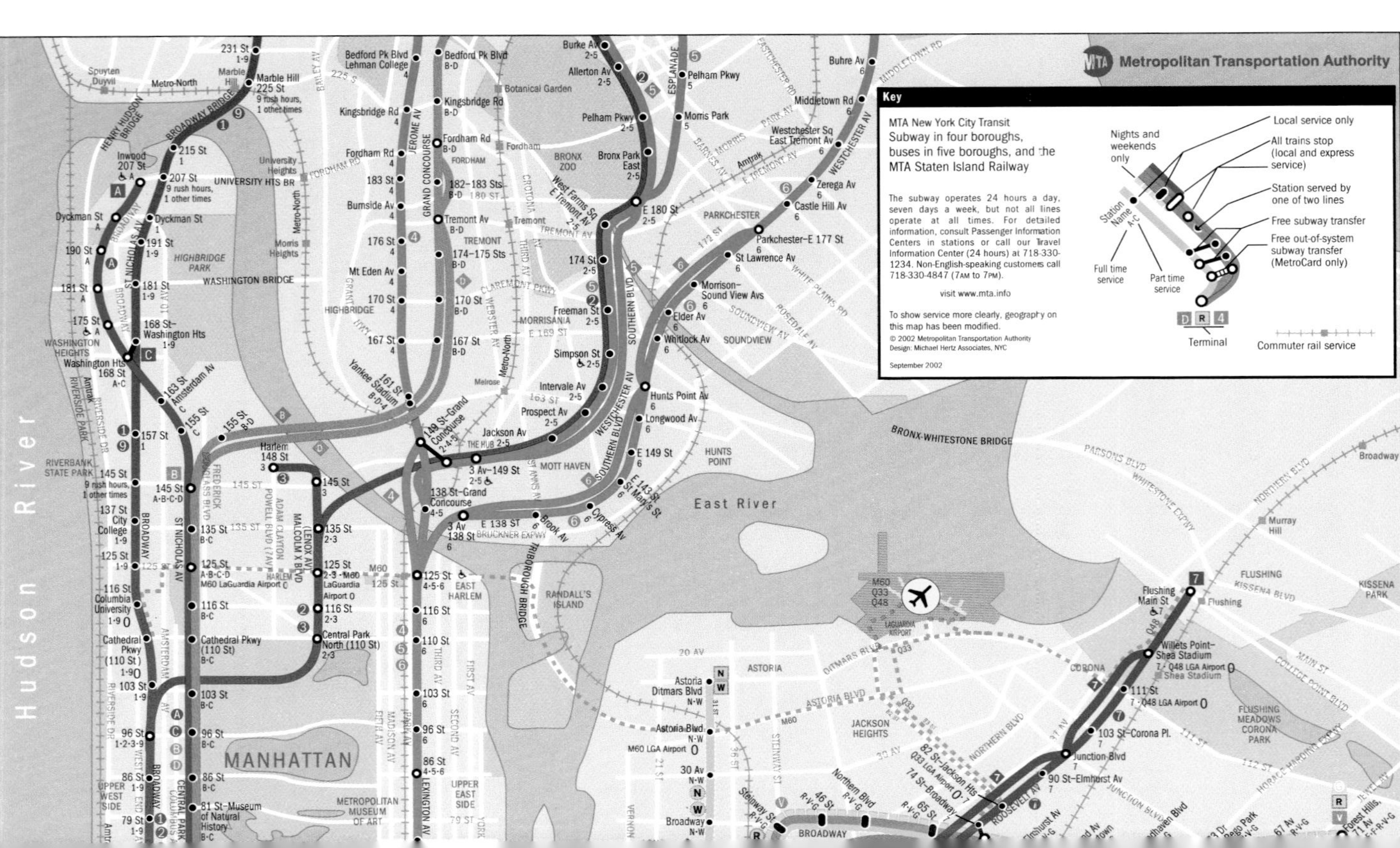

Metropolitan Transportation Authority
Key
MTA New York City Transit
Subway in four boroughs, buses in five boroughs, and the MTA Staten Island Railway
The subway operates 24 hours a day, seven days a week, but not all lines operate at all times. For detailed information, consult Passenger Information Centers in stations or call our Travel Information Center (24 hours) at 718-330-1234. Non-English-speaking customers call 718-330-4847 (7AM to 7PM).
visit www.mta.info
To show service more clearly, geography on this map has been modified.
© 2002 Metropolitan Transportation Authority
Design: Michael Hertz Associates, NYC
September 2002
Nights and weekends only
Local service only
All trains stop (local and express service)
Station served by one of two lines
Free subway transfer
Free out-of-system subway transfer (MetroCard only)
Station Name A·C
Full time service
Part time service
Terminal
Commuter rail service
Hudson River
East River
MANHATTAN
BRONX-WHITESTONE BRIDGE
TRIBOROUGH BRIDGE
WASHINGTON BRIDGE
HENRY HUDSON BRIDGE
BROADWAY BRIDGE
RANDALL'S ISLAND
LAGUARDIA AIRPORT
FLUSHING MEADOWS CORONA PARK
ASTORIA
JACKSON HEIGHTS
FLUSHING
CORONA
PARKCHESTER
SOUNDVIEW
HUNTS POINT
MOTT HAVEN
EAST HARLEM
UPPER EAST SIDE
UPPER WEST SIDE
WASHINGTON HEIGHTS
HIGHBRIDGE PARK
BRONX ZOO
METROPOLITAN MUSEUM OF ART

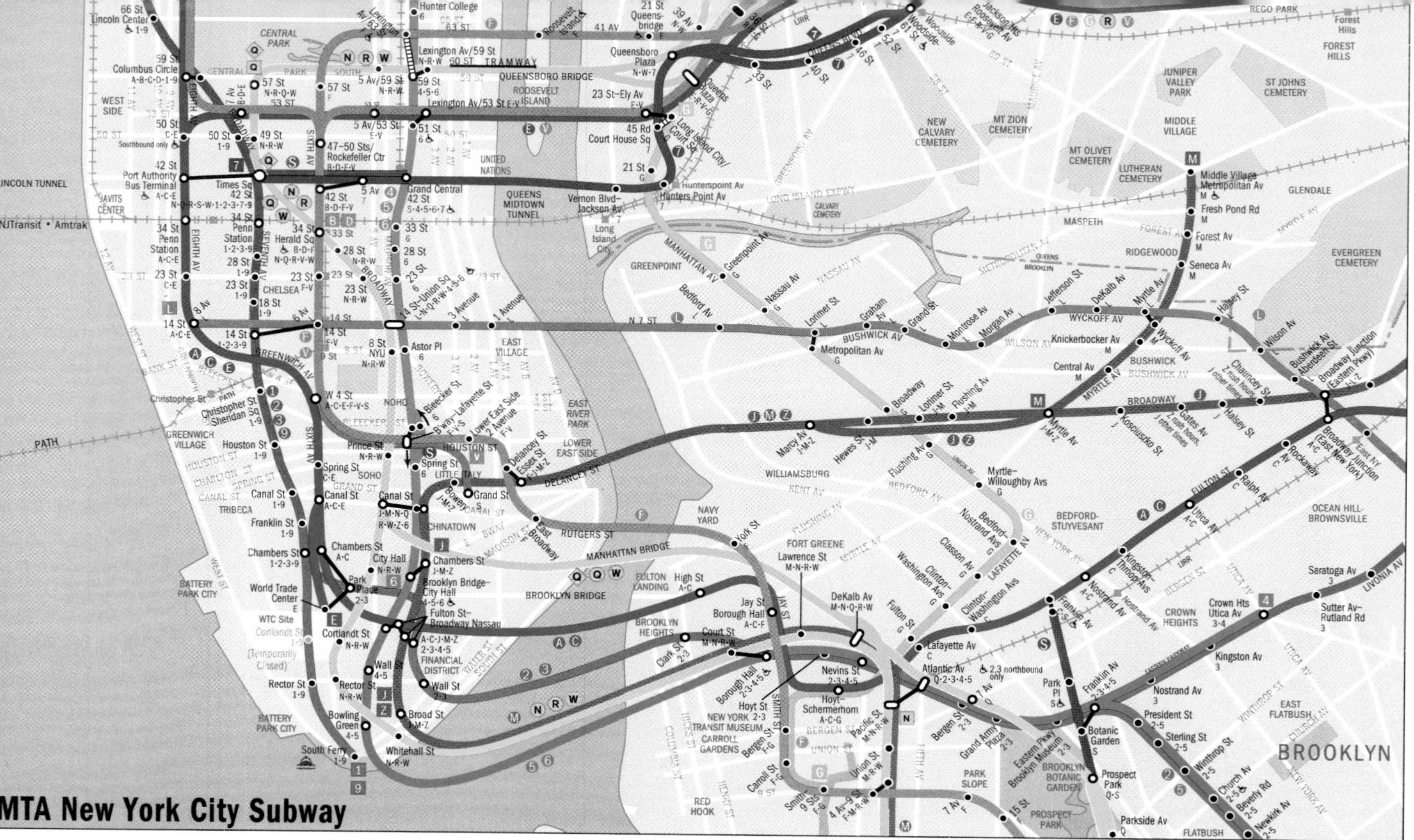

MTA New York City Subway

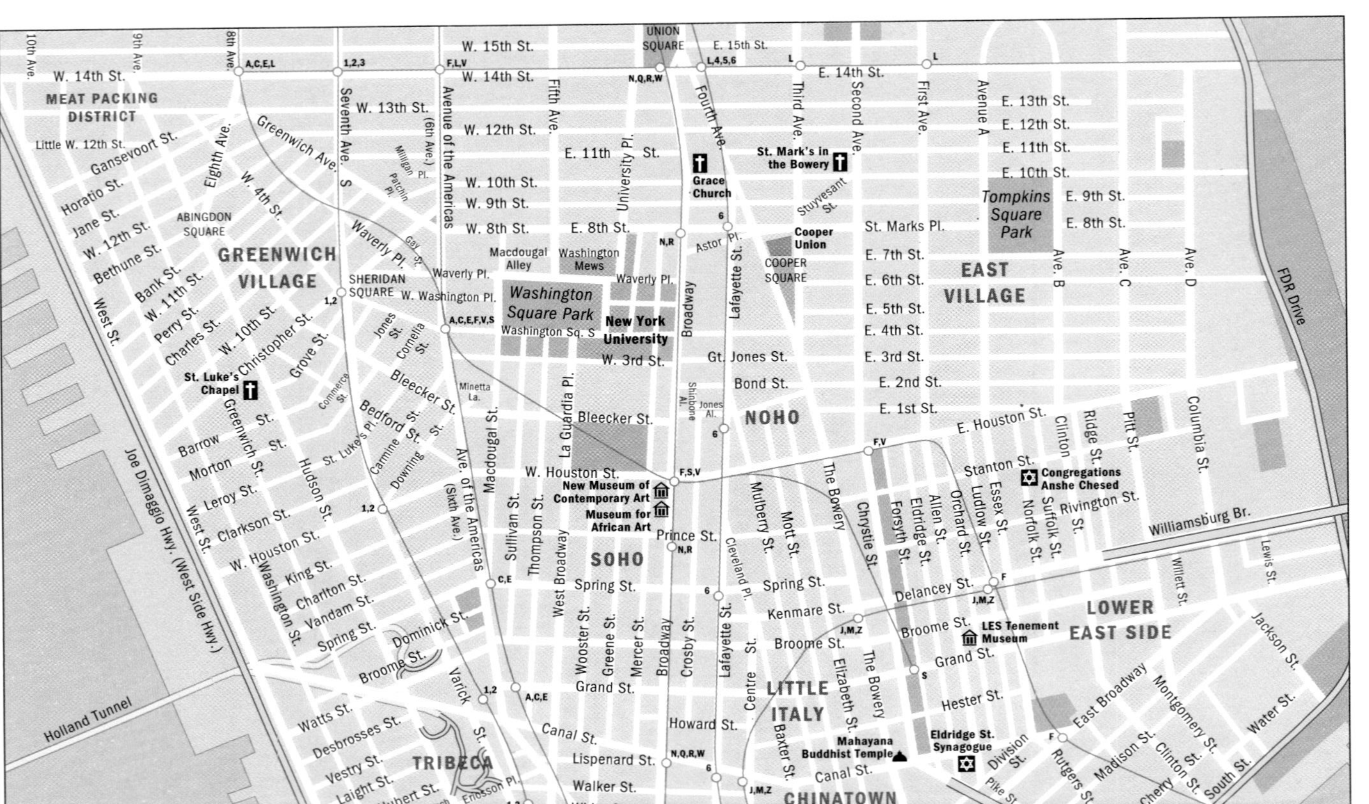

MEAT PACKING DISTRICT
GREENWICH VILLAGE
EAST VILLAGE
NOHO
SOHO
LITTLE ITALY
CHINATOWN
TRIBECA
LOWER EAST SIDE
UNION SQUARE
ABINGDON SQUARE
SHERIDAN SQUARE
COOPER SQUARE
Washington Square Park
Tompkins Square Park
New York University
St. Mark's in the Bowery
Grace Church
Cooper Union
St. Luke's Chapel
New Museum of Contemporary Art
Museum for African Art
Congregations Anshe Chesed
LES Tenement Museum
Eldridge St. Synagogue
Mahayana Buddhist Temple
FDR Drive
Joe Dimaggio Hwy. (West Side Hwy.)
Holland Tunnel
Williamsburg Br.
10th Ave.
9th Ave.
8th Ave.
Eighth Ave.
Seventh Ave. S
Avenue of the Americas
(6th Ave.)
Ave. of the Americas
(Sixth Ave.)
Fifth Ave.
Fourth Ave.
Third Ave.
Second Ave.
First Ave.
Avenue A
Ave. B
Ave. C
Ave. D
W. 15th St.
W. 14th St.
W. 13th St.
W. 12th St.
W. 10th St.
W. 9th St.
W. 8th St.
E. 15th St.
E. 14th St.
E. 13th St.
E. 12th St.
E. 11th St.
E. 10th St.
E. 9th St.
E. 8th St.
E. 7th St.
E. 6th St.
E. 5th St.
E. 4th St.
E. 3rd St.
E. 2nd St.
E. 1st St.
E. Houston St.
W. Houston St.
W. 3rd St.
Little W. 12th St.
Gansevoort St.
Horatio St.
Jane St.
W. 12th St.
Bethune St.
Bank St.
W. 11th St.
Perry St.
Charles St.
W. 10th St.
Christopher St.
Grove St.
W. 4th St.
Greenwich Ave.
Waverly Pl.
Gay St.
Milligan Pl.
Patchin Pl.
W. Washington Pl.
Washington Sq. S
Washington Mews
Macdougal Alley
University Pl.
Broadway
Astor Pl.
Lafayette St.
Stuyvesant St.
St. Marks Pl.
Gt. Jones St.
Bond St.
Shinbone Al.
Jones Al.
Bleecker St.
La Guardia Pl.
Minetta La.
Macdougal St.
Sullivan St.
Thompson St.
West Broadway
Wooster St.
Greene St.
Mercer St.
Crosby St.
Prince St.
Spring St.
Grand St.
Howard St.
Lispenard St.
Walker St.
Canal St.
Cleveland Pl.
Kenmare St.
Broome St.
Centre St.
Baxter St.
Mulberry St.
Mott St.
Elizabeth St.
The Bowery
Chrystie St.
Forsyth St.
Eldridge St.
Allen St.
Orchard St.
Ludlow St.
Essex St.
Norfolk St.
Suffolk St.
Clinton St.
Ridge St.
Pitt St.
Columbia St.
Stanton St.
Rivington St.
Delancey St.
Hester St.
Division St.
Pike St.
Rutgers St.
East Broadway
Madison St.
Montgomery St.
Cherry St.
South St.
Water St.
Jackson St.
Willett St.
Lewis St.
Jones St.
Cornelia St.
Commerce St.
Bedford St.
St. Luke's Pl.
Carmine St.
Downing St.
Barrow St.
Morton St.
Leroy St.
Clarkson St.
Hudson St.
Greenwich St.
W. Houston St.
King St.
Charlton St.
Vandam St.
Washington St.
Spring St.
Dominick St.
Broome St.
Varick St.
Watts St.
Desbrosses St.
Vestry St.
Laight St.
Hubert St.
Ericsson Pl.
West St.
A,C,E,L
1,2,3
F,L,V
N,Q,R,W
L,4,5,6
L
N,R
6
A,C,E,F,V,S
1,2
F,V
F,S,V
C,E
A,C,E
J,M,Z
F
S

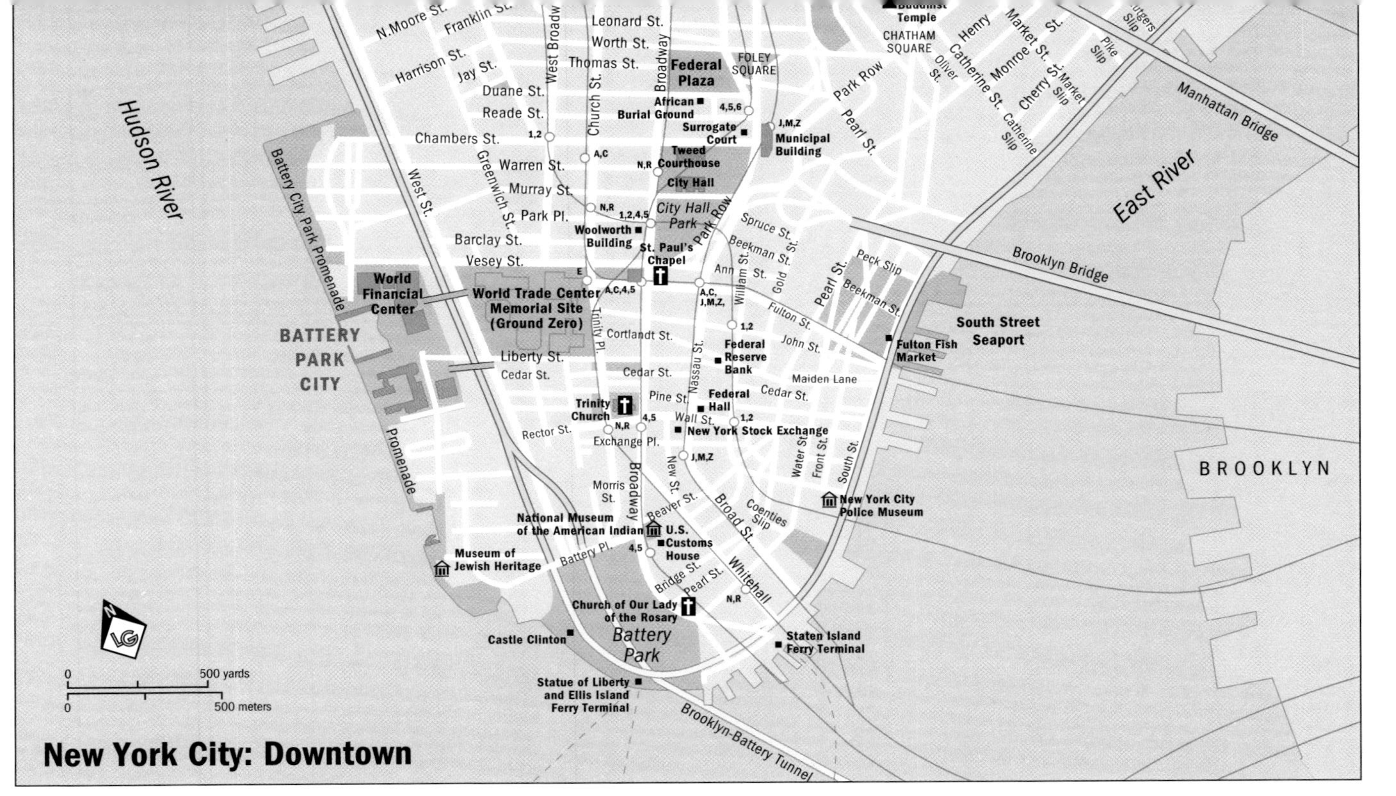
New York City: Downtown
Hudson River
East River
BROOKLYN
BATTERY PARK CITY
Battery City Park Promenade
Promenade
World Financial Center
World Trade Center Memorial Site (Ground Zero)
West St.
N.Moore St.
Franklin St.
Harrison St.
Jay St.
Duane St.
Reade St.
Chambers St.
Warren St.
Murray St.
Park Pl.
Barclay St.
Vesey St.
Greenwich St.
West Broadway
Church St.
Broadway
Leonard St.
Worth St.
Thomas St.
Federal Plaza
FOLEY SQUARE
African Burial Ground
Surrogate Court
Municipal Building
Tweed Courthouse
City Hall
City Hall Park
Park Row
Woolworth Building
St. Paul's Chapel
Trinity Pl.
Cortlandt St.
Liberty St.
Cedar St.
Trinity Church
Rector St.
Exchange Pl.
Pine St.
Wall St.
Nassau St.
Federal Reserve Bank
Federal Hall
New York Stock Exchange
Maiden Lane
John St.
Fulton St.
William St.
Ann St.
Gold St.
Spruce St.
Beekman St.
Pearl St.
Peck Slip
South Street Seaport
Fulton Fish Market
Water St.
Front St.
South St.
New York City Police Museum
New St.
Broad St.
Beaver St.
Coenties Slip
Morris St.
National Museum of the American Indian
U.S. Customs House
Museum of Jewish Heritage
Battery Pl.
Bridge St.
Whitehall
Church of Our Lady of the Rosary
Battery Park
Castle Clinton
Statue of Liberty and Ellis Island Ferry Terminal
Staten Island Ferry Terminal
Brooklyn-Battery Tunnel
Brooklyn Bridge
Manhattan Bridge
CHATHAM SQUARE
Temple
Henry
Market St.
Monroe St.
Cherry St.
Catherine St.
Oliver St.
Catherine Slip
Market Slip
Pike Slip
1,2
A,C
N,R
1,2,4,5
E
A,C,4,5
4,5,6
J,M,Z
A,C, J,M,Z,
4,5
0
500 yards
500 meters

W. 60th St.
St. Paul the Apostle
W. 59th St.
W. 58th St.
W. 57th St.
COLUMBUS CIRCLE
Central Park
Carnegie Hall
W. 56th St.
W. 55th St.
W. 54th St.
W. 53rd St.
NYC & Company Convention & Visitors Bureau
W. 52nd St.
W. 51st St.
W. 50th St.
W. 49th St.
W. 48th St.
W. 47th St.
W. 46th St.
W. 45th St.
W. 44th St.
W. 43rd St.
W. 42nd St.
W. 41st St.
W. 39th St.
W. 34th St.
W. 31st St.
W. 30th St.
W. 29th St.
W. 28th St.
W. 27th St.
W. 23rd St.
W. 14th St.
Twelfth Ave.
Eleventh Ave.
Tenth Ave.
Ninth Ave.
Eighth Ave.
Seventh Ave.
Dyer Ave.
Joe Dimaggio Hwy.
Intrepid Sea-Air-Space Museum
Schubert Theater
New York Times Building
TIMES SQUARE
Port Authority Bus Terminal
Lincoln Tunnel
Jacob K. Javits Convention Center
HELL'S KITCHEN
GARMENT DISTRICT
General Post Office
Madison Square Garden
Penn Station
Chelsea Hotel
General Theological Seminary
Cushman Row
CHELSEA
Hudson River
0 500 yards
0 500 meters
New York City: Midtown

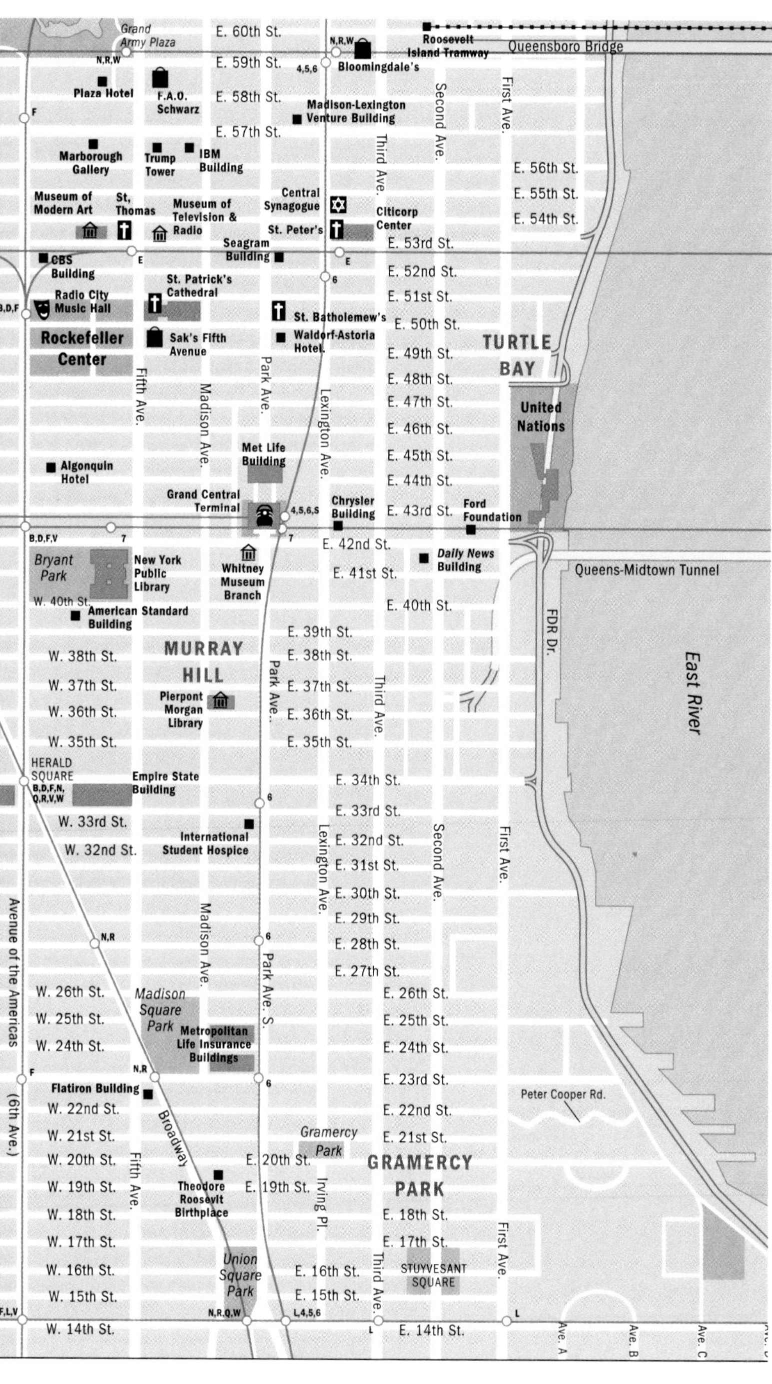

Grand Army Plaza
E. 60th St.
Roosevelt Island Tramway
Queensboro Bridge
E. 59th St.
Bloomingdale's
Plaza Hotel
F.A.O. Schwarz
E. 58th St.
Madison-Lexington Venture Building
E. 57th St.
Second Ave.
First Ave.
Third Ave.
Marborough Gallery
Trump Tower
IBM Building
E. 56th St.
E. 55th St.
E. 54th St.
Museum of Modern Art
St, Thomas
Museum of Television & Radio
Central Synagogue
St. Peter's
Citicorp Center
Seagram Building
E. 53rd St.
CBS Building
St. Patrick's Cathedral
E. 52nd St.
E. 51st St.
Radio City Music Hall
St. Batholemew's
E. 50th St.
Rockefeller Center
Sak's Fifth Avenue
Waldorf-Astoria Hotel
TURTLE BAY
E. 49th St.
E. 48th St.
Fifth Ave.
Madison Ave.
Park Ave.
Lexington Ave.
E. 47th St.
United Nations
E. 46th St.
Met Life Building
E. 45th St.
Algonquin Hotel
E. 44th St.
Grand Central Terminal
Chrysler Building
E. 43rd St.
Ford Foundation
E. 42nd St.
Bryant Park
New York Public Library
Whitney Museum Branch
Daily News Building
E. 41st St.
Queens-Midtown Tunnel
W. 40th St.
American Standard Building
E. 40th St.
FDR Dr.
E. 39th St.
MURRAY HILL
W. 38th St.
E. 38th St.
East River
W. 37th St.
E. 37th St.
Pierpont Morgan Library
W. 36th St.
E. 36th St.
W. 35th St.
E. 35th St.
HERALD SQUARE
Empire State Building
E. 34th St.
E. 33rd St.
W. 33rd St.
International Student Hospice
W. 32nd St.
E. 32nd St.
E. 31st St.
E. 30th St.
E. 29th St.
E. 28th St.
E. 27th St.
Avenue of the Americas (6th Ave.)
Park Ave. S.
W. 26th St.
E. 26th St.
Madison Square Park
W. 25th St.
E. 25th St.
Metropolitan Life Insurance Buildings
W. 24th St.
E. 24th St.
E. 23rd St.
Flatiron Building
Peter Cooper Rd.
W. 22nd St.
E. 22nd St.
Broadway
W. 21st St.
Gramercy Park
E. 21st St.
W. 20th St.
E. 20th St.
GRAMERCY PARK
W. 19th St.
Theodore Roosevlt Birthplace
E. 19th St.
Irving Pl.
W. 18th St.
E. 18th St.
W. 17th St.
E. 17th St.
Union Square Park
W. 16th St.
E. 16th St.
STUYVESANT SQUARE
W. 15th St.
E. 15th St.
W. 14th St.
E. 14th St.
Ave. A
Ave. B
Ave. C

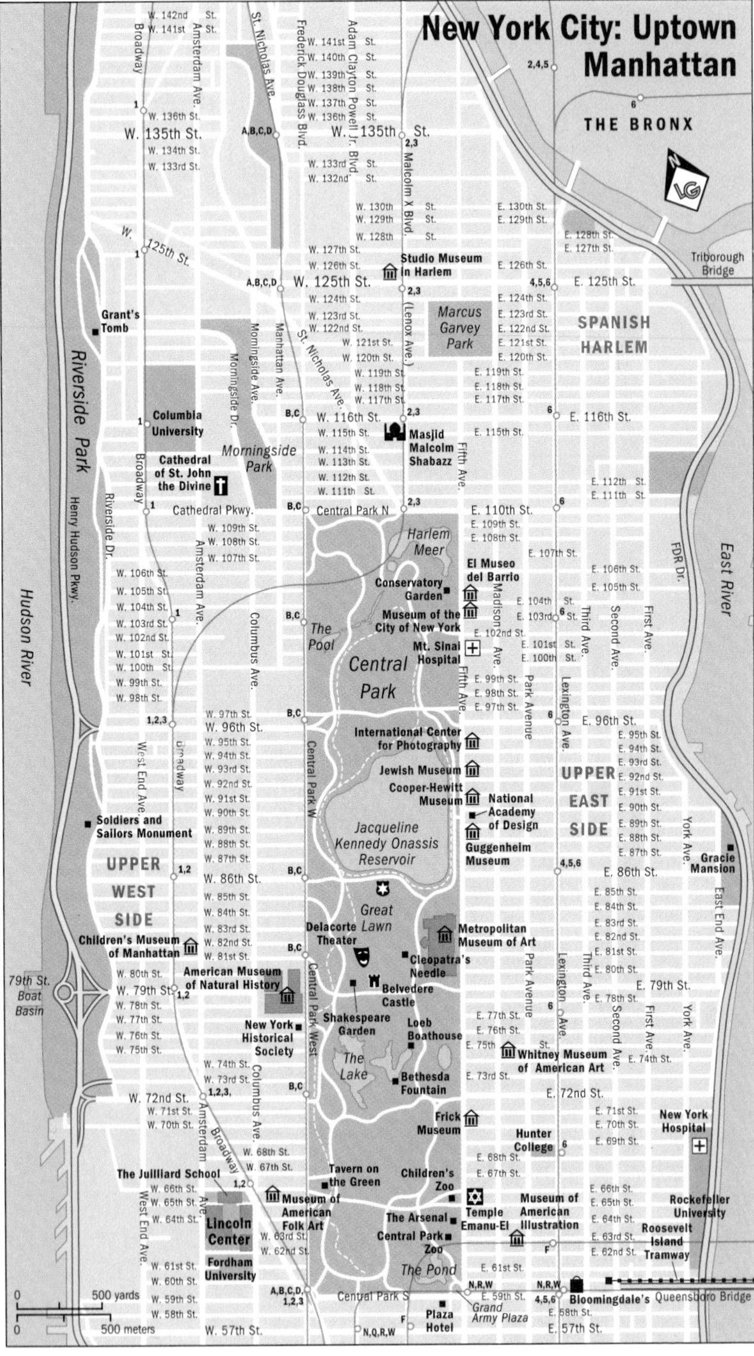

New York City: Uptown Manhattan
THE BRONX
SPANISH HARLEM
UPPER EAST SIDE
UPPER WEST SIDE
Hudson River
East River
Riverside Park
Central Park
Morningside Park
Marcus Garvey Park
Harlem Meer
The Pool
Jacqueline Kennedy Onassis Reservoir
Great Lawn
The Lake
The Pond
Grant's Tomb
Columbia University
Cathedral of St. John the Divine
Studio Museum in Harlem
Masjid Malcolm Shabazz
El Museo del Barrio
Conservatory Garden
Museum of the City of New York
Mt. Sinai Hospital
International Center for Photography
Jewish Museum
Cooper-Hewitt Museum
National Academy of Design
Guggenheim Museum
Metropolitan Museum of Art
Cleopatra's Needle
Belvedere Castle
Delacorte Theater
Shakespeare Garden
Loeb Boathouse
Bethesda Fountain
Whitney Museum of American Art
Frick Museum
Hunter College
Children's Zoo
Temple Emanu-El
Museum of American Illustration
The Arsenal
Central Park Zoo
Museum of American Folk Art
Tavern on the Green
Soldiers and Sailors Monument
Children's Museum of Manhattan
American Museum of Natural History
New York Historical Society
The Juilliard School
Lincoln Center
Fordham University
Gracie Mansion
New York Hospital
Rockefeller University
Roosevelt Island Tramway
Queensboro Bridge
Triborough Bridge
Bloomingdale's
Plaza Hotel
Grand Army Plaza
79th St. Boat Basin
Henry Hudson Pkwy.
FDR Dr.
Broadway
Amsterdam Ave.
Columbus Ave.
Central Park W
West End Ave.
Riverside Dr.
Morningside Dr.
Morningside Ave.
Manhattan Ave.
St. Nicholas Ave.
Frederick Douglass Blvd.
Adam Clayton Powell Jr. Blvd.
Malcolm X Blvd. (Lenox Ave.)
Fifth Ave.
Madison Ave.
Park Avenue
Lexington Ave.
Third Ave.
Second Ave.
First Ave.
York Ave.
East End Ave.
W. 135th St.
W. 125th St.
W. 116th St.
Cathedral Pkwy.
Central Park N
W. 96th St.
W. 86th St.
W. 79th St.
W. 72nd St.
W. 57th St.
Central Park S
E. 125th St.
E. 116th St.
E. 110th St.
E. 96th St.
E. 86th St.
E. 79th St.
E. 72nd St.
E. 57th St.
500 yards
500 meters

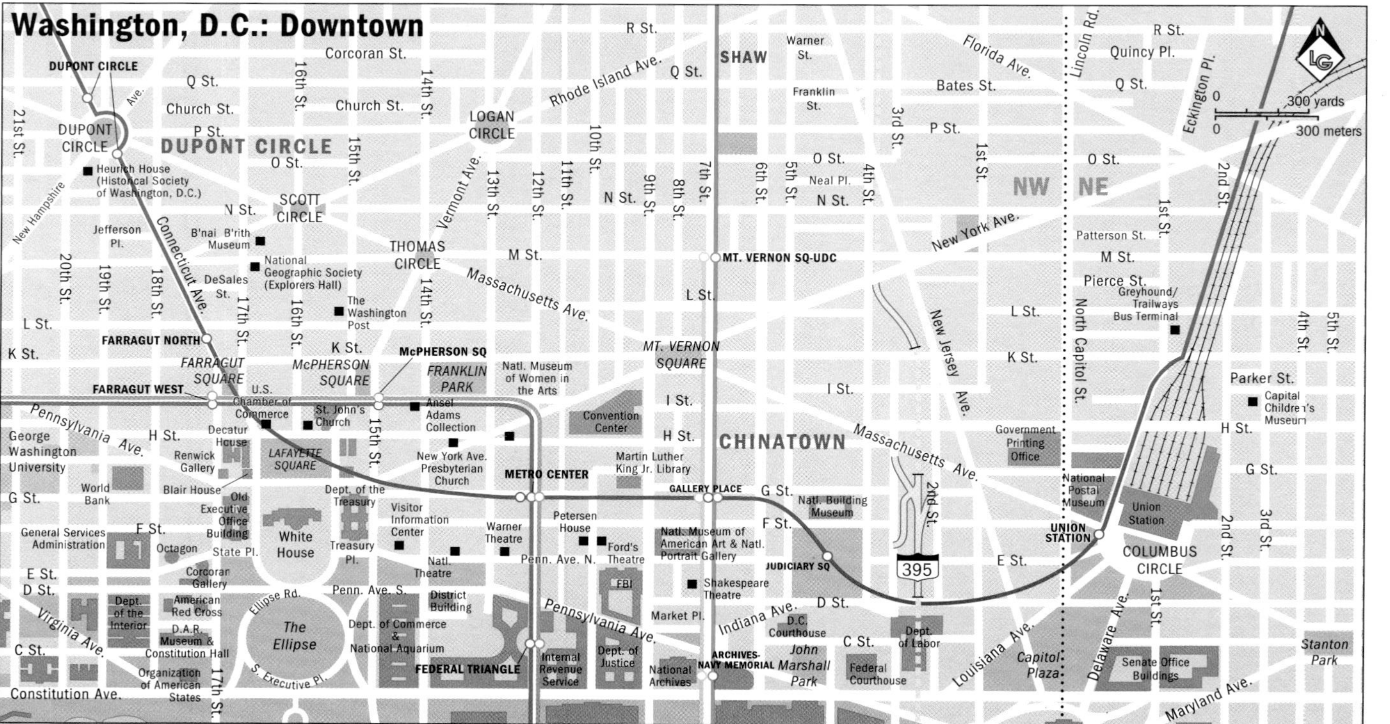
Washington, D.C.: Downtown
DUPONT CIRCLE
DUPONT CIRCLE
Heurich House (Historical Society of Washington, D.C.)
New Hampshire Ave.
Connecticut Ave.
SCOTT CIRCLE
LOGAN CIRCLE
THOMAS CIRCLE
Vermont Ave.
Rhode Island Ave.
Massachusetts Ave.
B'nai B'rith Museum
National Geographic Society (Explorers Hall)
The Washington Post
DeSales St.
Jefferson Pl.
FARRAGUT NORTH
FARRAGUT WEST
FARRAGUT SQUARE
McPHERSON SQ
McPHERSON SQUARE
FRANKLIN PARK
Natl. Museum of Women in the Arts
MT. VERNON SQUARE
MT. VERNON SQ-UDC
SHAW
CHINATOWN
Convention Center
Martin Luther King Jr. Library
METRO CENTER
GALLERY PLACE
JUDICIARY SQ
UNION STATION
Union Station
COLUMBUS CIRCLE
National Postal Museum
Government Printing Office
Greyhound/ Trailways Bus Terminal
Capital Children's Museum
NW
NE
U.S. Chamber of Commerce
St. John's Church
Ansel Adams Collection
New York Ave. Presbyterian Church
Decatur House
Renwick Gallery
Blair House
LAFAYETTE SQUARE
White House
Old Executive Office Building
Dept. of the Treasury
Treasury Pl.
Visitor Information Center
Warner Theatre
Natl. Theatre
Petersen House
Ford's Theatre
FBI
Natl. Museum of American Art & Natl. Portrait Gallery
Natl. Building Museum
Shakespeare Theatre
D.C. Courthouse
John Marshall Park
Dept. of Labor
Federal Courthouse
Capitol Plaza
Senate Office Buildings
Stanton Park
ARCHIVES-NAVY MEMORIAL
National Archives
Dept. of Justice
Internal Revenue Service
FEDERAL TRIANGLE
District Building
Dept. of Commerce & National Aquarium
The Ellipse
Ellipse Rd.
S. Executive Pl.
George Washington University
World Bank
General Services Administration
Octagon
Corcoran Gallery
American Red Cross
D.A.R. Museum & Constitution Hall
Dept. of the Interior
Organization of American States
Pennsylvania Ave.
Penn. Ave. N.
Penn. Ave. S.
Indiana Ave.
Louisiana Ave.
Delaware Ave.
Maryland Ave.
Virginia Ave.
Constitution Ave.
New York Ave.
New Jersey Ave.
Florida Ave.
Lincoln Rd.
Eckington Pl.
North Capitol St.
Market Pl.
State Pl.
395
R St.
Q St.
Quincy Pl.
Corcoran St.
Church St.
P St.
O St.
N St.
Neal Pl.
M St.
L St.
K St.
I St.
H St.
G St.
F St.
E St.
D St.
C St.
Bates St.
Warner St.
Franklin St.
Patterson St.
Pierce St.
Parker St.
21st St.
20th St.
19th St.
18th St.
17th St.
16th St.
15th St.
14th St.
13th St.
12th St.
11th St.
10th St.
9th St.
8th St.
7th St.
6th St.
5th St.
4th St.
3rd St.
2nd St.
1st St.
0 300 yards
0 300 meters
N
LG

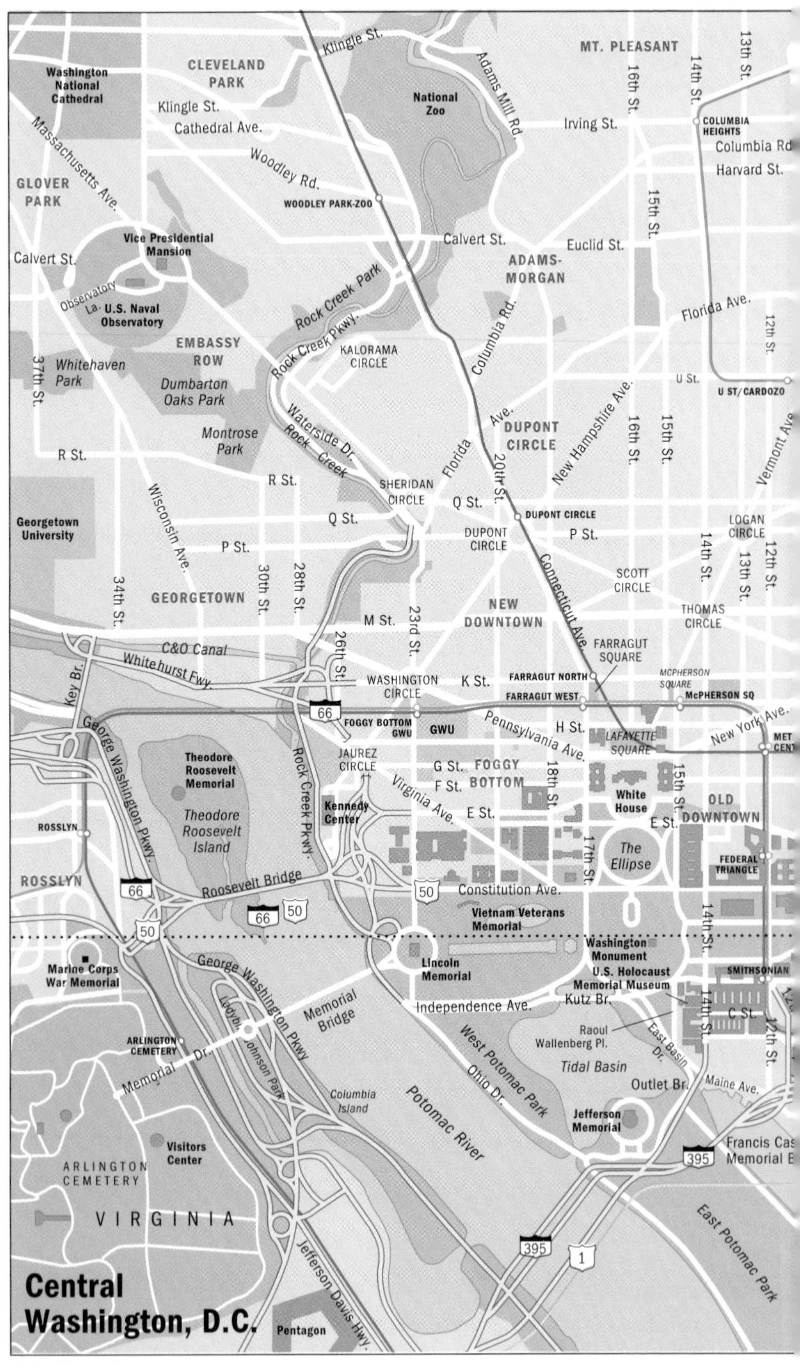
Central Washington, D.C.
CLEVELAND PARK
MT. PLEASANT
GLOVER PARK
ADAMS-MORGAN
EMBASSY ROW
DUPONT CIRCLE
GEORGETOWN
NEW DOWNTOWN
FOGGY BOTTOM
OLD DOWNTOWN
ROSSLYN
VIRGINIA
Washington National Cathedral
National Zoo
Vice Presidential Mansion
U.S. Naval Observatory
Observatory La.
Whitehaven Park
Dumbarton Oaks Park
Montrose Park
Georgetown University
KALORAMA CIRCLE
SHERIDAN CIRCLE
DUPONT CIRCLE
LOGAN CIRCLE
SCOTT CIRCLE
THOMAS CIRCLE
FARRAGUT SQUARE
MCPHERSON SQUARE
LAFAYETTE SQUARE
WASHINGTON CIRCLE
JAUREZ CIRCLE
GWU
Theodore Roosevelt Memorial
Theodore Roosevelt Island
Kennedy Center
White House
The Ellipse
Vietnam Veterans Memorial
Lincoln Memorial
Washington Monument
U.S. Holocaust Memorial Museum
Raoul Wallenberg Pl.
Tidal Basin
Jefferson Memorial
Marine Corps War Memorial
Visitors Center
ARLINGTON CEMETERY
Columbia Island
Potomac River
West Potomac Park
East Potomac Park
Francis Cas Memorial B
Pentagon
Ladybi. Johnson Park
COLUMBIA HEIGHTS
WOODLEY PARK-ZOO
U ST/CARDOZO
DUPONT CIRCLE
FARRAGUT NORTH
FARRAGUT WEST
McPHERSON SQ
FOGGY BOTTOM GWU
MET CENT
ROSSLYN
FEDERAL TRIANGLE
SMITHSONIAN
ARLINGTON CEMETERY
Klingle St.
Cathedral Ave.
Woodley Rd.
Massachusetts Ave.
Adams Mill Rd.
Irving St.
Columbia Rd
Harvard St.
Calvert St.
Euclid St.
Rock Creek Park
Rock Creek Pkwy.
Columbia Rd.
Florida Ave.
U St.
Waterside Dr.
Rock Creek
New Hampshire Ave.
Vermont Ave.
R St.
Q St.
P St.
Wisconsin Ave.
Connecticut Ave.
M St.
C&O Canal
Whitehurst Fwy.
K St.
Key Br.
H St.
Pennsylvania Ave.
New York Ave.
George Washington Pkwy.
G St.
F St.
E St.
Virginia Ave.
Roosevelt Bridge
Constitution Ave.
Independence Ave.
Kutz Br.
C St.
East Basin Dr.
Memorial Bridge
Memorial Dr.
Ohio Dr.
Outlet Br.
Maine Ave.
Jefferson Davis Hwy.
37th St.
34th St.
30th St.
28th St.
26th St.
23rd St.
20th St.
18th St.
17th St.
16th St.
15th St.
14th St.
13th St.
12th St.
66
50
395
1

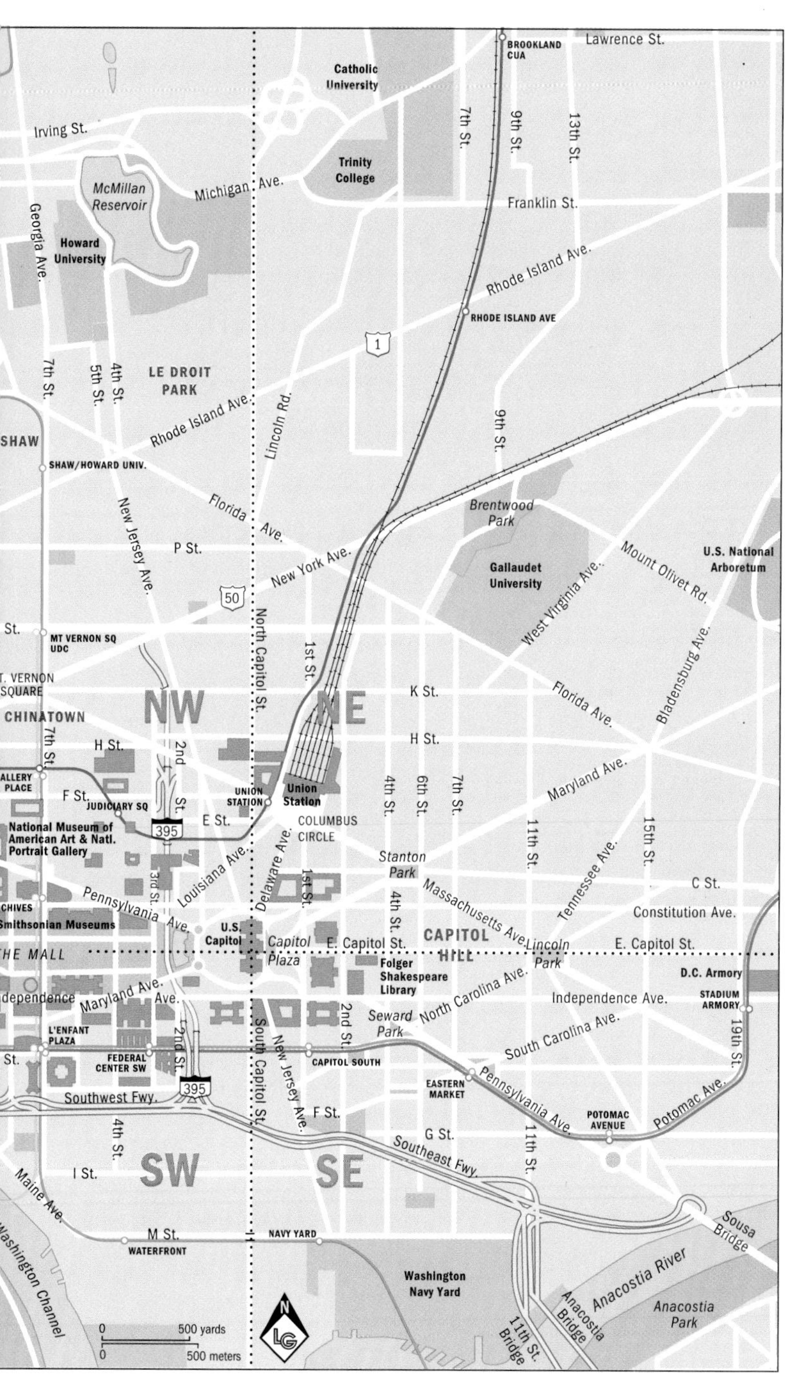

BROOKLAND CUA
Lawrence St.
Catholic University
Irving St.
7th St.
9th St.
13th St.
Trinity College
McMillan Reservoir
Michigan Ave.
Franklin St.
Georgia Ave.
Howard University
Rhode Island Ave.
RHODE ISLAND AVE
1
7th St.
5th St.
4th St.
LE DROIT PARK
Rhode Island Ave.
Lincoln Rd.
9th St.
SHAW
SHAW/HOWARD UNIV.
Florida Ave.
New Jersey Ave.
Brentwood Park
P St.
New York Ave.
Gallaudet University
Mount Olivet Rd.
U.S. National Arboretum
West Virginia Ave.
50
North Capitol St.
1st St.
Bladensburg Ave.
St.
MT VERNON SQ UDC
T. VERNON SQUARE
NW
NE
K St.
Florida Ave.
CHINATOWN
H St.
7th St.
H St.
2nd St.
GALLERY PLACE
F St.
JUDICIARY SQ
UNION STATION
Union Station
4th St.
6th St.
7th St.
Maryland Ave.
E St.
395
COLUMBUS CIRCLE
National Museum of American Art & Natl. Portrait Gallery
Louisiana Ave.
Delaware Ave.
11th St.
Tennessee Ave.
15th St.
Stanton Park
3rd St.
1st St.
C St.
Massachusetts Ave.
Pennsylvania Ave.
4th St.
Constitution Ave.
RCHIVES
Smithsonian Museums
U.S. Capitol
Capitol Plaza
E. Capitol St.
CAPITOL HILL
Lincoln Park
E. Capitol St.
THE MALL
Folger Shakespeare Library
D.C. Armory
Maryland Ave.
North Carolina Ave.
Independence Ave.
STADIUM ARMORY
ndependence Ave.
2nd St.
Seward Park
South Carolina Ave.
L'ENFANT PLAZA
2nd St.
South Capitol St.
New Jersey Ave.
19th St.
St.
FEDERAL CENTER SW
CAPITOL SOUTH
395
EASTERN MARKET
Pennsylvania Ave.
Southwest Fwy.
Potomac Ave.
F St.
4th St.
POTOMAC AVENUE
G St.
11th St.
Southeast Fwy.
I St.
SW
SE
Maine Ave.
Sousa Bridge
M St.
WATERFRONT
NAVY YARD
Washington Channel
Washington Navy Yard
Anacostia River
Anacostia Park
Anacostia Bridge
11th St. Bridge
0
500 yards
0
500 meters
N
LG

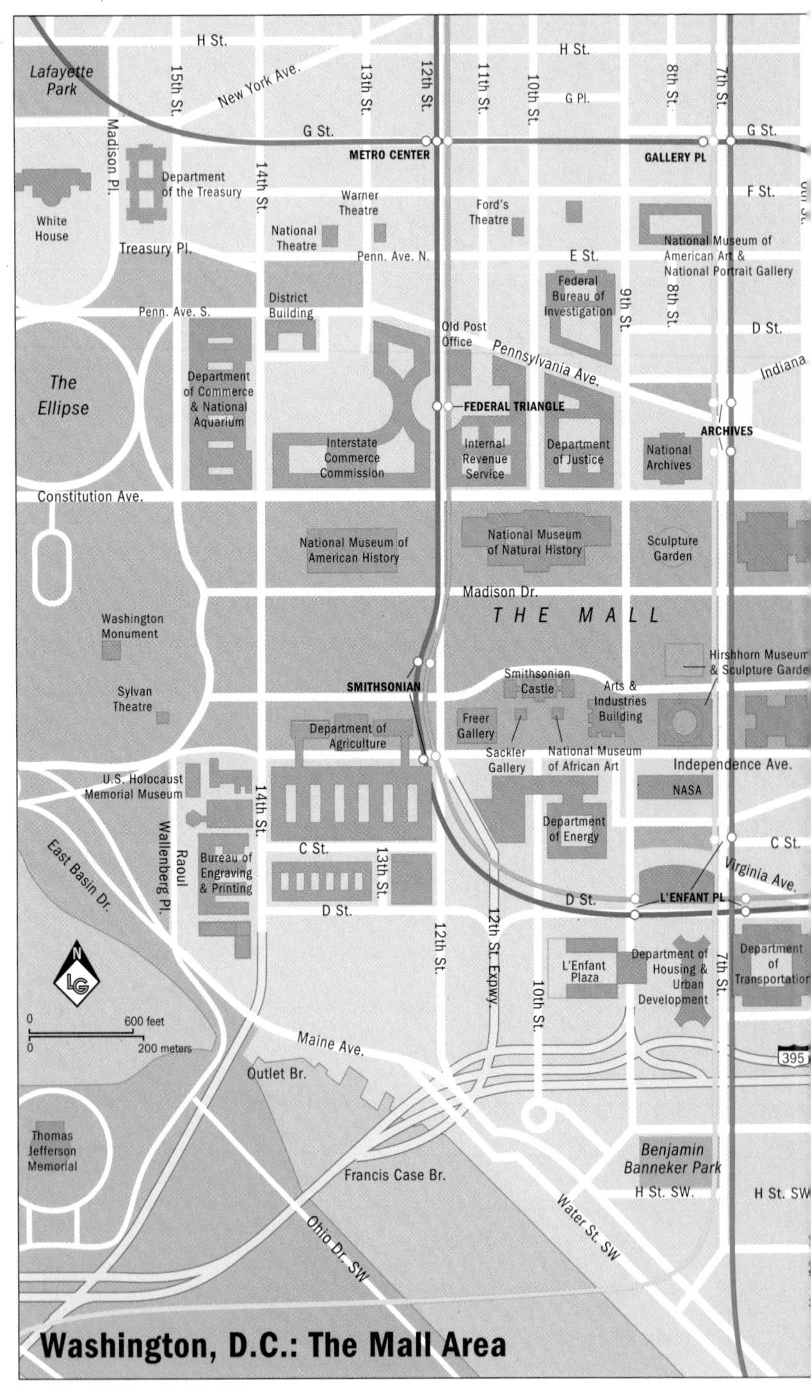

Washington, D.C.: The Mall Area
Lafayette Park
H St.
New York Ave.
G St.
G Pl.
F St.
E St.
D St.
C St.
15th St.
14th St.
13th St.
12th St.
11th St.
10th St.
9th St.
8th St.
7th St.
Madison Pl.
METRO CENTER
GALLERY PL
Department of the Treasury
White House
Treasury Pl.
Warner Theatre
National Theatre
Ford's Theatre
Penn. Ave. N.
Penn. Ave. S.
National Museum of American Art & National Portrait Gallery
Federal Bureau of Investigation
District Building
Old Post Office
Pennsylvania Ave.
Indiana
The Ellipse
Department of Commerce & National Aquarium
FEDERAL TRIANGLE
ARCHIVES
Interstate Commerce Commission
Internal Revenue Service
Department of Justice
National Archives
Constitution Ave.
National Museum of American History
National Museum of Natural History
Sculpture Garden
Madison Dr.
THE MALL
Washington Monument
Hirshhorn Museum & Sculpture Garden
Smithsonian Castle
SMITHSONIAN
Sylvan Theatre
Arts & Industries Building
Department of Agriculture
Freer Gallery
Sackler Gallery
National Museum of African Art
Independence Ave.
U.S. Holocaust Memorial Museum
NASA
Department of Energy
East Basin Dr.
Raoul Wallenberg Pl.
Bureau of Engraving & Printing
Virginia Ave.
L'ENFANT PL
12th St. Expwy.
L'Enfant Plaza
Department of Housing & Urban Development
Department of Transportation
0
600 feet
200 meters
Maine Ave.
395
Outlet Br.
Thomas Jefferson Memorial
Francis Case Br.
Benjamin Banneker Park
H St. SW.
H St. SW
Water St. SW
Ohio Dr. SW

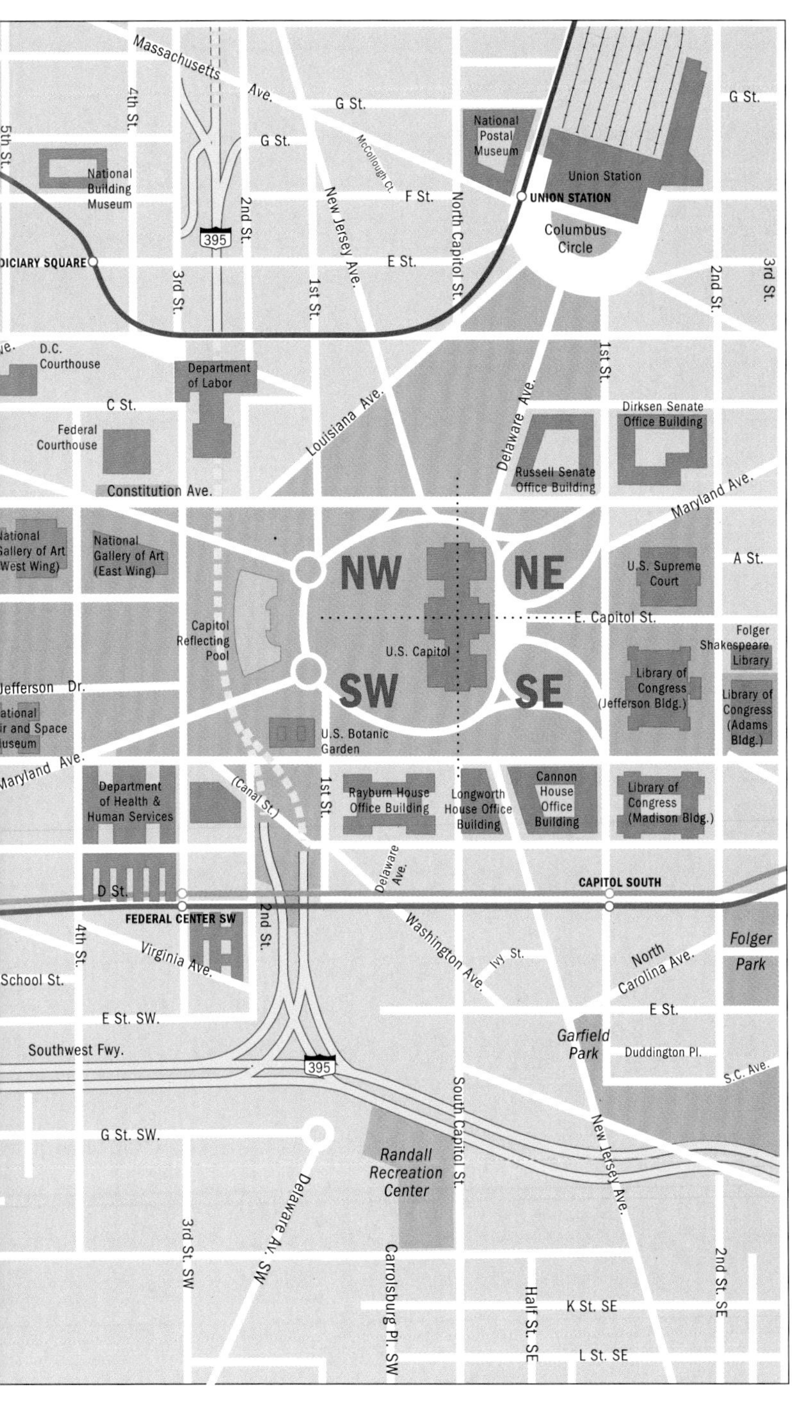

Massachusetts Ave.
G St.
G St.
G St.
5th St.
4th St.
National Building Museum
National Postal Museum
McCollough Ct.
Union Station
UNION STATION
F St.
2nd St.
New Jersey Ave.
North Capitol St.
395
Columbus Circle
JUDICIARY SQUARE
E St.
3rd St.
1st St.
2nd St.
3rd St.
D.C. Courthouse
Department of Labor
1st St.
C St.
Louisiana Ave.
Delaware Ave.
Dirksen Senate Office Building
Federal Courthouse
Russell Senate Office Building
Constitution Ave.
Maryland Ave.
National Gallery of Art (West Wing)
National Gallery of Art (East Wing)
NW
NE
U.S. Supreme Court
A St.
E. Capitol St.
Capitol Reflecting Pool
Folger Shakespeare Library
U.S. Capitol
Jefferson Dr.
SW
SE
Library of Congress (Jefferson Bldg.)
Library of Congress (Adams Bldg.)
National Air and Space Museum
U.S. Botanic Garden
Maryland Ave.
Department of Health & Human Services
(Canal St.)
1st St.
Rayburn House Office Building
Longworth House Office Building
Cannon House Office Building
Library of Congress (Madison Bldg.)
Delaware Ave.
CAPITOL SOUTH
D St.
FEDERAL CENTER SW
2nd St.
Washington Ave.
4th St.
Virginia Ave.
Ivy St.
North Carolina Ave.
Folger Park
School St.
E St. SW.
E St.
Garfield Park
Southwest Fwy.
Duddington Pl.
395
S.C. Ave.
South Capitol St.
G St. SW.
New Jersey Ave.
Delaware Av. SW
Randall Recreation Center
3rd St. SW
Carrolsburg Pl. SW
Half St. SE
K St. SE
L St. SE
2nd St. SE

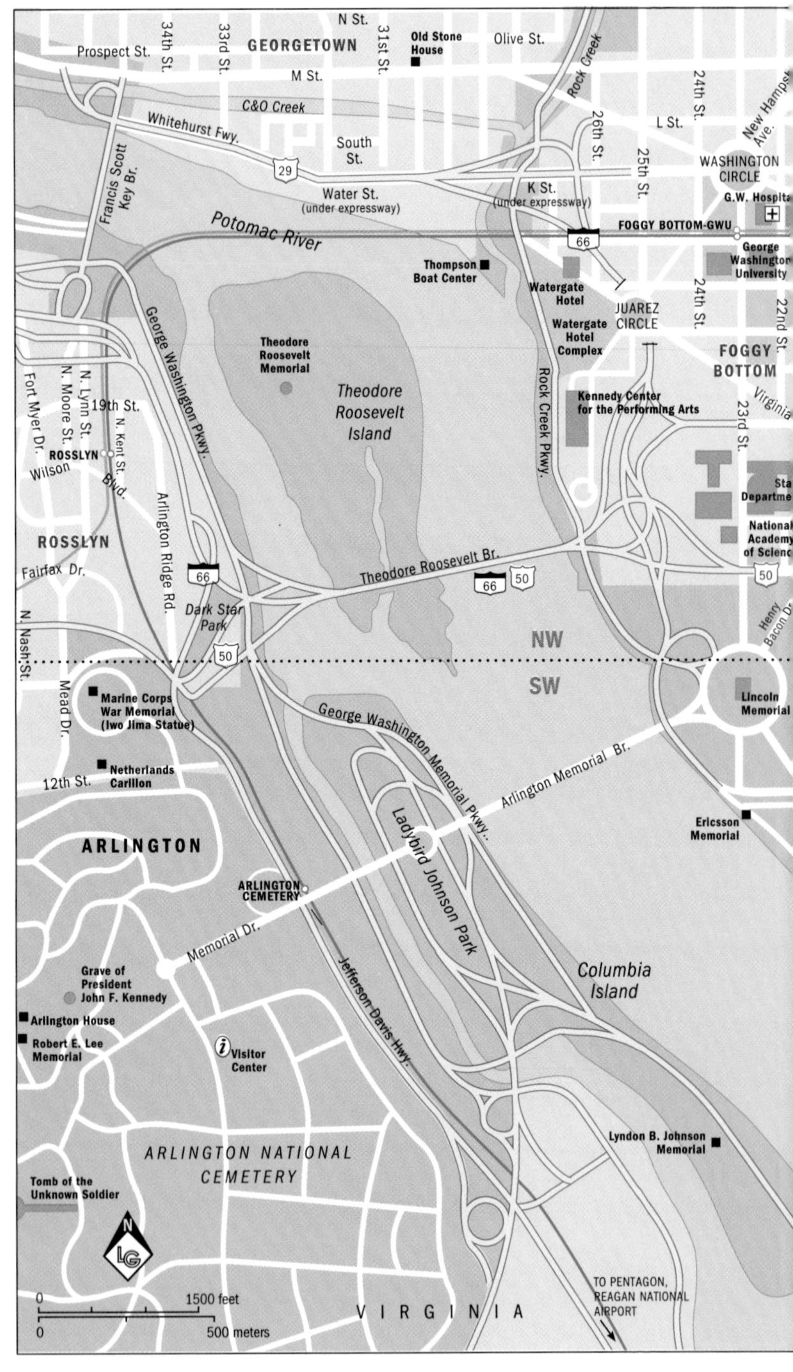

GEORGETOWN
N St.
Prospect St.
34th St.
33rd St.
31st St.
Old Stone House
Olive St.
M St.
Rock Creek
24th St.
New Hampshire Ave.
C&O Creek
Whitehurst Fwy.
South St.
26th St.
L St.
25th St.
WASHINGTON CIRCLE
29
Water St.
(under expressway)
K St.
(under expressway)
G.W. Hospital
Francis Scott Key Br.
Potomac River
66
FOGGY BOTTOM-GWU
George Washington University
Thompson Boat Center
Watergate Hotel
JUAREZ CIRCLE
Watergate Hotel Complex
24th St.
22nd St.
George Washington Pkwy.
Theodore Roosevelt Memorial
FOGGY BOTTOM
Theodore Roosevelt Island
Rock Creek Pkwy.
Kennedy Center for the Performing Arts
Virginia
23rd St.
Fort Myer Dr.
N. Moore St.
N. Lynn St.
19th St.
N. Kent St.
ROSSLYN
Wilson Blvd.
Arlington Ridge Rd.
National Academy of Sciences
ROSSLYN
Fairfax Dr.
Theodore Roosevelt Br.
50
Dark Star Park
Henry Bacon Dr.
N. Nash St.
NW
SW
Mead Dr.
Marine Corps War Memorial (Iwo Jima Statue)
George Washington Memorial Pkwy.
Lincoln Memorial
Netherlands Carillon
12th St.
Arlington Memorial Br.
Ladybird Johnson Park
Ericsson Memorial
ARLINGTON
ARLINGTON CEMETERY
Memorial Dr.
Jefferson Davis Hwy.
Columbia Island
Grave of President John F. Kennedy
Arlington House
Robert E. Lee Memorial
Visitor Center
Lyndon B. Johnson Memorial
ARLINGTON NATIONAL CEMETERY
Tomb of the Unknown Soldier
N
LG
0
1500 feet
0
500 meters
VIRGINIA
TO PENTAGON, REAGAN NATIONAL AIRPORT

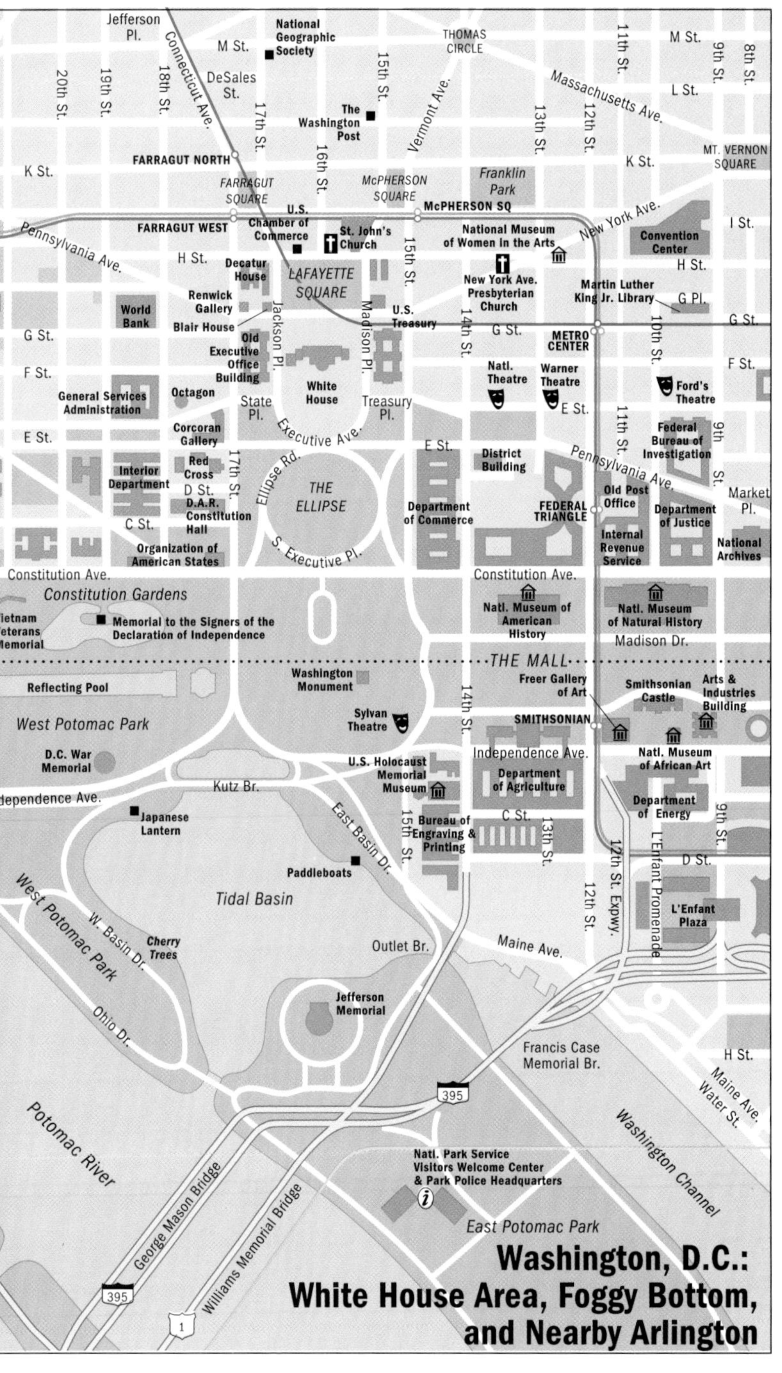

Washington, D.C.: White House Area, Foggy Bottom, and Nearby Arlington

Washington, D.C. Metro

Glenmont
Wheaton
Forest Glen
Silver Spring (MARC)
Takoma
Greenbelt
College Park-U of MD (MARC)
Prince George's Plaza
West Hyattsville
Fort Totten
Shady Grove
Rockville (MARC)
Twinbrook
White Flint
Grosvenor-Strathmore
Medical Center
Bethesda
Friendship Heights
Tenleytown-AU
Van Ness-UDC
Cleveland Park
Woodley Park-Zoo/Adams Morgan
Dupont Circle
Farragut N
U St/ African-American Civil War Memorial/ Cardozo
Georgia Av-Petworth
Columbia Hts
Shaw-Howard U.
Mt.Vernon Sq/7th St Convention Ctr
Brookland-CUA
Rhode Island Av
New York Av
Judiciary Sq
Union Station (VRE & MARC)
New Carrollton (MARC)
Landover
Cheverly
Deanwood
Minnesota Ave
Stadium-Armory
Benning Rd
Capitol Hts
Addison Rd
Summerfield
Largo Town
CAPITAL BELTWAY
MONTGOMERY CO.
DISTRICT OF COLUMBIA
Vienna/Fairfax-GMU
Dunn Loring/Merrifield
West Falls Church-VT/UVA
East Falls Church
Ballston/MU
Virginia Sq/GMU
Clarendon
Court House
FAIRFAX CO.
ARLINGTON CO.
Rosslyn
Foggy Bottom-GWU
Farragut W
McPherson Sq.
Metro Center
Gallery Place-Chinatown
Federal Triangle
Archives-Navy Memorial
Smithsonian
L'Enfant Plaza (VRE)
Federal Ctr SW
Capitol S
Eastern Market
Potomac Av
Potomac River
Anacostia R.
Arlington Cemetery
Waterfront
Navy Yard
Anacostia
Congress Hts
Southern Av
Naylor Rd
Suitland
Branch Av
Pentagon
Pentagon City
Crystal City (VRE)
National Airport
DISTRICT OF COLUMBIA
PRINCE GEORGE'S CO.
Braddock Rd
CITY OF ALEXANDRIA
King St. (VRE & MARC)
Van Dorn St (VRE)
Eisenhower Ave
Huntington
Franconia-Springfield (VRE)
N
LG

McPherson Sq
Mt.Vernon Sq/ 7th St Convention Ctr
New York Av
Foggy Bottom-GWU
Farragut W
Metro Center
Gallery Place-Chinatown
Judiciary Sq
Union Station (VRE & MARC)
Federal Triangle
Archives-Navy Memorial
Stadium-Armory
Smithsonian
Potomac River
L'Enfant Plaza (VRE)
Potomac Av
Eastern Market
Capitol S
Federal Center SW
Arlington Cemetery
Anacostia River
Waterfront-SEU
Navy Yard

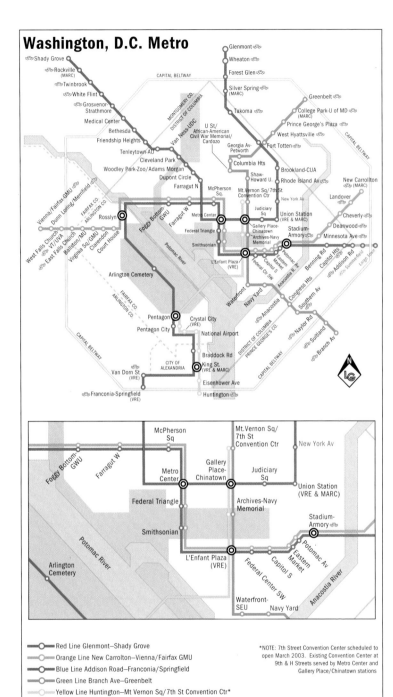

Red Line Glenmont–Shady Grove
Orange Line New Carrollton–Vienna/Fairfax GMU
Blue Line Addison Road–Franconia/Springfield
Green Line Branch Ave–Greenbelt
Yellow Line Huntington–Mt Vernon Sq/7th St Convention Ctr*
Station in service  Transfer station Future station Parking

*NOTE: 7th Street Convention Center scheduled to open March 2003. Existing Convention Center at 9th & H Streets served by Metro Center and Gallery Place/Chinatown stations

L.A.: Westside

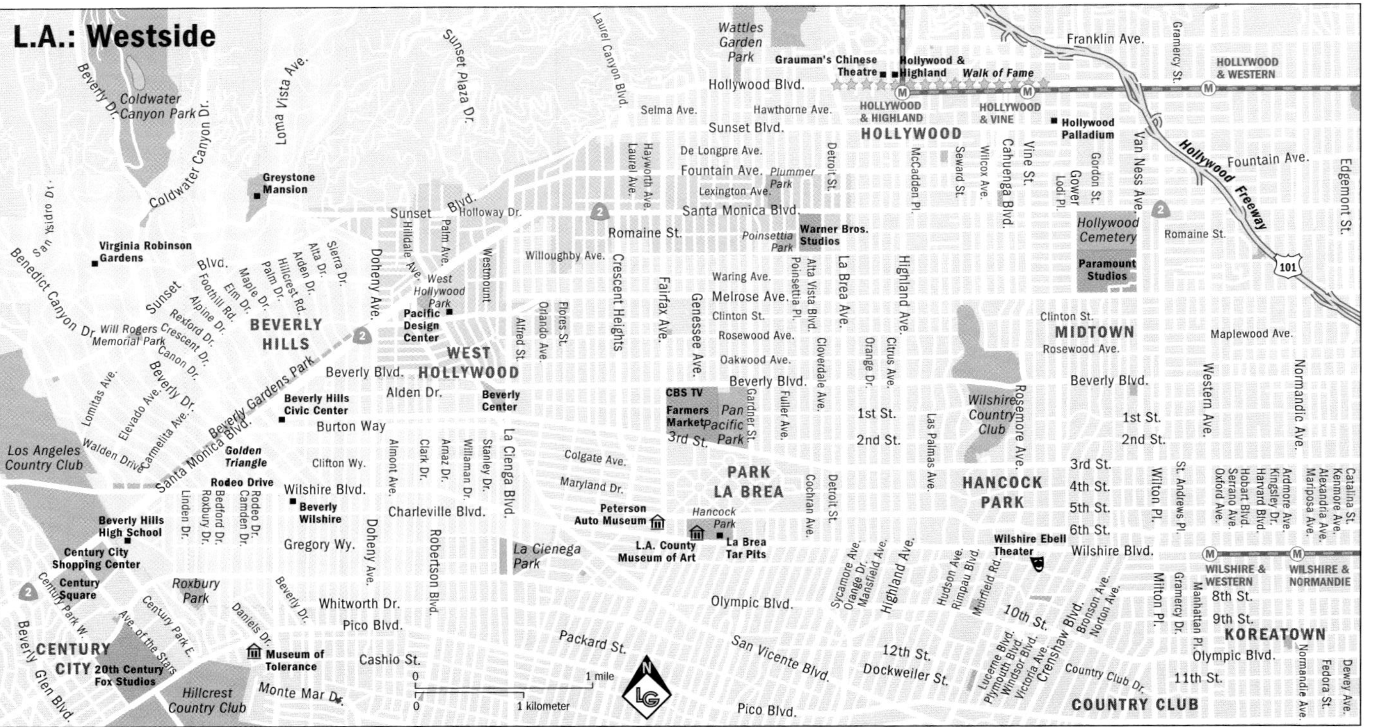

Wattles Garden Park
Grauman's Chinese Theatre
Hollywood & Highland
Walk of Fame
Franklin Ave.
Gramercy St.
HOLLYWOOD & WESTERN
Hollywood Blvd.
HOLLYWOOD & HIGHLAND
HOLLYWOOD & VINE
HOLLYWOOD
Hollywood Palladium
Hollywood Freeway
101
Fountain Ave.
Edgemont St.
Selma Ave.
Hawthorne Ave.
Sunset Blvd.
De Longpre Ave.
Fountain Ave.
Plummer Park
Lexington Ave.
Santa Monica Blvd.
Poinsettia Park
Warner Bros. Studios
Detroit St.
McCadden Pl.
Seward St.
Wilcox Ave.
Cahuenga Blvd.
Vine St.
Lodi Pl.
Gower
Gordon St.
Van Ness Ave.
Hollywood Cemetery
Paramount Studios
Romaine St.
Laurel Canyon Blvd.
Laurel Ave.
Hayworth Ave.
Romaine St.
Willoughby Ave.
Crescent Heights
Fairfax Ave.
Genessee Ave.
Waring Ave.
Melrose Ave.
Clinton St.
Rosewood Ave.
Oakwood Ave.
Poinsettia Pl.
Alta Vista Blvd.
La Brea Ave.
Cloverdale Ave.
Highland Ave.
Orange Dr.
Citrus Ave.
Clinton St.
MIDTOWN
Rosewood Ave.
Maplewood Ave.
Beverly Blvd.
Beverly Blvd.
Western Ave.
Normandic Ave.
CBS TV
Farmers Market
Pan Pacific Park
3rd St.
Gardner St.
Fuller Ave.
1st St.
2nd St.
Las Palmas Ave.
Wilshire Country Club
Rosemore Ave.
1st St.
2nd St.
3rd St.
4th St.
5th St.
6th St.
Wilshire Blvd.
PARK LA BREA
HANCOCK PARK
Cochran Ave.
Detroit St.
Hancock Park
La Brea Tar Pits
L.A. County Museum of Art
Peterson Auto Museum
Colgate Ave.
Maryland Dr.
Wilshire Ebell Theater
Wilton Pl.
St. Andrews Pl.
Oxford Ave.
Serrano Ave.
Hobart Blvd.
Harvard Blvd.
Kingsley Dr.
Ardmore Ave.
Mariposa Ave.
Alexandria Ave.
Kenmore Ave.
Catalina St.
WILSHIRE & WESTERN
WILSHIRE & NORMANDIE
8th St.
9th St.
KOREATOWN
Olympic Blvd.
11th St.
Milton Pl.
Gramercy Dr.
Manhattan Pl.
Normandie Ave.
Fedora St.
Dewey Ave.
Sycamore Ave.
Orange Dr.
Mansfield Ave.
Highland Ave.
Hudson Ave.
Rimpau Blvd.
Muirfield Rd.
10th St.
Crenshaw Blvd.
Bronson Ave.
Norton Ave.
Lucerne Blvd.
Plymouth Blvd.
Windsor Blvd.
Victoria Ave.
Country Club Dr.
COUNTRY CLUB
12th St.
Dockweiler St.
San Vicente Blvd.
Olympic Blvd.
Packard St.
Pico Blvd.
0
1 mile
0
1 kilometer
LG
N
Beverly Dr.
Coldwater Canyon Park
Coldwater Canyon Dr.
Loma Vista Ave.
Sunset Plaza Dr.
Greystone Mansion
San Ysidro Dr.
Virginia Robinson Gardens
Benedict Canyon Dr.
Sunset Blvd.
Foothill Rd.
Elm Dr.
Maple Dr.
Palm Dr.
Hillcrest Rd.
Arden Dr.
Alta Dr.
Sierra Dr.
Alpine Dr.
Rexford Dr.
Crescent Dr.
Canon Dr.
Will Rogers Memorial Park
BEVERLY HILLS
Doheny Ave.
Sunset Blvd.
Holloway Dr.
Hilldale Ave.
Palm Ave.
West Hollywood Park
Westmount
Pacific Design Center
WEST HOLLYWOOD
Alfred St.
Orlando Ave.
Flores St.
Beverly Blvd.
Alden Dr.
Beverly Center
Beverly Hills Civic Center
Burton Way
Beverly Gardens Park
Lomitas Ave.
Elevado Ave.
Beverly Dr.
Carmelita Ave.
Walden Drive
Santa Monica Blvd.
Los Angeles Country Club
Golden Triangle
Clifton Wy.
Almont Ave.
Clark Dr.
Arnaz Dr.
Willaman Dr.
Stanley Dr.
La Cienga Blvd.
Rodeo Drive
Linden Dr.
Roxbury Dr.
Bedford Dr.
Camden Dr.
Rodeo Dr.
Wilshire Blvd.
Beverly Wilshire
Charleville Blvd.
Gregory Wy.
Doheny Ave.
Robertson Blvd.
La Cienega Park
Beverly Hills High School
Century City Shopping Center
Century Square
Roxbury Park
Century Park W.
Ave. of the Stars
Century Park E.
Daniels Dr.
Beverly Dr.
Whitworth Dr.
Pico Blvd.
Museum of Tolerance
Cashio St.
CENTURY CITY
20th Century Fox Studios
Hillcrest Country Club
Monte Mar Dr.
Beverly Glen Blvd.
2

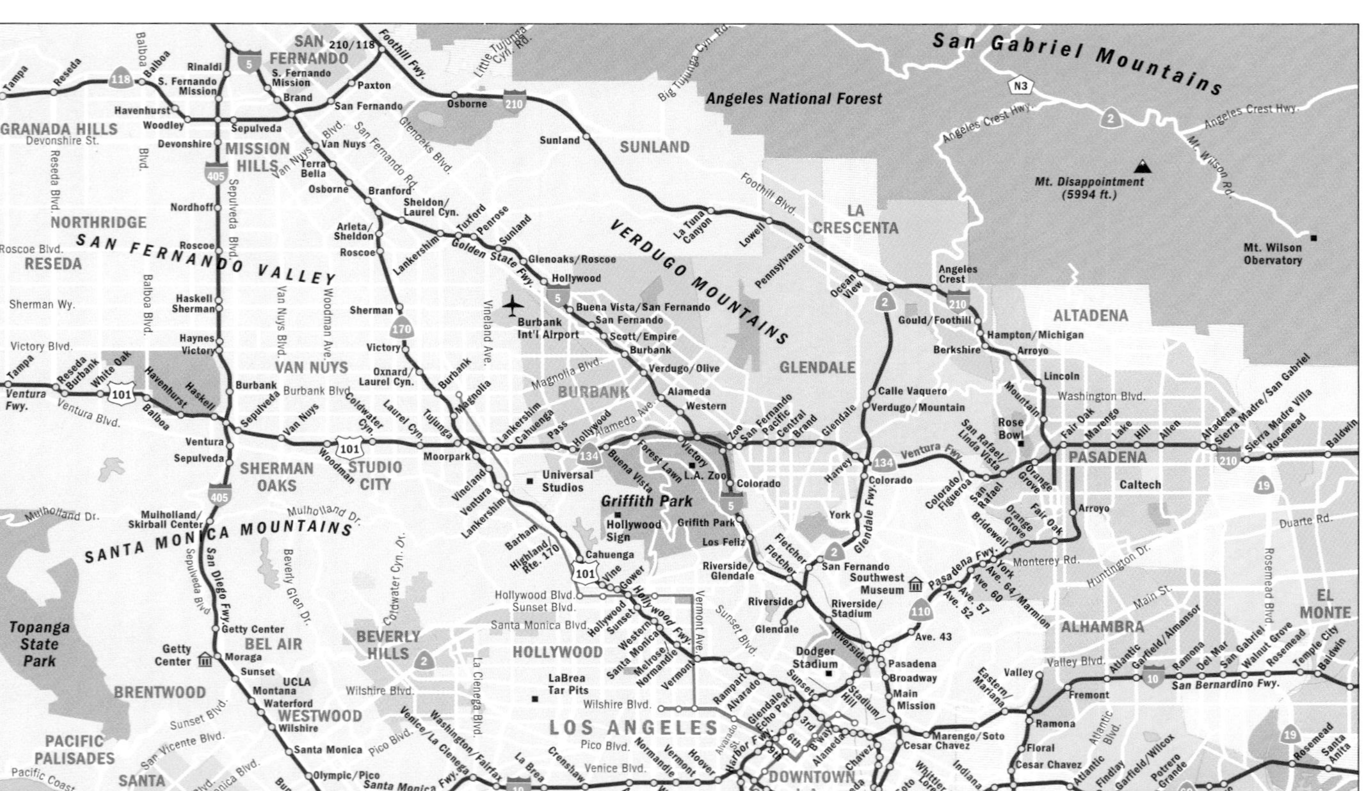

San Gabriel Mountains
Angeles National Forest
Mt. Disappointment (5994 ft.)
Mt. Wilson Observatory
Angeles Crest Hwy.
Mt. Wilson Rd.
Big Tujunga Cyn. Rd.
Little Tujunga Cyn. Rd.
SAN FERNANDO
GRANADA HILLS
MISSION HILLS
NORTHRIDGE
RESEDA
SAN FERNANDO VALLEY
VAN NUYS
SUNLAND
LA CRESCENTA
VERDUGO MOUNTAINS
GLENDALE
BURBANK
ALTADENA
PASADENA
Caltech
Rose Bowl
SHERMAN OAKS
STUDIO CITY
Universal Studios
Griffith Park
Hollywood Sign
L.A. Zoo
Forest Lawn
SANTA MONICA MOUNTAINS
Topanga State Park
BEL AIR
Getty Center
BEVERLY HILLS
HOLLYWOOD
LaBrea Tar Pits
LOS ANGELES
Dodger Stadium
Southwest Museum
DOWNTOWN L.A.
ALHAMBRA
EL MONTE
BRENTWOOD
WESTWOOD
UCLA
PACIFIC PALISADES
SANTA MONICA
Burbank Int'l Airport
Foothill Fwy.
Golden State Fwy.
Ventura Fwy.
San Diego Fwy.
Hollywood Fwy.
Glendale Fwy.
Pasadena Fwy.
San Bernardino Fwy.
Santa Monica Fwy.
Pomona Fwy.
Roscoe Blvd.
Sherman Wy.
Victory Blvd.
Ventura Blvd.
Devonshire St.
Sepulveda Blvd.
Van Nuys Blvd.
Woodman Ave.
Vineland Ave.
Burbank Blvd.
Magnolia Blvd.
Foothill Blvd.
Washington Blvd.
Mulholland Dr.
Beverly Glen Dr.
Coldwater Cyn. Dr.
Sunset Blvd.
Hollywood Blvd.
Santa Monica Blvd.
Wilshire Blvd.
Pico Blvd.
Venice Blvd.
La Cienega Blvd.
Vermont Ave.
San Vicente Blvd.
Pacific Coast
Huntington Dr.
Monterey Rd.
Main St.
Valley Blvd.
Rosemead Blvd.
Duarte Rd.
Atlantic Blvd.

Metropolitan
Los Angeles
Metro Green Line
Metro Blue Line
Metro Red Line
0 2 miles
0 2 kilometers
Pacific Ocean
Santa Monica State Beach
Muscle Beach
VENICE
CULVER CITY
PLAYA DEL REY
Dockweiler State Beach
Los Angeles Int'l Airport (LAX)
EL SEGUNDO
El Porto County Beach
Manhattan County Beach
MANHATTAN BEACH
HERMOSA BEACH
REDONDO BEACH
Redondo County Beach
Torrance County Beach
PALOS VERDES ESTATES
ROLLING HILLS
RANCHO PALOS VERDES
SAN PEDRO
LOMITA
TORRANCE
GARDENA
HAWTHORNE
INGLEWOOD
SOUTH CENTRAL
WATTS
COMPTON
HUNTINGTON PARK
DOWNEY
PARAMOUNT
NORWALK
LAKEWOOD
CERRITOS
CARSON
WILMINGTON
LONG BEACH
NAPLES
WHITTIER
Long Beach Int'l Airport
Queen Mary
U.S Naval Weapons Station
Seal Beach Nat'l Wildlife Refuge
Los Angeles Co.
Orange Co.
Harbor Fwy.
Imperial Fwy.
Gardena Fwy.
Artesia Fwy.
San Diego Fwy.
Long Beach Fwy.
Santa Ana Fwy.
San Gabriel River Fwy.
Pacific Coast Hwy.
Imperial Hwy.
Vista Del Mar
Palos Verdes Dr. West
Palos Verdes Dr. North
Hawthorne Blvd.
Sepulveda Blvd.
Manchester Ave.
Century Blvd.
El Segundo Blvd.
Rosecrans Ave.
Artesia Blvd.
W 190th St.
Del Amo Blvd.
Carson St.
Florence Ave.
Slauson Ave.
Firestone Blvd.
Alameda St.
Wilmington Ave.
Central Ave.
Vermont Ave.
Western Ave.
Crenshaw Blvd.
La Cienega Blvd.
La Brea Ave.
Figueroa St.
Main St.
Long Beach Blvd.
Atlantic Blvd.
Lakewood Blvd.
Bellflower Blvd.
Clark Ave.
Downey Ave.
Paramount Blvd.
Cherry Ave.
Orange Ave.
Bloomfield Ave.
Pioneer Blvd.
Alondra Blvd.
7th St.
Katella Ave.
Seal Beach Blvd.
Washington Blvd.
Rosemead Blvd.
Venice Blvd.
MLK Jr. Blvd.
Vernon Ave.
Van Ness Ave.
Sepulveda/Imperial
Nash
Aviation
Imperial
Hawthorne
Prairie
Crenshaw
Vermont
Harbor Fwy.
Long Beach
M.L. King Jr.
Garfield
Lakewood
Bellflower
Firestone
Norwalk
Rosecrans
El Segundo
Inglewood
Redondo Beach
Artesia
Western
Normandie
Figueroa/Main
Torrance
Carson
220th
223rd
Sepulveda
Pacific Coast
Anaheim
C St.
J. S. Gibson
Pacific/Channel
Front/Harbor
Seaside/Ferry
Henry Ford
New Dock
Seaside/Ocean
Ocean
Shoreline
Harbor Scenic
9th
7th
Willow
Wardlow
Del Amo
Alameda
Santa Fe
Atlantic
Alondra
Paramount
Downey
Clark
Studebaker
Pioneer
Bloomfield
Park Plaza
Carmenita/183rd
South
Lincoln/Carson
Cerritos/Spring
Willow/Katella
7th Seal Beach
C.S.U. Long Beach
Bellflower/Los Coyotes
Woodruff
Stearns/Palo Verde
Lakewood/Willow
Spring
Cherry
Orange
Acacia
Central
Avalon
Main
Washington/Venice
Culver
Sawtelle/Braddock
Jefferson
Centinella
Lincoln
Mindanao
Slauson
Jefferson Sepulveda
Howard Hughes
La Tijera
Florence/Manchester
La Cienega/Manchester
Century
Vernon
51st
Gage
Florence
Manchester
Washington
Atlantic/Bandini
Eastern
Washington Garfield
Paramount
Rosemead
Telegraph
Washington/Norwalk
Slauson/Pioneer
Beverly
Whittier
Pioneer/Imperial
Firestone/Rosecrans
Lincoln/Olympic

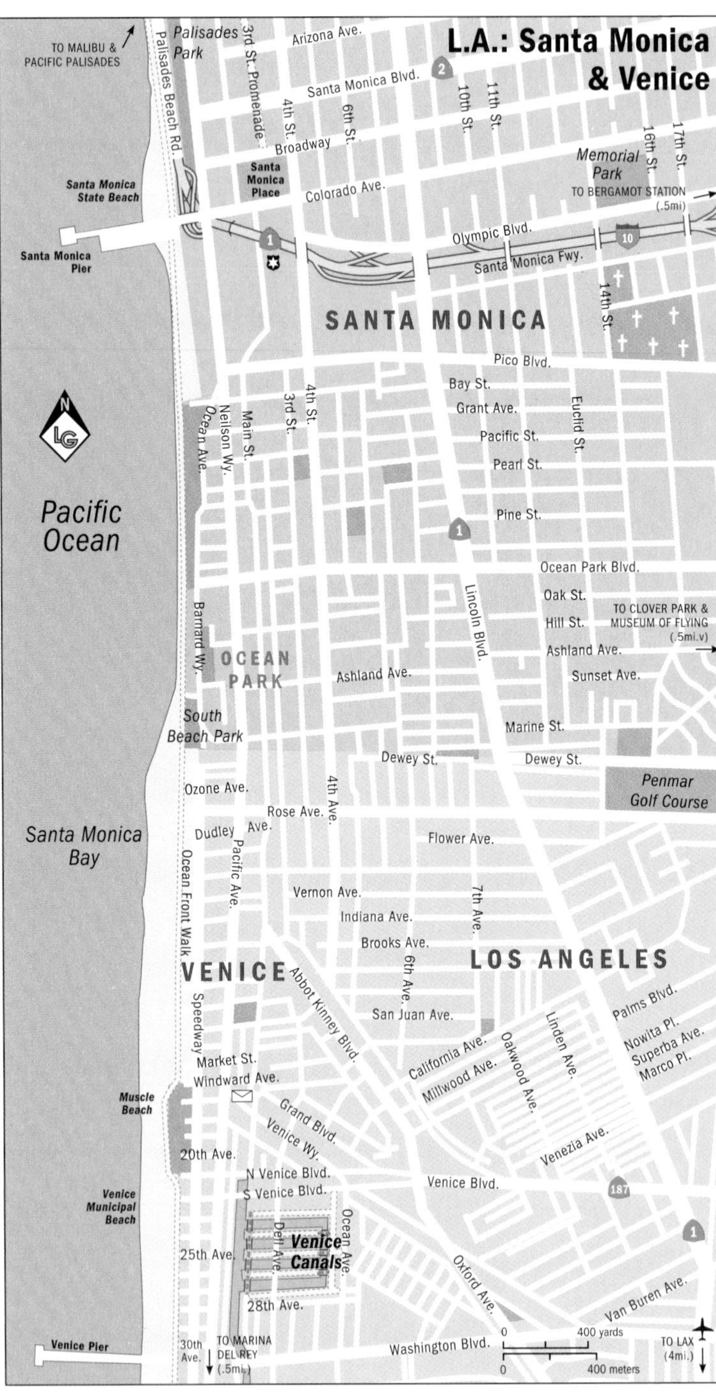

L.A.: Santa Monica & Venice
TO MALIBU & PACIFIC PALISADES
Palisades Park
Palisades Beach Rd.
3rd St. Promenade
Arizona Ave.
Santa Monica Blvd.
4th St.
6th St.
10th St.
11th St.
16th St.
17th St.
Broadway
Memorial Park
Santa Monica Place
Colorado Ave.
TO BERGAMOT STATION (.5mi)
Santa Monica State Beach
Santa Monica Pier
Olympic Blvd.
Santa Monica Fwy.
14th St.
SANTA MONICA
Pico Blvd.
Bay St.
Grant Ave.
Pacific St.
Pearl St.
Euclid St.
Ocean Ave.
Neilson Wy.
Main St.
3rd St.
4th St.
Pine St.
Pacific Ocean
Ocean Park Blvd.
Oak St.
Hill St.
Ashland Ave.
Sunset Ave.
TO CLOVER PARK & MUSEUM OF FLYING (.5mi.v)
Lincoln Blvd.
Barnard Wy.
OCEAN PARK
Ashland Ave.
South Beach Park
Marine St.
Dewey St.
Dewey St.
Penmar Golf Course
Ozone Ave.
Rose Ave.
4th Ave.
Dudley Ave.
Santa Monica Bay
Flower Ave.
Ocean Front Walk
Pacific Ave.
Vernon Ave.
Indiana Ave.
7th Ave.
Brooks Ave.
6th Ave.
VENICE
LOS ANGELES
Abbot Kinney Blvd.
Speedway
San Juan Ave.
Palms Blvd.
Nowita Pl.
Superba Ave.
Marco Pl.
Linden Ave.
Oakwood Ave.
California Ave.
Millwood Ave.
Market St.
Windward Ave.
Muscle Beach
Grand Blvd.
Venice Wy.
Venezia Ave.
20th Ave.
N Venice Blvd.
S Venice Blvd.
Venice Blvd.
Venice Municipal Beach
Venice Canals
Dell Ave.
Ocean Ave.
25th Ave.
Oxford Ave.
28th Ave.
Van Buren Ave.
Venice Pier
30th Ave.
TO MARINA DEL REY (.5mi.)
Washington Blvd.
0
400 yards
0
400 meters
TO LAX (4mi.)

Vancouver

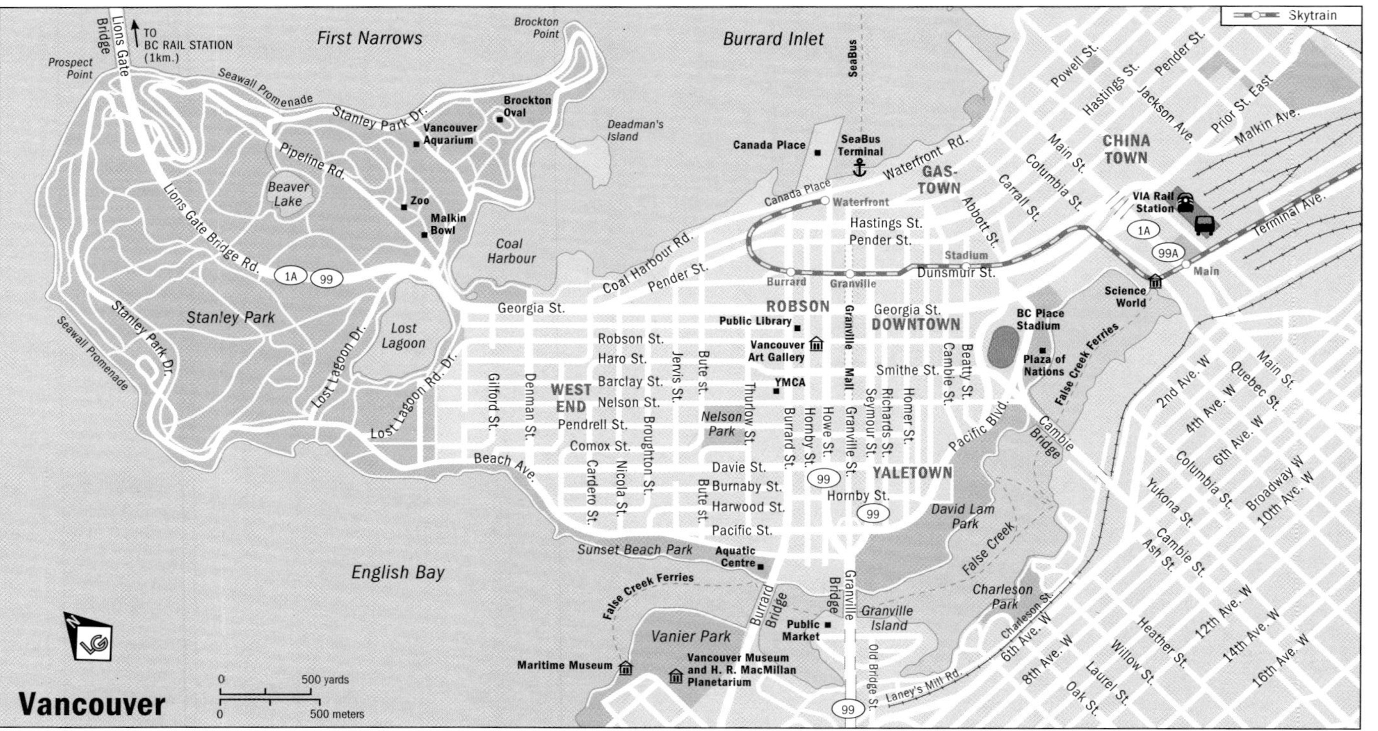
Skytrain
Lions Gate Bridge
TO BC RAIL STATION (1km.)
Prospect Point
First Narrows
Brockton Point
Burrard Inlet
SeaBus
Seawall Promenade
Stanley Park Dr.
Brockton Oval
Vancouver Aquarium
Deadman's Island
Canada Place
SeaBus Terminal
Pipeline Rd.
Beaver Lake
Zoo
Malkin Bowl
Coal Harbour
Lions Gate Bridge Rd.
1A
99
Stanley Park
Lost Lagoon
Lost Lagoon Dr.
Lost Lagoon Rd. Dr.
Coal Harbour Rd.
Pender St.
Georgia St.
Canada Place
Waterfront
Waterfront Rd.
GAS-TOWN
Hastings St.
Pender St.
Burrard
Granville
Stadium
Dunsmuir St.
ROBSON
Public Library
Vancouver Art Gallery
Granville Mall
Georgia St.
DOWNTOWN
YMCA
Robson St.
Haro St.
Barclay St.
Nelson St.
WEST END
Pendrell St.
Comox St.
Gilford St.
Denman St.
Jervis St.
Bute st.
Broughton St.
Cardero St.
Nicola St.
Nelson Park
Thurlow St.
Burrard St.
Hornby St.
Howe St.
Granville St.
Seymour St.
Richards St.
Homer St.
Smithe St.
Cambie St.
Beatty St.
Davie St.
Burnaby St.
Harwood St.
Bute st.
Pacific St.
Hornby St.
YALETOWN
Beach Ave.
Sunset Beach Park
Aquatic Centre
English Bay
False Creek Ferries
Vanier Park
Maritime Museum
Vancouver Museum and H. R. MacMillan Planetarium
Burrard Bridge
Public Market
Granville Bridge
Granville Island
Old Bridge St.
David Lam Park
False Creek
Charleson Park
Charleson St.
Laney's Mill Rd.
Pacific Blvd.
Cambie Bridge
BC Place Stadium
Plaza of Nations
False Creek Ferries
Science World
Powell St.
Hastings St.
Pender St.
Jackson Ave.
Prior St. East
Malkin Ave.
CHINA TOWN
Main St.
Columbia St.
Carrall St.
Abbott St.
VIA Rail Station
1A
99A
Main
Terminal Ave.
2nd Ave. W
4th Ave. W
6th Ave. W
Main St.
Quebec St.
Columbia St.
Broadway W
10th Ave. W
Yukona St.
Cambie St.
Ash St.
12th Ave. W
14th Ave. W
16th Ave. W
Heather St.
Willow St.
Laurel St.
Oak St.
6th Ave. W
8th Ave. W
0
500 yards
500 meters

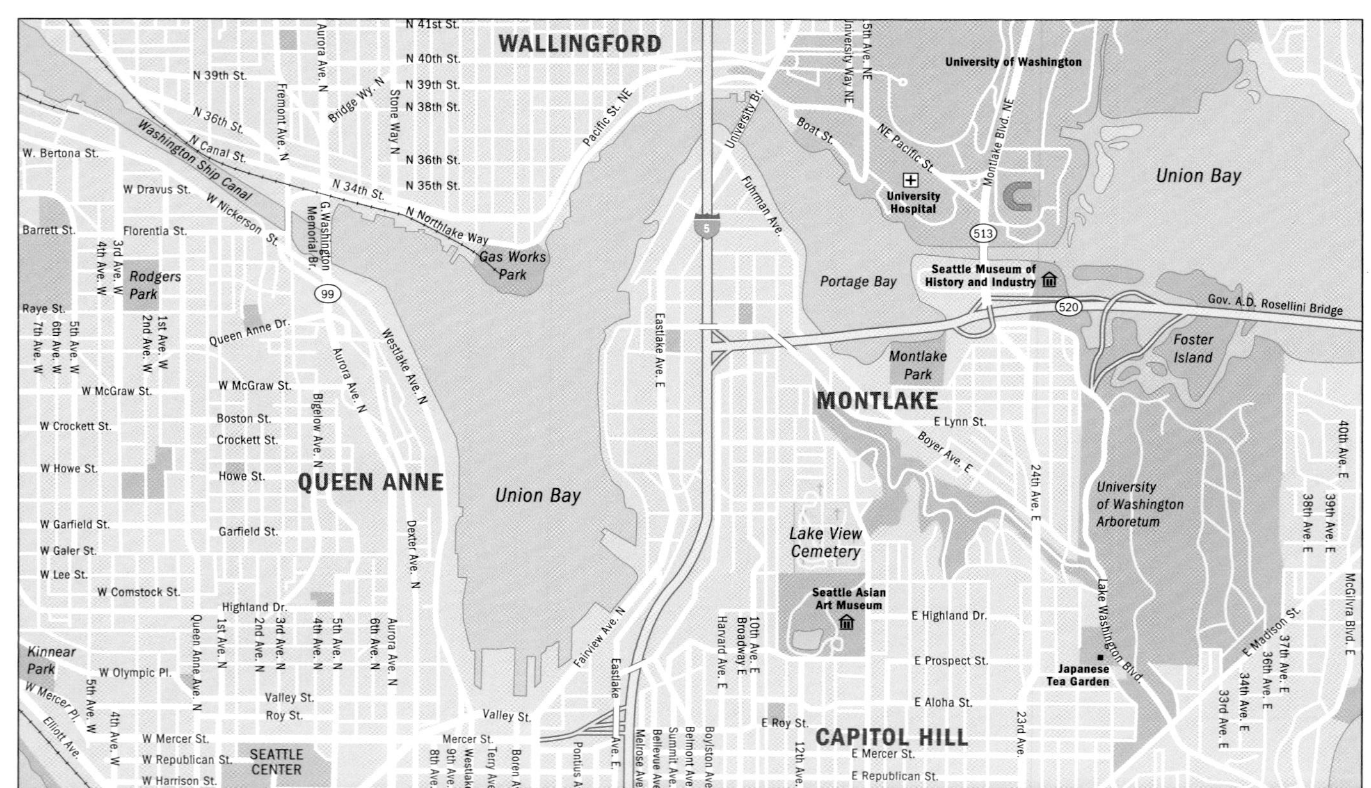

WALLINGFORD
University of Washington
Union Bay
N 41st St.
N 40th St.
N 39th St.
N 38th St.
N 36th St.
N 35th St.
N 39th St.
N 36th St.
N Canal St.
Washington Ship Canal
W. Bertona St.
W Dravus St.
W Nickerson St.
N 34th St.
N Northlake Way
Aurora Ave. N
Fremont Ave. N
Bridge Wy. N
Stone Way N
Pacific St. NE
University Br.
Boat St.
NE Pacific St.
Montlake Blvd. NE
University Way NE
15th Ave. NE
University Hospital
Fuhrman Ave.
Barrett St.
Florentia St.
G.Washington Memorial Br.
Gas Works Park
Rodgers Park
3rd Ave. W
4th Ave. W
Portage Bay
Seattle Museum of History and Industry
Gov. A.D. Rosellini Bridge
Foster Island
Raye St.
7th Ave. W
6th Ave. W
5th Ave. W
2nd Ave. W
1st Ave. W
Queen Anne Dr.
Aurora Ave. N
Westlake Ave. N
Eastlake Ave. E
Montlake Park
MONTLAKE
W McGraw St.
W McGraw St.
W Crockett St.
Boston St.
Crockett St.
Bigelow Ave. N
E Lynn St.
Boyer Ave. E
W Howe St.
Howe St.
QUEEN ANNE
Union Bay
24th Ave. E
University of Washington Arboretum
40th Ave. E
39th Ave. E
38th Ave. E
W Garfield St.
Garfield St.
Dexter Ave. N
Lake View Cemetery
W Galer St.
W Lee St.
W Comstock St.
Highland Dr.
Seattle Asian Art Museum
E Highland Dr.
Lake Washington Blvd.
McGilvra Blvd. E
E Madison St.
Kinnear Park
W Olympic Pl.
Queen Anne Ave. N
1st Ave. N
2nd Ave. N
3rd Ave. N
4th Ave. N
5th Ave. N
6th Ave. N
Aurora Ave. N
Fairview Ave. N
Harvard Ave. E
10th Ave. E
Broadway E
E Prospect St.
Japanese Tea Garden
37th Ave. E
36th Ave. E
34th Ave. E
33rd Ave. E
W Mercer Pl.
5th Ave. W
4th Ave. W
Elliott Ave.
Valley St.
Roy St.
Valley St.
Eastlake Ave. E.
E Aloha St.
E Roy St.
CAPITOL HILL
23rd Ave.
W Mercer St.
W Republican St.
W Harrison St.
SEATTLE CENTER
Mercer St.
8th Ave.
9th Ave.
Westlake
Terry Ave.
Boren Av
Pontius Av
Melrose Ave.
Bellevue Ave
Summit Ave.
Belmont Ave.
Boylston Ave.
12th Ave.
E Mercer St.
E Republican St.

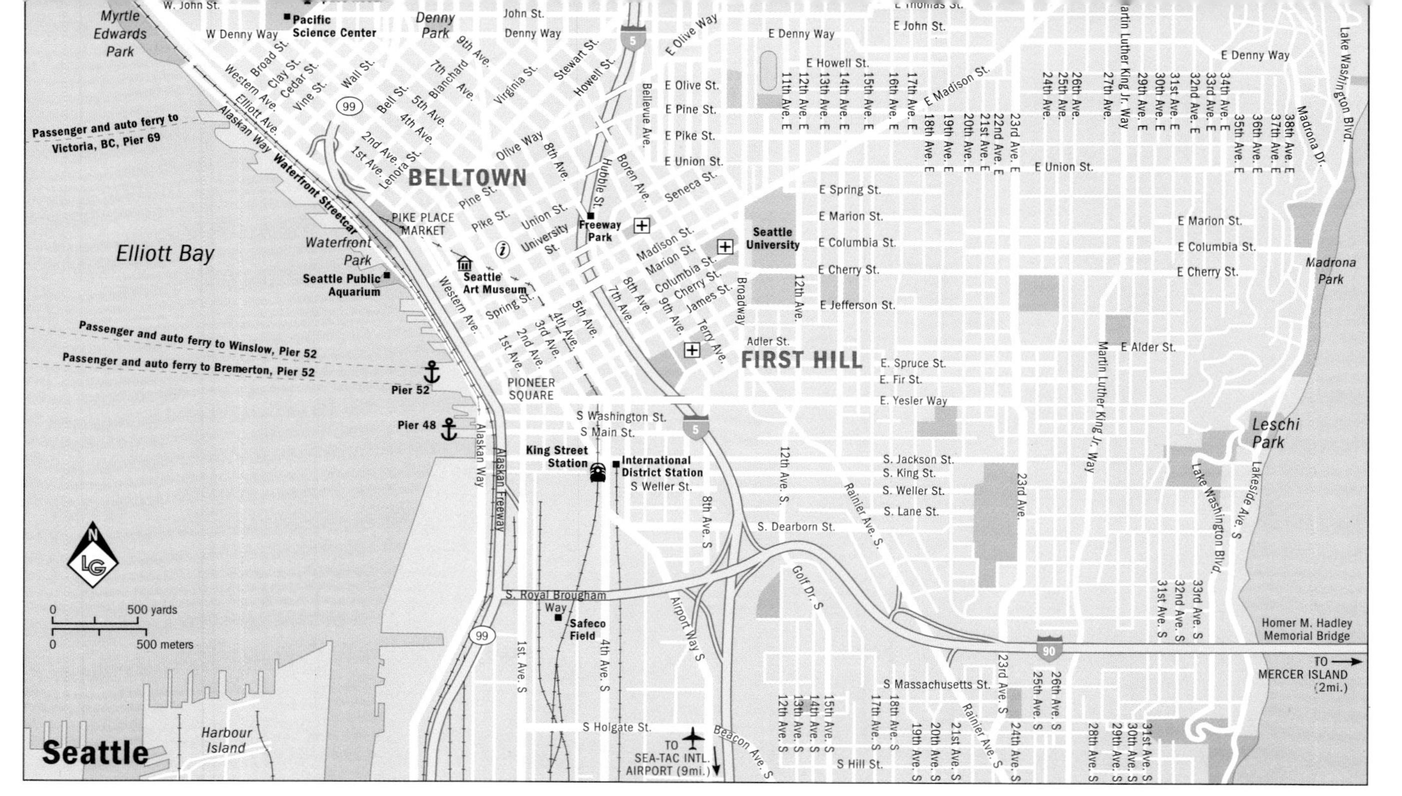
Seattle
BELLTOWN
FIRST HILL
PIONEER SQUARE
Elliott Bay
Myrtle Edwards Park
Denny Park
Waterfront Park
Madrona Park
Leschi Park
Harbour Island
Pacific Science Center
PIKE PLACE MARKET
Seattle Art Museum
Seattle Public Aquarium
Freeway Park
Seattle University
King Street Station
International District Station
Safeco Field
Pier 52
Pier 48
Passenger and auto ferry to Victoria, BC, Pier 69
Passenger and auto ferry to Winslow, Pier 52
Passenger and auto ferry to Bremerton, Pier 52
Homer M. Hadley Memorial Bridge
TO MERCER ISLAND (2mi.)
TO SEA-TAC INTL. AIRPORT (9mi.)
0 500 yards
0 500 meters
Alaskan Way
Alaskan Freeway
Waterfront Streetcar
Western Ave.
Elliott Ave.
Lake Washington Blvd.
Lakeside Ave. S
Madrona Dr.
Martin Luther King Jr. Way
Rainier Ave. S
Airport Way S
Golf Dr. S
Beacon Ave. S
S. Royal Brougham Way
Broadway
E Madison St.
E Denny Way
E Olive Way
E Union St.
S Massachusetts St.
S Holgate St.
S Hill St.

Portland
Bus Route
Streetcar
MAX
Fareless Square
Union Station (Amtrak)
Greyhound Station
Chinese Classical Garden
Old Town
Portland Saturday Market
Skidmore Fountain
CHINATOWN
Powell's Book Store
U.S. Outdoor Store
Transit Mall
PIONEER COURTHOUSE SQUARE
Library
Galleria
Mall
Morrison
Yamhill Dist.
Oak
Portland Art Museum
Portland Building
City Hall
Portland State University
Civic Stadium
PGE Park
King's Hill
Goose Hollow
TO WASHINGTON PARK ZOO (.7mi.)
Rose Garden Arena
Rose Quarter TC
Convention Center
Oregon Convention Center
Lloyd Center
Willamette River
Steel Bridge
Burnside Bridge
Morrison Bridge
Hawthorne Bridge
TO OREGON MUSEUM OF SCIENCE AND INDUSTRY (50yd.)
TO REED COLLEGE (2mi.)
TO (2mi.)
NW Lovejoy St.
NW Kearney St.
NW Johnson St.
NW Irving St.
NW Hoyt St.
NW Glisan St.
NW Flanders St.
NW Everett St.
NW Davis St.
NW Couch St.
W Burnside St.
NW 23rd Ave.
NW 22nd Ave.
NW 21st Ave.
NW 20th Ave.
NW 19th Ave.
NW 18th Ave.
NW 17th Ave.
NW 16th Ave.
NW 15th Ave.
NW 14th Ave.
NW 13th Ave.
NW 12th Ave.
NW 11th Ave.
NW 10th Ave.
NW 9th Ave.
NW Park Ave.
NW 8th Ave.
NW Broadway Ave.
NW 6th Ave.
NW 5th Ave.
NW 4th Ave.
NW 3rd Ave.
NW 2nd Ave.
NW 1st Ave.
NW Front Ave. (Naito Pkwy.)
Couch Park
SW Ankeny St.
SW Pine St.
SW Oak St.
SW Stark St.
SW Washington St.
SW Alder St.
SW Morrison St.
SW Yamhill St.
SW Main St.
SW Taylor St.
SW Salmon St.
SW Jefferson St.
SW Madison St.
SW Columbia St.
SW Clay St.
SW Market St.
SW Mill St.
SW Montgomery St.
SW 23rd Ave.
SW 22nd Ave.
SW 21st Ave.
SW 17th Ave.
SW 16th Ave.
SW 15 th Ave.
SW 14th Ave.
SW 13th Ave.
SW 12th Ave.
SW 11th Ave.
SW 10th Ave.
SW 9th Ave.
SW Park Ave.
SW Broadway
SW 6th Ave.
SW 5th Ave.
SW 4th Ave.
SW 3rd Ave.
SW 2nd Ave.
SW 1st Ave.
SW Front Ave. (Naito Pkwy.)
NE Multnomah St.
NE Hassalo St.
NE Holladay St.
NE 7th Ave.
NE Oregon St.
NE Irving St.
Lloyd Blvd.
NE Glisan St.
NE Flanders St
NE Everett St.
NE Davis St.
NE Couch St.
E Burnside St.
SE Ankeny St.
SE Ash St.
SE Pine St.
SE Oak St.
SE Stark St.
SE Washington St.
SE Alder St.
SE Morrison St.
SE Belmont St.
SE Yamhill St.
SE Taylor St.
SE Salmon St.
SE Main St.
SE Madison St.
SE Hawthorne Blvd.
SE Sandy Blvd
SE 1st Ave.
SE 2nd Ave.
SE 3rd Ave.
SE Martin Luther King Jr. Blvd.
SE Grand Ave.
SE 6th Ave.
SE 7th Ave.
SE 8th Ave.
SE 9th Ave.
SE 10th Ave.
SE 11th Ave.
12th Ave. SE
SE 13th Ave.
SE 14th Ave.
SE 15th Ave.
SE 16th Ave.
SE 17th Ave.
SE 18th Ave.
SE 19th Ave.
20th Ave.
Water Ave.
99E
5
84
30
405
26
N
LG
0
500 yards
500 meters

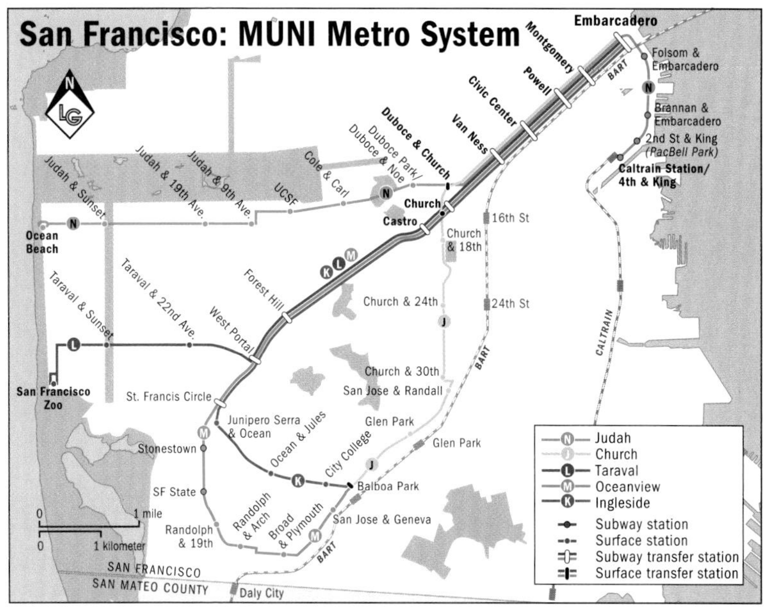

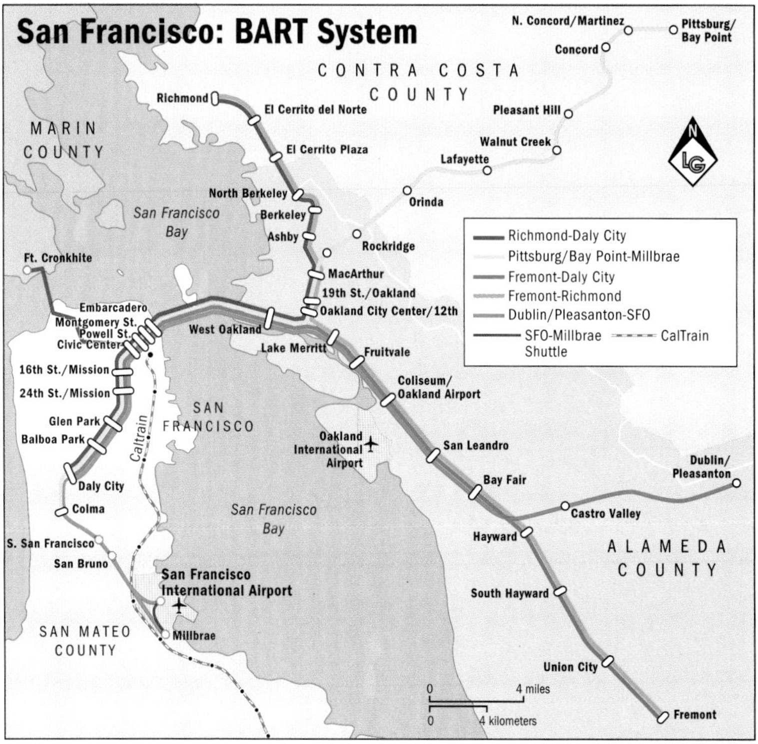

San Francisco: MUNI Metro System
Embarcadero
Montgomery
Powell
Civic Center
Van Ness
Duboce & Church
Duboce Park/
Duboce & Noe
Cole & Carl
UCSF
Judah & 9th Ave.
Judah & 19th Ave.
Judah & Sunset
Ocean Beach
Church
Castro
Church & 18th
16th St
24th St
Church & 24th
Forest Hill
West Portal
Taraval & 22nd Ave.
Taraval & Sunset
San Francisco Zoo
St. Francis Circle
Church & 30th
San Jose & Randall
Glen Park
Junipero Serra & Ocean
Ocean & Jules
City College
Stonestown
SF State
Balboa Park
Randolph & 19th
Randolph & Arch
Broad & Plymouth
San Jose & Geneva
Daly City
SAN FRANCISCO
SAN MATEO COUNTY
Folsom & Embarcadero
Brannan & Embarcadero
2nd St & King (PacBell Park)
Caltrain Station/ 4th & King
BART
CALTRAIN
0 1 mile
0 1 kilometer
Judah
Church
Taraval
Oceanview
Ingleside
Subway station
Surface station
Subway transfer station
Surface transfer station
San Francisco: BART System
CONTRA COSTA COUNTY
MARIN COUNTY
SAN FRANCISCO
SAN MATEO COUNTY
ALAMEDA COUNTY
San Francisco Bay
N. Concord/Martinez
Pittsburg/Bay Point
Concord
Pleasant Hill
Walnut Creek
Lafayette
Orinda
Rockridge
Richmond
El Cerrito del Norte
El Cerrito Plaza
North Berkeley
Berkeley
Ashby
MacArthur
19th St./Oakland
Oakland City Center/12th
West Oakland
Lake Merritt
Fruitvale
Coliseum/ Oakland Airport
Oakland International Airport
San Leandro
Bay Fair
Hayward
South Hayward
Union City
Fremont
Castro Valley
Dublin/ Pleasanton
Ft. Cronkhite
Embarcadero
Montgomery St.
Powell St.
Civic Center
16th St./Mission
24th St./Mission
Glen Park
Balboa Park
Daly City
Colma
S. San Francisco
San Bruno
San Francisco International Airport
Millbrae
Caltrain
Richmond-Daly City
Pittsburg/Bay Point-Millbrae
Fremont-Daly City
Fremont-Richmond
Dublin/Pleasanton-SFO
SFO-Millbrae Shuttle
CalTrain
0 4 miles
0 4 kilometers

San Francisco Transportation

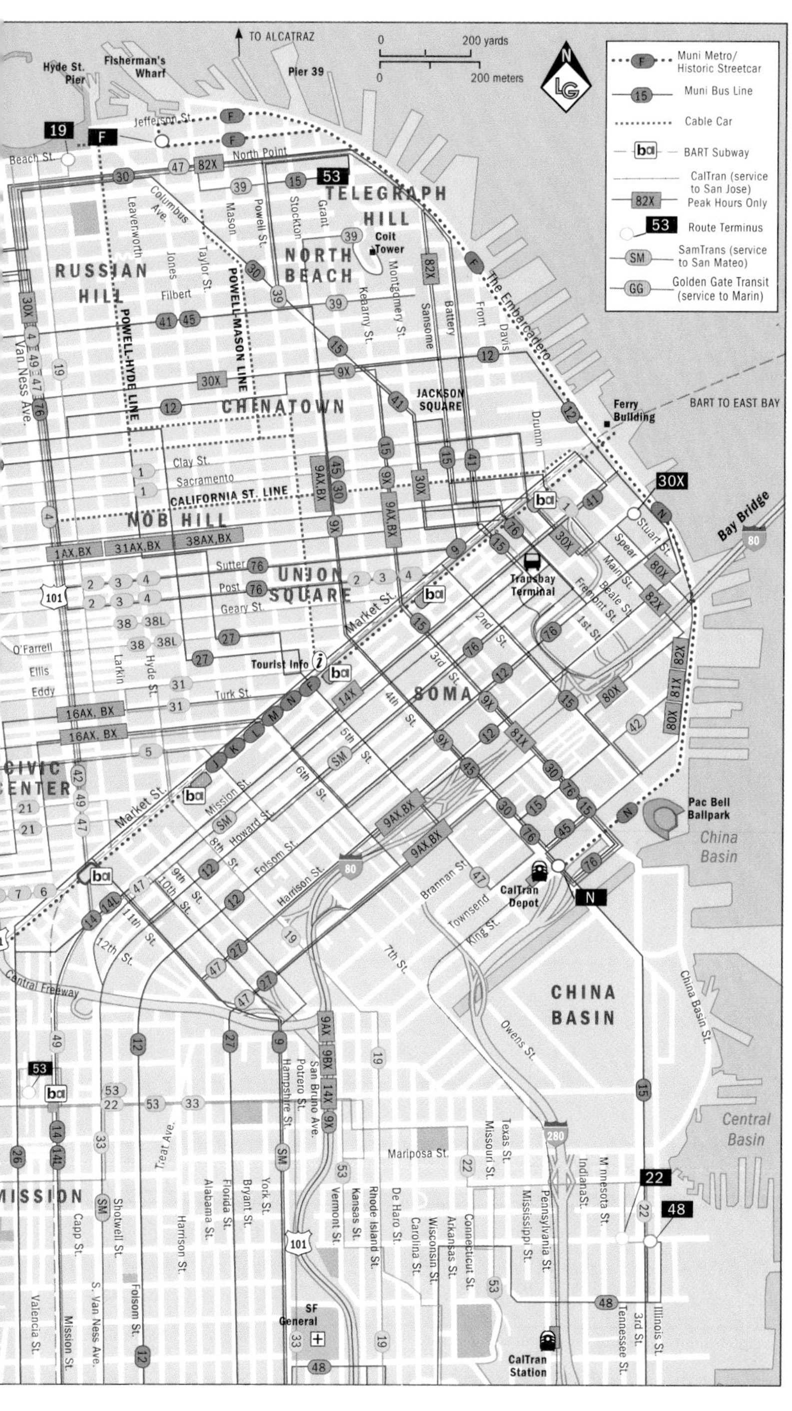

TO ALCATRAZ
0 200 yards
0 200 meters
Muni Metro/ Historic Streetcar
Muni Bus Line
Cable Car
BART Subway
CalTran (service to San Jose)
Peak Hours Only
Route Terminus
SamTrans (service to San Mateo)
Golden Gate Transit (service to Marin)
Hyde St. Pier
Fisherman's Wharf
Pier 39
TELEGRAPH HILL
Coit Tower
RUSSIAN HILL
NORTH BEACH
POWELL-HYDE LINE
POWELL-MASON LINE
CHINATOWN
JACKSON SQUARE
Ferry Building
BART TO EAST BAY
CALIFORNIA ST. LINE
NOB HILL
UNION SQUARE
Transbay Terminal
Bay Bridge
Tourist Info
SOMA
CIVIC CENTER
Pac Bell Ballpark
China Basin
CalTran Depot
CHINA BASIN
Central Freeway
Central Basin
MISSION
SF General
CalTran Station
The Embarcadero
Market St.
Van Ness Ave.

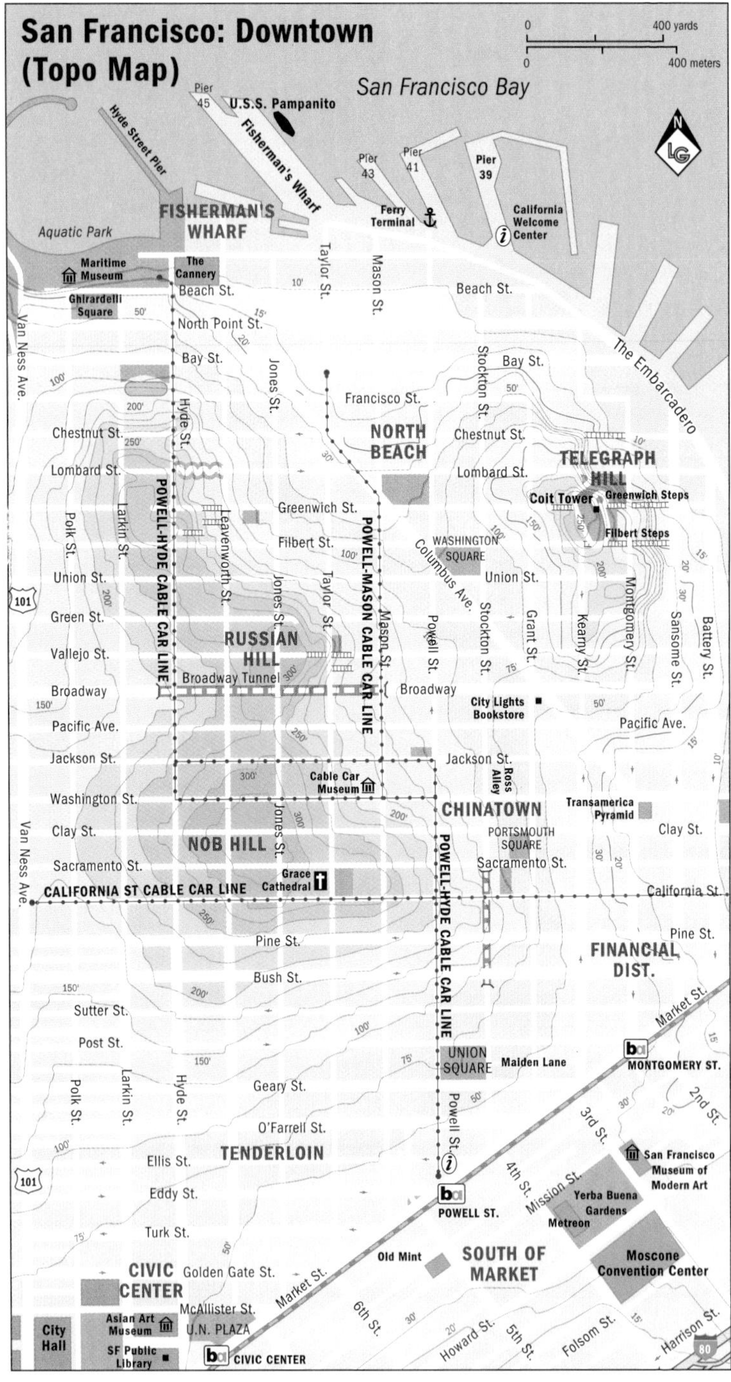
San Francisco: Downtown (Topo Map)
San Francisco Bay
Fisherman's Wharf
North Beach
Telegraph Hill
Russian Hill
Nob Hill
Chinatown
Financial Dist.
Union Square
Tenderloin
Civic Center
South of Market
Aquatic Park
Maritime Museum
The Cannery
Ghirardelli Square
U.S.S. Pampanito
Hyde Street Pier
Ferry Terminal
California Welcome Center
Pier 45
Pier 43
Pier 41
Pier 39
The Embarcadero
Coit Tower
Greenwich Steps
Filbert Steps
Washington Square
City Lights Bookstore
Ross Alley
Transamerica Pyramid
Portsmouth Square
Cable Car Museum
Grace Cathedral
Broadway Tunnel
Powell-Hyde Cable Car Line
Powell-Mason Cable Car Line
California St Cable Car Line
Maiden Lane
Montgomery St.
Powell St.
Civic Center
San Francisco Museum of Modern Art
Yerba Buena Gardens
Metreon
Moscone Convention Center
Old Mint
City Hall
Asian Art Museum
SF Public Library
U.N. Plaza
Van Ness Ave.
Polk St.
Larkin St.
Hyde St.
Leavenworth St.
Jones St.
Taylor St.
Mason St.
Powell St.
Stockton St.
Grant St.
Kearny St.
Montgomery St.
Sansome St.
Battery St.
Columbus Ave.
Beach St.
North Point St.
Bay St.
Francisco St.
Chestnut St.
Lombard St.
Greenwich St.
Filbert St.
Union St.
Green St.
Vallejo St.
Broadway
Pacific Ave.
Jackson St.
Washington St.
Clay St.
Sacramento St.
California St.
Pine St.
Bush St.
Sutter St.
Post St.
Geary St.
O'Farrell St.
Ellis St.
Eddy St.
Turk St.
Golden Gate St.
McAllister St.
Market St.
Mission St.
Howard St.
Folsom St.
Harrison St.
2nd St.
3rd St.
4th St.
5th St.
6th St.
101
80
0 400 yards
0 400 meters

Boston MBTA
Oak Grove
Malden
Wellington
Sullivan Square
Community College
North Station
Haymarket
State*
Downtown Crossing
Chinatown
NE Medical Center
Alewife
Davis
Porter
Harvard
Central
Kendall/MIT
Charles/MGH
Park St
South Station
Broadway
Andrew
JFK/UMass
Savin Hill
Fields Corner
Shawmut
Ashmont
Cedar Grove
Butler
Milton
Central Ave
Valley Rd
Capen St
Mattapan
North Quincy
Wollaston
Quincy Center
Quincy Adams
Braintree
Wonderland
Revere Beach
Beachmont
Suffolk Downs
Orient Heights
Wood Island
Airport
Maverick
Aquarium
Gov't Center
Bowdoin
Logan International Airport
Lechmere
Science Park
Arlington
Boylston
Copley
Hynes/ICA
Kenmore
Fenway
Longwood
Brookline Village
Brookline Hills
Beaconsfield
Reservoir
Chestnut Hill
Newton Centre
Newton Highlands
Eliot
Waban
Woodland
Riverside
Cleveland Circle
Boston College
Prudential
Symphony
Back Bay
Mass Ave
Ruggles
Roxbury Crossing
Jackson Sq
Stony Brook
Green St
Forest Hills
Heath
Museum of Fine Arts
Brigham Circle
E. Berkeley St
Melnea Cass Blvd
Dudley Sq
To Quincy & Hull
To Hingham
LEGEND
Transit lines & stop
Commuter rail & station
Terminal station
Free interchange with other lines
Accessible Station
Parking
*Chinatown: Accessible July 2002
*State: Not accessible for Blue line inbound.
Boston Harbor Ferry Services
1 Lovejoy Wharf to Charlestown Navy Yard
2 Lovejoy Wharf to U.S. Courthouse to World Trade Center
3 Long Wharf to Charlestown Navy Yard
4 Hingham Ship Yard to Rowes Wharf, Boston
5 Quincy Shipyard and Pemberton Point, Hull to Long Wharf, Boston
For schedule & fare information, call (617) 222-3200 or visit our website at www.mbta.com
© MBTA 2002

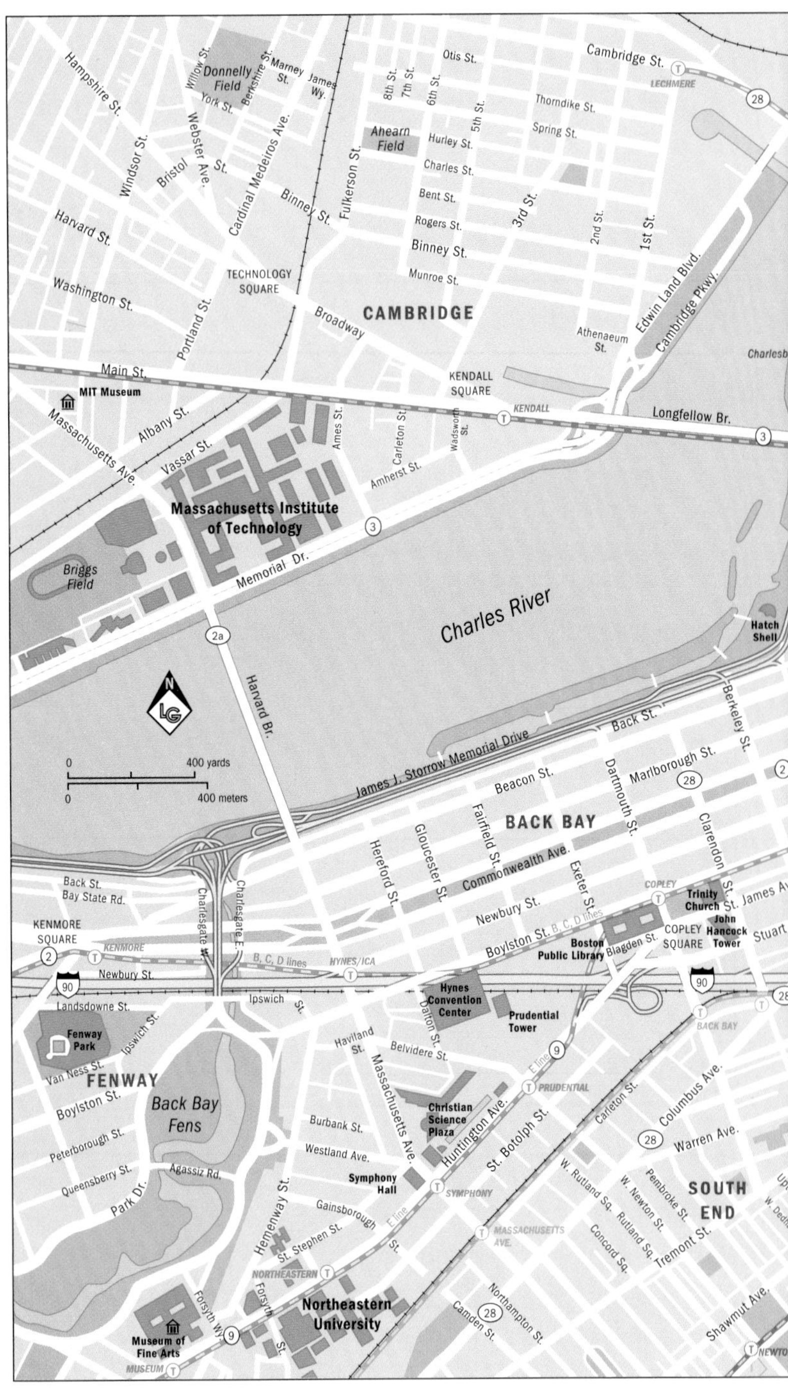

Hampshire St.
Donnelly Field
Willow St.
Berkshire St.
Marney St.
James Wy.
York St.
Otis St.
Cambridge St.
LECHMERE
8th St.
7th St.
6th St.
5th St.
Thorndike St.
Spring St.
Ahearn Field
Hurley St.
Charles St.
Bent St.
Rogers St.
Binney St.
Munroe St.
Windsor St.
Bristol St.
Webster Ave.
Cardinal Medeiros Ave.
Binney St.
Fulkerson St.
3rd St.
2nd St.
1st St.
Harvard St.
Washington St.
TECHNOLOGY SQUARE
Portland St.
Broadway
CAMBRIDGE
Edwin Land Blvd.
Cambridge Pkwy.
Athenaeum St.
Main St.
KENDALL SQUARE
MIT Museum
KENDALL
Longfellow Br.
Massachusetts Ave.
Albany St.
Vassar St.
Ames St.
Carleton St.
Wadsworth St.
Amherst St.
Massachusetts Institute of Technology
Memorial Dr.
Briggs Field
Charles River
Hatch Shell
Harvard Br.
0
400 yards
400 meters
James J. Storrow Memorial Drive
Back St.
Berkeley St.
Beacon St.
Dartmouth St.
Marlborough St.
BACK BAY
Fairfield St.
Gloucester St.
Hereford St.
Clarendon St.
Commonwealth Ave.
Exeter St.
Back St.
Bay State Rd.
Charlesgate W.
Charlesgate E.
COPLEY
Trinity Church
St. James Ave.
Newbury St.
John Hancock Tower
KENMORE SQUARE
KENMORE
Boylston St.
B, C, D lines
Boston Public Library
Blagden St.
COPLEY SQUARE
Stuart St.
HYNES/ICA
Newbury St.
Landsdowne St.
Ipswich St.
Hynes Convention Center
Dalton St.
Prudential Tower
Fenway Park
Ipswich St.
Van Ness St.
FENWAY
Haviland St.
Belvidere St.
BACK BAY
E line
PRUDENTIAL
Massachusetts Ave.
Christian Science Plaza
Huntington Ave.
Boylston St.
Back Bay Fens
Burbank St.
Westland Ave.
St. Botolph St.
Carleton St.
Columbus Ave.
Warren Ave.
Peterborough St.
Queensberry St.
Agassiz Rd.
Park Dr.
Symphony Hall
SYMPHONY
W. Rutland Sq.
W. Newton St.
Pembroke St.
SOUTH END
Upton
W. Dedham
Hemenway St.
Gainsborough St.
MASSACHUSETTS AVE.
Rutland Sq.
Concord Sq.
Tremont St.
St. Stephen St.
NORTHEASTERN
Forsyth St.
Forsyth Wy.
Northeastern University
Northampton St.
Camden St.
Shawmut Ave.
Museum of Fine Arts
MUSEUM
NEWTON

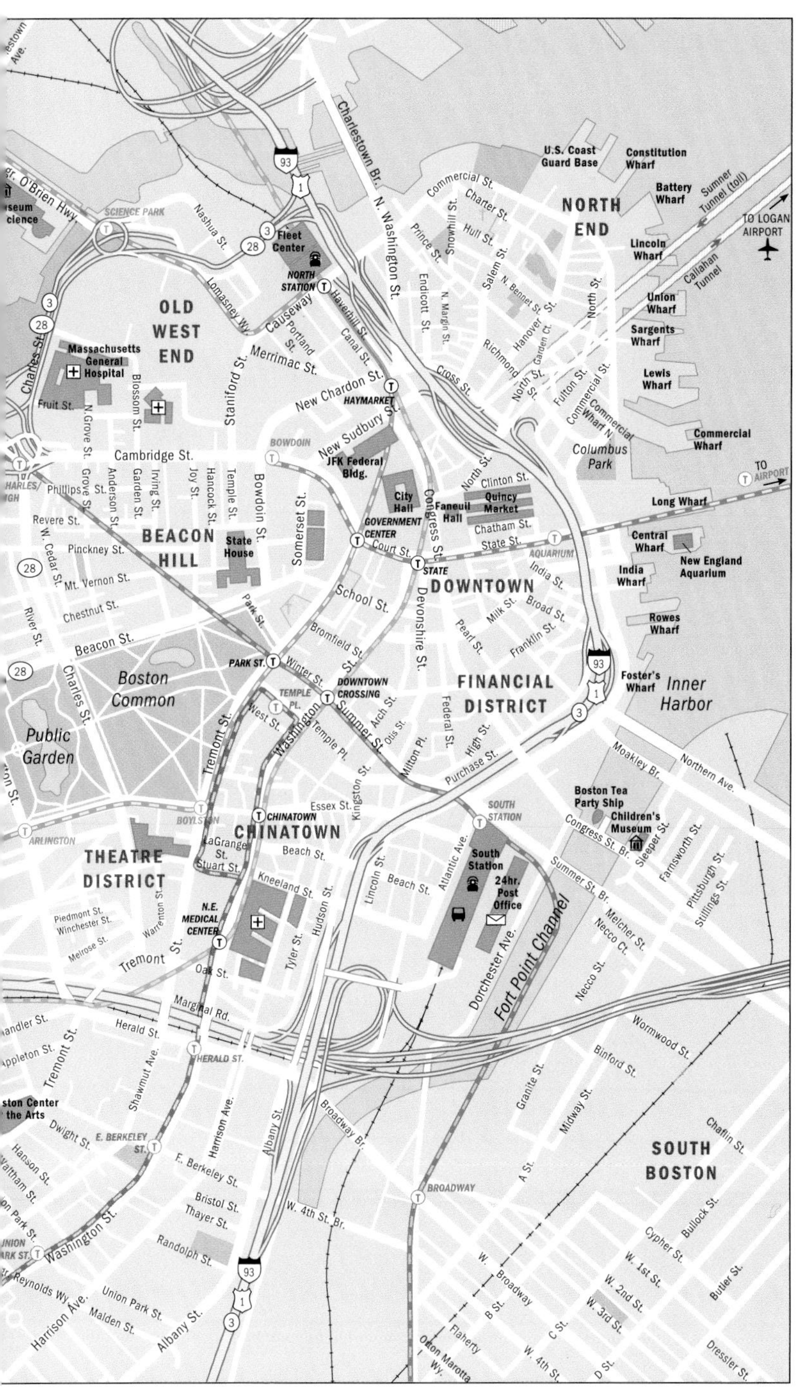

NORTH END
OLD WEST END
BEACON HILL
DOWNTOWN
FINANCIAL DISTRICT
CHINATOWN
THEATRE DISTRICT
SOUTH BOSTON
U.S. Coast Guard Base
Constitution Wharf
Battery Wharf
Lincoln Wharf
Union Wharf
Sargents Wharf
Lewis Wharf
Commercial Wharf
Long Wharf
Central Wharf
India Wharf
Rowes Wharf
Foster's Wharf
New England Aquarium
Inner Harbor
Sumner Tunnel (toll)
Callahan Tunnel
TO LOGAN AIRPORT
TO AIRPORT
Fleet Center
NORTH STATION
SCIENCE PARK
Massachusetts General Hospital
HAYMARKET
BOWDOIN
JFK Federal Bldg.
City Hall
GOVERNMENT CENTER
Faneuil Hall
Quincy Market
STATE
AQUARIUM
State House
PARK ST.
DOWNTOWN CROSSING
TEMPLE PL.
Boston Common
Public Garden
BOYLSTON
ARLINGTON
CHINATOWN
N.E. MEDICAL CENTER
SOUTH STATION
South Station
24hr. Post Office
Boston Tea Party Ship
Children's Museum
Fort Point Channel
Columbus Park
HERALD ST.
E. BERKELEY ST.
BROADWAY
Charlestown Br.
N. Washington St.
Commercial St.
Charter St.
Hull St.
Prince St.
Snowhill St.
Salem St.
N. Bennet St.
Endicott St.
N. Margin St.
Hanover St.
North St.
Garden Ct.
Richmond St.
Fulton St.
Commercial St.
Cross St.
Nashua St.
Lomasney Wy.
Causeway St.
Portland St.
Canal St.
Haverhill St.
Merrimac St.
Staniford St.
New Chardon St.
New Sudbury St.
Cambridge St.
Blossom St.
Fruit St.
N.Grove St.
Charles St.
Phillips St.
Grove St.
Anderson St.
Garden St.
Irving St.
Joy St.
Hancock St.
Temple St.
Bowdoin St.
Somerset St.
Revere St.
W. Cedar St.
Pinckney St.
Mt. Vernon St.
Chestnut St.
River St.
Beacon St.
Park St.
Court St.
Congress St.
North St.
Clinton St.
Chatham St.
State St.
India St.
Broad St.
Milk St.
Pearl St.
Franklin St.
School St.
Bromfield St.
Devonshire St.
Winter St.
Washington St.
West St.
Tremont St.
Temple Pl.
Summer St.
Arch St.
Otis St.
Milton Pl.
Federal St.
High St.
Purchase St.
Kingston St.
Essex St.
Beach St.
LaGrange St.
Stuart St.
Kneeland St.
Hudson St.
Lincoln St.
Atlantic Ave.
Piedmont St.
Winchester St.
Melrose St.
Warrenton St.
Tremont St.
Oak St.
Tyler St.
Marginal Rd.
Herald St.
Chandler St.
Appleton St.
Shawmut Ave.
Harrison Ave.
Albany St.
Broadway Br.
Dwight St.
Hanson St.
Waltham St.
E. Berkeley St.
Bristol St.
Thayer St.
Randolph St.
W. 4th St. Br.
Washington St.
Reynolds Wy.
Union Park St.
Malden St.
Harrison Ave.
Albany St.
Dorchester Ave.
Moakley Br.
Northern Ave.
Congress St. Br.
Sleeper St.
Farnsworth St.
Pittsburgh St.
Stillings St.
Summer St. Br.
Melcher St.
Necco Ct.
Necco St.
Wormwood St.
Binford St.
Granite St.
Midway St.
A St.
Chaffin St.
Bullock St.
Cypher St.
W. 1st St.
W. 2nd St.
W. 3rd St.
Butler St.
W. Broadway
B St.
C St.
W. 4th St.
D St.
Dressler St.
Flaherty Wy.
Otton Marotta Wy.
93
1
3
28

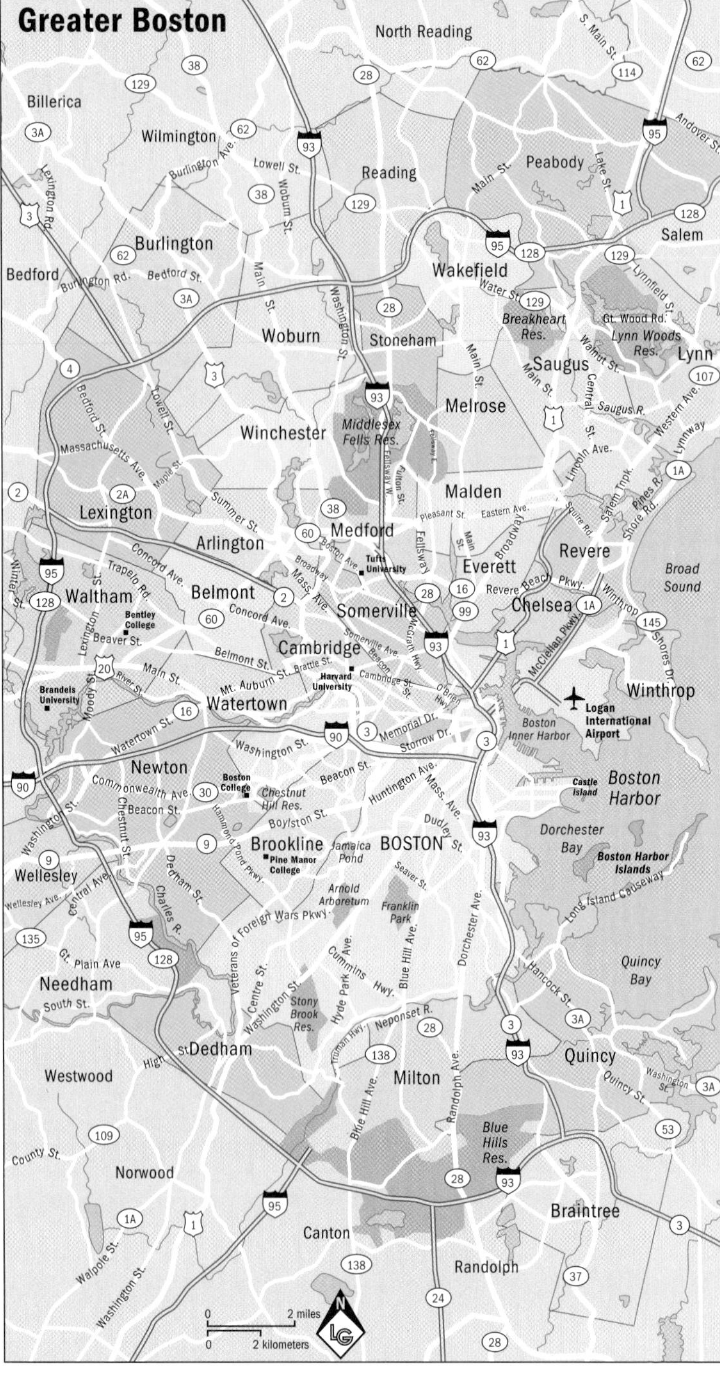
Greater Boston
North Reading
Billerica
Wilmington
Reading
Peabody
Salem
Burlington
Bedford
Wakefield
Woburn
Stoneham
Saugus
Lynn
Melrose
Winchester
Malden
Lexington
Medford
Arlington
Revere
Everett
Waltham
Belmont
Somerville
Chelsea
Cambridge
Winthrop
Watertown
Logan International Airport
Newton
Boston Harbor
Brookline
BOSTON
Wellesley
Needham
Dedham
Westwood
Milton
Quincy
Norwood
Canton
Braintree
Randolph
Broad Sound
Dorchester Bay
Quincy Bay
Boston Harbor Islands
Boston Inner Harbor
Castle Island
Middlesex Fells Res.
Breakheart Res.
Lynn Woods Res.
Chestnut Hill Res.
Jamaica Pond
Arnold Arboretum
Franklin Park
Stony Brook Res.
Blue Hills Res.
Tufts University
Bentley College
Brandeis University
Harvard University
Boston College
Pine Manor College
0 2 miles
0 2 kilometers

■ THE RESOURCE FOR THE INDEPENDENT TRAVELER

"The guides are aimed not only at young budget travelers but at the indepedent traveler; a sort of streetwise cookbook for traveling alone."

—The New York Times

"Unbeatable; good sight-seeing advice; up-to-date info on restaurants, hotels, and inns; a commitment to money-saving travel; and a wry style that brightens nearly every page."

—The Washington Post

"Lighthearted and sophisticated, informative and fun to read. [Let's Go] helps the novice traveler navigate like a knowledgeable old hand."

—Atlanta Journal-Constitution

"A world-wise traveling companion—always ready with friendly advice and helpful hints, all sprinkled with a bit of wit."

—The Philadelphia Inquirer

■ THE BEST TRAVEL BARGAINS IN YOUR PRICE RANGE

"All the dirt, dirt cheap."

—People

"Anything you need to know about budget traveling is detailed in this book."

—The Chicago Sun-Times

"Let's Go follows the creed that you don't have to toss your life's savings to the wind to travel—unless you want to."

—The Salt Lake Tribune

■ REAL ADVICE FOR REAL EXPERIENCES

"The writers seem to have experienced every rooster-packed bus and lunar-surfaced mattress about which they write."

—The New York Times

"A guide should tell you what to expect from a destination. Here Let's Go shines."

—The Chicago Tribune

"[Let's Go's] devoted updaters really walk the walk (and thumb the ride, and trek the trail). Learn how to fish, haggle, find work—anywhere."

—Food & Wine

LET'S GO PUBLICATIONS

TRAVEL GUIDES

Alaska 1st edition **NEW TITLE**
Australia 2004
Austria & Switzerland 2004
Brazil 1st edition **NEW TITLE**
Britain & Ireland 2004
California 2004
Central America 8th edition
Chile 1st edition
China 4th edition
Costa Rica 1st edition
Eastern Europe 2004
Egypt 2nd edition
Europe 2004
France 2004
Germany 2004
Greece 2004
Hawaii 2004
India & Nepal 8th edition
Ireland 2004
Israel 4th edition
Italy 2004
Japan 1st edition **NEW TITLE**
Mexico 20th edition
Middle East 4th edition
New Zealand 6th edition
Pacific Northwest 1st edition **NEW TITLE**
Peru, Ecuador & Bolivia 3rd edition
Puerto Rico 1st edition **NEW TITLE**
South Africa 5th edition
Southeast Asia 8th edition
Southwest USA 3rd edition
Spain & Portugal 2004
Thailand 1st edition
Turkey 5th edition
USA 2004
Western Europe 2004

CITY GUIDES

Amsterdam 3rd edition
Barcelona 3rd edition
Boston 4th edition
London 2004
New York City 2004
Paris 2004
Rome 12th edition
San Francisco 4th edition
Washington, D.C. 13th edition

MAP GUIDES

Amsterdam
Berlin
Boston
Chicago
Dublin
Florence
Hong Kong
London
Los Angeles
Madrid
New Orleans
New York City
Paris
Prague
Rome
San Francisco
Seattle
Sydney
Venice
Washington, D.C.

COMING SOON:

Road Trip USA

USA

WITH COVERAGE OF CANADA

2004

Jeremy Todd Editor
Kristin Kitchen Associate Editor
Erin Probst Associate Editor
N. MacDonald Snyder Associate Editor

Researcher-Writers

Ann Brown
Nina Jacobi
Jennifer Jue-Steuck
Neill Sharp Myers
Tom O'Donnell
Seth Robinson
Heather Schofield
Chris Schonberger
Chris Snyder
Jennie Wei

Brian J. Emeott Map Editor
Ariel Fox Managing Editor

Macmillan

HELPING LET'S GO If you want to share your discoveries, suggestions, or corrections, please drop us a line. We read every piece of correspondence, whether a postcard, a 10-page email, or a coconut. **Address mail to:**

Let's Go: USA
67 Mount Auburn Street
Cambridge, MA 02138
USA

Visit Let's Go at **http://www.letsgo.com,** or send email to:

feedback@letsgo.com
Subject: "Let's Go: USA"

In addition to the invaluable travel advice our readers share with us, many are kind enough to offer their services as researchers or editors. Unfortunately, our charter enables us to employ only currently enrolled Harvard students.

Published in Great Britain 2004 by Macmillan, an imprint of Pan Macmillan Ltd.
20 New Wharf Road, London N1 9RR
Basingstoke and Oxford
Associated companies throughout the world
www.panmacmillan.com

Published in the United States of America by St. Martin's Press.

ISBN: 1-4050-3322 3
First edition
10 9 8 7 6 5 4 3 2 1

Let's Go: USA is written by Let's Go Publications, 67 Mount Auburn Street, Cambridge, MA 02138, USA.

ADVERTISING DISCLAIMER All advertisements appearing in Let's Go publications are sold by an independent agency not affiliated with the editorial production of the guides. Advertisers are never given preferential treatment, and the guides are researched, written, and published independent of advertising. Advertisements do not imply endorsement of products or services by Let's Go, and Let's Go does not vouch for the accuracy of information provided in advertisements.

If you are interested in purchasing advertising space in a Let's Go publication, contact: Let's Go Advertising Sales, 67 Mount Auburn St., Cambridge, MA 02138, USA.

HOW TO USE THIS BOOK

ORGANIZATION. Welcome to *Let's Go USA 2004!* This book will walk you (and probably ride with you) state by state and province by province through the USA and Canada, starting on the east coast and heading west. The black tabs on the side of the book should help you find your way around.

PRICE RANGES AND RANKINGS. Our researchers list establishments in order of value from best to worst. Gay establishments, if they do not have their own section, are listed at the end of each . Our particular favorites are denoted by the Let's Go thumb's up (☒). Since the best value is not always the cheapest price, we have incorporated a system of price ranges for the guide. (p. xiv)

PHONE CODES & TELEPHONE NUMBERS. 3-digit area codes for each region appear opposite the name of the region and are denoted by the ☎ icon. Phone numbers in text are also preceded by the ☎ icon. Ten-digit dialing is noted when necessary.

SPECIAL FEATURES. *Let's Go* veterans might notice unfamiliar features popping up as they move through the book. This year USA has two unique sidebars:

Your Own Way - This feature tries to get at Americana in a way our other coverage can't. Through these you'll hear about Carhenge in Nebraska, the world's tackiest (and possibly best) roadside stand, and other choice Americana that may not be on the typical itinerary.

The Great Outdoors - A spotlight on America's ever-vanishing frontier—these articles will take you back to nature with the some of the best hiking, sight-seeing, and sun-catching the continent has to offer.

WHEN TO USE IT

TWO MONTHS BEFORE. The first chapter, **Discover** the United States and Canada, contains some of the best America has to offer travelers, as well as Suggested Itineraries that can help you plan your trip. The **Essentials** section contains practical information on planning a budget, making reservations, and renewing a passport, and has other useful tips about traveling in the US and Canada.

ONE MONTH BEFORE. Take care of insurance, and write down a list of emergency numbers. Read through our coveage and be sure you understand the transportation requirements of your itinerary. Make any reservations if necessary; many campsites fill up very quickly, as do hostels and hotels during special events.

TWO WEEKS BEFORE. Leave an itinerary and a photocopy of important documents with someone at home. Take some time to peruse the **Life and Times** (p. 9) section, which has info on history, culture, and recent political events.

ON THE ROAD. With a wide variety of informative and entertaining **Features** scattered throughout the guide, **Roadtrip** suggestions, a **Scholarly Article** on regional American dialects, and the inside scoop on the best values and tricks of the traveler, we aim to give you the most comprehensive, up-to-date take on the USA and Canada possible. Hit the road with us, and prepare for the ride of your life.

A NOTE TO OUR READERS The information for this book was gathered by *Let's Go* researchers from May through August of 2003. Each listing is based on one researcher's opinion, formed during his or her visit at a particular time. Those traveling at other times may have different experiences since prices, dates, hours, and conditions are always subject to change. You are urged to check the facts presented in this book beforehand to avoid inconvenience and surprises.

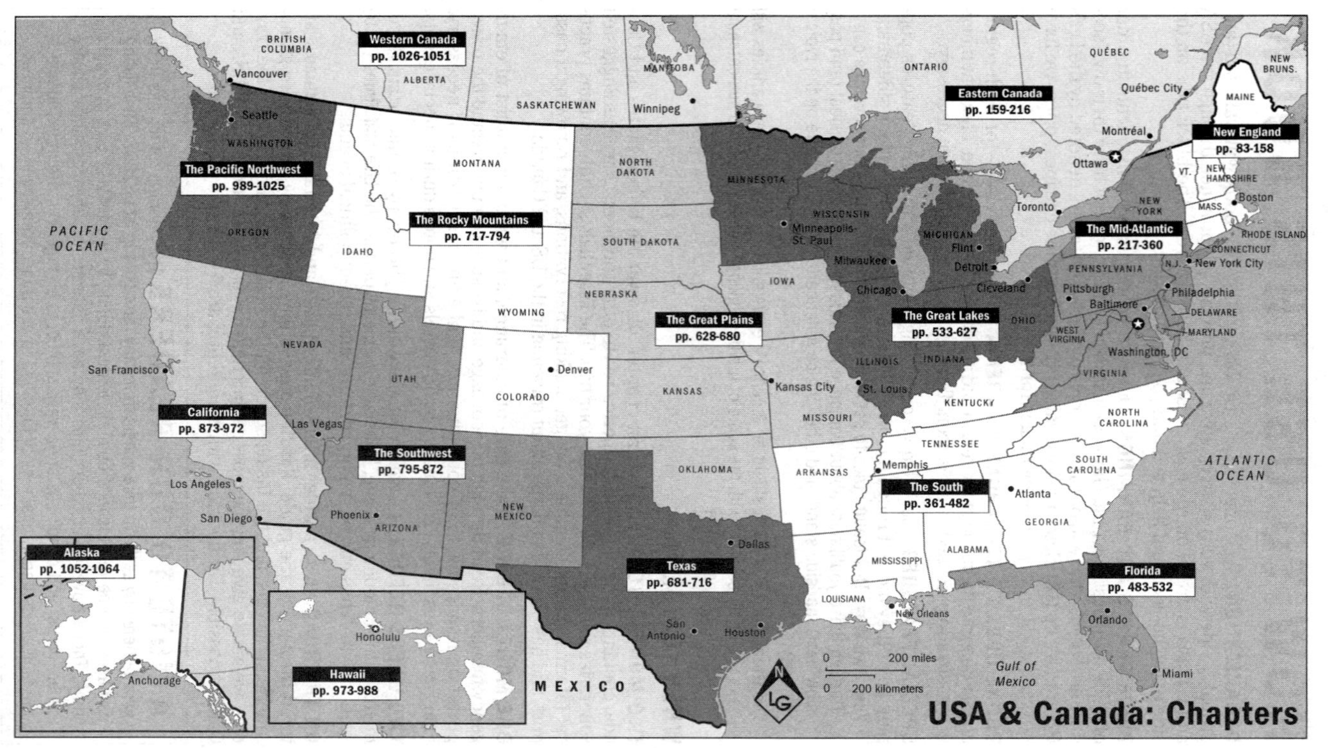
USA & Canada: Chapters
Western Canada
pp. 1026-1051
Eastern Canada
pp. 159-216
New England
pp. 83-158
The Mid-Atlantic
pp. 217-360
The Pacific Northwest
pp. 989-1025
The Rocky Mountains
pp. 717-794
The Great Plains
pp. 628-680
The Great Lakes
pp. 533-627
California
pp. 873-972
The Southwest
pp. 795-872
The South
pp. 361-482
Texas
pp. 681-716
Florida
pp. 483-532
Alaska
pp. 1052-1064
Hawaii
pp. 973-988
BRITISH COLUMBIA
ALBERTA
SASKATCHEWAN
MANITOBA
ONTARIO
QUÉBEC
NEW BRUNS.
Vancouver
Winnipeg
Québec City
Montréal
Ottawa
Toronto
MAINE
VT.
NEW HAMPSHIRE
MASS.
Boston
RHODE ISLAND
CONNECTICUT
NEW YORK
N.J.
New York City
PENNSYLVANIA
Pittsburgh
Philadelphia
Baltimore
DELAWARE
MARYLAND
Washington, DC
WEST VIRGINIA
VIRGINIA
NORTH CAROLINA
SOUTH CAROLINA
GEORGIA
Atlanta
KENTUCKY
TENNESSEE
Memphis
ALABAMA
MISSISSIPPI
LOUISIANA
New Orleans
Orlando
Miami
OHIO
Cleveland
MICHIGAN
Flint
Detroit
INDIANA
ILLINOIS
Chicago
St. Louis
WISCONSIN
Milwaukee
MINNESOTA
Minneapolis-St. Paul
IOWA
MISSOURI
Kansas City
ARKANSAS
OKLAHOMA
KANSAS
NEBRASKA
SOUTH DAKOTA
NORTH DAKOTA
Dallas
San Antonio
Houston
MONTANA
WYOMING
COLORADO
Denver
IDAHO
UTAH
NEVADA
Las Vegas
NEW MEXICO
ARIZONA
Phoenix
WASHINGTON
Seattle
OREGON
San Francisco
Los Angeles
San Diego
PACIFIC OCEAN
ATLANTIC OCEAN
Gulf of Mexico
MEXICO
Honolulu
Anchorage
0 200 miles
0 200 kilometers
N
LG

CONTENTS

RESEARCHER-WRITERS

Ann Brown *Texas, Oklahoma, Kansas*

A native Texan and damn proud of it, Ann Brown poured local knowledge, attention to detail, and an eye for style into her copy, resulting in vastly improved coverage of her little slice of America. Whether tracking down the hottest clubs in Kansas City, basking in Dodge City's gentle warming glow, or talking up a tight-lipped visitors center rep in Austin, Ann expected the best out of her route, and got it.

Nina Jacobi *Upper South*

A former Let's Go Editor, Nina revolutionized the coverage of her home region, discovering classic Americana throughout the South. A long-term Raleigh-Durham resident, she combined local knowledge and extraordinary dedication to uncover the soft underbelly of the North Carolina coast, the Tennessee mountains, and Kentucky's horse country, even discovering a hitherto unknown love of barbecue along the way.

Jennifer Jue-Steuck *Mid-Atlantic*

This researcher was so nice, we credited her twice. A film and gender studies scholar, Jennifer produced copy fit to make any editor weep. After a whirlwind tour of Washington, D.C, she took to the asphalt, traversing the mid-Atlantic in pursuit of hidden deals and budget steals. Whether strapping on her hiking boots in the Shenandoah Valley or going sophisticated in Philly's art museums, Jennifer proved herself an upbeat and indefatigable researcher.

Neill Sharp Myers *Deep South*

A true southerner, Neill's sense of all things authentic made her perfect for revamping our coverage of Dixie. As she charmed her way across the south, this Bowling Green, KY native befriended the most colorful of characters and uncovered the region's hidden gems. Tenacious and driven, Neill weathered hurricanes and head-colds alike, allowing nothing to come between her and the pursuit of perfect coverage.

Tom O'Donnell *Great Plains, Minnesota*

A veteran Let's Go researcher, Tom easily moved from one Central America to another. He swiftly covered his route while attempting to disguise both his Connecticut origins and love for John Deere tractors. With his down-to-earth, laid-back approach, Tom won over the hearts of old ladies at visitors centers everywhere. He juggled friendly folk and copious copy with ease, finding time to sip coffee in all the cafes between St. Paul and Omaha.

Seth Robinson *Florida, Georgia, South Carolina*

An L.A. native and history buff, Seth brought a trendlicious attitude and a reverent appreciation to our Southern coverage. He braved near muggings, Yogi the cockroach, a heinous sunburn, and Confederate flags, but never lost his energy, enthusiasm, or penchant for wacky analogies. From sampling Krispy Kreme in Atlanta to unleashing his wilderness self in the Everglades, Seth discovered the magic in the South and brought it to our text—fo' sho'.

Heather Schofield *New England*

A champion rower and outdoor enthusiast, Heather discovered a new side of New England. From the lush White Mountains to tranquil Acadia, she found fantastic wilderness and gourmet pizza wherever she went,. Tracking down both the Ironmen of Lake Placid, NY and the Old Man of Franconia Notch, NH, Heather effortlessly provided her editors with tremendously detailed coverage of the Northeast.

Chris Schonberger *Great Lakes*

In the course of tracking down Larry Bird memorabilia, this Connecticut native discovered a new home in the Midwest. Throughout the college towns and industrial cities, Chris burned the candle at both ends, combining long days researching with nights out on the town. From the waterslides of the Wisconsin Dells to the nightlife of Ann Arbor, MI, Chris brought out the wild side of America's Great Lakes.

Jennie Wei *The Rockies*

We're not sure whether Jennie was more charmed by the Rockies or the Rockies were more charmed by her. In either case, the affection was mutual, as Jennie's notes from the front more than made clear. From a cold reception on Pike's Peak to a hot-and-bothered Glacier National Park, Jennie proved that she could brave whatever Nature threw at her, and come out of it with magnificent research and stories to make those of us trapped in the office tremendously jealous.

Chris Snyder *Eastern Canada*

In a sordid triangle, Chris fell in love with Canada, and we fell in love with Chris. (It remains to be seen whether Canada loves us.) Taking time out of his busy crew schedule, Chris marched across Eastern Canada invigorating, expanding, and reorganizing his coverage with gusto. While the beauty of the majestic Canadian wilderness dazzled this outdoors enthusiast, his editors were dazzled by Chris' perfect prose.

REGIONAL RESEARCHER-WRITERS

Sheila Baynes, Eric Brown, Noam Katz, Mark Kirby, Jason Unger *Alaska and the Yukon*

Kristin Hoelting, Lucas Laursen, Brendan J. Reed, Taylor Terry, Bryden Sweeney Taylor *Southwest USA*

Jay Gierak, Kristin McCloskey, Aaron Rudenstine, Andrew Price *California*

Dave Dodman, Jennifer Jue-Steuck, Bradley Olson *Washington, D.C.*

Monique C. James, Angela E. Kim, James M. Schaffer *New York City*

Caitlin Casey, Heather Jackie Thomason, Jordan Blair Woods *San Francisco and Bay Area*

REGIONAL EDITORS

Greg D. Schmeller *Editor, Let's Go Adventure Guide: Alaska*
Shelley Jiang *Associate Editor, Let's Go Adventure Guide: Alaska*
Charles L. Black *Editor, Let's Go Adventure Guide: Southwest USA*
Robert Cacace *Associate Editor, Let's Go Adventure Guide: Southwest USA*
Jennie Lin *Editor, Let's Go: California*
Dan Song *Associate Editor, Lets Go: California*
Dunia Dickey *Editor, Let's Go: Washington, D.C.*
David A. Parker *Editor, Let's Go: New York City*
Michael B. Murphy *Editor, Let's Go: San Francisco*
Miranda I. Lash *City Guide Associate Editors*
Megan Moran-Gates

CONTRIBUTING WRITERS

Professor Bert Vaux is PhD in Linguistics and currently teaches at the University of Wisconsin-Milwaukee. He has written extensively, and taught popular classes on linguistics and dialects at Harvard University.

Ben Davis was the editor of *Let's Go: Turkey 2002.*

Stephanie L. Smith was a Researcher-Writer for *Let's Go: California 1997* and *New Zealand 1998.* She worked as a freelancer for CitySearch Los Angeles, reviewing restaurants, bars, and attractions,

ACKNOWLEDGMENTS

TEAM USA THANKS: Our ever vigilant and truly magnificent RW's, Ariel and Brian, Tor and Amelia, salacious leers and wily deers, Leonard and Rod, google and God, and, last but not least, Randy, for teaching us to fly.

KRISTIN THANKS: Team USA (Jeremy, the funniest person I know; Mac, the most argumentative; Erin, the cutest; Ariel, the most patient); Mr. and Mrs. OZ (Tor, for mangoes and mumbles; Amelia, for coffees and cassowaries); Chris, Seth, and Tom (for being the best RWs ever); my family (for letting me spend a summer away from home); Ed, Khalda, and Mike (for being a wonderful summer posse); Tom (for fun weekends); and countless indie rock bands (for keeping the office sane but silly). BELIEVE!

ERIN THANKS: Jeremy, for his amazing leadership/falsetto; Kristin, for organization and laughs; Mac, for leering salaciously; Ariel, for guidance; Oz, for you are delicious; Neill and Jennifer, for being perfect; and my family, for making long weekends wonderful.

MAC THANKS: Jeremy, for the constant stream of abuse; Kristin, for saving the book; Erin, for the suppression of Rod; Tor and Amelia, for entertainment and fake countries; Ariel, for restraint; my RWs, for making my life easy; James, despite his heritage; my family, for endless support; and Marietta, for everything.

JEREMY THANKS: Kristin, Mac, and Erin, for sundry tropicalia; Ariel for divine intervention; the happy accident of Tor and Amelia's close company; my parents; Diane for general book-savery; Kryptonite, for nothing; Leonard Cohen; and Monique, for her sad eyes, open spirit, and enormous reservoirs of love.

BRIAN THANKS: Ben Davis for making my job far easier, but Jeremy's far harder. Nathaniel & Mapland for keeping me awake on those late nights/early mornings. Christine Y. for answering my pestering questions all summer.

Editor
Jeremy Todd
Associate Editor
Kristin Kitchen, Erin Probst, N. MacDonald Snyder
Managing Editor
Ariel Fox
Map Editor
Brian J. Emeott
Typesetter
Christine C. Yokoyama

Publishing Director
Julie A. Stephens
Editor-in-Chief
Jeffrey Dubner
Production Manager
Dusty Lewis
Cartography Manager
Nathaniel Brooks
Design Manager
Caleb Beyers
Editorial Managers
Lauren Bonner, Ariel Fox, Matthew K. Hudson, Emma Nothmann, Joanna Shawn Brigid O'Leary, Sarah Robinson
Financial Manager
Suzanne Siu
Marketing & Publicity Managers
Megan Brumagim, Nitin Shah
Personnel Manager
Jesse Reid Andrews
Researcher Manager
Jennifer O'Brien
Web Manager
Jesse Tov
Web Content Director
Abigail Burger
Production Associates
Thomas Bechtold, Jeffrey Hoffman Yip
IT Directors
Travis Good, E. Peyton Sherwood
Financial Assistant
R. Kirkie Maswoswe
Associate Web Manager
Robert Dubbin
Office Coordinators
Abigail Burger, Angelina L. Fryer, Liz Glynn
Director of Advertising Sales
Daniel Ramsey
Senior Advertising Associates
Sara Barnett, Daniella Boston
Advertising Artwork Editors
Julia Davidson, Sandy Liu
President
Abhishek Gupta
General Manager
Robert B. Rombauer
Assistant General Manager
Anne E. Chisholm

PRICE RANGES >> USA

Our researchers list establishments in order of value from best to worst; our favorites are denoted by the Let's Go thumbs-up (☒). Since the best value is not always the cheapest price, we have incorporated a system of price ranges for quick reference. Our price ranges are based on a rough expectation of what you will spend. For **accommodations,** we base our price range off the cheapest price for which a single traveler can stay for one night. For **restaurants** and other dining establishments, we estimate the average amount that you will spend in that restaurant. The table below tells you what you will *typically* find in the United States at the corresponding price range; keep in mind that a particularly expensive ice cream stand may still only be marked a ❷, depending on what you will spend.

ACCOMMODATIONS	RANGE	WHAT YOU'RE *LIKELY* TO FIND
❶	under $30	Camping; most dorm rooms, such as HI or other hostels or university dorm rooms. Expect bunk beds and a communal bath; you may have to provide or rent towels and sheets.
❷	$30-45	Upper-end hostels or small bed and breakfast. You may have a private bathroom, or there may be a sink in your room and communal shower in the hall.
❸	$46-70	A small room with a private bath. Should have decent amenities, such as phone and TV. Breakfast may be included in the price of the room.
❹	$71-100	Similar to 3, but may have more amenities or be in a more touristed area.
❺	over $100	Large, posh hotels. If it's a 5 and it doesn't have the perks you want, you've paid too much.
FOOD		
❶	under $6	Mostly sandwich shops or greasy spoons. Don't worry about tucking your shirt in.
❷	$6-8	Sandwiches, appetizers at a bar, or low-priced entrees. You may have the option of sitting down or getting take-out.
❸	$9-12	Mid-priced entrees, possibly coming with a soup or salad. Tip'll bump you up a couple dollars, since you'll probably have a waiter or waitress.
❹	$13-16	A somewhat fancy restaurant or steakhouse. Either way, you'll have a special knife. Some restaurants in this range have a dress code, and many may look down on t-shirt and jeans.
❺	over $16	Food with foreign names and a decent wine list. Slacks and dress shirts may be expected. Don't order PB&J.

PRICE RANGES >> CANADA

Our researchers list establishments in order of value from best to worst; our favorites are denoted by the Let's Go thumbs-up (☒). Since the best value is not always the cheapest price, we have incorporated a system of price ranges for quick reference. Our price ranges are based on a rough expectation of what you will spend. For **accommodations,** we base our price range off the cheapest price for which a single traveler can stay for one night. For **restaurants** and other dining establishments, we estimate the average amount that you will spend in that restaurant. The table below tells you what you will *typically* find in the Canada at the corresponding price range; keep in mind that a particularly expensive ice cream stand may still only be marked a ❷, depending on what you will spend.

ACCOMMODATIONS	RANGE	WHAT YOU'RE *LIKELY* TO FIND
❶	under CDN$45	Camping; most dorm rooms, such as HI or other hostels or university dorm rooms. Expect bunk beds and a communal bath; you may have to provide or rent towels and sheets.
❷	CDN$45-67	Upper-end hostels or a small bed and breakfast. You may have a private bathroom, or there may be a sink in your room and communal shower in the hall.
❸	CDN$68-105	A small room with a private bath. Should have decent amenities, such as phone and TV. Breakfast may be included in the price of the room.
❹	CDN$106-150	Similar to 3, but may have more amenities or be in a more touristed area.
❺	over CDN$150	Large, posh hotels. If it's a 5 and it doesn't have the perks you want, you've paid too much.
FOOD		
❶	under CDN$7	Mostly sandwich shops or greasy spoons. Don't worry about tucking your shirt in.
❷	CDN$7-12	Sandwiches, appetizers at a bar, or low-priced entrees. Generally sit-down places; take-out may be an option.
❸	CDN$13-18	Mid-priced entrees, possibly coming with a soup or salad. Tip'll bump you up a couple dollars, since you'll probably have a waiter or waitress.
❹	CDN$19-24	A somewhat fancy restaurant or steakhouse. Either way, you'll have a special knife. Some restaurants in this range have a dress code, and many may look down on t-shirt and jeans.
❺	over CDN$24	Food with foreign names and a decent wine list. Slacks and dress shirts may be expected. Don't order poutine.

ABOUT LET'S GO

GUIDES FOR THE INDEPENDENT TRAVELER

Budget travel is more than a vacation. At *Let's Go*, we see every trip as the chance of a lifetime. If your dream is to grab a knapsack and a machete and forge through the jungles of Brazil, we can take you there. Or, if you'd rather enjoy the Riviera sun at a beachside cafe, we'll set you a table. If you know what you're doing, you can have any experience you want—whether it's camping among lions or sampling Tuscan desserts—without maxing out your credit card. We'll show you just how far your coins can go, and prove that the greatest limitation on your adventure is not your wallet, but your imagination. That said, we understand that you may want the occasional indulgence after a week of hostels and kebab stands, so we've added "Big Splurges" to let you know which establishments are worth those extra euros, as well as price ranges to help you quickly determine whether an accommodation or restaurant will break the bank. While we may have diversified, our emphasis will always be on finding the best values for your budget, giving you all the info you need to spend six days in London or six months in Tasmania.

BEYOND THE TOURIST EXPERIENCE

We write for travelers who know there's more to a vacation than riding double-deckers with tourists. Our researchers give you the heads-up on both world-renowned and lesser-known attractions, on the best local eats and the hottest nightclub beats. In our travels, we talk to everybody; we provide a snapshot of real life in the places you visit with our sidebars on topics like regional cuisine, local festivals, and hot political issues. We've opened our pages to respected writers and scholars to show you their take on a given destination, and turned to lifelong residents to learn the little things that make their city worth calling home. And we've even given you Alternatives to Tourism—ideas for how to give back to local communities through responsible travel and volunteering.

OVER FORTY YEARS OF WISDOM

When we started, way back in 1960, Let's Go consisted of a small group of well-traveled friends who compiled their budget travel tips into a 20-page packet for students on charter flights to Europe. Since then, we've expanded to suit all kinds of travelers, now publishing guides to six continents, including our newest guides: *Let's Go: Japan* and *Let's Go: Brazil.* Our guides are still annually researched and written entirely by students on shoe-string budgets, adventurous travelers who know that train strikes, stolen luggage, food poisoning, and marriage proposals are all part of a day's work. Even as you read this, work on next year's editions is well underway. Whether you're reading one of our new titles, like *Let's Go: Puerto Rico* or *Let's Go Adventure Guide: Alaska*, or our original best-seller, *Let's Go: Europe*, you'll find the same spirit of adventure that has made *Let's Go* the guide of choice for travelers the world over since 1960.

GETTING IN TOUCH

The best discoveries are often those you make yourself; on the road, when you find something worth sharing, please drop us a line. We're Let's Go Publications, 67 Mt. Auburn St., Cambridge, MA 02138, USA (feedback@letsgo.com).

For more info, visit our website: www.letsgo.com.

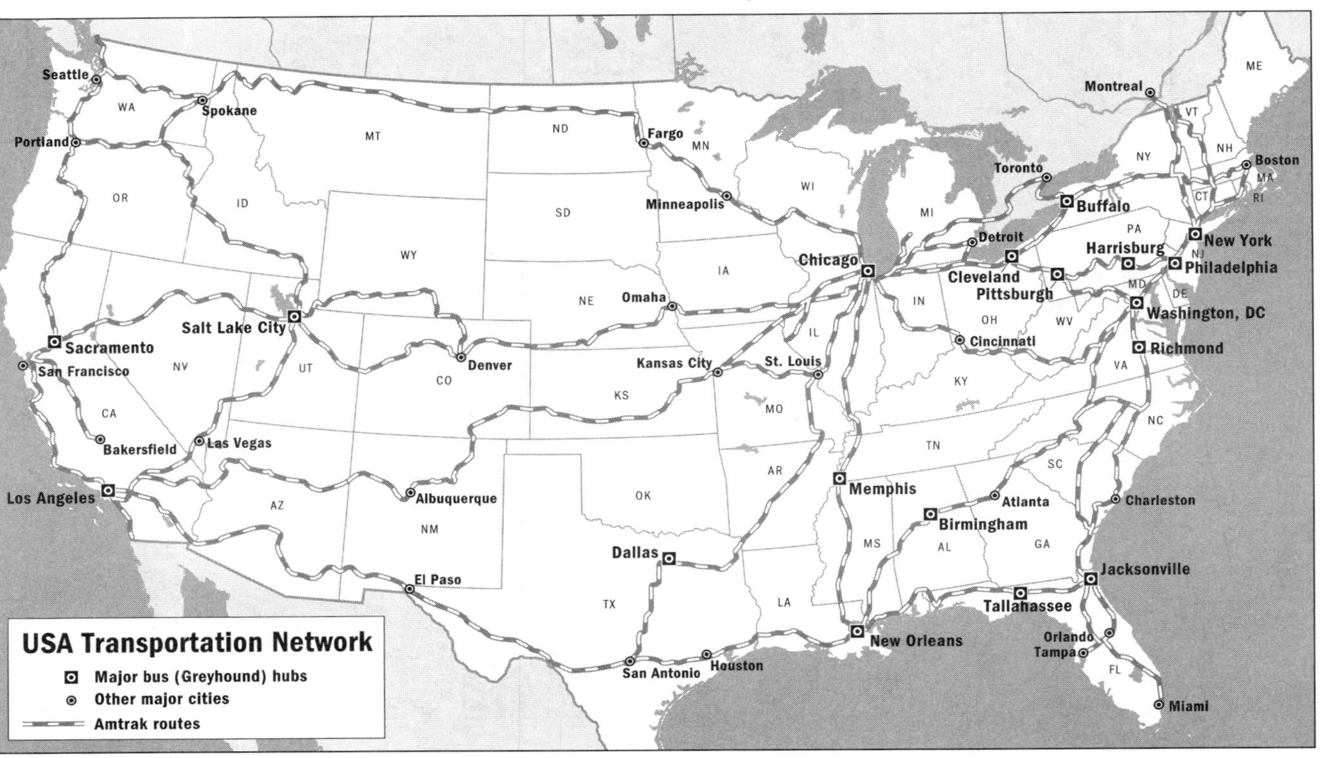
USA Transportation Network
Major bus (Greyhound) hubs
Other major cities
Amtrak routes
Seattle
Spokane
Portland
WA
OR
ID
MT
ND
SD
WY
NE
Fargo
MN
Minneapolis
WI
IA
MI
Sacramento
San Francisco
Salt Lake City
NV
UT
CA
Bakersfield
Las Vegas
Los Angeles
Denver
CO
AZ
Albuquerque
NM
El Paso
Omaha
Kansas City
KS
St. Louis
MO
OK
Dallas
TX
San Antonio
Houston
AR
LA
Chicago
IL
IN
OH
Cincinnati
KY
TN
Memphis
MS
New Orleans
AL
Birmingham
Atlanta
GA
SC
Tallahassee
Jacksonville
Orlando
Tampa
FL
Miami
Charleston
NC
VA
Richmond
Washington, DC
WV
MD
DE
Pittsburgh
Cleveland
Detroit
Toronto
Buffalo
PA
Harrisburg
Philadelphia
NJ
New York
NY
CT
RI
MA
Boston
NH
VT
ME
Montreal

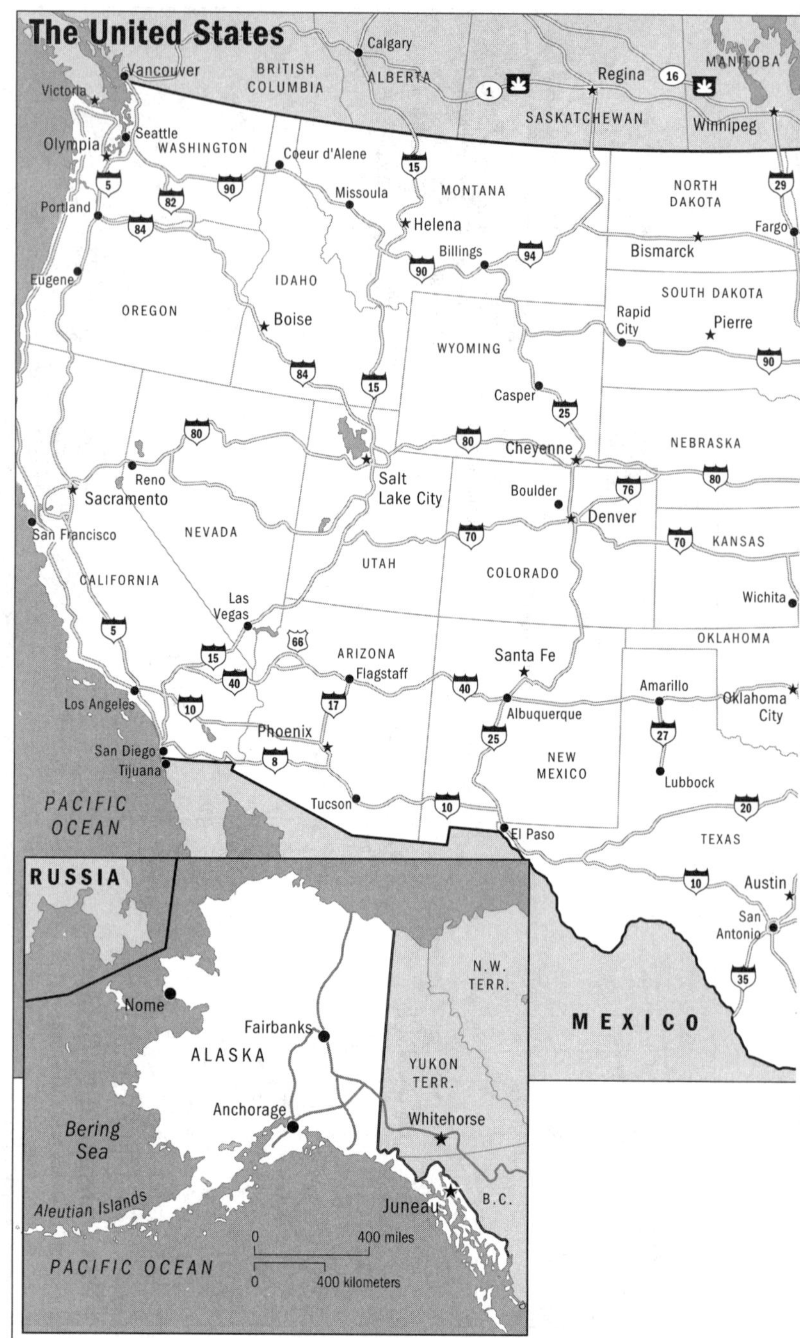
The United States
Vancouver
Victoria
BRITISH COLUMBIA
Calgary
ALBERTA
Regina
SASKATCHEWAN
MANITOBA
Winnipeg
Seattle
Olympia
WASHINGTON
Coeur d'Alene
Missoula
MONTANA
Helena
Portland
Billings
NORTH DAKOTA
Fargo
Bismarck
Eugene
IDAHO
OREGON
Boise
SOUTH DAKOTA
Rapid City
Pierre
WYOMING
Casper
NEBRASKA
Cheyenne
Reno
Sacramento
Salt Lake City
Boulder
Denver
San Francisco
NEVADA
UTAH
COLORADO
KANSAS
CALIFORNIA
Wichita
Las Vegas
ARIZONA
Santa Fe
OKLAHOMA
Flagstaff
Amarillo
Oklahoma City
Los Angeles
Albuquerque
Phoenix
San Diego
Tijuana
NEW MEXICO
Lubbock
PACIFIC OCEAN
Tucson
El Paso
TEXAS
Austin
San Antonio
MEXICO
RUSSIA
Nome
N.W. TERR.
Fairbanks
ALASKA
YUKON TERR.
Anchorage
Whitehorse
Bering Sea
Aleutian Islands
Juneau
B.C.
0
400 miles
0
400 kilometers
PACIFIC OCEAN

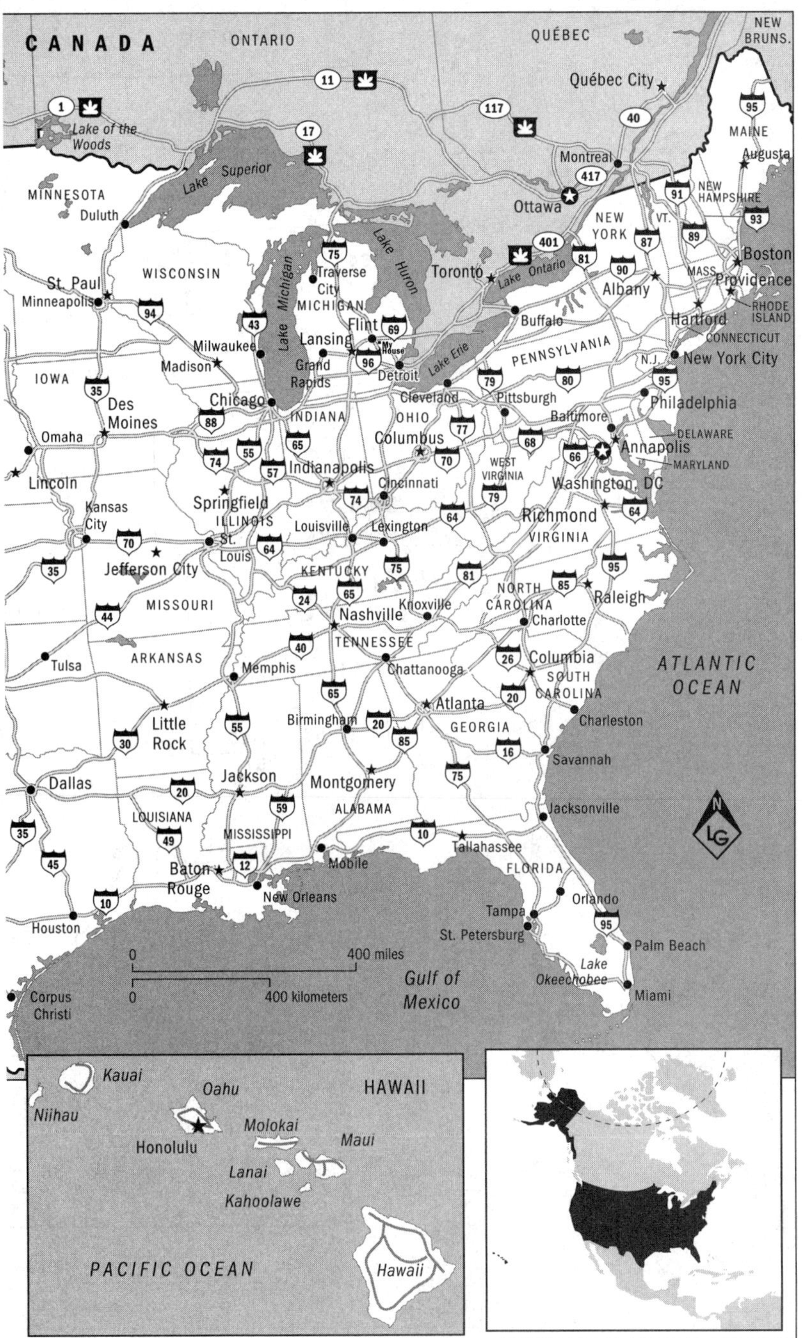
CANADA
ONTARIO
QUÉBEC
NEW BRUNS.
Québec City
Lake of the Woods
Lake Superior
MINNESOTA
Duluth
Montreal
Ottawa
MAINE
Augusta
NEW HAMPSHIRE
VT.
NEW YORK
Boston
MASS.
Providence
RHODE ISLAND
Hartford
CONNECTICUT
Toronto
Lake Ontario
Albany
Buffalo
WISCONSIN
St. Paul
Minneapolis
Lake Michigan
Lake Huron
Traverse City
MICHIGAN
Flint
My House
Lansing
Grand Rapids
Detroit
Lake Erie
PENNSYLVANIA
N.J.
New York City
Milwaukee
Madison
IOWA
Des Moines
Chicago
INDIANA
Cleveland
OHIO
Pittsburgh
Philadelphia
Baltimore
DELAWARE
Annapolis
MARYLAND
Omaha
Lincoln
Columbus
Indianapolis
WEST VIRGINIA
Washington, DC
Cincinnati
Kansas City
Springfield
ILLINOIS
Richmond
VIRGINIA
St. Louis
Louisville
Lexington
Jefferson City
KENTUCKY
MISSOURI
NORTH CAROLINA
Raleigh
Knoxville
Nashville
Charlotte
TENNESSEE
Tulsa
ARKANSAS
Memphis
Chattanooga
Columbia
SOUTH CAROLINA
ATLANTIC OCEAN
Atlanta
Little Rock
Birmingham
GEORGIA
Charleston
Savannah
Dallas
Jackson
Montgomery
ALABAMA
Jacksonville
LOUISIANA
MISSISSIPPI
Tallahassee
Mobile
FLORIDA
Baton Rouge
New Orleans
Orlando
Tampa
St. Petersburg
Houston
Palm Beach
0
400 miles
400 kilometers
Gulf of Mexico
Lake Okeechobee
Miami
Corpus Christi
LG
Kauai
Oahu
HAWAII
Niihau
Molokai
Honolulu
Maui
Lanai
Kahoolawe
PACIFIC OCEAN
Hawaii

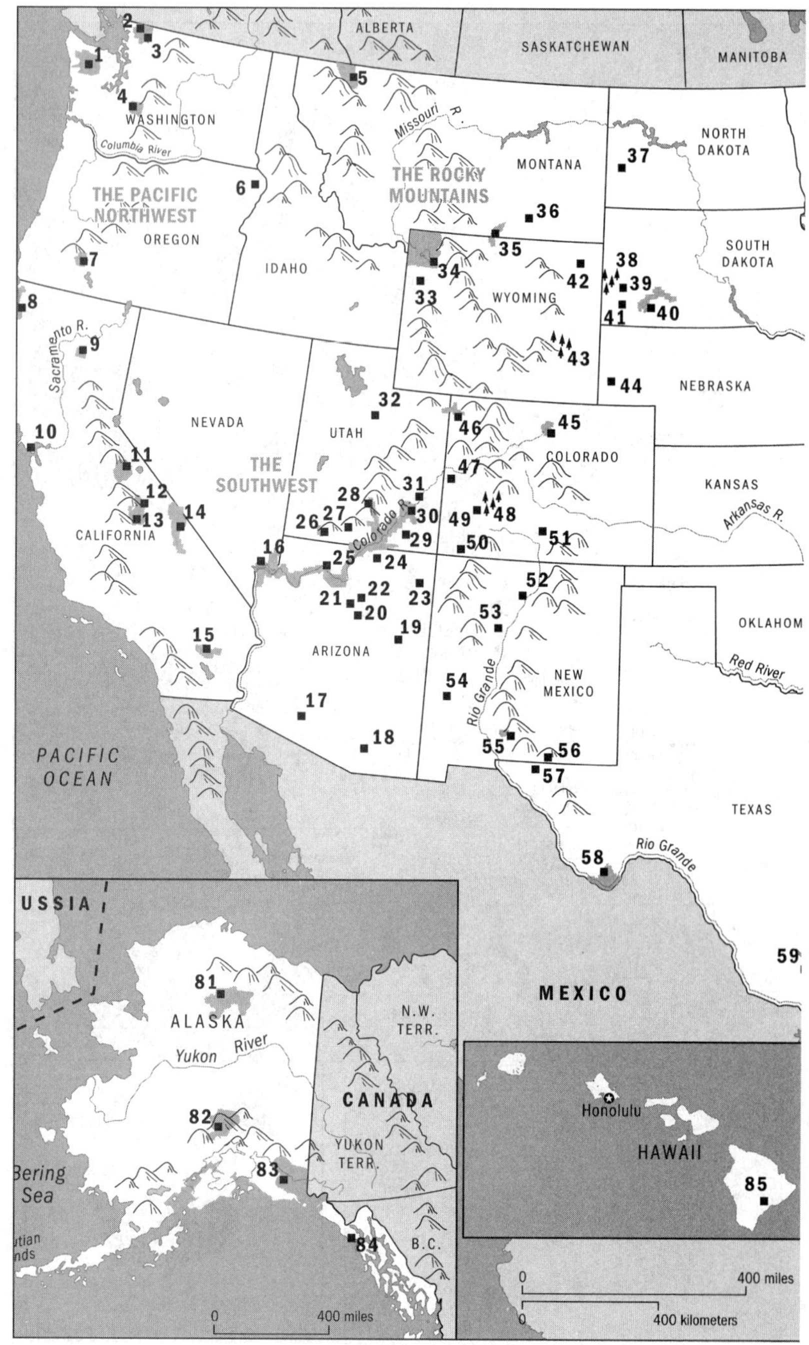

ALBERTA
SASKATCHEWAN
MANITOBA
WASHINGTON
Columbia River
THE PACIFIC NORTHWEST
OREGON
IDAHO
Missouri R.
THE ROCKY MOUNTAINS
MONTANA
NORTH DAKOTA
SOUTH DAKOTA
WYOMING
NEBRASKA
Sacramento R.
NEVADA
UTAH
THE SOUTHWEST
COLORADO
KANSAS
Arkansas R.
Colorado R.
CALIFORNIA
ARIZONA
NEW MEXICO
OKLAHOM
Red River
Rio Grande
TEXAS
PACIFIC OCEAN
MEXICO
USSIA
ALASKA
Yukon River
N.W. TERR.
CANADA
YUKON TERR.
B.C.
Bering Sea
Honolulu
HAWAII
0
400 miles
400 kilometers

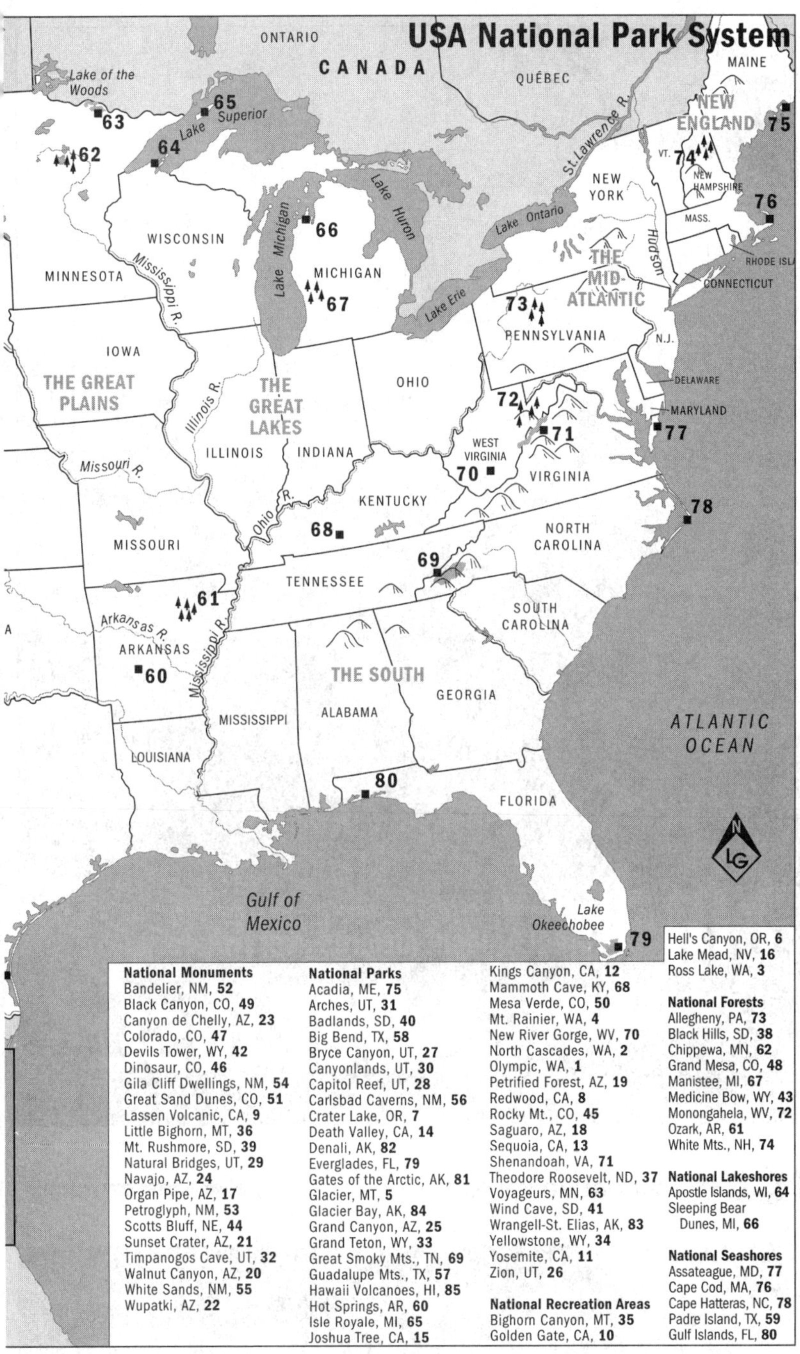

USA National Park System
ONTARIO
CANADA
QUÉBEC
MAINE
Lake of the Woods
Lake Superior
St. Lawrence R.
NEW ENGLAND
VT.
NEW HAMPSHIRE
MASS.
RHODE ISL
CONNECTICUT
NEW YORK
Lake Ontario
Lake Huron
Lake Michigan
Lake Erie
Hudson
THE MID-ATLANTIC
WISCONSIN
MINNESOTA
MICHIGAN
Mississippi R.
PENNSYLVANIA
N.J.
DELAWARE
MARYLAND
IOWA
THE GREAT PLAINS
Illinois R.
THE GREAT LAKES
OHIO
ILLINOIS
INDIANA
WEST VIRGINIA
VIRGINIA
Missouri R.
KENTUCKY
Ohio R.
MISSOURI
NORTH CAROLINA
TENNESSEE
SOUTH CAROLINA
Arkansas R.
ARKANSAS
THE SOUTH
GEORGIA
ALABAMA
MISSISSIPPI
LOUISIANA
ATLANTIC OCEAN
FLORIDA
Gulf of Mexico
Lake Okeechobee
LG
National Monuments
Bandelier, NM, 52
Black Canyon, CO, 49
Canyon de Chelly, AZ, 23
Colorado, CO, 47
Devils Tower, WY, 42
Dinosaur, CO, 46
Gila Cliff Dwellings, NM, 54
Great Sand Dunes, CO, 51
Lassen Volcanic, CA, 9
Little Bighorn, MT, 36
Mt. Rushmore, SD, 39
Natural Bridges, UT, 29
Navajo, AZ, 24
Organ Pipe, AZ, 17
Petroglyph, NM, 53
Scotts Bluff, NE, 44
Sunset Crater, AZ, 21
Timpanogos Cave, UT, 32
Walnut Canyon, AZ, 20
White Sands, NM, 55
Wupatki, AZ, 22
National Parks
Acadia, ME, 75
Arches, UT, 31
Badlands, SD, 40
Big Bend, TX, 58
Bryce Canyon, UT, 27
Canyonlands, UT, 30
Capitol Reef, UT, 28
Carlsbad Caverns, NM, 56
Crater Lake, OR, 7
Death Valley, CA, 14
Denali, AK, 82
Everglades, FL, 79
Gates of the Arctic, AK, 81
Glacier, MT, 5
Glacier Bay, AK, 84
Grand Canyon, AZ, 25
Grand Teton, WY, 33
Great Smoky Mts., TN, 69
Guadalupe Mts., TX, 57
Hawaii Volcanoes, HI, 85
Hot Springs, AR, 60
Isle Royale, MI, 65
Joshua Tree, CA, 15
Kings Canyon, CA, 12
Mammoth Cave, KY, 68
Mesa Verde, CO, 50
Mt. Rainier, WA, 4
New River Gorge, WV, 70
North Cascades, WA, 2
Olympic, WA, 1
Petrified Forest, AZ, 19
Redwood, CA, 8
Rocky Mt., CO, 45
Saguaro, AZ, 18
Sequoia, CA, 13
Shenandoah, VA, 71
Theodore Roosevelt, ND, 37
Voyageurs, MN, 63
Wind Cave, SD, 41
Wrangell-St. Elias, AK, 83
Yellowstone, WY, 34
Yosemite, CA, 11
Zion, UT, 26
National Recreation Areas
Bighorn Canyon, MT, 35
Golden Gate, CA, 10
Hell's Canyon, OR, 6
Lake Mead, NV, 16
Ross Lake, WA, 3
National Forests
Allegheny, PA, 73
Black Hills, SD, 38
Chippewa, MN, 62
Grand Mesa, CO, 48
Manistee, MI, 67
Medicine Bow, WY, 43
Monongahela, WV, 72
Ozark, AR, 61
White Mts., NH, 74
National Lakeshores
Apostle Islands, WI, 64
Sleeping Bear Dunes, MI, 66
National Seashores
Assateague, MD, 77
Cape Cod, MA, 76
Cape Hatteras, NC, 78
Padre Island, TX, 59
Gulf Islands, FL, 80

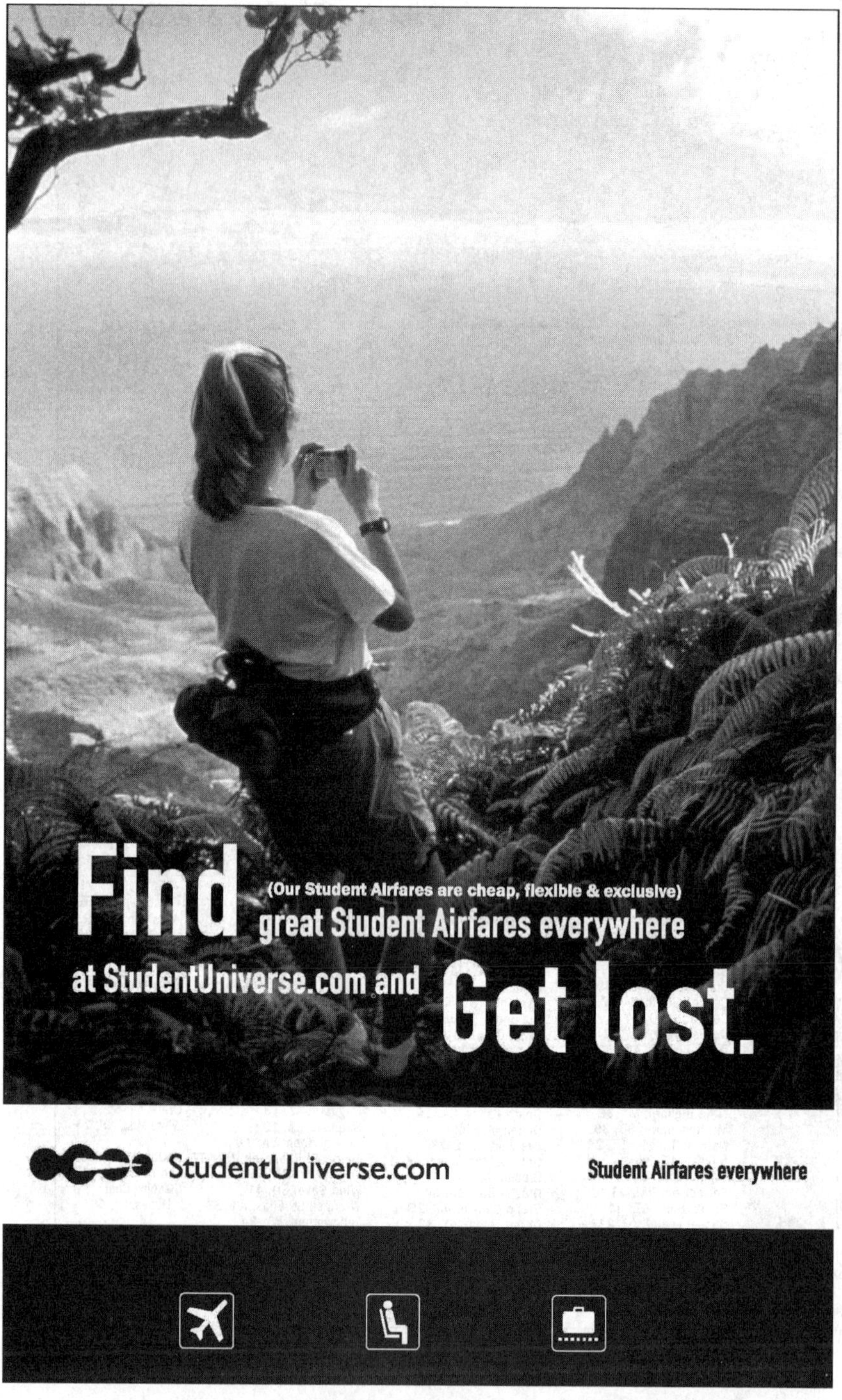
Find
(Our Student Airfares are cheap, flexible & exclusive)
great Student Airfares everywhere
at StudentUniverse.com and Get lost.
StudentUniverse.com
Student Airfares everywhere

DISCOVER THE USA & CANADA

Stretching from below the Tropic of Cancer to above the Arctic Circle, the United States is a country defined by open spaces and an amazing breadth of terrain. From sparse deserts to lush forests and snow-capped peaks to rolling fields of grain, the American landscape sprouts new views in every region.

Culturally as well as geographically, America is a nation of contrasts. The United States is formed by disunited peoples; centuries of immigration have created a country that cannot be said to value diversity so much as it is comprised by it. This diversity is reflected in every aspect of the American experience—from Cajun cuisine to the Harlem Renaissance, experiencing America involves experiencing the intermingling of different visions. To the north, Canada's cultural makeup reflects a similar confluence of immigrant cultures.

While transportation options throughout the United States and Canada are plentiful, the most rewarding way to see the countries is still by car. Whether driving cross-country or simply over the river and through the woods, the road trip is the definitive American travel institution.

USA FACTS AND FIGURES

POPULATION: 291,497,439.

LARGEST CITIES: New York City, Los Angeles, Chicago, Houston, Philadelphia.

COMMON LAST NAMES: Smith, Johnson, Williams, Jones, Davis.

MILES DRIVEN EACH YEAR: 1½ trillion (to the sun and back 7500 times).

COMMMON PET NAMES: Patches, Misty, Buster, Princess, Bear, Sheba.

TV'S PER HOUSE: 2.4.

WHEN TO GO

In general, the US tourist season comprises the summer months between Memorial Day and Labor Day (May 31-Sept. 6, 2004); the Canadian tourist season starts around mid-June. National parks flood with visitors during the high season, but cities are less affected by seasonal variation. For regions where winter sports are big or where winters are mild, the tourist season is generally inverted (Dec.-Apr.).

THINGS TO DO

Neither the following few pages nor this book's one thousand pages can do justice to the vibrant, diverse offerings of the North American continent. No two trips to the New World are the same, and visitors to several regions may feel like they've visited different countries. There are, however, a few common themes in the US and Canada that deserve mention and that should be a part of any thorough exploration.

SCENIC DRIVES

News commentator and stalwart American patriot Charles Kuralt once said, "Thanks to the interstate highway system, it is now possible to travel from coast to coast without seeing anything." The interstate system is the fastest, most efficient, most sensible way of driving through America—and also the most frustratingly nondescript. In contrast, the incredible network of backroads in the US affords a genuine view of the country. Unobstructed by vision-blocking soundproofers and gas-spewing trailers, a single rest stop on a back road can possess more character than 100 mi. of strip malls. The **Blue Ridge Parkway, VA** (p. 350), connects two national parks—Shenandoah and Great Smoky Mountains—passing tremendous green mountains and rustic Appalachian wilderness. In the North, the **Lake Superior North Shore Drive, MN** (p. 618) traces the dramatic shore of the most massive Great Lake, revealing waterfalls, lighthouses, and forests. Connecting San Antonio with Austin, TX, the **Texas Hill Country Drive** (p. 688) goes deep into the heart of broad-rim hat and dusty jean country, where the landscape is dotted with thriving immigrant communities and pristine vineyards. Just outside Phoenix, AZ, the **Apache Trail** (p. 844) curves around the stark cactus-laden desert mountains that loom over deep blue artificial lakes. The **San Juan Skyway** (p. 745), in southern CO, ascends to breathtaking heights under snow-capped mountains and past bottomless gorges. **Going-to-the-Sun Road** (p. 767), in the Waterton-Glacier Peace Park, MT, skirts mountainous landscape as it passes bubbling waterfalls and steep escarpments before descending into the rainforest. A diamond in the rough that is the interstate highway system, **I-87** quietly winds through the tree-carpeted Adirondacks of the Eastern US (p. 267).

MUST-SEE CITIES

Sure, everyone knows the major cities: New York has...well, everything; nothing tops the vivacity, glamour, great weather, and unbeatable smog of Los Angeles; and the multicultural metropolis of Toronto offers unparalleled opportunities. However, the real reasons to buckle up for the great American journey are the smaller, less obvious cities and towns. The magnificent fortifications and twisting alleyways of **Québec City, QC** (p. 192) testify to the city's unmatched old-world character. The "staid" American Midwest boasts **Minneapolis-St. Paul, MN** (p. 605), a sprawling and unsung urban center with the sights and diversity to rival even the most famous of American cities. Travelers to **Savannah, GA** (p. 440) are rewarded with lush gardens, antebellum homes, and Southern charm by the bucketful. The legendary nightlife of **Austin, TX** (p. 687) thrives on the city's mix of Southwestern grit, collegiate energy, and a unique, relaxed style. Only the most liberal-minded and fun-loving traveler need stop in the eclectic town of **Boulder, CO** (p. 727), a place of all sorts of Rocky Mountain highs. Countless adventurers find a warm welcome in **Flagstaff, AZ** (p. 829), perhaps the greatest crossroads in the US. The bohemian metropolis of **Portland, OR** (p. 1012), known as the microbrewery capital of North America, is worth seeing for its bohemian open-air market alone.

COLLEGE TOWNS

America's colleges, from sprawling state universities to tiny liberal-arts academies, have engendered unique communities with youthful vitality and alternative spirit. Lost between the twin giants of New York and Boston, the smaller college town of **Providence, RI** (p. 146), beckons with a slower, more inviting pace. The mountain hamlet of **Middlebury, VT** (p. 109) combines rural charm with a touch of youthful rowdiness. An increasingly diverse student community gives the Southern establishment a run for its money in **Charlottesville, VA** (p. 346), a gorgeous town known for its rolling hills and splendid architecture. **Missoula, MT** (p. 763) has become one of the most fascinatingly cosmopolitan cities in the Prairie. Perhaps the most famous American college town, **Berkeley, CA** (p. 945) has become a city in its own right, but has managed to do so without sacrificing its collegiate charms.

AMERICANA

America vaunts the biggest, smallest, and zaniest of almost everything. Kitschy roadside attractions dot the country's dusty roads, putting on public display a vast and truly baffling material culture—for a modest fee. Out west in Polson, MT (p. 766), the **Miracle of America Museum** enshrines reg'lar old American living. **Wall Drug's** (p. 636) notorious billboards lure tourists to the Badlands of South Dakota from as far away as Amsterdam—that's right, in Holland—and have turned their marketing ploy into a cultural phenomenon. Evidence of American architectural ingenuity can be found at the **Corn Palace** in Mitchell, SD (p. 634); this gargantuan structure is rebuilt every year with a fresh crop. America also claims the world's largest **folding pocketknife** in Natchitoches, LA (p. 476) and **wooden cross** in Petoskey, MI (p. 568). Bigger and brighter still are the casinos of **the Strip** in Las Vegas, NV (p. 795) and **the Boardwalk** in Atlantic City, NJ (p. 275). It is difficult to imagine a tribute to the American value of individual rights that stands so proud as **"The Tree That Owns Itself"** in Athens, GA (p. 435). And, of course no tour of American kitsch would be complete without a trip to the heart and soul of all Americana—**Graceland** (p. 388).

NATIONAL PARKS

From haunting red buttes to endless pitch-black caves, the national parks of the US and Canada protect some of the most phenomenal natural beauty in the world. While much of the land's beauty can be seen along the byways, the truly miraculous works of nature are cared for by the National Park Service. The easternmost park in the US, **Acadia National Park, ME** (p. 92) features unspoiled rocky beaches and dense pine forests. **Shenandoah National Park, VA** (p. 348) made its way into history as America's first land reclamation project, and today lures travelers with its mountain vistas. **Great Smoky Mountains National Park, TN** (p. 378), the largest national park east of the Mississippi, also holds the International Biosphere Reserve and World Heritage Site.

The most popular parks, however, lie out west. Arguably the most famous (and most crowded) park in the US, **Yellowstone National Park, WY** (p. 774), has

TOP TEN LIST

MUSEUMS WORTH MENTIONING

1. **House on the Rock,** Madison, WI. Eclectic doesn't even begin to describe this wonderland of oddness.
2. **Experience Music Project,** Seattle, WA. Mixing one man's fanaticism for rock 'n roll with Microsoft's technological flair, the EMP blurs the borders between museum and fun-park.
3. **Voodoo Museum,** New Orleans, LA. This mystifying museum has a suggested donation that is *strongly* recommended.
4. **Carhenge,** Alliance, NE. America at its most grotesquely automotive; the name says it all.
5. **National Ornamental Metal Museum,** Memphis, TN. From the ornate front gate to the blacksmith on premises, this museum practices what it preaches–shiny metal things.
6. **Salvador Dalí Museum,** St. Petersburg, FL. All the Dalí you could ever want, in a convenient, not-at-all-related-to-Dalí location.
7. **Federal Bureau of Investigation,** Washington, D.C. A surprisingly informative tour with insights into criminology and an awesome cane-gun.
8. **Bata Shoe Museum,** Toronto, ON. Footloose and fancy-free, this museum sold its soul to the devil, and the devil was shoes.
9. **Golden Gate Cookie Company,** San Francisco, CA. Learn the sexy side of the future at this working fortune cookie factory.
10. **Black Hole,** Los Alamos, NM. You won't be able to pull yourself away from this collection of antiquated surplus equipment from the Los Alamos National Laboratory.

attractions such as the Old Faithful geyser. **Grand Canyon National Park, AZ** (p. 821) wows visitors with...well, the Grand Canyon, while **Yosemite National Park, CA** (p. 964) draws hordes of trekkers, trailers, and tourists with its steep mountains and stunning waterfalls. Smaller—but no less breathtaking—are the otherworldly hoodoos (pillar-like rock formations) of **Bryce Canyon National Park, UT** (p. 816), the varied and dramatic terrain of **Waterton-Glacier International Peace Park, MT** (p. 767), and the awesome mountains of **Grand Teton National Park, WY** (p. 783).

Canada also possesses a highly developed and well-maintained national park system. At **Fundy National Park, NB** (p. 170) the world's largest tides ebb and flow, while nearby **Kouchibouguac National Park** (p. 172) features sandy beaches and acres of marshland. On Newfoundland, the UNESCO world heritage site of **Gros Morne National Park** (p. 178) sees more moose than tourists...for now. The Canadian Rockies also play host to gorgeous parklands, including the expansive ice fields of **Jasper National Park, AB** (p. 1044). The isolated **Pacific Rim National Park, BC** (p. 1033) offers some of the best hiking, surfing, and diving on the continent.

LET'S GO PICKS

BEST OPPORTUNITIES FOR PUBLIC BATHING: Hot springs are a therapeutic diversion from the hard work of travel; some of the best are in **Calistoga, CA** (p. 954). For skinny dippin', try **Austin, TX**'s Hippie Hollow (p. 687).

BEST SUN SPOTS: For a great East Coast sunrise, head to Cadillac Mountain in **Acadia National Park, ME** (p. 92). For a sunset celebration, go to the pier in **Clearwater, FL** (p. 496).

BEST PLACE TO APPEASE THE GODS OF BUDGET TRAVEL: Eating on the cheap is made easy at Cleveland, OH's **Massimo da Milano**(p. 536), where hungry travelers can get a heap of Italian food on the fly for $3.

BEST PLACE TO BE A BUDGET TRAVEL AGNOSTIC: The Abbey (p. 426), in Atlanta, GA, doesn't want to let go of its roots as a Methodist Church, despite the fact that the building now houses a world-class restaurant. Feel deliciously naughty as monk-resembling servers send you to culinary heaven and your pocketbook to hell.

BEST GATORS: America's most impressive creatures. Get up close and scarily personal in places like **Nachitoches, LA** (p. 476); the **Everglades, FL** (p. 515); **St. Augustine, FL** (p. 502), and **Myrtle Beach, SC** (p. 666).

MOST APPETIZING BEER NAMES: Montana's **Moose Drool** (p. 780), South Carolina's **Mullet** (p. 420), and Louisiana's **funkybuttjuice** (p. 470) definitely rank among the nation's finest name-impaired beverages.

BIG ART: Everything's big in America. Twenty-seven factory buildings are needed to hold the exhibits at the **Museum of Contemporary Art** in North Adams, MA (p. 143). The **world's largest painting,** a 360° mural, is housed in Atlanta, GA (p. 423). Still unfinished, the sculpture of **Crazy Horse** (p. 641) will be 563 ft. when completed, thus making the 60 ft. presidential heads on nearby **Mt. Rushmore** (p. 640) seem like child's play.

LONGEST PUB STREET: George St., NF (p. 210). Learn to drink (and drink some more) like a Canadian.

BEST WAY TO ESCAPE AMERICA (OTHER THAN CANADA): Tibetan cuisine, rare in the US, is served in Bloomington, IN (p. 550) at the **Snow Lion** restaurant, owned by the Dalai Lama's nephew. Made in Tajikstan and shipped to Boulder, CO (p. 734), the building of the **Dushanbe teahouse** is a gift between sister cities–a tasty tribute to international relations.

SUGGESTED ITINERARIES

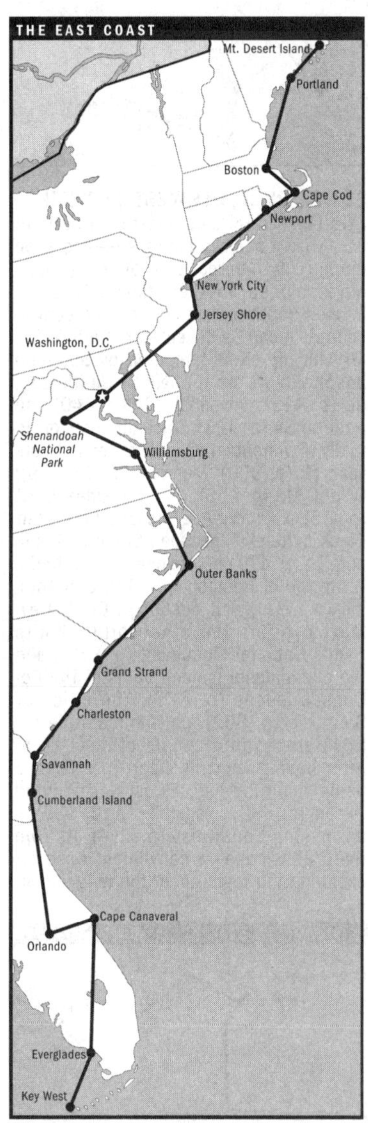

EAST COAST: MAINE TO THE FLORIDA KEYS (6 WEEKS) I-95 and the sometimes commercial, sometimes scenic U.S. 1 parallel each other from the northern wilds of Maine down to the gorgeous Florida Keys. Despite the many state-levied tolls, this strip gives a true cross-section of American life and culture, and encourages on-a-whim diversions. Begin on Mt. Desert Island, ME (p. 88) where mountain and ocean meet with spectacular results, then head down the coast. The youthful Portland, ME (p. 84) will whet your appetite for city life, and the thriving culture of Boston, MA (p. 114) will satisfy it. Cape Cod (p. 135) awaits with pristine beaches, while Newport, RI (p. 149) preserves the must-see summer estates of America's wealthiest industrialists. From there, cruise over to larger-than-life New York City (p. 217). The Jersey Shore (p. 275) deals out boardwalks and beaches for a quintessential summer experience. Washington, D.C. (p. 319) merits a few days, as does the placid Shenandoah National Park (p. 348). See colonial history acted out in Williamsburg, VA (p. 340), or find solitude on long stretches of sand in the Outer Banks (p. 407). The more built-up Grand Strand (p. 420) and the city of Charleston, SC (p. 413) beckon partyers back to the mainland. Savannah (p. 440) will leave Georgia on your mind, but Disney World (p. 487) will leave you blissfully mind-numb. Give the Space Coast of Florida (p. 500) a fly-by, and make a stop to explore the vast, mysterious Everglades (p. 515). Celebrate the end of your journey with umbrella drinks on sugar-white beaches in Key West (p. 519).

THE NORTH: TRACING THE US-CANADIAN BORDER (6 WEEKS) Crossing the continent at higher latitudes affords travelers time in the unique cities and less touristed parks of the North. Begin north of the border and take a whirlwind tour of Canada's cosmopolitan eastern cities. Québec City (p. 192) and Montréal (p. 180) are predominantly French-speaking and overflow with culture. Toronto (p. 200) boasts huge ethnic quarters and refreshing tidiness for such a big city. Cross the border at the spectacular Niagara Falls (p. 263) and motor over to the

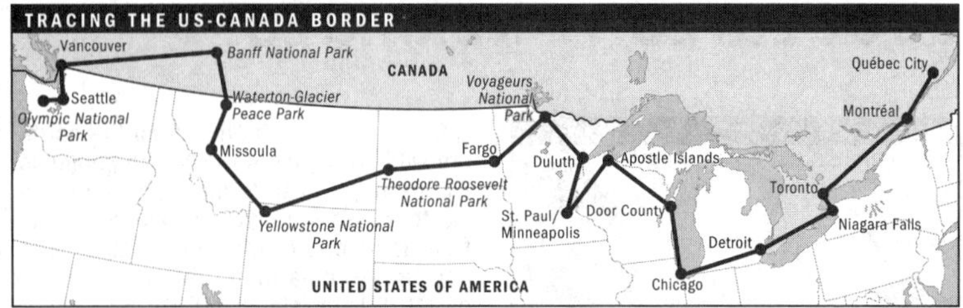

oft-stigmatized and underestimated city of Detroit (p. 552). Sail on to the Windy City of Chicago (p. 572). Wind down in the friendly and scenic lakeside communities of Wisconsin in Door County (p. 600) and the Apostle Islands (p. 603). Next, head to the surprisingly hip twin cities of St. Paul and Minneapolis (p. 605). The charming city of Duluth, MN (p. 614) combines a thriving shipping industry with endless waterfront recreation. Before leaving Minnesota, park the car and boat into the unspoiled expanse of Voyageurs National Park (p. 618). Speed out to the breathtaking Theodore Roosevelt (p. 631) and Yellowstone (p. 774) National Parks. Young and fresh, Missoula, MT (p. 763) provides a much-needed stop before heading north to Waterton-Glacier Peace Park (p. 772) and the popular Banff National Park (p. 1042) in Canada. Out on the Pacific coast, visit the lively city scenes of Vancouver (p. 1024) and Seattle (p. 988), or the serene wilderness of one of world's last remaining old-growth temperate rainforests at Olympic National Park (p. 1004).

SOUTH BY SOUTHWEST (8 WEEKS)

Striking straight across the American South from sea to shining sea—and even dipping into Mexico—this route highlights old-fashioned Southern flavor, Mexican-infused Southwestern culture, and canyon country. It can be driven year-round. Warm up with big cities tempered by Southern hospitality in the triangle of Charleston, SC (p. 413), Savannah, GA (p. 440) and Atlanta, GA (p. 423). Trace the roots of virtually all American musical styles in Nashville, TN (p. 370); Memphis, TN (p. 385); Oxford, MS (p. 456); and New Orleans, LA (p. 458). Experience the unadulterated Cajun culture of the Deep South in Acadiana, LA (p. 477) before heading out to the Texan trio of Houston (p. 702), San Antonio (p. 681), and Austin (p. 687). New Mexico offers the otherworldly White Sands National Monument (p. 869), and the phenomenal mineral baths of Truth or Consequences (p. 867). The cities of Santa Fe (p. 852) and Albuquerque (p. 861) are worth a couple of days each. After having your fill, head to Arizona's astonishing Petrified Forest and Painted Desert (p. 838). Flagstaff, AZ (p. 829) is an inviting Southwestern city in its own right, and makes a convenient base for exploring the region near the magnificent

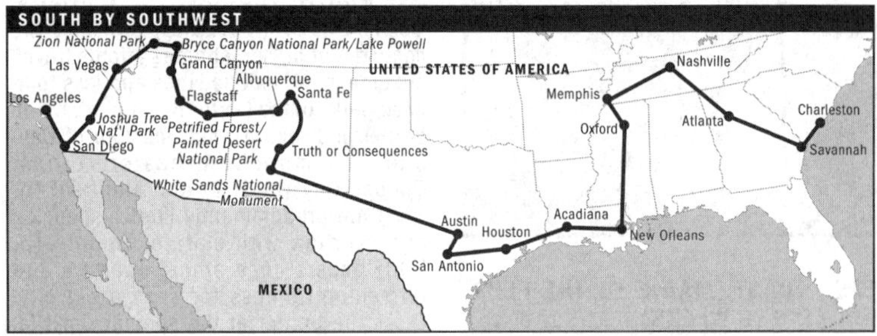

Grand Canyon (p. 821). The idyllic wilderness of Utah's Zion National Park (p. 818) and the startling rock pillars of Bryce Canyon (p. 816) provide travelers with a last gasp of clean air and natural beauty before the plunge into the glitz of Las Vegas (p. 795). In California, Joshua Tree National Park (p. 913) is a worthy stop in the desert on the way to the Pacific coast. Savor sunny San Diego (p. 903) before becoming star-struck in glamorous Los Angeles (p. 873).

THE AMERICAN WEST (3-6 WEEKS) Saddle up; the American West has blown the minds of generations of wanderers. Sidle up to the region with tours of Tucson, AZ (p. 845), Phoenix, AZ (p. 839), and Flagstaff, AZ (p. 829). Hit the must-see Grand Canyon (p. 821) from the South Rim, and then mosey through the more tranquil Bryce Canyon (p. 816) and Zion (p. 818) National Parks in Utah. Climb on toward Albuquerque, NM (p. 861) and Santa Fe, NM (p. 852) on the way to more mountainous terrain. Spend some time in the authentic Western towns of Durango (p. 746) and Telluride, CO (p. 743). After taking on the mile-high city of Denver (p. 718) and the youthful Boulder (p. 727), get lost among the peaks of Rocky Mountain National Park (p. 730). Stop over in Cheyenne, WY (p. 791) for a boot-stompin' good time on your way to the impressive Tetons (p. 783). The immensely popular Yellowstone National Park (p. 774) warrants an extra couple of days. The towns of Bozeman (p. 761) and Missoula, MT (p. 763), culturally straddling East and West, make pleasant and unique stops for the weary. Cap off your trip with the purple mountains' majesty of rugged Glacier National Park (p. 767).

THE AMERICAN WEST

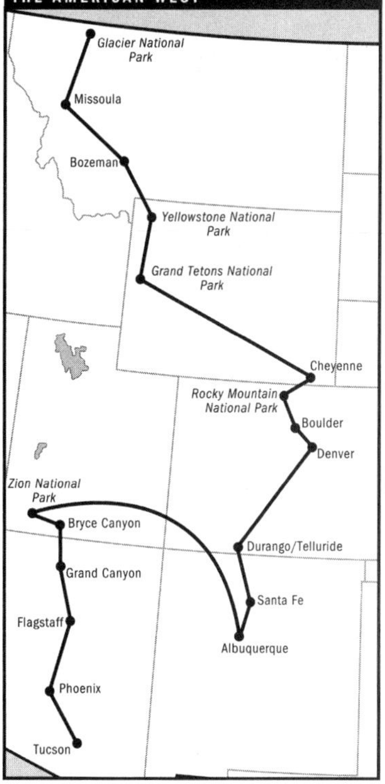

THE WEST COAST: FROM L.A. TO VANCOUVER (2-6 WEEKS). A tour of the West Coast provides the most mountainscapes, oceanfront property, and cosmopolitan bang for your buck. Between sunny, boisterous Los Angeles, CA and lush, mellow Vancouver, BC lies much natural (and artificial) diversion. Los Angeles (p. 873), America's western outpost of high culture, provides access to Hollywood (p. 878), famous art, and beach culture. Las Vegas, NV (p. 795), Tijuana, Mexico (p. 910), and Joshua Tree National Park, CA (p. 913) are worthy side trips. The 400 mi. stretch of shore-hugging Rte. 1 between L.A. and San Francisco is pure California: rolling surf, secluded beaches, dramatic cliffs, and eccentric locals. San Francisco (p. 924), a groovin' city in itself, is only 3-4hr. from Yosemite National Park (p. 964). From San Fran, the slightly inland Rte. 101 hits Napa Valley wine country (p. 952) before reuniting with Rte. 1 (and the coast) and passing through the primordial Redwood National Park (p. 959). After the park, rejoin I-5 for a trip through Oregon to Portland (p. 1012). A side trip to Crater Lake (p. 1020) is well worth it. Before getting too settled with a

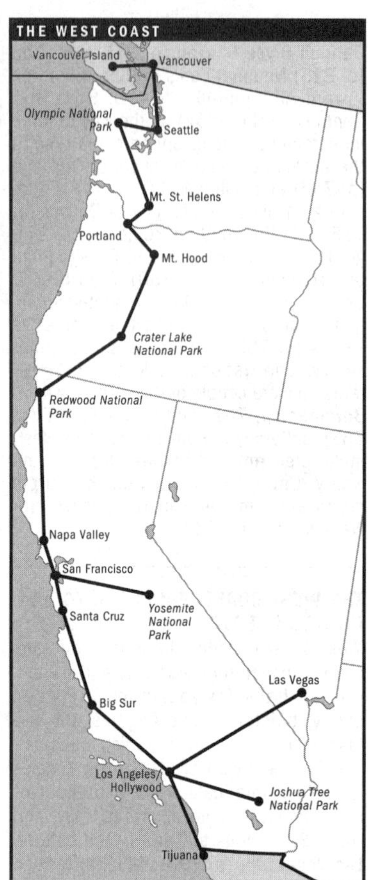

cappucino in Seattle (p. 988), commune with nature at Mt. St. Helens (p. 1007) and Olympic National Park (p. 1004), or trek over to Vancouver, BC (p. 1024) for access to the outdoor havens of Vancouver Island (p. 1033).

LIFE & TIMES

THE UNITED STATES

HISTORY

BRIDGE OVER TROUBLED WATER. Archaeologists estimate that the first Americans crossed the Bering Sea from Siberia by **land bridge** during the last Ice Age, somewhere from 10,000 to 15,000 years ago. Scientists have raised different theories to explain this migration. Whether it was the pursuit of nomadic bison, a shift in living conditions in Asia, or simple wanderlust that drove them over the land bridge, the Asiatic peoples gradually came to inhabit all corners of their new continent.

A BRAVE NEW WORLD. Though no one is entirely certain, it is likely that the earliest Europeans to stumble upon the "New World" were sea voyagers blown off-course by storms. History textbooks place the "discovery" of the Americas some time later in 1492, when **Christopher Columbus** found his voyage to the East blocked by Hispaniola in the Caribbean Sea. Optimistically believing that he had reached the spice islands of the East Indies, he dubbed the inhabitants "Indians." Columbus' arrival unleashed the unhappy tide of European conquest, bringing murder, disease, forced conversion, and other calamities to Native Americans.

In the centuries after Columbus' voyage, many Europeans high-tailed it to the New World in search of gold and silver. Even though most were unsuccessful, colonial fever took hold. The Spanish expanded into the Southern regions of the modern-day US, while the French and Dutch created more modest empires to the north. The English, meanwhile, successfully settled the east coast of the New World. After a few failed attempts, the English finally managed to establish a colony at **Jamestown** in 1607. Their success hinged on a strain of indigenous weed called tobacco, which quickly became all the rage in England. English settlement also spread to the northern regions of North America. In the years following 1620, a group of religious separatists known as **Puritans** fled to present-day Massachusetts for social as well as economic reasons.

INDEPENDENCE DAY. In order to protect her holdings in the Americas, Great Britain entered into the French and Indian War in 1754. Although ultimately successful, the struggle more than doubled Great Britain's government expenditures and raised awareness of the high price of colonialism. In order to offset the burden of this price on British taxpayers, the powers that were decided to shift more responsibility onto the American colonies, who had previously been taxed lightly. These new taxes angered colonists, who rallied against "taxation without representation." The leaders of the First Continental Congress were divided as to a course of action, but continued fighting between colonists and British troops convinced the Second Continental Congress to prepare the 13 colonies for war. In 1776, a **Declaration of Independence** was drafted. **July 4th,** the date on which the declaration was adopted, remains the most important national holiday for Americans. After eight years of fighting up and down the Eastern seaboard, British troops sailed off, and the colonists had a country of their own.

LIFE, LIBERTY, & THE CONSTITUTION. After achieving its independence, the country experimented with a loose confederated government until 1787, when the state legislatures sent a distinguished group of 55 men to draft what was to become the **Constitution.** The **Bill of Rights,** a set of 10 constitutional amendments passed shortly after the Constitution, has remained a cornerstone of the American political system. This document included the rights to free speech, freedom of the press, and freedom of religion. The original words of the document's authors are still interpreted differently according to the political climate of each era. Therein lies the power of the Constitution: it has the ability to be both timeless and timely, to represent the hopes of the nation's founders while accommodating the values of subsequent generations.

MANIFEST DESTINY. Looking beyond the Mississippi River, President Thomas Jefferson purchased the **Louisiana Territory** from Napoleon in 1803 for less than $0.03 an acre. The next year, Jefferson sent the Lewis and Clark expedition to explore the territory and to find an aqueous trade route to the Pacific Ocean. Lewis and Clark never did find a trade route, but they did chart the vast extent of land that lay west of the Mississippi. Droves of people migrated west in covered wagons along the grueling Oregon Trail in search of land, fortune, and a new life.

The **Homestead Act** of 1862 prompted the cultivation of the Great Plains by distributing government land to those who would farm it and live on it. This large-scale settlement led to bloody battles with the Sioux, Hunkpapas, and Cheyenne tribes who had long inhabited the Plains. From 1866 to 1891, the US fought a continuous war, in which the Native Americans eventually were routed—their land taken away, and their communities relegated to reservations. This series of conflicts provided the basis for much of the legend surrounding the **Wild West**.

AMERICA'S PECULIAR INSTITUTION. The first **Africans** were brought to America in 1619, prisoners aboard a Dutch slave ship headed for Jamestown, Virginia. The infusion of African slave labor led to the decline of indentured servitude, a system by which poor Europeans would provide 7 years of labor in exchange for their Atlantic crossing. From the late 16th century and into the 17th century, as the demand for cheap labor increased, white settlers systematically invaded and terrorized Native American communities in search of slaves. As Native Americans suffered fatally from European diseases, colonial America relied heavily on the African slave trade to fill the gap. Thousands of Africans were taken from their homes and forced across the Atlantic to be auctioned in the US, a harrowing journey known as the **Middle Passage.** This practice would last until 1807, when the slave trade was abolished. Slave ownership, one of the most brutal aspects of American history, would continue until the late 19th century.

Slavery exacerbated existing ideological differences between the North and the South. Because the federal government was designed to be relatively weak in order to prevent the "tyranny" of pre-Revolution days from reoccurring, each state could decide to allow or prohibit slavery independently. As the Northern states became more insistent that territories and new states should be kept free of slavery, the Southern states counteracted by citing the Revolutionary ideal of states' rights to self-determination. Northern abolitionists also joined with free African Americans to form the covert **Underground Railroad,** an escape route in which "conductors" secretly transported slaves in covered wagons into the free northern states. Southerners who invaded the North to retrieve their "property" fueled existing tensions between these two separate halves of a nation split by socioeconomic differences. It would take a fierce and bloody conflict to decide which region would prevail.

"A HOUSE DIVIDED": THE CIVIL WAR. Tensions between the North and South came to a head when **Abraham Lincoln,** an anti-slavery Congressman from Illinois, was elected President in 1860. In response, South Carolina, a hotbed of pro-slavery sentiment, seceded from the Union and was followed by 10 other Southern states. These rebellious states quickly united as the **Confederate States of America,** under the presidency of Jefferson Davis. Lincoln, however, refused to accept the secession, thereby setting the stage for war. On April 12, 1861, Southern troops fired on Fort Sumter in the harbor of Charleston, SC, and the Civil War began. For 4 years the country endured a savage and bloody conflict, fought by the North to restore the Union and by the South to break it.

Lincoln led the North to eventual victory, but the price was high. The war claimed more American lives than all others, and many families were divided against each other as brothers took up different uniforms and loyalties. Lincoln himself was assassinated on April 14, 1865, by a Southern sympathizer named John Wilkes Booth.

RECONSTRUCTION & INDUSTRIALIZATION. The period after the war brought Reconstruction to the South and Industrial Revolution to the North. The North's rapid industrialization rendered it a formidable contender in the world economy, while the South's agricultural economy began a slow decline. Injured and embittered by the war and dependent on an outdated agricultural tradition, Southerners struggled to readjust to the new economic and social situations forced upon them. The newly freed blacks faced a difficult transition from plantation to free life. **Jim Crow** laws, imposed by white politicians espousing a doctrine of segregation, impeded blacks' free exercise of their civil rights and prohibited them from frequenting the same establishments and schools as whites. Even drinking fountains were classified according to race. Though black colleges were founded and a few prominent blacks were able to gain some degree of political power, many were relegated to a life of share-cropping for white landowners.

During the North's **"Gilded Age"** of the 1870s, captains of industry such as Cornelius Vanderbilt, Andrew Carnegie, and John D. Rockefeller built commercial empires and enormous personal fortunes amid an atmosphere of widespread political and economic corruption. The burden of the concentration of massive wealth in a few hands landed most heavily on the powerless masses—on hapless farmers toiling in a dying agricultural economy and on workers facing low wages, violent strike break-ups, and unsafe working conditions. Yet the fruits of the industrial age, including railroads, telegraphs, and telephones, made transportation and communication across the vast nation much easier.

IMPERIALISM & WWI. The racism expressed in Jim Crow laws and Native American genocide didn't end at domestic borders. The United States' victory in the **Spanish-American War** in 1898 validated America's sense of military superiority, and the belief that its influence should be extended worldwide. The United States caught imperial fever, acquiring colonies in the Philippines, Puerto Rico and Guam. Meanwhile, large industrial monopolies came under attack from the Progressive Party. A new breed of journalists, the "muckrakers," began exposing the corruption rampant in big business and government.

In 1901, **Teddy Roosevelt,** following the assassination of William McKinley, succeeded to the presidency, bringing a youthful, progressive approach to the goverment. In response to the corrupt, monopolistic practices of big business, Roosevelt promoted anti-trust reforms to regulate large companies. In foreign affairs, Roosevelt established the US as an international police power, and recommended that the nation "speak softly and carry a big stick."

After vowing to keep the US out of "Europe's War," President **Woodrow Wilson** reluctantly entered **World War I** in its closing stages. US troops landed in Europe in 1917 and fought until Germany's defeat the next year. Though the metal-consuming war jump-started America's industrial economy and established the United States as a major international power, the toll of the Great War—10 million people dead, including 130,174 Americans—disillusioned and shocked the nation.

ROARING 20S, GREAT DEPRESSION, & WWII. Americans returned their attentions to their own continent, bursting with money but ruffled by the winds of change. Labor unrest and racial tension were blamed on communist influences, and the US would experience increased paranoia of communism (a **"Red Scare"**) over the course of 1919. The same year, the perceived moral decline of America was addressed with the immensely unpopular **Prohibition,** which outlawed all alcohol. Among the younger generations, however, restrictive conventions were exuberantly tossed aside. In this free-wheelin', booze-smugglin' **"Jazz Age,"** women shucked their undergarments aside and bared their shoulders to dance the Charleston.

During this period, women **suffragists** mobilized for the right to vote, putting intense pressure on politicians at every level of the government. These efforts eventually met with success in 1920 with the passage of the 19th Amendment, which extended the right to all women.

The economic boom of the **"Roaring 20s"** was driven largely by overextended credit. The facade crumbled on "Black Thursday," October 24, 1929, when the New York Stock Exchange crashed, launching the **Great Depression.** In an urbanized, mechanized age, millions of workers (25-50% of the work force) were left unemployed and struggled to provide food and housing for their families. The United States, like the rest of the developed world, rebounded slowly, with poor economic conditions existing for almost a full decade despite the progressive **"New Deal"** policies initiated by President **Franklin D. Roosevelt.** As such, the Depression imprinted a generation of Americans with a compulsion to hoard, an appreciation of savings, and a skepticism of economic speculation.

In the aftermath of the Depression, as Nazi-led Germany plowed through Europe, anxious Americans largely stood aside and watched, largely unaware of the horrifying policies adopted by the Nazi administration. Only the Japanese attack on Pearl Harbor, Hawaii on December 7, 1941, brought America reluctantly into **World War II.** The war was waged on two fronts, as the Allied powers fought both the Germans in Europe and the Japanese in the Pacific. The European front was resolved with the German surrender on May 8, 1945, less than a year after the immense **D-Day** invasion of continental Europe in June, 1944. The war in the Pacific continued until August, when the US dropped two newly developed **nuclear bombs** on Japan, at Hiroshima on August 6, 1945, and at Nagasaki three days later, killing 80,000 civilians and revolutionizing the stakes of global conflict in the future.

THE COLD WAR. Spared the wartime devastation faced by Europe and East Asia, and empowered by nationalist pride, the US economy boomed in the post-war era and secured the nation's status as the world's dominant economic and military power. While the 1950s are often nostalgically recalled as a time of prosperity, traditional values, and contentment, the decade certainly experienced its fair share of tumult and angst.

While Elvis Presley shook his hips and Americans sported Buddy Holly glasses, the ideological gulf between the two nuclear powers—the democratic, capitalist America and the totalitarian, communist Soviet Union—initiated a half-century of **Cold War** between the two nations. Tension with the Soviet Union heightened as President Harry Truman responded to the Soviet with a hostile foreign policy of **communist containment.** Exploiting rising anti-Communist feeling, the House Un-American Activities Committee, led by Senator Joseph McCarthy, conducted witch-hunts delving into every aspect of American public life, with special focus on Hollywood and the media as a whole. The power of McCarthy and the HUAC waned as the vast majority of accusations were proven to be groundless.

Fear of communism also led ultimately to American military involvement in Asia, where the successful Maoist revolution in China had created a series of imitators in surrounding countries. From 1950 to 1953, the United States fought the **Korean War** on behalf of the South Koreans, who had been attacked by the communist North Korean government. The precedents set in Korea were carried over to the Vietnam conflict. The Soviet launch of Sputnik, the first artificial satellite, in 1957 rekindled fears that communist regimes were surpassing America in many ways. The **Cuban Missile Crisis** in 1962, during which President John F. Kennedy negotiated the removal of Soviet missiles from a Cuban base and narrowly avoided nuclear war, reinforced the popular perception that the United States must protect the world from Soviet invasion.

In 1963, Lee Harvey Oswald assassinated **President Kennedy** during a parade in Dallas, Texas. The assassination of the young, charismatic President mirrored America's larger loss of innocence and optimism. Throughout the rest of the decade, cultural strife, stemming from the long-fought Civil Rights movement and the bloody, controversial Vietnam War, altered the nation's social fabric.

ALL YOU NEED IS LOVE ... AND PROTEST. Driven by the dictates of the containment policy instituted after WWII, the United States became embroiled in Vietnamese politics. This culminated in a large-scale deployment of combat troops in 1965 to protect the South Vietnamese state from the aggression of Ho Chi Minh's communist government to the north. The **Vietnam War** became a symbol for America's credibility as a protector of nations struggling with communism, making retreat difficult even when it became apparent that the situation in Vietnam was more complex than originally expected and that victory was unlikely. Though most Americans supported the war at first, opposition grew as it dragged on and its moral premises were questioned. The use of TV and photographic media to cover the war contributed to the harsh and hopeless perception of the situation in Vietnam. The mantra "Make Love, Not War," shouted by long-haired, scantily-clad bodies rolling in the mud at the 1969 **Woodstock** music festival, came to symbolize the hippie generation. The developing opposition to the conflict among the young catalyzed wrenching generational clashes that eventually culminated in the shooting of anti-war protestors by the National Guard at **Kent State** in 1970.

The Vietnam War was not the only cause that captured the hearts and lungs of idealistic young Americans. **Rosa Parks'** refusal to give up a bus seat in Montgomery, Alabama, in 1955 sparked a period of feverish activity in the **Civil Rights movement,** in which African Americans strove for legal equality. The struggle was characterized by countless demonstrations, marches, and sit-ins in the heart of a defiant and often violent South. Activists were drenched with fire hoses, arrested, and even killed by local mobs and policemen. The movement peaked with the March on Washington in 1963, where **Dr. Martin Luther King, Jr.** delivered his famous "I Have A Dream" speech, calling for non-violent racial integration. The tone of the Civil Rights movement changed as blacks became fed up with peaceful moderation and turned to the more militant rhetoric of **Malcolm X,** a converted Black Muslim who espoused separatist "Black Power." The gun-toting Black Panthers resorted to terrorist tactics to assert the rights of African-Americans.

The second wave of the **women's movement** accompanied the Civil Rights movement. Sparked by Betty Friedan's landmark book *The Feminine Mystique,* American women sought to change the delineation between men's and women's roles in society, and demanded access to male-dominated professions and equal pay. The sexual revolution, fueled by the introduction of the birth control pill, heightened debate over a woman's right to choose to have an abortion. The 1973 Supreme Court decision *Roe v. Wade* legalized abortion, but the battle between abortion opponents and pro-choice advocates still divides the nation today.

Despite a spate of Civil Rights legislation and anti-poverty measures passed under President Lyndon B. Johnson's **Great Society** agenda, the specter of the war overshadowed his presidency. By the end of these tumultuous years, the nation had dropped 7 million tons of bombs on Indochina—twice the amount used against America's World War II enemies—and victory was still out of reach. Thus, under President Richard Nixon, America admitted defeat and extracted the last of its troops from Vietnam.

In 1972, five burglars were caught breaking into the Democratic National Convention Headquarters in the **Watergate** apartment complex. Their botched attempt to bug the Democratic offices eventually led to a broader scandal involving the President himself. Caught by his own audiotape, Nixon fought Congress but ultimately resigned from the Presidency.

By the mid-1970s, America was firmly disillusioned with the idealistic counterculture of the previous decade. More frivolous forms of fun, such as dancing in platform shoes and powder blue suits under flashing colored lights—a phenomenon known as **"disco"**—became the mark of a generation that just wanted to have fun. Unfortunately, the international situation continued to be tenuous. The oil-rich Arab nations boycotted the US, causing an **energy crisis** that drove up gas prices, frustrated autophile Americans, and precipitated an economic recession.

THE 1980S. In 1980, **Ronald Reagan,** a politically conservative actor and former California governor, was elected to the White House. Reagan knew how to give the people what they wanted: money. He cut government spending on public programs and lowered taxes. Though the decade's conservatives did embrace certain right-wing social goals like school prayer and the campaign against abortion, the Reagan revolution was essentially economic. **Reaganomics** handed tax breaks to big business, spurred short-term consumption, and deregulated savings and loans. Yet all was not well—whereas the US had been a creditor nation in 1980, the end of the decade saw the nation as the world's largest debtor.

On the foreign policy front, Reagan aggressively expanded the military budget and sent weapons and aid to right-wing "freedom fighters" in Guatemala, Nicaragua, and Afghanistan, a policy that would come back to haunt the US in the decades to come.

THE 1990S: "SLICK WILLY". The US remained an active police force in the world through the early 1990s, as President Bush Sr. instigated **"Operation Desert Storm"** in 1990 as a response to Iraq's invasion of neighboring Kuwait. The war freed Kuwait, but its popularity in the US was compromised by the recession that followed. The public replaced Bush in the 1992 Presidential election with the young, saxophone-tooting Democrat **Bill Clinton,** who promised a new era of government activism after years of laissez-faire rule.

Meanwhile, Clinton's young administration began to find itself plagued with its own problems: a suspicious Arkansas real estate development called **Whitewater,** an alleged extramarital affair with Gennifer Flowers, and accusations of sexual harassment from Paula Jones. Yet Clinton's public approval remained high, especially after the nation supported him in a struggle against the Congressional Republicans whose attempts to balance the budget led to two government shutdowns between 1995 and 1996. Clinton was re-elected in 1996.

A new scandal erupted in 1998, as reports of an inappropriate relationship between Clinton and 24-year-old White House intern **Monica Lewinsky** were plastered across American newspapers, magazines, and television. Clinton initially denied the allegations, but he later admitted that he lied. Eventually, he was **impeached** for perjury and obstruction of justice on the recommendation of Independent Counsel Kenneth Starr. The resulting trial in the Senate ended with a vote for informal censure over conviction, and Clinton remained in office.

RECENT NEWS

SEPTEMBER 11, 2001. On September 11th, the most severe terrorist attack in US history occurred when four planes were hijacked. The site of the most violent crash was the World Trade Center in New York City, where approximately 3000 lives were taken. Osama bin Laden and the Taliban, the Islamic ruling body of Afghanistan, were deemed responsible for the attacks. Since September 11th, President Bush (Jr.) has waged a "War on Terrorism" designed to identify and capture known terrorists, particularly those of Al-Qaeda, an international terrorist network. The "War on Terrorism" became controversial among the US public when President Bush instituted military tribunals and US Attorney General John Ashcroft threatened the civil liberties of immigrants and non-citizens under sweeping measures like the Patriot Acts.

ECONOMIC RECESSION. The first months of the Bush administration witnessed a sharp decline in the stock market, ending six years of economic prosperity under Bill Clinton. Inflated technology stocks plummeted in value, causing the NASDAQ to fall. Further economic trouble came after September 11th when the travel industry saw a dramatic decrease in travelers resulting from fears of terrorism. Today the unemployment rate hovers near 6.4%, the highest in almost ten years. In recent months, the US economy has shown signs of rebounding, but the reality of a recession remains.

INCREASING UNILATERALISM. As a byproduct of the "War on Terrorism," the general direction of American policy has moved away from reliance on international organizations (i.e. the UN). Rather, as attempts to act in concert with such institutions have met with frustration and failure, the American government has begun to act on its own, as demonstrated by the recent war in Iraq. This policy has been met with hostility by many countries, especially those in continental Europe, and has increased overall tension around the world.

CULTURE

FOOD

There is much more to American food than McDonald's and KFC. Due to the geographic and ethnic diversity of the States, however, it is not easy to nail down exactly what American food is. The truth is that real American food is best found at the regional level, where agricultural production, immigration patterns, and local culture have resulted in food that goes beyond the fast food stereotype.

NORTHEAST. America's English settlers first landed in the Northeast, combining their staples of meats and vegetables with uniquely American foodstuffs such as turkey, maple syrup, clams, lobster, cranberries, and corn. The results yielded such treasures as Boston brown bread, Indian pudding, New England clam chowder, and Maine boiled lobster. The shellfish in the Northeast is second to none.

SOUTHEAST. Be prepared for some good ol' home cookin'. Fried chicken, biscuits, mashed potatoes, grits, and collard greens are some of the highlights of Southeastern cuisine. Ham biscuits provide a savory supplement to lunch and dinner dishes.

LOUISIANA. Chefs in New Orleans are among the best in the country, and creole or Cajun cooking tantalizes the taste buds. Locals and tourists alike regard smothered crawfish, fried catfish, jambalaya (rice cooked with ham, sausage, shrimp, and herbs), and gumbo (a soup with okra, meat, and vegetables) as delicacies. The faint of taste buds beware: Cajun and creole cooking bring in the heat.

TEXAS. From beef, to pork, to beef again, Texans like to throw it on the grill. Eat at any of the many barbecue joints, though, and they'll tell you that the real secret's in the sauce. For those in the mood for something ethnic, enchiladas, burritos, and fajitas are scrumptious Tex-Mex options.

SOUTHWEST. Strongly influenced by Mexican cuisine, the Mexican foodstuffs of corn, flour, and chilies are the basic components of Southwestern grub. Salsa made from tomatoes, chilies, and *tomatillos* adds a spicy notes to nearly all dishes, especially cheese- and chicken-filled quesadillas and ground beef tacos.

CUSTOMS & ETIQUETTE

TABLE MANNERS. In the US, good table manners means quiet eating. Loud chewing, talking with food in your mouth, or slurping are seen as rude, and burping is not seen as complimentary to the chef. Servers at sitdown restaurants usually expect to be tipped 15%.

PUBLIC BEHAVIOR. Dress in the US tends to be more modest than in Europe. Toplessness, particularly in women, should be avoided. The most acceptable forms of public affection are hugging and holding hands. Kissing in public will usually draw a few glances. Although most cities are tolerant of homosexuality, gay or lesbian couples should be aware that they may receive unwanted attention for public displays of affection, especially in rural areas.

GESTURES. One of the most offensive gestures in the US is extending your middle finger at someone. Otherwise known as "giving someone the finger," this gesture is considered not only rude, but obscene. On the other hand, a "thumbs up" gesture is a sign of approval and a widely recognized signal for hitchhiking.

THE ARTS

While early US artistic endeavors owed much to age-old European traditions, it did not take long for hearty American individualism to make its mark on the global canon. From the 19th century Transcendentalist literature of New England to the unique musical stylings of bluegrass and jazz, America has established itself time and again as an innovator in the world of creative arts.

LITERATURE

THE FIRST FEW PAGES. The first best-seller printed in America, the *Bay Psalm Book*, was published in Cambridge, MA, in 1640. Reflecting the Puritanical culture of much of 17th- and 18th-century America, it was religious in nature. Very few enduring classics were created until the early 1800s, when artists began to explore the unique American experience in their writing. **James Fenimore Cooper**'s *Last of the Mohicans* (1826), **Nathaniel Hawthorne**'s *The Scarlet Letter* (1850), and **Herman Melville**'s *Moby Dick* (1851)—among the first great American novels—all feature strong yet innocent individualists negotiating the raw American landscape. By the mid-19th century, the work of **New England Transcendentalists** like **Henry David Thoreau** *(Walden)* and **Ralph Waldo Emerson** embodied a spirit of anti-materialism by focusing on self-reflection and a retreat into nature. Later in the century, **Mark Twain** became one of America's best-loved storytellers with his homespun tales out of Hannibal, Missouri. His *Adventures of Huckleberry Finn* (1885) uses a young boy's journey to express social criticism and a treatment of the human spirit.

Literature also provided 19th-century American women the opportunity both to express themselves and to comment critically on their society. In 1852, **Harriet Beecher Stowe** published *Uncle Tom's Cabin*, an exposé of slavery that, according to some scholars, may have contributed to the outbreak of the Civil War. Poet **Emily Dickinson** secretly scribbled away in her native Amherst, Massachusetts, home; her untitled, unpunctuated, and uncapitalized verses weren't discovered until after her death in 1886.

EARLY 20TH CENTURY EXPLORATIONS. The 1920s marked a time of economic prosperity, while a reflective, self-centered movement fermented in American literature. **F. Scott Fitzgerald's** works *(The Great Gatsby)* portray restless individuals who are financially secure but unfulfilled by their conspicuous consumption. During this tumultuous time, many writers moved abroad in search of refuge; this **Lost Generation** included Fitzgerald, **Ernest Hemingway** (*The Sun Also Rises*), **T.S. Eliot** (The Waste Land), **Ezra Pound,** and **e.e. cummings,** whose sophisticated works conveyed the contemporary American experience. The **Harlem Renaissance,** a gathering of African-American artistic energy in New York City, fed off the excitement of the Jazz Age. **Langston Hughes, Nella Larsen,** and **Zora Neale Hurston** (*Their Eyes Were Watching God*) brought awareness of an African-American presence to a broad audience while revealing the depths of black creativity and intellectualism.

As America struggled to recover from the Great Depression, the plight of decaying agricultural life and faltering industry of the Deep South and West began to infiltrate literature. **William Faulkner** (*The Sound and the Fury*) juxtaposes avant-garde stream-of-consciousness techniques with subjects rooted in the rot and decay of the rural South. Nobel prize recipient **John Steinbeck,** best known for his 1939 novel *The Grapes of Wrath*, depicts the condition of migrant laborers in the Great Plains and California. The plays of **Tennessee Williams** (*A Streetcar Named Desire*) often portray family dynamics within lower-class, uprooted Southern families. In his remarkable autobiography, *Black Boy* (1945), **Richard Wright** recounts growing up black in the Jim Crow South.

POST-WAR MALAISE. In the conformist 1950s, literature provided alternative commentary on America's underlying social problems. **Ralph Ellison**'s *Invisible Man*, published in 1952, confronted a broad audience with the division between white and black identities in America. In 1955, **Vladimir Nabokov,** a Russian émigré, redefined English prose style for a whole generation of writers with his controversial story about unconventional love, *Lolita.* **Gwendolyn Brooks,** the first black writer to win a Pulitzer Prize, published intense poetry that highlighted social problems such as abortion, gangs, and drop-outs. The **Beats,** spearheaded by cult heroes **Jack Kerouac** (*On the Road*) and **Allen Ginsberg** (Howl), lived wildly and proposed a more free-wheeling attitude. Playwright **Arthur Miller** delved into the American psyche with *Death of a Salesman* (1949), in which he explored the frailty of the mythical American dream.

As conventions of society found themselves increasingly questioned in the 1960s, writers began to explore more outrageous material. **Anne Sexton** uncovered the depths of her own mental breakdown, while **Sylvia Plath** paved the way for feminist authors, exposed her psychological deterioration and hinted at her suicide in *The Bell Jar* (1963). The essays and stories of **James Baldwin** (*The Fire Next Time*) warned both white and black Americans about the self-destructive implications of racial hatred. **Flannery O'Connor** exposed the eerie, grotesque underbelly of the contemporary South in her stories, such as "A Good Man is Hard to Find."

In more recent fiction, the search for identity and the attempt to reconcile artistic and social agendas has continued. **E.L. Doctorow's** *Ragtime* (1975) evokes vibrant images of a turn-of-the-century America, weaving together historical and fictional figures. **Toni Morrison** (*Beloved*) won the Nobel Prize for her visceral interpretations of the tension between gender, ethnic, and cultural identities. **Don DeLillo's** *White Noise* (1985) carries on the American absurdist tradition by heating up to the tune of a chemical holocaust. Many stories have also focused on the fast pace and commercialism of modern society. In *Bright Lights Big City* (1987), **Jay McIntire** exposes the fast-living Wall Street of the 1980s, while the plays of **David Mamet** (*Glengarry Glen Ross*) are known for explosively confronting the gritty underside of American business. Among most recent authors, the prolific **Philip Roth** *(American Pastoral)* continues to disassemble the American dream, while **Kinky Friedman** reimagines the detective story with his own quirky spin.

MUSIC

The United States has given birth to a plethora of musical genres, whose styles and songs have intermingled to produce the many distinct styles that can be heard today. **Scott Joplin** meshed African-American harmony and rhythm with classical European style to develop the first American piano form, ragtime. From this rich, upbeat, piano-banging dance music of the 19th century to the Deep South's tradition of mournful blues, early African-American music defined soul. As soul and gospel music evolved into rhythm and blues, jazz, and funk, American music came to reflect the legacy of a resilient African-American voice.

SINGIN' THE BLUES. The blues can be described as the epitome of soul music. As with ragtime, black Southerners were primarily responsible for the blues, which was originally a blend of Northwest African slave calls and Native American song and verse forms. Blues songs were popularized by **W.C. Handy;** his "St. Louis Blues" remains one of the most recorded songs ever. As Southern blacks migrated to industrial centers during the early 20th century, the blues, augmented by the contributions of women like **Mamie Smith, Billie Holiday,** and **Bessie Smith,** found an audience in the North. The blues heavily influenced the development of other popular American musical styles, most notably jazz and rock 'n' roll.

AND ALL THAT JAZZ. Ragtime, blues, and military brass combined in New Orleans in the early 20th century to create America's classical music, jazz. Jazz's emphasis on improvisation and unique tonal and harmonic rules distinguished it from all other previous genres. The work of all-time jazz greats like **Louis Armstrong** and **Ella Fitzgerald** influenced the later work of classical composers; **Leonard Bernstein's** classical orchestrations and **George Gershwin's** jazzy theatrical style can both trace their roots and distinctly American sound to the ragtime tradition. Early jazz also led to the era of big band music, during which the incomparable **Duke Ellington** and the swing orchestra of **Glenn Miller** reigned supreme.

O, BROTHER. Country music has its roots in the Appalachian Mountains, among a poor rural white population that was putting a new spin on ancestral European folk traditions. Sentimental, often spiritual lyrics were placed to simple melodies to create a characteristically honest American sound. The genre owes much of its attitude and sound to classic heroes: **Hank Williams** cultivated an air of tragic, honky-tonk mystique, while **Johnny Cash** left his mark with a brazen, devil-may-care honesty. Commercially, country didn't catch on until it was given a boost by radio, and Nashville's famous 1930s program the **Grand Ole Opry.** Today, country artists like **Willie Nelson** and **Emmylou Harris** have captured both Southern and Northern audiences; roadtrippers should be aware that country music now dominates the radio waves across the country.

Another similar genre carrying on a distinctly American style is folk. Folk music has often embraced political and social activism through its direct lyrics and honest spirit. **Woody Guthrie's** diverse music touched upon issues of patriotism in the midst of the Great Depression ("This Land is Your Land") as well as commenting on union labor organization issues. Thanks to artists like **Bob Dylan** and **Joan Baez,** folk music popularly caught on in the sixties and spoke to social protesters across the nation. The **Grateful Dead** also grew out of folk music; more than just a band, they were an entire lifestyle that celebrated drugs and counterculture. Folk still survives today in coffee shops and on street corners, as folk musicians remain some of the most lucid social commentators.

PUT ANOTHER DIME IN THE JUKEBOX, BABY. No one can say exactly how rock 'n' roll was started, although it originally grew out of African-American traditions of gospel and rhythm and blues. One thing is for certain, though: **Elvis Presley** was the first to be crowned "King." His rock kingdom of **Graceland** is a popular attraction for Memphis tourists. During the 50's and 60's rock 'n' roll's driving, danceable rhythms, rebellious attitude, and fascination with electric instruments would dominate the popular music charts. Rock 'n' roll reflected the new post-WWII optimism and innocence throughout America, as teenagers looked for something more exciting and daring to express their style. The genre has produced most of America's more famous music icons—before Elvis, there were **Chuck Berry** and **Jerry Lee Lewis,** who ushered in a new era of poodle skirts and slicked-back hair. Today, the general category of "rock" could be divided chronologically into oldies (the **Beach Boys, Buddy Holly**), classic rock **(Bruce Springsteen, Pink Floyd)**, and modern rock.

The 1970s will be forever remembered for being the era of disco. Disco divas like **Gloria Gaynor** ("I Will Survive") and funk bands like **Parliament Funkadelic** dominated the American nightlife and fostered a culture that celebrated dancing, drugs, and excess. The 1980s witnessed a rap revolution, spawned by East Coast stars **Public Enemy, Run-DMC** and the **Beastie Boys,** which is still going strong today. The eighties also ushered in the popularity of "hair bands" like **Poison** and punk rockers like **The Ramones,** not to mention a little entertainer named **Madonna.** In the early nineties, grunge music escaped from the garage to the national spotlight largely because of Seattle's **Nirvana** and **Pearl Jam,** while hip-hop acts like the late **Notorious B.I.G.** inspired imitators around the world. The West Coast birthed the "gangsta rap" movement **(Dr. Dre, Snoop Doggy Dogg)** in the 90's as well, sparking much debate over the promotion of violence and excessive misogyny in its lyrics.

DIRTY POP. The late 1990s and new millennium have been dominated by a resurgence of bubblegum pop and dance tunes. The new MTV generation of consumer teens has sustained the popularity of young singers like **Britney Spears** and boy bands such as ***N-Sync.** Although many criticize the genre for being full of copycat songs with essentially the same musical structure and dance beat, legions of screaming fans, weaned on the energetically choreographed music videos of current superstars, don't seem to mind.

FILM

SILENT FILMS & PRE-CODE TALKIES. Before sound was wedded to image in the first "talkie"—*The Jazz Singer*, 1927—silent films ruled the screen. Though silent films quickly went out of fashion once sound entered the picture, they still hold a place of prominence in film history and the hearts of film buffs. **Hollywood,** California, owing to its sunny, film-friendly climate, proximity to a variety of photogenic terrain, and previous prominence as a theater center, quickly became the center of the movie business. By the period just after WWI, actors like Charlie Chaplin, Buster Keaton, and Mary Pickford were household names. Free from the control of domineering studios, these film artists brought a playful, exuberant, and innovative attitude to their work. Films such as *Sunrise* and *The Crowd*, meanwhile, combined innovative cinematography and compelling stories that remain vibrant to this day.

Between 1930 and 1934 American cinema enjoyed a rollicking, saucy period of artistic freedom that came to be known as Pre-Code Hollywood. Movies from this period bristled with robust doses of sex, violence, and brash humour. Films such as *Freaks*, *Morocco*, and *Scarface* took advantage of the free-spirited times and portrayed aspects of life that would soon be ignored when pressure to clean up the screen brought about the enforcement of the moral Production code in 1934.

CLASSIC ERA. It was not long, before the wild success of the movies gave rise to the expansion of the **studio system.** Giant production houses like Paramount, MGM, and Warner took up residence on the West Coast and turned movies into big business. American film's **golden age** took place during the height of the studio era, fueled by those who transcended the studio system's confines. Victor Fleming's *Gone with the Wind* (1939), a Civil War epic, was the first large-scale movie extravaganza, redefining the bounds of cinematic scope. Frank Capra, in his probing morality plays like *It's a Wonderful Life* (1946) and *Mr. Smith Goes to Washington* (1939), brought a conscience to entertainment. Michael Curtiz's *Casablanca* (1942), starring the moody Humphrey Bogart, fine-tuned the art of creating cinematic romance. In 1941, Orson Welles unveiled his intricate masterpiece, *Citizen Kane*, a landmark work whose innovations expanded contemporary ideas about the potential of film. Fantasy, however, still sold tickets: Walt Disney's animated *Snow White* (1937) and Fleming's *The Wizard of Oz* (1939) kept producers well-fed.

PRETTY BOYS, MONSTERS, & BOMBSHELLS. Heightened tensions with the Soviet Union and conflicts with communism abroad led to widespread communist witch-hunts at home. The film industry, under government pressure, took up the policy of **blacklisting** any artists with suspected, or even rumored, ties to communism. The resulting constant paranoia, as well as dwindling box office returns brought about by competition with television, eventually stimulated the production of a slew of movies that were sensational enough to draw crowds back to the theaters. Films such as *Invasion of the Body Snatchers* and *The Incredible Shrinking Man* used the genre of **science fiction** to grapple with cultural anxieties about communism and nuclear weapons while larger than life **westerns** such as *High Noon* and *The Searchers* galloped across the screens. Meanwhile, Alfred Hitchcock *(Rear Window, North by Northwest)* and the ever-free-thinking Orson Welles *(The Lady from Shanghai)* threw an element of suspense into the mix.

The 1950s also saw the emergence of a cult of **glamour** surrounding the most luminous stars. Cloaked in glitz and scandal, sex symbols Marilyn Monroe, James Dean *(Rebel Without a Cause)*, Elizabeth Taylor, and Rock Hudson drew audiences to movies by name recognition alone. Along with actors Marlon Brando *(A Streetcar Named Desire)* and Audrey Hepburn *(Breakfast at Tiffany's)*, these stars brought their own personal mystique to the screen, while adding much to the art of cinematic performance.

SOCK IT TO ME. The 1960s and early 1970s saw widespread social upheaval and tension between generations. The existing studio system proved entirely incapable of responding to the demands of the young, more liberal-thinking audiences. Rethinking their battle plans, many studios enlisted directors influenced by the French New Wave as well as artists from other media to direct features, including Sidney Lumet, John Frankenheimer, and Robert Altman. With the studios more willing to take a gamble, and the introduction of a movie ratings board (MPAA) to replace censorship, the work of a number of innovative filmmakers began to enter the mainstream. Stanley Kubrick, in *Dr. Strangelove* (1964), *2001: A Space Odyssey* (1968), and *A Clockwork Orange* (1971), brought a literary importance to filmmaking. Dennis Hopper's *Easy Rider* (1969), a film about countercultural youth rebellion, and the acclaimed documentary *Woodstock* (1970) opened the door to social critique. Meanwhile, during the first half of the 1970s the short-lived genre of blaxploitation—sensationalized portrayals of urban African-American lifestyles—enjoyed its time in the limelight with films such as *Shaft*, and *Superfly*.

Throughout the 1970s, experimentalism largely gave way to more polished treatment of equally serious issues. Film-schooled directors like Martin Scorsese *(Taxi Driver)*, Francis Ford Coppola *(The Godfather)*, and Michael Cimino *(The Deer Hunter)* brought technical skill to their exploration of the darker side of humanity. An influx of foreign filmmakers, like Milos Forman *(One Flew Over the Cuckoo's Nest)* and Roman Polanski *(Chinatown)*, introduced a new perspective to American film.

TAKING CARE OF BUSINESS. Driven by the global mass distribution of American cinema and the development of high-tech special effects, the late 1970s and 1980s witnessed the revitalization of the **blockbuster.** Directors like George Lucas with the *Star Wars* trilogy, and Steven Spielberg with *E.T.* (1982) and *Raiders of the Lost Ark* (1981), created enormously successful movies whose success spanned the globe. Though such films were often criticized for their over-reliance on special effects and lack of story line, they almost single-handedly returned Hollywood to its former status as king.

Despite the profit-orientation of Hollywood, quite a bit of highly imaginative work came out of the period, including Rob Reiner's *This is Spinal Tap*, a hilarious send-up of popular music, as well as David Lynch's *Blue Velvet*, a disturbing exploration of the primal terror beneath the tranquil surface of suburbia.

INDIE FEVER. The revival of the blockbuster continued strong into the 1990s, with such high-budget money makers as the dinosaur extravaganza *Jurassic Park* and the decadent marine love-story *Titanic* drawing the largest crowds.

Yet the recognition of independent, or **indie,** films—films that are either produced independently of any major studio or at least do not follow standard studio conventions—marks the most interesting turn for cinema in the last several years. Brothers Joel and Ethan Coen have created some of the most creative and original work of late, including the gruesome comedy *Fargo* and the hilarious, off-beat *The Big Lebowski.* Quentin Tarantino's cool yet hyper-charged action *(Reservoir Dogs, Pulp Fiction)*, Paul Thomas Anderson's emotionally charged and frequently sprawling storytelling style *(Boogie Nights, Magnolia)*, and Wes Anderson's darkly quirky humor *(Rushmore, The Royal Tenenbaums)* have all injected new life into American cinema.

FINE ARTS

American art has often been dismissed as a pale reflection of European trends. Despite this stereotype, it has a rich history rooted in the country's expansion from colonial America to the present day. Its raw and uncontrolled nature is reflected not only in the grandiose 19th-century landscape paintings that sought to capture the beauty of the untamed West, but also in the unwieldy lines and shapes of American 20th-century **abstract expressionism.**

PAINTING. Portraiture flourished in colonial America. John Singleton Copley, Charles Willson Peale, and Gilbert Stuart rendered intimate likenesses of iconic revolutionary figures, from Paul Revere to George Washington. In the first half of the 19th century, Thomas Cole and Frederic Edwin Church produced ambitious landscapes with didactic overtones. Later, **Winslow Homer's** vibrant watercolors captured the wild side of nature in sweeping seascapes, while softer American Impressionists such as Childe Hassam depicted the effects of light in New England city scenes. The turn of the 20th century saw an emphasis on adulterated realism and the depiction of urban life; the group of painters known as the Ash Can School, led by Robert Henri, promoted "art for art's sake." By the 1940s, abstract expressionism, originating in Europe, had been reborn in the US. Country-wide anxiety over international unrest and the threat of war bore heavily on the American psyche. In drip paintings and figurative images, painters like **Jackson Pollock** and **Mark Rothko** reflected the ironic mix of swaggering confidence and frenetic insecurity that characterized Cold War America. Ushering in the age of **pop art, Roy Lichtenstein** and **Andy Warhol** used mass-produced, cartoonish images to satirize the icons of American popular culture. The 1980s art boom, stationed around private galleries in New York City and L.A., ushered in a decade of slick, idyllic paintings and the kitschy sculptures of Jeff Koons.

PHOTOGRAPHY. Beginning in the early 20th century, photography became the medium of choice for artists with a social conscience. **Jakob Riis** and **Lewis Hine** photographed the urban poor and child laborers, while **Walker Evans** and **Dorothea Lange** captured destitute farmers during the Great Depression. **Robert Frank's** snapshots caught the social transitions and tensions of 1960s America. In the 1970s, photography came into its own as the back-to-basics 35mm photographs pushed the boundaries of defined art, with the stills of Diane Arbus, Garry Winogrand, and Cindy Sherman.

ARCHITECTURE & PUBLIC ART. American architecture of earlier days may have scraped together the leftovers of passé European styles, but the 20th-century architect **Frank Lloyd Wright** gave America its own architectural mode. His works, including the Fallingwater house in Pennsylvania (see p. 304) and the Robie House in Chicago (see p. 583), demonstrate an angular aesthetic and attention to environmental cohesiveness. Contemporary architects like Frank Gehry have moved the craft of architecture into the 21st century with feats of seemingly impossible engineering and optical effects.

In most American cities, public art has an established role. Not only do sculptures and installations adorn city parks and the lobbies of public buildings, but experiential walk-through environments like **Maya Lin's** Vietnam Veterans Memorial in Washington, D.C. (see p. 327) are often commissioned in large cities.

THE MEDIA

America is wired. Images, sounds, and stories from the television, radio, Internet, and magazines infiltrate every aspect of the American lifestyle. Fads have been popularized and fortunes have been made thanks solely to the power of mass media, but because of this intense power, constant debate rages over who should be held responsible for content. Despite controversy about policing the industry, American consumption of new media is continually growing.

TELEVISION. Television sets are found in 99% of US homes. Competition between the six national **networks** (ABC, CBS, NBC, Fox, UPN, and WB), cable television, and satellite TV has triggered exponential growth in TV culture over the past few years. Some of the most popular shows airing during prime time (8-11pm EST) include the political drama *The West Wing* (NBC), the hip comedy *Scrubs* (NBC), the tech-savvy *CSI: Crime Scene Investigation* (CBS), and the bitingly witty cartoon *The Simpsons* (Fox). One need not be bound to the networks, however, as **cable** provides special-interest channels that cover every subject from cooking to sports to science fiction. Meanwhile, **premium stations** air recently released movies along with regular programming; one favorite is HBO, which boasts the pleasingly off-beat *Curb Your Enthusiasm* and the mobster drama *The Sopranos*. Travelers will find that some hotel rooms come equipped with basic cable, while others offer premium stations or even pay-per-view channels.

Although **reality television** surged in popularity a few years ago, many network programs have suffered from the effects of an over-saturated market in 2003, and even the granddaddy of them all, *Survivor* (CBS), has dropped in popularity. Still, cable station MTV seems to have gotten it right, as teenagers and young adults spend hours glued to reality programs *The Real World* and (shudder) *Sorority Life*. Special comedy programs also dominate much of TV-land. Americans and Canadians alike have contributed to the successes of the long-running *Saturday Night Live* (NBC), while late-night television is sustained by the comic stylings of talk-show hosts like David Letterman on *The Late Show* (CBS) and Conan O'Brien's *Late Night* (NBC). Daytime programming is less-watched and less-respected but still fills the hours with tawdry soap operas and frequently trashy talk shows.

Television is the point of entry to **world wide news** for most Americans. Twenty-four hour news coverage is available on CNN, MSNBC, and Fox News, all cable stations. Each major network presents local and national nightly news (usually at 5 and/or 11pm EST), while prime-time "newsmagazines" like *60 Minutes* (CBS), *Dateline* (NBC), and *20/20* (ABC) specialize in investigative reports and exposés.

The Public Broadcasting Station (PBS) is commercial-free, funded by viewer contributions, the federal government, and corporate grants. Its repertoire includes educational children's shows like *Sesame Street*, nature programs, mystery shows, and British comedies.

PRINT. Despite the onset of more sophisticated technologies like TV and the Internet, Americans still cherish the feel of glossy pages and the smell of newsprint. Today, newsstands crowd city corners and transportation terminals throughout the country. Publications cover all areas of society, culture, and politics; whether it's for lounging away a Sunday afternoon at home or passing time in a doctor's waiting room, print media dominate the market.

Some of the most well-respected daily newspapers include *The New York Times* and *The Washington Post,* although every city has at least one major paper. Another popular rag, *USA Today,* is a more informal daily. Fashion magazines such as *Cosmopolitan* and men's magazines like *Maxim* feature articles and photos about sex and fashion, while *The New Yorker* amuses its subscribers with short stories and essays. Entertainment magazines such as *People* chronicle American gossip, while *Rolling Stone* focuses on the music industry. Those interested in the ups and downs of the stock market swear by the *Wall Street Journal* and *Forbes;* those who prefer statistics about their favorite sports franchise surf the pages of *Sports Illustrated.* Ranging from trashy tabloids like the *National Enquirer* to the most influential and respected news organs, American media is notably diverse and frequently subject to criticism for being exploitative and sensational. Despite this, many Americans consume and trust their news sources without question.

RADIO. Before television transformed American culture, the radio was the country's primary source of entertainment and news. Classic comedy programs like *The Jack Benny Show* and the crackly news coverage of Edward R. Murrow amused and informed Americans for decades. Even though the moving images and crisper sounds of television have reduced radio's earlier, widespread popularity, it remains a treasured medium. Radio is generally divided into AM and FM; talk radio comprises most of the low-frequency AM slots, and the high-powered FM stations feature most of the music. Each broadcaster owns a four-letter call-name, with "W" as the first letter for those east of the Mississippi River (as in WJMN), and "K" to the west (as in KPFA).

The more intellectually minded listen to **National Public Radio (NPR).** Full of classical music and social pundits debating important issues, the station gives even *Car Talk,* a show about car repair, an academic flair. Supplying the country's regional needs, local area channels give up-to-the-minute news reports and air a wide range of music, from country western to the latest pop. College radio stations often play more alternative styles of music to appeal to younger listeners.

SPORTS & RECREATION

For Americans, sports are inseparable from commercialism and regional allegiances. Dressed in colorful uniforms and covered with face-paint, Americans fill stadiums or lounge at home to cheer on their local teams.

(AMERICAN) FOOTBALL. Nowhere is the commercialism of American sports more spectacularly displayed than in the **Super Bowl.** Every January, the **National Football League (NFL)** season ends in grandiose style with a championship featuring the league's two best teams and commercial campaigns costing millions of dollars. The American-rules game is especially dear to middle America, where the padded warriors of the gridiron are applauded for their brute athleticism.

BASEBALL. The slow, tension-building game of baseball captures the hearts of dreaming Little League children and earns its place as America's national pastime. Baseball in the US and Canada centers on the Major League Baseball (MLB) season. With teams in most major cities, the MLB baseball season ends with the World Series, a seven game series between the leagues' two best teams.

BASKETBALL. Professional basketball teams hail from almost every major city, making up the **National Basketball Association (NBA).** NBA players have come a long way since the first teams were playing with peach baskets and Converse All-Star sneakers. Today, professional basketball games are fast-paced, aerial shows. Women have gotten into the game with the **WNBA**, a young but growing league. Enthusiasm for college hoops, however, often surpasses that for the pros. Sticking with their school allegiances, many Americans are known to live and die by—and bet large amounts of money on—their college's basketball team in the NCAA tournament, fondly called **March Madness.**

ICE HOCKEY. Though not as popular as other sports in the US, hockey is somewhat a national religion for Canadians. The **National Hockey League (NHL),** comprised of both American and Canadian teams, features great ice hockey and some of the best fights in professional sports. As NHL teams vie for the **Stanley Cup,** the tension of competition often results in crowd-pleasing team brawls.

OTHER SPORTS. Other sports claim smaller niches of the American spectatorship. Both golf and tennis have internationally publicized tournaments known as the **US Open**. The horse racing of the **Kentucky Derby** hones the betting strategies of seasoned gamblers and tries the tolerance of seasoned boozers. **NASCAR auto racing** draws droves of fans to Daytona Beach, Florida in February with the Daytona 500. Here, the cars tear around a banked track hundreds of times, while wide-eyed and open-mouthed fans throw down countless beers and hot dogs. **Major League Soccer (MLS)** is an up-and-coming but not yet widely followed sports in the United States.

HOLIDAYS & FESTIVALS

USA: NATIONAL HOLIDAYS

DATE IN 2004	HOLIDAY
January 1	New Year's Day
January 19	Martin Luther King, Jr. Day
February 16	Presidents Day
May 31	Memorial Day
July 4	Independence Day
September 6	Labor Day
October 11	Columbus Day
November 11	Veterans Day
November 25	Thanksgiving
December 25	Christmas Day

CANADA: NATIONAL HOLIDAYS

DATE IN 2004	HOLIDAY
January 1	New Year's Day
April 11	Easter Sunday
April 12	Easter Monday
May 24	Victoria Day
July 1	Canada Day
September 6	Labour Day
October 11	Thanksgiving
November 11	Remembrance Day
December 25	Christmas Day
December 26	Boxing Day

FESTIVALS 2004

From music to magic, culture to kitsch, the USA and Canada are home to a remarkably varied selection of festivals. Some of the most popular American and Canadian festivals are listed below, along with the page numbers of their respective descriptions in the guide. This list is far from exhaustive; refer to the Sights and Entertainment sections of specific cities for more festivals.

USA	
January	**Western Stock Show and Rodeo,** Denver, CO (p. 724)
	Winter Carnival, St. Paul, MN (p. 613)
February	**Mardi Gras,** New Orleans, LA (p. 470)
	Oregon Shakespeare Festival, (through October) Ashland, OR (p. 1021)
March	**South by Southwest,** Austin, TX (p. 694)
April	**New Orleans Jazz and Heritage Festival,** New Orleans, LA (p. 470)
	Fiesta San Antonio, San Antonio, TX (p. 686)
May	**Memphis in May International Festival,** Memphis, TN (p. 386)
	Spoleto Festival USA, Charleston, SC (p. 418)
June	**Portland Rose Festival,** Portland, OR (p. 1017)
	Chicago Blues Festival, Chicago, IL (p. 586)
	Summerfest, Milwaukee, WI (p. 594)
	Aspen Music Festival, (through August), Aspen, CO (p. 736)
	Tanglewood, Lenox, MA (p. 145)
July	**Frontier Days,** Cheyenne, WY (p. 792)
	Aquatennial, Minneapolis, MN (p. 613)
August	**Newport Folk Festival and JVC Jazz Festival,** Newport, RI (p. 151)
	Elvis Week, Memphis, TN (p. 388)
September	**La Fiesta de Santa Fe,** Santa Fe, NM (p. 857)
October	**Hot Air Balloon Festival,** Albuquerque, NM (p. 864)
November	**Macy's Thanksgiving Day Parade,** New York, NY (p. 232)
CANADA	
January	**Annual Polar Bear Swim,** Vancouver, BC.
February	**Winterlude,** Ottawa, ON (p. 215)
	Winter Carnival, Québec City, QC (p. 197)
May	**Stratford Shakespeare Festival** (through Nov.), Stratford, ON.
	Canadian Tulip Festival, Ottawa, ON (p. 215)
July	**Nova Scotia International Tattoo Festival,** Halifax, NS.
	International Jazz Festival, Montréal, QC (p. 190)
August	**Canadian National Exhibition,** Toronto, ON.

ADDITIONAL RESOURCES

GENERAL HISTORY

Manliness and Civilization, Gail Bederman. A cultural history of gender and race in America from 1880 to 1917, this book investigates the way ideas of manhood changed at the turn of the century by focusing on the lives of Theodore Roosevelt, educator G. Stanley Hall, Ida B. Wells, and Charlotte Perkins Gilman.

Lies My Teacher Told Me, James W. Loewen. This work, subtitled "Everything Your American History Textbook Got Wrong," exposes misrepresentations and misinterpretations of common historical accounts, attempting to correct fallacies and provide more thorough context for well-known facts.

Regeneration Through Violence, Richard Slotkin. This work discusses the significance of the West in American culture, focusing on ways in which the challenges presented by the ever-advancing American frontier permanently shaped American culture.

A People's History of the United States, Howard Zinn. With a broad scope spanning from Columbus' first steps in the New World to the first term of President Clinton, Zinn's massive book focuses on previously ignored figures, giving a voice to marginalized Americans and providing a new perspective to major historical events.

DOCUMENTARIES

Eyes on the Prize, Henry Hampton. A stunning, heart-wrenching series of films on the American Civil Rights movement. 1987.

The Civil War, Ken Burns. Presents a multiplicity of perspectives –from firsthand accounts of frontline soldier to modern historians, on the War Between the States. 1990.

Paris is Burning, Jennie Livingston. A look into the lives of a community of NYC drag queens in the 1980s who wrestle with class, gender, and sexual identities as they compete on the ball scene. 1990.

The Atomic Cafe, A playful, quirky, and intelligent look at 1960s footage on how to survive a nuclear attack, and how radiation effects people and the environment. 1982.

Harlan County, USA. Barbara Kopple. Delves into the struggles of a Kentucky miner's strike. 1976.

Gimme Shelter, Albert and David Maysles. Tells the story of the last stages of the Rolling Stones 1969 tour of the US, including a shocking look at the violence at their Altamont concert, an incident that came to mark the end of 1960s innocence. 1970.

CANADA

Geographically speaking, Canada is the second largest country in the world, sprawling over almost 10 million square kilometers (3.85 million sq. mi.). Still, nearly 32 million people—roughly the population of California—inhabit Canada's 10 provinces and three territories. Well over half the population crowds into the southern provinces of Ontario and Québec, while the newly declared northern territory, Nunavut, has under 30,000 people. Framed by the Atlantic to the east and the Pacific to the west, Canada extends from fertile southern farmlands to frozen northern tundra. The early French and English colonists were both geographically and culturally distant from one another. To this day, **anglophones** and **francophones** fight to retain political dominance in the Canadian government. The concerns of the First Nation peoples and an increasing immigrant population have also become intertwined in the struggle.

O CANADA! A BRIEF HISTORY

Although archaeologists are uncertain about the exact timing, recent data indicates that the **first Canadians** arrived at least 10,000 years ago by crossing the Asian-Alaskan land bridge. Their descendents flooded the continent, fragmenting into disparate tribes. The cold, barren North gained many hardy Inuit groups, while tribes like the Haida thrived in the bountiful rivers and forests of the West.

The prairies and grasslands of the central continent, supporting large populations of buffalo, found Assiniboine and Sioux populations. Algonquin and Micmac natives prospered in eastern forests and coasts, respectively.

The first **Europeans** known to explore the area were the Norse, led by Leif Erickson, who temporarily set up camp in northern Newfoundland around the year 1000. England came next; John Cabot sighted Newfoundland in 1497 when he came across the Grand Banks, a legendary rich fishing spot and long-kept secret of Atlantic fishermen. Jacques Cartier landed at the gulf of the St. Lawrence River in 1534, claiming the mainland for the French crown. He initiated a vibrant fur trade that would persist for centuries between the French and the Micmac natives, and, upon visiting an Iroquoi nation, adapted "Kanata" (the word for "village") as the name of the land. Cartier's actions touched off a rivalry between England and France that persisted until Britain's 1759 capture of Québec in the Seven Years' War and France's total capitulation four years later.

During the Revolutionary War, when the thirteen colonies on the American seaboard opted for independence and revolted from Britain, the Canadian settlements—upper and lower Canada (modern Ontario and Québec) and the maritimes (Newfoundland, Nova Scotia, New Brunswick, and Prince Edward Island)—remained loyal to the crown. Their populations boomed as thousands of Empire Loyalists fled the newly-formed United States to remain within the British Empire. In early America, there was hope that the breach could be repaired and that the Canadian colonies could be induced to enter the Union. The federalist papers included articles arguing for the unconditional right of statehood to any British North American colony willing to enter the Union. During the War of 1812, Thomas Jefferson anticipated the wholehearted entry of the Canadians—English and French—into the ranks of the US. Tensions between the US and the British North American colonies continued right up until the Civil War, which diverted American expansionist interest permanently from the North.

The movement to unify the British North American colonies gathered speed after the American Civil War, when US military might and economic isolationism threatened the independent and continued existence of the British colonies. On March 29, 1867, Queen Victoria signed the **British North America Act (BNA),** uniting Nova Scotia, New Brunswick, Upper Canada, and Lower Canada. Provinces were granted power over local affairs, and Canada could now pass its own laws—though because it still was a dominion of the British, it needed Parliament's approval on constitutional changes. Canada at last had its country—and its day: the BNA was proclaimed on **July 1, Canada Day**.

Since that time, Canada has expanded both territorially and economically. The years following consolidation witnessed sustained economic growth and expansion, with westward travelers trekking toward the Pacific in search of gold. These pioneers were greatly aided by the new trans-continental railway, completed in 1885 with labor dangerous and difficult by 15,000 Chinese immigrants. Following completion of the Canadian-Pacific Railroad, the Chinese workers, no longer employed, followed the rail lines and scattered across the country, establishing significant communities throughout Canada.

Participation in WWI earned the Dominion international respect and a charter membership in the League of Nations. It joined the United Nations in 1945 and was a founding member of the **North Atlantic Treaty Organization** in 1949. The Liberal government of the following decade created a national social security system and a national health insurance program. Pierre Trudeau's government repatriated Canada's constitution in 1982, freeing the nation from Britain in constitutional legality (though Elizabeth II remains nominal head of state). Free to forge its own alliances, the country signed the controversial **US-Canada Free**

Trade Agreement (FTA) in 1989 and the **North American Free Trade Agreement (NAFTA)** in 1994 under the leadership of Conservative Brian Mulroney, allowing for a dramatic increase in trade with the US.

In recent years, Canada has faced internal political tensions as well as an ever-increasing pressure to Americanize. Mulroney strove hard to mold a strong, unified Canada, but he will probably go down in Canadian history as the leader who nearly tore the nation apart in an effort to bring it together. His numerous attempts to negotiate a constitution that all ten provinces would ratify (Canada's present constitution lacks Québec's support) consistently failed, fanning the flames of century-old regional tensions and precipitating to his resignation in 1993. Most recently, landmark decisions to legalize gay marriage and growing momentum behind decriminalized marijuana initiatives have been seen by some commentators as signs of massive social change in the nation.

The **québécois separatist movement** has a long and not entirely pleasant history. Though francophone nationalism has roots as far back as the colonial period, the separatist impulse truly took hold in 1960, when nationalist Liberals took power in Québec. The national Official Language Act of 1969 set the French language on equal footing with English in government and throughout the country in an attempt to elevate Canadian nationalism and put an end to the separatism rampant in Québec. In 1970's October Crisis, after a decade of bombings and robberies, the Front de Liberation du Québec kidnapped two Canadian officials, killing one. The crisis, which prompted Trudeau to declare a brief period of martial law, brought the issue of Québec's separation to a head. Support for the newly formed Parti Québécois was not universal, however, and a 1980 referendum saw 60% of *québécois* opposed to separation from the Dominion. In a more recent (1996) referendum, however, separation was rejected by a mere 1.2% margin. The struggle for an independent Québec remains an actively debated issue in both the cultural and parliamentary arenas.

Canada has also locked horns with its **aboriginal peoples,** known as the First Nations. The Inuit and other peoples in the Northwest Territories have struggled for more political representation and have been largely successful: the 1999 creation of Nunavut represented a huge gain for First Nations in the north. The newly formed territory covers approximately 2 million sq. km (770,000 sq. mi.). About 85% of the region's 26,000 inhabitants are Inuit. While Nunavut's government mirrors that of the other provinces and territories, the new territory's political system is greatly influenced by Inuit customs and beliefs.

In addition to fretting over the independence wishes of their numerous constituents, Canadian policy-makers continue to struggle for Canada's **cultural independence** from the US. Media domination by their southern neighbor has put a bit of a strain on Canadian pride, so much so that Canada's radio stations are required by law to play 30% Canadian music. The US also poses another, more dangerous threat to Canadian well-being: each year, the country loses thousands of young professionals to the US, where taxes are lower and wages higher.

CANUCK CULTURE

Canada has two official languages, English and French. The *québécois* pronunciation of French can be perplexing to European speakers, and the protocol is less formal. There are also numerous native languages. Inuktitut, the Inuit language, is widely spoken in Nunavut and the Northwest Territories.

Most noted **Canadian literature** is post-1867. The opening of the Northwest and the Klondike Gold Rush (1898) provided fodder for the adventure tale—Jack London (*The Call of the Wild, White Fang*) and Robert Service (*Songs of a Sourdough,*

The Trail of '98) both authored stories of prospectors and wolves based on their mining experience in the north. On Prince Edward Island, L.M. Montgomery penned one of the greatest coming-of-age novels, *Anne of Green Gables* (1908). Prominent contemporary English-language authors include poet and novelist Margaret Atwood, best known for the futuristic best-seller *The Handmaid's Tale* (1986), and Sri Lankan-born novelist Michael Ondaatje, whose *The English Patient* (1992) received the prestigious Booker Prize. Canada also boasts three of the world's most authoritative cultural and literary critics: Northrop Frye, Hugh Kenner, and pop phenom Marshall McLuhan. Comparatists Clément Moisan and Philip Stratford have written extensively on the dynamic between English and French literature in Canada. The *québécois* literary tradition is becoming more recognized, and has been important in defining an emerging cultural and political identity.

Canada's contributions to the world of **popular music** encompass a range of artists and genres. Canadian rockers include Neil Young, Joni Mitchell, Leonard Cohen, Rush, Cowboy Junkies, Barenaked Ladies, k.d. lang, Bryan Adams, and the Tragically Hip. Chart-toppers of the last few years include the inimitable (and who would want to?) Céline Dion, Sarah McLachlan, Our Lady Peace, country crossover Shania Twain, Alanis Morissette, Sum 41, and MTV punk-poster-child Avril Lavigne. Canada is also home to *québécois* folk music and several world-class orchestras, including the Montréal, Toronto, and Vancouver Symphonies.

On the silver screen, Canada's National Film Board (NFB), which finances many documentaries, has gained worldwide acclaim since its creation in 1939. The first Oscar given to a documentary went to the NFB's 1941 *Churchill Island.* Recent figures of note include indie director Atom Egoyan, whose haunting film *The Sweet Hereafter* (1997) scored two Oscar nominations. *Québécois* filmmakers have also met with success. Director Denys Arcand caught the world's eye at Cannes with the striking *Jésus de Montréal* (1989), a reflection of the filmmaker's disillusionment with the Church, and the Oscar-nominated movie *Le déclin de l'empire américain* (1985). Most recently, *Atanarjuat: The Fast Runner* (2001), the first feature film in the Inuit language Inuktitut, gained international acclaim and the Golden Camera award at the Cannes Film Festival.

The *Toronto Globe and Mail* is Canada's national newspaper, distributed six days a week across the entire country. Every Canadian city has at least one daily paper; the weekly news magazine is *Maclean's.* The publicly owned **Canadian Broadcasting Corporation (CBC)** provides two national networks (one in English, one in French) for both radio and TV. The CBC is supplemented by a private broadcaster, CTV, as well as specialty cable channels and American networks. Canadian television has produced many great comedians: Dan Akroyd, John Candy, Eugene Levy, Mike Myers, Catherine O'Hara, and Martin Short.

In the realm of sports, Canada possesses an athletic heritage befitting its northern latitudes. Popular sports include ice skating, skiing, and the perennial cult favorite, ice hockey. Canadians also enjoy a spirited game of **curling,** which involves pushing a 20kg stone across a sheet of ice. Some of Canada's other popular sports are derived from those of the First Nations. Lacrosse, the national game of Canada, was played long before the Europeans arrived. Sports played in the United States have crossed the border in full force; in addition to the **Canadian Football League (CFL),** Canada has one NBA team (the Toronto Raptors) and two Major League Baseball outfits (the Montreal Expos and the Toronto Blue Jays).

ESSENTIALS

FACTS FOR THE TRAVELER

ENTRANCE REQUIREMENTS

Passport (p. 33). Required for citizens of all foreign countries except Canada.
Visa (p. 33). Visitors from most of Europe, Australia, and New Zealand can travel in the US for up to 90 days without a visa, although you may need to show a return plane ticket. Citizens of South Africa need a visa.
Inoculations (p. 41). Be sure immunizations are up to date.
Work Permit (p. 33). Required for all foreigners planning to work in the US.
Driving Permit (p. 63). Required for all those planning to drive.

EMBASSIES & CONSULATES

US EMBASSIES & CONSULATES ABROAD

Contact the nearest embassy or consulate to obtain information regarding visas and permits to the United States. Offices are only open limited hours, so call well before you depart. The US State Department provides contact information for US diplomatic missions on the Internet at http://foia.state.gov/MMS/KOH/keyofficers.asp. Foreign embassies in the US are located in Washington, D.C., but there are consulates in the Southwest that can be helpful in an emergency. For a more extensive list of embassies and consulates in the US, consult the web site www.embassy.org.

AUSTRALIA. Embassy and Consulate: Moonah Pl., Yarralumla **(Canberra),** ACT 2600 (☎02 6214 5600; http://usembassy-australia.state.gov/consular). **Other Consulates:** MLC Centre, Level 59, 19-29 Martin Pl., **Sydney,** NSW 2000 (☎02 9373 9200; fax 9373 9184); 553 St. Kilda Rd., **Melbourne,** VIC 3004 (☎03 9526 5900; fax 9510 4646); 16 St. George's Terr., 13th fl., **Perth,** WA 6000 (☎08 9202 1224; fax 9231 9444).

CANADA. Embassy and Consulate: Consular Section, 490 Sussex Dr., **Ottawa,** P.O. Box 866, Station B, Ottowa, Ontario K1P 5T1 (☎613-238-5335; www.usembassycanada.gov). **Other Consulates** (☎1-900-451-2778 or www.amcits.com): 615 Macleod Trail SE, Room 1000, **Calgary,** AB T2G 4T8 (☎403-266-8962; fax 264-6630); 1969 Upper Water St., Purdy's Wharf Tower II, Ste. 904, **Halifax,** NS B3J 3R7 (☎902-429-2480; fax 423-6861); 1155 St. Alexandre, **Montréal,** QC H3B 1Z1 (mailing address: P.O. Box 65, Postal Station Desjardins, Montréal, QC H5B 1G1) (514-398-9695; fax 981-5059); 2 Place Terrasse Dufferin, behind Château Frontenac, B.P. 939, **Québec City,** QC G1R 4T9; 360 University Ave., **Toronto,** ON M5G 1S4 (☎418-692-2095; fax 692-2096); 1075 W. Pender St., Mezzanine (mailing address: 1095 W. Pender St., 21st fl.), **Vancouver,** BC V6E 2M6 (☎604-685-4311; fax 685-7175).

IRELAND. Embassy and Consulate: 42 Elgin Rd., Ballsbridge, **Dublin** 4 (☎01 668 8777 or 668 7122; www.usembassy.ie).

NEW ZEALAND. Embassy and Consulate: 29 Fitzherbert Terr. (or P.O. Box 1190), Thorndon, **Wellington** (☎04 462-6000; http://usembassy.org.nz). **Other Consulate:** 23 Customs St., Citibank Building, 3rd fl., **Auckland** (☎09 303-2724; fax 366-0870).

SOUTH AFRICA. Embassy and Consulate: 877 Pretorius St., **Pretoria,** P.O. Box 9536, Pretoria 0001 (☎012 342-1048; http://usembassy.state.gov/pretoria). **Other Consulates:** Broadway Industries Center, Heerengracht, Foreshore, **Cape Town** Mailing address: P.O. Box 6773, Roggebaai, 8012 (☎021 342-1048; fax 342 2244); 303 West St., Old Mutual Building, 31st fl., **Durban** (☎031 305-7600; fax 305-7691); No. 1 River St., Killarney, **Johannesburg,** P.O. Box 1762, Houghton, 2041 (☎011 644-8000; fax 646-6916).

UK. Embassy and Consulate: 24 Grosvenor Sq., **London** W1A 1AE (☎020 7499 9000; www.usembassy.org.uk). **Other Consulates**: Queen's House, 14 Queen St., Belfast, **N. Ireland** BT1 6EQ (☎0289 032 8239; fax 9024 8482); 3 Regent Terr., Edinburgh, **Scotland** EH7 5BW (☎0 131 556 8315; fax 557 6023).

CANADIAN EMBASSIES & CONSULATES

AUSTRALIA. Embassy and Consulate: Commonwealth Ave., **Canberra** ACT 2600 (☎02 6270 4000; fax 6273 3285; www.dfait-maeci.gc.ca/australia). **Other Consulates:** 267 St. George's Terr., **Perth** WA 6000 (☎08 9322 7930; fax 9261 7706); 111 Harrington St., 5th fl., **Sydney** NSW 2000 (☎02 9364 3000; fax 9364 3098).

IRELAND. Embassy and Consulate: 65 St. Stephen's Green, Dublin 2 (☎01 417 4100; fax 01 417 4101).

NEW ZEALAND. Embassy and Consulate: 61 Molesworth St., 3rd fl., Thorndon, **Wellington.** Mailing Address: P.O. Box 12049 Thorndon, Wellington (☎04 473-9577; fax 471 2082; www.dfait-maeci.gc.ca/newzealand). **Other Consulates:** Street Address: Jetset Centre, 9th fl., 44-48 Emily Pl., **Auckland.** Mailing Address: P.O. Box 6186, Auckland (☎09 309-3690; fax 307 3111).

SOUTH AFRICA. Embassy and Consulate: 1103 Arcadia St., Hatfield 0028, **Pretoria.** Mailing Address: Canadian High Commission, Private Bag X13, Hatfield 0028, Pretoria (☎012 422-3000; fax 422 3052). **Other Consulates:** Reserve Bank Bldg., 60 St. George's Mall, 19th fl., **Cape Town** 8001. Mailing Address: P.O. Box 683, Cape Town 8000 (☎021 423-5240; fax 423 4893); 14 Nuttall Gardens, Morningside, **Durban** 4001. Mailing Address: P.O. Box 712, Durban 4000 (☎031 303 9695; fax 309 9694).

UK. Embassy and Consulate: Canada House, Trafalgar Sq., **London** SW1Y 5BJ (☎0 207 258 6600; www.dfait-maeci.gc.ca/london). **Other Consulates:** Unit 3, Ormeau Business Park, 8 Cromac Ave., **Belfast,** N. Ireland BT7 2JA (☎02 891 272 060; fax 272 060); Port Rd., Rhoose, **Vale of Glamorgan,** Wales CF62 3BT (☎1446 719 172; fax 710 856); 30 Lothian Rd., **Edinburgh,** Scotland EH1 2DH (☎0131 220 4333; fax 245 6010).

US. Embassy and Consulate: 501 Pennsylvania Ave. NW, **Washington, D.C.** 20001 (☎202-682-1740; http://canadianembassy.org). **Other Consulates:** 3 Copley Pl., #400, **Boston** MA 02116 (☎617-262-3760; fax 262-3415); 2 Prudential Plaza, 180 N. Stetson Ave., #2400, **Chicago** IL 60601 (☎312-616-1860; fax 616-1878); 750 N. St. Paul Street, #1700, **Dallas** TX 75201 (☎214-922-9806; fax 922-9815); 550 S. Hope St., 9th fl., **Los Angeles** CA 90071-2627 (☎213-346-2700; fax 346-2767); 200 S. Biscayne Blvd. #1600, **Miami** FL 33131 (☎305-579-1600; fax 374-6774); 1251 Ave. of the Americas, **New York** NY 10020-1175 (☎212-596-1628; fax 596-1793); 555 Montgomery St., #1288, **San Francisco** CA 94111 (☎415-834-3180, fax 834-3189).

CONSULAR SERVICES IN THE US & CANADA

IN WASHINGTON, D.C. (US)

Australia, 1601 Massachusetts Ave., 20036 (☎202-797-3000; www.austemb.org). **Ireland,** 2234 Massachusetts Ave., 20008 (☎202-462-3939; www.irelandemb.org). **New Zealand,** 37 Observatory Circle, 20008 (☎202-328-4800; www.nzemb.org). **UK,** 3100 Massachusetts Ave., 20008 (☎202-588-7800; www.britainusa.com/consular/embassy). **South Africa,** 3051 Massachusetts Ave., 20008 (☎202-232-4400; www.saembassy.org/usaembassy).

IN OTTAWA, ONTARIO (CANADA)

Australia, 50 O'Connor St., #710, K1P 6L2 (☎613-236-0841; www.ahc-ottawa.org). **Ireland,** 130 Albert St., K1P 5G4 (☎613-233-6281; fax 233-5835). **New Zealand,** 99 Bank St., #727, K1P 6G3 (☎613-238-5991; www.nzhcottawa.org). **UK,** 80 Elgin St., K1P 5K7(☎613-237-1303; www.britainincanada.org). **South Africa,** 15 Sussex Drive, K1M 1M8 (☎613-744-0330; www.southafrica-canada.com).

DOCUMENTS & FORMALITIES

PASSPORTS

REQUIREMENTS. All foreign visitors except Canadians need valid passports to enter the United States and to re-enter their own country. The US does not allow entrance if the holder's passport expires in under 6 months; returning home with an expired passport is often illegal, and may result in a fine. Canadians need to demonstrate proof of citizenship, such as a citizenship card or birth certificate.

NEW PASSPORTS. Citizens of Australia, Canada, Ireland, New Zealand, and the United Kingdom can apply for a passport at any post office, passport office, or court of law. Citizens of South Africa can apply for a passport at any Home Affairs office. Any applications must be filed well in advance of the departure date, although most passport offices offer rush services for a very steep fee.

PASSPORT MAINTENANCE. Be sure to photocopy the page of your passport with your photo, as well as your visas, traveler's check serial numbers, and any other important documents. Carry one set of copies in a safe place, apart from the originals, and leave another set at home. Consulates also recommend that you carry an expired passport or an official copy of your birth certificate in a part of your baggage separate from other documents. If you lose your passport, immediately notify the local police and the consulate of your home government. To expedite its replacement, it helps to have a photocopy. In some cases, a replacement may take weeks to process, and it may be valid only for a limited time. Any **visas** stamped in your old passport will be irretrievably lost. In an emergency, ask for **temporary traveling papers** that will permit you to re-enter your home country.

VISAS, INVITATIONS, & WORK PERMITS

VISAS. Citizens of South Africa and most other countries need a visa—a stamp, sticker, or insert in your passport specifying the purpose of your travel and the permitted duration of your stay—in addition to a valid passport for entrance to the US. See http://travel.state.gov/visa_services.html and www.unitedstatesvisas.gov for more information. To obtain a visa, contact a

US embassy or consulate; recent security measures have made the visa application process more rigorous, and therefore lengthy. Apply well in advance of your travel date.

Canadian citizens do not need to obtain a visa for admission to the US. Citizens of Australia, New Zealand, and most European countries can waive US visas through the **Visa Waiver Program.** Visitors qualify if they are traveling only for business or pleasure (*not* to work or study), are staying for fewer than 90 days, have proof of intent to leave (e.g., a return plane ticket), possess an I-94W form, are traveling on particular air or sea carriers, and possess a machine readable passport from a nation of which they are a citizen. See http://travel.state.gov/vwp.html for more information.

If you lose your I-94 form, you can replace it by filling out form I-102, although it's very unlikely that the form will be replaced within the time of your stay. The form is available at the nearest **Bureau of Citizenship and Immigration Services (BCIS)** office (www.bcis.gov), through the forms request line (☎800-870-3676), or online (www.bcis.gov/graphics/formsfee/forms/i-102.htm). **Visa extensions** are sometimes granted with a completed I-539 form; call the same forms request line or get it online at http://www.immigration.gov/graphics/formsfee/forms/i-539.htm.

All travelers, except Canadians, planning a stay of more than 90 days also need to obtain a visa. Admission as a visitor does not include the right to work, which is authorized only by a **work permit.** Entering the US to study requires a special visa. For more information, see **Alternatives to Tourism,** p. 72.

IDENTIFICATION

When you travel, always carry two or more forms of identification with you, including at least one photo ID; a passport combined with a driver's license or birth certificate is usually adequate. Never carry all your IDs together. Split them up in case of theft or loss, and keep photocopies of them in your bags and at home.

TEACHER, STUDENT, & YOUTH IDENTIFICATION. The **International Student Identity Card (ISIC),** the most widely accepted form of student ID, provides discounts on sights, accommodations, food, and transport; access to a 24hr. emergency helpline (in North America call ☎877-370-4742; elsewhere call US collect ☎715-345-0505); and insurance benefits for US cardholders (see **Insurance,** p. 44). The ISIC is preferable to an institution-specific card (such as a university ID) because it is more likely to be recognized and honored abroad. Applicants must be degree-seeking students of a secondary or post-secondary school and must be at least 12 years of age. Because of the proliferation of fake ISICs, some services (particularly airlines) require additional proof of student identity, such as a school ID or a letter signed by your registrar and stamped with your school seal.

The **International Teacher Identity Card (ITIC)** offers teachers the same insurance coverage and similar but limited discounts. For travelers who are 25 years old or under but are not students, the **International Youth Travel Card** (**IYTC;** formerly the **GO 25** Card) offers many of the same benefits as the ISIC.

Each of the cards costs $22 or equivalent. ISIC and ITIC cards are valid for 16 months; IYTC cards are valid for one year. Many student travel agencies (see p. 58) issue the cards, including STA Travel in Australia and New Zealand; Travel CUTS in Canada; USIT in the Republic of Ireland and Northern Ireland; SASTS in South Africa; Campus Travel and STA Travel in the UK; and Council Travel and STA Travel in the US. For more information, contact the **International Student Travel Confederation (ISTC),** Herengracht 479, 1017 BS Amsterdam, The Netherlands (☎31 20 421 28 00; www.istc.org).

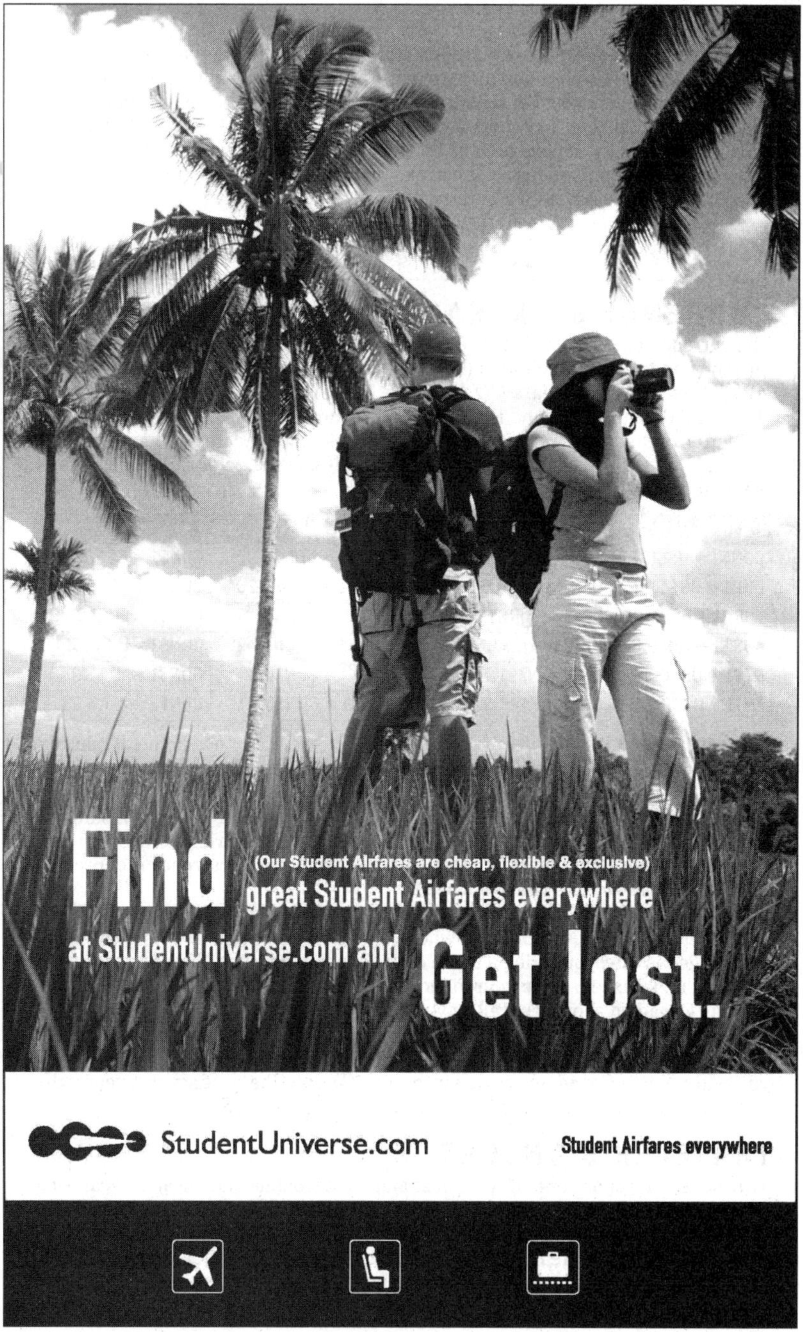

Find
(Our Student Airfares are cheap, flexible & exclusive)
great Student Airfares everywhere
at StudentUniverse.com and Get lost.
StudentUniverse.com
Student Airfares everywhere

CUSTOMS

Upon entering the US, you must declare certain items from abroad and pay a duty on the value of those articles that exceeds the US customs allowance. Note that goods and gifts purchased at duty-free shops abroad are not exempt from duty or sales tax at your point of return and thus must be declared as well; "duty-free" merely means that you need not pay a tax in the country of purchase. Upon returning, you must similarly declare all articles acquired abroad and pay a duty on the value of articles in excess of your home country's allowance.

MONEY

CURRENCY & EXCHANGE

The currency chart below is based on August 2004 exchange rates between local currency and Australian dollars (AUS$), Canadian dollars (CDN$), Irish pounds (IR£), New Zealand dollars (NZ$), South African Rand (ZAR), British pounds (UK£), US dollars (US$), and European Union euros (EUR€). Check the currency converter on financial web sites such as www.bloomberg.com and www.xe.com, or a large newspaper for the latest exchange rates. Dates below are correct as of September 2003.

US DOLLARS	
CDN$1 = US$0.71	US$1 = CDN$1.40
UK£1 = US$1.57	US$1 = UK£0.64
EUR€1 = US$1.09	US$1 = EUR€1.03
AUS$1 = US$0.64	US$1= AUS$1.56
NZ$1 = US$0.57	US$1 = NZ$1.75
ZAR1 = US$0.14	US$1 = ZAR7.29

CANADIAN DOLLARS	
US$1 = CDN$1.40	CDN$1 = US$0.71
UK£1 = CDN$2.20	CDN$1 = UK£0.45
EUR€1 = CDN$1.53	CDN$1 = EUR€0.66
AUS$1 = CDN$0.90	CDN$1= AUS$1.11
NZ$1 = CDN$0.80	CDN$1 = NZ$1.25
ZAR1 = CDN$0.19	CDN$1 = ZAR5.23

As a general rule, it's cheaper to convert money in the US than at home. While currency exchange will probably be available in your arrival airport, it's wise to bring enough foreign currency to last for the first 24 to 72 hours of a trip.

When changing money abroad, try to go only to banks or other establishments that have at most a 5% margin between their buy and sell prices. Since you lose money with every transaction, **convert large sums** (unless the currency is depreciating rapidly), **but no more than you'll need.**

If you use traveler's checks or bills, carry some in small denominations (the equivalent of $50 or less) for times when you are forced to exchange money at disadvantageous rates, but bring a range of denominations since charges may be levied per check cashed. Store your money in a variety of forms.

Many Canadian shops, as well as vending machines and parking meters, accept US coins at face value. Stores often convert the price of your purchase for you, but they are not legally obligated to offer a fair exchange. In almost all circumstances, you will receive Canadian change in return. (During the past several years, the Canadian dollar has been worth roughly 30% less than the US dollar.)

TRAVELER'S CHECKS

Traveler's checks are one of the safest and least troublesome means of carrying funds. American Express and Visa are the most widely recognized brands. Many banks and agencies sell them for a small commission. Check issuers provide refunds if the checks are lost or stolen, and many provide additional services, such as toll-free refund hotlines abroad, emergency message services, and stolen credit card assistance. They are readily accepted in the US. Ask about toll-free refund hotlines and the location of refund centers when purchasing checks, and always carry emergency cash.

American Express: Checks available with commission at select banks, at all AmEx offices, and online (www.americanexpress.com; US residents only). American Express cardholders can also purchase checks by phone (☎888-269-6669). AAA (see p. 63) offers commission-free checks to its members. Checks available in US, Australian, British, Canadian, Japanese, and Euro currencies. *Cheques for Two* can be signed by either of 2 people traveling together. For purchase locations or more information contact AmEx's service centers: In the US and Canada ☎800-221-7282; in the UK ☎0800 587 6023; in Australia ☎800 68 80 22; in New Zealand 0508 555 358; elsewhere US collect ☎801-964-6665.

Visa: Checks available (generally with commission) at banks worldwide. For the location of the nearest office, call Visa's service centers: In the US ☎800-227-6811; in the UK ☎0800 51 58 84; elsewhere UK collect ☎44 020 7937 8091. Checks available in US, British, Canadian, Japanese, and Euro currencies.

Travelex/Thomas Cook: In the US and Canada call ☎800-287-7362; in the UK call ☎01733 294 87.

CREDIT, DEBIT, & ATM CARDS

Where they are accepted, credit cards often offer superior exchange rates. Credit cards may also offer services such as insurance or emergency help, and are sometimes required to reserve hotel rooms or rental cars. **MasterCard** and **Visa** are the most welcomed; **American Express** cards work at some ATMs and at AmEx offices and major airports.

ATM cards are widespread in the US. Depending on the system that your home bank uses, you can most likely access your personal bank account from abroad. ATMs get the same wholesale exchange rate as credit cards, but there is often a limit on the amount of money you can withdraw per day (around $500), and typically a surcharge of $1-5 per withdrawal.

Debit cards are a relatively new form of purchasing power that are as convenient as credit cards but have a more immediate impact on your funds. A debit card can be used wherever its associated credit card company (usually Mastercard or Visa) is accepted, yet the money is withdrawn directly from the holder's checking account. Debit cards often also function as ATM cards and can be used to withdraw cash from associated banks and ATMs throughout the US. Ask your local bank about obtaining one.

The two major international money networks are **Cirrus** (to locate ATMs US ☎800-424-7787 or www.mastercard.com) and **Visa/PLUS** (to locate ATMs US ☎800-843-7587 or www.visa.com). Most ATMs charge a transaction fee that is paid to the bank that owns the ATM.

GETTING MONEY FROM HOME

If you run out of money while traveling, the easiest and cheapest solution is to have someone back home make a deposit to your credit card or cash (ATM) card. Failing that, consider **wiring money.** It is possible to arrange a **bank money transfer,** which means asking a bank back home to wire money to a bank in the US. This is the cheapest way to transfer cash, but it's also the slowest, usually taking several days or more. Note that some banks may only release your funds in local currency, potentially sticking you with a poor exchange rate; inquire about this in advance. Money transfer services like **Western Union** are faster and more convenient than bank transfers—but also much pricier. Western Union has many locations worldwide. To find one, visit www.westernunion.com, or call in the US ☎800-325-6000, in Canada ☎800-235-0000, in the UK ☎0800 83 38 33, in Australia ☎800 501 500, in New Zealand ☎800 27 0000, in South Africa ☎0860 100031. Money transfer services are also available at **American Express** and **Thomas Cook** offices.

COSTS

The cost of your trip will vary considerably, depending on where you go, how you travel, and where you stay. The most significant expenses will probably be your round-trip **airfare** to the US (see **Getting to the US: By Plane,** p. 57) and a **railpass** or **bus pass.** Before you go, spend some time calculating a reasonable per-day **budget** that will meet your needs.

STAYING ON A BUDGET. Accommodations start at about $12 per night in a hostel bed, while a basic sit-down meal costs about $10 depending on the region. If you stay in hostels and prepare your own food, you'll probably spend from $30-40 per person per day. A slightly more comfortable day (sleeping in hostels/guesthouses and the occasional budget hotel, eating one meal a day at a restaurant, going out at night) would run $50-65. A gallon of gas now costs about $1.60 ($0.40 per L), but prices vary widely according to state gasoline prices. In Canada, gas costs CDN$0.70 per L (CDN$2.65 per gallon).

TIPS FOR SAVING MONEY. Some simpler ways include searching out opportunities for free entertainment, splitting accommodation and food costs with other trustworthy fellow travelers, and buying food in supermarkets rather than eating out. Do your **laundry** in the sink (unless you're explicitly prohibited from doing so). With that said, don't go overboard with your budget obsession. Though staying within your budget is important, don't do so at the expense of your health or a great travel experience.

TIPPING & BARGAINING

In the US, it is customary to tip waitstaff and cab drivers 15-20% (at your discretion). Tips are usually not included in restaurant bills, unless you are in a party of six or more. At the airport and in hotels, porters expect at least a $1 per bag tip to carry your bags. Tipping is less compulsory in Canada; a good tip signifies remarkable service. Bargaining is generally frowned upon and fruitless in both countries.

TAXES

In the US, sales tax is similar to the European Value-Added Tax and ranges from 4-10% depending on the item and the place. In many states, groceries are not taxed. *Let's Go* lists sales tax rates in the introduction to each state; usually these taxes are not included in the prices of items.

In Canada, you'll quickly notice the 7% goods and services tax (GST) and an additional sales tax in some provinces. See the introductory sections for info on provincial taxes. Visitors can claim a rebate of the GST they pay on accommodations of less than 1 month and on most goods they buy and take home, so be sure to save your receipts and pick up a GST rebate form while in Canada. Total purchases must be at least CDN$200 and made within 10 months of the date of the purchase; further goods must be exported from Canada within 60 days of purchase. A brochure detailing restrictions is available from local tourist offices or through Revenue Canada, Visitor's Rebate Program, 275 Pope Rd. #104, Summerside, PE C1N 6C6 (☎902-432-5608 or 800-668-4748).

SAFETY & SECURITY

EMERGENCY = ☎911. For emergencies in the US and Canada, dial ☎911. This number is toll-free from all phones, including coin phones. In a few remote communities, 911 may not work. If it does not, dial ☎0 for the operator. In national parks, it is usually best to call the park warden in case of emergency.

PERSONAL SAFETY

EXPLORING. Crime is mostly concentrated in the cities, but being safe is important no matter where you are. St. Louis, MO; Atlanta, GA; Detroit, MI; Gary, IN; and Baltimore, MD are the most dangerous cities in the United States, but that does not mean you should not visit them. Common sense and a little bit of thought will go a long way in helping you to avoid dangerous situations. Wherever possible, *Let's Go* warns of neighborhoods that should be avoided when traveling alone or at night.

Tourists are especially vulnerable to crime because they carry large amounts of cash and tend not to be as street-savvy as locals. Avoid unwanted attention by blending in as much as possible; the gawking camera-toter is a more obvious target for thieves than the low-profile traveler. Familiarize yourself with your surroundings before setting out, and carry yourself with confidence. Check maps in shops and restaurants rather than on the street. *Be sure someone at home knows your itinerary, and never admit that you are traveling alone.*

When walking at night, stick to busy, well-lit streets and avoid dark alleyways. If you feel uncomfortable, leave as quickly and directly as you can, but don't allow fear of the unknown to turn you into a hermit.

SELF DEFENSE. There is no sure-fire way to avoid all the threatening situations you might encounter while traveling, but a good self defense course will give you concrete ways to react to unwanted advances. **Impact, Prepare,** and **Model Mugging** can refer you to local self-defense courses in the US (☎800-345-5425). Visit the web site at www.impactsafety.org for a list of nearby chapters. Workshops (2-3hr.) start at $50; full courses (20hr.) run $350-500.

DRIVING. If you are using a **car,** learn local driving signals and wear a seatbelt. Children under 40 lb. should ride only in specially-designed carseats, available for a small fee from most car rental agencies. Study route maps before you hit the road and if your car breaks down, wait for the police to assist you. For long drives in desolate areas, invest in a cellular phone and a roadside assistance program (see p. 63). Be sure to park your vehicle in a garage or well-traveled area, and use a steering wheel locking device in larger cities. *Sleeping in your car is one of the most dangerous (and often illegal) ways to get your rest.*

Interstate **public transportation** is generally safe. Occasionally, bus or train stations can be dangerous; *Let's Go* warns of these stations where applicable. Within major US cities, the quality and safety of public transportation vary considerably. It is usually a good idea to avoid subways and intra-city buses late at night; if you must use these forms of transportation, try to travel in a large group.

Let's Go does not recommend **hitchhiking** under any circumstances; see **Getting Around,** p. 61 for more info.

TERRORISM. In light of the September 11, 2001 terrorist attacks, there is an elevated threat of further terrorist activities in the United States. Terrorists often target landmarks popular with tourists; however, the threat of an attack is generally not specific or great enough to warrant avoiding certain places or modes of transportation. Stay aware of developments in the news and watch for alerts from federal, state, and local law enforcement officials. Also, allow extra time for airport security and do not pack sharp objects in your carry-on luggage, as they will be confiscated. For more information on the terror threat to the US, visit www.terrorismanswers.com.

TRAVEL ADVISORIES. The following government offices provide travel information and advisories by telephone, by fax, or via the web:

Australian Department of Foreign Affairs and Trade: ☎1300 555135, in Australia; ☎ 61 2 6261 1555 from outside; www.dfat.gov.au.

Canadian Department of Foreign Affairs and International Trade (DFAIT): In Canada and the US call ☎800-267-8376, elsewhere dial ☎613-944-4000; www.dfait-maeci.gc.ca. Call for their free booklet, *Bon Voyage...But.*

New Zealand Ministry of Foreign Affairs: ☎04 439 8000; www.mft.govt.nz/travel/index.html.

United Kingdom Foreign and Commonwealth Office: ☎0870 6060290; www.fco.gov.uk.

US Department of State: ☎202-647-5225, faxback service 202-647-3000; http://travel.state.gov. For *A Safe Trip Abroad,* call ☎202-512-1800.

FINANCIAL SECURITY

PROTECTING YOUR VALUABLES. There are a few steps you can take to minimize the financial risk associated with traveling. First, **bring as little with you as possible.** Second, buy a few combination **padlocks** to secure your belongings either in your pack or in a hostel or train station locker. Third, **carry as little cash as possible.** Keep your traveler's checks and ATM/credit cards in a **money belt**—not a "fanny pack"—along with your passport and ID cards. Fourth, **keep a small cash reserve separate from your primary stash.** This should be about $50 sewn into or stored in the depths of your pack, along with your traveler's check numbers and important photocopies.

CON ARTISTS & PICKPOCKETS. In large cities **con artists** often work in groups, and children are among the most effective. Beware of certain classic sob stories that require money. **Never let your passport or bags out of your sight.** Beware of **pickpockets** in city crowds, especially on public transportation. Also, be alert in public telephone booths: if you must say your calling card number, do so very quietly; if you punch it in, make sure no one can look over your shoulder.

ACCOMMODATIONS & TRANSPORTATION. Never leave your belongings unattended; crime occurs in even the most demure-looking hostel or hotel. Bring your own **padlock** for hostel lockers, and don't ever store valuables in any locker.

Be particularly careful on **buses** and **trains;** horror stories abound about determined thieves who wait for travelers to fall asleep. Carry your backpack in front of you where you can see it. When traveling with others, sleep in alternate shifts. When alone, use good judgement in selecting a train compartment: never stay in an empty one, and use a lock to secure your pack to the luggage rack. Try to sleep on top bunks with your luggage stored above you (if not in bed with you), and keep important documents and other valuables on your person. If traveling by **car,** don't leave valuables alone while you are away.

DRUGS & ALCOHOL

In the US, the drinking age is 21; in Canada it is 19, except in Alberta, Manitoba, and Québec, where it is 18. Drinking restrictions are particularly strict in the US. Younger travelers should expect to be asked to show government-issued identification when purchasing any alcoholic beverage. Drinking and driving is prohibited everywhere, not to mention dangerous and idiotic. Open beverage containers in your car will incur heavy fines; a failed Breathalyzer test will mean fines, a suspended license, imprisonment, or all three. Most localities restrict where and when alcohol can be sold. Sales usually stop at a certain time at night and are often prohibited entirely on Sundays. Narcotics like marijuana, heroin, and cocaine are highly illegal in the US and Canada. If you carry prescription drugs while you travel, keep a copy of the prescription with you, especially at border crossings.

HEALTH

BEFORE YOU GO

In your **passport**, write the names of any people you wish to be contacted in case of a medical emergency, and list any allergies or medical conditions. Matching a prescription to a foreign equivalent is not always easy, safe, or possible, so carry up-to-date, legible prescriptions or a statement from your doctor stating the medication's trade name, manufacturer, chemical name, and dosage. While traveling, be sure to keep all medication with you in your carry-on luggage. For tips on packing a basic **first-aid kit** and other health essentials, see p. 45.

IMMUNIZATIONS & PRECAUTIONS

Travelers over two years old should make sure that the following vaccines are up to date: MMR (for measles, mumps, and rubella); DTaP or Td (for diptheria, tetanus, and pertussis); OPV (for polio); HbCV (for haemophilus influenza B); HBV (for hepatitis B); and Varicella (for chickenpox, for those who are susceptible). For recommendations on immunizations and prophylaxis, consult the CDC (see below) in the US or the equivalent in your home country, and check with a doctor for guidance.

USEFUL ORGANIZATIONS & PUBLICATIONS

The US **Centers for Disease Control and Prevention** (**CDC;** ☎877-FYI-TRIP/394-8747; www.cdc.gov/travel) maintains an international travelers' hotline and an informative web site. The CDC's comprehensive booklet *Health Information for International Travel*, an annual rundown of disease, immunization, and general health advice, is free online or $29 via the Public Health Foundation (☎877-252-1200). For detailed information on travel health, including a country-by-country overview of diseases (and a list of travel clinics in the US), try the **International Travel Health Guide,** by Stuart Rose, MD ($29.95; www.travmed.com). For general health info, contact the **American Red Cross** (☎202-303-4498; www.redcross.org).

MEDICAL ASSISTANCE ON THE ROAD

Medical care in the US and Canada is among the best in the world. In case of medical emergency, dial ☎**911** from any phone and an operator will send out paramedics, a fire brigade, or the police as needed. Emergency care is also readily available in the US and Canada at any emergency room on a walk-in basis. If you do not have insurance, you will have to pay for medical care (see **Insurance** p. 44). Appointments are required for non-emergency medical services.

If you are concerned about obtaining medical assistance while traveling, you may wish to employ special support services. The *MedPass* from **GlobalCare, Inc.,** 6875 Shiloh Rd. East, Alpharetta, GA 30005, USA (☎800-860-1111; www.globalems.com), provides 24hr. international medical assistance, support, and medical evacuation resources. The **International Association for Medical Assistance to Travelers** (**IAMAT;** US ☎716-754-4883, Canada ☎519-836-0102; www.cybermall.co.nz/NZ/IAMAT) has free membership, lists English-speaking doctors worldwide, and offers detailed info on immunization requirements and sanitation. If your regular **insurance** policy does not cover travel abroad, you may wish to purchase additional coverage (see p. 44).

Those with medical conditions (such as diabetes, allergies to antibiotics, epilepsy, heart conditions) may want to obtain a **Medic Alert** membership (first year $35, annually thereafter $20), which includes a stainless steel ID tag, among other benefits, like a 24hr. collect-call number. Contact the Medic Alert Foundation, 2323 Colorado Ave, Turlock, CA 95382, USA (☎888-633-4298; outside US ☎209-668-3333; www.medicalert.org).

ONCE IN US & CANADA

ENVIRONMENTAL HAZARDS

Heat exhaustion and dehydration: Heat exhaustion leads to nausea, excessive thirst, headaches, and dizziness. Avoid it by drinking plenty of fluids, eating salty foods (e.g., crackers), and abstaining from dehydrating beverages (e.g., alcohol and caffeinated beverages). Continuous heat stress can eventually lead to heatstroke, characterized by a rising temperature, severe headache, delirium and cessation of sweating. Victims should be cooled off with wet towels and taken to a doctor. Heat exhaustion can be a problem even in temperate locations during the summer and year-round in certain areas of the South and Southwest.

Sunburn: If you are planning on spending time near water, in the desert, or in the snow, you are at risk of getting burned, even through clouds. If you get sunburned, drink more fluids than usual and apply an aloe-based lotion. Severe sunburns can lead to sun poisoning, a condition that affects the entire body, causing fever, chills, nausea, and vomiting. Sun poisoning should always be treated by a doctor.

Hypothermia and frostbite: A rapid drop in body temperature is the clearest sign of overexposure to cold. Victims may also shiver, feel exhausted, have poor coordination or slurred speech, hallucinate, or suffer amnesia. *Do not let hypothermia victims fall asleep.* To avoid hypothermia, keep dry, wear layers, and stay out of the wind. When the temperature is below freezing, watch out for frostbite. If skin turns white or blue, waxy, and cold, do not rub the area. Drink warm beverages, stay dry, and slowly warm the area with dry fabric or steady body contact until a doctor can be found.

Altitude Sickness: In order to avoid altitude sickness, allow your body a couple of days to adjust to less oxygen. Altitude sickness/acute mountain sickness (AMS) is characterized by headaches, loss of appetite, fatigue, dizziness, and confusion. Those suffering from AMS should stop ascending in all cases and consider descending in altitude. Travelers should take AMS into account in all high altitude regions, especially the Rocky Mountains. Alcohol is more potent and UV rays are stronger at high elevations.

INSECT-BORNE DISEASES

Many diseases are transmitted by insects—mainly mosquitoes, fleas, ticks, and lice. Be aware of insects in wet or forested areas, especially while hiking and camping; wear long pants and long sleeves, tuck your pants into your socks, and use a mosquito net. Use insect repellents such as DEET and soak or spray your gear with permethrin (licensed in the US for use on clothing). **Ticks**—responsible for Lyme and other diseases—can be particularly dangerous in rural and forested regions of the Northeast, the Great Lakes, and the Pacific coast.

Lyme disease: A bacterial infection carried by ticks and marked by a circular bull's-eye rash of 2 in. or more. Later symptoms include fever, headache, fatigue, and aches and pains. Antibiotics are effective if administered early. Left untreated, Lyme disease can cause problems in joints, the heart, and the nervous system. If you find a tick attached to your skin, grasp the head with tweezers as close to your skin as possible and apply slow, steady traction. Removing a tick within 24hr. greatly reduces the risk of infection. Do not try to remove ticks by burning them or coating them with nail polish remover or petroleum jelly.

FOOD- & WATER-BORNE DISEASES

Prevention is the best tactic: be sure that your food is properly cooked and the water you drink is clean. The tap water in the United States and Canada is treated to be safe for drinking. Always wash your hands before eating.

Traveler's diarrhea: Results from drinking untreated water or eating uncooked foods. Symptoms include nausea, bloating, and urgency. Try quick-energy, non-sugary foods with protein and carbohydrates to keep your strength up. Over-the-counter anti-diarrheals (e.g. Imodium) may counteract the problems. The most dangerous side effect is dehydration; drink 8 oz. of water with ½ tsp. of sugar or honey and a pinch of salt, try uncaffeinated soft drinks, or eat salted crackers. If you develop a fever or your symptoms don't go away after 4-5 days, consult a doctor. Consult a doctor immediately for treatment of diarrhea in children.

Dysentery: Results from a serious intestinal infection caused by certain bacteria. The most common type is bacillary dysentery, also called shigellosis. Symptoms include bloody diarrhea (sometimes mixed with mucus), fever, and abdominal pain and tenderness. Bacillary dysentery generally only lasts a week, but is highly contagious. Amoebic dysentery, which develops more slowly, is a more serious disease and may cause long-term damage if left untreated. A stool test can determine which kind you have; seek medical help immediately. Dysentery can be treated with the drugs norfloxacin or ciprofloxacin (commonly known as Cipro).

Giardiasis: Transmitted through parasites (microbes, tapeworms, etc. in contaminated water and food) and acquired by drinking untreated water from streams or lakes. Symptoms include stomach cramps, bloating, fatigue, weight loss, flatulence, nausea, and diarrhea.

OTHER INFECTIOUS DISEASES

Rabies: Transmitted through the saliva of infected animals; fatal if untreated. By the time symptoms (thirst, malaise, fever, headache and muscle spasms) appear, the disease is in its terminal stage. If you are bitten, wash the wound thoroughly, seek immediate medical care, and try to have the animal located. A rabies vaccine, which consists of 3 shots given over a 28-day period, is available but is only semi-effective.

Hepatitis B: A viral infection of the liver transmitted via bodily fluids or needle-sharing. Symptoms, which may not surface until years after infection, include jaundice, loss of appetite, fever, and joint pain. A 3-shot vaccination sequence is recommended for health-care workers, sexually-active travelers, and anyone planning to seek medical treatment abroad. The vaccination must begin 6 months before traveling.

Hepatitis C: Like Hepatitis B, but the mode of transmission differs. IV drug users, those with occupational exposure to blood, hemodialysis patients, and recipients of blood transfusions are at the highest risk, but the disease can also be spread through sexual contact or sharing items like razors and toothbrushes that may have traces of blood on them.

AIDS, HIV, & STDS

For detailed information on **Acquired Immune Deficiency Syndrome (AIDS)** in the United States and Canada, call the **US Centers for Disease Control's** 24hr. hotline at ☎800-342-2437, or contact the **Joint United Nations Programme on HIV/AIDS (UNAIDS),** 20, ave. Appia, CH-1211 Geneva 27, Switzerland (☎41 22 791 3666; www.unaids.org).

The Council on International Educational Exchange's pamphlet *Travel Safe: AIDS and International Travel* is posted on their web site (www.ciee.org/travel-safe.cfm), along with links to other online and phone resources. According to US law, HIV positive persons are not permitted to enter the US. However, HIV testing is conducted only for those who are planning to immigrate permanently. Travelers from areas with particularly high concentrations of HIV positive persons or those with AIDS may be required to provide more info when applying. Travelers to Canada who are suspected of being HIV positive will be required to submit to HIV testing.

Sexually transmitted diseases (STDs) such as gonorrhea, chlamydia, genital warts, syphilis, and herpes are easier to catch than HIV and can be just as deadly. **Hepatitis B** and **C** can also be transmitted sexually (see p. 43). Though condoms may protect you from some STDs, oral or even tactile contact can lead to transmission. If you think you may have contracted an STD, see a doctor immediately.

INSURANCE

Medical insurance (especially university policies) often covers costs incurred abroad; check with your provider. **US Medicare** does not cover foreign travel, with the exception of travel to Canada and Mexico. **Canadians** are protected by their home province's health insurance plan for up to 90 days after leaving the country; check with the provincial Ministry of Health or Health Plan Headquarters for details. **Homeowners' insurance** (or your family's coverage) often covers theft during travel and loss of travel documents (passport, plane ticket, railpass, etc.) up to $500.

Travel insurance generally covers four basic areas: medical/health problems, property loss, trip cancellation/interruption, and emergency evacuation. Although your regular insurance policies may well extend to travel-related accidents, you may consider purchasing travel insurance if the cost of potential trip cancellation/interruption or emergency medical evacuation is greater than you can absorb. Prices for travel insurance purchased separately generally run about $40 per week for full coverage.

ISIC and **ITIC** (see p. 34) provide basic insurance benefits, including $100 per day of in-hospital sickness for up to 60 days, $3000 of accident-related medical reimbursement, and $25,000 for emergency medical transport. Cardholders have access to a toll-free 24hr. helpline (run by the insurance provider **TravelGuard**) for medical, legal, and financial emergencies (US and Canada ☎877-370-4742). **American Express** (US ☎800-528-4800) grants some cardholders automatic car rental insurance (collision and theft, but not liability) and ground travel accident coverage of $100,000 on flight purchases made with the card.

INSURANCE PROVIDERS. STA (see p. 58) offers a range of plans that can supplement your basic coverage. Other private insurance providers in the US and Canada include: **Access America** (☎866-807-3982; www.accessamerica.com); **Berkely Group** (☎800-797-4514; www.berkely.com); **GlobalCare Insurance Services Inc.** (☎800-821-2488; www.globalcare-cocco.com); **Travel Assistance International** (☎800-821-2828; www.travelassistance.com). Providers in the **UK** include **Columbus Direct** (☎020 7375 0011; www.columbusdirect.co.uk). In **Australia,** try **AFTA** (☎02 9264 3299; www.afta.com.au).

PACKING

PACK LIGHTLY. Lay out only what you absolutely need, then take half the clothes and twice the money. If you plan to do a lot of hiking, also see the section on Camping & the Outdoors, p. 9.

LUGGAGE. If you plan to cover most of your itinerary by foot, a sturdy frame backpack is unbeatable. Toting a suitcase or trunk is fine if you plan to live in one or two cities or can store things in your car, but otherwise can be burdensome. In addition to your main piece of luggage, a daypack (a small backpack or courier bag) is a must.

CLOTHING. The climate in the US and Canada varies widely according to region. For most places, it's a good idea to bring a warm jacket or wool sweater, a rain jacket (Gore-Tex® is both waterproof and breathable), sturdy shoes or hiking boots, and thick socks. Flip-flops or waterproof sandals are must-haves for grubby hostel showers. If you have room, you may also want to add one outfit beyond the jeans and t-shirt uniform, and maybe a nicer pair of shoes. Remember also that if you plan to visit any religious or cultural sites, you'll need something besides tank tops and shorts to be respectful.

WASHING CLOTHES. Laundromats are common in North America, but it may be cheaper and easier to use a sink. Bring a small bar or tube of detergent soap, a small rubber ball to stop up the sink, and a travel clothesline.

CONVERTERS & ADAPTERS. In the United States and Canada, electricity is 110 volts AC. 220/240V electrical appliances are not compatible with 110V current. Appliances from anywhere outside the US and Canada need an **adapter** (which changes the shape of the plug) and a **converter** (which changes the voltage; $20). Don't make the mistake of using only an adapter (unless appliance instructions explicitly state otherwise). For more on all things adaptable, check out http://kropla.com/electric.htm.

CELLULAR PHONES. A cell phone can be a lifesaver (literally) on the road; it is highly recommended that travelers carry one, especially when traveling alone.

FIRST-AID KIT. For a basic first-aid kit, pack: bandages, pain reliever, antibiotic cream, a thermometer, a Swiss Army knife, tweezers, moleskin, decongestant, motion-sickness remedy, diarrhea or upset-stomach medication (Pepto Bismol or Imodium), an antihistamine, sunscreen, insect repellent, and burn ointment.

FILM. Film and developing in the United States are affordable (about $10 for a roll of 24 color exposures), so it is relatively easy to develop your film while traveling. Less serious photographers may want to bring a **disposable camera** or two rather than an expensive permanent one. Despite disclaimers, airport security X-rays can fog film, so buy a lead-lined pouch at a camera store or ask security to hand-inspect it. Always pack film in your carry-on luggage, since higher-intensity X-rays are used on checked luggage.

OTHER USEFUL ITEMS. For safety purposes, you should bring a **money belt** and small **padlock.** Basic **outdoors equipment** (plastic water bottle, flashlight, compass, waterproof matches, pocketknife, sunglasses, sunscreen, hat) may also prove useful. **Quick repairs** of torn garments can be done on the road with a needle and thread; also consider bringing electrical tape for patching tears. **Other things** you're liable to forget are an umbrella, sealable **plastic bags** (for damp clothes, soap, food, shampoo, and other spillables), an **alarm clock,** safety pins, rubber bands, and garbage bags.

IMPORTANT DOCUMENTS. Don't forget your passport, traveler's checks, ATM and/or credit cards, adequate ID, and photocopies of all the aforementioned in case these documents are lost or stolen (see p. 34). Also check that you have any of the following that might apply to you: a hosteling membership card (see p. 46); driver's license (see p. 34); travel insurance forms; and/or rail or bus pass (see p. 61).

ACCOMMODATIONS

HOSTELS

Hostels are generally laid out dorm-style, often with large single-sex rooms and bunk beds, although some offer private rooms for families and couples. They sometimes have kitchens and utensils for your use, bike or moped rentals, storage areas, transportation to airports, breakfast, and laundry facilities. There can be drawbacks: some hostels close during certain daytime "lockout" hours, have a curfew, don't accept reservations, impose a maximum stay, or, less frequently, require that you do chores. In the USA and Canada, a dorm bed in a hostel will average around ($15-25) and a private room around ($40-50).

HOSTELLING INTERNATIONAL

Joining the youth hostel association in your own country (listed below) automatically grants you membership privileges in **Hostelling International (HI),** a federation of national hosteling associations. HI hostels are scattered throughout USA and Canada. Many accept reservations via the **International Booking Network,** which takes worldwide reservations online and over the phone (☎202-783-6161; www.hostelbooking.com). HI's umbrella organization's web page (www.iyhf.org), which lists the web addresses and phone numbers of all national associations, can be a great place to begin researching hostelling in a specific region.

Most HI hostels also honor **guest memberships**—you'll get a blank card with space for six validation stamps. Each night you'll pay a nonmember supplement (one-sixth the membership fee) and earn one guest stamp; get six stamps, and you're a member. A new membership benefit is the Free Nites program, which allows hostelers to gain points toward free rooms. Most student travel agencies (see p. 58) sell HI cards, as do all of the national hosteling organizations listed below. All prices listed below are valid for **one-year memberships** unless otherwise noted.

BOOKING HOSTELS ONLINE. One of the cheapest and easiest ways to ensure a bed for a night is by reserving online. Our web site features the **Hostelworld** booking engine; access it at **www.letsgo.com/resources/accommodations.** Hostelworld offers bargain accommodations everywhere from Argentina to Zimbabwe with no added commission.

Hostelling International-American Youth Hostels (HI-AYH), 8401 Colesville Road, Suite 600, Silver Spring, MD, 20910 (☎301-495-1240; fax 495-6697; www.hiayh.org). $28, over 55 $18, under 18 free.

Australian Youth Hostels Association (AYHA), (www.yha.org.au) AUS$52, under 18 AUS$16.

Hostelling International-Canada (HI-C), 205 Catherine St. #400, Ottawa, ON K2P 1C3 (☎613-237-7884; www.hihostels.ca). CDN$35, under 18 free.

An Óige (Irish Youth Hostel Association), 61 Mountjoy St., Dublin 7 (☎830 4555; www.irelandyha.org). €25, under 18 €10.5.

pictures - reports - friends - discounts

Youth Hostels Association of New Zealand (YHANZ), P.O. Box 436, 166 Moorhouse Ave., Level 1, Moorhouse City, Christchurch (☎03 379 9970; www.yha.org.nz). NZ$40, under 18 free.

Hostels Association of South Africa, 3rd fl. 73 St. George's House, Cape Town 8001 (☎021 424 2511; www.hisa.org.za). R79, under 18 R40.

Scottish Youth Hostels Association (SYHA), 7 Glebe Crescent, Stirling FK8 2JA (☎ 870 1 55 32 55; www.syha.org.uk). UK£6, under 18 £2.50.

Youth Hostels Association (England and Wales), Trevelyon House, Dimple Rd., Matlock, Derbyshire DE4 3YH, UK (☎01629 5962600; www.yha.org.uk). UK£13.50, under 18 UK£6.75.

OTHER TYPES OF ACCOMMODATIONS

YMCAS & YWCAS

Young Men's Christian Association (YMCA) lodgings are usually cheaper than a hotel but more expensive than a hostel. Not all YMCA locations offer lodging; those that do are often located in urban downtowns. Many YMCAs accept women and families; some will not lodge those under 18 without parental permission.

YMCA of the USA, 101 North Wacker Drive, Chicago, IL 60606 (☎888-333-9622 or 800-872-9622; www.ymca.net). Provides a listing of the nearly 1000 Ys across the US and Canada. Offers info on prices, services available, telephone numbers and addresses.

YMCA Canada, 42 Charles St. E, 9th fl., Toronto, ON M4Y 1T4 (☎202-467-0801; www.ymca.ca), offers info on Ys in Canada.

YWCA of the USA, Empire State Building, 350 Fifth Ave. #301, New York, NY 10118 (☎212-273-7800; fax 213-273-7939; www.ywca.org), provides information on a wide range of services offered by the organization, including the occasional lodging option.

HOTELS

Hotel rooms in the US vary widely in cost depending on the region in which the hotel is located. The cheapest hotel single in the Northeast would run you about $60 per night, while it is possible to stay for $30 in a comparable hotel in the South, West, or Midwest regions. You'll typically have a private bathroom and shower with hot water, though some cheaper places may offer shared restrooms.

BED & BREAKFASTS (B&BS)

For a cozy alternative to impersonal hotel rooms, B&Bs (private homes with rooms available to travelers) range from the acceptable to the sublime. Rooms in B&Bs generally cost ($70-90) for a single and ($90-110) for a double in the US and Canada. For more info on B&Bs, see **Bed & Breakfast Inns Online,** P.O. Box 829, Madison, TN 37116 (☎615-868-1946; www.bbonline.com), **InnFinder,** 6200 Gisholt Dr. #105, Madison, WI 53713 (☎608-285-6600; www.innfinder.com), or **InnSite** (www.innsite.com).

UNIVERSITY DORMS

Many **colleges and universities** open their residence halls to travelers when school is not in session (May -Sept.); some do so even during term-time. Getting a room may take a couple of phone calls and require advanced planning, but rates tend to be low, and many offer free local calls and Internet access.

CAMPING & THE OUTDOORS

Camping is probably the most rewarding way to slash travel costs. Considering the sheer number of public lands available for camping in both the United States and Canada, it may also be the most convenient. Well-equipped campsites (usually including prepared tent sites, toilets, and water) go for $10-25 per night in the US and CDN$10-30 in Canada. **Backcountry camping,** which lacks all of the above amenities, is often free but can cost up to $20 at some national parks. Most campsites are first come first served.

USEFUL PUBLICATIONS & RESOURCES

A variety of publishing companies offer hiking guidebooks to meet the educational needs of novice or expert. For information about camping, hiking, and biking, write or call the publishers listed below to receive a free catalog.

Family Campers and RVers/National Campers and Hikers Association, Inc., 4804 Transit Rd., Bldg. #2, Depew, NY 14043 (☎/fax 716-668-6242). Membership fee ($25) includes their publication *Camping Today.*

Sierra Club Books, 85 Second St., 2nd fl., San Francisco, CA 94105-3441 (☎415-977-5500; www.sierraclub.org/books). Publishes general resource books on hiking, camping, and women traveling in the outdoors, as well as books on hiking in Arizona, Florida, Arkansas, the Rockies, the California Desert, and hikes of northern California.

The Mountaineers Books, 300 Third Ave W. Seattle, WA 98119 (☎206-284-8484; www.mountaineers.org). Over 400 titles on hiking (the *100 Hikes* series), biking, mountaineering, natural history, and conservation.

ESSENTIALS

Wilderness Press, 1200 Fifth St., Berkeley, CA 94710 (☎800-443-7227 or 510-558-1696; www.wildernesspress.com.) Over 100 hiking guides/maps, mostly for the western US.

Woodall Publications Corporation, 2575 Vista Del Mar Dr., Ventura, CA 93001 (☎800-680-6155; www.woodalls.com). Woodall publishes the annually updated *Woodall's Campground Directory* ($11) as well as regional directories for the US and Canada.

NATIONAL PARKS

National Parks protect some of the most spectacular scenery in North America. Though their primary purpose is preservation, the parks also host recreational activities such as ranger talks, guided hikes, marked trails, skiing, and snowshoe expeditions. For info, contact the **National Park Service,** 1849 C St. NW, Washington, D.C. 20240 (☎202-208-6843; www.nps.gov).

Entrance fees vary. The larger and more popular parks charge a $4-20 entry fee for cars and sometimes a $2-7 fee for pedestrians and cyclists. The **National Parks Pass** ($50), available at park entrances, allows the passport-holder's party entry into all national parks for one year._National Parks Passes can also be bought by writing to National Park Foundation, P.O. Box 34108, Washington, D.C. 20043 (send $50 plus $3.95 shipping and handling) or online at www.nationalparks.org. For an additional $15, the Parks Service will affix a **Golden Eagle Passport** hologram to your card, which will allow you access to sites managed by the US Fish and Wildlife Service, the US Forest Service, and the Bureau of Land Management. US citizens or residents 62 and over qualify for the lifetime **Golden Age Passport** ($10 one-time fee), which entitles the holder's party to free park entry, a 50% discount on camping, and 50% reductions on various recreational fees for the passport holder. Persons eligible for federal benefits on account of disabilities can enjoy the same privileges with the **Golden Access Passport** (free).

ESSENTIALS

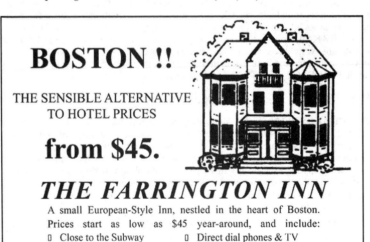

Most national parks have both backcountry and developed **camping.** Some welcome RVs, and a few offer grand lodges. At the more popular parks in the US and Canada, reservations are essential, available through MISTIX (☎800-365-2267; http://reservations.nps.gov) no more than five months in advance. Indoor accommodations should be reserved months in advance. Campgrounds often observe first come, first served policies, and many fill up by late morning.

NATIONAL FORESTS

Often less accessible and less crowded, **US National Forests** (www.fs.fed.us) are a purist's alternative to parks. While some have recreation facilities, most are equipped only for primitive camping—pit toilets and no water are the norm. When charged, entrance fees are $10-20, but camping is generally free or $3-4. Necessary wilderness permits for backpackers can be obtained at the US Forest Service field office in the area. *The Guide to Your National Forests* is available at all Forest Service branches, or call or write the main office (USDA, Forest Service, P.O. Box 96090, Washington, D.C. 20090; ☎202-205-8333). This booklet includes a list of all national forest addresses; request maps and other info directly from the forest(s) you plan to visit. Reservations, with a one-time $16.50 service fee, are available for most forests, but are usually only needed during high season at the more popular sites. Call up to one year in advance to National Recreation Reservation Center (☎877-444-6777; international 518-885-3639; www.reserveusa.com).

CANADA'S NATIONAL PARKS

Less trammeled than their southern counterparts, these parks boast at least as much natural splendor. Park entrance fees range from CDN$3-7 per person, with family and multi-day passes available. Reservations are offered for a limited number of campgrounds with a CDN$7 fee. For these reservations, or for info on the over 40 parks and countless historical sites in the network, call Parks Canada (☎888-773-8888) or consult the web page (http://parkscanada.pch.gc.ca). Regional passes are available at relevant parks; the best is the Western Canada Pass, which covers admission to all the parks in the Western provinces for a year (CDN$35 per adult, CDN$70 per group—up to seven people).

WILDERNESS SAFETY

THE GREAT OUTDOORS. Stay warm, stay dry, and stay hydrated. The vast majority of life-threatening wilderness situations can be avoided by following this simple advice. Prepare yourself for an emergency, however, by always packing raingear, a hat and mittens, a first-aid kit, a reflector, a whistle, high energy food, and extra water for any hike. Dress in wool or warm layers of synthetic materials designed for the outdoors; never rely on cotton for warmth, as it is useless when wet. See **Health,** p. 41, for information about outdoor ailments and basic medical concerns.

WILDLIFE. If you are hiking in an area that might be frequented by **bears,** keep your distance. No matter how cute bears appear, don't be fooled—they're powerful and dangerous animals. If you see a bear at a distance, calmly walk (don't run) in the other direction. If the bear pursues you, back away slowly while speaking in low, firm tones. If you are attacked by a bear, get in a fetal position to protect yourself, put your arms over your neck, and play dead. In all situations, remain calm and don't make any loud noises or sudden movements. Don't leave food or other scented items (trash, toiletries, the clothes that you cooked

ENVIRONMENTALLY RESPONSIBLE TOURISM. The idea behind responsible tourism is to leave no trace of human presence behind. A campstove is the safer (and more efficient) way to cook than using vegetation, but if you must make a fire, keep it small and use only dead branches or brush rather than cutting vegetation. Make sure your campsite is at least 150 ft. (50m) from water supplies or bodies of water. If there are no toilet facilities, bury human waste (but not paper) at least four inches (10cm) deep and above the high-water line, and 150 ft. or more from any water supplies and campsites. Always pack your trash in a plastic bag and carry it with you until you reach the next trash receptacle. For more information on these issues, contact one of the organizations listed below.

Earthwatch, 3 Clock Tower Pl., #100, Box 75, Maynard, MA 01754 (☎800-776-0188 or 978-461-0081; fax 978-461-2332; info@earthwatch.org; www.earthwatch.org).

Ecotourism Society, P.O. Box 668, Burlington, VT 05402 (☎802-651-9818; fax 802-651-9819; ecomail@ecotourism.org; www.ecotourism.org).

National Audobon Society, Nature Odysseys, 700 Broadway, New York, NY 10003 (☎212-979-3000; fax 212-979-3188; audobon@neodata.com; www.audobon.org).

Tourism Concern, Stapleton House, 277-281 Holloway Rd., London N7 8HN, UK (☎020 7753 3330; fax 020 7753 3331; info@tourismconcern.org.uk; www.tourismconcern.org.uk).

in) near your tent.Putting these objects into canisters is now mandatory in some national parks in California, including Yosemite. **Bear-bagging,** hanging edibles and other good-smelling objects from a tree out of reach of hungry paws, is the best way to keep your toothpaste from becoming a condiment. Bears are also attracted to any **perfume,** as are bugs, so cologne, scented soap, deodorant, and hairspray should stay at home.

Poisonous **snakes** are hazards in many wilderness areas in the US and Canada and should be carefully avoided. The two most dangerous are coral and rattlesnakes. Coral snakes reside in the Southwestern US and can be identified by black, yellow, and red bands. Rattlesnakes live in desert and marsh areas and will vigorously shake the rattle at the end of their tail when threatened. Don't attempt to handle or kill a snake; if you see one, back away slowly. If you are bitten, apply a pressure bandage and ice to the wound and immobilize the limb. Seek immediate medical attention for any snakebite that breaks the skin.

Mountain regions in the north provide the stomping grounds for **moose.** These big, antlered animals have been known to charge humans, so never feed, walk toward, or throw anything at a moose. If a moose charges, get behind a tree immediately. If it attacks you, get on the ground in a fetal position and stay very still.

For more info, see *How to Stay Alive in the Woods* (Macmillan Press, $8).

CAMPING & HIKING EQUIPMENT

WHAT TO BUY...

Good camping equipment is both sturdy and light. Camping equipment is generally more expensive in Australia, New Zealand, and the UK than in North America.

Sleeping Bag: Sleeping bags come in a number of materials and varieties specialized for season. Prices range $80-210 for a summer synthetic to $250-300 for a good down winter bag.

Tent: The best tents are free-standing (with their own frames and suspension systems), set up quickly, and only require staking in high winds. Good 2-person tents start at $90, 4-person at $300. Seal the seams of your tent with waterproofer, and make sure to check that it has a rain fly.

Backpack: Internal-frame packs mold better to your back, keep a lower center of gravity, and flex adequately to allow you to hike difficult trails. **External-frame packs** are more comfortable for long hikes over even terrain, as they keep weight higher and distribute it more evenly. Sturdy backpacks cost anywhere from $125-420—this is one area in which it doesn't pay to economize.

Boots: Be sure to wear hiking boots with good **ankle support.** They should fit snugly and comfortably over 1-2 pairs of wool socks and thin liner socks. Break in boots over several weeks first in order to spare yourself painful and debilitating blisters.

Other Necessities: Synthetic layers, like those made of polypropylene, and a **pile jacket** will keep you warm even when wet. A **"space blanket"** will help you to retain your body heat and doubles as a groundcloth ($5-15). Plastic **water bottles** are virtually shatter- and leak-proof. Bring **water-purification tablets** for when you can't boil water. For those places that forbid fires or the gathering of firewood, you'll need a **camp stove** (the classic Coleman starts at $40) and a propane-filled **fuel bottle** to operate it. Also don't forget a **first-aid kit, pocketknife, insect repellent, calamine lotion,** and **waterproof matches** or a **lighter.**

CAMPERS & RVS

Much to the chagrin of outdoors purists, the US and Canada are havens for the corpulent, home-and-stove on wheels known as **recreational vehicles (RVs).** Most national parks and small towns cater to RV travelers, providing campgrounds with large parking areas and electric outlets ("full hook-up"). The costs of RVing compare favorably with the price of staying in hotels and renting a car (see **Rental Cars,** p. 64), and the convenience of bringing along your own bedroom, bathroom, and kitchen makes it an attractive option.

ORGANIZED ADVENTURE TRIPS

Organized adventure tours offer another way of exploring the wild. Activities include hiking, biking, skiing, canoeing, kayaking, rafting, and climbing. Consult tourism bureaus, which can suggest parks, trails, and outfitters. Other good sources for organized adventure options are the stores and organizations specializing in camping and outdoor equipment listed above.

The National Outdoor Leadership School (NOLS), 284 Lincoln St., Lander, WY 82520-2848 (☎800-710-6657; admissions@nols.edu; www.nols.edu), offers educational wilderness trips all over the world, including many to the U.S. They also offer courses in wilderness medicine training and leave no trace ethics.

Outward Bound, 100 Mystery Point Rd., Garrison, NY 10524 (☎866-467-7651; www.outwardbound.com), offers expeditionary courses in outdoor education throughout the U.S. and overseas. Courses range from several days to over 40 days, and include special focuses, such as life & career renewal and couples.

The Sierra Club, 85 Second St., 2nd fl. San Francisco, CA 94105 (☎415-977-5500; national.outings@sierraclub.org; www.sierraclub.org/outings), plans many adventure outings at all of its branches throughout the US.

TrekAmerica, P.O. Box 189, Rockaway, NJ 07866 (☎800-221-0596; www.trekamerica.com), recently merged with AmeriCan Adventures, operates small group active adventure tours throughout the US, including Alaska and Hawaii, and Canada. These tours are for 18- to 38-year-olds, and run 1-9 weeks.

KEEPING IN TOUCH

BY MAIL

SENDING MAIL WITHIN THE US & CANADA

First-class letters sent and received within the US take 1-3 days and cost $0.37; Priority Mail packages up to 1 lb. generally take 2 days and cost $3.85, up to 5 lb. $7.70. All days specified denote business days. For more details, visit the US Postal Service at www.usps.com. For Canadian mailing information, visit Canada Post at www.canadapost.ca.

SENDING MAIL FROM THE US & CANADA

Airmail is the best way to send mail home from the US. **Aerogrammes,** printed sheets that fold into envelopes and travel via airmail, are available at post offices. Write "par avion" on the front. The cost is $0.70; simple postcard is also $0.70. A **standard letter** can be sent abroad in about 4-7 business days for $1.50. For packages up to 4 lb., use **Global Priority Mail,** for delivery to major locations in 3-5 days for a flat rate ($5).

If regular airmail is too slow, **Federal Express** (800-247-4747) can get a letter from New York to Sydney in 2 business days for a whopping $35. By **US Express Mail,** a letter would arrive within 4 business days and would cost $15.

Surface mail is by far the cheapest and slowest way to send mail. It takes 1-3 months to cross the Atlantic and 2-4 to cross the Pacific—appropriate for sending large quantities of items you won't need to see for a while.

RECEIVING MAIL

Mail can be sent via **General Delivery** to almost any city or town with a post office. Address letters to:

Elvis PRESLEY
General Delivery
Post Office Street Address
Memphis, TN 38101 or Kelowna, BC V1Z 2H6
USA or CANADA

The mail will go to a special desk in the central post office, unless you specify a post office by street address or postal code. It's best to use the largest post office, since mail may be sent there regardless of what is written on the envelope. It is usually safer and quicker to send mail express or registered. When picking up your mail, bring a form of photo ID, preferably a passport.

BY TELEPHONE

CALLING HOME FROM THE US & CANADA

A **calling card** is probably your cheapest bet. Calls are billed collect or to your account. You can often also make **direct international calls** from pay phones, but if you aren't using a calling card, you may need to drop your coins as quickly as your words. Where available, prepaid phone cards (see below) and occasionally major credit cards can be used for direct international calls, but they are still less cost-effective.

PLACING INTERNATIONAL CALLS. To call the US or Canada from home or to call home dial:

1. The **international dialing prefix.** To dial out of **Australia,** dial 0011; the **Republic of Ireland, New Zealand,** or the **UK,** 00; **South Africa,** 09.
2. The **country code** of the country you want to call. To call **Australia,** dial 61; **Canada** or the **US,** 1; the **Republic of Ireland,** 353; **New Zealand,** 64; **South Africa,** 27; the **UK,** 44.
3. The **city/area code.** *Let's Go* lists the city/area codes for cities and towns opposite the city or town name, next to a ☎.
4. The **local number.**

ESSENTIALS

CALLING WITHIN THE US & CANADA

The simplest way to call within the country is to use a coin-operated pay phone. You can also buy prepaid phone cards, which carry a certain amount of phone time. Phone rates typically tend to be highest in the morning, lower in the evening, and lowest on Sunday and late at night.

Let's Go has recently partnered with ekit.com to provide a calling card that offers a number of services, including email and voice messaging. Before purchasing any calling card, always be sure to compare rates with other cards, and to make sure it serves your needs (a local phonecard is generally better for local calls, for instance). For more information, visit www.letsgo.ekit.com.

TIME DIFFERENCES

4AM	7AM	10AM	NOON	2PM	10PM
Vancouver Seattle San Francisco Los Angeles	Toronto Ottawa New York Boston	London (GMT)	Hanoi Bangkok Jakarta Phnom Penh	China Hong Kong Manila Singapore	Sydney Canberra Melbourne

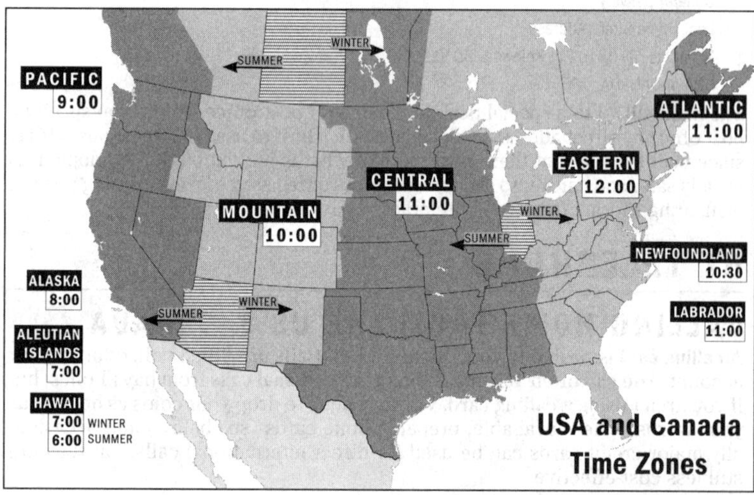

USA and Canada Time Zones

BY EMAIL & INTERNET

Most public libraries in the US and Canada offer free Internet access, and Internet cafes abound. Check the **Practical Information** sections of major cities for establishments with Internet access. For lists of additional cybercafes in the US and Canada, check out www.cybercaptive.com.

GETTING THERE

BY PLANE

When it comes to airfare, a little effort can save you a bundle. If your plans are flexible enough to deal with the restrictions, courier fares are the cheapest. Tickets bought from consolidators and standby seating are also good deals, but last-minute specials, airfare wars, and charter flights often beat these fares. The key is to hunt around, to be flexible, and to ask persistently about discounts. Students, seniors, and those under 26 should never pay full price for a ticket.

AIRFARES

Airfares to the US and Canada peak during the summer; holidays are also expensive. It is cheapest to travel midweek (M-Th morning), as round-trip flights run $40-50 cheaper than weekend flights. **Fares** for round-trip flights to the US or Canadian east coast from Western Europe range from $100-400 in the off season. A round-trip flight from Australia will tend to the $900-1500 range.

ESSENTIALS

Not fixing a return date ("open return") or arriving in and departing from different cities ("open-jaw") can be pricier than round-trip flights. Patching one-way flights together is the most expensive way to travel. Flights between major cities or regional hubs will tend to be cheaper.

If the US or Canada is only 1 stop on a more extensive globe-hop, consider a round-the-world (RTW) ticket. Tickets usually include at least 5 stops and are valid for about a year; prices range $1200-5000. Try **Northwest Airlines/KLM** (US ☎800-447-4747; www.nwa.com) or **Star Alliance,** a consortium of 22 airlines including United Airlines (US ☎800-241-6522; www.staralliance.com).

BUDGET & STUDENT TRAVEL AGENCIES

While knowledgeable agents specializing in flights to the US and Canada can make your life easy and help you save, they may not spend the time to find you the lowest possible fare—they get paid on commission. Travelers holding **ISIC and IYTC cards** (see p. 34) qualify for big discounts from student travel agencies. Most flights from budget agencies are on major airlines, but in peak season some may sell seats on less reliable chartered aircraft.

USIT, 19-21 Aston Quay, Dublin 2 (☎01 602 1600; www.usitworld.com) Ireland's leading student/budget travel agency has 22 offices throughout Northern Ireland and the Republic of Ireland. Offers programs to work in North America.

CTS Travel, 30 Rathbone Pl., London W1T 1GQ, UK(☎020 7290 0630; www.ctstravel.co.uk). A British student travel agent with offices in 39 countries including the US, Empire State Building, 350 Fifth Ave., Suite 7813, New York, NY 10118 (☎877-287-6665; www.ctstravelusa.com).

STA Travel, 7890 S. Hardy Dr., Ste. 110, Tempe AZ 85284, USA (24hr. reservations and info ☎800-781-4040; www.sta-travel.com). A student and youth travel organization with over 150 offices worldwide (check their web site for a listing of all their offices), including US offices in Boston, Chicago, L.A., New York, San Francisco, Seattle, and Washington, D.C. Ticket booking, travel insurance, railpasses, and more. In the UK, walk-in office 11 Goodge St., **London** W1T 2PF or call 0207-436-7779. In New Zealand, Shop 2B, 182 Queen St., **Auckland** (☎09 309 0458). In Australia, 366 Lygon St., **Carlton** Vic 3053 (☎03 9349 4344).

Travel CUTS (Canadian Universities Travel Services Limited), 187 College St., **Toronto,** ON M5T 1P7 (☎416-979-2406; www.travelcuts.com). Offices across Canada and the United States in Seattle, San Francisco, Los Angeles, New York and elsewhere. Also in the UK, 295-A Regent St., London W1B 2H9 (☎0207 255 2191).

FLIGHT PLANNING ON THE INTERNET.

Many airline sites offer special last-minute deals on the Web. Other sites do the legwork and compile the deals for you—try www.bestfares.com, www.flights.com, www.lowestfare.com, www.onetravel.com, and www.travelzoo.com.

StudentUniverse (www.studentuniverse.com), **STA** (www.sta-travel.com) and **Orbitz.com** provide quotes on student tickets, while **Expedia** (www.expedia.com) and **Travelocity** (www.travelocity.com) offer full travel services. **Priceline** (www.priceline.com) allows you to specify a price, and obligates you to buy any ticket that meets or beats it; be prepared for antisocial hours and odd routes. **Skyauction** (www.skyauction.com) allows you to bid on both last-minute and advance-purchase tickets.

An indispensable resource on the Internet is the *Air Traveler's Handbook* (www.cs.cmu.edu/afs/cs/user/mkant/Public/Travel/airfare.html), a comprehensive listing of links to everything you need to know before you board a plane.

COMMERCIAL AIRLINES

The commercial airlines' lowest regular offer is the **APEX** (Advance Purchase Excursion) fare, which provides confirmed reservations and allows "open-jaw" tickets. Generally, reservations must be made 7 to 21 days ahead of departure, with 7- to 14-day minimum-stay and up to 90-day maximum-stay restrictions. These fares carry hefty cancellation and change penalties (fees rise in summer). Book peak-season APEX fares early; by May you will have a hard time getting your desired departure date. Use **Microsoft Expedia** (www.expedia.com) or **Travelocity** (www.travelocity.com) to get an idea of the lowest published fares, then use the resources outlined here to try and beat those fares.

AIR COURIER FLIGHTS

Those who travel light should consider courier flights. Couriers help transport cargo on international flights by using their checked luggage space for freight. Generally, couriers must travel with carry-ons only and deal with complex flight restrictions. Most flights are round-trip only, with short fixed-length stays (usually one week) and a limit of a one ticket per issue. Most of these flights also operate only out of major gateway cities: New York, Los Angeles, San Francisco, or Miami in the US; and Montreal, Toronto, or Vancouver in Canada. Generally, you must be over 21 (in some cases 18). In summer, the most popular destinations usually require an advance reservation of about 2 weeks (you can usually book up to two months ahead). Super-discounted fares are common for "last-minute" flights (3 to 14 days ahead).

STANDBY FLIGHTS

Traveling standby requires considerable flexibility in arrival and departure dates and cities. Companies dealing in standby flights sell vouchers rather than tickets, along with the promise to get to your destination (or near your destination) within a certain window of time (typically 1-5 days). You call in before your specific window of time to hear your flight options and the probability that you will be able to board each flight. You can then decide which flights you want to try to make, show up at the appropriate airport at the appropriate time, present your voucher, and board if space is available. Vouchers can usually be bought for both one-way and round-trip travel. You may receive a monetary refund only if every available flight within your date range is full; if you opt not to take an available (but perhaps less convenient) flight, you can only get credit toward future travel. Carefully read agreements with any company offering standby flights as tricky fine print can leave you in a lurch. To check on a company's service record in the US, call the Better Business Bureau (☎212-533-6200). It is difficult to receive refunds, and clients' vouchers will not be honored when an airline fails to receive payment in time.

TICKET CONSOLIDATORS

Ticket consolidators, or **"bucket shops,"** buy unsold tickets in bulk from commercial airlines and sell them at discounted rates. The best place to look is in the Sunday travel section of any major newspaper (such as *The New York Times*), where many bucket shops place tiny ads. Call quickly, as availability is typically extremely limited. Not all bucket shops are reliable, so insist on a receipt that gives full details of restrictions, refunds, and tickets, and pay by credit card (in spite of the 2-5% fee) so you can stop payment if you never receive your tickets. For more info, see www.travel-library.com/air-travel/consolidators.html.

CHARTER FLIGHTS

Charters are flights a tour operator contracts with an airline to fly extra loads of passengers during peak season. Charter flights fly less frequently than major airlines, make refunds particularly difficult, and are almost always fully booked. Schedules and itineraries may also change or be cancelled at the last moment (as late as 48 hours before the trip, and without a full refund), and check-in, boarding, and baggage claim are often much slower. However, they can also be cheaper.

Discount clubs and **fare brokers** offer members savings on last-minute charter and tour deals. Study contracts closely; you don't want to end up with an unwanted overnight layover. **Travelers Advantage,** Trumbull, CT, USA (☎877-259-2691; www.travelersadvantage.com; $60 annual fee includes discounts and cheap flight directories) can provide more information.

GETTING AROUND

BY TRAIN

Locomotion is still one of the least expensive (and most pleasant) ways to tour the US and Canada, but discounted air travel may be cheaper, and much faster, than train travel. As with airlines, you can save money by purchasing your tickets as far in advance as possible, so plan ahead and make reservations early. It is essential to travel light on trains; not all stations will check your baggage.

AMTRAK

Amtrak is the only provider of intercity passenger train service in the US. (☎800-872-7245; www.amtrak.com.) Most cities have Amtrak offices which directly sell tickets, but tickets must be bought through an agent in some small towns. The web site lists up-to-date schedules, fares, arrival and departure info, and makes reservations. **Discounts** on full rail fares are given to: senior citizens (15% off), Student Advantage cardholders (15% off; call ☎800-962-6872 to purchase the $20 card), travelers with disabilities (15% off), ages 2-15 accompanied by a paying adult (50% off), children under 2 (free), and current members of the US armed forces, active-duty veterans, and their dependents (25% off; www.veteransadvantage.com). "Rail SALE" offers online discounts of up to 90%. Amtrak also offers some **special packages**—check the web site or call for more information.

VIA RAIL

VIA Rail, 3 Place Ville-Marie, Suite 500, Montreal, Quebec H3B 2C9 (☎888-842-7245 or 800-561-3449 from the US; www.viarail.ca), is Amtrak's Canadian analog. **Discounts** on full fares are given to: full-time students with ISIC cards (35% off full fare), seniors 60 and over (10% off), ages 2-11 accompanied by an adult (50% off), and ages 12-17 (35% off). Reservations are required for first-class seats and sleep car accommodations. The **Canrailpass** allows unlimited travel on 12 days within a 30-day period. Between early June and early October, a 12-day pass costs CDN$719 (seniors and youths and students with an ISIC, CDN$647). Low-season passes cost CDN$448 (seniors, youths, and students; CDN$403). Add CDN$39-61 per extra day up to 3 days. Call for info on seasonal promotions.

BY BUS

Buses generally offer the most frequent and complete service between the cities and towns of the US and Canada. Often a bus is the only way to reach smaller locales without a car. In rural areas and across open spaces, however, bus lines tend to be sparse. *Russell's Official National Motor Coach Guide* ($16 including postage) is an invaluable tool for constructing an itinerary. Updated each month, Russell's Guide has schedules of every bus route (including Greyhound) between any two towns in the United States and Canada. Russell's also publishes two semiannual Supplements which are free when ordered with the main issue; **A Directory of Bus Lines and Bus Stations,** and a series of **Route Maps** (both $9 if ordered separately). To order any of the above, write **Russell's Guides, Inc.,** P.O. Box 178, Cedar Rapids, IA 52406 (☎319-364-6138; fax 362-8808).

GREYHOUND

Greyhound (☎800-231-2222; www.greyhound.com) operates the most routes in the US, and provides service to parts of Canada. Schedule information is available at any Greyhound terminal or agency and on their web page.

Advance purchase fares: Reserving space far ahead of time ensures a lower fare, but expect smaller discounts between June 5 and Sept. 15. Fares are often lower for 14-day, 7-day, or 3-day advance purchases. For 3-day advance purchase M-Th, 2 people ride for the price of 1 ticket. Call for up-to-date pricing or consult their web page.

Discounts on full fares: Senior citizens with a Greyhound Senior Club Card (10% off); children ages 2-11 (50% off); Student Advantage card holders (up to 15% off); disabled travelers and their companions receive two tickets for the price of one; active and retired US military personnel and National Guard Reserves (10% off with valid ID). With a ticket purchased 3 or more days in advance during the spring and summer months, a friend can travel along for free (with some exceptions).

Ameripass: ☎800-454-7277. Allows adults unlimited travel through the US. 7-day pass $229, 10-day pass $279, 15-day pass $349, 30-day pass $459, 45-day pass $519, 60-day pass $625. Student discounts available. Children's passes are half-price. Before purchasing an Ameripass, total up the separate bus fares between towns to make sure that the pass is more economical or at least worth the flexibility it provides.

International Ameripass: For travelers from outside North America. ☎800-454-7277 for info. 7-day pass ($219), 10-day pass ($269), 15-day pass ($329), 30-day pass ($439), 45-day pass ($489), or 60-day pass ($599). International Ameripasses are not available at the terminal; they can be purchased in foreign countries at Greyhound-affiliated agencies; telephone numbers are listed on the web site. Passes can also be ordered at the web site, or purchased by calling ☎800-229-9424 in the US.

GREYHOUND CANADA TRANSPORTATION

Greyhound Canada Transportation, (☎800-661-8747; www.greyhound.ca), is Canada's main intercity bus company. The web site has full schedule info.

Discounts: Seniors 10% off; students 25% off with an ISIC; 10% off with other student cards; if reservations are made at least 7 days in advance, a friend travels half off, while children under 16 ride free with an adult.

Canada Pass: Unlimited travel from the western border of Canada to Montréal on all routes for North American residents, including some links to northern US cities. 7-day advance purchase required. 7-day pass CDN$264, 10-day pass CDN$334, 15-day pass CDN$415, 21-day pass CDN$455, 30-day pass CDN$515, 45-day pass CDN$575, 60-day pass CDN$655. Discovery Passes are available for non-US, non-Canadian travelers.

BY CAR

"I" (as in "I-90") refers to Interstate highways, "U.S." (as in "U.S. 1") to US highways, and "Rte." (as in "Rte. 7") to state and local highways. For Canadian highways, "TCH" refers to the Trans-Canada Hwy., while "Hwy." or "autoroute" refers to standard automobile routes.

INTERNATIONAL DRIVING PERMIT

If you do not have a license issued by a US state or Canadian province or territory, you might want an International Driving Permit (IDP)—it may help with police if your license is not written in English. You must carry your home license with your IDP at all times. You must be 18 to obtain an IDP, it is valid for a year, and must be issued in the country in which your license originates.

CAR INSURANCE

Most credit cards cover standard insurance. If you rent, lease, or borrow a car, you will need a **green card,** or **International Insurance Certificate,** to certify that you have liability insurance and that it applies abroad. Green cards can be obtained at car rental agencies, car dealers (for those leasing cars), some travel agents, and some border crossings. Rental agencies may require you to purchase theft insurance in countries that they consider to have a high risk of auto theft.

AUTOMOBILE CLUBS

Most automobile clubs offer free towing, emergency roadside assistance, travel-related discounts, and random goodies in exchange for a modest membership fee. Travelers should strongly consider membership if planning an extended roadtrip.

American Automobile Association (AAA). Provides emergency road service (☎800-222-4357) in the US. Free trip-planning services, maps, and guidebooks, and 24hr. emergency road service anywhere in the US. Free towing and commission-free American Express Traveler's Checks from over 1000 offices across the country. Discounts on Hertz car rental (5-20%), Amtrak tickets (10%), and various motel chains and theme parks. Basic membership $48, Associate Membership $25. To sign up, call ☎800-564-6222 or go to www.aaa.com.

Canadian Automobile Association (CAA), 1145 Hunt Club Rd., #200, Ottawa, ON K1V 0Y3 (☎800-222-4357; www.caa.ca). Affiliated with AAA (see above), the CAA provides the same membership benefits, including 24hr. emergency roadside assistance, free maps and tourbooks, route planning, and various discounts. Basic membership is CDN$69 and CDN$34 for associates; call ☎800-564-6222 to sign up.

ON THE ROAD

While driving, be sure to buckle up—seat belts are **required by law** in many regions of the US and Canada. The **speed limit** in the US varies considerably from region to region. Most urban highways have a limit of 55 mph (89kph), while rural routes range from 65 mph (104kph) to 75 mph (120kph). Heed the limit; not only does it save gas, but most local police forces and state troopers make frequent use of radar to catch speed demons. The **speed limit in Canada** is 50kph (31mph) in cities and 80kph (49 mph) on highways. On rural highways the speed limit may be 100kph (62 mph).

HOW TO NAVIGATE THE INTERSTATES

In the 1950s, President Dwight D. Eisenhower envisioned a well-organized **interstate highway system.** His dream has been realized: there is now a comprehensive, well-maintained, efficient means of traveling between major cities and between states. Luckily for travelers, the highways are named with an intuitive numbering system. Even-numbered interstates run east-west and odd ones run north-south, decreasing in number toward the south and the west. North-south routes begin on the West Coast with I-5 and end with I-95 on the East Coast. The southernmost east-west route is I-4 in Florida. The northernmost east-west route is I-94, stretching from Montana to Wisconsin. Three-digit numbers signify branches of other interstates (e.g., I-285 is a branch of I-85) that often skirt around large cities.

! DRIVING PRECAUTIONS. When traveling in the summer or in the desert, bring substantial amounts of water (a suggested 5 L of **water** per person per day) for drinking and for the radiator. For long drives to unpopulated areas, register with police before beginning the trek, and again upon arrival at the destination. Check with the local automobile club for details. When traveling for long distances, make sure tires are in good repair and have enough air, and get good maps. A **compass** and a **car manual** can also be very useful. You should always carry a **spare tire** and **jack, jumper cables, extra oil, flares, a flashlight (torch),** and **heavy blankets** (in case your car breaks down at night or in the winter). If you don't know how to **change a tire,** learn before heading out, especially if you are planning on traveling in deserted areas. Blowouts on dirt roads are exceedingly common. If you do have a breakdown, **stay with your car;** if you wander off, there's less likelihood trackers will find you.

RENTING. Car rental agencies fall into two categories: national companies with hundreds of branches, and local agencies that serve only one city or region. National chains usually allow you to pick up a car in one city and drop it off in another (for a hefty charge, sometimes in excess of $1000). The drawbacks of car rentals include steep prices (a compact car rents for $25-45 per day) and high minimum ages for rentals (usually 25). Most branches rent to ages 21 to 24 with an additional fee, but policies and prices vary from agency to agency. **Alamo** (☎800-327-9633; www.alamo.com) rents to ages 21 to 24 with a major credit card for an additional $20 per day. **Enterprise** (☎800-736-8222; www.enterprise.com) rents to customers ages 21 to 24 with a variable surcharge. **Dollar** (☎800-800-4000; www.dollar.com) and **Thrifty** (☎800-367-2277; www.thrifty.com) locations do likewise for varying surcharges. **Rent-A-Wreck** (☎800-944-7501; www.rent-a-wreck.com) specializes in supplying vehicles that are past their prime for lower-than-average prices; a bare-bones compact less than 8 years old rents for around $20 to $25. There may be an additional charge for a **collision and damage waiver (CDW),** which usually comes to about $12-15 per day. Major credit cards (including MasterCard and American Express) will sometimes cover the CDW if you use their card to rent a car; call your credit card company for specifics.

Because it is mandatory for all drivers in the US, make sure with your rental agency that you are covered by **insurance.** Be sure to ask whether the price includes **insurance** against theft and collision. Some credit cards cover standard insurance. If you rent, lease, or borrow a car, and you are not from the US or Canada, you will need a **green card,** or **International Insurance Certificate,** to certify that you have liability insurance and that it applies abroad. Green cards can be obtained at car rental agencies, car dealerships, some travel agents, and some border crossings. If you are driving a conventional vehicle on an **unpaved road** in a rental car, you are almost never covered by insurance. National chains often allow one-way rentals, picking up in one city and dropping off in another, although there is often a steep additional charge. There is usually a minimum hire period and sometimes an extra drop-off charge of several hundred dollars.

AUTO TRANSPORT COMPANIES. These services match drivers with car owners who need cars moved from one city to another. Would-be travelers give the company their desired destination and the company finds a car that needs to go there. Expenses include gas, tolls, and your own living expenses. Some companies insure their cars; with others, your security deposit covers any breakdowns or damage. You must be over 21, have a valid license, and agree to drive about 400 mi. per day on a fairly direct route. The following are popular transport companies:

Auto Driveaway Co., 310 S. Michigan Ave., Chicago, IL 60604-4298 (☎800-346-2277/312-341-1900; www.autodriveaway.com).

Across America Driveaway, 9905 Express Dr., Unit #2, Highland, IN 46322 (☎800-619-7707; www.schultz-international.com).

BY BICYCLE

Before you pedal furiously onto the byways of America astride your banana-seat Huffy, remember that safe and secure cycling requires a quality helmet and lock. U-shaped **Kryptonite** or **Citadel** locks ($30-60) carry insurance against theft for 1 or 2 years if your bike is registered with the police. **Bike Nashbar,** P.O. Box 1455, Crab Orchard, WV 25827 (☎800-627-4227), will beat any nationally advertised in-stock price by $0.05, and ships anywhere in the US or Canada. Their techline (☎800-888-2710; open M-F 8am-6pm) fields questions about repairs and maintenance.

Adventure Cycling Association, P.O. Box 8308, Missoula, MT 59807 (☎800-755-2453; www.adv-cycling.org). A national, nonprofit organization that researches and maps long-distance routes and organizes bike tours (75-day Great Divide Expedition $2800, 6-9 day trip $650-800). Annual membership ($30), includes access to maps and routes and a subscription to *Adventure Cyclist* magazine

The Canadian Cycling Association, 702-2197 Riverside Dr., Ottawa, ON K1H 7X3 (☎613-248-1353; www.canadian-cycling.com). Provides info for cyclists of all abilities. Distributes *The Canadian Cycling Association's Complete Guide to Bicycle Touring in Canada.*

BY MOTORCYCLE

The wind-in-your-face thrill, burly leather, and revving crackle of a motorcycle engine unobscured by windows or upholstery has built up quite a cult following, but motorcycling is the most dangerous of roadtop activities. Of course, safety should be your primary concern. Helmets are essential; wear the best one you can find. Those considering a long journey should contact the **American Motorcyclist Association,** 13515 Yarmouth Dr., Pickering, OH 43147 (☎800-262-5646; www.ama-cycle.org), the linchpin of US biker culture. And of course, take a copy of Robert Pirsig's *Zen and the Art of Motorcycle Maintenance* (1974) with you.

BY THUMB

Let's Go urges you to consider the great risks and disadvantages of **hitchhiking** before thumbing it. Hitching means entrusting your life to a randomly selected person who happens to stop beside you on the road. While this may be comparatively safe in some areas of Europe and Australia, it is generally *not* so in the US or Canada. *Let's Go* does not recommend hitchhiking at all in the US and Canada. We strongly urge you to find other means of transportation and to avoid situations where hitching is the only option.

SPECIFIC CONCERNS

WOMEN TRAVELERS

Women exploring on their own inevitably face some additional safety concerns, but it's easy to be adventurous without taking undue risks. If you are concerned, consider staying in hostels which offer single rooms that lock from the inside or in religious organizations with rooms for women only. Stick to centrally located accommodations and avoid solitary late-night treks or metro rides.

Always carry extra money for a phone call, bus, or taxi. **Hitchhiking** is never safe for lone women, or even for two women traveling together. When on overnight or long train rides, if there is no women-only compartment, choose one occupied by women or couples. Look as if you know where you're going and approach older women or couples for directions if you're lost or uncomfortable.

Generally, the less you look like a tourist, the better off you'll be. Dress conservatively: trying to fit in can be effective, but dressing to the style of an obviously different culture may cause you to be ill at ease and a conspicuous target. Wearing a **wedding band** may help prevent unwanted overtures.

Your best answer to verbal harassment is no answer at all; feigning deafness, sitting motionless, and staring straight ahead at nothing in particular will do a world of good that reactions usually don't achieve. The extremely persistent can sometimes be dissuaded by a firm, loud, and very public "Go away!" Don't hesitate to seek out a police officer or a passerby if you are being harassed. Memorize the emergency numbers in places you visit, and consider carrying a keychain whistle. A self-defense course will prepare you for a potential attack and raise your level of awareness of your surroundings (see **Self Defense,** p. 39).

For general information, contact the **National Organization for Women (NOW),** 733 15th St. NW, 2nd Floor, Washington, D.C. 20005 (☎202-628-8669; www.now.org), which has branches across the US that can refer women travelers to rape crisis centers and counseling services.

TRAVELING ALONE

There are many benefits to traveling alone, including independence and greater interaction with locals. On the other hand, any solo traveler is a more vulnerable target of harassment and street theft. As a lone traveler, try not to stand out as a tourist, look confident, and be especially careful in deserted or very

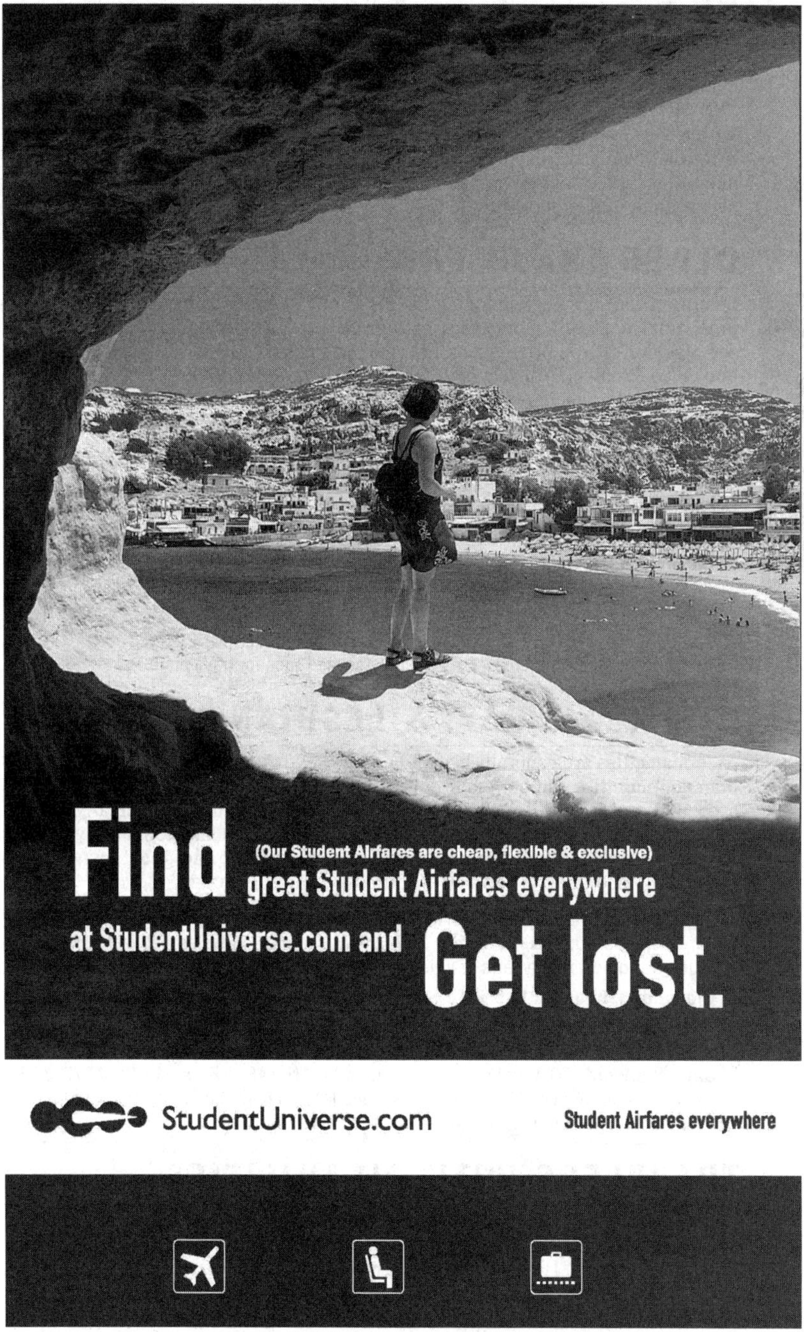
Find
(Our Student Airfares are cheap, flexible & exclusive)
great Student Airfares everywhere
at StudentUniverse.com and
Get lost.
StudentUniverse.com
Student Airfares everywhere

crowded areas. If questioned, never admit that you are traveling alone. Maintain regular contact with someone at home who knows your itinerary. For more tips, pick up *Traveling Solo* by Eleanor Berman (Globe Pequot Press, $18) or subscribe to **Connecting: Solo Travel Network,** 689 Park Road, Unit 6, Gibsons, BC V0N 1V7, Canada (☎604-886-9099; www.cstn.org; membership $35). To link up with a tour group, try **Contiki Holidays** (888-CONTIKI; www.contiki.com), which offers a variety of packages designed for 18- to 35-year-olds. Tours include accommodations, transportation, guided sightseeing and some meals; most average about $75 per day.

OLDER TRAVELERS

Senior citizens are eligible for a wide range of discounts on transportation, museums, movies, theaters, concerts, restaurants, and accommodations. If you don't see a senior citizen price listed, ask, and you may be delightfully surprised. The books *No Problem! Worldwise Tips for Mature Adventurers,* by Janice Kenyon (Orca Book Publishers, $16) and *Unbelievably Good Deals and Great Adventures That You Absolutely Can't Get Unless You're Over 50,* by Joan Rattner Heilman (NTC/Contemporary Publishing, $15) are both excellent resources. For more information, contact one of the following organizations:

Elderhostel, 11 Ave. de Lafayette, Boston, MA 02111 (☎877-426-8056; www.elderhostel.org). Organizes 1- to 4-week educational adventures for those 55+.

The Mature Traveler, P.O. Box 1543, Wildomar, CA 92595 (☎909-461-9598, www.thematuretraveler.com, subscription $30). Monthly newsletter with deals, discounts, tips, and travel packages for the senior traveler.

Walking the World, P.O. Box 1186, Fort Collins, CO 80522 (☎800-340-9255; www.walkingtheworld.com), runs walking-focused trips for travelers 50+.

BISEXUAL, GAY, & LESBIAN TRAVELERS

American cities are generally accepting of all sexualities, and thriving gay and lesbian communities can be found in most cosmopolitan areas. Most college towns are gay-friendly as well. Still, homophobia is not uncommon, particularly in rural areas. *Let's Go* includes local gay and lesbian info lines and community centers when available. Below are additional resources. **Out and About** (www.planetout.com) also offers a newsletter addressing travel concerns.

International Lesbian and Gay Association (ILGA), 81 rue Marché-au-Charbon, B-1000 Brussels, Belgium (☎+32 2 502 2471; www.ilga.org). Provides political information, such as homosexuality laws of individual countries.

Giovanni's Room, 1145 Pine St., Philadelphia, PA 19107 (☎215-923-2960; www.queerbooks.com). An international lesbian/feminist and gay bookstore with mail-order service (carries many of the publications listed below).

Gay's the Word, 66 Marchmont St., London WC1N 1AB, UK (☎+44 20 7278 7654; www.gaystheword.co.uk). The largest gay and lesbian bookshop in the UK, with both fiction and non-fiction titles. Mail-order service available.

TRAVELERS WITH DISABILITIES

Federal law dictates that all public buildings should be handicapped accessible, and recent laws governing building codes make disabled access more the norm than the exception. However, traveling with a disability still requires planning and

FURTHER READING: BISEXUAL, GAY, & LESBIAN

Spartacus International Gay Guide 2001-2002. Bruno Gmunder Verlag ($33).

Damron Men's Guide, Damron Road Atlas, Damron's Accommodations, and *The Women's Traveller.* Damron Travel Guides ($14-19). For more info, call ☎800-462-6654 or visit www.damron.com

Ferrari Guides' Gay Travel A to Z, Ferrari Guides' Men's Travel in Your Pocket, and *Ferrari Guides' Inn Places.* Ferrari Publications ($16-20). Purchase the guides online at www.ferrariguides.com.

The Gay Vacation Guide: The Best Trips and How to Plan Them, Mark Chesnut. Kensington Publishing Corporation ($15).

Gayellow Pages USA/Canada, Frances Green. Gayellow pages ($16). Visit Gayellow pages online at www.gayellowpages.com.

flexibility. Those with special needs should inform airlines and hotels of their disabilities when making reservations; some time may be needed to prepare special accommodations. Call ahead to restaurants, hotels, parks, and other facilities to find if they are handicapped accessible. US Customs requires a certificate of immunization against rabies for **guide dogs** entering the country.

In the US, Amtrak and major airlines will accommodate disabled passengers if notified at least 72hr. in advance. Hearing-impaired travelers may contact Amtrak using teletype printers (☎800-523-6590 or 800-654-5988). Greyhound buses will provide free travel for a companion; if you are alone, call Greyhound (☎800-752-4841) at least 48hr., but no more than 1 week, before you leave, and they will assist you. For information on transportation availability in individual US cities, contact the local chapter of the Easter Seals Society.

If you are planning to visit a national park or attraction in the US run by the National Park Service, obtain a free **Golden Access Passport,** which is available at all park entrances and from federal offices whose functions relate to land, forests, or wildlife. The Passport entitles disabled travelers and their families to free park admission and provides a 50% discount on all campsite and parking fees. For further reading, check out *Resource Directory for the Disabled,* by Richard Neil Shrout (Facts on File, $45).

USEFUL ORGANIZATIONS

Mobility International USA (MIUSA), P.O. Box 10767, Eugene, OR 97440 (voice and TDD ☎541–343-1284; www.miusa.org). Sells *A World of Options: A Guide to International Educational Exchange, Community Service, and Travel for Persons with Disabilities* ($35), and provides other useful travel info.

Society for Accessible Travel & Hospitality (SATH), 347 Fifth Ave., #610, New York, NY 10016 (☎212-447-7284; www.sath.org). An advocacy group that publishes free online travel information and the travel magazine *OPEN WORLD* ($18, free for members). Annual membership $45, students and seniors $30.

TOUR AGENCIES

Directions Unlimited, 123 Green Ln., Bedford Hills, NY 10507 (☎800-533-5343). Books individual and group vacations for the physically disabled; not an info service.

The Guided Tour Inc., 7900 Old York Rd., #114B, Elkins Park, PA 19027 (☎800-783-5841; www.guidedtour.com). Organizes travel programs for persons with developmental and physical challenges.

MINORITY TRAVELERS

While general attitudes towards race relations in the US and Canada differ drastically from region to region, racial and ethnic minorities sometimes face blatant and, more often, subtle discrimination and/or harassment. Verbal harassment is now less common than unfair pricing, false info on accommodations, or inexcusably slow or unfriendly service at restaurants. Report individuals to a supervisor and establishments to the **Better Business Bureau** for the region (www.bbb.org, or call the operator for local listings); contact the police in extreme situations. *Let's Go* always welcomes reader input regarding discriminating establishments.

FURTHER RESOURCES

United States Department of Justice (www.usdoj.gov/civilliberties.htm).

Go Girl! The Black Woman's Book of Travel and Adventure, Elaine Lee. Eighth Mountain Press ($18).

The African-American Travel Guide, Wayne Robinson. Hunter Publishing ($10).

TRAVELERS WITH CHILDREN

Family vacations often require that you slow your pace, and always require that you plan ahead. If you rent a car, make sure the rental company provides a car seat for younger children. **Be sure that your child carries some sort of ID** in case of an emergency of in case he or she gets lost. Tourist attractions, hotels, and restaurants often offer discounts for children. Children under two usually fly for 10% of the adult fare on overseas flights (this does not necessarily include a seat). International fares are usually discounted 25% for children two to 11. Also consult one of the following books:

Adventuring with Children: An Inspirational Guide to World Travel and the Outdoors, Nan Jeffrey. Avalon House Publishing ($15).

Backpacking with Babies and Small Children, Goldie Silverman. Wilderness Press ($10).

Gutsy Mamas: Travel Tips and Wisdom for Mothers on the Road, Marybeth Bond. Travelers' Tales, Inc. ($8).

Have Kid, Will Travel: 101 Survival Strategies for Vacationing With Babies and Young Children, Claire and Lucille Tristram. Andrews McMeel Publishing ($9).

Trouble-Free Travel with Children, Vicki Lansky. Book Peddlers ($9).

DIETARY CONCERNS

In the US and Canada, vegetarian options abound. *Let's Go* often indicates vegetarian options in restaurant listings; other places to look for vegetarian and vegan cuisine are local health food stores, as well as large natural food chains such as **Trader Joe's** and **Wild Oats.** Vegan options are more difficult to find in smaller towns and inland; be prepared to make your own meals. The **North American Vegetarian Society,** P.O. Box 72, Dolgeville, NY 13329 (☎518-568-7970; www.navs-online.org), publishes info about vegetarian travel, including *Vegetarian Journal's Guide to Natural Food Restaurants in the US and Canada* ($12). You might also try the Vegetarian Resource Group's web site, www.vrg.org/travel, or Jed Civic's *The Vegetarian Traveler: Where to Stay If You're Vegetarian, Vegan, Environmentally Sensitive* (Larson Publishing, $16).

Travelers who keep kosher should contact synagogues in larger cities for information on kosher restaurants. Your own synagogue or college Hillel should have access to lists of Jewish institutions across the nation. You may also consult the kosher restaurant database at www.shamash.org/kosher. A good resource is the *Jewish Travel Guide*, edited by Michael Zaidner (Vallentine Mitchell, $17). If you are strict in your observance, you may have to prepare your own food on the road.

THE WORLD WIDE WEB

Almost every aspect of budget travel is accessible via the web. Listed here are some budget travel sites to start off your surfing; other relevant web sites are listed throughout the book. Because web site turnover is high, use search engines (such as www.google.com) to strike out on your own.

OUR PERSONAL FAVORITE...

WWW.LETSGO.COM Our newly designed website now features online content of many of our guides. It also contains our newsletter, links for photos and streaming video, online ordering of our titles, info about our books, and a travel forum buzzing with stories and tips.

THE ART OF BUDGET TRAVEL

How to See the World: www.artoftravel.com. A compendium of great travel tips, from cheap flights to self defense to interacting with local culture.

Rec. Travel Library: www.travel-library.com. A fantastic set of links for general information and personal travelogues.

Lycos: travel.lycos.com. Introductions to cities and regions throughout the US and Canada, accompanied by links to applicable histories, news, and local tourism sites.

Shoestring Travel: www.stratpub.com. An alternative to Microsoft's huge site. A budget travel e-zine that features listings of home exchanges, links, and accommodations info.

INFORMATION ON THE US & CANADA

CIA World Factbook: www.odci.gov/cia/publications/factbook/index.html. Tons of vital statistics on the US and Canada's geography, government, economy, and people.

Tourism Offices Worldwide Directory: www.towd.com. Lists tourism offices for all 50 states and Canada, as well as consulate and embassy addresses.

ALTERNATIVES TO TOURISM

When we started out in 1961, about 1.7 million people were traveling internationally each year; in 2002, nearly 700 million trips were made, projected to be up to a billion by 2010. The dramatic rise in tourism has created an interdependence between the economy, environment, and culture of many destinations and the tourists they host. More than 50 million international travelers visit North America each year, and many of them arrive with agendas that are more complex than simply visiting tourist sights.

Those looking to **volunteer** in the US and Canada have many options. Despite its status as a leading industrial nation, the US unsurprisingly yet unfortunately displays extreme economic disparity across geographic regions and social classes. Mounting problems coupled with a growing social consciousness have led to a surge of volunteerism recently; thousands of organizations with specific causes now exist in the US and Canada with the aim of developing creative solutions to monumental problems. With the rich getting richer and the poor getting poorer, issues such as homelessness and hunger plague the US, while unchecked development and misguided environmental policies ravage natural resources. Troubled youth and neglected senior citizens seek guidance and assistance, and a poor public educational system and influx of immigrants has many Americans unable to read English at a proficient level. To top this off, those with perhaps more time and money at their expense have devoted their efforts to protecting and defending animals. You can participate in any of these numerous projects, either on an infrequent basis or as the main component of your trip. Later in this section, we recommend organizations that can help you find the opportunities that best suit your interests, whether you're looking to pitch in for a day or a year.

There are any number of other ways that you can integrate yourself with the communities you visit. Studying at a college or language program is one option. Many travelers also structure their trips by the work that they can do along the way—either odd jobs as they go, or full-time stints in cities where they plan to stay for some time.

FIND THE PATH. To read more on specific organizations that are working to better their communities, look for our **Giving Back** features throughout the book. We recommend **Alaska Native Heritage Center,** p. 63.

For more information about sustainable tourism, www.worldsurface.com features photos and personal stories of volunteer experiences. More general information is available at www.sustainabletravel.org. For those who seek more active involvement, Earthwatch International, Operation Crossroads Africa, and Habitat for Humanity offer fulfilling volunteer opportunities all over the world.

VOLUNTEERING

Though the US and Canada are considered wealthy in worldwide terms, there is no shortage of aid organizations to benefit the very real issues the countries do face. Volunteering can be one of the most fulfilling experiences you have in life, especially if you combine it with the thrill of traveling in a new place.

A NEW PHILOSOPHY OF TRAVEL

We at *Let's Go* have watched the growth of the 'ignorant tourist' stereotype with dismay, knowing that the majority of travelers care passionately about the state of the communities and environments they explore—but also knowing that even conscientious tourists can inadvertently damage natural wonders, rich cultures, and impoverished communities. We believe the philosophy of **sustainable travel** is among the most important travel tips we could impart to our readers, to help guide fellow backpackers and on-the-road philanthropists. By staying aware of the needs and troubles of local communities, today's travelers can be a powerful force in preserving and restoring this fragile world.

Working against the negative consequences of irresponsible tourism is much simpler than it might seem; it is often self-awareness, rather than self-sacrifice, that makes the biggest difference. Simply by trying to spend responsibly and conserve local resources, all travelers can positively impact the places they visit. Let's Go has partnered with **BEST** (**Business Enterprises for Sustainable Travel,** an affiliate of the Conference Board; see www.sustainabletravel.org), which recognizes businesses that operate based on the principles of sustainable travel. Below, they provide advice on how ordinary visitors can practice this philosophy in their daily travels, no matter where they are.

TIPS FOR CIVIC TRAVEL: HOW TO MAKE A DIFFERENCE

Travel by train when feasible. Rail travel requires only half the energy per passenger mile that planes do. On average, each of the 40,000 daily domestic air flights releases more than 1700 pounds of greenhouse gas emissions.

Use public mass transportation whenever possible; outside of cities, take advantage of group taxis or vans. Bicycles are an attractive way of seeing a community first-hand. And enjoy walking–purchase good maps of your destination and ask about on-foot touring opportunities.

When renting a car, ask whether fuel-efficient vehicles are available. Honda and Toyota produce cars that use hybrid engines powered by electricity and gasoline, thus reducing emissions of carbon dioxide. Ford Motor Company plans to introduce a hybrid fuel model by the end of 2004.

Reduce, reuse, recycle–use electronic tickets, recycle papers and bottles wherever possible, and avoid using containers made of styrofoam. Refillable water bottles and rechargable batteries both efficiently conserve expendable resources.

Be thoughtful in your purchases. Take care not to buy souvenir objects made from trees in old-growth or endangered forests, such as teak, or items made from endangered species, like ivory or tortoise jewelry. Ask whether products are made from renewable resources.

Buy from local enterprises, such as casual street vendors. In developing countries and low-income neighborhoods, many people depend on the "informal economy" to make a living.

Be on-the-road-philanthropists. If you are inspired by the natural environment of a destination or enriched by its culture, join in preserving their integrity by making a charitable contribution to a local organization.

Spread the word. Upon your return home, tell friends and colleagues about places to visit that will benefit greatly from their tourist dollars, and reward sustainable enterprises by recommending their services. Travelers can not only introduce friends to particular vendors but also to local causes and charities that they might choose to support when they travel.

Most people who volunteer in North America do so on a short-term basis, at organizations that make use of drop-in or once-a-week volunteers. These can be found in virtually every city, and are referenced both in this section and in our town and city write-ups themselves. The best way to find opportunities that match up with your interests and schedule may be to check with local or national volunteer centers.

More intensive volunteer services may charge you a fee to participate. These costs can be surprisingly hefty (although they frequently cover airfare and most, if not all, living expenses). Most people choose to go through a parent organization that takes care of logistical details and frequently provides a group environment and support system. There are two main types of organizations—religious and non-sectarian—although there are rarely restrictions on participation for either.

Before handing your money over to any volunteer or study abroad program, make sure you know exactly what you're getting into. It's a good idea to get the name of **previous participants** and ask them about their experience, as some programs sound much better on paper than in reality. The **questions** below are a good place to start:

-Will you be the only person in the program? If not, what are the other participants like? How old are they? How much will you be expected to interact with them?

-Is room and board included? If so, what is the arrangement? Will you be expected to share a room? A bathroom? What are the meals like? Do they fit any dietary restrictions?

-Is transportation included? Are there any additional expenses?

-How much free time will you have? Will you be able to travel around the region?

-What kind of safety network is set up? Will you still be covered by your home insurance? Does the program have an emergency plan?

HIV/AIDS OUTREACH

The UN estimates that there are 42 million people who have HIV/AIDS around the world. Each year, 5 million new cases of HIV appear, and each year, more than 3 million people die as a result of AIDS. Nearly one million people in the US are living with the disease, and one-fourth of them are unaware of it. Half of the 40,000 newly infected people each year in the US are under the age of 25. Many organizations exist in the US and Canada to combat these frightening numbers. With the help of volunteers, these groups promote the awareness and prevention of HIV/AIDS and provide support to those living with the disease.

Body Health Resources Corporation, 250 W. 57th St., New York, NY 10107 (www.thebody.com). The Body offers an extensive, informative web site about all things HIV/AIDS-related. Check out the "Helping and Getting Help" section for a listing of all the regional HIV/AIDS service organizations throughout the US and Canada that are in need of volunteers.

Washington AIDS International Foundation, 3224 16th St. NW, Washington, DC 20010 (☎202-745-0111; www.waifaction.org). Offers educational classes, meetings, seminars, conferences, and speeches targeted at youth and families to prevent the spread of HIV/AIDS and offers support to those already suffering from both diseases. Volunteers contribute to fundraising efforts as well as outreach. With a strong presence in DC and Maryland communities and schools, WAIF also has branches throughout the country, including a large chapter in San Francisco.

AIDS Action Committee, 294 Washington St., 5th floor, Boston, MA 02108 (☎617-437-6200; www.aac.org). Boston organization that trains volunteers to assist with hotlines, walk-in support, fundraising, local events, and a local resale store to benefit those with HIV/AIDS in the greater Boston area.

A Loving Spoonful, 100-1300 Richards St., Vancouver BC V6B 3G6 (☎604-682-6325; www.alovingspoonful.org). Deliver free meals to the homes of persons living with HIV/AIDS in the Greater Vancouver area. Public relations and fundraising opportunities for volunteers also available.

CONSERVATION

Protecting endangered species, battling air and water pollution, and conserving resources and habitats are only a few of the ways you can help save the earth by volunteering with a conservation group in North America.

National Parks Conservation Association, 1300 19th St. NW, Ste. 300, Washington, D.C. 20036 (☎800-628-7275; www.npca.org). Volunteer at any one of NPCA's 388 units (not only national parks, but also seashores, monuments, battlefields, and more) and help the land by picking up trash, giving tours, monitoring wildlife, and planting trees. From the Great Smoky Mountains to Alaska's Glacier Bay, there's something for everyone. For national parks, historic sites, and marine conservation areas in Canada, contact **Parks Canada,** 25 Eddy St., Hull QC K1A 0M5 (☎888-773-8888; www.parkscanada.gc.ca).

National Wildlife Federation, 11100 Wildlife Center Dr., Reston, VA 20190 (☎800-822-9919 or 703-438-6000; www.nwf.org). Become a Habitat Stewards Volunteer with the NWF and create or restore a wildlife habitat–from backyards to schools to refuges. Join FrogwatchUSA and collect data about frog and toad populations in the US while promoting the importance of wetland habitats and their diversity.

Natural Resources Conservation Service, Attn: Conservation Communications Staff, P.O. Box 2890, Washington, DC 20013 (☎202-720-3210; www.nrcs.usda.gov). Volunteer on farms and ranches, in classrooms, with organizations, or in offices to promote conservation and improve wildlife habitat. Give tours and speeches or organize exhibits with professionals and gain experience while helping the earth.

Earthwatch Institute, 3 Clock Tower Pl., Suite 100, Box 75, Maynard, MA 01754 (☎800-776-0188 or 978-461-0081; www.earthwatch.org). Arranges 1- to 3-week programs in the US and Canada to promote conservation of natural resources. Work side-by-side with leading scientists, studying everything from armadillos in Florida to climate change in the Arctic Circle.

WORKING WITH THE ELDERLY

More than 35 million persons over the age of 65 reside in the US. More than 3 million of them live below the poverty level, and more than two million older adults are classified as "near poor." Service groups catering to the elderly offer physical and spiritual nourishment to this often overlooked population.

Meals on Wheels Association of America, 1414 Prince St., Alexandria, VA 22314 (☎703-548-5558; www.mowaa.org). Buy, prepare, and deliver meals to the elderly and the poor. Public awareness and research projects also available. Programs in both the US and Canada; search the web site for the region you would like to serve.

National Hospice Foundation, 1700 Diagonal Rd., Suite 265, Alexandria, VA 22314 (☎703-516-4928; www.hospiceinfo.org). Offer emotional and spiritual support to those close to death and counseling to their families. Search by name, state, or ZIP code under "Find a Hospice" program to find a US hospice in need of volunteers.

HOMELESSNESS & HUNGER

Due to poverty, unemployment, a lack of affordable housing and health care, insufficient public assistance, domestic violence, and mental disorders, almost 4 million people experience homelessness in the US within any given year and nearly 34 million experience hunger. Many who suffer are children. There are numerous opportunities to get involved and make a difference.

US Department of Housing and Urban Development, 451 7th St. SW, Washington, D.C. 20410 (☎202-708-1112; www.hud.gov). Maintains a web site with listings of local homeless assistance programs, shelters, food banks, hospitals, and advocacy groups in every state (www.hud.gov/homeless/hmlsagen.cfm). **The National Coalition for the Homeless** boasts a similar directory online (www.nationalhomeless.org/local/local.html).

Homeless Veteran Program, a division of the **Department of Veterans Affairs** (800-827-1000; www.va.gov/homeless/). Provides outreach to homeless veterans living on the streets and in shelters, offering psychiatric care and information on health care and housing assistance. The web site lists program coordinators by state. AmeriCorps opportunities available.

Habitat for Humanity International, 121 Habitat St., Americus, GA 31709 (☎229-924-6935, x. 2551 or 2552; www.habitat.org). Volunteers build houses throughout the US and Canada (and in 85 other countries) for the benefit low-income families living in poverty. Projects take anywhere from 2 weeks to 3 years. Short-term program costs range $1200-4000.

America's Second Harvest, 35 E. Wacker Dr., #2000, Chicago, IL 60601 (☎800-771-2303 or 312-263-2303; www.2ndharvest.org). As the US's largest hunger organization, oversees more than 200 food banks throughout the country and feeds more than 23 million people. Sort and repackage salvaged food, tutor children, or prepare and serve food at shelters. To find food banks in Canada, contact the **Canadian Association of Food Banks,** 191 rue New Toronto St., Toronto ON M8V 2E7 (☎416-203-9241; www.cafb-acba.org).

LITERACY PROGRAMS

A quarter of American adults are not proficient in reading. Most experience difficulties because they did not finish high school, while others are immigrants or persons suffering from vision problems in need of special attention. Educational programs throughout the US and Canada offer instruction and support, bringing the joy of reading to all.

Proliteracy Worldwide, 1320 Jamesville Ave., Syracuse, NY 13210 (☎888-528-2224 or 315-422-9121; www.proliteracy.org). The world's largest adult volunteer literacy organization, with significant chapters in the US. Tutors teach basic literacy or English for Speakers of Other Languages (ESOL) to individuals and families. Mentoring positions available as well. Canadian volunteering through **Laubach Literacy of Canada,** 60-C Elizabeth St., Bedford QC J0J 1A0 (☎888-248-2898 or 450-248-2898; www.laubach.ca).

America's Literacy Directory, (☎800-228-8813; www.literacydirectory.org/volunteer.asp). A service of the National Institute for Literacy, this online directory allows you to search for volunteer opportunities with more than 5000 literacy programs in the US.

PREVENTION OF ANIMAL CRUELTY

Animal lovers should consider volunteering with shelters or animal rights associations to protect their furry friends. Opportunities abound in the US and Canada. Listed below are just a few options.

American Society for the Prevention of Cruelty to Animals (ASPCA), 424 E. 92nd St., New York, NY 10128 (☎212-876-7700; www.aspca.org). Promotes the humane treatment of animals through awareness programs, public policy efforts, shelter support, and animal medical treatment. Visit their web site and look under "How You Can Help" to find a list of shelters in need of volunteers, as well as opportunities at the ASPCA's headquarters in New York City. The ASPCA is partnered with **www.petfinder.com,** which also has a searchable database of shelters and rescue groups. In Canada, contact the **Canadian Society for the Prevention of Cruelty to Animals (CSPCA),** (☎514-735-2711; www.spca.com).

Justice for Animals, P.O. Box 33051, Raleigh, NC 27636 (☎919-787-5190; www.justiceforanimals.org). Conduct investigative work and write reports exposing animal cruelty in North Carolina's rodeos, circuses, fairs, parks, and shelters. Promotional and database work also available.

Animal Haven, 35-22 Prince St., Flushing, NY 11354 (☎718-886-3683; www.animalhavenshelter.org). Runs a shelter, adoption center, rehabilitation center, and animal training "university." From animal handlers to grant writers, Animal Haven welcomes volunteers.

YOUTH OUTREACH

The veritable birthplace of teenage angst, North America struggles to understand and connect with its youth. With over 25% of the population under the age of 18, this is no small task. Want to help? Contact one of these organizations.

Big Brothers Big Sisters of America, 230 N. 13th St., Philadelphia, PA 19107 (☎215-567-7000; www.bbbsa.org). Celebrating its 100th anniversary in 2004, this organization provides mentorship, friendship, and support to hundreds of thousands of American kids. Paired Bigs and Littles work on homework together, visit museums, participate in community service, or just hang out. In Canada, contact **Big Brothers Big Sisters of Canada,** 3228 South Service Rd., Suite 113E, Burlington ON L7N 3H8 (☎800-263-9133 or 905-639-0461; www.bbsc.ca).

The National Mentoring Partnership, 1600 Duke St., Suite 300, Alexandria, VA 22314 (☎703-224-2200; www.mentoring.org). A database of mentoring opportunities, including state and local mentoring partnerships and programs and volunteer centers.

STUDYING ABROAD

Study abroad programs range from basic language and culture courses to college-level classes, often for credit. In order to choose a program that best fits your needs, you will want to research all you can before making your decision—determine costs and duration, as well as what kind of students participate in the program and what sort of accommodations are provided.

In programs that have large groups of students who speak the same language, there is a trade-off. You may feel more comfortable in the community, but you will not have the same opportunity to practice a foreign language or to befriend other international students. For accommodations, dorm life provides a better opportunity to mingle with fellow students, but there is less of a chance to experience the local scene. If you live with a family, there is a potential to build lifelong friendships with natives and to experience day-to-day life in more depth, but conditions can vary greatly from family to family.

VISA INFORMATION

All foreign visitors are required to have a **visa** if they intend to study in the US or Canada. In addition, travelers must provide proof of intent to leave, such as a return plane ticket or an I-94 card. Foreign students who wish to **study** in the US must apply for either an M-1 visa (vocational studies) or an F-1 visa (for full-time students enrolled in an academic or language program). If English is not your native language, you will probably be required to take the Test of English as a Foreign Language (TOEFL), which is administered in many countries. The international students office at the institution you will be attending can give you specifics. Contact **TOEFL/TSE Publications** (www.toefl.org). **To obtain a visa,** contact a US or Canadian embassy or consulate. Check http://travel.state.gov/links.html for US listings and www.dfait-maeci.gc.ca/world/embassies/menu-en.asp for Canadian listings worldwide. Visa extensions are sometimes attainable with a completed I-539 form; call the Bureau of Citizenship and Immigration Service's (BCIS) forms request line (800-870-3676) or get it online at www.immigration.gov/graphics/formsfee/forms/i-539.htm. See http://travel.state.gov/visa_services.html and www.unitedstates.gov for more information. Recent security measures have made the visa application process more rigorous, and therefore lengthy. **Apply well in advance of your travel date.** The process may seem complex, but it's critical that you go through the proper channels–the alternative is potential deportation.

UNIVERSITIES

Most university-level study-abroad programs in the US are meant as language and culture enrichment opportunities, and therefore are conducted in English. A good resource for finding programs that cater to your particular interests is **www.studyabroad.com,** which has links to various semester abroad programs based on a variety of critera, including desired location and focus of study.

In order to live the life of a real American or Canadian college student, consider a visiting student program lasting either a semester or a full year. (While some institutions have trimesters, most American universities have fall semester Sept.-Dec. and spring semester Jan.-May. The Canadian school year often ends in Apr.) The best method by far is to contact colleges and universities in your home country to see what kind of exchanges they have with those in the US and Canada; college students can often receive credit for study abroad. A more complicated option for advanced English speakers is to enroll directly, full-time in a North American institution. The US hosts a number of reputable private universities, among them Stanford, Yale, Duke, and Harvard. Apart from these private institutions, each state maintains a public university system, and there are innumerable community, professional, and technical colleges. In Canada, all universities are public, with the most notable including the University of Toronto, McGill, Queen's, and Dalhousie. Tuition costs are high in the US (and in Canada for international students) and a full course of undergraduate study entails a four-year commitment.

LANGUAGE SCHOOLS

Unlike American universities, language schools are frequently independently run international or local organizations or divisions of foreign universities that rarely offer college credit. Language schools are a good alternative to university study if you desire a deeper focus on the language or a slightly less-rigorous courseload. These programs are also good for younger high school students that might not feel comfortable with older students in a university program. Some good programs include:

Eurocentres, 101 N. Union St. Suite 300, Alexandria, VA 22314, USA (☎703-684-1494; www.eurocentres.com) or in Europe, Head Office, Seestr. 247, CH-8038 Zurich, Switzerland (☎41 1 485 50 40; fax 481 61 24). Language programs for beginning to advanced students with homestays in the US.

Language Immersion Institute, 75 South Manheim Blvd., SUNY-New Paltz, New Paltz, NY 12561-2499, USA (☎845-257-3500; www.newpaltz.edu/lii). 2-week summer language courses and some overseas courses in English. Program fees are around $1000 for a 2-week course.

American Language Programs, 56 Hobbs Brook Rd., Weston, MA 02493 (☎781-888-1515; www.alp-online.com). ALP runs programs in Arizona, California, Florida, and Massachusetts that include home stay and intensive English training. $900-1080 per week (15-25hr.) for 1 person, $1600-1960 for 2 people.

Osako Sangyo University Los Angeles (OSULA) Education Center, 3921 Laurel Canyon Blvd., Los Angeles, CA 91604 (☎818-509-1484, ext.104 or 125; www.osula.com). Offers 12- to 24-week general and intensive English and Japanese classes in the suburbs of Los Angeles, in a residential college setting.

ART PROGRAMS

Those of a more creative persuasion can pursue artistic expression in the US—bohemian quarters of New York and San Francisco, as well as the wide open spaces of the American interior, beckon with artistic organizations of all stripes.

New York Film Academy, 100 E. 17th St., New York, NY 10003 (☎212-674-4300; www.nyfa.com). NYFA allows would-be actors, filmmakers, and screenwriters the chance to hone their skills on studio sets. Program lengths vary from 1 week to 1 year, with classes in acting, screenwriting, digital imaging, filmmaking, and 3-D animation. Program costs $2000-22,500.

University of Southern California School of Cinema-Television, Summer Production Workshop, 850 W. 34th St., Los Angeles, CA 90089-2211 (☎213-740-1742; www.usc.edu/schools/cntv/programs/spw). Boasting a luminous alumni list that includes Jedi boy George Lucas, screenwriter John Milius (*Apocalypse Now),* and producer Laura Ziskin (*Spider-Man*), the world-renowned film school offers summer workshops with classes in writing, digital imaging, directing, and producing. University housing is available, as are classes for students who have already logged some hours (or years) in the industry.

Arcosanti, HC 74 BOX 4136, Mayer, AZ 86333 (☎928-632-6233; www.arcosanti.org.) Founded by Frank Lloyd Wright's disciple Paolo Soleri, who still lives here, Arcosanti is an experimental community 70 mi. north of Phoenix based on Soleri's theory of "arcology"–the symbiotic relationship between architecture and ecology. It hosts 5-week workshops ($1050) in which participants help expand the settlement while learning about Soleri's project and developing their skills at construction and planning. For those with some background in construction or architecture, an expense-paid internship is available for a 3-month commitment.

Santa Fe Art Institute, P.O. Box 24044, Santa Fe, NM 87502 (☎505-424-5050; www.sfai.org). A world-class artistic center, the Santa Fe Art Institute offers weekend ($350), 1-week ($500), and 2-week ($900) workshops giving participants the opportunity to learn from professional resident artists in Santa Fe. Need-based scholarships are available for all workshops.

Denver Center Theater Company, 1245 Champa St., Denver, CO 80204 (☎303-893-4000; www.denvercenter.org). The Tony-award winning Denver Center Theatre Company offers a number of technical and administrative internships every year, as well as offering volunteering opportunities and inexpensive ($75-1500) theater workshops for all ages.

The Wilma Theater, 265 S. Broad St., Philadelphia, PA 19107 (☎215-893-9456; www.wilmatheater.org). Wilma offers unpaid internships and paid fellowships to young people with theater experience. Workshops on screenwriting, playwriting, acting, improv, and musical theater ($200) are also available.

WORKING

As with volunteering, work opportunities tend to fall into two categories. Some travelers want longterm jobs that allow them to get to know another part of the world as a member of the community, while others seek out short-term work to finance the next leg of their travels. In the US and Canada, people looking to work long-term should consider exchange programs. Short-term work is most often found in the service industry and agriculture.

Regardless of whether you are looking for temporary work or something more permanent, a good place to start your search is the local newspaper, which is usually the best source of up-to-date job information. Internet search engines like monster.com are also helpful. Before signing on, be sure you have the correct visa and working papers (see **Visa Information**).

LONG-TERM WORK

If you're planning on spending a substantial amount of time (more than 3 months) working in North America, search for a job well in advance. International placement agencies are often the easiest way to find employment abroad. **Internships,** usually for college students, are a good way to segue into working abroad, although they are often unpaid or poorly paid (many say the experience, however, is well worth it). Visit **www.aboutjobs.com** to peruse summer jobs, internships, and resort work. Be wary of advertisements or companies that claim the ability to get you a job abroad for a fee—often times the same listings are available online or in newspapers, or even out of date. It's best, if going through an organization, to use one that's somewhat reputable. Some good ones include:

Alliances Abroad Group, Inc., 3 Barton Skyway, Ste. 250, 1221 S. Mopac Expwy., Austin, TX 78746, US (☎ 512-457-8062; www.alliancesabroad.com). Organizes summer work in the service industry for university students ages 18-28.

Council Exchanges, 52 Poland St., London W1F 7AB, UK (☎44 020 7478 2000; US☎ 888-268-6245; www.councilexchanges.org) charges a $300-475 fee for arranging short-term working authorizations (generally valid for 3-6 months) and provides extensive information on different job opportunities in the US and Canada.

VISA INFORMATION

All foreign visitors are required to have a **visa** if they intend to work in the US or Canada. In addition, travelers must provide proof of intent to leave, such as a return plane ticket or an I-94 card. A **work permit** (or "green card") is also required. Your employer must obtain this document, usually by demonstrating that you have skills that locals lack. Friends in the US can sometimes help expedite work permits or arrange work-for-accommodations exchanges. **To obtain both visas and work permits,** contact a US or Canadian embassy or consulate. Check http://travel.state.gov/links.html for US listings and www.dfait-maeci.gc.ca/world/embassies/menu-en.asp for Canadian listings worldwide. Visa extensions are sometimes attainable with a completed I-539 form; call the Bureau of Citizenship and Immigration Service's (BCIS) forms request line (800-870-3676) or get it online at www.immigration.gov/graphics/formsfee/forms/i-539.htm. See http://travel.state.gov/visa_services.html and www.unitedstates.gov for more information. Recent security measures have made the visa application process more rigorous, and therefore lengthy. **Apply well in advance of your travel date.** The process may seem complex, but it's critical that you go through the proper channels—the alternative is potential deportation.

AU PAIR WORK

Au pairs are typically women, aged 18-27, who work as live-in nannies, caring for children and doing light housework in foreign countries in exchange for room, board, and a small spending allowance or stipend. Most former au pairs speak favorably of their experience, and how it allowed them to really get to know a foreign country without the high expenses of traveling. Drawbacks, however, often include long hours of constantly being on-duty and the somewhat mediocre pay. In the US, weekly salaries typically fall well below $200, with at least 45hr. of work expected. Au pairs are expected to speak English and have at least 200hr. of childcare experience. Much of the au pair experience really does depend on the family you're placed with. The agencies below are a good starting point for looking for employment as an au pair.

Accord Cultural Exchange, 750 La Playa, San Francisco, CA 94121, US (☎415-386-6203; www.cognitext.com/accord).

Childcare International, Ltd., Trafalgar House, Grenville Pl., London NW7 3SA, UK (☎44 020 8906 3116; fax 8906-3461; www.childint.co.uk).

InterExchange, 161 Sixth Ave., New York, NY 10013, US (☎212-924-0446; fax 924-0575; www.interexchange.org).

SHORT-TERM WORK

Traveling for long periods of time can get expensive; therefore, many travelers try their hand at odd jobs for a few weeks at a time to make some extra cash to carry them through another month or two of touring around. One popular option is to work several hours a day at a hostel in exchange for free or discounted room and/or board. Most often, short-term jobs are found by word of mouth, or simply by talking to the owner of a hostel or restaurant. Due to the high turnover in the tourism industry, many places are eager for help, if only temporary. *Let's Go* tries to list temporary jobs like these whenever possible; look in the practical information sections of larger cities.

FOR FURTHER READING ON ALTERNATIVES TO TOURISM

Alternatives to the Peace Corps: A directory of third world and U.S. Volunteer Opportunities, by Joan Powell. Food First Books, 2000 ($10).

How to Get a Job in Europe, by Sanborn and Matherly. Surrey Books, 1999 ($22).

How to Live Your Dream of Volunteering Overseas, by Collins, DeZerega, and Heckscher. Penguin Books, 2002 ($17).

International Directory of Voluntary Work, by Whetter and Pybus. Peterson's Guides and Vacation Work, 2000 ($16).

International Jobs, by Kocher and Segal. Perseus Books, 1999 ($18).

Overseas Summer Jobs 2002, by Collier and Woodworth. Peterson's Guides and Vacation Work, 2002 ($18).

Work Abroad: The Complete Guide to Finding a Job Overseas, by Hubbs, Griffith, and Nolting. Transitions Abroad Publishing, 2000 ($16).

Work Your Way Around the World, by Susan Griffith. Worldview Publishing Services, 2001 ($18).

Invest Yourself: The Catalogue of Volunteer Opportunities, published by the Commission on Voluntary Service and Action (☎ 718-638-8487).

NEW ENGLAND

New England fancied itself an intellectual and political center long before the States were United, and still does today. Students and scholars funnel into New England's colleges each fall, and town meetings still evoke the spirit of popular government that once inspired American colonists to create a nation. Numerous historic landmarks recount every step of the country's break from "Old" England.

The region's unpredictable climate can be particularly dismal during the harsh, wet winter from November to March, when rivers, campgrounds, and tourist attractions freeze up. Nevertheless, today's visitors find adventure in the rough edges that troubled early settlers, flocking to New England's dramatic, salty coastline to sun on the sand or heading to the slopes and valleys of the Green and White Mountains to ski, hike, bike, and canoe. In the fall, the nation's most brilliant foliage bleeds and burns, transforming the entire region into a kaleidoscope of color.

HIGHLIGHTS OF NEW ENGLAND

SEAFOOD. Head to Maine (see below) for the best lobster around, and don't forget to try New England clam "chowda" before you leave.

SKIING. Enthusiasts flock to the mountains of New Hampshire and Vermont; the most famous resorts include Stowe (p. 111) and Killington (p. 104).

Beaches. Cape Cod (p. 135) and Nantucket, MA (p. 141) have the region's best.

COLONIAL LANDMARKS. They're everywhere, but a walk along the Freedom Trail in Boston, MA (p. 114) is a great place to start.

SCENIC NEW ENGLAND. Take a drive along Rte. 100 in the fall, when the foliage is at its most striking, or hike the Appalachian Trail (p. 88) for a view on foot.

MAINE

Nearly a thousand years ago, Leif Erikson and his band of Viking explorers set foot on the coasts of Maine. Moose roamed the sprawling evergreen wilderness, the cry of the Maine coon cat echoed through towering mountains, and countless lobsters crawled in the ocean deep. A millennium has changed little. Forests still cover nearly 90% of Maine's land, an area larger than all the other New England states to the south. The inner reaches of the state stretch on for mile after uninhabited mile, while some more populated locales break up a harsh and jagged coastline.

PRACTICAL INFORMATION

Capital: Augusta.

Visitor Info: Maine Tourism Information, 59 State House Station, Augusta 04333 (☎207-623-0363 or 888-624-6345; www.visitmaine.com). **Maine Information Center,** in Kittery, 3 mi. north of the Maine-New Hampshire bridge (☎207-439-1319; open daily July-early Oct. 8am-6pm, mid-Oct. to June 9am-5:30pm). **Bureau of Parks and Lands,** State House Station #22 (AMHI, Harlow Bldg.), Augusta 04333 (☎207-287-3821; www.state.me.us/doc/parks). **Maine Forest Service,** Department of Conservation, State House Station #22, Augusta 04333 (☎207-287-2791).

Postal Abbreviation: ME. **Sales Tax:** 5%.

MAINE COAST

The Maine coast meanders 288 miles along the Atlantic Ocean with a multitude of rocky inlets and promontories that make for eye-catching scenery. The port towns are strung together by the two-lane U.S. 1, the region's only option for accessing most costal towns north of Portland. Although driving your own vehicle is the best way to truly explore the coast, be prepared to take your time; the traffic pace is often slow in the summer, especially through towns and villages.

PORTLAND ☎207

Portland, although a large industrial center, is also a center for the arts and a place to enjoy the outdoors. At night, the Victorian architecture in the Old Port Exchange forms a rather ironic backdrop to Portland's spirited youth culture. Teenagers and 20-somethings gather in bars, restaurants, and cafes near the wharf, and flood the streets in talkative groups and couples, even after stores close down. Outside the city, ferries run to the Casco Bay Islands while Sebago Lake provides sunning and water-skiing.

ORIENTATION & PRACTICAL INFORMATION. Downtown sits in the middle of the peninsula, along **Congress Street** between State St. and Pearl St. A few blocks south, along the waterfront lies the **Old Port,** between Commercial and Middle St. These two districts contain most of the city's sights and attractions. **I-295** (off I-95) forms the northwestern boundary of city. **Amtrak,** 100 Thompson Point Rd., on Connector Rd., off Congress St. (☎800-872-7245; www.thedowneaster.com), runs to Boston (2¾hr., 4 per day, $21). **Concord Trailways** (☎828-1151; office open daily 4:30am-9:30pm), in the same building, runs to Bangor (2½hr., 3 per day, $22) and Boston (2hr., 12 per day, $18). Metro buses run to and from the station (M-Sa every 20min., Su every hr.). **Greyhound/Vermont Transit,** 950 Congress St., on the western outskirts of town (☎772-6587), runs to Bangor (2½-3½hr., 5 per day, $20) and Boston (2hr., 6 per day, $15). *Be cautious here at night; the neighborhood is not entirely safe.* **Scotia Prince Cruises,** 468 Commercial St., sends ferries to Yarmouth, NS from the Portland International Marine Terminal, on Commercial St., near the Casco Bay Bridge. Boats run May to late October. Ferries depart Portland at 8pm for the 11hr. trip. (☎775-5611 or 800-341-7540. Cabins available. Fare May-late June and late Sept.-late Oct. $70, ages 5-14 $35; car $90, bike $10. Late June to late Sept. $90/45/110/20. Reservations strongly recommended.) **Metro Bus** services downtown Portland. Routes run 5:30am-11:45pm, individual routes may start later or end earlier. (☎774-0351. $1, seniors with Medicare card $0.50, under 5 free; transfers free.) **Visitors Information Bureau:** 245 Commercial St., between Union and Cross St. (☎772-5800. Open M-F 8am-5pm, Sa 10am-5pm.) **Internet Access: Portland Public Library.** 5 Monument Sq. (☎871-1700. Open M, W, F 9am-6pm, Tu and Th noon-9pm, Sa 9am-5pm.) **Post Office:** 400 Congress St. (☎871-8464. Open M-F 8am-7pm, Sa 9am-1pm.) **Postal Code:** 04101. **Area Code:** 207.

ACCOMMODATIONS. Portland has some inexpensive accommodations during the winter, but prices jump steeply during the summer, especially on weekends. Lodging in the smaller towns up and down the coast within 30min. of Portland can be a less expensive option. **The Inn at St. John ❹,** 939 Congress

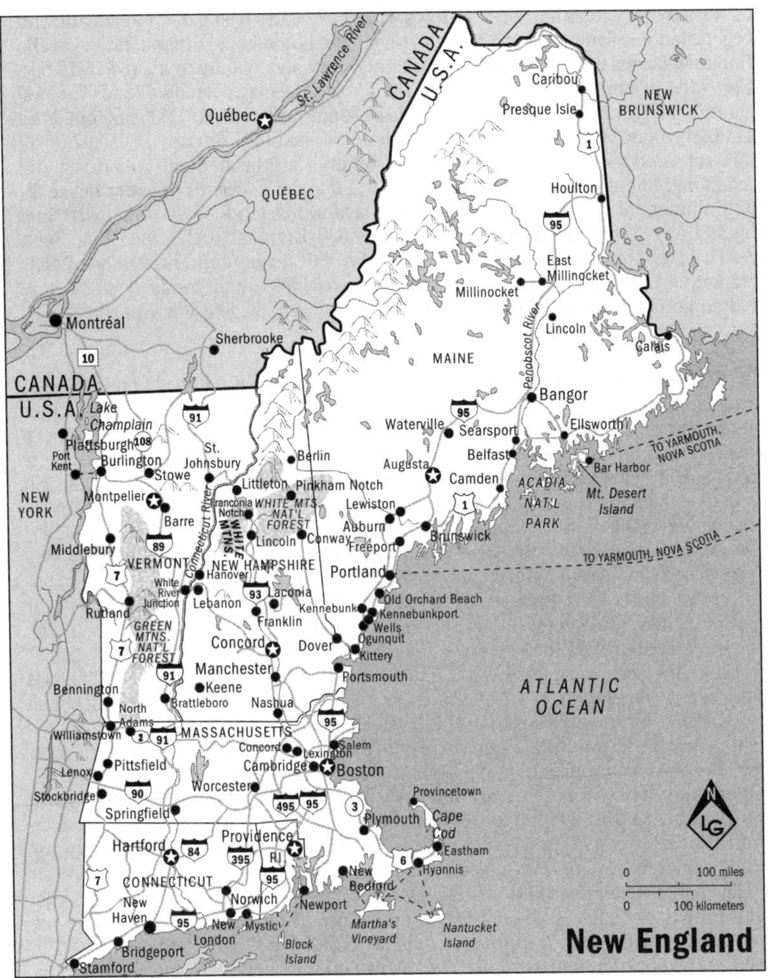

St., is not located in an especially appealing neighborhood, but its old-fashioned upscale decor makes it an elegant option. (☎773-6481 or 800-636-9127. Continental breakfast included. Bike storage, free local calls, and free parking. Rooms with private bath are available. Singles or doubles in summer M-Th $70-135, F-Su $115-175; winter M-Th $55-100, F-Su $60-115.) **Wassamki Springs ❶**, 56 Saco St., in Scarborough, is the closest campground to Portland. Winnebagos and brightly colored tents cluster among the trees and around a lake encircled by sandy beaches. (☎839-4276. Free showers and flush toilets. Reserve 2 weeks in advance, especially July-Aug. Open May to mid-Oct. Sites with water and electricity for 2 adults $28, with hookup $30; each additional person $5; lakefront sites $3 extra.)

FOOD. Portland's harbor overflows with the ocean's fruits, but non-aquatic and vegetarian fare isn't too hard to find either. The homemade, organic pizzas at the **Flatbread Company ❸,** 72 Commercial St., are tasty and healthy treats ($7.75-13.50). Enjoy the ocean view as your meal is fired in a huge clay oven. (☎772-8777. Open summer M-Th 11:30am-10pm, F-Sa 11am-10:30pm; winter M-Th 11:30am-9pm, F-Sa 11:30am-10pm.) **Federal Spice ❶,** 225 Federal St., just off Congress St., seasons all its wraps and soft tacos (all under $6) with fiery Caribbean, South American, and Asian ingredients. (☎774-6404. Open M-Sa 11am-9pm.) **Gilbert's Chowder House ❷,** 92 Commercial St., is the local choice for seafood. A large bowl of chowder in a bread bowl ($7-11) is a meal in itself. (☎871-5636. Entrees $10-21. Open June-Sept. Su-Th 11am-10pm, F-Sa 11am-11pm; Oct.-May call for hours.) The **Portland Public Market**, at Preble St. and Cumberland Ave., provides ethnic foods, seafood, and baked goods from over 20 small food vendors. (☎228-2000; www.portlandmarket.com. Open M-Sa 9am-7pm, Su 10am-5pm.)

SIGHTS. Offshore islands with secluded beaches and relatively undeveloped interiors lie just a ferry ride from the city proper. **Casco Bay Lines,** on State Pier near the corner of Commercial and Franklin, runs daily to **Long Island,** where waves crash on an unpopulated beach, and **Peaks Island,** as well as other islands. (☎774-7871; www.cascobaylines.com. Long Island: Operates M-Sa 5am-9:30pm, Su 7:45am-9:30pm. Round-trip $8, seniors and ages 5-9 $4. Peaks Island: Operates M-Sa 5:45am-11:30pm, Su 7:45am-11:30pm. Round-trip $6, seniors and ages 5-9 $3.) On Peaks Island, **Brad's Recycled Bike Shop,** 115 Island Ave., rents bikes. (☎766-5631. Open daily 10am-5pm. $5 per hr., $8.50 for 3hr., $12 per day.)

Try **Two Lights State Park,** across the Casco Bay Bridge accessed from State or York St., then south along Rte. 77 to Cape Elizabeth, for an uncrowded spot to picnic or walk alongside the ocean. (☎799-5871; www.state.me.us/doc/parks. $2.50.) While in the area, a trip to the still functioning **Portland Head Light** in **Fort Williams Park** is a scenic detour worth the time. From 77N turn right at the flashing signal onto Shore Rd. and proceed to the park. The **Portland Observatory,** 138 Congress St., is not only the last maritime signal tower in the US, it is also the best view in town. (☎774-5561; www.portlandlandmarks.org. Admission and tour $4, ages 6-16 $2. Open daily 10am-5pm; last tour 4:40pm.) While it takes about 8 days to brew a batch of beer at the **Shipyard Brewing Co.,** 86 Newbury St., it will only take 30min. to tour the brewery and try the free sample. (☎761-0807. Tours every 30min. during the summer M-F 3-5pm, Sa-Su noon-5pm; winter W-F 3-5pm, Sa noon-5pm. Free.)

The **Portland Museum of Art,** 7 Congress Sq., at the intersection of Congress, High, and Free St., collects 19th-century American art. The museum also includes the recently restored McLellan House, originally built in 1801. (☎775-6148 or 800-639-4067; www.portlandmuseum.org. Open June to mid-Oct. M-W and Sa-Su 10am-5pm, Th-F 10am-9pm; mid-Oct. to May closed M. $8, students and seniors $6, ages 6-12 $2; F 5-9pm free. Wheelchair-accessible.) The **Wadsworth-Longfellow House,** 489 Congress St., was the home of 19th-century poet Henry Wadsworth Longfellow. Presently, it stands as a museum of social history and US literature, focusing on late 18th- and 19th-century antiques as well as the life of the poet. (☎774-1822, ext. 208; www.mainehistory.org. Open June-Oct. M-Sa 10am-4pm, Su noon-4pm. $7, students and seniors $6, ages 5-17 $3. Price includes admission to a small neighboring history museum with rotating exhibits. Tours every 30-40min.)

ENTERTAINMENT & NIGHTLIFE. Signs for theatrical productions decorate Portland, and schedules are available at the Visitors Center (see **Practical Information,** p. 84). The **Portland Symphony** presents concerts renowned throughout the

Northeast. (☎842-0800. Tickets through Porttix located at 20 Myrtle St. Open M-Sa noon-6pm. Tickets may also be purchased online at www.porttix.com. Occasional 50% student discount.) Info on Portland's jazz, blues, and club scene packs the *Casco Bay Weekly* (www.cascobayweekly.com) and *FACE*, both of which are free. Traditionally on the first Sunday in June, the **Old Port Festival** (☎772-6828) fills the blocks from Federal to Commercial St. with as many as 50,000 people enjoying free public entertainment. Midday on Friday from early July to late August, the **Weekday Music Series** (☎772-6828; www.portlandmaine.com) hosts a variety of bands in Post Office Square between Middle and Exchange St.

The Old Port area, known as "the strip"—especially **Fore Street** between Union and Exchange St.—livens up after dark as shops stay open late and bars start serving beer. **Brian Boru,** 57 Center St., provides a mellow pub scene with top-notch nachos for $6. (☎780-1506. Su $2 pints. Open daily 11:30am-1am.) **Gritty MacDuff's,** 396 Fore St., brews its own beer ($3.50 pints) and entertains a largely local crowd with live music Sa and Su nights. (☎772-2739. Open daily 11:30am-1am.) **Una Wine Bar & Lounge**, 505 Fore St., mixes speciality martinis and serves wine by the taste, glass ($5-10), or bottle. (☎828-0300. Tapas $3-15. Open daily 4:30pm-1am).

SOUTH OF PORTLAND ☎207

KENNEBUNKPORT

Kennebunk and its coastal counterpart 8 mi. east, **Kennebunkport,** are popular hideaways for wealthy authors and artists—Kennebunkport reluctantly grew famous as the summer home of former President George Bush. Rare and used bookstores line U.S. 1 just south of Kennebunk, while art galleries fill the town. You could spend a day (and a fortune) exploring all the little shops in town. **Old Salt's Pantry ❶**, 5 Ocean Ave., provides breakfast and lunch fare with a homemade touch. The enormous muffins ($1.25), which can be grilled until warm and soft, are not to be missed. (☎967-3861. Open daily 9:30am-5:30pm.) For surfers, or those who just want to breathe the salty air and feel sand between their toes, the five **public beaches** in the area are all a short trip from town. (Parking fees depend upon beach, free to $10 per day, $20 per week.) Narrated scenic cruises aboard the **Deep Water II** sail frequently along the coast viewing wildlife and historic sites. (☎967-5595. 1½hr. $15, seniors $12.50, ages 3-12 $7.50. Ticket booth on Ocean Ave. in front of The Landing Restaurant.) The 55 ft. gaff-rigged **Schooner Eleanor,** leaving from Arundel Wharf, Ocean Ave., provides a relaxed 2hr. yachting experience. (☎967-8809. $38. Call for reservations and times.) The **Kennebunk-Kennebunkport Chamber of Commerce,** 17 U.S. 9/Western Ave., in Kennebunkport, has a free area guide. (☎967-0857; www.kkcc.maine.org. Open summer M-F 9am-5pm.) The Chamber of Commerce also operates a **hospitality center,** 2 Union Center, next to Ben and Jerry's. (☎967-0857. Open M-F 10am-9pm, Sa 9am-9pm, Su 10am-8pm.)

NORTHERN MAINE COAST ☎207

Much like the coastal region south of Portland, the north offers the traveler eye-catching cliffs, windswept ocean vistas, and quintessential New England small towns—for a price. Lodging in L.L. Bean country isn't cheap, but just passing through allows you to taste the area's proverbial milk and honey without buying the cow or the hive. U.S. 1 is northern coastal Maine's only thoroughfare, and traffic barely creeps along through the many small roadside hamlets.

CAMDEN

In the summer, khaki-clad crowds flock to Camden, 100 mi. north of Portland, to dock their yachts alongside the tall-masted schooners in Penobscot Bay. If you can't afford a private yacht, 2hr. **cruises** sail from the public landing, offering views of the many lighthouses and the abundant wildlife. (Schooner Olad ☎236-2323. Schooner Lazy Jack ☎230-0602. Both $25.) The **Camden-Rockport Lincolnville Chamber of Commerce** gives helpful information and provides an informative guide to the area. (☎236-4404 or 800-223-5459; www.camdenme.org. Open mid-May to mid-Oct. M-F 9am-5pm, Sa 10am-5pm, Su 10am-4pm; mid-Oct. to mid-May closed Su.) The **Camden Hills State Park ❶,** 1¼ mi. north of town on U.S. 1, is almost always full in summer, but sites are usually available for arrivals before 2pm. This secluded retreat also offers 25 mi. of trails, including a popular lookout from the top of Mt. Battie. (☎236-3109, reservations ☎800-332-1501 in ME only, ☎287-3824 out of state. Open mid-May to mid-Oct. Office open 7am-10pm. Free showers. Sites $20, ME residents $15; reservations $2 per day; day-use $3.) The **Good Guest House ❹,** 50 Elm St., offers two appealing rooms at reasonable rates. (☎236-2139. Private bath, full breakfast. Double bed $65, king size $75.) **Cappy's Chowder House ❸,** 1 Main St., offers up local seafood specialities (entrees $10-14) and homemade pies from its bakery. (☎236-2254. Open daily 11am-11pm, kitchen closes at 10pm.)

Maine Sports, on U.S. 1 in Rockport, just south of Camden, rents and sells a wide array of sea-worthy vehicles. (☎236-7120 or 800-722-0826. Open mid-June to Aug. daily 9am-8pm; Sept. to mid-June M-Sa 9am-6pm, Su 10am-5pm. Single kayaks $35-50; doubles $45-65. Canoes $35-40 per day.) The **Maine State Ferry Service,** 5 mi. north of Camden in Lincolnville, floats to Islesboro Island, a quiet residential island. (☎800-491-4883. 30min.; 5-9 per day, last return trip 4:30pm. Round-trip $5.25, with bike $10.25, car and driver $15. Parking $6 per day.) The ferry also has an agency at 517A Main St., on U.S. 1 in Rockland, that runs to Vinalhaven and North Haven. (☎596-2202. Rates and schedules change with weather; call ahead.)

NEW ENGLAND

THE APPALACHIAN TRAIL Stretching 2160 mi. from Mt. Katahdin, ME, to Springer Mountain, GA, the **Appalachian Trail (AT)** follows the path of the Appalachian Mountains along the eastern United States. Use of the AT is free, although only foot travelers may traverse it. The trail cuts through 14 states, 8 national forests, and 6 national parks. Generally, the AT is very accessible, crossed by roads along its entire length except for the northernmost 100 mi. Although many sections make excellent day hikes or overnights, about 2500 "through-hikers" attempt a continuous hike of the AT annually. Three-sided shelters (first come, first served) dot the trail, spaced about a day's journey apart. Hikers take advantage of streams and nearby towns to stock up on water and supplies. White blazes on rocks and trees mark the length of the main trail, while blue blazes mark side trails.

MT. DESERT ISLAND ☎207

Roughly half of Mt. Desert Island is covered by Acadia National Park, which harbors some of the last protected marine, mountain, and forest environments on the New England coast. During the summer the island is awash with tourists lured by thick forests and mountainous landscape. Bar Harbor, on the eastern side, is by far the most crowded and glitzy part of the island. Once a summer hamlet for the affluent, the town now welcomes a motley melange of R&R-seekers. Despite the exodus of the well-heeled wealthy to the secluded Northeast and Seal Harbor, the town still maintains its overpriced traditions.

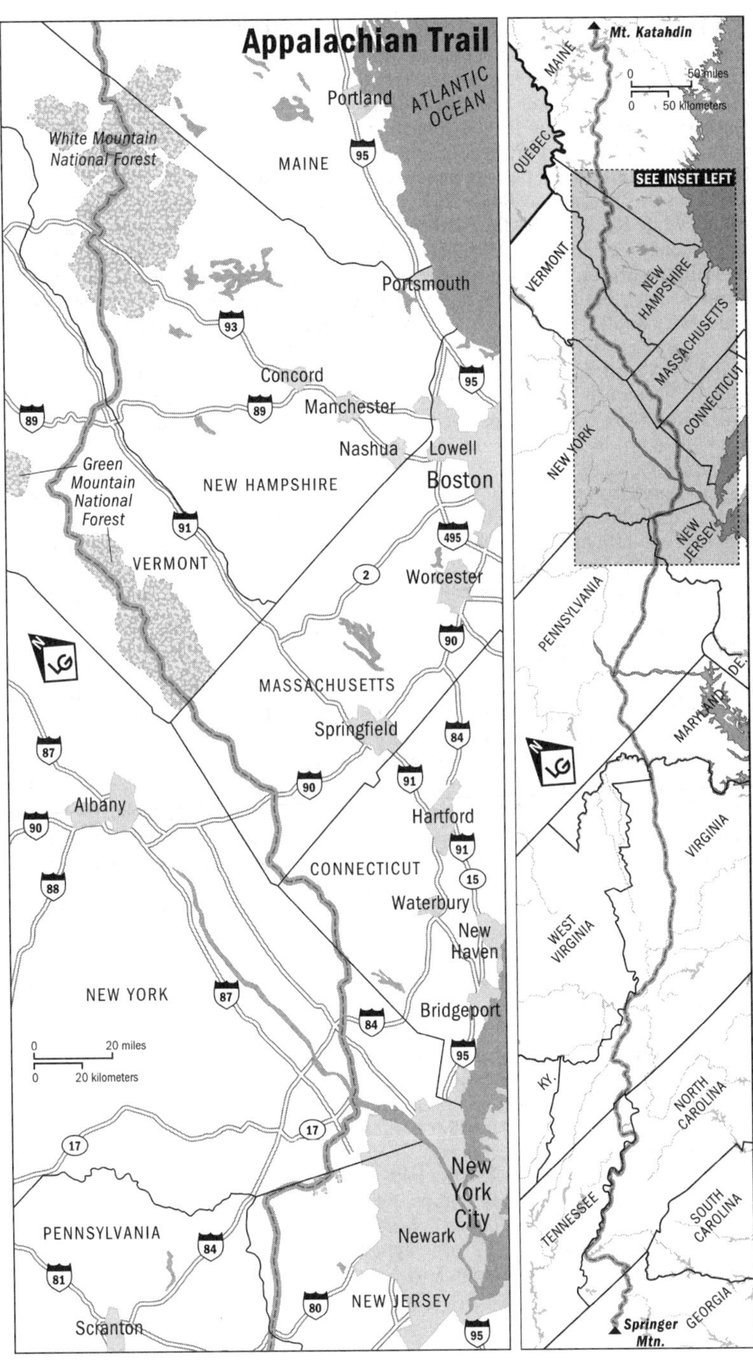
Appalachian Trail
Portland
ATLANTIC OCEAN
White Mountain National Forest
MAINE
Portsmouth
Concord
Manchester
Nashua
Lowell
Boston
Green Mountain National Forest
NEW HAMPSHIRE
VERMONT
Worcester
MASSACHUSETTS
Springfield
Albany
Hartford
CONNECTICUT
Waterbury
New Haven
NEW YORK
Bridgeport
0 20 miles
0 20 kilometers
New York City
Newark
PENNSYLVANIA
NEW JERSEY
Scranton
Mt. Katahdin
0 50 miles
0 50 kilometers
MAINE
QUÉBEC
SEE INSET LEFT
VERMONT
NEW HAMPSHIRE
MASSACHUSETTS
CONNECTICUT
NEW YORK
NEW JERSEY
PENNSYLVANIA
DE.
MARYLAND
VIRGINIA
WEST VIRGINIA
KY.
NORTH CAROLINA
TENNESSEE
SOUTH CAROLINA
GEORGIA
Springer Mtn.

ORIENTATION AND PRACTICAL INFORMATION. Mt. Desert Island is shaped roughly like a 16 mi. long and 13 mi. wide lobster claw. It promises not to hurt you. **Seal Harbor,** on Rte. 3, rests on the Southeast corner of the island. South on Rte. 198 near the cleft is **Northeast Harbor.** Across Somes Sound on Rte. 102 is **Southwest Harbor,** where fishing, lobster trapping and shipbuilding thrive. **Route 3** runs through Bar Harbor, becoming **Mount Desert Street** and then **Main Street. Mount Desert Street** and **Cottage Street** are the major streets for shops, restaurants, and bars in Bar Harbor. **Route 102** meanders through the western half of the island, while Rte. 3 circles the eastern half. There is a $10 park pass for cars.

Greyhound (☎288-3211 or 800-552-8737) leaves Bar Harbor once daily from the Villager Motel, 207 Main St., for Boston (7hr., $41) via Bangor (1½hr., $11). Fares are subject to change; call ahead. **Beal & Bunker** (☎244-3575; open late June-early Sept. daily 8am-4:30pm; call for winter hours) runs ferries from the Northeast Harbor town dock to Great Cranberry Island (15min.; 6 per day; $12, under 12 $6). **Bay Ferries,** 121 Eden St. (☎888-249-7245; www.catferry.com), runs to Yarmouth, NS. (3hr.; 1-2 per day; $55, seniors $50, ages 5-17 $25; cars $95, bikes $10. Reservations recommended, $5 fee if reserved by phone; car price does not include passengers. Ticket shop and tourist information in Bar Harbor, 4 Cottage St., ☎288-9432. Open daily 10am-9pm.) Free **Island Explorer** buses depart from Bar Harbor green and are a good way to get around the park and its campgrounds. The buses run approximately every 30min. from each stop. A schedule may be found in *Acadia Weekly*. **Acadia Bike & Canoe,** 48 Cottage St., in Bar Harbor, rents bikes, canoes and kayaks, and leads sea kayaking tours. (☎288-9605, for tours ☎800-526-8615. Open May-Oct. daily 8am-6pm. Bikes $14 per half-day, $19 per day; children $12. Canoes $30 per day, $25 each additional day; one-person kayaks $45 per day, tandems $55.)

Acadia National Park Visitors Center, 3 mi. north of Bar Harbor on Rte. 3, has a huge topographical map, a small bookstore, and rangers ready and willing to help. A free 15min. video introducing the park is shown every 30min. (☎288-5262. Open mid-June to mid-Sept. daily 8am-6pm; mid-Apr. to mid-June and mid-Sept. to Oct. 8am-4:30pm.) The **Park Headquarters,** 3 mi. west of Bar Harbor on Rte. 233, provides visitor info during the low-season. (☎288-3338. Open M-F 8am-4:30pm.) **Bar Harbor Chamber of Commerce,** 93 Cottage St. (☎288-5103; open June-Oct. M-F 8am-5pm, Nov.-May M-F 8am-4pm), operates an **info booth** at 1 Harbor Place on the town pier. (Open mid-May to mid-Oct. daily 9am-5pm.) **Hotlines: Downeast Sexual Assault Helpline** (☎800-228-2470; operates 24hr.). **Emergency: Acadia National Park Law Enforcement** (☎288-3369) **Internet Access: The Opera House,** 27 Cottage St. (☎288-3509. Open May-June daily 8am-11pm.; July-Oct. daily 7am-11pm. $2.25 first 15min., $0.10 each additional min.) **Post Office:** 55 Cottage St. (☎288-3122. Open M-F 8am-4:30pm, Sa 9am-noon.) **Postal Code:** 04609. **Area Code:** 207.

ACCOMMODATIONS. Though grand hotels and prices recall the island's exclusive resort days, reasonable establishments do exist, particularly on **Route 3** north of Bar Harbor where a large number of small motels dot the sides of the road. The perennially popular **Bar Harbor Youth Hostel ❶,** 321 Main St., accommodates 30 people in two dorm rooms and one family room that houses three people with a private bath. The hostel's friendly manager gives out free baked goods and discounts on kayak rentals. A book-swap and free movie nights keep travelers entertained. (☎288-5587. Linens free. Lockout 10am-5pm. Curfew 11pm. Reservations accepted if pre-payment as a check or money order is sent to P.O. Box 32, Bar Harbor. Open May-Nov. $21, nonmembers $25; family room

$55/65. Visa, cash, or travelers check only.) Sleep tight at **Hearthside ❺,** 7 High St., a back street B&B that is a short walk to downtown Bar Harbor. (☎288-4533. A/C and private bath; some rooms have fireplaces. Rooms in summer $100-150; low-season $70-100.)

Camping spots cover the island, especially on **Routes 102** and **198,** well west of town. **White Birches Campground ❶,** in Southwest Harbor, on Seal Cove Rd. 1 mi. west of Rte. 102, has 60 widely-spaced, wooded sites in a remote location that is ideal for hiking. (☎244-3797 or 800-716-0727. Free hot showers, bathrooms and heated pool. Coin-operated laundry. Reservations recommended, especially July-Aug. Open mid-May to mid-Oct. daily 8am-8pm. Sites for 1-4 people $21, with hookup $25; weekly $126/150; each additional person $4.) **Acadia National Park campgrounds** include **Blackwoods ❶,** 5 mi. south of Bar Harbor on Rte. 3. The 300 wooded sites are tightly packed in summer, but, when the throngs depart, the charm of the campground's thick, dark woods returns, as do the larger wildlife. (☎800-365-2267. Reservations recommended in summer. Mid-Mar. to Oct. $20; call for low-season rates. No hookups. Coin operated showers available at private facility located just outside of the campground.)

FOOD. To watch some flicks and munch on a few slices, head over to **Reel Pizza ❸,** 33 Kennebec Pl., at the end of Rodick off Main St. This movie theater/pizzeria shows two films each evening for $5 and serves up creative and delicious pizza pies ($7-19), such as the "Hawaii 5-O" with smoked ham, pineapple, green pepper, and macadamia nuts. The first three rows of the "theater" are comfy couches and chairs. (☎288-3828. Open daily 5pm to end of last screening.) The walls and ceilings at **Freddie's Route 66 Restaurant ❸,** 21 Cottage St., are absolutely crammed with 1950s memorabilia. The Cadillac burger with bleu cheese, bacon, lettuce, tomato and onion, as well as fries and coleslaw, is a well-spent $9. (☎288-3708. Open mid-May to mid-Oct. daily 11am-3pm and 4:30-10pm.) **Beal's ❸,** off Main St., at the end of Clark Point Rd. near the Coast Guard station, goes easy on the frills, offering lobster at superb prices on an outdoor, picnic-tabled patio overlooking the harbor. (☎244-3202 or 800-245-7178. Lobster 8.50 per pound. Open May-Oct. daily 7am-8pm; Nov.-Apr. 7am-4pm. Seafood sold year-round daily 9am-5pm.) **Ben and Bill's Chocolate Emporium ❶,** 66 Main St., near Cottage St., boasts 48 flavors of homemade ice cream, including—no kidding—lobster. (☎288-3281. Fudge $12 per lb. Cones $3-4. Open mid-Feb. to Jan. daily 9am-11:30pm.)

SIGHTS. The staff at the **Mount Desert Oceanarium,** at the end of Clark Pt. Rd. near Beal's in Southwest Harbor, have their sea schtick down. The main museum is small and geared for children, but the interactive exhibits fascinate all ages. Its sister oceanarium, off Rte 3. on the northeast edge of the island, teaches everything there is to know about lobsters with a museum and hatchery. (☎244-7330. Open mid-May to mid-Oct. M-Sa 9am-5pm. Main oceanarium $7, ages 4-12 $5. Ticket for both facilities $13/10.) For a relaxing drive with a stunning view, **Sargent Drive** runs along Somes Sound. Travelers on foot can head to **Bar Island** at low tide, when a gravel path, accessed via Bridge St., with tide pools is exposed for the two or three hours surrounding low tide. Tide times are published in the free and widely distributed *Acadia Weekly*. **Wildwood Stables,** along Park Loop Rd. in Seal Harbor, takes tourists around the island via horse and carriage. (☎276-3622. 1hr. tour $13.50, seniors $12.50, ages 6-12 $7, ages 2-5 $4. 2hr. tour $17.50/16.50/8/5. Reservations recommended. Wheelchair-accessible if notified in advance.)

ENTERTAINMENT AND NIGHTLIFE. Most after-dinner pleasures on the island are simple and cluster in Bar Harbor. **Geddy's Pub,** 19 Main St., gives a outdoorsy backdrop of weathered wooden signs, beat-up license plates, and moose head trophies to the dancing frenzy that breaks out nightly during the summer months as tables are moved aside for a DJ and dance floor. (☎288-5077. No cover. Live music daily 7-10pm. Open Apr.-Oct. daily 11:00am-1am; winter hours vary. Pub-style dinner, $10-17, served until 10pm.) Locals adore the **Lompoc Cafe & Brew Pub,** 36 Rodick St., off Cottage St., which features Bar Harbor Real Ale ($4), a free bocce court and live jazz, blues, Celtic, rock, and folk on Friday and Saturday nights. (☎288-9392. Th open mic. No cover. Open May-Oct. daily 11:30am-1am.)

ACADIA NATIONAL PARK ☎207

The jagged, rocky, oceanside perimeter of Acadia National Park's 41,000 acres is gradually obscured, then completely enveloped by thick pine forests further inland. Fern-shrouded streams and 120 mi. of hiking trails criss-cross the rugged, coastal terrain. Fearing the island would be overrun by cars, millionaire John D. Rockefeller, Jr. funded the creation of 57 mi. of carriage roads, now accessible to hikers, mountain bikers, and, in the winter, skiers. For information regarding which trails are groomed for skiing contact The Friends of Acadia (☎288-3340.) An ideal carriage road for biking is the **Eagle Lake Loop** (6½ mi.), which features gentle grades and a spectacular view of the lake. Touring the park by auto costs $10 for seven days, but is free by any other means of transportation. Seniors can purchase a $10 lifetime pass to the park, which entitles them to half-price camping at the park campgrounds. The *Biking and Hiking Guide to the Carriage Roads* ($6), available at the Visitors Center, and offers invaluable hiking directions. To spend the night in or near the park, see Mt. Desert Island's **Accommodations** (p. 90).

Precipice Trail (1½ mi.), one of the most popular and strenuous hikes, is closed June to late August to accommodate nesting peregrine falcons; be ready to use the iron ladders that are needed to complete the cliff and ledge trail. When the trail is closed, the birds may be viewed with telescopes provided by the park service daily 9am-noon in the trail parking lot. Other popular hikes on the eastern half of the island include **Mt. Champlaign/Bear Brook** (moderate, 2½ mi. round-trip) and the more strenuous **Beehive** (¾ mi. round-trip), both of which provide dramatic views of the Atlantic coastline. An easy ½ mi. amble along the **Bowl** trail from the summit of Mt. Champlaign rewards hikers with a view of Sand Beach and Otter Point. The top of Cadillac Mountain (1530 ft.) may be reached by hiking either the **Cadillac Mountain North** (4½ mi.) or **South Ridge** (7½ mi.), or by cruising up the paved **auto road.** Early birds can be among the first people in the US to see the sun rise from the summit. (Access road open from 1hr. before sunrise to midnight.)

About 4 mi. south of Bar Harbor on Rte. 3, **Park Loop Road** runs along the shore of the island, where great waves crash against steep granite cliffs, before eventually making a 27 mi. circuit of the eastern section of the island through tree shrouded pine forests. The sea comes into **Thunder Hole** with a bang about 2-3hr. before high tide when wave action is strong enough. Brave souls can test the chilly waters at **Echo Lake** along Rte. 102, or **Sand Beach** on the Park Loop along the eastern shore of the island. Also along Park Loop Rd. is **Jordan Pond House ❹,** a restaurant at the south edge of Jordan Pond where weary travelers can have afternoon tea (with 2 popovers; $7.25) on a lawn facing the pond. (☎276-3316. Lunch $10-18. Dinner $15-20. Open mid-May to late Oct. daily 11:30am-9pm; hours can vary.)

NEW HAMPSHIRE

There are two sides to New Hampshire: the rugged landscape and natural beauty of the White Mountains, and the tax-free outlets, tourist traps, and state liquor stores that line most of the highways. The first colony to declare its independence from Great Britain, New Hampshire has retained its backwoods libertarian charm along with its motto, "Live Free or Die!"

PRACTICAL INFORMATION

Capital: Concord.

Visitor Info: Office of Travel and Tourism, 172 Pembroke Rd. P.O. Box 1856, Concord 03302-1856 (☎603-271-2666 or 800-386-4664; www.visitnh.gov). **NH Parks and Recreation,** ☎271-3556; www.nhparks.state.nh.us. **Fish and Game Department,** 2 Hazen Dr., Concord 03301 (☎603-271-3421; www.wildlife.state.nh.us), furnishes info on regulations and licenses. **US Forest Service,** 719 North Main St., Laconia 03246 (☎603-528-8721; www.fs.fed.us/r9/white). Open M-F 8am-4:30pm.

Postal Abbreviation: NH. **Sales Tax:** 8% on meals and lodgings. **Area Code:** 603.

PORTSMOUTH ☎603

Although New Hampshire's seacoast is less than extensive, with only 13 mi fronting the Atlantic Ocean, the state makes the most of its toehold on the water. Portsmouth, once the colonial capital, is one of the nicest seaside towns in New England. As such, colonial history is an integral part of Portsmouth. Most buildings date to the 18th century. Although not large by any standards, Portsmouth is exceptionally cultured—and also exceptionally expensive. Being a port town, seafood reigns supreme, while a pint of local ale is the mainstay after dinner.

PRACTICAL INFORMATION. Just 57 mi. north of Boston, Portsmouth is situated at the junction of U.S. 1, 1A, and I-95. Leave the car in one of the inexpensive lots ($0.50-1 per hr.) downtown; the town is best navigated by foot. State St./U.S.1 and Congress St. are the two major roads that run northeast-southwest through town. The central intersecting road is Market St. which runs southeast-northwest. **Vermont Transit/Greyhound,** 22 Ladd St. (☎436-0163), inside Federal Tobacconists, heads to Boston (4 per day, 1¼hr., $15.50). **Seacoast Trolley** (☎431-6975) runs in summer every hr. 10am-5pm, with 14 stops around Portsmouth. (Fare $2.50 partial loop, $5 full loop with reboarding privileges.) **Taxi: Blue Star Taxi,** ☎436-2774. **Visitor Info: Greater Portsmouth Chamber of Commerce,** 500 Market St., outside downtown. (☎436-1118; www.portcity.org. Open M-W 8:30am-5pm, Th-F 8:30am-7pm, Sa-Su 10am-5pm.) The Chamber of Commerce runs an information kiosk in Market Sq. (Open May to mid-Oct. daily 10am-5pm.) **Medical Services: Portsmouth Regional,** 333 Borthwick Ave., a few miles from town. (☎436-5110 or 800-685-8282.) **Violence and Rape Hotline,** ☎800-336-3795. **Post Office:** 80 Daniel St. (☎431-2871. Open M-F 7:30am-5:30pm, Sa 8am-12:30pm.) **Postal Code:** 03801. **Area Code:** 603.

ACCOMMODATIONS & FOOD. Portsmouth is not exactly budget-friendly when it comes to hanging your hat; accommodation prices in town are steep. Try U.S. 1A south of Portsmouth for typically drab motels. Another alternative is **Camp Eaton ❷**, in York Harbor, ME, about 15 mi. north of Portsmouth off Rte. 1.

Although still expensive, the wooded sites are a relative bargain. The immaculate bathrooms and well-kept sites and grounds help to ease the pain. (☎207-363-3424. 2-person sites $37, low-season $23. Each additional person $6.)

Portsmouth offers a plethora of dining options, with many fine establishments of all varieties peppering Market St. Unfortunately, great deals may be in short supply. **The Friendly Toast ❷,** 121 Congress St., a block and a half from Market Sq., is a local landmark, cluttered with the most ghastly artifacts the 1950s could produce: mannequin limbs, pulp novels, formica furniture, and stroke-inducingly bad art. Menu items, such as the "mission burrito" ($7), are nearly impossible to finish. (☎430-2154. Entrees $6-8. Breakfast served all day. Open M-Th 7am-11pm, F 7am through Su 9pm.) **Cafe Brioche ❶,** 14 Market Sq., offers quick, easy, and tasty food. The daily soups ($2.50-3.50), such as curried sweet potato with wild rice, can spice up your day, and the spinach, feta, and olive quiche ($3.45) wakes up your taste buds. (☎430-9225. Open M-Th 6:30am-8pm, F-Su 6:30am-10pm.) At **Gilly's Lunchcart ❶,** 175 Fleet St., semi-inebriated folk trail out the door of a nearby pub and into the street for heavenly burgers and sandwiches into the wee hours of the night. During daylight hours, the Monday 11am-6pm "Dog Days" special offers $1 hotdogs. (Fries $1.75. Burger $2.25. Open M 11:30am-6pm, Tu-Su 11:30am-2:30am.)

SIGHTS & ENTERTAINMENT. Modern Portsmouth sells itself with its colonial past. The most prestigious example is **Strawbery Banke Museum,** on the corner of Marcy and Hancock St. The museum is a collection of buildings, each restored to display the region in various time periods. Museum employees frequent the various houses and shops in garb appropriate to their time period. To find the museum, follow the signs that lead toward the harbor and through a charming maze of shops. (☎433-1100; www.strawberybanke.org. Open May-Oct. M-Sa 10am-5pm, Su noon-5pm. $12, seniors $11, ages 7-17 $8; families $28. Tickets good for 2 consecutive days.) Right across the street, **Prescott Park** hugs the bank of the Piscataqua River. A great place to picnic, these small, well-tended gardens and lawns offer a pleasant respite with an amazing view. For something a little more challenging, try climbing aboard through the hatches of the **USS Albacore,** a research submarine built locally at the Portsmouth Navel Shipyard. (☎436-3680. Open May-Oct. daily 9:30am-5pm; winter hours vary. $5, over 62 or military with ID $3.50, ages 7-17 $2; families $10.) One of Portsmouth's oldest graveyards, North Cemetery, holds the burial sites of some of the city's most important skeletons including signers of the Declaration of Independence and the U.S. Constitution. **Gravestones by Dusk** offers a 1hr. historical tour of the cemetery. (☎436-5096. Open daily Apr.-Oct. $10 per person; $20 min. Times vary; call for reservations.) The **Music Hall,** 28 Chesnut St., a 125-year-old theater, shows main stream, independent, and foreign films during the summer. Be prepared for the occasional twist though—if you wear a toga to the *Animal House* showing, you get in for free. (☎436-2400. Box office open M-Sa noon-6pm or until 30min. after the show has started. $8; students, seniors, under 21, and military $6.)

NEW ENGLAND

NEW HAMPSHIRE SKI RESORTS ☎603

With abundant snow from November through April and a number of sizable mountains in the various ranges throughout the state, New Hampshire is a popular skiing destination for its long season. **Ski New Hampshire,** P.O. Box 10, Lincoln 03251, is a service that provides information and reservations for five resorts in the White Mountains. (☎745-9396 or 800-937-5493; www.skinh.com.) **Cranmore,** in North Conway (see p. 101), offers 39 trails and vacations complemented by great shopping. The Children's Summer Camps offer tennis, hiking, swimming, rock climbing, and gymnastics. (☎800-786-6754; www.cranmore.com. Lift operates M-F 9am-4pm, Sa-Su 8:30am-4pm. Lift tickets $35, ages 6-12 $19.) Located along U.S. 302 by North Conway, **Attitash** is expensive but has two mountains, 51 trails (evenly beginner, intermediate, and expert), and 25 acres of glades. Biking, horseback riding, waterslides, a climbing wall, trampolines, and an alpine slide keep summer visitors busy. (☎374-2368; www.attitash.com. Lift tickets $49, holidays $53; children $32. Slide open summer daily 10am-6pm. Single ride $12. Summer all-day value pack for all activities except golf and horseback riding $29, ages 2-7 $12.)

Just outside Pinkham Notch on Rte. 16, **Wildcat Mountain** offers 47 trails (25% beginner, 40% intermediate, 35% expert) and mountainscape views from its 4062 ft. peak. (☎888-754-9453; www.skiwildcat.com. Lift tickets M-F $42, Sa-Su $52; seniors and ages 13-17 $36/42; ages 6-12 $25/25. Gondola rides daily from late May-Oct. $9.50, ages 6-12 $4.50.) Three miles east of Lincoln on Rte. 112, **Loon Mountain** provides 43 trails. For warm-weather substitutes, biking and horseback riding are popular diversions. (☎745-8111; www.loonmtn.com. Lift tickets M-F $40, Sa-Su $47; ages 13-19 $33/41; under 13 $25/29.) Just off I-93 in Franconia Notch State Park, **Cannon Mountain** has 42 trails (15% beginner, 50% intermediate, 35% expert) at slightly lower prices than other local resorts and offers a two person pass for $40 on Tuesdays and Thursdays. Summer hiking, biking, canoeing, and swimming keep athletes in shape, while the Aerial Tramway (see p. 100) schleps those with a little less energy up the mountain. (☎823-8800; www.cannonmt.com. Lift tickets M-F $34, Sa-Su $45; ages 13-17 $23/37; seniors and under 13 $23/29.)

WHITE MOUNTAINS ☎603

NEW ENGLAND

Consisting of 780,000 acres of mountainous national forest maintained by the US Forest Service, the White Mountains provide an immense playground for outdoor enthusiasts. While many associate the mountains with skiing, hiking, and camping, warm-weather alternatives like canoeing, kayaking, and fishing make the White Mountains an attractive destination throughout the year. The White Mountain National Forest also holds dozens of geological wonders and preserves a refuge for some awe-inspiring and dangerous animals, like the moose and black bear.

ORIENTATION & PRACTICAL INFORMATION. The White Mountains can be daunting to an unfamiliar traveler, but with a good map and guide it is easily navigated. The immense forest, spanning both New Hampshire and Maine, is bordered by a dozen or so distinctive towns and contains several commercial ski resorts. Many of the region's highlights can be found within three areas: **Pinkham Notch** (see p. 98), in the northeast of the forest near Mt. Washington; **Franconia Notch Area** (see p. 99), northwest of the National Forest; and **North Conway** (see p. 101), a buzzing gateway town to the southeast.

Any unattended vehicle parked on White Mountain National Forest land must display a **parking pass,** sold by the US Forest Service and the AMC as well as the White Mountain Attraction Center; vehicles parked at national forest campground sites are an exception. (☎528-8721. $5 per week, $20 per year.) The **US Forest Service** operates four **ranger stations,** each providing free information on recreational opportunities, camping, safety precautions in the White Mountains, and any other questions you might have about the forest. **Pemigewasset/Ammonoosuc,** on Rte. 175 in Plymouth near Exit 25 of I-93, covers the southwest region of the forest. (☎536-

1315. Open M-F 8am-4:30pm.) **Androscoggin,** 2.5 mi. south of Gorham on Rte. 16, oversees the northern half. (☎466-2713. Open summer daily 8am-5pm; winter M-Sa 8am-4:30pm.) **Evans Notch,** 18 Mayville Rd., in Bethel, ME, covers the Maine section of the national forest. (☎207-824-2134. Open summer daily 8am-4:30pm; winter Tu-Sa 8am-4:30pm.) **Saco,** 100 yards west of the junction with Rte. 16 on Hwy. 112 (Kancamagus Hwy.), oversees the southeast section of the forest. (☎447-5448. Open daily 8am-4:30pm.)

The **White Mountain Attraction Center,** P.O. Box 10, N. Woodstock 03262, at Exit 32 from I-93, has info on recreation in the mountains. (☎745-8720. Open daily July-Sept. 8:30am-6pm; Apr.-July and Sept. to mid-Oct. 8:30am-5:30pm; mid-Oct. to Apr. 8:30am-5pm.) The **Appalachian Mountain Club (AMC)** is a nonprofit conservation and recreation organization that maintains 1400 mi. of trails in the Northeast as well as partnering with other organizations to upgrade and develop additional trails. They offer outdoors skills workshops, run programs to protect the environment, and provide lodging at backcountry huts, shelters, camps, and roadside lodges. The AMC's **Pinkham Notch Visitors Center,** 10 mi. north of Jackson on Rte. 16, is the area's best source of info on weather and trail conditions. They handle lodging reservations and have comprehensive information on White Mountain trails, safety, and eco-friendly "Leave No Trace" backpacking. (AMC headquarters: ☎617-523-0636; www.outdoors.org. Visitors Center: ☎466-2727. Open daily 6:30am-10pm.)

TRANSPORTATION. No matter which way you approach the White Mountains the scenery you pass on your way to your destination will be breathtaking. **Concord Trailways** (☎228-3300 or 800-639-3317), runs from Boston to Concord (30 Stickney Ave. 2 per day, $12.50), Conway (First Stop Market, W. Main St. 2 per day, $27), and Franconia (Kelly's Foodtown, Exit 38 off I-93. 1 per day, $28). For hikers, the **AMC** runs a **shuttle** between locations on the Appalachian Trail in the White Mountains. Consult AMC's *The Guide* for a complete map of routes and times or pick up a schedule at the AMC Pinkham Notch Visitor's Center. (☎466-2727. Service operates June to mid-Oct. daily 8am-4pm. Reservations highly recommended for all stops; required for some. $9.)

ACCOMMODATIONS. Other than ski resorts, most accommodations within the National Forest are controlled by the AMC. Just outside the borders of the forest, usually within an hour's drive from many of the hikes and attractions, plentiful accommodations range from hostels and motels to high-end resorts. For a guide and price range of the motels and hotels near the White Mountains, pick up the small, yellow *White Mountains Travel Guide*, available at any **info booth.**

The **AMC** operates seven full-service **huts** and one self-service hut, all of which lie on or close to the Appalachian Trail and are only accessible via trail. A free *AMC Huts and Lodges* brochure, available at the Pinkham Notch Visitors Center or from the AMC main line, has descriptions and locations. At the huts, all bunks are in co-ed bunkrooms. The huts are austere with no showers, electric lights, or electrical outlets at any of the huts. The **full-service ❸** huts provide bunk, mattress, pillow, and three wool blankets, as well as breakfast and dinner daily. There are toilets, washrooms separated by gender, and cold running water. Bring sleeping gear and a flashlight. At the **self-service ❶** huts, guests must provide their own food, but have use of a kitchen stocked with cookware. Blankets are not provided—bring a warm sleeping bag. (☎466-2727; www.outdoors.org. No pets. No smoking. Open June to mid-Sept. 3 huts open in winter, all become self-service during that time. Full service huts: AMC members $68, under 15 $44; nonmembers $69/46. Self-service huts: members $20, nonmembers $21.)

For car-accessible lodging, the AMC currently runs the **Joe Dodge Lodge** (see p. 98). In addition, the **Highland Center at Crawford Notch ❸,** off Rt. 302, is open year-round with 120 beds in both dorms and family rooms. The Highland Center also serves as an outdoor program center. (☎466-2727. $59 with breakfast and dinner, $43 without; double occupancy private rooms with breakfast and dinner $87 per person.) Another lodging option is the **White Mountains Hostel** (see p. 101).

CAMPING. The US Forest Service maintains 23 designated **National Forest campgrounds ❶,** all of which are accessible by car. Four remain open in winter, although only one has plowed access. All campgrounds keep sites available on a first come, first served basis, but some fill these slots quickly. On weekends, get to the campsite around check-out time (usually 10-11am) to snag a site. Bathrooms and firewood are usually available at campsites. (Reservations: ☎877-444-6777; www.reserveusa.com. Reservations accepted beginning Jan. 1 and must be made at least 1 week in advance. Sites $12-18; reservation charge $9, fee to change or cancel reservation $10. Cars parked at campsite do not require a parking pass.)

Camping is less expensive or free of charge at the many **backcountry campsites,** which are only accessible via hiking trails. Regulations prohibit camping and fires above the tree line (approximately 4000 ft.), within 200 ft. of a trail, certain bodies of water and a few specific roads, or within ¼ mi. of huts, shelters, tent platforms, lakes, streams, or roads. Rules are even more strict in the Great Gulf Wilderness—no wood or charcoal fires at all. There are also special regulations for a variety of other specific areas. Consult the US Forest Service's *Backcountry Camping Rules 2003-2004* for the complete run-down.

Finally, a plethora of private campgrounds, the majority of which cater to RVs and families, virtually surround the borders of the forest. A copy of *New Hampshire's Guide to Camping*, available from any highway rest stop or info booth in the state, provides a map, prices, and phone numbers of campgrounds.

No matter where you camp, **bears** are a threat. Stop by a ranger station or the AMC Visitors Center to pick up information on minimizing the risk of danger. Keep food hung and well away from sleeping areas. Do not keep anything with the scent of food on it in or near your tent (clothes worn while eating, for example). But animals are not only a danger when camping; **moose** can be problematic to drivers, so keep a watchful eye.

OUTDOOR ACTIVITIES. If you intend to spend a lot of time in the area and are planning to do a significant amount of **hiking,** the *AMC White Mountain Guide* ($22; available in the AMC Visitor's Center and most bookstores) is invaluable. The guide includes full maps and descriptions of all the mountain trails. Because weather in the mountains is highly unpredictable, hikers should bring three layers of clothing in all seasons: one for wind, one for rain, and at least one for warmth—preferably wool or a synthetic material like polypropylene or fleece, but not cotton. Carry insect repellent; black flies and swarms of mosquitoes can ruin a trip, particularly in June. Because dehydration can be a serious problem, always bring enough water. A high-calorie snack, like trail mix, is also a good idea.

After hiking, **cycling** is the next most popular way to tour the White Mountains. For help with planning, ask a ranger or consult *30 Bicycle Tours in New Hampshire* ($13; at local bookstores and outdoor equipment stores). **Great Glen Trails Outdoor Center,** across Rt. 16 from the Mt. Washington Auto Rd., rents bikes for use only on their trails. (☎466-2333. Open daily 8:30am-5pm. Trail fee (included in rental) $7. Bikes $15 for 2hr., half-day $20, full-day $30; under 18 $12/15/20.)

To see the National Forest with very little exertion, drive the **Kancamagus Scenic Highway (Route 12),** which connects the towns of Lincoln and Conway. The 35 mi. drive requires at least an hour, though the vistas typically lure drivers to the side of the road or to one of the many scenic outlooks for a picnic. Check gas at Lincoln, as no gas is available for 35 mi., then head east on the clearly marked Kanc to enjoy the scenic splendor stretching all the way to Conway.

PINKHAM NOTCH ☎603

Pinkham Notch, New Hampshire's easternmost notch, lies in the shadow of the tallest mountain in the Northeast—the 6288 ft. Mt. Washington. Pinkham's proximity to the peak makes it more crowded and less peaceful than some neighboring areas, but secluded areas can still be found not too far off the beaten path. The **AMC's Pinkham Notch Visitors Center** lies between Gorham and Jackson on Rte. 16.

Stretching from just behind the Pinkham Notch Visitors Center all the way up to the summit of Mt. Washington, **Tuckerman's Ravine Trail,** despite the deceiving 4¼ mi. distance, demands 4-5hr. of steep hiking each way. *Authorities urge caution when climbing—Mt. Washington claims at least one life every year.* Mt. Washington is one of the most dangerous small mountains in the world because of the highly unpredictable weather, including high wind speeds that reach hurricane force surprisingly frequently. It has never been recorded to be warmer than 72°F atop Mt. Washington, and the average temperature on the peak is a bone-chilling 26.9°F. The summit of Mt. Washington boasts the highest wind speed ever recorded at 231 mph. With proper measures, however, the trek up is stellar. Clouds cover often obscures the view from the top, but the vistas on the way up make up for it. Those lucky enough to hike on a clear day are rewarded with a view of five states and Canada. A less daunting option with more stable treadway for the steepest part of the ascent is the **Lion's Head Trail,** which diverges from the Tuckerman's Ravine Trail about 2 mi. into the hike. This trail is also the best winter ascent for those intrepid enough to make the hike in the snowy months.

Motorists can take the **Mt. Washington Auto Road,** a paved and dirt road that winds 8 mi. to the summit. Owners of vehicles that are sturdy enough to reach the top receive bragging rights in the form of a free "This Car Climbed Mt. Washington" bumper sticker; delay affixing it until your car has proven that its engine and brakes can handle the way down — tempting fate is never a good idea. The road begins 3 mi. north of the Visitors Center on Rte. 16. (☎466-3988. Road open daily June-Aug. 7:30am-6pm; May-June and Sept.-Oct. 8am-5pm. $18 per car and driver, free audio tour included; $7 each additional passenger, ages 5-12 $4.) If you are worried that your car might not make it or just want to enjoy the view, guided tours in vans are available through **Great Glen Stage Tours**, across Rte. 16 from the Auto Road. (☎466-2333. Open daily 8:30am-5pm. $24, seniors $22, ages 5-11 $11.)

Many of the region's lodging options are on or near Mt. Washington. Accessible by car, the **Joe Dodge Lodge ❸,** immediately behind the Pinkham Notch Visitors Center, offers over 100 comfortable bunks, including seven family rooms, as well as a small library and a larger living room. (☎466-2727. Breakfast and dinner included. In summer $55, under 16 $37; AMC members $52/34. Low-season $52/34; AMC members $49/33. 2-person private rooms $74/70, for 4 or more $97/89. Without meals members $35, nonmembers $37, children $23/25. Reservations recommended.) Situated about 2hr. up the Tuckerman Ravine Trail, **Hermit Lake Shelter ❶** has bathrooms but no showers, and sleeps up to 90 people on a first come, first served basis. Nightly passes sold at the Visitor's Center ($10). **Lakes of the Clouds** hut, just 1½ mi. from Mt. Washington's summit, is one of AMC's most popular huts.

FRANCONIA NOTCH AREA ☎603

Located in the northwestern expanse of the forest, Franconia Notch is not actually part of the White Mountain National Forest but rather a state park. Imposing granite cliffs, formed by glacial movements that began during an ice age 400 million years ago, tower on either side of the Franconia Notch Parkway (I-93) and create one of the more scenic spots in the White Mountains. Although one of the biggest attractions in the area, the famous rocky profile known as the "Old Man of the Mountain," collapsed in 2003, Franconia is still home to waterfalls, endless woodlands, and impressive natural rock formations that make it well worth a visit.

PRACTICAL INFORMATION. Most of the area highlights are directly accessible from I-93. The **Franconia Notch Chamber of Commerce,** on Main St. in Franconia, has maps of the region, brochures on nearby campgrounds, and a variety of other information about the area. (☎800-237-9007; www.franconianotch.org. Open mid-May to mid-Oct. Tu-Su 10am-5pm.) A note for those using old maps: the highway exit numbering system has recently changed. Old Exit 1 on the FN Parkway corresponds to new 34A, Exit 2 to 34B, and Exit 3 to 34C.

CAMPING & FOOD. The beauty of Franconia Notch makes it an ideal place for camping, but make sure to bring insect repellent if you plan to stay in the great outdoors. Nestled in the middle of Franconia Notch State Park, the always popular **Lafayette Place Campground ❶,** off I-93 S between Exits 34A and 34B, is an ideal place to pitch your tent. The scenic Pemi Trail winds away from the campground; follow it toward the Flume and the Basin to the South and toward Profile Lake and Cannon Mt. to the North. (☎823-9513; www.nhparks.state.nh.us. Reservations strongly recommended, $3. Must be made 3 days in advance at ☎271-3628. Open mid-May to mid-Oct. 2-person sites $16; $8 per additional adult, under 18 no extra charge.) Another excellent choice is the **Fransted Family Campground ❶,** 3 mi. north of the Notch on Rte. 18. Among the amenities are movie nights, a small beach, free volleyball, and 9-hole putt-putt golf. Facilities include showers, bathroom, and coin-operated laundry. (☎823-5675. Open May-Oct. Tent sites $20-26; with electricity and water $22-28; full hookup $29.) **Woodstock Inn & Station ❺,** on Rte. 3, offers a very comfortable—though expensive—alternative to camping. Jacuzzi and health club privileges included. (☎745-3951. Breakfast included. Rooms from $102; call for low-season rates.) Somewhat less expensive cabins and motels cluster along Rte. 3 between Lincoln and North Woodstock.

Polly's Pancake Parlor ❷, on Rte. 117 in Sugar Hill, just 2 mi. from Exit 38 off I-93, is a homey restaurant boasting a dining room overlooking Mt. Washington. The parlor serves up a stack of six superb pancakes for $6 or unlimited pancakes for $11. The hotcakes come topped with maple syrup or maple spread from the restaurant's own product line. (☎823-5575. Open mid-May to mid-Oct. daily 7am-3pm; Apr. and Nov. Sa-Su call for hours.) Even if the Inn's prices are too steep, the endless menu at the **Woodstock Inn Brewery ❸,** housed in the Inn & Station, is sure to please, with everything from not-so-standard sandwiches and salads ($6-8) to pasta ($10-14) and seafood from $12. (☎745-3951. Open daily 11:30am-10pm.)

SIGHTS. Traveling north from Lincoln on I-93, **The Flume,** Exit 34A on I-93, is a 2 mi. walk cutting through a spectacular granite gorge. Although only 12-20 ft. apart, the moss-covered canyon walls are 70-90 ft. high. Take a leisurely stroll over centuries-old covered bridges and past the 345 ft. Avalanche Falls. Tickets can be purchased from the **The Flume Visitors Center.** While at the center take in the excellent 15min. film acquainting visitors with the landscape and geological history of

IN RECENT NEWS

THE OLD MAN RESTS IN PEACE

The Old Man of the Mountain, a rock formation resembling a human face, had been a longstanding symbol of New Hampshire, prominently displayed on state license plates, quarters, and signs, and a popular attraction in the White Mountains. However, on the evening of May 2, 2003, the Old Man crumbled from his perch 1200 ft. above Profile Lake. His fall is believed to have been caused by the region's harsh weather conditions, including high winds, fog, heavy rains, and below freezing temperatures, which likely caused cracks to form in the surrounding rocks. The face of Cannon Mountain where the Old Man had rested for the last 10,000 years is now a sheer cliff.

Since his demise many have wondered how best to allow the legend to survive. In order to examine solutions to this dilemma Governor Craig Benson established an "Old Man Task Force" to examine possibilities for an 'enduring tribute' to the Old Man. The task force will not only create their own suggestions, but also consider suggestions submitted to oldman@nh.gov. As of now, the possibilities range from creating a new 'Old Man' out of rock, rubber and plastic to building a simple memorial. The task force will present its findings in late 2003; until then you'll catch locals making wistful looks at the Old Man's old home.

the area. (☎745-8391; www.flumegorge.com. Open daily May-June and Sept.-Oct. 9am-5pm; July-Aug. 9am-5:30pm. $8, ages 6-12 $5.) A 9 mi. paved **bike path** begins at the Visitors Center and parallels I-93 north through the park. To rent some wheels, check out **Cannon Mountain Bike Shop,** conveniently located at Exit 34B past the Tramway. (☎823-8800, ext. 710. Open mid-June to Sept. daily 9am-5pm; late May to mid-June Sa-Su 9am-5pm. $10 per hr., $20 half-day, $29 full day.) Between Exits 34A and 34B on I-93, visitors can find a well-marked turn-off for **The Basin.** Here a 5-10min. walk will take you to a 20 ft. whirlpool that has been carved out of a massive base of granite by a 15 ft. waterfall. (Wheelchair-accessible.)

For years Franconia has been well known as the home of the **Old Man of the Mountain,** but, in May, 2003, the profile fell from its perch. The viewing areas at Exit 34B on I-93 and between Exit 34A and 34B on I-93 are still open and provide a diagrammatic explanation of the Old Man's fall. A pleasant 10min. walk down the designated path from the parking lot at Exit 34B brings viewers to the banks of **Profile Lake,** which affords the best available view of the cliff where the Old Man used to rest. Also at Exit 34B, a small display of Old Man memorabilia and the history regarding his discovery and rising popularity can be found at the **Old Man of the Mountain Museum.** (☎823-7722, ext. 717. Open mid-May to mid-Oct. daily 9:30am-5pm. Free.) The 80-passenger **Cannon Mountain Aerial Tramway,** Exit 34B, climbs over 2000 ft. in 7min. and carries visitors to the summit of the Cannon Cliff, a 1000 ft. sheer drop into the cleft between Mt. Lafayette and Cannon Mountain. The tram offers unparalleled vistas of Franconia Notch along its ascent. Once at the top, a short walk will bring you to an **observation tower** (elevation over 4200 ft.) overlooking the Notch. (☎823-8800. Open mid-May to mid-Oct. and mid-Dec. to mid-Apr. daily 9am-5pm. Trains run every 15min. Round-trip $10, ages 6-12 $6. One-way $8.) In winter, the tram takes skiers up the mountain, which has 58 trails. (Ski pass M-F $34, Sa-Su $45.) Right next to the tramway station sits the one-room **New England Ski Museum,** with numerous old photographs and a display of skis through the ages. (☎823-7177. Open mid-May to mid-Oct. and mid-Dec. to mid-Apr. daily noon-5pm. Free.) On summer days, the lifeguard-protected beach at **Echo Lake,** just off Exit 34C on I-93, offers cool but sometimes crowded waters. The lake is accessible until 10pm. (☎823-8800, ext. 784. Lifeguard on duty mid-June to early Sept. daily 10am-5pm. $3, under 12 free. Free to all when lifeguard isn't on duty. Canoe or paddleboat rental ☎823-8800, ext. 783. $10 per hr. Last rental 4pm.)

HIKING. Myriad trails lead up into the mountains on both sides of Franconia Notch, providing excellent day hikes and views. The **Hiking Information Center** adjacent to Lafayette Place Campground is the best source in the area for hiking suggestions and safety tips. (Open daily 8am-4pm.) *In this area be prepared for severe weather, especially above 4000 ft.* The **Lonesome Lake Trail** (2 mi.), a relatively easy hike, winds from Lafayette Place Campground to **Lonesome Lake,** where the AMC operates its westernmost hut. The **Greenleaf Trail** (2½ mi.), which starts at the Aerial Tramway parking lot, and the **Old Bridle Path** (3 mi.), beginning from Lafayette Place and known for its stellar views, are more ambitious. Both lead up to the AMC's Greenleaf Hut, near the summit of Mt. Lafayette and overlooking Echo Lake. From Greenleaf, a 7½ mi. trek east along the **Old Bridle Path** and **Garfield Ridge** leads to the AMC's most remote hut, the **Galehead.** Beware that the Mt. Garfield summit is above the timberline, where storms may intensify quickly. Accessed from Lafayette Place, the **Falling Waters Trail,** with three waterfalls within 1½ mi. of the trailhead, is also a popular hike in the Notch. This area can occupy trekkers for days; make sure to get adequate supplies before starting out.

NEAR FRANCONIA: LOST RIVER GORGE

Outside of Franconia Notch State Park, Lost River Gorge, located 6 mi. west of North Woodstock on Rte. 112, is a glacial gorge with numerous caves, boulders, rock formations, and a winding stream. The reservation also maintains a nature garden and a forestry center with information about the area. The walk through the gorge is less than 1 mi., but can easily take over an hour; each creatively named cavern (such as the Lemon Squeeze) is open for exploration to those agile enough to wrench through. (☎745-8031; www.findlostriver.com. Open July-Aug. daily 9am-6pm; mid-May to June and Sept. to mid-Oct. 9am-5pm. Last ticket sold 1hr. before closing. Solid walking shoes recommended. $9.50, children 6-12 $6.50.)

NORTH CONWAY AND CONWAY ☎603

With its proximity to ski resorts in winter, foliage in the fall, and hiking and shopping year-round, the town of North Conway is one of New Hampshire's most popular vacation destinations. Rte. 16, the traffic-infested main road, houses outlet stores as well as a variety of smaller local shops. The town of Conway, 5 mi. south, has fewer touristy shops but several excellent meal and lodging options.

Numerous stores in the North Conway area rent outdoor equipment for the slopes, the water, and the roads. For ski goods in winter or biking gear during other seasons, **Joe Jones,** 2709 White Mtn. Hwy. at Mechanic St. in North Conway, has it all. (☎356-9411. Open July-Aug. daily 9am-8pm; Sept.-Nov. and Apr.-June Su-Th 10am-6pm, F-Sa 9am-6pm; Dec.-Mar. M-F 8:30am-6pm, Sa-Su 8:30am-8pm. Alpine skis, boots, and poles $20 for 1 day, $36 for 2 days; cross-country equipment $15/26; snowboards $20/38. Bikes $15 for 4hr., $25 for 8hr.) A second branch, **Joe Jones North,** lies a few miles north of town on Rte. 302. (☎356-6848.) **Eastern Mountain Sports (EMS),** just north on White Mtn. Hwy. in the lobby of the Eastern Slope Inn, sells camping equipment, and rents tents (2-person $15 for 1 day, $20 for 3 days; 4-person $20/25), sleeping bags ($15/20), snowshoes, packs, and skis. The knowledgeable staff happily provides free first-hand info on climbing and hiking, and offers a summer climbing school. (☎356-5433. Open June-Sept. M-Sa 8:30am-9pm, Su 8:30am-6pm; Oct.-May Su-Th 8:30am-6pm, F-Sa 8:30am-9pm.)

Located in the heart of Conway and maintained by incredibly friendly folk, the **White Mountains Hostel (HI-AYH) ❶,** 36 Washington St., off Rte. 16 at the intersection of Rte. 153, is kept meticulously clean and environmentally friendly. The hostel has 43 comfy bunks, a kitchen, and common room. Each bed comes with clean linen and a pillow. (☎447-1001. Light breakfast included. Laundry $3. Reception

7:30-10am and 5-10pm. Check-out 10am. Reservations recommended during the summer and peak foliage season. Bunks $22, nonmembers $25; private rooms $48.) The hostel at the beautiful **Cranmore Mt. Lodge ❶**, 859 Kearsarge Rd., in North Conway, has 22 bunks. The lodge is about 2 mi. from downtown, but the living room, pool, jacuzzi, cable TV, refrigerator, and duck pond that are at the disposal of guests justify the trip. A delicious full breakfast, included with each overnight stay, makes up for the tight bunkrooms and thin mattresses. Be sure to bring a warm blanket to ward off the nightly temperature drop. (☎356-2044 or 800-356-3596. Linen and towel $3. Check-in 3-11pm. Check-out 11am. Dorms $20.)

For sports fans who will appreciate the autographed bats and other sports paraphernalia, **Delaney's ❷**, to the North of town along Rt. 16, is the place to stop. (☎356-7776. Sandwich and fries $7-11. Open daily 11:30am-11pm.) Adjacent to Olympia Sports in the center of North Conway, **Morning Dew ❶**, caffeinates the local populace. This hole-in-the-wall coffee shack offers bagels ($1), juice ($1.50), and the daily paper in addition to a variety of coffees ($1-2.50), teas, and steamers. (☎356-9366. Open daily 7am-5pm.) A bagful of penny candy from **Zeb's General Store ❶** can help you keep up your energy while exploring the shop, which sells everything New England has to offer, from pure maple syrup to wooden signs and moose memorabilia. Thirsty tourists might wish to partake of the many varieties of their $1 homemade soda. (☎356-9294. Open daily mid-June to Dec. 9am-10pm; Jan.-May hours vary.) Several miles south in Conway, pink, green, and purple paint decorate the walls and ceilings of **Cafe Noche ❷**, 147 Main St., while colorful paper cut outs flutter through the air. From the multitude of authentic Mexican options, including many vegetarian options, local patrons recommend the Montezuma Pie (Mexican lasagna; $8.50) or the garden burger ($4.25). (☎447-5050. Open daily 11:30am-9pm.)

HANOVER ☎603

Home to the beautiful campus of Dartmouth College, the quiet little town of Hanover comes alive as students flood the streets and the many trails, paths, and waterways that make the area ideal for outdoor enthusiasts. The area is also peppered with colleges that boast outstanding cultural and historical attractions.

ORIENTATION & PRACTICAL INFORMATION. Located along the Connecticut River near the border with Vermont, and along Rte. 10 and 120, Hanover is easily accessible from both I-91 and I-89. Also in the area are **Lebanon** (5 mi. south on Rte. 120), **White River Junction** (4 mi. south on Rte. 10, encompassing the confluence of the White and Connecticut Rivers), and **Norwich** (1½ mi. northwest in Vermont). **Vermont Transit** (☎800-552-8737) runs buses from Hanover (in front of the Hanover Inn at 35 S. Main St.; buy tickets on the bus or from Garber Travel ☎643-2700) to Boston (4-5 per day, 3-4hr., $25) and Burlington (4-5 per day, 2½hr., $21-27). **Amtrak** (☎295-7160 for station information; ☎800-872-7245 for schedules and reservations), on Railroad Row off N. Main St. in White River Junction, rolls to New York (1 per day, 7hr., $61-67) and Burlington (1 per day, 2hr., $19-27). **Bike Rental: Dartmouth Outdoors Rentals,** in the basement of Robinson Hall by the town green on N. Main St. (☎646-1747; www.dartmouth.edu/~outrntls. Open M-F noon-6pm. Bikes $15 per day, $40 per week.) **The Hanover Chamber of Commerce,** 53. S. Main St., is ready and willing to answer any questions about the area. (☎643-3115; www.hanoverchamber.org. Open M-F 9am-4pm.) **Internet Access: Howe Library,** 13 E. South St. (☎643-0720. Open M-Th 10am-8pm, F noon-6pm, Sa 10am-5pm; Sept.-May Su 1-5pm as well.) **Post Office:** 50 S. Main St. (☎643-4544. Open M-F 8am-5:30pm, Sa 8am-noon.) **Postal Code:** 03755. **Area Code:** 603.

ACCOMMODATIONS & FOOD. Quality camping with wooded sites, free access to a pool, two beaches on a lake, tennis courts, and hiking is available at **Storr's Pond ❶,** two mi. north of Hanover off Rte. 10. (☎643-2134. Open May 15-Oct. 15. Reservations recommended. Sites for 1-4 people $20, each additional person $2; with electricity and water $25/3.) For those looking for a roof over their heads, **Sunset Motor Inn ❸** more than delivers. Just 2 mi. south of Hanover on Rte. 10, this small motel offers river views and some of the most reasonably priced accommodations in the area. (☎298-8721. A/C. $53-83 depending upon season and room type. Reservations recommended.)

For a hearty meal, try **Lou's ❶,** 30 S. Main St., where old photos of politicians and celebrities adorn the walls. Highly recommended are the $1 crullers—choose from glazed, cinnamon sugar, chocolate frosted, or jelly-filled. (☎643-3321. Most meals $5-7. Open M-F 6am-3pm, Sa-Su 7am-3pm.) Late-night munchies, travelers should head to **Everything But Anchovies ❷,** 5 Allen St., which serves "Ivy League Sandwiches and Subs" ($5-7), and pizzas ($13 for 14 in.). (☎643-6135. Open daily 7am-2am.)

SIGHTS. Virtually synonymous with Hanover is **Dartmouth,** the rural jewel in the Ivy League crown. (☎646-1110; www.dartmouth.edu.) The college offers **tours** starting from the **Admissions Office** in McNutt Hall on N. Main St. (☎646-2875. Open M-F 8am-4pm. Tours are free, times vary.) The **Hood Museum of Art,** on Wheelock St., houses collections that include African, Native American, and ancient Asian art, as well as a contemporary collection. (☎646-2808; www.hoodmuseum.dartmouth.edu. Open Tu and Th-Sa 10am-5pm, W 10am-9pm, Su noon-5pm. Free.)

With the Appalachian Trail passing through town, Hanover is an ideal base of operations for hiking. The **Dartmouth Outdoors Club,** in Robinson Hall on N. Main St., maintains hundreds of miles of trails, sells the *Dartmouth Outing Guide* ($15), and is a good source of information about area hiking. (☎646-2428. Open M-F 8am-4pm. More detailed maps $1-3.) (☎646-2429. Open Su-Th 2-6pm. Free.)

VERMONT

In 1609 Samuel de Champlain dubbed the area "green mountain" in his native French, and the name Vermont stuck. Today, the Green Mountain range defines Vermont, spanning the length of the state from north to south. Over the past few decades, ex-urbanite yuppies have invaded, creating tension between the original, pristine Vermont and the packaged Vermont of trendy businesses and outlet shops. Tourism is an issue of contention: with the extensive development of ski resorts in the state, visitors now descend upon the state in floods. But as holiday weekends end and the summer arrives, the foreign tide ebbs and the small towns dotting the sparsely populated mountains create a friendly, rural atmosphere.

PRACTICAL INFORMATION

Capital: Montpelier.

Visitor Info: Vermont Information Center, 134 State St., Montpelier 05602 (☎802-828-3237; www.vermontvacation.com). Open daily 7:45am-8pm. **Department of Forests, Parks, and Recreation,** 103 S. Main St., Waterbury 05671 (☎802-241-3670). Open M-F 7:45am-4:30pm. **Vermont Snowline** (☎802-229-0531; www.skivermont.com) gives snow conditions Nov.-May. 24hr.

Postal Abbreviation: VT. **Sales Tax:** 5%, meals and lodgings 9%. **Area Code:** 802.

VERMONT SKI RESORTS ☎802

Every winter, skiers pour into Vermont and onto the Northeast's finest slopes; in the summer and fall, these same inclines melt into the stomping grounds of hikers and cyclists. Towns surrounding each of the mountains make their livelihood on this annual avalanche, offering a range of tourist options. For information, contact **Ski Vermont,** 26 State St., P.O. Box 368, Montpelier 05601. (☎223-2439; www.skivermont.com. Open M-F 7:45am-4:45pm.) The Vermont Information Center (see **Practical Information,** above) provides helpful info. Cheaper lift tickets can be found during low-season—before mid-December and after mid-March.

Just north of Stowe on Rte. 108 W lies **Smuggler's Notch,** with three mountains, 72 trails, and the only triple-black-diamond run in the East. A hot spot in winter, the resort offers great package deals. In warm weather, tennis, golf, children's programs, hiking options, and convenient bookings for canoeing, kayaking, and fishing attract visitors. (☎644-8851 or 800-451-8752. Lift tickets $54, ages 7-18 $38, over 70 free. In winter, 5-day lodging and lift packages start at $125 per day, under 17 $109 per day.) Just down the road, the **Stowe Mountain Resort** offers one-day lift tickets for $60. Stowe offers 48 trails (16% beginner, 59% intermediate, 25% expert), and impressive summer facilities: a golf course and country club, alpine slides (single ride $11, ages 6-12 $8), a gondola ($12, seniors $10.50, ages 6-12 $7), a scenic toll road ($16 per car up to 6 passengers, each additional passenger $4) and a skate park (sk8r bois not included). (☎253-3000 or 800-253-4754. Attraction package with 5 alpine slide rides, 1 gondola ride, and use of the skate park $37, seniors and ages 6-12 $32.) West of Brattleboro on Rte. 100, in the town of West Dover, **Mount Snow** boasts 134 trails (25% beginner, 53% intermediate, 22% expert), 26 lifts, excellent snowmaking capabilities, and the first snowboard park in the Northeast. In the summer, mountain bikers take advantage of 45 mi. of trails. (☎800-245-7669. Open mid-Nov. to late Apr. M-F 9am-4pm, Sa-Su 8am-4pm; May-early Nov. daily 9am-4pm. Lift tickets M-F $49, Sa-Su $55; ages 13-19 $44/46; seniors and under 13 $31/33. $30 per day in summer.)

At the junction of U.S. 4 and Rte. 100 N, **Killington's** seven mountains and 205 trails cover the most terrain and entertain the East's longest ski and snowboarding season (mid-Oct. to early June). The summer also keeps a fair pace in Killington with hiking, biking, and fishing among other diversions (see below). (☎800-621-6867. Lift tickets M-F $59, Sa-Su $62; ages 13-18 $54; ages 6-12 $36.) For some of the most reasonable lift ticket prices in Vermont, head to **Burke,** off I-91 in northeastern Vermont. Burke features 40 trails (30% beginner, 40% intermediate, 30% expert). They operate a campsite in summer, when visitors can fish, hike, and bike 200 mi. of trails. (☎626-3322 for skiing information, ☎626-1390 for camping information. Lift tickets M-F $29, Sa-Su and holiday periods $45, ages 13-17 $24/35, under 13 $19/31. Tent sites $12; lean-tos $16.) Near the US-Canadian border in Vermont's Northeast Kingdom, **Jay Peak,** in Jay on Rte. 242, catches more snowfall than anywhere else in New England. With some of the East's best wood-skiing, Jay Peak is an appealing option for thrill-seekers (76 trails; 40% expert). (☎988-2611 or 800-451-4449. Lift tickets $54, half day $40; ages 7-17 $40/30.)

Other resorts include **Stratton** (☎297-2200 or 800-787-2886; 90 trails, 16 lifts), on Rte. 30 N in Bondville, and **Sugarbush** (☎583-6100 or 800-537-8427; www.sugarbush.com; 2 mountains, 115 trails, 17 lifts), in Warren. Cross-country resorts include the **Von Trapp Family Lodge** (see **Stowe,** p. 111); **Mountain Meadows,** Killington (☎775-7077; 90 mi. of trails); and **Woodstock** (☎457-1100; 40 mi. of trails).

KILLINGTON ☎802

Killington, at the base of 4241 ft. Mount Killington in the heart of the Green Mountains, attracts those who love the outdoors in all seasons. **The Killington Chamber of Commerce,** on U.S. 4 just west of the intersection with Killington Rd., is the best source of area information. (☎773-4181 or 800-337-1928; www.killingtonchamber.com. Open M-F 9am-5pm. Sept.-Oct. and Jan.-Mar. also Sa 9am-1pm.) **Vermont Transit** (☎775-1599), in the Killington Deli on Rte. 4 at the intersection with Rte. 100 N, runs to White River Junction (1hr., 2 per day, $7.50-8.50). The Bus leaves from the Transit Station to shuttle visitors to over 15 stops around town. (☎773-3244. From the Transit Station July-Sept. 10 per day 7:15am-7:15pm; Sept.-Dec. and Apr.-June 6 per day 7:15am-5:15pm; Jan.-Mar. 12 per day 7:15am-11:15pm. $2.) If you need of more flexible wheels, **Gramps Shuttle** (☎236-6600) will come to your aid.

In winter, the town rouses itself into a frenzy of activity centered on the resort and spreading down the slopes. Killington's offers a long season and 200 trails. To get geared up for the trips up and down the slopes, visit **The Basin Ski Shop,** 2886 Killington Rd. (☎422-3234. Open late Oct. to May M-Th 8:15am-9pm, F 8:15am-midnight, Sa-Su 7:15am-9pm; May-late Oct. M and Th-Sa 9:30am-6pm, Tu-W and Su 9:30am-5pm. Skis $25 per day.) During the green season the slopes and surrounding mountains turn into hiking and biking throughways. Many popular trails branch out from **Gifford Woods State Park** on Rte. 100, ¾ mi. from the intersection of Rte. 4 and Rte. 100 N. (☎775-5354. Park office open May to mid-Oct. M-F 8am-4:30pm, Sa 8am-noon. Day-use fee $2.50, ages 4-13 $2. Fishing licenses $15 per day, $41 per season.) The **Killington Resort Complex** also provides myriad summer recreational opportunities at its two mountain centers. (☎888-458-4637. All day adventure center pass $30, ages 6-12 and seniors $25; with mountain biking, including bike lift access, $40/35. Mountain bike rentals 2hr. $30, under 12 $15; 4hr. $35/17; full day $45/22.) Less expensive wheels can be rented at First Stop, at the intersection of Rte. 4 and Rte. 100 S. (☎422-9050. Open May-Sept. M and Th-Su 9am-6pm. Bikes $25 per day.)

Prices for lodging in the area are highly seasonal, with the low point in the summer months and the highest points over holiday weekends at the peak of ski season. **Beattie's Trailside Lodge ❸**, on Rte. 100 N 2½ mi. from the intersection with Rte. 4, is the best bargain in town. The seemingly endless perks include a full breakfast buffet, a four-course family style dinner, a big-screen TV in the lounge, and free bus tickets to the resort. (☎422-3532 or 800-447-2209; www.trailsidelodge.com. Early and late season $40-50 per person. Mid-winter and holidays up to $100 per person.) In summer, camping at one of 27 sites or 21 lean-tos at the **Gifford Woods State Park ❶** is a beautiful and inexpensive option. (☎775-5354 from May to mid-Oct., ☎800-299-3071 from Jan.-May. Sites $14; lean-tos $21. Each additional person $4.)

A plow car that formerly kept the rail track clear of snow now houses **Casey's Caboose ❷,** 2½ mi. up Killington Rd. from Rte. 4., a restaurant and bar that gives away 40,000 lb. of free wings every winter. Munch away on the raised deck or snuggle into one of the booths with a $3.75 pint. (☎422-3795. Open 3pm-midnight. Free wings daily 3-6pm.) **Johnny Boy's Pancake House ❶,** 923 Killington Rd., is the place to start the day with enormous breakfasts ($3.50-7.50) that will keep you energized all day. (☎422-4411. Open daily 7am-2pm.)

BURLINGTON ☎802

Tucked between Lake Champlain and the Green Mountains, the largest city in Vermont offers spectacular views of New York's Adirondack Mountains across the sailboat-studded waters of Champlain. Several colleges, including the University

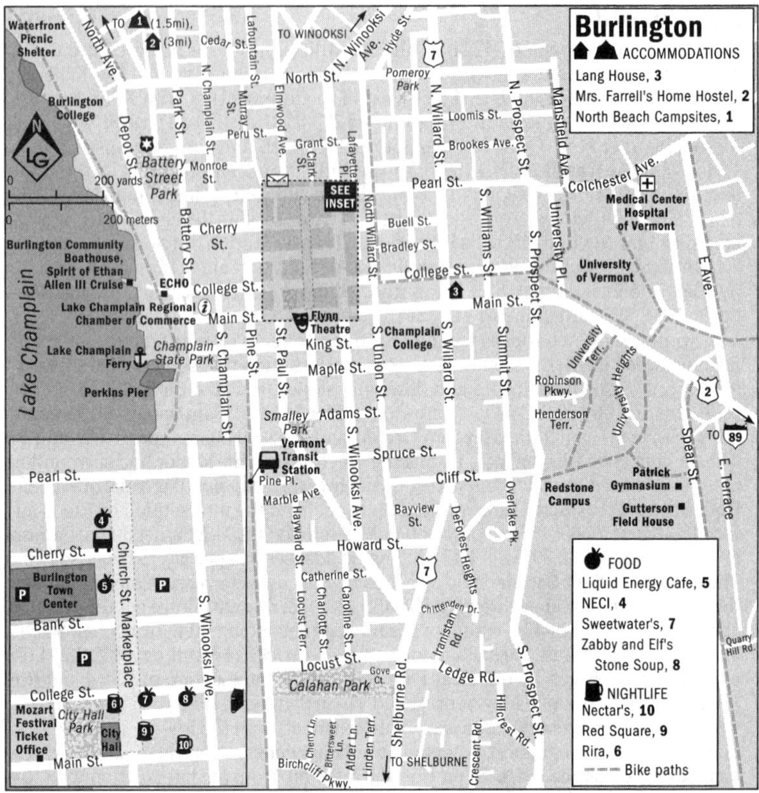

of Vermont (UVM), give the area a youthful, progressive flair. Along the bustling and pedestrian-friendly downtown marketplace of Church St., numerous cafes offer a taste of middle-class hippie atmosphere and a chance for people-watching.

PRACTICAL INFORMATION. Three miles east of Burlington, **Burlington International Airport** (☎863-1889) flies to a handful of major cities. **Chittenden County Transit Authority (CCTA)** runs U Mall/Airport shuttles to the airport. CCTA also services the downtown area with unbeatable access and frequent, reliable service. Connections to Shelburne and other outlying areas also run frequently; catch buses downtown at the intersection of Cherry and Church St. (☎864-2282; www.cctaride.org. Buses operate at least every 30min. M-Sa 6:15am-10:10pm, depending on routes. $1; seniors, disabled, and ages 6-18 $0.50.) **Amtrak,** 29 Railroad Ave., Essex Junction (☎879-7298 for station information, 800-872-7245 for schedules and pricing; open 1hr. before and after departures), 5 mi. east of Burlington on Rte. 15, chugs to New York (9hr., 1 per day, $62-68) and White River Junction (2hr., 1 per day, $19-27). **Vermont Transit,** 345 Pine St. (☎864-6811 or 800-552-8737; open daily 5:30am-7:30pm), runs buses to: Albany (4¾hr., 3 per day, $38); Boston (4¾hr., 4 per day, $44); Middlebury (1hr., 3 per day, $9); Montréal (2½hr., 5 per day, $26); White River Junction (2hr., 4 per day, $18). **Ski Rack,** 85 Main St., rents bikes. (☎658-3313 or 800-882-4530. Open July-Sept. M-Th 9am-

7pm, F 9am-8pm, Sa 9am-6pm, Su 10am-5pm; Oct.-June M-Sa 10am-7pm, Su 11am-5pm. Mountain bikes $10 per hr., $16 per 4hr., $22 per day; helmet and lock included. In-line skates $10 per 4hr., $14 per day. Kayaks $30-40 per day. Credit card required.) **Visitor Info: Lake Champlain Regional Chamber of Commerce,** 60 Main St., Rte. 100. (☎863-3489 or 877-686-5253; www.vermont.org. Open May to mid.-Oct. M-F 8am-5pm, Sa-Su 9am-5pm; mid-Oct. to May M-F 8am-5pm.) **Internet Access: Fletcher Free Library,** 235 College St. (☎864-7146. Open M-Tu and Th-F 8:30am-6pm, W 8:30am-9pm, Sa 9am-5pm, Su noon-6pm.) **Post Office:** 11 Elmwood Ave., at Pearl St. (☎863-6033. Open M-F 8am-5pm, Sa 8am-1pm.) **Postal Code:** 05401. **Area Code:** 802.

ACCOMMODATIONS. The Chamber of Commerce has the complete rundown on area accommodations, which on the whole tend toward more upscale lodgings. B&Bs are generally found in the outlying suburbs. Reasonably priced hotels and guest houses line **Shelburne Road (Route 7),** south of downtown, and **Main Street (Route 2),** east of downtown. **Mrs. Farrell's Home Hostel (HI-AYH) ❶,** 27 Arlington Ct., 3 mi. north of downtown via North Ave. and Heineberg Rd., is a welcoming abode for the homesick traveler. Six beds are split between a clean, comfortable basement and a lovely "summer cottage." (☎865-3730, call between 4-6pm. Check-in before 5pm. Dorms $17, nonmembers $20; cottage $40/43.) For an upscale experience, stay at the **Lang House ❺,** 360 Main St., a 4-year-old B&B only a 5-10min. walk from Church St. and downtown. Chefs from the New England Culinary Institute prepare a gourmet breakfast daily, and the view of Lake Champlain from the third floor rooms can be stunning. (☎652-2500 or 877-919-9799. Rooms with TV and A/C $135-195.) The **North Beach Campsites ❶,** on Institute Rd., 1½ mi. north of town by North Ave., have 137 sites with access to a pristine sandy beach on Lake Champlain. Take Rte. 127 to North Ave., or the "North Ave." bus from the main terminal on Pine St. The beach is open to non-campers, rents canoes and kayaks, and is a stellar spot for picnics. (☎862-0942 or 800-571-1198. Beach open 24hr. for campers; beach parking closes at 9pm. Lifeguards on duty mid June-Aug. 10am-5:30pm. Boat rentals from **Umiak;** canoe $15 per hr., kayak $10-15 per hr. ☎253-2317. Open daily 10am-5pm. Campgrounds open May to mid-Oct. Showers $0.25 per 5min. Sites $21; with water and electricity $27; full hookup $29. $5 parking fee for non-campers.) See **Champlain Valley** (p. 109) for more camping options.

FOOD. With approximately 85 restaurants in the **Church Street Marketplace** and its adjacent sidestreets, Burlington is a haven for hungry travelers. Visitors could eat in this food lover's paradise for weeks without hitting the same place twice—not bad for a city of only 40,000. A mostly vegetarian cafe, **Zabby and Elf's Stone Soup ❶,** 211 College St., specializes in hefty meals from the hot and cold bars ($6 per lb.) and sandwiches on freshly baked bread ($6-7). (☎862-7616. Open M 7am-7pm, Tu-F 7am-9pm, Sa 9am-7pm. No credit cards.) At the **Liquid Energy Cafe ❶,** 57 Church St., customers may concoct delicious smoothies ($3-5) from the long list of unconventional ingredients, many of which claim restorative powers. Custom-build yours to cure anything from acne to asthma, sit back in one of the sleek booths, and let your smoothie work its wonders. (☎860-7666. Open M-Th 7am-7pm, F-Sa 7am-8pm, Su 9am-7pm.) The **New England Culinary Institute ❹,** 25 Church St., known for its superb food at very reasonable prices, is a proving ground for student chefs. (☎862-6324. Dinner entrees from $14. Lunch M-Sa 11:30am-2pm; bistro M-Sa 2-4pm, Su brunch 11am-3pm; dinner M-Th 5:30-10pm, F-Sa 5:30-10:30pm, Su 5:30-9:30pm; winter dinner closes 30min.-1hr. earlier.) At **Sweetwater's ❷,** 120 Church St., incredibly high ceilings and vast wall paintings dwarf those who come for delicious soups

($3-6) and sandwiches ($6-9). When the warm weather rolls around, ask to be seated outdoors. (☎864-9800. Open M-F 11:30am-2am, Sa 11:30am-1am, Su 11:30am-midnight; bar open daily until midnight.)

SIGHTS. The **Shelburne Museum,** 7 mi. south of Burlington in Shelburne, houses one of the most impressive collections of Americana in the country. Ride the free trolley around the 45-acre museum to watch blacksmith demonstrations or visit a 19th-century general store and a 1906 paddleboat. A covered bridge, lighthouse, and 1950s house are displayed beside Degas, Cassat, Manet, Monet, Rembrandt, and Whistler paintings. (☎985-3346; www.shelburnemuseum.org. Open mid-May to late-Oct. daily 10am-5pm. Tickets valid for 2 days $18, ages 6-18 $9; after 3pm $10/5.)

Amateur historians delight in **South Willard Street,** where **Champlain College** occupies many of the Victorian houses that line the street. **City Hall Park,** in the heart of downtown, and **Battery Street Park,** on Lake Champlain near the edge of downtown, are charmingly pastoral and provide a wonderful escape to cool shade on hot summer days. With a stunning view across Lake Champlain, the **Burlington Community Boathouse,** at the base of College St., rents sailboats for a cruise on the lake and operates a small snack bar for those who just want to enjoy the view. (☎865-3377. Open mid-May to mid-Oct. 24hr.; rentals 10am-6pm. Sailboats $30-45 per hr.) The **Spirit of Ethan Allen III** runs a narrated, 500-passenger scenic cruise that departs from the boathouse at the bottom of College St. (☎862-8300; www.soea.com. Cruises late May to mid-Oct. daily 10am, noon, 2, 4pm; sunset cruise 6:30pm. $10, ages 3-11 $4. 1½hr. Sunset cruise $13/5. 2½hr.) Visitors have the opportunity to discover ecology, culture, and history at **ECHO,** 1 College St., a science center and lake aquarium near the water. The multitude of hands-on exhibits and interactive demos are fun for young and old alike. (☎864-1848; www.echovermont.org. Open M-W and F-Su 10am-5pm, Th 10am-8pm. $9, students and seniors $8, ages 3-17 $6.) The **Ethan Allen Homestead** rests northeast of Burlington on Rte. 127 in the Winooski Valley Park. In the 1780s, Allen, his Green Mountain Boys, and Benedict Arnold forced the surrender of Fort Ticonderoga and helped establish the state of Vermont. Now, 1hr. tours visit the cabin and tell the story of the daring frontiersman. (☎865-4556; www.sover.net/~eahome. Open June-Oct. M-Sa 10am-5pm, Su 1-5pm; Nov.-Apr. Sa 10am-5pm, Su 1-5pm; May daily 1-5pm. $5, seniors $4, ages 5-17 $2.50; families $14.)

FESTIVALS & NIGHTLIFE. With so many colleges and youth in the area, Burlington's nightlife scene is always alive and kicking. A pedestrian haven for tie-dye seekers, ice cream lovers, and those seeking a casual pint with friends, Church St. Marketplace nurtures off-beat puppeteers and musicians who entertain the crowds at all hours. Pick up a free *Seven Days* newspaper to get the skinny on what's happening around town. In the summer, the **Vermont Mozart Festival** brings Bach, Beethoven, and Mozart to local barns, farms, and meadows. (☎862-7352; www.vtmozart.com. Concerts July 18-Aug. 8, 2004.) The **Discover Jazz Festival** features over 1000 musicians each year, with past performers including Ella Fitzgerald, Dizzy Gillespie, and Betty Carter. (☎863-7992; www.discoverjazz.com. July 7-13, 2004. Some performances are free but others are sold through the Flynn Theater Box Office.) The **Champlain Valley Folk Festival,** located about halfway between Burlington and Middlebury, croons in early August. (☎800-769-9176; www.cvfest.org. Tickets $25-75.) The **Flynn Theater Box Office,** 153 Main St., handles sales for the Folk Festival and the Discover Jazz Festival. (☎863-5966; www.flynncenter.org. Open M-F 10am-5pm, Sa 11am-4pm.)

Nectar's, 188 Main St., rocks with inexpensive food, including the locally acclaimed gravy fries ($3), and nightly live tunes. (☎658-4771. No cover. Open M-Tu 11am-2:30am, W-F 6am-2:30am, Sa-Su 7am-2:30am.) One of Burlington's most popular night spots, the **Red Square,** 136 Church St., dishes out live music nightly. Bands play in the alley if the crowd gets large. (☎859-8909. No cover. Open daily 4pm-2am.) For a laidback pint, try **Rira,** 123 Church St., a traditional Irish pub. (☎860-9401. Beer $2.50-4.50. Open M-Sa 11:30am-2am, Su 11:30am-1am.)

DAYTRIP FROM BURLINGTON: CHAMPLAIN VALLEY. Stretching 100 mi. between Vermont's Green Mountains and New York's Adirondacks, **Lake Champlain** boasts plentiful opportunities for camping, biking, and hiking. Visitors can take a bridge or ferry across the lake; both offer fantastic views. The **Lake Champlain Ferry,** located on the dock at the bottom of King St., sails from Burlington to Port Kent, NY, and back. (☎864-9804; www.ferries.com. 1hr. July-Aug. 11-13 per day 7:30am-7:30pm; mid-May to late June and Sept. to mid-Oct. 9 per day 8am-6:35pm. $3.75, ages 6-12 $1.50; car and driver $13.75.) Throughout the day, service from Grand Isle to Plattsburg, NY and from Charlotte, VT to Essex, NY is also offered. (Each route $2.75, ages 6-12 $0.75; car and driver $7.75.)

Mount Philo State Park ❶, 15 mi. south of Burlington, off Rte. 7, offers pleasant, easy-to-moderate hiking and picnic facilities with a view of the surrounding countryside. Camping is offered on seven sites nestled on the side of the mountain among the trees. (☎425-2390 or for winter reservations ☎800-658-1622. 2-night min. stay. Open mid-May to mid-Oct. daily 10am-dusk. 7 sites without hookup $14; 3 lean-tos $21. Entrance fee $2.50, ages 4-13 $2.) The marsh of the **Missisquoi National Wildlife Refuge,** 2 mi. to the northwest of Swanton on Rte. 78 at the northern end of the lake, provides extensive lands for hiking, bird watching, kayaking, and canoeing in warm weather, and cross-country skiing and snowshoeing in the winter. (☎868-4781. Office open M-F 8am-4:30pm. Refuge open dawn-dusk. Free.)

Also north of the lake, **Burton Island State Park ❶** is accessible only by private boats and a ferry which runs five times daily from Kill Kare State Park, 35 mi. north of Burlington and 3½ mi. southwest of U.S. 7, near St. Albans Bay. This secluded park, devoid of cars, provides a tranquil place to hike, swim, and picnic. (☎524-6353 or 800-252-2363. Open late May-early Sept. daily 8am-8pm; call for schedule. Day-use $2.50, ages 4-13 $2. Ferry service $3 each way. $1 for a bike. 4-night min. stay. 17 tent sites $16; 26 lean-tos $23. Each additional person $4.) The state park on **Grand Isle ❶,** just off U.S. 2, north of Keeler Bay, also offers lakeside camping with a small rocky beach. (☎372-4300 summer, 800-252-2363 Jan.-May. Reservations strongly recommended, especially for summer weekends; 2-night min. stay required for reservations. Open mid-May to mid-Oct. 4-person sites $16; lean-tos $23. Each additional person $4. Cabin $46. Row boat and kayak rentals $5.25 per hr, $31.50 per day. No day-use.) Also along the Champlain Islands are myriad **biking trips** (☎597-4646; www.champlainbikeways.org), **state parks** available for day use (**Alburg Dunes** ☎796-4170; **Knight Point** ☎372-8389; **North Hero;** ☎372-8727; **Knight Island** ☎524-6353; www.vtstateparks.com), and the **Lipizzan Stallions.** These horses, known for their grace and amazing strength, perform four times weekly. (Champlain Islands Chamber of Commerce ☎372-8400 for more information; www.herrmannslipizzans.com. Performances Th-F 6pm, Sa-Su 2:30pm. Located 1½ miles past the drawbridge between Grand Isle and North Hero on Rte. 2 W. $15, seniors $12, ages 6-12 $8.)

MIDDLEBURY ☎802

"Vermont's Landmark College Town" surges with the energy and culture stimulated by the bohemian momentum of Middlebury College. The result is a traditional Vermont atmosphere tinged with both vitality and history.

NEW ENGLAND

PRACTICAL INFORMATION. Middlebury stretches along U.S. 7, 42 mi. south of Burlington. **Vermont Transit** stops at the Exxon station, 16 Court St., west of Main St. (☎388-9300. Station open daily 6am-10pm.) Buses run to: Albany (4hr., 3 per day, $31); Boston (6hr., 3 per day, $48); Burlington (1hr., 3 per day, $9); Rutland (1½hr., 3 per day, $8). The **Addison County Transit Resources** provide free shuttle service in the immediate Middlebury vicinity, making stops every hour at the town green, Marbleworks, along Rte.7 S, and Middlebury College. (☎388-1946. Runs daily 7am-8pm.) Exploring on foot is probably the easiest way around town, but for those who prefer wheels, the **Bike Center,** 74 Main St., rents bikes. (☎388-6666; www.bikecentermid.com. Open M-Th and Sa 9:30am-5:30pm, F 9:30am-8pm; June-Sept. also Su 1-4pm. Bikes from $15 per day.) The staff at the **Addison County Chamber of Commerce,** 2 Court St., has area info. (☎388-7951 or 800-733-8376; www.midvermont.com. Open M-F 9am-5pm; late Sept.-Oct. also Sa-Su 9am-5pm.) **Internet Access: Ilsley Public Library,** 75 Main St. (☎388-4095. Open M, W, F 10am-6pm; Tu and Th 10am-8pm; Sa 10am-4pm.) **Post Office:** 10 Main St. (☎388-2681. Open M-F 8am-5pm, Sa 8am-12:30pm.) **Postal Code:** 05753. **Area Code:** 802.

ACCOMMODATIONS. Lodging with four walls and no mosquitoes does not come cheaply in Middlebury. The **Sugar House Motor Inn ❸,** 1395 Rte. 7, 2 mi. north of Middlebury, offers basic motel rooms with free local calls, refrigerators, microwaves, and cable TV as well as a pool and grill. (☎388-2770 or 800-784-2746. Make reservations in advance. Rooms from $69.) For those weary of small roadside motels, the hospitality of the **Middlebury B&B ❹,** 174 Washington St., is a welcome change. The friendly owner and her two small dogs add to the homey atmosphere. (☎388-4851. Rooms $75-110.) The best budget accommodations are to be found in the great outdoors. **Branbury State Park ❶,** 7 mi. south on U.S. 7, then 4 mi. south on Rte. 53, stretches along Lake Dunmore, offering 40 sites and seven lean-tos among the idyllic fields and boulder-strewn hillsides. (☎247-5925. Open late May to mid-Oct. Sites $16; lean-tos $23. Showers $0.25 per 5min. Canoe rentals $5 per hr., $30 per day. Paddle boats $5 per 30min.)

FOOD & NIGHTLIFE. Middlebury's many fine restaurants cater chiefly to plump wallets, but the presence of students ensures the survival of less expensive options. A student favorite, **Noonie's Deli ❶,** 137 Maple St., in the Marbleworks building just behind Main St., makes terrific sandwiches ($4-5) on thick slices of homemade bread. (☎388-0014. Open M-Sa 8am-8pm.) Students also flock to **Mister Up's ❷,** a popular nighttime hangout on Bakery Ln., just off Main St. Sandwiches ($6-7) or selections from the extensive salad bar go down easily on the open-air riverside deck. (☎388-6724. Open M-Sa 11:30am-midnight, Su 11am-midnight.) Bright colors and larger-than-life murals deck the walls of **Amigos ❸,** 4 Merchants Row, which offers Mexican favorites. (☎388-3624. Lunch $6-8. Dinner entrees $8-18. Open M-Sa 11:30am-9:30pm, Su 4:30-9:30pm; bar open daily until 10:30pm.) Night owls should check out **Angela's Pub,** 86 Main St. Whether it's live music, the jukebox, or karaoke, this hot spot jumps with musical accompaniment and great beer specials (Th $1.50 pint of Budweiser) at night. (☎388-6936. Tu karaoke. W open mic. F live band. Sa DJ. No cover. Open Tu-F 4pm-2am, Sa 8pm-2am.) For a more mellow drinking atmosphere, try the **Two Brothers** next door at 88 Main St. (☎388-0002. Beer $1.75-5.50. No cover. Open daily 11:30am-2am.)

SIGHTS. Middlebury College hosts the town's cultural events; the concert hall in the college **Arts Center,** just outside of town on S. Main St., has a terrific concert series. The **box office** has details on events sponsored by the college. (☎443-6433.

Open Sept.-May M-F noon-5pm, also 1hr. before start of show. Many events free, most $5-10.) The center also hosts numerous other productions. Through the summer months, Middlebury's crack at an **International Film Festival** screens movies Saturday at 7 and 9:30pm in the Dana Auditorium. (☎443-5510; www.middlebury.due/ls/film. Free.) Tours from the **Admissions Office,** in Emma Willard Hall on S. Main St., showcase the picturesque campus. (☎443-3000. Tours Sept.-late May daily 9am, 1pm. Call for reservations. July-Aug. self-guided tour brochures available.) In the town proper, at the bottom of the hill on Mill St., the **Marbleworks Memorial Bridge** provides a terrific view of the crumbling mills that once generated the town's power. Too poor for a pint? Trek ¾ mi. north of town to the **Otter Creek Brewery,** 793 Exchange St., for free samples and a tour. (☎800-473-0727. Tours daily 1, 3, 5pm. Shop open 10am-6pm.) Fifteen miles east of the Middlebury College campus, the **Middlebury College Snow Bowl** (☎388-4356; www.middlebury.edu/~snowbowl) entertains skiers in winter with 14 trails and three lifts. (Lift tickets M-F $26, Sa-Su $35; students and seniors $20/25; preschool $6/6.) The **Henry Sheldon Museum of Vermont History,** 1 Park St., showcases, via an excellent 30-40min. tour, historical objects that profile lives of past Vermonters. (☎388-2117; www.henrysheldonmuseum.org. Open M-Sa 10am-5pm. $5, seniors $4.50, students $4, ages 6-18 $3.)

The outdoors surrounding Middlebury make for great—and scenic—hiking and paddling. Hiking information is provided in liberal quantities from the **Middlebury Ranger Station,** 1077 Rte. 7S. (☎388-4362. Open M-F 8am-4:30pm.) For paddling supplies, **Middlebury Mountaineer,** 3 Mill St., can meet your needs. (☎388-1749. One person kayak full day $40, tandem $50, car rack and PDF included. Open M-Sa 10am-5pm, Su noon-3pm.) Exercise your legs and your mind at the **Robert Frost Interpretive Trail,** an easy 1 mi. trail starting from a parking lot 2 mi. east of Ripton on Rte. 125. Excerpts from the poet's works are mounted on plaques along the path in spots similar to ones that might have inspired the poems' creation. (☎388-4362. Free.)

NEW ENGLAND

STOWE ☎802

Stowe curls gracefully up the side of Mt. Mansfield—Vermont's highest peak, at 4393 ft. A mecca for outdoor activities in all seasons, but especially skiing in the winter, the village tries very hard to live up to its aspirations as a ritzy European skiing hot spot. In fact, Stowe has something of an obsession with all things Austrian; nowhere is this more clear than in the proliferation of Austrian-type chalets and restaurants sprouting off the mountain's ascending road.

PRACTICAL INFORMATION. Stowe is 10 mi. north of I-89 Exit 10, 27 mi. southwest of Burlington. The ski slopes lie along **Mountain Road (Route 108),** northwest of Stowe. **Vermont Transit** (☎244-7689 or 800-872-7245; open M-Sa 5am-9pm, Su 6am-8pm) comes only as close as **Depot Beverage,** 1 River Rd., in Waterbury, 11 mi. from Stowe, and runs to Burlington (30min., 1 per day, $8-9) and Boston (4hr., 1 per day, $50-53). **Peg's Pick-up/Stowe Taxi** (☎253-9490 or 800-370-9490) will take you into Stowe for around $25 plus $5 for each additional passenger; call ahead. In winter, the **Stowe Trolley** runs up and down Mountain Rd. every 20-30min., picking up passengers. (☎253-7585. Trolley runs in winter 7:30am-10pm. $1, weekly pass $10, season pass $20. Daily 1½hr. tours leave from town hall July to mid-Oct. 11am. $2.) **Visitors Info: Stowe Area Association,** 51 Main St. (☎253-7321 or 800-247-8693; www.gostowe.com. Open June to mid-Oct. and mid-Dec. to Mar. M-Sa 9am-8pm, Su 9am-5pm; mid-Oct. to mid-Dec. and Apr.-June M-F 9am-5pm.) Pick up the free *Stowe Scene* newspaper and the *Vacation Planner* guide here for listings of local events and helpful information about recreation in the area. **Internet Access: Stowe**

Free Library, 90 Pond St. (☎253-6145. Open M, W, F 9:30am-5:30pm, Tu and Th 2-7pm, Sa 10am-3pm.) **Post Office:** 105 Depot St., off Main St. (☎253-7521. Open M-F 7:15am-5pm, Sa 9am-noon.) **Postal Code:** 05672. **Area Code:** 802.

ACCOMMODATIONS. Easy access is one of many reasons to stay at the **Stowe Bound Lodge ❶,** 645 S. Main St., located ½ mi. south of the intersection of Rte. 100 and 108. The friendly owners make travelers feel at ease with their engaging conversation and comfortable common space with a piano and fireplace. (☎253-4515. Private rooms with shared bath $20 per person.) **Foster's Place ❷,** 4968 Mountain Rd., offers dorm rooms with a lounge, laundry facilities, game room, outdoor pool, and hot tub/sauna in a recently renovated school building. (☎253-9448 or 800-330-4880. Reservations recommended. Singles $35-39, with private bath $49-59; quads $55. Call for seasonal rates.) A converted 19th-century farm house and adjacent motel, the **Riverside Inn ❸,** 1965 Mountain Rd., 2 mi. from town, offers a number of great perks and some of the best rates in town. The friendly owners allow free loan of their mountain bikes as well as use of the pool table and fireplace in the lodge. (☎253-4217 or 800-966-4217. Rooms $39-99.) **Smuggler's Notch State Park ❶,** 6443 Mountain Rd., 8 mi. west of Stowe, just past Foster's Place, keeps it simple with hot showers, tent sites, and lean-tos. The scanty amenities are more than made up for by the natural beauty and seclusion of the park's sites. (☎253-4014. Reservations recommended. Open late May to mid-Oct. 4-person sites $14; lean-tos $21. Each additional person $4.)

FOOD & NIGHTLIFE. The **Depot Street Malt Shoppe ❶,** 57 Depot St., is reminiscent of decades past. Sports pennants and vinyl records deck the walls, while rock 'n' roll favorites liven up the outdoor patio seating. The cost of a 1950s-style cherry or vanilla Coke has been adjusted for inflation, but prices remain reasonable. (☎253-4269. Meals $3-6. Open daily 11:30am-9pm.) Perfect for picnics, **Mac's Deli ❶,** located in Mac's Stowe Market, on S. Main St. ¼ mi. from the intersection of Rte. 100 and Rte. 108, has tasty sandwiches, subs, and wraps ($3-5) made with any of the meats and cheeses in the market's deli selection. They also serve piping hot soups for $2-3. (☎253-4576. No seating. Open M-Sa 7am-9pm, Su 7am-8pm.) Fans of little green men and all things not of this planet will enjoy **Pie in the Sky ❸,** 492 Mountain Rd. Their "Out of This World" pizzas include such works as the "Blond Vermonter" with olive oil, Vermont cheddar, apples, and ham. (☎253-5100. Pizza $8-17. Open daily 11:30am-10pm.)

For sports fans, the **Sunset Grille and Tap Room,** 140 Cottage Club Rd., off Mountain Rd., allows its guests to face off on the air hockey and pool tables while following numerous sporting events on over 15 TVs, including four big screens. The adjacent restaurant offers barbecue. (☎253-9281. Lunch $4-9. Dinner $10-15. Kitchen open daily 11:30am-midnight; bar open until 2am.) The M-F specials and six homemade microbrews served up in **The Shed,** 1859 Mountain Rd., make this brewery stand out. (☎253-4364. Tu night $2.50 pint night. Open daily 11:30am-midnight.) Head to the **Rusty Nail,** 1 mi. from town center on Mountain Rd., to dance the night away in a renovated barn. (☎253-6245. Tu open mic, Th karaoke, F-Sa live music. Cover $5-15. Open Tu 11:30am-midnight, W 11:30am-9pm, Th 11:30am-11pm, F and Sa 11:30am-2am, Su 11:30am-8pm.)

SKIING. Stowe's ski offerings include the Stowe Mountain Resort (☎253-3000 or 800-253-4754) and Smuggler's Notch (☎644-8851 or 800-451-8752; see Vermont Ski Resorts, p. 104). The hills are alive with the area's best cross-country skiing on 60km of groomed trails and 45km of backcountry skiing at the **Von Trapp Family Lodge,** 2 mi. off Mountain Rd., accessed from Luce Hill Rd. Budget traveler beware: prices for lodging climb to $960 in the high season. However, there's no charge to visit, and the lodge offers inexpensive rentals and lessons. (☎253-5719 or 800-826-7000. Trail fee $16, ski rentals $18, lessons $15-45 per hr. Ski school package includes all 3 for $40.) **AJ's Ski and Sports,** 350 Mountain Rd., rents ski equipment in winter. (☎253-4593 or 800-226-6257. Open winter Su-Th 8am-8pm, F-Sa 8am-9pm; summer daily 9am-6pm. Skis, boots, and poles: downhill $26 per day, $50 for 2 days; cross-country $15/28; snowboard and boots $22 per day.)

OUTDOOR ACTIVITIES. In summer, Stowe's frenetic pace drops off some, but it still burns with the energy of outdoor enthusiasts. **Action Outfitters,** 2160 Mountain Rd., can serve nearly all recreation needs. (☎253-7975. Open daily May-Oct. 9am-5pm; Oct.-May 8am-6pm. Mountain bikes $7 per hr., $16 half-day, $24 full day; in-line skates $6/12/18. Canoes $25 half-day, $30 full day.) Stowe's 5½ mi. asphalt **recreation path** runs parallel to the Mountain Rd.'s ascent and begins behind the church on Main St. in Stowe. Perfect for biking, skating, and strolling in the summer, the path accommodates cross-country skiing and snowshoeing in the winter. A few miles past Smuggler's Notch on Mountain Rd. (Rte. 108), the road shrinks to one lane and winds past huge boulders and 1000 ft. high cliffs.

Seasoned and aspiring fly fishermen should head to the **Fly Rod Shop,** 2½ mi. south of Stowe on Rte. 100, to pick up the necessary fishing licenses ($15 per day, $30 per week, $41 per year; $20 per year for VT residents), rent fly rods and reels, and enroll in the free fly fishing classes in the shop's pond. (☎253-7346 or 800-535-9763. Classes W 4-6pm and Sa 9am-11am. Open Apr.-Oct. M-F 9am-6pm, Sa 9am-4pm, Su 10am-4pm; Nov.-Mar. M-F 9am-5pm, Sa 9am-4pm, Su 10am-4pm. Rods and reels $15 per day.) **Umiak,** on Rte. 100, ¾ mi. south of Stowe Center, rents kayaks and canoes in the summer. During the snowy season, Umiak and runs guided moonlight snowshoeing tours ($39 per person) with wine and cheese served. (☎253-2317. Open daily 9am-6pm; winter hours vary. River trip $38 per person; rental and transportation to the river included. Kayaks $12 per hr., $24 for 4hr.; canoes $18/34.) Another popular diversion in the area is horseback riding. **Ziemke Glassblowing Studio,** 7 mi. south of Stowe along Rte. 100, allows free viewing of the entire glassblowing process—from a molten mass in the 2100°F furnace to finished vases, glasses, and candle holders. The wares being made are also for sale in the gallery. (☎244-6126. Open daily 10am-6pm. Glass $25-195.)

ME AND MY CHUNKY MONKEY After meeting in 7th grade gym class and devoting a number of intervening years to school and jobs, Ben Cohen and Jerry Greenfield enrolled in a $5 Penn State correspondence course in ice cream-making, converted a gas station into their first shop in 1978, and launched themselves on the road to a double-scoop success story. Today, **Ben and Jerry's Ice Cream Factory,** north of Waterbury on Rte. 100, is "One Sweet Whirled" for ice cream lovers. Whether you're into "Karamel Sutra" or just "Makin' Whoopie Pie," the 30min. tour of the facilities gives you a taste of the founders' passion. The tour tells Ben & Jerry's history, showcases the company's social consciousness, and awards a free sample at the end. *(☎882-2586; www.benjerry.com. Tours June daily every 20min. 9am-5pm; July to late Aug. every 10min. 9am-8pm; late Aug. to late Oct. every 15min. 9am-6pm.; Nov.-May every 30min. 10am-5pm. $3, seniors $2, under 12 free.)*

NEAR STOWE: ROUTE 100 GLUTTONY

Rte. 100 features a bona fide food fiesta south of Stowe. Begin at **Ben & Jerry's** (see **Me And My Chunky Monkey,** p. 113) and drive north on Rte. 100 towards Stowe. The first stop is the **Cabot Annex Store,** home to **Lake Champlain Choco-**

lates and the **Cabot Creamery Cooperative.** The annex is bursting at the seams with rich chocolate truffles and Vermont's best cheddar and provides free samples of both. (☎241-4150 for Lake Champlain Chocolates and ☎244-6334 for Cabot Creamery Cooperative. Open daily 9am-6pm.) Leave room for **Cold Hollow Cider Mill;** in addition to free samples of cider, jams, and jellies, you can pick up $0.40 doughnuts. (☎800-327-7537. Call for a cider-making schedule in Sept. and Oct. Open daily 8am-7pm.) Free fudge samples go down easy in the **Waterbury Center** next door. In the adjacent building, **Grand View Winery** offers wine and hard cider sampling for $1. (☎456-7012. Wine tasting daily 11am-5pm. Building open daily 9am-7pm.) Finally, maple is everywhere at **Stowe Maple Products.** March and April is syrup season, but they sell home-harvested goods all year. (☎253-2508. Open M-Sa 9am-5pm, Su 10am-4pm.)

MASSACHUSETTS

Massachusetts regards itself, with some justification, as the intellectual center of the nation. Since the 1636 establishment of Cambridge's Harvard College, the oldest college in America, Massachusetts has been a breeding ground for academics and literati. The undisputed highlight of the state is Boston, the birthplace of the American Revolution (a.k.a. the "Cradle of Liberty") and later self-proclaimed "Hub of the Universe," a small, diverse city packed full of cultural and historical attractions. Resplendent with bright colors during the fall, the Berkshire Mountains fill western Massachusetts with a charm that attracts thousands of visitors. The seaside areas—from Nantucket to Northern Bristol and including scenic Cape Cod, New England's premier vacation destination—illuminate the stark beauty that first attracted settlers to these shores.

PRACTICAL INFORMATION

Capital: Boston.

Visitor Info: Office of Travel & Tourism, 10 Park Plaza, Suite 4510, Boston, MA 02116 (☎617-973-8500 or 800-227-6277; www.mass-vacation.com). Free, comprehensive *Getaway Guide* available online or in person. Open M-F 8:45am-5pm.

Postal Abbreviation: MA. **Sales Tax:** 5%; no tax on clothing and pre-packaged food.

BOSTON ☎617

Perhaps more than any other American city, Boston reveals the limits of the "melting pot" metaphor. The corporate sanctuaries of the Financial District are visible from the winding streets of the North End. Aristocratic Beacon Hill is just across Boston Common from the nation's first Chinatown. The trendy South End abuts the less gentrified neighborhoods of Roxbury and Dorchester. While walking Boston's famed Freedom Trail will expose you to some of the earliest history of the US—in which the city played a starring role—wandering the streets of Boston's neighborhoods lends a glimpse of a still-evolving metropolis, where the lives of the 800,000 people who call Boston home are just as interesting as the colonial history that shaped their town. For more comprehensive coverage of the Boston area, see *Let's Go: Boston 2004*.

Boston

SEE COLOR INSERTS FOR MORE BOSTON MAPS

INTERCITY TRANSPORTATION

Airport: Logan International (☎800-235-6426; www.massport.com/logan), 5 mi. northeast of Downtown. T: Airport; a free shuttle connects all 5 terminals to the T stop. **Back Bay Coach** (☎888-222-5229; www.backbay-coach.com) runs door-to-door service to and from the airport (24hr. advanced reservation recommended). A **taxi** to downtown costs $15-20.

Trains: South Station, Summer St. at Atlantic Ave. T: South Station. Open 24hr. **Amtrak** runs frequent daily service to: **New York City** (3½-4½hr., $64-99); **Philadelphia** (5-6hr., $74-163); **Washington, D.C.** (6½-8hr., $81-176).

Buses: Buses depart South Station. T: South Station. Open 24hr.

Bonanza Bus (☎888-751-8800; www.bonanzabus.com) runs to: **Newport** (1½hr., 6-9 per day, $17); **Providence** (1hr., 7-9 per day, $8); **Woods Hole** (1½hr., 12-15 per day, $22).

Greyhound runs to: **New York City** (4½-6hr., every 30min., $30); **Philadelphia** (7-8hr., every hr., $55); **Washington, D.C.** (10-11hr., every 1-2hr., $66).

Peter Pan Trailways (☎800-237-8747; www.peterpanbus.com) runs to **Albany** (4-4½hr., 3 per day, $32-34).

Plymouth & Brockton St. Railway (☎508-746-0378; www.p-b.com) goes to **Plymouth** (1hr., $9) and all over **Cape Cod,** including **Hyannis** (1½hr., 35 per day, 7am-midnight, $14) and **Provincetown** (3¼hr., $23).

Vermont Transit (☎800-552-8737; www.vermonttransit.com) goes north to: **Burlington** (5hr., 5 per day, $50); **Montréal** (8hr., 6 per day, $62); **Portland** (2hr., 9 per day, $15).

NEW ENGLAND

ORIENTATION

Boston is the capital of Massachusetts and the largest city in New England. The city's patchwork of distinct neighborhoods is situated on a peninsula jutting into the Massachusetts Bay (bordered to the north and west by the **Charles River** and to the east by **Boston Harbor**). The city proper is centered on the grassy expanse of **Boston Common;** the popular **Freedom Trail** (p. 121) begins here and links most of the city's major sights. The Trail heads east through crowded **Downtown** (still the same compact 3 sq. mi. settled in 1630), skirting the city's growing **Waterfront** district to the southeast. The Trail then veers north to the charming **North End,** Boston's "Little Italy"—cut off from Boston proper by the **Fitzgerald Expressway (I-93)**—then crosses the river to historic **Charlestown.**

Boston Common is sandwiched between **Beacon Hill** to the north and **Chinatown** to the south. Much of Chinatown overlaps the nightlife-heavy **Theatre District** to the west. Just west of the Common are the grand boulevards and brownstones of the chic **Back Bay,** centered on beautiful Copley Sq. and home to Boylston St., a bar-hopper's paradise. The **Massachusetts Turnpike (I-90)** separates the Back Bay from the artsy and predominantly gay **South End,** to its south, which has a lion's share of the city's best restaurants. West of the Back Bay are **Kenmore Square** and **Fenway,** home to baseball's Red Sox, the city's major museums, and the clubs of Lansdowne St. South of the Fenway is vibrant, gay-friendly **Jamaica Plain,** filled with countless green spaces and cheap restaurants.

LOCAL TRANSPORTATION

Public Transit: Massachusetts Bay Transportation Authority or **MBTA** (☎222-5000; www.mbta.com). Known as the T, the subway has 5 colored lines–Red, Blue, Orange, Green, and Silver (Green splits into lettered lines B-E)–that radiate out from Downtown. "Inbound" trains head toward T: Park St. or T: Downtown Crossing; "outbound" trains head away from those stops. All T stops have maps and schedules. Lines run daily 5:30am-12:30am; "Night Owl" system of buses run F-Sa until 2:30am. Fare $1, ages 5-11 $0.40, seniors $0.20. **Visitor passes** for unlimited subway and bus use are good for 1 day ($6), 3 days ($11), or 7 days ($22). **MBTA Commuter Rail** trains run from T: North Station (Green/Orange) to: **Concord** (Fitchurg line; $4); **Plymouth** (Plymouth/Kingston line; 1hr., $5); **Salem** (Newburyport/Rockport line; 30min., $3).

Taxi: Boston Cab, ☎536-5010. **Checker Taxi,** ☎495-8294. **Town Taxi,** ☎536-5000.

Car Rental: Dollar Rent-a-Car (☎634-0006 or 800-800-3665), at the airport. Open 24hr. Under 25 $30 surcharge per day. 10% AAA discount. Must be 21+ with major credit card. All other agencies have desks at the airport.

PRACTICAL INFORMATION

Visitor Info: Greater Boston Convention and Visitors Bureau (☎536-4100; www.bostonusa.com) has a booth at Boston Common, outside T: Park St. Open M-F 8:30am-5pm. Downtown's **National Historic Park Visitor Center,** 15 State St. (☎242-5642), has Freedom Trail info and tours. T: State. Open daily 9am-5pm.

Tours: Boston Duck Tours (☎723-3825; www.bostonducktours.com). Wacky con-DUCK-tors drive WWII amphibious vehicles past major sights before splashing down in the Charles, offering cheesy commentary and vigorous quacking all the way. 1½hr. tours depart from the Prudential Ctr., T: Prudential, Apr.-Nov. daily every 30min. 9am-1hr. before sunset. $23, students and seniors $20, ages 3-11 $14. Tickets sold online; at the New England Aquarium, T: Aquarium; and the Prudential Ctr. M-Sa 8:30am-8pm, Su 8:30am-6pm. Credit cards accepted only at Aquarium and online.

Hotlines: Rape Crisis Center, ☎492-7273. 24hr. **BGLT Help Line,** ☎267-9001. M-F 6-11pm, Sa-Su 5-10pm.

Post Office: 25 Dorchester Ave. (☎654-5302), behind South Station at T: South Station (Red). Open 24hr. **Postal Code:** 02205. **Area Code:** 617. 10-digit dialing required.

ACCOMMODATIONS

Finding truly cheap accommodations in Boston is very hard. Rates and bookings are highest in summer and during college-rush times in September, late May, and early June. Reservation services promise to find discounted rooms, even during sold-out periods. Try **Boston Reservations** (☎332-4199), **Central Reservation Service** (☎800-332-3026 or 569-3800; www.bostonhotels.net), or **Citywide Reservation Services** (☎267-7424 or 800-468-3593; www.cityres.com). Traveler beware: all rooms in Boston come with a 12.45% **room tax,** not included the prices below.

HI–Boston Fenway (HI-AYH), 575 Commonwealth Ave. (☎267-8599), in Fenway. T: Kenmore, lets out on Comm. Ave. The best hostel in Boston, housed in a former luxury hotel, with 155 bright and airy 3-bed dorm rooms and a penthouse common room with a 360° view of Boston. Each room has private bath and A/C. Same lineup of freebies as HI-Boston (see below). Free linen. Check-out 11am. Open June-Aug. Dorm bed $35, nonmembers $38; 3-bed room $99. ❷

Oasis Guest House, 22 Edgerly Rd. (☎267-2262; www.oasisgh.com), at Stoneholm St., in Back Bay. From T: Hynes/ICA, exit onto Mass Ave., walking with the Virgin Megastore on your left, cross Boylston St. and turn right onto Haviland St.; the next left is Edgerly Rd. This rambling 30-room guest house is true to its name, serving as a calm respite from the traffic of the city. Continental breakfast daily 8-11am. Reservations recommended up to 2 months in advance. Apr. to mid-Nov. singles $59; doubles with shared bath $69, with private bath $89. Mid-Nov. to Mar. $80/90/125. ❸

Newbury Guest House, 261 Newbury St. (☎437-7666 or 800-437-7668; www.hagopianhotels.com), between Gloucester and Fairfield St. T: Hynes/ICA. In a central location, their 32 immaculately clean, bright, and tastefully decorated double rooms have some of the best amenities in the city; all rooms come with private bath and digital cable. Full complimentary breakfast daily 7:30-10:30am. Reception 24hr. Check-in 3pm. Check-out noon. Doubles Apr.-Oct. $125-190; Nov.-Mar. $99-125. ❺

HI—Boston (HI-AYH), 12 Hemenway St. (☎536-1027), in Back Bay. From T: Hynes/ICA, walk down Massachusetts Ave., turn right onto Boylston St., then left onto Hemenway St. Central location, spotless bathrooms, quiet dorms, and a full lineup of nightly events, including free movie screenings and complimentary entrance to museums and dance clubs. Free linen, lockers, and kitchen use. Laundry facilities. Check-in noon. Check-out 11am. Dorms $32, nonmembers $35. ❷

Beantown Hostel & Irish Embassy Hostel, 222 Friend St., 3rd fl. (☎723-0800), in Downtown. Exit T: North Station onto Causeway St. and turn left onto Friend St. These 2 connected, party-hardy hostels are Boston's cheapest. Co-ed and single sex dorms (110 beds). Beantown curfew 1:45am; Irish Embassy (above a pub) curfew-less. Free linen, lockers, and kitchen use. Laundry facilities. Free buffet summer Tu and Th 8pm. Check-out 10am. Dorms $25. Cash only. ❶

YMCA of Greater Boston, 316 Huntington Ave. (☎927-8040). T: Northeastern lets out onto Huntington Ave. in Back Bay. Access to world-class athletic facilities and Boston's nearby cultural attractions. A long-term men-only residence that is co-ed Sept. to mid-June with 2 floor of sterile, serviceable rooms (with shared hallway bathrooms). Breakfast included. Reception 24hr. Check-out 11am. 18+. Singles $45; doubles $65. ❷

NEW ENGLAND

FOOD

Once a barren gastronomical wasteland whose only claim to fame was baked beans, Boston is now a culinary paradise. Trendy bistros, fusion restaurants, and a globetrotting array of ethnic eateries have taken their place alongside the long-standing "chowda" shacks, greasy-spoons, soul-food joints, and welcoming pubs.

DOWNTOWN

Downtown is the most heavily touristed part of Boston, so expect mediocre food, big crowds, and high prices. The best and most affordable food options are the identical sandwich shops (sandwiches $5-7) found on almost every street corner and the more diverse food court inside **Quincy Market** (p. 121; most dishes $5-7). Downtown is also near the fresh seafood shops lining Boston's **Waterfront** district.

No Name, 15½ Fish Pier (☎338-7539), the next pier over from the World Trade Ctr. Take the free shuttle to the WTC from T: South Station. One of Boston's best and cheapest Waterfront seafood spots, with fish sent fin-flapping fresh from the boats to your table. Entrees $8-12. Open M-Sa 11am-10pm, Su 11am-9pm. Cash only. ❸

Sultan's Kitchen, 72 Broad St. (☎338-7819), at Custom House St. From T: State (Blue/Orange), walk against traffic down State St. and turn right onto Broad St. The most popular lunch-to-go spot in the Financial District, with long lines of suits queuing for savory Middle Eastern and Turkish delights ($2-5)—everything from falafel and hummus to more exotic fare like *taramasalata* (fish roe dip). Salads $2.75. Open M-F 11am-5pm, Sa 11am-3pm. $10 min. for credit cards. ❶

Legal Sea Foods, 255 State St. (☎227-3115), opposite the New England Aquarium, near T: Aquarium. Now a national chain, Legal Sea Foods remains Boston's finest seafood restaurant. High-quality cuisine at high prices (raw bar $8-9; entrees $18-30), alongside the best clam chowder ($3.75-4.50) in the city, if not the world. Open Su noon-10pm, M-Th 11am-10pm, F-Sa 11am-11pm. ❺

Durgin Park, Quincy Market (☎227-2038). T: Government Ctr. Boston's most touristed restaurant, Durgin Park has been serving (rightfully) rare old New England dishes—like fried seafood, Yankee pot roast, and Indian pudding—since 1827. Meat entrees $9-13. Lobster at market price. Open Su-Th 11:30am-midnight, F-Sa 11:30am-1am. ❹

NORTH END

Boston's Italian-American enclave is the place to go for authentic Italian fare, with over 100 nearly identical red sauce restaurants packed into 1 sq. mi. Quality doesn't vary drastically from place to place, but price does. Most establishments line **Hanover Street,** accessible from T: Haymarket. After dinner, follow the crowds to one of the countless Italian *caffès*. For *cannoli* to go ($2-3), try **Mike's Pastry,** 300 Hanover St., or **Modern Pastry,** 257 Hanover St.

Trattoria Il Panino, 11 Parmenter St. (☎720-1336), at Hanover St. The classic romantic North End *trattoria*—warm lighting, exposed brick, intimate seating, and jovial staff—with equally classic fare in gigantic portions. *Antipasti* $11-13. Pastas $10-15. Chicken dishes $16-17. Open Su-Th 11am-11pm, F-Sa 11am-midnight. ❹ Il Panino also runs the cheaper lunch counter **Il Panino Express,** down the street at 264 Hanover St. Calzones, 1 ft. subs, and salads $5-8. Open daily 11am-11pm. Cash only. ❷

L'Osteria, 104 Salem St. (☎723-7847). Turn left off Hanover St. onto Parmenter St., then right onto Salem St. A simple, reliable *trattoria* that serves all the robust Italian favorites found on Hanover St., but at lower prices. *Antipasti* $7-10. Pastas around $10. Chicken dishes $14-15. Open Su-Th noon-10pm, F-Sa noon-11pm. ❸

Pizzeria Regina, 11 Thatcher St. (☎227-0765). Turn left off Hanover St. onto Prince St., then left again onto Thatcher St. Since 1926, the North End's best pizza (and sassiest waitresses) has come gooey, greasy, and always piping hot. Worth the lengthy wait. Open Su-Th 11am-11pm, F-Sa 11am-midnight. Cash only. ❶

CHINATOWN

Chinatown is *the* place for filling and cheap Asian food (not just Chinese) anytime. Most places stay open until 3-4am, and even though "blue laws" only allow alcohol to be served until 2am, it's rumored that if you ask for "cold tea," you'll get a teapot filled with something that's brewed, but not from tea leaves. Establishments below are accessible from T: Chinatown.

Shabu-Zen, 16 Tyler St. (☎292-8828), off Beach St. Spartan Shabu-Zen is named for its signature do-it-yourself dish *shabu-shabu*. Waitresses offer plates of thinly sliced meats and vegetables that you cook yourself in pots of boiling hot water. 2-person combo plates $10-15, à la carte $5-8. Open daily noon-11pm. ❸

Jumbo Seafood Restaurant, 5-7-9 Hudson St. (☎542-2823). Greet your dinner swimming in the tanks by the entrance at the best of Chinatown's Hong Kong-style seafood spots, with huge plates, a light touch, and a glowing velvet mural on the wall. Dinner entrees $9-13. Lunch specials $5-6. Open Su-Th 11am-1am, F-Sa 11am-2am. ❸

Ginza, 16 Hudson St. (☎338-2261). Walk against traffic down Washington St., turn left at the parking lot onto Beach St., head several blocks down to Hudson St., and turn right. Ginza's sushi doesn't come cheap ($3-10—trust us, it's worth it), but their full lineup of sake bombs will ease whatever pain your bill might inflict. Open Su-M 11:30am-2am, Tu-Sa 11:30am-4am; closed M-F 2:30-5pm, Sa-Su 4-5pm. ❸

BACK BAY

The diverse eateries of the elegant Back Bay line chic **Newbury Street,** accessible from T: Hynes/ICA. Though Newbury is known as Boston's expensive shopping district, affordable restaurants can be found.

Kashmir, 279 Newbury St. (☎536-1695), at Gloucester St. The best Indian food in Boston. Marble floors, traditional carpets, and plush red seats create a setting as light and exotic as the subtly flavored curries ($12-15) and extensive vegetarian menu (entrees $11-13). All-you-can-eat buffet (11am-3pm) M-F $9, Sa-Su $12. Open M-F 11:30am-11pm, Sa-Su noon-11pm. ❹

Parish Café, 361 Boylston St. (☎247-4777), near T: Arlington. With outdoor seating, this lively bar is definitely not a secret among locals, who crowd tables and barstools to order sandwiches ($9-17) designed by the city's hottest chefs. Open Su noon-2am, M-Sa 11:30am-2am. ❸

Island Hopper, 91 Massachusetts Ave. (☎266-1618), at Newbury St. Encyclopedic menu lives up to its name, with a country-hopping array of Chinese and pan-Southeast Asian dishes–from General Gau's Chicken to Burmese Noodles. Entrees $8-16. Lunch specials $7-8. Open Su noon-11pm, M-Th 11:30am-11pm, F-Sa 11:30am-midnight. ❸

SOUTH END

Prices here continue to rise as lines grow ever longer, but the wait and hefty bill are worth it: the South End's restaurants creatively meld flavors and techniques from around the world to create amazing meals. Most eateries line **Tremont Street,** accessible from T: Back Bay.

Addis Red Sea, 544 Tremont St. (☎426-8727). Spicy, curry- and veggie-heavy Ethiopian cuisine in an intimate and sophisticated (but still casual) setting are not to be missed. All entrees are served utensil-free on traditional *mesob* tables, to be scooped up with spongy, slightly sour *injera* bread. Entrees $8-10. 2-person combos $11-17. Open Su noon-10pm, M-F 5-10:30pm, Sa noon-11pm. ❸

NEW ENGLAND

The Dish, 253 Shawmut Ave. (☎617-426-7866), at Milford St. The Dish attains the culinary and atmospheric perfection all casual neighborhood eateries aspire to. Upscale decor meets a low-key local clientele and a menu of gourmet and/or pseudo-Mediterranean updates on classic Americana, such as Cajun-style meatloaf and pork chops with pistachio and goat cheese. Entrees $11-17. Open daily 5pm-midnight. ❹

Flour, 1595 Washington St. (☎267-4300), at Rutland St. T: Newton St. Harvard-educated chef/owner Joanne Chang bakes the most mouth-watering cakes, cookies, and pastries ($1-3) in the city, all nothing short of transcendent. Gourmet sandwiches $6-7. Open Su 9am-3pm, M-F 7am-7pm, Sa 8am-6pm. ❷

Laurel, 142 Berkeley St. (☎424-6711), a few blocks up Columbus St. from T: Back Bay. Patrons receive artful culinary masterpieces ($10-14), like duck confit with sweet potatoes or shrimp and prosciutto ravioli, in huge portions. Open Su 11am-3pm, M-Th 11:30am-2:30pm and 5:30-10pm, F-Sa 11:30am-2:30pm and 5:30-11pm. ❸

JAMAICA PLAIN

Restaurants in "JP" are some of the best bargains in the city, with a variety of ethnic cuisines—the area's Mexican offerings are worth special note. Many places also cater to the neighborhood's large vegetarian and vegan population. The action is centered on **Centre Street,** which runs parallel to the Orange Line (between T: Jackson Sq. and T: Forest Hills).

Bella Luna, 405 Centre St. (☎524-6060). Turn right out of T: Stony Brook. Crispy gourmet pizza in a funky setting–complete with hand-decorated plates, local art on the walls, and crayons at the tables. Medium pizzas $7-14, large $9-18. Check out the **Milky Way Lounge & Lanes,** a bowling alley/karaoke bar upstairs. Open Su noon-10pm, M-W 11am-10pm, Th-Sa 11am-11pm. ❸

El Oriental de Cuba, 416 Centre St. (☎524-6464). Turn right out of T: Stony Brook. No Asian food here—the Oriental of this divey restaurant's name is the Cuban Oriente, home to a hearty, plantain-loving, meat-heavy cuisine. Don't miss the pressed Cuban sandwiches ($5), plantains and beans, or Puerto Rican *mofongo* (mashed garlicky plantains). Entrees $7-10. Open Su 8am-8pm, M-Sa 8am-9pm. ❸

Jake's Boss BBQ, 3492 Washington St. (☎983-3701). Turn right out of T: Green St., then right again onto Washington St. The first solo effort by Boston's most respected pit-master, Kenton Jacobs (the "Jake" of the name), brings real down-home Texas smoked ribs and brisket to these cold northern reaches. Hefty sandwiches around $5.50. Boss dinners $7.50-9.50. Open Su-W 11am-10pm, Th-Sa 11am-11pm. ❷

SIGHTS

THE FREEDOM TRAIL

Passing through the landmarks that put the city on the map in colonial times, the 2½ mi. red-painted path of the Freedom Trail is a great introduction to Boston's history. Even on a trail dedicated to freedom, though, some sights charge admission. Starting at their **Visitors Center,** the National Park Service offers free guided tours of the portion of the Trail from the Old South Meeting House to the Old North Church. *(15 State St., opposite Old State House. ☎242-5642; www.thefreedomtrail.org. Tours mid-June to Aug. daily 10, 11am, 1, 2, 3pm; mid-Apr. to mid-June M-F 2pm. Arrive 30min. before tour start time to get a required ticket. Limit 30 people per tour.)* The Freedom Trail begins at another **Visitors Center,** on Boston Common, outside T: Park St.

BEACON HILL. The Trail first runs uphill to the **Robert Gould Shaw Memorial,** which honors the first black regiment of the Union Army in the American Civil War and their Bostonian leader, made famous by the movie *Glory*. Opposite the memorial is the gold-domed **Massachusetts State House.** *(☎727-3676. Open M-F 10am-4pm. Free; self-guided tour pamphlet available at entrance.)*

DOWNTOWN. Passing the **Park Street Church** *(☎523-3383)*, the trail reaches the **Granary Burial Ground,** where John Hancock, Samuel Adams, Elizabeth Goose (of "Mother Goose" fame), and Paul Revere rest. **King's Chapel & Burying Ground** is America's oldest Anglican church (they ran out of money before they could build a steeple); the latest inhabitants are Unitarian. The burying ground next door is the city's

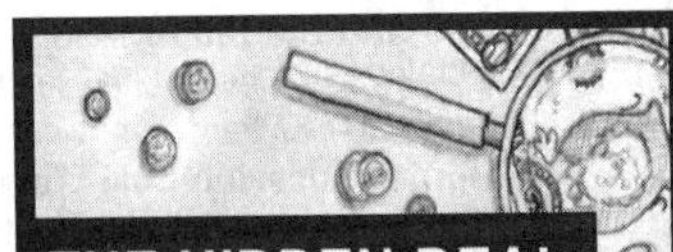

THE HIDDEN DEAL

TAKE ME OUT TO THE BALL GAME

Tiny Fenway Park sells out almost every night, and tickets—the most expensive in baseball—remain hard to come by. Illegal scalpers hawk billets at up to a 500% markup (though after games start, prices plummet).

But fear not: there *are* options for snagging choice seats without parting with a first-born. On game days, the box office sells obstructed-view and standing-room tickets beginning at 9am (line up early, especially for Sox-Yankees games). Obstructed-view seats in the infield are excellent, while standing-room seats offer tremendous views of the field. Risktakers can wait until a few hr. before a game, hoping the team will release the superb seats held for players' friends and families.

Seat quality varies widely. Avoid sections 1-7, unless you enjoy craning your neck for 3hr. The best "cheap" seats are sections 32-36 (32-33 are down the left-field line in the outfield grandstand, close enough to touch the famed Green Monster). Bleacher sections 34-36 have perfect sightlines for watching pitches, but most fans emerge lobster-red from the direct sunlight shining down on the seats.

first and the final resting place of midnight rider William Dawes. *(58 Tremont St. ☎227-2155. Chapel open summer daily 9am-4pm; winter Sa 9am-4pm. Burying Ground open daily summer 9am-5pm; winter 9am-3pm. Chapel $2. Burying Ground free.)* The Charles Bulfinch-designed **Old City Hall,** on School St., is the original site of the country's first public school, the Boston Latin School, which has since relocated to the Fenway. *(☎523-8678.)* Now a tourist trinket shop, the **Old Corner Bookstore** was once the heart of the city's intellectual and literary scene. *(1 School St. ☎367-4000.)* The **Old South Meeting House** was the site of the preliminary meeting that set the mood for the Boston Tea Party. *(310 Washington St. ☎482-6439. Open daily Apr.-Oct. 9:30am-5pm; Nov.-Mar. 10am-4pm. $5, students and seniors $4, ages 6-18 $1.)* Formerly the seat of British government in Boston, the **Old State House** now serves as a fascinating museum chronicling the history of Boston and its place in American history. *(206 Washington St. ☎720-1713. Open daily July-Aug. 9am-6pm; Sept.-June 9am-5pm. $5, students and seniors $4, ages 6-18 $1.)* The Trail passes a circle of bricks marking the site of the **Boston Massacre** en route to **Faneuil Hall** and **Quincy Market,** Boston's most visited tourist sights. A former meeting hall and current mega-mall, the complex is home to a food court and carts selling generally low quality baubles. *(Faneuil Hall ☎242-5675. Open daily 9am-5pm. Tours every 30min. on the 2nd fl.)*

NORTH END. Heading into the Italian-American North End, the Trail crawls through Big Dig rubble to the **Paul Revere House.** *(19 North Sq. ☎523-2338. Open mid-Apr. to Oct. daily 9:30am-5:15pm; Nov.-Dec. and mid-Apr. daily 9:30am-4:15pm; Jan.-Mar. Tu-Su 9:30am-4:15pm. $2.50, students and seniors $2, ages 5-17 $1.)* The **Old North Church** is where Robert Newman was instructed by Revere to hang lanterns—"one if by land, two if by sea"—warning patriots in Charlestown that the British were coming. The church itself still houses such Revolutionary relics as George Washington's hair and tea from the Boston Tea Party. *(193 Salem St. ☎523-6676. Open daily mid-June to Sept. 9am-6pm; Oct. to mid-June 9am-5pm. Suggested donation $3.)* **Copp's Hill Burying Ground,** up Hull St. from the church, is a final resting place for numerous colonial Bostonians, and was a key vantage point in the Battle of Bunker Hill.

CHARLESTOWN. The Battle of Bunker Hill is the focus of much of the rest of the Trail, which heads across the Charles River to the **USS Constitution** (a.k.a. "Old Ironsides") and its companion museum. *(☎426-1812. Ship open Tu-Su 10am-4pm. Museum open daily May-Oct. 9am-6pm; Nov.-Apr. 10am-5pm. Free.)* The Trail winds through residential Charlestown toward the suggestive **Bunker Hill Monument,** which is actually on Breed's Hill—fitting given that the entire Battle of Bunker Hill was actually fought on Breed's Hill. A grand view awaits at the top of the monument's 294 steps. *(Monument Sq. Open daily summer 9am-6pm; winter 9am-5pm. Free.)* The Trail loops back to Boston from Monument Sq., passing **City Square,** the site of the Puritans' original settlement, begun in 1629 when they first arrived in the Boston area.

DOWNTOWN

In 1634, Massachusetts Bay colonists designated the **Boston Common** as a place for their cattle to graze. These days, street vendors, runners, and tourists roam the green, and many congregate near the **Frog Pond,** a wading pool in summer and an ice-skating rink in winter. *(T: Park St.)* Across Charles St. from the Common is the lavishly laid out **Public Garden,** the nation's first botanical garden. Bronze versions of the title characters from the children's book *Make Way for Ducklings* (in the book, they live in the Public Garden) point the way to the **Swan Boats,** graceful paddle-boats that float around a quiet willow-lined pond. *(☎522-1966. $2.50, ages 2-15 $1 for a 15min. ride. Boats open daily spring and summer 10am-5pm, weather permitting.)*

Just steps from the Common is the pedestrian mall at **Downtown Crossing.** The city's biggest budget shopping district is centered around legendary **Filene's Basement,** a chaotic three-floor bargain feeding frenzy. *(426 Washington St. T: Downtown Crossing. ☎542-2011. Open M-F 9:30am-8pm, Sa 10am-5pm, Su 11am-7pm.)*

BEACON HILL

Looming snootily over the Common is aristocratic Beacon Hill, an exclusive residential neighborhood that was the first spot on the Shawmut Peninsula settled by Puritans. Antique shops, pricey cafes, and ritzy boutiques now line charming **Charles Street,** the neighborhood's main artery. For generations, the Hill was home to Boston's intellectual, political, and social elite, christened the "Boston Brahmins." For a taste of Brahmin life, visit the **Nichols House,** preserved as it was in the 19th century. *(55 Mt. Vernon St., off Charles St. T: Charles/MGH. ☎227-6993. Open May-Oct. Tu-Sa noon-4:30pm; Nov.-Apr. Th-Sa noon-4:30pm. $5. Entrance by 30min. guided tour only, given every 30min.; last tour 4pm.)* Quiet **Louisburg Square,** between Mt. Vernon and Pinckney St., was the birthplace of door-to-door Christmas caroling.

The city was the first in America to outlaw slavery, and many blacks moved to the Beacon Hill era after the Civil War. The **Black Heritage Trail** is a free 2hr. (1½ mi.) walking tour through Beacon Hill sights that were important during Boston's abolitionist era. The tour begins at the foot of Beacon Hill, near the Shaw Memorial (p. 121), and ends at the free **Museum of Afro-American History.** *(46 Joy St. ☎720-2991. Museum open June-Aug. daily 10am-4pm; Sept.-May M-Sa 10am-4pm. Heritage Trail tours June-Aug. daily 10am, noon, 2pm; Sept.-May by appointment.)* Also at the foot of the hill is the cheesy **Bull & Finch Pub,** 84 Beacon St., the inspiration for the bar in *Cheers.*

WATERFRONT

The Waterfront district is made up of the wharves along Boston Harbor from South Station to the North End. The excellent **New England Aquarium** presents cavorting penguins, an open animal infirmary, and a bevy of briny beasts in a four-story, 200,000 gallon tank. *(Central Wharf at T: Aquarium. ☎973-5200. Open July-Aug. M-Tu and F 9am-6pm, W-Th 9am-8pm, Sa-Su 9am-7pm; Sept.-June M-F 9am-5pm, Sa-Su 9am-6pm. $15.50, over 60 $13.50, ages 3-11 $8.50. IMAX $7.50, over 60 and ages 3-11 $6.50.)* The Long Wharf, north of Central Wharf, is the departing point for **Boston Harbor Cruises,** which leads history-minded sightseeing cruises and various whale-watching excursions; they also charter boats to the Harbor Islands. *(☎227-4321. Open late May-Sept. Cruises: Sightseeing 45min.-1½hr.; 3 per day; $17, students and seniors $15, under 12 $12. Whale-watching 3hr., $29/25/23.)*

BACK BAY

Now one of Boston's most desirable and eminently walkable districts, the Back Bay was an uninhabitable tidal flat tucked into the "back" corner of the bay until the late 19th century. Today the elegant Back Bay is lined with stately brownstones and spacious, shady promenades laid out in an easily navigable grid. Cross-streets are labeled alphabetically from Arlington to Hereford St. Running through the Back Bay, **Newbury Street,** accessible from T: Hynes/ICA, is an eight-block parade of everything fashionable and form-fitting.

COPLEY SQUARE. Named for painter John Singleton Copley, Copley Sq. is popular with both lunching businessmen and busy Newbury St. tourists looking for a place to rest their feet. The square is dominated by H.H. Richardson's Romanesque fantasy, **Trinity Church,** reflected in the 14 acres of glass used in I.M. Pei's stunning **John Hancock Tower.** The tower is now closed to the public. *(T: Copley. Church ☎536-0944. Open daily 8am-6pm. $4.)* Facing the church, the dramatic **Boston Public**

Library is disguised as a museum; don't miss John Singer Sargent's recently restored *Triumph of Religion* murals or the hidden courtyard. Of the library's 7 million odd books, 128 are copies of *Make Way for Ducklings*. *(☎536-5400. Open M-Th 9am-9pm, F-Sa 9am-5pm; Oct.-May also Su 1-5pm. Free. Free Internet Access. Free 1hr. art and architecture tours M 2:30pm, Tu and Th 6pm, F-Sa 11am; additional tour Oct.-May Su 2pm.)* The 50th fl. of the **Prudential Center** mall next door to Copley Sq. is home to the **Prudential Skywalk,** which offers a 360° view of Boston from a height of 700 ft. *(T: Prudential. ☎859-0648. Skywalk open daily 10am-10pm. $7, over 62 and ages 3-10 $4.)*

CHRISTIAN SCIENCE PLAZA. Down Massachusetts Ave. from Newbury St., the 14-acre Christian Science Plaza is the most well-designed and underappreciated public space in Boston. This epic expanse of concrete, centered on a smooth reflecting pool, is home to the Byzantine-revival "Mother Church," a.k.a. **First Church of Christ, Scientist,** a Christian denomination of faith-based healing founded in Boston by Mary Baker Eddy. *(T: Symphony. Green-E line. ☎450-3790. Open June-Aug. M-Sa 10am-4pm; Sept.-May M-F 10am-4pm. Entrance by free 30-45min. tours. Tours depart on the hr. M-F 10am-3:30pm, Su 11:30am; no tour W noon.)* The adjacent **Mary Baker Eddy Library,** another of Boston's library/museum hybrids, has exhibits on Mrs. Eddy's life and a surreal "hologram fountain," where holographic words pour out of a spout and crawl all over the walls. The **Mapparium,** a glowing, humming, multistory stained-glass globe, depicts the world as it was in 1935, and the globe's perfect acoustics let you whisper in the ear of Pakistan and hear it in Suriname. *(☎222-3711. Open Tu-F 10am-9pm, Sa 10am-5pm, Su 11am-5pm. $5; students, seniors, and children $3.)*

JAMAICA PLAIN

Jamaica Plain offers everything quintessentially un-Bostonian: ample parking, good Mexican food, and Mother Nature. Although it's one of Boston's largest green spaces (over 265 acres), many Boston residents never make it to the lush fields of the **Arnold Arboretum.** A popular spot for bikers, skaters, and joggers, the Arboretum has heaps of flora and fauna from all over the world, including over 500 lilacs that bloom but once, on the second or third Sunday in May—a.k.a. Lilac Sunday. *(T: Forest Hills. ☎524-1718. Open daily dawn-dusk.)* The Arboretum is the next-to-last link in Frederick Law Olmsted's Emerald Necklace, a ring of nine parks around Boston. Near the Arboretum, **Jamaica Pond** is a glacier-made pond (Boston's largest), a popular illicit skinny-dipping spot, and a great place for a quick sail. *(T: Green St. Boathouse ☎522-6258. Sailboats and rowboats $10-15 per hr.)* For an "educational" end to your JP junket, swing by the **Sam Adams Brewery.** At the end of the tour, those 21+ learn how to "taste" beer and can even try brews currently being tested in their labs. *(30 Germania St. T: Stony Brook. ☎522-9080. Tours May-Aug. W and Th 2pm; F 2, 5:30pm; Sa noon, 1, 2pm. Sept.-Apr. Th 2pm; F 2, 5:30pm; Sa noon, 1, 2pm. Free.)*

MUSEUMS

If you're planning a museum binge, consider a **CityPass** (www.citypass.com), which covers admission to the JFK Library, MFA, the Museum of Science, Harvard's Museum of Natural History (p. 130), the Aquarium (p. 123), and the Prudential Center Skywalk (p. 123). Passes, available at museums or online, are valid for nine days. ($30.25, ages 3-17 $18.50.)

Museum of Fine Arts, 465 Huntington Ave. (☎267-9300; www.mfa.org), in Fenway. T: Museum. The exhaustive MFA showcases a globe-spanning array of artwork from every tradition known to mankind—from samurai armor to contemporary American art to medieval instruments. The ancient Egyptian and Nubian galleries (lots of mummies), Impressionist paintings (the largest collection outside France), and the colonial portrait gallery (includes the painting of George Washington found on the $1 bill) are in the collection. Open M-Tu and Sa-Su 10am-4:45pm, W-F 10am-9:45pm (Th-F only West Wing open after 5pm). $15; students and seniors $13; ages 7-17 M-F $6.50, after 3pm free. W after 4pm and all-day Su free, Th-F after 5pm $2 off.

Isabella Stewart Gardner Museum, 280 Fenway (☎566-1401), in Fenway. T: Museum. This astounding private collection remains exactly as eccentric Mrs. Gardner arranged it over a century ago—empty frames even remain where stolen paintings once hung. The Venetian-style *palazzo* architecture gets as much attention as the Old Masters, and the courtyard garden alone is worth the price of admission. Highlights include an original of Dante's *Divine Comedy* and Titian's *Europa,* considered the most important Italian Renaissance work in North America. Open Tu-Su 11am-5pm. M-F $10, Sa-Su $11; students $5; under 18 and individuals named "Isabella" free.

John F. Kennedy Library & Museum (☎929-4500 or 877-616-4599), Columbia Point, just off I-93 in Dorchester, south of Boston. From T: JFK/UMass, take free shuttle #2 "JFK Library" (daily every 20min. 8am-5:30pm). Housed since 1993 in a glass tower designed by I.M. Pei, the JFK Library is a thoughtful monument to Boston's favorite son, 35th US President John Francis Fitzgerald Kennedy. Exhibits trace JFK's career from the campaign trail to his assassination. Plenty of exhibits on his fashion-plate wife Jackie. Open daily 9am-5pm. $8, students and seniors $6, ages 13-17 $4, under 12 free.

Institute of Contemporary Art (ICA), 955 Boylston St. (☎266-5152). in Back Bay. T: Hynes/ICA. Boston's lone outpost of the avant-garde attracts major and minor contemporary artists. Thought-provoking exhibits rotate every 3-4 months. Open W and F noon-5pm, Th noon-9pm, Sa-Su 11am-5pm. $7, students and seniors $5. Th 5-9pm free.

Sports Museum of New England, Fleet Ctr. (☎624-1235), in Downtown. T: North Station. A must for all who understand or want to understand Boston's fanatical sports obsession. Interactive exhibits each dedicated to a different Boston sports franchise. Archival footage, authentic gear, and reconstructions of lockers belonging to Boston's all-time greats. Don't miss Larry Bird's size 14 shoes. Open by tour only, usually M-Th on the hr. 11am-3pm, Su noon and 2pm. $6, seniors and ages 6-17 $4, under 6 free.

Museum of Science, Science Park (☎723-2500). T: Science Park. Seeks to educate and entertain children of all ages with countless interactive exhibits. The must-sees are the giant *Tyrannosaurus rex*; the wacky Theater of Electricity; and the Soundstair, stairs that sing when you step on them. An IMAX Theater and trippy

IN RECENT NEWS

KICKED TO THE CURB

Smokers beware, you will have to start keeping those lighters holstered in Boston. As of May 5, 2003, smoking is banned citywide in all public establishments, including bars and restaurants. Despite some public support, local establishments aren't looking forward to enforcing the ban. Many owners are expressing economic concerns linking smoking to private consumption. They argue that by restricting smoking, especially at bars, patrons will spend less time at establishments and not consume as much (say, alcohol) as they would have otherwise.

Across the Charles River, the city of Cambridge tried to capitalize on the Boston smoking ban, since the ban did not include provisions for Cambridge. Restaurants and bars tried to draw patrons away from Boston with a "We're Still Smoking" campaign. That, however, ended on June 9, 2003, when a new piece of legislation was passed extending the smoking ban to Cambridge. With Cambridge smoke-free, the prediction is that soon all of Massachusetts will implement bans, and smokers visiting Boston and environs will have to take their habit curbside before lighting up.

laser shows are at the Hayden Planetarium. Open Sept.-June Sa-Th 9am-5pm, F 9am-9pm; July-Aug. Sa-Th 9am-7pm, F 9am-9pm. $13, seniors $11, ages 3-11 $10. IMAX or laser show tickets $8.50, seniors $7.50, ages 3-11 $6.50; $3.50 discount on shows after 6pm.

ENTERTAINMENT

The best publications for entertainment and nightlife listings are the *Boston Phoenix* (published every Th; free from streetside boxes) and the *Boston Globe* Calendar section ($0.50, included with Thursday *Boston Globe*). In addition to selling tickets to most major theater shows, **Bostix** sells half-price, day-of-show tickets for select shows from booths at Faneuil Hall (p. 122) and Copley Sq. (p. 123); the web site and booths post which shows are on sale each day. (☎723-5181; www.artsboston.org. Tickets daily 11am. Cash only.)

THEATER

Boston's tiny two-block Theater District, near T: Boylston, west of Chinatown, was once the nation's premier pre-Broadway tryout area. Today it remains a stop for touring Broadway and West End productions, not to mention a sexy nightlife district. The **Charles Playhouse,** 74 Warrenton St., is home to the wacky whodunit *Shear Madness* and the dazzling performance *Blue Man Group*. (*Shear:* ☎426-5225. $34; *Blue Man:* ☎426-6912. $43-53. Half-price student rush tickets available 1hr. before showtime. Volunteer to usher *Blue Man Group* and watch for free.) The giant **Wang Center,** 270 Tremont St., hosts various Broadway productions and the nation's most-watched performance of the Christmastime favorite *The Nutcracker*. (☎482-9393 or 800-447-7400. Box office open M-Sa 10am-6pm.) For more avant-garde productions, check out the **Boston Center for the Arts,** 539 Tremont St. (☎426-2787), in the South End, near T: Back Bay.

CLASSICAL MUSIC

Modeled on the world's most acoustically perfect music hall (the Gewandhaus in Leipzig, Germany), **Symphony Hall,** 301 Massachusetts Ave., T: Symphony, is home to both the well-respected **Boston Symphony Orchestra (BSO)** and its light-hearted sister the **Boston Pops.** The NYC Met's James Levine will take over the position of BSO conductor this year. Every 4th of July, the Pops gives a free evening concert at the Esplanade's **Hatch Shell,** near T: Charles/MGH, bursting with patriotic music, fireworks, and a performance of Tschaikovsky's *1812 Overture* using real cannons. (☎266-1200. Box office open daily 10am-6pm. BSO: Season Oct.-Apr. $25-90; general seating at open rehearsals W night and Th morning $12. Rush Tu and Th 5pm, F 9pm $8. Pops: Season May-July. $15-69.)

SPORTS

Tourists may think of Boston as the Freedom Trail, but Bostonians know that—despite the supposed "Curse of the Bambino" placed on the Boston Red Sox by Babe Ruth—the true heart of the city beats within the gates of storied **Fenway Park.** The nation's oldest, smallest, and most expensive baseball park, Fenway is also home to the Green Monster (the left field wall) and one of only two manual scoreboards left in the major leagues (the other is at Chicago's Wrigley Field; p. 583). Get tickets from the **Ticket Office,** 4 Yawkey Way, T: Kenmore. (☎482-4769. Bleachers $10-20, grandstands $27-44, field boxes $70.) If you are a basketball or hockey fan, head to the **Fleet Center,** 50 Causeway St., at T: North Station. Built on the site of the legendary Boston Garden, this complex hosts concerts and games for basketball's **Celtics** and hockey's **Bruins.** (☎624-1750. Box office open summer M-F 10am-5pm; in season daily 10am-7pm. Celtics $10-140. Bruins $19-99.)

Raced every Patriot's Day (third M in Apr.), the **Boston Marathon,** the nation's oldest foot race, is a 26.2 mi. run that snakes from Hopkinton, MA in the west, passes over "Heartbreak Hill," and ends amid much hoopla at Copley Sq. For over 100 years, the marathon has attracted runners and spectators from all over the world. Since 1965, the **Head of the Charles Regatta** (www.hocr.org)—the world's largest crew regatta—has drawn preppies to the banks of the river every October.

NIGHTLIFE

Before you set out to paint the town red, there are a few things to keep in mind. Boston bars and clubs are notoriously strict about age requirements (usually 21+), so bring back-up ID. Arcane zoning laws require that all nightlife shuts down by 2am. The T stops running at 1am, so bring extra cash for the taxi ride home, or catch the "Night Owl" bus service, which runs until 2:30am F-Sa.

DANCE CLUBS

Boston is a town for pubbers, not clubbers. What few clubs Boston has are on or near Kenmore Sq.'s **Lansdowne Street,** near T: Kenmore.

Avalon, 15 Lansdowne St. (☎262-2424). The flashy, trashy grand dame of Boston's club scene and the closest Puritan Boston gets to Ibiza. World-class DJs, amazing light shows, gender-bending cage dancers, and throngs of hotties pack the giant dance floor. Su gay night. Th-Sa 19+, Su 21+. Cover $15-20. Open Th-Su 10pm-2am.

Pravda 116, 116 Boylston St. (☎482-7799), in the Theatre District. T: Boylston. The caviar, red decor, long lines, and 116 brands of vodka may recall Mother Russia, but capitalism reigns supreme at commie-chic Pravda, the favored haunt of Boston's yuppified 20-somethings. Full house/top 40 dance club and 2 bars (1 made of ice). 21+. Cover W $15, F-Sa $10. Bars open W-Sa 5pm-2am; club W and F-Sa 10pm-2am.

Sophia's, 1270 Boylston St. (☎351-7001). From T: Kenmore, walk down Brookline Ave., turn left onto Yawkey Way, then right onto Boylston St. Far from Lansdowne St. in distance and style, Sophia's is a fiery Latin dance club with 4 floors of salsa, merengue, and Latin music from a mix of live bands and DJs. Trendy, international crowd. 21+. Cover $10; no cover before 9:30pm W-Th and Sa. Open W-Sa 5pm-2am.

Axis, 13 Lansdowne St. (☎262-2437). Smaller, less popular little sister of Avalon has a similar techno beat and identical sweaty college crowd. Popular drag shows M night, hosted by sassy 6 ft. drag diva Mizery. M 18+, Th-Sa 19+. Cover M $7, Th $5, F $20, Sa $10. Open M and Th-Sa 10pm-2am. Upstairs from Axis is a new club called **ID.** 19+. Cover $15. Open Th-Sa same hours as Axis.

BARS AND PUBS

Boston's large student population means the city is filled with great bars and pubs. Most tourists stick to the many faux Irish pubs around **Downtown,** while the **Theatre District** is the premier after-dark destination of the city's international elite. The shamelessly yuppie meat markets on Back Bay's **Boylston Street** are also popular.

Bukowski's Tavern, 50 Dalton St. (☎437-9999), in Back Bay off Boylston St., 1 block south of T: Hynes/ICA. Named for boozer poet Charles Bukowski, Bukowski's casual atmosphere and 99+ bottles of beer on the wall (plus 15 on tap) is the antithesis of Boylston St. chic. Pints $3-20. 21+. No cover. Open daily until 2am. Cash only.

Mantra/OmBar, 52 Temple Pl. (☎542-8111), in Downtown. T: Temple Pl. Seductive. Scandalous. Incomprehensible...and that's just the bathroom, which has 1-way mirrored stalls and ice cubes in the urinals. Pricey fusion restaurant by day, Mantra becomes OmBar by night, complete with a thumping bar in the bank vault downstairs and a smoke-free "hookah den" upstairs—a surreal Ottoman hideaway with plush couches. Cocktails $9. Open M-Sa 5:30pm-2am.

Delux Café, 100 Chandler St. (☎338-5258), at Clarendon St. 1 block south of T: Back Bay, in the South End. Dine or drink (or both) among kooky decorative distractions, like Elvis shrines, blinking Christmas trees, and continuously looped cartoons. Popular with everyone from bike messengers to businessmen. Cocktails $4-5. No cover. Open M-Sa 5pm-1am; food until 11:30pm. Cash only.

Emily's/SW1, 48 Winter St. (☎423-3649), in Downtown. T: Park St. A fun college crowd throngs to this hopping dark Top 40 dance club that was catapulted to fame as the hangout of choice for the cast of MTV's *Real World: Boston*, who lived across the Common in Beacon Hill. Beer $4. Cover $5. Open Tu-Th until midnight, F-Sa until 2am.

Purple Shamrock, 1 Union St. (☎227-2060), in Downtown. From T: Government Ctr., walk through City Hall Plaza to Congress St. This faux pub is popular with college kids. Karaoke Tu starts 9-10pm. 21+. Cover Th-Sa $5. Open daily until 2am.

The Littlest Bar, 47 Province St. (☎523-9766), in Downtown. T: Park St. This very cozy, predominantly local watering hole draws curious tourists and celebrities (note the "Seamus Heaney peed here" sign) hoping for a spot inside what is, in fact, the littlest bar in Boston (just 16 ft. from end to end). Open daily 8:30am-2am. Cash only.

LIVE MUSIC

The live music scene in Boston is impressive—no surprise for the town that gave the world such rockin' acts as Aerosmith, the Dropkick Murphys, and the Mighty Mighty Bosstones. The best acts often play across the river in **Cambridge** (p. 131).

Wally's Café, 427 Massachusetts Ave. (☎424-1408), at Columbus Ave. in the South End. Turn right out of T: Massachusetts Ave. or T: Symphony. Established in 1947, Wally's is Boston's longest-standing jazz joint—and it only improves with age. Live music daily 9pm-2am. 21+. No cover. Cash only.

Paradise Rock Club, 969 Commonwealth Ave. (☎617-562-8800), in Kenmore Sq. Visible from T: Pleasant St., which runs along Commonwealth Ave. This smoky, spacious, Asian fetish-themed venue has been known to host well-known national and international rock acts, including U2 and Soul Asylum. 18+. Cover $10-20.

GAY & LESBIAN NIGHTLIFE

For up-to-date listings of gay and lesbian nightlife, pick up a free copy of the South End-based *Bay Windows*, a gay weekly available everywhere, or check the lengthy listings in the free *Boston Phoenix* and *Improper Bostonian*.

The **South End's** bars and late-night restaurants, accessible from T: Back Bay, are all gay-friendly (sorry ladies, these are mostly spots for the boys). The sports bar **Fritz,** 26 Chandler St. (☎482-4428), and divey **The Eagle,** 520 Tremont St. (☎542-4494), are exclusively for gay men. Boston's other major exclusively gay bar/clubs are the Theatre District's **Vapor/Chaps,** 100 Warrenton St. (☎695-9500); **Jacque's,** 77-79 Broadway (☎426-8902); and **Europa/Buzz,** 51 and 67 Stuart St. (☎482-3939). In Fenway is **Ramrod,** 1256 Boylston St. (☎266-2986), a Leather & Levis spot that spawned a non-fetish dance club known as **Machine.** Popular gay nights at straight clubs include Avalon's Sunday bash (p. 127)—preceded by the early evening "T-Dance" at Vapor—and sassy drag night at Axis on Monday (p. 127).

Lesbians flock to **Jamaica Plain's** bookstores and cafés, many of which are queer-owned. On Thursdays, the girls all trek out to **Midway Café,** 3496 Washington St. (☎524-9038), south of T: Green St. (Orange), for the popular (and very cruisy) **Dyke Night.** On Fridays, queer women flock to **"Circuit Girl"** at Europa/Buzz, then rest on Saturday in preparation for Sunday's **"Trix"** lesbian night at Machine.

OUTDOOR ACTIVITIES

For such a major urban center, Boston has a surprising number of green spaces and outdoor opportunities—thanks largely to the **Emerald Necklace,** a continuous string of nine parks ringing the city. Designed by Frederick Law Olmsted (1822-1903), who also created New York's Central Park (p. 223) and San Francisco's Golden Gate Park (p. 935), the Necklace runs from Boston Common and the Public Garden along the Commonwealth Avenue Mall, the Back Bay Fens and Riverway, Jamaica Plain's Olmsted Park, Jamaica Pond, and Arnold Arboretum (p. 124), ending finally at far-flung Franklin Park. The spots in Jamaica Plain, especially the Arboretum, are the most popular with bikers, skaters, runners, and picnickers.

The **Charles River** separates Boston from Cambridge and is popular with outdoors enthusiasts. Though swimming is strongly discouraged, runners, bikers, and skaters crowd the **Charles River Esplanade** park, which runs along the Charles' banks. The Esplanade is home to the **Hatch Shell,** where Boston's renowned 4th of July festivities take place. Rent watercraft from **Charles River Canoe & Kayak,** beyond Eliot Bridge in the west. (☎462-2513. Canoes $12 per hr., $48 per day; kayaks $13/52. Open May-Oct. Th 4pm to 30min. before sunset, F 1pm to 30min. before sunset, Sa-Su and holidays 10am to 30min. before sunset.)

Serious hikers should consider the **Harbor Islands National Park,** made up of the 30-odd wooded islands floating in Boston Harbor that are ringed with pristine beaches and blanketed with miles of hiking trails. The most popular islands include Lovell's (with the islands' best beach) and Bumpkin (wild berry paradise). **Boston Harbor Cruises** runs ferries from Long Wharf at T: Aquarium to George's Island. (☎223-8666; www.bostonislands.com. Open May-Oct. daily 9am-sunset, hours vary by island. Ferries run daily May-June and Sept.-Oct. 10am, 2, 4pm; July-Aug. on the hr. 9am-5pm. Ferry ticket $8, seniors $7, children $6; includes free shuttles to other islands from George's Island.)

NEAR BOSTON

CAMBRIDGE ☎617

Although it is separated from Boston by only a small river, Cambridge (pop. 100,000)—often referred to as Boston's "Left Bank" for its liberal politics and Bohemian flair—has always been worlds away from conservative Boston in both history and temperament. The city has thrived as an intellectual hotbed since the colonial era, when it became the home of prestigious **Harvard University,** the nation's first college. The **Massachusetts Institute of Technology (MIT),** the country's foremost school for the study of science and technology, moved here in the early 20th century. Cambridge's counterculture vibe has died down since its 1960s heyday, but the city remains a vibrant place, with dozens of bookstores and shops, a large student population, and superior food and nightlife options.

PRACTICAL INFORMATION. Across the Charles River from Boston, Cambridge is best visited as a daytrip, easily reached by a 10min. T ride from Downtown. Accommodations are expensive; it's best to stay in Boston. Cambridge's main artery, **Massachusetts Avenue ("Mass Ave."),** runs parallel to the T's Red Line, which makes stops along the street. The **Kendall/MIT** stop is just across the river from Boston, near MIT's campus. The Red Line continues to: **Central Square,** a bar-hopper's paradise; **Harvard Square,** the city's chaotic heart; and largely residential **Porter Square.** Harvard Sq. sits at the intersection of Mass. Ave., Brattle St., JFK St., and Dunster St. The **Cambridge Office For Tourism** runs a booth outside T:

Harvard (Red) with plenty of maps and info. (☎441-2884; www.cambridge-usa.org. Open M-F 9am-5pm, Sa 10am-3pm, Su 1-5pm.) **Internet Access: Adrenaline Zone,** 40 Brattle St., in Harvard Sq. (☎876-1314. Open Su-Th 11am-11pm, F-Sa 11am-midnight. $5 per hr.) **Post Office:** 770 Mass Ave. (☎876-0550), in Central Sq., and 125 Mt. Auburn St. (☎876-3883), in Harvard Sq. (Both open M-F 7:30am-6pm, Sa 7:30am-3pm.) **Postal Code:** 02138. **Area Code:** 617. 10-digit dialing required.

FOOD. Cambridge is a United Nations of ethnic eateries, from Mexican to Tibetan. Most visitors stick to the spots in Harvard Sq. The all-you-can-eat lunch buffets ($7-9, served daily 11:30am-3pm) at Cambridge's many Indian restaurants are as much cherished local institutions as Harvard or MIT. One of the best is **Tanjore ❷,** 18 Eliot St. (☎868-1900), off JFK St. **Darwin's Limited ❷,** 148 Mt. Auburn St., is a 5min. walk from Harvard Sq. proper: exit the T onto Brattle St. and turn right at the Harvard Sq. Hotel onto Mt. Auburn St.; it's six to seven blocks up on the left. The Bohemian staff at his deli counter (with attached cafe) craft Boston's best gourmet sandwiches ($5-6.25), served on fresh bread and named after nearby streets. (☎354-5233. Open Su 7am-7pm, M-Sa 6:30am-9pm. Cash only.) Indian restaurants are a rupee a dozen in Cambridge, but **Punjabi Dhaba ❷,** 225 Hampshire St., in Inman Sq., stands above the rest with its incredibly cheap, spicy menu. (☎547-8272. Veggie dishes $5; huge combos $8. Open daily noon-midnight. Cash only.) For over 40 years, **Bartley's Burger Cottage ❸,** 1246 Mass Ave., has been serving some of the area's juiciest burgers, named after famous folk. Try the Ted Kennedy, a "plump liberal" burger. (☎354-6559. Burgers $8-12. Open M-Tu and Sa 11am-9pm; W-F 11am-10pm. Cash only.) **Emma's Pizza ❷,** 40 Hampshire St. (☎617-864-8534), opposite the 1 Kendall Sq. complex, dishes up the best gourmet pizza in Boston. (☎864-8534. Combos $15-20. 6-slice 12 in. pies $8; 8-slice 16 in. pies $11. Open Tu-F 11:30am-10pm, Sa 4-10pm.) Cool off with a so-smooth-it's-illegal scoop from **Toscanini's ❶,** 1310 Mass Ave. Will it be burnt caramel or cassis sorbet? (☎354-9350. Scoop $3. Open Su-Th 8am-10pm, F-Sa 8am-11pm.)

SIGHTS. Harvard Sq. is of course named after **Harvard University.** The student-led tours offered by **Harvard Events & Information,** Holyoke Ctr. Arcade (across Dunster St. from the T), are the best way to tour the university's dignified red-brick-and-ivy campus and learn about its sometimes tumultuous history. (☎495-1573; www.harvard.edu. Open M-Sa 9am-5pm. Tours Sept.-May M-F 10am, 2pm, Sa 2pm; June-Aug. M-Sa 10, 11:15am, 2, 3:15pm.) **Harvard Yard,** just off Mass Ave., is the heart of undergraduate life and the site of commencement. The massive **Harry Elkins Widener Memorial Library,** in Harvard Yard, houses nearly 5 million of Harvard's 13.3 million book collection, making it the world's largest university library collection.

Harvard's many museums are well worth a visit. The disorganized **Arthur M. Sackler Museum,** 485 Broadway, at Quincy St. just off Mass. Ave., has four floors of East Asian, pre-Columbian, Islamic, and Indian treasures. Across the street, the **Fogg Art Museum,** 32 Quincy St., offers a small survey of North American and European work from the Middle Ages to the early 20th century, with a strong Impressionist collection and several great van Gogh portraits. Inside the Fogg, the excellent **Busch-Reisinger Museum** is dedicated to modern German work. (All 3 museums: ☎495-9400. Open M-Sa 10am-5pm, Su 1-5pm. $6.50, students and seniors $4, under 18 free. Sa 10am-noon free.) Continue your artistic education next door at the Le Corbusier-designed **Carpenter Center,** 24 Quincy St., which displays the hottest contemporary art by both students and professionals. The **Harvard Film Archive (HFA),** in the basement of the Carpenter, has a great art-house film series. Schedules are posted outside the door. (Carpenter ☎495-3251. Open M-Sa 9am-11pm, Su noon-11pm. Galleries free. HFA ☎495-4700. $7, students and seniors $5.) The **Harvard Museum of Natural History,** 26 Oxford St., has interesting exhibits on botany, comparative zoology, and geology, including the famous **Glass Flowers**—over 3000 incredibly lifelike, life-sized glass models of plants. (☎495-3045. Open daily 9am-5pm. $7.50, students and seniors $6, ages 3-18 $5. Su 9am-noon and Sept.-May W 3-5pm free.)

Kendall Sq., T: Kendall/MIT, is home to the **Massachusetts Institute of Technology (MIT),** the world's leading institution dedicated to the study of science. Free campus tours begin at the **MIT Info Center,** 77 Mass Ave., in Lobby 7/Small Dome building, and include visits to the Chapel and Kresge Auditorium, which touches the ground in only three places. (☎253-1000; www.mit.edu. Tours M-F 10am, 2pm.) The **MIT Museum,** 265 Mass Ave., features cutting-edge technological wonders in dazzling multimedia exhibitions. Highlights include a gallery of "hacks" (elaborate, if nerdy, campus pranks) and the world's largest hologram collection. (☎253-4444. Open Tu-F 10am-5pm, Sa-Su noon-5pm. $5; students, seniors, and ages 5-18 $2.)

ENTERTAINMENT. Some of the Boston area's best live music spots are in Central Sq., T: Central. **The Middle East,** 472-480 Mass. Ave. (☎864-3278), and **T.T. the Bear's Place,** 10 Brookline St. (☎492-2327), at Mass Ave., feature live music every night from the nation's hottest indie rock acts. Harvard Sq.'s **Club Passim,** 47 Palmer St., at Church St., off Mass Ave., is a folk music legend: a 17-year-old Joan Baez premiered here, while Bob Dylan played between sets, and countless acoustic acts have hit this intimate venue before making it big. (☎492-7679. Open mic Tu 7pm. Cover $10-20. Box office open daily 6:30-10pm.)

NIGHTLIFE. On weekend nights, **Harvard Square** is equal parts gathering place, music hall, and three-ring circus, with tourists, locals, and pierced suburban punks enjoying the varied street performers, from magicians to Andean flute players. During the school year, stressed Harvard students unwind as much as they can in the square's many bars, but Cambridge's best nightlife options are in **Central Square,** a bar-hopper's heaven not yet overrun by yuppies or tourists. Most bars are open until 1am, with some staying open until 2am on the weekends. The harem-like **Enormous Room,** 567 Mass. Ave., unmarked save an outline of a bull elephant on the window, is too seductive to resist. Amidst sultry arabesque lighting and couches and floor pillows for lounging, a well-scrubbed mixed crowd jives to music from a hidden DJ. (☎491-5550. Beer $4. Mixed drinks $6-9. Cash only.) **The People's Republik,** 878-880 Massachusetts Ave. Cheeky chalkboards outside entice passersby to drop in for a drink ("Drink beer—It's cheaper than gasoline"), and proletarians do indeed choose beer over vodka at this Communist-themed dive. (☎491-6969. Beer $2-4; cocktails $4-4.50. No cover. Open Su-W noon-1am, Th-Sa noon-2am. Cash only.) **The Field,** 20 Prospect St., off Mass. Ave., is the best of Central Sq.'s many faux Irish pubs. An attractive crowd gathers in three warmly and eclectically decorated rooms. (☎354-7345. Beer and mixed drinks $3.75-4.50.) A typical-looking Irish pub on the outside, **The Phoenix Landing,** 512 Mass. Ave., literally throbs with the sounds of some of the area's best electric and downtempo grooves. (☎576-6260. Su and W-Th 19+, M-Tu and F-Sa 21+. Cover $3-5.) **The Good Life,** 720 Mass. Ave., is a snazzy nightspot with a casual crowd and high-class atmosphere—jazz, plush booths, and 1950s-era cocktails. (☎868-8800. Drinks $5-7.)

LEXINGTON ☎781

"Stand your ground. Don't fire unless fired upon, but if they mean to have a war, let it begin here," said Captain John Parker to the colonial Minutemen on April 19, 1775. Although no one is certain who fired the "shot heard 'round the world," the American Revolution did indeed erupt in downtown Lexington. The site of the fracas lies in the center of town at **Battle Green,** where a Minuteman Statue still stands guard. The fateful command itself was issued from across the street at the

Buckman Tavern, 1 Bedford St. (☎862-5598), which housed the Minutemen on the eve of their decisive battle. The nearby **Hancock-Clarke House,** 36 Hancock St. (☎861-0928), and the **Munroe Tavern,** 1332 Mass. Ave. (☎862-1703), also played significant roles in the birth of the Revolution. All three can be seen on a 30min. tour that runs continuously. (All open Mar.-Nov. M-Sa 10am-5pm, Su 1-5pm Call ahead, as hours often change. $5 per site, ages 6-16 $3; combo ticket for all 3 $12/7.) The **Museum of Our National Heritage,** 33 Marrett Rd. (Rte. 2A), emphasizes a historical approach to understanding popular American life, especially at the time of the Revolution. (☎861-6559. Open M-Sa 10am-5pm, Su noon-5pm. Free.)

The road from Boston to Lexington is easy. Drive straight up Mass Ave. from Boston or Cambridge, or bike the excellent **Minuteman Trail** to downtown Lexington (access off Mass Ave. in Arlington, or Alewife St. in Cambridge). MBTA bus #62/76 from T: Alewife runs to Lexington (20min., $0.75). An excellent model and description of the Battle of Lexington decorates the **Visitors Center,** 1875 Mass. Ave., opposite Battle Green. (☎862-1450. Open daily May-Oct. 9am-5pm; Nov.-Apr. 10am-4pm.) **Area code:** 781.

CONCORD ☎978

Concord, site of the second conflict of the American Revolution, is famous both for its military history and for its status as a 19th-century intellectual center. The period rooms at the **Concord Museum,** 200 Lexington Rd., on the Cambridge Turnpike, move through Concord's three centuries of history. Highlights include the original lamp from Paul Revere's midnight ride and an exhibit of Ralph Waldo Emerson's study, which is curiously missing from his well-preserved 19th-century home across the street. (☎369-9609. Open Apr.-Dec. M-Sa 9am-5pm, Su noon-5pm; Jan.-Mar. M-Sa 11am-4pm, Su 1-4pm. $7, students and seniors $6, ages 5-18 $3; families $16. Emerson House by 30min. guided tour only. $6, seniors and ages 7-17 $4.) Down the road from the museum, the **Orchard House,** 399 Lexington Rd., was once home to the multi-talented Alcotts, whose daughter Louisa May wrote *Little Women.* (☎369-4118. Open Apr.-Oct. M-Sa 10am-4:30pm, Su 1-4:30pm; Nov.-Mar. M-F 11am-3pm, Sa 10am-4:30pm, Su 1-4:30pm. $8, students and seniors $7, ages 6-17 $5; families $20. Guided tour only.) Farther down the road lies **Wayside,** 455 Lexington Rd., the former residence of the Alcotts and Hawthornes. (☎369-6975. Open May-Oct. Th-Tu 10am-5pm. $4, under 17 free. Guided tour only.) Today, Alcott, Hawthorne, Emerson, and Thoreau reside on "Author's Ridge" in the **Sleepy Hollow Cemetery** on Rte. 62, three blocks from the center of town.

The spot from which "the shot heard 'round the world" was fired is over the **Old North Bridge.** From the parking lot, a 5min. walk brings visitors to the **North Bridge Visitors Center,** 174 Liberty St., to learn about the town's history, especially its involvement in the Revolutionary War. (☎369-6993. Open daily Apr.-Oct. 9am-5pm; Nov.-Mar. 9am-4pm.) The **Minuteman National Historical Park,** off Rte. 2A between Concord and Lexington, best explored along the adjacent 5½ mi. **Battle Road Trail,** includes an impressive **Visitors Center** that organizes battle reenactments and screens a multimedia presentation on the "Road to Revolution." (☎781-862-7753. Off Rte. 2A between Concord and Lexington. Open daily Apr.-Nov. 9am-5pm; Dec.-Mar. 9am-4pm.) Concord, north of Boston, is served by the Fitchburg commuter rail train ($4) that runs from T: North Station. **Area Code:** 978.

NEAR CONCORD: WALDEN POND ☎978

In 1845, Thoreau retreated 1½ mi. south of Concord "to live deliberately, to front only the essential facts of life" (though the harsh essence of *his* life was eased from time to time by his mother's home cooking; she lived within walking distance of his cabin). In 1845, he published his thoughts on his time here under the title *Walden*, now considered one of the major works of the Transcendentalist movement. The **Walden Pond State Reservation,** 915 Walden St., off Rte. 126, draws picnickers, swimmers, and boaters and is mobbed in summer. No camping, pets, or "novelty flotation devices" allowed. Although visiting after the pond closes is forbidden, it has become something of a rite of passage for local college students to break in after dark and go skinny-dipping. (☎369-3254. Open daily dawn-dusk. Parking $5.) When Walden Pond is swarming with "classy" flotation devices, head east from Concord center on Rte. 62 to another of Thoreau's haunts, **Great Meadows National Wildlife Refuge,** on Monsen Rd. (☎443-4661. Open daily dawn-dusk. Free.)

SALEM ☎978

Salem is generally considered the Halloween headquarters of the world, and though it has much more to offer, it isn't trying that hard to free itself from that stereotype. The **Salem Witch Museum,** 19½ Washington Sq. N., gives a melodramatic but informative multimedia presentation detailing the history of the infamous 17th-century witch trials. It also presents an interesting exhibit on the role of scapegoating throughout history. (☎744-1692. Open daily July-Aug. 10am-7pm; Sept.-June 10am-5pm. $6, seniors $5.50, ages 6-14 $4. Cash only.) Escape the witch kitsch at the **Witch Trials Memorial,** off Charter St., where engraved stones commemorate the trials' 19 victims.

Salem's **Peabody Essex Museum,** East India Sq., on the corner of Essex and New Liberty St., recalls the port's prouder past, its leading role in Atlantic whaling and merchant shipping. Admission includes tours of four historic Salem houses. (☎800-745-4054 or 745-9500. Open Su-W and F-Sa 10am-7pm, Th 10am-9pm. $12, seniors $10, students $8, under 17 free.) Built in 1668 and officially named the Turner-Ingersoll Mansion, Salem's **House of Seven Gables,** 54 Turner St., became the "second most famous house in America" after the release of Concord-born Nathaniel Hawthorne's Gothic romance of the same name. (☎744-0991. Open July-Oct. daily 10am-7pm; Nov.-Dec. and Feb.-Jun. M-Sa 10am-5pm, Su noon-5pm. $10, seniors $9, ages 5-12 $6.50, under 5 free. By 30min. guided tour only.)

The **Salem Visitors Center,** 2 New Liberty St., has free maps, public restrooms, historical displays, and a gift shop. (☎740-1650. Open daily July-Aug. 9am-6pm; Sept.-June 9am-5pm.) Salem, 20 mi. northeast of Boston, is accessible by the Newburyport/Rockport commuter rail train (30min., $3) from Boston's North Station, by MBTA bus #450 or 455 (45min., $0.75) from T: Haymarket, or by car from I-95 or U.S. 1 N. to Rte. 128 and Rte. 114. **Area code:** 978.

PLYMOUTH ☎508

Despite what textbooks say, the Pilgrims' first step onto the New World was *not* at Plymouth. They stopped first at Provincetown (see p. 137), then promptly left because the soil was inadequate. **Plymouth Rock** is a small stone that has dubiously been identified as the rock on which the Pilgrims disembarked, the second time. It served as a symbol of liberty during the American Revolution and since then, has moved three times before ending up at its current home, beneath an extravagant portico on Water St., at the foot of North St. After several vandalization episodes, and one dropping (in transit) it's cracked, and under "tight" security.

Three miles south of town off Rte. 3A, the historical theme park **Plimoth Plantation** recreates the Pilgrims' early settlement. In the **Pilgrim Village,** costumed actors play the roles of actual villagers carrying out their daily tasks, while **Hob-**

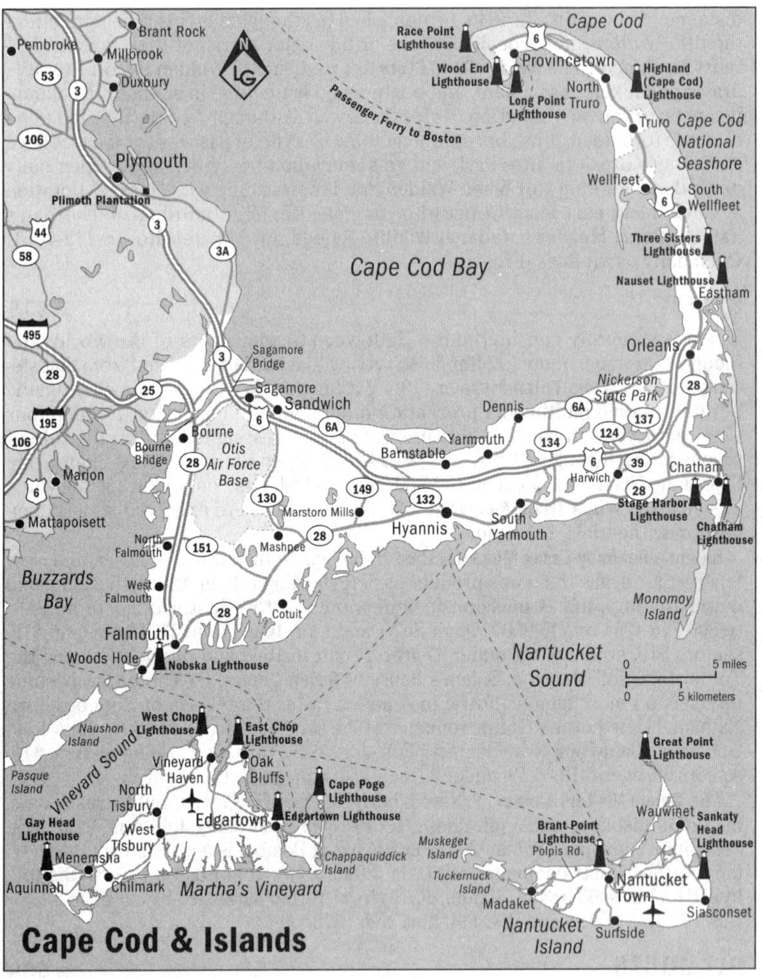

bamock's Homesite represents a Native American village of the same period. (☎746-1622. Open Apr.-Nov. daily 9am-5pm. $20, ages 6-12 $12; $2 AAA discount.) Docked off Water St., the **Mayflower II** is a 1950s scale replica of the Pilgrims' vessel and is staffed by actors to recapture the atmosphere of the original ship. (Open Apr.-Nov. daily 9am-5pm. $8, ages 6-12 $6. Admission to both sights $22, students and seniors $20, ages 6-12 $14; $3 AAA discount.)

Plymouth, 40 mi. southeast of Boston, is best explored by car; take Exit 6A from Rte. 3, off I-93. **Plymouth & Brockton Bus** (☎746-0378) runs from T: South Station to the Exit 5 Info Ctr. (1hr., $9). Plymouth/Kingston commuter rail train goes from T: North Station to the Cordage Park Station (1hr., 3-4 per day, $5). From the info center and Cordage Park Station, catch a local GATRA bus ($0.75, seniors and children $0.35) to Plymouth center. **Plymouth Visitors Center** is at 170 Water St. (☎747-7525 or 800-872-1620. Open Apr.-May and Sept.-Nov. daily 9am-5pm; June 9am-6pm; July-Aug. 9am-9pm.) **Area code:** 508.

NEW ENGLAND

CAPE COD & ISLANDS ☎508

Writer Henry David Thoreau once said in his book *Cape Cod*: "[the Cape] is wholly unknown to the fashionable world, and probably will never be agreeable to them." Heh. Now New England's premier vacation destination, this thin strip of land draws tourists by the droves with its charming small towns and diverse, sun-drenched landscapes—everything from cranberry bogs and sandy beaches to deep freshwater ponds carved by glaciers and desert-like dunes sculpted by the wind. Though parts of the Cape are known as the playground of the rich and famous—and the peninsula is in general geared toward bigger spenders—it can be an option for budget travelers, thanks to an emphasis on free activities, like sunbathing and hiking, and a decent hostel and budget B&B system.

ORIENTATION

Stretching out into the Atlantic Ocean south of Boston, Cape Cod resembles a bent arm, with **Falmouth** and **Woods Hole** at its armpit, **Hyannis** at its bicep, **Chatham** at its elbow, the **National Seashore** tattooed on its forearm, and **Provincetown** at its clenched fist. The southern islands **Martha's Vineyard** (p. 139) and **Nantucket** (p. 141) are accessible by ferries from Woods Hole or Hyannis.

Cape locations can be confusing. **Upper Cape** refers to the suburbanized, more developed area closer to the mainland. Proceeding eastward away from the mainland and curving up along the Cape, you travel **Down Cape** through **Mid-Cape** (where the Cape's two hostels are, near **Eastham** and **Truro**), finally hitting the **Lower Cape** and the National Seashore. In summer, traffic to and from the Cape is hell: vacationers drive out on Friday and return Sunday afternoon, so avoid traveling then.

Cycling is the best way to travel the Cape's gentle slopes. The park service has free trail maps and the highly recommended and detailed *Cape Cod Bike Book* ($3), also available at most Cape bookstores. The 135 mi. **Boston-Cape Cod Bikeway** connects Boston to Provincetown, and the trails that line either side of the **Cape Cod Canal** in the National Seashore rank among the country's most scenic, as does the 25 mi. **Cape Cod Rail Trail** from Dennis to Wellfleet. For discount coupons good throughout the Cape, pick up a free *Official 2004 Guide to Cape Cod* or *Cape Cod Best Read Guide*, available at most Cape info centers. **Area code:** 508.

FALMOUTH & WOODS HOLE ☎508

Coming from Boston, Falmouth and Woods Hole are the first true Cape towns day-trippers encounter. Unlike other places on the Cape, these towns sustain a decent-sized year-round population and in summer tend to have less of a touristed feel, as most people bypass them to drive farther up the Cape or catch the ferry to the Islands. The beach reigns proudly as the main attraction, but at times, it can become a bit of a social scene. Check out **Chapoquoit,** south of Old Silver, on the western shore of North Falmouth to avoid the scene and relax peacefully, or **Falmouth Heights** on the southern shore of Falmouth, along Grand Ave. if you have the goods and feel like showing off. **Old Silver** beach and **Stoney** beach are also popular destinations, but lack the extreme nature of the other two. Accommodations are plentiful and nearly identical. The **Village Green Inn ❹,** 40 Main St., is maybe the best, most lauded accommodation on the Cape, with peaceful rooms, attentive service, and an excellent breakfast. (☎548-5621 or 800-237-1119. Doubles $90-175; 2-person suites $150-235. Third person additional $30.) For inexpensive, diet-busting fried seafood ($5-12), check out the **Clam Shack ❷,** 227 Clinton Ave., an always-busy, lively spot right on the water. (☎540-7758. Open June-Aug. daily 11:30am-8pm.) After-hours don't miss **Captain Kidd's,** 77 Water St. in Woods Hole. It's a local bar with no gimmicks, just strong drinks and a view of the harbor. (☎548-8563. Open daily 11am-1am.) **Bonanza Bus** (☎888-751-8800; www.bonanzabus.com) leaves from Logan Airport and South Station in Boston and stops at Falmouth Bus Station, on Depot St. (1½hr.; one-way $22, round-trip $40.) The bus continues on to the ferry terminal in Woods Hole for the same price.

HYANNIS ☎508

Hyannis is not the Cape Cod most people expect. Though JFK spent his summers in nearby Hyannisport, Hyannis proper is little more than a transportation hub (ferries to Nantucket depart from here) with a depressing Main St. and tacky mall—a far cry from the quaint villages farther out on the Cape. What it lacks in cuteness it partly makes up in watersports. **Kalmus Park Beach,** on Ocean St. in Hyannisport, is popular with windsurfers, while **Orrin Keyes Beach,** on Sea St., attracts more of a local crowd. **Veteran's Park Beach,** off Ocean St., is great for families. All have parking ($10), lifeguards, bathhouses, snack bars, picnic areas, and wheelchair accessibility. If you're bored or hungry, make sure to visit the **Cape Cod Potato Chip Factory,** 100 Breeds Hill Rd., for history, a tour, and a free bag of those delicious kettle-cooked chips. (☎775-3358. Tours M-F 9am-5pm. Free.) Hyannis is full of cookie-cutter motels and inns. The immense **Hyannis Inn Motel ❸,** 473 Main St., has large, clean rooms with cable TV and mini-fridges. (☎775-0255. Open mid-Mar. to mid-Oct. Doubles $62-126; deluxe rooms $72-141, with whirlpool $97-165.) For inexpensive, delicious sandwiches ($4-6), head to **Box Lunch ❶,** 357 Main St., a local Cape Cod chain. (☎790-5855. Open M-F 9am-6pm, Sa 10am-10pm, Su 10am-5pm.) Identical upscale seafood restaurants line Main St., with entrees averaging $12-20. **Plymouth & Brockton** (☎746-0378) runs from Boston's South Station to the brand new Hyannis Transportation Center, off Main St. (1½hr.; M-F 24 per day 7am-midnight, Sa-Su 17 per day 7am-midnight; $14.)

CAPE COD NATIONAL SEASHORE ☎508

As early as 1825, the Cape had suffered so much man-made damage that the town of Truro required local residents to plant beach grass and keep their cows off the dunes. These conservation efforts culminated in 1961, when the National Park Service created the Cape Cod National Seashore. The seashore includes much of the Lower and Outer Cape from Provincetown south to Chatham. The National Seashore has six beaches: **Coast Guard** and **Nauset Light,** in Eastham; **Marconi,** in Wellfleet; **Head of the Meadow,** in Truro; and **Race Point** and **Herring Cove,** in Provincetown. There are 11 self-guided nature trails and three bike trails. Parking at the beaches is expensive. (In summer Sa-Su and low-season holidays $10 per day, $30 per season; different rates for Marconi and Head of the Meadow.) Among the best of the seashore's 11 self-guided **nature trails** are the **Great Island Trail** and the **Atlantic White Cedar Swamp Trail.** The Great Island Trail, in Wellfleet, traces an 8 mi.loop through pine forests and grassy marshes and has views of the bay and Provincetown. The **Atlantic White Cedar Swamp Trail,** a 1¼ mi. walk, starts at Marconi Station in south Wellfleet and trickles past swampy waters and under towering trees. There are also three bike trails: **Nauset Trail** (1½ mi.), **Head of the Meadow Trail** (2 mi.), and **Province Lands Trail** (5 mi.). Park rangers at the **National Seashore's Salt Pond Visitors Center,** at Salt Pond, off Rte. 6 in Eastham, provide maps, schedules for guided tours, and additional information about the park. (☎255-3421. Open daily July-Aug. 9am-5pm; Sept.-June 9am-4:30pm.) Camping in the National Seashore is illegal. Eastham's **Mid-Cape Hostel (HI-AYH) ❶,** 75 Goody Hallet Dr., close to the bike path known as the **Cape Cod Rail Trail,** features communal bungalow living in a woodsy location. From Rte. 6, take the Rock Harbor Exit at the Orleans Ctr. rotary, turn right onto Bridge Rd., then right again onto Goody Hallet Dr. By P&B bus, ask the drive to let you off as close as possible, and call the hostel for the "shortcut" directions along walking paths. (☎255-2785 or ☎888-901-2085. Shared bathrooms, kitchen, and barbecue facilities. Bike rental $5 per day. 7-day max. stay. Open late June-early Sept. Dorms $19, nonmembers $22.) **Truro Hostel (HI-AYH) ❶,** 111 North Pamet Rd., in Truro, sits on a bluff overlooking the ocean, and offers a large kitchen, porch, and access to Ballston Beach all in a turn-of-the-century converted Coast Guard station. Men sleep downstairs; women sleep upstairs. From Rte. 6, take the Pamet Rd. exit, which becomes North Pamet Rd. Free linen. Check-in 4-9pm. Check-out 7:30-10am. Curfew 10pm. Members $22, nonmembers $25. (☎508-349-3889 or 888-901-2086. Open late June-early Sept. 8-10am and 4-10pm.) **Plymouth & Brockton** (☎746-0378) runs buses from Boston's South Station through the towns on the seashore (2½hr.; $18, round-trip $35). By car, take Rte. 3 to Rte. 6 west, cross the Sagamore Bridge, and follow signs.

PROVINCETOWN ☎508

At first glance, Provincetown may seem like a typical Cape Cod village with a slight cosmopolitan twist. What sets it apart is its popularity as one of the premier gay and lesbian communities and vacation spots on the East Coast. The first landing site of the Pilgrims in 1620, Provincetown was a key fishing and whaling center in the 1800s, attracting a large Portuguese population. In the early 20th century, the town's popularity soared with resident artists and writers like Norman Mailer, Tennessee Williams, and Edward Hopper. Provincetown's tradition of tolerance and open-mindedness soon began to attract the gay community, who now fill the town to its rim in summer. Though far from inexpensive, P-town has better options for outdoors, dining, and nightlife than much of Cape Cod. It's easily accessible by public transportation and just as easily navigated on foot.

ORIENTATION & PRACTICAL INFORMATION. Most people in P-town are very sure of their orientation, but maybe you need help. **Commercial Street,** the town's main drag—home to countless art galleries, novelty shops, and trendy bars and eateries—runs along the harbor, centered on **MacMillian Wharf. Bradford Street,** the other main street, runs parallel to Commercial St., one block inland. Standish St. divides P-town into the **East End** and **West End.** Take the **Provincetown Shuttle** to outlying areas including Herring Cove Beach and North Truro. Buy tickets on the bus or at the Chamber of Commerce. (☎800-352-7155. Late June-Aug. daily every hr. 7am-9am, every 20min. 9am-12:30am. $1; seniors, ages 6-16 $0.50, under 6 free. 1-day pass $3; seniors, disabled, and children $1.50.) **Plymouth & Brockton** (☎746-0378) runs buses from Boston's South Station to Provincetown (3¼hr.; $23 one-way, $45 round-trip). All but officially known as the "Fairy Ferry," **Boston Harbor Cruises** (☎617-227-4321 or 877-733-9425; www.bostonharborcruises.com) runs catamarans from Long Wharf, near T: Aquarium in Boston. (1½hr. $28, round-trip $49; students and seniors $21/35.) Rent bikes from **Ptown Bikes,** 42 Bradford St. (☎487-8735. Open daily 9am-7pm. 2hr. min. $3.50 per hr., $10-17 per day.) **Gail Force Bikes,** 144 Bradford St., also has bikes. (☎487-4849. Open daily July-Aug. 8am-8pm; June and Sept. 9am-6pm; May and Oct. 9am-5pm. $3-4 per hr., $14-19 per day.) The **Provincetown Chamber of Commerce,** 307 Commercial St., is on MacMillian Wharf. (☎487-3424; www.ptownchamber.com. Open June-Sept. daily 9am-7pm; reduced low-season hours.) Head to the **Province Lands Visitors Center,** on Race Point Rd. off Rte. 6, for park info. (☎508-487-1256. Open May-Oct. daily 9am-5pm.)

ACCOMMODATIONS. Provincetown teems with expensive places to rest your head. **Somerset House ❺,** 378 Commercial St., is a fun and fabulous 12-room guesthouse with a very social, sassy atmosphere—and with a motto like

NEW ENGLAND

"Get Serviced," you'd expect nothing less. (☎487-0383 or 800-575-1850. Doubles June-Aug. $110-245; Sept.-May $75-177. Nov.-Apr. 50% off second day. 10% discount with *Let's Go*.) **Dexter's Inn ❹,** 6 Conwell St., just off Bradford St., offers hotel-quality rooms for quite reasonable prices, plus a lush garden, large sundeck, and free parking. (☎487-1911. Mid-June to mid-Sept. 4-night min. stay. Mid-June to mid-Sept. $75-125; late May to mid-June and mid-Sept. to mid-Oct. $70-90; mid-Oct. to late May $50-65.) **Sunset Inn ❹,** 142 Bradford St., was the inspiration for Edward Hopper's painting *Rooms for Tourists*. It's lost some of the romance of Hopper's painting, but still has simple and well-kept rooms, plus a "clothing optional" sundeck. (☎487-9810 or 800-965-1801. June-Sept. rooms with shared bath $79-89; Apr.-May and Oct. $59-99.) The only truly budget accommodation is **Outermost Hostel ❶,** 28 Winslow St., with 5 cramped cottages. (☎487-4378. Linen $3. Key deposit $10. Reception 8-9:30am and 5:30-10pm. Open May to mid-Oct. Dorms $20.)

FOOD. Sit-down meals in Provincetown tend to be expensive. A number of fast food joints line the Commercial St. extension (next to MacMillian Wharf) and the Aquarium Mall, farther west on Commercial St. Get groceries at the **Grand Union,** 28 Shankpainter Rd., in the West End. (☎487-4903. Open M-Sa 7am-11pm, Su 7am-10pm.) Though the post office theme at the **Post Office Café ❸,** 303 Commercial St., is somewhat inconsistently executed, the seafood, pasta, and sandwiches are consistently good. Their clambake special (1¼ lb. lobster and steamers) is the best deal in town. (☎487-3892. Entrees $7-20. Open daily 8am-midnight.) **Tofu A Go-Go ❷,** 338 Commercial St., is a casual restaurant with deliciously fresh vegetarian, vegan, and macrobiotic options. (☎487-6237. Entrees $5-8. Open June-Aug. daily 11am-9pm; call for Apr.-May and Sept.-Oct. hours.) **Karoo Kafe ❷,** 338 Commercial St., is a self-described "fast food safari," serving up South African and Mediterranean favorites from falafel to tofu with *peri-peri* sauce. (☎487-6630. Most entrees $5-7. Open June-Aug. daily 11am-9pm; Mar.-May and Sept.-Nov. lunch hours only.) **Café Edwidge ❸,** 333 Commercial St., delivers an elegant but casual dining experience in an airy candlelit dining room or outdoor terrace. Though the dinner menu is delicious, it's the Edwidge's breakfast that draws crowds. (☎487-4020. Breakfast $6-10. Dinner $8-22. Open late June-Aug. 8am-1pm and 6-10pm; mid-May to late June and Sept. to mid-Oct. Sa-Su 8am-1pm and 6-10pm.)

SIGHTS. The **Pilgrim Monument,** the tallest all-granite structure in the US at 253 ft., and the **Provincetown Museum,** on High Pole Hill just north of the center of town, commemorate the Pilgrims' first landing. Hike up to the top of the tower for stunning views of the Cape and the Atlantic. (☎487-1310. Open daily July-Aug. 9am-6:15pm; Apr.-June and Sept.-Nov. 9am-4:15pm. $7, ages 4-12 $3, under 4 free.) A large bas-relief **monument,** in the small park at Bradford St. and Ryder St. behind the town hall, depicts the signing of the Mayflower Compact on Nov. 11, 1620 in Provincetown Harbor.

OUTDOOR ACTIVITIES. Provincetown's miles of shoreline provide spectacular scenery and more than enough space to catch some sun. **National Seashore** park (2 mi. from town) stretches out from Race Point Rd. with its beaches, forest, and sand dunes. At **Race Point Beach,** waves roll in from the Atlantic, while **Herring Cove Beach,** at the west end of town, offers calm, protected waters. The **Visitors Center** offers free daily guided tours and activities during the summer. Directly across from Snail Rd. on Rte. 6, an unlikely path leads to a world of rolling **sand dunes;**

look for shacks where writers such as Tennessee Williams, Norman Mailer, and John Passos spent their days. At the west end of Commercial St., the 1¼ mi. **Breakwater Jetty** takes you away from the crowds to a secluded peninsula, where there are two working lighthouses and the remains of a Civil War fort.

Today, Provincetown seafarers have traded harpoons for cameras, but they still enjoy whale-hunting—**whale-watching cruises** rank among P-town's most popular attractions. Most companies guarantee whale sightings. (A 3hr. tour—a 3hr. tour—$18-20. Discount coupons at the Chamber of Commerce.) **Boston Harbor Cruises Whale Watch** (☎617-227-4321 or 877-733-9425), **Dolphin Fleet** (☎349-1900 or 800-826-9300), and **Portuguese Princess** (☎487-2651 or 800-422-3188) all leave from MacMillian Wharf.

NIGHTLIFE. Nightlife in P-town is almost totally gay- and lesbian-oriented. The establishments listed are 21+. **Crown & Anchor,** 247 Commercial St., is a complex with a restaurant, two cabarets, the chill Wave video bar, and the techno-filled Paramount dance club, where the boys flock nightly. (☎487-1430. Beer $3-4. Mixed drinks $4-8. Sa "Summer Camp." Cover $10; no cover for Wave. Open summer daily 11pm-1am; low-season Sa-Su 11pm-1am.) Founded in 1798 by gay whalers, the **Atlantic House,** 6 Masonic Pl., just off Commercial St., still attracts its fair share of seamen. Choose from three different scenes: the low-key "little bar;" the Leather & Levis "macho bar;" and the "big room," where you too can be a dancing queen. (☎487-3821. Beer $3. Mixed drinks $4. Cover $10. Open daily 9pm-1am; "little bar" 11am-1am.) The only major club for women is **Vixen,** 336 Commercial St., with a casual bar out front and a steamy dance floor out back. (☎487-6424. Beer $3. Mixed drinks $5-7. Cover $5. Bar open daily noon-1am; club open daily 10pm-1am.) Don't be fooled by the traditional decor at **Governor Bradford,** 312 Commercial St.; the Governor has a wild side, hosting drag karaoke nightly 9:30pm. (☎487-2781. Beer $3-4. Mixed drinks $4-8. No cover. Open daily 11am-1am.)

NEW ENGLAND

MARTHA'S VINEYARD ☎508

Martha's Vineyard is a favorite summertime escape from Boston, although such escape doesn't come cheap. In the past decade, the Vineyard has become one of the most popular vacation destinations for the area's rich and famous; From July to August, the population swells to over 105,000—up from the 15,000 year-round Islanders. Savvy travelers might consider a weekend visit to the Vineyard in the spring and fall, when many private and town beaches are open, and B&B and inn prices plunge.

TRANSPORTATION. The island is accessible by ferry or airplane only; the latter is prohibitively expensive (flights begin at $130 each way), so stick to ferries. **Bonanza Bus** (☎888-751-8800) runs from Boston's South Station to Woods Hole on Cape Cod (1½hr., $20), where the **Steamship Authority** (☎693-9130 on Martha's Vineyard, ☎477-8600 elsewhere) sends 12-17 boats per day to either **Vineyard Haven** (45min.; daily 7am-9:30pm; $5.50, ages 5-12 $2.75, cars $55; bikes additional $3) or **Oak Bluffs** (45min., May-Oct. 10:45am-6:15pm, same prices as Vineyard Haven). **Martha's Vineyard Regional Transit Authority** runs summer shuttles between and within the six towns on the island (☎693-9440. $1.) Pick up a free **schedule and map** of all 15 routes at the ferry terminal, Chamber of Commerce, or info booths. **Bikes** are the cheapest way to get around; rent from **Anderson's,** in Oak Bluffs, on Circuit Ave. (☎693-9346. Open daily July-Aug. 8am-6pm; Apr.-June and Sept.-Oct. 9am-5pm. $15 per day.) **Taxi: AdamCab,** ☎800-281-4462. **Atlantic Cab,** ☎877-477-8294. **All Island,** ☎800-693-8294.

ORIENTATION & PRACTICAL INFORMATION. Six communities make up Martha's Vineyard. The rural towns of West Tisbury, Chilmark, and Aquinnah (Gay Head) take up the western side of the island, called **up-island** because sailors tack up-wind to get to it. The three **down-island** towns are Oak Bluffs, Edgartown, and **Vineyard Haven.** Only Oak Bluffs and Edgartown sell alcohol. Vineyard Haven has the main ferry port and the **Chamber of Commerce,** on Beach Rd. (☎693-0085. Open June-Oct. Su noon-4pm, M-F 9am-5pm, Sa 10am-4pm; Nov.-May M-F 9am-5pm, Sa 10am-2pm.) **Post Office:** Across from the Chamber of Commerce. (☎693-2818. Open M-F 8:30am-5pm, Sa 9:30am-1pm.) **Postal Code:** 02568. **Area Code:** 508.

ACCOMMODATIONS. Budget accommodations are almost nonexistent in the Vineyard; always reserve far in advance. **Martha's Vineyard Hostel (HI-AYH) ❶,** Edgartown-West Tisbury Rd., right next to a bike path in West Tisbury, has the 74 cheapest beds on the island, and is the best hostel in Massachusetts. From Vineyard Haven, take MVRTA bus #3 or 3a to West Tisbury and then #6 to the hostel. (☎693-2665 or 888-901-2087. Free linen. Lockers $0.75. Bike rental $15 per day. Open Apr.-Nov. Dorms $18-24, nonmembers $21-27.) **Nashua House ❹,** 30 Kennebec Ave., in Oak Bluffs, is cozy and convenient with 15 rooms (all with shared bath) in an old Victorian. From the ferry terminal, walk straight ahead along Lake Ave. and turn left onto Kennebec Ave. (☎693-0043. Singles and doubles with shared bath $79-109; each additional person $20.) **Attleboro House ❹,** 42 Lake Ave., in Oak Bluffs, has a homey, no-frills atmosphere in one of Oak Bluffs' famous gingerbread houses, built in 1874. From the ferry terminal, walk 4 blocks straight down Lake Ave. (☎693-4346. Open June to mid-Sept. Doubles $75-115; suites $115-200; each additional person $15.)

FOOD. Vineyard food is mostly mediocre and overpriced, though cheap lunch places dot Vineyard Haven and Oak Bluffs. Popular seafood shacks sell fried fish, clams, and shrimp for $10-15. **Aquinnah Shop Restaurant ❺,** 27 Aquinnah Cir., in Aquinnah, offers a picturesque meal outdoors overlooking the cliffs. The food is good, and the scenery better. (☎645-3867. Entrees $18-26, seafood $12-15. Open July-Aug. daily 8am-9pm; Apr.-June and Sept.-Oct. M-Th 8am-3pm, F-Su 8am to sunset.) **The Bite ❷,** Basin Rd., near the beach in Menemsha, features phenomenal service in a low-key setting that is topped only by their decadent fried seafood. (☎645-9239. Entrees $8-16. Open summer daily 11am-9pm; spring and fall M-F 11am-3pm, Sa-Su 11am-7pm. Cash only.) **Fresh Pasta Shoppe ❸,** 206 Upper Main St., in Edgartown, is actually known for serving the best pizza ($10-16) around. (☎627-5582. Open May-Oct. Su 4-9pm, M-Sa 11am-9pm; stays open later if busy.) **Linda Jean's Restaurant ❷,** 34 Circuit Ave., in Oak Bluffs, is popular with locals for their cheap breakfasts (under $7) and friendly service. (☎693-4093. Sandwiches $3-5. Entrees $10. Open daily 6am-8pm.) **Mad Martha's ❶,** 117 Circuit Ave., in Oak Bluffs with branches in Edgartown and Vineyard Haven, is an island institution serving outstanding $3 homemade ice cream. (☎693-9151. All branches open summer daily 11am-11pm. Cash only.)

SIGHTS. Oak Bluffs, 3 mi. west of Vineyard Haven on Beach Rd., is the most youth-oriented of the Vineyard villages. A tour of **Trinity Park,** near the harbor, includes the famous **Gingerbread Houses,** elaborate pastel Victorian cottages, and the **Flying Horses Carousel,** the oldest carousel in the nation. Snatch the brass ring and win a free ride. (☎693-9481. Open June-Aug. daily 10am-10pm. $1.) **Chicama Vineyards,** a 1 mi. walk up a dirt road from the MVRTA #3 bus stop, in West Tisbury, has free tours and wine tastings. (☎693-0309; www.chicamavineyards.com. Open June-Oct. Su 1-5pm, M-Sa 11am-5pm; Nov.-May M-Sa 1-4pm. Tours June-Oct. Su 2, 4pm, M-Sa noon, 2, 4pm.) **Vineyard Haven** has more boutiques and fewer tacky t-shirt shops than some of the other towns on the island.

OUTDOOR ACTIVITIES. Exploring the Vineyard can involve more than pedaling around—hit the beach or trek down one of the great trails. **Felix Neck Wildlife Sanctuary,** on the Edgartown-Vineyard Haven Rd., offers five trails that meander through 350 acres and lead to water. (☎627-4850. Office open June-Sept. Su 12:30-4pm, M-F 8am-4pm, Sa 9am-4pm; Oct.-May Su 12:30-3pm, Tu-F 8am-4pm, Sa 9am-4pm. Gate opens with the office and closes around 7pm. $4, seniors and ages 3-12 $3.) **Menemsha Hills Reservation,** off North Rd. in Menemsha, has 4 mi. of trails along the rocky Vineyard Sound beach, leading to the island's second highest point. **Cedar Creek Tree Neck,** off Indian Hill Rd. on the western shore, harbors 250 acres of headland with trails throughout, while the Long Point park in West Tisbury preserves 633 acres and a shore on the Tisbury Great Pond. The 20-acre **Polly Hill Arboretum,** 809 State Rd., in West Tisbury, is a must for anyone with an interest in flora and fauna. (☎696-9538. Open summer Th-Tu 7am-7pm, low-season sunrise to sunset. $5, under 12 free.)

Two of the best beaches on the island, **South Beach,** at the end of Katama Rd., 3 mi. south of Edgartown (shuttle from Edgartown $2), and **State Beach,** on Beach Rd. between Edgartown and Oak Bluffs, are free and open to the public. South Beach boasts sizable surf but an occasionally nasty undertow. State Beach's warmer waters once set the stage for parts of *Jaws*, the granddaddy of classic beach-horror films. For the best sunsets on the island, stake out a spot at **Aquinnah Beach,** New England's best clothing-optional spot, or **Menemsha Town Beach.** The native Wampanoag frequently saved sailors shipwrecked on the breathtaking **Gay Head Cliffs,** near Aquinnah. The 100,000-year-old precipice shines brilliantly and supports one of the island's five **lighthouses,** a favorite sunset spot. (☎645-2211. Open F-Su 1½hr. before sunset to 30min. after sunset. $3, under 12 free.)

NANTUCKET ☎508

Nantucket has entered modern lore as Martha's Vineyard's conservative little sister. Rampant affluence has given the island's residents an influential stance in fighting for the preservation of its charms: dune-covered beaches, wildflowers, cobblestone streets, and spectacular bike paths. Even with all this privilege, it is possible to enjoy a stay on the island without holding up a convenience store.

PRACTICAL INFORMATION. As any fan of the American TV show *Wings* (set in Nantucket's Tom Nevers Field airport) knows, flights are out-of-reach pricey, so take one of the ferries from Hyannis, on Cape Cod (both are near the bus station). **Hy-Line Cruises,** Ocean St. Wharf (☎778-2600), runs to Straight Wharf on slow boats (2hr.; in summer 3 per day, low-season 1-3 per day; $13.50, ages 5-12 $6.75) and fast boats (1hr., year-round 6 per day, $33/25). The **Steamship Authority,** South St. Wharf (☎477-8600), goes to Steamboat Wharf on slow boats (2hr.; May-Oct. 6 per day; Oct.-Dec. 3 per day; $13, ages 5-12 $6.50) and fast boats (1hr.; year-round 5 per day 6am-7:20pm, $26/19.50). Both charge $5 extra for bikes.

Steamship Authority ferries dock at Steamboat Wharf, which becomes **Broad Street** inland. Turn left off Broad St. onto S. Water St. to reach **Main Street,** at the base of which **Hy-Line** ferries dock. **Nantucket Regional Transit Authority** (☎228-

7025; www.town.nantucket.ma.us) has shuttle buses to destinations throughout the island. Buses to **Siasconset** and **Surfside** leave from Washington and Main St. (near the lamppost). Buses to **Miacomet** leave from Washington and Salem St., a block up from Straight Wharf; and those to **Madaket** and **Jetties Beach** leave from Broad St., in front of the Peter Foulger Museum. (Buses every 30min. 7am-11:30pm; Surfside bus every 40min. 10am-5:20pm. Fare $0.50-2, seniors half-price, under 6 free.) Bikes are the best way to see Nantucket. The cheapest rentals are at **Cook's Cycle,** 6 S. Beach St., right off Broad St. (☎228-0800. Open Apr.-Nov. daily 9am-5pm. $20 per day.) Get bus maps at **Nantucket Visitor Services,** 25 Federal St., off Broad St. (☎228-0925. Open summer daily 9am-6pm; winter M-Sa 9am-5:30pm.)

ACCOMMODATIONS. There once was a hostel on Nantucket—and there still is. Across the street from the beach the **Nantucket Hostel (HI-AYH) ❶,** 31 Western Ave., a 3½ mi. bike ride from town at the end of the unlit Surfside Bike Path, is housed in a gorgeous 128-year-old lifesaving station, with 3 large, clean, single-sex dorm rooms. (☎228-0433 or 888-901-20-84. Taxi to the hostel $8. Full kitchen. Free linen. Check in 5-10pm. Lockout 10am-5pm. Curfew 10pm. 7-day max. stay. Open Apr.-Oct. Dorms $22, nonmembers $25.) Unfortunately, most other accommodations on Nantucket are expensive; cheap options are listed with the **Nantucket Accommodations Bureau** (☎228-9559) or **Nantucket & Martha's Vineyard Reservations** (☎800-649-5671). **Nesbitt Inn ❹,** 21 Broad St., one block from the wharf, is the oldest and one of the least expensive inns on Nantucket. Small rooms with fan, sink, and shared baths explain the low price, but guests are kept comfortable with a fireplace, deck, common room with TV, and continental breakfast. (☎228-0156. Reception 7am-10pm. Open Mar.-Dec. Singles $75; doubles $85, with king-sized bed $95; quads $125. Mar.-Apr. and Oct.-Dec. $20 less.)

FOOD. Sit-down restaurants are pricey (entrees average $15-20). The cheapest options are the takeout places on Steamboat Wharf. Get groceries at the **A&P** off Straight Wharf. (☎228-9756. Open M-Sa 7am-10pm, Su 7am-7pm.) **Something Natural ❶,** 50 Cliff Rd., just outside town on Cliff Rd., has the best sandwiches on the island, each served on delectable, freshly baked bread. (☎228-0504. Full sandwich—big enough for 2—$7-8; ½ sandwich $4-5. Open Su-Th 8am-6pm, F-Sa 8am-6:30pm.) **The Atlantic Café ❸,** 15 S. Water St., is nautical *and* nice, with an aquatic theme, friendly employees, and American pub fare. (☎228-0570. Sandwiches $8-15. Entrees $13-22. Open May-Oct. daily 11:30am-1am; Nov.-Apr. Tu-Su 11:30am-1am. Food until 11pm.) The sandwich shop **Henry's ❶** is the first place visitors see getting off the ferry at Steamboat Wharf. (☎228-0123. Sandwiches $4-5.25. Open May to mid-Oct. daily 8am-10pm. Cash only.)

SIGHTS. The popular **Nantucket Whaling Museum,** 7 Broad St., explores the glories and hardships of the old whaling community. Next door, the **Peter Foulger Museum** has a rotating exhibit on Nantucket history. (Whaling Museum ☎228-1736, Peter Foulger ☎228-1894; www.nha.org. Both open June-early Oct. M-Sa 10am-5pm, Su noon-5pm; early Oct.-May Sa-Su noon-4pm. Whaling museum $10, ages 6-17 $6, under 6 free. Admission to Foulger Museum only available with a History Ticket: $15, ages 6-17 $8, under 7 free; families $35.) For a panorama of the island, climb the 92 stairs to the top of the bright white **Congregational Church Tower,** 62 Centre St., the third right off Broad St. On a clear day, visitors can see 14 mi. out to sea. (☎228-0950. Open mid-June to Oct. M-Sa 10am-4pm; Apr. to mid-June F-Sa 10am-2pm. $2.50, ages 5-12 $0.50.)

OUTDOOR ACTIVITIES. The silky public beaches of Nantucket are the highlight of the island. The northern beaches (Children's, Jetties, and Dionis) are calmer than the southern beaches (Cisco, Surfside, Nobadeer). **Madaket** is one of the few places on the eastern seaboard where you can see the sun set over the ocean. **Dionis** and **Jetties** near town are the most popular (and busiest) beaches, while **Siasconset** and **Wauwinet** to the east are isolated and quiet. The biggest waves are at **Nobadeer** and **Cisco,** which is headquarters for **Nantucket Island Surf School** (☎560-1020; www.surfack.com. Rentals $40 per day, $25 per ½ day. Lessons $65 for a 1hr. private lesson, $80 for a 2hr. group lesson). **Nantucket Community Sailing,** at Jetties Beach, rents water craft. (☎228-6600. Open late June-Aug. daily 9am-5pm. Kayaks $15 per hr., $80 per day.) **Barry Thurston's,** 5 Salem St., at Candle St., left off Straight Wharf, rents rods and reels. (☎228-9595. Open Apr.-Dec. M-F 8am-6pm, Su 8am-5pm. Equipment $20 per 24hr.)

There are two popular bike routes on Nantucket. From Steamboat Wharf, turn right on N. Water St., and bear left onto Cliff Rd., headed for **Madaket Beach** (6¼ mi. each way). Many combine this with the **Sanford Farm hike,** a single trail made up of several loops running through the brushy flatlands and hills of the old Sanford Farm, a preserved area at the heart of the island. A longer bike route runs to **Siasconset** (8¼ mi.) from the Straight Wharf. Head up Main St. and turn left onto Orange St.; signs to the bike path begin after the rotary. To see more of the island, return from Siasconset Beach on the **Polpis Road** path (10 mi.).

WESTERN MASSACHUSETTS

THE BERKSHIRES ☎413

Within easy driving distance from Boston and New York and distinguished by stunning autumn foliage, the Berkshires are an attractive destination for a weekend getaway. Sprinkled with small New England towns, the mountains offer picturesque ice cream shops, country stores, and scenic rural drives, as well as pristine colleges, art museums, and spas.

ORIENTATION AND PRACTICAL INFORMATION

Comprising the western third of Massachusetts, the **Berkshire** region is bordered to the north by Rte. 2 (the Mohawk Trail) and Vermont and to the south by the Mass. Pike and Connecticut. **Peter Pan Bus Lines** (☎800-343-9999) runs buses from Boston to Springfield, where there is a **Bonanza** connection to Williamstown and a transfer in Pittsfield. (4hr., daily 10am, $33). **Visitor Info: Berkshire Visitors Bureau,** 3 Hoosac St. in Adams. (☎743-4500 or 800-237-5747; www.berkshires.org. Open M-F 8:30am-5pm.) The **Pittsford Visitor Center**, 121 South St. in Pittsford, can also provide information about the region. (☎395-0105. Open M-Th and Sa 9am-5pm, F 9am-8pm, Su 11am-3pm.) Within the 100,000-acre domain of the 12 state parks in Berkshire County there are innumerable hiking and camping opportunities. For info, stop by the **Region 5 Headquarters,** 740 South St., in Pittsfield. (☎442-8928. Open M-F 8am-5pm.) **Area Code:** 413.

NORTH ADAMS

Formerly a large industrial center, North Adams once had 100 trains per day pass through its state-of-the-art Hoosac Tunnel, but the prestige, popularity, and economic prosperity of the city declined over the years. Bolstered by a new art museum, however, the city is on the upswing again as it finds new uses for its many factory buildings. The five-year-old **Mass MoCA,** 1040 Mass MoCA Way, comprises 27 old factory buildings and is the largest center for contemporary visual and performing arts in the country. The museum, known for pushing limits and exceeding typical boundaries, exhibits art that, because of its size and complexity, can't be exhibited anywhere else in the US. (☎662-2111; www.massmoca.org. Open June-Oct. daily 10am-6pm; Nov.-May Su-W 11am-5pm. June-Oct. $9, ages 6-16 $3; Nov.-May $7, students and seniors $5, ages 6-16 $2.) The **Contemporary Artists Center,** 189 Beaver St. (Rte. 8 N), also displays stunning modern art. (☎663-9555. Open W-Sa 11am-5pm, Su noon-5pm. Free.)

The **Western Gateway,** on the Furnace St. bypass off Rte. 8, is a small complex that consists of a visitors center, a railroad museum, a gallery, and one of Massachusetts' five Heritage State Parks. (☎663-6312. Open daily 10am-5pm. Live music summer Th 7pm. Donations accepted.) On Rte. 8, ½mi. north of downtown North Adams, lies **Natural Bridge State Park,** home to a white marble bridge over a 60 ft. deep chasm formed during the last Ice Age. The bridge is not the only attraction in the park; the glacial potholes and the 30 ft. waterfall flowing through the chasm are also impressive sights. (May-Oct. ☎663-6392; Nov.-Apr. ☎663-8469. Open late May to mid-Oct. daily 9am-5pm. Parking $2.) **Clarksburg State Park ❶,** 1199 Middle Rd., a few mi. north of town on Rte. 8, has 44 wooded campsites and over 346 acres of woods and water. (☎664-8345. Camping $12, MA residents $10; day-use fee $5. No lifeguard on duty.) The **Visitors Center** on Union St. (Rte. 2/Rte. 8), on the east side of town, is easily accessed by following Rte. 2 east from Mass MoCA. (☎663-9204. Open daily 10am-4pm.)

WILLIAMSTOWN

With a purple cow named "Ephs" (after college founder Ephraim Williams) as a mascot and a lively student population, **Williams College** injects youthful vigor into an otherwise quaint little town. Maps of the scenic campus are available from the admissions office, 33 Stetson Ct., in Bascom House. (☎597-2211; www.williams.edu. Open M-F 8:30am-4:30pm. Tours daily; contact the office for a schedule as times change frequently.) While on campus, pay a visit to an impressive college collection at the **Williams College Museum of Art,** 15 Lawrence Hall Dr., #2. Housing over 12,000 pieces in both permanent and rotating exhibits, the museum focuses on American and contemporary art but encompasses a spectrum ranging from medieval works to modern art. (☎597-2429; www.williams.edu/wcma. Open Tu-Sa 10am-5pm, Su 1-5pm. Free. Wheelchair-accessible.)

Located ½ mi. down South St. from the rotary, the **Clark Art Institute**, 225 South St., displays an impressive collection of 19th-century French paintings as well as a variety of 14th- to 19th-century American and European art. The Institute, with 140 acres of grounds, also encourages patrons to enjoy a picnic in the gardens or explore the many trails. (☎458-2303; www.clarkart.edu. Open July-Aug. daily 10am-5pm; Sept.-June Tu-Su 10am-5pm. Nov.-May free; June-Oct. $10, students with ID and children under 19 free. Wheelchair-accessible.) As the summer heats up, so do the stages at the Williamstown Theater. Check out the Tony-award winning **Williamstown Theater Festival,** which hosts plays and musicals on three stages, one of which is free. (☎597-3400, info line 597-3399; www.wtfestival.org. Box office open June-Aug. Tu-Sa 11am-after curtain, Su 11am-4pm. Performances Tu-Su. Main Stage $20-48; Nikos Stage $21-23, F afternoons $3.) The Williamstown Chamber of Commerce operates a **Visitors Information Booth** with abundant information about cultural events in the area as well as a helpful guide to lodging and restaurants. (☎485-9077; www.williamstownchamber.com. Open July-Aug. daily 10am-6pm; Sept. F-Su 10am-6pm.)

The wooded hills surrounding Williamstown beckon from the moment visitors arrive. The **Hopkins Memorial Forest** (☎597-2346) offers 2425 acres of free hiking and cross-country skiing on 15 mi. of trails. Take Rte. 7 N (North St.), turn left on Bulkley St., follow Bulkley to the end, and turn right onto Northwest Hill Rd. For bike, snowshoe, or cross-country ski rentals, check out **The Mountain Goat,** 130 Water St. (☎458-8445. Bike and ski rentals $25 per day, $35 for 2 days. Open M-W and F-Sa 10am-6pm, Th 10am-7pm, Su 11am-5pm.)

Many affordable motels cluster along Rte. 2 east of town. The welcoming **Maple Terrace Motel ❹,** 555 Main St. (Rte. 2), with beautifully planted gardens, bright rooms with cable TV and VCRs, a heated outdoor pool, and continental breakfast, is one of the best choices in town. (☎458-9677. Rooms summer $79-108; low-season $53-63. Reservations strongly recommended.) Comfortable **Chimney Mirror Motel ❷,** 295 Main St., is a less expensive and correspondingly less lavish choice, but does offer A/C and breakfast. (☎458-5202. Rooms summer Su-Th $68-78, F-Sa $89-99; low-season $52-65.) For affordable meals, take a stroll to 28 Spring St. where you will find **Pappa Charlie's Deli ❶.** Once there, sink your teeth into $5 celebrity-themed sandwiches such as the "Gwyneth Paltrow"—an eggplant parmigiana with a side salad. (☎458-5969. Open Su-Th 8am-8pm, F-Sa 8am-9pm, Su 9am-8pm. Cash only.) Serving up Herrell's ice cream ($1.75-2.50) and incredibly thick milkshakes ($3.25) as well as delightful lunchtime specials, **Lickety Split ❶,** 69 Spring St., is hopping in the early afternoon. (☎458-1818. Sandwiches $5. Quiche $3.50. Open Feb.-Nov. M-Sa 11:30am-10pm, Su noon-10pm.; Dec.-Jan. M-Sa 11:30am-4pm; lunch until 3pm. Cash only.)

LENOX

Tanglewood, an enormous and scenic musical complex on Rte. 7, a short distance west of Lenox Center on West St. (Rte. 183), is one of the Berkshires' greatest treasures. Tanglewood showcases a variety of concerts spanning many musical genres, but as the summer home of the **Boston Symphony Orchestra,** its bread-and-butter is top-notch classical music. For a great evening or a relaxing Sunday afternoon, lawn tickets and picnics are the way to go. Chamber concerts, generally performed by the young musicians training at Tanglewood over the summer, entertain regularly in the evenings. The Boston Pops give four summer concerts. The summer ends with a **jazz festival** in late August. (☎637-5165; www.bso.org. Orchestral concerts held late June to late Aug. F 8:30pm with 6pm prelude, Sa 8:30pm, Su 2:30pm; open rehearsals Sa 10:30am. Auditorium or "Music Shed" $17-90; lawn seats $15-18, under 12 free. Students with valid ID half-price lawn tickets. Call for schedule.)

Though best known for her works of fiction such as *Ethan Frome*, **Edith Wharton** also dabbled in architecture, designing and building her own home in 1902. Newly restored and containing three acres of formal gardens and stables, **The Mount,** 2 Plunkett St., at the southern junction of Rte. 7 and 7A, offers tours, special events, and a lecture series. (☎637-1899; www.edithwharton.org. Open late May-Nov. daily 9am-5pm; tours M-F every hr. and Sa-Su every 30min. 9:30am-3:30pm. $16, students $8, under 12 free. Special events $16 if reserved ahead, $18 at the door.) Shakespeare's works never go out of style at **Shakespeare & Company,** 70 Kemble St. (Rte. 7A). Enjoy enchanting productions of the Bard's plays, as well as those written by Berkshires authors like Wharton, James, and Hawthorne, at the new Founders Theater. (☎637-3353; www.shakespeare.org. Box office open Apr.-Nov. daily 10am-2pm or until performance. $8-50.) At **Pleasant Valley Wildlife Sanctuary,** amble through the 1500 acres and 7 mi. of trails containing hardwood forest, meadows, wetlands, and the slopes of Lenox Mountain. (☎637-0320; www.massaudubon.org. Open July-

Sept. daily dawn-dusk. Nature Center open late Oct.-late June M 9am-4pm, Tu-Sa 9am-5pm, Su 10am-4pm; July-late Oct. Su-M 10am-4pm, Tu-Sa 9am-5pm. From Pittsfield, take Rte. 20 S to W. Dugway Rd. Follow W. Dugway 1½ mi. to the Nature Center. $4, ages 3-12 $3.)

STOCKBRIDGE

Stockbridge, like many of the other small towns in the Berkshires, teems with culture, natural beauty, and history. Bring back memories of days gone by at the **Norman Rockwell Museum,** 9 Glendale Rd. (Rte. 183), where you can visit the artist's studio and see the largest single collection of his original works, including many *Saturday Evening Post* covers. (☎298-4100; www.nrm.org. Open May-Oct. daily 10am-5pm; Nov.-Apr. M-F 10am-4pm, Sa-Su 10am-5pm. $12, students $7, under 18 free.) Travelers can spend a pleasant afternoon at the 15-acre **Berkshire Botanical Gardens,** enjoying soothing aromas and stunning flower arrangements. (☎298-3926; www.berkshirebotanical.org. At the intersection of Rte. 2 and 183. Open May-Oct. daily 10am-5pm. $7, seniors and students $5, under 12 free.) The Gilded Age produced mansions not only in Newport, but also in the Berkshires. **Naumkeag,** 5 Prospect Hill Rd., is the not-to-be-missed 44-room Choate family mansion and lavish gardens, built in 1885. (☎298-3239; www.thetrustees.org. Open daily 10am-5pm, last tour at 4pm. Admission and tour $10, ages 3-12 $3. Admission to the garden only, no tour $8/3.)

RHODE ISLAND

Founded in 1636 by religious outcast Roger Williams, Rhode Island exudes pure New England charm. Small, elegant hamlets speckle more than 400 miles of winding coastline, while numerous bike trails and small highways traverse the scenic interior. Only 48 miles north to south, this small state packs a lot of punch. Scenic Providence and historic Newport make a strong case for staying a while longer.

PRACTICAL INFORMATION

Capital: Providence.

Visitor Info: Providence/Warwick Convention and Visitors Bureau: 1 Sabin St., in downtown. (☎274-1636 or 800-233-1636; www.visitrhodeisland.com. Open M-Sa 9am-5pm.) **Division of Parks and Recreation,** 2321 Hartford Ave., Johnston 02919. (☎401-222-2632. Open M-F 8:30am-4pm.)

Postal Abbreviation: RI. **Sales Tax:** 7%.

PROVIDENCE ☎401

Located at the mouth of the Seekonk River, Providence is a compact and easily walkable city. Cobbled sidewalks, historic buildings, and modern art sculptures share space in the heart of downtown, while the surrounding area supports a plethora of inexpensive restaurants and shops. The home of two world class institutes of higher education, Providence seamlessly blends the hustle and bustle of a busy state capital with the more laidback feel of a college town.

TRANSPORTATION. T.F. Green Airport, south of the city at Exit 13 off I-95, is a Southwest Airlines hub. **Amtrak,** 100 Gaspee St., operates from a white station southeast of the state capitol. (☎800-872-7245. Wheelchair-accessible.

Open daily 5am-10:45pm; ticket booth open 5am-9:45pm.) Trains run to: Boston (1hr., high-speed Acela 40min.; 11 per day, Acela 10 per M-F, 3 per Sa-Su; $9, Acela $30) and New York (4hr., Acela trains 3¼hr.; 10 per day, Acela 10 per M-F, 2 per Sa-Su; $56, Acela $88). **Greyhound** has an info and ticket booth in Kennedy Center. (☎454-0790. Ticket window open 6:30am-8pm.) To: Boston (1hr.; 8 per M-F, 12 per Sa-Su, round-trip $13.50) and New York (5hr., 8 per M-F, 11 per Sa-Su, round-trip $41). **Bonanza Bus,** 1 Bonanza Way, at Exit 25 off I-95 and at the RIPTA information booth in Kennedy Center (☎888-751-8800; station open daily 4:30am-11pm, Kennedy Center ticket window 7am-6pm daily), has service to: Boston (1hr., 18 per day, $14) and New York (4hr.; 7 per day; $59, students $49). **Rhode Island Public Transit Authority (RIPTA),** 265 Melrose St., runs an **info booth** at Kennedy Plaza that provides free bus maps. (☎781-9400; www.ripta.com. Terminal open 6am-8pm. Ticket window M-F 7am-6pm; Sa 9am-noon, 1-5pm.) RIPTA's service includes Newport and a variety of other points. (Hours vary, buses run daily 5am-midnight; $0.25-5, base fare $1.25, within downtown Providence $0.50.) **Providence Link,** run by RIPTA, has trolleys ($0.50) that run through the city with stops at major sights. **Yellow Cab** (☎941-1122) provides taxi service in the Providence metro area.

ORIENTATION & PRACTICAL INFORMATION. I-95 and the **Providence River** run north-south and split Providence into three sections. West of I-95 is **Federal Hill;** between I-95 and the Providence River is **Down City;** and east of Providence is **College Hill,** home to **Brown University** and **Rhode Island School of Design (RISD).** Walking - the three main areas are within 15min of each other - or taking the Providence Link are the best ways to see the city during daylight hours.

Providence/Warwick Convention and Visitors Bureau: 1 Sabin St., in downtown. (☎274-1636 or 800-233-1636. Open M-Sa 9am-5pm.) The **Providence Preservation Society,** 21 Meeting St., at the foot of College Hill, provides pamphlets and detailed info on historic Providence. (☎831-7440. Open M-F 8:30am-5pm.) **Internet Access: Providence Public Library,** 225 Washington St. (☎455-8000. Open M-Th 9am-8pm, F-Sa 9am-5:30pm. Free.) **Post Office:** 2 Exchange Terr. (☎421-5214. Open M-F 7:30am-5:30pm, Sa 8am-2pm.) **Postal Code:** 02903. **Area Code:** 401.

ACCOMMODATIONS. Downtown motel rates make Providence an expensive overnight stay. Rooms fill up well in advance for the graduation season in May and early June. Head 10 mi. south on I-95 to **Warwick** or **Cranston** for cheaper motels or to **Seekonk, MA** on Rte. 6. Catering largely to the international visitors of the universities, the stained-glass-windowed **International House of Rhode Island ❸,** 8 Stimson Ave., off Hope St. near the Brown campus, has three comfortable, unique, and welcoming rooms. Reservations are required and should be made far in advance. Amenities include a fridge, private bath and TV in each room, as well as a shared kitchen and laundry facilities. (☎421-7181. Reception open Aug.-May M-F 9:30am-5pm; June-July M-F 8:30am-4pm. Singles $50, students $35; doubles $60/45; $5 per night discount for stays of 5 nights or more; $550 per month, students $450 per month.) The **Gateway Motor Inn ❸,** 50 Mink St., on Rte. 6 about 1 mi. after entering Seekonk, MA, has clean, comfortable, unexceptional rooms. (☎508-336-8050. Free continental breakfast. Singles $59; doubles $65; $6 for each additional person.) The nearest **campgrounds** lie 30min. from downtown. One of the closest, **Colwell's Campground ❶,** in nearby Coventry, provides showers and hookups for 75 sites along the Flat River Reservoir, a perfect place to swim or water ski. From Providence, take I-95 S. to Exit 10, then head west 8½ mi. on Rte. 117 to Peckham Ln. (☎397-4614. Check-in 9am-3pm. Sites $16, with electricity $18.)

FOOD. Providence provides a wide variety of delicious, inexpensive culinary options for the budget traveler. **Atwells Avenue,** on Federal Hill just west of downtown, has a distinctly Italian flavor; **Thayer Street,** on College Hill to the east, is home to off-beat student hangouts and ethnic restaurants; and **Wickenden Street,** in the southeast corner of town, has a diverse selection of inexpensive eateries.

Geoff's Superlative Sandwiches ❶, 163 Benefit St., in College Hill, attracts a diverse clientele with about 85 creatively-named sandwiches ($5-7), such as the "Buddy Cianci," the "Wacko," and the "Embryonic Journey," a sandwich that contains egg salad, bacon, and melted cheddar. Grab a green treat from the huge pickle barrel to complement your meal. (☎751-2248. Open M-F 8am-9pm, Sa-Su 9:30am-9pm.) **Julian's ❸,** 318 Broadway, near Federal Hill, is a funky sit-down eatery with plenty of vegetarian options and art on the walls. (☎861-1770. Wraps and sandwiches $5-8. Dinner entrees $11-22. Live music Tu and Su. Open M 9am-5pm, Tu-F 9am-1am, Sa 9am-3pm and 5pm-1am, Su 9am-3pm and 6pm-1am.) **Loui's Family Restaurant ❶,** 286 Brook St., serves eclectic breakfast and lunch fare to scores of local college students. (☎861-5225. Open daily 5:30am-3pm.)

SIGHTS. A jaunt down Benefit St. in College Hill reveals notable historic sights and art galleries. The world-renowned RISD occasionally shows the work of its students and professors at the **RISD Museum of Art,** 224 Benefit St. The museum's three floor maze of well-lit galleries also exhibits a smattering of Egyptian, Indian, Impressionist, medieval, and Roman artwork, as well as a gigantic 12th-century Japanese Buddha. (☎454-6500; www.risd.edu/museum.cfm. Open Tu-Su 10am-5pm. $6, students $3, seniors $5, ages 5-18 $2. Free Su 10am-1pm, every 3rd Th 5-9pm, F noon-1:30pm, and last Sa of month 11am-4pm.) Established in 1764, **Brown University** incorporates several 18th-century buildings, including the **Carliss-Brackett House,** 45 Prospect St., now the Office of Admission for Brown. (☎863-2378; www.brown.edu/admission. Free 1hr. walking tours of the campus leave from here M-F 9am-4pm. Open M-F 8am-4pm.) From atop the hill, gaze at the stunning marble dome of the **Rhode Island State Capitol.** (☎222-3938; www.state.ri.us/tours/tours.htm. Open M-F 8:30am-4:30pm. Free guided tours hourly M-F 9am-noon. Reservations recommended for groups. Pick up one of the self-guide booklets available in room 38 in the basement, M-F 8:30am-3:30pm.)

The **John Brown House Museum,** 52 Power St., is steeped in tranquil elegance. The 1hr. tour includes a brief video introducing the house and the families that have occupied it. The knowledgeable tour guides provide information regarding all aspects of the house. (☎331-8575. Open Tu-Sa 10am-5pm, Su noon-4pm. $7, students and seniors $5.50, ages 7-17 $3; families $18.) The factory that started the industrial revolution in America is preserved in Pawtucket at the **Slater Mill Historic Site,** 67 Roosevelt Ave. Situated by the rushing waters of the Blackstone River, the site has a large waterwheel and working water-powered machinery. (☎725-8638; www.slatermill.org. Open June-Nov. Su 1-5pm, Tu-Sa 10am-5pm. Call for winter hours. Continuous tours (included in price of admission) last 1½ hr. $8, seniors $7, ages 6-12 $6, under 6 free.) In addition to founding Rhode Island, in 1638 Roger Williams founded the *first* **First Baptist Church of America.** Rarely crowded, its 1775 incarnation stands today at 75 N. Main St. (☎454-3418; www.fbcia.org. Free guided tours are available after the Su service. Open M-F 10am-noon and 1-3pm, Sa 10am-noon. Free.)

ENTERTAINMENT & NIGHTLIFE. For film, theater, and nightlife listings, read the "Weekend" section of the *Providence Journal* or the *Providence Phoenix*. Between 10 and 15 summer evenings per year, floating and stationary bonfires spanning the entire length of the downtown rivers are set ablaze during **Water Fire,** a public art exhibition and festival. (☎272-3111; www.waterfire.org. Free.) The regionally acclaimed **Trinity Repertory Company,** 201 Washington St., typically offers $12 student rush tickets on the day of performances. (☎351-4242. $32-48.) The **Providence Performing Arts Center,** 220 Weybosset St., hosts a variety of high-end productions such as concerts and Broadway musicals. (☎421-2787. Box office open M-F 10am-6pm, Sa noon-5pm. $26-68. Half-price tickets for students and seniors sometimes available 1hr. before weekday showtimes; call ahead to confirm.) The **Cable Car Cinema and Cafe,** 204 S. Main St., one block down from Benefit St., shows arthouse and foreign films in a small theater outfitted with comfy couches. A friendly staff serves up sandwiches ($4-5) and offers a variety of vegan baked goods, ice cream, and beverages. (☎272-3970. 2 shows per evening, times vary. $8, M-W students $6. Cafe open M-F 7:30am-11pm, Sa-Su 9am-11pm.)

Brownies, townies, and RISDs rock the night away at several hot spots throughout town. Something's going on every night at **AS220,** 115 Empire St., between Washington and Westminster St., a non-profit, totally uncensored cafe/bar/gallery/performance space. (☎831-9327. Cover under $10, usually around $6. Open M-F 10am-1am, Sa 1-6pm and 7pm-1am, Su 7pm-1am.) **Trinity Brewhouse,** 183 Fountain St., behind Trinity Repertory Theatre, offers award-winning beer as well as a live blues band on Wednesday nights. (☎453-2337. Open M-Th 11:30am-1am, F 11:30am-2am, Sa noon-2am, Su noon-1am.) Head over to the **Custom House Tavern,** 36 Weybosset St., in Down City, to hear local talent perform rock, jazz, or funk. (☎751-3630. Open M-Th 11:30am-1am, F 11:30am-2am, Sa 8pm-2am, Su 8pm-1am.)

NEWPORT ☎401

Money has always found its way into Newport. Once a center of trans-Atlantic shipping, the coastal town later became the summer home of America's elite seeking to leave the hustle and bustle of urban life behind. As a result, Newport sports some of the nation's most opulent mansions. Today, Newport is a high-priced tourist town, but its numerous arts festivals, awe-inspiringly extravagant mansions, and natural beauty are reason enough to visit.

PRACTICAL INFORMATION. Running parallel to the shore, **Thames Street** is home to the tourist strip and the wharves, while **Bellevue Avenue** contains many of Newport's mansions. A virtual mecca of information, the **Newport County Convention and Visitors Bureau,** 23 America's Cup Ave., two blocks from Thames St., in the Newport Gateway Center, should be one of your first stops in Newport. (☎845-9123 or 800-976-5122; www.gonewport.com. Open Su-Th 9am-5pm, F-Sa 9am-6pm.) **Bonanza Buses** (☎846-1820) depart from the Gateway Center as do the buses of **Rhode Island Public Transit Authority** (**RIPTA;** see p. 146). If using the RIPTA bus, parking at the Center is a cheap option ($1 per day). **Ten Speed Spokes,** 18 Elm St., rents bikes. (☎847-5609. Open M-F 10am-6pm, Sa 10am-5pm, Su noon-5pm. Bikes $5 per hr., $25 per day. Credit card and photo ID required.) **Internet Access: Public Library,** 300 Spring St. (☎849-8720. Open M 11am-8pm, Tu-Th 9am-8pm, F, Sa 9am-6pm. Free.) **Post Office:** 320 Thames St. (☎847-2329. Open M-F 8:30am-5pm, Sa 9am-1pm.) **Postal Code:** 02840. **Area Code:** 401.

ACCOMMODATIONS. With over 250 guest houses and inns scattered throughout the city, small, private lodging abounds in Newport. Those willing to share a bathroom or forego a sea view might find a double for $75. Many hotels and guest houses book solid two months in advance for summer weekends, especially during the well-known festivals. For less expensive lodging it is best to head out of town a bit. Rte. 114 (W. Main Rd.) hosts a variety of chain motels about 4 mi. from Newport. Family-owned and built **Twin Lanterns ❶**, 1172 W. Main Rd., 7 mi. north of Newport, is relatively inexpensive and offers a homey setting. In the process of renovating, they currently offer eight clean one-room cabins with two single beds, A/C, TV and private bathrooms, as well as eight tent sites with hot shower facilities. (☎682-1304 or 866-682-1304. Tent sites $15. Cabins $50.) A few minutes from Newport's harborfront, the **Newport Gateway Hotel ❺**, 31 W. Main Rd., in Middletown, has clean, comfortable doubles with A/C and cable TV. (☎847-2735. Su-Th $65-99, F-Sa $159-195.) **Fort Getty Recreation Area ❶**, on Fort Getty Rd. on Conanicut Island, provides peaceful lodging as well as much needed wallet relief. (☎423-7211. Showers and beach access. Reservations recommended 1-2 months in advance. Tent sites late May-Oct. $20; RV sites $30.)

FOOD. While many Newport restaurants are pricey, cheap food can be found. Your best bet is on Thames St., where inexpensive eateries and ice cream parlors line the street. The vegetarian friendly **Panini Grill**, 186 Thames St. offers tasty grilled sandwiches ($5-6) and is open to satisfy late night cravings. (☎847-7784. Open Su-Th 11am-9:30pm, F-Sa 11am-2am). A drive north down W. Main Rd. reveals typical chains and the **Newport Creamery ❷**, 208 W. Main. Rd., which serves breakfast and lunch fare as well as ice cream. (☎846-2767. Dinner $6-10. Open 6:30am-11pm.) Good, hearty breakfasts ($7-8) like the "Portuguese Sailor" (chorizo sausage and eggs) are prepared before your eyes at the **Franklin Spa ❶**, 229 Spring St. (☎847-3540. Open M-W 6am-2pm, Th-Sa 6am-3pm, Su 7am-1:30pm.) Acquaint yourself with and promptly devour some choice mollusks at **Flo's Clam Shack ❸**, 4 Wave Ave., across from the east end of Easton Beach. Seafood platters with coleslaw and fries $8-14. (☎847-8141. Open Su-Th 11am-9pm, F-Sa 11am-10pm; call for low-season hours.)

SIGHTS. George Noble Jones built the first "summer cottage" in Newport in 1839, thereby kicking off the creation of an extravagant string of palatial summer estates. Most of the mansions lie south of downtown on Bellevue Ave. A self-guided walking tour or, in select mansions, a guided tour by the **Preservation Society of Newport**, 424 Bellevue Ave., provides a chance to ogle at the decadence. (☎847-1000; www.newportmansions.org. Open summer daily 9am-5pm, winter M-F 9am-5pm.) The five largest mansions are the **Elms**, 367 Bellevue Ave., **Chateau-sur-Mer**, 474 Bellevue Ave., **Rosecliff**, 548 Bellevue Ave., the **Marble House**, 596 Bellevue Ave., and the **Breakers**, 44 Ochre Point Ave. Of these, the Marble House, containing over 500,000 cubic ft. of marble, silk walls, and gilded rooms is the must-see. The enormous, ornate Breakers and the Elms, surrounded by striking formal gardens, are also well worth checking out. (☎847-1000. Mansions open M-F 10am-5pm. $10-15 per house, ages 6-17 $4. Combination tickets for 2-5 houses available, $22-31.)

Newport's gorgeous beaches are frequently as crowded as the streets. The most popular sandy spot is **Easton's Beach**, or First Beach, on Memorial Blvd. (☎848-6491. Parking late May to early Sept. M-F 10am-9pm $8, before 10am $6, Sa-Su $10.) Other beaches line Little Compton, Narragansett, and the shore between Watch Hill and Point Judith; for more details inquire at the **Visitors Center.** Starting at Easton's Beach or Bellevue Ave., the **Cliff Walk** traverses Newport's eastern shore as a 3½ mi. walking/running trail (www.cliffwalk.com). Wildflowers and a rocky shoreline mark one side while gorgeous mansions border the other side of the trail. **Fort Adams State Park**, south of town on Ocean Dr., 2½ mi. from the Visitors Center, offers hot showers, picnic areas, and multiple fishing piers. (☎847-2400; www.fortadams.org. Park open sunrise to sunset.) While in the Fort Adams area, **Ocean Drive** is a breathtaking 10min. car ride along the coast.

The oldest synagogue in the US, the restored **Touro Synagogue,** 85 Touro St., dates back to 1763. (☎847-4794; www.tourosynagogue.org. Tours only, May-June and Sept.-Oct. every 30min. M-F 1-2:30pm, Su 11am-3pm; July-Aug. Su-F 10am-5pm. Call for low-season tour schedule. Last tour begins 30min. before closing. Free.) The **Tennis Hall of Fame,** 194 Bellevue Ave., which contains a brief history of the sport, numerous displays of tennis champions, and displays such as a colorful exhibit of tennis ball canisters through history, will make die-hard fans and relative novices feel right at home. (☎849-3990; www.tennisfame.com. Open daily 9:30am-5pm. $8, students and seniors $6, under 17 $4, families $20.)

ENTERTAINMENT. From June through August, Newport gives lovers of classical, folk, jazz, and film each a festival to call their own. Festival tickets, as well as accommodations, fill up months ahead of time, so start looking early if you want to attend. Bring a picnic to Fort Adams State Park and partake in the festivities of one of the oldest and best-known jazz festivals in the world, the **Newport Jazz Festival.** Also at Fort Adams State Park, folk singers entertain at the **Newport Folk Festival,** where former acts include Bob Dylan, Joan Baez, and the Indigo Girls. (Both festivals ☎847-3700; www.festivalproductions.net. Jazz Festival Aug. 13-15, 2004; Folk Festival Aug. 6-8, 2004. Tickets $50 per day, under 12 $5.) The **Newport Music Festival** brings classical musicians from around the world for over 60 concerts during two weeks in July. The concerts take place in the ballrooms and on the lawns of the mansions. (☎846-1133; box office ☎849-0700; www.newportmusic.org. July 9-25, 2004. Box office open daily 10am-6pm. Tickets $35-40.) Over the course of six days in June, the **Newport International Film Festival** screens over 70 feature, documentary, and short films in the **Jane Pickens Theater** and the **Opera House Cinema** (☎846-9100; www.newportfilmfestival.com.)

A number of pubs and clubs line Thames St., making it a happening area at night. Be sure to bring proper ID, as area clubs are very strict. If you are willing to brave the long lines, **The Rhino Bar and Grille's Mamba Room,** 337 Thames St., is the place to dance the night away. (☎846-0707. Cover $10-20. Open W-Sa 9pm-1am.) **One Pelham East,** 274 Thames St., showcases alternative bands. (☎324-6111. Live music nightly. Cover $3-20. Open daily 3pm-1am.) Don't be fooled by the name of **The Newport Blues Cafe,** 286 Thames St.; it plays a variety of live music ranging from blues to rock to reggae. (☎841-5510. Cover free to $15. Open 6pm-1am; dinner until 10pm; live music after 9:30pm.) For a pint ($4) at the best pub in town head over to **Aidan's,** 1 Broadway. (☎845-9311. Open 11:30am-1am daily.)

NEAR NEWPORT: BLOCK ISLAND

A popular daytrip 20 mi. southwest of Newport, sand-blown **Block Island** possesses an untamed natural beauty. More than one-third of the island is protected open space; local conservationists hope to increase this figure to 50%. All beaches are free, but, when on foot, many are a hike from the ferry stops. The **Interstate Navigation Company** (☎783-4613) provides **ferry service** to Block Island from: Galilee Pier in Point Judith. (1¼hr.; 8-9 per day; one way $8.30, seniors $8, ages 5-11 $4. Cars by reservation $26, driver and passengers must pay regular fare; bikes $2.25.); New London, CT. (2hr.; mid-June to mid-Sept.; M-Th and Sa-Su one per day, F two per day; $15, ages 5-11 $9, seniors $13.50, bike $3.50, cars by reservation $28.00); and Newport (2hr.; July-Aug.; 1 daily; $8.25, senior $7.75, ages 5-11 $3.65, bike $2.30).

The island does not permit camping; it's best to take a daytrip unless you're willing to shell out at least $60, and probably much more for a room in a guest house. Most moderately priced restaurants hover near the ferry dock in Old Harbor, but a few others are located in New Harbor, 1 mi. inland. The **Block Island Chamber of Commerce** (☎466-2982) is located at the ferry dock in Old Harbor. (Lockers and an ATM available in the visitors center next door. Open summer daily 9am-5pm; low-season hours vary.) **Area Code:** 401.

Rebecca's Seafood Restaurant ❶, on Water St., across from the dock, opens early for breakfast and stays open late to serve up some of the cheapest eats in the area in a picturesque white and green building. (☎466-5411. Sandwiches $4-6. Open M-Th 7am-8pm, F-Su 7am-2am.) Decadent sweets ($2.50-5) are to be found at **Juice 'n' Java ❶** on Dodge St. (☎466-5220. Open daily 7am-midnight.)

Cycling is the ideal way to explore the tiny island; **Aldo's Rental's,** on Chapel St. behind the Harborside Inn, offers a variety of options. (☎466-5018. Mountain bikes $7 per hr., $25 per day; mopeds $35 per hr., $85 per day; cars/SUVs $55-80 per 2hr., $90-155 per day; kayaks $15 per hr. $35 per half-day. Open mid-May to mid-Oct. daily 8am-6pm. Coupons available in the Block Island Times or at the rental booth.)

A trip to **North Light,** the granite lighthouse that rests on the northern tip of the island 4 mi. from town, makes for a pleasant excursion. The lighthouse was restored as a maritime museum in 1993, and requires a ¾ mi. hike along the shore. (Open July 5-Labor Day daily 10am-4pm. $2.)

CONNECTICUT

Connecticut is like a patchwork quilt; industrialized centers like Hartford and New Haven are interspersed with serene New England villages, a vast coastline, and lush woodland beauty. Home to Yale University and the nation's first law school, Connecticut has a rich intellectual history. Make no mistake, Connecticut knows how to let its hair down—this is the state that also brought us the lollipop, the three-ring circus, and the largest casino in the United States.

PRACTICAL INFORMATION

Capital: Hartford.

Visitor info: Connecticut Vacation Center, 505 Hudson St., Hudson 06106 (☎800-282-6863; www.ctbound.org). Open M-F 8am-4:30pm.)

Postal Abbreviation: CT. **Sales Tax:** 6%.

HARTFORD ☎860

Hartford may be the world's insurance capital, but it has more to offer travelers than financial protection, including several high-quality museums and historical sites, a lively theater scene, and the only hostel in all of Connecticut and Rhode Island. As Mark Twain—a prized former resident of 17 years—boasted, "of all the beautiful towns it has been my fortune to see, this is the chief."

PRACTICAL INFORMATION. Hartford marks the intersection of the **Connecticut River, I-91,** and **I-84.** Union Place, between Church and Asylum St. along Spruce St., houses **Amtrak** (☎727-1778; office open M-F 6am-7:30pm, Sa-Su 6:30am-7:30pm), which runs trains to New York ($36-41) and New Haven ($12-14), as well as **Greyhound** (☎724-1397; station open daily 5:45am-10pm). Greyhound runs buses to: New York (2½hr., 21 per day, $24); Boston (2hr., 12 per day, $23); New Haven (1½hr., 3 per day, $11); and Mystic (1hr., 1 per day, $11). **Visitor Info: Greater Hartford Welcome Center,** 45 Pratt St. (☎244-0253 or 800-446-7811. Open M-F 9am-5pm.) The **Old State House,** 800 Main St., also provides tourist info. (☎522-6766. Open M-F 10am-4pm, Sa 11am-4pm.) **Internet Access: Hartford Public Library.** 500 Main St. (☎695-6300. Open M-Th 10am-8pm, Sa 10am-5pm; Oct.-May also open Su 1pm-5pm.) **Connecticut Transit Information Center,** at State and Market St. (☎525-9181; www.cttransit.com. Open M-Sa 6:30am-6:30pm, Su 7am-6pm. Buses within the city $1, seniors $0.50, students $0.75.) **Taxi: Yellow Cab,** ☎666-6666. **Post Office:** 80 State House Sq. (☎240-7553. Open M-F 8am-5pm.) **Postal Code:** 06103. **Area Code:** 860.

ACCOMMODATIONS & FOOD. The cozy **Mark Twain Hostel (HI-AYH) ❶,** 131 Tremont St., offers welcoming accommodations, with a kitchen, common room, and pleasant front porch, in a residential area not far from the center of town. Head west on Farmington Ave., then turn right on Tremont St., or take the "Farmington Ave." bus west. (☎523-7255. Laundry $2.50. Check-in 5-10pm. Reservations recommended. Dorms $18, nonmembers $21.) Located across the street from the verdant Bushnell Park, the **YMCA ❶,** 160 Jewell St., provides basic dormitory-like accommodations in the heart of downtown. The use of the Y's facilities including the gym, pool, squash and racquetball courts are included. (☎246-9622. $10 key deposit. Must be 18+ with ID. Check-in 7:30am-10pm. Check-out noon. No reservations. Singles $20, with private bath $25.) Many restaurants lie within a few blocks of downtown. Pick up a copy of the **Greater Hartford Visitor's Guide** from the Welcome Center for a helpful listing of eateries and a map with each restaurant plotted. Hartford's oldest eatery, the **Municipal Cafe ❶,** 485 Main St., is a friendly lunch diner with bimonthly comedy improv shows at night. Although the diner dates back to 1924, the sandwiches ($3.50-4.25) and entrees ($6-7) are always fresh. (☎241-1111. Open M-F 10am-2:30pm. Improv alternating W nights at 6:30pm. Cover $3.) **Black-Eyed Sally's BBQ & Blues ❷,** 350 Asylum St., serves down-home southern cooking. Enjoy some Jambalaya ($16) under a picture of two jolly dancing pigs advertising "Free Ribs 2nd Tuesday of Next Week." (☎278-7427. Sandwiches $7-9. Half-rack of ribs $14. Open M-Th 11:30am-10pm, F 11:30am-11pm, Sa 5pm-11pm, Su 5-9pm. Live blues W-Sa nights. W no cover. Th-Sa cover $5-15.)

SIGHTS. The **Wadsworth Athenaeum,** 600 Main St., has collections of contemporary and Baroque art, including one of three Caravaggios in the US. Rotating exhibitions, a breathtaking collection of Hudson River School landscapes, and a collection of German and French porcelain. (☎278-2670; www.wadsworthathenaeum.org. Open Tu-F 11am-5pm, Sa-Su 10am-5pm. $9, seniors $7, age 13-18 and students with ID $5; additional $6 for special exhibits. Free Sa before noon. Call ahead for tour and lecture info.) Designed by Charles Bulfinch in 1796, the gold-domed **Old State House,** 800 Main St., housed the state government until 1878. Now, historic actors welcome tourists into the small chambers and provide information about significant happenings in the structure, such as Reverend Hooker's sermon urging an elected government in 1638 and the beginning of the Amistad trial in 1839. On a lighter note, take a peek at the museum of oddities contained within the Old State House that includes a crocodile, a tiger and a two-headed calf. (☎522-6766; www.ctosh.org. Open M-F 10am-4pm, Sa 11am-4pm. Free.) Ride around until dizzy on the vintage 1914 **carousel**, complete with an organ, at Jewell St. in the lush **Bushnell Park**, (☎585-5411. Open May-Oct. T-Su 11am-5pm. $0.50 per ride). Just west of the central city, at 351 Farmington Ave, rests the Mark Twain House, complete with an orientation exhibit and 20 minute video about the author and his times. An entertaining tour of the intricately textured **Twain** homestead, where the author penned parts of *The Adventures of Huckleberry Finn* and *Tom Sawyer*, recalls Twain's life. From the Old State House, take any "Farmington Ave." bus west. (☎247-0998. Open M-W and F-Su 10am-6pm, Th 10am-8pm; Jan.-Apr. closed Tu. $16, seniors $14, students $12, ages 6-12 $8.) The **Harriet Beecher Stowe House,** 77 Forest St. adjacent to Twain's home offers tours of spacious abode with information about the life and times of the author—whom Abraham Lincoln called "the little lady that started the big war"— who wrote *Uncle Tom's Cabin.* (☎522-9258; www.hartnet.org/stowe. Open June to mid-Oct. Tu-Sa 9:30am-4:30pm, Su noon-4:30pm; mid-Oct. to late May closed M. $6.50, seniors $6, ages 6-16 $2.75.)

ENTERTAINMENT. The **Hartford Stage Company,** 50 Church St., a Tony Award-winning regional troupe, stages productions of traditional masterpieces, American classics, and contemporary works. (☎527-5151; www.hartfordstage.org. $20-60. Call for showtimes.) **TheaterWorks,** 233 Pearl St., is an off-Broadway-style theater that presents a variety of recent plays. (☎527-7838. $18-25. Performances Tu-Sa 8pm, Su 2:30pm.) For more show options, head to **The Bushnell,** 166 Capitol Ave., home of Hartford's symphony, ballet, and opera companies as well as a venue for Broadway hits, jazz, and family favorites. (☎987-5900; www.bushnell.org. Box office open M-Sa 10am-5pm, Su noon-4pm. Rush and student rate tickets sometimes available.) The **Austin Arts Center**, 300 Summit St. on the Trinity College campus, stages dance, music, and theater performances by both students and professional groups throughout the academic year. (☎297-2199; www.trinitycoll.edu. Performances Sept.-May. Many free, some ticketed.)

NEW HAVEN ☎203

A city with a bad reputation that has proven hard to drop, New Haven has been working hard to improve itself—with generally impressive results. Home to Yale University, the city continues to tackle town and gown tensions, but the new New Haven, and especially the area around Yale's campus, now sustains a healthy assortment of ethnic restaurants, art galleries, pizza dives, and coffee shops supported by students and townies alike.

PRACTICAL INFORMATION. New Haven lies at the intersection of **I-95** and **I-91,** 40 mi. south of Hartford, and is laid out in nine squares surrounded by radial roads. Between Yale University and City Hall, the central square, called **the Green,** provides a pleasant place to sit and relax. *At night, don't wander too far from the immediate downtown and campus areas; some of the surrounding sections can be extremely unsafe.* **Amtrak,** at Union Station on Union Ave., Exit 1 off I-91 (☎773-6177; ticket office open daily 6:30am-9:30pm), runs to: New York (1½hr., 20 per day, $36); Boston (2½hr., 16 per day, $48); Washington, D.C. (5½hr., 20 per day, $74); Mystic (1hr., 3-4 per day, $28). Also at Union Station, **Greyhound** (☎772-2470; ticket office open daily 7am-8pm) runs frequently to: New York (2½hr., 11 per day, $20); Boston (3½-5hr., 11 per day, $29); Providence (2½hr., 11 per day, $20). The **New Haven Trolley Line** services the immediate downtown area and Yale campus. (☎288-6282. Runs every 15min. M-Sa 11am-6pm. Free.) **Taxi: MetroTaxi,** ☎777-7777. **Greater New Haven Convention and Visitors Bureau,** 59 Elm St. (☎777-8550; www.newhavencvb.org. Open M-F 8:30am-5pm.) **Internet Access: New Haven Public Library,** 133 Elm St. Free access with photo ID. (☎946-8130. Open June to mid-Sept. M-Th 10am-6pm, F 10am-5pm; mid-Sept. to June M noon-8pm, Tu-Th 10am-8pm, Sa 10am-5pm.) **Post Office:** 170 Orange St. (☎752-3283. Open M-F 7:30am-5pm, Sa 8am-noon.) **Postal Code**: 06510. **Area Code:** 203.

ACCOMMODATIONS. Inexpensive lodgings are sparse in New Haven; the hunt intensifies and prices jump around Yale Parents Weekend (mid-October) and Commencement (early June). Head 10 mi. south on I-95 to **Milford** for affordable motels. **Hotel Duncan ❸,** 1151 Chapel St., located in the heart of Yale's campus, exudes old-fashioned charm at affordable rates. Guests enjoy spacious rooms and ride in the oldest manually operated elevator in the state. (☎787-1273. Reservations recommended F-Su. Singles $44-50; doubles $60-70.) **Hammonasset Beach State Park ❶,** 20min. east on I-95 N from New Haven, Exit 62 in Madison, offers 558 sites just a few minutes from woods and a long sandy beach. (☎245-1817. Office open mid-May to Oct. daily 8am-10:30pm. Sites $15. Day use M-F $10, Sa-Su $14.)

FOOD. For great authentic Italian cuisine, work your way along Wooster St., in Little Italy, 10min. east of downtown. **Pepe's ❸,** 157 Wooster St., claims to be the originator of the first American pizza, originally known as "tomato pie" in the 1920s. Try a small red or white sauce clam pie for $9. (☎865-5762. Open M and W-Th 4-10pm, F-Sa 11:30am-11pm, Su 2:30-10pm.) After finishing some slices head next door to **Libby's ❶,** 139 Wooster St., for one of the dozen types of cannolis ($1.50-2) available. (☎772-0380. Open M and W-Th 11:30am-10pm, F-Sa 11:30am-11pm, Su 11:30am-9pm.) No condiments are allowed at **Louis' Lunch ❶,** 263 Crown St. Cooked vertically in original cast iron grills, these burgers ($4)—and burgers are all they make—are too fine for ketchup or mustard. (☎562-5507. Open Tu-W 11am-4pm, Th-Sa 11am-2am.) Indian restaurants dominate the neighborhood southwest of downtown, near Howe St. The all-you-can-eat lunch buffet ($8) and lunch entrees ($4-6) at **Tandoor ❷,** 1226 Chaple St., a diner-style restaurant decorated with holiday lights regardless of season, are some of the best deals in town. (☎776-6620. Dinner entrees $8-14. Open daily 11:30am-3pm and 5-10:30pm.) For Thai cuisine, head to Chaple St.

SIGHTS. The majority of the sights and museums in New Haven are located on or near the **Yale University** campus. Most of the campus buildings were designed in the English Gothic or Georgian Colonial styles, many of them with intricate moldings and a few with gargoyles. The **Yale Visitors Center,** 149 Elm St., faces the Green and is the starting point for **campus tours.** (☎432-2300; www.yale.edu. Open M-F 9am-4:45pm, Sa-Su 10am-4pm. Free 1¼hr. campus tours M-F 10:30am, 2pm, Sa-Su 1:30pm.) Bordered by Chapel, College, Grove, and High St., the charming Old Campus contains Connecticut Hall, which, raised in 1753, is the university's oldest remaining building. One block north, on the other side of Elm St., **Sterling Memorial Library,** 120 High St., is designed to resemble a monastery—even the telephone booths are shaped like confessionals. The design is not entirely without a sense of humor, though—the Cloister Hall has carved stone corbels portraying sleeping, smoking, and lounging students using the library for anything but studying. (☎432-1775. Free Internet. Open June-Sept. M-W and F 8:30am-5pm, Th 8:30am-10pm, Sa 10am-5pm; Sept.-June M-Th 8:30am-midnight, F 8:30am-5pm, Sa 8:30am-7pm, Su 8:30am-midnight.) Paneled with Vermont marble cut thin enough to be translucent, **Beinecke Rare Book and Manuscript Library,** 121 Wall St., is a massive modern structure containing 600,000 rare books and manuscripts. The building protects one of the five Gutenberg Bibles in the US and holds an extensive collection of John James Audubon's prints. (☎432-2977. Open M-Th 8:30am-8pm, F 8:30am-5pm, Sa 10am-5pm.)

Open since 1832, the **Yale University Art Gallery,** 1111 Chapel St., at York St., holds over 100,000 pieces from around the world, including works by Monet, Van Gogh, Matisse, and Picasso. (☎432-0600. Open Tu-W and F-Sa 10am-5pm, Th 10am-8pm, Su 1-6pm. Self-guided audio tours available. Free.) The **Peabody Museum of Natural History,** 170 Whitney Ave., Exit 3 off I-91, houses Rudolph F. Zallinger's Pulitzer Prize-winning mural depicting the "Age of Reptiles" in a room also containing dinosaur skeletons. Check out the 100-million-year-old eight ft. turtle and a mummy residing in the "House of Eternity." (☎432-5050. Open M-Sa 10am-5pm, Su noon-5pm. $5, seniors and ages 3-15 $3.) Outside of the campus area and accessed from East Rock Rd. northeast of the city, **East Rock Park** provides an excellent sunset view of New Haven and the Long Island Sound from an overlook 325 ft. above sea level. (☎782-4314.)

NIGHTLIFE. **Toad's Place,** 300 York St., has hosted gigs by Bob Dylan, the Rolling Stones, and George Clinton. Also a popular dance spot with students, Toad's hosts dance parties Wednesday and Saturday nights during the school year. (☎562-5694, recorded info ☎624-8623. Box office open daily 11am-6pm; buy tickets at the bar after 8pm. $5-35 cover for shows. $5 cover for dance nights. Open Su-Th 8pm-1am, F-Sa 8pm-2am; closed when there is not a show.) **Bar,** 254 Crown St., is a hip hangout, replete with pool table, lounge room, dance floor/theater, five homemade beers brewing in tanks in the bar, and brick-oven pizza. The party every Tuesday night attracts a large gay crowd. (☎495-8924. Cover Tu $3, Sa $6. Open Su-Tu 4pm-1am, W-Th 11:30am-2:30am, F 11:30am-2am, Sa 5am-2am.)

MYSTIC & THE CONNECTICUT COAST ☎860

In the days when Herman Melville's white whale Moby Dick became legend, Connecticut's coastal towns were busy seaports full of dark, musty inns packed with tattooed sailors swapping stories. Today, prim-and-proper vacationers and sailing enthusiasts venture to the Connecticut coast seeking brighter, more commodious accommodations and a whale of a good time.

Located along the Mystic River, **Mystic Seaport,** 1 mi. south on Rte. 27 from I-95 at Exit 90, offers a look back at 18th-century whaling Connecticut. In the 17 acres of recreated village, actors in period dress entertain visitors with educational skits, a functioning wood-only shipyard, and three splendid ships open to exploration. (☎888-973-2767; www.mysticseaport.org. Open Apr.-Oct. daily 9am-5pm; Nov.-Mar. 10am-4pm. $17, seniors $16, ages 6-12 $9.) A few dollars more entitles visitors to a **Sabino Charters'** cruise along the Mystic River on an authentic 1908 coal-fired steamboat. (☎572-5351. 30min. trips on the ½hr. mid-May to early Oct. daily 10:30am-3:30pm. $5, ages 6-12 $4. 1½hr. cruise 4:30pm. $10, ages 6-12 $9.) The **Mystic Aquarium and Institute for Exploration,** 55 Coogan Blvd., at Exit 90 off I-95, takes visitors underwater through real-time video feeds from marine sanctuaries around the US, and boasts an impressive menagerie of seals, penguins, sharks, and beluga whales. (☎572-5955; www.mysticaquarium.org. Open July-early Sept. 9am-6pm; early Sept.-July daily 9am-5pm. $16, seniors $15, ages 3-12 $11.) Only 1½ mi. east of downtown, the **Denison Pequotsepos Nature Center,** 109 Pequotsepos Rd., offers indoor exhibits about the wildlife that populates the 8 mi. of trails and excellent bird watching. (☎536-1216; www.dpnc.org. Visitor center open M-Sa 9am-5pm, Su 10am-4pm. Park open dawn-dusk. $6, seniors and ages 6-12 $4.)

It is almost impossible to find budget-friendly lodgings in Mystic, and reservations need to be made well in advance. At the intersection of Rte. 27 and I-95, the **Old Mystic Motor Lodge ❹,** 251 Greenman Ave., offers standard motel rooms with TV, mini-fridges, microwaves, and a continental breakfast. (☎536-9666. Rooms $89-99.) Reasonably priced rooms with TV, A/C, mini-fridges, and microwaves are also available at the **Windsor Motel ❷**, 345 Gold Star Hwy. (Rte. 184), in Groton. (☎445-7474. Singles $45, F-Sa $75; doubles $55/85.) Close to Mystic, the option-filled **Seaport Campgrounds ❶**, on Rte. 184, 3 mi. north on Rte. 27 from Mystic offers a pool, mini-golf course, a pond for fishing, and playground area. (☎536-4044. Open mid-Apr. to mid-Nov. Sites with water and electricity mid-May to mid-Sept. $33; Apr. to mid-May and mid-Sept. to mid-Nov. $26. Each each additional adult $7. Seniors and AAA members 10% discount.)

The popular **Mystic Pizza ❷**, 56 W. Main St., has been serving its "secret recipe" pizzas for 30 years. The pizzeria's renown stems largely from the 1988 Julia Roberts movie *Mystic Pizza* that was filmed here. (☎536-3737. Small pizza $6; large $11. Open 11am-11pm.) Locals cite **Cove Fish Market,** in a shack 1 mi. east of downtown on Old Stonington Rd., for its good seafood. (☎536-0061. Entrees $6-12. Crab-patty burger $3. Open mid-May to early Sept. daily 11am-8pm. Fish market open year-round M-Sa 10am-7pm, Su 10am-6pm.) Although many head to the casinos for nightlife, there are several places to kick back a cold one in Mystic. The younger crowd heads to the **Margarita's,** 12 Water St. downtown. (☎536-4589. A student ID will get you 2-for-1 deals on food on W. Happy Hour with $4.50 margaritas 4-7pm. Open Su-Th 4pm-1am, F-Sa 4pm-2am; kitchen closes M-Th 10pm, F-Su 11pm.)

Amtrak (☎800-872-7245), with a depot ½ mi. east of Mystic on Rte. 1, runs to: **Boston** (1½hr., 3 per day, $39-42); **New York** (3hr., 4 per day, $47-58); **New Haven** (1hr., 3 per day, $28-31). The **Mystic Tourist and Information Center,** Bldg. 1d in Old Mystick Village, off Rte. 27, has a friendly staff. (☎536-1641; www.visitmystic.com. Open mid-June to Sept. M-Sa 9am-6pm, Su 10am-5pm; Sept.-early June M-Sa 9am-5:30pm, Su 10am-5pm.) **Internet Access: Mystic & Noank Library,** 40 Library St., in Mystic. (☎536-7721. Open M-W 10am-9pm, Th-Sa 10am-5pm; mid-June to early Sept. closes Sa 1pm. $0.25 per 15min.) **Post Office:** 23 E. Main St. (☎536-8143. Open M-F 8am-5pm, Sa 8:30am-12:30pm.) **Postal Code:** 06355. **Area Code:** 860.

AHOY THERE. Groton, west of Mystic on 1-95 and the base of General Dynamics, which builds submarines for the US Navy, is home to the first nuclear submarine ever built. The **Nautilus,** manufactured in 1954, now rests at the Naval Submarine Base, on Rte. 12 north of I-95, where you may clamber your way through the retired sub while listening to an audio tour. The connected **Submarine Force Museum** details the development of the US submarine fleet, from its humble beginnings to the high-tech wonders of the modern fleet. While there, take a look through one of the three working periscopes to view the harbor. (☎694-3174 or 800-343-0079; www.ussnautilus.org. Open mid-May to late Oct. M and W-Su 9am-5pm, Tu 1-5pm; Nov. to mid-May M and W-Su 9am-4pm. Free.)

NEW ENGLAND

CONNECTICUT CASINOS

Foxwoods and Mohegan Sun, two tribally owned casinos in southeast Connecticut, bring a little bit of sin to the suburbs. Although they each have their own style, they share a tendency towards decadence that make them both worth a traveler's while, especially if said traveler can afford to lose a few dollars.

The 4.7 million square ft. **Foxwoods** complex contains not only a casino complete with 6500 slot machines, blackjack, craps, poker, and all the other usual suspects, but also three hotels, a spa, nightlife and entertainment areas, shopping, and food. Over ten bus companies run to Foxwoods from surrounding areas. (For specific info ☎888-287-2369 or www.foxwoods.com/by_bus.html.) The 1450-seat **Fox Theatre** hosts a variety of live performances; past appearances include Frank Sinatra, Bill Cosby, and the Dixie Chicks. (☎800-200-2882. Prices and performance times vary.) **Greyhound** provides service to Foxwoods from New York. (625 8th Ave. ☎800-231-2222 or 212-971-6300. 9-12 buses daily. $23.) Driving is also convenient with free parking at the resort. From I-95 take Exit 92 to Rte. 2 West, and from I-84 take Exit 55 to Rte. 2 East. Once on Rte. 2 follow the signs to the casino.

While winning or losing money on the floor is uncertain, paying handsomely for lodging in the casino complex is a sure thing. The **Two Trees Inn ❺,** a short shuttle ride from the casino, is the least expensive of the three hotels in the complex. (☎800-442-1000. Rooms $99-210). A better option for those who aren't cleaning up are the campgrounds that speckle the roadside along Rte. 2.

Mohegan Sun offers two of the world's largest casinos in distinctive environments as well as a wide variety of services, entertainment, lodging, and shopping. The entire complex is contained in one enormous interconnected sleek structure that is at odds with the interior design, which reflects the culture and heritage of the Mohegan Tribe. With free parking and shuttles from each of the Mohegan Sun's four lots, driving is the most convenient way to access the casino. From I-395 take Exit 79A to Rte. 2A East. Once on Rte. 2A follow the signs to the casino. (For specific information ☎888-226-7711.) A variety of bus lines also services the casino from many points in the northeast. (☎888-770-0140.)

EASTERN CANADA

All prices in this chapter are listed in Canadian dollars unless otherwise noted.

Centuries of immigration and ethnic cross-pollination have forged a unique cultural landscape in the eastern provinces of this vast nation. The gleaming, ultramodern metropolis of Toronto—the United Nation's "most international city"—is in many ways the epitome of diversity, while the city of Québec is a living tribute to Old World charm. Many travelers follow the sound of jazz to Montréal, where flashy festivals, sexy nightlife, and a vibrant bilingual arts scene complement some of the finest dining this side of the Atlantic. Cape Breton and Newfoundland's rolling hills resound with the strains of Celtic music, and the islands' fjords and forests promise blissful tranquility and amazing vistas. The port city of Halifax draws from the best of both worlds, with a colorful nightlife coexisting with charming coastal villages. As an added bonus, Canada can be enjoyed on the cheap; due to a favorable exchange rate, American dollars go 25% further in Canada.

HIGHLIGHTS OF EASTERN CANADA

FOOD. Fresh seafood abounds, particularly on Prince Edward Island (p. 172), while ethnic diversity makes for fabulous dining in the neighborhoods of Toronto (p.).

COASTAL TOWNS. Say "cheese" in the picture-perfect towns of St. John's, NF (p.) and Peggy's Cove, NS (p.).

NIGHTLIFE. Québec offers up terrific nightlife opportunities in Montréal (p. 180), while pubs dominate in Halifax, NS (p.). What's more, the drinking age is 18 in the province of Québec, making the region a large draw for college students from the US.

WILDERNESS. Glacier-carved valleys and unspoiled trails make Gros Morne National Park a hiker's dream (p. 200).

NOVA SCOTIA

Around 1605, French colonists joined the indigenous Micmac Indians in the Annapolis Valley and on the shores of Cape Breton Island. During the American Revolution, Nova Scotia declined the opportunity to become the 14th American state, instead establishing itself as a refuge for fleeing British loyalists. Subsequent immigration waves infused Pictou and Antigonish Counties with a Scottish flavor. This diversity is complemented by the four breathtaking geographies found in the province: the rugged Atlantic coast, the lush Annapolis Valley, the calm Northumberland Strait, and the glorious highlands of Cape Breton Island.

PRACTICAL INFORMATION

Capital: Halifax.

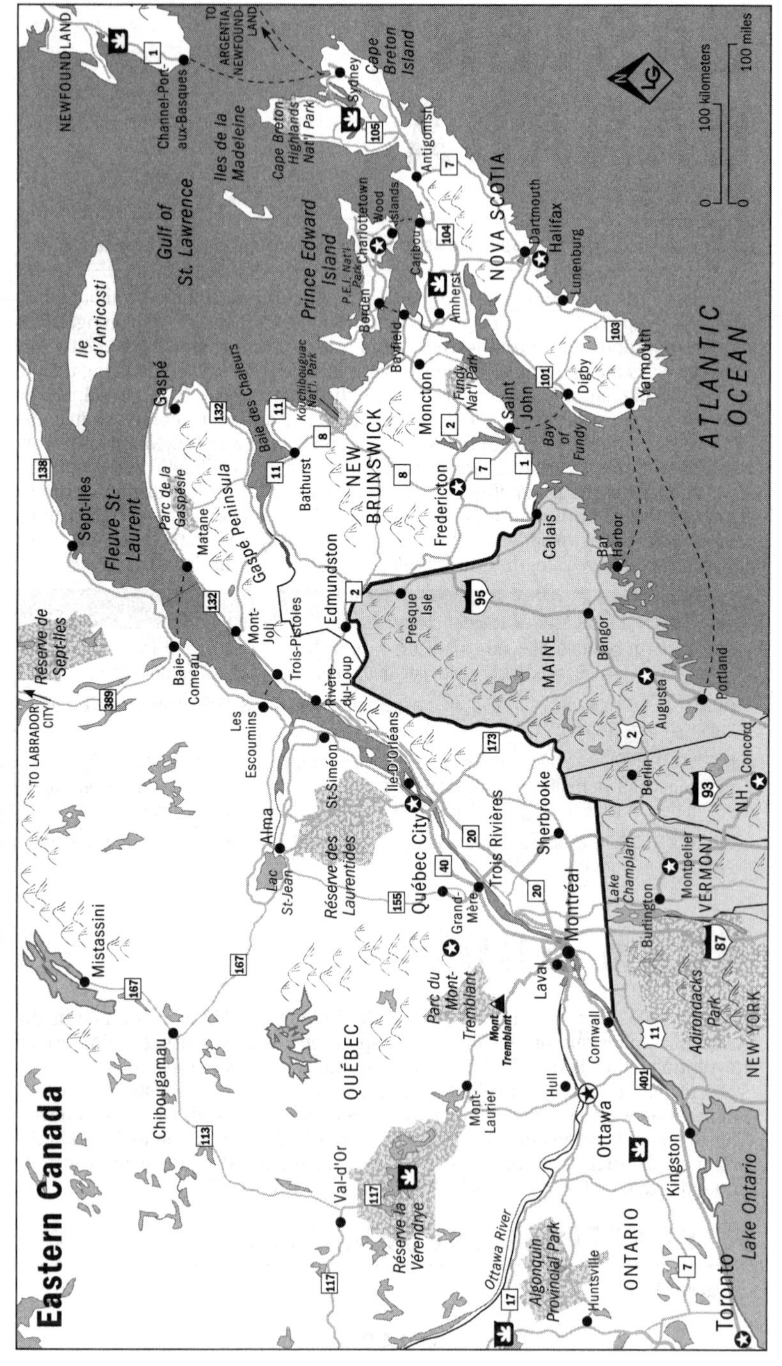
Eastern Canada
NEWFOUNDLAND
Channel-Port-aux-Basques
TO ARGENTIA, NEWFOUNDLAND
Sydney
Cape Breton Island
Cape Breton Highlands Nat'l Park
Iles de la Madeleine
Antigonish
NOVA SCOTIA
Dartmouth
Halifax
Lunenburg
Yarmouth
Digby
Gulf of St. Lawrence
Prince Edward Island
Charlottetown
Wood Islands
P.E.I. Nat'l Park
Borden
Caribou
Amherst
Ile d'Anticosti
Gaspé
Baie des Chaleurs
Kouchibouguac Nat'l. Park
Bayfield
Moncton
Fundy Nat'l Park
Saint John
Bay of Fundy
ATLANTIC OCEAN
Sept-Iles
Fleuve St-Laurent
Parc de la Gaspésie
Matane
Gaspé Peninsula
Bathurst
NEW BRUNSWICK
Fredericton
Calais
Bar Harbor
Edmundston
Trois-Pistoles
Mont-Joli
Réserve de Sept-Iles
Baie-Comeau
Les Escoumins
Rivière-du-Loup
Presque Isle
MAINE
Bangor
Augusta
Portland
TO LABRADOR CITY
St-Siméon
Ile-D'Orléans
Québec City
Alma
Lac St-Jean
Réserve des Laurentides
Trois Rivières
Sherbrooke
Berlin
Concord
NH.
Grand-Mère
Montréal
Lake Champlain
Montpelier
Burlington
VERMONT
Mistassini
Chibougamau
QUÉBEC
Parc du Mont-Tremblant
Mont Tremblant
Laval
Cornwall
Adirondacks Park
NEW YORK
Hull
Ottawa
Mont-Laurier
Val-d'Or
Réserve la Vérendrye
Ottawa River
Algonquin Provincial Park
Huntsville
ONTARIO
Kingston
Toronto
Lake Ontario
100 kilometers
100 miles
0
0

Visitor Info: Nova Scotia Department of Tourism and Culture, P.O. Box 456, Halifax B3J 2R5 (☎902-425-5781 or 800-565-0000; www.explore.gov.ns.ca).

Drinking Age: 19. **Postal Abbreviation:** NS. **Sales Tax:** 15% HST.

HALIFAX ☎902

The first permanent British settlement in Canada, Halifax was founded in 1749 as a base for military excursions against the French fortress of Louisbourg. The town's fortifications were continually revamped as new threats emerged—the Americans and their Revolution, then Napoleon, and finally the War of 1812. The Citadel that now presides on a hill just above the city was designed in 1818. With the threat of war having passed, this buzzing seaport still attracts considerable attention. These days, however, the first-rate nightlife, natural beauty, and maritime heritage are the major attractions.

ORIENTATION & PRACTICAL INFORMATION. The major north-south thoroughfare, **Barrington Street,** runs straight through downtown. Approaching the Citadel and the Public Garden, **Sackville Street** cuts east-west parallel to **Spring Garden Road,** Halifax's shopping thoroughfare. Downtown is flanked by the blue-collar North End and the arboreal South End, on the ocean. **Halifax International Airport,** 35min. from downtown via Hwy. 102; take Exit 6. (☎873-1223; www.hiaa.ca.) **Zinck's Bus Company** runs shuttles to and from major downtown hotels. (☎873-2091. Shuttles daily 7:15am-11pm. One-way $12, round-trip $20.) Taxis to downtown cost about $40. **VIA Rail,** 1161 Hollis St. (☎888-842-7245; www.viarail.com; open daily 9am-5:30pm), at South St. in the South End, near the harbor, has trains to Montréal (19hr.; 1 per day, no train Tu; $156) and Québec City (15½hr.; 1 per day, no train Tu; $130). For public transportation, **Metro Transit** is efficient and thorough. (☎490-4000. Buses run daily roughly 6am-midnight. $1.65, seniors and ages 5-15 $1.15, under 5 free.) Metro Transit also operates the **Dartmouth-Halifax Ferry,** on the harbor front. The 12min. ride to Dartmouth is a cheap way to see Halifax from the sea. (For rates and phone, see Metro Transit, above. Ferry runs every 15-30min. M-Sa 6:30am-midnight, Su 10:30am-midnight.) **FRED (Free Rides Everywhere Downtown)** operates June-August. (☎490-4000. Daily 11am-6pm.) **Taxi: Yellow Cab,** ☎420-0000. **Visitor Info: Halifax International Visitors Centre,** 1595 Barrington St. (☎490-5946; www.explore.gov.ns.ca. Open July-Aug. daily 8:30am-8pm; June and Sept. 8:30am-7pm; low-season M-F 8:30am-4:30pm. Free Internet access.) **Currency Exchange:** Banks offer the best rates in town. In times of desperation, the casino (at the waterfront) is open 24hr. and will change money. **Medical Services: Victoria General Hospital,** 1278 Tower Rd. (☎473-2700.) **Hotlines: Sexual Assault,** ☎425-0122. **Crisis Help Line,** ☎421-1188. Both 24hr. **Public Library:** 5381 Spring Garden Rd. (☎490-5804. Open Tu-Th 10am-9pm, F-Sa 10am-5pm, Sept.-May also Su 2-5pm.) **Post Office:** 1680 Bedford Row. (☎494-4670. Open M-F 7:30am-5:15pm.) **Postal Code:** B3J 1T0. **Area Code:** 902.

SALTY SIGHTSEEING While it's tough to find cheap accommodations in Nova Scotia, it's even harder to find adequate transportation. Don't despair—Salty Bear Adventure Travel offers a unique 3-day travel pass that will take you from Halifax, through Cape Breton's Cabot Trail, across the ferry to P.E.I.'s Charlottetown, and back again for $189. Included is door-to-door service between sights and hostels, all ferry fares and park fees, and not least the company of local guides. (☎866-458-2327; www.saltybear.ca. Departs Halifax hostels Tu and F 8am.)

THE LOCAL LEGEND

GRAVEYARD OF THE ATLANTIC

Infamous rocky coastlines, horrible winter weather, dense fog, and fierce gales have succeeded in sinking hundreds of ships in the waters off Nova Scotia—leaving behind wreckage and fostering local lore.

The most famous ship of all time—the *Titanic*—hit an iceberg near Halifax on April 14, 1907 and sank, dispelling the belief that it was invincible. Rescue ships set sail from Halifax expecting to find no survivors in the chilly Atlantic waters. These "death ships" carried back hundreds of bodies, and today Halifax is the largest living memorial to the tragedy, with 150 graves from the *Titanic*. The Maritime Museum of the Atlantic also houses a unique collection of artifacts found floating in the water among the victims.

On December 6, 1917, the *Mont Blanc,* a French ship heavy with acid and TNT, collided with the *Imo,* a Belgian relief shop. The *Mont Blanc* began to burn, and the crew made it safely to shore in lifeboats. Meanwhile, the ship had drifted towards shore, coming to rest at the Halifax wharf. Before anyone could put out the blaze, the biggest explosion before the atomic age ripped throuhgh downtown Halifax, killing hundreds instantly. The blast was felt nearly 500km away and leveled 2.5 square km of downtown. In all, nearly 2000 people lost their lives.

ACCOMMODATIONS. Affordable summer accommodations are plentiful, but reservations are a good idea during the summer months. Expect crowds during major events, such as the Tattoo Festival (see **Entertainment,** below). The **Halifax Backpackers Hostel ❶,** 2193 Gottingen St., attached to a coffee shop, exemplifies the grassroots community spirit that makes Halifax worth visiting. The enthusiastic owners are eager to organize pub outings and ad-hoc games of ultimate frisbee. (☎431-3170; www.halifaxbackpackers.com. TV/VCR in common room, full kitchen, Internet access, bike rental/storage, and laundry. F-Sa live music. $10 key deposit. Check-in noon-10pm, but someone is at the phone 24hr. Dorms $20; singles $50; family room $65. Rooms almost always co-ed.) The **Halifax Heritage House Hostel (HI-C) ❶,** 1253 Barrington St., is a 5min. walk from the heart of downtown. Behind the brick facade is a spacious 65-bed hostel with TV room, kitchen, laundry facilities, Internet access, and four- to eight-bed dorms. Plenty of activities keep backpackers busy. (☎422-3863. Office open 7am-1am. $5 key deposit. Check-in after 2pm. Reservations highly recommended. Dorms $18, nonmembers $23; singles $50; doubles $57.) Just a short distance from pubs and clubs, **St. Mary's University ❶,** 5865 Gorsebrook Ave., has hundreds of newly-renovated dorm-style rooms in the summer. (☎520-5049 or 888-347-5555. Free linen, towels, and local calls. Free Internet in library. No kitchen or common room access. Reception 24hr. Reservations recommended. Open May to mid-Aug. Singles $34.25, students $20; doubles $53.) **Laurie Provincial Park ❶,** 25km north of Halifax on Hwy. 2, offers rustic campsites among the pine groves of Grand Lake. (☎861-1623. Running water and outhouses, but no showers. Check-in before 10:30pm. Open June-Sept. Sites $14.)

FOOD. Dozens of downtown restaurants double as nightspots after dusk. Grab a bite before 9 or 10pm, as most places close their doors (and kitchens) when the sun goes down. After eating, let the drinking and music commence. **The Economy Shoe Shop ❸,** 1663 Argyle St., with a breezy streetside patio and a huge indoor atrium, brings a wonderfully haphazard flair to decor and food. It also doubles as an immense bar at night. Make a meal of the mountainous nachos ($8) or have a proper seafood or steak dinner ($7-20). (☎423-8845. Open daily noon-2am.) Part deli, part gelato stand, and part restaurant, **The Italian Gourmet ❶,** 5431 Doyle St., just off Spring Garden Rd., is 100% delicious, offering plates of mouth-watering lunch specials ($8) and original sandwich creations ($4-5) at their deli counter. (☎423-7880. Gelato $3. Open M

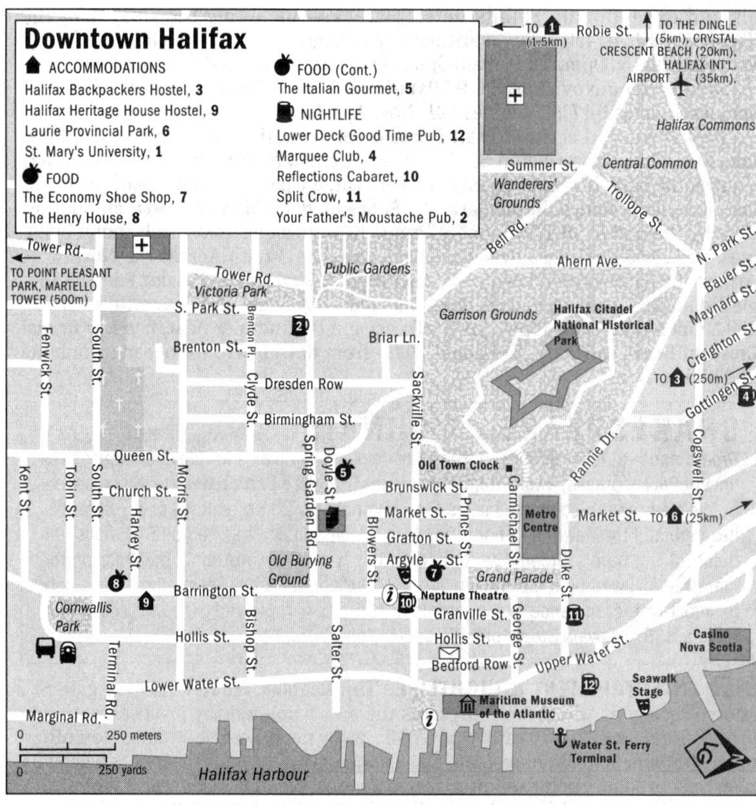

and Sa 9am-7pm, Tu-F 9am-8pm, Su 10am-6pm.) **The Henry House ❽**, 1222 Barrington St., produces its own microbrewed beers. The "Peculiar" brew (pints $6) is a sweet and potent complement to the hearty $6 beef-and-beer stew. (☎423-5660. Open M-Sa 11:30am-1am, Su noon-11pm.)

SIGHTS. Citadel Hill, the city's major landmark, offers a fine view of the city and harbor and houses the star-shaped **Halifax Citadel National Historical Park,** on Sackville St., as well as the old **Town Clock.** A 1hr. film tells the history of the British fortress. Come any day to see the preparation for the **noonday cannon firing.** Guided tours lasting 45min. are the best way to take in the stories about the fort's history. (☎426-5080. Partially wheelchair-accessible. Open daily mid-June to early Sept. 9am-6pm; mid-May to mid-June and early Sept. to mid-Oct. 9am-5pm. $9, seniors $7.75, ages 6-16 $4.25; families $22.50. Nov.-Apr. admission free, no tours. Parking $3.25.) The **Halifax Public Gardens,** across from the Citadel, near the intersection of South Park and Sackville St., are ideal for picnicking. The Roman statues, Victorian bandstand, exquisite horticulture, and overfed loons on the pond are all properly British, in that they have no capacity for displaying emotion. (www.region.halifax.ns.ca. Open daily 8am-sunset. Concerts July-Sept. Su 2pm.) The **Maritime Museum of the Atlantic,** 1675 Lower Water St., on the waterfront, documents the often-tragic maritime history of Nova Scotia with beautiful ship models and exceptional exhibits on shipwrecks—including the sinking of the *Titanic*. (☎424-7490; www.maritime.museum.gov.ns.ca. Open May-Oct. M and W-Sa 9:30am-5:30pm, Tu 9:30am-8pm, Su in May-Oct. 1-5:30pm and June-Sept. 9:30am-5:30pm; Nov.-Apr. Tu 9:30am-5pm, W-Sa 9:30am-5pm, Su 1-5pm. $8, seniors $7, ages 6-17 $4; families $21. Nov.-Apr. free.)

The 186 wooded acres of **Point Pleasant Park** is at the southern tip of Halifax; take bus #9 from Barrington St. downtown. Leased to the city of Halifax for 999 years at the bargain rate of one shilling per year, the park remains one of England's last imperial holdings. In the park, the **Prince of Wales Martello Tower,** an odd fort built by the British in 1797, honors Prince Edward's obsession with round buildings. (☎426-5080. Open July-Sept. daily 10am-6pm. Free.) Across the Northwest Arm of the harbor from downtown, **The Dingle** or **Sir Sandford Fleming Park,** on Dingle Rd., offers walking trails through manicured gardens and grassy hills. (☎490-4894. Open daily 5am-10pm. Free.) To escape the summer heat, head to **Crystal Crescent Beach,** off Hwy. 349 about 20km from downtown, for ocean swimming and hiking trails.

SHAKESPEARE AT SUNRISE *A Midsummer Night's Dream* ends—at least in the script—at daybreak, as the play's four lovers, hapless victims of Puck's pranks, awake from what seems like just a bad dream. The Shakespeare by the Sea theater company makes the playwright's vision a reality. For 3 years, they have greeted the dawn of Canada Day (July 1) with an unrehearsed and hilarious rendition of the bard's *Dream,* performed outdoors on the waterfront. The 4am performance is followed by a rousing rendition of "O Canada," a continental breakfast, and, for most of the audience, a long nap. *(☎425-7777; www.shakespearebythesea.ca. Tickets $35. Seawalk Stage, outside Casino Nova Scotia.)*

ENTERTAINMENT & NIGHTLIFE. The **Neptune Theater,** 1593 Argyle St., known locally as "the Jewel," presents the area's noteworthy professional stage productions. (☎429-7070 or 800-565-7345; www.neptunetheatre.com. Box office open M-F 9am-5pm, Sa noon-5pm. $20-60; student and senior discounts available; rush tickets 30min. before shows.) Halifax's most popular festival and the world's largest indoor annual festival is the **Nova Scotia International Tattoo,** held the first week of July. Marching bands and kilted bagpipers attend the festival for its military pageantry, music, dance, and comedy. (☎420-1114; www.nstattoo.ca. Tickets $18-45.) The **Atlantic Jazz Festival** (☎492-2225 or 800-567-5277; www.jazzeast.com. Tickets $15-30.) jams for a week in late July with ticketed and free concerts featuring over 400 artists from around the world. In mid-September, street performers display random talents from magic tricks to chalk art at **Buskerfest** (☎429-3910). Also in mid-September, the **Atlantic Film Festival** (☎422-3456) shows Canadian and international films. The **Halifax Event Line** (☎490-5946) has more info.

Halifax boasts an intoxicating nighttime scene—the pub per capita ratio is "the highest in North America," which makes bar-hopping common and easy. The free *Coast,* available at bars and cafes, lists special goings-on. Many bars have Happy Hour with $1-2 drinks. The **Split Crow,** 1855 Granville St., is a Halifax institution, boasting 4 of its own microbrews and live Celtic music every night. (☎422-4366. Happy Hour daily 9-10pm. Cover $3. Open daily 11am-1am.) Amid nautical decor, the **Lower Deck Good Time Pub,** in the Privateer's Warehouse, on Upper Water St., offers excellent maritime music nightly. (☎425-1501. W $0.25 wing night. Cover $2-5. Open daily 11am-12:30am.) The best rock acts in town head to the **Marquee Club,** 2037 Gottingen St., which sports an avant-garde atmosphere (mannequins dangling from the ceiling and car doors plastered to the walls) and a hip, young clientele. (☎429-3020. Live acts Tu and Th-Sa. Cover $3-4. Upstairs club open W-Sa

8pm-3:30am, downstairs Tu-Sa 8pm-3:30am.) Near the universities, **Your Father's Moustache Pub,** 5686 Spring Garden Rd., has the best patio in town—on the roof three floors above the street. (☎423-6766. W rib night, $9.95 for a full rack. Happy Hour M-Th 4:30-7pm, F 4:30-8pm, with $2.75 bottles and $2 shots. Open M-W and Su 10am-midnight, Th and Sa 10am-1am, F 10am-2am.) The city's best sound system throbs at **Reflections Cabaret,** 5184 Sackville St., a "labels-free" environment where pounding bass overtakes gay and straight dancers alike. (☎422-2957. W drag night, cabaret performances two Su per month. Open nightly until 4am.)

LIGHTHOUSE ROUTE ☎902

A drive along Nova Scotia's Lighthouse Route reveals some of the province's richest history and scenery: picturesque fishing villages perched on wave-battered rocks give way to sandy beaches; seaside forests and ocean caves can be found minutes from the crafts shops of local artisans. The Atlantic Ocean is the source of the region's spirit, as well as income. Leave at least a full day to drive along the 350km route between Halifax and Yarmouth.

MAHONE BAY

The larger town of Mahone Bay is famous for its local crafts and folk art; take Hwy. 333 to Hwy. 3 and head west for about 90km. The **Tourist Office** is at 165 Edgewater St. (☎624-6151. Open daily July-Aug. 9am-7pm; June and Sept. 9am-6pm; May and Oct. 9am-5pm.) Main St. is lined with art galleries and artisans' workshops, many of which are open for demonstrations. In addition, Mahone Bay has a collection of great restaurants. For huge sandwiches ($3-6) and homemade desserts ($4), head to the **Saltspray Cafe ❶,** 621 South Main St. (☎624-0457. Cup of seafood chowder, $4.25. Open daily 7am-9pm.) The **Wooden Boat Festival** (☎624-0348; www.woodenboatfestival.org), a celebration of the region's nautical heritage, happens the first weekend in August and includes a boat-building contest and race.

LUNENBURG

Only 10km south of Mahone Bay, dark-trimmed Victorian houses and the occasional German flag hint at Lunenburg's status as Canada's oldest German settlement. The town may be better known for producing the undefeated racing schooner **Bluenose II,** which now adorns the Canadian dime and Nova Scotia's license plate. (☎800-763-1963. Call for tours.) Explore ocean-going history and commercial fishing species at the **Fisheries Museum of the Atlantic,** 68 Bluenose Dr., by the harborfront. (☎634-4794; www.fisheries.museum.gov.ns.ca. Open mid-May to late Oct. daily 9:30am-5:30pm; low-season, aquarium open M-F 8:30am-4:30pm. $9, seniors $7, ages 6-17 $3; families $22; low-season free.) For more info, consult the **Tourist Office,** on Blockhouse Hill Rd. (☎634-8100; www.explorelunenburg.ca. Open daily May-June 9am-7pm; July-Aug. 9am-8pm; Sept.-Oct. 9am-6pm.)

YARMOUTH

The port of Yarmouth, 339km from Halifax on the southwestern tip of Nova Scotia, has a major **ferry terminal,** 58 Water St., where boats set out across the Bay of Fundy to Maine. (Open daily 8am-5pm.) All ferry and cruise prices are listed in US dollars: **Bay Ferries** provides service to Bar Harbor, ME. (☎742-6800 or 888-249-7245; www.catferry.com. 2½hr.; 2 per day; low-season 1 per day. $55, seniors $50, ages 5-12 $25; low-season $45/40/20. Bikes $20; automobiles from $85, depending on length and height, passengers and driver not included. $3 departure/arrival tax. Reservations recommended.) **Scotia Prince Cruises** sail 11hr. from Yarmouth to Portland, ME. (☎800-845-4073 or 866-412-5270; www.scotiaprince.com. To Portland: daily, 9am Atlantic time. To Yarmouth: daily, 8pm Eastern time. Late June to

Oct. $90, ages 5-12 $45; low-season $70/35. Bikes $20/10; autos $110/90. $9 passage charge per person. Car fares do not include passengers and driver.) The **Visitors Center,** 228 Main St., up the hill from the ferry terminal, houses both **Nova Scotia Information** (☎742-5033) and **Yarmouth Town and County Information.** (☎742-6639. Both open May to mid-Oct. Su-Tu and Th-Sa 7:30am-9pm, W 7:30am-5pm.)

CAPE BRETON ISLAND ☎902

Located north of Halifax and set against the awesome canvas of the Atlantic Ocean, Cape Breton Island offers wonderful vistas and overflows with Acadian and Gaelic heritage. To top it all off, the impressive mountains and valleys of Cape Breton Highlands National Park accentuate the Island's natural grandeur.

PRACTICAL INFORMATION. The **Port Hastings Visitor Information Centre,** just up the hill from the Canso Causeway in Port Hastings, provides helpful advice. Pick up a copy of *Dreamers and Doers* to find out the latest happenings. (☎625-4201. Open daily mid-June to Aug. 8am-8:30pm; Apr. to mid-June and Sept.-Jan. 9am-5pm.) **Acadia Bus Lines,** 99 Terminal Rd., in Sydney (☎564-5533 or 800-567-5151; open M-F 6:30am-11pm, Sa-Su 6:30am-6pm), runs buses to Halifax (6hr., 2 per day, $40-60). **Transit Cape Breton** (☎539-8124) provides public transportation in Sydney, Glace Bay, and Waterford. A number of privately-owned **shuttle companies** service the smaller communities on the island; check the *Cape Breton Post* and the Visitors Center for listings. **Taxi: Citywide,** ☎539-4004, in Sydney. **Internet Access: Baddeck Public Library,** 526 Chebucto St. (☎295-2055. Open M 1-5pm, Tu and F 1-5pm and 6-8pm, Th 5-8pm, Sa 10am-noon and 1-5pm. Free.) **Medical Services: Victoria County Memorial Hospital,** 30 Margaree Rd., Baddeck. (☎295-2112.) **Hotlines: Distress Line,** ☎567-2911. **Post Office:** 17 Archibald Ave., North Sydney. (☎267-1177. Open M-F 8:30am-5pm, Sa 9am-noon.) **Postal Code:** B2A 2W0. **Area Code:** 902.

ACCOMMODATIONS & FOOD. The town of Baddeck, north of Port Hastings, charms visitors with a quaint downtown and great seafood. You'll find immaculate rooms, a perfect location, and a great price at the **Tree Seat B&B ❸,** 555 Chebucto St., next to the Bell Museum. The friendly owners serve a healthy (and filling) country-style continental breakfast. (☎295-1996. Check-in 4pm. Open May-Oct. Singles $50-80.) **Cabot Trail Hostel ❶,** the only hostel on the Cabot Trail, is in Pleasant Bay, 23849 Cabot Trail. Frequent barbecue and lobster dinners, whale-watching packages, and pick-up service from Baddeck make this a great stopover. (☎224-1976; www.cabottrail.com/hostel. Linen included. Laundry $2. Kitchen. Free Internet. Dorm beds $20.) Don't blow through Cape Breton without sampling the area's excellent seafood. At **Baddeck Lobster Suppers ❸,** 17 Ross St., the famished have a choice of salmon plates ($18-22) or a 1 lb. lobster meal ($28), both of which come with as much chowder and mussels as you can eat. (☎295-3307. Lunch $3-8. Open daily 11:30am-1pm and 4-9pm.) Sweet tooths should find their way to **SleepyCats Sweets ❶,** 503 Chebucto St., where a heaping waffle cone of homemade ice cream only costs $3.75. (☎295-2062. Open daily 11am-10pm.)

SIGHTS & ENTERTAINMENT. Cape Breton's most appealing quality is its natural splendor. The best way to take in the surrounding scenery is the **Cabot Trail,** a drive that winds along steep rocky cliffs by the coast and takes as long as two days to complete. Start in Baddeck, on the Trans-Canada Hwy. 70km north of Port Hastings; for the best views, follow the Trail counter-clockwise. The Trail's northern segment winds through **Cape Breton Highlands National Park** (see below); visits from May to mid-Oct. require a parks pass ($5, seniors $4.25, ages 6-16

$2.50; families $12.50). Beaches around Ingonish can be crowded in the summer. For long sandy beaches without the crowds, turn off the Trail in Cape North and go 5km in the direction of Meat Cove to **Cabot's Landing Beach.** The adventurous may wish to go all the way to **Meat Cove** (at the end of an 8km dirt road), a tiny fishing village with incredible ocean vistas for whale watching, several hiking trails, kayak rentals, and a **campground** ❶ where the price is more than justified by the view. (☎383-2379. Kayaks $15 per hr., $5 each hr. thereafter. Sites $18 per night. Showers.) Off shore is **Saint Paul Island;** known as the "Graveyard of the Gulf," it is the site of over 300 shipwrecks. In the summer months, warm waters support huge plankton populations, making the waters off Cape Breton a popular summer resort for playful whales. **Wesley's Whale Watch,** in Pleasant Bay, runs traditional "Cape Island" tours on a fishing trawler, as well as more intense "Zodiac" excursions on a speedy rubber boat. Wesley's refunds for trips that come up whale-less. (☎224-1919 or 866-999-4253; www.novascotiawhales.com. Each tour 2hr., 5 per day. Cape Island $24, children $12; wheelchair-accessible. Zodiac $36/18. Reservations required for Zodiac and recommended for Cape Island.) The views from the Trail as you descend from the highlands into **Chéticamp** are picture-worthy. If you want to view the coast by kayak, stop in at **Scotia Sea Kayaking,** in Chéticamp. Tours range from afternoon jaunts to three-day excursions. (☎235-2679 or 800-564-2330. Half-day tours $45, ages 13-17 $35, ages 6-12 $25; food and camping equipment rental included. Reservations recommended.) Chéticamp, an Acadian village, also specializes in traditional folk art, and collectors will find no shortage of local galleries. As you make your way back into Baddeck, stop in at the **Alexander Graham Bell Museum,** 559 Chebacto St. Visitors can learn about Bell's passion for inventions, his work with the deaf, and the creative genius of the "queerest man fooling around the live-long day," as his neighbors here once referred to him. (☎295-2069. Open daily June 9am-6pm; July to mid-Oct. 8:30am-6pm; mid-Oct. to June 9am-5pm; Nov.-Apr. by appointment only. $5.75, seniors $5, ages 6-16 $3; families $14.50.)

Near Sydney on the southern shore of the island, the **Fleur-de-lis Trail** covers important historical sites. The **Fortress of Louisbourg,** 30km south of Sydney, is a reconstruction of the Fortress as it stood in 1744, before being destroyed by the British twice in the succeeding decades. Actors in period dress reenact military exercises, and visitors are treated to a taste of 18th-century cuisine. (☎733-2280. Open daily May-June and Sept. 9:30am-5pm (guided tours only); July-Aug. 9am-6pm. $14, seniors $12, ages 6-16 $7; families $34.) At the **Glace Bay Miner's Museum,** 42 Birkley St., 35km north of Louisbourg, retired miners lead visitors on a 1hr. tour of a 1930s-era coal mine. (☎849-4522; www.minersmuseum.com. Open June-Sept. M and W-Su 10am-6pm, Tu 10am-7pm; Sept.-June M-F 9am-4pm. $8, children $5; families $20.) In mid-October, the **Celtic Colours International Festival** brings musicians from all over the world to Cape Breton for a week of concerts. One of the highlights is the world's biggest square dance, with several thousand feet stomping in unison. (☎562-6700 or 877-285-2321; www.celtic-colours.com.)

CAPE BRETON HIGHLANDS NATIONAL PARK

Exploring the national park area on foot or bike reveals mountain passes, steep descents, and rocky coastal vistas that dwarf visitors in their grand majesty. There are 25 hiking and walking trails ranging from 20min. family strolls to challenging overnight adventures. The **Corney Brook Trail** (8km, 2-3hr.), a particularly beautiful trail of intermediate difficulty, reveals a small, secluded waterfall to patient hikers. **North Bay Beach,** near Ingonish, is a great spot for a picnic or a supervised dip in clear water. A parks pass is required mid-May to mid-October. ($5, seniors $4.25, ages 6-16 $2.50; families $12.50). There are two **Visitors Centers,** one at the east entrance to the park in Ingonish and the other at the west entrance just beyond Chéticamp. (☎224-2306. Both open daily July-Aug. 8am-8pm; Sept.-Oct. and mid-May to June 9am-5pm.) The park also has six serviced **campgrounds ❶** and one wilderness area. The two largest areas have 100-200 sites each and are open all year. The others have approximately 10-20 sites each and are summer camping only. (No reservations accepted. Sites $21; with hookup $23-27. In winter $17. Wilderness camping $8 per person.) Wildlife in the park is abundant, with moose sightings particularly common. *For the love of God, do not feed the moose.*

NEW BRUNSWICK

Powerful South Indian Ocean currents sweep around the tip of Africa and ripple thousands of kilometers through the Atlantic before coming to a spectacular finish at New Brunswick. The Bay of Fundy is home to the world's highest tides, which can rise and fall as much as 53 ft. Away from the ocean's violent influence, vast unpopulated stretches of timeless wilderness swathe the land. While over a third of the province's population is French-speaking (New Brunswick is Canada's only officially bilingual province), English is widely used throughout the province.

PRACTICAL INFORMATION

Capitol: Fredericton.

Visitor Info: Department of Tourism and Parks, P.O. Box 12345, Campbellton, NB E3N 3T6 (☎800-551-0123; www.tourismnewbrunswick.ca).

Drinking Age: 19. **Postal Abbreviation:** NB. **Sales Tax:** 15% HST.

SAINT JOHN ☎506

The city of Saint John (never abbreviated, in order to distinguish it from St. John's, Newfoundland) was literally founded overnight on May 18, 1783, by the United Empire Loyalists, a band of roughly 10,000 American colonists holding allegiance to the British crown. Today, the town draws thousands of nature enthusiasts who flood here to witness the Bay of Fundy's tides and the "Reversing Falls."

ORIENTATION & PRACTICAL INFORMATION. Saint John's downtown (known locally as "uptown") is bounded by **Union Street** to the north, **Princess Street** to the south, **King Square** to the east, and **Market Square** and the harbor to the east. Fort Latour Harbour Bridge (toll $0.25) on Hwy. 1 links Saint John to West Saint John, as does Hwy 100. Reasonably priced parking lots are located at Water St. and Chipman Hill; free parking can be found outside of downtown. **Via Rail** (☎888-842-6141) has a station in Moncton that services eastern Canada; take the SMT bus from Saint John to reach the station. **SMT,** 300 Union St. (☎648-3500; www.acadianbus.com; open daily 7am-9pm) sends buses to: **Halifax** (6-6½hr.; 2-4 per day; $72); **Moncton** (2hr; 2-4 per day; $26); **Montréal** (12hr.; 1 per day; $105). **Saint John Transit** runs local transit until roughly 12:30am. The main bus stop is in King Sq. (☎658-4700. $2, under 15 $1.75.) They also offer a 2hr. tour of the city, leaving from Reversing Falls, the Rockwood Park Campsite, and Barbours General Store at Loyalist Plaza. (Late June to early Oct. $16, ages 6-14 $5.) **NFL Bay Ferries** (☎888-249-7245), on Lancaster St., Exit 120 from Hwy. 1, float to **Digby, NS.** (3hr.; 1-2 per day; $20, seniors $17.50, ages 5-12 $10; cars $70, plus $7 fuel surcharge.) The **City Centre Information Centre,** at Market Sq., has info. (☎658-2855 or 866-463-8639; www.tourismsaintjohn.com. Open daily June-Aug. 9am-8pm; Sept.-Nov. 9am-6pm; Nov.-May 9:30am-6pm.) **Taxi: Century Taxi,** ☎696-6969. **Post Office:** Station B, 41 Church Ave. W, in West Saint John. (☎672-6704. Open M-F 8am-5pm.) **Postal Code:** E2M 4P0. **Area Code:** 506.

ACCOMMODATIONS. There are a number of nearly identical motels on the 100 to 1300 blocks and farther along the 1700 block of **Manawagonish Road,** in the western part of town. Singles cost $35-50. The **University of New Brunswick at Saint John ❶,** on Tucker Park Rd., offers neat, furnished rooms a 10min. drive from downtown. Take Somerset St. onto Churchill Blvd. and turn left. (☎648-5755. Reception 24hr. Open May-Aug. Singles $30, students $19; doubles $45/36.) The warm and spacious **Earle of Leinster Bed and Breakfast ❸,** 96 Leinster St., two blocks from the city center, offers 7 four-star rooms and 2 "backpacker" rooms, each with a private bath, cable, VCR, fridge, and microwave. Take Exit 122, turn left at Union St., right on Wentworth St., and then left on Leinster. (☎652-3275; http://earlofleinster.tripod.com. Laundry, pool table, breakfast. Reception closes at 10pm. In summer single backpacker room $55; regular room $100.) Partially wooded tent sites at the **Rockwood Park Campground ❶,** off Lake Dr. S in Rockwood Park; take the "University" bus to Mt. Pleasant. (☎652-4050. Showers, laundry, phones, and Internet. Open May-Sept. Sites $17, with hookup $23; weekly $80/110.)

FOOD. The butcher, baker, fishmonger, produce dealer, and cheese merchant sell fresh goodies at **Old City Market,** 47 Charlotte St., between King and Brunswick Sq. The market may be the best place to get your daily **dulse,** sun-dried seaweed from the Bay of Fundy that is best described as "ocean jerky." (Dulse, $3.74 per bag. Market, ☎658-2820. Open M-Th 7:30am-6pm, F 7:30am-7pm, Sa 7:30am-7pm, Sa 7:30am-5pm.) **Incredible Edibles Cafe ❹,** 42 Princess St., more than deserves its name; the well-traveled chef infuses creativity into every Italian, Thai, Indian, and Eastern European dish. (☎633-7554. Open daily 10:30am-11pm.) **Billy's Seafood Company ❸,** 49-51 Charlotte St., is a delicious splurge for lobster-lovers. (☎672-3474. Fresh Malpeque oysters 6 for $13. Fish and chips $7 lunch, $11 dinner. Open M-Th 11am-10pm, F-Sa 11am-11pm, Su 4-10pm.) **Reggie's Restaurant ❶,** 26 Germain St., a local institution, specializes in "self-serve" all-American homestyle fare: burgers, big breakfasts, and milkshakes. The plentiful breakfast special ($5) is served all day. (☎657-6270. Open M-Tu 6am-7pm, Sa 6am-5pm, Su 7am-5pm.)

SIGHTS. Saint John's main attraction is the **Reversing Falls,** a natural phenomenon caused by the powerful Bay of Fundy tides (for more on the tides see **Fundy,** p. 170). Though the name suggests gravity-defying walls of water running uphill, the "falls" actually refer to the rapids at the mouth of the Saint John River, which run upstream with the force of the tides. Two hours before and after high tide, patient spectators see the flow of water at the nexus of the river and harbor slowly halt and change direction. As amazing as the event itself is the huge number of people captivated by it. The **Reversing Falls Tourist Centre,** 200 Bridge St., at the west end of the Hwy. 100 bridge, in the restaurant, distributes tide schedules and shows a 17min. film on the phenomenon. Take the westbound "East-West" bus from the Scotia Bank facing Billy's Seafood. (☎658-2937. Open daily May to mid-June 9am-6pm; mid-June to mid-Oct. 8am-8pm. Screenings every 15min. $2.) At **Reversing Falls Jet-Boat,** in Fallsview Park, thrill-seekers might consider riding the falls in a jet boat or running through the rapids in a plastic bubble. (☎643-2300. Wheelchair-accessible. Open M-W and F 9am-5pm, Su noon-5pm; winter closed M. $6, seniors $4.75, students $3.25.) Nature buffs will be delighted to find over 12km of wooded trails, six vibrant ecosystems, and scenic bay views in the **Irving Nature Park,** a 600-acre eco-preserve at the end of Sand Cove Rd. W. (☎653-7367. Open daily dawn-dusk. Free.)

FUNDY NATIONAL PARK ☎506

Twice each day, the world's largest tides withdraw over one kilometer into the Bay of Fundy, leaving a variety of aquatic lifeforms high and dry. The dramatic contrast between the two tidescapes and the rapidity with which the waters rise and fall (1m per 3 min.) draw thousands of tourists each year to Fundy National Park. Visitors to the park in chillier September and October will avoid the crush of vacationers.

PRACTICAL INFORMATION. The park charges an entrance fee, payable at any entrance. ($5 per day, seniors $4.25, ages 6-16 $2.50; families $12.50.) **Park Headquarters,** P.O. Box 1001, Alma, in the southeastern corner of the Park, includes an administrative building and the **Visitors Center.** (☎887-6000. Open mid-June to early Sept. daily 8am-10pm; mid-May to mid-June and early Sept. to early Oct. daily 8am-4:30pm; mid-Oct. to early May M-F 8am-noon and 12:30-4:30pm.) Another Visitors Center, **Wolfe Lake Information,** is at the northwest entrance, off Hwy. 114. (☎432-6026. Open late June to early Sept. daily 10am-6pm.) No public transportation serves Fundy; the nearest bus depots are in Moncton and Sussex. The free park newspaper *Salt and Fir,* available at the entrance stations and Visitors Centers, includes a map of trails and campgrounds. **Weather Info:** ☎887-6000.

CAMPING. The park operates five **campgrounds** and over 700 sites. Getting a site is seldom a problem, but finding one at your campground of choice may be difficult. Sites with hookup are available at Headquarters and the Chignecto North campgrounds only. (☎800-414-6765. Reservations are highly recommended.) **Headquarters Campground ❶** is closest to civilization with a washer and dryer, kitchen, shower, and playground, but is usually in highest demand. (Summer sites $21, with hookup $27; winter, $13/19. Wheelchair-accessible.) **Chignecto North Campground ❶,** off Hwy. 114, 5km inland from the headquarters, provides more private, wooded sites, with biking and hiking trails nearby. (Open mid-May to mid-Oct. Sites $21, with hookup $25-27. Wheelchair-accessible.) **Chignecto South Campground ❶,** across the highway from Chignecto North, provides basic overflow sites when the northern campground is full. (Open late June-late Aug. Sites $21.) **Point Wolfe Campground ❶,** along the scenic coast, 7km west of headquarters, stays cooler and more insect-free than the inland campgrounds and has direct access to several beautiful oceanside hikes. (Open late June-late Aug. Sites $21.) Year-round wilderness camping is also available in some of the most scenic areas of the park, including **Goose River ❶** along the coast. The campsites, all with fireplaces, wood, and outhouses, require reservations and permits. (☎887-6000. $8 per person per night, $56 per season.) More domestic alternatives exist only in the town of Alma, where a few clean but spartan motels line Main Street. If you're lucky and find a room during peak season, expect to pay about $75 per night. Otherwise, nearby Moncton is your best bet.

FOOD. A trip into Alma is worthwhile if only for a sticky bun ($1) from **Kelly's Bake Shop ❶.** Just follow the smell of home-baked goodness to 8587 Main St. Replenish lost hiking calories (and then some!) with fresh bread, cookies, pies, and peanut butter balls. (☎887-2460. Open July-Aug. 7am-8pm; Sept.-June 10am-5pm.) Refuel with basic groceries or a home-cooked meal at **Harbor View Market and Coffee Shop ❶,** 8598 Main St., in Alma. The breakfast special of 2 eggs, toast, bacon, and coffee sets customers back a mere $4.50. (☎887-2450. Open July-Aug. daily 7am-10pm.) For seafood caught locally and hauled in daily, **Collins Lobster ❷,** 20 Ocean Dr., just behind Kelly's Bake Shop, is a local favorite. The takeout lobster ($8 per lb. live, $8.50 cooked) is a fine catch. (☎887-2054. Open daily 10am-5pm.)

OUTDOOR ACTIVITIES. The park maintains 120km of trails year-round. Though no rental outfits serve the island, about 35km are open to mountain bikes. *Salt and Fir* contains detailed descriptions of all trails, including where to find waterfalls and ocean views. Moose are most common along Hwy. 114 between Wolfe Lake and Caribou Plain. Hike the easy **Caribou Plain Trail** (3½km loop) at dusk and you'll likely spot several of the beasts dining in the swamps. Deer live throughout the park and thieving raccoons run thick; the peregrine falcons are harder to spot. *Never feed the animals, and keep a respectful distance when watching them. Drivers should beware of moose and deer crossing Hwy. 114 after dark.* Most recreational facilities operate only during the summer season (mid-May to early Oct.) and include daily free interpretive programs. The park staff leads beach walks, junior naturalists programs, and evening theater and campfire gatherings. Visitors can take a 3hr. nocturnal tour through the woods. (Call for event times and prices.) The best place to experience **Fundy's tides** in the park is at Alma Beach, on Hwy. 114 between Alma and park headquarters. A boardwalk and informative signs explain the phenomenon and local geography. 40km north on Hwy. 114, the **Hopewell Rocks** are the Bay of Fundy's most picturesque creations. The "flowerpot" rocks appear to be miniature islands at high tide but become four-story sandstone monoliths when the tide goes out nearly 1km. Visitors can explore the rocks at low tide or kayak among them at high tide. (☎734-3429; www.thehopewellrocks.ca. $6, seniors $5, ages 5-18 $4; families $15. Open mid-May to mid-Oct.; hours vary, approx. 8am-7pm. Kayaks ☎734-2660. 2hr. guided tour $45, children $40. Open early June to early Sept. Call for tour times.)

MONCTON ☎506

This pleasant town was a controversial choice to host the 1999 Francophone Summit. The summit stoked the fires of urban renewal, and today Moncton is a rapidly growing bilingual city boasting a revived downtown and a couple of the most peculiar natural attractions to be found in all of Eastern Canada.

The **Petitcodiac River** that flows through the center of Moncton is usually nothing more than red mud flats, but twice a day the tidal bore rushes in as two dramatic waves, raising the river at the rate of 3m per hour. (The initial wave is much more impressive in the spring and fall; in summer it's no more than a few inches high.) This strange phenomenon is best viewed near the end of Main St. at the suitably named **Tidal Bore Park,** where tide schedules are available. **Magnetic Hill,** at the corner of Mountain Rd. and Trans-Canada Hwy., wows visitors with its seemingly outright defiance of physics. Though a bit hokey, the thrill of rolling "uphill" is well worth the cost. (☎853-3540. Open daily mid-May to mid-June 9am-6pm; mid-June to July 9am-7pm; July-Sept. 9am-8pm. $5 per car.) **The Acadian Museum,** at the Université de Moncton, tells the story of the 17th-century Acadian settlers through displays of everyday artifacts and crafts. An **art gallery** attached to the museum showcases works by up-and-coming local artists in the "picture province." (☎858-4088. Open M-F 10am-5pm, Sa-Su 1-5pm. $2, students and seniors $1. Su free.)

The cozy, charming **Downtown Bed & Breakfast ❸,** 101 Alma St., is conveniently located, well-priced, and exceedingly friendly. Featuring a sunny patio and a French toast breakfast worth getting up for, Downtown also has fast, free Internet access, which is otherwise nonexistent in Moncton. (☎855-7108. Shared but spacious bath, towels, and TV/VCR in common room. Singles $65; doubles $75. Tax included.) Although there are no registered hostels in Moncton, the **Université de Moncton ❷** rents well-appointed rooms for summer travelers at three of its residences. Reception is at Résidence Lefebvre, near the center of campus. Take the #5 bus from Highland Square. (☎858-4015. Sink, fridge, and microwave in most rooms. Parking $5 per day. Singles without bath $41, students $20; with bath $75/52.)

The Pump House ❶, 5 Orange Ln., a firehouse-themed brewery, churns out eight original beers on-site. Plenty of vegetarian options and brick oven pizzas ($4-9) satisfy any hunger. (☎855-2337. Open daily 11am-midnight.) **Graffiti ❷,** 897 Main St., designs filling portions of Greek and Mediterranean fare. (☎382-4299. Souvlaki dishes $6-7. Chicken couscous $10. Open Su-Th 11am-11pm, F-Sa 11am-midnight.)

The **Greater Moncton International Airport,** (☎856-5444; www.gma.ca) 5km outside of town, has flights to major cities. **SMT,** 961 Main St. (☎859-5060; open daily 9am-8:30pm), runs **buses** to Halifax (4hr.; 3 per day; $47). **Codiac Transit** is the local bus line. (☎857-2008. Open M-F 6am-4:30pm. Operates M-Sa 7am-6pm.) **Air Cab** (☎857-2000) runs from the airport to town for $15. The **Tourist Information Center,** in the Treitz Prince Lewis House in Tidal Bore Park, informs. (☎800-363-4558; www.gomoncton.com. Open daily late May 8:30am-4:30pm; early June 9am-7pm; late June to Aug. 9am-8pm; low-season hours vary.) **Post Office:** 281 St. George St. (☎857-7240. Open M-F 8am-5:30pm.) **Postal Code:** E1C 1G9. **Area Code:** 506.

NEAR MONCTON: KOUCHIBOUGUAC NATIONAL PARK

Unlike Fundy's rugged forests and high tides, **Kouchibouguac National Park** (KUSH-uh-buh-kwak) features warm lagoon waters, salt marshes, peat bogs, and white sandy beaches. Bask in the sun along the 25km stretch of barrier islands and sand dunes, or float down canoe waterways. Kouchibouguac is home to the warmest Atlantic waters north of Virginia, and swimmers enjoy the surf and a view at **Kellys Beach,** 11km from the Visitor Center. Hikers have a variety of **trails** to choose from, including a leisurely self-guided nature walk down the Bog Trail (3.6km loop) and the more challenging Kouchibouguac River Trail (22km loop). Wildlife is abundant, and sightings of moose and deer are common at dusk (although mosquitoes are an annoyance). **Ryans Rental Center,** between the South Kouchibouguac Campground and Kellys Beach, rents canoes, kayaks, and bikes. (☎876-8918. Open late June-Aug. daily 8am-9pm; May Sa-Su 8am-5pm. Canoes or kayaks $7 per hr., $30 per day; bikes $5/26.) The park runs two campgrounds in summer. Reservations are recommended and must be made at least 3 days in advance. (☎876-1292 for reservations. $8 reservation fee applies.) **South Kouchibouguac ❶** has 311 sites with showers. (Late June-early Sept. $22, with hookup $26; mid-May to late June and early Sept. to mid-Oct. $18/23.) **Côte-à-Fabien ❶** has 32 sites ($14) but no showers. Low-season campers stay at **primitive sites ❶** within the park and campgrounds outside the park ($8 per night). The **Visitors Center** is at the park entrance on Hwy. 117, just off Hwy. 11, 90km north of Moncton. (☎876-2443. Entrance fee $5, seniors $4.25, children $2.50; families $12.50. Open daily mid-June to mid-Sept. 8am-8pm; mid-Sept. to mid-June 9am-5pm. Park administration open M-F 8am-4:30pm.)

PRINCE EDWARD ISLAND

Prince Edward Island, host to the 1864 conference that set Canada on the path to nationhood, is the smallest province in Canada. More commonly called "P.E.I." or "the Island," it attracts most of its visitors with the beauty made famous by the novel *Anne of Green Gables.* The fictional work did not exaggerate the wonders of natural life on the island; the soil, made red by its high iron-oxide content, contrasts with the green crops, turquoise waters, and purple lupin. Some of Canada's finest beaches stretch across the shores, while quaint towns checker the island.

PRACTICAL INFORMATION

Capital: Charlottetown.

Ferries: Northumberland Ferry (☎888-249-7245; www.nfl-bay.com from P.E.I. and Nova Scotia), in Wood Islands, 61km east of Charlottetown on the Trans-Canada Hwy. To **Caribou, NS** (1¼hr.; 4-9 per day; $12, seniors $10; vehicles $50).

Toll Bridges: Confederation Bridge connects the cities of Borden, P.E.I., and Bayfield, NB, across the Northumberland Strait. Tourists pay no fee crossing into P.E.I., but must shell out a $38.75 passenger car toll when leaving.

Visitor Info: P.E.I. Visitor Information Centre, P.O. Box 940, Charlottetown C1A 7M5 (☎368-4444 or 888-734-7529; www.peiplay.com). Open daily June 8am-8pm; July-Aug. 8am-10pm; Sept. to mid-Oct. 9am-6pm; mid-Oct. to May M-F 9am-4:30pm.

Drinking Age: 19. **Postal Abbreviation:** PEI. **Sales Tax:** 10% PST, plus 7% GST.

CHARLOTTETOWN ☎902

Most of Charlottetown's sights center on its role in Canadian history as the site of the Charlottetown Confederation Conference. In addition to history, the Prince Edward Island National Park contains incredible coastal vistas, sandy beaches, and wind-swept cliffs (see **Cavendish,** p.). The town is also home to the **University of Prince Edward Island (UPEI).** The historical and urban center of the province, Charlottetown is one of the most visited spots on Prince Edward Island.

ORIENTATION & PRACTICAL INFORMATION. Queen Street and **University Avenue** are the main thoroughfares, straddling **Confederation Centre** on the west and east, respectively. The most popular beaches—**Cavendish, Brackley,** and **Rustico Island**—lie on the north shore in the middle of the province opposite Charlottetown. The longest continuous marine span bridge in the world, **Confederation Bridge** meets P.E.I. at Borden-Carleton, 56km west of Charlottetown on Hwy. 1. **Charlottetown-Cavendish Shuttles** (☎566-3243) picks up passengers at the Info Center (call for other points) and drops them off in Cavendish. (45min. July-Aug. 4 per day; June and Sept. 2 per day. $10, same-day round-trip $18.) **Taxi: City Cab,** ☎892-6567. **Bike Rental: MacQueens,** 430 Queen St. (☎368-2453. Open M-Sa 8:30am-5:30pm. Hybrid road and mountain bikes $25 per day, $125 per week; youth-size bikes $12.50/50. Must have credit card or $100 deposit for reservations.) **Visitor Info: P.E.I. Visitor Information Center,** 178 Water St. (See **Practical Information,** above.) **Internet Access: Confederation Center Library,** at Queen St. in Confederation Center. (☎368-4647. Open Tu-Th 10am-8pm, F-Sa 10am-5pm, Su 1-5pm. Free.) **Hotlines: Island Help Line,** ☎800-218-2885 (24hr.). **Rape Crisis Center,** ☎800-289-5656. **Post Office:** 135 Kent St. (☎628-4400. Open M-F 8am-5:15pm.) **Postal Code:** C1A 7K2. **Area Code:** 902

EASTERN CANADA

ACCOMMODATIONS. B&Bs and country inns crowd every nook and cranny of the province; some are open year-round, but the most inexpensive are closed low-season. Many of the island's Visitors Centers, including Charlottetown's, display daily vacancy listings for accommodations. Charlottetown's cheapest non-camping option is the **UPEI,** off Belvedere Ave., a dorm-style B&B without the Victorian frills in three residence halls: **Marian Hall** ❷ offers singles with shared baths (May-June $32, July-Aug. with breakfast $38); **Bernadine Hall** ❸ has singles and doubles with in-room sinks (singles $46/51; doubles $48/58); and **Blanchard Hall** ❹ has two-bedroom apartments (May-Aug. $76). Check-in is at Bernadine Hall. (☎566-0442. Linen and towels included. Open 24hr.) Find all the comforts of home at **City Gardens Bed & Breakfast** ❸, 114 Nassau St., near Queen St.: a quiet backyard, TV room, Internet, and a hot breakfast. (☎892-7282. 4 rooms $40-75. Cash only.)

FOOD & NIGHTLIFE. The quest for food often boils down to the search for **lobster** (from around $9 per lb.). Fresh seafood, including world-famous **Malpeque oysters** (around $9 per half-dozen, $15 for a full dozen), is sold along the shores of the island, especially in North Rustico on the north shore. Home to a world-class culinary school, Charlottetown's restaurants tend to be excellent and relatively inexpensive. In fact, the best deal in town is to be had at the **Canadian Culinary Institute ❷** itself, 4 Sydney St. First-year students cook up gourmet entrees and serve them cafeteria style. Entrees $3.53. Full lunch with salad, dessert, and beverage $8. (☎894-6857. Open M-F 11:30am-1pm. Arrive early to avoid the large line.) The young clientele at **Beanz ❶,** 52 University Ave., washes down homemade sandwiches ($4) and scrumptious cinnamon rolls ($1) with great espresso ($1.50). (☎892-8797. Open M-F 6:30am-6pm, Sa 8am-6pm, Su 9am-5pm.) After the sun goes down, head to **Baba's Lounge,** 81 University Ave., upstairs, for local brews ($4), live rock (Tu, Th-Sa), and an eclectic open mic night (W). (☎892-7377. Cover varies, usually no more than $5. Open M-Sa noon-2am, Su noon-midnight.)

SIGHTS. Province House, the proud centerpiece of Charlottetown's **Confederation Square,** was the site of the first meeting to discuss Canadian union. Fully restored to its 19th-century Victorian appearance, the House is still the seat of P.E.I.'s provincial government. (☎566-7626. 15min. video. Free self-guided tours. Open year-round; in summer daily 9am-5pm.) Also in Confederation Square, the **Confederation Centre of the Arts** houses an **art gallery** highlighting Canadian art from every province. The museum has a great collection of works by Robert Harris as well as the scrapbooks and manuscripts of Lucy Maud Montgomery. (☎628-1864; www.confederationcentre.com. Open mid-June to mid-Oct. daily 9am-5pm; mid-Oct. to mid-June Tu-Sa 11am-5pm, Su 1-5pm. Donations accepted.) Pushing the boundary between historical narration and garish multimedia spectacle, **Founder's Hall,** 6 Prince St., transports visitors "back in time" to the 1864 conference with wireless headsets and video reenactments. (☎368-1864; www.foundershall.ca. Open mid-May to late June and Sept. to mid-Oct. M-Sa 9am-5pm, Su 9am-4pm; late June-Aug. M-Sa 9am-8pm, Su 9am-4pm. $7, seniors $5.50, ages 6-17 $3.75.)

Some of Canada's finest **beaches** are to be found on P.E.I. The stretches of beach on the eastern coast are less touristed than those in the west, perhaps due to the rougher surf. *At all beaches, high winds and riptides make solo swimming dangerous.* **Basin Head Beach,** 95km east of Charlottetown, makes a relaxing daytrip, with over 11km of uncrowded white sand. **Lakeside,** a beach 35km east of Charlottetown on Hwy. 2, is unsupervised and often deserted on summer weekdays. Trot along the surf atop a sturdy steed from **Lake Circle T Trails,** located beside the golf course in Lakeside. (☎961-3060. Open July-Aug. daily 9am-8pm. Guided horse rides $15 per hr.) Celtic concerts and Scottish *ceilidhs,* with bagpipes and traditional dance, are held throughout the summer at the **College of Piping,** 619 Water St. E., in Summerside. Call for a full schedule. (☎877-224-7473. *Ceilidhs* nightly July-Aug. $12, seniors $11, students and children $7.)

CAVENDISH ☎902

GREEN GABLES. Green Gables House, off Hwy. 6 in Cavendish just west of Hwy. 13, is a shrine for readers—a surprising number of whom are from Japan—who adore Lucy Maud Montgomery's *Anne of Green Gables.* The traditionally furnished house is the spitting image of Anne Shirley's home in the novel (as well it should be—it was restored and redecorated to mirror the book's descriptions). (☎963-7874. Open daily July-Aug. 9am-8pm; May-June and

Sept.-Oct. 9am-5pm. $5.75, seniors $5, ages 6-16 $3; families $14.50.) Back towards Charlottetown on Hwy. 6 is the **Lucy Maud Montgomery House,** a calmer and less touristed site that retains the serenity and quiet beauty of Cavendish as Montgomery knew it. Visitors are treated to a small museum (run by descendants of the author) and a picturesque walking tour of the ruins of Montgomery's childhood home. (☎963-2231; www.peisland.com/lmm. Open daily June and Sept. to mid-Oct. 10am-5pm; July-Aug. 9am-7pm. $2, ages 6-16 $1.) Serious Anne afficionados will also want to make a trip to **Avonlea,** a life-size recreation of Anne's town. Actors in period dress re-enact scenes from the novel throughout the day. (☎963-3050; www.avonlea.ca. $17, seniors $15, ages 6-16 $13; families $45. Open mid-June to late Sept. daily 9am-5pm.) A **Visitor Center** for the town of Cavendish, Green Gables, and the park is located at the intersection of Hwy. 6 and 13. (☎963-7830; www.peiplay.com. Open mid-June to mid-Aug. daily 8am-9pm; call for low-season hours.)

After a long day of sightseeing, calm yourself with the spectacular sunset view from the dining room of **Café on the Clyde ❷,** down Hwy. 13 in nearby New Glasgow. The potato pie ($10) is a perennial favorite, as are the generous slices of fresh berry pies ($3.50-4.50). (☎964-4303. Open daily 8am-9pm.) Find peace and quiet at the **Country House Inn ❸,** on Gulf Shore Rd. in the National Park 5 km south from the Hwy. 13 gate. Beautiful ocean views, easy beach access, and a huge buffet-style breakfast make this a perfect base for exploring Cavendish. (☎963-2055; www.cavendishbeachresort.com/countryhouseinn. Free bikes and passes for beaches and national park. Open June-Oct. 3-night min. stay. Singles $50-60.)

PRINCE EDWARD ISLAND NATIONAL PARK. Wind-sculpted sand dunes, red sea cliffs, and saltwater marshes undulate along the park's terrain, which is home to many of the Island's 300 species of birds. Eleven easy **trails** of varying length meander along meadows and floating boardwalks. An entrance fee is required (mid-June to Sept. $5, seniors $4.25, children $2.50, families $12.50; low-season $3/2.50/1.50/7.50). The park operates three **campgrounds ❶** during the summer and one low-season. Reservations are strongly recommended and must be made at least three days in advance. Nature walks, campfires, and slide shows entertain campers at all three campgrounds in July and August. (☎672-6350 for info; 800-414-6765 for reservations. Showers, laundry facilities, and beach access. Park facilities open mid-May to Oct. From June to mid-Oct., sites $21-22, with hookup $25-27; low-season free.) Privately-owned campgrounds also fill the island.

NEWFOUNDLAND

Perched off the Eastern shore of North America, Newfoundland had the earliest encounter with European civilization on the continent. In the 10th century, 500 years before Columbus, Viking seafarers established an outpost on the north shore of the island. The region's legendary stock of codfish later lured British and Irish colonists to Newfoundland's craggy coast. Over the next few centuries, Newfoundland developed a distinct maritime culture, with elements from Irish and British seafaring traditions to form a unique music, accent, and way of life. Geographic remoteness hardly dampened the Islanders' enthusiasm for Great Britain—Newfoundland was the last province to join, reluctantly, the Confederation. It maintains an independent spirit as well as gorgeous vistas, rugged fjords, the longest pub street in North America, and the friendliest folks east of Iowa.

PRACTICAL INFORMATION

Capital: St. John's.

Visitor Info: Tourism Newfoundland & Labrador, P.O. Box 8730, St. John's A1B 4K2 (☎800-563-6353; www.gov.nf.ca/tourism).

Newfoundland Ferries: Marine Atlantic (☎800-341-7981) runs service from **North Sydney, NS** to **Argentia** (14hr.; late June to mid-Sept. 3 per week, late Sept. M only; $69, seniors $62, ages 5-12 $35; bicycles $22; automobiles $146) and **Port aux Basques** (6-8hr., 1-3 per day, $25/23/13/11/73). Prices for vehicles are in addition to passenger fare. Reservations highly recommended. Arrive at least 1hr. early.

Drinking Age: 19. **Postal Abbreviation:** NF. **Sales Tax:** 15% HST.

ST. JOHN'S ☎709

One of the oldest ports in North America, St. John's has grown from a 16th-century strategic harbor to the capital of Canada's easternmost province. The city's heart continues to be its harbor, crammed with freighters and fishing boats from around the world. Despite this traffic, the hilly downtown—stacked full of brightly colored rowhouses—has maintained a hospitable, residential feel while also sustaining countless pubs, quality restaurants, and swank Scandinavian clothing stores.

ORIENTATION & PRACTICAL INFORMATION. The Trans-Canada Hwy. becomes **Kenmount Road** as it enters the city and is packed with strip malls, fast food restaurants, and chain motels. From the end of Kenmount Rd., **Freshwater Road** leads into the downtown core, where **Harbour Drive, Water Street,** and **Duckworth Road** run parallel to one another and host the lion's share of stores, pubs, and restaurants. Driving downtown is a confusing affair; walking is a much better option. **St. John's International Airport** (☎758-8581; www.stjohnsairport.com) has daily flights from Halifax, Montréal, and Toronto. Taxi service from the airport to downtown is about $15. **DRL Coachlines,** (☎888-269-1852; www.drlgroup.com/coachlines) a regional firm, runs buses from the Memorial University student center to Port aux Basques (13hr.; 1 per day; $97) on the far end of the island. Numerous **local taxi shuttles** service the more remote communities; ask at the Visitors Center. **St. John's Metrobus** buses locally within the city. (☎570-2020. Buses daily 6:30am-11pm. $1.75, children $1.25, under 3 free.) **Canary Cycles,** 294 Water St., rents bikes for $20 per day. (☎579-5972; www.canarycycles.com. Helmet $5. Credit card required.) From June to September, a **Visitors Center** sits in a converted railcar on Harbour Dr. (☎576-8514. Open daily 9am-5pm.) Another info center is open year-round at City Hall, 35 New Gower St. (☎576-8104. Open M-F 9am-4:30pm.) **Medical Services: General Hospital,** 300 Prince Philip Pkwy. (☎737-6300.) **Hotlines: Crisis Line,** ☎737-4668. **Sexual Assault Line,** ☎726-1411. 24hr. **Post Office:** 354 Water St. (☎758-1003. Free **Internet access.** Open M-F 8am-5pm.) **Postal Code:** A1C 1C0. **Area Code:** 709.

ACCOMMODATIONS. Most of the accommodations in St. John's take the form of Victorian B&Bs. Although quality is very high and the charm is undeniable, the prices (starting at $55 and going straight up) discourage many budget travelers. There are a few less-pricey options, but demand often far outstrips supply; be sure to make reservations if visiting in July and August. **The Downtown International Hostel ❶,** 25 Young St., has a great location, clean rooms, and a friendly atmosphere that often results in impromptu group trips to the pubs on George St. (☎754-7658; downtownhostel@yahoo.com. Well-equipped kitchen.

Internet access. With only 5 beds, reservations are highly recommended. Dorms $20; private rooms $30.) **Memorial University ❶**, on Livyers Loop off Prince Phillip Dr., rents comfortable dorm rooms 10min. from downtown. (☎737-7933. Free linen and parking. Towels $2. Laundry facilities. Check-in daily 3pm-midnight, on call 24hr. Open May-Aug. Singles $19, non-students $30; doubles $32/39.) **The Roses B&B ❹**, 9 Military Rd., two streets from Duckworth St., has a gorgeous harbor view and rooms that are downright proper. (☎726-3336. Open year-round. Singles $70; doubles $80.)

FOOD. The golden-arches school of American cuisine can be found along Kenmount Rd. near the University. Hipper restaurants cluster around Water St. For the budget-minded, **Mustang Sally's Cafe ❶**, 7 Queen St., at George St., satisfies the palate and the wallet. Choose your own ingredients for the well-known quesadillas and wraps ($5-7). (☎754-9727. Open M-Th and Su 10am-11pm, F-Sa 10am-4am.) **The Classic Cafe ❷**, 364 Duckworth St., takes a classy approach to traditional lunch and dinner favorites. (☎579-4444. Chicken and fish entrees $13-20. Salads and sandwiches $4-9. Open M-F 11am-2pm and 5-10pm, Sa 9am-11pm, Su 9am-3pm and 5-11pm.) For a bite of homestyle local food, **Velma's Traditional Newfoundland Food ❸**, 264 Water St., does amazing things with cod. (☎576-2264. Cod tongues $17. Open M-F 8:30am-9:30pm, Sa 8am-10pm, Su 9am-9pm.)

SIGHTS. A trip up **Signal Hill**, on Signal Hill Rd. just east of Duckworth St., grants gorgeous views of the harbor, the city, and the bleak expanse of the Atlantic Ocean. On the way up the hill, the newly opened **Geocentre** offers a hands-on look at global and local geology using impressive multimedia exhibits. (☎737-7880; www.geocentre.ca. Open M-Sa 9:30am-5pm, Su 1-5pm; mid-Oct. to May closed M. $6, seniors and students $5, ages 5-17 $3; families $5.) Close to the top of the hill, the **Queen's Battery** commands a strategic position at the entrance of the harbor. The battery's six 32 lb. cannons protected the harbor during the 1860s, but by then St. John's had already been subjected to numerous bloody battles between the French and the English. The hill also has seen its share of significant peaceful moments, earning its name by being the site where Marconi received the first trans-Atlantic radio transmission in 1901. **Cabot Tower,** at the peak of the hill, houses an exhibit about Marconi and his technological breakthrough. The top of the tower offers the best view in town, encompassing the harbor, Cape Spear, and—if you're lucky—frolicking whales. (Tower open daily 8:30am-9pm.) Four times a week during the summer, the **Signal Hill Tattoo** reenacts 19th-century military exercises. Cast members sell tickets at the **Interpretation Centre,** which houses an exhibit on 500 years of Newfoundland history. (☎772-5367. Interpretation Centre open daily mid-June to Labor Day 8:30am-8pm; low-season 8:30am-5pm. Exhibits $3.50, seniors $3, ages 6-16 $1.75; families $8.75. Combination pass for Signal Hill and Cape Spear: $5.50/5/3/14. Tattoo reenactment $3.50.) On the way down the hill, the **North Head Walking Trail** takes hikers right to the edge of the entrance to the harbor.

Eleven kilometers out of town on Blackhead Rd., off Water St., **Cape Spear** promontory is the easternmost land in North America. Two white lighthouses (one of which is the oldest surviving lighthouse in Canada) stand out against a green, rocky point and the slate-gray Atlantic. Paths meander around the jagged shore, up through the heath, and past two run-down bunkers from World War II to the lighthouses. (☎772-4210. Visitors Center open May-Oct. daily 10am-6pm. Lighthouse $3.50, seniors $3, ages 6-16 $1.75; families $8.75.) The **Irish Loop,** a daylong scenic drive around the southern tip of the Avalon Peninsula, grants views of passing icebergs, seasonal Atlantic Puffin, and the rugged Avalon Peninsula Reserve. For thrills by sea rather than land, head to Cape Broyle on the

Irish Loop and dive into a sea kayak. **Stan Cook Sea Kayaking,** 67 Circular Rd., a family-run tour operation, has tours for all skill levels. (☎579-6353 or 888-747-6353. 2½hr. $52, 4hr. $75, all day $105. Ages 10 and up.) In St. John's, **Dee Jay Charters** runs whale-watching charters out of the harbor, next to the Visitors Center's train car. (☎753-8687. 2½hr. 3 trips daily. $25, ages 11-16 $10, under 10 free. Reservations recommended.)

WINDY WEATHER The weather in St. John's can be so extreme (winds at Signal Hill reach 140kph, and gusts hit 200kph) that locals have developed a vocabulary to describe it. "Caplin Weather" refers to wet, foggy weather, common in June and July. In the winter, "growlers" loom in the waters off St. John's—large, unstable icebergs that are particularly dangerous to boats because of their low profile.

ENTERTAINMENT & NIGHTLIFE. The entertainment options in St. John's are surprisingly varied. Traditional Newfoundland dinner parties ("times") include folk music, dancing, and occasionally theater; check at the Visitors Center for listings. More organized theater may be had just off Water St. at the converted **Longshoremen's Protective Union Hall (LSPU Hall),** 3 Victoria St. (☎753-4531). Every other summer, St. John's hosts the **Soundsymposium** (☎754-5409; www.soundsymposium.com), a festival of experimental and bizarre music. The next one is scheduled for July 8-18, 2004. The daily performance of the **Harbour Symphony** is the world's only symphony of boat whistles; the sound can carry for 12 mi. The first Wednesday of every August brings the oldest continuing sporting event in North America, the **Royal St. John's Regatta,** to Quidi Vidi Lake. (☎576-8921.)

Less organized fun can be had in the legendary pub scene. **George Street,** or Pub Street, contains the longest continuous chain of pubs and bars in North America and has themes and music to suit any partygoer's tastes. **The Ship Inn,** 265 Duckworth St. at Solomon's Lane, is legendary in St. John's for its phenomenal live music and relaxed feel. (☎753-3870. Occasional cover. Live music Tu-Su. Pints $5-6. Open daily noon-2am.) **O'Reilly's Irish Pub,** 15 George St., packs in the 20-somethings with a heaping helping of Newfoundland music, which tends to be a mixture of traditional Celtic and modern pop styles. Tu is open mic night. (☎722-3735. Open Su-Th noon-2am, F-Sa noon-3am.) The psychadelic **Bar None,** 164 Water St., upstairs from the alley, attracts a young crowd with its mix of rock and alternative tunes. (☎579-2110. Pints $5.75. Open M-W 2pm-2am, Th-Su 2pm-3am.)

GROS MORNE NATIONAL PARK ☎709

On precisely the opposite side of Newfoundland from St. John's, Gros Morne encompasses more than 1800 square kilometers of fjords, conifer forests, and glacier-carved valleys. Designated a UNESCO world heritage site in 1987, Gros Morne preserves some of the wildest scenery and animal life in North America.

THIS AIN'T BULLWINKLE. Moose are a common sight throughout Newfoundland, and not always a welcome one; they pose a serious hazard to drivers. Each year, dozens of people are killed in moose collisions. Most accidents occur between dusk and dawn, when the moose are active. Avoid driving at these times, and use extreme caution if you must drive.

ORIENTATION & PRACTICAL INFORMATION. Tucked against the Gulf of St. Lawrence on the west coast of Newfoundland, Gros Morne is reached by taking the **430 spur (Viking Trail)** off the Trans-Canada Hwy. in Deer Lake. There is no public transportation to Gros Morne. **DRL Coachlines** (☎888-269-1852) runs a daily bus from St. John's to Port-aux-Basques, with a stop in Deer Lake. From there, **Pittman's Shuttle Service** (☎634-4710) will take you into the park. Inside the park, the town of **Rocky Harbour** is the main service center. The main **Visitors Center** is at the center of the park, near Rocky Harbour; pick up a free copy of *Tuckamore*—the invaluable park guide—and some good advice. (☎458-2066. Open daily mid-June to Aug. 9am-9pm; May to mid-June and Sept. to mid-Oct. 9am-5pm; mid-Oct. to Jan. M-F 9am-4pm.) Separated from Rocky Harbour and the northern portion of the park by Bonne Bay, the southernmost region of Gros Morne has beautiful hiking trails and the new **Discovery Centre,** with exhibits on Gros Morne's geology and conservation. (☎453-2490. Open daily mid-June to Aug. 9am-6pm; May to mid-June and Sept. to mid-Oct. 9am-5pm.) This part of the park is about 70km from Rocky Harbour on Hwy. 431. The **Bonne Bay Water Taxi,** between Norris Point Wharf and Woody Point Wharf, is a quicker option. (☎458-2730. 3 departures daily. One-way $5, student $3; families $8; round-trip $8/5/15.) From mid-May to mid-October, there are entrance fees for the National Park, charged at either the entrance kiosk or the Visitors Center. (Daily pass $7.50, seniors $6, ages 6-16 $3.75; families $15.)

CAMPING. Gros Morne contains five developed **campgrounds** ❶ comprising over 300 sites. Although the park is rarely full, campers planning to visit during the busy months of July and August would be wise to reserve a site at their desired campground. (☎800-414-6765. $15 reservation fee.) The developed campgrounds contain the usual amenities: running water, pit toilets, and close proximity to picnic grounds. In addition, Trout River, Lomond, Berry Hill, and Shallow Bay sport playgrounds, showers, and hot water. **Shallow Bay, Green Point,** and **Lomond** campgrounds are on the coast with unsupervised beach access; Lomond has a boat launch. **Trout River** campground is on a pond and has swimming and a sheltered boat launch. **Berry Hill** campground is set off the beach, close to a number of trailheads. Campgrounds are open mid-June to mid-Sept., with the exception of Lomond (open mid-May to mid-Oct.) and Green Point (open year-round; no water Oct.-Apr.). **Backcountry camping** is allowed along some of the longer trails with a permit. Campers pay a reduced entry fee to the park, but must pay a daily rate for camping. (Entry for campers $5.50, seniors $4.25, ages 6-16 $3; families $11. Campsites $21, except at Green Point $13; backcountry camping $8 per person.) For the less rugged and more frugal, the **Juniper Campground** ❶, in Rocky Harbour, runs a small **hostel.** The friendly travelers who end up here are often generous in offering rides to St. John's or Port-aux-Basques. (☎458-2917. Kitchen. Dorms $12.)

OUTDOOR ACTIVITIES. The easiest way to take in the Gros Morne scenery is onboard a **boat tour** of the fjords and shoreline. **Bon Tours** runs the most popular tour, at Western Brook Pond. (☎458-2730. 2hr., plus 3km walk from parking lot to dock. Wheelchair-accessible. In July and Aug., 3 tours daily. $35, ages 12-16 $16, under 12 $10; families $75. Reservations required.) Those more interested in self-propulsion can rent a **kayak** from Norris Point, just south of the Visitors Center. (☎458-2722. 2hr. kayak rental $25; 8hr. $35; 24hr. $40. 2½hr. tours $45, seniors $40, ages 16 and under $35; families $140; full-day tours $105/95/80/224.) There are hundreds of kilometers of trails to enjoy. Park interpreters lead many fascinating guided hikes; check *Tuckamore* for schedules. **Gros Morne Mountain** (16km, 7-8hr.) among the park's most rigorous hikes. Though it is possible to complete the hike in 1 day, primitive campsites line the route. The view from the peak is awe-inspiring but closed until July 1 due to preservation efforts. The **Tablelands Trail** (6km, 2hr.) is less demanding and affords a remarkable view of a tundra-like landscape.

QUÉBEC

Originally populated by French fur trading settlements along the St. Lawrence River, Québec was ceded to the British in 1759. Ever since, anti-federalist elements within *québécois* society have rankled under national government control. Visitors may be tipped off to the underlying struggles by the occasional cry for "Liberté!" scrawled across a sidewalk, but the tensions are mostly kept behind closed doors. Instead, Montréal's renowned nightlife and Québec City's centuries-old European flair distinguish Québec among Canada's provinces.

PRACTICAL INFORMATION

Capital: Québec City.

Visitor Info: Tourisme Québec, C.P. 979, Montréal H3C 2W3 (☎800-363-7777, in Montréal 514-873-2015; www.tourisme.gouv.qc.ca). Open daily 9am-5pm. **Canadian Parks Service,** Québec Region, 3 Passage du D'or, C.P. Box 6060, Haute-Ville GIR 4V7 (☎800-463-6769, in Québec City 418-648-4177).

Drinking Age: 18. **Postal Abbreviation:** QC. **Sales Tax:** 7.5% PST, plus 7% GST.

MONTRÉAL ☎514

This island city has been coveted territory for over 300 years. Wars and sieges dominated Montréal's early history as British forces strove to wrest it from French control. Today, the invaders are not British, French, or American generals, but rather visitors eager to experience a diverse city with a cosmopolitan air. Though only an hour from the US border, Montréal has grown to be the second largest French-speaking city in the world. Fashion that rivals Paris, a nightlife comparable to London, and cuisine from around the globe all attest to a prominent European legacy. Whether attracted to Montréal's global flavor or its large student population, it is hard not to be swept up by the vibrancy coursing through the *centre-ville*.

EASTERN CANADA

INTERCITY TRANSPORTATION

Airports: Dorval (☎394-7377; www.admtl.com), 25min. from downtown by car. Many area hostels run airport shuttles for about $11; call hostels in advance for information. By Métro, take bus #211 from the Lionel Groulx (green and orange lines) to Dorval Train Station, then transfer to bus #204. **L'Aérobus** (☎931-9002) runs a minivan to Dorval from 777 rue de la Gauchetière Ouest, at rue de l'Université, stopping at any downtown hotel if notified in advance. Vans run daily every 30min. 3:30am-11pm. $11, under 5 free. Taxi to downtown $30-35. Another airport, **Mirabel International** (☎450-476-3010 or 800-465-1213), is 45min. from downtown by car. Taxi to downtown $70.

Trains: Gare Centrale, 895 rue de la Gauchetière Ouest, under Queen Elizabeth Hotel. Métro: Bonaventure. Served by **VIA Rail** (☎989-2626 or 800-561-9181; www.viarail.com), open daily 7am-midnight. To: **Ottawa** (2hr., 4-5 per day, $43); **Québec City** (3hr., 4 per day, $57); **Toronto** (4-5½hr., 8 per day, $105). Buy discount tickets 5+ days in advance. Luggage regulations require large pieces to be checked at least 30min. before departure– arrive 45min. before departure if you have luggage. **Amtrak** (☎800-842-7275), open daily 8am-5pm. To **New York** (9-12hr., 2 per day, $62).

Buses: Station Centrale, 505 bd. de Maissonneuve Est (☎843-4231). Métro: Berri-UQAM; follow the gray "Autobus-Terminus" signs upstairs. Open 24hr. **Voyageur** (☎842-2281; www.voyageur.com), to **Ottawa** (2hr., every hr. 6am-midnight, $35) and

Toronto (7-9hr., 7 per day, $85). **Orléans Express** (☎395-400; www.orleansexpress.com), to **Québec City** (3-4hr., 21 per day, $38). **Greyhound USA** (☎287-1580), to **Boston** (7hr., 5 per day, $61) and **New York City** (9hr., 7 per day, $70).

Carpooling Service: Allô Stop, 4317 rue St-Denis (☎985-3032; www.allostop.com). Open Sa-W 9am-6pm, Th-F 9am-7pm. Matches passengers with member drivers; part of the rider fee goes to the driver. To **Québec City** ($15) and **Sherbrooke** ($9). Riders and drivers fix their own fees for rides over 1000 mi. Annual membership fee required ($6).

ORIENTATION

Two major streets divide the city, making orientation simple. The one-way **Boulevard St-Laurent** (also called **"le Main,"** or **"The Main"**) runs north through the city, splitting Montréal and its streets east-west. The Main also serves as the unofficial French/English divider; English **McGill University** lies to the west, while **St-Denis,** a street running parallel to St-Laurent, lies to the east and defines the French student quarter (also called the *quartier latin* and the "student ghetto"). **Rue Sherbrooke,** which is paralleled by **de Maisonneuve** and **Ste-Catherine** downtown, runs east-west almost the entire length of Montréal. The **Underground City** runs north-south, stretching from **rue Sherbrooke** to **rue de la Gauchetière** and **rue St-Antoine.** A free map from the tourist office helps navigation. **Parking** is expensive and often difficult to find along the streets. Try parking lots on the city's outskirts for reasonable prices.

NEIGHBORHOODS

When first founded, Montréal was limited to the riverside area of present-day **Vieux-Montréal.** It has since evolved from a settlement of French colonists into a hip, cosmopolitan metropolis. A stroll along **rue Ste-Catherine,** the flashy commercial avenue, is a must. This is where European fashion teases Canada, overheard conversations mix English and French, and upscale retail shops intermingle with tacky souvenir stores and debaucherous nightclubs. Its assortment of peep shows and sex shops has earned it the nickname "Saint-Vitrine" (holy windows).

A small **Chinatown,** occupies rue de la Gauchetière, just north of Métro: Place d'Armes. **Little Greece,** a fairly long walk from downtown, is just southeast of the Outremont Métro. At the northern edge of the town's center, **Little Italy** occupies the area north of rue Beaubien between rue St-Hubert and Louis-Hémon. Rue St-Denis, home to the city's elite at the turn of the century, still serves as the **Quartier Latin's** main street. Restaurants of all flavors are clustered along rue Prince Arthur. Nearby, **Square St-Louis** hosts a beautiful fountain and sculptures. **Boulevard St-Laurent,** north of Sherbrooke, is perfect for walking or biking. A little further north, **Jean-Talon** is home to Greek, Slavic, Latin American, and Portuguese immigrants among others. The area around the intersection of ch. de la Côte-des-Neiges and rue Jean-Brillant, near l'Université de Montréal comprises a small neighborhood full of fun cafes and strolling shoppers. Many attractions between **Mont-Royal** and the **Fleuve St-Laurent** are free. **Le Village,** the gay village, is located along rue Ste-Catherine Est between rue St-Hubert and Papineau. Both the Quartier Latin and the area along rue St-Denis foster a very liberal, gay-friendly atmosphere.

LOCAL TRANSPORTATION

Public Transit: STM Métro and Bus (☎288-6287; www.stm.info). The world's most advanced public transit system when it was built for the 1976 World's Fair, Montréal's Métro is still comprehensive, logical, and safe. The 4 Métro lines and most buses run daily 5:30am-12:30am; some have early morning schedules as well. Get maps at the tourist

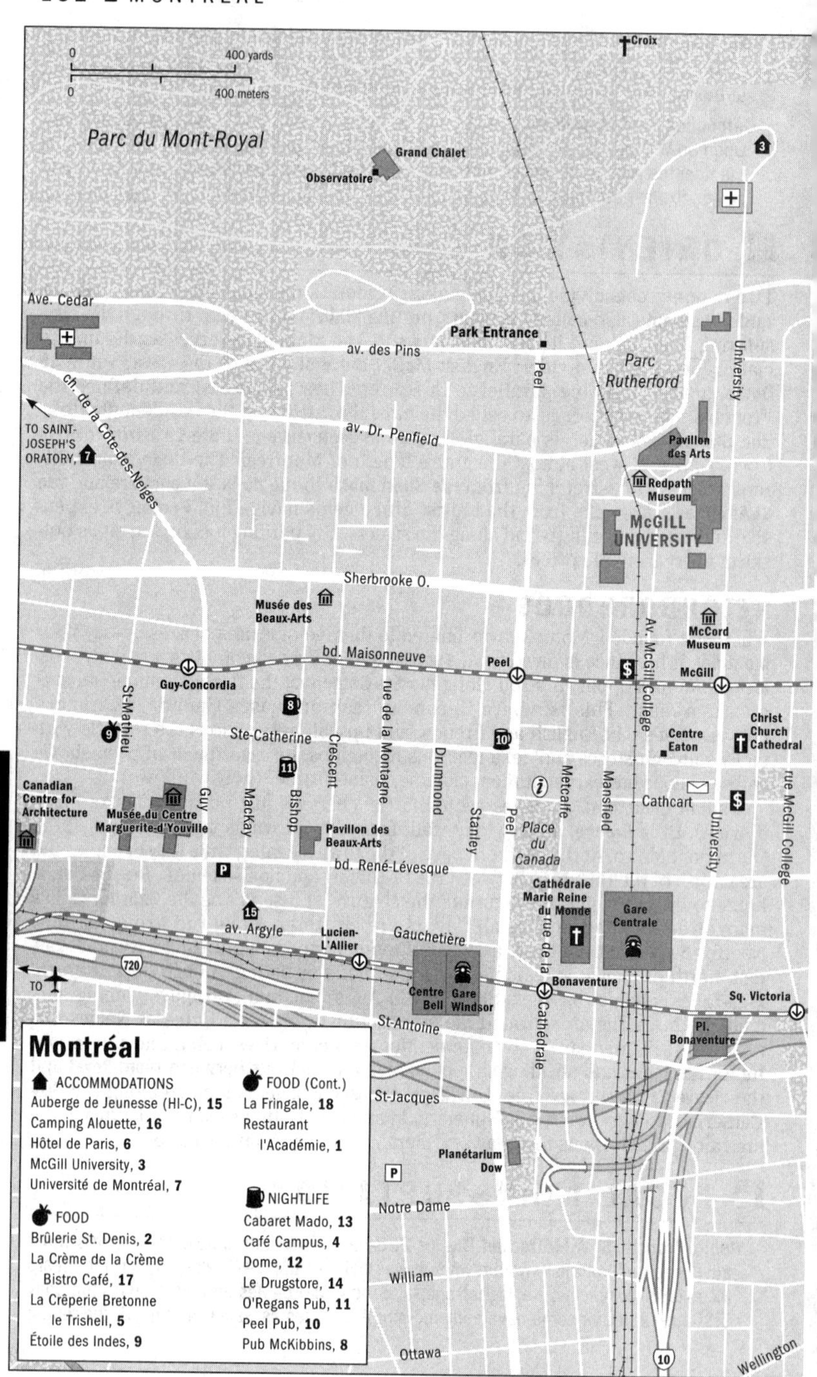

Parc du Mont-Royal
Grand Châlet
Observatoire
Croix
Ave. Cedar
Park Entrance
av. des Pins
Parc Rutherford
University
ch. de la Côte-des-Neiges
TO SAINT-JOSEPH'S ORATORY, 7
av. Dr. Penfield
Peel
Pavillon des Arts
Redpath Museum
McGILL UNIVERSITY
Sherbrooke O.
Musée des Beaux-Arts
McCord Museum
bd. Maisonneuve
Guy-Concordia
Peel
McGill
Av. McGill College
St-Mathieu
Ste-Catherine
Crescent
rue de la Montagne
Drummond
Centre Eaton
Christ Church Cathedral
Canadian Centre for Architecture
Musée du Centre Marguerite-d'Youville
Guy
MacKay
Bishop
Pavillon des Beaux-Arts
Stanley
Peel
Metcalfe
Mansfield
Place du Canada
Cathcart
University
rue McGill College
bd. René-Lévesque
Cathédrale Marie Reine du Monde
Gare Centrale
av. Argyle
Lucien-L'Allier
Gauchetière
rue de la Cathédrale
720
TO
Centre Bell
Gare Windsor
Bonaventure
Sq. Victoria
St-Antoine
Pl. Bonaventure
St-Jacques
Planétarium Dow
Notre Dame
William
Ottawa
10
Wellington
Montréal
ACCOMMODATIONS
Auberge de Jeunesse (HI-C), 15
Camping Alouette, 16
Hôtel de Paris, 6
McGill University, 3
Université de Montréal, 7
FOOD
Brûlerie St. Denis, 2
La Crème de la Crème Bistro Café, 17
La Crêperie Bretonne le Trishell, 5
Étoile des Indes, 9
FOOD (Cont.)
La Fringale, 18
Restaurant l'Académie, 1
NIGHTLIFE
Cabaret Mado, 13
Café Campus, 4
Dome, 12
Le Drugstore, 14
O'Regans Pub, 11
Peel Pub, 10
Pub McKibbins, 8

Parc Jeanne-Mance
av. du Parc
TO LITTLE GREECE
Duluth
TO LITTLE ITALY,
MONT ROYAL
JEAN TALON
THÉÂTRE DU RIDEAU VERT, NAT'L THEATRE SCHOOL OF CANADA
Théâtre d'Aujourd'hui
Roy
av. des Pins
Sherbrooke
SQUARE SAINT-LOUIS
Prince Arthur
TO OLYMPIC PARK, BIODÔME
QUARTIER LATIN
Milton
Sherbrooke E.
St-Denis
Berri
St-Hubert
Musée juste pour rire
Sherbrooke O.
bd. St-Laurent
Bibliothèque Nationale du Québec
Ontario
Théâtre Saint-Denis
Pl.-des-Arts
St-Laurent
Berri-UQAM
bd. Maisonneuve
Place des Arts
LE VILLAGE
Musée d'Art Contemporain
UNIVERSITÉ QUÉBEC À MONTRÉAL
Ste-Catherine
Théâtre du Nouveau Monde
TO 13 (25m), 14 (200m)
St-Alexandre
rue de Bleury
Jeanne-Mance
St-Urbain
bd. René-Lévesque
CHINATOWN
Gauchetière
TO 16 (20km)
av. Viger
Place-d'Armes
Champ-de-Mars
SQUARE VIGER
Palais de Congrès
720
Musée Artur Pascal
Berri
St-Antoine
Parc Champs-de-Mars
Palais de Justice
Vieux Palais de Justice
Hôtel de Ville de Montréal
TO ÎLE SAINTE-HÉLÈNE, LE VIEUX FORT, LA RONDE
St-Jacques
PL. D'ARMES
Notre-Dame
VIEUX-MONTRÉAL
St-Vincent
Jacques-Cartier
Musée du Château Ramezay
St-Paul
Chapelle Notre-Dame-de-Bon-Secours
St-Sulpice
St-François-Xavier
Centaur Theatre
Basilique Notre-Dame de Montréal
St-Paul
Marché Bonsecours
Tour de l'Horloge
Pl. Royale
rue de la Commune
VIEUX-PORT
Centre d'Histoire de Montréal
Quai Jacques Cartier
Quai de l'Horloge
St-Jean
Pointe à Callière
IMAX
Quai King Edward
Fleuve St-Laurent
McGill
St-Pierre
Quai Alexandra
Musée Marc-Aurèle-Fortin
Le Pélican

EASTERN CANADA

office or any Métro station. Buses are well-integrated; transfer tickets (*correspondances*) from bus drivers are valid as subway tickets and vice versa. Fare for métro or bus $2.25, 6 tickets $9.50. Between Apr. and Oct., buy a Tourist Card at any downtown station, Sherbrooke, Mont-Royal, Pie-IX, Jean-Talon, or Longueuil. 1-day unlimited access $7, 3-day $14.

Taxi: Taxi Coop de Montréal, ☎725-9885. **Champlain Taxi Inc.,** ☎273-2435.

Car Rental: Via Route, 1255 rue MacKay (☎871-1166; www.viaroute.com), at Ste-Catherine. Open M-W 7am-7pm, Th-F 7am-9pm, Sa 7:30am-5pm, Su 9am-7pm.

Bike Rental: Ça Roule, 27 de la Commune Est (☎866-0633; www.caroulemontreal.com). Métro: Place d'Armes. Open daily 10am-8pm; closes at 6pm or earlier in bad weather. Bikes $20-25 per day; rollerblades $20 per day; protective gear included. ID required. Much of the Métro system allows bikes during designated hours. Before trying, check the policy of the route.

PRACTICAL INFORMATION

Visitor Info: Infotouriste, 1001 rue de Square-Dorchester (☎877-266-5687; www.tourisme-montreal.org), on Ste-Catherine between rue Peel and rue Metcalfe. Métro: Peel. Open July-Aug. daily 8:30am-8pm; Sept.-June 9am-6pm. In **Vieux-Montréal,** 174 rue Notre-Dame Est, at Pl. Jacques Cartier. Open daily July-Aug. 9am-7pm; low-season 9am-5pm.

Currency Exchange: Custom House, 905 bd. Maisonneuve (☎844-1414). Métro: McGill. Open M-F 8:30am-6pm, Sa 9am-4pm. **Calforex,** 1250 rue Peel (☎392-9100). Métro: Peel. Flat $2.75 fee. Open M-W 8:30am-7pm, Th-Sa 8:30am-9pm, Su 10am-6pm; low-season Sa 10am-7pm. Rue Ste-Catherine is lined with other small *bureaux de change*—watch out for high commissions.

Hotlines: Tél-Aide, ☎935-1101. **Sexual Assault Hotline,** ☎934-4504. Both operate 24hr. **Gay and Lesbian Hotline,** ☎866-5090. Operates daily 7-11pm. **Rape Crisis,** ☎278-9383. Operates M-F 9:30am-4:30pm; call Tél-Aide after hours.

Internet Access: Bibliothèque Nationale du Québec, 1700 rue St-Denis (☎873-1100). Métro: Berri UQAM. 2 computers with free access; sign-up required. Open M-F 9am-5pm. **Internet cafes** are plentiful in Montréal and generally charge $2 for 30min.

Post Office: 685 rue Cathcart (☎395-4539). Open M-F 8am-6pm. **Postal Code:** H3B 3B0. **Area Code:** 514 for the island of Montréal, 450 for the north and south shores.

ACCOMMODATIONS

The **Infotouriste** (☎877-266-5687) is the best resource for info about hostels, hotels, and *chambres touristiques* (rooms in private homes or small guest houses). Inquire about B&Bs at the **Downtown Bed and Breakfast Network ❶,** 3458 av. Laval, H2X 3C8, near Sherbrooke; the managers run their own modest hideaway and maintain a list of 80 other homes downtown. (☎289-9749 or 800-267-5180; www.bbmontreal.qc.ca. Open daily 9am-9pm. Singles $40-75; doubles $45-90.) The least expensive *maisons touristiques* and hotels cluster around **rue St-Denis,** which abuts Vieux Montréal. Canada Day and the Grand Prix in July make accommodations scarce, even outside the city. Reserve well in advance.

Auberge de Jeunesse, Montréal Youth Hostel (HI-C), 1030 rue MacKay (☎843-3317; www.hostellingmontreal.com). Métro: Lucien-L'Allier; from the station exit, cross the street and head right. The hostel is down the first real street on the left, across from the parking lot. Airport shuttle drivers will stop here if asked. With a full bathroom in every room, a complete kitchen, laundry facilities, pool tables, Internet access, and a *petit café* whipping up quality eats, the Montréal Youth Hostel is synonymous with heaven.

The 240 beds (4-10 per room) fill quickly in summer; reservations are strongly recommended. Pub crawl Tu and F 8:30pm. Linen $2.30; no sleeping bags. 1-week max. stay. Reception 24hr. Check-in 1pm. Check-out 11am. Dorms $22, nonmembers $26; private doubles $29/34 per person. ❶

McGill University, Bishop Mountain Hall, 3935 rue de l'Université (☎398-6367; www.mcgill.ca/residences/summer, or reserve.residences@mcgill.ca). Métro: McGill. Follow Université along the edge of campus; when the road seems to end in a parking lot at the top of the steep hill, bear right–it is the circular grey stone building with lots of windows. Kitchenettes on each floor. 1000 beds. Free Internet access, common room with TV, towels and linen provided, and laundry facilities. Full breakfast M-Th 7:30-9:30am $7; continental breakfast $4.50. Reception daily 7am-10pm; there is a guard for late check-in. Check-in 3pm. Check-out noon. Open mid-May to mid-Aug. Singles $45, students and seniors $40; weekly $235/200. ❷

Université de Montréal, Residences, 2350 rue Edouard-Montpetit (☎343-6531; www.resid.umontreal.ca). Métro: Edouard-Montpetit. Follow the signs up the steep hill. Located in a tranquil, remote neighborhood on the edge of a beautiful campus, the East Tower affords a great view. Recently renovated. Linen provided. Free local calls. Laundry facilities. TV lounge. Cafe with basic foods open M-F 7:30am-2:30pm. Parking $10. Reception 24hr. Check-in noon. Check-out noon. Open mid-May to early Aug. Singles $35; doubles $45. Students 10% off. ❶

Hôtel de Paris, 901 rue Sherbrooke Est (☎522-6861 or 800-567-7217; www.hotel-montreal.com). Métro: Sherbrooke. This European-style 19th-century flat houses a score of pleasant hotel rooms with private bath, TV, telephone, and A/C. Some rooms contain kitchenettes. There are also about 100 hostel beds, which, while cheaper than the hotel rooms, are not as good a deal as Montréal's other hostels. Linen $3. Single-sex dorm rooms $20; hotel rooms $80-155. ❶/❹

Camping Alouette, 3449 rue de l'Industrie (☎450-464-1661 or 888-464-7829; www.campingalouette.com), 30km from the city. Follow Autoroute 20 south, take Exit 105, and follow the signs. The privacy missing from Montréal's bustling hostels is omnipresent at these secluded campsites. Nature trail, pool, laundry facilities, a small store, volleyball courts, a dance hall, and a daily shuttle to and from Montréal (30min., $12 round-trip). Sites for 2 $22, with hookup $33; each additional person $2. ❶

BON APPÉTIT

Montréal is a diner's city, where chic restaurants rub shoulders with funky cafés, and everyone can find something to fit their taste. Expect nothing less than excellent food, but don't hold your breath for speedy service. **Chinatown** and **Little Italy** boast outstanding examples of their culinary heritage, and **rue Prince Arthur** adds a cheerful blend of Greek and Polish to the mix. The western half of **Ste-Catherine** and the area of **Boulevard St-Laurent** north of Sherbrooke offer a large range of choices. By far the best and affordable restaurants cluster on **rue St-Denis.**

Many restaurants, even upscale ones, have no liquor license; head to the nearest ***dépanneur*** or **SAQ** (*Societé des alcools du Québec*) to buy wine to have with dinner. Do like the locals: buy a bottle of wine and head to rue Prince Arthur's pedestrian mall for a relaxed meal on one of the many outdoor patios. All restaurants are required by law to post their menus outside. For further guidance, consult the free *Restaurant Guide*, published by the **Greater Montréal Convention and Tourism Bureau** (☎844-5400), which lists over 130 restaurants by type of cuisine.

If you feel like cooking, head to one of the **markets.** (All markets open M-W 8am-6pm, Th 8am-8pm, F 8am-9pm, Sa-Su 8am-5pm.) **Marché Jean-Talon,** 7075 rue Casgrain (☎277-1558, Métro: Jean Talon), has a vibrant selection of ethnic goodies in addition to an incredible outdoor market full of fruits and veggies, while the **Marché Maisonneuve,** 4445 rue Ontario Est (☎937-7754, Métro: Pie-IX), is great for produce and traditional *québécois* gems.

Restaurant l'Académie, 4051 rue St-Denis (☎849-2249), on the corner of av. Duluth. Métro: Sherbrooke. An elegant culinary heaven where lunchtime indulgence is reasonably priced, and the atmosphere is refined without being stuffy. L'Académie is most recognized for their *moules et frites,* which are mussels steamed and served in a variety of sophisticated sauces (around $10). Open daily noon-10pm. ❷

Brûlerie St. Denis, 3967 rue St-Denis (☎286-9158). Métro: Sherbrooke. A fun student cafe where the food and coffee are excellent, the waiters are friendly, and the patrons seem to already know each other. While adventurous types will find themselves quickly caught up in conversation, you won't feel out of place sitting with a newspaper. Café du jour $1.50. Bagel "Belle Hélène" $4.50. Shockingly large slices of raspberry cheesecake $5.25. Open daily 8am-11pm. ❶

Étoile des Indes, 1806 Ste-Catherine Ouest (☎932-8330), near St-Mathieu (parking on St-Mathieu). A local favorite for Indian food. Their spicy Bangalore *phal* dishes are only for the brave, but the homemade cheese in their *paneer* plates is for everyone. The Butter Chicken ($10) is phenomenal, and regulars come from as far away as Philadelphia just to have it. Dinners $5-15. Lunch specials including soup $6-9. Open M-Sa noon-2:30pm and 5-11pm, Su 5-11pm. ❷

La Fringale, 312 rue St-Paul Ouest (☎842-4491), in Vieux Montréal. Reminiscent of a warmly lit farmhouse, this acclaimed restaurant serves traditional French cuisine with a country air. Entrees $20-35. Open M-F 11am-midnight, Sa-Su 5pm-midnight. ❺

La Crêperie Bretonne le Trishell, 3470 rue St-Denis (☎281-1012). Métro: Sherbrooke. Montréalers have been known to line up for a taste of le Trishell's melt-in-your-mouth crêpes and fondues. Fresh strawberry crêpe $6.75. Open M-W 11:30am-11pm, Th-F 11:30am-midnight, Sa noon-midnight, Su noon-11pm. ❶

La Crème de la Crème Bistro Café, 21 rue de la Commune Est (☎874-0723), in Vieux-Montréal. A cozy brick cafe on the waterfront which combines Greek cuisine and Provençal decor, La Crème de la Crème serves up tasty baguette sandwiches (with salad $7-9) and generous slices of cake ($4). Open June-Sept. daily 11am-midnight; Oct.-June opens at 11am, hours vary with the weather. ❷

SIGHTS

MONT-ROYAL, LE PLATEAU, & THE EAST

Package tickets *(forfaits)* for the Biodôme, Funiculaire, and Gardens/Insectarium are a decent deal. Tickets are good for 30 days, so you can pace yourself. *(Any 2 sights $17, students and seniors $12.75, children 5-17 $8.50. All 3 sights $25/19/12.50.)*

BIODÔME. The fascinating **Biodôme** is the most recent addition to Olympic Park. Housed in the former Olympic Vélodrome, the Biodôme is a "living museum" in which four complete ecosystems have been reconstructed: the Tropical Forest, the Laurentian Forest, the St-Laurent marine ecosystem, and the Polar World. Stay alert to spot some of the more elusive of the 6200 vertebrates subsisting here. *(4777 av. Pierre-de-Coubertin. Métro: Viau. ☎868-3000; www.biodome.qc.ca. Open summer daily 9am-6pm; low-season 9am-5pm. $10.50, students and seniors $8, ages 5-17 $5.25.)*

ST. JOSEPH'S. The dome of **St. Joseph's Oratory,** the second highest dome in the world after St. Peter's Basilica in Rome, stands in testimony to the chapel's grandeur. An acclaimed religious site that attracts pilgrims from all over the globe, St. Joseph's is credited with a long list of miracles and unexplained healings. The

Votive Chapel, where the crutches and canes of thousands of healed devotees hang for all to see, keeps warm with the heat of 10,000 candles. *(3800 ch. Queen Mary. Métro: Côte-des-Neiges. ☎733-8211; www.saint-joseph.org. Open daily 6am-9:30pm.)*

OLYMPIC PARK. The world's tallest inclined tower (*le Tour Olympique* or *le Tour de Montréal*) is the crowning glory of **Olympic Park,** built for the 1976 summer Olympic games. Take the **Funiculaire** to the top of the tower for a breathtaking view of Montréal. *(3200 rue Viau. Métro: Viau, Pie-IX. ☎252-4141. 4 tours of the stadium offered daily, 2 in French and 2 in English. Tour $5.50, students and seniors $5, ages 5-17 $4.25; tour not included in* forfait *package—see above. Funiculaire open daily mid-June to Sept. 9am-9pm; early Sept. to mid-June 9am-5pm. $10, students and seniors $7.50, ages 5-17 $5.)*

BOTANICAL GARDENS & INSECTARIUM. A free shuttle runs to the **Jardin Botanique (Botanical Gardens).** The Japanese and Chinese landscapes showcase the largest *bonsai* and *penjing* collections outside of Asia. Beware: the gardens also harbor an **insectarium** with astounding collections of mounted and live exotic bugs, including at least a dozen fist-sized spiders. *(4101 rue Sherbrooke Est. Métro: Pie-IX. ☎872-1400; www.ville.montreal.qc.ca/jardin or /insectarium. Open daily late June-early Sept. 9am-6pm; Sept.-June 9am-4pm. $10.50, students and seniors $8, ages 5-17 $4.25.)*

PARC DU MONT-ROYAL. Designed by Frederick Law Olmstead, creator of New York's Central Park, the 127-year-old **Parc du Mont-Royal** surrounds and includes Montréal's namesake mountain. Though the hike from rue Peel up the mountain is longer than it looks, the view of the city from the observation points rewards the hardy. The 30m cross at the top of the mountain is a replica of the cross placed there in 1643 by de Maisonneuve, the founder of Montréal. In winter, locals gather here to ice-skate, toboggan, and cross-country ski. In summer, Mont-Royal welcomes joggers, cyclists, picnickers, and amblers. *(The park is bordered by ch. Remembrance, bd. Mont-Royal, av. du Parc, and ch. de la Côte des Neiges. Métro: Mont-Royal or Bus #11. ☎844-4928. Tour info ☎843-8240. Guided tours M-F 9am-5pm from Smith House, 1260 ch. Remembrance, between Beaver Lake and Chalet du Mont-Royal. Open daily 6am-midnight.)*

CATHÉDRALE MARIE REINE DU MONDE. A scaled-down replica of St. Peter's in Rome, **Cathédrale Marie Reine du Monde** stirred tensions when it was built as a Roman Catholic basilica in the heart of Montréal's Anglo-Protestant area. *(On the block bordered by René-Lévesque, Cathédrale, and Mansfield. ☎866-1661. Open M-F 6am-7pm, Sa 7:30am-8:30pm, Su 8am-7pm. At least 4-5 masses offered daily. Free.)* Across rue Cathédrale, **Place du Canada** comprises a lovely park and modest war memorial.

MCGILL. The **McGill University** campus extends up Mont-Royal and is composed predominantly of Victorian-style buildings set on pleasant greens. Stop by the **McGill Welcome Center** for a tour. *(Burnside Hall Building, Room 115. ☎398-6555. Open M-F 9am-5pm, Sa tours offered in July and Aug. Call for details.)* The campus includes the site of the 16th-century Native American village of **Hochelaga** and the **Redpath Museum of Natural History,** containing rare fossils and two genuine Egyptian mummies. *(Main gate at rue McGill and Sherbrooke. Métro: McGill. Museum: ☎398-4086; www.mcgill.ca/redpath. Open July-Aug. M-Th 9am-5pm, Su 1-5pm; Sept.-late June M-F 9am-5pm, Su 1-5pm. Free.)*

THE UNDERGROUND CITY

Not content with being one of the best shopping spots on the planet, Montréal has set its sights lower. Thirty kilometers of tunnels link Métro stops and form the ever-expanding "prototype city of the future," connecting railway stations, two bus terminals, restaurants, cinemas, theaters, hotels, two universities, two department stores, 1700 businesses, 1615 housing units, and 2000 boutiques. Here, residents bustle through the hallways of this sprawling, mall-like, "sub-urban" city. At the McGill stop lie some of the Underground City's finest and most navigable offerings. The **Promenades de la Cathédrale** take their name from their above-ground neighbor, **Christ Church Cathedral.** However, the primary subterranean shopping complex is more interested in your pocketbook than your soul. (635 rue Ste-Catherine Ouest. Church: ☎843-6577. Open daily 8am-6pm. Promenades: ☎849-9925.) To find the shopping wonderland **Place Bonaventure,** follow signs marked "Restaurants et Commerce" through the maze of shops under rue de la Gauchetière Ouest. The tourist office supplies treasure maps of the tunnels and underground attractions. (900 rue de la Gauchetière Ouest. Métro: Bonaventure. ☎397-2325. Shops open daily 9am-9pm.)

VIEUX MONTRÉAL

In the 17th century, the city of Montréal, struggling with Iroquois tribes for control of the area's lucrative fur trade, erected walls encircling the settlement for defense. Today the remnants of those ramparts delineate the boundaries of Vieux Montréal, the city's first settlement, on the stretch of river bank between **rue McGill, Notre-Dame,** and **Berri.** The fortified walls that once protected the quarter have crumbled, but the beautiful 17th- and 18th-century mansions of politicos and merchants have retained their splendor. **Guidatour** leads official **walking tours** of Vieux Montréal, departing from the Basilique Notre-Dame-de-Montréal. *(☎844-4021 or 800-363-4021; www.guidatour.qc.ca. 1½hr. tours daily from mid-June to late Sept. 11am, 1:30, 4pm in English, and 11am in French; from late May to mid-June and in early October tours leave on Sa-Su. $13.50, seniors and students $11.50, ages 6-12 $5.50.)*

BASILIQUE NOTRE-DAME DE MONTRÉAL. Towering above the Place d'Armes and its memorial to Maisonneuve is the most beautiful church in Montréal. One of North America's largest churches and a historic center for the city's Catholic population, the neo-Gothic **Basilique Notre-Dame de Montréal** has hosted everyone from Québec separatists to the Pope. Don't miss the Sacred Heart Chapel's bronze altarpiece and the sound-and-light spectacular *Et la lumière fut*—"And then there was light." *(110 rue Notre-Dame Ouest. Métro: Place-D'Armes. ☎842-2925; www.basiliquenddm.org. Open M-Sa 8am-5pm, Su 1:30-4pm. Free for prayer; entrance $3, ages 7-17 $1. Light show Tu-Th 6:30pm, F 6:30pm and 8:30pm, Sa 7pm and 8:30pm. $10, seniors $9, ages 1-17 $5.)*

CHAPELLE NOTRE-DAME-DE-BON-SECOURS. Marguerite Bourgeoys was the first teacher in Montréal, the founder of the first order of non-cloistered nuns, and the driving force behind the construction of the first stone chapel, built on the waterfront as a sailor's refuge. This chapel now houses the museum that bears her name, which displays archaeological treasures illuminating Montréal's history. *(400 rue St-Paul Est. Métro: Champ-de-Mars. ☎282-8670; www.marguerite-bourgeoys.com. Museum and chapel open May-Oct. Tu-Sa 10am-5pm; Nov. to mid-Jan. Tu-Su 11am-3:30pm. $6, seniors $4; call for child, group, and family rates.)*

CHÂTEAU RAMEZAY. The grand **Château Ramezay** presides over Vieux-Montréal as a testament to the power of the French viceroy for whom it was built. Constructed in 1705, converted to a museum in 1895, and renovated in the summer of 2002, the Château is a living record of Québec's heritage. The Governor's garden and the basement exhibit recreating the interior of an 18th-century home are both noteworthy. *(280 rue Notre-Dame Est. Métro: Champ-de-Mars. ☎861-3708; www.chateauramezay.qc.ca. Open June-Sept. daily 10am-6pm; Oct.-May Tu-Su 10am-4:30pm. $7, seniors $6, students $5, under 18 $4; families $15. Tours available by reservation. Fully wheelchair-accessible.)*

ÎLE STE-HÉLÈNE & ST-LAURENT

By car, take either of two bridges to Île Ste-Hélène: the Pont Jacques Cartier or the Pont de la Concorde. To avoid traffic and the hassle of finding parking, take the yellow Métro line to Île Ste-Hélène and catch bus #167 to the island's attractions. The best among many good reasons to visit Île Ste-Hélène, **La Ronde** amusement park boasts a free-fall drop and the tallest wooden roller coaster in the world. (Métro: Jean-Drapeau. ☎397-2000; www.laronde.com. Rides open daily 10am-10:30pm, grounds open until midnight; low-season hours vary. Unlimited 1-day pass $30.) Every Saturday night in June and July, La Ronde hosts the **Mondial SAQ,** the world's most prestigious fireworks competition—view the sky explosions free from Mont-Royal or the crowded Pont Jacques-Cartier. (Tickets ☎800-361-4595, info ☎397-2000; www.montrealfeux.com. Tickets $30-40, children $20.) Originally built in 1820 to defend Canada's inland waterways from imperialistic Americans, **Le Vieux Fort** now protects the **Stewart Museum,** which documents the discovery and colonization of North America. It houses a large collection of weapons, war instruments, and strategic maps and stages a musket firing by costumed colonials. (Métro: Jean-Drapeau. ☎861-6701; www.stewart-museum.org. Open mid-May to mid-Oct. daily 10am-6pm; late Oct. to early May W-M 10am-5pm. Musket firing in summer daily 3pm. $10, students and seniors $8, under 7 free; families $20.)

MUSEUMS

McCord Museum, 690 rue Sherbrooke Ouest (☎398-7100; www.mccord-museum.qc.ca). Métro: McGill or bus #24. Extracting the story of Canada's history from everyday objects, the McCord's exhibits range from toys to wedding gowns, lawn ornaments to photographs. Absorbing displays chronicle Montréal's development and quirks. The museum features a unique First Nations collection, Canada's most important costume collection, and an immense photographic archive. Open June-Sept. M-Sa 10am-6pm, Su 10am-5pm; Oct.-May Tu-Sa 10am-6pm, Su 10am-5pm. $10, seniors $7, students $5, ages 7-12 $3; families $19.

Musée des Beaux-Arts, 1380 and 1379 rue Sherbrooke Ouest (☎285-1600; www.mmfa.qc.ca). Métro: Guy-Concordia. Located about 5 blocks west of the McGill entrance, the museum's small permanent collection features art from ancient cultures to 20th-century works, including Inuit art. Don't miss the collection of creative decorative arts, which includes an 18th-century French sleigh and a cactus hat stand. From Apr. 15-Aug. 29, 2004, the museum will feature the drawings of Jean Cocteau; from Sept. 16-Dec. 12, 2004, works from the collection of Max Stern; from Sept. 30-Dec. 19, 2004, Renaissance and Rococo pieces from the Wadsworth Atheneum. Open Tu-Su 11am-6pm. Guided tours W and Su 1:30 (French), 2:30pm (English). Permanent collection free. Temporary exhibits $12, students and seniors $6, under 12 $3; W 5:30-9pm half-price.

Pointe-à-Callière: Montréal Museum of Archaeology and History, 350 Place Royale (☎872-9150; www.pacmusee.qc.ca), off rue de la Commune near Vieux-Port. Métro: Place d'Armes. This museum and national historic site uses the products of more than 10 years of archaeological digs in an innovative underground tour of the city's past incarnations. Open late June-early Sept. M-F 10am-6pm, Sa-Su 11am-6pm; low-season Tu-F 10am-5pm, Sa-Su 11am-5pm. $10, seniors $7.50, students $6, ages 6-12 $3.50, under 5 free. Fully wheelchair-accessible.

Musée d'Art Contemporain, 185 rue Ste-Catherine Ouest (☎847-6226; www.macm.org), at Jeanne-Mance. Métro: Place-des-Arts. Canada's premier modern art museum concentrates on the work of Canadian artists. The current rotation of the museum's 6000 piece collection focuses on developments of the 1940s, 50s, and 60s. Open Tu and Th-Su 11am-6pm, W 11am-9pm. $6, seniors $4, students $3, under 12 free; W 6-9pm free.

Canadian Centre for Architecture, 1920 av. Baile (☎939-7026; www.cca.qc.ca). Métro: Guy-Concordia or Atwater. Houses one of the world's most important collections of architectural prints, drawings, photographs, and books. Guided tours Sa-Su 2pm (French) and 3:30pm (English). Open Tu-W and F-Su 11am-6pm, Th 11am-9pm. $6, seniors $4, students $3, under 12 free; Th after 5:30pm free.

ENTERTAINMENT

THEATER

Montréal lives up to its cultured reputation with a vast selection of theater in both French and English. The **Théâtre du Nouveau Monde,** 84 rue Ste-Catherine Ouest, stages only French productions. (☎878-7878, ticket info 866-8668; www.tnm.qc.ca. Métro: Place-des-Arts. Tickets $36-42.) In mid-July, however, the theater is turned over to the bilingual **Festival Juste pour Rire/Just for Laughs** (☎790-4242; www.hahaha.com). The friendly **Théâtre du Rideau Vert,** 4664 rue St-Denis, puts on both *québécois* works and French adaptations of English plays. (☎844-1793; www.rideauvert.qc.ca. Métro: Mont-Royal. Tickets $20-40.) The hip **Théâtre d'Aujourd'hui,** 3900 rue St-Denis, produces original, eccentric *québécois* shows. (☎782-3900; www.theatredaujourdhui.qc.ca. Métro: Sherbrooke. Tickets $25, students $20, Th 2 for 1 admission.) The hyper-competitive, well-renowned **National Theatre School of Canada,** 5030 rue St-Denis, stages excellent "school plays" throughout the academic year. (☎842-7954; www.ent-nts.qc.ca. Most shows free.) The city's exciting **Place des Arts,** 260 bd. de Maisonneuve Ouest (☎842-2112; www.pda.qc.ca), at rue Ste. Catherine Ouest and Jeanne Mance, houses the **Opéra de Montréal** (☎985-2258; www.operademontreal; tickets $40-125), the **Montréal Symphony Orchestra** (☎842-9951, www.osm.ca; tickets $18-83), and **Les Grands Ballets Canadiens** (☎849-0269; www.grandsballets.qc.ca; tickets $25-85). **Théâtre Saint-Denis,** 1594 rue St-Denis (☎849-4211), hosts Broadway-style traveling productions. Theatergoers should peruse the *Calendar of Events,* available at tourist offices and newspaper stands, or call **Tel-Spec** for ticket info. (☎790-2222; ww.tel-spec.com. Open M-Sa 9am-9pm, Su noon-6pm.) **Admission Ticket Network** has tickets. (☎790-1245 or 800-361-459; www.admission.com. Open daily 8am-1am. Credit card required.)

MUSIC, FESTIVALS, & SPORTS

Montréal might also be in the running for festival capital of the world. To keep track of all the offerings, pick up a copy of *Mirror* (in English) or *Voir* (in French) in any theater and many bars and cafes. In summer, keep your eyes peeled for ***ventes-trottoirs,*** "sidewalk sales" that shut down a major Montréal street for a day and night of pedestrian-only outdoor fun. In mid-June, Montréal reels from the effects of its always-entertaining **Fringe Festival** (☎849-3378; www.montreal-fringe.ca), with theater, dance, and music events at various spots throughout the Plateau Mont-Royal. It wouldn't be Montréal without the high-spirited **Fête Nationale** (☎849-2560; www.cfn.org), on St-Jean-Baptiste Day, June 24, a celebration of Québec pride through local music performances and cultural events.

Two of Montréal's signature summer festivals draw crowds from all over the world. In early June, Montréal swoons during the **Mondial de la Bière,** when over 300 brands of beer, port, scotch, and whiskey are available for tasting. (☎722-9640; www.festivalmondialbiere.qc.ca. Day pass $10.) The first week of July, jazz fiends take over the city for the **Montréal International Jazz Festival** (☎871-1881; www.montrealjazzfest.com). From Bobby McFerrin to Ray Charles, the show brings together a variety of over 300 performers. Events cluster near Métro station **Place-des-Arts.** One month later, **Divers/Cité** (☎285-4011; www.diverscite.org), a gay pride week, rocks the city in and around Emilie-Gamelin Park.

Montréal also has its share of sporting events. Between October and April, hockey's **Montréal Canadiens** (nicknamed Les Habitants—"the locals"—or Les Habs) play at the **Centre Bell,** 1250 rue de la Gauchetière Ouest. (Info ☎989-2841, tickets ☎790-1245. Métro: Bonaventure. Call in advance to reserve tickets, $23-150.) Dress and behavior at games can be quite formal. Get in on the action during the one-day **Tour de l'Île,** an amateur cycling event with over 45,000 participants. (☎521-8356. Register by Apr. to participate.)

Like much of the city, Vieux Montréal is best seen at night. Street performers, artists, and *chansonniers* in various *brasseries* set the tone for lively summer evenings of clapping, stomping, and singing along. Real fun goes down on **St-Paul,** near the corner of St-Vincent. For a sweet Sunday afternoon, **Parc Jeanne-Mance** reels with bongos, dancing, and handicrafts. (May-Sept. noon-7pm.)

NIGHTLIFE

Combine a loosely enforced drinking age of 18 with thousands of taps flowing unchecked till 3am and the result is the unofficially titled "nightlife capital of North America." Most pubs and bars offer a Happy Hour, usually 5-8pm, when bottled drinks may be two-for-one and mixed drinks may be double their usual potency. In summer, restaurants spill onto outdoor patios. Avoid crowds of drunken American college students by ducking into one of the laidback local pubs along **rue St-Denis** north of Ste-Catherine. Alternatively, *be* a drunken American college student on **rue Ste-Catherine,** especially around **rue Crescent.** Tamer fun can be found in the pedestrian-only section of **rue Prince Arthur** at **rue St-Laurent.**

Café Campus, 57 rue Prince Arthur (☎844-1010; www.cafecampus.com). Unlike the more touristy meat-market discothèques, this hip club gathers a friendly student and twenty-something crowd. Regular theme nights include: Su French music, Th "Tabasko" (Latin groove), and the fun and happy Tu Retro (hits from the 1980s and 90s). Drinks $4-5.50. Cover $2-5, live music $5-15. Open daily 8:30pm-3am.

Pub McKibbins, 1426 rue Bishop (☎288-1580). Fine fermented drinks are served within the warmly lit walls of this Irish pub. Trophies and brass tokens ornament the walls and dartboards entertain the crowds, while a fieldstone fireplace warms the quarters in winter. Ground yourself with the Shepard's Pie ($9) before the next Guinness ($7). Irish jam nights M-Tu, folk music W, live Irish bands Th-Sa. Open daily 11am-3am; kitchen closes 10pm.

Peel Pub, 1107 rue St-Catherine Ouest (☎844-7296), downstairs, at rue Peel. Chicken wings and pitchers of beer are this friendly sports bar's specialty. The comfortable tables and laidback atmosphere make this a great place for relaxed conversations after a day on the streets. Pitchers $10.50. Happy hr. daily 3-7pm. Open daily 8am-3am.

O'Regans Pub, 1224 rue Bishop (☎866-8464), south of rue Ste-Catherine. The best fish and chips in town ($9.25). The tartan stools and cozy booths are quickly claimed F-Su, when live traditional Irish music filters into the street. W Celtic jam night. Open daily noon-3am; kitchen closes 9pm.

The Dome, 32 rue Ste-Catherine Est (☎875-5757), at the corner of St-Laurent. Attracts an international crowd to bump and grind. Music varies, but count on a staple of hip-hop and R&B. Cover $5. Open F-Sa 10pm-3am.

GAY & LESBIAN NIGHTLIFE

Most of Montréal's gay and lesbian hot spots can be found in the **gay village,** along rue St-Catherine between St-Hubert and Papineau. While most of the village's establishments cater to men, there are a few lesbian-friendly locales.

Le Drugstore, 1366 rue Ste-Catherine Est (☎524-1960). Métro: Beaudry. A 3-story gay megaplex basking in the glow of multicolored neon lights. Crowd is mostly male, though women are welcome. Ground floor is wheelchair-accessible. Open daily 8am-3am.

Cabaret Mado, 1115 St-Catherine Est (☎525-7566). Métro: Beaudry. This cabaret is the home of the wildest drag shows in town. Come Tu for "le Mardi a Mado." Straight-friendly, especially weekends. Drinks $4-5. Cover varies. Open daily 4pm-3am.

QUÉBEC CITY ☎418

Dubbed the Gibraltar of America because of the stone escarpments and military fortifications protecting the port, Québec City—generally shortened to just Québec [KAY-beck]—sits high on the rocky heights of Cape Diamant, where the St. Laurence narrows and is joined by the St. Charles River. Passing through the portals of North America's only walled city is like stepping into a European past. Horse-drawn carriages greet visitors on the winding maze of streets in the Old City (Vieux Québec) and there are enough sights and museums to satisfy even the most voracious history buff. Canada's oldest city also boasts a thriving French culture, standing apart from Montréal as the center of true *québécois* heritage.

TRANSPORTATION

Airport: Jean Lesage International Airport (☎640-2700; www.aeroportdequebec.com) is about 15min. away from downtown but inaccessible by public transit. Taxi to downtown $25.

Trains: VIA Rail, 450 rue de la Gare du Palais (☎692-3940), in Québec City. Open M-F 5:30am-8:30pm, Sa-Su 7:30am-8:30pm. To: **Montréal** (3hr.; 4 per day; $57); **Ottawa** (via Montréal, 5-8hr., 4 prt day, $83); **Toronto** (4-7hr., 5 per day, $105). Discounts for students, seniors, and ages 2-11.

Buses: Orléans Express, 320 rue Abraham Martin. (☎525-3000). Open M-Sa 5:30am-1am, Su 6:30am-1am. To: **Montréal** (3-4hr.; at least every hr. 5:30am-11:30pm; $38) and the **US** via Montréal.

Public Transit: Société de Transport de la Communauté Urbaine de Québec (STCUQ), 270 rue des Rocailles (route and schedule info ☎627-2511). Known as RTC for Réseau de Transport de la Capitale. Open M-F 6:30am-10pm, Sa-Su 8am-10pm. Buses generally operate daily 6am-1am. $1.95, students and seniors $1.35, children free.

Taxi: Taxi Coop Québec, ☎525-5191. **Taxi de Luxe,** ☎564-0555.

Driver/Rider Service: Allô Stop, 665 rue St-Jean (☎522-0056), will match you with a driver heading for Montréal ($15). Must be a member ($6 per year, drivers $7). Open M-Tu and Sa-Su 9am-6pm, W-F 9am-7pm.

Car Rental: Solimpax, 900 bd Pierre Bertrand (☎681-0678). Open M-F 7am-8pm, Sa-Su 8am-4pm.

Bike Rental: Velo Passe-Sport, 22 côte du Palais (☎692-3643; www.velopasse-sport.com). $12 for 2hr., $18 for 4hr., $22 for 8hr. Open Apr.-May and Sept.-Oct. W-Su 9:30am-5:30pm; June Tu-Su 9am-6pm; July-Aug. daily 8am-8pm.

ORIENTATION & PRACTICAL INFORMATION

Québec's main thoroughfares service both the *Vieux Québec* (Old City) and the more modern city outside it, and generally run parallel in an east-west direction. Within **Vieux Québec,** the main streets are **St-Louis, Ste-Anne,** and **St-Jean.** Most streets in Vieux Québec are one way. The major exception is **rue d'Auteuil,** bordering the walls inside Vieux Québec. Outside the walls, both St-Jean and St-Louis continue. St-Jean eventually joins ch. Ste-Foy, and St-Louis becomes **Grande Allée. Boulevard René-Lévesque,** the other major street outside the walls, runs between St-Jean and St-Louis. The **Basse-ville** (lower town) is

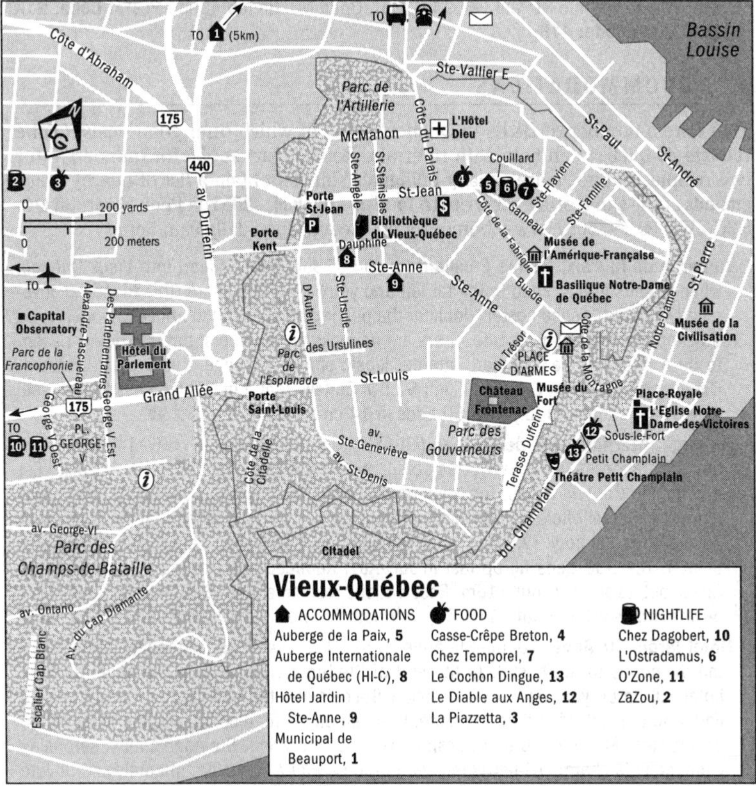

separated from the **Haute-ville** (upper town, a.k.a. Old Québec) by an abrupt cliff roughly paralleled by rue St-Vallier Est. Street parking in the city can be difficult; look along rue d'Auteuil or park in the lower town. Pricey garages are plentiful (about $14 per 24hr. of parking).

Visitor Info: Bureau d'information touristique du Vieux-Québec, 835 av. Wilfred Laurier (649-2608; www.quebecregion.com), in the Old City just outside the walls. Open late June-Aug. daily 8:30am-7:30pm; Sept. to Oct. daily 8:30am-6:30pm; mid-Oct. to late June M-F 9am-5pm, Sa 9am-6pm, Su 10am-4pm. **Cre Touriste de Québec,** 12 rue Ste-Anne (☎877-266-5687; www.bonjourquebec.com), across from Château Frontenac, deals primarily with provincial tourism; they can also help with hostel or tour reservations. Open daily late June-Aug. 8:30am-7:30pm; Sept.-mid June 9am-5pm.

Hotlines: Tél-Aide, ☎686-2433. Operates daily noon midnight. **Viol-Secours (sexual assault line),** ☎522-2120. Counselors on duty M-F 9am-4pm and on-call 24hr. **Gay hotline,** ☎888-505-1010.

Medical Services: L'Hôtel Dieu, 11 côte du Palais (☎525-4444), just down the hill from rue St-Jean.

Internet Access: Bibliothéque du Vieux-Québec, 37 rue Ste-Angéle (☎691-6357). Open Tu and Th noon-8pm, W and F noon-5pm, Sa-Su 1-5pm.

Post Office: 300 rue St-Paul (☎694-6175). Open M-F 8am-5:45pm. **Postal Code:** G1K 3W0. **Area Code:** 418.

ACCOMMODATIONS

There are a number of B&Bs in Québec, many of which offer good deals. **Centre Touriste de Québec** can help with referrals. Rooms start at $55 for one or $75 for two people, and hosts are usually bilingual. You can obtain a list of nearby **campgrounds** at the same office, or write to **Tourisme Québec,** 1255 rue Peel, Montréal QC, H3C 2W3. (☎266-5687; www.bonjourquebec.com. Open daily 9am-5pm.)

Auberge de la Paix, 31 rue Couillard (☎694-0735). Take St-Jean into Vieux Québec; when it splits into 3, keep to the far left and you'll be on Couillard. This friendly, conveniently located "peace hostel" (look for the peace sign suspended above the door) is as tidy and modern as they come. There are no locks on the doors, but this doesn't seem to be a problem. New kitchen, Internet kiosk, smoking lounge, patio, and courtyard. Continental breakfast 8-10am. Linen $2.50. Curfew 2am, but 24hr access to facilities. Reservations required July-Aug. 60 beds in 14 co-ed rooms $19.50. ❶

Auberge Internationale de Québec (HI-AYH), 19 rue Ste-Ursule (☎694-0755). From the bus station, take rue St-Nicolas uphill; stay with it as it changes to rue St Vallier Est and then to Côte du Palais. Turn right onto St-Jean, then left onto Ste-Ursule. This newly renovated hostel offers traditional dorm beds as well as doubles and family rooms with private bath. Laundry, TV, living room, kitchen, Internet access, cafe, bar, and in-house theater. The 300 beds fill up fast in July-Aug. Reduced-rate parking at a city garage. Check-out 11am. Lockout 11pm. Reservations recommended. $20, nonmembers $24; private rooms without bath $46/50; with bath $65/69; family rooms $110/114. ❶

Hôtel Jardin Ste-Anne, 10- rue Ste-Anne (☎694-1720; www.jardinsteanne.com). Follow the directions to the hostel. At the end of Ste-Ursule, turn left on Ste-Anne, and the hotel will be on your right. By car, follow St-Louis into the old city, turn left on rue du Fort, and the first left will be Ste-Anne. Bear left as the road splits, and the hotel will be on your left. Modern and quiet despite its central location, Ste-Anne's most surprising commodity is charm. 18 newly renovated rooms with A/C, cable, Internet, and private bath. Garage parking $10. Continental buffet breakfast $5. Reservations recommended at least 34 weeks ahead in summer. Budget rooms $69-135, depending on season. ❹

Municipal de Beauport, 95 rue de la Serenité (☎641-6112), in Beauport. Take Autoroute 40E, get off at Exit 321 at rue Labelle onto Hwy. 369, turn left, and follow the signs marked "camping." Bus #55 will also take you to this pleasant 136-site campground on a hill over the Montmorency River. Swimming pool, laundry facilities, and plenty of picnic tables. Canoes $8 per hr. Free showers. Open June-early Sept. Sites $21, with hookup $26; $125/155 per week. ❶

EASTERN CANADA

L'HAUTE CUISINE

In general, rue Buade, St-Jean, and Cartier, as well as the **Place Royale** and **Petit Champlain** areas, offer the widest selection of food and drink. The **Grande Allée** may sing a siren's song to the hungry, but its prices might encourage you to keep strolling. A walk down St-Jean away from the old city reveals a host of fun restaurants, ice creameries, and food markets. One of the most filling yet inexpensive meals is a *croque monsieur*, a large, open-faced sandwich with ham and melted cheese (about $7). French onion soup, slathered with melted cheese, can be found in virtually every restaurant and cafe. It usually comes with baguettes or *tourtiére*, a thick meat pie. Other specialties include the ever-versatile crêpe.

Casse-Crêpe Breton, 1136 rue St-Jean (☎692-0438), is probably the best deal in town. To start, create your own mix-and-match dinner crêpe ($4-7), then top it off with a delightful dessert crêpe stuffed with fresh fruit or other sugary fillings ($4). Grab a spot at the counter to watch the chef in action. Open daily 7am-11pm. ❶

La Piazzetta, 707 rue St-Jean (☎529-7489), a few blocks from the city walls. Drawing inspiration from the *Commedia dell'Arte,* Piazzetta injects a wild carnival atmosphere into its Italian creations. Sit down in one of the wildly shaped chairs and enjoy the popular *pizza Generosa* (with ham and swiss cheese; $16.25). Open M-Th and Su 11am-11pm, F-Sa 11am-midnight. ❸

Le Diable aux Anges, 28 bd. Champlain and 39 rue du Petit-Champlain (☎6294674)> Absorb the European aura of its dimly lit, colonial interior. A number of traditional *québécois* dishes and sinfully-named desserts add variety to this bistro cafe. Ask for the breakfast menu and try the Bagel Oeuforique (topped with cream cheese, fried egg, ham, and tomato; $9). Open daily 9am-11pm. ❷

Chez Temporel, 25 rue Couillard (694-1813). Stay off the touristy path at this genuine *café québécois,* discreetly tucked in a side alley off rue St-Jean, near the Auberge de la Paix. Besides the usual cafe staples, it offers some unique coffee drinks ($4.50). Alcoholic drinks available with food. Salads and soups $5-8. Excellent quiches $6. Open daily 7am-2am. ❶

Le Cochon Dingue, 46 bd. Champlain (692-2013), which means "crazy pig," is quickly becoming a culinary landmark on Québec for its quirky take on traditional French favorites. Go hog-wild with an extra slice of strawberry cheesecake ($5.25) after your *croque monsieur* ($9.50). Open June-Aug. M-F 7am-midnight, Sa-Su 8am-midnight; Sept.-May M-F 7am-11pm, Sa-Su 8am-11pm. ❷

SIGHTS

Inside the **Fortifications of Québec,** a 6.5km stretch of wall surrounding Vieux Québec, are most of the city's historic attractions. Monuments are clearly marked and explained, usually in French; you'll get more out of the town by consulting the free *Québec City and Area Tourist Guide,* which outlines several suggested walking tours and is available at any Visitors Center. Although it takes one to two days to explore all of Vieux Québec's narrow, hilly streets and historic sites on foot, this is by far the best way to absorb its charm. The ubiquitous **horse-drawn carriage tours,** while pricey ($60 per tour), can be fun. Find carriages on the Grande Allée, or call *Calèches duVieux Québec.* (☎683-9222.) The **Funiculaire** carries passengers between Upper-Town, Place Royal, and the Quartier Petit-Champlain. (☎692-1132 Open 7:30am-midnight. $1.50.)

BATTLEFIELDS. The **Parc des Chaps-de-Bataille,** or **Plains of Abraham,** adjacent to the Citadel along av. George-VI, accessible from Grande Allée, has on its ground an astounding assortment of historical, cultural, and natural offerings. The **Discovery Pavillion,** near St-Louis Gate and the Manège Militaire, is the primary information desk for the park and houses the new multimedia **Canada Odyssey,** a virtual tour of Canadian military, agricultural, and natural history. *(Pavilion: ☎648-4071. Wheelchair-accessible. Open daily mid-June to mid-Oct. 8:30am-5:30pm, mid-Oct. to mid-Jun. 8:30am-5pm. Canada Odyssey: ☎648-4071; www.canadaodyssey.com. Open daily mid-June to mid-Oct. 10am-5:30pm, mid-Oct. to mid-June 10am-5pm. $6:50, seniors and ages 13-17 $5.50, families $20.)* To enjoy the beautiful natural setting of the battlefields, visit the **Jardin Jeanne d'Arc,** a serene spot with over 150 flower species. The **Martello Towers** present a look at the more personal side of military history, including exhibits in Tower 1 on the day-to-day lives of soldiers and in Tower 2 the "Council of War," an award-winning period mystery dinner. *(Tower 1: Open mid-June to Aug. daily 10am-*

5:30pm; Sept to mid-Oct. Sa-Su 10am-5:30pm or by reservation. $4, seniors and ages 13-17 $3, families $12. "Council of War:" ☎649-6157. Runs July-Aug. Sa in French, Su in English at 6pm; also on some holidays. $31.75, seniors and ages 13-17 $28.75. Reservations required.)

PETIT-CHAMPLAIN. One of old Québec's highlights is the crowded thoroughfare of **Rue du Petit-Champlain.** Along either side of this narrow passageway, visitors will find a host of cafes, craft shops, trendy boutiques, and restaurants. Each evening, the **Téâtre Petit Champlain** presents *québécois* music, singing, and dancing. *(68 rue du Petit-Champlain. ☎692-2631. Most shows $20-30.)* Dating back to 1688, **L'Eglise Notre-Dame-des-Victoires** is the oldest church in Canada. *(32 rue Sous-le-Fort. ☎692-1650. Open May to mid-Oct. M-Sa 9am-5pm, Su 1-5pm; mid-Oct. to Apr. daily 10am-4pm. Free.)*

INSIDE THE WALLS. The **Château Frontenac,** with its grand architecture and green copper roofs, is perhaps the most recognizable structure in the city and is thought to be the most photographed hotel in the worlds. A costumed guide leads visitors through the former Governor's Palace. *(1 rue des Carrièrres. ☎691-2166. Tours daily May to mid-Oct. every hr. 10am-6pm; mid-Oct. to May Sa-Su noon-5pm; reservations highly recommended. $7, seniors $6.25, ages 6-16 $4.50.)* With its shimmering golden altar and ornate stained-glass windows, the **Basilique Notre-Dame de Québec** is one of the oldest and most stunning cathedrals in North America. The Basilique shows a light show, the "Act of Faith," which relays the history of the church. *(At rue de Buade and Ste-Famille. ☎694-4000; www.patrimonie-religieux.com. Basilique open daily 9:30am-3:30pm. Free. Shows May-Oct. M-F hourly 3:30-8:30pm. $7.50, students and seniors $5, families $20.)*

CAP DIAMANT. A climb to the top of Cap Diamant reveals a perfect view of the city. Just north is the **Citadel,** an active military base and the largest North American fortification still guarded by troops. *(On rue St-Louis at Côte de la Citadelle. ☎694-2815. Open daily Apr. to mid-May 10am-4pm; mid-May to mid-June 9am-5pm; mid-June to Aug. 9am-6pm; Sept. 9am-4pm; Oct. 10am-3pm. Changing of the guard late-June to Sept 1 daily at 10am. Beating of the retreat F-Su 6pm. $6pm. $6, seniors $5, under 18 $3; families $14.)*

PARLIAMENT HILL. Finished in 1886, the **Assemblée Nationale,** just outside the wall of the city, was designed in the style of Louis XIV. Lively debates can be observed from the visitor's gallery; free simultaneous translation earphones are available for both English and French speakers. *(At ave. Dufferin and Grand Allée Est. ☎643-7239; www.assnat.qc.ca. Open late June-early Sept. M-F 9am-4:30pm, Sa-Su 10am-4:30pm; mid-Sept to mid-June M-F 9am-4:30pm. 30min. tours free. Reservations recommended.)* The **Capitol Observatory** offers breathtaking views of the city from 221m (725 ft.) above sea level, the highest observation spot in town. *(1037 rue de la Chevrotière, off Grande Allée. ☎644-9841; wwww.observatoirecapiale.org. Open daily late-June to mid-Oct. 10am-5pm; winter Tu-Su 10am-5pm. $5, students and seniors $4.)*

EASTERN CANADA

MUSEUMS. The **Musée de l'Amérique-Française,** on the grounds of the **Québec Seminary,** across the street from the Basilica, is an excellent museum whose informative exhibits recount the details of Francophone settlement in North America. *(2 côte de la Fabrique. ☎692-2843; www.mcq.org. Open daily late June-Sept 9:30am-5pm; winter Tu-Su 10am-5pm. $4, students and seniors $3.)* The **Centre d'Interprétation Place-Royale** provides free 45min. tours of the **Place-Royale,** home to the oldest permanent European settlement in Canada (dating from 1608). *(27 rue Notre-Dame. Take rue Sous-le-Fort from the bottom of the Funiculaire. ☎646-3167; www.mcq.org. Open June-Sept. daily 9:30am-5pm; winter Tu-Su 10am-5pm.)* The **Musée de la Civilisation** celebrates the unique cultural heritage of Québec as seen through everyday objects, interactive exhibits, and elaborate dioramas. In 2004, the museum will recreate a Roman-empire era Gaulish village. Follow the series of signs at the bottom of the Funiculaire. *(85 rue Dalhousie. ☎643-2158; www.mcq.org. Wheelchair-accessible. Open late June-early Sept. daily 9:30am-6:30pm;*

mid-Sept to mid-June Tu-Su 10am-5pm. $7, seniors $6, students $4, children $2.) Housed in an old jail on the grounds of the battlefields, the **Musée du Québec** houses eclectic modern and colonial art, focusing on the works of *québécois* artists. A permanent tactile exhibit is designed for blind visitors. Don't miss the view from the top of the turret, or the Picasso ceramics exhibit in summer 2004. *(☎643-2150. Wheelchair-accessible. Open June-early Sept. M-Tu and Th-Su 10am-6pm, W 10am-9pm; mid-Sept. to May Tu and Th-Su 10am-5pm, W 10am-9pm. Free; special exhibits $10, seniors $9, students $5, ages 12-16 $3.)* A sound-and-light show allows visitors to experience the battle of the Plains of Abraham on a 400 sq. ft. model of 1759 Québec at the popular **Musée du Fort.** *(10 rue Ste-Anne. ☎692-2175. Open Feb.-Mar. Th-Su 11am-4pm; Apr.-June and Sept.-Oct. daily 10am-5pm; July-Aug. daily 10am-6pm. $7.50, seniors $5.50, students $4.50.)*

 FESTIVALS

Images of "Le Bonhomme de Neige" plaster the snow-covered city in anticipation of the raucous annual **Winter Carnival** (☎521-5555; www.carnaval.qc.ca), which will break the tedium of northern winters January 30-February 15, 2004. The 37th annual **Summer Festival,** or **Festival d'Été** (☎888-992-5200; www.infofestival.com), with free outdoor concerts, packs hostels and crowds the streets in early July. Throughout the summer, the **Plein Art** (☎694-0260; with metiers-d-art.cqc.ca) exhibition floods the Pigeonnier on the Grande-Allée with arts and crafts. Now in its 12th season, the **Edwin Bélanger Bandstand,** on the Plains of Abraham, hosts free outdoor concerts through the summer. (☎648-4050; www.ccbn-nbc.gc.ca.) In early June, **Le Grand Rire "Bleue"** brings comedy to the streets with shows and strolling performers throughout the city. (☎647-2525; www.grandrirebleu.com.) But Québec's most festive day of the year—eclipsing even Canada Day—is June 24, **la Fête nationale du Québec** or St-Jean-Baptiste Day (☎640-0799; www.snqc.qc.ca). This celebration of *québécois* culture features several free concerts, a bonfire, and 5 million rip-roaring drunk acolytes of John the Baptist.

NIGHTLIFE

The Grande Allée's many restaurants are interspersed with *bar discothéques*, where twenty-somethings dance until dawn. Quebéc City's young, visible punk contingent clusters around rue St-Jean and several nearby sidestreets, but more laidback nightclubs find a niche here, too.

THE HIDDEN DEAL

FACE THE MUSIC

In the mood for music, Québec City style? Step into a *boîte aux chansons*, or "song bar," where live local musicians serenade the crowd every night (for animatronics see Disney World, p. 487). The musicians are all singer-guitarists, and many are young songwriters waiting for their big break. The selection ranges from rock and pop favorites *à la québécoise*—with hits by francophone stars like Jean Leloup and Daniel Bélanger—to original works by the artist of the night. Sometimes American oldies and *québécois* folk work their way into the program, and believe us, a bar full of Québeckers singing "California Dreamin'" is an experience not to be missed. The local favorite seems to be Les Yeux Bleux, where *chansonniers* sing from a candlelit stage dripping with the red wax of concerts past. Everyone feels like a regular in this cozy nook; a strange combination of enthusiasm and lack of pressure make this an ideal introduction to the *boîte aux chansons* phenomenon.

1117½ rue St-Jean. ☎694-9118. No cover. 2-for-1 beer May-Aug. F-Sa before 9pm and Su-Th before 10pm. Open daily 8pm-3am; arrive between 9-10pm for 10pm shows.

Chez Dagobert, 600 Grande Allée Est (☎522-0393; www.dagobert.ca), saturates the air with techno and dance sounds that can be heard for blocks. 2 dance floors and an adjoining bar give plenty of room to mingle. Live rock nightly. Outside bar open daily 2pm-2am; inside club 10pm-3am.

O'Zone, 570 Grande Allée (☎529-7932). is a bit less hectic than its neighbors. Folks linger at the bars (both the conventional and the fusion sushi) before going to the second story dance floor for rock, dance, and hip-hop. Special beer-plus-4 sushi pieces $5. Open M-F 11am-3am.

ZaZou, 811 rue St-Jean (☎524-4982), knows how to throw a dance party, with loud music thumpin' and zebra-print booths jumpin'. F is the biggest night of the week, although karaoke is popular, too. A gay bar, the crowd tends to be very mixed and straight-friendly. Cover $1 F-Sa. Open daily 2pm-3am.

L'Ostradamus, 29 rue Couillard (☎694-9560), injects live jazz and techno into its smoke-drenched, "spiritual" ambience. Cover $2-5. Open daily 8pm-3am.

DAYTRIP FROM QUÉBEC CITY

ÎLE-D'ORLÉANS.

Originally named in honor of the god of wine (and sex), the **Île-d'Orléans** was first called Île de Bacchus because of the multitude of wild grapes fermenting there. The island, about 5km downstream from Québec on the St-Laurent, was cut off from the mainland until 1935, when the present bridge was built. Known as the "Garden of Québec" for its abundant agricultural products, the Île D'Orléans has retained its pastoral way of life and a reputation for cider, chocolate, and maple products. A summer visit rewards tourists with fragrant apple blossoms, while a fall stopover reveals splendid autumn foliage. The 7000 inhabitants inhabit a landscape that ranges from wide pastures in the northern half to denser forests toward the south. The best way to see the Île-d'Orléans is by car, since the island is not accessible by public transportation or bicycle. Take Hwy. 75 to Autoroute 440 Est, on to Hwy. 368, and cross the bridge to the island. Stop at the tourist office (on your right, about 1km after the bridge ends) and pick up a tourist guide (☎828-9411. Guide book $1. In-car audio guide $10). A full circuit of the island covers 67km and takes about 1½hr. Many of the island's cider presses and farms are open for tours; consult the tourist office. B&Bs are everywhere on the island, but for a more authentic experience, stay at the **Auberge Le P'tit Bonheur ❶,** 186 côte Lafleur in St-Jean, a 350 year-old farmhouse that offers sugar shack recreations, horseback riding, snowshoeing, cross-country skiing, and outdoors accommodations in a traditional wigwam for those so inclined. (☎829-2588. Kitchen, TC room, and outdoor barbecue. Homecooked lunches $6. Dinners $10. Bikes $40 per day. Dorm rooms $19; singles with private bath $60.) On the way out of Île-d'Orléans, turn east onto Hwy. 138 to view the splendid **Chute Montmorency** (Montmorency Falls). In winter, vapors from the falls form a frozen mist that screens the running water. (☎663-3330.)

ONTARIO

Existing in uneasy political tension with French Québec, this populous central province raises the ire of peripheral regions of Canada with its high concentration of power and wealth. In the south, world-class Toronto shines—multicultural,

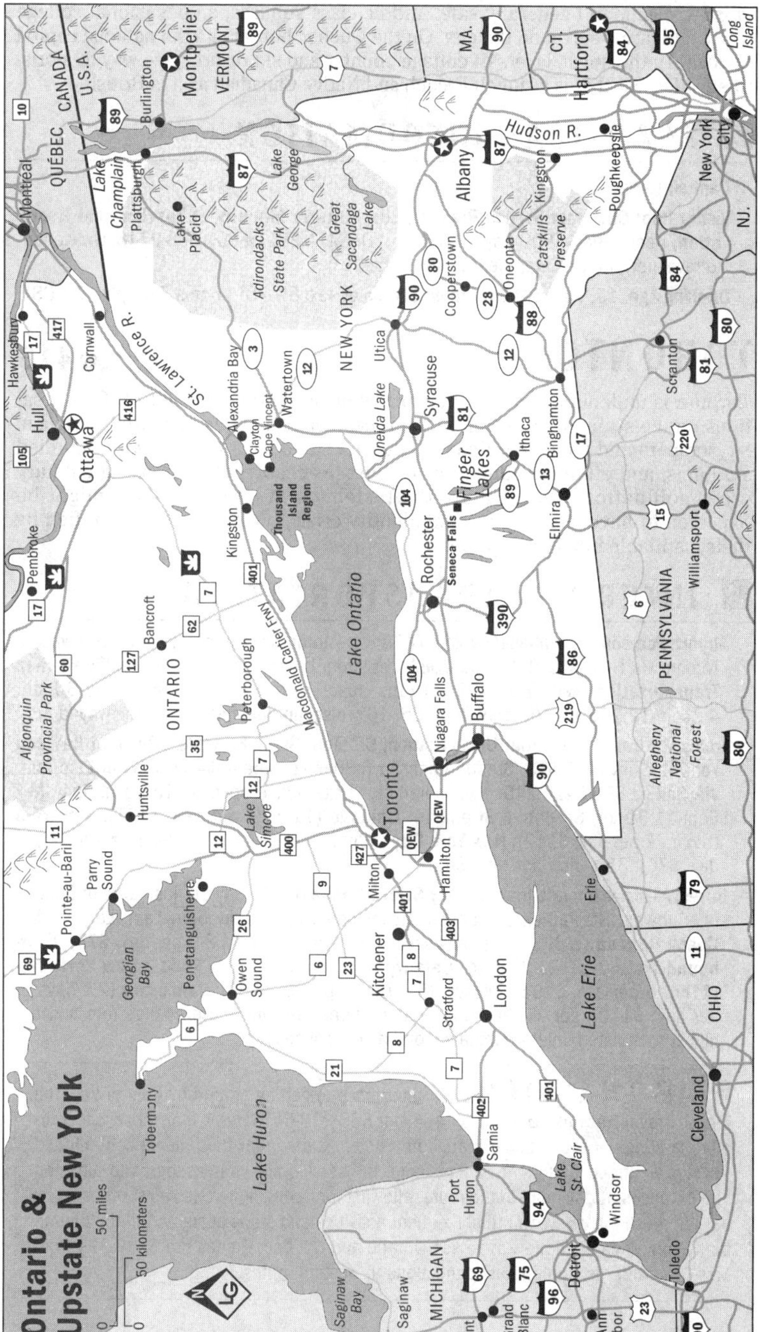

Ontario & Upstate New York

0 — 50 kilometers
0 — 50 miles

vibrant, clean, and generally safe. Middle-class suburbs, an occasional college town, and farms surround the city. On the Québec border sits the national capital Ottawa. To the north, layers of cottage country and ski resorts give way to a pristine wilderness that is as much French and Native Canadian as it is British.

PRACTICAL INFORMATION

Capital: Toronto.

Visitor Info: Customer Service Branch of the **Ontario Ministry of Tourism and Recreation,** Hearst Block, 900 Bay St., Toronto, ON M7A 2E1 (☎800-668-2746; www.ontariotravel.net), in the Eaton Centre, lower level 1.

Drinking Age: 19. **Postal Abbreviation:** ON. **Sales Tax:** 8% PST (rooms 5%), plus 7% GST.

TORONTO ☎416

Toronto is undeniably among the world's most multicultural cities. Conversations on the street are as often in Cantonese or Punjabi as they are in English. Skyscrapers and a bustling financial district stand back to back with fan-filled stadiums, and ethnic communities coexist peaceably, often creating culinary cross-pollinations that titillate the tastebuds. A city so diverse might be expected to have something of an identity crisis, but residents are unified by their justifiable hometown pride.

INTERCITY TRANSPORTATION

Airport: Pearson International (☎247-7678; www.torontoairport.ca), about 20km west of Toronto via Hwy. 401. Take bus #58A west from Lawrence W subway. **Pacific Western Transportation** (☎905-564-6333) runs buses to downtown hotels every 30min. 4:25am-12:25am. $15, round-trip $26. 10% discount for students on one-way fare.

Trains: All trains leave from **Union Station,** 65 Front St. (☎888-842-7245), at Bay and York St. Subway: Union. Station open Su 6:30am-12:45am, M-Sa 5:30am-12:45am. **VIA Rail** (☎888-842-7245; www.viarail.ca). Ticket office open Su 7am-11:30pm, M-F 6am-11:30pm, Sa 6am-6:30pm. To: **Chicago** (11hr., 1 per day, $137); **Montréal** (5½hr., 7 per day, $112); **New York City** (12hr., 1 per day, $115); **Windsor** (4hr., 4 per day, $78). 35% discount with ISIC.

Buses: All buses operate from the **Bay Street Terminal,** 610 Bay St., just north of Dundas St. Subway: St. Patrick or Dundas. Ticket office open daily 5am-1am. Lockers $2. **Coach Canada** (☎393-7911) has service to **Montréal** (7hr., 8-9 per day, $78). **Greyhound** (☎367-8747) goes to: **Calgary** (2 days, 3 per day, $161); **New York City** (11hr., 6 per day, $105); **Ottawa** (5½-7hr., 9 per day, $60); **Vancouver** (2½ days, 3 per day, $170). For all Greyhound routes, fares vary with the exchange rate and are higher than listed unless purchased one day in advance.

EASTERN CANADA

SKIP THE TRAIN An alternative to getting around by train or bus, the Moose Travel Network (☎905-853-4762 or 888-816-6673; www.moosenetwork.com) offers a series of expeditions throughout Eastern Canada for the independent-minded traveler. Founded by former backpackers, the service allows passengers to jump on and off buses at any point in the route, allowing for flexible itineraries as short as a few days and as long as five months. Frequent activities and stops at sights "off the beaten path" make this a unique way to see Ontario and Québec. Routes run $239-399 from May-Oct., with discounted rail connections to western routes.

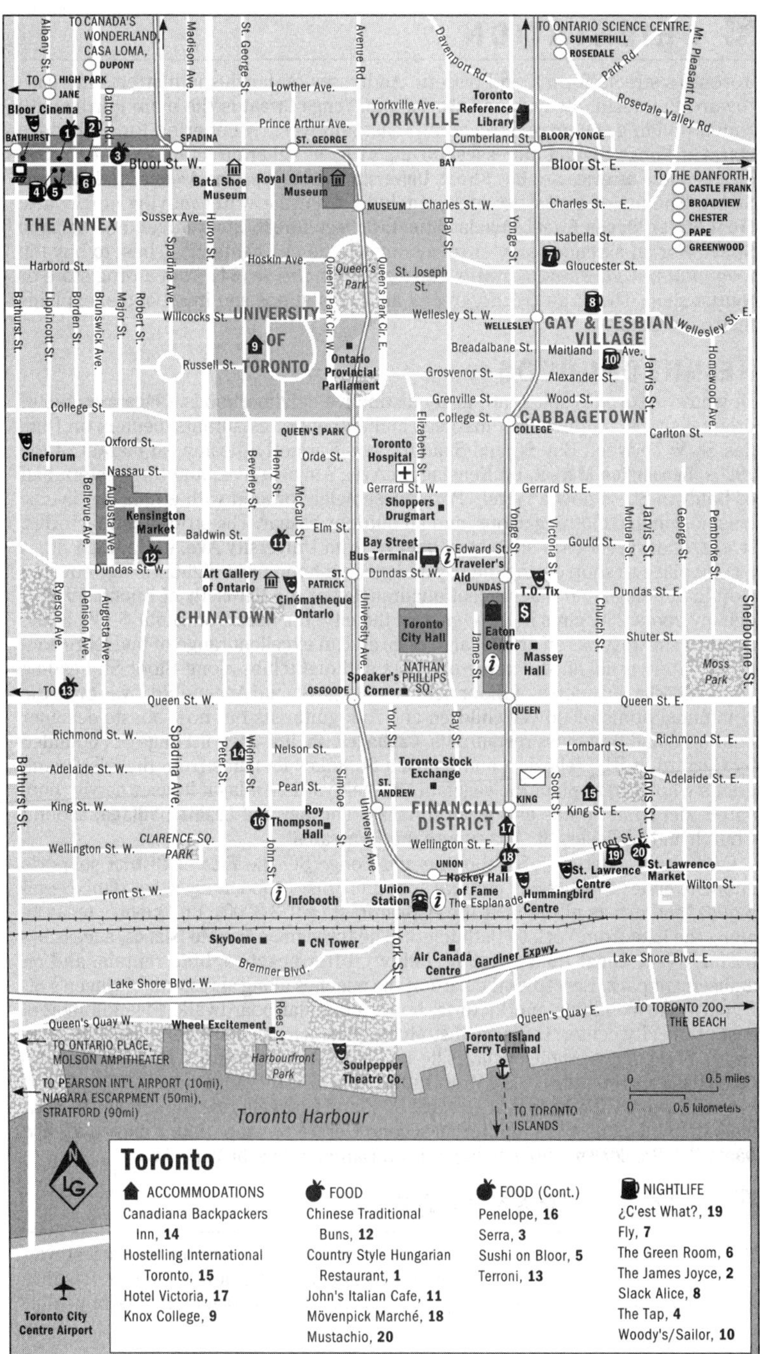

EASTERN CANADA

ORIENTATION

Toronto's streets form a grid pattern. Addresses on north-south streets increase toward the north, away from **Lake Ontario. Yonge Street** is the main north-south route, dividing the cross streets into east and west. Numbering for both sides starts at Yonge St. and increases moving away in either direction. West of Yonge St., the main arteries are **Bay Street, University Avenue, Spadina Avenue,** and **Bathurst Street.** The major east-west routes include, from the water moving northward, **Front Street, Queen Street, Dundas Street, College Street, Bloor Street,** and **Eglinton Street.** For an extended stay or travel outside the city center, it is best to buy the *Downtown and Metro Toronto Visitor's Map Guide* ($4) from a drug store or tourist shop. The *Ride Guide,* free at all TTC stations and info booths, explains metro area transit.

NEIGHBORHOODS

Downtown Toronto splits into many distinctive neighborhoods. **Chinatown,** full of oriental shops, outdoor fruit markets, and authentic restaurants, centers on Dundas St. W between Bay St. and Spadina Ave. Formerly the Jewish market of the 1920s, **Kensington Market,** on Kensington Ave., Augusta Ave., and the western half of Baldwin St., is now a largely Portuguese neighborhood with ethnically diverse cuisine, vintage clothing shops, and an outdoor bazaar. The strip of old factories, stores, and warehouses on **Queen Street W,** from University Ave. to Bathurst St., is a good place to shop during the day and go club-hopping at night. The ivy-covered Gothic buildings and magnificent quadrangles of the **University of Toronto (U of T)** occupy about 200 acres in the center of the city. **The Annex,** on Bloor St. W, at the Spadina subway, has an artistic ambience and an excellent range of budget restaurants. Afterwards, hit the numerous bars and nightclubs along Bloor St. heading west. **Yorkville,** just north of Bloor between Yonge St. and Avenue Rd., was once the communal home of flower children and folk guitarists but now boasts designer boutiques and first-class restaurants. **Cabbagetown,** just east of Yonge St., bounded by Gerrard St. E, Wellesley, and Sumach St., takes its name from the Irish immigrants who used to plant the vegetable in their yards. Today it houses newly renovated Victorian homes and several parks. The **Gay and Lesbian Village,** around Church and Wellesley St., has superb outdoor cafes.

On Front St. between Sherbourne and Yonge St., the **Theater District** supports enough venues to whet any cultural appetite. Music, food, ferry rides, dance companies, and artists all dock at the **Harbourfront** (☎973-3000), on Queen's Quay W along the lake from York to Bathurst St. The three main **Toronto Islands,** accessible by ferry (see **Local Transportation,** below), offer beaches, bike rentals, and an amusement park. East from the harbor, the beaches along and south of Queen's St. E, between Woodbine and Victoria, boast a popular boardwalk. Five kilometers east of the city center, the rugged stretch of **Scarborough Bluffs** rises over the lakeshore. Three more ethnic enclaves lie 15-30min. from downtown by public transit. **Corso Italia** surrounds St. Clair W at Dufferin St.; take the subway to St. Clair W and bus #512 west. **Little India** is at Gerrard St. E and Coxwell; ride the subway to Coxwell, then take bus #22 south to the second Gerard St. stop. Better known as **"the Danforth," Greektown** (subway: Pape) is on Danforth Ave. at Pape Ave.

LOCAL TRANSPORTATION

The **Toronto Transit Commission's (TTC)** subway and streetcars are the easiest way to get around the city, but if you must drive, avoid rush hour (4-7pm). A flashing green light means that you can go straight or turn left freely, as the opposing traffic has a red light. Pedestrians should exercise caution when crossing the streets; they do not necessarily have the legal right of way. **Parking** on the street is hard to find and usually carries a 1hr. limit. Day parking generally costs inbound daytrippers $3-4 at outlying subway stations; parking overnight at the subway stations is prohibited. The cheapest parking downtown can be found at city-run lots (look for the green P), where 24hr. parking is usually around $9. Free parking can be found in **Cabbagetown,** on the residential streets just west of Parliament St. City officials have begun to enforce traffic and parking regulations zealously—don't tempt them. Towing is a common occurrence, even for locals; the **non-emergency police number** (☎808-2222) has an answering system to help recover towed cars.

Ferries: Toronto Island Ferry Service (☎392-8194, recording ☎392-8193). Ferries to Centre Island, Hanlans Point, and Wards Island leave from the foot of Bay St. Service daily every 30min.; call for exact schedule. Round-trip $6; students, seniors, and ages 15-19 $3.50; ages 2-14 $2.50.

Public Transit: Toronto Transit Commission (☎393-4636; www.ttc.ca) has a network of 2 long and 2 short subway lines connected to many bus and streetcar routes. Buses are required to stop anywhere along a route at a female passenger's request 9pm-5am. Subway runs M-Sa 6am-1:30am, Su 9am-1:30am. Buses cover subway routes after 1:30am. Fare $2.25, 10 tokens for $19; students and seniors $1.50; under 13 $0.50, 10 tokens for $4.25. M-Sa 1-day travel pass $7.75. Su and holidays unlimited travel for families $7.75. Transfers among subway, bus, and streetcar lines is free, but passengers must obtain a transfer slip from the driver when they board the train or bus.

Taxi: Co-op Cabs, ☎504-2667.

Car Rental: National Car Rental (800-522-9696; www.national.com) has an office in Union Station. About $60 per day for 21- to 24-year olds and $35 per day for those above 24. Open Su 8:30am-10pm, M-F 7am-10pm, Sa 7am-5pm.

Bike Rental: Wheel Excitement, 5 Rees St. (☎260-9000) on the beach near York St. $12 per hr.; each additional hr. $3, $27 per day. Open M-F 10am-5pm, Sa-Su 10am-6pm.

PRACTICAL INFORMATION

Visitor Info: The **Metropolitan Toronto Convention and Visitors Association (MTCVA),** 207 Queens Quay W. (☎203-2600 or 800-363-1990; www.torontotourism.com), mails out information packets and provides a comprehensive automated phone system for answering questions. Ontario's **Ministry of Tourism and Recreation,** in the Eaton Center, Level 1 (☎800-668-2746; www.ontariotravel.net), provides maps and information on day trips or travel to the rest of Ontario. **Traveler's Aid** (☎366-7988), which provides general information, free maps, and hotel/hostel reservations, has locations in the bus station (open daily 9:30am-9:30pm), Union Station (open daily 10am-2pm), and 3 locations in Pearson International Airport.

Currency Exchange: Toronto Currency Exchange, 277 Yonge St. (☎864-1441), across from the Eaton Center, offers the best rates around. Open Su 11am-7pm, M-Sa 10am-9pm.

Hotlines: Rape Crisis, ☎597-8808. Open 24hr. **Toronto Gay and Lesbian Phone Line,** ☎964-6600. Operates M-F 7-10pm.

Medical Services: The Toronto Hospital, 200 Elizabeth St. (☎340-3111).

Toronto Reference Library: 789 Yonge St. (☎395-5577; www.tpl.toronto.on.ca.). Subway: Bloor/Yonge. Free **Internet** access and a rare collection of Sir Arthur Conan Doyle paraphernalia. Open M-Th 10am-8pm, F-Sa 10am-5pm.

Post Office: Adelaide Station, 31 Adelaide St. E (☎214-2352). Subway: King. Open M-F 8am-5:45pm. **Postal Code:** M5C 2J0. **Area Code:** 416 (city), 905 (outskirts). In text, 416 unless noted otherwise.

ACCOMMODATIONS

Cut-rate hotels concentrate around Jarvis St. and Gerrard St. The **University of Toronto Housing Service** provides a web site listing of budget sleeping options in several of its colleges. (☎978-8045; http://eir.library.utoronto.ca/studenthousing.) The **Downtown Association of Bed and Breakfast Guest Houses** places guests in renovated Victorian homes. (☎483-8822; www.bnbinfo.com.)

Hostelling International Toronto (HI-AYH), 76 Church St. (☎971-4440 or 877-848-8737; www.hihostels.ca), at King St. Subway: King. Chic decor, brand-new facilities, and a hip staff make travelers feel at home in the heart of downtown Toronto. Kitchen, outdoor patio, pool tables, Internet access, and pub crawls. Linen $2 (free with ISIC). A/C. Laundry $3. Reception 24hr. Check-in after noon. Check-out 11am. Reservations recommended in summer. Dorms $22, nonmembers $26; private rooms $70/74. ❶

Canadiana Guest House & Backpackers Inn, 42 Widmer St. (☎598-9090 or 877-215-1225; www.canadianalodging.com), off Adelaide St. W. Subway: Osgoode. An assortment of young, adventurous professionals populate the themed rooms of Canadiana, whose wooden beds and classy furnishings create a calm, refined atmosphere. Frequent evening barbecues ($2.25) and outings (such as sailing and bowling). 110 beds, A/C, kitchen, and Internet access. Linen included. Lockers $1. Laundry $3. Limited parking. Check-in 8am-2am. Check-out 10:30am. 6- to 8-bed dorms $25; 4-bed dorms $28; private doubles $65. 10% discount for ISIC or HI cardholders. ❶

Hotel Victoria, 56 Yonge St. (☎363-1666 or 800-363-8228; www.hotelvictoria-toronto.ca), between Wellington St. and King St. Subway: King. This small, stately hotel is the second oldest in town, offering an unbeatable location and 48 elegant rooms. Continental breakfast, private bath, TV, A/C, baggage storage, free newspapers, and health club privileges. During peak tourist season, standard rooms $135; deluxe rooms $159 and up. Reservations strongly suggested. ❺

Knox College, 59 St. George St. (☎978-0168; knox.residence@utoronto.ca). Subway: St. George. This genteel Presbyterian seminary boasts huge rooms, beautiful Gothic architecture, and a location right on the U of T campus. Office open M-F 9am-4pm. Reserve rooms at least 3 weeks in advance. Open mid-May to late Aug. Singles $55, students $45; doubles $80/70. ❸

FOOD

With over 6000 metropolitan-area restaurants trying to out-cook each other, an amazing meal is found on almost any street in Toronto. "L.L.B.O." (for "Liquor Licensing Board of Ontario") signs indicate that alcohol is available. **Baldwin Street,** at McCaul St., is home to a quiet row of diverse restaurants offering excellent food at reasonable prices. For fresh produce and cheap ethnic food, try **Kensington Market,** between Baldwin St. and Dundas St. W west of Spadina Ave. The **Saint Lawrence Market,** at King and Sherbourne St., six blocks east of the King subway stop, is a great place for meats and produce. (Open T-Th 8am-6pm, F 8am-7pm, Sa 5am-5pm.)

THE ANNEX

Serra, 378 Bloor St. W (☎922-6999). Subway: Spadina. Cool but not intimidating, slightly upscale but not exorbitant, and delicious beyond all expectations, Serra is an oasis amid the bustle of the Annex. Rigatoni with prosciutto and black olives $13, scrumptious créme brûlée $7. Open M-F noon-10pm, Sa-Su 5-10pm. ❸

Country Style Hungarian Restaurant, 450 Bloor St. W (☎537-1745). Subway: Bathurst. Plan to arrive famished and leave stuffed—the generous cooks load your plate with enough schnitzel ($12) and other traditional Hungarian goodies to feed you for days. Daily specials $9.50-$12. Raspberry soda $2. Open daily 11am-10pm. ❷

Sushi on Bloor, 515 Bloor St. W (☎516-3456). Subway: Bathurst. One of the many sushi joints crowding into the Annex, Sushi on Bloor is often packed with loyal patrons when other places are empty. Pleasant atmosphere and friendly staff. Fresh sushi (6 pieces) $4-5. Lunch and dinner specials from $5.50. Open Su noon-10pm, M-Th noon-10:45pm, F-Sa noon-11pm. ❶

WEST QUEEN ST./KENSINGTON MARKET

Terroni, 720 Queen St. W (☎504-0320). Subway: Osgoode, then transfer to westbound street car. Named for a derogatory description of Southern Italians (*terroni* means "people of the earth"), Terroni brings fine dining down to earth with a relaxed ambience and a snug outdoor patio. Imagine someone's no-nonsense Italian granny catering a Fortune 500 luncheon to get an idea of the food here. They're most famous for their pizzas ($9-13). The deli section, stocked with pastas, olives, and Italian meats, is also well worth a look. Open daily 11am-11pm. ❷

Chinese Traditional Buns, 536 Dundas St. (☎299-9011). At Kensington Market, hidden down a flight of stairs. Subway: St. Patrick. The best deal in Chinatown serves doughy buns stuffed with tasty meats or vegetables, then steamed and served in a bamboo basket. The Gou-Bu-Li buns (6 for $3) and jellied bean curd soup ($1.50) make a delicious and filling lunch. Open daily 9:30am-10pm. ❶

John's Italian Cafe, 27 Baldwin St. (☎596-8848). West of McCaul St. Subway: St. Patrick. This local favorite in a quiet residential neighborhood serves up fancy pizzas ($18) and generous plates of gnocchi with pesto ($11). Upstairs, the bar specializes in jazzy relaxation. Open daily 11:30am-2am. ❸

THEATER/ST. LAWRENCE DISTRICT

Penelope, 225 King St. W (☎351-9393 or 877-215-4026). Subway: St. Andrew. Attentive service and mouth-watering food in the relaxing atmosphere of a Grecian resort. Succulent roast lamb $13. Open M-W 11:30am-10pm, Th-F 11:30am-11:30pm, Sa 4:30-11:30pm. ❷

Mövenpick Marché, 161 Bay St. (☎366-8986), in BCE Place at Yonge St. and Front St. Subway: King. A combination restaurant and produce market the size of some department stores (and every bit as complex), Mövenpick allows diners to browse through 14 culinary stations in order to customize their meals. Avoid lines by taking a meal to go. Entrees $8-10. Open daily 7am-2am. ❷

Mustachio, downstairs in the St. Lawrence Market (☎368-5241). Subway: King. No-nonsense service and enormous sandwiches make for an unbeatable meal on the go. The veal and eggplant parmigiana ($5) overflows with freshly-cooked fixin's. Foccaccia sandwiches $3.75. Open T-Th 8am-6pm, F 8am-7pm, Sa 5am-5pm. ❶

SIGHTS

One of Toronto's most interesting activities is also its cheapest thrill: walking through the busy streets. For an organized expedition, the **Royal Ontario Museum** leads 14 **free walking tours.** (☎586-5513; www.rom.on.ca. Tours June-Sept. W 6pm and Su 2pm. Destinations and meeting places vary; call for specific info.) Free 1hr. walking tours of the **University of Toronto,** Canada's largest university, depart from the **Nona MacDonald Visitors Centre** at King's College Circle. (☎978-5000. Tours June-Aug. M-F 11am and 2pm, Sa-Su 11am. Historical tours available June-Aug. M-F 10:30am-2:30pm.) A self-guided **Discovery Walk,** highlighting the interconnected parks of downtown Toronto, starts in front of **City Hall.** (☎338-0338. 2hr.)

CN TOWER. Toronto's **CN Tower** stands as the world's tallest free-standing structure. It also contains the world's highest wine cellar and longest metal stairway. The mammoth concrete symbol of human ingenuity is visible from nearly every corner of the city. The tower offers a heavenly view, and despite the frightening void below, trusting souls lie down on the observation deck's sturdy glass floor. *(301 Front St. W. Subway: Union. ☎360-8500; www.cntower.ca. Tower open Su-Th 10am-10pm, F-Sa 10am-11pm; inside attractions 11am-7pm. $19, seniors $17, ages 4-12 $14; additional $7.50 for the Sky Pod. Combined admission to tower, attractions, and Sky Pod also available.)*

GOVERNMENT. Curving twin towers and a two-story rotunda make up the innovative **City Hall**. In front of City Hall, **Nathan Phillips Square** is home to a reflecting pool that becomes a skating rink in winter. Numerous events, including live music every Wednesday *(June to early Oct. noon-2pm)*, also happen on the square. *(Subway: Osgoode. ☎338-0338. Open M-F 8:30am-4:30pm. Brochures available for self-guided tours.)* The Ontario government meets in the stately **Provincial Parliament Buildings,** at Queen's Park in the city center. *(Subway: Queen's Park. ☎325-7500. Free 30min. tours late May-early Sept. daily 9am-4pm. Call ahead for Parliamentary schedule. Free gallery passes available at south basement door when the House is in session, usually Sept.-Dec. and Mar.-June.)*

GOT SOMETHING TO SAY? When knowing you've got the right to free speech just isn't enough, head to the Speaker's Corner, at the southwest corner of Nathan Phillips Square. The City Council of Toronto has dedicated the small pulpit to the Concept of Free Speech: "The public may mount the dais and speak, or challenge another speaker to debate." Be careful what you say, though, as the city bears no responsibility for all the risks associated with speaking your mind.

SPADINA HOMES. Straight from a fairy tale, **Casa Loma,** a castle atop a hill near Spadina, is a classic tourist attraction. More than 90 rooms, an eerie underground tunnel, and two imposing towers add to the grandeur of this display of late-Victorian opulence. The Norman Tower offers an incredible view of downtown Toronto. *(Subway: Dupont, then walk a few blocks north. ☎923-1171; www.casaloma.org. Open daily 9:30am-4pm. Free self-guided audio tour. $10, seniors and ages 14-17 $6.50, children $6. Parking $2.30 per hr.)* Visitors are treated to a tour of 19th-century Toronto next door at the **Spadina Museum,** an 80-acre estate relic from 1866. *(285 Spadina Rd. ☎392-6910. Open Apr.-Dec. Tu-Su noon-5pm. $5, seniors and ages 12-17 $3.25, ages 6-11 $3.)*

WILDLIFE. The **Metro Toronto Zoo** keeps over 5000 animals in a 710-acre park that re-creates the world's seven geographic regions and features the new Gorilla Rainforest. *(Meadowvale Rd. off Exit 389 on Hwy. 401. Take bus #86A from Kennedy Station. ☎392-5900. Open mid-Mar. to mid-May and early Sept. to mid-Oct. 9am-6pm; late May to early Sept. 9am-7:30pm; mid-Oct. to mid-Mar. 9:30am-4:30pm. Last entry 1hr. before closing. $18, ages 4-14 $10, seniors $12. Parking $6.)*

HOCKEY. No trip to Toronto is complete without a visit to the **Hockey Hall of Fame,** the cathedral for Canada's religiously-devoted sports fans. A beautiful stained glass dome in the 148-year-old **Great Hall** houses hockey's Holy Grail, the Stanley Cup. If not in the mood for idle veneration, interactive exhibits provide an opportunity for more active enjoyment. *(30 Yonge St. In BCE Place. Subway: BCE Place. ☎360-7765. Open mid-June to early Sept. M-Sa 9:30am-6pm, Su 10am-6pm; mid-Sept. to early June M-F 10am-5pm, Sa 9:30am-6pm, Su 10:30am-5pm. $12, seniors and under 18 $7.)*

 MUSEUMS

Art Gallery of Ontario (AGO), 317 Dundas St. (☎979-6648; www.ago.net), at McCaul St. Subway: St. Patrick. Showcases an enormous collection of Western art from the Renaissance to the 1990s, with a particular focus on the works of Canadian artists. Check out the spectacular exhibition of Henry Moore's sculptures– the largest collection outside of Britain. Open Tu and Th-F 11am-6pm, W 11am-8:30pm, Sa-Su 10am-5:30pm. $12, students with ID and seniors $9, ages 6-15 $6; W 6-8:30pm free. Admission to special exhibits extra; call for specifics.

Royal Ontario Museum (ROM), 100 Queen's Park (☎586-8000; www.rom.on.ca), at Bay St. Subway: Museum. Houses a must-see Egyptian exhibit, an extensive dinosaur collection, and a realistic bat-cave. Open M-Th and Sa 10am-6pm, F 10am-9:30pm, Su 11am-6pm. Admission varies according to current exhibition, up to $20 for adults; students, seniors, and children less; call for details. F after 4:30pm free.

Bata Shoe Museum, 327 Bloor St. (☎979-7799; www.batashoemuseum.ca). Subway: St. George or Spadina. Walk a mile in a medieval knight's metal boots or in the tiny Chinese slippers that once contained bound feet. The diverse collection of approximately 10,000 shoes focuses on the often stepped-over role of footwear in human culture. Open M-W and F-Sa 10am-5pm, Th 10am-8pm, Su noon-5pm. $6, students and seniors $4, ages 2-14 $2, families $13; 1st Tu of every month free.

Ontario Science Center, 770 Don Mills Rd. (☎696-3147; www.ontariosciencecentre.ca), at Eglinton Ave. E, Subway: Pape, then take the #25 bus, presents more than 650 interactive exhibits showcasing humanity's greatest innovations. "Truth" is an exhibit that challenges visitors to re-evaluate their points of view regarding several "scientifically-proven" facts. Open daily 10am-5pm. $13, seniors and ages 13-17 $9, ages 5-12 $7; with Omnimax film $18/12/10.

HOW LONG IS *YOUR* (STREET)? With its quality cuisine and culture, Toronto has nothing to prove, but the city holds two of the world's more interesting world records. One, for the world's longest street, goes to Yonge Street, which runs 1900km (1190 mi.) from the shores of Lake Ontario to Rainy River, a small mining town in northern Ontario. The second, for the world's tallest building, goes to the CN Tower. At 553m (1815'5"), it also contains the world's highest observation deck. We get the point, guys.

EASTERN CANADA

ENTERTAINMENT

The monthly *Where Toronto*, free at tourist booths, gives the lowdown on arts and entertainment. **T.O. Tix,** 208 Yonge St., at the corner of Dundas St., sells half-price tickets on performance day. (Subway: Yonge. ☎536-6468. Open Tu-Sa noon-7:30pm; arrive before 11:45am for first dibs.)

Ontario Place, 955 Lakeshore Blvd. W, features cheap summer entertainment, including rides and an IMAX theater. (☎314-9811, recording ☎314-9900; www.ontarioplace.com. Hours vary; open mid-June to Sept. 10am-8pm. All-day pass $28, children $14, seniors $16.) Top pop artists perform in the **Molson Amphitheater,** 909 Lakeshore Blvd. W. (☎260-5600. Tickets through Ticketmaster $20-125.) **Roy Thompson Hall,** 60 Simcoe St., at King St. W, is both Toronto's premier concert hall and the home of the **Toronto Symphony Orchestra** from September to June. (☎593-4828, box office ☎872-4255; www.tso.ca. Subway: St. Andrews. Open M-F 10am-6pm, Sa noon-5pm, Su 2hr. before performances. $25-85, matinees $25-50. $15 rush tickets available on concert days M-F 11am and Sa

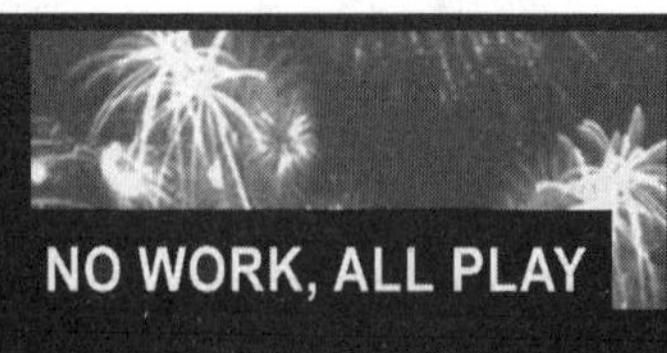

NO WORK, ALL PLAY

SALVAGING STRATFORD

In 1832, British settlers in Canada picked a nice spot on a river and founded a town. The innkeeper kept a picture of Shakespeare on his wall. Soon, his inn became the Shakespeare Inn, and not long after, the river was christened the Avon. After the railroad industry came and went in this town of Stratford, a local newspaperman had an idea to revitalize the economy. In June 1953, Alec Guinness read the opening lines to *Richard III* from a makeshift stage, and the **Stratford Shakespeare Festival** was born.

Today the festival is one of the most important theater festivals in the world, attracting over 600,000 visitors each year between early May and early November. The **Stratford Repertory Theatre** is now the largest in North America, putting on 16 productions throughout the festival. The event has featured plays by Samuel Beckett, Anton Chekov, Tennessee Williams, and, of course, the Bard himself. In addition to plays, visitors are treated to backstage tours, talks with the actors, and the serenity of Stratford's gardens.

From Toronto, take Rte. 401 west to Kitchener, then follow Rte. 7 west to Stratford. For the 2004 calendar of events, visit www.stratfordfestival.ca or call ☎800-567-1600. Tickets $50-100, with discounts for seniors and students. Rush tickets and matinee discounts also available.

1pm.) The **Hummingbird Centre,** 1 Front St. East at Yonge St., stages touring Broadway shows, popular music concerts, and an assortment of ethnic festivals. (☎393-7469; www.hummingbirdcentre.com. Subway: Union. Box office open M-F 10am-6pm and Sa 10am-1pm.)

The **St. Lawrence Centre,** 27 Front St. E, stages excellent drama and chamber music recitals. (☎366-7723. Box office open summer M-Sa 10am-6pm; winter performance days 10am-8pm, non-performance days 10am-6pm. Some student and senior discounts.) **CanStage** performs free summer Shakespeare (Tu-Su 8pm, $15 donation suggested) at **High Park,** on Bloor St. W, at Parkside Dr. Year-round shows at the St. Lawrence Centre include new Canadian works and classics. (Subway: High Park. Box office ☎368-3110; www.canstage.com. Open M-Sa 10am-6pm. Call for schedule.) Several blocks west in the Harbourfront Centre, the **Soulpepper Theatre Company,** 231 Queen's Quay W, presents famous masterpieces. (☎973-4000; www.soulpepper.ca. $21-45, students $25, rush tickets $18.)

Canada's answer to Disney is **Canada's Wonderland,** 9580 Jane St., 1hr. from downtown at Rt. 400 and Rutherford Rd. One shot of white-knuckle thrill rides, one shot of refreshing water rides, served with a dash of happy-go-lucky. (☎905-832-7400; www.canadas-wonderland.com. Open late June to early Sept. daily 10am-10pm; fall Sa-Su, times vary. Waterpark open summer daily 11am-7pm. $49, seniors and ages 3-6 $24.) The park is accessible by **Go Bus** (☎869-3200; one-way $4) from the Yorkdale or York Mills subway station.

From April to early October, the **Toronto Blue Jays** play hardball at the enormous, modern **Sky Dome,** at Front and Peter St. (Subway: Union, follow the signs. ☎341-2222, tickets ☎341-1234; www.skydome.com. $7-45.) To get an inside look at the Sky Dome, take the tour. (☎341-2770. Times vary. $12.50, seniors and under 16 $8.50, youth $7.) The Sky Dome is also the home to the **Toronto Argonauts** (tickets ☎545-1777; www.argonauts.on.ca. $16-48) of the Canadian Football League, as well as concerts (☎341-3663) and other events throughout the year. Hockey fans head for **The Air Canada Centre,** 40 Bay St., to see the **Maple Leafs.** (Subway: Union. ☎815-5500; www.mapleleafs.com and www.theaircanadacentre.com. Tickets $30-160.)

Film fans choose the **Bloor Cinema,** 506 Bloor St. W (☎516-2330; www.bloorcinema.com), at Bathurst St., or the **Cinémateque Ontario,** 317 Dundas St. W (☎923-3456; www.bell.ca/cinematheque), in the AGO's Jackman Hall. Toronto's rich cultural offerings include several world-class **festivals** (☎800-363-1990; www.torontotourism.com). The 10-day **Toronto International Film Festival** (☎968-3456; www.e.bell.ca/filmfest), in early September, is one of the most prestigious festivals on the art-house circuit, with its showings of classic, Canadian, and foreign films. In June, the **Toronto International Dragon Boat Race Festival** (☎595-1739; www.torontodragonboat.com), on Toronto's Centre Island, continues a 2000-year-old Chinese tradition replete with great food and performances. In late August, the **Canadian National Exhibition (CNE),** one of North America's largest annual fairs, brings an international carnival to Exhibition Place. (☎263-3800; www.theex.com. Open daily 10am-midnight. $10, seniors and under 6 $7.) In the last week of June, the city also rocks with one of the three largest gay and lesbian **Pride Week** celebrations in the world (☎927-7433; www.pridetoronto.com), while in early July the **Toronto Street Festival** (☎338-0338; www.toronto.ca/special_events) and the **Fringe Theatre Festival** (☎966-1062; www.fringetoronto.com) come to the city.

NIGHTLIFE

Toronto offers a seemingly limitless selection of bars, pubs, dance clubs, and late-night cafes. The city stops alcohol distribution nightly at 2am, which is when most clubs close down. New clubs are always opening on trendy **Queen Street W** in the **Entertainment District,** on **College Street W,** and on **Bloor Street W.** The free entertainment magazines *Now* and *Eye* come out every Thursday. The gay scene centers on **Wellesley** and **Church Street.** For info, pick up the free, biweekly *Xtra.* All are available in bars or in streetside dispensers.

THE ANNEX

The James Joyce, 386 Bloor St. (☎324-9400). Subway: Spadina. Live Celtic music every night, pool tables, and unmistakable Irish conviviality make the Joyce the best place in the Annex to nurse a pint of Guinness ($6.25). Hot poppers $4. Open daily noon-2am.

The Green Room, 296 Brunswick Ave. (☎929-3253), from Bloor St., walk down Brunswick Ave. and turn right into the alley. Subway: Bathurst. Think abandoned coffee shop colonized by transient artists and musicians and you'll have a feel for this smoky hidden gem. Quesadillas $4. Pints $5. Open daily 11am-2am.

Tap, 513 Bloor St. W. (☎533-5321). Subway: Bathurst. Colored lights and first-rate rock tunes fill the velvety darkness of this popular hangout. Pints $5. Sa after 10pm Moe Berg of Guilty Pleasures spins. Open daily 6pm-3am.

DOWNTOWN

The Second City, 56 Blue Jays Way (☎343-0011 or 888-263-4485), at Wellington St., just north of the Sky Dome. Subway: Union. One of North America's wackiest, most creative comedy clubs that has spawned comics Dan Akroyd, John Candy, Martin Short, Mike Myers, and a hit TV show (SCTV). Free improv sessions M-Th 9:30pm and Sa midnight. Shows M-Th 8pm $21, F-Sa 8 and 10:30pm $28. Su touring company's production $14. Student tickets Su-Th $13. Reservations strongly recommended.

¿C'est What?, 67 Front St. E (☎867-9499). Subway: Union. This mellow, slightly upscale cafe/pub is a great showcase for local and underground musical talent, as well as local alcohol—try their homemade microbrews ($6-8) and wines ($7) while listening. Sa jazz 4-7pm. Open daily 11:30am-2am.

THE GAY & LESBIAN VILLAGE

Woody's/Sailor, 465-467 Church St. (☎972-0887), by Maitland St. Subway: Wellesley. *The* gay bar in the Church and Wellesley area, famous throughout Canada. Don't miss "Bad Boys Night Out" Tu and "Best Chest" Th at midnight. Bottled beer $4.75. No cover. Open daily noon-2am.

Slack Alice, 562 Church St. (☎969-8742). Subway: Wellesley. The best of both worlds: Tuscan and Thai dishes served with a refined air turns to energetic dancing on F-Sa. The crowd is mostly gay and lesbian, but very straight-friendly. Happy Hour 4-7pm and all day on Tu. Entrees $9-27. Pints $5. Open daily 11am-2am.

Fly, 8 Gloucester St. (☎410-5426), just east of Yonge St. Subway: Wellesley. The ultimate dancing experience. Canada's best DJ's come to spin for the throngs of sweaty dancers who feast on free food platters, energy drinks ($4), and abundant alcohol. Known as the best gay club in town, the crowd is fairly diverse. Arrive early to avoid long entrance lines. Covers vary; expect $10-40. Open Sa 10pm-wee hours (often 7am).

DAYTRIP FROM TORONTO

NIAGARA ESCARPMENT

The Niagara Escarpment passes west of Toronto as it winds its way from Niagara Falls to Tobermory at the tip of the Bruce Peninsula. Along this rocky 725km ridge, the **Bruce Trail** snakes through parks and private land. Hikers are treated to spectacular waterfalls, breathtaking vistas, and unique flora and fauna. The Escarpment areas around Milton are most easily accessible from Toronto. Go west on Rte. 401 and exit at Rte. 25 (exit #320), go north on Rte. 25, and turn left at Campbellville. Follow signs to Hilton Falls, Rattlesnake Point, Crawford Lake, and Mount Nemo. Entrance is $3-6. Open 8.30am-sundown. For info, write or call the **Niagara Escarpment Commission,** 232 Guelph St., Georgetown, ON L7G 4B1 (☎905-877-5191; www.escarpment.org). Camping reservations are available (☎888-668-7275). Those planning extensive trips to the Escarpment should contact the **Bruce Trail Association,** P.O. Box 857, Hamilton, ON L8N 3N9 (☎905-529-6821; www.brucetrail.org).

OTTAWA ☎613

Legend has it that in the mid-19th century, Queen Victoria chose Ottawa as Canada's capital by closing her eyes and pointing a finger at a map. In reality, perhaps political savvy, rather than blind chance, guided her to this once remote logging town. As a stronghold for neither the French nor English, Ottawa was the perfect compromise. Forced to attempt to forge national unity while preserving local identities, Ottawa continues to play cultural diplomat to larger Canada.

TRANSPORTATION

Airport: Ottawa International (☎248-2125; www.ottawa-airport.ca), 20-30min. south of the city off Bronson Ave. Take bus #97 from MacKenzie King Bridge. A **hotel shuttle** (☎260-2359) runs between the airport and downtown hotels every 30min. 5am-12:35am; call for other pickups. $12, seniors and students $11; $20 round-trip.

Trains: VIA Rail, 200 Tremblay Rd. (☎244-8289; www.viarail.ca), east of downtown, off the Queensway at Alta Vista Rd. Ticket office open M-F 5am-9pm, Sa 6:30am-7:30pm, Su 8:20am-9pm. To: **Montréal** (2hr., 4-5 per day, $46); **Québec City** via Montréal (7hr., 2 per day, $89); **Toronto** (4hr., 5 per day, $66). 35% discount with ISIC.

Buses: Voyageur, 265 Catherine St. (☎238-5900), between Kent and Lyon St. Serves primarily Eastern Canada. Station open daily 5:30am-2:30am. To **Montréal** (2½hr.; every hr. 6am-midnight; $33, students and seniors $21). **Greyhound** (☎237-7038) leaves from the same station, bound for Western Canada and southern Ontario, and runs to **Québec City** via **Montréal** (6hr.; every hr.; $64-71) and **Toronto** (5hr.; 8 per day; $54-60). Service to the US goes through Montréal or Toronto. Blue **Hull City** buses (☎819-770-3242) connect Ottawa to Hull, Québec, across the river.

Public Transit: OC Transpo, 1500 St. Laurent (☎741-4390; www.octranspo.com). Buses based at Rideau Centre. $2.50, ages 6-11 $1.25; express (green buses) $3.50.

Taxi: Blue Line Taxi, ☎238-1111. **Capital,** ☎744-3333.

Car Rental: Avis (☎739-3334) and **Budget** (☎729-6666) have locations in the airport. **Discount** (☎310-2277) has a downtown location on Gladstone Ave. at Kent St.

Bike Rental: RentABike (☎241-4140; www.cyberus.ca/~rentabike/) has a convenient location directly behind Rideau Hall. $8 per hr., $23 per day. Helmet, lock, and map included. Open Apr. 1-Oct. 1 daily 9am-6pm.

ORIENTATION

The **Rideau Canal** divides Ottawa into the eastern lower town and the western upper town and is lined with bike paths and walkways. The canal itself is a major access route and the world's longest skating rink during the winter. West of the canal, Parliament buildings and government offices line **Wellington Street,** one of the city's main east-west arteries, running directly into the heart of downtown. **Laurier Avenue** is the only other east-west street permitting traffic from one side of the canal to the other. East of the canal, Wellington St. becomes **Rideau Street,** surrounded by a fashionable shopping district. North of Rideau St., the **Byward Market** hosts a summertime open-air market and most of Ottawa's nightlife. **Elgin Street,** a primary north-south artery stretching from Hwy. 417 (the Queensway) to the War Memorial just south of Wellington near Parliament Hill, is also home to a few pubs and nightlife spots. **Bank Street,** which runs parallel to Elgin three blocks to the west, services the town's older shopping area. Parking downtown is hard to find, and Ottawa is notorious for prompt ticketing of vehicles. On weekends, **park for free** in the World Exchange Plaza, on Queen St. between O'Connor and Metcalfe.

PRACTICAL INFORMATION

Visitor Info: National Capital Commission Information Center, 90 Wellington St. (☎239-5000 or within Canada ☎800-465-1867; www.capcan.ca), opposite the Parliament Bldg. Open daily early May-early Sept. 8:30am-9pm; early Sept. to early May 9am-5pm. For info on Hull, in the Québec province, contact the **Association Touristique de l'Outaouais,** 103 rue Laurier, Hull (☎819-778-2222 or 800-265-7822; www.outaouais-tourism.ca). Open mid-June to Sept. M-F 8:30am-8pm, Sa-Su 9am-6pm; Oct.-early June M-F 8:30am-5pm, Sa-Su 9am-4pm.

Hotlines: Rape Crisis, ☎562-2333. **Ottawa Distress Centre,** ☎238-3311 (English). **Sexual Assault Support Centre,** ☎738-3762. **Gayline-Telegai,** ☎238-1717.

Currency Exchange: Custom House Currency Exchange, 153 Sparks St. (☎234-6005 or 800-242-3147; www.customhouse.com), behind the tourist office, changes money at competitive rates. $2 flat service charge, waived for groups of 5 or more. Open May-Sept. M-Sa 9am-7pm, Su 10am-5pm; Oct.-Apr. M-F 9am-5pm.

Medical Services: Ottawa General Hospital, 501 Smyth Rd. (☎737-7777), 1km south of downtown.

Internet Access: Ottawa Public Library, 120 Metcalf St. (☎236-0301). 30min. free Internet access. Open M-Th 10am-9pm, F noon-6pm, Sa 10am-5pm.

Post Office: 59 Sparks St. (☎844-1545), at Elgin St. Open M-F 8am-6pm. **Postal Code:** K1P 5A0. **Area Code:** 613 in Ottawa; 819 in Hull. In text, 613 unless noted otherwise.

ACCOMMODATIONS

In downtown Ottawa, economical options exist only if you avoid hotels. Advance reservations are strongly recommended, especially if staying through Canada Day (July 1). **Ottawa Bed and Breakfast** represents 10 B&Bs in the Ottawa area. (☎563-0161. Singles $49-54, doubles $59-64.)

University of Ottawa Residences, 90 University St. (☎564-5400 or 877-225-8664), in the center of campus, an easy walk from downtown. From the bus and train stations, take bus #95. The best deal in town. Clean, spacious dorms in a concrete landscape. Free linen and towels. Parking $10 per day. Check-in 4:30pm. Check-out 10:30am. Open early May-late Aug. Singles $40, students $30; doubles $60/45. Rooms for up to 4 people in New Residence $99, including kitchenette and tasty breakfast. ❶

Ottawa International Hostel (HI-C), 75 Nicholas St. (☎235-2595), in downtown Ottawa. The site of Canada's last public hanging, the former Carleton County Jail now "incarcerates" travelers in tiny cells. Private showers, kitchen, Internet access, laundry facilities, lounges, jail tours, and a friendly, tongue-in-cheek atmosphere. Linen $2.50. Key deposit $2. Parking $5 per day. 24hr. reception. Check-in 1pm. Check-out 11am. Winter doors locked 1-7am. Dorms $20, nonmembers $24; private rooms from $53/57. ❶

Gatineau Park, (☎819-827-2020, reservations 819-456-3016), northwest of Hull. 3 rustic campgrounds within 1hr. of Ottawa: **Lac Philippe Campground,** 248 sites with facilities for family camping, trailers, and campers; **Lac Taylor Campground,** 33 semi-rustic sites; and **Lac la Pêche Campground,** 36 campsites accessible only by canoe. For Lac Philippe and Lac Taylor, arrive 1:30-9:30pm; depart before 11am; camping permit $24. For Lac la Pêche, arrive between 1:30pm and sunset; camping permit $20. $5 reservation fee for all sites. Take Hwy. 5 north and exit at Old Chesea. Follow signs to the Visitors Center or, for the campsites, follow Hwy. 5 to its end, then take Hwy. 105 north 10km to Hwy. 366 W. Follow signs to the campgrounds. ❶

FOOD

Ottawa's **Byward Market,** on Byward St. between York and George St., is full of tables with produce and plants, chatty locals, and sweet maple syrup. (☎562-3325. Open in warmer weather daily 8am-5pm; boutiques open later.) Byward Market, York, George, and Clarence St. are packed with cafes, great restaurants, and bars.

Medithéo, 77 Clarence St. (☎562-2500; www.meditheo.com). Whether it's the exotic atmosphere, the scintillating cuisine, or that third glass of sangria ($7), the world looks different from the inside of this unique eatery. With 5 dishes stacked one above the other, the vegetarian Mazzeh sampler ($19) is a good way to treat yourself to a wide variety of Mediterranean flavors. Entrees $17-25. Complete the experience with a smoke on an ornate shisha pipe, $15. Open M-F 11am-11pm, Sa-Su 11am-2am. ❹

Mamma Grazzi's Kitchen, 25 George St. (☎241-8656). This little Italian hideaway is in a stone building in one of the oldest parts of Ottawa. The thin-crust pizza ($9-15) is well worth the wait. Hours vary; in general, Su-Th 10:30am-10pm, F-Sa 10:30am-11pm. ❷

Byward Café, 55 Byward Market (☎241-2555), at the bottom of the market, at George St. Fun pop background music and a huge array of savory treats bring both young and old to eat, drink, and relax on the breezy covered patio. Panini sandwiches around $4.50. Open summer daily 8am-11pm; winter 8am-6pm. ❶

D'Arcy McGee's Irish Pub, 44 Sparks St. (☎230-4433; www.darcymcgees.ca). Whether lured in by the traditional Celtic music or chased in by the traditional Canadian rain, visitors to D'Arcy's are never sorry they came. Hearty pub food $8-15. Live music W nights. Open Su-Tu 11am-1am, W-Sa 11am-2am. ❷

SIGHTS

THE HUB. Parliament Hill, on Wellington at Metcalfe St., towers over downtown with its distinguished Gothic architecture. Warm your hands over the **Centennial Flame** at the south gate, lit in 1967 to mark the 100th anniversary of Confederation.

The Prime Minister can be spotted at the central Parliament structure, **Centre Block,** which contains the House of Commons, Senate, and Library of Parliament. (The library is closed until 2005.) Free tours of Centre Block depart every 30min. from the white **Infotent** by the Visitors Center. *(☎992-4793. Tours mid-May to Sept. M-F 9am-8pm, Sa-Su 9am-5pm; Sept. to mid-May daily 9am-3:30pm, leaving from the main entrance to Centre Block. Infotent open daily mid-May to mid-June 9am-5pm; mid-June to Aug. 9am-8pm.)*

When Parliament is in session, you can watch Canada's officials debate. Visitors with luck and stamina may be able to see **Question Period,** the most interesting debates of the day. *(☎992-4793 or 866-599-4999; www.parl.gc.ca. Mid-Sept. to Dec. and Feb. to mid-June M-Th 2:15-3pm, F 11:15am-noon. Arrive about 2hr. in advance to obtain passes.)* On display behind the library, the bell from Centre Block is one of few remnants of the original 1859-66 structure that survived a 1916 fire. According to legend, the bell crashed to the ground after chiming at midnight on the night of the blaze. Today, daily concerts chime out on the carillon of 53 bells hanging in the Peace Tower. *(1hr. concerts June-Sept. M-F 2pm. 15min. concerts Sept.-June M-F noon.)*

Those interested in trying to make a statuesque soldier smile should attend the 30min. **Changing of the Guard** on the broad lawns in front of Centre Block. *(☎993-1811. Late June to late Aug. daily 10am, weather permitting.)* At dusk, Centre Block and its lawns transform into the background for **Sound and Light,** which relates the history of the Parliament Buildings and the nation. *(☎239-5000. Shows mid-May to early Sept. Performances alternate between French and English; call for show times.)* Several blocks west along Wellington St. stand the **Supreme Court of Canada** and the **Federal Court.** *(☎995-5361; www.ssc-csc.gc.ca. Open daily June-Aug. 9am-5pm; Sept.-May hours vary. Free tours every 30min.; tours alternate between French and English. No tours Sa-Su noon-1pm.)*

CONFEDERATION SQUARE. East of the Parliament Buildings at the junction of Sparks, Wellington, and Elgin St. stands **Confederation Square** and the enormous **National War Memorial,** dedicated by King George VI in 1939. The structure, a lifesize representation of Canadian troops marching under the watchful eye of the angels of liberty, symbolizes the triumph of peace over war—an ironic message on the eve of WWII. At **Nepean Point,** several blocks northwest of Rideau Centre and the Byward Market, behind the National Gallery of Canada, share a panoramic view of the capital with a statue of explorer Samuel de Champlain. Legend has it that the astrolobe he holds was discovered in the waters of the Ottawa River.

ROYALTY. The **Governor General,** the Queen's representative in Canada, resides at **Rideau Hall.** Take a guided tour of the house, gardens, and art collection—many visitors even run into the ever-gracious Governor General. *(1 Sussex Dr. ☎991-4422 or 800-465-6890; www.gg.ca. Free 45min. guided tours 10am-3pm; self-guided tours 3-4:30pm.)* See the production of collectors' "loonies" ($1 coins) at the **Royal Canadian Mint.** *(320 Sussex Dr. ☎993-8990 or 800-276-7714. In summer, tours leave every 15min. M-F 9am-8pm, Sa-Su 9am-5:30pm. In winter, daily 9am-5pm. $3, Sa-Su $1.50; children free.)*

OUTDOOR ACTIVITIES. Ottawa has managed to avoid the traditional urban vices of pollution and violent crime; the many parks and recreation areas have visitors go to is **Gatineau Park** (see **Accommodations,** p. 212), occupying 356 sq. km in the northwest. Don't miss the spectacular fall foliage. *(Information ☎819-827-2020, rentals ☎819-456-3016; www.canadascapital.gc.ca/gatineau. Bikes and a variety of boats available at lakes Philippe and la Pêche. Bikes $8 per hr., $30 per day, $35 per 24hr.; boats $10/30/38. Open daily mid-June to Labor Day, Sa-Su thereafter.)* Artificial **Dow's Lake,** accessible by the Queen Elizabeth Driveway, extends off the Rideau Canal south of Ottawa. **Dow's Lake Pavilion** rents pedal boats, canoes, and bikes in summer and ice skates and sleighs during the winter. *(101 Queen Elizabeth Driveway, near Preston St. ☎232-1001. Open mid-May to Sept. daily 8am-8pm. Rentals by the hr. and ½hr., prices vary.)*

MUSEUMS

Canadian Museum of Civilization, 100 Laurier St., Gatineau, QC (☎819-776-7000; www.civilization.ca). Housed in a striking sand dune-like structure across Port Alexandra Bridge from the National Gallery, the museum offers life-sized dioramas and architectural recreations exploring 1000 years of Canadian history. Open Apr.-Oct. M-W and F-Su 9am-6pm, Th 9am-9pm; low-season hours vary. $10, seniors $7, students $6, ages 2-12 $4; families $22. Th free after 4pm; Su half-price.

National Gallery, 380 Sussex Dr. (☎990-1985 or 800-319-2787; national.gallery.ca). A spectacular glass-towered building adjacent to Nepean Pt. holds the world's most comprehensive collection of Canadian art. The facade is a modern reinterpretation of the nearby neo-Gothic Library of Parliament. Don't miss Rideau Chapel, an entire church reconstructed inside the Gallery. Open May-Oct. M-W and F-Su 10am-5pm, Th 10am-8pm; low-season closed M-T. Free; special exhibits $11, seniors and students $9.25, teens 12-19 $4.50, children free. Reservations available for special exhibits (☎888-541-8888).

Canadian Museum of Contemporary Photography, 1 Rideau Canal (☎990-8257; www.cmcp.gallery.ca), on the steps between the Château Laurier and the Ottawa Locks. Showcases an impressive rotation of temporary exhibits, including everything from minimalist modernism to documentary photo essays. Open M-W and F-Su 10am-5pm, Th 10am-8pm; low-season W and F-Su 10am-5pm, Th 10am-8pm. Free.

Canadian War Museum, 330 Sussex Dr. (☎776-8600; www.warmuseum.ca), next to the National Gallery. Documents the history of the Canadian armed forces, from colonial skirmishes to UN Peacekeeping missions. See Hitler's armored car and walk through a mock WWI trench. Open M-W and F-Su 9:30am-5pm, Th 9:30am-8pm; mid-Oct. to May closed M. $4, students and seniors $3, children $2, families $9; Th after 4pm free; Su half-price. Free for Canadian veterans, current military personnel, retired military personnel, and their families.

Canadian Museum of Nature, 240 McLeod St. (☎566-4700; www.nature.ca), at Metcalfe St. A multimedia exploration of the natural world. For something creepy-crawly, check out the bug exhibit, where nothing bites...hard. Open May to early Sept. M-W and F-Su 9:30am-5pm, Th 9:30am-8pm; low-season hours vary. $8, students and seniors $7, ages 3-12 $3.50, families $13; Sa free before noon.

FESTIVALS

Ottawans seem to celebrate everything, even the bitter Canadian cold. All-important **Canada Day,** July 1, involves fireworks, partying in Major's Hill Park, concerts, and all-around merrymaking. During the first three weekends of February, **Winterlude** (☎239-5000 or 800-465-1867; www.canadascapital.gc.ca/winterlude.) lines the Rideau Canal. Ice sculptures and a working ice cafe illustrate how it feels to be an Ottawan in the winter—frozen. For three weeks in early May, the **Tulip Festival** (☎567-4447 or 800-668-8547; www.tulipfestival.ca) explodes with a kaleidoscope of more than a million buds around Dow's Lake, while pop concerts and other events center around Major's Hill Park. Music fills the air during the **Dance Festival** (☎947-7000; www.canadadance.ca), in late June, and the **Jazz Festival** (☎241-2633; www.ottawajazzfestival.com), in late July; both hold free recitals and concerts.

NIGHTLIFE

Many of Ottawa's nightclubs have been bought out recently due to increasing crime (mostly old-fashioned bar brawls). Now that nightspots can serve alcohol until 2am, the capital city is where it's at.

The Honest Lawyer, 141 George St. (☎562-2262), near Dalhousie St. If you were to mix an arcade, a college library, and a law office, this cavernous bar is what you'd get. A bowling alley, pool table, and foosball table round out this classy sports bar. The 130 oz. "Beerzooka" is, well, a lot of beer ($35). M wing night ($7 all-you-can-eat). F-Sa 21+. Open M-F 11:30am-2am, Sa 3pm-2am, Su 6pm-2am.

Zaphod, 27 York St. (☎562-1010; www.zaphodbeeblebrox.com), in Byward Market. Named after a character in *The Hitchhiker's Guide to the Universe,* this popular alternative rock club shows local musicians in spacey atmospherics. Pangalactic Gargle Blasters $6.50. Live bands W-Sa. Cover $2-10 depends on performer. Open daily 4pm-2am.

The Lookout, 41 York St. (☎789-1624), next to Zaphod's on the second floor. A hoppin' gay club with intense dancing. During daylight hours, the club shows local art exhibits. Though the Thursday evening crowd is mostly male, women flock in on Fridays. Sa is house party night. Open daily noon-2am.

MID-ATLANTIC

From the Eastern seaboard of New York south through Virginia, the mid-Atlantic states claim many of the nation's major historical, political, and economic centers. This region has witnessed the rotation of US capitals: first Philadelphia, PA; then Princeton, NJ; Annapolis, MD; Trenton, NJ; New York City, and finally Washington, D.C. During the Civil War, the mid-Atlantic even housed the Confederacy's capital, Richmond, VA. Urban centers cover much of the land, but the great outdoors have survived. The Appalachian Trail meanders through the region, and New York's Adirondacks compose the largest national park outside of Alaska.

HIGHLIGHTS OF THE MID-ATLANTIC

NEW YORK, NY. The Big Apple combines world-class museums (p. 238) with top-notch arts and entertainment venues (p. 242).

WASHINGTON, D.C. The impressive Smithsonian Museum (p. 331), the White House (p. 329), the Capitol (p. 326), and a slew of monuments (p. 327) comprise some of the coveted attractions of the nation's capital.

SCENIC DRIVES. The long and winding Blue Ridge Pkwy. (p. 350) is justifiably famous.

HISTORIC SITES. Harper's Ferry, WV (p. 353) and Gettysburg, PA (p. 299) are the best places to relive the Civil War. Philadelphia, PA (p. 281) abounds with colonial landmarks.

NEW YORK

This state offers a little bit of everything: the excitement of New York City, the grandeur of Niagara Falls, and the fresh natural beauty of the Catskills and the Adirondacks. While "The City" attracts cosmopolitan types looking for adventure year-round, those seeking a more mellow New York experience head upstate. Here, surrounded by the beauty of some of the state's landscape, you may find it difficult to remember that smog and traffic exist. The cities of upstate New York have a sweet natural flavor contrasting the tang of the Big Apple.

PRACTICAL INFORMATION

Capital: Albany.

Visitor Info: Division of Tourism, 1 Commerce Plaza, Albany 12245 (☎518-474-4116 or 800-225-5697; www.iloveny.state.ny.us). Operators available M-F 8:30am-5pm. **New York State Office of Parks and Recreation and Historic Preservation,** Empire State Plaza, Agency Bldg. 1, Albany 12238 (☎518-474-0456). Open M-F 9am-5pm.

State Fossil: Eurypterus remipes. **Postal Abbreviation:** NY. **Sales Tax:** 7-9%, depending on county.

NEW YORK CITY ☎212

Since its earliest days, New York has scoffed at the timid offerings of other American cities. It boasts the most immigrants, the tallest skyscrapers, the biggest museum in the Western Hemisphere, and plenty of large landfills. Even the vast

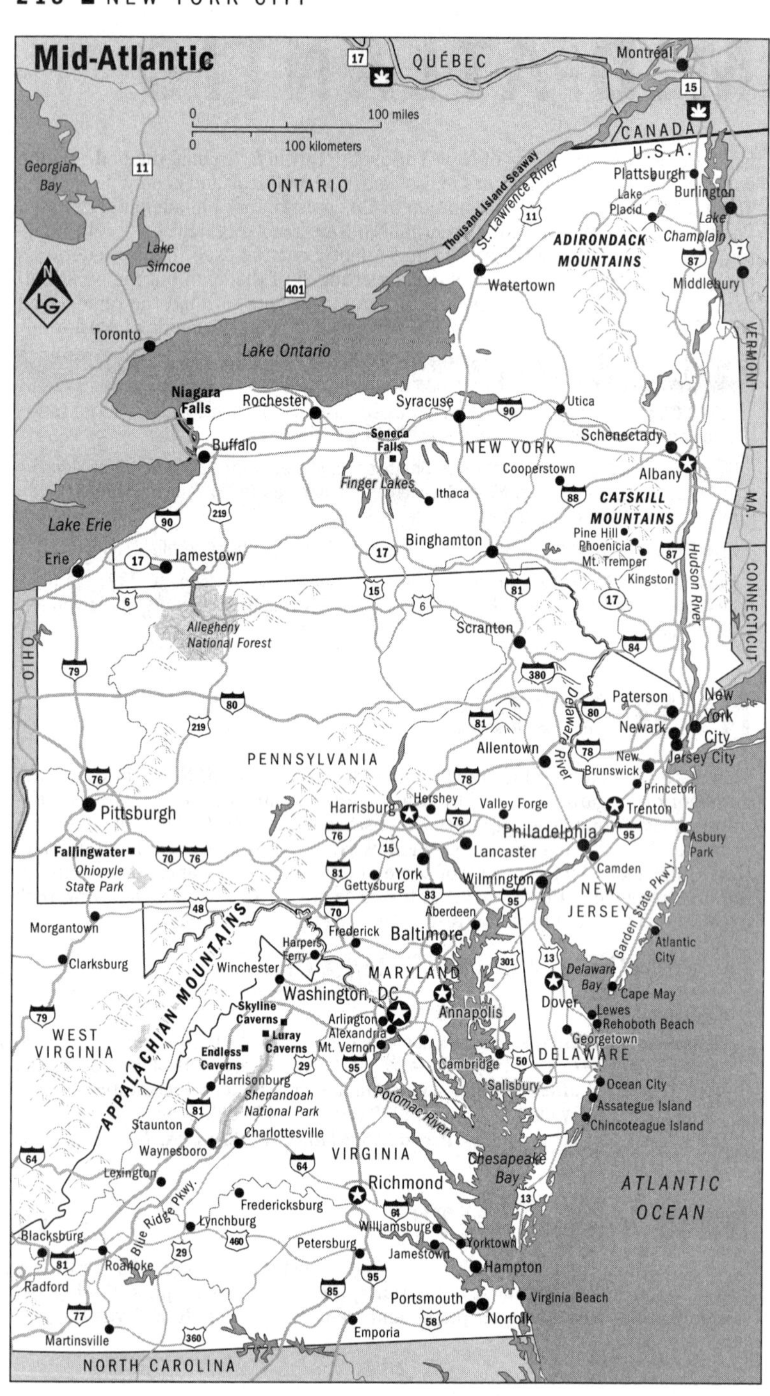

MID-ATLANTIC

blocks of concrete have their own gritty charm. With a population of eight million, New York City's five boroughs teem with something much better than fresh air: constant, varied, and thrilling action. There's flamenco at an outdoor cafe, jazz in a historic speakeasy, house and techno in a flashy club. For the coverage this city deserves, see our city guide, *Let's Go: New York City 2004.*

New Yorkers were awakened to both horror and heroism on September 11, 2001, when Osama bin Laden's suicide hijackers crashed two large airplanes into the two towers of the World Trade Center. The city has returned to normal with resilience, but it hasn't forgotten. Corporate skyscrapers and government buildings are heavily guarded, and several sites are closed indefinitely. Nevertheless, don't let security measures keep you from appreciating *the* ultimate big city.

INTERCITY TRANSPORTATION

Airports: 3 airports serve the New York metropolitan area.

John F. Kennedy Airport (JFK) (☎718-244-4444), at the end of the Van Wyck Expwy., in southern Queens. JFK handles most international and many domestic flights. The airport is 15 mi. from Midtown Manhattan, but the drive can take 1hr. Bus service available 24hr. from any airport terminal to the Howard Beach-JFK subway station (1-1¼hr., every 15-20min., $2). From there, take the Far Rockaway A train to Manhattan (1hr.). Taxis to Manhattan are $35 (plus tolls and tip).

LaGuardia Airport (☎718-533-3400), off Exit 7 on the Grand Central Pkwy., in northern Queens. LaGuardia is 9 mi. from Midtown Manhattan; the drive is around 20-25min. Domestic flights leave from here. The MTA M60 bus connects to Manhattan subway lines 1 at 110th St./Broadway; A, B, C, D at 125th St./St. Nicholas Ave.; 2, 3 at 125th St./Lenox (Sixth) Ave.; 4, 5, 6 at 125th St./Lexington Ave. The Q33 bus goes to Jackson Heights/Roosevelt Ave. in Queens for E, F, G, R, V, 7; the Q48 bus goes to 74th St.-Broadway in Queens for E, F, G, R, V, 7. (Allow at least 1½hr. for all routes. M60 runs daily 5am-1am, Q33 and Q48 24hr.; all buses $2.) Taxis to Manhattan are $16-26 (plus tolls and tip).

Newark Liberty International Airport (☎973-961-6000), 16 mi. west of midtown in Newark, NJ, on I-95 at Exit 14. Domestic and international flights. Olympia Airport Express (☎973-964-6233) travels from the airport to Port Authority, Grand Central Terminal, and Penn Station 24hr., leaving every 15-30min. (Trip takes 40-50min. $11.) Bus #107 by the New Jersey Transit Authority (☎973-762-5100) covers Newark, Newark International Airport (North Terminal), and Port Authority (25min., every 30-45min. 6am-midnight;,$3.60).

Trains: Grand Central Terminal, 42nd St. and Park Ave. (Subway: 4, 5, 6, 7, S to 42nd St.-Grand Central), handles **Metro-North** (☎800-638-7646) commuter lines to Connecticut and NY suburbs. **Amtrak** (☎800-872-7245) runs out of **Penn Station,** 33rd St. and Eighth Ave. (Subway: 1, 2, 3 to 34th St.-Penn Station/Seventh Ave.; A, C, E to 34th St.-Penn Station/Eighth Ave.) To: **Boston** (4-5hr., $64); **Philadelphia** (1½hr., $48); **Washington, D.C.** (3-4hr., $72). The **Long Island Railroad (LIRR)** (☎718-217-5477) and **NJ Transit** (☎973-762-5100) commuter rails also chug from Penn Station. Nearby at 33rd St. and Sixth Ave., **PATH** (☎800-234-7284) trains depart for New Jersey.

Buses: Greyhound (☎800-231-2222) buses leave the **Port Authority Terminal,** 42nd St. and Eighth Ave. (☎564-8484; subway: A, C, E to 42nd St.-Port Authority). *Watch for con artists and pickpockets, especially at night.* Both companies cover: **Boston** (4-6hr., $42); **Philadelphia** (2-3hr., $21); **Washington, D.C.** (4½hr., $42).

ORIENTATION

NYC is comprised of **five boroughs:** the Bronx, Brooklyn, Manhattan, Queens, and Staten Island. Flanked on the east by the East River (actually a strait) and on the west by the Hudson River, **Manhattan** is a sliver of an island, measuring only 13 mi. long and 2½ mi. wide. **Queens** and **Brooklyn** are on the other side of the East River. Residential **Staten Island,** southwest of Manhattan, has repeatedly sought secession from the city. North of Manhattan sits the **Bronx,** the only borough connected by land to the rest of the US.

BOROUGHS

MANHATTAN

Above 14th Street, Manhattan is an organized grid of avenues running north-south and streets east-west. Streets run consecutively, and their numbers grow as you travel north. Avenues are slightly less predictable: some are numbered while others are named. The numbers of the avenues increase as you go west. **Broadway,** which follows an old Algonquin trail, defies the rectangular pattern, cutting diagonally across the island, veering east of Fifth Ave. at 23rd St. **Central Park** and **Fifth Avenue** (south of 59th St., north of 110th St.) separate the city into the East Side and West Side. **Washington Heights** is located north of 155th St.; **Morningside Heights** (above 110th St. and below 125th St.) is sandwiched between **Harlem** (150s to 110th St.) and the glamorous **Upper West Side** (110th St. to 59th St., west of Central Park). The museum-heavy **Upper East Side** is across Central Park, above Fifth Ave., Times Square, and the Theater District in **Midtown** (59th St. to 42nd St.). **Lower Midtown** (41st St. to 14th St.) includes **Herald Square, Chelsea,** and **Union Square.**

Below 14th Street, the city dissolves into a confusing tangle of old, narrow streets that aren't numbered south of Houston St. The rebellious, bohemian **East Village** and **Alphabet City** are grid-like, with alphabetized avenues from Ave. A to Ave. D, east of First Ave. More established but still intellectual **Greenwich Village,** only slightly less confusing, is especially complicated west of Sixth Ave. Moving south, trendy **SoHo** (South of Houston St.) and **TriBeCa** (Triangle Below Canal St.) are just west of historically ethnic enclaves **Little Italy, Chinatown,** and the **Lower East Side.** The **Financial District/Wall Street area** at the tip of Manhattan, set over the original Dutch layout, is full of narrow, winding, one-way streets.

BROOKLYN

The **Brooklyn-Queens Expressway (BQE)** pours into the **Belt Parkway** and circumscribes Brooklyn. Ocean Pkwy., Ocean Ave., Coney Island Ave., and diagonal Flatbush Ave. run from the beaches of southern Brooklyn (**Coney Island** and **Brighton Beach**) to the heart of the borough in **Prospect Park.** The streets of western Brooklyn (including **Park Slope**) are aligned with the western shore and thus collide at a 45-degree angle with central Brooklyn's main arteries. In northern Brooklyn (including **Williamsburg, Greenpoint, Brooklyn Heights,** and **Downtown Brooklyn**), several avenues—Atlantic Ave., Eastern Pkwy., and Flushing Ave.—travel from downtown Brooklyn east into Queens.

QUEENS

The streets of Queens resemble neither the orderly grid of Upper Manhattan nor the haphazard angles of Greenwich Village; instead, a mixed bag of urban planning techniques has resulted in a logical—but extremely complicated—system. Streets generally run north-south and are numbered from west to east, from 1st St. in **Astoria** to 271st St. in **Glen Oaks.** Avenues run perpendicular to streets and are numbered from north to south, from Second Ave. to 165th Ave. The address of an establishment or residence often tells you the closest cross-street (for example, 45-07 32nd Ave. is near the intersection with 45th St.). Pick up the very useful Queens Bus Map, free and available on most Queens buses.

THE BRONX

Major highways cut the Bronx up into pieces. The **Major Deegan Expressway (I-87)** runs up the western border of the borough, next to the Harlem River. The **Cross-Bronx Expressway (I-95)** runs across the borough before turning north on its easternmost edge. Up the center of the borough runs the **Bronx River Parkway.** Several avenues run north-south, including **Jerome Avenue** on the western side of the borough and **White Plains Road** and **Boston Road** to the east. Streets running east-west include **Tremont Avenue, Fordham Road,** and the **Pelham Parkway.**

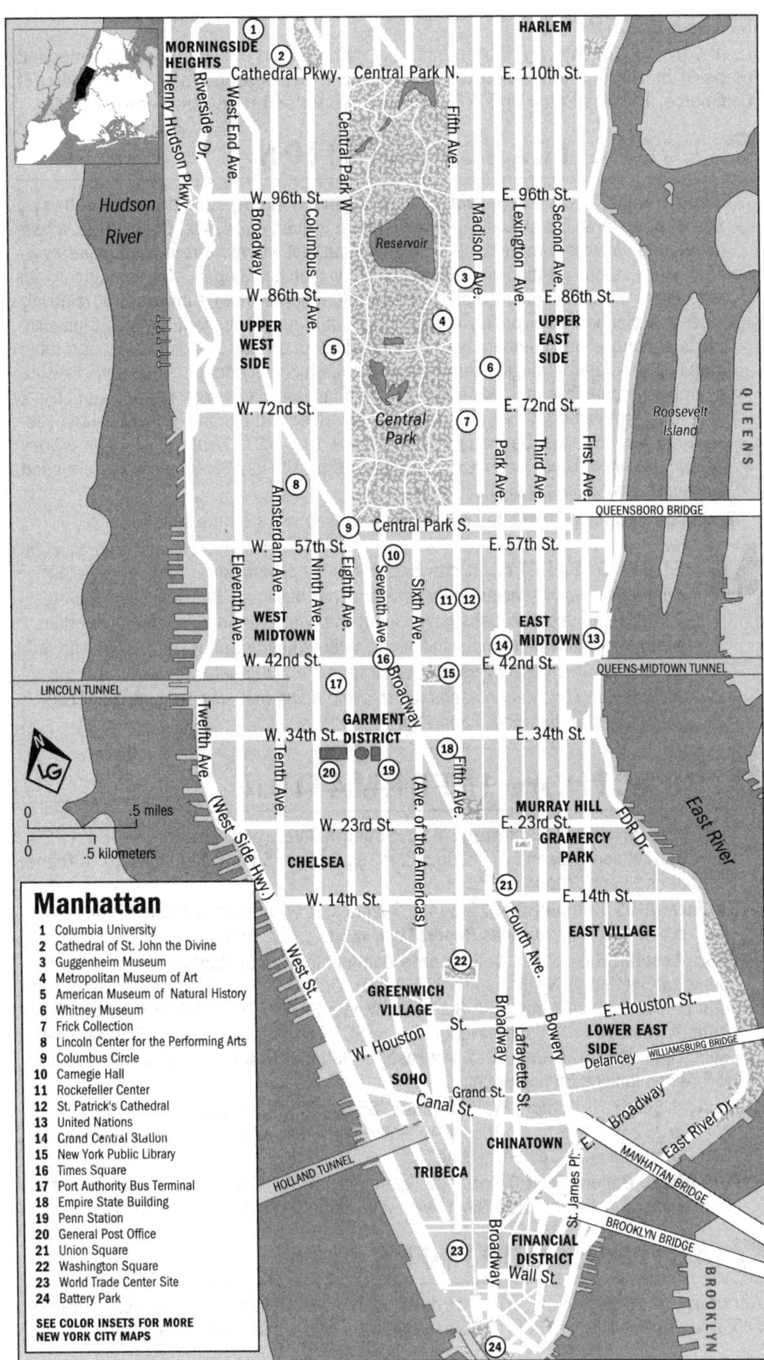

Manhattan

1 Columbia University
2 Cathedral of St. John the Divine
3 Guggenheim Museum
4 Metropolitan Museum of Art
5 American Museum of Natural History
6 Whitney Museum
7 Frick Collection
8 Lincoln Center for the Performing Arts
9 Columbus Circle
10 Carnegie Hall
11 Rockefeller Center
12 St. Patrick's Cathedral
13 United Nations
14 Grand Central Station
15 New York Public Library
16 Times Square
17 Port Authority Bus Terminal
18 Empire State Building
19 Penn Station
20 General Post Office
21 Union Square
22 Washington Square
23 World Trade Center Site
24 Battery Park

SEE COLOR INSETS FOR MORE NEW YORK CITY MAPS

STATEN ISLAND

Unlike the rest of the city, Staten Island is quite spread out. Pick up much-needed maps of Staten Island's bus routes as well as other pamphlets at the **Chamber of Commerce,** 130 Bay St. (☎718-727-1900), left from the ferry station onto Bay St.

LOCAL TRANSPORTATION

Public Transit: The **Metropolitan Transit Authority (MTA)** runs the city's subways, buses, and trains. The extensive subway system is open daily 24hr. Once inside, a passenger may transfer onto any other train without restrictions. Subway maps are available in any station. Station entrances lit by green globes are open 24hr.; entrances with red globes are somehow restricted. **Buses,** often slower than subways, but relatively safer and cleaner, stop roughly every 2 blocks and run throughout the city. Blue signposts announce bus numbers; glass-walled shelters display bus schedules and route maps. In the outer boroughs, some buses are run by independent contractors. Be sure to grab a borough bus map. **MetroCards,** the dominant currency for subway and buses, have a pre-set value (every $15 gets you 1 free ride) and can make free bus and subway transfers but must be made within 2hr. The 1-day ($7), 7-day ($21), and 30-day ($70) "Unlimited Rides" MetroCards (as opposed to $2 "Pay-Per-Ride" cards) are good for tourists visiting many sights.

Taxi: Most people in Manhattan hail yellow (licensed) cabs on the street.

SUBWAY SAFETY. In crowded stations, pickpockets find work; violent crimes occasionally occur in stations that are deserted. Stay alert and stick to well-lit areas; most stations have clearly marked "off-hours" waiting areas that are under observation and significantly safer. When boarding, pick a car with a number of other passengers in it, or sit near the middle of the train, in the conductor's car. *For safety reasons, try to avoid riding the subways outside of central Manhattan between 1 and 7am.*

PRACTICAL INFORMATION

Visitor Info: NYC & Company, 810 Seventh Ave., at 53rd St. (☎484-1222; www.nycvisit.com). Open M-F 8:30am-6pm, Sa-Su 9am-5pm. Other locations in Grand Central and Penn Station.

Hotlines: AIDS Hotline 800-825-5448. Operates daily 9am-9pm. **Crime Victims' Hotline,** ☎577-7777. **Sex Crimes Report Line,** ☎267-7273. Both 24hr.

Bi-Gay-Lesbian Resources: Callen-Lorde Community Health Center, 356 W. 18th St., between Eighth and Ninth Ave. (☎271-7200). Open M 12:30-8pm, Tu and Th-F 9am-4:30pm, W 8:30am-1pm and 3-8pm. **Gay Men's Health Crisis-Geffen Clinic,** 119 W. 24th St., between Sixth and Seventh Ave. (☎807-6655). Walk-in counseling M-F 10am-6pm. Open M-F 11am-8pm. **Gay and Lesbian National Hotline,** ☎989-0999. Operates M-F 4pm-midnight, Sa noon-5pm.

Medical Services: Doctors Walk-in Clinic, 55 E. 34th St., between Park and Madison Ave. (☎252-6001, ext. 2). Open M-Th 8am-8pm, F 8am-7pm, Sa 9am-3pm, Su 9am-2pm. Last walk-in 1hr. before closing.

Post Office: General Post Office, 421 Eighth Ave., at W. 32nd St. (☎330-3002). Open 24hr. General Delivery at 390 Ninth Ave., at W. 30th St. **Postal Code:** 10001.

ACCOMMODATIONS

Accommodations in New York are very expensive. A night in a hostel averages $25; in a cheap hotel, $60-80. A mid-range hotel room can easily cost over $120.

Area codes: 212, 347, or 646 (Manhattan); 718 (other 4 boroughs); 917 (cell phones). All New York City calls made within and between all five area codes must be dialed using 10-digit dialing. *In listings, area code is 212 except where otherwise noted.*

HOSTELS

Jazz on the Park, 36 W. 106th St./Duke Ellington Blvd. (☎932-1600; www.jazzhostel.com), between Manhattan Ave. and Central Park W. Subway: B, C to 103rd St./Central Park W. Clean, brightly-colored hostel with funky decor and 210 beds. A/C and lockers. Live jazz in the downstairs lounge, all-you-can-eat barbecues on the terrace on Sa in summer ($5), and Su gospel brunches. Internet access $1 per 5min. Linen, towels, and breakfast included. 24hr. laundry on premise. Check-in and check-out 11am. Reservations essential June-Oct. Dorms $27; private rooms (full or bunk bed) $80. ❶

New York International HI-AYH Hostel, 891 Amsterdam Ave. (☎932-2300; www.hinewyork.org), at 103rd St. Subway: 1 to 103 St./Broadway; B, C to 103rd St./Central Park W. Largest US youth hostel in a block-long landmark building, with 90 dorm-style rooms and 624 beds. Soft carpets, spotless bathrooms, and A/C. Kitchens, dining rooms, communal TV lounges, and large outdoor garden. Internet access. Linen and towels included. 2-week max. stay. Check-in noon. Check-out 11am. Credit card reservations required. Nov.-Apr. 10- to 12-bed dorms $29, 6- to 8-bed dorms $32, 4-bed dorms $35; May-Oct. $31/34/37. Family rooms with queen and 2 bunks available. ❶

Central Park Hostel, 19 W. 103rd St. (☎678-0491; www.centralparkhostel.com), between Manhattan Ave. and Central Park W. Subway: B, C to 103rd St./Central Park W. Clean rooms with A/C and a nice TV lounge downstairs in this 5-story walk up brownstone. Shared bathrooms. Lockers available. Linen and towels provided. Key deposit $2. 13-night max. stay. Dorms $25; private doubles $75. ❶

Sugar Hill International House, 722 St. Nicholas Ave. (☎926-7030), at 146th St. Subway: A, B, C, D to 145th St./St. Nicholas Ave. Passport ID required (Americans allowed). Brownstone with large and spacious rooms (25-30 beds total, 6-8 beds per room), a garden out back, and a quiet family feel. Friendly staff is a living library of Harlem history and culture. All-female room available. Free Internet access. Facilities include kitchens, stereo, and library. Key deposit $10. 2-week max. stay. Call in the morning. Check-in 9am-9pm. Check-out 11am. Reserve 1 month ahead during low-season, no reservations accepted July-Sept. Dorms $20-25; doubles $50-60. ❶

Big Apple Hostel, 119 W. 45th St. (☎302-2603; fax 302-2605; www.bigapplehostel.com), between Sixth and Seventh Ave. Subway: 1, 2, 3, 7, 9, N, Q, R, S, W to 42nd St.-Times Sq. This centrally located hostel is the budget traveler's best option. Clean, carpeted rooms, kitchen with refrigerator, luggage room, big deck (closed 2-6am) with grill, common rooms, and laundry facilities. Americans accepted with out-of-state photo ID or other convincing proof that they're tourists. Safe deposit available at reception ($0.25). Internet access $1 per 8min. 3-week max. stay. Reception 24hr. Check-in and check-out 11am. No reservations accepted Aug.-Sept. except through web site or by fax—send credit card number. Dorm-style room with shared bath $33 (same-sex available for single travelers, mixed for groups of friends); singles/doubles $90. ❷

Chelsea International Hostel, 251 W. 20th St. (☎647-0010; www.chelseahostel.com), between Seventh and Eighth Ave., in Chelsea. Subway: 1, 9 to 23rd St./Seventh Ave.; C, E to 23rd St./Eighth Ave. Enclosed hostel with funky youth travelers (mostly Scandinavians and other Europeans, but Americans allowed, too). Congenial staff offers pizza W night. Backyard garden. Extremely safe neighborhood, with police station across the street. Sparsely-furnished, smallish, utilitarian rooms. Kitchens, laundry room, TV rooms. Internet access $0.19 per min. Key deposit $10. Check-in 8am-6pm, passport required. Check-out 1pm. Reservations recommended. 4- and 6-person dorms $25; doubles with double or bunk bed $60. ❶

GUEST HOUSES & B&BS

Akwaaba Mansion, 347 MacDonough St. (☎718-455-5958; www.akwaaba.com), in Bedford-Stuyvesant. Subway: A, C to Utica Ave. This 1860 Victorian-style B&B won an award from the New York Landmarks Preservation Society, and there are frequent fashion and advertising shoots here. *Akwaaba,* an African word meaning "welcome," contains 18 rooms each with their own theme; all are decorated in African cultural decor. Library, TV room, tree-shaded patio, wrap-around sun porch, and breakfast in an elegant dining room. F jazz and Su brunch with Southern/African cuisine ($10). Rooms comfortably accommodate 2. All include private bath and A/C. Check-in 4-7pm. Check-out 11am. Reserve at least 1 month ahead. Rooms $120-135; weekends $135-150. ❺

Bed & Breakfast on the Park, 113 Prospect Park W. (☎718-499-6115; www.bbnyc.com), between 6th and 7th St., in Prospect Park. Subway: F to Seventh Ave./Ninth St., then 2 blocks east and 2 blocks north. A magnificently restored brownstone jam-packed with Victoriana, this decadent, aromatic opiate of a hotel lacks only adequate horse stables and gas lighting. Classy furnishings (rococo armoires, oriental carpets, damask) are museum-quality, but feel free to fall asleep on them. Gourmet breakfast in not-so-common room. 8 doubles (2 with shared bath) $100-375. ❺

HOTELS

Gershwin Hotel, 7 E. 27th St. (☎545-8000; www.gershwinhotel.com), between Madison and Fifth Ave. Subway: N, R to 28th St./Broadway. An absolute gem of a first-rate boutique hotel, with stunning pop art decor—there are genuine Warhol pieces in the lobby. Offers spaces for poetry, comedy, concerts, and open mic nights, and has its own art gallery. Private rooms with bathrooms, cable TV, A/C, and phones. Internet $1 per 4min. Reception 24hr. Check-in 3pm. Check-out 11am. Dorm rooms available: 8- to 12-bed dorms $29-59 per bed. Economy room (single or double occupancy) $99; standard room (single or double occupancy) $129; superior rooms $159-179; family room $219-250; triples and quads add $10 per person. $15 extra for Th-Sa. ❹

Carlton Arms Hotel, 160 E. 25th St., between Third and Lexington Ave. (☎679-0680; www.carltonarms.com). Subway: 6 to 23rd St./Park Ave. S. Map 12, E4, 25. For the unconventional and truly hip; bold, dramatic artwork covers every nook and cranny from the bathroom to the closets. Each room is decorated by a different artist. 11C is the "good daughter/bad daughter" room—half the room is festooned in teenybopper posters, the other half in horror-movie pics. 54 spacious rooms. Check-in noon. Check-out 11:30am. Reserve for summer 2 months ahead; confirm 10 days ahead. Singles $60, with bath $75; doubles $80-95; triples $99-110; quads $105-117. Pay for 7+ nights up front and get a 10% discount. ❸

Hotel Stanford, 43 W. 32nd St. (☎563-1500 or 800-365-1114; www.hotelstanford.com), between Fifth Ave. and Broadway. Subway: B, D, F, N, Q, R, V, W to 34th St.-Herald Sq. This Korean District hotel has impeccable rooms with A/C, bathrooms, cable TV, phones, and refrigerators. On the first floor, beautiful, immaculate Korean bakery and bustling 24hr. Korean eatery. Check-in 3pm. Check-out noon. Reservations recommended. Singles $120-150; doubles, twins $150-180; suites $200-250. ❺

ThirtyThirty, 30 E. 30th St. (☎689-1900 or 800-497-6028; www.stayinny.com), between Park Ave. S. and Madison Ave. Subway: N, R to 28th St./Broadway; 6 to 28th St./Park Ave. S. Sleek, modern hotel in a prime location at relatively budget prices. Pet friendly. All rooms have A/C, cable TV, and phones. Check-in 3pm. Check-out 11am. Singles $125; doubles $165; suites $245. ❺

Larchmont Hotel, 27 W. 11th St. (☎989-9333), between Fifth and Sixth Ave. Subway: 4, 5, 6, L, N, Q, R, W to 14th St.-Union Sq. Spacious, clean rooms in a whitewashed brownstone on a quiet block. A/C, closets, desks, TVs, and wash basins in all rooms. Shared bath. Continental breakfast included. Check-in 3pm. Check-out noon. Reserve 5-6 weeks ahead. Singles $70-95; doubles $90-125. ❹

Chelsea Pines Inn, 317 W. 14th St. (☎929-1023; www.chelseapinesinn.com), between Eighth and Ninth Ave. Subway: A, C, E to 14th St.; L to Eighth Ave. This fabulous gay-owned and operated inn is a friendly, amenity-laden haven of cozy rooms decorated with vintage film posters. Gorgeous garden and "greenhouse" out back. All rooms with A/C, cable TV, phones, refrigerators, and showers. Continental breakfast included, with homemade bread. Reservations are essential. 3-day min. stay on weekends. Rooms with private showers and shared toilet $99-169; with queen-size bed and private bath $129-159, with queen-size bed, private bath, day bed, stereos and breakfast area $139-169. Extra person $20. Call for special summer rates (beginning at $79). ❹

FOOD

New York will dazzle you with its culinary bounty. City dining, like the population, spans the globe, ranging from sushi bars and Italian eateries to French bistros.

CHINATOWN

Doyers Vietnamese Restaurant, 11-13 Doyers St. (☎693-0725), between Bowery and Pell St.; follow the steps downstairs. The inexpensive noodle soups, cool summer rolls, and thin rice noodle dishes bring back many repeat customers. Try the squid. Serves beer. Open daily 11am-9:30pm. ❶

Fried Dumpling, 106 Mosco St. (☎693-1060), between Mulberry and Mott St. For half the price of a ride on the subway, you can get either 5 dumplings or 4 pork buns. Only other items on the menu are soy milk ($1) and a very good hot-and-sour soup ($1). ❶

Joe's Shanghai, 9 Pell St. (☎233-8888), between Bowery and Mott St. From fried turnip cakes ($3.25) to crispy whole yellowfish ($13), this branch of the Queens legend serves Shanghai specialties. Serves beer. Open daily 11am-11:15pm. Cash only. ❷

Chinatown Ice Cream Factory, 65 Bayard St. (☎608-4170), at Elizabeth St. Yummy homemade ice cream in exotic flavors like lychee, taro, ginger, red bean, and green tea. 1 scoop $2.20, 2 for $4, 3 for $4.80. Open summer M-Th 11:30am-11:30pm, F-Su 11:30am-midnight; fall-spring daily noon-11pm. ❶

LITTLE ITALY & NOLITA

Lombardi's Coal Oven Pizza, 32 Spring St. (☎941-7994), between Mott and Mulberry St. in Little Italy. Claims to be oldest pizzeria in the US (est. 1905). Large pie feeds 2 ($13.50). Open M-Th 11:30am-11pm, F-Sa 11:30am-midnight, Su 11:30am-10pm. Cash only. ❸

ON THE MENU

CITY OF BAGELS

NYC's bagels are legendary. Crisp on the outside and chewy on the inside, a bagel is a New York breakfast tradition and a great snack. Here are three of the best places to buy a bagel in the city:

H&H Bagels, 2239 Broadway, at 80th St. (☎212-595-8003; www.handhbagel.com). Map 17, C4, 29. H&H has fed Upper West Siders for years with bagels ($0.95) that are reputedly the best in Manhattan. Be forewarned: H&H doesn't have a toaster and only sells spreads in tubs. **Also at:** 639 W. 46th St., between 11th and 12th Ave. (☎212-595-8000). Both locations open 24hr. ❶

Ess-a-Bagel, 831 Third Ave., between 50th and 51st St. (☎212-980-1010). Real New-York-style deli. Bagels $0.70, $8.40 for a baker's dozen. Open M-F 6am-9pm, Sa-Su 8am-5pm. ❶

La Bagel Delight, 252 7th Ave., at 5th St., Brooklyn (☎718-768-6107). With four locations in Brooklyn, the Italian Stallions of La Bagel are an institution throughout the borough. Also at: 90 Court St., 122 7th Ave., and 3623 Ft. Hamilton Pkwy. All locations open M-F 6am-6pm, Sa-Su 6am-6pm. ❶

Rice, 227 Mott St. (☎226-5775), between Prince and Spring St. Subway: 6 to Spring St.; F, S, V to Broadway-Lafayette St.; N, R to Prince St. Serves all kinds of rices, from basmati to Bhutanese red ($1-3.50), with wide selection of fixings (mango chutney $1, ratatouille and chicken satay $4-9.50). Open daily noon-midnight. Cash only. ❷

Cafe Gitane, 242 Mott St. (☎334-9552), at Prince St. This fashionable cafe is a prime spot to see and be seen. Salads $5.25-9. Tasty grilled eggplant with goat cheese and pesto on rice pilaf $8. Tiramisu $4.50. Open daily 9am-midnight. Cash only. ❷

Cafe Habana, 229 Elizabeth St. (☎625-2002), between Prince and Spring St. Inexpensive but retro stylish. *Tostadas de pollo* $7.50. Cuban sandwiches $6.50. Vegetarian plate $7. Grilled steak $10.50. Open daily noon-midnight. ❷

LOWER EAST SIDE

Paul's Boutique, 99 Rivington St. (☎646-805-0384), at Ludlow St. Subway: F, J, M, Z to Delancey St.-Essex St.; F, V to Lower East Side/Second Ave. Like Fred Flintsone driving around with bare feet, croissant sandwiches with fresh mozzarella ($4) and huge salads ($6.50) satisfy. Beer and wine make for a good lazy afternoon. Open M-Th 9am-10pm, F-Sa 9am-midnight, Su 9am-8pm. ❶

Katz's Delicatessen, 205 E. Houston St. (☎254-2246), between Orchard and Ludlow St. Subway: F, V to Lower East Side-Second Ave. A neighborhood institution since 1888, every president in the last 3 decades has had a Katz salami. Orgasmic food (as Meg Ryan confirmed in *When Harry Met Sally*) includes knishes and franks ($2.40). Sandwiches $10. Open Su-Tu 8am-10pm, W-Th 8am-11pm, F-Sa 8am-3am. ❸

Kossar's Bialys, 367 Grand St. (☎473-4810), between Essex and Norfolk St. Subway: F, J, M to Delancey St. New York's best bialy emporium. You can get 2 onion bialys (a kind of Polish bagel) for a buck, or 13 for $6. Open all night on Sa, Kossar's offers LES' cheapest late-night nosh. Open Su-Th 6am-10pm, F 6am-4:30pm, Sa 11pm-6am. ❶

GREENWICH VILLAGE

Salaam Bombay, 317 Greenwich St. (☎226-9400), at Reade St. Subway: 1, 2, 3, 9 to Chambers St. The best Indian restaurant in the 5 boroughs. Ask the extremely personable manager for nightly recommendations. Try the lamb chops ($23) or chicken tikka ($12). Unbeatable weekend buffet $13. Full bar. Open M-F 11:30am-3pm and 5:30-10:45pm, Sa-Su noon-3pm and 5:30-10:45pm. ❹

Corner Bistro, 331 W. 4th St. (☎242-9502), on the corner of Jane St., at Eighth Ave. Subway: A, C, E, L to 14th St./Eighth Ave. Unbelievable hamburgers ($4.50-5.50) and cold beer ($2-3). Open M-Sa 11:30am-4am, Su noon-4am. Cash only. ❶

John's Pizzeria, 278 Bleecker St. (☎243-1680), between Seventh Ave. S. and Morton St. Subway: 1, 9 to Christopher St. Widely regarded as Manhattan's best pizzeria; a great place to sit down and enjoy a pie. 2 sizes—small and large $10-20. No slices. Open M-Th 11:30am-11:30pm, F-Sa 11:30am-12:30am, Su noon-11:30pm. Cash only. ❸

EAST VILLAGE

Second Ave. Delicatessen, 156 Second Ave. (☎677-0606), at 10th St. Subway: 6 to Astor Pl. The Lebewohl family has maintained this definitive, strictly kosher New York deli (no outside food allowed) since 1954. Famous chopped liver ($6.50), babka ($3.25), kasha varnishkes ($4), mushroom barley ($4), and pastrami/corned beef sandwiches ($8-11). Open M-Sa 10am-8:30pm, Su 11am-7pm. ❷

Bendix Diner, 167 First Ave. (☎260-4220), between E. 10th and E. 11th St. Subway: 6 to Astor Pl.; L to First Ave. A severely funked-up diner. "Thai Chow and American Grub" (pad thai, curry soups, fried chicken). Huge entrees $6-13. Everything is good except the water. Just kidding. That's good too. Open M-F 9am-11pm, Sa-Su 9am-midnight. ❷

Frank, 88 Second Ave. (☎420-1232), between E. 5th and 6th St. Subway: 6 to Astor Pl. Let's be Frank. We will be an Italian bistro that paradoxically needs a lot more space (because there is always a wait to eat), yet derives an essential charm from the closeness of its quaint quarters. Our food will be as good as beer is to an alcoholic reneging on rehab. Pasta, entrees, specials $10-15; cheaper at lunchtime. A wine list more artful than souffle. Wait! Let's not *be* Frank, *Let's Go* to Frank. Open M-Th 10:30am-4pm and 5pm-1am, F-Sa 10:30am-4pm and 5pm-2am, Su 10:30am-4pm and 5pm-midnight. ❸

CHELSEA

Chat 'n' Chew, 10 E. 16th St. (☎243-1616), between Fifth Ave. and Union Sq. W. Subway: 4, 5, 6, L, N, Q, R, W to 14th St.-Union Sq. Heaping plates of macaroni and cheese ($8), classic grilled cheese with tomato ($6), cornmeal fried oysters ($6). "Not your Mother's Meatloaf" $11. Open M-Th 10am-midnight, F-Sa 10:30am-11:30pm, Su 10:30am-11pm. ❷

Kang Suh, 1250 Broadway (☎564-6845), between Fifth and Sixth Ave. Subway: B, D, F, N, Q, R, V, W to Herald Sq. The real deal: homestyle Korean cookin' with quick, efficient service. The delectable *hwe dup bap* (spicy sashimi salad with rice; $17) and the stellar juicy barbecue draw Koreans in hordes. Open 24hr. ❸

THEATER DISTRICT

Island Burgers and Shakes, 766 Ninth Ave. (☎307-7934), between 51st and 52nd St. Playful, refreshing decor and good music. The burgers are so good that Island sells more than 150 lb. of meat a day. $5-8 for 1 of the more than 50 hamburgers on the menu (or craft your own). Also chicken, salads, stuff to drink. No fries, but it's OK (there are other sorts of potato products). Open Sa-Th noon-10:30pm, F noon-11pm. ❷

Original Fresco Tortillas, 536 Ninth Ave. (☎465-8898), between 39th and 40th St. Tiny 9-seater with great, cheap homemade food: fajitas/tacos $1-2, huge burritos $4-5. No artificial spices or MSG. Open M-F 11am-11pm, Sa-Su noon-10pm. ❶

Becco, 355 W. 46th St. (☎397-7597), between Eighth and Ninth Ave. Gourmet cuisine that makes you forget your budget. 70 wines priced at $20 per bottle allow for moderate splurges. $17 *prix-fixe* lunch (dinner $22) gets you a gourmet antipasto platter or Caesar salad, plus unlimited servings of the 3 pastas of the day. $16 food min. per person for dinner, $14 for lunch. Open daily noon-3pm and 5pm-midnight. ❹

UPPER EAST SIDE

Barking Dog Luncheonette, 1678 Third Ave. (☎831-1800), at 94th St. Subway: 6 to 96th St. Big, tasty portions. "Mom's Lovin' Meatloaf" $11. Salads $5-11. Sandwiches $6-8. Specials (M-F 5-7pm) include soup/salad and dessert. Open daily 8am-11pm. ❷

Le Pain Quotidien, 1131 Madison Ave. (☎327-4900), between 84th and 85th St. Subway: 4, 5, 6 to 86th St./Lexington Ave. Boutique bakery with some of NYC's freshest bread. Pick up a *baguette à l'ancienne* ($2.50), or sit for a meal at trademark communal wooden tables. Open M-F 7:30am-7pm, Sa-Su 8am-7pm. ❶

UPPER WEST SIDE

H&H Bagels, 2239 Broadway (☎595-8003), at 80th St. H&H has fed Upper West Siders for years with bagels ($0.95) that are reputedly the best in Manhattan. Be forewarned: H&H doesn't have a toaster and only sells spreads in tubs. Open 24hr. ❶

Zabar's, 2245 Broadway (☎787-2000), between 80th and 81st St. Subway: 1, 2 to 79th St. This Upper West Side institution sells high-class groceries (fancy cheese, smoked salmon) and bagels. Open M-F 8am-7:30pm, Sa 8am-8pm, Su 9am-6pm. ❶

Big Nick's Burger Joint and Pizza Joint, 2175 Broadway (☎362-9238), at 77th St. Subway: 1, 2 to 79th St. Cramped but clean source of tried-and-true pizza, plate-sized burgers ($5-6.75), and breakfast dishes from a vast menu. Free delivery. Open 24hr. Another location at 70 W. 71st St., at Columbus Ave. (☎799-4444). ❷

Gray's Papaya, 2090 Broadway (☎799-0243), at 72nd St. Subway: 1, 2, 3 to 72nd St./Broadway. Cheap, lively takeout with amazing deals on hot dogs. Never-ending "recession special" sells 2 franks and 1 fruit drink (banana daiquiri, pineapple, piña colada, papaya) for a mere $2.45. Open 24hr. ❶

HARLEM & MORNINGSIDE HEIGHTS

La Marmite, 2264 Frederick Douglass Blvd. (Eighth Ave.) (☎666-0653), between 121st and 122nd St. Subway: B, C to 116th St.; A, B, C, D to 125th St./St. Nicholas Ave. Serves authentic French and African cuisine in a cramped, colorful setting. Be prepared for the bite in the spices. Popular lunch dishes (available until 4pm) include *thiebou djeun* ($8), a Senagalese dish of fried rice served with fish and vegetables. Famous *dibi* ($9) and *poisson grille* ($9) on dinner menu. Entrees $8-12. Open daily 24hr. ❷

Amir's Falafel, 2911A Broadway (☎749-7500), between 113th and 114th St. Subway: 1 to 110th St., 116th St./Broadway. Small and simple, with cheap Middle Eastern staples like *shawarma,* and *mousaka* for vegetarians and meat-lovers alike. Sandwiches $3-5, vegetarian platters $5.50. Open daily 11am-11pm. Cash only. ❶

Sylvia's, 328 Lenox (Sixth) Ave. (☎996-0660), at 126th St. Subway: 3 to 125th St./ Lenox (Sixth) Ave. For 40 years, Sylvia has accented her "World-Famous Talked-About BBQ Ribs Special" with sweet spicy sauce ($11). Salmon croquette, pork chop, fried chicken leg, collard greens, and candied yams ($7). Free live jazz and R&B Sa 11am-4pm. Su gospel brunch 11am-4pm. Open M-Sa 8am-10:30pm, Su 12:30-8pm. ❷

BROOKLYN

Santa Fe Grill, 60 Seventh Ave. (☎718-636-0279), at Lincoln Pl. Subway: Q to Seventh Ave.; 2, 3 to Grand Army Plaza. Bottomless chips and salsa, strong margaritas with little plastic dolphins and mermaids floating in them, and a menu on which every single thing is so good that ordering can be impossible; you can't miss with the bocados especiales, $13. Open M-Th 5-11pm, F 5pm-midnight, Sa 3pm-midnight, Su 3-11pm. ❸

Grimaldi's, 19 Old Fulton St. (☎718-858-4300), between Front and Water St. Subway: A, C to High St. Delicious thin-crust pizza with fresh mozzarella, sold only by the pie. Sinatra haunts both decor and jukebox. Small pies $12, large $14; toppings $2 each. Open M-Th 11:30am-11pm, F-Sa noon-midnight, Su noon-11pm. Cash only. ❸

QUEENS

Flushing Noodle, 135-42 Roosevelt Ave. (☎718-353-1166), in Flushing. Subway: 7 to Flushing-Main St. One of Flushing's finest Chinese noodle shops. Noodles $3.75-5. Lunch specials $5 (11am-3:30pm). Open daily 9am-10pm. ❶

Jackson Diner, 37-47 74th St. (☎718-672-1232), in Jackson Heights, between 37th and 38th Ave. Subway: E, F, G, R, V to Jackson Heights/Roosevelt Ave. Delicious Indian food in colorful, almost-trendy setting. Great *saag gosht* (lamb with spinach, tomato, ginger, and cumin; $11). Lunch specials $6-7.50. Weekend lunch buffet $9 (11:30am-4pm). Open M-F 11:30am-10pm, Sa-Su 11:30am-10:30pm. Cash only. ❷

SIGHTS

THE STATUE OF LIBERTY & ELLIS ISLAND

The Statue of Liberty stands at the entrance to New York Harbor, long a symbol of hope for millions of immigrants fresh from the arduous voyage across the Atlantic. In 1886, the French government presented Frederic-Auguste Bartholdi's sculpture to the US as a sign of goodwill. The actual statue is now off-limits to tourists, but Liberty Island still offers a superb view of the monument. While the Statue embodies the American Dream, the Ellis Island museum chronicles the harsh realities of immigrant life in the New World. *(Subway: 4, 5 to Bowling Green; N, R to Whitehall St. ☎363-3200. Ferry Information: ☎269-5755. Ferries run in a loop, Battery Park-Liberty Island-Ellis Island, daily every 30min. 9am-3:50pm. Tickets for ferry, the Statue of Liberty, and Ellis Island: $10, seniors $8, ages 4-12 $4, under 4 free.)*

FINANCIAL DISTRICT & CIVIC CENTER

The southern tip of Manhattan is a financial powerhouse: the Wall St. area, less than ½ mi. long, has one of the highest concentrations of skyscrapers in the world. Crooked streets retain the city's original Dutch layout; lower Manhattan was the first part of the island to be settled. *(Subway: 1, 2, to Wall St./William St.; 4, 5 to Bowling Green, Wall St./Broadway; N, R to Rector St., Whitehall St.; 1, 2, 4, 5, A, C, J, M, Z to Fulton St./Broadway-Nassau St.; J, M, Z to Broad St.)*

FINANCIAL DISTRICT. Once the northern border of the New Amsterdam settlement, Wall St. is named for the wall built in 1653 to shield the Dutch colony from British invasion. By the early 19th century, the area was the financial capital of the US. On the southwest corner of Wall and Broad St. stands the **New York Stock Exchange.** This 1903 temple to capitalism sees billions of dollars change hands daily. The exchange, founded in 1792 at 68 Wall St., is now off-limits to tourists.

WALL STREET. Around the corner, at the end of Wall St., stands the seemingly ancient **Trinity Church,** with its delicately crafted steeple towering anomalously amid the Financial District's canyons. *(74 Trinity Place. ☎602-0800.)* **Bowling Green,** the city's first park, lies at the intersection of Battery Pl., Broadway, and Whitehall St. The site of the city's first "mugging," it's also where Peter Minuit purchased Manhattan for the equivalent of $24. The Beaux Arts **U.S. Custom House,** 1 Bowling Green, overlooks the park. *(1 Bowling Green St. ☎668-6624.)*

WORLD TRADE CENTER MEMORIAL SITE (GROUND ZERO). Words cannot describe the sadness of the empty lot where the World Trade Center once stood. One day, the space will be filled with a memorial, a revitalized transit hub, even a new skyscraper or two. Today, however, the poignancy of the landscape lies in the profound sense of loss reflected in its vacancy. It must be seen to be understood.

CIVIC CENTER. Fittingly, the city's center of government is located north of its financial district, as the city tries to keep tabs on unscrupulous dealings. Perhaps the finest piece of architecture in the city is **City Hall.** This elegant structure where New York's mayor keeps his offices is also the neighborhood's center; around it are courthouses, civic buildings, and federal buildings. The building's interior is closed indefinitely to the public. *(Broadway at Murray St., off Park Row.)* The **Woolworth Building,** a sumptuous, 1913 Neo-Gothic skyscraper built for $15.5 million to house F.W. Woolworth's five-and-dime store empire, looms south of City Hall. Arches and mosaics adorn the resplendent lobby of this "Cathedral of Commerce." *(233 Broadway, between Barclay St. and Park Pl.)* A block and a half south on Broadway lies **St. Paul's Chapel;** Manhattan's oldest public building in continuous use hasn't missed a day since George Washington prayed here on his inauguration day. *(Between Vesey and Fulton St. ☎602-0747. Open M-F 9am-3pm, Su 7am-3pm. Su mass 8am.)*

SOUTH STREET SEAPORT. The shipping industry thrived at the **South Street Seaport** for most of the 19th century, when New York was the most important port city in the US. During the 20th century, bars, brothels, and crime flourished. Now a 12-block "museum without walls," South Street Seaport features old schooners, sailboats, and houses. Visit the Seaport Museum Visitors Center for info on attractions. *(Between FDR Dr. and Water St., and between Beekman and John St. Subway: 1, 2, 4, 5,*

A, C, J, M, Z to Fulton St./Broadway-Nassau St. Visitors Center: 12 Fulton St. ☎748-8600. Open Apr.-Sept. W-M 10am-6pm; Oct.-Mar. W-M 10am-5pm. Admission to ships, shops and tours $5, under 12 free. Walking around the museum is free.) The **Fulton Fish Market,** the largest fresh-fish market in the country (and a notorious former mafia stronghold), lies on South St., on the other side of the overpass. *(☎748-8786. Market opens at 4am. Market tours May-Oct. 1st and 3rd W of each month, 6am. $12. Reservations required, call around 1 week in advance. Walking around the fish market free.)*

CHINATOWN & LITTLE ITALY

Mott and **Pell Street,** the unofficial centers of Chinatown, brim with Chinese restaurants and commercial activity. Chinese-style baby jackets, bamboo hats, and miniature Buddhas crowd the storefronts. **Canal Street** abounds in low-priced, creatively labeled merchandise (those are *not* Rolexes). **Mulberry Street** remains the heart of the Little Italy, which has been largely taken over by Chinatown in recent decades. *(Subway to Chinatown: J, M, Z to Canal St./Centre St.; N, Q, R, W to Canal St./ Broadway; 4, 6 to Canal St./ Lafayette St. Subway to Little Italy: 6 to Spring St./Lafayette St.; J, M, Z to Canal St./Centre St.; N, Q, R, W to Canal St./ Broadway; 4, 6 to Canal St./Lafayette St.; S to Grand St.; F to E. Broadway; F, V, S to Broadway-Lafayette St.)*

LOWER EAST SIDE

The Lower East Side was once the most densely settled area in New York. The Irish came in the mid-1800s, Eastern Europeans in the 50 years preceding WWI, African-Americans and Puerto Ricans post-WWII, and Latin Americans and Asians in the 1980s and 90s. Main thoroughfares like E. Broadway reflect the area's multicultural roots. Orchard St., an historic shopping area that fills up on Sundays, still has traces of the Jewish ghetto. *(Subway: F, V to Lower East Side-Second Ave.; F to E. Broadway; F, J, M, Z to Delancey St.-Essex St.)*

LOWER EAST SIDE SIGHTS. The Lower East Side Visitors Center is a source of maps and brochures, and also organizes a free area shopping tour. *(261 Broome St., between Orchard and Allen St. ☎226-9010. Open daily 10am-4pm.)* At the **Lower East Side Tenement Museum,** tours lead through three meticulously restored apartments of immigrant families. *(90 Orchard St. ☎431-0233. Call for info on tours of tenements and neighborhood. $8-9, students and seniors $6-7.)* The **Eldridge Street Synagogue** *(12 Eldridge St. ☎219-0888)* and **Congregation Anshe Chesed** *(172-176 Norfolk St., at Stanton St. ☎865-0600)* are two splendid old synagogues.

SOHO. The architecture in the area **South of Houston**—with Canal St. on the south, Broadway on the west, and Crosby St. on the east—is American Industrial, notable for its cast-iron facades. Inhabited by New York's prospering *artistes*, SoHo is filled with galleries (see Galleries, p. 240), chic boutiques, and very expensive shopping. *(Subway: C, E to Spring St./Ave. of the Americas; 6 to Spring St./Lafayette St.; N, R to Prince St.; 1, 2 to W. Houston St.; F, S, V to Broadway-Lafayette St.)*

TRIBECA. TriBeCa, or **Triangle Below Canal Street,** has been anointed (by resident Robert DeNiro and others) as the hottest neighborhood in the city. Inside the industrial warehouses are trendy lofts, restaurants, bars, and galleries—without the upscale airs. Admire the cast-iron edifices lining White St., Thomas St., and Broadway, the Federal-style buildings on Harrison St., and the shops, galleries, and bars on Church and Reade St. *(Subway: 1, 2 to Canal St./Varick St., Franklin St., Chambers St./W. Broadway; C, E to Canal St./Ave. of the Americas; A, C to Chambers St./Church St.)*

GREENWICH VILLAGE

Once a staid high-society playground in the mid-19th century, the Village (west of Broadway, between Houston and 14th St.) has undergone a relentless process of cultural ferment that layered grime, activism, and artistry atop its quaint, meandering streets. The last 40 years brought the Beat movement, the homosexual community around Christopher St., and the punk scene; the gentrification process of the 1980s and 90s made the Village a fashionable and comfortable settlement for wealthier New Yorkers with more spunk than their uptown counterparts. *(Subway: A, C, E, F, V, S to W. 4th St.; A, C, E, L to 14th St./Eighth Ave.; 1, 2, 3 to 14th St./Seventh Ave.; F, L, V to 14th St./Ave. of the Americas (Sixth Ave.); 4, 5, 6, L, N, Q, R, W to 14th St.-Union Sq.; 1, 2 to Houston St., Christopher St.; N, R to 8th St.-NYU; L to Sixth Ave., Eighth Ave.; 6 to Bleecker St.)*

WASHINGTON SQUARE. Washington Square Park has a rich history. By the beginning of the 20th century, it had already served as a potter's field for the burial of the poor and unknown (around 15,000 bodies lie buried here); a hanging-grounds during the Revolutionary War; a park and parade ground; and the center of New York's elite social scene during the mid-1800s. On the north side of the park is **The Row,** a stretch of 1830s stately brick residences that were soon populated by writers, dandies, and professionals. At the north end of the Park stands the **Washington Memorial Arch,** built in 1889 to commemorate the centennial of George Washington's inauguration. **New York University,** the country's largest private university, has some of the Village's least appealing contemporary architecture. On the park's southeast side, where Washington Sq. S meets LaGuardia Pl., NYU's **Loeb Student Center** sports pieces of scrap metal representing birds in flight.

WEST VILLAGE. The area of Greenwich Village west of 6th Ave. boasts eclectic summer street life and excellent nightlife. A visible gay community thrives around **Sheridan Square,** at the intersection of Seventh Ave., W. 4th St., and Christopher St. The 1969 Stonewall Riot, arguably the beginning of the modern gay rights movement, started here. The neighborhood is a magnet for literary pilgrimages. **Chumley's,** a former speakeasy, was a hangout for such authors as Ernest Hemingway and John Dos Passos. *(86 Bedford St., between Grove and Barrow St. ☎675-4449. Open Su-Th 5pm-midnight, F-Sa 5pm-2am.)* Off 10th St. and Sixth Ave. you'll see an iron gate and street sign marking **Patchin Place.** e.e. cummings, Theodore Dreiser, and Djuna Barnes lived in the 145-year-old buildings that line this path. The Village's narrowest building, **75½ Bedford Street,** only 9½ ft. in width, housed writer Edna St. Vincent Millay in the 1920s, when she founded the nearby **Cherry Lane Theater,** 38 Commerce St. Actors Lionel Barrymore and Cary Grant also appreciated the cramped quarters.

EAST VILLAGE & ALPHABET CITY

The East Village—north of Houston St., east of Broadway, and south of 14th St.—was carved out of the Bowery and the Lower East Side in the early 1960s, when artists and writers moved here to escape high rents in Greenwich Village. Today East Village's wide-ranging population includes punks, hippies, ravers, rastas, guppies, goths, and beatniks. The tensions of gentrification have forged the East Village into one of the city's most politicized neighborhoods. *(Subway: 6 to Astor Pl., Bleecker St.; L to First Ave., Third Ave.; F, V to Lower East Side-Second Ave.)*

EAST VILLAGE. Full of pot-smoking flower children and musicians in the 1960s, **St. Mark's Place** hosted the punk scene's teens in the late 1970s. Nowadays, those youths still line the street—in their "old-tattooed-geezer" incarnations. The present-day St. Mark's Pl. is a drag full of tiny ethnic eateries, street level shops, sidewalk vendors selling trinkets of all kinds, and tattoo shops. Simmering with street life, **Astor Place,** at the intersection of Lafayette, E. 8th St., and Fourth Ave., is distinguished by a large black cube balanced on its corner.

ALPHABET CITY. East of First Ave. and south of 14th St., the avenues run out of numbers and adopt letters. During the area's heyday in the 1960s, Jimi Hendrix played open-air shows here to bright-eyed love children. The area was once ravaged by drug-related crime, but locals have done an admirable job of making the neighborhood livable again, starting a number of community gardens. Alphabet City's extremist Boho activism has made the neighborhood chronically ungovernable; police officers in 1988 set off a riot when they attempted to evict a band of the homeless and their supporters in **Tompkins Square Park.** *(E. Seventh St. and Ave. A.)*

LOWER MIDTOWN

UNION SQUARE. At the intersection of Fourth Ave. and Broadway, Union Square and the surrounding area sizzled with high society before the Civil War. Today, the park hosts the **Union Square Greenmarket,** a pleasant farmers market. *(Between Broadway and Park Ave., and 14th and 17th St. Subway: 4, 5, 6, L, N, Q, R, W to 14th St.-Union Sq.)* The photogenic **Flat Iron Building** is the world's first skyscraper. Originally named the Fuller Building, it was nicknamed after its dramatic wedge shape (imposed by the intersection of Broadway, Fifth Ave., 22nd St., and 23rd St.).

CHELSEA. Home to some of the most fashionable clubs, bars, and restaurants in the city, Chelsea (west of Fifth Ave., between 14th and 30th St.) boasts a large BGLT community, a growing artsy-yuppie population, and innovative **art galleries** (see **Museums and Galleries,** p. 238) fleeing high SoHo rents. *(Subway: 1, 2, 3 to 14th St./Seventh Ave.; A, C, E, L to 14th St./Eighth Ave.; C, E to 23rd St./Eighth Ave.; 1, 2 to 23rd St./Seventh Ave.; 1 to 28th St./Seventh Ave.)* The historic **Hotel Chelsea,** between Seventh and Eighth Ave., has sheltered such artists as Sid Vicious of the Sex Pistols. Countless writers have sought inspiration here, including Vladimir Nabokov, and Dylan Thomas. *(222 W. 23rd St., between Seventh and Eighth Ave. ☎243-3700.)*

HERALD SQUARE AREA. Herald Square is located between 34th and 35th St., between Broadway and Sixth Ave. The area is a center for shopping. *(Subway: B, D, F, N, Q, R, W to Herald Sq.)* The **Empire State Building,** now the city's tallest building after the WTC tragedy, dominates postcards, movies, and the city's skyline. The limestone and granite structure stretches 1454 ft. into the sky, and its 73 elevators run through 2 mi. of shafts. The nighttime view from the top is spectacular. *(350 Fifth Ave., at 34th St. Observatory: ☎736-3100. Open daily 9:30am-midnight; last elevator up at 11:30pm. $9, seniors $7, under 12 $4. Skyride: ☎279-9777. Open daily 10am-10pm. $11.50, seniors and ages 4-12 $8.50.)* East on 34th St. stands **Macy's.** This Goliath of department stores sponsors the **Macy's Thanksgiving Day Parade,** a NYC tradition buoyed by ten-story Snoopys, marching bands, and floats. *(Between 7th Ave. and Broadway, in Herald Sq.)* The **Garment District,** surrounding Macy's, but selling cheaper clothing, was once a red-light district, and purportedly contained the world's largest concentration of apparel workers during the 1930s. *(Between Broadway and Eighth Ave.)*

MIDTOWN

East of Eighth Ave., from about 42nd St. to 59th St., lie Midtown's mammoth office buildings, posh hotels, and high-brow stores. *(Subway: 4, 5, 6, 7, S to 42nd St.-Grand Central; E, V, 6 to 51st St.; 4, 5, 6, N, R, W to 59th St.-Lexington Ave.; F to Lexington Ave./63rd St.; B, D, F, V, 7 to 42nd St.-Bryant Park; B, D, F, V to 47th-50th St.-Rockefeller Center; 1, 2, 3, 7, N, Q, R, S, W to 42nd St.-Times Square; A, C, E to 42nd St.-Port Authority; E, V to Fifth Ave./53rd St.; 1, 2 to 50th St./Broadway.)*

FIFTH AVENUE. A monumental research library in the style of a classical temple, this main branch of the **New York Public Library,** between 40th and 42nd St., contains the world's seventh largest research library and an immense reading room. *(42nd St. and Fifth Ave. ☎869-8089.)* The pleasant **Bryant Park** behind the library features free, extremely popular summertime cultural events, like classic film screenings, jazz concerts, and live comedy. *(☎484-1222 for events schedule. Open daily 7am-9pm.)* Designed by James Renwick, the twin spires of **St. Patrick's Cathedral** stretch 330 ft. into the air. New York's most famous church is the largest Catholic cathedral in the US. *(51st. St. ☎753-2261.)* On 59th St., at the southeast corner of Central Park, sits the legendary **Plaza Hotel,** constructed in 1907 at an astronomical cost. Its 18-story, 800-room French Renaissance interior flaunts five marble staircases, countless ludicrously named suites, and a two-story Grand Ballroom.

ROCKEFELLER CENTER. The main entrance to Rockefeller Center is on Fifth Ave. between 49th and 50th St. **The Channel Gardens,** so named because they sit between the **Maison Française** on the left and the **British Empire Building** on the right, usher the pedestrian toward **Tower Plaza.** This sunken space, topped by the gold-leafed statue of Prometheus, is surrounded by the flags of over 100 countries. During spring and summer an **ice-skating rink** lies dormant beneath an overpriced cafe. The rink, which is better for people-watching than for skating, reopens in winter in time for the **annual Christmas tree lighting,** one of New York's greatest traditions. **Tours of Rockefeller Center** are available through NBC. *(Tours meet at 30 Rockefeller Plaza, at W. 49th St. between Fifth and Sixth Ave. ☎664-3700. 1¼hr. Every hr. M-Sa 9am-4pm, Su 10am-4pm. No children under 6. $10, seniors and ages 6-16 $8, groups over 3 $8.)*

Behind Tower Plaza is the **General Electric Building,** a 70-story skyscraper. **NBC,** which makes its home here, offers an hour-long tour that traces the history of the network, from their first radio broadcast in 1926 through the heyday of TV programming in the 1950s and 60s to today's sitcoms. The tour visits six studios including the infamous 8H studio, home of *Saturday Night Live. (30 Rockefeller Plaza. ☎664-3700 for tours. Every 30min. M-Sa 8:30am-5pm, Su 9:30am-4:30pm. No children under 6. $17.50, seniors and ages 6-16 $15, groups over 3 $15.)* A block north is **Radio City Music Hall.** Narrowly escaping demolition in 1979, this Art Deco landmark received a complete interior restoration shortly thereafter. Radio City's main attraction is the Rockettes, a high-stepping long-legged troupe of dancers. Tours of the Music Hall take the visitor through The Great Stage and various rehearsal halls. *(50th St. at Sixth Ave. ☎247-4777. $17, under 12 $10; group discounts available.)*

PARK AVENUE. A luxurious boulevard with greenery running down its center, **Park Avenue** from 45th St. to 59th St. is lined with office buildings and hotels. Completed in 1913, the **Grand Central Terminal** has a richly classical main facade on 42nd St.; on top stands a beautiful sculpture of Mercury, Roman god of transportation. An info booth sits in the middle of the commuter-filled Concourse. *(Between 42nd and 45th St.)* Several blocks uptown is the *crème de la crème* of Park Avenue hotels, the **Waldorf-Astoria.** *(Between 49th and 50th St.)* The **Seagram Building,** Ludwig Mies Van der Rohe's dark, gracious modern monument, stands a few blocks uptown. *(375 Park Ave., between 52nd and 53rd St.)*

UNITED NATIONS AREA. The **United Nations,** a "center for harmonizing the actions of nations" founded in 1945 in the aftermath of WWII, is located in international territory along what would be First Ave. The UN complex consists of the Secretariat Building (the skyscraper), the General Assembly Building, the Hammarskjöld Library, and the Conference Building. The only way into the General Assembly Building is by guided tour. *(First Ave., between 42nd and 48th St. ☎963-4475. 1hr. tours depart every 15min. from the UN visitor's entrance at First Ave. and 46th St. M-F 9:15am-4:45pm, Sa-Su 9:30am-4:45pm. $8.50, seniors $7, students $6, ages 4-14 $5; disabled 20% discount. Under 4 not admitted.)* At the **Chrysler Building,** a spire influenced by radiator grille design tops this Art Deco palace. *(On 42nd St. and Lexington Ave.)*

TIMES SQUARE & THEATER DISTRICT. At the intersection of 42nd St., Seventh Ave., and Broadway, the city offers up one of the world's largest electronic extravaganzas. **Times Square** may have given New York its reputation as a dark metropolis covered with strip clubs, neon, and filth, but today the smut has been replaced by teeming masses of smiling people with fanny packs, 30 ft. tall flatscreens announcing the conquests of reality TV, and a creepy homogeneity totally unbecoming to New York's true spirit. But it doesn't really matter what we think: at some point, whether you like it or not, you'll probably be one of the nearly 40 million people who pass through Times Square every year. Good luck.

57TH STREET & CENTRAL PARK SOUTH. Several luxury hotels, including the **Essex House,** the **St. Moritz,** and **the Plaza,** overlook Central Park from their perch on Central Park S, between Fifth and Eighth Ave., where 59th St. should be. Amid 57th St.'s galleries and stores is New York's musical center, **Carnegie Hall** (see p. 245). A $60 million restoration program has returned the 1891 building to its earlier splendor. *(881 Seventh Ave., at W. 57th St. ☎247-7800 or 903-9765. 1hr. tours M-F 11:30am, 2, 3pm. $6, students and seniors $5, under 12 $3.)*

CENTRAL PARK

Once an 843-acre squatting-place for the very poor, Central Park was founded in the mid-18th century, when some wealthy New Yorkers—longing for their own European-style playground—advocated the creation of a public space to ameliorate social ills. Frederick Law Olmsted collaborated with Calvert Vaux to design the park in 1858. Their Greensward plan took 15 years and 20,000 workers to implement, and the result is a beautiful park very well-used by New Yorkers.

Central Park is fairly safe during the day, but less so at night. Don't be afraid to go to events in the Park at night, but take large paths and go with someone. Do not wander the darker paths at night, especially if you are a woman. In an **emergency,** use one of the call-boxes located throughout the park. **24hr. Police Line,** ☎570-4820.

Expansive fields such as the **Sheep Meadow,** from 66th to 69th St., and the **Great Lawn,** from 80th to 85th St., complement developed spaces such as the **Mall,** between 66th and 71st St., the **Shakespeare Garden,** at 80th St., and the **Imagine Mosaic,** commemorating the music and dreams of John Lennon on the western side of the park at 72nd St. Don't miss the park's free summertime performances at **Central Park Summerstage** and **Shakespeare in the Park.** *(☎360-3444; parks and recreation info 360-8111, M-F 9am-5pm. Free park maps at Belvedere Castle, located mid-park at 79th St.; the Charles A. Dana Discovery Center, at 110th St. near 5th Ave.; the North Meadow Recreation Center, mid-park at 97th St.; and the Dairy, mid-park near 65th St.)*

UPPER EAST SIDE

Since the late 19th and early 20th centuries, when some of New York's wealthiest citizens built elaborate mansions along **Fifth Avenue,** the Upper East Side has been home to the city's richest residents. Today, some of these park side mansions have been turned into museums, such as the Frick Collection and the Cooper-Hewitt Museum. They are just two of the world-famous museums that line **Museum Mile,** from 82nd to 104th St. on Fifth Ave. (see p. 238). **Park Avenue** from 59th to 96th St. is lined with dignified apartment buildings. Lexington and Third Ave. are commercial, but as you go east, the neighborhood becomes more and more residential. *(Subway: N, R, W to Fifth Ave./59th St. 4, 5, 6, N, R, W to 59th St.-Lexington Ave.; F to Lexington Ave./63rd St.; 6 to 68th St., 77th St., 96th St.; 4, 5, 6 to 86th St./Lexington Ave.)*

UPPER WEST SIDE

While Central Park West and Riverside Dr. flank the Upper West Side with residential quietude, Columbus Ave., Amsterdam Ave., and Broadway buzz with action. Organic fruit and progressive politics dominate the area between 59th and 110th St., west of Central Park. *(Subway: 1, 2, A, B, C, D to 59th St.-Columbus Circle; 1, 2 to 66th St., 79th St., 86th St./Broadway; 1, 2, 3 to 72nd St., 96th St./Broadway; B, C to 72nd St./Central Park W, 81st St.; B, C to 86th St., 96th St./Central Park W.)*

LINCOLN CENTER. Broadway intersects Columbus Ave. at **Lincoln Center,** the cultural hub of the city (see p. 244). The airy architecture reinterprets the public plazas of Rome and Venice, but the Center's performance spaces for opera, ballet, and classical music take center stage. *(Between 62nd and 66th St.)*

MORNINGSIDE HEIGHTS. Above 110th St. and below 125th St., between Amsterdam Ave. and the Hudson River, **Morningside Heights** finds itself caught between the chaos of Harlem and the bourgeois glamour of the Upper West Side. *(Subway: 1 to Cathedral Pkwy. (110th St.), 116th St.-Columbia University, 125th St./Broadway.)* The centerpiece of **Columbia University's** urban campus is the majestic Roman Classical Low Library, which looms over College Walk, the school's central promenade that bustles with academics, students, and crackpots. *(Morningside Dr. and Broadway, from 114th to 120th St.)* The still-unfinished cathedral of **St. John the Divine,** under construction since 1892, is the largest in the world. It features altars and bays dedicated both to the sufferings of Christ and to the experiences of immigrants, victims of genocide, and AIDS patients. *(1047 Amsterdam Ave., between 110th and 113th St. ☎316-7540; tours ☎932-7347. Open M-Sa 7:30am-6pm, Su 7:30am-6pm. Suggested donation $2, students and seniors $1. Tours Tu-Sa 11am, Su 1pm. $5.)* **Riverside Church,** near Columbia has an observation deck in its tower and an amazing view, as well as the world's largest carillon (74 bells), a gift of John D. Rockefeller, Jr. *(490 Riverside Dr., at 120th St. ☎870-6792. Open M-F 9am-4:30pm. Bell tower: open Tu-Sa 10:30am-5pm, Su 9:45-10:45am and noon-4pm. Observation deck: Tu-Sa $2, students and seniors $1. Call for free tours.)* **Grant's Tomb,** a huge presidential grave commemorating the Union Civil War general, lies at 122nd St. and Riverside Dr. *(Open daily 9am-5pm. Free.)*

HARLEM

Over the years Harlem has entered the popular psyche as the archetype of America's frayed edges. Manhattan's largest neighborhood extends from 110th Street to the 150s, between the Hudson and East Rivers. Harlem began its transformation into a black neighborhood between 1910-1920. The 1920s brought prosperity and the artistic Harlem Renaissance movement; Civil Rights and radical Black Power activism came in the 1960s. Today, thanks to community activism and economic boom in recent decades, Harlem is thriving after a period of decline. *(Subway: 6 to 103rd St., Central Park N (110th St.), 116th St. at Lexington Ave.; 4, 5, 6 to 125th St./Lexington Ave.; 2, 3 to Central Park N (110th St.), 116th St., 125th St., 135th St. at Lenox (Sixth) Ave.; 3 to 145th St./Lenox (Sixth) Ave., 148th St.; B, C to Cathedral Pkwy. (110th St.), 116th St., 135th St. at Central Park W; A, B, C, D to 125th St., 145th St./Central Park W; A, B, C, D to 145th St./St. Nicholas Ave.; 1 to 137th St., 145th St. at Broadway.)*

SUGAR HILL. African-Americans with "sugar" (a.k.a. money) moved here in the 1920s and 30s; musical legends Duke Ellington and W.C. Handy lived in the neighborhood, while leaders W.E.B. DuBois and Thurgood Marshall both inhabited 409 Edgecombe. Some of the city's most notable gangsters operated here—Wesley Snipes starred as one in the film *Sugar Hill.* The area is the birthplace of Sugarhill Records, the rap label that created the Sugarhill Gang; their 1979 *Rapper's Delight* became the first hip-hop song to reach the Top 40. *(143rd to 155th St., between St. Nicholas and Edgecombe Ave. Subway: A, B, C, D to 145th St./St. Nicholas Ave.)*

WASHINGTON HEIGHTS. North of 155th St., **Washington Heights** affords a taste of urban life with an ethnic flavor. Eat a Greek dinner, buy Armenian pastries and vegetables from a South African, and discuss the Talmud with a **Yeshiva University** student. Fort Tryon Park is home to **The Cloisters,** a museum specializing in medieval art. *(Subway: C to 155th St./St. Nicholas Ave., 163rd St.; 1, A, C to 168th St.-Broadway; A to 175th St., 181st St., 190th St.; 1, to 181st St./St. Nicholas Ave., 191st St.)*

BROOKLYN

Part of NYC since 1898, Brooklyn is now the most populous borough. In the coverage below, neighborhoods are arranged from north to south.

WILLIAMSBURG & GREENPOINT. Home to a growing number of artists, Williamsburg's galleries match its artsy population (see **Galleries,** p. 240). **Greenpoint,** bounded by Java St. to the north, Meserole St. to the south, and Franklin St. to the west, is Brooklyn's northernmost border with Queens and home to a large Polish population. The birthplace of Mae West and the Union's Civil War ironclad the USS *Monitor*, Greenpoint features charming Italianate and Grecian houses built during the 1850s shipbuilding boom. *(Subway: L to Bedford Ave.; G to Nassau Ave.)*

FULTON LANDING. Fulton Landing hearkens back to days when the ferry—not the subway or the car—was the primary means of transportation between Brooklyn and Manhattan. Completed in 1883, the nearby **Brooklyn Bridge**—spanning the gap between lower Manhattan and Brooklyn—is the product of elegant calculation, careful design, and human exertion. A walk across the bridge at sunrise or sunset is one of the most exhilarating strolls New York City has to offer. *(From Brooklyn: entrance at the end of Adams St., at Tillary St. Subway: A, C to High St./Cadman Plaza E. From Manhattan: entrance at Park Row. Subway: J, M, Z, 4, 5, 6 to Brooklyn Bridge-City Hall.)*

DOWNTOWN. Brooklyn Heights, a well-preserved 19th-century residential area, sprang up with the development of steamboat transportation between Brooklyn and Manhattan in 1814. Rows of posh Greek Revival and Italianate houses in this area essentially created New York's first suburb. **Montague Street,** the main drag, has the stores, cafes, and mid-priced restaurants of a cute college town. **Downtown** is the location of Brooklyn's **Civic Center,** and holds several grand municipal buildings. *(Subway: M, N, R, 1, 2, 4, 5 to Court St.-Borough Hall.)*

PROSPECT PARK. Park Slope is a residential neighborhood with charming brownstones. Neighboring **Prospect Park** is the borough's answer to Manhattan's Central Park. (Frederick Law Olmsted and Calvert Vaux designed the park in the mid-1800s.) It has a zoo, an ice skating rink, a children's museum, and plenty of wide open spaces. In the middle of Grand Army Plaza, the 80-ft.-high **Memorial Arch,** built in the 1890s to commemorate the North's Civil War victory, marks one of the park's entrances. *(Bounded by Prospect Park W, Flatbush Ave., Ocean Ave., Parkside Ave., and Prospect Park SW. Subway: 1, 2 to Grand Army Plaza; F to 15 St.-Prospect Park; Q, S to Prospect Park. ☎ 718-965-8951; events hotline ☎ 718-965-8999.)*

BROOKLYN BOTANIC GARDEN. Adjacent to the park, this 52-acre fairyland features the **Fragrance Garden for the Blind** (with mint, lemon, violet, and other appetizing aromas) and the more formal **Cranford Rose Garden.** *(1000 Washington Ave.; other entrances on Eastern Pkwy. and on Flatbush Ave. ☎ 718-623-7000. Open Apr.-Sept. Tu-F 8am-6pm, Sa-Su 10am-6pm; Oct.-Mar. Tu-F 8am-4:30pm, Sa-Su 10am-4:30pm. $3, students and seniors $1.50, under 16 free. Free Tu all day and Sa 10am-noon, seniors free every F.)*

CONEY ISLAND. Once an elite resort (until the subway made it accessible to the masses), **Coney Island** is now fading. The **Cyclone,** 834 Surf Ave., built in 1927, was once the most terrifying rollercoaster in the world. Meet sharks, and other beasties at the **New York Aquarium.** *(Surf Ave. and W. 8th St. Subway: F, Q, W to Coney Island-Stillwell Ave.; F, Q to W. 8th St.-NY Aquarium; Q to Ocean Pkwy., Brighton Beach. ☎ 718-372-5159. Open mid-June to Sept. daily noon-midnight; late Mar. to mid-June F-Su noon-midnight. $5.)*

QUEENS

ASTORIA & LONG ISLAND CITY. In the northwest corner of Queens lies Astoria, where Greek-, Italian-, and Spanish-speaking communities mingle amid lively shopping districts and cultural attractions. Long Island City is just south, across the river from the Upper East Side. The **Isamu Noguchi Garden Museum,** the **Museum for African Art,** and the juggernaut **MoMa** (see **Museums,** p. 238) have all temporarily relocated to Long Island City. *(Astoria is located in the northwestern corner of Queens, across the river from Manhattan. Long Island City is located southwest of Astoria. Subway: All N and W stops between 36th Ave. and Astoria Ditmars Blvd. G, R, V to 36th St. or Steinway St.)*

SOCRATES SCULPTURE PARK. Led by sculptor Mark di Suvero, artists transformed this one time abandoned landfill into an artistic exhibition space with 35 stunning day-glo and rusted metal abstractions. *(At the end of Broadway, across the Vernon Blvd. intersection. ☎718-956-1819. Park open daily 10am-dusk.)*

FLUSHING & FLUSHING MEADOWS PARK. Flushing boasts colonial neighborhood landmarks, a bustling downtown, and a huge Asian immigrant population. Nearby **Flushing Meadows-Corona Park** was the site of the 1939 and 1964 World's Fair, and now holds **Shea Stadium** (home of the Mets), the **USTA National Tennis Center** (where the US Open is played), and the simple yet interesting **New York Hall of Science.** *(47-01 111th St. at 48th Ave. ☎718-699-0005. Open July-Aug. M-W 9:30am-2pm, Th-F 9:30am-5pm, Sa-Su 10:30-6pm; Sept.-June Tu-W 9:30am-2pm, Th-Su 9:30am-5pm. $7.50; students, seniors, and ages 5-17 $5. Parking $6.)* The **Unisphere,** a 380-ton steel globe in front of the New York City Building, is the retro-futuristic structure featured in the 1997 movie *Men In Black*. *(Subway to Flushing: 7 to Main St.-Flushing. Subway to Flushing Park: 7 to 111th St. or Willets Point-Shea Stadium.)*

THE BRONX

The relentless stream of immigration, once Italian and Irish but now mostly Hispanic and Russian, has created vibrant ethnic neighborhoods (including a Little Italy that puts its Manhattan counterpart to shame).

YANKEE STADIUM. In 1923, Babe Ruth's success as a hitter inspired the construction of the Yankees' own ballpark. Inside the 11.6-acre park (the field itself measures only 3½ acres), monuments honor Yankee greats like Lou Gehrig, Joe DiMaggio, and Babe Ruth. *(E. 161st St., at River Ave. Subway: 4, B, D to 161st St. ☎718-293-6000. Tours daily at noon. $10, seniors and under 15 $5.)*

THE BRONX ZOO. The most popular reason to come to the Bronx is the **Bronx Zoo/Wildlife Conservation Park.** The largest urban zoo in the US, it houses over 4000 animals. Soar into the air on the **Skyfari** aerial tramway ($2) that runs between Wild Asia and the **Children's Zoo,** or ride a camel. *(Subway: 2, 5 to West Farms Sq.-E. Tremont Ave. Follow Boston Rd. for 3 blocks until the Bronx Park S. gate. Bus: Bx9, Bx12, Bx19, Bx22, and Q44 pass various entrances to the zoo. ☎718-367-1010. Open M-F 10am-5pm, Sa-Su 10am-5:30pm. $11, seniors $7, ages 2-12 $6;.W free, donation suggested.)*

NEW YORK BOTANICAL GARDEN. Located adjacent to the Zoo, the city's most extensive botanical garden (250 acres) includes a 40-acre **hemlock forest,** kept in its natural state. Although it costs an extra few dollars to enter, the different ecosystems in the gorgeous domed greenhouse **Conservatory** are worth a visit. *(Bronx River Pkwy. Exit 7W and Fordham Rd. Subway: 4 to Bedford Park Blvd.-Lehman College; B, D to Bedford Park Blvd. Walk 8 blocks east or take the Bx26 bus. Bus: Bx19 or Bx26. Train: Metro-North Harlem line goes from Grand Central Terminal to Botanical Garden station. ☎718-817-8700. Open Tu-Su Apr.-Oct. 10am-6pm; Nov.-Mar. 10am-4pm. $3, students and seniors $2, children 2-12 $1; W all day and Sa 10am-noon free. Call for tours.)*

BELMONT. Arthur Ave. is the center of this uptown **Little Italy,** which is home to wonderful homestyle southern Italian cooking. To get a concentrated sense of the area, stop into **Arthur Avenue Retail Market,** 2334 Arthur Ave., between 186th and Crescent St. The recent Kosovar influx has put Kosovar flags in the fronts of many stores and eateries. *(Centering on Arthur Ave. and E. 187th St., near the Southern Blvd. entrance to the Bronx Zoo. Subway: B, D to Fordham Rd./Grand Concourse; then walk 11 blocks east to Arthur Ave. and head south.)*

STATEN ISLAND

Staten Island has a lot to offer, but tourism here is often limited. Its many parks are vast and lush, and there are beaches, historical sites and lovely gardens. The **Staten Island Ferry** (leaves from South Ferry in Manhattan; Subway: N, R to Whitehall St. or 1, 9 to South Ferry) is itself a sight not to be missed; it offers the best and cheapest ($0) tour on NY's upper harbor. The beautiful 19th-century **Snug Harbor Cultural Center** houses the **Newhouse Center for Contemporary Art,** a small art gallery with a summer sculpture show, and the **Staten Island Botanical Gardens.** *(1000 Richmond Terr. Bus S40. ☎ 718-448-2500. Free tours of the grounds Apr.-Nov. Sa-Su 2pm, starting at the Visitors Center. Botanical Garden: ☎ 718-273-8200. Open daily dawn-dusk.)*

MUSEUMS

For listings of upcoming exhibits consult *Time Out: New York, The New Yorker, New York* magazine and Friday's *The New York Times* (Weekend section). Most museums are closed on Monday and jam-packed on weekends. Many request a "donation" in place of an admission fee—don't be embarrassed to give as little as a dollar. Most are free one weeknight.

UPPER WEST SIDE

American Museum of Natural History, Central Park West (☎ 769-5100), between 77th and 81st St. Subway: B, C to 81st St. You're never too old for the Natural History Museum, one of the world's largest museums devoted to science. The main draw is the fourth floor dinosaur halls, which display real fossils in 85% of the exhibits (most museums use fossil casts). Perhaps the most impressive part of the museum is the sparkling Hayden Planetarium within the Rose Center for Earth and Space. Wheelchair-accessible. Open daily 10am-5:45pm; Rose Center also open F until 8:45pm. Suggested donation $10, students and seniors $7.50, children $6.

New York Historical Society, 2 W. 77th St. (☎ 873-3400), at Central Park West. Subway: 1, 2 to 79th; B, C to 72nd St./Central Park W, 81st St. Founded in 1804, this is New York's oldest continuously operated museum. The Neoclassical building houses both a library and museum. Wheelchair-accessible. Open Memorial Day-Labor Day Tu-Su 11am-6pm, Labor Day-Memorial Day Tu-Su 11am-5pm. $6, students and seniors $4, children free.

UPPER EAST SIDE

Metropolitan Museum of Art, 1000 Fifth Ave. (☎ 535-7710, concerts and lectures 570-3949, wheelchair info 535-7710), at 82nd St. Subway: 4, 5, 6 to 86th St./Lexington Ave. The largest in the Western Hemisphere, the Met's art collection boasts over 2 million works spanning 5000 years. Highlights are the Egyptian Art holdings (including the completely reconstructed Temple of Dendur), the awesome European paintings collection, and extensive exhibits of American art. The Costume Institute houses over 75,000 international costumes and accessories from the 17th century to the present, as well as the recently overhauled collection of Greek and Roman art. Open Su and Tu-Th 9:30am-5:15pm, F-Sa 9:30am-8:45pm. Suggested donation $10, seniors and students $5.

Guggenheim Museum, 1071 Fifth Ave. (☎ 423-3500), at 89th St. Subway: 4, 5, 6 to 86th St./Lexington Ave. The Guggenheim's most famous exhibit is surely the building itself, an inverted white quasi-ziggurat, designed by Frank Lloyd Wright and hailed as a modern masterpiece. Interdependent gallery spaces make up a spiral design that recalls a citrus fruit's membrane or a shopping mall's parking garage. The large collection of modern and postmodern paintings includes significant works in Cubism, Surrealism, American Minimalism, and Abstract Expressionism. Open Su-W and Sa 10am-5:45pm, Th 11am-6pm, F 9:30am-8:30pm. $15, students and seniors $10, under 12 free.

Frick Collection, 1 E. 70th St. (☎288-0700), at Fifth Ave. Subway: 6 to 68th St. Henry Clay Frick left his house and art collection to the city, and the museum retains the elegance of his chateau. The Living Hall displays 17th-century furniture, Persian rugs, Holbein portraits, and paintings by El Greco, Rembrandt, Velázquez, and Titian. The courtyard is inhabited by elegant statues surrounding the garden pool and fountain. Wheelchair-accessible. Open Tu-Sa 10am-6pm, Su 1-6pm. $10, students and seniors $5. Under 10 not allowed, under 16 must be accompanied by an adult.

Museum of the City of New York, 1220 Fifth Ave (☎534-1672)., at 103rd St. Subway: 6 to 103rd St./Lexington Ave. This fascinating museum details the history of the Big Apple, from the construction of the Empire State Building to the history of Broadway theater. Cultural history of all varieties is on parade—don't miss the model ships, NYC paintings, hot pants, and Yankees World Series trophies. Open W-Sa 10am-5pm, Su noon-5pm. Suggested donation $7; students, seniors, and children $4.

The Jewish Museum, 1109 Fifth Ave. (☎423-3200), at 92nd St. Subway: 6 to 96th St. The gallery's permanent collection details the Jewish experience throughout history using ancient Biblical artifacts and ceremonial objects, as well as contemporary masterpieces by Marc Chagall, Frank Stella, and George Segal. Open M-W 11am-5:45pm, Th 11am-9pm, F 11am-3pm, Su 10am-5:45pm. $8, students and seniors $5.50, members and under 12 free. Th 5-9pm pay-what-you-wish.

Whitney Museum of American Art, 945 Madison Ave. (☎570-3676), at 75th St. Subway: 6 to 77th St. The only museum with a historical mandate to champion the works of living American artists has assembled the largest collection of 20th- and 21st-century American art in the world, including Jasper Johns' *Three Flags* and Frank Stella's *Brooklyn Bridge*. Open W-Th and Sa 11am-6pm, F 1-9pm, Su 11am-6pm. $12, students and seniors $9.50, under 12 free. F 6-9pm pay-what-you-wish.

MIDTOWN

Museum of Television and Radio, 25 W. 52nd St. (☎621-6600), between Fifth and Sixth Ave. Subway: B, D, F, V to 47th-50th St.-Rockefeller Center/Sixth Ave. or E, V to Fifth Ave./53rd St. More archive than museum, this shrine to modern media contains over 100,000 easily accessible TV and radio programs. The museum also hosts a number of film screenings that focus on topics of social, historical, or artistic interest. Open Tu-W and F-Su noon-6pm, Th noon-8pm; F until 9pm for theaters only. Suggested donation $10, students and seniors $8, under 13 $5.

DOWNTOWN

New Museum of Contemporary Art, 583 Broadway (☎219-1222), between Princeton and W. Houston St. Subway: N, R to Prince St.; C, E to Spring St./Ave. of the Americas (Sixth Ave.); 6 to Spring St./Lafayette St.; F, S, V to Broadway-Lafayette St. One of the world's premier museums of modern art, with the newest (and, usually, the most controversial) in contemporary art. Open Tu-W and F-Su noon-6pm, Th noon-8pm. $6, students and seniors $3, under 18 free. Th 6-8pm $3.

BROOKLYN

Brooklyn Museum of Art, 200 Eastern Pkwy. (☎718-638-5000), at Washington Ave. Subway: 1, 2 to Eastern Pkwy.-Brooklyn Museum. If it weren't for the Met, the BMA would be New York's largest and most magnificent museum. It's enormous Oceanic and New World art collection takes up the central 2-story space on the first floor. You'll find outstanding Ancient Greek, Roman, Middle Eastern, and Egyptian galleries on the third floor. Open W-F 10am-5pm, Sa-Su 11am-6pm. Open first Sa of month 11am-11pm. Suggested donation $6, students and seniors $3, under 12 free. First Sa of month free.

QUEENS

Museum of Modern Art (MoMa), 45-20 33rd St. (☎708-9400), at Queens Blvd., in Long Island City. Subway: 7 to 33rd St./Queens Blvd. Relocated to Queens until its Manhattan location at 11 W. 53rd St. finishes renovations in early 2005, the MoMa still boasts one of the world's most impressive collections of post-Impressionist, late 19th-century, and 20th-century art. Some of the collection's most renowned works are Picasso's *Les Demoiselles d'Avignon,* Rodin's *John the Baptist,* and van Gogh's *Starry Night.* Open Sa-M and Th 10am-5pm, F 10am-7:45pm. $12, students and seniors $8.50, under 16 free. F 4-7:45pm pay what you wish.

Museum for African Art, 36-01 43rd Ave. (☎966-1313), Long Island City. Subway: 7 to 33rd St./Queens Blvd. Features 2 major exhibits a year, along with several smaller exhibitions of stunning African and African-American art on such themes as storytelling, magic, religion, and mask-making. Objects on display span centuries and come from all over Africa. Many hands-on, family-oriented workshops on traditional African activities (e.g., weaving and drumming) also offered. Open Tu-F 10:30am-5:30pm, Sa-Su noon-6pm. $5, students and seniors $2.50. Su free.

GALLERIES

New York's galleries provide a riveting—and free—introduction to the contemporary art world. To get started, pick up a free copy of *The Gallery Guide* at any major museum or gallery. Published every 2 to 3 months, it lists the addresses, phone numbers, and hours of nearly every showplace in the city. Most galleries are open Tuesday to Saturday, from 10 or 11am to 5 or 6pm. Galleries are usually only open on weekend afternoons in the summer, and many are closed from late July to early September.

SOHO

Artists Space, 38 Greene St., 3rd fl. (☎226-3970), at Grand St. Subway: 1, 2 to Canal St./Varick St.; A, C, E to Canal St./Ave. of the Americas (Sixth Ave.). Nonprofit gallery open since 1972. Its space is usually divided into several small exhibits by emerging artists. Slide file of unaffiliated artists gives those without backing a chance to shine. Open Tu-Sa 11am-6pm. Slide file open by appointment F-Sa.

The Drawing Center, 35 Wooster St. (☎219-2166), between Grand and Broome St. Subway: 1, 2 to Canal St./Varick St.; A, C, E to Canal St./Ave. of the Americas (Sixth Ave.). Specializing in original works on paper, this nonprofit space sets up high-quality exhibits. Historical and contemporary works—everything from Picasso to Kara Walker—on rotation. Open Tu-F 10am-6pm, Sa 11am-6pm; closed Aug. Suggested donation $3.

Exit Art, 548 Broadway, 2nd fl. (☎966-7745), between Prince and Spring St. Subway: 6 to Spring St./Lafayette St.; C, E to Spring St./Ave. of the Americas (Sixth Ave.). Fun, friendly, and happening "transcultural" and "transmedia" non-profit space, featuring experiments in the presentation of visual art, theater, film, and video. Open Tu-F 10am-6pm, Sa 11am-6pm. Suggested donation $5.

CHELSEA

Dia Center for the Arts, 548 W. 22nd St. (☎989-5566), between Tenth and Eleventh Ave. Subway: C, E to 23rd St./Eighth Ave. 4 floors of longer-term (3-9 months) exhibits cover a balanced range of media and styles. The roof holds an ongoing video installation piece, *Rooftop Urban Park Project*, as well as a cafe with a decent view of Chelsea. Open mid-Sept. to mid-June W-Su noon-6pm. $6, students and seniors $3.

The Museum at the Fashion Institute of Technology, Seventh Ave. (☎217-5800), at 27th St. Subway: 1, 2 to 18th St./Seventh Ave. Changing exhibits pertain to all things sartorial, from photography to mannequin displays. Open Tu-F noon-8pm, Sa 10am-5pm. Free.

Sonnabend, 536 W. 22nd St. (☎627-0489), between Tenth and Eleventh Ave. Subway: C, E to 23rd St./Eighth Ave. Originally from SoHo, this famous gallery has shown works by well-known US and European artists for 40 years. Open Tu-Sa 10am-6pm; closed Aug.

UPPER EAST SIDE

The upper east side is a ritzy neighborhood with chi-chi showplaces to match. The **Fuller Building,** 41 E. 57th St., between Park and Madison Ave., harbors 12 floors of galleries. (Most open M-Sa 10am-5:30pm; Oct.-May most closed M.)

Pace Gallery, 32 E. 57th St. (Pace Prints and Primitive ☎421-3237, Pace-MacGill ☎759-7999, Pace Wildenstein ☎421-3292), between Park and Madison Ave. Subway: N, R to Fifth Ave./59th St.; 4, 5, 6 to 59th St./Lexington Ave. 4 floors dedicated to the promotion of widely disparate forms of art. Open Oct.-May Tu-Sa 9:30am-6pm; June-Sept. M-Th 9:30am-6pm, F 9:30am-4pm.

Sotheby's, 1334 York Ave. (☎606-7000, ticket office 606-7171), at 72nd St. Subway: 6 to 68th St. One of the city's most respected auction houses, offering everything from Degas to Disney. Auctions open to anyone, but the more popular require a ticket (first come, first served). They also have several galleries for works soon to be auctioned off. Open Labor Day-late June M-Sa 10am-5pm, Su 1-5pm; late June-Labor Day closed Sa-Su.

Leo Castelli, 59 E. 79th St. (☎249-4470), between Park and Madison Ave. Subway: 6 to 77th St. Showing a selection of contemporary artists such as Jasper Johns and Ed Ruscha. Open mid-Aug. to late June Tu-Sa 10am-6pm; late June to mid-Aug. Tu-F 11am-5pm. Occasionally closed between exhibitions; call ahead.

WILLIAMSBURG

Lunar Base, 197 Grand St. (☎718-599-2905), between Bedford St. and Driggs Ave. Subway: L to Bedford Ave. Amid many other nearby galleries, this new gallery boasts bold abstract and contemporary works from international artists. Open Th-Su 1-7pm.

Pierogi, 177 N. 9th St. (☎718-599-2144), between Bedford and Driggs Ave. Subway: L to Bedford Ave. Hosts 2 big-name solo shows a month, but the front files still display hundreds of affordable works by emerging artists. Open M and F-Su noon-6pm.

The Williamsburg Art and Historical Center, 135 Broadway, 2nd fl. (☎718-486-7372), between Bedford and Driggs Ave. Subway: J, M, Z to Marcy Ave.; L to Bedford Ave. The epicenter of the Williamsburg arts scene, this historic building's beautiful second-floor gallery exhibits the work of local and international artists. A monthly musical performance and biannual international show keep this Center bustling with artists from all backgrounds. Theater and music events also featured. Open Sa-Su noon-6pm.

LONG ISLAND CITY

P.S.1 Contemporary Art Center, 22-25 Jackson Ave. (☎718-784-2084), at 46th Ave., in Long Island City. Subway: 7 to 45th Rd.-Courthouse Sq.; E, V to 23rd St. Ely Ave.; G to 21st St./Jackson Ave. P.S.1, the first public school in then-independent Long Island City, was converted into a cutting-edge art space with rotating exhibits. Wheelchair-accessible. Open W-Su noon-6pm. Suggested donation $5, students and seniors $2.

New York Center for Media Arts, 45-12 Davis St. (☎718-472-9414), off Jackson Ave., in Long Island City. Subway: E, V to 23rd St.-Ely Ave.; G to 21st St.; 7 to 45th Rd.-Courthouse Sq. Spacious converted warehouse featuring rotating installations of multimedia artwork. Exhibits rotate every few months. Open Th-Su noon-6pm.

SHOPPING

There is no easier place to blow your dough than NYC—stores run the gamut from the world's (second) largest department store to sidewalk stands peddling bootleg Top 40 selections. Here's a quick, style-conscious walking tour of the city.

The best place to start is downtown on the **Lower East Side,** where hip, new designers sell their uneven hemlines and poly-nylon-rubber-day-glo shirts on Orchard, Stanton, and Ludlow St. Next stop is **Chinatown,** where you can pick up a (fake) Kate Spade from any of the million vendors along Canal St. Not to worry: they'll stick the label on for you. Pick up other imitation items right off the sidewalk, from CDs to Polo shirts. Walk up to **SoHo** to spend some major cash, this time on hip but established designers. Wooster, Prince, and West Broadway are home to the likes of Rowley and Sui, but Broadway is cheaper, with the NYC staple Canal Jeans Co. between Spring and Prince St. **Greenwich Village** has a mishmash of offerings: the city's largest comic book store (Forbidden Planet), Cheap Jack's Vintage Clothing, and the city's best used bookstore (The Strand, 828 Broadway, at 12th St.). Just east of Broadway is the more risqué **East Village,** a den of tattoo parlors, silver trinkets, sex shops, and cheap CD stores centered on St. Mark's Pl. Find some fashionable enclaves on 9th St. farther east, and a number of good vintage stores all over. In **Herald Square** you'll find department stores like Macy's. Designer flagships line **Fifth Avenue** between 42nd and 59th St.; peruse them for a look at the really unattainable—Chanel, Armani, Prada, Louis Vuitton, and Tiffany's alongside elite department stores like Bergdorf, Saks, and Bloomingdale's. To keep the kids quiet while you shop at Versace, try F.A.O. Schwarz on 5th Ave. at 58th St. **Uptown** has everything, from cute boutiques along **Columbus Avenue** on the West Side to the cheapest kicks and FuBu gear on 125th St. in **Harlem.**

ENTERTAINMENT

Publications with noteworthy entertainment and nightlife sections are the *Village Voice*, *Time Out: New York*, *New York* magazine, and the Sunday edition of *The New York Times*. *The New Yorker* has the most comprehensive theater survey.

THEATER

Broadway tickets usually start from $50, but many money-saving schemes exist (see **Cheap Seats,** p. 243). **TKTS,** Duffy Square, at 47th St. and Broadway, sells tickets for many Broadway and some larger off-Broadway shows at a 25-50% discount on the day of the performance. The lines begin to form an hour or so before the booths open, but they move fairly quickly. More tickets become available as showtime approaches, so you may find fewer possibilities if you go too early. (☎768-1818. Tickets sold M-Sa 3-8pm for evening performances, W and Sa 10am-2pm for matinees, Su 11am-7pm for matinees and evening performances.)

The **Theatre Development Fund** (☎221-0885) offers discount vouchers for off- and off-off-Broadway productions, as well as for other events sponsored by small, independent production companies. Those eligible—students, teachers, performing-arts professionals, retirees, union and armed forces members, and clergy—must first join the TDF mailing list by paying $20. Once you are a member, which may take 6-8 weeks after you mail in the application, you can purchase 4 vouchers for $28. These are redeemable at the box office of any participating production.

You may reserve full-price tickets over the phone and pay by credit card using **Tele-Charge** (☎239-6200 or outside NYC 800-432-7250) for Broadway shows; **Ticket Central** (☎279-4200) for off-Broadway shows; and **Ticketmaster** (☎307-4100 or outside NYC 800-755-4000) for all types of shows. All three services have a per-ticket service charge, so ask before purchasing. You can avoid these fees if you buy tickets directly from the box office.

Shakespeare in the Park (☎539-8750) is a New York summer tradition. From June through August, two plays are presented at the **Delacorte Theater** in Central Park, near the 81st St. entrance on the Upper West Side, just north of the main road. Tickets are free, but lines form extremely early.

CHEAP SEATS To The budget traveler, the Great White Way's major theatrical draws may seem locked away in gilded Broadway cages. Never fear, however, *Let's Go* is here! Er, that is to say, you can find cheap tickets, compadre. Should Ticketmaster and TKTS (see above) fail, other avenues remain open to you.

Rush Tickets: Some theaters distribute them on the morning of the performance; others make student rush tickets available 30min. before showtime. Lines can be extremely long, so get there *early*. Call the theater before to find out their policy.

Cancellation Line: No rush luck? Some theaters redistribute returned or unclaimed tickets several hours before showtime. You might have to sacrifice your afternoon—but, come on, Dame Edna is worth it! Once again, call ahead.

Hit Show Club: 630 9th Ave. (☎581-4211), between 44th and 45th St. This free service distributes coupons redeemable at the box office for 30% or more off regular ticket prices. Call for coupons via mail or pick them up them up at the club office.

Standing-room Only: Sold on the day of show, these tend to be around $15 or $20. Call first, as some theaters can't accommodate standing room.

EXPERIMENTAL/PERFORMANCE SPACES

Knitting Factory, 74 Leonard St. (☎219-3006), between Broadway and Church St. Subway: 1, 2 to Franklin St. This multi-level performance space features several shows nightly, from avant-garde and indie rock to jazz and hip-hop. Summertime jazz festival. Cover $5-25. Box office open M-F 10am-2am, Sa noon-2am, Su 2pm-2am. Tickets available by phone M-F 10am-4pm, Sa noon-4am, Su 2pm-4am. Bar open 6pm-4am.

The Kitchen, 512 W. 19th St. (☎255-5793; www.thekitchen.org), between Tenth and Eleventh Ave. Subway: C, E to 23rd St./Eighth Ave. Features experimental and avant-garde film and video, as well as concerts, dance performances, and poetry readings in unassuming spot. Ticket prices vary. Box office open M-F 10am-5pm.

JAZZ JOINTS

The **JVC Jazz Festival** puts on all-star performances from June to July. Tickets go on sale in early May, but many events are outdoors and free. Check the newspaper or call ☎501-1390. Annual festivals sponsored by major corporations draw local talent and industry giants. The concerts take place throughout the city (some free), but center at TriBeCa's **Knitting Factory** (see above).

Smoke, 2751 Broadway (☎864-6662), between 105th and 106th St. This sultry cocktail lounge jumps with excellent jazz 7 nights a week. Although slightly congested, the intimate space swells with music and an animated atmosphere. Jam sessions M 10pm, Th midnight. W funk, Su Latin jazz. Happy Hour daily 5-8pm. Cover Th-Sa $10-20. $10 drink min. Open daily 5pm-4am.

Detour, 349 E. 13th St. (☎533-6212), between First and Second Ave. Subway: L to First Ave. Great nightly jazz and no cover—a perfect mix. Happy Hour (2-for-1 drinks) daily 4-7pm. Mixed drinks $6, bottled beer $4. 1-drink min. Open Su-Tu 4pm-2am, W-Su 4pm-4am. Wheelchair-accessible.

Apollo Theatre, 253 W. 125th St. (☎531-5301; box office 531-5305), between Frederick Douglass and Adam Clayton Powell Blvd. Subway: A, B, C, D to 125th St. This Harlem landmark has heard Duke Ellington, Count Basie, Ella Fitzgerald, and Billie Holliday. A young Malcolm X shined shoes here. W Amateur Night ($13-30) is legendary. Order tickets through Ticketmaster (☎307-7171) or at the box office. Open M-Tu and Th-F 10am-6pm, W 10am-8:30pm.

ROCK, POP, PUNK, FUNK

New York City has a long history of producing bands on the vanguard of popular music and performance, from the Velvet Underground to Sonic Youth. **Music festivals** provide the opportunity to see tons of bands at a (relatively) low price. The **CMJ Music Marathon** (☎877-633-7848) runs for four nights in late October or early November, including over 400 bands and workshops on the alternative music scene. **The Digital Club Festival** (☎677-3530), a newly reconfigured indie-fest, visits New York in late July. The **Macintosh New York Music Festival** presents over 350 bands over a week-long period in July.

Southpaw, 125 Fifth Ave. (☎718-230-0236), between Sterling and St. John's Pl., Brooklyn. Subway: M, N, R, to Union St.; Q to Seventh Ave.; 2, 3 to Bergen St. New club in Park Slope hosts DJs, local musicians, and well-known talent. 2003 highlights included Sleater-Kinney, Elliott Smith, and Luna.

SOBs (Sounds of Brazil), 204 Varick St. (☎243-4940), at W. Houston St. Subway: 1, 9 to Houston St. Dinner club with some of NYC's best live music. Weekly "Basement Bhangra" has exploded in the past year, and SOBs continues to attract hip-hop's best talent. Recent acts include Talib Kweli, Blackalicious, and Black Eyed Peas. Box office (located next door at 200 Varick St.) open M-F 11am-5pm, Sa noon-6pm. Cash only.

Mercury Lounge, 217 E. Houston St. (☎260-4700), between Essex and Ludlow St. This converted gravestone parlor has attracted an amazing number and range of big-name acts, from folk to pop to noise. Past standouts include spoken-word artist Maggie Estep, Morphine, and Mary Lou Lord. Cover varies. Box office open M-Sa noon-7pm. Cash only.

FILMS

Many films open in New York weeks before they're distributed elsewhere, and the response of Manhattan audiences and critics can shape a film's success or failure. Big-screen fanatics should check out the cavernous **Ziegfeld,** 141 W. 54th St., one of the largest screens left in America. (☎765-7600. Subway: 1, 9 to 51st St. Tickets $9.50, seniors and children $6.) The city's best independent theater is **BAMRose Cinemas,** at the Brooklyn Academy of Music, 30 Lafayette Ave., Brooklyn. (☎718-636-4100. Subway: 1, 2, 4, 5, Q to Atlantic Ave.; M, N, R, W to Pacific St. Tickets $10, students $7, children and seniors $6.)

OPERA & DANCE

You can do it all at **Lincoln Center;** as the world's largest cultural complex, many of the city's best opera, dance, and performance groups reside here. (Between 62nd and 66th St., between Ninth and Tenth Ave. ☎875-5456. Subway: 1, 2 to 66th St.) Check *The New York Times* listings. The **Metropolitan Opera Company's** premier outfit performs on a Lincoln Center stage as big as a football field. You can stand in the orchestra for $16 or all the way back in the Family Circle for $12. (☎362-6000. Season Sept.-May M-Sa. Box office open M-Sa 10am-8pm, Su noon-6pm. Tickets from $195; upper balcony around $65.)

Alongside the Met, the **New York City Opera** has come into its own. "City" has a split season (Sept.-Nov. and Mar.-Apr.) and keeps its ticket prices low. (☎870-5630. Box office open M 10am-7:30pm, Tu-Sa 10am-8:30pm, Su 11:30am-7:30pm.

Tickets $25-92; $10 student and senior rush tickets the morning of the performance.) **Dicapo Opera Theatre,** 184 E. 76th St., between Third and Lexington Ave., is a small company that garners standing ovations after every performance. (☎288-9438. Subway: N, R to 23rd St./Broadway. Tickets around $40.)

The **New York State Theater** in Lincoln Center is home to the late George Balanchine's **New York City Ballet.** Tickets for the *Nutcracker* in December sell out almost immediately. (☎870-5570. Season Nov.-Mar. Tickets $16-88.) The **American Ballet Theater** dances at the Metropolitan Opera House. (☎477-3030, box office 362-6000. Tickets $17-75.) **City Center,** 131 W. 55th St. (☎581-1212), has the city's best dance, from modern to ballet, including the **Alvin Ailey American Dance Theater.** The dance company **De La Guarda** (think disco in a rainforest with an air show overhead) performs at 20 Union Sq. E. (☎239-6200. Standing-room only. $45-50, some $20 tickets sold 2hr. before show. Box office open Tu-Th 1-8:15pm, F 1-10:30pm, Sa 1-10pm, Su 1-7:15pm.) Other dance venues include **Dance Theater Workshop,** 219 W. 19th St. (☎924-0077), between Seventh and Eighth Ave.; **Joyce Theater,** 175 Eighth Ave. (☎242-0800), between 18th and 19th St.; and **Thalia Spanish Theater,** 41-17 Greenpoint Ave. (☎718-729-3880), between 41st and 42nd St. in Queens.

CLASSICAL MUSIC

Lincoln Center has the most selection in its halls. The **Great Performers Series,** featuring famous and foreign musicians, packs the Avery Fisher and Alice Tully Halls and the Walter Reade Theater from October until May (see above for contact info; tickets from $10). **Avery Fisher Hall** presents the annual **Mostly Mozart Festival.** Show up early; there are usually recitals 1hr. before the main concert that are free to ticketholders. (☎875-5766. July-Aug. Tickets $25-50.) The **New York Philharmonic** begins its regular season in mid-September. Students and seniors can sometimes get $10 tickets the day of; call ahead. Check about seeing morning rehearsals. (☎875-5656. Tickets $10-60.) For a few weeks in late June, the Philharmonic holds **free concerts** on the Great Lawn in Central Park, at Prospect Park in Brooklyn, at Van Cortlandt Park in the Bronx, and elsewhere. (☎875-5709.) Free outdoor events at Lincoln Center occur all summer. (☎875-5928.)

Carnegie Hall, on Seventh Ave., at 57th St., sometimes offers rush tickets (☎247-7800. Box office M-Sa 11am-6pm, Su noon-6pm. Tickets $10-60.) A good, cheap way to absorb New York musical culture is to visit a music school. Except for opera and

THE LOCAL LEGEND

LITERARY LEGACIES

Since **William Bradford** founded the country's first newspaper (the *New York Gazette*) in 1725, New York City has been America's literary capital. **Herman Melville** and **Washington Irving** were both born in Lower Manhattan; Irving gave New York its ever-enduring pen- (and movie-) name, **Gotham. Walt Whitman,** born in South Huntington, Long Island, edited the controversial **Brooklyn Eagle** newspaper. **Edgar Allen Poe** lived in uptown poverty in the rural Bronx. Starving **Greenwich Village** novelists such as **Willa Cather, John Reed,** and **Theodore Dreiser** helped establish the city's literary center; **e.e. cummings** and **Djuna Barnes** both lived off 10th St. at **Patchin Place. Edna St. Vincent Millay** lived at Bedford St., where she founded the **Cherry Lane Theatre.** Midtown's legendary **Algonquin Hotel** witnessed the 1919 **Round Table** weekly lunch meetings attended by such noted wits such as **Robert Benchley, Dorothy Parker, Alexander Woollcott,** and **Edna Ferber.**

The area surrounding Columbia University witnessed the 1920s flowering of the **Harlem Renaissance:** novelists **George Schuyler, Claude McKay** and **Zora Neale Hurston,** as well as poet **Langston Hughes** and his circle, set the stage for next-generation black writers like **Ralph Ellison** and **James Baldwin.**

ballet productions ($5-12), concerts are usually free and frequent. The best options are the **Juilliard School of Music,** Lincoln Center (☎769-7406), the **Mannes College of Music,** 150 W. 85th St. (☎580-0210), and the **Manhattan School of Music,** 120 Claremont Ave. (☎749-2802).

SPORTS

Most cities are content to have one major-league team in each big-time sport. New York opts for the Noah's Ark approach: two baseball teams, two hockey teams, NBA and WNBA basketball teams, two football teams... and one lonely soccer squad. The beloved **Mets** bat at **Shea Stadium** in Queens. (Subway: 7 to Willets Point-Shea Stadium. ☎718-507-6387. $13-30.) The **Yankees** play ball at **Yankee Stadium** in the Bronx. (Subway: 4, B, D to 161st St. ☎718-293-4300. $8-65.) Both the **Giants** and the **Jets** play football across the river at **Giants Stadium** in East Rutherford, NJ (☎201-507-8900; tickets from $25), and the **New York/New Jersey Metrostars** play soccer in the same venue. The **Knickerbockers** (that's the **Knicks** to you), as well as the WNBA's **Liberty,** play basketball at **Madison Square Garden** (☎465-5800; from $22 and $8, respectively), and the **Rangers** play hockey there (from $25). The **Islanders** hit the ice at the **Nassau Veterans Memorial Colisseum** in Uniondale. (☎516-794-9300. Tickets $27-70.) New York also hosts a number of other world-class events. Get tickets 3 months in advance for the prestigious **US Open,** held in late August and early September at the USTA Tennis Center in Flushing Meadows, Queens. (☎888-673-6849. $33-69.) On the first Sunday in November, 2 million spectators witness the 30,000 runners of the **New York City Marathon.** The race begins on the Verrazano Bridge and ends at Central Park's Tavern on the Green. (☎860-4455.)

NIGHTLIFE

BARS

LOWER EAST SIDE

bOb Bar, 235 Eldridge St. (☎777-0588), between E. Houston and Stanton St. Subway: F, V to Lower East Side-Second Ave. Small and laidback, with a hip-hop-inclined crowd and graffiti-esque paintings covering the walls. Happy Hour F 7-10pm, $3 beers. While Tu alternates between Latin, reggae, and hip-hop (free), Th, F, Sa are strictly hip-hop. Anti-thugwear dress code in effect (no sports apparel, sports shoes, or hats). Cover $5 after 10pm; women $3. Open daily 7pm-4am.

Kush, 183 Orchard St. (☎677-7328), between E. Houston and Stanton St. Subway: F, J, M, Z to Delancey St.-Essex St.; F, V to Lower East Side/Second Ave. In the words of the Brazilian reclining upon the plush sofa in the dim corner while puffing his hookah ($15, various flavors): "This is a genuine displacement of the heart of the Middle East to the core of the Big Apple." Tu live music and belly dancing. DJs a few nights a week. Weekend nights are more "semite-nomad meets the brothers of Sig-Chi" feel than straight up grove of the Silk Road. Open daily 7pm-2am (sometimes until 4am). Opens 6pm in winter.

Lotus Lounge, 35 Clinton St. (☎253-1144), at Stanton St. Subway: F, J, M, Z to Delancey St.-Essex St. The ceilings are high, the slats are of soft wood, and the lanterns are lit at Lotus Lounge. Bookshelves stretch across the back for a chill afternoon of knowledge acquisition. Beer $4-5 ($2 specials frequently). Live DJs every night. A cafe 8am-4pm. A bar 4pm-4am.

SOHO AND TRIBECA

Milady's, 160 Prince St. (☎226-9069), at Thompson St. Subway: C, E to Spring St./Ave. of the Americas (Sixth Ave.). A rough in the overbearing SoHo diamond mine. Down-to-earth neighborhood haunt with a cast of affable regulars and, supposedly, SoHo's only pool table. Everything under $6. Good, inexpensive food served M-Th 11am-midnight, F-Sa 11am-1am, Su 11am-11pm. Bar open daily until 4am.

Circa Tabac, 32 Watts St. (☎941-1781), between Sixth Ave. and Thompson St. Subway: C, E to Spring St./Ave. of the Americas (Sixth Ave.). Claims to be the world's first, and perhaps only, cigarette lounge. The war on smoking has spread even to downtown NYC, but Circa Tabac remains a haven for cigarette lovers. Decor recalls a Prohibition-era speakeasy: a jazz soundtrack accompanies protective curtains and Art Deco pieces. State-of-the-art air purifiers and odor killers keep the air clear. 180 kinds of cigarettes ($5-25) available. Open Su-W 5pm-2am, Th-Sa 5pm-4am.

GREENWICH VILLAGE

The Whitehorse Tavern, 567 Hudson St. (☎243-9260), at W. 11th St. Subway: 1, 2 to Christopher St. Dylan Thomas drank himself to death here, pouring 18 straight whiskeys through an already tattered liver. Boisterous students and locals squeeze into one of New York's oldest bars to pay the poet homage by tattering their own livers. Outdoor patio. Beer $3.50-5. Open Su-Th 11am-2am, F-Sa 11am-4am.

The Village Idiot, 355 W. 14th St. (☎989-7334), between Eighth and Ninth Ave. Subway: A, C, E, L to 14th St./Eighth Ave. Honky-tonk, New York style. Cheap beer ($1.50 mugs of MGD), loud country music, and a vibe as close to a roadhouse as this city gets. As if the customers' drunken antics or the bras hanging from the bar weren't enough, the (female) staff occasionally dances on the bar. Open daily noon-4am.

EAST VILLAGE

Niagara, 112 Ave. A (☎420-9517), at E. 7 St. Subway: 6 to Astor Pl.; L to First Ave. Is a famous NY state waterfall an appropriate name for a bar? Maybe "bustling, art-filled space with beautiful dark wood furniture, industrious bartenders, and a downstairs lounge called 'Lei Lounge' which features a second DJ and a pretty lady dancing (tastefully) on the weekends" would be more appropriate. But perhaps Lei Lounge is an unacceptable moniker, thereby illegitimizing the whole name altogether... Just accept "Niagara" and accept the $5 beers and weekly art shows (Th). Open daily 4pm-4pm.

Tribe, 132 First Ave. (☎979-8965), at St. Mark's Pl. Subway: 6 to Astor Pl. Behind the frosted glass windows lies a chic, friendly bar with colorful but subtle back lighting. Comfortable lounging areas. Before midnight: super chill. Then it rapidly evolves into a party. Beer $5; cocktails $5-10. DJ nightly 10pm: lots of hip-hop and old school; Tu Salsa/Latin. Open daily 5pm-4am.

Delft, 14 Ave. B (☎260-7100), between E. 2nd and E. 3rd St. Subway: F, V to Lower East Side/2nd Ave. Hopping joint, excellent DJs nightly. Basement lounge area often devolves into dancing. Young, attractive crowd never quite as good looking as the bartenders. Beer $6, drinks $8-10. Open daily 7pm-4am.

d.b.a., 41 First Ave. (☎475-5097), between E. 2nd and 3rd St. Subway: F, V to Lower East Side-Second Ave. For the serious beer drinker. With 19 premium beers on tap (around $5), well over 100 bottled imports and microbrews, classy bourbons and whiskeys ($6), and 45 different tequilas, this extremely friendly space lives up to its motto—"drink good stuff." Mellow jazz and sassy crowd. Popular outdoor beer garden open until 10pm. Su morning brunch: free bagels and lox while it lasts. Open daily 1pm-4am.

CHELSEA & UNION SQUARE

Billiard Club, 220 W. 19th St. (☎206-7665), between Seventh and Eighth Ave. Subway: 1, 2 to 23rd St./Seventh Ave. This pool hall's red felt tables await both the hustlin' type and those who just enjoy a game of eight-ball. Low-lying lounge ottomans and a 10 ft. square TV screen greet the rest. $13 per hour before 6pm, $14 after. 21+ to play after 6pm. Open M-Th 1pm-2am, F-Sa 1pm-4am, Su 2pm-2am.

The Half King, 505 W. 23rd St. (☎462-4300), at Tenth Ave. Subway: C, E to 23rd St./ Eighth Ave. Named after a mysterious and brutal Seneca Chief, this restaurant/bar has quickly become the hot spot for journalists, writers, and filmmakers on the West Side. Rotating photojournalism exhibits, weekly reading series, and a secluded patio keep everyone happy whether they're dining on a filet of salmon with asparagus ($13) or downing a pint of beer ($4.50). Open Su-Th 9am-noon, F-Sa 9am-4am.

UPPER EAST SIDE

The Big Easy, 1768 Second Ave. (☎348-0879), at 92nd St. Subway: 6 to 96th St./Lexington. A post-grad hangout for those who miss their college glory years. With 2 beirut (a.k.a beer pong) tables in back, "Power Hour" of $1 Bud drafts nightly 11pm-midnight, and well drinks 11pm-midnight, this place can get "sloppy" in the best sense of the word. Open daily 5pm-4am.

American Spirits, 1744 Second Ave. (☎289-7510), between 90th and 91st St. Subway: 4, 5, 6 to 86th St./Lexington Ave. Cozy sports bar. Beer $4-5, mixed drinks $7-8. Karaoke Tu and Th; live music every third Sa of the month. Happy Hour M-F 4-8pm with $2 drafts and $3 well drinks. Open daily 3pm-4am.

UPPER WEST SIDE

The Evelyn Lounge, 380 Columbus Ave. (☎724-2363), at 78th St. Subway: B, C to 81st St. A somewhat upscale bar for the after-work set, with fireplaces and settees creating a homey setting. Drinks ($9 martinis) are a bit pricey, but comfy couches and classy hipsters make them worthwhile. Enticing bar menu $7-14. Downstairs features a DJ W-Sa, spinning hip-hop F-Sa. Open M-Th 6pm-4am, F-Su 5pm-4am.

Potion Lounge, 370 Columbus Ave. (☎721-4386), between 77th and 78th St. Subway: 1 to 79th; B, C to 81st St. A silvery-blue lounge complete with local art on the walls, bubbles rising through pipes in the windows, and velvety sofas. The lounge takes its name from the colorful layered drinks ("potions" $10) it serves. Draft beers $5-6, martinis $9. DJs on weekends. Open Tu-Sa 6pm-4am.

BROOKLYN

Galapagos, 70 N. 6th St. (☎718-782-5188), between Kent and Wythe St. Subway: L to Bedford Ave. Once a mayonnaise factory, this space is now one of the hipper cultural spots in the city. Great bar in an interesting futuristic decor, complete with an enormous reflecting pool, Vaudeville performances on M, and weekly film series (Su 7, 9:30pm, M 8:30pm; $5 cover). DJs Tu-Sa. Occasional $5 cover. Happy Hour M-Sa 6pm-8pm. Open Su-Th 6pm-2am, F-Sa 6pm-4am.

The Gate, 321 Fifth Ave. (☎718-768-4329), at Third St. A few short years ago, Park Slope was a nightlife wasteland. The Gate's good selection of beers (all around $3), welcoming atmosphere, and large patio (always filled) paved the way for the Fifth Ave. renaissance. Open M-Th 4pm-4am, F-Su noon-4am.

Loki Lounge, 304 Fifth Ave. (☎718-965-9600), at Second St. Don't be put off by Loki's dark exterior: inside is one of Brooklyn's best bars. laidback, comfortable, and staffed by good bartenders, Loki is a bar that does all the important things well. With occasional live music. Open daily 4pm-4am.

Pete's Candy Store, 709 Lorimer St. (☎718-302-3770), between Frost and Richardson St. Subway: L to Lorimer St. A labor of the owner's love, this hand-painted bar includes a small performance room in the back and a "make-out" hallway. A lively local crowd flocks to the soda-shop-turned-bar for the nightly free live music. Tu Bingo and W Quiz-Off (both 7-9pm) are extremely popular, but it's the Bucket of Joy (Stoli, Red Bull, 7-Up and straws) that makes this place more than worth the walk ($6). M night poetry readings; among the best in the city. Open Su-Tu 5pm-2am, W-Sa 5pm-4am.

Union Pool, 484 Union Ave. (☎718-609-0484), off Skillman Ave. One of the funkiest places in Brooklyn. The backyard has a fountain, butterfly chairs, picnic tables, and restored Ford pickups from the 50s. The bar, an old pool supply depot, is owned, run, and populated by close friends, so whimsical events from circus performances, local film festivals, and barbecues are frequent. Live DJ nightly 10pm. Live music a few times a week, usually 9pm. $2 pints of Yuengling. Open daily 5pm-4am.

DANCE CLUBS

Club scenes are about carefree crowds, unlimited fun, and huge pocketbook damage. It can pay to call ahead to put your name on the guest list. Come after 11pm unless you crave solitude, but the real party starts around 1 or 2am. A few after-hours clubs keep at it until 5-6am. **All clubs listed are 21+ unless otherwise noted.**

Centrofly, 45 W. 21st St. (☎627-7770), between Fifth and Sixth Ave. Subway: 1, 2 to 23rd St./Seventh Ave.; 6 to 23rd St./Park Ave. S; F, V to 23rd St./Ave. of the Americas (Sixth Ave.); N, R to 23rd St./Broadway. Where the beautiful people and music aficionados come to dance to the latest house and techno, often by big-name DJs. All seating, except for champagne room, is waitress service. Cover $10-20. Mixed drinks $8-10. Open M-Sa 10pm-5am.

Filter 14, 432 W. 14th St. (☎366-5680), at Washington St. Subway: A, C, E, L to 14th St./Eighth Ave.; 1, 2, 3 to 14th St./Seventh Ave. Leave the pretension behind: everyone here is all about the music. Intimate, no-frills club with some of the best house—from progressive to experimental to soul—in the city. Funky crowd, but dress code not strictly in effect. Cover $5-12. Open Tu-Sa 10pm-4am.

Nell's, 246 W. 14th St. (☎675-1567), between Seventh and Eighth Ave. Subway: A, C, E, L to 14th St./Eighth Ave.; 1, 2, 3 to 14th St./Seventh Ave. With various themes from Cuban Salsa to Comedy, this bar/club packs in a diverse crowd. Mingle upstairs, dance downstairs. Leather couches and dark wood recall a 1930s bar. Metal detector policy in effect. No sneakers, jeans, or work boots. Hours and cover vary daily.

Spa, 76 E. 13th St. (☎388-1060), between Broadway and Fourth Ave. Subway: 4, 5, 6, L, N, Q, R, W to 14th St.-Union Sq. Don't be intimidated by the doorperson's earpiece or the Herculean-sized bouncers. Dress funky and walk in with attitude. Booths around large, lit-up dance floor; waterfall behind one of the bars. Lots of Plexiglass. Tu is a popular night. Cover Su and Tu-Th $20, F-Sa $25. Open Tu-Sa 10pm-4am.

Webster Hall, 125 E. 11th St. (☎353-1600), between Third and Fourth Ave. Subway: 4, 5, 6, L, N, Q, R, W to 14th St.-Union Sq. This popular (if somewhat mainstream) club offers 4 floors dedicated to R&B/hip-hop, 70s and 80s/Top 40, house/techno/trance, and Latin. Sports bar and coffee bar to boot. One of the only 19+ clubs in the city. Cover Th $20 for men, free for women; F-Sa $30. www.websterhall.com has guest passes that get you $10-15 off. Open Th-Sa 10pm-6am.

GAY & LESBIAN NIGHTLIFE

Gay nightlife in New York is centered in **Chelsea,** especially along Eighth Ave. in the 20s, and in the **West Village,** on Christopher St. **Park Slope** in Brooklyn is home to a large lesbian community.

GREENWICH VILLAGE

Bar d'O, 29 Bedford St. (☎627-1580), at Downing St. Subway: 1, 2 to Christopher St. Mixed, cozy, dimly-lit bar/lounge. Go early for the atmosphere, around midnight for the shows. Don't leave in the middle of a show, or you'll be in for a nasty tongue-lashing. Superb performances by drag divas Raven O and Joey Arias Tu and Sa-Su 11pm. M night is "Pleasure" for lesbians. Cover $5-7. Open Sa-Su 6pm-4am, M-F 6pm-3am.

Stonewall Inn, 53 Christopher St. (☎463-0950), at Seventh Ave. S. Subway: 1, 2 to Christopher St. Heroic bar of the 1969 Stonewall Riots. Join the diverse crowd in this renovated bar to toast the brave drag queens who fought back. 3 bars. 2-for-1 Happy Hour M-F 3-9pm. Sa-Su $4 Cosmos. Cover for special shows. Open daily 3pm-4am.

Henrietta Hudson, 438 Hudson St. (☎243-9079), between Morton and Barrow St. Subway: 1, 2 to Christopher St. A young, clean-cut lesbian crowd presides at this neighborhood bar. Also gay male and straight friendly. 2-for-1 Happy Hour M-F 4-7pm. M Karaoke, W-Sa DJ, Su Tea dance. Cover $5 Su-F after 9pm, Sa after 7pm. Open M-F 4pm-4am, Sa 1pm-4am, Su 3pm-4am.

EAST VILLAGE

The Cock, 188 Ave. A (☎946-1871), at E. 12th St. Subway: L to First Ave. A crowded boy bar with a full offering of nightly gay-oriented diversions. Call for the always changing entertainment fare. Computerized lights and "X-rated go-go boys." M drinks $3. Open Tu-Su 10pm-4am, M 9pm-4am.

Boiler Room, 86 E. 4th St. (☎254-7536), between First and Second Ave. Subway: F, V to Lower East Side-Second Ave. Popular locale catering to alluring alternative types, NYU students, and eager refugees from the sometimes stifling Chelsea clone scene. Formerly predominantly gay male bar, now more mixed crowd. Terrific jukebox and pool table give the evening a democratic spin. Open daily 4pm-4am.

Wonder Bar, 505 E. 6th St. (☎777-9105), between Ave. A and B. Subway: L to First Ave.; 6 to Astor Pl. or Bleecker St. "Mostly gay" bar with mostly college crowd. 80% male, but women welcome. 2-for-1 Happy Hour daily 6-8pm. Open daily 6pm-4am.

CHELSEA

SBNY, 50 W. 17th St. (☎691-0073), between Fifth and Sixth Ave. Subway: 1, 2 to 18th St./Seventh Ave.; F, V to 23rd St./Ave. of the Americas (Sixth Ave.). One of the most popular gay mega-bars, the newly-renamed Splash Bar New York (formerly known simply as Splash) has an enormous 2-floor complex. Cool, almost sci-fi decor provides a sleek backdrop for a very crowded scene. Drinks $4-7. Cover varies, peaking at $7. Open Su-Th 4pm-4am, F-Sa 4pm-5am.

La Nueva Escuelita, 301 W. 39th St. (☎631-0588), at Eighth Ave. Subway: A, C, E to 42nd St.-Port Authority. Latin dance club with merengue, salsa, soul, hip-hop, and arguably the best drag shows in New York. Largely, but not entirely, gay Latin crowd. F, starting at 10pm, is He/She Bar, with go-go gals, performances, and special events. Cover Th $5, F $12, Sa $15, Su 7-10pm $8, after 10pm $10. Her/She ☎631-1093; $8 before midnight, $10 after. Open Th-Sa 10pm-5am, Su 7pm-4am.

LONG ISLAND ☎631

Long Island, a sprawling suburbia stretching 120 mi. east of Manhattan, is both a home to over 2.7 million New Yorkers (excluding those who live in Queens and Brooklyn) and a sleepy summertime resort for wealthy Manhattanites. It is both expensive and difficult to navigate without a car.

PRACTICAL INFORMATION. Long Island Railroad (LIRR) services the island from Penn Station in Manhattan (34th St. at Seventh Ave.; subway: 1, 2, 3 to 34th St.-Penn Station/Seventh Ave.; A, C, E to 34th St.-Penn Station/Eighth Ave.) and stops in Jamaica, Queens (subway: E, J, Z) before proceeding to "points east." (☎718-217-5477. $4.75-15.25; lower in off-peak hours.) To reach **Fire Island,** take the LIRR to Sayville, Bayshore, or Patchogue. The **Sayville ferry** serves Cherry Grove, the Pines, and Sailor's Haven. (☎589-0810. Round-trip $9-11, under 12 $5.) The **Bay Shore ferry** sails to Fair Harbor, Ocean Beach, Ocean Bay Park, Saltaire, and Kismet. (☎516-665-3600. Round-trip $11.50, under 12 $5.50.) The **Patchogue ferry** shuttles to Davis Park and Watch Hill. (☎516-475-1665. Round-trip $11, under 12 $4.25.) The Hamptons are accessible by LIRR or by car. Take the Long Island Expwy. to Exit 70, go south to Rte. 27 (Sunset Hwy. or Montauk Hwy.), and head east to Montauk (approx. 50 mi. on Rte. 27). Towns are located either directly off, or on, the highway. **Long Island Convention and Visitors Bureau** has four locations throughout the island. Call ☎951-2423 or 877-386-6654 for locations and hours. **Area Code:** 631 and 516. In listings, 631 unless otherwise noted.

FIRE ISLAND

A gay hot spot off Long Island's shores, Fire Island is a 32 mi. long barrier island buffering the South Shore from the roaring waters of the Atlantic. Cars are allowed only on the easternmost and westernmost tips of the island; there are no streets, only "walks." A hip countercultural enclave during the 1960s and home to the disco scene of the 1970s, the island's communities still party loud.

Two prominent Fire Island resort hamlets, **Cherry Grove** and **Fire Island Pines** (called **"the Pines"**), host largely gay communities—and parties that rage late into the night. Crowded "streets," or wooden pathways, border spectacular Atlantic Ocean beaches. Weekdays provide an opportunity to enjoy the island's beauty and charm in a low-key setting, Thursdays and Sundays offer an ideal balance of sanity and scene, while Fridays and Saturday see mounting crowds and prices.

Gay nightlife on Fire Island has a very established rhythm that may be confusing to newcomers. Since neither Cherry Grove nor the Pines are very big, it's best just to ask around, either at your hotel or restaurant. More commercial than the Pines, the roadless Grove is lined with narrow, raised boardwalks leading to the small, uniformly shingled houses overflowing with men. Lesbian couples, however, make up the majority of the town's population. A night in Cherry Grove usually begins at the **Ice Palace,** attached to the **Cherry Grove Beach Hotel,** where you can disco until dawn. (☎597-6600. Open daily Sept.-June noon-10pm; July-Aug. noon-4am). Most go to the Pines for late-night partying; you can catch a water taxi from the docks at Cherry Grove, or walk 10min. up the beach. The Pines has traditionally looked down its nose at its uninhibited neighbor. Houses here are spacious and often stunningly modern. Unfortunately, the Pines' active and upscale nighttime scene has a bit of a secret club feel to it—you need to be in the know or somehow be able to look like you are. **Tea Dance** (a.k.a. "Low Tea", 5-8pm) takes place inside and around the Yacht Club bar/club beside the Botel hotel (☎597-6500). Move on to disco **High Tea** at 8pm in the **Pavilion** (☎597-6131), the premier disco in Cherry Grove, but make sure you have somewhere to disappear to during "disco naptime" (after 10pm). You can unabashedly dance until dawn at the **Island Club and Bistro** (☎597-6001), better known as the Sip-and-Twirl. The Pavilion becomes hot again late-night on weekends, including Sundays during the summer.

THE HAMPTONS & MONTAUK

West Hampton, Southampton, Bridgehampton, and East Hampton make up the entity known as **the Hamptons,** where the upper crust of society roam the sidewalks before heading to the beach for the afternoon. As a result of the clientele, the prices are high here. Try going to **Montauk,** at the eastern tip of Long Island, for slightly cheaper accommodations. While lodging anywhere on the South Fork requires some research and often reservations, clean rooms can be had at **Tipperary Inn ❺,** 432 West Lake Ln., accessible via the S-94 bus to Montauk Dock. The Inn provides A/C, TV, phone, and fridge. (☎668-2010. Rooms for 2-6 people summer $125-160; low-season $75-95.)

Many beaches in the Hamptons require a permit to park, but anyone can walk on for free. Sights include the **Montauk Point Lighthouse and Museum,** off Rte. 27 at the far eastern tip of the island, which was built in 1796 by special order of President George Washington. (☎668-2544. Open June-Sept. M-F and Su 10:30am-6pm, Sa 10:30am-7:30pm; other months call for info. $6, seniors $5, under 12 $3.) Whaling buffs shouldn't miss the **Sag Harbor Whaling Museum,** at the corner of Main and Garden St. in Sag Harbor. (☎725-0770. Open May-Sept. M-Sa 10am-5pm, Su 1-5pm. $3, seniors $2, ages 6-13 $1. Tours by appointment $2.)

THE CATSKILLS ☎845

According to the legend, the Catskills, ideal for quiet solitude and rest, cradled Rip Van Winkle during his century-long repose. In an anomalous blip in the tranquility of the mountain region, the infamous Woodstock rock festival was brought to the small town of Bethel, NY in 1969 bringing the town celebrity status overnight. Today, following age old tradition, the region's best attractions are the miles of pristine hiking and skiing trails, the small villages, and the crystal-clear fishing streams of the state-managed **Catskill Forest Preserve.**

PRACTICAL INFORMATION. Traveling from **I-87,** follow **Rte. 28 W** for the easiest way to explore the region. **Adirondack/Pine Hill Trailways** provides excellent service through the Catskills. The main stop is in **Kingston,** 400 Washington Ave., on the corner of Front St. (☎331-0744 or 800-858-8555. Ticket office open M-F 5:45am-11:30pm, Sa-Su 6:15am-11:30pm.) Buses run to **New York City** (2hr.; 10-15 per day; $20). Other stops in the area include **Hunter, Pine Hill, Delhi,** and **Woodstock;** each connects with **Albany, New York City, Copperstown,** and **Utica.** Two stationary **tourist cabooses** dispense info, including the extremely useful *Ulster County: Catskills Region Travel Guide;* cabooses are located at the traffic circle in Kingston and on Rte. 209 in Ellenville. (Open May-Oct. daily 9am-5pm, but hours vary occasionally depending on volunteer availability.) **Area code:** 845, unless otherwise noted.

MID-ATLANTIC

CATSKILL FOREST PRESERVE

The nearly 300,000 acre **Catskill Forest Preserve** contains many small towns and outdoor adventure opportunities. Ranger stations distribute free permits for **backcountry camping,** which are necessary for stays over three days or in groups of 10 or more. Hiking trails are for the most part maintained, but some of the lesser used paths sometimes fall into disrepair. The lean-tos are also maintained, but can become crowded. For more info, call the **Dept. of Environmental Conservation** (☎256-3000). Most of the **campgrounds** sit at gorgeous trailheads that mark great day-long jaunts. Reservations are vital in summer, especially on weekends. The **Office of Parks** (☎518-474-0456) distributes brochures on the campgrounds. Required permits for **fishing** (out-of-state residents $15 per day, $25 per week) are available in sporting goods stores and at many campgrounds. **Ski season** runs from November to April, with slopes down numerous mountainsides along Rte. 28 and Rte. 23A.

MT. TREMPER

Kaleidoworld, in Catskill Corners on Rte 28, is a blast to the past through the reflective lenses of the two largest kaleidoscopes in the world, the larger of the two measuring a whopping 60 ft. The 5-10min. of glimmering images flitting around in your head will leave ex-flower-children muttering "I can see the music!" (☎688-5800. Open Su-Th 10am-5pm, F-Sa 10am-7pm. $8 for both kaleidoscopes, $ 5 for one; seniors $7/5; under 12 free.) The **Kenneth L. Wilson Campground ❶** has 76 sites nestled in a tranquil forest. The small lake in the park allows for canoeing, kayaking, and the use of paddle boats as well as providing a picturesque panorama on a mountainous background. From Rte. 28 exit onto Rte. 212. From Rte. 212 make a hard right onto Wittenburg Rd./County Rte. 40 and follow Rte. 40 5 mi. to the campground. (☎679-7020. Registration 8am-9pm. Reservations recommended for the weekend. Sites $17. $2.75 registration fee. Day use $6 per car, $1 on foot or bike. Canoes and kayaks $15 per 4 hr. Paddleboats $5 per hour. Lifeguard on duty M-F 9:30am-5:45pm, Sa-Su 9:30am-6:45pm.)

PHOENICIA

Phoenicia is a central, small town in the Catskills. The **Esopus Creek,** to the west, has great trout fishing, and **The Town Tinker,** 10 Bridge St., rents inner tubes for river-riding through the small ripples and rapids. (☎688-5553. Inner tubes $10 per day, with seat $12. Driver's license or $15-50 deposit required. Tube taxi transportation $5 per trip on either the railroad, see below, or a bus. Life jackets required $3. Wetsuit $15. Package with seated tube, life jacket, and 1 time transport $20; package plus wetsuit $30. Open mid-May to Sept. daily 9am-6pm; last rental 3:30-4pm.) A drier and more sedate alternative for seeing the countryside is the wheezing, 100-year-old **Catskill Mountain Railroad,** which follows Esopus Creek for three scenic mi. from Bridge St. to Mt. Pleasant. (☎688-7400. 40min. Runs Sa-Su and holidays, 1 per hr. May-Sept. 11am-5pm, Sept.-Oct. noon-4pm. $5, round-trip $8; ages 4-11 any ride $5.) At the 65 ft. high **Sundance Rappel Tower,** off Rte. 214, visitors work their way back down to the solid ground under their own steam power. (☎688-5640. 4 levels of lessons; beginner 3-4hr., $22. Must be at least group of 8 for a lesson. Reservations required.) A 12 mi. round-trip hike to the 4180 ft. summit of **Slide Mt.** lends a view of New Jersey, Pennsylvania, and the Hudson Highlands; for a trip to the peak, head to Woodland Valley campground (see below). Nestled in the woods, the **Zen Mountain Monastery,** off Rte. 40 north of Rte. 28, houses 35-40 Buddhists living and working together while partaking in Zen training. (☎688-2228. Office open Tu 2-5pm, W-Sa 8:30am-5pm. Meditation training sessions W 7pm and Su 8:45am. Free, but $5 suggested donation on Su because lunch is provided.) Customers line up outside of **Sweet Sue's,** on Main St., on Saturday mornings to sample her thick french toast and stacks of nine inch pancakes ($7-9). (☎688-7852. Open Th-M 7am-3pm.)

With 72 sites, the secluded **Woodland Valley campground ❶,** on Woodland Valley Rd. off High St., 7 mi. southeast of Phoenicia, has a small stream, showers, and access to many hiking trails. (☎688-7647. Office open daily 8am-9pm. Open late May-early Oct. Sites $15. $2.75 registration fee.) Surrounded by mountains and decorated with delicate paintings on the exterior walls, the **Cobblestone Motel ❸,** on Rte. 214, has friendly managers, an outdoor pool, and newly renovated rooms with refrigerators. (☎688-7871. Queen $56; queen and single $61; 2 doubles or queens with futon and kitchen $85-95; 2 bedroom cottage with kitchen $109. 3 bedroom cottage with kitchen $129.)

PINE HILL

Pine Hill sits near **Belleayre Mt.,** which offers hiking trails "**Sky Rides**" on a chairlift to the summit during the summer, as well as both downhill and cross-country ski slopes when the snow starts to fall. (☎254-5600 or 800-942-6904. Lift tickets M-F $33, Sa-Su $42; ages 13-22 and 62+ $30/34. Equipment rental $21. Sky ride $8, ages 13-17 and seniors $5. Open mid June-mid Oct. Sa-Su 10am-6pm.) **Belleayre Music Festival,** held at the Belleayre Mt. ski resort, hosts a series of classical, jazz, country, opera, and folk concerts in July and August. (☎800-942-6904. Lawn tickets $12-15, occasional free concerts.) The **Belleayre Beach at Pine Hills,** ½ mi. south of Pine Hills on Rte. 28, provides abundant warm weather recreation including swimming from a sand beach, hiking, volleyball, and a playground. (☎800-942-6904. Open late May-mid June Sa-Su 10am-6pm, mid June-Sept. M-F 10am-6pm, Sa-Su 10am-7:30pm. Beach has lifeguards while park is open. $6 per car. $1 per person on foot.) Having undergone major renovations recently, **Belleayre Hostel ❶** is a lodging bargain. Some rooms have their own TV and kitchens but shared amenities include-kitchen access, picnic area, grill, trail maps, outdoor fire place stocked with wood, and sporting equipment. Also shared is the large recreation building with a pool table, table tennis, a big screen TV, Nintendo, a computer with games and Internet access, and an air hockey table. Follow the small green "Hostel" sign from Main St._(☎254-4200. Laundry $2. Check-in 4-11pm. Check-out 11am. Reservations strongly recommended. Bunks $20, under 17 accompanied by adult $10; private/family rooms for 3-8 $50-120 depending upon the number of bunks in the room; cabins for up to 4 $75-90; brand-new cabins with kitchenettes for up to 8 $150; cabin for up to 8 with full kitchen and wrap around porch $200.)

ALBANY ☎518

While Albany—the capital of New York State and the oldest continuous European settlement in the original 13 colonies—proclaims itself "the most livable city in America," it is hardly a booming tourist town. On weekdays, downtown shops and restaurants thrive on the purses of politicians, but weekends find the plaza and capital buildings deserted.

PRACTICAL INFORMATION. Amtrak, 525 East St., across the Hudson from downtown Albany (☎462-5710; station open M-F 4:30am-midnight, Sa-Su 5am-midnight; ticket counter M-F 4:30am-10pm, Sa-Su 5am-10pm), has service to Buffalo (5hr., 4 per day, $50-79) and New York City (2½hr., 12-13 per day, $43-50). **Greyhound,** 34 Hamilton St. (☎434-8461 or ☎800-231-2222; station open 24hr, ticket window open daily 12:05am-11:30pm), runs buses to Buffalo (6hr., $51) and New York City (3hr., $32). *Be careful here at night.* From the same station, **Adirondack Trailways** (☎436-9651 or 800-855-8555) connects to Kingston (1hr., 7 per day, $10) and Lake Placid (4hr., 1-2 per day, $27). For local travel, the **Capital District Transportation Authority** (**CDTA;** ☎482-8822) serves Albany ($1), Schenectady ($1.35), and Troy ($1.25). Schedules are available at the Amtrak and bus stations. The **Albany Visitors Center,** 25 Quackenbush Sq., at Clinton Ave. and Broadway, runs trolley tours of downtown and provides self-guided walking tours. (☎434-0405; www.albany.org. Open M-F 9am-4pm, Sa-Su 10am-4pm. Trolley tours July-Aug. 1 per day; time varies; arrive 20min. early. Trolley tours $10, seniors $5.) **Internet Access: Albany Public Library,** 161 Washington St. (☎427-4300. Open June-Sept. M-Th 9am-9pm, F 9am-6pm, Sa 9am-5pm, Sept.-June also open Su 1pm-5pm.) **Post Office:** 45 Hudson Ave. (☎462-1359. Open M-F 8am-5:30pm.) **Postal Code:** 12207. **Area Code:** 518.

ACCOMMODATIONS & FOOD. Pine Haven Bed & Breakfast ❸, 531 Western Ave., is truly a haven for weary travelers. Standing at the convergence of Madison and Western Ave., with ample parking in the rear, the large Victorian house offers gorgeous rooms with phone, TV, and A/C in an inviting setting. (☎482-1574. Breakfast included. Reservations required. Rooms $59-89.) **Red Carpet Inn ❸,** 500 Northern Blvd., located between the downtown and the airport, provides laundry facilities and clean rooms with A/C and cable TV. (☎462-5562. Rooms $50-55.) **Thompson's Lake State Park ❶,** on Rte. 157 north of East Berne, 18 mi. southwest of

Albany, offers the closest camping, with 140 sites within easy walking distance of a lake with fishing, boating, and a sandy swimming beach. Follow I-85 out of Albany, turn right on Rte. 157, and look for signs. (☎872-1674. Sites $16 for the first night, $13 each night after. Row boats $5 per hr., $20 per day. Paddle boats $4 per 30min. Lifeguard on duty June-Sept. M-F 10am-6pm, Sa-Su 10am-7pm.)

Two areas have good concentrations of restaurants. **Lark Street** is full of ethnic eats and coffeeshops with a young, college-town atmosphere, while **South Pearl Street** is dotted with traditional American eateries. Around lunch time the portable lunch carts that set up shop along State St. near the Empire State Plaza and the State Capitol are a good source of inexpensive grub. In the city proper, the best eating option involves doing not-so-hard time with pizzas, sandwiches, and burgers alongside Al Capone Amber Ale at the **Big House Brewing Company ❷,** 90 N. Pearl St., at Sheridan St. (☎445-2739. Entrees $6-7. Happy Hour 4-7pm. Live bands F. Kitchen open Tu-W 4-9pm, Th-Sa 4-10:30pm. Bar open Tu-W until 1am, Th-Sa until 3am; later depending on crowds.) Located inside the Honest Weight Food Co-op, the **Stone Soup Deli ❶,** 484 Central Ave., invites visitors to wash down one of its healthy sandwich and salad combinations ($4.75) with one of a variety of $2-3 organic shakes. (☎482-2667. Open M-F 7am-8pm, Sa 7am-6pm, Su 10am-6pm.)

SIGHTS & ENTERTAINMENT. Albany's sights are centered around the **Rockefeller Empire State Plaza,** between State and Madison St., a modernist Stonehenge that took 900,000 cubic yards of concrete and 232,000 tons of steel to create. The plaza houses state offices, a bus terminal, a post office, multiple information centers, a large display of modern art, and a food court. (Parking $2 Sa-Su all day and M-F after 2pm.) The New York State Information Center, in the north concourse, is the departure spot for **Plaza Tours** which visit the buildings, memorials, and certain works of art. (Information center: ☎474-2418. Open M-F 8:30am-5pm. Tours: ☎473-7521. M-F 11am and 1pm. Free.) The huge flying saucer at one end of the Plaza is the **Empire Center for the Performing Arts,** also known as "The Egg," a venue for professional theater, dance, and concerts. (☎473-1845. Box office open June-Sept. M-F 10am-4pm; Sept.-late May M-F 10am-5pm, Sa noon-3pm. $8-32.) Across the street, the huge **New York State Museum** has in-depth exhibits examining the state's history, people, and wildlife. (☎474-5877. Open daily 9:30am-5pm. Donations accepted.) Between the museum and the Egg, an elevator ride up the 42 floors of the **Corning Tower** provides a 60 mi. view on clear days. (☎474-2418. Open daily 10am-2:30pm. Photo ID required. Free.) The **Capitol Repertory Theatre,** 111 N. Pearl St., stages some of Albany's best theater including both plays and musicals. (☎445-7469. Box office open M-Sa 10am-5pm. $31-39.) Offering concerts, plays, comedy, and musicals, the variety of the **Palace Theatre,** 19 Clinton St., can't be beaten. (☎465-4663. Box office open M-F 10am-6pm; Sept.-June Sa 10am-2pm. $15-60.) In use since 1899, the magnificent **New York State Capitol,** adjacent to the Plaza, has provided New York politicians with luxury quarters for over a century. Tours leave from the New York Travel Information Center; no backpacks allowed on tour. (☎474-2418. Tours begin M-F 10am, noon, 2, 3pm, Sa-Su 11am, 1pm, 3pm. Free.)

Bounded by State St. and Madison Ave. north of downtown, **Washington Park** has tulip gardens, tennis courts, and plenty of room for celebrations and performances. The **Park Playhouse** stages free musical theater in the pastoral setting from July to mid-August. (☎434-2035. Open Tu-Su 8pm.) Folks come **Alive at Five** to free concerts at the **Tricentennial Plaza,** across from Fleet Bank on Broadway or in the ampitheater in the **Hudson Riverfront Park.** (☎434-2032. Concerts June-July Th 5-8pm.) The biggest summer event, the annual **Tulip Festival** (☎434-2032; May 7-9, 2004), in Washington Park, celebrates the town's Dutch heritage and the blooming of the over 100,000 tulips with song, dance, fine arts, crafts, a Tulip Queen crowning, and food vendors. For more events, call the **Albany Alive Line** (☎434-1217).

Biking aficionados traverse the **Mohawk-Hudson Bikeway** (☎386-2225), which passes along old railroad grades and canal towpaths as it weaves through the capitol area. Maps available at the Visitors Center. For rentals, check out the **Down Tube Cycle Shop,** 466 Madison Ave. (☎434-1711. Open Apr.-Sept. M-F 11am-7pm, Sa 10am-5pm; Sept.-Apr. M-F 10am-6pm. Full-day $25, 2 days $35.)

COOPERSTOWN ☎607

For earlier generations, Cooperstown recalled images of Leatherstocking, the frontiersman hero of novelist James Fenimore Cooper, who roamed the woods around Lake Otsego in his youth. Tiny Cooperstown now evokes a different source of American legend—baseball. Tourists file through the Baseball Hall of Fame, eat in baseball-themed restaurants, and sleep in baseball-themed motels.

PRACTICAL INFORMATION. Cooperstown is accessible from **I-90** and **I-88** via **Rte. 28.** The town is only four blocks by five blocks and is centered around **Main St.** which is chock full of baseball memorabilia shops and restaurants. Street parking is rare in Cooperstown; park in the three free lots just outside of town on Maple St. off Glen Ave. (Rte. 28), Rte. 28 south of town, or adjacent to the Fenimore Art Museum. From these lots, it's an easy 5-20min. walk to Main St. (Rte. 31). **Trolleys** also leave from the lots every 20min., dropping riders off at major stops in town, including the **Hall of Fame,** the **Farmer** and **Fenimore museums, Doubleday Field,** the **Pine Hall Trailways** stop, and the **Chamber of Commerce.** (Trolleys run late June to early Sept. daily 8:30am-9pm; early June to mid-June and mid-Sept. to mid-Oct. Sa-Su 8:30am-6pm. All-day pass $2, children $1.) **Pine Hall Trailways** (☎547-2519 or 800-858-8555) picks up visitors at AAA Tri-County Motor Club at the corner of Elm St. and Chestnut St. and travels to Kingston (3½hr., 2 per day, $22) and New York City (5½hr., 2 per day, $43). **Cooperstown Area Chamber of Commerce and Visitor Information Center,** 31 Chestnut St., on Rte. 28 near Main St., proffers information about the sights in the area. (☎547-9571; www.cooperstownchamber.org. Generally open June-Sept. daily 9am-7pm, Sept-June daily 9am-5pm; hours vary, call ahead.) **Internet Access: Village Library of Cooperstown,** 22 Main St. (☎547-8344. Open M-T and Th-F 9am-5pm, W 9am-8pm, Sa 10am-2pm.) **Post Office:** 40 Main St. (☎547-2311; open M-F 8:30am-5pm, Sa 8:30am-noon). **Postal Code:** 13326. **Area Code:** 607.

ACCOMMODATIONS. Lodging is expensive year round, but accommodation seekers really strike out during peak season between late June and mid-Sept. The cheapest options are to camp or travel in the low-season when many motels and guest houses slash rates by $20-50. The **Mohican Motel ❹,** 90 Chestnut St., offers well-kept rooms, cable TV, and A/C at relatively affordable prices. (☎547-5101. 2- to 6-person rooms late June to early Sept. Su-F $84-104, Sa $129-151; Apr. to late June and early Sept-late Oct. Su-F $56-62, Sa $76-82.) The beautiful pine forests and lakeside view of **Glimmerglass State Park ❶,** 8 mi. north of Cooperstown on Rte. 31 on the north shore of Lake Otsego, with 43 campsites, including 4 handicapped sites, make it an ideal camping location. Daytime visitors and campers alike can hike and bike in the 600 rolling acres of forests or swim, fish, and boat in the cool water. (☎547-8662. Park open 8am-dark. Showers, dumping station; no hookups. Beach opens at 11am. Lifeguard on duty 11am-7pm. Day-use $7 per vehicle. Sites $13. $2.75 registration fee.) **Cooperstown Beaver Valley Campground ❶** has wooded sites, cabins, a pool, recreation area, small pond, baseball diamond, and boat rentals. Drive south of town 5 mi.

on Rte. 28 and follow the signs. (☎293-8131 or 800-726-7314. Sites $28-30, with hookup $31. Cabins without indoor plumbing or linens $58-63. Boat rentals $5 per hour, $20 per day.)

FOOD. The **Doubleday Cafe ❶,** 93 Main St., serves all three meals amidst a mix of eye-catching memorabilia of the Babe and other baseball greats. (☎547-5468. Omelette with toast $2-4. Chili $3. Open June-Sept. Su-Th 7am-10pm, F-Sa 7am-11pm; Sept.-June Su-Th 7am-9pm, F-Sa 7am-10pm; bar closes after kitchen.) For elegant but affordable dining, **Hoffman Lane Bistro ❸,** 2 Hoffman Ln., off Main St. across from the Hall of Fame, has airy rooms with tasteful artwork and checkered black-and-white tablecloths. Their gourmet appetizers and sandwiches ($6-8) leave customers rooting for more. (☎547-7055. Entrees $13-20. Kitchen open daily June to late Aug. 12pm-3pm and 5pm-10pm. Sept.-June 5pm-10pm; bar open Su-Th until 1am, F-Sa until 2am.) A Cooperstown institution, **Schneider's Bakery ❶,** 157 Main St., has been satisfying those with a sweet tooth and creating $0.45 "old-fashioneds"—doughnuts less greasy and a tad smaller than their commercial cousins—since 1887. (☎547-9631. Open M-Sa 6:30am-5:30pm.)

SIGHTS. With almost 400,000 visitors per year, the **National Baseball Hall of Fame and Museum,** on Main St., is an enormous, glowing monument to America's national pastime. Containing 35,000 pieces of memorabilia, the building is home to priceless artifacts—everything from the bat with which Babe Ruth hit his "called shot" home run in the 1932 World Series to the infamous jersey worn by 3 ft. 7in. St. Louis Brown Eddie Gaedel. The museum begins with exhibits tracing the game to ancient Egyptian rituals but also features a 13min. multimedia tribute to the sport, a candid display on African-American ballplayers' experiences in the Negro Leagues, and the recently added "Women in Baseball" exhibits. (☎547-7200 or 888-425-5633; www.baseballhalloffame.org. Open Apr.-Oct. daily 9am-9pm; Oct.-Apr. 9am-5pm. $9.50, seniors $8, ages 7-12 $4.)

The biggest event of the year, with over 20,000 visitors expected, is the annual **Hall of Fame Induction Weekend.** On either the last weekend of July or the first weekend of August new members of the Hall Of Fame are inducted with appropriate pomp and circumstance. Ceremonies take place on the field adjacent to the **Clark Sports Center** on Susquehanna Ave., a 10min. walk south from the Hall. Admission to the event is free; the autographs of the 40-50 Hall of Famers who return for the event are not. The annual **Hall of Fame Game** between two rotating Major League teams doesn't just have to be in your field of dreams. Held in the delightfully intimate Doubleday Field the game is played every June. Both events, but especially the induction weekend, see enormous crowds, so rooms must be reserved months in advance.

Overlooking a pristine lawn and Lake Otsego, **Fenimore Art Museum,** on Lake Rd./Rte. 80 about one mi. from Main St., houses a collection of American folk art, Hudson River School paintings, James Fenimore Cooper memorabilia, unusual traveling exhibits, and an impressive array of Native American art. (☎547-1400 or 888-547-1450; www.nysha.org. Open June-Oct. daily 10am-5pm; Apr.-May and Oct.-Dec. Tu-Su 10am-4pm. $9, seniors $8, ages 7-12 $4.) Jump in a time machine by walking across the street to the **Farmer's Museum,** which contains a complete 1850's farming village with live demonstrations as well as museum displays about farming past and present. (☎547-1450; www.farmersmuseum.org. Open daily June-Oct. 10am-5pm; Apr.-May and Oct.-Dec. Tu-Su 10am-4pm. $9, seniors $8, ages 7-12 $4.) Nine mi. north of Cooperstown on Lake Rd./Rte. 80, the **Glimmerglass Opera** stages summer performances specializing in new and little known works as well as new takes on well known operas. (☎547-2255. M-Th $28-92. F-Su $56-104.)

ITHACA & THE FINGER LAKES ☎607

According to Iroquois legend, the Great Spirit laid his hand upon the earth to bless it, and the impression of his fingers resulted in the Finger Lakes: Canandaigua, Cayuga, Seneca, and eight others. Regardless of the lake's origins, the results are spectacular with not only lakes but over 1,000 waterfalls to feed them; 150 of those which are within 10 mi. of Ithaca. Students from Ithaca College and Cornell University tote bookbags amongst Ithaca's ruggedly carved gorges and cascading streams, while north of Ithaca, a divine nectar flows—the rich wine of the area's acclaimed vineyards.

PRACTICAL INFORMATION. Downtown Ithaca centers around **Ithaca Commons,** a pedestrian area lined with shops and restaurants. Atop a steep hill, **Collegetown** is an area of hole-in-the-wall bars, take out restaurants and diners adjacent to Cornell's campus and overflowing with students. **Ithaca Bus Terminal,** 710 W. State St., at Rte. 13 (☎272-7930; open daily 6:30am-6pm), houses **Short Line** (☎277-8800) with service to New York (5hr., 8 per day, $39) and **Greyhound** (☎272-7930), with service to: Buffalo (3½hr., 3 per day, $29); New York City (5hr., 3 per day, $39); and Philadelphia (8hr., 3 per day, $54). Although Ithaca sits not far from the base of Cayuga Lake, **Tompkins Consolidated Area Transit (T-CAT;** ☎277-7433) is the only choice for getting there without a car. Buses stop at Ithaca Commons; westbound buses also stop on Seneca St. and eastbound buses stop on Green. (Buses run daily; times vary by route. $1.50-3, students and seniors $0.75.) The **Ithaca/Tompkins County Convention and Visitors Bureau,** 904 E. Shore Dr., has the best map of the area ($3), hotel and B&B listings, and brochures. While there, make sure to pick up a copy of the invaluable *Ithaca Gorges & Waterfalls* guide containing listings for outdoors recreation, lodgings, restaurants, maps, and much more._(☎272-1313 or 800-284-8422. Open mid-May-early Sept. M-F 9am-5pm, Sa 10am-5pm, Su 10am-4pm; mid-Sept. to early May M-F 9am-5pm. Unmanned Visitor's Center in the Clinton House, 116 N. Cayuga St. Open M-F 10am-5:30pm, Sa 10am-2pm, 3pm-5pm.) **Internet Access: Tompkins County Public Library,** 101 E. Green St. (☎272-4557. Open Sept.-June M-Th 10am-9pm, F-Sa 10am-5pm, Su 1pm-5pm. July-Aug. closed weekends.) **Post Office:** 213 N. Tioga St., at E. Buffalo. (☎800-275-8777. Open M-F 8:30am-5pm, Sa 8:30am-1pm.) **Postal Code:** 14850. **Area Code:** 607.

ACCOMMODATIONS. Budget accommodations are not too hard to come by in Ithaca. Camping in one of the nearby state parks or negotiating a good price at a bed & breakfast are usually the best deals in town, but the relatively inexpensive roadside motels that line the many roads entering and leaving the city are also a good option. The Visitor's Bureau can provide more in depth information about all of these lodging options. By far the best bargain in Ithaca is the **Elmshade Guest House ❷,** 402 S. Albany St., at Center St. just five blocks from Ithaca Commons. The tasty continental breakfast that often earns mention in the guest register along with impeccably clean and well-decorated rooms and cable TV make for a very pleasant stay. From the bus station, walk up State St. and turn right onto Albany St. (☎273-1707. Reservations recommended. Singles with shared bath $45; doubles $60-65; apartment with kitchenette $85.) Nearby state parks offer camping as well as day use. On lake Cayuga and enclosing a waterfall plummeting 215 ft., a distance greater than the Niagara Falls drop, **Taughannock Falls State Park ❶,** north on Rte. 89, has one of the best locations in the area. (☎387-6739. Sites $13, $19 with electricity. Cabins for 4 people $40 per night, $160 per week. $2.75 registration fee. Day use $7.) The huge foaming waterfall commands the entrance to the campsite at **Buttermilk Falls ❶,** on Rte. 13 south of Ithaca. The closest park to Ithaca, Buttermilk has 46 sites and miles of trails following Buttermilk Creek through the woods. (☎273-5761. Sites $13. $2.75 registration fee. Day use $7.)

FOOD. Restaurants in Ithaca center on Ithaca Commons and Collegetown. With a new menu everyday and ethnic nights on Sundays with food exclusively from one country, **Moosewood Restaurant ❷,** 215 N. Cayuga, at Seneca St. in the Dewitt Mall, features an amazing selection of wonderfully fresh and creative vegetarian options. (☎273-9610. Lunch $6.50-7; dinner $10-16. Live music 3-4 nights weekly. Open Sept.-May M-Th 11:30am-3pm and 5:30pm-8:30pm, F and Sa 11:30am-3pm and 5:30pm-9pm, Su 5:30pm-8:30pm; June-Oct. M-Th 11:30am-3pm and 5:30pm-9pm, F-Sa 11:30am-3pm and 6pm-9:30pm, Su 5:30pm-8:30pm.) Tasting is the theme at **Just a Taste ❸,** 116 N. Aurora St., near Ithaca Commons. Wines are served as quarter glasses in groups of 4-6 wines known as a flight ($6-11). A smorgasbord of tempting *tapas* ($2.50-7.50 each), desserts, and beers, which can be enjoyed on the outdoor patio during the summer months, rounds out the menu. (☎277-9463. Open Su-Th 2:30pm-4:30pm and 5:30-10pm, F-Sa 2:30pm-4:30pm and 5:30-11pm.) **Kope's Garage ❷,** 110 N. Aurora St. is the perfect place to park yourself for a meal among the many license plates and posters of ancient cars. (☎273-9108. Sandwiches $5-7. Entrees $10-17. Open M-Th 11:30am-9:30pm, F-Sa 11:30am-10:30pm.) At **Gino's NY Pizzeria**,106 N. Aurora St., a 16oz. soda and the two largest slices of pizza you will ever attempt to consume ($3) could keep you going all the way to New York. (☎277-2777. Open Su-Th 10:30am-10pm, F-Sa 10:30am-2am.)

SIGHTS. **Cornell University,** youngest of the Ivy League schools, sits on a steep hill in Ithaca between two tremendous gorges. Accessed down a steep flight of steps across University Ave. from the Johnson Art Museum, the suspension bridge above Fall Creek provides a heart-pounding walk above one gorge, while the **College Avenue Stone Arch Bridge** above Cascadilla Creek has a brilliant sunset view. The **Information and Referral Center,** in the 2nd floor lobby of Day Hall on East Ave. offers **campus tours** and has info on campus sights and activities. (☎254-4636. Open M-F 8am-5pm; telephone staffed Sa 8am-5pm and Su noon-1pm. Tours Apr.-Nov. M-F 9, 11am, 1, and 3pm; Sa 9am, 10:30am, and 1pm; Su 1pm. Dec.-Mar. daily 1pm.) The funky, box-like cement edifice rising from the top of the hill houses Cornell's **Herbert F. Johnson Museum of Art,** at the corner of University Ave. and Central Ave. With works by Giacometti, Matisse, O'Keeffe, Picasso, and Degas, the collection, although small, is impressive; the 5th floor Asian art exhibit and the rooftop sculpture garden both yield amazing views. (☎255-6464. Open Tu-Su 10am-5pm. Free. If using museum parking, a permit obtained from the front desk is required during the museum's hours of operation. Parking is metered, but the permit is free.) The extensive **botanical gardens** and **arboretum** that compose the **Cornell Plantations** lie serenely in the northeast corner of campus. Visitors can ramble through the Slim Jim Woods, drive to the Grossman Pond, or take the short hike to a lookout point that provides a view of campus and the surrounding area. (☎255-3020. Open daily sunrise to sunset. Free. Free parking permit that can be obtained in the visitors center is required at the botanical gardens M-F 8:30am-4:30pm.) An amble around the 1½ mi. **Founder's Loop** takes you through the heart of campus. The *Passport to the Trails of Tompkins County* ($1), listing 14 trails and available from the Visitors Bureau, is a comprehensive guide to navigating the landscape. A community gathering place on weekends, the **Ithaca Farmer's Market**, 3rd St. off Rt. 13, has much more than just produce under its eves. Ethnic food stalls, fresh produce, cider tastings, and hand-crafted furniture are among the products brought to market from vendors up to 30 mi. from the city. (☎273-7109. Open Apr.-Dec. Sa 9am-2pm; June-Oct. Su 10am-2pm.)

The fertile soil and cool climate of the Finger Lakes area has made it the heart of New York's wine industry. Designated **wine trails** provide opportunities for wine tasting and vineyard touring—locals say that the fall harvest is the best time to visit. (For more information contact the Ithaca Chamber of Commerce, see p. 258) The closest trail to Ithaca, the **Cayuga Trail** (☎800-684-5217; www.cayugawinetrail.com), contains 15 vineyards, 11 of which are located along Rte. 89 between Seneca Falls and Ithaca. Other wineries are found on the **Seneca Lake Trail** (☎877-536-2717; www.senecalakewine.com), with 25 wineries encircling the lake on Rte. 414 (east side) and 14 (west side). The **Keuka Trail** (☎800-440-4898; www.keukawinetrail.com), with eight wineries along Rte. 54 and 76, is also easily accessible from Ithaca. Some wineries offer free picnic facilities and tours. All give free tastings; some require purchase of a glass for a nominal charge.

NIGHTLIFE. Collegetown, centering on College Ave., harbors student hangouts and provides access to a romantic path along the gorge starting near the College Ave. Stone Arch Bridge. Split down the middle, **Stella's,** 403 College Ave., has two entrances: one leads to a red-walled cafe serving decadent drinks such as "The Tasteful Hedonist" with 2 shots of espresso, steamed milk, swiss chocolate and a cherry ($4); the other heads to a blue-walled jazz bar with funky countertops. (☎277-1490. Food served daily 11am-12:30am. Coffeeshop open summer M-F 6am-1am, Sa-Su 10am-1am. Jazz bar open daily 11am-1am. No cover.) In an ironic twist, the **Rongovian Embassy to the USA ("The Rongo"),** on Rte. 96 in Trumansburg about 10 mi. north of Ithaca, is a music club serving Mexican food (entrees under $11) and playing local music worth the drive. A huge wall map allows travelers to plot a trip to "Nearvarna," "Fat City," and other fictitious destinations in the nation of Rongovia. (☎387-3334. Beer $2.50-3.75. Cover $5-free. Bar open F-Sa 6pm-1am; live music occasionally on other nights.) Housed in a traditional art house theater and fitting for the campus of an Ivy League University the **Cornell Cinema,** 104 Willard Straight Hall on the Cornell campus, shows old films, new indies, and the occasional blockbuster. (☎255-3522. Open late Aug. to late July, 1-2 showings nightly. $6, undergraduates and seniors $5, graduate students and under 13 $4.) With red and purple plush curtains and masks on the walls, it's Mardi Gras all year long at **Maxie's Supper Club,** 635 W State St. While there, spice up your evening with a Cajun Bloody Mary ($6) featuring horseradish and cajun seasoning. (☎272-4136. Raw bar and "mini-plates' $5-10. Entrees $14-24. Raw bar open daily 4pm-12am; kitchen open Su-Th 5pm-12am, F-Sa 5pm-1am; bar open daily 4pm-1am.) The **Hangar Theatre,** 2 mi. from downtown at the Rte. 89 N. Treman Marina entrance, puts together a professional array of musicals and plays, with events in "The Wedge", a free experimental theater in the same building before and after the mainstage show. (☎273-8588. Shows T-Th and Su 7:30, F-Sa 8pm; matinees Sa 3pm, and some Su 3pm. $10-30.) With a kitchen sink full of unique shows, the intimate 73-seat **Kitchen Theatre,** 116 N. Cayuga, hosts everything from one-man shows to full plays. (☎272-0403. $16-20.) In the same building, the **Ticket Center at Clinton House** sells tickets to events at the Hangar Theatre, the Kitchen Theatre and many of the local college theater events. (☎273-4497 or 800-284-8422. Open M-Sa 10am-5:30pm.) A local student favorite, **Ruloff's,** 411 College St., exudes a classic college bar atmosphere. At 5:30, during Happy Hour, and at half past midnight, the bartender spins the "wheel of fortune" to pick the night's drink special. (☎272-6067. Beer $2.50-4. Open M-Sa 11:30am-1am, Su 10am-1am.) For a night on the town, the free *Ithaca Times*, available at many stores and restaurants, has complete listings of entertainment options.

BUFFALO ☎716

Buffalo loves its underdogs. The city's less-than-glorious sports teams aren't the only fiercely defended competitors; even the last stragglers of the Nissan Buffalo Marathon, run every Memorial Day weekend, draw enthusiastic cheers. Don't underestimate this city, though: by day, Buffalo is a cultural powerhouse with historic architecture and impressive art collections; by night, the top-notch theater district and boisterous club scene could compete with those of cities twice Buffalo's size. From the downtown skyline to funky Elmwood Village, Buffalo balances small-town warmth with big-city culture.

TRANSPORTATION. **Buffalo Niagara International Airport,** 4200 Genesee St. (☎630-6000; www.buffaloairport.com), 10 mi. east of downtown down Hwy. 33. Take the Metro Link Airport-Downtown Express (#204) from the **Transportation Center,** 181 Ellicott St., at N. Division St. **Airport Taxi Service** (☎ 633-8294 or 800-551-9369; www.buffaloairporttaxi.com) offers shuttles to downtown for $15. Call for reservations. **Amtrak,** 75 Exchange St. (☎856-2075; office open M-F 6am-3:30pm), at Washington St., runs to: New York (8hr., 4 per day, $96) and Toronto (4hr., 1 per day, $33). **Greyhound,** 181 Ellicott St., at N. Division St. (☎855-7533 or 800-231-2222; station open 24hr.), in the Buffalo Metropolitan Transportation Center sends buses to: New York (8½hr., 14 per day, $69); Boston (11½hr., 9 per day, $59); Niagara Falls, ON (1hr., 12 per day, $4); Toronto (2½hr., 12 per day, $16). The **Niagara Frontier Transit Authority** (**NFTA;** ☎855-7211; www.nfta.com) offers bus and rail service in the city ($1.50-2.25; seniors, children, and disabled riders $0.65-0.95) with additional buses to Niagara Falls, NY and free rides on the Main St. Metrorail. **Taxi: Cheektowaga Taxi** (☎822-1738). Airport service from downtown about $25. **Car Rental:** Most major chains have a rental desk in the airport. **Enterprise** rents to licensed drivers 18+. Call for reservation information. (☎565-0002; www.enterprise.com. Open Su-F 7:30am-9pm, Sa 8am-9pm.)

PRACTICAL INFORMATION. **Visitors Center:** 617 Main St., in the Theater District. (☎852-2356 or 800-283-3256; www.visitbuffaloniagara.com. Open Su noon-4pm, M-Sa 10am-4pm.) **Buffalo and Erie County Public Library:** 1 Lafayette Sq. at Washington St., offers Internet access with $1 temporary library membership. (☎858-8900. Open Su 1-5pm, M-W and F-Sa 8:30am-6pm, Th 8:30am-8pm.) **Bi-Gay-Lesbian Resources: Pride Buffalo, Inc.,** 266 Elmwood Ave., Suite 207. (879-0999; www.pridebuffalo.org); **PFLAG,** P.O. Box 617. (☎883-0384; www.pflag-buffalo-niagara.org) **Police:** ☎853-2222 (non-emergency). **Hotlines: Suicide, Rape, Crisis, and Emergency Mental Health.** (☎834-3131. 24hr.) **Medical Services: Buffalo General Hospital,** 100 High St. Take the Metro Rail to the Allen-Hospital stop, go up Main St. and turn right on High St. (☎859-5600) **Post Office:** 701 Washington St. (☎856-4604. Open M-F 8:30am-5:30pm, Sa 8:30am-1pm.) **Postal Code:** 14203. **Area Code:** 716.

ACCOMMODATIONS. Budget lodgings are a rarity in Buffalo, but chain motels can be found near the airport and **I-90,** 8-10 mi. northeast of downtown. The bright and comfortable **Hostel Buffalo (HI-AYH) ❶,** 667 Main St., offers 50 beds and spotless floors in a centrally-located neighborhood. Friendly staff make travelers feel at home and offer free movie showings nightly. (☎852-5222; hostel@hotmail.com. Wheelchair-accessible. Free linen, access to kitchen and common rooms, pool table, and laundry facilities. Reception 9-11am and 5pm-midnight. Check-in 5pm. Check-out 11am. Dorms $19, nonmembers $22; 2 private doubles available $56/63 without bath, $59/66 with bath; add $10 for each additional adult and $5 for each additional child. Reservations recommended after Labor Day.) The **Lenox Hotel & Suites ❸,** 140 North St., at Delaware Ave., take bus #11 or #25 to North St., offers clean, functional rooms only 5min. away from the Allentown nightlife. (☎884-1700; www.lenoxhotelandsuites.com. Cable TV, A/C, kitchens available, but not wheelchair-accessible. Singles from $59; doubles from $69. Student discount $10-20, depending on season.)

THE LOCAL LEGEND

BUFFALO'S WINGS

In Buffalo, they're called "chicken wings." Everywhere else, they're called "Buffalo wings." Either way, it all started out as a big accident.

Late one night in 1964, Teressa Bellisimo was working in the kitchen of the **Anchor Bar & Restaurant** when her son, the bartender, asked her to whip up something for him and a group of her ravenous friends. She thought for a moment, then remembered the plate of chicken wings she had set aside as too meaty for soup stock. She dumped them in the deep frier, then covered them with an impromptu sauce and served them with celery and bleu cheese dressing. *Voila!* Buffalo wings were born.

Since then, Buffalo wings have gone from bar food to main attraction. July 29, 1977 was declared **"Buffalo Wing Day"** in the city of Buffalo. These days, the **National Buffalo Wing Festival** (www.buffalowing.com) packs Buffalo's Dunn Tire Park full of wing chefs and admirers every Aug. The Anchor Bar now serves over 1000lb. of chicken wings a day and exports its special sauce to countries worldwide.

1047 Main St. ☎886-8920. 10 wings $7, 20 wings $11, bucket of 50 $23. Live jazz Sa-Su after 10pm. Open M-Th 11am-11pm, F-Sa 11am-1am, Su noon-11pm. ❷

FOOD & NIGHTLIFE. Up Elmwood Ave. in historic Allentown, **Gabriel's Gate ❷,** 145 Allen St., with its rustic furniture, mounted animal heads, and big chandelier, is a friendly restaurant reminiscent of a saloon. Enjoy the garden *souvlaki* ($7) or "Richmond Ave." burger ($4) from the comfy shaded patio. (☎886-0602. Open M-Th 11:30am-1am, F-Sa 11:30am-2am, Su noon-1am.)

Downtown bars and clubs are concentrated on **Chippewa Street** and **Franklin Street,** but live music can be found at just about every Buffalo establishment. Expect parties to start around midnight and last until 4am. Pick up a copy of *Artvoice* (www.artvoice.com) for complete event listings in Buffalo. With its hip atmosphere, **Quote,** 263 Delaware Ave., at Chippewa St., has been called Buffalo's "Best New Nightclub" by *Artvoice.* Wednesday is "Flip Night"—buy a drink, flip a coin, and if you call it, your drink is only $1. (☎854-2853. 21+. Sa cover $3. Open W-F 3:30pm-4am, Sa-Su 9pm-4am.) Across the intersection, **City SPoT,** 227 Delaware Ave., is the place to go for anything from a cup of plain coffee or tea to specialty espresso drinks and ice blended shakes. A side room features acoustic acts with local songwriters. (☎856-2739. Open 24hr.) **Club Marcella,** 622 Main St., with two dance floors and drag shows Wednesday and Sunday, caters to a primarily gay crowd. (☎847-6850; www.clubmarcella.com. F-Sa hip-hop. 18+. Cover usually $3, but varies. Open Su and W-Sa 9pm-4am.) **Nietzsche's,** 248 Allen St., is to Buffalo what CBGB's was to New York. Ani DiFranco and 10,000 Maniacs got their break here, and music feels like it's burned into the walls. Live rock or jazz acts every night. (☎886-8539; www.nietzsches.com. Cover varies. Open daily noon-4am. Kitchen closes at 1am.) Farther up Elmwood Ave., between Virginia Ave. and Forest Ave., is **Elmwood Village,** full of funky boutiques, coffee shops, and ethnic restaurants.

SIGHTS & ENTERTAINMENT. The **Albright-Knox Art Gallery,** 1285 Elmwood Ave., take bus #20, houses an internationally recognized collection of over 6000 modern pieces, including works by Picasso and Rothko. (☎882-8700; www.albrightknox.org. Open Tu-Sa 11am-5pm, Su noon-5pm. $6, seniors and students $5, families $12; Sa 11am-1pm free.) Next to the Gallery is **Delaware Park,** the center of Buffalo's park system, which was designed by Frederick Law Olmsted. Frank Lloyd Wright also designed several important houses in the area. Architecture buffs can take a 2hr. self-guided **walking tour** of historic downtown Buffalo. Pick up a free copy of *Walking Buffalo* at the tourist office. The Allentown Village

Society organizes the popular **Allentown Art Festival** (☎881-4269; www.allentownartfestival.org), a two-day celebration of local artists, June 12-13, 2004. The **Buffalo Niagara Guitar Festival** (☎845-7156; www.guitarfestival.com) is America's first and largest all-guitar music festival and features such luminaries as Bo Diddley. From September to January, **Ralph Wilson Stadium** (☎648-1800; www.buffalobills.com), in Orchard Park, hosts the NFL's **Buffalo Bills,** while hockey's **Buffalo Sabres** slap the puck at the **HSBC Arena,** 1 Seymour H. Knox III Plaza, from September to April (☎855-4444 ext. 82; www.sabres.com).

NIAGARA FALLS ☎716

One of the seven natural wonders of the world, Niagara Falls also claims the title of one of the world's largest sources of hydroelectric power—not to mention daredevil risk-takers. Since 1901, when 63-year-old Annie Taylor was the first to survive the plunge, the Falls have attracted many thrill-seekers. Modern-day Taylors beware—heavy fines and possible death await the daring. For those of a more sane disposition, outlet shopping and neon drenched storefronts beckon.

TRANSPORTATION

Trains: In America, Amtrak, at 27th and Lockport St. (☎285-4224), 1 block east of Hyde Park Blvd. Taxis meet each incoming train ($7-10 to downtown), or wait for bus #52 (runs frequently). Runs to: **New York City** (M-Th and Sa $63, F and Su $75) and **Toronto** (M-Th and Sa $22, F and Su $29). Open daily 7am-4:30pm. **In Canada, VIA Rail Canada,** 4267 Bridge St. (☎888-842-7245), take the Niagara Falls Shuttle (see **Public Transit**) from downtown, runs to: **New York** (Amtrak; 1 per day; M-Th and Sa CDN$97, F and Su CDN$115) and **Toronto** (2 per day; CDN$30, CDN$20 with ISIC). Open M-F 6am-8pm, Sa-Su 7am-8pm.

Buses: Niagara Falls Bus Terminal, at 4th and Niagara St. (☎282-1331), sells **Greyhound** tickets for direct service to: **New York** (1 per day, $69) and **Toronto** (2 per day, $17), or for use in Buffalo. Open M-F 9am-4pm, Sa-Su 9am-noon. To get a bus in Buffalo, take bus #40 "Grand Island" from the Niagara Falls bus terminal to the **Buffalo Transportation Center,** 181 Ellicott St. (1 hr., 19 per day, $2.25). In Canada, the **Bus Terminal,** across from the Train Station at 4267 Bridge St. (☎357-2133), sends Greyhound buses to: **Toronto** (2hr., 23 per day, CDN$23). Open daily 7am-10:30pm.

Public Transit: Niagara Frontier Metro Transit System, (☎285-2002; www.nfta.com), provides local city transit ($1.50). **ITA Buffalo Shuttle** (☎800-551-9369) has service from Niagara Falls info center and major hotels to Buffalo Airport ($50). On the Canadian side, the **Niagara Falls Shuttle** (☎356-1179.) runs between the bus and train stations, downtown, and other touristy areas. June 20-Aug. 31 every 30min. 8:45am-2am, All-day pass CDN$6.

Taxi: Blue United Cab, ☎285-9331. Travelers should beware of taxi drivers who charge full fare for each rider. **Niagara Falls Taxi,** ☎905-357-4000, in Canada.

Bike Rental: Bikes & Hikes, 526 Niagara St. (☎278-0047; www.bikesandhikes.com). $12 for 2hr. rental including helmet, lock, and map for self-guided tour.

ORIENTATION & PRACTICAL INFORMATION

Niagara Falls spans the US-Canadian border (addresses given here are in New York, unless noted). Take **U.S. 190** to the Robert Moses Pkwy., which leads directly to the falls and downtown. On the **American** side, **Niagara Street** is the main east-west artery, ending in the west at **Rainbow Bridge,** which crosses to

Canada (pedestrian crossings $0.50, cars $2.50; tolls only charged going into Canada). North-south streets are numbered, increasing toward the east. Budget motels line **Route 62 (Niagara Falls Boulevard)** outside of town. On the **Canadian** side, most attractions are scattered along **Niagara Parkway (River Road)**, and the main entertainment and shopping district is **Clifton Hill** between Victoria Ave. and River Rd. Customs procedures, while still casual in tone, are taken extremely seriously since September 11th. Many businesses in the Niagara area accept both American and Canadian currency.

Visitor Info: Orin Lehman Visitors Center (☎278-1796), in front of the Falls' observation deck; the entrance is marked by a garden. Open daily 7am-10:15pm. **Niagara Falls Tourism,** (☎800-563-2557 or 905-356-6061; www.discoverniagara.com), has info on the Canadian side. In Canada, tune in to 105.1FM for tourist info.

Internet Access: Public Library, in America, 1425 Main St., take Bus #50 up Main St. (Open M-W 9am-9pm, Th-Sa 9am-5pm.)

Sexual Assault Crisis Line: ☎905-682-4584.

Medical Services: In America, **Niagara Falls Memorial Medical Center,** 621 10th St. (☎278-4000). In Canada, **Greater Niagara General Hospital,** 5546 Portage Rd. (☎905-358-0171).

Post Office: 615 Main St. (☎285-7561). Open M-F 8:30am-5pm, Sa 8:30am-2pm. **Postal Code:** 14302. **Area Code:** 716 (NY), 905 (ON). In text, 716 unless otherwise noted.

ACCOMMODATIONS

Many newlyweds spend part of their honeymoon by the awesome beauty of the Falls, which are especially romantic at night. Cheap motels (from $25) advertising free wedding certificates line **Lundy's Lane** on the Canadian side and **Route 62** on the American side, while many moderately priced B&Bs overlook the gorge on **River Road** between the Rainbow Bridge and the Whirlpool Bridge on the Canadian side. Reservations are always recommended.

Hostelling International Niagara Falls (HI-AYH), 4549 Cataract Ave., Niagara Falls, ON (☎905-357-0770 or 888-749-0058). Just off Bridge St., about 2 blocks from the bus station and VIA Rail. Once a lodging house for railroad workers, this well-equipped hostel now enjoys a "laidback" atmosphere, thanks to its cheerful staff of self-described hippies and its convivial, rainbow-colored interior. Organized activities include pancake breakfasts, Su music jams, and barbecues. Lockers CDN$2. Linen CDN$2 (free with ISIC). Laundry facilities, kitchen, and Internet access. CDN$5 key deposit. Bike Rentals CDN$15 per day. Reception 24hr. Check-out 10:30am. Quiet hours 11pm-7am. Reservations recommended May-Nov. Dorm rooms CDN$18; nonmembers CDN$23; singles $50/54; family rooms $25/29. ❶

Hostelling International Niagara Falls (HI-AYH), 1101 Ferry Ave. (☎282-3700). From the bus station, walk east on Niagara St., then turn left onto Memorial Pkwy.; the hostel is at the corner of Ferry Ave. *Avoid walking alone on Ferry Ave. at night.* 44 beds in a friendly old house. Kitchen, TV lounge, and limited parking. Family rooms available. Linen $1.75. Check-in 7:30-9:30am and 4-11pm. Lockout 9:30am-4pm. Curfew 11:30pm; lights out midnight. Open Feb. to mid-Dec. Dorms $15, nonmembers $18. Credit cards not accepted. ❶

Rainbow House Bed & Breakfast, 423 Rainbow Blvd. (☎282-1135 or 800-724-3536; www.rainbowhousebb.com). From Niagara St. walk down 4th and turn left at Rainbow Blvd. Offers four flowery rooms and a quiet garden for weary travelers. Breakfast, refreshments, A/C, TV, bag storage, and wedding chapel. Checkout 11am. Singles, doubles, and triples. Summer $85, low-season $75. ❸

Niagara Glen-View Tent & Trailer Park, 3950 Victoria Ave., Niagara Falls, ON (☎800-263-2570). Take the Niagara Falls Shuttle from downtown or the bus station. Hiking trail across the street. Ice, showers, laundry facilities, groceries, and pool. Office open daily 8am-11pm. Sells tickets for People Mover and Adventure Pass. Park open May to mid-Oct. June-Sept. campsites CDN$35, with hookup CDN$42; May and Oct. $28/35. MC/V accepted. ❷

FOOD

Backpackers and locals alike flock to **The Press Box Restaurant ❶,** 324 Niagara St., for enormous meals at microscopic prices. On Mondays and Wednesdays, feast on $1 spaghetti. (☎284-5447. Open daily 9am-11pm.) At the newly-renovated **Top of the Falls Restaurant ❹,** on Goat Island, take the trolley to Terrapin Point, the food is excellent, but the view is even better. Every table has a spectacular view of Horseshoe Falls. (☎278-1796. Dinners $15-20. Vegetarian options available. Open M-Th 11am-9pm, F-Su 11am-11pm.) On the Canadian side, the oldest restaurant in town is still a local favorite. **Simon's Restaurant ❷,** 4116 Bridge St., ON, one block from the hostel, serves huge breakfasts (CDN$6), giant homemade muffins (CDN$0.69), and homestyle dinners. (☎905-356-5310. Open Su 5:30am-2pm, M-Sa 5:30am-8pm.) **George's Family Restaurant ❶,** 420 Niagara St., look for the orange building across from the casino, has been serving big breakfasts ($4) and burgers ($2.50) to the local crowd for 18 years. (☎284-5766. Open Su-M and W-Sa 8am-2pm, T 8-11am.)

DO YOU FEEL LUCKY? On the Canadian side of the border, glitzy casinos are almost as popular as the Falls themselves. In the past, Americans would crowd over to the Canadian side of the Falls to visit the casinos, leaving the American side's economy to stagnate. But on New Year's Eve, 2002, the **Seneca Niagara Casino,** 310 4th St. at Niagara St. (☎299-1100; www.snfgc.com), changed all that. The casino's success has brought much-needed revenue to the City of Niagara and has lured gamblers back to the America. Expect this trend to continue: the Seneca plans to expand rapidly, with a hotel and even an arena planned for construction in the near future.

SIGHTS

While the most popular attraction is (of course) the Falls, entrepreneur and tourist offices on both sides of the border have made sure to provide plenty of competition. In Canada, the gambling and entertainment industry keeps tourists occupied, while the American side enjoys a full calendar of historical and cultural festivals (☎800-338-7890; www.niagara-usa.com).

AMERICAN SIDE. For over 150 years, the **Maid of the Mist** boat tour has entertained visitors with the awe-inspiring (and wet) views from the foot of both falls. *(☎284-8897. Open daily 10am-6pm. Tours leave in summer daily every 30min. $10.50, ages 6-12 $6.25, $1 for entrance to observation deck only.)* The **Cave of the Winds Tour** hands out souvenir (read: ineffective) yellow raincoats and sandals for a drenching hike to the base of the Bridal Veil Falls, including an optional walk to Hurricane Deck where gale-force waves slam down from above. *(☎278-1730. Open May to mid-Oct.; hours vary depending on season and weather conditions. Trips leave every 15min. Must be at least 42 in. $8, ages 6-12 $7.)*

The **Master Pass,** available at the park's Visitors Center, covers admission to the theater; Maid of the Mist; the Cave of the Winds Tour; the **Niagara Gorge Discovery Center**, in Prospect Park, which has gorge trail hikes and a simulated elevator ride through the geologic history of the Falls; the **Aquarium,** which houses the endangered Peruvian Penguin; and the **Niagara Scenic Trolley,** a tram-guided tour of the park and the best transportation between the sites on the American side. *(Master Pass $28, ages 6-12 $19. Discovery Center: ☎278-1780. Open daily May-Sept. 9am-7pm; Sept.-May 9am-5pm. $5, children $3. Film every 30min. Aquarium: 701 Whirlpool St., across from Discovery Center. ☎285-3575; www.aquariumofniagara.org. Open July-Aug. daily 9am-7pm., low-season daily 9am-5pm. $7, children and seniors $5. Trolley: ☎278-1730. Open May-Aug. daily 9am-10pm. Runs very 10-20min. $5, children $3.)*

Three miles north on Robert Moses Pkwy., the **Niagara Power Project** features hands-on exhibits, displays, and videos on energy, hydropower, and local history. *(5777 Lewiston Rd. ☎286-6661. Open daily 9am-5pm. Call ahead to arrange a guided tour. Free.)* Eight miles north in **Lewiston, NY,** the 150-acre state **Artpark,** at the foot of 4th St., focuses on visual and performing arts, offering opera, musicals, pops concerts, and rock shows. *(☎800-659-7275. Shows May-Aug.; call for schedule. Box office open M-F 10am-4pm, later on event days. Shows at 8pm. $15-40.)* **Old Fort Niagara** was built for French troops in 1726 and was the site of battles during the French and Indian War and the American Revolution. *(Follow Robert Moses Pkwy. north from Niagara Falls. ☎745-7611. Open June-Aug. daily 9am-8pm; low-season hours vary. $7, seniors $6, ages 6-12 $4.)*

CANADIAN SIDE. On the Canadian side of Niagara Falls (across Rainbow Bridge), **Queen Victoria Park** provides the best view of **Horseshoe Falls.** Starting 1hr. after sunset, the Falls are illuminated for 3hr. every night, and a free fireworks display lights up the sky every Friday and Sunday at 10pm, May 16-Sept. 1. Parking close to the park is expensive (CDN$12). Farther down Niagara Pkwy., across from the Greenhouse, parking is CDN$3 per hour. **People Movers** efficiently and comfortably take you through the 30km area on the Canadian side of the Falls, stopping at attractions along the way. *(☎877-642-7275. Mid-June to early Sept. daily 9am-11pm; low-season hours vary. CDN$6, children CDN$3.)* Bikers, in-line skaters, and walkers enjoy the 32km **Niagara River Recreation Trail,** which runs from Fort Erie to Fort George and passes many historical sights dating back to the War of 1812.

Far above the crowds and excitement, **Skylon Tower** has the highest view (on a clear day all the way to Toronto) of the Falls at 236m.; the tower's **Observation Deck** offers a calming, unhindered vista. *(5200 Robinson St. ☎356-2651. Open June-Oct. daily 8am-11pm; winter hours change monthly. CDN$10, seniors CDN$9, children CDN$6, families $27.)* The **Adventure Pass** includes entrance to the **Maid of the Mist** boat tour; **Journey Behind the Falls,** a tour behind Horseshoe falls; **White Water Walk,** a long boardwalk next to the famous Niagara River Rapids; the **Butterfly Conservatory,** on the grounds of the world-famous Niagara Parks Botanical Gardens; CDN$2 discounts for the **Spanish Aero Car,** an aerial cable ride over the rapids' whirlpool waters; and all-day transportation on the People Movers. *(Pass: CDN$32, children $19. www.niagararparks.com has details and sells passes online. Maid of the Mist: ☎357-7393. CDN$13, children CDN$8. In summer open daily 9:30am-7:45pm. Trips every 15min. Journey: ☎354-1551. CDN$7, children, CDN$4. In summer open daily 9am-7:30pm. Walk: ☎374-1221. CDN$6, children CDN$3. In summer open daily 9am-8pm. Guided tours available. Conservatory: ☎358-0025. CDN$8.50, children CDN$4. In summer open 9am-7:30pm, call for updated times. Aero Car: ☎354-5711. CDN$6, children CDN$3. In summer open daily 9am-8pm.)*

Meanwhile, commercialism can be as much of a wonder as any natural sight. The Canadian side of the Falls offers the delightfully tasteless **Clifton Hill,** a collection of wax museums, funhouses, and overpriced shows. **Ripley's Believe It or Not Museum** displays wax model wonders and a selection of medieval torture devices. *(4960 Clifton Hill. ☎356-2238. Open summer daily 9am-2am; low-season hours vary. CDN$10, children CDN$5.50, seniors CDN$8.)*

NORTHERN NEW YORK

THE ADIRONDACKS ☎518

Demonstrating uncommon foresight, the New York State legislature established the **Adirondack Park** in 1892, preserving a six million-acre swath of mainly mountainous terrain, much of it designated as "forever wild." Thousands of miles of gorgeous trails carve through the park and more than 2500 glittering lakes and ponds are fed by 30,000 miles of rivers and streams. Despite being within one days drive of over 60 million people, the immense dimensions of the park allow the Adirondacks to be one of the few places in the Northeast where hikers can still spend days without seeing another soul.

PRACTICAL INFORMATION. Adirondacks Trailways (☎800-858-8555) services the region. From Albany, buses set out for Lake Placid and Lake George. From the Lake George bus stop at Lake George Hardware, 35 Montcalm St., buses go to: Albany (4 per day, $11.65); Lake Placid (1-2 per day, $15.30); and New York City (4-5 per day, $41). The **Adirondack Mountain Club (ADK)** is the best source of info on outdoor activities in the region. Two booklets available through the ADK and not to be missed are the *Adirondacks Waterways* and the *Adirondack Great Walks and Day Hikes* guides, which detail hundreds of hikes and paddles of all difficulty levels throughout the park. Offices are located at 814 Goggins Rd., Lake George 12845 (☎668-4447; www.adk.org; open M-Sa 8:30am-5pm), and at Adirondack Loj Rd., P.O. Box 867, Lake Placid 12946. (☎523-3441. Open Su-Th and Sa 8am-8pm, F 8am-10pm.) The Lake Placid ADK has an education program center which can provide the scoop on outdoor skills classes such as canoeing, rock climbing, whitewater kayaking, and wilderness medicine. For the latest backcountry info including, but not limited to, weather, trail closings, and safety concerns, visit ADK's **High Peaks Information Center,** 3 mi. east of Lake Placid on Rte. 73, then 5 mi. down Adirondack Loj Rd. in the Loj itself. The center also has washrooms (showers $0.25 per min.) and sells basic outdoor equipment, trail snacks, and a variety of helpful guides to the mountains for $11-25, including the ADK guides specific to each region of the mountains. Educational programs that teach backcountry skills of all kinds via one to three day excursions, as well as free lectures and guided hikes are also run from the center. (☎523-3441. Open Oct.-May Su-Th 8am-5pm, F-Sa 8am-8pm; May-Oct. Su-Th 8am-6pm, F-Sa 8am-8pm. Parking fee $9. Educational programs $30-150 including food and equipment.) **Area Code:** 518.

ACCOMMODATIONS AND FOOD. Lodging tends to cluster around the many small towns throughout the mountains, most of which are located on the shores of one of the many bodies of water. The ADK also runs two lodges near Lake Placid. The **Adirondack Loj ❷,** at the end of Adirondack Loj Rd., off Rte. 73, lures in hikers looking for a place to rest their sore feet. The log cabin has 46 bunks and a den decorated with skis and a moose trophy. Heated by an imposing fieldstone fireplace in the winter, the cozy den is the perfect place to warm chilled limbs after exploring the wilderness trails on skis and snowshoes. In summer, guests swim, fish, and canoe on Heart Lake, located 100 ft. from the lodge's doorstep. (☎523-3441. Breakfast included; lunch $5.50, dinner $14. Reservations highly recommended. Bunks $34-45; low-season $30-39. Private room $110/95 per night. Lean-tos $26/13; campsites $23/10; canvas cabin $32/29; 4-person wood cabins $100/85; 16-person $320/272. Snowshoe rentals $10 per day; cross-country ski rentals $20 per day. Canoe or kayak rental 8am-8pm; $5 per hr., guests $3. Parking $9

THE BIG SPLURGE

A BIRD'S EYE VIEW

As the extent of the Adirondacks is immense, much of the park is largely inaccessible except on foot, or for those who have wings. **Helms Aero Service** provides visitors with the latter, opening great expanses of the park to less hardy souls unwilling to hike the great distances involved. Seaplanes with pontoons are able to land on many of the backcountry lakes that are extremely difficult to reach on foot. With 14 regular drop-offs, any traveler can find his ideal lake for a camping and fishing trip. Canoes can even be brought in to many of the locations.

The flights are not limited to those in search of the biggest fish in the forest. Sightseeing tours also fly over Long Lake with a view of waterfalls at the southern tip, glide through the High Peaks up close, and highlight the "great camps" of the gilded age, the summer houses built by such magnates as the Vanderbilts and J.P. Morgan.

Helms Aero Service, *located on Rte. 30, in Long Lake (☎624-3931). Open late Apr.-Nov 8am-dusk. Fishing: Reserve in advance. Generally $45-80 each way for 2 passengers and gear. Sightseeing: $45 min. for 2 adults for 15min. tour of Long Lake. $20 each additional adult, $10 each additional child up to 5 people. $130 for up to 5 people for High Peaks or Great Camps tours.*

except those staying at the lodge or campground for whom parking is free.) Two miles east of Tupper Lake, **Northwood Cabins ❸**, 92 Tupper-Sara Hwy., rents nine white and blue cabins, all heated and with a TV, and some with kitchenettes and a fireplace. (☎359-9606 or 800-727-5756. Open mid-May to mid-Oct. Cabins $42-68.) For a more rustic experience (read: no showers), hike 3½ mi. from the closest trailhead to the **John's Brook Lodge ❷**, in Keene Valley. From Lake Placid, follow Rte. 73 for 15 mi. through Keene to Keene Valley, turn right at the Ausable Inn, and drive five miles to the parking lot at the end of the dirt road ($5 per car for parking). The hike runs over rolling hills, but the meal waiting at the end is it. John's Brook, including three included meals provided daily, is no secret—beds fill completely on weekends. (Call the Adirondack Loj for reservations, ☎523-3441. No showers. Blankets, but not linens, provided. July to early Sept. bunks $38-41.) The **White Birch Cafe ❷**, 6 Demars Blvd., in Tupper Lake, serves up good, fresh food at reasonable prices. (☎359-8044. Sandwiches $6-8. Open M and W-Su 11am-8pm.)

The **Backcountry Camping** rules have recently changed in sections of the eastern half of the park. In designated areas camping is prohibited except at prescribed sights and campfires are banned within the entire section. The areas affected by this change are identified on the new maps sold by the ADK and can be purchased at the High Peaks Information Center ($8). Otherwise, camping is free anywhere on public land in the backcountry as long as it is at least 150 ft. away from a trail, road, water source, or campground, and below 4000 ft. in altitude. Inquire about the location of free trailside shelters before planning a hike in the forest. Contact the **Department of Environmental Conservation's** (☎402-9428) office for backwoods camping for more details.

SIGHTS. Of the six million acres in the Adirondacks Park, 40% is open to the public, offering a slew of outdoor activities. The other 60% is privately owned by logging companies, residents, and outdoors clubs. The fourteen **scenic byways** that connect many of the small villages and towns nestled among the mountains serve both as means of transport and as recreation. The rivers, streams, ponds, and lakes in the area also carry kayakers, canoers, and seasonal whitewater rafters through the breathtaking landscape. The 2000 mi. of winding trails that pass through the forest provide spectacular mountain scenery for hikers, snowshoers, and cross-country skiers. A number of the trails that wind their way through the highest peaks begin at Adirondack Loj at the end of Adirondack Loj road three mi. east of town along Rte. 73. Outdoor enthusiasts with a full day to spend hiking should consider conquering Phelps Mountain, a 9 mi. round-trip journey with unusual views of the surrounding peaks. **Mount Marcy,** a 7½ mi. hike to the state's highest peak (5344 ft.) is a day trip that finishes with a commanding view. For a great view accompanying a short hike, Mt. Jo is a good bet. The steep 2 mi. round trip journey provides views of the surrounding peaks and Heart Lake in the valley below. Saranac Lake hosts a ten day no-holds-barred carnival every winter. Lake George also hosts a carnival on weekends in February. (Lake George Chamber of Commerce: 2176 Rte. 9. ☎668-5755. Open daily 9am-5pm.) In late June, Tupper hosts the **Tin Man Triathlon,** a 1¼ mi. swim, 56 mi. bike ride, and 13 mi. run through town. (Tupper Lake Chamber of Commerce: 60 Park St. ☎359-3328 or 888-887-5253. Open daily 9am-5pm). Lake Placid goes the distance with an **IronMan Triathlon,** doubling the distances of the Tin Man.

Experienced rock climbers and those who want to break into the sport should consult the experienced staff at the **Mountaineer,** in Keene Valley, between I-87 and Lake Placid on Rte. 73. The Mountaineer reels in all types of alpine enthusiasts as it hosts the **Adirondack International Mountainfest,** a weekend of clinics and classes for all manner of mountain sport. (☎576-2281. Open summer Su-Th 9am-5:30pm, F 9am-7pm, Sa 8am-7pm; low-season M-F 9am-5:30pm, Sa 8am-5:30pm, Su 9am-5:30pm. Snowshoes $15 per day, ice-climbing boots and crampons $20, rock shoes $12. Mountainfest occurs the weekend of Martin Luther King Day weekend.) The **Adirondack Park Visitor Interpretive Center,** just west of Newcomb on Rte. 28 N draws both naturalists and those just hoping to spot a little wildlife in the forest. While there can be no guarantee of seeing wildlife in the park, moose, bears, minx, and otter are often found along the parks trails. (☎582-2000. Visitors center open daily 9am-5pm; trials open dawn to dusk. Free.) The 21 exhibit **Adirondack Museum**, off Rte. 30 in Blue Mountain Lake, showcases the history, culture, and lifestyles of the Adirondacks through the ages. The collection of 25 boats and the complete, richly decorated railcar are among the more impressive exhibits. (☎352-7311; www.adirondackmuseum.org. Open late May to mid-Oct. daily 10am-5pm. $14; seniors $13; students, military, and ages 7-17 $7; under 6 free.)

Stroll down **Ausable Chasm,** a gorge cut deep into the earth by the roaring Ausable River, 12 mi. south of Plattsburgh on Rte. 9. The chasm includes numerous waterfalls and is surrounded by the Adirondack forest seemingly untouched by the years. At the conclusion of the walk the flatter water provides the opportunity for rafting through a labyrinth of age-old rock formations. (☎537-1211; www.ausablechasm.com. Open mid May to late June daily 9:30am-4pm; late June to Sept. Su-Th 9:30am-5pm, F-Sa 9:30am-6:30pm. $16 for entrance to the walkway, senior and ages 12-19 $14, ages 5-11 $12. $24/22/20 for entrance and raft trip.) Further south along the shores of Lake Champlain, one mi. east of the town of Ticonderoga, lies **Fort Ticonderoga,** a critical strategic point in early wars for control of the colonies, and once referred to as "the key to the continent." Today the fort has been restored, houses a museum, provides daily historical talks and musket demonstrations, and stages reenactments of historical battles, occasionally with as many as 1000 reenactors. (☎585-2821; www.fort-ticonderoga.org. Open May to late Oct. daily 9am-5pm. $12, seniors $11, ages 7-12 $6.)

LAKE PLACID ☎518

Tucked away among the High Peaks Mountains, Lake Placid lives and breathes winter sports, but still maintains a lively summer schedule full of outdoors events. Host to the Olympic Winter Games in both 1932 and 1980, this modest town has seen thousands of pilgrims and, aside from the manifold motels, has remained charmingly unchanged by its popularity. World-class athletes train year-round in the town's extensive facilities, lending an international flavor and an Olympic aura, which distinguish Lake Placid from its Adirondack neighbors.

PRACTICAL INFORMATION. Lake Placid sits at the intersection of Rte. 86 and Rte. 73 in the northeastern quarter of the park. **Adirondack Trailways** (☎800-225-6815) stops at 326 Main St., in front of the Coffee Cup Cafe and has extensive service in the area. Destinations include Lake George ($15), the Albany airport ($27), and New York City ($63). The **Placid Xpress** shuttle makes rounds around the town every 15 to 20 minutes including stops at the various parking areas including free municipal lots. (☎523-2445. Map of route available at the Visitors Bureau. Runs July-Sept. 7:30am-10pm. Free.)

The Lake Placid that exists today is a product of its rich Olympic past. The **Olympic Regional Development Authority,** 218 Main St., Olympic Center, operates the sporting facilities. (☎523-1655 or 800-462-6236. Open M-F 8:30am-5pm.) Also in the Olympic Center is the **Lake Placid-Essex County Visitors Bureau,** which provides information about food, lodging and attractions in the area. (☎523-2445; www.lakeplacid.com. Open M-F 8am-5pm, Sa-Su 9am-4pm, closed Su in the spring and fall.) **Weather Info:** ☎523-1363. **Internet Access: Lake Placid Public Library,** 67 Main St. (☎523-3200. Open M-F 11am-5pm, Sa 11am-4pm. No email.) **Mountain Mama's,** 26 Main St., also provides two high speed connections. (☎523-9327. Open T-Su 10am-5pm. $5 per hour, $5 minimum.) Visitors Bureau. (See above. Limited to 15 min. if people are waiting.) **Post Office:** 201 Main St. (☎523-3071. Open M-F 8:30am-5pm, Sa 8am-noon.) **Postal Code:** 12946. **Area Code:** 518.

ACCOMMODATIONS. If you avoid the resorts on the west end of town, both lodgings and food can be had cheaply in Lake Placid. A remnant of the Olympic days, many inexpensive motels line Rte. 86 and 73 just east of town. The Visitor's Center can provide suggestions to fit your needs. With a prime location not far from the Olympic Center, the friendly and helpful owners of the **High Peaks Hostel ❶,** 333 Main St., will make any traveler feel right at home in one of their 28 bunks or 4 private rooms. The homemade breakfasts, well-equipped kitchens, and great community atmosphere more than make up for slightly crowded bunk arrangments. (☎523-4951. Bunks $20, private rooms $48.) The **Jackrabbit Inn and Hostel ❶,** 3½ mi. east of town on Rte. 73, also offers affordable rooms and bunks in a bunkhouse with a lounge and a kitchen. (☎523-0123 or 800-584-7006. Bunks $20, Motel rooms $40-75.)

CAMPING. Two state park campgrounds, some of the nicest in the area, are within 10 mi. of Lake Placid. **Meadowbrook State Park ❶,** 5 mi. west of town on Rte. 86 in Ray Brook, has shady wooded campsites that are relatively secluded. (☎891-4351. Sites $11 plus $3 registration fee. Day use $4 per car, $1 walk in.) **Wilmington Notch State Campground ❶,** about 9 mi. east of Lake Placid on Rte. 86, also offers shady, although somewhat more crowded sites, as well as a a 35ft waterfall within a five minute walk of the campground. (☎946-7172. Open May-mid Oct. Sites $11-13. Day use $4 per car.) An hour from Lake Placid, 12 mi. south of Plattsburgh on Rte. 9, lies one of the state's most beautiful campgrounds, **Ausable Point ❶.** Dotted with wildflowers and situated on the banks of Lake Champlain with a sandy beach, the park is ideal both for camping and for day use. (☎561-7080. Make reservations for weekends and holidays. $3 first night only registration fee, sites $17, with electricity $20. Day use $6 per car. Lifeguard on duty June-late Aug. M-F 10am-7pm, Sa-Su 10am-8pm.)

FOOD & NIGHTLIFE. Lake Placid Village, concentrated primarily along Main St., has a number of reasonably priced dining establishments. The **Hilton Hotel's** ❷ lunch buffet, 1 Mirror Lake Drive, serves all-you-can-eat sandwiches, soups, salads, and a hot entree for only $8 in a room overlooking the lake from above the town. (☎523-4411. Buffet daily noon-2pm.) With a great selection of coffees and teas, **Aroma Round** ❶, 18 Saranac Ave., can get you moving in the morning with a cool breeze on the outside deck, or round out the day with a warm beverage ($1.50-3) around their small fireplace. (☎523-3818. Open daily 7am-10pm.) The **Brown Dog Deli and Wine Bar** ❹, 3 Main St., builds tasty sandwiches ($6-8) with meats and cheeses on their homemade bread. For a treat, try the multiple course meals accompanied by wine pairings on Saturday evenings. (☎523-3036. Entrees $15-18. Sa evening meals $15-30. Open daily 11am-10pm.) The **Black Bear Restaurant** ❷, 157 Main St., dishes out meals from the grill as well as a few vegetarian and vegan options and smoothies. The organic salad bar with ten different soups each day ($6.50) is also a popular choice. (☎523-9886. Daily specials $15. Breakfast $3-7. Lunch special $8. Open daily 6am-9pm.) On the shore of Mirror Lake where US national canoeing and kayaking teams can often be seen practicing, **The Cottage** ❷, 5 Mirror Lake Dr., creates sandwiches and salads (all under $9) that can be served on the outside deck to receive the best view. (☎523-9845. Kitchen open daily 11:30am-10pm; bar open until midnight or 1am, depending on the crowd.) One of Lake Placid's few late-night hot spots, **Wise Guys,** 3 School St., boasts both a sports bar and a dance club. (☎523-4446. No cover M-F, Sa-Su up to $3. Bar open M-F 3pm-3am, Sa-Su noon-3am. Club open Th-Sa 9pm-3am.)

SIGHTS. The **Olympic Center,** in downtown Lake Placid, houses the 1932 and 1980 hockey arenas, as well as the petite, memorabilia-stuffed **Winter Olympic Museum.** The museum, packed full with a 5min. introductory video, ice skates through the ages, bobsleds used in former olympics, and medals among the many exhibits is a walk through time and down memory lane. (☎523-1655 ext. 226; www.orda.org. Open daily 10am-5pm. $4, seniors $3, ages 7-12 $2. **Public skating**: ☎523-1655. M-F 8-9:30pm. $5, children and seniors $4; skate rental $3.) During the summer, purchase tickets to watch ski jumpers and aerial freestylists practice for upcoming competitions by sailing down astroturf-covered ramps onto astroturf-covered hillsides or into a swimming pool in the Olympic Jumping Complex, just east of town on Rte. 73. To see the situation from the jumper's perspective travelers can take a chairlift and an elevator to the top of the ramp for a look down. (☎523-2202. Open 9am-4pm. $5, with chairlift $8; seniors $3, children $5.) About 5 mi. east of town on Rte. 73, the **Verizon Sports Complex** at **Mt. Van Hoevenberg** offers bobsled rides down the actual 1980 Olympic track. In colder weather, the bobsleds run on ice and will set you back a chilly $30 per ride. In warmer weather, the sleds grow wheels to rocket down the side of the mountain but cost the same. If coasting down the side of the mountain at high speeds isn't for you, consider the narrated trolley tours that drive more slowly up and down the mountain for a view of the tracks. (☎523-4436. Open W-Su 10am-12:30pm and 1:30-4pm. Winter bobsled runs Dec.-Mar.; summer Apr.-Nov. Must be at least 48 in. tall; under 18 need a parent. Trolley tours 9am-4pm. $5, seniors and ages 7-12 $4.) While at the complex, consider whipping yourself into shape Olympian-style at the cross-country skiing venue. Hosting people with skis strapped to their feet when the ground is white, and those with two wheels ready to handle the mountainous terrian underneath them when the greenery returns, this venue is always in use. Cross-country ski and bike rentals are available inside the complex. (☎523-1176. Open for skiing daily 9am-4:30pm, last rental 4pm. $14 per day trail fee, seniors and ages 7-12 $12, ages 70+ free. Equipment rental $16, under 18 $12. Open for biking mid-June to early

Sept. daily 10am-5pm; early Sept.-early Oct. Sa-Su 10am-5pm. Bikes $30 per day; trail fee—not included in rental—$6 per day, $10 per 2 days; helmet required, and included with bike rental, $3 per day.)

For those planning to take in all or most of Lake Placid's Olympic attractions, the **Olympic Sites Passport** is the best bargain. For $19 per person, the pass includes entrance to the Olympic Jumping Complex (including chairlift and elevator ride), the trolley tour of the bobsledding complex, a $5 coupon toward a bobsled ride on Mt. Van Hoevenberg, admission to the Winter Sports Museum, and choice of either the **Scenic Gondola Ride** to the top of Little Whiteface or access to the **Veterans Memorial Highway** that climbs Whiteface Mountain. Purchase a passport at any Olympic venue or at the **Olympic Center Box Office** in Lake Placid. (☎523-1655 or 800-462-6236.) After touring the Olympic venues, get outfitted for your own sporting adventures at **High Peaks Cyclery,** 331 Main St. Renting and selling all manner of bicycles, climbing gear, camping equipment, skis, snowshoes, and much more, the experts there can make sure you are prepared for any outing. If you aren't ready to head out alone, inquire about the many adventure programs and guide services offered as well. (☎523-3764. Open daily 9am-6pm. Bikes $25-40 per day. Tent $15-20 per day. Cross-country skis $15 per day. Snowshoes $15 per day. Inquire about prices for guided tours.)

Departing from **Lake Placid Marina, tour boat cruises** motor around the 16 mi. perimeter of the lake in long, sleek, turn-of-the-century boats, providing glimpses of the stately homes that line the shores as well as illuminating the history of the area. (☎523-9704. Cruises depart mid-May to late June M-F 10:30am, 2:30pm, Sa-Su 10:30am, 2:30, 4pm. Late June-Sept. daily 10:30am, 1pm, 2:30pm, 4pm. Sept-mid Oct. daily 10:30am, 1:30pm, 3:00pm. $7.50, seniors $6.50, children $5.50. Arrive at least 15min. early.) For an old-fashioned mode of transportation, step into a horse drawn carriage from **Mirror Lake Carriage Tours,** located at the northern end of Main St. across from the Hilton. The 35min. tour circles the picturesque lake. (☎523-5352. Open June to mid-Oct. daily 10am-11pm. $12, ages 3-11 $8.) Immediately adjacent, at 1 Main St., is **Mirror Lake Boat Rentals** where visitors may rent a variety of boats in which to drift, paddle, and motor your way around the lake. (☎524-7890. Open May to mid-Oct. 10am-dark. $18 per hour for paddle boats, canoes, and hydrobikes; $35 per hour for sailboats and electric cruisers.) For a cool dip in the waters, head down to the **Mirror Lake Public Beach** on Parkside Dr. (☎523-3109. Lifeguards on duty late June to Sept. 9am-7pm, weather permitting. Free.)

To climb to the 4,867 ft. summit of Whiteface Mountain without breaking a sweat, drive your car up the **Veterans Memorial Highway,** 11 mi. east of Lake Placid on Rte. 86. The alpine-style tollbooth five mi. from the summit has info about the highway and the short self-guided nature walk that is required to reach the summit. Stop at one or two of the nine parking areas on the way up for spectacular mountain vistas before reaching the observation deck and weather station at the summit. (☎946-7175. Open July-Sept. daily 8:30am-5pm; mid-May to July and Sept. to mid-Oct. 9am-4pm, longer if weather permits. Car and driver $9; motorcycle and driver $6; $4 per passenger.) Sip selections of the award winning wine produced by Finger Lake-based **Swedish Hill Winery,** 1 mi. east of downtown on Rte. 73. After sampling there, bring your glass with you to complete your tasting tour with another eight tastes at the **Goose Watch Winery,** 123 Main St. in the Alpine Mall, for only an additional $0.01. (☎523-2498. Open M-Sa 10am-6pm, Su noon-6pm. 8 tastes and a wineglass $3.) Just eight mi. east of town on Rte. 86, 700 ft. of waterfalls cascade down through the small picturesque **High Falls Gorge.** Accessible in all seasons, winter admission comes with ice cleats for steady footing and hot chocolate to warm chilled bones. (☎946-2278; www.highfallsgorge.com. Open 9am-5:30pm, last admission 5pm. Summer $9, ages 4-12 $5; call for winter rates.)

THOUSAND ISLAND SEAWAY ☎315

Spanning 100 miles from the mouth of Lake Ontario to the first of the many locks on the St. Lawrence River, the Thousand Island region of the St. Lawrence Seaway forms a natural US-Canadian border. Surveys conducted by the US and Canadian governments determined that there are 1,864 islands in the Seaway, with requirements being that at least one square foot of land must sit above water year-round and two trees should grow on it. The islands, which feature granite cliffs, shady trees, and sandy beaches, are surprisingly variable for a relatively small region and, thus, interesting to tour. The Thousand Island region is also a fisherman's paradise, with some of the world's best bass and muskie catches.

PRACTICAL INFORMATION. The Thousand Island region hugs the St. Lawrence River under two hr. from Syracuse by way of **I-81 N.** From southwest to northeast, **Cape Vincent, Clayton,** and **Alexandria Bay** ("Alex Bay" to locals) are the main towns in the area. Cape Vincent, the smallest of the three, and Clayton are quieter than the more touristy Alex Bay. For Wellesley Island, Alexandria Bay, and the eastern 500 islands, stay on I-81 until you reach Rte. 12 E. For Clayton and points west, take Exit 47 and follow Rte. 12 until you reach Rte. 12 E. **Greyhound,** 540 State St., in Watertown (☎788-8110; open M-F 9am-1pm, 3-4pm, and 6:10-6:30pm; Sa-Su only at departure times), runs to: Albany (6hr., 2 per day, $41); New York City (8hr., 2 per day, $47.50); and Syracuse (1¾hr., 2 per day, $12). **Thousand Islands Bus Lines** (☎287-2790) leaves from the same station for Alexandria Bay ($5.60) and Clayton ($3.55), with departures for both M-F 1pm. Return trips leave Clayton from Gray's Florist, 234 James St. (departs daily 8:45am), and Alexandria from the Dockside Cafe, 17 Market St. (departs daily 8:30am).

The **Clayton Chamber of Commerce,** 517 Riverside Dr., hands out the free and helpful *Clayton Vacation Guide* and *Thousand Islands Seaway Region Travel Guide.* (☎686-3771; www.1000islands-clayton.com. Open mid-June to mid-Sept. daily 9am-5pm; mid-Sept. to mid-June M-F 9am-4pm.) The **Alexandria Bay Chamber of Commerce,** 7 Market St., is just off James St. and offers the Alexandria Bay Vacation Guide to aid your travel in the area. (☎482-9531; www.alexbay.org. Open May-Sept. M-F 8am-6pm, Sa 10am-5pm.) The **Cape Vincent Chamber of Commerce,** 175 James St., by the ferry landing, welcomes visitors and distributes a Cape Vincent Vacation Guide. (☎654-2481; www.capevincent.org. Open May-Oct. Tu-Sa 9am-5pm; late May to early Sept. Su-M 10am-4pm.) **Internet Access:** In Clayton, **Hawn Memorial Library,** 220 John St. (☎686-3762. Open M and Th-F 10am-5pm. T and W 10am-8pm, Sa 9am-12pm.) In Alexandria Bay, **Macsherry Library,** 112 Walton St. (☎482-2241. Open M-Th 9am-12pm, 1pm-5pm, 7pm-9pm; F-Sa 9am-12pm, 1pm-5pm.) **Cape Vincent Community Library,** 157 N. Real, at Gouvello St. (☎654-2132. Open Tu and Th 9am-8pm, F-Sa 9am-1pm.) **Clayton Post Office:** 236 John St. (☎686-3311. Open M-F 9am-4:30pm, Sa 9am-noon.) **Postal Code:** 13624. **Alexandria Bay Post Office:** 13 Bethune St. (☎482-9521. Open M-F 8:30am-5pm, Sa 9am-12pm.) **Postal Code:** 13607. **Cape Vincent Post Office:** 362 Broadway St., across from the village green. (☎654-2424. Open M-F 8am-1pm and 2-4:30pm, Sa 9:30-11:30am.) **Postal Code:** 13618. **Area code:** 315.

ACCOMMODATIONS. Along the western edge of the Seaway in Cape Vincent, near where Lake Ontario meets the St. Lawrence River stands the **Tibbett's Point Lighthouse Hostel (HI-AYH) ❶,** 33439 County Rte. 6. Take Rte. 12 E into town, turn left onto Broadway, and follow the river until the road ends. The lighthouse is still active, and when windy, as it often is, the hypnotic rhythm of the waves buffeting the shore lulls visitors to sleep at night. (☎654-3450. Full kitchen with microwave. Linen $1. Check-in 7am-9am and 5pm-10pm. Reservations strongly recommended on weekends in July and August. Open mid-May to late Oct. Dorms $14, nonmembers $17.) The **Bayview Motel ❷,** 42823 Rte. 12 between Alex Bay and Clayton, offers clean no-frills rooms, although with air-conditioning and TVs, for reasonable rates. (☎482-4906. Open May to mid-Oct. Rooms $39-59.) There are numerous state and private campgrounds in the area, especially along Rte. 12 E. Sites, however, are quite close together and fill up well in advance on weekends. **Burnham Point State Park ❶,** on Rte. 12 E, 4½ mi. east of Cape Vincent and 11 mi. west of Clayton, has a wonderful view of the water, and three picnic areas among the 49 sites, but lacks a beach and is therefore often one of the less crowded campgrounds. (☎654-2324. Showers. Wheelchair-accessible. Open late May-early Sept. daily 8am-10pm. Sites $13-19, with electricity $19-23. Boat dockage $6 per day. $2.75 surcharge for each registration. Day use $6 per car.) **Wellesley Island ❶,** across the $2 toll bridge on I-81 N before Canada, boasts 2,600 acres of marshes and woodland with hiking. The pristine sand beach in the park near the marina is perfect for a pleasant dip in the water on a warm day. (☎482-2722. 430 sites plus cabins. Showers and small museum. Sites $13-19, with electricity $19, full hookup $25. Registration fee $2.75. Cabins with 4 beds, refrigerator, stove, microwave, and picnic table. $40-51. Day use $7 per car. Boat rentals $15 per day for rowboats and canoes. $60 per day plus gas for 16 foot motor boats. Lifeguard mid-June to early Sept. daily 11am-8pm.)

Food options in the Thousand Island Seaway tend towards the generic. However, **Aubrey's Inn ❷,** 126 S. James St. in Cape Vincent serves up some of the best deals in the seaway beside an indoor mural of the Tibbett's Point Lighthouse. (☎654-3754. Breakfast $1.50-6. Most entrees $7-9. Open daily 7am-10pm.)

EXPLORING THE SEAWAY. Of the three significant towns on the western half of the seaway, Clayton and Cape Vincent tend to be the quieter and less expensive two, while Alex Bay has a larger tourist population and a more bustling atmosphere. Some of the most popular activities in the area are the scenic tours of the waterways and riding ferries. With fact-packed live narrations, **Uncle Sam Boat Tours,** 604 Riverside Dr., in Clayton (☎686-3511), and 47 James St., in Alexandria Bay (☎482-2611 or 800-253-9229), delivers good views of the islands and the plush estates that call them home, including the famous **Boldt Castle** on Heart Island. While only a three hr. scenic tour leaves from Cape Vincent, a variety of tours highlight the Seaway from Alexandria Bay. (Tours leave Cape Vincent July-Sept., Alex Bay May to late Oct. daily $9-30, ages 4-12 $4.50-20; prices vary with type and duration of tour. Tours do not cover the price of admission to the castle; $4.75, ages 4-12 $3. Lunch and dinner cruises must be reserved in advance.) **Ferries** from Cape Vincent to **Wolfe Island,** a quaint island with a strawberry farm and golf course among its attractions, are a stepping stone on the way to Kingston in Canada. (☎783-0638. Leave from the Cape Vincent Ferry Dock along Club St. Ferries run May to mid-Oct., 10 per day. $2 per person, $8 per car and driver, bicycles $2. Picture ID may be required.) In Alexandria Bay, **Empire Boat Lines,** 5 Fuller St., sends out scenic tours on smaller boats able to come very close to the islands. The tours include scenic tours, tours to Boldt Castle, and the only regular service to the newly renovated and opened **Singer Castle** chock full of secret rooms and passageways. (☎482-8687 or 888-449-2539. Tours $12.50-27.50, ages 7-14 $6.50-21. Tour prices do not include castle admission. Boldt Castle $4.75, ages 4-12 $3. Singer Castle $10, ages 6-12 $6.) Fishing trips and charters, are the preferred way to explore the islands and waterways for many.

Catch a fish or at least tell the tale of the big one that got away with **1000 Islands Fishing Charters,** 335 Riverside Dr. in Clayton. Offering both drift fishing trips with larger group of people and private charters with only your party on the boat, 1000 Islands can accommodate your preferences. (☎686-3030 or 877-544-4241. Trips July to late Aug. Reservations required. Drift trip $35 per person for 3hr., $45 per person for 5hr. Tackle and bait included. Private Charter $75-160 per person dependant upon the number of people in the group, 7½hr. Tackle included, bait included on some trips.) For those not content to see the waters from above, check out **Hunt's Dive Shop,** 40782 Rt. 12 between Alex Bay and Clayton, for an underwater peek at one or more of the many wrecks that line of floor of the seaway. (☎686-1070. Minimum two people, $65 per person. Equipment rentals $50 per person. Open May-Sept. daily 9am-5:30pm.)

Endorsed by maniacal boaters, the **Antique Boat Museum,** 750 Mary St., in Clayton, houses practically every make and model of hardwood, freshwater, and recreational boat ever conceived as well as offering inexpensive rentals for a variety of skiffs and sailboats. (☎686-4104. Open mid-May to mid-Oct. daily 9am-5pm. $6, students $2, seniors $5, under 5 free.) **French Creek Marina,** 250 Wahl St. (☎686-3621), off Strawberry Lane just south of the junction of Rte. 12 and Rte. 12 E, rents 14 ft. fishing boats ($50 per day), launches boats ($5), and provides overnight docking ($20). **Fishing licenses** are available at sporting goods stores, bait shops, or at the **Town Clerk's Office,** 405 Riverside Dr., in Clayton. (☎686-3512. Open M-F 9am-noon and 1-4pm. $15 per day, $25 per week, $40 per season.)

NEW JERSEY

Travelers who refuse to get off the interstates envision New Jersey as a conglomeration of belching chemical plants and ocean beaches strewn with garbage and gamblers. This false impression unfairly camouflages the state's quieter delights. The interior blooms with fields of corn, tomatoes, and peaches, and placid sandy beaches outline the southern tip of the state. The state shelters quiet hamlets, the Pine Barrens forest, and two world-class universities—Rutgers and Princeton. And, if nothing else will convince you that New Jersey is worth a look, bear in mind that Bruce Springsteen calls "the garden state" home.

PRACTICAL INFORMATION

Capital: Trenton.

Visitor Info: State Division of Tourism, 20 W. State St., P.O. Box 826, Trenton 08625 (☎609-292-2470; www.visitnj.org). **New Jersey Department of Environmental Protection and Energy,** 401 E. State St., Trenton 08625 (☎609-292-2797).

Postal Abbreviation: NJ. **Sales Tax:** 6%; no tax on clothing.

ATLANTIC CITY ☎609

For over 50 years, board-gaming strategists have been wheeling and dealing with Atlantic City geography, passing "Go" to collect their $200 and buying properties in an effort to control this coastal city as reincarnated on the *Monopoly* board. Meanwhile the opulence of Boardwalk and Park Place gradually faded into neglect and then into mega-dollar tackiness. Casinos rose from the rubble of the boardwalk in the 1970s, and nowadays Atlantic City's status is defined by waves of urban professionals looking for a fast buck and quick tan.

TRANSPORTATION

Atlantic City lies halfway down New Jersey's eastern seashore, accessible via the **Garden State Parkway** and the **Atlantic City Expressway,** and easily reached by train from Philadelphia or New York.

Airport: Atlantic City International (☎645-7895 or 800-892-0354; www.acairport.com). Located just west (20min.) of Atlantic City in Pamona.

Trains: Amtrak, 1 Atlantic City Expressway (☎800-872-7245), is open daily 6am-9pm. To **New York** (5½hr., 11 per day, $54) and **Philadelphia** (2½hr., 30 per day, $48). Or **New Jersey Transit** (☎800-772-2222).

Buses: Greyhound (☎340-2000). Buses travel between **New York** Port Authority and most major casinos (2½-3hr., round-trip from $26). Greyhound also has service from casinos to **Philadelphia** (18 per day, round-trip $14). **New Jersey Transit** (☎215-569-3752 or 800-582-5946) offers hourly service from the station on Atlantic Ave. between Michigan and Ohio St. to **New York** ($25, seniors $23). **Gray Line Tours** (☎800-669-0051; www.nycsightseeing.com; terminal open 24hr.) offers daytrips from **New York** (2½hr, $27).

Taxi: Atlantic City Airport Taxi (☎383-1457 or 877-568-8294). $25 flat rate from Atlantic City to the airport.

ORIENTATION & PRACTICAL INFORMATION

Attractions cluster on and around the **Boardwalk,** which runs east-west along the Atlantic Ocean. Running parallel to the Boardwalk, **Pacific** and **Atlantic Avenue** offer cheap restaurants, hotels, and convenience stores. *Atlantic Ave. can be dangerous after dark, and any street farther out can be dangerous even by day.* Getting around is easy on foot on the Boardwalk. **Parking lots** near the boards run $3-7.

Visitor Info: The **Visitors Center on the Atlantic Expressway,** 1 mi. after the Pleasantville Toll Plaza, (☎449-7130) offers pamphlets, brochures, and general help with the added bonus of free parking. Open daily 9am-5pm. Also helpful is the **Atlantic City Convention Center and Visitors Bureau,** 2314 Pacific Ave. (☎888-228-4748; www.atlanticcitynj.com.) Open daily 9am-5pm. On the Boardwalk, try the Bureau's **Visitor Info Center** at Mississippi St. (☎888-228-4748; www.atlanticcitynj.com.) Open daily 9:30am-5:30pm, Memorial Day to Labor Day also Th-Su 9:30am-8pm.

Medical Services: Atlantic City Medical Center, 1925 Pacific Ave. at Michigan. (☎344-4081.)

Hotlines: Rape and Abuse Hotline, ☎646-6767. **Gambling Abuse,** ☎800-426-2537. Both 24hr.

Post Office: 1701 Pacific Ave. (☎345-4212), at Illinois Ave. Open M-F 8:30am-6pm, Sa 8:30am-12:30pm.) **Postal Code:** 08401. **Area Code:** 609.

Free Parking: Meterless parking is available on some residential streets. Try Oriental Ave. at New Jersey Ave. near the Garden Pier Historic Museum for free 3hr. parking with easy walking distance to the Boardwalk. *Be careful at night: this area is more desolate than other parts of the city.*

Alternative Forms of Transportation: Rolling Chair Rides are found along the boardwalk as frequently as yellow cabs in Manhattan. (☎347-7500.) **Atlantic City Trolley Tours**, 821 Shunpike Rd., in Cape May. (☎884-7392 or 866-872-6737; www.gatrolley.com. Runs June to mid-Sept.)

ACCOMMODATIONS

Inn of the Irish Pub, 164 St. James Pl. (☎344-9063; www.theirishpub.com), between New York Ave. and Tennessee, near the Ramada Tower, has spacious, clean rooms. Enjoy the porch's relaxing rocking chairs and refreshing Atlantic breeze. The downstairs bar offers lively entertainment and a friendly atmosphere. Key deposit $7. Doubles with shared bath $45-52, with private bath $75-90; quads with shared bath $85-99. ❸

Comfort Inn, 154 South Kentucky Ave. (☎348-4000), between Martin Luther King Blvd. and New York Ave., near the Sands (see p. 277). Basic rooms with king-size or 2 queen-size beds and—true to Atlantic City swank—a jacuzzi. Breakfast, free parking, and a heated pool. Rooms with ocean views $20 extra, but come with fridge, microwave, and a bigger jacuzzi. Reserve well in advance for Sa-Su and holidays. Sept.-May rooms $59-69; June-Aug. $89-159. ❹

Red Carpet Motel, 1630 Albany Ave. (☎348-3171). A bit out of the way, off the Atlantic Expwy. on the way into town, the Red Carpet provides standard, comfortable, uninspiring rooms and free shuttles to the boardwalk and casinos. Cable TV, restaurant in lobby. Doubles $39-59; quads $55-79. Prices can jump to $130 on summer weekends. *Be careful in the surrounding neighborhood after dark.* ❸

Shady Pines Campground, 443 S. 6th Ave. (☎652-1516), in Absecon, 6 mi. from Atlantic City. Take Exit 12 from the Expwy. This leafy, 140-site campground sports a pool, playground, laundry, firewood service, and new showers and restrooms. Call ahead for summer weekend reservations. Open Mar.-Nov. Sites with water and electricity $33. ❷

FOOD

Although not recommended by nutritionists, $0.75 hot dogs and $1.50 pizza slices are all over the Boardwalk. Some of the best deals in town await at the casinos, where all-you-can-eat lunch ($7) and dinner ($11) buffets abound. Tastier, less tacky food can be found a little farther from the seashore.

Inn of the Irish Pub, 164 St. James Pl. (☎345-9613; www.theirishpub.com), may not serve the healthiest food, but it tastes damn good. Start off with a 20th St. sampler (buffalo wings, fried mozzarella, potato skins, and chicken thumbs; $7). The daily lunch special (11:30am-2pm) includes a pre-selected sandwich and a cup of soup for $2. All-you-can-eat Su brunch $7. $6 dinner specials M-F 2-8pm and Sa-Su until 8pm. Domestic drafts $1. Open 24hr. Cash only. ❷

White House Sub Shop, 2301 Arctic Ave. (☎345-8599 or 345-1564 for pick-up; www.whitehousesubshop.com), at Mississippi Ave. Sinatra was rumored to have had these immense subs ($4-12) flown to him while he was on tour. Pictures of White House sub-lovers Joe DiMaggio, Wayne Newton, and Mr. T adorn the walls. Italian subs and cheesesteaks $6-12. Open Su-Th 10am-10pm, F-Sa 10am-11pm. Cash only. ❷

Tony's Baltimore Grille, 2800 Atlantic Ave. (☎345-5766), between Pacific and Baltic, at Iowa Ave. Tourists can't resist the old-time Italian atmosphere with personal jukeboxes, not to mention the $3-8 pasta and pizza. Seafood platter $12. Open daily 11am-3am. Bar open 24hr. Cash only. ❷

Sundae Ice Cream (☎347-8424), between South Carolina and Ocean Ave. on the Boardwalk, makes over 20 flavors of ice cream and yogurt ($2.50). The chocolate chip cookie dough is terrific. If it's too chilly for dessert, try the coffee, tea, or hot cocoa ($1). Funnel cake $3.50. Open Su-Th 10am-midnight, F-Sa 10am-3am. Cash only. ❶

CAINO, THE BOARDWALK, & BEACHES

All casinos on the Boardwalk fall within a dice toss of one another. The farthest south is the elegant **Hilton** (☎347-7111 or 800-257-8677; www.hiltonac.com), between Providence and Boston Ave., and the farthest north is the gaudy **Showboat** (☎343-4000 or 800-621-0200; www.harrahs.com), at Delaware Ave. and Boardwalk. Donald Trump's glittering **Trump Taj Mahal Hotel and Casino,** 1000 Boardwalk at Virginia Ave. (☎449-1000; www.trumptaj.com), is too ostentatious to be missed; neglected payments on this tasteless tallboy cast the financier into his billion dollar tailspin. In true *Monopoly* form, Trump owns three other hotel

THE LOCAL STORY

HIGH DIVING HORSES

Before gambling took center stage in Atlantic City, vacationers flocked there in pursuit of a different sort of entertainment. Back then, the main attraction was a high diving horse act. Here, Atlantic City historian Allen "Boo" Pergament tells the story behind the legend.

LG: Who invented the act?
AP: William "Doc" Carver, frontiersman, army scout, fellow showman and friend of famed Buffalo Bill, Deadeye Dick, and others, accidentally fell while crossing the Platte River. Years later, after having delved into the world of Wild West Shows, Doc used his brush with death and decided to train young women and horses to dive from a high platform
LG: How did the act come to the Steel Pier?
AP: Unfortunately, Doc passed away just before his act opened in Atlantic City, but [it] went into the annals of history as the most memorable and famous act in town. 5000 spectators would end their adventures on the Steel Pier with dread-filled and delighted anticipation as a horse ran up an L-shaped platform to meet a young woman who would jump on its back seconds before it plunged 40ft. into a pool of water below. From 1929 to 1978, audiences could count on the high diving horse act every summer.

casinos in the city: the recently remodeled **Trump Plaza,** at Mississippi and the Boardwalk (☎441-6000 or 800-677-7378; www.trumpplaza.com); **Trump World's Fair** (☎800-473-7829), on the Boardwalk; and **Trump Castle** (☎441-2000; www.trumpmarina.com), on Huron Blvd. at the Marina. In summer, energetic partiers go to "rock the dock" at Trump Castle's indoor/outdoor bar/restaurant, **The Deck** (☎877-477-4697). Many a die is cast at **Caesar's Boardwalk Resort and Casino,** 2100 Pacific Ave. (☎348-4411; www.caesarsatlatincity.com) at Arkansas Ave. The **Sands** (☎441-4000; www.acsands.com), at Indiana Ave., stands tall and flashy with its seashell motif. The newest casino in town is **The Borgata** (☎866-692-6742; www.theborgata.com), a golden scintillation near the Trump Marina Hotel Casino and Harrah's in the Marina District that has been in the works since 2000. All are open 24hr.

There's something for everyone in Atlantic City—thanks to the Boardwalk. Those under 21 **gamble for prizes** at one of the many arcades that line the Boardwalk, including **Central Pier Arcade & Speedway**, at the Boardwalk and Tennessee (☎345-5219). It feels like real gambling, but the teddy bear in the window is easier to win than the convertible on display at Caesar's. The historic **Steel Pier** (☎898-7645 or 866-386-6659; www.steelpier.com), the Boardwalk at Virginia Ave., juts into the coastal waters with a ferris wheel that spins riders over the Atlantic. It also offers the rest of the usual amusement park suspects: roller coaster, carousel, and games of "skill" aplenty. (Open daily noon-midnight; call the Taj Mahal for winter hours. Rides $2-5 each.) When and if you tire of spending money, check out the historic **Atlantic City Beach.** For more water fun, visitors invariably stumble upon at least one of the piers occupied by **Morey's Piers & Raging Waters Waterparks,** on the Boardwalk at 25th Ave., Schellenger, and Spencer (☎522-3900 or 888-667-3971; www.moreyspiers.com). Just west of Atlantic City, **Ventnor City** offers more tranquil shores.

CAPE MAY ☎609

At the southern extreme of New Jersey's coastline, Cape May is the oldest seashore resort in the US, and the money here is no younger. Once the summer playground of Upper Eastside New Yorkers, the town still shows the signs of affluent infiltration in the elegant restaurants of Beach Ave. but is no longer characterized by it. Meanwhile, the resort's main attraction continues to be the sparkling white beaches which shun the commercialism of more modern beach towns.

ORIENTATION & PRACTICAL INFORMATION. Despite its geographic isolation, Cape May is easily accessible by car or bus. Start digging for loose change as you follow the tollbooth-laden **Garden State Parkway** as far south as it goes (most tolls $0.35). Watch for signs to Center City until on Lafayette St. Alternatively, take the slower, scenic **Ocean Drive** 40 mi. south along the shore from Atlantic City. **Route 55** brings beachgoers from Philadelphia. **NJ Transit** (☎215-569-3752 or 973-762-5100) makes a stop at the bus depot on the corner of Lafayette and Ocean St. It runs to: Atlantic City (2hr., 18 per day, $4); New York City (4½hr., 3 per day, $30); Philadelphia (3hr., 18 per day, $15). If you're coming from the D.C. area, the 1¼hr. **Cape May-Lewes Ferry** presents a pleasant and more direct alternative to an otherwise potentially long and laborious 3-4hr. drive. (☎800-643-3779. Reservations required; call at least 2hr. in advance. Passenger cars $20-25.) **Cape May Seashore Lines** runs four old-fashioned trains per day to attractions along the 26 mi. stretch to Tuckahoe. (☎884-2675. $8, children $5.) Bike the beach with the help of **Shields' Bike Rentals,** 11 Gurney St. (open daily 7am-7pm; $4 per hr., $9 per day; tandems $10/30; surreys $24 per hr.), or **Steck's Bike Rentals,** 251 Beach Dr. (☎884-1188. Open daily May-Nov. 7am-7pm. $5 per hr., $12 per day, $42 per week.) Other services include: **Welcome Center:** 609 Lafayette St. (☎884-9562. Open daily 9am-4:30pm.) **Chamber of Commerce:** 513 Washington St. Mall. (☎884-5508; www.capemaychamber.com. Open M-F 9am-5pm, Sa-Su 10am-6pm.) **Washington Street Mall Information Booth** at Ocean St. (☎800-275-4278; www.capemaymac.org. Open summer daily 9:15am-4pm and 6-9pm; call for low-season hours.) **Post Office:** 700 Washington St. (☎884-3578. Open M-F 9am-5pm, Sa 8:30am-12:30pm.) **Postal Code:** 08204. **Area Code:** 609.

ACCOMMODATIONS. Sleeping does not come cheaply in Cape May. Luxurious hotels and Victorian B&Bs along the beach run $85-250 per night. Farther from the shore, prices drop. Although the **Hotel Clinton ❷,** 202 Perry St. at S. Lafayette St., may lack stately suites and A/C, the Italian family-owned establishment offers 16 breezy rooms, the most affordable rates in town, and priceless warmth from the charismatic proprietors. (☎884-3993. Open mid-June to Sept. Reservations recommended. Singles $35; doubles $45. Cash only.) Next door, the **Parris Inn ❷,** 204 Perry St., rents a variety of spacious, comfortable rooms and apartments (some much nicer than others) less than 3 blocks from the beach, most with private baths, A/C, and TV. (☎884-8015. Open mid-Apr. to Dec. Singles summer $45-65; doubles $65-125; low-season rates...well, they're lower.) For an elegant stay less than a block from the beach in the heart of a line of colorful Victorian homes and B&Bs, **Poor Richard's Inn ❹,** 17 Jackson St. offers a European-style breakfast and antique-laden rooms. (☎884-3536; www.poorrichardsinn.com. Some shared baths. Check-in 1-10pm. Check-out 10:30am. Memorial Day-Oct. $75-165; low-season $65-150.) Campgrounds line U.S. 9 just north of Cape May. In a prime seashore location, **Cape Island Campground ❷,** 709 Rte. 9, is connected to Cape May by the Seashore Line (see above). The fully equipped campground features mini-golf, two pools, a playground, a store, and laundry facilities. (☎800-437-7443; www.capeisland.com. Full hookup. Sites $38.)

FOOD & NIGHTLIFE. Cape May's cheapest food is the generic pizza and burger fare along **Beach Avenue.** Shell out a few more clams for a more substantial meal at one of the posh beachside restaurants. Crawling with pedestrians hunting for heavenly fudge and saltwater taffy, the **Washington Street Mall** supports several popular food stores and eateries. Start the morning off right with a gourmet breakfast on the porch of the **Mad Batter ❹,** 19 Jackson St. Try a stack of blueberry blintz crêpes with warm syrup ($7.50), or choose from a variety of steak and seafood options ($14-25) for lunch or dinner. (☎884-5970; www.madbatter.com. Open daily 8am-10pm.) A meal at the pub-like **Ugly Mug ❷,** 426 Washington St. Mall, is worth battling through the initially suffocating smokescreen. Fresh air can be had on the patio as patrons inhale a New England cup o' chowder for $2.25 or the ever-popular "oceanburger" for $5.75. (☎884-3459. Free pizza M 10pm-2am. Open M-Sa 11am-2am, Su noon-2am; hot food served until 11pm.)

The rock scene collects around **Carney's,** on Beach Ave. between Jackson and Decatur St., with nightly entertainment in the summer beginning at 10pm. Themed parties include "Island Tropics" and "Animal House." (☎884-4424. Su jams 4-9pm. Open daily 11:30am-2am.) A chic crowd congregates at **Cabana's,** at the corner of Decatur St. and Beach Ave. across from the beach. You'll have to find a lot of sand dollars if you want an entree ($16-22), but there is no cover for the nightly blues or jazz. (☎884-8400; www.cabanasonthebeach.com. Acoustic sessions Sa 4-6:30pm. Open daily noon-2am.) **Magic Brain Cybercafe,** 31 Perry St., is the best place in town to grab a quick meal and check email. The spotless new Internet cafe greets you with an amicable staff, and an auspicious location less than one block from the beach. (☎884-8188; www.magicbraincybercafe.com. Internet access $7 per 30min. Cash only. Open daily 8am-10pm.)

HITTING THE BEACH. Cape May's sands actually sparkle, studded with the famous Cape May "diamonds" (actually quartz pebbles). A **beach tag** is required for beachgoers over 11. Tags are available from roaming vendors or from the **Beach Tag Office,** located at Grant and Beach Dr. (☎884-9522. Open daily 9:30am-5:30pm. Tags required June-Sept. daily 9:30am-5:30pm. $4, 3-day $8, weekly $11, seasonal $17.) Those in search of exercise and a spectacular view of the seashore can ascend the 199 steps to the beacon of the 1859 **Cape May Lighthouse** in **Cape May Point State Park,** west of town at the end of the point. (Lighthouse ☎884-5404. Visitors Center ☎884-2159. Park open daily 8am-dusk. Free. Lighthouse open Apr.-Nov. daily 9am-8pm; Dec.-Mar. Sa-Su 8am-dusk. $4, ages 3-12 $1. Visitors Center open daily July-Aug. 8am-8pm; Sept.-June 8am-4:30pm.) Three trails commence at the Visitors Center: the red (½ mi., wheelchair-accessible), yellow (1¼ mi., moderate and flat), and the blue trails (2 mi., moderate and flat, last leg takes hikers along the oceanfront back to the start) boast excellent bird watching and clearly marked paths through marsh and oceanside dunes. The behemoth bunker next to the lighthouse is a WWII gun emplacement, used to scan the shore for German U-boats. In summer, several shuttles run the 5 mi. from the bus depot on Lafayette St. to the lighthouse ($5, ages 3-12 $4). Due to the unusually close proximity of freshwater ponds adjacent to the oceanside, even migratory birds flock to Cape May for a break from the long, southbound flight. Sneak a peak at more than 300 types of feathered vacationers at the **Cape May Bird Observatory,** 701 E. Lake Dr., on Cape May Point, a birdwatcher's paradise. Bird maps, field trips, and workshops are available, along with advice about where to go for the best birdwatching. (☎884-2736; www.njaudubon.org. Open Tu-Su 10am-5pm.) For a look at some larger creatures, including dolphins and whales, **Cape May Whale Watch and Research Center** offers tours. (☎888-531-0055. $17-22, ages 7-12 $8-12.) **South End Surf Shop,** 311 Beach Ave., rents beach necessities. (☎898-0988. Open Apr.-Sept. daily 9am-4pm. Surfboard $20 per day.) For those thinking of doing a little wave jumping, rent boats, waverunners, and kayaks from **Cape May Watersports,** 1286 Wilson Dr. (☎884-8646. Open daily 8am-sunset. Boats $50-60 per 4hr., waverunners $50 per hr., kayaks $15 per hr.)

PENNSYLVANIA

Established as a colony to protect Quakers from persecution, Pennsylvania has clung to the ideals of freedom from the drafting of the Declaration of Independence in Philadelphia to the present. In 1976, Philadelphia groomed its historic shrines for the nation's bicentennial, and today the colonial monuments serve as the centerpiece of the city's ambitious renewal. Pittsburgh, the steel city with a raw image, was once dirty enough to fool streetlights into burning during the day, but has begun a cultural renaissance as of late. Removed from the noise of its urban areas, Pennsylvania's landscape has retained much of the rustic beauty first discovered by colonists centuries ago, from the farms of Lancaster County to the gorges of the Allegheny Plateau.

PRACTICAL INFORMATION

Capital: Harrisburg.

Visitor Info: Pennsylvania Travel and Tourism, 453 Forum Bldg., Harrisburg 17120 (☎800-847-4872; www.experiencepa.com).

Bureau of State Parks, Rachel Carson State Office Bldg., 400 Market St., Harrisburg 17108 (☎888-727-2757; www.dcnrstate.pa.us/stateparks). Open M-Sa 7am-5pm.

Postal Abbreviation: PA. **Sales Tax:** 6%.

PHILADELPHIA ☎215

With his band of Quakers, William Penn founded the City of Brotherly Love in 1682. But it was Ben, not Penn, that transformed the town into the urban metropolis it is today. Benjamin Franklin, ingenious American ambassador, inventor, and womanizer, almost singlehandedly built Philadelphia into an American colonial capital. Sightseers will eat up Philly's historic attractions, world-class museums, and architectural accomplishments—not to mention the native cheesesteaks (a staple here) and the endless culinary choices of the city's ethnic neighborhoods.

INTERCITY TRANSPORTATION

Airport: Philadelphia International (☎800-745-4283 or 937-6800; www.phl.org), 8 mi. southwest of Center City on I-76. The 20min. **SEPTA Airport Rail Line** (☎580-7800; www.septa.org) runs from Center City to the airport. Trains run from Market East Station to the airport daily every 30min 4:25am-11:25pm; from the airport (Terminal E) to city stations 5:09am-12:09am. $5.50 each way at window. Last train from airport 12:09am. A taxi to downtown costs about $20.

Trains: Amtrak, 30th St. Station (☎800-872-7245), at Market St. in University City. Station open 24hr. To: **Baltimore** (2hr., M-F 19 per day, $43-44); **Boston** (7hr., 9 per day, $74); **New York** (2hr.; 31 per day; $48-52, express trains $90); **Pittsburgh** (8hr., 2 per day, $39-76); **Washington, D.C.** (2hr., 19 per day, $45-51). Ticket office open M-F 5:10am-10:30pm, Sa-Su 6:10am-10:30pm.

Buses: Greyhound, 1001 Filbert St. (☎931-4075 or 800-231-2222), at 10th and Filbert downtown, 1 block north of Market. Station open daily 24hr. To: **Atlantic City** (2hr., 18 per day, $10); **Baltimore** (2hr., 10 per day, $18.50); **Boston** (7hr., 16 per day, $55); **New York** (2hr., 28 per day, $21); **Pittsburgh** (7hr., 9 per day, $38-41);

Washington, D.C. (3hr., 10 per day, $22). **New Jersey Transit** (☎569-3752 or 800-772-3606; office open M-F 8am-5pm) is in the same station. To **Atlantic City** (1½hr., 14 per day, $6.60) and other points on the New Jersey shore.

ORIENTATION

Penn planned his city as a logical and easily accessible grid, though the prevalence of one-way streets can cause a migraine behind the wheel. As an incentive for visitors to walk, Philadelphia has posted, at almost every corner, a map with the handy-dandy "you are here" star, along with arrows indicating directions to specific destinations. The north-south streets ascend numerically from the **Delaware River,** flowing from **Penn's Landing** and **Independence Hall** on the east side to the **Schuylkill River** (SKOO-kill) on the west. The first street is **Front;** the others follow consecutively from 2 to 69 across the Schuylkill River. This **Center City** area is distinguished from poorer South and Northeast Philly and affluent Northwest Philly. The intersection of **Broad (14th)** and **Market Street** is the focal point of Center City, marked by the ornate City Hall. Be warned: street addresses often refer to alleys not pictured on standard maps of the city. The **SEPTA transportation map,** available free from the tourist office, is probably the most complete map of the city.

Driving is not a great way to get around town. However, parking near the historic sights is about $10 per day, and lower-priced options scatter at farther but walkable distances. Meterless 2hr. parking spaces can sometimes be found in the Washington Sq. district or on the cobblestones of Dock St. Most lots require vehicles to be in by 9-10am and out by 6-7pm. At 2nd St., between Market and Chestnut St., a **Central Parking System** lot is a good deal. (Early bird special $6.50. Max. day rate $11. Su flat rate $8.) In centrally-located Chinatown, park in the lot on Arch St. between 9th and 10th St. for $6. To park near Center City or the Rodin Museum, the parking lot directly behind **The Free Library of Philadelphia** offers a $5 flat rate on weekends. A final option is to park outside the city and ride Philly's **buses** and **subway** to major downtown destinations (see **Local Transportation**, below). *Public transportation can be unsafe after dark.*

NEIGHBORHOODS

The **Historic District** stretches from Front to 6th St. and from Race to South St. The hip **Washington Square District** runs from 6th to Broad St. and Market to South St. The affluent **Rittenhouse Square District** lies directly to the west. **Chinatown** comprises the blocks around 10th and Arch St., while the **Museums District** takes up the northwest quadrant bordered by Market and Broad St. Across the Schuylkill River, **University City** includes the sprawling campuses of the **University of Pennsylvania** and **Drexel University.**

LOCAL TRANSPORTATION

Public Transit: Southeastern Pennsylvania Transportation Authority (SEPTA), 1234 Market St. (☎580-7800). Extensive bus and rail service to the suburbs. Buses serve the 5-county area. Most operate 5am-2am, some 24hr. 2 major subway routes: the blue east-west **Market Street line** (including 30th St. Station and the historic area) and the orange north-south **Broad Street line** (including the stadium complex in south Philadelphia). *The subway is unsafe after dark; buses are usually safer.* Pick up a free SEPTA system map at any subway stop. $2, transfers $0.60. Unlimited all-day pass for both $5.50, unlimited weekly pass $18.75, unlimited month pass $70. Note: **the subway closes around midnight,** when all-night shuttle service begins; shuttles stop at the major subway stops about every 10-15min. until the subway reopens in the morning.

Downtown Philadelphia

ACCOMMODATIONS
Antique Row B&B, **18**
Bank St. Hostel (HI), **9**
Chamounix Hostel (HI), **6**
La Reserve, **19**

FOOD
Abner's Cheesesteaks, **14**
Alma de Cuba, **15**
Basset's Ice Cream, **5**
Famous 4th St. Deli, **23**
Jamaican Jerk Hut, **20**
Jim's Steaks, **21**
Lombardi's, **11**

FOOD (Cont.)
Pink Rose Pastry Shop, **22**
Rangoon, **4**
Ray's Tea House and Café, **3**
Sang Kee Peking Duck House, **1**
Singapore, **2**
Smokey Joe's, **13**
Tandoor India Restaurant, **12**

NIGHTLIFE
The Five Spot, **8**
Khyber, **10**
Moriarty's, **17**
Warmdaddy's, **7**
Woody's, **16**

0 200 yards
0 200 meters
Mt. Vernon St.
TO EASTERN STATE PENITENTIARY
TO TEMPLE UNIVERSITY
Greene St.
TO BOATHOUSE ROW
Philadelphia Museum of Art
23rd St.
Spring Garden St.
18th St.
SPRING GARDEN
611
Spring Garden St. Bridge
Fairmount Park
Hamilton St.
TO PHILADELPHIA ZOO
Rodin Museum
76
Schuylkill
Free Library of Philadelphia
Callowhill St.
N. Broad St.
13th St.
12th St.
11th St.
Callowhill St.
Front St.
Benjamin Franklin
676
30
River
Fels Planetarium
LOGAN CIRCLE
RACE–VINE
CHINATOWN
Franklin St.
676
Benjamin Franklin Bridge
Please Touch Museum
Race St.
Academy of Natural Sciences
Parkway
Pennsylvania Academy of Fine Art
Race St.
Convention Center
Trocadero Theater
Shoe Museum
Afro-American Historical and Cultural Museum
Independence National Historical Park
Elfreth's Alley
U.S. Mint
OLD CITY
Betsy Ross House
Delaware River
Arch St.
Cherry St.
Amtrak
Arch St.
PARKWAY/MUSEUM DISTRICT
Masonic Temple
Arch St.
Reading Terminal Market
Greyhound
CHINATOWN
Independence St.
Christ Church Burial Ground (Ben Franklin's Grave)
Christ Church
30th St.
John F. Kennedy Blvd.
Filbert St.
Philadelphia Visitors Center
2ND ST.
TO 6
Market St.
CITY HALL
City Hall
Juniper St.
21st St.
20th St.
30TH ST.
15TH ST.
S. Penn Sq.
13TH ST.
11TH ST.
8TH AND MARKET ST.
Liberty Bell Pavilion
5TH ST.
Franklin Court
Bank St.
95
Penn's Landing
DREXEL UNIVERSITY
Mütter Museum
CENTER CITY
Balch Institute
Atwater Kent Museum
Chestnut St.
19th St.
17th St.
16th St.
15th St.
AVENUE OF THE ARTS
Chestnut St.
Independence Hall and Congress Hall
Delaware Ave.
Sansom St.
Sansom St.
JEWELERS ROW
Carpenters' Hall
2nd St.
Independence Seaport Museum
TO UNIVERSITY OF PENNSYLVANIA
23rd St.
22nd St.
Walnut St.
Walnut St.
Norman Rockwell Museum
RITTENHOUSE SQUARE
WALNUT–LOCUST
WASHINGTON SQUARE
HISTORIC DISTRICT
Dock St.
Locust St.
Curtis Institute of Music
Academy of Music
Tomb of the Unknown Soldier
SOCIETY HILL
Barnegar
25th St.
24th St.
RITTENHOUSE SQUARE DISTRICT
Spruce St.
Merriam Theater
S. Broad St.
10th St.
WASHINGTON SQUARE DISTRICT
Spruce St.
Mattis St.
Delancey Pl.
Rosenbach Museum and Library
18th St.
Pine St.
ANTIQUE ROW
Pine St.
9th St.
8th St.
7th St.
6th St.
5th St.
4th St.
3rd St.
HEAD HOUSE SQUARE
Front St.
U.S.S. Becuna
U.S.S. Olympia
Lombard St.
LOMBARD SOUTH
Lombard St.
South St.
TO VETERAN'S STADIUM
South St.
TO MUMMER'S MUSEUM
TO AIRPORT

MID-ATLANTIC

Tours: In the tourist area, convenient, purple **Phlash** buses hit all major sights. (☎580-7800. July-Aug. daily 10am-8pm every 10-12min. $1, seniors and under 5 free. Day-pass $3.) **Philadelphia Sight-Seeing Tours** provide informative guides and a knowledgeable trolley driver. Hop on and off all day or take the 1½hr. tour in one go. (☎925-8687. Runs every 30min: $20, ages 6-12 $5; extra day $6/3.) For more extensive coverage of the city, try the double-decker buses of **The Big Bus Company.** (☎866-324-4287. Runs every 30min. $25, children $10.) Last but far from least, **Ride the Ducks** offers a land and water tour in one. (☎227-3825. $20, ages 3-12 $11.)

Taxi: Yellow Cab, ☎922-8400. **City Cab,** ☎492-6500.

Car Rental: Alamo, ☎492-3960 or 800-327-9633.

Bike Rental: Frankenstein Bike Work, 1529 Spruce St. (☎893-4467). Open May-Sept. M-Sa 10:30am-6:30pm. Call ahead for Su service. Cruisers $12 for 4hr., $20 per day.

PRACTICAL INFORMATION

Visitor Info: The **City Visitor Center** and the **National Park Service Visitors Center** (☎965-2305 or 800-537-7676; www.independencevisitorcenter.com) are both at 5th St., between Market and Chestnut St. Pick up maps, schedules, brochures, and the free *Gazette* for upcoming city events. Open summer daily 9am-6pm; winter 9am-5pm.

Hotlines: Suicide and Crisis Intervention, ☎686-4420. **Youth Crisis Line,** ☎787-0633. **Women Against Abuse,** ☎386-7777. All 24hr.

Bi-Gay-Lesbian Resources: Gay and Lesbian Peer Counseling Services, ☎732-8255. Operates M-F 6-9pm. **William Way Lesbian, Gay, and Bisexual Community Center** (☎732-2220; www.waygay.org) has info about gay events and activities. Open M-F 11:30am-10pm, Sa 11:30am-7pm, Su 10:30am-7pm.

Internet Access: The Free Library of Philadelphia (see p. 291).

Post Office: 2970 Market St. (☎895-8980.), at 30th St., across from the Amtrak station. Open daily 6am-midnight. **Postal Code:** 19104. **Area Code:** 215.

ACCOMMODATIONS

Aside from its two hostels, inexpensive lodging in Philadelphia is uncommon, but if arrangements are made a few days in advance, comfortable rooms close to Center City can be had for around $60. The motels near the airport at Exit 9A on I-95 sacrifice location for the most affordable rates in the area. The personable proprietors at **Antique Row Bed and Breakfast** and **La Reserve** (see below) will recommend rooms if they're full. **Bed and Breakfast Connections/Bed and Breakfast of Philadelphia,** in Devon, PA, books rooms in Philadelphia and southeastern Pennsylvania. (☎610-687-3565; www.bnbphiladelphia.com. Open M-F 9am-5pm. Reserve at least a week in advance; one-time registration fee $10. Singles $60-90; doubles $75-250.)

MID-ATLANTIC

Chamounix Mansion International Youth Hostel (HI-AYH), 3250 Chamounix Dr. (☎878-3676 or 800-379-0017; www.philahostel.org), in West Fairmount Park. Take bus #38 from lower Market St. to Ford and Cranston Rd.; take Ford Rd., turn left on Chamounix Dr., and follow to hostel. A young, energetic staff maintains uncommonly lavish hosteling in a converted mansion. Kitchen, laundry, TV/VCR, piano, and bikes. Free parking, discounted bus tokens, and free summer Philadelphia Orchestra passes. Internet access $1 per 5min. Linen $3. Check-in 8-11am and 4:30pm-midnight. Lockout 11am-4:30pm. Curfew midnight. Dorms $15, nonmembers $18. ❶

Bank Street Hostel (HI-AYH), 32 S. Bank St. (☎922-0222 or 800-392-4678; www.bankstreethostel.com). From the bus station, walk down Market St.; it's in an alleyway between 2nd and 3rd St. This social hostel in the historic district offers A/C, a big screen TV, free coffee and tea, laundry facilities, kitchen, and pool table. 70 beds.

Late sleepers beware of the 9am musical wake-up call blasted from the extensive speaker system. Internet access $1 per 4min. Linen $3. Lockout 10am-4:30pm. Curfew Su-Th 12:30am, F-Sa 1am. Cannot reserve rooms via phone; must mail payment in advance—call for details. Dorms $18, nonmembers $21. Cash only. ❶

Antique Row Bed and Breakfast, 341 S. 12th St. (☎592-7802; www.antiquerowbnb.com). Enchanting traditional B&B at the heart of colonial rowhouses. The engaging owner offers her guests expert restaurant referrals and serves her own hearty breakfast. 4 apartments geared toward longer visits with TV, utilities, and laundry. Free local calls. Rooms $75-100; reduced rates for longer stays. ❹

La Reserve (a.k.a. **Bed and Breakfast Center City**), 1804 Pine St. (☎735-1137; www.centercitybed.com). Take I-676, to the 23rd St. Exit and bear right. 10 blocks down, turn left onto Pine. Entertains guests with an extravagant dining room that is often the site of lively dinner parties and visits from local musicians. Personable owner is a reliable source of Philadelphia advice and sidesplitting humor. Full breakfast. Plush doubles $80-130. ❹

Timberlane Campground, 117 Timberlane Rd. (☎856-423-6677; www.timberlanecampground.com), 15 mi. from Center City, across the Delaware River in Clarksboro, NJ, is the closest campsite to Philadelphia. Take U.S. 295 S to Exit 18B (Clarksboro), follow straight through the traffic light ½ mi. and turn right on Friendship Rd. Timber Ln. is 1 block on the right. Reservations recommended. Sites $24; full hookup $30. ❶

FOOD

Street vendors are at the forefront of Philly specialties, hawking cheesesteaks, hoagies, cashews, and soft pretzels. Ethnic eateries gather in several specific areas: hip **South Street,** between Front and 7th St.; **18th Street** around Sansom St.; and **2nd Street,** between Chestnut and Market St. The nation's third largest **Chinatown** is bounded by 11th, 8th, Arch, and Vine St., and offers well-priced vegetarian restaurants. For the carnivorous, no Philly visit is complete without a cheesesteak. The quintessential Philly cheesesteak rivalry squares off at 9th and Passyunk Ave., in South Philadelphia; **Pat's King of Steaks** ❷ (☎468-1546; www.patskingofsteaks.com), the legendary founder of the cheesesteak, faces the larger, more neon **Geno's Steaks** ❷, (☎389-0659; www.genosteaks.com). Both offer cheesesteaks for $5-6 and stay open 24hr.

Fresh fruit and other foodstuffs pack the mobbed streets of the immense **Italian Market,** which spans the area around 9th St. below Christian St. Philadelphia's original farmer's market (since 1893), the **Reading Terminal Market,** at 12th and Arch St. across from the Pennsylvania Convention Center, is the largest indoor market in the US. Stocking globally diverse food, the market is a fabulous lunch spot. (☎922-2317; www.readingterminalmarket.org. Open M-Sa 8am-6pm; Amish merchants W-Th 8am-3pm, F-Sa 8am-5pm.)

HISTORIC DISTRICT

Famous 4th Street Delicatessen, 700 S. 4th St. (☎922-3274), at Bainbridge St. This delicatessen rivals New York's finest. A landmark since 1923, the Delicatessen has earned its stellar reputation by serving favorites, like hot corned beef sandwiches ($7.50), in its antique original dining room. The cookies and lemonade make for a delicious treat. Open M-Sa 8am-6pm, Su 8am-4pm. ❷

Jim's Steaks, 400 South St. at 4th St. (☎928-1911; www.jimsteaks.com). Though the place looks a little run-down on the outside, the inside bustles with activity. Customers arrive in droves for the authentic Philly hoagie ($3.50-5) and fries ($1.25), and pass the time in line by inspecting the impressive wall of fame. Open M-Th 10am-1am, F-Sa 10am-3am, Su noon-10pm. ❶

Pink Rose Pastry Shop, 630 S. 4th St. (☎592-0565; www.pinkrosepastry.com), at Bainbridge St. across from the Delicatessen. Friendly students serve up the widest selection of homemade delicacies at intimate tables graced with freshly-cut flowers. The sour cream apple pie ($4.50) is unforgettable, while white chocolate raspberry mousse cake ($5.50) with a latte ($2.75) leaves diners crooning for more. Open M-Th 8am-10pm, F 8am-11pm, Sa 9am-11pm, Su 9am-10pm. ❶

CHINATOWN

Singapore, 1006 Race St. (☎922-3288), between 10th and 11th St. Health-conscious food fanatics flock to this restaurant for the vegetarian roast pork with black bean sauce ($6.50) or the tofu pot with assorted vegetables ($7). Open daily 11am-11pm. ❷

Rangoon, 112-114 9th St. (☎829-8939), between Cherry and Arch St. Simple pink and plastic decor belies the complex, spicy scents of Burmese cuisine wafting onto the sidewalk. The crisp lentil fritters ($9) and tasty mint kebab ($9) earn this place its reputation as the best Chinese in Chinatown. Open daily 11:30am-9:30pm. ❸

Sang Kee Peking Duck House, 238 9th St. (☎925-7532), near Arch St. Locals pack the large, new dining room for the extensive menu. Shrimp seaweed soup $5. Entrees $6-10. Open Su-Th 11am-11pm, F-Sa 11am-midnight. ❷

Ray's Cafe and Tea House, 141 N. 9th St. (☎922-5122), is ideal for quick snacks on the run, long tête-à-têtes, or spending quiet time curled up with your favorite read. Delectable dishes such as bok choy ($7) or rice noodle soup ($7) are for hungrier folk. For lighter fare, the mango bubble tea ($3), smooth and light, is excellent. Open M-Th 9am-9:30pm, F 9am-10:30pm, Sa 11:30am-10:30pm, Su 11:30am-9pm. Cash only. ❷

CENTER CITY

Jamaican Jerk Hut, 1436 South St. (☎545-8644), near Broad St. This tropical paradise brightens an otherwise bleak block. While chefs jerk Negril garlic shrimp ($15) to perfection, Bob Marley tunes jam in the backyard veranda. The vegetable stir fry, with crisp, colorful, and crunchy cooked vegetables over a bed of jasmine rice and 2 fried bananas ($7-9), is sure to please. BYOB. Live music F-Sa 7pm; cover $2. Open M-Th 11am-10pm, F-Sa 11am-11pm, Su 5-10pm. ❸

Alma de Cuba, 1623 Walnut St. (☎988-1799; www.almadecubarestaurant.com), near Rittenhouse Sq. Trendy spot for hot Latin food. Try the sancocho de pollo soup (coconut-chicken broth with poached chicken slices, yucca, carrots, cilantro, green peas, and a touch of lime juice) for $6. For dinner, cilantro honey mustard glazed salmon ($23) is served over a banana-lentil sald with fresh horseradish cream. Happy Hour M-F 5-7pm. Live Cuban jazz W 9pm-midnight. Salsa Su 8pm. Open M-Th 5-11pm, F-Sa 5pm-midnight, Su 5-10pm. ❹

Bassett's Ice Cream (☎925-4315), in Reading Terminal Market at 12th and Arch St. Established in 1861, Bassett's is the oldest ice creamery in the state, and some say the best in the nation. Originals such as tomato ice cream may be archaic remnants of the olden days, but modern finds—such as peach, mocha chip, and rum raisin—also await. 2 scoops $2.50, 3 scoops $3.25. Open M-Sa 8am-6pm. ❶

Lombardi's, 132 S. 18th St. (☎564-5000; www.lombardisoriginalpizza.com), off Rittenhouse Sq. between Sansom and Chestnut St., makes some of the best pizza this side of Italy. Established in 1905, this hometown favorite uses a coal oven to cook its crusts to perfection. Original pizza with fresh mozzarella, basil, and homemade meatballs $16. White pizza topped with green leaf spinach $17. Fresh salads $6-8. Pastas $7-11. Open Su-W 11:30am-10pm, Th-Sa 11:30am-11pm; M-F closed 4-5pm. Cash only. ❹

UNIVERSITY CITY

Tandoor India Restaurant, 106 S. 40th St. (☎222-7122), between Chestnut and Walnut St. Every college may havbe a good, cheap Indian restaurant nearby, but this is one of the best. Northern Indian cuisine with bread fresh from the clay oven. Lunch buffet daily 11:30am-3:30pm ($6); dinner buffet daily 4-10pm ($9). 20% student discount with valid ID. Open daily 11:30am-10:30pm. ❷

Smokey Joe's, 210 S. 40th St. (☎222-0770), between Locust and Walnut St. Hearty meals at student-friendly prices make it the most popular UPenn bar and restaurant. Franklin Field Deal offers any burger, choice of soup, chicken tenders, cheesefries, mozzarella sticks, poppers, chicken fingers, wings, or nachos & cheese, plus free refills on soda for $9.50. Open daily 11am-2am; closed the second week of Aug. ❷

Abner's Cheesesteaks, 3813 Chestnut St. (☎662-0100; www.abnerscatering.com), at 38th St. Local fast food in a bright, spacious, and cleaner-than-average joint attracts the professional set for lunch and tipsy UPenn students deep into the night. Cheesesteak, large soda, and fries $6.20. Open Su-Th 11am-midnight, F-Sa 11am-3am. ❷

SIGHTS

INDEPENDENCE MALL

REVOLUTIONARY SIGHTS. The **Independence National Historical Park,** a small green bounded by Market, Walnut, 2nd, and 7th St., is comprised of a rash of historical buildings. At night, the **Lights of Liberty Show** illuminates the American Revolution in a breathtaking way. A 1hr., ½ mi. guided tour through the Park—with an elaborate audio program—narrates the happenings of the Revolution while an impressive, $12 million laser light show illuminates five key sites in the downtown area. *(Park: ☎597-8974, or 965-2305 8:30am-5pm. Open daily June-Aug 9am-6pm; Sept.-May 9am-5pm. Free. Light Show: PECO Energy Liberty Center at the corner of 6th and Chestnut St. Tu-Sa. ☎877-462-1776; www.lightsofliberty.org. $17.76, seniors and students $16, ages 6-12 $12. Underground parking lot available on 6th St. between Arch and Market St. underneath the Visitors Center.)* Instead of wandering blindly through the Park, begin your trip down American history memory lane at the newly renovated and impressive **Visitors Center** (see **Practical Information,** p. 284). They dispense detailed maps and brochures, offer a small exhibit detailing each historical site, and provide electronic trip-planners that cater to the desires of each individual visitor. One of the most popular of Philadelphia's historic landmarks, **Independence Hall** abounds with revolutionary tourism. After Jefferson drafted the Declaration of Independence, the delegates signed the document here in 1776 and reconvened in 1787 to ink their names onto the US Constitution. Today, knowledgeable park rangers take visitors on a brief but informative tour through the nation's first capitol building. *(Between 5th and 6th St. on Chestnut St. Open daily 9am-5pm; arrive early in summer to avoid a long line. Free guided tours every 15min. Tickets distributed exclusively at the Visitors Center.)* The US Congress first assembled in nearby **Congress Hall.** While soaking up the history, guests can take a rest in one of the plush Senate chairs. *(At Chestnut and 6th St. Open daily 9am-5pm.)* The predecessor to the US Congress, the First Continental Congress united against the British in **Carpenters' Hall,** which is now a mini-museum heralding the carpenters responsible for such architectural achievements as Old City Hall and the Pennsylvania State House. *(320 Chestnut St. ☎925-0167. Open Mar.-Dec. Tu-Su 10am-4pm; Jan.-Feb. W-Su 10am-4pm.)* The **Portrait Gallery in the Second Bank** features portraits of Thomas Jefferson, Martha Washington, and Noah Webster. *(At the time of press, this was closed for renovations; please go to www.gophila.com for up-to-date details.*

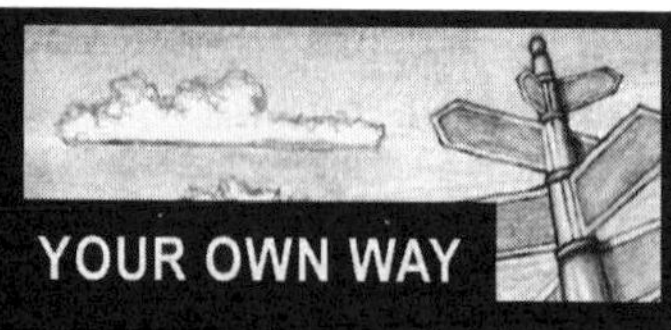

YOUR OWN WAY

ART AND THE CITY

When it comes to public artwork, Philadelphia stands alone as the most philanthropic American city. Because of a citywide ordinance passed in 1959, 1% of the cost of any public building is reserved for the purchase of public art. As a result, the city has thousands of pieces produced by world-class artists, and a trip to Philly would be incomplete without visiting some of the more famous ones.

Across from City Hall, Claes Oldenburg's pop art icon, The Clothespin, has graced the city since 1976 as a tangible reminder of the beauty and symbolic meaning behind seemingly mundane objects. Down 15th St. in Kennedy Plaza, the Philadelphia LOVE sign is perhaps the most celebrated pop artwork in the city. When asked why he tilted his "O," Robert Indiana, the designer (who happened to be on his 4th marriage at the time), explained that love is never perfect. Take a moment to ponder your own interpretation alongside the world's most pensive piece of art, Auguste Rodin's The Thinker, located outside the Rodin museum. Made of bronze and limestone, The Thinker has graced the corner of 22nd St. and the Parkway since 1929.

At the corner of 3rd and Arch St. Normally open daily 10am-3pm. $3, under 17 free.) North of Independence Hall rests the country's most revered bell. While freedom may still ring at the **Liberty Bell Pavilion,** the (cracked) Liberty Bell does not. *(On Market St., between 5th and 6th St. ☎597-8974. Open daily 9am–5pm. Free.)* The new **National Constitution Center,** stunning, modern, and gorgeous, provides visitors with an in-depth look at the significant history of the American Constitution. *(525 Arch St. in Independence Historical National Park. ☎409-6600 or 866-917-1787; www.nationalconstitutioncenter.org. 17min. multimedia presentation prior to entrance; last shown 4:10pm. Open daily 9:30am-5pm. $6, seniors and under 12 $5.)*

OTHER SIGHTS. The rest of the park preserves residential and commercial buildings of the Revolutionary era. On the northern edge of the Mall, a white molding demonstrates the size and location of Ben Franklin's home in **Franklin Court.** The original abode was unsentimentally razed by the statesman's heirs in 1812 in order to erect an apartment complex. The home contains an underground museum, a 20min. movie, a replica of Franklin's printing office, and a working post office, the first post office in the nation and the only one not to fly the American flag—as there wasn't one in 1775. *(318 Market St., between 3rd and 4th St. ☎965-2305. Open summer daily 9am-5pm. Free.)* On a more somber note, a statue of the first American president and army general presides over the **Tomb of the Unknown Soldier,** in Washington Sq., where an eternal flame commemorates the fallen heroes of the Revolutionary War.

Adjacent to the house where Jefferson drafted the Declaration of Independence, the **Balch Institute for Ethnic Studies at the Philadelphia Historical Society** is an academic glimpse into America's social history, including the plight of African slaves and of Japanese Americans during WWII. *(1300 Locust St. ☎732-6200; www.balchinstitute.org. Open M-Tu and Th-F 1-5:30pm, W 1-8:30pm. $6; students, seniors, and under 12 $3. Sa 10am-noon free.)*

Across the street, the **Atwater Kent Museum** offers rare Pennsylvania artifacts, such as the wampum belt received by William Penn from the Lenni Lenape at Shakamaxon in 1682, and, of course, more Franklin exhibits. *(15 S. 7th St. ☎685-483; www.philadelphiahistory.org. Open M and W-Su 10am-5pm. $5, seniors and ages 13-17 $3, under 13 free.)*

OUTSIDE INDEPENDENCE MALL

COLONIAL MADNESS. A penniless Ben Franklin arrived in Philadelphia in 1723 and strolled by the colorful and clustered rowhouses that line the narrow **Elfreth's Alley,** near 2nd and Arch St. The vigorous neighborhood—the oldest continuously inhabited street in America—now houses a museum that provides a glimpse into the daily lives of Philadelphia's patriots. *(126 Elfreth's Alley. ☎574-0560; www.elfrethsalley.org. Open Feb.-Dec. Tu-Sa 1-4pm, Su noon-5pm; Jan. Sa 10am-4pm, Su noon-4pm. $2, ages 5-18 $1. Last tour 4:40pm.)* The **Betsy Ross House**—home of one of the most celebrated female patriots—conveys, through child-oriented, first-person placards, the skills that led seamstress Betsy Ross to sew America's first flag in 1777. *(239 Arch St. ☎686-1252; www.betsyrosshouse.org. Open Apr.-Sept. daily 10am-5pm; Oct.-Mar. Tu-Su 10am-5pm. Suggested donation $2, children $1. Cash only.)*

OTHER SIGHTS. For those who like to get off on the right foot, the Temple University School of Podiatric Medicine houses the **Shoe Museum,** founded in 1976. The sixth floor collection of 900 pairs features footwear from the famous feet of Reggie Jackson, Lady Bird Johnson, Julius Erving, Nancy Reagan, and others. *(At 8th and Race St. ☎625-5243. Tours W and F 9am-noon. Tours are free but limited; visitors must call to make an appointment.)* The powder-blue **Benjamin Franklin Bridge,** considered the longest suspension bridge in the world when it opened on July 1, 1926, off Race and 5th St., connects Philadelphia to New Jersey, and provides an expansive view of the city for those not afraid of heights. The bridge adds a touch of urban art after dark as its sweeping expanse is highlighted by hundreds of color-changing lights.

SOCIETY HILL & THE WATERFRONT

Society Hill proper begins on Walnut St., between Front and 7th St., east of Independence Mall. Though Independence Mall may end at Walnut St., its history continues to preside over 200-year-old townhouses and cobblestone walks illuminated by electric "gaslights."

HISTORICAL SIGHTS. Flames don't have a chance in **Head House Square,** at 2nd and Pine St., which holds the distinction of being America's oldest firehouse and marketplace and now houses restaurants and boutiques. Bargain hunters can test their haggling skills at an outdoor arts and craft fair. *(☎790-0782. Open June-Aug. Sa noon-11pm, Su noon-6pm. Free workshops Su 1-3pm.)* Each January, sequin- and feather-clad participants join in a rowdy New Year's Day Mummer's parade; south of Head House Sq., the **Mummer's Museum** swells with the glamour of old costumes. *(1100 S. 2nd St., at Washington Ave. ☎336-3050; www.riverfrontmummers.com/museum.html. Free string band concerts Tu 8pm. Open May-Sept. Tu 9:30am-9:30pm, W-Sa 9:30am-4:30pm, Su noon-4:30pm; July-Aug. closed Su. Oct.-Apr. Tu-Sa 9:30am-4:30pm, Su noon-4:30pm. $3.50; students, seniors, and under 12 $2.50.)*

ON THE WATERFRONT. A looming, neon sign at the easternmost end of Market St. welcomes visitors to **Penn's Landing,** the largest freshwater port in the world. Philadelphian shipbuilding, cargo, and immigration unfold at the **Independence Seaport Museum.** Kids can get their sea legs at the "Boats Float" exhibit. Near the museum a host of old ships bobs at the dock, including the USS *Olympia*, the oldest steel warship still afloat, and the USS *Becuna*, a WWII submarine. *(☎925-5439; www.phillyseaport.org. Open daily 10am-5pm. Museum and ships $8, seniors $6.50, children $5.)* Finish the waterfront day in relaxing fashion at a free **waterfront concert.** *(☎629-3257; www.pennslanding.com. Big bands Apr.-Oct. Th 8pm. Children's theater Su.)*

CENTER CITY

As the financial and commercial hub of Philly, Center City barely has enough room to accommodate the professionals who cram into the area bounded by 12th, 23rd, Vine, and Pine St. Rife with activity during the day, the region retires early at night.

ART & ARCHITECTURE. The country's first art museum and school, the **Pennsylvania Academy of Fine Art** has permanent displays of artwork by Winslow Homer and Mary Cassatt, while current students show their theses and accomplished alumni get their own exhibits each May. *(118 N. Broad St., at Cherry St. ☎972-7600; www.pafa.org. Open Tu-Sa 10am-5pm, Su 11am-5pm. Tours 45min.-1hr.; M-F 11:30am-1:15pm, Sa-Su noon-1:45pm. $5, students and seniors $4, ages 5-18 $3. Special exhibits $8/7/5.)* Presiding over Center City, the granite and marble **City Hall** took 30 years to build (a bit longer than the expected 5 years) and is currently undergoing a $125 million cleaning project. It remains the nation's largest working municipal building and, until 1908, it reigned as the tallest building in the US, aided by the 37 ft. statue of William Penn stretching toward the heavens. A law prohibited building anything higher than Penn's hat until entrepreneurs overturned it in the mid-1980s. A commanding view of the city still awaits visitors in the building's tower. *(At Broad and Market St. ☎686-2840. Open M-F 9:30am-4:30pm. City Hall tour daily 12:30pm, ends at the tower 2pm. Tower Tour every 15min. daily 9:15am-4:15pm. 5 people only per tour; reservations recommended. Suggested donation $1.)*

RITTENHOUSE SQUARE

Masons of a different ilk left their mark in the brick-laden **Rittenhouse Square District,** a ritzy neighborhood southeast of Center City. This part of town cradles the musical and dramatic pulse of the city, housing several performing arts centers.

RITTENHOUSE MUSEUMS. For the best results, completely digest lunch before viewing the bizarre and often gory medical abnormalities displayed at the highly intriguing **Mütter Museum.** Among the potentially unsettling fascinations are a wall of skulls and human horns. The museum also contains an exhibit on infectious diseases such as the Black Death and AIDS and displays a Level 4 biohazard suit. *(19 S. 22nd St. ☎563-3737, ext. 211; www.collphyphil.org/muttpg1.shtml. Open daily 10am-5pm. $9; seniors, students, and ages 6-18 $6.)* Just south of the square, the more benign **Rosenbach Museum and Library** permanently displays the original manuscript of James Joyce's *Ulysses* and the collected illustrations of Maurice Sendak among rotating exhibits. *(2010 Delancey St. ☎732-1600; www.rosenbach.org. Open Tu and Th-F 10am-5pm, W 10am-8pm, Sa-Su 10am-5pm. Guided 1¼hr. tours Tu-Su 11am-4pm, W 6:30pm. Exhibition and tour $8, students and seniors $5.)*

PARKWAY/MUSEUM DISTRICT

Once nicknamed "America's Champs-Elysées," the **Benjamin Franklin Parkway** has seen better days. While it sports an international flag row cutting through Philadelphia's streets, the surrounding areas suffer from a lack of care. Nevertheless, the Parkway supports some of Philly's finest cultural attractions. Of the city's five original town squares, **Logan Circle** was the sight of public executions until 1823 but now delights hundreds of children who felicitously frolic in its **Swann Memorial Fountain.** Designed by Alexander Calder, the fountain represents the Wissahickon Creek, the Schuylkill River, and the Delaware River, the three bodies of water surrounding the city.

SCIENCE. A modern assemblage of everything scientific, the highly-interactive **Franklin Institute** would make the old inventor proud. The newly installed skybike allows kids and adults to explore scientific theories while pedaling across a tightrope suspended nearly four stories high. *(At 20th St. and Ben Franklin Pkwy. ☎448-1200; www.fi.edu. Open daily 9:30am-5pm. $12.75, seniors and ages 4-11 $10. IMAX Theater ☎448-1111. $8. Museum and IMAX $16, children $13.)* Part of the Institute, the newly renovated **Fels Planetarium** flashes lively laser shows on Friday and Saturday nights. *(222 N. 20th St. ☎448-1388. $6, seniors and ages 4-11 $5. Exhibits and laser show $12.75/*

10.50. Exhibits and both shows $14.75/12.50.) Opposite Fels, the **Academy of Natural Sciences** allows budding archaeologists to try their hand at digging up dinosaur fossils. *(1900 Ben Franklin Pkwy., at 19th St. ☎299-1000; www.acnatsci.org. Open M-F 10am-4:30pm, Sa-Su 10am-5pm. $9, seniors and military $8.25, ages 3-12 $8. AAA $1 discount. Wheelchair-accessible.)* For a little family fun, visit the **Please Touch Museum,** where kids can romp around in the Alice In Wonderland Funhouse, play miniature golf in the Science Park, or hone their broadcasting skills in the Me On TV workshop. *(210 N. 21st St. ☎963-0667; www.pleasetouchmuseum.org. Open daily July-Aug. 9am-5pm; Sept.-June 9am-4:30pm. $9. Su 9-10am free.)*

ART. Sylvester Stallone may have etched the sight of the **Philadelphia Museum of Art** into the minds of movie buffs everywhere when he bolted up its stately front stairs in *Rocky* (1976), but it is the artwork within that has earned the museum its fine reputation. The world-class collection includes Cezanne's *Large Bathers* and Toulouse-Lautrec's *At the Moulin Rouge*, as well as extensive Asian, Egyptian, and decorative art collections. *(Benjamin Franklin Pkwy. and 26th St. ☎763-8100; www.philamuseum.org. Open Tu, Th, Sa-Su 10am-5pm; W and F 10am-8:45pm. Tours daily 10am-3pm. Live jazz, fine wine, and light fare F 5:30-8:30pm. $9; students, seniors, and ages 5-18 $7; Su free.)* A casting of *The Gates of Hell* outside the **Rodin Museum** guards the portal of human passion, anguish, and anger in the most extensive collection of the prolific sculptor's works this side of the Seine. One of the five original castings of *The Thinker* (1880) marks the museum entrance from afar. *(At Benjamin Franklin Pkwy. and 22nd St. ☎763-8100; www.rodinmuseum.org. Open Tu-Su 10am-5pm. 1hr. guided audio tour available for $5 in the giftshop. Free guided tour Su 1pm. $3 suggested donation.)*

BOOKS AND INMATES. The Free Library of Philadelphia scores with a library of orchestral music and one of the nation's largest rare book collections. The user-friendly library is conveniently divided into subject rooms. Philadelphia art students frequently seek sketching subjects and inspiration amid the classical architecture of the building. *(At 20th and Vine St. ☎686-5322; www.library.phila.gov. Open M-Th 9am-9pm, F 9am-6pm, Sa 9am-5pm.)* In a reversal of convention, guests pay to get into prison at the castle-like **Eastern State Penitentiary,** once a ground-breaking institution of criminal rehabilitation. Tours twist through the smoldering dimness Al Capone once called home and fascinating stories tell of daring inmates and their attempted escapes. *(2124 Fairmount Ave. at 22nd St. ☎236-3300; www.easternstate.org. Tours every hr. 10am-4pm. Last entry 4pm. Open W-Su 10am-5pm. $9, students and seniors $7, ages 7-12 $4, under 7 not permitted.)*

UNIVERSITY CITY

The **University of Pennsylvania** *(www.upenn.edu)* and **Drexel University** *(www.drexel.edu)*, across the Schuylkill from Center City, are in west Philly within easy walking distance of the 30th St. subway station. The Penn campus, a thriving assemblage of luscious green lawns and red brick quadrangles, contrasts sharply with the dilapidated buildings surrounding it. Ritzy shops and hip cafes spice up 36th St. A statue of the omnipresent Benjamin Franklin, who founded the university in 1740, greets visitors at the entrance to the Penn campus on 34th and Walnut St. *Much of the area surrounding University City is unsafe at night.*

U-CITY SIGHTS. The **University Museum of Archaeology and Anthropology** journeys through three floors of the world's major cultures under a beautiful stone and glass rotunda. *(At 33rd and Spruce St. ☎898-4001; www.upenn.edu/museum. Open Tu-Sa 10am-4:30pm, Su 1-5pm. $5, students and seniors $2.50.)* In 1965, Andy Warhol had his first one-man show at the cutting-edge **Institute of Contemporary Art.** *(118 S. 36th at Sansom St. ☎898-7108; www.icaphila.org. Open during academic terms W-F noon-8pm, Sa-Su 11am-5pm. $3; students, seniors, and artists $2. Su 11am-1pm free.)* North of the University area, the **Philadelphia Zoo,** the oldest zoo in the country, houses more than 2000 animals, including lowland gorillas, bearded pigs, and giant anteaters, and the new, kid-friendly walk through the Galapagos. *(3260 South St. at 34th and Girard St. ☎243-1100; www.phillyzoo.org. Open daily Feb.-Nov. 9:30am-5pm; Dec.-Jan. 9:30am-4pm. $15, seniors and ages 2-11 $13. Parking $7.)*

ENTERTAINMENT

The **Academy of Music,** at Broad and Locust St., was modeled after Milan's La Scala and hosts the six yearly productions of the **Pennsylvania Ballet.** (☎551-7000; www.paballet.org. $20-85.) The **Philadelphia Orchestra,** located at the stunning **Kimmel Center,** 260 S. Broad St., performs from September to May. (☎790-5800 or 893-1999; www.kimmelcenter.org. Box office open daily 10am-6pm and until performance begins. $5 tickets go on sale at the Locust St. entrance 45min. before F-Sa concerts. $8 student rush tickets Tu and Th 30min. before show.)

With 5000 seats under cover and 10,000 on outdoor benches and lawns, the **Mann Music Center,** on George's Hill near 52nd and Parkside Ave. in Fairmount Park, hosts big name entertainers like Tony Bennett and Willie Nelson, as well as a variety of jazz and rock concerts. (☎893-1999 for tickets or 546-7900 for general info; www.manncenter.org. Tickets available at the Academy of Music box office. Free lawn tickets for June-Aug. orchestra concerts available from the Visitors Center, at 16th and JFK Blvd., on the day of a performance. Pavilion seats $10-32.) **The Trocadero,** 1003 Arch St. at 10th St., at 120 years old, is the oldest operating Victorian theater in the US and hosts local as well as big-name bands. (☎922-5486; www.thetroc.com. Tickets $6-16. Advance tickets through Ticketmaster. Box office open M-F noon-6pm, Sa noon-5pm.) The **Robin Hood Dell East,** on Ridge Ave. near 33rd St. in Fairmount Park, brings in top names in pop, jazz, and gospel in July and August. During the school year, however, theatrical entertainment bustles. The students of the world-renowned **Curtis Institute of Music,** 1726 Locust St., give free concerts. (☎893-5252; www.curtis.edu. Mid-Oct. to Apr. M, W, F 8pm.) **Merriam Theater,** 250 S. Broad St. in Center City, stages performances ranging from student works to Broadway hits; past performers include Katherine Hepburn, Laurence Olivier, and Sammy Davis, Jr. (☎732-5446. Box office open M-Sa 10am-5:30pm.) The **Old City,** from Chestnut to Vine and Front to 4th St., comes alive for the **First Friday** celebration, when streets fill with live music and art galleries, museums, and restaurants open their doors to entice visitors with free food and sparkling wine. (☎800-555-5191; www.oldcity.org. Oct.-June. First F each month.)

Philly gets physical with plenty of sports venues, and four professional teams play just a short ride away on the Broad St. subway line. Baseball's **Phillies** (☎463-1000; www.phillies.com) will begin play at the new **Citizens Bank Park,** on Pattison Ave. between 11th and Darien St., in April 2004. Football's **Eagles** (☎463-5500l; www.philadelphiaeagles.com) play at **Lincoln Financial Field,** at Broad St. and Pattison Ave. Across the street, fans fill the **First Union Center** (☎336-3600) on winter nights to watch the NBA's **76ers** (☎339-7676; www.sixers.com) and the NHL's **Flyers** (☎755-9700; www.philadelphiaflyers.com). General admission tickets for baseball and hockey start at $10; football and basketball tickets go for $15-50.

NIGHTLIFE

Check the Friday *Philadelphia Inquirer* for entertainment listings. The free Thursday *City Paper* and the Wednesday *Philadelphia Weekly* have weekly listings of city events. A diverse club crowd jams to the sounds of live music on weekends along **South Street** toward th e river. Many pubs line **2nd Street** near Chestnut St., close to the Bank St. hostel. Continuing south to Society Hill, especially near **Head House Square,** a slightly older crowd fills dozens of streetside bars and cafes.

Delaware Avenue, or **Columbus Boulevard,** running along Penn's Landing, has recently become a trendy local hot spot full of nightclubs and restaurants that attract droves of yuppies and students. Gay and lesbian weeklies *Au Courant* (free) and *PGN* ($0.75) list events throughout the Delaware Valley. Most bars and clubs that cater to a gay clientele congregate along **Camac, South 12th,** and **South 13th Street.**

The Khyber, 56 S. 2nd St. (☎238-5888; www.thekhyber.com). A speakeasy during the days of Prohibition, the Khyber now legally gathers a young crowd to listen to a range of punk, metal, and hip-hop music. The ornate wooden bar was shipped over from England in 1876. Vegetarian sandwiches $3. Happy Hour M-F 5-7pm. Live music daily 10pm. Cover $10. Open daily 11am-2am. Cash only.

Warmdaddy's (☎627-8400; www.warmdaddys.com), at Front and Market St. Though entrees tend to be pricey, Bayou dreamers will eat up this Cajun club renowned for its blues and diversity. Music and reduced-price entrees Su 3pm. $5 cover for Th midnight Happy Hour. Live music summer 7pm; winter 8:30pm. Cover F-Sa $10; varies during the week. Open Tu-Th 5:30pm-1am, F-Sa 7pm-2am; kitchen closes 1am.

The Five Spot, 5 S. Bank St. (☎574-0070), off Market St. between 2nd and 3rd St. The classically designed lounge encourages cool cats to drink heartily, while the cramped dance floor upstairs hosts swingers of all abilities. Th Latin dancing with free lessons. F-Sa DJ spins modern, rap, and R&B. 21+. Cover $5. Dress well. Open daily 9pm-2am.

Moriarty's, 1116 Walnut St. (☎627-7676; www.moriartysrestaurant.com), near 11th St and the Forest theater. This Irish pub draws a healthy crowd late into the night with a quiet, comfortable bar scene. Over 20 beers on tap, ESPN on the TV, and private booths galore. Grolsch $2 pints 3-5pm and midnight-2am daily. Open Su noon-2am, kitchen closes midnight; M-Sa 11am-2am, kitchen closes 1am.

Woody's, 202 S. 13th St. (☎545-1893; www.woodysbar.com), at Walnut St. An outgoing gay crowd frequents this lively club with a free cyber bar, coffee bar, and dance floor. Happy Hour daily 5-7pm. M karaoke. Tu Big Gay Divas night. Lunch daily noon-3:30pm; dinner daily 4-11pm. Bar open M-Sa 11am-2am, Su noon-2am. Cash only.

OUTDOOR ACTIVITIES

Philly's finest outdoor opportunities can be found in the resplendent **Fairmount Park** (www.phila.gov/fairpark). Ten times the size of New York City's Central Park, Fairmount is larger than any other city park and covered with bike trails and picnic areas, offering city-weary vacationers the adventure of the great outdoors and stirring vistas of the Schuylkill River. The Grecian ruins by the waterfall immediately behind the Art Museum are the abandoned **Waterworks,** built between 1819 and 1822. Free tours of the Waterworks' romantic architecture, technology, and social history meet on Aquarium Dr., behind the Art Museum. (☎685-4935; www.fairmountwaterworks.org. Open Sa-Su 1-3:30pm.) Farther down the river, Philly's place in the rowing world is evidenced by a line of crew clubs forming the historic **Boathouse Row.** The Museum of Art hosts $3 guided tours of Boathouse Row on Wednesday and Sunday, and trolley tours to some of the mansions in Fairmount Park. The area near Boathouse Row is also Philly's most popular in-line skating spot, and many joggers seeking recreation and a refreshing river breeze also crowd the local paths. In the northern arm of Fairmount Park, trails follow the secluded Wissahickon Creek for 5 mi., as the concrete city fades to a distant memory. The **Japanese House and Garden,** off Montgomery Dr. near Belmont Ave., is designed in the style of a 17th-century *shoin;* the authentic garden offers the utmost in tranquility. (☎878-5097; www.shofuso.com. Open May-Oct. Tu-F 10am-4pm, Sa-Su 11am-5pm; call for seasonal hours. Ask for the free 30-45min tour. $2.50, students and seniors $2.) *Some neighborhoods surrounding the park are not safe, and the park is not safe at night.*

DAYTRIP FROM PHILADELPHIA

VALLEY FORGE

In 1777-78, it was the frigid winter, not the British military, that almost crushed the Continental Army. When George Washington selected Valley Forge as the winter camp for his 12,000 troops after a defeat at Germantown in October, the General could not have predicted the fate that would befall his troops. Three arduous months of starvation, bitter cold, and disease nearly halved his forces. It was not until Baron Friedrich von Steuben arrived with fresh troops and supplies that recovery seemed possible. Renewed, the Continental Army left Valley Forge and its harrowing memory on June 19, 1778 to win the Battle of Monmouth.

The hills that once tormented the frost-bitten soldiers now roll through **Valley Forge National Historical Park.** (☎610-783-1077. Park open daily sunrise-sunset. Free.) Visitors can explore the park by car, foot, or bus. The 10 mi. self-guided **auto tour** (audio tapes $8, CDs $11), begins at the Visitors Center. Also beginning at the Visitors Center is the ¼ mi. guided **walking tour,** led by a knowledgeable park ranger. (Daily 10:50am and 1:50pm. Free.) The new 1½hr. **bus tour** also allows visitors to explore sites. (Summer F-Su. $15.50, ages 12-16 $12.50, under 12 $10.50.) All tours pass Washington's headquarters, reconstructed soldier huts and fortifications, and the Grand Parade Ground where the Continental Army drilled. The **Visitors Center,** 600 W. Germantown Pike, features a small museum and an 18min. film shown every 30min. (☎610-783-1077; www.nps.gov/vafo. Open daily 9am-5pm.) The park has three picnic areas but no camping. Joggers can take a revolutionary trip down a fairly flat, paved 6 mi. trail through deer-populated forests.

Valley Forge lies 30min. from Philadelphia by car. To get there, take I-76 west from Philly for about 12 mi. Get off at the Exit 24, then take Rte. 202 S for 1 mi. and Rte. 422 W for 1½ mi. to another Valley Forge exit. **SEPTA** runs buses to the Visitors Center daily; catch #125 at 16th and JFK ($3.50).

LANCASTER COUNTY ☎717

Lancaster County produces 30 eggs, six gallons of milk, and three pounds of pork per second—yet its chief industry is not agricultural. Economic success stems from the county's unusual composite of residents—the Amish, the Mennonites, and the Brethren. The simplicity of the undeveloped, unassuming Amish lifestyle fascinates a technologically dependent society. Thousands of visitors flock to this pastoral area every year to observe a modest way of life that eschews modern conveniences like motorized vehicles, television, electricity, washing machines, and cellular phones. Look, but don't shoot—many Amish have religious objections to being photographed.

ORIENTATION & PRACTICAL INFORMATION. Lancaster County covers an area almost the size of Rhode Island. County seat Lancaster City, in the heart of Dutch country, has red brick row houses huddled around historic **Penn Square.** The rural areas are mostly accessible by car (or horse and buggy), but it is easy to see the tourist sites with a bike or to walk the mile or two between public transportation drop-offs. Travelers beware: on the country roads of Lancaster, **Intercourse** suspiciously leads to **Paradise.** From Paradise, **U.S. 30 W** plots a straight course into **Fertility.** Because the area is heavily Mennonite, most businesses and all major attractions close on Sunday. **Amtrak,** 53 McGovern Ave. (☎291-5080; ticket office open daily 5:30am-10pm), in Lancaster City, runs to Philadelphia (1hr., 8-10 per day, $16) and Pittsburgh (6½hr., 2 per day, $48). **Capital Trailways** (☎397-4861; open daily 8am-10pm), in the same location, buses to

Philadelphia (3hr., 1 per day, $16) and Pittsburgh (6hr., 3 per day, $44). **Red Rose Transit,** 45 Erick Rd., serves Lancaster and some areas in the surrounding countryside. (☎397-4246. Buses run daily approximately 5am-6pm. $1.15, seniors free.) The **Pennsylvania Dutch Visitors Bureau,** 501 Greenfield Rd., on the east side of Lancaster City off Rte. 30, dispenses info on the region, including excellent maps and walking tours. A 15min. slide show makes Lancaster look a little more exciting than it actually is. (☎299-8901 or 800-735-2629; www.padutchcountry.com. Open daily June-Aug. 8am-6pm; Sept.-May 8:30am-5pm.) **Post Office:** 1400 Harrisburg Pike. (☎800-275-8777 or 396-6925. Open M-F 7:30am-7pm, Sa 9am-2pm.) **Postal Code:** 17604. **Area Code:** 717.

ACCOMMODATIONS. Hundreds of hotels and B&Bs cluster in this area, as do several working farms with guest houses; the Visitors Bureau can provide room information. As part of a religious outreach mission, the amicable staff at the **Mennonite Information Center** (see **Sights,** p. 296) will try to find a Mennonite-run guest house for about the same price. Camping can be found very easily. Hear the hooves and neighs of the Amish horses from dawn until late at night at the **Kendig Tourist Home ❶,** 105 N. Ronks Rd., left off Rte. 30 E, just past Flory's Campgrounds. The spotless rooms come with TV and A/C; some have private bath. (☎393-5358. Singles $26-36. Cash only.) The **Pennsylvania Dutch Motel ❸,** 2275 N. Reading Rd., at Exit 21 off the Pennsylvania Turnpike, has a helpful hostess and spacious, clean rooms with cable TV and A/C. (☎336-5559. Singles $46; doubles $50; low-season rates lower.) Jacuzzis, fireplaces, and a candlelit gourmet breakfast make for a lovely setting inside the Victorian-style **Intercourse Village Bed and Breakfast ❹,** Rte. 340 (Main St.). (☎800-644-0949 or 768-2626; www.amishcountryinns.com. Intercourse prices depend on size—rooms $120-126.) The wilderness setting at the **Sickman's Mill Campground ❶,** 671 Sand Hill Rd., off State Rd. 272, 6 mi. south of Lancaster, keeps things quiet. Amenities include hot showers, clean toilets, a playground, and firewood. Recreational activities include freshwater creek fishing, tours of the 19th-century mill, and river tubing. (☎872-5951. Office open daily 10:30am-9pm. Tours $4. Inner tube rental $6. Sites $15; with electricity $20. Cash or check only.)

FOOD. Amish food, wholesome and generous in portion, is characterized by a heavy emphasis on potatoes and vegetables. Palatable alternatives to high-priced "family-style" restaurants are the **Farmers Markets** and the **produce stands** that dot the roadway. **The Central Market,** in downtown Lancaster City at the northwest corner of Penn Sq. between the Heritage Center Museum and Fleet Bank, has been doing business since the 1730s. Nowadays, simply dressed Pennsylvania Dutch invade the city to sell affordable fresh fruit, meats, cheeses, vegetables, sandwiches, and desserts alongside more conventionally dressed vendors. (☎291-4739. Open Tu and F 6am-4pm, Sa 6am-2pm.) Lancaster restaurants surround the market. Though a chain, **Isaac's Restaurant and Deli ❷,** 44 N. Queen St., in Central Mall, is a culinary option worth considering. Personal pizzas with roasted red pepper and portabella mushroom ($7-9) aim to please, as does the Salty Eagle sandwich, with grilled ham, swiss, and honey mustard for $5.50. (☎394-5544. Open M-Th 10am-9pm, F-Sa 10am-10pm, Su 11am-9pm.) Across the street, **My Place ❶,** 12 N. Queen St., provides a slice of Italy in Amish country. The food makes up for what it lacks in atmosphere. (☎393-6405. Pizza slice $1.30. Huge cheesesteak hoagie $4. Generous salads $2-3. Open M-Th 10:30am-10pm, F-Sa 10:30am-11pm. Cash only.) At the **Amish Barn ❸,** 3029 Old Philadelphia Pike, quilts surround the tables where patrons feed on Amish specialties, like $2 chicken corn soup and $5 Amish apple dumpling. (☎768-8886; www.amishbarn.com. Entrees around $10. Open June-Aug. M-Sa 8am-9pm; spring and fall M-Sa 8am-8pm; call for winter hours.)

HERSHEY'S CANDYLAND Around the turn of the century, Milton S. Hershey, a Mennonite resident of eastern Pennsylvania, discovered how to mass market a rare and expensive luxury–chocolate. Today, the company that bears his name operates the world's largest chocolate factory, in Hershey, about 45min. from Lancaster. East of town at the amusement park **Hersheypark,** the **Chocolate World Visitors Center** presents a free, automated tour through a simulated chocolate factory. After the tour, visitors emerge into a pavilion full of chocolate cookies, discounted chocolate candy, and oh so fashionable Hershey sportswear. *(Theme Park: ☎534-3900; www.hersheypa.com. Open June M-F 10am-10pm; July-Aug. M-F 10am-10pm, Sa-Su 10am-11pm; May to early June and Sept. call for hours. $36, seniors and ages 3-8 $20; after 5pm $21, ages 3-8 and 55+ $18. Visitors Center: ☎800-437-7439. Opens with park and closes 2hr. earlier. Free; parking $6. Amex/D/MC/V.)*

SIGHTS. To develop an understanding and appreciation of Amish culture, visit the informative **The People's Place,** 3513 Old Philadelphia Pike, on Rte. 340 (Main St.), 11 mi. east of Lancaster City in Intercourse. The complex encompasses most of the block, with bookstores, craft shops, and an exhibit called **20Q**—for the 20 most-asked questions about the Amish—detailing the nuances of their unique lifestyle. The film *Who Are the Amish?* takes care of any lingering queries. (☎768-7171; www.thepeoplesplace.com. Open M-Sa June-Aug. 9:30am-7pm; Sept.-May 9:30am-5pm. Film shown every 30min. 9:30am-5pm. $5, seniors $4, under 12 $2.50. Film and 20Q $8/7/4.) From April-October every year, quilt and art fanatics flock here to see the **The People's Place Quilt Museum,** located in the building directly across the street from The People's Place. (☎768-7101 or 800-828-8218; www.ppquiltmuseum.com. Open M-Sa 9am-5pm.) To get the story from the people who live it, stop in the **Mennonite Information Center,** on Millstream Rd. off Rte. 30 east of Lancaster. The Mennonites, unlike the Amish, believe in outreach and established this center to help tourists distinguish between the two faiths. Exceptionally cordial hostesses will guide guests through the Biblical Tabernacle. (☎299-0954; www.mennoniteinfoctr.com. 2hr. private tours available.)

For the most authentic exploration of Amish country available in a car, wind through the fields off U.S. 340, near Bird-in-the-Hand. Cyclists can capture the simplistic spirit on the **Lancaster County Heritage Bike Tour,** a reasonably flat 46 mi. route past covered bridges and historic sites run by the Visitors Center. A visit to Lancaster is not complete without using the preferred mode of local transportation, the horse and buggy. **Ed's Buggy Rides,** 253 Hartman Bridge Rd., on Rte. 896, 1½ mi. south of U.S. 30 W in Strasburg, bumps along 3 mi. of scenic backwoods, covered bridges, and countryside. (☎687-0360; www.edsbuggyrides.com. Open daily 9am-5pm. $8, under 11 $4. Cash only.) **Amish Country Tours** offers 1½hr. trips that include visits to one-room schools, Amish cottage industries, breathtaking farmland vistas, and roadside stands. (☎786-3600. Tours given June-Oct. daily 10:30am, noon, 1:30, 3pm; May and Nov. Sa-Su 10:30am, 1:30pm. $15, ages 4-12 $7.) Old country crafts and food can be found from late June to early July at the **Pennsylvania Dutch Folk Life and Fun Festival,** in Kutztown, which offers an unusual combination of polka bands, pot pies, and petting zoos. (☎610-683-8707; www.kutztownfestival.com. $10 per day, under 12 free.)

Lancaster also attracts visitors with its many **outlet malls,** located along Rte. 30. For nighttime entertainment, the **Dutch Apple Dinner Theater,** 510 Centerville Rd., has hosted such performances as *Grease*, *Annie Get Your Gun*, *Pinocchio*, and *The Jungle Book*. (☎898-1900; www.dutchapple.com. Shows Tu-Su evenings, with selected matinee dates. $20, under 19 $15.)

GETTYSBURG ☎717

During perhaps the most memorable dates of the US Civil War, the three sweltering days of July 1-3, Union and Confederate forces clashed spectacularly at Gettysburg. The Union forces ultimately prevailed, though at a high price of over 50,000 casualties between North and South. President Lincoln arrived in Gettysburg 4 months later to dedicate the Gettysburg National Cemetery, where 979 unidentified Union soldiers still rest. Today, the National Soldier's Monument towers where Lincoln once delivered his legendary Gettysburg Address. Each year, thousands of visitors visit these fields and are reminded of the President's declaration: "these dead shall not have died in vain."

PRACTICAL INFORMATION. Inaccessible by Greyhound or Amtrak, Gettysburg is in south-central Pennsylvania, off U.S. 15, about 30 mi. south of Harrisburg. **Towne Trolley** makes in-town trips, but doesn't serve the battlefield. (Runs Apr.-Oct. $1.) The **Gettysburg Convention and Visitor's Bureau,** 31 Carlisle St., has walls of helpful maps and brochures, and provides the *Gettysburg Visitors Guide,* which is full of important facts and phone numbers. (☎800-337-5015 or 334-6274; www.gettysburg.com. Open M-F 8:30am-5pm, Sa-Su 9am-5pm.) **Post Office:** 115 Buford Ave. (☎800-275-8777 or 337-3781; www.usps.com. Open M-F 8am-4:30pm, Sa 9am-noon.) **Postal Code:** 17325. **Area Code:** 717.

ACCOMMODATIONS & FOOD. Follow Rte. 34 N to Rte. 233 to reach the closest hostel, **Ironmasters Mansion Hostel (HI-AYH) ❶,** 20 mi. from Gettysburg, within the entrance of Pine Grove Furnace State Park. Unusually large and luxurious, the building holds 46 beds in a tranquil, idyllic area. Spacious porches, an ornate dining room, and a decadent jacuzzi make this hostel seem more like a Club Med resort. (☎486-7575. Linen $2. Laundry. Internet access $3 per 15min. Reception 7:30-9:30am and 5-10pm. By reservation only Dec.-Feb. Dorms $14, nonmembers $17.) Multiple motels line Steinwehr Rd. near the battlefield, but finding summer rates below $100 is difficult anywhere in the downtown area. For those willing to sacrifice proximity to restaurants, stores, and attractions, the **Red Carpet Inn ❸,** 2450 Emmitsburg Rd., 4 mi. south of Military Park, has comfortable rooms with heat and A/C, large beds, and a pool. (☎334-1345 or 800-336-1345. Rooms $60-110, depending on season.) For a more elegant stay, **The Brickhouse Inn ❺,** 452 Baltimore St., offers mid-to-upscale B&B rooms in the best location in downtown. (☎338-9337 or 800-864-3463; www.brickhouseinn.com. Open Apr.-Nov. Gracious hosts and breakfast included. Check-in 3:30-8pm. Check-out 11am. Rooms $105-155.) **Artillery Ridge ❶,** 610 Taneytown Rd., 1 mi. south of the Military Park Visitors Center, maintains over 200 sites with access to showers, stables, laundry, a pool, nightly movies, a pond, and bike rentals. (☎334-1288; www.artilleryridge.com. Open Apr.-Nov. Sites $20; with hookup $28; with sewer and hookup $31. Each additional person $4, children $2.)

In addition to the scenic beauty of its battlefields, Gettysburg features an downtown area complete with quaint shops and lively restaurants. Hefty rations persist in the town's square and just beyond the entrance to the battlefield. In Gettysburg's first building (circa 1776), now the **Dobbin House Tavern ❸,** 89 Steinwehr Rd., patrons can create their own grilled burger ($6-7) under the candlelight and view an Underground Railroad shelter. For finer dining, the House also serves fresh cut steaks, seafood, lamb, veal, and other elegant entrees for $18-23. (☎334-2100; www.dobbinhouse.com. Open Su-Th 11:30am-9:30pm, F-Sa 11:30am-10pm; fine dining begins at 5pm, last seating 9:30pm.) For ice cream and fudge, **Kilwins ❶,** 37 Steinwehr Ave., takes guests to celestial heights with peppermint, mint chocolate chip, and other classic flavors ($3-4). Peanut lovers beware: the peanut fudge is as addictive as it is pricey ($12.75 per lb., free ½ lb. with 1 lb. purchase). (☎337-2252; www.kilwins.com. Open Su-Th 11am-10pm, F-Sa 11am-11pm.) Near the battlefield, **General Pickett's Restaurant ❸,** 571 Steinwehr Rd., charges $6-10 for a Southern-style, all-you-can-eat buffet. (☎334-7580. Open M-Sa 11am-3:15pm and 4:30-8pm, Su 11am-7:30pm.)

SIGHTS. Visitors can explore Gettysburg in many ways. A sensible start is the **National Military Park Visitors Information Center,** 97 Taneytown Rd., which distributes free maps for an 18 mi. self-guided driving tour. (☎334-1124, ext. 431; www.nps.gov/gett. Visitors Center open daily June-Aug. 8am-6pm; Sept.-May 8am-5pm. Park open daily 6am-10pm. Free.) An electronic map uses lights to show the course of the battle July 1-3, 1863, and is available to view inside the center. ($3, seniors $2.50, under 15 $2.) Prepare to spare a penny or two for a more in-depth look at the historic grounds. **Licensed battlefield guides** squeeze into the family wagon to personally guide visitors through the monuments and landmarks. (☎334-1124, ext. 431; www.gettsyburgtourguides.org. 2hr. tours 8am until 2hr. before dusk. 1-6 people $40, 7-15 people $60, 16-49 people $90. Arrive by 9am to ensure a time slot. Cash or travelers checks only.) If you are uncomfortable inviting a guide into your car, follow the free walking tour, purchase an audio tape driving tour ($10-40 in the Visitors Center Bookstore), or enjoy a 2hr. bus tour (departures 9:30am-4pm; $22, ages 4-11 $15). Bus tours to the Eisenhower house and farm are also available and include a 20min. house tour and self-guided tour of the grounds. (Departures every 30min. 9am-4pm. $7, ages 13-16 $4, ages 6-12 $2.50.)

The chilling sights and sounds of battle surround the audience at the **Cyclorama Center,** next to the Visitors Center. The center shows *Gettysburg 1863* (5min. after the hr.), *The American Civil War* (35min. after the hr.) and a 20min. light show (every 30min.) around a 9500 sq. ft. mural of the battle. (☎334-1124, ext. 422. Open daily 9am-5pm. $3, seniors $2.50, ages 6-16 $2. Last show 4:30pm. Cash or travelers check only.) Artillery Ridge Campgrounds (see **Accommodations,** above) conducts **horseback tours** by reservation. (1hr. horseback tour $28, 2hr. horseback and history tour $50. No one under age 8 or over 240lb.) Adjacent to the campground office is a meticulously detailed diorama of the Gettysburg battle, along with other exhibits. ($4.50, seniors and children $3.50.) **Historic Tours** trundles visitors around the battlefield in 1930 Yellowstone Park buses. (☎334-8000; www.gettysburg.com. 2½hr. tours $17, children $11, AAA/AARP $16.) Based on the chilling tales told by author Mark Nesbitt, candlelit **Ghosts of Gettysburg,** 271 Baltimore St., reawakens the war-ridden dead. (☎337-0445; www.ghostsofgettysburg.com. Walks Mar.-Nov. 8, 8:15, 9, 9:45pm; call for low-season times. $6, under 8 free.)

The grim **Jennie Wade House,** 528 Baltimore St., preserves the kitchen where Miss Wade, the only civilian killed in the battle of Gettysburg, was mortally wounded by a stray bullet. The hole in the wall, through which the fatal bullet traveled, is still visible today. Legend has it that unmarried women who pass their finger through the fatal bullet hole will be engaged within a year. (☎334-4100. Open May-Aug. daily 9am-9pm; Sept.-Dec. and Mar.-Apr. 9am-5pm. Admission includes a 35min. guided tour. Last tour 1hr. before close. $6, ages 4-11 $3.50.) Perhaps as frightening as the prospect of marriage are the uncomfortably lifelike Civil War scenes on display at the **American Civil War Museum,** 297 Steinwehr Ave., across from the Military Park entrance. (☎334-6245; www.e-gettysburg.cc. Open daily Mar.-Dec. 9am-8:15pm; Jan.-Feb. weekends and holidays only. $5.50, ages 13-17 $3.50, ages 6-12 $2.50, under 6 free. Cash or travelers checks only.)

For a more personal perspective of the effects of the Civil War and life in the 1800s, the **Schriver House,** 309 Baltimore St., a "Civil War museum dedicated to the *civilian* experience at Gettysburg," features the infectious energy of its tour guides and owner as well as relics discovered under the floor boards of the attic and diary entries from a wartime inhabitant. (☎337-2800; www.schriverhouse.com Open Apr.-Nov. M-Sa 10am-5pm, Su noon-5pm; Dec. and Feb.-Mar. Sa-Su noon-5pm. $6, seniors $5.45, ages 12 and under $4.)

PITTSBURGH ☎412

Those who come to the City of Steel expecting sprawling industry and hordes of soot-encrusted American Joes are bound to be disappointed. The decline of the steel industry has meant cleaner air and rivers, and a recent economic renaissance has produced a brighter urban landscape. Throughout renewals, Pittsburgh's neighborhoods have maintained strong and diverse identities—some ethnic, some intellectual, and some based in the counter culture. Admittedly, some of the old, sooty Pittsburgh survives in the suburbs, but one need only ride up the Duquesne Incline and view downtown from atop Mt. Washington to see how thoroughly Pittsburgh has entered a new age.

TRANSPORTATION

Airport: Pittsburgh International (☎472-5526; www.pitairport.com), 18 mi. west of downtown, by I-279 and Rte. 60 N in Findlay Township. The Port Authority's **28x Airport Flyer** bus serves downtown and Oakland from the airport. Operates daily every 30min. 6am-midnight. $2. **Airline Transportation Company** (☎321-4990 or 471-8900) runs downtown M-F every hr. 7am-11:30pm, reduced service Sa. $14. Taxi downtown $30.

Trains: Amtrak, 1100 Liberty Ave. (☎471-6170), at Grant St. on the northern edge of downtown, next to Greyhound and the post office. Generally safe inside, *but be careful walking from here to the city center at night.* Station open daily 6am-midnight. To: **Chicago** (9½-10hr., 1 per day, $81); **New York** (10-13hr., 4 per day, $54-93); **Philadelphia** (8-11½hr., 2-3 per day, $39-93).

Buses: Greyhound, 55 11th St. (☎392-6526), at Liberty Ave. Open 24hr. To **Chicago** (9-12hr., 12 per day, $56) and **Philadelphia** (6-8hr., 9 per day, $41).

Public Transit: Port Authority of Allegheny County (PAT) (☎442-2000). Within downtown, bus free until 7pm; subway between the 3 downtown stops free. Beyond downtown, bus $1.75, transfers $0.50, all-day weekend pass $4; subway $1.75. Ages 6-11 half-price for bus and subway. Schedules and maps at most subway stations.

Taxi: Yellow Cab, ☎665-8100.

ORIENTATION & PRACTICAL INFORMATION

Pittsburgh's downtown, the **Golden Triangle,** is shaped by two rivers—the **Allegheny** to the north and the **Monongahela** to the south—which flow together to form a third river, the **Ohio.** Streets in the Triangle that run parallel to the Monongahela are numbered one through seven. The **University of Pittsburgh** and **Carnegie Mellon University** lie east of the Triangle in Oakland. The **Wayfinder system** helps tourists and locals alike navigate the often confusing streets of the city. The 1500 color-coded signs point the way to major points of interest, business areas, and universities. Don't venture into one of Pittsburgh's many tight-knit neighborhoods without

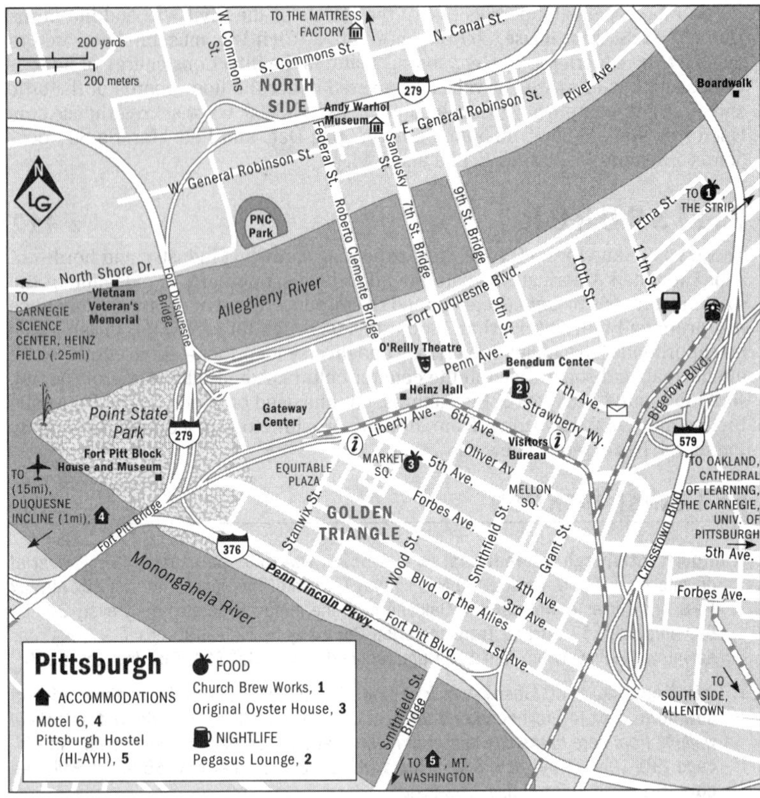

getting directions first—the city's streets and 40-odd bridges are notoriously difficult to navigate. *Be careful in the area north of PNC Park.* To stay oriented, pick up the detailed *Pittsburgh StreetMap* ($4) in any convenience store.

Visitor Info: Pittsburgh Convention and Visitors Bureau, 425 Sixth Ave., 30th fl. (☎281-7711 or 800-359-0758; www.pittsburgh-cvb.org). Open M-F 9am-5pm. There are 2 **Visitors Centers,** 1 downtown on Liberty Ave. (open M-F 9am-5pm) and 1 at the airport.

Hotlines: Rape Action Hotline, ☎765-2731. Operates 24hr. **Gay, Lesbian, Bisexual Center,** ☎422-0114. Operates M-F 6:30-9:30pm, Sa 3-6pm.

Internet Access: Carnegie Library of Pittsburgh, 4400 Forbes Ave. (☎622-3114). Open M-W 10am-8pm, Th-Sa 10am-6pm.

Post Office: 700 Grant St. (☎642-4472). Open M-F 7am-6pm, Sa 7am-2:30pm. **Postal Code:** 15219. **Area Code:** 412.

ACCOMMODATIONS

Pittsburgh Hostel (HI-AYH), 830 E. Warrington Ave. (☎431-1267), across the river and up a steep hill in Allentown, 1 mi. south of downtown. Take bus #52, "Allentown." Sparkling clean, grade-A hostel living with spacious dorms, laundry, kitchen, A/C, free parking, a well-stocked common room, and an elevator in a vault. Friendly, knowledgeable staff point visitors to their favorite 'Burgh spots. *Be careful walking around the neighborhood at night.* Linen $1, towels $0.50. Check-in 8-10am and 5pm-midnight. Lockout 10am-5pm. Dorms $19, nonmembers $22, under 18 $9.50; private rooms for 2 $43-48/49-54. Wheelchair-accessible. ❶

Motel 6, 211 Beecham Dr. (☎922-9400), off I-79 at Exit 60A, 10 mi. from downtown. Standard lodging with TV and A/C. Reservations suggested for weekends in the summer. Singles $30; doubles $36. $3 per extra person. ❷

Pittsburgh North Campground, 6610 Mars Rd. (☎724-776-1150), in Cranberry Township, 20min. north of downtown; take I-79 to the Cranberry/Mars Exit. The closest camping near Pittsburgh. 110 campsites, showers, swimming. Office open daily 8am-9pm. Tent sites for 2 $20; with hookup $27.50. $3 per each additional adult. ❶

FOOD

Aside from the pizza joints and bars downtown, **Oakland** is the best place to find a good inexpensive meal. Collegiate watering holes and cafes pack **Forbes Avenue** around the University of Pittsburgh, while colorful eateries and shops line **Walnut Street** in Shadyside and **East Carson Street** in South Side. The **Strip District** on Penn Ave. between 16th and 22nd St. (north of downtown along the Allegheny) bustles with Italian, Greek, and Asian cuisine. The Saturday morning **Farmers Market** sells an abundance of fresh produce and fish.

Spice Island Tea House, 253 Atwood St. (☎687-8821), in Oakland. Escape to this urban oasis and explore the world of tea and the cuisine of Asia. An extensive Pan-Asian menu covers everything from pad thai to more exotic dishes, while an encyclopedic tea list runs the gamut from cool thai iced tea ($1.75) with a splash of sweet milk to darjeeling fit for a king. The dim, candle-filled cafe is the perfect place to embark upon your journey. Entrees from $5. Open daily 11am-11pm. ❷

The Church Brew Works, 3525 Liberty Ave. (☎688-8200). You can pray to the beer gods at this unique brewery and restaurant, which makes its home in an abandoned church. The vaulted ceiling, beautiful stained-glass windows, and beer vat altar complement the contemporary American menu that includes favorites like Seven Onion Soup ($4.50) and Untraditional Pierogies ($6.50), stuffed with a different filling each day, as well as excellent pizzas ($11-14.25). A selection of quality homemade beers ($3.75 pint) make a perfect companion to any meal. Open M-Th 11:30am-11:45pm, F-Sa 11:30am-1am, Su noon-10pm. ❸

Primanti Brothers, 46 18th St. (☎263-2142), in the Strip District, is perhaps Pittsburgh's most famous culinary institution. Designed for truckers with big appetites and no time for side orders, the huge cheese steak sandwiches ($4.25) are piled high with coleslaw, tomato, and french fries, all stuffed between two thick slices of bread. Try it with cheese fries ($2.75) or a bowl of Pittsburgh-style chili ($2.50) and wash the whole thing down with an Iron City beer for the true 'Burgh experience. Open 24hr. 4 other locations in the city. ❶

La Fiesta, 346 Atwood St. (☎687-8424), in Oakland, serves fresh Mexican fare in a multi-colored, sombrero-filled setting. The lunch buffet is a great deal for $7 and the half-priced, late-night menu will cure any travelers' munchies without emptying their wallets. Open M-F 11:30am-1am, Sa-Su noon-1am. ❷

Dave & Andy's, 207 Atwood St. (☎681-9906). Always searching for new ways to push the envelope of ice cream flavordom, the inventive owners collect leftover hops from local breweries to create flavors like Vanilla Bean Golden Ale and Chocolate Bell Tower Malt. Along with their experimental masterpieces, an endless inventory of more common flavors are also made on site. Try one of the homemade waffle cones (from $2) and find an M&M surprise at the end. Open M-F 11:30am-10pm, Sa-Su noon-10pm. ❶

The Original Oyster House, 20 Market Sq. (☎566-7925). Pittsburgh's oldest and perhaps cheapest restaurant and bar serves seafood platters ($5-7) and fresh fish sandwiches ($2.50-5.50) in a smoky marble and wrought-iron bar, decorated with black-and-white photos of sports heroes and panoramic shots of Miss America pageants. Open M-Sa 9am-11pm. ❶

SIGHTS

GOLDEN TRIANGLE. The **Golden Triangle** is home to **Point State Park** and its famous 200 ft. fountain. The **Duquesne Incline,** in the South Side, carries visitors up a steep track, rising 400 ft. to offer a spectacular view of the city. *(1220 Grandview Ave. Access from W. Carson St. ☎381-1665. Open M-Sa 5:30am-12:45am, Su 7am-12:45am. One-way $1.75, children 6-11 $0.85, under 6 free.)* Founded in 1787, the **University of Pittsburgh** stands in the shadow of the 42-story **Cathedral of Learning,** at Bigelow Blvd. between Forbes and 5th Ave. in Oakland. The Cathedral features 26 "nationality classrooms" decorated by artisans from the city's many ethnic traditions, from austere 16th-century English to elaborate 18th-century African styles. In December, the rooms are decorated in various traditional holiday styles. *(☎624-6000; www.univ-relations.pitt.edu/natrooms. Cassette-guided tours M-F 9am-2:30pm, Sa 9:30am-2:30pm, Su 11am-2:30pm. $3, seniors $2, ages 8-18 $0.50.)*

CARNEGIE. Back when Pittsburgh was a bustling steel metropolis, Andrew Carnegie was its biggest robber baron—and its biggest benefactor. Carnegie's most spectacular gift, **The Carnegie,** across the street from the Cathedral of Learning, holds two museums. The **Natural History Museum** houses models of all seven continents, as well as an impressive collection of fossils and gems. After exploring the history of the earth, visitors can enter the **Art Museum** to see an impressive collection of artwork through the ages. *(4400 Forbes Ave. ☎622-3289; www.carnegiemuseums.org. Open Tu-Sa 10am-5pm, Su 1-5pm; July-Aug. also M 10am-5pm. $6, seniors $5, students and ages 3-18 $4.)* Closer to downtown, the **Carnegie Science Center,** next to Heinz Field, allows visitors to experience an earthquake, climb aboard a real WWII submarine, and navigate the solar system in the planetarium. Next door at the new **SportsWorks,** aspiring athletes can put their skills to the test as they clamber up a climbing wall, sprint against Jackie Joyner-Kersee, or attempt to hit a running receiver with a pass. *(1 Allegheny Ave. ☎237-3400; www.carnegiemuseums.org. Open Su-F 10am-5pm, Sa 10am-7pm. $14, seniors and ages 3-18 $10; Omnimax $8/6; combo $18/13.)*

OTHER SIGHTS. The **Andy Warhol Museum,** on the North Side, is the world's largest museum dedicated to a single artist. It supports seven floors of the Pittsburgh native's material, including pop portraits of Marilyn, bovine psychedelia in a room covered with pink cow wallpaper, "oxidations" created by urinating on metallic paint, and interactive pieces like *Silver Clouds*, a room where visitors can play among floating helium-filled metallic pillows. The museum also does a fantastic job of placing Warhol's work in its proper cultural context. *(117 Sandusky St. ☎237-8300; www.warhol.org. Open Tu-Th and Sa-Su 10am-5pm, F 10am-10pm. $8, students and ages 3-18 $4, seniors $7.)* From the Warhol, walk 20min. to **The Mattress Factory** in the North Side. A museum recognized as the best facility of site-specific installation art in the US, the factory serves as an experimental studio space and allows guests to literally walk into artwork. Call ahead for directions and be careful in the surrounding area. *(505 Sampsonia Way, off East Commons. ☎231-3169; www.mattress.org. Open Tu-F 10am-5pm, Sa 10am-7pm, Su 1-5pm. $8, students and seniors $5, under 12 free. Free Th.)* Near the Carnegie, the **Phipps Conservatory and Botanical Gardens** is packed with plants from around the world and allows visitors to walk amongst live butterflies. Other highlights include a beautiful Japanese courtyard garden and an impressive collection of orchids. *(1 Schenley Park. ☎622-6914; www.phippsconservatory.org. Open Tu-Su 9am-5pm. $6, seniors $5, students $4, children 3-13 $3. Tours daily*

11am.) At the **Pittsburgh Zoo and PPG Aquarium,** visitors can follow a circular path that winds through Asian forests, African savannahs, and tropical rainforests, offering up-close encounters with grizzly bears, Siberian tigers, and other exotic fauna. The aquarium houses spectacular sea creatures including sharks, stingrays, and eels. *(1 Wild Place. ☎800-4744-966; www.pittsburghzoo.com. Open daily June-Aug. 10am-6pm; Sept.-May 9am-5pm; Apr.-Nov. $8, seniors $7, children 2-13 $6; Dec.-Mar. $6, seniors and children 2-13 $5. Parking $3.50.)* East of town in Penn Hills, an eastern suburb of Pittsburgh, lies the first Hindu temple in the US. The **Sri Venkateswara (S.V.) Temple** is modeled after a temple in Andhra Pradesh, India, and has become a major pilgrimage site for American Hindus since its completion. Non-Hindus can walk through the Great Hall and observe prayer. *(1230 S. McCully Dr. ☎373-3380.)*

ENTERTAINMENT & NIGHTLIFE

Most restaurants and shops carry the weekly *City Paper* and *Pulp*, both great sources for free, up-to-date entertainment listings, nightclubs, and racy personals. The acclaimed **Pittsburgh Symphony Orchestra** performs September through May at **Heinz Hall,** 600 Penn Ave. (☎392-4900; www.pittsburghsymphony.org. Tickets $19-73; student rush 2hr. before performance $14.) The **Pittsburgh Public Theater** performs popular and original plays at the **O'Reilly Theater,** 621 Penn Ave. (☎316-1600; www.ppt.org. Tickets $28-47, students $12.) Broadway musicals light up the stage at the **Benedum Center**, 803 Liberty Ave. (☎456-6666; www.pittsburghclo.org. Matinees $12-36, evening shows $18-46.) Sports fans will not be disappointed in the 'Burgh. At brand new **PNC Park,** 115 Federal St., on the North Side, the **Pirates** (☎321-2827; tickets $9-35) step up to the plate from April through September. The **Steelers** (☎323-1200; tickets are very difficult to obtain.) storm the gridiron from September through December down the road at **Heinz Stadium.** The NHL's **Penguins** (☎800-642-7367; tickets $16-106) rock the winter ice at Mellon Arena.

For nightlife, the **Strip District** is relatively dense with revelers who flock to its larger bars and clubs, and a hip crowd fills **East Carson Street** on the South Side, which overflows on weekend nights. The **Station Square** complex just across the Smithfield St. Bridge from downtown offers a number of popular bars and clubs, as well as moderately priced restaurants.

Metropol and the more intimate **Rosebud,** 1600 Smallman St. (☎261-4512), in the Strip District, fill a spacious warehouse with 2 dance floors of oh-so-hip partygoers who come to see national and local acts. Cover $5. Doors open 8pm. Call for schedule.

Nick's Fat City, 1601-1605 E. Carson St. (☎481-6880), in the South Side, features popular local and regional rock 'n' roll bands and its stage has seen the likes of Prince and Bruce Springsteen. Cheap draughts of Yuengling (a favorite PA brew) and a bar full of guitars and other rock memorabilia round out the equation to make this a 'Burgh hot spot. Cover varies. Open Tu-Sa 11am-2am.

Jack's, 1117 E. Carson St. (☎431-3644), at S. 12th St., in the South Side. The only bar in the 'Burgh open 365 days a year packs in a rowdy but friendly crowd. M hot dogs $0.25. W wings $0.10. M-W $1 beers. 21+. Open M-Sa 7am-2am, Su 11am-2am.

Pegasus Lounge, 818 Liberty Ave. (☎281-2131), downtown, spins house on a multilevel dance floor and has drag shows for the gay and lesbian community. W drag shows. 21+. Tu and Th-F 18+. Open Tu-Sa 9pm-2am.

DAYTRIPS FROM PITTSBURGH

OHIOPYLE STATE PARK

Throngs come each year to raft Ohiopyle's 8 mi. of class III rapids. Some of the best whitewater rafting in the East, the rapids take about 5hr. to conquer. For novices, class I and II rapids ease rafts down sections of the river. Four outfitters front

Rte. 381 in "downtown" Ohiopyle: **White Water Adventurers** (☎800-992-7238), **Wilderness Voyageurs** (☎800-272-4141), **Laurel Highlands River Tours** (☎800-472-3846), and **Mountain Streams** (☎800-723-8669). Trip prices on the Youghhiogheny River ("The Yock" to locals) vary dramatically ($33-136 per person per day), depending on the season, day of the week, and difficulty. (Rentals: Rafts about $10-18 per person; canoes $21; inflatable kayaks about $20-26.) In order to float anything, you need a **launch permit** from the park office. (M-F free, Sa-Su $2.50. Call at least 30 days in advance for Sa permits. Rental companies provide free permits.) For guided trips, park in the lot on Dinnerbell Rd. across the street from the park office. At the end of the trip, a shuttle takes adventurers back to their car. Ohiopyle also offers great opportunities for biking, fishing, and rock climbing. Most outfitters rent equipment and offer guided excursions. (Bikes from $3 per hr., $70-76 full-day guided tour.) The **Visitors Center,** off Rte. 381 on Dinnerbell Rd. offers information on the park and surrounding areas. (☎329-8591. Open May-Oct. daily 10am-4:30pm.)

FALLINGWATER

Fallingwater, 8 mi. north of Ohiopyle on Rte. 381, is a masterpiece by the king of modern architecture, Frank Lloyd Wright. Designed in 1935 for Pittsburgh's wealthy Kaufmann family, "the most famous private residence ever built" exemplifies Wright's concept of organic architecture, incorporating original boulders into the structure and striking a perfect symbiosis with its surroundings. The house appears as though it will cascade over the waterfall it sits on, and the water's gentle roar can be heard in every room. (☎329-8501. Open mid-Mar. to Nov. Tu-Su 10am-4pm; also some weekends in Dec. and the first 2 weekends in Mar. 10am-3pm. Reservations required. Tours Tu-F $12, ages 6-18 $8; Sa-Su $15/10. Children under 6 must be left in child care, $2 per hr.) For a more intimate, quainter Frank Lloyd Wright home, head to the nearby **Kentuck Knob,** on Kentuck Rd., 6 mi. north of U.S. 40, where a guided tour exhibits the grounds, rustic home, and greenhouse. (☎329-1901. Open Tu-Su Mar.-Dec. 10am-4pm; Jan.-Feb. 11am-3pm. Tours Tu-F $10, ages 6-18 $8, Sa-Su $15/12. Call for reservations.)

DELAWARE

Tiny Delaware is a sanctuary from the sprawling cities of the Boston, New York, and Washington, D.C. Delaware was first to ratify the US Constitution on December 7, 1787, and proudly totes its tag as the "First State." The history of Delaware has been dominated by the wealthy DuPont clan, whose gunpowder mills became one of the world's biggest chemical companies. Tax-free shopping and scenic beach towns lure visitors to Delaware from all along the nation's eastern shores.

PRACTICAL INFORMATION

Capital: Dover.

Visitor Info: Delaware State Visitors Center, 406 Federal St., Dover 19901 (☎302-739-4266; www.destatemuseums.org/vc). Open M-F 8am-4:30pm, Su 1:30-4:30pm.

Postal Abbreviation: DE. **Sales Tax:** 8% on accommodations.

LEWES ☎302

Explored by Henry Hudson and founded in 1613 by the Dutch, Lewes (pronounced Lewis) was the first town in the first state and over the years has attracted colonists, pirates, fishermen, and now summer renters. The city hasn't changed much, with its unaltered Victorian houses, quiet streets, and a genuine lack of tourist culture. Lewes has plotted out a walking tour of its colonial attractions, but the main draw—especially for the older and wealthier set—remains its beautiful beach.

ORIENTATION & PRACTICAL INFORMATION. Automobile is the only sensible way to reach Lewes. From points north, **Route 1 S** brings you directly to **Savannah Road,** which bisects the town. From the west, travel east on **Route 404,** then take **Route 9 E** at Georgetown. This will land you at Rte. 1; continue south until Savannah Rd. The best public transportation option is the **Delaware Resort Transit** shuttle bus, which runs from the ferry terminal through Lewes to Rehoboth and Dewey Beach. (☎800-553-3278. Operates every 30min. late May-early Sept. daily 7am-3am. $1 per ride, seniors and disabled $0.40; day pass $2.) **Seaport Taxis** (☎645-6800) will take you door-to-door anywhere in Lewes for a small fee. Note that the beach is not in town—a bridge separates the two, and it's a long walk to the beach without a car. Thankfully, the beach has plenty of parking. The **Fisher-Martin House Information Center,** 120 Kings Hwy., offers everything a tourist would want to know, and then some. Ask about their nationally known annual garden tours. (☎645-8073 or 877-465-3937; www.leweschamber.com. Open M-F 10am-4pm, Sa 9am-3pm, Su 10am-2pm.) The **Post Office** is at 116 Front St. (☎644-1948. Open M-F 8:30am-5pm, Sa 8am-noon.) **Postal Code:** 19958. **Area Code:** 302.

ACCOMMODATIONS & FOOD. An Inn by the Bay ❺, 205 Savannah Rd., offers a delightful stay in a Victorian-style home. (☎644-8878; www.aninnbythebay.com. TV, VCR, A/C, refrigerators, and breakfast buffet. Summer rooms from $140; lower in winter.) From the bustle of Lewes' main thoroughfare, enter the secluded and classy **Zwaanendael Inn ❹,** 142 2nd St. A central location offers tight quarters at reasonable rates. (☎645-6466; www.zwaanendaelinn.com. Check-in 2pm. Check-out 11am. Summer rooms $85-145; lower in winter.) To reach the popular **Cape State Park ❶** from the north, bypass Savannah Rd. and continue on Rte. 1; signs mark the park on the left. Sites are only a short hike to the beach. (☎645-2103. Campground open Apr.-Nov. Park open year-round 7am-11pm. Sites $22, with water hookup $24. Parties over 4 require $2 extra per person.) The few restaurants in Lewes cluster primarily on 2nd St. Once a sea captain's house (circa 1895), **The Buttery ❸,** 2nd and Savannah St., is the best spot for fine dining and people-watching in Lewes. (☎645-7755. Lunch $7-15. Dinner $18-32. Su brunch 10:30am-2:30pm. Open daily for lunch 11am-2:30pm; for dinner from 5pm.) Voted "Best Ice Cream" in 2003 by *Delaware Today*, **Kings Homemade Ice Cream Shops ❶,** 201 2nd. St., is the toast (or should we say "topping") of the town. (☎645-9425. 1 scoop $2.25, 2 scoops $3.25. Open May-Oct. daily 11am-11pm.) Locals come to the wood-paneled **Rose and Crown Restaurant and Pub ❷,** 108 2nd St., to eat great burgers ($5-7) and, on weekends, jam to live blues and rock. (☎645-2373. Happy Hour daily 4-6pm, $1 off all drinks. Open daily 11am-1am.)

SIGHTS. Secluded among sand dunes and scrub pines 1 mi. east of Lewes on the Atlantic Ocean is the 4000 acre **Cape Henlopen State Park,** where kids frolic in the waves under the watchful eyes of lifeguards, parents, and young couples soaking up the rays from their lawn chairs. In addition to its expansive beach, the park is home to sparkling white "walking dunes," a 2 mi. paved trail ideal for biking or skating, and a well-preserved WWII observation tower. (☎645-8983. Park open daily 8am-sunset. $5 per car; bikes and walkers free.) First-come, first-serve bike rentals are free at the **Seaside Nature Center,** the park's museum on beach and ocean wildlife, which also holds weekly talks on local animals and leads hikes. (☎645-6852. Open daily July-Aug. 9am-5pm; Sept.-June 9am-4pm. Bike rental, with helmet, available 9am-3pm; 2hr. limit.) The **Zwaanendael Museum,** 102 Kings Hwy., is a bright two-floor space filled with relics of maritime history and exhibits on the settlement of Delaware, lighthouses, and shipwrecks. The museum building itself is, appropriately, a replica of the old town hall in Hoorn, Holland. (☎645-1148. Open Tu-Sa 10am-4:30pm, Su 1:30-4:30pm. Free.) The town has gathered some historic buildings into the **Historical Society Complex,** on Shipcarpenter St. near 2nd St. (☎645-7670. Open June-Aug. M and W-F 10am-4pm, Sa 10:30am-noon. $6.)

REHOBOTH BEACH ☎302

Rehoboth Beach lies between Lewes and Ocean City, both geographically and culturally. While Lewes tends to be quiet and family-oriented and Ocean City attracts rowdy underage high-schoolers, Rehoboth manages to balance its discount-boardwalk fun with serene, antique B&Bs. Well-heeled Washington families and a burgeoning gay population constitute the beach's summer crowd.

ORIENTATION & PRACTICAL INFORMATION. To reach Rehoboth, take **Route 1B** to **Rehoboth Avenue** and follow it to the water. When parking, beware of meter monitors constantly on the prowl. **Greyhound/Trailways,** 251 Rehoboth Ave. (☎227-7223 or 800-231-2222), stops next to the Chamber of Commerce. Buses go to and from Baltimore (5½hr., 1 per day, $32); Philadelphia (4hr., 2 per day, $32); Washington, D.C. (3½hr., 3 per day, $36). The **ferry** to Cape May is the best option for island-hopping. (☎644-6030 or 800-643-3779. Office open daily 8:30am-4:30pm. 8 per day. $8 per passenger, $25 per vehicle.) The **Rehoboth Beach Chamber of Commerce,** 501 Rehoboth Ave., a former railroad depot next to an imitation lighthouse, doles out info. (☎227-2233 or 800-441-1329; www.beach-fun.com. Open M-F 9am-5pm, Sa-Su 9am-1pm.) **Post Office:** 179 Rehoboth Ave., at 2nd St. (☎227-8406. Open M-F 9am-5pm, Sa 8:30am-12:30pm.) **Postal Code:** 19971. **Area Code:** 302.

ACCOMMODATIONS. Inexpensive lodgings abound in Rehoboth. The **Boardwalk Plaza Hotel ❸,** Lewes Boardwalk at Olive Ave., offers one-of-a-kind upscale lodging, complete with lobby parrots, Victorian decor, and rooftop and oceanside pools. (☎227-7169; www.boardwalkplaza.com. Check-in 3pm. Check-out 11am. Rooms $59-519. AAA, military, and AARP 10% discount in low season.) The comfortable porch at **The Abbey Inn ❸,** 31 Maryland Ave., is just a street away from the noise of Rehoboth Ave. (☎227-7023. 2-night min. stay. Open late May-early Sept. Singles and doubles with shared bath from $48; triples and quads with shared bath $61; suite with private bath $105. 15% surcharge on weekends.) **The Beach View Motel ❺,** 6 Wilmington Ave., 50 yd. from the boardwalk, has clean, nicely decorated rooms with refrigerator, telephone, microwave, and continental breakfast. (☎227-2999; www.beachviewmotel.com. Summer rooms $139-194; low-season $45-139.) **Big Oaks Family Campground ❶,** 1 mi. off Rte. 1 on Rd. 270, offers a rugged alternative to town lodging. (☎645-6838. Sites $32.)

FOOD. Rehoboth is known for its high-quality beach cuisine at bargain prices. **Eden ❺,** 122 Rehoboth Ave., is *the* haute cuisine destination in town. Though there is no jacket-and-tie formality, be prepared to spend big. (☎227-3330. Wasabi and sesame-crusted yellowfin tuna, seaweed salad, and pickled calamari $28. Open daily from 6pm.) **Cafe Papillon ❷,** 42 Rehoboth Ave., in the Penny Lane Mall, offers authentic European fare. French cooks speak the international language of good food and serve up fresh crêpes ($2.75-7), croissants ($2-3.50), and stuffed baguette sandwiches ($5-8). (☎227-7568. Open Apr.-June Sa-Su 8am-11pm; July-Oct. daily 8am-11pm.) The warm and inviting atmosphere at **Our Place Restaurant and Garden Patio ❸,** 37 Baltimore Ave., will make your stomach and your wallet happy. (☎227-4143. $9 Su brunch 9am-2pm. Open Apr.-June Th-M from 5pm; July-

Labor Day Th-Tu from 5pm; Oct.-Dec. and mid-Mar. to Apr. Sa-Su from 5pm.) **Royal Treat ❶**, 4 Wilmington Ave., flips up a stack of pancakes and bacon for just $5.90. (☎227-6277. Open daily June-Aug. for breakfast 8-11:30am; ice cream 1-11:30pm.)

NIGHTLIFE. Rehoboth party-goers head out early to maximize their time before 1am last calls. **The Summer House Saloon,** 228 Rehoboth Ave., across from City Hall, is a favorite flirtation spot. (☎227-3895; www.summerhousesaloon.com. Su 4-8pm half-price daiquiris. Th 9:30pm-1:30am live blues rock band, F 9pm-1am live DJ and dancing. Open May-Sept. M and Sa-Su 4pm-1am, Tu-F 5pm-1am.) Look for live music (F-Sa 10pm-1am) at **Dogfish Head Brewings & Eats,** 320 Rehoboth Ave. (☎226-2739; www.dogfish.com. Happy Hour with $2 homemade rum and gin drinks. Open May-Aug. M-Th 4pm-midnight, F 4pm-1am, Sa noon-1am, Su noon-11pm; Sept.-Apr. M and Th 4pm-midnight, F 4pm-1am, Sa noon-1am, Su noon-11pm.) **The Blue Moon,** 35 Baltimore Ave., an established hot spot, rocks to the sounds of techno music for a predominantly gay crowd. (☎227-6515. Happy Hour M-F 4-6pm. Su brunch with Bloody Mary bar $17. Open daily 4pm-1am.) **Cloud 9,** 234 Rehoboth Ave., is the heart of the gay scene in Rehoboth. (☎226-1999. Happy Hour daily 4-7pm. M half-price pasta. Th buy-one-get-one-free entrees. DJ F-M. Open Apr.-Oct. daily 4pm-1am; Nov.-Mar. Th-M 4pm-1am.)

MARYLAND

Once upon a time, folks on Maryland's rural eastern shore trapped crabs, raised tobacco, and ruled the state. Meanwhile, across the bay in Baltimore, workers loaded ships and ran factories. Then the federal government expanded, industry shrank, and Maryland had a new focal point: the Baltimore-Washington Pkwy. As a result, suburbs grew, Baltimore revitalized, and the "Old Line State" acquired a new, liberal urbanity. As D.C.'s generic suburbs continue to swell beyond the limits of Maryland's Montgomery and Prince George counties, Baltimore revels in its immensity, while Annapolis—the state capital—remains a small town of sailors.

PRACTICAL INFORMATION

Capital: Annapolis.

Visitor Info: Office of Tourism, 217 E. Redwood St., 9th fl., Baltimore 21202 (☎800-634-7386; www.mdisfun.org). **Department of Natural Resources,** 580 Taylor Ave., Annapolis 21401 (☎410-260-8367; www.dnr.state.md.us). Open M-F 8am-4:30pm.

Postal Abbreviation: MD. **Sales Tax:** 5%.

BALTIMORE ☎410

Nicknamed "Charm City" for its mix of small-town hospitality and big-city flair, Baltimore impresses visitors with its lively restaurant and bar scene, first-class museums, and loving attention to history. The true pulse of the city lies beyond the glimmering Inner Harbor, in Baltimore's overstuffed markets, coffee shops, and diverse citizenry. The city's southern heritage is evident in Roland Park, where friendly neighbors greet you from front porches in a "Bawlmer" accent. Birthplace of the *Star-Spangled Banner*, Baltimore lies just north of the nation's capital and is now home to two major sports teams that provide year-round spectacle—win or lose—for its proud residents.

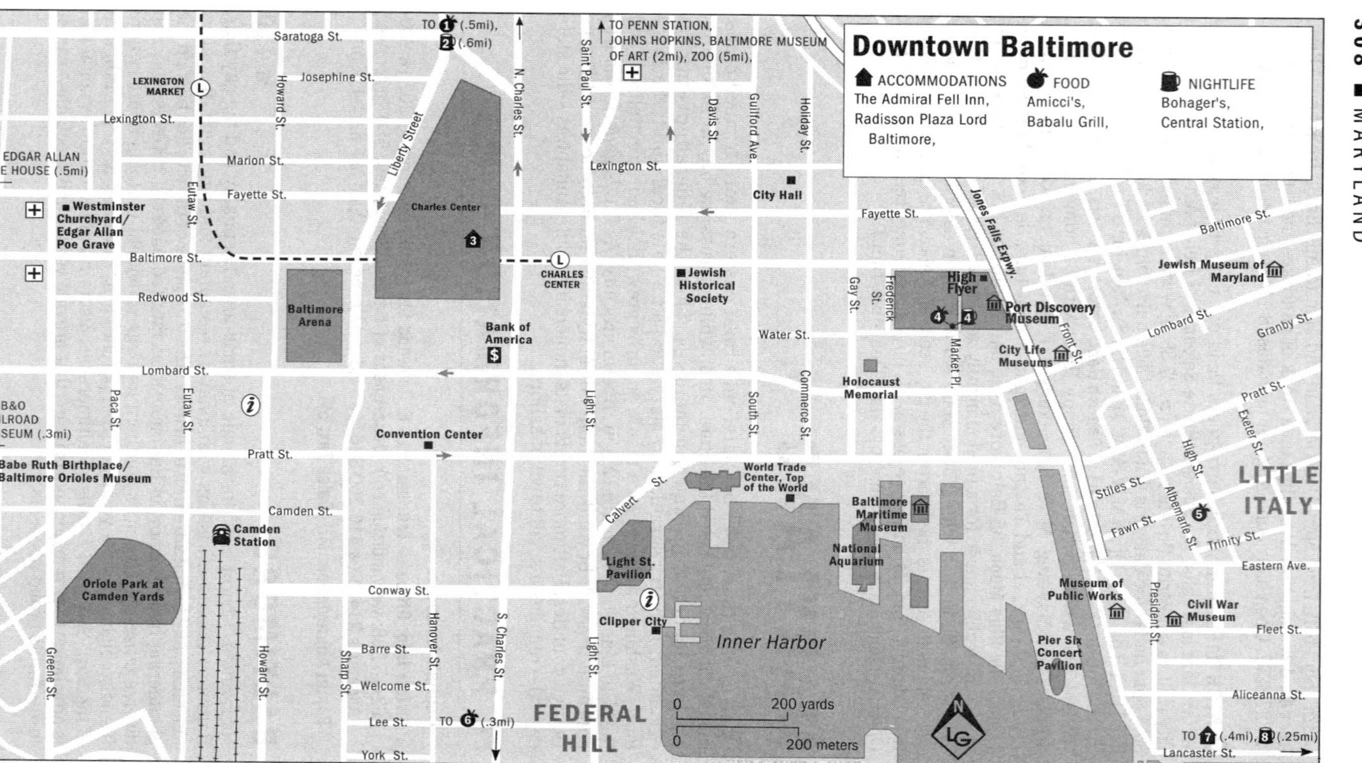
Downtown Baltimore
ACCOMMODATIONS
The Admiral Fell Inn, Radisson Plaza Lord Baltimore,
FOOD
Amicci's, Babalu Grill,
NIGHTLIFE
Bohager's, Central Station,
TO PENN STATION, JOHNS HOPKINS, BALTIMORE MUSEUM OF ART (2mi), ZOO (5mi),
TO (.5mi), (.6mi)
TO EDGAR ALLAN POE HOUSE (.5mi)
TO B&O RAILROAD MUSEUM (.3mi)
LEXINGTON MARKET
Westminster Churchyard/ Edgar Allan Poe Grave
Charles Center
CHARLES CENTER
Baltimore Arena
Bank of America
Convention Center
Babe Ruth Birthplace/ Baltimore Orioles Museum
Camden Station
Oriole Park at Camden Yards
City Hall
Jewish Historical Society
High Flyer
Port Discovery Museum
City Life Museums
Holocaust Memorial
Jewish Museum of Maryland
World Trade Center, Top of the World
Baltimore Maritime Museum
National Aquarium
Light St. Pavilion
Clipper City
Inner Harbor
Museum of Public Works
Pier Six Concert Pavilion
Civil War Museum
LITTLE ITALY
FEDERAL HILL
TO (.3mi)
TO (.4mi), (.25mi)
200 yards
200 meters
Saratoga St.
Josephine St.
Lexington St.
Marion St.
Fayette St.
Baltimore St.
Redwood St.
Lombard St.
Pratt St.
Camden St.
Conway St.
Barre St.
Welcome St.
Lee St.
York St.
Howard St.
Eutaw St.
Paca St.
Greene St.
Sharp St.
Hanover St.
Liberty Street
N. Charles St.
S. Charles St.
Saint Paul St.
Light St.
Calvert St.
Davis St.
Guilford Ave.
Holiday St.
South St.
Commerce St.
Water St.
Gay St.
Frederick St.
Market Pl.
Front St.
Jones Falls Expwy.
Granby St.
Exeter St.
High St.
Stiles St.
Fawn St.
Albemarle St.
Trinity St.
Eastern Ave.
President St.
Fleet St.
Aliceanna St.
Lancaster St.

TRANSPORTATION

Airport: Baltimore-Washington International (**BWI;** ☎859-7111; www.bwiairport.com), on I-195 off the Baltimore-Washington Pkwy. (I-295), about 10 mi. south of the city. Take MTA bus #17 to the Nursery Rd. Light Rail station. Airport **shuttles** to hotels (www.supershuttle.com) run daily every 30min. 5:45am-11:30pm. $11 to downtown-Baltimore. Shuttles leave for D.C. daily every hr. 5:45am-11:30pm ($26-34). **Amtrak** trains from BWI run to Baltimore ($5) and D.C. ($12). **MARC** commuter trains are cheaper but slower, and run M-F to Baltimore ($3.25) and D.C. ($5).

Trains: Penn Station, 1500 N. Charles St., at Mt. Royal Ave. Easily accessible by bus #3 or 11 from Charles Station downtown. **Amtrak** trains run every 30min.-1hr. To: **New York** (from $70); **Philadelphia** (from $43); **Washington, D.C.** (from $14). On weekdays, 2 **MARC commuter lines** (☎800-325-7245 in MD) connect Baltimore to D.C.'s Union Station (☎859-7400 or 291-4268) via **Penn Station** (with stops at BWI) or **Camden Station,** at Howard and Camden St. Open daily 5:30am-9:30pm; self-serve 24hr.

Buses: Greyhound (☎800-231-2222) has 2 locations: downtown at 210 W. Fayette St. (☎752-7682), near N. Howard St.; and 5625 O'Donnell St. (☎752-0908), 3 mi. east of downtown near I-95. Connections to: **New York** ($38); **Washington, D.C.** ($11); and **Philadelphia** ($20).

Public Transit: Mass Transit Administration (MTA), 300 W. Lexington St. (☎800-543-9809; 539-5000 for schedule info M-F 6am-7pm), near N. Howard St. Bus, Metro, and Light Rail service to most major sights in the city. Some buses run 24hr. Metro runs M-F 5am-midnight, Sa 6am-midnight. Light Rail runs M-F 6am-11pm, Sa 8am-11pm, Su 11am-7pm. One-way fare for all is $1.60, but higher on light rail to outer suburbs.

Water Taxi: Harbor Boating, Inc., 1732 Thames St. (☎563-3901 or 800-658-8947; www.thewatertaxi.com). Main stop at Inner Harbor; other stops at the harbor museums, Harborplace, Fells Point, Little Italy, and more. Apr.-Oct. stops every 15-18min.; Nov.-Mar. every 40min. Service May-Aug. M-Th 10am-11pm, F-Sa 10am-midnight, Su 10am-9pm; Apr. and Sept.-Oct. M-Th 10am-8pm, F-Sa 10am-midnight, Su 10am-8pm; Nov.-Mar. daily 11am-6pm. 1-day unlimited rides $6, ages 10 and under $3. Ticket includes coupons for Baltimore attractions.

Taxi: American Cab, ☎636-8300. **Arrow Cab,** ☎261-0000.

ORIENTATION & PRACTICAL INFORMATION

Baltimore lies 35 mi. north of D.C. and about 150 mi. west of the Atlantic Ocean. To get to Baltimore from D.C., take the **Baltimore-Washington Parkway. Exit 53** from **Route 395** leads right into the **Inner Harbor.** Without traffic, the trip takes less than an hour. The city is divided by **Baltimore Street** (east-west) and **Charles Street** (north-south). The **Inner Harbor,** at Pratt and Charles St., is home to historic ships, Baltimore's only shopping mall, and an aquarium. The museum-laden, artistic **Mount Vernon** neighborhood—served by city buses #3 and 11—occupies **North Charles Street,** north of Baltimore St., around **Monument Street** and **Centre Avenue. Little Italy**—served by city bus #10—sits a few blocks east of the Inner Harbor, past the **Jones Falls Expressway.** Continuing past Little Italy, a short walk to the southeast brings you to bar-happy **Fells Point**—also served by city bus #10. Old-fashioned **Federal Hill**—accessed by city buses #1 and 64—preserves Baltimore history, while the area east of **Camden Yards** has recently been re-urbanized.

Visitor Info: Baltimore Area Visitors Center, 451 Light St. (☎837-7024; www.baltimore.org). In a brand-new building, this user-friendly center provides maps, brochures with discounts, and the helpful *Quickguide.* Open M-Sa 9am-5pm, Su 10am-5pm.

Hotlines: Suicide, ☎531-6677. **Sexual Assault and Domestic Violence,** ☎828-6390. Both 24hr. **Gay and Lesbian,** ☎837-8888. Operates daily 7pm-midnight.

Internet Access: Enoch Pratt Free Library, 400 Cathedral St. (☎396-5430). Open M-W 10am-8pm, Th 10am-5:30pm, F-Sa 10am-5pm; Sept.-May also Su 1-5pm. Free.

Post Office: 900 E. Fayette St. (☎347-4202). Open M-F 7:30am-10pm, Sa 8:30am-5pm. **Postal Code:** 21233. **Area Code:** 410.

GOT THAT, HON? As *The Baltimore Sun* puts it, **hon** is a "provincial term of affection" in the city. In 1994, the mysterious **"Hon Man"** led a campaign to add the term to the "Welcome to Baltimore" sign on the Baltimore-Washington Pkwy. For 2 years, he repeatedly plastered placards saying "Hon" to it, only to have highway workers remove them. When state troopers caught him in the act, they extracted his promise never to hang a "Hon" sign again. With one relapse, he's kept his word.

ACCOMMODATIONS

Expensive hotels dominate the Inner Harbor, and reputable inexpensive hotels elsewhere are hard to find. For a convenient way to reserve bed and breakfasts, call **Amanda's Bed and Breakfast Reservation Service,** 1428 Park Ave. (☎800-899-7533; www.bedandbreakfast-maryland.com. From $65 per night. Open M-F 10am-5pm.)

Radisson Plaza Lord Baltimore, 20 W. Baltimore St. (☎539-8400 or 800-333-3333), between Liberty and Charles St. A national historic landmark built in 1928, this is the oldest functioning hotel in Baltimore. Rooms are large though sometimes shabby, but the location—just 6 blocks from the Inner Harbor—and its historic flavor prove an unbeatable combination. Reservations recommended. Fitness center. Parking $25 per night. Rooms $129-209. 10% AAA discount. ❺

The Admiral Fell Inn, 888 S. Broadway (☎522-7377 or 866-583-4162; www.harbormagic.com), at Thames St. A veritable portal to the past with themed rooms that include canopied beds and armoires. 2 ghosts—a Miss Rebecca Milowe and a Mr. Edgar Allan Poe—haunt the premises on a regular basis, though guests attest that their presence is felt the most Th-Su. Formerly a retreat where sailors used to rest after long sojourns at sea. Unlimited Internet access included with the mandatory Internet charge ($4 per day). Valet parking $15 per night. Rooms $169-259. 10% AAA and AARP discount. ❺

Capitol KOA, 768 Cecil Ave. N (☎923-2771 or 800-562-0248, from Baltimore 987-7477), in Millersville, between D.C. and Baltimore. Take Rte. 50E (John Hanson Hwy.) to Rte. 3 N (Robert Crain Hwy.). Bear right after 8 mi. onto Veterans Hwy.; then turn left under the highway onto Hog Farm Rd. and follow blue camping signs. Mostly RVs, some cabins, and a small wooded area for tents. Pool, volleyball courts, and bathroom/shower facilities. Free shuttle to MARC commuter train Odenton Station M-F; to New Carrollton Metro Sa-Su. Open Mar. 25-Nov. 1. Tent site for 2 $33; water and electricity $39; RV complete hookup $44; 1-room cabin $58; 2-room cabin $67. Additional adult $5. ❷

FOOD

Corks, 1026 S. Charles St. (☎752-3810). A hidden retreat that specializes in a vast array of strictly American wines and fine contemporary American cuisine made with classic French techniques and Asian influences. With a more formal air, the front room is ideal for dining with friends; dimly-lit, the larger back "cellar" is for sheer romance. Semi-formal attire. Open M-Th 5-10pm, F-Sa 5-11pm, Su 5-9:30pm. ❺

Babalu Grill, 32 Market Pl. (☎234-9898), in Power Plant Live. This new Cuban restaurant smacks of authenticity. Popular appetizers include Cuban-style turnovers with seasoned beef and avocado salsa ($6). Select a side of rice and beans ($4) or fried plantains ($5) to accompany boiled lobster, served hot on a bed of coconut rice ($29). Babalu turns into a hot salsa club at night ($5 cover 10-11pm, $10 cover after 11pm). Open for lunch Tu-F 11:30am-2:30pm; dinner M-Th 5-10pm, F-Sa 5-11pm, Su 4-9pm. Club open Th-Sa 10pm-2am. ❹

The Helmand, 806 N. Charles St. (☎752-0311). This unassuming Afghan restaurant is the best in town, with dishes like *kaddo borani* (pan-fried and baked baby pumpkin in a yogurt-garlic sauce; $3). Entrees up to $10. Vegetarians have a variety of options, and desserts are to satisfy all sweet tooths. Open Su-Th 5-10pm, F-Sa 5-11pm. ❷

Amicci's, 231 S. High St. (☎528-1096). Mediterranean flair is everywhere at this *ristorante,* from the menu to the Italian movie decor. Live large with the renowned antipasto for two ($9), and then try the veggie gnocchi ($12), or choose from 11 immense pasta dishes under $15. Open Su-Th 11:30am-10pm, F-Sa 11:30am-11pm. ❸

SIGHTS

Baltimore's gray harbor ends with a colorful bang in the **Inner Harbor,** a body of water surrounded by five blocks of eateries, museums, and boardable ships.

THE NATIONAL AQUARIUM. The **National Aquarium** is perhaps the one thing, besides its murder rate, that sets Baltimore apart from all other major American cities. Though a visit to the outdoor sea pool to watch slap-happy seals play is free to the general public, it is worth the time and money to venture inside. The eerie **Wings in the Water** exhibit showcases 50 species of stingrays in an immense backlit pool. In the steamy **Tropical Rainforest,** piranhas, parrots, and a pair of two-toed sloths peer through the dense foliage in a 157 ft. glass pyramid. At the **Marine Mammal Pavilion,** dolphins perform every hour on the half-hour. *(Pier 3, 501 E. Pratt St. ☎576-3800; www.aqua.org. Open M-Th 9am-5pm, F-Sa 9am-8pm, Su 9am-7pm. Remains open 2hr. after last entrance time. $17.50, seniors $14.50, ages 3-11 $9.50, under 3 free.)*

BALTIMORE MARITIME MUSEUM. Several ships grace the harbor by the aquarium, most of which belong to the Baltimore Maritime Museum. Visitors may clamber through the interior of the **USS Torsk,** the intricately-painted submarine that sank the last

ON THE MENU

FEELING CRABBY?

A long-time Maryland favorite, crab cakes are deep- or pan-fried patties of lump crabmeat and batter that together form a delectable entree. Most restaurants in the D.C. metro area serve crab cakes. The quality and size of said crab cakes vary widely among restaurants, and diners often pay up to $15 for just 2 crab cakes!

As such, *Let's Go* recommends this simple recipe for homemade crab cakes:

Ingredients:
1 pound backfin crab meat
1 egg, beaten
8 crumbled saltine crackers
2 tablespoons mayonnaise
1 teaspoon mustard
dash Worcestershire sauce

Preparation:
Carefully remove all cartilage from the crab meat. Put meat in a bowl and set it aside. Mix together all other ingredients. Gently mix in crab meat. Shape into 6 crab cakes. Put crab cakes on a plate, cover with wax paper, and refrigerate for an hour. In a large frying pan, heat about 1-2 tablespoons of vegetable oil. Sauté until golden brown (about 2-3 min. per side).

Let's Go recommends serving crab cakes on a bed of field greens drizzled with Hollandaise sauce and, of course, an ice cold beer.

WWII Japanese combat ship. You can also board one of the survivors of the Pearl Harbor attack, the Coast Guard cutter **Roger B. Taney,** and ascend the **octagonal lighthouse** on Pier 5. For these historic sites and more, purchase the **Seaport Day Pass,** which grants access to the **Maritime Museum,** the **Museum of Industry,** Baltimore's **World Trade Center,** and the **USS Constellation**—the last all-sail warship built by the US Navy. Water taxi service to and from attractions is included. *(Piers 3 and 5. ☎396-3453; http://baltomaritimemuseum.org. Open spring-fall Su-Th 10am-5:30pm, F-Sa 10am-6pm; winter F-Su 10:30am-5pm. Boats stay open 1hr. later than ticket stand. $6, seniors $5, ages 5-13 $3. Seaport Day Pass $16/13.50/9.)*

WALTERS ART GALLERY. Spanning 50 centuries in three buildings, the **Walters Art Gallery** houses one of the largest private art collections in the world. The Ancient Art collection features sculpture, jewelry, and metalwork from Egypt, Greece, and Rome, and is the museum's pride and joy. Byzantine, Romanesque, and Gothic art are also on display. At the **Hackerman House,** an exquisite townhouse/mansion attached to the Walters, rooms filled with dark wooden furniture, patterned rugs, and plush velvet curtains display art from China, Korea, Japan, and India. *(600 N. Charles St. Take bus #3 or 11. ☎547-9000; www.thewalters.org. Open Tu-Su 10am-5pm, first Th every month 10am-8pm. Tours W noon and Su 1:30pm. $8, seniors $6, students $5, 18 and under free. Admission to collection free Sa 10am-1pm and first Th of every month.)*

EDGAR ALLAN POE HOUSE. Horror pioneer Edgar Allan Poe was born in 1809 in what is now a preserved historical landmark in the heart of a rundown neighborhood. In between doses of opium, Poe penned famous stories such as *The Tell-Tale Heart* and *The Pit and the Pendulum,* as well as macabre poems like *The Raven* and *Annabel Lee.* The house contains period furniture and exhibits relating to Poe, all impeccably maintained by a staff eager to regale visitors with all sorts of Poe stories. *Steer clear of neighborhood at night. (203 N. Amity St., near Saratoga St. Take bus #15 or 23. From Lexington Market, walk on N. Lexington St. away from downtown and turn right on Amity St. It is the 2nd house on the right. ☎396-7932; www.eapoe.org. Open Apr.-July and Oct.-Dec. W-Sa noon-3:45pm; Aug.-Sept. Sa noon-3:45pm. $3, under 13 $1.)*

JOHNS HOPKINS UNIVERSITY. Approximately 3 mi. north of the harbor, prestigious **Johns Hopkins University (JHU)** spreads out from 33rd St. JHU was the first research university in the country and is currently a world leader in developments in medicine, public health, and engineering. The beautiful campus was originally the Homewood estate of Charles Carroll, Jr., the son of the longest-lived signer of the Declaration of Independence. One-hour campus tours begin at the **Office of Admissions** in Garland Hall. One mile north of the main campus, **Evergreen House** is an exercise in excess—even the bathroom of this elegant mansion is plated in 23-carat gold. Purchased in 1878 by railroad tycoon John W. Garret, the house, along with its collections of fine porcelain, impressive artwork, Tiffany silver, and rare books, was bequeathed to JHU in 1942. *(JHU: 3400 N. Charles St. Take bus #3 or 11. ☎516-8171; www.jhu.edu. Tours Sept.-May M-F 10am, noon, 3pm; call admissions for summer hours, ☎516-5589. Evergreen House: 4545 N. Charles St. ☎516-0341. Take bus #11. Open M-F 10am-4pm, Sa-Su 1-4pm. Tours every hr.; last tour 1hr. before close. $6, students $3, seniors $5.)*

ENTERTAINMENT

Much of Baltimore's finest entertainment can be enjoyed free of charge. At **Harborplace,** street performers are constantly amusing tourists with magic acts and juggling during the day. On weekend nights, dance, dip, and dream to the sounds of anything from country to calypso.

MUSIC

The **Baltimore Museum of Art** offers free summer jazz concerts (Sept.-May) in its sculpture garden. (☎466-0600.) More jazz can be found several times a week from May to October at the canvas-topped **Pier 6 Concert Pavilion.** (☎625-3100. Tickets $15-30.) For a more private performance from local artists and some big names, **Fletcher's** features everything from rock to rap to blues. Zydeco fans gather at **Harry's,** 1200 N. Charles St., a Vegas-style bar and performance space. (☎685-2828. Shows F-Sa. Cover $3-10. Open F 11am-2am, Sa 2pm-2am.) The **Baltimore Symphony Orchestra** plays at **Meyerhoff Symphony Hall,** 1212 Cathedral St., from September to May and during their month-long Summerfest. (☎783-8000. Box office open M-F 10am-6pm, Sa-Su noon-5pm, and 1hr. before performances. Tickets $15-52. Discounts available 1hr. before concerts.)

THEATER

The **Lyric Opera House,** 110 W. Mt. Royal Ave., near Maryland Ave., hosts the **Baltimore Opera Company** from October to April. (☎727-6000. Box office open M-F 10am-5pm. Tickets $24-109.) Broadway shows are performed all year at the **Mechanic Theater,** 25 Hopkins Plaza, at Baltimore and N. Charles St. (☎481-7328. Box office open daily 10am-5pm. Tickets $27-60.) The **Theater Project,** 45 W. Preston St., near Maryland St., experiments with theater, poetry, music, and dance. (☎752-8558. Box office open 1hr. before shows; call to charge tickets. Shows Th-Sa 8pm, Su 3pm. $15, seniors $10.) The **Arena Players,** the first black theater group in the country, performs comedies, drama, and dance at 801 McCullough St., at Martin Luther King, Jr. Blvd. (☎728-6500. Box office open M-F 10am-2pm. Tickets start at $15.) From June through September, the **Showcase of Nations Ethnic Festivals** celebrate Baltimore's ethnic neighborhoods with a different culture featured each week. Call the Baltimore Area Visitors Center for info. (☎837-7024.)

SPORTS

The beloved **Baltimore Orioles** play ball at **Camden Yards,** just a few blocks from the Inner Harbor at the corner of Russell and Camden St. (☎685-9800. Tickets $7-50.) The expansion-team Baltimore **Ravens,** successors to the defunct Baltimore Colts, matured fast enough to win the 2001 Super Bowl. They play in **Ravens Stadium,** adjacent to Camden Yards. (☎481-7328; www.ravenszone.net.)

 NIGHTLIFE

Nightlife in Mount Vernon tends more toward the classic bar populated by an older and more sophisticated set, while Fells Point and Power Plant Live are home to the college and 20-something scene. Be aware of the 1:30am last call.

Bohager's, 701 S. Eden St. (☎563-7220), between Spring and Eden St. in Fells Point. A tropical paradise for college students and folks who drink like them. Patrons jive to the sounds of DJs' island and house mixes under a retractable dome in the most dependably debauched club in Baltimore. Soap sud night Th 9pm-2am. $15 open bar F-Sa 8pm-1:45am. Open M-F 11:30am-2am, Sa-Su 3pm-2am.

Howl At The Moon, 34 Market Pl. (☎783-5111), in Power Plant Live. An amusing dueling-piano bar where the crowd runs the show. All songs are by request, and sing–(or perhaps "howl")–alongs are frequent. Cover $7. Beers $3-5. Mixed drinks $4-8. Open Tu-Th and Sa 7pm-2am, F 5pm-2am.

Central Station, 1001 N. Charles St. (☎752-7133), at Eager St. Chill under lights from the set of *A Few Good Men* or play some pool with a mixed gay/straight crowd. Newly constructed disco club next door is the scene for hot bumping and grinding W-Su.

Karaoke M 10pm-2am. Open mic Tu 11pm-2am. Tu Men's Night, Th Ladies' Night. $1 off beer Happy Hour (4-8pm daily). $2 Smirnoff Su 4pm-close. Club hours Tu-Th 8pm-close ($3 cover), F-Sa 8pm-close ($10 cover), Su 5pm-close ($3 cover). Open daily 3pm-2am.

ANNAPOLIS ☎410

Annapolis became the capital of Maryland in 1694, and in 1783 enjoyed a stint as temporary capital of the US (hot on the heels of Philadelphia, New York, and Trenton, NJ). It has walked the tightrope between a residential port town and a naval garrison dominated by its world-famous Naval Academy. The historic waterfront district retains its 18th-century appeal despite the presence of ritzy boutiques. Crew-cut "middies" ("midshipmen," a nickname for Naval Academy students) mingle with longer-haired students from St. John's and couples on weekend getaways amid the highest concentration of historical homes in America.

ORIENTATION & PRACTICAL INFORMATION. Annapolis lies southeast of U.S. 50, 30 mi. east of D.C. and 30 mi. south of Baltimore. The city extends south and east from two landmarks: **Church Circle** and **State Circle. School Street,** in a blatantly unconstitutional move, connects Church and State. **East Street** runs from the State House to the Naval Academy. **Main Street,** where food and entertainment congregate, starts at Church Circle and ends at the docks. Downtown Annapolis is compact and easily walkable, but finding a parking space—unless in an expensive lot or in the public garage ($7-11 per day)—can be tricky. Parking at the **Visitors Center** ($1 per hr., $8 max. weekdays, $4 max. weekend) is the best bet. There is also free weekend parking in State Lots A and B at the corner of Rowe Blvd. and Calvert St. **Greyhound** (☎800-231-2222) buses stop at the local Mass Transit Administration bus stop in the football field parking lot at Rowe Blvd. and Taylor St. Tickets are available from the bus driver; cash only. To: Baltimore (1hr., 5 per day, $10); Philadelphia (4hr., 2 per day, $20); Washington, D.C. (1-2hr., 4 per day, $14). The **Annapolis Department of Public Transportation** operates a web of city buses connecting the historic district with the rest of town. (☎263-7964. Buses run daily 5:30am-10pm. $0.75, seniors and disabled $0.35.) **Taxi: Annapolis Cab Co.,** ☎268-0022. **Checker Cab,** ☎268-3737. **Car Rental: Budget,** 2001 West St. (☎266-5030). **Annapolis and Anne Arundel County Conference and Visitors Bureau,** 26 West St., has free maps and brochures. (☎280-0445; www.visit-annapolis.org. Open daily 9am-5pm.) **Post Office:** 1 Church Cir. (☎263-9292. Open M-F 9am-5pm.) **Postal Code:** 21401. **Area Code:** 410.

ACCOMMODATIONS. The heart of Annapolis favors elegant and pricey B&Bs over cheap motels. Rooms should be reserved in advance, especially for weekends, spring graduations, and the summer. **Bed and Breakfasts of Maryland** is a good resource. (☎800-736-4667, ext. 15. Open M-F 9am-5pm, Sa 10am-3pm.) True to its name, six flags wave from the large front porch of **Flag House Inn ❺,** 26 Randall St., which has a prime location next to the Naval Academy. The complimentary full-cooked breakfast includes house specialities like blueberry french toast and baked orange croissants. (☎280-2721 or 800-437-4825; www.flaghouseinn.com. Rooms from $110.) **Scotlaur Inn ❹,** 165 Main St., sits atop Chick & Ruth's Delly. Ten tiny guest rooms with queen, double, or twin beds, A/C, TVs, and private baths grace this homey "bed & bagel." Most rooms include huge complimentary breakfast, courtesy of Chick & Ruth. (☎268-5665; www.scotlaurinn.com. Check-in 2pm. Check-out 11am. Rooms $80-150.)

FOOD. Most restaurants in the area cluster around **City Dock,** an area packed with people in summertime, especially Wednesday nights at 7:30pm when the spinnaker races finish at the dock. Luckily, the brisk business has yet to drive up prices. The best place to find cheap eats is the **Market House** food court at the center of City Dock, where a hearty meal costs under $5. A Swedish coffeehouse with an Idaho twist, **Potato Valley Cafe ❷,** 47 State Cir., across from the State House, specializes in oven-roasted baked potatoes ($5-7); one makes a filling meal. Choose from a wide variety of sour cream, cheese, bacon, or vegetable toppings. (☎267-0902. Open M-F 10am-5pm, Sa 11:30am-5pm.) An acclaimed menu and simple-chic design make **Aqua Terra ❺,** 164 Main St., a high-end NYC-style bistro serving contemporary American cuisine, a worthwhile splurge. Less expensive items include Vietnamese noodles with jumbo shrimp and bok choy ($19). (☎263-1985; www.aquaterra.com. Open M and F-Sa 5:30-11pm, Tu-Th 5:30-10pm, Su 5-9pm.) Locals flock to **Carrol's Creek Bar & Cafe ❷,** 410 Severn Ave., in the Annapolis City Marina Complex, for home-cooked food and cheap drinks overlooking the waterfront. Texas barbecue shrimp ($8) and Maryland crab soup ($5.25) are favorites. Happy Hour (M-F 4-7pm) features $2.50 domestic drafts and $2.50 rail drinks. (☎263-8102; www.carrolscreek.com. Open M-Sa 11:30am-4pm and 5-10pm, Su all-you-can-eat brunch ($19) 10am-1:30pm, dinner 3-9pm (10pm in summer).

SIGHTS. In many senses the **US Naval Academy,** 52 King George St., is Annapolis, and Annapolis is the Academy. The legendary military school, known in many circles simply as "Navy," turns harried, short-haired "plebes" (first-year students) into Naval-officer "middies" (midshipmen) through rigorous drilling and hazing. President Jimmy Carter and billionaire H. Ross Perot are among the Academy's celebrity alumni. Once at the Academy, the first stop should be the **Leftwich Visitors Center,** in the Halsey Field House, which doubles and triples as a food court and hockey rink. Tours include historic Bancroft Hall, the crypt, a dorm room, and the athletic facilities where the middies test their seafaring prowess on land. **King Hall,** the world's largest dining facility, turns into a madhouse at lunchtime, serving the entire student populace in under 20 frenzied minutes. On summer Saturdays, alumni weddings (sometimes 1 per hr.) take place in the Academy's **chapel.** (Chapel open M-Sa 9am-4pm, Su 1-4pm. Often closed in summer Sa for weddings.) Underneath the chapel is the final resting place of **John Paul Jones,** father of the United States Navy, who uttered the famous words, "I have not yet begun to fight!" as he rammed his sinking ship into a British vessel. (☎263-6933; www.usna.com. Tours every 30min. Apr.-Nov. M-F 10am-3pm, Sa 9:30am-3pm, Su 12:30-3pm; Dec.-Mar. M-Sa 10am-2:30pm, Su 12:30-2:30pm. $6.50, seniors $5.50, and students $4.50.)

FREUDIAN SLIPPING Like a pubescent rite of passage, first year "plebes" at the Naval Academy must shimmy up the **Herndon Monument,** a large, imposing obelisk in front of the chapel. At the starting gun's shot, the mob of plebes sprints toward the shaft. The hilariously humiliating event ends only when a hat is snatched off the top of the structure. Sounds easy, right? But it's not just wham, bam, thank you ma'am: the midshipmen lubricate the massive shaft with over 200 lb. of lard to prolong the event. The climactic grasping of the hat is never a quickie—one year, the spectacle lasted over 3hr.—a record for the Navy.

The historic **Hammond-Harwood House,** 19 Maryland Ave., an elegant 1774 building designed by Colonial architect William Buckland, retains period decor right down to the candlesticks. The house is most renowned for its impeccably preserved colonial doorway. The **William Paca House,** 186 Prince George St., was the first Georgian-style home built in Annapolis. Paca, an early governor of Maryland, was one of the original signers of the Declaration of Independence. The elegant house overlooks two acres of lush vegetation, and the garden hides shaded benches that gaze upon trellises, water lilies, and gazebos. Both houses feature historical exhibits on life in the late 1700s, stocked by archaeological digs on the grounds. (☎263-5553; www.hammondharwoodhouse.org. Open Mar.-Dec. M-Sa 10am-4pm, Su noon-4pm; Jan.-Feb. F-Sa 10am-4pm, Su noon-4pm. 45min. tours on the hr.; last tour 1hr. before closing. Hammond-Harwood: $6, students $5, under 12 $3. Paca: garden $5, house and garden $8. Uniformed armed service personnel free for both. Joint tickets $10.)

Built from 1772 to 1779, the Corinthian-columned **State House,** in the center of State Circle, is the oldest working capitol building in the nation. It was the US Capitol building from 1783-1784, and the Treaty of Paris was signed here on January 14, 1784. Visitors can explore the historical exhibits and silver collection or watch the state legislature bicker in two exquisite marble halls. The cordial State House guide, clad in authentic colonial garb, gladly fields questions. (90 State Cir. ☎974-3400. Open daily 9am-5pm; grounds 6am-11pm. Tours daily 11am, 3pm. State legislature mid-Jan. to mid-Apr. Free.)

ENTERTAINMENT & NIGHTLIFE. Locals and tourists generally engage in one of two activities: wandering along City Dock or schmoozing 'n' boozing at upscale pubs. The bars and taverns that line downtown Annapolis draw crowds every night. If you want more culture than drink can provide, Annapolis also has performance options. Theatergoers can check out **The Colonial Players, Inc.,** 108 East St., for innovative and often unknown works. (☎268-7373. Performance times and ticket prices vary; call ahead.) During the summer, the **Annapolis Summer Garden Theater** offers musical "theater under the stars" Th-Su at 8:30pm. Seating is free on the terraced lawn overlooking an open courtyard theater near the City Dock. (143 Compromise St. ☎268-9212; www.summergarden.com.) The **Naval Academy Band** performs on the City Dock every Tuesday night at 7:30pm (free).

As close as you can get to the water without falling in, **Pusser's Landing,** 80 Compromise St., facing City Dock, is a working pier with seats practically leaning over the water. Crowds are mixed during the day, but it attracts a more mature clientele at night. Make sure to look up at the impressive British-style tin ceiling while waiting for your food. (☎626-0004; www.pussers.com. $2-4 beers. Open daily 7am-2am.) Beer connoisseurs, midshipmen, and tourists enjoy 135 different ales, lagers, and stouts, including international microbrews, among the beer-history decor at **Ram's Head Tavern,** 33 West St. Happy Hour (M-F 4-7pm and after midnight daily) provides free food and reduced prices on drafts ($2). Free live music out back on the patio many evenings. For bigger-name bands, a dinner and show combination ticket gets you a 10% discount on your meal and a complimentary drink. (☎268-4545; www.ramsheadtavern.com. Open M-Sa 11am-2am, Su 10am-2am.) Locals and officers pack in under naval pilot-donated helmets and a two-story Ficus tree growing through **Irish McGarvey's,** 8 Market Space. Saddle up to the bar for Aviator Lager, the manliest-sounding beer in town. Parties in the summer invite patrons to dress tropical and enjoy frozen Zombies ($4) with their fish tacos ($5). Happy Hour (M and W 10pm-2am) features buffalo wings for $3-10, 32 oz. drafts for $3, and 10 oz. mugs for $1. (☎263-5700; www.mcgarveyssaloon.com. Th 6pm-1am house beer $1.50. Open M-Sa 11:30am-2am, Su 10am-2am.)

ASSATEAGUE & CHINCOTEAGUE ☎757

Crashing waves, windswept dunes, wild ponies galloping free—if it sounds like the stuff of a childhood fantasy, that's because it is. Local legend has it that ponies first came to Assateague Island by swimming ashore from a sinking Spanish galleon. A less romantic and more likely theory is that miserly colonial farmers put their horses out to graze on Assateague to avoid mainland taxes. Whatever their origins, the famous ponies now roam free across the unspoiled beaches and forests of the picturesque island, and, on the last Wednesday and Thursday in July, swim from Assateague to Chincoteague during Pony Penning.

ORIENTATION & PRACTICAL INFORMATION. Telling the two islands apart, especially since their names are sometimes used interchangeably, can often leave visitors bewildered. **Assateague Island** is the longer barrier island facing the ocean, while **Chincoteague Island** is nestled between Assateague and mainland Eastern Shore. Maryland and Virginia share Assateague Island, which is divided into three distinct parts. **Chincoteague Wildlife Refuge** is actually on Assateague. The best way to get to Chincoteague is by car; the best way to explore it is by bike. From D.C., take Rte. 50 E to Salisbury, MD, then take Rte. 13 S and turn left onto Rte. 175 E. **Visitor Info: Chincoteague Chamber of Commerce,** 6733 Maddox Blvd., in Chincoteague. (☎336-6161; www.chincoteague.com. Open M-Sa 9am-4:30pm.) **Post Office:** 4144 Main St. (☎336-2934. Open M-F 8am-4:30pm, Sa 8am-noon.) **Postal Code:** 23336. **Area Code:** 757.

ACCOMMODATIONS & FOOD. Due to Assateague's lack of civilization, visitors eat and sleep on **Chincoteague.** The dazzling **Hampton Inn & Suites ❺,** 4179 Main St., is the newest lodging in town. (☎336-1616. June-Aug. from $139. 10% AAA, AARP discount.) For breathtaking views, head to the waterfront **Island Motor Inn ❺,** 4391 Main St. (☎336-3141. June rooms from $125, higher in July-Aug. 10% AAA and senior discount low-season.) **Maddox Family Campground ❶,** just across from the Visitors Center, is a large, sprawling site. (☎336-3111. For full hookups, reserve at least 3 months in advance. Sites $28.) For coffee and light fare in a SoHo-esque atmosphere, stop by **Main St. Shop & Coffee House ❶,** 4288 Main St. (☎336-6782. Open Easter-Labor Day daily 8:30am-5pm; Labor Day-Thanksgiving Sa-Su 8:30am-5pm.) **AJ's on the Creek ❹,** 6585 Maddox Blvd., specializes in handcut steaks and grilled fish. (☎336-5888. Dinner entrees $15-25. Open summer M-Sa 11am-10pm; winter M-F 4-9pm, Sa 4-9:30pm.)

SIGHTS. The **Chincoteague National Wildlife Refuge** stretches across the Virginia side of the island. Avid bird-watchers flock here to see rare species such as peregrine falcons, snowy egrets, and black-crowned night herons. The **wild pony roundup,** held the last consecutive Wednesday and Thursday in July (after a monthlong carnival), brings hordes of tourists to Assateague. During slack tide, local firemen herd the ponies together and swim them from Assateague to Chincoteague Island, where the fire department auctions off the foals the following day. The adults swim back to Assateague and reproduce, providing next year's crop. Head to the refuge's Visitors Center, located just inside the refuge, to learn about biking, hiking, walking, and bird and nature tours. Guided wildlife bus tours are also available. ($12, children $8. Memorial Day-Labor Day daily 10am, 1, 4pm.) Trails include the 3 mi. pony-populated **Wildlife Loop** (open 3pm-dusk for cars, all day for pedestrians and bicyclists), the 1½ mi. **Woodland Trail** (cars not permitted), and the ¼ mi. **Lighthouse Trail** (pedestrians only). Follow Beach Rd. to its end to find the famous beach and sand dunes. Park rangers request that visitors resist the urge to feed the ponies, who, if overfed by guests, could starve in the winter months when visitors have left the islands. Also be careful to gawk from a safe distance—the ponies may appear harmless, but they aren't. (8231 Beach Rd. ☎336-6122; http://chinco.fws.gov. Absolutely no pets permitted. Park open daily May-Sept. 5am-10pm; Oct. and Apr. 6am-8pm; Nov.-Mar. 6am-6pm. Visitors Center open Memorial Day-Labor Day 9am-5pm; Labor Day-Memorial Day 8am-4:30pm. 7-day pass $10 per car.) The **Oyster & Maritime Museum** is the only non-profit museum in Chincoteague and contains numerous samples of sea creatures and shells. Don't miss the 1865 Barbier & Frenestre first order Fresnel lens from the old Assateague Lighthouse, one of only 21 in the US; retired in 1961, its light could be seen from 23 mi. away. (7125 Maddox Blvd. ☎336-6117. Open May-Sept. M-Sa 10am-5pm, Su noon-4pm; low-season hours vary. $3, ages 12 and under $1.50. Cash only.) The **Chincoteague Pony Centre** offers pony rides and showcases veterans of the pony swim. (6417 Carriage Dr. ☎336-2776. Heading north on Main St., turn right onto Church St., left onto Chicken City Rd., and right onto Carriage Dr. Open summer M-Sa 9am-10pm, Su 1-9pm. Rides M-Sa 9am-1pm and 3:30-6pm, Su 1-4pm. $5.)

OCEAN CITY ☎410

Ocean City is a lot like a kiddie pool—it's shallow and plastic, but can be a lot of fun if you're the right age, or just in the right mood. This 10 mi. strip of prime Atlantic beach packs endless bars, all-you-can-eat buffets, hotels, mini-golf courses, boardwalks, flashing neon, and sun-seeking tourists into a thin region between the ocean and the Assawoman Bay. The siren call of senior week beckons droves of recent high school and college graduates to alcohol and hormone-driven fun, turning O.C. into a city-wide block party in June. July and August cater more to families and professional singles looking for inexpensive fun in the sun.

ORIENTATION & PRACTICAL INFORMATION. Driving is the most sensible mode of transportation to reach the ocean resort. From the north, simply follow Rte. 1, which becomes **Coastal Highway (Philadelphia Avenue).** From the west, Rte. 50 also leads directly to Ocean City. If you're trekking to Ocean City from points south, take Rte. 113 to Rte. 50 and follow that to town. Ocean City runs north-south, with numbered streets linking the ocean to the bay. Most hotels are in the lower numbered streets toward the ocean; most clubs and bars are uptown toward the bay. **Trailways** (☎289-9307), at 2nd St. and Philadelphia Ave., sends **buses** to Baltimore (3½ hr., 3 per day, $32) and Washington, D.C. (5hr., 3 per day, $43). In town, **public buses** (☎723-1607) run the length of the strip and are the best way to get around town 24hr. a day ($2 per day for unlimited rides). The **Ocean City Visitors Center,** 4001 Coastal Hwy., at 40th St. in the Convention Center, gives out discount coupons. (☎800-626-2326; www.ococean.com. Open June-Aug. M-F 8:30am-5pm, Sa-Su 9am-5pm; Sept.-May daily 8:30am-5pm.) **E-Point Internet Cafe,** 1513 Philadelphia Ave., in the 15th St. Shopping Center complex, offers access. (☎289-9844. $2 per 15min., $1 for students, $3/2.50 for 30min., $6/4 for 1hr. Cash only.) **Post Office:** 7101 Coastal Hwy. (☎524-7611. Open M-F 9am-5pm, Sa 9am-noon.) **Postal Code:** 21842. **Area Codes:** 410, 443. In text, 410 unless otherwise noted.

ACCOMMODATIONS. The **Atlantic House Bed and Breakfast ❹,** 501 N. Baltimore Ave., offers free bike rentals, a full breakfast buffet, a great location, and a wholesome change of pace from the Ocean City motel trend. They even have complimentary beach chairs, umbrellas, and towels. (☎289-2333; www.atlantic-house.com. A/C, cable TV, hot tub, parking. Closed Dec.-Mar. except for Valentine's Day. May-Aug. rooms with shared baths from $80, with private bath $110-185. Rates drop in low-season.) Just a half block from the beach, the **Sea Spray Motel ❹,** 12 35th St., sports a dark wood interior and copious amenities. Some rooms have kitchens and porches; all rooms offer cable TV and A/C. (☎289-6648 or 800-678-5702; www.seaspraymotel.com. Gas grill access, laundry facilities. Rooms June-Sept. $80-175.) The only in-town camping option is **Ocean City Travel Park ❶,** 105 70th St. (☎524-7601. Tent sites $27-54; RVs $32-69.)

FOOD. Ocean City's cuisine is plentiful and cheap, so don't expect gourmet quality. **Reflections ❹,** 6600 Coastal Hwy., at 67th St., on the ground floor of the Holiday Inn, offers tableside cooking and fine dining, classic Las Vegas-style. (☎524-5252. Early Bird dinner entrees $10-19 (must be seated by 6pm); regular entrees from $20. Open daily 5-10:30pm.) For a little something that can't be found at 2am and isn't listed on a take-out menu glued to the back of a magnet, try the healthier and trendier food at **Coral Reef Cafe ❸,** 1701 Atlantic Ave., on the Boardwalk at 17th St. Crab dip with toasted focaccia ($10) and the New Orleans chicken wrap with mozzarella and homemade spicy cream cheese ($9) are just a couple of specialities worth the extra money. (☎289-6388; www.ocsuites.com. Open daily June-Sept. 7am-10pm; Oct.-May 7am-9pm.) With freshly caught food and a friendly atmosphere, **The Embers ❺,** 24th St. and Coastal Hwy., boasts the biggest seafood buffet in town. All the clams, oysters, Alaskan crablegs, prime rib, and steak you can eat are $26. (☎289-3322 or 888-436-2377; www.embers.com. Open daily 3-10pm.) **Brass Balls Saloon & Bad Ass Cafe ❶,** on the Boardwalk between 11th and 12th St., is known for its $1.25 Jello shots (after 10pm). The motto here is "Drink Hearty, Eat Healthy." Breakfast specials like the Oreo waffles ($5.25) or the $7 pizzas seem to defy the latter imperative, though the college crowds can't get enough of the "drink hearty" part. (☎289-0069; www.brassballssaloon.com. Open Mar.-Oct. daily 8:30am-2am.)

ENTERTAINMENT & NIGHTLIFE. Ocean City's star attraction is its beautiful **beach.** The wide stretch of surf and sand runs the entire ten miles worth of town and can be accessed by taking a left onto any of the numerous side streets off Philadelphia and Baltimore Ave. The breaking waves know no time constraints, but beach-goers are technically limited to 6am-10pm. When the sun goes down, hard-earned tans glow under the glaring lights of Ocean City's bars and nightclubs. The elder statesman of the bayside clubs, **Fager's Island,** 60th St., in the bay, has hordes walking the plank to its island location. Live rock, R&B, jazz, and reggae play nightly to accompany the 100+ beers. No one seems to know the source of the classical music tradition, but the *1812 Overture* booms at every sunset. Start the week at the Monday night deck party til 2am (6pm $5 cover, after 7pm $10). (☎524-5500. Happy Hour Tu-F with half-price drinks and appetizers. Open daily 11am-2am.) Professional party-goers will no doubt be impressed by **Seacrets,** on 49th St., a virtual entertainment mecca and amusement park for adults. This oasis features 10 bars, including two floating bars on the bay. Barefoot partygoers wander from bar to bar, sipping the signature frozen rum runner mixed with piña colada ($6) to the strains of live bands nightly. A magnificent sunset view ushers in early revelers for cocktails in the raft pool. (☎524-4900; www.seacrets.com. Cover $5-20. Open daily 11am-2am.) A new addition to the Ocean City scene, the **Party Block Complex,** 17th St. and Coastal Hwy., offers patrons one cover to flirt between four different clubs, from the laidback Oasis Bar to the flashy Rush Club.

WASHINGTON, D.C. ☎202

For outsiders, seeing D.C. as anything more than a passionless hub of politics and pomposity can present a serious challenge. Its residents and other D.C. enthusiasts, though, love the city because they know its true nature: a thriving international city filled with cultural offerings on par with the finest in the world. Political Washington is a whirlwind of endless press conferences and power lunches, potent memorials and presidential intrigues. Outside the federal enclave, Washington's neighborhoods flaunt cultural delights. Dupont Circle showcases easels of the masters beside those of budding artists, Adams Morgan embraces a banquet of ethnic offerings, and Bethesda rightly claims the most diverse restaurant scene. High culture bows and pirouettes on the Kennedy Center stage almost every night as local and big-name rock groups deafen their young audiences in the "New U" St. corridor. Political powerhouse, thriving metropolis, and intern party town, D.C. packs more punch per square mile than any other city. For expanded coverage of the D.C. area, check out *Let's Go: Washington, D.C. 2004*.

INTERCITY TRANSPORTATION

Airports: Ronald Reagan National Airport (☎703-417-8000; www.mwaa.com/national). Metro: National Airport. If you're flying to D.C. from within the US, this airport is your best bet, as it is on the Metro and closer to the city. Taxi from downtown $10-15. The **SuperShuttle** bus (☎800-258-3826; www.supershuttle.com) runs between National and the city (about $10 per person). **Dulles International Airport** (☎703-572-2700; www.mwaa.com/dulles) is much farther from the city. Taxis from downtown start at $40. The **Washington Flyer Coach Service** (☎888-927-4359; www.washfly.com) departs from Dulles every 30min. M-F 5:45am-10:15pm, Sa-Su 7:45am-10:15pm; from Metro: West Falls Church every 30min. M-F 6:15am-10:45pm, Sa-Su 8:15am-10:45pm ($8; discounts for groups of 3 or more, seniors, and international students). The **SuperShuttle** bus also runs from Dulles to downtown daily ($21).

Trains: Amtrak operates from Union Station, 50 Massachusetts Ave. NE (☎484-7540). To: **Baltimore** (50min., $14); **Boston** (7¾hr., $81); **New York** (3¾hr.; reserved $72; metroliner $137); **Philadelphia** (2hr., $45). Maryland's commuter train, **MARC** (☎800-543-9808), departs from Union to Baltimore ($6.50) and the suburbs.

ORIENTATION

Diamond-shaped D.C. stretches its tips in the four cardinal directions. The **Potomac River** forms the jagged southwest border, its waters flowing between the district and Arlington, VA. **North Capitol, East Capitol,** and **South Capitol Street** slice up the city into four quadrants: NW, NE, SE, and SW. The **Mall** stretches west of the Capitol. The suffixes of the quadrants distinguish otherwise identical addresses (e.g. 800 G St. NW and 800 G St. NE).

Washington's streets lie in a simple grid. Streets that run east-to-west are labeled alphabetically in relation to North Capitol/South Capitol St., which runs through the Capitol. Since the street plan follows the Roman alphabet, in which "I" and "J" are the same letter, there is no J St. After W St., east-west streets take on two-syllable names, then three-syllable names, then the names of trees and flowers. The names run in alphabetical order, but sometimes repeat or skip a letter. Streets running north-south are numbered all the way to 52nd St. NW and 63rd St. NE. Addresses on lettered streets indicate the number of the cross street. For instance, 1100 D St. SE is on the corner of D and 11th.

Major roads include **Pennsylvania Avenue, Connecticut Avenue, Wisconsin Avenue, 16th Street NW, K Street NW, Massachusetts Avenue, New York Avenue,** and **North Capitol Street.** D.C. is ringed by the **Capital Beltway** (**I-495**—except where it's part of I-95). The Beltway is bisected by **U.S. 1** and meets **I-395** from Virginia. The **Baltimore-Washington Parkway** connects Washington, D.C. to Baltimore. **I-595** trickles off the Capital Beltway towards Annapolis, and **I-66** heads west into Virginia.

NEIGHBORHOODS

Postcard-perfect, **Capitol Hill** symbolizes the democratic dream with the Capitol building, Supreme Court, and the Library of Congress. The **Mall** is flanked by the Smithsonian Museums and the National Gallery of Art, and monuments and

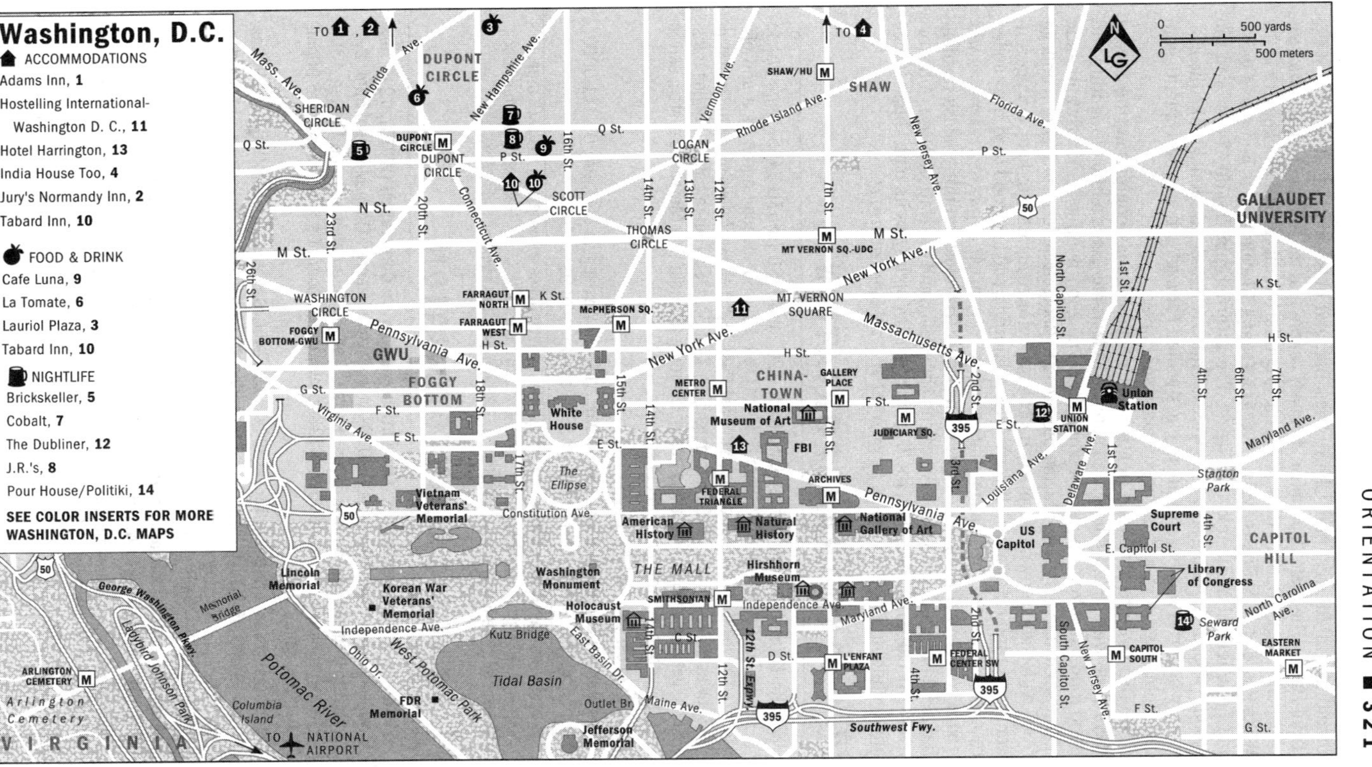

MID-ATLANTIC

memorials fill its west end. Cherry trees bud and blossom along the brink of the Tidal Basin. The **State Department, Kennedy Center,** and the infamous **Watergate Complex** make Foggy Bottom their stomping grounds, but this area's blockbuster is the **White House** at 1600 Pennsylvania Ave. The **Federal Triangle** area is home to a growing commercial and banking district. The International Trade Center and the Ronald Reagan Building share the wide avenues with federal agencies like the FBI. It's a wonderful (corporate) life in glass-walled **Farragut,** where government agencies, lobbying firms, and lawyers make their home.

There's more to D.C. than politics; the neighborhoods comprising the **Second City** bustle with sights, shops, and eateries. **Adams-Morgan** is a hub of nightlife and good food. **Chinatown,** more of a block than a neighborhood, offers fairly authentic Chinese cuisine. Fashionable and picturesque **Georgetown** has the feel of a college town with Georgetown University nearby and enough nightlife to keep college students tipsy and entertained. If you're hip, glamorous, and like good food surrounded by cutting edge art, then **Dupont Circle** is made for you. *At night, travelers should avoid walking through the circle.* The **Upper Northwest,** an upper-class residential neighborhood, is home to American University and the National Zoo. A historically African-American area, the **U District** parties nightly as its clubs blast trance and techno until the sun rises. *Be careful in this area at night.*

LOCAL TRANSPORTATION

Public Transit: Metro Center Line Exit, 12th and F St. (☎636-3425, general info ☎637-7000; open M-F 7:30am-6:30pm). $1.10-3.60, depending on time and distance traveled; 1-day Metro pass $6. **Fast Pass** ($30) allows 7 days of unlimited travel. Subway trains run M-F 5:30am-midnight, Sa 7am-3am, Su 7am-midnight. For bus transfers, get a pass on the platform *before* boarding the train. The **Metrobus** system serves Georgetown, downtown, and the suburbs. $1.20.

Taxi: Yellow Cab, ☎544-1212.

Car Rental: Bargain Buggies Rent-a-Car, 3140 N. Washington Blvd. (☎703-841-0000), in Arlington, VA. Open M-F 8am-7pm, Sa 9am-3pm, Su 9am-noon.

Bicycle Rental: Better Bikes (☎293-2080). Delivers bikes anywhere in the D.C. area. 10-speeds $25 per day, $95 per week; mountain bikes $38/135. Helmet, map, backpack, locks, and breakdown service included. $25 deposit. Cash only. Open 24hr.

PRACTICAL INFORMATION

Visitor Info: Washington, D.C. Convention and Tourism Corporation (WCTC), 1212 New York Ave. NW, Ste. 600 (☎789-7000; www.washington.org). Open M-F 9am-5pm. **D.C. Visitor Information Center,** in the Ronald Reagan International Trade Center, 1300 Pennsylvania Ave. NW (☎866-324-7386; www.dcvisit.com). Open M-F 8:30am-5:30pm, Sa 9am-4pm.

Hotlines: Rape Crisis Center, ☎333-7273. 24hr. **Gay and Lesbian National Hotline** (☎888-843-4564). Operates M-F 4pm-midnight, Sa noon-5pm. **Traveler's Aid Society,** ☎371-1937. Offices at Union Station, National and Dulles Airports, and downtown at 512 C St. NE. Hours vary.

Medical Services: Children's National Medical Center, 111 Michigan Ave. NW (☎884-5000). **Georgetown University Medical Center,** 3800 Reservoir Rd. NW (☎687-2000).

Internet Access: The Cyberstop Cafe, 1513 17th St. NW (☎234-2470), near P St. Open M-F 7am-midnight, Sa-Su 8am-midnight.

Post Office: 2 Massachusetts Ave. NE. (☎523-2368). Open M-F 7am-midnight, Sa-Su 7am-8pm. **Postal Code:** 20002. **Area Code:** 202.

ACCOMMODATIONS

In D.C., inexpensive lodgings are harder to come by than straight-talking politicians. The best escape from these ridiculous rates is staying outside the city or visiting in the low season. Don't forget that D.C. adds a 14.5% hotel tax to your bill.

HOSTELS

Hostelling International-Washington D.C. (HI-AYH), 1009 11 St. NW (☎737-2333; www.hiwashingtondc.org), 3 blocks north of Metro on 11th St. Metro: Metro Center. A friendly staff and reasonable rates make this an appealing choice. In the heart of D.C., 5 blocks from the White House and a 20min. walk from the National Mall. *Use caution in this area at night.* Reception 24hr. Check-in 2pm. Check-out 11am. Credit card required for reservation. Wheelchair-accessible. $29-32, nonmembers $32-35. ❷

India House Too, 300 Carroll St. (☎291-1195; www.dchostel.com), on the border of D.C. and Takoma Park. Metro: Takoma. Hostelers can come and go as they please, smoke and drink in certain areas, or fire up a barbecue in the backyard. Free linens and use of kitchen. A/C in some rooms. Satellite TV, laundry facilities, and free Internet access. Reservations preferred. Reception daily 8am-midnight. 7-night max. stay. 18+. Dorms $20; private rooms $40 (no private bath). Cash only. ❶

HOTELS & GUEST HOUSES

Adams Inn, 1744 Lanier Pl. NW (☎745-3600 or 800-578-6807; www.adamsinn.com), 2 blocks north of the center of Adams-Morgan. Complimentary continental breakfast, coffee, tea, apples, and cookies. Rooms have A/C and private sinks (some with private bath). Friendly, helpful staff. Limited parking $10 per night. Cable TV in common area, laundry facilities, and free Internet access. Reception M-Sa 8am-9pm, Su 1-9pm. Credit card needed to secure reservation. Check-in 3-9pm. Check-out noon. 2-night min. stay if staying Sa night. Singles $75, with private bath $85; each additional person $10. ❹

Tabard Inn, 1739 N St. NW (☎785-1277; www.tabardinn.com), between 17th and 18th St. 40 individually decorated rooms in 3 townhouses. Rooms have hardwood floors and stone-tile bathrooms as well as A/C, phone, and data port (but no TV). Patio, bar, and lounges. Breakfast and passes to the YMCA included. Reception 24hr. Singles $80-110, with private bath $110-190; each additional person $15. ❹

Jury's Normandy Inn, 2118 Wyoming Ave. NW (☎483-1350 or 800-424-3729; www.jurysdoyle.com), at Connecticut Ave., 2 blocks off Columbia Rd. Jury's offers stylish, spacious rooms with refrigerators, phones, cable TV, and complimentary electrical outlets. Free wine and cheese reception (Tu 5:30-7pm), complimentary coffee and cookies in the lobby every evening, and daily continental breakfast ($5.50). Exquisitely furnished lounge area and an outdoor patio add a touch of charm. 1 smoking floor. Limited underground parking $12 per night. Check-in 3pm. Check-out noon. Rooms $79-155; each additional person $15. AAA members typically save 10%. ❹

Hotel Harrington, 11th and E St. NW (☎628-8140 or 800-424-8532; www.hotel-harrington.com). Metro: Metro Center or Federal Triangle. For nearly 90 years, this hotel has offered clean rooms and a great location. Cable TV, A/C, and laundry. Parking $8.50 per day. Singles $89; doubles $99. $10 off if you call from the airport, train, or bus station; 10% off on stays of 5+ days. 10% off for students and AAA members. ❹

FOOD

How do you feast like a senator on an intern's slim budget? Savvy natives go grubbing at Happy Hours. Bars often leave out free appetizer platters to bait early evening clients (see **Nightlife,** p. 333). As for budget eateries, **Adams-Morgan** and **Dupont Circle** are home to the *crème de la crème* of ethnic cuisine. Suburban **Bethesda, MD** features over 100 different restaurants within a four-block radius.

ADAMS-MORGAN

The Diner, 2453 18th St. NW (☎232-8800). The Diner's hours and quintessential American food have earned it high esteem among local college kids and other late-night revelers. Enjoy omelettes ($6-8), pancakes (3 for $4.50), or burgers ($6-7.25). Kosher hot dogs offered. Vegetarian options available, including some vegan soups. Tu nights feature film screenings; each month typically has a different theme. Open 24hr. ❷

New Orleans Cafe, 2412 18th St. NW (☎234-0420). With Dixieland playing over its speakers, murals of jazz bands, and an owner whose friendliness epitomizes Southern hospitality, this cafe rewards its customers with all things (desirable) from N'awlins. Jambalaya and cajun linguine ($8-15), spicy gumbo soups ($4-8), and po' boy sandwiches ($5-9) await. Open Tu-F 11am-10pm, Sa-Su 10am-10pm. ❸

Pasta Mia Trattoria, 1790 Columbia Rd. NW (☎328-9114), near 18th St. Red-and-white checked tablecloths in an airy room complete dusky evenings devoted to Disney-worthy romance. Offers standard Italian fare; *pièce de résistance* is a large selection of huge pasta entrees ($9-10). No reservations; arrive early. Open M-Sa from 6:30pm. ❷

BETHESDA

Bacchus, 7945 Norfolk Ave. (☎301-657-1722), at Del Ray Ave. A superb Lebanese restaurant featuring 50 kinds of appetizers, all in the vicinity of $5; the *shawarma* ($7) is highly recommended. Open M-F noon-2pm and 5:30-10pm, Sa 5:30-10:30pm. ❷

Thyme Square Cafe, 4735 Bethesda Ave. (☎301-657-9077), at Woodmont Ave. Friendly service, colorful decorations, and healthy vegetarian salads, sandwiches, and pasta dishes radiate wholesomeness. A true vegan paradise. Try the avocado "PLT" (grilled portobello, lettuce, tomato, avocado, and eggless mayo on multi-grain bread; $9). Open Su-Th 11:30am-9:30pm, F-Sa 11:30am-10pm. ❷

Grapeseed, 4865 Cordell Ave. (☎301-986-9592), near Norfolk Ave. Grapeseed offers an unpretentious environment for experimentation in the intimidating field of wine tasting. Wine by the bottle, the glass, or the taste (a 3 oz. pour). Hosts wine tastings twice a month (Tu 5-7pm, $15). Open M-Th 5-10pm, F-Sa 5-11pm, Su 5-9pm. ❹

La Panetteria, 4921 Cordell Ave. (☎301-951-6433), near Norfolk Ave. La Panetteria offers excellent Northern Italian cuisine and unobtrusive service. Dishes like veal-stuffed tortellini in cream ($6.50) prove just as delicious as more expensive options. Lunch specials $7-12. Open M-Th 11:30am-10pm, F-Sa 11:30am-11pm, Su 4-10pm. ❸

CHINATOWN

Burma Restaurant, upstairs at 740 6th St. NW (☎638-1280), between G and H St. Burmese curries, unique spices, and a plethora of garnishes. Try the green tea salad ($7), followed by the squid (sautéed in garlic, ginger, and scallions; $8). Vegetarians enjoy the papaya and tofu salads ($6). Open M-F 11am-3pm and 6-10pm, Sa-Su 6-10pm. ❷

Hunan Chinatown, 624 H St. NW (☎783-5858). Upscale restaurant serving standard Chinese food; locals maintain that the cuisine is well worth the added expense. Serves Kung Pao chicken (lunch $7), tea smoked duck (dinner $14.50), and Hunan lamb (dinner $14). Open Su-Th 11am-10pm, F-Sa 11am-11pm. ❸

China Doll, 627 H St. NW (☎289-4755). Standard Chinese dishes and combination meals with soup, spring roll, and steamed rice (lunch $6-8; dinner $8 and up). Dim sum daily 11am-4pm. Open Su-Th 11am–10pm, F-Sa 11am-midnight. ❷

DUPONT CIRCLE

La Tomate, 1701 Connecticut Ave. NW (☎667-5505), at R St. This modern Italian bistro offers attentive service, a creative menu, and bread with fresh black olive spread waiting on the table. Pastas ($12.25-18) include the delectable *farfalle prosciutto e funghi*, a bowtie pasta with prosciutto, mushrooms, and a touch of cream ($12.50). Entrees $15-27. Reservations recommended. Open M-W 11:30am-11pm, F-Sa 11:30am-11:30pm, Su 11:30am-10pm. ❹

Tabard Inn, 1739 N St. NW (☎785-1277; www.tabardinn.com), between 17th and 18th St., in the hotel of the same name (see p. 325). This longtime Dupont secret offers a menu that changes daily and features locally-grown ingredients. Entrees ($19-26) include the grilled marinated ostrich steak with horseradish cream potato puree ($25). Casual dress in an unpretentious atmosphere. Open for breakfast M-F 7-10am; brunch Sa 11am-2pm, Su 10:30am-2pm; dinner Su-Th 6-9:30pm, F-Sa 6-10:30pm. ❺

Lauriol Plaza, 1865 18th St. NW (☎387-0035), at T St., between Dupont Circle and Adams Morgan. Lauriol occupies half the block with 3 magnificent floors of Mexican dining. Large entrees ($8-15), appetizers such as fried plantains and guacamole ($2.75-8), and excellent margaritas ($5, pitchers $23). Free parking. No reservations accepted, so get there early. Su brunch 11am-3pm. Open Su-Th 11:30am-11pm, F-Sa and holidays 11:30am-midnight. ❸

Cafe Luna, 1633 P St. NW (☎387-4005), near 17th St. This popular basement restaurant serves mostly vegetarian and low-fat fare. Breakfast ($2-5) served all day. Huge sandwiches ($4-6) satisfy almost any appetite. W and Su half-price pizzas, which are only $5-7 to begin with. Brunch Sa-Su 10am-3pm. Open M-Th 8am-11pm, F 8am-1am, Sa 10am-1am, Su 10am-11pm. ❶

GEORGETOWN

Clyde's of Georgetown, 3236 M St. NW (☎333-9180), between Potomac St. and Wisconsin Ave. Join the crowds at Clyde's for delicious sandwiches ($7-12), salads ($11-13), seafood ($13-17), and pasta ($13-15). Open M-Th 11:30am-2am, F 11:30am-3am, Sa 10am-3am, Su 9am-2am. ❹

Red Ginger, 1564 Wisconsin Ave. NW (☎965-7009). Serves flavorful, sometimes spicy Caribbean gourmet food, including the whole red snapper (with saffron rice and a mango pineapple chutney; $15) Weekend brunch offers complimentary champagne (Sa-Su 11:30am-5pm). Open Tu-F 4:30-11pm, Sa 11:30am-11:30pm, Su 11:30am-10pm. ❹

Patisserie Poupon, 1645 Wisconsin Ave. NW (☎342-3248), near Q St. Start the day with a mouthwatering buttery brioche, pear danish, or croissant ($1.30-2.25). Beautifully prepared tarts and cakes ($4-38). Sandwiches and salads $4-7. Coffee bar in back. Open Tu-Sa 8am-6:30pm, Su 8am-4pm. ❶

UPPER NORTHWEST

Yanni's, 3500 Connecticut Ave. NW (☎362-8871). Find homestyle Greek cooking in this airy restaurant, adorned with classical statues and murals of Greek gods. Try charbroiled octopus, crunchy on the outside and delicately tender within, served with rice and vegetables ($14). Entrees $9-18 (vegetarian options $9-12). Strong Greek coffee ($2.50) goes well with *baklava* ($5). Open daily 11:30am-11pm. ❸

THE BIG SPLURGE

MATISSE

Behind its unassuming façade, **Matisse Restaurant** reveals a dining area of which even the French impressionist himself would approve. The food options are also artistically conceived. For $75, patrons can order a 7-course "Chef's Table" individually customized to their tastes and personally prepared and served by the chef himself. From the cozy atmosphere of the restaurant's wine cellar, customers watch each course perpared before their eyes.

Those looking for less expensive options won't be disappointed, either. Matisse's truly unique entrees generally run $10-16 at lunch and $20-26 at dinner. If you stop by for Su brunch, start with warm porridge, strawberries, and cream ($5) and proceed with an oatmeal *soufflé* with sausage and maple syrup ($14).

Matisse is a favorite with the likes of Ted Koppel, Jim Lehrer, and even First Lady Laura Bush. Henry Kissinger's birthday party was also held here.

4934 Wisconsin Ave. NW., near Fessenden St. ☎244-5322. Open for lunch Tu-F 11:30am-2:30pm; brunch Su 11am-3pm; dinner M 5-9:30pm, Tu-Th 5:30-10pm, F 5:30-10:30pm, Sa 5:30-11pm, Su 5-9pm. ❹

Cactus Cantina, 3300 Wisconsin Ave. NW (☎686-7222), at Macomb St. near the Cathedral. Try the *fajitas al carbon* (half chicken, half beef; $12) followed by the dessert *cajeta* ($5.25) amidst displays of classic Native American dress and cowboy garb. A few vegetarian options available. Be prepared to wait for a table on weekends. Open Su 11am-11pm, M-Th 11:30am-11pm, F-Sa 11:30am-midnight. ❸

2 Amys Neapolitan Pizzeria, 3715 Macomb St. NW (☎885-5700), near Wisconsin Ave. and adjacent to Cactus Cantina. 2 Amys is named after the 2 owners' wives. Amid the pastel yellow and orange hues of the dining areas, superb, freshly cooked pizzas ($8-13) are served by a friendly waitstaff. The "Narcia" pizza (tomato, salami, roasted peppers, mozzarella, and garlic; $13) is excellent. Expect a wait. Open Tu-Sa 11:30am-11pm, Su noon-10pm. ❸

Mama Maria and Enzio's, 2313 Wisconsin Ave. NW (☎965-1337), near Calvert St. Amazing southern Italian cuisine with a casual, family atmosphere and exceptionally warm service. Shrimp in lemon sauce ($16) is worth the wait. Pizzas $9-12. Calzones $7. Cannoli $5. Lunch entrees $7-11. Reservations for parties of 3 or more. Open M-F 11:30am-3pm and 5-10:30pm, Sa 5-10:30pm, Su 4:30-5pm. ❸

SIGHTS

CAPITOL HILL

THE CAPITOL. The **US Capitol** may be an endless font of cynicism, but it still demands and justifies respect in terms of sheer grandeur. From the times of frontiersman Andrew Jackson (1829) to peanut-farmin' Jimmy Carter (1977), presidents were inaugurated here. The East Front entrance, facing the Supreme Court, brings visitors into the 180 ft. high rotunda, where soldiers slept during the Civil War. From the lower-level crypt, visitors can climb to the second floor for a view of the House or Senate visitors chambers. Americans may obtain a free gallery pass from the office of their representative or senator in the House or Senate office buildings near the Capitol. Foreigners may get one-day passes by presenting identification at the appointments desks in the crypt. *(Metro: Capitol South or Union Station. ☎225-6827; www.aoc.gov. Generally open M-Sa 9am-4:30pm. Access by 30min. guided tour only. Free, but tickets are required. Same-day tickets available at the Garfield Circle kiosk on the West Front, across from the Botanic Gardens. Kiosk is open from 9am until all tickets are distributed; get there about 45min.-1hr. before opening time to guarantee yourself a ticket.)*

The real business of Congress, however, is conducted in **committee hearings.** Most are open to the public; check the *Washington Post's* "Today in Congress" box for times and locations. The free **Capitol subway** (the "Capitol Choo-Choo") shuttles between the basement of the Capitol and the House and Senate office buildings; a buzzer and flashing light signal an imminent vote.

SUPREME COURT. In 1935, the justices of the **Supreme Court** decided it was time to take the nation's separation of powers literally and moved from their makeshift offices in the Capitol into a new Greek Revival courthouse across the street. Oral arguments are open to the public; show up early to be seated. *(1 1st St. Metro: Capitol South or Union Station. ☎479-3000; www.supremecourtus.gov. In session Oct.-June M-W 10am-noon and open 1-3pm for 2 weeks every month; courtroom open when Justices are on vacation. The "3min. line" shuffles visitors through standing gallery of the courtroom for a glimpse. Court open M-F 9am-4:30pm. Seating before 8:30am. Free.)*

LIBRARY OF CONGRESS. With over 126 million objects stored on 532 mi. of shelves (including a copy of *Old King Cole* written on a grain of rice), the **Library of Congress** is the largest library in the world. The collection was torched by the British in 1814 and then restarted from Thomas Jefferson's personal stocks. The collection is open to anyone of college age or older with a legitimate research purpose; a tour of the facilities and exhibits is available for tourists. The **Jefferson Building's** green copper dome and gold-leafed flame tops a spectacular octagonal reading room. *(1st St. SE. ☎707-5000; www.loc.gov. Great Hall open M-Sa 8:30am-5:30pm. Tours available. Visitors Center and galleries open daily 10am-5pm. Free.)*

UNION STATION. Trains converge at **Union Station,** two blocks north of the Capitol. Colonnades, archways, and domed ceilings hark back to imperial Rome—if Rome was filled with stores and a food court. *(50 Massachusetts Ave. NE. Metro: Union Station. ☎371-9441; www.unionstationdc.com. Shops open M-Sa 10am-9pm, Su 10am-6pm.)*

MONUMENTS

WASHINGTON MONUMENT. With a $9.4 million restoration project completed two years ago, this shrine to America's first president is even more impressive. Once nicknamed the "the Beef Depot monument" after the cattle that grazed here during the Civil War, the **Washington Monument** was built with rock from multiple quarries, which explains the stones' multiple colors. The beautiful **Reflecting Pool** mirrors Washington's obelisk. *(Metro: Smithsonian. Open Apr.-Aug. Labor Day-Mar. daily 9am-4:45pm; Apr.-Labor Day daily 8am-11:45pm. Tours every 30min. 9am-4:30pm; last tour 4:30pm. Admission to the monument by timed ticket. Free.)*

VIETNAM VETERANS MEMORIAL. Maya Lin, who designed the **Vietnam Veterans Memorial,** received a "B" when she submitted her memorial concept for a grade as a Yale senior. She went on to beat her professor in the public memorial design competition. In her words, the monument is "a rift in the earth—a long, polished black stone wall, emerging from and receding into the earth." The wall contains the names of the 58,132 Americans who died in Vietnam, indexed in books at both ends. *(Constitution Ave. at 22nd St. NW. Metro: Smithsonian or Foggy Bottom-GWU. ☎634-1568; www.nps.gov/vive. Open 24hr.)*

LINCOLN MEMORIAL. The **Lincoln Memorial,** at the west end of the Mall, recalls the rectangular grandeur of Athens' Parthenon. A seated Lincoln presides over the memorial and everything that takes place below it. From these steps, Martin Luther King, Jr. gave his "I Have a Dream" speech during the 1963 March on Washington. Though you may find Lincoln's lap inviting, climbing the 19 ft. president is a federal offense; a camera will catch you if the rangers don't. *(Metro: Smithsonian or Foggy Bottom-GWU. ☎426-6841; www.nps.gov/linc. Open 24hr.)*

KOREAN WAR MEMORIAL. The 19 colossal polished steel statues of the **Korean War Memorial** trudge up a hill, rifles in hand, with an eternal expression of weariness and fear frozen upon their faces. The statues are accompanied by a black granite wall with over 2000 sandblasted photographic images from this war, in which 54,000 Americans lost their lives. *(At the west end of the Mall, near Lincoln. Metro: Smithsonian or Foggy Bottom-GWU. ☎426-6841; www.nps.gov/kowa. Open 24hr.)*

FRANKLIN DELANO ROOSEVELT MEMORIAL. Occupying a stretch of West Potomac Park, the **Franklin Delano Roosevelt Memorial** deviates from the grand presidential tributes nearby, replacing their imposing marble statuary with sculpted gardens, cascading fountains, and thematic alcoves. Whether or not to display the disabled Roosevelt in his wheelchair was hotly debated when the memorial was being planned; as a compromise, Roosevelt is seated, as in a famous picture taken at Yalta. The memorial is laid out in four "rooms" of red granite, each representing a phase of FDR's presidency. *(Metro: a long walk from Smithsonian, but a short walk from the Jefferson or Lincoln Memorials. ☎426-6841; www.nps.gov/frde. Open 24hr.)*

JEFFERSON MEMORIAL. A 19 ft. hollow bronze statue of **Thomas Jefferson** stands enshrined in an open-air rotunda, encircled by massive Ionic columns and overlooking the Tidal Basin. Quotes from the Declaration of Independence, the Virginia Statute of Religious Freedom, and *Notes on Virginia* adorn the walls. *(Metro: A long walk from L'Enfant Plaza or Smithsonian. ☎426-6841; www.nps.gov/thje. Open 24hr.)*

SOUTH OF THE MALL

HOLOCAUST MEMORIAL MUSEUM. Opened in 1993, the privately-funded **Holocaust Memorial Museum** examines the atrocities of the Holocaust. Special exhibitions, which can be viewed without passes, include **The Wall of Remembrance,** a touching collection of tiles painted by American schoolchildren in memory of the 1.5 million children killed during the Holocaust, and the orientation film shown daily *(every 30min. 10:15am-4:15pm)*. The permanent gallery is divided into three chronologically organized floors. *(14th St. between C St. and Independence Ave. SW. Metro: Smithsonian. ☎488-0400; www.ushmm.org. Open daily 10am-5:30pm. Free. Not recommended for children under 11; kids can tour the exhibition "Daniel's Story," an account of Nazi occupation told from a child's perspective.)*

BUREAU OF ENGRAVING AND PRINTING. The buck starts here, arguably the birthplace of the good and bad of modern capitalism. The **Bureau of Engraving and Printing,** the largest producer of currency, stamps, and security documents in the world, offers guided tours of the presses that print $696 million in money and stamps each day. *(At 14th and C St. SW. Metro: Smithsonian. ☎847-2808; www.moneyfactory.com. Ticket booth opens M-F at 8am to distribute tickets for same-day tours 9am-2pm. Free.)*

FEDERAL TRIANGLE

NATIONAL BUILDING MUSEUM. Montgomery Meigs' Italian-inspired edifice remains one of Washington's most striking sights. The museum's exhibits, tucked below office space around the Great Hall, honor American achievements in urban planning, construction, and design. *(F St. NW, between 4th and 5th St. Metro: Judiciary Sq. ☎272-2448; www.nbm.org. Open M-Sa 10am-5pm, Su 11am-5pm. 45min. tours M-W 12:30pm; Th-Sa 11:30am, 12:30, 1:30pm; Su 12:30, 1:30pm. Suggested donation $5.)*

NATIONAL ARCHIVES. Visitors line up at the **National Archives** to view the original Declaration of Independence, US Constitution, and Bill of Rights. This building houses 16 million pictures and posters, 18 million maps, and billions of pages of text—about 2-5% of the documents the government produces each year. *(8th St. and Constitution Ave. NW. Metro: Archives-Navy Memorial. ☎501-5000; www.nara.gov. Open daily Apr.-Labor Day 10am-9pm; Sept.-Mar. 10am-5:30pm. Free.)*

FEDERAL BUREAU OF INVESTIGATION. The **J. Edgar Hoover Building** closed to visitors in August 2002 for extensive renovations. Tours will not resume until fall 2004. *(935 Pennsylvania Ave. NW. ☎324-3447; www.fbi.gov.)*

INTERNATIONAL SPY MUSEUM. Opened in 2002, Washington's newest museum is the culmination of more than 7 years of work and planning by some of the nation's foremost experts and practitioners in the intelligence community. With glowing neon lighting in the elevators and movie-set like backdrops in some historical exhibits, the museum can feel a bit campy, but it offers unparalleled insight into the world of espionage. *(800 F St. NW, at 9th St. Metro: Gallery Place-Chinatown. ☎393-7798; www.spymuseum.org. Open daily Apr.-Oct. 10am-8pm (last admission 7pm); Nov.-Mar. 10am-6pm (last admission 5pm). $13, seniors and military $12, children $10, under 5 free.)*

FORD'S THEATER. John Wilkes Booth shot President Abraham Lincoln during a performance at the preserved **Ford Theater.** Every president since 1868 has taken his chances and seen a play at the theater at least once a year. Of course, they avoid the unlucky box and sit front row center. National Park Rangers describe the events with animated gusto during a 15min. talk. *(511 10th St. NW. Metro: Metro Center. ☎426-6924; www.nps.gov/foth. Open daily 9am-5pm. Free.)*

OLD POST OFFICE. A classical masterpiece, the **Old Post Office** building rebukes its contemporary neighbors with arched windows, conical turrets, and a clock tower—all sheathing a shopping mall. *(Pennsylvania Ave. and 12th St. NW. Metro: Federal Triangle. ☎289-4224; www.oldpostofficedc.com. Tower open mid-Apr. to mid-Sept. M-Sa 9am-7:45pm, Su 10am-5:45pm; low season M-F 9am-4:45pm, Sa-Su 10am-5:45pm. Shops open M-Sa 10am-7pm, Su noon-6pm. Free.)*

CAPITAL CHILDREN'S MUSEUM. This huge, interactive museum is the ultimate escape from glass-encased artifacts. Visitors can brew hot chocolate and roll tortillas in a two-story mock-up of life in Mexico, or help with scientific demonstrations in the chemist-staffed laboratory. *(800 3rd St. NE, between H and I St. NE. Metro: Union Station. ☎675-4120; www.ccm.org. Open Memorial Day-Labor Day daily 10am-5pm, Labor Day-Memorial Day Tu-Su 10am-5pm. $7, seniors $5, children under 2 free.)*

NATIONAL MUSEUM OF WOMEN IN THE ARTS. In a former Masonic Temple, the **National Museum of Women in the Arts** tours works by the likes of Mary Cassatt, Georgia O'Keeffe, and Frida Kahlo. This museum is the only one in the world dedicated solely to the celebration of achievements of women in the visual, performing, and literary arts from the 16th century to the present. *(1250 New York Ave. NW. Metro: Metro Center. ☎783-5000; www.nmwa.org. Open M-Sa 10am-5pm, Su noon-5pm. $5-8, 60+ and students $3-6, 18 and under free. 1st Su and W of each month free.)*

WHITE HOUSE & FOGGY BOTTOM

WHITE HOUSE. With its simple columns and expansive lawns, the **White House** seems a compromise between patrician lavishness and democratic simplicity. Thomas Jefferson proposed a design of the building, but his entry lost to that of amateur architect James Hoban. Today's Presidential staff works in the West Wing, while the First Lady's cohorts occupy the East Wing. Staff who cannot fit in the White House work in the nearby **Old Executive Office Building.** The President's official office is the **Oval Office,** site of many televised speeches. *(1600 Pennsylvania Ave. NW. ☎456-7041; www.whitehouse.gov. Currently no tours are available to the public.)*

LAFAYETTE PARK. Historic homes surround **Lafayette Park** north of the White House. These homes include the Smithsonian-owned **Renwick Gallery** craft museum, which has some remarkable 1980s sculptures. *(17th St. and Pennsylvania Ave. NW. Metro: Farragut North, Farragut West, or McPherson Sq. ☎357-2700; www.nmaa.si.edu. Open daily 10am-5:30pm. Free.)* Once housed in the Renwick's mansion, the **Corcoran Gallery** now boasts larger quarters and displays American artists. *(17th St. between E St. and New York Ave. NW. ☎639-1700; www.corcoran.org. Open M, W, F-Su 10am-5pm, Th 10am-9pm. Free tours M and W-F noon, Sa-Su 2:30pm. $5, seniors $3, students $1; families $8.)* Nearby, the **Octagon,** a curious building designed by Capitol architect William Thornton, is reputedly filled with ghosts. Tour guides explain its history. *(Open Tu-Su 10am-4pm. $5, seniors and students $3.)*

KENNEDY CENTER. Completed in the late 1960s, the **John F. Kennedy Center for the Performing Arts** is a living monument to the assassinated president. The $78 million edifice boasts four major stages, a film theater, sumptuous red carpets, mirrors, crystal chandeliers, and 3700 tons of marble. *(25th St. and New Hampshire Ave. NW. Metro: Foggy Bottom-GWU. ☎467-4600; www.kennedy-center.org. Open daily 10am-midnight. Free tours leave from the level A gift shop, M-F 10am-5pm, Sa-Su 10am-1pm; call ☎416-8340.)* Across the street is Tricky Dick Nixon's **Watergate Complex.**

GEORGETOWN

DUMBARTON OAKS ESTATE. The former home of John Calhoun, **Dumbarton Oaks Mansion,** nestled in beautiful gardens, holds an impressive collection of Byzantine and pre-Columbian art, and was the site of the 1944 Dumbarton Oaks Conference that helped write the United Nations charter. *(1703 32nd St. NW, between R and S St. ☎339-6401, tour info 339-6409; www.doaks.org. Mansion open Tu-Su 2-5pm. Suggested donation $1. Gardens open daily Apr.-Oct. 2-6pm; Nov.-Mar. 2-5pm. Suggested donation $5, seniors and children $3.)*

GEORGETOWN UNIVERSITY. Archbishop John Carroll oversaw construction in 1788, and **Georgetown University** opened the following year, becoming the nation's first Catholic institution for higher learning. Today, approximately 50% of Georgetown's 6000 undergraduates are Catholic, and a Jesuit brother resides in every dorm, although students of many creeds attend. *(37th and O St. Campus tours offered year-round, M-Sa mornings; call ☎687-3600 for more info or log onto www.georgetown.edu.)*

UPPER NORTHWEST

NATIONAL ZOO. Founded in 1889 and designed by Frederick Law Olmsted, designer of both New York City's Central Park (see p. 234) and Boston's "Emerald Necklace" parks (see p. 114), the **National Zoo** is one of D.C.'s least crowded sights. Tigers, elephants, and gorillas (oh my!) await. Watch out for an unwelcome exhibit: local foxes visiting the zoo for lunch. In 2003, foxes were responsible for a number of bird killings, including that of a bald eagle who succumbed on July 4 to wounds allegedly sustained from a *foxus arielus hungrius*. *(3001 Connecticut Ave. Metro: Woodley Park-Zoo. ☎673-4800; www.si.edu/natzoo. Open daily May 1-Sept. 15 6am-8pm; Sept. 16-Apr. 30 6am-6pm. Free.)*

WASHINGTON NATIONAL CATHEDRAL. This church, the sixth-largest in the world, was built from 1907 to 1909. Rev. Martin Luther King, Jr. preached his last Sunday sermon from the pulpit, which has more recently hosted the Dalai Lama. The elevator rises to the Pilgrim Observation Gallery, revealing D.C. from the highest vantage point in the city. *(Massachusetts and Wisconsin Ave. NW. Metro: Tenleytown, then take a 30-series bus toward Georgetown; or walk up Cathedral Ave. from Metro: Woodley*

Park-Zoo. ☎537-6200; www.cathedral.org/cathedral. Open mid-May to Labor Day M-F 10am-8pm, Sa 10am-4:30pm, Su 8am-7:30pm; Labor Day to mid-May M-Sa 10am-4:30pm, Su 8am-7:30pm. Su 11am service. Shops open daily 9:30am-5pm. Free.)

DUPONT CIRCLE

ART GALLERY DISTRICT. A triangle of creativity, the **Art Gallery District** contains over two dozen galleries displaying everything from contemporary photographs to tribal crafts. Together they hold a joint open house the first Friday of each month (6-8pm), complete with free wine at each venue. *(Bounded by Connecticut Ave., Florida Ave., and Q St. www.artgalleriesdc.com.)*

PHILLIPS COLLECTION. **Phillips Collection,** a well-endowed house of contemporary work, was the first museum of modern art in the US. Visitors gape at Renoir's masterpiece, *Luncheon of the Boating Party*, and works by Delacroix, Miró, and Turner. *(1600 21st St, at Q St. NW. ☎387-2151; www.phillipscollection.org. Open Tu-W and F-Sa 10am-5pm, Th 10am-8:30pm; summer also Su noon-5pm. Permanent collection $8, students and seniors $6, under 19 free. Audio tours free with admission.)*

EMBASSY ROW. The stretch of Massachusetts Ave. between Dupont Circle and Observatory Circle is also called **Embassy Row.** Before the 1930s, Washington socialites lived along the avenue in extravagant edifices; status-conscious diplomats later found the mansions perfect for their purposes. Flags line the entrance to the **Islamic Center,** a brilliant white building where stunning designs stretch to the tips of spired ceilings. *(2551 Massachusetts Ave. NW. ☎332-8343. No shorts allowed; women must cover their heads, arms, and legs. Open daily 10am-5pm; prayers 5 times daily.)*

MUSEUMS

The Smithsonian Museums on the Mall constitute the world's largest museum complex. The **Smithsonian Castle,** on the south side of the mall, has an introduction to and info on the Smithsonian buildings. (☎357-2700; www.si.edu. Metro: Smithsonian or Federal Triangle. All Smithsonian museums except National Gallery of Art open daily 10am-5:30pm, extended summer hours determined annually. Castle open daily 9am-5:30pm. Museums free. Recorded audio tours available at some museums—usually for less than $5. Wheelchair-accessible.)

National Air and Space Museum (☎357-2700; www.nasm.edu), on the south side of the Mall across from the National Gallery, is the world's most popular museum with 7.5 million visitors per year. Airplanes and space vehicles dangle from the ceilings; the Wright brothers' original biplane hangs in the entrance gallery. Walk through the Skylab space station, the Apollo XI command module, and a DC-7.

National Gallery of Art (☎737-4215; www.nga.gov), east of Natural History, is not technically a part of the Smithsonian, but a close cousin due to its location on the mall. The West Building, the gallery's original home, contains masterpieces by such famous folks as Fra Angelico, Leonardo da Vinci, El Greco, Raphael, Rembrandt, Vermeer, and Monet. The gallery's newer addition, the East Building, is devoted to 20th-century art, with everyone from Magritte and Matisse to Man Ray and Miró, just to mention the "M"s. Together, the 2 buildings and the neighboring sculpture garden make up North America's most popular art museum, with 6 million visitors annually. Open M-Sa 10am-5pm, Su 11am-6pm.

Hirshhorn Museum and Sculpture Garden (☎633-4674; http://hirshhorn.si.edu), on the south side of the mall west of Air and Space. This museum is home to modern, post-modern, and post-postmodern works. The 4-story, slide-carousel-shaped brown building has outraged traditionalists since 1966. Each floor consists of 2 concentric circles: an outer ring of rooms with paintings and an inner corridor of sculptures.

Freer Gallery of Art (☎357-4880; www.asia.si.edu.), just west of the Hirshhorn, displays American and Asian art. The static (as dictated by Charles L. Freer himself) American collection focuses on works by James McNeill Whistler. The rotating Asian collections include bronzes, manuscripts, and jade pieces.

National Museum of American History (☎357-2700; http://americanhistory.si.edu), on the north side of the Mall. The museum earned the entire institute the nickname "the nation's attic" because of the clutter of old goods—from fiber-optic cable to harmonicas—that reside here behind Plexiglas. When the Smithsonian inherits quirky artifacts of popular history, like Dorothy's slippers from *The Wizard of Oz,* they end up here. Hands-on exhibits are geared toward children.

National Museum of Natural History (☎357-2700; www.mnh.si.edu). The MNH contains 3 crowded floors of rocks, animals, gift shops, and displays selected from the museum's 124 million possessions. The Hope Diamond and the dinosaurs are major attractions.

National Museum of African Art and the **Arthur M. Sackler Gallery** (African Art: ☎357-4600 M-F, 357-2700 Sa-Su; www.nmafa.si.edu. Sackler: ☎633-4880; www.asia.si.edu). Built in 1987, these two hide their treasures underground, behind the castle and below the beautifully landscaped, 4-acre **Enid A. Haupt Garden.** The Museum of African Art displays artifacts from sub-Saharan Africa, such as masks, textiles, ceremonial figures, and musical instruments. The Sackler Gallery showcases an extensive collection of illuminated manuscripts, Chinese and Japanese painting, jade miniatures, and friezes from Egypt, Phoenicia, and Sumeria.

ENTERTAINMENT

MUSIC

The D.C. punk scene is, or at least was, one of the nation's finest, but performers of every stripe frequently call on the city. The bigger, more mainstream events take place at the sports arenas: **RFK Stadium** in the summer and the **MCI Center** year-round. Tickets for many shows are available from **Protix** (☎410-481-6500, 703-218-6500, or 800-955-5566). In its 73rd season, the **National Symphony Orchestra** continues to delight D.C., primarily in the Kennedy Center's Concert Hall. D.C. also has a diverse and thriving jazz and blues scene, with venues perfect for anyone's budget. The **Kennedy Center** (see p. 330) and the **Smithsonian Museums** (see p. 331) often sponsor free shows, especially in the summer.

THEATER & DANCE

Arena Stage, 6th St. and Maine Ave. SW, is often called the best regional theater company in America. (☎488-3300; www.arenastage.org. Metro: Waterfront. Box office open M-Sa 10am-8pm, Su noon-8pm. Tickets $35-58. Discounts for students, seniors, and the disabled. A limited number of half-price tickets usually available 1½hr. before start of show.) The **Kennedy Center,** at 25th St. and New Hampshire Ave., offers scores of ballet, opera, and dramatic productions, most of them expensive. (☎416-8000, for rush tickets info ☎467-4600; www.kennedy-center.org. Tickets $10-75.) The company at **Shakespeare Theatre** at the Lansburgh, 450 7th St. NW at Pennsylvania Ave., will put on *Henry IV* from February-May 2004 and Rostand's *Cyrano de Bergerac* from June-July 2004. (☎547-1122; www.shakespearetheatre.org. Metro: Archives-Navy Memorial. Tickets $15-66. Discounts for students and seniors. $10 standing-room tickets available 1hr. before sold-out performances.) In the **14th Street theater district,** tiny repertory companies explore and experiment with enjoyable results; check *CityPaper* for listings. **Woolly Mammoth,** 1401 Church St. NW (☎393-3939; www.woollymammoth.net), Metro: Dupont Circle; **Studio Theater,** 1333 P St. NW (☎332-3300; www.studiotheatre.org), at 14th St., Metro: Dupont Circle; and **The Source Theatre,** 1835 14th St. NW (☎462-1073; www.sourcetheatre.com), between S and T St., Metro: U St. Cardozo, are all fine theaters in the neighborhood near Dupont Circle. Tickets run $10-38.

SPORTS

The 20,000-seat **MCI Center,** 601 F St. NW, in Chinatown, is D.C.'s premier sports arena. (☎628-3200: Metro: Gallery Pl.-Chinatown.) The **Washington Wizards** constantly serve as the league's laughingstock for both their poor play and lame mascot. (☎661-5065; www.washingtonwizards.com. Tickets $10-100.) The WNBA's **Washington Mystics** have been a disappointment since the league's inception 6 years ago, but star forward Chamique Holdsclaw makes the games entertaining and exciting. (www.wnba.com/mystics. Tickets $8-50.) The **Washington Capitals** skate from October through April. (☎661-5065; www.washingtoncaps.com. Tickets $10-100.) Three-time Superbowl champions the **Washington Redskins** draw crowds to **Fed-Ex Stadium,** Raljon Dr., in Raljon, MD, from September through December. (☎301-276-6050; www.redskins.com. Tickets $40-100.)

NIGHTLIFE

BARS & CLUBS

Talk about leading a double life. D.C. denizens who crawl through red tape by day paint the town red by night. If you find yourself taking Jell-O body shots off a beautiful stranger at an all-you-can-drink-fest, just don't say we didn't warn you. If you ache for a pint of amber ale, swing by the Irish pub-laden **Capitol Hill.** If you like girls (or boys) who wear Abercrombie & Fitch, hit up **Georgetown,** where youthful prepsters go to get happy. **Dupont Circle** is home to glam gay and lesbian nightlife, while **Adams-Morgan** plays host to an international crowd. To party *with* rock stars, head to none other than **U District** for the best live rock 'n' roll in all of D.C.

DUPONT & U DISTRICT

Brickskeller, 1523 22nd St. NW (☎293-1885). With over 1100 different bottled brews to choose from, the Brickskeller boasts the largest selection in the world ($3.25-19). "Beer-tails," mixed drinks made with beer, cost $3.25-6.50. Monthly tastings Sept.-May. Pub menu. Be warned: you will get laughed at for ordering Miller Lite. Open M-Th 11:30am-2am, F 11:30am-3am, Sa 6pm-3am, Su 6pm-2am.

Cafe Saint-Ex, 1847 14th St. NW (☎265-7839), at T St. Rockers playing at the nearby clubs usually come by Cafe Saint-Ex for drinks or dinner. The vintage aviation-themed bar attracts a truly mixed crowd: punk rockers and lawyers alike. Upstairs bar and patio. Downstairs Gate 54 lounge. Beer $2-5, rail drinks $6. 21+ after 10:30pm. No cover. Open M-F 5pm-2am, Sa-Su 11am-2am.

Eighteenth Street Lounge, 1212 18th St. NW (☎466-3922). 8 years old and still the mod-est of the mod, this progenitor of the now-swelling D.C. lounge scene draws musical tourists from around the globe to hear its top-shelf DJs. Plush couches, high prices, and an outdoor patio bar. The main attraction here are the DJs, most of whom are signed to ESL's own independent record label. Dress to impress. Cover generally $10-20, but no cover Tu. Open Tu-Th 5:30pm-2am, F 5:30pm-3am, Sa 9:30pm-3am.

The Big Hunt, 1345 Connecticut Ave. NW (☎785-2333). Leopard-print couches adorn this jungle-themed 3 floor bar, where the casual khaki-and-flip-flops crowd hunts for potential mates. Notorious pickup joint for college kids and Hill workers pretending they're still in college. 24 brews on tap ($3.75-5). Solid pub fare. Pool table. Happy Hour M-F 4-7pm. Open M-Th 4pm-2am, F 4pm-3am, Sa 5pm-3am, Su 5pm-2am.

2:K:9, 2009 8th St. (☎667-7750), at Florida Ave. This post-industrial club rolls out reams of red carpet in its enormous dance and performance space. A sea of black pants and dark shirts floods the martini lounge, 45 ft. bar, and 2 mega dance floors, which usually feature hip-hop and house. Women 18+, men 21+. Cover $5-15. Open Th-Sa 5pm-2am.

ADAMS MORGAN

Madam's Organ, 2461 18th St. NW (☎667-5370), near Columbia Rd. A 3 floor bar with an intimate rooftop patio. Live band plays nightly on first floor Pool tables. 2-for-1 drinks during Happy Hour (M-F 5-8pm), and redheads always drink half-price Rolling Rocks. Drafts $3.75-5.75; mixed drinks $4.75-6.75. 21+. Cover Su-Th $2-4, F-Sa $5-7. Open Su-Th 5pm-2am, F-Sa 5pm-3am.

Millie & Al's, 2440 18th St. NW (☎387-8131). Jukebox bar draws an ultra-casual crowd into its booths with cheap pizza, fries, subs, and $1 jello-shooter specials. Nightly specials 4-7pm. DJs play rock and hip-hop F-Sa. $3 burgers; $2.50 fries. Draft beers $2-3.50; bottles $3-4.25. 21+. No cover. Open M-Th 5:30pm-2am, F-Sa 4pm-3am.

The Reef, 2446 18th St. NW (☎518-3800). The newest hot spot on 18th St. 3 levels of drinking for a casual 20s crowd: jungle-themed first floor, aquarium-esque 2nd fl. lounge, and a massive roof deck. Rail drinks $5, 14 rotating bottled beers $3-6 each. Happy Hour daily 4-7:30pm. 21+ after 9pm. No cover. Open M-Th 4pm-2am, F-Sa 4pm-3am, Su 11am-3pm (brunch) and 4pm-2am.

CAPITOL HILL

The Dubliner, 520 N. Capitol St. NW (☎737-3773). Metro: Union Station. A subdued crowd enjoys Guinness and the house brew, Auld Dubliner Amber Ale ($5 a pint). Live Irish music often includes familiar pop melodies injected with an Irish twist (M-Sa 9pm, Su 7:30pm). A large patio turns lounge-style for celebrators as the night ticks on. Open Su-Th 7am-2am, F-Sa 7:30am-3am.

Pour House/Politiki, 319 Pennsylvania Ave. SE (☎546-1001). Metro: Capitol South. 3 levels and 3 names, but young attractive interns everywhere. A dark wood paneled, subterranean bar goes Hawaiian with tiki-style drinks and food with bamboo. "Top of the Hill" martini bar open upstairs Tu-Sa. Nightly drink specials and a free buffet Su-Th 4pm-1:30am. Open M-F 4pm-1:30am, Sa-Su 10am-2:30am.

GAY NIGHTLIFE

The *Washington Blade* is the best source of gay news and club listings; published every Friday, it's available in virtually every storefront in Dupont Circle.

J.R.'s, 1519 17th St. NW (☎328-0090), at Church St. D.C.'s busiest gay bar for good reasons: beautiful bartenders, fun events, and great drink deals. Packed every night with hordes of "guppies" (gay urban professionals). Happy Hour (M-W 5-8pm) brings $3 mini-pitchers, $2 rail drinks and domestic beers, and $1 sodas; the famous Power Hour follows (8-9pm), during which everything is half-price. Open M-Th 11:30am-2am, F-Sa 11:30am-3am, Su noon-2am.

Cobalt, 1639 R St. NW (☎462-6569), at 17th St. No sign marks this gay hot spot; look for the blue light and bouncer. Shirtless bartenders serve drinks ($4.75-5.75) to a young, preppy crowd who come to this second floor club. Open Tu-Th 10pm-2am, F-Sa 10pm-3am, Su 8:30pm-2am. Downstairs, **30°** is a lounge offering a more relaxed atmosphere with half-price martinis during Happy Hour (M-F 5-8pm). 21+. Open Su-Th 5pm-2am, F-Sa 5pm-3am.

Apex, 1415 22nd St. NW (☎296-0505), near P St. Formerly known as Badlands, this 2-story dance complex draws a young crowd. DJs always play a mix of house, trance, and Top 40 music. Th college night, $5 cover (free with student ID), $3 rail drinks. F $8 cover, drag karaoke starts 11pm. Sa "Liquid Ladies" night, $7 cover, $3 Long Island iced teas. 18+. Open Th-Sa from 9pm onward.

DAYTRIPS FROM D.C.

ARLINGTON, VA

The silence of the 612-acre **Arlington National Cemetery** honors those who sacrificed their lives in war. The **Kennedy gravesites** hold the remains of President John F. Kennedy, his brother Robert F. Kennedy, and his wife Jacqueline Kennedy Onassis. The Eternal Flame flickers above JFK's simple memorial stone. The **Tomb of the Unknowns** honors unidentified servicemen who died fighting for the US and is guarded by soldiers from the Army's Third Infantry. (Changing of the guard Apr.-Sept. every 30min. 8am-6pm; Oct.-Mar. every hr. 8am-4pm.) **Pierre L'Enfant,** originally buried within the District, was reinterred at Arlington along with soldiers from the Revolutionary War and the War of 1812. His distinctive grave on the hillside in front of **Arlington House,** once owned by Robert E. Lee, overlooks the city he designed. Lee's home is now a museum of antebellum life and provides one of the best views of D.C. from across the Potomac (open daily 9:30am-4:30pm). Farther down the hill among the plain headstones lies General of the Armies **John J. Pershing,** commander of US forces during WWI, who asked to be buried among his men. Arlington also holds the bodies of Arctic explorers **Robert E. Peary** and **Richard Byrd** and legendary populist attorney and presidential candidate **William Jennings Bryan. Memorial Day** each year brings a small American flag to each of the cemetery's gravesites; the President lays a memorial wreath at the Tomb of the Unknowns and makes a speech commemorating the day. The newest addition to the cemetery is the impressive **Women in Military Service for America Memorial.** A memorial recognizing the **September 11th Attacks** is being planned, as is a memorial dedicated to the crew of the lost space shuttle **Columbia.** (☎703-697-2131. Metro: Arlington Cemetery. Open daily Apr.-Sept. 8am-7pm; Oct.-May 8am-5pm. Free.)

Exit the cemetery through Weitzel Gate, and walk for 20min. to get to the **Iwo Jima Memorial,** based on Joe Rosenthal's Pulitzer Prize-winning photo of Marines straining to raise the US flag on Mt. Suribachi. The statistics on **the Pentagon,** the world's largest office building, are mind-boggling: five concentric and 10 radial hallways totalling 17½ mi., 7754 windows, 131 stairways, and four postal codes of its own. The wall that took the impact of the hijacked airplane on September 11, 2001 has been completely restored.

ALEXANDRIA, VA

Alexandria didn't become a tourist attraction until the 1980s, when city residents backed away from proposed high-rises and decided to revitalize Old Town. Capitalizing on original 18th-century architecture and the legacy of historical all-stars like George Washington and Robert E. Lee, the town re-cobbled the streets, rebricked the sidewalks, installed gardens, restored over 1000 original facades, and invited tall ships and contemporary shops. As a result, today, **Old Town Alexandria** is packed with tourists. Sights cluster along Washington and King St. Looming over western Alexandria, the lofty **George Washington Masonic National Memorial,** 101 Callahan Dr., is an imposing testament to the strength of masonry and the legacy of Washington, who was the only mason to have been a masonic chartermaster and US president at the same time. (☎703-683-2007.) Thirty-seven different Lees inhabited the **Lee-Fendall House,** 614 Oronoco St. (☎703-549-1789). Formerly a hotbed of political, business, and social life, the restored **Gadsby's Tavern,** 134 N. Royal St. (☎703-838-4242), takes you back to ye good olde days of hospitality, when as many as four hotel guests slept in one bed. The **Ramsay House Visitors Center,** 221 King St., cordially offers free maps and literature. The house, a 1724 building shipped upriver from Dumfries, VA, was the home of Scottish merchant and Lord Mayor William Ramsay. (☎703-838-4200; www.funside.com. Open daily 9am-5pm.)

MT. VERNON

George Washington's fabulous estate **Mount Vernon** is easily accessible in Fairfax County, VA. Visitors can see Washington's bedroom and tomb and the estate's fields, where slaves once grew corn, wheat, and tobacco. During his days as president, Washington dedicated his leisure time to beautifying the mansion's interior and administering the corps of slaves that ran the farm. The estate maintains 30-40% of Washington's original furnishings, which are now on display. To get there, take the Fairfax Connector 101 bus from the Huntington Metro stop, or take the George Washington Pkwy. south, which becomes Washington St. in Alexandria, to the entrance. (☎703-780-2000. Open daily Apr.-Aug. 8am-5pm; Sept.-Oct. and Mar. 9am-5pm; Nov.-Feb. 9am-4pm. $11, seniors $10.50, ages 6-11 $5, under 6 free.)

VIRGINIA

If Virginia is obsessed with its past, it has good reason. Many of America's formative experiences—the English settlement of North America, the boom in the slave trade, the final establishment of American independence, and much of the Civil War—took place in Virginia. More recently, the state has begun to abandon its Old South lifestyle in search of a cosmopolitan image. The western portion of the state, with its towering forests and fascinating underground caverns, provides a welcome respite from nostalgia and relentless Southern heat.

PRACTICAL INFORMATION

Capital: Richmond.

Visitor Info: Virginia Division of Tourism (motto: "Virginia is for lovers"), 901 E. Byrd St., Richmond 23219 (☎800-847-4882; www.virginia.org). Open M-F 8am-5pm. **Department of Conservation and Recreation,** 203 Governor St., Ste. 213, Richmond 23219 (☎804-786-1712; www.dcr.state.va.us). Open daily 8am-5pm.

Postal Abbreviation: VA. **Sales Tax:** 4.5%.

RICHMOND ☎804

Once known as the "Cradle of the Confederacy," Richmond has a survivor's history of conflicts, disasters, and triumphs. William Mayo created the blueprint for what would become Richmond, officially charted in 1742. Fire struck in 1781, and Richmond burned to the ground as a result of a British attack led by Benedict Arnold, but managed to persevere, indeed, to prosper. By 1946, Richmond's economy and industrial strength outpaced every other city's growth in the nation.

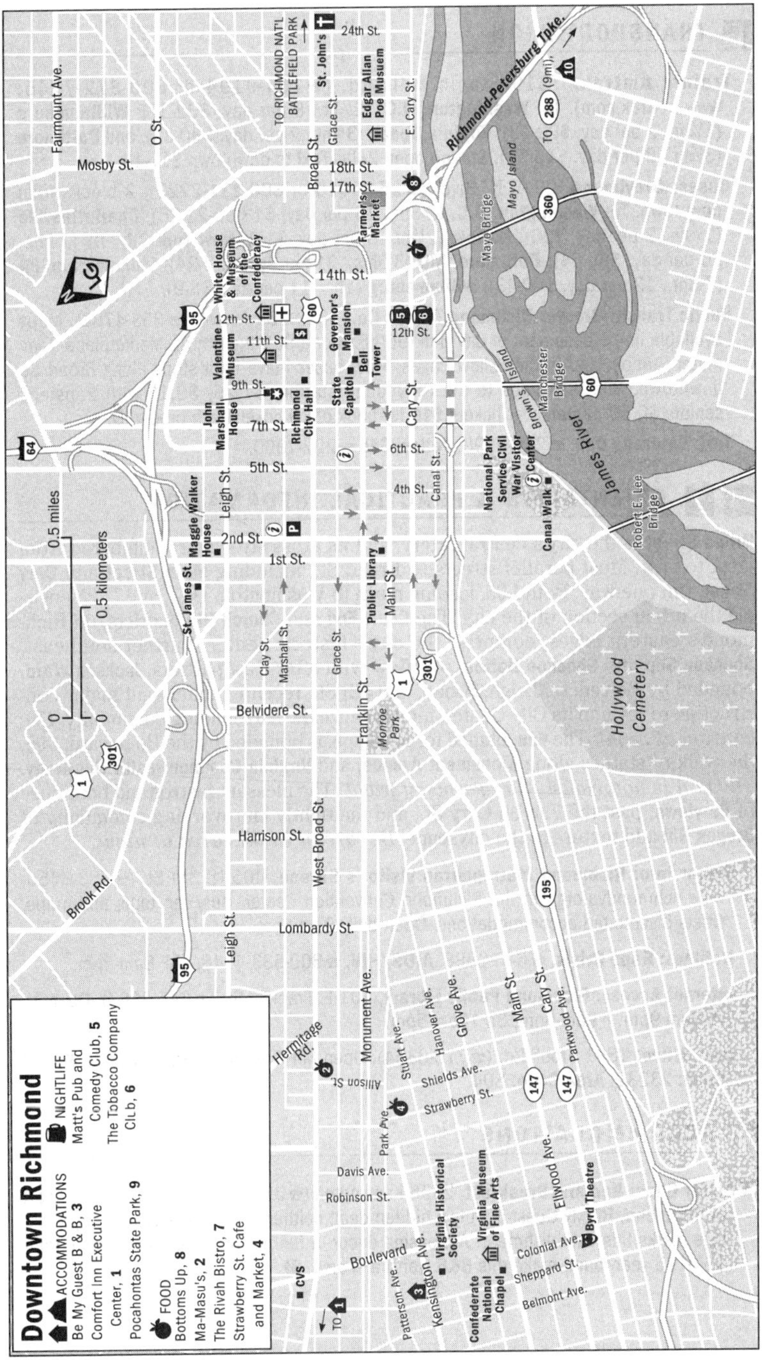

Downtown Richmond

ACCOMMODATIONS
Be My Guest B & B, **3**
Comfort Inn Executive Center, **1**
Pocahontas State Park, **9**

FOOD
Bottoms Up, **8**
Ma-Masu's, **2**
The Rivah Bistro, **7**
Strawberry St. Cafe and Market, **4**

NIGHTLIFE
Matt's Pub and Comedy Club, **5**
The Tobacco Company Club, **6**

0 — 0.5 miles
0 — 0.5 kilometers

Brook Rd.
Fairmount Ave.
Mosby St.
O St.
St. James St.
Maggie Walker House
John Marshall House
Valentine Museum
White House & Museum of the Confederacy
Leigh St.
Harrison St.
Belvidere St.
Lombardy St.
Clay St.
Marshall St.
1st St.
2nd St.
5th St.
7th St.
9th St.
11th St.
12th St.
14th St.
17th St.
18th St.
24th St.
TO RICHMOND NAT'L BATTLEFIELD PARK
Richmond City Hall
Broad St.
St. John's
West Broad St.
Grace St.
State Capitol
Governor's Mansion
Bell Tower
Farmer's Market
Edgar Allan Poe Musuem
CVS
TO 1
Hermitage Rd.
Allison St.
Robinson St.
Davis Ave.
Boulevard
Monument Ave.
Franklin St.
Monroe Park
Public Library
Main St.
Cary St.
4th St.
6th St.
Canal St.
E. Cary St.
Park Ave.
Patterson Ave.
Kensington Ave.
Stuart Ave.
Hanover Ave.
Grove Ave.
Strawberry St.
Shields Ave.
Virginia Historical Society
Confederate National Chapel
Virginia Museum of Fine Arts
Main St.
Cary St.
Ellwood Ave.
Parkwood Ave.
Colonial Ave.
Sheppard St.
Belmont Ave.
Byrd Theatre
National Park Service Civil War Visitor Center
Canal Walk
Brown's Island
Manchester Bridge
Mayo Bridge
Mayo Island
James River
Robert E. Lee Bridge
Hollywood Cemetery
Richmond-Petersburg Tpke.
TO 288 (9mi), 10

MID-ATLANTIC

TRANSPORTATION

Trains: Amtrak, 7519 Staple Mills Rd. (☎264-9194 or 800-872-7245; www.amtrak.com). To: **Washington, D.C.** (2¼hr., 8 per day, $32-37); **Williamsburg** (1¼hr., 2 per day, $22-23); **Virginia Beach** (3¼hr., 2 per day, $30-33); and **Baltimore** (3½hr., 8 per day, $43-51). Station open 24hr. **Taxi** to downtown $17-18.

Buses: Greyhound, 2910 N. Blvd. (☎254-5910 or 800-231-2222), 2 blocks from downtown. To: **Washington, D.C.** (2-3hr., 14 per day, $18.50-21.25); **Charlottesville** (1½hr., 2 per day, $20); **Norfolk** (2½hr., 8 per day, $17); **New York City, NY** (7-8hr., 20 per day, $60-64); **Baltimore, MD** (3-5hrs., 21 per day, $22-24); **Philadelphia, PA** (7-8hr., 12 per day, $40-43); **Williamsburg** (1hr., 11 per day, $8-9).

Public Transit: Greater Richmond Transit Co., 101 S. Davis Ave. (☎358-4782). Maps available in the basement of City Hall (900 E. Broad St.), the 6th St. Marketplace Commuter Station, and in the Yellow Pages. Most buses leave from stops along Broad St. downtown. Bus #24 goes to the Greyhound station. $1.25, $0.15 with transfers; seniors $0.50. Supersaver tickets $10 for book of 10 tickets with proper ID.

Taxi: Veterans Cab, ☎276-8990. **Yellow Cab** ☎222-7300.

ORIENTATION & PRACTICAL INFORMATION

Broad Street is the city's central artery, and its cross streets are numbered from west to east. Most parallel streets to Broad St., including **Main Street** and **Cary Street,** run one-way. Both I-95, leading north to Washington, D.C., and I-295 encircle the urban section of the city. The **Court End** and **Church Hill** districts, on Richmond's eastern edges, comprise the city's historic center. Further southeast, **Shockoe Slip** and **Shockoe Bottom** overflow with after-dark partiers. **Jackson Ward,** bounded by Belvedere, Leigh, Broad, and 5th St., recently underwent major construction to revamp its City Center and revitalize the surrounding community. *Use caution at night.* The **Fan,** named for its shape, is bounded by the Boulevard, I-95, the walk of statues along **Monument Avenue,** and **Virginia Commonwealth University.** *The Fan is notoriously dangerous at night.* The pleasant bistros and boutiques of **Carytown,** past the Fan on Cary St., and the tightly knit working community of **Oregon Hill** add texture to the cityscape. *Be careful in this area at night.*

Visitor Info: Richmond Metropolitan Visitor's Bureau, 405 N. 3rd St. (☎783-7450; www.richmondva.org), in the Richmond Convention Center. Bus/van tours and maps. Offers discounted accommodations. Open daily 9am-6pm.

Hotlines: Rape Crisis, ☎643-0888. **AIDS/HIV,** ☎800-533-4148. M-F 8am-5pm.

Internet Access: Richmond Public Library, 101 E. Franklin St. (☎646-4867). Open M-Th 9am-9pm, F 9am-6pm, Sa 10am-5pm.

Post Office: 1801 Brook Rd. (☎775-6304). Open M-F 7am-6pm, Sa 9am-2pm. **Postal Code:** 23232. **Area Code:** 804.

ACCOMMODATIONS

Be My Guest Bed and Breakfast, 2926 Kensington (☎358-9901). Located in the heart of Richmond, Be My Guest is truly a hidden deal: neither a sign nor a Yellow Pages listings marks this establishment. A pleasing decor, a full hot breakfast, and rooms from $60-125 year-round make this B&B worth a search. ❸

Comfort Inn Executive Center, 7201 W. Broad St. (☎800-221-2222 or 672-1108; www.choicehotels.com/hotel/va419). Take 64W to 95N, Exit 78, merge left, turn right on Robinhood Rd., then left on North Blvd. and right on Broad—it's on the left side of the road 6 mi. from downtown. Recently renovated, this hotel strikes the city's best balance between desirable accommodation and affordable prices. Singles $69 ($49 with Visitors Center discount); 2-room suites $139. ❸

Pocahontas State Park, 10301 State Park Rd. (☎796-4255, 800-933-7275 or 255-3867 for reservations; www.dcr.state.va.us/parks/pocahontas). Take I-95 south to Rte. 288; after 5 mi., connect to Rte. 10, exit on Ironbridge Rd. east, turn right on Beach Rd.; the Park is 4 mi. down on the right. Showers, biking, boating, picnic areas, and the second largest pool in Virginia. Rent a canoe, rowboat, kayak, or paddleboat ($6 per hr. or $22 per day). $20; all sites include water and electricity. ❶

FOOD

The Rivah Bistro, 1417 E. Cary St. (☎344-8222; www.rivahbistro.com), is where the stars dine when they come to town. Serving some of the best bistro food in the city, this classy establishment has a cosmopolitan flair thanks to its French-Moroccan chef. Delicacies include lobster ravioli ($20). Su brunch 10:30am-3pm. Open for lunch M-Sa 10:30am-4pm, dinner M-Th 4-10pm, F-Sa 4-11pm, Su 3-9pm. ❺

Strawberry Street Cafe and Market, 421 and 415 N. Strawberry St. (cafe ☎353-6860, market 353-4100; www.strawberrystreetcafe.com), offers an unlimited salad bar ($8), a brunch bar ($10; available Sa-Su until 3pm), and an array of Americana classics ($6-11). Lunch M-F from 11:30am, dinner daily from 5pm, brunch Sa-Su until 3pm. ❸

Ma-Masu's, 2043 W. Broad St. (☎355-8063; www.menus.com/mamusus). Ma-Masu, "Spiritual Mother" extraordinaire, introduces her guests to Liberian culture with a mural that reads, "It's okay to lick your fingers here." *Keli-willy* (fried plantains with spices and onions) and *toywah beans* $6, collard greens $2.50, coconut juice $2. Delivery available. Open Tu-Th noon-9pm, F noon-10pm, Sa 2-10pm. ❶

Bottoms Up, 1700 Dock St. (☎644-4400; www.bottomsuppizza.com), at 17th and Cary St. Named "Richmond's Best Pizza" 5 years in a row. Take a choose-your-own-pizza adventure, or go with the Chesapeake (spicy crab meat). Pizza $4-6.30 per slice. Open M-Tu 11am-10pm, Th 11am-midnight, F-Sa 11am-2am, Su 11am-11pm. ❶

SIGHTS

AROUND ST. JOHN'S CHURCH. St. John's Church is the site of Patrick Henry's famed 1775 "Give me liberty or give me death" speech. The church still serves as an active house of worship. *(2401 E. Broad St. ☎648-5015. 25min. tours M-Sa 10am-3:30pm, Su 1-3:30pm. Services Su 8:30 and 11am. Speech recreation summer Su 2pm, organ recital 1:30pm. Admission $5, seniors 62+ $4, ages 7-18 $3.)* Nearby is the **Edgar Allan Poe Museum,** in Richmond's oldest standing house (circa 1737), where visitors try to unravel the mysterious death of the morbid author. *(1914 E. Main St. ☎888-648-5523; www.poemuseum.org. Open Tu-Sa 10am-5pm, Su 11am-5pm. Tours on the hr., last tour 4pm. $6; students, seniors, and AAA $5; under 9 free.)*

CONFEDERATE SOUTH. The Civil War South is celebrated—yes, celebrated—at the **Museum of the Confederacy.** The poignant painting "Last Meeting of Lee and Jackson" and the collection of artifacts and documents detailing gruesome Confederate medical treatments are intriguing. Next door, the museum runs tours through the White House of the Confederacy, where a South-shall-rise-again attitude permeates the air. (*1201 E. Clay St.* ☎ *649-1861; www.moc.org. Open M-Sa 10am-5pm, Su noon-5pm. 45min. tours every ½hr. M, W, F-Sa 10:30am-4:30pm, Tu and Th 11:30am-4:30pm. Tours every 30min. M, W, F-Sa 10:30am-4:30pm, Tu, Th 11:30am-4:30pm. $9.50, seniors 62+ $9, ages 7-18 $5, under 7 free.)*

FAN DISTRICT. This old-world section of Richmond is home to the country's largest and best-preserved Victorian neighborhood. Stroll down **Monument Avenue,** a boulevard lined with gracious old houses and towering statues of Virginia heroes—a true Richmond memory lane. The statue of **Robert E. Lee** faces south toward his beloved Dixie; **Stonewall Jackson** faces north so that the general can perpetually scowl at the Yankees. The statue of African-American tennis hero **Arthur Ashe,** created a storm of controversy when built at the end of the avenue.

CARYTOWN. Located near the VCU campus, this nine-block stretch of **Cary Street** is full of little boutiques, charming restaurants, and culture. At dinnertime, Carytown welcomes an colorful mix of restaurant-goers.

VIRGINIA MUSEUM OF FINE ARTS. The **Virginia Museum of Fine Arts**—the South's largest art museum—features a collection by some of the world's most renowned painters: Monet, Renoir, Picasso, and Warhol, as well as treasures from ancient Rome, Egypt, and Asia. *(2800 Grove Ave.* ☎ *340-1400; www.vmfa.state.va.us. Open W-F, Sa-Su 11am-5pm. Free highlight tour 2:30, 6, 7pm. Suggested donation $5.)*

ENTERTAINMENT & NIGHTLIFE

One of Richmond's most entertaining diversions is the marvelous old **Byrd Theatre,** 2908 W. Cary St. Movie buffs buy tickets from a tuxedoed agent and on weekends are treated to a pre-movie Wurlitzer organ concert. (☎353-9911; www.byrdtheatre.com. All shows $2; Sa balcony open for $1 extra.) Free concerts abound downtown and at the **Nina Abody Festival Park.** *Style Weekly*, a free magazine available at the Visitors Center, and its younger counterpart, *Punchline*, found in most hangouts, both list concert lineups. Cheer on the **Richmond Braves,** Richmond's AAA minor-league baseball team, for a fraction of major-league prices. (☎359-4444; www.rbraves.com. Boxes $9, general $6, youth and seniors $3.)

Student-driven nightlife enlivens **Shockoe Slip** and sprinkles itself throughout the **Fan.** After dark, **Shockoe Bottom** turns into college-party central, with transient bars pumping bass-heavy music early into the morning. Aspiring socialites should head over to **The Tobacco Company Club,** 1201 E. Cary St., at the corner of 12th S., where an older crowd—and some young'uns trying to act older—drinks martinis, smokes cigars, and discusses the joys of oppressing the underclass. (☎782-9555; www.thetobaccocompany.com. Drink specials 8-9pm. Ladies Night Th. No bikini contests here (or tennis shoes, jeans, or boots). Cover $3 (dinner guests free). 21+. Open Th-Sa 8pm-2am.) **Matt's Pub and Comedy Club,** 109 S. 12th St., pours out a bit of Brit wit within dark wooden walls. (☎643-5653. Tex-Mex and pub cuisine $3-7. Microbrews and drafts $2.75-$3.60; cocktails $3.25. Stand-up comedy F 8, 10:30pm in winter and 9pm only in summer, Sa 8 and 11pm; reservations recommended. Cover $9.75 if charged. Open F-Sa 11:30am-2am.)

WILLIAMSBURG ☎757

Colonial Williamsburg is a blast from the past—a fife-and-drum corps marches down the streets, and costumed wheelwrights, bookbinders, and blacksmiths go about their tasks using 200-year-old methods. Travelers who visit in late fall or early spring will avoid the crowds, but also miss the special summer programs.

TRANSPORTATION

Airport: Newport News and Williamsburg International Airport, 20min. away in Newport News. Take state road 199 W to I-64 S. **Williamsburg Limousine Service** (☎877-0279). Shuttle service to airports only. $22.50 to Newport News; $65 to Norfolk. Cash only.

Trains: Amtrak (☎800-872-7245 or 229-8750; www.amtrak.com). From: **Baltimore** (5hr., 1 per day, $48-57); **Philadelphia** (6hr., 1 per day, $64); **New York** (7½-8hr., 1 per day, $81); **Richmond** (1hr., 1 per day, $22-23);

Buses: Greyhound (☎800-231-2222 or 229-1460; www.greyhound.com). From: **Baltimore** (via D.C.; 6-7hr., 3 per day, $52); **Norfolk** (1-2hr., 8 per day, $14.75); **Richmond** (1hr., 8 per day, $9.50); **Virginia Beach** (2½hr., 7 per day, $18.75); **Washington, D.C.** (3-4hr., 8 per day, $45.50). Ticket office open M-F 8am-noon and 1-5pm, Sa 8am-noon and 1-2pm.

Transportation Center, 408 N. Boundary St., behind the fire station, houses offices for Amtrak, Greyhound, and taxi service.

Public Transportation: James City County Transit (JCCT; ☎259-4093; www.williamsburgtransport.com). Bus service along Rte. 60, from Merchants Sq. west to Williamsburg Pottery or east past Busch Gardens. Operates M-Sa 6:30am-6:20pm. $1 plus $0.25 per zone change. **Williamsburg Shuttle** (R&R) provides service between **Colonial Williamsburg, Water Country USA,** and **Busch Gardens** every 30min. May 25-Sept. 3 daily 9am-10pm. All-day pass $2.

Taxi: Yellow Cab, ☎245-7777.

ORIENTATION & PRACTICAL INFORMATION

Williamsburg lies some 50 mi. southeast of Richmond. The **Colonial Parkway,** which connects the three towns, has no commercial buildings and is a beautiful route between historic destinations. Take I-64 and the Colonial Parkway exit to reach Colonial Williamsburg.

Visitor Info: Williamsburg Area Convention And Visitors Bureau, 201 Penniman Rd. (☎253-0192; www.visitwilliamsburg.com), ½ mi. northwest of the Transportation Center. Open M-F 8:30am-5pm. **Colonial Williamsburg Visitors Center,** 100 Visitors Center Dr. (☎800-447-8679 or 229-1000; www.colonialwilliamsburg.com), 1 mi. northeast of the Transport Center. Open daily 8:30am-7pm; winter hours vary.

Post Office: 425 N. Boundary St. (☎229-0838). Open M-F 8am-5pm, Sa 9am-2pm. **Postal Code:** 23185. **Area Code:** 757.

ACCOMMODATIONS

Bryant Guest House, 702 College Terr. (☎229-3320). From Scotland Rd., turn right onto Richmond Rd., then left onto Dillard St. 4 rooms with private baths, TV, and limited kitchen facilities in a stately, exquisitely landscaped brick home. Singles $35; doubles $45; 5-person suite $75. ❷

Liberty Rose, 1022 Jamestown Rd. (☎253-1260). For those who can afford it, this Victorian B&B will invite your romantic side to indulge. Check-in 3pm. Check-out 11am. Rates start at $185 per night. ❺

Lewis Guest House, 809 Lafayette St. (☎229-6116), a 10min. walk from the historic district, rents 2 comfortable rooms, including an upstairs unit with private entrance, kitchen, partial A/C, and shared bath. Rooms $25-35. Cash only. ❶

FOOD

The Old Chickahominy House, 1211 Jamestown Rd. (☎229-4689), 1½ mi. from the historic district on the Williamsburg-Jamestown border. For breakfast, enjoy a plate of Miss Melinda's pancakes with a side of smoked bacon ($8). Later on in the day, Becky's "complete luncheon" includes Virginia ham, hot biscuits, fruit salad, a slice of homemade pie, and iced tea or coffee ($7). Open M-F 8:30-10:30am and 11:30am-2:30pm, Sa-Su 8:30-10am and 11:45am-2pm. ❷

Chowning's Tavern, Duke of Gloucester St. (☎220-7012; http://intranetcwf.org). Quasi-historical dishes like "Ploughman's Pastie" (roasted turkey and melted cheddar cheese in a flaky pastry; $7.25) will have you chowing down George Washington-style. After 9pm, peanuts are at stake as patrons roll the dice against their servers. The merriment continues as costumed waiters sing 18th-century ballads and challenge guests to card games over light meals ($3.50-5.50). Cover $3. Open daily 11am-10pm. ❷

Berret's, 199 S. Boundary St. (☎253-1847), located at Merchant's Square (Colonial Williamsburg's shopping district). This popular establishment combines 2 restaurants in 1: the less expensive and more casual **Tap House Grill,** and the pricey and more formal **Berret's Restaurant and Bar.** Start off a spending binge at the Restaurant with baked escargot ($8), then try the Virginia ham and crabmeat combination ($24). Live music on terrace Su 6-9pm in summer. Tap House open daily from 4pm. Restaurant and bar open daily 11:30am-3pm and 5:30-10pm. ❺

SIGHTS

COLONIAL WILLIAMSBURG. Every day is a historical reenactment at Colonial Williamsburg. Though the site prides itself on its authenticity, the pristine paint on the houses and spotless garb on the "natives" gives the place more of an amusement park feel. Immersing yourself in the colonists' world doesn't require a ticket—visitors can enjoy the gorgeous gardens, march behind the fife-and-drum corps, lock themselves in the stocks, interact with the locals, and use the restrooms without ever doling out a dollar—the pay area is only a small part of the overall attraction. Two of the historic buildings—the **Wren Building** and the **Bruton Parish Church**—are free. The *Visitor's Companion* newsletter, printed on Mondays, lists free events, evening programs, and complete hours. *(☎800-447-8679; www.colonialwilliamsburg.org. Visitors Center open daily 8:30am-9pm. Most sights open 9:30am-5pm. Day pass $33, ages 6-12 $16.50; 2 consecutive days $39/19.50; under 6 free.)*

COLLEGE OF WILLIAM AND MARY. Spreading west from the corner of Richmond and Jamestown Rd., the College of William and Mary, founded in 1693, is the second-oldest college in the US (after Harvard, see p. 130) and has educated luminaries such as presidents Jefferson, Monroe, and Tyler. The Office of Admissions, in Blow Hall, offers free tours throughout the year. *(☎221-4223; www.wm.edu. Tours M-F 10am, 2:30pm, most Sa 10am.)*

DAYTRIPS FROM WILLIAMSBURG

JAMESTOWN & YORKTOWN

The "Historic Triangle" brims with US history. More authentic and less crowded than the Colonial Williamsburg empire, Jamestown and Yorktown show visitors where it all really began. At the Colonial National Park, southwest of Williamsburg on Rte. 31, you'll see the remains of the first permanent English settlement in America (1607), as well as exhibits on colonial life. The Visitors Center offers a hokey film, a 35min. "living history" walking tour (10:15am, 2:45pm; free with admission), and a 45min. audio tape tour ($2) for the Island Loop Route. (☎229-1733. Open daily 9am-5pm. Visitors Center closes 30min. before park. $5 for Yorktown segment, $6 for Jamestown segment, under 17 free; $9 joint pass.)

Nearby, the **Jamestown Settlement** contains a commemorative museum with changing exhibits, a reconstruction of James Fort, a Native American village, and full-scale replicas of the ships that brought the original settlers to Jamestown in 1607. (☎229-1607. Open daily June 15-Aug. 15 9am-6pm, rest of the year 9am-5pm. $10.75, ages 6-12 $5.25. Combination ticket including Yorktown Victory Center $16, ages 6-12 $7.75, under 6 free.)

The British defeat at **Yorktown** in 1781 signaled the end of the Revolutionary War. The Yorktown branch of **Colonial National Park** vividly recreates the significant last battle with an engaging film and an electric map. The **Visitors Center** rents cassettes and players ($2) for driving the battlefield's 3- or 5-mi. car route. (☎898-2410. Visitors Center open daily 9am-4:30pm. $5, under 17 free.) Brush up on your high school history as you listen to the rallying cries of revolutionary figures foretelling the independence won at Yorktown.

VIRGINIA BEACH ☎757

Virginia's largest city, once the capital of the cruising collegiate crowd, is now gradually shedding its playground image and maturing into a family-oriented vacation spot. Fast-food joints, motels, and cheap discount stores (hallmarks of every beach town) still abound, but culture now penetrates this plastic veneer.

TRANSPORTATION

Trains: Amtrak (☎800-872-7245 or 245-3589; www.amtrak.com). The nearest train station, in Newport News, runs 45min. bus service to and from the corner of 19th and Pacific St. Call ahead to reserve your train ticket. To Newport News from: **Baltimore,** (7hr., $58); **New York City,** (9hr., $83-115); **Philadelphia,** (8hr., $68-90); **Richmond,** (2hr., $30-33); **Washington, D.C.,** (6hr., $53-62); **Williamsburg** (2hr., $26-28).

Buses: Greyhound, 1017 Laskin Rd. (☎800-231-2222 or 422-2998; www.greyhound.com), station open M-Sa 7am-11am and 12:30-7pm. Connects with Maryland via the Bridge-Tunnel. ½mi. from the oceanfront area. From: **Richmond** (3¼hr., $18); **Washington, D.C.** (5½hr., $31.50); **Williamsburg** (2¼hr., $17.50).

Public Transportation: Virginia Beach Transit/Trolley Information Center (☎437-4768; www.vbwave.com), Atlantic Ave. and 24th St. Info on area transportation and tours, including trolleys, buses, and ferries. Trolleys transport riders to most major points in Virginia Beach. The Atlantic Avenue Trolley runs from Rudee Inlet to 42nd St. Open May-Sept. daily 8am-2am. Fare $1, seniors and disabled $0.25, kids under 38 in. free; 3-day passes $5, 5-day $8. Other trolleys run along the boardwalk, the North Seashore, and to Lynnhaven Mall.

Taxi: Yellow Cab, ☎460-0605. **Beach Taxi,** ☎486-4304.

Bike Rental: RK's Surf Shop, 305 16th St. (☎428-7363), in addition to aquatic equipment, rents bikes for $4 per hr. or $16 per day. Open daily June-Sept. 9am-10pm, Oct.-May 11am-6pm; bikes must be returned 2hr. before closing.

ORIENTATION & PRACTICAL INFORMATION

In Virginia Beach, east-west streets are numbered and the north-south avenues, running parallel to the beach, have ocean names. Prepare to feel like a thimble on a Monopoly board: **Atlantic** and **Pacific Avenue** comprise the main drag. **Arctic, Baltic,** and **Mediterranean Avenue** are farther inland. Virginia Beach uses a 10-digit phone number, so be sure to dial 757 before every local number.

Visitor Info: Virginia Beach Visitors Center, 2100 Parks Ave. (☎800-822-3224 or 491-7866; www.vbfunc.om), at 22nd St. Info on budget accommodations and area sights. Helpful, knowledgeable staff. Open daily June-Aug. 9am-8pm; Sept.-May 9am-5pm.

Internet Access: Virginia Beach Public Library, 4100 Virginia Beach Blvd. (☎431-3000). Open M-Th 10am-9pm, F-Sa 10am-5pm; Oct.-May also Su 1-5pm. Free.

Post Office: 501 Viking Dr. (☎340-0981). Open M-F 7:30am-6pm, Sa 10am-2pm. **Postal Code:** 23452. **Area Code:** 757.

ACCOMMODATIONS

Angie's Guest Cottage, Bed and Breakfast, and HI-AYH Hostel, 302 24th St. (☎428-4690; www.angiescottage.com). Barbara "Angie" Yates and her personable staff welcome predominantly young international and American guests with warmth, discounted trolley tokens, and great advice about the beach scene. Kitchen, lockers available. Linen $2. No A/C. Open Apr. 1-Sept. 30. Reservations recommended. Check-in 9am-9pm. Check-out 9:30-10am. 4-9 person dorms $19.80, HI-AYH members $16.45; low-season $15/12. Private rooms $36, 2 people $24 per person; less in low-season. ❶

First Landings, 2500 Shore Dr. (☎800-933-7275 or 412-2300 for reservations; www.dcr.state.va.us), about 8 mi. north of town on Rte. 60. In the State Park bearing the same name, beachfront sites thrive on the natural beauty of Virginia's shore. The park is extremely popular; call at least 11 months ahead for reservations. Picnic areas, a private swimming area on a sprawling beach, a bathhouse, and boat launching areas. Cabin rates Apr.-May and Sept.-Nov. $65-75; June-Aug. $85-95. ❸

The Castle Motel, 2700 Pacific Ave. (☎425-9330), is quite possibly the best bang for your buck as far as motels go. Spacious, clean rooms come with cable TV, refrigerator, shower and bath, desk, and two full beds. The beach is just 2 blocks away. Check-out 11am. 21+. Open May-Oct. Rates start at $69 on weekdays, $99 weekends. ❸

FOOD

Tropical Smoothie Cafe, 211 25th St. (☎422-3970; www.tropicalsmoothie.com). This new location is part of the burgeoning chain's recent growth. Smooth and silky smoothies ($3-5), medium-sized, healthy wraps ($5), and fresh salads ($4-5) served in a nondescript setting one block from the oceanfront. Open daily 9am-11pm. ❶

Cuisine and Co., 3004 Pacific Ave. (☎428-6700; www.cuisineandcompany.com). This sophisticated escape serves gourmet lunches and rich desserts. Treats include creamy tuna melts ($5), a chunky chicken salad ($5.50), and decadent cookies ($8 per lb.). Open between Labor Day-Memorial Day M-Sa 9am-7pm, Su 9am-6pm. ❶

The Happy Crab, 550 Laskin Rd. (☎437-9200). Dine on the screened porch overlooking a small harbor. Early-bird specials (daily 5-6:30pm) offer unbeatable seafood platters ($25) or huge 1-person servings big enough to split. Open Mar.-Sept. M-Th 11am-10pm, F-Su 11am-11pm; winter hours vary. ❹

SIGHTS

BACK BAY NATIONAL WILDLIFE REFUGE. Composed of islands, dunes, forests, marsh, ponds, and beaches, this remote but pristine national refuge is a sanctuary for an array of endangered species and other wildlife. With nesting bald eagles and peregrine falcons, the natural wonderland is open to the public for camping, hiking, fishing, and photography, and features a tram tour departing daily at 9am from Little Island City Park up the road. *(Take General Booth Blvd. to Princess Anne Dr.; turn left, then turn left onto Sandbridge Rd. and continue approximately 6 mi. Turn right onto Sandpiper Rd., which leads directly to the Visitors Center. ☎721-2412; www.backbay.fws.gov. Visitors Center open M-F 8am-4pm, Sa-Su 9am-4pm. Closed Dec.-Mar. Sa $5 per car, $2 per family on foot or bike. Tram daily 9am, return 12:45pm; trams run by volunteers; ☎721-7666 or 498-2473, www.bbrf.org. $6, seniors and under 12 $4.)*

FALSE CAPE STATE PARK. False Cape State Park got its name because back in the day (around the 17th century), ships used to touch shore there, mistakenly thinking that they had landed at the nearby Cape Henry (where America's first English settlers landed in 1607). The Back Bay tram stops at False Cape State Park, where walkers trek one mile to the beach. If you miss the 9am daily tram, prepare for an adventurous four-mile hike or canoe ride, as foot and water are the only ways to get where you want to go. **Kayak Eco Tours** offers kayak excursions to these areas. *(4001 Sandpiper Rd. ☎426-7128 or 800-933-7275, 888-669-8368 or 480-1999 for tours; www.dcr.state.va.us/parks. Campsites $9; reservations necessary.)*

VIRGINIA MARINE SCIENCE MUSEUM. Located a one-mile drive or 30min. walk south down Pacific Ave. (which becomes General Booth Blvd.), the Virginia Marine Science Museum houses Virginia's largest aquarium and is home to hundreds of species of fish, including crowd-pleasing sharks and stingrays. The museum also houses a six-story IMAX theater and offers excursion trips for dolphin observation in summer and whale watching in winter. *(717 General Booth Blvd. ☎425-6010, excursions 437-2628; www.vmsm.com. Open daily 9am-7pm; low-season 9am-5pm. $11, seniors $10, ages 4-11 $7. IMAX tickets $7.25/6.75/6.25. Combined museum and IMAX admission $16/13/10. Excursions $12, ages 4-11 $10.)*

NIGHTLIFE

Mahi Mah's, 615 Atlantic Ave. (☎437-8030; www.mahimahs.com), at 7th St. inside the Ramada Hotel. Sushi, wine tastings, live music, tiki parties, and oceanfront views. Well-dressed crowd. Outdoor band nightly. Open daily 7am-1am.

Chicho's, 2112 Atlantic Ave. (☎422-6011; www.chichos.com), on "The Block" of closet-sized college bars clustered between 21st and 22nd St. One of the hottest spots on the hot spot strip features gooey pizza ($2.25-3.25), tropical mixed drinks ($5-7), and live rock 'n' roll music M. Open May-Sept. W-Su noon-2am, M-Tu 6pm-2am; Oct.-Apr. M-F 6pm-2am, Sa-Su noon-2am.

Harpoon Larry's, 216 24th St. (☎422-6000; www.harpoonlarrys.com), at Pacific Ave., serves tasty fish in an everyone-knows-your-name atmosphere. The amicable bartender and manager welcome 20- and 30-somethings to escape the sweat and raging hormones of "The Block." Specials include crab cakes ($7) and rum runners (Tu $2). W $1.50 Coronas with $0.25 jalapeño poppers. Happy Hour (M-F 7-9pm) offers $1 domestic drafts and $2 rail drinks. Open May-Sept. daily noon-2am; low-season hours vary.

CHARLOTTESVILLE ☎434

Thomas Jefferson, composer of the Declaration of Independence and colonial Renaissance man, built his dream house, Monticello, high atop his "little mountain" just southeast of Charlottesville. Around his personal paradise, Jefferson endeavored to create the ideal community. In an effort to breed intellect and keep him busy in his old age, Jefferson humbly created the University of Virginia (UVA), now the core of a vibrant college town that still pays homage to its founder.

TRANSPORTATION

Airport: Charlottesville-Albemarle Airport (☎973-8342; www.gocho.com), 8 mi. north of Charlottesville, 1 mi. west of Rte. 29 on Airport Rd.

Trains: Amtrak, 810 W. Main St. (☎800-872-7245 or 296-4559; www.amtrak.com). Trains run once daily on the line to New Orleans. To **Washington, D.C.** (2hr., $20+). Ticket office open daily 6am-9:30pm.

Bus: Greyhound/Trailways, 310 W. Main St. (☎800-231-2222 or 295-5131; www.greyhound.com). To: **Baltimore** (5hr., $40+); **Richmond** (1¼hr., $15+); and **Washington, D.C.** (3hr., $20+).

Public Transit: Charlottesville Transit Service (☎296-7433). Bus service within city limits, M-Sa 6:30am-midnight. $0.75, seniors and disabled $0.35, under 6 free.

Taxi: Carter's Airport Taxi, ☎981-0170. **AAA Cab Co.,** ☎975-5555.

ORIENTATION & PRACTICAL INFORMATION

Charlottesville's streets are numbered from east to west, using compass directions; 5th St. NW is 10 blocks from (and parallel to) 5th St. NE. There are two downtowns: **The Corner,** on the west side across from the university, is home to student delis and coffeeshops. Historic **downtown,** about a mile east, is a tad higher on the price scale. The two are connected by east-west **University Avenue,** which starts as Ivy Rd. and becomes Main St. after the end of the bridge in The Corner district.

Visitor Info: Chamber of Commerce, 415 E. Market St. (☎295-3141), at 5th St. Within walking distance of Amtrak, Greyhound, and downtown. Maps, guides, and info about special events available. Open M-F 9am-5pm. **Charlottesville-Albemarle County Convention and Visitors Bureau** (☎977-1783), off I-64 on Rte. 20. The place to go for Jefferson-oriented activities. Open daily Mar.-Oct. 9am-5:30pm; Nov.-Feb. 9am-5pm. **University of Virginia Information Center** (☎924-7969), at the Rotunda in the center of campus, offers brochures, a university map, and tour information. Open daily 9am-4:45pm.

Hotlines: Region 10 Community Services, ☎972-1800. **Sexual Assault Crisis Center,** ☎977-7273. Both open 24hr. **Mental Health,** ☎977-4673. Open M-F 9am-6pm.

Internet Access: Jefferson Madison Regional Library, 201 E. Market St. (☎979-7151). Open M-Th 9am-9pm, F-Sa 9am-5pm, Su 1-5pm. Free.

Post Office: 513 E. Main St. (☎963-2661). Open M-F 8:30am-5pm, Sa 10am-1pm.

Postal Code: 22902. **Area Code:** 434.

ACCOMMODATIONS

Boar's Head Inn, 200 Ednam Dr. (☎800-476-1988 or 296-2181; www.boarsheadinn.com), is by far one of the classiest, most convenient, and costly places you can stay in town. Some B&B rates are more affordable starting at $118 per night. ❺

The Inn at Monticello, 1188 Scottsville Rd. (☎979-3593; www.innatmonticello.com), boasts the most auspicious location for those who want to mold their trip around visits to Jefferson's home. This 1850 manor-turned-B&B is within a 5min. drive of Monticello. Lovely antiques, elegant rooms, full breakfasts. Rooms $125-175. ❺

The Budget Inn, 140 Emmet St. (☎800-293-5144; www.budgetinn-charlottesville.com), is the closest motel to the university. 36 big rooms with lots of sunlight and cable TV. Rooms $40-90; each additional person $5. ❷

FOOD

littlejohn's, 1427 University Ave. (☎977-0588). During lunch hours, this deli becomes as overstuffed as its sandwiches. In the wee, wee hours of the morning, barflies trickle into littlejohn's to kick back and relax with the Easy Rider (baked ham, mozzarella, and cole slaw; $3.75). Many, many beers ($2-3). Open 24hr. ❶

Blue Light Grill and Raw Bar, 120 E. Main St. (☎295-1223; www.bluelightgrill.com), on the mall. Ideal for seafood lovers, this grill has a modern, uncluttered atmosphere with red walls and high ceilings. The grilled scallops with *haricots verts* ($19) are excellent. Open M 5:30-10pm, Tu-Sa 11:30am-2:30pm and 5:30-10pm. ❺

Chaps, 223 E. Main St. (☎977-4139), is a favorite for homemade ice cream. With a diner-that's-been-here-forever feel, the joint also serves cheap, simple grub. Open M-F 7am-10pm, Sa-Su 7am-11pm. Cash only. ❶

SIGHTS

UVA. Most activity on the grounds of the **University of Virginia** clusters around the **Lawn** and fraternity-lined **Rugby Road.** Monticello is visible from the lawn, a terraced green carpet that is one of the prettiest spots in American academia. Professors live in the Lawn's pavilions; Jefferson designed each one in a different architectural style. *(☎924-7969. Tours meet at Rotunda entrance facing the Lawn. Tours daily 10, 11am, 2, 3, 4pm; no tours on Thanksgiving, mid-Dec. to mid-Jan., and early to mid-May.)*

HISTORIC MANSIONS. Jefferson oversaw every stage of the development of his beloved **Monticello,** a home that truly reflects the personality of its brilliant creator. The house is a quasi-Palladian jewel filled with fascinating innovations, such as a fireplace dumbwaiter to the wine cellar and a mechanical copier. *(1184 Monticello Loop. ☎984-9822; www.monticello.org. Open Mar.-Oct. daily 8am-5pm; Nov.-Feb. 9am-4:30pm. $13, ages 6-11 $6.)* The partially reconstructed **Michie Tavern** has an operating grist mill and a general store. *(Just west of Monticello on the Thomas Jefferson Pkwy. ☎977-1234; www.michietavern.com. Open daily 9am-5pm; last tour 4:20pm. $8, seniors and AAA $7, ages 6-11 $3.)* Just outside Charlottesville, James Madison's **Montpelier** once supported his more than 100 slaves and property with tobacco, wheat, and corn crops. *(Rte. 20. ☎540-672-2728; www.montperlier.org. Open daily Apr.-Oct. 9:30am-4:30pm. $11, seniors and AAA $10, ages 6-14 $6.)* **Ash Lawn-Highland** was the 535-acre plantation home of President James Monroe. Although less distinctive than Monticello, Ash Lawn reveals more about family life in the early 19th century. *(1000 James Monroe Pkwy. Off Rte. 792, 2½ mi. east of Monticello. ☎293-9539; www.ashlawn-highland.org. Open daily Mar.-Oct. 9am-6pm; Nov.-Feb. 10am-5pm. Tour $9, seniors and AAA $8, ages 6-11 $5.)*

NIGHTLIFE

Buddhist Biker Bar and Grille, 20 Elliewood Ave. (☎971-9181). UVA students and local 20-somethings flock to this bar for its huge lawn and drink specials. The food ain't bad either–try the spinach dip ($5) or stuffed mushrooms ($3.75). Beer $2.50-4. M $1 beers, W $2 cocktails, Th live bluegrass. Open M-Sa 3:30pm-2am.

Baja Bean, 1327 W. Main St. (☎293-4507). Cheap burritos, tamales, and *chimichangas* for under $8 at this Mexican bar and restaurant. Every 5th of the month is the Cinco Celebration, a fiesta with $3 Coronas. W 9pm-midnight dance parties with lasers and DJ-fueled music. Dollar Night (Tu and Th 8pm) has many drinks for $1-3. Happy Hour (M-F 3-7pm) with $1.50 mudslide shooters, $1.75 Baja Gold drafts, $2 rail highballs, and $3 Rox Rum Ritas. Open daily 11am-2am; kitchen closes at midnight.

Orbit, 102 14 St. NW (☎984-5707). A hot new bar and restaurant popular with C-ville locals. The recently opened downstairs has a *2001: A Space Odyssey* theme, and the garage-door windows open on hot summer nights. Upstairs has 8 pool tables and another bar with extensive beers on tap, including numerous imports ($2.50-4.50). Tu after 5pm ladies shoot pool for free. Th $2 drafts. Occasional Su live acoustic music. Open daily 5pm-2am.

SHENANDOAH NATIONAL PARK ☎540

Shenandoah's amazing multihued mountains—covered with lush, green foliage in the summer and streaked with brilliant reds, oranges, and yellows in the fall—offer relaxation and recreation throughout the year. America's first great nature reclamation project, Shenandoah National Park had humble beginnings, starting out as a 280-acre tract of over-logged, over-hunted land that Congress authorized Virginia to purchase in 1926. In 1936 a decree from Franklin Roosevelt sought to improve the land and foster new life upon the slowly rejuvenating soil. Today, the national park spans 196,000 acres with 500 miles of trails and more plant species than all of Europe. Despite pollution problems, visitors can see miles of ridges and treetops on a clear day.

ORIENTATION & PRACTICAL INFORMATION

The park runs nearly 105 mi. along the famous **Skyline Drive,** which extends from Front Royal in the north to Rockfish Gap in the south before evolving into the **Blue Ridge Parkway.** Skyline Drive closes during (and following) bad weather. Mile markers are measured north to south and denote the location of trails and stops. Three major highways divide the park into sections: the **North Section** runs from Rte. 340 to Rte. 211; the **Central Section** from Rte. 211 to Rte. 33; and the **South Section** from Rte. 33 to I-64. A park pass is valid for seven days and is necessary for readmittance. (Most facilities close in winter; call ahead. Entrance fee $10 per vehicle; $5 per hiker, biker, or bus passenger; disabled persons free.) **Greyhound,** 101 E. Main St., at Tropical Thicket (☎800-231-2222; www.greyhound.com) sends two buses a day to Waynesboro, near the park's southern entrance, from Charlottesville ($8.50), Richmond ($26), and Washington, D.C. ($40). No bus or train serves Front Royal, near the park's northern entrance.

The **Dickey Ridge Visitors Center,** at Mi. 4.6, and the **Byrd Visitors Center,** at Mi. 51, answer questions and maintain small exhibits about the park, including eight documentary films about various park topics (10-40min.) which are shown upon request at the Byrd Visitor Center. (Dickey Ridge: ☎635-3566. Byrd: ☎999-3283.)

For both, www.nps.ogv/shen (for camp and park info) and www.visitshenandoah.com (for info and reservations). Both open Apr.-Dec. daily 8:30am-5pm, additional hours July-Sept. F-Sa 8:30am-6pm.) The station's rangers conduct informative presentations on local wildlife, guide short walks among the flora, and wax romantic during outdoor, lantern-lit evening discussions. Pick up a free *Shenandoah Overlook* visitor newsletter for a complete listing of programs. Comprehensive and newly updated, the *Guide to Shenandoah National Park and Skyline Drive* ($7.50 and worth every penny) is available at both Visitors Centers. (General info ☎999-2297, recorded message ☎999-3500. Operates daily 8am-4:30pm.) Send **mail** to: Superintendent, Park Headquarters, Shenandoah National Park, 3655 US Highway 211 E., Luray, 22835. (For emergencies call ☎800-732-0911.) **Area Code:** 540.

ACCOMMODATIONS

Bears Den Hostel ❶, 18393 Blue Ridge Mountain Rd., 35 mi. north of Shenandoah on Rte. 601, holds 20 travelers in its two dorm rooms. Take Rte. 340 N to Rte. 7 E and follow it for 10 mi. to 601 N; travel ½ mi. on 601 and turn right at the gate. In house convenience store. (☎554-8708. 5-day max stay. Reception 7:30-9:30am and 5-10pm. Check-out 9:30am. Front gate locked and quiet hours begin at 10pm. Camping $6 per person. Beds $13, nonmembers $18; private room for 2 $42.) The park also maintains three affordable "lodges" ($55)—essentially motels with nature-friendly exteriors. Reservations (☎554-8708 or 800-999-4714; info@bearsdencenter.org) up to 6 months in advance recommended. **Skyland ❸,** Mi. 42 on Skyline Drive, offers wood-furnished cabins and more upscale motel rooms. (☎999-2211. Cabins open Apr.-Oct. $55-108. Motel rooms open Mar.-Nov. $82-123.) **Big Meadows ❸,** Mi. 51, has similar services, with a historic lodge and cabins. (☎999-2221. Open late Apr. to Nov. Cabins $78-90; lodge $70-146.) **Lewis Mountain ❷,** Mi. 57, operates cabins. (Tent cabins $20, cabins $64-97.)

CAMPING

The park service (☎800-365-2267 from 10am-10pm; www.reservations.nps.gov) maintains four major campgrounds: **Mathews Arm ❶,** Mi. 22 ($16), with 177 sites, and convenient to nearby **Elkwallow,** Mi. 24, which has a gas station, eatery, and gift shop; **Big Meadows ❶,** Mi. 51 ($19); **Lewis Mountain ❶,** Mi. 58 ($20); and **Loft Mountain ❶,** Mile 80 ($16). The latter three have stores, laundry, and showers, but no hookups. Heavily wooded and uncluttered by RVs, Mathews Arm and Lewis Mountain are the best options. Reservations are possible only at Big Meadows.

The **Appalachian Trail (AT)** runs the length of the park. Twelve three-sided shelters are strewn at 8-10 mi. intervals along the AT. Unwritten trail etiquette usually reserves the cabins for those hiking large stretches of the trail. **Backcountry camping** is free, but you must obtain a permit at park entrances, Visitors Centers, or ranger stations. Camping without a permit or above 2800 ft. is illegal and unsafe. The **Potomac Appalachian Trail Club (PATC) ❶,** 118 Park St. SE, in Vienna, a volunteer organization, maintains six cabins in backcountry areas of the park. Bring lanterns and food; the primitive cabins contain only bunk beds, blankets, and stoves. (☎703-242-0693; www.patc.net. Headquarters open M-W 7-9pm, Th noon-2pm and 7-9pm, F noon-2pm. 1 group member must be 21+. Reservations required. Su-Th $15 per group, F-Sa $25.) Trail maps and the PATC guide can be obtained at the Visitors Center. The PATC puts out three topographical maps ($5 each).

BLUE RIDGE PARKWAY

DISTANCE: 469 mi.

SEASON: Spring, summer, and fall.

STATES: Virginia, North Carolina, and Tennessee

The beauty of unrestrained wilderness does not end at the southern gates of Shenandoah National Park. Jaws will continue to drop as travelers weave through the world's longest scenic drive–the 469 mi. Blue Ridge Parkway. Merging with Skyline Dr., the parkway winds through Virginia and North Carolina, connecting Shenandoah National Park (p. 348) in Virginia to the Great Smoky Mountains (p. 378) in Tennessee, and offering an endless array of stunning vistas along the way. Administered by the National Park Service, the parkway sprouts hiking trails, campsites, and picnic grounds with humbling mountain views. While still accessible in the winter, the Parkway lacks maintenance or park service from November to April. *The steep bending roads can be treacherous, exercise caution, especially during inclement weather.*

For general information, call the park service in Roanoke, VA (☎857-2490), or write to the **Blue Ridge Parkway Superindendent,** 199 Hemphill Knob Rd., Asheville, NC 28803 (☎828-298-0398; www.nps.gov/blri). Twelve **Visitors Centers** line the Parkway at Mi. 5.8, 63.8, 86, 169, 217.5, 294.1, 304.4, 316.4, 331, 364.6, 382, and 451.2. Pick up trail maps, or a free copy of *The Parkway Milepost* for info on ranger-led activities. (Most open daily 9am-5pm.) **Maximum Speed Limit:** 45 mph. **Emergency Number:** ☎800-727-5928. **Area Code:** 540, except where otherwise noted.

1 GEORGE WASHINGTON NATIONAL FOREST. From Shenandoah National Park, the Blue Ridge trails south from Waynesboro to Roanoke south through Virginia's 1.8 million acre George Washington National Forest. A **Visitors Center** (☎291-1806), 12 mi. off the Parkway at Mi. 70, at the intersection of Rte. 130 and Rte. 11 in Natural Bridge, distributes information on hiking, camping, canoeing, and swimming at **Sherando Lake ❶,** 4½ mi. off the Parkway at Mi. 16. In addition to its 65 campsites, the lake has some excellent fishing. (Site with hook-up $15; recreational user fee $8.)

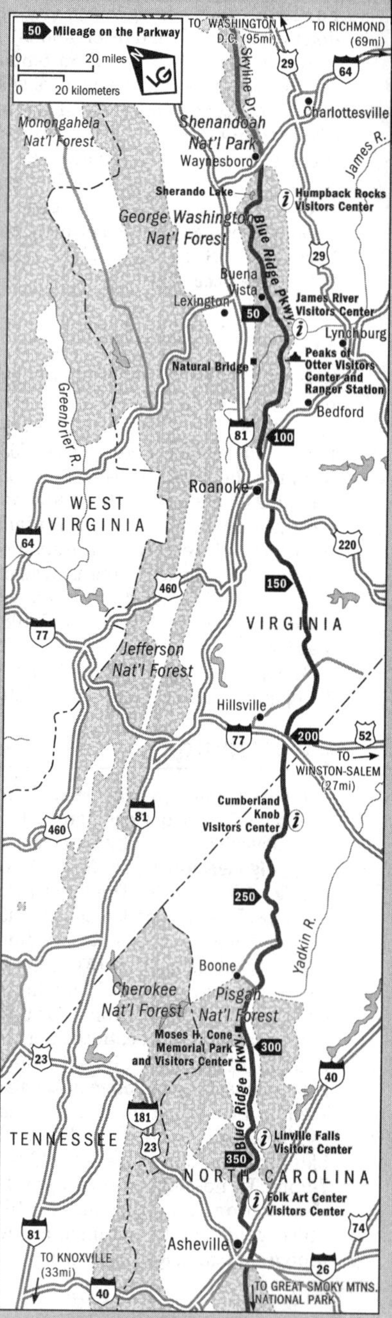

2. HUMPBACK ROCKS. Excellent hiking trails along the parkway vary in difficulty and duration, offering naturalists of all ages and abilities a chance to explore the peaks and valleys of the Blue Ridge. Whether moseying along easy trails through the scenic backdrop or scrambling up the more strenuous climbs through the Humpback Mountains, there is something for everyone. One of the less demanding trails, the **Mountain Farm Trail** (Mi. 5.9) is an easy 20min. hike that leads to the reconstructed homestead.

3 LEXINGTON. At the intersections of I-81 and I-64, the college town of Lexington drips with Confederate pride. Check out the Lee Chapel and Museum, at the center of the **Washington and Lee** campus, which holds Confederate General (and college namesake) Robert E. Lee's crypt along with the remains of his trusty horse Traveler. (☎463-8768; http://leechapel.wlu.edu. Open Apr.-Oct. M-F 9am-5pm, Su 1-5pm; Nov.-Mar. M-Sa 9am-4pm, Su 1-4pm. Free.) For accommodations and further attractions, contact the **Lexington Visitors Center,** 106 E. Washington St. (☎877-453-9822 or 463-3777; www.lexingtonvirginia.com). Other cities and towns along the Parkway also offer accommodations, primarily motels for around $35-55.

4 NATURAL BRIDGE. Across from the Visitors Center in George Washington National Forest, a water-carved **Arc de Triomphe,** hidden behind the entrance, towers 215 ft. above green-lined falls and an underground river. One of the seven natural wonders of the world, the 100 million-year-old **Natural Bridge** still bears the initials carved into the side by a vandalous George Washington. The nightly "Drama of Creation" light and sound show chronicles the biblical seven days of creation. (☎291-2121 or 800-533-1410; www.naturalbridgeva.com. Bridge open daily 8am-dark. Drama show Su-F 9pm, Sa 9, 10pm. $10; AAA $9; students, seniors and military $8; ages 6-15 $5. Wheelchair-accessible.)

5 PEAKS OF OTTER. Three- to five-mile hiking trails start from Peaks of Otter (Mi. 86), where visitors can among peaks as high as 4500 ft. The **Sharp Top** (1½ mi.; 3875 ft.), beginning at the Visitors Center, climbs to the to the peak of Sharp Top Mountain for an amazing panoramic view of the surrounding Blue Ridge Mountains. Those too tired to walk all the way can opt for the bus ride up. Other trails ascend **Flat Top Mountain** (4½ mi.; 4001 ft.) and **Harkening Hill** (3¼ mi.; 3350 ft.), providing a chance to traverse well-forested terrain.

6 LINN COVE VIADUCT. The majority of the Blue Ridge Parkway was completed by 1967, but a small stretch of 7½ mi. remained the "missing link" for 20 years. The imposing **Grandfather Mountain** blocked the road. In order to finish the parkway without damaging the mountain, a lengthy construction process was undertaken. Completed in 1987, a 1243 ft. stretch of road curves around the boulders at **Linn Cove**–a feat of engineering that cost around $10 million. The ¼ mi. **Linn Cove Viaduct Access Trail** (Mi. 304.4 in North Carolina) is wheelchair-accessible.

7 MOSES H. CONE MEMORIAL PARK. The sprawling estate at **Moses H. Cone Memorial Park** (Mi. 294.1) features a Visitors Center and a craft store in a historic manor, as well as 25 mi. of hiking and horse trails. Travelers can also rent canoes and rowboats at nearby **Price Lake** at Mi. 297. (☎828-295-3782. Visitors Center open June-Aug. daily 8:30am-6pm; May and Sept.-Oct. Sa Su 10am-6pm. Craft Store open mid-Mar. to late Nov. daily 9am-5pm. Canoes $4 for 1hr.; $3 each additional hr.; ☎828-963-5911.) The Park Service hosts a variety of ranger-led activities, including historical talks, campfire circles, guided nature walks, slide shows, and musical demonstrations; information is available at the Blue Ridge Visitors Centers.

8 MOUNT MITCHELL STATE PARK. Off of the Parkway at Mi. 355.4, **Mount Mitchell** reaches an elevation of 6684ft.–he highest peak east of the Mississippi River. Visitors can hike or drive to the top, where they'll find a park office, a small campground, a restaurant, an observation tower, and some sweet views. The park can be reached via N.C. 128. (Park gates open daily June-Aug. 8am-9pm; Apr.-May and Sept. 8am-8pm; Mar. and Oct. 8am-7pm.; Nov.-Feb. 8am-6pm. Summit is 5 mi. from Pkwy. Free. Office and restaurant hours vary.)

OUTDOOR ACTIVITIES

HIKING

The trails off Skyline Dr. are heavily used and generally safe for cautious day-hikers with maps, appropriate footwear, and water. The middle section of the park, from **Thorton Gap,** Mi. 32, to **South River,** Mi. 63, bursts with photo opportunities and stellar views, although it also tends to be crowded with tourists. Rangers recommend purchasing *Hiking Shenandoah Park* ($13), a guide detailing the distance, difficulty, elevation, and history of 59 hikes.

Whiteoak Canyon Trail (Mi. 42.6; 4½ mi., 4hr. return) is a strenuous hike that opens upon the second highest waterfall in the park (plunging an impressive 86 ft.), rewarding those who ascend the 1040 ft. of elevation with views of the ancient Limberlost hemlocks.

Limberlost Trail (Mi. 43; 1¼ mi., 1hr. return) slithers into a hemlock forest. Weaving through orchards, passing over a footbridge, and remaining relatively level, it is recommended for all ages and activity levels. No pets allowed. Wheelchair-accessible.

Old Rag Mountain Trail (Mi. 45; 8¾ mi., 6-8hr. return) starts outside the park. From U.S. 211, turn right on Rte. 522, then right on Rte. 231. Trail scrambles up 3291 ft. to triumphant views of the valley below. Be careful in damp weather, rocks can get slippery. Hikers 16 and older who have not paid Shenandoah admission must pay $3.

Stony Man Nature Trail (Mi. 41.7; 1½ mi., 1½hr. return) is a trail that offers independent hikers the opportunity to gain altitude, gradually climbing to the park's second-highest peak. The surrounding forests contain a vast variety of trees. No pets allowed.

OTHER ACTIVITIES

There are two other ways to explore Shenandoah: by boat and by beast. **Downriver Canoe Company** in Bentonville offers canoe, kayak, raft, and tube trips. From Skyline Dr. Mi. 20, follow U.S. 211 W for 8 mi., then take U.S. 340 N 14 mi. to Bentonville; turn right onto Rte. 613 and go 1 mi. (☎635-5526 or 800-338-1963; www.downriver.com. Open M-F 9am-6pm, Sa-Su 7am-7pm.) Guided **horseback rides** are available at the Skyland Lodge, Mi. 42. (☎999-2210; www.visitshenandoah.com. Riders must be 4 ft. 10 in. Open Mar.-late Nov. $20-22 per 1hr. ride. 1 day advance reservation required.)

DAYTRIPS FROM SHENANDOAH

LURAY CAVERNS

In 1878, three young boys discovered 64 acres of underground craftsmanship, now known as the **Luray Caverns,** at U.S. 211 off I-81 Exit 264. View mineral formations in the shape of fried eggs, shaggy dogs, and ice cream cones on the 1hr. guided tour through moist, 54°F tunnels. The unforgettable cathedral room has hosted some 350 weddings and includes the world's largest natural instrument: a 37-mallet organ created from 1954-1957 by Leeland W. Sprinkle, a Virginian organist, who tapped 3000 cave formations to derive the 37 sounds. On a peak day, roughly 40,000 visitors flood the cavern to see the wishing well, the *trompe-l'oeil au naturel* reflective pool, and the bleeding rock. Access to the automobile museum and an outdoor garden maze are included in the admission. Tours last approximately 1hr. Visitors are advised to bring a sweater and their camera. (☎743-6551; www.luraycaverns.com. Open mid-June to Aug. daily 9am-7pm; mid-Mar. to mid-June and Sept.-Oct. daily 9am-6pm; Nov. to mid-Mar. M-F 9am-4pm, Sa-Su 9am-5pm. $17, seniors $15, ages 7-13 $8.)

ENDLESS CAVERNS

Escape the tourist congestion of Luray Caverns to discover the beauty of infinity at **Endless Caverns,** 1800 Endless Caverns Rd. Follow signs from the intersection of U.S. 11 and U.S. 211 in New Market. Discovered in 1879, the caverns are considered "endless" because they encompass over 5 mi. of mapped cave passages with no visible end. Cave temperature is cool (55° F, but feels colder), and the tour is fairly strenuous; wear a jacket and sturdy shoes for the 1¾hr. long tour. (☎896-2283; www.endlesscaverns.com. Open daily mid-Mar. to mid-June 9am-5pm; mid-June to Labor Day 9am-6pm, Day After Labor Day to mid-Nov. 9am-5pm, mid-Nov. to mid-Mar. 9am-4pm. $14, AAA and AARP $13, ages 4-12 $5.50.)

SKYLINE CAVERNS

Smaller than Endless and Luray Caverns, **Skyline Caverns,** on U.S. 340, 1 mi. from the junction of Rte. 340 and Skyline Drive, contains an orchid-like garden of white rock spikes. Respect the formation—only one grows every 7000 years. Most remarkable are the anthodites, an extremely rare type of crystal. Notable tour stops include the Capitol Dome, the Wishing Well, Cathedral Hall, and Rainbow Falls, which pours 37 ft. from one of the three cavern streams. (☎635-4545 or 800-296-4545; www.skylinecaverns.com. Open mid-Mar. to mid-June M-F 9am-5pm, Sa-Su 9am-6pm; mid-June-Sept. M-F 9am-6:30pm, Sa-Su 9am-6pm; mid-Nov. to mid-Mar. daily 9am-4pm. $14; seniors, AAA, and military $12; ages 7-13 $7.)

WEST VIRGINIA

With 80% of the state cloaked in untamed forests, hope of commercial expansion and economic prosperity once seemed a distant dream for West Virginia. When the coal mines—formerly West Virginia's primary source of revenue—became exhausted, the state appeared doomed, until government officials decided to capitalize on the area's evergreen expanses, tranquil trails, and raging rivers. Today, thousands of tourists forge paths into West Virginia's breathtaking landscape.

PRACTICAL INFORMATION

Capital: Charleston.

Visitor Info: Dept. of Tourism, 2101 Washington St. E., Bldg. #17, Charleston 25305; P.O. Box 30312 (☎800-225-5982; www.callwva.com; operator M-F 7am-9pm, Sa-Su 9am-5pm). **US Forest Service,** 200 Sycamore St., Elkins 26241 (☎304-636-1800; www.fs.fed.us/r9/mnf). Open M-F 8am-4:45pm.

Postal Abbreviation: WV. **Sales Tax:** 6%.

HARPERS FERRY ☎304

A bucolic hillside town overlooking the Shenandoah and Potomac rivers, Harpers Ferry earned its fame when a band of abolitionists led by John Brown raided the US Armory in 1859. Although Brown was captured and executed, the raid brought the issue of slavery into the national spotlight. Brown's adamant belief in violence as the only means to overcome the problem of slavery soon gained credence, and the town became a major theater of conflict, changing hands eight times during the Civil War. Today, Harpers Ferry attracts more mild-mannered guests, as outdoor enthusiasts come to enjoy the town's surrounding wilderness.

ORIENTATION & PRACTICAL INFORMATION. Harper's Ferry is on West Virginia's border with Maryland. **Amtrak** (☎800-535-6406; www.amtrak.com), on Potomac St., sends one train per day to Washington, D.C. (1¾hr., $9-20); reservations are required, as no tickets are sold at the station. The same depot serves **MARC,** the **Maryland Rail Commuter** (☎800-325-7245; www.mtamaryland.com; open M-F 5:30am-8:15pm), offering a cheaper and more frequent service to Washington, D.C. (M-F 2 per day, $9). The **Appalachian Trail Conference** (**ATC,** see **Outdoor Activities,** p. 356) runs buses to Charles Town ($2). **The Outfitter,** 111 High St. (☎535-2087; www.theoutfitteratharpersferry.com), about halfway along the Appalachian Trail, rents bikes ($20 per day), sells outdoor apparel, and conducts informative hiking tours. For a more in depth perspective of the area, try the **Jefferson County Convention and Visitors Bureau** (www.jeffersoncountycvb.com). The **Cavalier Heights Visitors Center** is just inside the Harpers Ferry National Historic Park entrance, off Rte. 340. (☎535-6298; www.harpersferryhistory.org. Open daily 8am-5pm. Visitors must park here unless they are staying at an accommodation with parking located within walking distance of town. 3-day admission $5 per car, $3 per hiker or bicyclist. Shuttles leave the parking lot for town every 10min.; last pick-up 6:45pm.) The **Historic Town Area Visitor Information Center,** sister center of the Cavalier Heights Visitor Center, located at the end of Shenandoah St. near the intersection of High St, provides free tour info. (☎535-6298; www.harpersferryhistory.org. Open 8am-5pm.) **Post Office:** 1010 Washington St., on the corner of Washington and Franklin St. (☎535-2479 or 800-275-8777; www.usps.com. Open M-F 8am-4pm, Sa 9am-noon.) **Postal Code:** 25425. **Area Code:** 304.

ACCOMMODATIONS. Fishing fanatics might try **Anglers Inn ❺,** 867 Washington St., with mariner decor and combined stay and fly fishing/fishing packages available. All rooms come with a private bath. (☎535-1239; www.theanglersinn.com. Rooms $95-115.) Ragged hikers find a warm welcome at the social and spacious **Harpers Ferry Hostel (HI-AYH) ❶,** 19123 Sandy Hook Rd., at Keep Tryst Rd. off Rte. 340 in Knoxville, MD. This renovated auction house, complete with a backyard trail to Potomac overlooks, landscaped lawns, library, Internet access, fully stocked kitchen, shuttle pick up service, and $2 laundry, welcomes guests into four rooms with 37 well-cushioned beds. (☎301-834-7652; www.harpersferryhostel.org. 3-night max. stay. Check-in 7-9am and 6-10pm. Open mid-Mar. to mid-Nov. Camping $6/9, includes use of hostel kitchen and bathrooms. Beds $15, nonmembers $18.) The **Hillside Motel ❷,** 19105 Keep Tryst Rd., three mi. from town in Knoxville, MD, has 19 clean rooms inside a beautiful stone motel. Unfortunately, hitting the nearby local restaurant and liquor store may be the wildest activity on a Saturday night. (☎301-834-8144. Singles $40; doubles $50. Winter rates lower.) For a quainter stay, the charming **Harpers Ferry Guest House ❹,** 800 Washington St., is ideally located in the center of the historic district. (☎535-6955. M-Th $75, F-Su $95.) Without a doubt, the most splendid views of the confluence of rivers and mountains can be had at the **Historic Hilltop House Hotel ❹,** 400 East Ridge St., which sits on a cliff within walking distance of sights and attractions. Although the rooms are somewhat worn, the views more than compensate. (☎535-2132 or 800-338-8319; www.hilltophousehotel.net. Rates $70-155. AARP 10% discount. Ask about weekend murder mystery group parties.) For those who can afford to spend a few extra bucks, Camp along the **C&O Canal ❶,** where free camping sites lie 5 mi. apart, or in one of the five Maryland state park campgrounds within 30 mi. of Harpers Ferry. (Ranger station ☎301-739-4200.) **Greenbrier State Park ❶,** on Rte. 40 E off Rte. 66, has 165 campsites and outdoor recreation revolving around a lake. (☎301-791-4767 or 888-432-2267; http://reservations.dnr.state.md.us. Open May-Sept. Reservations required. Closed Nov.-Mar. Sites $20; with hookup $25.)

FOOD. Harpers Ferry has sparse offerings for hungry hikers on a budget. **Route 340** welcomes fast food fanatics with various chain restaurants. Those with a thing for caffeine can satiate coffee cravings at the new **Daily Grind ❷,** 180 High St., a happy little coffeehouse with a convenient location in historic Harper's Ferry. Be forewarned: this joint offers more than merely coffee; huge sandwiches ($6-7) or salads ($5) combined with a Chai smoothie ($4.50) are likely to engender shameless salivation. (☎535-1447. Open M-F 8am-5pm, Sa 8am-8pm, Su 8pm-6pm.) Nearby Charles Town's **La Mezzaluna Cafe ❸,** Somerset Village Suite B3 off Rt. 340S just 5min. from Harper's Ferry, boasts surprisingly delicious Italian favorites in a spacious setting. Pasta entrees $9-14 come with house salad. (☎728-0700. Lunch Tu-Sa 11am-3pm; dinner Tu-Th 4-9pm, F-Sa 4-10pm, Su 2:30-9pm.) Across the street from the Hillside Motel, the **Cindy Dee Restaurant ❶,** 19112 Keep Tryst Rd., at Rte. 340, fries enough chicken ($5) to clog all your arteries, and their homemade apple dumplings ($2.75) are delectable. (☎301-695-8181. Open daily 7am-9pm.) The historic area, especially High St. and Potomac St., caters to the luncher with either burgers and fries or salads and steaks, but vacates for dinner. For nightlife and varied cuisine, the tiny **Shepherdstown,** 11 mi. north of Harpers Ferry, is practically a bustling culinary metropolis in these quiet parts. From the Ferry, take Rte. 340 S for 2 mi. to Rte. 230 N or bike 13 mi. along the C&O towpath.

Coffee addicts flock to **Lost Dog,** 134 E. German St., which brews 30 different blends of coffee and over 50 kinds of tea in an hip and happening atmosphere. (☎876-0871. Open Su-Th 6:30am-8pm, F-Sa 6:30am-9pm.) Amid the colonial architecture of E. German St., the **Mecklinburg Inn,** 128 E. German St., provides rock 'n' roll and Rolling Rock for $1.75 on open mic night every Tuesday from 9pm to midnight. (☎876-2126. Happy Hour M-F 4:30-6:30pm. 21+ after 5pm. Open M-Th 3pm-12:30am, F 3pm-1:30am, Sa 1pm-2am, Su 1pm-12:30am. No credit cards.)

SIGHTS. The **Harpers Ferry National Historic Park,** comprising most of historic Harper's Ferry, is composed of several museums, all of which are included with admission to the park. (☎535-6298. Open daily summer 8am-6pm; winter 8am-5pm. 3-day admission $5 per car; $3 per pedestrian, bike, or motorcycle.) Parking in historic Lower Town is nonexistent; it's necessary to park at the Visitors Center and board the free, frequently-running bus to town, or walk about 20min. The bus stops at **Shenandoah Street,** where a barrage of replicated 19th-century shops greets visitors; for example, the **Dry Goods Store** displays clothes, hardware, liquor, and groceries that would have been sold over 100 years ago. Check out their free 1850s price list to compare prices then and now. The **Harpers Ferry Industrial Museum,** on Shenandoah St., describes the methods used to harness the powers of the Shenandoah and Potomac rivers and details the town's status as the endpoint of the nation's first successful rail line. The unsung stories of the Ferry captivate visitors at **Black Voices from Harpers Ferry,** on the corner of High and Shenandoah St., where well-trained actors play fettered slaves expressing their opinions of John Brown and his raid. Next door on High St., the plight of Harpers Ferry's slaves is further elaborated in the **Civil War Story.** Informative displays detail the importance of Harpers Ferry's strategic location to both the Union and Confederate armies. A ticket is required to enter some of the exhibits. In addition, the park offers occasional reenactments of Harpers Ferry's history.

The **John Brown Museum,** on Shenandoah St., just beyond High St., is the town's most captivating historical site. A 30min. video chronicles Brown's raid of the armory with a special focus on the moral and political implications of his actions. A daunting, steep staircase hewn into the hillside off High St. follows the **Appalachian Trail** to **Upper Harpers Ferry,** which has fewer sights but is laced with interesting historical tales. Allow 45min. to ascend past **Harper's House,** the restored home of town founder Robert Harper, and **St. Peter's Church,** where a pastor flew the Union Jack during the Civil War to protect the church. Just a few steps uphill from St. Peter's lie the archeological ruins of **St. John's Episcopal Church** (built 1852, rebuilt after the Civil War, then abandoned in 1895), used as a hospital and barracks during the Civil War.

OUTDOOR ACTIVITIES. After digesting the historical significance of Harpers Ferry, many choose to soak up the town's outdoors. Go to the park's Visitors Center for trail maps galore. The moderate difficulty **Maryland Heights Trail,** located across the railroad bridge in the Lower Town of Harpers Ferry, wanders 4 mi. through steep Blue Ridge Mountains that include precipitous cliffs and glimpses of crumbling Civil War-era forts. The strenuous 7½ mi. **Loudon Heights Trail** starts in Lower Town off the Appalachian Trail and leads to Civil War infantry trenches and scenic overlooks. For more moderate hiking, the 2½ mi. **Camp Hill Trail** passes by the Harper Cemetery and ends at the former Stoner College. History dominates the **Bolivar Heights Trail,** starting at the northern end of Whitman Ave.

The **Chesapeake & Ohio Canal** towpath, off the end of Shenandoah St. and over the railroad bridge, serves as a lasting reminder of the town's industrial roots and is the point of departure for a day's bike ride to Washington, D.C. The **Appalachian Trail Conference,** 799 Washington St., at Washington and Jackson St., offers catalogs with deals on hiking books and trail info (☎535-6331; www.appalachiantrail.org. Open mid May-Oct. M-F 9am-5pm, Sa-Su and holidays 9am-4pm; Nov. to mid-May M-F 9am-5pm. Membership $30, seniors and students $25.)

River & Trail Outfitters, 604 Valley Rd., 2 mi. out of Harpers Ferry off Rte. 340, in Knoxville, MD, rents canoes, kayaks, inner tubes, and rafts. They also organize everything from scenic daytrips to placid rides down the Shenandoah River ($21) to wild overnights. (☎301-695-5177; www.rivertrail.com. Canoes $55 per day. Raft trips $50-60 per person, children under 17 $40. Tubing $32 per day.) At **Butt's Tubes, Inc.,** on Rte. 671 off Rte. 340, adventurers can buy a tube for the day and sell it back later. (☎800-836-9911; www.buttstubes.com. Open M-F 10am-3pm, last pickup 5pm; Sa-Su 10am-4pm, last pickup 6pm. $12-20.) Horse activities in the area include a variety of recreational trips offered through **Elk Mountain Trails.** (☎301-834-8882; www.elkmountaintrails.com. Rides $20-68. No credit cards.)

MONONGAHELA NATIONAL FOREST ☎304

Mammoth Monongahela National Forest sprawls across the eastern portion of the state, sustaining wildlife (including nine endangered species), limestone caverns, weekend canoers, fly fisherman, spelunkers, and skiers. Over 500 campsites and 600 mi. of wilderness hiking trails lure adventurers to this outdoor haven. Surrounded by a luscious green thicket, Monongahela's roads are indisputably scenic, and the beauty of **Route 39** from Marlinton down to Goshen, VA, past Virginia's swimmable Maury River, is unsurpassed. The **Highland Scenic Highway (Route 150)** runs near the Nature Center and stretches 43 mi. from Richwood to U.S. 219, 7 mi. north of Marlinton. Tempting as it is to gaze at the forest's splendor, driving through the winding and often foggy roads can be treacherous.

Aside from displaying an informative wildlife exhibit that includes hissing rattlesnakes and carnivorous plants, the **Cranberry Mountain Nature Center** (see below) conducts free weekend tours of the **Cranberry Glades** from June to August Sa-Su at 2pm (tours last 30min.-1hr.). Wrapping around the glades is the **Cow Pasture Trail** (6 mi.), which passes a WWII German prison camp. Two popular short hikes in the area are the panoramic, **High Rocks Trail** (4 mi.; 1-15% grade with narrow dirt path; not recommended for lone hikers), leading off of the Highland Scenic Hwy., and the awesome **Falls of Hills Creek** (2 mi.), off Rte. 39/55 south of Cranberry Mountain Nature Center, with three falls ranging in height from 25-63 ft. Small concrete pathway leads to a long cascade of wooden steps down to falls. Good knees are a must.

Those with several days might choose to hike, bike, or cross-country ski a part of the **Greenbrier River Trail** (75 mi., 1° grade), which runs from Cass to North Caldwell; the trailhead is on Rte. 38 off U.S. 60. Lined with numerous access points and campgrounds, the trail offers multiple vistas and arguably the highest concentration of butterflies in West Virginia. **Watoga State Park** (☎799-4087; www.watoga.com), in Marlinton, has maps and a lake. Downhill delights abound in **Canaan Valley** with the 54 trails at **Snowshoe Resort,** just outside the National Forest. (☎572-1000; www.snowshoemtn.com. Open Dec.-Mar. daily 8:30am-10pm. M-F lift tickets $38, students and seniors $30; Sa-Su $44. Ski rental $26, children $18. Prices subject to change.) A few minutes down the road, travelers may cross a babbling stream and travel up the impeccably landscaped driveway to **Morning Glory Inn ❹,** off Rt. 219N, which offers gargantuan B&B rooms with cathedral-like wood beam ceilings, modern and cozy decor, whirlpool tubs, and a sprawling porch. (☎572-5000 or 866-572-5700; www.morningloryinn.com. Check-in 2pm. Check-out 11am. Prices are per person based on double-occupancy Mar.-Christmas Su-Th $80, F-Sa $85; Jan.-Mar Su-Th $100, F-Sa $150.) In summer, **mountain biking** is the outdoor activity of choice, though the abundant trout that flow through the Williams and Cranberry rivers make for great **fishing.** For all types of gear, try **Elk River,** off Rte. 219 in Slatyfork. Trails to the National Forest begin right outside the door, and the outfitter gives year-round fly fishing tours while running a rustic B&B. (☎572-3771; www.ertc.com. Inn $50-115 per night. Rates for equipment and guided trips vary extensively.) Travel north to **Cass Scenic Railroad State Park,** off Rt. 28/92, for novel train rides on the surviving 11 mi. of the once burgeoning 3000 mi. lumber railroad lines of West Virginia. Ascend to 4842 ft. on original "Shay and Heisler-type steam logging locomotives." Special rides include the "Scary Train" on Halloween, and the Saturday "Dinner Train" in summer. (☎456-4300 or 800-225-5982; www.cassrailroad.com. M-F 8am-4pm, Sa-Su 9am-5pm.) Science and physics lovers will certainly appreciate the **National Radio Astronomy Observatory,** off Rte. 28/92, which houses **The Robert C. Byrd Green Bank Telescope,** the largest fully steerable telescope in the world. Free tours take experts and laymen alike to the base of the large and looming, 17 million lb. telescope. (☎456-2150; www.gb.nrao.edu. Tours late May to mid-Oct. 9am-6pm on the hr.)

Each of Monongahela's six districts has a campground and a recreation area, with ranger stations off Rte. 39 east of Marlinton and in the towns of Bartow and Potomack. (Open M-F 8am-4:30pm.) The forest **Supervisor's Office,** 200 Sycamore St., in Elkins, distributes a full list of sites and fees, and provides info about fishing and hunting. (☎636-1800. Open M-F 8am-4:45pm.) Established sites are $5; backcountry camping is free, but register at the **Cranberry Mountain Nature Center,** near the Highland Scenic Hwy. at the junction of Rte. 150 and Rte. 39/55. (☎653-4826 or 653-8564; www.fs.fed.us/r9/mnf. Open Apr.-Nov. daily 9am-5pm.) **Cranberry Campground ❶,** in the Gauley district, 13 mi. from Ridgewood on Forest Rd. 76, has hiking trails through cranberry bogs and campsites ($8). Most public transportation in the forest area goes to White Sulphur Springs at the forest's southern tip. **Amtrak,** 315 W. Main St. (☎800-872-7245, www.amtrak.com for reservations, no ticket office, buy tickets in advance online or via phone), across from the Greenbrier Resort, runs trains Su, W, and F to Washington, D.C. from Charlottesville ($23), Hinton ($55), and White

Sulphur Springs ($50). If you request it, an extra stop may be made in downtown Alderson. **Greyhound** (☎800-231-2222; www.greyhound.com) will drop passengers off along Rte. 60 but does not run outbound from the forest. **Area Code:** 304.

NEW RIVER GORGE ☎304

The New River Gorge is an electrifying testament to the raw beauty and power of nature. One of the oldest rivers in the world, the **New River** carves a narrow gorge through the **Appalachian Mountains,** creating precipitous valley walls that tower an average of 1000 ft. above the white waters. These steep slopes remained virtually untouched until 1873, when industrialists drained the region to uncover coal and timber. With the coal mines now defunct, the gorge has come full circle, becoming once again an animal filled natural marvel.

PRACTICAL INFORMATION. **Amtrak** runs through the heart of the gorge, stopping on Rte. 41 N in Prince and Hinton. (☎800-872-7245 or 253-6651; www.amtrak.com. Trains Su, W, F. Prince: Open Su, W, F 9:30am-9pm. Hinton: Open Su, W, F 11am-1:30pm and 4:30-6:30pm.) **Greyhound** stops at 105 Third St. in Beckley. (☎800-231-2222 or 253-8333; www.greyhound.com. Open M-F 7am-8:30pm, Sa 7am-noon and 3-8:30pm, Su 7-9am and 4-8:30pm.) Bike tours, rentals, and repairs are available at **New River Bike and Pouring,** 103 Keller Ave., off U.S. 19 in Fayetteville. (☎574-2453 or 800-890-2453; www.newriverbike.com. Open daily 9am-6pm. Bike $25 half-day, $35 full-day.)

The park operates four **Visitors Centers.** Off Rte. 19 near Fayetteville at the northern extreme of the park, **Canyon Rim** has information on all park activities. (☎574-2115. Open daily June-Aug. 9am-8pm; Sept.-May 9am-5pm.) **Grandview,** on Rte. 9 near Beckley, attracts visitors in May when the rhododendrons are in bloom. (☎763-3145. Open daily May-Sept. 10am-8pm; Sept.-May 9am-5pm.) The other Visitors Centers are **Hinton,** on Rte. 20, and **Thurmond,** on Rte. 25 off I-19. (Hinton: ☎466-1597. Thurmond: ☎465-8550. Both open daily 9am-5pm.) Area information, including Bridge Day info and 10min. video, is also available at the **New River Convention and Visitors Bureau,** 310 Oyler Ave., in Oak Hill. (☎465-5617; www.newrivercvb.com. Open daily 9am-5pm.) **Area Code:** 304.

ACCOMMODATIONS. Budget motels can be found off **I-77** in Beckley ($45-60), while smaller lodges and guest houses are scattered throughout Fayetteville. (Accommodations and tourist info ☎800-225-5982. Operates M-F 7am-9pm and Sa-Su 9am-5pm.) The **Whitewater Inn ❷,** on the corner of Appalachian Dr. off U.S. 19, features small but clean rooms at affordable rates. (☎574-2998. No in-room phones. Rooms $35-45.) **Canyon Rim Ranch ❹,** off Gatewood Rd. next to Cunard Access, offers bunkhouses with A/C and shared bath. Visitors must supply their own linens, blankets, and towels. (☎574-3111; www.canyonrimranch.com. Bunkhouses $15 per person for parties of 6+; for fewer than 6 people, bunkhouses $89 per night.) Many raft companies operate private campgrounds, while four public campgrounds stake a claim in the area. The most central public campground, **Babcock State Park ❶,** on Rte. 41 south of U.S. 60, 15 mi. west of Rainelle, is the largest public campground in the Gorge and has 26 shaded sites and a range of cabins. Recreational activities include swimming, horseback riding, basketball, and tennis. (☎438-3004 or 800-225-5982 (ask to be transferred to Babcock State Park); www.babcockst.com. Sites $13; with electricity $17. Cabins $55-100.) For a complete package, check out family oriented **ACE Adventure Center,** off Minden Rd. in the town of Oak Hill. Boasting lakes, paths, bike races and rentals, a massage center, bunks, camp sites, classy chalets, horseback riding, whitewater rafting, and a lakeside lodge restaurant, this amazing complex is so large that visitors are handed maps to navigate. (☎888-223-7238 or 469-2651; www.aceraft.com. Campsites $9 per person; bunkhouses $12 per person; cabin tents $33; cabins $95.)

SIGHTS. Where Rte. 19 crosses the river at the park's northern end, the manmade grandeur of the **New River Gorge Bridge,** the second highest bridge in the US, overlooks the Canyon Rim cut out of the gorge. Best seen on foot, the bridge towers 876 ft. above New River and claims the world's largest single steel arch span. The Visitors Center at this site offers a decent vista, but for something more adventurous, descend the zig-zag wooden stairs to the lower level lookout. On **Bridge Day,** the third Saturday in October, thousands of extreme sports enthusiasts leap off the bridge by bungee or parachute as onlookers enjoy the festival's food and crafts. (☎800-927-0263; www.wvbridgeday.com.) Retired coal miners lead tours down a mine shaft at the **Beckley Exhibition Coal Mine,** on Ewart Ave. in Beckley at New River Park. Explore the mining industry by riding behind a 1930s engine through 150 ft. of underground passages. A jacket is suggested, as the tunnels are chilly. (☎256-1747; www.exhibitioncoalmine.com. Open Apr.-Oct. daily 10am-6pm; last tour leaves 5:30pm. $12, seniors $10.50, ages 4-12 $8.50.)

OUTDOOR ACTIVITIES. The **New River Gorge National River** runs north from Hinton to Fayetteville, falling over 750 ft. in 50 mi. As a way to conserve its magnificent natural, scenic, and historic value, the New River Gorge has been protected by the park service since 1958. A state information service, **West Virginia Division of Tourism** (☎800-225-5982; www.callwva.com) connects you to some of nearly 20 outfitters on the New River and the rowdier Gauley River. Brochures are at the **New River Convention and Visitors Bureau** (see **Practical Information,** above). **USA Raft,** at the intersection of Rte. 16 and 19 in Fayetteville, runs cheap express trips. (☎800-346-7238; www.usaraft.com. New River: Su-F $49, Sa $59. Gauley River: upper portion $69-79, lower portion $58-68.)

Though the renowned rapids draw the most tourists, the park's numerous trails provide hikers with an appreciation for the river and its coal industry. The most rewarding trails are the **Kaymoor Trail** (2 mi.) and the **Thurmond Minden Trail** (6½ mi., only 3 mi. round-trip to main overlook). Kaymoor starts at the bridge on Fayette Station Rd. and runs past the abandoned coke ovens of Kaymoor, a coal mining community that shut down in 1962. From Rte. 19 S Exit Main St., turn left, and take the overpass above Rte. 19, then make a left on Minden Rd., which is across from the Speedway Gas Station, turn right at the "Old Minden Store Rd." sign and, of the possible dirt paths, take the one closed off from vehicles with a small gate. Thurmond Minden, fairly flat with a 3.5% grade, has vistas of the New River, Dunloup Creek, and the historic community of Thurmond, but is unclearly marked in some areas.

Horseback riding trips are another way to explore the gorge. **New River Trail Rides** leads 2hr. rides, sunset trips, and overnight adventures year-round from their stables off Wonderland Rd., adjacent to the ACE campgrounds. (☎888-742-3982 or 465-4819; www.ridewva.com. Rides start at $39 for 2½hr. and include a Sunset Ride, Scenic Overlook Ride (departures 9:30am, 1, 3:30pm, and sunset), and a Waterfall Excursion Ride, the "Guide's Favorite" (8:30am departure, 3½hr., $59). Hayrides 1-1½hr.; $15, kids under 6 free; min. of 6 people.) All levels of experience can take advantage of the Gorge's spectacular rock climbing with **New River Mountain Guides** (☎574-3872 or 800-732-5462), at Wiseman and Court St. in downtown Fayetteville. For a vertical challenge, climb the **Endless Wall,** which runs southeast along the New River and offers great river views from a height of 1000 ft. The wall is accessible from a trail off the parking lot at Canyon Rim Visitors Center (see **Practical Information,** p. 358). **New River Bike &**

Touring Company, 103 Keller Ave. (☎866-301-2453 or 574-2453; www.newriver-bike.com) in the heart of downtown Fayetteville, offers tours (full day $95 includes complimentary lunch, half-day $65) and bike rentals (half-day $25, full day $35). For a different perspective, the new **Jetboat Rides**, located at Hawks Nest State Park off Rte. 60, will whisk you downstream. (☎469-2525 or 800-225-5982; www.newriverjetboats.com. Trips last ½hr. Adults $16, 60+ $14, kids ages 5-16 $6, under 5 free.)

THE SOUTH

The American consciousness has become much more homogeneous since the 1860s, when regional strife ignited the bloodiest conflict in the nation's history. Yet marked differences persist between North and South, as much in memory as in practice: what's known as "the Civil War" up North is here still sometimes referred to as "The War Between the States." And outside the area's commercial capitals—Atlanta, Nashville, Charlotte, and New Orleans—Southerners continue to live slower-paced and friendlier lives than their northern cousins.

Perhaps the greatest unifying characteristic of the South is its legacy of extreme racial division: slavery continues to leave its mark on Southern history, and the Civil Rights movement of the 1950s and 1960s remains too recent to be comfortably relegated to textbooks. At the same time, racial tensions and interactions have inspired many strands of American culture rooted in the South, from great literature to nearly *all* American music: gospel, blues, jazz, country, R&B, and rock 'n' roll. The south's cultural pedigree belies its generally poor economic status; its architecture, cuisine, and language all borrow from Native American, English, African, French, and Spanish influences. Landscapes are equally varied—nature blessed the region with mountains, marshlands, sparkling beaches, and fertile soil.

HIGHLIGHTS OF THE SOUTH

FOOD. Some of the best Southern barbecue is at Dreamland in Mobile, AL (p. 451). New Orleans, LA (p. 458) has spicy and delicious Cajun cuisine. Southern "soul food" completes the spirit–Nita's Place, Savannah, GA (p. 440) will take you higher.

MUSIC. Make time for Tennessee–Nashville (p. 370) is the perfect place to get into country music, but if you're already a believer, you'll be heading to Graceland (p. 388).

CIVIL RIGHTS MEMORIALS. The Martin Luther King Center in Atlanta, GA (p. 423) and the Birmingham Civil Rights Institute, AL (p. 449) won't fail to move you.

OLD SOUTH. Charm and elegance. Nowhere is the antebellum way of life so well-kept as in stately Charleston, SC (p. 413) or Savannah, GA (p. 440).

KENTUCKY

Legendary for the duels, feuds, and stubborn spirit of its earlier inhabitants (such as the infamous Daniel Boone), Kentucky invites travelers to kick back, take a shot of local bourbon, and relax amid rolling hills and bluegrass. The state also boasts an extensive network of caves, including the longest known cave in the world. Today, the spirit of Kentucky can be boiled down into one pastime: going fast. The state is home to the signature American sports car, the Corvette, and to the world's premier horse race, the Kentucky Derby. Louisville tends to ignore its vibrant cultural scene and active nightlife at Derby time, and Lexington devotes much of its most beautiful farmland to breeding champion racehorses.

PRACTICAL INFORMATION

Capital: Frankfort.

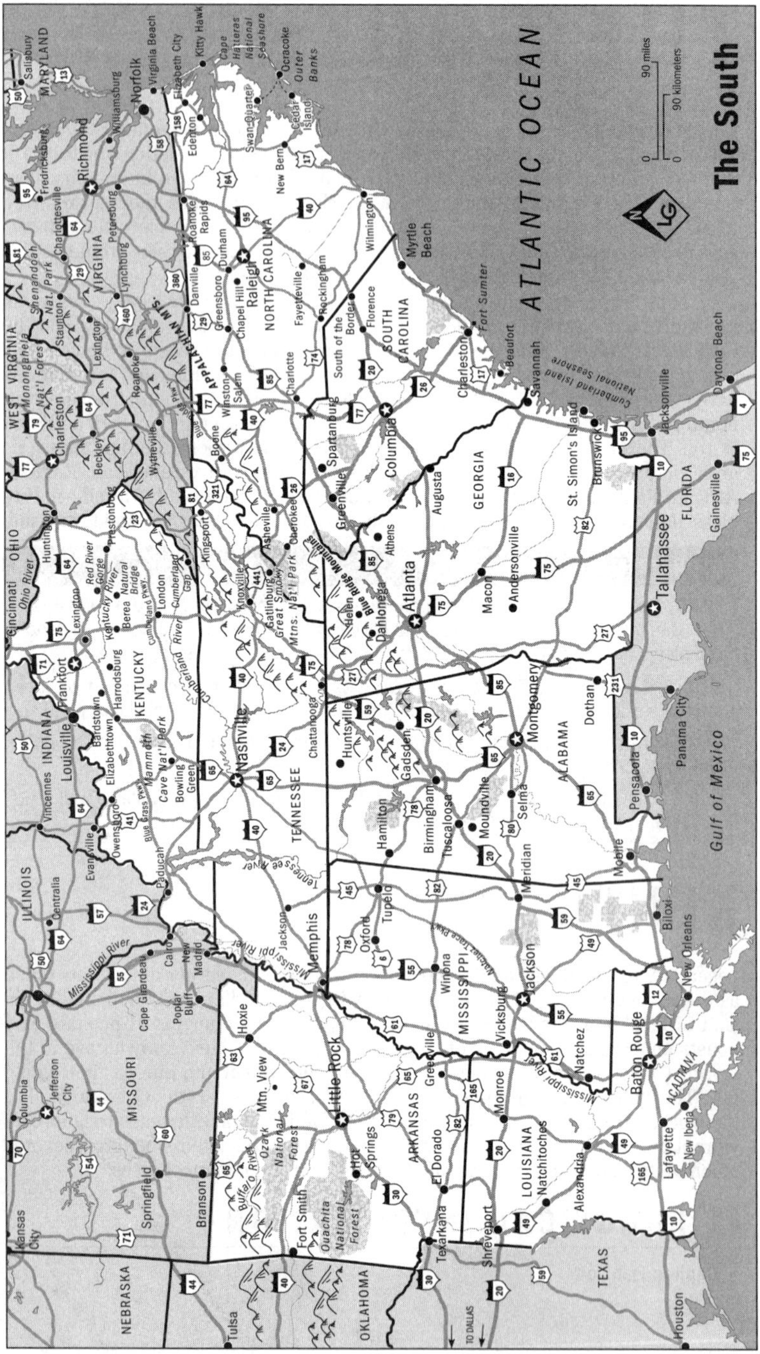
The South
ATLANTIC OCEAN
Gulf of Mexico
0 90 miles
0 90 kilometers
KENTUCKY
TENNESSEE
NORTH CAROLINA
SOUTH CAROLINA
GEORGIA
FLORIDA
ALABAMA
MISSISSIPPI
LOUISIANA
ARKANSAS
VIRGINIA
WEST VIRGINIA
MARYLAND
OHIO
INDIANA
ILLINOIS
MISSOURI
OKLAHOMA
TEXAS
NEBRASKA
APPALACHIAN MTS.
Blue Ridge Mountains
Great Smoky Mtns. Nat'l Park
Mammoth Cave Nat'l Park
Shenandoah Nat. Park
Ohio River
Mississippi River
Tennessee River
Cumberland River
Kentucky River
Louisville
Frankfort
Lexington
Nashville
Memphis
Atlanta
Richmond
Norfolk
Raleigh
Columbia
Charleston
Savannah
Tallahassee
Montgomery
Jackson
Little Rock
Baton Rouge
New Orleans
Birmingham
Chattanooga
Knoxville
Bowling Green
Paducah
Owensboro
Cincinnati
Huntington
Cumberland Gap
Red River Gorge
Natural Bridge
Berea
Bardstown
Elizabethtown
Harrodsburg
London
Cumberland Pkwy.
Blue Grass Pkwy.
Daytona Beach
Jacksonville
Pensacola
Mobile
Biloxi
Houston
Tulsa
Kansas City
Springfield
Branson
Hot Springs
Shreveport
Myrtle Beach
Fort Sumter
TO DALLAS

Visitor Info: Kentucky Dept. of Travel, Capital Plaza Tower, 500 Mero St., Suite 2200, Frankfort 40601 (☎502-564-4930 or 800-225-8747; www.kentuckytourism.com). **Kentucky State Parks,** Capital Plaza Tower, 500 Mero St., Suite 1100, Frankfort 40601 (☎800-255-7275; www.kystateparks.com).

Postal Abbreviation: KY. **Sales Tax:** 6%.

LOUISVILLE ☎502

Louisville (pronounced "Lua-Vul" by locals) is caught between two pasts. One left a legacy of smokestacks, stockyards, and crumbling structures; the other shines with beautiful Victorian neighborhoods, ornate buildings, and the elegant, twin-spired Churchill Downs. Visitors can spend lazy afternoons browsing through used book stores or hunting for bargains at independent boutiques; by night, bars and clubs heat up around the city. Louisville's premier attraction, however, remains the Kentucky Derby. The nation's most prestigious horse race, this extravagant event will pack the city with visitors on May 1, 2004.

ORIENTATION & PRACTICAL INFORMATION. Interstates through the city include **I-65** (north-south expressway), **I-71,** and **I-64.** The easily accessible **Watterson Expressway (I-264)** rings the city, while the **Gene Snyder Freeway (I-265)** circles farther out. In central downtown, **Main Street** and **Broadway** run east-west, and **Preston Highway** and **19th Street** run north-south. The **West End,** beyond 20th St., is a rough area. The **Louisville International Airport** (☎367-4636; www.louintlairport.com) is 15min. south of downtown on I-65; take bus #2 into the city. A taxi downtown is $15.40. **Greyhound,** 720 W. Muhammad Ali Blvd. (☎561-2801; open 24hr.), between 7th and 8th St., runs to: Chicago (6hr., 7 per day, $39); Cincinnati (2hr., 11 per day, $19.50); Indianapolis (1¾hr., 8 per day, $17). **Transit Authority River City's (TARC)** extensive bus system serves most of the metro area. (☎585-1234; www.ridetarc.org. Schedules vary by route; buses run as early as 4:30am until as late as 11:30pm. $0.75, M-F 6:30-8:30am and 3:30-5:30pm $1. Transfers free.) Two free trolley routes service Main St./Market St. (M-F 6:45am-6:30pm; Sa 10am-6pm) and 4th St. (M-F 7am-11pm, Sa 9:30am-10pm) downtown. **Taxi: Yellow Cab,** ☎636-5511. **Bike rental: Highland Cycle,** 1737 Bardstown Rd. (☎458-7832. Open M-F 9am-5:30pm, Sa 9am-4:30pm. Bikes from $5 for 1hr., $15 for 24hr.) **Visitor Info: Louisville Visitor Information Center,** 3rd and Market St., in the Kentucky International Convention Center. (☎584-3732; www.gotolouisville.com. Open M-F 9am-5pm, Sa 9am-4pm, Su noon-4pm.) **Internet Access: Louisville Free Public Library,** 301 York St. (☎574-1611), dow town. Open M-Th 9am-9pm, F-Sa 9am-5pm, Su 1-5pm. **Hotlines: Rape H** 7273. **Crisis Center,** ☎589-4313. Both operate 24hr. **Gay/L** Operates daily 6-10pm. **Post Office:** 835 S. 7th **Postal Code:** 40203. **Area Code:** 502.

HITCHIN' POSTS. Lodging in downto Budget motels are on **I-65** near the airport ana. **Newburg Road,** 6 mi. south, is also a bud make reservations 6 to 12 months in advan around January, the Visitors Center helps tra

Travelodge ❷, 3315 Bardstown Rd., near U strip, has spacious, comfy rooms at good rat parking, free local calls, continental breakfast, on premises. Singles $45; doubles $51. Winter **Rocking Horse Manor ❹,** 1022 S. 3rd St., combine with the comforts of a B&B—including feather

NO WORK, ALL PLAY

HORSE PLAY

Each year, the Kentucky Derby Festival kicks off with 64 tons of fireworks at **Thunder Over Louisville,** the largest fireworks show in North America, and continues for 3 weeks with balloon and steamboat races, concerts, and a parade. All of this is a mere prelude to the climactic 80,000 mint juleps consumed on the first Saturday in May at the nation's most prestigious horse race, the **Kentucky Derby.** The rollicking, week-long extravaganza leading up to the big day corrals over 500,000 visitors. The 1¼ mi. race itself, held every year since 1875, pits North America's finest Thoroughbreds against each during "the most exciting two minutes in sports." When the horses leave the gate, the stands are mesmerized; after all, $20 million ride on each Derby Day, a figure that only includes betting at the track--a total of over $138 million was placed on the Derby Day races in 2003.

A 1- to 10-year wait stands
...tween you and a ticket for the
... for the Roses" (from $65);
... have to send a written
... o Churchill Downs to be
... a lottery. Never fear,
...erby morning, gen-
...ckets are sold for
...y spots in the
...areas ($40).
... but these
...ry good
...any of
...see

and beverages, and a full gourmet breakfast. (☎583-0408; www.rockinghorse-bb.com. Cable TV, private baths, whirlpool tubs. No children. German spoken. Rooms from $79.) **Louisville Metro KOA ❶,** 900 Marriot Dr., across the river in Indiana, has campsites convenient to downtown. (☎812-282-4474. Sites for 2 $24; with hookup $29. $4 per extra person, under 18 $2.50. Cabins for 2 $39.)

OATS & HAY. Louisville's food is varied, but good budget fare can be hard to find in the heart of downtown. **Bardstown Road** is lined with cafes, budget eateries, and local and global cuisine, while **Frankfort Road** is rapidly catching up to Bardstown with restaurants and chi-chi cafes of its own. Downtown, **Theater Square,** at Broadway and 4th St., has several restaurants that serve various lunch options.

At **Molly Malone's Irish Pub and Restaurant ❷,** 933 Baxter Ave., fantastic pub fare and salads ($7.50-9) are served up on a lovely patio. (☎473-1222. Burgers and sandwiches $6.50-8.50; entrees $8-14. Beer from $2.50. Open M-Th 11am-1:30am, F 11am-4am, Sa noon-4am, Su noon-2am.) Local vegetarians love **Zen Garden ❷,** 2240 Frankfort Ave., a small, quiet restaurant that prepares excellent vegetarian Asian dishes. (☎895-9114. Entrees $6.50-9.50. Open M-Th 11am-10pm, F-Sa 11am-11pm.) **Mark's Feed Store ❷,** 1514 Bardstown Rd., serves award-winning barbecue in a dining room decorated with checkered tablecloths and metal animal feed ads. (☎459-6275. Sandwiches $4-5, with a cup of burgoo (beef stew) $5.50; barbecue dinners under $8. M free dessert after 4pm; Tu kids eat free. Open Su-Th 11am-10pm, F-Sa 11am-11pm.)

NOT JUST A ONE-HORSE TOWN. The small record stores, independent cafes, boutiques, and antique shops on the **Highlands** strip can easily fill an afternoon with shopping or browsing. The strip runs along Baxter Ave. and Bardstown Rd. between Broadway and Trevilian Way. (Buses #17 and 23.) Nearby, the **American Printing House for the Blind,** 1839 Frankfort Ave., has a small but fascinating museum on the development of Braille and other lesser-known systems for aiding the blind. The facility is one of the leading production plants for materials the visually-impaired. (☎895-2405; www.aph.org. Open M-F 8:30am-4:30pm; guided tours of the plant M-Th 10am and 2pm. Both museum and tours free. Wheelchair-accessible.) The world's tallest baseball bat (120 ft.) leans against the **Louisville Slugger Factory and Museum,** 800 W. Main, operated by the Hillerich and Bradsby Co. Inside, visitors can wander through a museum about the history of the illustrious baseball bat, watch a video, and even go on a tour of the factory to learn how Sluggers are made. At the tour's end, visitors receive a free miniature bat. (☎588-7228; www.sluggermuseum.org. Open Dec.-Mar. M-Sa 9am-5pm; Apr.-Nov. M-Sa 9am-5pm, Su noon-5pm; last tours 4pm. $6, seniors 60+ $5, children 6-12 $3.50.)

HORSIN' AROUND. The free weekly arts and entertainment newspaper, *Leo*, is available at most downtown restaurants and at the Visitors Center. Broadway shows, comedy acts, and big-name music performances play in the lavish Spanish Baroque interior of **Louisville Palace,** 625 S. 4th Ave. (☎583-4555. Tickets $20-100.) On the **"First Friday"** of every month, over a dozen of Louisville's downtown galleries treat visitors to special openings and refreshments until 9pm. Trolleys provide free transportation between galleries from 5-9:30pm. The **Kentucky Shakespeare Festival,** at the amphitheater in Central Park in Old Louisville, runs during June and July. (☎583-8738; www.kyshakes.org. Performances 8pm. Free.)

Clubs cluster on Baxter Ave. near Broadway. **Phoenix Hill Tavern,** 644 Baxter Ave., cranks out blues and rock with live bands and DJs on three stages, including a deck and roof garden. (☎589-4957; www.phoenixhill.com. Beer from $3. W college night, beer from $0.75; Th ladies night; F Happy Hour 5-8pm. 21+. Cover $2-5. Open W-Th and Sa 8pm-4am, F 5pm-4am.) **@tmosphere,** 917 Baxter Ave., is one of the area's hottest bars. The lounge is open daily; the dance floor in the back is open (and packed) Thursday through Saturday. (☎458-5301; www.atmospherenightclub.com. Th ladies night. 21+. Cover Sa $5. Open daily 11am-4am.)

Downtown nightlife centers around clubs that combine multiple venues. Get four clubs for the price of one at **O'Malley's Corner**—and a karaoke bar to boot. If you don't dig the country-western or disco dance floors, just migrate to the hip-hop or Top 40 rooms. (133 W. Liberty St., entrance at the corner of Jefferson and 2nd. ☎589-3866; www.omalleyscorner.com. Th-F line dancing lessons 7-9pm; drink specials all night. F ladies night, ladies free before 11pm. 21+. Cover $3-10, includes all clubs. Open Th-Sa 7pm-3:30am.) For gay nightlife, make **The Connection,** 120 S. Floyd St. This huge club combines an amazing six venues under one roof. The different bars have different theme nights and varying hours, but at least one is open daily 5pm-4am. (☎585-5752. Cover includes all bars, free-$5. Drinks from $3.25. Happy hour daily 5-10pm. 21+. Dance Bar open F-Su 9pm-5am; showroom with drag shows F-Su 10pm-3am.)

a horse. General admission ticket-holders do participate in the spectacle surrounding the race and peek at the famous hats worn by ladies in the crowd.

Festival Information *(☎584-6383; www.kdf.com).* ***Derby Information*** *(☎636-4402; www.kentuckyderby.com).*

Even if you miss the Derby, be sure to visit **Churchill Downs.** No bets are necessary to admire the twin spires, the colonial columns, the gardens, and the sheer scale of the track. Races are held here from late April through July and in November. The **Kentucky Derby Museum** offers a short film on a 360° screen, a simulated horse race, tips on betting, a chance to see a thoroughbred, and free tours of the Downs every day.

Churchill Downs, *700 Central Ave. (☎636-4400), 3 mi. south of downtown.* ***Kentucky Derby Museum,*** *704 Central Ave. (☎637-1111; www.derbymuseum.org), at Gate One at Churchill Downs. Open Dec. to mid-Mar. M-Sa 9am-5pm, Su noon-5pm; mid-Mar. to Nov. M-Sa 7am-5pm with exhibits opening 8am, Su noon-5pm. Churchill Downs tours every hr. on the half hr., last tour 4:15pm; no extra charge. Backside tours of stable areas mid-Mar. to Nov. M-Sa 7am-1pm, Su 12:30, 2pm; $5 extra. $8, seniors $7, ages 5-12 $3. Wheelchair-accessible.*

NEAR LOUISVILLE

BARDSTOWN. Kentucky's second-oldest city, 17 mi. east on Rte. 245 from I-65 Exit 112, will charm visitors with its historic downtown district. The real attractions, however, are the bourbon distilleries that lie outside of town. Bardstown, once home to 22 distilleries, is still proudly known as the "Bourbon Capital of the World." It all started in 1791, when Kentucky Baptist Reverend Elijah Craig left a fire unattended while heating oak boards to make a barrel for his aging whiskey. The boards were scorched, but Rev. Craig carried on, and bourbon was born in that first charred wood barrel. Today, 90% of the nation's bourbon hails from Kentucky, and 60% of that is distilled in Nelson and Bullitt Counties.

Jim Beam's American Outpost, 15 mi. west of Bardstown in Clermont, off Rte. 245, treats visitors to free samples of the world's best selling bourbon (M-Sa), as well as lemonade, coffee, and bourbon candies. Peek into a warehouse that holds aging bourbon, check out an authentic moonshine still and Jeremiah Beam's historic home, or watch a video about the company's 200-year history. You're also welcome to relax on the rocking chairs on the porch. (☎543-9877. Open M-Sa 9am-4:30pm, Su 1-4pm. Free.) Visitors can take a factory tour at **Maker's Mark Distillery,** 19 mi. southeast of Bardstown on Rte. 52 E in Loretto. Any day but Sunday, buy a bottle of bourbon in the gift shop, and you can hand-dip it yourself in the label's trademark red wax. (☎865-2099; www.makersmark.com. Tours every hr. M-Sa 10:30am-3:30pm, and Mar.-Dec. Su 1:30-3:30pm. Complimentary samples of bourbon chocolates. Free.) Bardstown also hosts the **Kentucky Bourbon Festival** every September, with several days of tours, events, and bourbon-drinking (☎800-638-4877; www.kybourbonfestival.com). **Visitor Info: Bardstown Visitors Information Center,** 107 E. Stephen Foster Ave. (☎348-4877 or 800-638-4877; www.visitbardstown.com. Open summer M-F 8am- 5pm, Sa-Su 10am-6pm; winter M-F 8am-5pm.)

BOWLING GREEN. Auto enthusiasts inevitably pay their respects to the home of the classic American sports car, the Corvette. The extensive **National Corvette Museum,** 350 Corvette Dr., off I-65 Exit 28, displays 'Vettes from the original chrome-and-steel '53 to futuristic concept cars; featured cars rotate constantly. (☎800-538-3883; www.corvettemuseum.com. Open daily 8am-5pm. Tours daily 10am and 2pm at no extra charge; subject to change. $8, seniors 55+ $6, ages 6-16 $4.50; families $20; AAA and military discounts. Wheelchair-accessible.) To see their production in action, visit the **General Motors Corvette Assembly Plant,** across Duncan Hines Blvd. from the museum. If you're lucky, you may even get a chance to test-start one of the mint condition products. (☎270-745-8287; www.bowlinggreenassemblyplant.com. Tours M-F 9am, 1pm; plant closed for the first 2 weeks of July and through Dec. 7+. Closed-toed shoes required. Free.)

MAMMOTH CAVE NATIONAL PARK ☎270

Hundreds of enormous caves and narrow passageways cut through **Mammoth Cave National Park,** 80 mi. south of Louisville in the cave region of central Kentucky. From I-65, turn off at Exit 48 (Park City) or Exit 53 (Cave City) and follow signs to the Visitors Center for tours and camping. With over 365 mi. of mapped caves, Mammoth Cave comprises the world's longest network of cavern corridors—over three times longer than any other known cave system. Tours depart from the Visitors Center. (☎758-2328 or 800-967-2283; www.nps.gov/maca/home.htm. Open daily 7:30am-7pm; low-season 8am-4:30pm. Tour times vary; call for schedules.) The **Historic Tour** gives visitors a feeling for the caves and a chance to see many of the historic and cultural sights that lie within their walls. (Approximately 2hr.; 2mi. $10, youth $5.) The **Frozen Niagara Tour** focuses on the cave's impressive geological features. (2hr.; ¾mi. $10, youth $5.) The **Discovery Tour** consumes a bit less time and money. The ½hr. self-guided tour leads straight to one of the largest rooms in the cave. (Visitors admitted 10am-2pm. $4, youth $2.50.)

Above ground, the 52,000-acre park also features numerous walking, biking, and horseback riding trails, as well as fishing and canoeing. Camping with bath houses, a camp store, and laundry is available at the pleasant **Headquarters Campground ❶**, near the Visitors Center. (☎758-2212. RVs allowed, but sites have no hookups. Open Mar.-Nov. Sites $16.) To escape the crowds, check out **Maple Springs Campground ❶**, across the river from the Visitors Center by ferry, or by a 35 mi. detour. (No hookups. Sites $25. Open Mar.-Nov.) Reservations are recommended for both campgrounds (☎800-967-2283; http://reservations.nps.gov). **Backcountry camping** permits can be obtained for free at the Visitors Center. For those who choose not to camp, charming rooms await at the **Mammoth Cave Hotel ❸**, next to the Visitors Center. (☎758-2225. Woodland Cottages with bath but no A/C or heat for 1 person $36, for 2 $45. Hotel Cottages with A/C, heat, and TV but no phone $52/59. Available lodgings vary with season. Hotel singles from $62; doubles from $68. AAA 10% off.) **Greyhound** travels to Cave City, just east of I-65 on Rte. 70.

LEXINGTON ☎859

Though the Kentucky Derby takes place in Louisville, Lexington is the state's real horse country. Green pastures roll away from the city, and the beautiful Keeneland Race Track hosts some of the country's most exciting races in April and October. Farms that have raised some of the most famous racehorses in the world surround the city in scenic "bluegrass country" for which eastern Kentucky is famous. Downtown, visitors will find a collection of graceful historic mansions, once home to Lexington's most famous and influential residents. The basketball powerhouse University of Kentucky's students help create an active nightlife.

TRANSPORTATION

Airport: Blue Grass Airport, 4000 Terminal Dr. (☎425-3114; www.bluegrassairport.com), off of Man O' War Blvd. about 6 mi. southwest of downtown. Ritzy downtown hotels run shuttles, but there is no public transportation. Taxi to downtown about $15.

Buses: Greyhound, 477 New Circle Rd. NW (☎299-0428). Open daily 7:30am-11pm. To: **Cincinnati** (1½hr., 7 per day, $20); **Knoxville** (4hr., 4 per day, $45); **Louisville** (2-6hr., 5 per day, $17.50).

Public Transit: LexTran (☎253-4636; www.lextran.com). Buses leave from the Transit Center, 220 E. Vine St., on a long block between Limestone and Rose St., 6am-12:30am. Serves the university and city outskirts. Most routes run 5am-midnight. $1, ages 5-18 $0.80, seniors and disabled $0.50; transfers free.

Taxi: Lexington Yellow Cab, ☎231-8294.

ORIENTATION & PRACTICAL INFORMATION

I-64 and **I-75** pass Lexington to the northeast. **New Circle Road (Route 4, U.S. 60 bypass, U.S. 421 bypass,** and **U.S. 25 bypass)** loops around the city, intersecting with many roads that connect the downtown district to the surrounding towns. **High, Vine,** and **Main Street,** running east-west, and **Limestone** and **Broadway Street,** running north-south, are the major routes through downtown. Beware of the curving one-way streets downtown and near the **University of Kentucky (UK)** to the south.

Visitor Info: Lexington Convention and Visitors Bureau, 301 E. Vine St. (☎233-7299 or 800-845-3959; www.visitlex.com), at Rose St. Open summer M-F 8:30am-5pm, Sa 10am-5pm, Su noon-5pm; low-season closed Su.

Hotlines: Crisis Intervention, ☎253-2737 or 800-928-8000. **Rape Crisis,** ☎253-2511 or 800-656-4673. Both 24hr.

Medical Services: Saint Joseph East Hospital, 150 N. Eagle Creek Dr. (☎967-5000). **Lexington Women's Diagnostic Center,** 701 Bob-o-link Dr. (☎277-8485).

Internet Access: Lexington Public Library, 140 E. Main St. (☎231-5500), at Limestone St. Open M-Th 9am-9pm, F-Sa 9am-5pm, Su 1-5pm.

Post Office: 210 E. High St. (☎254-6156). Open M-F 8am-5pm. **Postal Code:** 40507. **Area Code:** 859.

ACCOMMODATIONS

The cheapest places to stay are outside the city on New Circle Rd. or near I-75. The Visitors Bureau (see above) can help find lodging.

Microtel, 2240 Buena Vista Dr. (☎299-9600), off I-75 at Exit 110 (Winchester Rd./Rte.60). Take bus #7. Pleasant motel rooms with window seats, about 3½ mi. from downtown. A/C, data ports, and cable TV. Wheelchair-accessible rooms available. Singles Su-Th $40, F-Sa $47; doubles $45/52. ❷

Extended Stay America, 2750 Gribbin Dr. (☎266-4800 or 800-398-7829; www.extstay.com). From New Circle Rd., turn off at Exit 15 and take Richmond Rd. away from the city center; turn right onto Patchen Dr. and left onto Gribbin Dr. Spacious rooms include fully equipped kitchenettes, cable TV with HBO, data ports, and free local calls. Pool and on-site laundry facilities. Singles from $45; doubles from $50. ❷

Kentucky Horse Park Campground, 4089 Ironworks Pkwy. (☎259-4257 or 800-370-6416 ext. 257; www.kyhorsepark.com), 10 mi. north of downtown off I-75 at Exit 120. Well manicured campsites with laundry facilities, bath houses, modem, playground, basketball/volleyball/tennis courts, and swimming pool. Tent sites are on a rolling open field, while RV sites nicely mix shade and lawn. Apr.-Oct. tent sites $15; hookup $23, seniors $20. Nov.-Mar. $13/19/16.50. ❶

FOOD & NIGHTLIFE

Alfalfa Restaurant ❷, 557 S. Limestone St. near UK, treats customers to hearty international dishes and live jazz or folk. The menu includes delicious sandwiches on homemade bread ($3.50-6.75), filling salads ($5-8), and plenty of vegetarian and vegan options. "Starving Student" specials are $4 with a student ID. (☎253-0014; www.alfalfarestaurant.com. Live music Tu-Th 7-9pm, F-Sa 8-10pm. No cover. Open M 11am-2pm, Tu-Th 11am-2pm and 5:30-9pm, F 11am-2pm and 5:30-10pm, Sa 10am-2pm and 5:30-10pm, Su 10am-2pm.) **Atomic Cafe ❸,** 265 N. Limestone St., excites the taste buds with excellent Caribbean fare. Gourmands will love the coconut shrimp ($15) while on weekends toes tap to live reggae on an outdoor patio. (☎254-1969. Salads and sandwiches $4.50-7.50; beer from $2.50. Live music F-Sa 9:30pm; cover $3-5. Open Tu-Sa 4pm-1am; kitchen closes at 11pm.)

In general, those looking for a good time after dark hit the area around Main St. west of Limestone St. and the eastern fringes of UK. For specifc info, read the "Weekender" section of the Friday *Herald-Leader*. Cold beer and handtossed pizza are plentiful at **Pazzo's Pizza Pub,** 385 S. Limestone Rd., at Euclid St. Buy a pitcher on Wednesday night and get two free pints. (☎255-5125; www.pazzospizzapub.com. Outdoor patio. Beer from $2.25; 10-in. specialty pizzas $7-11. Open

M-Sa 11am-1am, Su noon-10pm; kitchen open Su-W until 10pm, Th-Sa until 11pm.) **The Bar,** 224 E. Main St., a popular disco cabaret/lounge complex, caters to gays and lesbians. (☎255-1551; www.thebarcomplex.com. Happy Hour M-Sa 4-7pm. DJs spin W-Sa 11pm-close. 21+. Cover F-Sa $5 after 8pm. Open M-Th 4pm-1am, F-Sa 4pm-3:30am.)

SIGHTS

HORSE ATTRACTIONS. Lexington **horse farms** are gorgeous places to visit; the Visitors Bureau can help arrange tours of open farms. **Kentucky Horse Park** is one of Lexington's main attractions, entertaining visitors with live horse shows, horse-drawn trolley tours of the grounds, and a film about man's relationship with horses. Admission includes access to two museums: the **International Museum of the Horse** traces the role of the horse in history, while the **American Saddlebred Museum** educates visitors about Kentucky's oldest native breed. You can also watch as employees feed, groom, and exercise the horses on this working farm. The last weekend in April, the horse park hosts the annual Rolex tournament qualifier for the US equestrian team. *(4089 Ironworks Pkwy. Off Ironworks Pike, Exit 120 from I-75. ☎233-4303 or 800-678-8813; www.kyhorsepark.com. Open mid-Mar. to Oct. daily 9am-5pm; Nov. to mid-Mar. W-Su 9am-5pm. Apr.-Oct. $12, ages 7-12 $6.50; Nov.-Mar. $9/7; live horse shows and 15min. horse-drawn tours included. 45min. horseback ride additional $14; ages 7 and up. Pony rides $4; ages 12 and under. Parking $2. Wheelchair-accessible.)*

The **Keeneland Race Track,** west of the city off U.S. 60, ranks among the country's most beautiful racing facilities. Every April, the final prep race for the Kentucky Derby is held here. Visit in April or October to catch a race at the track, or come watch the horses during their morning workouts and explore the impressive grounds during the rest of the year. A $4 cafeteria-style breakfast and the chance to chat with a jockey or horse owner may make the **Track Kitchen** the best breakfast deal in town. *(4201 Versailles Rd., across U.S. 60 from the airport. ☎254-3412 or 800-456-3412; www.keeneland.com. Races Oct. and Apr.; tickets $2.50. Workouts free and open to the public mid-Mar. to Nov. 6-10am. Breakfast daily 5:30-11am; closed first 2 weeks in Feb.)*

CITY ATTRACTIONS. A few blocks northeast of the town center, in the area surrounding **Gratz Park,** a small, peaceful neighborhood of gorgeous old houses stands as a throwback to a time when plantation owners escaped the suffocating heat of the fields in milder Lexington. Deep porches, stone foundations, and rose-covered trellises distinguish these estates, which line Market and N. Mill St. between 2nd and 3rd St. The Federal style **Hunt Morgan House** stands at the end of the park across from the Carnegie Literacy Center. Built in 1814 by hemp merchant John Wesley Hunt—the first millionaire west of the Alleghenies—the house was once home to many notable characters, including Nobel laureate Thomas Hunt Morgan and Confederate General John Hunt Morgan, the "Thunderbolt of the Confederacy." As legend has it, Gen. Hunt Morgan, while being pursued by Union troops, rode his horse up the front steps and into the house, leaned down to kiss his mother, and rode out the back door. A small museum devoted to Civil War artifacts and memorabilia now occupies two rooms on the second floor. In the week before Halloween, Gratz Park "ghost tours" begin at the Hunt Morgan House in the evenings, entertaining visitors with tales of the neighborhood's many other-worldly inhabitants. *(201 N. Mill St. At W. 2nd St. ☎233-3290; www.bluegrasstrust.org/hunt-morgan. Guided tours only, 15min. past the hr. Open Mar.-Nov. Tu-Sa 10am-4pm, Su 2-5pm. $5, students $3.)*

WHISKEY BUSINESS All bourbon is whiskey, but not all whiskey is bourbon. So what makes bourbon so special? It's all in the making, codified by the US government. For alcohol to be bourbon, it must fulfill these six requirements:

1. It must be aged in a new white oak barrel, flame-charred on the inside. (Scotch, on the other hand, must be aged in used barrels.)
2. It must age at least 2 years in that barrel.
3. It must be at least 51% corn.
4. It cannot be distilled over 160 proof (80% alcohol).
5. It cannot go into the barrel over 125 proof.
6. It can have no additives or preservatives.

TENNESSEE

In the east, the mountains of Tennessee stretch skyward at Great Smoky National Park, while the land in the west settles out into the wide Mississippi River. But the varied terrain of the Volunteer State has one unifying factor: music. From the twang of eastern bluegrass to the woes of Nashville country, from the roguish jazz and gut-wrenching blues of Memphis to the roots of rock 'n' roll at Graceland, music is the soul of the state. Others might argue that the heart of the state can be found in Jack Daniels Tennessee Whiskey, but the spirit is bottled back up and redeemed by Tennessee's Bible-producing business, the largest in the world.

PRACTICAL INFORMATION

Capital: Nashville.

Visitor Info: Tennessee Department of Tourist Development, 320 6th Ave. N., Nashville 37243 (☎615-741-2159 or 800-462-8366; www.tnvacation.com). Open M-F 8am-4:30pm. **Tennessee State Parks Information,** 401 Church St., Nashville, 37243 (☎800-421-6683; www.tnstateparks.com). Open M-F 8am-4:30pm.

Postal Abbreviation: TN. **Sales Tax:** 9.25%.

NASHVILLE ☎615

Nashville bears a number of unusual nicknames. Known as "the Athens of the South," the city is home to an array of Greek architecture—including a full-scale replica of the Parthenon in Centennial Park. This area has also been called the "buckle of the bible belt," a reference to the Southern Baptists who make their home here. But Nashville's most popular moniker by far is "Music City USA," and for good reason: this town has long been known as the banjo-pickin', foot-stompin' capital of country music. Be prepared to have a rollicking good time in a city [illegible] music and beer are available in abundance 24 hours a day.

[illegible]ATION

[illegible]n (☎275-2098; www.flynashville.com.), 8 mi. south of downtown. [illegible]ntown, take I-40E and turn off at Exit 216A. **Gray Line Tours** runs an [illegible]275-1180) to major downtown hotels daily 6am-11pm. $11, round-[illegible] downtown $20.

Buses: Greyhound, 200 8th Ave. S. (☎255-3556), at Demonbreun St. downtown. Borders on a rough neighborhood, but the station is well-lit. Station open 24hr. To: **Birmingham** (3½hr., 8 per day, $27.50); **Chattanooga** (2½hr., 5 per day, $18.50); **Knoxville** (3½hr., 7 per day, $24); **Memphis** (4hr., 7 per day, $29).

Public Transit: Metropolitan Transit Authority (MTA) (☎862-5950; www.nashvillemta.org). Buses operate on limited routes. Times vary route to route, but none run M-F before 5:30am or after 11:15pm; Sa-Su less frequent service. $1.45, express fare $1.75, downtown service $0.25, transfers $0.10; children 4 and under free. Weekly pass $14.70.

Taxi: Nashville Cab, ☎242-7070. **Music City Taxi,** ☎262-0451.

ORIENTATION & PRACTICAL INFORMATION

Nashville's streets are fickle, often interrupted by curving parkways and one-way streets. Names change without warning. **Broadway,** the main east-west thoroughfare, runs through downtown, then veers left after passing over I-40; **West End Avenue** continues straight ahead. Broadway joins **21st Avenue** after a few blocks, passing through **Vanderbilt University.** In the downtown area, numbered avenues run north-south, parallel to the Cumberland River. The curve of **James Robertson Parkway** encloses the north end, becoming **Main Street** on the other side of the river (later **Gallatin Pike**) and turning into **8th Avenue** in the center of downtown. *The area south of Broadway between 2nd and 7th Ave. can be unsafe at night.*

Visitor Info: Nashville Visitor Information Center, 501 Broadway (☎259-4747; www.nashvillecvb.com), in the Gaylord Entertainment Center, off I-65 at Exit 84, James Robertson Pkwy. Open M-Sa 8:30am-5:30pm, Su 10am-5pm. Discounted attraction ticket packages and info on upcoming events.

Hotlines: Crisis Line, ☎244-7444. **Rape Hotline,** ☎256-8526. Both 24hr. **Gay and Lesbian Switchboard,** ☎297-0008; www.rainbowcommunitycenter.org. Operates nightly 6-9pm.

Internet Access: Nashville Public Library, 615 Church St. (☎862-5800), between 6th and 7th Ave. Open M-Th 9am-8pm, F 9am-6pm, Sa 9am-5pm, Su 2-5pm.

Post Office: 901 Broadway (☎255-3613), in the same building as the Frist Center for the Visual Arts. Open M-F 8:30am-5pm. **Postal Code:** 37202. **Area Code:** 615.

ACCOMMODATIONS

Finding a room in downtown Nashville can be expensive, especially in summer. To help defray the cost, the Visitors Center offers several deals on motel rooms. Additionally, budget motels concentrate around **West Trinity Lane** and **Brick Church Pike,** off I-65 at Exits 87A and 87B. Travelers can also find dirt-cheap hotels around **Dickerson Road** and **Murfreesboro,** but the neighborhood is somewhat seedy. Closer to downtown, several motels huddle on **Interstate Drive** over the Woodland St. Bridge.

Cat's Pajamas Bed & Breakfast, 818 Woodland St. (☎650-4553; www.bbonline.com/tn/catspajamas), across the river, just over 1 mi. from downtown. With funky decor and a full breakfast featuring organic foods, this hip little B&B provides a welcome break from stuffy inns and anonymous hotel rooms. Creative, socially conscious hosts are very helpful in orienting visitors. Small fridge upstairs, separate guest entrance, Internet hook-up available. Check-in 3-6pm or by other arrangement. Rooms with shared bath $90, with private bath $110. ❹

Cumberland Inn, 150 W. Trinity Ln. (☎226-1600 or 800-704-1028). Coming from downtown on I-65N, take Exit 87A and turn right at the bottom of the ramp. Though the rooms are a bit dingy, these rates are among Nashville's lowest. A/C, HBO, guest washing machine and dryer, free coffee; some rooms with fridge. Singles $30; doubles $35. AAA, AARP 10% off. ❶

Nashville Holiday Travel Park, 2572 Music Valley Dr. (☎889-4225 or 800-547-4480), near Opryland USA, has a wooded area for tenting and crowded RV sites. Bath houses, laundry facilities, pool, Internet access, mini-golf, playground, basketball court, and game room. Sites for 2 $23; water and electricity $41.50; full hookup $45. Each additional person over 11 $4. ❶

FOOD

In Nashville, music influences even the local delicacies. **Goo-Goo Clusters** (peanuts, pecans, chocolate, caramel, and marshmallow), sold in specialty shops throughout the city, bear the initials of the Grand Ole Opry. Nashville's other finger-lickin' traditions, barbecue or fried chicken followed by pecan pie, are no less sinful. Restaurants catering to collegiate tastes and budgets cram **21st Avenue, West End Avenue,** and **Elliston Place,** near Vanderbilt.

Loveless Cafe, 8400 Rte. 100 (☎646-9700; www.lovelesscafe.com). Follow West End Ave. out of the downtown area; it will become Harding Pike. Rte. 100 will split off after the Belle Meade Plantation. A Nashville tradition. Feast on a plate of country ham ($10) or fried chicken ($11), served with nationally renowned made-from-scratch biscuits and homemade preserves. Brunch on Sa and Su is all-you-can-eat (9am-1pm; $9, children under 10 $5). Reservations recommended. Open Su-Th 8am-8pm, F-Sa 8am-9pm. ❸

SATCO (San Antonio Taco Company), 416 21st Ave. S. (☎327-4322). Great Mexican food and great deals. This student hangout sells fajitas for $1.25-1.50 and tacos for $1. Taco salad $5. Single beers from $2; bucket of 6 from $10. Open summer Su-W 11am-midnight, Th-Sa 11am-1am; winter Su-W 11am-11pm, Th-Sa 11am-midnight. ❶

Pancake Pantry, 1796 21st Ave. (☎974-8991), serves up big stacks of steaming, delicious pancakes in all different varieties, from traditional buttermilk to orange-walnut or apricot-lemon (most $5.45). Other breakfast and lunch items also available. Open M-F 6am-3pm, Sa-Su 6am-4pm. ❶

Jack's Bar-B-Que, 416 Broadway (☎254-5715; www.jacksbarbque.com), is a bit of a legend—both for the flashing neon-winged pigs above the door and the succulent, tender pork. Sandwiches $3-5. Plates $7-11. Open summer M-W 10:30am-8pm, Th 10:30am-9pm, F-Sa 10:30am-10pm, Su noon-6pm; winter Th 10:30am-8pm, F-Sa 10:30am-10pm. Another location at 334 W. Trinity Ln., ☎228-9888. ❷

SIGHTS

GRAND OLE COUNTRY LOVIN'. Country music drives this city. The first stop of any traveler—country fan or not—should be the state-of-the-art **Country Music Hall of Fame,** where visitors can view live performances or design their own CDs of country hits. Travelers should leave plenty of time to wander through the well-crafted displays on the history of country, listen to samples from greats like Johnny Cash and Patsy Cline, and watch videos of performances and interviews with modern artists. An extra $10 will upgrade tickets to include a guided tour of RCA's **Studio B,** where over 1000 American Top 10 hits have been recorded. *(222 5th Ave. S. ☎416-2001; www.countrymusichalloffame.com. Open daily 10am-6pm. $16, seniors $14, college students $10, ages 6-17 $8, under 6 free.)* After sampling the history of country music, two-step over to the **Ryman Auditorium,** the site of the legendary **Grand Ole Opry** radio show for more than 30 years. The Opry eventually had to

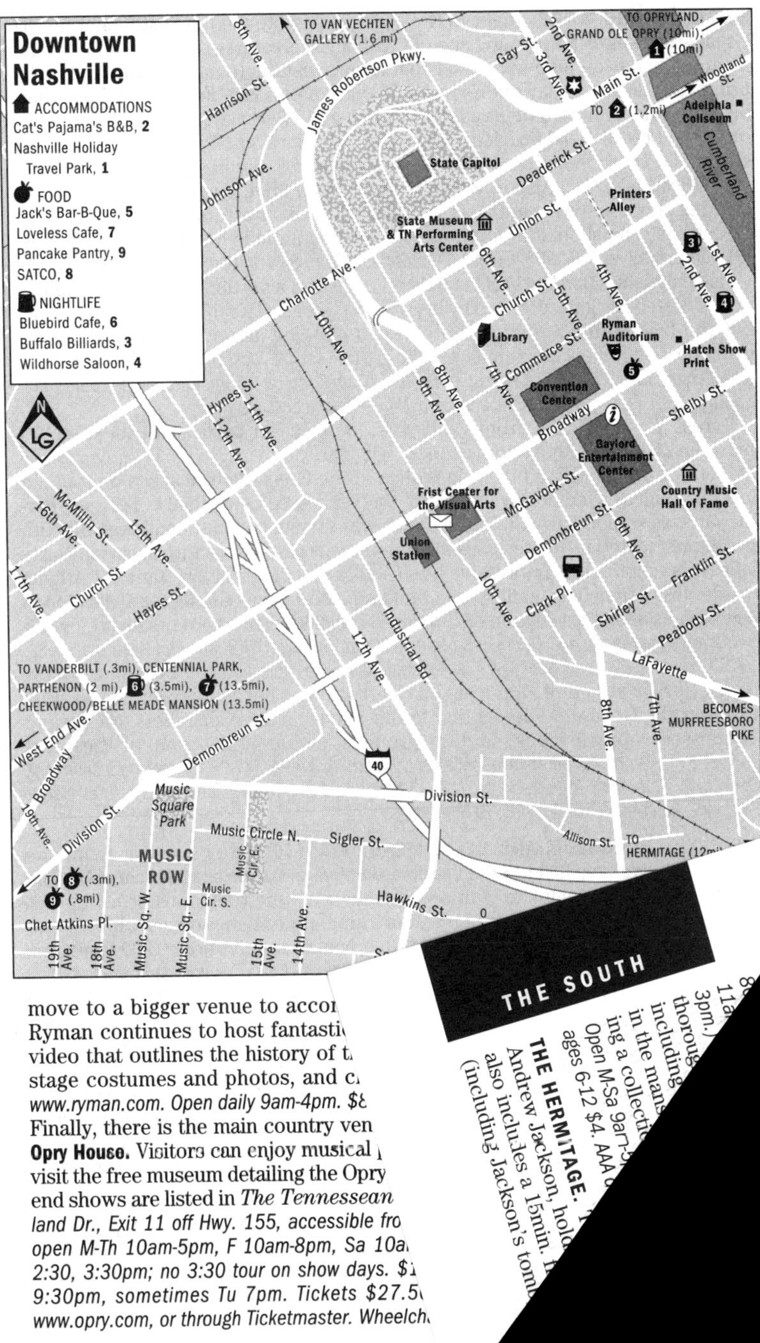

move to a bigger venue to acco
Ryman continues to host fantasti
video that outlines the history of t
stage costumes and photos, and c
www.ryman.com. Open daily 9am-4pm. $8
Finally, there is the main country ven
Opry House. Visitors can enjoy musical
visit the free museum detailing the Opry
end shows are listed in *The Tennessean*
land Dr., Exit 11 off Hwy. 155, accessible fro
open M-Th 10am-5pm, F 10am-8pm, Sa 10a
2:30, 3:30pm; no 3:30 tour on show days. $1
9:30pm, sometimes Tu 7pm. Tickets $27.5
www.opry.com, or through Ticketmaster. Wheelch

MUSEUMS AND MORE. Right in the heart of downtown, the **Frist Center for the Visual Arts** inspires both young and old with an interesting array of rotating exhibits and a hands-on learning center that allows visitors to paint, draw, and make prints. On the last Friday of every month, the center hosts "Frist Friday," a gathering with music, hors d'oeurves, and drinks. *(919 Broadway. ☎244-3340; www.fristcenter.org. Open M-W and F-Sa 10am-5:30pm, Th 10am-8pm, Su 1-5pm. $6.50, students and seniors 65+ $4.50, 18 and under free. Wheelchair-accessible. Frist Fridays 5:30-9pm, galleries open 6-8pm; free; 21+.)* Also downtown, **Hatch Show Print,** one of the oldest poster printing shops in the country, is well-known for its posters of Grand Old Opry celebrities. The shop still operates today, using antique letterpress techniques. *(316 Broadway. ☎256-2805. Open M-F 9:30am-5:30pm, Sa 10:30am-5:30pm. Free.)*

Fisk University's Carl Van Vechten Gallery consists of a portion of the private collection of Alfred Steiglitz, donated by his widow Georgia O'Keeffe. The Gallery is tiny, but the fascinating Steiglitz photographs hanging among works by Picasso, Cezanne, and Renoir are a must-see for art-lovers. *(At Jackson St. and D.B. Todd Blvd., off Jefferson St. ☎329-8720. Open summer Tu-F 10am-5pm, Sa 1-5pm; winter Tu-F 10am-5pm, Sa-Su 1-5pm. Free, but donations accepted. Wheelchair-accessible.)*

Across West End Ave. from Vanderbilt, the pleasant **Centennial Park** stretches between 25th and 28th Ave. A visit here will clarify why Nashville is known as the "Athens of the South": a full-scale replica of the Greek **Parthenon** sits on top of a low hill. Built as a temporary exhibit for the Tennessee Centennial in 1897, the Parthenon was so popular with locals that it was maintained and finally rebuilt with permanent materials in the 1920s. As out-of-place as the structure seems in Nashville, it is nonetheless impressive—especially the 42-ft. golden statue of Athena inside. In its first floor gallery, the building also houses the **Cowan Collection of American Paintings,** a selection of 19th- and early 20th-century American art. *(☎862-8431; www.parthenon.org. Open Tu-Sa 9am-4:30pm, Su 12:30-4:30pm; Oct.-Mar. closed Su. $3.50, seniors 62+ and ages 4-17 $2. Wheelchair-accessible.)* At the **Capitol,** a stately Greek Revival structure atop a hill on Charlotte Ave. north of downtown, visitors can tour the Governor's Reception Room, the legislative chambers, the former Tennessee Supreme Court, and the grounds, including the tomb of President James K. Polk. *(On Charlotte Ave. between 6th and 7th Ave. ☎741-0830; www.tnmuseum.org. Open daily 8am-4pm. Tours every hr. M-F 9-11am and 1-3pm; self-guided tours also available. Free. Wheelchair-accessible. Photo ID required.)*

CHEEKWOOD MUSEUM AND BELLE MEADE MANSION. For a break from the bustle of downtown, head to the **Cheekwood Botanical Garden and Museum of Art.** The well-kept gardens, complete with a woodland sculpture trail, are a peaceful spot for a stroll. The museum features American and contemporary sculpture and painting and a collection of English and American decorative arts. *(1200 Forrest Park Dr., off of Page Rd., between Rte. 100 and Belle Meade Blvd 8 mi. southwest of town. ☎356-000; www.cheekwood.org. Audio tours available for museum. Open Tu-Sa 9:30am-4:30pm, Su m-4:30pm. $10, students and ages 6-17 $5; maximum family charge $25; half price after* The nearby **Belle Meade Plantation** was once one of the nation's most famed hbred nurseries. The lavish 1853 mansion has hosted seven US presidents, the 380 lb. William Howard Taft, who allegedly spent some time lodged ion's bathtub. Today, visitors can explore the house and grounds, includ- n of antique carriages. *(5025 Harding Rd. ☎356-0501 or 800-270-3991. pm, Su 11am-5pm. 2 guided tours per hr.; last tour 4pm. $10, seniors $8.50, iscount. Partially wheelchair-accessible.)*

he **Hermitage,** the graceful manor of seventh US president s an impressive array of the original furnishings. Admission lm about Jackson's life, access to the house and grounds), and a visit to the nearby **Tulip Grove Mansion** and the

Hermitage Church. *(4580 Rachel's Ln. Exit 221A off I-40, continue 4 mi. on Old Hickory Blvd; entrance is on the right. ☎ 889-2941; www.thehermitage.com. Open daily 9am-5pm. Tours of mansion run regularly, guided garden tours at 10am - 2pm, guided farm tours at 11am - 3pm; self-guided tours also available; all included in admission. $12, students 13-18 and seniors 62+ $11, ages 6-12 $5; families $34. AAA discount. Partially wheelchair-accessible.)*

ENTERTAINMENT

The hordes of visitors that converge upon Nashville have turned the **Grand Ole Opry** (see above) into a grand American institution. However, there are other great forms of entertainment in the capital city as well. The **Tennessee Performing Arts Center,** 505 Deaderick St. at 6th Ave. N., hosts the Nashville Symphony, opera, ballet, Broadway shows, and other theater productions. (☎255-2787; www.tpac.org. Tickets $15-75. Wheelchair-accessible.) Listings for the area's music and events fill the free *Nashville Scene* and *Rage*, available at most area establishments. The Visitors Center hands out a list of gay and lesbian establishments.

Two major-league franchises dominate the Nashville sports scene. The National Football League's **Tennessee Titans** play at **Adelphia Coliseum,** 460 Great Circle Rd., across the river from downtown. (☎565-4200. Tickets $12-52.) The **Nashville Predators,** a new National Hockey League team, face-off at the **Gaylord Entertainment Center,** 501 Broadway. (☎770-2040; tickets available through Ticketmaster. $10-85.)

NIGHTLIFE

Nightlife downtown centers on Broadway and 2nd Ave., where bars and tourist attractions draw large crowds. Parking can sometimes be difficult on summer evenings, especially when something is going on at the Gaylord Entertainment Center. Near Vanderbilt, **Elliston Place** hops with college-oriented music venues.

Bluebird Cafe, 4104 Hillsboro Rd. (☎383-1461; www.bluebirdcafe.com), in the strip mall in Green Hills. Coming from 21st Ave., it will be on your left after you cross Richard Jones Rd. This famous bird sings original country and acoustic every night. Country stars Garth Brooks and Kathy Mattea started their careers here. $7 per person food/drink min. if sitting at a table. Cover after 9:30pm usually $4-10; no cover Su. Open M-Sa 5:30pm, Su 6pm until the singing stops (usually between 11pm and 1am). Early show 6:30pm. Reservations recommended Tu-Sa.

Wildhorse Saloon, 120 2nd Ave. N. (☎902-8211; www.wildhorsesaloon.com). Bring your cowboy boots and hat, and two-step through the night in this huge country dance hall. Dance lessons M-F 7-9pm, Sa-Su 2-9pm. Live music Tu-Sa. Cover after 7pm $4-6. Open Su-Th 11am-1am, F-Sa 11am-3am.

Buffalo Billiards, 154 2nd Ave. N. (☎313-7665; buffalobilliards.com). A popular bar with pool tables and a fun, relaxed atmosphere. Th features $2 drafts all night; Happy Hour M-F 4-8pm; Su free pool and $2.50 drafts. Beer from $3. 21+. Open M-W 4pm-2am, Th-F 4pm-3am, Sa-Su 1pm-3am. Upstairs, **Havana Lounge** is a popular hip-hop club; the dance floor is often packed. 21+. Cover $5. Open W-Sa.

KNOXVILLE ☎865

Knoxville was settled after the Revolutionary War and named for Washington's Secretary of War, Henry Knox. This was once the capital of the "Territory South of the River Ohio"—the land that would eventually become Tennessee. In 1982, the city hosted the World's Fair, attracting some 10 million visitors, and is still home to the 26,000 students of the University of Tennessee (UT). Shaded by the stunning Great

Smoky Mountains and hemmed in by vast lakes created by the Tennessee Valley Authority, Knoxville is a friendly, easily navigated city with great restaurants, unusual sights, and a surprisingly happening nightlife scene.

PRACTICAL INFORMATION. Downtown stretches north from the **Tennessee River,** bordered by **Henley Street** and **World's Fair Park** to the west. The **McGhee Tyson Airport** (☎342-3000; www.tys.org) lies near the intersection of U.S. 140 and Hwy. 129, about 10 mi. south of downtown. **Greyhound,** 100 E. Magnolia Ave. (☎522-5144; open 24hr.), at Central St., sends buses to: Chattanooga (2hr., 5 per day, $14.50); Lexington (4hr., 6 per day, $42); Nashville (3-3½hr., 7 per day, $24). *Avoid this area at night.* Public transit **KAT** buses cover the city. (☎637-3000; www.kat-bus.com. M-F 6:15am-6:15pm, Sa-Su reduced service. 4 night routes run M-F 8:45pm-midnight, Sa 6:45pm-midnight, Su 10:15am-6:30pm; fare includes shuttle service to destinations far from drop-off point if you call a day ahead. $1, ages 4 and under free; transfers $0.20.) Four free **trolley** lines run throughout the city: Blue runs to the Coliseum, Blount Mansion, and the Women's Basketball Hall of Fame; Orange heads downtown and westward to World's Fair Park and UT; Green travels between the Fort Sanders neighborhood and UT; the Late Line serves UT, the Strip, Market Square, and the Old City. (Blue Line: M-F 5:50am-6:20pm; Orange Line: M-F 7am-6:15pm; Green Line: M-F 7am-6pm; Late Line: F-Sa 8pm-3:30am.)

At the **Gateway Regional Visitor Center,** 900 Volunteer Landing Ln., by the river on the southeast side of downtown, visitors can watch a short video and check out exhibits about the region. (☎971-4440 or 800-727-8045; www.knoxville.org. Apr.-Oct. M-Sa 9am-6pm, Su 1-5pm; Nov.-Mar. M-Sa 9am-5pm.) **Internet Access: Lawson McGhee Public Library,** 500 W. Church Ave. (☎215-8750. Open June-Aug. M-Th 9am-8:30pm, F 9am-5:30pm, Su 1-5pm; Sept.-May M-Th 9am-8:30pm, F 9am-5:30pm, Sa-Su 1-5pm.) **Post Office:** 501 W. Main Ave. (☎521-1070. Open M-F 7:30am-5:30pm.) **Postal Code:** 37901. **Area Code:** 865.

ACCOMMODATIONS. Many not-quite-budget motels sit along **I-75** and **I-40,** just outside the city. A much better option is the **Knoxville Hostel (HI-AYH) ❶**, 404 E. Fourth Ave., just a short walk from the restaurants and clubs of the Old City. The hostel features not only clean rooms, a kitchen, and a comfortable common room, but also free Internet access, a continental breakfast, and even bathrobes for guests. *Be cautious around this neighborhood at night. If you arrive at the Greyhound station, call the hostel and they will pick you up.* (☎546-8090; knoxnumberone@aol.com. Free local calls. Laundry. Ask about shuttle service to Gatlinburg. Office usually open 7:30-11:30am and 4-8pm. $12, nonmembers $15.) The standard rooms at **Scottish Inns ❶**, 201 Callahan Rd., at Exit 110 off I-75, are more expensive and farther from downtown, but do allow more privacy. (☎689-7777. Free local calls, A/C, HBO, continental breakfast, and nice outdoor pool. Singles Su-Th $29, F-Sa $44; doubles $39/49. AAA, AARP $2 off.) **Volunteer Park Family Campground ❶**, 9514 Diggs Gap Rd., at Exit 117 off I-75, is 12 mi. from the city and offers a pool, laundry, a convenience store, and weekly live music in summer. (☎938-6600 or 800-238-9644; www.volpark.com. Music Tu and F nights in summer. Tent sites $18, with water and electricity $20; full hookup $25. Rates are for 2 adults and 2 children, additional person $3. Sites half price mid-Nov. to mid-Apr.)

FOOD. **Market Square,** a popular plaza to the east of World's Fair Park, presents restaurants, fountains, and shade, but shuts down at night. The other center for chowing,, browsing, and carousing, **Old City,** spreads north up Central and Jackson St. and stays active later than Market Sq. Part of Cumberland Ave. along campus proper, **The Strip** is lined with student hangouts, bars, and restaurants, and is dominated by fast food chains. **The Tomato Head ❶**, 12 Market Sq., prepares delicious gourmet pizzas (slices $1.85-4) and sandwiches ($4.25-6), with vegetarian and vegan options galore. (☎637-4067. Open M 11am-3pm, Tu-Th 11am-10pm, F-Sa 11am-11pm, Su 10am-9pm.) Don't miss one of the terrific croissant sandwiches at the **11th Street Espresso House ❶**, 1016 Laurel Ave., in an old Victorian house near the Knoxville Museum of Art. The porch is the perfect spot to enjoy a cup of coffee. (☎546-3003. Sandwiches $4.75. Salads $3.50-5.25. Coffee drinks $1.50-3.50. W poetry night 8pm; occasional live music. Open M-Sa 9am-midnight, Su 10am-10pm.) The **Crescent Moon Cafe ❷**, 718 S. Gay St., near the intersection with Main Ave., serves budget- and health-friendly wraps and salads with a gourmet twist. (☎637-9700. Most meals $7. Open M-Th 8am-2pm, F 8am-2pm and 5-8pm.)

SIGHTS. The must-see **Museum of Appalachia,** 16 mi. north of Knoxville at I-75 Exit 122 in Norris, showcases one-of-a-kind artifacts and exudes true Appalachian charm. The museum consists of a number of old buildings relocated from the surrounding countryside, including barns, corn cribs, a smokehouse, and the cabin where Mark Twain was conceived. Visitors will also be treated to live mountain music. Presenting both the tools of everyday Appalachia living and the stories of the people who used them, the museum is a testament to the region's unique culture. The annual **Tennessee Fall Homecoming Festival** held here on the second full weekend in October draws 400 musicians, as well as writers, craftspeople, and huge crowds. (☎494-7680; www.museumofappalachia.com. Open Jun.-Aug. daily 8am-8pm; low-season closing times as early as 5pm. Live music Apr.-Dec. 9:30am-4:30pm. $12, seniors and AAA $10, ages 6-12 $5; families $28; higher during festival.)

The **Women's Basketball Hall of Fame,** 700 Hall of Fame Dr., traces the history of women's involvement in the sport and inspires aspiring ballplayers. Visitors can watch a short video, listen to interviews with current stars, and even shoot some hoops. (☎633-9000; www.wbhof.com. Open M-Sa 10am-7pm, Su 1-6pm. $8, seniors and ages 6-15 $6; AAA $2 off. Wheelchair-accessible.) Nearby, the **James White Fort,** 205 E. Hill Ave., preserves portions of the original stockade built in 1786 by the founder of Knoxville. Guided tours give visitors the scoop on the lives of the first white settlers in the area. (☎525-6514. Open Mar. to mid-Dec. M-Sa 9:30am-5pm; Jan.-Feb. M-F 10am-4pm. Continuous tours until 1hr. before close; admission by tour only. $5, seniors and AAA $4.25, ages 7-12 $2.) History buffs will also want to see the **Blount Mansion,** 200 W. Hill Ave., the home of William Blount, who served as the first Governor of the Territory South of the River Ohio. Tours of the cozy house, built in 1792, include a short video. (☎525-2375 or 888-654-0016; www.blountmansion.org. Open Apr.-Dec. M-Sa 9:30am-5pm; Jan.-Mar. M-F 9:30am-5pm. Guided tours on the hr. 10am-4pm. $5, AAA and seniors $4.45, ages 6-17 $2.50.)

The self-guided **Cradle of Country Music Tour** ambles through the eastern end of downtown, lingering periodically at hallowed ground where country triumphs and heartaches left their mark. Sights include the theater where Roy Acuff made his first public performance and the hotel where Hank Williams spent his last night. Maps and information are available at the Gateway Regional Visitor Center.

World's Fair Park, just west of downtown, recently underwent major reconstruction, adding a vast swath of greenery stretching toward the river and expanding the Convention Center. The **Knoxville Museum of Art,** 1050 World's Fair Park Dr., houses high-caliber changing exhibits and a small but dynamic permanent collection of modern and postmodern art. The museum often hosts "Alive after Five" on Fridays, with live jazz or blues, free popcorn, catered food, and a cash bar. (☎525-6101; www.knoxart.org. Open Tu-W noon-8pm, Th-F noon-9pm, Sa-Su 11am-5pm. $5, ages 17 and under free. Wheelchair-accessible. Alive after Five some F 5:30-9pm, $6.)

ENTERTAINMENT & NIGHTLIFE. Knoxville is a great place to visit for college sports fans; UT's **football** and **women's basketball** consistently rank among the top teams of their respective leagues. (☎974-2491; www.utsports.com. Football tickets $38, basketball $8-14.) If sports aren't your thing, the **Bijou Theatre,** 803 S. Gay St., hosts musicals, concerts, theater, and dance performances. (☎522-0832, after-hours 868-8710; www.bijoutheatercenter.com. Tickets $25-28. Wheelchair-accessible.) **Sundown in the City,** a free outdoor concert series, brings some big name bands to Market Square on Thursday nights during the summer. (☎523-2665; www.concertwire.com. June-Oct. Th 6-10pm. $3 suggested donation.) The annual **Dogwood Arts Festival** brings crafts, food, and live entertainment to Market Square every April. Festivities also include a parade and a bicycling competition. (☎637-4561; www.dogwoodarts.com. Apr. 16-19, 2004. Free.)

The Old City is the center of Knoxville's nightlife, with several cool bars and music venues; the Strip and Market Square also host a number of popular bars. The hip **Blue Cats,** 125 E. Jackson St., draws some big live music acts. (☎544-4300; www.bluecatslive.com. Cover varies; doors usually open at 9pm. Beer from $2.75.) On Saturday nights, the club hosts **Fiction,** Knoxville's hottest dance party. (☎329-0039; www.fictionfx.com. 18+. Cover $3-5. Sa 10pm-3am at Blue Cats.) **Preservation Pub,** 28 Market Sq., a fabulous, friendly bar, serves some serious brew (from $2.75). Check out the great quotes on the walls. (☎524-2224; www.preservationpub.com. Live music nightly except Tu and Su. Happy hour daily 4-7pm. 21+ after 10pm. No cover. Open M-F 11am-3am, Sa 4pm-3am, Su 6pm-1am.) **Barley's Taproom and Pizzeria,** 200 E. Jackson Ave., in the Old City, is also a good spot for a beer, especially on Mondays, with $2 drafts all day, and on Wednesday evenings, when a live bluegrass radio program is recorded on stage. (☎521-0092. Beer from $1.75. Live music almost daily. Cover $5 or less. Happy Hour daily noon-6pm. Open M-Sa 11:30am-late, Su noon-midnight.) For goings-on around the town, pick up a free copy of *Metro Pulse* or log onto www.metropulse.com.

GREAT SMOKY MOUNTAINS ☎865

The largest wilderness area in the eastern US, Great Smoky Mountains National Park encompasses over 500,000 acres of gray-green Appalachian peaks bounded by the misty North Carolina and Tennessee valleys. Black bears, wild hogs, wild turkeys, and salamanders make their home here, along with more than 1500 species of flowering plants. Conifer forests line the mountain ridges at elevations of over 6000 ft. Spring sets the mountains ablaze with wildflowers and azaleas; in June and July, rhododendrons bloom. By mid-October, the mountains are a vibrant quilt of autumnal color. Sadly, the area has not remained untouched by human presence. Fifty years ago, a visitor at Newfound Gap could see 113 miles on average; today, poorer air quality has cut visibility to only 14 miles.

ORIENTATION & PRACTICAL INFORMATION

The Newfound Gap Road (U.S. 441) is the only road connecting the Tennessee and North Carolina sides of the park. On the Tennessee side, Gatlinburg and Pigeon Forge lie just outside of the park; both are oppressively touristy, especially in the
hs. Townsend, to the west near Cades Cove, is less crowded. In
a, the town of Cherokee lies near the park entrance on U.S. 441. Bry-
the Deep Creek campground, is quieter. The free *Smokies Guide*
k's tours, lectures, activities, and changing natural graces.

iters: Sugarlands (☎436-1291), on Newfound Gap Rd. 2 mi. south of
TN, next to the park's headquarters, shows a well done 20min. video on the
ecology of the park. There is also an exhibit on regional plants and animals.

Open daily June-Aug. 8am-7pm; Apr.-May and Sept.-Oct. 8am-6pm; Mar. and Nov. 8am-5pm; Dec.-Feb. 8am-4:30pm. On the North Carolina side of the park, **Oconaluftee** (☎828-497-1900), about 2 mi. north of Cherokee, shares its grounds with an outdoor **Mountain Farm Museum** made up of historic buildings relocated from throughout the park in the 1950s. Open daily 8am-7pm; low-season hours vary.

Buses: East Tennessee Human Resource Agency (ETHRA), 298 Blair Bend Rd., (☎800-232-1565; www.ethra.org), in Loudon, offers door-to-door van transportation from Knoxville and other towns in the vicinity. Operates M-F 8am-4:30pm. Call at least 48hr. in advance to schedule a trip. $2 and up.

Park Info Line, ☎436-1200; www.nps.gov/grsm. Operates daily 8am-4:30pm. **Emergency Hotline,** ☎436-1294. **Area Code:** 865.

ACCOMMODATIONS

Motels, lining Rte. 441 and Rte. 321, decrease in price with distance from the park. Small motels cluster in both Cherokee and Gatlinburg. Prices soar on weekends. Visitors can gamble on motels, but in general it is better to splurge on a B&B, stay in hostel-style accommodations near the park, or camp within the park itself. Beautiful B&Bs and some good restaurants can be found in Bryson City, NC, about 15min. from the park's main entrance on U.S. 441.

Ten **campgrounds** ❶ lie scattered throughout the park, each with tent sites, limited trailer space, water, and bathrooms with flush toilets. There are no showers or hookups. **Smokemont, Elkmont,** and **Cades Cove,** the largest and most popular campgrounds, accept reservations from mid-May to late October. (Sites $17-20 during reservation period; $14 rest of the year.) The rest are first come, first served; visitors centers have info about availability. (Sites $12-14.) In summer, reserve spots as early as your travel plans allow. (☎800-365-2267, park code GRE; http://reservations.nps.gov. Open daily 10am-10pm.) Cades Cove and Smokemont are open year-round, while the other campgrounds open between March and May and close in October or November. **Backcountry camping** requires a **permit,** free at ranger stations and Visitors Centers. Many of the park's 100 primitive backcountry sites require reservations. (☎436-1231. Office open daily 8am-6pm.)

Folkestone Inn, 101 Folkestone Rd. (☎828-488-2730 or 888-812-3385; www.folkestone.com), in Bryson City, runs right up to the park with gorgeous rooms and a backdrop of gentle mountains. Total relaxation in this remote hide-away is inescapable, especially after a fantastic full breakfast. Follow signs for Deep Creek Campground. Most rooms with deck or balcony. 2-night min. stay on weekends May-Oct. Children must be 10 or older. Check-in 3-9pm. Check-out 11am. Be sure to call ahead. Rooms for 1 person $82-132; for 2 $88-138. Each extra person $12. ❹

LeConte Lodge (☎429-5704; www.leconte-lodge.com), at the top of Mount LeConte, is the only lodging within the park. These rustic cabins can only be reached by a minimum 5 mi. hike. The shortest and steepest route is the Alum Cave trail (5 mi. one-way). A sunrise at nearby Myrtle Point is a fabulous way to begin a day in the Smokies. The Lodge is popular; in the summer, you'll need to reserve months in advance to secure a bed. No electricity, phones, TV, or showers. Open late Mar. to mid-Nov. $83, ages 4-10 $66.50; prices include 6pm dinner and breakfast. ❹

Charleston Inn, 208 Arlington Ave. (☎828-488-4644; www.charlestoninn.com). From Main St., go straight through the intersection with Veteran's Blvd. and continue up the hill; it will be on your right. This gorgeous, modern B&B is within walking distance of the shops and restaurants of Bryson City. Welcoming innkeepers, full breakfast. Rooms with A/C and private baths, most with TV, some with jacuzzi. 2-night min. stay on weekends during peak season. Check-in 3-8pm; call if arriving later. Check-out 11am. Rooms for 1 or 2 people $95-135, cabin $155. ❹

Nantahala Outdoor Center (NOC), 13077 U.S. 19 W. (☎800-232-7238), 13 mi. southwest of Bryson City, just south of the National Park, beckons with cheap beds and three restaurants. They also arrange whitewater rafting. Showers, kitchen, and laundry facilities. Call ahead. Bunks in simple cabins $14. Platform tents $5 per person. ❶

FOOD

Mountain Perks, 9 Depot St. (☎828-488-9561), in Bryson City across from the train station. Take Everett St. from Main St.; it will be on the corner on the right, 3 blocks down. Live music gets the crowds going F 7pm. Orgasmic desserts $2-3.25, scrumptious oversized wraps $6.50-11.50, creative coffee drinks $0.75-4, and amazing salads $4.25-6.75. Open M-Sa 7am-3pm, also sometimes F 7-9pm. ❷

Smokin' Joe's Bar-B-Que, 8303 Rte. 73, (☎448-3212), in Townsend. Authentic Tennessee cookin' is the order of business here. With succulent, slow-cooked meats and homemade side dishes, Joe's smokes the competition. Dinners ($7-12) come with meat, 2 sides, and bread–enjoy one on the porch next to the river. Sandwiches $2.50-4.50. Beer from $2.50. Open summer Su-Th 11am-9pm, F-Sa 11am-10pm; low-season hours vary. ❷

Pizza by the River (☎828-488-5651), on Hwy. 19, 1½ mi. past Nantahala Outdoor Center, 14½ mi. southwest of Bryson City. This roadside stand is a local favorite, serving up excellent pizza. Outdoor deck overlooks the waters of the Nantahala. Slices $2.50-3 (before 4pm), 11 in. pies $10, sandwiches $6. Open Apr. to mid-Oct. Su-Th 11am-8pm, F-Sa 11am-9pm. ❷

OUTDOOR ACTIVITIES

HIKING

Over 900 mi. of hiking trails and 170 mi. of road meander through the park. Rangers at the Visitors Centers will help devise a trip appropriate for your ability. Trail maps and a guide to day hikes in the area are also available at the Visitors Centers ($1 each). The Great Smokies are known for phenomenal **waterfalls,** and many of the park's most popular hikes culminate in stunning cascade vistas. Other trails reward hikers with fantastic views of the surrounding mountains. Less crowded areas not accessible from Rte. 441 include **Cosby** and **Cataloochee,** both on the eastern edge of the park. The following distances and times for hikes are round-trip. *Wherever you go, bring water and don't feed the bears.*

Rainbow Falls (5½ mi., 4hr.) is a moderate to strenuous hike that reveals the Smokies' highest single-plunge waterfall. The park's most popular hike.

Laurel Falls (2½ mi., 2hr.) is one of the easier (and more crowded) hikes on the Tennessee side of the park, following a paved trail through a series of cascades before reaching the 60 ft. falls.

Ramsay Cascades (8 mi., 5hr.) is a strenuous hike leading to cascades that fall 100 ft. down the mountainside. The trailhead is in the Greenbrier area–from Gatlinburg, the park entrance is 4¾ mi. east on Hwy. 321; the trailhead is 4¾ mi. from the entrance.

Chimney Tops (4 mi., 2hr.) is a steep scramble leading up to two 4755 ft. rock spires, where breathtaking views await.

BIKING

Biking is permitted along most roads within the park, with the exception of the Roaring Fork Motor Nature Trail. The best opportunities for cyclists are at the **Foothills Parkway, Cades Cove,** and **Cataloochee.** On Wednesday and Saturday mornings from May to mid-September, the 11 mi. Cades Cove Loop is closed to car traffic to allow bicyclers full use of the road (dawn-10am). While the Smokies boast no mountain biking trails, a few gravel trails in the park, including the **Gatlinburg Trail** and the **Oconaluftee River Trail,** allow bicycles. Bike rental is available at **Cades Cove Campground Store.** (☎448-9034. $4 per hr., $20 per day. Open June to mid-Aug. daily 9am-7pm, no rental after 4:30pm. Late Aug. M-F 9am-5pm, no rental after 2:30pm; Sa-Su 9am-7pm, no rental after 4:30pm. Open daily Apr.-May and Sept.-Oct. 9am-5pm, no rental after 2:30pm. Bike rental begins W and Sa 7am.)

FISHING

Forty species of fish swim in the park's rivers and streams. The Smokies permit fishing in open waters year-round from 30min. before sunrise to 30min. after sunset. All anglers over 12 (over 15 in North Carolina) must possess a valid Tennessee or North Carolina **fishing license.** The park itself does not sell licenses; check with local Chambers of Commerce, sports shops, and hardware stores for purchasing information. Visitors Centers have brochures about fishing regulations.

RIDING

Over 500 mi. of the park's trails are open to horses. Five drive-in **horse camps** are located within the park, providing facilities for travelers with horses: **Anthony Creek, Big Creek, Cataloochee, Round Bottom,** and **Tow String.** (Reservations required: ☎800-362-2267; http://reservations.nps.gov. Open mid-Mar. to Oct. $20-25 per night.) There are also four **riding stables** where visitors can take guided rides through scenic trails. (Cades Cove Riding Stable: ☎448-6286; open mid-Mar. through Oct. Smokemont Riding Stable: ☎828-497-2373; open mid-Apr. through Oct. Smoky Mountain Riding Stable: ☎436-5634; open mid-Mar. through Nov. Sugarlands Horseback Riding Stable: ☎430-5020; open mid-May through Nov. All $20 per hr., age and weight restrictions vary.)

AUTO TOURS

For the less hairy-chested, the park offers a number of auto tours, allowing visitors to appreciate diverse wildlife and spectacular vistas without lacing up their hiking boots. The **Cades Cove Loop, Newfound Gap Road,** and **Roaring Fork** auto tours are favorites. Pamphlets and maps are available in the Visitors Centers ($1 each). The **Cataloochee** auto tour ($0.50) goes through the area where elk have been reintroduced onto the park land. Throughout the park, motorists can stop at the **quiet walkways** and **nature trails** for a short stroll through the forest. Most walks are less than 1 mi. in length.

NEAR SMOKY MOUNTAINS: CHEROKEE RESERVATION

The **Cherokee Indian Reservation,** on the southeast border of the national park, features a number of museums, shops, attractions, and a 24hr. dry casino, concentrated in the town of Cherokee itself. Three historical attractions stand in marked contrast to the miles of rampant commercialism. For an in-depth look at the history and traditions of the Cherokee people, visit the **Museum of the Cherokee Indian,** at the corner of Drama Rd. and Tsali Blvd. (U.S. 441). (☎828-497-3481; www.cherokeemuseum.org. Open June-Aug. M-Sa 9am-7pm, Su 9am-5pm; Sept.-May daily 9am-5pm. $8, ages 6-13 $5; AAA $7.20/4; AARP $7.20.) From May to October, the reservation offers tours of the **Oconaluftee Indian Village,** 276 Drama Rd., a recreated mid-18th-century Cherokee village. Tours educate visitors about traditional Cherokee crafts, political organization, and village life. (☎828-497-2315; www.oconalufteevillage.com. Open mid-May to late Oct. daily 9am-5:30pm. $13, ages 6-13 $6. Combination tickets with Museum $17/9. Wheelchair-accessible.)

"Unto these Hills," an outdoor drama, chronicles the story of the Cherokee people from the arrival of the first European explorers to the Trail of Tears. Though the play verges on melodrama at some points, it nonetheless provides a good historical overview (with some impressive pyrotechnics to boot). Follow signs from Rte. 441. (☎828-497-2111, 866-554-4557; www.untothesehills.com. Show mid-June to late Aug. M-Sa 8:30pm, pre-show singing at 7:45pm. Tickets $16-18, child $8-18.) For less somber entertainment, roll the dice at **Harrah's Cherokee Casino,** 777 Casino Dr. off of Hwy. 19 N. (☎800-427-7247 or 828-497-7777; www.harrahs.com. 21+. Open 24hr.) The **Cherokee Visitors Center,** 498 Tsali Blvd. (Rte. 441), provides information; follow signs. (☎800-438-1601 or 828-497-9195; www.cherokee-nc.com. Open mid-June to late Aug. 8:15am-8am; low-season hours vary.)

CHATTANOOGA ☎423

Chattanooga is a city of superlatives and firsts; it is home to the first-ever tow truck, the world's largest fresh-water aquarium, the original Coca-Cola bottling factory, and the world's steepest passenger railway. But it was a different kind of train that made Chattanooga famous—the city was once a major transportation hub; builders completed the Terminal Station for the legendary "Chattanooga Choo-Choo" almost a century ago. Technology eventually replaced the train system, but visitors continued to stream in. The creation of Ruby Falls and Rock City Gardens has increased tourism further. Today, these attractions and other kid-friendly activities around town make Chattanooga an ideal family destination. American history fans will be interested in the decisive Civil War battles that took place in this area, and everyone will enjoy the undeniable natural beauty of the "Scenic City."

PRACTICAL INFORMATION. Chattanooga straddles the Tennessee/Georgia border at the junction of I-24, I-59, and I-75. Downtown, Lookout Mountain, and the Bluff View Art District compose the town's distinct parts. The **Chattanooga Metropolitan Airport** lies about 5mi. east of downtown. (☎855-2200; www.chattairport.com.) **Greyhound,** 960 Airport Rd. (☎892-1277; open daily 6:30am-9:30pm), buses to: Atlanta (2hr., 9 per day, $18-19); Knoxville (2hr., 4 per day, $14-15); Nashville (3hr., 5 per day, $18-19). **Chattanooga Area Transportation Authority (CARTA)** operates a free downtown electric shuttle service with stops on every block between the aquarium and the Holiday Inn. (☎629-1473; www.carta-bus.org. Shuttles run M-F 6am-9:30pm, Sa 9am-9:30pm, Su 9am-8:30pm. Wheelchair-accessible.) **Visitors Center:** 2 Broad St., next to the aquarium. (☎800-322-3344; www.chattanoogafun.com. Discounted attraction tickets. Open daily 8:30am-5:30pm.) **Internet Access: Public Library,** 1001 Broad St., at 10th St. (☎757-5310. Open daily M-Th 9am-9pm, F-Sa 9am-6pm.) **Post Office:** 900 Georgia Ave., between Martin Luther King Blvd. and 10th St. (☎267-6208. Open M-F 8am-4:30pm.) **Postal Code:** 37402. **Area Code:** 423.

ACCOMMODATIONS. The usual budget hotels congregate east of the city on I-24/I-75. Closer to town there are a few budget accommodations off of **Broad Street.** These chains are your best bet for inexpensive lodgings in Chattanooga, unless you want to camp. The **Ramada Inn Downtown ❸,** 100 W. 21st St., Exit 178 off I-24, has clean, standard rooms in a convenient location. (☎265-3151; www.stadiuminn.com. A/C, cable TV, HBO, continental breakfast, and pool. Rooms from $49; low-season from $39. AAA, AARP 10% off.) Though a bit on the expensive side, **Chanticleer Inn ❹,** 1300 Mockingbird Ln., just down the street from Rock City, is worth every penny. Guests are treated to exceptional hospitality, gorgeous scenery, and a hearty breakfast. The well-appointed rooms occupy small stone cottages; some have fireplaces or whirlpool tubs. (☎706-820-2002; www.stayatchanticleer.com. A/C, cable TV, Internet access, and pool. Rooms $99-159. AAA discount.) **Best Holiday Trav-L-Park ❶,** 1709 Mack Smith Rd., occupies a Civil War battlefield. From Chattanooga, take I-24E to I-75S and turn off at Exit 1. Turn right at the top of the ramp, then left at the next light; it's ½ mi. down. (☎706-891-9766 or 800-693-2877; www.chattacamp.com. Full bathhouse; laundry, playground, game room, and pool available. Sites with 30 amp hook-up $25; 50 amp $27; cabins $36. AARP 10% off.) Nearby **Lake Chickamauga** is also surrounded by campgrounds.

FOOD. In the Bluff View Art District, **Rembrant's Coffee House ❶,** 204 High St., offers gourmet sandwiches and salads at great prices. The lovely brick patio, complete with a fountain, is the perfect spot to unwind with a good book while sampling the incredible pastries (under $4) or sipping a mug of coffee. (☎265-5033, ext. 3. Sandwiches and salads $3-6. Open daily M-Th 7am-10pm, F 7am-11:30pm, Sa 8am-11:30pm, Su 8am-10pm.) The **Pickle Barrel ❶,** 1012 Market St., downtown, serves up satisfying sandwiches ($4.25-6.25) and gourmet daily specials. Choose between the lively downstairs area, with names of past customers carved into the tabletops, and the open-air deck upstairs. (☎266-1103. Spicy black bean burger $5.25. 21+ after 9pm, except families. Open M-Sa 11am-3am, Su noon-3am.) **Jack's Alley** is lined with several places to eat, including **Sticky Fingers ❷,** 420 Broad St., the best place in town for ribs ($13). Enjoy a heaping mound of hickory-smoked barbecue with baked beans and homemade slaw ($9) or a filling salad ($7-8). The $7 Sunday brunch features an all-you-can-eat buffet. (☎265-7427; www.stickyfingersonline.com. Open daily 11am-10pm.)

SIGHTS. Downtown Chattanooga, a small area between 10th St. and the river, is crammed with attractions, shops, and restaurants. The **Tennessee Aquarium,** 1 Broad St., on Ross' Landing, is the largest fresh-water aquarium in the world. The aquarium entertains visitors with an IMAX screen, mesmerizing seahorses, and some intensely ugly fish. (☎800-322-3344; www.tnaqua.org. Open summer M-Th 10am-6pm, F-Su 10am-8pm; low-season daily 10am-6pm. $14, ages 3-12 $7.50; IMAX $7.75/5.25; both $18/10.50. 1¼hr. behind-the-scenes tour daily 3pm, $7/5.) Almost as fascinating, the **International Towing and Recovery Hall of Fame and Museum,** 3315 S. Broad St., chronicles the creation and life of the tow truck. Even if you're not interested in cars, this museum is worth seeing as a testament to human ingenuity. (☎267-3132; www.internationaltowingmuseum.org. Open M-F 10am-4:30pm, Sa-Su 11am-5pm. $8, seniors and ages 6-18 $6, under 6 free.) At the **Creative Discovery Museum,** 321 Chestnut St., children can climb, splash and dig through interactive exhibits on everything from music to dinosaurs. (☎756-2738; www.cdmfun.org. $8, ages 2-12 $6, under 2 free. Open Mar.-May M-Sa 10am-5pm, Su noon-5pm; Memorial Day-Labor Day daily 10am-6pm; Sept.-Feb. M-Tu and Th-Sa 10am-5pm, Su noon-5pm; last admission 1hr. before close. Wheelchair-accessible.)

The **Bluff View Art District** is a small neighborhood of upscale shops and cafes, anchored by the **Hunter Museum of American Art,** 10 Bluff View Ave. From downtown, take 4th St. to High St. and turn left. The engrossing exhibits include a well-done contemporary section and a fantastic display of classical American painting, all inside the grand mansion. (☎267-0968; www.huntermuseum.org. Open Tu-Sa 9:30am-5pm, Su noon-5pm, first F of each month 9:30am-8pm. $5, seniors $4, students $3, ages 3-12 $2.50; free on first F. Wheelchair-accessible.) Across the street is the **Houston Museum,** 201 High St. This amazing collection is the life work of Anna Houston, a bit of an eccentric who lived in a barn that she constructed herself and supposedly married as many as 10 times. She bequeathed her belongings, including music boxes and an amazing glass collection, to a committee that started a museum in this picturesque house on the banks of the river. To see the exhibits, visitors must join a 45min. tour. (☎267-7176. Open M-F 9:30am-4pm, Sa noon-4pm. $7.)

One of the most popular destinations in Chattanooga is **Lookout Mountain.** Take S. Broad St. and follow the signs; the route to the attractions is well-marked. Billed as "America's most amazing mile," the **Incline Railway** is the world's steepest passenger railway, chugging visitors up an insane 72.7% grade to an observation deck. The deck is also accessible by car, allowing you to soak in the incredible views for free. (☎629-1411; www.CARTA-Bus.org. Open daily June-Aug. 8:30am-8:50pm; Sept.-Oct. and Mar.-May 9am-5:15pm; Nov.-Feb. 10am-6pm. One-way $8; round-trip $9; ages 3-12 $3.50/4.50.) The nature trail at **Rock City Gardens** combines the natural spectacle of scenic lookouts and narrow rock passages with decidedly less organic additives: the trail has been outfitted with strategically placed shops and finishes at a cave decked out with colorful elves and fairy tale dioramas. The gardens, founded by Garnet Carter—the man who also invented miniature golf—were once promoted by advertisements painted on barn roofs. The expansive view from the observation points reveals seven states on a clear day. (☎706-820-2531 or 800-854-0675; www.seerock-city.com. Open daily at 8:30am, closes Jan.-May 5pm, Jun.-Aug. 8pm, Sept. to mid-Nov. 6pm. Open mid-Nov. to Dec. until 4pm and in evenings 6-9pm for the "Enchanted Garden of Lights." $13, ages 3-12 $7.) One thousand feet inside the mountain, the **Ruby Falls** cavern formations and a 145 ft. waterfall—complete with colored lights and sound effects—add a little pizzazz to a day of sightseeing. The waterfall is impressive, but be prepared to endure long waits and narrow passageways crowded with tourists. (☎821-2544; www.rubyfalls.com. Open daily 8am-8pm. 1hr. tour $13, ages 3-12 $6.) An array of combination packages for various attractions are available; inquire at any ticket window.

ENTERTAINMENT & NIGHTLIFE. For entertainment listings and information on local events, check the "Weekend" section of the Friday *Chattanooga Times Free Press*. Most of the city's nightlife options are downtown, especially in the area surrounding **Jack's Alley,** which runs from Broad St. to Market St., between 4th and 5th St. There are several bars off of the commercialized alley, but **Taco Mac's,** 423 Market St., offers the best selection with over 50 beers on tap. (☎267-8226. Outdoor seating available. Beer from $2.85. Happy Hour M-F 4-7pm. Open M-F 11am-3am, Sa-Su noon-3am.) Nearby, the popular **Big River Grille and Brewing Works,** 222 Broad St., offers six original beers, plus seasonal ales and lagers. (☎267-2739. Pints $3.25. Happy Hour M-F 4-7pm. Pool tables; live music Th-Sa. Open Su-Th 11am-12:30 or 1am, F-Sa 11am-2am.) The rooftop bar at the **Tortilla Factory,** 203 W. 2nd St., is a great spot to sip a cold one in nice weather. (☎756-6399. Beer from $3; select beers $2 on Tu. Roof 21+ after 9pm. Open daily 5pm-2:30am; downstairs restaurant open Su-Th 11am-11pm, F-Sa 11am-midnight.) **Rhythm and Brews,** 221 Market St., is the town's best live music venue. (☎267-4644; www.rhythm-brews.com. Beer from $3.25. Open mic W. 21+. Cover $5-20. Usually open W-Sa 8pm-whenever.)

e **Chattanooga Lookouts,** a minor league baseball farm team for the Reds, play at w **BellSouth Park,** at 2nd and Chestnut St. (☎267-2208. Tickets $4-8, seniors der 12 $2.) For nine nights in June, the riverfront shuts down for live rock, blues, jazz, and reggae during the **Riverbend Festival.** (☎756-221; www.river-ival.com. $24.) The mountains surrounding Chattanooga also offer plenty ınities for **whitewater rafting;** ask at the visitors center for details.

MOUNTAINS OF FUN A mythical American village created by Dolly Parton in the Tennessee hills, **Dollywood** dominates Pigeon Forge. The park celebrates the cultural legacy of the east Tennessee mountains and the country songmistress herself, famous for some mountainous topography of her own. In Dolly's world, craftspeople demonstrate their skills and sell their wares, 30 rides offer thrills and chills, and country singers perform. Nearby, visitors can make waves at **Dolly's Splash Country.** *(1020 Dollywood Ln. ☎865-428-9488; www.dollywood.com. Park open Apr.-Dec. Open daily June to mid-Aug. , most days 9am-8pm, but hours vary. $40, seniors $37, ages 4-11 $30, including tax; enter after 3pm during the summer and get in free the next day. Splash Country $29/24.50/23.50, including tax. Discount coupons available at tourist centers and motels.)*

MEMPHIS ☎901

Music is the pulse of Memphis. Ever since masters like John Coltrane played in the bars, this city has been much more than just a place to get terrific barbecue—the neighborhoods of Memphis, particularly Beale St., have seen the creation of jazz, blues, soul, and rock 'n' roll over the last century. Today, most visitors make the Memphis pilgrimage to see Graceland, the former home of Elvis Presley and one of the most deliciously tacky spots in the US. There's plenty to do after you've paid your respects to the king; unusual museums, fantastic ribs, and live music every night of the week are just some of the reasons you might want to stay a few days.

BLUE SUEDE SHOES

Airport: Memphis International, 2491 Winchester Rd. (☎922-8000; www.mscaa.com), south of the southern loop of I-240. Taxi fare to the city around $22–negotiate in advance. Operated by MATA, **DASH** runs buses frequently from the airport.

Trains: Amtrak, 545 S. Main St. (☎526-0052), at G.E. Patterson Ave., on the southern edge of downtown. *The surrounding area can be unsafe.* The Main St. Trolley line runs to the station. Ticket office hours M-F 5am-2:45pm, Sa-Su 5-6:30am, and daily 9:30-11:45pm. To: **Chicago** (10½hr., 1 per day, $155); **Jackson** (4½hr., 1 per day, $48); **New Orleans** (8½hr., 1 per day, $90).

Buses: Greyhound, 203 Union Ave. (☎523-9253), at 3rd St. downtown. *The area can be unsafe at night.* Open 24hr. To: **Chattanooga** (7-10hr., 4 per day, $38); **Jackson** (4-6hr., 6 per day, $32-39); **Nashville** (4hr., 13 per day, $27-29).

Public Transit: Memphis Area Transit Authority, or **MATA,** (☎274-6282; www.matatransit.com), corner of Auction Ave. and Main St. Bus routes cover most suburbs but run infrequently. Major routes run on Front, 2nd, and 3rd St. Buses run M-F beginning between 4:30 and 6am and stopping between 7 and 11pm, depending on the route. Sa-Su service less frequent. $1.25, transfers $0.10. Refurbished 19th-century **trolley cars** cruise Main St. and the Riverfront. Main St.: M-Th 6am-midnight, F 6am-1am, Sa 9:30am-1am, Su 10am-6pm. Riverfront: M-Th 6:30am-midnight, F 6:30am-1am, Sa 9:50am-1am, Su 10:20am-6pm. $0.60, M-F 11am-1:30pm $0.30; seniors $0.30; under 5 free. 1-day pass $2.50, 3-day $6. MATA also operates the **Downtown Airport Shuttle (DASH),** which runs between the airport and 9 downtown hotels M-Sa 7:30am-5pm, Su 8:30am-4:30pm. One-way $15, round-trip $25. Info ☎522-1677.

Shuttles: Sun Studio and Graceland both offer free shuttle service between attractions. The Elvis Express, operated by Graceland, runs between Graceland and Beale St. The Sun Studio shuttle transports travelers between Graceland, Sun Studio, and the Rock-n-S[illegible] museum. Call attractions for further info.

Taxi: City Wide, ☎722-8294. **Yellow Cab,** ☎577-7700. Expect a long wait.

ON THE SOUTHSIDE, HIGH UP ON THE RIDGE

Downtown, named avenues run east-west and numbered ones run north-south. **Madison Avenue** divides north and south addresses. Two main thoroughfares, **Poplar** and **Union Avenue** are east-west; **2nd** and **3rd Street** are the major north-south routes downtown. **I-240** and **I-55** encircle the city. **Bellevue** becomes **Elvis Presley Boulevard** and leads south straight to Graceland. **Midtown** lies east of downtown.

Visitor Info: Tennessee Welcome Center, 119 Riverside Dr. (☎543-5333; www.memphistravel.com), at Jefferson St. Open daily 7am-11pm. The uniformed **blue suede brigade** roaming the city will happily give directions or answer questions—just stay off of their shoes.

Hotlines: Crisis Line, ☎274-7477. 24hr. **Gay/Lesbian Switchboard,** ☎324-4297. Operates daily 7:30-11pm.

Internet Access: Cossitt Branch Public Library, 33 S. Front St. (☎526-1712), downtown at Monroe. Open M-F 10am-5pm. Farther away but with longer hours, the **Main Library** is at 3030 Poplar Ave. (☎415-2700). Open M-Th 9am-9pm, F-Sa 9am-6pm, Su 1-5pm.

Post Office: 1 N. Front St. (☎576-2037) Open M-F 8:30am-5pm. **Postal Code:** 38103. 555 S. 3rd St. (☎521-2559) Open M-F 8:30am-5:30pm, Sa 10am-2pm. **Postal Code:** 38101. **Area Code:** 901.

SINCE MY BABY LEFT ME, I GOT A NEW PLACE TO DWELL

A few downtown motels have prices in the budget range; more lodgings are available near Graceland at **Elvis Presley Boulevard** and **Brooks Road.** For the celebrations of Elvis' historic birth (Jan. 8) and death (Aug. 16), as well as for the Memphis in May festival, book rooms 6 months to 1 year in advance.

American Inn, 3265 Elvis Presley Blvd. (☎345-8444), Exit 5B off I-55, close to Graceland. Despite the Inn's shabby exterior, you can't help falling in love with the large, clean, comfy rooms and the Elvis-themed mural in the lobby. Cable TV, A/C, pool, and continental breakfast. Kings $35; doubles $46. ❷

Homestead Studio Suites Hotel, 6500 Poplar Dr. (☎767-5522). Though about 16mi. from downtown, these impeccably clean rooms come with a full kitchen, data ports, and access to laundry facilities–visitors will feel like they are living in their own apartment. The surrounding area also offers plenty of dining options. Queens $70; doubles $80. Weekly rates $50/60 per night. AAA, AARP discount. ❸

The Peabody Hotel, 149 Union Ave. (☎529-4000 or 800-732-2639; www.peabodymemphis.com). A definite splurge for definite luxury. Known as one of the mid-South's grandest hotels since 1869, the Peabody has hosted the likes of William F..., Charles Lindbergh, and Presidents Andrew Johnson and William McKinley—...ourse, the famous Peabody Ducks. Today, guests are treated to beautifully-... rooms, high tea in the grand lobby, and access to a fitness center, a spa and ...elegant restaurants. Singles from $199; doubles from $229. ❺

...eland RV Park and Campground, 3691 Elvis Presley Blvd. (☎396-7125 or ...6), beside the Heartbreak Hotel, a 2min. walk from Graceland. No privacy, ...n is great. Advance reservations are a good idea. Pool, laundry facilities, ... to Beale St. Sites $22, with water and electricity $31, full hookup $34; ... people, each additional person $4. ❶

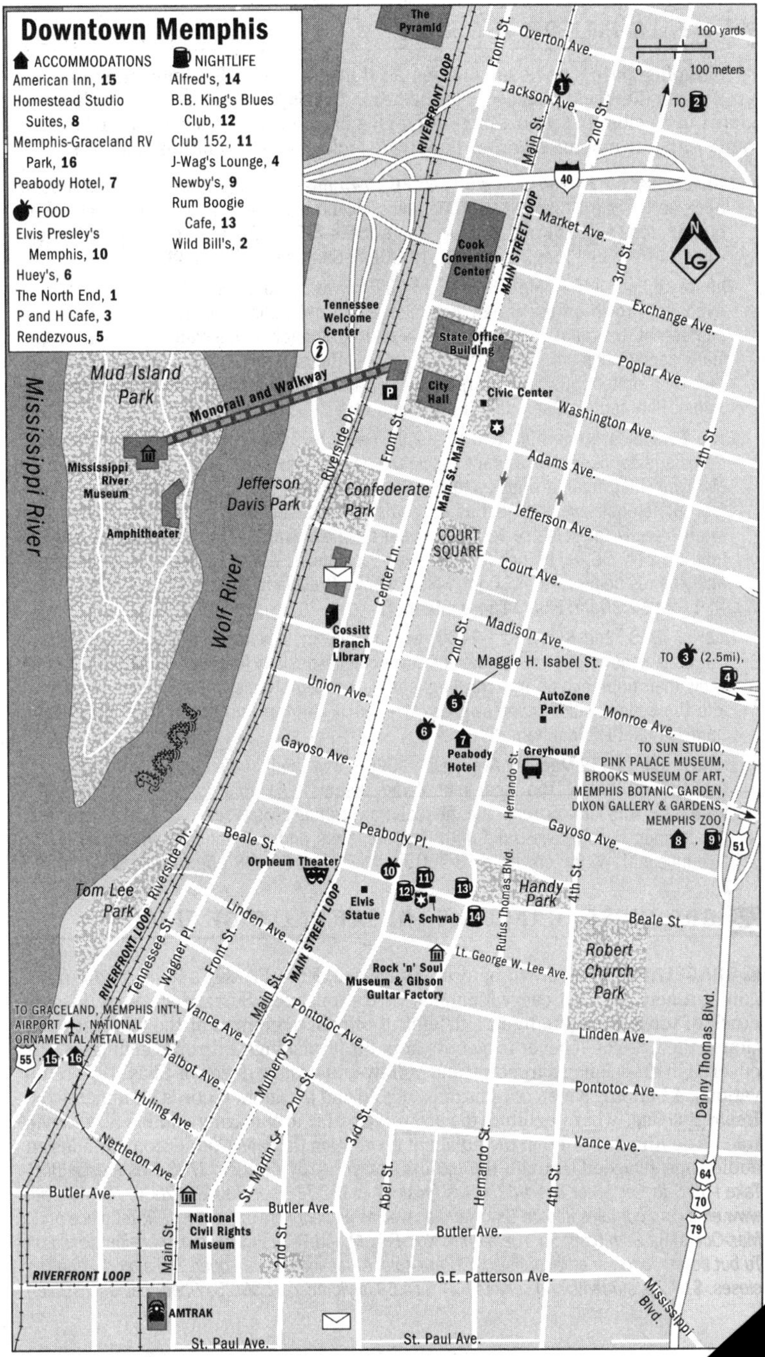

Downtown Memphis

ACCOMMODATIONS
- American Inn, **15**
- Homestead Studio Suites, **8**
- Memphis-Graceland RV Park, **16**
- Peabody Hotel, **7**

FOOD
- Elvis Presley's Memphis, **10**
- Huey's, **6**
- The North End, **1**
- P and H Cafe, **3**
- Rendezvous, **5**

NIGHTLIFE
- Alfred's, **14**
- B.B. King's Blues Club, **12**
- Club 152, **11**
- J-Wag's Lounge, **4**
- Newby's, **9**
- Rum Boogie Cafe, **13**
- Wild Bill's, **2**

The Pyramid
Mud Island Park
Mississippi River
Mississippi River Museum
Amphitheater
Monorail and Walkway
Wolf River
Jefferson Davis Park
Confederate Park
Tennessee Welcome Center
Cook Convention Center
State Office Building
City Hall
Civic Center
COURT SQUARE
Cossitt Branch Library
AutoZone Park
Peabody Hotel
Greyhound
Orpheum Theater
Elvis Statue
A. Schwab
Rock 'n' Soul Museum & Gibson Guitar Factory
Handy Park
Robert Church Park
Tom Lee Park
National Civil Rights Museum
AMTRAK
RIVERFRONT LOOP
MAIN STREET LOOP
Main St. Mall

TO 2
TO 3 (2.5mi), 4
TO SUN STUDIO, PINK PALACE MUSEUM, BROOKS MUSEUM OF ART, MEMPHIS BOTANIC GARDEN, DIXON GALLERY & GARDENS, MEMPHIS ZOO, 8, 9
TO GRACELAND, MEMPHIS INT'L AIRPORT, NATIONAL ORNAMENTAL METAL MUSEUM, 15, 16

0 100 yards
0 100 meters

THE SOUTH

MEALS FIT FOR THE KING

In Memphis, barbecue is as common as rhinestone-studded jumpsuits; the city even hosts the **World Championship Barbecue Cooking Contest** in May. Don't fret if gnawing on ribs isn't your thing—Memphis has plenty of other Southern restaurants with down-home favorites like fried chicken, catfish, chitlins, and grits.

Rendezvous, 52 S. 2nd St. (☎523-2746; www.hogsfly.com). The entrance is around back on Maggie H. Isabel St. A Memphis legend, serving large portions of charcoal-broiled ribs ($15.75) and cheaper sandwiches ($3-6.50); look for the long line up. Open Tu-Th 4:30-11pm, F 11:30am-11:30pm, Sa noon-11:30pm. ❸

The North End, 346 N. Main St. (☎526-0319; www.thenorthendonline.com), at Jackson Ave., downtown on the trolley line. Serves up delicious tamales, wild rice blends, stuffed potatoes and creole dishes in a relaxed, friendly atmosphere (all $3-11). Specialty sandwiches on homebaked bread $5-9. The orgasmic hot fudge pie is known as "sex on a plate" ($3.75). Happy Hour daily 4-7pm. Live music Th-Su 8pm; karaoke Th 10pm. Pool tables. Open daily 11am-3am. ❷

Elvis Presley's Memphis, 126 Beale St. (☎527-6900; www.elvis.com). This large, Graceland-sponsored restaurant specializes in Elvis' favorites, like fried dill pickle chips ($6) and fried peanut butter and banana sandwiches ($6.25). Apparently, the King's food preferences were almost as eccentric as his tastes in decor. More standard and artery-friendly fare also served; hearty sandwiches, wraps and burgers with a heap of fries are $7-9.50. Su brunch features live gospel music 11am-2pm. Live blues and rockabilly bands begin Tu-Th 8:30pm, F-Sa 9:30pm. Graceland shuttles stop here. Open Su-Th 11am-12:30am, F-Sa 11am-1:30am. ❷

Huey's, 77 S. 2nd St. (☎527-2700; www.hueys.cc), downtown. Relaxed and casual, Huey's is consistently voted a favorite by locals, especially for burgers ($4.50). Patrons show their appreciation by scrawling graffiti across the walls and launching toothpicks into the ceiling with straw-blowguns. Live music Su 4pm; no cover. Open M-F 11am-3am, Sa-Su 11:30am-3am. ❶

P and H Cafe, 1532 Madison Ave. (☎726-0906; www.pandhcafe.com). The initials stand for Poor and Hungry. The "beer joint of your dreams" grills food for wallet-watchers. The waitresses and kitschy decor are the real draw. During Elvis Week in Aug., P and H hosts the famous "Dead Elvis Ball," with impersonators and live bands. Sandwiches $3-5. Live music M, W, Sa; cover Sa $3-5. Open M-F 11am-3am, Sa 5pm-3am. ❶

GOODNESS, GRACIOUS, GREAT BALLS OF FIRE!

GRACELAND. Bow down before **Graceland,** Elvis Presley's home and a paragon of Americana that every Memphis visitor must see. Surrender yourself to the crush of tourists swarming in a delightful orgy of gaudiness at the tackiest mansion in the US. You'll never forget the faux-fur furnishings, mirrored ceilings, walls covered in green shag carpeting, and yellow-and-orange decor of Elvis' 1974 renovations. A blinding sheen of hundreds of gold and platinum records illuminates the **Trophy Building,** where exhibits discuss Elvis' stint in the army and his 30+ movie roles. The King is buried in the adjacent **Meditation Gardens.** Admission includes an au[illegible]our; proceed through the exhibits at your own pace. *(3763 Elvis Presley Blvd. [illegible]5 S to Exit 5B or bus #43, "Elvis Presley." ☎332-3322 or 800-238-2000. The web site [illegible].com contains info on Graceland as well as all peripheral attractions. Ticket office open [illegible] M-Sa 9am-5pm, Su 10am-4pm; Nov.-Feb. M and W-Su 10am-4pm, mansion closed on [illegible]ets for other attractions sold 10am-4pm. Attractions remain open 2hr. after ticket office [illegible]6.25, students and seniors 62+ $14.63, children 7-12 $6.25. Wheelchair-accessible.)*

MORE ELVIS. If you love him tender, love him true, then visit the peripheral Elvis attractions across the street from the mansion. **Walk a Mile in My Shoes,** a free 20min. film screened every 30min., traces Elvis' career from the early (slim) years through the later (fat) ones. The **Elvis Presley Automobile Museum** houses a fleet of Elvis-mobiles including pink and purple Cadillacs and motorized toys aplenty. *($7.25, students and seniors 62+ $6.53, children 7-12 $3.25.)* Visitors to **Elvis' Custom Jets** can walk through the King's private plane, the *Lisa Marie*, complete with a blue suede bed equipped with a gold-plated seatbelt, and peek into the bright interior of the tiny *Hound Dog II* Jetstar. *($6.25, seniors $5.63, children $3.25.)* The **Sincerely Elvis** exhibit offers a glimpse into Elvis' private side, displaying his wedding announcements, a collection of Lisa Marie's toys, and items from his wild wardrobe, as well as an incredible array of memorabilia and heaps of fan letters. *($5.25, seniors $4.73, children $2.75.)* The **Platinum Tour Package** discounts admission to the mansion and all attractions. *($25.25, students and seniors $22.73, ages 7-12 $12.25.)*

Every year during the week of August 16 (the date of Elvis' death), millions of the King's cortege get all shook up for **Elvis Week,** an extended celebration that includes trivia contests, a fashion show, and a candlelight vigil. The festivities attract Elvis impersonators from around the world. The days surrounding his birthday, January 8, are ushered in with speeches by local politicians and birthday cake.

MUSIC: THE MEMPHIS HEARTBEAT. No visit to Memphis is complete without a visit to **Sun Studio,** where rock 'n' roll was conceived. In this legendary one-room recording studio, Elvis was discovered, Johnny Cash walked the line, Jerry Lee Lewis was consumed by great balls of fire, and Carl Perkins warned everyone to stay off his blue suede shoes. Tours go through a small museum area and proceed to the studio itself, where visitors listen to the recording sessions that earned the studio its fame. *(706 Union Ave. ☎800-441-6249; www.sunstudio.com. Open daily 10am-6pm. 35min. tours every hr. on the ½hr. $9.50, under 12 free; AAA discount.)* Long before Sam Phillips and Sun Studio produced Elvis and Jerry Lee Lewis, historic **Beale Street** saw the invention of the blues and the soul hits of the Stax label. For an idea of how all these different elements influenced each other and American culture at large, head over to the must-see **Rock 'n' Soul Museum.** The numerous artifacts on display include celebrity stage costumes and B.B. King's famous guitar, "Lucille." Best of all, the audio tour contains a hundred complete songs, from early blues classics to Isaac Hayes' *Shaft* theme song. *(145 Lt. George W. Lee Ave. 1 block south of Beale St. ☎543-0800; www.memphisrocknsoul.org. Open daily 10am-6pm. $8.50, seniors 60+ $7.50, ages 5-17 $5; audio tour included. Wheelchair-accessible.)* The **Gibson Guitar Factory,** in the same building, offers tours detailing the various stages of the guitar-making process. *(www.gibsonmemphis.com. Tours last 25min. Su-W 1, 2pm, Th-Sa every hr. 11am-2pm. $10; ages 12 and up only.)*

UNIQUE MUSEUMS. On April 4, 1968, Dr. Martin Luther King Jr. was assassinated at the **Lorraine Motel** in Memphis. Today, the powerful **National Civil Rights Museum** occupies the original building. Relive the courageous struggle of the Civil Rights movement through photographs, videos, and interviews in this moving exhibit, which ends in Dr. King's motel room. *(450 Mulberry St. ☎521-9699; www.civilrightsmuseum.org. Open June-Aug. M and W-Sa 9am-6pm, Su 1-6pm; Sept.-May M and W-Sa 9am-5pm, Su 1-5pm. Feb. open Tu. $10, students with ID and seniors 55+ $8, ages 4-17 $6.50. Free M after 3pm. 1hr. audio tours included with admission, child's version available.)* South of downtown, the **National Ornamental Metal Museum,** the only institution of its kind in the US, displays fine metalwork from international artists. Get a better idea of the artistic process at the working blacksmith shop behind the museum, alongside a sculpture garden overlooking the impressive Mississippi River. Check out the front gate as you walk in. *(374 Metal Museum Dr. Exit 12C from I-55. ☎774-6380; www.metalmuseum.org. Open Tu-Sa 10am-5pm, Su noon-5pm. $4, seniors 62+ $3, stu-*

dents $2.) The **Pink Palace Museum and Planetarium** is a child-oriented science and history museum housed in a grand (and yes, pink) mansion. Visitors are treated to a bit of Memphis history, an IMAX theater, planetarium shows, and some funky exhibits, including a shrunken head display. The mansion was originally built as the dream home of Piggly-Wiggly founder Clarence Saunders, who relinquished the house after losing his fortune on Wall Street. *(3050 Central Ave. ☎320-6362; www.memphismuseums.org. Open M-Th 9am-6pm, F-Sa 9am-9pm, Su noon-6pm. $8, seniors 60+ $7.50, children 3-12 $5.50; IMAX film $7.25/6.75/5.75; planetarium show $4.25/3.75/3.75. Package deals available; exhibits, IMAX, and planetarium $16.50/15/13. Wheelchair-accessible.)* **A. Schwab,** a small, family-run department store (circa 1876), still offers old-fashioned bargains, including deals on postcards, souvenirs, and 44 types of suspenders. The mezzanine houses a "museum" of ancient cash registers and never-sold relics from baby dolls to butter churns. Elvis bought some of his ensembles here. *(163 Beale St. ☎523-9782. Open M-Sa 9am-5pm. Free tours upon request.)*

AQUAMMODATIONS Every day at 11am the **Peabody Hotel** rolls out the red carpet, and the ducks that live in their own luxury rooftop "palace" ride down the elevator, with the help of a personal attendant, and waddle over to a large fountain in the center of the floor to the tune of John Phillip Sousa's *Stars and Stripes Forever* or *King Cotton March*. The procession is repeated, in reverse, when the ducks retire at the start of cocktail hour at 5pm. *(149 Union Ave. Downtown. ☎529-4000.)*

OVERTON PARK. The **Brooks Museum of Art,** in the southwest corner of Overton Park east of downtown, showcases a diverse collection of paintings and decorative arts. Visitors often particularly enjoy the galleries devoted to unique visiting exhibits. On the first Wednesday of each month, the museum hosts a celebration *(6-9pm, $5)* with food, films, live music, and drinks. *(1934 Poplar Ave. ☎544-6200; www.brooksmuseum.org. Open Tu-F 10am-4pm, Sa 10am-5pm, Su 11:30am-5pm, first W of each month 10am-9pm. $6, seniors 65+ $5, students with ID and youth 7-17 $2; W usually free. Audio tour $3/2/2. Wheelchair-accessible.)* Also in the park is the small but impressive **Memphis Zoo.** The cat park is a roar and the China section is one of only four places in the US where you can see giant pandas. Kids will enjoy watching the sea lion show *(daily 10:30am, 2:30pm)* or taking a spin on the endangered species carousel. *(2000 Prentis Place. ☎276-9453; www.memphiszoo.org. Open daily Mar.-Oct. 9am-6pm, Jun.-Aug. Sa until 9pm; Nov.-Feb. daily 9am-5pm; last admission 1hr. before close. $10, seniors 60+ $9, ages 2-11 $6. Giant pandas $3; parking $3. Wheelchair-accessible.)*

MUD ISLAND RIVER PARK. A quick walk or monorail ride over the Mississippi to **Mud Island** allows you to stroll and splash along the **River Walk,** a scale model of the Mississippi River the length of five city blocks. Free tours of the River Walk run several times daily. Also on the island, the **Mississippi River Museum** charts the history and culture of the river over the past 10,000 years with videos, musical recordings, and life-sized replicas of steamboats and ironclads. *(Monorail leaves from 125 N. Front St. every 10min., round-trip $2; pedestrian bridge free. ☎576-7241 or 800-507-6507; www.mudisland.com. Park open Mar.-May and Sept.-Oct. Tu-Su 10am-5pm; Jun.-Aug. daily 10am-8pm; last admission 1hr. before close. 3-5 tours daily. Museum $8, seniors 60+ $6, children 5-12 $5. Wheelchair-accessible.)* Visitors can also paddle around on the Mississippi or peddle through the streets of downtown Memphis. *(1hr. kayak rental $15 for 1 person, for 2 people $20; 1hr. canoe for 2 people $20. 2hr. bicycle rental $10.)*

PARKS & GARDENS. Memphis has almost as many parks as museums. The 96-acre **Memphis Botanic Garden,** with 22 distinct gardens, is the perfect place to take a long stroll. Relish the fantastic 57 variety rose garden, the sensory garden, or the peaceful Japanese garden. *(750 Cherry Rd. In Audubon Park off Park Ave. ☎685-1566; www.memphisbotanicgarden.com. Open Mar.-Oct. M-Sa 9am-6pm, Su 11am-6pm; Nov.-Feb. M-Sa 9am-4:30pm, Su 11am-4:30pm. $5, seniors 62+ $4, children 3-12 $3. Free every Tu after noon. Wheelchair-accessible.)* Across Park Ave., the **Dixon Gallery and Gardens** flaunts an impeccable garden accented with an impressive range of sculptures, and a collection of European art with works by masters including Renoir, Degas, and Monet. *(4339 Park Ave. ☎761-2409; www.dixon.org. Open Tu-F 10am-4pm, Sa 10am-5pm, Su 1-5pm. $7, seniors 60+ $6, students and children $3. Gallery audio tour $3; free self-guided tour for gardens available. Seniors free on Tu.)*

ARE YOU LONESOME TONIGHT?

W.C. Handy's 1917 "Beale St. Blues" claims that "You'll find that business never closes 'til somebody gets killed." Beale St. has changed a lot since Handy's day; today's visitors are more likely to encounter the Hard Rock Cafe and all the mega-commercialism that comes with it than the rough-and-tumble juke joints of old. Despite all the change, the strip between 2nd and 4th St. is still the place visitors come for live music. Few clubs have set closing times. On Friday nights, a $10 wristband lets you wander in and out of any club on the strip. You can save a few bucks by buying a drink at one of the many outdoor stands and soaking up the blues and acrobatics of street performers as you meander from show to show. The free *Memphis Flyer* and the "Playbook" section of the Friday morning *Memphis Commercial Appeal* can tell you what's goin' down in town.

ENTERTAINMENT

The majestic **Orpheum Theatre,** 203 S. Main St., hosts Broadway shows and big-name performers. On Fridays during the summer months, the grand old theater shows classic movies with an organ prelude and a cartoon. (☎525-3000; www.orpheum-memphis.com. Box office open M-F 9am-5pm and before shows. Movies 7:15pm; $6, children under 12 and seniors $5. Concerts and shows $15-55.) Just as things are really beginning to heat up in the South, the legendary **Memphis in May** (☎525-4611) celebration hits the city, continuing throughout the month with concerts, art exhibits, food contests, and sporting events. The **Beale Street Music Festival,** also in May, features some of the biggest names from a range of musical genres.

BEALE STREET BLUES

Rum Boogie Cafe, 182 Beale St. (☎528-0150). One of the first clubs on Beale St., Rum Boogie still rocks with homegrown blues and a friendly ambience. Check out the celebrity guitars hanging from the ceiling and the original Stax Records sign. Live music begins Su-Th 8pm, F-Sa 9pm. Happy Hour M-F 5-7pm. 21+ Su-Th after 9pm, F-Sa after 8pm. Cover M-Th after 8pm $3, F-Sa after 9pm $5. Open daily 11am-2am.

Club 152, 152 Beale St. (☎544-7011), one of the most popular clubs on Beale, offers 3 floors of dancing and drinks. Live music acts range from blues to techno; DJs spin dance and techno upstairs. Check out the "mood elevator." Beer from $3. 21+. Cover $3 on Th, $5-8 on F, $5-10 on Sa. Open M-W 6pm-3am, Th-Sa 6pm-5am, Su 7pm-2am; winter closed M-Tu.

B.B. King's Blues Club, 143 Beale St. (☎524-5464; www.bbkingsclub.com). The laid-back atmosphere and live blues bands make this place a popular joint for locals, visitors, and celebrities alike. B.B. himself still shows up for some meals, and occasionally plays a show. Entrees $7-19. Cover $5-7, when B.B. plays $50-150. Open Su-Th 10am-1:30am, F-Sa 10am-3am.

Alfred's, 197 Beale St. (☎525-3711; www.alfreds-on-beale.com), is a favorite with locals and offers karoake, live music, and DJs spinning hiphop into the wee hours. Outdoor patio. 21+ after 10pm. Cover F-Sa $5. Open Su-Th 11am-3am, F-Sa 11am-5am.

NIGHTLIFE OFF BEALE STREET

For a collegiate climate, try the **Highland Street** strip near **Memphis State University.**

Newby's, 539 S. Highland St. (☎452-8408; www.newbysmemphis.com), is a dark, loud, lively college bar with pool tables, comfy red booths, and an outdoor patio. Live bands play everything from rock to reggae almost every night beginning at 10pm. Beer from $3. Happy Hour 3-10pm daily. 21+. Cover usually $3-5. Open daily 3pm-3am.

Wild Bill's, 1580 Vollintine Ave. (☎726-5473), a neighborhood restaurant and music joint, lies off the beaten track. This small, dark hole in the wall stands in stark contrast to the touristed, trendy places downtown. Live music F-Sa 11pm, Su 10pm. Cover F-Su $5. Open M-Th 7am-11pm, F-Su 7am until late.

J-Wag's Lounge, 1268 Madison (☎725-1909), is a relaxed gay-friendly bar with pool, darts, and a several drink specials. During "Beer Bust," M-F 10am-2pm, patrons who'd rather booze than eat lunch can select from 5 all-you-can-drink drafts. Several years ago, J-Wag's was featured in the movie *The People vs. Larry Flynt*. Drag shows F and Sa 3am. Happy Hour daily noon-7pm. Cover F-Sa midnight-4am $3. Open 24hr.

DAYTRIP FROM MEMPHIS

THE MISSISSIPPI DELTA

South of Memphis, U.S. 61 runs to Vicksburg through the swamps and flatlands of the Mississippi Delta region, where cotton was king and the blues were born. With the exception of the abundant casinos brought in roughly a decade ago to alleviate some of the economic depression of the Delta, the past seems not so very far away in many of the towns 61 passes through, and **Clarksdale, MS,** 70 mi. south of Memphis in the heart of the Delta, is no exception. Here some of the most famous musicians were born and are now glorified at festivals and in museums. The **Delta Blues Museum,** 1 Blues Alley, housed in the old train depot at the intersection of John Lee Hooker Ln., off 3rd. St., displays regional artwork, photographs, and rare Delta artifacts, including harmonicas owned by Sonny Boy Williamson and a guitar fashioned by ZZ Top from a log cabin Muddy Waters once lived in. 2004 marks the silver anniversary of the museum; call to inquire about special events and exhibits. (☎662-627-6820; www.deltabluesmuseum.org. Open Mar.-Oct. M-Sa 9am-5pm; Nov.-Feb. M-Sa 10am-5pm. $6, ages 6-12 $3.) If you do make it to the museum, take a minute to walk over to **Ground Zero ❶,** 0 Blues Alley, for a plate lunch complete with beverage cornbread and dessert for only $6. On the weekend, stay late for local tunes. (☎621-9009. Open for lunch M-Sa 11am-2pm; for dinner W-F 5pm-close and Sa 6pm-close.) For some of the area's best barbecue, try **Abe's ❷,** 616 State St., where a pulled pork sandwich is only $3 and ribs cost $10. (☎624-9947. Open Su-Th 9am-9pm, F-Sa 9am-10pm.) Twenty miles north on U.S. 49, across the river in Arkansas, lies

'he legendary King Biscuit Time radio show was first broadcast here in

first weekend of October, the town hosts the **King Biscuit Blues Festi-**

rgest free blues festival in the South. The **Delta Cultural Center,** 141

, displays exhibits on the rich land and poor people that figure so

'y in regional culture. (☎870-338-4350 or 800-358-0972; www.deltacul-

.com. Open M-Sa 10am-5pm, Su 1-5pm. Free.)

NORTH CAROLINA

North Carolina brings to mind fields of tobacco, pastel sunsets, and rocking chairs on porches—and these generalizations aren't far from the truth. Travelers will find, however, that they won't want to just sit around sipping sweet tea; the state boasts a surprising number of natural and cultural attractions. Outdoorsy types will revel in the awesome landscapes and laidback culture of the Western mountains, where thrill-seekers can find snowboarding, mountain-biking, and white-water rafting opportunities galore. The cities of the central Piedmont region combine the cosmopolitanism of the North with the slower pace of the South, drawing travelers with a variety of cultural activities and important historical sights. This area is home to some of the nation's top universities, as well as the Research Triangle, which sees cutting-edge innovations in medicine and technology. Charlotte, meanwhile, has the distinction of being the country's second-largest financial center. No traveler should come to North Carolina without spending a few days relaxing on the gorgeous beaches, where great surfing and fresh fish come in equal parts. Despite its marked diversity, one thing can be said for the whole of the "Tarheel State"—natural beauty and southern hospitality are the rule.

PRACTICAL INFORMATION

Capital: Raleigh.

Visitor Info: Dept. of Commerce, Travel and Tourism, 301 N. Wilmington St., Raleigh 27601 (☎919-733-4171 or 800-847-4862; www.visitnc.com). **Division of Parks and Recreation,** 512 N. Salisbury St., Archdale Building 7th fl., Room 732 (☎919-733-4181; parkinfo@ncmail.net).

Postal Abbreviation: NC. **Sales Tax:** 6.5%.

THE TRIANGLE ☎919

A trio of towns—Raleigh, Durham, and Chapel Hill—sporting large universities and top-notch scientists, "the Triangle" was born in the 1950s with the creation of the spectacularly successful Research Triangle Park. As a result, the area is alive with students, scholars, and things to do. **Raleigh,** the state capital and home to North Carolina State University (NC State), is a historic town that has recently revamped its tourist attractions. **Durham,** formerly a major tobacco producer, now supports medical research projects devoted to finding cancer cures. The University of North Carolina (UNC), chartered in 1789 as the nation's first state university, is located just 20 mi. down the road in **Chapel Hill.** College culture infuses the area with a hip music scene, popular bars, and a plethora of quirky stores.

TRANSPORTATION

Airport: Raleigh-Durham International (☎840-2123; www.rdu.com), 15 mi. from both downtown Raleigh and Durham, between U.S. 70 and I-40 on Aviation Blvd. From Durham, take Exit 284B from I-40E or Exit 292 from U.S. 70E. From Raleigh, take Exit 285 from I-40W or Exit 292 from U.S. 70W. A taxi to downtown Raleigh or Durham costs about $27.50. Triangle Transit Authority offers van shuttle service from RDU to surrounding areas; see **Public Transit** below.

Trains: Amtrak, 320 W. Cabarrus St., Raleigh (☎833-7594), 4 blocks west of the Civic Ctr. Open 24hr. To: **Durham** (40min., 2 per day, $4-7), **New York,** (10hr., 2 per day, $66-144), **Richmond** (3½hr., 2 per day, $22-51) and **Washington D.C.** (5½hr., 2 per day, $34-80). In Durham, station at 400 W. Chapel Hill St. (☎956-7932). Open daily 7am-9pm. To **Raleigh** (40min., 2 per day, $4-7).

Buses: Greyhound has stations in both Raleigh and Durham. **Raleigh:** 314 W. Jones St. (☎834-8275). Open 24hr. To: **Chapel Hill** (1¼hr., 4 per day, $11); **Charleston** (7½hr., 4 per day, $53); **Durham** (40min., 9 per day, $6.50). **Durham:** 820 W. Morgan St. (☎687-4800), 1 block off Chapel Hill St. downtown, 2½ mi. northeast of Duke. Open daily 7:30am-9:30pm. To **Chapel Hill** (25min., 4 per day, $8) and **Washington, D.C.** (6hr., 6 per day, $50).

Public Transit: Affordable public transportation between the cities is available through **Triangle Transit Authority** (☎549-9999; www.ridetta.org). Buses run approximately M-F 6am-10pm, Sa 6am-5:30pm. $1.50. **Capital Area Transit,** Raleigh (☎828-7228). Buses run M-Sa 5am-midnight. $0.75; transfers free. **Durham Area Transit Authority (DATA),** Durham (☎683-3282; www.ci.durham.nc.us/departments/works/divisions/data.cfm). Most routes start downtown at 521 Morgan St. Operates daily; hours vary by route; fewer on Su. $0.75; seniors, under 18, and disabled $0.35; children under 43 in. free; transfers free. There is also a free shuttle between Duke's east and west campuses (☎684-2218). **Chapel Hill Transit,** Chapel Hill (☎968-2769; www.ci.chapel-hill.nc.us/transit). Buses run 5:40am-8pm. Free.

Taxi: Cardinal Cab, (☎828-3228).

PRACTICAL INFORMATION

Visitor Info: Capital Area Visitor Center, 301 N. Blount St. in Raleigh (☎733-3456; www.visitraleigh.com). Open M-F 10am-4pm, Sa-Su 1-4pm. **Durham Convention and Visitors Bureau,** 101 E. Morgan St. (☎800-772-BULL; www.durham-nc.com). Open M-F 8:30am-5pm, Sa 10am-2pm. **Chapel Hill Visitors Center,** 501 W. Franklin St., near Carrboro. (☎968-2060 or 888-968-2062; www.chocvb.org.) Open M-F 8:30am-5pm, Sa 10am-2pm.

Hotlines: Rape Crisis, ☎919-403-6562. 24hr.

Internet Access: State Library, 109 E. Jones St., in Raleigh, 1 block south of the Visitor Center (☎733-3683). Open M-F 10am-5pm. **Durham County Public Library,** 300 N. Roxboro St., near the Visitors Center (☎560-0100). Open M-Th 9am-9pm, F 9am-6pm, Sa 9:30am-6pm. Sept.-May also open Su 2-6pm. **Chapel Hill Public Library,** 100 Library Rd. (☎968-2777). Open M-Th 10am-9pm, F 10am-6pm, Sa 9am-6pm, Su 1-8pm. From the university area, go down Frankin St. toward Durham and take a left on Estes St.; it's immediately on your right.

Post Office: Raleigh: 311 New Bern Ave. (☎832-1604). Open M-F 8am-5:30pm, Sa 8am-noon. **Postal code:** 27611. **Durham:** 323 E. Chapel Hill St. (☎683-1976). Open M-F 8:30am-5pm. **Postal code:** 27701. **Chapel Hill:** 125 S. Estes St. (☎967-6297). Open M-F 8:30am-5:30pm, Sa 8:30am-noon. **Postal code:** 27514. **Area Code:** 919.

ACCOMMODATIONS

Raleigh's budget lodging can be found on Capital Blvd., in the Crabtree area, about 2½ mi. northeast of town, about a mile inside the I-440 beltline. Reasonably priced accommodations are harder to come by in Chapel Hill.

Homestead Suites, 4810 Bluestone Dr. (☎510-8551; www.homesteadhotels.com), off Glenwood Ave. in Raleigh just northwest of Crabtree Valley Mall, has new, comfortable rooms with kitchenettes, A/C, cable TV, free local calls, and Internet access. Laundry facilities and extensive room service available. Free access to local gym included. Queens $46; 2 queen beds or king with pull-out couch $56; for stays of a week or longer, nightly rates drop to $36/46. ❷

Best Value Carolina Duke Inn, 2517 Guess Rd. (☎286-0771 or 800-438-1158 for reservations), just off I-85 at Exit 175 in Durham, provides travelers with clean, budget-priced rooms. Laundry facilities, pool, A/C, cable TV, free local calls, and breakfast included. Doubles have fridges and microwaves. DATA bus access across the street; complimentary shuttle to RDU. Wheelchair-accessible. Singles $40-43; doubles $48; large family rooms $60. 10% AARP/AAA discount. ❷

Falls Lake State Recreation Area (☎676-1027), about 12 mi. north of Raleigh, off Rte. 98, has four campgrounds; call for directions. Main campground Holly Point is adjacent to the lake and has 2 swimming beaches, showers, boat ramps, and a dump station. Gates close Jun.-Aug. 9pm; Apr.-May and Sept. 8pm; Mar. and Oct. 7pm; Nov.-Feb. 6pm. Reservations taken with 2 weeks notice for stays of more than 7 days. $12, with hookup $17. No credit cards. ❶

FOOD

The area's major universities have spawned a swath of affordable and interesting eateries; Raleigh's **Hillsborough Street** and **Capital Boulevard,** Durham's **9th Street,** and Chapel Hill's **Franklin Street** all cater to a college (read: budget-oriented) crowd. In Raleigh, travelers can find good dining options in **City Market,** a collection of shops, cafes, and bars a few blocks southeast of the capitol. In Durham, **Brightleaf Square,** about a mile east of 9th St. on Main St., is a complex of renovated brick tobacco warehouses that now holds galleries, shops, and many quality restaurants.

RALEIGH

The Rockford, 320½ Glenwood Ave. (☎821-9020), near the intersection with Hillsborough St., is a trendy second-floor restaurant serving inexpensive, delicious food. The ABC sandwich—slices of cheddar and granny smith with strips of bacon on whole wheat—is a favorite ($6.75). All entrees $7 or less; beer from $2.50. Open M-W 11:30am-2pm and 6pm-midnight, Th-Sa 11:30am-2pm and 6pm-2am, Su 6pm-midnight. ❶

Irregardless Cafe, 901 W. Morgan St. (☎833-8898; www.irregardless.com), just after Morgan splits off of Hillsborough St. The selection of excellent dishes with a gourmet twist changes daily, specializing in seafood and a variety of vegetarian and vegan options. Frequent live music. Entrees $14-20. Lunch $6-12. Open for lunch Tu-Sa 11:30am-2:30pm; for dinner Tu-Th 5:30-9:30pm, F 5:30-10pm, Sa 5:30 to at least 11pm with dancing beginning at 9:30pm; Su brunch 10am-2pm. ❸

DURHAM

The Mad Hatter's Cafe and Bake Shop, 1802 W. Main St. (☎286-1987; www.madhattersbakeshop.com), 1 block from 9th St., offers a wide selection of delicious dishes in generous portions, including handmade pizza, Asian noodle soups, and wraps. The pleasant, modern restaurant also has an outdoor patio area. Sandwiches $6-8. Occasional live music. Open M-Th 7am-9pm, F-Sa 7am-11pm, Su 8am-4pm. ❷

Pao Lim Asian Bistro and Bar, 2505 Chapel Hill Blvd. (☎419-1771), near the intersection with University Dr., prepares some of the area's best Asian cuisine. Entrees from $7.50; lunch specials around $5.50. Open M-Th 11:30am-9:30pm, F 11:30am-10pm, Sa noon-10pm, Su noon-9:30pm. ❷

Francesca's, 706 9th St. (☎286-4177), farther down 9th St., dishes up delectable desserts for around $3. Be sure to sample some of the homemade gelato for $2.50. Open M-Th 11am-11pm, F-Sa 11am-midnight, Su 11am-10pm. ❶

CHAPEL HILL

Skylight Exchange, 405½ W. Rosemary St. (☎933-5550; delivery 929-6354), entrance in an alley off of Rosemary, a block over from Franklin. This eclectic and comfortable restaurant doubles as a used book/music store. Specialty sandwiches $3-8, coffee and a refill $1.25. The Exchange becomes "Nightlight," a bar, M-Sa at 9pm. Beer from $1.50. Trivia night M 9pm. Live music about 4 nights a week at 10pm; see http://dyss.net/nightlight for schedules. Open M-Sa 11am-2am, Su 11am-11pm. ❶

Cosmic Cantina, 128 W. Franklin St. (☎960-3955), inside the shopping complex, is a great stop for authentic, cheap, and quick Mexican fare ($3-8). Margaritas $3, pitcher of sangria $12. Another location in **Durham,** 1920½ Perry St. (☎286-1875), at the end of the shops on 9th St., is a student hot spot. Both open daily 11am; closing varies and can be as late as 4am. ❶

Ramshead Rathskellar, 157½ E. Franklin St. (☎942-5158). The dimly-lit interior of "the Rat" has seen more than 50 years of Tarheels come and go. M nights feature all-you-can-eat pasta for $5.30, including unlimited bread, salad, and iced tea. Sandwiches under $7. Ask to sit in the "cave." Open Su-Th 11am-9pm, F-Sa 11am-10:30pm. ❸

SIGHTS

RALEIGH. Downtown Raleigh offers a number of worthwhile, free attractions. Across from the **capitol building,** in the center of downtown Raleigh, are two first-rate museums. Kids will enjoy the **Museum of Natural Sciences,** home to "Willo," a rare dinosaur fossil with an iron concretion within the ribcage—possibly a fossil of the creature's heart. Also impressive is the skeleton of a 15 ft. giant ground sloth unearthed near Wilmington. The **North Carolina Museum of History** looks back through North Carolina history via an ever-changing array of special exhibits, as well as the N.C. Sports Hall of Fame and an exhibit on past and present health care systems in the state. Program and tour info is available on the web site. *(Museum of Natural Sciences: 11 W. Jones St. ☎733-7450. Open M-Sa 9am-5pm, Su noon-5pm. Free. Audio tour $4. Museum of History: 5 E. Edenton St. ☎715-0200; www.ncmuseumofhistory.org. Open Tu-Sa 9am-5pm, Su noon-5pm. Free.)* **Artspace,** 201 E. Davie St., is a collection of 46 artists' studios open to the public, with three exhibition galleries featuring work by regional, national, and international artists. *(☎821-2787; www.artspacenc.org. Open Tu-Sa 10am-6pm, first F of each month 10am-10pm, studio hours vary. Free.)*

Stretching east from the Visitors Center, **Historic Oakwood** is a Victorian neighborhood featuring some of Raleigh's most notable architecture, with attractive homes constructed in the late 19th and early 20th centuries. This neighborhood and the adjacent **Oakwood Cemetery** make a pleasant setting for a walk or drive, a calming escape from the bustle of the city center. *(Historic Oakwood is bordered by Franklin, Watauga, Linden, Jones, and Person St. Free self-guided walking tour available at the Visitors Center. Entrance to the cemetery is at 701 Oakwood Ave; ☎832-6077. Open daily 8am-5pm; free maps available in the cemetery office, near the gates.)*

DURHAM. Durham's main attractions center around the Duke family and their principle legacy, **Duke University,** which is divided into East and West Campuses. The majestic, neo-gothic **Duke Chapel,** completed in the early 1930s, looms grandly at the center of West Campus. Over a million pieces of stained glass and a host of statues depicting both Christian and Southern figures grace the chapel. *(☎684-2572. Open daily Sept.-May 8am-10pm; June-Aug. 8am-8pm. Free. Self-guided tour available.)* Nearby on Anderson St., the gorgeous **Sarah P. Duke Gardens** showcase both native and non-native plants on more than 55 lush acres, complete with ponds and a vine-draped gazebo. *(☎684-3698. Open daily 8am-dusk. Free.)* At the other end of Durham, the **Museum of Life and Science,** 433 Murray Ave., off of N. Duke St., is a must-see for families with children. Visitors can romp through the musical playground, pet barn animals, ride a train through the Nature Park, and explore hands-on exhibits about everything from bubbles to outer space. In the **Magic Wings Butterfly House,** over 1000 species of butterflies from around the world flutter among tropical plants. *(☎220-5429; www.ncmls.org. Open M-Sa 11am-5pm, Su noon-5pm; Memorial Day-Labor Day, Su open until 6pm. $8.50, seniors 65+ $7.50, children 3-12 $6, under 3 free; includes butterfly house. Train $1.50; ride 1½ mi.)*

Nearby, at the **Duke Homestead,** visitors can explore the original farm, home, and factories where Washington Duke first planted and processed tobacco. The seeds sown here would eventually grow into the key to the city's prosperity: Duke's sons founded the American Tobacco Company, which came to dominate the industry for decades, putting Durham on the map and generating enough profits to found the university. Tours include an early factory, a curing barn, and a packhouse as well as the restored home. The adjoining **Tobacco Museum** explains the history of the tobacco industry and displays fascinating old cigarette advertisements. *(2828 Duke Homestead Rd., off Guess Rd. ☎477-5498. Open Tu-Sa 10am-4pm. Free. Free 45min. Homestead tours depart 15min. after the hr.)*

The 1988 movie *Bull Durham* was filmed in the **Durham Bulls'** ballpark. The AAA farm team for the Tampa Bay Devil Rays still plays here, minus Kevin Costner. *(Take "Durham Bulls Stadium" Exit off I-40. ☎687-6500; www.durhambulls.com.)* Travelers visiting the area during June and July should not miss a modern dance performance at the **American Dance Festival,** hosted annually at Duke. *(☎684-6402; www.americandancefestival.org. Tickets $18-36.)*

CHAPEL HILL. Chapel Hill and neighboring Carrboro are virtually inseparable from the beautiful campus of the **University of North Carolina at Chapel Hill.** The university's **Dean Dome** hosts a variety of sporting events and concerts. *(Tickets available through Ticketmaster.)* Until 1975, NASA astronauts trained at UNC's **Morehead Planetarium;** of the 12 astronauts who have walked on the moon, 11 worked here. Today, Morehead gives live sky shows as well as multimedia presentations on outer space in the 68 ft. domed Star Theater. The planetarium also houses small exhibits on outer space. *(250 E. Franklin St. ☎549-6863; www.morehead.unc.edu. Open mid-June through mid-Aug. Su-W 12:30-5pm and 7-9:45pm, Th-Sa 10am-5pm and 7-9:45 pm; mid-Aug. through mid-Jun. Su-Tu 12:30-5pm, W-Sa 10am-5pm and 7-9:45pm; call for show times. $4.50; students, seniors, and children $3.50. Exhibits free.)* Further information about campus attractions, including the **Ackland Art Museum** and **Coker Arboretum,** can be found in the Visitors Center, in the planetarium's west lobby, or at www.unc.edu.

ENTERTAINMENT & NIGHTLIFE

Pick up a free copy of the weekly *Spectator* and *Independent* magazines, available at many restaurants and bookstores, for listings of Triangle events. Additional info on cultural happenings in Raleigh can be found at www.raleighnow.com. Chapel Hill offers the Triangle's best nightlife, especially in terms of music. A number of popular bars line Franklin St., and several live music clubs congregate near the western end of Franklin St., where it becomes Main St. in the neighboring town of Carrboro. **Cat's Cradle,** 300 E. Main St., in Carrboro, is the area's main venue, hosting a wide variety of local and national acts. Recent performers include John Mayer and Dispatch. (☎967-9053; www.catscradle.com. Cover and show times vary based on performer.) One block closer to campus, just off Franklin St., **Go! Room 4,** 100-F Brewer Ln. (☎969-1400), features local acts. Another nearby club, **Local 506,** 506 W. Franklin St., focuses on indie rock. (☎942-5506; www.local506.com. 21+. Cover around $5.)

Nightlife options are also plentiful in Raleigh; the area around Glenwood by Hillsborough St. is home to a number of popular, trendy bars. **Mitch's Tavern,** 2426 Hillsborough St., a second floor bar across from N.C. State, is a favorite among students and locals for a late-night brew. The dark, smoky charm of the tavern's interior led the producers of *Bull Durham* to select this as the set for two scenes. (☎821-7771; www.mitchs.com. Pints $2, pitchers $7. Open daily 11am-2am.) **Greenshields,** 214 E. Martin St., at Blount St. in City Market, brews their own beer in a fun, relaxed environment. (☎829-0214. Pints $3.50. Open M-W 11:30am-11pm, Th 11:30am-midnight, F-Sa 11:30am-1am, Su 11:30am-10pm.)

For dancing, head to **Five Star,** 511 W. Hargett St., in downtown Raleigh. This popular Chinese restaurant becomes a nightclub at around 10pm. (☎833-3311. F-Sa 21+. Cover $5 after 10:30pm. Open daily 5:30pm-2am; live DJs Th-Sa beginning at 10pm.) Both **Retail Bar,** 14 W. Martin St., and **Legends,** 330 W. Hargett St., are gay-friendly. (Retail ☎828-7622; www.retailbar.com. 21+. Cover F-Sa $5. Open Tu-Th 8pm-2am, F 8pm-2:30am, Sa 8pm-3am. Legends ☎831-8888; www.legends-club.com. Cover $2-6, under 21 up to $10. Open daily 9pm-3am, later on F-Sa. M and Th gothic, Su drag show at 11:30pm and 12:45am.)

In Durham, **George's Garage,** 737 9th St., arguably the area's best sushi restaurant, stays open til the wee hours serving drinks. Ask about nightly specials. (☎286-4131. Dancing F-Sa. Cover F-Sa $3. Bar open Su-Th 4pm until at least 12:30am, sometimes until 2am, F-Sa 4pm-2am.)

WINSTON-SALEM ☎336

Winston-Salem was, as its name suggests, originally two different towns. Salem was the center of the Moravian movement, driven by religious fervor, dedication to education, and the production of crafts. Winston, meanwhile, rose to prominence as a major center of tobacco production, home to the famous tobacco mogul R.J. Reynolds. As the two towns merged, a dynamic, bustling little city was born. Today, the skyline of Winston-Salem (including some rather suggestive buildings) testifies that to the twin town's continued prominence.

PRACTICAL INFORMATION. The **Piedmont Triad International Airport** (☎721-0088; www.ptia.org), at Exit 210 off of I-40, about 20min. from the city, is the closest airport serving commercial flights. The **Amtrak Connector** van service takes passengers from the Best Western Salem Inn, 127 S. Cherry St., across from the Visitor Center, to the Amtrak Station in Greensboro. (Info ☎800-298-7246. Departs 8:35am daily. Return trips available at night, arriving 8:05pm.) The **Greyhound** station, 250 Greyhound Ct., is downtown at Exit 110A off of Hwy. 52N. (☎724-1429. Open daily 8:30am-12:30am.) **Winston-Salem Transit Authority** has a main depot on 5th St. between Liberty and Trade St. (☎727-2000. Fare $1, transfers free. Buses operate M-F 6:30am-11:30pm, Sa 8am-6:30pm.) **Winston-Salem Visitor Center:** 200 Brookstown Ave. (☎777-3796, 800-331-7018; www.visitwinstonsalem.com. Open daily 8:30am-5pm.) **Internet Access: Public Library,** 660 W. 5th St., at Spring St. downtown. (☎727-2264. Open M-W 9am-9pm, Th-F 9am-6pm, Sa 9am-5pm; Sept.-May also open Su 1-5pm.) **Post Office:** 1500 Patterson Ave. (☎721-1749. Open M-F 8:30am-5pm.) **Postal Code:** 27101. **Area Code:** 336.

ACCOMMODATIONS. There are scores of motels that are perfect for the budget traveler at Exit 184 off I-40, on the way into town. On the northern side of the city, budget motels center around Hwy. 52, just past Patterson Ave. Most rooms run $39-69. **Motel 6 ❷,** 3810 Patterson Ave., offers some of the least expensive lodging available in the city. Though a bit far from downtown, the clean rooms are a great value, with A/C, HBO, data ports, a pool, laundry facilities. (☎661-1588. Singles $32; doubles $38; additional adults $3. AARP 10% off.) The **Colonel Ludlow Inn ❺,** 434 Summit St., at W. 5th St. a few blocks from downtown, will reward those in the mood for a splurge. The luxurious rooms are outfitted with jacuzzis, stereos, TVs, stocked refrigerators, bathrobes, and a full breakfast brought to your door. (☎777-1887 or 800-301-1887; www.bbinn.com. Exercise room and pool table. Reception 8am-9pm. Rooms for 1 person Su-Th $109, for 2 $109-169; F-Sa $129-189. Room without jacuzzi for 1 person Su-Th $79, for 2 $89; F-Sa $99.)

FOOD. Winston-Salem is the birthplace of national doughnut company **Krispy Kreme,** and no visit to the city would be complete without stopping by the **Krispy Kreme Shop ❶,** 259 S. Stratford Rd., where you can watch the famous doughnuts being made fresh on site and feel your heart clog at no extra cost. (☎724-2484. Doughnuts $0.69-0.79. Open M-Th 5:30am-11pm, drive-thru til midnight, F-Sa 5:30am-midnight, drive-thru til 1am, Su 5:30am-11pm.) In the heart of the Old Salem Village, the romantic **Old Salem Tavern ❺,** 736 Main St., will delight the taste buds with imaginative dishes served by waiters and waitresses in traditional Moravian garb. Lunch entrees range from quiche and salad ($6.25) to Southern-style catfish ($8.25), while dinner fare is a bit more fancy, with selections such as the $18 pan-seared duck with honey lavender glaze. (☎748-8585. Open for lunch Su-F 11:30am-2pm, Sa 11:30am-2:30pm; for dinner M-Th 5-9pm, F-Sa 5-9:30pm.) **The West End Cafe ❷,** 926 W. 4th St., is a laidback local favorite with something for everyone, including sandwiches and creative entrees that change seasonally. (☎723-4774. Salads $4.75-8. Burgers $4.50-6. Dinner entrees $9-21. Open M-F 11am-10pm, Sa noon-10pm.)

SIGHTS. **Old Salem Village** takes visitors back in time to a working Moravian village. The Moravians, an early Protestant group, came to North Carolina from the present-day Czech Republic in order to live in political and religious harmony. Today, the restored village outlines their fascinating history and traditions. The area stretches south from downtown and includes a Visitor Center, a number of museums, and a multitude of traditional Moravian homes and buildings, including shoemaker and gunsmith shops. The neat **Museum of Early Southern Decorative Art (MESDA),** in the **Frank L. Horton Museum Center,** 924 S. Main St., showcases artifacts and decorative arts from around the Southeast, representing the period from 1690-1820. The museum is "ropes free," meaning the rooms are reconstructed to look and feel the same as the rooms in historical Southern homes. (1hr. guided tours only, leave every 30min. M-Sa 9:30am-3:30pm, Su 1:30-3:30pm.) The **Toy Museum,** in the same building, displays antique toys spanning 1700 years. Most attractions require an admission ticket; passes good for all Old Salem attractions can be purchased at the **Old Salem Visitor Center Complex,** 601 Old Salem Rd., at the **Boys School,** located at the intersection of Main and Academy St., or at the Horton Museum Center. ($20, ages 6-16 $10; 2-day pass $23/10; includes audio walking tour.) Alternatively, you can buy a ticket good for any two attractions ($14/7). Tickets for individual attractions are not available; only the **Children's Museum**—a period-themed play area in the Horton Museum Center—offers admission separate from these combination passes (ages 4 and up $5). (Old Salem general info ☎888-653-7253; www.oldsalem.org. AAA $2 off adult prices; look for other coupons on the web site. Visitor Center open M-Sa 8:30am-5:30pm, Su 12:30-5:30pm. Most attractions open M-Sa 9am-5pm, Su 1-5pm.)

Winston-Salem's other premier attraction is **Reynolda House,** 2250 Reynolda Rd., on the other side of town, perhaps one of the South's most famous homes. (☎758-5150 or 888-663-1149; www.reynoldahouse.org. Open Tu-Sa 9:30am-4:30pm, Su 1:30-4:30pm; no admittance after 4pm. $8, seniors and AAA $7, students and ages 21 and younger free. Wheelchair-accessible.) Now affiliated with Wake Forest Uni-

YOUR OWN WAY

PITSTOP PARADISE

When does a shopping center make it onto a state map? When it offers 11 amusement rides, indoor mini-golf, multiple video arcades, a lawn ornament superstore, and an enormous statue of a man sporting an oversized yellow sombrero. The statue bestrides the driveway in colossal fashion—motorists steer their cars between his legs. Part amusement park, part tacky gift shop, part fireworks superstore, and all neon, **South of the Border** glows on I-95 just over the state line outside of Dillon, South Carolina. This landscape of asphalt and flashing lights is studded with statues of cacti and sombrero-wearing dinosaurs. Other inexplicably awesome attractions include a 22-story Sombrero Tower with a glass elevator.

Pedro's playland has a number of shops peddling all imaginable kinds of trinkets. Comb through the bins and you'll find handcuffs, hula hoops, incense, salt-water taffy, and foam-front baseball caps. One shop has an entire section devoted to back-scratchers. If the flashing lights become too much, just stroll over to the Mexico Shop for a pair of ridiculously oversized sunglasses. Among the shops crammed with assorted junk, Pedro's resort does offer a drug store, a post office, gas pumps, and a grocery store for more practical purchases.

versity, the 1917 house is credited to the vision of Katherine Smith, the wife of tobacco giant R.J. Reynolds. In its heyday, the household was completely self-sufficient, with a working "village" on the grounds. The mansion is now home to an impressive collection of American art, but the manor's true allure is the two acres of gardens that surround it. The **Reynolda Gardens,** created for the enjoyment of the public as well as the Reynolds family, remain one of the most beautiful spots in Winston-Salem. (☎758-5593. Open dawn-dusk. Free.)

ENTERTAINMENT & NIGHTLIFE. Look for listings of local events in the free weekly newspaper, *Go Triad.* On weekends from May to August, the city hosts **Alive After Five** every Thursday evening (Corpening Plaza, 100 W. 2nd St.), **Fourth Street Jazz and Blues** every Friday evening (W. 4th St.), and **Summer on Trade** every Saturday evening (6th and Trade St.). Check out www.winstonsalemevents.com for more info. You'll find quality live music and some big name bands at **Ziggy's,** 433 Baity St., off University Pkwy. near the Coliseum. (☎748-1064; www.ziggyrock.com. Beer from $2. Cover $5-25. Open Tu-Su 8pm-2am, bands start around 9pm.) Good musicians also rock out at **The Garage,** 110 W. 7th St., at Trade St. (☎777-1127; www.the-garage.ws. Beer from $2. Cover usually around $5-6, additional $1 if under 21. Open Th-Sa 9pm-2am, sometimes also W.)

CHARLOTTE ☎704

Named long ago after the wife to England's King George III, Charlotte is still referred to as the "Queen City" today. Gold prospectors flooded this area after the precious ore was discovered here in 1799; searches yielded nuggets weighing as much as 28 pounds. Though this first gold rush in North America was short-lived, money has continued to drive the city: a branch of the US Mint was established here in 1837, and Charlotte is now the second-largest financial center in the nation. The biggest city in the Carolinas, the Queen City has expanded both out and up; skyscrapers gleam in the bustling uptown area. For visitors, the city offers top-notch museums, ritzy clubs, and a variety of professional sports.

ORIENTATION. The nucleus of Charlotte, the busy uptown area, is easily maneuverable with streets laid out in a simple grid pattern. Numbered streets run southeast to northwest, intersected by perpendicular named streets. **Tryon Street,** running north-south, and **Trade Street,** bisecting the city from east to west, are the major crossroads. I-77 crosses the city north-south, providing access to uptown via W. Trade St. Uptown can also be reached from I-277, which circles the city, and is called the **John Belk Freeway** to the south of uptown and the **Brookshire Freeway** to the north.

PRACTICAL INFORMATION. The **Charlotte-Douglas International Airport,** about 7 mi. west of the city on Josh Birmingham Pkwy., accessible from the Billy Graham Pkwy., is as a hub for US Airways (☎359-4027; www.charlotteairport.com). **Amtrak,** 1914 N. Tryon St. (☎376-4416), and **Greyhound,** 601 W. Trade St. (☎372-0456), stop in Charlotte. Both stations are open 24hr. The **Charlotte Area Transit System (CATS),** operates local buses; the central terminal is at 310 E. Trade St. (☎336-3366; www.ridetransit.org. Most buses operate M-Sa 5:30am-1:30am, Su 7am-1:30am. $1, $1.40 for express service in outlying areas; most transfers free, local to express transfers $0.40.) Within the uptown area, CATS runs **Gold Rush,** free shuttles that resemble old-fashioned cable cars. **Visitors Center:** 500 S. College St., Ste. 300. (☎800-722-1994; www.visitcharlotte.org. Open M-F 8:30am-5pm, Sa 9am-3pm.) **Hotlines: Rape Crisis,** ☎375-9900. **Suicide Line,** ☎358-2800. Both 24hr. **Gay/Lesbian Hotline,** ☎535-6277. Operates Su-Th 6:30-9:30pm. **Internet Access: Public Library of Charlotte and Mecklenburg County,** 310 N. Tryon St., in uptown (☎336-2572). Open M-Th 9am-9pm, F-Sa 9am-6pm, Su 1-6pm. **Post Office:** 201 N. McDowell. (☎333-5135 Open M-F 7:30am-6pm, Sa 10am-1pm.) **Postal Code:** 28204. **Area Code:** 704.

ACCOMMODATIONS & FOOD. There are several clusters of budget motels in the Charlotte area: on Independence Blvd. off the John Belk Freeway; off I-85 at Sugar Creek Rd., Exit 41; off I-85 at Exit 33 near the airport; and off I-77 at Clanton St., Exit 7. The **Continental Inn ❷,** 1100 W. Sugar Creek Rd., Exit 41 off of I-85, has immaculate, inviting rooms. (☎597-8100. A/C, cable TV, free HBO, continental breakfast. Su-Th singles $36, F-Sa $40; doubles $46/52. 10% discount for AAA/AARP.) **Homestead Studio Suites Hotel ❸,** 710 Yorkmont Rd., near the airport, provides clean, spacious rooms with full kitchenettes and high-speed Internet connections as well as on-site coin-operated laundry facilities and free access to a local health club. (☎676-0083; www.homesteadhotels.com. Queens $56, kings $61; 2 queen beds $66. Weekly $287/327/367. 10% discount for AAA/AARP.)

Two areas outside of uptown offer attractive dining options. North Davidson **("NoDa"),** around 36th St., is home to a small artistic community inhabiting a set of historic buildings. South from city center, the **Dilworth** neighborhood, along East and South Blvd., is

Tired travelers can get some shut-eye at the **South of the Border Motor Hotel,** with bright rooms and A/C, HBO, and fridges. A **campground** has laundry, playgrounds, and bathhouses. For a full-service restaurant, try the **Sombrero Room** (with cowskin patterned vinyl seats) or the **Peddler Steakhouse** (the roof is a giant sombrero).

In recent years, the Mexico-themed resort complex has come under criticism for promoting stereotypes about Latinos. Visitors will quickly see why: the sleepy Mexican mascot, Pedro, can't seem to keep his eyes open or form a sentence in English. His frenetic misspellings pepper the famous billboards that have drawn travelers here for decades. The billboards, which dominate the sides of I-95 for dozens of miles in either direction, advertise S.O.B. with a variety of horrible puns ("You never sausage a place!").

To witness America at its most overwhelmingly tacky (think 8 ft. pink flamingoes), head to South of the Border. Trust us—you can't miss it.

South of the Border *is located at the North Carolina/South Carolina line on I-95/U.S.301-501 (Hotel reservations ☎800-845-6011; in SC ☎800-922-6064; www.pedroland.com). Motor Hotel rooms from $39. Pool, sauna, tennis courts. Wheelchair-accessible. Campground tent sites $13, full-hookup $19. Rides open Su-Th 10am 10pm, F-Sa 10am-11pm. Restaurant hours vary.*

lined with restaurants serving everything from ethnic cuisine to pizza and pub fare. In NoDa, the hip, heavily-pierced staff at the **Fat City Deli ❷,** 3027 N. Davidson St., serves up satisfying sandwiches ($5-7) and salads ($4-6.50). Patrons can take in the breeze on the outdoor patio or the beats of live bands (W-Sa nights) and DJs (M-Tu nights). (☎343-0240; www.fatcitydeli.net. Open daily 11:30am-2am, kitchen closes at 1am.) For a slightly pricier option uptown, the hip **Cosmos Cafe ❹,** 300 N. College St., at E. 6th St., has a versatile menu covering everything from spring rolls and sushi to wood-fired pizzas. The restaurant becomes a popular yuppie bar around 10:30pm; swing by Wednesday nights for superb gourmet martinis at half price. (☎372-3553; www.cosmoscafe.com. Pizzas $8.25-10. Mezes and tapas $5.25-9. Tapas are half price M-F 5-7pm. Tu Latin night with free salsa lessons. Open M-F 11am-2am, Sa 5pm-2am.) The best spot to find organic health food is **Talley's Green Grocery ❶,** 1408-C East Blvd., an upscale market behind Outback Steakhouse. Cafe Verde, in the back of the store, offers excellent sandwiches and hearty prepared dishes. (☎334-9200; www.talleys.com. Sandwiches $6. Open M-Sa 8:30am-9pm, Su 10am-7pm.) **Thomas Street Tavern ❷,** 1218 Thomas Ave., is a favorite local pub with pool, foosball, and an extensive beer menu. Follow E. 10th St. out of uptown; after E. 10th becomes Central Ave., turn right on Thomas Ave. (☎376-1622. Grill items $5.25-7.25. Sandwiches around $6. Pizzas $6-8. Open M-Sa 11am-2am, Su noon-2am.) The fun and quirky **Smelly Cat Coffeehouse ❶,** 514 E. 36th St., in NoDa, serves delectable desserts and coffee drinks. To add a sugar rush to your caffeine high, order the "Muddy Kitten" ($4), a combination of ice cream, chocolate, and espresso. (☎374-9656. Bagels $0.80. Ice cream $2.25. Open M-Th 7am-10pm, F-Sa 7am-midnight, Su 9am-5pm. Live music some weekends.)

SIGHTS. Charlotte has a number of worthwhile museums, most of them located in the uptown area. The **Levine Museum of the New South,** 200 E. 7th St., is a fantastic new hands-on museum that explores the history of the Charlotte and Carolina Piedmont area. (☎333-1887. Open Tu-Sa 10am-5pm, Su noon-5pm. $6; students, seniors, and ages 6-18 $5; under 6 free.) A single price of admission will grant you access to both the **Mint Museum of Craft and Design,** 220 N. Tryon St., in uptown, and the **Mint Museum of Art,** 2730 Randolph Rd., about 2½ mi. southeast. The craft and design museum features contemporary work in glass, wood, and fiber. Check out the impressive chandelier in the lobby. The art museum, meanwhile, focuses on more traditional painting and ceramics. This building, relocated from its original position, once functioned as Charlotte's mint; visitors can peruse coins once produced here. (Both museums: ☎337-2000; www.mintmuseum.org. Craft and Design open Tu-Sa 10am-5pm, Su noon-5pm; art museum Tu 10am-10pm, W-Sa 10am-5pm, Su noon-5pm. $6, students and seniors 62+ $5, ages 6-17 $3. Audio tour $2. Craft and Design free on 1st F of every month 5-8pm. Art free every Tu 5-10pm.) Kids will delight at the exhibits in **Discovery Place,** 301 N. Tryon St., a hands-on science museum. (☎372-6261 or 800-935-0553; www.discoveryplace.org. Open Jun.-Aug. M-Sa 10am-6pm, Su 12:30-6pm; Sept.-May M-F 9am-5pm, Sa 10am-6pm, Su 1-5pm. Museum $7.50, seniors 60+ $6.50, ages 6-12 $6, ages 3-5 $5. OmniMax Theater $7.50/6.50/6/5. Museum and OmniMax $13/11/10/8.)

ENTERTAINMENT & NIGHTLIFE. In addition to having a number of professional sports teams, Charlotte is a mecca for the fastest-growing sport in national popularity—stock car racing. The **Lowe's Motor Speedway,** Exit 49 off of I-85, hosts several major NASCAR events each year. To witness the action yourself, call ☎800-455-3267 for tickets and schedule information, or look online at www.gospeedway.com. Charlotte's WNBA team, the **Sting,** shoots hoops in the Coliseum. (Tickets ☎877-962-2849; www.ticketmaster.com or www.charlottesting.com. Coliseum box office open M-F 10am-5pm, game day 10am-game time. Tickets $8-53.) Football fans can catch an NFL game when the **Carolina Panthers** play in Ericsson Stadium, 800 S. Mint St. (Ticket information ☎358-7407; www.panthers.com. Stadium tours available; $4, seniors $3, children 5-15 $2.) Ten miles to the south, the Charlotte **Knights** play AAA minor league baseball at Knights Castle, off I-77 S at Exit 88. (Tickets ☎364-6637; www.charlotteknights.com. Box office open M-F and game day Sa 10am-5pm. $6-9.)

To check out nightlife, arts, and entertainment listings, grab a free *Creative Loafing* in one of Charlotte's shops or restaurants, visit www.charlotte.creativeloafing.com, or look over the E&T section of the *Charlotte Observer*. For live rock bands, pool, and foosball, head to **Amos' Southend,** 1423 S. Tryon St. (☎377-6874; www.amossouthend.com. Cover $3-35. Open Th-Sa, sometimes W; doors usually open at 9pm.) **The Evening Muse,** 3227 N. Davidson St., in NoDa, is a laid-back venue for a wide variety of musical acts, from acoustic and jazz to rock. (☎376-3737; www.theeveningmuse.com. Beer from $1.50. Cover usually around $5. Open Tu-Th 6pm-midnight, F-Sa 6pm until people go home.)

Many of Charlotte's hippest clubs can be found uptown, especially on College St. around 6th and 7th St. At the progressive dance club **Mythos,** 300 N. College St., DJs spin hip-hop, dance, and house music. (☎375-8765; www.mythosclub.com. Upscale dress. 21+. Open Th 10pm-2:30am, $5 before 11pm, $10 after; F 10pm-4am, cover varies; Sa 10pm-late, before 2am $10, after 2am $12.) Nearby at **Have a Nice Day Cafe,** 314 N. College St., you can groove to pop, rap, and disco in a newly renovated club decorated with 70s memorabilia. (☎373-2233; www.thenewcafe.com. 21+. Cover $5-7. Open W and F-Sa 9pm-2am.)

CAROLINA MOUNTAINS

The sharp ridges and rolling slopes of the southern Appalachian range create some of the most spectacular scenery in the Southeast. Scholars, ski bums, farmers and artists all find reasons to call this gorgeous region home. The well named High Country stretches between Boone and Asheville, 100 mi. to the southwest. The central attraction of the mountains is the Blue Ridge Parkway (see p. 16), a road through the mountains from northern Virginia to southern North Carolina maintained by the National Park Service. Views from many of the Parkway's scenic overlooks are staggering, particularly on days when the peaks are wreathed in mist. To the south lies the Great Smoky Mountains National Park (see p. 378), with myriad opportunities for hiking, biking, rafting, and relaxing. From the high places of Western North Carolina, you'll be able to take in whole landscapes at once.

ASHEVILLE ☎828

Hazy blue mountains, deep valleys, and spectacular waterfalls form the impressive backdrop to this small, friendly city. Once a popular retreat for the nation's well-to-do, Asheville hosted enough Carnegies, Vanderbilts, and Mellons to fill a 1920s edition of *Who's Who on the Atlantic Seaboard*. The population these days tends more toward dreadlocks, batik, and vegetarianism, providing funky nightlife and festivals all year. In contrast to the laidback locals, Asheville's sights are fanatically maintained and its downtown meticulously preserved, making for a pleasant respite from the Carolina wilderness.

PRACTICAL INFORMATION. The **Asheville Regional Airport** is at Exit 9 off I-26, 15 mi. south of the city. (☎684-2226; www.flyavl.com.) **Greyhound,** 2 Tunnel Rd. (☎253-8451; open daily 8am-9pm), 2 mi. east of downtown near the Beaucatcher Tunnel, sends buses to: Charlotte (2½-3½hr., 5 per day, $23-25); Knoxville (2-2½hr., 8 per day, $27-29); Raleigh (8-8½hr., 5 per day, $53-57). The **Asheville Transit System** handles bus service within city limits. Pick up a copy of bus schedules and routes from the Visitors Center or visit the **Asheville Transit Center,** 49 Coxe Ave., by the Post Office. (☎253-5691. Hours vary by route, all M-Sa between 5:30am and 9pm. $0.75, transfers $0.10; short trips in downtown free. Discounts for seniors, disabled, and multi-fare tickets.) The **Chamber of Commerce and Visitor Center,** 151 Haywood St., Exit 4C off I-240, on the northwest end of downtown, dispenses a wealth of knowledge to visitors. (☎800-257-1300; www.exploreasheville.com. Open M-F 8:30am-5:30pm, Sa-Su 9am-5pm.) **Internet Access: Pack Memorial Library,** 67 Haywood St. (☎255-5203. $2 for 55min. Open M-Th 10am-8pm, F 10am-6pm, Sa 10am-5pm; Sept.-May also Su 2-5pm.) **Post Office:** 33 Coxe Ave., off Patton Ave. (☎271-6429. Open M-F 7:30am-5:30pm, Sa 9am-1pm.) **Postal Code:** 28802. **Area Code:** 828.

ACCOMMODATIONS. The cheapest lodgings are on **Tunnel Road,** east of downtown—and be warned, they are not very cheap. Slightly more expensive options can be found on **Merrimon Avenue,** just north of downtown. The **Log Cabin Motor Court ❸,** 330 Weaverville Hwy., 5 mi. north of downtown, provides immaculate, inviting cabins with HBO and laundry. Some also have fireplaces, kitchenettes, wireless Internet, and A/C. (☎645-6546; www.cabinlodging.com. Reception 10am-8pm. By reservation only Jan.-Mar. Cabins with 1 bedroom and bath $50, with kitchenette $70; 2 bedrooms and bath $90-115. AAA, military 10% off.) **Motel 6 ❷,** 1415 Tunnel Rd., Exit 55 off of I-40, has basic rooms at some of Asheville's lowest rates. (☎299-3040. A/C, HBO, data ports, pool, free local calls, laundry, and coffee. Singles $29-47, depending on the season; doubles $33-53. AARP discount.) **Powhatan Lake Campground ❶,** 375 Wesley Branch Rd., 12 mi. southwest of Asheville off Rte. 191, is in the Pisgah National Forest, offering wooded sites on a 10-acre trout lake. (☎667-0391 or 877-444-6777. No hookups, but hot showers. Gates close 10pm. Open Apr.-Oct. Sites $15-18.)

FOOD. Downtown Asheville is packed with excellent places to eat. At the **Laughing Seed Cafe ❷,** 40 Wall St., downtown, the extensive menu of international vegetarian dishes will leave you stumped. (☎252-3445. Entrees $7-9.50. Sandwiches $5-7.50. Dinner specialties $12.50-15. Smoothies around $4. Open M and W-Th 11:30am-9pm, F-Sa 11:30am-10pm, Su 10am-9pm.) If you're looking for a bite to eat without the hassle, try the quirky, laidback **Beanstreets ❶,** 3 Broadway St., which serves coffee ($1-4), sandwiches ($3.50-5.50), and omelettes ($3-4.75) on cheerfully mismatched tables. (☎255-8180. Open mic Th 9-11:30pm, live music most F 9pm. Open M-W 7:30am-6pm, Th-F 7:30am-midnight, Sa 9am-midnight, Su 9am-4pm.) Anyone with a sweet tooth must indulge at **Old Europe ❶,** 18 Battery Park Ave., near Wall St. The incredible cakes and pastries are handmade by the Hungarian owners. (☎252-0001. Cookies under $1. Pastries under $4. Beer $3. Coffee drinks $1.21-3.20. Open M-F 8:30am-midnight, Sa-Su 9:30am-midnight.)

SIGHTS. George Vanderbilt's palatial **Biltmore Estate,** 1 Approach Rd., just north of I-40 Exit 50, was constructed in the 1890s and is the largest private home in America. A self-guided tour of the house and grounds can take all day; try to arrive early. (☎225-1333 or 800-543-2961; www.biltmore.com. Estate entrance open daily 8:30am-5pm. Winery open Jan.-Oct. M-Sa 11am-7pm, Su noon-7pm. Audio guide $6.50. Rooftop tour $14. Trail rides $45. Carriage rides $35. Wheelchair-accessible.) If Biltmore is a bit more than your wallet can take, check out the free scenery at the **Botanical Gardens,** 151 W. T. Weaver Blvd. (☎252-5190; www.ashevillebotanicalgardens.org. Open daily dawn-dusk.) The

Thomas Wolfe Memorial, 52 N. Market St., between Woodfin and Walnut St., celebrates one of the early 20th century's most influential American authors. (☎253-8304; www.wolfememorial.com. 30min. tours every hr. on the ½hr. Open Apr.-Oct. Tu-Sa 9am-5pm, Su 1-5pm; Nov.-Mar. Tu-Sa 10am-4pm, Su 1-4pm. $1, students $0.50.) The **Asheville Art Museum** displays 20th-century American artwork. (☎253-3227; www.ashevilleart.org. Open Tu-Th and Sa 10am-5pm, F 10am-8pm, Su 1-5pm. $6; students, seniors, and ages 4-12 $5. Wheelchair-accessible.) 25 mi. southeast of Asheville on U.S. 64/74A, the scenic setting for *Last of the Mohicans* rises up almost ½ mi. in **Chimney Rock Park.** After driving to the base of the Chimney, take the 26-story elevator to the top or walk up for a 75 mi. view. (☎625-9611 or 800-277-9611; www.chimneyrockpark.com. Ticket office open daily summer 8:30am-5:30pm; winter 8:30am-4:30pm. Park open 1½hr. after office closes. $12, ages 4-12 $5.50.)

NIGHTLIFE & ENTERTAINMENT. The downtown area, especially the southeast end around the intersection of Broadway and College St., offers music, munchies, and movies. **Jack of the Wood,** 95 Patton Ave., heats up at night with locally brewed ales and awesome live celtic, bluegrass, and old-time mountain music. (☎252-5445; www.jackofthewood.com. Beer $3. M trivia night 8pm. 21+ after 9pm. Cover F-Sa $5. Open M-F 4pm-2am, Sa noon-2am, Su 3pm-2am.)Indie and art-house flicks play at the **Fine Arts Theatre,** 36 Biltmore Ave. (☎232-1536; www.fineartstheatre.com. $7, matinees and seniors $5.) Summer shouldn't be anyone's season of discontent, not with free **Shakespeare in Montford Park,** at the Hazel Robinson Amphitheater. (☎254-4540; www.montfordparkplayers.org. Performances June-early Aug. F-Su 7:30pm.) The free weekly paper, *Mountain Xpress*, and *Community Connections*, a free gay publication, have listings.

BOONE ☎828

Nestled among the breathtaking mountains of the High Country, Boone serves as a base for exploring this rugged landscape. **Grandfather Mountain,** near the intersection of U.S. 221 and the Blue Ridge Parkway (Mi. 305), provides some nice hikes and splendid views. Hiking or camping on Grandfather Mt. requires a permit ($6), available at the park entrance or at several area stores, including the **Mast General Store,** 630 W. King St., downtown. (☎262-0000. Open M-Sa 10am-6pm, Su noon-5pm.) The free *Grandfather Mountain Trail Map and Backcountry Guide*, available anywhere permits are sold, details area hikes. At the top of the mountain, a private park features a mile-high suspension bridge, a museum, and a small zoo. (☎800-468-7325; www.grandfather.com. $12, seniors $11, ages 4-12 $6. Open daily Apr.-Oct. 8am-7pm; Nov.-Mar. 8am-5pm; ticket sales stop 1hr. before close. Wheelchair-accessible.) Near Boone, the **Wilson Creek** area offers waterfalls, swimming holes, and trails. **Linville Gorge** is perfect for backcountry camping and rock climbing. For more info, call the ranger's office (☎737-0833).

Boone also boasts some of the best downhill skiing in the Southeast. **Sugar Mountain,** off Hwy. 184 in Banner Elk (☎800-784-2768; www.skisugar.com), and **Ski Beech,** 1007 Beech Mt. Pkwy. (☎800-438-2093; www.skibeech.com), also off Hwy. 184, are the largest resorts. **Appalachian Ski Mountain,** off U.S. 221/321 in Blowing Rock (☎800-322-2373; www.appskimtn.com) is a bit smaller. **Boone Appalcart** (see below) runs a free winter shuttle from Boone to Sugar Mountain. Call ☎800-962-2322 for info about daily ski conditions.

In the town of Todd, 11 mi. north of Boone at the edge of Ashe County, the **Todd General Store** hosts live mountain music concerts on Saturday afternoons during the summer months. From downtown Boone, take 421S and turn left on Hwy. 194;

continue 11 mi. and make a right onto Todd Railroad Grade Rd.; it's on the left after ½ mi. (☎336-877-1067. Most free, some concerts up to $10. Times vary; call for schedules.) ASU's **Appalachian Cultural Museum,** on University Hall Dr. off of Blowing Rock Rd. (U.S. 321), seeks to break down stereotypes with exhibits on crafts, storytelling, and even NASCAR. (☎262-3117. $4, seniors $3.50, ages 10-18 $2. Open Tu-Sa 10am-5pm, Su 1-5pm. Wheelchair-accessible.)

Catering primarily to vacationing families, Boone and the surrounding towns have more than their share of expensive motels and B&Bs. The neighboring community of Blowing Rock offers plenty of pricey inns. In Boone, the **Boone Trail Motel ❷,** 275 E. King St./U.S. 421, just south of downtown, is close to the action and features clean, if not particularly luxurious rooms. (☎264-8839. A/C, HBO. No room phones. Office usually open 9am-1am. Singles $25-40; doubles $30-60.) Along the Parkway near Boone, the **Julian Price Campground ❶,** Mi. 297, has spectacular tent and RV sites. Sites around Loop A are on a lake. (☎963-5911. Flush toilets and water; no hookups or showers. Open May-Oct. Sites $14.)

King St. offers lots of great little restaurants. The small, hip **Black Cat ❶,** 127 S. Depot St. right off of King St., makes excellent burritos. (☎263-9511. Burritos, quesadillas, and nachos from $3.75. Margaritas $3.50. Live music F-Sa. Open Su-Th 11:30am-9pm, F-Sa 11:30am-10pm.) **Our Daily Bread ❷,** 627 W. King St., serves sandwiches, salads, and vegetarian specials, all $5.25-7.25. (☎264-0173. Open M-F 11am-6pm, Sa 11am-5pm, Su noon-5pm.) Fans of vegetarian fare will be in heaven at **Angelica's ❷,** 506 W. King St. (☎265-0809. Sandwiches $7.50. Vegetarian sushi $6-9. Smoothies $4. Open Su-Th 11am-9pm, F-Sa 11am-9:30pm.) For a cold beer or a game of pool, head to **Murphy's Pub,** 747 W. King St. (☎264-5117. Beer from $1.75. 21+. Live music usually W-Sa; cover $3-5. Open daily 11am-2am.)

The Boone Bowling Center, 261 Boone Heights Dr., doubles as the **Greyhound** terminal (☎264-3167) and sends buses to Charlotte (2½hr., 1 per day, $25). **Boone AppalCart,** 274 Winklers Creek Rd., provides local bus service. (☎264-2278. Hours vary by route. Fare $0.50.) **Visitor Info: Boone Area Chamber of Commerce,** 208 Howard St. (☎800-852-9506; www.boonechamber.com. Open M-F 9am-5pm.) The **North Carolina High Country Host Visitor Center,** 1700 Blowing Rock Rd./U.S. 321, has regional info. (☎800-438-7500; www.mountainsofnc.com. Open M-Sa 9am-5pm, Su 9am-3pm.) **Internet Access: Watauga County Public Library,** 140 Queen St., at N. Depot St. one block up from King St. (☎264-8784. Open M-Th 9am-7pm, F-Sa 9am-5pm.) **Post Office:** 680 W. King St. (☎262-1171. Open M-F 9am-5pm, Sa 9am-noon.) **Postal Code:** 28607. **Area Code:** 828.

NORTH CAROLINA COAST

Lined with barrier islands that shield inlanders from Atlantic squalls, the Carolina Coast has a history as stormy as the hurricanes that pummel its beaches. England's first attempt to colonize North America ended in 1590 with the peculiar disappearance of the Roanoke Island settlement, known today as the "Lost Colony." Later on, the coast earned the title "Graveyard of the Atlantic"; over 1000 ships have foundered on the Outer Banks' southern shores, leaving hundreds of wrecks for scuba divers to explore. The same wind that sank ships lifted the world's first powered flight in 1903, with some assistance from Orville and Wilbur Wright. Flying now forms the basis of much of the area's recreational activities: hang-gliding, paragliding, windsurfing, kiteboarding, and good ol' kite-flying.

OUTER BANKS ☎252

Locals claim that the legendary pirate Blackbeard once roamed the waters off the Outer Banks; some speculate that his treasures still lie beneath these beaches. But whether or not you dig up Blackbeard's loot, you'll find other gems on the these islands, from significant historical sights to gorgeous stretches of sand. The northern half of Bodie Island, especially the three contiguous towns of Kitty Hawk, Kill Devil Hills, and Nags Head, are heavily trafficked and dense with stores. Farther south on Rte. 12, however, the pristine beaches remain largely undeveloped; national park status has preserved much of the islands' original beauty. Ocracoke Island, despite its growing popularity with visitors, retains its community charm.

ORIENTATION

The Outer Banks consist of four narrow islands strung along the northern half of the North Carolina coast. **Bodie Island,** the northernmost island, is joined to the mainland by US 158 and serves as most travelers' point of entry. For much of Bodie Island, Rte. 12 (known as the Beach Road) and US 158 (called the Bypass) run parallel. **Roanoke Island** lies between the southern end of Bodie and the mainland. US 64 runs from the mainland to **Manteo** on Roanoke by bridge; another bridge connects Roanoke to Bodie just south of Nags Head at **Whalebone Junction.** From the junction, where US 64 runs into Rte. 12, the **Cape Hatteras National Seashore** stretches south for 70 miles. Rte. 12 continues south through the park, connecting Bodie to the great sandy elbow that is **Hatteras Island** by another bridge. **Ocracoke Island,** the southernmost island, is linked by ferry to Hatteras Island and towns on the mainland. Both Hatteras and Ocracoke are almost entirely park land. Directions to locations on Bodie Island are usually given in terms of distances in miles from the Wright Memorial Bridge. There is **no public transit** on the Outer Banks. Hectic traffic calls for extra caution and travel time.

TRANSPORTATION & PRACTICAL INFORMATION

Ferries: Free ferries run between **Hatteras** and **Ocracoke** (40 min., daily 5am-midnight; no reservations accepted). Toll ferries run between **Ocracoke** and **Cedar Island,** east of New Bern on Rte. 12, which becomes U.S. 70 (2¼hr.; $1 per pedestrian, $3 per cyclist, $15 per car). Toll ferries also travel between Ocracoke and **Swan Quarter,** on U.S. 264 (2½hr.). Call ahead for schedules and reservations: for ferries from Ocracoke ☎800-345-1665, from Cedar Island ☎800-856-0343, from Swan Quarter ☎800-773-1094. General info and reservations at ☎800-293-3779 or www.ncferry.org.

Taxi: Beach Cab (☎441-2500 or 800-441-2503), for Bodie Island and Manteo. **Coastal Cab** (☎449-8787).

Bike Rental: Ocean Atlantic Rental (☎441-7823), in Nags Head.

Visitor Info: Outer Banks Welcome Center on Roanoke Island, 1 Visitors Center Cir., (☎877 298-4373; www.outerbanks.org), at the base of the bridge to the mainland in Manteo; info for all the islands except Ocracoke. Open daily 9am-5:30pm; info by phone M-F 8am-6pm, Sa-Su 10am-4pm. Hotel and ferry reservations. **Aycock Brown Welcome Center** (☎261-4644), Mi. 1.5 on US 158 in Kitty Hawk. Open daily 9am-5:30pm. **Cape Hatteras National Seashore Information Centers: Whalebone Junction** (☎441-6644), on Rte. 12 at the north entrance to the park. Open Apr.-Nov. daily 9am-5pm. **Bodie Island** (☎441-5711), on Rte. 12 at Bodie Island Lighthouse. Open

June-Aug. daily 9am-6pm; Sept.-May 9am-5pm. **Hatteras Island** (☎995-5209), on Rte. 12 at the Cape Hatteras Lighthouse. Open summer daily 9am-6pm; winter 9am-5pm. **Ocracoke Island** (☎928-4531), next to the ferry terminal at the south end of the island. Open daily 9am-5pm. Park info online at www.nps.gov/caha.

Internet Access: Dare County Library, 400 Mustian St. (☎441-4331), in Kill Devil Hills, 1 block west of U.S. 158, just south of the Wright Memorial. Open M and Th-F 9am-5:30pm, Tu-W 10am-7pm, Sa 10am-4pm.

Post Office: 3841 N. Croatan Hwy. (☎261-2211), in Kitty Hawk. Open M-F 9am-4:30pm, Sa 10am-noon. **Postal Code:** 27949. **Area Code:** 252.

ACCOMMODATIONS & FOOD

Most motels line **Route 12** and **U.S. 158** on crowded Bodie Island. For more privacy, go farther south; **Ocracoke** is the most secluded. On all three islands, rooming rates are highest from Memorial Day to Labor Day, especially on weekends. It's a good idea to make reservations as far in advance as possible.

CAMPING

Sleeping on the beach may result in fines, so try one of the four lovely **campgrounds ❶,** owned by the National Park Service that are practically on the shore. These oceanside sites, which lie off of Rte. 12 along the Cape Hatteras National Seashore, are open only during the warmer months. The northernmost is **Oregon Inlet,** on the southern tip of Bodie Island; **Cape Point,** in Buxton, and **Frisco** both lie near the elbow of Hatteras Island close to the lighthouse. The **Ocracoke** campground, at the southern end of the Outer Banks, is located 3 mi. north of Ocracoke Village. All four have sites that include water, restrooms, cold-water showers, picnic tables, and grills. (☎473-2111. All sites $18. RVs allowed, no hookups available. Cape Point open late May to early Sept.; all others open mid-Apr. to mid-Oct.)

BODIE ISLAND

Outer Banks International Hostel (HI-AYH) ❶, 1004 W. Kitty Hawk Rd., is the best deal in the northern islands. This clean and friendly hostel has 60 beds, two kitchens, A/C, volleyball, shuffleboard, Internet access ($5 for 30min.), and laundry facilities. (☎261-2294; www.outerbankshostel.com. Members $16, nonmembers $19; private rooms $15 plus $16/19 per person. Camping spot on the grounds $17 for 2 adults, $4 each additional person; tent rental $6. Children under 12 half price; children under 5 free.) The **Nettlewood Motel ❸,** 1718 Beach Rd., near Mi. 7, offers clean and comfortable rooms with private access to an uncluttered strip of beach. (☎441-5039. TV, A/C, heat, refrigerators, and pool. Doubles are equipped with a kitchenette. Mid-June to late Aug. singles M-F $55, Sa-Su $75, doubles $99/150; mid-May to mid-June and late Aug.-late Sept. singles $40/50; doubles $55/75. Jan. to mid-May and Oct.-Nov. singles $35/40; doubles $45/55. Weekly rates available.)

For a bite to eat, the fun and lively **Chilli Peppers ❸,** Mi. 5.5 on U.S. 158, specializes in fresh seafood and Tex-Mex. (☎441-8081; www.chillipeppers.com. Spicy fish quesadilla $7 during lunch. Sandwiches from $7. Dinner entrees $15 and up. Open M-Sa 11:30am-2am, Su 11:30am-10:30pm; dinner served until 11pm.) **Tortuga's Lie ❸,** Mi. 11 on Beach Rd. in Nags Head, serves Caribbean-influenced seafood, sandwiches, pasta, and grill items in a casual setting. Try an order of Coco Loco Chicken for $9. (☎441-7299; www.tortugaslie.com. W sushi night. Open daily 11:30am-10pm. No reservations, usually a wait for dinner.) The **Outer Banks Brewing Station ❸,** Mi. 8.5 on U.S. 158, offers original beers, a diverse menu, and live music in the evenings. (☎449-2739; www.obbrewing.com. Entrees $6-8. Seafood

$10-14. Pints $3.50. $1 off appetizers 3-5pm. Open daily 11:30am-2am.) The oceanfront deck at **Quagmires ❸,** M.P. 7.5 on Beach Rd., is another popular spot to grab a drink after a day in the sun. (☎441-9188; www.quags.com. Local seafood and Mexican specialties $7-18. Beers from $2.50. Open daily 11:30am-2am.)

OCRACOKE

Hatteras Island is almost exclusively park land, so there are few lodging options other than pitching a tent at one of the area's many campgrounds. For sturdy walls, head to Ocracoke, where accommodations and restaurants all cluster on the island's southern tip in tiny **Ocracoke Village.** For pleasant, wood-paneled rooms at some of Ocracoke's lowest prices, **Blackbeard's Lodge ❹,** 111 Back Rd., is a nice option. Turn right off of Rte. 12 just before the boat filled with seashells. The swing and rocking chairs on the front porch provide a perfect spot to relax and watch the world go by. (☎928-3421; reservations 800-892-5314; www.blackbeardslodge.com. Game room, A/C, cable TV, and heated pool. Rooms from $75; lower in winter.) The bright rooms at the **Sand Dollar Motel ❹,** 70 Sand Dollar Rd. in Ocracoke, exude a beach-cabin allure. (☎928-5571. Open Apr.-late Nov. Refrigerators, microwaves, A/C, cable TV, pool, and breakfast. Queen bed $70, 2 double beds $75; 3 double beds $85; winter rates vary.)

Sea lovers can sail on over to **Jolly Roger ❷,** on Rte. 12 by the harbor in Ocracoke, for waterfront dining and a laidback atmosphere. Inhale the sea breeze along with locally caught fresh fish specials (market price) and sandwiches for $4-8. (☎928-3703. Beer from $2.50 a pint or $6.50 a pitcher. Open Apr.-Oct. daily 11am-10pm.) Occupying a counter along the back wall of Styron's General Store (est. 1920) at the corner of Lighthouse and Creek Rd. in Ocracoke, the **Cat Ridge Deli ❷,** 300 Lighthouse Rd., specializes in Thai-influenced cuisine. (☎928-3354. Wraps around $6. Closed Jan.-Mar. Open daily 10:30am-7pm; in low-season 10:30am-5pm.)

SIGHTS

The **Wright Brothers National Memorial,** Mi. 8 on U.S. 158, marks the spot where Orville and Wilbur Wright took to the skies in history's first powered flight. Exhibits in the Visitors Center document humanity's journey from the first airplane to the first moon landing. (☎441-7430. Open June-Aug. daily 9am-6pm; Sept.-May 9am-5pm. $3 per person, under 16 free.) At the nearby **Jockey's Ridge State Park,** Mi. 12 on U.S. 158, **Kitty Hawk Kites** (☎441-4124 or 877-359-8447; www.kittyhawk.com) takes aspiring hang-gliding pilots under its wing. Beginner lessons including flights start at $85. Those preferring to explore things at ground level can slide down the tallest dunes on the east coast, comprised of some 30 million tons of sand. (Park ☎441-7132. Open summer daily 8am-8:45pm; low-season hours vary. Free.)

Roanoke Island is a locus of historical and cultural draws. Facing the Manteo Waterfront, **Roanoke Island Festival Park** (follow signs from the highway), staffed largely by actors in 16th-century garb, features *Elizabeth II*, a replica of a 16th-century English merchant ship. (☎475-1500; www.roanokeisland.com. Park and museum open summer daily 10am-7pm; ship open daily 10am-6:30pm. Winter hours vary; park closed Jan.-Feb. $8, students $5, 5 and under free; last tickets sold at 6pm.) In summer, students from the North Carolina School of the Arts perform jazz and ballet at the Park's outdoor pavilion ($5 donation suggested). Farther down U.S. 64, the **Fort Raleigh National Historic Site,** 1409 National Park Rd., marks the place where the English first attempted to settle in the New World. Settlers occupied this area beginning in 1585, but a lack of supplies and tensions with local tribes forced them return to England. A second colony, established in 1587, disappeared without explanation around 1590. During the summer, actors perform **The Lost Colony,** a musical version of the settlers' story, in a theater overlooking the sound by the Fort Raleigh site. (☎473-2127 or 866-468-7630; www.thelostcolony.org. Shows June-Aug. M-Sa 8:30pm. $16, seniors $15, under 11 $8. Fort Raleigh Visitors Center open daily 9am-5pm, in summer 9am-6pm.) Nearby, flowers release their perfumes in the romantic **Elizabethan Gardens,** where visitors can wander among fountains and antique statues. (☎473-3234; www.elizabethangardens.org. Open June-Aug. M-Sa 9am-8pm, Su 9am-7pm; low-season hours vary. $6, seniors 62+ $5, youth 6-18 $2, under 5 free with adult.)

SCENIC DRIVE: CAPE HATTERAS NATIONAL SEASHORE

Get two shores for the price of one along the 70 mi. expanse of the Cape Hatteras National Seashore: one faces out to the Atlantic Ocean and another looks across the Pamlico Sound to North Carolina's mainland. Dotted with dunes, stunted trees, and occasional stretches of marshland, the park's main appeal is this unique landscape. Driving south from Hatteras to Ocracoke, the water of the sound reaches out to the horizon to the right, while magnificent, largely empty beaches lie over the dunes on the left.

Route 12 is the main artery of the park, running from the northern entrance of the park at Whalebone Junction on Bodie Island to the town of Ocracoke. A 40min. stretch from Hatteras to Ocracoke is covered by a free ferry (see **Transportation and Practical Information,** above). For its entire length, Rte. 12 is a paved two-lane road. Total transport time from Whalebone to Ocracoke is about 2½hr.

All of the major attractions of the park are accessible and clearly marked from Rte. 12. The chief of these are the Outer Banks' three **lighthouses** on Bodie, Hatteras, and Ocracoke Islands. The tallest brick lighthouse in North America is the 198 ft. Cape Hatteras lighthouse, built in 1870. Due to beach erosion, the lighthouse was relocated by 2900 ft. in 1999. To scale the tower for an impressive view, you'll have to join one of the self-guided tours. (Open Apr.-Sept. Every 20min. daily 9am-5:40pm; lasts 20min. Ticket sales begin 8:15am. Adults $4; children under 12, disabled, and seniors 62+ $2.) Duck into the Visitors Center to check out a section of the original lens, which resembles a disco ball on steroids. (☎995-5209. Open summer daily 9am-6pm, winter 9am-5pm.) Another set of attractions along Rte. 12 serves to remind visitors that lighthouses have a value apart from the picturesque—various **shipwrecks** can be seen from the shore. Visibility varies over time; ask a ranger at one of the Visitors Centers for info on the best wrecks to view. For a schedule of the various daily programs run at the Visitors Centers located at each lighthouse, pick up a copy of the free paper *In The Park.*

The seashore's rich wildlife is on display at the **Pea Island National Wildlife Refuge** on the northern tip of Hatteras Island. Adjoining the **Visitors Center** is the marsh-country **Charles Kuralt Nature Trail,** which affords trekkers a chance to glimpse grackles, pelicans, and the Carolina salt marsh snake. The ½ mi. **North Pond Wildlife Trail,** also beginning at the Visitors Center, is fully handicapped accessible. (Visitors Center ☎987-2394. Usually open summer daily 9am-4pm; winter Sa-Su only. Beaches in the Refuge are open only during daylight.) Farther south, the **Pony Pasture,** on Rte. 12 in Ocracoke, acts as the stomping ground for a herd of semi-wild horses, said to be descendants of horses left here by shipwrecked explorers in the 16th or 17th century.

WILMINGTON ☎910

Located at the mouth of the Cape Fear River and only a few miles from the beaches of the Atlantic, Wilmington has long been an important center for shipping and industry on the Carolina coast. Home to the largest film production facility east of L.A., the city is sometimes referred to as "Wilmywood" and "Hollywood East." Since 1983, over 400 feature films and TV projects have been shot along the picturesque Cape Fear coast, including all six seasons of the hit TV series *Dawson's Creek*. But even if you don't catch a glimpse of the celebrities, the historic downtown area has plenty to offer, from important historic memorials to excellent restaurants and picturesque views of the waterfront.

PRACTICAL INFORMATION. Wilmington International Airport, 1740 Airport Blvd., is off 23rd St. about 2 mi. north of Market St. (☎341-4333; www.airport-wilmington.com). The **Greyhound** terminal, 201 Harnett St. (☎762-6073; open M-F 9-11am, 1-4:30pm, 8:30-9pm; Sa-Su 9-10am, 2-4pm, 8:30-9pm), between 3rd and Front St. about a mile north of downtown, departs to Charlotte (9hr., 2 per day, $41-44) and Raleigh (3hr., 2 per day, $29). The Wilmington Transit Authority (☎343-0106; www.wavetransit.com) runs **local buses** (M-Sa 7am-7pm; $0.75, seniors 65+ $0.35) and a **free trolley** that travels along Front St. between Orange and Red Cross St. A **river taxi** ferries passengers across the river between downtown and the U.S.S. North Carolina. (☎343-1611. Memorial Day-Oct. daily 10am-5pm. Round-trip $2. Sightseeing tours also available at 11am and 3pm; adults $8, children $4. Leaves from the foot of Market St.) **Taxi: Port City Taxi,** ☎762-1165. **Visitors Center:** 24 N. 3rd St., at the corner of 3rd and Princess. (☎341-4030 or 800-222-4757; www.cape-fear.nc.us. Open M-F 8:30am-5pm, Sa 9am-4pm, Su 1-4pm.) There is also an **information kiosk** at the foot of Market St. by the waterfront. (Open daily Apr.-May and Sept.-Oct. 9am-4:30pm; Jun.-Aug. 9:30am-5pm.) **Internet Access: New Hanover County Library,** 201 Chestnut St., at the intersection with 3rd St., one block from the Visitors Center. (☎798-6302. Open M-W 9am-8pm, Th-Sa 9am-5pm, Su 1-5pm.) **Post Office:** 152 N. Front St., at the intersection with Chestnut St. (☎313-3293. Open M-F 9am-5pm, Sa 9am-noon.) **Postal code:** 28401. **Area code:** 910.

ACCOMMODATIONS & FOOD. Wilmington's best lodging comes in the form of B&Bs; you'll find most of them conveniently located in the historic downtown area. Though rooms are more expensive than at budget motels, the personalized experience, unique rooms, added bonuses, and convenient location may make Wilmington's B&Bs worth the extra cash. Space is limited so be sure to reserve as far in advance as your travel plans allow, especially during the summer. **Catherine's Inn ❺,** 410 S. Front St., offers gorgeous rooms, a two-story porch overlooking the Cape Fear River, a sunken garden with a gazebo, a full country breakfast, and warm hospitality. (☎251-0863 or 800-476-0723; www.catherinesinn.com. Private bath, off-street parking; Internet access; complimentary wine, beer, and sodas. Check-in 3-5pm. Queen rooms for 1 person $85, for 2 $100-110; kings $95/115-125.) For those who prefer the less expensive motels, you'll find nearly every chain you can think of on Market St. between College Rd. and 23rd St. Weekend rates often run $10-20 higher than weekday prices. **Travel Inn ❷,** 4401 Market St., provides clean, basic rooms for some of the lowest rates available. (☎763-8217. Pool, cable TV with free HBO. Rooms summer M-F $35-39, Sa-Su $59-79; winter, from $35. 10% discount for AAA/AARP.) If the B&Bs are full and you're looking for a room downtown, try the **Best Western Coastline Inn ❹,** 503 Nutt St. These large, comfortable rooms all overlook the river. (☎763-2800; www.coastlineinn.com. Data ports, fitness center, free Internet access and fax, bike rental, breakfast brought to your door. Rooms Apr.-Oct. M-F $89, Sa-Su $129-149; Oct.-Apr. $79/99-109. Suites $20 more. 10% discount for AAA/AARP.) The **Carolina Beach State Park ❶,** about 18 mi. south of the city on U.S. 421, offers campsites, as well as hiking, picnic areas, and a marina. (☎458-8206. Restrooms, hot showers, laundry facilities, water, and grills. No RV hookups. Sites $12.)

Quality restaurants are plentiful in historic downtown Wilmington, catering to a wide variety of tastes. The trendy **Caffè Phoenix ❸**, 9 S. Front St., serves excellent Mediterranean dishes. (☎343-1395. Salads from $7.50. Lunch sandwiches $7.50-9. Seafood $16.50-21. Open M-Th 11:30am-10pm, F-Sa 11:30am-11pm, Su 10:30am-10pm. Coffee shop open M-Sa 7-10am.) **Nikki's ❶**, 16 S. Front St., is known for having the area's best vegetarian food in a casual atmosphere. (☎772-9151. Sandwiches $4.25-7. Wraps around $6.50. Sushi from $3.50. Open M-Sa 11am-4pm and Th-Sa 6-10pm.) Up Market St., **Indochine ❷**, 7 Wayne Dr., dishes up generous portions of delicious Thai and Vietnamese fare. (☎251-9229. Entrees from $8. Outdoor garden seating available. Open Tu-Sa 11am-2pm and Tu-Su 5-10pm.)

SIGHTS. No visit to Wilmington would be complete without an afternoon at the relaxing, largely residential **Wrightsville Beach.** From downtown, take Market St. to Eastwood Rd., which will bring you to the bridge. Wilmington is also home to the largest movie and TV production facility east of Hollywood, **Screen Gems Studios,** 1223 N. 23rd St., near the airport. Guided studio tours provide a fascinating behind-the-scenes glimpse of the industry—and a chance to check out parts of the set of *Dawson's Creek*. (☎343-3433; www.screengemsstudios.com. Tours last 1hr. Sa-Su noon, 2pm. Schedules can vary; call for details. $12, seniors $7.50, children under 12 $5.) Art aficionados shouldn't miss the **Louise Wells Cameron Art Museum,** 3201 S. 17th St., at the intersection with Independence Blvd., which features work by American masters, including one of the world's major collections of works by artist Mary Cassatt. (☎395-5999; www.cameronartmuseum.com. Open Tu-Sa 10am-5pm, Su 10am-4pm. $5, children 6-18 $2, 5 and under free; families $12.) You can also tour the bowels of the massive **Battleship North Carolina,** moored in the Cape Fear River across from downtown, at the junction of Hwy. 17, 74, 76, and 421. This massive warship, with a crew of 2339, participated in every major naval offensive in the Pacific during WWII. (☎251-5797; www.battleshipnc.com. Open daily mid-May to mid-Sept. 8am-8pm, mid-Sept. to mid-May 8am-5pm; ticket sales end 1hr. before closing. $9, seniors 65+ and military $8, children 6-11 $4.50, 5 and under free.) For a change of pace, take a stroll through the **New Hanover County Arboretum,** 6206 Oleander Dr., which includes a Japanese garden with a traditional teahouse. (☎452-6393. Open daily dawn-dusk. Free.)

ENTERTAINMENT & NIGHTLIFE. For the local word about what's going on, pick up a free copy of *Encore* or *The Outrider*, weekly newpapers with event listings, available in most hotels and cafes. Wilmington's historic **Thalian Hall,** 310 Chestnut St., offers a wide range of entertainment, from theater, dance, and music to comedy acts. (Box office ☎343-3664 or 800-523-2820; www.thalianhall.com. Box office open M-F noon-6pm, Sa-Su 2-6pm. For building tour info ☎343-3660.)

Downtown Wilmywood is jumping on Friday and Saturday nights; most bars and clubs cluster around Front St. For low-key chilling with pool tables and a young, hip crowd, head to **Blue Post,** 15 S. Water St., by Dock St. at the back corner of the parking lot. (☎343-1141. Beer from $2.50. 21+. Open M-F 3pm-2am, Sa-Su 2pm-2am.) The **Reel Cafe,** 100 S. Front St., offers a rooftop bar, a dance floor, and live music on the courtyard patio. (☎251-1832; www.thereelcafe.com. Weekends 21+. Cover $5 or less, Sa ladies free. Open daily 4pm-2am; food served til 2am. Rooftop bar open Th-Su, dance floor F-Sa.) Are your socks dirty? Spend an evening at **Soapbox,** 255 N. Front St., a "Laundro-Lounge" where you can do your laundry as you booze. (No, we aren't kidding.) You'll find foosball, pool, and live music here, as well as a number of ironing boards. (☎251-8500. Spoken word on last W of every month, 8pm. Tu is "TeeVee Show", featuring short, local, independent films. Cover varies. Open daily 10am-2am.) Take in the view from **Level 5,** 21 N. Front St. on the fifth floor, a popular rooftop bar. (☎342-0272. Comedy acts Tu-Th, live music F, DJ on Sa. 21+, 18+ for shows. Cover $2-5. Open daily 5pm-2am.) **Kefi's Tavern,** 2012 Eastwood Rd., offers live rock, reggae, and punk shows near Wrightsville Beach. (☎256-3558. Open M-Sa 2pm-2am. Cover varies, usually about $7. 21+ after 9pm.)

SOUTH CAROLINA

To some, South Carolina's pride in the Palmetto State may seem extreme. Inspired by the state flag, the palmetto tree logo decorates hats, bottles and bumper stickers across the landscape. This pride is justified, though, by the unrivaled beaches of the Grand Strand and the stately elegance of Charleston. Columbia, though less well known, offers an impressive artistic and cultural experience without the smog and traffic that plague other cities of the New South. Tamed for tourists and merchandising, the Confederate legacy of the first state to secede from the Union is groomed as a cash cow. In recent years, South Carolina has been in the national news for its refusal to remove the Confederate flag from the statehouse. In July 2000, state legislators approved moving the flag from the Statehouse dome to the lawn, a change condemned by many as a meaningless halfway measure.

PRACTICAL INFORMATION

Capital: Columbia.

Visitor Info: Department of Parks, Recreation, and Tourism, Edgar A. Brown Bldg., 1205 Pendleton St., #106, Columbia 29201 (☎803-734-1700; www.travelsc.com). **South Carolina Forestry Commission,** 5500 Broad River Rd., Columbia 29212 (☎803-896-8800).

Postal Abbreviation: SC. **Sales Tax:** 5-7%.

CHARLESTON ☎843

Built on rice and cotton, Charleston's antebellum plantation system yielded vast riches now seen in its numerous museums, historic homes, and ornate architecture. An accumulated cultural capital of 300 years flows like the long, distinctive drawl of the natives. Several of the south's most renowned plantations dot the city, while two venerable educational institutions, the **College of Charleston** and **the Citadel,** add a youthful eccentricity. Horse-drawn carriages, cobblestone streets, pre-Civil War homes, beautiful beaches, and some of the best restaurants in the Southeast explain why Charleston often heads the list of the nation's top destinations.

TRANSPORTATION

Trains: Amtrak, 4565 Gaynor Ave. (☎744-8264), 8 mi. west of downtown. Open daily 6am-10pm. To: **Richmond** (6¾hr., 2 per day, $129); **Savannah** (1¾hr., 2 per day, $38); **Washington, D.C.** (9½hr., 2 per day, $171).

Buses: Greyhound, 3610 Dorchester Rd. (☎747-5341 or 800-231-2222 for schedules and fares), in N. Charleston. *Avoid this area at night.* Station open daily 8am-9:30pm. To: **Charlotte** (5-9hr., 3 per day, $41-43); **Myrtle Beach** (2½hr., 2 per day, $23-25); **Savannah** (2¾hr., 2 per day, $24-26). **CARTA's** "Dorchester/Waylyn" bus goes into town from the station area; return "Navy Yard: 5 Mile Dorchester Rd." bus.

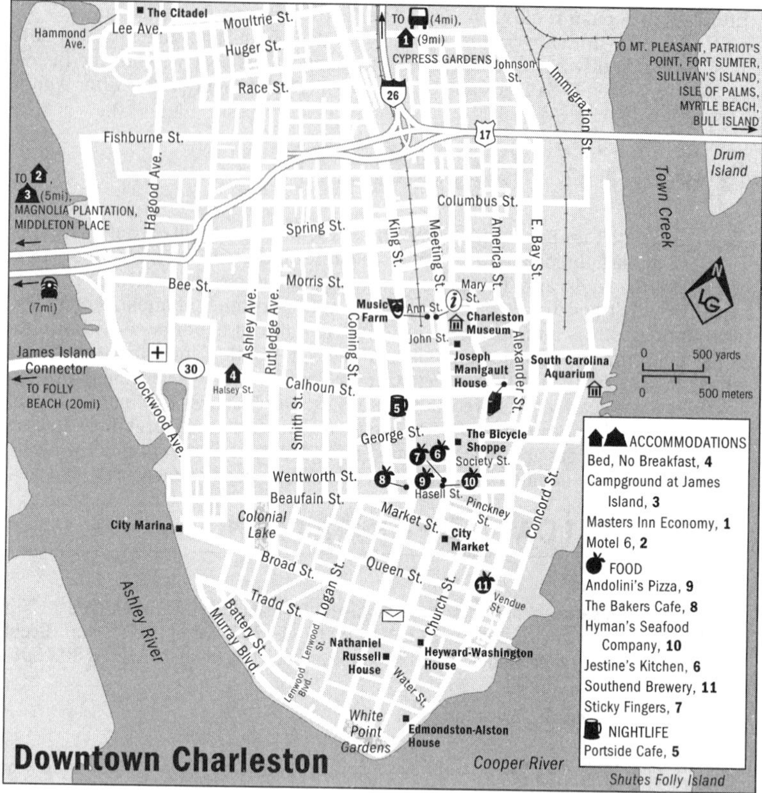

Public Transit: CARTA, 36 John St. (☎724-7420). $1, seniors $0.50, disabled $0.25; 1-day pass $3, 3-day $7. CARTA's **Downtown Area Shuttle (DASH)** is made up of trolley routes that circle downtown. Operates daily 8am-11pm. Same fares apply. Visitors Center has schedules.

Taxi: Yellow Cab, ☎577-6565.

Bike Rental: The Bicycle Shoppe, 280 Meeting St. (☎722-8168), between George and Society St. Open M-Sa 9am-7pm, Su 1-5pm. $5 per hr., $20 per day.

ORIENTATION & PRACTICAL INFORMATION

Old Charleston lies at the southernmost point of the mile-wide peninsula below **Calhoun Street.** The major north-south routes through the city are **Meeting, King,** and **East Bay Street.** The area north of the Visitors Center is run-down and uninviting. **Savannah Highway (U.S. 17)** cuts across the peninsula going south to Savannah and north across two towering bridges to Mt. Pleasant and Myrtle Beach. There are plenty of metered parking spaces, and plenty of police officers giving tickets.

Visitor Info: Charleston Visitors Center, 375 Meeting St. (☎853-8000 or 800-868-8118; www.charlestoncvb.com), across from Charleston Museum. Open daily Apr.-Oct. 8:30am-5:30pm; Nov.-Mar. 8:30am-5pm.

Medical Services: Charleston Memorial Hospital, 326 Calhoun St. (☎577-0600).

Hotlines: Crisis Line, ☎744-4357 or 800-922-2283. 24hr. general counseling and referral. **People Against Rape,** ☎745-0144 or 800-241-7273. 24hr.

Internet Access: Public Library, 68 Calhoun St. (☎805-6801). Open M-Th 9am-9pm, F-Sa 9am-6pm, Su 2-5pm.

Post Office: 83 Broad St. (☎577-0690). Open M-F 8:30am-5:30pm, Sa 9:30am-2pm. Also houses a cute little postal museum. **Postal Code:** 29402. **Area Code:** 843.

ACCOMMODATIONS

Motel rooms in historic downtown Charleston are expensive. Cheap motels are a few miles out of the city, around Exits 209-211 on I-26 W in N. Charleston, or across the Ashley River on U.S. 17 S in Mt. Pleasant.

Bed, No Breakfast, 16 Halsey St. (☎723-4450). The only budget option within walking distance of downtown, this charming 2-room inn offers guests a luxuriously affordable way to stay in the historic heart of the city. Shared bathroom. Reservations recommended. Rooms $60-95. No credit cards. ❸

Masters Inn Economy, 6100 Rivers Ave. (☎744-3530 or 800-633-3434), at Exit 211B off I-26, 11 mi. from downtown, offers spacious and comfortable rooms at some of the lowest prices in Charleston. A/C, cable TV, pool, free local calls, and laundry. Singles Su-Th $39, F-Sa $43; doubles $43/49. ❷

Motel 6, 2058 Savannah Hwy. (☎556-5144), 5 mi. south of town. Be sure to call ahead and reserve one of these clean rooms; the immensely popular motel is often booked solid for days. Rooms Su-Th $44, F-Sa $54; each additional person $6. ❸

Campground at James Island County Park (☎795-4386 or 800-743-7275). Take U.S. 17 S to Rte. 171 and follow the signs. Spacious, open sites. The spectacular park features 16 acres of lakes, bicycle and walking trails, and a small water park. Bike and boat rental. Primitive sites $13; tent sites $19; hookup $26. Seniors 10% discount. ❶

FOOD

Charleston has some of the best food in the country. While most restaurants cater to big-spending tourists, there are plenty of budget-friendly opportunities to sample the Southern cooking, barbecue, and fresh seafood that have made the low country famous. Alluring options await on nearly every street.

Hyman's Seafood Company, 215 Meeting St. (☎723-6000). Since 1890, this casual restaurant has offered 15-25 different kinds of fresh fish daily ($7-15), served in any one of 8 styles. Po' boy sandwich with oyster, calamari, crab, or scallops $7-8. No reservations; expect long waits. Open daily 11am-11pm. ❸

Southend Brewery, 161 E. Bay St. (☎853-4677). Outstanding ribs ($13-20), eclectic pizzas ($8-10), and home-brewed beers ($3.50)—not to mention the opportunity to color on the paper tablecloths with crayons—entice many to frequent this 3-story brewhouse. Happy Hour daily 4-7pm. Open Su-W 11:30am-10pm, Th-Sa 11:30am-11pm; bar open daily until 1am. ❸

Jestine's Kitchen, 251 Meeting St. (☎722-7224). Serving up some of the best southern food in Charleston, Jestine's has become a local favorite with its daily Southern blue plate specials ($7-10) and "blue collar special" (peanut butter and banana sandwich; $3). Open Tu-Th 11am-9:30pm, F-Sa 11am-10pm, Su 11am-9pm. ❷

Andolini's Pizza, 82 Wentworth St. (☎722-7437), just west of King St. Perfectly hidden from the uber-trendy King St. shoppers, Andolini's creates amazing pizza at unbeatable prices. A large slice with any topping, a salad, and a drink runs a measly $5. Large thin-crust cheese pie $11. Calzones from $5. Open M-Th 11am-11pm, F-Sa 11am-midnight, Su noon-10pm. ❷

Sticky Fingers, 235 Meeting St. (☎853-7427). Voted the best barbecue in town on numerous occasions, Sticky Fingers has become a Charleston legend, now spread throughout the South, for its mouth-watering ribs ($12-26)—prepared in 5 different ways. The Carolina combo lets diners enjoy ribs, barbecue, chicken, and all the sides for a paltry $13. Open M-Sa 11am-11pm, Su 11am-10pm. ❹

The Bakers Cafe, 214 King St. (☎577-2694). Delighting local patrons for the past 23 years, this upscale cafe cooks up elegant morning and midday meals. Poached eggs ($6-10), as well as a variety of sandwiches ($8-9) and entrees ($6-11), make the Bakers Cafe an irresistible way to beat the heat. Open daily 8am-3pm. ❷

SIGHTS

Charleston's ancient homes, historical monuments, churches, galleries, and gardens can be seen by foot, car, bus, boat, trolley, or horse-drawn carriage—or on one of the nine ghost tours. **City Market,** downtown at Meeting St., stays abuzz in a newly restored 19th-century building. (Open daily from about 9am-5pm.)

PLANTATIONS AND GARDENS. The 300-year-old **Magnolia Plantation and Gardens** is by far the most majestic of Charleston's plantations, not to mention the oldest major public garden in the country. Visitors can enjoy the Drayton family's staggering wealth by exploring their 50 acres of gorgeous gardens with 900 varieties of camelia and 250 varieties of azalea. Other attractions include a hedge maze, bike and canoe rental, swamp, and bird sanctuary. *(On Rte. 61, 10 mi. out of town off U.S. 17. ☎571-1266 or 800-367-3517. Open Feb.-Nov. daily 8am-5:30pm; call for winter hours. Gardens $12, seniors $11, ages 13-19 $9, ages 6-12 $6; with house admission $19/18/16/13; with nature trail $18/17/15/10; with swamp garden $17/16/13/9. Canoes or bikes $5 per 3hr.)* A bit farther down the road, **Middleton Place** is a more manicured plantation with working stables, gardens, house, restaurant, and inn. *(On Rte. 61, 14 mi. northwest of downtown. ☎556-6020 or 800-782-3608; www.middletonplace.org. Wheelchair-accessible. Open daily 9am-5pm. Gardens $20, seniors $19, under 16 $12; house tour additional $10. AAA discount.)* Even farther out, but well worth the trip, **Cypress Gardens** lets visitors paddle their own boats out onto the eerie, gator-filled swamps. *(3030 Cypress Gardens Rd. Off Rte. 52. ☎553-0515; www.cypressgardens.org. Open daily 9am-5pm. $9, ages 6-12 $3.)*

CHARLESTON MUSEUM & HISTORIC HOMES. Across the street from the Visitors Center stands the **Charleston Museum,** the country's oldest museum, which boasts outstanding exhibits on the Revolutionary War and the Civil War, as well as an exhaustive look into the history of the Low Country. *(360 Meeting St. ☎722-2996; www.charlestonmuseum.org. Wheelchair-accessible. Open M-Sa 9am-5pm, Su 1-5pm. $8, children $4.)* Built in 1772, the **Heyward-Washington House** was home to Thomas Heyward, Jr., a signer of the Declaration of Independence. The house, which was rented to George Washington during his 1791 trip through the South, features timeless pieces of American furniture and a lush surrounding garden. Also managed by the Charleston Museum is the **Joseph Manigault House,** a stunning piece of neo-classical architecture built in 1803. Be sure to check out the Gate Temple, a gorgeous outdoor vestibule that leads to the front door and porch. Although a combo ticket is available for the museum and these two historic houses, just pick one house and save the money. *(Heyward-Washington House: 87 Church St. ☎722-0354. Joseph Manigault House: 350 Meeting St. ☎723-2926. Both houses open M-Sa 10am-5pm, Su*

1-5pm. 1 house $8, ages 3-12 $4; museum and 1 house $12; museum and 2 houses $18.) The **Nathaniel Russell House** and **Edmondston-Alston House** are both examples of the late Federal style of architecture, with the former boasting a "free-flying" staircase and masterful iron balconies and the latter a lush garden and stunning view of the Charleston Harbor. *(Nathaniel Russell: 51 Meeting St. ☎724-8481. Open M-Sa 10am-5pm, Su 2-5pm. $7, under 6 free. Edmondston-Alston: 21 E. Battery. ☎722-7171 or 800-782-3608. Open Su-M 1:30-4:30pm, Tu-Sa 10am-4:30pm. $10. Neither house is wheelchair-accessible.)*

PATRIOT'S POINT & FORT SUMTER. Climb aboard four Naval ships, including a submarine and the giant aircraft carrier *Yorktown*, in **Patriot's Point Naval and Maritime Museum,** the world's largest naval museum. *(40 Patriots Point Rd. Across the Cooper River in Mt. Pleasant. ☎884-2727; www.state.sc.us/patpt. Open daily Apr.-Sept. 9am-6pm, ships close 7:30pm; Oct.-Mar. 9am-5pm, ships close 5:30pm. $12.50, seniors and military $11, ages 6-11 $6.)* From Patriot's Point in Mt. Pleasant, **Fort Sumter Tours** has boat excursions to the National Historic Site where Confederate soldiers bombarded Union forces in April 1861, turning years of escalating tension into openly hostile war. There is a dock at Liberty Square next to the South Carolina Aquarium in Charleston. *(Tours: ☎881-7337. Fort Sumter: ☎883-3123; www.nps.gov/fosu. 2¼hr. total tour, 1hr. is at the Fort. 1-3 tours per day from each location. $12, seniors $11, ages 6-11 $6.)*

BEACHES. Folly Beach is popular with students from the Citadel, College of Charleston, and University of South Carolina. *(Over the James Bridge and U.S. 171, about 20 mi. southeast of Charleston. ☎588-2426.)* The more wide open **Isle of Palms** extends for miles down toward the less-crowded **Sullivan's Island.** *(Isle of Palms: Across the Cooper Bridge, drive 10mi. down Hwy. 17 N, and turn right onto the Isle of Palms Connector. ☎886-3863.)*

SOUTH CAROLINA AQUARIUM. This extremely interesting aquarium has quickly become Charleston's greatest attraction. Although a bit overpriced, its exhibits showcase aquatic life from the region's swamps, marshes, and oceans. Stare down the fishies at the 330,000-gallon Great Ocean Tank, which boasts the nation's tallest viewing window. *(At the end of Calhoun St. on the Cooper River, overlooking the harbor. ☎720-1990; www.scaquarium.org. Wheelchair-accessible. Open daily mid-June to mid-Aug. 9am-6pm; mid-Aug. to mid-June 9am-5pm. $14, seniors $12, ages 3-11 $7.)*

BULL ISLAND. To get away from human civilization, take a ferry to Bull Island, a 5000-acre island off the coast of Charleston. The boat is often greeted by dolphins swimming in some of the cleanest water on the

NO WORK, ALL PLAY

AFRICA, SOUTH CAROLINA

Every Memorial Day weekend, almost 100,000 people from the world over come to the small, quiet town of Beaufort, South Carolina, to pay homage to the culture and history that emerged when Africans were shipped to America as slaves many generations ago.

Known as the **Gullah Festival,** the gathering is a 5-day celebration of African traditions that has attracted droves of tourists, scholars, and locals since its humble creation in 1986. African storytellers captivate visitors, who also watch seductive African dance, listen to the harmonizing strains of live gospel and jazz music, and enjoy a multitude of authentic African dishes. A former slave market is memorialized in a special ceremony. Basket weaving and boat building exhibitions have also made their way into the festival, showcasing the very same techniques that were used centuries ago. Festival organizers have made a point to reach out to a younger audeince in recent years, adding to the schedule a Miss Gullah Festival Pageant and a Gullah Golf Tournament.

For more info, call ☎843-522-1998.

planet. Once on the island there are 16 mi. of hiking trails populated by 278 different species of birds. *(☎881-4582. ½hr. ferries depart from Moore's Landing, off Seewee Rd., 16 mi. north of Charleston off U.S. 17. Departs Mar.-Nov. Tu and Th-Sa 9am, 12:30pm; returns Tu and Th-Sa noon, 4pm; departs Dec.-Feb. Sa 10am; returns 3pm. Round-trip $30, under 12 $15.)*

ENTERTAINMENT & NIGHTLIFE

With nearby colleges and a constant tourist presence, Charleston's nightlife beats strong. Free copies of *City Paper*, in stores and restaurants, list concerts and other events. Big-name bands take center stage nightly at the **Music Farm,** 32 Ann St. (☎853-3276. Tickets $5-25.) Charleston's trendiest flock to the **Portside Cafe,** 462 King St., where prepped-out collegiates marinate under a warm Southern sky while grooving to the nightly live music. (☎722-0409. Sandwiches under $7. Barbecue from $8. Open M-F 6:30pm-4am, Sa 6:30pm-2am.) The city will explode with music, theater, dance, and opera, as well as literary and visual arts events, when Charleston hosts the 28th **Spoleto Festival USA,** the nation's most comprehensive arts festival. Founded in 1977 and dedicated to young artists, the celebration is the American counterpart to the Festival of Two Worlds in Spoleto, Italy. (☎722-2764; www.spoletousa.org. May 28-June 13, 2004. $10-75.)

COLUMBIA ☎803

Much ado is made over Columbia's Civil War heritage, and understandably so, as Old South nostalgia brings in big tourist dollars. However, locals point out that more antebellum buildings have been lost to developers in the last century than were burned by Sherman and his rowdy troops. Still, the town is the heart of the nation's "rebel" child, and a defiant spirit is cultivated in Columbia's bars, businesses, and citizens. Southern pride and passion are perpetuated at the **University of South Carolina (USC),** where "Gamecocks" roam the campus' sprawling green spaces and fascinating museums.

ORIENTATION & PRACTICAL INFORMATION. The city is laid out in a square, bordered by Huger and Harden St. running north-south and Blossom and Calhoun St. east-west. **Assembly Street** is the main drag, running north-south through the heart of the city, and **Gervais Street** is its east-west equivalent. The Congaree River marks the city's western edge. *The Beltline offers little for tourists and, for safety purposes, is best avoided.*

Columbia Metropolitan Airport, 3000 Aviation Way (☎822-5000; www.columbiaairport.com), is in West Columbia. A taxi to downtown costs about $13-15. **Amtrak,** 850 Pulaski St. (☎252-8246; open daily 10pm-5:30am), sends one train per day to: Miami (15hr., $142); Savannah (2½hr., $41); Washington, D.C. (10hr., $117). **Greyhound,** 2015 Gervais St. (☎256-6465), at Harden St., sends buses to: Atlanta (5hr., 7 per day, $49.50); Charleston (2½ hr., 2 per day, $26.25); Charlotte (2hr., 3-4 per day, $16-18). **Connex TCT** runs transit through Columbia, with most main routes departing from pickup/transfer depots at Sumter and Laurel St. and at Assembly and Taylor St. (☎217-9019. Runs daily 5:30am-midnight; call for schedules. $0.75; seniors and disabled, except 3-6pm, $0.25; under 6 free. Free transfers.) **Taxi: Capital City Cab,** ☎233-8294. **Visitor Info: Columbia Metropolitan Convention and Visitors Bureau,** 9000 Assembly St., has maps and info. (☎545-0000; www.columbiacvb.com. Open M-F 9am-5pm, Sa 10am-4pm.) For info on USC, try the **University of South Carolina Visitors Center,** 937 Assembly St. (☎777-0169 or 800-922-9755. Open M-F 8:30am-5pm, Sa 9:30am-12:30pm. Free parking pass.) **Medical Services: Palmetto Richland Memorial Hospital,** 5 Richland Medical Park. (☎434-7000.) **Internet Access: Richland**

County Public Library, 1431 Assembly St. (☎799-9084. Open M-Th 9am-9pm, F-Sa 9am-6pm, Su 2-6pm.) **Post office:** 1601 Assembly St. (☎733-4643. Open M-F 7:30am-6pm.) **Postal Code:** 29201. **Area Code:** 803.

ACCOMMODATIONS. Generally, the cheapest digs lie farthest from the city center. A conveniently short drive from downtown, the **Masters Inn ❷,** 613 Knox Abbott Dr., offers free local calls, morning coffee, a pool, and cable TV. Take Blossom St. across the Congaree River, where it becomes Knox Abbott Dr. (☎796-4300. Singles $33-36; doubles $35-38.) Inexpensive motels also line the three interstates (I-26, I-77, and I-20) that circle the city. **Knights Inn ❷,** 1987 Airport Blvd., Exit 133 off I-26, has many amenities for a low price. Rooms have refrigerators, microwaves, cable TV, A/C, free local calls, and pool access. (☎794-0222. Singles and doubles Su-Th $35, F-Sa $39. 10% senior discount.) After exploring all that Columbia has to offer, guests at the **Adams Mark Hotel ❹,** 1200 Hampton St., retreat to enormous rooms to take full advantage of one of downtown's classiest establishments. This full-service hotel comes complete with an indoor pool, fitness center, and three restaurants, making a great trip to Columbia even better. (☎771-7000. Rooms from $80.) The 1400 acres of **Sesquicentennial State Park ❶** include swimming and fishing, a nature center, hiking trails, and 87 wooded sites with electricity and water. Public transportation does not serve the park; take I-20 to the Two Notch Rd./U.S. 1, Exit 17, and head 3 mi. northeast (☎788-2706. Open daily Apr.-Oct. 7am-9pm; Nov.-Mar. 8am-6pm. Campsites $16. Entrance $1.50 per person.)

FOOD. It's little wonder that **Maurice's Piggie Park ❶,** 800 Elmwood Ave., 1600 Charleston Hwy., and nine other SC locations, holds the world record for "Most BBQ sold in one day." Maurice's cash "pig" is his exquisite, mustard-based sauce that covers the $5 Big Joe pork barbecue sandwich. (☎256-4377. Open M-Sa 10am-10pm.) Gamecocks past and present give highest marx to **Groucho's ❷,** 611 Harden St., where the famous "dipper" sandwiches ($6) have been delighting patrons for over 60 years. (☎799-5708. Open M-Sa 11am-4pm.) In the heart of downtown lies the **Hampton Street Vineyard ❹,** 1201 Hampton St., a casually elegant bistro that serves up delectable dishes to a mostly local clientele. Enjoy the Chilean salmon ($15) or the grilled duck ($16) in the candle-lit interior while watching the bustle of downtown Columbia on the sidewalk patio. (☎252-0850. Open M-F 11:30am-2pm and 6-10pm.) Charge over to the **Rhino Room ❹,** 807 Gervais St., for some of the best and most diverse food in town—from baby lamb ($10) to pepper strip steak ($17). Patrons often glimpse politicians on their lunch or dinner breaks. (☎931-0700. Open M-Sa 11:30am-2pm and 5:30-10pm.)

SIGHTS. Bronze stars mark the impact of Sherman's cannonballs on the **Statehouse,** an Italian Renaissance high-rise. Home to South Carolina's key governmental proceedings, the marble interior fittingly houses the state's official mace and sword. Survey the surrounding grounds, which have monuments and sculptures scattered throughout the lush and tranquil gardens. (On Sumter, Assembly, and Gervais St. ☎734-2430. Wheelchair-accessible. Open M-F 9am-5pm, Sa 10am-5pm; first Su each month 1-5pm. Free tours available.) Across Sumter St. from the Statehouse is the central green of the USC campus—the **Horseshoe.** Here, students play frisbee, sunbathe, study, and nap beneath a canopy of shade trees. At the head of the green, sitting at the intersection of Bull and Pendleton St., **McKissick Museum** explores the folklore of South Carolina and the Southeast through history, art, and science. (☎777-7251; www.cla.sc.edu/mcks. Open May-Aug. M-F 9am-4pm, Sa-Su 1-5pm; Sept.-Apr. Tu-W and F 9am-4pm, Th 9am-7pm, Su 1-5pm. Free.) The **South Carolina Confederate Relic Room and Museum,** 301 Gervais St., traces South Carolina's military history and houses an exhaustive collection of Civil War artifacts and displays. (☎737-8095; www.state.sc.us/crr. Wheelchair-accessible. Open Tu-Sa 10am-5pm. $3, under 21 free.) Two 19th-century mansions, the **Robert Mills Historic House and Park** and the **Hampton-Preston Mansion,** 1616 Blanding St., two blocks east of Bull St., compete as examples of antebellum opulence and survivors of Sherman's Civil War rampage. Both have been lovingly restored with period fineries. (☎252-1770; www.historiccolumbia.org. Tours every hr. Su 1-4pm, Tu-Sa 10am-3pm. Tours $5; students, military, and AAA $4; under 5 free. Buy tickets at Mills House Museum Shop.) For a broader experience of 19th-century life, stop by the **Manns-Simons Cottage,** once owned by a freed slave, and the **Woodrow Wilson Boyhood Home,** 1705 Hampton St. (Open Su 1-4pm, Tu-Sa 10am-4pm. Tickets at the Mills House Museum Shop.)

One of the top ten zoos in the country, **Riverbanks Zoo and Garden,** on I-126 at Greystone Blvd., northwest of downtown, recreates natural habitats to house over 2000 species. After ogling the adorable koalas and wallabies at the newly added Koala Knockabout, be sure to say hello to the zoo's newest additions—adorable Siberian tiger cubs. (☎779-8717; www.riverbanks.org. Open M-F 9am-5pm, Sa-Su 9am-6pm. $7.75, students $6.50, seniors $6.25.)

NIGHTLIFE. Columbia's nightlife centers around the collegiate **Five Points District,** at Harden and Devine St., and the blossoming, slightly more mature **Vista area,** on Gervais St. before the Congaree River. The oldest bar in Columbia, **Group Therapy,** 2107 Greene St., helps locals drown their sorrows the old-fashioned way. Try the Mullet (warm Jack Daniels with a touch of Budweiser; $7), and you'll never need to see a shrink again. (☎256-1203. Open daily 4:30pm-late.) Across the street at **Big Al's,** 749 Saluda Ave., a sleek and suave local crowd shoots pool, smokes stogies, and downs drinks in this dark and smoky den. (☎758-0700. Open M-F 5pm-late, Sa 5pm-2am, Su 9pm-2am.) In the Vista, the **Art Bar,** 1211 Park St., attracts a funky crowd to match its ambience. Glow paint, Christmas lights, kitschy 1950s bar stools, and a troop of life-size plastic robots are complemented by an eclectic music line-up. (☎929-0198. Open M-F 8pm-late, Sa-Su 8pm-2am.) The weekly publication *Free Times* gives details on Columbia's club and nightlife scene. *In Unison* is a weekly paper listing gay-friendly nightspots.

MYRTLE BEACH & THE GRAND STRAND ☎843

Each summer, millions of Harley-riding, RV-driving Southerners make Myrtle Beach the second-most-popular summer tourist destination in the country. During spring break and early June, Myrtle Beach is thronged with rambunctious students on the lookout for a good time. The rest of the year, families, golfers, shoppers, and others partake in the unapologetic tackiness of the town's theme restaurants, amusement parks, and shops. The pace slows significantly on the rest of the 60 mi. Grand Strand. South of Myrtle Beach, Murrell's Inlet is the place to go for good seafood, Pawley's Island is lined with beach cottages and beautiful private homes, and Georgetown, once a critical Southern port city, showcases white-pillared 18th-century-style rice and indigo plantation homes.

ORIENTATION & PRACTICAL INFORMATION. Most attractions are on **Kings Highway (Route 17),** which splits into a Business Route and a Bypass 4 mi. south of Myrtle Beach. **Ocean Boulevard** runs along the ocean, flanked on either side by cheap pastel motels. Avenue numbers repeat themselves after reaching 1st Ave. in the middle of town; note whether the Ave. is "north" or "south." Also, take care not to confuse north **Myrtle Beach** with the town **North Myrtle Beach,** which has an almost identical street layout. **Route 501** runs west toward Conway, **I-95,** and—most importantly—the factory outlet stores. Unless otherwise stated, addresses on the Grand Strand are for Myrtle Beach. **Greyhound,** 511 7th

Ave. N (☎448-2471; open daily 9am-1:45pm and 3-6:45pm), runs to Charleston (2½hr., 2 per day, $24-25). **The Waccamaw Regional Transportation Authority (WRTA),** 1418 3rd Ave., provides minimal busing; pick up a copy of schedules and routes from the Chamber of Commerce or from area businesses. (☎488-0865. Runs daily 5am-2am. Local fares $0.75-2.) WRTA also operates the **Ocean Boulevard Lymo,** a bus service that shuttles tourists up and down the main drag. (☎488-0865. Runs daily 8am-midnight. Unlimited day pass $2.50.) Rent bikes at **The Bike Shoppe,** 715 Broadway, at Main St. (☎448-5335. Open M-F 9am-6pm, Sa 9am-5pm. Beach cruisers $5 per half-day, $10 per day; mountain bikes $10/15.) **Visitor Info: Myrtle Beach Chamber of Commerce,** 1200 N. Oak St., parallel to Kings Hwy., at 12th N. (☎626-7444 or 800-356-3016; www.mbchamber.com. Open daily 8:30am-5pm.) **Mini Golf:** absolutely everywhere. **Medical Services: Grand Strand Regional Medical Center,** 809 82nd Pkwy. (☎692-1000.) **Internet Access: Chapin Memorial Library,** 400 14th Ave. N. (☎918-1275. Open M and W 9am-6pm, Tu and Th 9am-8pm, F-Sa 9am-5pm; in summer Sa hours 9am-1pm.) **Post Office:** 505 N. Kings Hwy., at 5th Ave. N. (☎626-9533. Open M-F 8:30am-5pm, Sa 9am-1pm.) **Postal Code:** 29577. **Area Code:** 843.

ACCOMMODATIONS. There are hundreds of motels lining Ocean Blvd., with those on the ocean side fetching higher prices than those across the street. Cheap motels also dot Rte. 17. From October to March, prices plummet as low as $20-30 a night for one of the luxurious hotels right on the beach. Call the **Myrtle Beach Lodging Reservation Service,** 1551 21st Ave. N., #20, for free help with reservations. (☎626-9970 or 800-626-7477. Open M-F 8:30am-5pm.) Across the street from the ocean, the family-owned **Sea Banks Motor Inn ❷,** 2200 S. Ocean Blvd., has immaculate rooms with mini-fridges, cable TV, laundry, and pool and beach access. (☎448-2434 or 800-523-0603. Mid-Mar. to mid-Sept. singles $45; doubles $75. Mid-Sept. to mid-Mar. $22/28.) The **Hurl Rock Motel ❷,** 2010 S. Ocean Blvd., has big, clean rooms with access to a pool and hot tub. (☎626-3531 or 888-487-5762. 25+. Singles $45; doubles $54-89. Low-season as low as $25/28.) **Huntington Beach State Park Campground ❶,** 3 mi. south of Murrell's Inlet on U.S. 17, is located in a diverse environment including lagoons, salt marshes, and a beach. *Be careful: gators come within yards of the sites.* (☎237-4440. Open daily Apr.-Oct. 6am-10pm; Nov.-Mar. 6am-6pm. Tent sites Apr.-Oct. $12; water and electricity $25; full hookup $27. Nov.-Mar. $10/21/23. Day-use $4.)

FOOD. The Grand Strand tempts hungry motorists to leave the highway with over 1800 restaurants serving every type of food in every type of setting imaginable. Massive family-style, all-you-can-eat joints beckon from beneath the glow of every traffic light. **Route 17** offers countless steakhouses, seafood buffets, and fast food restaurants. Seafood, however, is best on **Murrell's Inlet.** With license plates adorning the walls and discarded peanut shells crunching underfoot, the **River City Cafe ❶,** 404 21st Ave. N., celebrates a brand of American informality bordering on delinquency. Peruse the enthusiastic signatures of patrons on tables and walls as you polish off a burger ($3-6) or knock back a $3 beer. (☎448-1990. Open daily 11am-10pm.) While most of the restaurants in Broadway at the Beach seem to sacrifice food quality for elaborate decor, **Benito's ❸,** in the "Caribbean Village" part of the complex, serves up delightful stuffed shells ($10) and delectable calzones ($6) that will make you forget the screaming children and blaring lights outside. (☎444-0006. Open daily 11am-10:30pm.) Take a break from Ocean Dr. at **Dagwood's Deli ❷,** 400 11th. Ave.N., where beach bums and businessmen come together to enjoy a "Shag" (ham, turkey, and swiss cheese; $5) or a Philly cheesesteak ($5-7). Be prepared to wait. (☎448-0100. Open M-Sa 11am-9pm.)

SIGHTS & NIGHTLIFE. The boulevard and the beach are both "the strand," and while you're on it, the rule is see and be seen. Fashionable teens strut their stuff, low riders cruise the streets, and older beachgoers showcase their sunburns. Coupons are everywhere—never pay full price for any attraction in Myrtle Beach. Pick up a copy of the *Monster Coupon Book*, *Sunny Day Guide*, *Myrtle Beach Guide*, or *Strand Magazine* at any tourist info center or hotel.

The colossal **Broadway at the Beach,** Rte. 17 Bypass and 21st Ave. N. (☎444-3200 or 800-386-4662), is a sprawling 350-acre complex determined to stimulate and entertain with theaters, a water park, mini golf, 20 restaurants, nightclubs, 100 shops, and other attractions. Within Broadway, the **Butterfly Pavilion,** the first facility of its kind in the nation, showcases over 40 species of butterflies in free flight. (☎839-4444. Wheelchair-accessible. Open daily 10am-11pm. $11, seniors $10, ages 3-12 $8.) South Carolina's most visited attraction is Broadway's **Ripley's Aquarium,** where guests roam through a 330 ft. underwater tunnel and gaze upward at the ferocious sharks and terrifying piranha swimming above. (☎916-0888 or 800-734-8888; www.ripleysaquarium.com. Wheelchair-accessible. Open daily 9am-11pm. $15, ages 5-11 $9, ages 2-4 $3.) The reptile capital of the world is the amazing **Alligator Adventure,** Rte. 17 in North Myrtle Beach at Barefoot Landing, where even the most ardent Animal Planet fans are mesmerized by the exotic collection of snakes, lizards, and frogs, and the hourly gator feedings. Don't miss the the park's 20 ft., 2000lb. resident, Utan—the world's largest reptile. (☎361-0789. Wheelchair-accessible. Open daily 9am-10pm. $14, seniors $12, ages 4-12 $9.)

Most visitors to Myrtle Beach putter over to one of the many elaborately themed **mini golf** courses on Kings Hwy. The **NASCAR Speedpark,** across from Broadway at the Beach on the Rte. 17 Bypass, provides 7 different tracks of varying difficulty levels, catering to the need for speed. (☎918-8725. Open daily 10am-11pm. Unlimited rides $25, under 13 $15.) The 9100-acre **Brookgreen Gardens,** Rte. 17 opposite Huntington Beach State Park south of Murrell's Inlet, provide a tranquil respite from the touristy tackiness that dominates Myrtle Beach. Over 500 American sculptures—each more captivating than the last—are scattered throughout the grounds beneath massive oaks. Guided tours of the gardens and wildlife trail are offered in addition to summer drama, music, and food programs. (☎235-6000; www.brookgreen.org. Wheelchair-accessible. Open daily 9:30am-5pm. 7-day pass $12, seniors and ages 13-18 $10, 12 and under free.)

For a night on the town, the New Orleans-style nightclub district of **Celebrity Square,** at Broadway at the Beach, facilitates stepping out with ten nightclubs, ranging in theme from classic rock to Latin. Elsewhere, **Club Millennium 2000,** 1012 S. Kings Hwy. (☎445-9630), and **2001,** 920 Lake Arrowhead Rd. (☎449-9434), bring clubbers a hot-steppin' odyssey. (21+. Cover varies. Open daily 8pm-2am.)

GEORGIA

Georgia has two faces; the rural southern region contrasts starkly with the sprawling commercialism of the north. But the state somehow manages to balance its many different identities. Cosmopolitan Atlanta boasts of Coca-Cola and Ted Turner's CNN, both of which have networked the globe, while Savannah fosters a different, distinctively antebellum atmosphere. And while collegiate Athens breeds "big" bands, Georgia's Gold Coast offers a slow-paced seaside existence. This state of countless contradictions was called home by two former presidents as well: Jimmy Carter's hometown of Plains and Franklin D. Roosevelt's summer home in Warm Springs both stand on red Georgia clay. No matter where you go in Georgia, one thing remains constant—the enduring Southern hospitality.

PRACTICAL INFORMATION

Capital: Atlanta.

Visitor Info: Department of Industry and Trade, Tourist Division, 285 Peachtree Center Ave., Atlanta 30303 (☎404-656-3590 or 800-847-4842; www.georgia.org), in the Marriot Marquis 2 Tower, 10th fl. Open M-F 8am-5pm. **Department of Natural Resources,** 205 Butler St. SE #1352, Atlanta 30334 (☎404-656-3530 or 800-864-7275). **US Forest Service,** 1800 NE Expwy., Atlanta 30329 (☎404-248-9142). Open W-Su 11am-7:30pm.

Postal Abbreviation: GA. **Sales Tax:** 4-7%, depending on county.

ATLANTA ☎404

An increasingly popular destination for recent college graduates weary of more fast-paced cities, Atlanta strives to be cosmopolitan with a smile. Northerners, Californians, the third-largest gay population in the US, and a host of ethnicities have diversified this unofficial capital of the South while giving it a distinctly un-Southern feel. A national economic powerhouse, Atlanta holds offices for 400 of the Fortune 500 companies, including the headquarters of Coca-Cola, Delta Airlines, the United Parcel Service, and CNN. Nineteen colleges, including Georgia Tech, Morehouse College, Spelman College, and Emory University, also call "Hotlanta" home. The city is equally blessed with hidden gems; getting lost on Atlanta's streets reveals a endless number of trendy restaurants and beautiful old houses.

INTERCITY TRANSPORTATION

Flights: Hartsfield International Airport (☎530-2081; www.atlanta-airport.com), south of the city. MARTA (see **Public Transit**) is the easiest way to get downtown, with rides departing from the Airport Station (15min., every 8min. daily 5am-1am, $1.75). **Atlanta Airport Shuttle** (☎524-3400) runs vans from the airport to over 100 locations in the metropolis and outlying area (every 15min. daily 7am-11pm, shuttle to downtown $14). Taxi to downtown $20.

Train: Amtrak, 1688 Peachtree St. NW (☎881-3062), 3 mi. north of downtown at I-85, or 1 mi. north of Ponce de Leon on Peachtree St. Take bus #23 from "Arts Center" MARTA station. To **New Orleans** (10½hr., 1 per day, $52-119) and **New York** (19hr., 3 per day, $197). Open daily 7am-9:30pm.

Buses: Greyhound, 232 Forsyth St. SW (☎584-1728), across from "Garnett" MARTA station. To: **New York** (18-23hr., 14 per day, $91); **Savannah** (5hr., 6 per day, $45); **Washington, D.C.** (15hr., 12 per day, $75-79). Open 24hr.

ORIENTATION

Atlanta sprawls across ten counties in the northwest quadrant of the state at the junctures of I-75, I-85 (the city "thru-way"), and I-20. **I-285** (the "Perimeter") circumscribes the city. Maneuvering around Atlanta's main thoroughfares, arranged much like the spokes of a wheel, challenges even the most experienced native. **Peachtree Street** (one of over 100 streets bearing that name in Atlanta), is a major north-south road; **Spring Street** (which runs only south) and **Piedmont Avenue**

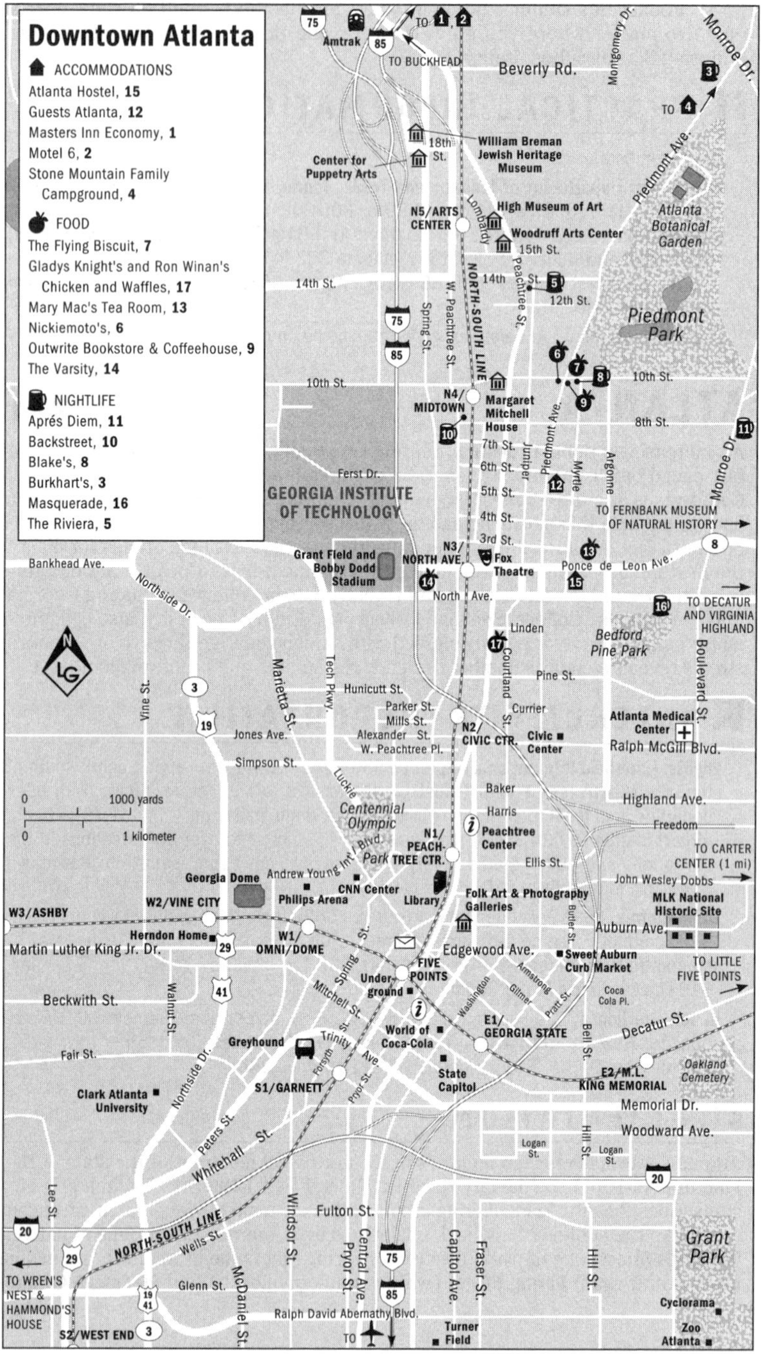

Downtown Atlanta

ACCOMMODATIONS

Atlanta Hostel, **15**
Guests Atlanta, **12**
Masters Inn Economy, **1**
Motel 6, **2**
Stone Mountain Family Campground, **4**

FOOD

The Flying Biscuit, **7**
Gladys Knight's and Ron Winan's Chicken and Waffles, **17**
Mary Mac's Tea Room, **13**
Nickiemoto's, **6**
Outwrite Bookstore & Coffeehouse, **9**
The Varsity, **14**

NIGHTLIFE

Aprés Diem, **11**
Backstreet, **10**
Blake's, **8**
Burkhart's, **3**
Masquerade, **16**
The Riviera, **5**

(which runs only north) are parallel to Peachtree. On the eastern edge **Moreland Avenue** traverses the length of the city, through Virginia Highland, Little Five Points (L5P), and East Atlanta. **Ponce de Leon Avenue** is the major east-west road, and will take travelers to most major destinations (or intersect with a street that can). To the south of "Ponce" runs **North Avenue**, another major east-west street. Navigating Atlanta requires a full arsenal of transportation strategies, from walking to public transportation to driving. The outlying areas of Buckhead, Virginia Highlands and L5P are easiest to get to by car, but once you've arrived, the restaurant and bar-lined streets encourage walking. Atlanta's most popular attractions, centered in downtown and midtown, are best explored using MARTA.

NEIGHBORHOODS

Sprouting out of downtown Atlanta, the **Peachtree Center** and **Five Points MARTA** stations deliver hordes of tourists to shopping and dining at **Peachtree Center Mall** and **Underground Atlanta.** Downtown is also home to **Centennial Olympic Park** as well as Atlanta's major sports and concert venues. Directly southwest of downtown, the **West End,** an African-American neighborhood, is the city's oldest historic quarter. From Five Points, head northeast to **Midtown,** from Ponce de Leon Ave. to 17th St., for museums and **Piedmont Park.** East of Five Points at Euclid and Moreland Ave., the **Little Five Points (L5P)** district is a local haven for artists and youth subculture. North of L5P, **Virginia Highland,** a trendy neighborhood east of Midtown and Piedmont Park, attracts yuppies and college kids. **Buckhead,** a swanky area north of Midtown on Peachtree St., houses designer shops and dance clubs.

LOCAL TRANSPORTATION

Public Transit: Metropolitan Atlanta Rapid Transit Authority, or **MARTA** (☎848-4711; schedule info M-F 6am-11pm, Sa-Su 8am-10pm). Clean, uncrowded trains and buses provide hassle-free transportation to Atlanta's major attractions. Rail operates M-F 5am-1am, Sa-Su and holidays 6am-12:30am in most areas. MARTA tokens for both trains and buses $1.75. Bus hours vary. Exact change or a token from a station machine needed; transfers free. Unlimited weekly pass $13. Pick up a system map at the **MARTA Ride Store,** Five Points Station downtown, or at the airport, Lindbergh, or Lenox stations. The majority of trains, rail stations, and buses are wheelchair-accessible.

Taxi: Atlanta Yellow Cab, ☎521-0200. **Checker Cab,** ☎351-8255.

Car Rental: Atlanta Rent-a-Car, 3185 Camp Creek Pkwy. (☎763-1110), just inside I-285 2½ mi. east of the airport. Ten other locations in the area including 2800 Campelton Rd. (☎344-1060) and 3129 Piedmont Rd. (☎231-4898). $25 per day, $0.24 per mi. over 100 mi. 21+ with major credit card.

PRACTICAL INFORMATION

Visitor Info: Atlanta Convention and Visitors Bureau, 233 Peachtree St. NE, Peachtree Center #100 (☎521-6600 or ☎800-285-2682; www.atlanta.net), downtown. Open M-F 8:30am-5:30pm. Automated **information service** ☎222-6688. For maps, stop in at the **Visitors Center,** 65 Upper Alabama St. (☎521-6688), on the upper level of Underground Atlanta MARTA: Five Points. Open M-Sa 10am-6pm, Su noon-6pm.

Bi-Gay-Lesbian Resources: The Atlanta Gay and Lesbian Center, 170 11th St. (☎874-9890; www.aglc.org). **Gay Yellow Pages,** ☎892-6454.

Hotlines: Rape Crisis Counseling, ☎616-4861. Staffed 24hr.

Medical Services: Piedmont Hospital, 1968 Peachtree Road NW. (☎605-5000).

Public Library: Central Library, 1 Margaret Mitchell Square (☎730-1700). Open Su 2-6pm, M-Th 9am-9pm, F-Sa 9am-6pm. Internet access available upon registering for a free PC-access card.

Post Office: Phoenix Station (☎521-2963), at the corner of Forsyth and Marietta St., one block from MARTA: Five Points. Open M-F 9am-5pm. **Postal Code:** 30303. **Area Code:** 404 inside the I-285 perimeter, 770 outside. In text, 404 unless otherwise noted. 10-digit dialing required.

Safety is no less a concern in Atlanta than it is in any other major city. While recent efforts to beef up police presence in high-risk areas of the city are having an effect, travelers—especially women—should be careful to avoid walking alone in much of the city, and should excercise special caution in the West End and Midtown areas.

ACCOMMODATIONS

Atlanta Hostel, 223 Ponce de Leon Ave. (☎875-9449 or 800-473-9449; www.hostel-atlanta.com), in Midtown. From MARTA: North Ave., exit onto Ponce de Leon and walk about 3½ blocks east to Myrtle St., or take bus #2. Look for the sign that reads "Woodruff Inn: Bed and Breakfast" (the building's original name). This family-owned-and-operated establishment offers visitors immaculate dorm-style rooms in a cozy home that resembles a B&B. Enjoy complimentary breakfast on the patio, TV, laundry, pool table, kitchen, and Internet access ($1 for 10 min.). No sleeping bags allowed, but free blankets are distributed. Free lockers. Linen $1. Dorms $18; private rooms $39-49. ❶

Guests Atlanta, 811 Piedmont Ave. NE (☎872-5846 or 800-724-4381; www.guestsatlanta.com). Nestled on a shaded lane in the heart of Midtown, Guests Atlanta is comprised of three gorgeous Victorian mansions. Beautiful, clean rooms with TV, Internet access, and breakfast. Laundry available. Reservations recommended in summer. Singles $70; doubles $90. ❹

Masters Inn Economy, 3092 Presidential Pkwy. (☎770-454-8373 or 800-633-3434), off Chamblee Tucker Rd. in Doraville; Exit 94 off I-85. Clean, large rooms with king-size beds, local calls, cable TV, and pool. Singles M-Th and Su $40, F-Sa $44; doubles $44/49.2 *Be very cautious and aware in this area, especially if you are traveling alone.* ❷

Motel 6, 2820 Chamblee Tucker Rd. (☎770-458-6626), Exit 94 off I-85 in Doraville. Spacious and tidy rooms. Free local calls, morning coffee, and A/C. Under 18 stay free with parents. Singles $45. *Be very cautious and aware in this area, especially if you are traveling alone.* ❷

Stone Mountain Family Campground (☎770-498-5710), on US 78. Perfect for those who want to get away from the commotion of the city, this expansive campground offers stunning sites (many of which are on the lake), bike rentals, and a free laser show. Internet access also available. Max. stay 2 weeks. Sites $20-28. Full hookup $32-37. Entrance fee $7 per car. ❶

FOOD

From Vietnamese to Italian, fried to fricasseed, Atlanta cooks up ample options for any craving. "Soul food," designed to nurture the spirit as well as the body, nourishes the city. Have a taste of the South and dip cornbread into "pot likker," water used to cook greens. Visit one of the legendary "Chicken and Waffles" restaurants, where the uncommon combination makes for a terrific meal. For sweet treats, you can't beat the Atlanta-based **Krispy Kreme Doughnuts** ❶, whose glazed delights

($0.60) are a Southern institution. The factory store, 295 Ponce de Leon Ave. NE (☎876-7307), continuously bakes their wares. (Open Su-Th 5:30am-midnight, F-Sa 24hr.; drive-through daily 24hr.) A depot for soul food's raw materials since 1923, the **Sweet Auburn Curb Market,** 209 Edgewood Ave., has an eye-popping assortment, from cow's feet to ox tails. (☎659-1665. Open M-Sa 8am-6pm.)

BUCKHEAD

Fellini's Pizza, 2809 Peachtree Rd. NE (☎266-0082). Under the watchful eye of three gargoyles (and one angel), Fellini's welcomes hungry customers with its bright yellow awnings, spacious deck (complete with fountain), and mouth-watering pizza. If Hotlanta has become too warm, enjoy your slice ($1.45, toppings $0.40 each) or pie ($9.50-11) in the brick-walled interior, which manages to combine a romantic atmosphere and classic rock. Open M-Sa 11:30am-2am, Su 12:30pm-midnight. Cash only. ❷

Buckhead Diner, 3073 Piedmont Rd. (☎262-3336). Don't let the traditional silver and neon exterior fool you. With its own dress code (business casual), valet parking, and high-profile clientele, the Buckhead Diner is not the typical late-night junction eatery. With menu options like grilled lamb ($18), oak-fired Atlantic salmon ($20), and the award-winning chocolate banana cream pie ($6), you'll never look at diners the same. Open M-Sa 11am-midnight, Su 10am-10pm. ❹

MIDTOWN

Gladys Knight's and Ron Winans's Chicken and Waffles, 529 Peachtree St; MARTA North Ave. (☎874-9393), screams soul. Situated on the southern border of Midtown, this joint serves up incredible dishes like the Midnight Train (4 southern-fried chicken wings and a waffle; $8). Among the side dishes are collard greens ($3), cinnamon raisin toast ($1), and corn muffins ($1). Enjoy an Uptown (sweetened iced tea and lemonade, $2) in one of the deep brown leather booths while relaxing to the smooth musical stylings of R&B all-stars. Open M-Th 11am-11pm, F-Sa 11am-4am, Su 11am-8pm. ❷

The Varsity, 61 N. Ave. NW (☎881-1707; www.thevarsity.com), at Spring St. MARTA: North Ave. Established in 1928, the Varsity has been delighting patrons for generations with its unique assembly-line food preparation and delicious diner food. Young and old alike flock to the the world's largest drive-in where they enjoy the Varsity's hamburgers ($1), classic coke floats ($2), and famous onion rings ($2). Most items around $2. Open Su-Th 10am-11:30pm, F-Sa 10am-12:30am. ❶

THE BIG SPLURGE

SPIRITUAL PROVISIONS

At one Atlanta church, the minister has been replaced by a maitre-d'ushering the faithful into the house of worship, where dinner tables and wine stand in for pews and holy water.

From 1915 to 1967, **the Abbey** served the spiritually hungry. Today, it is an elegant restaurant providing a different kind of sustenance. Halls that once resonated with the good word now echo with jovial conversation and light jazz music. The restaurant does not cast off its divine origins entirely—candles still adorn the walls (and the tables), and waiters serve patrons while cloaked in traditional monks' robes.

The ambience is only half the delight; the Abbey's four-course meals could convert any palate. Begin your meal with an Abbey fall salad or butternut squash bisque (both $7) before moving onto the heavenly entrees, which include poached Maine lobster ($38) and grilled beef tenderloin ($30). Finish off with the blissful triple decadent mousse ($7) or *chocolat l'Abbaye* (Godiva cappuccino and Godiva chocolate liqueur; $10). Sample the Abbey's fine wines, imbibed by the glass ($7-12) or the bottle ($23-2700). Dining at the Abbey may very well be your most gratifying church visit yet.

163 Ponce de Leon, at Piedmont. ☎876-8831; www.theabbeyrestaurant.com. MARTA: North Ave. Open daily 6-10pm. ❺

Mary Mac's Tea Room, 224 Ponce de Leon Ave. (☎876-1800; www.marymacs.com), at Myrtle. MARTA: North Ave or take the "Georgia Tech" bus north. Whether you're sipping the house specialty tea ($1.25) or enjoying the baked turkey, you'll appreciate the stellar service and charming tea rooms that await you at this Midtown treasure. All entrees come with 2 side dishes and run $9. Open M-Sa 11am-8:30pm, Su 11am-3pm. ❸

10TH ST.

Nickiemoto's, 990 Piedmont Ave. (☎253-2010). Plates of sushi—referred to as "edible art"—delight both the taste buds and the eyes. Combo plates from $10.50. Open M-Th 11:30am-11pm, F 11:30am-midnight, Sa noon-midnight, Su noon-11pm. ❸

Outwrite Bookstore & Coffeehouse, 991 Piedmont Ave. (☎607-0082). With rainbow-wigged mannequin heads gracing the windows, its own coffee shop, and remarkably friendly service, this unique gay and lesbian establishment has a relaxed and stylish air. Try the espresso specialty drink "Shot in the Dark" ($2) to go along with your bagel ($1), then retreat with your favorite book to the deck where comfy furniture awaits. Open daily 9am-11pm. ❶

The Flying Biscuit, 1001 Piedmont Ave. (☎874-8887). Packed with loyal patrons—mostly young professionals and families—who swear by its breakfast feasts, the Flying Biscuit is the place to take that first meal of the day. Enjoy the Flying Biscuit Breakfast ($7) and the signature Delio (double espresso mochaccino; $4) on the sun-drenched patio or at the granite-topped bar, and your day will be off to the right start. Open Su-Th 7am-10pm, F-Sa 7am-11pm. ❷

VIRGINIA HIGHLAND

Doc Chey's, 1424 N. Highland Ave. (☎888-0777), serves up heaping mounds of noodles at fantastic prices ($6-8). The pan-Asian restaurant is ultra-popular among young Atlanta locals. Try the delicious Chinese Lo Mein ($6) or the unique spicy tomato ginger noodle bowl ($8), one of Doc's originals. Open Su-Th 11:30am-10pm, F-Sa 11:30am-11pm. ❷

Fontaine's Oyster House, 1026½ N. Highland Ave. (☎872-0869). Oysters are the name of the game at Fontaine's; have them on the half-shell (6 for $5) or eat them roasted in one of eight ways ($8-15). All oystered out? Sink your teeth into some fried alligator, crawfish, or shrimp (combos $7-12). Shuck your favorite seafood down at the bar or on the beautiful balcony patio. Open M and W-F 10:30am-4am, Tu 4pm-4am, Sa 11:30am-3am, Su 10:30am-midnight; kitchen closes M-Sa midnight, Su 11:30pm. ❸

Everybody's, 1040 N. Highland Ave. (☎873-4545), receives high accolades for selling Atlanta's best pizza. Their inventive pizza salads, a colossal mound of greens and chicken on a pizza bed ($12), use the freshest of ingredients. Be sure to try Everybody's unique pizza sandwiches ($8-9). Open M-Th 11:30am-11pm, F-Sa 11:30am-1am, Su noon-10:30pm. ❸

SIGHTS

SWEET AUBURN DISTRICT

MARTIN LUTHER KING, JR. Some of the most powerful sights in the city run along Auburn Ave. in Sweet Auburn. Reverend Martin Luther King, Jr.'s birthplace, church, and grave are all part of the 23-acre **Martin Luther King, Jr. National Historic Site.** The **Visitors Center** houses poignant displays of photographs, videos, and quotations oriented around King's life and the struggle for civil rights. *(450 Auburn Ave. NE. MARTA: King Memorial. ☎331-5190; www.nps.gov/malu. Open June-Aug. daily 9am-6pm; Sept.-May 9am-5pm. Free.)* The Visitors Center administers tours of the **Birthplace of MLK.** *(501 Auburn Ave. Tours every 30 min. June-Aug; every hr. Sept-May. Arrive early to sign up;*

advance reservations not accepted.) Across the street from the Visitors Center stands **Ebenezer Baptist Church,** where King gave his first sermon at age 17 and co-pastored with his father from 1960 to 1968. *(407 Auburn Ave. ☎688-7263. Open June-Aug. M-Sa 9am-6pm, Su 1-6pm; Sept.-May M-Sa 9am-5pm, Su 1-5pm.)* Next door at the **Martin Luther King, Jr. Center for Nonviolent Social Exchange** lies the beautiful blue reflecting pool with an island on which King is laid to rest in a white marble tomb. The center's Freedom Hall holds a collection of King's personal articles (including his Nobel Peace Prize medal), an overview of his role model, Gandhi, and an exhibit on Rosa Parks. *(449 Auburn Ave. NE. ☎331-5190. Open June-Aug. daily 9am-6pm; Sept.-May 9am-5pm. Free.)* Plaques lining Sweet Auburn point out the architecture and prominent past residents of this historically black neighborhood.

DOWNTOWN & AROUND

From March to November, the **Atlanta Preservation Center** offers walking tours of six popular areas, including Druid Hills, the setting of *Driving Miss Daisy.* Other popular tour destinations include Inman Park, Atlanta's first trolley suburb, and Historic Downtown, Atlanta's earliest high-rise district. *(537 Peachtree St. NE. ☎876-2041; www.preserveatlanta.com. $7, students and seniors $5. Call ahead to arrange wheelchair-accessible tours.)*

GRANT PARK. In Grant Park, directly south of Oakland Cemetery and Cherokee Ave., is the world's largest painting (42 ft. tall and 358 ft. in circumference). The 117-year-old Cyclorama takes visitors back in time, revolving them on a huge platform in the middle of the "1864 Battle of Atlanta." An engrossing combination of sight and sound, no history buff can afford to miss this experience. *(800 Cherokee Ave. SE. Take bus #31 or 97 from Five Points. MARTA: M.L. King Memorial. ☎624-1071. Wheelchair-accessible. Open June-Sept. daily 9:30am-5:30pm; Oct.-May 9:30am-4:30pm. $6, seniors $5, ages 6-12 $4.)*

ZOO ATLANTA. Next door to the park, the zoo delights visitors young and old with a spectacular array of animals. Komodo dragons, Allen the orangutan, two giant pandas of Chengdu, and a Sumatran tiger are just a few of the specimens waiting here, leering salaciously. *(800 Cherokee Ave. SE. Take bus #31 or 97 from Five Points. ☎624-5600; www.zooatlanta.org. Wheelchair-accessible. Open Apr.-Oct. M-F 9:30am-4:30pm, Sa-Su 9:30am-5:30pm; Nov.-Mar. daily 9:30am-4:30pm. $15, seniors $11, ages 3-11 $10.)*

WORLD OF COCA-COLA (WOCC). Two blocks from the capitol, the World of Coca-Cola details the rise of "the real thing" from its humble beginnings in Atlanta to its position of world domination. Uncap the secrets of Coke as you walk through two floors of Coca-Cola history and memorabilia, complete with a demonstration by a "soda jerk" and TVs that continuously play old Coca-Cola advertisements. The real highlight, however, comes at the tour's end, as visitors get to sample 46 flavors of Coke from around the world, from the long-lost Tab to Mozambique's "Krest." *(55 Martin Luther King, Jr. Dr. MARTA: Five Points. ☎676-5151; www.woccatlanta.com. Wheelchair-accessible. Open June-Aug. M-Sa 9am-6pm, Su 11am-6pm; Sept.-May M-Sa 9am-5pm, Su noon-6pm. $6, seniors $4, ages 6-12 $3.)*

UNDERGROUND ATLANTA. Adjacent to the WOCC, this redeveloped part of Atlanta gets down with six subterranean blocks of mall and over 120 chain restaurants, shops, and night spots. Once a hot spot for alternative music, the underground now resembles a carnival-like labyrinth of marketing and merchandise. *(Descend at the entrance beside the Five Points subway station. ☎523-2311. Shops open June-Sept. M-Sa 10am-9:30pm, Su 11am-7pm; Oct.-May M-Sa 10am-9pm, Su noon-6pm. Bars and restaurants close later.)*

CNN. Overlooking beautiful Centennial Park is the global headquarters of Ted Turner's 86-million-viewer success, **Cable News Network (CNN).** Check out the 1hr. studio tour, which reveals "the story behind the news." Sit inside a replica control room, learn the secrets of teleprompter magic, and peer into the renowned CNN newsroom. *(At Techwood Dr. and Marietta St. MARTA: Omni/Dome/GWCC Station at W1. ☎827-2300; www.cnn.com/studio tour. Elevator tours available for visitors in wheelchairs with 24hr. notice. 45min. tours every 20min. daily 9am-6pm. $8, seniors $6, ages 5-12 $5.)*

OLYMPIC PARK. Follow Andrew Young International Blvd. (known to locals as "International") to its end and you will find **Centennial Olympic Park,** a 21-acre state park that serves both as a public recreation area and a lasting monument to the 1996 Olympic Games. Enormous "Hermes Towers" and an array of flags (each representing a nation that has hosted one of the modern Olympic Games) surround the park and its well-known **Fountain of Rings,** which enthralls (and soaks) children and adults alike. Check out one of the 20min. fountain shows (daily 12:30, 3:30, 6:30, 9pm) in which the water dances to symphonic melodies and dazzling lights. *(265 Park Avenue West, NW. MARTA: Peachtree Center ☎223-4412; www.centennialpark.com. Wheelchair-accessible.)*

CARTER PRESIDENTIAL CENTER. A charming garden and a circle of state flags surrounding the American flag welcome visitors to this self-guided museum, located just north of Little Five Points. The museum relates the works, achievements, and events of Jimmy Carter's life and presidency through a variety of films and exhibits. Highlights of the tour include a replica of Carter's Oval Office and his Nobel Peace Prize medal. Attached to the museum, the **Jimmy Carter Library,** one of only 11 Presidential libraries in the country, serves as a depository for historical materials from the Carter Administration. *(441 Freedom Pkwy. Take bus #16 to Cleburne Ave. ☎331-0296; www.jimmycarterlibrary.org. Wheelchair-accessible. Museum open M-Sa 9am-4:45pm, Su noon-4:45pm; grounds open daily 6am-9pm. $7, seniors $5, under 16 free.)*

STATE CAPITOL. Situated on the corner of Washington and Mitchell is the **Georgia State Capitol Building,** a wondrous structure built in 1889 with Georgia's own resources: Cherokee marble, Georgian oak, and steel. Inside, the Georgia Capitol Museum displays the political and cultural history of the state from Native American times onward. *(☎656-2844; www.sos.state.ga.us. Tours available M-F every hr. 10am-2pm. Capitol and museum open M-F 8am-5pm. Free.)*

WEST END

AFRICAN-AMERICAN HISTORY. Dating from 1835, the West End is Atlanta's oldest neighborhood. Experience several eccentric twists on the "historic home" tradition at the **Wren's Nest.** Home to author Joel Chandler Harris, who popularized the African folktale trickster Brer Rabbit, the Wren's Nest offers a glimpse into middle-class life as it was at the beginning of the 20th century. *(1050 R.D. Abernathy Blvd. Take bus #71 from West End Station/S2. ☎753-7735. Wheelchair-accessible. Open Tu-Sa 10am-2:30pm. Tours every hr. on the ½hr. $7, ages 4-12 $4, seniors and ages 13-19 $5.)* The **Hammonds House,** the home-turned-gallery of Dr. Otis Hammonds, a renowned African-American physician and art lover, displays unique contemporary and historic works in Georgia's only collection dedicated entirely to African-American and Haitian art. *(503 Peeples St. SW. ☎752-8730; www.hammondshouse.org. Wheelchair-accessible. Open Tu-F 10am-6pm, Sa-Su 1-5pm. $2, students and seniors $1.)* Born a slave, Alonzo F. Herndon became a prominent barber and founder of Atlanta Life Insurance Co., eventually attaining the status of Atlanta's wealthiest African-American in the early 1900s. A Beaux-Arts Classical mansion, the **Herndon Home** was built in 1910 and today is dedicated to the legacy of Herndon's philanthropy. *(587 University Pl. NW. Take bus #3 from Five Points station to the corner of Martin Luther King, Jr. Dr. and*

Maple, walk 1 block west, turn right on Walnut, and walk 1 block. ☎581-9813; www.herndonhome.org. Wheelchair-accessible. Tours every hr. $5, students $3. Open Tu-Sa 10am-4pm.)

MIDTOWN

WOODRUFF ARTS CENTER. Cultural connoisseurs, the **Woodruff Arts Center (WAC)** is your place. To the west of Piedmont Park, Richard Meier's award-winning buildings of glass, steel, and white porcelain are matched only by the treasures they contain. Within the WAC, the **High Museum of Art** features a rotation of incredible temporary exhibits, which have included the works of Pablo Picasso, Edgar Degas, Edward Hopper, and Ansel Adams. The museum has recently begun construction of three new galleries (expected to be completed in 2005), which will house much of the American collection and showcase the museum's photography section. *(1280 Peachtree St. NE. MARTA: Arts Center and exit Lombardy Way. WAC: ☎733-4200. High Museum of Art: ☎733-4400; www.high.org. Open Tu-Su 10am-5pm. $13, students with ID and seniors $10, ages 6-17 $8.)* The **Folk Art & Photography Galleries,** part of the High Museum, house additional and more esoteric exhibits. *(30 John Wesley Dobbs Ave. NE. One block south of MARTA: Peachtree Center. ☎577-6940. Wheelchair-accessible. Open M-Sa 10am-5pm, and the first Th of every month 10am-8pm. Free.)*

MARGARET MITCHELL HOUSE. Located between the 10th St. district and Midtown, the apartment where Mitchell wrote her Pulitzer-Prize-winning novel, *Gone with the Wind*, now welcomes the public. Tour the house and view her typewriter and autographed copies of the book. Across the street you'll find the **Gone with the Wind Movie Museum,** which includes the door to Tara Plantation, the portrait of Scarlett at which Clark Gable hurled a cocktail onscreen (complete with stain), as well as other original props and memorablia from the movie. *(990 Peachtree St., at 10th and Peachtree St. adjacent to MARTA: Midtown. ☎249-7015; www.gwtw.org. Open daily 9:30am-5pm. 1hr. tours every 45min. $12, students and seniors $9, ages 6-17 $5.)*

WILLIAM BREMAN JEWISH HERITAGE MUSEUM. The largest Jewish museum in the Southeast, featuring a powerful Holocaust exhibit and a gallery tracing the history of the Atlanta Jewish community from 1845 to the present. *(1440 Spring St. NW. From MARTA: Peachtree Center Station, walk 3 blocks north to 18th St. and Spring St. ☎873-1661; www.atlantajewishmuseum.com. Wheelchair-accessible. Open M-Th 10am-5pm, F 10am-3pm, Su 1-5pm. $5, students and seniors $3, under 7 free.)*

CENTER FOR PUPPETRY ARTS. Across the street from the Jewish Heritage Museum, this is one attraction destined to entertain all ages. Go "behind the scenes" and learn about the history of world puppetry, complete with an original Izzy (Atlanta's Olympic mascot) and authentic Punch and Judy figures. The highlight of the tour is the Jim Henson exhibit, which showcases some of the puppetmaster's famous creations. *(1404 Spring St. NW., at 18th St. ☎873-3391; www.puppet.org. Wheelchair-accessible. Open Tu-Sa 9am-5pm, Su 11am-5pm. $8, students and seniors $7. Puppet workshop ages 5 and over $5.)*

FERNBANK MUSEUM OF NATURAL HISTORY. Sporting outstanding dinosaur and sea-life exhibits, an IMAX theater, and numerous interactive discovery centers, the Fernbank is one of the best science museums in the Southeast. *(767 Clifton Rd. NE. Off Ponce de Leon Ave.; take bus #2 from North Ave. or Avondale Station. ☎929-6300; www.fernbank.edu/museum. Wheelchair-accessible. Open M-Sa 10am-5pm, Su noon-5pm. Museum $12, students and seniors $11, ages 3-12 $10; IMAX film $10/9/8; both attractions $17/15/13.)* The adjacent **R.L. Staton Rose Garden** blossoms from spring until December. *(Corner of Ponce de Leon Ave. and Clifton Rd.)*

BUCKHEAD

A drive through **Buckhead,** north of Midtown and Piedmont Park, off Peachtree St. near W. Paces Ferry Rd., uncovers Atlanta's Beverly Hills—the sprawling mansions of Coca-Cola bigwigs and other specimens of high culture. Conducive to wining and dining, the area is strung with dance clubs and restaurants frequented by Atlanta's twenty-somethings.

BUCKHEAD ATTRACTIONS. One of the most exquisite residences in the Southeast, the Greek Revival **Governor's Mansion** has elaborate gardens and one of the finest collections of furniture from the Federal Period. *(391 W. Paces Ferry Rd. ☎261-1776. Tours Tu-Th 10-11:30am. Free.)* In the same neighborhood, the **Atlanta History Center** traces Atlanta's development from a rural area to an international cityscape. Its Civil War Gallery spotlights the stories of both Confederate and Union soldiers, while the Folklife Gallery expounds on Southern culture from grits to banjos. Also on the grounds are exquisite mansions from the early 20th century, including the **Swan House,** a lavish Anglo-Palladian Revival home built in 1928 (undergoing restoration until 2005), and the **Tullie Smith Farm,** an 1845 Yeoman farmhouse. 33 acres of trails and gardens abutting the homes are perfect for an afternoon stroll. *(130 W. Paces Ferry Rd. NW. ☎814-4000; www.atlantahistorycenter.com. Wheelchair-accessible. Open M-Sa 10am-5:30pm, Su noon-5:30pm. $10, students and seniors $8, ages 6-17 $5; tours of the houses free with museum admission.)*

ENTERTAINMENT

For hassle-free fun, buy a MARTA pass (see **Practical Information,** p. 423) and pick up the city's free publications on music and events. *Creative Loafing*, *Music Atlanta*, the *Hudspeth Report*, or "Leisure" in the Friday edition of the *Atlanta Journal and Constitution* contain the latest info and are available in most coffee shops and on street corners. Check for free summer concerts in Atlanta's parks.

The **Woodruff Arts Center** (see **Midtown,** p. 431) houses the Atlanta Symphony, the Alliance Theater Company, the Atlanta College of Art, and the High Museum of Art. **Atlantix,** 65 Upper Alabama St., MARTA: Five Points, sets you up with half-price rush tickets to dance, theater, music, and other attractions throughout the city. (☎678-318-1400. Walk-up service only. Tu 11am-3pm, W-Sa 11am-6pm, Su noon-3pm.) The **Philips Arena,** 100 Techwood Dr. (☎878-3000 or 800-326-4000), hosts concerts, the **Atlanta Hawks** basketball team, and the **Atlanta Thrashers** hockey team. The pride and joy of Atlanta, the National League's **Atlanta Braves,** play at **Turner Field,** 755 Hank Aaron Dr., MARTA: West End or bus #105, where a Coke bottle over left field erupts with fireworks after home runs. (☎522-7630; Ticketmaster 800-326-4000. $5-15, $1 skyline seats available game day.) 1hr. tours of Turner Field include views of the diamond from the $200,000 skyboxes. (☎614-2311. Open non-game days M-Sa 9:30am-3pm, Su 1-3pm; evening-game days M-Sa 9:30am-noon; no tours afternoon-game days; low-season M-Sa 10am-2pm. $8, under 13 $4.) See the **Atlanta Falcons** play football at the **Georgia Dome,** MARTA: Omni/Dome/World Congress Center, the world's largest cable-supported dome. Tours are available by appointment. (☎223-8687. Open daily 10am-4pm. $2; students, seniors, and ages 3-12 $1.)

Six Flags Over Georgia, 275 Riverside Pkwy., at I-20 W, is one of the largest amusement parks in the nation. Take bus #201 "Six Flags" from Hamilton Homes. Check out the 54 mph "Georgia Scorcher" roller coaster and the "Superman" roller coaster, with a pretzel-shaped inverted loop. (☎770-948-9290. Open mid-May to Aug. M-F 10am-9pm, Sa 10am-10pm; low-season hours vary. $40, seniors and under 4 ft. $25. Parking $10-12.)

NIGHTLIFE

Atlanta's rich nightlife lacks a true focal point. Fortunately, it also lacks limits; young people can be found partying until the wee hours and beyond. Scores of bars and clubs along Peachtree Rd. and Buckhead Ave. in **Buckhead** cater to a younger crowd. Pricier **Midtown** greets the glitzy and the glamorous. Alternative **L5P** plays hosts to bikers and goths, while **Virginia Highland** and up-and-coming **East Atlanta** feature an eclectic mix of all of types imaginable.

BARS & PUBS

The Vortex, 438 Moreland Ave. (☎688-1828), in L5P. An incredible restaurant that doubles as an even cooler bar, Vortex is the no-nonsense spot for serious eaters and drinkers. With burgers named "Coronary Bypass" ($8) and "Italian Stallion" ($7), you'll need a drink like the "Bitch on Wheels" ($8) to make it through the night. Open M-Sa 11am-2am, Su 11am-midnight.

Blind Willie's, 828 N. Highland Ave. NE (☎873-2583). Blind Willie's is the quintessential blues club: the brick-lined interior is dark and cramped, and the bar serves mostly beer ($3-4) to its ardently loyal patrons. Despite its hole-in-the wall status, Blind Willie's continues to be an Atlanta legend. Live blues, zydeco, and folk music starts around 10pm. Cover $5-10. Open Su-Th 8pm-2am, F 8pm-3am, Sa 8pm-2:30am.

Masquerade, 695 North Ave. NE (☎577-8178, concert info 577-2007), occupies an original turn-of-the-century mill. The bar has 3 levels: "heaven," with live music from touring bands; "purgatory," a more laidback pub and pool house; and "hell," a dance club with everything from techno to 1940s big band jazz. An outside space provides dancing under the stars, while the 4000-seat amphitheater caters to metal and punk tastes. 18+. Cover $3-8 and up. Open W-Su 8pm-4am.

Eastside Lounge, 485 Flat Shoals Ave. SE (☎522-7841). If the streets of East Atlanta seem empty, it's because everyone is packed into this suave hideout. Couches near the bar and tables in the small upstairs offer rest for the weary, but be prepared to stand with the rest of the trendsetters. DJ spins F-Sa. Open M-Sa 7pm-3am.

Flatiron, 520 Flat Shoals Ave. (☎688-8864). Set on the corner of Glenwood and Flat Shoals, this L5P hot spot is a favorite with locals who are tired of the bohemian scene. Beer $3-4. Open Su-Th 11am-2am, F-Sa 11am-3pm.

Steamhouse, 3041 Bolling Way (☎233-7980). For those who like raw oysters ($8 for a dozen on the half shell) with their beer ($4), Steamhouse has plenty of both. A great place for a lazy hot summer evening–the party often spills out onto the patio. Open daily 11:30am-2am.

Aprés Diem, 931 Monroe Dr. (☎872-3333). By day, this delectable bistro serves up chicken focaccia ($8) and iced cappuccinos ($3) on its sunny patio. By night, crowds flock to its hip international and gay-friendly bar. Enjoy house choices Cosmopolitans and Sour Apple Martinis ($7) at this local favorite. Open Su 11am-midnight, M-Th 11:30am-midnight, F 11:30am-2am, Sa 11am-2am.

DANCE CLUBS

Tongue & Groove, 3055 Peachtree Rd. NE (☎261-2325). The club that has been taking Atlanta by storm, Tongue and Groove has been the recipient of praise from both the media and locals alike. Whether you decide to kick back at one of the 2 gorgeous bars or shake it on the dance floor, you're guaranteed to have fun. W Latin night. Th house. F hip-hop. Sa Euro night. Cover for men W and F $5, Sa $10; for women W $5, Sa $10 after midnight. Open T and Th-F 10pm-4am, W 9pm-4am, Sa 10pm-3am.

Chaos, 3067 Peachtree Rd. NE (☎995-0064). One of the largest and newest clubs in Buckhead, Chaos manages to avoid the cheesy commercialism of some of its neighbors. M hip-hop; other nights Top 40 and techno. Cover $10 for men. Dress to impress; jeans and baseball caps won't cut it here. 21+. Open M-F 9pm-4am, Sa 9pm-3am.

The Riviera, 1055 Peachtree St. NE (☎607-8050). For some good, old-fashioned Midtown fun, head over to the glitzy "Riv" for a night of flamboyant dancing, drinking, and pool. Call ahead for a schedule of live local bands. Cover $15. Open daily 8pm-6am.

GAY & LESBIAN NIGHTLIFE

Most of Atlanta's gay culture centers around **Midtown** and several blocks north in **Ansley Square,** near Piedmont and Monroe. In Atlanta, straight and gay often party together, and some of the city's best all-around joints are rainbow-colored. For information on gay happenings and special events in Hotlanta, check out the free *Southern Voice* newspaper, available everywhere.

Backstreet, 845 Peachtree St. NE (☎873-1986) in Midtown, is Atlanta's most popular gay club and *the* hangout for the city's late-night partiers. One of the oldest clubs in the area, the behemoth Backstreet still rocks out with a vast dance floor, several balconies, and three full bars. Required quarterly "membership" $10. Cover F-Sa $5. Open 24hr.

Blake's, 227 10th St. (☎892-5786). Midtown males flock to this friendly bar, where see-and-be-seen is a way of life. The well-known bar is also a popular destination for the young lesbian crowd. Open daily 3pm-2am.

Burkhart's, 1492 Piedmont Ave. NE (☎872-4403), in Ansley Sq. This multi-bar hot spot has become a favorite of gay Atlanta. Two stories of drinking and dancing promote a relaxed approach to fun. 21+. Open M-F 4pm-3am, Sa-Su 2pm-4am.

OUTDOOR ACTIVITIES

In the heart of Midtown, **Piedmont Park** is a hotbed of fun, free activities. Look for the **Dogwood Festival** (www.dogwood.org), an art festival, in the spring and the **Jazz Festival** (www.atlantafestivals.com) in May. In June, the park celebrates with the **Gay Pride Festival** (www.atlantapride.org), and on July 4th, Atlanta draws 55,000 people to the world's largest 10K race, the famed Peachtree Road Race. Every summer Turner Broadcasting and HBO present **"Screen on the Green,"** a series of free films projected once a week in the meadow behind the Visitors Center. The **Atlanta Botanical Garden** occupies the northern end of the park and provides a tranquil refuge from the hustle-and-bustle of everyday Atlanta life. Stroll through 15 acres of landscaped gardens, a hardwood forest with trails, and an interactive children's garden focusing on health and wellness. The Garden is also home to the Storza Woods and the **Dorothy Chapman Fuqua Conservatory,** which houses some of the world's rarest and endangered plant species. (345 Piedmont Ave. NE. Take bus #36, MARTA: Arts Center Station; on Su, bus #31 Lindburgh from Five Points. ☎876-5859; www.atlantabotanicalgarden.org. Open Apr.-Sept. Tu-Su 9am-7pm; Oct.-Mar. Tu-Su 9am-6pm. $10, seniors $7, students $5; Th free after 3pm.)

Sixteen miles east of the city on US 78 Georgia's number one natural attraction, **Stone Mountain Park,** provides a respite from the city with beautiful scenery and the remarkable **Confederate Memorial.** Carved into the world's largest mass of granite, the 825 ft. "Mt. Rushmore of the South" profiles Jefferson Davis, Robert E. Lee, and Stonewall Jackson. The hike up the **Confederate Hall Trail** (1½ mi.) provides a spectacular view of Atlanta. The mountain is surrounded by a 3200-acre historic park. On summer nights, be sure to check out the dazzling laser show that illuminates the side of the mountain. (Take bus #120 "Stone Mountain" from MARTA: Avondale. ☎770-498-5600 or 800-317-2006; www.stonemountainpark.com. Park gates open daily 6am-midnight. Attractions open summer daily 10am-8pm; low-season 10am-5pm. $19, ages 3-11 $15. Laser show daily 9:30pm; free.)

ATHENS ☎706

In the grand Southern tradition of naming college towns after great classical cultural centers, Athens is perhaps the most successful at living up to its namesake. Of course, the only Greeks around here live in the University of Georgia's (UGA) frat houses, and the city is better known for its production of rock stars than philosophers or mathematicians—the university and surrounding bars have been the spawning ground for hundreds of popular bands, including R.E.M. and the B-52s. Residents of all ages and walks of life make Athens feel more like a miniature city than a college town.

PRACTICAL INFORMATION. Situated 70 mi. northeast of Atlanta, Athens can be reached from I-85 via U.S. 316, which runs into U.S. 29. Although there is a commuter airport (☎549-5783), it's easier to fly into Atlanta and take a **commuter shuttle** (☎800-354-7874) to various points in and around Athens ($30). **Southeastern Stages,** 220 W. Broad St. buses to Atlanta and Augusta. (☎549-2255. Call for schedules. Open M-F 7:15am-7:15pm, Sa-Su 7:40am-1pm.) The **Athens Transit System** runs "The Bus" every 30min. on loops around downtown, UGA, and surrounding residential areas. (☎613-3430. Buses M-F 6:15am-7:15pm, Sa 7:30am-7pm. $1, seniors 50¢, ages 6-18 75¢; transfers free.) UGA's **Campus Transit System** runs everywhere on campus and to some stops downtown. (☎369-6220. Open daily 7am-12:45am. Free.) **Taxi: Alfa Taxi,** ☎583-8882. Two blocks north of the UGA campus is the **Athens Welcome Center,** 280 E. Dougherty St., in the Church-Waddel-Brumby House. (☎353-1820. Open M-Sa 10am-6pm, Su noon-6pm.) The **UGA Visitors Center,** at the intersection of College Station and River Rd. on campus, provides info on UGA attractions. (☎542-0842. Open M-F 8am-5pm, Sa 9am-5pm, Su 1-5pm.) **Medical Services: Athens Regional Medical Center,** 1199 Prince Ave. (☎549-9977.) **Hotlines: Crisis Line,** ☎353-1912. **Community Connection,** ☎353-1313. **Post Office:** 575 Olympic Dr. (☎800-275-8777. Open M-F 8:30am-4:30pm.) **Postal Code:** 30601. **Area Code:** 706.

ACCOMMODATIONS. Accommodations are usually reasonably priced, but rates rise for football weekends. For an upscale gem, check out **The Foundry Park Inn ❺,** 295 E. Dougherty Street at Thomas, on one of Athens' oldest historic sites. Thoughtfully decorated rooms and suites are available year-round. (☎549-7020; www.foundryparkinn.com. Rooms from $90.) The **Perimeter Inn ❷,** 3791 Atlanta Hwy., 5 mi. from downtown, is a reasonably priced, comfortable, independently-owned motel with a Spanish flair. (☎548-3000 or 800-934-2963. Singles $38; doubles $44.) Within walking distance of the campus and downtown, the posh **Magnolia Terrace Guest House ❹,** 277 Hill St., between Milledge Ave. and Prince St., is a simple B&B with seven luxurious rooms and a full breakfast in the morning. (☎548-3860. Rooms M-F $95, Sa-Su up to $150.) **Watson Mill Bridge State Park ❶,** 650 Watson Mill Rd., 21 mi. east of Athens, is the best place in the area to camp, with horse and hiking trails, canoe and boat rentals, and plenty of fishing. (☎783-5349 or 800-864-7275. Park open daily 7am-10pm; office 8am-5pm. Sites $15, with water and electricity $17; secluded primitive sites $20.)

FOOD. The **Last Resort Grill ❸,** 174 and 184 W. Clayton St., at the corner of Hull St., is an eclectic lunch-and-dinner restaurant with a gourmet atmosphere and reasonable prices. Order a fried green tomato sandwich ($4.75) and receive a delicious, artful presentation on a gigantic white plate, or indulge in desserts that are widely considered the best in Athens. (☎549-0810. Lunches $5-10. Dinners $10-20. Open Su-Th 11am-3pm and 5-10pm, F-Sa 5-11pm; bar until 2am.) R.E.M. fans that wonder what "automatic for the people" means should ask Dexter Weaver, the owner of **Weaver D's Fine Foods ❶,** 1016 E. Broad St., to whom the phrase originally belongs. Weaver D's is a tiny restaurant that serves pork chop sandwiches ($4.25)

THE LOCAL LEGEND

THE TREE THAT OWNS ITSELF

Most trees can only dream of the gift given to the white oak that sits at the corner of Dearing and Finley Street in Athens, Georgia: the gift of self-ownership. That's right, this famed Tree That Owns Itself has the deed to both itself and the land within 8 ft. of its trunk. It is doubly lucky in that, unlike most property holders, it pays no taxes and is beloved by local citizens.

Legend holds that Colonel William H. Jackson, a professor at the University of Georgia, owned the land on which the tree stood and enjoyed its shade and "magnificent proportions" so much that he willed it the land around it. Although the deed has never been tested in the courts, it's true legitimacy seems irrelevant. Local residents not only acknowledge the tree's ownership of itself, but actually take it as an obligation to see that the oak is protected. In fact, in 1942 when the original oak (estimated to have been around 400 years old) fell in a terrible storm, the Junior Ladies' Garden Club collected acorns from the site in order to grow a sucessor. They were successful, and in 1946 the sapling that is now today's Tree That Owns Itself was planted.

and soul-food lunches ($5-6) out of a small roadside house. R.E.M. was one of Weaver's biggest fans and repaid him for the use of his phrase as their 1992 album title by inviting him to the Grammy Awards. (☎353-7797. Open M-Sa11am-6pm.) **The Grill ❷,** 171 College St., is Athens' version of the all-night burger-and-malt joint that is vital to the life of every college town. In addition to the standard mega-burger platter ($7) and luscious malts ($3.25), the Grill also has a mean vegetarian side. (☎543-4770. Open 24hr.)

SIGHTS. The University of Georgia, chartered in 1785 as the first land-grant college in the US, is the very reason Athens exists and tops its list of tourist attractions. The campus Visitors Center, at the corner of College Station and River Rd. in south campus, has self-guided tours, maps, and helpful answers. (☎542-0842. Open M-F 8am-5pm, Sa 9am-5pm, Su 1-5pm.) The campus begins downtown on Broad St., where The Arch guards the official entrance to the institution. Sanford Stadium is the home turf of UGA's "Dawgs," the white English bulldogs that serve as the school's mascot. Butts-Mehre Heritage Hall, on the corner of Pinecrest Dr. and Rutherford St., houses the school's athletic offices and the Heritage Museum, which celebrates generations of UGA athletes—and white English bulldogs. (☎542-9036. Open M-F 8am-5pm, Sa-Su 2-5pm.) Also on campus, the Georgia Museum of Art, 90 Carlton St., in the Performing and Visual Arts Complex off East Campus Dr., is an impressive state-funded collection of over 7000 works of art. (☎542-4662. Open Tu and Th-Sa 10am-5pm, W 10am-9pm, Su 1-5pm. Free, $1 suggested donation.)

Beyond the university, Athens boasts a wealth of historic sites, homes, and artifacts chronicling the town's genteel and wealthy history. The many lush gardens and arboretums encourage long walks and picnics. Maps and tours of the city's historic areas and green spaces are available at the Athens Welcome Center (see **Practical Information,** p. 435), the oldest residence in town. The **US Navy Supply Corps School and Museum,** 1425 Prince Ave., was originally a teacher's college, then a Carnegie library, and is now one of only 11 official U.S. Navy Museums. Exhibits of ship models, uniforms, and all manner of Navy flotsam are on display. (☎354-7349. Visitors must call ahead. Open M-F 9am-5:15pm. Free.) The city's most elaborate garden, the **State Botanical Garden of Georgia,** 2450 S. Milledge Ave., houses 313 acres of trails, a tropical conservatory, and a Day Chapel. (☎542-1244. Open daily 8am-sunset, Visitors Center open Tu-Sa 9am-4:30pm, Su 11:30am-4:30pm. Free.)

If you hesitate to bequeath your property to undeserving offspring, consider making your favorite plant an heir. Professor William H. Jackson set the legal precedent when he willed to a beloved oak tree all the land within 8 ft. of its trunk. Today, **The Tree That Owns Itself** (see p. 24) flourishes at the intersection of Finley and Dearing St., near Broad St. downtown. By far Athens' best Civil War relic, **The Double-Barreled Cannon** was a great idea that failed spectacularly. On the grounds of City Hall, at Washington and College St., the two barrels face northward threateningly.

ENTERTAINMENT & NIGHTLIFE. Athens has cradled hundreds of fledgling bands in all styles of music over the years. R.E.M. is arguably Athens' most well-known homegrown band, but those plugged into the music world will know that most musicians show up in Athens at one point or another to play in a true-blue music mecca. In late June, **Athfest** takes over the town. (☎548-2516. 1 day $10, both days $15.) Take a look at Athens' free weekly newspaper, *Flagpole Magazine*, available everywhere downtown, to find out which bands are playing where. If you're broke, tune in to **WUOG 90.5,** one of the nation's last bastions of real college radio. The students who run the station play tons of local music, and liven it with unscripted, unplanned, and often incoherent commentary. R.E.M. got their start at **The 40 Watt Club,** 285 W.Washington St., a real Athens institution. Born in 1979 as a raucous Halloween party lit by a single 40 watt bulb, the club has had numerous incarnations and locations, but currently kicks with live music most nights. (☎549-7871. Cover $5-15. Open daily 10pm-3am.) If you want to do something other than listen to music, Athens lives up to its name theatrically as well as academically. **The Classic Center,** 300 N. Thomas St., hosts Broadway productions, all sorts of entertainers and concerts, and the Athens Symphony. (☎357-4444. Call for schedules and ticket prices.) **The Morton Theater,** 195 W. Washington St., was built in 1910 as a Vaudeville Theater and was entirely African-American owned and operated. Today it is a fully restored, high-tech performing arts center home to all sorts of theater and music. (☎613-3770. Call for schedules and ticket prices.) **Jittery Joe's,** 1210 S. Millege Rd., offers a classy coffeeshop atmosphere. (☎208-1979. Open M-Th 6:30am-midnight, F 6:30am-1am, Sa 8:30am-1am, Su 8:30am-midnight.)

MACON ☎478

Before Macon was officially established in 1823, the area along the banks of the Ocmulgee River was the heart of the Creek Native American territory before President Andrew Jackson forced them to move to Oklahoma to make way for white settlers in the "Trail of Tears." White men turned the sacred ground into a port city that became one of Georgia's cultural centers. In the 20th century, Macon developed into a magnet for many of Georgia's top musicians, most of whom performed at the Douglass Theater, one of the greatest venues for black performers in the country. Today, Macon is a mix of small-town south and big-city ambition.

ORIENTATION & PRACTICAL INFORMATION. Macon sits at the intersection of I-75 and I-16, about 75 mi. southwest of Atlanta. **I-475** makes a large arc west of downtown, branching off of I-75. Downtown is a grid with numbered streets running east-west and named streets running north-south. The town is actually set at a 45° angle, so north means northwest, and south means southeast. **Riverside Drive** is a main artery parallel to I-75 and the river. **Martin Luther King Boulevard (MLK)** runs east-west through the heart of downtown. Shops, bars, and restaurants cluster on **Cherry Street,** the main north-south thoroughfare. West of downtown, MLK Blvd. becomes Houston (HOUSE-ston) Ave., which feeds onto Eisenhower Pkwy. North of town along Riverside Dr. lie more shopping centers and pricier hotels.

Greyhound, 65 Spring St. (☎743-2868; open daily 4:30am-midnight), runs to Athens (8hr., 2 per day, $68); Atlanta (1½hr., 12 per day, $15.25); Birmingham (5-6hr., 7 per day, $50). **Macon-Bibb County Transit Authority (MTA-MAC),** 1000 Terminal Dr., operates 20 buses throughout the downtown area and the **MITSI** trolley. (☎746-1387. Operates M-Sa 5:30am-11pm. $0.75, students $0.50, seniors $0.35; transfers $0.25. Trolley $0.25.) Services include: **Hotlines: Crisis Line,** ☎745-9292. **Medical Services: Medical Center of Central Georgia,** 777 Hemlock St. (☎633-1000), downtown. **Internet access: Washington Memorial Library,** 1180 Washington St., at the corner of College St. (☎744-0800. Open M-Th 9am-9pm, F-Sa 9am-6pm, Su 1:30-5pm.) **Visitors Info: Macon-Bibb Country Convention and Visitors Bureau,** 200 Cherry St., at the southern tip of downtown. (☎743-3401 or 800-768-3401; www.maconga.org. Open M-Sa 9am-5pm. Free parking.) **Post Office:** 451 College St. (☎752-8432. Open M-F 8am-6pm, Sa 9am-2pm.) **Postal Code:** 31213. **Area Code:** 478.

ACCOMMODATIONS. Macon has many hotels, but forces you to make a tough choice: surrender to the chain motels, pay outrageous prices, or gamble with questionable safety. The chains are plentiful along Riverside Dr. (just off of I-75 north of town) and on Eisenhower Pkwy. (west of town near I-475). The low rates and quality amenities at Masters Inn ❷, Exit 160 off I-75 at Pio Nono Ave., make it a good bet in a convenient location. (☎788-8910 or 800-633-3434. Free local calls, continental breakfast, and pool. Singles $35-37; doubles $39-43.) To be close to downtown attractions without completely breaking the bank, check out one of the only downtown hotel facilities, The Crowne Plaza ❹, 108 First St. Though it is a chain and still has a somewhat cookie-cutter feel, rooms here come with all of the amenities and are very clean. The proximity to downtown is the real value. (☎478-746-1461 or 800-227-6963. Rooms from $69.)

FOOD. **Jeneane's Cafe ❶,** 524 Mulberry St., serves lightning-fast lunch to the noontime crowd in the most personal, efficient, sweetie-eat-your-vegetables way imaginable. Desserts are concocted daily by a retired pastry chef, and though the teal plastic cafeteria seats might remind you of a high school cafeteria, the food won't. (☎743-5267. Meat-and-vegetable lunch plate $5. Open M-F 6:30am-2:30pm.) **Len Berg's Restaurant ❶,** 240 Post Office Alley, walk south down Walnut St., is a 1908 sit-down lunch counter where all food costs less than $7. (☎742-9255. Open M-F 11am-2:30pm.) Since 1916, **Nu-Way Weiners ❶,** 430 Cotton Ave., has been serving up some of the tastiest dogs ($1.34) in the South. (☎743-1368. Open M-F 6am-7pm, Sa 7am-6pm.)

SIGHTS. Macon is a tour-planner's dream—the entire downtown is compact and walkable, and the major museums are all within one block of each other. The **Georgia Music Hall of Fame,** 200 MLK Blvd, at the end of Mulberry St., will overwhelm you with its mind-boggling collection of inductees, including Ray Charles, The Allman Brothers, Gladys Knight, James Brown, and the Indigo Girls. From some of Little Richard's wacky suits to Lynyrd Skynyrd's keyboard and cassette case, the Hall of Fame has priceless treasures and memorabilia. (☎750-0350. Open M-Sa 9am-5pm, Su 1-5pm. $8; students with ID, seniors, and AAA $6; ages 4-16 $3.50.) The **Georgia Sports Hall of Fame,** 301 Cherry St., is another lavishly designed showcase of Georgia talent. It includes relics from the life of Hank Aaron and a basketball court that visitors can play on in between ooh-ing at exhibits. (☎752-1585. Open M-Sa 9am-5pm, Su 1-5pm. $6; students, seniors, and military $5; ages 6-16 $3.50.)

The **Tubman African American Museum,** 340 Walnut Ave., is the South's largest museum that is exclusively devoted to African-American art, history, and culture. Beginning in ancient Africa, the museum traces the ancestry and legacy of African-Americans by showcasing art, music, and great historical figures from every era of history. (☎743-8544. Open M-Sa 9am-5pm, Su 2-5pm. $3, under 12 $2.) An impressive National Park, the **Ocmulgee National Monument,** 1207 Emery Hwy., across the river from downtown, protects some of the gigantic mounds, prehistoric trenches, and village sites of the five distinct Indian groups that inhabited it for over 12,000 years. (☎752-8257. Park and Visitors Center open daily 9am-5pm. Free.)

Macon has many historical houses, including **Cannonball House,** 856 Mulberry St., the city's only casualty of the Civil War. (☎745-5982. Open M-Sa 10am-5pm. $3, children $2.) **Hay House,** 934 Georgia Ave., near downtown, is the most opulent of all the city's magnificent dwellings. The gigantic Italian Renaissance Revival mansion was built in 1860 and boasts wide marble hallways, crystal chandeliers, and plenty of pomp to awe visitors. (☎742-8155. Open M-Sa 10am-4:30pm, Su 1-4:30pm. $8, students $4, seniors and AAA $7.)

ENTERTAINMENT & NIGHTLIFE. The biggest event of Macon's year is the annual **Cherry Blossom Festival,** March 19-28, 2004. The city hosts thousands of visitors, who come to admire the 265,000 Yoshino Cherry trees blooming in every backyard and on every street. With its median of cherry trees, 3rd St. is the center of the celebration. Over 500 mostly free events—like concerts, tours, and parades—keep the masses tickled pink. After the blossoms fade, there are still plenty of amusements. The **Macon Little Theater,** 4220 Forsyth Rd., puts on musicals and plays year-round. (☎471-7529. Box office open M-Sa 10am-5pm. Most shows $16, seniors $14, under 23 $11.)

Macon has more bars and nightclubs than you'd expect from a small southern town—but hey, this *is* where Little Richard grew up. Entertainment clusters along Cherry St. downtown. The free *Synergy Magazine,* available outside stores and in newsstands downtown, has entertainment listings. Gay-friendly and open to all, **Club Synergy,** 425 Cherry St., has 2 dance floors, DJs from all over, a full bar, and a willingness to occasionally flood itself for the odd beach party theme. (☎755-9383. Cover $5-7. Open W-Sa 8pm until late.) **River Front Bluez,** 550 Riverside Dr., in a shack by the side of the road, is a great place to hear gritty, down-and-out blues. (☎741-9970. Live bands W-Sa around 9pm.) If upscale plush clubbing is your thing, go to **Déa,** 420 Martin Luther King Blvd. This swank outfit's dress code is a small price to pay for feeling like a movie star as you strut into the dark interior. (☎755-1620. Cover varies, but can be quite high. Open W-Sa 8pm-3am.)

ANDERSONVILLE ☎229

Fifty-five miles south of Macon and 10 mi. northeast of Americus on Rte. 49, the **Andersonville National Historic Site** preserves the location where 45,000 Union soldiers were confined in a primitive prison pen without food, water, or shelter in 1864 near the end of the Civil War. Nearly 13,000 men died horrible deaths within the camp's wooden walls due to the barbaric conditions and severe overcrowding—at one point more than 32,000 men were confined in a space intended to hold 10,000. On the grounds, the excellent **National Prisoner of War Museum,** 496 Cemetery Rd., memorializes the experience of American POWs with artifacts, interactive video testimonials, recordings, photographs, and journals. The museum is extraordinarily sobering as you pass actual rations that kept men alive for days, view myriad portrayals of horrible suffering and amazing strength, and finally exit into a small memorial in the sunlight. Also on the grounds, the **Andersonville National Cemetery** is a fitting place to end the visit. (☎924-0343, ext. 201. Park open daily 8am-5pm; museum 8:30am-5pm. Special talks daily 11am and 2pm. Museum audio tours $1.) Directly across Rte. 49 from the park exit is the tiny town of Andersonville. The **Welcome Center,** 114 Main St., doubles as a dusty little museum stuffed with bric-a-brac. To the left of the monument in the middle of town and up the street a quarter mile on the left, the **Andersonville Restaurant** ❶ (the only one in town) serves an unpretentious buffet lunch for $6.25 and chatty conversation for free. (☎928-8480. Open M-Sa 11am-2pm and 5pm-9pm, Su 11am-2pm.)

SAVANNAH ☎912

In February 1733, General James Oglethorpe and a ragtag band of 120 vagabonds founded the city of Savannah and the state of Georgia. General Sherman later spared the city during his rampage through the South. Some say he found Savannah too pretty to burn—presenting it instead to President Lincoln as a Christmas gift. Today, that reaction is believable to anyone who sees Savannah's stately old trees and Federalist and English Regency houses interwoven with spring blossoms.

ORIENTATION & PRACTICAL INFORMATION. Savannah rests on the coast of Georgia at the mouth of the **Savannah River,** which runs north of the city along the border with South Carolina. The city stretches south from bluffs overlooking the river. The restored 2½ sq. mi. **downtown historic district,** bordered by East Broad St., Martin Luther King Jr. Blvd., Gwinnett St., and the river, is best explored on foot. *Do not stray south of Gwinnett St.; the historic district quickly deteriorates into an unsafe area.* A parking pass ($8) allows 2-day unlimited use of all metered parking, city lots, and garages. **Savannah/Hilton Head International Airport,** 400 Airways Ave. (☎964-0514; www.savannahairport.com), at Exit 104 off I-95, serves coastal Georgia and the Low Country of South Carolina. **Amtrak,** 2611 Seaboard Coastline Dr. (☎234-2611; open Sa-Th 4:30am-12:15pm and 5pm-12:45am, F 4:30am-12:45am), chugs to Charleston (1½hr., 1 per day, $38). **Greyhound,** 610 W. Oglethorpe Ave. (☎232-2135; open 24hr.), at Fahm St., sends buses to: Atlanta (6hr., 5 per day, $36-38); Charleston (3hr., 2 per day, $24-26); Jacksonville (2½hr., 13 per day, $19-20). **Chatham Area Transit (CAT),** 124 Bull St. (☎233-5767), in the Chatham County Court House, runs buses and a free shuttle through the historic area. (Open daily 7am-11pm. Shuttle M-Sa 7am-9pm, Su 9:40am-5pm. $0.75, seniors $0.37; no transfers. Weekly pass available at Parking Services Office 100 E. Bryan St., $12.) **Hotlines: Rape Hotline,** ☎233-7273, 24hr. **Taxi: Yellow Cab,** ☎236-1133. The **Savannah Visitors Center,** 301 Martin Luther King Jr. Blvd., at Liberty St. in a lavish former train station, offers a reservation service for local inns and hostels. (☎944-0455; reservation service ☎877-728-2662; www.savannahgeorgia.com. Open M-F 8:30am-5pm, Sa-Su 9am-5pm.) **Medical Services: Georgia Regional Hospital,** 1915 Eisenhower Dr. (☎356-2045.) **Internet Access: Public Library,** 2002 Bull St. (☎652-3600. Open M-Th 9am-9pm, F-Sa 9am-6pm, Su 2-6pm.) **Post Office:** 2 N. Fahm St., at Bay St. (☎235-4610. Open M-F 7am-6pm, Sa 9am-3pm.) **Postal Code:** 31402. **Area Code:** 912.

ACCOMMODATIONS. Downtown motels cluster near the historic area, Visitors Center, and Greyhound station. For those with cars, **Ogeechee Road (U.S. 17)** has several budget options. **The Eliza Thompson House ❺,** 5 W. Jones St., is the premier bed and breakfast in Savannah, located in the heart of downtown minutes from the city's beautiful, bustling squares. Built in 1847, this historic inn welcomes guests with complimentary wine, coffee, and dessert hours. (☎236-3620 or 800-348-9378. Reservations recommended. 25 rooms from $140.) **Thunderbird Inn ❷,** 611 W. Oglethorpe Ave., has the least expensive rooms downtown. The modest exterior belies the clean rooms and pleasant furnishings within. (☎232-2661. TV, A/C, large bathrooms. Singles Su-Th $40, F-Sa $50. 5% off with mention of *Let's Go.*) **Savannah International Youth Hostel (HI-AYH) ❶,** 304 E. Hall St., is unfortunately the best option for budget travelers wishing to stay in the historic district. This small bare-bones inn, near an unsafe part of town, offers little more than a bed and a roof but is located only minutes from some of Savannah's greatest sights. (☎236-7744. Linen $1. Bike rental $10. Check-in 7-10am and 5-11pm; call for late-night check-in. Lockout 10am-5pm. 3-night max. stay. Open Mar.-Oct. Dorms $18; private rooms $35-$45.) **Skidaway Island State Park ❶** is 6 mi. southeast of downtown off Diamond Causeway; follow Liberty St. east from downtown until it becomes Wheaton St., turn right on Waters Ave., and follow it to Diamond Causeway. (☎598-2300 or 800-864-7275. Bathrooms, heated showers, electricity, and water. Open daily 7am-10pm. Check-in before 10pm. Sites $18; with hookup $20.)

FOOD. **Nita's Place ❸,** 129 E. Broughton St., gives reason enough to come to Savannah. You can read enthusiastic letters from satisfied customers pressed beneath the glass tabletops while you experience the uplifting power of fantastic soul food. The dessert-like squash casserole, a delight beyond description, will make you a believer. (☎238-8233. Entrees $10-13. Open M-Th 11:30am-3pm, F-Sa 11:30am-3pm and 5-8pm.) **Wall's BBQ ❶,** 515 E. York Ln., in an alley between York St. and Oglethorpe Ave., serves up mouth-watering barbecue in a hidden hole-in-the-wall location. Don't plan on devouring your delicious barbecue sandwich or ribs ($4.50-12) here; most locals know to order and then relish their incredible meal in one of the neighboring squares. (☎232-9754. Baked deviled crabs $3. Open Th-Sa 11am-9pm.) **Mrs. Wilkes Boarding House ❸,** 107 W. Jones St., is a Southern institution where friendly strangers gather around large tables for homestyle atmosphere and soul food. Fried chicken, butter beans, and superb biscuits are favorites. (☎232-5997. All-you-can-eat $12. Open M-F 8-9am and 11am-3pm.) **Clary's Cafe ❶,** 404 Abercorn St., has been serving up some of Savannah's best breakfasts since 1903. The famous weekend brunch features $4 malted waffles. (☎233-0402. Open M-Tu and Th-F 7am-4pm, W 7am-5pm, Sa-Su 8am-4:30pm.)

SIGHTS & ENTERTAINMENT. Most of Savannah's 21 squares contain some distinctive centerpiece. Elegant antebellum houses and drooping vine-wound trees often cluster around the squares, adding to the classic Southern aura. Bus, van, and horse carriage **tours** leave from the Visitors Center, but walking can be more rewarding. (Tours daily every 10-15min. $13-15.) Two of Savannah's best-known historic homes are the **Davenport House,** 324 E. State St., on Columbia Sq., and the **Owens-Thomas House,** 124 Abercom St., one block away on Oglethorpe Sq. Built in 1820, the Davenport House is nearly exactly as Isaiah Davenport left it in the mid-19th century, complete with the original furniture, cantilevered staircase, and exemplary woodwork. The Owens-Thomas House is similar, but the carriage house, holding artifacts and relating stories about slave life, is free. (Davenport: ☎236-8097; www.davenportsavga.com. Open M-Sa 10am-4pm, Su 1-4pm. $7, ages 7-18 $3.50. Owens-Thomas: ☎233-9743. Open M

THE LOCAL STORY

SAVANNAH'S BOOK

The news of Danny Hansford's death spread through the quiet town of Savannah like wildfire. When residents discovered that Hansford—a prominent member of the upper echelons of local society—had been murdered at the well-to-do Mercer House in Monterey Square, they could not believe their ears.

As is the case with all good hearsay, the story of the murder soon took on many forms, each told from a unique perspective. John Berendt, a New York writer, caught wind of the murder, trial, and all-around commotion and decided to write a book portraying the incredible fervor that erupted.

Berendt's *Midnight in the Garden of Good and Evil* (1994) eloquently tells the complex and fascinating story through the eccentric characters of a Southern belle, a scandalous drag queen, and the prim and proper ladies of the Married Woman's Card Club.

Since the release of "the Book" (as it is now called by locals), tourism has skyrocketed, pumping over $100 million into Savannah's economy. And while residents may become tired of seeing tourists roaming the streets and squares of Savannah clutching "the Book" in their arms, it will at least give them something to talk about.

"The Book" Gift Shop, *127 E. Gordon St. ☎233-3867. Open M-Sa 10:30am-5pm, Su 12:30-4pm.*

noon-5pm, Tu-Sa 10am-5pm, Su 1-5pm; last tour 4:30pm. $8, seniors $7, students $4, ages 6-12 $2.) The **Green Meldrim House,** 14 W. Macon St., on Madison Sq., is a Gothic Revival mansion that served as General Sherman's Savannah headquarters following his famed "march to the sea." It was from this house that Sherman wrote the famous telegram to President Lincoln, giving him the city as a gift. (☎232-1251. Open Tu and Th-F 10am-4pm, Sa 10am-1pm. Tours every 30min. $5, students $2.)

Savannah's four forts once protected the city's port from Spanish, British, and other invaders. The most intriguing, **Fort Pulaski National Monument,** 15 mi. east of Savannah on U.S. 80 E and Rte. 26, marks the Civil War battle where Union forces first used rifled cannons to decimate the Confederate opposition. (☎786-5787. Partially wheelchair-accessible. Open daily summer 9am-7pm; low-season 9am-5pm. $3, under 16 free.)

Special events in Savannah include the annual **NOGS Tour of the Hidden Gardens of Historic Savannah** (☎238-0248), in late April, when private walled gardens are opened to the public who can partake of a special Southern teatime. Green is the theme of the **St. Patrick's Day Celebration on the River,** a five-day, beer- and fun-filled party that packs the streets and warms celebrants up for the annual **St. Patrick's Day Parade,** the second-largest in the US. (Celebration: ☎234-0295. Parade: ☎233-4804. Mar. 17, 2004. Begins 10:15am.) **First Friday for the Arts** (☎232-4903) occurs on the first Friday of every month in City Market, when visitors meet with residents of a local art colony. **First Saturday on the River** (☎234-0295) brings arts, crafts, entertainment, and food to historic River St. each month. A free paper, *Connect Savannah,* found in restaurants and stores, has the latest in news and entertainment.

NIGHTLIFE. The waterfront area on **River Street** brims with endless ocean-front dining opportunities, street performers, and a friendly pub ambience. At **Kevin Barry's Irish Pub,** 117 W. River St., the Guinness flows and the entire bar jigs with live Irish folk music. (☎233-9626. Music W-Sa after 8:30pm. Cover $2. Open M-F 2pm-3am, Sa 11:30am-3am, Su 12:30pm-2am.) If sugary drinks are your pleasure, head to **Wet Willies,** 101 E. River St., for its casual dining and irresistible frozen daiquiris. (☎233-5650. Drinks $4-6. Open Su-Th 11am-1am, F-Sa 11am-2am.) Local college students eat, drink, and shop at the restaurants and stores of **City Market,** the largest Historic District in the US. (Jefferson at W. St. Julian St.) Delivering better than the rest, **Malone's Bar and Grill,** 27 W. Barnard St., serves up dancing, drinks, and live music. The lower floor opens up to a game room, while techno and rap beat upstairs Friday and Saturday nights. (☎234-3059. Happy Hour daily 4-8pm. F-Sa top level 18+. Open M-Sa 11am-3am, Su noon-2am; kitchen closes 1am.) For the best alternative scene and a gay- and lesbian-friendly atmosphere check out **Club One,** 1 Jefferson St. near Bay St, where the Lady Chablis, a character featured in *Midnight in the Garden of Good and Evil* (see p. 359), performs regularly. (☎232-0200. Cover $3-10. Open M-Sa 5pm-3am, Su 5pm-2am.)

ALABAMA

Forty years later, the "Heart of Dixie" is still haunted by its controversial role in the Civil Rights movement of the 1960s, when Governor George Wallace fought a vicious campaign opposing integration. Today, the state's efforts to de-emphasize this past and broaden its image have resulted in a series of important monuments and homages to the tumult of the Civil Rights movement. Testaments to many of Alabama's less contentious legacies also shine through. While the state's rich colonial past, Native American heritage, and legacy of immigration are on full display,

Alabama has much to offer the present and the future; its unique cuisine, nationally acclaimed gardens, and unparalleled festivals should serve as the passport for escaping the unpleasant past.

PRACTICAL INFORMATION

Capital: Montgomery.

Visitor Info: Alabama Bureau of Tourism and Travel, 401 Adams Ave., Montgomery 36104 (☎334-242-4169 or 800-252-2262; www.touralabama.org). Open M-F 8am-5pm. **Division of Parks,** 64 N. Union St., Montgomery 36104 (☎800-252-7275). Open daily 8am-5pm.

Postal Abbreviation: AL. **Sales Tax:** 4%, plus a substantial county tax.

MONTGOMERY ☎334

Today, Montgomery stands still and quiet, in sharp contrast to its turbulent past as the first capital of the Confederacy and the birthplace of America's Civil Rights movement. Montgomery's role in the movement took off in 1955, when local authorities arrested Rosa Parks, a black seamstress and activist, because she refused to give up her seat to a white man on a city bus. The success of the ensuing bus boycott, organized by local minister Dr. Martin Luther King, Jr., encouraged nationwide reform. Montgomery now relies on its prominent past to overcome a rather nondescript present—Civil Rights movement battlegrounds and memorials are the main attractions.

ORIENTATION & PRACTICAL INFORMATION. Downtown follows a grid pattern. Major east-west routes are Madison Ave. downtown and Vaughn Rd. south of **I-65;** main north-south roads are Perry St. and Decatur St., which becomes Norman Bridge Rd. farther south. Dexter Ave. is Montgomery's main street, running east-west up an imposing hill to the Capitol. West of downtown, **I-65** runs north-south and intersects **I-85,** which forms downtown's southern border. A ring road, varyingly called East, South, West, and North Boulevard, encircles both downtown and the outlying neighborhoods. **Greyhound,** 950 W. South Blvd. (☎1-800-231-2222; open 24hr.), at Exit 168 on I-65 and a right onto South Blvd., runs to: Atlanta (3hr., 9 per day, round-trip $31); Birmingham (2hr., 7 per day, round-trip $35); Mobile (3hr., 8 per day, round trip $31.50); Selma (55min., 5 per day, round-trip $28); Tuskegee (45min., 9 per day, round-trip $19). **Montgomery Area Transit System** runs local buses. (M-F 6am-6pm. "Fixed route" bus $1.) Call one day in advance to schedule a pick-up and **Demand and Response Transit (DART)** service will send a bus to your exact location if they can accommodate you. (☎262-7321. $2.) **The Lightning Route Trolley** arrives every 25min. at well-marked stops near downtown attractions. (M-Sa 9am-6pm. Adults, $0.25 per stop, seniors and disabled with MAP card, $0.10. Day pass $1, seniors $0.50.) **Taxi: Yellow Cab,** ☎262-5225; **New Deal Cab,** ☎262-4747. **Visitors Center:** 300 Water St., in Union Station. (☎262-0013; www.visitingmontgomery.com. Open M-Sa 8:00am-5pm, Su noon-4pm.) **Hotlines: Council Against Rape,** ☎286-5987. Operates 24hr. **Post Office:** 135 Catoma St. (☎263-4974. Open M-F 7:30am-5:30pm, Sa 8am-noon.) **Public Library:** Main Branch, 245 High St. (Between McDonough and Lawrence St.) (584-7144. Open M-Th 9am-9pm, F-Sa 9am-6pm, Su 1-6pm.) **Postal Code:** 36104. **Area Code:** 334.

ACCOMMODATIONS. For those with a car, South Blvd., Exit 168 off I-65, overflows with inexpensive beds, while most exits off I-85 lead to standard, more expensive chains. Beware—the cheapest of the cheap can be fairly seedy. If you're looking to stay close to downtown attractions in the historic part of town, the **Red**

IN RECENT NEWS

HELLO MY NAME IS BISCUIT AND I AM A BASEBALL TEAM

In a league awash with Braves, Mudcats, and Devil Rays, the Montgomery Biscuits cannot help but stand out. And that, it seems, it just the idea. Chosen by franchise-owners after Montgomery citizens entered a contest to name the team, folks have been talking about the less-than-intimidating moniker ever since. The national and international press are waiting expectantly for the Biscuits to take the field. Already, Monte Meyers, retail manager of the team's store, The Biscuit Basket, has received orders for team merchandise from as far away as Great Britain and British Columbia (*Montgomery Advertiser*, June 23, 2003). What's more, the list for the Early Bird Ticket Program has been steadily expanding. The true test, however, will come when the Biscuits take the field in April 2004. Montgomeryites are keeping their fingers crossed that their fresh team will rise to the occasion.

For more information on the Montgomery Biscuits and to order tickets or merchandise, call ☎334-323-2255, or check out www.biscuitsbaseball.com.

Bluff Cottage ❹, 551 Clay St., is a B&B worth the price tag. Themed rooms, full baths, Internet, TV, bathrobes, and flowers add to the cottage's allure. (☎264-0056 or 888-551-2529; www.redbluffcottage.com. Singles $90; doubles $95.) The **Embassy Suites Hotel ❹**, 300 Tallapoosa St., right across the street from the Visitors Center, usually has room in one of their 237 suites. All come standard with dataports, two cable TVs, wet bar, fridge, coffeemaker, and microwave. Complimentary breakfast, restaurant, lounge, pool, and sauna. (☎269-5055; www.embassysuites.com. Call for rates, generally starting at $99.) Travelers with less to spend should check out the **Comfort Inn ❸**, 1035 W. South Blvd, Exit 168 off of I-65 South, which has exceptionally clean rooms, continental breakfast, A/C, microfridge, microwave, free local calls, a pool, and cable TV. (☎281-5090. Singles $64; doubles $69. AAA and AARP discounts available.) The site of a 1763 French stronghold, **Fort Toulouse Jackson Park ❶**, 12 mi. north of Montgomery on Ft. Toulouse Rd., off U.S. 231, has 39 sites with water and electricity under hanging Spanish moss in beautiful woods. (☎567-3002. Registration daily 8am-5pm. In spring and fall, reservations are recommended at least 2 weeks in advance. Sites $11; with hookup $14. Seniors $8/11.)

FOOD. In a tiny pink house filled with heavenly paintings and posters, **Martha's Place ❶**, 458 Sayre St., is a true Bible Belt gem. Fried chicken, pork chops, collard greens, and black-eyed peas are all included in Martha's gigantic, authentic soul food lunch. Don't miss the pound cake and sweet tea. (☎263-9135. Traditional lunch $5.50. 4-vegetable plate $4. Open M-F 11am-3pm.) Even though the center of Montgomery life has moved from Dexter Ave., **Chris' Hot Dogs ❶**, 138 Dexter Ave., the oldest restaurant in town, has continued to make hot dogs ($1.60) like nobody else since 1917. Hamburgers, grilled cheese and other authentic diner fare are also available. (☎265-6850. Open M-Th and Sa 10am-7pm, F 10am-8pm. Cash and local checks only.) **Jimmy's Uptown Grille ❸**, 540 Clay St, offers flavors that are a little more exotic (think lamb and elk) and well-worth the extra bucks. Take in the old house' ambience at the bar in front, conveniently open until 2am or later. (☎265-8187. Open M-Sa 4pm. Kitchen closes at 9:30pm. Reservations recommended on weekends.) **Tomatinos ❷**, 1036 E. Fairview Ave., in Old Cloverdale, just across the street from the Capri theatre (see **Nightlife** p. 445), specializes in flavorful homeade pizzas and calzones. Whole wheat dough is made fresh daily. Prices at this relaxed, locally-owned Italian spot range from $6.50 for a small cheese pizza to $13.75 for a large. A large selection of beer ($1.75-

3.75) and wine (bottle $22) is also available. Cap off the meal next-door at the adjoining bakery, **Cafe Louisa ❶**, where gelato is only $3 and espresso costs $1.75. (☎264-4241. Open M-F 11am-10pm, Su 4-10pm). Eat with the old guard of Montgomery society at **The Sahara Restaurant ❷**, 511 East Edgemont Ave. Amidst oil paintings of revered local residents, tuxedoed waiters serve $20 dinners of whole grilled fish and filet mignon. (☎262-1215. Blue-plate southern lunch with veggies, beverage, and dessert $6-9. Open M-Sa 11am-10pm.)

SIGHTS. The **State Capitol**, at Bainbridge St. and Dexter Ave., is, as any self-respecting state capitol should be, an imposing Greek Revival structure sporting marble floors, cantilevered staircases, and neat echo chambers. On the front steps, a bronze star commemorates the spot where Jefferson Davis took the oath of office as president of the Confederacy. (☎242-3935. Open M-F 9am-5pm, Sa 9am-4pm. Guided tours available. Free.) Only two football fields away is the 112-year-old **King Memorial Baptist Church**, 454 Dexter Ave., where Martin Luther King Jr. was pastor for six years. (☎263-3970. Open Sa 1:30-2pm for walkthrough. Guided tours M-Th, F 10am and 2pm; F 10am.) Maya Lin, the architect who designed the Vietnam Veterans Memorial in Washington, D.C. (p. 319), also designed Montgomery's newest sight—the **Civil Rights Memorial**, 400 Washington Ave., in front of the Southern Poverty Law Center. The outdoor monument, over which water continuously flows, pays tribute to activists who died fighting for civil rights. (Open 24hr. Free. Wheelchair-accessible.) **Alabama Department of Archives and History**, 624 Washington Avenue, is not only a housing institute for important state documents, but also a museum. Come here to explore Civil War and civil rights history or, for younger visitors, to interact with the past in the "Hands-On Gallery." And if you do nothing else, be sure to visit the second floor exhibit of Spider Martin's **Selma to Montgomery: A March for the Right to Vote** photography exhibit. Twenty-two of Martin's images—from Bloody Sunday to the 54 mi. march from Selma to Montgomery—are housed here, courtesy of the artist. (☎242-4365. Museum open M-F 8am-5pm, Sa 9am-5pm. Free admission. Wheelchair-accessible.) The **Rosa Parks Library and Museum**, 252 Montgomery St., was dedicated 45 years after Rosa Parks refused to give up her bus seat on December 1, 1955. The museum uses video, artifacts, audio, and an actual 1955 Montgomery bus to recreate that fateful day and the subsequent events that rocked the city and the nation. (☎241-8661. Open M-F 9am-5pm, Sa 9am-3pm. $5.50, under 12 $3.50.) The **Hank Williams Museum**, 118 Commerce St., across from the Montgomery Civic Center, features the Montgomery native's outfits, memorabilia, and even the '52 Cadillac in which he died at the young age of 29. (☎262-3600. Open M-Sa 9am-6pm, Su 1-4pm. $7, under 12 $2.) **Old Alabama Town**, 301 Columbus St., at Hull St., reconstructs 19th-century Alabama with over 40 period buildings, including a pioneer homestead, an 1892 grocery, and an early African-American church. (☎240-4500. Tickets sold M-Sa 8am-3pm; grounds open until 4:30pm. $7, seniors $6.30, ages 6-18 $3.) A modest exterior hides the quirky **F. Scott and Zelda Fitzgerald Museum**, 919 Felder Ave., off Carter Hill Rd. at Dunbar. The curator will be happy to show you photographs, Zelda's paintings, and some of Scott's original manuscripts, not to mention evidence of the couple's stormy marriage and many love letters. (☎264-4222. Open W-F 10am-2pm, Sa-Su 1-5pm. Free.) The **Montgomery Museum of Fine Arts**, 1 Museum Dr., part of the Blount Cultural Park, houses a collection of 19th- and 20th-century American paintings including works by southern painters such as Georgia O'Keefe and Edward Hopper. (☎244-5700. Open Tu-W and F-Sa 10am-5pm, Th 10am-9pm, Su noon-5pm. Free, but donations appreciated.)

ENTERTAINMENT & NIGHTLIFE. The nationally acclaimed **Alabama Shakespeare Festival**, considered by many to be Montgomery's leading attraction, is staged at the **Carolyn Blount Theater** on the grounds of the 300-acre private estate, **Wynton M. Blount Cultural Park;** take East Blvd. 15min. southeast of downtown to

Vaughn Rd., or Exit 6 off I-85, onto Woodmere Blvd. The theater also hosts contemporary plays; the 2004 season includes *The Secret Garden, Macbeth, Proof, Steel Magnolia, Titus Andronicus,* and *Disguises.* (☎271-5353 or 800-841-4273. www.asf.net. Box office open M-Sa 10am-6pm, Su noon-4pm; performance nights until 9pm. $12-40, under 25 with ID $10, seniors half-price 1hr. prior to show.) For regional music, head to Montgomery's locally-owned **1048 bar**, at 1104 E. Fairview Ave. to enjoy a beer listen to the best acts in town. (☎834-1048. Domestics, $2.75, Imports, $3.50, Makers on the rocks, $4.75. Open Su-F 4pm-4am, Sa 4pm-2am.) **Gator's Blues Bayou,** 5040 Vaughn Rd., at Vaughn Plaza, does delta, acoustic, blues, and rock in its cafe and nightclub. (☎274-0330. Live music Tu-Sa, usually 8pm until late. Kitchen open M-F 11am-2pm and 5-10pm, Sa 5-10pm, Su 11am-2pm.) Montgomery's only independent movie theater, the **Capri Theater,** 1045 E. Fairview (☎262-4858), shows inspired arthouse films. Call for times and current showings. The Thursday *Montgomery Advertiser, The Buzz,* and the monthly *King Kudzu* list other entertainment options.

NEAR MONTGOMERY

TUSKEGEE

After Reconstruction, "emancipated" blacks in the South remained segregated and disenfranchised. **Booker T. Washington,** a former slave, believed that blacks could best improve their situation through hard work and learning a trade, and the curriculum of the college he founded reflected that philosophy. "What we need we will ourselves create," Washington asserted, a claim made concrete by the fact that virtually the entire school was made through student labor. Today, a more academically-oriented **Tuskegee University** (☎727-8347 for tours) fills 160 buildings on 5000 acres, while the buildings of Washington's original institute comprise a national historical site. On campus, the **George Washington Carver Museum** has exhibits and informative films on its namesake. Artist, teacher, scientist, and head of the Tuskegee Agricultural Dept., Carver improved the daily lives of Macon County's poor by discovering hundreds of practical uses for common, inexpensive products like the peanut. (☎727-3200. Open daily 9am-4:30pm. Free.) Across the street from the campus lies **The Oaks,** a restoration of Washington's home. (Tours available daily every 2hr. 10am-4pm; call to schedule.) To get to Tuskegee, take I-85 toward Atlanta, get off at Exit 32, and follow the signs. **Greyhound** (☎727-1290) runs from Montgomery (45min., 6 per day, $8-9). **Area Code:** 334.

SELMA

Selma, perhaps more than anywhere else in Alabama, is haunted by the past. The small, historic Southern town was shaped by two momentous events that took place 100 years apart. As a stronghold for the Confederate armies, its fall in 1865 marked a decisive victory for the North. A century later, Selma gained notoriety during the Voting Rights movement. In the Selma of 1964, state-imposed restrictions gave only 1% of eligible blacks the right to vote. In 1965, civil rights activists organized an ill-fated march on the state capitol that was quashed by billy club-swinging troops. Their spirits battered but not destroyed, the marchers kept trying. A third attempt resulted in the 54 mi. trek from Selma to Montgomery that Dr. King declared the "greatest march ever made on a state capitol in the South." Six months later, Congress passed the Voting Rights Act, which prohibited states from using prerequisites to disqualify voters on the basis of color.

Nowadays, though, the city has a lot more to it than these bloody conflicts. Selma has the largest historical district in Alabama, with over 1200 historic structures, and calls itself home to one of America's most unique festivals, the **Tale Tellin' Festival.** Storytellers and yarn-spinners from across the South converge on Selma during the second Friday and Saturday in October. The **National Voting**

Rights Museum & Institute, 1012 Water Ave., houses memorabilia relating to the Voting Rights Act of 1965 and continues to disseminate information about voting rights and responsibilities. (☎418-0800. Open Tu-F 9am-5pm, Sa-M by appointment. Donations suggested.) The **Brown Chapel AME Church and King Monument,** 410 Martin Luther King St., served as the headquarters for many civil rights meetings during the Movement and was the starting point for the march to Montgomery. (☎874-7897. Tours available by appointment M-Sa 10am-4pm, Su 1-4pm.) **The Old Depot Museum,** 4 Martin Luther King Jr. St., explores the history of Selma with artifacts of past and present, some dating back thousands of years to the area's original inhabitants. Check out their photography collection by the 19th century Alabama native Mary Morgan Keipp. (☎874-2197. Open M-Sa 10am-4pm, Su by appointment. $4, seniors $3; students 19-25, $2; students 6-18, $1.) Downtown Selma is bordered by **Jeff Davis Avenue** to the north and the **Alabama River** to the south. **U.S. 80,** which becomes **Broad Street,** runs straight through town. **Greyhound,** 434 Broad St. (☎874-4503; open daily 7am-10pm), runs to Montgomery (1hr., 6 per day, $12). **Visitors Center:** 2207 Broad St. (☎875-7485; www.selmashowcase.com. Open daily 8am-8pm.) **Internet Access:** Selma/Dallas County Public Library, 1103 Selma Ave. (874-1727. Open M-Sa 9am-5pm. Free Internet access with library card.) **Post Office:** 1301 Alabama Ave. (☎874-4678. Open M-F 8am-4:40pm, Sa 8am-noon.) **Postal Code:** 36703. **Area Code:** 334.

BIRMINGHAM ☎205

For most people, Birmingham recalls the struggle for black Civil Rights in the 1960s. Leaders like Martin Luther King, Jr. and Fred Shuttleworth faced some of their toughest fights in what was labeled "Bombingham" after dozens of bombs rocked the city in the early 1960s. Today's Birmingham, Alabama's largest city, has turned the corner and focused its efforts on building a substantial medical research community. The city does not shy from its stormy past, however, and some of the most powerful civil rights monuments in the South are located downtown.

TRANSPORTATION

Airport: Birmingham International Airport (☎595-0533; www.bhamintlairport.com), Exit 129 off I-20/59.

Trains: Amtrak, 1819 Morris Ave. (☎324-3033), south of 1st Ave. N at 19th St. Open daily 9am-5pm. 1 train per day to **Atlanta** (5hr., $27) and **New Orleans** (7hr., $32).

Buses: Greyhound, 618 19th St. N (☎252-7190). Open 24hr. To: **Atlanta** (3hr., 12 per day, $22); **Mobile** (5½-8hr., 6 per day, $42); **Montgomery** (2hr., 6 per day, $18); **Nashville** (3½-5½hr., 6 per day, $28).

Public Transit: Metropolitan Area Express (MAX) and **Downtown Area Rapid Transit (DART)** (☎521-0101). MAX: M-F most routes 6am-6pm. $1, students $0.60; transfers free. DART trolley runs to downtown tourist destinations. Most routes daily 10am-midnight. $0.50, some routes free.

Taxi: Yellow Cab, ☎252-1131.

ORIENTATION

Downtown Birmingham is organized in a grid, with numbered avenues running east-west and numbered streets running north-south. Richard Arrington Jr. Blvd. is the one exception, running along what would have been called 21st St. Downtown is divided by railroad tracks running east-west through the center of the city—thus, avenues and streets are designated "N" or "S." Avenue numbers decrease as they near the railroad tracks (with 1st Ave. N and S running alongside them), while street numbers grow from 11th St. at the western edge of downtown to 26th St. at the east. **20th Street** is the main north-south thoroughfare. **I-65** to the west, **I-20/59** to the north, and **Route 31** to the east form a U around downtown, leaving the southern side exposed. Five Points, the center of youthful nightlife, is at the intersection of 20th St. S and 11th Ave. S, while the **University of Alabama-Birmingham** is just to the northeast, between 6th and 10th Ave., west of 20th St. S. While most of the city is pancake-flat, the southeastern edge climbs up suddenly into the bluffs, and the streets curl, wind, and become both very confusing and very beautiful. Birmingham's three interstates are readily accessible; **I-20** approaches from Atlanta to the east; **I-65** runs north to Nashville and south to Mobile; and **I-59** runs northeast from New Orleans into the heart of the city.

Visitor Info: Greater Birmingham Convention and Visitors Center, 2200 9th Ave., N, 1st fl. (☎458-8000; www.sweetbirmingham.com), will answer your questions and try to sell you Birmingham tote bags. Open M-F 8:30am-5pm.

Hotlines: Crisis Center, ☎323-7777. **Rape Response,** ☎323-7273. Both 24hr.

Internet Access: Birmingham Public Library, 2100 Park Place (☎226-3610), at the corner of Richard Arrington Jr. Blvd near the Visitors Center. Tell them you're from out-of-town to get a sign-on code. Open M-Tu 9am-8pm, W-Sa 9am-6pm, Su 2-6pm.

Post Office: 351 24th St. N (☎800-275-8777). Open M-F 6am-11pm. **Postal Code:** 35203. **Area Code:** 205.

ACCOMMODATIONS

Relatively cheap hotels and motels dot the Greater Birmingham area along the various interstates. The closer to downtown, the more expensive the room.

The Hospitality Inn, 2127 7th Ave. S (☎322-0691), four blocks north of Five Points and near the University, is one of the best deals in the city with clean, wood-paneled rooms, a convenient location, and a pleasant staff. Singles or 2 twin beds $39; 2 double beds $46. Wheelchair-accessible. ❷

Delux Inn and Suites, 7905 Crestwood Blvd. (☎956-4440 or 800-338-9275), Exit 132 off I-20, then left on Crestwood, in the eastern section of town. Comfortable rooms with A/C, cable TV, continental breakfast, and a pool make this motel one of the better deals for its price. Rooms for 1-4 people $59. ❸

Oak Mountain State Park (☎620-2527 or 800-252-7275), 15 mi. south, off I-65 in Pelham at Exit 246. Alabama's largest state park, with 10,000 acres of horseback riding, golfing, and hiking, and an 85-acre lake with a beach and fishing. Sites $10.75; with water and electricity $14.50; full hookup $16.75. Parking $2. ❶

FOOD

An old streetcar suburb near the University of Alabama-Birmingham, **Five Points South,** at the intersection of 20th St. S and 11th Ave. S, is the best place to eat.

Bahama Wing, 321 17th St. N (☎324-9464), in downtown. A hole-in-the-wall that's so local, you'll be the only diner who doesn't live two doors down. It is *the* place for tasty and cheap wings, from 2 pieces served with a slice of toasted white bread and fries ($1.75) to 15 pieces ($10.50). These aren't your usual wings; they come in dozens of flavors ranging from Spicy Jerk to Bahama Breeze. Catfish dinner $7.25. Open M-W 11am-7 pm, Th-Sa 11am-10pm. ❷

MOUNDVILLE When white settlers first came across **Moundville,** 60 mi. southwest of Birmingham on I-59/20, they believed they had come across the city of some lost classical race. Archaeologists eventually placed the two dozen flat-topped earthen mounds, the highest at 58 ft., as the work of the same Mississippian civilization that built **Effigy Mounds** in Iowa (see p. 651). From AD 1000-1500, the site was the ceremonial capital of the Mississippian people. The exact purposes of the mounds and the causes of their builders' disappearance are unknown. In addition to the mounds, the park contains the **Jones Archeological Museum,** where exhibits and artifacts from the mounds are on display, and a model **Indian Village** features life-size dioramas on the daily life of the Moundville Indians. Every year during the first full week of October, the **Moundville Native American Festival** is held on the grounds and features Native American dances, crafts, storytelling, and celebration.

Fish Market Restaurant, 611 Richard Arrington Jr. Blvd. S (☎322-3330). Birmingham's oldest seafood wholesaler doubles as a no-frills joint with cheap catches. Fish entrees $8-9. Open M-Th 10am-9pm, F-Sa 10am-10pm. ❷

Jim 'N Nick's Barbecue, 744 29th St. S (☎323-7082), near the corner of Clairmont Ave. and University Blvd., roasts chicken, pork, and beef barbecue sandwiches ($3.50) on a hickory wood fire in a brick pit out back. Get a big dinner barbecue platter for $9, and finish it off with a tasty piece of homemade pie. Open summer M-Th and Sa 10:30am-9pm, F 10:30am-10pm, Su 11am-9pm; winter M-Sa 10:30am-9pm, Su 11am-8pm. ❷

SIGHTS

CIVIL RIGHTS. Birmingham's efforts to reconcile itself with its ugly past have culminated in the **Birmingham Civil Rights District,** a nine-block tribute to the battles and bombings that took place there. The district is centered around **Kelly Ingram Park,** the sight of numerous Civil Rights protests. Commemorative statues and sculptures now grace the green lawns. *(At 5th and 6th Ave. N between 16th and 17th St. Park open daily 6am-10pm.)* The **Sixteenth Street Baptist Church** served as the center of Birmingham's Civil Rights movement. Four young black girls died in the church in a September 1963 bombing by white segregationists, spurring protests in the nearby park. A small exhibit in the church's basement chronicles its past. *(1530 6th Ave. N. ☎251-9402. Open Tu-F 10am-4pm, Sa by appointment. $2 suggested donation.)* Across the street from the church, the powerful **Birmingham Civil Rights Institute** traces the nation's Civil Rights struggle through the lens of Alabama's segregation battle. Traditional displays and documentary footage balance the imaginative exhibits and disturbing artifacts from the Jim Crow era, like the burnt-out shell of a torched Greyhound bus. *(520 16th St. N. ☎328-9696. Open Tu-Sa 10am-5pm, Su 1-5pm. $8, students $4, seniors $5, under 18 free; Su free.)*

4TH AVENUE. In the heart of the old historic black neighborhood, now known as the **4th Avenue District** is the **Alabama Jazz Hall of Fame.** Jazz greats from Erskine Hawkins to Sun Ra and his Intergalactic Arkestra to the magnificent Ella Fitzgerald each get a small display on their life work. *(1631 4th Ave. N, in the Carver Theater 1 block south of Kelly Ingram Park. ☎254-2731. Open Tu-Sa 10am-5pm, Su 1-5pm. Free.)* Bama's sports greats, from Willie "The Say Hey Kid" Mays to runner Carl Lewis, are immortalized in the **Alabama Sports Hall of Fame.** *(2150 Civic Center Blvd., at the corner of 22nd St. N. ☎323-6665. Open M-Sa 9am-5pm, Su 1-5pm. $5, students $3, seniors $4, children under 6 free.)* Two blocks away, the **Birmingham Museum of Art** is the largest municipal art museum in the South, containing over 18,000 works and a sculpture garden. *(2000 8th Ave. N. ☎254-2565. Open Tu-Sa 10am-5pm, Su noon-5pm. Donations appreciated.)*

SMELTING. Birmingham remembers its days as the "Pittsburgh of the South" at the **Sloss Furnaces National Historic Landmark.** Although the blast furnaces closed 20 years ago, they stand as the only preserved example of 20th-century iron-smelting in the world. Ballet, drama, and music concerts are held in a renovated furnace shed by the stacks. *(10 32nd St. N. Adjacent to the 1st Ave. N overpass off 32nd through 34th St. downtown. ☎324-1911. Open Tu-Sa 10am-4pm, Su noon-4pm. Tours Sa-Su 1, 2, 3pm. Free.)*

OTHER SIGHTS. For a breather from the heavy-duty ironworks, revel in the marvelously sculpted grounds of the **Birmingham Botanical Gardens.** Spectacular floral displays, an elegant Japanese garden, and an enormous greenhouse vegetate on 67 acres. *(2612 Lane Park Rd. Off U.S. 31. ☎414-3900. Garden Center open daily 8am-5pm; gardens dawn to dusk. Free.)* If you prefer cogs and grease to petals and pollen, the **Mercedes-Benz U.S. International Visitors Center** is a 24,000 sq. ft. museum that spares no technological expense while celebrating the history of all things Mercedes. You can tag along on a tour of the nearby factory. *(I-20/59 off Exit 89 on Mercedes Dr. at Vance St. ☎507-2266 or 205-507-2253. Open M-F 9am-5pm, first Sa of every month 10am-3pm. $4, seniors and children $3. Under 12 not allowed on factory tour.)*

ENTERTAINMENT & NIGHTLIFE

Opened in 1927, the **Historic Alabama Theater,** 1817 3rd Ave. N, is booked 300 nights of the year with films, concerts, and live performances. Their organ, the "Mighty Wurlitzer," entertains the audience pre-show. (☎251-0418. Order tickets at the box office 1hr. prior to show. Open to the public M-F 9am-4pm. Free. Showtimes generally 7pm, Su 2pm. Films $6, seniors and under 12 $5. Organ plays ½hr. before the official show time.) Those lucky enough to visit Birmingham in the middle of May can hear everything from country to gospel to big name rock groups at **City Stages.** The 3-day festival, held on multiple stages in the blocked-off streets of downtown, is the biggest event all year and includes food, crafts, and children's activities. (☎251-1272 or 800-277-1700; www.citystages.org. $20, weekend pass $30.)

Nightlife centers around **Five Points South,** at 20th St. S and 11th Ave. S. On spring and summer nights, many grab outdoor tables, loiter by the fountain until late, or rock in one of the many lively nightclubs nearby. The hippest people jam at **The Nick,** 2514 10th Ave. S, at the corner of 24th St., which locals call "the place." (☎252-3831. Happy Hour M-F 3-9pm. Live music most nights. Cover $5-10; usually free M. Open M-F 3pm to late, Sa 8pm-6am.) Live bands, from reggae to alternative, entertain a collegiate crowd at **The Hippodrum,** 2007 Highland Ave. (☎933-6565. Live music Tu-Sa. Hours and cost vary.) For more info on bands and times, the free *Birmingham Weekly* and the biweekly *black & white* are available in many stores and shops downtown.

HUNTSVILLE ☎256

Huntsville, 80 mi. north of Birmingham, was the first English-speaking settlement in Alabama and the location of the state's Constitutional Convention in 1819. Far more momentous, however, was the 1950 decision to locate the nation's rocket program here, as initially proposed by Wernher von Braun. The 363 ft. replica of a Saturn V rocket at the **US Space and Rocket Center,** Exit 15 off I-565, is easily recognizable for miles. This self-proclaimed "fun center of the universe" features space-flight simulators, an IMAX theater, and tours of the Marshall Space Flight Center. (☎837-3400. Open daily 9am-5pm. $17, ages 3-12 $12.)

Miles of budget motels and chain restaurants cluster on **University Drive,** north-west of downtown, and also at the exits near the airport. To peruse possible lodgings, get off I-565 at Exit 19 and head northwest to University Dr. Another option is the **Southland Inn ❷,** 3808 Governors Dr., off I-565 between Exits 15 and 17. Convenient, yet out of the way of the crush and bustle of University Dr., these simple but functional rooms and the small outdoor pool make it a good deal. (☎539-9391. 1 night $33; 2 nights $45. Inquire about special rates for longer stays.) **Wild Rose Cafe ❷**, 121 N Side Sq., a traditional lunch counter, serves quality meat-and-three (vegetables, that is) platters for $7. (☎539-3658. Open M-F 7-9:30am and 11am-2:30pm.)

Greyhound, 601 Monroe St. (☎534-1681; open daily 7:30am-11:45pm), runs buses to Birmingham (2¼hr., 5 per day, $15); Memphis (7hr., 5 per day, $50); and Nashville (2hr., 6 per day, $15). A convenient **tourist shuttle** runs between downtown, museums, points on University Dr., and the Space and Rocket Center. The trolley can also make hotel pickup stops by reservation. (Every hr. M-F 6:40am-6:40pm, Sa 8:40am-7:10pm. $1, all-day pass $2. Wheelchair-accessible.) **Huntsville Shuttle** runs 11 routes. (☎532-7433. Runs M-F 6am to 6pm. $1; students, seniors, and children under 7 $0.50; transfers free.) **Visitors Center:** 700 Monroe St., in the Von Braun Center. (☎551-2230. Open M-Sa 9am-5pm, Sun noon-5pm.) **Area Code:** 256.

MOBILE ☎251

Although Bob Dylan lamented being stuck here, Mobile (mo-BEEL) has had plenty of fans in its time—French, Spanish, English, Sovereign Alabama, Confederate, and American flags have each flown over the city since its founding in 1702. This historical diversity is revealed in local architecture as well as in the local population: antebellum mansions, Italianate dwellings, Spanish and French forts, and Victorian homes line azalea-edged streets. Today, Mobile offers an untouristed version of New Orleans. The site of the very first Mardi Gras, the city still hosts a three-week long Fat Tuesday celebration—sans the hordes that plague its Cajun counterpart.

ORIENTATION & PRACTICAL INFORMATION. The downtown district borders the Mobile River. **Dauphin Street,** which is one-way downtown, and **Government Boulevard (U.S. 90),** which becomes **Government Street** downtown, are the major east-west routes. **Airport Boulevard, Springhill Road,** and **Old Shell Road** are secondary east-west roads. **Royal Street** and **Broad Street** are major north-south byways. **Water Street** runs along the river downtown, becoming the **I-10 causeway.** A road variously called **I-65 East/West Access Road, Frontage Road,** and the **Beltline** lies west of downtown. **Amtrak,** 11 Government St. (☎432-4052), next to the convention center, currently sends passengers to Atlanta via Motorcoach, a Greyhound bus that honors Amtrak tickets. **Greyhound,** 2545 Government Blvd., at Pinehill St. west of downtown, runs buses to: Atlanta (6-9hr., 2 per day, $46); Birmingham (6hr., 5 per day, $43); Montgomery (3hr., 7 per day, $30); New Orleans (3hr., 8 per day, $26). **Metro Transit** has major depots at Bienville Sq. and the Royal St. parking garage, near the Adams Mark Hotel. (☎344-5656. Runs every hr. M-F 6am-6pm, reduced service on Sa. $1.25, seniors and disabled $0.60; transfers $0.10.) **Moda!** runs free, electric **trolleys** with A/C to most of the sights downtown, including the Visitors Center. (☎208-7540. Operates M-F 7am-6pm.) Services include: **Taxi: Yellow Cab,** ☎476-7711; **Cab Service Inc.,** ☎342-0024. **Visitor Info: Fort Condé Info Center,** 150 S. Royal St., in a reconstructed French fort near Government St., is an island oasis in the stormy sea of traveling. (☎208-7304. Open daily 8am-5pm.) **Post Office:** 168 Bay Shore Ave. (☎478-5639. Open M-F 9am-4:30pm.) **Postal Code:** 36607. **Area Code:** 251.

ACCOMMODATIONS. Few accommodation options exist in the historic part of downtown Mobile. While there are some larger, more expensive chains in the area, there is only one **Malaga Inn ❹**, 359 Church St., at Claiborne (right in front of the Civic Center), where you can experience Mobilian charm in all its pink-stuccoed glory. Rooms have private baths, telephones, and cable TV. (☎438-4701; www.malagainn.com. Continental breakfast. Rooms $79-150. Some are wheelchair-accessible.) A modest (approx. 7 mi.) drive from downtown, a slew of affordable motels line I-65 on Beltline, from Exit 5A (Spring Hill Rd.) to Exit 1 (Government Blvd.), and Rte. 90 west of downtown. **Olsson's Motel ❷,** 4137 Government Blvd., Exit 1B off I-65, 2 has fun, quirky perks like recliners and four-poster beds. (☎661-5331. Singles $35 plus tax; doubles $39 plus tax.) **Family Inn ❷,** 980 S. Beltline Rd., is the best of the chain lodgings. (☎344-5500. Free local calls, continental breakfast, and cable TV. Su-Th $39; F-Sa $49, but travelers should inquire about the 8 rooms that typically go for $30 per night.) **Mobile's I-10 Kampground ❶,** 6430 Theodore Dawes Rd., 7½ mi. west on I-10, south off Exit 13, is a shady and relatively quiet spot, disturbed occasionally by the starting up of one of the many RV's. (☎653-9816 or 800-272-1263. 150 shady sites, pool, and laundry facilities. Tent sites $15; RV hookup $21. Each additional person $1.)

FOOD & NIGHTLIFE. Mobile's Gulf location means fresh seafood and Southern cookin'. **Wintzell's Oyster House ❸,** 605 Dauphin St., is a long-time local favorite that offers oysters "fried, stewed, or nude" in rooms covered with thousands of signs professing bits of wit and wisdom in the words of the late Mr.Wintzell himself. (☎432-4605. Happy Hour specials M-F 4-7pm with $0.25 raw oysters. Meals $8-14. Open M-Sa 11am-10pm, Su noon-8pm.) For turf, follow the cloud of wood smoke to **Dreamland ❷,** 3314 Old Shell Rd. Their famous ribs, cooked over the open fire in the large dining room, will stick to yours. (☎479-9898. Half-slab $9. Half-chicken $6.50. Open M-Sa 10am-10pm, Su 11am-9pm.) **The Brick Pit ❷,** 5456 Old Shell Rd is dedicated to "serious barbeque" and all pulled pork is smoked for 30 hours. (☎343-0001. Half slab ribs $9, pulled pork sandwich $5.50. Open Tu-Th 11am-8pm, F-Sa 11am-9pm.) To taste a bit of the simple American goodness that Mobilians have been enjoying since 1924, head to the **Dew Drop Inn ❶,** 1808 Old Shell Rd., Mobile's oldest restaurant, for a hamburger ($2.25), hot dog ($2.25), or fried chicken ($7). Mull over your options as you sip your coke from the classic little green bottle. (☎273-7872. Open M-F 11am-8pm, Sa 11am-3pm.)

Mobile's late-night scene is a bit one-dimensional—downtown, pool is the name of the game. The **Lower Dauphin Street Entertainment District** is a fancy name for the downtown block of bars, each of which has a couple of pool tables, 20 or more youngish locals, and drinks for under $5. Most places close around 2 or 3am. Or, if you're tired of the downtown scene head to the **Bubble Lounge,** 5546 Old Shell Rd., where you can sip a top shelf martini ($7) or just enjoy the funky, dimly-lit atmosphere. (☎341-5556. Open Su-M 6pm-2am, or later.) Savor the last moments of your day at **Carpe Diem,** 4072 Old Shell Rd., just slightly west of I-65. Because this colorful and locally-beloved coffee house has their own roaster, the grounds used to make the coffee you sip ($1.70 and up) will never be more than 2 weeks old. (☎304-0448. Open Su 8am-10pm, M-F 6am-11pm, Sa 7am-11pm). Check the weekly *Lagniappe* for other entertainment options

SIGHTS. Mobile's attractions lie scattered inland, around downtown, and near the bay. The **Museum of Mobile,** 111 S. Royal St., is a new attraction that celebrates and documents "Mobilian" history in all its glory. Exhibits cover "The Founding of Mobile" and the fate of the slave ship *Clotilda* alongside the private hoards of prominent Mobile families. (☎208-7569. Open M-Sa 9am-5pm, Su 1-5pm. $5, students $3, seniors $4; families $20.) Mobile's attractions lie scattered inland, around downtown, and near the bay. The **MuseuBienville Square,** at the intersection of Dauphin and Conception St., is the main hangout for locals. Eight separate historic districts, all marked by extensive signage in the downtown area, display the evidence of the city's varied architectural and cultural influences. In particular, the buildings of the **Church Street East Historic District** showcase Federal, Greek Revival, and Victorian architecture. The staff at the Fort Condé Visitors Center gives several walking and driving tours of these neighborhoods and will design one especially for you. Several spectacular mansions and houses have been converted into museums. In the **DeTonti Historical District,** north of downtown, brick townhouses with wrought-iron balconies surround the restored **Richards-DAR House Museum,** 256 North Joachim St. The house's ornate iron lace is some of the most elaborate of its era. (☎208-7320. Open M-F 11am-3:30pm, Sa 11am-4pm, Su 1-4pm. Tours $5, children $2. Free tea and cookies.) And not too far away, adjacent to the Historic DeTonti District, is the **African-American Archives-Museum,** 564 Dr. Martin Luther King, Jr. Ave. Housed in what was the first African-American Library, you can sort through portraits, biographies, books, carvings, and other artifacts that represent the lives of numerous African-Americans from the Mobile area and abroad. (☎433-8511. Open M-F 8am-4pm, Sa 10am-2pm. Free admission and parking.) **Oakleigh Historical Complex,** 350 Oakleigh Pl., 2½ blocks south of Government St. at George St., contains the grandiose **Oakleigh House Museum,** the working-class **Cox-Deasy House Museum,** and the **Mardi Gras Cottage Museum.** The houses attempt to portray the everyday and festival lives of various classes of Mobilians in the 1800s. (☎432-1281. Open M-Sa 9am-3pm. Tours every 30min., last tour 3:30pm. $10, seniors and AAA $9, ages 6-11 $5.) The **Bragg-Mitchell Mansion,** 1906 Springhill Ave., complete with tall white columns, is the most plantation-like of Mobile's old homes. (☎471-6364. Open for tours Tu-F 10am-3:30pm. $5.) The **USS Alabama,** moored 2½ mi. east of town at Battleship Park (accessible from I-10 and Government St.'s Bankhead Tunnel), earned nine stars from battles fought in WWII. Open passageways let landlubbers explore the ship's depths. The park also houses a collection of airplanes and the *USS Drum,* a submarine that visitors can walk through. (☎433-2703. Open Apr.-Sept. daily 8am-7pm. Coupon available at Fort Condé Visitors Center, $2 AAA discount. Parking $2.) **Bellingrath Gardens,** 12401 Bellingrath Gardens Rd., Exit 15A off I-10, was voted one of America's top five formal garden displays for its lush rose and oriental gardens, bayou boardwalk, and 900-acre setting. (☎800-247-8420. Open daily 8am-dusk; ticket office closes 5pm. Gardens $9, ages 5-11 $5.25.) Early spring is the time to be in Mobile. Azaleas bloom in a pink line beginning at the Visitors Center, marking the 27 mi. **Azalea Trail,** which twists through the city. In February, Mobile's **Mardi Gras,** the oldest one in the country and the precursor to the debauchery that is New Orleans, erupts with parades, costumes, an Out-of-Towners ball, and the crowning of the Mardi Gras King and Queen. To add more fuel to the Fat Tuesday fire, in 2005 the **Mardi Gras Museum** will open in Mobile; call the Visitors Center for details. The *Mobile Traveler* and *Mobile Bay Monthly,* available at Fort Condé Visitors Center, has an updated list of all Mobile attractions.

MISSISSIPPI

More than any other state, Mississippi is tied to its past. The legacy of cotton, a dependence upon slavery, and subsequent racial strife and economic ruin are easily visible here; some tout the state as "the closest you can get to the past." Despite its tribulations, Mississippi has had a number of remarkable triumphs, having produced some of the nation's greatest literary giants, among them William Faulkner, Eudora Welty, Tennessee Williams and Willie Morris. Perhaps most notably, Mississippi is the American home of the blues. The Crossroads state has yielded the likes of Robert Johnson, Bessie Smith, W.C. Handy, Muddy Waters, and B.B. King, whose riffs would eventually spread upriver and throughout the world.

PRACTICAL INFORMATION

Capital: Jackson.

Visitor Info: Division of Tourism, P.O. Box 1705, Ocean Springs 39566 (☎800-927-6378; www.visitmississippi.org). **Department of Parks,** P.O. Box 451, Jackson 39205 (☎800-467-2757).

Postal Abbreviation: MS. **Sales Tax:** 7%.

JACKSON ☎601

Jackson makes a concerted effort to overcome Mississippi's troubled, bloody past and lingering backwater image. Impressive museums and sights line Pascagoula and State St. downtown, and as the state's political and cultural capital, Jackson strives to bring the world to its people. North Jackson's lush homes and plush country clubs epitomize wealthy Southern living, while shaded campsites, cool reservoirs, and national forests invite outdoor exploration. Just don't arrive on a Sunday—true to its deep Southern roots, Jackson will be closed for a rest.

ORIENTATION & PRACTICAL INFORMATION. West of I-55 and north of I-20, downtown is bordered on the north by **High Street,** on the south by **South Street,** and on the west by **Lamar Street.** North-south **State Street** bisects the city. **Jackson International Airport,** 100 International Dr. (☎939-5631; www.jmaa.com), lies east of downtown off I-20. **Amtrak,** 300 W. Capitol St. (☎355-6350; open daily 10:15am-5:15pm), runs to Memphis (4½hr., 7 per week, $33) and New Orleans (4hr., 7 per week, $21). **Greyhound,** 201 S. Jefferson St. (☎353-6342; open 24hr.), sends buses to Memphis (5hr.; 5 per day; $30-32), Montgomery (5hr., 7 per day, $50-53), and New Orleans (4½hr., 4 per day, $27-29). *Avoid this area at night, as it can be unsafe.* **Jackson Transit System (JATRAN)** provides limited public transportation. Maps are posted at most bus stops and available at JATRAN headquarters, 1025 Terry Rd. (☎948-3840. Open M-F 8am-4:30pm. Transit runs at least every 30min. M-F 5:30am-6:30pm; every hr. Sa 7am-6pm. $1, transfers free.) **Taxi: City Cab,** ☎355-8319. **Visitor Info: Jackson Convention and Visitors Bureau,** 921 N. President St., downtown. (☎960-1891 or 800-354-7695; www.visitjackson.com. Open M-F 8am-5pm.) **Hotlines: Rape,** ☎982-7273. 24hr. **Post Office:** 401 E. South St. (☎351-7096. Open M-F 7am-6pm, Sa 8am-noon.) **Postal Code:** 39205. **Area Code:** 601.

ACCOMMODATIONS. If you have a car, head for the motels along **I-20** and **I-55**, where the interstate is crawling with the standard mid-range chains. **Parkside Inn ❷,** 3720 I-55 N, at Exit 98B off the access road, is the area's cheap and surprisingly clean motel. (☎982-1122. Pool, cable TV, and close to the airport. Singles $35; doubles with microwave and fridge $38-49.) For another budget option, check in at the **Tarrymore Motel ❷,** 1651 Terry Rd., at the intersection of Hwy. 80. Although a bit grungy, it's a great deal. Just don't stay here if you don't have a car; *the neighborhood between the motel and downtown isn't safe to walk through.* (☎355-0753. All rooms $35.) To rough it, head to **Timberlake Campgrounds ❶.** Take I-55 N to Lakeland East (Exit 98B), turn left after 6 mi. onto Old Fannin Rd. and go 4 mi.; it's inside the Barnett Reservoir. (☎992-9100. Office open daily 8am-5pm. Tent sites $13, seniors $10. Hookup May-Sept. $19/16; Oct.-Apr. $13/10.)

FOOD & NIGHTLIFE. For the real Jackson scene, check out **Mayflower ❸,** 123 W. Capitol St., which has been serving gourmet fresh-from-the-Gulf seafood dishes in a relaxed, diner-like atmosphere since 1935. (☎355-4122. Filet $11. Flounder $16. Open M-Th 11am-2:30pm and 4:30pm-9:30pm, F 11am-2:30-pm and 4:30-10pm, Sa 4:30-9:30pm.) Also downtown, the **George Street Grocery ❷,** 416 George St., off of West St., is packed with state politicians by day and students by night. (☎969-3573. All-you-can-eat Southern lunch buffet $8. Live music Th-Sa 9pm-2am. Restaurant open M-Th 11am-9pm, F 11am-2am, Sa 5-10pm.) **Two Sisters ❸,** 707 N. Congress St., just around the corner from George St., offers yet another Southern smorgasbord in a delightful old creaky-staired home. Take all you want of it for $9.50. (☎353-1180. Open Su-F 11am-2pm.) **Hal & Mal's Restaurant and Brew Bar,** 200 S. Commerce St., near the corner of State and Pascagoula, stages live music in an old, relic-strewn warehouse. (☎948-0888. Cover F-Sa under $5. Restaurant open M 11am-3pm, Tu-F 11am-10:30pm, Sa 5-10:30pm. Bar open M-Th until 11pm, F-Sa until 1am.) On Thursday, pick up the *Clarion-Ledger* for a list of weekend events.

SIGHTS. A museum absolutely unique to Jackson, **International Museum of Muslim Cultures (IMMC),** 117 E. Pascagoula St. was created initially as a temporary satellite to an exhibit at the Mississippi Art Museum, but became permanent in response to overwhelming community enthusiasm. (☎960-0440; www.muslimmuseum.org. Open M-Th and Sa-Su 9:30am-5pm, F 9:30am-12:30pm. $7; students, seniors, children, and disabled $4.) The **Mississippi Museum of Art (MMA),** 201 E. Pascagoula St., at Lamar St., will amaze you with its spacious galleries that display over 3100 works of art, from regional and local to rotating national and international exhibits. (☎960-1515; www.msmuseumart.org. Open M and W-Sa 10am-5pm, Tu 10am-8pm, Su noon-5pm. $5, seniors $4, students $3, ages 6-17 $2. Prices may vary; call ahead.) Adjacent to the MMA, the out-of-this-world **Russell C. Davis Planetarium,** 201 E. Pascagoula, shows both movies and astronomy shows accompanied by music and lasers. (☎960-1550. Shows daily. Call ahead. $5.50, seniors and under 12 $4.) The **Old Capitol Museum,** at the intersection of Capitol and State St., houses an excellent, Smithsonian-caliber collection documenting Mississippi's turbulent history. (☎359-6920. Open M-F 8am-5pm, Sa 9:30am-4:30pm, Su 12:30-4:30pm. Free.) The **New State Capitol,** 400 High St., between West and President St., was completed in 1903, and a recent restoration project preserved the buildings *Beaux Arts* grandeur. (☎359-3114. Self-guided tours M-F 8am-5pm. Free.) Tour the grandiose **Governor's Mansion,** 300 E. Capitol St., one of only two inhabited governor's mansions in the country. (☎359-6421. Tours every 30min. Tu-F 9:30-11am. Free.)

VICKSBURG ☎601

Vicksburg's green hills and prime location on the Mississippi River were host to one of the major battles of the Civil War. President Lincoln, referring to Vicksburg, said the Civil War would "never be brought to a close until that key is in our pocket." After a 47-day siege, the Confederacy surrendered to Ulysses S. Grant's army on July 4, 1863. The city held quite a grudge—it refused to celebrate the Fourth of July until the late 1940s. Today, the battlefield is the town's main attraction—though it has a quirky, only-in-America underbelly that is easily overlooked.

PRACTICAL INFORMATION. A car is necessary in Vicksburg. The bus station, the Visitors Center, downtown, and the far end of the sprawling military park mark the city's extremes; no public transportation runs between them. **Greyhound** (☎638-8389; open daily 7am-8:30pm) pulls out at 1295 S. Frontage Rd. for Jackson (1hr., 6 per day, $11.25). The **Tourist Information Center,** on Clay St., across from the military park entrance, west off I-20, has an extremely helpful map of sights, accommodations, and restaurants. (☎636-9421 or 800-221-3536; www.vicksburgcvb.org. Open summer daily 8am-5:30pm; winter M-F 8am-5pm, Sa-Su 8am-4pm.) **Post Office:** 3415 Pemberton Blvd., is off U.S. 61 S. (☎636-1022. Open M-F 8:30am-5pm, Sa 9am-noon.) **Postal Code:** 39180. **Area Code:** 601.

ACCOMMODATIONS. Vicksburg is a Bed and Breakfast town. The **Battlefield Inn ❸,** 4137 I-20 Frontage Rd., is built on part of the actual battlefield—complete with cannons—right next to the National Military Park. (☎800-359-9363. Singles $60; doubles $65. Pool, laundry, grill, mini golf, on-site restaurant, and free buffet breakfast.) Rooms at the **Beechwood Motel ❶,** 4449 E. Clay St., include cable

TV, microwave, and fridge. (☎636-2271. Singles $30; doubles $33.) Close to the military park, with a free shuttle to all the casinos, is **Battlefield Kampground ❶,** 4407 I-20 Frontage Rd., off Exit 4B. (☎636-2025. Pool, playground, and laundry. Tent sites $12, with water and electricity $15, full hookup $18. Motel rooms $25.)

FOOD & NIGHTLIFE. At **Walnut Hills ❸,** 1214 Adams St., just north of Clay St., noontime is "dinnertime." All-you-can-eat round table dinners of catfish, ribs, okra, snap peas, biscuits, and iced tea cost $12. (☎638-4910. Round table dinners Su-F 11am-2pm. Open M-F 11am-9pm, Su 11am-2pm.) If you're tired of the typical Southern spread, head to **Jacques' ❸,** 4137 I-20 N. Frontage Rd, inside the Battlefield Inn (see above) for some of the most flavorful food in the region—from gnocchi to calamari. (☎638-5811, ext. 1222. Most entrees $12. Karaoke W and F.) While downtown, indulge in home-cooked meals at **Burger Village ❶,** 1220 Washington St. (☎638-0202. Meals $4.25-5.25. Open Tu-Sa 9am-4pm.) Wannabe high-rollers tired of jamming can get lost in one of the four **casinos** that line the river.

SIGHTS. Vicksburg is a mecca for thousands of touring schoolchildren, Civil War buffs, and Confederate and Union army descendents. Memorials and combat site markers riddle the grassy 1700-acre **Vicksburg National Military Park,** lending the grounds a sacred air. The park sits on the eastern and northern edges of the city with its Visitors Center on Clay St., about ½mi. west of I-20 Exit 4B. Driving along the 16 mi. path, there are three options: taking a self-guided tour with a free map available at the entrance, using an informative audio tour, or hiring a guide to narrate the sights. (☎636-0583; www.nps.gov/vick. Park center open daily 8am-6pm. Grounds open summer daily 7am-7pm; winter 7am-5pm. $5 per car. Tape $6, CD $15, live guide $30.) Within the park, the sunk and saved Union **USS Cairo Museum** contains artifacts salvaged in the early 1960s from the old ironclad. (☎636-2199. Usually open daily Apr.-Oct. 9:30am-6pm; Nov.-Mar. 8:30am-5pm. Free with park fee.) The **Old Courthouse Museum,** 1008 Cherry St., is an excellent source of Civil War knowledge. During the 1863 siege of Vicksburg, Confederate troops used the cupola as a signal station and held Union prisoners in the courtroom. It now houses a collection of Jefferson Davis memorabilia and a restored courtroom. (☎636-0741; www.oldcourthouse.org. Open Apr.-Sept. M-Sa 8:30am-5pm, Su 1:30-5pm; Oct.-Mar. M-Sa 8:30am-4:30pm, Su 1:30-5pm. $3, seniors $2.50, under 18 $2.)

Vicksburg also has a bunch of attractions not related to the war. Most can be found on **Washington Street,** running along the river as the town's tiny commercial main street. The **Corner Drug Store,** 1123 Washington St., is a fully operating modern pharmacy—on one half of the floor. On the other half, the owner has created a very elaborate 1800s drug store museum, displaying the store as it was set up a century ago, complete with archaic drugs like cocaine, arsenic, opium, and "haschissh." All sorts of old implements adorn the walls, and a small collection of Civil War battle paraphernalia and old moonshine jugs sits in one corner. (☎363-2756. Open M-Sa 8am-6pm, Su 9:30-11:30am. Free.) Down the street, the **Biedenharn Museum of Coca-Cola Memorabilia,** 1107 Washington St., is a good place to grab an ice cream cone. Standing in a 1900 soda fountain, learn everything there is to know about the bottling of "the ideal brain tonic"—Coca-Cola. (☎638-6514. Open M-Sa 9am-5pm, Su 1:30-4:30pm. $2.25, age 6-12 $1.75. AAA discount.)

OXFORD ☎662

When westward explorers first came to this quaint townsite in northern Mississippi, they decided to name it "Oxford" in hopes of getting the state government to open a university here. The plan worked brilliantly, eventually landing Oxford the **University of Mississippi (Ole Miss).** The school gained notoriety in the early 1960s, when James Meredith attempted to be the first black student to enroll. Mississippi

Governor Ross Burnett openly defied federal law, banning Meredith until the National Guard arrived. Underneath its rough past, Oxford is the "little postage stamp of native soil" that William Faulkner decided "was worth writing about."

ORIENTATION & PRACTICAL INFORMATION. Oxford is 30 mi. east of I-55 on Rte. 6 (Exit 243), 55 mi. south of Memphis, and 140 mi. north of Jackson. Main east-west roads are **Jackson Avenue** and **University Avenue,** while **Lamar Boulevard** runs north-south. The center of town is **Courthouse Square,** at the intersection of Jackson Ave. and Lamar St., and bordered by Van Buren Ave. **Oxford Tourism Info Center,** 111 Courthouse Sq., offers free audio walking tours and loads of info on Faulkner. (☎234-4680 or 800-758-9177. Open M-F 9am-5pm. The little house next door is open Sa-Su 10am-2pm.) **Greyhound,** 2625A W. Oxford Loop (☎234-0094; open M-F 8:30am-5pm, Sa 8:30am-noon), runs to Memphis (2hr., 1 per day, $20); Nashville (9hr., 1 per day, $60); and New Orleans (14 hr., 2 per day, $79). **Internet Access: Public Library,** 401 Bramlett Blvd., at Jackson Ave. (☎234-5751. Open M-Th 9:30am-8pm, F-Sa 9:30am-5:30pm, Su 2-5pm.) **Post Office:** 401 McElroy Dr. (☎234-5615. Open M-F 9am-5pm, Sa 9:30am-12:30pm.) **Postal Code:** 38655. **Area Code:** 662.

ACCOMMODATIONS. Spend a night in Southern comfort at the **Oliver-Britt House Inn ❹,** 512 Van Buren Ave., an unpretentious B&B. Five comfortable but small rooms fit in this turn-of-the-century house. (☎234-8043. Breakfast on weekends. Rooms Su-Th $70-105, F-Sa $70-115; football weekends $20 more.) The town's best independently-owned budget hotel is **Johnson's Inn ❷,** 2305 W. Jackson Ave., west of town off Hwy. 6. It sports spacious, relatively new rooms with microwaves and fridges, cable TV, and free local calls. (☎234-3611. Singles $35; doubles $38.) **Wall Doxy State Park ❶,** 23 mi. north of town on Rte. 7, is a scenic spot with an expansive lake. (☎252-4231 or 800-467-2757. Sites with water and electricity $9; RV sites with dump stations $13. Cabins $52-58 per night. 3-night min. stay for cabins. Entrance fee $2 per car.)

FOOD & ENTERTAINMENT. Food is best found in **Courthouse Square** at Jackson Ave. and Lamar Blvd. It's hip to be square at **Square Books ❶,** 160 Courthouse Sq. The unofficial heart of this literary college town, Square Books is one of the best independent bookstores in the nation. Read upstairs while tasting basic coffee drinks ($2) and pastries ($1-2) or on a balcony overlooking the downtown area. (☎236-2262. Open M-Th 9am-9pm, F-Sa 9am-10pm, Su 10am-6pm.) **Ajax Diner ❷,** 118 Courthouse Sq., cooks excellent meat-and-vegetable platters ($7) accompanied by jalapeño cornbread. (☎232-8880. Open M-Sa 11:30am-10pm.) The **Bottletree Bakery ❷,** 923 Van Buren Ave., serves large deli sandwiches ($7-8) and fresh pastries in a relaxed atmosphere with brightly painted walls and recycled furniture. (☎236-5000. Open Tu-F 7am-4pm, Sa 9am-4pm, Su 9am-2pm.) At night, live music rolls from **Proud Larry's ❸,** 211 S. Lamar Blvd., where hand-tossed pizzas are served up piping hot. (☎236-0050. Dinners $8-10. Cover $5-7. Music M-W and Su 10pm-midnight, F-Sa 10pm-1am. Kitchen open M-Sa 11am-10pm, Su 11:30am-3pm.) For local listings, check the free weekly *Oxford Town.*

SIGHTS. Faulkner remains the South's favorite son, and his home, **Rowan Oak,** just south of downtown on Old Taylor Rd, off S. Lamar Blvd., is Oxford's biggest attraction. Entranced by the home's history (it had belonged to a Confederate general), Faulkner bought the place in 1930 and named the property after the Rowan tree, a symbol of peace and security. The plot outline of his 1954 novel *A Fabl*[illegible] etched in pencil on the walls of the study. (☎234-3284. The house is cu[illegible] closed for renovations. Grounds open sunrise to sunset. Free self-guided[illegible]

Outside of Faulkner, Oxford's sights are all affiliated with another symbol of Southern intellectualism—Ole Miss. The town's covered sidewalks and tall cedar trees make it a fitting home for the **Center for the Study of Southern Culture,** a University department in the old Barnard Observatory. Here, visitors can pick up pamphlets or attend conferences, including the ever-popular annual **Faulkner & Yoknapatawpha Conference** (July 25-29, 2004). Other conferences and festivals sponsored by the center include **The Oxford Conference on the Book,** in April, which celebrates a different important author each year, and the **Southern Foodways Symposium,** which brings people together in late October to discuss weighty academic subjects, like barbecue and other Southern food traditions. (☎915-5993; www.olemiss.edu/depts/south. Center open M-F 8am-5pm. Free.) The big event scheduled for 2004 is the completion of the **Civil Rights Memorial** that will "commemorate equality in education" on the grounds of the Ole Miss Campus. Blues buffs will revel in the **Ole Miss Blues Archive,** on the 2nd fl. of the main campus library on University Circle, which has one of the largest collections of blues memorabilia in the world. (☎915-7408. Open M-F 9am-5pm. Free.)

LOUISIANA

After exploring the Mississippi River valley in 1682, Frenchman René-Robert Cavalier proclaimed the land "Louisiane," in honor of Louis XIV. The name has endured three centuries, though French ownership of the vast region has not. The territory was tossed between France, England, and Spain before Thomas Jefferson and the US snagged it in the Louisiana Purchase of 1803. Nine years later, a smaller, redefined Louisiana was admitted to the Union. Each successive government lured a new mix of settlers to the bayous: Spaniards from the Canary Islands, French Acadians from Nova Scotia, Americans from the East, and free blacks from the West Indies. Louisiana's multinational history, Creole culture, Catholic governmental structure (under which counties are called "parishes"), and Napoleonic legal system are unlike anything found in the other 49 states.

PRACTICAL INFORMATION

Capital: Baton Rouge.

Visitor Info: Office of Tourism, P.O. Box 94291, Baton Rouge 70804 (☎225-342-8100 or 800-261-9144; www.louisianatravel.com). Open M-F 8am-4:30pm.

Office of State Parks, P.O. Box 44426, Baton Rouge 70804 (☎225-342-8111 or 888-677-1400; www.lastateparks.com). Open M-F 8:30am-4:30pm.

Postal Abbreviation: LA. **Sales Tax:** 8%.

NE... RLEANS ☎504

... by the French, *La Nouvelle Orléans* was ceded secretly to the ...; the citizens didn't find out until 1766. Spain returned the city to ...ime for the United States to grab it in the Louisiana Purchase of ... of cultural cross-pollination have resulted in a vast melange of ...rds, Victorian verandas, Cajun jambalaya, Creole gumbo, and ... The city's nickname, "The Big Easy," reflects the carefree atti... of this fun-loving place where food and music are the two rul-

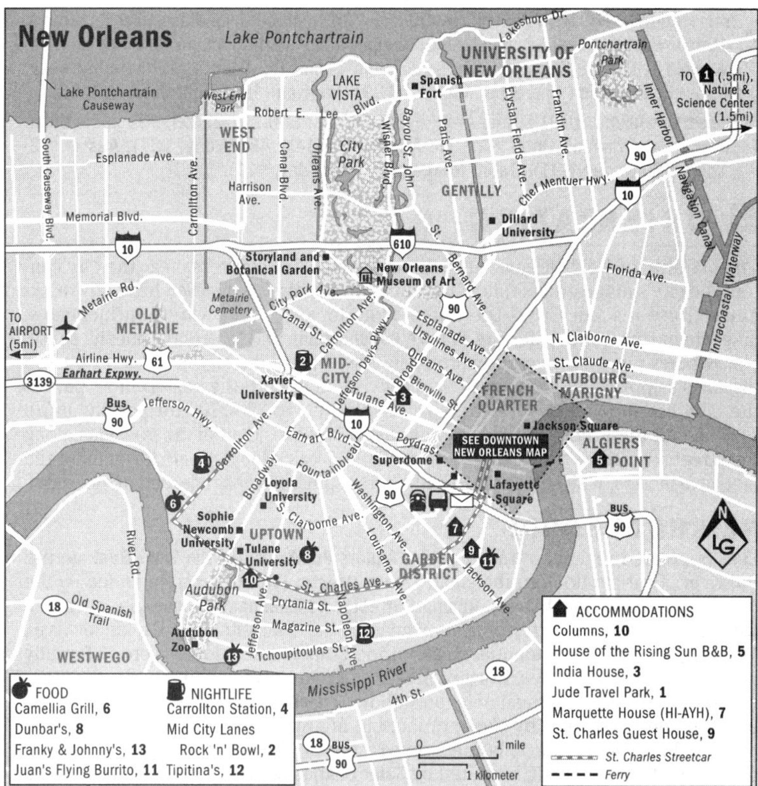

ing passions. New Orleans has its own style of cooking, a distinct accent, and colorful way of making music—at the start of the 20th century, its musicians invented the musical style that came to be known as jazz. While New York may claim to be "the city that never sleeps," "N'awlins" holds the title for "the city that won't stop partying." The only thing that stifles this vivacity is the heavy, humid air that slows folks to a near standstill during the summer. But when the day's heat retreats into the night, the city jumps with drinking and dancing into the early morning. Come late February, there's no escaping the month-long celebration of Mardi Gras, the peak of the city's already festive mood.

INTERCITY TRANSPORTATION

Airport: Louis Armstrong New Orleans International Airport, 900 Airline Dr. (☎465-2303), 15 mi. west of the city. Cab fare to the Quarter is set at $24 for 1-2 people; $10 each additional person. The **Louisiana Transit Authority,** 118 David Dr. (☎818-1077), runs buses from the airport to Elk St. downtown M-Sa every 15-30min. 5:10am-6:40pm. After 6:40pm, buses go to Tulane Ave. and Carollton Ave. (mid-city) until 11:30pm. Station open M-F 8am-4pm. $1.50; exact change needed. Pick-up on the upper level, near the exit ramp.

Trains: Amtrak, 1001 Loyola Ave. (☎800-872-7245), in the Union Passenger Terminal, a 10min. walk to Canal St. via Elk. Station open daily 6am-10pm. Ticket office open M, W, F-Sa 6:15am-8:30pm; Tu, Th, Su 6:15am-11pm. To: **Atlanta** (12hr., 7 per week, $50-89); **Houston** (9hr., 3 per week, $50-89); **Jackson** (4hr., 7 per week, $18-36).

Buses: Greyhound, 1001 Loyola Ave. (☎524-7571 or 800-231-2222), also in the Union Passenger Terminal. Open 24hr. To: **Atlanta** (12-14hr., 8per day, $67); **Austin** (12-15hr., 56 per day, $91); **Baton Rouge** (2hr., 9 per day, $11).

ORIENTATION

The majority of New Orleans' attractions live in close quarters, near the city center. The city's main streets follow the curve of the **Mississippi River,** hence the nickname "the Crescent City." Directions from locals reflect watery influences—lakeside means north, referring to **Lake Ponchartrain,** and "riverside" means south. Uptown lies west, up river; downtown is down river. The city is concentrated on the Mississippi's east bank, but **"The East"** refers only to the easternmost part of the city. **Parking** in New Orleans is relatively easy (☎299-3700 for parking info). Throughout the French Quarter (and in most other residential areas), signs along the streets designate "2hr. residential parking" areas. Many streets throughout the city have meters, which become free M-F after 6pm, on weekends, and on holidays.

NEIGHBORHOODS

Less populated regions of the city, like **Algiers Point,** are on **the West Bank** across the river. Tourists flock to the small **French Quarter (Vieux Carré),** bounded by the Mississippi River, **Canal Street, Rampart Street,** and **Esplanade Avenue.** Streets in the Quarter follow a grid pattern. Just northeast of the Quarter across Esplanade Ave., **Faubourg Marigny** is a residential neighborhood that has developed a crop of trendy nightclubs, bars, and cafes. Northwest of the Quarter across Rampart St., the little-publicized African-American neighborhood of **Tremé** has a storied history, but has been ruined somewhat by the encroaching highway overpass and the housing projects lining its Canal St. border. *Be careful in Tremé at night.* Uptown, the residential **Garden District,** bordered by **Saint Charles Avenue** to the north and **Magazine Street** to the south, is distinguished by its elegant homes. The scenic **Saint Charles Streetcar route,** easily picked up at Canal St. and Carondelet St., passes through parts of the **Central Business District** ("CBD" or "downtown"), the Garden District via St. Charles Ave., and the **Uptown** and **Carrollton** neighborhoods along **South Carollton Avenue** and past **Tulane** and **Loyola Universities**. For a detailed guide to all of the city's neighborhoods, pick up *Historic Neighborhoods of New Orleans*, a pamphlet available at the Jackson Sq. Visitors Center.

LOCAL TRANSPORTATION

Public Transit: Regional Transit Authority (RTA), 6700 Plaza Dr. (☎248-3900). Open M-F 8am-5pm. Most buses pass Canal St., at the edge of the French Quarter. Major buses and streetcars run 24hr., but are notoriously irregular and often don't come at all after midnight. Most buses and streetcars $1.25 in exact change. Express buses and the Riverfront Streetcar $1.50, seniors and disabled passengers $0.40; transfers $0.25. 1-day pass $5, 3-day pass $12; passes sold at major hotels in the Canal St. area. Office has bus schedules and maps.

Taxi: United Cabs, ☎522-0629 or 800-232-3303. **Checker Yellow Cabs,** ☎943-2411.

Bikes: French Quarter Bicycles, 522 Dumaine St. (☎529-3136), between Decatur and Chartres St. $5 per hr., $20 per day, $87.50 per week; includes lock, helmet, and map. Credit card or $200 cash deposit required. Open M-F 11am-7pm, Sa-Su 10am-6pm.

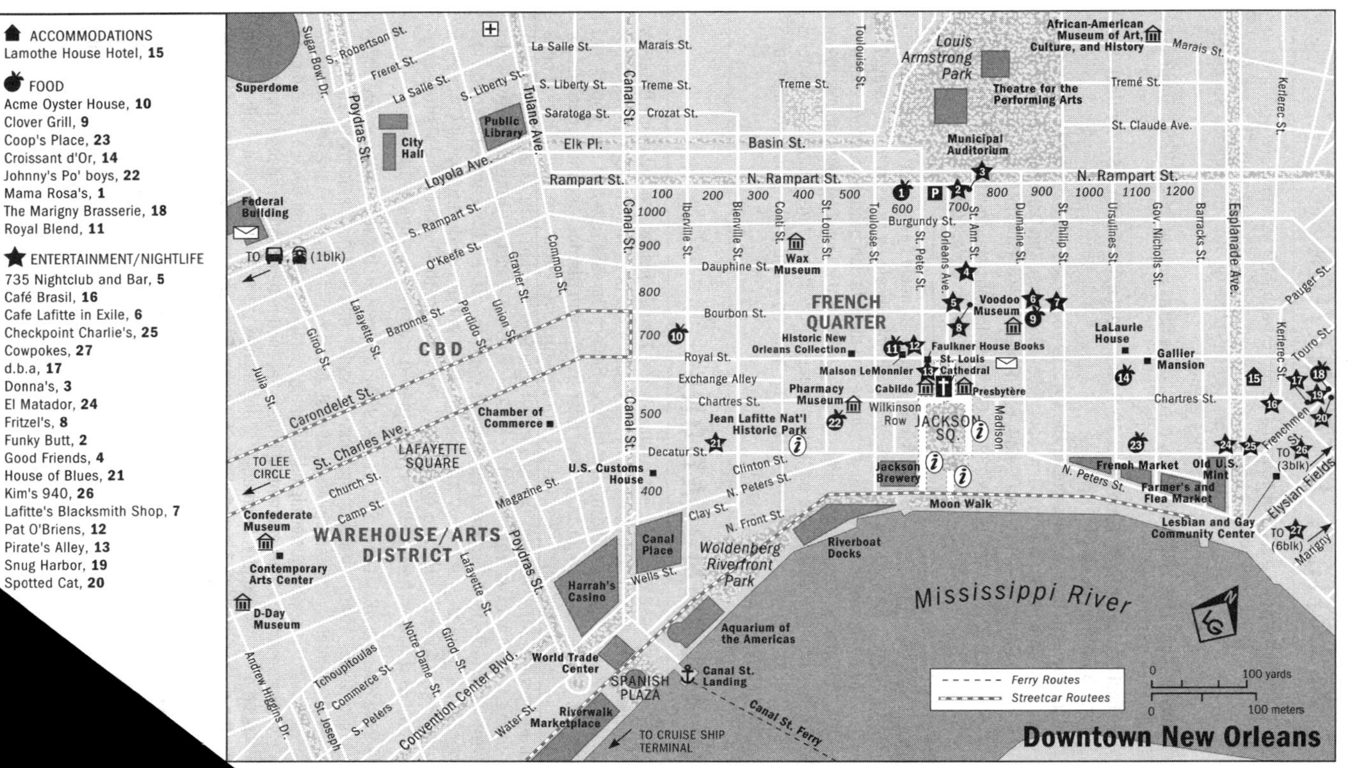
Downtown New Orleans
ACCOMMODATIONS
Lamothe House Hotel, 15
FOOD
Acme Oyster House, 10
Clover Grill, 9
Coop's Place, 23
Croissant d'Or, 14
Johnny's Po' boys, 22
Mama Rosa's, 1
The Marigny Brasserie, 18
Royal Blend, 11
ENTERTAINMENT/NIGHTLIFE
735 Nightclub and Bar, 5
Café Brasil, 16
Cafe Lafitte in Exile, 6
Checkpoint Charlie's, 25
Cowpokes, 27
d.b.a, 17
Donna's, 3
El Matador, 24
Fritzel's, 8
Funky Butt, 2
Good Friends, 4
House of Blues, 21
Kim's 940, 26
Lafitte's Blacksmith Shop, 7
Pat O'Briens, 12
Pirate's Alley, 13
Snug Harbor, 19
Spotted Cat, 20
Ferry Routes
Streetcar Routees
0
100 yards
0
100 meters
Superdome
Federal Building
City Hall
Public Library
Louis Armstrong Park
Theatre for the Performing Arts
Municipal Auditorium
African-American Museum of Art, Culture, and History
FRENCH QUARTER
CBD
LAFAYETTE SQUARE
WAREHOUSE/ARTS DISTRICT
Mississippi River
JACKSON SQ.
Voodoo Museum
Wax Museum
Historic New Orleans Collection
Faulkner House Books
St. Louis Cathedral
Maison LeMonnier
Cabildo
Presbytère
Pharmacy Museum
Jean Lafitte Nat'l Historic Park
Wilkinson Row
Madison
LaLaurie House
Gallier Mansion
French Market
Old U.S. Mint
Farmer's and Flea Market
Lesbian and Gay Community Center
Jackson Brewery
Moon Walk
Riverboat Docks
Woldenberg Riverfront Park
Aquarium of the Americas
Canal St. Landing
Canal St. Ferry
SPANISH PLAZA
World Trade Center
Riverwalk Marketplace
Harrah's Casino
Canal Place
U.S. Customs House
Chamber of Commerce
Confederate Museum
Contemporary Arts Center
D-Day Museum
TO LEE CIRCLE
TO CRUISE SHIP TERMINAL
TO (1blk)
TO 26 (3blk)
TO 27 (6blk)
Canal St.
N. Rampart St.
Rampart St.
Basin St.
Elk Pl.
Tulane Ave.
Loyola Ave.
Poydras St.
Esplanade Ave.
Bourbon St.
Royal St.
Chartres St.
Decatur St.
Dauphine St.
Burgundy St.
N. Peters St.
St. Charles Ave.
Carondelet St.
Convention Center Blvd.
Elysian Fields
Frenchmen St.
Marigny

PRACTICAL INFORMATION

Visitor Info: Metropolitan Convention and Visitors Bureau, 529 St. Ann St. (☎568-5661 or 800-672-6124; www.neworleanscvb.com), by Jackson Sq. in the French Quarter. Open daily 9am-5pm. Beware of false Visitors Centers in the Quarter–the Jackson Sq. center is the only official center in the French Quarter.

Hotlines: Cope Line, ☎523-2673, for crises. **Rape Crisis Hotline,** ☎483-8888. **Domestic Violence Hotline,** ☎486-0377. All 24hr.

Medical Services: Charity Hospital, 1532 Tulane Ave. (☎903-3000). **LSU Medical Center,** 433 Bolivar St. (☎568-4806).

Internet Access: New Orleans Public Library, 219 Loyola Ave. (☎529-7323), 1½ blocks west of Canal St. Open M-Th 10am-6pm, F-Sa 10am-5pm. **The Contemporary Arts Center,** 900 Camp Rd., and **Royal Blend,** 621 Royal St., also have Internet.

Post Office: 701 Loyola Ave. (☎589-1714), near the bus station. Open M-F 7am-8pm, Sa 8am-5pm, Su noon-5pm. **Postal Code:** 70113. **Area Code:** 504.

SAFETY IN NEW ORLEANS. Travelers should be aware of New Orleans' capacity for quick change–safe and decidedly unsafe areas are often separated by a block or less, and areas that are usually safe can become dangerous in a heartbeat. The tenement areas directly north of the French Quarter and northwest of Lee Circle pose particular threats to personal safety. At night, stick to busy, well-lit roads. Never walk alone after dark and make some attempt to downplay the tourist image.

ACCOMMODATIONS

Finding inexpensive yet decent rooms in the **French Quarter** can be as difficult as staying sober during Mardi Gras. Luckily, other parts of the city compensate for the absence of cheap lodging downtown. Several **hostels** cater to the young and almost penniless, as do guest houses near the **Garden District.** Accommodations for Mardi Gras and the Jazz Festival get booked up to a year in advance. During peak times, proprietors will rent out any extra space, so be sure you know what you're paying for. However, rates tend to sink in the low-season (June to early Sept.) when business is slow, and negotiation can pay off. As for campers, there are oodles of campsites to discover, but even those get pricey during Mardi Gras. Pick up a copy of the *Louisiana Official Tour Guide* at the Jackson Sq. Visitors Center; it has the most comprehensive, unbiased campsite listings available.

India House, 124 S. Lopez St. (☎821-1904), at Canal St. between N. Broad and Jeffer- What this bohemian haunt lacks in tidiness it makes up for in character. pictures of past guests fight for space on the walls. Commu- s, sleeping), comfy couches, and backyard patio com- ng house that used to be a brothel. Kitchen, pool, turtle t, A/C, and lounge areas. No key deposit–hell, no keys; posit $5. Dorms $15, peak times $18; weekly $90. Pri-

Prytania St. (☎523-6556). This is the romantic boarding dream of. Located in the Garden District, one of New eighborhoods, the clean and character-filled rooms of this mented by the large, leafy courtyard and continental break- breakfast room overlooking the pool. With no phones or TVs, ontemplate the beauty of New Orleans and chat with the folks rge antique signs hang haphazardly in the hallway, and the friendly staff lives out back. Small, single "backpacker" rooms $30-35, with A/C and private bath $55. Rooms with 1 queen-sized bed or 2 twins $65-95, depending on season. During Jazz Fest and Mardi Gras, rooms $100-150. ❶

House of the Rising Sun Bed and Breakfast, 335 Pelican Ave. (☎888-842-2747), across the river from the Canal St. ferry dock. Located in historic, residential Algiers Point, only minutes away from the French Quarter and downtown (via the ferry), this house and the nearby riverfront streets are a pleasant contrast to the faster pace of the Quarter. Run by two extraordinarily knowledgeable hosts—one English, one Cajun—they offer "Cajun and Cockney hospitality" out of their charming, thoughtfully decorated home. Rooms Sept.-May $95; June-Aug. $75; up to $150 around Mardi Gras. ❹

Marquette House New Orleans International Hostel (HI-AYH), 2249 Carondelet St. (☎523-3014), in the Garden District. A wonderful hostelling experience, especially for hostel virgins, due to its no-alcohol policy, cleanliness, and slight strictness. Extremely large, semi-rustic private rooms are also available at reasonable prices. 200 beds, A/C, kitchen (no stove), study rooms, Internet access $0.10 per min. Very quiet. Wheelchair-accessible. Linen $2.50. No lockout or curfew. Key deposit $5. Dorms $18, nonmembers $20; private rooms with queen-sized bed and pull-out sofa $50/53. Each additional person after 2 people $10. Weekly rates available. ❷

Columns, 3811 St. Charles Ave. (☎899-9308), has a magnificent c. 1893 front porch. Known for its easy-going elegance and classy comfortability, this is one of New Orleans stellar hidden gems. Rates are high, but the atmosphere and full Southern breakfast make it well worth the price. If your pockets aren't that deep, simply stop by for a cocktail and a swing. Rooms $115-200. ❺

Lamothe House Hotel, 622 Esplanade Ave. (☎947-1161 or 800-367-5858), is an imposing 1839 pink townhouse across the street from the French Quarter. 20 rooms feature antique furniture, cable TV, phones, A/C, and full bathrooms. A continental breakfast complete with pastries and coffee is served in the house's decadent dining room, and the large pool is an ideal place to enjoy the complimentary afternoon sherry. Rooms May-Sept. and Dec. $79; Oct.-Nov. and Jan.-Apr. $129. 4 Behind the big pink building is the smaller **Marigny Guest House,** 621 Esplanade Ave. (☎944-9700), built in 1890, with simpler rooms starting at $59. ❸

CAMPING

Jude Travel Park and Guest House, 7400 Chef Menteur Hwy. (U.S. 90) (☎241-0632 or 800-523-2196), just east of the eastern junction of I-10 and U.S. 90, Exit 240B. Bus #98 "Broad" drives past the front gate to #55 "Elysian Fields," which heads downtown. Pool and hot tub, showers, laundry, 24hr. security, and shuttle bus to French Quarter. 46 tent/RV sites $20. 5-room guest house available $75-120 per person per night. ❶

St. Bernard State Park, 501 St. Bernard Pkwy. (☎682-2101), 18 mi. southeast of New Orleans; take I-10 Exit 246A, turn left onto Rte. 46, travel for 7 mi., then turn right on Rte. 39 S. for 1 mi. 51 sites with water and electricity, as well as swimming pools and walking trails. Office open daily 7am-9pm. Sites $12. ❶

FOOD

If the eats in the Quarter prove too trendy, touristy, or tough on the bud[illegible] are plenty of other options, most notably on **Magazine Street** and in[illegible] area, both of which are accessible via the St. Charles Streetcar.

FRENCH QUARTER

Clover Grill, 900 Bourbon St. (☎598-1010). The Clover has bee[illegible] since 1950, serving greasy and delicious burgers ($4 and u[illegible] can-made hubcap (makes 'em cook faster), as well as brea[illegible]

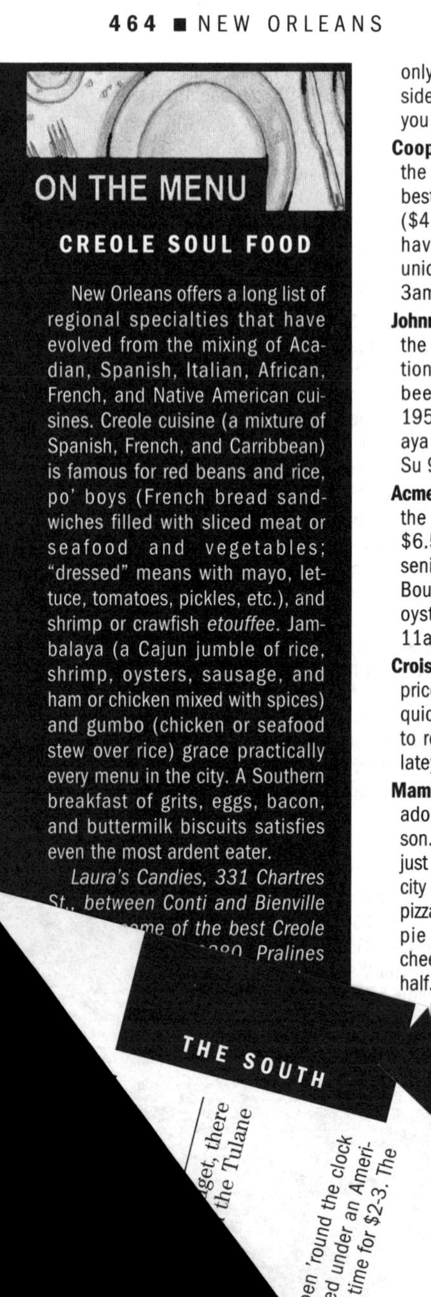

ON THE MENU

CREOLE SOUL FOOD

New Orleans offers a long list of regional specialties that have evolved from the mixing of Acadian, Spanish, Italian, African, French, and Native American cuisines. Creole cuisine (a mixture of Spanish, French, and Carribbean) is famous for red beans and rice, po' boys (French bread sandwiches filled with sliced meat or seafood and vegetables; "dressed" means with mayo, lettuce, tomatoes, pickles, etc.), and shrimp or crawfish *etouffee*. Jambalaya (a Cajun jumble of rice, shrimp, oysters, sausage, and ham or chicken mixed with spices) and gumbo (chicken or seafood stew over rice) grace practically every menu in the city. A Southern breakfast of grits, eggs, bacon, and buttermilk biscuits satisfies even the most ardent eater.

Laura's Candies, 331 Chartres St., between Conti and Bienville ... ome of the best Creole ... 80. Pralines

only place in New Orleans where bacon comes with a side of sexual innuendo—"You can beat our prices, but you can't beat our meat." Open 24hr. ❶

Coop's Place, 1109 Decatur St. (☎525-9053), near the corner of Ursuline St., has some of the Quarter's best Southern cooking. Their gumbo is thick and spicy ($4.25 per bowl), their beer-battered alligator bits ($8) have won awards, and their jambalaya ($8) has a unique flavor found nowhere else. Open Su-Th 11am-3am, F-Sa 11am-4am. ❷

Johnny's Po' Boys, 511 St. Louis St. (☎524-8129), near the corner of Decatur St. This French Quarter institution, with 40 varieties of the famous sandwich, has been the place to grab a po' boy ($4-7.50) since 1950. Decent Creole fare is also on the menu. Jambalaya $4.25. Gumbo $6.25. Open M-F 8am-4:30pm, Sa-Su 9am-4pm. ❷

Acme Oyster House, 724 Iberville St. (☎522-5973). At the bar, patrons slurp fresh oysters (6 for $4, 12 for $6.50) shucked before their eyes by Hollywood, the senior shucker. Acme is at least partly responsible for Bourbon St. debauchery—their motto is "Eat Louisiana oysters, love longer." Open Su-Th 11am-10pm, F-Sa 11am-11pm. ❶

Croissant d'Or, 617 Ursulines St. (☎524-4663). Fair-priced and delicious French pastries, sandwiches, and quiches are served to the local crowd that comes here to read the morning paper. Croissants $1.60. Chocolatey delights $2. Open M-Sa 7am-5pm. ❶

Mama Rosa's, 616 N. Rampart St. (☎523-5546). Locals adore this casual Italian *ristorante*, and with good reason. Served right across from Louis Armstrong Park and just down the street from some of the best sounds of the city (see Donna's and Funky Butt p. 473), Mama Rosa's pizza is some of the best you'll ever eat. 14 in. cheese pie $9. The "outrageous *muffuletta*" (deli meats, cheeses, and olive salad on Italian bread) $6.50 for a half. Open Su-Th 11am-10pm, F-Sa 11am-11pm. ❷

...l Blend, 621 Royal St. (☎523-2716). The quiet ...tyard provides an escape from the hustle of Royal ...d the ubiquitous chain coffee stores in the Quar-...er 20 hot and iced coffees available, as well as ...selection of teas and fresh-baked treats. Light ...croissant sandwiches, quiches, and salads) $5-...es $1-2. Internet cafe upstairs, $3 for 15min. ...-Th 9am-8pm, F-Sa 9am-midnight. ❶

...DE THE QUARTER

...Flying Burrito, 2018 Magazine St. (☎569-...), makes some of the best burritos on the planet. ...$5.75, get the "gutter punk" burrito, a meal the size ...your head, and wash it down with some Mexican ...ers ($2.50) from their full-service bar. Open M-Sa ...1am-11pm, Su noon-10pm. ❶

Franky and Johnny's, 321 Arabella St. (☎899-9146), southwest of downtown toward Tulane on the corner of Tchoupitoulas St. A noisy and popular local hangout where you can sample alligator soup ($3 a cup) or crawfish pie ($4). Feb.-June boiled crawfish $6-11 for 2 lb. Open Su-Th 11am-10pm, F-Sa 11am 'til the cows come home. ❷

The Marigny Brasserie, 640 Frenchmen St. (☎945-4472), at Royal St. in Marigny. More upscale eats on one of the best streets to hear good sounds in all of New Orleans. Experience a slightly more sophisticated side of raucous "N'awlins"—dine surrounded by women in gorgeous dresses and waiters with inscrutable foreign accents. Some of the city's famous favorite dishes are embellished here; mushroom-crusted salmon ($18) is a swanky version of the classic cajun blackened redfish. Open Su-Th 5:30-11pm, F-Sa 5:30pm-1am; Su brunch 10:30am-3:30pm. ❺

Dunbar's, 4927 Freret St. (☎899-0734), on the corner of Robert St. Take St. Charles Ave. west to Jackson St., turn right on Jackson and then left onto Freret. Residents call it the best place to get mama-just-cooked-it soul food—better, they'll tell you, than any place in the Quarter. Gumbo meal $5.50. Specials, like the seafood platter, $15. Open M-Sa 7am-9pm. ❸

Camellia Grill, 626 S. Carrollton Ave. (☎866-9573). Take the St. Charles Streetcar to the Tulane area; Camellia is across the tracks. Classic, counter-service diner where cooks don't mind telling the whole restaurant about their marital problems. Big drippin' plates, crowds, and excellent service. Chef's special omelette $7. The aptly-named "whole meal" sandwiches $6-7. Open M-Th 9am-1am, F-Sa 8am-3am, Su 8am-1am. ❷

SIGHTS

FRENCH QUARTER

Allow *at least* a full day in the Quarter. The oldest section of the city is famous for its ornate wrought-iron balconies—French, Spanish, and uniquely New Orleans architecture—and raucous atmosphere. Known as the **Vieux Carré** (ve-yuh ca-RAY), or Old Square, the historic district of New Orleans offers dusty used bookstores, voodoo shops, museums, art galleries, bars, and tourist traps. **Bourbon Street** is packed with touristy bars, strip clubs, and pan-handlers disguised as clowns. **Decatur Street** has more mellow cafes and bars, and if you're searching for some bona fide New Orleans tunes, head northeast of the Quarter to Frenchmen St., a block of bars that some locals say is what Bourbon St. was like 20 years ago.

ROYAL STREET. A streetcar named "Desire" once rolled down Royal St., now one of the French Quarter's most aesthetically pleasing avenues. Pick up the *French Quarter Self-Guided Walking Tour* from the Visitors Center on St. Ann St. to begin an informed jaunt past balconies of wrought-iron oak leaves and acorns, as well as Louisiana's oldest commercial and government buildings. Highlights of Royal St. are the **Maison LeMonnier,** known as the "first skyscraper," a towering three stories high, and the **LaLaurie House,** rumored to be haunted by the souls of the slaves abused by the LaLaurie family. *(LeMonnier: 640 Royal St.; LaLaurie: 1140 Royal St.)*

JACKSON SQUARE. During the day, much of the activity in the French Quarter centers around Jackson Sq., a park dedicated to Gen. Andrew Jackson, victor of the Battle of New Orleans. The square swarms with artists, mimes, musicians, psychics, magicians, and con artists. Catch a horse-drawn tour of the Quarter for $10; wait on the Decatur St. side. The oldest Catholic cathedral in the US, **Saint Louis Cathedral** possesses a simple beauty. Fully operational since 1718, services are still performed. *(615 Pere Antoine Alley. ☎525-9585. Cathedral open daily 6:30am-6:30pm. Tours every 15-20min. Free.)* Behind the cathedral lies **Cathedral Garden,** also known as **Saint Anthony's Garden,** bordered by **Pirate's Alley** and **Père Antoine's Alley.** Legend has it that the former was the site of covert meetings between pirate Jean Lafitte and

Andrew Jackson as they conspired to plan the Battle of New Orleans. In reality, the alley wasn't even built until 16 years later. Pirate's Alley is also home to **Faulkner House Books,** where the late American author wrote his first novel, *Soldier's Pay.* Upholding the literary tradition, the small bookshop is a treasure-trove of Faulkner's essays and books, alongside an extensive catalogue of other Southern writers. *(624 Pirate's Alley. ☎524-2940. Open daily 10am-6pm.)*

FRENCH MARKET. The historical French Market takes up several city blocks just east of Jackson Sq., toward the water along N. Peters St. *(☎522-2621. Shops open daily 9am-8pm.)* The market begins at the famous **Café du Monde** (see p. 463) and for the first block or two is a normal strip mall of touristy shops housed in a historical building. Down by Gov. Nicholls St., the market becomes the outdoor **Farmer's Market,** which never closes and has been selling "most anything that grows" since 1791. Beyond the Farmer's Market is the **Flea Market,** where vendors sell everything from feather boas to woodcarvings. For a map of the whole strip, stop at the **Visitors Center.** *(700 Decatur St., Under Washington Artillery Park. ☎596-3424. Open daily 8:30am-5pm. Flea Market open daily 8:30am-5pm.)*

OTHER ATTRACTIONS. The **Jean Lafitte National Historical Park and Preserve Visitors Center** conducts free walking tours through the Quarter. *(419 Decatur St. ☎589-2636. 1½hr. tour daily 9:30am. Come early; only the first 25 people are taken. Daily presentations on regional topics 3pm. Office open daily 9am-5pm.)* It's always a great night to stroll the **Moon Walk,** alongside the Mighty Mississippi. The walk offers a fantastic riverside view and a chance for jokes at Michael Jackson's expense. *Be extremely careful in this area at night.* At the southwest corner of the Quarter, the **Aquarium of the Americas** houses an amazing collection of sea life and birds. Among the 500 species are black-footed penguins, endangered sea turtles, and extremely rare white alligators. *(1 Canal St. ☎565-3033. Open daily May-Aug. 9:30am-7pm; Sept.-Apr. 9:30am-6pm. $14, seniors $10, ages 2-12 $6.50.)* The steamboat **Natchez** breezes down the Mississippi on 2hr. cruises with live jazz and narration on riverside sights. An Audubon Adventure Passport includes a steamboat ride from the Aquarium and the Audubon Zoo upriver, a ticket to the IMAX theater, and a Grey Line daytime tour or cemetery and ghost walking tour. *(Departs near the Aquarium and across from Jackson Brewery. ☎586-8777 or 800-233-2628. Departs 11:30am, 2:30pm. $55 per person.)*

OUTSIDE THE QUARTER

WATERFRONT. The **Riverwalk,** a multimillion-dollar conglomeration of overpriced shops overlooking the port, stretches along the Mississippi. *(☎522-1555. Open M-Sa 10am-9pm, Su 11am-7pm.)* Take a chance on the newly opened **Harrah's New Orleans Casino,** at Canal St. and the river. An endless Mardi Gras of slot machines suck down depressingly less endless buckets of quarters. *(☎800-427-7247. 21+. Open 24hr.)* For an up-close view of the Mississippi River and a unique New Orleans district, take the free **Canal Street Ferry** to Algiers Point. The Algiers of old was home to many of New Orleans' African-Americans and was the birthplace of many of the city's famous jazz museums. Once called "The Brooklyn of the South," it is now a quiet, beautiful neighborhood to explore by foot. Stop at the **Dry Dock Cafe,** just off the ferry landing, to pick up a map of the area. At night, the ferry's outdoor observation deck affords a panoramic view of the city's sights. *(Departs daily every 30min. 5:45am-midnight, from the end of Canal St. Cars $1 round-trip.)*

WAREHOUSE ARTS DISTRICT. Relatively new to the downtown area, the **Warehouse Arts District,** centered roughly at the intersection of Julia and Camp St., contains several revitalized warehouse buildings turned contemporary art galleries, as well as many of the city's museums. The galleries feature widely attended exhibition openings the first Saturday of every month. On **White Linen Night,** the first Saturday in August, thousands take to the streets donning their fanciest white finery.

(☎ 522-1999; www.neworleansartsdistrictassociation.com for Arts District info.) In an old brick building with a modern glass-and-chrome facade, the **Contemporary Arts Center** mounts exhibits ranging from puzzling to cryptic. *(900 Camp St. ☎ 528-3805; www.cacno.org. Internet access. Open Tu-Su 11am-5pm. Exhibits $5, students and seniors $3, under 12 free. Th free.)* In the rear studio of the **New Orleans School of Glassworks and Printmaking Studio,** observe students and instructors transform blobs of molten glass into vases and sculptures. *(727 Magazine St. ☎ 529-7277. Open winter M-Sa 10am-6pm; summer M-F 10am-5:30pm. Free.)* **The Jonathan Ferrara Gallery** hosts an annual "No Dead Artists: A Juried Exhibition of New Orleans Art Today" every April. Ferrara was nationally recognized for his involvement in "Guns in the Hands of Artists," a 1996 program in which people turned in guns to be made into works of art. His gallery hosts all sorts of local artists. *(841 Carondelet St. ☎ 522-5471. Open Tu-Sa noon-6pm. Free.)* Just west of the Warehouse District, the **Zeitgeist Multi-Disciplinary Arts Center** offers films, theatrical and musical performances, and art exhibitions. Alternative, experimental, and provocative, the center states their mission as, "Something for and against everyone!" *(1724 Oretha Castle Haley Blvd., 4 blocks north of St. Charles St. ☎ 525-2767.)* A few blocks west on St. Charles St., in **Lee Circle,** stands a bronze Confederate Gen. Robert E. Lee, continuing to stare down the Yankees: he faces due North.

BEFORE YOU DIE, READ THIS: Being dead in New Orleans has always been a problem. Because the city lies 4-6 ft. below sea level, a 6 ft. hole in the earth fills up with 5 ft. of water. At one time coffins literally floated in the graves, while cemetery workers pushed them down with long wooden poles. One early solution was to bore holes in the coffins allowing them to sink. Unfortunately, the sight of a drowning coffin coupled with the awful gargling sound of its immersion proved too much for the families of the departed. Burial soon became passé, and stiffs were laid to rest in beautiful raised stone tombs. Miles and miles of these ghastly structures now fill the city's graveyards and ghost stories.

SAINT CHARLES STREETCAR. Much of the Crescent City's fame derives from the **Vieux Carré,** but areas uptown have their fair share of beauty and action. The **Saint Charles Streetcar** still runs west of the French Quarter, passing some of the city's finest buildings, including the 19th-century homes along **Saint Charles Avenue.** *Gone With the Wind*-o-philes will recognize the whitewashed bricks and elegant doorway of the house on the far right corner of Arabella St.—it's a replica of Tara. But frankly, my dear, it's not open to the public. For more views of fancy living, get off the streetcar in the **Garden District,** an opulent neighborhood around Jackson and Louisiana Ave.

CITY PARK. Brimming with golf courses, ponds, statues, Greek Revival gazebos, softball fields, a stadium, and **Storyland,** a theme park for kids, City Park is a huge green wonderland of non-alcoholic activities. The **New Orleans Botanical Garden** is also found here. *(1 Palm Dr., at the northern end of Esplanade Ave. ☎ 482-4888. Maps at Jackson Sq. Visitors Center.)*

HISTORIC HOMES & PLANTATIONS

Called the "Great Showplace of New Orleans," **Longue Vue House and Gardens** epitomizes the grand Southern estate with lavish furnishings, opulent decor, and sculpted gardens inspired by the Spanish Alhambra. *(7 Bamboo Rd., off Metairie Rd. ☎ 488-5488. Tours every hr. M-Sa 10am-4:30pm, Su 1-5pm. $10, seniors $9, students $5, under 5 free. Tours available in English, French, German, Spanish, Italian, and Japanese.)* On the way to Longue Vue, pause for a peek at the 85 ft. tall monument among the raised tombs in the **Metairie Cemetery,** where country/rock legend Gram Parsons is buried. Across from downtown New Orleans, **River Road** curves along the Mississippi River accessing several plantations preserved from the 19th century. *Great River*

Road Plantation Parade: A River of Riches, available at the New Orleans or Baton Rouge Visitors Centers, contains a good map and descriptions of the houses. Pick carefully, since a tour of all the privately owned plantations is expensive. Those below are listed in order from New Orleans to Baton Rouge.

HERMANN-GRIMM HISTORIC HOUSE. Built in 1831, the house exemplifies French style, replete with a large central hall, guillotine windows, a fan-lit entrance, and original parterre beds. On Thursdays from October to May, volunteers demonstrate period cooking in an 1830s Creole kitchen. *(820 St. Louis St. ☎525-5661. Tours every hr. M-F 10am-4pm; last tour 3:30pm. $6, ages 8-18 $5.)*

GALLIER HOUSE MUSEUM. The elegantly restored residence of James Gallier, Jr., the city's most famous architect, displays the taste and lifestyle of the wealthy in the 1860s. *(1118-1132 Royal St. ☎525-5661. Open M-F 10am-4pm; last tour 3:30pm. $6; students, seniors, and ages 8-18 $5; under 8 free.)*

SAN FRANCISCO PLANTATION HOUSE. Beautifully maintained since 1856, the San Francisco is an example of Creole style with a bright blue, peach, and green exterior. *(Rte. 44, 2 mi. northwest of Reserve, 42 mi. from New Orleans on the east bank of the Mississippi. Exit 206 off I-10. ☎535-2341 or 888-322-1756. Tours daily Mar.-Oct. 9:40am-4:30pm; Nov.-Feb. 10am-4pm. $10, ages 12-17 $5, ages 6-11 $3. First tour leaves 9:40am, last tour 4pm.)*

LAURA: A CREOLE PLANTATION. Laura, unlike the others on the riverbank, was owned and operated by slave-owning Creoles who lived a life entirely apart from that of white antebellum planters. Br'er Rabbit hopped into his first briar patch here, the site of the first recorded "Compair Lapin" West African stories. A valuable, entirely unique look at plantation life in the south. *(2247 Hwy. 18/River Rd., at the intersection of Rte. 20 in Vacherie. ☎225-265-7690 or 888-799-7690. Tours based on the "memories" of the old plantation home daily 9:30am-4pm. $10.)*

OAK ALLEY. The name Oak Alley refers to the magnificent lawn-alley bordered by 28 evenly spaced oaks corresponding to the 28 columns surrounding the Greek Revival house. The Greeks wouldn't have approved, though: the mansion is bright pink. *(3645 Rte. 18., between St. James and Vacherie St. ☎800-442-5539. Tours daily every 30min. Mar.-Oct. 9am-5:30pm; Nov.-Feb. 9am-5pm. $10, ages 13-18 $6, ages 6-12 $4.)*

NOTTOWAY. The largest plantation home in the South, Nottoway is often called the "White Castle of Louisiana." A 64-room mansion with 22 columns, a large ballroom, and a three-story stairway, it was the first choice for filming *Gone with the Wind*, but the owners wouldn't allow it. *(30970 Hwy. Rte. 405., between Bayou Goula and White Castle, 18 mi. south of Baton Rouge on the southern bank of the Mississippi. ☎225-545-2730 or 888-323-8314. Open daily 9am-5pm. Admission and 1hr. tour $10, under 12 $4.)*

MUSEUMS

New Orleans Pharmacy Museum, 514 Chartres St. (☎565-8027), between St. Louis and Toulouse St. This apothecary shop was built by America's first licensed pharmacist in 1823. On display in the old house are 19th-century "miracle drugs" like cocaine and opium, voodoo powders, a collection of old spectacles, the still-fertile botanical garden, and live leeches. Open Tu-Su 10am-5pm. $2, students and seniors $1, under 12 free.

National D-Day Museum, 945 Magazine St. (☎527-6012), in the Historic Warehouse District on the corner of Magazine St. and Andrew Higgins Dr. Founded by renowned historian Stephen Ambrose and dedicated in 2000 by Tom Hanks and Stephen Spielberg, this museum lives up to its hype. An engaging, exhaustive, and moving study of WWII in its entirety, the museum confronts the lesser-known, gruesome Pacific battles and the prickly, ugly issues of race and propaganda. The project is remarkable, especially for its unbiased scrutiny. Open daily 9am-5pm. $10; students, seniors, and military with ID $6; ages 5-17 $5; military in uniform free.

African-American Museum of Art, Culture, and History, 1418 Governor Nicholls St. (☎565-7497), 4 blocks north of Rampart St. in Tremé. In an 1829 Creole-style villa rescued from blight in 1991, this museum displays a wide variety of changing and permanent exhibits showcasing local and national African-American artists, along with important historical themes. Slightly off the beaten path and well worth the trek, the museum reveals a different New Orleans from the showy one of the French Quarter. Open M-F 10am-5pm, Sa 10am-2pm. $5, seniors $3, ages 4-17 $2.

Louisiana State Museum, P.O. Box 2448, New Orleans 70176 (☎800-568-6968; lsm.crt.state.la.us). The "State Museum" really oversees 8 separate museums, 6 of which are in New Orleans. The **Cabildo,** 701 Chartres St., portrays the history of Louisiana from Indian times to the present and holds Napoleon's death mask. The **Arsenal,** 615 St. Peter (enter through the Cabildo), studies the history of the Mississippi River and New Orleans as a port city. The **Presbytère,** 751 Chartres St., features a gigantic and very interactive exhibit about the history of Mardi Gras. The **1850 House,** 523 St. Ann St., on Jackson Sq., is–you guessed it–a recreated house from the time period. **Madame John's Legacy,** 632 Dumaine St., showcases a rare example of Creole architecture as well as an exhibit on contemporary self-taught Louisiana artists. The **Old US Mint,** 400 Esplanade, focuses not only on currency, but on the history of jazz in an exhibit that includes Satchmo's first horn. All open Tu-Su 9am-5pm. Old US Mint, Cabildo, Presbytère: $5; students, seniors, and active military $4. 1850 House, Mme. John's Legacy: $3/2. Under 12 free for all museums. 20% discount on tickets to 2 or more museums.

New Orleans Museum of Art (NOMA) (☎488-2631; www.noma.org) in City Park, at the City Park/Metairie Exit off I-10. This magnificent museum houses art from North and South America, one of the 5 best glass collections in existence, opulent works by the jeweler Fabergé, a strong collection of French paintings, and some of the best African and Japanese cultural collections in the country. Be sure to check out the newly opened sculpture garden. Open Tu-Su 10am-5pm. $6, seniors $5, ages 3-17 $3. Call for tickets to special exhibits.

The Voodoo Museum, 724 Dumaine St., in the Quarter. At this quirky haunt, learn why all those dusty shops in the Quarter are selling *gris-gris* and alligator parts. A priest or a priestess will be glad to do a reading or a ritual for a fee, or visitors can just walk through the rooms full of portraits and artifacts for the basic entrance fee. Open daily 10am-7:30pm. $7; students, seniors, and military $5.50; high school students $4.50; ages 12 and under $3.50.

Musée Conti Wax Museum, 917 Conti St. (☎525-2605 or 800-233-5405), between Burgundy and Dauphine St. A great mix of the historically important, sensationally infamous, and just plain kitschy history of New Orleans in 31 tableaux. Perennial favorites include a voodoo scene and a mock-up of Madame LaLaurie's torture attic. Open M-Sa 10am-5:30pm, Su noon-5:30pm. $6.75, seniors $6.25, under 17 $5.75.

Confederate Museum, 929 Camp St. (☎523-4522), in a brownstone building called Memorial Hall, just south of Lee Circle at Howard St. and the I-10 Camp St. Exit. The state's oldest museum is a wood-beamed, ancient hall lined with Confederate uniforms, flags, and a substantial amount of Jefferson Davis memorabilia. Open M-Sa 10am-4pm. $5, students and seniors $4, under 12 $2.

GIRLS GONE WILD French quarter shops sell beads for $1-5, but why buy them when you can *earn* them? The best bead bartering locations are strung along the 700th block of Bourbon St., especially near the balconies above the Cat's Meow and Tricou House. Women (and even men) who flash body parts on the street are compensated with beads. Only in New Orleans is exposing oneself so colorfully rewarded.

ENTERTAINMENT

THEATER & MUSIC

Le Petit Théâtre du Vieux Carré, 616 St. Peters St., is one of the city's most beloved and historical theaters. The oldest continuously operating community theater in the US, the 1789 building replicates the early 18th-century abode of Joseph de Pontalba, Louisiana's last Spanish governor. About five musicals and plays go up each year, as well as three fun productions in the "Children's Corner." (☎522-9958. Box office open M-Sa 10:30am-5:30pm, Su noon-5pm. $20 for plays, $26 for musicals.)

Uptown tends to house authentic Cajun dance halls and popular university hangouts, while the **Marigny** is home to New Orleans' alternative/local music scene. Check out *Off Beat*, free in many local restaurants; *Where Y'At*, another free entertainment weekly; or the Friday *Times-Picayune* to find out who's playing where. Born at the turn of the century in **Armstrong Park,** traditional New Orleans jazz still wails nightly at the tiny, historic **Preservation Hall,** 726 St. Peters St. With only two small ceiling fans trying to move the air around, most people can only stay for one set, meaning you can usually expect to find a place to listen. (Daytime ☎522-2841 or 800-785-5772; after 8pm ☎523-8939. No food or drink allowed. Cover $5. Doors open at 8pm; music 8:30pm-midnight.) Keep your ears open for **Cajun** and **zydeco** bands, which use accordions, washboards, triangles, and drums to perform hot dance tunes and saccharine waltzes. Anyone who thinks couple-dancing went out in the 50s should try a *fais-do-do*, a traditional dance that got its name from the custom parents had of putting their children to sleep before dancing the night away. (*Fais-do-do* is Cajun baby talk for "to make sleep.")

FESTIVALS

New Orleans' **Mardi Gras** celebration is the biggest party of the year, a world-renowned, epic bout of lascivious debauchery that fills the three weeks leading up to Ash Wednesday—the beginning of Lent and a time of penance and deprivation in the Catholic tradition. Mardi Gras, which literally means "Fat Tuesday," is an all-out hedonistic pleasure-fest before 40 days of purity. Parades, gala, balls, and general revelry take to the streets as tourists pour in by the plane-full (flights into the city and hotel rooms fill up months in advance). In 2004, Mardi Gras falls on February 24th, and the biggest parades and bulk of the partying will take place the two weeks prior to that. The ever-expanding **New Orleans Jazz and Heritage Festival** (Apr. 22-May 2, 2004) attracts 7000 musicians from around the country to the city's fairgrounds. The likes of Aretha Franklin, Bob Dylan, and Wynton Marsalis have graced this festival. Less drunken than its Mardi Gras counterpart, music plays simultaneously on 12 stages in the midst of a food and crafts festival; the biggest names perform evening riverboat concerts. (☎522-4786; www.nojazzfest.com.)

NIGHTLIFE

BARS

FRENCH QUARTER

Lafitte's Blacksmith Shop, 941 Bourbon St. (☎522-9377), at Phillip St. Appropriately, one of New Orleans' oldest standing structures is a bar—one of the oldest bars in the US. Built in the 1730s, the building is still lit by candlelight after sunset. Named for the scheming hero of the Battle of New Orleans, it offers shaded relief from the elements of the city and a dim hiding place for celebrities. Live piano 8pm until late. Beers $4-5. Open daily 10 or 11am to 4 or 5am.

Funky Butt, 714 N. Rampart St. (☎558-0872), is an awesome hideout to hear some late live jazz and marvel at the wonder of the *derrière.* Walk in to face a gigantic, languorous nude painting and hear the strains of a live band 5 ft. from the door. Stay to sip a funky-buttjuice ($6) and sit with only a score of people in the tiny space alongside the band. 7pm house band. Sets nightly 10pm and midnight. Cover $5-10. Open daily 7pm-2am.

Donna's, 800 N. Rampart St. (☎596-6914). As one fan says, this is "the place where you can sit and watch New Orleans roll by." On the edge of the French Quarter, right where the gay bars face the projects, the extremes of the city swirl together in front of Donna's. Brass bands play inside, and the smell of ribs and chicken wafts out as customers sit on the sidewalk and take it all in. Open M and F-Su 6:30pm-1:30am.

Fritzel's, 733 Bourbon St. (☎561-0432), between Orleans and St. Ann, was opened over 30 years ago by a German proprietor who wanted to give musicians of all abilities the chance to play. Since its opening, it has hosted some of the best jazz in the Quarter every night and, although cocktails are still Bourbon St. pricey ($6 for most beers), there's no cover. Open daily 11am-2am.

Pat O'Brien's, 718 St. Peters St. (☎525-4823). Housed in the 1st Spanish theater in the US, this busy bar, one of the most famous in the French Quarter, bursts with rosy-cheeked patrons who carouse in a courtyard lined with plants and flowers. Home of the original Hurricane. If you're feeling sentimental, purchase your first in a souvenir glass ($9, without glass $6). Open M-Th 10am-4am, F-Su 10am-5am.

Pirate's Alley, 622 Pirate's Alley (☎586-0468), down the alley on your left when facing the front of St. Louis Cathedral. Alley cats will rub your ankles as you sip a white russian ($6). Its location on a side street in the Quarter, compounded by the plain wooden walls and awnings, make this bar feel like a safehaven in what can be a sensory-overload city. Open daily 10am-4am. *Do not pet the kitties, they don't know what love is.*

OUTSIDE THE QUARTER

The Spotted Cat, 623 Frenchmen St. (☎943-3887), is what you might have imagined—or wished—most New Orleans bars would be like: cheap beer (or $20 bottles of champagne, if you're looking to live the high life) and passion-filled trumpets, voices, and piano solos that pour out the open front door onto the sidewalk. The wooden walls and floors make for excellent acoustics as well as ambience. "Early" band 6:30pm, "late" band 10:00pm. Never a cover, just a 1-drink min. (domestics $2 during Happy Hour). Open daily 4pm-late.

THE LOCAL STORY

GENDER JAMBALAYA

Crystal, 60, is a leading member of the BGLT community in New Orleans. A transsexual, she says she was one of the first to bring about awareness that there are transgendered people—"common, everyday people"—in the community. Today, she is active in many organizations serving the BGLT community.

Q: Would you say that New Orleans is the most gay-friendly city in the US?

A: Yes, most definitely. New Orleans has always been a melting pot, because it was a port, and so much of the world came in. Everyone in a neighborhood had to live and work together, and you had to learn to accept those who were different.

Q: How does gay life in New Orleans differ from other cities?

A: The New Orleans community is unique—the whole community works very well together. Those who are just cross-dressers often don't have a ton of places to go. But you'll notice we don't have any "segregated" bars, that is, between men and women, leather and trans, etc. I used to work at one of the biggest women's bars in New Orleans, and I'd be at the door and we'd have people from New York and San Fran who were amazed that there were men, women, everybody else in the bar. "Oh, we don't do this at home." Well, that's your problem. That's what we do here.

Snug Harbor, 626 Frenchmen St. (☎949-0696), near Decatur St. Regulars include big names in modern jazz like Charmaine Neville and Ellis Marsalis. Cover is sometimes steep ($12-18), but the music, played in the beautiful and intimate cypress "jazz room" is some of the best in the city. All ages. Shows nightly 9, 11pm. Reservations and advance ticket purchase recommended, especially for weekend events. Restaurant open Su-Th 5-11pm, F-Sa 5pm-midnight; bar until 1am. The kitchen closes early some nights depending on the act; call ahead to find out if they are serving.

Checkpoint Charlie's, 501 Esplanade (☎949-7012), is a combination bar, laundromat, and restaurant that feels like a cozy neighborhood coffeeshop or a wild nightclub, depending on where you're standing. In one night here you can drink while you wash your clothes, listen to a poetry slam over jazz, buy a used book, or have a greasy burger while shooting a game of pool. Live music nightly, usually starting around 10pm. Beer $2-3, pitchers $7.50. Burgers $5-7. No cover. Food served 24hr.

Carrollton Station, 8140 Willow St. (☎865-9190), at Dublin St. A cozy neighborhood club with live music, antique bar games, and friendly folks. As one of the regulars says, this is "a place with character full of characters." 12 beers on tap ($2-5) and well-stocked bar. Music F-Sa at 10pm. Cover varies, usually $5-8. Open daily 3pm-6am.

d.b.a., 618 Frenchmen St. (☎942-3731), next to Snug Harbor. Try one of the beers on tap in their wood-paneled bar. Live music most nights at 10pm. Monthly beer and tequila tastings. No cover. 1-drink min. Open M-F 4pm-4am, Sa-Su 4pm-5am.

DANCE CLUBS

FRENCH QUARTER

El Matador, 504 Esplanade Ave. (☎569-8361). A mix of patrons and a wide range of musical styles make this nightclub a good place to relax and start the night. Usually no cover, but it varies according to the fame of the band. Live flamenco show Sa 7:30pm. Open M-Th 9pm until late, F-Su 4pm-late.

House of Blues, 225 Decatur St. (☎529-2624). A sprawling complex with a large music/dance hall (capacity over 1000) and a balcony and bar overlooking the action. Concerts nightly 9:15pm. 18+. Cover usually $5-10, big names up to $30. Restaurant open Su-Th 11am-11pm, F-Sa 11am-midnight.

735 Nightclub and Bar, 735 Bourbon St. (☎581-6740). Dance music and a hip mixed crowd keep this club energized well into the night. Techno, progressive house, and trance play downstairs, with 80s music on the back patio every Th. 18+. Cover $5, under 21 $10. Open W-Su 2pm-3am.

OUTSIDE THE QUARTER

Tipitina's, 501 Napoleon Ave. (☎895-8477). The best local bands and some big national names—such as the Neville Brothers and Harry Connick, Jr.—play so close you can almost touch them. Su 5-9pm feature Cajun *fais-do-dos* (see p. 470). 18+. Cover $4-25. Music usually W-Su 10:30pm; call ahead for times and prices.

Mid City Lanes Rock 'n' Bowl, 4133 S. Carrollton Ave. (☎482-3133), in the mini-mall at Tulane Ave. Since 1941, this place has attracted the few, the lucky, and the multitasking partiers. The "home of Rock 'n' Bowl" is a bowling alley by day and traditional dance club by night (you can bowl at night, too). Lanes $12 per hr. plus $1 for shoes. Drinks $2.50-3.50. Live music Tu-W 8:30pm, local zydeco Th 9:30pm, F-Sa 10pm. 18+ at night when the bar gets hopping. Cover $3-10. Open daily noon to around 1 or 2am.

Cafe Brasil, 2100 Chartres St. (☎949-0851). Unassuming by day, Brasil is full on weekend nights with regulars and out-of-towners who come to see a wide variety of New Orleans talent. All ages. Cover F-Sa after 11am $6-10. Open daily 7pm-late.

GAY & LESBIAN ACTIVITIES

New Orleans also has a vibrant gay scene, rivalling and perhaps surpassing that of San Francisco. Gay establishments cluster toward the northeast end of Bourbon St., and St. Ann St. is known to some as the **"Lavender Line."** The oldest bar in the city was gay-friendly farther back than anybody can remember—meaning that, yes, one of the first bars on American soil was a de facto gay bar.

Facts like this only skim the surface of gay history in New Orleans. Luckily, someone is keeping track: Robert Batson, "history laureate" of New Orleans, leads the **Gay Heritage Tour**—a walking tour through the French Quarter—leaving from Alternatives, 909 Bourbon St. It lasts for 2½hr. and is perhaps the best possible introduction to New Orleans for anyone, gay or straight. (☎945-6789. W and Sa 2pm. $20 per person. Reservations required.)

As for gay nightlife, to find the real lowdown, get a copy of *The Whiz Magazine*, a locally produced guide to BGLT nightlife; there's always a copy on top of the radiator in Cafe Lafitte in Exile. *Ambush* and *Eclipse* are more impersonal, mass-produced gay entertainment mags that can be found at many French Quarter businesses. For info and tailored entertainment and community fact sheets, go to the **Lesbian and Gay Community Center of New Orleans,** 2114 Decatur St., in Marigny. (☎945-1103. Open M-W 2-8pm, Th-F noon-8pm, Sa 11am-6pm, Su noon-6pm. Report hate crimes to ☎944-4325.)

NIGHTLIFE

Cafe Lafitte in Exile, 901 Bourbon St. (☎522-8397). This is where it all started. Exiled from Laffite's Blacksmith Shop in 1953 when Lafitte's came under new management, the ousted gay patrons trooped up the street to found this haven, the oldest gay bar in America. On the opening night, surrounded by patrons dressed as their favorite exile, Cafe Lafitte in Exile lit an "eternal flame" (it still burns today) that aptly represents the soul of the gay community in New Orleans. Today, though Cafe Lafitte has video screens, occasional live music, pageants, and shows, it's still the same old neighborhood gathering place at heart. Open 24hr.

Kim's 940, 940 Elysian Fields Ave. (☎944-4888, for guest house info 258-2224). If you're a girl, go here. This new bar/dance club/guest house has quickly become the center of the New Orleans lesbian circuit, which is much smaller than the male-oriented nightlife. Dancing, drinking, and flirting mesh alongside the official BGLT Pride events and gatherings Kim's often hosts. All are welcome. Live DJ Th-Sa. Cover F $3, Sa $5. Open daily 4pm until everyone goes home.

Good Friends, 740 Dauphine St. (☎566-7191). This is a gay "Cheers" episode. A cozy, friendly neighborhood bar full of locals who are all too happy to welcome in a refugee from Bourbon St. They host the occasional pool tournament, drink specials, and "hot buns" contest, but usually things are pretty calm. Open 24hr.

Cowpokes, 2240 St. Claude Ave. (☎947-0505), 1 block off Elysian Fields in Marigny. Line dancing, country-western games, 10-gallon hats, and spurs can be as wholesome as you want to make them. Both cowgirls and pardners are welcome. Th ladies' night, country line dancing lessons and 2-for-1 drinks 8-11pm. Open Su-Th 4pm-1am, F-Sa 4pm-2am.

OUTDOOR ACTIVITIES

The St. Charles Streetcar eventually makes its way to **Audubon Park,** near **Tulane University.** Audubon contains lagoons, statues, stables, and the award-winning **Audubon Zoo,** 6500 Magazine St., where white alligators swim in a recreated Louisiana swamp. Tigers, elephants, rhinos, sea lions, among others are grouped into exhibit areas that highlight historical and natural regions of the globe, while peacocks roam the walkways freely. Free museum shuttle between park entrance and zoo every 15min. (☎581-4629. Zoo open winter daily 9:30am-5pm; in summer M-F 9:30am-5pm, Sa-Su 9:30am-6pm. $10, seniors $6, ages 2-12 $5.)

One of the most unique sights in the New Orleans area, the coastal wetlands along Lake Salvador make up a segment of the **Jean Lafitte National Historical Park** called the **Barataria Preserve,** 7400 Barataria Blvd. South of New Orleans, take Business 90 to Rte. 45. (☎589-2330. Daily park-sponsored foot tour through the swamp 11am. Open daily 7am-5pm; extended summer hours. **Visitors Center** open daily 9am-5pm. Free.) Many commercial boat tours operate around the park; **Cypress Swamp Tours** will pick you up from your hotel for free. (☎581-4501 or 800-633-0503. 2hr. tours 9:30, 11:30am, 1:30, 3:30pm. $22, ages 6-12 $12. Call for reservations.)

BATON ROUGE ☎225

Once the site of a tall cypress tree marking the boundary between rival Native American tribes, Baton Rouge ("red stick") has blossomed into Louisiana's second largest city. State politics have shaped this town—it was once home to notorious governor, senator, and demagogue "Kingfish" Huey P. Long. The presence of **Louisiana State University (LSU)** adds an element of youth and rabid Tigertown loyalty. Baton Rouge has a simple meat-and-potatoes flavor, albeit spiced with a history of political corruption, that stands in contrast to the sauciness of New Orleans.

ORIENTATION AND PRACTICAL INFORMATION. From east to west, the main streets in Baton Rouge are N. Foster Dr., N. Acadian Thwy., and 22nd St. Baton Rouge Terr., Florida St., and Government St. run perpendicular to these, beginning in the north. Close to downtown, **Greyhound,** 1253 Florida Blvd. (☎383-3811 or 800-231-2222; open 24hr.), at 13th St., sends buses to Lafayette (1hr., 12 per day, $12.25) and New Orleans (2hr., 8 per day, $11). *The area is unsafe at night.* **Buses: Capitol Transportation,** ☎389-8282. **Taxi: Yellow Cab,** ☎926-6400. **Visitor Info: State Capitol Visitors Center,** on the first floor of the State Capitol. (☎342-7317. Open daily 8am-4:30pm.) **Baton Rouge Convention and Visitors Bureau,** 730 North Blvd. (☎382-3595; www.bracvb.com. Open M-F 8am-5pm.) For community information, including weather, call **Community Connection** (☎267-4221). **Internet Access: State Library of Louisiana,** 701 N. Fourth St., a beautiful library with free, fast Internet access—most often without a wait. (☎342-4915. Open daily 8am-4:30pm.) **Post Office:** 750 Florida Blvd., off River Rd. (☎800-275-8777. Open M-F 7:30am-5pm, Sa 8am-12:30pm.) **Postal Code:** 70821. **Area Code:** 225.

ACCOMMODATIONS. For the budget savvy who just need a place to rest their heads before heading out to the swamp, check out the newly built and locally-owned **Highland Inn ❷,** 2605 S. Range Ave., at I-12 Exit 10 in Denham Springs, 15min. from downtown. Only one year old, the building still gleams. (☎225-667-7177. Cable TV, continental breakfast, free local calls, and pool. Singles $44; doubles $49.) To get to the **Motel 6 ❷,** 10445 Rieger Rd., take the Siegen Ln. Exit from I-10, a 10min. drive from downtown. Newly renovated, exceptionally clean rooms make this chain experience worth the soul sacrifice. Suprisingly, pets are welcome. (☎291-4912. Cable TV, complimentary coffee, free local calls, pool, and kids under 18 stay free. Singles $35; doubles $39.) **KOA Campground ❶,** 7628 Vincent Rd., 1 mi. off I-12 at the Denham Springs Exit, keeps 110 well-maintained sites, clean facilities, and a big pool. (☎664-7281 or 800-562-5673. Sites $19; full RV hookup $28, 50 amp $30. 2 Kabins $35.)

FOOD. Downtown, sandwich shops and cafes line 3rd St.; the casinos boast some of the city's best cuisine. If you're just in the mood for some simple, small-town fare, check out the **Frostop ❶,** 402 Government St., downtown, easily spotted by the giant, gracefully-aging root beer can out front. Grilled cheese tastes great for $1.87, burgers $3, and a variety of seafood platters for $8-10. The Frostop also has an amazing selection of floats, shakes, sundaes, and malts for $2-4. (☎344-1179. Open M-F 10am-7pm, Sa 11am-7pm.) Head to LSU at the intersection of Highland Rd. and Chimes St., off I-10, for cheap chow and an abundance of bars and smoothie shops. **Louie's Cafe ❷,** 209 W. State St., grills up fabulous omelettes ($5.25-10) and some great veggie fare in a cross between college hangout and mama's kitchen. (☎346-8221. Veggie po' boy $6.75. Open 24hr.) When you want a good sit-down meal, check out **The Chimes ❸,** 3357 Highland Rd., at (surprise) Chimes St. A big restaurant and bar where you can sample a brew from almost every country, Chimes stocks 120 brews with 30 on tap. Start the meal with an appetizer of Louisiana alligator (farm-raised, marinated, fried, and served with Dijon mustard sauce) for $7.50, then dig into some $8 crawfish *étoufée.* (☎383-1754. Seafood and steak entrees $8-14. Open M-Sa 11am-2am, Su 11am-11:45pm.)

SIGHTS. In a move reminiscent of Ramses II, Huey Long ordered the construction of the striking **Louisiana State Capitol,** now referred to as "the new Capitol"—a magnificent, modern, and somewhat startling skyscraper completed over a mere 14 months in 1931 and 1932. Called "the house that Huey built," the building was meant to raise Louisiana's image and prestige and pave Long's path to the presidency of the US. It's ironic that Long was assassinated inside it 3 years later; toward the back of the first floor a display marks the exact spot of the shooting. The **observation deck,** on the 27th floor, provides a fantastic view of the surrounding area. (☎342-5914. Open daily 8am-4pm. Last tour at 3pm. Free.) The **Old State Capitol,** 100 North Blvd., resembles a cathedral with a fantastic cast-iron spiral staircase and domed stained glass. Inside are interactive political displays urging voter responsibility alongside exhibits about Huey P. and Louisiana's tumultuous (and often corrupt) political history. (☎800-488-2968. Open Tu-Sa 10am-4pm, Su noon-4pm. $4, seniors $3, students $2.) The **Old Governor's Mansion,** 502 North Blvd., may look a little familiar—the venerable Huey Long insisted that his governor's residence resemble his ultimate goal—the White House. Inside, a museum displays many of Long's personal belongings including a book he wrote, somewhat prematurely, called *My First Days in the White House.* (☎387-2464. Open Tu-F 10am-4pm, but hours may vary. $5, seniors $4, students $3.)

The **Louisiana Art and Science Museum (LASM),** 100 S. River Rd., is a large, expanding complex and a strange combination of art gallery and hands-on science museum that recently opened a state-of-the-art planetarium. From June 2 to Aug. 1, 2004, LASM will exhibit *The Land Through a Lens: American Photography from the Smithsonian Institution.* (☎344-5272. Open Tu-F 10am-3pm, Sa 10am-4pm, Su 1-4pm. $4; students, seniors, and children $3. First Su of every month free.) At the **USS Kidd and Nautical Center,** 305 S. River Rd., at Government St. and the Mississippi River, you can check out the *Destroyer Kidd,* which was hit directly by a kamikaze during its career and has been restored to its WWII glory. (☎342-1942. Open daily 9am-5pm. $6, children $3.50.)

The **LSU Rural Life Museum,** 4560 Essen Ln., just off I-10 at Exit 160, depicts the life of 18th- and 19th-century Creoles and working-class Louisianans through their original furnished shops, cabins, and storage houses. Right next door, explore the lakes, winding paths, and flowers of the **Windrush Gardens.** (☎765-2437. Both open daily 8:30am-5pm. $5, seniors $4, ages 5-12 $3.)

NATCHITOCHES ☎318

Be careful not to say it how it's spelled; pronounced *NAK-ah-tish*, the oldest city in Louisiana was founded in 1714 by the French to facilitate trade with the Spanish in Mexico. The town was named after the original Native American inhabitants of the region. With its strategic location along the banks of the Red River, Natchitoches should have become a major port city, much like New Orleans. A big logjam, however, changed the course of the city's history, redirecting the Red River and leaving the town high and dry, with only a 36 mi. long lake running along historic downtown. More recently, the town was the setting of the 1988 movie *Steel Magnolias*, which cast most of the townspeople as extras.

ORIENTATION & PRACTICAL INFORMATION. Downtown Natchitoches is tiny. **Highway 6** enters town from the west off I-49 and becomes **Front Street,** the main drag, where it follows the **Cane River,** running north until it becomes Hwy. 6 again. **Second Street** runs parallel to Front St., and the town stems out across the lake from those two streets. Historic homes highlight the town, while the plantations lie from 7 to 18 mi. south of town, off **Route 1 South.** Both the plantations and Rte. 1 follow the Cane River. **Greyhound,** 331 Cane River Shopping Center (☎352-8341; open M-F 8am-5pm), sends buses to: Dallas (6hr., 3 per day, $55); Houston (8-10hr., 2 per day, $59); New Orleans (6½hr., 3 per day, $49). Visitor info is at **Natchitoches Convention and Visitors Bureau,** 781 Front St. (☎352-8072 or 800-259-1714; www.natchitoches.net. Open M-F 8am-6pm, Sa 9am-5pm, Su 10am-4pm.) The **Post Office** is at 240 Saint Denis St. (☎352-2161. Open M-F 8am-4:30pm, Sa 9-11am.) **Postal Code:** 71457. **Area Code:** 318.

ACCOMMODATIONS. Natchitoches isn't a cheap town. As the "B&B Capital" of Louisiana, Natchitoches abounds with cozy rooms in historic homes (nearly 40 total), and the ambiance comes with a higher price. Beware of Christmas time; during the annual **Festival of Lights** (see below), room rates as much as triple, and reservations are booked months in advance. The **Natchitoches Convention and Visitors Bureau** has a handy listing of all the B&Bs in town.

An authentic taste of Natchitoches can be had at the elegant and more than reasonably-priced **Chaplin House Bed and Breakfast ❸,** 434 Second St. The proprietors of this exquisitely restored and decorated 1892 home boast a wealth of local knowledge. (☎352-2324; www.natchitoches.net/chaplin. Full continental breakfast. Singles $55; doubles $80.) One of the best deals is the **Fleur de Lis Bed and Breakfast ❸,** 336 Second St., near the southern end of town, an adorable, gingerbready Victorian with a whimsical pastel exterior and quirky flavor all its own. (☎352-6621 or 800-489-6621. Rooms Jan.-Nov. $65-85; Dec. $100.)

West of town, you'll find the well-furnished **Microtel Inn ❸,** 5335 Rte. 6 W. (☎214-0700 or 888-771-7171. A/C, cable TV, fridges, pool access, and continental breakfast. Singles $52; doubles $60. 10% AAA discount.) Further out, the 600,000-acre **Kisatchie National Forest ❶** offers basic outdoor living with trails and scenic overlooks. The park is about 25 mi. south of the Rte. 6 Ranger Station near Natchitoches, and many of its sites, though equipped with bathhouses, are primitive. The **Kisatchie Ranger District,** 106 Rte. 6 W, ¼ mi. past the Microtel Inn, has maps, camping information, and park conditions, and provides help finding the well-hidden sites. (☎352-2568. Open M-F 8am-4:30pm. Sites $2-3.)

FOOD & NIGHTLIFE. Lasyone's ❷, 622 2nd St., is the place to go for down-home cooking. Their specialty is meat pie ($2.75; with salad bar and veggies $7.25), and travelers can get an eyeful of the 5 ft. model in the window before enjoying a more manageable size. (☎352-3353. Lunch specials $6. Open M-Sa 7am-6pm.) **Ma Mere's ❶,** 612 Front St., also has meat pies ($2.25), an array of deli sandwiches ($5), and several specialty fudges and sweets ($2-3). Sit outside or in. (☎352-1606. M-Sa 9am-5:30pm, Su 9am-3pm.) **Mama's Oyster House ❸,** 606 Front St., is a downtown staple, cooking up lunch gumbo for $9 a bowl and oyster po' boys for $7. For dinner, fried crawfish ($12) complements the live entertainment on the first and third Friday of each month. (☎356-7874. Open M-Sa 11am-10pm.) Drink with a friendly, local crowd at **Pioneer Pub,** 812 Washington St., opposite the Visitors Center. (☎352-4884. Live music Sa at 9pm. Open daily 11am-2am, or until the crowd leaves.)

SIGHTS & ENTERTAINMENT. Much of Natchitoches' charm lies on the Cane River Lake along **Front Street,** where coffeeshops, casual restaurants, and antique stores fill the storefronts of historical buildings that date back to the mid-19th century. To see Natchitoches' landmarks—including many of the *Steel Magnolias* filming sites—from the comfort of a large, green trolley, take a 1hr. ride with the **Natchitoches Transit Company,** 100 Rue Beau Port, next to the tourist center just off Front St. (☎356-8687. Call for departure times. $8, seniors $7, ages 3-12 $5.)

Many of the popular tourist destinations are in the **Cane River National Heritage Area,** the plantation-dotted countryside around Natchitoches. The Visitors Center has information about all the plantations and a free tourist newspaper, *Historic Natchitoches,* which lists points of interest in the area. To see the next generation of handbags, drive out to **Bayou Pierre Gator Park & Show,** 8 mi. north of Natchitoches off Rte. 1 N (look for the big school bus in the shape of a gator off Rte. 1). Originally a conservation project, the park now entertains visitors with regular feeding shows, a snake house, an aviary, and a nutria (swamp rats the size of small dogs) exhibit. (☎354-0001 or 877-354-7001. Open daily mid-Apr. to Oct. 10am-6pm; call for winter hours, when the alligators are hibernating. $6.50, ages 3-12 $4.75.) A string of plantation homes line the Cane River, south of downtown along Rte. 1. The **Melrose Plantation,** 14 mi. south on Rte. 1, then left on Rte. 493, is unique in origin—its female founder was an ex-slave. The African House, one of the outhouses, is the oldest structure of Congo-like architecture on the North American continent. (☎379-0055. Open daily noon-4pm. $6, ages 13-17 $4, ages 6-12 $3.)

While Natchitoches may not see a white Christmas, she'll most definitely see a bright one. The town's residents spend months putting up some 300,000 Christmas bulbs, only to be greeted in turn by 150,000 camera-toting tourists flocking like moths to the **City of Lights** display, held during the **Christmas Festival of Lights.** The month-long exhibition peaks the first weekend in December when a carnival-like atmosphere—complete with a fair, fireworks, and parade—fills the air. (☎800-259-1714; www.christmasfestival.com. Nov.25-Jan. 6, 2004.)

ACADIANA

Throughout the early 18th century, the English government in Nova Scotia became increasingly jealous of the prosperity of French settlers (Acadians) and deeply offended by their refusal to kneel before the British Crown. During the war with France in 1755, the British rounded up the Acadians and deported them by the shipload in what came to be called *le grand dérangement,* "the Great Upheaval." The "Cajuns" (as they are known today) of St. Martin, Lafayette, New Iberia, and St. Mary parishes are descendants of these settlers. In the 1920s, Louisiana passed laws forcing Acadian schools to teach in English. Later, during the oil boom of th 1970s and 1980s, oil executives and developers envisioned the Acadian cent Lafayette as the Houston of Louisiana and threatened to flood the area w culture. Even so, the proud people of southern Louisiana have re homogenization, and, in fact, the state is officially bilingual.

LAFAYETTE ☎337

The center of Acadiana, Lafayette is ripe for ripping up the dance floors to soul-moving zydeco, getting to know the sweet simple flavor of boiled crawfish, and experiencing the strange splendor of the magnificent Atchafalaya Basin. Get beyond the highway's chains and into downtown on Jefferson St., and there is no question that Cajuns rule the roost. Dance floors heat up every night of the week, and many locals continue to answer their phones with a proud *bonjour*.

ORIENTATION & PRACTICAL INFORMATION. Lafayette stands at a crossroads. **I-10** leads east to New Orleans and west to Lake Charles; **US 90** heads south to New Iberia and the Atchafalaya Basin, and north to Alexandria and Shreveport; **US 167** runs north into central Louisiana. Most of the city is west of the **Evangeline Thruway (U.S. 49/U.S. 90),** which runs north-south. **Jefferson Boulevard** intersects Evangeline Thwy. and is the main street through town. **Johnston Street** delineates the east border of downtown with many fast-food restaurants. **Amtrak,** 133 E. Grant St. (☎800-872-7245), sends three trains per week to: Houston (5½hr., $35); New Orleans (4hr., $21); and San Antonio (10hr., $55). **Greyhound,** 315 Lee Ave. (☎235-1541; open 24hr.), buses to: Baton Rouge (1hr., 12 per day, $12.25); New Iberia (30min., 2 per day, $7.75); and New Orleans (3½hr., 10 per day, $16.25). Amtrak and Greyhound will move to a new, central terminal in late 2003; call for details. The **Lafayette Bus System,** 1515 E. University St., is centered at Lee and Garfield St. (☎291-8570. Infrequent service M-Sa 6:30am-6:30pm; service until 11pm on some routes. Buses approximately every 30min. $0.75, ages 5-12 $0.50, seniors and disabled $0.35.) **Taxi: Yellow/Checker Cab Inc.,** ☎234-2111. **Visitor Info: Lafayette Parish Convention and Visitors Commission,** 1400 N. Evangeline Thwy. (☎232-3808; www.lafayettetravel.com. Open M-F 8:30am-5pm, Sa-Su 9am-5pm.) **Medical Services: Lafayette General Medical Center,** 1214 Coolidge Ave. (☎289-7991). **Post Office:** 1105 Moss St. (☎269-7111. Open M-F 8am-5:30pm, Sa 8:30am-noon.) **Postal Code:** 70501. **Area Code:** 337.

ACCOMMODATIONS & FOOD. Inexpensive hotels line the Evangeline Thwy. **Travel Host Inn South ❷,** 1314 N. Evangeline, rents out clean rooms with cable TV, microwaves, fridges, continental breakfast, and an outdoor pool. (☎233-2090. Singles $32; doubles $36.) Close to the center of Lafayette, **Acadiana Park Campground ❶,** 1201 E. Alexander, off Louisiana Ave., has 75 sites with access to tennis courts and a soccer field. (☎291-8388. Office open Sa-Th 8am-5pm, F 8am-8pm. Full hookup $9.) The lakeside **KOA Lafayette ❶,** 5 mi. west of town on I-10 at Exit 97, has over 200 sites and offers a store, mini-golf course, and two pools. (☎235-2739. Office open daily 7:30am-8:30pm. Sites $19; with water and electricity $27; full hookup $29.)

It's not hard to find reasonably priced Cajun and Creole cuisine in Lafayette, a city that prides itself on its food. Of course, music is also a priority, and can be found live in most of those same restaurants at night. Since 1927, **Dwyer's Cafe ❶,** 323 J... a diner with stained glass and murals on the walls, has been the ... to get breakfast or lunch. They serve a bang-up breakfast (grits, ..., juice, and coffee) for $4. At lunch locals saunter in from the ... lunch (different every day) of gigantic proportions for $7. ...-F 5am-4pm, Sa-Su 5am-2pm.) In central Lafayette, **Chris' Po' ...** ...n St., offers seafood platters ($7-10) and—whaddya know— ...5. (☎234-1696. F night live blues and Cajun in the spring and ...am-8:30pm, F 10:30am-9pm.) **The Filling Station ❶,** 900 Jeffer-... name. Occupying the shell of an old gas station, the restau-... ...urritos and burgers for scandalously low prices. A popular,

relaxing local hangout with outdoor tables, their full bar will fill your tank nicely, too. (☎291-9625. Burritos $3. Margaritas $4.50. Kitchen open M-F 11am-9pm; bar open until people empty out.)

SIGHTS. Driving through south-central Louisiana means driving over America's largest swamp, the Atchafalaya Basin. The **Atchafalaya Freeway** (I-10 between Lafayette and Baton Rouge) crosses 32 mi. of swamp and cypress trees. Follow signs to **McGee's Landing,** 1337 Henderson Rd., which sends three 1½hr. **boat tours** into the Basin each day. (☎228-2384. Tours daily 10am, 1, 3pm. Spring and fall sunset tours by reservation. $12, seniors and under 12 $6, under 2 free.) The **Acadian Cultural Center,** 501 Fisher Rd. (take Johnston St. to Surrey, then follow the signs), is a unit of the **Jean Lafitte National Historical Park and Preserve** that runs throughout the delta region of Louisiana. The Acadian Center has a dramatic 40min. documentary chronicling the arrival of the Acadians in Louisiana, as well as a new film on conservation efforts in the Atchafalaya swamp and terrific bilingual exhibits on Cajun history and culture. (☎232-0789. Open daily 8am-5pm. Shows every hr. 9am-4pm. Free.) Next door, a "living museum" re-creates the Acadian settlement of **Vermilionville,** 1600 Surrey St., with music, crafts, food, actors in costume, and dancing on the Bayou Vermilion banks. (☎233-4077 or 800-992-2968. Live bands Su 1-4pm. Cajun cooking demos daily 10:30am, 12:30, 1:30pm. Open Tu-Su 10am-4pm. Admission closes at 3pm. $8, seniors $6.50, ages 6-18 $5.) **Acadian Village,** 200 Greenleaf Rd., features authentic 19th-century Cajun homes with a fascinating array of artifacts and displays. While at the village, view a small collection of Native American artifacts at the **Native American Museum,** or see the collection of 19th-century medical paraphernalia at the **Doctor's House.** (☎981-2489 or 800-962-9133. Both open daily 10am-5pm. $7, seniors $6, ages 6-14 $4.) Closer to downtown, **Saint John's Cathedral Oak,** 914 St. John St., shades an entire lawn with spidery branches reaching from a trunk 19 ft. in circumference. The largest branch weighs an astonishing 72 *tons*.

ENTERTAINMENT & NIGHTLIFE. While in Lafayette, be sure to take advantage of the many local festivals and music performances, though be warned that hotel rates rise sharply with the noise level. Lafayette kicks off **Downtown Alive!,** a 12-week annual concert series held at the 700 block of Jefferson St., playing everything from New Wave to Cajun and zydeco. (☎291-5566. Apr.-June and Sept.-Nov. F 5:30pm, music 6-8:30pm.) The **Festival International de Louisiane** is the largest outdoor free francophone fes-

THE HIDDEN DEAL

I SAW YOU STANDING ALONE

For one of the best lodging experiences in the South, travelers of all stripes should head straight downtown to the Blue Moon Guest House. As you walk in, take a gander at the bottle tree in the backyard, check out the walkway paved with (fake) doubloons, or immerse yourself in the local art showcased on the surrounding walls. Chat with the hosts about their world travels in French, or let them tell about the music scene in Lafayette. The Blue Moon offers spacious common areas, a deck, backyard, and an attached "saloon" where local and out-of-town bands whoop it up Thursday through Saturday. (Of course, they're done by 11pm to give sleepy guests and neighbors some shut-eye.) Kitchen, Internet access ($3 per day), beautiful baths, large, air-conditioned dorms, and spacious, comfy private rooms are a steal. The Blue Moon Saloon, in the backyard of the hostel, is quickly making a name for itself as a nice place to have a beer and watch some local or out-of-town bands at close range.

(215 E. Convent St. Take Exit 103A from I-10, turn south on Johnston and left on Convent. ☎234-3442. Check-in 8am-noon and 5-10pm. Check-out 11am. Lockout 10am-5pm. Dorms $15; private rooms $40-55, on festival weekends $70. ❶)

tival in the US, transforming Lafayette into a gigantic, French-speaking fairground for one wild weekend in April. Book a hotel or campground well in advance; prices will likely double. (☎232-8086. April 21-25, 2004.) The **Festival de Musique Acadienne et Creole** began with the idea of educating Acadiana youth about their Cajun culture. It now attracts some of the state's best Cajun and Zydeco musicians. (☎232-3737. Sept 17-19, 2004.) The **Breaux Bridge Crawfish Festival** in nearby Breaux Bridge, 10 mi. east on I-10, stages crawfish races, live music, dance contests, cook-offs, and a crawfish-eating contest. (☎332-6655. April 30-May 2, 2004.)

To find the best zydeco in town, pick up a copy of *The Times*, free at restaurants and gas stations. On Sunday afternoons, the place to be is **Angelle's Whiskey River Landing,** 1365 Henderson Levee Rd., in Breaux Bridge, where live Cajun music heats up the dance floor on the very lip of the levee looking out over the swamp. (☎228-8567. Live music Sa 9pm-1am, Su 1-4pm.) **Hamilton's Zydeco Club,** 1808 Verot School Rd., is one of the best places in Lousiana to cut loose at night with live Cajun bands and wild dancing. (☎991-0783. Open sporadically; call or drive by to see the marquee for upcoming events and times.) **Grant Street Dance Hall,** 113 Grant St., features bands playing everything from zydeco to metal. (☎237-8513. 18+. Cover usually $5-10. Only open days of shows; call ahead.) **Randol's,** 2320 Kaliste Saloom Rd., romps with live Cajun and zydeco music nightly and doubles as a restaurant. (☎981-7080. Open Su-Th 5-10pm, F-Sa 5-11pm.)

ARKANSAS

Encompassing the Ozark and Ouachita mountains, the clear waters of Hot Springs, and miles of lush pine forests, "the Natural State" lives up to its nickname. The state's subcultures are as varied as its geography. The bluesy Mississippi Delta region seeps into east Arkansas, while the northern Ozark mountains support a close-knit, no-nonsense community with a rich heritage all its own. All across Arkansas, however, travelers are easily accepted into the friendly family.

PRACTICAL INFORMATION

Capital: Little Rock.

Visitor Info: Arkansas Department of Parks and Tourism, One Capitol Mall, Little Rock 72201 (☎501-682-7777 or 800-628-8725; www.arkansas.com). Open M-F 8am-5pm.

Postal Abbreviation: AR. **Sales Tax:** 6%.

LITTLE ROCK ☎501

Located squarely in the middle of the state along the Arkansas River, Little Rock became a major trading city in the 19th century. A small rock just a few feet high served as an important landmark for boats pushing their way upstream, and, lo and behold, Little Rock was born. The capital was the focus of a nationwide civil rights controversy in 1957, when Governor Orval Faubus and local white segregationists violently resisted nine black students who entered Central High School under the shields of the National Guard. Fortunately, Little Rock has since become a more integrated community with outdoor markets and a thriving downtown.

PRACTICAL INFORMATION. Little Rock is at the intersection of **I-40** and **I-30,** 140 mi. west of Memphis. Downtown, numbered streets run east-west, while named streets run north-south. Major thoroughfares are **Main** and **Martin Luther**

King Jr. Street. Near the river, Markham is 1st St. and Capitol is 5th St. The east side of Markham St. is now President Clinton Ave. and moves through the hopping **Riverwalk** district. North Little Rock is essentially a separate city across the river from Little Rock proper. **Greyhound,** 118 E. Washington St. (☎372-3007), at Poplar St., is in North Little Rock; take bus #7 or 18. Buses run to: Memphis (2½hr., 8 per day, $26); New Orleans (12½hr., 4 per day, $83); and St. Louis (8½hr., 1 per day, $51). **Amtrak,** 1400 W. Markham St., at Victory St. (☎372-6841; open Sa-Tu 11pm-7:30am, W-F 11pm-8am), runs from Union Station Square; take bus #1 or 8. Trains run to Dallas (6½hr., $60); Malvern, near Hot Springs (1hr., $10); and St. Louis (7hr., $53). **Central Arkansas Transit (CAT)** operates an extensive and tourist-friendly bus system through downtown and the surrounding towns. Go to the **River Cities Travel Center,** 310 E. Capitol St., to catch buses and trolleys and get detailed route and schedule info. (☎375-1163. Buses run M-Sa every 30-40min. 6am-6pm, some routes until 10pm; Su 9am-4pm. $1.10, seniors $0.50; transfers $0.10.) CAT also runs **free trolleys** from the business district to River Market. (M-F 7am-7:30pm.) Take the 6th or 9th St. exit off I-30 and follow the signs to **Little Rock Visitor Information Center,** 615 E. Capitol Ave., in the newly renovated Curran Hall. (☎370-3290 or 877-220-2568; www.littlerock.com. Open daily 8am-6pm.) **Internet Access** is available at the **Main Library,** 100 Rock St., near River Market. (☎918-3000. Open M-Th 9am-8pm, F-Sa 9am-6pm, Su 1-5pm. Free.) **Post Office:** 600 E. Capitol St. (☎375-5155. Open M-F 7am-5:30pm.) **Postal Code:** 72701. **Area Code:** 501.

ACCOMMODATIONS. The historic **Capital Hotel ❺,** 111 W. Markham St., at Louisiana, is by far the nicest accommodation in Little Rock. Hailed for its beauty and stellar dining by the Clinton clan, the hotel is a Little Rock stronghold. (☎800-766-7666. Singles $124-440. Full buffet breakfast.) Budget motels are particularly dense on I-30 southwest of town and at the intersection of I-30 and I-40 in North Little Rock. The **Cimarron Motel ❷,** 10200 I-30, off Exit 130, has basic rooms and a pool. (☎565-1171. Key deposit $5. Singles $30; doubles $35.) **King Motel ❶,** 10420 I-30, near the Cimarron, has relatively comfortable, cheap rooms without frills. (☎565-1501. Key deposit $5. Singles $25; doubles $30.) **Maumell Park ❶,** 9009 Pinnacle Valley Rd., on the Arkansas River, has 129 sites near the beautiful Pinnacle Mountain State Park. From I-430, take Rte. 10 (Exit 9) west 3 mi., turn right on the Pinnacle Valley Rd., and continue for 3 mi. (☎868-9477. Sites with water and electricity $16. Boat launch $2; free for campers.)

FOOD & NIGHTLIFE. The city is obviously pouring money into the downtown **River Market,** 400 President Clinton Ave., and people are responding. The downtown lunch crowd heads here for a wide selection of food shops, coffee stands, delis, and an outdoor **Farmers Market.** (☎375-2552. Market hall open M-Sa 7am-6pm; many shops only open for lunch. Farmer's Market Tu and Sa 7am-3pm.) Near Market Hall, **The Flying Fish ❷,** 511 President Clinton Ave., has quickly become downtown's favorite hangout. Hungry patrons clamor for catfish baskets (2 fillets $5.50), po' boy sandwiches (oyster and catfish po' boys $6.50), and on-tap brewskies. (☎375-3474. Open daily 11am-10pm.) Just past the Hillcrest area, **Pizza D'Action ❶,** 2919 W. Markham, boasts some of the tastiest pizza and eclectic crowds in the area. Live music most nights. (☎666-5403. Pizza $5-15. Cheeseburgers and sandwiches $4. Wide selections of beer and liquor.) **Vino's ❶,** 923 W. 7th St., at Chester St., is Little Rock's original microbrewery/nightclub with tasty Italian fare and a clientele ranging from lunchtime's corporate businessmen to midnight's pierced and dyed punks. (☎375-8466. Cheese pizza slices $1.15. Calzones from $5.50. Live music Th-Sa. Cover $5-12. Open M-W 11am-10pm, Th 11am-11pm, F 11am-midnight, Sa 11:30am-midnight, Su 1-9pm.)

SIGHTS. Tourists can visit **"Le Petite Roche,"** the actual little rock of Little Rock, at Riverfront Park at the north end of Rock St. From underneath the railroad bridge at the north end of Louisiana St., look straight down, the rock is part of the embankment. Little Rock's most important attraction lies at the corner of Daisy L. Gatson Bates Dr. (formerly 14th St.) and Park St. **Central High School** remains a fully functional (and fully integrated) school; it's therefore closed to visitors. But in a restored Mobil station across the street, a **Visitors Center,** 2125 Daisy L. Gatson Bates Dr., contains an excellent exhibit on the "Little Rock Nine." (☎374-1957. Open M-Sa 10am-4pm, Su 1-4pm. Free.) The **MacArthur Museum of Arkansas Military History,** 503 E. 9th St., on the grounds of the Arkansas Arts Center, is a little gem. Located in the birthplace of Gen. Douglass MacArthur, it contains a small but in-depth exhibit of military artifacts. (☎376-4602; www.arkmilitaryheritage.com. Open Tu-Sa 10am-4pm, Su 1-4pm. Free.) The **Arkansas Art Center,** 501 East 9th St., is a huge complex that'll keep your aesthetic senses tingling for hours. This is not your ordinary selection of landscapes and still lifes; one of the most prominent sculptures, *Heavy Dog Kiss*, has a huge human head kissing a huge dog head. (☎372-4000; www.arkarts.com. Open Tu-Sa 10am-5pm, Su 11am-5pm. Suggested donation $5.)

In the middle of downtown, the **Arkansas Territorial Restoration,** 200 E. Third St., displays life in 19th-century Little Rock as period actors show off old-time tricks of Arkansas frontier living. (☎324-9351; www.arkansashistory.com. Open M-Sa 9am-5pm, Su 1-5pm. $2.50, seniors $1.50, under 18 $1.) When the Legislature is not in seecion, visitors are free to explore the **State Capitol,** at the west end of Capitol St. (☎682-5080. Open M-F 7am-5pm, Sa-Su 10am-5pm.) Construction of the **Clinton Presidential Library** (☎370-8000) is slated to finish sometime in 2004. Next to the River Market district, the Library will update the old Little Rock skyline. Visit www.clintonpresidentialcenter.com for a look at the building's plans.

FLORIDA

Ponce de León landed in St. Augustine in 1513, in search of the elusive Fountain of Youth. Although the multitudes who flock to Florida today aren't seeking fountains, many find their youth restored in the Sunshine State—whether they're dazzled by Disney World or bronzed by the sun on the state's seductive beaches. Droves of senior citizens also migrate to Florida—jokingly referred to as heaven's waiting room—where the sun-warmed air is just as therapeutic as de León's fabled magical elixir. Florida's recent population boom has strained the state's natural resources; commercial strips and tremendous development have turned pristine beaches into tourist traps. Still, it is possible to find a deserted spot on the peninsula on which to plop down with a paperback and get some sand in your toes.

HIGHLIGHTS OF FLORIDA

BEACHES. White sand, lots of sun, clear blue water. Pensacola (p. 531) and St. Petersburg (p. 496) win our thumbs-up for the best of the best.

DISNEY WORLD. Orlando's cash cow...er, mouse (p. 487). What else is there to say?

EVERGLADES. The prime Florida haunt for fishermen, hikers, canoers, bikers, and wildlife watchers (p. 515). Check out the unique mangrove swamps.

KEY LIME PIE. This famous dessert hails from the Florida Keys (p. 518).

PRACTICAL INFORMATION

Capital: Tallahassee.

Visitor Info: Florida Division of Tourism, 126 W. Van Buren St., Tallahassee 32301 (☎888-735-2872; www.flausa.com). **Division of Recreation and Parks,** 3900 Commonwealth Blvd., #536, Tallahassee 32399 (☎850-488-9872).

Postal Abbreviation: FL. **Sales Tax:** 6%. **Accommodations Tax:** 11%.

CENTRAL FLORIDA

ORLANDO ☎407

When Walt Disney was flying over the small towns of Central Florida in search of a place to put his Florida operation, he marveled at the endless number of lakes and streams that dominate the Orlando area. Amidst this beautiful setting, he foresaw a world full of thrill-packed amusement rides and life-sized, cartoonish figures. While Orlando is older than Disney World, most of the city's resources are dedicated to supporting the tourism industry that is the lifeblood of the economy. Theme parks, hotels, diners, and other kitschy treats line every major street; even downtown Orlando, 20 mi. from Disney, overflows with tourist attractions.

TRANSPORTATION

Airport: Orlando International, 1 Airport Blvd. (☎825-2001; www.orlandoairports.net). From the airport take Rte. 436 N, exit to Rte. 528 W/Bee Line Expwy., then head east on I-4 for downtown, and west on I-4 to the attractions, including Disney and Universal. City bus #42 and 51 make the trip for $1. **Mears Motor Shuttle** (☎423-5566) has

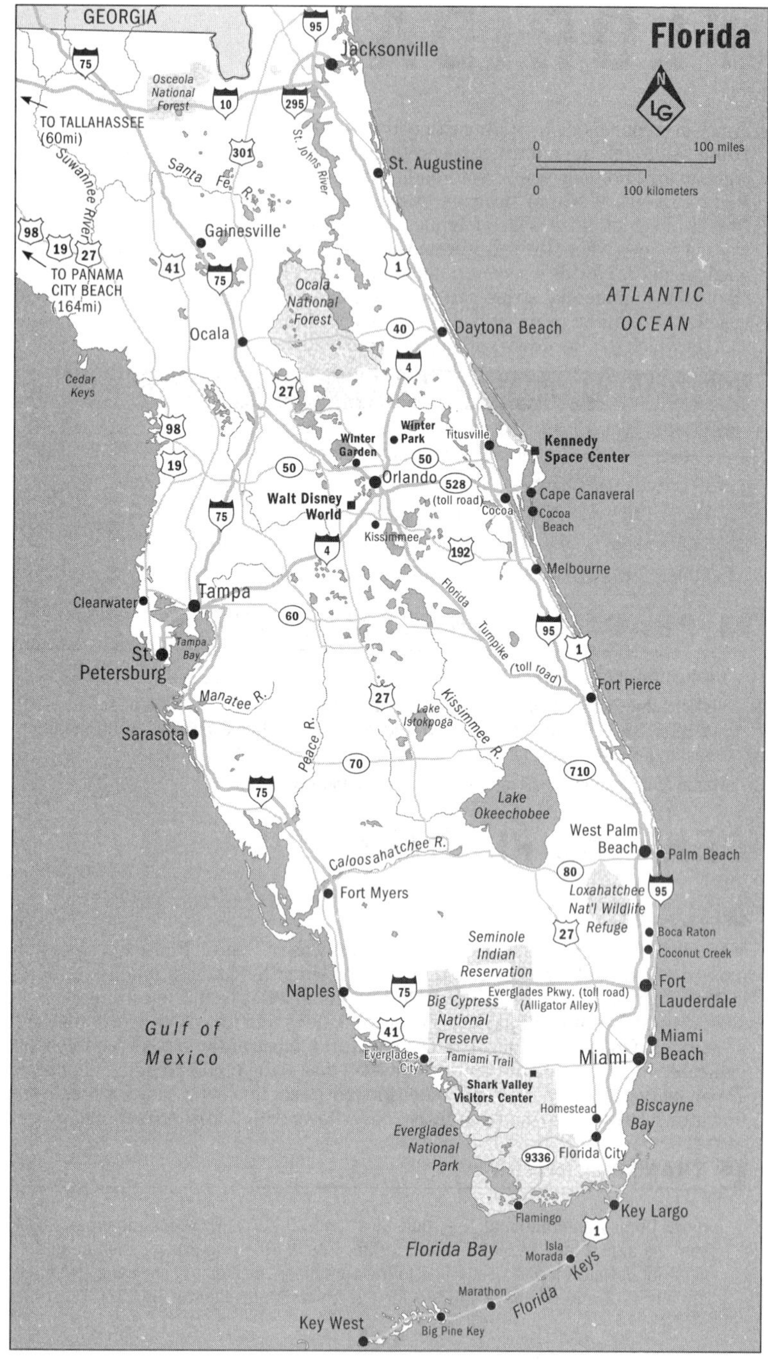
Florida
GEORGIA
ATLANTIC
OCEAN
Gulf of
Mexico
0
100 miles
0
100 kilometers
Jacksonville
Osceola
National
Forest
TO TALLAHASSEE
(60mi)
Suwannee River
Santa Fe R.
St. Johns River
St. Augustine
Gainesville
TO PANAMA
CITY BEACH
(164mi)
Ocala
National
Forest
Ocala
Daytona Beach
Cedar
Keys
Winter
Park
Titusville
Winter
Garden
Kennedy
Space Center
Orlando
(toll road)
Cape Canaveral
Walt Disney
World
Cocoa
Cocoa
Beach
Kissimmee
Melbourne
Florida
Turnpike
(toll road)
Tampa
Clearwater
Tampa
Bay
St.
Petersburg
Fort Pierce
Manatee R.
Kissimmee R.
Lake
Istokpoga
Sarasota
Peace R.
Lake
Okeechobee
West Palm
Beach
Palm Beach
Caloosahatchee R.
Fort Myers
Loxahatchee
Nat'l Wildlife
Refuge
Seminole
Indian
Reservation
Boca Raton
Coconut Creek
Fort
Lauderdale
Naples
Everglades Pkwy. (toll road)
(Alligator Alley)
Big Cypress
National
Preserve
Miami
Beach
Miami
Everglades
City
Tamiami Trail
Shark Valley
Visitors Center
Homestead
Biscayne
Bay
Everglades
National
Park
Florida City
Flamingo
Key Largo
Florida Bay
Isla
Morada
Florida Keys
Marathon
Key West
Big Pine Key
95
75
10
295
301
98
19
27
41
1
40
4
50
528
192
60
70
710
80
9336

booths at the airport for transportation to most hotels (price varies depending on destination, about $15 per person). No shuttle reservations are necessary from the airport; for return, call 1 day in advance.

Trains: Amtrak, 1400 Sligh Blvd. (☎843-7611), 3 blocks east of I-4. Take S. Orange Ave., head west on Columbia, then take a right on Sligh. Station open daily 7:30am-7pm. To **Jacksonville** (3-4hr., 3 per day, $34).

Buses: Greyhound, 555 N. John Young Pkwy. (☎292-3440), just south of W. Colonial Dr. (Rte. 50). Open 24hr. To **Jacksonville** (2½-4hr., 9 per day, $25-27) and **Kissimmee** (40min., 8 per day, $7-8).

Public Transit: LYNX, 445 W. Amelia St., Suite 800 (☎841-2279 or 800-344-5969). Downtown terminal between Central and Pine St., 1 block west of Orange Ave. and 1 block east of I-4. Buses operate daily 6am-9pm, hours vary with route. $1, seniors and under 18 $0.25; transfers $0.10. Weekly pass $10. Look for signposts with a colored paw. Serves the airport, downtown, and all major parks. The Lynx **Lymmo** is a free downtown transportation service with 11 stations and 8 stops scattered along and around Magnolia Ave. Look for markers with the "Lymmo" name.

Taxi: Yellow Cab, ☎699-9999.

ORIENTATION & PRACTICAL INFORMATION

Orlando lies at the center of hundreds of small lakes, toll highways, and amusement parks. **Orange Blossom Trail (Route 17/92 and 441)** runs north-south and **Colonial Drive (Route 50)** east-west. The **Bee Line Expressway (Route 528)** and the **East-West Expressway (Route 408)** exact several tolls for their convenience. The major artery is **I-4,** which actually runs north-south through the center of town, despite being labeled an east-west highway. The parks—**Disney World, Universal Studios,** and **Sea World**—await 15-20 mi. southwest of downtown; Winter Park is 3-4 mi. northeast.

Visitor Info: Orlando Official Visitor Center, 8723 International Dr., #101 (☎363-5872; www.orlandoinfo.com), southwest of downtown; take bus #8. Get the free "Magic Card" for discounts at sites, restaurants, and hotels. Open daily 8am-7pm. Tickets sold 8am-6pm.

Hotlines: Rape Hotline, ☎740-5408. **Crisis Hotline,** ☎843-4357.

Internet Access: Orlando Public Library, 101 E. Central Blvd. (☎835-7323). Open M-Th 9am-9pm, F-Sa 9am-6pm, Su 1-6pm. Internet access $5 for 7-day unlimited use.

Post Office: 46 E. Robinson St. (☎425-6464), downtown. Open M-F 7am-5pm. **Postal Code:** 32801. **Area Code:** 407. 10-digit dialing required.

ACCOMMODATIONS

With more than 110,000 hotel rooms from which to choose, there are plenty of options for all tastes and wallet sizes. Prices rise as you approach Disney World. **Irlo Bronson Memorial Highway (U.S. 192)** runs from Disney World to downtown Kissimmee, and is probably the best place to find a deal. Public transportation goes from Kissimmee to the major parks. **International Drive (I-Drive),** a north-south thoroughfare that parallels the interstate, is the center of Orlando's lodging world. Most accommodations provide free transportation to Universal and Disney.

The Courtyard at Lake Lucerne, 211 N. Lucerne Circle E (☎648-5188 or 800-444-5289), 30min. from Disney. From I-4, take Exit 82C onto Anderson St., right on Delaney Ave., and right on N. Lucerne Circle. Listed in the National Registry of Historic Places, this ridiculously beautiful B&B offers its guests lavish rooms, complimentary wine upon arrival, and a nightly cocktail hour. All rooms have TV and phone, and 6 have whirlpool tubs. Of the 4 homes, the Wellborn is the best deal, with 15 1-bedroom Art Deco suites for $89-115. Other rooms $89-225. ❺

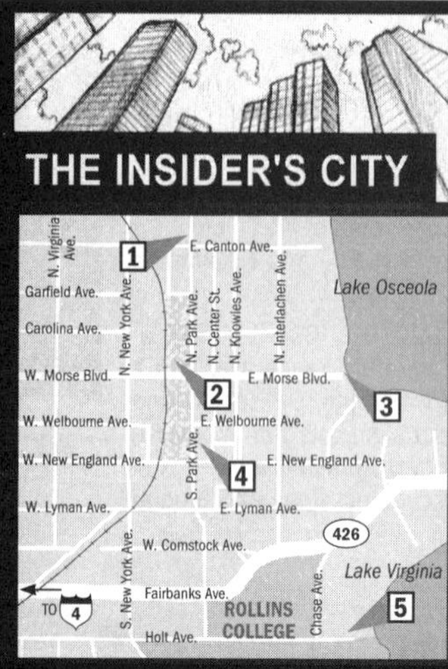

AFTERNOON ON THE AVE.

Orlando's theme parks worn you out? Head north to the small residential city of Winter Park (Exit 87 off I-4) for a dose of culture, shopping, and nature on Park Avenue.

1 The **Charles Hosmer Morse Museum of American Art,** 445 N. Park Ave., has the world's largest collection of works by interior-design and stained-glass guru Louis C. Tiffany.

2 Unwind at **Central Park.** From Mar. 19-21, 2004, the park will host the 45th annual **Winter Park Sidewalk Arts Festival.**

3 Climb aboard a **Scenic Boat Tour**—a 1hr. journey on Winter Park's lakes and canals, with a close-up look at local plant life and spectacular mansions.

4 At **Pannullo's ❹,** 216 S. Park Ave., indulge in delicious pasta dishes ($12-14).

5 The free **Cornell Fine Arts Museum,** 1000 Holt Ave. at Rollins College, showcases fine art spanning from the Renaissance to today.

Disney's All-Star Resorts (☎934-7639), in Disney World. From I-4, take Exit 64B and follow the signs to Blizzard Beach—the resorts are just behind it. Disney's All Star Movie, Music, and Sports Resorts, the "value resorts," are a great deal for large groups. Large theme decorations, from surfboards to cowboy boots, adorn the courtyards. Each of the hotels has 2 pools, a food court, a pool bar, and laundry facilities. Get info and tickets at the Guest Services Desk to avoid long lines at park gates. Free parking and Disney transportation. A/C, phone, TV. Rooms $77-124; under 18 free with adult. ❹

Motel 6, 7455 W. Irlo Bronson Hwy. (U.S. 192) (☎396-6422), in Kissimmee. Close to public transportation and a slew of chain restaurants, Motel 6 offers immaculate, spacious rooms at unbeatable prices. Rooms have free local calls, HBO, morning coffee, laundry facilities, and outdoor pool. Rooms $30, each additional person $4. ❶

Fort Summit KOA (☎863-424-1880 or 800-424-1800), 11 mi. west of Disney in Baseball City. From I-4, take Exit 55 to U.S. 27; then go south on Frontage Rd. Palm trees and oaks provide shade, while a pool, hot tub, Internet access, horseback riding, frequent bingo games, cookouts, and ice cream socials provide entertainment. Tent sites $22-27; RVs $30-34; cabins $39-46. Discounts for KOA, AAA, and AARP. ❶

FOOD

Most eating in the Orlando area is either fine dining or done on-the-run. Prices are exorbitant inside theme parks; pack some food if you have space. Cheap buffets and ethnic eateries line International Dr., U.S. 192, and Orange Blossom Trail.

Cafe Trastevere, 825 N. Magnolia Ave. (☎839-0235), in downtown Orlando. At this intimate Italian bistro, the too-good-to-be-true Bruschetta Michelangelo ($4.50) and savory Pollo Trastevere ($8.25) will leave you dreaming of Rome. W half-price wine 4-10pm. Tu and Th free wine with dinner 5-7pm. Open M-F 11:30am-10pm, Sa 5-10pm. ❸

Pebbles Restaurant, 12551 State Rd. 535 (☎827-1111), Lake Buena Vista, in the Crossroads Plaza. A local favorite, this Orlando chain cooks up tasty Florida cuisine in a casual atmosphere. Refreshingly original dishes like seared crab cake with mango tartar sauce ($10) and baked *chèvre* with tomato concasse and garlic bread ($6). Open M-Th 11am-11pm, F 11am-midnight, Sa noon-midnight, Su noon-11pm. ❷

Barney's Steak and Seafood, 1615 E. Colonial Dr. (☎896-6864), near Mills Ave. Locals flock to this upscale restaurant for the legendary surf and turf dinner ($28). If land and sea are too much to handle at once, check out the first-class salad bar before sampling the salmon ($18) or sirloin steak ($15). No collarless shirts, hats, or flip-flops. Happy Hour M-F 11am-7pm. Music Su-Tu 5:30pm. Open M 11:30am-4pm and 5-9pm, Tu-F 11:30am-4pm and 5-10pm, Sa 5-10pm, Su 4-9pm. ❺

Viet Garden, 1237 E. Colonial Dr. (☎896-4154), near Mills Ave. This little gem serves up delectable Vietnamese and Thai cuisine. Savor the array of garnished rice dishes, which feature combinations of chicken, beef, and shrimp ($5-9). Open Su-Th 10am-9pm, F-Sa 10am-10pm. ❶

Azteca's, 809 N. Main St. (☎933-8155), in Kissimmee at Orange Blossom Trail and U.S. 192. Whether en route to Orlando or simply unwinding in Kissimmee, be sure to stop by Azteca's for overwhelming amounts of delicious Mexican food. Lunch specials M-F $4. Open Tu-Th 11am-10pm, F-Sa 11am-11pm, Su 11am-9pm. ❶

Beefy King, 424 N. Bumby Ave. (☎894-2241), just south of E. Colonial Dr. Voted "Best Beefy Experience" by *Florida Magazine,* this family eatery has been pleasing residents for 30 years with its fantastic sandwiches ($2-4) served at an old-fashioned luncheon counter. Open M-F 10am-5:30pm, Sa 11am-3pm. ❶

ENTERTAINMENT & NIGHTLIFE

Check the Calendar section in Friday's *Orlando Sentinel* for happenings around town; the free *Orlando Weekly* is also a source for entertainment listings. Relatively inexpensive bars line **North Orange Avenue,** the city's main drag. For more tourist-oriented attractions, head to the bright lights and neon signs of **International Drive,** where mini-golf, Ripley's Believe It or Not, the world's largest McDonald's, and Wonderworks (a science funhouse in an upside-down building) await.

SAK Comedy Lab, 380 W. Amelia St. (☎648-0001), at Hughey Ave. downtown. Despite its trademark family-friendly, clean humor, SAK still manages to produce top-notch hilarity that all audiences can enjoy. Shows Tu and W 9pm, Th-F 8 and 10pm, Sa 8, 10pm, midnight. $5-13.

Tabu, 46 N. Orange Ave. (☎648-8363) in downtown Orlando, provides a haven for twenty-somethings in search of the South Beach scene. Tu college night. Th women get in and drink free. Stylish dress. Usually 18+. Cover $5-10. Open Tu-Sa 10pm-3am.

Jax 5th Ave. Deli and Ale House, 11 S. Court Ave. (☎841-5322), downtown, is a laid-back bar that stocks 250 brands of beer. A friendly and knowledgeable staff will help you choose from the dazzling displays. Deli and pub food $5-10. Live jazz Sa nights. Open M-Th 11am-1am, F 11am-2am, Sa noon-2am.

Back Booth, 37 W. Pine St. (☎999-2570), downtown Orlando. Catch up-and-coming local bands ranging from jazzy funk to ska punk. Cover $3-10. Shows usually 9 or 10pm; call for schedule.

WALT DISNEY WORLD ☎407

Disney World is the Rome of central Florida: all roads lead to it. The name is more apt than one might imagine, as Disney indeed creates a "world" of its own among lakes, forests, hills, and streams. Within this Never-Neverland, theme parks, resorts, theaters, restaurants, and nightclubs all work together to make fun the buzzword. Of course, the only setback is that magical amusement comes at a price—everything in Walt Disney's World costs almost thrice as much as in the real world. In the end, the corporate empire that is Disney leaves no one unhappy or bored, and despite the expense, WDW wins the prize of best park in the US.

PRACTICAL INFORMATION

Disney dominates **Lake Buena Vista,** 20 mi. west of Orlando via I-4. (☎824-4321 or 939-4636; www.disneyworld.com.) The one-day entrance fee ($52, ages 3-9 $42) admits visitors to one of the parks, allowing them to leave and return to the same park later in the day. A better option, the **Park-Hopper Pass** buys admission to all four parks for several days. (4-day $208, ages 3-9 $167; 5-day $239/192.) The **Park Hopper Plus** includes a set number of days of admission plus free access to other Disney attractions. (5-day with 2 extras $269/216; 6-day with 3 extras $299/240; 7-day with 4 extras $329/264.) The Hopper passes need not be used on consecutive days, never expire, and allow for unlimited transportation between attractions. Attractions that charge separate admissions include **Typhoon Lagoon** ($31/25), **Pleasure Island** ($21, 18+ unless with adult), **Blizzard Beach** ($31/25), and **Disney's Wide World of Sports Complex** ($10/8). For descriptions, see **Other Disney Attractions** (p. 491). *Never pay full fare for a Disney park. Official Tourist Info Centers and sell Park Hopper passes for an average $10-15 less.*

Disney World opens its gates 365 days a year, but hours fluctuate by season. Expect the parks to open at 9am and close between 7 and 11pm, but call beforehand—the schedule is set a month in advance. Prepare for crowds (and afternoon thunderstorms) in summer, but the enormously crowded peak times are Christmas, Thanksgiving, and the month around Easter. The parks are least crowded in January. The **FASTPASS** option at all of the theme parks allows you to bypass long lines on popular rides. Simply insert your park entrance ticket into a FASTPASS station, and you will receive a ticket telling you when to return, usually 30min. to 2hr. later.

THE PARKS

MAGIC KINGDOM

Seven lands comprise the Magic Kingdom: **Main Street, USA; Tomorrowland; Fantasyland; Liberty Square; Frontierland; Adventureland;** and **Mickey's Toontown Fair.** More than any of the other Disney parks, the Kingdom is geared toward children.

MAIN STREET, USA. As the entrance to the "Most Magical Place on Earth," Main Street captures the spirit and bustle of early 20th-century America, with vendors peddling their wares and a daily parade. The aroma of freshly baked cookies and cakes beckons from **Main Street Bakery,** and the **Emporium** is a one-stop shop for Magic Kingdom souvenirs. A horse-drawn trolley carries visitors up Main St. to **Cinderella's Castle,** Disney's own Statue of Liberty, where there are frequent dancing and singing shows by your favorite Disney characters.

TOMORROWLAND. In the 1990s, Tomorrowland received a neon facelift that skyrocketed it out of the space-race days of the 1960s and into a futuristic intergalactic nation. The indoor roller coaster **Space Mountain** dominates the landscape, providing thrills and chills in the blackness of outer space. **Buzz Lightyear's Space Ranger Spin** equips *Toy Story* fans with laser cannons to fight the Evil Emperor Zurg. A science experiment gone wrong, the frightening **ExtraTERRORestrial Alien Encounter** has an angry alien breathing down your neck.

MICKEY'S TOONTOWN & FANTASYLAND. Visitors can meet all their favorite characters at the **Hall of Fame** and **Mickey's Country House.** Bring an autograph book and camera to the **Judge's Tent** to meet Mickey, but expect a long line of fans. **Fantasyland** brings some of Disney's all-time favorite animated films to life. Soar above London and Neverland in a pirate ship sprinkled with pixie dust at **Peter Pan's**

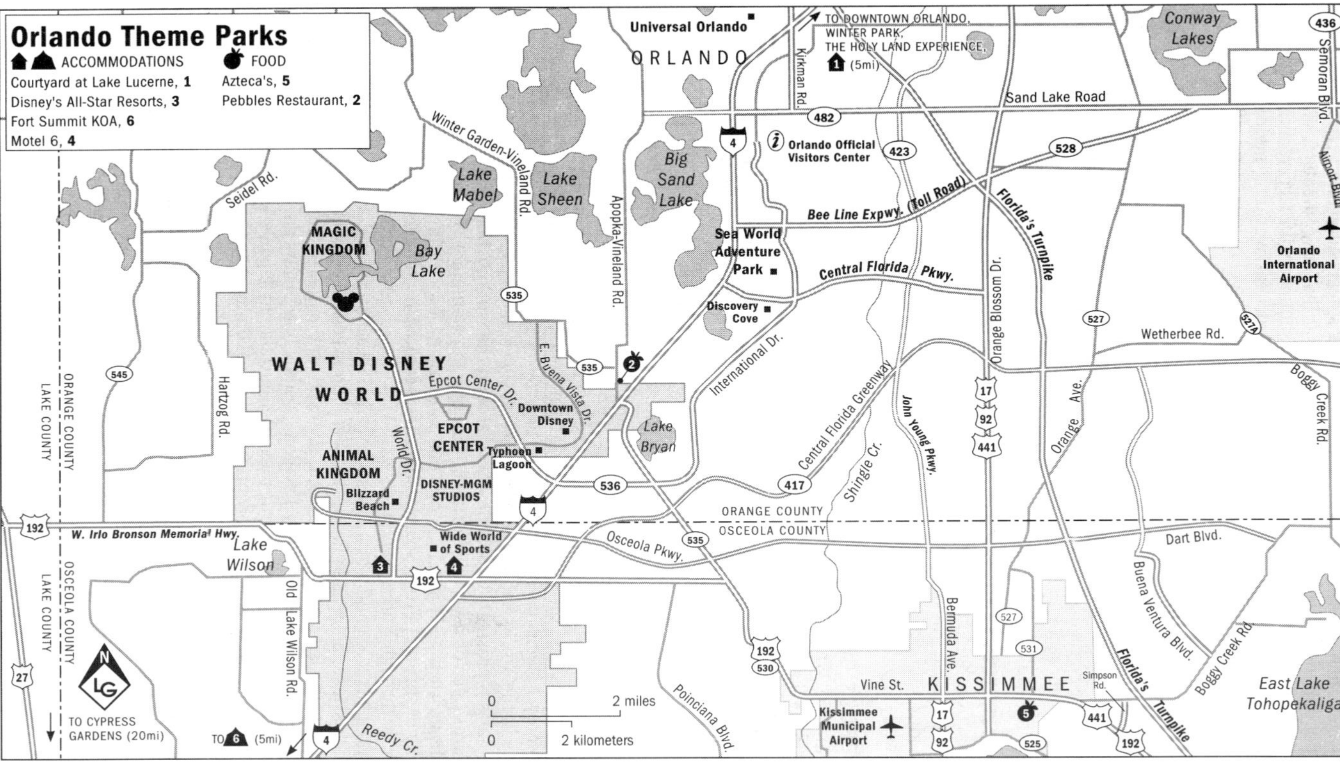
Orlando Theme Parks
ACCOMMODATIONS
Courtyard at Lake Lucerne, 1
Disney's All-Star Resorts, 3
Fort Summit KOA, 6
Motel 6, 4
FOOD
Azteca's, 5
Pebbles Restaurant, 2
Universal Orlando
ORLANDO
TO DOWNTOWN ORLANDO, WINTER PARK, THE HOLY LAND EXPERIENCE, (5mi)
Kirkman Rd.
Conway Lakes
Semoran Blvd.
Sand Lake Road
Orlando Official Visitors Center
Airport Blvd.
Winter Garden-Vineland Rd.
Lake Mabel
Lake Sheen
Big Sand Lake
Apopka-Vineland Rd.
Seidel Rd.
Bee Line Expwy. (Toll Road)
Florida's Turnpike
Orlando International Airport
MAGIC KINGDOM
Bay Lake
Sea World Adventure Park
Central Florida Pkwy.
Discovery Cove
Orange Blossom Dr.
Wetherbee Rd.
WALT DISNEY WORLD
E. Buena Vista Dr.
International Dr.
Boggy Creek Rd.
Epcot Center Dr.
Downtown Disney
Central Florida Greenway
John Young Pkwy.
Orange Ave.
EPCOT CENTER
Lake Bryan
ANIMAL KINGDOM
World Dr.
Typhoon Lagoon
Shingle Cr.
DISNEY-MGM STUDIOS
Blizzard Beach
ORANGE COUNTY
OSCEOLA COUNTY
LAKE COUNTY
W. Irlo Bronson Memorial Hwy.
Lake Wilson
Wide World of Sports
Osceola Pkwy.
Dart Blvd.
Old Lake Wilson Rd.
Bermuda Ave.
Buena Ventura Blvd.
Boggy Creek Rd.
East Lake Tohopekaliga
Vine St.
KISSIMMEE
Simpson Rd.
Kissimmee Municipal Airport
Poinciana Blvd.
0 2 miles
0 2 kilometers
TO CYPRESS GARDENS (20mi)
TO 6 (5mi)
Reedy Cr.

Flight, then dance with dwarves at **Snow White's Scary Adventures.** Board a honey pot and journey into the Hundred Acre Wood at **The Many Adventures of Winnie the Pooh,** where you will withstand a blustery day, bounce with Tigger, and encounter bizarre Heffalumps. For some saccharine but heartwarming melodies, meet mechanical children from around the world on the classic boat ride **"it's a small world."** Rest in peace, "Mr. Toad's Wild Ride."

LIBERTY SQUARE & FRONTIERLAND. Welcome to Americana, Disney-style. Liberty Sq. introduces visitors to the educational and political aspects of American history, while Frontierland showcases the America of cowboys and Indians. **The Hall of Presidents** is a fun exhibit on US heads of state, from George Washington to George W. Bush. Next door, the spooky **Haunted Mansion** houses 999 happy ghouls. In Frontierland, take a lazy raft ride over to **Tom Sawyer Island** and explore, or take on the two thrill rides—**Splash Mountain** and **Big Thunder Mountain Railroad.**

ADVENTURELAND. Sail on the classic **Pirates of the Caribbean** (yo ho, yo ho!) and uncover hidden treasures, or fly on the **Magic Carpets of Aladdin** for an aerial view of the park. One of the original rides from the park's opening, **The Jungle Cruise** provides a tongue-in-cheek take on exploration, touring the world's amazing rivers while supplying good wet fun and lots of bad puns.

EPCOT CENTER

In 1966, Walt dreamed up an "Experimental Prototype Community Of Tomorrow" (EPCOT), which would evolve constantly to incorporate new ideas from US technology—eventually becoming a self-sufficient, futuristic utopia. At present, Epcot splits into **Future World** and the expansive **World Showcase.** After a day of walking around EPCOT, it's no wonder that some joke that the true acronym is "Every Person Comes Out Tired."

The trademark 180 ft. high geosphere (or "golfball") at the entrance to Future World houses the **Spaceship Earth** attraction, in which visitors board a "time machine" for a tour through the evolution of communications. **Body Wars** takes visitors on a tour of the human body (with the help of a simulator), while at nearby **Test Track** riders experience life in the fast lane on one of Disney's fastest and longest rides. See the world from a different perspective at the immensely popular **Honey, I Shrunk the Audience,** which boasts stellar 3D effects.

In the World Showcase, architectural styles, monuments, and typical food and crafts represent 11 countries from around the world, while people in traditional dress perform various forms of cultural entertainment. The best cultural film, **Impressions de France** has gorgeous panoramic views of the country accompanied by captivating French classical music. **Maelstrom** is an amusing and thrilling boat ride through Norway, complete with Vikings and trolls. Every night at 9pm, Epcot presents a magnificent mega-show called **IllumiNations** with music, dancing fountains, laser lights, and fireworks. World Showcase also specializes in regional cuisine. The all-you-can-eat meat, seafood, and salad buffet ($19) at **Restaurant Akershus ❹,** in the Norway Pavilion, is actually a Disney dining bargain. Watch a dexterous chef prepare your meal at your table in Japan's **Mitsukoshi Teppanyaki Dining Room ❸,** a moderately priced theatrical dining experience.

DISNEY-MGM STUDIOS

Disney-MGM Studios sets out to create a "living movie set." Restaurants resemble their Hollywood counterparts, and movie characters stroll the grounds signing autographs. MGM is built around several stunt shows and mini-theatricals; plan your day according to the ones you want to see. Enter the greatest scenes in movie history at the **Great Movie Ride,** inside a replica of Mann's Chinese Theater. **The Twi-**

light Zone Tower Of Terror drops guests 13 stories in a runaway elevator. The thrilling, twisting, "limo" ride that is **Rock 'n' Roller Coaster** will take you from 0 to 60 mph in less than 3 seconds; it's also the only Disney attraction to take you upside down. Based on the hit TV game show, **Who Wants to Be a Millionaire? Play It!** replicates the real show, save affable host Regis Philbin. **The Indiana Jones Epic Stunt Spectacular** shows off some of the greatest scenes from the trilogy in live action. **The Magic of Disney Animation,** a tour that introduces you to actual Disney animators, explains how Disney animated films are created and offers a sneak peak at the sketches of upcoming Disney flicks.

DISNEY'S ANIMAL KINGDOM

If fake plastic characters and make-believe are getting to be too much, the Animal Kingdom is a heavy dose of reality. **Kilimanjaro Safaris** depart for the exotic Harambe preserve where elephants, hippos, giraffes, and other creatures of the African savannah roam. A **Maharajah Jungle Trek** drops riders among tigers, tapirs, and bats. Animal Kingdom is not all about immersion in foreign lands. Like any Disney park, shows and rides make up a large part of the attraction (the park's catchphrase is NAHTAZU: "not a zoo"). **DINOSAUR** puts travelers in the middle of the early Cretaceous, while the coaster **Primeval Whirl** puts you in a dinosaur's jaws. Another 3-D spectacular, **It's Tough to be a Bug!** put on by the cast of the animated flick *A Bug's Life* is sure to entertain all ages and species.

OTHER DISNEY ATTRACTIONS

Besides the four main parks, Disney offers several other draws with different themes and separate admissions. **Blizzard Beach** is a water park built on the premise of a melting mountain. Ride a ski lift to the fastest water-slide in the world, plummeting down a 120 ft. descent. **Typhoon Lagoon,** a 50-acre water park, centers on the nation's largest wave-making pool and the 7 ft. waves it creates. As well as eight water slides, the lagoon has a creek for inner-tube rides and a saltwater coral reef stocked with tropical fish and harmless sharks. Water parks fill up early on hot days; late arrivals might get turned away. With more than nine sports venues for over 30 sports, **Disney's Wide World Of Sports Complex** is a hubbub of athletic activity. Catch the Atlanta Braves in spring training, or test your skills at punting and passing at the **NFL Experience.** The larger-than-life **Downtown Disney** is a neon conglomeration of theme restaurants, nightlife, and shopping encompassing the **Marketplace, Pleasure Island,** and the **West Side.** In the Marketplace at the **LEGO Imagination Center,** take a photo with large LEGO sculptures or try creating your own. In the West Side, **Cirque Du Soleil** presents La Nouba, a breathtaking blend of circus acrobatics and theater—with a pricetag that will also take your breath away. *($82, ages 3-9 $72.)* Next door, the high-tech interactive games of **Disney Quest** guarantee a "virtually" exciting time. *($31, ages 3-9 $25.)* **Pleasure Island** is hedonistic Disney with an attitude. Party at eight nightclubs—from comedy to jazz to 80s pop. *(Open daily 8pm-2am. 18+ unless accompanied by parent. $21.)*

LIFE BEYOND DISNEY ☎407

The big non-Disney theme parks band together in competition with Mickey. "Flex-Tickets," combine admission prices to various parks at a discount. A four-park ticket ($187, ages 3-9 $152) covers Sea World, both Universal Studios parks, and Wet 'n Wild, and allows 14 consecutive days of visiting with free transportation. The five-park ticket ($223/187) adds Busch Gardens in Tampa (see p. 495) and also lasts 14 consecutive days. Universal City Travel (☎800-224-3838) sells tickets.

THE PARKS

UNIVERSAL ORLANDO

A relatively sugar-free alternative to Disney World is Universal: nothing magical, just movie rides that thrill, spin, and make you squeal. With two parks (**Universal Studios Florida** and **Islands of Adventure**), three resort hotels, and an entertainment complex called **CityWalk,** Universal now stands toe-to-toe with the "other park." *(I-4 Exit 74B or 75A. ☎363-8000. Open daily 9am, closing times vary. CityWalk open until 2am. Each park $53, ages 3-9 $43. CityWalk is ungated and free. Parking $7.)*

UNIVERSAL STUDIOS FLORIDA. The first park to "ride the movies" showcases a mix of rides and behind-the-scenes extravaganzas. Live the fairy tale courtesy of "OgreVision" at **Shrek 4-D,** the park's newest attraction. **Back to the Future...The Ride,** a staple of any Universal visit, utilizes seven-story OmniMax surround screens and spectacular special effects. A studio tour of **Nickelodeon** offers an interactive look at the sets, stages, and slime.

ISLANDS OF ADVENTURE. This park encompasses 110 acres of the most technologically sophisticated rides in the world and typically has short wait times. Five islands portray different themes, ranging from cartoons to Jurassic Park to Marvel Superheroes. **The Amazing Adventures of Spider Man** is the crown jewel; new technology and several patents sprung from its conception. A fast-moving car whizzes around a 3-D video system as you and Peter Parker find the stolen Statue of Liberty. The most entertaining island is **Seuss Landing,** home of the **Green Eggs & Ham Cafe** ❷ (green eggs and ham-wich $5.60). **The Cat in the Hat** turns the classic tale into a ride on a wild couch that loops its way through the story. If that's too tame, the **Dueling Dragons** is the world's first inverted, dueling roller coaster.

CITYWALK. The free CityWalk greets the eager tourist upon entering Universal Studios. A mix of unique restaurants, a few clubs, and free evening parking make it an appealing alternative to Pleasure Island. **The NASCAR Cafe, Jimmy Buffet's Margaritaville,** and **Emeril's** are a few of the pricey theme restaurants that line the main street. Clubs on the walk include **Bob Marley's** and **The Groove.** *(21+. Cover $4-5.)*

SEA WORLD

One of the largest marine parks in the US, **Sea World Adventure Park** makes a splash with marine-themed shows, rides, and exhibits. In recent years, it has transformed itself from a repository of cutting-edge marine technology to a full-fledged park emphasizing the mystery and dark side of sea creatures. Eels, barracudas, sharks, and other beasties lick their chops in **Terrors of the Deep,** the world's largest collection of dangerous sea creatures. **The Shamu Adventure** thrills with amazing aquatic acrobatics executed smartly by a family of Orcas and their trainers. Whale belly flops send waves of 52°F salt water into the cheering "soak zone." The park's first thrill ride, **Journey to Atlantis,** gets rave reviews, as does **Kraken,** a floorless roller coaster billed as the highest, fastest, and longest coaster in Orlando. *(12 mi. southwest of Orlando off I-4 at Rte. 528/Beeline Expwy. Take bus #8. ☎351-3600. Open daily 9am-7pm; extended hours in summer. $52, ages 3-9 $43. Parking $7.)* Orlando's newest vacation destination is the adjacent **Discovery Cove.** Swim with dolphins, snorkel among tropical fish, and frolic in an aviary with more than 200 birds. *(☎877-434-7268. Open daily 9am-5:30pm. $119-399. Reservations required.)*

THE HOLY LAND EXPERIENCE

Step back in time at this small, controversial park billed as a "living biblical museum." Take in the architecture and sights of ancient Jerusalem, and watch as costumed performers reenact biblical scenes. The **Scriptorium** is a one-of-a-kind museum displaying valuable artifacts, scrolls, and manuscripts relating to the Bible. *(655 Vineland Rd. I-4 Exit 78. ☎872-2272. Open M-Th 10am-5pm, F-Sa 10am-6pm, Su noon-6pm. $30, ages 4-12 $20.)*

CYPRESS GARDENS

The botanical gardens of **Cypress Gardens** feature over 8000 varieties of plants and flowers amidst winding walkways and electric boat rides, while hoop-skirted Southern Belles patrol the grounds. Despite all the pretty flowers, the **water-ski shows** attract the biggest crowds and the loudest applause. *(Southwest of Orlando in Winter Haven; take I-4 southwest to Rte. 27 S, then Rte. 540 W. ☎863-324-2111. Open daily 9:30am-5pm. $37, ages 6-12 $24.)*

BLUE SPRING STATE PARK

Orange City's 3000-acre state park, 32 mi. northeast of Orlando, is home to some of Florida's most pristine flora and fauna. Hike along the **Blue Spring Trail** for a scenic view of the legendary spring itself (a constant 72°F), or come face-to-face with Florida's most prized (and endangered) mammal, the **manatee,** as you scuba, snorkel, or swim in one of the park's numerous clear lakes and springs. *(2001 W. French Ave., Exit 114 off I-4. ☎386-775-3663. Partially wheelchair-accessible. Open daily 8am-dusk. $2-4 entrance fee for vehicles, $1 for pedestrians and bicyclists.)*

TAMPA ☎813

Even with beautiful weather and ideal beaches, Tampa has managed to avoid the plastic pink flamingos that plague its Atlantic Coast counterparts. While Busch Gardens is Tampa's main theme park and primary tourist attraction, the rest of the bay city provides a less commercial vacation spot. Ybor City (EE-bor), Tampa's Cuban district, is a seething hotbed of energy and activity, where sun-bleached tourists can find many of Tampa's best restaurants, bars, and clubs. Downtown is home to Tampa's cultural gems.

ORIENTATION & PRACTICAL INFORMATION. Tampa wraps around Hillsborough Bay and sprawls northward. **Nebraska Avenue** and **Dale Mabry Road** parallel **I-275** as the main north-south routes; **Kennedy Boulevard, Columbus Street,** and **Busch Boulevard** are the main east-west arteries. With some exceptions, numbered streets run north-south and numbered avenues run east-west. **Ybor City** is bounded roughly by Nuccio Pkwy. on the north, 22nd St. on the south, Palm St. on the east, and 5th St. on the west. *Be careful not to stray outside these boundaries; the area can be dangerous.*

Tampa International Airport (☎870-8770; www.tampaairport.com) is 5 mi. west of downtown, Exit 39 off I-275. HARTline bus #30 runs between the airport and downtown Tampa. **Amtrak,** 601 Nebraska Ave. (☎221-7600; open daily 6am-10:30pm), at the end of Zack St., Two blocks north of Kennedy St., runs to: Miami (5hr., 1 per day, $49). **Greyhound,** 610 E. Polk St. (☎229-2174; open daily 5am-midnight), sends buses to: Atlanta (11-14hr., 9 per day, $61-65); Miami (7-10hr., 10 per day, $36-38); Orlando (2-3hr., 7 per day, $15-16). **Hillsborough Area Regional Transit (HARTline)** provides public transportation. Buses #3, 8, and 46 run to Ybor City from downtown. (☎254-4278. $1.25, seniors and ages 5-17 $0.60; exact change required.) The **Tampa Town Ferry** (☎223-1522) runs between many attractions along the Alaia and Hillsborough Rivers. The free **Tampa-Ybor Trolley** runs during lunchtime; schedules are available at the Visitors Center. **Visitor Info: Tampa Bay Convention and Visitors Bureau,** 400 N. Tampa St., Ste 2800. (☎223-1111 or 800-448-2672; www.visittampabay.com. Open M-F 8:30am-5:30pm.) **Hotlines: Crisis Hotline,** ☎234-1234. **Helpline,** ☎251-4000. **Internet Access:** John F. Germany Public Library, 900 N. Ashley Dr. (273-3652), downtown. (Open M-Th 9am-9pm,

NO WORK, ALL PLAY

HALLOWEEN FIESTA

Every year, during the last weekend in Oct., more than 100,000 people (including Randy Constan) flock to Tampa to participate in one of the nation's biggest and best street parties. Held in the notoriously festive town of Ybor City, Guavaween is a Latin-style celebration of Halloween.

In the 19th century, Tampa residents attempted to cultivate a guava industry on the Gulf coast. Though the effort failed, guavas became synonymous with the region. Local newspaper columnist Steve Otto noted that, if New York City could be the "Big Apple," then certainly Tampa could be known as the "Big Guava."

The analogy stuck, and for the last 20 years, "Mama Guava" has kicked off the Guavaween bash by leading the legendary "Mama Guava Stumble Parade" through the streets of Ybor. Concerts and costume contests abound during the festival, with winners taking home up to $1000 in prizes. Modeled after New Orleans' Mardi Gras celebration, Guavaween recently has toned down its wild antics and now appeals to partiers and families alike, with the "silly scavenger hunt" entertaining children during the day. Don't be fooled, though—sin and skin still prevail when the sun goes down, and the countdown to the next Guavaween begins the following Monday.

For more info, call ☎813-242-4828 or 888-293-4770.

F 9am-6pm, Sa 9am-5pm, Su 10am-6pm.) **Post Office:** 401. S Florida Ave. (☎223-4332. Open M-F 8:30am-4:30pm.) **Postal Code:** 33601. **Area Code:** 813.

ACCOMMODATIONS. In Tampa, chain hotels and motels hug I-275 and can be found at most exits. Motels are particularly abundant along bustling Busch Blvd. **Villager Lodge ❷,** 3110 W. Hillsborough Ave., conveniently located 5 mi. from the airport at Exit 30 off I-275, has 33 small rooms with A/C, cable TV, and pool access. (☎876-8673. Singles $40; doubles $55; each additional person $5.) **Super 8 Motel ❸,** 321 E. Fletcher Ave., 3 mi. from Busch Gardens in northwest Tampa, offers clean rooms with cable TV, pool access, and breakfast; some rooms have a fridge and stove. (☎933-4545. Singles M-F $47, Sa-Su $52; doubles $54/58. Students with ID 10% discount.) With spacious, comfortable rooms, the full-service **Baymont Inn ❹,** 9202 N. 30th St., is a great alternative to the motels that line E. Busch Blvd. (☎930-6900 or 877-229-6668. A/C and fridge in every room. Singles $74; doubles $79.)

FOOD. Tampa is blessed with many inexpensive restaurants. Heading that list is **Skipper's Smokehouse ❷,** 910 Skipper Rd., off Nebraska Ave., a tremendous backcountry eatery whose thatched hut/restaurant is complemented by an adjacent oyster bar (21+) and the popular "Skipper Dome," where guests can enjoy the legendary gator tail sandwich ($5.50) while grooving to the beats of nightly blues, zydeco, reggae, and cajun concerts. (☎971-0666. Cover depends on concerts. Happy Hour Th-F 4-8pm. Restaurant and bar open Tu 11am-10pm, W-F 11am-11pm, Sa noon-11pm, Su 1-10pm.) **Bernini ❹,** 1702 E. 7th Ave., serves up piping hot pizzas ($10-15), savory pasta dishes ($16-24), and the house favorite, Crispy Duck ($22). Hungry customers enjoy their meals under photos and replicas of the eponymous sculptor's works. (☎248-0099. Open M-Th 11:30am-10pm, F 11:30am-11pm, Sa 4pm-11pm, Su 5-10pm.) Those looking for something light should find their way to **Joffery's Coffee Company ❷,** 1616 7th Ave., which offers an array of magnificent sandwiches ($6-8) and coffees ($2-4) perfect for post-clubbin' grubbin'. (☎248-5282. Open M-Tu 7am-6pm, W 7am-10pm, Th 7am-midnight, F 7am-3am, Sa 8:30am-3am, Su 9am-6pm.) Tampa's gulf shore heritage is evident at **Cafe Creole ❸,** 1330 E. 9th Ave., an Ybor City joint known for oysters and jambalaya. (☎247-6283. Entrees $6-18. Live jazz nightly. Happy Hour Tu-F 4-7pm. Open Tu-Th 11:30am-10:30pm, F 11:30am-11:30pm, Sa 5-11:30pm.)

SIGHTS. Tampa blossomed through the success of Ybor City, a planned community once known as the cigar capital of the world. Early 20th-century stogie manufacturer Vincent Martínez Ybor employed a wide array of immigrants, and the city soon flourished under the influence of intermingled Cuban, Italian and German heritages. The **Ybor City State Museum,** 1818 9th Ave., details the rise and fall of the tobacco empire and the workers who drove it. Exhibits include a detailed look at 19th- and early 20th-century Ybor life, while an entire display is dedicated to the art of hand-rolled cigars, complete with a viewing of a cigar roller at work. (☎247-6323; www.ybormuseum.org. Open daily 9am-5pm. $2, under 6 free. Neighborhood walking tours Sa 10:30am, $4.)

The **Florida Aquarium,** 701 Channelside Dr., invites you to get up close and personal with fish from Florida's various lagoons. Head into the wetlands exhibit to gape at gators, turtles, and fighting river otters, and then make your way over to the coral reef, where menacing sharks and enigmatic jellyfish haunt the waters. Wild dolphins of the gulf stage a meet 'n' greet on Dolphin Quest Eco-Tours of Tampa Bay. (☎273-4000; www.flaquarium.net. Open daily 9:30am-5pm. $15, seniors $12, ages 3-12 $10. 1.5hr. Eco-Tours M-F 2pm; Sa-Su noon, 2, and 4pm. $18/17/13. Combo tickets available.) Built in 1891, Henry B. Plant's Tampa Bay Hotel was once considered the most luxurious resort in all the South. After serving as Army headquarters during the Spanish-American War and then becoming part of the University of Tampa, a wing of the lavish hotel is open today as the **Henry B. Plant Museum,** 401 W. Kennedy Blvd. View restored bedrooms, card rooms, and authentic artifacts from the opulent mansion, complete with Edison carbon-filament lighting and continuous classical music. (☎254-1891; www.plantmuseum.com. Open Tu-Sa 10am-4pm, Su noon-4pm. Free; suggested donation $5.) Downtown, the **Tampa Museum of Art,** 600 N. Ashley Dr., houses a noteworthy collection of ancient Greek and Roman works, a sculpture display that overlooks the scenic Hillsborough River, and a series of changing, family-oriented exhibits. (☎274-8130; www.tampagov.net/dept_museum. Open Tu-W and F-Sa 10am-5pm, Th 10am-8pm, Su 11am-5pm. Tours Th 5-8pm, Sa 10am-noon. $7, seniors $6, ages 6-18 $3. Free Sa 10am-noon and Th 5-8pm.)

Anheiser Busch's addition to the world of Floridian theme parks, **Busch Gardens,** 3000 E. Busch Blvd., is the most prized weapon in the arsenal of Tampa tourism. Thrill-seekers head for the park's famous rollercoasters Kumba, Montu, and Gwazi, while those without steel stomachs watch 2500 animals roam, fly, slither, and swim through the African-themed zoo areas. The "Edge of Africa" safari experience remains among the park's most popular attractions. (☎987-5082 or 888-800-5447; www.buschgardens.com. Hours vary, usually open daily 9:30am-7pm. $52, ages 3-9 $43. Parking $7.) Nearby, **Adventure Island,** 10001 Malcolm McKinley Dr., serves as the local water park. (☎987-5660; www.adventureisland.com. Open June-Aug. daily; Sept.-Oct. Sa-Su. Hours vary, usually M-Th 9am-7pm, F-Su 9am-8pm. $30, ages 3-9 $28. Parking $5. Busch Gardens/Adventure Island combo ticket $60, ages 3-9 $50.)

ENTERTAINMENT & NIGHTLIFE. Brief yourself on city entertainment with the *Tampa Weekend* or *Weekly Planet*, found free in local restaurants, bars, and street corners. Gay travelers should check out the free *Stonewall.* Every year in the first week of February, the **Jose Gasparilla,** a fully rigged pirate ship loaded with hundreds of exuberant "buccaneers," invades Tampa, kicking off a month of parades and festivals. Thousands pack Ybor City every October for **"Guavaween"** (☎621-7121), a Latin-style Halloween celebration.

With over 35 clubs and bars in a small area, **Ybor City** has everything you need if debauchery is on your agenda. Most nighttime hangouts are located on bustling 7th Ave., though fun can be found on 8th Ave. and 9th Ave. as well. *Use* *caution when walking down side streets.* During the week, many restaurants close at 8pm, and clubs don't open until 10pm. **Coyote Ugly Saloon,** 1722 7th Ave., is the newest and hottest club to hit the Ybor strip. Taking its cue from the movie, the rowdy bar serves up mostly single liquor shots with complementary bar dancing and body licking. Their motto? "You will get drunk, you will get ugly." (☎228-8459. Happy Hour daily 5-7pm. 21+. Open M-Sa 5pm-3am.) Tampa's trendy crowd congregates at **Velvet,** 1430 E. 7th St. The swanky bar serves up a mean martini while the erudite, perched on sleek couches, puff on cigars to a "lounge funk" beat. (☎247-2711. 21+. Open F-Sa 9pm-3am.) **The Castle,** 2004 N. 16th St., at 9th St., caters to the goth scene, but is open to all who want to enter the sanctum. (☎247-7547. M 80s night, Th music video night, F-Sa goth nights. 18+. Cover $3-5. Open M and Th-Sa 9:30pm-3am.) Latin, high-energy dance has swept aside country line-dancing at **Spurs,** 1915 7th Ave. (☎247-7787. Open Th-Sa and Su 7:30pm-3am.)

ST. PETERSBURG & CLEARWATER ☎727

Across the bay, 22 mi. southwest of Tampa, St. Petersburg caters to a relaxed community of retirees and young singles. The town enjoys 28 mi. of soft white beaches, emerald-colored water, and about 361 days of sunshine per year. The St. Petersburg-to-Clearwater stretch caters to beach bums and city strollers alike. While the outdoor scenery draws crowds, indoor activities are equally captivating—museum exhibits on Salvador Dalí and John F. Kennedy more than rival the sunset.

ORIENTATION & PRACTICAL INFORMATION. In St. Petersburg, **Central Avenue** parallels numbered avenues, running east-west in the downtown area. **34th Street (U.S. 19), I-275,** and **4th Street** are major north-south thoroughfares. The beaches line a strip of barrier islands on the far west side of town facing the Gulf. Several causeways, including the **Clearwater Memorial Causeway (Route. 60),** access the beaches from St. Pete. Clearwater sits at the far north of the strip. **Gulf Boulevard** runs down the coastline, through Belleair Shores, Indian Rocks Beach, Indian Shores, Redington Shores, Madeira Beach, Treasure Island, and St. Pete Beach. The stretch of beach past the huge pink Don Cesar Hotel, in St. Pete Beach, and Pass-a-Grille Beach have the best sand, and less pedestrian and motor traffic. **St. Petersburg Clearwater International Airport** (☎453-7800; www.fly2pie.com), off Roosevelt Blvd. sits across the bay from Tampa. **Airport Super Shuttle** runs shuttles. (☎572-1111. $19.) **Greyhound,** 180 9th St. N at 2nd Ave. N in St. Pete (☎822-1497; open daily 4:30am-11:30pm), sends buses to Clearwater (½hr., 7 per day, $8-9) and Orlando (3-4hr., 5 per day, $15-16). The Clearwater station is at 2811 Gulf-to-Bay Blvd. (☎796-7315. Open daily 6am-9pm.) **Pinellas Suncoast Transit Authority (PSTA),** handles public transit; most routes depart from Williams Park at 1st Ave. N and 3rd St. N. (☎530-9911. $1.25, students $0.75, seniors $0.60. 1-day unlimited pass $3.) To reach Tampa, take express bus #100X M-F from the Gateway Mall ($1.50). A **beach trolley** runs up and down the shore. (Daily every 20-30min. 5am-10pm, $1.25. A 1-day unlimited bus pass is $3.) Jump on and off the **Looper Trolley** ($1), which also runs a 1½hr. tour of downtown St. Pete (☎893-7111). **Visitor Info: St. Petersburg Area Chamber of Commerce,** 100 2nd Ave. N. (☎821-4069; www.stpete.com. Open M-F 8am-5pm, Sa 10am-5pm, Su noon-5pm.) **The Pier Information Center,** 800 2nd Ave. NE. (☎821-6443. Open M-Sa 10am-8pm, Su 11am-6pm.) **Hotlines: Rape Crisis** (☎530-7233); **Helpline** (☎344-5555). **Taxi**: Yellow Cab (☎799-2222); Bats Taxi (☎367-5702) **Internet Access:** St. Petersburg Main Library, 3745 9th Ave. N. (☎893-7724). Open M-Th 9am-9pm, F-Sa 9am-6pm, Su 10am-6pm. **Medical Services: Bayfront Medical Center,** 701 6th St. S. (☎823-1234). **Post Office:** 3135 1st Ave. N, at 31st St. (☎322-6696. Open M-F 8am-6pm, Sa 8am-12:30pm.) **Postal Code:** 37370. **Area Code:** 727.

ACCOMMODATIONS. St. Petersburg and Clearwater offer two hostels, and many cheap motels line **4th Street N** and **U.S. 19** in St. Pete. Some establishments advertise singles for as little as $25, but these tend to be very worn-down. To avoid the worst neighborhoods, stay on the north end of 4th St. and the south end of U.S. 19. Several inexpensive motels cluster along **Gulf Boulevard**. Tucked away off the sandy Clearwater shore, the **Clearwater Beach International Hostel (HI-AYH) ❶,** 606 Bay Esplanade Ave., off Mandalay Ave. at the Sands Motel in Clearwater Beach, features a common room with TV and a pool, in addition to nearby volleyball and tennis courts. (☎443-1211. Internet access $1 per 8min. Linen and key deposit $5. Office hours 9am-noon and 5-9pm. Dorms $13, nonmembers $14; private rooms $30-40. Surcharge for credit card payments.) A hidden gem, the **St. Petersburg Youth Hostel ❶,** 326 1st Ave. N, is a beachfront inn situated in the historic downtown Kelly Hotel. Call ahead to make sure there is room in the hostel, which consists of one four-person room with private bath. (☎822-4141. Common room, TV, and A/C. Youth hostel card or student ID required. Bunks $20. Hotel rooms $43.) The **Treasure Island Motel ❷,** 10315 Gulf Blvd., across the street from the beach, has big rooms with A/C, fridge, color TV, pull-out couch, and use of a beautiful pool. Catch dinner off a pier in back. (☎367-3055. Singles and doubles from $40.) **Fort De Soto County Park ❶,** 3500 Pinellas Bayway S, composed of five islands, has the best camping around, and ranks among the best parks in Florida. It centers around the Spanish Fort De Soto, which may be explored by day. Reservations must be made either at the park office, 501 1st Ave. N, Ste. A116, or at the Parks Dept., 631 Chestnut St. in Clearwater. (☎582-2267. 2-night min. stay. 14-night max. Front gate locked 9pm. Curfew 10pm. Aug.-Dec. $23; Jan.-July $33. Park office: ☎582-7738. Open daily 8am-4:30pm. Parks Dept.: ☎464-3347. Open daily 8am-5pm.)

FOOD. St. Petersburg's cheap, health-conscious restaurants cater to its retired population, and generally close by 8 or 9pm. **Dockside Dave's ❷,** 13203 Gulf Blvd. S, in Madeira Beach, is one of the best-kept secrets on the islands. The half-pound grouper sandwich (market price, around $8) is simply sublime. (☎392-9399. Open M-Sa 11am-10pm, Su noon-10pm.) City polls have ranked **Tangelo's Bar and Grille ❷,** 226 1st Ave. N, as a superb Cuban restaurant. Their imported sauce accents the $5.50 Oaxacan *mole negro* chicken breast sandwich. (☎894-1695. Open M 11am-6pm, Tu-Th 11am-8pm, F-Sa 11am-9pm.) Also in St. Pete is the **Fourth Street Shrimp Store ❷,** 1006 4th St. N—a purveyor of all things shrimp. (☎822-0325. Filling shrimp taco salad $7. Open Su-Th 11am-9pm, F-Sa 11am-9:30pm.) After a long day of relaxing under the unrelenting Clearwater sun, make your way over to **Frenchy's Cafe ❸,** 41 Baymont St., and cool off with a salted magarita ($3). If beach volleyball has you hungry, try the boiled shrimp, which comes dusted in secret seasonings for $13. The original grouper burger ($7) is also a fine choice. (☎446-3607. Open M-Th 11:30am-11pm, F-Sa 11:30am-midnight, Su noon-11pm.)

SIGHTS. Grab a copy of *See St. Pete* or the *St. Petersburg Official Visitor's Guide* for the lowdown on area events, discounts, and useful maps. Downtown St. Pete is cluttered with museums and galleries that make it worth the effort to leave the beach. For an incredible history experience, head over to the **Florida International Museum**, 100 2nd St. N, where eye-opening and intriguing exhibits await. The **Cuban Missile Crisis: When the Cold War Got Hot** exhibit allows visitors to relive the terrifying Cold War era of the 1960s, recounting day-by-day the tenuous Cuban Missile Crisis. **John F. Kennedy: The Exhibition** provides a comprehensive look at JFK's personal and political life. (☎822-3693 or 800-777-9882; www.floridamuseum.org. Wheelchair-accessible. Open M-Sa 10am-5pm, Su noon-5pm; ticket office closes 4pm. $12, seniors $11, students $6, seniors $11.) The highlight of St. Petersburg is the exhaustive **Salvador Dalí Museum,** 1000 3rd St. S, the largest private collection of the Surrealist's work in the world. The South's most visited museum houses 95 of Dali's oil paintings and provides exceptional guided tours offering fascinating views into the life and works of the enigmatic artist. (☎823-3767 or 800-442-3254; www.salvadordalimuseum.org. Wheelchair-accessible. Open M-W and F-Sa 9:30am-5:30pm, Th 9:30am-8pm, Su noon-5:30pm. $10, students $5, seniors $7, under 10 free. Free tours daily 12:15, 1:30, 2:30, 3:45pm.) The **Florida Holocaust Museum,** 55 5th St. S, traces Jewish life and anti-Semitism from early Europe to the present. (☎820-0110 or 800-960-7448; www.flholocaustmuseum.org. Open M-F 10am-5pm, Sa-Su noon-5pm. $8, students and seniors $7, under 19 $3.)

Beaches are the most worthwhile—but not the only—attraction along the coastline. The nicest beach may be **Pass-a-Grille Beach,** but its parking meters eat quarters by the bucketful. Check out **Clearwater Beach,** at the northern end of the Gulf Blvd. strand, where mainstream beach culture lives in a fantastic white sand beach setting. The **Sunsets at Pier 60 Festival** brings arts and entertainment to Clearwater Beach, but the sunsets draw the crowds. (☎449-1036; www.sunsetsatpier60.com. Festival open daily 2hr. before sundown until 2hr. after.)

NIGHTLIFE. St. Pete caters to those who want to end the night by 9 or 10pm; most visitors looking for nightlife either head to Tampa or to the beach. Clearwater hotels, restaurants, and parks often host free concerts. Free copies of *Weekly Planet* or *Tampa Tonight/Pinellas Tonight* grace local restaurants and bars. **Beach Nutts,** 9600 W. Gulf Blvd., Treasure Island, has fresh grouper ($10), while the porch has a spectacular view of the beach and bands play nightly. (☎367-7427. Open daily 11am-2am.) Locals wind down with a beer and a game of pool at the **Beach Bar,** 454 Mandalay Ave. If not in the mood for darts, walk around the corner and find your groove on the dance floor. (☎ 446-8866. Dancing F-Sa 9pm-2am. 21+. Bar open daily 10am-2am.) The younger crowd likes to make a dash for the mainland and party at **Liquid Blue,** 22 North Ft. Harrison St., Clearwater's premier techno nightspot. (☎446-4000. 18+. Cover varies. Open Tu-Sa 9pm-2am.)

ATLANTIC COAST

DAYTONA BEACH ☎386

When locals first started auto-racing on the hard-packed sands in Daytona Beach more than 60 years ago, they were combining two aspects of life that would come to define the town's entire mentality: speed and sand. Daytona played an essential role in the founding of the **National Association of Stock Car Auto Racing (NASCAR)** in 1947, and the mammoth Daytona International Speedway still hosts several big races each year. While races no longer occur on the sand, 23 mi. of Atlantic beaches still pump the lifeblood of the community.

ORIENTATION. Daytona Beach lies 53 mi. northeast of Orlando and 90 mi. south of Jacksonville. **I-95** parallels the coast and the barrier island. **Atlantic Avenue (Route A1A)** is the main drag along the shore, and a scenic drive up A1A goes to St. Augustine and Jacksonville. **International Speedway Boulevard (U.S. 92)** runs east-west, from the ocean, through the downtown area, and to the racetrack and airport. Daytona Beach is a collection of smaller towns; many street numbers are not consecutive and navigation can be difficult. To avoid the gridlock on the beach, arrive early (8am) and leave early (around 3pm). Visitors must pay $5 to drive onto the beach, and police strictly enforce the 10 m.p.h. speed limit. Free parking is plentiful during most of the year but sparse during spring break (usually mid-Feb. to Apr.), Speedweeks, Bike Week, Biketoberfest, and the Pepsi 400. See p. 500 for festival dates.

PRACTICAL INFORMATION. Amtrak, 2491 Old New York Ave. (☎734-2322; open daily 8:30am-7pm), in DeLand, 24 mi. west on Rte. 92, tracks to Miami (7hr., 1 per day, $97). **Greyhound,** 138 S. Ridgewood Ave. (☎255-7076; open daily 6:30am-10:30pm), 4 mi. west of the beach, goes to Jacksonville (2hr., 11 per day, $16-17) and Orlando (1½hr., 7 per day, $10-11). **Volusia County Transit Co. (VOTRAN),** 950 Big Tree Rd., operates local buses and a trolley that covers Rte. A1A between Granada Blvd. and Dunlawton Ave. All buses have bike racks. On beach areas where driving is prohibited, free beach trams transport beachgoers. (☎761-7700. Service M-Sa 6am-8pm, Su 7am-6:30pm. Trolley M-Sa noon-midnight. $1, seniors and ages 6-17 $0.50. Free maps available at hotels.) **Taxi: Yellow Cab,** ☎255-5555. **Visitor Info: Daytona Beach Area Convention and Visitors Bureau,** 126 E. Orange Ave., on City Island. (☎255-0415 or 800-544-0415; www.daytonabeachcvb.org. Open M-F 9am-5pm.) **Rape Crisis Line,** ☎255-2102. **Medical Services: Halifax Medical Center,** 303 N. Clyde Morris Blvd. (☎904-254-4000.) **Internet Access: Volusia County Library Center** 105 E. Magnolia Ave. (☎257-6036. Open M and W 9:30am-5:30pm, Tu and Th 9:30am-8pm, F-Sa 9:30am-5pm.) **Post Office:** 220 N. Beach St. (☎226-2618. Open M-F 8am-5pm, Sa 9am-noon.) **Postal Code:** 32115. **Area Code:** 386.

ACCOMMODATIONS. Almost all of Daytona's accommodations front **Atlantic Avenue (Route A1A),** either on the beach or across the street; those off the beach offer the best deals. Daytona has peak and low-season rates. Spring break and race events drive prices to absurdly high levels, but low-season rates are more motel-like. Almost all the motels facing the beach cost $35 for a low-season single; on the other side of the street it's $25. The **Camellia Motel ❷,** 1055 N. Atlantic Ave. (Rte. A1A), across the street from the beach, is an especially welcoming retreat with cozy, bright rooms, free local calls, cable TV, and A/C. (☎252-9963. Reserve early. Singles $30; doubles $35. During spring break, singles $100; each additional person $10. Kitchens additional $10.) For a truly unique sleeping experience, try the **Travelers Inn ❷,** 735 N. Atlantic Ave. Each of the 22 rooms has a different theme— find the force with Yoda in the *Star Wars* room or rock out with Jimi Hendrix or the Beatles in their rooms. (☎253-3501 or 800-417-6466. Singles $29-49; doubles $39-59; each additional person $10. With kitchens $10 more. Prices triple during special events.) The **Boardwalk Inn ❹,** 301 S. Atlantic Ave, is Daytona's newest addition to the beachfront. Each suite comes equipped with cable TV, microwaves, and a host of other amenities; add the Olympic-sized swimming pool, spa, and exercise room, and guests will have little incentive to get out and explore all that Daytona has to offer. (☎253-8300. Spring and summer rooms $90-110; winter $60-80.) **Tomoka State Park ❶,** 2099 N. Beach St., 8 mi. north of Daytona in Ormond Beach, has 100 sites under a tropical canopy. Enjoy salt-water fishing, nature trails, and a sculpture museum. (☎676-4050, for reservations ☎800-326-3521. Open daily 8am-dusk. Sites Nov.-Apr. $17; with electricity $19. May-Oct. $11/13. Seniors 50% discount. $3.25 entrance fee for vehicles, $1 for pedestrians and bicyclists.)

FOOD. One of the most famous (and popular) seafood restaurants in the area is **Aunt Catfish's ❸,** 4009 Halifax Dr., at Dunlawton Ave. next to the Port Orange Bridge. Order anything that resides under the sea and you're in for a treat, though the lobster and crab receive the most praise. Most entrees $9-15. Salads ring in under $9. (☎767-4768. Open M-Sa 11:30am-9:30pm, Su 9am-9:30pm.) **Sweetwater's ❺,** 3633 Halifax Dr., in Port Orange, has been a long-time local favorite, voted everything from Best Seafood to Best Early Bird Special to Best Waterfront View. Feast upon the $18 Hungry Seaman dinner, a marine cornucopia of fish, shrimp, scallops, and lobster scampi. (☎761-6724. Open daily 11:30am-10pm.) From frog legs ($10) to flounder ($10), **B&B Fisheries ❸,** 715 E. International Speedway, doesn't mess around when it comes to serving up some of Daytona's best seafood.

Don't worry landlovers, B&B also dishes out incredible slabs of steak from $10. (☎252-6542. Open M-F 11am-8:30pm, Sa 4-8:30pm.) **The Dancing Avocado Kitchen ❶,** 110 S. Beach St., offers a delicious alternative to the Daytona seafood-and-grill scene. Enjoy the belly dancer sandwich (avocado, hummus, lettuce, tomato, and olives; $5.50) or the signature symphony salad ($6) in this organically delightful eatery. (☎947-2022. Open M-Sa 8am-4pm.)

START YOUR ENGINES. The center of the racing world, the **Daytona International Speedway** hosts NASCAR's Super Bowl: the Daytona 500 (Feb. 15, 2004). **Speedweek** (Jan. 31-Feb. 15, 2004) precedes the legendary race, while the **Pepsi 400** (for those who think young) heats up the track July 3, 2004. Next door, **Daytona USA,** 1801 W. International Speedway Blvd., includes a new simulation ride, an IMAX film on the history of Daytona, and a fun teaching program on NASCAR commentating. The breathtaking **Speedway Tour** is a unique chance to see the garages, grandstands, and famous 31° banked turns up close. The **Richard Petty Driving Experience** puts fans in a stock car for a ride-along at 150 mph. (☎947-6800; NASCAR tickets 253-1223. Open daily 9am-7pm. $16, seniors $13, ages 6-12 $8. Tours every ½hr. daily 9:30am-5:30pm, $7. Richard Petty: ☎800-237-3889. 16+. $106.) **Bike Week** draws biker mamas for various motorcycle duels, and **Biketoberfest** brings them back for more. (Bikeweek: Feb. 27-Mar. 7, 2004; www.bikeweek.com. Biketoberfest: Oct. 21-24, 2004; www.biketoberfest.com.)

NIGHTLIFE. When spring break hits, concerts, hotel-sponsored parties, and other events answer the call of students. News about these travels fastest by word of mouth, but the *Calendar of Events* and *SEE Daytona Beach* make good starting points. On mellow nights, head to the boardwalk to play volleyball or shake your groove-thing at the **Oceanfront Bandshell,** an open-air amphitheater constructed entirely of *coquina* rock. Dance clubs thump along Seabreeze Blvd. just west of N. Atlantic Ave. **Razzle's,** 611 Seabreeze Blvd., caters to the traditionally scandalous Spring Break crowd with its high energy dance floors, flashy light shows, and nightly drink specials. (☎257-6326. Cover around $5. Open daily 7pm-3am.) **Ocean Deck,** 127 S. Ocean Ave., stands out among the clubs with its live music on the beach and nightly drink specials. Chow down on the "shipwreck" (shrimp, crab, oysters and clams; $10) while grooving to the nightly reggae, jazz, and calypso, with rock on Su. (☎253-5224. Music nightly 9:30pm-2:30am. 21+ after 9pm. Open daily 11am-3am; kitchen until 2am.)

COCOA BEACH & CAPE CANAVERAL ☎321

Cape Canaveral and the surrounding "Space Coast" were a hot spot during the Cold War. Once the great Space Race began, the area took off—it became the base of operations for every major space exploration, from the Apollo moon landings to the current International Space Station effort. The towns of Cocoa Beach and nearby Melbourne provide typical beach atmosphere, including the surfer's Mecca, **Ron Jon Surf Shop,** 4151 N. Atlantic Ave, where you'll find two floors of boards, shirts, shorts, and sunscreen. (☎799-8888. Open 24hr.) During summer launch dates, tourists pack the area and hotel prices follow NASA into the stratosphere.

ORIENTATION & PRACTICAL INFORMATION. The Space Coast, 50 mi. east of Orlando, consists of mainland towns Cocoa and Rockledge, oceanfront Cocoa Beach and Cape Canaveral, and Merritt Island. Both **I-95** and **U.S. 1** run north-south on the mainland, while **Route A1A (North Atlantic Avenue)** is the beach's main drag. **Greyhound,** 302 E. Main St. (☎636-6531; station open daily 7am-5:30pm), in Cocoa, 8 mi. inland, runs to Daytona (1¾hr., 4 per day, $15-16) and Orlando (1hr., 5 per day, $10-11). **Space Coast Area Transit (SCAT)** has North Beach and South

Beach routes and stops at every town in Brevard County. Surfboards are allowed inside buses. (☎633-1878. Operates M-F 6am-6:45pm, Sa-Su service on some routes. $1; students, seniors, and disabled $0.50; transfers free.) **Blue Dolphin Shuttle** connects Cocoa Beach with the Orlando Airport; call in advance. (☎433-0011. $60.) **Taxi: Checker Taxi,** ☎777-9339. **Visitor Info: Cocoa Beach Chamber of Commerce,** 400 Fortenberry Rd., on Merritt Island. (☎459-2200; www.cocoabeachchamber.com. Open M-F 8:30am-5pm.) **Space Coast Office of Tourism,** 8810 Astronaut Blvd. (A1A), #102. (☎407-868-1126 or 800-936-2326. Open M-F 8am-5pm.) **Medical Services: Cape Canaveral Hospital,** 701 W. Cocoa Beach Cswy. (☎799-7111). **Internet Access: Cocoa Beach Public Library,** 550 N. Brevard Ave. (☎868-1104. Open M-W 9am-9pm, Th 9am-6pm, F-Sa 9am-5pm, Su 1-5pm.) **Post Office:** 500 N. Brevard Ave., Cocoa Beach. (☎783-4800. Open M-F 8:30am-5pm, Sa 8:30am-noon.) **Postal Code:** 32931. **Area Code:** 321 (...lift-off!). 10-digit dialing required.

ACCOMMODATIONS & FOOD. Wary of wild teenagers, most hotels in Cocoa Beach rent rooms only to guests who are 21+. Across from the beach, **Motel 6 ❷,** 3701 N. Atlantic Ave. (A1A), offers clean, comfortable rooms at cheaper rates than most accommodations in the area. (☎783-3103. A/C, TV, pool, laundry, and shuffleboard. 21+. Singles $43; F-Sa $6 each additional person.) Behind the bus station and the water tower, the **Dixie Motel ❷,** 301 Forrest Ave., is a family-owned establishment with clean rooms, floor-to-ceiling windows, A/C, cable TV, and a swimming pool. (☎632-1600. Laundry available. 21+. Rooms Nov.-Apr. from $55, May-Oct. from $40.) Party-hard teenagers and vacationing families alike flock to the **Cocoa Beach Comfort Inn ❸,** 3901 N. Atlantic Ave., which offers visitors enormous rooms with all the perks. Pool, A/C, cable TV, coffee makers, and, in some rooms, a wet bar. (☎783-2221. 18+. Rooms Nov.-Apr. from $80; May-Oct. from $60.) Pitch your tent at scenic **Jetty Park Campgrounds ❶,** 400 E. Jetty Rd., at the northern tip of Cape Canaveral. (☎783-7111. Reserve 3 months ahead, especially before shuttle launches. Jan.-Apr. primitive sites $19; with water and electricity $23; full hookup $26. May-Dec. $17/21/24.) Bikini contests, live rock and reggae, karaoke, delicious drink specials, and tasty seafood make **Coconut's on the Beach ❸,** 2 Minutemen Causeway at A1A, a popular hangout. Try the classic crab cake for lunch ($7) or the coconut-crusted mahi-mahi for dinner ($15), while chilling on the deck and ogling surfers. Key lime pie is $3. Call for monthly events schedule. (☎784-1422. Open M-Sa 11am-1:30am, Su 10am-1:30am.) Lines awaiting "famous" New York-style pizza stream out the door of **Bizzarro ❶,** 4 1st Ave., off A1A in Indialantic. (☎724-4799. Sicilian slice $1.50. Open M-Th 11am-9pm, F-Sa 11am-11pm, Su noon-9pm.) The **Tea Room ❶,** 6211 N. Atlantic Ave. (A1A), combines home cookin' and a little TLC to start your day off right. (☎783-5527. Daily breakfast specials around $3. Pastries $0.50-1.25. Open M-F 7am-2pm, Sa-Su 8am-2pm.)

THE FINAL FRONTIER. All of **NASA's** shuttle flights take off from the **Kennedy Space Center,** 18 mi. north of Cocoa Beach on Rte. 3, accessible by car via Rte. 405E off I-95, or Rte. 528E from the Beeline Expwy. From Cocoa Beach, take Rte. A1A until it turns west onto Rte. 528, then follow Rte. 3 N. The recently renovated **Kennedy Space Center Visitors Complex (KSC)** provides a huge welcoming center, complete with two 3-D IMAX theaters, a Rocket Garden, and exhibits on the latest in-space exploration. KSC offers two tours of their 220 sq. mi. grounds. The **Kennedy Space Center Tour** hits the three main attractions: the LC 39 Observation Gantry, Apollo/Saturn V Center, and the International Space Station Center. (Departs regularly 9am-2:15pm.) Meet a real space pioneer face-to-face at the daily **Astronaut Encounter,** when astronauts past and present discuss their otherworldly experiences. The **NASA Up Close Tour** provides access to facilities that are restricted on the standard tour. Check out the shuttle launch pad, the gigantic VAB building (where the shuttle is put together), and the Crawler Transporter. Check NASA's **launch schedule**—

you may have a chance to watch the space shuttles *Endeavor*, *Atlantis*, or *Discovery* thunder off into the blue yonder above the Cape. A combo package will get you admission to the Visitors Complex and transportation to a viewing area to watch the fiery ascension. (☎452-2121; 449-4444 for launch info; www.kennedyspacecenter.com. Open daily 9am-5:30pm. Standard KSC grounds tour $28, ages 3-11 $18. "Maximum Access" tour, including admission to the Astronaut Hall of Fame, $33, ages 3-11 $23. Up Close tour additional $20. Launch combo $17.)

Surrounding the NASA complex, the **Merritt Island National Wildlife Refuge** teems with sea turtles, manatees, wild hogs, otters, and over 300 species of birds. Exit 80 off I-95, east on Garden St. to SR 402. (☎861-0667. Open daily dawn to dusk. Visitors Center open M-F 8am-4:30pm, Sa-Su 9am-5pm.) **Canaveral National Seashore,** on the northeastern shore of the wildlife refuge, covers 67,000 acres of undeveloped beach and dunes. Take Rte. 406 E off U.S. 1 in Titusville. (☎407-867-0677. Open Apr.-Oct. daily 6am-8pm; Nov.-Mar 6am-6pm. Closed 3 days before and 1 day after NASA launches. $5 per car, $1 per pedestrian/bicyclist.)

ST. AUGUSTINE ☎904

Spanish adventurer Pedro Menéndez de Aviles founded St. Augustine in 1565, making it the first European colony in North America and the oldest continuous settlement in the United States. Thanks to preservation efforts, much of St. Augustine's Spanish flavor remains intact. This city's pride lies in its provincial cobblestone streets, *coquina* rock walls, and antique shops rather than in its token beaches. Forget L.A.'s high-priced plastic surgeons—eternal youth comes cheap around these parts—about $5.75, to be exact, in the form of admission to the famed Fountain of Youth.

ORIENTATION & PRACTICAL INFORMATION

Most of St. Augustine's sights conveniently lie within a 10-15min. walk from the hostel, motels, and bus station. Narrow streets and frequent one-ways can make driving unpleasant. Parking is available at the Visitors Center all day for just $3. The city's major east-west routes, **King Street** and **Cathedral Place,** run through downtown and become the Bridge of Lions that leads to the beaches. **San Marco Avenue,** or **Avenida Menendez,** runs north-south. **Castillo Drive** grows out of San Marco Ave. near the center of town. **Saint George Street,** a north-south pedestrian route, contains most of the shops and many of the sights in town. **Greyhound,** 100 Malaga St. (☎829-6401; open daily 7:30am-8:30pm), has service to Daytona Beach (1¼hr., 6 per day, $13-14) and Jacksonville (1hr., 6 per day, $9-10). If the station is closed, the driver accepts cash. **Public Transit: Public Street Corner,** offers bus service; expect a bus every ½hr. at the Greyhound station, where all routes converge. (☎823-4816 for schedules and info. Operates daily 6am-5pm. $1.) **Sightseeing Trains,** 170 San Marco Ave., shuttle travelers on a red trolley that hits all the major attractions on their 20 stops. (☎829-6545 or 800-226-6545. Operates every 15-20min. 8:30am-5pm. $12, ages 6-12 $5. Ticket good for 3 consecutive days.) **Taxi: Ancient City Taxi,** ☎824-8161. **Visitors Center:** 10 Castillo Dr., at San Marco Ave. From the bus station, walk three blocks north on Riberia St., then right on Orange St. (☎825-1000. Open daily 8:30am-5:30pm.) **Post Office:** 99 King St. (☎829-8716. Open M-F 8:30am-5pm, Sa 9am-1pm.) **Postal Code:** 32084. **Area Code:** 904.

ACCOMMODATIONS

Pirate Haus Inn and Hostel, 32 Treasury St. (☎808-1999 or 877-466-3864), just off Saint George St., is hands-down the place to stay, with spacious dorms, beautiful private rooms, helpful management, and a great location. From Rte. 16 E, go south on

U.S. 1, make a left on King St. and then left on Charlotte St.; parking is available in the metered lot behind the inn. Weary travelers are pampered by a lively common room, big lockers, Internet access, and a tasty pancake breakfast. A/C and free lockers. Key/linen deposit $5. Office hours 8-10am and 6-10pm, no lockout for registered guests. Dorms $15, nonmembers $17; private rooms $46. Under 13 free. ❶

Casablanca Inn, 24 Avenida Menendez (☎829-0928), in the historic downtown district, stands out among the many B&Bs in St. Augustine. Feast upon the enormous 2-course breakfast and unwind on the porch, which offers rocking chairs and a spectacular view of the river. Large rooms boast cable TV, pleasant artwork, and—perhaps inexplicably—fireplaces. Rooms $100-160. ❺

Sunrise Inn, 512 Anastasia Blvd. (☎829-3888), is the best option among the many motels along Rte. A1A. A/C, cable TV, phones, and pool. Check-in/check-out 10am. Singles Su-Th $28, F-Sa $38; doubles $33/43. ❷

Seabreeze Motel, 208 Anastasia Blvd. (☎829-8122), has clean rooms with refrigerators and pool access. A/C, cable TV, and free local calls. Kitchenette available. Singles M-F $40, Sa-Su $45, holidays and special events $60; doubles $45/50/65. ❷

Anastasia State Recreation Area, on Rte. A1A, 4 mi. south of the historic district. From town, cross the Bridge of Lions and turn left past the Alligator Farm. Nearby, Salt Run and the Atlantic Ocean provide opportunities for great windsurfing, fishing, swimming, and hiking. (☎461-2033. Office open daily 8am-dusk. Reservations recommended F-Sa. Sites $18; with electricity $20. Vehicle entrance fee $3.25, pedestrians $1. ❶

FOOD & NIGHTLIFE

The bustle of daytime tourists and the abundance of budget eateries make lunch in St. Augustine's historic district a delight, especially among the cafes and bars of **Saint George Street.** The **Bunnery Bakery and Cafe ❶,** 121 Saint George St., is an always-packed cafe that leaves patrons in a lull of bakery bliss. Locals and tourists alike flock to the Bunnery for its hearty breakfasts ($2-6) and then return for delectable panini sandwiches ($4-7) at lunch. (☎829-6166. Open 8am-6pm. No credit cards.) Frankly, my dear, you'll get more BBQ than you can handle at **Scarlett O'Hara's ❷,** 70 Hypolita St. at Cordova St. Monster "Big Rhett" burgers ($6) and full slabs of ribs ($15) are consumed by patrons who, after discovering this gem, will never go hungry again. Live music, usually rock or reggae, entertains nightly. (☎824-6535. Happy Hour M-F 4-7pm. Occasional $2 cover. Open daily 11am-12:30am.) **Pizzalley's ❶,** 117 St. George St., is the best pizza place in the historic district. Scarf down a piping hot slice ($2) or a tremendous sub ($5-$7) in this cramped but worthwhile eatery. (☎825-2627. Open daily 11am-9pm.)

St. Augustine supports a variety of bars, many on Rte. A1A S and Saint George St. *Folio Weekly* contains event listings. Local string musicians play on the two stages in the **Milltop,** 19½ Saint George St., a tiny yet illustrious bar above an old mill in the restored district. (☎829-2329. Music daily 1pm until closing. Cover varies. Open M-Sa 11am-1am, Su 11am-10pm.) Sample your choice of 24 drafts at the **Oasis Deck and Restaurant,** 4000 Rte. A1A S at Ocean Trace Rd. (☎471-3424. Gator tail $6. Seafood sandwich $3-7. Happy Hour 4-7pm. Live rock or reggae M-Sa 8pm-12:30am, Su 7-11:30pm. Open daily 6am-1am.) Cheap flicks and bargain eats await at **Pot Belly's,** 36 Granada St. Screening just-out-of-theaters movies, this combination pub, deli, and cinema serves a range of sandwiches ($3-6), junk food ($1-3) and brew ($7.50 for a pitcher) to the in-house tables, ensuring that viewers never have to miss that crucial moment. (☎829-3101. Movie tickets $4.75. Shows 6:30, 8:45pm.)

SIGHTS

FOUNTAIN OF YOUTH. No trip to St. Augustine would be complete without a trek down beautiful Magnolia Dr. to the **Fountain of Youth,** the legend that sparked Ponce de León's voyage to the New World. A guided tour goes through hundreds of years of Spanish conquistador history in minutes. To fully capture the historical significance of the place, take a swig of the sulfury libation and try to ignore the fact that the water now runs through a pipe. *(11 Magnolia Ave. Go right on Williams St. from San Marco Ave. and continue until it dead-ends into Magnolia Ave. ☎829-3168 or 800-356-8222. Open daily 9am-5pm. $5.75, seniors $4.75, ages 6-12 $2.75.)*

SPANISH HERITAGE. The oldest masonry fortress in the continental US, **Castillo de San Marcos National Monument** has 14 ft. thick walls built of *coquina*, the local shell-rock. The fort, a four-pointed star complete with drawbridge and moat, contains a museum, a large courtyard surrounded by quarters for the garrison, a jail, a chapel, and the original cannon brought overseas by the Spanish. *(1 Castillo Dr., off San Marco Ave. ☎829-6506. Open daily 8:45am-5:15pm, last admission 4:45pm. Occasional tours; call ahead. $5, ages 6-16 $2.)* One of the most religiously significant sights in the US is **La Leche Shrine and Mission of Nombre de Dios,** the birthplace of American Catholicism. The first Mass in the US was held here over 400 years ago. A 208 ft. cross commemorates the city's founding, and the shaded lawns make for a peaceful stroll. *(27 Ocean St. Off San Marco Ave. ☎824-2809. Open M-F 8am-5pm, Sa 9am-5pm, Su 9:30am-5pm. Mass M-F 8:30am, Sa 6pm, Su 8am. Donation suggested.)*

HISTORICAL SIGHTS. Not surprisingly, the oldest continuous settlement in the US holds some of the nation's oldest artifacts. The **Gonzalez-Alvarez House** is the oldest house on the National Registry of Historic Places. Constructed in the 17th century, the tiny house now serves as a tourist haven containing exhibits on the Spanish, British, and American heritage of the area. *(14 Saint Francis St. ☎824-2872; www.oldcity.com/oldhouse. Partially wheelchair-accessible. Open daily 9am-5pm, last admission 4:30pm. $6, students $4, seniors $5.50; families $14.)* Step into the past at the **Oldest Store Museum,** a former general store showcasing over 100,000 turn-of-the-century items, from a high-wheel bicycle to a Model T. *(4 Artillery Ln. ☎829-9729. Open M-Sa 10am-4pm, Su noon-4pm. $5, ages 6-12 $1.50.)* For the best view of the nation's oldest city and its surrounding waters, climb the 219 stairs of the **St. Augustine Lighthouse and Museum,** one of only six lighthouses in the state open to the public. Tour the 19th-century tower and keeper's house to learn about marine archaeological studies in the surrounding waters. *(81 Lighthouse Ave. Off Rte. A1A across from the Alligator Farm. ☎829-0745. Open daily 9am-6pm. Tower, grounds, and house $6.50, seniors $5.50, ages 7-11 $4. House and grounds $4/3/2.)*

RESTORED HOTELS. Take a student-guided tour through **Flagler College,** a small liberal arts institution housed in the restored Spanish Renaissance-style **Ponce de Leon Hotel.** Constructed by railroad and Standard Oil tycoon Henry Flagler in 1888, the hotel served as the luxury playground for America's social elite. Celebrity heavyweights such as John Rockefeller and Will Rogers once strolled through the gorgeous interior, much of which was designed by Louis Comfort Tiffany. *(☎823-3378; www.flagler.edu. Wheelchair-accessible. Tours mid-May to mid-Aug. daily on the hr. 10am-4pm. $4, under 12 $1.)* In 1947, Chicago publisher and art lover Otto Lightner converted the Alcazar Hotel into the **Lightner Museum** to hold an impressive collection of cut, blown, and burnished glass, as well as old clothing and oddities like nun and monk beer steins. Today, the museum's eccentricity remains its strongest feature, as it houses everything from a stuffed lion to a Russian bath steamroom. *(75 King St. ☎824-2874; www.lightnermuseum.org. Wheelchair-accessible. Open daily 9am-5pm. 18th-century musical instruments play daily 11am-2pm. $6, students and ages 12-18 $2.)*

JUST FOR FUN. Across the Bridge of Lions, the **St. Augustine Alligator Farm** allows visitors to get up close and personal with some of nature's finest reptiles. The park, which has been delighting visitors since 1893, is the only place in the world where all 23 known crocodilian species live. *(On Rte. A1A S. ☎824-3337. Open daily 9am-8pm. Presentations every hr. Feeding daily 1:30pm. $14.25, ages 5-11 $8.50. Discounts for AAA/CAA, military, and seniors.)* A mouth-watering adventure of a different sort awaits at **Whetstone Chocolates.** Tour the only chocolate factory in Florida, learn the intricate production process, and enjoy a free sample of their product—just don't drool on the glass. *(2 Coke Rd., off State Rd. 312 just east of U.S. 1. ☎825-1700. Open M-Sa 10am-5:30pm. Free.)*

JACKSONVILLE ☎904

At almost 1000 square miles, Jacksonville is geographically the largest city in the continental US. Without theme parks, star-studded beaches, or tropical environs, Jacksonville struggles to shine through the cluttered tourist offerings of southern Florida. The city, however, still draws visitors with its family-oriented attractions, and its downtown is undergoing a massive makeover to prepare for the 2005 Super Bowl. Tourists can anticipate a more accessible and exciting Jacksonville in the near future, but for now, expect the construction which will bring that about.

ORIENTATION & PRACTICAL INFORMATION. Three highways intersect in Jacksonville, making driving around the city relatively easy. **I-95** runs north-south, while **I-10** starts in the downtown area and heads west. **I-295** forms a giant "C" on the western half of the city, and **Arlington Expressway** becomes **Atlantic Boulevard (Route 10)** heading to the beach. The St. Johns River snakes throughout the city. **Airport: Jacksonville International,** 2400 Yankee Clipper Dr. (☎741-4902; www.jaxairports.org), 18 mi. north of the city on I-95, Exit 127B. **Amtrak,** 3570 Clifford Ln. (☎766-5110; open 24hr.), off I-95 at Exit 20th St. W, sends coaches to Orlando (3½hr., 2 per day, $34). Take Northside 4 Moncreif Bus A to get to the terminal. **Greyhound,** 10 N. Pearl St. (☎356-9976, open 24hr.), at Central Station Skyrail stop downtown, buses to Atlanta (6-8hr., 8 per day, $41-43) and Orlando (3-5hr., 11 per day, $24-26). **Jacksonville Transportation Authority** runs throughout the city from the main station at State and Union downtown. (☎630-3181. Operates daily 5am-10pm. $0.75.) The **Skyway** monorail is the best way to maneuver downtown. (☎630-3181. Operates M-F 6am-11pm, Sa 10am-11pm. $0.35.) **Taxi: Yellow Cab,** ☎260-1111. **Visitor Info: Jacksonville and the Beaches Convention and Visitors Bureau,** 201 E. Adams St., downtown. (☎798-9111 or 800-733-2668; www.jaxcvb.com. Open M-F 8am-5pm.) **Hotlines: Rape Crisis,** ☎355-7273. **Internet Access: Jacksonville Main Public Library,** 122 N. Ocean St. (☎630-2665. Open M-Th 9am-8pm, F-Sa 9am-6pm, Su 1-6pm.) **Post Office:** 311 W. Monroe St. (☎353-3445. Open M-F 8:30am-5pm, Sa 9am-1pm.) **Postal Code:** 32202. **Area Code:** 904.

ACCOMMODATIONS & FOOD. Inexpensive hotels abound along I-95 to the north and south of the city and on the Arlington Expwy. heading to the ocean. Bare-bones but clean, the **Best Value Inn ❷,** 1057 Broward Rd., off I-95 at the Broward Rd. Exit, north of the city, has large, comfortable rooms with TV and A/C. If a long day at the beach has left you feeling a bit lethargic, head over to the adjoining **Red Hare Restaurant ❷,** where you'll find good eats at better prices (entrees $5-10, Su brunch buffet $6). (☎757-0990. Rooms $40.) Just steps from the sands of Jacksonville Beach, **Fig Tree Inn Bed and Breakfast ❹,** 185 4th Ave. S, offers five differently themed rooms brimming with antiques. Enjoy your breakfast or afternoon tea on the front porch of this beach-style shingle cottage. (☎246-8855 or 877-217-9830. Rooms $75-140.) **Kathryn Abbey Hanna Park ❶,** 500 Wonderwood Dr., in Mayport, has 293 wooded sites near the beach, all with full hookup, along with 4 cabins with A/C. Twenty miles of bike paths and a water playground are also on sight. (☎249-4700. Cabins 2-night min. stay. Reception 8am-9pm. Reservations recommended for cabins. Tent sites $13.50; RVs $18; cabins $34.)

Breakfast fans rejoice at **Famous Amos Restaurant** ❷, 375 Atlantic Blvd., where the day's most important meal is deliciously cooked up morning, noon, and night ($2-7). For a more traditional lunch or dinner meal, Famous Amos offers heaping portions of chicken, steak, and stew ($5-10). (☎249-3025. Open 24hr.) Locals take a break from the rays at the **Beachside Seafood Market and Restaurant** ❷, 120 N. 3rd St. (Rte. A1A) by 2nd Ave., where the cooks fry up fish sandwiches and baskets ($4-6) using their own fresh catches. (☎241-4880. Open M-Sa 11am-6:30pm, Su 11am-5pm.) For an elegant bistro with a casual twist, head over to **Benny's Steak and Seafood** ❺, at Jacksonville Landing, where the mostly local clientele take on the Collossal Cowboy (22 oz. ribeye, $30) and fresh grouper ($19) in the classy interior or on the waterfront deck. (☎301-1014. Open Su-Th 11am-10pm, F-Sa 11am-midnight.)

SIGHTS. At the **Anheuser-Busch Brewery Tour,** 111 Busch Dr., off I-95 10min. north of downtown, visitors from all over the globe unite under the banner of brewsky. Most are awed by their sneak peak at the brewing process, though all are blown away by the "hospitality room," in which 21+ beer-lovers get to sample any 2 of Busch's 12 beers; designated drivers enjoy free soda and pretzels. (☎696-8373; www.budweisertours.com. Wheelchair-accessible. Open M-Sa 9am-4pm, hourly tours. Free.) **Fort Caroline National Memorial,** 12713 Fort Caroline Rd., was the sight of a 1565 battle between Spanish and French Huguenot forces—the first armed conflict between European powers over new world settlement. Today visitors can try their hand at storming a replica of the fort; the less aggressive can peruse the museum's Native American and French artifacts. (☎641-7155. Open daily 9am-5pm. Free.) The fort occupies a small patch of the **Timucuan Ecological and Historic Preserve,** 13165 Mt. Pleasant Rd., where 46,000 serene acres of saltwater marshes and tidal creeks teem with fish, dolphins, and eagles. (☎641-7155. Open daily 8am-dusk. Free.) The beautiful grounds of the **Cummer Museum of Art and Gardens,** 829 Riverside Ave., line the St. Johns River south of downtown. Indoors, the Renaissance, Baroque, and American colonial exhibits impress art connoisseurs, while children delight in the exciting hands-on art education center. Upcumming shows highlight works by Edward Hopper (opening Feb. 2004) and Georgia O'Keefe (opening Oct. 2004). (☎356-6857; www.cummer.org. Wheelchair-accessible. Open Tu and Th 10am-9pm, W and F-Sa 10am-5pm, Su noon-5pm. $6, seniors $4, students $3. Free Tu 4-9pm; college students with ID free Tu-F after 1:30pm.)

ENTERTAINMENT & NIGHTLIFE. Acts ranging from Ringo Starr to the Dixie Chicks to Gilbert and Sullivan theater have performed at the historic **Florida Theatre,** 128 E. Forsyth St. (☎355-2787), built in 1927. The theater hosts more than 300 performances a year; check out www.floridatheatre.com for upcoming shows. A different kind of popular culture thrives at the **Alltel Stadium** (☎633-2000), East Duval and Haines St., home to the NFL's Jaguars. Much of Jacksonville's nightlife centers around **Jacksonville Landing,** Main St. and Independent Dr., a riverfront area packed with restaurants, bars, shopping, and live entertainment. (☎353-1188. Open M-Th 10am-8pm, F-Sa 10am-9pm, Su noon-5:30pm.) Next door, wolf down some Not 'cho Average Nachos ($8) while taking in the game at **Legends Sports Bar.** During Monday Night Football you can chase your chips down with $4 pitchers of beer. (☎353-4577. Open daily 11am-2am.)

BEACHES. Miles of uncrowded white sands can be found at **Jacksonville Beach,** as well as neighboring **Atlantic Beach, Neptune Beach,** and **Ponte Vedra Beach.** To reach the Atlantic take Rte. 90/Beach Blvd. or Rte. 10/Atlantic Blvd. east from downtown for about 30min. Fishermen stake out spots on the Jacksonville Beach Pier, while golfers take advantage of the more than 20 area golf courses. The Boardwalk is abuzz with activity, from musical festivals to sand-castle building contests. Surfing and volleyball tournaments take place in May. Staple Florida attractions are nearby, including a dog track, mini golf, go-karts, and a water park.

SOUTH FLORIDA

MIAMI ☎305

Miami's Latin heart pulses to the beat of the largest Cuban population this side of Havana—speaking Spanish is very useful. Beautiful buildings and beautiful people have established the city as a tourist haven. When it's cold in New York or smoggy in Los Angeles, Miami Beach seems to be the preferred hangout for an inordinate number of celebrities and the hopping nightclub scene lets the average Joe enjoy a lifestyle along with them. But it's not all bikinis and sand—Miami is the starting point for one of America's greatest natural habitats, the Everglades, as well as the gateway to the Florida Keys and the Caribbean.

When visiting Miami, it is best to avoid Liberty City, which is considered to be an unsafe area and offers visitors little in the realm of tourism. When partying in South Beach, be advised to stay north of 6th St.; the area quickly deteriorates into an unsafe neighborhood. Also, many residents of SoBe–which has long been considered a gay-friendly area–complain that homosexuals are still verbally berated. It is best to be vigilant at all times.

TRANSPORTATION

Airport: Miami International (☎876-7000; www.miami-airport.com), at Le Jeune Rd. and NW 36th Ave., 7 mi. northwest of downtown. Bus #7 runs downtown; many others make downtown stops. From downtown, take bus "C" or "K" to South Beach. Taxi to Miami Beach $24.

Trains: Amtrak, 8303 NW 37th Ave. (☎835-1223), near the Northside Metrorail station. Bus "L" goes directly to Lincoln Rd. Mall in South Beach. Open daily 6:30am-10pm. To: **Charleston** (13-14hr., 2 per day, $64-149); **New Orleans** (24hr., 3 per week, $206-387); **Orlando** (5hr., 2 per day, $33-64).

Buses: Greyhound, Miami Station, 4111 NW 27th St. (☎871-1810). To: **Atlanta** (17-19hr., 13 per day, $85.50); **Fort Lauderdale** (1hr., every hr., $5); **Key West** (5hr., 4 per day, $30.25); **Orlando** (5-9hr., 10 per day, $36). Open 24hr.

Public Transit: Metro Dade Transportation (☎770-3131; info M-F 6am-10pm, Sa-Su 9am-5pm). The extensive **Metrobus** network converges downtown, where most long trips transfer. Over 100 routes, but the major, lettered bus routes A, C, D, G, H, J, K, L, R, S, and T serve Miami Beach. After dark, some stops are patrolled (indicated with a sign). Buses run M-F 4am-2:30am. $1.25, transfers $0.25; students, seniors, and disabled $0.60/0.10. Call for weekend schedule. Exact change only. The **Metrorail** services downtown's major business and cultural areas. Rail runs daily 5am-midnight. $1.25, rail-to-bus transfers $0.50. The **Metromover** loop downtown is linked to the Metrorail stations. Runs daily 5am-midnight. $0.25, seniors $0.10; free transfers from Metrorail. **Tri-Rail** (☎800-874-7245) connects Miami, Fort Lauderdale, and West Palm Beach. Trains run M-Sa 4am-8pm, Su 7am-8pm. M-F $6.75, Sa-Su $4; students, seniors, and

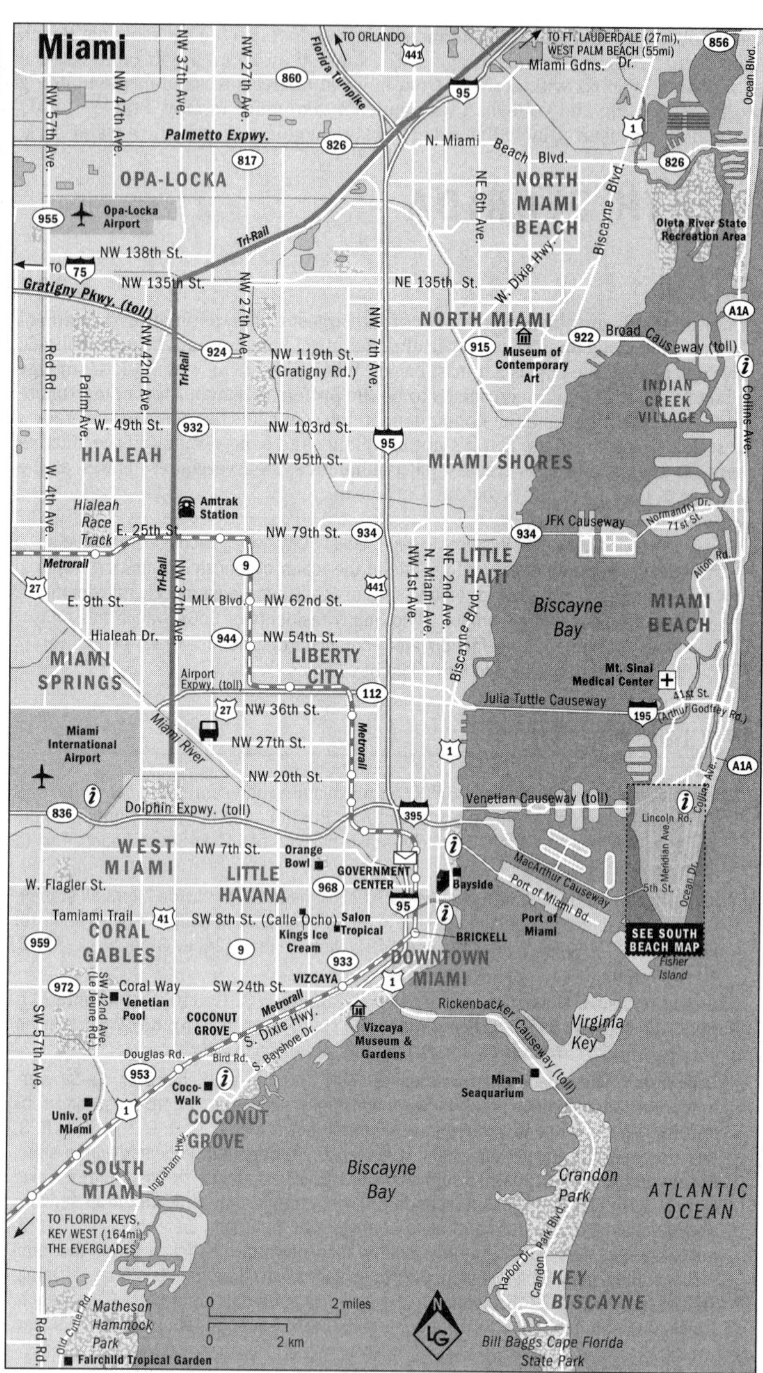
Miami
TO ORLANDO
TO FT. LAUDERDALE (27mi), WEST PALM BEACH (55mi)
Florida Turnpike
Miami Gdns. Dr.
Ocean Blvd.
NW 57th Ave.
NW 47th Ave.
NW 37th Ave.
NW 27th Ave.
Palmetto Expwy.
N. Miami Beach Blvd.
OPA-LOCKA
NORTH MIAMI BEACH
NE 6th Ave.
Biscayne Blvd.
Opa-Locka Airport
Oleta River State Recreation Area
Tri-Rail
NW 138th St.
TO
NW 135th St.
NE 135th St.
W. Dixie Hwy.
Gratigny Pkwy. (toll)
NORTH MIAMI
Broad Causeway (toll)
Museum of Contemporary Art
Red Rd.
NW 42nd Ave.
Parlm Ave.
NW 27th Ave.
NW 119th St. (Gratigny Rd.)
NW 7th Ave.
INDIAN CREEK VILLAGE
Collins Ave.
W. 49th St.
NW 103rd St.
HIALEAH
NW 95th St.
MIAMI SHORES
W. 4th Ave.
Hialeah Race Track
Amtrak Station
E. 25th St.
NW 79th St.
JFK Causeway
Normandy Dr.
71st St.
Metrorail
LITTLE HAITI
NE 2nd Ave.
N. Miami Ave.
NW 1st Ave.
Alton Rd.
E. 9th St.
MLK Blvd.
NW 62nd St.
Biscayne Bay
MIAMI BEACH
Hialeah Dr.
NW 54th St.
MIAMI SPRINGS
LIBERTY CITY
Airport Expwy. (toll)
Mt. Sinai Medical Center
Julia Tuttle Causeway
41st St. (Arthur Godfrey Rd.)
Miami International Airport
Miami River
NW 36th St.
NW 27th St.
NW 20th St.
Dolphin Expwy. (toll)
Venetian Causeway (toll)
Lincoln Rd.
Meridian Ave.
Ocean Dr.
5th St.
WEST MIAMI
NW 7th St.
Orange Bowl
GOVERNMENT CENTER
Bayside
MacArthur Causeway
Port of Miami Bd.
Port of Miami
W. Flagler St.
LITTLE HAVANA
Tamiami Trail
SW 8th St. (Calle Ocho)
Salon Tropical
Kings Ice Cream
CORAL GABLES
BRICKELL
SEE SOUTH BEACH MAP
Fisher Island
DOWNTOWN MIAMI
VIZCAYA
SW 24th St.
Coral Way
SW 42nd Ave. (Le Jeune Rd.)
Venetian Pool
SW 57th Ave.
COCONUT GROVE
Metrorail
S. Dixie Hwy.
Vizcaya Museum & Gardens
Rickenbacker Causeway (toll)
Virginia Key
Douglas Rd.
Bird Rd.
S. Bayshore Dr.
Miami Seaquarium
Coco-Walk
Univ. of Miami
COCONUT GROVE
Ingraham Hwy.
SOUTH MIAMI
Biscayne Bay
Crandon Park
ATLANTIC OCEAN
TO FLORIDA KEYS, KEY WEST (164mi), THE EVERGLADES
Crandon Park Blvd.
Harbor Dr.
KEY BISCAYNE
Matheson Hammock Park
Old Cutler Rd.
Red Rd.
0 2 miles
0 2 km
Bill Baggs Cape Florida State Park
Fairchild Tropical Garden

ages 5-12 50% off. The **Electrowave** (☎843-9283) offers shuttles along Washington Ave. from S. Pointe to 17th St. Pick up a brochure or just hop on in South Beach. Runs M-W 8am-2am, Th-Sa 8am-4am, Su and holidays 10am-2am. $0.25.

Taxi: Metro, ☎888-8888. **Central Cab,** ☎532-5555.

Bike Rental: Miami Beach Bicycle Center, 601 5th St. (☎531-4161), at the corner of Washington Ave., Miami Beach. Open M-Sa 10am-7pm, Su 10am-5pm. $5 per hr., $20 per day, $70 per week. Credit card or $200 cash deposit required.

ORIENTATION

Three highways crisscross the Miami area. **I-95,** the most direct north-south route, merges into **U.S. 1 (Dixie Highway)** just south of downtown. U.S. 1 runs to the Everglades entrance at Florida City and then continues as the Overseas Hwy. to Key West. **Route 836 (Dolphin Expressway),** a major east-west artery through town, connects I-95 to **Florida's Turnpike,** passing the airport in between.

When looking for street addresses, pay careful attention to the systematic street layout; it's easy to confuse North Miami Beach, West Miami, Miami Beach, and Miami addresses. Streets in Miami run east-west, avenues north-south; both are numbered. Miami divides into NE, NW, SE, and SW quadrants; the dividing lines downtown are **Flagler Street** (east-west) and **Miami Avenue** (north-south). Some numbered roads also have names. Get a map that lists both numbers and names.

Several causeways connect Miami to **Miami Beach.** The most useful is **MacArthur Causeway,** which becomes 5th St. Numbered streets run east-west across the island, increasing as you go north. In South Beach, **Collins Avenue (A1A)** is the main north-south drag; parallel are the club-filled **Washington Avenue** and the beachfront **Ocean Avenue.** The commercial district sits between 6th and 23rd St. One-way streets, traffic jams, and limited parking make driving around **South Beach (SoBe)** frustrating. Tie on your most stylish sneakers and enjoy the small island at your leisure. It only takes about 20min. to walk up Collins Ave. from 6th to 16th St., not counting all the time you spend checking out the funky fashion stores and restaurants.

Back in Miami, the heart of **Little Havana** lies between SW 12th and SW 27th Ave.; take bus #8, 11, 17, or 37. One block north of **Calle Ocho** (SW 8th St.), **W. Flagler Sreet.** is a hub of Cuban business. **Coconut Grove,** south of Little Havana, centers on the shopping and entertainment district on **Grand Avenue** and **Virginia Street. Coral Gables,** an upscale residential area, rests around the intersection of **Coral Way (SW 24th St.)** and **Le Jeune Road,** also known as **SW 42nd Avenue.** Though public transportation is reliable and safe, a car can be useful to get around the city and its suburbs.

PRACTICAL INFORMATION

Visitor Info: Miami Beach Visitors Center, 420 Lincoln Rd. (☎672-1270; www.miamibeachchamber.com). Open M-F 9am-6pm, Sa-Su 10am-4pm. **Info booth,** 401 Biscayne Blvd. (☎539-2980), downtown outside of Bayside Marketplace. Open daily 10am-6:30pm. In South Beach, **Coconut Grove Chamber of Commerce,** 2820 McFarlane Ave. (☎444-7270). Open M-F 9am-5pm. **Greater Miami Convention and Visitors Bureau,** 701 Brickell Ave. (☎539-3000 or 800-283-2707), 27th fl. of Barnett Bank Bldg., downtown. Open M-F 9am-5pm.

Hotlines: Crisis Line, ☎358-4357. 24hr. **Gay Hotline,** ☎759-5210. **Abuse Hotline,** ☎800-342-9152.

Medical Services: Mt. Sinai Medical Center, 1300 Alton Rd., in Miami Beach (☎674-2121). **Rape Treatment Center and Hotline** (☎585-7273), at Jackson Memorial Hospital, 1611 NW 12th Ave. Open 24hr.

Internet Access: Miami Public Library, 101 W. Flagler St. (☎375-2665), across from the Museum of Art. Open M-W and F-Sa 9am-6pm, Th 9am-9pm, Su 1-5pm. 45min. free. **Kafka's Cafe,** 1464 Washington Ave. (☎673-9669), in Miami Beach. Open daily 8am-midnight. 8am-noon and 8pm-midnight $3 per hr., noon-8pm $6 per hr.

Post Office: 500 NW 2nd Ave. (☎639-4284), in downtown Miami. Open M-F 8am-5pm, Sa 9am-1:30pm. **Postal Code:** 33101. **Area Code:** 305.

ACCOMMODATIONS

Cheap rooms abound in South Beach, and choosing a place to stay is all about attitude. Hostels in Miami Beach are the cheapest option for people traveling alone. If young bohemian isn't your thing, cruise farther down Collins Ave. to the funky, hot-pink Art Deco hotels. Get a discount when you stay more than two nights in one of the trendy **South Beach Group Hotels,** including Whitelaw, Mercury, Shelly, Chelsea, Chesterfield, and Lily. In general, high season for Miami Beach runs late December through mid-March; during the low-season, hotel clerks are often quick to bargain. The **Greater Miami and the Beaches Hotel Association,** 407 Lincoln Rd. #10G, can help you find a place to crash. (☎531-3553; www.gmbha.com. Open M-F 9am-5pm.) The Miami Beach Visitors Center (see **Practical Information,** above) can get you the cheapest rates. Camping is not allowed on Miami Beach.

Banana Bungalow, 2360 Collins Ave. (☎538-1951), at 23rd St. along the northern edge of the Art Deco district. Banana Bungalow is known as "party central"–the pool and fully-stocked bar keep the young and hip crowd occupied all day and long into the night. The activity desk provides opportunities for canoeing, kayaking, and clubbing as well as free guest passes for the club *du jour.* All rooms have A/C and cable TV, though not all the fixtures work. Free coffee, tea, and toast in the well-equipped communal kitchen. Game room with pool table and arcade games. Free lockers in dorms. Key/linen deposit $20. Internet access $0.20 per min. Dorms $17-19; private rooms $50-85. ❶

Whitelaw Hotel-Lounge, 808 Collins Ave. (☎398-7000). From 7-9pm, bright white leather and chrome greet beautiful party people lured into the hotel's lobby by complimentary cocktails. Plush down comforters, continental breakfast, TV, A/C, refrigerator, free Internet access, free airport shuttle, and VIP guest passes to any club in SoBe. Doubles Apr.-Dec. $70; Jan.-Mar. $125. ❹

Chesterfield Hotel, 855 Collins Ave. (☎531-5831). Deep house music pumps through this uber-chic retreat, where the motto is "our rooms were made for sharing." Fabulous amenities, great location, and a surprisingly helpful "hipper-than-thou" staff. Continental breakfast, TV, A/C, free Internet access, free airport shuttle, bar, cafe, and free VIP passes to any area club. Doubles Apr.-Nov. $90, third night is free; Dec.-Mar. $125. ❹

The Tropics Hotel/Hostel, 1550 Collins Ave. (☎531-0361), across the street from the beach. From the airport, take bus "J" to 41st St., transfer to bus "C" to Lincoln Rd., walk 1 block south on Collins, and it's next to the parking garage. A respite from the intense SoBe scene, this quiet refuge offers guests large, comfortable rooms with A/C, private baths, pool access, and an outdoor kitchen. Lockers at front desk; none in rooms. Free linen. Laundry. Key deposit $10. Internet access $0.20 per min. Dorms $16; singles or doubles $40-50. ISIC discount. ❶

The Clay Hotel and International Hostel (HI-AYH), 1438 Washington Ave. (☎534-2988 or 800-379-2529), in the heart of the Art Deco district; take bus "C" from downtown. This historic Mediterranean-style building, once the center of Al Capone's Miami gambling syndicate and often featured on the TV series *Miami Vice,* now hosts a largely international crowd. Kitchen, laundry facilities, and A/C. Dorms come with phone and fridges; some have TV. Lockers $1 per day. Linen/key deposit $10. Internet access $6 per hr. 4- to 8-bed dorms $16, nonmembers $17; private rooms $43-79. ❶

Miami Beach International Travelers Hostel (9th St. Hostel), 236 9th St. (☎534-0268 or 800-978-6787), at Washington Ave. From the airport, take bus "J" to 41st and Indian Creek, then transfer to bus "C" or "K." An excellent option for the budget-conscious traveler, this inn welcomes a constant stream of vivacious visitors, here to take advantage of the hostel's proximity to some of SoBe's hottest clubs and serene beaches. Laundry and common room with TV and movie library. Internet access $8 per hr. 4-bed dorms with A/C and bath $13, nonmembers $15. Singles or doubles $55; low-season $36. ❶

FOOD

The food in Miami is just like the people: fun, exciting, and very diverse. Four-star restaurants owned by celebrities and renowned chefs are just as prevalent as four-choice sandwich counters renowned for their affordability. The South Beach strip along Ocean Drive houses an eclectic mix of tourist traps like **Hard Rock Café,** star-gazing favorites like **Joia** and **Tantra,** and booty-shaking pseudo-clubs like **Mango.** Go at least one block inland from the beach to find more wallet-pleasing prices.

Macarena, 1334 Washington Ave. (☎531-3440), in Miami Beach. Dance your way to wonderful food in an atmosphere that's intimate and festive. This eatery serves up authentic Latin American delights while captivating dancers provide the entertainment. *Paella* big enough for two ($14, lunch $7) and the best rice pudding ever ($5.50) make for perfect Spanish treats. Wine comes from their own vineyards. W and F Flamenco dancing. Th ladies night. Sa live salsa. Lunch daily 12:30-3:30pm; dinner Su-Tu 7pm-1am, W-Th 7pm-1:30am, F-Sa 7pm-5am. ❸

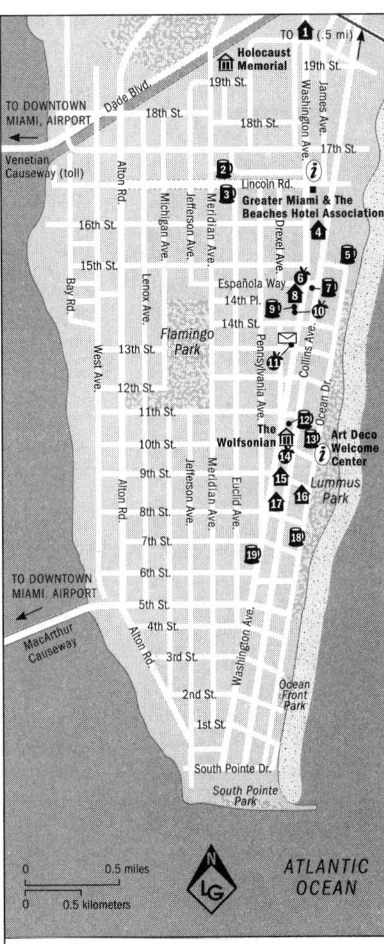

South Beach

ACCOMMODATIONS
Banana Bungalow, **1**
Chesterfield Hotel, **16**
The Clay Hotel and Int'l Hostel, **8**
Miami Beach Int'l Travelers Hostel, **15**
The Tropics Hotel/Hostel, **4**
Whitelaw Hotel-Lounge, **17**

FOOD
Fairwind Seafood, **14**
Flamingo Cafe, **10**
Macarena, **11**
Taystee Bakery, **6**

NIGHTLIFE
Bash, **19**
Billboard, **5**
Clevelander, **13**
Crobar, **7**
Laundry Bar, **2**
Liquid, **9**
Score, **3**
Twist, **12**
Wet Willies, **18**

ON THE MENU

CUBAN CUISINE

Bienvenidos a Miami, where the streets are lined with myriad delectable South American and Cuban *restaurantes* and *dulcerias* (sweet shops). Here is a guide to help new diners through *desayuno* (breakfast), *almuerzo* (lunch), and *cena* (dinner).

For breakfast, try *huevos rancheros*—a platter of fried eggs topped with spicy salsa.

For lunch, try a Cuban sandwich, which boasts ham, roast pork, and Swiss cheese on Cuban bread. It is heated and pressed flat, melting the cheese and making the bread warm and crispy.

A favorite dinner choice among Cubans, *boliche* is a beef roast stuffed with *chorizo* (hardened sausage), onions, green peppers, and spices.

Argentinian *empanadas* are turnovers filled with ham, beef, or cheese.

Don't let the direct translation of *vaca frita* ("fried cow") repulse you. This traditional Cuban dish is slowly roasted beef sauteed with onions, green peppers, and spices.

A popular dessert is *flan,* a rich custard made with eggs and baked in a pan of dark, caramelized sugar.

For a sweet treat, try *maduros*—caramelized plantains.

Fairwind Seafood, 1000 Collins Ave. (☎531-0050), across from the Essex House. One of the best kept secrets in South Beach, Fairwind creates masterful seafood dishes at suprisingly low prices. Try the superb *sashimi* tuna salad with mango salsa ($9.50), seafood pasta ($10.50), and Key Lime Creme Brulée ($4). Happy Hour daily 4-7pm. Open daily 7am-6am. ❸

Flamingo Cafe, 1454 Washington Ave. (☎673-4302), near the Clay Hostel in Miami Beach. Far and away the biggest bang for your buck, this friendly cafe produces overwhelming amounts of food for staggeringly low prices. Breakfast plate (eggs, toast, and meat) $2. Beef tacos and salad $2.75. *Frijoles con queso* $2.75. Lunch specials $5-7. Open M-Sa 7am-9:30pm. ❶

Taystee Bakery, 1450 Washington Ave. (☎538-4793). A haven for anyone with a South American sweet-tooth, Taystee has a large selection of super-cheap, no sugar/no salt baked goods. Guava pastries $1. *Empanadas* $1.50. *Pan cubano* sandwiches $4. Open M-Sa 6:30am-7:30pm. ❶

The Rascal House, 17190 Collins Ave. (☎947-4581). For food just like your gramma used to make before she got mean, head over to the Rascal House where genuinely concerned waitresses will make sure you don't come back skinny. Be careful not to fill up on the 5 plates of complementary treats at breakfast (bagels, muffins, breads, and croissants)—the breakfast, lunch, and dinner meals ($3-10) can be quite overwhelming. Open Su-Th 6:30am-1am, F-Sa 6:30am-2am. ❷

Bissaleh Cafe, 17608 Collins Ave. (☎682-2224). Whether you're enjoying the authentic Israeli dips platter ($4) in the highly-charged interior or smoking hookah under the midnight moon ($7), Bissaleh's Middle East charm will leave you completely enchanted. Open Su-Th noon-2am, Sa sunset-3am. ❷

King's Ice Cream, 1831 SW 8th St./Calle Ocho (☎643-1842), in Miami. Break from the Little Havana heat with a refreshing (and delicious) tropical fruit *helado* (ice cream). Flavors include a regal coconut (served in its own shell), *mamey,* and mango ($1 for a small cup). Open M-Sa 10am-11pm, Su 1-11pm. ❶

SIGHTS

SOUTH BEACH. South Beach is the reason to come to Miami. The liberal atmosphere, hot bodies, Art Deco design, and excellent sand make these 17 blocks seem like their own little world. *(Between 6th and 23rd St.)* **Ocean Drive** is where Miami's hottest come to see and be seen. Bars and cafes cram this tiny strip of land, which is part fashion show and part raging party. The **Art Deco Welcome Center** offers 1½hr. guided walking tours of the area's most notable architecture and provides free maps. *(1001 Ocean Dr. ☎531-3484. Open M-F 11am-6pm, Sa 10am-10pm, Su 11am-10pm. Tours Th 6:30pm and Sa 10:30am. $15.)* Walking tours start at the **Oceanfront Auditorium.** *(1001 Ocean Dr., at 10th St. ☎672-2014. 1½hr. tours Th 6:30pm and Sa 10:30am; $10. 1¼hr. self-guided tours daily 11am-4pm; $5.)* The **Holocaust Memorial** commemorates the 6 million Jews who fell victim to genocide in WWII. Marvel at the 42ft. bronze arm protruding from the ground, whose base is supported by dozens of sculpted figures struggling to escape persecution. *(1933-45 Meridian Ave. ☎538-1663. Wheelchair-accessible. Open daily 9am-9pm. Free.)* Part of Florida International University, **The Wolfsonian** examines the cultural impact of art and design from 1885 to 1945, exhibiting over 70,000 objects. It includes an exhaustive look at propaganda from WWII, an array of political cartoons, and a series of original Norman Rockwell paintings. *(1001 Washington Ave. ☎531-1001; www.wolfsonian.org. Wheelchair-accessible. Open M-Tu and F-Sa 11am-6pm, Th 11am-9pm, Su noon-5pm. $5, students and seniors $3.50. Free Th 6-9pm.)* Visit the new home of **Parrot Jungle Island,** on Watson Island in Biscayne Bay. Since 1936, visitors have walked among free-flying parrots, strutting flamingos, and swinging orangutans. Also on site are the Parrot Bowl amphitheater, the Serpentarium, the clay cliffs of Manu Encounter, and the Treetop Ballroom. *(1111 Parrot Jungle Tr. From downtown Miami, take the MacArthur Causeway east toward South Beach. Parrot Jungle Tr. is the first exit after the bridge. ☎258-6453; www.parrotjungle.com. Open daily 10am-6pm. $24; seniors, military, and students $22; ages 3-10 $19. Parking $6.)*

COCONUT GROVE. A stroll through the lazy streets of **Coconut Grove** uncovers an unlikely combination of haute boutiques and tacky tourist traps. People-watching abounds at the open-air mall, **CocoWalk,** along Grand Ave. On the bayfront between the Grove and downtown stands the **Vizcaya Museum and Gardens.** Built in 1916 for the affluent James Deering, the 70-room Italian villa features European antiques, tapestries, and art and is surrounded by 10 acres of lush gardens. *(3251 S. Miami Ave. ☎250-9133; www.vizcayamuseum.com. Partially wheelchair-accessible. Open daily 9:30am-5pm; last entry 4:30pm. $10, ages 6-12 $5. $1 off for ISIC holders. Gardens free.)*

BAYSIDE. On the waterfront downtown, Miami's sleek **Bayside** shopping center hops nightly with talented street performers. Stores and restaurants cater mostly to cruise ship guests and tourists with money to burn, though a tour through the center and its surrounding statues makes it a worthwhile trip. *(Open M-Th 10am-10pm, F-Sa 10am-11pm, Su 11am-9pm.)*

CORAL GABLES. In addition to hosting the **University of Miami,** scenic **Coral Gables** boasts one of the most beautiful planned communities in the region. Nearby, the family-friendly **Venetian Pool,** founded in 1923, draws tourists and local families alike to its 800,000 gallon oasis. Waterfalls and Spanish architecture dress up this swimming hole, which is always crowded on hot summer weekends. *(2701 DeSoto Blvd. ☎460-5356. Partially wheelchair-accessible. Open summer M-F 11am-7:30pm, Sa-Su 10am-4:30pm; Nov.-Mar. hours vary. $9, ages 3-12 $5; $6/3.)*

NORTH MIAMI. The **Museum of Contemporary Art (MOCA),** is known for its often eccentric exhibits and displays. Having played host to Versace dresses and steel drummers alike, MOCA supports uncommon means of artistic expression. *(770 NE 125th St. ☎893-6211; www.mocanomi.org. Wheelchair-accessible. Open Tu-Sa 11am-5pm, Su noon-5pm. Free.)*

ENTERTAINMENT & NIGHTLIFE

For the latest on Miami entertainment, check out the "Living Today," "Lively Arts," and Friday "Weekend" sections of the *Miami Herald*. Weekly *Oceandrive*, *New Times*, *Street*, and *Sun Post* list local happenings. *TWN* and *Miamigo*, the major gay papers, are available free in paperboxes along Ocean Dr. **Performing Arts and Community Education (PACE)** manages more than 400 concerts each year (jazz, rock, soul, dixieland, reggae, salsa, and bluegrass); most are free. **Carnaval Miami,** the nation's largest Hispanic festival, fills 23 blocks of Calle Ocho in early Mar. with salsa dancing and the world's longest conga line.

Nightlife in the Art Deco district of South Miami Beach starts late (usually after midnight) and continues until well after sunrise. Gawk at models, stars, and beach bunnies while eating dinner at one of Ocean Blvd.'s open cafes or bars, then head down to **Washington Avenue,** between 6th and 18th St., for some serious fun. Miami Beach's club scene is transient; what's there one week may not be there the next. Many clubs don't demand covers until after midnight, and often the $20+ door charge includes an open bar. Most clubs have dress codes and everyone dresses to the nines, even on so-called "casual" nights. If discos aren't your thing, pull up a stool at one of the frat-boy party bars along the beach.

Crobar, 1445 Washington Ave. (☎531-8225). One of the hottest clubs in South Beach, Crobar's always-packed dance floor is crawling with the local chic and out-of-town trendy. Su gay night. 21+. Reduced cover until 11:30pm. Open daily 10pm-5am.

Wet Willies, 760 Ocean Dr. (☎532-5650), pours a constant stream of strong, cheap daiquiris. If you're 21+, check out the outdoor bar upstairs, a great place to enjoy your "Call-a-Cab" or "Attitude Improvement" while surveying SoBe from above. 21+. No cover. Open daily noon-2am.

Clevelander, 1020 Ocean Dr. (☎531-3485). Clevelander serves up its famous "Miami Vice" ($7) to a clientele as diverse as the strip. The combination of bar and pool has been known to induce the occasional collegiate "wet T-shirt contest"–though cleaner fun prevails more often than not. 21+. No cover. Open daily 11am-3am.

Bash, 655 Washington Ave. (☎538-2274). The large indoor dance floor grooves to house and progressive while the courtyard in back jams to worldbeat. Th fashion shows. F Brazilian parties. 21+. Cover Th $10, F-Su $20. Open Th-Su 10pm-5am.

Liquid, 1439 Washington Ave. (☎532-9154). The beautiful and famous go to this ultra-chic club, owned by Madonna's brother Michael Ciccone and her chum Ingrid Casares. 21+. Cover $20. Open daily 10pm-5am.

Billboard (☎538-2251), 15th St. and Ocean Dr. Shake that healthy butt at SoBe's #1 hip-hop palace. Look for special appearances by stars like Ginuwine, Usher, and the Neptunes. Ladies free until 11pm. Open daily 10pm until late.

GAY & LESBIAN NIGHTLIFE

South Beach's vibrant gay scene takes to the street at night in search of the new "it club." Gay and mixed clubs in the area have bragging rights as the most trendy, amorphous hot spots, attracting a large crowd of both gay and straight partiers.

Twist, 1057 Washington Ave. (☎538-9478), is a popular 2-story club with an outdoor lounge, rockin' dance floor, and 6 bars. Straight couples welcome. 21+. Cover varies. Open daily 1pm-5am.

Laundry Bar, 721 Lincoln Ln. (☎531-7700). Men and women alike flock to the unusual Laundry Bar, where the chic and friendly clientele sip cocktails to the beat of DJ-spun house music and the hum of real laundry machines. 21+ starting at 10pm. No cover. Open 7am-5am.

Score, 727 Lincoln Rd. Mall (☎535-1111). Mostly men frequent this multi-bar hot spot, where an always packed dance floor sits under the watchful eye of Adonis himself. 21+. No cover. Open daily M-Sa 3pm-5am, Su 3pm-2am.

THE EVERGLADES ☎305

Encompassing the entire tip of Florida and spearing into Florida Bay, Everglades National Park spans 1.6 million acres of one of the world's most unique and fragile ecosystems. Vast prairies of sawgrass range through broad expanses of shallow water, creating the famed "river of grass," while tangled mazes of mangrove swamps wind up the western coast. To the south, delicate coral reefs lie below the shimmering blue waters of the bay. A host of species found nowhere else in the world inhabits these lands and waters: American alligators, dolphins, sea turtles, and various birds and fish, as well as the endangered Florida panther, Florida manatee, and American crocodile. Unfortunately, the mosquito is the most prevalent and noticeable Everglades species.

AT A GLANCE

AREA: 1,508,508 Acres.

CLIMATE: Subtropical Grassland.

HIGHLIGHTS: Be terrified by the denizens of the Everglades Alligator Farm, be amazed by the flora and fauna of Anhinga Trail, and sleep it off at the amazing Everglades International Hostel.

CAMPING: Reservations must be made in person, at least a day in advance, at Flamingo and Gulf Coast Visitor's Centers. Sites $14. $10 for back-country camping up to 6 people per campsite.

FEES: $10 per private automobile, good for seven days.

ORIENTATION & PRACTICAL INFORMATION

The main entrance to the park, the **Ernest Coe Visitors Center,** 40001 Rte. 9366, sits just inside the eastern edge of the Everglades. (☎242-7700. Open daily 8am-5pm.) Rte. 9366 cuts 40 mi. through the park past campgrounds, trailheads, and canoe waterways to the **Flamingo Visitors Center** (☎239-695-2945; open daily in summer 8am-5pm; winter 7:30am-5pm) and the heavily developed Flamingo Outpost Resort. At the northern end of the park off U.S. 41 (Tamiami Trail), the **Shark Valley Visitors Center** provides access to a 15 mi. loop through a sawgrass swamp that can be accessed by foot, bike, or a 2hr. tram. **Shark Valley** is an ideal site for those who want a taste of the freshwater ecosystem but aren't inclined to venture too deep into the park. (☎221-8776. Open daily 8:30am-6pm. Tram tours May-Nov. daily 9:30, 11am, 1, 3pm; Dec.-Apr. every hr. 9am-4pm: $10, seniors $9, under 12 $5.50. Reservations recommended. Wheelchair-accessible with reservations. Bike rental daily 8:30am-3pm. $4.25 per hr., including helmets.) The **Gulf Coast Visitors Center,** 800 Copeland Ave. S, in Everglades City in the northwestern end of the park, provides access to the western coastline and the vast river network throughout the park. (☎239-695-3311. Open summer daily 8:30am-5pm; extended hours in winter.) **Entrance fees** vary, depending on the area of the park. (Ernest Coe $10 car per day, $5 per pedestrian or bike. Shark Valley $8/4. Gulf Coast free.) Log onto www.nps.gov/ever/ for all the details. For other area information on lodgings and local discounts, check out the **Tropical Everglades Visitors Center,** on U.S. 1 in Florida City. (☎245-9180 or 800-388-9669. Open daily 9am-5pm.) **Emergency: Park headquarters,** ☎247-7272. **Area Code:** 305.

Summer visitors can expect mosquitoes aplenty when visiting the Everglades. Stay away from swampy areas during sunrise and sunset. The best time to visit is winter or spring when heat, humidity, storms, and bugs are at a minimum and wildlife congregate in shrinking pools of evaporating water. *Wear long-sleeve clothing and bring insect repellent.*

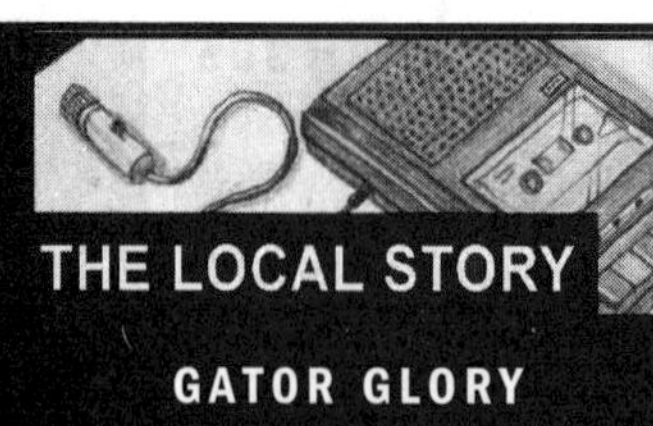

THE LOCAL STORY

GATOR GLORY

Julio Aguilar has been an animal trainer for 7 years at the Everglades Alligator Farm, where he cares for and performs with some of the largest and most intimidating reptiles in the world.

LG: What's been your scariest encounter with an alligator?
JA: I was working with one of the 9 ft. show gators, named Godzilla, and I was going to do one of the usual techniques I do during the shows. But when I dropped down, he turned around and tried to bite me on the head. So I almost lost my head there.
LG: What are the differences between crocodiles and alligators?
JA: Alligators have broad, round snouts that look like an upside-down letter "U," while crocodiles have longer and skinnier snouts that look like a letter "V." Alligators are usually black, while crocs can be green, brown, or grayish.
LG: What do you feed the gators?
JA: Alligators are strictly carnivores, and we feed them about 6000-7000 lb. of chicken per month.
LG: What should someone do if they ever encounter an alligator or crocodile?
JA: The best thing to do is to relax and try not to resist because as soon as that alligator or crocodile feels a little bit of tension, he usually goes into a "death roll"—and that's when your hand is going to come off.

ACCOMMODATIONS & FOOD

Outside the eastern entrance to the park, **Florida City** offers some cheap motels along U.S. 1. The **Everglades International Hostel (HI-AYH) ❶**, 20 SW 2nd Ave., off Rte. 9336 (Palm Dr.), presents a far better option. After venturing into the Everglades on one of the hostel-guided tours ($25-30), hang out with fellow travelers in the gazebo, the gardens, or the kitchen house, which has a large-screen TV with a free video collection. (☎248-1122 or 800-372-3874; www.evergladeshostel.com. Free Internet access. Laundry. Bike rental $5. Canoe rental $20. Linen $2. Dorms $13, with A/C $14, nonmembers $17/18; Private rooms $33/35, nonmembers $36/38.) The only option for lodging inside the park, **Flamingo Lodge ❸**, 1 Flamingo Lodge Hwy., has large rooms with A/C, TV, private baths, and a great view of the Florida Bay. (☎800-600-3813. Continental breakfast included in summer. Reservations recommended. Singles and doubles May-Oct. $65; Nov.-Dec. and Apr. $79; Jan.-Mar. $95.) A few **campgrounds ❶** line Rte. 9336. All sites have drinking water, grills, dump sites, and restrooms, but none have hookups. (☎800-365-2267. Reservations required Nov.-Apr. Sites in winter $14.; in summer free.) **Backcountry camping** inside the park is accessible primarily by boat (see **Boating,** below). Required **permits** are available on a first come, first served basis at the Flamingo and Gulf Coast Visitors Centers. (Applications must be made in person at least 24hr. in advance. Dec.-Apr. $10 for 1-6 people; May-Nov. free.)

Near the Gulf Coast Visitors Center, motels, RV parks, and campgrounds encircle Everglades City. The **Barron River Villa, Marina, and RV Park ❶** offers 67 RV sites, 29 on the river, and tiny motel rooms with TV and A/C. (☎800-535-4961. RV sites May-Sept. full hookup $18, on the river $20; Oct.-Apr. $28/34. Motel rooms May-Aug. $41; Sept.-Dec. $49; Jan.-Apr. $57.)

Right across the street from the hostel, **Rosita's ❶,** 199 Palm Dr., has the best Mexican food in the area. Breakfast eggs ($4) can get you ready for a long day of exploring the park. Come back to relax with some great *chiles rellenos* or cheese enchiladas. (☎246-3114. Open daily 8:30am-9pm.) The pinnacle of eateries in Homestead, the vegan-friendly **Main St. Cafe ❷,** 128 N. Krome Ave., serves up great sandwiches ($4-6) in a charming deli-style restaurant that doubles as a comedy club on the weekends. (☎245-7575. Th teen open mic 8-11pm; F open mic 7pm-midnight; Sa folk and acoustic rock 7pm-midnight. Open M-W 11am-4pm, Th-Sa 11am-midnight.) Located at the southern end of Homestead, **Farmers' Market Restaurant ❸,** 300 N. Krome Ave., delivers on its promise of "good home cooking." Enjoy hearty portions and small-town service at this local favorite for a traditional, all-American breakfast ($4-6), lunch ($5-8) or dinner for $8-13. (☎242-0008. Open daily 5:30am-9pm.)

OUTDOOR ACTIVITIES

The park is swamped with fishing, hiking, canoeing, biking, and wildlife-watching opportunities. Forget swimming; alligators, sharks, and barracuda patrol the waters. From November through April, the park sponsors amphitheater programs, canoe trips, and ranger-guided Slough Slogs (swamp tours).

HIKING

The Everglades are accessible to travelers more interested in scenery than exercise through a series well-developed short trails.. A good choice is the **Pa-hay-okee Overlook,** located 13 mi. from the main entrance off Rte. 9336. Wheelchair-accessible, it rewards its visitors with a stunning view of the park after only a ¼,mile hike. One of the best hiking trails, the famous **Anhinga Trail,** begins at the Royal Palm Visitors Center, 4 mi. inside the park from the main entrance, and is also wheelchair-accessible. Moderately difficult, this trail grants explorers up-close encounters with alligators, anhinga birds, and turtles and is best traversed December to March. For a more difficult trail, head over to Long Pine Key (6 mi. from the main entrance), where the **Long Pine Key Trail** ventures through 10 mi. of slash pine forests. Another arduous hike is the **Mahogany Hammock Trail** (20 mi. from the main entrance and wheelchair-accessible). Though this trail offers hikers incredible routes through freshwater prairie and pineland, mosquitoes have the run of the land during the summer season, making it most enjoyable during the winter months.

BOATING

If you really want to experience the Everglades, start paddling. The 99 mi. **Wilderness Waterway** winds its way from the northwest entrance to the Flamingo station in the far south. Noteworthy **camping** ❶ spots along the way include chickees (wooden platforms elevated above mangrove swamps), beaches, and groundsites. (In winter $10; in summer free.) **Everglades National Park Boat Tours**, at the **Gulf Coast Visitors Center**, rents canoes ($24) and is the best option for guided boat tours. The **Ten Thousand Island Cruise** ($16) is a 1½hr. tour through the Everglades' myriad tiny islands, and patrons often get to see bald eagles, dolphins, and manatees. The **Mangrove Wilderness Cruise** ($25) is a 2hr. cruise through the inland swamps that brings its six passengers face-to-face with the most prominent local residents: alligators. (☎239-695-2591 or 800-445-7724. Tours every 30min.) For those who would rather do their own paddling, **Hell's Bay Canoe Trail,** located about 29 mi. from the entrance, is the premier spot for canoeing. For more information on navigating the park's waterways, consult the rangers at the **Flamingo Visitor Center**.

BIKING

While the Everglades mostly caters to those with walking sticks and canoeing paddles, it does offer some excellent biking opportunities. The best route can be found at the **Shark Valley Visitors Center,** where a 15 mi. loop awaits the adventurous. The trail peaks at an incredible observation tower that offers great views of the park's rivers of grass, alligators, and the occasional wily fawn. (Bike rentals $5.25 per hr.)

GARDENS & GATORS

For a truly bizarre time, head up U.S. 1 to the **Coral Castle,** 28655 South Dixie Hwy., in Homestead. Over 20 years, Latvian immigrant Ed Leedskalnin turned hundreds of tons of dense coral rock into a garden of magnificent sculptures. The incredible sight has since been studied by anthropologists who thought it might explain how humans built the Egyptian pyramids. (☎248-6344; www.coralcastle.com. Wheelchair-accessible. Open M-Th 9am-6pm, F-Su 9am-7pm. Guided tours daily. $7.75, ages 7-12 $5, seniors $6.50. Discounts at visitors center.) View gators, crocs, and snakes at the **Everglades Alligator Farm,** 40351 SW 192 Ave., 4 mi. south of Palm Dr. Though ultra-touristy, this is the best place to see thousands of gators, from little hatchlings clambering for a piece of the sun to 18-footers clambering for a piece of you. (☎247-2628 or 800-644-9711; http://everglades.com. Wheelchair-accessible. Open May-Sept. daily 9am-6pm. Wildlife shows—free with admission—11am, 2, 5pm. $9, ages 4-10 $5)

KEY LARGO ☎305

Over half a century ago, Hollywood stars Humphrey Bogart and Lauren Bacall immortalized the name "Key Largo" in their hit movie. Quick-thinking locals of Rock Harbor, where some of the scenes were shot, soon changed the name of their town to Key Largo to attract tourists. It worked. Key Largo is now the gateway to the rest of the enchanting, laidback islands. While some (older) visitors still come to see the relics of the moviemaking past, more are drawn to Key Largo's greatest natural assets: the coral reefs and the incredible fishing. Pennekamp State Park was the country's first completely underwater park, and divers of all abilities flock to the isle for the chance to glimpse at the reef ecosystem and the numerous shipwrecks. Don't believe the hype; sharks are scarce here.

ORIENTATION & PRACTICAL INFORMATION. The **Overseas Highway (U.S. 1)** bridges the divide between the Keys and the southern tip of Florida, stitching the islands together. Mile markers section the highway and replace street addresses. **Biking** along U.S. 1 is treacherous due to fast cars and narrow shoulders; instead of riding, bring your bike on the bus. Beer flows freely in the Keys, and drunk driving has become a problem recently—stay alert when on the roads. **Greyhound** (☎871-1810; open daily 8am-6pm), Mi. 102 at the Howard Johnson, goes to Key West (3 hr., 4 per day, $26-29) and Miami (1¾hr., 3 per day, $12.50-14.50). Most bus drivers are willing to stop at mile markers along the side of the road. Tiny Greyhound signs along the highway indicate bus stops (usually hotels), where you can buy tickets or call the **info line** on the red phones provided. **Taxi: Mom's Taxi,** ☎852-6000. **Visitor Info: Key Largo Chamber of Commerce/Florida Keys Visitors Center,** 106000 U.S. 1, Mi. 106 (☎451-1414 or 800-822-1088; www.keylargo.org. Open daily 9am-6pm.) **Medical Services: Mariners Hospital,** Mi. 91.5 (☎852-2354). **Post Office:** 100100 U.S. 1, Mi. 100. (☎451-3155. Open M-F 8am-4:30pm.) **Postal Code:** 33037. **Area Code:** 305.

ACCOMMODATIONS. **Ed and Ellen's Lodgings ❸,** 103365 U.S. 1, Mi. 103.4 (on Snapper Ave.), has clean, large rooms with cable TV, A/C, and kitchenettes. Ed, the humorous and ever-present owner, is tremendously helpful with everything from restaurant suggestions to diving and snorkeling reservations. (☎451-9949 or 888-333-5536. Doubles $59-79; low-season $49-59. Each additional person $10. Rates increase on weekends, holidays, and lobster season.) A few lodgings near downtown Key Largo boast reasonable rates. The **Bay Cove Motel ❸,** 99446 Overseas Hwy, Mi. 99.5, borders a small beach on the bay side of the island. Rooms have cable TV, A/C, and mini-fridges. (☎451-1686. Doubles $50-80, depending on season.) The waterside **Hungry Pelican ❸,** Mi. 99.5, boasts and explosion of bougainvillea vines, tropical birds in the trees, and cozy rooms with double beds, fridges, and cable TV. Free use of paddle boats, canoes, and hammocks. (☎451-3576. Continental breakfast. Rooms $50-115; each additional person $10.) Reservations are strongly recommended for the popular **John Pennekamp State Park Campground ❶**(see **Sights,** below). The 47 sites are clean, convenient, and well worth the effort required to obtain them. One-half are available through advance registration, and the others are given out first come, first served. Pets are not allowed. (☎451-1202. Bathrooms and showers. 14 day max. stay. Open 8am-dusk. $24; with electricity $26.)

FOOD. Seafood restaurants of varying price, quality, specialty, and view litter the Overseas Hwy. The neighboring island Islamorada boasts one of the best seafood restaurants in all the Keys. The **Islamorada Fish Company, ❷,** Mi. 81.5, offers an incredible array of seafood sandwiches ($7-10) and entrees ($13-18), which patrons enjoy under the pristine island sunset. When you finish, be sure to taste the legendary Key Lime Pie ($3). (☎664-9271 or 800-258-2559. Open daily 11am-9pm, sometimes later). Tucked away on a quiet residential street, **Calypso's ❷,** 1 Seagate Dr., at Oceanbay near Mi. 99.5, offers delectable Buffalo Shrimp ($7), or opt for an equally delicious dolphin fish sandwich ($7). (☎451-0600. Open M and W-Th noon-10pm, F-Sa noon-11pm.) For a scrumptious breakfast in Key Largo, head to **The Hideout Restaurant ❷,** Mi. 103.5 at the end of Transylvania Ave. on the ocean side. Plate-size pancakes (two for $3) and not-soon-forgotten raisin toast ($3) make this the affordable meal you can't afford to miss. Stop by this hidden treasure on Friday nights for all-you-can-eat fish fest—complete with hush puppies, beans, conch fritters, and free Bud Light—for a paltry $10. (☎451-0128. Open Sa-Th 11:30am-2pm, F 11:30am-2pm and 5-9pm.) **Mary Mac's Kitchen ❶,** Mi. 99 on the bay side, cooks up lunches for its eager patrons, who enjoy their famous steak sandwiches ($4-5) and overwhelming hamburgers ($4). (☎451-3722. Open daily 10:30am-5pm).

SIGHTS. Key Largo is the self-proclaimed "Dive Capital of the World" and many diving instructors offer their services via highway billboards. The best place to go is the nation's first underwater sanctuary, **John Pennekamp State Park,** Mi. 102.5. The park extends 3 mi. into the Atlantic Ocean, safeguarding a part of the coral reef that runs the length of the Keys. (☎451-1202; www.pennecamppark.com. $2.50 per vehicle with 1 occupant, 2 occupants $5; each additional person $0.50. Walk- or bike-in $1.50.) Stop by the park's **Visitors Center** for complimentary maps, boat and snorkeling tour info, and hourly films on the park. To see the reefs, visitors must take their own boat or rent. (☎451-9570, for reservations 451-6325. Deposit required. Open daily 8am-5pm. 19ft. motor boat $28 per hr. Canoes $10 per hr.) **Scuba trips** depart from the Visitors Center. (☎451-6322. 9:30am and 1:30pm. $37 per person for a 2-tank dive. Deposit required.) A **snorkeling tour** also allows you to partake of the underwater quiet. (☎451-1621. 2½hr. total, 1½hr. water time. Tours 9am, noon, 3pm. $26, under 18 $20; equipment $5. Deposit required.) Head to any of the local marinas to charter a spot on a **fishing boat.** To avoid paying a commission, hang out on the docks and ask one of the friendly captains yourself. A relatively new addition, **Glass Bottom Boat Tours,** provides a crystal clear view of the reefs without wetting your feet. (☎451-1621. 2½hr. Tours 9:15am, 12:15, 3pm. $18, under 12 $10.) Located at Mi. 100 on the ocean side, the **Holiday Inn Hotel** also offers a plethora of scuba, snorkel, and boat trips. The best known is the **Key Largo Princess,** which offers 2hr. glass bottom boat tours ($18). Aside from its always active dock, the hotel has become a tourist destination, as it houses the **African Queen,** the original boat on which Humphrey Bogart and Katherine Hepburn sailed in the movie of the same title.

KEY WEST ☎305

The small "last island" of the Florida Keys, Key West has always drawn a cast of colorful characters since its days of pirates, smugglers, and treasure hunters. Henry Flagler, Ernest Hemingway, Tennessee Williams, Truman Capote, and Jimmy Buffett have all called the quasi-independent "Conch Republic" home. Today thousands of tourists hop on the Overseas Hwy. to glimpse the past, visit the over 300 bars, and kick back under the sun. The crowd is as diverse as Key

West's past: families spend a week enjoying the water; twenty-somethings come to party and work; and a swinging gay population finds a haven of clubs and resorts oriented exclusively to them. Key West is as far south as you can get in the continental US. This is the end of the road—enjoy it.

TRANSPORTATION

Buses: Greyhound, 3535 S. Roosevelt Blvd. (☎296-9072), at the airport. Open daily 8am-6pm. To **Miami** (4½hr., 3 per day, $32-36).

Public Transit: Key West Port and Transit Authority (☎292-8161), at City Hall, has clockwise ("Old Town") and counterclockwise ("Mallory Sq. Rte.") routes. Service daily every 1½hr. 7am-10:30pm. $0.75, students and seniors $0.35.

Bike rental: The Bicycle Center and Keys Moped & Scooter, 523 Truman Ave. (☎294-4724), rents wheeled adventures. Open daily 9am-6pm. Bikes $4 per half-day, $30 per week. Mopeds $18 per day, $23 per 24hr. Electric cars $29 per hr.

Taxi: Keys Taxi, ☎296-6666.

ORIENTATION & PRACTICAL INFORMATION

Key West lies at the end of **Overseas Highway (U.S. 1),** 155 mi. southwest of Miami (3-3½hr.). The island is divided into two sectors; the eastern part, known as **New Town,** harbors tract houses, chain motels, shopping malls, and the airport. Beautiful old conch houses fill **Old Town,** west of White St. **Duval Street** is the main north-south thoroughfare in Old Town; **U.S. 1** (Truman Avenue) is a major east-west route. A car is the easiest way to get to Key West, though driving in town is neither easy nor necessary. *Do not park overnight on the bridges.*

Visitor Info: Key West Welcome Center, 3840 N. Roosevelt Blvd. (☎296-4444 or 800-284-4482), just north of the intersection of U.S. 1 and Roosevelt Blvd., is a private reservation service. Open M-Sa 9am-7:30pm, Su 9am-6pm. Key West Chamber of Commerce, 402 Wall St. (☎294-2587 or 800-527-8539; www.keywestchamber.org), in old Mallory Sq. Open M-F 8:30am-6:30pm, Sa-Su 8:30am-6pm.

Bi-Gay-Lesbian Resources: The Key West Business Guild Gay and Lesbian Information Center, 728 Duval St. (☎294-4603), is helpful for locating exclusively gay guesthouses. Open M-F 9am-5pm.

Hotlines: Help Line, (☎296-4357) Operates 24hr.

Internet Access: Internet Isle Cafe, 118 Duval St. (☎293-1199). $8 per hr. Open daily 8am-11pm.

Post Office: 400 Whitehead St. (☎294-2557), one block west of Duval St. at Eaton St. Open M-F 8:30am-5pm, Sa 9:30am-noon. **Postal Code:** 33040. **Area Code:** 305.

ACCOMMODATIONS

Key West is packed virtually year-round, particularly from January through March, so reserve rooms far in advance. **Pride Week** (www.pridefestkeywest.com) each June is a particularly busy time of the year. In Old Town the multi-colored 19th-century clapboard houses capture the charming flavor of the Keys. B&Bs dominate, and "reasonably priced" means over $50. Some of the guest houses in Old Town are for gay men exclusively.

Casablanca Hotel, 900 Duval St. (☎296-0815), in the center of the main drag. This charming B&B once hosted Humphrey Bogart and James Joyce. Pool, A/C, cable TV, breakfast, and large bathrooms. Call ahead for reservations during Fantasy Fest. Dec.-May $89-200; June-Nov. $79-89. ❸

Caribbean House, 226 Petronia St. (☎296-1600 or 800-543-4518), has festive Caribbean-style rooms with A/C, cable TV, free local calls, fridge and comfy double beds. Continental breakfast. Reservations not accepted for cottages. Rooms in winter $69; in summer from $49.Cottages $69/89. ❸

Wicker Guesthouse, 913 Duval St. (☎296-4275 or 800-880-4275), has a pastel decor, private baths, A/C, and cable TV. Most rooms have kitchenettes. No phones. Kitchen, pool access, free parking, and breakfast included. Reservations recommended; ask for summer specials. Rooms June-Dec. $89-105; late Dec. to May $130-150. ❹

Eden House, 1015 Fleming St. (☎296-6868 or 800-533-5397), just 5 short blocks from downtown, is a brightly painted hotel with a hostel-like atmosphere. Clean, classy rooms with bath. Pool, jacuzzi, hammock area, and kitchens. Bike rentals $10 per day. Happy Hour daily 4-5pm. Summer rooms with shared bath $105; low-season $80. ❺

Boyd's Campground, 6401 Maloney Ave. (☎294-1465), sprawls over 12 oceanside acres and provides full facilities, including showers. Take a left off U.S. 1 onto Macdonald Ave., which becomes Maloney. Sites for 2 in summer $42-60, with water and electricity $52-70, full hookup $57-75; winter $45-70/55-80/60-85; each additional person $8. Waterfront sites additional $6-14. ❷

FOOD

Expensive and trendy restaurants line festive **Duval Street.** Side streets offer lower prices and fewer crowds.

Blue Heaven, 729 Thomas St. (☎296-8666), one block from the Caribbean House. Feast upon the town's best grub: healthy breakfasts with fresh banana bread ($2-9); Caribbean or Mexican lunches ($2.50-10); and heavenly dinners ($9-19) that include plantains, corn bread, and fresh veggies. Open M-Sa 8am-3pm and 6-10:30pm, Su 8am-1pm and 6-10:30pm. ❸

El Siboney, 900 Catherine St. (☎296-4184). Breaking with the unfortunate Key West tradition of overpriced food, this Cuban establishment serves up heaping mounds of beans, rice, and meat– all for around $7. Open M-Sa 11am-9:30pm. ❷

Rooftop Cafe, 308 Fronts Ave. (☎294-2042), at Tifts Ave. This quaint Cuban eatery overlooks the passing tourist trains and scandalous skin shows. The chicken bella vista salad ($11) and the steak largo hueso ($12), however, seem to keep patrons' minds on their food. Open daily 9am-11pm. ❸

Karr Breizh Creperie, 512½ Duval St. (☎296-1071). It would be easy to miss this small creperie if not for the alluring aroma emanating from the charming, open-air cafe. Watch as the owner creates a delightful array of delicious French crepes, from banana and apple to Nutella ($4-7). For a less sinful delight, try the local favorite, goat cheese salad ($6). Open daily 9am-11pm. ❷

Grand Cafe, 314 Duval St. (☎292-4816). With its tucked-in patio and elegant interior, the Grand Cafe provides refuge from the often hectic Duval St. Try one of the gourmet pizzas ($10-12) or garden fresh salads ($5-10), and your break from hedonism will surely be justified. Open daily 11am-11pm. ❸

SIGHTS

ON LAND. Because of limited parking, traversing Key West by bike or moped is more convenient and comfortable than driving. For those inclined towards riding, the **Conch Tour Train** is a 1½hr. narrated ride through Old Town. *(Leaves from Mallory Sq. at 3840 N or from Roosevelt Blvd., next to the Quality Inn. ☎294-5161. Runs daily 9am-4:30pm. $18, ages 4-12 $9.)* **Old Town Trolley** runs a similar narrated tour—but you can get on and off throughout the day at nine stops. *(☎296-6688. Tours 9am-5:30pm. Full tour 1½hr. $18, ages 4-12 $9.)* No one can leave Key West without a visit to the

Ernest Hemingway Home, where "Papa" wrote *For Whom the Bell Tolls* and *The Snows of Kilimanjaro*. Take a tour with hilarious guides who relate Hemingway and Key West history, then traipse through on your own among 60 descendants of Hemingway's cat, half of which have extra toes. *(907 Whitehead St. ☎294-1136; www.hemingwayhome.com. Partially wheelchair-accessible. Open daily 9am-5pm. $10, ages 6-12 $6.)* Tucked into the affluent Truman Annex Gated Community, the **Harry S Truman Little White House Museum** provides a fascinating look at both President Truman and his get-away in Key West. *(111 Front St. ☎294-9911; www.trumanlittlewhitehouse.com. Partially wheelchair-accessible. Open daily 9am-5pm. $10, children $5; includes tour.)* In addition to its serene garden, the **Audubon House** shelters fine antiques and a collection of original engravings by naturalist John James Audubon. *(205 Whitehead St. ☎294-2116; www.audubonhouse.com. Not wheelchair-accessible. Open daily 9:30am-5pm. $8, students $7.50, ages 6-12 $3.50, seniors $5.)*

ON WATER. The **glass-bottomed boat** *Fireball* cruises to the reefs and back. *(☎296-6293. 2-2½hr. cruises daily noon, 2, and 6pm. Tickets $20, at sunset $25; ages 5-12 $10/12.50.)* The **Mel Fisher Maritime Heritage Society Museum** showcases the amazing discovery and salvage of the Spanish galleon *Atocha*, which sank off the Keys in the 17th century with millions in gold and silver. The museum also has an entire floor dedicated to the study of the harsh 17th- and 18th-century slave trade. *(200 Greene St. ☎294-2633; www.melfisher.org. Open daily 9:30am-5pm; last film 4:30pm. $9, students $4.50, ages 6-12 $3.50.)* The **Key West Shipwreck Historeum Museum,** located in Mallory Sqaure, boasts the remains of the Isaac Allerton, the 594-ton ship that sunk to the bottom of the Atlantic in 1856. Get a glimpse into the lives of classic adventurers by surveying authentic artifacts and the original cargo that the Allerton was carrying. The museum's **Lookout Tower,** which stands 65ft. tall, offers one of the best views of the island. *(1 Whitehead St. 292-8990; www.shipwreckhistoreum.com. Open daily 9:45am-4:45pm.)* Down Whitehead St., past the Hemingway House, you'll come to the southernmost point in the continental US at the fittingly named **Southernmost Beach.** A small, conical monument marks the spot: "90 miles to Cuba." Locals and tourists alike take part in the daily tradition of watching the sun go down. At the **Mallory Square Dock,** street entertainers and kitsch-hawkers work the crowd, while boats parade in revue during the **Sunset Celebration.**

NIGHTLIFE

The free *Island News*, found in local restaurants and bars, lists dining spots, music, and clubs. Nightlife in Key West revs up at 11pm and winds down in the wee daylight hours. The action centers around upper **Duval Street.** Key West nightlife reaches its annual exultant high the third week of October during **Fantasy Fest** (☎296-1817; www.fantasyfest.net), when decadent floats filled with drag queens, pirates, and wild locals take over Duval St.

Capt. Tony's Saloon, 428 Greene St. (☎294-1838), the oldest bar in Key West and reputedly one of Tennessee Williams' preferred watering holes, has been serving since the early 1930s. Bras and business cards festoon the ceiling. Live entertainment daily. Open M-Sa 10am-2am, Su noon-2am.

Rick's, 202 Duval St. (☎296-4890). An unabashed meat market, Rick's boasts well-placed body shots and a hot clientele. Happy Hour, with $2 longneck Buds, daily 3-6pm. W and Th $7 all-you-can-drink nights. Open M-Sa 11am-4am, Su noon-4am.

Sloppy Joe's, 201 Duval St. (☎294-5717). For the best party you'll most likely forget, stop by Hemingway's favorite hangout and be blown away by the house specialty, the Hurricane ($7). Grab the *Sloppy Joe's News* to learn the latest on upcoming entertainment. 21+. Open M-Sa 9am-4am, Su noon-4am.

Margaritaville, 500 Duval St. (☎292-1435). Find your lost shaker of salt in this Jimmy Buffet-inspired bar that specializes in, yes, margaritas ($6). Open daily 10am-2am.

GAY & LESBIAN NIGHTLIFE

Known for its wild, outspoken gay community, Key West hosts more than a dozen fabulous drag lounges, night clubs, and private bars for the gay man's enjoyment. Most clubs also welcome straight couples and lesbians, but check with the bouncer before entering. Most gay clubs line Duval St. south of Fleming Ave. Check out *Celebrate!*, for extensive coverage of the Key West gay and lesbian community.

Aqua, 711 Duval St. (☎294-0555), has become the hottest drag club in Key West. You're likely to see many wide-eyed tourists checking out the singing beauties. Next door, **KWEST MEN,** 705 Duval St. (☎292-8500), is a sweaty, scandalous dance club, where boys in G-strings gyrate on the dance floor. No cover. 21+. Drag show nightly 10pm. Tu amateur night. Open 4pm-4am.

The Bourbon Street Pub, 724 Duval St. (☎296-1992). This strip dance club is so hot, you'll soon find yourself shirtless, too. No cover. Open 4pm-4am. Its sister club, 801 Bourbon, 801 Duval St. (☎294-4737), is also very popular. Open daily 11am-4am.

FORT LAUDERDALE ☎954

City streets and highways may be fine for most city's transportation needs, but Fort Lauderdale adds a third option: canals. Intricate waterways connect ritzy homes with the intracoastal river—owning a yacht (over 40,000 in town) is both practical and stylish. "The Venice of America" also boasts 23 miles of beach, making Fort Lauderdale fun even for those who can't afford a yacht. For the aquaphobic, trendy Las Olas Blvd. has some of the best shopping in south Florida.

TRANSPORTATION

Airport: Fort Lauderdale/Hollywood International, 1400 Lee Wagoner Blvd. (☎359-6100; www.fort-lauderdale-fll.com), 3½ mi. south of downtown on U.S. 1. Or take I-595 E from I-95 to Exit 12B. Buses to and from the airport go through Broward Transit Central Terminal (☎367-8400). Take bus #11 south to the airport, and #1 from the airport.

Trains: Amtrak, 200 SW 21st Terr. (☎587-6692), just west of I-95, ¼ mi. south of Broward Blvd. Take bus #22 from downtown. Open daily 7:15am-9:15pm. To **Orlando** (4¾hr., 2 per day, $29-56).

Buses: Greyhound, 515 NE 3rd St. (☎764-6551), 3 blocks north of Broward Blvd. downtown. *Be careful in this area, especially at night.* Open 24hr. To: **Daytona Beach** (7hr., 4 per day, $35.50); **Miami** (1hr., 17 per day, $5); **Orlando** (5½hr., 6 per day, $33.50).

Public Transit: Broward County Transit (BCT), ☎357-8400. Central Terminal located at NW 1st Ave. and Broward Ave. downtown. Buses #11 and 36 run north-south on A1A through the beaches. Operates daily 6am-11pm. $1; seniors, under 18, and disabled $0.50; transfer $0.15. 1-day passes ($2.50), 7-day passes ($9), 10-ride passes ($8). Schedules available at hotels, libraries, and the central terminal. **City Cruiser** (☎761-3543) loops through downtown and the beach strip between Sunrise Blvd. and Las Olas Blvd. F-Sa every 30min. 6pm-1am. Free. **Tri-Rail** (☎728 8445 or 800-874-7245) connects West Palm Beach, Fort Lauderdale, and Miami. Trains run M-F 4am-10pm, Sa-Su 7am-5pm. Schedules available at airport, motels, or Tri-Rail stops. $2-6; children, disabled, students, and seniors with Tri-Rail ID 50% discount.

Taxi: Yellow Cab ☎777-7777. **Public Service Taxi** ☎587-9090.

Bike Rental: Mike's Cyclery, 5429 N. Federal Hwy. (☎493-5277). Open M-F 10am-7pm, Sa 10am-5pm. A variety of bicycles $20 per day, $50 per week; racing bikes slightly more. Credit card deposit required.

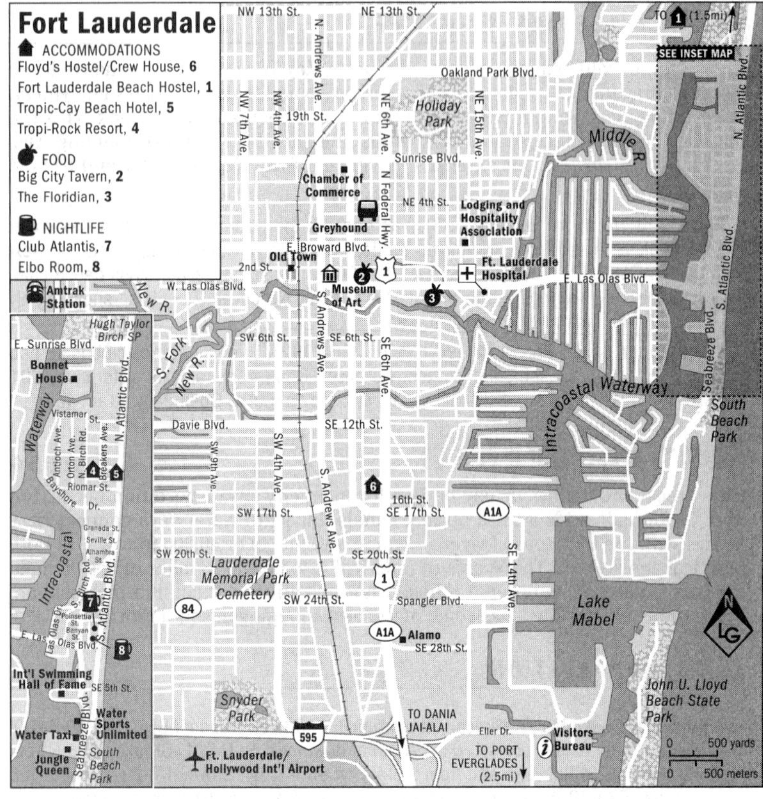

ORIENTATION

North-south I-95 connects West Palm Beach, Fort Lauderdale, and Miami. Rte. 84/I-75 (Alligator Alley) slithers 100 mi. west from Fort Lauderdale across the Everglades to small cities on Florida's Gulf Coast. Florida's Turnpike runs parallel to I-95. Fort Lauderdale is bigger than it looks. The city extends westward from its 23 mi. of beach to encompass nearly 450 sq. mi. Streets and boulevards are east-west and avenues are north-south. All are labeled NW, NE, SW, or SE according to a quadrant. The two major roads in Fort Lauderdale are **Broward Boulevard,** running east-west, and **Andrews Avenue,** running north-south. The brick-and-mortar downtown centers around **U.S. 1 (Federal Highway)** and **Las Olas Boulevard,** about 2 mi. west of the oceanfront. Between downtown and the waterfront, yachts fill the ritzy inlets of the **Intracoastal Waterway. The Strip** (a.k.a. Rte. A1A, Fort Lauderdale Beach Blvd., 17th St. Causeway, Ocean Blvd., or Seabreeze Blvd.) runs 4 mi. along the beach between Oakland Park Blvd. to the north and Las Olas Blvd. to the south.

PRACTICAL INFORMATION

Visitor Info: Greater Fort Lauderdale Convention and Visitors Bureau, 1850 Eller Dr. #303 (☎765-4466, 800-227-8669, or 527-5600 for 24hr. travel directions and hotel info; www.sunny.org), in the Port Everglades, has the useful *Superior Small Lodgings,* a comprehensive and detailed list of low-priced accommodations. Open M-F 8:30am-5pm. **Chamber of Commerce,** 512 NE 3rd Ave. (☎462-6000), 3 blocks off Federal Hwy. at 5th St. Open M-F 8am-5pm.

Hotlines: First Call for Help, ☎467-6333. **Sexual Assault and Treatment Center,** ☎761-7273. Both 24hr.

Medical Services: Fort Lauderdale Hospital, 1601 E. Las Olas Blvd., at SE 16th Ave. (☎463-4321).

Public Library: 100 S. Andrews Ave. (☎357-7444). Open M-Th 9am-9pm, F-Sa 9am-5pm, Su noon-5:30pm.

Post Office: 1900 W. Oakland Park Blvd. (☎527-2028). Open M-F 7:30am-7pm, Sa 8:30am-2pm. **Postal Code:** 33310. **Area Code:** 954.

ACCOMMODATIONS

Thank decades of spring breakers for the abundance of hotels lining the beachfront. Generally, it is easy to find an available room at any time of the year, depending on how much you are willing to pay. High-season runs from mid-February to early April. Motels just north of the strip and a block west of A1A are the cheapest. Many hotels offer low-season deals for under $35. The **Greater Fort Lauderdale Lodging and Hospitality Association,** 1412 E. Broward Blvd., provides a free directory of area hotels. (☎567-0766. Open M-F 9am-5pm.) The *Fort Lauderdale News* and the *Miami Herald* occasionally sport listings by local residents who rent rooms to tourists in spring. Sleeping on the well-patrolled beaches is illegal. Instead, check out one of the outstanding hostels in the area.

Fort Lauderdale Beach Hostel, 2115 N. Ocean Blvd. (A1A) (☎567-7275), between Sunrise and Oakland Park Blvd. Take bus #11 from the central terminal. After a long day of tanning and swimming at the adjacent beach, backpackers mingle in the tropical courtyard, the TV-equipped common room, and the well-stocked kitchen. A/C, ping-pong, grill, free Internet access, and local phone calls. Call ahead for free daytime pickup from anywhere in Fort Lauderdale. Breakfast included. Free lockers. Linen deposit $10. Reservations suggested Dec.-June. Dorms $16-18. ❶

Floyd's Hostel/Crew House, 445 SE 16th St. (☎462-0631). From downtown take bus #1 or 40 and get off at 17th St. Call ahead for free pickup in the Fort Lauderdale area. Floyd's is a homey hostel catering to international travelers and boat crews. The owners got engaged thanks to *Let's Go: USA 1995*. We're just that good. Free food, cable TV, linen, lockers, laundry, and Internet access. Check-in by midnight or call for special arrangement. Passport or American driver's license required. 4-bed dorms $18, $115 per week. Private rooms in winter $55; in summer $40. ❶

Tropic-Cay Beach Hotel, 529 N. Ft. Lauderdale Beach Blvd. (A1A) (☎564-5900 or 800-463-2333), directly across from the beach; take bus #11 or 44. Don't be fooled by the lackluster exterior; Tropic-Cay is hands-down the best deal on the beach. Before heading back to their super clean, extremely large rooms, party-hard guests return from late-night ruckus to the outdoor patio bar and central pool, where fun continues long into the night. Tropic-Cay is one of the most crowded party spots on the beach, so be sure to call ahead. Kitchens available. During spring break, you must be 21+ to rent. Key deposit $10. Doubles Sept.-May $59-99; May-Sept. $35-59; $10 per extra person. ❸

Tropi-Rock Resort, 2900 Belmar St. (☎564-0523 or 800-987-9385), 2 blocks west of A1A at Birch Rd.; take bus #11 or 44. A few blocks inland from the beach, this yellow-and-orange hotel provides a resort atmosphere at affordable prices. The lush hibiscus garden with caged birds surrounding the pool and Tiki bar sings with a little more privacy and luxury than neighboring motels. Gym, Internet access, tennis courts, free local calls, and refrigerators. Rooms mid-Dec. to Apr. $85-160; Apr. to mid-Dec. $65-105. AAA discount available. ❹

FOOD

Though clubs along the strip offer massive quantities of free Happy Hour grub—wieners, chips, and hors d'oeuvres come on surfboard-sized platters—most bars have hefty cover charges (from $5) and drink minimums (from $3).

The Floridian, 1410 E. Las Olas Blvd. (☎463-4041), is a local favorite, serving up heaping portions of french toast ($5), cheeseburgers ($5), and veggie burger platters ($7). Try the house specialty–the Floridian (grilled tuna salad sandwich, $6)–with one of the to-die-for milkshakes ($4), and you might never want to leave. Open 24hr. ❷

Big City Tavern, 609 E. Las Olas Blvd. (☎727-0307). An elegant eatery in the heart of the Las Olas strip, the refined Big City Tavern creates delectable dishes without the accompanying pretention. Enjoy almond crusted trout ($15) or 12 oz. New York steak ($28) in the brick-lined interior or on the tranquil patio. Open daily 11am-10pm. ❺

Squiggy's N.Y. Style Pizza, 207 SW 2nd St., in Old Town (☎522-6655). Whether you're between bars or looking for a treat before heading home, Squiggy's is the place for those late-night munchies. Gooey slices of Sicilian pie ($2, after 8pm $2.50) will certainly please you and the honey you met grooving under the strobe lights. Open M 11am-11:30pm, Tu-W 11am-3am, Th-Su 11am-4am. ❶

SIGHTS

Most visitors flock to Fort Lauderdale to lounge on the sunny beaches. When floating in the crystal-clear waves of the Atlantic, it's easy to forget the city's other notable attractions. Cruising down the palm-lined shore of Beachfront Ave. (A1A), biking through a nature preserve, or boating through the winding intracoastal canals reveals the less sandy side of Fort Lauderdale.

ON THE WATERFRONT. Fort Lauderdale Beach doesn't have a dull spot on it, but most of the action is between Las Olas Blvd. and Sunrise Blvd. The latest on-the-beach mall, **Las Olas Waterfront,** boasts clubs, restaurants, and bars. *(2 SW 2nd St.)* The **Water Taxi** offers a relaxing way to beat the rush-hour traffic and maneuver through town. The friendly captains will drive right up to any Las Olas restaurant or drop you off anywhere along the Intracoastal Waterway of New River. Alternatively, ride through the entire route for an intimate viewing of the fabulous, colossal houses along the canal. Special packages include a canal pub crawl to Ft. Lauderdale's best bars. *(651 Seabreeze Blvd./A1A. ☎467-6677; www.watertaxi.com. Call 30min. before pick-up. Open 9am-midnight. $4, seniors and under 12 $2; 1-day unlimited pass $5, 3-day pass $7; pub crawl $15.)* If traveling with a family or young children, take a tour aboard the tourist-targeted **Jungle Queen.** The captain's commentary acquaints you with the changing scenery as the 550-passenger riverboat cruises up the New River. *(801 Seabreeze Blvd. At the Bahia Mar Yacht Center, on Rte. A1A, 3 blocks south of Las Olas Blvd. ☎462-5596; www.junglequeen.com. 3½hr. tours daily 10am, 2, 7pm. $13.50, ages 2-10 $9.25; 7pm tour $30/17, dinner included.)* **Water Sports Unlimited** is the best beach spot for water-sport rentals and trips. Sail the ocean on a boat *($95 for 2 hr.)* or enjoy its serene blue water from above on a parasailing trip *($60-70)*. Speed boats and wave runners also available. *(301 Seabreeze Blvd./Rte. A1A. ☎467-1316. Open daily 9am-5pm.)*

ON DRY LAND. Get lost in an oasis of subtropical trees and animals in the middle of urban Fort Lauderdale at **Hugh Taylor Birch State Park.** Bike, jog, canoe, or drive through the 3½ mi. stretch of mangroves and royal palms, or relax by the fresh lagoon filled with herons, gophers, tortoises, and marsh rabbits. *(3109 E. Sunrise Blvd., west off A1A. ☎564-4521. Open 8am-dusk. $3.25 per vehicle, $1 entrance fee. Canoes $5.30 per hr. Cabins and primitive sites available by reservation; call ahead.)* Anointed by Guinness as the "fastest game in the world," Jai Alai still remains mostly unknown to Americans outside the state of Florida. Take a break from the beach heat and watch a match at **Dania Jai-Alai,** which sports one of the largest *frontons* (courts) in the state. *(301 E. Dania Beach Blvd. Off U.S. 1, 10min. south of Fort Lauderdale. ☎927-2841. Games Tu and Sa noon, 7:15pm, W-F 7:15pm, Su 1pm. General admission $1.50, reserved seats from $2.50.)* Cast your line at the **International Game Fishing Association's Fishing Hall of Fame and Museum,** where a gallery of odd-looking fish, a timeline of American fishing, the inside scoop on fishing hot spots, and an interactive reeling exercise amaze even the most avid fisherman. For the true fish fetishist, check out the large wooden replicas of world-record catches adorning the museum's ceiling and the film *Journeys* in the big screen theater. *(300 Gulf Stream Way. Off I-95 at Griffin Rd., Exit 23. ☎922-4212; www.igfa.org/museum. Wheelchair-accessible. Open daily 10am-6pm. $5, seniors $4.50, children $4. IGFA members free.)* For a different kind of high-seas adventure, doggy-paddle on over to the **International Swimming Hall of Fame and Musuem,** where exhibits on the sport and some of its greatest athletes await. *(1 Hall of Fame Dr. ☎462-6536; www.ishof.org. Wheelchair-accessible. Open daily 9am-5pm. $3; students, seniors, and military $1.)* Fort Lauderdale's **Museum of Art,** 1 E. Las Olas Blvd., is home to an extensive collection of American painter William Glacken's work and remarkable temporary exhibits, which have included everything from surrealists to photojournalists. *(☎468-3283; www.museumofart.org. Wheelchair-accessible. Open T-Su 11am-5pm. Tours Sa-Su 1:30pm. $7, seniors $6, children and students $5.)*

 NIGHTLIFE

Ask any local and they'll tell you that the *real* nightlife action is in **Old Town.** Two blocks northwest of Las Olas on 2nd St. near the **Riverwalk** district, the 100 yards of Old Town are packed with raucous bars, steamy clubs, cheap eats, and a stylish crowd. Considerably more expensive, and geared specifically toward tourists, the **Strip** houses several popular nightspots across from the beach.

Tarpon Bend, 200 SW 2nd St. (☎523-3233). Always the busiest place on the block. Starched shirts from the office converge with flirty black tube tops around the icy beer tubs of "the Bends." Bottle beers $3-4, "draft of the month" $1. W Ladies drink free until 11pm. Open daily 11:30am-1am, sometimes later.

The Voodoo Lounge, 111 SW 2nd St. (☎522-0733). A well-dressed and well-known party in lush red VIP rooms, this upscale club offers a more refined aproach to fun. The pretentious bouncers and velvet rope may seem out of character for the beach crowd, but this club has something for everyone. Su Drag shows, W Ladies night. F-Sa 21+. Cover F-Sa $10. Open M, W, and F-Su 10pm-4am.

Rush Street, 220 SW 2nd St. (☎524-1818). A young crowd flocks to Rush Street, where mini-skirted ladies mingle with beach bums and fashion-conscious men alike. All get down on the dance floor, which rocks the house with neon lights and blaring music. No cover. Lunch M-F 11am-2pm. Open M-Th 5:30-10pm, F-Sa 5:30-11pm, Su 4:30-9pm.

Elbo Room (☎463-4615), on prime real estate at the corner of A1A and Las Olas Blvd. The booming sidewalk bar, chock full of scantily clad beach beauties, is one of the most visible and packed scenes on the strip. Live local rock music nightly. Open M-Th 11am-2am, F-Sa 11am-3am, Su noon-2am.

Club Atlantis, 219 S. Ft. Lauderdale Beach Blvd. (☎779-2544), is a popular hangout for sin-seeking teens. Mud wrestling and scandalous grinding fill the dance floors. 18+. Cover varies. Open daily 9pm-4am.

PALM BEACH & WEST PALM BEACH ☎561

Nowhere else in Florida is the line between the "haves" and the "have-nots" as visible as at the intracoastal waterway dividing aristocratic vacationers on Palm Beach Island from blue-collar residents of West Palm Beach. Five-star resorts and guarded mansions reign over the "Gold Coast" island, while auto repair shops and fast food restaurants characterize the mainland. Budget travel may be difficult here, but the region still offers some unique museums and stunning houses.

ORIENTATION & PRACTICAL INFORMATION. Palm Beach is located approximately 60 mi. north of Miami and 150 mi. southeast of Orlando. **I-95** runs north-south through the center of West Palm Beach, then continues south to Fort Lauderdale and Miami. The more scenic coastal highway, **A1A,** also travels north-south, crossing over Lake Worth at the Flagler Memorial Bridge to Palm Beach. Large highways cut through urban areas and residential neighborhoods; finding your way around can be a bit confusing. Stick to the major roads like north-south **Highway 1** (which turns into S. Dixie Hwy.) **A1A,** east-west **Palm Beach Lakes Boulevard,** and **Belvedere Road.** The heart of downtown West Palm Beach is **Clematis Street,** across from the Flagler Memorial Bridge, and **City Place,** 222 Lakeview Ave. (☎835-0862); both contain affordable restaurants and nightclubs.

Palm Beach International Airport (☎471-7420; www.pbia.org), at Belvedere and Australian Ave., Exit 51 from I-95 N, is 2½ mi. east of downtown West Palm Beach. The Tri-Rail stops at the airport, as does bus #44 from the downtown West Palm Beach Quadrille. **Amtrak,** 201 S. Tamarind Ave., is east of I-95 in the downtown West Palm Beach Quadrille. (☎832-6169. Open daily 7:30am-8:45pm.) Trains chug to **Orlando** (4hr., 2 per day, $21) and **Atlanta** (20hr., 3 per day, $270-350). **Greyhound** leaves from the same station heading to **Orlando** (4hr., 8 per day, $30) and **Miami** (2hr., 15 per day, $21). **Public Transit: Palm Tran,** 3201 Electronics Way, has 35 routes from North Palm Beach Gardens to Boca Raton, with #41 and #42 traveling through the Palm Beach area. The major hub is at the intersection of Quadrille Blvd. and Clematis St. in downtown West Palm Beach. Schedules available on all buses, at the main office, or at any public library. (☎841-4200 or 877-870-9489. $1.25; students under 21, seniors, and disabled $0.60; 1-day pass $3/2.) **Tri-Rail** connects West Palm Beach to Fort Lauderdale and Miami and leaves from the train station on Tamarind. (☎954-788-7936 or 800-874-7245. Hours vary by route: generally M-F 4am-10pm, Sa-Su 7am-5pm. $2-6; students, seniors, and disabled half-price; under 4 free.) **Taxi: Yellow Cab** ☎689-2222. **Visitor Info: Palm Beach County Convention and Visitors Bureau,** 1555 Palm Beach Lakes Blvd. (☎471-3995; www.palmbeachfl.com. Open M-F 8:30-5:30.) **Medical Services: Columbia Hospital,** 2201 45th St. (☎842-6141). **Hotlines: Helpline** ☎615-4029. 24hr., **Teenline** ☎930-1234. 24hr. **Internet Access: Clematis St. News Stand,** 206 Clematis St. (☎832-2302. Open Su-W 7:30am-10pm, Th-Sa 7:30am-midnight. $8 per hr.) **Post Office:** 640 Clematis St., in West Palm Beach. (☎833-0929. Open M-F 8:30am-5pm.) **Postal Code:** 33401. **Area Code:** 561.

ACCOMMODATIONS. Catering to the rich and famous (with an emphasis on *rich*) who flock to Palm Beach during the winter months, extravagant resorts and hotels are arguably the most notable attraction lining the Gold Coast. While the idea of mingling with royalty might sound like a fairytale come true, the words "budget" and "hostel" will only receive blank stares from receptionists. Many reasonably priced B&Bs are booked far in advance; reserve a room before you arrive. West Palm Beach is the best bet for an affordable room near the action, but the absolute cheapest options are the chain hotels near the highway. Built in 1922 by a former Palm Beach mayor and elegantly restored in 1990, **Hibiscus House Bed & Breakfast ❹,** 501 30th St., in West Palm Beach at the corner of Spruce St. west of Flagler Dr., is affordable without sacrificing luxury. Sleep in one of nine antique-decorated bedrooms and wake up to a two-course gourmet breakfast served on Waterford crystal. Each room has a terrace, TV, phone, and A/C. (☎863-5633 or 800-203-4927. Call ahead for reservations. Rooms Dec.-Mar. $100-270; Apr.-Nov. $75-135.) **Hotel Biba ❹,** 32 Belvedere Rd., in West Palm Beach, bus #44, is fun, funky, and eclectic. Don't be fooled by its lackluster turquoise exterior; Hotel Biba is a hip hotel that has become a haven for those budget-conscious travelers with a sense of style. Beautiful bodies lounge on the pool deck and gather in the garden bar for drinks in the evening. (☎832-0094. Breakfast included. Rooms Dec.-Mar. $109-129; Apr.-Nov. $79-109.) **Heart of Palm Beach Hotel ❺,** 160 Royal Palm Way, in Palm Beach, bus #41, welcomes visitors with cool pinks and greens. Palm Beach's most inexpensive hotel still manages to embody the prestige of the nearby beaches and ritzy Worth Ave. (☎655-5600. Internet access, refrigerators, TV, heated pool, free parking. Call ahead for reservations. Rooms Dec.-Mar. $199-399; Apr.-Nov. $89-169; under 18 stays free with parents.)

FOOD & NIGHTLIFE. Clematis St. in downtown West Palm Beach offers a lively option for travelers on the cheap. A mixture of pool hall, sports bar, concert venue, and meat market, **Spanky's ❷,** 500 Clematis St., is West Palm Beach's notoriously fun night spot. Enjoy cold beer (pitchers $5) and tasty bar food in this enormous venue, whose closing time is marked only by a question mark. Every night is a different theme and drink special, like Island Tuesdays with $0.75 Coronas and $2 Rum Runners. (☎659-5669. Beer-battered onion rings $4. Hot wings 12 for $8. Open M-F at 11:30am, Sa noon, Su 1pm; closes when the place empties out.) Voted "Best Burger" and "People's Choice" in a recent cook-off, **O'Shea's Irish Pub and Restaurant ❷,** 531½ Clematis St., at Rosemary St., will modify any dish to fit vegetarian needs. Locals and those nostalgic for Dublin flock here for the live nightly music, usually Irish rock or folk, and Mrs. O'Shea's $7.50 savory chicken pie. (☎833-3865. Open Su-Tu 11am-10pm, W-Th 11am-midnight, F-Sa 11am-1am.) For a respite from West Palm Beach's bar-and-grill scene, **Maision Carlos ❹,** 207 Clematis St., is your best bet. This elegant French and Italian bistro serves both lunch ($7-15) and dinner ($12-25) to its hungry clientele, who savor their pasta and meat under the indoor umbrellas and low-hanging lights. (☎659-6524. Open M-Sa for lunch 11:30am-2:30pm, for dinner 5:30-10pm.)

Known for exclusive dinner parties and black tie galas, nightlife on Palm Beach is an invitation-only affair. You won't find a disco or "local bar" anywhere along the ritzy downtown area. You will, however, find **Sprinkles Ice Cream & Sandwich Shop ❶,** 279 Royal Poinciana Way, the best bargain for a hungry stomach. Customers line up for a scoop of homemade ice cream ($3.75) in a hand-dipped cone. (☎659-1140. French bread pizza $5.50. Open Su-Th 10am-10pm, F-Sa 10am-11pm.)

SIGHTS. Perhaps one of West Palm Beach's greatest treasures is the **Norton Museum of Art,** 1451 S. Olive Ave. Well-known for its collection of European, American, contemporary, and Chinese art, the museum boasts works by Cezanne, Matisse, O'Keeffe, and Pollock. Be sure to stop by the central garden, which features its own fountain of youth. (☎832-5196; www.norton.org. Wheelchair-accessible. Open May-Sept. Tu-Sa 10am-5pm, Su 1-5pm; Nov.-Apr. M-Sa 10am-5pm, Su 1-5pm. $6, ages 13-21 $2, under 13 free. Tours M-Su 2-3pm; lectures M-F 12:30-1pm. Free. Self-guided audio tour $4.) If you're visiting in early spring, catch the training seasons of the **Montreal Expos** and **Atlanta Braves,** who make their winter home at **Municipal Stadium,** 1610 Palm Beach Lakes Blvd. (☎683-6012. Call for times and schedules.)

In Palm Beach, just walking around can be one of the most enjoyable (and affordable) activities. Known as the "Rodeo Drive of the South," **Worth Avenue,** between S. Ocean Blvd. and Coconut Row, outfits Palm Beach's rich and famous in the threads of fashion heavyweights like Gucci, Polo, and Armani. Walk or drive along **Ocean Boulevard** to gawk at the spectacular, enormous mansions owned by celebrities and millionaires. One particularly remarkable complex is **The Breakers,** 1 S. County Rd., a sizable Italian Renaissance resort. Even if you can't afford the bare-minimum $270 price tag for a night of luxury, live vicariously though a guided tour. (☎659-8440 or 888-273-2537. Tour W 3pm. $10.)

Of course, a trip to Palm Beach County is incomplete without relaxing on one of its picturesque beaches. Although most of the beachfront property in Palm Beach is private, more public beaches can be found in West Palm Beach. Good options on Palm Beach include the popular **Mid-town Beach,** 400 S. Ocean Blvd., and **Phipps Ocean Park,** 2185 S. Ocean Blvd. (☎585-9203).

NORTH FLORIDA

PANAMA CITY BEACH ☎850

Panama City Beach is the place to find everything touristy, beachy, and kitschy crammed into a 27 mi. long strip running along the Gulf of Mexico. Regardless of whether you're in college or not, the "PCB" experience is the essence of a spring-break rampage. As the heart of the "Redneck Riviera," there is no pretension or high culture here—just miles and miles of parties and loud, thumping bass in high season. Warm-as-a-bath turquoise water, roller coasters, surf shops, and water parks round out the entertainment possibilities.

ORIENTATION & PRACTICAL INFORMATION. After crossing Hathaway Bridge from the east, **Thomas Drive** and **Front Beach Road** (marked as Alt. U.S. 98) fork off from U.S. 98 and run along the gulf. This becomes the **"Miracle Strip,"** the main drag of PCB. Beware the sunset and late-night rush; this two-lane road grinds to a standstill at busy times. Regular Rte. 98 becomes **Panama Beach Parkway** and is the less-trafficked "express route" around the strip. **Greyhound,** 917 Harrison Ave. (☎785-6111; open M-Sa 7am-9pm, Su 7am-11am, 1:15-4:15pm and 6:45pm-8:30pm), stops at the junction of U.S. 98 and 79 and continues on to Atlanta (9hr., 4 per day, $47-51) and Orlando (8-11hr., 3 per day, $62-65). **Bay Town Trolley,** 1021 Massalina Dr., shuttles along the beach. (☎769-0557. M-F 6am-6pm. $1, students and seniors $0.50; $1 to cross bridge.) **Taxi: Yellow Cab,** ☎747-8294. **Panama City Beach Convention and Visitors Bureau,** 17001 Panama City Beach Pkwy., at U.S. 98 and 79, has a free **Internet** kiosk. (☎800-722-3224; www.pcbeach.com. Open daily 8am-5pm.) **Hotlines: Domestic Violence and Rape Crisis,** ☎763-0706. **Crisis and Mental Health Emergency,** ☎769-9481. Both 24hr. **Post Office:** 421 Jenks Ave. (☎763-6509. Open M-F 8am-5pm, Sa 9am-noon.) **Postal Code:** 32401. **Area Code:** 850.

ACCOMMODATIONS. Depending on the location and time of year, rates range from outrageous to extremely outrageous. High-season runs from the end of April until early September and typically means rooms from $100; rates drop in fall and winter. The **South Pacific Motel ❷,** 16701 Front Beach Rd., is definitely one of the best deals on the beach, thanks to a secret treasure: two motel rooms that are 20 paces away from the surf and go for $45 in peak season. The rest of the rooms are also relatively cheap, even in summer, and the family-owned ambience makes it a nice contrast to the impersonal strip. (☎234-2703 or 800-966-9439. Pool, private beach, and cable TV. In summer 2 of the rooms $45; doubles $70; 2-bedroom apartments $97.) **The Palmetto ❸,** 17255 Front Beach Rd., is another safe and sunny place to take up residence on your vacation. (☎234-2121. Indoor/outdoor pool, shuffleboard, TV, on-site laundry, and A/C. Rooms $98; low-season from $55.) **Travelodge ❷,** 9424 Front Beach Rd., ½ mi. from the beach, has clean, spacious rooms with two double beds, free cable TV, and coffee. (☎235-1122 or 800-578-7878. Rooms Su-Th $45-59; F-Sa $79-89.) Camp on the beach at **Saint Andrews State Recreation Area ❶,** 4607 State Park Ln., at the east end of Thomas Dr. Call up to 11 months in advance for reservations at this extremely popular campground. All 176 sites are beneath the pines and near the water. (☎233-5140, for reservations ☎800-326-3521. Sites $17; with electricity or waterside $19; winter $10/12. Each additional person $2, each additional car $3.)

FOOD & NIGHTLIFE. Buffets stuff the Strip and Thomas Dr. "Early bird" specials (usually 4-6pm) get you the same food at about half the price. **Scampy's ❷,** 4933 Thomas Dr., is a notable exception to the strip's often low-quality food, offering delicious, cooked-rather-than-reheated seafare in a smaller, less harried atmosphere than the mega-troughs. (☎235-4209. 18 lunch specials $4-8. Seafood salad $9. Dinner entrees $11-20. Open Su-Th 11am-10pm, F-Sa 11am-11pm.) At night, many of the restaurants on the Strip turn into bars and clubs, and most have live bands. Cool off at **Sharky's ❷,** 15201 Front Beach Rd., with a Hurricane or a Sharkbite specialty drink ($5.25). More adventurous spirits will savor their signature appetizer, "shark bites" (fried shark cubes; $7). Raw oysters go for $2 per dozen daily 4-6pm. (☎235-2420. Live performers on the beach deck most nights. Cover $8. Kitchen open daily 11:30am-11pm; club open until 2am.)

The back patio bar at **Harpoon Harry's,** 12627 Front Beach Rd., overlooks the beach. Build a midnight sandcastle after having a drink. (☎234-6060. Open daily 11am-2am.) The largest club in the US (capacity 8000) and MTV's former Spring Break headquarters, **Club LaVela,** 8813 Thomas Dr., has eight clubs and 48 bar stations under one jammin' roof. Live bands work the Rock Pavilion every night. Wet T-shirt, bikini, and male hard body contests fill the weekends and every night during Spring Break. (☎234-3866. 18+. No daytime cover; nightly cover varies. Open daily 10am-4am.) Next door, **Spinnaker,** 8795 Thomas Dr., contains a restaurant, a pool deck, and a playground for kids. This enormous beach clubhouse hosts live bands throughout the week. (☎234-7882. Fresh seafood $8-20. Live music Th-Su 10:30pm. Happy Hour daily 9-11pm. 21+, during spring break 18+. Cover $5-15. Restaurant open daily 11am-10pm; club 10pm-4am.)

SIGHTS & ENTERTAINMENT. Over 1000 acres of gators, nature trails, and beaches make up the **Saint Andrews State Recreation Area** (see **Accommodations,** above; open daily 8am-sunset; $4 per car). **The Glass Bottom Boat** takes visitors on a dolphin-watching excursion and sails to Shell Island from **Treasure Island Marina,** 3605 Thomas Dr. (☎234-8944. 3hr. trips 9am, 1, 4:30pm. $15, seniors $14, under 12 $8.) Also in the Marina, the world's largest speed boat, the **Sea Screamer,** 3601 Thomas Dr., cruises the Grand Lagoon. (☎233-9107. In summer 4 cruises per day; spring and fall departures vary, call for times. $15, ages 4-12 $10.) Sister to the Screamer is the **Sea Dragon,** an authentic pirate ship that takes swashbucklers on Pirate Cruises. (☎234-7400. 2hr. cruises in daytime, evening, and sunset; call ahead for times. $16, seniors $14, ages 3-14 $12, under 2 $5.) An assortment of dolphin shows, parasailing outfits, and amusement parks line **Front Beach Road Miracle Strip Amusement Park** and **Shipwreck Island Water Park,** 12000 Front Beach Rd. (Amusement park: ☎234-5810. Open summer Su-F 6-11pm, Sa 1-11:30pm; spring and fall hours vary. $18, seniors $12, under 35 in. free. Water park: ☎234-0368. Open summer daily 10:30am-5:30pm; spring and fall hours vary. $24, seniors $14. Admission to both parks $33.)

PENSACOLA ☎850

Pensacola's military-infused population and reputation for conservatism have been a part of the city's make-up since before the Civil War, when three forts on the shores of Pensacola formed a defense to guard the deep-water ports. Most visitors, however, will be drawn to the area for its sugar-white beaches and the secluded, emerald waters along the **Gulf Island National Seashore.**

For those seeking solace from sunburn, the **National Museum of US Naval Aviation,** inside the Naval Air Station, at Exit 2 off I-10, provides ample diversion. The excitement of more than 130 planes of past and present, dangling from the ceiling or parked within arm's reach, will have aspiring pilot soaring. (☎452-3604. Open daily 9am-5pm. 1½hr. tours daily 9:30, 11am, 1, 2:30pm. Free.) An the **Naval Live Oaks Area,** 1801 Gulf Breeze Pkwy., relaxing paths meander through a forest that John Quincy Adams established as the first and only naval tree reservation in the US. (☎934-2600. Open daily 8am-5:30pm.) Pay $1 to cross the Pensacola Beach Bridge to **Santa Rosa Island** for some of the best beaches around. A hodgepodge of military bunkers from different wars, **Fort Pickens,** where Apache leader Geronimo was once imprisoned in the late 1800s, commands the western part of Santa Rosa. Visitors explore the ruins and sunbathe on the beautiful secluded seashore. (Park open daily 7am-10pm. Visitors Center open daily Mar.-Oct. 9:30am-5pm; Nov.-Feb. 8:30am-4pm. $8.)

Hotels along the beach cost at least $65 and get more expensive in summer. The **Five Flags Inn ❹,** 299 Fort Pickens Rd., is one of the better beachfront deals, offering free local calls, gulfside rooms, beach patio and pool, and coffee. (☎932-3586. Rooms May-Aug. $99; Sept.-Oct. $75; Nov.-Dec. $55; Feb.-May $75.) Also offering good beachside rates is the **Sandpiper Gulf Aire Inn ❷,** 21 Via De Luna. The inn offers motel rooms, kitchenettes, and villas for prices that will help you sleep even better in the newly renovated rooms. Private beach, pool, and cable TV. (☎800-301-5925; www.gulfairemotel.com. Rooms $69-89; low-season from $39.) Cheaper options lie inland, north of downtown at the exits of I-10 and I-110, a 15min. drive from the beach. Clean and well-furnished, the **Civic Inn ❷,** 200 N. Palafox St., is near downtown and budget friendly. (☎432-3441. A/C, TV. Singles Su-Th $40, F-Sa $48; doubles $48/68.) At the western edge of Santa Rosa Island, the **Fort Pickens Campground ❶** on the Gulf Islands National Seashore offers sites within walking distance of gorgeous beaches. (☎934-2622 for camping info, ☎800-365-2267 for reservations. All have electricity and water. Sites $20.)

Hopkins House ❷, 900 Spring St. in historic Pensacola, has incredibly popular, all-you-can-eat family-style dinners ($8) on Tuesday and Friday evenings, as well as regular lunch and breakfast specials. (☎438-3979. Open Tu-Su 7-9:30am and 11:15am-2pm. Open for dinner Tu and F 5:15-7:30pm.) **Jerry's Drive-In ❶,** 2815 E. Cervantes, has been serving up the best of American diner fare—its hamburgers ($2) were voted best along the Gulf Coast--since 1939. (☎433-9910. Open M-F 10am-10pm, Sa 7am-10pm. Cash only.) **Tre Fratelli ❸,** 304 Alcaniz St., a Sicilian restaurant and pizzeria, concocts fantastic pasta sauces. (☎438-3663. Pasta $8-13. Pizza $10-15. Open M-Sa 11am-3pm and 5-10pm.) **The Coffee Cup ❶,** 520 E. Cervantes. Oversized omlettes ($4-$6.20) will fill you up for the day, as will the famous pork chops ($5). (☎432-7060. Open M-Sa 6am-2pm.)

The city buttresses Pensacola Bay. **Palafox Street,** which becomes one-way near the bay, and **I-110** are the main north-south byways. **Government, Gregory,** and **Main Street** run east-west. **Main Street** becomes **Bayfront Parkway** along the edge of the bay and runs over the **Pensacola Bay Bridge.** On the other side, **Pensacola Beach Road** leads to Santa Rosa Island and Pensacola Beach, while **Gulf Breeze Parkway** trails along the coast. **Amtrak,** 980 E. Heinburg St. (☎433-4966 or 800-872-7245; open M, W, F midnight-1pm, Tu and Th 5:30am-1pm, Sa 5:30am-8:30am), stops by on its east-west route between New Orleans (7hr., 3 per week, $30-65) and Orlando (13hr., 3 per week, $50-108). **Greyhound,** 505 W. Burgess Rd. (☎476-4800; open 24hr.), heads to: Atlanta (9-14hr., 5 per day, $51); New Orleans (4-7hr., 2 per day, $44); Orlando (9hr., 7 per day, $62). A **trolley** runs two lines through downtown. Stops line Palafox St. (M-F 9am-3pm; $0.25). During the summer, two free Tiki Trolley shuttles run along the beach. (F-Sa 10am-3am, Su 10am-10pm.) Services include: **Taxi: Yellow Cab,** ☎433-3333. **Visitor Info: Pensacola Convention and Visitors Bureau,** 1401 E. Gregory St., near the Pensacola Bay Bridge. (☎800-874-1234; www.visitpensacola.com. Open daily 8am-5pm.) **Post Office:** 101 S. Palafox St. (☎439-0169. Open M-F 8:30am-5pm.) **Postal Code:** 32501. **Area Code:** 850.

GREAT LAKES

Though the region's alternate name--the Midwest--evokes a bland image of cornfields and small-town, white-picket-fence America, the states that hug the five Great Lakes encompass a variety of personalities. The world's largest freshwater lake, Lake Superior and its unpopulated, scenic coast cradle some of the most stunning natural features in the region—from the dense forests in northern Wisconsin to the waterfalls of the Upper Peninsula in Michigan. Along the Michigan, Indiana, and Illinois coast, Lake Michigan hosts sand dunes and a paradise of swimming, sailing, and deep-water fishing. Minneapolis and St. Paul have the panache of any coastal metropolis, while Chicago dazzles with a stunning skyline, incredible culinary offerings, and world-class museums.

HIGHLIGHTS OF THE GREAT LAKES

FOOD. Wisconsin cheese, Chicago pizza (p. 578), "pasties" in Michigan's Upper Peninsula (p. 569), and Door County's fishboils (p. 601) are some regional specialties.

RECREATIONAL ACTIVITIES. Canoeing and kayaking are popular in the northern reaches of the Great Lakes; Grand Traverse Bay (p. 565) is an recreation hot spot.

SCENIC VISTAS. Reach the top of the Log Slide in MN (p. 571) or the Dune Climb in MI (p. 564), and you'll never want to come down.

SCENIC DRIVES. In MI, see the Lake Michigan shore on U.S. 31 and Rte. 119 (p. 620); Brockway Mountain Dr. (p. 572); or the dirt roads of Pictured Rocks State Park (p. 570). In MN, drive Rte. 61 N from Duluth along the Lake Superior shore (p. 620).

OHIO

Of all the Great Lake states, Ohio probably most closely resembles the traditional definition of "Middle America." The state's perfect farmland is a patchwork of cornfields and soybean plants, and three cities—Cincinnati, Cleveland, and Columbus—are home to millions of Ohioans. Away from the big cities, small towns cultivate a friendly atmosphere while liberal colleges challenge a practical, traditional Midwestern identity.

PRACTICAL INFORMATION

Capital: Columbus.

Visitor Info: State Office of Travel and Tourism, 77 S. High St., 29th fl., Columbus 43215 (☎614-466-8844; www.ohiotourism.com). Open M-F 8am-5pm. **Ohio Tourism Line** (☎800-282-5393).

Postal Abbreviation: OH. **Sales Tax:** 6%.

CLEVELAND ☎216

Ridiculed for having a river so polluted it caught fire (twice) and branded "Mistake on the Lake," Cleveland has gone to great lengths over the past decade to correct its beleaguered image. Early in the 90s, new football and baseball stadiums catalyzed the downtown makeover, which reached its zenith in 1995 with the arrival of

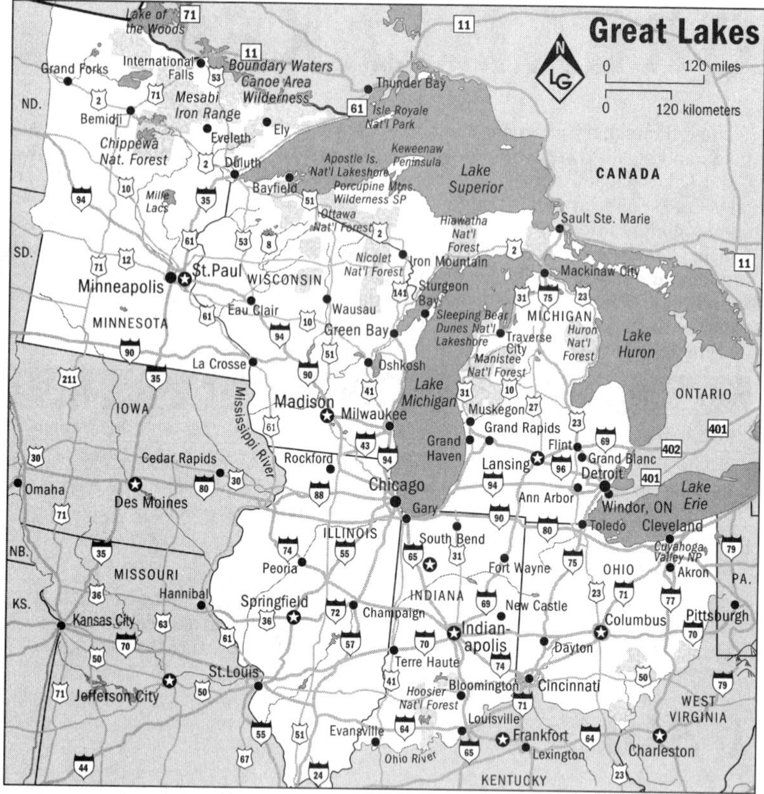

the Rock and Roll Hall of Fame. Meanwhile, the lake and river were cleaned, the city skyline was redefined, and the deserted factories and warehouses of the Flats were transformed into bustling bars and nightclubs. Modern sculptures and flower-lined streets now give the downtown a sense of vitality, while colorful neighborhoods and fine museums complement the city center.

TRANSPORTATION

Airport: Cleveland Hopkins International (☎265-6030; www.clevelandairport.com), 10 mi. southwest of downtown in Brook Park. RTA line #66X "Red Line" to Terminal Tower. Taxi to downtown $20.

Trains: Amtrak, 200 Cleveland Memorial Shoreway NE (☎696-5115), across from Brown Stadium east of City Hall. Open daily midnight-7am and noon-7:30pm. To **Chicago** (6½-7½hr., 12 per day, $75-92) and **Pittsburgh** (3hr., 2 per day, $33-40).

Buses: Greyhound, 1465 Chester Ave. (☎781-1841), at E. 14th St., 7 blocks from Terminal Tower. Near RTA bus lines. To: **Chicago** (6½-7½hr., 14 per day, $42-45); **Cincinnati** (4½-6½hr., 10 per day, $35-38); **New York City** (9hr., 11 per day, $70-75); **Pittsburgh** (2½-4½ hr., 11 per day, $22-24). Most eastbound buses stop over in Pittsburgh.

Public Transit: Regional Transit Authority (RTA), 315 Euclid Ave. (☎621-9500). Open M-F 7am-6pm. Bus lines, connecting with Rapid Transit trains, travel from downtown to most of the metropolitan area. Service daily 5am-midnight; call for info on "owl" (after midnight) service. Train $1.50. Bus $1.25, express $1.50, downtown loop $0.75, 1-day pass $3. Travelers with cars staying outside of the downtown area can park for free at one of the many park and rides and take the train to Terminal Square for $1.50. The **Waterfront Line** serves the Science Center, Rock and Roll Hall of Fame, and the Flats.

Taxi: Americab, ☎429-1111.

ORIENTATION & PRACTICAL INFORMATION

Terminal Tower, in **Public Square,** at the intersection of Detroit Ave. and Ontario St., forms the center of downtown and splits the city east and west. Many street numbers correspond to the distance of the street from Terminal Tower; e.g., E. 18th St. is 18 blocks east of the Tower. To reach Public Sq. from **I-90** or **I-71,** take the Ontario St./Broadway exit. From **I-77,** take the 9th St. Exit to Euclid Ave., which runs into Public Sq. *While the downtown area and* ***University Circle,*** *home of* ***Case Western University,*** *are relatively safe, the area between the two around 55th St. can be rough.* **The Flats,** along both banks of the Cuyahoga River, and **Coventry Road,** in Cleveland Heights, are the happening spots for food and nightlife.

Visitor Info: Cleveland Convention and Visitors Bureau, 3100 Tower City Ctr. (☎621-4110 or 800-321-1001; www.travelcleveland.com), in Terminal Tower. Open M-F 10am-4pm.

Hotlines: Rape Crisis Line, ☎619-6192 or 619-6194. Operates 24hr.

Internet Access: Cleveland Public Library, 525 Superior Ave (☎623-2904). 15min. limit if crowded. Open M-Sa 9am-6pm, Su 1-5pm; closed Su in summer.

Post Office: 2400 Orange Ave. (☎443-4494, after 5pm ☎443-4096.) Open M-F 7am-8:30pm, Sa 8:30am-3:30pm. **Postal Code:** 44101. **Area Code:** 216; 440 or 330 in suburbs. In text, 216 unless noted otherwise.

ACCOMMODATIONS

With hotel taxes (not included in the prices listed below) as high as 14.5%, cheap lodging is hard to find in Cleveland. **Cleveland Private Lodgings,** P.O. Box 18557, Cleveland 44118, will place you in a home around the city for as little as $45. (☎321-3213; my.en.com/~privlodg/. Call M-F 9am-noon or 3-5pm. Allow 2-3 weeks for a letter of confirmation; for faster response, correspond by e-mail.) Those with cars might consider staying in the suburbs or near the airport, where prices tend to be lower. Most accommodations will not rent to those under 21.

Cuyahoga Valley Stanford Hostel (HI-AYH), 6093 Stanford Rd. (330-467-8711), in Peninsula, 22 mi. south of Cleveland in the Cuyahoga Valley National Park. Housed in a 19th-century farm house, this idyllic hostel offers clean, comfortable dorms with the comforts of country living, including a kitchen, living room, and access to miles of trails. Linens $3. Lockout 10am-5pm. Dorms $16, under 18 with guardian half price. ❶

Motel 6, 7219 Engle Rd. (☎440-234-0990), off Exit 235 on I-71, 15 mi. southwest of the city, has comfy rooms with cable TV and A/C. Located near restaurants, stores, and a park-and-ride lot. 21+. Singles Su-Th $46, F-Sa $56; doubles $52/62. ❸

Knights Inn, 22115 Brookpark Rd. (☎440-734-4500), at Exit 9 off I-480; take the first 2 rights after the freeway. Standard motel rooms, free local phone calls, continental breakfast, free shuttle to airport. 21+. Singles $40; doubles $45. Weekly rate $175. ❷

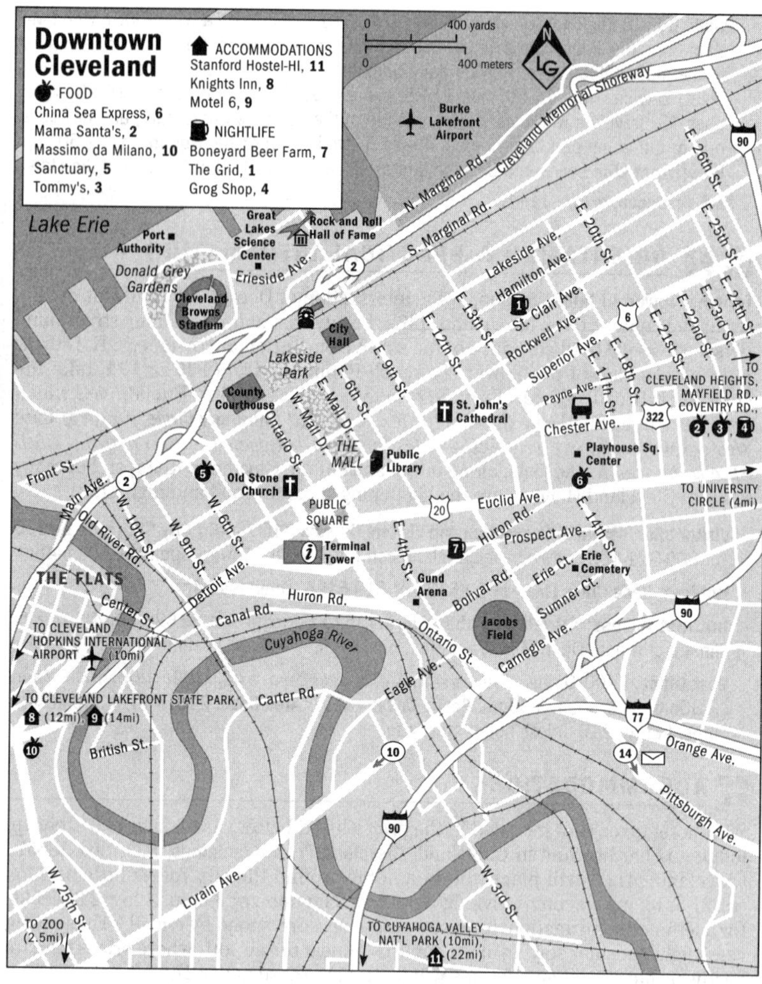

FOOD

The delis downtown satiate most hot corned beef cravings, but Cleveland has more to offer elsewhere. A hip, young crowd heads to the cafes and colorful shops of **Coventry Road,** in **Cleveland Heights.** The sounds of Italian crooners fill the sidewalks of **Little Italy,** around **Mayfield Road,** where visitors can shop in the tiny stores before settling down to a delicious Italian meal. Over 100 vendors hawk produce, meat, and cheese at the old-world style **West Side Market,** 1979 W. 25th St., at Lorain Ave. (☎771-8885. Open M and W 7am-4pm, F-Sa 7am-6pm.)

Tommy's, 1824 Coventry Rd. (☎321-7757), in Cleveland Heights. Take bus #9X east to Mayfield and Coventry Rd. Tommy's whips up tantalizing veggie cuisine, including a variety of falafels ($5.40-6.10). The extensive menu also offers non-vegetarian options. Entrees from $5. Open M-Th 7:30am-10pm, F-Sa 7:30am-11pm, Su 9am-10pm. ❶

Mama Santa's, 12305 Mayfield Rd. (☎231-9567), in Little Italy just east of University Circle, has kept hordes of college students and courting couples happy for over 40 years with its sumptuous Sicilian pizzas, authentic pasta dishes, and welcoming atmosphere. Lasagna and *cavatelli* with meatballs both $7. Pizzas $5.25-6.25. Open M-Th 11am-10:30pm, F-Sa 11am-11:30pm; closed most of Aug. ❷

China Sea Express, 1507 Euclid Ave (☎861-0188), downtown, has Chinese food worth more than its price. A delicious all-you-can-eat lunch buffet is $5.75 and includes wonton soup, lo mein, General Tso's chicken, crab rangoon, and all of the expected Chinese staples. Open Su-Th 11am-9pm, F-Sa 11am-10pm. Buffet served 11am-3pm. ❷

Sanctuary, 1810 W. 6th St. (☎575-1983), downtown, is an artsy diner serving big burgers ($4.50), breakfast all day, and wings with every sauce imaginable. Open M-W 8am-2pm, Th 8am-9pm, F-Sa 8am-11:30pm, Su 10am-2pm; bar open F-Sa until 2:30am. ❷

SIGHTS

DOWNTOWN. The aspirations of a new Cleveland are revealed in the new downtown—a self-declared "Remake on the Lake." One of the city's centerpieces is I.M. Pei's glass pyramid housing the **Rock and Roll Hall of Fame,** where music blaring from outdoor speakers invites visitors into a dizzying retrospective of rock music. Take a tour through rock history on the "Mystery Train," listen to the "500 Songs that Shaped Rock and Roll," and ogle memorabilia—from Elvis' jumpsuits to Jimi Hendrix's guitar—sure to wow fans of any era. *(1 Key Plaza. ☎781-7625; www.rockhall.com. Open M-Tu and Th-Su 10am-5:30pm, W 10am-9pm; also June-Aug. Sa 10am-9pm. $18, students $16, seniors $14, ages 9-11 $11, under 9 free.)* Next door, the **Great Lakes Science Center** educates with interactive exhibits. Hang-glide over the Grand Canyon, deliver a weather forecast, and step inside a giant steel cauldron. *(601 Erieside Ave. ☎694-2000; www.glsc.org. Open Su-Th 9:30am-5:30pm, Sa 9:30am-6:45pm. Science center or OMNIMAX $8, seniors $7, ages 3-17 $6; both $11/10/8. Parking for Hall of Fame and Science Center $7.)* **Cleveland Lakefront State Park** is a 14 mi. park near downtown with beaches, bike trails, and great picnic areas. The soft sand at Edgewater Beach beckons sunbathers and swimmers. *(Accessible via Lake Ave., Cleveland Memorial Shoreway, or Lakeshore Blvd. ☎881-8141. Open daily 6am-11pm.)*

THE WILD SIDE. Another great place to escape the urban jungle is the **Cleveland Metroparks,** which extend into the Cuyahoga Valley. The **Cleveland**

THE HIDDEN DEAL

EXTRA VALUE MEAL

When it comes to lunch, the words "fast" and "$3" usually evoke images of golden arches and super-sized fries, but **Massimo da Milano,** an elegant Italian eatery near downtown in Cleveland's up-and-coming Ohio City area, has redefined fast food with its fantastic lunch buffet. Instead of a bag of greasy fries and a hamburger, $3 will get you a big plastic box and soup container waiting to be filled with a smorgasbord of Italian specialties. The menu varies slightly each day, but the buffet always includes two soups, four hot pastas, freshly made pizza, salad, bread, Italian meats and cheeses, and a selection of desserts. Stuff the sizable box and soup container with as much food as you possibly can; you only get one crack at the buffet. Also, be ready to eat on the go: your $3 doesn't buy you a seat in the restaurant.

If you decide to bypass the buffet and splurge a bit more on a meal in Massimo's main dining room, you won't be disappointed. Veal parmesan ($17), crispy calamari ($7), and linguini tossed with a selection of seafood ($18) are just a few of the classic Italian dishes on offer.

***Massimo da Milano,** 1400 W 25th St. (☎696-2323), just across the Detroit St. bridge. Open for lunch M-F 11:30am-2:30pm; dinner M-Sa by reservation only. The lunch buffet is served M-F 11am-2:30pm.*

Metroparks Zoo, 5 mi. south of downtown on I-71 at the Fulton Rd. Exit, allows visitors to walk through the African Savannah and the Northern Trek, catching glimpses of Siberian tigers, red pandas, and Madagascar hissing cockroaches. One of the zoo's highlights is a replica Rainforest, which houses Bornean orangutans. *(☎661-6500; www.clemtzoo.com. Open daily 10am-5pm. $9, children 2-11 $4, under 2 free.)*

UNIVERSITY CIRCLE. While much has been made of Cleveland's revitalized downtown, the city's cultural nucleus still lies in **University Circle,** a part of Case Western University's campus, 4 mi. east of the city. The **Cleveland Museum of Art** boasts a grand hall of armor—part Medieval, part Asian—along with a survey of art from the Renaissance to the present. An exceptional collection of Impressionist and modern works is highlighted by nine Picasso pieces. *(11150 East Blvd. ☎421-7340; www.clevelandart.org. Open Tu, Th, Sa-Su 10am-5pm, W and F 10am-9pm. Free.)* Nearby, the **Cleveland Museum of Natural History** sends visitors to the stars in the planetarium, while those dreaming of a different kind of sparkle can explore the new gallery of gems. The outdoor Wildlife Center and Woods Gardens display plants and wildlife indigenous to Ohio, from barn owls to bobcats. *(1 Wade Oval Dr. ☎231-4600; www.cmnh.org. Open June M-Sa 10am-5pm, Su noon-5pm; July-Aug. M and F-Sa 10am-5pm, Tu-Th 10am-7pm, Su noon-5pm; Sept.-May M-Tu and Th-Sa 10am-5pm, W 10am-10pm, Su noon-5pm. $7; students, seniors, and ages 7-18 $5; ages 3-6 $4.)* Reopened in the summer of 2003 after a $40 million renovation, the **Cleveland Botanical Garden** provides a peaceful respite from urban life with traditional Victorian and Japanese gardens. *(11030 East Blvd. ☎721-1600. Open Apr.-Oct. M-Sa 9am-dusk, Su noon-dusk. Free.)*

ENTERTAINMENT & NIGHTLIFE

Football reigns supreme in Cleveland, where the **Browns** grind it out on the gridiron at **Cleveland Browns Stadium** during the winter. (☎241-5555. Tickets from $25.) Baseball's **Indians** hammer the hardball at **Jacobs Field,** 2401 Ontario St. (☎420-4200. Tickets from $5.) If you can't catch a game, the best way to see the field is on a 1hr. **stadium tour.** (☎420-4385. Tours April to June and Sept. M-F 1, 2pm, Sa when the Indians are away every hr. 10am-2pm; mid-June to Aug. M-Sa every hr. 10am-2pm. $6.50, seniors and under 15 $4.50.) The **Cavaliers** hoop it up from November to April at **Gund Arena,** 1 Center Ct. (☎420-2000.) In summer, the WNBA's **Rockers** play in the same building. (☎263-7625.)

The **Cleveland Orchestra** performs at impressive **Severance Hall,** 11001 Euclid Ave. (☎231-7300; www.clevelandorch.com. Box office open Sept.-May M-F 9am-6pm, Sa 10am-6pm. From $25.) **Playhouse Square Center,** 1519 Euclid Ave. (☎771-4444), a 10min. walk east of Terminal Tower, is the second-largest performing arts center in the US. Inside, the **State Theater** hosts the **Cleveland Opera** (☎575-0900; www.clevelandopera.org) and the renowned **Cleveland Ballet** (☎426-2500) from October to June. (Box office open M 10am-5pm, Tu-Su 10am-8pm.)

Most of Cleveland's nightlife is centered in **the Flats,** which has recently been transformed into a haven of beer and debauchery. For info on clubs and concerts, pick up a copy of *Scene* or the *Free Times*. The *Gay People's Chronicle* and *OUTlines* are available at gay clubs, cafes, and bookstores.

Grog Shop, 2785 Euclid Heights Blvd. (☎321-5588), at Coventry Rd. in Cleveland Heights, is a mainstay of Cleveland's alternative music scene. A move to a larger, less dingy location in the summer of 2003 had some purists waxing nostalgic about an era lost, but the Grog continues to host the best in underground rock and hip-hop night after night. Cover varies. Open M-F 7pm-2:30am, Sa-Su 1pm-2:30am.

The Grid, 1437 St. Claire Ave. (☎623-0113), entertains a predominantly gay crowd with a space-aged dance floor, four bars, and male strippers on select nights. M karaoke, Tu drag show. Free parking. 18+. Cover F-Sa after 11pm $5, ages 18-20 $10. Open M-Sa 5pm-2:30am, Su 4pm-2:30am; dance floor open F until 3am, Sa until 4am.

Boneyard Beer Farm, 748 Prospect Ave. (☎575-0226), in the Gateway District, rears over 120 beers from around the world for a clientele of brew lovers. Skull and crossbones decor, faux cow-skin chairs, and barrels of peanuts make this a great place to enjoy a brew. Beers $3-6.50. Open M-Sa 4pm-2:30am, Su 7pm-2:30am.

DAYTRIPS FROM CLEVELAND

CUYAHOGA VALLEY NATIONAL PARK

Just 10 mi. south of Cleveland lies the northern edge of the scenic **Cuyahoga Valley National Park.** The park's lifeline is the **Cuyahoga River,** which winds 30 mi. through dense forests and open farmland, passing stables, aqueducts, and mills along the way. The best way to see the soothing natural beauty of the park is by hiking or biking its long trails. The **Ohio & Erie Canal Towpath Trail** runs through shaded forests and past the numerous locks used in the canal during its heyday, when it served as a vital link between Cleveland and the Ohio River.

For wheels, go to **Century Cycles,** 1621 Main St. in Peninsula. (☎330-657-2209. Open M-Th 10am-8pm, F-Sa 10am-6pm, Su 10am-5pm. $6 per hr.) To see the park by rail, hop on the **Cuyahoga Valley Scenic Railroad,** which runs along the river's banks from Peninsula, Independence, and Akron. (☎330-657-2000. Open Feb.-Dec. $11-20, seniors $10-18, children $7-12. Call ahead for reservations.) In the summer, the **Cleveland Orchestra** performs outdoor evening concerts at the **Blossom Music Center,** 1145 W. Steels Corners Rd., in Cuyahoga Falls. (☎33-920-8040. Lawn seating $22-70.) In winter, **Boston Mills/Brandywine Ski Resorts** boasts 16 lifts, snow tubing, and night skiing on both sides of the Cuyahoga. (☎330-467-2242. Boston Mills: 7100 Riverview Rd., in Peninsula. Brandywine: 1146 W Highland Rd., in Sagamore Hills. 8hr. lift ticket $39, seniors and ages 5-12 $34.)

CEDAR POINT AMUSEMENT PARK

Consistently ranked the "best amusement park in the world" by *Amusement Today*, **Cedar Point Amusement Park,** off U.S. 6, 65 mi. west of Cleveland in Sandusky, earns its superlatives. Many of the world's highest and fastest roller coasters reside here. The towering **Top Thrill Dragster** takes the cake in both categories, launching thrill-seekers 420 ft. before plummeting down at 120mph on an arc that seems to defy the laws of physics. Fifteen other coasters, including the enormous **Millennium Force** (310 ft., 90 mph), offer a grand old adrenaline rush. (☎419-627-2350 or 800-237-8386; www.cedarpoint.com. Laser light shows in summer nightly at 10pm. Open June-Aug. daily 10am-11pm; Sept.-early Oct. hours vary. Parking $8. $44, seniors $30, children 3 and older or shorter than 4 ft. $22.)

FOOTBALL HALL OF FAME

The **Pro Football Hall of Fame,** 2121 George Halas Dr. NW, in Canton, 60 mi. south of Cleveland, Exit 107A from I-77, honors the pigskin greats. Bronze busts of football luminaries line the Hall of Heroes, while interactive exhibits test sports fans' knowledge of the game. O.J. Simpson's jersey and helmet are displayed, but not his glove. (☎330-456-8207; www.profootballhof.com. Open daily June-Aug. 9am-8pm; early Sept.-late May 9am-5pm. $12, seniors $8, ages 6-14 $6.)

COLUMBUS ☎614

Rapid growth, huge suburban sprawl, and some gerrymandering have nudged Columbus' population beyond that of Cincinnati or Cleveland. Columbus has refused to let its size affect its character, however—the city is still a showcase of America without glitz, fame, pretentiousness, or smog. Friendly neighborhoods, down-to-earth people, and impressive museums make Columbus a pleasant stop for any traveler heading across the US.

ORIENTATION & PRACTICAL INFORMATION. Columbus is laid out in an easy grid. **High Street,** running north-south, and **Broad Street,** running east-west, are the main thoroughfares, dividing the city into quadrants. Most of the city's activity is centered around High St., which heads north from the office complexes of downtown to the lively galleries in the Short North. It ends in the collegiate cool of **Ohio State University (OSU),** America's largest university, with over 60,000 students. South of downtown, schnitzel is king at the historic **German Village.**

Port Columbus International Airport, 4000 International Gtwy. (☎292-8266; www.port-columbus.com), is 8 mi. east of downtown. Taxi to downtown about $17. **Greyhound,** 111 E. Town St. (☎221-2389 or 800-231-2222), offers service from downtown to: Chicago (7-11hr., 6 per day, $51); Cincinnati (2-3½hr., 10 per day, $17); Cleveland (2-4½hr., 11 per day, $20-25). The **Central Ohio Transit Authority (COTA),** 177 S. High St., runs local transportation until 11pm or midnight, depending on the route. (☎228-1776. Office open M-F 8:30am-5:30pm. $1.10, express $1.50.) **Taxi: Yellow Cab,** ☎444-4444. **Greater Columbus Visitors Center,** 111 S. 3rd St., on the 2nd fl. of City Center Mall. (☎221-6623 or 800-345-2657; www.surpriseitscolumbus.com. Open M-Su 11am-6pm.) **Internet Access: Columbus Metropolitan Library,** 96 S. Grant St. (☎645-2275. Open M-Th 9am-9pm, F 9am-6pm, Sa 9am-6pm, Su 1-5pm.) **Post Office:** 850 Twin Rivers Dr. (☎469-4521. Open M-F 7am-8pm, Sa 8am-2pm.) **Postal Code:** 43215. **Area Code:** 614.

ACCOMMODATIONS & FOOD. Those under the age of 21 will have a hard time finding accommodations in Columbus; a city ordinance prevents hotels from renting to underaged visitors. Nearby suburbs are your best bet to dodge the ban. In the summer, **OSU ❷** offers cheap, clean rooms on North Campus with A/C, free local calls, private bathroom, microwave, and a fridge, close to endless nightlife and food options. (☎292-9725. Open mid-June to mid-Aug. Singles $36-44; doubles $18-22 per person.) The newly-remodeled **German Village Inn ❸,** 920 S. High St., close to downtown, offers clean, well-appointed rooms with cable TV, A/C, and free local calls. (☎443-6506. 21+. Rooms $60; each additional person $6.) **Motel 6 ❷,** 5910 Scarborough Dr., 15min. from downtown off I-70 at Exit 110A, is a standard chain option. (☎755-2250. Singles $37-45; each additional adult $6.)

For great budget eats, there's no beating the **North Market,** 59 Spruce St. in the Short North Arts District, which is packed with fresh produce and food vendors selling everything from barbecue to sushi. (☎463-9664. Meals around $5. Open M 9am-5pm, Tu-F 9am-7pm, Sa 8am-5pm, Su noon-5pm. Hours of individual vendors may vary.) High St. also features a variety of tasty budget options. The **J&G Diner ❷,** 733 N. High St., in the Short North District, serves filling Belgian waffles ($4) and "hippie" ($6.50) or "rabbi" ($7.50) omelettes amid provocative paintings of a green-clad bombshell. (☎294-1850. Open M-F 10:30am-10pm, Sa 9am-10pm, Su 9am-9pm.) Next door, an eclectic crowd sips their lattes at the **Coffee Table ❶,** 731 N. High St., which serves great espresso drinks (from $1.55) and seems to have an Elvis infatuation. (☎297-1177. Open M-Th 7am-midnight, F 7am-10pm, Sa 8am-10pm.) **Bernie's Bagels and Deli ❶,** 1896 N. High St., serves healthy sandwiches ($3-5) and all-day breakfast in a subterranean dive, with live music seven nights a week. (☎291-3448. Open daily 11am-2:30am.) You might find yourself waxing poetic about your meal at **Haiku Poetic Art and Food ❸,** 800 N. High Street, where sushi chefs produce their edible art amid chic Japanese decor. Noodle dishes ($10-13), such as udon tempura, are also excellent. (☎294-8168. Open M-Th 11am-11pm, F-Sa 11am-midnight, Su 4-10pm.)

SIGHTS. OSU rests 2 mi. north of downtown. **The Wexner Center for the Arts,** 1871 N. High St., by 15th Ave., was the first public building by controversial modernist architect Peter Eisenman. The museum is under renovation and scheduled to reopen in the fall of 2004, but until then much of its avant-garde collection is scattered throughout various venues around the city. Performance spaces host dance, music, and theater productions. (☎292-3535; www.wexarts.org. Exhibits open Feb.-June Tu-W and F-Sa 10am-6pm, Th 10am-9pm, Su noon-6pm. $3, students and seniors $2. Th 5-9pm free. Films $5, students and seniors $4, under 12 $2. Call for info on satellite locations. Wheelchair-accessible.) The **Columbus Museum of Art,** 480 E. Broad St., hosts a growing collection of contemporary American art and one of the most renowned collections of early Modern art in the country. Other highlights include a collection of local folk art and a great children's exhibit that allows kids to walk into a Dutch Studio. (☎221-6801; www.columbusmuseum.org. Open Tu-W and F-Su 10am-5:30pm, Th 10am-8:30pm. $6, students and seniors $4, ages 6-18 $4. Th free. Parking $3.) The submarine-shaped **Center of Science and Industry (COSI),** 333 W. Broad St., allows visitors to explore space from the safety of an armchair, create their own short stop-animation film, and revert to the old school with arcade games like Pong, Centipede, and Space Invaders. A seven story Extreme Screen shows action-packed films. (☎228-2674; www.cosi.org. Open M-Sa 10am-5pm, Su noon-6pm. $12, seniors $10, ages 2-12 $7. Extreme Screen $6. Combo $17/15/10. Wheelchair-accessible.) Nearby, James Thurber's childhood home, the **Thurber House,** 77 Jefferson Ave., off E. Broad St., guides visitors through the major events of the famous *New Yorker* writer's life. It also serves as a literary center, hosting seminars with authors like John Updike. (☎464-1032. Open daily noon-4pm. Free. Tours Su $2.50, students and seniors $2.)

The **Short North Arts District** is packed with galleries that are great for browsing. The eccentric **Gallery V,** 694 N. High St., exhibits contemporary paintings and sculptures along with handcrafted jewelry from all over the US. (☎228-8955. Open Tu-Sa 11am-5pm. Free.) The **Thomas R. Riley Galleries,** 642 N. High St., specializes in elaborate, three-dimensional glass sculptures. (☎228-6554. Open Tu-Sa 11am-6pm, Su noon-5pm. Free.) On the first Saturday of each month from 6 to 10pm, the Short North district is packed with an eclectic crowd for the free **Gallery Hop Night.**

For some good Germanica, march down to the **German Village,** south of Capitol Sq. This area, first settled in 1843, is now the largest privately funded historical restoration in the US, full of stately homes and beer halls. At **Schmidt's Sausage Haus ❸,** 240 E. Kossuth St., lederhosen-clad waitresses serve Bavarian specialities like huge sausage platters ($9.25-10.25) while traditional oompah bands (Schnickel-Fritz, Schnapps, and Squeezin' 'n' Wheezin') lead polkas. (☎444-6808. Polkas summer W-Th 7-10pm, F-Sa 8-11pm; no W show in winter. Open M-Th 11:30am-10pm, F-Sa 11:30am-11pm, Su 4-10pm.) One block west, **Schmidt's Fudge Haus,** 220 E. Kossuth St., mixes up savory fudge and chocolate concoctions named for local celebrities. (☎444-2222. Open M-Th noon-4pm, F-Sa noon-7pm, Su noon-3pm.) The **German Village Society Meeting Haus,** 588 S. 3rd St., provides info on happenings. (☎221-8888. Open M-F 9am-4pm, Sa 10am-2pm; shorter hours in winter.) About 10 mi. north of downtown on Rte. 745 in Dublin, the surreal **Field of Corn,** 4995 Rings Rd., contains 109 concrete ears of corn, each 7 ft. tall, that pay homage to the town's agrarian roots and suggest a subtle indictment of modern development.

ENTERTAINMENT & NIGHTLIFE. Four free weekly papers available in shops and restaurants—*The Other Paper*, *Columbus Alive*, *The Guardian*, and *Moo*—list arts and entertainment options. The 2002 National Champion **Ohio State Buckeyes** play football in the historic horseshoe-shaped **Ohio Stadium.** Major League Soccer's **Columbus Crew** (☎447-2739) kicks off at **Crew Stadium.** Columbus' brand-new NHL hockey team, the **Blue Jackets** (☎246-3350), plays winter games in Nationwide Arena. The **Clippers,** a minor league affiliate of the NY Yankees, swing away from April to early September. (☎462-5250. Tickets $5-8.)

If you're feeling bored, Columbus has a sure cure: rock 'n' roll. Bar bands are a Columbus mainstay, and it's hard to find a bar that doesn't have live music on the weekend. Bigger national acts stop at the **Newport,** 1722 N. High St. (☎228-3580. Tickets $5-40.) To see smaller alternative and local bands before they hit the big time, head to **Little Brothers**, 1100 N. High St. (421-2025. 18+. Covers $5-30. Open daily 8pm-2am.) Beer chugging and pool playing replace traditional study techniques at the **Library,** 2169 N. High St., a bar that attracts a mix of locals and students. (☎299-3245. Beers $2-3. Open M-Sa 3pm-2:30am, Su 7pm-2:30am.) South from Union Station is the **Brewery District,** where barley and hops have replaced coal and iron in the once industrial area.

NEAR COLUMBUS

One hour south of Columbus, the area around **Chillicothe** (CHILL-i-caw-thy) features several American Indian cultural sites. The **Hopewell Culture National Historical Park,** 16062 Rte. 104, swells with 23 Hopewell burial mounds spread over 13 acres that serve as one of the few keys to a 2000-year-old culture. A museum provides theories about the mounds and their origin. (☎740-774-1126; www.nps.gov/hocu. Museum open daily Sept.-May 8:30am-5pm; June-Aug. extended hours. Grounds open dawn-dusk. $5 per car, $3 per pedestrian.) For a more lively presentation of Native American life, head to the **Sugarloaf Mountain Amphitheater,** on the north end of Chillicothe off Rte. 23. Between mid-June and late August the theater presents *Tecumseh*, a drama reenacting the life of the Shawnee leader. A tour explains how the stuntmen dive off a 21 ft. cliff. (☎775-0700 or 866-775-0700. Shows M-Sa 8pm. M-Th $14, under 10 $7; F-Sa $16/8. Tour $3.50/2.50.) After seeing the sights, travelers can enjoy **Scioto Trail State Park ❶,** 12 mi. south of Chillicothe off U.S. 23, with walk-in **camping.** (☎740-663-2125. Sites $12, with electricity $16.)

CINCINNATI ☎513

Founded in 1788 as a frontier outpost on the Ohio River, Cincinnati quickly emerged as a vital gateway between the South and the West, and by 1860 it was the sixth largest city in the US. Industry thrived as major trade routes passed through the city, and a profusion of meat-packing plants earned Cincinnati the nickname "Porkopolis," providing a slightly less flattering alternative to Longfellow's more regal title, "Queen City of the West." Located just across the river from Kentucky, Cincinnati continues to straddle its dualistic past: in many ways it is an archetypical Northern industrial city, but it has the feel—and sometimes the accent—of a Southern city. Nevertheless, its stellar ballet, brand-new baseball stadium, and world-famous chili make Cincinnati a highlight of the region.

TRANSPORTATION

Airport: Greater Cincinnati International (☎859-767-3151; www.cvgairport.com), in Kentucky, 12 mi. south of Cincinnati and accessible by I-75, I-71, and I-74. **Jetport Express** shuttles to downtown. (☎859-767-3702. $12, $16 round-trip.) The **Transit Authority of Northern Kentucky,** or **TANK** (☎859-331-8265), also offers shuttle services.

Trains: Amtrak, 1301 Western Ave. (☎651-3337), in Union Terminal. Open M-F 9:30am-5pm and Tu-Su 11pm-6:30am. To **Chicago** (12hr., 2 per day, $19-36) and **Indianapolis** (3hr., 1 per day, $21-28). *Avoid the area to the north, especially Liberty St.*

Buses: Greyhound, 1005 Gilbert Ave. (☎352-6012), past the intersection of E. Court and Broadway. Open 24hr. To: **Cleveland** (4-6hr., 9 per day, $35); **Columbus** (2-3hr., 9 per day, $17); **Louisville, KY** (2hr., 10 per day, $20).

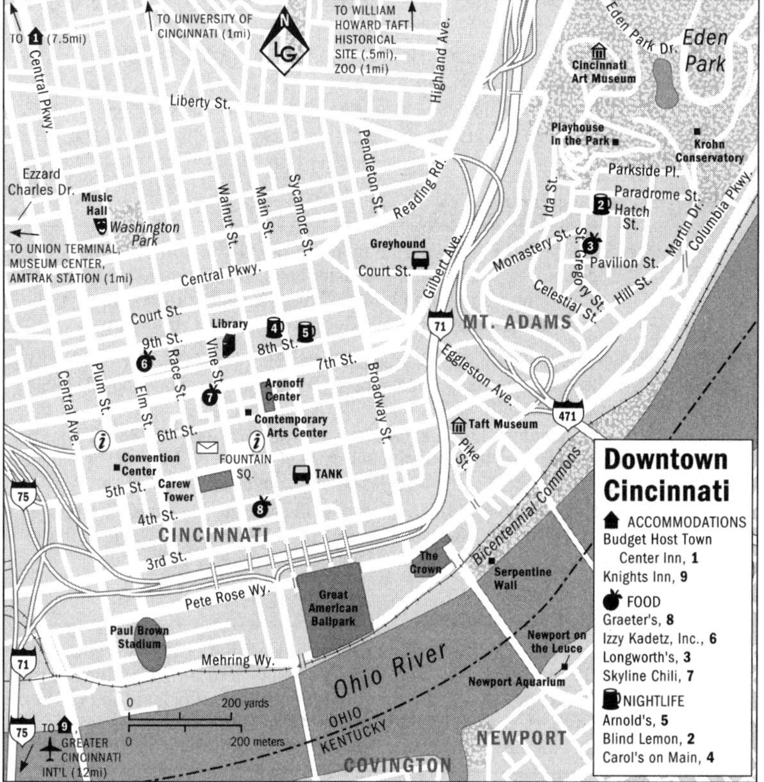

Public Transit: Cincinnati Metro and **TANK,** both in the bus stop in the Mercantile Center, 115 E. 5th St. (☎621-9450). Open M-F 8am-5pm. Most buses run out of Government Sq., at 5th and Main St., to outlying communities. Summer $0.50; winter $0.65, winter rush-hour $0.80; extra to suburbs. Office has schedules and info.

Taxi: Yellow Cab, ☎241-2100.

ORIENTATION & PRACTICAL INFORMATION

The downtown business district is a simple grid centered around **Fountain Square,** at **5th** and **Vine Street.** Cross streets are numbered and designated E. or W. by their relation to Vine St. **Downtown** is bounded by Central Pkwy. on the north, Broadway on the east, 3rd on the south, and Central Ave. on the west. The **University of Cincinnati** spreads out from the Clifton area north of the city. **Cinergy Field,** the **Serpentine Wall,** and the **Riverwalk,** all to the south, border the Ohio River. *Be careful outside of the downtown area at night, especially north of Central Pkwy.*

Visitor Info: Cincinnati Convention and Visitors Bureau, 300 W. 6th St. (☎621-2142 or 800-246-2987; www.cincyusa.com). Open M-F 8:30am-5:30pm. **Visitor Center at Fifth Third Center,** 511 Walnut St., on Fountain Sq., offers brochures on sights all over the area. Staff can also help find discounted tickets to shows and various sights. Free Internet access. Open M-Sa 10am-5pm, Su noon-5pm.

Hotlines: Rape Crisis Center, 216 E. 9th St., downtown (☎872-9259). **Gay/Lesbian Community Switchboard,** ☎591-0222. Both 24hr.

Internet Access: Cincinnati Public Library, 800 Vine St. (☎369-6900). Open M-W 9am-9pm, Th-Sa 9am-6pm, Su 1-5pm.

Post Office: 525 Vine St., on the Skywalk. (☎684-5667. Open M-F 8am-5pm, Sa 8am-1pm.) **Postal Code:** 45202. **Area Codes:** 513; Kentucky suburbs 859. In text, 513 unless noted otherwise.

ACCOMMODATIONS

Cheap hotels are scarce in downtown Cincinnati. About 30 mi. north of Cincinnati, in **Sharonville,** budget motels cluster along **Chester Road.** Twelve miles south of the city, inexpensive accommodations line I-75 at Exit 184. Closer to downtown, the motels at **Central Parkway** and **Hopple Street** offer good, mid-priced lodging.

Knights Inn-Cincinnati/South, 8048 Dream St. (☎859-371-9711), in Florence, KY, just off I-75 at Exit 180, has homey rooms. Cable TV, A/C, and outdoor pool. 21+. Singles $36-40; doubles $40-45. ❷

Budget Host Town Center Inn, 3356 Central Pkwy. (☎283-4678 or 800-283-4678), Exit 3 off I-75, 10min. from downtown and the University of Cincinnati. The rooms are quite faded. Pool, A/C, and cable TV. 21+. Singles $45-60; doubles $50-65. ❸

Stonelick State Park (☎625-6593), 25 mi. east of the city, outside the I-275 loop, has 115 campsites at the edge of Stonelick Lake and provides welcome relief from Cincinnati's pricey lodgings. Sites $14; with electricity $18; lakeside $20. ❶

FOOD

Cincinnati's greatest culinary innovation is its chili, which consists of noodles topped with meat, cheese, onions, and kidney beans—and a distinctive secret ingredient. The city has also given rise to a number of noteworthy fast-food chains. Fine restaurants and bars can be found in **Mount Adams,** while moderately priced chains cluster at the **Newport on the Levee** and **Covington Landing** across the river.

Skyline Chili, everywhere. Locations all over Cincinnati, including 643 Vine St. (☎241-2020), at 7th St., dish up the best beans in town. The secret ingredient has been debated for years—some say chocolate, but curry is more likely. 5-way large chili $5.89. Cheese coney dog $1.30. Open M-F 10am-8pm, Sa 11am-4pm. ❶

Graeter's, 41 E. 4th St. (☎381-0653), between Walnut and Vine St. downtown, as well as 14 other locations. Since 1870, Graeter's has blended their specialty giant chocolate chips into dozens of different ice cream flavors. Sandwiches ($3-5) and baked goods also served. Single cone $1.85. Open M-F 7am-6pm, Sa 7am-5pm. ❶

Izzy Kadetz Inc., 800 Elm St. (☎721-4241), downtown. Known to locals as "Izzy's," this Jewish-style deli does a roaring lunch trade with great reubens ($5.60) and corned beef sandwiches ($6.10) served with a big, fluffy potato pancake. Open M-Sa 7am-8pm. ❷

Longworth's, 1108 St. Gregory St. (☎651-2253), in Mt. Adams. A mainstay of the laid-back Mt. Adams neighborhood, Longworth's packs a restaurant, a bar, and a nightclub into one building. The simple, hearty fare includes satisfying burgers (from $5.75), pizzas (from $8), and pastas ($8.75-11.25). Live bands jam on the first floor while DJs spins 80s pop on the dance floor upstairs. Open M-Sa 11am-2am, Su noon-2am. ❷

SIGHTS

DOWNTOWN. Downtown Cincinnati orbits around the **Tyler Davidson Fountain,** at 5th and Vine St., a florid 19th-century masterpiece. To the east, the expansive garden at **Procter and Gamble Plaza** is just one mark that the giant company has left on its hometown. Around **Fountain Square,** business complexes and shops are connected by a series of skywalks. The observation deck at the top of **Carew Tower,** Cincinnati's tallest building, provides the best view in the city. *(441 Vine St. ☎241-3888. $2, children $1.)* Close to Fountain Sq., the **Contemporary Arts Center** recently moved to its brand-new, ultra-modern structure, which boasts six floors of avant-garde art. The fantastic "UnMuseum" on the sixth floor displays contemporary art for children, including a giant, robotic metal tree that responds to the presence of visitors. *(44 E. 6th St. ☎345-8420; www.contemporaryartscenter.org. Open M 11am-9pm, Tu-W 11am-6pm, Th 11am-9pm, F 11am-6pm, Sa noon-6pm, Su 11am-6pm. $6.50, students $4.50, seniors $5.50, children 3-13 $3.50. M 5-9pm free. Audio tour $3. Wheelchair-accessible.)*

EDEN PARK. Eden Park provides a nearby respite from the city with rolling hills, a pond, and cultural centers. *(Northeast of downtown and Mt. Adams. Take bus #49 to Eden Park Dr. Open daily 6am-10pm.)* The collections at the elegant **Cincinnati Art Museum,** inside the park, span 5000 years, including Near Eastern artifacts, Chagall's Expressionism, and Andy Warhol's rendition of infamous Cincinnati baseball great Pete Rose. The "Cincinnati Wing" explores the city's artistic legacy. *(953 Eden Park Dr. ☎721-5204; www.cincinnatiartmuseum.org. Open Tu and Th-Su 11am-5pm, W 10am-9pm. Free. Free tours M-F 1pm, Sa 1, 2pm, Su 1, 2, 3pm. Special exhibits cost extra.)* The nearby **Krohn Conservatory** is one of the largest public greenhouses in the world, boasting a lush rainforest and a butterfly garden. *(950 Eden Park Dr. ☎421-5707; www.cinci-parks.org. Open daily 10am-5pm. Donations accepted. Wheelchair-accessible.)* For more outdoor fun, head to the **Cincinnati Zoo,** where standard inhabitants like elephants and gorillas are neighbors to rare manatees. *(3400 Vine St. ☎281-4700; www.cincinnati-zoo.org. Call for seasonal schedules. $11.50, seniors $9, children 2-12 $6. Parking $6.50.)*

MUSEUM CENTER. Built in 1933, the enormous Art Deco **Union Terminal** is now Cincinnati's cultural center, housing three major museums and an Omnimax theater. The **Cincinnati History Museum** begins with huge scale models of the city before leading visitors through exhibits charting Cincinnati's past, from its beginnings as a trading post to its emergence as the "Queen City" and beyond. A giant mastodon skeleton welcomes visitors into the **Museum of Natural History and Science,** where intrepid explorers can uncover the secrets of the Ice Age and descend into the damp, dark depths of a cave to see bats, cave beetles, and other subterranean creatures. Kids are in control at the **Cinergy Children's Museum,** where little 'uns clamber through caves and across bridges in a giant playscape and shoot balls out of catapults and funnels. *(1301 Western Ave. ☎287-7000; www.cincymuseum.org. Open M-Sa 10am-5pm, Su 11am-6pm. Admission to 1 museum or Omnimax $6.75, children 3-12 $4.75; 2 attractions $9.75/6.75; 3 attractions $12.75/8.75; 4 attractions $15.75/10.75.)*

OTHER SIGHTS. Just across the river from downtown, the spectacular **Newport Aquarium** offers full immersion in a water world with glass tunnels that blur the separation between visitors and toothy sharks. Stingrays, sea turtles, and penguins frolic, and the stunning Jellyfish Gallery—featuring blue-lit aquariums in a chandeliered room with classical music—resembles a living artwork. *(Located at Newport on the Levee. ☎800-406-3474; www.newportaquarium.com. Open summer daily 10am-7pm; winter hours vary. $16, seniors $14, children 3-12 $10.)* 1 mi. north of downtown, the **William Howard Taft National Historic Site** is the birthplace and childhood home of the ex-President and Supreme Court Justice. A tour guides visitors through three fully restored rooms in the house, while exhibits detail Taft's childhood and political career. *(2038 Auborn Ave. ☎684-3262; www.nps.gov/wiho. Tours daily 8am-4pm. Free.)*

ENTERTAINMENT

The free newspapers *City Beat*, *Everybody's News*, and *Downtowner* list the happenings around town. The community of **Mount Adams** supports a thriving arts and entertainment district. Perched on its own wooded hill in Eden Park, the **Play-**

house in the Park, 962 Mt. Adams Circle, performs theater in the round. (☎421-3888. Performances mid-Sept. to June Tu-Su. $26-40. Senior rush tickets 2hr. before show, students 15min. before show; all rush tickets $15.)

The **Music Hall,** 1243 Elm St. (☎721-8222), hosts the **Cincinnati Symphony Orchestra** and the **Cincinnati Pops Orchestra** from September through May. (☎381-3300. $17-63.) The **Cincinnati Opera** also sings here. (☎888-533-7149. $12-90.) For updates on these and more, call **Dial the Arts** (☎621-4744). The symphony's summer season (June-July) tunes up at **Riverbend,** near Coney Island. The **Cincinnati Ballet Company** (☎621-5219) is at the **Aronoff Center for the Arts,** 650 Walnut St., which also hosts a Broadway series. (☎241-7469. Ballet performances Nov.-Mar. $12-47, matinees $9-40; musicals $15-65. Broadway Oct.-May. $25-65. Wheelchair-accessible.)

In Mason, off I-71 at Exit 24, **Paramount's King Island** cages **The Beast,** the world's longest wooden roller coaster, which spreads its tentacles over 35 acres. (☎573-5800 or 800-288-0808; www.pki.com. Open late May-late Aug. Su-F 9am-10pm, Sa 9am-11pm. $43, seniors and ages 3-6 $26. Parking $8.) Sports fans watch baseball's **Reds** (☎381-7337; $5-30) at the **Great American Ball Park,** 100 Main St., and football's **Bengals** (☎621-8383; $35-50) at **Paul Brown Stadium** five blocks west.

NIGHTLIFE

Overlooking downtown from the east, the winding streets of **Mount Adams** have spawned some off-beat bars and music venues, creating a relaxed environment removed from the bustling city below.

Blind Lemon, 936 Hatch St. (☎241-3885), at St. Gregory St. Live blues and rock fill the cavernous tavern where Jimmy Buffet started. During the colder months, bonfires on the outdoor courtyard create a perfect atmosphere. Drafts $2. Live music M-Sa 9:30pm, Su 8pm. Bonfires Oct.-Mar. Th-Sa. 21+. Open Su-W 8:30am-1am, Th-Sa 9:30am-2am.

Arnold's, 210 E. 8th St. (☎421-6234), between Main and Sycamore St. This wood-paneled mainstay provides good domestic beer ($2.50-3.75). After 9pm, Arnold's offers music in the courtyard. Pasta and sandwiches $4-20. Music Tu-Sa. Open M-Th 11am-10pm, F 11am-11pm, Sa 11am-1am, Su 8am-1pm; bar open M-Sa until 1am.

Carol's On Main, 825 Main St. (☎651-2667), inserts funk and style into downtown Cincinnati. Drawing theater groups and thirtysomething yuppies, this trendy restaurant/bar is known for great food and late hours. **Plush,** a cabaret upstairs, thumps to hip-hop and indie rock. Entrees $6-8.75. Kitchen open M-Tu 11:30am-11pm, W-F 11:30am-1am, Sa-Su 4pm-1am; bar closes M-Tu 1:30am, W-Su 2:30am.

INDIANA

The cornfields of southern Indiana's Appalachian foothills give way to expansive plains in the industrialized north, where Gary's smokestacks spew black clouds over the waters of Lake Michigan, and urban travel hubs string along the interstates. Despite its official motto—"The Crossroads of America"—Indiana is a modest, slow-paced state, where farms roll on and on, big cities are a rarity, and countless Hoosier school kids grow up dreaming of becoming the next Larry Bird.

PRACTICAL INFORMATION

Capital: Indianapolis.

Visitor Info: Indiana Division of Tourism, 1 N. Capitol Ave., #700, Indianapolis 46204 (☎800-289-6646; www.state.in.us/tourism). **Division of State Parks,** 402 W. Washington, #W-298, Indianapolis 46204 (☎317-232-4125).

Postal Abbreviation: IN. **Sales Tax:** 5%.

Time Zone: Eastern Standard Time. *With the exception of a few counties in the northwest and southwest corners, most of Indiana does not observe Daylight Savings Time.*

INDIANAPOLIS ☎317

Surrounded by flat farmland, Indianapolis feels like a model Midwestern city. Folks shop and work all day among downtown's skyscrapers before returning to sprawling suburbs. Life ambles here—until May, that is, when 400,000 spectators overrun the city and the road warriors of the Indianapolis 500 claim the spotlight.

DRIVER'S MANUAL. The city is laid out in concentric circles, with a dense central cluster of skyscrapers and low-lying outskirts. The very center of Indianapolis is just south of **Monument Circle,** at the intersection of **Washington Street (U.S. 40)** and **Meridian Street.** Washington St. divides the city north-south; Meridian St. divides it east-west. **I-465** circles the city and provides access to downtown. **I-70** cuts through the city east-west. Meter parking is abundant along the edge of the downtown area and near the Circle Centre Mall.

Indianapolis International Airport (☎487-7243; www.indianapolisairport.com) is located 7 mi. southwest of downtown off I-465, Exit 11B; take bus #8 "West Washington." Taxi to downtown around $17. **Amtrak,** 350 S. Illinois St. (☎263-0550; open daily 7am-2:30pm and 11pm-6:30am), behind Union Station, rolls to Chicago (5hr., 1 per day, $16-31). **Greyhound,** 350 S. Illinois St. (☎267-3071; open 24hr.), buses to: Bloomington (1hr., 2 per day, $14); Chicago (3-4hr., 11 per day, $26); Cincinnati (2-5hr., 4 per day, $17). **Indy Go,** 209 N. Delaware St., runs routes throughout the city, as well as shuttles to special events. (☎635-3344. Office open M-F 8am-6pm, Sa 9am-4pm. $1, under 6 free.) **Taxis Yellow Cab,** ☎487-7777. **Visitor Info: Indianapolis City Center (Visit Indy),** on the first floor of Circle Centre Mall, dispenses info and downtown maps. (☎237-5200 or 800-323-4639; www.indy.org. Free **Internet Access.** Open M-F 10am-5:30pm, Sa 10am-5pm, Su noon-5pm.) **Hotlines: Rape Crisis Line,** ☎800-221-6311; 24hr. **Gay/Lesbian Switchboard,** ☎251-7955; operates daily 7-11pm. **Post Office:** 125 W. South St., across from Amtrak. (☎464-6376. Open M-W and F 7am-5:30pm, Th 7am-6pm.) **Postal Code:** 46204. **Area Code:** 317.

PIT STOP. Budget motels line the I-465 beltway, 5 mi. from downtown. Make reservations a year in advance for the Indy 500, which drives rates up drastically in May. Head to **Motel 6 ❷,** 6330 Debonair Ln., at Exit 16A off I-465, for clean, pleasant rooms with A/C and cable TV. (☎293-3220. Singles $35; doubles $40.) Though occasionally hard to come by, the rooms at the **Methodist Tower Inn ❸,** 1633 N. Capitol Ave., are the cheapest ones close to downtown. A short walk from Monument Circle, the inn provides large rooms with TV and A/C. (☎925-9831. Singles $63; doubles $67.50. Each additional person $5.) Live in the lap of luxury in the **Renaissance Tower Historic Inn ❸,** 230 E. 9th St., which offers reasonable overnight rates for rooms with cable TV, A/C, kitchenette, and stately canopy beds. (☎261-2652 or 800-676-7786. Rooms $59 per night, $260 per week; call for availability.) Especially busy during the state fair, the **Indiana State Fairgrounds Campgrounds ❶,** 1202 E. 38th St., bus #4 or 39 from downtown, has 170 sod-and-gravel sites, mostly packed by RVs. To get close to nature, go elsewhere. (☎927-7520. Sites $16; full hookup $19.)

HIGH-OCTANE FUEL. Ethnic food stands, produce markets, and knick-knack vendors fill the spacious **City Market,** 222 E. Market St., a renovated 19th-century building. Meals start around $5. (☎630-4107. Open M-W and F 6am-6pm, Th 6am-8pm, Sa 6am-4pm.) Moderately priced restaurants cluster in Indianapolis' newly constructed **Circle Centre,** 49 West Maryland St. (☎681-8000). Massachusetts Ave. houses some of the liveliest restaurants and bars in the city; in the summer, crowded outdoor patios seat diners every night. **Bazbeaux Pizza ❷,** 334 Massachusetts Ave. (☎636-7662) and 832 E. Westfields Blvd. (☎255-5711), serves Indianapolis' favorite pizza. The Tchoupitoulas pizza, topped with a concoction of shrimp, is a Cajun masterpiece (from $11). Construct your own wonder ($6) from a choice of 53 toppings. (Both locations open Su-Th 11am-10pm, F-Sa 11am-11pm.) **The Abbey ❷,** 771 Massachusetts Ave. (☎269-8426) and 923 Indiana Ave. (☎917-0367), is a popular coffee shop, offering wraps and sandwiches ($6-7) along with vegetarian options. Sip cappuccinos in velvet chairs for $2.25. (Both locations open M-Th 8am-midnight, F 8am-1am, Sa 11am-1am, Su 11am-midnight.) For the best Mexican food in town, head to **Don Victor's ❷,** 1032 S. East St., which offers burrito and enchilada platters ($6), as well as more authentic dishes such as *menudo* and *pozole*. The Fiesta Platter ($21; serves 2) is a good way to sample various dishes. (☎637-4397. Live mariachi F and Su. Open Su-Th 11am-9pm, F-Sa 11am-10pm.)

SUNDAY DRIVE. The newly restored canal at **White River State Park,** near downtown, entices locals to stroll, bike, or nap on the banks. Bikes can be rented at **Bike Indy,** 801 W. Washington St. (☎435-1675. Open June-Aug. M-Su 9:30am-dark; Sept.-Oct. F-Su 9:30am-dark; May F-Sa 9:30am-dark. $7 per hr., $20 full day.) Near the park entrance, the **Eiteljorg Museum of American Indians and Western Art,** 500 W. Washington St., features an impressive collection of art depicting the Old West, including works by Georgia O'Keeffe and Frederick Remington. The museum also offers a collection of Native American artifacts from across the United States. (☎636-9378; www.eiteljorg.org. Open Tu-Sa 10am-5pm, Su noon-5pm; May-Sept. also M 10am-5pm. Tours daily 1pm. $7, seniors $6, students and ages 5-17 $4.) Next door, the **Indiana State Museum,** 650 W. Washington St., allows visitors to follow the "Hoosier Heritage Trail" through in-depth exhibits on Indiana history—so in-depth, in fact, that it starts off with the beginning of the earth itself and wraps up with profiles of Indiana's most famous citizens, from Larry Bird to Axl Rose. (☎232-1637; www.indianamuseum.org. Open M-Sa 9am-5pm, Su 11am-5pm. $7, seniors $6.50, children $4. IMAX $8.50/7/6. Combo $12.25/10.75/7.)

No sports fan should miss the **NCAA Hall of Champions,** 700 W. Washington St., which covers all 28 college sports. Relive the passion of the Final Four in the March Madness Theater and try your hand at hitting a clutch shot in the 1930s-style gymnasium, marked out with famous game-winners. (☎735-6222; www.ncaahallofchampions.org. Open M-Sa 10am-5pm, Su noon-5pm. $7, students $4, under 6 free.) It may be far from downtown, but the **Indianapolis Museum of Art,** 1200 W. 38th St., is worth a visit. In the midst of renovation, the museum's beautiful 152 acres offer nature trails, a historic home, botanical gardens, a greenhouse, and a theater. The museum's collection includes extensive collections of American, African, and Neo-Impressionist works. (☎923-1331; www.ima-art.org. Open Tu-W and F-Sa 10am-5pm, Th 10am-8:30pm, Su noon-5pm. Free; special exhibits $5.)

A majestic stained-glass dome graces the marbled interior of the **State House,** 200 W. Washington St., between Capitol and Senate St. (☎233-5293. Open M-F 8am-4pm. 2-5 1hr. guided tours per day. Free.) Animal lovers should check out the seemingly cageless **Indianapolis Zoo,** 1200 W. Washington St., which holds large whale and dolphin pavilions. (☎630-2001; www.indyzoo.com. Open June-Aug. daily 9am-5pm; Sept.-May 9am-4pm. $10.75, seniors $7.75, ages 2-12 $6.75. Parking $3.) Kids will get a kick out of the fun-filled **Indianapolis Children's Museum,** 3000 N. Meridian St., the largest children's museum in the world. Explore an Egyptian tomb and ride a carousel. (☎334-3322; www.childrensmuseum.org. Open Mar.-Aug. daily 10am-5pm; Sept.-Feb. Tu-Su 10am-5pm. $9.50, seniors $8, children $4.)

DAYS OF THUNDER. The country's passion for fast cars reaches fever pitch during the **500 Festival** (☎636-4556), an entire month of parades and hoopla leading up to race day at the **Indianapolis Motor Speedway,** 4790 W. 16th St., off I-465 at the Speedway Exit, bus #25. The festivities begin with time trials in mid-May and culminate with the "Gentlemen, start your engines" of the **Indianapolis 500** the Sunday before Memorial Day. In quieter times for the track, buses full of tourists drive around the 2½ mi. track at slightly tamer speeds. (☎481-8500; www.indy500.com. Track tours daily 9am-4:40pm. $3, ages 6-15 $1.) The **Speedway Museum,** at the south end of the infield, houses **Indy's Hall of Fame** and a large collection of cars that have tested their mettle on the storied track over the years. (☎484-6747. Open daily 9am-5pm. $3, ages 6-15 $1.) Tickets for the race go on sale the day after the previous year's race and usually sell out within a week.

IN THE FAST LANE. The **Walker Theatre,** 617 Indiana Ave., a 15min. walk northwest of downtown, used to house the headquarters of African-American entrepreneur Madame C.J. Walker's beauty enterprise. Today the national historic landmark hosts arts programs, including the biweekly **Jazz on the Avenue.** (☎236-2099. Tours M-F 9am-5pm. Jazz F 6-10pm. $5.) The **Indianapolis Symphony Orchestra** performs from late June to August in the **Hilbert Circle Theater** on Monument Circle. (☎639-4300; www.indyorch.org. Box office open M-F 9am-5pm, Sa 10am-2pm.)

Sports fans have more for which to be thankful than just the speedway. Basketball fans watch the **Pacers** (☎917-2500) hoop it up from November to April at the **Conseco Fieldhouse,** 125 S. Pennsylvania St. (Tickets $10-92.) The WNBA's **Indiana Fever** (☎239-5151) take over in the summer. (Tickets $8-90.) Football's **Colts** (☎239-5151) take to the gridiron at the **RCA Dome,** 100 S. Capital Ave. (Tickets $15-149.)

Somewhat bland by day, the **Broad Ripple** area, 6 mi. north of downtown at College Ave. and 62nd St., transforms into a center for nightlife after dark. Partiers fill the clubs and bars and spill out onto the sidewalks until about 1am on weekdays and 3am on weekends. The **Jazz Cooker,** 925 E. Westfield Blvd., heats up when the Steve Ball Trio begins jamming. Attached to the Jazz Cooker, **Monkey's Tale** is a relaxed bar where a great jukebox spins tunes. (☎253-2883. Music F-Sa 7-10pm. Bar open M-Sa until 3am, Su until 12:30am.) **Vogue,** 6259 N. College Ave., is the hottest club in town and hosts national acts. (☎255-2828. 21+. Covers $3-5; ladies free F. Open W 9pm-3am, F-Sa 10pm-3am. Shows 8pm; call

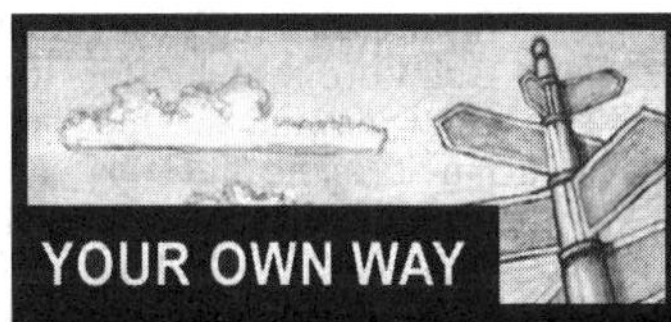

YOUR OWN WAY

FAMOUS HOOSIERS

For an introduction to Indiana's rich basketball tradition, head to the **Indiana Basketball Hall of Fame,** about 50 mi. east of Indianapolis in New Castle. There you can listen to legendary coach John Wooden give his famed locker room speech about the "Pyramid of Success," which defines the hard-nosed, purist mentality of Indiana basketball. A small exhibit on Oscar Robertson and a shrine-like collection of Larry Bird relics allow visitors to pay homage to Indiana's basketball legends, but the focus of the museum is on the high school teams that are the foundation of the state's mania. Tons of memorabilia—from jerseys and trophies to newspaper clippings and banners—as well as highlight reels of classic games capture the passion of Indiana basketball, while the Hall of Fame commemorates those who have made significant contributions to Indiana's basketball legacy. Fittingly, some of the more modern features of the museum, including a theater, interactive quiz, and a basketball hoop with five seconds on the scoreboard that allows you to attempt a game-winning shot, are sporadically out of order, but the museum is worth the trip for passionate basketball fans who enjoy Indiana's simple love of the game.

***Hall of Fame,** 1 Hall of Fame Court, New Castle, IN (☎765-529-1891). Open Tu-Sa 10am-5pm, Su 1pm-5pm. $4, ages 5-12 $2.*

for schedule.) For local and alternative acts, head to the nearby **Patio,** 6308 N. Guildford, which offers live music every night on a small stage. (☎233-0799. 21+. Cover around $5. Open 9pm-close.) Downtown, the **Slippery Noodle,** 372 S. Meridian St., is the oldest bar in Indiana, as well as one of the country's best venues for live blues every night. (☎631-6974. 21+. Cover Th-Sa $5. Open M-F 11am-3am, Sa 12:30pm-3am, Su 4pm-12:30am.)

BLOOMINGTON ☎812

The region's rolling hills create an exquisite backdrop for Bloomington's most prominent institution, Indiana University (IU). The college town atmosphere, nightlife hot spots, and die-hard fans of Hoosier basketball help Bloomington compete with its northern neighbor, Indianapolis. Additionally, a strong Tibetan influence adds a unique flavor to this laidback town.

ORIENTATION & PRACTICAL INFORMATION. Bloomington lies south of Indianapolis on Rte. 37. **North Walnut** and **College Street** are the main north-south thoroughfares. The town centers on **Courthouse Square,** which is surrounded by restaurants, bookshops, and bars. **Greyhound,** 219 W. 6th St. (☎332-1522; station open M-F 9am-5pm, Sa-Su noon-4pm), connects Bloomington to Chicago (5hr., 2 per day, $52) and Indianapolis (1hr., 2 per day, $16). **Bloomington Transit** sends buses on seven routes through both the town and the IU campus. Service is infrequent; call ahead. (☎332-5688. $0.75, seniors and ages 5-17 $0.35.) The campus also has a shuttle ($0.75). **Taxi: Yellow Cab** (☎336-4100) charges by zone. The **Visitors Center,** 2855 N. Walnut St., offers free local calls and a helpful staff. (☎334-8900 or 800-800-0037. Open Apr.-Oct. M-F 8:30am-5pm, Sa 9am-4pm; Nov.-Mar. M-F 8:30am-5pm, Sa 10am-3pm. Brochure area open 24hr.) **Internet Access: Monroe County Public Library,** 303 E. Kirkwood Ave. (☎349-3050. Open M-Th 9am-9pm, F 9am-6pm, Sa 9am-5pm, Su 1-5pm.) **Post Office:** 206 E. 4th St., two blocks east of Walnut St. (☎334-4030. Open M and F 8am-6pm, Tu-Th 8am-5:30pm, Sa 8am-1pm.) **Postal Code:** 47404. **Area Code:** 812.

ACCOMMODATIONS. Budget hotels are located around the intersection of N. Walnut St. and Rte. 46. Though rooms are often in short supply, the recently renovated **College Motor Inn ❸,** 509 N. College Ave., has an elegant exterior and pleasant rooms with cable TV and free local calls. (☎336-6881. Reservations recommended. Singles from $55; doubles from $62. Prices rise for weekends and special events.) If no space is available, you can always turn to **Motel 6 ❷,** 1800 N. Walnut, which has one of its more attractive locations just north of downtown. (☎332-0820. Cable TV, A/C, pool. Singles Su-Th $39, F-Sa $45; doubles $45/51.) Usually rooms at the **Scholar's Bed & Breakfast ❹,** 801 N. College Ave., rent for over $100, but deals can be found on weekdays, when the lush rooms with TV/VCR, A/C, and private baths drop in price. Gourmet breakfast included. (☎332-1892. Check-in 4-6pm. Call for room availability. Rooms from $75.) **Paynetown "Peyton" State Recreation Area ❶,** 10 mi. southeast of downtown on Rte. 446, has open campsites on Lake Monroe with access to trails, a beach, and a wheelchair-accessible fishing dock. Boat rental available. (☎837-9490. Primitive sites $7; with shower $12; with electricity $15. Vehicle registration $5, IN residents $3. For boats call ☎837-9909. Kayaks and canoes $9 per hr., $25 per 8hr. with $25 deposit; fishing boats $25 per hr.)

FOOD. Downtown Square hosts a wealth of veggie-heavy restaurants, bookstores, and offbeat clothing and record shops in a four block stretch on Kirkwood Ave., near College Ave. and Walnut St. **Snow Lion ❷,** 113 S. Grant St., owned by the Dalai Lama's nephew, is one of only a few Tibetan restaurants in the country. Spicy dishes and authentic decor transport diners. An extensive Pan-Asian menu is also available. (☎336-0835. Entrees $7-9. Tibetan Butter Tea $1.50. Open daily 11am-10pm.) **The Laughing Planet Cafe ❶**, 322 E. Kirkwood Ave., in the Kenwood Manor Building, serves up bean-heavy burritos ($3.50-6) and other organic delights made from local produce in a cafe setting. (☎323-2233. Open daily 11am-9pm.) Downstairs, beans of a different variety are served at the colorful **Soma ❶**. Sip lattes ($2.50) and smoothies ($3.40) on comfy orange couches with Midwest hipsters. (☎331-2770. Open summer M-Sa 7am-10pm, Su 8am-11pm. Call for winter hours.) Locals pack into the booths at **Trojan Horse ❶**, 1010 W. Kirkwood St., a Greco-American tavern with great gyros ($4.65-6.45), falafel ($4.65), and burgers ($3.35). (☎332-1101. Open M-Th 11am-11pm, F-Sa 11am-midnight).

SIGHTS. Designed by I.M. Pei, IU's architecturally striking **Art Museum**, E. 7th St., on campus, maintains an excellent collection of Oriental and African artwork, along with varied European art. (☎855-5445; www.indiana.edu/~iuam. Open Tu-Sa 10am-5pm, Su noon-5pm.) Nearby, the **Mathers Museum of World Cultures**, 416 N. Indiana St., near E. 8th St., has a vast collection of artifacts from around the world that serve as the foundation for changing exhibits on the technologies and dress of various cultures. (☎855-6873; www.indiana.edu/~mathers. Open Tu-F 9am-4:30pm, Sa-Su 1-4:30pm. Tours every 30min. F-Sa noon-4:30pm, Su 1-4:30pm. Free.) **Oliver Winery**, 8024 N. State Rd. 37, not only has flowery, fountain-filled grounds, but also offers free tastings of its wines, including blackberry wine, a local favorite. (☎876-5800 or 800-258-2783; www.oliverwinery.com. Open M-Sa 10am-6pm, Su noon-6pm.) A large Tibetan influence in Bloomington is evidenced by a temple and a retreat. The **Tibetan Cultural Center**, 3655 Snoddy Rd., offers meditation. (☎334-7046. Grounds open Sa-Su noon-4pm. Center open Su noon-3pm.)

NIGHTLIFE. Bloomington's nightlife scene is just what you'd expect from a Midwestern college town: it's all about beer and rock. **The Crazy Horse**, 214 W. Kirkwood Ave., drafts an alcohol army of 80 beers and cooks up Bloomington's best burgers from $5. (☎336-8877. Open M-W 11am-1am, Th-Sa 11am-2am, Su noon-midnight.) **Nick's**, 423 E. Kirkwood Ave., looks like a quaint English pub, but is full of IU students guzzling beer and watching sports. (☎332-4040. Beers from $2. 21+ after 8pm. Open M-Sa 11am-2am, Su noon-midnight.) **Bullwinkle's**, 201 S. College Ave., has drag shows; a mixed clientele grooves on the dance floor. (☎334-3232. Drag shows M and W 11pm, 1am. Open M and W-Th 9pm-3am, F-Sa 8pm-3am.)

MICHIGAN

Pressing up against four of the Great Lakes, two peninsulas present visitors with two distinct Michigans. The sparsely populated Upper Peninsula hangs over Lake Michigan, housing moose, wolves, and the stunning waterfalls of the Hiawatha National Forest. Campers and hikers have recently begun discovering the U.P., and the resplendent forests now entertain backpackers and families alike. In the Lower Peninsula, beach bums hang out in the many quaint communities along the western coast of the state, sunning and boating along some of Michigan's 3000 miles of coastline. Those craving an urban environment head to Ann Arbor, the intellectual center of the state, or to industrial Detroit for world-class museums.

PRACTICAL INFORMATION

Capital: Lansing.

Visitor Info: Michigan Travel Bureau, 333 S. Capitol St., Ste. F, Lansing 48909 (☎888-784-7328; www.michigan.org). **Department of Parks and Recreation,** Information Services Ctr., P.O. Box 30257, Lansing 48909 (☎517-373-9900). State parks requires a motor vehicle permit; $4 per day, $20 annually. Call ☎800-447-2757 for reservations.

Postal Abbreviation: MI. **Sales Tax:** 6%.

DETROIT ☎313

Long the ugly step-sister of America's big cities, Detroit has nowhere to go but up. Violent race riots in the 1960s caused a massive flight to the suburbs; the population has more than halved since 1967, turning much of the city into a post-industrial urban wasteland riddled with boarded-up buildings and empty parking lots. The decline of the auto industry in the late 1970s added unemployment to the city's ills. The unmistakable sound of Motown kept Detroit funky through the 60s but has long since fizzled out. Today, the five gleaming towers of the riverside Renaissance Center symbolize the hope of a city-wide effort to revitalize downtown Detroit. Despite the poverty and violence that plague Detroit, the tourism industry focuses on the city's jewels. Top-notch museums cluster in the cultural center of the city, while professional sports and a music scene inherited from Motown entertain both locals and travelers. Across the river, Windsor, Ontario exudes a cosmopolitan flavor from its streets packed with bars and restaurants.

TRANSPORTATION

Airport: Detroit Metropolitan (☎734-247-7678; www.metroairport.com), 2 mi. west of downtown, off I-94 at Merriman Rd. in Romulus. **Checkered Sedan** (☎800-351-5466) offers taxi service to downtown for $42.

Trains: Amtrak, 11 W. Baltimore St. (☎873-3442). Open daily 5:45am-11:30pm. To **Chicago** (6hr., 3 per day, $23-41) and **New York** (16hr., 2 per day, $72-163). For Canadian destinations, **VIA Rail,** 298 Walker Rd., Windsor, ON (☎519-256-5511 or 800-561-3949). To **Toronto** (4hr.; 4 per day; CDN$78, 40% off with ISIC card).

Buses: Greyhound, 1001 Howard St. (☎961-8011). Station open 24hr.; ticket office open daily 6am-12:30am. To: **Ann Arbor** (1½hr., 5 per day, $7.50); **Chicago** (5½-7½hr., 7-8 per day, $37.50); **Cleveland** (4-6hr., 11 per day, $28.50). *At night, the area is unsafe.*

Public Transit: Detroit Department of Transportation (DOT), 1301 E. Warren St. (☎933-1300). Serves downtown, with limited service to the suburbs. Many buses stop service at midnight. $1.50, some short routes $0.50; transfers $0.25. An ultramodern elevated tramway, **People Mover,** 150 Michigan Ave., circles the Central Business District on a 2¾ mi. loop; worth a ride just for the view of the riverfront and downtown architecture. (☎962-7245 or 800-541-7245.) Runs M-Th 7am-11pm, F 7am-midnight, Sa 9am-midnight, Su noon-8pm. $0.50. **Southeastern Michigan Area Regional Transit (SMART),** 600 Woodward Ave. (☎962-5515), runs bus service to the suburbs 4am-midnight. Times vary depending on route. $1.50, transfers $0.25.

Taxi: Checker Cab, ☎963-7000.

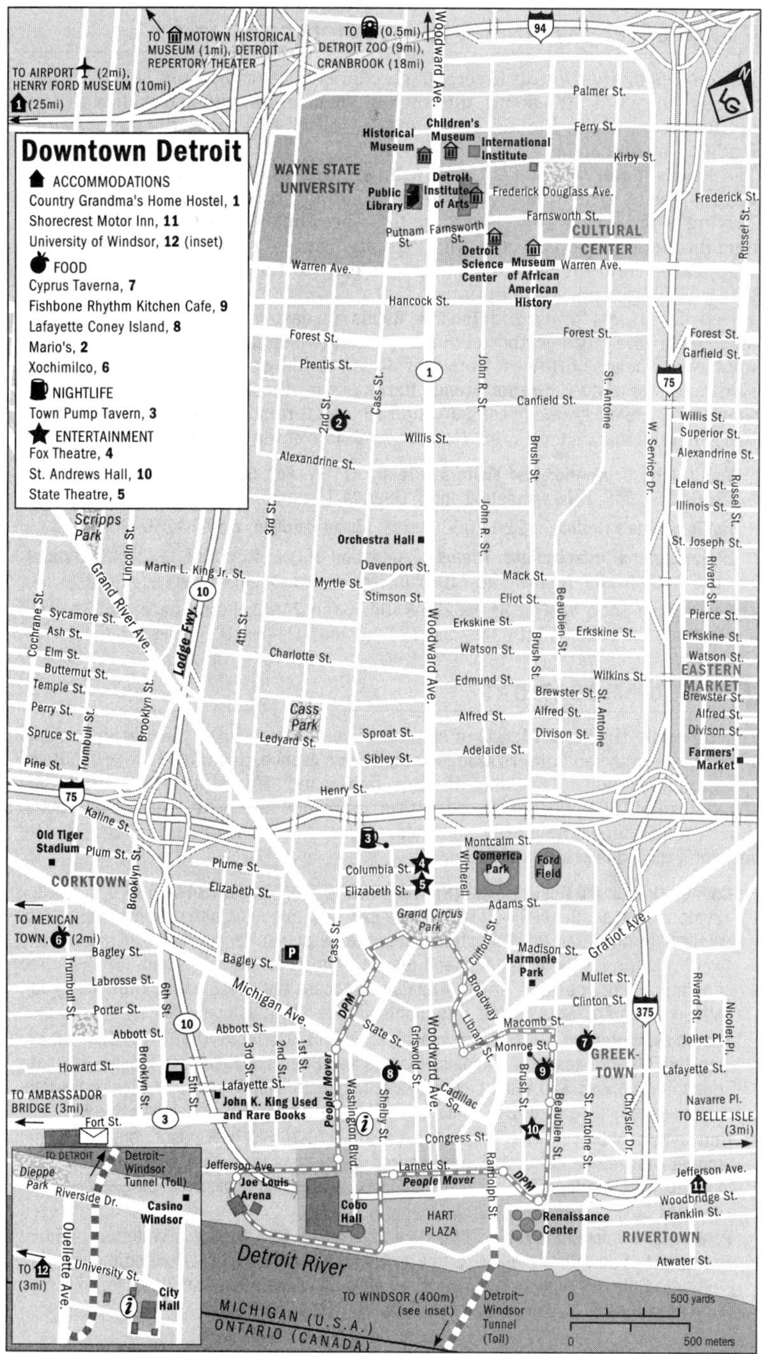
Downtown Detroit
ACCOMMODATIONS
Country Grandma's Home Hostel, 1
Shorecrest Motor Inn, 11
University of Windsor, 12 (inset)
FOOD
Cyprus Taverna, 7
Fishbone Rhythm Kitchen Cafe, 9
Lafayette Coney Island, 8
Mario's, 2
Xochimilco, 6
NIGHTLIFE
Town Pump Tavern, 3
ENTERTAINMENT
Fox Theatre, 4
St. Andrews Hall, 10
State Theatre, 5
TO MOTOWN HISTORICAL MUSEUM (1mi), DETROIT REPERTORY THEATER
TO AIRPORT (2mi), HENRY FORD MUSEUM (10mi), 1 (25mi)
TO (0.5mi), DETROIT ZOO (9mi), CRANBROOK (18mi)
Woodward Ave.
94
Palmer St.
Ferry St.
Kirby St.
Historical Museum
Children's Museum
International Institute
WAYNE STATE UNIVERSITY
Public Library
Detroit Institute of Arts
Frederick Douglass Ave.
Frederick St.
Farnsworth St.
Putnam St.
Detroit Science Center
Museum of African American History
CULTURAL CENTER
Warren Ave.
Russel St.
Hancock St.
Forest St.
Garfield St.
Prentis St.
Cass St.
2nd St.
3rd St.
4th St.
John R. St.
St. Antoine
Canfield St.
Willis St.
Superior St.
Alexandrine St.
Brush St.
W. Service Dr.
Leland St.
Illinois St.
St. Joseph St.
Rivard St.
Scripps Park
Lincoln St.
Orchestra Hall
Martin L. King Jr. St.
Davenport St.
Myrtle St.
Stimson St.
Mack St.
Eliot St.
Grand River Ave.
Lodge Fwy.
Cochrane St.
Sycamore St.
Ash St.
Elm St.
Butternut St.
Temple St.
Perry St.
Spruce St.
Pine St.
Trumbull St.
Brooklyn St.
Charlotte St.
Erkskine St.
Watson St.
Edmund St.
Wilkins St.
Beaubien St.
Pierce St.
EASTERN MARKET
Brewster St.
Alfred St.
Divison St.
Adelaide St.
Farmers' Market
Cass Park
Ledyard St.
Sproat St.
Sibley St.
Henry St.
75
Kaline St.
Old Tiger Stadium
Plum St.
Plume St.
CORKTOWN
Montcalm St.
Comerica Park
Ford Field
Witherell
Columbia St.
Elizabeth St.
Adams St.
Grand Circus Park
TO MEXICAN TOWN, 6 (2mi)
Bagley St.
Madison St.
Harmonie Park
Gratiot Ave.
Clifford St.
Broadway
Labrosse St.
Porter St.
Abbott St.
6th St.
Michigan Ave.
DPM
State St.
Library St.
Mullet St.
Clinton St.
Macomb St.
375
Monroe St.
GREEKTOWN
Joliet Pl.
Nicolet Pl.
Howard St.
1st St.
Griswold St.
Lafayette St.
5th St.
John K. King Used and Rare Books
People Mover
Washington Blvd.
Shelby St.
Cadillac Sq.
Chrysler Dr.
Navarre Pl.
TO AMBASSADOR BRIDGE (3mi)
Fort St.
TO BELLE ISLE (3mi)
Congress St.
Randolph St.
TO DETROIT
Detroit-Windsor Tunnel (Toll)
Dieppe Park
Riverside Dr.
Casino Windsor
Jefferson Ave.
Joe Louis Arena
Cobo Hall
Larned St.
HART PLAZA
Renaissance Center
Woodbridge St.
Franklin St.
RIVERTOWN
Ouellette Ave.
University St.
TO 12 (3mi)
City Hall
Detroit River
Atwater St.
MICHIGAN (U.S.A.)
ONTARIO (CANADA)
TO WINDSOR (400m) (see inset)
Detroit-Windsor Tunnel (Toll)
0
500 yards
500 meters

ORIENTATION & PRACTICAL INFORMATION

Detroit lies on the Detroit River, which connects Lake Erie and Lake St. Clair. Across the river to the south, the town of **Windsor, ON,** can be reached by tunnel just west of the Renaissance Center (toll $2.50), or by the Ambassador Bridge. Detroit can be a dangerous town, but it is typically safe during the day. The **People Mover** surrounds the downtown area where businesses and sports venues cluster; the area it encircles is generally safe during business hours. Driving is the best way to negotiate this sprawling city, where good and bad neighborhoods alternate on a whim. Though streets tend to end suddenly and reappear several blocks later, parking is easy to find and driving avoids less safe public transportation options.

Detroit's streets form a grid. **The Mile Roads** run east-west as major arteries. **Eight Mile Road** is the city's northern boundary and the beginning of the suburbs. **Woodward Avenue** heads northwest from downtown, dividing city and suburbs into "east side" and "west side." **Gratiot Avenue** flares out northeast from downtown, while **Grand River Avenue** shoots west. **I-94** and **I-75** pass through downtown. For a particularly helpful map, check *Visit Detroit,* available at the Visitors Bureau.

Visitor Info: Convention and Visitors Bureau, 211 W. Fort St., 10th fl. (☎202-1800 or 800-338-7648; www.visitdetroit.com). Open M-F 9am-5pm.

Hotlines: Crisis Hotline, ☎224-7000. **Sexual Abuse Helpline,** ☎876-4180. Both 24hr.

Bi-Gay-Lesbian Organizations: Triangle Foundation of Detroit, ☎537-3323. **Affirmations,** 195 W. 9 Mile Rd. (☎248-398-7105), in Ferndale, has a large library and nightlife info.

Post Office: 1401 W. Fort St. (☎226-8304. Open 24hr.). **Postal Code:** 48233. **Area Codes:** 313 (Detroit); 810, 248, and 734 (suburbs). In text, 313 unless noted.

ACCOMMODATIONS

Detroit's suburbs harbor loads of chain motels. Those near the airport in **Romulus** tend to be pricey, and others along **East Jefferson Avenue,** near downtown, can be of questionable quality. For a mix of convenience and affordability, look along **Telegraph Road** off I-94, west of the city. If the exchange rate is favorable, good deals can be found across the border in **Windsor.** *Visit Detroit* lists accommodations by area and includes price ranges.

Country Grandma's Home Hostel (HI-AYH), 22330 Bell Rd. (☎734-753-4901), in New Boston, 6 mi. south of I-94 off I-275. Take Exit 11B, turn right, and then make an immediate right onto Bell Rd. Though inaccessible by public transportation, Grandma's is worth the trip for the hospitality and respite from urban Detroit. 7 beds, kitchen, free parking. Bring your own linen. Wheelchair-accessible. Reservations required; call ahead. Open Apr.-Sept. Dorms $15, nonmembers $18. Cash only. ❶

Shorecrest Motor Inn, 1316 E. Jefferson Ave. (☎568-3000 or 800-992-9616), is ideally located 3 blocks east of the Renaissance Center. Rooms include A/C, fridges, and data ports. Key deposit $20 when paying by cash. Free parking. Wheelchair-accessible. Reservations recommended. 21+. Clean, comfortable singles $69; doubles $89. ❸

University of Windsor, 401 Sunset Ave. (☎519-973-7074), in Windsor, rents functional rooms with refrigerators, A/C, and shared bathrooms from early May-late Aug. Free Internet access and use of university facilities. Wheelchair-accessible. Singles CDN$32; doubles CDN$37. ❷

Pontiac Lake Recreation Area, 7800 Gale Rd. (☎248-666-1020), in Waterford, 45min. northwest of downtown; take I-75 to Rte. 59 W, turn right on Will Lake northbound, and left onto Gale Rd. Huge wooded sites in rolling hills, just 4 mi. from the lake. 176 sites with electricity $11. Vehicle permit $4. ❶

 FOOD

Although many restaurants have migrated to the suburbs, there are still some budget dining options in town. The downtown area doesn't offer much after 5pm, but ethnic neighborhoods provide interesting choices. At the **Greektown** People Mover stop, Greek restaurants and excellent bakeries line one block of Monroe St., near Beaubien St. To snag a *pierogi*, cruise Joseph Campau Ave. in **Hamtramck** (Ham-TRAM-eck), a Polish neighborhood northeast of Detroit. **Mexican Town,** just west of downtown, is packed with Mexican restaurants, markets, and nightspots. No traveler should miss the **Eastern Market,** at Gratiot Ave. and Russell St., an 11-acre produce-and-goodies festival. (☎833-1560. Open Sa 4am-5pm.)

Cyprus Taverna, 579 Monroe St. (☎961-1550), serves *mousaka* ($9) and other Greek specialties in the heart of Greektown. If you're tired of the flaming cheese routine, try *haloumi,* a fried Cypriot cheese delivered warm to the table. Lunch specials from $5.25. Dinner entrees $9-13. Open Su-Th 11am-1:30am, F-Sa 11am-4am. ❸

Mario's, 4222 2nd St. (☎832-6464), downtown, is an elegant, old-fashioned Italian eatery. If the whole table can agree on 1 of the 6 specialty dinners ($30 per person), the meal will be prepared tableside by one of the capable chefs (2½hr. is suggested for optimal service). All meals include antipasto platters, salad, and soup. Live bands and ballroom dancing shake the place up on the weekends, and free shuttle service takes customers to and from major sporting and theater events. Entrees from $16. Open M-Th 11:30am-11pm, F 11:30am-midnight, Sa 4pm-midnight, Su 2-10pm. ❺

Lafayette Coney Island, 118 W. Lafayette St. (☎964-8198). Detroit's most famous culinary establishment, Lafayette doles out its coney dogs ($2.10) and chili cheese fries ($2.45) to loyal customers. Brusque service—and the antacids you'll need—is worth it for a perfect dog. Open M-Th 7:30am-4am, F-Sa 7:30am-5am, Su 9:30am-4am. ❶

Xochimilco, 3409 Bagley St. (☎843-0129), draws the biggest crowds in Mexican Town with cheap, delicious enchiladas and burrito platters ($5-8). Muraled walls, great service, and warm chips with your salsa are just a few of the details that separate Xochimilco (so-she-MO-ko) from its competition. Open daily 11am-2am. ❷

Fishbone's Rhythm Kitchen Cafe, 400 Monroe St. (☎965-9600), in Greektown, brings the spice of Mardi Gras to the Motor City, with zydeco music and an oyster bar and Cajun specialities like deep-fried alligator ($9), jambalaya ($14), and seafood gumbo ($5.25). . Open M-F 6:30am-1am, Sa 6:30am-2am, Su brunch 10am-2pm. ❸

 SIGHTS

Sections of Detroit and the surrounding area allow visitors a chance to explore everything from books to wildlife while enjoying the city's public parks. For wandering book lovers, **John K. King Used and Rare Books,** 901 W. Lafayette St., is a four-floor maze of over a million books on every topic imaginable. Friendly and knowledgeable staff help guide new customers through the impressive warehouse. (☎961-0622. Open M-Sa 9:30am-5:30pm.)

DETROIT ZOO. You'll find exotic animals like tigers and red pandas roaming the suburban grounds of the **Detroit Zoological Park.** The park features the National Amphibian Conservation Center, while the all-new Arctic Ring of Life exhibit features polar bears and a trek through the Tundra. *(8450 W. Ten Mile Rd., just off the Woodward Exit of Rte. 696 in Royal Oak. ☎248-398-0900; www.detroitzoo.org. Open May-June and Sept.-Oct. daily 10am-5pm; July-Aug. M-Tu and Th-Su 10am-5pm, W 10am-8pm; Nov.-Mar daily 10am-4pm. $9, seniors and ages 2-12 $6. Parking $4.)*

ONE HELL OF A PREP SCHOOL. Fifteen miles north of Detroit in posh Bloomfield Hills, **Cranbrook's** scholarly campus holds public gardens, several museums, and an art academy. Far and away the best of the lot is the **Cranbrook Institute of Science,** 39221 N. Woodward Ave., with a planetarium and rotating exhibits emphasizing educational fun. The new Bat Zone houses bats, owls, and other nocturnal creatures and offers daily demonstrations. *(☎248-645-3209 or 877-462-7262; www.cranbrook.edu. Open M-Th and Sa-Su 10am-5pm, F 10am-10pm. $7, seniors and ages 2-12 $5. Planetarium shows $3, under 2 $1. Bat Zone $3/1; free with general admission.)*

BELLE ISLE. The best escape from Detroit's urban wasteland is the 1000-acre **Belle Isle,** where a conservatory, nature center, aquarium, maritime museum, and small zoo allow animal lovers to drift from sight to sight. *(3 mi. from downtown via the MacArthur Bridge at the foot of E. Grand Blvd. ☎852-4078. Isle accessible daily 6am-10pm; attractions 10am-5pm. $2 per sight, ages 2-12 $1; zoo $3/1.)*

MUSEUMS

Motown Historical Museum, 2648 W. Grand Blvd. (☎875-2264; www.motownmuseum.com). "Dexter Avenue" bus. Housed in the apartment where entrepreneur and producer Berry Gordy founded Hitsville, USA, and created the unmistakable Motown sound. Upstairs, an impressive collection of memorabilia includes the piano used by the legendary Motown artists and the hat and gloves donned by Michael Jackson in "Thriller." Downstairs, Studio A—where the Jackson 5, Marvin Gaye, and Smokey Robinson recorded—has been meticulously preserved, right down to the sheet music, vending machine, and telephones. Open summer Tu-Sa 10am-6pm; winter Tu-Sa 10am-5pm. $8, under 13 $5.

Detroit Institute of Arts, 5200 Woodward Ave. (☎833-7900; www.dia.org). The majority of the museum's extensive collection of American art is on tour while renovations continue for the new American Wing, set to open in 2006. However, there is an extensive collection of traditional Dutch and Flemish art in an elaborate setting, as well as an impressive modern collection boasting works by Picasso, Van Gogh, and Matisse. Among the highlights of the museum is Diego Rivera's monumental mural "Detroit Industry," which fills an entire room and pays homage to the city and its industrial past. Open W-Th 10am-4pm, F 10am-9pm, Sa-Su 10am-5pm; first F of each month 11am-9pm. Suggested donation $4, students and children $1.

Henry Ford Museum, 20900 Oakwood Blvd. (☎271-1620; www.hfmgv.org), off I-94 in Dearborn. Take SMART bus #200 or 250. Housing full-scale planes, trains, and automobiles, the museum's enormous exhibit hall explores "100 Years of the Automobile in American Life." The impressive display details the major cultural changes that cars have brought about in American history. The premises boast the convertible in which President Kennedy was assassinated, the bus in which Rosa Parks sat up front, and the chair in which Lincoln was shot. Next door, experience a microcosm of America at **Greenfield Village,** where over 80 historic edifices salute American ingenuity. Visit the factory where Thomas Edison researched. Museum and village open M-Sa 9am-5pm, Su noon-5pm; village closed Jan.-Mar. Museum $14, seniors $13, ages 5-12 $10. Village $18/17/12. Combination pass $24/12/18. IMAX $10/9/8.50.

Museum of African American History, 315 E. Warren Rd. (☎494-5800; www.maah-detroit.org), features a poignant core exhibit that begins with the slave trade and then moves through African-American history, ending in a bittersweet display of modern African-American culture. Open W-Sa 9:30am-5pm, Su 1-5pm. $5, under 17 $3.

Detroit Science Center, 5020 John R St. (☎577-8400; www.sciencedetroit.org). Children can learn about waves while strumming a stringless harp or take virtual trips through the rings of Saturn in the planetarium. Open mid-Sept. to early June M-F 9:30am-3pm, Sa-Su 10:30am-6pm; mid-June to early Sept. M-F 9:30am-5pm, Sa-Su 10:30am-6pm. $7, seniors and ages 2-12 $6; IMAX additional $4.

ENTERTAINMENT

Music has always filled the streets of Detroit, with the city's sidewalk performers carrying on the Motown legacy. Though the era of Motown has come and gone, a vibrant music scene still dominates the Motor City. The **Detroit Symphony Orchestra** performs at **Orchestra Hall,** 3711 Woodward Ave., at Parsons St. (☎962-1000, box office ☎576-5111; www.detroitsymphony.com. Open M-F 10am-6pm. Tickets $10-25. Half-price student and senior rush tickets 1½hr. prior to show.)

Celebrated dramatic works are performed in the newly renovated and restored **theater district,** clustered around Woodward Ave. and Columbia St. The **Fox Theatre,** 2211 Woodward Ave., near Grand Circus Park, features high-profile dramas, comedies, and musicals in a 5000-seat theater that occasionally shows epic films. (☎983-3200. Box office open M-F 10am-6pm. $25-100; movies under $10.) The **State Theater,** 2115 Woodward Ave. (☎961-5450, for tickets call 248-645-6666), hosts a variety of popular concerts. Beyond the theater district, the acclaimed **Detroit Repertory Theater,** 13103 Woodrow Wilson Ave., puts on four productions a year. (☎868-1347. Shows Th-F 8:30pm, Sa 3, 8:30pm, Su 2, 7:30pm. Tickets from $17.)

Sports fans also won't be disappointed in Detroit. During the dog days of summer, baseball's **Tigers** round the bases in the newly built **Comerica Park,** 2100 Woodward Ave. (☎471-2255. $5-60.) Football's **Lions** hit the gridiron next door at **Ford Field,** 200 Brush St. (☎800-616-7627. $35-54.) Inside the **Joe Louis Arena,** 600 Civic Center Dr., the 2002 Stanley Cup champion **Red Wings** play hockey. (☎645-6666. $20-40.) Thirty minutes outside Detroit in Auburn Hills, basketball's **Pistons** hoop it up at **The Palace at Auburn Hills,** 2 Championship Dr. (☎248-377-0100. $10-60.)

FESTIVALS & NIGHTLIFE

Detroit's numerous **festivals** draw millions of visitors. Most outdoor events take place at **Hart Plaza,** a downtown oasis that hugs a scenic expanse of the Detroit River. A new and rousingly successful downtown tradition, the **Detroit Electronic Music Festival** (☎393-9200; www.demf.org) has lured over one million ravers to Hart Plaza on Memorial Day weekend. Jazz fans jet to the riverbank during Labor Day weekend for the four-day **Ford Detroit International Jazz Festival** (☎963-7622; www.detroitjazzfest.com), which features more than 70 acts on three stages and mountains of international food at the World Food Court. A week-long extravaganza in late June, the international **Freedom Festival** (☎923-7400), celebrates the friendship between the US and Canada. The continent's largest fireworks display ignites the festivities on both sides of the border. On the Detroit side, food and a bandstand dominate the festival, while Windsor provides a carnival complete with rides and cotton candy. **Detroit's African World Festival** (☎494-5853) brings over a million people to Hart Plaza on the third weekend in August for free reggae, jazz, and gospel concerts. The nation's oldest state fair, the **Michigan State Fair** (☎369-8250), at Eight Mile Rd. and Woodward Ave., beckons with bake-offs, art, and livestock birth exhibits during the 2 weeks before Labor Day.

For info on the trendiest nightspots, pick up a free copy of *Orbit* in record stores and restaurants. The *Metro Times* also contains complete entertainment listings. *Between the Lines*, also free, has BGLT entertainment info. Head to **Harmonie Park,** near Orchestra Hall, for some of Detroit's best jazz. Alternative fans should check out **Saint Andrews Hall,** 431 E. Congress St., Detroit's mainstay for local and national alternative acts. **Shelter,** the dance club downstairs in St. Andrews Hall, draws young, hip crowds on non-concert nights. (☎961-6358. St. Andrews 18+; Shelter 21+. Shows F-Su. Advance tickets through Ticketmaster $7-12.) On Saturdays, the State Theater (see Entertainment, p. 557) houses **Ignition,** a giant party that enlists DJs from a local radio station to play alternative dance music. (2115 Woodward Ave. 18+. Cover starts at $5. Sa 9pm-2am.) If all you want is a good pint, try the **Town Pump Tavern,** 100 Montcalm St., behind the State Theater. Good beer abounds at this watering hole, which is cloaked in ivy and features a mock study with comfy leather chairs. (☎961-1929. Open daily 11am-2am.) The bars and clubs along **Ouellette Avenue** in Windsor (see below) attract young party kids looking to take advantage of Ontario's lower drinking age.

NEAR DETROIT: WINDSOR, ON ☎519

Combining cultural highlights, natural attractions, and a vibrant nightlife, Windsor offers tourists an alternative to the grittier city across the river. Outdoor cafes, tree-lined streets, and lively shopping give Windsor a pleasant European feel. Its many bars, favorable exchange rates, and drinking age (19) lure Detroiters of all ages across the river, creating a cosmopolitan mix on the crowded streets.

For a small industrial city, Windsor scores big with its collection of contemporary art. Stroll through the "museum without walls" at the **Odette Sculpture Garden,** part of a 6 mi. long riverfront green area between the Ambassador Bridge and Curry Ave. Visitors are enchanted by native totem poles next to unusual modern sculptures. (☎253-2300. Open daily dawn-dusk. Free.) The city's other major exhibit space, **The Art Gallery of Windsor,** 401 Riverside Dr. W, provides a showcase for a rotating cast of Canada's best modern artists. (☎977-0013; www.artgalleryofwindsor.com. Open W-Th noon-5pm, F noon-9pm, Sa-Su 11am-5pm. Free.) Beauty of the natural type is on display at **Point Pelee National Park of Canada,** 407 Robson St., Leamington, ON, 45 mi. southeast of downtown. Visitors look for the butterflies flying through the park's tall grass. (☎322-2365. Open daily Apr. and June to mid-Oct. 6am-9:30pm; mid-Oct. to Mar. 7am-6:30pm; May 5am-9:30pm. CDN$5, students CDN$2.50, seniors CDN$4.25; families CDN$12.50. Rates are lower in winter. Guided butterfly tours in Sept. W-Su CDN$10.)

Locals come from miles around to eat finger-lickin' good barbecue at the **Tunnel Bar-B-Q ❸,** 58 Park St. E, across from the tunnel exit. The terrific half-strip rib dinner (CDN$14) is recommended in particular. (☎258-3663. Open Su-Th 8am-2am, F-Sa 8am-4am.) The rest of Windsor's culinary and nightlife activity is centered along Ouelette (OH-let) Ave. downtown. Family-run **Aar-D-Vark Blues Cafe,** 89 University Ave. W, offers a Canadian take on a traditional Chicago blues joint. Pink aardvarks lead customers into the graffittied bar. (☎977-6422. Live music Tu-Su. Open M-F noon-2am, Sa 4pm-2am, Su 7pm-2am.) For the traveler who prefers the clank of quarters to the beat of drums, the **Casino Windsor,** 377 Riverside Dr., offers three floors of gambling in a glimmering new building and draws thousands of American gamers looking to cash in on good exchange rates. Test Lady Luck 24hr. a day. (For reservations ☎800-991-8888, for info ☎800-991-7777. 19+.)

Canada's national rail service, **VIA Rail,** 298 Walker Rd. (☎256-5511 or 800-561-3949; ticket window open M-Sa 5:15am-9pm, Su 6am-9pm), provides service to Toronto (4hr.; 4-5 per day; CDN$62, 40% discount with ISIC). **Transit Windsor,** 3700 North Service Rd. E, sends buses throughout the city. (☎944-4111. CDN$2.25, seniors and students CDN$1.55.) **Taxi: Veteran's Cab,** ☎256-2621. **Visitor Info: The Convention and Visitors Bureau of Windsor, Essex County, and Pelee Island,** 333 Riverside Dr. W, #103. (☎255-6530 or 800-265-3633; www.city.windsor.on.ca/cvb. Open M-F 8:30am-4:30pm.) The **Ontario Travel Center,** 110 Park St., offers brochures, maps, and help from a knowledgeable staff. (☎973-1338. Open daily 8am-8pm.) **Post Office:** City Centre, corner of Park St. and Ouellette Ave. (☎253-1252. Open M-F 8am-5pm.) **Postal Code:** N9A 4K0. **Area Code:** 519.

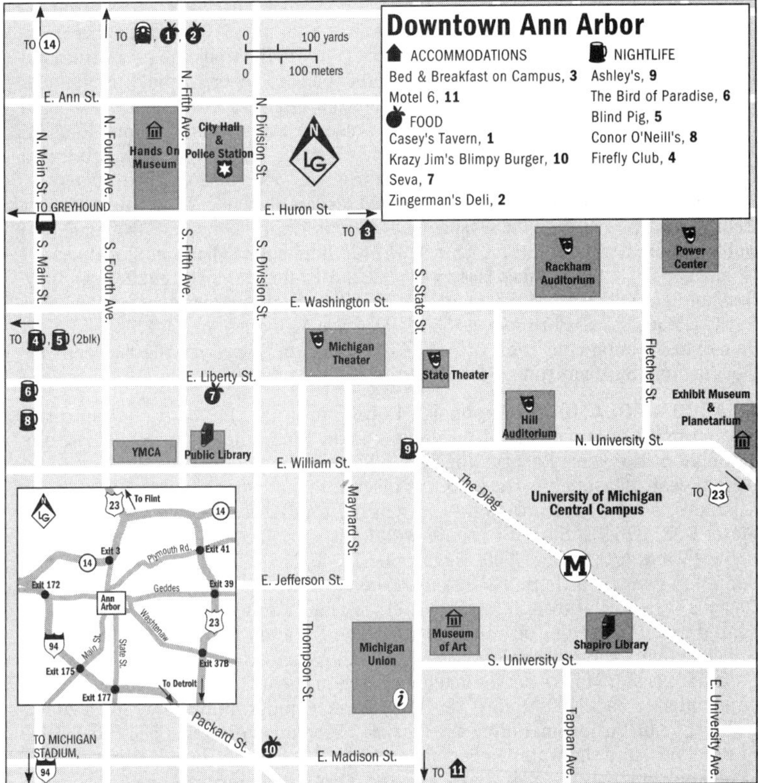

ANN ARBOR ☎734

Ann Arbor's namesakes, Ann Rumsey and Ann Allen—the wives of two of the area's early pioneers—supposedly enjoyed sitting under grape arbors. Now known to locals as "A2," the town has managed to prosper without losing its relaxed charm, despite being tucked between several major industrial hubs. Meanwhile, the huge and well-respected University of Michigan adds a hip college collage of young liberal Middle Americans. Ann Arbor is the prototype for a great college town, and is well worth a visit for anyone traveling in the area.

ORIENTATION & PRACTICAL INFORMATION. Ann Arbor's streets lie in a grid, but watch out for the *slant* of Packard St. and Detroit St. **Main Street** divides the town east-west, and **Huron Street** cuts it north-south. The central campus of the **University of Michigan (U of M)** lies east of Main St. and south of E. Huron, a 5min. walk from downtown. Although street meter parking is plentiful, authorities ticket ruthlessly. Downtown Ann Arbor is very walkable, and a car is generally unnecessary. One-way streets and frequent dead-ends also make driving stressful.

Amtrak, 325 Depot St. (☎994-4906; ticket window open daily 7:15am-11:30pm), sends trains to Chicago (4hr., 3 per day, $23-41) and Detroit (1hr., 3 per day, $9-12). **Greyhound,** 116 W. Huron St. (☎662-5511; open M-Sa 8am-6:30pm, Su 8-9am and noon-6:30pm), sends buses to: Chicago (5-7hr., 4-5 per day, $32-37.50); Detroit (1-1½hr., 3-4 per day, $9-10); Grand Rapids (4-5hr., 2 per day, $19.50). **Ann Arbor Transportation Authority (AATA),** 331 S. 4th Ave., provides public transit in Ann Arbor and a few neighboring towns. (☎996-0400. Station open M-F 7:30am-9pm. Buses run M-F 6am-11pm, Sa-Su 8am-6pm. $1, ages 6-18 $0.50.) AATA's **Nightride** provides safe door-to-door transportation. (☎663-3888 to reserve; the wait is 15-45min. Runs M-F 11pm-6am, Sa-Su 7pm-7:30am. $3.) **Checker Sedan** runs between Ann Arbor and the Detroit Metro Airport. (☎800-351-5466. One-way $46. Reserve in advance.)

Visitor Info: Ann Arbor Area Convention and Visitors Bureau, 120 W. Huron St., at Ashley. (☎995-7281 or 800-888-9487; www.annarbor.org. Open M-F 8:30am-5pm.) **Hotlines: Sexual Assault Crisis Line,** ☎483-7273. **University of Michigan Sexual Assault Line,** ☎936-3333. **S.O.S. Crisis Line,** ☎485-3222. All 24hr. **University of Michigan Gay/Lesbian Referrals,** ☎763-4186. Operates M-F 9am-5pm. **Internet Access: Ann Arbor Public Library,** 343 S. Fifth Ave. (☎324-4200. Open M 10am-9pm, Tu-F 9am-9pm, Sa 9am-6pm, Su noon-6pm.) **Post Office:** 2075 W. Stadium Blvd. (☎665-1100. Open M-F 7:30am-5pm, Sa 10am-1pm.) **Postal Code:** 48103. **Area Code:** 734.

ACCOMMODATIONS. Expensive hotels, motels, and B&Bs cater to the many business travelers and college sports fans who flock to Ann Arbor throughout the year. Reservations are always advisable, especially during the school year. Reasonable rates exist at discount chains farther out of town or in Ypsilanti, 5 mi. southeast along I-94. On the outskirts of Ann Arbor, good ol' **Motel 6 ❸,** 3764 S. State St., rents well-kept, standard rooms equipped with cable TV and A/C. (☎665-9900. Singles Su-Th $46, F-Sa $56; doubles $52/62.) For something with a little more character, head to the homey **Bed & Breakfast On Campus ❹,** 921 E. Huron St., which offers six handsome guest rooms, each decorated in a distinct period furnishing with books and artwork reflective of the era. The living room provides a TV, piano, and a selection of movies, while full gourmet breakfasts are served each morning in the atrium. All rooms with private baths. (☎994-9100. Rooms $85-115.) Seven campgrounds lie within a 20 mi. radius of Ann Arbor, including the **Pinckney Recreation Area ❶,** 8555 Silver Hill, in Pinckney, and the **Waterloo Recreation Area ❶,** 16345 McClure Rd., in Chelsea. (Pinckney ☎426-4913. Waterloo ☎475-8307. Both campgrounds: primitive sites $6; with water and electricity $14. $4 vehicle permit.)

FOOD. Where there are students, there are cheap eats. The cheapest cram the sidewalks of **State** and **South University Street,** while the more upscale line **Main Street.** **Zingerman's Deli ❸,** 422 Detroit St., is an institution in Ann Arbor and is world famous for its gourmet breads, cheeses, and huge deli sandwiches, which come in over 40 varieties ($9-12). Expect a line out the door during the lunchtime rush. While you're there, try **Zingerman's Next Door** for baked goods, desserts, homemade gelato, and espresso drinks. (☎663-3354. Open daily 7am-10pm.) Enjoy meatless delights at Ann Arbor's long-established veggie haven **Seva ❸,** 314 E. Liberty St. Its earthy decor complements a menu that offers Mexican entrees, stir-fry dishes, goat cheese ravioli, and all points in between. (☎662-1111. Entrees $8-13. Open Su-Th 10am-9pm, F 10:30am-10pm, Sa 9am-10pm.) The truly hungry should head to **Casey's Tavern ❷,** 304 Depot St., across from the train station, for gigantic portions. The Caesar Steak Sandwich ($8) has locals and travelers alike raving. (☎665-6775. Sandwiches $6.65-8.25. Open M-Th 11am-11pm, F-Sa 11am-midnight.) **Krazy Jim's Blimpy Burger ❶,** 551 S. Division St., near campus, caters to the college crowd with gorgeously greasy "cheaper than food" burgers (from $1.70). Krazy Jim does not take kindly to poor ordering technique, so make sure to acquaint yourself with the "Helpful Hints for Blimpy Virgins" before stepping to the counter. (☎663-4590. Open daily 11am-10pm.)

SIGHTS & ENTERTAINMENT. Most of Ann Arbor's cultural attractions are provided by the university. The **University of Michigan Museum of Art (UMMA),** 525 S. State St., packs a collection of African and Chinese artifacts, early European painting, and pieces of American interior design into a small but stately building. Works by Picasso and Monet highlight the museum's cache. (☎763-8662; www.umich.edu/~umma. Open Tu-W and F-Sa 10am-5pm, Th 10am-9pm, Su noon-5pm. Free.) The **University of Michigan Exhibit Museum of Natural History,** 1109 Geddes Ave., displays T-Rex and Mastodon skeletons (Michigan's official state fossil) along with other exhibits on everything from anthropology to zoology. The planetarium offers indoor star-gazing on weekends. (☎764-0478; www.exhibits.lsa.umich/edu. Open M-Sa 9am-5pm, Su noon-5pm. Museum free; planetarium $3.50.) Outside the university, museum-goers who can't keep their hands to themselves will love the **Ann Arbor Hands-On Museum,** 220 E. Ann St., which houses four floors of exhibits designed to be touched, twisted, and turned. Let your inner child loose as you test the mechanics of a car, explore the technology behind the Internet, and make your way up a climbing wall. (☎995-5437; www.aahom.com. Open M-Sa 10am-5pm, Su noon-5pm. $7; students, seniors, and ages 2-17 $5.)

Artists and chefs peddle handmade paper, unique clothing, and gourmet food in a trio of historic brick buildings at the **Kerrytown shops,** on Detroit St. Browsing never hurts, even if the prices are a little steep. (☎662-5008. Open M-F 8am-7pm, Sa 7am-6pm, Su 9am-5pm.) In front of the shops, growers haul their crops, baked goods, and perennials to the popular **Farmers Market,** 315 Detroit St. (☎994-3276. Open May-Dec. W and Sa 7am-3pm; Jan.-Apr. Sa 8am-2pm.) Paintings and pottery take over the market space on Sundays, when local artists display their creations at the **Artisans Market.** (Open May-Dec. Su 11am-4pm.) Book lovers should scour the many **bookshops** along S. Main St. for unusual or inexpensive finds.

It's nigh impossible to get tickets for a Wolverine football game at U of M's 115,000 capacity stadium, but fans can give it a shot by calling the athletics office (☎764-0247). As tens of thousands of students depart for the summer, locals indulge in a little celebration. The **Ann Arbor Summer Festival** (☎647-2278) draws crowds from mid-June to early July for comedy, dance, and theater productions from national and local acts, as well as musical performances including jazz, country, and classical. The festival includes nightly outdoor performances followed by popular movies at **Top of the Park,** on top of the Fletcher St. parking structure, next to the Health Services Building. The **County Events Hotline** (☎930-6300) has more info, and the Visitor Center has schedules. In late July, thousands pack the city to view the work of nearly 600 artists at the **Ann Arbor Summer Art Fair** (☎995-7281; www.artfair.org). Classical music lovers should contact the **University Musical Society,** in the Burton Memorial Clock Tower at N. University and Thouper, for info on area performances. (☎764-2538 or 800-221-1229. Open M-F 10am-5pm. $12-67.)

NIGHTLIFE. Free in restaurants and music stores, the monthly *Current*, *Agenda*, *Weekender Entertainment*, and the weekly *Metrotimes* print up-to-date nightlife and entertainment listings. For BGLT info pick up a copy of *OutPost* or *Between the Lines*. The hottest spot in town for live music, the **Blind Pig,** 208 S. First St., feels its way through the night with rock 'n' roll, hip-hop, blues, and swing. (☎996-8555. 19+. Cover $3-10, under 21 $2 extra. Open daily 3pm-2am.) The **Firefly Club,** 207 S. Ashley St., offers an intimate setting for all varieties of jazz from traditional big band to modern avant garde. (☎665-9090. Latin jazz every Th. Su jazz brunch 10am-2pm. 21+. Cover $3-20. Open M-W 7pm-2am, Th-Sa 5pm-2am, Su 8pm-2am.) Tucked away under the Zydeco Cajun Restaurant, **The Bird of Paradise,** 312 S. Main St., straightens up and flies right with live jazz every night. (☎662-8310. Cover $3-25. Open daily 7:30pm-2am. Music starts at 8:30-9pm.) Mingle with locals and students at **Conor O'Neill's,** 318 S. Main St., Ann Arbor's "Best Pick-Up Joint," where the food and beer are as authentically Celtic as the bartenders. (☎665-2968.

Open daily 11am-2am.) **Ashley's,** 338 S. State St., is a beer drinker's heaven with over 60 brews on tap, all described in detail in the encyclopedic drinks menu. (☎996-9191. Pints $4.25-6. Open daily 11:30am-2am.)

GRAND RAPIDS ☎616

From its humble beginning as one of many fur trading posts, Grand Rapids worked hard to distinguish itself from its neighbors. While many towns stuck to their tourist friendly and time-warped aesthetics, Grand Rapids plowed ahead to become a city of concrete and tall buildings. In recent years, Grand Rapids has experienced something of a renaissance, branching out from its days as the "Furniture City" to become a diverse metropolis with a growing nightlife scene and fine museums. Close to both Chicago and Detroit, the city acts as a hub for travelers.

PRACTICAL INFORMATION. Most of Grand Rapids' streets are neatly gridded. The town is quartered by the north-south Division St. and the east-west Fulton St. **Amtrak,** 507 Wealthy St., at Market, has service to Chicago (4hr., 1 per day, $30). The station only opens when trains pass through. Tickets can be purchased at the station by credit card or on the train. **Greyhound,** 190 Wealthy St. (☎456-1709; station open daily 6:45am-10pm), connects to Ann Arbor (3hr., 1 per day, $18-21); Chicago (4½hr., 3 per day, $27-29); Detroit (3½-4½hr., 5 per day, $22.50). **Grand Rapids Transit Authority (GRATA),** 333 Wealthy St. SW, sends buses throughout the city and suburbs. (☎776-1100. Runs M-F 5:45am-11:15pm, Sa 6:30am-9:30pm, Su 8am-7:45am. $1.25, seniors $0.60; 10-ride pass $9.) **Taxi: Veterans Taxi,** ☎459-4646. The **Grand Rapids/Kent County Convention and Visitors Bureau,** 140 Monroe Center St., 3rd Fl. (☎459-8287 or 800-678-9859; www.visitgrandrapids.org; open M-F 9am-5pm) and the **West Michigan Tourist Association,** 1253 Front Ave. NW (☎456-8557 or 800-442-2084; www.wmta.org; open M-Th 8:30am-5pm, F 8:30am-6pm, Sa 9am-1pm), furnish general info. **Hotlines: Suicide, Drug, Alcohol, and Crisis Line,** ☎336-3535. Operates 24hr. **Internet Access: Grand Rapids Public Library,** 1100 Hynes SW, Ste. B (☎988-5400. Open summer M-Th 9am-9pm, F-Sa 9am-5:30pm, Su 1-5pm; low-season M-Th 9am-9pm, F-Sa 9am-5:30pm.) **Post Office:** 2929 Michael St. (☎532-2109. Open M-F 9am-5:30pm, Sa 9am-12:30pm.) **Postal Code:** 49503. **Area Code:** 616.

ACCOMMODATIONS. Be warned that there is a city ordinance that prohibits renting hotel rooms to people under 21. Most of the cheaper motels and restaurants are south of the city along Division and 28th St. **The Grand Rapids Inn ❷,** 250 28th St. SW, offers serviceable rooms with cable TV at rock-bottom prices. The motel is located on a busy road and the area can be noisy, but it's still one of the best deals in the area. (☎452-2131. Pool and free coffee. Singles from $33; doubles from $40.) Just 12 mi. northeast of downtown, **Grand Rogue Campgrounds ❶,** 6400 W. River Dr., has 82 wooded, riverside sites and offers fishing and kayaking opportunities. Take Rte. 131 north to Comstock Park Exit 91, then head left on W. River Dr. for 4 mi. (☎361-1053. Rustic sites $17.50, no hookups $22.50; with hookups $29.50.)

FOOD & NIGHTLIFE. Throngs of locals pack the **Beltline Bar and Café ❶,** 16 28th St. SE, for Grand Rapids' most popular Mexican food. "Wet" burritos, the house specialty, are drenched in Beltline's tasty burrito sauce and start at $5.69. (☎245-0494. Open M-W 7am-midnight, Th-Sa 10am-1am, Su noon-10:30pm.) The **Four Friends Coffeehouse ❶,** 136 Monroe Ctr., has excellent coffee concoctions (from $1.25), fresh muffins ($1.60), and delicious paninis ($4.75) in a trendy atmosphere. (☎456-5356. Live music F-Sa during the school year. Open June-Aug. M-Th 7am-10pm, F 7am-midnight, Sa 8am-midnight. Low-season open an hour later F and S.) Near Four Friends, the smell of freshly baked breads lures the lunch crowd into **Blake's Turkey Sandwich Shoppe ❶,** 102 Monroe Ctr., where you'll be giving thanks for the plentiful selection of tasty turkey sandwiches (from $4.85) and soups ($2). For those who can't wait until November, a full turkey dinner is served for just $6.30. (☎774-2220. Open M-F 7:30am-5:30pm, Sa 11am-3pm.) The **Grand Rapids Brewing Company ❷,** 3689 28th St. SE, makes tasty burgers ($6) and steaks. (☎285-5970. Handcrafted beer $3.50. Open M-Th 11am-midnight, F-Sa 11am-1am, Su 11am-11pm; kitchen closes Su-Th at 10pm, F-Sa at 11pm.)

Detailed listings on events and nightlife in Grand Rapids can be found in *On the Town* or *In the City;* both are available in most shops, restaurants, and kiosks. The artsy **Eastown District** once housed the bulk of the local music scene, but much of the nightlife has moved into the downtown area. The focal point of activity is now a set of chic bars and restaurants housed in the **B.O.B.** (Big Old Building), 20 Monroe Ave., a spacious brick structure with a balcony and plenty of bar space. Inside, **Bob's House of Brews** serves up the beers (W-Sa 5-10pm) and **Dr. Grins Comedy Club** takes care of the laughs. (Shows F 9pm, Sa 8, 10:30pm). Other options include a martini bar and a tapas restaurant, to name a few. Live performances go on every night in one or more of the spaces. (☎356-2000.) The wild **Diversions,** 10 Fountain St. NW, draws a primarily gay clientele, but clubbers of all types are drawn to the dance floor, where DJs spin every night from 10pm. The club also features a video bar and restaurant. (☎451-3800. Karaoke M, W, F-Sa 10pm. Ages 18-20 cover Su-Th $5, F-Sa $10; 21+ F-Sa $3. Open daily 8pm-2am.) For an the alternative crowd, there's a buzz at **Skelletone's,** 133 S. Division Ave., a "caffeinated music cafe" serving up late-night java with a stiff shot of punk rock. (☎356-1926. Covers $2-8. Open M-Tu and Sa 8pm-1am, W-Th 8pm-2am, F 8pm-3am.)

SIGHTS. The largest sculpture garden in the Midwest, the **Frederik Meijer Gardens and Sculpture Park,** 1000 E. Beltline NE, exhibits over 100 sculptures, from classical to modern abstract, among 125 acres of beautifully maintained gardens and nature trails. Inside, the conservatory harbors a tropical rainforest, a Victorian courtyard, and a display of weird and wonderful carnivorous plants. The collection highlight is the 24 ft. "American Horse," which pays homage to a lost Da Vinci sculpture. (☎957-1580; www.meijergardens.org. Open June-Aug. M-W and F-Sa 9am-5pm, Th 9am-9pm, Su noon-5pm; Sept.-May M-Sa 9am-5pm, Su noon-5pm. $8, seniors $7, students and ages 5-13 $4. Audio tours $1. Train tours $2, children $1. Depart 9:30am-4pm every ½ hr.) The riverfront **Public Museum of Grand Rapids,** 272 Pearl St. NW, showcases everything from automobiles to the history of housewifery, and includes such marvels as a 76 ft. whale skeleton, a large antique carousel, and a planetarium. The museum also offers an intriguing exhibit exploring the furniture industry that has long defined Grand Rapids. (☎456-3977; www.grmuseum.com. Open Tu-Sa 9am-5pm. $7, seniors $6, ages 3-17 $2.50. Carousel $1. Planetarium $2.) Across the street, **The Ford Museum,** 303 Pearl St. NW, pays homage to former US President Gerald Ford in his hometown. The museum focuses on the volatility of American culture during his presidency. Among the museum's highlights are a full-scale replica of the Oval office, a chance to deliver a campaign speech from a teleprompter, and the original tools used in the Watergate break-in. (☎451-9263; www.ford.utexas.org. Open daily 9am-5pm. $5, seniors $4, under 16 free.) Also downtown, the **Grand Rapids Art Museum,** 155 N. Division Ave., at Pearl St., boasts an impressive collection of works spanning from the Renaissance to modern art. (☎831-1001; www.gramonline.org. Open Su-Th 11am-6pm, F 11am-9pm. $6, students and seniors $5, ages 6-17 $3.) Architecture enthusiasts shouldn't miss the **Meyer May House,** 450 Madison Ave. SE, a 1908 Prairie School masterpiece that is considered the most complete Frank Lloyd Wright restoration in existence. (☎246-4821. Open Tu and Th 10am-2pm, usually Su 1-5pm. Tours depart Visitor's Center every hr. Free.)

LAKE MICHIGAN SHORE

The freighters that once powered the rise of Chicago still steam along the coast of Lake Michigan, but these days they are greatly outnumbered by pleasure boats cruising along the coast. Valleys of sand beckon sunbathers, while hikers trek through the virgin forests of Michigan's state parks. When autumn comes, the weather forbids swimming, but inland, nature takes over with a vibrant display of fruit harvests—from cherries in July to apples in September. Almost every town holds a festival celebrating a local fruit or blossom. Snow covers much of the coast in winter, drawing snowmobile, skiing, and ice skating enthusiasts. The coastline stretches 350 miles north from the Indiana border to the Mackinac Bridge; its southern end is a scant two hours from downtown Chicago.

PRACTICAL INFORMATION

Many of the region's attractions lie in the small coastal towns that cluster around **Grand Traverse Bay** in the north. **Traverse City,** at the southern tip of the bay, is famous as the "cherry capital of the world." Fishing is best in the Au Sable and Manistee Rivers. The main north-south route along the coast is U.S. 31. Numerous green "Lake Michigan Circle Tour" signs lead closer to the shoreline, providing an excellent view of the coast. Coastal accommodations can be quite expensive; for cheaper lodging, head inland. Determined travelers can occasionally find a good deal lakeside, and numerous camping options exist during the summer months. Based in Grand Rapids, the **West Michigan Tourist Association,** 1253 Front Ave. NW, hands out info on the area. (☎456-8557 or 800-442-2084; www.wmta.org. Open M-Th 8:30am-5pm, F 8:30am-6pm, Sa 9am-1pm.) **Area Code:** 616 and 231.

CENTRAL MICHIGAN SHORE

SLEEPING BEAR DUNES ☎231

The Sleeping Bear Dunes lie along the western shores of the Leelanau Peninsula, 20 mi. west of Traverse City on Rte. 72. The town of **Empire,** while not the metropolis its name implies, serves as the gateway to the **Sleeping Bear Dunes National Lakeshore,** an expanse including both the Manitou Islands and 25 mi. of lakeshore on the mainland. Near the historic Fishtown shops at the end of River St., **Manitou Island Transit,** in Leland, makes daily trips to South Manitou from June to August. (☎256-9061. Check-in 9:15am. May and Sept.-Oct. service M, W, F-Su. Daily trips to North Manitou July to mid-Aug. June 1-15 3 per week, June 15-30 5 per week. Call ahead for May and Sept.-Nov. schedule. Round-trip $25, under 12 $14. Reservations recommended.) **Camping** is available on both islands with the purchase of a **permit** ($5), though there is an entrance fee ($7 for 7 days; available at the Visitors Center). The Manitou Islands do not allow any wheeled vehicles, including cars and bikes. Hardcore **backpackers** looking for an adventure can camp on both Manitou islands. On South Manitou, a small village near the dock provides shopping and a rest area for day hikers. North Manitou Island travelers should take note—once the daily boat leaves for the day, hikers are cut off from the modern world until the next morning. *In bad weather, the ferry won't venture to the island until the weather clears, even if that is several days later.*

Willing climbers can be king of the sandhill at **Dune Climb,** 5 mi. north of Empire on Rte. 109. From there, a 2½ mi. hike over sandy hills leads to Lake Michigan. If you'd rather let your car do the climbing, drive to an overlook along the 7 mi. **Pierce Stocking Scenic Drive,** off Rte. 109 just north of Empire, where a 450 ft. sand cliff descends to the cool water below. (Open mid-May to mid-Oct. daily 9am-10pm.) For maps and info on the numerous cross-country skiing, hiking, and mountain biking trails in the lakeshore area, stop by the **National Parks Service Visitors Center,** 9922 Front St., in Empire. (☎326-5134. Open daily June-Aug. 9am-6pm; Sept.-May 9am-4pm.)

The Sleeping Bear Dunes have four **campgrounds: DH Day ❶** (☎334-4634), 1 mi. west of Glen Arbor on Rte. 109, with 88 primitive sites ($10); **Platte River ❶** (☎325-5881 or 800-365-2267), off the southern shore, with 179 sites and showers ($14, with electricity $19); and two backcountry campsites, **Whitepine ❶** and **Valley View ❶,** accessible by 1½-2½ mi. trails (no reservations; $5 permit required, available at Visitors Center or at any campground). The Platte River, at the southern end of the lakeshore, and the Crystal River, at the northern end, are ideal for canoeing or lazy floating. **Riverside Canoes,** 5042 Scenic Hwy. (Rte. 22), at Platte River Bridge, also organizes 2½hr. canoe and kayak excursions, as well as relaxed tubing trips. (☎325-5622; www.canoemichigan.com. Open May-early Oct. daily 8am-10pm. Inner tubes $6 for 1hr., $14 for 2hr.; canoes $30; kayaks $22. Includes shuttle to river. Prices higher for trips on more advanced Upper Rapids.)

GREAT LAKES

TRAVERSE CITY ☎231

Traverse City offers the summer vacationer a slew of sandy beaches and picturesque orchards—half of the nation's cherries are produced in the surrounding area. Swimming, boating, and scuba diving interests focus on Grand Traverse Bay, and the scenic waterfront makes for excellent biking. The **TART** bike trail runs 8 mi. along E. and W. Grand Traverse Bay, while the 30 mi. loop around Old Mission Peninsula, north of the city, provides great views of the Bay. **McLain Cycle and Fitness,** 750 E. 8th St. and 2786 Garfield Rd. N, rents bikes and other outdoor equipment and dispenses biking info. (☎941-7161. Open summer M-F 9am-6pm, Sa 9am-5pm, Su 11am-4pm; low-season closed Su. $10 per 2hr., $15 per day, $30 Sa-Su.)

Many attractions in Traverse City focus on the area's fruit. The annual **National Cherry Festival** (☎947-4230; www.cherryfestival.org), held the first full week in July, is a rousing tribute to the annual cherry harvest. In early to mid-July, five orchards near Traverse City let visitors pick their own cherries, including **Amon Orchards,** 10 mi. north on U.S. 31. (☎938-9160. Open daily 9am-6pm. $4 per quart.) More sophisticated fruit connoisseurs can indulge their taste buds at one of the area's many well-respected wineries. The scenic **Château Grand Traverse,** 12239 Center Rd., 8 mi. north of Traverse City on Rte. 37, has free tours and tastings. (☎223-7355 or 800-283-0247. Open June-Aug. M-Sa 10am-7pm, Su noon-6pm; May and Sept.-Oct. M-Sa 10am-6pm, Su noon-5pm; Nov.-Apr. M-Sa 10am-5pm, Su noon-5pm. Tours in summer every hr. noon-4pm. Call for low-season tour hours.)

East Front St. (U.S. 31) is lined with motels, but it is nearly impossible to find a room for under $50 in the busy summer months. One of the cheaper options is the **Restwood Motel ❸,** 1566 Hwy. 31, which offers small, serviceable rooms with cable TV and close proximity to the bay and state park. (☎938-1130. Rooms Su-Th from $30, F-Sa from $59; winter rates from $25.) **Northwestern Michigan College ❷,** 1701 E. Front St., West and East Halls, has some of the cheapest beds in the city. Rooms are sparsely furnished but offer all the comfort of college life, including laundry, a common room, and access to outdoor basketball courts, volleyball nets, and a track. (☎995-1409. Linen $10. Reserve several weeks in advance. Open early June-Aug. Singles $28; doubles $36; triples $45.) For those who prefer to commune with nature—or at least with 300 other campers—**Traverse City State Park ❶,** 1132 U.S. 31 N, 2 mi. east of town, has 344 wooded sites across the street from the beach. (☎922-5270 or 800-447-2757. Toilet and shower facilities. Sites with hookup $20; cabins $37. $4 vehicle permit fee.)

Front St. downtown offers a range of appealing food options. **Poppycock's ❷,** 128 E. Front St., is a vegetarian-friendly bistro that doles out gourmet sandwiches ($6.50-9) and pastas ($8-14). (☎941-7632. Open summer M-W 11am-10pm, Th 11am-midnight, F-Sa 11am-12:30pm, Su noon-8pm; low-season M-Th 11am-9pm, F-Sa 11am-10pm.)

The smell of freshly baked goods tempts the hungry into **The Omelette Shoppe ❷,** 124 Cass St. This bustling bakery and breakfast joint specializes in gooey cinnamon buns and 18 varieties of omelettes (around $6.50), including Italian-style frittatas. (☎946-0912. Pancakes $4-5. Sandwiches $5-7. Open M-F 6:30am-2:30pm, Sa-Su 7am-3pm. Another location at 1209 E. Front St. (☎946-0590), in the Campus Plaza complex. Open M-Sa 7am-3pm, Su 10am-3pm.) For all things cherry, from cherry pie to cherry salsa, head to the **Cherry Stop,** 211 E. Front St., a gourmet grocer and gift shop celebrating the city's favorite fruit. (☎929-3990 or 800-286-7209. Open M-Sa 10am-6pm, Su 11am-4pm.) No Anglophile should miss **Cousin Jenny's ❶,** 129 S. Union St., a purveyor of pasties that takes the portable meat pies back to their Cornish roots. Try the breakfast bobby, a 6 oz. pasty stuffed with eggs, hash browns, and other goodies. (☎941-7281. Pasties $4.59 for 10 oz., $5.59 for 16 oz. Open M-F 7:30am-6pm, Sa 7:30am-5pm. Bobbies served 7:30am-10:30am.) The **U & I Lounge,** 214 E. Front St., is the hottest bar in town, thanks in part to the tasty local beer. (☎946-8932. Sandwiches $5-6. Hot dogs $2.50. Open M-Sa 11am-2am, kitchen closes 1:35am; Su noon-2am, kitchen closes 1:15am.) For more entertainment info, pick up the weekly *Northern Express* at corner kiosks around the city.

Indian Trails and **Greyhound,** 3233 Cass Rd. (☎946-5180 or 800-231-2222), run to Detroit (8-9hr.; M and Th-Su 2 per day, Tu-W 1 per day; $46) and the Upper Peninsula via St. Ignace (3hr., 1 per day, $18). Call the **Bay Area Transportation Authority** and they'll pick you up; a 24hr. notice is preferred. (☎941-2324. Available M-Sa 6am-1:30am, Su 8am-1:30am. $2, seniors $1.) **Traverse City Convention and Visitors Bureau:** 101 West Grandview Pkwy. (U.S. 31 N). (☎947-1120 or 800-872-8377; www.tcvisitor.com. Open M-Sa 9am-6pm, Su 11am-3pm.) **Post Office:** 202 S. Union St. (☎946-9616. Open M-Sa 6am-7pm.) **Postal Code:** 49684. **Area Code:** 231.

NORTHERN MICHIGAN SHORE

STRAITS OF MACKINAC ☎231

Mackinac is pronounced "mack-i-NAW"; only fur'ners say "mack-i-NACK." The five-mile **Mackinac Bridge** ("Mighty Mac"), connecting **Mackinaw City** to St. Ignace in the Upper Peninsula, is the third longest suspension bridge in the US and the tenth longest in the world. A local tradition not to be missed is the annual **Labor Day Bridge Walk,** where Michigan's governor leads thousands across the bridge from Mackinaw City to St. Ignace. Near the bridge in Mackinaw City, **Colonial Michilimackinac Fort** still guards the straits between Lake Michigan and Lake Huron. (☎436-4100. Open daily early May to mid-Oct. 9am-5pm; mid-July to late Aug. 9am-6pm. $9, ages 6-17 $5.75.) **Historic Mill Creek,** which includes a working sawmill and nature trails, is located 3½ mi. south of Mackinaw City on Rte. 23. (☎436-4100. Open early May to mid-Oct. daily 9am-5pm; mid-July to late Aug. 9am-6pm. $7, ages 6-17 $4.25.) Historic Mill Creek, Fort Michilimackinac, and Fort Mackinac (on Mackinac Island, see p. 567) form a trio of State Historic Parks in the area. Colonial enthusiasts should buy a **Combination Pack,** good for seven days from date of purchase, for unlimited daily admission to all three. ($18, ages 6-17 $10.50. Available at all 3 sights.)

Lakeshore accommodation options abound on Rte. 23, south of the city. The best lodging deals in the area lie across the Mackinac Bridge on the **I-75 Business Loop** in St. Ignace. Five minutes from the docks, the **Harbor Light Motel ❷,** 1449 State St. on I-75, rents newly refurbished rooms with cable TV, A/C, and refrigerator. A volleyball net and the occasional bonfire on the beach make this a good bet for travelers. (☎906-643-9439. Summer singles $45; doubles $47. Low-season $30/32.) For an outdoor escape, campers can crash at one of the 600 sites of **Mackinac Mill Creek Campground ❶,** 3 mi. south of town on Rte. 23. The grounds provide beach access, fishing, and biking trails. Public showers, pool, and Internet access also on site. (☎436-5584. Sites $15; full hookup $17.50. Cabins $40.)

Family-oriented restaurants cluster around Central St., near Shepler's Dock in Mackinaw City. **Cunningham's ❸**, 312 E. Central St., serves huge homemade pasties ($6.50), pies, and fresh fish in a relaxed atmosphere. (☎436-8821. Dinner specials $8.50. Open May to mid-Oct. Open daily in spring 8am-8pm; summer 8am-10pm; in fall 8am-9pm.) At the laidback **Audie's ❷**, 314 N. Nicolet St., huge sandwiches ($6.50-8) at affordable prices keep visitors happy. For fine dining, try their **Chippewa Room,** which serves steaks and seafood ($14-34) in a more upscale setting. (☎436-5744. Open daily 7:30am-10pm. Chippewa Room open daily 5-10pm.) For the best pasties in town, head to the **Mackinaw Pastie & Cookie Co. ❶**, 117 W. Jamet St., two blocks south of Colonial Michilimackinac, which serves up six variations of the U.P.'s favorite meat pie. (☎231-436-8202. Pasties $4.55-6.10. Open daily 9am-9pm. Other location at 516 S. Huron.)

For transportation outside the city, **Indian Trails** (☎800-292-3831 or 800-231-2222) has a flag stop at City Hall, 102 S. Huron. One bus runs north and one south each day; buy tickets at the next station. The **Michigan Department of Transportation Welcome and Travel Information Center,** on Nicolet St. off I-75 at Exit 338, has loads of helpful info on lodging, food, and area attractions. (☎436-5566. Open daily mid-June to Aug. 8am-6pm; Sept. to mid-June 9am-5pm. Free reservation service.)

GREAT LAKES

MACKINAC ISLAND ☎231

Mackinac Island, a 16min. ferry ride from the mainland, has long been considered one of Michigan's greatest treasures. Victorian homes and the prohibition of cars on the heavily touristed island—and the resulting proliferation of horse-drawn carriages—give Mackinac an aristocratic air with a decidedly equine aroma. Travelers flock to the island for its stunning parks, museums, and coastal, old-world charm. Escape the touristy Main St. for a quiet look at what made the island popular in the first place—its beautiful fauna and rolling hills.

Fort Mackinac is one of the island's main draws. (☎436-4100. Open daily early May to mid-Oct. 9:30am-6pm; mid-July to late Aug. 9am-7pm. $9, ages 6-17 $5.75, under 6 free.) Tickets to the Fort also allow access to four museums of island history that are housed in refurbished period buildings. Travelers with a sweet tooth flock to the birthplace of Mackinac Fudge (½ lb. $5.50), the tantalizing aroma of which wafts out of storefronts all over the island and along the entire Michigan coastline. **Mackinac Island Carrige Tours,** Main St., cart guests on tours all over the island in horse-drawn buggies, showcasing architectural wonders such as the ritzy Grand Hotel. (☎906-847-3307; www.mict.com. Open daily 9am-5pm. $16.50, ages 4-11 $7.50.) For those who would rather take the reins in their own hands, **Jack's Livery Stable,** off Grande Ave. on Mahoney Ave., rents saddle horses and horses with buggies. (☎847-3391. Saddle horses $30 first hr., $25 each additional hr. 2-person horse and buggie $45 per hr.) Bicycles are the best way to see the island's beaches and forests. Rental shops line Main St. by the ferry docks and generally offer identical rates. ($4 per hr., $20 per day.) Encompassing 80% of the island, **Mackinac Island State Park** features a circular 8¼ mi. shoreline road for biking and hiking.

Hotel rates on the island are exorbitantly high; the mainland is the place to stay. For food, **Mighty Mac ❶**, Main St., cooks it cheap, with ¼ lb. burgers for under $4. (☎847-8039. Open daily 8am-8pm.) The **Pink Pony ❸**, also on Main St., serves handmade pastas, fresh salads, and fish dishes under the watchful eye of the pink-colored horses on the wall. (☎906-847-3341. Entrees from $10. Open daily 8am-10pm.)

Transportation to the island via ferry is quick and pleasant, providing terrific views of the Mackinac Bridge. Three ferry lines leave Mackinaw City (in summer every 30min. Su-Th 8am-10pm, F-Sa 8am-11pm) and St. Ignace with overlapping schedules, though service from St. Ignace is less frequent. **Shepler's** (☎800-828-6157) offers the fastest service. Catamarans operated by **Arnold Transit Co.** are also a fun way to jet to the island. (☎847-3351 or 800-542-8528. Check at the ticket counter for exact times. Round-trip $16, under 16 $8; bikes $6.50.) The invaluable *Mackinac Island Locator*

Map ($1) and the *Discover Mackinac Island* book ($2) can be found at the **Mackinac Island Chamber of Commerce and Visitors Center,** on Main St. (☎906-847-3783; www.mackinacisland.org. Open daily June-Sept. 8am-6pm; Oct.-May 9am-5pm.)

SCENIC DRIVE: NORTHERN MICHIGAN SHORE DRIVE

Cherry trees, tranquil lake shores, and intimate resort villages dot the Northern Michigan Shore. Once used by Native Americans and French traders to peddle goods, the route now guides visitors through the diversity of Michigan's natural beauty. Heading north, the drive begins in Michigan's coastal beach communities before moving through lush forest.

U.S. 31 winds its way 65 mi. north from Traverse City to Petoskey, where the tortuous Rte. 119 takes over and completes the 31 mi. journey to Cross Village. It takes about 3hr. to do justice to the drive, stopping along the way to admire both the natural and fabricated wonders that line the route. Although the roads are generally well maintained, drivers should exercise special caution on the spectacular 27 mi. stretch of Rte. 119 between Cross Village and Harbor Springs, known as the **Tunnel of Trees.** This patch of road is extremely narrow and twists through many sharp curves, necessitating slow speeds and care in passing.

North of Traverse City, tiny towns form the center of picturesque orchard communities. Twelve miles outside of the city, lush cherry orchards line the road around **Acme.** Twenty miles north of Acme, then west on Barnes Park Rd., the village of **Torch Lake** harbors pristine, isolated beaches on **Grand Traverse Bay** at **Barnes County Park.** More cherry trees line the route north of **Atwood,** one of the most prolific areas of the cherry harvest. Though many towns along the route are easily missed, they are worth the stop; many have small antique and unique clothing shops.

Rolling hills and increasingly elaborate homes mark the entrance into **Charlevoix** (SHAR-le-voy), a resort village that inhabits the narrow strip of land between Lake Michigan and Lake Charlevoix. The resort community that once served as the setting for Ernest Hemingway's Nick Adams stories now inspires yachting and sunbathing. The **Charlevoix Area Chamber of Commerce,** 408 Bridge St., dispenses info on golfing, boating, and shopping in the area. (☎547-2101; www.charlevoix.org. Open M-F 9am-5pm, Sa 10am-4pm.) Lodging rarely comes cheap in this coastal resort town, but the **Colonial Motel ❷,** 6822 U.S. 31 S, is a good option offering cable TV, use of grill and picnic area, and easy access to the state park. (☎547-6637. Open May-Oct. Singles Su-Th $35-45, F-Sa $65-75; low-season rates lower. Special rates for longer stays.) Campers who don't mind doing without showers and electricity can bask in 81 rustic sites on the shores of Lake Michigan at **Fisherman's Island State Park ❶,** on Bells Bay Rd., 5 mi. south of Charlevoix on U.S. 31. The park offers 5 mi. of undeveloped shoreline and rewards hikers who trek through the forest with a spectacular beach. (☎547-6641 or 800-447-2757. Rustic sites $6; vehicle permit $4.) Charlevoix also serves as the gateway to **Beaver Island,** one of the the Great Lakes' best-kept secrets. Hiking, boating, biking, and swimming abound on the 53 sq. mi. island, a 2hr. ferry trip from shore. **Ferries** depart from 102 Bridge St., in Charlevoix. (☎547-2311 or 888-446-4095; www.bibco.com. 1-4 per day. Round-trip $33, ages 5-12 $17; bikes $16.) The **Beaver Island Chamber of Commerce** can be found just north of the ferry dock. (☎448-2505; www.beaverisland.org. Open summer M-F 8am-4pm, Sa 10:30am-2:30pm; low-season M-F 8am-noon.)

PETOSKEY ☎231

Eighteen miles north of Charlevoix, the slightly larger resort town of Petoskey is best known for its Petoskey Stones—fossilized coral from an ancient sea that remain strewn about the area's beaches. Another vacation haunt of Hemingway, the town honors him with a small collection of memorabilia, including signed first editions, childhood photos, and a typewriter, at the **Little Traverse History Museum,**

100 Depot Ct. (☎347-2620. Open summer M-F 10am-4pm, Sa-Su 1-4pm. $1. Students and children free.) Nearby, off northbound U.S. 31, the gazebo and grassy areas of **Sunset Park Scenic Overlook** are unbeatable places to watch the sunset.

Budget accommodations are hard to come by, but the major chains clump at the junction of U.S. 31 and U.S. 131. If you don't mind roughing it, the **Petoskey State Park ❶,** 5 mi. north of downtown off Rte. 191, has 160 sites along the Little Traverse Bay. (☎347-2311 or 800-447-2757. Open April-early Nov. Sites with electrical hookup $20. Cabins $32.) Petoskey's **Gaslight District,** just off U.S. 31 downtown, features local crafts and foods in period shops. In the heart of the district, an outdoor collage of coffee cups lures the hungry into the **Roast and Toast Cafe ❶,** 309 E. Lake St. Large sandwiches ($4.25-6) and a huge array of coffee concoctions and Italian sodas (from $1.50) ensure that everyone leaves satisfied. (☎347-7767. Open mic Su 6-8pm. Open M-Th 7am-7pm, F-Su 7am-8pm.) The **City Park Grill ❷,** 432 E. Lake St., sells sandwiches ($6-8) in an elegant setting befitting the quaint town. (☎347-0101. Live music W-Sa 10pm. Cover $3 Th-Sa. Kitchen open Su-Th 11:30am-10pm, F-Sa 11:30am-11pm; bar closes Su-W midnight, W 1am, Th-Sa 2am.)

Although it lies 20 mi. east of Petoskey in a remote woodland just outside Indian River, the **Cross in the Woods,** 7078 Rte. 68 (☎238-8973), is worth seeing. A 31 ft. bronze Jesus, cleaved onto a 55 ft. tall wooden cross, forms a monument to both the religious fervor of Middle America and the country's obsession with size.

UPPER PENINSULA

A multi-million-acre forestland bordered by three of the world's largest lakes, Michigan's Upper Peninsula (U.P.) is among the most scenic, unspoiled stretches of land in the world. Vacationers in the Upper Peninsula escape urban life in a region where cell phones don't work and locals laugh if you ask about nearest Internet access. Dominated by the **Hiawatha National Forest,** the U.P. is a wonderland of hiking, biking, hunting, and kayaking. Those who are less adventurous can enjoy the countless scenic outlooks in the region's parks. Deposits of copper have colored the cliffs with a tapestry of colors that draws visitors from all over the state.

Only 24,000 people live in the U.P.'s largest town, **Marquette.** Here hikers enjoy numerous treks, including Michigan's section of the **North Country Trail,** a scenic trail extending from New York to North Dakota. The **North Country Trail Association,** 49 Monroe Ctr. NW, Ste. 200B, Grand Rapids 49503 (☎616-454-5506), provides details on the path. A vibrant spectrum of foliage makes autumn a beautiful time to hike; in the winter, skiers and snowmobilers replace hikers as layers of snow blanket the trails. After the ice thaws, dozens of pristine rivers beckon canoers. Those who heed the call of the water should contact the **Michigan Association of Paddlesport Providers,** P.O. Box 270, Wellston 49689 (☎231-862-3227), for canoeing tips.

Outside the major tourist towns, motel rooms in the U.P. generally start around $24. The peninsula has 200 **campgrounds** (☎800-447-2757; www.michigan.gov/dnr). Bring extra blankets—temperatures in these parts drop to 50°F, even in July. For regional cuisine, indulge in the Friday night **fish-fry**—all-you-can-eat whitefish, perch, or walleye buffets served in most restaurants. The local ethnic specialty is a **pasty** (*PASS-tee*), a meat pie imported by Cornish miners in the 19th century.

PRACTICAL INFORMATION

Helpful **Welcome Centers** surround the U.P. at its six main entry points: **Ironwood,** 801 W. Cloverland Dr. (☎932-3330; open daily June-Sept. 8am-6pm; Oct.-May 8am-4pm); **Iron Mountain,** 618 S. Stephenson Ave. (☎774-4201; open daily 8am-4pm); **Menominee,** 1343 10th Ave. (☎863-6496; open daily 8am-4pm); **Marquette,** 2201 U.S. 41 S (☎249-9066; open daily 9am-6pm); **Sault Sainte Marie,** 943 Portage Ave. W (☎632-

8242; open daily 9am-5pm); and **Saint Ignace,** on I-75 N north of the Mackinac Bridge (☎643-6979; open daily June-Aug. 8am-6pm; Sept.-May 9am-5pm). The **Upper Peninsula Travel and Recreation Association** (☎800-562-7134; info line staffed M-F 8am-4:30pm) publishes the invaluable *Upper Peninsula Travel Planner.* For additional help planning a trip, write or call the **US Forestry Service** at the **Hiawatha National Forest,** 2727 N. Lincoln Rd., Escanaba 49829 (☎786-4062). **Area Code:** 906.

SAULT SAINTE MARIE & THE EASTERN U.P. ☎906

The shipping industry rules in gritty Sault ("Soo") Ste. Marie, where "the locks" are the primary attraction for both tourists and prospective residents. Back in the day, St. Mary's River, the only waterway linking Lake Superior to the other Great Lakes, dropped 21 vertical feet over one mile in this area, rendering the river impassable by boat. In 1855, entrepreneurs built the first modern locks, an advancement that opened up industrial opportunities that led the region to relative economic prosperity. Now the busiest in the world, the city's four locks float over 12,000 ships annually, lowering them through successive, emptying chambers. Raging rapids still exist on the Canadian side of the river, juxtaposing the tamed water of the locks, but a plan is currently underway to build two new locks there.

On the American side of the bridge, a 2hr. **Soo Locks Boat Tour** leaves from both 1157 and 515 E. Portage Ave., and introduces travelers to the mechanics of the locks' operation. (☎632-6301 or 800-432-6301; www.soolocks.com. Call for departure times. Open mid-May to mid-Oct. $18, ages 13-18 $16, ages 4-12 $8.50, under 4 free. Call ahead for specific dock.) The **Soo Locks Park,** accessed from Portage Ave., gives visitors a close-up view of the 1000 ft. supertankers that use the locks. (Open daily 6am-midnight). For a panoramic view of the locks, visitors can ascend the **Tower of History,** 326 E. Portage Ave., which has three levels of observation decks and exhibits tracing the city's history. (☎632-3658. Open daily mid-May to mid-Oct. 10am-6pm. $4, ages 13-18 $2.) On the waterfront, at the end of Johnston St., lies the **Museum Ship Valley Camp,** a 1917 steam-powered freighter turned tribute to the sailing industry. A theater and the **Marine Hall of Fame** highlight the museum. (☎632-3658. Open daily July-Aug. 10am-8pm; mid-May to June and Sept. to mid-Oct. 10am-6pm. $8, ages 6-16 $4.) The **Soo Locks Visitor Center,** 300 W. Portage Ave. in the park, dispenses info. (☎253-9101. Open May-Nov. daily 7am-11pm).

MIDDLE OF THE PENINSULA ☎906

The western branch of the **Hiawatha National Forest** dominates the middle of the Peninsula, offering limitless wilderness activities and rustic **campsites ❶.** (Pit toilets, no showers; first come, first served. Sites $7-11.) **Rapid River,** on Rte. 2, is home to the southern office of the western branch of Hiawatha National Forest. Those looking for comic relief should stop by **Da Yooper's Tourist Trap,** 490 N. Steel St., 12 mi. west of Marquette on U.S. 41. This little theme park is the ultimate collection of tacky Americana. The lawn holds the world's largest operational chainsaw and biggest rifle, while the backyard pays homage to Yoopers (U.P. residents) of the past. (☎800-628-9978. Open M-F 9am-9pm, Sa 9am-8pm, Su 9am-7pm. Free.)

In the north, the lakefront town of **Munising,** on Rte. 28, accesses the forest and the not-to-be-missed **Pictured Rocks National Lakeshore,** where water saturated with copper, manganese, and iron oxide paints the cliffs with multicolored bands. Various overlooks within the park offer spectacular glimpses of the rocks, but the **Pictured Rocks Boat Cruise,** at the city dock in Munising, gives the best view. (☎387-2379; www.picturedrocks.com. 3hr. tour $25, ages 6-13 $10, under 6 free; rates subject to change.) The forest and lakeshore share a **Visitors Center** at the intersection of M-28 and Rte. 58 in Munising. (☎387-3700. Open mid-May to mid-Oct. daily 8am-6pm; mid-Oct. to mid-May M-Sa 9am-4:30pm.) Heading east from Munising, Rte. 58—a bumpy, partially unpaved gem of a road—weaves along the lakeshore, eventually ending up in Grand Marais. Ask about road conditions at the Visitors Center.

For a paved (but less scenic) alternative from Munising to Grand Marais, go east on Rte. 28, then north on Rte. 77. **Miner's Falls,** 10 mi. east of Munising off Rte. 58, rewards visitors with a staggering, rocky waterfall. Two miles farther up the road, **Miner's Castle Overlook** allows trekkers to walk up to the edge of the cliffs and see the colorful rocks across the deep blue water of the lake. Twenty miles east of Miner's Castle off Rte. 58, visitors can stroll, birdwatch, or collect smooth stones along the shore at **Twelve Mile Beach ❶.** (Running water, toilets. Self-registered rustic campsites $10.) From atop the sandy **Log Slide,** 5 mi. west of Grand Marais on Rte. 58, hikers are rewarded with a magnificent view of Lake Superior.

As an alternative to the campsites at Twelve Mile Beach, **backcountry camping permits ❶** for 1-6 people ($15) are available from the **Munising** or **Grand Sable Visitors Center,** 2 mi. west of Grand Marais on Rte. 58. (☎494-2660. Open mid-May to early Oct. daily 9am-7pm.) For non-campers, the **Poplar Bluff Cabins ❷,** Star Rte. Box 3118, 12 mi. east of Munising on Rte. 28, then 6 mi. south from Shingleton on Rte. 94, have small, functional lakeview cottages with kitchens. (☎452-6271. Free use of boats on lake. Cabins $50-60 per night, $350 per week.)

West of the city, the uncrowded eastern branch of the Hiawatha offers unparalleled natural attractions. At **Tahquamenon Falls State Park** (☎492-3415), on Rte. 123, the Upper and Lower Falls cascade down copper tinted cliffs. Amateur voyageurs can explore the Lower Falls via **canoe** ($10 per half-day) or **rowboat** ($12 per person). The less daring can gawk at the 50 ft. Upper Falls. North of Tahquamenon, over **300 shipwrecks** protected in an Underwater Preserve lie off **Whitefish Point,** affording divers an unbeatable opportunity to search for sunken treasure. Those who like to stay dry can explore the history of maritime disaster in the **Shipwreck Museum,** which contains descriptions of ships that have fallen victim to Lake Superior's fury, as well as artifacts from the wrecks. (☎888-492-3747 or 800-635-1742; www.shipwreckmuseum.com. Open May-Oct. daily 10am-6pm. $8.50, children $5.50; families $23.) The town of **Paradise,** at the eastern border of the Hiawatha, serves as the entrance point to the Shipwreck Museum, lighthouse, and beaches.

KEWEENAW PENINSULA ☎906

As the northern-most part of Michigan, the Keweenaw (KEE-wa-naw) Peninsula—with its lush forests, low mountains, and smooth stone beaches—doesn't seem like part of the Midwest. The peninsula once basked in the glory of a copper mining boom, but when mining petered out, the land was left barren and exploited. Now, with the help of reforestation efforts, Keweenaw has become a haven for outdoor enthusiasts. Towering pines shade hiking trails while state parks provide beaches and camping grounds for those looking to get back to nature. In the winter, visitors don skis and snowshoes to trek across the mountains.

The **Porcupine Mountain Wilderness State Park ❶,** affectionately known as "The Porkies," hugs Lake Superior at the base of the peninsula. (☎885-5275. Reservations required for cabins. Rustic sites $9; with toilets, showers, and electricity at the Union $19; 2- to 8-person rustic cabins $45-55.) The **Visitors Center,** near the junction of Rte. 107 and South Boundary Rd. inside the park, provides required **permits** good for all Michigan state parks. (☎885-5208. Open mid-May to mid-Oct. daily 10am-6pm. Permits $4 per day, $20 per yr.) Eight miles inside the park on Rte. 107, **Lake of the Clouds** outlook leads visitors to a ledge, where woods give way to a view of the lake etching out a path between rugged cliffs and mountains in the Big Carp River valley. **Summit Peak,** off South Boundary Rd., allows visitors to ascend a lookout tower offering stunning vistas of Lake Superior and the untouched forests of the park. Farther east, at the end of South Boundary Rd., the **Presque Isle Falls** are a great place to relax and listen to the water rushing past. From the park, paths lead into the **Old Growth Forest,** the largest tract of uncut forest between the Rockies and the Adirondacks. Among the most popular trails is the **Lake Superior Trail** (17 mi.), which traces the lakefront before reaching the falls.

The twin towns of **Houghton** and **Hancock** link the Porkies to the rest of Keweenaw. Eight miles north of Hancock on Rte. 203, **McLain State Park** ❶ is home to some of the area's best camping. The campground rests along a 2 mi. agate beach and harbors an impressive lighthouse. (☎482-0278. 103 sites with electricity $19; cabins $37-50. Required vehicle permit $4 per day.) From the state park, U.S. 41 winds north through Keweenaw. Drivers and bikers can take Rte. 26, off Rte. 41, to access the most scenic path to the tip of the peninsula, winding through small lakeside villages and desolate ghost towns where copper miners once toiled. Rising 1337 ft. above sea level, the breathtaking **Brockway Mountain Drive** (6 mi.), between Eagle Harbor and Copper Harbor, offers a panoramic view of the pine-covered peaks and lake-filled valleys of the Upper Peninsula. In **Copper Harbor,** the northernmost town in Michigan, the **Keweenaw Adventure Company,** 145 Gratiot St., provides kayaks and bikes to those who wish to explore the wild side of Keweenaw. (☎289-4303. 2½hr. intro paddle $29; bike rentals $27 for half day, $40 per day.)

ILLINOIS

At first glance, Illinois is a state with dual personalities. In the northern part of the state, Chicago gleams as a Midwestern metropolis with top-notch museums, stunning architecture, and suburban sprawl stretching into two neighboring states. Once removed from suburbia, a second Illinois—the "Land of Lincoln"—reaches outward with endless corn fields and small towns. Illinois, in its politics and its culture, is a compromise between these contrasting landscapes, and can claim to exist as a mix of urban chic and rural values as perhaps no other state can.

PRACTICAL INFORMATION

Capital: Springfield.

Visitor Info: Illinois Office of Tourism, 77 E. Randolph Ave., Chicago 60607 (☎800-226-6632; www.enjoyillinois.com). **Springfield Office of Tourism,** 109 N. 7th St., Springfield 62701 (☎800-545-7300).

Postal Abbreviation: IL. **Sales Tax:** 6.25-8.75%, depending on the city.

CHICAGO ☎312

From the renowned museums and shopping that dot the downtown lakefront to the varied and vibrant music and comedy scenes, Chicago's charms please almost any visitor. Retaining some of the flavor of its industrial legacy, Chicago today is both a contemporary city and a place acutely aware of its historical roots. A symbol of industrialized city life in middle America since the late 1800s, Chicago continues to wear the mantle admirably—travelers can expect to find a city of many voices, diverse neighborhoods, and spectacular food and entertainment options.

INTERCITY TRANSPORTATION

Airports: O'Hare International (☎773-686-2200; www.ohare.com), off I-90. Although O'Hare is only 18 mi. away, the drive from downtown can take up to 2hr., depending on traffic. The Blue Line **Rapid Train** runs between the Airport El station and downtown (40min.-1hr., $1.50). **Midway Airport** (☎773-767-0500), on the western edge of the South Side, often offers less expensive flights. To get downtown, take the El Orange Line from the Midway stop. **Airport Express** (☎888-284-3826) connects to downtown hotels from O'Hare (45min.-1hr., daily every 5-10min. 6am-11:30pm, $20) and Midway (30-45min., every 10-15min. M-F 6am-10:30pm, Sa-Su 6am-11pm; $15).

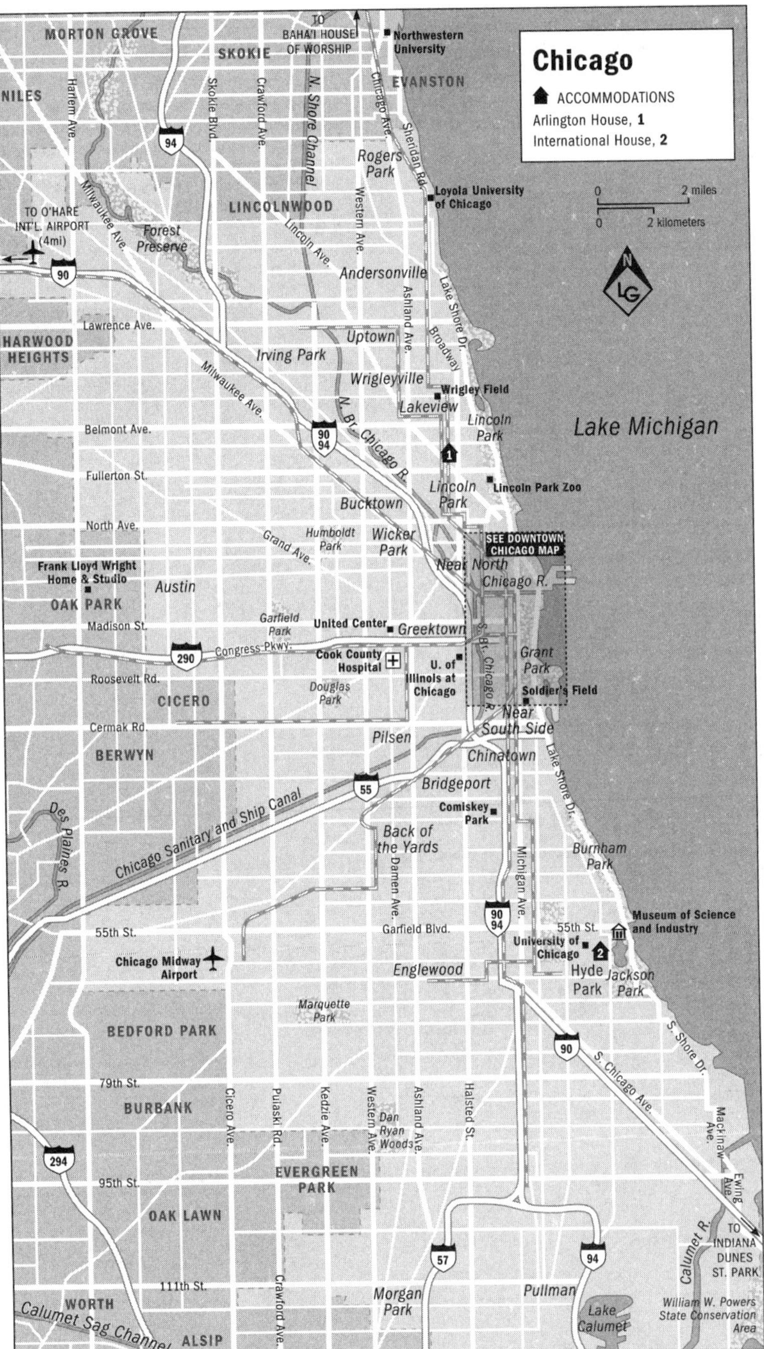
Chicago
ACCOMMODATIONS
Arlington House, 1
International House, 2
0
2 miles
0
2 kilometers
N
LG
Lake Michigan
MORTON GROVE
SKOKIE
TO BAHA'I HOUSE OF WORSHIP
Northwestern University
EVANSTON
NILES
Harlem Ave.
Skokie Blvd.
Crawford Ave.
N. Shore Channel
Chicago Ave.
Sheridan Rd.
94
Rogers Park
Loyola University of Chicago
LINCOLNWOOD
Western Ave.
TO O'HARE INT'L. AIRPORT (4mi)
Milwaukee Ave.
Forest Preserve
Lincoln Ave.
90
Andersonville
Ashland Ave.
Lake Shore Dr.
Lawrence Ave.
HARWOOD HEIGHTS
Uptown
Broadway
Irving Park
Wrigleyville
Wrigley Field
Milwaukee Ave.
Lakeview
Lincoln Park
Belmont Ave.
90
94
N. Br. Chicago R.
1
Fullerton St.
Lincoln Park
Lincoln Park Zoo
Bucktown
North Ave.
Grand Ave.
Humboldt Park
Wicker Park
SEE DOWNTOWN CHICAGO MAP
Frank Lloyd Wright Home & Studio
Near North
Chicago R.
Austin
OAK PARK
Garfield Park
United Center
Greektown
Madison St.
290
Congress Pkwy.
Cook County Hospital
U. of Illinois at Chicago
S. Br. Chicago R.
Grant Park
Roosevelt Rd.
Douglas Park
Soldier's Field
CICERO
Near South Side
Cermak Rd.
Pilsen
BERWYN
Chinatown
Lake Shore Dr.
55
Bridgeport
Chicago Sanitary and Ship Canal
Comiskey Park
Des Plaines R.
Back of the Yards
Damen Ave.
Michigan Ave.
Burnham Park
Museum of Science and Industry
90
94
55th St.
Garfield Blvd.
55th St.
University of Chicago
2
Chicago Midway Airport
Englewood
Hyde Park
Jackson Park
Marquette Park
BEDFORD PARK
90
S. Shore Dr.
S. Chicago Ave.
79th St.
BURBANK
Cicero Ave.
Pulaski Rd.
Kedzie Ave.
Western Ave.
Dan Ryan Woods
Ashland Ave.
Halsted St.
Mackinaw Ave.
294
EVERGREEN PARK
Ewing Ave.
95th St.
OAK LAWN
TO INDIANA DUNES ST. PARK
Calumet R.
57
94
111th St.
Crawford Ave.
Morgan Park
Pullman
WORTH
William W. Powers State Conservation Area
Lake Calumet
Calumet Sag Channel
ALSIP

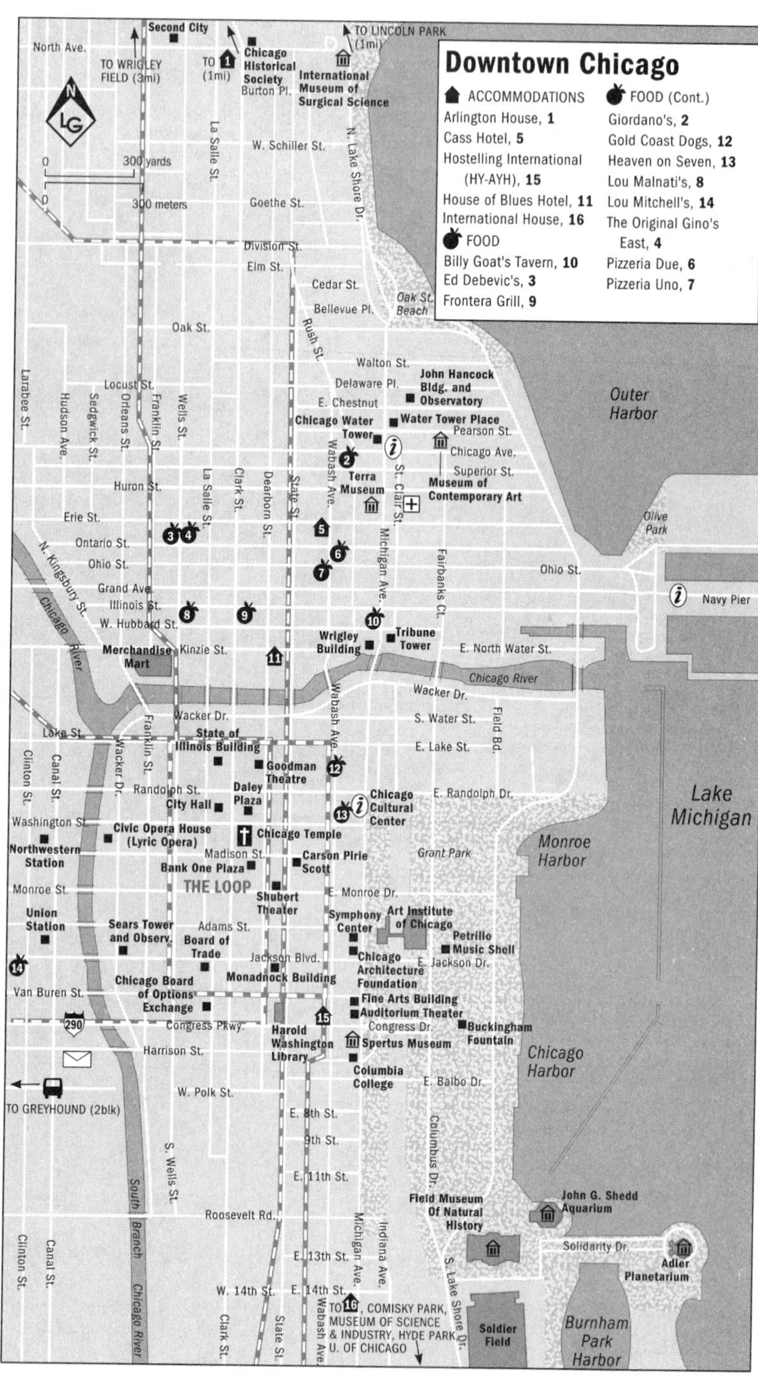
Downtown Chicago
ACCOMMODATIONS
Arlington House, 1
Cass Hotel, 5
Hostelling International (HY-AYH), 15
House of Blues Hotel, 11
International House, 16
FOOD
Billy Goat's Tavern, 10
Ed Debevic's, 3
Frontera Grill, 9
FOOD (Cont.)
Giordano's, 2
Gold Coast Dogs, 12
Heaven on Seven, 13
Lou Malnati's, 8
Lou Mitchell's, 14
The Original Gino's East, 4
Pizzeria Due, 6
Pizzeria Uno, 7
Second City
TO WRIGLEY FIELD (3mi)
TO (1mi)
Chicago Historical Society
International Museum of Surgical Science
TO LINCOLN PARK (1mi)
North Ave.
Burton Pl.
W. Schiller St.
Goethe St.
Division St.
Elm St.
Cedar St.
Bellevue Pl.
Oak St. Beach
Oak St.
Walton St.
Delaware Pl.
E. Chestnut
John Hancock Bldg. and Observatory
Water Tower Place
Chicago Water Tower
Pearson St.
Chicago Ave.
Superior St.
Terra Museum
Museum of Contemporary Art
Huron St.
Erie St.
Ontario St.
Ohio St.
Grand Ave.
Illinois St.
W. Hubbard St.
Kinzie St.
Merchandise Mart
Wrigley Building
Tribune Tower
E. North Water St.
Chicago River
Wacker Dr.
S. Water St.
E. Lake St.
Lake St.
State of Illinois Building
Goodman Theatre
Randolph St.
Daley Plaza
City Hall
Chicago Cultural Center
E. Randolph Dr.
Washington St.
Civic Opera House (Lyric Opera)
Chicago Temple
Northwestern Station
Madison St.
Bank One Plaza
Carson Pirie Scott
Grant Park
Monroe St.
THE LOOP
Shubert Theater
E. Monroe Dr.
Union Station
Sears Tower and Observ.
Adams St.
Board of Trade
Symphony Center
Art Institute of Chicago
Petrillo Music Shell
Jackson Blvd.
Chicago Architecture Foundation
E. Jackson Dr.
Monadnock Building
Chicago Board of Options Exchange
Van Buren St.
Fine Arts Building
Auditorium Theater
Congress Pkwy.
Congress Dr.
Buckingham Fountain
Harold Washington Library
Spertus Museum
Harrison St.
Columbia College
E. Balbo Dr.
TO GREYHOUND (2blk)
W. Polk St.
E. 8th St.
9th St.
E. 11th St.
Roosevelt Rd.
Field Museum of Natural History
John G. Shedd Aquarium
Solidarity Dr.
Adler Planetarium
E. 13th St.
W. 14th St.
E. 14th St.
TO 16, COMISKY PARK, MUSEUM OF SCIENCE & INDUSTRY, HYDE PARK, U. OF CHICAGO
Soldier Field
Burnham Park Harbor
Chicago Harbor
Monroe Harbor
Lake Michigan
Outer Harbor
Olive Park
Navy Pier
Ohio St.
Field Bd.
Columbus Dr.
S. Lake Shore Dr.
N. Lake Shore Dr.
Fairbanks Ct.
St. Clair St.
Michigan Ave.
Indiana Ave.
Wabash Ave.
State St.
Dearborn St.
Clark St.
La Salle St.
Wells St.
S. Wells St.
Franklin St.
Orleans St.
Sedgwick St.
Hudson Ave.
Larabee St.
Locust St.
N. Kingsbury St.
Rush St.
Wacker Dr.
Clinton St.
Canal St.
South Branch Chicago River
0 300 yards
0 300 meters
290

Trains: Amtrak, Union Station, 225 S. Canal St. (☎558-1075), at Adams St. just west of the Loop. Amtrak's nationwide hub. Getting there by bus is easiest; buses #1, 60, 125, 151, and 156 all stop at the station. Otherwise, take the El to State and Adams St., then walk 7 blocks west on Adams. Luggage storage at desk $1.50 per day. Station open 6:30am-9:30pm; tickets sold daily 6am-9pm. To: **Detroit** (8hr., 3 per day, $31-57); **Milwaukee** (1½hr., 6 per day, $20); **New York** (20hr., 2 per day, $90-165).

Buses: Greyhound, 630 W. Harrison St. (☎408-5980), at Jefferson and Desplaines Ave. Take the El to Linton, or buses #60, 125, 156, or 157 to the terminal. Station and ticket office open 24hr. To: **Detroit** (6-7hr., 7 per day, $27-35); **Indianapolis** (3½-4½hr., 10 per day, $29-31); **Milwaukee** (2hr., 12 per day, $14). **Van Gelder** in Union Station (☎608-752-5407 or 800-747-0994) runs to **Madison** (3-4hr., 4 per day, $22).

ORIENTATION

Chicago has overtaken the entire northeastern corner of Illinois, running along 29 mi. of the southwest Lake Michigan shorefront. Quite literally, all roads lead to Chicago; the city sits at the center of a web of interstates, rail lines, and airplane routes; most cross-country traffic swings through the city. A good map is essential for navigating Chicago; pick up a free one at the tourist office or any CTA station.

The flat, sprawling city's grids usually make sense. Navigation is pretty straightforward, whether by car or by public transportation. At the city's center is the **Loop** (p. 581), Chicago's downtown business district and the public transportation system's hub. The block numbering system starts from the intersection of State and Madison, increasing by about 800 per mi. The Loop is bounded loosely by the Chicago River to the north and west, Wabash Ave. to the east, and Congress Pkwy. to the south. Directions in *Let's Go* are usually from downtown. South of the Loop, east-west street numbers increase toward the south. Many ethnic neighborhoods lie in this area (see **Neighborhoods** below), but farther south, avoid the struggling South Side. Most of the city's best spots for food and nightlife jam into the first few miles north of the Loop. Beware the 45mph speed limit on **Lake Shore Drive,** a scenic freeway hugging Lake Michigan that offers express north-south connections.

To avoid driving and parking in the city, daytrippers can leave their cars in one of the suburban park-and-ride lots ($1.75); call CTA (see above) for info. Parking downtown costs around $8-15 per day. Check out the lots west of the South Loop and across the canal from the **Sears Tower** (p. 581), for the best deals.

It is a good idea to stay within the boundaries made apparent by tourist maps. Aside from small pockets such as Hyde Park and the University of Chicago, areas south of the loop and west of the little ethnic enclaves are mostly industrial or residential and pose a safety threat to the unwary tourist. **Cabrini Green** (bounded by W. Armitage Ave. on the north, W. Chicago Ave. on the south., Sedgwick St. on the east, and Halsted St. on the west) was once the site of an infamously dangerous public housing development and sits within tourist map borders. (Although, the neighborhood is now part of a city experiment in mixed-income housing.) Other unsafe neighborhoods are usually outside of them.

NEIGHBORHOODS

The diverse array of communities that composes the Windy City justifies its title as a "city of neighborhoods." North of the Loop, LaSalle Dr. loosely defines the west edge of the posh **Near North** area; here, most activity is centered along the **Magnificent Mile** of Michigan Ave. between the Chicago River and Oak St. A trendy restaurant and nightlife district, **River North** lines N. Clark St., just north of the Loop and west of Michigan Ave. The primarily residential **Gold Coast** shimmers on N. Lakeshore Dr. between Oak St. and North Ave. The **Bucktown/Wicker Park** area—at the intersection of North, Damen, and Milwaukee Ave.—is the place to be for artsy, cutting-edge cafes and nightlife. **Lincoln Park,** a hotbed of activity, revolves around the junction of N. Clark St., Lincoln Ave., and Halsted St. To the north, near the 3000 block of N. Clark St. and N. Halsted St., sits **Lakeview,** a gay-friendly area teeming with food and nightlife that becomes **Wrigleyville** in the 4000 block. **Andersonville,** 5 mi. farther up N. Clark St. north of Foster Ave., is the center of the Swedish community, though immigrants from Asia and the Middle East have recently settled here.

The near south and west sides are filled with other vibrant ethnic districts. While much of the German community has scattered, the beer halls and restaurants in the 3000 and 4000 blocks of N. Lincoln Ave. keep the torch of German culture burning. The former residents of **Greektown** have also moved, but S. Halsted St. still houses authentic Greek restaurants. *The area is bustling and safe until the restaurants close, at which point tourists wisely clear out.* Although nearby **Little Italy** has fallen prey to the encroachments of **University of Illinois at Chicago (UIC),** good dining options remain. Jewish and Indian enclaves center on Devon Ave., from Western Ave. to the Chicago River. The **Pilsen** neighborhood, around 18th St., offers a slice of Mexico and a developing art community. Chicago's Polish population is the largest of any city outside of Warsaw; those seeking Chicago's famous Polish cuisine should go to N. Milwaukee Ave. between blocks 2800 and 3100.

LOCAL TRANSPORTATION

Public Transit: The **Chicago Transit Authority (CTA),** 350 N. Wells, 7th fl. (☎836-7000 or 888-968-7282; www.transitchicago.com), runs efficient trains, subways, and buses. The **elevated rapid transit train system,** called the **El,** encircles the Loop. The El operates 24hr., but check ahead for schedules, as *late-night service is infrequent and unsafe in many areas.* Some buses do not run all night; call the CTA for schedules and routes. Many routes are "express," and different routes may run along the same track. Helpful CTA maps are available at many stations and at the Chicago Visitor Information Center. Train and bus fare is $1.50; add $0.25 for express routes. Transfers ($0.30) allow for up to 2 more rides on different routes during the following 2hr. Buy **transit cards** ($1.50 min.), for fares and transfers at all CTA stations, on the Internet, and at some museums. CTA also offers a variety of consecutive-day passes for tourists, available at airports and Amtrak stations, ranging from $5-18, depending on length of pass. On Sa from early May-late Oct., a **Loop Tour Train** departs on a free 40min. elevated tour of the downtown area (tickets must be picked up at the **Chicago Cultural Center;** see p. 576. Tours start at 11:35am, 12:15, 12:55, 1:35pm).

METRA, 547 W. Jackson St. (☎836-7000; www.metrarail.com), distributes free maps and schedules for its extensive commuter rail network of 11 rail lines and 4 downtown stations. Open M-F 8am-5pm. Fare $2-6.60, depending on distance.

PACE (☎836-7000; www.pacebus.com) runs the suburban bus system. Many free or cheap shuttle services run throughout the Loop, with schedules available most places.

Taxi: Yellow Cab, (☎829-4222; www.yellowcabchicago.com). **Flash Cab,** (☎773-561-4444; www.flashcab.com).

Car Rental: Dollar Rent-a-Car (☎800-800-4000; www.dollar.com), at O'Hare and Midway St. Call for specific price information; must be 21 with major credit card to rent; under-25 surcharge $18 per day.

PRACTICAL INFORMATION

Visitor Info: Chicago has 3 visitor centers, each located in a well-known landmark. **Chicago Cultural Center,** 77 E. Randolph St. (☎744-6630), at Michigan Ave., has map and tour information. Open M-W 10am-7pm, Th 10am-9pm, F 10am-6pm, Sa 10am-5pm, Su 11am-5pm.

Water Works Visitor Center, 163 E. Pearson St. (☎744-2400), at Michigan Ave., is located in the Water Tower Pumping Station. Open daily 7:30am-7pm. On the lake sits the **Navy Pier Info Center,** 700 E. Grand Ave. (☎595-7437). Open Su-Th 10am-10pm, F-Sa 10am-noon.

Bi-Gay-Lesbian Resources: Gay and Lesbian Hotline (☎773-929-4357). Operates 6-10pm. For current info on events and nightlife, pick up the *Windy City Times* or *Gay Chicago* at Lakeview's **Unabridged Books,** 3251 N. Broadway (☎773-883-9119).

Medical Services: Northwestern Memorial Hospital, 251 E. Huron St. (☎908-2000), near Michigan Ave.; **emergency division** at 250 E. Erie St. (☎926-5188). Open 24hr.

Internet Access: Free at the **Chicago Public Library.** Main branch at 400 S. State St., at Congress. Open M-Th 9am-7pm, F-Sa 9am-5pm, Su 1-5pm.

Post Office: 433 W. Harrison St. (☎800-275-8777), at the Chicago River. Free parking. Open 24hr. **Postal Code:** 60607. **Area Code:** 312 (downtown) or 773 (elsewhere in Chicago); 708, 630, or 847 (outside the city limits). In text, 312 unless noted.

GREAT LAKES

ACCOMMODATIONS

Find a cheap place to rest your head at one of Chicago's many hostels. The motels on **Lincoln Avenue** in Lincoln Park are moderately priced. Motel chains off the interstates, about 1hr. from downtown, are out of the way and more expensive. **At Home Inn Chicago** (☎800-375-7084) offers a reservation and referral service for many downtown B&Bs. Most have a two-night minimum stay, and rooms average $120. Travelers should be aware of Chicago's 15% tax on most accommodation rates.

Arlington House, 616 W. Arlington Pl. (☎773-929-5380 or 800-467-8355), off Clark St. The friendly, social atmosphere and brilliant location ensure a lively stay in this Lincoln Park hostel. Newly renovated dorms are tidy and pleasant with clean bathrooms. The common room is consistently packed with fellow guests. Located on a quiet, safe residential street near food and nightlife. Kitchen, TV room, and laundry. Linen and deposit $10. Dorms $21; private singles with shared bath $50, with private bath $51. ❶

Hostelling International–Chicago (HI-AYH), 24 E. Congress Pkwy. (☎360-0300; www.hichicago.org), off Wabash Ave. in the Loop. The location offers easy access to the major museums during the day, but *be careful on the deserted streets of the Loop at night.* Student center, library, kitchen, and organized activities give the hostel a lively social atmosphere. Laundry and Internet access. All rooms with A/C. Reservations recommended. Dorms $29, nonmembers $37.50. ❶

House of Blues Hotel, 330 N. Dearborn St. (☎245-0333). If you're going to spend money on accommodations in Chicago, this unique hotel, with its eclectic mix of Gothic, Moroccan, Indian, and American folk art influences, is hard to beat. The colorful fusion of architectural and decorative styles is complemented by excellent service and prime location near entertainment and food. Spacious, vibrant rooms come with big bathrooms. TV, VCR, CD player, in-room Internet access. Free music F and Sa in lobby bar. Access to Crunch gym: $15. Rooms from $129 but increase during peak season. ❺

Cass Hotel, 640 N. Wabash Ave. (☎787-4030 or 800-227-7850), just north of the Loop. Take the El to State St. Reasonable rates and a convenient location near the Magnificent Mile make this newly renovated hotel a favorite find of the budget-conscious. The $2 breakfast at the coffeeshop is a great deal. Parking available ($26 per day). Laundry room, TV, A/C, and private bath. Key deposit $5 if paying cash. Reservations recommended. Wheelchair-accessible. Singles from $79, doubles from $84. ❹

International House, 1414 E. 59th St. (☎773-753-2270), in Hyde Park, off Lake Shore Dr. Take the Illinois Central Railroad from the Michigan Ave. station (20min.) or METRA South Shore Line to 59th St. and walk a ½ block west. On the grounds of the University of Chicago; *avoid walking alone off-campus at night.* Common areas and an outdoor courtyard filled with the activity of a diverse group of students augment neat, spacious singles with shared bath. Linen provided. Laundry, tennis courts, game room, weight room, and cafeteria. Reservations with credit card required. Rooms $50. ❸

FOOD

Chicago's many culinary delights, from pizza to po' boy sandwiches, are among its main attractions. One of the best guides to city dining is the monthly *Chicago* magazine, which includes an extensive restaurant section, indexed by price, cuisine, and quality. It can be found at tourist offices and newsstands everywhere.

PIZZA

No trip to Chicago would be complete without sampling deep-dish pizza. Over the years, several deep-dish empires have competed to conquer the Windy City. Each local has a preference, but these samplings should provide a good overview.

Lou Malnati's, 439 N. Wells St. (☎828-9800), at Hubbard downtown. A Chicago mainstay for over 30 years, Lou's is a sports-themed chain offering deep-dish masterpieces. Pizzas take 30min. There are more than 20 branches throughout the Chicago area. Pizzas $4.50-20. Open M-Th 11am-11pm, F-Sa 11am-midnight, Su noon-10pm. ❷

Giordano's, 730 N. Rush St. (☎951-0747), is the home of the famous stuffed crust. An absurdly overfilled pizza, with heaps of cheese and other toppings sizzling inside it, is $11-22. The "not less famous" thin crust pie ($7-21) is also satisfying. Lines can be long, but customers can pre-order while they wait. Open M-Th 11am-midnight, F-Sa 11am-1am, Su noon-midnight. Call for other locations throughout the city. ❸

Pizzeria Uno, 29 E. Ohio St. (☎321-1000), at Wabash. It may look like any other Uno's, but rest assured this first restaurant is of a different order than its younger siblings. Lines are long, but the world-famous pies have a made-from-scratch taste worth the wait. Individual-sized pies ($5) only take 25min. **Pizzeria Due,** 619 N. Wabash Ave (☎943-2400), is on the opposite street corner and offers the same menu in the lower level of a Victorian mansion. Uno open M-F 11:30am-1am, Sa 11:30am-2am, Su 11:30am-11:30pm. Due open Su-Th 11am-1:30am, F-Sa 11am-2am. ❷

The Original Gino's East, 633 N. Wells St. (☎266-5421), at Ontario. Stake your claim on the customer-decorated walls of this legendary deep-dish joint. Pizza $9-23. Mini-pizza weekday lunch special $4. Open daily 11am-11pm. ❹

'ROUND THE LOOP

Many of Chicago's best restaurants, from ragin' Cajun to tried-and-true German, inhabit the streets of the Loop.

Lou Mitchell's, 565 W. Jackson Blvd. (☎939-3111), 2 blocks west of the Sears Tower. This retro diner has been stuffing faithful customers for over 75 years. Start the day with "meltaway pancakes" that take up the whole plate ($5.25) or hearty omelettes served simmering in the skillet ($6.50-8.50). Lines are long but customers are appeased with donut holes while they wait. Cash only. Open M-Sa 5:30am-3pm, Su 7am-3pm. ❶

Heaven on Seven, 111 N. Wabash Ave. (☎263-6443), 7th fl. of the Garland Bldg. This is paradise: Cajun-style. Mardi Gras and voodoo decor compliment the endless hot sauce and spicy cuisine perfectly. The line is long, but the jambalaya is fantastic. Open M-F 8:30am-5pm, Sa 10am-3pm. Cash only. Other locations at 600 N. Michigan Ave. (☎280-7774) and 3478 N. Clark St. (☎773-477-7818). ❸

Billy Goat's Tavern, 430 N. Michigan Ave. (☎222-1525), underground on lower Michigan Ave. Escape the glitzy storefronts of the Magnificent Mile by descending into this no-frills bar and diner, where gruff service is part of the charm. Delicious "cheezeborgers" $2.75. Open M-F 6am-2am, Sa 10am-3am, Su 11am-2am. ❶

Gold Coast Dogs (☎527-1222), on Wabash Ave. between Randolph and Lake St. Hot dogs are sacred in Chicago, but only when topped Second City-style with a veritable salad of relish, onions, pickles, and tomatoes. Locals rank Gold Coast as the best. "One Magnificent Dog" will set you back $2.19. Open M-F 7am-10pm, Sa-Su 11am-8pm. ❶

RIVER NORTH

River North houses some of the trendiest eateries in town, as well as Chicago's pizza institutions (see **Pizza,** above).

Ed Debevic's, 640 N. Wells St. (☎664-1707), at Ontario, serves great burgers ($7) and shakes ($4) with attitude; don't be surprised if your waiter shouts at you from behind the counter. This faux 1950s diner trades heavily in kitsch, from poodle-skirt waitresses to "The World's Smallest Sundae" ($1 with souvenir cup). Sit in a booth or at the counter while the staff dances and a DJ spins tunes. Open mid-June to Aug. Su-Th 11am-10pm, F-Sa 11am-midnight; Sept.-June Su-Th 11am-9pm, F-Sa 11am-11pm. ❷

Frontera Grill, 455 N. Clark St. (☎661-1434), between Illinois and Hubbard St. Take El Red Line to Grand/State. A delightful departure from chain tacos and burritos, Frontera delivers what many claim is the best authentic Mexican cuisine in the region. Entrees ($14-18) change every month but are always superb. The usual 1hr. wait is bearable if you snag a bar seat and order appetizers (from $5). Lunch Tu-Th 11:30am-2:30pm, Sa 10:30am-2:30pm. Dinner Tu 5:20-10pm, W-Th 5-10pm, F-Sa 5-11pm. ❹

SOUL FOOD

Head to the **South Side** for good, cheap soul food, like ribs, fried chicken, and collard greens. *Be very careful south of the Loop,* though, especially after dark. **Wicker Park,** to the north, is another option for satisfying soul food.

Army & Lou's, 422 E. 75th St. (☎773-483-6550), on the South Side. Locals come here for some of the best southern fare around, served in an upscale setting. Fried chicken and 2 sides $9; mixed greens and ham $8. Open M and W-Su 9am-10pm. ❷

Dixie Kitchen & Bait Shop, 5225 S. Harper St. (☎773-363-4943). Tucked in a parking lot on 52nd St. in Hyde Park, this place is a local hot spot. Fried green tomatoes ($5) and oyster po' boy sandwiches ($8) are among Dixie's southern highlights. Fried catfish $11. Blackened Voodoo beer $2. Open Su-Th 11am-10pm, F-Sa 11am-11pm. ❷

The Smokedaddy, 1804 W. Division St. (☎773-772-6656), north of the Loop in Wicker Park. Fantastic ribs ($10) and pulled pork sandwiches ($6) merit the neon "WOW" sign out front. Live blues nightly. Open M-F 11:30am-1:30am, Sa-Su 11:30am-2am. ❷

GREEKTOWN

The Parthenon, 314 S. Halsted St. (☎726-2407). Look in the window around dinner time and you will see meat slowly roasting on a spit. The staff converses in Greek, the murals transport you to the Mediterranean, and the food wins top awards. The tasty Greek Feast family-style dinner ($17 per person) includes everything from *saganaki* (flaming goat cheese) to baklava. Open Su-F 11am-1am, Sa 11am-2am. ❸

Rodity's, 222 S. Halsted St. (☎454-0800), between Adams St. and Jackson Blvd. With slightly cheaper fare than the other Greektown options (daily specials under $9), Rodity's prepares more than generous portions of *spanakopita* ($8) and other delectable Greek treats. Open Su-Th 11am-midnight, F-Sa 11am-1am. ❷

LINCOLN PARK

Cafe Ba-Ba-Reeba!, 2024 N. Halsted St. (☎935-5000), just north of Armitage. Hard to miss with its colorful facade and bustling interior, the sprawling Ba-Ba-Reeba pleases an upbeat crowd with unbeatable *tapas* ($4-8) and hearty Spanish *paellas* ($10-15 per person). During the summer sip sangria ($3.50) on the outdoor terrace. Lunch Sa-Su noon-5pm. Dinner Su-Th 5-10pm, F-Sa 5pm-midnight. Reservations recommended. ❸

Potbelly Sandwich Works, 2264 N. Lincoln Ave. (☎773-528-1405), between Belden and Webster. This laidback deli, appropriately decorated with a potbelly stove and furnished with cozy booths, offers delicious subs ($4). Yogurt smoothies and thick shakes $2. Open daily 11am-11pm. Call for additional locations. ❶

Penny's Noodle Shop, 950 W. Diversey Ave. (☎773-281-8448), at Sheffield Ave. One of the best budget options in town, Penny's delivers generous portions of Asian noodles (all under $6) to scores of locals who pack the place at all hours. No reservations; sit at the counter or prepare to wait. Open Su-Th 11am-10pm, F-Sa 11am-10:30pm. Call for additional locations. ❷

ANDERSONVILLE

Kopi, A Traveler's Cafe, 5317 N. Clark St. (☎773-989-5674), near Foster St., a 10min. walk from the Berwyn El. Kopi provides a friendly refuge and caffeine fix for travelers. Sip on espresso ($1.35) while browsing the extensive travel library. Music M nights. Open M-Th 8am-11pm, F 8am-midnight, Sa 9am-midnight, Su 10am-11pm. ❶

Ann Sather, 5207 N. Clark St. (☎773-271-6677). The last authentic Swedish diner left in the neighborhood delights locals with their wildly popular and addictively gooey cinnamon rolls ($4). Open M-F 7am-3:30pm, Sa-Su 7am-5pm. Call for other locations. ❶

BUCKTOWN/WICKER PARK

Kitsch'n on Roscoe, 2005 W. Roscoe St. (☎773-248-7372), at Damen Ave. in nearby Roscoe Village. The joint's title is a good indication of the campy experience this breakfast and lunch spot has to offer. Try the "Kitsch'n Sink Omelette" ($7) or enjoy "Jonny's Lunch Box" (soup, sandwich, fruit, and a snack cake served in a lunch box, $6.50) on kitschy theme tables. Meals $3-12. Open Tu-Sa 9am-10pm, Su 9am-3pm. ❷

OLD TOWN

Flat Top Grill, 312 W. North Ave. (☎787-7676). You're the chef at this do-it-yourself stir-fry joint. Start with noodles or rice and then produce your own culinary masterpiece from a selection of fresh vegetables, meats, and sauces. Don't worry, though—there are a host of suggested recipes for clueless cooks. One bowl $8. Open Su-Th 11:30am-10pm, F-Sa 11:30am-11pm. Call for other locations. ❸

Nookies, 1746 N. Wells St. (☎337-2454). Satisfying locals for 30 years, this neighborhood diner has passed the test of time with its hearty, old-fashioned breakfasts. Start the day right with cornflakes-crusted French toast ($5) and a cup o' joe. Open M-Sa 6:30am-10pm, Su 6:30am-9pm. Cash only. Other locations at 2114 (☎773-327-1400) and 3334 N. Halsted (☎773-248-9888). ❷

WRIGLEYVILLE

Mia Francesca, 3311 N. Clark St. (☎773-281-3310), is a bustling urban trattoria specializing in Northern Italian cuisine. The menu is always changing but the food is consistently excellent. Eat in one of the two busy dining rooms or escape to the more serene courtyard and coach house in the back, but don't miss the fantastic fried calamari ($5). Entrees $10-20. Open Su-Th 5-10:30pm, F-Sa 5-11pm. Reservations recommended. ❹

SIGHTS

Only a fraction of Chicago's eclectic sights are revealed by tourist brochures, bus tours, and strolls through the downtown area. Sights range from well-publicized museums to undiscovered back streets, from beaches and parks to towering skyscrapers. To see it all requires some off-the-beaten path exploration.

THE LOOP

When the **Great Fire of 1871** burned Chicago's downtown, the city was forced to modernize its structures and build up rather than out. As a result, the functional became the fabulous, producing one of the most concentrated clusters of architectural treasures in the world.

TOURS. Visitors can view the architecture via **walking tours** organized by the **Chicago Architecture Foundation.** One tour of early skyscrapers and another of modern architecture start at the foundation's gift shop and last 2hr. Highlights include Louis Sullivan's arch, classic Chicago windows, and Mies van der Rohe's revolutionary skyscrapers. *(224 S. Michigan Ave. ☎922-8687; www.architecture.org. Historic Skyscrapers May-Oct. M and Sa-Su 10am, 2:30pm, Tu-F 10am. Modern skyscrapers May-Oct. M and Sa-Su 11am, 1:30pm, Tu-F 1:30pm. $12 for 1 tour, $18 for both. Call for info on special tours.)*

SEARS TOWER. A few blocks west on Jackson, the **Sears Tower** is undoubtedly Chicago's most immediately recognizable landmark. The Tower is the second-tallest building in the world (first, in the minds of Chicagoans), standing 1454 ft. tall, and on a clear day, visitors to the 103rd fl. **Skydeck** can see three states. *(233 S. Wacker Dr.; enter on Jackson. ☎875-9696; www.sears-tower.com. Open daily May-Sept. 10am-10pm; Oct.-Apr. 10am-8pm. $9.50, seniors $7.75, youth $6.75. Lines are long, usually at least 1hr.)*

THE PLAZA. The **Bank One Building and Plaza** is one of the world's largest bank buildings. It leads gazes skyward with its diamond-shaped, diagonal slope. Back on the ground, Marc Chagall's vivid mural *The Four Seasons* lines the block and defines a public space used for concerts and lunchtime entertainment. The mosaic is a fabulous sight at night, when it is lit by various colored bulbs. Two blocks north, the Methodist **Chicago Temple,** the world's tallest church, sends its Babelesque steeples heavenward. *(77 W. Washington St., at the corner of Clark and Washington St. ☎236-4548. Tours M-Sa 2pm, after mass Su. Free.)*

STATE STREET. State and Madison St., the most famous intersection of "State Street, that great street," forms the focal point of the Chicago street grid as well as another architectural haven. Louis Sullivan's beloved **Carson Pirie Scott** store is adorned with exquisite ironwork and an extra-large Chicago window. Sullivan's other masterpiece, the **Auditorium Building,** sits several blocks south at the corner of Congress St. and Michigan Ave. Once Chicago's tallest building, it typifies Sullivan's obsession with form and function, housing a hotel and an opera house with some of the world's finest acoustics. Murals and marble mosaics adorn the interior.

OTHER ARCHITECTURAL WONDERS. Burnham and Root's **Monadnock Building** deserves a glance for its alternating bays of purple and brown rock. *(53 W. Jackson Blvd.)* Just to the southeast, the **Sony Fine Arts Theatre** screens current arthouse and foreign films in the grandeur of the **Fine Arts Building.** *(418 S. Michigan Ave. ☎939-2119. Open M-Th. $8.25; students $6; seniors, children, and matinees $5.)* The $144 million **Harold Washington Library Center** is a researcher's dream, as well as a postmodern architectural delight. *(400 S. State St. ☎747-4300. Open M-Th 9am-7pm, F-Sa 9am-5pm, Su 1-5pm. Tours M-Sa noon, 2pm, Su 2pm.)* On the north side of the Loop, at Clark and Randolph, the glass **State of Illinois Building** offers an elevator ride to the top that gives a thrilling (and free) view of a sloping atrium, circular floors, and hundreds of employees.

SCULPTURE. In addition to its architectural masterpieces, Chicago is decorated with a fantastic collection of outdoor sculpture. Large, abstract designs punctuate downtown corners, making a walking tour a terrific way to spend an afternoon. The Chicago Cultural Center sells the *Loop Sculpture Guide* for $4 (see p. 576). The piece known simply as "The Picasso," at the foot of the **Daley Center Plaza,** was the first monumental modern statue to be placed in the Loop, eventually becoming an unofficial symbol of the city. *(Intersection of Washington and Dearborn St. ☎443-3054.)* Directly across Washington St. rests surrealist Joan Miró's *Chicago*, the artist's gift to the city. *(69 W. Washington St.)* Two blocks north on Clark St., Jean Dubuffet's *Monument with Standing Beast* stands guard in front of the State of Illinois Building (see above). Three blocks south on Dearborn at Adams, Alexander Calder's *Flamingo*, a stark red structure, stands in front of the Federal Center Plaza. Calder's other Chicago masterpiece, *The Universe*, swirls in the lobby of the Sears Tower.

NEAR NORTH

MAGNIFICENT MILE. Chicago's row of glitzy shops along N. Michigan Ave. between the Chicago River and Oak St. can magnificently drain the wallet. Several of these retail stores were designed by the country's foremost architects and merit a look. The plain **Chicago Water Tower** and **Pumping Station** stick out among the ritzy stores at the corner of Michigan and Pearson Ave. Built in 1867, these were the sole structures in the area to survive the Great Chicago Fire. The Pumping Station houses a tourist center (see p. 576). Across Pearson St., expensive, trendy stores pack **Water Tower Place,** the first urban shopping mall in the US. One block north, the **John Hancock Building** rockets toward the sky in black steel and glass.

TRIBUNE TOWER. North of the Loop along the lake, just past the Michigan Ave. Bridge, lies the city's ritziest district. The Tribune Tower, a Gothic skyscraper just north of the bridge, overlooks this stretch. The result of an international design competition in the 1920s, the tower is now home to Chicago's largest newspaper, *The Chicago Tribune. (435 N. Michigan Ave.)*

THE MART. Over 8 mi. of corridors fill the nearby Merchandise Mart. As one of the largest commercial buildings in the world (25 stories high and two blocks long), it even has its own postal code. The first two floors house a public mall, while the remainder contain private showrooms where design professionals converge to choose home and office furnishings. **Tours at the Mart** guides visitors through the building. *(Entrance on N. Wells or Kinzie St., north of the river. Bus #114. ☎644-4664. 2hr. tours Th-F 1:30pm. $12, seniors $10, students $9.)*

NAVY PIER. Big, bright, and always festive, Navy Pier captures the carnival spirit 365 days a year. No small jetty, the mile-long pier has it all: a concert pavilion, dining options, nightspots, sightseeing boats, a spectacular ferris wheel, a crystal garden with palm trees, and an IMAX theater. Now *that's* America. From here, explorers can rent bicycles to navigate the Windy City's streets. *(600 E. Grand Ave. Take El Red Line to Grand/State and transfer to a free pier trolley bus. Bike rental open daily June-Sept. 8am-11pm; May 8am-8pm; Apr. and Oct. 10am-7pm. $9 per hr., $34 per day.)*

OLD TOWN. The bells of the pre-fire **Saint Michael's Church** ring 1 mi. north of the Magnificent Mile in **Old Town,** a neighborhood where eclectic shops and nightspots fill revitalized streets. Architecture buffs should explore the W. Menomonee and W. Eugenie St. area. In early June, the **Old Town Art Fair** attracts artists and craftsmen nationwide. *(Take bus #151 to Lincoln Park and walk south down Clark or Wells St.)*

NORTH SIDE

LINCOLN PARK. Urban renewal has made **Lincoln Park** a popular choice for wealthy residents. Bounded by Armitage to the south and Diversey Ave. to the north, Lincoln Park offers a lakeside community of harbors and parks. Cafes and nightspots pack its tree-lined streets. For some of Chicago's liveliest clubs and restaurants, check out the area around N. Clark St., Lincoln Ave., and N. Halsted St.

LAKEVIEW. North of Diversey Ave. on N. Clark St., the streets of Lincoln Park become increasingly diverse as they melt into the community of Lakeview around the 3000 block. In this self-proclaimed "gay capital of Chicago," supermarket shopping plazas alternate with tiny markets and vintage clothing stores, while apartment towers and hotels spring up between aging two-story houses. Lakeview dance clubs form a center of Chicago nightlife. Polish diners share blocks with Korean restaurants, and Mongolian eateries face Mexican bars in this ethnic enclave.

WRIGLEYVILLE. Around the 4000 block of N. Clark, Lakeview shifts into **Wrigleyville.** Even though the **Cubs** (p. 587) haven't won a World Series since 1908, Wrigleyville residents remain fiercely loyal to their hometown team. Tiny, ivy-covered **Wrigley Field** is the North Side's most famous institution. A pilgrimage here is a must for the baseball aficionado interested in seeing the country's most patient fans. Tours of the historic park are available when the Cubs are away. *(1060 W. Addison St., just east of the junction of Waveland Ave. and N. Clark St. ☎773-404-2827. Tours $15.)*

NEAR WEST SIDE

The Near West Side, bounded by the Chicago River to the east and Ogden Ave. to the west, assembles a cornucopia of vibrant ethnic enclaves.

HULL HOUSE. Aside from great food options, the primary attraction on the Near West Side lies a few blocks north on Halsted, where activist Jane Addams devoted her life to the historic Hull House. This settlement house bears witness to Chicago's (and Addams') pivotal role in turn-of-the-century reform in America. Although the house no longer offers social services, it has been painstakingly restored as a small museum. *(800 S. Halsted St. Take El Blue Line to Halsted/U of I or bus #8 "Halsted." ☎413-5353; www.uic.edu/jaddams/hull/hull_house.html. Open Tu-F 10am-4pm, Su noon-4pm. Free.)*

SOUTH OF THE LOOP

HYDE PARK AND THE UNIVERSITY OF CHICAGO. Seven miles south of the Loop along the lake, the scenic campus of the ivy-clad **University of Chicago** dominates the **Hyde Park** neighborhood. The university's efforts at revitalizing the area have resulted in a community of scholars and a lively campus life amidst the degenerating neighborhoods surrounding it. University police patrol the area bounded by 51st St. to the north, Lakeshore Dr. to the east, 61st St. to the south, and Cottage Grove to the west—but *don't test these boundaries, even during the day.* Lakeside Burnham Park, east of campus, is *fairly safe during the day, but not at night.* The impressive **Oriental Institute, Museum of Science and Industry** (see **Museums,** p. 584), and **DuSable Museum of African-American History** are all in or near Hyde Park. On the first weekend in June, the **Arts Fest** (http://artsfest.uchicago.edu) showcases the diverse cultural offerings of the area. *(From the Loop, take bus #6 "Jefferson Express" or the METRA Electric Line from the Randolph St. Station south to 59th St.)*

ROBIE HOUSE. On campus, Frank Lloyd Wright's famous **Robie House,** designed to resemble a hanging flower basket, is the seminal example of his Prairie-style house. Now in the midst of a 10-year restoration project designed to return Robie House to its original 1910 state, the house will remain open to visitors during all stages of renovation. *(5757 S. Woodlawn, at the corner of 58th St. ☎773-834-1847. Tours M-F 11am-3pm, Sa-Su 11am-3:30pm. $9, seniors and ages 7-18 $7.)*

WEST OF THE LOOP

OAK PARK. Gunning for the title of the most fantastic suburb in the US, Oak Park sprouts off of Harlem St. *(10 mi. west of downtown, I-290 W to Harlem St.)* Frank Lloyd Wright endowed the downtown area with 25 of his spectacular homes and buildings, all of which dot the Oak Park Historic District. His one-time home and workplace, the **Frank Lloyd Wright House and Studio,** offers an unbeatable look at his interior and exterior stylings. *(951 Chicago Ave. ☎708-848-1976; www.wrightplus.org. Open daily 10am-5pm. 45min. tours of the house M-F 11am, 1, 3pm; Sa-Su every 20min. 11am-3:30pm. 1hr. self-guided tours of Wright's other Oak Park homes, with a map and* *audio cassette, available daily 10am-3:30pm. Guided tours Mar.-Nov. Sa-Su every hr. 11am-4pm; Dec.-Feb. Sa-Su every hr. noon-2pm. $9, seniors and under 18 $7; combination interior/exterior tour tickets $14/10.)* Visitors should also stop by the former home of Ernest Hemingway. Throughout the year, fans flock to the **Ernest Hemingway Birthplace and Museum** to take part in the many events honoring an architect of the modern American novel. The museum features rare photos of Hemingway, his childhood diaries, letters, and other memorabilia. *(Birthplace: 339 N. Oak Ave. Museum: 200 N. Oak Park Ave. ☎ 708-848-2222. House and museum open Th-F and Su 1-5pm, Sa 10am-5pm. Combined ticket $7, seniors and under 18 $5.50.)* Swing by the **Visitors Center** for maps, guidebooks, tours, and local history. *(158 Forest Ave. ☎ 708-524-7800; www.visitoakpark.com.)*

MUSEUMS

Chicago's museums range from some of the largest collections in the world to one-room galleries. The first five listings (known as the **Big Five**) provide a diverse array of exhibits, while a handful of smaller collections target specific interests. Lake Shore Dr. has been diverted around Grant Park, linking the Field Museum, Adler, and Shedd. This compound, known as **Museum Campus,** offers a free shuttle between museums. Visitors who plan on seeing the Big Five, plus the Hancock Observatory, can save money by purchasing a **CityPass** that grants admission to the sights and provides discount coupons for food and shopping. ($49, ages 3-11 $38; available at each attraction and good for 9 days.)

Art Institute of Chicago, 111 S. Michigan Ave. (☎ 443-3600; www.artic.edu/aic), at Adams St. in Grant Park; take the El Green, Brown, Purple, or Orange Lines to Adams. It's easy to feel overwhelmed in this expansive museum, whose collections span four millennia of art from Asia, Africa, Europe, and beyond. Make sure to see Chagall's stunning *America Windows*—the artist's blue-stained glass tribute to the country's bicentennial—between visits to Wood's *American Gothic,* Hopper's *Nighthawks,* and Monet's *Haystacks*. Open M and W-F 10:30am-4:30pm, Tu 10:30am-8pm, Sa-Su 10am-5pm. $10, students and children $6, under 6 free; free Tu.

Field Museum of Natural History, 1400 S. Lake Shore Dr. (☎ 922-9410; www.fmnh.org), at Roosevelt Rd. in Grant Park; take bus #146 from State St. Sue, the largest *Tyrannosaurus Rex* skeleton ever unearthed, towers over excellent geology, anthropology, botany, and zoology exhibits. Other highlights include Egyptian mummies, Native American halls, and a dirt exhibit. Open daily 9am-5pm. $8; students, seniors, and ages 3-11 $4; under 3 free.

Shedd Aquarium, 1200 S. Lake Shore Dr. (☎ 939-2438; www.sheddnet.org), in Grant Park. The world's largest indoor aquarium has over 6600 species of fish in 206 tanks. The Oceanarium features beluga whales, dolphins, seals, and other marine mammals in a giant pool that appears to flow into Lake Michigan. See piranhas and tropical fish of the rainforest in the *Amazon Rising* exhibit or get a rare glimpse of seahorses in the oceanarium exhibit *Seahorse Symphony*. Also, check out the sharks at the new Wild Reef exhibit. Open June-Aug. M-W and F-Su 9am-6pm, Th 9am-10pm (Oceanarium and *Seahorse Symphony* 9am-8pm); Sept.-May M-F 9am-5pm, Sa-Su 9am-6pm. Feedings M-F 11am, 2, 3pm. Combined admission to Oceanarium and Aquarium $21, seniors and ages 3-11 $15. Tour of Oceanarium $3.

Museum of Science and Industry, 5700 S. Lake Shore Dr. (☎ 773-684-1414; www.msichicago.org), at 57th St. in Hyde Park. Take bus #6 "Jeffrey Express," the #10 "Museum of Science and Industry" bus (runs daily in summer, Sa-Su and holidays rest of year), or METRA South Shore line to 57th St. The Museum features the *Apollo 8* command module, a full-sized replica of a coal mine, and a host of interactive exhibits on topics from DNA to the Internet. Stop by the *Yesterday's Main Street* exhibit for a scoop at the 1920s-style ice cream parlor. Omnimax shows completely immerse you in another world. Open Sept.-May daily 9:30am-4:30pm; June-Aug. 9:30am-5:30pm. Call for a schedule of Omnimax shows. Admission $9, seniors $7.50, ages 3-11 free; with Omnimax $15/10/12.50. Parking $8 per day.

Adler Planetarium, 1300 S. Lake Shore Dr. (☎922-7827; www.adlerplanetarium.org), on Museum Campus in Grant Park. Aspiring astronauts can discover their weight on Mars, read the news from space, and explore a medieval observatory. Open daily 9:30am-4:30pm. Admission and choice of sky show $13, seniors $12, ages 4-17 $11. Some exhibits $5 extra. Sky show daily on the hr. $5.

Chicago Historical Society, 1601 Clark St. (☎642-4600; www.chicagohs.org), at the south end of Lincoln Park. Immerse yourself in Chicago's rich history, from its early days as a wilderness outpost to its emergence as a city of skyscrapers. *A House Divided: America in the Age of Lincoln* tells the story of Honest Abe's days in Illinois and explores the consequences of slavery. Open M-Sa 9:30am-4:30pm, Su noon-5pm. $5, seniors and students 17-22 $3, children 6-7 $1. Call for tour information.

Museum of Contemporary Art, 220 E. Chicago Ave. (☎280-2660; www.mcachicago.org), 1 block east of Michigan Ave.; take #66 "Chicago Ave." bus. The beautiful view of Lake Michigan is the only unchanging feature in the MCA's ultra-modern exhibition space. Pieces from the outstanding permanent collection rotate periodically. Call to see what is on display—their extensive collection includes works by Calder, Warhol, Javer, and Nauman. Open Tu 10am-8pm, W-Su 10am-5pm. $8, students and seniors $6, under 12 free; free Tu.

Terra Museum of American Art, 664 N. Michigan Ave. (☎664-3939; www.terramuseum.org), between Huron and Erie St. Wedged between the posh shops on N. Michigan, this is one of only a few galleries to showcase exclusively American art from colonial times to the present. Includes works from Hopper, Inness, and the celebrated Hudson River School. Open Tu 10am-8pm, W-Sa 10am-6pm, Su noon-5pm. Free. Tours Tu-F noon, 6pm, Sa-Su noon, 2pm.

Spertus Museum, 618 S. Michigan Ave. (☎322-1747; www.spertus.edu/museum.html), near Harrison St. downtown; take El Red Line to Harrison. A moving Holocaust Memorial is the only permanent exhibit at this small museum that features Jewish art and history. Open Mar.-Dec. Su-W 10am-5pm, Th 10am-8pm, F 10am-3pm. Artifact center open Su-Th 1-4:30pm. $5; students, seniors, and children $3; free F.

International Museum of Surgical Science, 1524 N. Lake Shore Dr. (☎642-6502; www.imss.org), at North Ave. A sculpture of a surgeon holding his wounded patient marks the entrance to this unique museum, a harrowing journey through the history of surgery. Highlights, if that's the right word, include a fascinating collection of gallstones and bladderstones. Open Tu-Su 10am-4pm. $6, students and seniors $3; free Tu.

ENTERTAINMENT

The free weeklies *Chicago Reader* and *New City*, available in many bars, record stores, and restaurants, list the latest events. The *Reader* reviews all major shows with times and ticket prices. *Chicago* magazine includes theater reviews alongside exhaustive club, music, dance, and opera listings. *The Chicago Tribune* includes an entertainment section every Friday. *Gay Chicago* provides info on social activities as well as other news for the area's gay community.

THEATER

One of the foremost theater centers of North America, Chicago's more than 150 theaters feature everything from blockbuster musicals to off-color parodies. Downtown, the recently formed Theater District centers around State St. and Randolph, and includes the larger venues in the city. Smaller theaters are scattered throughout Chicago. Most tickets are expensive. Half-price tickets are sold on the day of performance at **Hot Tix Booths,** 108 N. State St., and on the 6th fl. of 700 N.

Michigan Ave. Purchases must be made in person. (☎977-1755. Open M-F 10am-7pm, Sa 10am-6pm, Su noon-5pm.) **Ticketmaster** (☎559-1212) supplies tickets for many theaters; ask about discounts at all Chicago shows. The "Off-Loop" theaters on the North Side put on original productions, with tickets usually under $18.

Steppenwolf Theater, 1650 N. Halsted St. (☎335-1888; www.steppenwolf.org), where Gary Sinise and the eerie John Malkovich got their start and still stop by. Tickets Su-Th $40, F-Sa $45; half-price Tu-F after 5pm, Sa-Su after noon. Box office open Su-M 11am-5pm, Tu-F 11am-8pm, Sa 11am-9pm.

Goodman Theatre, 170 N. Dearborn (☎443-3800; www.goodman-theatre.org), presents consistently solid original works. Tickets around $40-60; half-price after 6pm or after noon for matinees; $12 for students after 6pm or after noon for matinees. Box office open M-F 10am-5pm; 10am-8pm show nights, usually W-Su.

Bailiwick Repertory, 1225 W. Belmont Ave. (☎773-327-5252; www.bailiwick.org), in the Theatre Bldg. A mainstage and experimental studio space. Tickets from $10. Box office open W noon-6pm, Th-Su noon-showtime.

GREAT LAKES

COMEDY

Chicago boasts a plethora of comedy clubs. The most famous, **Second City,** 1616 N. Wells St. (☎642-8189; www.secondcity.com), at North Ave., spoofs Chicago life and politics. Alums include Bill Murray, John Candy, and John Belushi. Most nights a free improv session follows the show. At next door **Second City Etc.,** 1608 N. Wells St. (☎642-6514), a group of up-and-coming comics offers more laughs. (Tickets $18. Shows for both M-Th 8:30pm, F-Sa 8 and 11pm, Su 8pm. Box office open daily 10:30am-10pm. Reservations recommended for weekend shows.) Watch improv actors compete to bust your gut at **Comedy Sportz,** 2851 N. Halsted. Two teams of comedians create sketches based on audience suggestions, all in the spirit of competition. (☎773-549-8080. Tickets $17. Shows Th 8pm, F-Sa 8, 10:30pm.)

DANCE, CLASSICAL MUSIC, AND OPERA

Ballet, comedy, live theater, and musicals are performed at **Auditorium Theatre,** 50 E. Congress Pkwy. (☎922-2110; www.auditoriumtheatre.org. Box office open M-F 10am-6pm.) From October through May, the sounds of the **Chicago Symphony Orchestra** resonate throughout **Symphony Center,** 220 S. Michigan Ave. (☎294-3000; www.chicagosymphony.org.) **Ballet Chicago** pirouettes throughout theaters in Chicago. (☎251-8838; www.balletchicago.org. Tickets $12-45.) The acclaimed **Lyric Opera of Chicago** performs from September through March at the **Civic Opera House,** 20 N. Wacker Dr. (☎332-2244; www.lyricopera.org.) While other places may suck your wallet dry, the **Grant Park Music Festival** affords a taste of the classical for free. From mid-June through late August, the acclaimed **Grant Park Symphony Orchestra** plays a few free evening concerts per week at the Grant Park **Petrillo Music Shell.** (☎742-4763; www.grantparkmusicfestival.com. Usually W-Su; schedule varies.)

FESTIVALS

The city celebrates summer on a grand scale. The **Taste of Chicago** festival cooks for eight days through July 6th. Seventy restaurants set up booths with endless samples in Grant Park, while crowds chomp to the blast of big name bands. The Taste's fireworks are the city's biggest. (Free entry, food tickets $0.50 each.) The first week in June, the **Blues Festival** celebrates the city's soulful music. The **Chicago Gospel Festival** hums and hollers in mid-June, and Nashville moves north for the **Country Music Festival** at the end of June. The **¡Viva Chicago!** Latin music festival steams up in late August, while the **Chicago Jazz Festival** scats over Labor Day weekend. All festivals center at the Grant Park

Petrillo Music Shell. The Mayor's Office's **Special Events Hotline** (☎744-3370; www.ci.chi.il.us/SpecialEvents/Festivals.htm) has more info.

The regionally famous **Ravinia Festival** (☎847-266-5100; www.ravinia.org), in the northern suburb of Highland Park, runs from late June to early September. During the festival's 14-week season, the Chicago Symphony Orchestra, ballet troupes, folk and jazz musicians, and comedians perform. On certain nights, the Orchestra allows students free lawn admission with student ID. (Shows 8pm, occasionally 4:30 and 7pm—call ahead. Round-trip on the METRA costs about $7; the festival runs 1½hr every night. Charter buses $12. Lawn seats $10-15, other $20-75.)

SPORTS

The National League's **Cubs** step up to bat at **Wrigley Field,** 1060 W. Addison St., at N. Clark St., one of the few ballparks in America to retain the early grace and intimate feel of the game. (☎773-404-2827; www.cubs.com. $10-22.) The **White Sox,** Chicago's American League team, swing on the South Side at new **Comiskey Park,** 333 W. 35th St. (☎674-1000. $12-24.) The **Bears** of the NFL play at the newly renovated **Soldier Field,** 425 E. McFetridge Dr. (☎888-792-3277. $45-65.) The **Bulls** have won three NBA championships at the **United Center,** 1901 W. Madison, just west of the Loop. (☎943-5800. $30-450.) Hockey's **Blackhawks** skate onto United Center ice when the Bulls aren't hooping it up. (☎455-4500. $25-100.) **Sports Information** (☎976-4242) has up-to-the-minute info on local sports events.

NIGHTLIFE

"Sweet home Chicago" takes pride in the innumerable blues performers who have played here. Jazz, folk, reggae, and punk clubs throb all over the **North Side.** The **Bucktown/Wicker Park** area stays open late with bars and clubs. Aspiring pickup artists swing over to **Rush Street** and **Division Street.** Full of bars, cafes, and bistros, **Lincoln Park** is frequented by singles and young couples, both gay and straight. The vibrant center of gay culture is between 3000 and 4500 **North Halsted Street.** Many of the more colorful clubs and bars line this area. For more upscale raving and discoing, there are plenty of clubs near **River North,** in Riverwest, and on Fulton St.

BARS AND BLUES JOINTS

The Green Mill, 4802 N. Broadway Ave. (☎773-878-5552). El Red Line: Lawrence. Founded as a Prohibition-era speakeasy, Mafiosi-to-be can park themselves in Al Capone's old seat. This authentic jazz club draws

IN RECENT NEWS

CLUBBING CATASTROPHE

On February 17, 2003, a regular night of clubbing turned deadly as 21 people died and over 50 more were injured in the popular E2 nightclub on South Michigan Ave. Witnesses allege that when a fight broke out between two women around 2am, security guards fired pepper spray into the crowd, which prompted a wild stampede towards the doors. The narrow staircase leading to the exit was jammed with frantic patrons, many of whom were crushed to death at the top of the steps. According to city officials, the club was in violation of an order barring use of the second floor, but the lawyer for one of the clubs' owners says that there was "confusion" about the order. On September 23, 2003, the owners of E2, along with two others associated with the club, were charged with involuntary manslaughter. All four defendants have pleaded not guilty.

The backlash from the incident has been tremendous as authorities have begun an initiative to enforce safety standards in clubs and bars throughout the city. Many clubs have been randomly inspected and shut down for failing to conform to requirements. Even the Green Mill jazz club, one of the oldest and most famous nightclubs in the country, has been warned to limit attendance to the 106 person maximum mandated by its license.

The city's crackdown has, if anything, been topped by club owners attempting to limit crowds and avoid violations. Don't expect to talk your way into a Chicago club without a valid I.D. any time soon—stricter security measures show no signs of going away.

late-night crowds after other clubs shut down. The cover-free jam sessions on weekends after main acts finish are reason enough to chill until the wee hours. Cover $5-15. Open M-Sa noon-5am, Su noon-4am.

Kingston Mines, 2548 N. Halsted St. (☎773-477-4647), across the street from B.L.U.E.S. One of the oldest clubs in town, this is the place to see big names. Mick Jagger and Bob Dylan have been known to frequent this raucous blues joint. Live blues on 2 stages daily starting at 9:30pm. Cover $8-15. Open Su-F 8pm-4am, Sa 8pm-5am.

The Hideout, 1354 W. Wabansia Ave. (☎773-227-4433). El Brown Line: Clybourn and North. Nestled in a municipal truck parking lot, this is the insider's rock club. Some weekends, the lot fills with "kid's shows" for families still able to rock. Arrangements with a record company have established the club as one of the best places to catch rising alt-country acts. Tu-F cover $5-10. Open M 8pm-2am, Tu-F 4pm-2am, Sa 7pm-3am.

B.L.U.E.S., 2519 N. Halsted St. (☎773-528-1012). Fullerton El: Howard, Dan Ryan. Crowded and intimate with unbeatable music. Albert King, Bo Diddley, Wolfman Washington, and Dr. John have played here. Live music every night 9:30pm-2am. 21+. Cover M-Th $6-8, F-Sa $8-10. Open Su-F 8pm-2am, Sa 8pm-3am.

DANCE CLUBS

Berlin, 954 W. Belmont Ave. (☎773-348-4975). El Red or Brown line: Belmont, in Lakeview. Anything goes at Berlin, a gay-friendly mainstay of Chicago's nightlife. Crowds pulsate to house/dance music amid drag contests and disco nights. W ladies night. 21+. Cover F-Sa after midnight $5. Open M-F 4pm-4am, Sa 2pm-5am, Su 4pm-2am.

Funky Buddha Lounge, 728 W. Grand Ave. (☎666-1695). El Blue Line: Chicago, just west of River North. Trendy, eclectic dance club where hip-hop and funk blend with leopard and velvet decor. W Soul and R&B night. Cover $10 for women, $20 for men. Free before 10pm. Open M-W 10pm-2am, Th-F 9pm-2am, Sa 9pm-3am, Su 6pm-2am.

Smart Bar, 3730 N. Clark St. (☎773-549-4140), downstairs from the Metro. Resident DJ spins punk, techno, hip-hop, and house. 21+. Cover $5-25; Metro (see above) concertgoers free. Opening times vary (around 10pm); closes M-Th and Su 4am, F-Sa 5am.

The Apartment, 2251 N. Lincoln Ave. (☎773-348-5100), lets you party in the killer city pad that you've always craved. Sit on sofas in front of the fireplace and play Playstation 2, lounge in the luxurious master bedroom, or chat in the faux kitchen. A bathtub filled with beer keeps the good times rolling. No cover. Open W-Th 9pm-2am, F-Sa 9pm-3am.

OUTDOOR ACTIVITIES

A string of lakefront parks fill the area between Chicago proper and Lake Michigan. On sunny afternoons dog walkers, in-line skaters, and skateboarders storm the shore. Close to downtown, the two major parks are Lincoln and Grant. **Lincoln Park** extends across 5 mi. of lakefront on the north side with winding paths, natural groves of trees, and asymmetrical open spaces. The **Lincoln Park Zoo** is usually filled with children fascinated by the zoo's caged gorillas and lions. (☎742-2000; www.lpzoo.com. Open daily 10am-5pm; in summer M-F 10am-5pm, Sa-Su 10am-7pm. Free.) Next door, the **Lincoln Park Conservatory** provides a veritable glass palace of plants from varied ecosystems. (☎742-7736. Open daily 9am-5pm. Free.)

Grant Park, covering 14 lakefront blocks east of Michigan Ave., follows the 19th-century French park style: symmetrical and ordered with corners, a fountain, and wide promenades. The Grant Park Concert Society hosts free summer concerts in the **Petrillo Music Shell,** 520 S. Michigan Ave. (☎742-4763). Colored lights illuminate **Buckingham Fountain** from 9 to 11pm. On the north side, Lake Michigan lures swimmers and sun-bathers to **Lincoln Park Beach** and **Oak St. Beach.** Beware, though: the rock ledges are restricted areas, and swimming from them is illegal. Although the beaches are patrolled 9am-9:30pm, they can be unsafe after dark. The **Chicago Parks District** (☎742-7529) has further info.

Starting from Hyde Park in the south, **Lake Shore Drive** offers sparkling views of Lake Michigan all the way past the city and one of the best views of the downtown skyline. At its end, Lake Shore becomes **Sheridan Road,** which twists and turns its way through the picturesque northern suburbs. Just north of Chicago is **Evanston,** a lively, affluent college town (home to **Northwestern University**) with an array of parks and nightclubs. Ten minutes farther north is upscale **Wilmette,** home to the ornate and striking **Baha'i House of Worship,** 100 Linden Ave., at Sheridan Rd. This architectural wonder is topped by a stunning nine-sided dome. (☎847-853-2300. Open June-Sept. daily 10am-10pm; Oct.-May 10am-5pm. Services M-Sa 12:15pm, Su 1:15pm).

The **Indiana Dunes State Park** and **National Lakeshore** lie simultaneously 45min. east of Chicago on I-90 and in a different world. The State Park's gorgeous dune beaches on Lake Michigan provide hikes through dunes, woods, and marshes. Info about the State Park is available at their office, 1600 N. 25 E. in Chesterton, IN (☎219-926-1952). Obtain Lakeshore details at their **Visitors Center,** 1100 N. Mineral Springs Rd., in Porter, IN (☎219-926-7561).

GREAT LAKES

SPRINGFIELD ☎217

Springfield, "the town that Lincoln loved," was a hotbed of political activity during the antebellum years, and attracted the attention of the entire nation when it hosted the epic Lincoln-Douglass debates of 1858. Happily, many Lincoln sights are free. (Info line ☎800-545-7300.) The **Lincoln Home Visitors Center,** 426 S. 7th St., screens a film and doles out free tickets to tour the **Lincoln Home,** at 8th and Jackson St. (☎492-4241. Open daily 8:30am-5pm. 10min. tours every 5-10min. from the front of the house. Arrive early to avoid the crowds.) The **Old State Capitol,** where Lincoln gave his prophetic "House Divided" speech in 1858, also held the Lincoln-Douglass debates. (☎785-7961. Open daily Mar.-Oct. 9am-5pm, Nov.-Feb. 9am-4pm. Last tour 1hr. before closing. Donation suggested.) Lincoln, his wife Mary Todd, and three of their sons rest in the monumental **Lincoln Tomb,** 1500 Monument Ave., at Oak Ridge Cemetery. (☎782-2717. Open daily Mar.-Oct. 9am-5pm, Nov.-Feb. 9am-4pm.) The **Dana-Thomas House,** 301 E. Lawrence Ave., was one of Frank Lloyd Wright's early experiments in the Prairie Style and still features Wright's original fixtures. (☎782-6776. Open W-Su 9am-4pm. 1hr. tours every 15-20min. Suggested donation $3, under 18 $1.)

Bus service to the cheap lodgings off I-55 and U.S. 36 on Dirksen Pkwy. is limited. Rooms downtown should be reserved early for holiday weekends and the **State Fair** in mid-August. For a comfortable stay without a hefty price, head to the **Pear Tree Inn ❸,** 3190 S. Dirksen Pkwy., which offers rooms with cable TV, A/C, and free local calls. (☎529-9100. Breakfast included. Rooms from $46.) Interesting cuisine is sparse in Springfield, though there are a few exceptions. **Cozy Drive-In ❶,** 2935 S. 6th St., is a staple of historic Rte. 66 and birthplace of the "Cozy Dog," or corndog ($1.60). Today, it's a family-owned diner devoted to roadside memorabilia and great food. (☎525-1992. Burger $1.70. Open M-Sa 8am-8pm.) The colorful **Cafe Brio ❹,** 524 E. Monroe, is an inventive eatery with seasonal cuisine. (☎544-0574. Entrees $10-20. Open M-Th 11am-10pm, F-Sa 11am-11pm, Su 11am-3pm.)

Amtrak, (☎753-2013; station open daily 6am-9:30pm) at 3rd and Washington St., near downtown, runs trains to Chicago (3½hr., 4 per day, $22-45) and St. Louis (2hr., 4-5 per day, $11-20). **Greyhound,** 2351 S. Dirksen Pkwy. (☎800-231-2222; depot open M-F 8am-1pm and 2-8:15pm, Sa-Su 8am-noon and 2-4pm), on the eastern edge of town, rolls to: Chicago (4-6hr., 5 per day, $39); Indianapolis (8-10hr., 2 per day, $48); St. Louis (2hr., 4 per day, $27). For local transportation, try **Springfield Mass Transit District,** 928 S. 9th St. (☎522-5531. Buses operate M-Sa 6am-6pm. $0.75, seniors $0.35; transfers free.) The **downtown trolley** system is designed for tourists. (☎528-4100. Trolleys run W-Su 9am-4pm; call ahead to confirm hours. Hop-on/off $10, seniors $9, ages 5-12 $5; circuit $5.) **Taxi: Lincoln Yellow Cab,** ☎523-4545. **Visitor Info: Springfield Convention and Visitors Bureau,** 109 N. 7th St. (☎789-2360 or 800-545-7300; www.visit-springfieldillinois.com. Open M-F 8am-5pm.) **Internet Access: Lincoln Library,** 326 S. 7th St. (☎753-4900. Open June-Aug. M-Th 9am-9pm, F 9am-6pm, Sa 9am-5pm; Sept.-May also open Su noon-5pm.) **Post Office:** 411 E. Monroe, at Wheeler. (☎788-7470. Open M-F 7:45am-5pm.) **Postal Code:** 62701. **Area Code:** 217.

WISCONSIN

Hospitality is served up with every beer and every piece of Wisconsin cheddar sold in the Great Lakes' most wholesome party state. A wide variety of wily creatures make themselves at home in the thick woods of Wisconsin's extensive park system, while the state's favorite animal—the cow—grazes near highways. Along the shoreline, fishermen haul in fresh perch, and on rolling hills farmers grow barley for beer. Visitors to "America's Dairyland" encounter cheese-filled country stores en route to the ocean-like vistas of Door County, as well as the ethnic *fêtes* (not to mention other, less refined beer bashes) of Madison and Milwaukee.

PRACTICAL INFORMATION

Capital: Madison.

Visitor Info: Division of Tourism, 123 W. Washington St., P.O. Box 7976, Madison 53707 (☎608-266-2161 or 800-432-8747; www.tourism.state.wi.us).

Postal Abbreviation: WI **Sales Tax:** 5-5.5%, depending on county.

MILWAUKEE ☎414

Home to beer and countless festivals, Milwaukee is a city with a reputation for *gemütlichkeit* (hospitality). Ethnic communities throw rollicking, city-wide parties each summer weekend, from the traditional Oktoberfest to the Asian Moon festival. When the weather turns cold, the city celebrates with the International Arts Festival Milwaukee, during which galleries and museums extend their hours. Milwaukee's 1500 bars and taverns fuel the revelry with as much beer as anyone could ever need. Aside from merrymaking, the city boasts top-notch museums, German-inspired architecture, and a long expanse of scenic lakeshore.

TRANSPORTATION

Airport: General Mitchell International Airport, 5300 S. Howell Ave. (☎747-5300; www.mitchellairport.com). Take bus #80 from 6th St. downtown (30min.). **Limousine Service,** ☎769-9100 or 800-236-5450. 24hr. pickup and dropoff from most downtown hotels. $10, round-trip $18. Reservations required.

Trains: Amtrak, 433 W. St. Paul Ave. (☎271-0840), at 5th St. downtown. In a fairly safe area, but less so at night. To **Chicago** (1½hr., 7 per day, $20) and **St. Paul** (6½hr., 1 per day, $45-98). Open M-Sa 5:30am-10pm, Su 7am-10pm.

Buses: Greyhound, 606 N. 7th St. (☎272-2156), off W. Michigan St., 3 blocks from the train station. To **Chicago** (2-3hr., 13 per day, $13) and **Minneapolis** (7-9hr., 6 per day, $49). Station open 24hr.; office open daily 6:30am-11:30pm. **Coach USA Milwaukee**

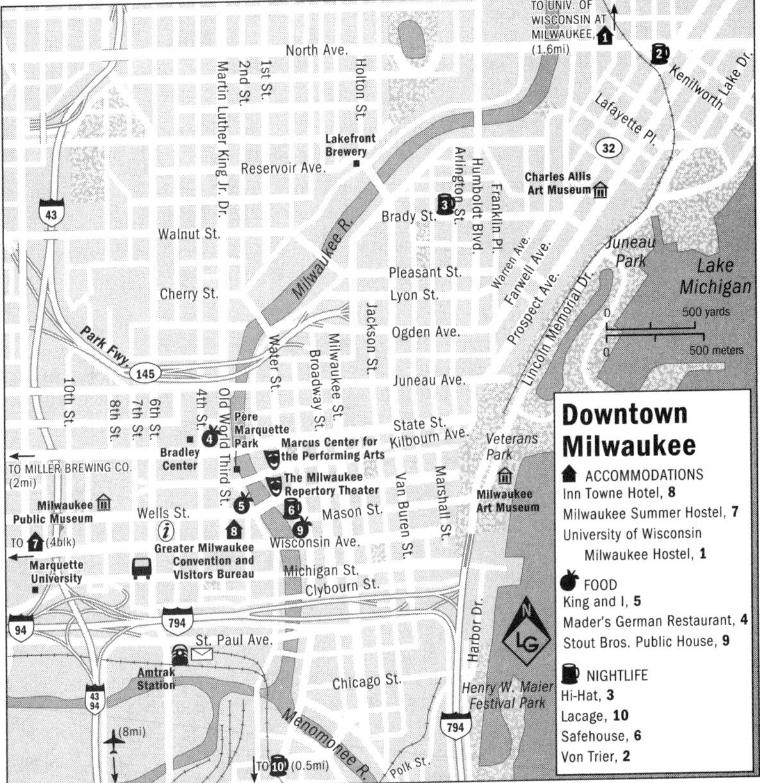

(☎262-544-6503), in the same terminal, covers southeastern Wisconsin. **Badger Bus,** 635 N. James Lovell St. (☎276-7490 or 608-255-1511), across the street, burrows to **Madison** (1½hr., 6 per day, $10). Open daily 6:30am-10pm. *Be cautious at night.*

Public Transit: Milwaukee County Transit System, 1942 N. 17th St. (☎344-6711). Efficient metro area service. Most lines run 5am-12:30am. $1.50, seniors and children $0.75; weekly pass $11. Fare includes transfer that can be used 1hr. after first ride. Free maps at the library or at Grand Ave. Mall. Call for schedules. The **Trolley** (☎344-6711) runs 2 services. The River Route connects Brady St. and the Third Ward, and the Lake Valley Route runs between the Potawatomi Bingo Casino and the lake, with service to the Festival Park during ethnic festivals. $0.50, seniors $0.25. Open June-Aug. Su-Th 10am-6:30pm, F-Sa 10am-midnight; Sept.-May M-Sa 10am-6:30pm.

Taxi: Veteran, ☎291-8080. **Yellow Taxi,** ☎271-6630.

ORIENTATION & PRACTICAL INFORMATION

Most of Milwaukee's action is downtown, which lies between **Lake Michigan** and **10th Street.** Address numbers increase north and south from **Wisconsin Avenue,** the center of east-west travel. Most north-south streets are numbered, increasing from Lake Michigan toward the west. The **interstate system** forms a loop around Milwaukee: **I-43 S** runs to Beloit; **I-43 N** runs to Green Bay; **I-94 E** is a straight shot to Chicago; **I-94 W** goes to Madison and then Minneapolis/St. Paul; **I-794** cuts through the heart of downtown Milwaukee; and **I-894** connects with the airport.

Visitor Info: Greater Milwaukee Convention and Visitors Bureau, 400 W. Wisconsin Ave. (☎273-7222 or 800-554-1448; www.milwaukee.org), in the Midwest Express Center lobby. Open year-round M-F 9am-5pm; summer also Sa 9am-2pm, Su 11am-3pm.

Hotlines: Crisis Intervention, ☎257-7222. **Rape Crisis Line,** ☎542-3828. Both operate 24hr. **Gay People's Union Hotline,** ☎562-7010. Operates daily 7-10pm.

Post Office: 345 W. St. Paul Ave. (☎270-2308), south along 4th Ave. from downtown, by the Amtrak station. Open M-F 7:30am-8pm. **Postal code:** 53201. **Area code:** 414.

ACCOMMODATIONS

Downtown lodging options tend to be expensive; travelers with cars should head out to the city's two hostels. **Bed and Breakfast of Milwaukee** (☎277-8066) finds rooms in picturesque B&Bs from $55 around the area.

Milwaukee Summer Hostel (HI), 1530 W. Wisconsin Ave. (☎288-3232), in McCormick Hall on Marquette University's campus. Take bus #10 or 30 down Wisconsin to 16th St. This hostel offers small, sparsely furnished rooms, but the central location and low prices make it a good summer option. Laundry, kitchen facilities, free Internet access, and parking nearby (Su-Th $3.50, F-Sa free). Check-in 5-10pm. Check-out 8-11am. Open June to mid-Aug. Dorm beds $17, nonmembers $20; Private rooms $37/40. ❶

University of Wisconsin at Milwaukee (UWM), Sandburg Hall, 3400 N. Maryland Ave. (☎229-4065 or 299-6123). Take bus #30 north to Hartford St. Close to East Side restaurants and bars, the UWM sports spotless, dorm suites, divided into singles and doubles. Laundry facilities and free local calls. Parking $6.50. 2-day advance reservations required. Open June to mid-Aug. Singles with shared bath $36; doubles $60. ❷

Wellspring Hostel (HI-AYH), 4382 Hickory Rd. (☎262-675-6755), in Newburg. Take I-43 N to Rte. 33 W to Newburg and exit on Main St.; Hickory Rd. intersects Newburg's Main St. just northwest of the Milwaukee River. The idyllic setting on a riverside farm, is well worth the 45min. drive. Well-kept with 10 beds, kitchen, and nature trails. Linens $1 each. Office open daily 8am-8pm. Dorms $15-18. ❶

Inn Towne Hotel, 710 N. Old World Third St. (☎224-8400 or 800-528-1234), downtown. This centrally located Best Western offers spacious rooms with complimentary continental breakfast, exercise facilities, cable TV, and A/C. Proximity to Water St. offers endless food and nightlife options. Parking $10 per day. Rooms from $79. ❹

FOOD

From *wurst* to *bier*, Milwaukee is best known for its German traditions. Restaurants are scattered along nearly every street in the city, particularly downtown, where most adopt continental attitudes and hefty prices to match their 100 years of experience. In addition to its German influences, the city takes advantage of its location and diverse population. Nearby Lake Michigan provides the main ingredient to a local favorite called the **Friday night fish fry.** Polish and Serbian influences dominate the **South Side,** and good Mexican food prevails in **Walker's Point,** at National and 5th St. **East Side** eateries are cosmopolitan and quirky, with a mix of ethnic flavors. Downtown, the Riverwalk project has revitalized the **Water Street Entertainment District,** which boasts hot new restaurants for a range of palates. On the north end of the Riverwalk, **Water Street** is home to the city's best brew-pubs. For those who prefer to skip straight to the sweet stuff, the Dairy State's deservedly famous frozen custard is the way to go.

Mader's German Restaurant, 1037 N. Old World Third St. (☎271-3377). Mader's is a local favorite with *schnitzels* and *sauerbraten* worth the steep prices. Suits of armor, steins, and guns conjure up images of Bavaria. Entrees from $12. Open M-Th 11:30am-9pm, F-Sa 11:30am-10pm, Su 10:30am-9pm. Reservations recommended. ❸

La Fuente, 625 S. 5th St. (☎271-8595), on the South Side. Locals flock here for authentic Mexican food and the best margaritas in town ($6.50-7.50). Murals, mariachi music, and a patio add to the laidback atmosphere. Lunches from $4. Dinner entrees $6-11. Open Su-Th 10am-10pm, F-Sa 10am-11:30pm. ❷

Stout Bros. Public House, 777 N. Water St. (☎273-2337), downtown. One of Milwaukee's many brew pubs, this restaurant serves up hearty sandwiches ($7-8) and homemade beers in a restored 1874 bookbinder's building. Try "The Yank," their creamy flagship ale ($3.25). Open M 11am-10pm, Tu-Sa 11am-11pm, Su 11am-3pm. ❷

King and I, 823 N. 2nd St. (☎276-4181). The lunch buffet ($7) is a favorite at this authentic Thai place. Entrees $11-17. Open M-F 11:30am-10pm, Sa 5-11pm, Su 4-9pm. Buffet served M-F 11:30am-2:30pm. ❸

GREAT LAKES

SIGHTS

BREWERIES. Although many of Milwaukee's breweries have left, the city's name still evokes images of a cold one. No visit to the city would be complete without a look at the yeast in action. The **Miller Brewery,** a corporate giant that produces 43 million barrels of beer annually, offers a free 1hr. tour with three generous samples. *(4251 W. State St. ☎931-2337; www.millerbrewery.com. Under 18 must be accompanied by an adult. ID required. Open M-Sa 10am-5:30pm; 2 tours per hr., 3 during busy days; winter M-Sa 10am-5pm, call for tour schedule.)* For a taste of Milwaukee's microbreweries, take a 3hr. **Riverwalk Boat Tour.** The tour's pontoon boat, appropriately titled the *Brew City Queen*, travels to the Milwaukee Alehouse, the Lakefront Brewery, and the Rock Bottom Brewery. *(Tours start from Père Marquette Park on Old World Third St. between State and Kilbourn. ☎283-9999. Tours Sa-Su, call for times. $12.)* Some microbreweries offer their own tours as well. The **Lakefront Brewery** produces five popular year-round beers and several seasonal specials. Sip samples while watching the beer being made before your eyes. The Lakefront Palm Garden restaurant, a huge hall that recalls the era of brewery-run *biergartens*, also cooks up a mean Friday night fish fry. *(1872 N. Commerce St. ☎372-8800; www.lakefrontbrewery.com. Tours F 3, 6, 7pm; Sa 1, 2, 3pm. $5 with souvenir mug, $2 non-beer drinkers. ID required without legal guardian.)* One of the state's most renowned microbreweries, **Sprecher Brewing** still believes in Old World brewing techniques. The 1hr. tour, which includes a visit to an old lager cellar and the Rathskellar museum of beer memorabilia, is followed by four beer samples. *(701 W. Glendale, 5 mi. north of the city on I-43, then east on Port Washington St. ☎964-2739; www.sprecherbrewery.com. Tours F 4pm, Sa 1, 2, 3pm; Jun.-Aug. additional tours M-Th. Call for tour times. $2, under 21 $1. Reservations required.)*

MUSEUMS. Several excellent museums dot the shores of Milwaukee. The **Milwaukee Art Museum** is a sculpture in and of itself with its cylindrical elevators and windows that frame a spectacular view of Lake Michigan. Moveable, sail-like wings jut out from the building, which houses a wide spectrum of works, including Haitian folk art and 19th-century German paintings. Don't skip the basement, which contains one of the most complete furniture collections in the country. *(700 N. Art Museum Dr., on the lakefront downtown. ☎224-3200; www.mam.org. Free audio tour available. Open Tu-W and Sa 10am-5pm, Th noon-9pm, F 10am-9pm. $6, students and seniors $4, under 12 free.)* Visitors can wander through the cobbled streets of Old Milwaukee and venture into a replica of a Costa Rican rainforest at the **Milwaukee Public Museum.** *(800 W. Wells St., at N. 8th St. ☎278-2702; www.mpm.edu. Open daily 9am-5pm. Free tours M-Sa noon, Su 1pm. $6.75, seniors $5.50, children $4.50, under 3 free. Free M. IMAX Theater $4.50, seniors and children $4. Parking available.)* The intimate **Charles Allis Art Museum** combines East Asian artifacts with Classical antiques in a stately, refurbished 1910 mansion. *(1801 N Prospect Ave. at E. Royal Pl., 1 block north of Brady. Take bus #30, 31, or River Rte. Trolley. ☎278-8295; www.cavtmuseums.org. Open W 1-5pm and 7-9pm, Th-Su 1-5pm. $5, students and seniors $3, children free.)*

PARKS. Better known as "The Domes," the **Mitchell Park Horticultural Conservatory** recreates a desert and a rainforest and mounts seasonal floral displays in three seven-story conical glass greenhouses. *(524 S. Layton Ave., at 27th St. Take bus #10 west to 27th St., then #27 south to Layton. ☎649-9830. Open daily 9am-5pm. $4.50, seniors and ages 6-17 $3, under 6 free.)* The **Boerner Botanical Gardens** cultivate gorgeous blossoms and host open-air concerts on Thursday nights. *(9400 Boerner Dr., in Whitnall Park. ☎525-5600. Open May-Sept. daily 8am-sunset. $4, seniors $3, age 6-17 $2.)* For an escape from the city, visit one of the many parks along the waterfront.

OTHER SIGHTS. A road warrior's nirvana, locally headquartered **Harley-Davidson** gives 45min. tours of its engine plant that will enthrall any aficionado. *(11700 W. Capitol Dr. ☎342-4680. Tours June-Aug. M-F 9:30, 11am, 1pm; Sept.-Dec. M, W, F 9:30, 11am, 1pm. Call ahead; the plant sometimes shuts down in summer. Reservations required for groups larger than 5. Closed shoes must be worn.)* For a brush with Olympic glory, amateur ice skaters should head to daily open skates at the **Pettit National Ice Center.** Home to the US speedskating team, the Pettit includes several hockey and figure-skating rinks. *(500 S. 84th St., at I-94, next to the state fairgrounds. ☎266-0100. Call for open skating schedules. $6, seniors and children $5. Skate rental $2.50.)*

ENTERTAINMENT

Music comes in almost as many varieties as beer in Milwaukee. The modern **Marcus Center for the Performing Arts,** 929 N. Water St., across the Milwaukee River from Père Marquette Park, is the area's major arts venue. Throughout the summer, the center's Peck Pavilion hosts **Rainbow Summer,** a series of free lunchtime concerts performed by both professional and local bands. (☎273-7121; www.marcuscenter.org. Concerts M-F noon-1:15pm. Call for additional evening performances.) The music moves indoors during the winter with the **Milwaukee Symphony Orchestra,** the **Milwaukee Ballet,** and the **Florentine Opera Company.** (☎273-7121. Symphony $17-52, ballet $13-62, opera $15-80. Ballet and symphony offer half-price student and senior rush tickets. Box office open M-F 11:30am-9pm, Sa-Su noon-9pm.) From September through May the **Milwaukee Repertory Theater,** 108 East Wells St., opens its three stages, offering a mix of innovative shows and classics. (☎224-9490; www.milwaukeerep.com. $8-50; students and seniors $2 off, as well as half-price rush 30min. before shows. Box office open M-Sa 10am-6pm, Su noon-6pm.)

Baseball's **Brewers** team step up to bat at **Miller Park,** at the interchange of I-94 and Rte. 41 (☎902-4000 or 800-933-7890; www.milwaukeebrewers.com. Tickets $5-35. Tours April-Sept. Tu-F 11:30am-1:30pm every hr., Sa 10:30am-1:30pm every ½hr., Su 11:30am-1:30pm every ½hr. $6, seniors and children under 14 $3.), while the NBA's **Bucks** hoop it up at the **Bradley Center,** 1001 N. 4th St. (☎227-0500).

FESTIVALS

Summertime livens up Milwaukee's scene with countless free festivals and live music events. On any given night, a free concert is happening; call the **Visitors Bureau** (☎273-7222) to find out where. On Thursdays in summer, **Cathedral Park Jazz** (☎272-0993) jams for free in **Cathedral Square Park,** at N. Jackson St. between Wells and Kilbourn St. In Père Marquette Park, between State and Kilbourn St., **River Flicks** (☎270-3560) screens free movies at dusk Thursdays in August.

Locals line the streets in mid-July for **The Great Circus Parade** (☎608-356-8341), a recreation of turn-of-the-century processions, complete with trained animals, daredevils, and 65 original wagons. During the 11 days of **Summerfest,** the largest of Milwaukee's festivals, daily life halts as a potpourri of musical acts, culinary specialties, and a crafts bazaar takes over. (☎273-3378 or 800-273-3378; www.summerfest.com. Late June-early July. Tickets M-Th $9, F-Su $10.) In early August, the **Wisconsin State Fair** rolls into the fairgrounds, next to the Pettit National Ice Center, toting 12 stages along with exhibits, rides, fireworks, and a pie-baking contest. (☎266-7000 or 800-884-3247; www.wsfp.state.wi.us. $7, seniors $5, ages 7-11 $3.) Ethnic festivals also abound during festival season and are held in the **Henry W. Maier Festival Park,** on the lakefront downtown. The most popular are: **Polish Fest** (☎529-2140; www.polishfest.org) and **Asian Moon** (☎483-8530; www.asianmoon.org), both in mid-June; **Festa Italiana** (☎223-2193; www.festaitaliana.com) in mid-July; **Bastille Days** (☎271-7400; http://bastille.easttown.com) around Bastille Day (July 14); and **German Fest** (☎464-9444; www.germanfest.com) in late July. (The Milwaukee County Transit Trolley runs a Lakefront extension to the festivals. Most festivals $7, under 12 free; some free plus price of food.) Pick up a copy of the free weekly *Downtown Edition* or call ☎800-554-1448 for more information.

NIGHTLIFE

Milwaukee never lacks something to do after sundown. The downtown business district becomes desolate at night, but the area along **Water Street** between Juneau and Highland Ave. offers hip, lively bars and clubs. Nightspots that draw a college crowd cluster around the intersection of **North Avenue** and **North Farwell Street,** near the UW campus. Running east-west between Farwell St. and the Milwaukee River, **Brady Street** is lined with the hottest bars and coffeehouses. **S. 2nd Street** is a fairgrounds for eclectic, trendy nightclubs, lounges, and the city's best gay bars.

Safehouse, 779 N. Front St. (☎271-2007), across from the Pabst Theater downtown. A wooden sign labeled "International Exports, Ltd." welcomes guests to this bizarre world of spy hideouts and secret passwords. A briefing with "Moneypenny" in the foyer is just the beginning of the intrigue. The "Ultimate Martini" is propelled through a maze of plastic tubes before it is served just how Mr. Bond likes it—"shaken, not stirred" ($12.75 with souvenir shaker and glass). Draft beer $2.75; 24oz. specialty drinks $6.50-7.50. Cover $1-3. Open M-Th 11:30am-1:30am, F-Sa 11:30am-2am, Su 4pm-midnight.

Von Trier, 2235 N. Farwell Ave. (☎272-1775), at North Ave. Flower boxes and a brick facade invite customers into this German-style *biergarten*. The intricate wood carvings, big oak bar, and stein-lined walls create a laidback atmosphere for enjoying some serious beer. The bar boasts a vast selection of imports from all over the world, but the house special is German weiss ($5). Open Su-Th 4pm-2am, F-Sa 4pm-2:30am.

Hi-Hat, 1701 Arlington St. (☎225-9330), at Brady St. Jazz be-bops from speakers above the cavernous, candlelit bar, which mixes some of the meanest cocktails in town. The restaurant occasionally plays host to live jazz and DJs on weekends, and swing and jazz are played on various nights throughout the week. The Su brunch is a local favorite ($9-13). M-W swing and jazz. Open daily 4pm-2am, Su 10am-2am, brunch 10am-3pm.

Lacage, 801 S. 2nd Ave. (☎383-8330). The largest nightspot in town boasts 7 bars, 2 dancefloors, and a loyal 20- and 30-something gay clientele. Lacage considers themselves "straight-friendly," and crowds are often mixed. DJs spin to keep 2 large floors grooving. F and Su the bar splits: dancing on one side and drag shows on the other. Downstairs, the upscale bistro **E.T.C.** serves tapas ($8-12) and screens live jazz. Cover W $2, Th $3, F-Sa $5. Open Su-Th 9pm-2am, F-Sa 9pm-2:30am.

MADISON ☎608

Locals in Madison refer to their city as "The Isthmus." For those who have forgotten their seventh-grade geography, that's a narrow strip of land that connects two larger landmasses. In other words, it's a rather awkward place to build a city. As a

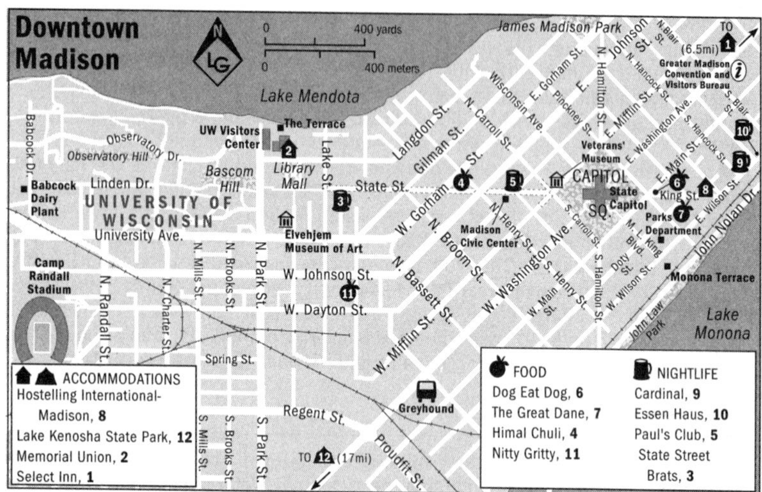

result, the Capitol and the University of Wisconsin-Madison share very close living quarters. The odd coupling, though, has proven fruitful as Madison's peculiar flavor is a fine blend of mature stateliness and youthful vigor.

ORIENTATION

Madison's main attractions are centered around the Capitol and the University of Wisconsin-Madison. **State Street,** which is reserved for pedestrians, bikers, and buses, connects the two and serves as the city's hub for eclectic food, shops, and nightlife. **Lake Monona** to the southeast and **Lake Mendota** to the northwest lap at the shores of the isthmus. The northeast and southwest ends of the isthmus are joined by **Washington Avenue (U.S. 151),** the city's main thoroughfare. **I-90** and **I-94** are joined through the city, but separate on either side of it. I-94 E goes to Milwaukee, then Chicago; I-94 W goes to Minneapolis/St. Paul; I-90 E goes direct to Chicago through Rockford, IL; I-90 W goes to Albert Lea, MN.

PRACTICAL INFORMATION

Airport: Dane County Regional Airport, 4000 International Ln. (☎246-3380). Cabs to downtown $7-12. **Greyhound,** 2 S. Bedford St. (☎257-3050), has buses to **Chicago** (3-4hr.; 6 per day; M-Th $21, F-Su $23) and **Minneapolis** (5-6hr.; 4 per day; M-Th $38, F-Su $40). **Badger Bus** (☎255-6771; www.badgerbus.com) is located at the same address and offers service to **Milwaukee** (90min., 8 per day, $14). **Van Galder** (☎752-5407 or 800-747-0994; www.vangalderbus.com) leaves from the UW Memorial Union, 800 Langdon St., to **Chicago** (3-4hr., 4 per day, $22). **Madison Metro Transit System,** 1101 E. Washington Ave. (☎266-4466), serves downtown, campus, and environs ($1.50). **Greater Madison Convention and Visitors Bureau:** 615 E. Washington Ave. (☎255-2537 or 800-373-6376; www.visitmadison.com. Open M-F 8am-5pm.) **Internet Access: Madison Public Library,** 201 W. Mifflin St. (☎266-6300. Open M-W 8:30am-9pm, Th-F 8:30am-6pm, Sa 9am-5pm; Oct.-Apr. also open Su 1-5pm.) **Taxi: Union Cab,** ☎242-2000. **Post Office:** 3902 Milwaukee St., at Rte. 51 (☎246-1228. Open M-F 8am-6pm, Sa 9am-2pm.) **Postal Code:** 53714. **Area Code:** 608.

ACCOMMODATIONS

Motels stretch along Washington Ave. (U.S. 151) near the intersection with I-90, with rooms starting at $40 per weeknight and rising dramatically on weekends. From the Capitol, bus routes #6 and 7 shuttle the 5 mi. between the Washington Ave. motels and downtown. Prices steepen downtown, starting around $60.

Hostelling International–Madison (HI-AYH), 141 S. Butler St. (☎441-0144; www.madisonhostel.org), at King St. This well-located hostel is a good bet for social travelers. Cheerful setting and spotless rooms. Kitchen, laundry, Internet access. Office hours 7:45am-10pm. Dorms $16, nonmembers $19; private rooms $35/38. ❶

Memorial Union, 800 Langdon St. (☎262-1583), on the UW campus next to Union Terrace. Large, elegant rooms with excellent lake and city views. Cable TV, A/C, and free parking. Call ahead; the 6 rooms fill up–especially on football weekends–up to a year in advance. No-frills **college cafeterias** here dole out the quickest, cheapest food in town, with meals from $5-8. Rooms from $62. ❸

Select Inn, 4845 Hayes Rd. (☎249-1815), near the junction of I-94 and U.S. 151. Large rooms with cable TV, A/C, and whirlpool. Continental breakfast included. Summer singles from $46; doubles from $57. Winter $39/46. ❸

Lake Kegonsa State Park, 2405 Door Creek Rd. (☎873-9695), 20min. south on I-90 in Stoughton. Pleasant sites in a wooded area near the beach. Showers, flush toilets. Park open year-round 6am-11pm; campground open May 1-Oct. 31. Sites $9, WI residents $7; $11/9 Sa-Su. Parking permits $10/5 per day. ❶

FOOD

Fine dining establishments pepper Madison, spicing up the university and Capitol areas. **State Street** hosts a variety of cheap restaurants, including chains and Madison originals; at its west end, vendors peddle international delicacies, including Thai, Cuban, and East African treats.

The Great Dane, 123 East Doty St. (☎284-0990), near the Capitol. This popular, spacious brewpub serves hearty sandwiches, burgers, and other pub favorites ($7-18) along with a host of hand-crafted beers. The newspaper-style menu describes both the brewing process and the beers offered. Open Su-Th 11am-2am, F-Sa 11am-2:30am. ❷

Himal Chuli, 318 State St. (☎251-9225). This storefront stirs up Nepalese favorites, such as *tarkari, dal,* and *bhat.* In English, that's terrific veggie meals and lentil soup ($3). Flavorful meat dishes also available. Meals $6-13. Open daily 11am-9:30pm. ❷

WALKING IN A WATER WONDERLAND

Water-sliding in northern Wisconsin may sound unpleasant, but once the clarification of "indoor" is provided, it begins to seem more reasonable. Over the past decade, the free-wheeling entrepreneurs at the **Wisconsin Dells** have created the largest concentration of indoor water parks in the world. This might seem like a dubious distinction, but it has turned the Dells into one of the leading attractions in Wisconsin.

The largest of these water wonderlands is the **Kalahari Resort,** which is, in fact, the biggest indoor water park in the world, covering 125,000 sq. ft. with wave pools, lazy rivers, and some of the wildest water slides around. The Tasmanian Twister shoots sliders through a tube into a giant funnel before dumping them into a swirling pool of water. The gravity-defying Botswana Blast sends rafters uphill into a clear tube towering over the entire park before letting them race down a series of twists and turns to the bottom. So, grab your suit, hop on a slide, and let 'er rip. It's the least you can do to commemorate the ingenious Americans who wedded water with Wisconsin.

*The **Wisconsin Dells** are on I-94, 125 mi. west of Milwaukee. **Kalahari Indoor Waterpark,** 1305 Kalahari Dr. (☎608-254-5466 or 877-253-5466). Open Su-Th 9am-10pm, F-Sa 9am-11pm. $35.*

Nitty Gritty, 223 N. Frances St. (☎251-2521), at Johnston St. Burgers, beer, and birthdays abound at this popular college grill, which celebrates a gazillion birthdays each day with balloons and free beer (for the birthday person only). Just don't wear your birthday suit; they will totally throw you out. "Gritty Burger" $6.20. Entrees $5-10. Open M-Th 11am-2am, F-Sa 11am-2:30am, Su 5pm-midnight. ❷

Dog Eat Dog, 106 King St. (☎441-9464), near the Capitol. Madison's only authentic Chicago-style hot dog stand serves up succulent weiners ($2.50) with all the works—relish, cucumbers, tomatoes, and hot peppers. Delicious cheese fries ($3.25) are worth the damage they entail. Open M-Sa 11am-8pm.Cash only. Also at 1225 Regent St. ❶

SIGHTS

INSIDE MADISON

With its double nature as a seat of government and home to a thriving college scene, the isthmus has an eclectic mix of sights. The imposing **State Capitol,** at the center of downtown, boasts beautiful ceiling frescoes and mosaics. (☎266-0382. Open daily 6am-8pm. Free tours from the ground floor info desk M-Sa on the hr. 9-11am and 1-3pm, Su 1-3pm.) Facing the Capitol is the **Veterans Museum,** 30 W. Mifflin St., which contains exhibits tracing US military history from the Civil War to WWII with a focus on Wisconsin-born soldiers and infantry units. (☎267-1799; http://museum.-dva.state.wi.us. Open Mar.-Sept. M-Sa 9am-4:40pm, Su noon-4pm. Free.) Close to the Capitol at the end of Martin Luther King, Jr. Blvd. is the **Monona Terrace Community and Convention Center,** 1 John Nolen Dr., Frank Lloyd Wright's impressive 352,610 sq. ft. structure overlooking the lake. The beautiful roof-top gardens offer the city's best views of the Capitol and Lake Monona. (☎261-4000; www.mononaterrace.com. Open daily 8am-5pm. 45min. guided tours available daily from the Gift Shop. Call for times. $3.) Every Saturday and Wednesday morning from late April to early November, visitors swarm the Capitol grounds for the **Dane County Farmers' Market,** where farmers sell fresh-picked crops and Madison radicals advocate animal rights. (☎800-373-6376; www.madfarmmkt.org. W 8:30am-1:30pm, Sa 6am-2pm.)

The **University of Wisconsin-Madison (UW)** itself has a few noteworthy museums. One of the state's most acclaimed art museums, the **Elvehjem Museum of Art** (EL-vee-hem) boasts an astounding collection of Ancient Greek vases and several galleries of American and European painting. (800 University Ave. ☎263-2246; www.lvm.wisc.edu. Open Tu-F 9am-5pm, Sa-Su 11am-5pm. Free. Tours Th 12:30pm permanent galleries, Su 2pm temporary galleries.) UW produces its own brand of ice cream at the **Babcock Dairy Plant,** 1605 Linden Dr., at Babcock Dr., where visitors can watch their favorite flavor being made. (☎262-3045. Store open M-F 9:30am-5:30pm, Sa 10am-1:30pm.) Also part of UW, the outdoor **Olbrich Botanical Gardens** and indoor **Bolz Conservatory,** 3330 Atwood Ave., house a plethora of plant life. The Gardens showcase floral settings, from butterfly-attracting plants to an English herb garden, and an exquisite Thai Pavilion—unique in the continental USA—constructed entirely without nails. (☎246-4550; www.olbrich.org. Gardens open Apr.-Sept. daily 8am-8pm; Oct.-Mar. 9am-4pm. Free. Conservatory open M-Sa 10am-4pm, Su 10am-5pm. $1, under 5 free; free W and Sa 10am-noon.) Aspiring botanists can trek along the 20 mi. of trails amongst the 1240 acres of the **University Arboretum,** 1207 Seminole Hwy., off Beltline Hwy. (☎263-7760. Grounds open daily 7am-10pm; Visitors Center open M-F 9:30am-4pm, Sa-Su 12:30-4pm.) For more info visit the **UW Visitors Center,** 716 Langdon St., on the west side of the Memorial Union (☎263-2400).

OUTSIDE MADISON

Some of Madison's most unique sights are far from the town proper. Forty-five minutes west of Madison off U.S. 14, the **House on the Rock,** 5754 Rte. 23, in Spring Green, is an unparalleled multilevel house built into a chimney of rock. The 40-acre complex of gardens, fantastic architecture, kitsch, and collections features a 200 ft. fiberglass whale engaged in an epic struggle with an octopus and the world's largest carousel—of its 269 animals, not one is a horse. (☎935-3639; www.thehouseontherock.com. Open daily mid-Mar. to late May and Sept.-Oct. 9am-6pm; late May-Aug. 9am-7pm. $19.50, ages 7-12 $11.50, ages 4-6 $5.50, under 3 free.) Nine miles north of the House on the Rock, Frank Lloyd Wright's famed **Taliesin** home and school hugs the hills and valley that inspired his style of organic architecture. (On Rte. 23 at Rte. C in Spring Green. ☎588-7900; www.taliesinpreservation.org. Open May-Oct. daily 8:30am-5:30pm. Shuttle tours offered in Apr. and Nov. Sa-Su 10am-4pm. 4 1-4hr. walking tours per day $10-70. Call for exact rates and schedules.)

BARABOO'S BIZARRE The Greatest Show on Earth is in Baraboo, Wisconsin—permanently. Twenty miles northwest of Madison along the Baraboo River, a swath of bank has been set aside by the State Historical Society to honor the one-time winter home of the world-famous **Ringling Brothers** circus. The **Circus World Museum** packs a full line-up of events from big-top performances to street parades. *(426 Water St. ☎356-8341; www.circusworldmuseum.com. Open summer daily from 9am-6pm. Big top shows 11am, 3:30pm. $15, seniors $13, ages 5-11 $8.)* Baraboo, however, has more to offer than plumed horse parades. The **fantastical sculpture garden of Dr. Evermor** lies just south of Baraboo on Rte. 12. Here, Tom Every, a self-taught artist and welder, transforms industrial scrap metal into whimsical creatures—including a full orchestra of musical birds made from old instruments. The centerpiece is a massive palace/rocketship structure, *Forevertron*, which has been recognized by *Guinness* as the largest junk sculpture in the world. *(For more info, call Eleanor Every at ☎592-4735 or 219-7830. Open daily 10:30am-5:30pm. Free.)*

ENTERTAINMENT

20,000 music-lovers flood the Square on Wednesday nights in June and July when the Wisconsin Chamber Orchestra performs free **Concerts on the Square.** (☎257-0638. 7pm.) Leading out from the Capitol, **State Street** exudes a lively college atmosphere, sporting many offbeat clothing stores and record shops, as well as a host of bars and restaurants. The **Madison Civic Center,** 211 State St. (☎266-9055; www.madcivic.org) is undergoing extensive remodeling and expansion to be completed in 2005. The Civic Center remains open during construction and continues to stage frequent performances in the Oscar Mayer Theatre, and hosts the **Madison Symphony Orchestra.** (☎257-3734; www.madisonsymphony.org. Office open M-F 11am-5:30pm, Sa 11am-2pm. Season runs late Aug.-May. Tickets from $23-67.) The building is also home to the rotating contemporary exhibits and permanent modern collection of the **Madison Art Center.** (☎257-0158; www.madisonartcenter.org. Open Tu-Th 11am-5pm, F 11am-9pm, Sa 10am-9pm, Su 1-5pm. Free.) The **Madison Repertory Theatre,** also located in the Civic Center, performs classic and contemporary works. (☎266-9055; www.madisonrep.org. Showtimes vary; tickets $6.50-22. Box office open M-F 11am-5:30pm, Sa 11am-2pm or until show, Su if show.) Students and locals pass their days and nights hanging out at UW's gorgeous, lakeside **Union Terrace.** (800 Langdon St. ☎265-3000.) The terrace is home to free weekend concerts year-round, which take place on the lakeshore in the summer, and move indoors in the winter.

NIGHTLIFE

Fueled by the 40,000-plus students who pack this aptly labelled party school, Madison's nightlife scene is active and boozetastic. Clubs and bars are scattered throughout the isthmus, particularly along **State Street** and **U.S. 151.**

Essen Haus, 514 E. Wilson St. (☎255-4674), off U.S. 151. This lively German bar and restaurant is the only place in town where college girls dance the polka with octogenarians. Round up a crew and pass around the infamous "beer boot." On the menu, traditional German fare (bratwurst $6) rubs shoulders with American cuisine. Incredible beer selection (from $1.50). Open Tu-Th 4pm-2am, F-Sa 4pm-2:30am, Su 3-10pm.

Cardinal, 418 E. Wilson St. (☎251-0080). A benchmark of Madison's gay scene, Cardinal also attracts straight clubbers who come for its wide array of themed dance nights every day of the week, from goth industrial and electronic underground to Latin jazz and 80s hits. Cover $3-5. Open M-Th 8pm-2am, F-Sa 8pm-2:30am.

State Street Brats, 603 State St. (☎255-5544). Head to "Brats" for the true wild and crazy college bar experience. 2 floors of frat-house fun with a wide list of Wisconsin microbrews. Brats and burgers ($3-8) anchor the menu. Open Tu and Th-Sa 11am-2am, M, W, Su 11am-close.

Paul's Club, 212 State St. (☎257-5250). Mingle under the branches of the full-size oak tree that adorns the bar at Paul's Club, a laidback lounge that offers refuge from the drunken hijinks of State St. Enticing leather couches provide a great place to chat with the trendy crowd. Open Su-Th 4pm-2am, F 4pm-2:30am, Sa noon-2:30am.

OUTDOOR ACTIVITIES

Madison's many parks and lakeshores offer endless recreational activities. There are 10 gorgeous public **beaches** for swimming or strolling along the two lakes (☎266-4711 for more info). Back on dry land, **bicycling** is possibly the best way to explore the city and surrounding park lands. Madison, in fact, is the bike capital of the Midwest, with more bikes than cars traversing the landscape. **Budget Bicycle Center,** 1230 Regent St. (☎251-8413), loans out all types of two-wheel transportation ($10 per day, $30 per week, tandems $10-30 day). Hikers and picnickers should head to **Picnic Point** on Lake Mendota. A bit of a hike off University Bay Dr., this spot provides great views of the college. For other city parks, the **Parks Department,** 215 Martin Luther King Jr. Blvd., in the Madison Municipal Building, can help with specific park info. (☎266-4711. Office open M-F 8am-4:15pm; park open daily 4am-dusk. Admission to Madison parks is free.)

DOOR COUNTY ☎920

Jutting out like a thumb from the Wisconsin mainland between Green Bay and Lake Michigan, the Door Peninsula exudes a coastal spirit unlike any other in the nation's heartland. The rocky coastline, azure waters, and towering pines resemble a northeastern fishing village more than a Midwestern getaway. Door County beckons to both campers and vacationers with miles of bike paths, national and state parks, beaches, and quaint country inns. Despite its undeniable popularity as a tourist destination, the Door has managed to carefully avoid commercialism and maintain its unique local flavor. Its 12 villages swing open on a summer-oriented schedule; visitors are advised to make reservations for accommodations and campsites if they plan to be on the peninsula during a weekend in either July or August.

ORIENTATION & PRACTICAL INFORMATION. Door County begins north of **Sturgeon Bay,** where Rte. 42 and 57 converge and then split again. Rte. 57 hugs the eastern coast; Rte. 42 runs up the west. The peninsula's west coast, tends to be more expensive, while the colder, calmer east coast contains most of the park area. From south to north along Rte. 42, **Egg Harbor, Fish Creek, Ephraim, Sister Bay,** and **Ellison Bay** are the largest towns. During the summer, the days are warm, but temperatures can dip to 40°F at night, even in July. Public transportation only comes as close as **Green Bay,** 50 mi. southwest of Sturgeon Bay, where **Greyhound** has a station at 800 Cedar St. (☎432-4883. Open M-F 6:30am-5pm; Sa-Su 6:30-6:50am, 10am-noon and 3:30-5:10pm.) and runs to **Milwaukee** (2½hr., 5 per day, $20). Reserve tickets at least a day in advance. **Door County Chamber of Commerce:** 6443 Green Bay Rd., on Rte. 42/57 entering Sturgeon Bay. (☎743-4456 or 800-527-3529; www.doorcountyvacations.com. Open Apr.-Oct. M-F 8:30am-5pm, Sa-Su 10am-4pm; Nov.-Mar. M-F 8:30am-4:30pm.) **Post Office:** 359 Louisiana, at 4th St. in Sturgeon Bay. (☎743-2681. Open M-F 8:30am-5pm, Sa 9:30am-noon.) **Postal Code:** 54235. **Area Code:** 920.

ACCOMMODATIONS. Unique, country-style lodgings crowd Rte. 42 and 57; reservations for July and August should be made far in advance. The **Century Farm Motel ❸,** 10068 Rte. 57, 3 mi. south of Sister Bay on Rte. 57, rents cozy two-room cottages hand-built in the 1920s. The motel, situated on a chicken and buffalo farm, is removed from the tourist activity of the Door's towns and offers fantastic peak season prices. (☎854-4069. A/C, TV, and fridge. Open mid-May to mid-Oct. $50-60. Cash only.) Relaxed and convenient, the **Lull-Abi Motel ❸,** 7928 Egg Harbor Rd./Rte. 42 in Egg Harbor, soothes visitors with spacious rooms, a patio, an indoor whirlpool, as well as free coffee and bicycles. (☎868-3135. Open May-late Oct. Doubles $59-109. Suites with wet bar and refrigerator $69-109.)

CAMPING. Except for the restricted **Whitefish Dunes,** the area's **state parks** ❶ offer outstanding camping ($10, WI residents $8; F-Sa $12/10). All state parks require a **motor vehicle permit** ($3 per hour; $10/5 per day; $30/20 per yr.). **Peninsula State Park,** just past Fish Creek village on Rte. 42, contains 20 mi. of shoreline and 17 mi. of trails alongside the largest of the state park campgrounds. (☎868-3258. 469 sites with showers and toilets. Make reservations far in advance, or come in person to put your name on the waiting list for one of 70 walk-in sites.) The relatively uncrowded **Potawatomi State Park,** 3740 Park Dr., sits just outside Sturgeon Bay off Rte. 42/57. (☎746-2890. 125 campsites, 19 open to walk-ins.) Highlighted by hidden coves, **Newport State Park,** 7 mi. from Ellison Bay off Rte. 42, is a wildlife preserve at the tip of the peninsula. Sites are accessible by hiking only. (☎854-2500. 16 sites, 3 open to walk-ins.) The untamed **Rock Island State Park** offers 40 remote sites near Washington Island. (☎847-2235. Open late May to mid-Oct.)

FOOD. Food from the lake and Scandinavian customs dominate Door County fare. Many people visit the region just for **fishboils,** a Scandinavian tradition, in which cooks toss potatoes, spices, and whitefish into a large kettle over a wood fire. To remove the fish oil from the top of the water, the boilmaster throws kerosene into the fire, producing a massive fireball; the cauldron boils over, signaling chow time. The **Bayside Tavern ❶,** on Rte. 42 in Fish Creek, cooks up spicy, Cincinnati-style chili ($4) and speciality burgers ($4-7). At night, Bayside becomes a lively bar. (☎868-3441. Live music M and Sa. Open mic Th. Sa cover $3-5. Open Su-Th 11am-2am, F-Sa 11am-2:30am.) Door County's best-known fishboils bubble up at **The Viking Grill ❸,** in Ellison Bay. (☎854-2998. Open daily 6am-8pm, fishboils mid-May to Oct. 4:30-8pm. $13.75, under 12 $10.25.) Drop in on **Al Johnson's Swedish Restaurant ❸,** 700-710 Bayshore Dr., in the middle of Sister Bay on Rte. 42, for Swedish pancakes ($6.25), served with lingonberries. The restaurant is hard to miss; just look for the goats grazing atop the sod-covered roof. (☎854-2626. Open daily 6am-9pm; in low-season 7am-8pm. Entrees $14-18.) Fish Creek's local favorite **Sister Bay Bowl and Supper Club ❷,** 504 Bayshore Dr., rolls out generous portions along with a six-lane bowling alley. (☎854-2841 Entrees from $5, bowling from $3. Open daily 11:30am-2pm and 5-10pm; winter 11:30am-2pm and 5-9pm.)

SIGHTS. Most of Door County's sights are located on the more populated West Side. At the base of the peninsula, Sturgeon Bay houses the intriguing **Door County Maritime Museum,** at 120 N. Madison St., downtown. The museum offers insight into the area's ship-building and water-charting history with antique boats and interactive exhibits. (☎743-5958; www.dcmm.org. Open May-Oct. daily 9am-6pm. $3.) **Door Peninsula Winery,** 5806 Rte. 42, in Sturgeon Bay, invites vine-lovers into a former school house that now produces award-winning fruit wine. (☎743-7431 or 800-551-5049; www.dcwine.com. 15-20min. tours and free tastings in summer 9am-6pm; low-season 9am-5pm. Tours $1.50.) The **Skyway Drive-In,** on Rte. 42 between Fish Creek and Ephraim, screens double features at great prices. (☎854-9938. Current release double feature $6, ages 6-11 $3. Call for schedules.) Just south of the Skyway, Peninsula State Park houses the outdoor **American Folklore Theatre,** where a local troupe performs original, Wisconsin-themed shows. (☎869-2329; www.americanfolktheatre.com. $12, ages 13-19 $6.50, ages 6-12 $3.50.)

The shipping town of **Green Bay,** 50 mi. south of Sturgeon Bay at the foot of the Door peninsula, is best known as home to the Green Bay Packers. Chances of snagging a ticket to a Packer's game are slim, but the appropriately green and yellow **Lambeau Field** is worth a look. (☎496-5719. Tickets $32-39.)

OUTDOOR ACTIVITIES. Biking is the best way to take in the largely untouched lighthouses, rocks, and white-sand beaches of the Door's rugged eastern coastline. Village tourist offices have free bike maps. **Whitefish Dunes State Park,** off Rte. 57, glimmers with extensive sand dunes, hiking/biking/skiing trails, and a well-kept wildlife preserve. (Open daily 8am-8pm. $7 vehicle permit required.) Just north of the Dunes off Rte. 57 on Cave Point Rd., the rugged **Cave Point County Park** has some of the best views on the peninsula. (Open daily 6am-9pm. Free.) In **Baileys Harbor,** 3 mi. north of Lakeside, waves and wind have carved miles of sand ridges along the coastline. **Ridges Sanctuary,** north of Baileys Harbor off Rte. Q, has trails meandering through the 30 ridges, which are separated by wetlands called swales. The unique ecosystem is home to a thriving population of plants and fauna, including a number of endangered species. Also offered are birdwatching opportunities and a boreal forest at **Toft's Point.** (☎839-2802. Nature center open daily 9am-4pm. $2.) **Baileys Harbor Ridges Beach,** an uncrowded stretch of sand that allows for secluded swimming, adjoins the sanctuary on Ridges Rd.

Accessed via Cana Island Rd. off Rte. Q, **Cana Island Lighthouse** juts out from the lake, compelling visitors to cross the rocky path (at low tide) or wade through the frigid waters (at high tide) to reach its oft-photographed shores. There is no access to the lighthouse itself but the island provides an expansive view of the bay. (No phone. No facilities. Open daily 10am-5pm. $3, children $1.)

The West Side's recreational offerings are fewer than the East Side's, but they are no less exciting. **Peninsula State Park,** in Fish Creek, is a popular spot for tourists. Visitors rent boats and ride bicycles along 20 mi. of shoreline road. More crowded than east coast beach options, **Nicolet Beach** (inside the park) attracts sunbathers from all over the peninsula. One mile and 110 steps up from the beach, **Eagle Tower** offers the highest view of the shore. On a clear day, the tower allows a glimpse of Michigan's shores across the waters of Green Bay. (Open daily 6am-11pm. Vehicle permit required. $3 per hr., $10 per day.) Across from the Fish Creek entrance to Peninsula State Park, **Nor Door Sport and Cyclery,** 4007 Rte. 42, rents out bikes and winter equipment. (☎868-2275. Open M-F 9am-6pm, Sa-Su 9am-5pm. Bikes $5 per hr., $20 per day. Cross-country skis $10 per day.)

APOSTLE ISLANDS ☎715

The National Lakeshore protects 21 of the breathtaking islands off the coast of Wisconsin, as well as a 12 mi. stretch of mainland shore. Bayfield, a tiny mainland town, serves as the access point to the islands. Tourism is focused on the mainland and Madeline Island where coastal inns draw families looking for a back-to-nature weekend. Backpackers pour into town on their way to and from hikes, kayakers explore island caves, and sailers delight in the clear waters. Adventure companies allow summer tourists with all levels of outdoor experience to enjoy the kayaking, hiking, and camping among the unspoiled sandstone bluffs.

PRACTICAL INFORMATION. Most excursions begin in the sleepy mainland town of **Bayfield** (pop. 686), in northwest Wisconsin on the Lake Superior coast. The **Bay Area Rural Transit (BART),** 300 Industrial Park Rd., 21 mi. south on Rte. 13 in Ashland, offers a shuttle to Bayfield. (☎682-9664. 4 per day M-F 7am-5pm. $1.80, students $1.50, seniors $1.10.) **Bayfield Chamber of Commerce,** 42 S. Broad St. (☎779-3335 or 800-447-4094; www.bayfield.org. Open M-Sa 8:30am-5pm, Su 10am-2pm. Lobby with free local phone open 24hr.) **National Lakeshore Headquarters Visitors Center,** 410 Washington Ave., distributes hiking info and **camping permits.** (☎779-3398. Open mid-May to mid-Sept. daily 8am-6pm; mid-Sept. to mid-May W-Su 8am-4:30pm. Permits for up to 14 consecutive days $15.) For **short-term work** picking apples and raspberries, contact the **Bayfield Apple Company,** on County J Rd. near the intersection of Betzold Rd. (☎779-5700 or 800-363-4526. Open May-Jan. daily 9am-6pm.) **Post Office:** 22 S. Broad St., Bayfield. (☎779-5636. Open M-F 9am-4:30pm, Sa 9am-11am.) **Postal Code:** 54814. **Area Code:** 715.

ACCOMMODATIONS. In summer months, the budget pickings are slim for Bayfield. On weekends in July and August, rooms should be booked weeks in advance. The **Seagull Bay Motel ❸,** off Rte. 13 at S. 7th St., offers spacious, smoke-free rooms with cable TV and a lake view. (☎779-5558. Mid-May to mid-Oct. from $60-90; mid-Oct. to mid-May $35-65.) **Greunke's First Street Inn ❹,** 17 Rittenhouse Ave., has been accommodating guests for 139 years. Quaint country rooms and a homey atmosphere make this a great place to experience Bayfield hospitality. (☎779-5480 or 800-245-3072. Open May-Oct. Rooms $55-105.) **Dalrymple Park ❶,** ¼ mi. north of town on Rte. 13, has 30 campsites in a grand setting under tall pines on the lake. (Open mid-May to mid-Oct. No showers; self-regulated; no reservations. Sites $15.) **Apostle Islands Area Campground ❶,** ½ mi. south of Bayfield on County Rd. J off Rte. 13, has 55 campsites buried in the woods of Bayfield. (☎779-5524. Open early May-early Oct. July-Aug. reservations recommended 1 month in advance. Sites $15, with hookup $20, with full sewer and cable $27.) The Chamber of Commerce has info on **guest houses** (from $35).

FOOD. The bright pink exterior is just the beginning at **Maggie's ❷,** 257 Manypenny Ave., where satisfying burgers ($6) and the best fajitas ($10) complement the Mardi Gras and flamingo decor. (☎779-5641. Open Su-Th 11am-10pm, F-Sa 11am-11pm.) Down the street is Maggie's breakfast counterpart, **Egg Toss Cafe ❷,** 41 Manypenny Ave., which serves a variety of breakfasts and sandwiches ($5-7) in a patio setting. (☎779-5181. Open daily 6am-3pm.) One of the oldest establishments in Bayfield, **Greunke's Restaurant ❸,** 17 Rittenhouse Ave., at 1st St., has been serving hungry fisherman for over a century. These days, it specializes in huge breakfasts by day ($4-6) and famous fishboils by night. Check out the still-working Wurlitzer jukebox and photos of celebrity customers. (☎779-5480. Fishboils W-Su 6:30-8pm. $11, children $6. Open M-Sa 6am-10pm, F-Su 7am-9:30pm.)

SIGHTS & OUTDOOR ACTIVITIES. Though often overshadowed by Bayfield and Madeline Island (see below), the other 21 islands have their own subtle charms. The **sandstone quarries** of Basswood and Hermit Islands and the abandoned logging and fishing camps on some of the other islands serve as silent reminders of a more prosperous era. The restored **lighthouses** on Sand, Raspberry, Long, Michigan, Outer, and Devil's Islands offer spectacular views. **Sea caves,** carved out by thousands of years of wind and water, create a spectacular sight on several islands. The **Apostle Islands Cruise Service** runs narrated 3hr. tours that provide a brief look at these various sights and a sampling of the history and lore of the islands. From late June to early September, the cruise service runs an inter-island shuttle. (☎779-3925 or 800-323-7619. Tours of the archipelago depart the Bayfield City Dock mid-May to mid-Oct. daily 10am. Call for additional tours and departure times. $26, children $15. Reservations recommended.)

The best beach on the mainland is **Bay View Beach,** just south of Bayfield along Rte. 13, near Sioux Flats. Look carefully for the hard-to-find dirt road marked Bayview Park Rd. to enter this serene beach. **Trek and Trail,** at 1st and Washington St., rents bikes and kayaks and runs various kayaking tours of the islands. (☎800-354-8735. Bikes $5 per hr., $20 per day. 4hr. kayak rental from $20, all equipment included, but renters must complete $50 kayaking safety course. Tours from $50.)

Bayfield's apples attract visitors after the summer hikers leave. The population swells to 40,000 during the **Apple Festival** in the first full weekend of October, when natives and tourists alike gather for the street fairs. The **Bayfield Apple Company** has fresh-picked fruit and tasty jam (see p. 603). Locals flock to **Big Top Chautauqua,** 3 mi. south of Bayfield off Hwy. 13 on Ski Hill Rd., to see national acts such as Willie Nelson and the ever-popular "house shows," original musicals about life in northern Wisconsin. (☎373-5552 or 888-244-8386; www.bigtop.org. Open June-Sept. Shows Su-Th 7:30pm, F-Sa 8:15pm. Tickets can be purchased at the Bayfield Branch Box Office, Rittenhouse Ave. and 1st St., next to Greunke's. Reserved seating $18, general admission $12, children 12 and under $8.)

MADELINE ISLAND ☎715

Several hundred years ago, the Ojibwe tribe came to Madeline Island from the Atlantic in search of the megis shell, a light in the sky purported to bring prosperity and health. Today, the island maintains its allure, housing a colony of artists alongside relaxing beaches frequented by thousands of summer visitors.

The **Madeline Island Motel ❹,** on Col. Woods Ave. across from the ferry landing, has private patios as well as clean rooms named for local historical figures. (☎747-3000. Mid-June to Oct. doubles $95; Oct.-May $70-80.) Rooms in the area fill during the summer; call ahead for reservations. Madeline Island has two campgrounds. **Big Bay Town Park ❶,** 6½ mi. from La Pointe off Big Bay Rd., sits next to tranquil Big Bay Lagoon. (☎747-6913. No reservations. Open mid-May to mid-Oct. Sites $10, with electricity $13.) Across the lagoon, **Big Bay State Park ❶** rents 60 primitive sites. (☎747-6425, for reservations ☎888-475-3386. Reservations $4. Sites $10-12. Daily vehicle permit $10, WI residents $5.)

Tom's Burned Down Cafe ❷, 1 Middle Rd., may look like a garage sale with bizarre sculptures out front, but the lively bar serves healthy food, including many vegan options, and hosts the islands' artist community. (☎747-6100. Open daily Su-Th 10am-2am, F-Sa 10am-2:30am. Live music on Sa-Su. Sandwiches $7, pizzas $9.) **Grampa Tony's ❷**, 814 Main St., has something for everyone: pizza (from $7), subs ($5-7), ice cream ($2.50), and espresso drinks. (☎747-3911. Open daily 7am-9pm.)

With roughly five streets, Madeline Island is easy to navigate. **Visitor Info: Madeline Island Chamber of Commerce,** on Middle Rd. (☎747-2801 or 888-475-3386; www.madelineisland.com. Open M-F 9:15am-4:30pm, Sa-Su 10am-3pm.) For pamphlets about the island, visit the chamber's booth near the ferry landing in Bayfield. **Madeline Island Ferry Line** shuttles between Bayfield and La Pointe on Madeline Island. (☎747-2051. June-Sept. daily every 30min. 9:30am-6pm, every hr. 6:30-9:30am and 6-11pm. 1-way $4, ages 6-11 $2; bikes $1.75; cars $9.25. Mar.-June and Sept.-Dec. ferries run less frequently and prices drop.) In winter, the state highway department builds a road across the ice. During transition periods, the ferry service runs **windsleds** between the island and the mainland. At **Motion to Go,** 102 Lake View Pl., on Middle Rd., about one block from the ferry, "Moped Dave" rents scooters and bikes. (☎747-6585. Open May-June 9am-6pm; July-Aug. daily 8am-8pm; Sept. to mid-Oct. 9am-7pm. Mopeds $17.50 per hr.; mountain bikes $7 per hr., $26 per day.) The **Post Office** is just off the dock on Madeline Island in La Pointe. (☎747-3712. Open M-F 9am-4:20pm, Sa 9:30am-12:50pm.) **Postal Code:** 54850. **Area Code:** 715.

MINNESOTA

In the 19th century, floods of German and Scandinavian settlers forced native tribes out of the rich lands now known as Minnesota, a name derived from a Dakota word meaning "sky-tinted waters." Minnesota's white pioneers transformed the southern half of the state into a stronghold of commercial activity; however, the north has remained largely untouched, an expanse of wilderness quilted with over 15,000 lakes. Attempts at preserving this rugged frontier have helped raise awareness about Minnesota's natural resources and the culture of the Ojibwe, the state's Native American antecedents.

PRACTICAL INFORMATION

Capital: St. Paul.

Visitor Info: Minnesota Office of Tourism, 100 Metro Sq., 121 7th Pl. E., St. Paul 55101 (☎800-657-3700; www.exploreminnesota.com). Open M-F 8am-5pm.

Postal Abbreviation: MN. **Sales Tax:** 6.5%.

MINNEAPOLIS & ST. PAUL ☎612

Native son Garrison Keillor wrote that the "difference between St. Paul and Minneapolis is the difference between pumpernickel and Wonder bread." Indeed, the story of the Twin Cities is one of contrast: St. Paul is accurately described as a conservative, Irish-Catholic town, while Minneapolis has an equally well deserved reputation as a young metropolis of the future. Minneapolis' theaters and clubs rival those of New York, while the traditional capitol and the cathedral reside in St. Paul. In both cities, consumer culture, the bohemian youth world, corporate America, and an international community thrive together.

TRANSPORTATION

Airport: Minneapolis-St. Paul International (☎726-5555; www.msairport.com), 15min. south of the cities on Rte. 5, off I-494 in Bloomington. From the airport, take bus #7 to Washington Ave. in Minneapolis or bus #54 to St. Paul. **Airport Express** (☎827-7777) shuttles to both downtowns and to some hotels roughly every 30min. Operates 4:30am-11pm. To **Minneapolis** ($13) and **St. Paul** ($10).

Trains: Amtrak, 730 Transfer Rd. (☎651-644-6012 or 800-872-7245), on the east bank off University Ave. SE, between the Twin Cities. City bus #7 runs from the station to St. Paul, and #16 connects to both downtowns. Open daily 6:30am-11:30pm. To **Chicago** (8hr., 1 per day, $87-105) and **Milwaukee** (6hr., 1 per day, $81-97).

Buses: Greyhound, 29 9th St. N. (☎371-3325; open daily 5:30am-1am), in Minneapolis downtown. In St. Paul, 950 Hawthorne Ave. (☎651-222-0507; open daily 6:15am-9pm), 2 blocks west of the capitol. To: **Chicago** (9-12hr.; 9 per day; $58); **Milwaukee** (7-9 hr.; 7 per day; $49-52). Both routes depart from Minneapolis and St. Paul stations.

Public Transit: Metropolitan Transit Commission, 560 6th Ave. N (☎373-3333; www.metrotransit.org), serves both cities. Most major lines end service by 12:45am; some buses operate 24hr. $1.25; seniors, ages 6-12, and disabled $0.75. Peak fare (M-F 6-9am and 3:30-6:30pm) $1.75/1.25. Express lines $2.25/1.75. Bus #16 connects the 2 downtowns 24hr. (50min.); bus # 94 (B, C, or D) takes 30min.

Taxi: Yellow Taxi, ☎824-4444 in Minneapolis; ☎651-222-4433 in St. Paul.

PRACTICAL INFORMATION

Curves and one-way streets tangle both of the downtown areas; even the numbered grids in the cities are skewed, making north-south and east-west designations tricky. Downtown Minneapolis lies about 10 mi. west of downtown St. Paul via **I-94. I-35** splits in the Twin Cities, with **I-35 W** serving Minneapolis and **I-35 E** serving St. Paul. **I-494** runs to the airport and the Mall of America, while **I-394** heads to downtown Minneapolis from the western suburbs. **Hennepin Avenue** and the pedestrian **Nicollet Mall** are the two main roads in Minneapolis; St. Paul has no real main thoroughfares. Paying to park in lots or garages is the only option in both downtowns.

Visitor Info: Minneapolis Convention and Visitors Association, 40 S. 7th St. (☎661-4700; www.minneapolis.org), near Hennepin Ave., on the 1st. fl. of the City Center. Open M-Sa 10am-6pm, Su noon-5pm. **St. Paul Convention and Visitors Bureau,** 175 W. Kellogg, #502 (☎800-627-6101 or 651-265-4900; www.stpaulcvb.org), in the River Centre. Open M-F 8am-4:30pm.

Hotlines: Crime Victim Center Crisis Line, ☎340-5400. **Rape/Sexual Assault Line,** ☎825-4357. Both open 24hr. **Gay-Lesbian Helpline,** ☎822-8661 or 800-800-0907. Open M-F noon-midnight, Sa 4pm-midnight. **Gay-Lesbian Information Line,** ☎822-0127. Open M-F 2-10pm, Sa 4-10pm.

Internet Access: Minneapolis Public Library, 250 Marquette Ave. (☎630-6000; www.mplib.org). Open M-F 9:30am-6pm, Sa 10am-6pm. **St. Paul Public Library,** 90 W. 4th St. (☎651-266-7000; www.stpaul.lib.mn.us). Open M 11:30am-8pm, Tu-W and F 9am-5:30pm, Th 9am-8pm, Sa 11am-4pm.

Post Office: 100 S. 1st St., Minneapolis (☎349-0359), at Marquette Ave. on the river. Open M-F 7am-11pm, Sa 9am-1pm. 180 E. Kellogg Blvd., St. Paul (☎651-293-3268). Open M-F 8:30am-5:30pm, Sa 9am-noon. **Postal Codes:** Minneapolis 55401, St. Paul 55101. **Area Codes:** Minneapolis 612, St. Paul and eastern suburbs 651, southwestern suburbs 952, northwestern suburbs 763. In text, 612 unless otherwise noted.

ACCOMMODATIONS

The Twin Cities are filled with unpretentious, inexpensive accommodations. Minneapolis caters to a younger crowd and consequently has cheaper hotels; St. Paul offers finer establishments for those with thicker wallets. The Visitors Centers have lists of **B&Bs,** while the **University of Minnesota Housing Office** (☎624-2994; www.umn.edu/housing/offcampus.htm) keeps a list of local rooms ($15-60) that rent on a daily or weekly basis. The section of I-494 at Rte. 77, near the Mall of America, is lined with budget chain motels from $40. The nearest private campgrounds are about 15 mi. outside the city; the closest state park camping is in the **Hennepin Park** system, 25 mi. away. Call **Minnesota State Parks** (☎651-296-6157 or 888-646-6367) or the **Minnesota Alliance of Campground Operators** (☎651-778-2400).

Downtown St. Paul
FOOD
Cossetta, 2
Mickey's Diner, 1
CAFES
Cafe Latte, 3
Mississippi St.
L'Orent St.
Pine St.
Broadway
Wall St.
Wacouta St.
Sibley St.
E. 11th St.
E. 10th St.
E. 9th St.
E. 8th St.
E. 7th St.
E. 6th St.
E. 7th Pl.
Robert St.
Minnesota St.
Cedar St.
E. 5th St.
E. 4th St.
Kellogg Blvd.
Wabasha St.
Mississippi River
Penn Ave.
Arch St.
University Ave.
Jackson St.
Empire St.
Winter St.
Capitol Hts.
Park St.
Rice St.
State Capitol
Union Bus Depot
Constitution Ave.
Columbus Ave.
E. 12th St.
Ireland Blvd.
Minnesota History Center
W. 6th St.
5th St.
St. Peter St.
Market St.
Landmark Center
Ordway Center
Washington
St. Paul Public Library
Science Museum of Minnesota
River Centre
Chestnut St.
Walnut St.
Exchange St.
Sherman St.
Shepard Rd.
Cathedral of St. Paul
James J. Hill House
Summit Ave.
Grand Ave.
W. 7th St.
TO AMTRAK
TO MINNEAPOLIS (10mi)
0 300 yards
0 300 meters

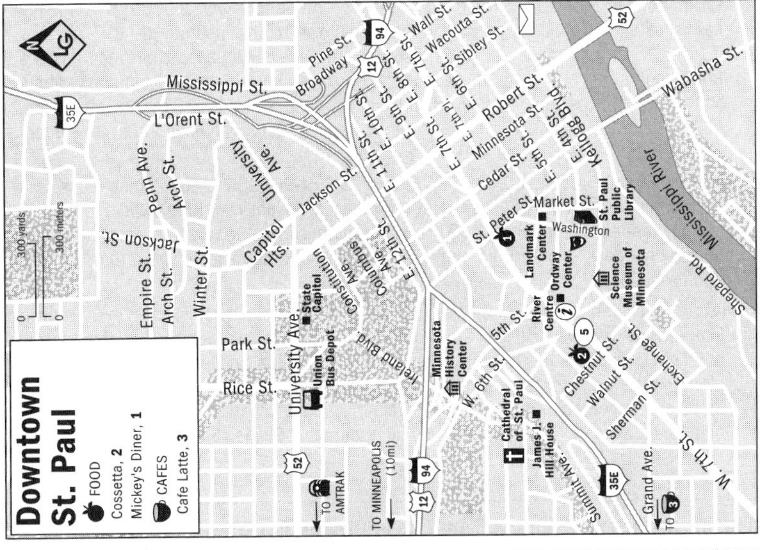

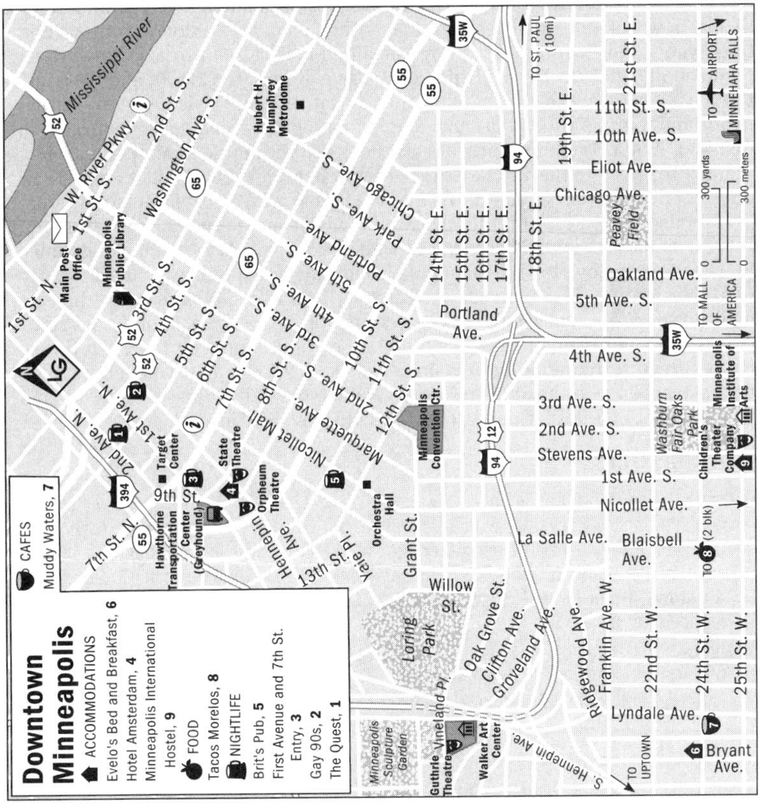

Downtown Minneapolis
ACCOMMODATIONS
Evelo's Bed and Breakfast, 6
Hotel Amsterdam, 4
Minneapolis International Hostel, 9
FOOD
Tacos Morelos, 8
NIGHTLIFE
Brit's Pub, 5
First Avenue and 7th St. Entry, 3
Gay 90s, 2
The Quest, 1
CAFES
Muddy Waters, 7
Mississippi River
W. River Pkwy.
1st St. N.
1st St. S.
2nd St. S.
Washington Ave. S.
Main Post Office
Minneapolis Public Library
3rd St. S.
4th St. S.
5th St. S.
6th St. S.
7th St. S.
8th St. S.
9th St.
10th St. S.
11th St. S.
12th St. S.
13th St.
Hubert H. Humphrey Metrodome
Chicago Ave. S.
Park Ave. S.
Portland Ave.
5th Ave. S.
4th Ave. S.
3rd Ave. S.
2nd Ave. S.
Marquette Ave.
Nicollet Mall
Hennepin Ave.
1st Ave. N.
2nd Ave. N.
7th St. N.
Target Center
State Theatre
Orpheum Theatre
Hawthorne Transportation Center (Greyhound)
Orchestra Hall
Minneapolis Convention Ctr.
Yale Pl.
Grant St.
Willow St.
Loring Park
Oak Grove St.
Clifton Ave.
Groveland Ave.
Vineland Pl.
Minneapolis Sculpture Garden
Guthrie Theatre
Walker Art Center
S. Hennepin Ave.
TO UPTOWN
14th St. E.
15th St. E.
16th St. E.
17th St. E.
18th St. E.
19th St. E.
21st St. E.
Portland Ave.
TO ST. PAUL (10mi)
11th St. S.
10th Ave. S.
Eliot Ave.
Chicago Ave.
Peavey Field
Oakland Ave.
5th Ave. S.
4th Ave. S.
3rd Ave. S.
2nd Ave. S.
Stevens Ave.
1st Ave. S.
Nicollet Ave.
La Salle Ave.
Blaisbell Ave.
Washburn Fair Oaks Park
Minneapolis Institute of Arts
Children's Theater Company
TO MALL OF AMERICA
TO AIRPORT, MINNEHAHA FALLS
TO (2 blk)
Ridgewood Ave.
Franklin Ave. W.
22nd St. W.
24th St. W.
25th St. W.
Lyndale Ave.
Bryant Ave.
0 300 yards
0 300 meters

GREAT LAKES

Minneapolis International Hostel, 2400 Stevens Ave. S. (☎522-5000; www.minneapolishostel.com), Minneapolis, south of downtown by the Institute of Arts. Take bus #17 or 18 from Nicollet Mall to 24th St. and walk 2 blocks east to Stevens. Visitors from around the country and the world lend this clean hostel a strong community atmosphere. Internet access, kitchen, living room, porch, and patio. Check-in after 1pm. Check-out before 11am. Reservations recommended. Beds with linen $20, with student or Hosteling ID $19; singles $29. ❶

Evelo's Bed and Breakfast, 2301 Bryant Ave. (☎374-9656), in south Minneapolis, just off Hennepin Ave. Take bus #17 from downtown to Bryant Ave. Kind owners rent out 3 lovingly tended rooms in this 1897 Victorian home. Fresh flowers in each room, continental breakfast, shared bathroom. Reservations and deposit required. Singles $55; doubles $70. ❸

Hotel Amsterdam, 828 Hennepin Ave. (☎288-0459; www.gaympls.com), in downtown Minneapolis, between 8th and 9th St. Located above the Saloon nightclub, this friendly hotel offers visitors easy access to downtown action and attractions. The colorful lounge offers guests a place to meet other travels, watch TV, or access the Internet. "The inn that's out" is geared toward the BGLT community, but all are welcome. Reservations recommended. Private rooms with communal bathrooms. Singles $44; doubles $50-65. ❷

FOOD

The Twin Cities' cosmopolitan, cultured vibe is reflected in the culinary choices. Posh restaurants share the streets with intimate cafes. **Uptown** Minneapolis, near Lake St. and Hennepin Ave., offers plenty of funky restaurants and bars where the Twin Cities' young socialites meet after work. In downtown Minneapolis, the **Warehouse District,** on 1st Ave. N between 8th St. and Washington Ave., and **Nicollet Mall,** a 12-block pedestrian stretch of Nicollet Ave., attract locals and tourists with shops and simple food options ranging from burgers to Tex-Mex. While grabbing a bite to eat, check out the statue of **Mary Tyler Moore,** famous for turning the whole world on with her smile, at Nicollet and 7th St. South of downtown, Nicollet turns into **Eat Street,** a 17-block stretch of international cuisine. In St. Paul, the upscale **Grand Avenue,** between Lexington and Dale, is lined with laidback restaurants and bars, while **Lowertown,** along Sibley St. near 6th St. downtown, is a popular nighttime hot spot. Near the University of Minnesota (U of M) campus between the downtowns, **Dinkytown,** on the east bank of the river, and the **Seven Corners** area of the **West Bank,** on Cedar Ave., caters to student appetites—including late night cravings. In the Twin Cities, many forego restaurants for area **cafes** (see p. 609). For do-it-yourselfers, pick up fresh produce at the **St. Paul Farmers Market,** on Wall St., between E. 4th and 5th St. (☎651-227-6856. Open late Apr. to mid-Nov. Sa 6am-1pm.)

MINNEAPOLIS

Chino Latino, 2916 Hennepin Ave. (☎824-7878), at Lake St., Uptown. A curtain of gold sequins dances above the outside entrance, but beware: "no iron gut, no service" at this Latin-Asian fusion. The trendiest restaurant in town packs in the young, see-and-be-seen, hipper-than-thou crowds with its *satay* bar ($7-9) and pu pu platter ($28; serves an army). Open M-Sa 4:30pm-1am, Su 11am-1am. Reservations strongly recommended for dinner. ❸

Figlio, 3001 Hennepin Ave. (☎822-1688), at W. Lake St. in the Calhoun Square complex, Uptown. Dishing up Italian with flare, Figlio has been awarded the honor of "Best Late Night Dining" by Twin City residents for many years for its scrumptious sandwiches (from $8), pastas and pizzas (from $11), and seafood (from $15). When the end (of your meal) is near, be sure to indulge in the "Death By Chocolate" dessert ($6). Open Su-Th 11:30am-1am, F-Sa 11:30am-2am. ❸

Bryant-Lake Bowl, 810 W. Lake St. (☎825-3737), at Bryant St. near Uptown. Built in the 1930s, this funky bowling alley/bar/cabaret is also—surprise—a really good, inexpensive restaurant. The "BLB Scramble" (a breakfast dish of eggs and vegetables; $5.25), ravioli, soups, and sandwiches ensure that the stylish patrons throw strikes with pleasantly full stomachs. Bowling $3. Entrees $6-15. Open daily 8am-1am. ❷

Tacos Morelos, 14 26th St. W (☎870-0053), at Nicollet Ave. Hispanophiles can practice their Spanish at this award-winning, authentic Mexican establishment. Try the 3 amigos enchiladas (1 enchilada with each of 3 sauces; $10), or gorge on their famous tacos ($2 each). Entrees from $6. Open Su-Th 9am-10pm, F-Sa 9am-2am. ❷

ST. PAUL

Cafe Latte, 850 Grand Ave. (☎651-224-5687), at Victoria St. More gourmet than its prices and cafeteria-style setup would suggest, meals at this cafe/bakery/pizza wine bar are consistently wonderful, and desserts are to die for. Chicken-salsa chili ($5), turtle cake ($4), and daily specials fill the 2 spacious floors with chic, hungry locals. Open M-Th 9am-11pm, F-Sa 9am-midnight, Su 9am-10pm. ❶

Mickey's Diner, 36 W. 7th St. (☎651-222-5633), at St. Peter St. A 1939 diner on the National Register of Historic Places. Mickey's offers food that outshines its bright history and chrome-and-vinyl decor. Take a spin at a counter stool, or groove to some oldies on the juke box at each booth. Steak and eggs from $6. Pancakes $3.75. 2 eggs $2.25. Omelette $6. Open 24hr. ❶

Cossetta, 211 W. 7th St. (☎651-222-3476). What began as an Italian market in 1911 is today a cafeteria-style dining experience. Try the veal parmigiana ($9) or Cossetta's famous pizza ($11-21). Open Su-Th 11am-9pm, F-Sa 11am-10pm; winter closes Su at 8pm. ❷

CAFES

Cafes are an integral part of the Twin Cities' nightlife. Particularly in Uptown Minneapolis, quirky coffeehouses caffeinate the masses and draw crowds as large as any bar. Come hungry, since most complement their java with some of the cheapest food in town.

Uncommon Grounds, 2809 Hennepin Ave. S. (☎872-4811), at 28th St., Uptown. The self-described "BMW of coffeeshops" uses secret ingredients to make the tastiest coffees ($2-5) and teas around. With velour booths and relaxing music in a smoke-free interior, this coffeeshop lives up to its name. Open M-F 5pm-1am, Sa-Su 10am-1am.

Pandora's Cup and Gallery, 2516 Hennepin Ave. (☎381-0700), at 25th St., Uptown. This 2-story coffee house offers great coffee, tasty sandwiches (portabella and swiss $5.25) and Internet access ($1 for 6min.). The tragically hip sip their espresso ($1.35-2) and munch on peanut butter and jelly "sammiches" ($2) on retro furniture throughout the house or on 1 of the 2 outdoor patios. $1 minimum. Open daily 7am-1am.

Muddy Waters, 2401 Lyndale Ave. S (☎872-2232), at 24th St., Uptown. The linoleum tables and vinyl chairs of this "caffeine canteen" recall a smoky 1950s diner, but the music, stylish mosaic, outstanding coffee ($2), and pierced staff keep it on the cutting edge. Spaghetti-o's with half a bagel ($4), Pop-Tarts ($1.50), and cheese sandwiches ($5) are just the beginning of the eclectic menu. Open M-F 7am-1am, Sa-Su 8am-1am.

Plan B Coffeehouse, 2717 Hennepin Ave. (☎872-1419), between 27th and 28th St., Uptown, has an intellectual bent, as evidenced by its sign—the periodic table. The desk toward the back may be littered with boring dictionaries, but the animated conversation, artwork, and mismatched furniture tell a different story. Try the "tripper's revenge" ($3.75). Smoking allowed. Open Su-Th 9am-midnight, F-Sa 9am-1am.

SIGHTS

MINNEAPOLIS

LAKES & RIVERS. In the land of 10,000 lakes, Minneapolis boasts many of its own; the city contains 22 lakes, 150 parks, and 100 golf courses. **Lake Calhoun,** on the west end of Lake St., Uptown, is the largest of the bunch and a recreational paradise. Scores of in-line skaters, bicyclists, and runners loop the lake on all but the coldest days. Ringed by stately mansions, the serene **Lake of the Isles** is an excellent place to commune with Canadian geese. Just southeast of Lake Calhoun on Sheridan St., **Lake Harriet** lures the locals with tiny paddleboats and a bandshell with nightly free concerts in summer. The city maintains 28 mi. of lakeside trails around the three lakes for strolling and biking. **Calhoun Cycle Center,** three blocks east of Lake Calhoun, rents out bikes for exploring the paths. *(1622 W. Lake St. ☎827-8231. Open M-Th 10am-8pm, F-Su 9am-9pm. $15-25 per ½ day, $24-40 per day. Must have credit card and driver's license.)* At the northeast corner of Lake Calhoun, the **Minneapolis Park & Recreation Board** handles canoe and rowboat rentals. *(2710 W. Lake St. ☎370-4964. Open daily 10am-8pm. Canoes $6 per hr.; rowboats $11 for 4hr. $10 deposit.)* **Minnehaha Park** allows a gander at the impressive **Minnehaha Falls,** immortalized in Longfellow's *Song of Hiawatha. (Park is near the airport; take bus #7 from Hennepin Ave. downtown. Falls are off Minnehaha Ave. at Minnehaha Pkwy.)*

MUSEUMS. Lakes are only the beginning of Minneapolis' appeal—locals and visitors have plenty to do during the (at least) 6 months of frigid winter. The **Minneapolis Institute of Arts,** south of downtown, boasts more than 100,000 art objects spanning 5000 years, including Rembrandt's *Lucretia* and the world-famous *Doryphoros*, Polykleitos' perfectly proportioned man. *(2400 3rd Ave. S. ☎870-3131; www.artsmia.org. Open Tu-W and F-Sa 9am-5pm, Th 9am-9pm, Su noon-5pm. Free.)* A few blocks southwest of downtown, the world-renowned, not-to-be-missed **Walker Art Center** counts daring exhibits by Lichtenstein, Rothko, and Warhol among its amazing galleries of contemporary art. *(725 Vineland Pl. at Lyndale Ave. ☎375-7622; www.walkerart.org. Open Tu-W and F-Sa 10am-8pm, Th 10am-9pm, Su 11am-5pm. $6; students, seniors, and ages 12-18 $4. Th and 1st Sa of the month free.)* Next to the Walker lies the **Minneapolis Sculpture Garden,** the largest urban sculpture garden in the US. The tongue-in-cheek, postcard-friendly **Spoonbridge and Cherry** is the highlight of the worthwhile gardens. The adjacent **Cowles Conservatory** houses an array of plants and a Frank Gehry fish sculpture. *(Gardens open daily 6am-midnight; conservatory open Tu-Sa 10am-8pm, Su 10am-5pm. Both free.)* Gehry also holds the honor of having designed the Cities' most unique and controversial structure: the **Weisman Art Museum,** on the East Bank of the U of M campus. The undulating metallic pseudo-building was the rough draft for his famous Guggenheim Bilbao and hosts an inspired collection of modern art, including works by O'Keeffe, Warhol, and Hartley. Check out the walk-through apartment replica, by Edward and Nancy Reddin Kienholz, that engages all the senses by asking viewers to eavesdrop at each door. *(333 E. River Rd. ☎625-9494. Open Tu-W and F 10am-5pm, Th 10am-8pm, Sa-Su 11am-5pm. Free.)*

ST. PAUL

ARCHITECTURE. St. Paul's history and architecture are among its greatest assets. Mark Twain once said that the city "is put together in solid blocks of honest bricks and stone and has the air of intending to stay." Nowhere is this more evident than along **Summit Avenue,** the nation's longest continuous stretch of Victorian houses, including a childhood home of novelist **F. Scott Fitzgerald** and the Minnesota **Governor's Mansion.** *(Fitzgerald: 599 Summit Ave. Currently a private residence. Governor's Mansion: 1006 Summit Ave. ☎651-297-8177. Tours May-Oct. F 1-3pm. Reservations required. Free.)* Also on Summit, the magnificent home of railroad magnate **James J. Hill**—the largest and most expensive home in the state when it was completed in 1891—offers 1¼-hr. tours every 30 min. *(240 Summit Ave. ☎651-297-2555. Open W-Sa 10am-3:30pm. Reservations preferred. $6, seniors $5, ages 6-15 $4. Wheelchair-accessible.)* **Walking Tours of Summit Avenue,** lasting 1½hr., depart from the Hill House and explore the architectural and social history of the area. *(☎651-297-2555. Sa 11am and 2pm. $4-6.)* Golden horses top the ornate **State Capitol,** the world's largest unsupported marble dome. *(75 Constitution Ave. ☎651-296-2881. Open M-F 9am-5pm, Sa 10am-4pm, Su 1-4pm. Tours on the hr. Free.)* A scaled-down version of St. Peter's in Rome, the **Cathedral of St. Paul,** at the end of Summit Ave, overlooks the capitol. St. Paul's is currently undergoing a $35 million renovation to replace the original copper roof. *(239 Selby Ave. ☎651-228-1766. Mass M-Th 7:30am, 5:15pm; F 7:30am; Sa 8am, 7pm; Su 8, 10am, noon, 5pm. Tours M, W, F 1pm. Open M-Th 7am-5:30pm, F 7am-4pm, Sa 7am-7pm, Su 7am-5pm.)*

HISTORY & SCIENCE. Along the river, the innovative and exciting **Minnesota History Center** houses 10 interactive, hands-on exhibit galleries on Minnesota history that entertain young and old alike. Learn how Minnesotans cope with their extreme seasons in "Weather Permitting," or admire Prince's "Purple Rain" attire in "Sounds Good to Me: Music in Minnesota." *(345 Kellogg Blvd. W. ☎651-296-6126; www.mnhs.org. Open Sept.-May Tu 10am-8pm, W-Sa 10am-5pm, Su noon-5pm; July-Aug. M and W-Sa 10am-5pm, Tu 10am-8pm, Su noon-5pm. Free, with a pay parking lot. Wheelchair-accessible.)* Downtown's **Landmark Center** is a grandly restored 1894 Federal Court building replete with towers and turrets, a collection of pianos, a concert hall, and four courtrooms. *(75 W. 5th St. ☎651-292-3225. Open M-W and F 8am-5pm, Th 8am-8pm, Sa 10am-5pm, Su 1-5pm. Free tours Th 11am, Su 1pm.)* Out front, **Rice Park,** the oldest park in Minnesota, is an ideal place for a stroll or a picnic. The **Science Museum of Minnesota** includes a beautiful atrium, a new exhibit on the human body, and an expanded Paleontology Hall. The "Virtual River Pilot" allows visitors to take a ride on the Mississippi River. *(120 West Kellogg Blvd. ☎651-221-9444; www.smm.org. Open M-W 9:30am-5pm, Th-Sa 9:30am-9pm, Su 10:30am-5:30pm. $8, seniors and ages 4-12 $6.)*

SHOP 'TIL YOU DROP Welcome to the largest mall in America—the Mall of America. With more than 520 specialty stores and 60 restaurants and nightclubs extending for over 2 mi., the Mall of America is the consummation of an American love affair with all that is obscenely gargantuan. Don't settle for just shopping and eating, though; the complex also boasts a movie megaplex, an aquarium, and the rollercoaster and ferris wheel of the largest indoor amusement park in the world. The Mall is a great idea for a day of mind-numbing entertainment or a good old-fashioned shopping spree. *(60 E. Broadway, Bloomington. From St. Paul, take I-35 E south to I-494 W to the 24th Ave. exit. Metro Transit express buses depart every half hour for the Mall. ☎952-883-8800; www.mallofamerica.com. Open M-Sa 10am-9:30pm, Su 11am-7pm.)*

AMUSEMENTS. Located on 500 wooded acres out in suburban Apple Valley, the **Minnesota Zoo** houses local and exotic animals in their natural habitats, including 15 endangered and threatened species, a Tiger Lair exhibit, and the new World of Birds show. *(13000 Zoo Blvd. Take Rte. 77 S to Zoo exit and follow signs. ☎952-431-9500 or 800-366-7811; www.mnzoo.org. Open June-Aug. daily 9am-6pm; Sept. and May M-F 9am-4pm, Sa-Su 9am-6pm; Oct.-Apr. daily 9am-4pm. $11, seniors $7.25, children $6.)* In Shakopee, even the most daring thrill-seekers can get their jollies at **Valleyfair,** a quality amusement park with five coasters and the heart-stopping Power Tower, which drops over 10 stories. *(1 Valleyfair Dr. Take Rte. 169 south to Rte 101 W. ☎800-386-7433; www.valleyfair.com. Open June-Aug. daily; May and Sept. select days. Call for hours, usually 10am-10pm. $32, ages over 60 and under 48 in. $16, under 3 free. Parking $7.)*

ENTERTAINMENT

Second only to New York in number of theaters per capita, the Twin Cities are always full of drama and music. Summer is an amazing time to visit, as most parks offer free concerts and shows on the weekends. Music is an important part of the cities—the thriving alternative, pop, and classical music scenes fill out the wide range of cultural options. For more info, read the free *City Pages* (www.citypages.com), available at libraries, most cafes, and newsstands around town.

THEATER

The renowned repertory **Guthrie Theater,** 725 Vineland Pl., Minneapolis, adjacent to the Walker Art Center just off Hennepin Ave., draws praise for its mix of daring and classical productions. (☎377-2224; www.guthrietheater.org. Season Aug.-June. Box office open M-F 9am-8pm, Sa 10am-8pm, Su hours vary. $16-44, students and seniors $5 discount. Rush tickets 15min. before show $12.50; line starts 1-1½hr. before show.) Touring Broadway shows take the stage at either the historic **State Theatre,** 805 Hennepin Ave., in downtown Minneapolis, or across the street at the **Orpheum Theatre,** 910 Hennepin Ave. N (both box offices ☎339-7007; www.state-orpheum.com). For family-oriented productions, the **Children's Theater Company,** 2400 3rd Ave. S., next to the Minneapolis Institute of Arts, comes through with first-rate plays. (☎874-0400. Season Sept.-June. Box office open in season M-Sa 9am-5pm; in summer M-F 9am-4pm. $15-28; students, seniors, and children $9-22. Rush tickets 15min. before show $11.) The ingenious **Théâtre de la Jeune Lune,** 105 1st St. N, stages critically acclaimed, off-the-beaten-path productions in an old warehouse. (☎332-3968; box office ☎333-6200. Open M-F 10am-6pm. $10-26.) **Brave New Workshop,** 3001 Hennepin Ave., in Uptown, stages satirical comedy shows and improv in an intimate club. (☎332-6620; www.bravenewworkshop.com. Box office open M-W 9:30am-5pm, Th-F 9:30am-9pm, Sa 10am-11pm. $15-22.)

MUSIC

The Twin Cities' vibrant music scene offers everything from opera and polka to hip-hop and alternative. **Sommerfest,** a month-long celebration of Viennese music put on by the **Minnesota Orchestra,** is the best of the cities' classical options during July and August. **Orchestra Hall,** 1111 Nicollet Mall, downtown Minneapolis, hosts the event. (☎371-5656 or 800-292-4141; www.minnesotaorchestra.org. Box office open M-Sa 10am-6pm. $15-65. Student rush tickets 30min. before show $10.) Nearby, **Peavey Plaza,** on Nicollet Mall, holds free nightly concerts and occasional film screenings. The **Saint Paul Chamber Orchestra,** the **Schubert Club,** and the **Minnesota Opera Company** all perform at St. Paul's glass-and-brick **Ordway Center For The Performing Arts,** 345 Washington St., which also hosts touring Broadway productions. (☎651-224-4222; www.ordway.org. Box office open M-F 9am-6pm, Sa 11am-5pm, Su 11am-4pm. $15-85.) Bands gravitate to the studio complex of the artist Prince, formerly and currently known as **Paisley Park,** just outside the city in Chanhassen.

SPORTS

The puffy **Hubert H. Humphrey Metrodome,** 900 S. 5th St., in downtown Minneapolis, houses baseball's **Minnesota Twins** (☎375-7454; www.twinsbaseball.com) and football's **Minnesota Vikings** (☎338-4537; www.vikings.com). The NBA's **Timberwolves** (☎337-3865; www.timberwolves.com) and WNBA's **Lynx** (☎673-8400, www.wnba.com/~lynx) howl at the **Target Center,** 601 1st Ave. (☎673-0900), between 6th and 7th St. in downtown Minneapolis. The expansion NHL team, the **Wild,** takes to the ice at St. Paul's **RiverCentre** (☎651-222-9453; www.wild.com). The soccer craze hits the Midwest with the minor-league **Thunder,** at the **National Sports Center** (☎763-785-5600) in suburban Blaine.

FESTIVALS

Both to liven up the dreary cold days and to celebrate the coming of summer, the Twin Cities celebrate countless festivals. From Jan. 21 to Feb. 8, 2004, the **St. Paul Winter Carnival,** near the state capitol, cures cabin fever with ice sculptures, ice fishing, skating contests, and an ice palace. On the 4th of July, St. Paul celebrates the **Taste of Minnesota** with fireworks, concerts, and regional and ethnic cuisine from hordes of local vendors. The **Minneapolis Riverfront Fourth of July Celebration and Fireworks** is a day for the family with trolley rides, concerts, food, and fireworks. (☎378-1226; www.mississippimile.com.) On its coattails rides the 10-day **Minneapolis Aquatennial,** with concerts and art exhibits glorifying the lakes. (☎518-3486.) In the 2 weeks prior to Labor Day, everyone heads to the nation's largest state fair, the **Minnesota State Fair,** at Snelling and Como St. in St. Paul. With cheese curds and walleye-on-a-stick, the fair provides a sampling of the area's flavor. (☎651-642-2200; www.mnstatefair.org. $8, seniors and ages 5-12 $7, under 5 free.)

 NIGHTLIFE

Minneapolis' vibrant youth culture feeds the Twin Cities' nightlife. The post-punk scene thrives in the Land of 10,000 Aches: Soul Asylum, Hüsker Dü, and The Replacements all rocked here before they went big. A cross-section of the diverse nightlife options can be found in the downtown **Warehouse District** on Hennepin Ave.; in **Dinkytown,** by the U of M, and across the river on the **West Bank** (bounded on the west by I-35 W. and to the south by I-94), especially on **Cedar Avenue.** The Twin Cities card hard, even for cigarettes.. The top floor of the **Mall of America** (see **Shop 'til You Drop,** p. 611) invites bar-hopping until the wee hours.

The Quest, 110 5th St. (☎338-3383; www.thequestclub.com), between 1st Ave. N and 2nd Ave. N in the Warehouse District. Once owned by Prince, this upper-class poppin' dance club pays homage to his purple highness with purple windows and lots of funk. Live salsa on M and house music draw in a young, cosmopolitan crowd. Cover $5-10. Hours vary, so call ahead.

Brit's Pub, 1110 Nicollet Mall (332-8032; www.britspub.com), between 11th and 12th, allows patrons to play a game of boccie on their English Garden Park on the rooftop. 18 different beers ($4-5), the "Earl of Sandwich" sandwich ($8), and fish and chips ($12) add to the English flavor. Open M-Su 11am-1am.

First Avenue and 7th St. Entry, 701 1st Ave. N (☎338-8388; www.first-avenue.com), downtown Minneapolis, rocks with the area's best live music several nights a week, including concerts with the hottest rock bands in the nation. Music from grunge to hip-hop to world beat. Cover $6-10, for concerts $6-30. Usually open M-Th 8pm-2am, F-Sa 9pm-3am, Su 7pm-2am.

The Gay 90s, 408 Hennepin Ave. (☎333-7755; www.gay90s.com), at 4th St., claims the seventh highest liquor consumption rate of all clubs in the nation. This superplex hosts thousands of gay and lesbian partiers in its 8 bars and showrooms, though the straight crowd is sizeable. Tu-Su drag shows upstairs starting at 9:30pm. W-Th and Su 18+, M-Tu and F-Sa 21+. Cover after 9pm $3-5. Open M-Sa 8am-2am, Su 10am-2am.

DULUTH ☎218

In picturesque Duluth, the people are friendly, the parks are manicured, and the location on the shore of Lake Superior is amazing. As the largest freshwater port in the world, Duluth harbors huge ships from over 60 different countries. The popularity of Canal Park and the Aerial Lift Bridge have enticed microbreweries, restaurants, theaters, and museums to occupy the old factories down on the wharf, turning a once-overlooked tourist destination into a worthwhile tourism spot.

PRACTICAL INFORMATION. Greyhound, 4426 Grand Ave. (☎722-5591; ticket office open daily 6:30am-5:30pm), stops 3 mi. west of downtown; take bus #1 "Grand Ave. Zoo" from downtown. Buses run only to Minneapolis (3½hr.; 3 per day; $24). The **Duluth Transit Authority,** 2402 W. Michigan St., buses within the city. (☎722-7283. Peak fare M-F 7-9am and 2:30-6pm $1, students $0.75; off-peak $0.50.) The **Port Town Trolley** moves tourists around. (☎722-7283. Runs June-Aug. daily 11am-7pm. $0.25.) **Convention and Visitors Bureau:** 100 Lake Place Dr., at Endion Station in Canal Park. (☎722-4011 or 800-438-5884; www.visitduluth.com. Open M-F 8:30am-5pm.) **Crisis Line:** ☎723-0099. **Internet Access: Duluth Public Library,** 520 W. Superior St. (☎723-3836. Open May-Sept. M-Th 10am-8:30pm, F 10am-5:30pm; Oct.-Apr. M-Th 10am-8:30pm, F 10am-5:30pm, Sa 10am-4pm. 1 hr. free each day.) **Post Office:** 2800 W. Michigan St. (☎723-2555. Open M-F 8am-5pm, Sa 9am-1pm.) **Postal Code:** 55806. **Area Code:** 218.

ACCOMMODATIONS. Motel rates rise and rooms fill during the warm months. The **Chalet Motel ❸,** 1801 London Rd., 2 mi. west of downtown, offers decent rooms with A/C near scenic Leif Erickson Park, which overlooks Lake Superior. (☎728-4238 or 800-235-2957. Apr.-Sept. singles M-F $45, Sa-Su $55. Doubles $58/68. Prices lower in winter.) A few miles south of town, the warm **Duluth Motel ❷,** 4415 Grand Ave., houses visitors in affordable, well-kept rooms right across from the Greyhound station. (☎628-1008. In summer $40-60; winter $10-50.) **Voyageur Lakewalk Inn ❸,** 333 East Superior St., lies off the Lakewalk with rooms overlooking Lake Superior. (☎722-3911. Summer rooms Su-Th $48, F-Sa $63; winter $35/45.) With a decidedly less urban feel, the rocky **Jay Cooke State Park ❶,** southwest of Duluth on I-35 Exit 242, draws in travelers with hiking, snowmobiling, cross-country skiing, and 80 campsites among the tall trees of the St. Louis River Valley. (☎384-4610 or 800-246-2267. Open daily 9am-9pm. Office open daily 9am-4pm. Reservations recommended; $8.50 reservation fee. Backcountry sites $7, sites with showers $12, with electricity $15; vehicle permit $7 per day.)

FOOD & NIGHTLIFE. Fitger's Brewery Complex, 600 E. Superior St., and the **Canal Park** region, south from downtown along Lake Ave., feature plenty of pleasant eateries. **The Brewhouse ❷,** 600 E. Superior St. in Fitger's Brewery Complex, has home-brewed beer, including Big Boat Oatmeal Stout ($2.75), and pub food from $5. (☎726-1392. Live entertainment F-Sa. Open daily 11am-1am; grill closes 10pm.) The **DeWitt-Seitz Marketplace,** in the middle of Canal Park Dr., has slightly pricier restaurants. The friendly staff at the **Blue Note Cafe ❷,** 357 Canal Park Dr., serves delicious sandwiches ($5-8) and desserts ($2-4) in a quiet coffeehouse setting. (☎727-6549. Live music F-Sa. Open May-Sept. M-Th 9:30am-9pm, F-Sa 9:30am-10pm, Su 9:30am-8pm; call for winter hours.) Located in an old pipe-fitting factory in Canal Park, **Grandma's Sports Garden ❷,** 425 S. Lake Ave., is the most popular place in town. Casual dining, an upstairs patio and a half-price Happy Hour (M-F 3-6pm) keep people coming over the river and through the woods to Grandma's. (☎722-4724. Bar open daily 9pm-1am. Restaurant open daily June-Aug. 11am-10pm; Sept.-May 11:30am-10pm.)

SIGHTS & ENTERTAINMENT. Duluth's proximity to majestic **Lake Superior** is its biggest draw. Nearly 400 mi. across, it is the largest body of fresh water in the world. Many visitors head down to **Canal Park** to watch the big ships go by at the **Aerial Lift Bridge.** Accompanied by deafening horn blasts, this unique bridge climbs 138 ft. in 1min. to allow vessels to pass; late afternoon is prime viewing time. Ships load at the **Ore Docks Observation Platform,** 35th Ave. W. and Superior St. downtown, and are tracked by the **Boatwatcher's Hotline** (☎722-6489; www.lsmma.com). The **Duluth Shipping News** (☎722-3119; www.duluthshipping-news.com) is published daily, usually available by 3pm at the **Lake Superior Maritime Visitors Center,** by the Aerial Lift Bridge at Canal Park. The Visitors Center prepares extensive displays on commercial shipping in Lake Superior. (☎727-2497. Open daily 10am-9pm.) Canal Park also serves as the beginning and end of the looped **Duluth Lakewalk,** a beautiful 4 mi. promenade.

A 39-room neo-Jacobian mansion built on iron-shipping wealth, **Glensheen Historical Sites,** 3300 London Rd., lies on the eastern outskirts of town and provides visitors with a glimpse of Duluth's most prosperous period. (☎726-8910 or 888-454-4536. Open May-Oct. daily 9:30am-4pm; Nov.-Apr. F-Su 11am-2pm. $9.50, seniors and ages 12-15 $7.50, ages 6-11 $4.50. Reservations recommended.) Waterfront tours aboard the giant steamer **William A. Irvin,** and her companion tug boat *Lake Superior*, reveal more of Duluth's shipping past. The *Irvin*, docked at Duluth's Downtown Waterfront, is longer than two football fields and was the "Queen of the Lakes" in her prime. (☎722-5573; www.williamirvin.com. Open May and Sept. to mid-Oct. Su-Th 10am-4pm, F-Sa 10am-6pm; June-Aug. Su-Th 9am-6pm, F-Sa 9am-8pm. $6.75, students and seniors $5.75, ages 3-12 $4.50.) Across the road from the *William A. Irvin* is the **Duluth OMNIMAX Theatre.** (☎727-0022. $6.75; seniors and students $5.75; children 12 and under $4.50.) Across the Aerial Lift Bridge, **Park Point** has excellent but cold swimming areas (Lake Superior's water averages 39°F), parks, and sandy beaches. The scenic **Willard Munger State Trail** links West Duluth to Jay Cooke State Park, providing 14 mi. of paved path perfect for bikes and skates; the **Willard Munger Inn,** 7408 Grand Ave., rents both. (☎624-4814 or 800-982-2453. Bikes and inline skates $15 for 2hr.; $20 for 4hr.)

Great Lakes Aquarium and Freshwater Discovery Center, 353 Harbor Dr., is America's first and only all-freshwater aquarium. The Isle Royale exhibit holds over 85,000 gallons of water and is just one of over 50 fascinating displays. (☎740-3474; www.glaquarium.org. Open Memorial Day to Sept. 10am-6pm. $10, seniors $9, children 4-17 $7, under 4 free. Parking $3.) **The Depot,** 506 W. Michigan St., a former railroad station, houses four museums including the **Lake Superior Railroad Museum,** which allows visitors to enjoy the North Shore Scenic Railroad trip. (☎727-8025; www.duluthdepot.org. Open June-Aug. daily 9:30am-6pm; Sept.-May M-Sa 10am-5pm, Su 1-5pm. All museums and a trolley ride $8.50, families $23.50.)

CHIPPEWA NATIONAL FOREST ☎218

Gleaming white strands of birch lace the pine forests of the Chippewa National Forest, home to the highest density of breeding bald eagles in the continental US. The national forest shares territory with the **Leech Lake Indian Reservation,** home of 3725 Ojibwe tribespeople. The Ojibwe, mistakenly called Chippewa, migrated from the Atlantic coast in the 18th century and, in the mid-19th century, were forced onto reservations such as Leech Lake by the US government.

Cheap, plentiful, and available in varying degrees of modernity, **camping ❶** is the way to stay in the forest. The Forest Office (see below) has info on 23 campgrounds and more than 400 free primitive recreation sites. Billboards for private campgrounds line the edges of Rte. 71 along the western border of the forest. For those who prefer more permanent forms of shelter, **Stony Point Resort ❺,** 8724 Stoney Point Camp Trail NW, 7 mi. east of Walker off Rte. 200 then 4 mi. north on Onigum Rd., rents modern lakeside cottages and cabins. (☎547-1665 or 800-338-9303; www.stonypointresort.com. Open May-Sept. Rates for 4 or 6 from $115; $20 for each additional person.) Next door, the **National Forest Campground ❶** provides a budget-friendly alternative. (☎877-444-6777. Self-regulated sites $18.)

For the northbound traveler, **Walker,** a small town in the southwest corner of the park and reservation, is an ideal gateway to the forest. Known as the "Fishing Capital of Minnesota," it draws thousands of tourists each summer. The **Leech Lake Area Chamber of Commerce** is on Rte. 371 downtown. (☎547-1313 or 800-833-1118; www.leech-lake.com. Open May-Sept. M-F 9am-5pm, Sa 10am-1pm; Oct.-Apr. M-F 9am-5pm.) The **Forest Office,** just east of town on Rte. 371, has the dirt on outdoor activities. (☎547-1044. Open M-F 7:30am-4:30pm.) **Back Street Bike & Ski Shop**, 200 10th St. S. (☎547-2500) has bikes, in-line skates, and cross country skis, while **Adventure Tours and Rentals,** 32326 Wolf Lake Rd. (☎800-635-8858), provides canoes and kayaks to explore the lakes. **Greyhound** runs to Minneapolis (4½hr., daily 12:20pm, $43); buy tickets from the driver. **Post Office:** 515 Michigan Ave. (☎547-1123. Open M-F 9am-4pm, Sa 9-11:30am.) **Postal code:** 56484. **Area code:** 218.

WHERE IT ALL BEGINS Near Chippewa, step across the Mighty Mississippi at its source at the **Beginning of the Mississippi,** in **Lake Itasca State Park,** 30 mi. west of Chippewa National Forest on Rte. 200. Discovered in 1832 by Henry Rowe Schoolcraft and his Native American guide Ozawinib, the headwaters take their name from the Latin *veritas caput*—"true head." The park also boasts the oldest and largest tree in Minnesota. More like a vacation home than a cheap place to spend the night, the **Mississippi Headwaters Hostel (HI-AYH) ❶** within the park stays open in the winter to facilitate access to the park's excellent cross-country skiing. *(☎266-3415; www.himinnesota.org. Laundry, kitchen, multiple bathrooms. Linen $2-4. $7 per day vehicle permit. Private rooms available. 2-night min. stay some weekends. Check-in Su-Th 5-10pm, F-Sa 5-11pm. Check-out M-F 10am, Sa-Su noon. Dorms $15-17, nonmembers $18-20.)* The **park office,** through the north entrance and down County Rd. 122, has camping info. *(☎266-2100. Office open M-F 8am-4:30pm, Sa-Su 8am-4pm; mid-Oct. to Apr. M-F 8am-4:30pm. Ranger on call after hours.)*

IRON RANGE ☎218

Lured by the cry of "Gold!", the miners that rushed to join loggers and trappers in this area soon set their sights on iron. Today, the 120 mi. of wilderness and over 500 majestic lakes along the Iron Trail serve as a retreat for the nature fanatic and as a corridor to the Boundary Waters, the Mississippi Headwaters, and the north shores of Lake Superior. Although these days the closest one can get to the mining techniques of old is on a tour of the Soudan Underground Mine, Iron Rangers continue to celebrate their heritage with exhibitions of past industrial glory.

EVELETH

The town of Eveleth, 10 mi. east of Chisolm on Rte. 53, has produced more elite hockey players than any other city of its size in the country. As such, it is the home of the **US Hockey Hall of Fame,** 801 Hat Trick Ave. Focusing on collegiate and Olympic success, the Hall honors American-born players of the hardest hitting sport. (☎744-5167 or 800-443-7825; www.ushockeyhall.com. Open M-Sa 9am-5pm, Su 10am-3pm. $6, seniors and ages 13-17 $5, ages 6-12 $4, under 6 free.) Further proof that they take their hockey seriously in Eveleth is the 107ft. **World's Largest Hockey Stick,** at Grant and Monroe St. Follow the signs marked "Big Stick."

SOUDAN

For those who feel the need to dig deeper, the town of Soudan, 50 mi. northeast of Chisolm on Rte. 169, features an unforgettable journey ½ mi. underground in a high-speed elevator (or "cage") at the **Soudan Underground Mine State Park,** off Rte. 1. The oldest and deepest iron ore mine in the state, the "Cadillac of Underground Mines" offers fascinating tours given by retired miners and their families. Visitors go by train almost a mile into the underground maze to experience the dark, difficult lives of ore workers in the Iron Range. Bring sturdy shoes and a jacket—it's always a chilly 50°F underground. (☎753-2245. Park open June-Sept. daily 9am-6pm; tours every 30min. 10am-4pm. $7, ages 5-12 $5, 4 and under free; $7 state park vehicle permit required.) Next door, the **McKinley Park Campground ❶,** overlooking Lake Vermilion, gives visitors the opportunity to relax. Semi-private campsites are available, with restrooms, showers, laundry facilities, bait and tackle, and firewood. (☎753-5921; www.mckinleypark.net. Reservations required. Open May-Sept. Sites $15, with electricity $20. Overnight car parking $3.)

ELY

The charming town of Ely serves as a launching pad into the **Boundary Waters Canoe Area Wilderness** (**BWCAW;** see **Boundary Waters,** p. 620), and thus supports its share of wilderness outfitters and attractions. The **International Wolf Center,** just north of downtown at 1396 Rte. 169, houses five gray wolves, offers BWCAW permits, and has displays on *canis lupus*. (☎365-4695 or 800-359-9653; www.wolf.org. Open July-Aug. daily 9am-7pm; May-June and Sept. to mid-Oct. daily 9am-5pm; mid-Oct. to Apr. Sa-Su 10am-5pm. $7, seniors $6, ages 6-12 $3.25. Call for wolf presentation times.) **Stony Ridge Resort ❶,** 60 W. Lakeview Pl., off Shagawa Rd., has RV and tent campsites and cabins. (☎365-6757. RV and tent sites with water, electricity, and showers $15; 1-bedroom cabins from $75. Canoe rental $20 per day.)

FOLLOW THE YELLOW BRICK ROAD Best remembered as gingham-checked Dorothy in the cinematic classic *The Wizard of Oz*, Judy Garland was born "Frances Gumm" somewhere over the rainbow in Grand Rapids, MN, 40 mi. southwest of Chisolm. Today, the white house and garden are preserved at the **Judy Garland Birthplace and Museum.** The Judy Garland Museum proper is connected to the house and has interactive exhibits and galleries about America's sweetheart. Tour the premises, or drop by in June to mingle with Munchkins at the annual **Judy Garland Festival.** To get there, click your heels three times, or travel south on Hwy. 169 in Grand Rapids to 2727 S. Pokegama Ave. *(☎800-664-5839; www.judygarlandmuseum.com. Open mid-May to mid-Oct. daily 10am-5pm. $3.)*

VOYAGEURS NATIONAL PARK ☎218

Voyageurs National Park sits on Minnesota's boundary with Ontario, accessible almost solely by boat. Named for the French Canadian fur traders who once traversed the area, the park invites today's voyagers to leave the auto-dominated world and push off into the longest inland lake waterway on the continent. As the traders did, modern travelers can also canoe to reach these northern woods. Preservation efforts have kept the area much as it was in the late 18th century, with wolves, bear, deer, and moose roaming freely. Summer visitors explore the seven hiking trails the park offers, while winter visitors bundle up to cross-country ski and snowmobile. The dangers of undeveloped wilderness still remain. Water should be boiled for at least 10min.; some fish contain mercury. Ticks bearing Lyme disease have been found as well.

The **Oberholtzer Trail** at Rainy Lake leads hikers to two overlooks that showcase the range of flora found in the park. For adventures with moose, visitors should consider the **Cruiser Lake Trail system,** accessible from either Rainy Lake or Kabetogama Lake, which also offers hiking on the cliffs and canoeing. A wheelchair-accessible trail, at Ash River, leads to a nice view of Kabetogama Lake and serves as the starting point for the **Blind Ash Bay Trail.**

Many of the campsites in the park are accessible only by water. Several car-accessible sites lie outside Voyageurs in the state forest, including **Woodenfrog ❶,** about 4 mi. from Kabetogama Lake Visitors Center on Rte. 122, and **Ash River ❶,** 3 mi. from the Visitors Center on Rte. 129. (☎753-2245. Primitive sites $9.) The **Ash Trail Lodge ❺,** 10 mi. east of Rte. 53 on Rte. 129, is a good option for the wilderness-challenged, offering 17 roomy cabins, a restaurant and bar, and lots of socializing in a wooded environment. (☎374-3131 or 800-777-4513; www.ashtraillodge.com. 3-night min. stay, $300-1200.) **International Falls,** the inspiration for Rocky and Bullwinkle's hometown of Frostbite Falls, has other lodging options and a few attractions outside Voyageurs. For traditional indoor accommodations, Rte. 53 is loaded with motels. The friendly **Tee Pee Motel ❷,** 1501 2nd Ave., at Rte. 53, provides homey rooms with cable TV, fridge, and A/C. (☎283-8494 or 800-850-1518. Singles $40; doubles $50.) **International Voyageurs RV Campground ❶,** 5 min. south of town on Rte. 53 at City Rd. 24, offers campsites with showers and laundry. (☎283-4679. RV sites for 1-2 people with full hookup $18. Tent sites $12. Additional person $2.)

The **International Falls Convention and Visitors Bureau,** 301 2nd Ave., downtown, hands out travel info on the area. (☎800-325-5766; www.intlfalls.org. Open M-F 8am-5pm.) The park can be accessed through **Crane Lake, Ash River, Kabetogama Lake,** or **Rainy Lake** (all east of Rte. 53) or through **International Falls,** at the northern tip of Rte. 53, just below Ft. Frances, ON. There are three visitors centers in the park: **Rainy Lake,** at the end of Rte. 11, 12 mi. east of International Falls (☎286-5258; open mid-May to Sept. daily 9am-5pm, Oct. to mid-May W-Su 9am-4:30pm); **Ash River,** 8 mi. east of Rte. 53 on Rte. 129, then 3 mi. north (☎374-3221; open mid-May to Sept. daily 9am-5pm); and **Kabetogama Lake,** 1 mi. north of Rte. 122 (☎875-2111; open mid-May to Sept. daily 9am-5pm). *Rendezvous*, the visitors guide to the park, provides all the information needed to have an adventurous trip. Voyageurs offers cruises, canoe trips, ranger-led hikes and talks about the park; call any visitors center for info, or toll free ☎888-381-2873, or log onto www.nps.gov/voya.

SCENIC DRIVE: NORTH SHORE DRIVE

Vast and mysterious, Lake Superior defines the landscape of Northeastern Minnesota with its jagged, glacier-carved edges and seemingly limitless surface. Scenic overlooks on the lake's North Shore provide harrowing views of the crashing waves below. Inland, the **Sawtooth Mountains** hover over the lake with stunning rock formations and tall, sweeping birch trees.

The true Lake Superior North Shore extends 646 mi. from Duluth to Sault Ste. Marie, ON, but **Route 61,** winding 150 mi. along the coast from Duluth to Grand Portage, gives travelers an abbreviated version of the spectacular journey. Most of the small fishing towns along the shore maintain Visitors Centers, of which the **R.J. Houle Visitor Information Center,** 1330 Hwy. 61, 21 mi. from Duluth up Rte. 61 in picturesque **Two Harbors,** is the *crème de la crème*. The friendly staff offers advice and personal anecdotes about each town on the Minnesota stretch of the North Shore. (☎834-4005 or 800-554-2116. Open June to mid-Oct. M-Sa 9am-5pm, Su 9am-3pm; mid-Oct. to May W-Sa 9am-1pm.) Rte. 61 is often congested with boat-towing pickup trucks and family-filled campers on summer weekends. Accommodations flanking the roadside fill up fast in summer; make reservations early. Bring warm clothes—temperatures can drop as low as 40°F, even on summer nights.

Striking views of the jagged cliffs that descend to the massive lake are the greatest appeal of Rte. 61. State parks along the route not only offer looks at the shore but also boast stunning attractions of their own. Camping at **Gooseberry Falls State Park ❶** is an appealing lodging option. (☎834-3855. Park open daily 8am-10pm; Visitors Center open daily 9am-7pm. Primitive sites with shower $12; vehicle permit $7 per day.) Gooseberry Falls offers 18 mi. of trails and five waterfalls. Three of the falls are located near the Visitor Center and are wheelchair-accessible. Those looking for more excitement can take a ½ mi. trail to the spectacular rocky shore.

Eight mi. down the road, the **Split Rock Lighthouse** takes visitors back to the lake's industrial heyday and offers a spectacular birds-eye view atop a 130 ft. cliff. Visitors can enter the lighthouse, light keeper's home, and fog-signal building, restored to look as they did during operation in the 1920s. (☎226-6372 or 888-727-8386; www.mnhs.org. Open mid-May to mid-Oct. daily 9am-6pm. $6, seniors $5, ages 6-12 $4. 45min. tours offered every hr. on the hr.) If the waterfalls at Gooseberry were not exciting enough, the **Tettegouchie State Park** is home to the tallest waterfall in Minnesota. It is a ¾ mi. hike to the falls, but the trail is not difficult and well worth the effort. (☎226-6365. Park open daily 8am-10pm; Visitors Center open 9am-7pm.) Rte. 61 becomes more convoluted as it enters the **Lake Superior National Forest** and passes over countless winding rivers and creeks toward Tofte, where the 1526 ft. **Carlton Peak** dominates the landscape. The **Coho Cafe ❷,** in Tofte on Rte. 61, serves delicious pastries, pastas, and pizzas as well as strong coffee for the weary traveler. (☎663-8032. Sandwiches $8. Open May-Oct. daily 7am-9pm.) The pine-paneled **Cobblestone Cabins ❸,** off Rte. 61, 2 mi. north of Tofte, provide guests with eight cabins and access to a cobblestone beach, canoes, a wood burning sauna, and kitchenettes. (☎633-7957. Open May-Oct. Cabins $30-80.)

GRAND MARAIS ☎218

Near the north end of the 150 mi. scenic drive lies the picture perfect fishing resort village and former artists' colony of Grand Marais. This popular tourist spot is a great place to sleep, eat, and enjoy the scenery. **The Grand Marais Visitor Information Center,** 13 N. Broadway, can be found next to the City Hall off Rte. 61. (☎387-2524 or 888-922-5000; www.grandmaraismn.com. Open M-Sa 9am-5pm.) The family owned **Nelson's Traveler's Rest ❷,** on Rte. 61, ½ mi. west of town, provides fully-equipped cabins with fireplaces and lake views. (☎387-1464 or 800-249-1285; www.travelsrest.com. Open mid-May to mid-Oct. Call in advance. Single cabins from $35; doubles from $49.) **Grand Marais Recreation Area RV Park-Campground ❶,** off Rte. 61 on 8th Ave W., has 300 wooded and mostly primitive sites by the lake. (☎387-1712 or 800-998-0959. Office open daily 6am-10pm. Reservations recommended. Open May to mid-Oct. Primitive sites May-June and Sept.-Oct. $16; with water and electricity $20. July- Aug. $21/25. Rates apply for parties of 2; $2.50 per each additional person per day. Discounted use of municipal pool.)

Cheap and popular with locals and fishermen, **South of the Border Cafe ❶,** 4 W. Rte. 61, specializes in huge breakfasts and satisfying diner food. The bluefin herring sandwich costs $3.25. (☎387-1505. Breakfast under $7. Open daily 5am-2pm.) Though equally popular, the **Angry Trout Cafe ❹** is a bit more expensive, serving only organic dishes ranging from Alaskan Cod ($18) to Mushroom Ravioli ($17). (☎387-1265. Open seasonally Su-Th 11am-8:30pm, F-Sa 11am-9pm.) z

BOUNDARY WATERS. Grand Marais also serves as a gateway to the **Boundary Waters Canoe Area Wilderness (BWCAW),** a designated wilderness area comprising 1.2 million acres of lakes, streams, and forests. The BWCAW is understandably finicky about when, where, and how many people it will allow to enter; phoning ahead is essential. One mile south of Grand Marais, the **Gunflint Ranger Station** distributes permits and has tourist information. (☎387-1750. Open May-Sept. daily 6am-6pm; Oct.-Apr. M-F 8am-4:30pm.) Make reservations with National Recreation Reservation Service. (☎877-444-6777. Reservation fee $12. Day permits free. Camping permits $10 per adult per trip, children $5. Seasonal passes $40.) The **Gunflint Trail (County Road 12)** runs northwest from town for 60 mi. to Lake Saganaga, on the border of Canada. This developed road offers access to amazing trails and lakes for nature enthusiasts and serves as the eastern entrance into the BWCAW. **The Gunflint Trail Association** has hosts spread throughout the trail. (☎800-338-6932; www.gunflint-trail.org.) At Rte. 61 and Wisconsin St. is the **Gunflint Trail Information Center,** which offers information about the trail as well as the BWCAW. (☎387-3191. Open daily 9am-5pm.) **The Golden Eagle Lodge Campground ❶,** on the Gunflint Trail, offers nine sites with water and electric hookups and rents canoes, bikes, and boats. (☎800-346-2203; www.golden-eagle.com. $22 for site with 2 people. $3 each additional person. Reservations necessary.)

AMERICAN DIALECTS[1]

Many people believe that regional variation in the US is disappearing, thanks to the insidious and pervasive influence of television and mainstream American culture. There is hope for those of us who relish linguistic and cultural diversity, though: recent research by William Labov at the University of Pennsylvania and by Scott Golder and myself at Harvard University has found that regional variation is alive and well, and along some dimensions is even increasing between the major urban centers.

Consider, for instance, the preferred cover term for sweetened carbonated beverages. As can be seen in the map below, Southerners generally refer to them as coke, regardless of whether or not the beverages in question are actually made by the Coca-Cola Company; West and East coasters (including coastal Florida, which consists largely of transplanted New Yorkers) and individuals in Hawaii and the St. Louis, Milwaukee, and Green Bay spheres of influence predominantly employ soda. The remainder of the country prefers pop.

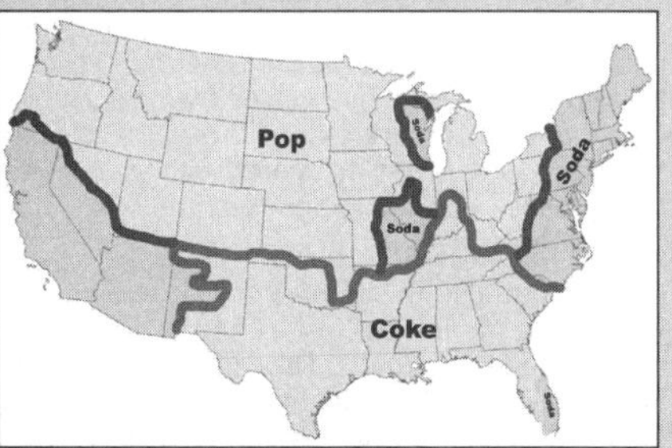

National television advertisements and shows generally employ soda, presumably due to the concentration of media outlets in soda areas New York and California, but this has had no effect on the robust regional patterns. (The three primary terms do appear, however, to be undermining traditional local expressions such as tonic in Boston and cocola in the South.)

Another deeply entrenched, regionally conditioned food product is the long sandwich made with cold cuts. Its unmarked form in the US is submarine sandwich or just sub. Pennsylvanians (and New Jerseyites in the Philadelphia sphere of influence) call it a hoagie, New Yorkers call it a hero, western New Englanders call it a grinder, Mainers call it an Italian sandwich, and people in the New Orleans area call it a po' boy.

Confrontation between traditional regional terms and newer interlopers has created subtle variations in meaning in some areas. In the Boston sphere of influence, for instance, grinder is commonly relegated to hot subs, whereas sub is used for cold ones. Similarly, in stores in northern Vermont grinder refers to large (12-in.) subs, whereas hoagie is used for their small (6-inch) counterpart. Many in the Philadelphia area divide up the sub domain in the same manner as Boston, but hoagie is used for the cold version and steak sandwich for the hot one.

In other cases, the dialectal picture is so evenly distributed that there is no clear national standard, as with the terms for the machine out of which one drinks water in schools and other public spaces.

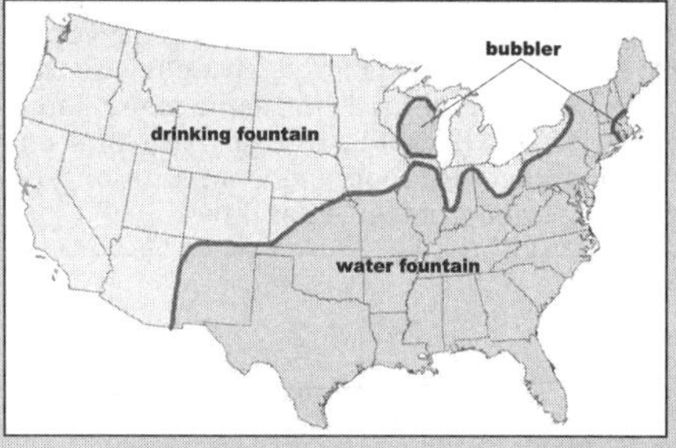

The preferred term in the southeastern half of the US is water fountain, whereas in the northwestern half it's drinking fountain. If you're in eastern Wisconsin or the Boston area, be sure to elicit bubbler from the locals.

These examples should suffice to show that regional variation is alive and well in the US. But where did these differences come from, and how have they resisted the influence of the American media juggernaut? The second question has a relatively straightforward answer: humans are generally unaware of the properties of their language, and normally assume that the way they behave and speak is the way everyone else does and should behave and speak. You, for example, were probably

[1]The maps employed in this chapter were designed by Prof. Vaux on the basis of previously published materials (primarily William Labov's forthcoming *Atlas of North American English* and Frederick Cassidy's *Dictionary of American Regional English*) and his online survey of English dialects. Specific references are available on request by emailing the author at vaux@post.harvard.edu. Please note that all generalizations made here reflect statistical predominance, not absolute invariance. One can find individuals who say *soda* in the South, for example, but these are in the minority.
The examples adduced in this chapter are primarily lexical, due to the difficulty of conveying subtleties of pronunciation in a publication intended for non-linguists.

unaware before reading this that a large swathe of the US doesn't share your term for water fountains. Since humans are generally unaware of the idiosyncrasies of their own speech, it is to be expected that they would typically fail to notice that what is said on TV differs from their own forms.

SETTLEMENT PATTERNS & THE ORIGINS OF THE AMERICAN DIALECTS

The other question, involving the origins of linguistic variation, can be answered in part by considering the history of US settlement by speakers of English.

The continental US was settled by three main waves of English speakers: Walter Raleigh brought settlers primarily from the southwest of England to form the Chesapeake Bay Colony in 1607; Puritans from East Anglia came to the Massachusetts Bay Colony in 1620; and Scots-Irish, Northern English, and Germans came to America through Philadelphia in large numbers beginning in the 18th century. Settlers then moved horizontally westward across the country from these three hearths, giving rise to the three main dialect areas in the US: the South, the North, and the Midlands. The fourth area on the map, the West, contains a mixture of features imported from the other three.

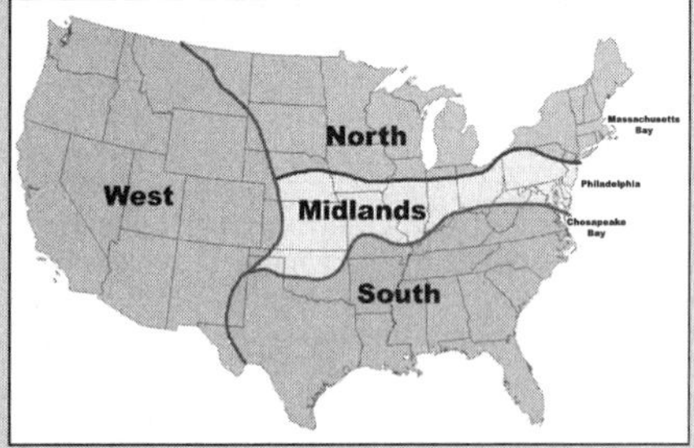

The particular linguistic variables on which these dialect divisions are based in many cases can be connected to dialect differences in the areas of England from which the various settlers came. The original English-speaking settlers in New England, for example, came from East Anglia in the southeast of England. There, in the 17th century (and still today), "r"s were only pronounced before vowels, and "r"s were (and still are) inserted inside certain vowel sequences, as in draw[r]ing and John F. Kennedy's famous Cuba[r] and China[r]. The New England lengthening of "a" in words like aunt ("ahnt") and bath ("bahth") was also imported from the British dialect of East Anglia.

Other features cannot be connected to British antecedents so transparently, but nicely demonstrate the North/South/Midlands boundary. One of my favorite examples is the large wasplike critter that is usually seen when it stops by puddles to collect mud, which it then rolls into a ball and carries off to construct a nest. Northerners call this a mud wasp, midlanders and westerners call it a mud dauber, and southerners call it a dirt dauber. Another such example is the small freshwater lobster-like critter, which is a crayfish in the North, a crawdad in the Midlands, and a crawfish or mudbug in the South.

The North breaks into two main areas, the Northeast and the Inland North. The Northeast and its crony, southeast coastal Florida, are roughly the home of sneakers; the rest of the country uses tennis shoes or gym shoes as the generic term for athletic shoes. The Inland North is most famous for pop and for the so-called "Rust Belt Vowel Shift." This is a change in the pronunciation of most of the American vowels that produces what is perceived by most Americans as "Midwestern," even though it is also found in eastern Rust Belt cities such as Rochester, Syracuse, and Utica, New York.

The Midlands region is home not only to mud dauber, but also to the oft-noted regionalisms warsh and the needs X-ed construction, as in the car needs warshed. The Midlands and the South together are home to catty-corner (diagonally across from), which in the North is normally kitty-corner. (My personal favorite expression for this concept is kitty wampus, which is used by a handful of individuals in the Upper Midwest.)

The South is home to the "pin-pen merger" ("i" and "e" are pronounced identically before "m," "n," and "ng"), preservation of the contrast in pronunciation between "w" and "hw" (as in witch and which respectively), use of y'all to address a group of individuals, multiple modal constructions (as in I might could do that), nekkid for "naked," and commode for "toilet."

The inland part of the South features gems such as rolling for the act of covering a house and/or its front yard in toilet paper. In the rest of country, this is generally called tp'ing or toilet papering. (It's wrapping in the Houston area.)

AMERICAN DIALECTS YOU HAVE TO HEAR

Since, as we have just seen, regional variation is alive and well in the US, where should one go to hear the most satisfying range of dialects? Here are some of my favorites, which also provide a representative sample of the main dialect groups in the country. (If you get to one of these locales and have trouble finding a really juicy local accent, try a police station, working-class bar, or farm.)

THE NORTHEAST

No linguistic tour of the Northeast would be complete without visiting the two main linguistic spheres of influence in the area, Boston and New York City. Though locals would probably die rather than admitting it, the two actually share a large number of linguistic features, such as pronouncing can (is able) differently than can (container), wearing sneakers and drinking soda, having no word for the roly poly/potato bug/sow bug/doodlebug (though the critter itself is just as rampant in the Northeast as anywhere else in the country), and pronouncing route to rhyme with moot and never with out.

Perhaps the most striking feature shared by these two areas is the behavior of "r": it disappears when not followed by a vowel (drawer is pronounced draw), and conversely gets inserted when between certain vowels (drawing comes out as drawring). Because these dialects don't allow "r" to follow a vowel within a syllable, they end up preserving vowel contrasts that were neutralized before "r" in other dialects. This is heard in the "3 Maries": Mary, marry, and merry are each pronounced differently, whereas in most of the country all three are homophonous. Similarly mirror and nearer have the same first vowel in most of the US, but not in Boston and New York. Bostonians and New Yorkers pronounce words like hurry, Murray, furrow, and thorough with the vowel of hut, whereas most other Americans use the vowel in bird. And of course there's the first vowel in words like orange and horrible, which in most of the US is the same as in pore, but in Boston and New York is closer to the vowel in dog.

NEW YORK CITY

Though New York shares many important features with Boston and other parts of the Northeast, it is also in many ways a linguistic island, undergoing little influence from the rest of the country and-despite the ubiquity of New York accents on TV and in movies-propagating almost none of its peculiarities to the outside world. Its lack of linguistic influence can be connected to its stigmatization: two surveys in 1950 and the 1990s found that Americans considered New York to have the worst speech in the country.

When you visit the New York City area (including neighboring parts of New Jersey and Long Island), be sure to listen for classic New Yorkisms. This includes the deletion of "h" before "u" (e.g. huge is pronounced yuge, and Houston becomes Youston), and the rounding of "a" to an "o"-like vowel before "l" in words like ball and call (the same vowel also shows up in words like water, talk, and dog). New Yorkers who don't have a thick local accent may not have these particular features, but they are sure to have other shibboleths like stoop (small front porch or steps in front of a house), on line instead of in line (e.g. We stood on line outside the movie theater for three hours), hero for sub, pie for pizza, and egg cream for a special soft drink made with seltzer water, chocolate syrup, and milk. You can also tell New Yorkers by their pronunciation of Manhattan and forward: they reduce the first vowel in the former (it comes out as Mn-hattan), and delete the first "r" in the latter (so it sounds like foe-ward). Believe it or not, it is also common in the New York area to pronounce donkey to rhyme with monkey (which makes sense if you consider the spelling), even though they typically aren't aware that they are doing so.

NEW ENGLAND

Moving up the coast to New England, we find that most people don't actually sound like John F. Kennedy, but they do all use cellar for basement (at least if it's unfinished), bulkhead for the external doors leading out of the cellar, and rotary for what others call a roundabout or traffic circle. New England itself is divided by the Connecticut River into two linguistically distinct areas, Eastern and Western.

Eastern New England: Boston

You can hear great Eastern New England speech almost anywhere in Maine, New Hampshire, Rhode Island, or Massachusetts, especially if you stay away from more affluent areas in the bigger cities, but I'll focus here on the Boston area. (Revere, South Boston, Somerville, and Dorchester are traditionally considered to harbor especially thick local accents.) Thanks to park your car in Harvard Yard and Nomar Garciaparra many Americans are familiar with the Boston pronunciation of -ar-, which generally comes out as something very similar to the Southern pronunciation of -ay- (Boston park sounds like Southern pike). The sequence -or- also has an interesting outcome in many words, being pronounced like the vowel in off. For instance, the Boston pop group LFO, in their 1999 song "Summer Girls," rhymed hornet with sonnet.

In the domain of vocabulary, be sure to get a frappe (or if you're in Rhode Island, a cabinet), a grinder, harlequin ice cream with jimmies or shots on it, and of course a tonic. (Frappes are milkshakes, harlequin is Neapolitan ice cream, and jimmies and shots are sprinkles.) You might also want to visit a package store (or packie for short) to buy some alcohol, or a spa to buy cigarettes and lottery tickets. There aren't many spas (small independent convenience stores, equivalent to party stores in Michigan, as used in the movie True Romance) left in the area at this point, but you can still find a few that haven't been replaced by 7-11 in Boston, Cambridge, Somerville, Allston, and Watertown.

The towns where you'll hear the best Boston accents (and classic local terms like wicked and pissa) also feature many triple deckers, three-family houses with three front porches stacked on top of one another. These seem to be less common in Connecticut, but if you happen to pass through that area, be sure to look out for tag sales (yard sales). Connecticut is also home to the term sleepy seed for the gunk that collects in the corner of your eye after you've been sleeping; not all Connecticutians have this expression, but your trip will have been worthwhile if you find someone who does.

Western New England: Vermont

West of the Connecticut River, I recommend you head up to the Northeast Kingdom in Vermont. Here you'll find the best Canadian features south of the border, thanks to the heavy French Canadian representation in the area, including toque ("tuke") for a woolen winter hat (known as a toboggan in some other parts of the country); poutin (put-SIN) for french fries coated with gravy and cheese curds, and sugar pie. This is also the land of the skidoo (snowmobile), the skidder (giant machine with jaws used to haul logs), and the camp (summer cabin, typically on a body of water). If you're wise enough to visit the Northeast Kingdom, be sure to check out how they pronounce the "a" and the "t" in the name of the local town Barton.

THE MIDLANDS

Pennsylvania

As you head out of the Northeast, you should try to stop through Pennsylvania, which is unique among the fifty states for having a significant number of dialect features peculiar to it. Some of these are due to the Pennsylvania Dutch presence in the region (redd up "clean up," gumband "rubber band" (cf. German Gummi "rubber"; now limited to parts of western Pennsylvania), toot "bag," rootch "scootch up (in a bed)"); the reasons for the restriction of other terms to Pennsylvania are less clear. To this category belongs hoagie, which as we already saw is limited to Pennsylvania plus the parts of New Jersey in Philadelphia's sphere of influence. Pennsylvania also shows extreme internal diversity: Philadelphia groups with the Northeastern dialects (e.g. in preferring soda), whereas Pittsburgh is tied to the Inland North (pop), the Midlands (many of my relatives there use the needs warshed construction), and the Appalachian region, of which it is the northernmost extremity.

Philadelphia and its satellites in southern New Jersey are perhaps best known for their pronunciation of water, which comes out as something like wooder. This conveniently shows up in the local term water ice, which refers to something between Italian ice and a snow cone. Residents of the Philly sphere of influence are also more likely than other Americans to bag school rather than skip school or play hooky. When you make your trip to Philly to hear these choice linguistic tidbits and you run short of money, be sure to ask where the MAC machine is, not the ATM or cash machine.

You should also make a special effort to visit the opposite end of the state, anchored by the beautiful city of Pittsburgh, which (unknown to most Americans) has its own distinctive dialect. Here the "aw" sound is replaced by something approaching "ah," as in dahntahn for downtown; "ay' similarly loses its "y" in certain situations, as in Pahrts for Pirates and Ahrn City for Iron City. The "o" in this region is very rounded in words like shot, and comes out sounding a lot like the New York vowel in ball. It is also popular to delete the "th-" at the beginning of unstressed words in certain collocations, such as up 'ere (for up there), like 'at, and 'n 'at (for and that, which western Pennsylvanians are fond of ending sentences with).

In terms of vocabulary, Pittsburgh and environs have some real whoppers, such as yins or you 'uns, used to address a group of two or more people; jagoff meaning "a jerk or loser" (shared with Chicagoland); jumbo "bologna sandwich"; and slippy "slippery."

These days many Pittsburgh residents don't have the traditional dialect, but you're sure to come across at least a few of the items just discussed. You'll have even better luck if you visit some of the unknown small towns in western Pennsylvania such as Franklin, Emlenton, and Oil City, which have satisfying variants of the Pittsburgh speech patterns and also happen to be unusually scenic.

Cincinnati

From Pittsburgh you're in striking distance of Cincinnati, one of the better representatives of the Midlands dialect region. Here, instead of inserting "r," as we saw in Boston and New York, they insert "l": saw comes out as sawl, drawing as drawling, and so on. In the Cincinnati area one can also find drive-through liquor stores (and for some people, regular liquor stores) referred to as pony kegs. (Elsewhere in the US, on the other hand, pony keg usually refers to a small keg.)

THE RUST BELT

Milwaukee

Moving westward, the next interesting dialect zone is the Inland North or Rust Belt, within which I recommend Milwaukee, WI (not to be confused with Zilwaukee, MI.) Here, in the land so eloquently etymologized by Alice Cooper in *Wayne's World*, you will find-especially if you visit an area where there hasn't been much immigration, such as West Allis-not only the classic speech features identified with the Midwest (as canonized for example in the Da Bears skit on "Saturday Night Live"), but also features characteristic of areas other than the Midwest (freeway, otherwise associated with the West Coast; bubbler, most familiar from the Boston area; soda, otherwise characteristic of the West and East coasts). Milwaukeeans share some features with the rest of Wisconsin: they pronounce Milwaukee as Mwaukee and Wisconsin as W-scon-sin rather than Wis-consin; they refer to annoying Illinoisans as FIB's or fibbers (the full form of which is too saucy to explain here), and they eat frozen custard and butter burgers. They also share some features with the Upper Midwest, notably pronouncing bag as baig and using ramp or parking ramp for "parking garage" (the same forms surface in Minnesota and Buffalo). Milwaukee is also known for the cannibal sandwich, raw ground sirloin served on dark rye bread and covered with thin-sliced raw onions.

Milwaukee is only an hour and a half drive north of Chicago, yet it lacks many of the classic Chicagoisms, such as jagoff, gaper's block (a traffic jam caused by drivers slowing down to look at an accident or other diversion on the side of the road), black cow (root beer with vanilla ice cream, known elsewhere as a root beer float), expressway, and pop. It also differs from the more northern reaches of Wisconsin with respect to many of the classic Upper Midwestern features so cleverly reproduced in the movie Fargo, such as the monophthongal "e" and "o" in words like Minnesota and hey there. You can find the occasional inhabitant of Wisconsin's northern border with Minnesota who has Upper Midwest terms like pasties, whipping shitties (driving a car in tight circles, known elsewhere as doing donuts), hotdish (elsewhere called a casserole), and farmer matches (long wooden matches that light on any surface), but for the most part these are less commonly used than in Minnesota and the Dakotas (and the Upper Peninsula of Michigan in the case of pasties).

THE WEST

The San Fernando Valley

Moving ever westward, we come next to the West Coast. Here it is more difficult to find hardcore traditional dialects, largely because the West was settled relatively recently, and by individuals from a wide variety of different locales; one is hard-pressed to find any Californian (or other Westerner) whose family has been there for more than two generations. Perhaps the best place to start is the San Fernando Valley of California, home of the Valley Girl. Many of the Valley Girl quirks immortalized in Frank Zappa's 1982 song "Valley Girl" and the 1995 film Clueless are now profoundly out of favor, such as gnarly, barf out, grodie (to the max), gag me with a spoon, rad, for sure, as if, and bitchin'. Others are now ubiquitous throughout the US, such as totally, whatever, sooo X (as in, That's so like 5 years ago), and the use of like to report indirect speech or state of mind (as in, I was like, "No way!"). Others are still used in the area but have yet to infiltrate the rest of the country, such as flip a bitch or bust a bitch (make a U-turn) and bag on (make fun of, diss).

And if you're interested in figuring out whether someone's from northern or southern California, I recommend seeing if they use hella or hecka to mean "very" (e.g. that party was hella cool; characteristic of northern California), and if they refer to freeway numbers with or without "the" before them (Southern Californians refer to "the 5", "the 405", and so on, whereas northern Californians just use "5" and "405").

THE SOUTH

Looping back around the country we come to the South, which is perhaps the most linguistically distinct and coherent area in the US. This is not only home to obvious cases like y'all, initial stress on Thanksgiving, insurance, police, and cement, and the other features mentioned above, but also showcases feeder road (small road that runs parallel to a highway), wrapping (tp'ing), doodlebug (the crustacean that rolls into a ball when you touch it) in the Houston area, and party barns (drive-through liquor stores) in Texas (bootlegger, brew thru, and beer barn are also common terms for this in the South). The South as a whole differs from the rest of the country in pronouncing lawyer as law-yer, using tea to refer to cold sweet tea, and saying the devil's beating his wife when it rains while the sun is shining (elsewhere referred to as a sunshower, or by no name at all). The South is so different from the rest of the country that almost anywhere you go you will hear a range of great accents, but I especially recommend the Deep South (start with Mississippi or Alabama) and New Orleans.

New Orleans

Louisiana is famous for the Cajuns, a local group descended from the Acadians, French

Louisiana is famous for the Cajuns, a local group descended from the Acadians, French people who were exiled from Nova Scotia and settled in southern Louisiana in the 1760s. Some Cajuns still speak their own special creole, Cajun French, and this in turn has influenced the English dialect of the region. This can be seen in local expressions such as: by my house for "in/at my place" (e.g. he slept by my house last night), which is claimed to be based on the French expression chez moi; make dodo meaning "to sleep," based on Cajun French fais do do; make groceries meaning "do grocery shopping," cf. French faire le marché; and lagniappe, French for "a little something extra," e.g., when your butcher gives you a pound and two ounces of hot sausage but only charges you for a pound.

Some of the creole elements that have made their way into the local English dialect may be of African rather than French origin, such as where ya stay (at)? meaning "'where do you live?", and gumbo, referring to a traditional southern soup-like dish, made with a rich roux (flour and butter) and usually including either sea food or sausage. The word gumbo is used in Gullah (an English-based creole spoken on the Sea Islands off the Carolina coast) to mean okra, and appears to have descended from a West African word meaning okra.

The New Orleans dialect of English also includes words drawn from other sources, such as yat (a typical neighborhood New Orleanian), neutral ground (the grassy or cement strip in the middle of the road), po' boy (basically a sub sandwich, though it can include fried oysters and other seafood and may be dressed, i.e. include lettuce, tomatoes, pickles, and mayonnaise), hickey (a knot or bump you get on your head when you bump or injure it), and alligator pear (an avocado).

HAWAII

Last but not least we come to Hawaii, which in many ways is the most interesting of the fifty states linguistically. Many Americans are aware of Hawaiian, the Austronesian language spoken by the indigenous residents of the Hawaiian Islands before the arrival of colonizers from Europe and Japan. Fewer, however, know of the English-based creole that has arisen since that time, known as Hawaiian Pidgin English, Hawaiian Creole English, or just Pidgin. This variety of English is spoken by a fairly large percentage of Hawaiians today, though they tend not to use it around haole (Caucasian) tourists.

Pidgin combines elements of all of the languages originally spoken by settlers, including Portuguese (cf. where you stay go? meaning "where are you going?", or I called you up and you weren't there already meaning "I called you up and you weren't there yet"), Hawaiian (haole, makapeapea "sleepy seed," lanai "porch," pau "finished"), Japanese (shoyu "soy sauce"), and even Californian/surfer (dude, sweet, awesome, freeway). They also have some English expressions all their own, such as shave ice (snowcone) and cockaroach (cockroach).

The syntax (word order) of Pidgin differs significantly from that of mainland English varieties, but resembles the English creoles of the Caribbean in important ways. This includes deletion of the verb be in certain contexts (e.g. if you one girl, no read dis meaning "if you're a girl, don't read this"), lack of inversion of the subject and finite verb in questions and subordinate clauses (e.g. doctah , you can pound my baby? Meaning "doctor, can you weigh my baby?", or how dey came up wid dat? meaning "how did they come up with that?"), null subjects (e.g. cannot! meaning "I can't!", or get shtrawberry? meaning "do you have strawberry [flavor]?"), and the use of "get" to express existential conditions ("there is," "there are"), as in get sharks? meaning "are there sharks [in there]?".

IN CONCLUSION

This tour only begins to scratch the surface of the range of English varieties to be found in the US, but it should provide enough fodder to keep you busy for a while on your travels, and with any luck will enable you to provide some entertainment for your hosts as well. And if the info I've provided here isn't enough to sate your thirst for American dialects, I urge you to visit the Sea Islands, where Gullah is still spoken, Tangier Island in Chesapeake Bay, and Ocracoke Island, off the coast of North Carolina. Each of these islands features a variety of English that will shock and titillate you; I'll leave the details for you to discover.

Bert Vaux is PhD in Linguistics and currently teaches at the University of Wisconsin-Milwaukee. He has written extensively, and taught popular classes on linguistics and dialects at Harvard University .

GREAT PLAINS

In 1803, the Louisiana Purchase doubled America's size, adding French territory west of the Mississippi at the bargain price of $0.04 per acre. Over time, the plains spawned legends of pioneers and cowboys and of Native Americans struggling to defend their homelands. The arrival of railroad transportation and liberal land policies spurred an economic boom, until a drought during the Great Depression transformed the region into a dust bowl. Since the 1930s, the region has struggled to settle on an effective course of development. Modern agriculture has reclaimed the soil, and the heartland of the US now thrives on the trade of farm commodities. The Plains are also a vast land of prairies, where open sky stretches from horizon to horizon, broken only by long, thin lines of trees. Grasses and grains paint the land green and gold. The land rules here, as its inhabitants know. While signs of humanity are unmistakable—checkerboard farms, Army posts, and railroad corridors—the region's most staggering sights are the works of nature, from the Badlands and the Black Hills to the mighty Missouri and Mississippi Rivers.

HIGHLIGHTS OF THE GREAT PLAINS

NATIONAL PARKS AND MONUMENTS. Discover the uncrowded gems of Theodore Roosevelt National Park, ND (p. 631), and the Badlands, SD (p. 635), or join the crowds in the Black Hills around Mt. Rushmore (p. 639).

HISTORICAL SITES. Scotts Bluff National Monument, NE (p. 657), and Chimney Rock, NE (p. 657) will fascinate anyone interested in the pioneers.

NORTH DAKOTA

An early visitor to Fargo declared, "It's a beautiful land, but I doubt that human beings will ever live here." Posterity begs to differ. The stark, haunting lands that intimidated settlers eventually found willing tenants, and the territory became a state along with South Dakota on Nov. 2, 1889. The event was not without confusion—Benjamin Harrison concealed the names when he signed the two bills, so both Dakotas claim to be the 39th state. North Dakota lies too far north to attract throngs of summer tourists, but awe-inspiring beauty greets those who do visit.

PRACTICAL INFORMATION

Capital: Bismarck.

Visitor Info: Tourism Department, 400 E. Broadway, #50, Bismarck 58501 (☎800-435-5663; www.ndtourism.com). **Parks and Recreation Department,** 1835 Bismarck Expwy., Bismarck 58504 (☎328-5357; www.ndparks.com). **Game and Fish Department,** 100 N. Bismarck Expwy., Bismarck 58501 (☎328-6300). State offices open M-F 8am-5pm.

Postal Abbreviation: ND **Sales Tax:** 7%.

BISMARCK ☎701

In Bismarck, the people are friendly, the streets are clean, and the scenery is spectacular. Located at the center of the Lewis and Clark Trail, it is the most comfortable North Dakotan city in which to relax, enjoy the scenery, and learn about

Great Plains
Regina
SASKATCHEWAN
MANITOBA
Winnipeg
CANADA
U.S.A.
ONTARIO
Lake of the Woods
Thunder Bay
International Falls
Lake Superior
MICHIGAN
Williston
Minot
Devils Lake
Lake Sakakawea
NORTH DAKOTA
Grand Forks
Theodore Roosevelt Nat'l Park
Washburn
Mandan
Bismarck
Jamestown
Moorhead
Fargo
Duluth
MONTANA
MINNESOTA
WISCONSIN
Aberdeen
SOUTH DAKOTA
Watertown
St. Paul
Minneapolis
Deadwood
Lake Oahe
Pierre
Rapid City
Wall
Black Hills
WYOMING
Mount Rushmore National Memorial
Badlands Nat'l Park
Mitchell
Sioux Falls
Rochester
Mississippi River
Madison
Crazy Horse Memorial
Wounded Knee
Missouri River
Yankton
Spirit Lake
Okoboji
Sheldon
Effigy Mounds National Monument
Dubuque
Sioux City
IOWA
Ames
Cedar Rapids
Carhenge
NEBRASKA
Scotts Bluff
Chimney Rock
Des Moines
Davenport
Iowa City
Grand Island
Omaha
Platte River
Osceola
Burlington
Peoria
Kearney
Hastings
Lincoln
ILLINOIS
Springfield
MISSOURI
Hannibal
Waconda Lake
KANSAS
Topeka
Independence
Columbia
Oakley
Lawrence
Kansas City
St. Louis
COLORADO
Jefferson City
Garden City
Great Bend
Hutchinson
Dodge City
Wichita
Springfield
Branson
Blackwell
NEW MEXICO
Tulsa
Tahlequa
ARKANSAS
Oklahoma City
Memphis
TN.
Amarillo
Shawnee
Little Rock
Lawton
OKLAHOMA
Ardmore
Lubbock
MISSISSIPPI
TEXAS
Ft. Worth
Dallas
Shreveport
Abilene
Jackson
LOUISIANA
150 miles
225 kilometers
LG
N

pioneer culture. The city was founded on land that defies the notion that all prairies are monotonous: seas of yellow wildflowers, grids of green farmland, and fields of golden wheat blend with surprising harmony.

ORIENTATION & PRACTICAL INFORMATION. Bismarck is on I-94, halfway between Fargo and Theodore Roosevelt National Park. The **Missouri River** separates Bismarck from Mandan, its neighbor to the west. **Washington** and **9th Street** are the main north-south thoroughfares and are intersected by **Main, Divide,** and **Interstate Avenue.** The **Bismarck Municipal Airport** (☎222-6502), is on Airport Rd., 2 mi. southeast of the city. **Greyhound,** 3750 E. Rosser Ave. (☎223-6576; open daily 9am-1pm and 5-8pm), runs buses to Fargo (4hr., 3 per day, $33-35) and Billings (7½hr., 3 per day, $67-71). **Taxi: Taxi 9000** (☎223-9000). **Hospital: St. Alexius Medical Center,** 900 East Broadway Ave. (☎530-7000; Emergency and Trauma Center 530-7001.) **Internet Access: Bismarck Public Library,** 515 N. 5th St. (☎222-6410. Free for 1hr., email $0.50 per ½hr. Open June-Aug. M-Th 9am-9pm, F 9am-6pm, Sa 9am-5pm, Su 1-5pm; Sept.-May M-F 9am-9pm, Sa 9am-5pm, Su 1-5pm.) The **Bismarck-Mandan Visitors Center,** 1600 Burnt Boat Dr., Exit 157 off I-94, distributes the *Bismarck-Mandan Visitors Guide.* (☎800-767-3555; www.bismarck-mandancvb.org. Open June-Aug. M-F 7:30am-7pm, Sa 8am-6pm, Su 10am-5pm; Sept.-May M-F 8am-5pm.) **Post Office:** 220 E. Rosser Ave. (☎221-6501. Open M-F 7:45am-5:50pm, Sa 10am-noon.) **Postal Code:** 58501. **Area Code:** 701.

ACCOMMODATIONS & FOOD. Budget motels abound off I-94 at Exit 159. The best value around is the **Select Inn ❷,** 1505 Interchange Ave., Exit 159 off I-94, which provides clean and spacious rooms, laundry access, and continental breakfast. (☎800-641-1000. Coupons in the *Bismarck-Mandan Visitors Guide.* Singles $45; doubles $52. AAA discount.) The **Expressway Inn ❸,** 200 E. Bismarck Expressway, offers hotel rooms at motel prices. (☎222-2900 or 800-456-6388. Singles $38; doubles and weekends $46.) Camping is relaxing in the beautiful **Fort Abraham Lincoln State Park ❶** (see **Sights,** below), 7 mi. south on Rte. 1806 in Mandan. Tent sites line the banks of the Missouri River and have an amazing view of the surrounding prairie. (☎663-9571 or 800-807-4723. Reservations necessary. Primitive sites $7, with electricity $12; vehicle fee $74.)

YOU ARE NOW ONLY SIX PAGES FROM WALL DRUG.

With an enormous menu of pasta, chicken, seafood, and sandwiches ($5-10), the Italian restaurant **Walrus ❷,** 1136 N. 3rd. St., in Arrowhead Plaza, is a local favorite. The Italian sausage pizziola ($6.50) is a house specialty. (☎250-0020. Open M-Sa 10:30am-1am.) **Peacock Alley Bar and Grill ❷,** 422 E. Main Ave., delivers Cajun, Italian and American meals in their scrumptious salads ($5-7), sandwiches ($6-8), and pastas ($8) in the historic Patterson Hotel—the tallest building in the state when it was built in 1910. (☎255-7917. Open for brunch Sa 10am-12:30pm, Su 9am-1pm; lunch M-F 11am-2pm; dinner M 5:30-9pm, Tu-Sa 5:30-10pm. Bar open until 1am.) Housed in the old Northern Pacific train depot, **Fiesta Villa ❷,** 411 E. Main Ave., serves quesadillas, tacos, and other Mexican fare. The nearby railroad tracks rattle the foundation while the authentic homemade sauces and margaritas shake things up. (☎222-8075. Entrees $6-9. Open Su-Th 11am-10pm, F-Sa 11am-11pm. Patio open until 1am on busy evenings.)

SIGHTS. The **North Dakota State Capitol,** 600 E. Boulevard Ave, is an efficient 19-story office-style building that was built between 1932 and 1934 for only $2 million. Inside, visitors can view examples of Art Deco architecture in the beautiful Memorial Hall. The observation deck on the 19th floor is a perfect place to see the prairie and the Capitol's 130 acres of well-manicured grounds. (☎328-2580. Open M-F 7am-5:30pm. 30-45min. tours leave Sept.-May M-F every hr. 8-11am and 1-4pm; June-Aug. M-F 8-11am and 1-4pm, Sa 9-11am and 1-4pm, Su 1-4pm. Free.) Next door to the Capitol is the **North Dakota Heritage Center,** 612 E. Boulevard Ave., an excellent museum with exhibits ranging from triceratops to tractors. (☎328-2666; www.state.nd.us/hist. Open M-F 8am-5pm, Sa 9am-5pm, Su 11am-5pm. Free.) On Rte. 1806 in Mandan along the Missouri River lies North Dakota's oldest state park, **Fort Abraham Lincoln State Park,** which was occupied by the Mandan Indians until their failed battle with smallpox. Lewis and Clark came through in 1804, and General George Armstrong Custer, commanding the 7th Cavalry, took up residence here. Now, Fort Lincoln houses an "On-a-Slant" Mandan Indian village with several reconstructed earthlodges, as well as replicas of the cavalry post and Custer's Victorian-style home. (☎663-3069. Open June-Aug. Buildings open daily 9am-7pm; park 9am-9:30pm. $5, students $3; vehicle fee $5.)

A daytrip from Bismarck will satisfy the curiosity of those interested in the Corps of Discovery, the expedition led by Captains Meriwether Lewis and William Clark. The **Lewis and Clark Interpretive Center,** 38 mi. north of Bismarck at the junction of Rte. 83 and Rte. 200A, along the Lewis and Clark Trail, presents an overview of the explorers' wilderness journey. Visitors can don buffalo robes and a cradle board, just like those Sakajawea once wore, or simulate trading with Native Americans using an interactive computer program. Two miles away at **Fort Mandan,** modern-day trailblazers can enter a replica of the rugged riverside lodgings that sheltered the expedition during the winter of 1804. (☎462-8535 or 877-462-8535; www.fortmandan.com. Center open daily June-Aug. 9am-7pm; Sept.-May 9am-5pm. Fort open daily 8:30am-sunset. Admission to both $5, students $3.)

ENTERTAINMENT & NIGHTLIFE. The **Bismarck Symphony** (☎258-8345) plays in the magnificent **Belle Mehus Auditorium,** 201 N. 6th St. The symphony celebrates holidays in style—8000 people turn up for their Fourth of July concert on the Capitol steps. From October to April, musical programs can be heard on select Sunday afternoons. **Borrowed Buck's Roadhouse,** 118 S. 3rd St., has a full dance floor and a live DJ every night. Rock music is the focus, but on Wednesday the venue changes to country hoe-down for the "Dance Ranch." Live bands take the stage once or twice a month. (☎224-1545. 21+. Open M-F 4pm-1am, Sa noon-1am.) If only one night of country a week isn't enough, look no farther than **Lonesome Dove,** 3929 Memorial Hwy. on the border of Mandan. The real country joint in Bismarck, Lonesome Dove has a large dance floor and live, toe-tappin' country music W-Su. (☎663-2793. Open daily noon-1am.)

I-94, ROAD OF CONCRETE WONDERS Two gargantuan concrete monuments separated by 131 mi. of interstate symbolize the past and present of North Dakota. Looming on the horizon in Jamestown, ND, at Exit 258, is **the world's largest buffalo**—a towering 24 ft. monument to the animals that once roamed the Plains. Across the highway, a herd of real buffalo regards their concrete brother apathetically from behind a protective fence. In New Salem, ND, 33 mi. west of Bismarck, at Exit 127, Salem Sue, **the world's largest Holstein Cow** (38 ft. tall and 50 ft. long), keeps an eye on the interstate and the spectacular patchwork fields of the Plains. ($1 suggested donation.)

THEODORE ROOSEVELT NATIONAL PARK ☎701

After his mother and wife died on the same day, pre-White House Theodore Roosevelt moved to his ranch in the Badlands for spiritual renewal. He was so influenced by the buttes and gorges, horseback riding, big-game hunting, and cattle ranching in this "place of grim beauty" that he later claimed, "I never would have been President if it weren't for my experiences in North Dakota." Roosevelt established numerous national parks, monuments, and bird refuges. Roosevelt National Park was created in 1947 as a monument to his conservationist efforts.

ORIENTATION & PRACTICAL INFORMATION. The park is split into **north** and **south units.** AM 1610 offers information about both parts of the park. The north unit is located off of I-85 and the entrance to the more-developed south unit is just north of I-94 in **Medora,** a revamped tourist haven filled with ice cream parlors and gift "shoppes." The park entrance fee ($5 per person, under 17 free; $10 max. per vehicle) covers admission to both the north and south units for 7 days. The **South Unit's Visitors Center,** in Medora, maintains a mini-museum displaying Roosevelt's guns, spurs, and old letters, as well as a 13min. film detailing his relationship with the land. (☎623-4466. Open daily late June to Sept. 8am-8pm; Sept. to mid-June 8am-4:30pm.) The **North Unit's Visitors Center,** located next to the park entrance, has an interesting exhibit on the nature and wildlife in the park. (☎842-2333. Open daily 9am-5:30pm.) For more info, write to **Theodore Roosevelt National Park,** P.O. Box 7, Medora 58645, call the Visitors Center, or check out www.nps.gov/thro.

Greyhound serves Medora from Western Edge Books at the corner of Broadway and Fourth St., with buses to Bismarck (3½hr., 3 per day, $25-27) and Billings (6hr., 2 per day, $52-55). There is no ticket office in Medora; buy your ticket during the **Dickinson** layover. **Dakota Cyclery,** 275 3rd Ave., rents bikes. (☎623-4808 or 888-321-1218; www.dakotacyclery.com. Open daily 9am-6pm. $20-30 per half-day; full-day $30-45.) The Cyclery also leads 2-, 4-, and 8hr. bike tours of the plains and badlands by reservation. Off-road biking is not allowed in either unit of Theodore Roosevelt National Park.

Medora lacks a real pharmacy and grocery store. However, both the **Ferris Store,** 251 Main St. (☎623-4447; open daily 8am-8pm), and **Medora Convenience and Liquor,** on Pacific Ave. at Main St. (☎623-4479; open daily 7am-10pm), sell basic pharmaceutical goods, food, and cooking items. There is a 24hr. **Walmart** (☎225-8504) in Dickinson, 30 mi. east on I-94. **South unit time zone:** Mountain (2hr. behind Eastern). **North unit time zone:** Central (1hr. behind Eastern). **Post Office:** 355 3rd Ave., in Medora. (☎623-4385. Open M-Sa 8am-7pm. Window service M-F 8am-noon and 12:30-4:30pm, Sa 8:15-9:45am.) **Postal Code:** 58645. **Area Code:** 701.

ACCOMMODATIONS & FOOD. Free backcountry camping permits are available from the Visitors Centers. **Cottonwood Campgrounds ❶** lies 5 mi. after the South Unit visitor center on the Scenic Loop Dr. In the north, **Juniper Campground ❶,** 5 mi. west of the north unit entrance, is in a beautiful valley. Be cautious as the campground is frequented by buffalo all year. Both campgrounds have toilets and running water in the summer, but only pit toilets in the winter, and no hook-ups. (Sites $10; during winter $5.) It is difficult to find cheap lodging in Medora without camping and most places are closed during the winter months. The **Medora Motel ❸,** 400 E. River Rd. S, offers the cheapest rates and has A/C, cable TV, and an outdoor heated swimming pool. (☎800-633-6721. Register at the Badlands Motel on Pacific Ave. Open Memorial Day-Labor Day. Singles $59; doubles $66; family units $95. Children free.) Teddy Roosevelt was known to bunk down at the rustic **Rough Riders Hotel ❹,** 301 3rd Ave. The hotel's room rates are a little steep, but the restaurant serves reasonable breakfasts ($4-7), lunches ($4-10), and dinners ($12-20) in upscale surroundings. (☎623-4444, ext. 497. Open daily 7am-9pm. In winter, B&B only. Singles $76; doubles $89.) Teddy himself addresses the public everyday on the Rough Riders balcony at 3:30pm. The **Iron Horse Saloon ❸,** 160 Pacific Ave., offers great American standards year-round. (☎623-9894. Breakfast and lunch $4-7. Dinner $7-15. Open daily June-Sept. 6am-1am; Oct.-May 10:30am-1am.) On the corner of Main St. and Broadway, Medora's **Fudge & Ice Cream Depot** ❶ offers a sweet retreat from the heat. (☎623-4444, ext. 152. One scoop $2, two scoops $2.50. Open daily 11am-7:30pm during the summer.)

ENTERTAINMENT. The popular **Medora Musical** is a comical singing, dancing, and theatrical experience, attracting hordes nightly to celebrate the glory of the West, America, and Teddy Roosevelt himself. The patriotic show, held in the open-air **Burning Hills Amphitheatre** west of town, incorporates pyrotechnics, magicians, horses, and Argentine Gauchos. (Show runs early June to late Aug. daily 8:30-10:30pm. $21-23, students $13-14.) Before the show, at the Tjaden Terrace, cast members from the musical serenade the audience as they clog their arteries at a rowdy western cook out. At the **Pitchfork Steak Fondue** ❺, the "chef" puts ten steaks on a pitchfork and dips them into a vat of boiling oil for five minutes. (Daily at 6:30pm. Reservations required. $20, half steak $16. Buffet only $12 and pre-schoolers $4.) Tickets for both the musical and the fondue are available at the Burning Hills Amphitheatre, 335 4th St., at the **Harold Schafer Heritage Center.** (☎800-633-6721; www.medora.com. Open daily 10am-6pm.)

OUTDOOR ACTIVITIES. The **south unit** is busier and more crowded than the north unit and includes a 36 mi. **scenic automobile loop,** from which all sights and trails are accessible. **Painted Canyon Overlook,** seven mi. east of Medora off I-94, has its own **Visitors Center** with picnic tables, public phone, restrooms and a breathtaking panoramic view of the Badlands, while the occasional buffalo roams through the parking lot. (☎575-4020. Open daily June-Aug. 8am-6pm; mid-Apr. to late May and early Sept. to mid-Nov. 8:30am-4:30pm. Free.) The **Painted Canyon Trail** is a worthwhile one mi. hiking loop that winds gently through shady wooded areas and scorching buttes. **Peaceful Valley Ranch,** seven mi. into the park, offers horseback excursions. (☎623-4568. 1½hr. trail rides leave in summer daily 8:30am-2pm;

The seclusion of Theodore Roosevelt Park provides ample opportunity for wildlife contact, but be careful not to surprise the buffalo; one ranger advises singing while hiking so they can hear you coming. Also beware of rattlesnakes and black widow spiders living in prairie dog burrows. Even if you avoid the creepy-crawlies, stay on guard; prairie dogs have bites more menacing than their barks.

evening ride 6pm. 8-9 per day. $20.) The **Ridgeline Trail** is a relatively flat self-guided ½ mi. hiking trail. Signs along the way describe the ecology and geology of the terrain. For a little more exercise try the **Coal Vein Trail.** This ¾ mi. trail traces a seam of lignite coal that ignited and burned from 1951 to 1977; the searing heat of the blaze served as a natural kiln, baking the adjacent clay and sand. The beautiful **Buck Hill** is accessible by car, but a short climb up a steep paved path to an elevation of 2855 ft. yields an unforgettable 360° view of the Badlands landscape that should not be missed. Constant winds morph the soft sands of **Wind Canyon,** while a short dirt path leads along the bluffs giving a closer look at the canyon walls and the river below. The third largest **petrified forest** in the US is a day's hike into the park; if you prefer to drive, ask a ranger for directions and expect to walk about ¾ mi. Tours leave roughly every 45min. from the South Unit's Visitors Center for TR's **Maltese Cross Cabin,** built circa 1883. (Tours in summer 8:45am-4:15pm.) For more info on hiking, pick up a copy of the *Backcountry Guide* ($2) at one of the Visitors Centers. In **emergencies** call ☎623-4562 or 911.

The newly developed **Maah Daah Hey Trail** connects the north and south units through the scenic Little Missouri Badlands. This 120 mi. trail does not allow mechanized equipment, including bikes, in the park. Most would probably prefer to drive to the **north unit,** which is 70 mi. from the south unit on U.S. 85. Equally as scenic as the south unit, it is infinitely more conducive to hiking and exploring. Most of the land is wilderness, resulting in unlimited **backcountry hiking** possibilities. For those eager to escape the crowds, but reluctant to leave the car, the north unit boasts a **14 mile scenic drive.** The drive connects the entrance and Visitors Center to **Oxbow Overlook** and is as unsullied as possible. The 1 mi. **Little Mo Trail** weaves through woodlands and badlands, and ¾ of the one mi. trail is wheelchair-accessible. The 11 mi. **Buckhorn Trail** is a long but relatively easy walk that includes a visit to a prairie dog town. Seasoned hikers and adventurers will thrive on the challenging 16 mi. **Achenbach Trail** that features vertical drops and uphill climbs as it winds around the Little Missouri River, visible from the **River Bend Outlook.**

SOUTH DAKOTA

With fewer than ten people per square mile, South Dakota has the highest ratio of sights to people in all of the Great Plains. Colossal carvings such as Mt. Rushmore and the Crazy Horse Memorial and stunning natural spectacles like the Black Hills and the Badlands make tourism the state's largest industry. Buffalo roam parts of the state as do adventure-seeking tourists. Small and patient, down-to-earth and friendly, South Dakota is the highlight of the Plains.

PRACTICAL INFORMATION

Capital: Pierre.

Visitor Info: Department of Tourism, 711 E. Wells Ave., Pierre, SD 57501 (☎605-773-3301 or 800-732-5682; www.travelsd.com). Open M-F 7am-7pm. **US Forest Service,** 330 Mt. Rushmore Rd., Custer 57730 (☎605-673-4853). Open M-F 7:30am-4:30pm. **Game, Fish, and Parks Department,** 523 E. Capitol Ave., Foss Bldg., Pierre 57501 (☎605-773-3391, for campground reservations ☎800-710-2267; www.campsd.com), has info on state parks and campgrounds. Open M-F 8am–5pm.

Postal Abbreviation: SD. **Sales Tax:** 4%.

SIOUX FALLS ☎605

South Dakota's eastern gateway, Sioux Falls, is your typical "nice guy"—quiet, friendly, clean-cut, and a little boring—more of a place to catch your breath than a destination in itself. The city's namesake rapids are at Falls Park, north of downtown. The **Sioux River Greenway Recreation Trail** circles the city from Falls Park in the northeast to the Elmwood golf course in the northwest as it follows the Big Sioux River. Sioux Falls also boasts a small-scale casting of **Michelangelo's** *David*, located in Fawick Park at 10th St. and 2nd Ave. At **Buffalo Ridge,** 5 mi. west of Sioux Falls at Exit 390 on I-90, you can visit a dilapidated yet endearing ghost town with over 50 educational exhibits portraying life in the Old West. Catch a glimpse of the ghost of Comanche, Custer's horse, and witness the mechanized murder of Bill Hickock in the saloon. A herd of over 50 buffalo also makes appearances near the town from time to time. (☎528-3931; www.buffaloridgesd.com. Open early Apr.-Oct. sunrise to sunset. $4, children 5-12 $3.) The **Corn Palace,** 604 N. Main St., in Mitchell, 70 mi. west of Sioux Falls on I-90, poses as a regal testament to the "a-maize-ing" power of corn. Dating back to 1892, the structure is refurbished with a new mural every year using 600,000 pieces of corn in nine colors and 3000 bushels of grains and grasses. (☎996-5031 or 800-257-2676; www.cornpalace.org. Open June-Aug. daily 8am-9pm; May and Sept. 8am-5pm; Oct.-Apr. M-F 8am-5pm. Free.) During summer, the **Wells Fargo Falls Park Light and Sound Show,** at the Visitors Center, enhances the natural beauty of Sioux Falls with a little help from modern technology. (Memorial Day to Labor Day nightly starting ½hr. after sunset. Free.)

Budget motels flank 41st St. at Exit 77 off I-29. The **Select Inn ❷,** 3500 Gateway Blvd., is a particularly good value. (☎361-1864 or 800-641-1000. Continental breakfast included. Singles $42; doubles $50; AAA discounts.) There are a number of state parks nearby. **Split Rock City Park ❶,** 20 mi. northeast in Garretson, has the cheapest camping. From I-90 E, take Exit 406, Rte. 11 N. (Corson), and drive 10 mi. to Garretson; turn right at the sign for Devil's Gulch; the park will be on your left before the tracks. (☎594-6721. Pit toilets and drinking water. Sites $6.) Phillips Ave., between 9th and 12th St., houses coffeehouses and restaurants. **Soda Falls ❶,** at the back of **Zandbroz Variety Store,** 209 S. Phillips Ave., has everything from fantastic sandwiches ($2-4) and sundaes ($3-4) to free gift-wrapping. The lunch counter was built in the 1920s from some of the first marble used in the Dakotas. (☎331-5137. Open M-Sa 9am-8pm, Su noon-5pm.) **Coffee 'N Clay ❶,** 324 S. Phillips Ave., is a colorful establishment that offers good sandwiches ($5) and strong coffee. (☎367-1100. Open M-Th 7am-9pm, F 7am-10pm, Sa 8am-10pm, Su 9am-6pm.)

Nitwits Comedy Club, 431 N. Phillips Ave., showcases local talent along with Hollywood imports. (☎274-9656 or 888-798-0277; www.nitwitscomedy.com. Cover $10. Box office opens W-F 6pm, Sa 3pm, Su 5pm. Club office open Tu-F 10am-6pm. Showtimes W-Sa 7:30pm, F-Sa 10pm.) Dance the night away at the **ACME DRINK COMPANY,** 305 N. Main Ave., where clubbers spill onto the patio. (☎339-1131. W 18+, Th-Sa 21+. Cover W $5, Th-Sa no cover. Open W 9pm-1am, Th-Sa 8pm-2am.)

Jack Rabbit Buses, 301 N. Dakota Ave. (☎336-0885 or 800-678-6543; open daily 7:30am-5pm), hop to: Minneapolis (6hr., 3 per day, $50); Omaha (4hr., 3 per day, $37); Rapid City (9hr., 1 per day, $86). **Sioux Falls Transit** buses run throughout the city. (☎367-7183. Buses operate M-F 5:40am-6:55pm, Sa 7:45am-6:45pm. $1; transfers free.) The **Sioux Falls Trolley** offers free rides around downtown Sioux Falls. (☎367-7183. Runs Apr.-Sept. M-Sa.) **Taxi: Yellow Cab,** ☎336-1616. **Medical Services: Avera McKennan Hospital & University Health Center,** 800 E. 21st St. (☎322-8000.) **Visitors Center:** in Falls Park, between Main Ave. and Weber Ave. on Falls Park Dr. (☎367-7430; www.siouxfallschamber.com. Open mid-Apr. to Sept. daily 9am-9pm; Oct. to mid-Apr. Sa-Su 9am-5pm.) The free climb up the Visitors Center's observation tower has an aerial view of the falls. **Internet Access: Sioux Falls Public Library,** 201 N. Main Ave., at 8th St. (☎367-7081. Open June-Aug. M-Th 9:30am-9pm, F 9:30am-6pm, Sa 9:30am-5pm; Sept.-May M-Th 9:30am-9pm, F 9:30am-6pm, Sa 9:30am-5pm, Su 1-5pm.) **Post Office:** 320 S. 2nd Ave. (☎357-5001. Open M-F 7:30am-5:30pm, Sa 8am-1pm.) **Postal Code:** 57104. **Area Code:** 605.

THE BADLANDS ☎605

When faced with the mountainous rock formations suddenly appearing out of the prairie, early explorers were less than enthusiastic. General Alfred Sully called these arid and treacherous formations "Hell with the fires out," and the French translated the Sioux name for the area, *mako sica*, as *les mauvaises terres:* "bad lands." Late spring and fall in the Badlands offer pleasant weather that can be a relief from the extreme temperatures of mid-summer and winter; however, even at their worst, the Badlands are worth a visit. Deposits of iron oxide lend layers of marvelous red and brown hues to the present land, and the colorful moods of the Badlands change with the time, season, and weather. According to geologists, they erode about 2 in. every year. At that rate they will disappear in 500,000 years—hurry and visit before it's too late.

PRACTICAL INFORMATION

Badlands National Park lies about 50 mi. east of Rapid City on I-90. The **entrance fee** comes with a free copy of *The Prairie Preamble* with trail map. ($10 per car, $5 per person on bike, foot, or motorcycle.) **Driving tours** of the park can start at either end of

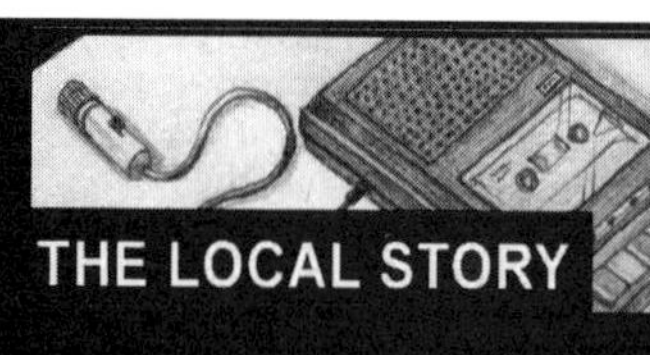

THE LOCAL STORY

WALL DRUG

Ted Hustead is the third-generation president of Wall Drug, the world's largest drug store. With nearly 200 enticing billboards across South Dakota and countless others across the world, Wall Drug, with its western memorabilia, clothing, and artwork, has become a major tourist attraction.

In 1936, my grandmother came up with an idea in the middle of summer... She said, "Ted, we've got to let the people know that we have a business here, the people that are going past Wall on their way to Mt. Rushmore and Yellowstone on dusty, dirty Highway 14... Let's put up a sign and advertise free ice water; it's 110 degrees today." My grandpa thought it was a little corny, but he was up for trying anything. He hired a couple local people and made a series of signs and put them on the edge of town: "Slow down the ol' hack–Wall Drug, just across the railroad track. Free ice water." That summer, they had to hire nine ladies just to wait on all the customers that started pouring into this business...

Wall Drug, *510 Main St. (605-279-2175; www.walldrug.com). Open daily 6am-10pm.*

Rte. 240, which winds through wilderness in a 32 mi. detour off I-90 Exit 110 or 131. The **Ben Reifel Visitors Center,** 5 mi. inside the park's northeastern entrance, serves as the Park Headquarters. (☎433-5361. Open daily mid-Apr. to mid-June 8am-5pm; mid-June to mid-Aug. 7am-7pm; mid-Aug. to mid-Sept. 8am-6pm; mid-Sept. to mid-Oct. 8am-5pm; mid-Oct. to Apr. 9am-4pm.) Another ranger station, the **White River Visitors Center,** is located 55 mi. to the southwest, off Rte. 27, in the park's less-visited southern section. (☎455-2878. Open June-Aug. daily 10am-4pm.) Both Visitors Centers have potable water and restrooms. The **National Grasslands Visitors Center (Buffalo Gap),** 708 Main St., in Wall, has films and an exhibit on the complex ecosystem of the surrounding area. (☎279-2125. Open daily June-Aug. 7am-8pm; Sept.-May 8am-4:30pm.) For info, write to Badlands National Park, P.O. Box 6, Interior, SD 57750 (www.nps.gov/badl). **Area Code:** 605. **Time Zone:** Mountain (2hr. behind Eastern).

ACCOMMODATIONS

In addition to standard lodging and camping, **backcountry camping** (½ mi. from the road and out of sight) allows an intimate introduction to this austere landscape, but be sure to bring water. Campers are strongly urged to contact one of the rangers at the Visitors Center before heading out. Wherever you sleep, don't cozy up to bison; they are really, really dangerous.

Cedar Pass Lodge, 1 Cedar St. (☎433-5460; www.cedarpasslodge.com), next to the Ben Reifel Visitors Center inside the park, rents cabins with A/C and showers. Reservations recommended. Open mid-Apr. to mid-Oct. 1 person $48, additional person $4. ❸

Badlands Inn, at Exit 131 off I-90, (☎433-5401 or 800-341-8000; www.badlandsinn.com) south of the Ben Reifel Visitors Center in Interior on Rte. 4 . Each of the rooms offers a view of the Badlands and access to an outdoor pool. Open mid-May to mid-Sept. Singles $32-40, with 2 people $37-50; doubles $40-57. ❷

Cedar Pass Campground, south of the Ben Reifel Visitors Center. It's best to get there early in summer, since sites fill before evening. Sites with water and restrooms $10. ❶

Sage Creek Campground, 13 mi. from the Pinnacles entrance south of Wall, take Sage Creek Rim Rd. off Rte. 240. You sleep in an open field where there are pit toilets, no water, and fires are not allowed–but hey, it's free. ❶

FOOD

Cedar Pass Lodge Restaurant (☎433-5460) is in the park. Brave diners try the $3.65 buffalo burger. Open daily mid-May to late Oct. 7am-9pm; low-season 8am-4pm. ❶

Cuny Table Cafe (☎455-2957), in Buffalo Gap, 8 mi. west of the White River Visitor Center on Rte. 2, only a short detour from Wounded Knee, provides your stomach with more loving fare. Cuny doesn't advertise, because it doesn't need to—the food does all the talking. Indian Tacos (home-cooked fry bread piled with veggies, beans, and beef) $5. Cash only. Open daily 5am-5pm. ❶

A&M Cafe (☎433-5340), just 2 mi. south of the Ben Reifel Visitors Center on Rte. 44, outside the park in Interior, is a small but hectic cafe that has generous breakfasts and ample sandwich platters for $3-6. Open daily 6:30am-9:30pm. ❶

OUTDOOR ACTIVITIES

The 244,000-acre park protects large tracts of prairie and stark rock formations. The Ben Reifel Visitors Center has an 18min. video on the Badlands as well as a wealth of info on nearby activities and camping. Park rangers offer free talks and daily excursions in summer. Check the handy *Prairie Preamble* for schedules.

HIKING

Hiking is permitted throughout the entire park, although officials discourage climbing on the formations and request sticking to high-use trails. Rangers can aid hikers in forming backcountry hiking itineraries that respect the park. The south unit is mostly uncharted territory, and the occasional found path is most likely the tracks of livestock. For backcountry hikers, it's a good idea to bring a compass, a map, and lots of water. Despite the burning heat in summer, long pants are advisable to protect from poison ivy, stinging and biting insects, and the park's one venomous snake—the prairie rattlesnake. Five hiking trails begin off Loop Rd. near the Ben Reifel Visitor Center:

Door Trail (¾ mi., 20min.) is wheelchair-accessible for the first 100m. The rest of the trail cuts through buttes and crevices for spectacular views of the surrounding countryside. Self-guide brochure ($0.50) available at the start of the trail.

Window Trail (¼ mi., 10min.), more of a scenic overlook than an actual hike, consists of a wheelchair-accessible ramp with a splendid view.

Cliff Shelf Nature Trail (½ mi., 30min.) also has self-guide brochures ($0.50). This moderate trail consists of stairs, a boardwalk, and unpaved paths. It is the best bet for coming face-to-face with wildlife.

Notch Trail (1½ mi., 1½-2hr.) demands surefootedness through a canyon and a willingness to climb a shaky ladder at a 45° angle. Not for the faint of heart, the trail blazes around narrow ledges before making its way to the grand finale: an unbelievable view of the Cliff Shelf and White River Valley.

DRIVING

A scenic drive along **Route 240/Loop Road** is an excellent introduction to the entire northern portion of the park. This scenic byway makes its way through rainbow-colored bluffs and around hairpin turns, while providing views of many distinct types of Badlands terrain. The gravel **Sage Creek Rim Road,** west of Rte. 240, has fewer people and more animals. Highlights are the Roberts Prairie Dog Town and the park's herds of bison and antelope; across the river from the Sage Creek campground lies another prairie dog town and some popular bison territory.

RIDING

Travelers interested in exploring the area on horseback can check out **Badlands Trail Rides,** 1½ mi. south of the Ben Reifel Visitors Center on Rte. 377. While the trails do not lead into the park, they do cover territory on the park's immediate outskirts. All levels are welcome, and a full introduction is given before the ride. (☎433-5453. Open summer daily 8am-7pm. $15 for 30min. ride; $20 for 1hr. ride.)

RAPID CITY ☎605

Rapid City's location makes it a convenient base from which to explore the surrounding attractions. Mount Rushmore, Crazy Horse, the Black Hills, and the Badlands are all within an hour's drive of downtown Rapid City. The area welcomes three million tourists each summer, over 60 times the city's permanent population. Be sure to pick up a map of the **Rapid City Star Tour** at the Civic Center or any motel and then follow the signs. The route leads to 12 free attractions, including a jaunt up Skyline Drive for a bird's-eye view of the city and the seven concrete dinosaurs of **Dinosaur Park,** and a magical trip to **Storybook Island,** a kids' amusement park inhabited by the Gingerbread Man, the Three Little Pigs, and other childhood pals. You can also check out America's largest Berlin Wall exhibit, featuring two pieces of the wall, at the **Dahl Fine Arts Center,** 713 7th St. (☎394-4101. Open Su 1-5pm, Tu-Sa 10am-5pm. Free.). Runners, walkers, and bikers traverse the 8 mi. **Rapid City Recreational Path** along Rapid Creek.

Rapid City accommodations are more expensive during the summer and motels often fill weeks in advance, especially during the first two weeks in August when nearby Sturgis hosts its annual **motorcycle rally** (see p. 640). Needless to say, reservations are a good idea. Winter travelers benefit from an abundance of low-season bargains. Large billboards guide the way to **Big Sky Motel ❸**, 4080 Tower Rd., 5min. south of town on a service road off Mt. Rushmore Rd. The rooms are very clean and many have great views. (☎348-3200 or 800-318-3208. No phones. Singles $48; doubles $64. Lower low-season; call for rates. AAA discounts.) **Camping ❶** is available at **Badlands National Park** (see p. 635), **Black Hills National Forest** (see p. 639), and **Custer State Park** (see p. 642).

The Millstone Family Restaurant ❷, 2010 W. Main St., at Mountain View Rd., cooks up large portions of chicken ($6.25-7.65), spaghetti and meatballs ($7.85), and pork ribs ($8.50). Try the steak and salad bar combo for $7.65. (☎343-5824. Open daily 6am-11pm.) The cosmopolitan **Once Upon a Vine ❷,** 507 6th St., has the city's best wine selection. The chef puts together delectable sandwiches ($6.50-7.75) and gourmet pizzas ($7.75) for discerning taste buds. Dinner comes with a higher price tag (up to $18) and fewer selections. (☎343-7802. Cafe open Tu-Th 11:30am-2pm and 5-8pm, F 11:30am-2pm and 5-10pm, Sa 5-10pm. Wine bar open Tu-Th 11:30am-9pm, F 11:30am-11pm, Sa 5-11pm.) **Pauly's Sub Co. ❶,** 711 Omaha St., serves hot, cold, and vegetarian subs deli-style for the visitor on the run. Gyros cost $3.50, and subs run $2.29-6.19. (☎343-8020. Open M-Sa 10am-8pm, Su 11am-8pm.) Nightlife options line **Main Street** between 6th St. and Mt. Rushmore Rd. For a beer as black as the Hills, toss back a Smokejumper Stout ($3) at the **Firehouse Brewing Company,** 610 Main St. The company brews five beers in-house and serves sandwiches, burgers, and salads for $6-10 in the restored 1915 firehouse or outside on their heated patio. (☎348-1915; www.firehousebrewing.com. Open M-Th 11am-10pm, F-Sa 11am-11pm, Su 4-9pm. Extended hours during the summer.) After dinner at the firehouse, head upstairs to **The Brew Haha Comedy Club** for some good laughs and poor puns.

The Rushmore Plaza Civic Center, 44 Mt. Rushmore Rd., hosts concerts and sporting events. (☎394-4111 or 800-468-6463; www.gotmine.com.) The **Journey Museum** traces the history of the Great Plains of the West. (☎394-6923; www.journeymuseum.org. Open Memorial Day-Labor Day M-Su 9am-5pm. In the winter, starting Sept. 5th, M-Sa 10am-5pm, Su 1-5pm. $6, seniors $5, students $4.)

Driving in Rapid City is easy; roads are laid out in a sensible grid pattern. **Saint Joseph Street** and **Main Street** are the main east-west thoroughfares, and **Mount Rushmore Road (Route 16)** is the main north-south route. Downtown Rapid City is located off Exit 57 on 1-90. Many north-south roads are numbered, and numbers increase from east to west, beginning at **East Boulevard. The Rapid City Regional Hospital** (☎719-8100) is located at 353 Fairmont Blvd. The Airport Express Shuttle

(☎399-9999) can get you quickly to the **Rapid City Regional Airport** (☎393-9924), off Rte. 44, 8½ mi. east of the city. **Rapid Taxi Inc.** (☎348-8080) will take you around town. **Jack Rabbit Lines** scurries east from the Milo Barber Transportation Center, 333 6th St. (☎348-3300), downtown, with one bus daily to: Omaha (12hr., $106); Pierre (4hr., $34-36); Sioux Falls (10hr., $96). **Powder River Lines,** also in the Center, runs once daily to Billings (8hr., $61) and Cheyenne (8hr., $70). (Station open M-F 8am-5pm, Sa-Su 10am-noon and 2-5pm.) **Rapid Ride** runs city buses. Pick up a schedule at the terminal in the Milo Barber Transportation Center. (☎394-6631. Operates M-F 6:25am-5:30pm. $1, seniors $0.50.) **Visitor Info: Rapid City Chamber of Commerce and Visitors Information Center,** 444 Mt. Rushmore Rd., in the Civic Center. (☎343-1744; www.rapidcitycvb.com. Open M-F 8am-5pm.) **Internet Access: Rapid City Public Library,** 610 Quincy St., at 6th St. (☎394-4171. Open Labor Day-Memorial Day M-Th 9am-9pm, F-Sa 9am-5:30pm; Sept.-May M-Th 9am-9pm, F-Sa 9am-5:30pm, Su 1-5pm. 1hr. per day. Free.) **Post Office:** 500 East Blvd., east of downtown. (☎394-8600. Open M-F 8am-5:30pm, Sa 8:30am-12:30pm.) **Postal code:** 57701. **Area code:** 605.

BLACK HILLS REGION

The Black Hills, so-called for the hue that the pine-covered slopes take on when seen from a distance, have long been thought sacred by the Sioux. The Treaty of 1868 gave the Black Hills and the rest of South Dakota west of the Missouri River to the tribe, but when gold was discovered in the 1870s, the US government snatched back 6000 square miles. Today, the area attracts millions of visitors annually with a trove of natural treasures, including Custer State Park, Wind Cave National Park, and Jewel Cave National Monument, while the monuments of Mt. Rushmore and Crazy Horse illustrate the clash of the two cultures that reside here.

BLACK HILLS NATIONAL FOREST ☎605

The Black Hills region holds over 130 attractions—including reptile farms and even a Flintstones theme park—but the greatest sights are the natural ones. Most of the land in the Black Hills is part of the Black Hills National Forest and exercises the "multiple use" principle—mining, logging, ranching, and recreation all take place in close proximity. The forest itself provides opportunities for backcountry hiking, swimming, biking, and camping, as do park-run campgrounds and private tent sites. In the hills, the **Visitors Center,** on I-385 at Pactola Lake, offers a great view of the lake, a wildlife exhibit with a bald eagle, maps of the area, and details on backcountry camping. (☎343-8755. Open Memorial Day-Labor Day daily 8:30am-6pm.) **Backcountry camping** in the national forest is free. Camping is allowed 1 mi. away from any campground or Visitors Center and at least 200 ft. off the side of the road (leave your car in a parking lot or pull off). Open fires are prohibited, but controlled fires in provided grates are allowed. Good **campgrounds** ❶ include: **Pactola,** on the Pactola Reservoir just south of the junction of Rte. 44 and U.S. 385; **Sheridan Lake,** 5 mi. northeast of Hill City on U.S. 385 (north entrance for group sites, south entrance for individuals); and **Roubaix Lake,** 14 mi. south of Lead on U.S. 385. (Sites at all 3 $17-19.) Pactola closes in the winter, but Roubaix keeps 13 sites open. All National Forest campgrounds are quiet and wooded, offering fishing, swimming, and pit toilets. No hookups are provided. (☎877-444-6777; www.forestrecreationmanagement.com for reservations.) The national forest extends into Wyoming, and a **ranger station** can be found in Sundance. (☎307-283-1361. Open M-F 7:30am-5pm, Sa 9am-3pm.) The Wyoming side of the forest permits campfires and horses, and draws fewer visitors. The hostel in **Deadwood** (see p. 643) is the cheapest and best indoor accommodation in these parts.

I-90 skirts the northern border of the Black Hills from Spearfish in the west to Rapid City in the east. **U.S. 385** twists from Hot Springs in the south to Deadwood in the north. The road is certainly beautiful, but don't expect to get anywhere fast. These winding routes hold drivers to half the speed of the interstate. Unless astride a flashy piece of chrome and steel, steer clear of the Hills in early August, when over 12,000 motorcyclists converge on the area for the **Sturgis Rally**. Winter in the Black Hills offers stellar skiing and snowmobiling. Unfortunately, many attractions close or have limited hours, and most resorts and campgrounds are closed in winter. The **Black Hills Visitor Information Center** is at Exit 61 off I-90 in Rapid City. (☎355-3700. Open summer daily 7am-8pm; low-season 8am-5pm.)

MOUNT RUSHMORE ☎605

Mount Rushmore National Memorial boasts the faces that launched a thousand minivans. Historian Doane Robinson originally conceived of this "shrine of democracy" in 1923 as a memorial for Western heroes; sculptor Gutzon Borglum chose four presidents instead. Borglum initially encountered opposition from those who felt the work of God could not be improved, but the sculptor defended the project's size, insisting that "there is not a monument in this country as big as a snuff box." In 1941, the 60 ft. heads of Washington, Jefferson, Roosevelt, and Lincoln were finished. The 465 ft. tall bodies were never completed—work ceased when US funds were diverted to WWII. The disembodiment doesn't seem to perturb the millions of visitors who come here every year.

From Rapid City, take U.S. 16 and 16A to Keystone, and Rte. 244 up to the mountain. The memorial is 2 mi. from downtown Keystone. Remote parking is free, but spots are limited and the lot fills early. There is an $8 per car "annual parking permit" for the lot adjacent to the entrance. The **Info Center** details the monument's history and has ranger tours. A state-of-the-art **Visitors Center** chronicles the monument's history and the lives of the featured presidents in addition to showing a film that explains how the carving was accomplished—about 90% of the sculpting was done with dynamite. (Info center ☎574-3198. Visitors Center ☎574-3165. Wheelchair-accessible. Both open summer daily 8am-10pm; low-season 8am-5pm.)

From the Visitors Center, it is ½ mi. along the planked wooden **Presidential Trail** to **Borglum's Studio.** Visitors can stare at Borglum's full-bodied plaster model of the carving as well as tools and designs for Mt. Rushmore. (Open summer daily 9am-6pm.) During the summer, the **Mount Rushmore Memorial Amphitheater** hosts an evening program. (☎574-2523; www.nps.gov/moru. Patriotic speech and film 9pm, light floods the monument 9:30-10:30pm. Trail lights extinguished 11pm.)

For a look at American presidents in a different medium, check out the **National Presidential Wax Museum,** Hwy. 16A in downtown Keystone. (☎666-4455; www.presidentialwaxmuseum.com. Open daily May-Sept. 9am-9pm; last self-guided tours leave 8pm. $9, seniors $7, ages 6-12 $6.)

Horsethief Campground ❶ lies 2 mi. west of Mt. Rushmore on Rte. 244 in the Black Hills National Forest. Former President George Bush fished here in 1993; rumor has it that the lake was overstocked with fish to guarantee presidential success. (☎877-444-6777; www.reserveusa.com. Water and flush toilets in the woods. Reservations recommended on weekends. Sites $19, lakeside sites $21.) The commercial **Mt. Rushmore KOA/Palmer Gulch Lodge** ❷, 7 mi. west of Mt. Rushmore on Rte. 244, has campsites for two and cabins with showers, stoves, pool, spa, laundry, nightly movies, a small strip mall, car rental, and free shuttle service to Mt. Rushmore. (☎574-2525 or 800-562-8503; www.palmergulch.com. Make reservations early, up to 2 months in advance for cabins. Open May-Oct. Sites June-Aug. $27; with water and electricity $34; cabins $49-56; May and Sept.-Oct. $23/30/42-49.)

CRAZY HORSE MEMORIAL ☎605

In 1947, Lakota Chief Henry Standing Bear commissioned sculptor Korczak Ziolkowski to sculpt a memorial to Crazy Horse as a reminder to whites that Native Americans have their own heroes. A famed warrior who garnered respect by refusing to sign treaties or live on a government reservation, Crazy Horse was stabbed by a treacherous white soldier in 1877. The **Crazy Horse Memorial,** which at its completion will be the world's largest sculpture, will stand as a spectacular tribute to the revered Native American leader.

The first blast rocked the hills on June 3, 1948, and on the memorial's 50th anniversary, the completed face (all four of the Rushmore heads could fit inside it) was unveiled. Ziolkowski believed that Crazy Horse should be a project funded by those who believed in the memorial—not taxpayers. The sculptor went solo for years, twice refusing offers of $10 million in federal funding. Today, his wife Ruth and seven of their 10 children carry on the work, with admission prices funding 85% of the cost. Part of Crazy Horse's arm is now visible, and eventually, his entire torso and head, as well as part of his horse, will be carved into the mountain.

The memorial, 17 mi. southwest of Mt. Rushmore on U.S. 385/U.S. 16, includes the **Indian Museum of North America,** the **Sculptor's Studio-Home,** and the **Native American Educational and Cultural Center,** where native crafts are displayed and sold. The orientation center shows a moving 17min. video entitled "Dynamite and Dreams." The view of Crazy Horse from the visitor center is a distant but impressive one. During the first full weekend of June, visitors have the opportunity to trek 6¼ mi. up to the face. Otherwise, expect to pay $3 to take a bus to the base of the mountain. (☎673-4681; www.crazyhorse.org. Open May-Sept. daily 7am-dark; Oct.-Apr. 8am-dark. Monument lit nightly about 10min. after sunset for 1hr. $9; under 6 free; $19 per carload.)

WIND CAVE & JEWEL CAVE ☎605

In the cavern-riddled Black Hills, the subterranean scenery often rivals the aboveground sites. Local entrepreneurs may attempt to lure you into the holes in their backyards, but the government owns the area's prime underground real estate: **Wind Cave National Park** (☎745-4600; www.nps.gov/wica), adjacent to Custer State Park (p. 642) on U.S. 385, and **Jewel Cave National Monument** (☎673-2288, tour reservations ☎800-967-2283; www.nps.gov/jeca), 13 mi. west of the U.S. 385/U.S. 16 junction, in Custer. There is no public transportation to the caves. Bring a sweater on all tours—Wind Cave remains a constant 53°F, while Jewel Cave is 49°F.

WIND CAVE. Wind Cave was discovered by Tom Bingham in 1881 when he heard the sound of air rushing out of the cave's only natural entrance. The wind was so strong, in fact, that it knocked his hat off. When Tom returned to show his friends the cave, his hat got sucked in. Air forcefully gusts in and out of the cave due to changes in outside pressure. Scientists estimate that only 5% of a potential 2000 mi. of passageways have been discovered. Within the 100 mi. that have been explored, geologists have found a lake over 200 ft. long in the cave's deepest depths. Wind Cave is unique in that it does not house the typical crystal formations of stalagmites and stalactites. Instead, it is known for housing over 95% of the world's "boxwork"—a honeycomb-like lattice of calcite covering its walls. Five **tours** cover a range of caving experience. (☎745-4600. Tours June-Aug. daily 8:40am-6pm; less frequently in winter.) The **Garden of Eden Tour** (1hr., ¼ mi., 5 per day, 150 stairs) is the least strenuous. ($6, seniors and ages 6-16 $3, under 6 free.) The **Natural Entrance Tour** (1¼hr., ½ mi., 11 per day, 300 stairs) and the **Fairgrounds Tour** (1½hr., ½ mi., 8 per day, 450 stairs) are both moderately strenuous, and one of the two leaves about every 30min. ($8, seniors and ages 6-16 $4, under 6 free.)

Light your own way on the more rigorous **Candlelight Tour.** (Limited to 10 people. 2hr. June-Aug. 10:30am, 1:30pm. $9, seniors and children $4.50. Under 8 not admitted. "Non-slip" soles on shoes required.) The rather difficult **Wild Cave Tour,** an intro to basic caving, is limited to 10 people ages 16 and over who can fit through a 10 in. high passageway. (Parental consent required for under 18. 4hr. tour daily 1pm. $20, seniors $10. Reservations required.) In the afternoon, all tours fill up about 1hr. ahead of time, so buy tickets in advance. **Wind Cave National Park Visitors Center** at RR1, P.O. Box 190, Hot Springs, can provide more info. (☎745-4600. Open June to mid-Aug. daily 8am-7pm; winter hours vary. Parts of some tours are wheelchair-accessible.) The **Elk Mountain Campground ❶,** 1 mi. north of the Visitors Center, is an excellent site in the woods that rarely fills up during the summer. (Potable water and restrooms. Sites mid-May to mid-Sept. $12; mid-Sept. to late Oct. and Apr. to mid-May $6.) Backcountry camping is allowed in the northwestern sector of the park. Campers must have a permit, which is free and can be obtained at the Visitors Center.

JEWEL CAVE. Distinguishing itself from nearby Wind Cave's boxwork, the walls of Jewel Cave are covered with a layer of calcite crystal. The **Scenic Tour** (1¼hr., ½ mi., 723 stairs.) highlights chambers with the most interesting crystal formations. (Leaves in summer roughly every 20min. 8:30am-6pm; in winter call ahead. $8, ages 6-16 $4, under 6 free.) The **Lantern Tour** is an illuminating journey lasting 1¾hr. Walk, duck, and stoop by candlelight through the many tunnels. (Summer every hour 9am-5pm; in winter call ahead. $8, ages 6-16 $4.) Reservations, pants, a long-sleeve shirt, knee-pads, sturdy boots, and a willingness to get down and dirty are required for the 3-4hr. **Spelunking Tour,** limited to five people over age 16. (June-Aug. daily at 12:30pm. $27. Must be able to fit through an 8½ in. by 2 ft. opening.) The **Visitors Center** has more info. (☎673-2288. Open daily June to mid-Aug. 8am-7:30pm; Oct. to mid-May 8am-4:30pm.) Behind the Visitors Center, Jewel Cave offers visitors picnic tables and two alluring hiking trails. The **Roof Trail** is short, but provides a memorable introduction to the Black Hills' beauty while trekking across the "roof" of Jewel Cave. The bucolic 3½ mi. **Canyons Trail** winds through small canyons and fields and up forested hills before returning to the Visitors Center.

CUSTER STATE PARK ☎605

Peter Norbeck, governor of South Dakota in the late 1910s, loved to hike among the thin, towering rock formations that haunt the area south of Sylvan Lake and Mt. Rushmore. In order to preserve the land, he created Custer State Park. The spectacular **Needles Highway (Route 87)** within the park follows his favorite hiking route. Norbeck designed this road to be especially narrow and winding so that newcomers could experience the pleasures of discovery. **Iron Mountain Road (U.S. 16A)** from Mt. Rushmore to near the Norbeck Visitors Center (see below) takes drivers through a series of tunnels, "pigtail" curves, and switchbacks. The park's **Wildlife Loop Road** twists past prairie dog towns, popular bison wallows, and wilderness areas near prime hiking and camping territory. If you're "lucky," one of Custer's 1500 **bison** will approach your car. Don't get out—bison are dangerous.

The park requires an **entrance fee.** (7 day pass May-Oct. $5 per person, $12 per carload; Nov.-Apr. $2.50/6.) The **Peter Norbeck Visitors Center,** on U.S. 16A, ½ mi. west of the State Game Lodge, serves as the park's info center. Learn to date a tree (only then will you fully understand the heartbreak of being dumped by a sycamore), explore the history of the park, and gather information on trails, campgrounds, and the park's greatest feature: bison. (☎255-4464; www.custerstatepark.info. Open Apr.-May and mid-Oct. to Nov. daily 9am-5pm; June-Aug. 8am-8pm; Sept. to mid.-Oct. 8am-6pm.) The Visitors Center can also give information about **primitive camping,** which is available for $2 per person per night in the **French Creek Natural Area ❶.** Eight **campgrounds ❶** have sites with showers and restrooms. No hookups are provided; only the Game Lodge Campground offers two electricity-accessible sites. (☎800-710-2267; daily 7am-9pm. Over 200 of the 400+ sites can be reserved; the entire park fills in summer by 3pm. Sites $13-18. $5 non-resident users fee.) Motels in the surrounding area include the convenient **Chalet Motel ❷**, 933 Mt. Rushmore Rd./16A, just west of the Stockade Lake entrance to the park in Custer. One-, two-, or three-bedroom units with kitchenettes are available; no phones are installed. (☎673-2393 or 800-649-9088. Reservations recommended. Rooms from $42.) Food is available at all park lodges, but the general stores in Custer, Hermosa, and Keystone are usually cheaper. **The Bank Coffee House ❶**, 548 Mt. Rushmore Rd., in Custer, serves $3-5 sandwiches (until 2pm) and $3 pie. Internet access and, obviously, coffee available. (☎673-5698. Open June-Aug. daily 7am-10pm; Sept.-May M-Sa 6am-9pm.)

At 7242 ft., **Harney Peak** is the highest point east of the Rockies and west of the Pyrenees. Waiting at the top are a few mountain goats and a great view of the Black Hills. Bring water and food, wear good shoes, and leave as early in the morning as possible. **Sunday Gulch Trail** offers the most amazing scenery of all the park's trails—rivers, boulders, and creatures await the adventurous. For less extreme hikers, the park provides 30 lower-altitude trails. You can also hike, fish, paddle boat, or canoe at popular **Sylvan Lake,** on Needles Hwy. (☎574-2561. Kayaks $4 per person per 30min.) Fishing is allowed anywhere in the park, but a South Dakota fishing license is required. ($7, non-residents $12.) One hour horse rides are available at **Blue Bell Lodge,** on Rte. 87 about 8 mi. from the south entrance. (☎255-4531, stable ☎255-4571. Reservations recommended. $18, under 12 $15.) Mountain bikes can be rented at the **Legion Lake Resort,** on U.S. 16A, 6 mi. west of the Visitors Center. (☎255-4521. $10 per hr., $25 per half-day, $40 per day.) The strong granite of the Needles makes for great rock climbing. For more info contact **Granite Sports/Sylvan Rocks,** at the corner of Elm and Main St. in Hill City. (☎574-2121. Open summer daily 10am-8:30pm; low-season hours vary.)

DEADWOOD ☎605

Gunslingers **Wild Bill Hickok** and **Calamity Jane** sauntered into this town during the height of the Gold Rush in the summer of 1876. Bill stayed just long enough—two months—to spend eternity here. Jane and Bill now lie side-by-side in the **Mount Moriah Cemetery,** just south of downtown, on Cemetery St. off Rte. 85. ($1, ages 5-12 $0.50. Open year round.) **Saloon #10,** 657 Main St., was forever immortalized by the murder of Wild Bill Hickok. Hickok was shot holding black aces and eights, thereafter infamous to poker players as a "dead man's hand." His death chair is on display and every summer the shooting is reenacted on location. (☎578-3346 or 800-952-9398; www.saloon10.com. Saloon open daily 8am-2am. Reenactments summer daily 1, 3, 5, 7pm.) Assassin Jack McCall is apprehended by authorities outside of Saloon #10. (Summer Tu-Su 7:45pm.) **Random shootouts** happen daily along Main St. at 2, 4, and 6pm—listen for gunshots and the sound of Calamity Jane's whip. **Alkali Ike Tours** offers 1hr. narrated bus tours of the Deadwood region. Tickets are sold at the booth on Main St., just outside Saloon #10. (☎578-3147. July-Aug. 5 tours per day. $6.50, ages 7-13 $3.50, under 7 free. AARP discount.) **Trolleys** ($0.50) circle downtown and provide a cheap alternative to the tours, look for signs on each block of Main St. to pick one up.

Gambling takes center stage in this authentic western town—brazen casinos line **Main Street,** and many innocent-looking establishments have slot machines and poker tables waiting in the wings. Children are allowed in the casinos until 8pm. There's live music outside the **Stockade** and 24hr. gambling at the **Buffalo Saloon,** 658 Main St. (☎578-1300). For the fun of gambling without the high stakes, many casinos offer nickel slot machines. Even those who lose most of their money at the gambling tables can afford to stay at **Hostelling International Black Hills at the Penny Motel (HI-AYH) ❶,** 818 Upper Main St. Look for the Penny Motel sign. A great kitchen with free pasta, rice, and cooking necessities, comfortable beds with linen, super clean rooms, and a friendly owner await visitors. Free Internet, a book swap, and private bathrooms are the icing on the cake. (☎578-1842 or 877-565-8140; www.pennymotel.com. Dorms $13, nonmembers $16; 1 private room $36. Motel rooms $46-$78; winter $29-$56.) The Penny Motel also rents bikes. ($5 per hr. $14 half day; $24 full day.) The **Whistlers Gulch Campground ❶,** off U.S. 85, has a pool, laundry facilities, and showers. (☎578-2092 or 800-704-7139. Sites $20, full hookup $30.) Cheap eats abound in Deadwood, but remember, you get what you pay for. All restaurants provide cheap specials allowing diners to eat for as little as $2 a meal. The **Deadwood History and Information Center,** 3 Siever St., can help with any questions. (☎578-2507 or 800-999-1876; www.deadwood.org. Open daily in summer 8am-7pm; winter 9am-5pm.) **Free parking** is available in the Sherman St. parking lot on Rte. 85 heading toward Lead. **Area code:** 605.

IOWA

Named for the Ioway Native Americans who farmed along the state's many river banks, Iowa contains one-fourth of all US Grade A farmland. Farming is *the* way of life in Iowa, a land where men are measured by the size of their John Deere tractors. The state ripples with gentle hills between the two great rivers that sculpt its eastern and western boundaries. The Mississippi River Valley in Eastern Iowa offers amazing views of the Mighty Miss from limestone bluffs. Despite its distinctly American landscape, Iowa preserves its European heritage in small towns that maintain their German, Dutch, and Scandinavian traditions.

PRACTICAL INFORMATION

Capital: Des Moines.

Visitor Info: Iowa Tourism Office, 200 E. Grand Ave., Des Moines, 50309 (☎800-345-4692 or 515-242-4705; www.traveliowa.com).

Postal Abbreviation: IA. **Sales Tax:** 5%; some towns add an additional 1-2%.

DES MOINES ☎515

Des Moines hums with the activity of its affable residents. The Skywalk, a second-floor maze of passageways connecting buildings downtown, is without equal in the Midwest. A beautiful system of parks traces the area's rivers and presents a welcome contrast to the now-bustling downtown area. From the "BarbeQlossal" **World Pork Expo** (June 10-12, 2004; ☎847-838-6772; www.worldpork.org) to world-class art, Des Moines' offerings run the gamut from kitsch to cosmopolitan.

TRANSPORTATION

Airport: Des Moines International, 5800 Fleur Dr. (☎256-5100; www.dsmairport.com), at Army Post Rd. 5 mi. southwest of downtown; M-F take bus #8 "Havens." Taxi to downtown $11-15.

Buses: Greyhound, 1107 Keo Way (☎243-1773 or 800-231-2222), at 12th St., just northwest of downtown; take bus #4 "Urbandale." To: **Iowa City** (2hr., 7 per day, $22); **Omaha** (2hr.; 8 per day; M-Th $23, F-Su $25); **Chicago** (8hr.; 10 per day; M-Th $38, F-Su $40); **St. Louis** (10hr.; 5 per day; M-Th $67, F-Su $71). Station open 24hr.

Public Transit: Metropolitan Transit Authority (MTA), 1100 MTA Lane (☎283-8111; www.dmmta.com), south of the 9th St. viaduct. Open M-F 8am-5pm. Buses run M-F approximately 6am-11pm, Sa 6:45am-5:50pm. $1, seniors (except M-F 3-6pm) and disabled persons $0.50 with MTA ID card; transfers $0.10. Routes serve Clive, Des Moines, Urbandale, West Des Moines, and Windsor Heights. Maps at the MTA office and web site as well as the public library.

Taxi: Yellow Cab, ☎243-1111.

Car Rental: Enterprise, 5601 Fleur Dr. (☎285-2525), just outside the airport, with speedy airport pickup. **Budget** (☎287-2612) and **National** (☎256-5353) have booths at the baggage claim in the airport.

ORIENTATION & PRACTICAL INFORMATION

I-80 and U.S. 65 encircle Des Moines; I-235 bisects the circle from east to west. Numbered streets run north-south, named streets east-west. Addresses begin with zero downtown at the **Des Moines River** and increase as you move east or west; **Grand Avenue** divides addresses north-south. Other east-west thoroughfares, moving northward, are **Locust Street, University Avenue** (home to Drake University), and **Hickman Road.** Parking garages and on-street metered parking allow downtown Des Moines to be explored easily by foot. Note that Des Moines and West Des Moines are different places, and the numbered streets within each are not the same.

Visitor Info: Greater Des Moines Convention and Visitors Bureau, 405 6th Ave., Ste. 201, (☎286-4960 or 800-451-2625; www.seedesmoines.com), along Locust in the Skywalk. Open M-F 8:30am-5pm. Up a few blocks is the **Chamber of Commerce,** 700 Locust St. (☎286-4950). Open M 9am-5pm, Tu-Th 8am-5pm, F 8am-4pm.

Medical Services: Mercy Medical Center, 111 6th Ave., downtown (☎243-2584). Open 24hr.

Internet Access: Des Moines Public Library, 100 Locust St. (☎283-4152; www.desmoineslibrary.com), and all other branches. Free 1hr. per day with the option of signing up a day in advance. Open M-W 10am-9pm, Th-F 10am-6pm, Sa 10am-5pm. Also open Oct.-Apr. Su 10am-5pm.

Post Office: 1165 2nd Ave. (☎283-7585), downtown, just north of I-235. Open M-F 7:30am-5:30pm. **Postal Code:** 50318. **Area Code:** 515.

ACCOMMODATIONS

Downtown Des Moines is cluttered with high-end hotels, but numerous cheap accommodations are sprinkled along Fleur Dr. by the airport, off I-80, and on Merle Hay Rd., 5 mi. northwest of downtown. Campgrounds are located west of the city off I-80. Remember the 7% hotel tax, and be sure to make reservations a few months in advance for visits during the **State Fair** in August and at least one month in advance during the high school sports tournament season in March.

The Carter House Inn, 640 20th St. (☎288-7850; www.carter-house.com), at Woodland St. in historic Sherman Hill. This beautifully reconstructed 19th-century Victorian home houses a 4-room B&B. Each room is elegantly furnished and immaculate. A large home-cooked breakfast is served on fine china by candlelight, with classical music playing in the background. Rooms $70-100; call ahead for availability. Student discounts around 15% can be arranged. ❹

Motel 6, 4817 Fleur Dr. (☎287-6364), 10min. south of downtown at the airport. Simple, clean, secure rooms with free local calls, morning coffee, and HBO. Singles $45; doubles $52. AARP discount available. 2 wheelchair-accessible rooms. ❷

Iowa State Fairgrounds Campgrounds, E. 30th St. (☎261-0678) at Grand Ave. Take bus #1 "Fairgrounds" to the Grand Ave. gate and follow East Grand Ave. straight east through the park. 1800 campsites on 160 acres. No fires. Check-in until 10pm. Open mid-Apr. to Oct. Reservations accepted only during the State Fair in Aug. Sites with water and electricity $18; full hookup $20. Fee collected in the morning. ❶

FOOD

Good eating places tend to cluster on **Court Avenue** downtown. Warm weather lures street venders peddling gyros, hot dogs, and pizza to **Nollen Plaza,** on Locust St. between 3rd and 4th Ave. West Des Moines boasts an assortment of budget eateries along Grand Ave. and in the antique-filled **Historic Valley Junction.** The **Farmers Market** (☎243-6625) sells loads of fresh fruit and vegetables, baked goods, and ethnic food on Saturday mornings (mid-May-Oct. 7am-noon), and Court Ave. between 1st and 4th St. is blocked off for the extravaganza. The Skywalk also houses many joints that serve food cafeteria-style.

Big Daddy's Bar-B-Q, 1000 E. 14th St. (☎262-0352), just north of I-235, sends several people to the hospital every year with its killer sauces, which, according to locals, are "just that damn hot." The adventurous—or insane—are encouraged to try the "Last Supper," "ER," or "Code Blue" sauces; the "Final Answer" is reserved for only the highest pain thresholds. Rib platters for 2 $9; beef, pork, or ham sandwiches $4; cornbread $0.75 per slice. Open Tu-Sa 11am-5pm; takeout Tu-Th 11am-6pm, F-Sa 11am-7pm. ❷

Noah's Ark Ristorante, 2400 Ingersoll Ave. (☎288-2246). One day in 1946, restaurant owner Noah Lacona was repairing the roof of his establishment when a friend passed by and teased, "Are you working on Noah's Ark?" The name stuck, and since then, Noah and his family have been serving up Italian cuisine. Savor pastas ($8-10), steaks ($13-24), seafood ($13-17), or Noah's famous Neopolitan pizzas ($7-9) in a dining area as dark, cozy, and eclectic as a family den. Open M-Th 11am-11pm, F-Sa 11am-1am. ❹

Raccoon River Brewery Co., 200 10th St., (☎362-5222), at Mulberry St. This friendly brewery offers fresh beer and food, as well as a relaxing outdoor patio for grabbing meals during the summer months. The motley menu has something for everyone, ranging from BBQ chicken pizza ($10) to yellowfin tuna ($17). Leave room for a delicious white chocolate raspberry brownie ($5) Live music on weekends starting at 10:30pm. Open M-Th 11am-midnight, F 11am-2am, Sa noon-2am. ❹

Bauder's Pharmacy and Fountain, 3802 Ingersoll Ave. (☎255-1124), at 38th St. A throwback to the good old days serving old-fashioned ice cream. Wax nostalgic while enjoying simple sandwiches ($2-4) at the authentic lunch counter or pop from the soda fountain. Ice cream $1.50 per scoop; shakes, floats, and malts $2.75. Open M-F 8:30am-7pm, Sa 9am-4pm, Su 10am-2pm. ❶

SIGHTS

The inspiring **State Capitol,** E. 9th St. and Grand Ave., combines elegance with politics. Its impressive architecture includes a grand stairway and mosaic artwork—all newly renovated. The gold-domed building also offers a clear view of the Des Moines skyline. (☎281-5591. Open M-Sa 9am-4pm.) Located at the base of the

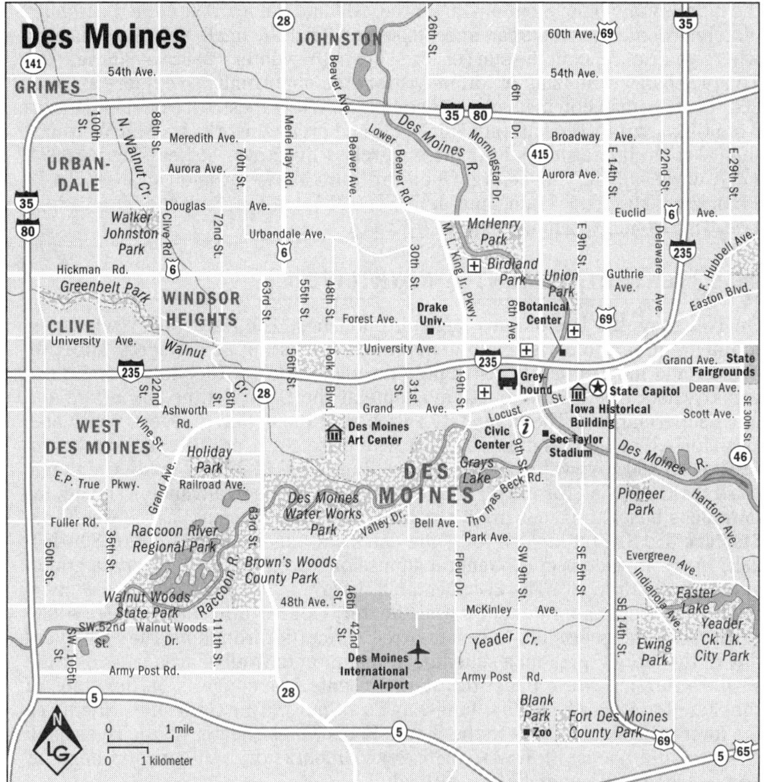

Capitol complex parking lot, the **State of Iowa Historical Building,** 600 E. Locust St., addresses the history of Iowa, Native American culture, and conservation through interactive exhibits. The most exciting is "A Few of Our Favorite Things," which showcases 100 creations from the past century that have changed the way Iowans live, from jazz to Jell-O. The building also houses the state historical library and archives and a roof-top restaurant with a panoramic view. (☎281-5111; www.iowahistory.org. Open Sept.-May Tu-Sa 9am-4:30pm, Su noon-4:30pm; June-Aug. also open M 9am-4:30pm. Free.) Built on urban renewal land east of the Des Moines River, the geodesic greenhouse and outdoor gardens of the **Botanical Center,** 909 E. River Dr., house exotic flora and fauna. (☎323-8900; www.botanicalcenter.com. Open M-Th 10am-6pm, F 10am-9pm, Sa-Su 10am-5pm. $1.50, seniors $0.75, students $0.50.)

Most cultural sights cluster west of downtown on Grand Ave. The phenomenal **Des Moines Art Center,** 4700 Grand Ave., is composed of three unique contemporary buildings designed by world-renowned architects Eliel Saarinen, I.M. Pei, and Richard Meier. In addition to a collection of African tribal art, the museum houses modern masterpieces by Monet, Matisse, and Picasso, along with an expansive collection of Pop, Minimalist, and contemporary paintings and sculptures by Andy Warhol, Eva Hesse, and Jeff Koons. (☎277-4405; www.desmoinesartcenter.org. Open Tu-W and F-Sa 11am-4pm, Th and 1st F of the month 11am-9pm, Su noon-4pm. Free.) Behind the Art Center lie the immaculately groomed **Rose Garden** and **Greenwood Pond**—a small, still-water lagoon where you can relax in the sun (or ice skate in the winter). **Salisbury House,** 4025 Tonawanda Dr., off 42nd St., offers visitors the opportunity to explore an early 20th-century mansion in its original condition. With tapestries from Persia, rugs from China, art by Sir Anthony Van Dyck, and original works by Walt Whitman, this 42-room home shows how the upperclass lived over 80 years ago. (☎274-1777; www.salisburyhouse.org. Open for tours Mar.-Apr. and Oct.-Nov. Tu-Sa 11am, 2pm; May Tu-F 11am, 2pm; June-Sept. M-F 11am, 1, 2pm and Su 1, 2, 3pm; Dec. Tu-F 2pm. $7, seniors $6, ages 6-12 $3.)

ENTERTAINMENT & NIGHTLIFE

On Thursday, the Des Moines Register publishes "The Datebook," (www.desmoinesregister.com/entertainment) a helpful listing of concerts, sporting events, and movies that is distributed throughout town. Cityview, a free local weekly, lists free events and is available at the Civic Center box office and most supermarkets. The **Iowa State Fair,** one of the nation's largest, captivates Des Moines for 11 days in mid-August with prize cows, crafts, cakes, and corn. (☎800-545-4692; www.iowastatefair.org. Runs Aug. 12-22, 2004 with the theme "Still the One." Call for prices and to purchase tickets in advance.) Tickets for **Iowa Cubs** baseball games are a steal; Chicago's farm team plays at **Sec Taylor Stadium,** 350 SW 1st St. Call for game dates and times. (☎243-6111 or 800-464-2827; www.iowacubs.com. General admission $6, children $4; reserved grandstand $8, children $6.) The **Civic Center,** 221 Walnut St. (☎246-2328; www.civiccenter.org), sponsors concerts and theater, call for info. **Jazz in July** (☎280-3222; www.metroarts.org) presents free concerts throughout the city every day of the month; pick up a schedule at restaurants, Wells Fargo banks, or the Visitors Bureau. **Music Under the Stars** presents free concerts on the steps of the State Capitol (☎283-4294; June-July Su 7-9pm.) In June and July, **Nitefall on the River** brings music acts to the Simon Estes Amphitheater on the river bank at E. 1st and Locust St. (☎237-1386; www.dmparks.org. All concerts begin at 7pm. $8, children under 12 free with adult.)

Court Avenue, in the southeast corner of downtown, serves as the focal point for much of Des Moines' nightlife scene. **Java Joe's,** 214 4th St., is the place to hear Des Moines' best up-and-coming bands. This hip, mellow coffeehouse with Internet access ($1 per 10min.), sells exotic coffee blends, and beer ($2.50-3). Vegetarians will delight in the creative array of sandwiches, all for $3-7. Call for schedule of live music and open mic nights. (☎288-5282; www.javajoescoffeehouse.com. Open M-Th 7:30am-11:30pm, F-Sa 7:30am-1am, Su 9am-11pm.) **Buzzard Billy's,** 100 Court Ave., on the first floor of an old brick commercial warehouse, has the best patio in town. Young professionals enjoy microbrews on tap ($4), martinis, and exotic Cajun food. (☎280-6060; www.buzzardbillys.com. Open M-Th 11am-10pm, F-Sa 11am-11pm, Su 11am-9pm.)

DAYTRIPS FROM DES MOINES

PELLA

Forty-one miles east of Des Moines on Hwy. 163, Pella blooms in May with its annual **Tulip Time Festival,** a time of Dutch dancing, a parade, concerts, and glockenspiel performances. (☎888-746-3882. May 6-8, 2004; www.pellatuliptime.com.) For a dose of Dutch culinary culture, visit the **Jaarsma Bakery,** 727 Franklin St. (☎641-628-2940. Pecan rolls 2 for $1.60. Almond poppyseed cakes 4 for $1.39. Open M-Sa

6am-6pm.) Also open year-round, the **Pella Historical Village,** 507 Franklin St., is the site of America's tallest working windmill. (☎641-628-4311. Open Jan.-Mar. M-F 9am-5pm, Sa 10am-3pm; Apr.-Dec. M-Sa 9am-5pm. $7, students K-12 $1.)

PRAIRIE CITY

Twenty miles east of Des Moines on Hwy. 163 at Hwy. 117, the **Neal Smith National Wildlife Refuge,** a veritable time machine, transports visitors 150 years back in time to Iowa's prairie days, when nearly 31 million acres of tallgrass prairie graced the Iowa plains. Today, only one-tenth of one percent of that remains. The Neal Smith National Wildlife Refuge restores 8600 acres of this endangered landscape—the largest tallgrass prairie ecosystem in the US. The refuge is home to bison, elk, and a learning center that is particularly kid-friendly. In August, the big bluestem grass grows up to 6 ft. (☎994-3400. Learning Center open M-Sa 9am-4pm, Su noon-5pm. Trails and auto tour open daily sunrise to sunset. Free.)

MADISON COUNTY

Fifteen miles southwest of Des Moines off I-35 at Exit 65 lies Madison County, immortalized in the novel and movie *The Bridges of Madison County.* **Winterset,** the county seat, welcomed American tough guy John Wayne into the world in 1907 when he was christened Marrion Robert Morrison. The **John Wayne Birthplace,** 216 S. 2nd St., has been converted to a museum featuring two rooms of memorabilia (including the Duke's eye patch from *True Grit*) and two rooms authentically furnished in turn-of-the-century style. (☎462-1044; www.johnwaynebirthplace.org. Open daily 10am-4:30pm. $2.50, seniors $2.25, children $1.) **Francesca's House,** 3271 130th St., used in the film, has been left exactly as it was in the movie. (☎515-981-5268. Open May-Oct. 10am-6pm.) The county's famous covered bridges are celebrated each year at the **Madison County Covered Bridge Festival,** held the second full weekend in October. For more information on the bridges and their locations, visit the **Madison County Chamber of Commerce,** 73 Jefferson St. (☎462-1185 or 800-298-6119; www.madisoncounty.com. Open M-F 9am-5pm, Sa 9am-4pm, Su 11am-4pm.)

IOWA CITY ☎319

Home to the **University of Iowa** and its Hawkeyes, Iowa City is an energetic and youthful place to visit. Downtown is known for its inexpensive restaurants, trendy shops, and coffee houses, while an active nightlife scene and the college football following keep the college kids entertained. In the summer, cultural activities abound, from the Iowa Arts Festival in June (☎337-7944; www.iowaartsfestival.com) to the Iowa City Jazz Festival in July (☎358-9346; www.iowacityjazzfestival.com).

ORIENTATION & PRACTICAL INFORMATION. Iowa City is off I-80, 114 mi. east of Des Moines. North-south **Madison** and **Johnson Street** and east-west **Market** and **Burlington Street** mark off downtown. **Greyhound** and **Burlington Trailways** are both located at 404 E. College St. (☎337-2127. Station open M-F 6:30am-8pm, Sa-Su 10am-8pm.) Buses travel to: **Des Moines** (2-4hr.; 7 per day; M-Th $21, F-Su $22); **Chicago** (6hr.; 8 per day; M-Th $40, F-Su $42); **St. Louis** (10-11hr.; 2 per day; M-Th $68, F-Su $69); **Minneapolis** (8-12hr.; 5 per day; M-Th $59, F-Su $62). The **Cambus** runs daily all over campus and downtown and is free. (☎335-8633. Operates M-F 5am-midnight, Sa-Su noon-midnight; summer M-F 6:30am-6pm, Sa-Su noon-6pm.) **Iowa City Transit** runs a free downtown shuttle daily from 7:30am-6:30pm as well as other routes. (☎356-5151. Operates M-F 6:30am-10:30pm, Sa 6:30am-7pm. $0.75; children 5-12 $0.50; seniors with pass $0.35 9am-3:30pm, after 6:30pm, and Sa.)

The friendly **Convention and Visitors Bureau,** 408 1st Ave., sits across the river in Coralville off U.S. 6. (☎337-6592 or 800-283-6592; www.icccvb.org. Open M-F 8am-5pm, Sa-Su 10am-4pm.) More area info is available at the University of Iowa's **Campus Information Center,** in the **Iowa Memorial Union** at Madison and Jefferson St. (☎335-3055. Open Sept.-May M-F 8am-8pm, Sa 10am-8pm, Su noon-4pm; June-Aug. M-F 8am-5pm.) **Medical Services: Mercy Iowa City,** on Market St. at Van Buren St. Open 24hr. Mercy On Call (☎358-2767 or 800-358-2767) is staffed daily from 7am-midnight with registered nurses to answer all questions. **Internet Access: Iowa City Public Library,** 123 S. Linn St., allows 1hr. of Internet per day. (☎356-5200; www.icpl.org. Open M-Th 10am-9pm, F-Sa 10am-6pm, Su 1-5pm.) Iowa City's neo-futuristic lounge, **Serendipity Laundry Cafe,** 702 S. Gilbert St., also offers Internet access ($0.10 per min.), as well as laundry facilities, tanning beds, copiers, scanners, fax machines, pool tables, drinks, and sandwiches. (☎354-4575. Open daily 10am-2am; summer hours 10am-midnight.) **Post Office:** 400 S. Clinton St. (☎354-1560; open M-F 8:30am-5pm, Sa 9:30am-1pm). **Postal Code:** 52240. **Area Code:** 319.

ACCOMMODATIONS & FOOD. One mile from Exit 244 on 1-80 and 6 blocks from downtown is **Haverkamp's Linn Street Homestay ❷,** 619 N. Linn St. An unbeatable value, this 1908 bed and breakfast contains three reasonably priced rooms filled with classic antiques; call ahead for reservations. (☎337-4636; www.bbhost.com/haverkampslinnstbb. Rooms $35-50.) Cheap motels line U.S. 6 in **Coralville,** 2 mi. west of downtown, and **1st Avenue** at Exit 242 off I-80. The cheapest of the bunch is the **Big Ten Inn ❷,** 707 1st Ave., off U.S. 6, which provides clean and comfortable rooms with HBO and a lounge for all visitors. (☎351-6131. Singles $38; doubles $50.) Nearby is the **Capri Motor Lodge ❷,** 705 2nd St., which offers morning coffee, as well as a microwave, fridge, foldout couch, and cable TV in each room. (☎354-5100. Singles $43; doubles $51.) **Kent Park Campgrounds ❶,** 15 mi. west on U.S. 6, has 86 secluded sites near a lake with fishing, boating, and swimming. (☎645-2315. Check-in by 10:30pm. $10, with electricity $15.)

Downtown boasts cheerful, moderately-priced restaurants and bars. At the open-air **Pedestrian Mall,** on College and Dubuque St., musicians serenade passersby and vendors man their food carts, sometimes until 3am. **Hamburg Inn #2 Inc. ❷,** 214 N. Linn St., serves breakfast all day. "The Burg," as it is more commonly known, is Iowa City's oldest family owned-restaurant. The decor is simple, but the menu is varied, from pie shakes ($4.50) to tuna steaks ($8). Nearly everything on the menu is under $8. (☎337-5512. Open daily 6am-11pm.) **The Pita Pit ❶,** 113 Iowa Ave., offers a refreshing combination of colorful walls and delicious, energizing pitas. The Club ($5) and the Hummus ($4) are two popular pitas. (☎351-7482; www.pitapit.com. Open M-W 11am-3am, Th-Sa 11am-4am, Su noon-midnight.) **Masala ❷,** 9 S. Dubuque St., Iowa City's award-winning vegetarian Indian restaurant, may just have the best deals in town with their $6.25 lunch buffet and a $5 Monday dinner special. Student discounts are given. (☎338-6199. Open daily 11am-2:30pm and 5-10pm.) Iowa City's only Greek restaurant is **The Parthenon ❹,** 320 E. Burington St., where columns emerge from the cool, blue walls and Grecian urns and sculptures are sprinkled throughout. Savor the warm pita bread, and sup upon mousaka (the national dish of Greece; $11), classic salads ($6-9), steaks ($15-20), or seafood ($13-40). Vegetarian dishes are also served. (☎358-7777. Open for lunch M-Sa 11:30am-2pm; dinner M-Th 4:30-9pm, F-Sa 4:30-10pm, Su 4-8pm.)

SIGHTS. The University of Iowa's **Museum of Natural History,** at Jefferson and Clinton St., details the ecology, geology, and Native American culture of Iowa, complete with whimsical but informative dioramas and a large collection of stuffed mammals and birds. Don't miss the reproduction of the giant ground sloth that roamed Iowa's woods many centuries ago. (☎335-0482; www.uiowa.edu/~nathist. Open M-Sa 9:30am-4:30pm, Su 12:30-4:30pm. Free.) A short drive from downtown lies the **Plum Grove Historic Home,** 1030 Carroll St. Explore the 1844 home and garden of Robert Lucas, the first governor of the Iowa Territory. (☎351-5738; www.jccniowa.org/~jchsweb. Open Memorial Day-Oct. W-Su 1-5pm. Free.) In West Branch, 15 min. northeast of the city (Exit 254 on I-80; follow signs), lies the **Herbert Hoover National Historic Site.** Over 100 acres beautifully recreate the feel of an 1870s American town. Take a walking tour of the 31st President's birthplace cottage, his father's blacksmith shop, and the schoolhouse and Quaker meeting-house he attended. A ½ mi. prairie trail includes the graves of President and Mrs. Hoover, while the fascinating **Herbert Hoover Presidential Library-Museum** chronicles the life and term of the 31st president. (☎643-2541; www.nps.gov/heho. Open daily 9am-5pm. $3, seniors $1, under 16 free. Wheelchair-accessible.)

NIGHTLIFE. Ever the college town, Iowa City is loaded with places to get drunk on the cheap. Many bars double as dance clubs, and loud music seems to be the common denominator downtown. The Pedestrian Mall overflows with bar-hopping college students during the school year. **The Union Bar,** 121 E. College St., brags that it's the "biggest damn bar in college football's 'Big Ten.'" (☎339-7713. Drinks $3-5. 18+ with college ID. Cover usually $5. Open Tu-Sa 8pm-2am.) Local musicians play Th-Sa 9:30pm (only F and Sa in the summer) in **The Sanctuary,** 405 S. Gilbert St. Escape into a restaurant and bar with 120 beers and comfortable sofas. (☎351-5692; www.sanctuarypub.com. Live music on F and Sa. Food $5-18. Cover varies. Bar open M-Sa 4pm-2am; restaurant open M-Tu 4-11pm, W-Sa 4pm-midnight.) **The Sports Column,** 12 S. Dubuque St., draws a crowd every night with their laidback attitude, swingin' music, and nightly specials. Th dollar draft night, Sa two-for-one. (☎356-6902. Open until 2am.) In summer, the **Friday Night Concert Series** (☎354-0863; 6:30-9:30pm) offers everything from jazz to salsa to blues, while **Just Jazz Saturdays** (6:30-9:30pm) features exactly what it advertises. Both events take place on the Pedestrian Mall.

IS THIS HEAVEN, RAY? Movie buffs and baseball fanatics alike may want to go the distance to the **Field of Dreams** in Dyersville, where the movie *Field of Dreams* was shot. In the film, a mysterious voice directs a farmer (played by Kevin Costner) to build a baseball field amidst Iowa's acres of corn. Bring your own bat, ball, and glove so you can try to hit one into the stands, er, stalks. *(28995 Lansing Rd. Take Rte. 20 west from Dubuque to Rte. 136 N.; go right after the tracks for 3 mi. ☎888-875-8404 or 563-875-8404.Open Apr.-Nov. daily 9am-6pm. Free.)*

EFFIGY MOUNDS

Mysterious and striking, the Effigy Mounds were built by Native Americans as early as 1000 BC. The enigmatic effigies are low-lying mounds of piled earth formed into distinct geometric and animal shapes for burial and ceremonial purposes. Though they once covered much of the Midwest, farmers' plows have ensured that only a scattering of them remain, mostly in western Wisconsin and eastern Iowa. One of the largest concentrations of intact mounds composes the **Effigy Mounds National Monument,** 151 Rte. 76, 100 mi. west of Madison in Marquette, Iowa, located on more than 2500 acres along the Mississippi River. Offering striking views of the river from high, rocky bluffs, the 11 mi. of trails winding through the park explore the lives of these indigenous people and the social and spiritual meanings the mounds had for them. Take Rte. 18 W from Madison. (☎319-873-3491; www.nps.gov/efmo. Visitors Center open June-early Sept. daily 8am-6pm; closes earlier in the fall. Guided tours are available June-early Sept.; call ahead for times.) 7 mi. south on Rte. 76 in McGregor is **Pike's Peak State Park ❶.** Follow Hwy. 34 from the south end of McGregor's Main St. up the twisty road 1.5 mi. Pike's Peak boasts amazing views and over 70 campgrounds. (☎563-873-2341.

Reservations not accepted. Check-out 4pm. Sites $11, with electricity $16. $8/13 Labor Day through Memorial Day. Sewage and water additional $3.) **Wyalusing State Park ❶**, just across the Mississippi and 10 mi. south of Prairie du Chien in Wisconsin, offers more than 110 campsites overlooking the stunning confluence of the Wisconsin River and the mighty Mississippi as well as its own assortment of mounds and trails. (☎608-996-2261 or 888-947-2757; www.wyalusing.org. Campsites $10; summer weekends $12. Electricity an additional $3 per night.)

SPIRIT LAKE & OKOBOJI ☎712

In attempts to rival its neighbors, Iowa boasts its own Great Lakes. **Spirit Lake, West Okoboji Lake,** and **East Okoboji Lake** are all popular vacation destinations. West Okoboji Lake ranks with Switzerland's Lake Geneva and Canada's Lake Louise as one of the world's beautiful blue-water lakes, carved out by a glacier 10,000 years ago and continuously replenished with spring water.

It's hard to miss the **amusement park** in **Arnold's Park,** off Rte. 71, with its roller coaster, kiddie rides, and ice cream shops. (☎332-2183 or 800-599-6995; www.arnoldspark.com. Open Memorial Day-Labor Day. Hours vary, usually daily 11am-10pm. $16, children 3-4 ft. tall and seniors $12, under 3 ft. free. Individual ride tickets $1.50-4.50.) The park's **Roof Garden** hosts open air concerts, including an annual **Blues and Zydeco Festival** each June (call the park for info). One block west of the amusement park, **Abbie Gardner Historic Log Cabin,** 34 Monument Dr., is a museum with artifacts, paintings, and a 13min. video explaining the origins of the dispute between encroaching settlers and members of the Sioux that eventually led to the Spirit Lake Massacre of March 1857. (☎332-7248. Open June-Oct. 1 M-F noon-4pm, Sa-Su 9am-4pm. Free, but donation suggested.) Theater buffs can catch productions by the **Stephens College Okoboji Summer Theater.** (☎332-7773. Box office open M 10am-6pm, Tu-Sa 10am-9pm, Su 1-7pm. $11-13.) For a dose of the outdoors, hike, skate, or bike **The Spine,** a 14½ mi. trail that runs through the area. Rent bikes at **Okoboji Bikes,** on Rte. 71 in Fox Plaza just south of the amusement park. (☎332-5274. Open M-F 10am-6pm, Sa 10am-5pm, Su noon-5pm. Half-day $15, full day $25.) **Orleans Beach,** on Hwy. 327, ½ mi. east of the Hwy. 276 junction, offers a long stretch of sand with a diving platform. For aquatic fun, rent kayaks, boats, and jetskis at **Funtime Rentals Okoboji,** on U.S. 71. (☎332-2540. Open daily 9am-9pm.)

Budget accommodations in the immediate lake area are scarce, especially in summer. Cheap motels line U.S. 71 in Spencer, about 15 mi. south of Okoboji. **The Northland Inn ❸,** at the junction of Rte. 9 and Rte. 86, just north of West Okoboji Lake, offers wood-paneled rooms and a continental breakfast. (☎336-1450. May-Sept. 1 bed $50; 2 beds $60; Oct.-Apr. $23-28/38.) Pitch your tent year-round at tranquil **Marble Beach Campground ❶** (☎336-4437, winter ☎337-3211), in the state park on the shores of Spirit Lake. Other camping options include **Emerson Bay ❶** (☎332-3805) and **Gull's Point ❶** (☎332-3870), both off Rte. 86 on West Okoboji Lake. (Sites at all 3 campgrounds $11; with electricity $16.) The **Koffee Kup Kafe ❶,** off U.S. 71 in Arnold's Park, serves up an all-day power breakfast (eggs, bacon, pancakes, hash browns, and juice) for $5.75. Those craving simpler fare can try a variety of tasty pancakes for $1-3. (☎332-7657. Open daily 6am-2pm.) A local lunch spot, **Tweeter's ❷,** off U.S. 71 in Okoboji, grills burgers ($6-10), tosses salads ($5-7), and melts sandwiches ($5-8) in a family-dining atmosphere. (☎332-9421. Open daily Apr.-Oct. 10am-midnight; Nov.-Mar. 10am-11pm.) **Okoboji Spirit Center,** 243 W. Broadway Ave., houses an informative welcome center, museum, and theater. (☎322-2107 or 800-270-2574; www.vacationokoboji.com. Open June-Aug. M-Sa 9am-9pm, Su 10am-6pm; Sept.-May M-F 9am-5pm.) In Spirit Lake, **Post Office:** 1513 Hill Ave. (☎336-1383. Open M-F 8:30am-5pm, Sa 9-10am.) **Postal Code:** 51360. **Area Code:** 712.

NEBRASKA

Nebraska often has it rough—imagine having to deal with persistent accusations of being "boring," "endless," or "the Great American Desert." In actuality, the landscape is the state's greatest attraction. Central Nebraska features the Sandhills, a breathtakingly immense windblown dune region with cattle, ranches, windmills, and tiny towns. The Panhandle offers Western-style mountains and canyons, historical trails, and National Monuments. For the more urbane traveler, Omaha and Lincoln feature quality sports, fine music, and some of the best damn meat in America. While the urge might be to speed through the Cornhusker State, patient travelers will be rewarded with a true Great Plains experience.

PRACTICAL INFORMATION

Capital: Lincoln.

Visitor Info: Nebraska Tourism Office, 700 S. 16th St., Lincoln 68509 (☎402-471-3796 or 800-228-4307; www.visitnebraska.org). Open M-F 8am-5pm. **Nebraska Game and Parks Commission,** 1212 Deer Park Blvd., Omaha 68108 (☎402-595-2144). Open M-F 8am-5pm.

State Soft Drink: Kool-Aid. **Postal Abbreviation:** NE. **Sales Tax:** 5-6.5%, depends on city.

OMAHA ☎402

Omaha is a city of seemingly endless sprawl, stretched out over miles and miles of the Nebraska prairie. The heart of the city, however, is refreshingly compact. Omaha's museums, world-renowned zoo, and sports complex are the envy of other medium-sized cities. The Old Market in downtown lures visitors with a surprisingly large concentration of quiet cafes, breweries, and nightclubs. Recently, a burgeoning indie rock scene has put Omaha musicians in the national spotlight. Overall, the town seems to settle comfortably into its role as a gateway to the West, while down-to-earth residents still manage to embody that small-town spirit common to Midwestern America.

ORIENTATION & PRACTICAL INFORMATION. Omaha rests on the west bank of the **Missouri River,** brushing up against Iowa's border. While the city wears a facade of geometric order, it is actually an imprecise grid of numbered streets (north-south) and named streets (east-west). **Dodge Street** (Rte. 6) divides the city east-west. **I-480/Rte. 75** (the Kennedy Expwy.) intersects with **I-80,** which runs across the southern half of town. *At night, avoid N. 24th St., Ames Ave., and the area north of I-480.* **Eppley Airfield,** 4501 Abbott Dr., has domestic flights. (☎422-6817; www.eppleyairfield.com.) **Amtrak,** 1003 S. 9th St. (☎342-1501; open 10:30pm-8am), at Pacific St., chugs to Chicago (10hr., 1 per day, $86) and Denver (9hr., 1 per day, $132). **Greyhound,** 1601 Jackson St. (☎341-1906; open 24hr.), runs to: Des Moines (2-2½hr.; 10 per day; M-Th $23, F-Su $26); Lincoln (1hr., 7 per day, $10/11); St. Louis (9hr., 3 per day, $75/79). **Metro Area Transit (MAT),** 2222 Cumming St., handles local transportation. Get schedules at 16th and Douglas St. near the Greyhound station, Park Fair Mall, and the library. (☎341-0800. Open M-F 8am-4:30pm. $1.25, transfers $0.05.) Catch a **taxi** with **Happy Cab** (☎339-8294). The **Greater Omaha Convention and Visitors Bureau,** 6800 Mercy Rd., #202, at the Ak-Sar-Ben complex off S. 72nd St. north of I-80, has tourist info. (☎444-4660 or 866-937-6624; www.visitomaha.com. Open M-F 8am-4:30pm.) **Hotlines: Rape Crisis,** ☎345-7273. 24hr. **First Call for Help,** ☎330-1907. M-F 8am-5pm. **Internet Access: Omaha Library,** 215

S. 15th St., between Douglas and Farnham. (☎444-4800. Open M-Th 9am-9pm, F-Sa 9am-5:30pm, Su 1-5pm.) **Post Office:** 1124 Pacific St. (☎348-2543. Open M-F 7:30am-6pm, Sa 7:30am-noon.) **Postal Code:** 68108. **Area Code:** 402.

ACCOMMODATIONS. Motels in downtown Omaha are not particularly budget-friendly. For better deals, look west my friend; start around L St. and 60th and head west from there. The **Satellite Motel ❷,** 6006 L St., south of I-80 Exit 450 (60th St.), is a round two-story building with lots of personality. Clean, wedge-shaped rooms come equipped with fridge, microwave, coffee-maker, and cable TV. (☎733-7373. Singles $40; doubles $46.) For a taste of the countryside and a friendly game of croquet, go to the first B&B in Nebraska, **Bundy's Bed and Breakfast ❶,** 16906 S. 255th St., 20 mi. southwest of Omaha in Gretna. Take Exit 432 off I-80, follow Hwy. 6 west for 4 mi., and take a right on 255th St. before the Linoma Lighthouse. (☎332-3616. No smoking, drinking, or children. 4 rooms with shared bath. Singles $25; doubles $45.) Outdoorsfolk should set up camp at the **Haworth Park Campground ❶,** in Bellevue on Payne St. at the end of Mission Ave., south of downtown. Take the exit for Rte. 370 E off Rte. 75, turn right onto Galvin Rd., left onto Mission Ave., and right onto Payne St. before the toll bridge. Tent sites are separate from the RV area but not entirely out of view. (☎291-3379 or 293-2098. Showers, toilets, and shelters. Open daily 6am-10pm, but stragglers can enter after hours; reservations recommended. Check-out 3pm. Tent sites $7; with hookup $9. RV sites $15.)

FOOD. It's no fun being a chicken, cow, or vegetarian in Omaha, where there is a fried chicken joint on every block and a steakhouse in every district. Once a warehouse area, the brick streets of the **Old Market,** on Jackson, Howard, and Harney St. between 10th and 13th, now feature popular shops, restaurants, and bars. The **Farmers Market** (☎345-5401) is located at 11th and Jackson St. (Open mid-July to mid-Aug. W 4-8pm, Sa 8am-12:30pm; mid-May to mid-Oct. Sa 8am-12:30pm.) At **La Buvette ❷,** 511 11th St., in the Old Market, vegetarians unwind over plates of hummus ($5), and struggling artists find inspiration in a glass of wine (from $3). (☎344-8627. Open M-Th 9am-10pm, F-Sa 9am-midnight, Su 11am-8pm.) If you want to find out what all the beeftastic hubbub's about, sink your teeth into some USDA prime grade beef at **Omaha Prime ❺,** 415 S. 11th St., in the Old Market. Their steak and chops will cost you $25-40, but keep in mind that only 5% of all beef holds the coveted honor of being "prime." (☎341-7040. Open M-Sa 5-9pm.) **M's Pub ❷,** 422 S. 11th St., in the Old Market, offers a patio for relaxed outdoor meals (try the crab cake sandwich for $10), while inside the trendy working crowd sips beer for $4.50. (☎342-2550; www.mspubomaha.com. Open M-Sa 11am-midnight, Su 5-11pm.) **La Casa ❸,** 4432 Leavenworth St., flaunts the best Italian food and pizzas ($6-18) in Omaha. (☎556-6464. Open Tu-Th 11am-2pm and 5-10pm, F 11am-2pm and 5-10:30pm, Sa 5-10:30pm, Su 4:30-9:30pm.) **Délice European Cafe ❶,** 1206 Howard St., at 12th St. in the Old Market, sells scrumptious pastries and deli fare ($2-6) in a bright, spacious bakery. They also serve wine and beer ($2.50-6.50), making the meal appropriately European, and the patio affords shaded views of the Court St. area. (☎342-2276. Open M-Th 7:30am-9pm, F-Sa 7:30am-11pm, Su 7:30am-6pm.)

SIGHTS. With the world's largest desert dome, indoor rainforest, nocturnal exhibit, and gorilla sperm bank, the always evolving **Henry Doorly Zoo,** 3701 S. 10th St. (reached by exiting I-80 at 13th St., at Bert Murphy Blvd.), is naturally the number one tourist attraction in Nebraska. The Hubbard Gorilla Valley will open in spring 2004 to allow more room for the great apes and to aid in conservation and breeding. (☎733-8401; www.omahazoo.com. Open daily 9:30am-5pm. $9, over 62 $7.50, ages 5-11 $5.25.) Just down the road at the **Wildlife Safari Park,** drive your all-terrain vehicle (or beat-up Chevette) 4½ mi. through a nature preserve inhabited by bison, pronghorns, moose, wolves, and other beasts. (☎944-9453. Open Apr.-Oct. daily 9:30am-5pm. $10 per car. Sa-Su guided tram tours an additional $1.)

The **Durham Western Heritage Museum,** 801 S. 10th St., occupies the former Union Train Station, an impressive Art Deco structure. Climb aboard an old steam engine or lounge car on the Track Level, learn about Omaha's neighborhoods in the historical galleries, or indulge in a malted milkshake at the authentic soda fountain. (☎444-5071; www.dwhm.org. Open Tu-Sa 10am-5pm, Su 1-5pm. $5, seniors $4, ages 3-12 $3.50.) Nebraska's largest art museum is Omaha's **Joslyn Art Museum,** 2200 Dodge St., which displays a impressive collection of 19th- and 20th-century American and European art. Dance for joy around the original plaster cast of Degas' famous sculpture *Little Dancer,* complete with an authentic billowing tutu. (☎342-3300; www.joslyn.org. "Jazz on the Green" mid-July to mid-Aug. Th 7-9pm. Open Tu-Sa 10am-4pm, Su noon-4pm. $6, students and seniors $4, ages 5-17 $3.50; Sa 10am-noon. Free.) See the gargantuan remnants of US airpower from the past half-century in the equally enormous **Strategic Air and Space Museum,** Exit 426 off I-80 in Ashland. The museum displays military aircraft, including a B-52 bomber, as well as exhibits on military history. Bunker down in a 1950s bomb shelter, or practice your duck-and-cover technique in a 1960s classroom. (☎827-3100 or 800-358-5029; www.strategicairandspace.com. Open daily 9am-5pm. Guided tours 11am, 2pm. $7, seniors and military $6, ages 5-12 $3. AAA discount.)

GREAT PLAINS

ENTERTAINMENT & NIGHTLIFE. At **Rosenblatt Stadium,** across from the zoo on 13th St., you can watch the **Omaha Royals** round the bases from April to early September. (☎738-5100; www.oroyals.com. General admission $4, reserved seat $6, box seat $8. Wheelchair-accessible.) The stadium has also hosted the NCAA College Baseball World Series (June 18-28, 2004) every June since 1950. In late June and early July, **Shakespeare on the Green** stages free performances in Elmwood Park, on 60th and Dodge St. (☎280-2391. Th-Su 8pm.)

Punk and progressive folk have found a niche at the several area universities; check the windows of the **Antiquarian Bookstore,** 1215 Harney St., and **Homers,** 114 Howard St., in the Old Market, for the scoop on shows. Several good bars await nearby. **The Dubliner,** 1205 Harney St., below street level, stages live traditional Irish music on Friday and Saturday evenings. (☎342-5887. Cover $2-3. Open M-Sa 11am-1am, Su 1pm-1am.) The **13th Street Coffee Company,** 519 S. 13th St., keeps more than 20 types of beans on hand and brews three different varieties every day. The hopelessly romantic, or just plain hopeless, can imbibe Love Poison—white chocolate mocha with hot cinnamon. (☎345-2883. Coffee $2-6. Live music most weekends; call ahead for details. Free Internet access. Open M-Th 6:30am-11pm, F 6:30am-midnight, Sa 8am-midnight, Su 9am-11pm.) **The Max,** 1417 Jackson St., is one of the most popular gay bars in the state. With five bars, a disco dance floor, DJ, fountains, and patio, the Max is Omaha's gay haven. (☎346-4110; www.themaxomaha.com. Happy Hour daily 4-9pm. 21+. Cover F-Sa $5, Su $3. Open daily 4pm-1am.) For country tunes and line dancing, head to **Guitars and Cadillacs,** 10865 W. Dodge Rd., near the junction of I-680. Follow the signs for Old Mill Rd. (☎333-5500. F-Sa 1-3am after-hours dancing for those 18+. Open Th 8pm-1am, F 6pm-3am, Sa 7pm-3am, and Su 6pm-midnight.)

LINCOLN ☎402

The spirit of Lincoln rises and falls with the success of its world-famous college football team, the Nebraska Cornhuskers. Many youngsters spend their childhoods running wind sprints, weightlifting, and practicing, all for the dream of stepping onto the celebrated field. Off the field, however, life goes on. Lincoln houses the Nebraska state legislature, the only one-house legislature in the Union, as well as quality restaurants and scenic parks.

ORIENTATION & PRACTICAL INFORMATION. Lincoln's grid makes sense—numbered streets increase as you go east, and lettered streets progress through the alphabet as you go north. **O Street** is the main east-west drag. It becomes Hwy. 6 west of the city, and Rte. 34 east. **R Street** runs along the south side of the **University of Nebraska-Lincoln (UNL).** Most downtown sights lie between 7th and 16th St. and M and R St. Here, parking options abound, with metered, on-street, and garage parking available. **Lincoln Municipal Airport,** 2400 W. Adams St. (☎458-2480; www.lincolnairport.com), is located 5 mi. northwest of downtown off Cornhusker Hwy.; take Exit 399 off I-80. **Amtrak,** 201 N. 7th St. (☎476-1295; open Su-Th 11:30pm-7am), runs once daily to: Chicago (12hr., $94); Denver (7hr., $89); and Omaha (1hr., $16). Prices vary with availability. **Greyhound,** 940 P St. (☎474-1071; ticket window open M-F 7:30am-6pm, Sa 9:30am-3pm), sends buses to: Chicago (12hr.; 5 per day; M-Th $54, F-Su $58); Denver (9-18hr., 5 per day, $77/81); Kansas City (6-10hr., 3 per day, $52/56); Omaha (1 hr., 3 per day, $10/11). **StarTran,** 710 J St., handles public transportation. Schedules are available on the bus, at the office on J St., and at many locations downtown. All downtown buses connect at 11th and O St., two blocks east of Historic Haymarket. (☎476-1234. Buses run M-F 5am-7pm, Sa 6:30am-7pm. $1, seniors and ages 5-18 $0.50.) **Taxi: Yellow Cab,** ☎477-4111. **Visitors Center:** 201 N. 7th St., at P St. in Lincoln Station. (☎434-5348 or 800-423-8212; www.lincoln.org. Open May-Sept. M-F 9am-8pm, Sa 8am-4pm, Su noon-4pm; Oct.-Apr. M-F 9am-6pm, Sa 10am-4pm, Su noon-4pm.) **Medical Services: Bryan-LGH Medical Center East,** 1600 S. 48th St. (☎489-0200 or 481-3142.) **Internet Access: Lincoln Public Library,** 136 S. 14th St., at N St. (☎441-8500. Open M-Th 10am-9pm, F-Sa 10am-6pm, Su 1:30-5:30pm.) **Post Office:** 700 R St. (☎458-1844. Open M-F 7:30am-6pm, Sa 9am-1pm.) **Postal Code:** 68501. **Area Code:** 402.

ACCOMMODATIONS. There are few inexpensive motels downtown. Cheaper places are farther east around the 5600 block of Cornhusker Hwy. (U.S. 6). The **Cornerstone Hostel (HI-AYH) ❶,** 640 N. 16th St., at U St. just south of Vine St., on frat row, is conveniently located in a church basement in the university's downtown campus. It rarely fills up, and while the basement can get stuffy in summer, the sounds of the organ drifting from upstairs will take your mind off the heat. (☎476-0926. 9 beds in 2 single-sex rooms. Lockers available. Full kitchen and laundry facilities. Free parking and linen. No curfew. Dorms $10, nonmembers $13.) **The Great Plains Budget Host Inn ❷,** 2732 O St., at 27th St., has large rooms with fridges and coffee makers. Take bus #9 "O St. Shuttle." (☎476-3253 or 800-288-8499. Free parking and kitchenettes available. Singles $42; doubles $48. 10% AAA discount.) Experience the elegance of the **Atwood House Bed and Breakfast ❺,** 740 S. 17th St., at G St., two blocks from the Capitol. With antiques nestled in every corner and whirlpool baths awaiting in most suites, this 1894 mansion provides a relaxing respite and a hot breakfast for the weary traveler. (☎438-4567 or 800-884-6554; www.atwoodhouse.com. Suites $115-179.) To get to the pleasant **Camp-A-Way ❶,** 200 Ogden Rd., near 1st and Superior St., take Exit 401 or 401a from I-80, then Exit 1 on I-180/Rte. 34. Though next to a highway, the 87 sites are peaceful and shaded. (☎476-2282 or 866-719-2267; www.camp-a-way.com. Showers, laundry, pool, and convenience store. Reservations recommended during fair time in Aug. Sites $15; with water and electricity $20; full hookup $26.)

FOOD & NIGHTLIFE. Historic Haymarket, 7th to 9th St. and O to R St., is a renovated warehouse district near the train tracks with cafes, bars, restaurants, and a **farmers market.** (☎435-7496. Open mid-May to mid-Oct. Sa 8am-noon.) **Lazlo's Brewery and Grill ❹,** 710 P St., prides itself on fresh fish ($10-20), ground beef, and freshly brewed beers ($4). The servers, thankfully, are not so fresh. (☎434-5636. Burgers $5-7. Steak and chops $15-21. Open Su-Th 11am-10pm, F-Sa 11am-11pm.) Get breakfast at **Kuhl's ❶,** 1038 O St., a diner at 11th St. The Lincoln special—two eggs; toast; hash browns; and ham, bacon, or sausage—sets the local standard at $5.75. (☎476-1311. Breakfasts $3-6. Open M-F 6am-7pm, Sa 6am-4pm, Su 7am-3pm.) **Maggie's Bakery and Vegetarian Vittles ❶,** 311 N. 8th St., sustains Lincoln's vegetarians and vegans with $1.50-2 pastries, $4-6 wraps, and $6 lunch specials. (☎477-3959. Open M-F 8am-3pm.) **Billy's ❸,** 1301 H St., offers fresh fish and meat ($11-18) in a historic setting. (☎474-0084. Lunch $6-12. Open M-F 11am-2pm and 5-10pm, Sa 5-10pm.)

Nightspots abound in Lincoln, particularly those of the sports bar variety. With as many as ten bars per block, it's clear Lincoln is a college town. For the biggest names in Lincoln's live music scene, try the suitably dark and smoky **Zoo Bar,** 136 N. 14th St., where blues is king. (☎435-8754. Cover $2-10. Open M-Sa 3pm-1am, Su 5-11pm.) Those more interested in the college sports bar scene should head to **Iguana's,** 1426 O St. (☎476-8850. Open M-Sa 7pm-1am.) **Duffy's Tavern,** 1412 O St., showcases up-and-coming local rock bands as well as national acts. (☎474-3543. Nightly drink specials. Open M-Sa 4pm-1am, Su 6pm-1am.)

GREAT PLAINS

SIGHTS. The "Tower on the Plains," the 400 ft. **Nebraska State Capitol Building,** at 15th and K St., wows with its streamlined exterior and detailed interior highlighted by a beautiful mosaic floor. Although outside renovations continue, the inside remains untouched and remarkable. The 19 ft. statue "The Sower" sits atop the building. (☎471-0448. Open M-F 9am-4pm, Sa 10am-5pm, Su 1-4pm. Free 30min. tours every hr. except noon.) The **Museum of Nebraska History,** on Centennial Mall, a renamed portion of 15th St., has a phenomenal collection of headdresses, moccasins, jewelry, and other artifacts in its permanent exhibit on Plains Indians. (☎471-4754. Open M-F 9am-4:30pm, Sa-Su 1-4:30pm. Free; $2 donation recommended.) The **University of Nebraska State Museum,** 14th and U St., in Morrill Hall, boasts an amazing fossil collection that includes Archie, the largest mounted mammoth in any American museum. (☎472-2642; www.museum.unl.edu. Open M-Sa 9:30am-4:30pm, Su 1:30-4:30pm. $4, ages 5-18 $2, under 5 free.) In the same building, the **Mueller Planetarium** lights up the ceiling with several daily shows. (☎472-2641; www.spacelaser.com. Laser shows F-Sa. Planetarium $6, under 19 $4; laser shows $5/4.) For a wheel-y good time, coast on over to the **National Museum of Roller Skating,** 4730 South St., at 48th St., to learn the history of the sport. (☎483-7551, ext. 16; www.rollerskatingmuseum.com. Open M-F 9am-5pm. Free, but donations appreciated.)

Come August, the **Nebraska State Fair** offers car races, tractor pulls, and plenty of rides, in addition to livestock, crafts, and fitter family contests. (☎474-5371; www.statefair.org. Aug. 28 to Sept. 6, 2004. $6, ages 6-12 $2.) **Pioneers Park,** 3201 S. Coddington Ave., ¼ mi. south of W. Van Dorn, is a sylvan paradise perfect for a prairie picnic. The **Pioneers Park Nature Center** has bison and elk within its sanctuary and is also the starting point for 6 mi. of trails. (☎441-7895. Park open sunrise-sunset. Nature Center open June-Aug. M-Sa 8:30am-8:30pm, Su noon-8:30pm; Sept.-May M-Sa 8:30am-5pm, Su noon-5pm. Free. Wheelchair-accessible.)

SCOTTS BLUFF & CHIMNEY ROCK ☎308

Known to the Plains Indians as *Me-a-pa-te* ("hill that is hard to go around"), the imposing clay and sandstone highlands of **Scotts Bluff National Monument** were landmarks for people traveling the Mormon and Oregon Trails in the 1840s. For some time the bluff was too dangerous to cross, but in the 1850s a single-file wagon trail was opened just south of the bluff through narrow **Mitchell's Pass,** where traffic wore deep marks in the sandstone. Today, a half-mile stretch of the original **Oregon Trail** is preserved at the pass, complete with a pair of covered wagons. Tourists can gaze at the distant horizons to the east and west as pioneers once did. The **Visitors Center,** at the entrance on Rte. 92, relates the multiple and contradictory accounts of the mysterious death of Hiram Scott, the fur trader who gave the Bluffs their name. Don't miss the 12min. slide show about life on the Oregon Trail. (☎436-4340; www.nps.gov/scbl. Open summer daily 8am-7pm; winter 8am-5pm. $5 per carload, $3 per motorcycle.) To get to the top of the bluffs, hike the challenging **Saddle Rock Trail** (1½ mi. each way) or motor up **Summit Drive.** At the top, you'll find two short **nature trails.** Guide books ($0.50) are available at the trailheads and the Visitors Center. The **North Overlook** is a ½ mi. paved walk with a view of the North Platte River Valley. The **South Overlook** (¼ mi.) provides a spectacular view of Scotts Bluff.

Take U.S. 26 to Rte. 71 to Rte. 92; the Monument is on Rte. 92 about 2 mi. west of **Gering** (*not* in the town of Scotts Bluff). A 1¼ mi. bike trail links Gering with the base of the bluffs. From July 8-11, 2004, expect festive folk to pack the towns near Gering for the carnival, craft show, and chili cook-off of the 83rd annual **Oregon Trail Days** festival. (☎436-4457; www.oregontraildays.com.) Twenty miles east on Rte. 92, just south of Bayard, the 475 ft. spire of **Chimney Rock,** visible from more than 30 mi. away, served as another landmark that inspired travelers on the Oregon Trail. Unfortunately, there is no path up to the base of the rock due to the rough terrain and rattlesnakes. The Nebraska State Historical Society operates a **Visitors Center.** (☎586-2581; www.nps.gov/chro. Open summer daily 9am-5pm; winter Tu-Su 9am-5pm. $3, under 18 free.) For an extra historical delight, continue down the road past the Visitors Center, take a right onto Chimney Rock Rd., and follow the gravel road ½ mi. to its end. Here you will find the first graveyard of settlers on the Oregon Trail and a closer view of the rock itself. **Area Code:** 308. **Time Zone:** Mountain.

KANSAS

Boasting America's largest tallgrass prairie, as well as junctures of the Anne Chisolm, Santa Fe, and Oregon Trails, Kansas epitomizes rural America. Vast stretches of farmland dotted with cattle make up the majority of the landscape, while several small cities offer more urban amenities. Steeped in Civil War and Wild West history, Kansas provides myriad opportunities for the history buff and antique collector. I-70, which cuts horizontally through the state, has been dubbed "the Main Street through America's Central Park." Also, as highway signs remind every traveler, this heartland has plenty of heart to go around—because "every Kansas farmer feeds 101 people—and you."

PRACTICAL INFORMATION

Capital: Topeka.

Visitor Info: Division of Travel and Tourism: 350 Speedway Blvd., Kansas City 66111 (☎913-299-2253 or 800-252-6727; www.travelks.com). Open daily 8am-6pm. **Kansas Department of Wildlife and Parks,** 512 SE 25th Ave., Pratt 67124 (☎620-672-5911; www.kdwp.state.ks.us). Open M-F 8am-5pm.

Postal Abbreviation: KS. **Sales Tax:** 5.3% or higher, depending on city.

STUCK IN THE MIDDLE Have you ever wanted to be at the center of the action? Two miles northwest of Lebanon, KS, sits a stone monument marking the geographic center of the United States. Established in 1898 by government surveyors, the site became the "historical" center of the contiguous states after Alaska and Hawaii joined the Union in 1959.

WICHITA ☎316

Wichita made a name for itself in the early 19th century as home to the Wild West's long arm of the law. In the 20th century, its economy took off as it became a center of aviation manufacturing and an agricultural commodities hub for the southern and central Plains. With several renowned museums and performing art companies, today's Wichita is the cultural center of Kansas. Downtown emits a suburban vibe, while Old Town has become the nightlife mecca for party-seeking yuppies.

ORIENTATION & PRACTICAL INFORMATION. Wichita lies on I-35, 170 mi. north of Oklahoma City and 200 mi. southwest of Kansas City. A small, quiet downtown makes for easy walking and parking. **Broadway Street** is the major north-south artery. **Douglas Avenue** separates the numbered east-west streets to the north from the named east-west streets to the south. Running east-west, **Kellogg Avenue (U.S. 54)** serves as an expressway through downtown and as a main commercial strip. The closest **Amtrak** station, 414 N. Main St. (☎283-7533; open M-F midnight-8am), 30 mi. north of Wichita in the town of Newton, sends trains to Dodge City (2½hr., 1 per day, $26-51) and Kansas City (4hr., 1 per day, $33-64). **Greyhound,** 308 S. Broadway St., two blocks east of Main St. (☎265-7711; open daily 3am-6pm), runs to: Denver (14hr., 2 per day, $72); Kansas City (4hr., 3 per day, $33); Oklahoma City (4hr., 3 per day, $32). **Wichita Transit,** 214 S. Topeka St., runs 18 bus routes in town. (☎265-7221. Open M-F 6am-6pm, Sa 7am-5pm. Buses run M-F 5:45am-6:45pm, Sa 6:45am-5:45pm. $1, ages 6-17 $0.75, seniors and disabled $0.50; transfers $0.10.) **Visitor Info: Convention and Visitors Bureau,** 100 S. Main St., at Douglas Ave. (☎265-2800 or 800-288-9424; www.visitwichita.com. Open M-F 8am-5pm.) **Internet Access: Public Library,** 223 S. Main St. (☎261-8500. Open M-Th 10am-9pm, F-Sa 10am-5:30pm, Su 1-5pm.) **Post Office:** 330 W. 2nd St. N, at N. Waco St. (☎267-7710. Open M-F 7:30am-5pm, Sa 9am-noon.) **Postal Code:** 67202. **Area Code:** 316.

GREAT PLAINS

ACCOMMODATIONS. Wichita offers a bounty of cheap hotels. S. Broadway St. has plenty of mom-and-pop places, *but be wary of the surrounding areas.* The chains line **East and West Kellogg Avenue,** 5-8 mi. from downtown. Only 10 blocks from downtown, the **Mark 8 Inn ❷,** 1130 N. Broadway St., has small, comfortable rooms with free local calls, cable TV, A/C, fridge, and laundry facilities. (☎265-4679 or 888-830-7268. Singles $34; doubles $37.) **Wichita Inn ❷,** 8220 E. Kellogg Ave., is your next best bet, offering cable, continental breakfast, TV/VCR, and micro-fridge. (☎685-8291. Singles $42; doubles $46.) **USI Campgrounds ❶,** 2920 E. 33rd St., right off Hillside Rd., is the most convenient of Wichita's hitchin' posts, with laundry, showers, and storm shelter—in case there's a twister a-comin'. (☎838-0435. No tents. RV sites $21.)

FOOD. Beef is what's for dinner in Wichita. If you eat only one slab here, get it from **Doc's Steakhouse ❸,** 1515 N. Broadway St., bus #13 "N. Broadway," where the most expensive entree—a 17 oz. T-bone with salad, potato, and bread—is only $11. (☎264-4735. Open M-Th 11:30am-9:30pm, F 11:30am-10pm, Sa 4-10pm.) The **Old Town** area is a good choice for lunch. Several restaurants offer $5 buffets and other specials. **Hog Wild Pit Bar-B-Q ❶,** 1200 S. Rock Rd. (also at 233 S. West St. and 662 E. 47th St.), has dine-in, drive-thru, and carry-out lip-smackin' Kansas goodness. Six-dollar dinners include choice of meat, two sides, and bread. (☎618-7227. Sandwiches $4. Open daily 11am-8pm.) **North Broadway Street,** around 10th St., offers authentic Asian food, mostly Vietnamese. **Saigon ❷,** 1103 N. Broadway St., creates good and greasy Vietnamese fare. (☎262-8134. Noodles with chicken and an egg roll $6. Open daily 10am-9pm.)

SIGHTS. Wichita's four **Museums on the River** are within a few blocks of each other; take the trolley or bus #12 to "Riverside." Walk through the rough and tumble cattle days of the 1870s in the **Old Cowtown,** 1871 Sim Park Dr., which is lined with many original buildings. (☎264-6398; www.old-cowtown.org. Open Apr.-Oct. M-Sa 10am-5pm, Su noon-5pm; Nov.-Mar. Sa 10am-5pm, Su noon-5pm. $7, seniors $6.50, ages 12-17 $5, ages 4-11 $3.50, under 3 free; Tu-W seniors 2-for-1. Call for special events info.) The **Mid-America All-Indian Center and Museum,** 650 N. Seneca St., boasts Native American artifacts, the outdoor **Indian Village,** and the **Gallery of Nations,** which includes a regal display of Native American tribal flags. The late Blackbear Bosin's awe-inspiring sculpture *Keeper of the Plains* stands guard over the confluence of the Arkansas and Little Arkansas Rivers. The center hosts the annual **Mid-America All-Indian Intertribal Powwow,** featuring dancing, food, arts, and crafts. Call for dates. (☎262-5221. Open M-Sa 10am-5pm, Su 1-5pm. $3, ages 6-12 $2.)

Exploration Place, 300 N. McLean Blvd., Wichita's newest and most impressive piece of riverfront architecture, houses the city's interactive museum. Excavate area fossils, touch a 20 ft. tornado, or examine the miniature display of early 1950s Kansas landmarks. (☎263-3373 or 877-904-1444; www.exploration.org. Open Tu-Su 9am-5pm. Also open M during summer noon-6pm. $8, seniors $7.50, ages 5-15 $6, ages 2-4 $3.) **Botanica,** 701 N. Amindon St., the Wichita botanical gardens, contains a wide collection of flora from the Americas and Asia. Though Kansas may be completely landlocked, Botanica hosts an amazing array of aquatic plants in the Jaynew Milburn Aquatic Collection. (☎264-0448; www.botanica.org. Open M-Sa 9am-5pm, Su 1-5pm. $6, students $3, seniors $5.)

BOOZE, BOOTS, & BOVINES In its heyday in the 1870s, Dodge City, KS ("the wickedest little city in America") was a haven for gunfighters, prostitutes, and other lawless types. At one time, the main drag had one saloon for every 50 citizens. Disputes were settled man-to-man, with a duel, and the slower draw ended up in Boot Hill Cemetery, so named for the boot-clad corpses buried there. Legendary lawmen Wyatt Earp and Bat Masterson earned their fame cleaning up the streets of Dodge. Today, the town's most conspicuous residents, about 50,000 cows, reside on the feedlots on the east part of town. Whoop it up during the **Dodge City Days,** complete with rodeo, carnival, and lots of steak. You'll know when you're getting close. *(☎620-227-3119; www.dodgecitydays.com. July 30-Aug. 8, 2004.)*

LAWRENCE ☎785

Lawrence was founded in 1854 by anti-slavery advocates to ensure that Kansas became a free state. Now home to the flagship **University of Kansas (KU),** Lawrence offers numerous first-rate artistic, architectural, historical, cultural, and social activities. KU's **Watkins Community Museum of History,** 1047 Massachusetts St., whets the appetites of Kansas history buffs. (☎841-4109; www.dchsks.org. Open Tu-Sa 10am-4pm, Su 1:30-4pm. Free.) The main attractions, however, are two tours through downtown Lawrence. A 1½hr. driving tour beginning at 1111 E. 19th St., **Quantrill's Raid: The Lawrence Massacre** traces the events leading up to the murder of over 200 men by pro-slavery vigilantes on August 21, 1863. The second tour, **House Styles of Old West Lawrence,** provides a look at gorgeous 19th century homes. There is a walking (45min.) and a driving (25min.) tour. Maps are at the Visitors Center, Chamber of Commerce, and library.

Inexpensive motels are hard to come by in Lawrence. The best place to look is around Iowa and 6th St., just west of campus. Three blocks from downtown, the **Halcyon House Bed and Breakfast ❸,** 1000 Ohio St., is extremely close to local attractions and good parking. (☎841-0314. Breakfast included. Rooms $49.) The traditional **Westminster Inn and Suites ❸,** 2525 W. 6th St., offers many amenities, including a pool, to make stays more comfortable. (☎841-8410. Breakfast included. Singles M-Th $49, F-Su $55; doubles $59/65. $5 AAA discount. 2 wheelchair-accessible rooms.)

Downtown Lawrence features both traditional barbecue joints and health-conscious offerings. The **Wheatfields Bakery and Cafe ❷,** 904 Vermont St., serves up large sandwiches ($6.50) on French bread, olive loaf, or focaccia. Vegetarians will enjoy the $5 zucchini, sprouts, and roasted red pepper sandwich, slathered in herb cream cheese. (☎841-5553. Open M-Sa 6:30am-8pm, Su 7:30am-4pm.) **Cafe Nova ❶,** 745 New Hampshire St., percolates several varieties of coffee each day; sweeteners range from maple syrup to sweet cream. (☎841-3282. Internet access $2 per hr. Open M-F 8am-11pm, Sa-Su noon-11pm.) The **Free State Brewing Company ❷,** 636 Massachusetts St., the first legal brewery in Kansas and a popular local hangout, brews over 50 beers yearly and always has at least five on tap. (☎843-4555. Beer $2.50. Sandwiches $6. Pasta dishes $8-10. M $1.25 beer. Open M-Sa 11am-midnight, Su noon-11pm.) For live music and a neighborhood bar atmosphere, head down to the well-equipped **Jazzhaus,** 926½ Massachusetts St. Performers range from local groups to the occasional regional act. (☎749-3320. Cover after 9pm $2-8, depending on show; Tu $1.50, but no live music. Open daily 4pm-2am; music begins 9pm.)

Lawrence lies just south of I-70 in northeastern Kansas. There is an unstaffed **Amtrak** station at 413 E. 7th St.; trains chug to Chicago (10hr., 1 per day, $55-107). **Greyhound,** 2447 W. 6th St. (☎843-5622; ticket window open M-F 7:30am-4pm, Sa 7:30am-noon), runs buses to: Dallas (13-15hr., 5 per day, $59-82); Denver (12-13hr., 3 per day, $59-79); Kansas City, MO (1hr., 3 per day, $12-14). The **Lawrence Transit System (the "T"),** 930 E. 30th St., has schedules in local businesses, in the library, and on every bus. (☎832-3465. Open M-F 6am-8pm, Sa 7am-8pm. $0.50, seniors and disabled $0.25.) **Visitors Center:** 402 N. 2nd St., at Locust St. (☎865-4499 or 888-529-5267. Open Oct.-Mar. M-Sa 9am-5pm, Su 1-5pm; Apr.-Sept. M-F 8:30am-5:30pm, Su 1-5pm.) **Lawrence Chamber of Commerce:** 734 Vermont St. #101. (☎865-4411; www.lawrencekansas.org. Open M-F 8am-5pm.) **Internet Access: Public Library,** 707 Vermont Ave. (☎843-3833. Open M-F 9am-9pm, Sa 9am-6pm, Su 2-6pm.) **Post Office:** 645 Vermont St. (☎843-1681. Open M-F 8am-5:30pm, Sa 9am-noon.) **Postal Code:** 66045. **Area Code:** 785.

YOUR OWN WAY

NO AVOIDING IT

One hundred fifty miles west of Wichita on Route 54 lies the infamous Buffalo Capital of the World, the Cowboy Capital, the Queen of the Cowtowns, the Wickedest Little City in America, and the Beautiful Bibulous Babylon of the Frontier—in other words, Dodge City, Kansas. There's no let-up in Old West nostalgia from cradle-to-grave here—even the cemetery is devoted to those who died in real West shoot-outs.

Downtown Dodge City boasts a replicated Old West town where visitors can amble through the saloon, depot, and curios store. The real treasure, though, lies uphill in Boot Hill Cemetery. Though it was only used for a short while, it was the right short while to be a cemetery, as treacherous outlaws, brave lawmen, and assorted passers-by provided plenty of coffin fodder. Boot Hill remains the most famous burial ground in all Western lore.

Summer brings Dodge City Days, usually the last week in July, when round-ups, parades, and dances carry on late into the night. Come see the crowing of Miss Rodeo Kansas, and enjoy warm cornbread and beans from the ubiquitous chuck wagons.

For more information, visit www.dodgecity.org.

MISSOURI

Nestled in the middle of the country, Missouri serves as the gateway to the west while hugging the Midwest and South, blending the three identities into a state that defies regional stereotyping. Its large cities are defined by wide avenues, long and lazy rivers, numerous parks, humid summers, and blues and jazz wailing into the night. In the countryside, Bible factory outlets stand amid fireworks stands and barbecue pits. Missouri's patchwork geography further complicates its characterization. In the north, near Iowa, amber waves of grain undulate. Along the Mississippi, towering bluffs inscribed with Native American pictographs evoke western canyonlands, while in Hannibal, spelunkers enjoy the winding limestone caves that inspired Mark Twain.

PRACTICAL INFORMATION

Capital: Jefferson City.

Visitor Info: Missouri Division of Tourism, P.O. Box 1055, Jefferson City 65102 (☎573-751-4133 or 800-877-1234; www.missouritourism.org). Open M-F 8am-5pm; toll-free number operates 24hr. **Dept. of Natural Resources,** Division of State Parks, P.O. Box 176, Jefferson City 65102 (☎573-751-2479 or 800-334-6946). Open M-F 8am-5pm.

Postal Abbreviation: MO. **Sales Tax:** 6-7% depending on the county.

ST. LOUIS ☎314

Directly south of the junction of three rivers—the Mississippi, Missouri, and Illinois—St. Louis marks the transition between Midwest and West. The silvery Gateway Arch pays homage to American expansion, while another great US tradition, baseball, thrives at Busch Stadium. Innovative musicians influenced by great St. Louis blues and ragtime players of the past crowd bars and cafes. Sprawling and diverse, St. Louis offers visitors both high-paced life in a city and lazy days spent floating on the Mississippi.

TRANSPORTATION

Airport: Lambert-St. Louis International (☎426-8000; www.lambert-stlouis.com), 12 mi. northwest of the city on I-70. MetroLink and Bi-state bus #66 "Maplewood-Airport" provide easy access to downtown ($1.25). Taxis to downtown $20. A few westbound Greyhound buses stop at the airport.

Trains: Amtrak, 550 S. 16th St. (☎331-3000). Office open daily 6am-1am. To **Chicago** (6hr., 3 per day, $21-59) and **Kansas City** (5½hr., 2 per day, $25-52).

Buses: Greyhound, 1450 N. 13th St. (☎231-4485), at Cass Ave. From downtown, take Bi-State bus #30, less than 10min. away. *Be cautious at night.* To **Chicago** (6-7½hr., 9 per day, $34) and **Kansas City** (4½-5hr., 5 per day, $32).

Public Transit: Bi-State (☎231-2345) runs local buses. Info and schedules available at the **Metroride Service Center,** in the St. Louis Center. (☎982-1485.) Open M-F 6am-8pm, Sa-Su 8am-5pm. **MetroLink,** the light-rail system, runs from 5th St. and Missouri Ave., in East St. Louis, to Lambert Airport. Operates M-Sa 5am-midnight and Su 6am-11pm. Travel for free in the "Ride Free Zone" (from Laclede's Landing to Union Station) M-F 11:30am-1pm. Bi-State or MetroLink $1.25, transfers $0.10; seniors and ages 5-12 $0.50/0.05. Day pass $4, available at MetroLink stations. **Shuttle Bugs,** small buses painted like ladybugs, cruise around Forest Park and the Central West End. Operates M-F 6:45am-6pm, Sa-Su 10am-6pm. $1.25. The **Shuttle Bee** buzzes around Forest Park, Clayton, Brentwood, and the Galleria. Operates M-F 6am-11:30pm, Sa 7:30am-10pm, Su 9:30am-6:30pm. $1.25.

Taxi: Yellow Cab, ☎361-2345.

ORIENTATION & PRACTICAL INFORMATION

I-64 (U.S. 40) runs east-west through the entire metropolitan area. Downtown is defined as the area east of Tucker between **Martin Luther King** and **Market Street,** which runs north-south and divides the city. Numbered streets parallel the Mississippi River, increasing to the west. The historic **Soulard** district borders the river south of downtown. **Forest Park** and **University City,** home to **Washington University** and old, stately homes, lie west of downtown; the Italian neighborhood called **The Hill** rests south of these. St. Louis is a driving town: parking comes easy, wide streets allow for lots of meters, and private lots are often cheap (from $2 per day).

While the safety situation in St. Louis has shown improvement of late, visitors are still well advised to keep a heads up; areas in North County can be dangerous at night, and East St. Louis—across the river in Illinois—is generally to be avoided.

Visitor Info: St. Louis Visitors Center, 308 Washington Ave. (☎241-1764). Open daily 9:30am-4:30pm. The *Official St. Louis Visitors Guide* and the monthly magazine *Where: St. Louis,* both free, contain helpful info and good maps. A second **information center** is inside the America's Convention Center. Open M-F 8:30am-5pm, Sa 9am-2pm.

Hotlines: Rape Hotline, ☎531-2003. **Suicide Hotline,** ☎647-4357. **Kids Under 21 Crisis,** ☎644-5886. All 24hr. **Gay and Lesbian Hotline,** ☎367-0084. Operates M-Sa 6-10pm.

Medical Services: Barnes-Jewish Hospital, 216 S. Kingshighway Blvd. (☎747-3000). **Metro South Women's Health Center,** 2415 N. Kingshighway Blvd. (☎772-1749).

Post Office: 1720 Market St. (☎436-4114. Open M-F 8am-8pm, Sa 8am-1pm.) **Postal Code:** 63101. **Area Code:** 314 (in St. Louis), 636 (in St. Charles), 618 (in IL); in text, 314 unless noted otherwise.

ACCOMMODATIONS

Most budget lodging is far from downtown. For chain motels, try Lindbergh Blvd. (Rte. 67) near the airport, or the area north of the I-70/I-270 junction in Bridgeton, 5 mi. beyond the airport. Watson Rd. near Chippewa is littered with cheap motels; take bus #11 "Chippewa-Sunset Hills" or #20 "Cherokee."

Huckleberry Finn Youth Hostel (HI-AYH), 1908 S. 12th St. (☎241-0076), at Tucker Blvd., 2 blocks north of Russell Blvd. in the Soulard District. Take bus #73 "Carondelet." A full kitchen, free parking, unbeatable prices, and proximity to Soulard bars make the cramped, weathered dorms tolerable. Ask about work opportunities; occasionally the owner hires hostelers to do odd jobs. Linen $2. Key deposit $5. Reception daily 8-10am and 6-10pm. Check-out 9:30am. Dorm-style rooms $19, nonmembers $21. ❶

Royal Budget Inn, 6061 Collinsville Rd., Fairmont City, IL (☎618-874-4451), 20min. east of the city off I-55/I-70 Exit 6. Clean, 1-bed purple-lit rooms with a Taj Mahal flavor make for an unusual budget option. $2 key deposit. Rooms $40. ❷

The Mayfair, 806 St. Charles St. (☎421-2500). Constructed at the height of the Jazz Age, the Mayfair has hosted famous musicians and politicians, from Irving Berlin to Harry Truman. Standard rooms are spacious with marble-topped sinks and soft queen-sized beds. Suites have a sitting room in addition to bedrooms. Rooms from $109; suites from $119. ❺

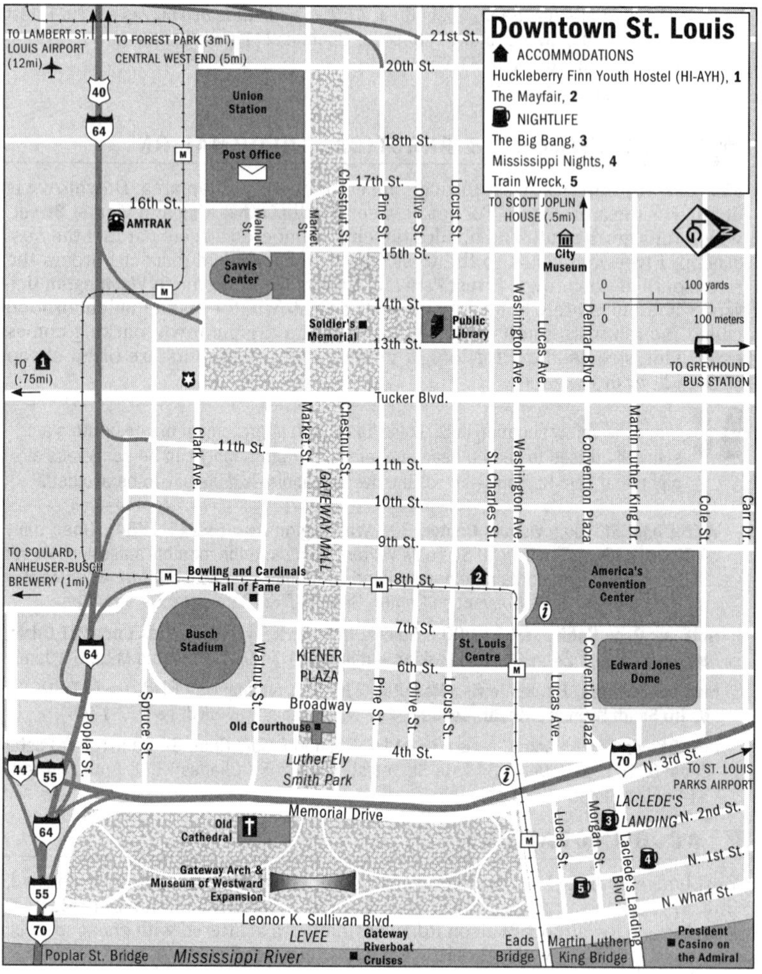

Dr. Edmund A. Babler Memorial State Park, 20 mi. west of downtown, just north of Hwy. 100 (☎636-458-3813 or 877-422-6766), has tent and RV sites and a shower house. Tent sites $8. RV sites with electric hookup $14.

FOOD

In St. Louis, the difference of a few blocks can mean vastly different cuisine. The area surrounding **Union Station,** at 18th and Market St. downtown, is being revamped with hip restaurants and bars. The **Central West End** offers coffeehouses and outdoor cafes. A slew of impressive restaurants waits just north of Lindell Blvd. along **Euclid Avenue;** take the MetroLink to "Central West End" and walk north, or catch the Shuttle Bug. St. Louis' historic Italian neighborhood, **The Hill,** southwest of downtown and just northwest of Tower Grove Park, produces plenty of inexpensive pasta; take bus #99 "Lafayette." Cheap Thai, Philippine, and Vietnamese restaurants spice the **South Grand** area, at Grand Blvd. just south of Tower Grove Park; board bus #70 "Grand." Coffee shops and unique restaurants cluster on **University City Loop,** on Delmar Blvd. between Skinker and Big Bend Blvd.

Blueberry Hill, 6504 Delmar Blvd. (☎727-0880), on the Loop. Eclectic rock 'n' roll restaurant with 9 different rooms including the "Elvis Room." Walls decked with record covers, Howdy Doody toys, a *Simpsons* collection, and giant baseball cards. Call ahead to find out if Chuck Berry is playing; he usually jams in the "Duck Room" 1 W each month. Big, juicy burgers $5. Live bands F-Sa and some weeknights 9:30pm. 21+ after 9pm. Cover $4-15. Kitchen open daily 11am-9pm. ❷

In Soo, 8423 Olive Blvd. (☎997-7473), is home to some of the best pot stickers ($5) and vegetable moo-shu ($9) you'll ever taste. The chef's wife meticulously manages every aspect of the restaurant, intermittently chiding customers, hugging them, and personally wrapping their moo-shoo pancakes. Open M and W-Su 11:30am-10pm. ❷

Ted Drewe's Frozen Custard, 4224 S. Grand Blvd. (☎352-7376) and 6726 Chippewa (☎481-2652), on Rte. 66. *The* place for the St. Louis summertime experience since 1929. Those patient enough to get through the line are rewarded by the "chocolate chip cookie dough concrete shake," ($1.70-3.80). Both locations open daily May-Aug. 11am-midnight; Chippewa St. site also Sept.-Dec. and Feb.-May 11am-11pm. ❶

Mangia Italiano, 3145 S. Grand Blvd. (☎664-8585). Fresh pasta made on site for $5-9. A handpainted mural and mismatched tables add a touch of flair to the trendy bistro. Jazz weekend nights. Kitchen open M-F noon-10pm and Sa-Su 12:30-10:30pm; bar open until 3am. ❷

Arcelia, 2001 Park Ave. (231-9200). Big combination platters ($5.50-10.25) feature usual suspects like burritos and enchiladas, but this bustling Mexican eatery also offers more authentic dishes such as *mole de pollo* and *menudo*. Open M-Th 10am-2pm and 5-10pm, F-Su 10am-10pm. ❷

Kaldi's Coffeehouse and Roasting Company, 700 De Mun Ave. (☎727-9955), in Clayton. An eclectic crowd sips espresso drinks (from $1) and munches on fresh baked goods, sandwiches, and veggie delights at this top-notch coffeeshop. Panini $5. Hummus plate $4.50. Open daily 7am-11pm. ❶

Imo's, 4479 Forest Park Ave. (☎535-4667), makes the city's favorite St. Louis-style thin crust pizza and receives shout-outs from native rap superstar Nelly. Pizzas from $6.40. Numerous other locations throughout the city. Open M-Th 11am-midnight, F-Sa 11am-1am, Su 11am-11pm. ❷

Cha Yoon Elixir Bar, 4 N. Euclid Ave. (☎367-2209), is a chic sushi joint offering fresh fish and an encyclopedic tea menu. Lounge on leather couches and sip tieguanyin oolong ($6 per pot), which is said to be hand-picked by monkeys who are trained to reach the most inaccessible tea trees. No, really. Open M-Th 11am-10pm, F-Sa 11am-11pm, Su 5-9pm. ❸

SIGHTS

JEFFERSON EXPANSION MEMORIAL. At 630 ft., the **Gateway Arch**—the nation's tallest monument—towers gracefully over all of St. Louis and southern Illinois, serving as a testament to the city's historical role as the "Gateway to the West." The ground-level view is impressive, and the arch frames downtown beautifully from the Illinois side, but the 4min. ride to the top in quasi-futuristic elevator modules is more fun. Waits are shorter after dinner or in the morning, but are uniformly long on Saturday. Beneath the arch, the underground **Museum of Westward Expansion** adds to the appeal of the grassy park complex known comprehensively as the **Jefferson Expansion Memorial.**

The museum radiates out in a semi-circle from a statue of a surveying Jefferson, celebrating the Louisiana Purchase and Westward expansion. *(☎982-1410; www.gatewayarch.com. Museum and arch open daily summer 8am-10pm; winter 9am-6pm. Tram $8, ages 13-16 $5, ages 3-12 $3. Museum free.)* Scope out the city from the water with **Gateway Riverboat Cruises;** tours leave from the docks in front of the arch. *(☎621-4040, arch and riverboat line ☎800-878-7411. 1hr. riverboat tours daily; call for departure times. $10, ages 3-12 $4. Discounts on combination arch/riverboat tickets. Limited wheelchair access.)* Across the street but still part of the Memorial, the magnificently ornate **Old Courthouse,** where the Dred Scott case began, has been restored as a museum detailing the case as well as the story of St. Louis' growth. *(11 N. 4th St. ☎655-1600. Open daily 8am-4:30pm. Tours summer every hr.; winter less frequently. Free. Limited wheelchair access.)*

ST. LOUIS HISTORY. It's a strike either way at the **International Bowling Museum and Hall of Fame** and the **St. Louis Cardinals Hall of Fame Museum,** which share a home across from Busch Stadium. The mildly amusing bowling museum traces the largely speculative history of the sport and allows visitors to bowl, while the baseball museum exhibits memorabilia from the glory days of St. Louis hardball. The museum also offers stadium tours. *(111 Stadium Plaza. ☎231-6340. Open Apr.-Sept. daily 9am-5pm, game days until 6:30pm; Oct.-Mar. Tu-Su 11am-4pm. Museums or stadium tour $6, ages 5-12 $4, both $8.50/7.50. Wheelchair-accessible.)* Historic **Union Station,** 1 mi. west of downtown, houses a shopping mall, food court, and entertainment center in a magnificent structure that was once the nation's busiest railroad terminal. *(At 18th and Market St. Metrolink to Union Station. ☎421-6655; www.stlouisunionstation.com. Open M-Sa 10am-9pm, Su 10am-6pm.)* "The Entertainer" lives on at the **Scott Joplin House,** just west of downtown near Jefferson St., where the ragtime legend tickled the ivories and penned classics from 1900 to 1903. The 45min. tour delves into Joplin's long-lasting influence on American music. *(2658 Delmar Blvd. ☎340-5790. Apr.-Oct. M-F tours every 30min. 10am-4pm, Su noon-5pm.; Nov.-Mar. M-Sa 10am-4pm, Su noon-5pm. $2.50, ages 6-12 $1.50. Wheelchair-accessible.)*

SOUTH OF DOWNTOWN. Soulard is bounded by I-55 and Seventh St. In the early 1970s, the city proclaimed this area a historic district because it once housed German and East European immigrants, many of whom worked in the breweries. Today, it is an attractive, tree-lined neighborhood packed with 19th-century brick townhouses. The district surrounds the bustling **Soulard Farmers Market,** where fresh, inexpensive produce abounds. *(730 Carroll St. From downtown, travel south on Broadway or 7th St. to Lafayette. Take bus #73 "Carondelet." ☎622-4180. Open W-Sa 7am-7pm; hours vary among merchants.)* At the end of 12th St., the **Anheuser-Busch Brewery,** the largest brewery in the world, holds court and produces the "King of Beers." The 1½hr. tour includes a glimpse of the famous Clydesdales and two beer samples. *(1127 Pestalozzi St., at 12th and Lynch St. Take bus #40 "Broadway" south from downtown. ☎577-2626; www.budweisertours.com. Tours June-Aug. M-Sa 9am-5pm, Su 11:30am-5pm; Sept.-May M-Sa 9am-4pm, Su 11:30am-4pm. Wheelchair-accessible.)*

The internationally acclaimed 79-acre **Missouri Botanical Garden** thrives north of Tower Grove Park on grounds left by entrepreneur Henry Shaw. The Japanese Garden is guaranteed to soothe the weary traveler. *(4344 Shaw Blvd. From downtown, take I-44 west, or ride MetroLink to "Central West End" and take bus #13 "Union-Missouri Botanical Gardens" to the main entrance. ☎800-642-8842; www.mobot.org. Open daily 9am-5pm; also June-Aug. M 9am-8pm. $7, seniors $5, under 12 free. Guided tours daily 1pm. Wheelchair-accessible.)* **Grant's Farm,** the former home of President Ulysses S. Grant, is now zoo. The tram-ride tour crosses terrain inhabited by over 1000 free-roaming animals, including elephants, zebras, and more of Anheuser's Clydesdale collection. *(3400 Grant St. Take I-55 west to Reavis Barracks Rd. and turn left onto Gravois. ☎843-1700; www.grantsfarm.com. Open mid-May to Aug. Tu-F 9am-3:30pm, Sa 9am-4pm, Su 9:30am-4pm; Sept.-Oct. W-F 9:30am-2:30pm, Sa-Su 9:30am-3:30pm; early Apr.-early May W-F 9am-3pm, Sa 9am-3:30pm, Su 9:30am-3:30pm. Free. Parking $5.)*

FOREST PARK. Forest Park contains three museums, a zoo, a 12,000-seat amphitheater, a grand canal, and countless picnic areas, pathways, and flying golf balls. *(Take MetroLink to Forest Park and catch the Shuttle Bug. All Forest Park sites are wheelchair-accessible.)* Marlin Perkins, the late host of TV's *Wild Kingdom*, turned the **St. Louis Zoo** into a world-class institution, featuring black rhinos, Asian elephants, and a top-notch penguin and puffin environment. *(☎781-0900; www.stlzoo.com. Open daily late May to early Sept. 8am-7pm; Sept.-May 9am-5pm. Free. Children's Zoo $4, under 2 free.)* Atop **Art Hill,** a statue of France's Louis IX, the city's namesake, raises his sword in front of the **St. Louis Art Museum,** which contains masterpieces of Asian, Renaissance, and Impressionist art. *(☎721-0072; www.slam.org. Open Tu-Th and Sa-Su 10am-5pm, F 10am-9pm. Main museum free; special exhibits usually $10, students and seniors $8, ages 6-12 $6; F free. Free tours W-Su 1:30pm.)* The **Missouri History Museum** focuses on the city's cultural heritage and has a small exhibit on the 1904 World's Fair. *(Located at Lindell and DeBaliviere. ☎454-3124; www.mohistory.org. Open M and W-Su 10am-6pm, Tu 10am-8pm. Main museum free. Special exhibits usually $5, seniors and students $4, Tu 4-8pm free.)* The **St. Louis Science Center** features an Omnimax theater, a planetarium, and over 700 interactive exhibits. Program the behavior of a virtual fish, gape at mind-boggling visual tricks, and build your own arch. *(5050 Oakland Ave. ☎289-4444; www.slcs.org. Main museum free. Omnimax $7, seniors and ages 2-12 $6. Planetarium $6/5. Open early June to Aug. M-Th and Sa 9:30am-5:30pm, F 9:30am-9:30pm, Su 11:30am-5:30pm; Sept.-May M-Th and Sa 9:30am-4:30pm, F 9:30am-9:30pm, Su 11:30am-4:30pm.)*

GREAT PLAINS

CENTRAL WEST END. From Forest Park, head east a few blocks to gawk at the Tudor homes of the **Central West End.** The vast **Cathedral Basilica of St. Louis** is a unique amalgam of architectural styles; visitors are enchanted by the intricate ceilings and mosaics depicting Missouri church history. *(4431 Lindell Blvd. MetroLink stop "Central West End" or bus #93 "Lindell" from downtown. ☎533-0544. Open daily summer 7am-7pm; low-season 7am-dusk. Tours M-F 10am-3pm, Su after noon Mass. Call to confirm hours. Wheelchair-accessible.)* At a shrine of a different sort, monster truck enthusiasts pay homage to **Bigfoot,** the "Original Monster Truck," who lives with his descendants near the airport. *(6311 N. Lindbergh St. ☎731-2822. Open M-F 9am-6pm, Sa 9am-3pm. Free.)* Northwest of the Central West End, the sidewalks of the **Loop** are studded with gold stars on the **St. Louis Walk of Fame,** which features local luminaries from Maya Angelou to Ike and Tina Turner. *(6504 Delmar Blvd. ☎727-7827; www.stlouiswalkoffame.org.)*

OTHER SIGHTS. The slightly surreal **City Museum** is constructed from salvaged parts of area buildings and contains a weird and wonderful amalgam of architectural styles. The "Museum of Mirth, Mystery and Mayhem" keeps the archaic tradition of freakshows alive while the outdoor "Monstrocity," which is made entirely of recycled parts and includes two planes, a firetruck, a ferris wheel, sky tunnels, and a gothic tower with gargoyles, is far and away the coolest playscape ever. *(701 N. 15th St., downtown. ☎231-2489; www.citymuseum.org. Open Sept.-May W-F 9am-5pm, Sa 10am-5pm, Su 11am-5pm; June-Aug. Tu-Th 9am-5pm, F 9am-1am, Sa 10am-1am, Su 11am-5pm. Main museum $7.50, museum and "Monstrocity" $10, museum and skatepark $10.)*

ENTERTAINMENT

Founded in 1880, the **St. Louis Symphony Orchestra** is one of the country's finest. **Powell Hall,** 718 N. Grand Blvd., holds the 101-member orchestra in acoustic and visual splendor. (☎534-1700. Performances late Sept.-early May Th-Sa 8pm, Su 3pm. Box office open late May to mid-Aug. M-F 9am-5pm; mid-Aug. to late May M-Sa 9am-5pm; and before performances. Tickets $10-95, students half-price.)

St. Louis offers theatergoers many choices. The outdoor **Municipal Opera,** the "Muny," presents hit musicals on summer nights in Forest Park. (☎361-1900. Box office open June to mid-Aug. daily 9am-9pm. Tickets $8-54.) Productions are also regularly staged by the **St. Louis Black Repertory,** 634 N. Grand Blvd. (☎534-3807), and by the **Repertory Theatre of St. Louis,** 130 Edgar Rd. (☎968-4925). The **Fox Theatre,** 537 N. Grand, was originally a 1930s movie palace, but now hosts Broadway shows, classic films, and Las Vegas, country, and rock stars. (☎534-1111. Open M-Sa 10am-6pm, Su noon-4pm. Tours Tu, Th, Sa 10:30am. Tu $5, Th and Sa $8; under 12 $3. Call for reservations.) **Metrotix** has tickets to most area events. (☎534-1111. Open daily 9am-9pm.)

A recent St. Louis ordinance permits gambling on the river for those over 21. The **President Casino on the Admiral** floats below the Arch on the Missouri side. (☎622-1111 or 800-772-3647; www.presidentscasino.com. Open M-Th 8am-4am, F-Su 24hr. Entry tax $2.) On the Illinois side, the **Casino Queen** claims "the loosest slots in town." (☎618-874-5000 or 800-777-0777; www.casinoqueen.com. Open daily 9am-7am.) Parking for both is free, and both are wheelchair-accessible. **Six Flags St. Louis,** 30min. southwest of St. Louis on I-44 at Exit 261, reigns supreme in the kingdom of amusement parks. The brand-new "Xcalibur" catapaults thrill-seekers 113 ft. into the air while spinning in circles, and the vaunted "Boss" wooden roller coaster features a 570° helix. (☎636-938-4800. Hours vary by season. $39, seniors and under 48 in. $24.) The **St. Louis Cardinals** play ball at **Busch Stadium.** (☎421-3060. $9-55.) The **Rams,** formerly of L.A., take to the field at the **Edward Jones Dome.** (☎425-8830. $40-49.) The **Blues** hockey team slices ice at the **Savvis Center** at 14th St. and Clark Ave. (☎843-1700. Tickets from $15.)

NIGHTLIFE

Music rules the night in St. Louis. The *Riverfront Times* (free at many bars and clubs) and the *Get Out* section of the *Post-Dispatch* list weekly entertainment. The *St. Louis Magazine*, published annually, lists seasonal events. For beer and live music, often without a cover charge, St. Louis offers **Laclede's Landing,** a collection of restaurants, bars, and dance clubs housed in 19th-century industrial buildings north of the Arch on the riverfront. In the summer, bars take turns sponsoring "block parties," with food, drink, music, and dancing in the streets. (☎241-5875. 21+. Generally open 9pm-3am, with some places open for lunch and dinner.) Other nightlife hot spots include the bohemian **Loop** along Delmar Blvd., **Union Station** and its environs, and the less touristy and gay-friendly **Soulard** district.

Brandt's Market & Cafe, 6525 Delmar Blvd. (☎727-3663), a Loop mainstay, offers live jazz, along with beer, wine, espresso, and a varied menu. During the summer, specials are served outside, while musicians jam in the dark interior. This is because they want to keep the customers away from the horrible Who cover bands inside that make patrons' ears bleed all over the floor. Bring paper towels, just in case. Open M-Th 11am-midnight, F-Sa 11am-1am, Su 11am-10pm.

The Pageant, 6161 Delmar Blvd. (☎726-6161). Line up early for a spot in the fantastic 33,000 sq. ft. nightclub, which hosts national acts. Call for ticket and cover prices. 18+. Doors usually open 7pm. The classy **Halo Bar** is open daily 5pm-3am and features live DJs.

Mississippi Nights, 914 N. 1st St. (☎421-3853), at Laclede's Landing. St. Louis' favorite place for music since 1979 has a history of bringing in the best national acts of all genres. Covers from $6. Doors usually open 7-8pm.

The Big Bang, 807 N. 2nd St. (☎241-2264), at Laclede's Landing. Dueling pianists lead the crowd in a rock 'n' roll sing-along show. Beer from $3.25. Cover Su-Th $3, F-Sa $6. Open Su-Th 7pm-3am, F-Sa 5pm-3am.

Train Wreck, 720 N. 1st St. (☎436-1006), at Laclede's Landing, features a multi-level entertainment center with a nightclub, restaurant, and sports bar. Alternative cover bands F-Sa nights. Cover $3. Open Su-Th 11am-10pm, F-Sa 11am-3am.

Clementine's, 2001 Menard St. (☎664-7869), in Soulard, contains a crowded restaurant and St. Louis' oldest gay bar (established in 1978). Open M-F 10am-1:30am, Sa 8am-1:30am, Su 11am-midnight.

HANNIBAL ☎573

Hannibal anchors itself on the Mississippi River 100 mi. west of Springfield and 100 mi. northwest of St. Louis. Founded in 1819, Hannibal slept in obscurity until Mark Twain used his boyhood home as the setting of *The Adventures of Tom Sawyer.* Tourists now flock to Hannibal to imagine Tom, Huck, and Becky romping around the quaint streets and nearby caves. Hannibal has seen its popularity wane over the years and seems content to rest on its laurels, but it is still an irresistible stop for any traveler with a Mark Twain fixation.

Start the Mark Twain tour at the annex of the **Mark Twain Boyhood Home and Museum,** 208 Hill St. (☎221-9010), which screens a 10min. video and houses an assortment of memorabilia to commemorate the events of the witty wordsmith's life. Across the street sit the **Pilaster House** and **Clemens Law Office,** where a young Twain awoke one night to find a murdered man lying on the floor next to him. Restored rooms are accompanied by audio segments explaining their significance to Twain's life and his novels. Farther down Main St., the **New Mark Twain Museum** takes visitors on an interactive tour through the author's novels. Upstairs, the highlight of the museum is the collection of Norman Rockwell illustrations entitled *Tom and Hucks.* The impressive display contains paintings, original sketches, and Rockwell's anecdotes about the drawings. (☎221-9010. Open June-Aug. daily 8am-6pm; May daily 8am-5pm; Nov.-Feb. M-Sa 10am-4pm, Su noon-4pm; Mar. M-Sa 9am-4pm, Su noon-4pm; Apr. and Sept.-Oct. daily 9am-5pm. Single ticket covers all sites; $6, ages 6-12 $3.) The **Mark Twain Riverboat,** at Center St. Landing, steams down the Mississippi for a 1hr. sightseeing cruise that is part history, part folklore, and part advertisement for the land attractions. (☎221-3222. Late May-early Sept. 3 per day; May and Sept.-Oct. 1 per day. $10, ages 5-12 $7; dinner cruises 6:30pm $28/20.) The **Mark Twain Cave,** 1 mi. south of Hannibal on Rte. 79, winds through the complex series of caverns Twain explored as a boy and is an amazing geological formation. A 1hr. tour guides visitors to the author's favorite spots and details the myths and legends associated with the cave. Graffiti from as early as the 1830s, including Jesse James' signature, still marks the walls. The cave tour includes the only section of the cave christened by Twain, **Aladdin's Castle,** the picturesque spot where Tom and Becky were "married." (☎221-1656. Open June-Aug. daily 8am-8pm; Apr.-May and Sept.-Oct. 9am-6pm; Nov.-Mar. 9am-4pm. 1hr. tour $12, ages 5-12 $6.) From June to August, nearby **Cameron Cave,** Hwy. 79 S, provides a slightly longer and far spookier lantern tour. (Tickets available at Mark Twain Cave. $14, ages 5-12 $7. Discount tickets available for both caves.) Every 4th of July weekend, 100,000 fans converge on Hannibal for the fence-painting, frog jumping fun of the **Tom Sawyer Days** festival (☎221-2477).

As befits a state bordering the Deep South, Hannibal is home to some tasty barbecue establishments. Even though catfish ($10) is the specialty at **Bubba's ❷,** 101 Church St., a former warehouse that dishes out good food and Southern hospitality, the pit-smoked barbecue pork and beef sandwiches (from $4.50) are not to be missed. Sandwiches with home-style vegetable sides like cole slaw and jambalaya are $5.50. (☎221-5552. Open daily 11am-9pm.) Cool down with an ice cream (from $1.50) at the **Main Street Soda Fountain ❶,** 207 S. Main St., home to a 100-year-old soda fountain. (☎248-1295. Open Tu-Su 11am to late evening.)

The **Hannibal Convention and Visitors Bureau,** 505 N. 3rd St., offers free local calls and information. (☎221-2477; www.visithannibal.com. Open M-F 8am-6pm, Sa 9am-6pm, Su 9:30am-4:30pm.) **Post Office:** 801 Broadway. (☎221-0957. Open M-F 8:30am-5pm, Sa 8:30am-noon.) **Postal Code:** 63401. **Area Code:** 573.

KANSAS CITY ☎816

With more miles of boulevard than Paris and more working fountains than Rome, Kansas City looks and acts more European than one might expect from the "Barbecue Capital of the World." When Prohibition stifled most of the country's fun in the 1920s, Mayor Pendergast let the good times continue to roll. The Kansas City of today maintains its big bad blues-and-jazz reputation in a metropolis spanning two states: the highly suburbanized town in Kansas (KCKS) and the quicker-paced commercial metropolis in Missouri (KCMO).

TRANSPORTATION

Airport: Kansas City International (☎243-5237; www.kansas-city-mci.com), 18 mi. northwest of KC off I-29. Take bus #129. **KCI Shuttle** (☎243-5000 or 800-243-6383) services downtown, Westport, Crown Center, and Plaza in KCMO and Overland Park, Mission, and Lenexa in KCKS. Departs daily every 30min. 4:30am-midnight. $14. Taxi to downtown $42-46.

Trains: Amtrak, 30 W. Pershing Rd. (☎421-3622), in the newly renovated Union Station. Take bus #27. Open daily 7am-midnight. To **Chicago** (8-12hr., 2 per day, $38-100) and **St. Louis** (6-13hr., 3 per day, $25-58).

Buses: Greyhound, 1101 N. Troost (☎221-2835). Take bus #25. *Stay alert—the terminal is in an unsafe area.* Open summer 24hr., winter daily 5:30am-midnight. To **Chicago** (12-18hr., 5-6 per day, $47-50) and **St. Louis** (6hr., 3 per day, $29-31).

Public Transit: Kansas City Area Transportation Authority (Metro), 1200 E. 18th St. (☎221-0660), near Troost St. Buses run 4:30am-midnight. $1, seniors and disabled $0.50; free transfers. $1.20 to Independence, MO.

Taxi: Yellow Cab, ☎471-5000.

ORIENTATION & PRACTICAL INFORMATION

The KC metropolitan area sprawls interminably, making travel difficult without a car. Most sights worth visiting lie south of downtown on the Missouri side or in the 18th and Vine Historic District. *All listings are for KCMO, unless otherwise indicated.* Although parking around town is not easy during the day, there are many lots that charge $5 or less per day. **I-70** cuts east-west through the city, and **I-435** circles the two-state metro area. KCMO is laid out on a grid with numbered streets running east-west from the Missouri River well out into suburbs, and named streets running north-south. **Main Street** divides the city east-west.

Visitor Info: Convention and Visitors Bureau of Greater Kansas City, 1100 Main St., #2550 (☎221-5242 or 800-767-7700; www.visitkc.com), 25th fl. of the City Center Sq. Bldg. Open M-F 8:30am-5pm. Other locations in the Plaza (open M-Sa 10am-6pm, Su 11am-5pm) and Union Station (open M-Sa 10am-10pm, Su noon-5pm). **Missouri Tourist Information Center,** 4010 Blue Ridge Cut-Off (☎889-3330 or 800-877-1234); follow signs from Exit 9 off I-70. Open daily 8am-5pm, except on days when the Chiefs are playing at home.

Hotlines: Rape Crisis Line, ☎531-0233. **Gay and Lesbian Hotline,** ☎931-4470. **General Crisis Hotline,** ☎741-8700. 24hr.

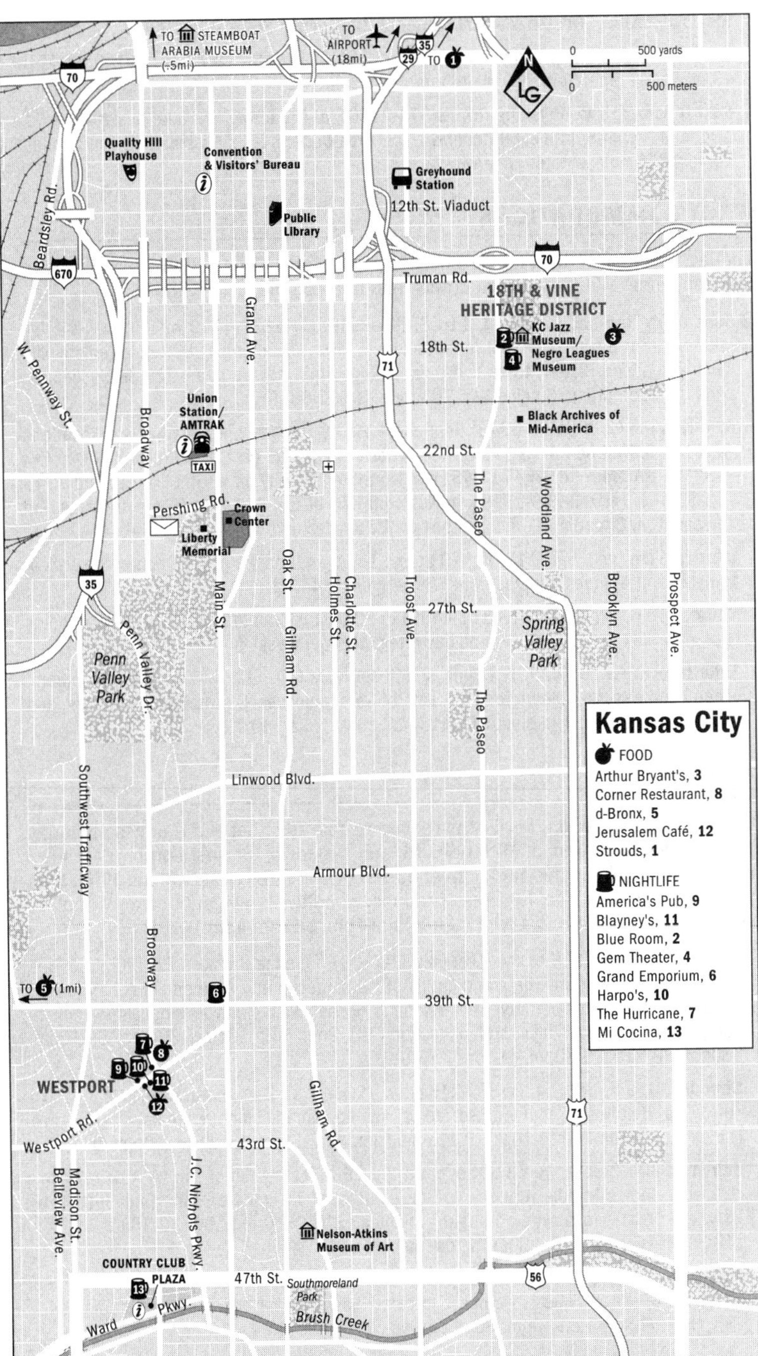
TO STEAMBOAT ARABIA MUSEUM (.5mi)
TO AIRPORT (18mi)
TO 1
500 yards
500 meters
Quality Hill Playhouse
Convention & Visitors' Bureau
Greyhound Station
12th St. Viaduct
Public Library
Beardsley Rd.
Truman Rd.
18TH & VINE HERITAGE DISTRICT
KC Jazz Museum/ Negro Leagues Museum
18th St.
Grand Ave.
W. Pennway St.
Union Station/ AMTRAK
TAXI
Broadway
Black Archives of Mid-America
22nd St.
Pershing Rd.
Crown Center
Liberty Memorial
The Paseo
Woodland Ave.
Main St.
Oak St.
Charlotte St.
Holmes St.
Troost Ave.
27th St.
Brooklyn Ave.
Prospect Ave.
Spring Valley Park
Penn Valley Dr.
Penn Valley Park
Gillham Rd.
Linwood Blvd.
Southwest Trafficway
Armour Blvd.
TO 5 (1mi)
39th St.
WESTPORT
Westport Rd.
43rd St.
J.C. Nichols Pkwy.
Madison St.
Belleview Ave.
Nelson-Atkins Museum of Art
COUNTRY CLUB PLAZA
47th St.
Southmoreland Park
Ward Pkwy.
Brush Creek
Kansas City
FOOD
Arthur Bryant's, 3
Corner Restaurant, 8
d-Bronx, 5
Jerusalem Café, 12
Strouds, 1
NIGHTLIFE
America's Pub, 9
Blayney's, 11
Blue Room, 2
Gem Theater, 4
Grand Emporium, 6
Harpo's, 10
The Hurricane, 7
Mi Cocina, 13

Medical Services: Truman Medical Center, 2301 Holmes St. (☎404-1000).

Internet Access: Kansas City Public Library, 311 E. 12th St. (☎701-3400). Open M-Th 9am-8pm, F 9am-6pm, Sa 10am-5pm, Su 1-5pm.

Post Office: 315 W. Pershing Rd. (☎374-9100), at Broadway St.; take bus #40 or 51. Open M-F 8am-5pm. **Postal Code:** 64108. **Area Code:** 816 in Missouri, 913 in Kansas; in text 816 unless noted otherwise.

ACCOMMODATIONS

The least expensive lodgings are near the interstates, especially I-70, and toward Independence, MO. Downtown hotels tend to be on the pricey side.

Serendipity Bed and Breakfast, 116 S. Pleasant St. (☎833-4719 or 800-203-4299), 20min. from downtown KC in Independence, MO. A charming 1887 home replete with Victorian decor. Historic tours and train pickups are available in a 1928 Buick, weather and time permitting. Singles $45-70; doubles $80-85. ❷

American Inn (☎800-905-6343) dominates the KC budget motel market with locations at 4141 S. Noland Rd. (☎373-8300); Woods Chapel Rd. (☎228-1080), off I-70 at Exit 18; 1211 Armour Rd. (☎471-3451), in North Kansas City off I-35 at Exit 6B; and 7949 Splitlog Rd. (☎913-299-2999), in KCKS off I-70 at Exit 414. The rooms are large and pleasant. A/C, cable TV, and outdoor pools. Singles and doubles from $40. ❷

Interstate Inn (☎229-6311), off I-70 at Exit 18. A great deal if you get one of the walk-in singles and doubles. Singles from $29; doubles $44. ❷

YMCA, 900 N. 8th St. (☎913-371-4400) in KCKS. Take bus #1 or 4. A variety of rooms **for men.** Key deposit $10. No nightly rates; $84 per week. ❶

Lake Jacomo (☎795-8200), 22 mi. southeast of KCMO. Take I-470 south to Colbern, then head east on Colbern for 2 mi. Lots of water activities, 33 forested campsites, and marina. Sites $10; with electricity $18; full hookup $22. ❶

FOOD

Kansas City rustles up a herd of barbecue restaurants that serve unusually tangy ribs. The **Westport** area, at Westport Rd. and Broadway St. just south of 40th St., has eclectic menus, cafes, and coffeehouses. Ethnic fare clusters along **39th Street** just east of the state line. For fresh produce, visit **City Market,** at 5th and Walnut St. along the river. (☎842-1271. Open Su-F 9am-4pm, Sa 6am-4pm.)

Arthur Bryant's, 1727 Brooklyn Ave. (☎231-1123). Take the Brooklyn Exit off I-70 or bus #110 from downtown. The grand-daddy of KC barbecue and a perennial candidate for best barbecue in the country. Bryant's "sandwiches" are a carnivore's delight—wimpy triangles of bread drowning in pork perfection ($9). Open M-Th 10am-9:30pm, F-Sa 10am-10pm, Su 11am-8:30pm. ❷

Strouds, 1015 E. 85th St. (☎333-2132), at Troost Ave., 2 mi. north of the Holmes Exit off I-435. Belt bustin' soul food served up with homemade cinnamon rolls. Chicken fried steak $12. Open M-Th 4-10pm, F 11am-11pm, Sa 2-11pm, Su 11am-10pm. ❸

d-Bronx, 3904 Bell St. (☎531-0550), on the 39th St. restaurant row. A New York deli transplanted to Middle America, d-Bronx has over 35 kinds of subs (half-sub $4-6, whole $8-12) and powdered sugar brownies ($1.50). Open M-W 10:30am-9pm, Th 10:30am-10pm, F-Sa 10:30am-11pm. ❷

Jerusalem Cafe, 431 Westport Rd. (☎756-2770). In a city of beef, vegetarians can find refuge here. Sandwiches with rice and salad $5-7. Try the popular falafel hummus for $5. Open M-Sa 11am-10pm, Su noon-8pm. ❷

Corner Restaurant, 4059 Broadway St. (☎931-6630), in the heart of Westport. A greasy spoon famous for its plate-sized pancakes ($2-3). Biscuits and gravy $4. Lunch specials $6. Open M-W 7am-3pm, Th-Sa 7am-11pm. ❶

SIGHTS

18TH & VINE. Jazz once flourished in the recently designated **18th and Vine Historic District.** The **American Jazz Museum** brings back the era with classy displays, music listening stations, neon dance hall signs, and everything from Ella Fitzgerald's eyeglasses to Louis Armstrong's lip salve. Swinging in the same building, the **Negro Leagues Baseball Museum** recalls the segregated era of America's pastime with photographs, interactive exhibits, and bittersweet nostalgia. *(1616 E. 18th St. Take bus #108 "Indiana." Jazz museum: ☎474-8463; www.americanjazzmuseum.com. Baseball museum: ☎221-1920; www.nlbm.com. Both open Tu-Sa 9am-6pm, Su noon-6pm. 1 museum $6, under 12 $2.50; both museums $8/4.)* Nearby, the **Black Archives of Mid-America** holds a large collection of paintings and sculpture by African-American artists and focuses on local black history. *(2033 Vine St. ☎483-1300; www.blackarchives.org. Open M-F 9am-4:30pm. Tours 10am. $2, under 17 $0.50.)*

OTHER MUSEUMS. The **Nelson-Atkins Museum of Art** contains one of the best East Asian art collections in the world and a sculpture park with 13 pieces by Henry Moore. The museum is under renovation until further notice, so call ahead for exhibit closings. *(4525 Oak St., 3 blocks northeast of Country Club Plaza. Take bus #147, 155, 156, or 157. ☎561-4000; www.nelson-atkins.org. Open Tu-Th 10am-4pm, F 10am-9pm, Sa 10am-5pm, Su noon-5pm. Enjoy live jazz inside the Museum's Rozzelle Court Restaurant F 5:30-8:30pm. Free walking tours Sa 11am-2pm, Su 1:30-3pm. Admission is free while the construction is going on, except for special exhibits.)* When the *Arabia* sank in the Missouri River, it was quickly buried in the silt-filled banks. 150 years later, the course of the river shifted, and excavations along the banks yielded 200 tons of treasure. Bottles of bourbon, plates, stationery, clothing, and most of the original logs from the ship now find rest at the **Arabia Steamboat Museum.** *(400 Grand Blvd. ☎471-1856; www.1856.com. Open M-Sa 10am-6pm, Su noon-5pm. $9.75, seniors $9.25, ages 4-12 $4.75.)*

THE PLAZA & CROWN CENTER. A few blocks to the west of the Nelson-Atkins Museum, at 47th St. and Southwest Trafficway, **Country Club Plaza,** known as "the Plaza," is the oldest and perhaps most picturesque shopping center in the US. Modeled after buildings in Seville, Spain, the Plaza boasts fountains, sculptures, hand-painted tiles, reliefs of grinning gargoyles, and yuppies roaming in their natural habitat—chain coffee shops. *(☎753-0100. Take buses #139, 151, 155, 156, or 157. Free concerts June-Aug. F-Sa.)* **Crown Center,** headquarters of Hallmark Cards, houses a maze of restaurants and shops and the children's **Coterie Theatre.** In the winter, the **Ice Terrace** is KC's only public outdoor ice-skating rink. On the third level of the center, see how cards and accessories are made at the **Hallmark Visitors Center.** *(2405 Grand Ave., 2 mi. north of the Plaza near Pershing Rd. Take bus #140, 156, 157, or any trolley. Crown Center: ☎274-5916. Coterie: ☎474-6785. $8, under 18 $6. Ice Terrace: ☎274-8412. Rink open Nov.-Dec. Su-Th 10am-9pm, F-Sa 10am-11pm; Jan.-Mar. daily 10am-9pm. $5, under 13 $4; rentals $1.50. Visitors Center: ☎274-3613, recording 274-5672; http://hallmarkvisitorscenter.com. Open M-F 9am-5pm, Sa 9:30am-4:30pm.)*

ENTERTAINMENT

From Sept. to May, the **Missouri Repertory Theatre,** 50th and Oak St., stages American classics. (☎235-2700. Box office open M-F 10am-5pm; call for weekend hours. Tickets range from $10-47, students and seniors $3 off.) **Quality Hill Playhouse,** 303

W. 10th St., produces off-Broadway plays and revues from September to June. (☎421-1700. Tickets around $22, students and seniors $2 off.) From late June to mid-July, the **Heart of America Shakespeare Festival** in Southmoreland Park, 47th and Oak St., puts on free shows. (☎531-7728; www.kcshakes.org. Most nights 8pm.) In Shawnee Mission, KS, the **New Theatre Restaurant,** 9229 Foster St., stages dinner theater productions of classic comedies and romances and attracts nationally recognized actors. Take Metcalf Ave. and turn into the Regency Park Center between 91st and 95th St. (☎913-649-7469. Box office open M-Sa 9am-6pm, Su 11am-3pm. Tickets $22-44, buffet meal included.)

Sports fans stampede to **Arrowhead Stadium,** at I-70 and Blue Ridge Cutoff, home to football's **Chiefs** (☎920-9400 or 800-676-5488; tickets $51-70) and soccer's **Wizards** (☎920-9300; tickets $12-17). Next door, a water-fountained wonder, **Kauffman Stadium** houses the **Royals,** Kansas City's baseball team. (☎921-8000 or 800-676-9257. Tickets $5-22. A stadium express bus runs from downtown and Country Club Plaza on game days.)

NIGHTLIFE

In the 1920s, jazz musician Count Basie and his "Kansas City Sound" reigned at the River City bars. Twenty years later, saxophonist Charlie "Bird" Parker spread his wings and soared, asserting Kansas City's prominence as a jazz music roost to be reckoned with. The restored **Gem Theater,** 1615 E. 18th St., stages old-time blues and jazz. (☎842-1414. Box office open M-F 10am-4pm.) Across the street, the **Blue Room,** 1600 E. 18th St., cooks four nights a week with some of the smoothest acts in town. (☎474-2929. Cover F-Sa $5. Bar open M and Th 5-11pm, F 5pm-1am, Sa 7pm-1am.) The **Grand Emporium,** 3832 Main St., twice voted the best blues club in the US, has live music five nights a week. (☎531-1504. Live music M and W-Sa. Cover up to $15, depending on act. Open M and Sa noon-2am, Tu-F 11am-2am--or when show ends.) For something besides jazz, bars and dancing hot spots cluster in the Westport area.

Blayney's, 415 Westport Rd. (☎561-3747). Canned R&B on the dance floor, live music on the outdoors deck. Cover $2-6. Open Tu-Th 8pm-3am, F 6pm-3am, Sa 5pm-3am.

America's Pub, 510 Westport Rd. (☎531-1313). Kansas City bachelorette party headquarters. While the dance floor is usually packed, the elevated barstools provide a chance to relax. Th $1 drinks. Cover $6. Open W-Sa 8pm-3am.

The Hurricane, 4048 Broadway St. (☎753-0884), hosts everything from open mic M to hip-hop Th. Cover $5-10. Open M-F 3pm-3am, Sa-Su 5pm-3am.

Harpo's, 4109 Pennsylvania Ave. (☎753-3434). The keystone of Westport nightlife. The live music and $0.25 beer on Tu attract collegiates and co-eds ready to party hearty. Cover Tu and Sa $2-3. Open daily 11am-3am.

Mi Cocina, 620 W. 48th St. (☎960-6426). The place to see and be seen in Kansas City. The trendy latino music accompanies couture-clad fashionistas. Forgo the pricey Mexican food, and swill on one of their infamous margaritas ($8.50). Open M-Th 11am-10pm, F-Sa 11am-3am, Su noon-10pm.

BRANSON ☎417

Back in 1967, the Presley family had no idea the impact the tiny theater they opened on **West Route 76,** a little road nestled in the gorgeous Missouri end of the Ozark mountains, would have. Now, more than 30 years later, over 7 million tourists clog Branson's strip each year to visit the "live country music capital of the Universe." Billboards, motels, and giant showplaces call to the masses that visit Branson to embrace a collage of all things plastic, franchised, and "wholesome."

Branson boasts over 30 indoor theaters and a few outdoor ones as well, all housing family variety shows, magic acts, comedians, plays, and straight-up music. Box office prices for most shows run $20-50, depending on who's playing. Never pay full price for a show or attraction in Branson—coupon books, including the *Sunny Day Guide* and the *Best Read Guide*, offer dozens of discounts.

To see a real, live battle between the North and the South, head to Dolly Parton's **Dixie Stampede,** 1 mi. west of Hwy. 65 on 76 Country Blvd, where "a friendly competition" between Yankees and Rebs is staged on the backs of ostriches, horses, and other animals that lend themselves to trick riding. Ticket prices include a full four course "feast" to be enjoyed while simultaneously taking in the explosions of red, white, and blue. (☎800-520-5544. Shows daily 4:40, 7:10pm. $44, ages 4-11 $24. AAA discounts available.) Big-name country acts, such as Loretta Lynn and Billy Ray Cyrus, play the **Grand Palace,** 2700 W. Rte. 76. (☎336-1220 or 800-884-4536. Feb.-Dec. $35-50, children $12-15.) One of Branson's more unique shows is **The Shepherd of the Hills,** on Rte. 76 W, an outdoor drama/dinner that tells the story of a preacher stranded in the Ozark mountains and his growing relationship with the simple people of the area. (☎334-4191 or 800-653-6288. M-Sa Apr.-Oct. $26, under 17 $13. Price includes dinner, show, and tour of complex and its viewing tower.)

Competition is fierce among accommodations, and consumers win out most of the time. Motels along Rte. 76 generally start around $25, but prices often increase from July to September. Less tacky inexpensive motels line Rte. 265, 4 mi. west of the strip, and Gretna Rd. at the west end of the strip. **Budget Inn ❶,** 315 N. Gretna Rd., has slightly dim but spacious rooms close to the action. (☎334-0292. A/C, free local calls, cable TV, and pool access. Rooms from $25.) For a more colorful option, **JR's Motor Inn ❷,** 1944 W. 76 Country Blvd., has an on-site coffeeshop, free continental breakfast, and pool. (☎800-837-8531. Rates from $48-59.) **Indian Point ❶,** at the end of Indian Point Rd., south of Rte. 76 and west of town, has lakeside sites with swimming and a boat launch. (☎338-2121 or 888-444-6777. Reception daily 9am-7pm. Sites $12, powered $16.)

For small-town, affordable eats, head downtown to the **Branson Cafe ❶,** 120 W. Main. Burger and fries are only $4.45, and breakfast and homestyle lunch platters will set you back about $8. (☎334-3021.Open M-Sa 5:30am-8:00pm.) **Uncle Joe's Barbeque ❷,** 2819 W. Hwy. 76, right next to Uncle Joe's Jazz, serves BBQ sandwiches for $6 and tenderloin for $7. (☎334-4548. Jazz nightly. Open M-Su 11am-10pm.)

JUST A BUNCH OF JUNKIES

Every year, junkaholics flock to Searcy County during the first weekend of August for "The Largest Yard Sale West of the Mississippi." Located approximately 70 mi. south of Branson on Hwy. 65, this celebration began just 10 years ago when local residents of Marshall, AR wanted to see if there was enough interest to sustain a community-wide yard sale. To their delight, it turns out that everybody loves junk, and the festival just keeps getting bigger.

Arrive at 5pm Friday, the official opening time, to see the first of the hundreds of yard sales get set up as thousands of shoppers descend upon the area. Saturday is the main day of the 'Fest and yard sales go from sun-up to late afternoon. Kettle corn and lots of homemade treats are plentiful for non-junkies looking to take in the scene.

For more information, contact the Searcy County Chamber of Commerce at ☎870-448-5788; www.searcycountychamber.com.

Branson is impossible without a car, but infuriating with one. Especially on weekends, endless traffic jams clog Hwy. 76, the two-lane road that runs by all the attractions. Avoid peak tourist times, like Saturday nights. **Jefferson Shuttle,** 155 Industrial Park Dr. (☎339-2550), in Hollister, across the river from Branson, behind Lowe's Home Improvement Center, runs once daily to Kansas City ($39) via Springfield, MO ($11). Branson's low-season runs from January to March, when many attractions close. Beware of fake "tourist information centers"—they are trying to sell you something. The real info center is the **Branson Chamber of Commerce and Convention and Visitors Bureau Welcome Center,** 269 Rte. 248, west of the Rte. 248/65 junction. (☎334-4139 or 800-961-1221; www.explorebranson.com. Open M-Sa 8am-5pm, Su 10am-4pm; extended hours in summer.) **Area Code:** 417.

OKLAHOMA

Oklahoma is a state that remembers its distinctive, though not always glamorous, history. Originally dubbed "Indian Territory," Oklahoma was the designated relocation area for the "Five Civilized Tribes" traveling the Trail of Tears. In 1889, the tribes were forced onto reservations even farther west when Oklahoma was opened up to white settlers known as Sooners. Today, Oklahoma celebrates its Indian heritage through museums, artwork, and cultural events. Also a state rich in African-American heritage, Oklahoma played a substantial role in the Civil War. Present day Oklahoma City mourns its losses from the second worst terrorist attack on American soil and honors the victims with a striking national memorial.

PRACTICAL INFORMATION

Capital: Oklahoma City.

Visitor Info: Oklahoma Tourism and Recreation Department, 15 N. Robinson Ave., #801, Oklahoma City 73152 (☎405-2406 or 800-652-6552; www.travelok.com), in the Concord Bldg. at Sheridan St. Open M-F 8am-5pm.

Postal Abbreviation: OK. **Sales Tax:** 4.5%. **Tolls:** Oklahoma is fond of toll-booths, so keep a wad of bills (and a roll of coins for unattended booths) handy.

TULSA ☎918

Though Tulsa is not Oklahoma's political capital, it is in many ways the center of the state. First settled by Creek Native Americans arriving on the Trail of Tears, Tulsa's location on the banks of the Arkansas River made it a logical trading outpost. Contemporary Tulsa's Art Deco skyscrapers, French villas, Georgian mansions, and distinctively large Native American population reflect its varied heritage. Rough-riding motorcyclists and slick oilmen, seeking the good life on the Great Plains, have recently joined the city's cultural mélange.

ORIENTATION & PRACTICAL INFORMATION. Tulsa is divided neatly into 1 sq. mi. quadrants. Downtown surrounds the intersection of **Main Street** (north-south) and **Admiral Boulevard** (east-west). Numbered streets lie in ascending order north or south from Admiral. Named streets run north-south in alphabetical order; those named after western cities are west of Main St., while eastern cities lie to the east. **Tulsa International Airport** (☎838-5000; www.tulsaairports.com), just northeast of downtown, is accessible by I-244 or U.S. 169. **Greyhound,** 317 S. Detroit

Ave. (☎584-4428; open 24hr.), departs to: Dallas (5-7hr., 8 per day, $39-52); Kansas City (5hr., 3 per day, $51-56); Oklahoma City (2hr., 7 per day, $17-18); St. Louis (9-11 hr., 6 per day, $49-80). **Metropolitan Tulsa Transit Authority,** 510 S. Rockford Ave., runs local buses. (☎582-2100. Call center open M-Sa 4:30am-9pm, Su 9am-5pm. Buses operate daily 5am-12:30am. $1.25, seniors and disabled $0.60, under 5 free; transfers $0.05.) **Taxi: Yellow Checker Cab,** ☎582-6161. **Medical Services: Hillcrest Medical Center,** 1120 S. Utica Ave. (☎579-1000). **Center for Women's Health** (☎749-4444), located within Hillcrest. **Visitor Info: Tulsa Convention and Visitors Bureau:** Williams Center Tower Two, 2 W. 2nd St., #150. (☎585-1201 or 800-558-3311; www.visittulsa.com. Open M-F 8am-5pm.) **Internet Access: Tulsa Public Library,** 400 Civic Center, at 4th and Denver. (☎596-7977. Open June-Aug. M-Th 9am-9pm, F-Sa 9am-5pm, Sept.-Apr. also Su 1-5pm.) **Post Office:** 333 W. 4th St. (☎732-6651. Open M-F 7:30am-5pm.) **Postal Code:** 74103. **Area Code:** 918.

ACCOMMODATIONS. Decent budget accommodations are scarce downtown. Close to downtown, the **Victorian Inn ❷,** 114 E. Skelly Dr., offers rooms with free local calls, cable TV, fridge, and whirlpool. (☎743-2009. Check-out 11am. Singles $38; doubles $42.) Members of the fairer sex need not apply at the best deal in town—the **male only YMCA ❶,** 515 S. Denver Ave. (☎583-6201. Pool, track, weight rooms, and racquetball courts. Deposit $20. Rooms $20 per day.) Visitors can also try the budget motels around the junction of **I-44** and **I-244** (Exit 222 off I-44); take bus #17 "Southwest Blvd." **Georgetown Plaza Motel ❶,** 8502 E. 27th St., off I-44 at 31st and Memorial St., rents clean, frayed rooms with free local calls and cable TV. (☎622-6616. Singles $28-31; doubles $34.) The **Gateway Motor Hotel ❷,** 5600 W. Skelly Dr., at Exit 222C, may have dated pea-green decor but has an inviting personality and, better yet, extremely cheap rooms. (☎446-6611. Singles $28-35; doubles $34.) The 250-site **Mingo RV Park ❶,** 801 N. Mingo Rd., at I-244 and Mingo Rd., provides laundry and showers in a semi-urban setting. (☎832-8824 or 800-932-8824. Reception daily 8am-7pm. Full hookup $25.)

FOOD & NIGHTLIFE. Most downtown restaurants cater to lunching businesspeople, closing at 2pm on weekdays and altogether on weekends. **Nelson's Buffeteria ❶,** 514 S. Boston Ave., is an old-fashioned diner that has served its blue plate special (2 scrambled eggs, hash browns, biscuit and gravy; $3) and famous chicken-fried steak ($6) since 1929. (☎584-9969. Open M-F 6am-2pm.) After lunch, S. Peoria Ave. is the place to go. Located in a converted movie theater, **The Brook Restaurant ❷,** 3401 S. Peoria, has classic Art Deco appeal. A traditional menu of chicken, burgers, and salads ($6-8) is complemented by an extensive list of signature martinis for $4.50-5.25. (☎748-9977. Open M-Sa 11am-1am, Su 11am-11pm.) For really extended hours, try **Mama Lou's Restaurant ❶,** 5688 W. Skelly Dr. Mama serves breakfast all day, the most popular dish being the #1—2 eggs, 4 bacon strips, 4 sausage links, 2 biscuits, and fruit for $4.35. (☎445-1700. Open 24hr.)

Read the free *Urban Tulsa,* at local restaurants, and *The Spot* in the Friday *Tulsa World* for up-to-date specs on arts and entertainment. Good bars line an area known as **Brookside,** in the 3000s along S. Peoria Ave., and 15th St. east of Peoria. At the **Suede Lounge,** 3340 S. Peoria Ave., a 23+ martini lounge/champagne bar, imbibe your lip-smacking libation while watching beautiful people dance to a combination of live music and canned tunes. (☎744-0896. Cover $0-10. Open Tu-Sa 7pm-2am.) A true Tulsan-style sports bar and grill, **Boston's,** 1738 Boston Ave., serves up everything from chips and salsa ($3) to chicken fried steak ($8), accompanied by eclectic tunes. On Tuesdays enjoy "Red Dirt" music, a distinctive Oklahoman sound. (☎583-9520. Cover $5. Open M-F 11am-2am.)

SIGHTS & ENTERTAINMENT. Perched atop an Osage foothill 2 mi. northwest of downtown, the **Thomas Gilcrease Museum,** 1400 Gilcrease Museum Rd., houses the world's largest collection of Western American art, as well as 250,000 Native American artifacts. Take the Gilcrease Exit off Rte. 412 or bus #47. (☎596-2700 or 888-655-2278; www.gilcrease.org. Open Tu-Su 10am-4pm. $3 requested donation.) The **Philbrook Museum of Art,** 2727 S. Rockford Rd., presents international art alongside remnants of the oil-rich Oklahoma of the 1920s in a renovated 23-acre Italian Renaissance villa, complete with a grassy sculpture garden. Bus #5 "Peoria."(☎749-7941 or 800-324-7941; www.philbrook.org. Open Tu-W and F-Sa 10am-5pm, Th 10am-8pm, Su 11am-5pm. $5, students and seniors $3, under 13 free.) The ultra-modern, gold-mirrored architecture of **Oral Roberts University,** 7777 S. Lewis Ave., rises out of an Oklahoma plain about 6 mi. south of downtown between Lewis and Harvard Ave.; take bus #12. In 1964, Oral had a dream in which God commanded him to "Build Me a University," and thus Tulsa's biggest tourist attraction was born. The **Visitors Center,** in the Prayer Tower, has free tours. (☎495-6807; www.oru.edu. Open June-Aug. M-Sa 9am-5pm, Su 1-5pm; Sept.-May M-Sa 10am-4:30pm, Su 1-4:30pm.)

Tulsa thrives during the **International Mayfest** (☎582-6435) in mid-May. August brings both **Jazz on Greenwood,** which includes ceremonies and concerts at Greenwood Park, 300 N. Greenwood Dr., as well as the **Intertribal Powwow,** at the Tulsa Fairgrounds Pavilion (Expo Sq.), which attracts Native Americans and thousands of onlookers for a 3-day festival of food, crafts, and nightly dance contests. (☎744-1113. $5; families $16.)

NEAR TULSA: TAHLEQUAH

The Cherokees, suffering from the loss of nearly one-quarter of their population along the Trail of Tears, began anew by placing their capital in Tahlequah, 66 mi. southeast of Tulsa on Rte. 51. In the center of town, on Cherokee Sq., stands the capitol building of the **Cherokee Nation,** 101 S. Muskogee Ave. (Rte. 51/62/82). Built in 1870, the building, along with other tribal government buildings like the Supreme Court building and the Cherokee National Prison, formed the highest authority in Oklahoma until the state was admitted to the Union in 1907.

The **Cherokee Heritage Center,** 4 mi. south of town on Rte. 82, reminds visitors of the injustice perpetrated against Native Americans. In the Center's **Ancient Village,** local Cherokees recreate a 16th-century settlement with ongoing demonstrations of skills like bow-making and basket-weaving. Next door, the well-executed **Cherokee National Museum** presents a wealth of information on the Trail of Tears using artifacts and personal histories. (☎456-6007 or 888-999-6007; www.cherokeeheritage.org. Village and Museum open May-Oct. daily 10am-5pm; Feb.-Apr. M-Sa 10am-5pm; Nov.-Dec. M-Sa 10am-5pm, Su 1-5pm. $8.50, under 13 $4.25. 10% AAA discount.) Across from the northeast corner of Cherokee Sq., the **Visitors Center,** 123 E. Delaware St., offers free maps of the major sites downtown. (☎456-3742. Open M-F 9am-5pm.)

OKLAHOMA CITY ☎405

In the late 1800s, Oklahoma's capitol was a major transit point on cattle drives from Texas to the north, and today its stockyards are a fascinating window into a world not often seen by outsiders. Lying along the Santa Fe Railroad, the city was swarmed by over 100,000 homesteaders when Oklahoma was opened to settlement in 1889, and it continues to celebrate American Westward expansion at one of the nation's largest museums devoted to the West. A shadow looms over the city, though—the psychic by-product of the national memorial commemorating the victims of the 1995 Federal Building bombing.

ORIENTATION & PRACTICAL INFORMATION Oklahoma City is constructed as a nearly perfect grid. **Santa Fe Avenue** divides the city east-west, and **Reno Avenue** slices it north-south. Cheap and plentiful parking makes driving the best way to go. **Will Rogers World Airport** (☎680-3200; www.flyokc.com), is on I-44 southwest of downtown, Exit 116B. **Amtrak** has an unattended station at 100 S. E.K. Gaylord Blvd., and rumbles to Fort Worth (4½ hr., 1 per day, $23-38). To get to the **Greyhound** station, 427 W. Sheridan Ave. (☎235-4083; open 24hr.), at Walker St., take city bus #4, 5, 6, 8, or 10. *Be careful at night; the area is unsafe.* Buses run to: Fort Worth (4-8 hr., 5-9 per day, $38-40); Kansas City, MO (6-9hr., 6 per day, $72-77); Tulsa (2hr., 7 per day, $17). **Oklahoma Metro Transit** has bus service; all routes radiate from the station at 200 N. Shartel St. Their office, 300 SW 7th St., distributes free schedules. (☎235-7433. Open M-F 8am-5pm. Buses run M-Sa 6am-7:30pm. $1.25, seniors and ages 6-17 $0.60.) Look for the **Oklahoma Spirit** trolley ($0.25) downtown and in Bricktown. **Taxi: Yellow Cab,** ☎232-6161. The **Oklahoma City Convention and Visitors Bureau,** 189 W. Sheridan Ave., at Robinson St., has city info. (☎297-8912 or 800-225-5652; www.okccvb.org. Open M-F 8:30am-5pm.) **Internet Access: Oklahoma City Public Library,** 131 Dean McGee Ave. (☎231-8650. Open M and W-F 9am-6pm, Tu 9am-9pm, Sa 9am-5pm.) **Post Office:** 305 NW 5th St. (☎800-275-8777. Open M-F 7am-9pm, Sa 8am-5pm.) **Postal Code:** 73102. **Area Code:** 405.

ACCOMMODATIONS. Ten minutes from downtown and 5min. from a huge mall and plenty of eateries, **Flora's Bed and Breakfast ❸,** 2312 NW 46th St., has two traditional rooms available. (☎840-3157. Doubles $70.) Other cheap lodging lies along the interstate highways, particularly on I-35 north of the I-44 junction. **The Royal Inn ❷,** 2800 S. I-35, south of the junction with I-40, treats you to modest rooms and free local calls. (☎672-0899. Singles $35; doubles $45.) Behind a strip mall, the 172 sites of **Abe's RV Park ❶,** 12115 I-35 Service Rd., have a pool, laundry, and showers. Take southbound Frontage Rd. off Exit 137; it's ¼ mi. to the red and white "RV" sign. (☎478-0278. Open daily summer 8am-8pm; low-season 8am-6pm. Sites $23.) A more scenic option, **Lake Thunderbird State Park ❶** offers campsites near a beautiful lake fit for swimming and fishing. Take I-40 east to Choctaw Rd. (Exit 166), go south 10 mi. until the road ends, then make a left, and drive another mile. (☎360-3572. Showers available. Office open M-F 8am-5pm, with a host for late or weekend arrivals. Sites $8-10; with water and electricity $16-$23; huts $45.)

FOOD & NIGHTLIFE. Oklahoma City contains the largest cattle market in the US, and beef tops most menus. Most downtown eateries close early in the afternoon after they've served business lunchers. Restaurants with longer hours lie east of town on Sheridan Ave. in the Bricktown district and north of downtown along Classen Blvd. and Western Ave. Asian restaurants congregate around the intersection of Classen and NW 23rd St. **Pho Pasteur ❷,** 2800 N. Classen Blvd., #108, has Vietnamese and Chinese food in a classy setting. (☎524-2233. Beef noodle soups $5. Chicken noodle $5. Open daily 9am-9pm.) Everyone's fighting for the rights to the late Leo's recipes at **Leo's Original BBQ ❶,** 3631 N. Kelley St., a classic hickory-smoking outfit in the northwest reaches of town. (☎424-5367. Beef sandwich and baked potato $4.20. Open M-Sa 11am-9pm.)

OKC nightlife is growing by leaps and bounds—head to Bricktown to get into the thick of it all. **The Bricktown Brewery,** 1 N. Oklahoma St., at Sheridan Ave., brews five beers daily. (☎232-2739. Live music Tu and F-Sa 9pm. Upstairs 21+. Cover $5-15 during live music. Open Su-M 11am-10pm, Tu-Th 11am-midnight, F-Sa 11am-1:30am.) **City Walk,** 70 N. Oklahoma, houses seven theme clubs under one roof. Enjoy the tropical Tequila Park, line dance inside the City Limits, or sing along at Stooge's piano bar. (☎232-9255. Cover $5-8. Open Th-Sa 8pm-2am.)

SIGHTS & ENTERTAINMENT. Monday morning is the time to visit the **Oklahoma City Stockyards,** 2500 Exchange Ave. (☎235-8675), the busiest in the world. Take bus #12 from the terminal to Agnew and Exchange Ave. Cattle auctions (M-Tu) begin at 8am and may last into the night. Visitors enter free of charge via a catwalk that soars over cow pens and cattle herds from the parking lot northeast of the auction house. The auction is as Old West as it gets; beware of tight jeans and big hair.

Plant lovers should make a bee-line for **Myriad Gardens,** 301 W. Reno Ave., with 17 acres of vegetation ranging from desert to rainforest. Or cross the **Crystal Bridge,** a 70 ft. diameter glass cylinder, perched over a tropical ravine. (☎297-3995. Gardens: Open daily 7am-11pm. Free. Crystal Bridge: Open M-Sa 9am-6pm, Su noon-6pm. $5, students and seniors $4, ages 4-12 $3.) The **National Cowboy and Western Heritage Museum,** 1700 NE 63rd St., the city's most popular tourist attraction, features an extensive collection of Western art and exhibits on rodeo, Native Americans, and frontier towns. (☎478-2250; www.nationalcowboymuseum.org. Open daily 9am-5pm. $8.50, seniors $7, ages 6-12 $4, under 6 free.)

The **Oklahoma City National Memorial,** at 5th and Harvey St. downtown, is a haunting remembrance to the victims of the 1995 bombing of the Murrah Federal Building. Outside lies the Field of Empty Chairs (one for each of the 168 victims), a stone gate, and a reflecting pool. This is especially powerful at night when each chair is lit. Indoors, a museum tells the story of the bombing through photographs, videos, and testimonials. (☎235-3313. Museum open M-Sa 9am-6pm, Su 1-6pm. $7, seniors $6, students $5, under 6 free.) Oklahoma City hosts the **Red Earth Festival** (☎427-5228; June 4-6, 2004), the country's largest celebration of Native American culture. Early summer 2004 will also find the 19th annual **Charlie Christian Jazz Festival** entertaining music lovers. (Call the Black Liberated Arts Center, Inc., ☎424-2552, for more info.) The **Cox Business Convention Center** (☎236-8666) hosts art fairs and dance competitions. Fall visitors should check out the **World Championship Quarter Horse Show** (☎948-6800) in mid-November.

TEXAS

Covering an area as long as the stretch from North Carolina to Key West, Texas has more the brawn of a country than a state. The fervently proud, independent citizens of the "Lone Star State" seem to prefer it that way: where else do you see "Don't Mess With Texas" on official road signs and "No firearms allowed" at restaurants and museums? After revolting against the Spanish in 1821 and splitting from Mexico in 1836, the Republic of Texas stood alone until 1845, when it entered the Union as the 28th state. The state's unofficial motto proclaims that "everything is bigger in Texas." This truth is evident in prolific wide-brimmed hats, styled and sculpted ladies' coifs, boat-sized American autos, giant ranch spreads, countless steel skyscrapers, and oil refineries the size of small towns.

HIGHLIGHTS OF TEXAS

FOOD. Drippin' barbecue and colossal steaks reign supreme in the state where beef is king and vegetables are for the cows. Some of the best beef awaits in Dallas (p. 695) and Amarillo (p. 710).

SAN ANTONIO. Remember the Alamo! A city rich with Spanish heritage (p. 710).

RODEOS/COWBOYS. The ol' West lives on in Fort Worth (p. 701) and at the Mesquite Rodeo in Dallas (p. 700), with the finest rope-riders in the land.

PRACTICAL INFORMATION

Capital: Austin.

Visitor Info: Texas Transportation Information Centers, ☎800-452-9292. For a free guidebook, call **Texas Tourism** ☎800-888-8839; www.traveltex.com. **Texas Parks and Wildlife Department,** Austin Headquarters Complex, 4200 Smith School Rd., Austin 78744 (☎512-389-4800 or 800-792-1112).

Postal Abbreviation: TX. **Sales Tax:** 6-8.25%.

SAN ANTONIO ☎210

Though best known as the home of the Alamo—the symbol of Texas' break from Mexico—San Antonio today is more defined by its integration of Anglo and Hispanic cultures. Using this cultural amalgamation to its economic advantage, San Antonio annually attracts 8 million tourists with a variety of sights and offerings. The region's early Spanish influence can be seen in missions originally built to convert Indians to Catholicism and in La Villita, once a village for the city's original settlers that is now a workshop for local artisans. Mexican culture is on display in Market Square, where mariachi bands entertain weekend revelers. Visit one of San Antonio's galleries for exquisite displays of Southwestern art. The blend of diverse cultures comes together in the eateries and shops of the vibrant Riverwalk.

TRANSPORTATION

Airport: San Antonio International Airport, 9800 Airport Blvd. (☎207-3411; www.sanantonio.gov/airport), north of town. Accessible by I-410 and U.S. 281. Bus #2 ("Airport") connects the airport to downtown at Market and Alamo. Taxi to downtown $14-16.

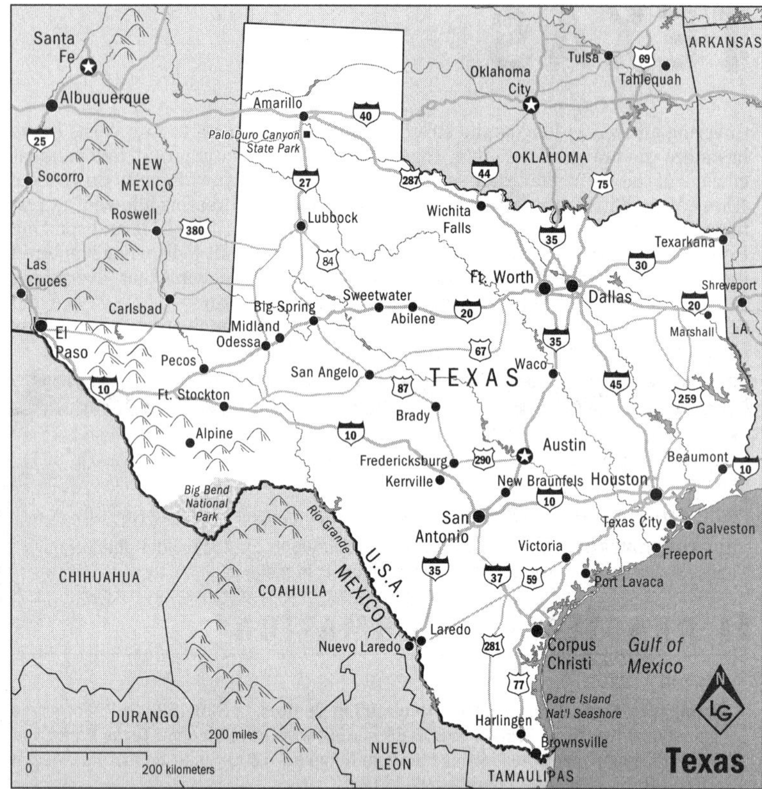

Trains: Amtrak, 350 Hoefgen St. (☎223-3226), facing the northern side of the Alamodome. To: **Dallas** (9hr., 1 per day, $25); **Houston** (5hr., 3 per week, $26); and **Los Angeles** (29hr., 3 per week, $110). Open daily 11am-10:30pm.

Buses: Greyhound, 500 N. Saint Mary's St. (☎270-5824). To **Dallas** (5-7hr., 19 per day, $31) and **Houston** (3-4hr., 15 per day, $22). Open 24hr.

Public Transit: VIA Metropolitan Transit, 1021 San Pedro (☎362-2020). Buses operate daily 5am-midnight; many routes stop at 6pm. Infrequent service to outlying areas. $0.80, transfers $0.15. 1-day passes $2, available at 260 E. Houston St.

Taxi: Yellow Checker Cab, ☎226-4242.

PRACTICAL INFORMATION

Visitor Info: 317 Alamo Plaza (☎207-6748; www.sanantoniocvb.com), downtown across from the Alamo. Open daily 8:30am-6pm. Free maps and brochures.

Hotlines: Rape Crisis, ☎349-7273. Operates 24hr. **Supportive Services for the Elderly and Disabled,** ☎337-3550. Referrals and transportation.

Medical Services: Metropolitan Methodist Hospital, 1310 McCullough Ave. (☎208-2200).

Internet Access: San Antonio Public Library, 600 Soledad St. (☎207-2534). Open M-Th 9am-9pm, F-Sa 9am-5pm, Su 11am-5pm.

Post Office: 615 E. Houston St. (☎800-275-8777), 1 block from the Alamo. Open M-F 9am-5pm. **Postal Code:** 78205. **Area Code:** 210.

ACCOMMODATIONS

For cheap motels, try **Roosevelt Avenue,** a southern extension of Saint Mary's St., and **Fredericksburg Road.** Inexpensive motels also line **Broadway** between downtown and Brackenridge Park. Drivers should follow **I-35 North** or the **Austin Highway** to find cheaper and often safer lodging within a 15 mi. radius of town.

Bullis House Inn San Antonio International Hostel (HI-AYH), 621 Pierce St. (☎223-9426), 2 mi. north of downtown on Broadway, right on Grayson. From the bus station, walk to Navarro St. and take bus #11 or 15 to Grayson and New Braunfels; walk 2 blocks west. Located next door to Fort Sam Houston on Government Hill, this spacious, ranch-style hostel includes a pool, kitchen, and Internet access. Fills quickly in summer. Breakfast $5. Linen $2. Key deposit $10. Reception daily 8am-10pm. No curfew. Dorms $20, nonmembers $23. For a slightly more upscale option, Bullis' main house has been renovated into a B&B, with each room including cable and a queen bed or larger. Without breakfast, rooms range from $51-81; homefries with that? $59-89. ❶/❸

Capri Motel, 1718 Roosevelt Ave. (☎533-2583), about 2 mi. south of downtown along the mission trail. Somewhat dated, but clean rooms. HBO. Singles $40; doubles $50. ❷

Alamo KOA, 602 Gembler Rd. (☎224-9296 or 800-562-7783), 6 mi. from downtown. Take bus #24 "Industrial Park" from the corner of Houston and Alamo downtown. From I-10 E, take Exit 580/W.W. White Rd., drive 2 blocks north, then take a left onto Gembler Rd. Well-kept grounds with lots of shade. Most sites include grill and patio. Showers, laundry facilities, pool, hot tub, and free movies. Reception daily 7:30am-9:30pm. Sites $28, full hookup $31; each additional person $4. ❶

TEXAS

FOOD

Expensive cafes and restaurants surround the **Riverwalk.** North of town, Asian restaurants open onto **Broadway** across from Brackenridge. On weekends, hundreds of carnival food booths crowd the walkways of **Market Square.** If you come late in the day, prices drop and vendors are willing to haggle. (☎207-8600. Open daily June-Aug. 10am-8pm; Sept.-May 10am-6pm.) The Texas original, **Pig Stand** diners offer cheap, decent grub in multiple locations; the branches at 801 S. Presa, off S. Alamo, and 1508 Broadway (both near downtown) stay open 24hr.

Mi Tierra, 218 Produce Row (☎225-1262), in Market Sq. Perpetually smiling mariachi musicians serenade patrons. Try the Puebla plate which includes a quarter of a chicken smothered in mole poblano, with rice and beans ($10). Lunch specials $6. Grab dessert on the run from the bakery. Jumbo pineapple biscuits $0.75. Open 24hr. ❷

Madhatters, 320 Beauregard St. (☎212-4832). Located in the lovely King William area of downtown, Madhatters provides the best tea this side of the rabbit hole. Serving 60 exotic hot teas, $4 breakfasts, and $5 lunches on cleverly shabby chic china, there's no need to ask Alice—this place is an adventure everyone should experience. Open M-F 7am-9pm, Sa 9am-9pm, Su 9am-4pm.❶

Rosario's, 910 S. Alamo St. (☎223-1806), at S. Saint Mary's St. Mexican cafe and cantina offers classic Tex-Mex cuisine with several vegetarian options. Lunch draws a business crowd, but evenings are more laidback with live music F-Sa nights. Open M 11am-3pm, Tu-Th 11am-10pm, F 11am-1:30am, Sa 11am-11pm. ❷

Liberty Bar, 328 E. Josephine St (☎227-1187). A friendly local hangout with daily specials and sandwich plates ($6-9). Try the Karkade (iced hibiscus and mint tea with fresh ginger and white grape juice). Open M-Th 11am-10:30pm, F-Sa 11am-midnight, Su 10:30am-10:30pm. ❷

Josephine St. Steaks/Whiskey, 400 Josephine St. (☎224-6169). At Hwy. 281 and Josephine St., rough hewn home cookin' is the daily special. Try the chicken fried steak sandwich ($8), or the popular T-bone, ($12). Lunch specials ($5-8) include an entree served with a garden salad and 1 side. Open M-Th 11am-10pm, F-Sa 11am-11pm. ❸

G/M Steakhouse, 211 Alamo Pl. (☎223-1523). Grab a cheap 'n greasy breakfast here (2 eggs with bacon and a biscuit $3) before hitting the sights, or drop in for lunch (burger and fries $3). Open M-F 7am-10:30pm, Sa-Su 7am-11pm. ❶

SIGHTS

Much of historic San Antonio lies in the present-day downtown and surrounding areas. The city may seem diffuse, but almost every major site or park is within a few miles of downtown and accessible by public transportation.

DOWNTOWN

THE ALAMO. Built as a Spanish mission during the colonization of the New World, **The Alamo** has come to signify the bravery of those who fought for Texas' independence and to serve as a touchstone of Lone Star pride. For 12 days in 1836, Texan defenders of the Alamo, outnumbered 20 to 1, held their ground against Mexican attackers. The morning of the 13th day saw the end of the defiant stand as the strains of the infamous *deguello* were heard. (Literally "throat-cutting" in Spanish, the *deguello* is military music that had come to signify annihilation of the enemy in Mexican history.) All 189 men were killed. The massacre served to unite Texans behind the independence movement, and "Remember the Alamo!" became the rallying cry for Sam Houston's ultimately victorious forces. After languishing for decades (including use as an arms depot during the Civil War), the site is presently under the care of the Daughters of the Republic of Texas and the locus of the city's downtown. *(At the center of Alamo Plaza near Houston and Alamo St. ☎225-1391; www.thealamo.org. Open M-Sa 9am-5:30pm, Su 10am-5pm. Free.)*

TEXAS

OTHER MISSIONS. The San Antonio Missions National Historical Park *(www.nps.gov/saan)* preserves the five missions along the river that once formed the soul of San Antonio. To reach the missions, follow the brown and white "Mission Trail" signs beginning on S. Saint Mary's St. downtown. **Mission San José** (a.k.a. the "Queen of the Missions") has remnants of its own irrigation system, a gorgeous sculpted rose window, and numerous restored buildings. **Mission Concepción** is the oldest unrestored stone church in North America, and traces of the once-colorful frescoes are still visible. **Mission San Juan Capistrano** and **Mission San Francisco de la Espada,** smaller and simpler than the others, evoke the isolation of such outposts. Between them lies the Espada Aqueduct, the only remaining waterway built by the Spanish. *(Bus #42 stops within walking distance of Mission Concepción and right in front of Mission San José. The main Visitors Center is located at Mission San José. ☎534-8833 for info on all missions. San José: 6701 San José Dr., off Roosevelt Ave. ☎922-0543. 4 Catholic masses held each Su 7:45, 9, 10:30am, and a noon "Mariachi Mass." Concepción: 807 Mission Rd., 4 mi. south of the Alamo off E. Mitchell St. ☎534-1540. San Juan: 9101 Graf St. ☎534-0749. San Francisco: 10040 Espada Rd. ☎627-2021. All missions open daily 9am-5pm. Free.)*

SECULAR SAN ANTONIO

DISTRICTS. Southwest of the Alamo, black signs indicate access points to the 2½ mi. **Paseo del Río (Riverwalk),** a series of shaded stone pathways that follow a winding canal built by the WPA in the 1930s. Lined with picturesque gardens, shops, and cafes, the Riverwalk connects most of the major downtown sights and is the

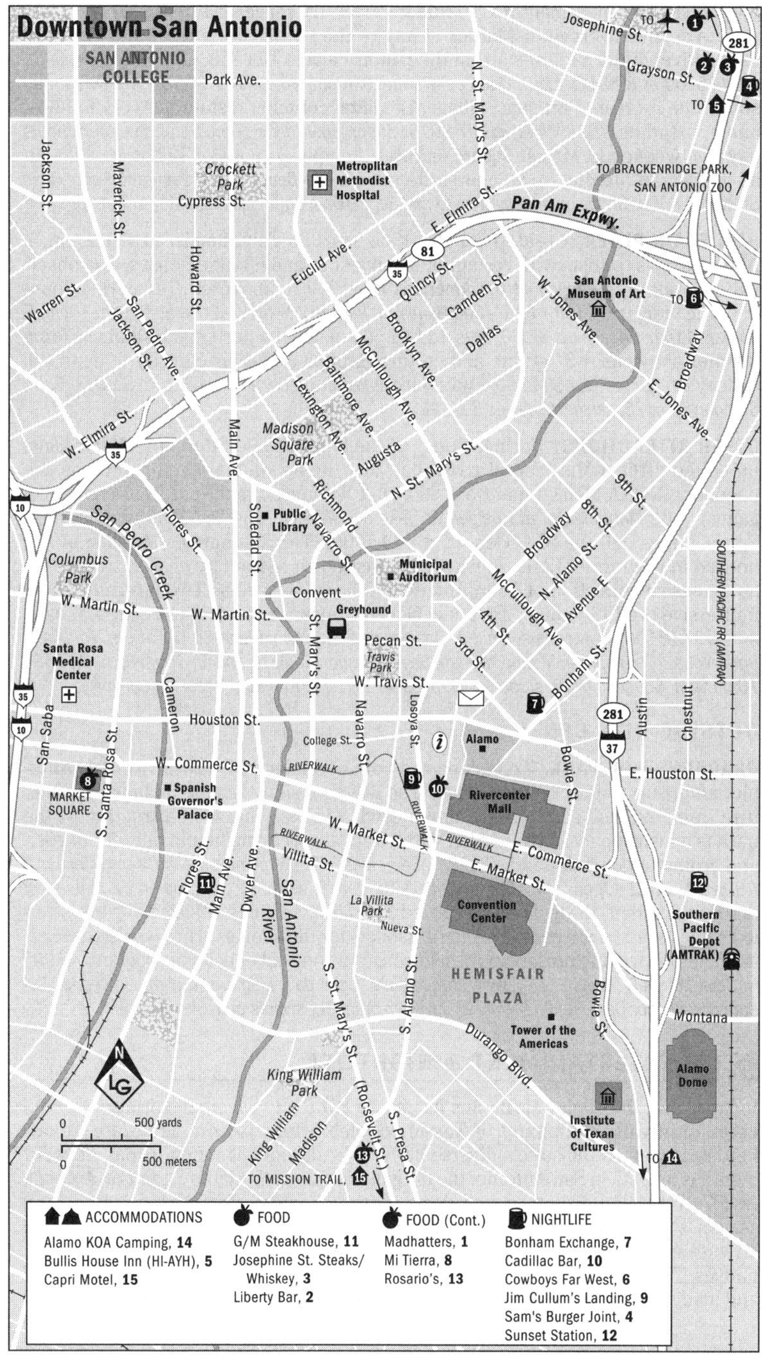
Downtown San Antonio
SAN ANTONIO COLLEGE
Park Ave.
Josephine St.
Grayson St.
TO BRACKENRIDGE PARK, SAN ANTONIO ZOO
N. St. Mary's St.
Crockett Park
Cypress St.
Metroplitan Methodist Hospital
Jackson St.
Maverick St.
Howard St.
E. Elmira St.
Pan Am Expwy.
Euclid Ave.
Quincy St.
Camden St.
W. Jones Ave.
San Antonio Museum of Art
Warren St.
San Pedro Ave.
Jackson St.
Brooklyn Ave.
Dallas
McCullough Ave.
Baltimore Ave.
Lexington Ave.
Broadway
E. Jones Ave.
W. Elmira St.
Main Ave.
Madison Square Park
Augusta
N. St. Mary's St.
9th St.
8th St.
Richmond
Flores St.
San Pedro Creek
Public Library
Soledad St.
Navarro St.
Broadway
N. Alamo St.
Municipal Auditorium
Columbus Park
Convent
McCullough Ave.
Avenue E
W. Martin St.
W. Martin St.
Greyhound
4th St.
Santa Rosa Medical Center
St. Mary's St.
Pecan St.
3rd St.
Travis Park
Bonham St.
W. Travis St.
SOUTHERN PACIFIC RR (AMTRAK)
Cameron
Houston St.
Losoya St.
Austin
Chestnut
San Saba
S. Santa Rosa St.
College St.
Alamo
Bowie St.
W. Commerce St.
RIVERWALK
Navarro St.
E. Houston St.
MARKET SQUARE
Spanish Governor's Palace
Rivercenter Mall
RIVERWALK
W. Market St.
RIVERWALK
RIVERWALK
E. Commerce St.
Villita St.
E. Market St.
Flores St.
Main Ave.
Dwyer Ave.
San Antonio River
La Villita Park
Convention Center
Nueva St.
Southern Pacific Depot (AMTRAK)
S. St. Mary's St.
S. Alamo St.
HEMISFAIR PLAZA
Bowie St.
Montana
Tower of the Americas
Durango Blvd.
Alamo Dome
King William Park
Institute of Texan Cultures
King William
Madison
(Roosevelt St.)
S. Presa St.
0 500 yards
0 500 meters
TO MISSION TRAIL
ACCOMMODATIONS
Alamo KOA Camping, 14
Bullis House Inn (HI-AYH), 5
Capri Motel, 15
FOOD
G/M Steakhouse, 11
Josephine St. Steaks/Whiskey, 3
Liberty Bar, 2
FOOD (Cont.)
Madhatters, 1
Mi Tierra, 8
Rosario's, 13
NIGHTLIFE
Bonham Exchange, 7
Cadillac Bar, 10
Cowboys Far West, 6
Jim Cullum's Landing, 9
Sam's Burger Joint, 4
Sunset Station, 12

hub of San Antonio's nightlife. To ride the river, try **Yanaguana Cruise Services.** Buy tickets at the Rivercenter Mall or at any of the hotels along the walk; board at either Rivercenter or across from the Hilton Palacio Del Rio. *(315 E. Commerce St. ☎244-5700 or 800-417-4139. Open daily 9am-10:30pm. $6, seniors $4.25.)* A few blocks south, the recreated artisans' village, **La Villita,** contains restaurants, craft shops, and art studios. *(418 Villita. ☎207-8610. Shops open daily 10am-6pm; restaurant hours vary.)* On weekends, **Market Square** features the upbeat tunes of Tejano bands with a backbeat of buzzing frozen margarita machines. *(Between San Saba and Santa Rosa St. ☎207-8600. Shops open daily June to mid-Sept. 10am-8pm; mid-Sept.-May 10am-6pm.)*

HEMISFAIR PLAZA. Created for the 1968 World's Fair, **HemisFair Plaza,** on S. Alamo, draws tourists with restaurants, museums, and historic houses. The observation deck of the **Tower of the Americas** rises 750 ft. above the Texas Hill Country—the view is best at night. *(600 HemisFair Park. ☎207-8617. Open Su-Th 9am-10pm, F-Sa 9am-11pm. $4, seniors $2.50, ages 4-11 $1.50.)* Inside the park, the **Institute of Texan Cultures** showcases 27 ethnic and cultural groups and their contributions to the history of Texas. *(☎458-2300; www.texancultures.utsa.edu/public. Open Tu-Sa 9am-5pm, Su noon-5pm. $5, seniors $3, ages 3-12 $2.)*

OTHER ATTRACTIONS. Former home of the San Antonio Spurs, the **Alamodome,** modelled after a Mississippi riverboat, now hosts special events such as the upcoming NCAA Men's Final Four 2008 and Women's Final Four 2010 basketball games. *(100 Montana St., at Hoefgen St. Take bus #24 or 26. ☎207-3600.)* For info on Spurs games call the SBC Center *(☎444-5000)*. The **San Antonio Museum of Art,** housed in the former Lone Star Brewery just north of the city center, showcases an extensive collection of Latin American folk art, as well as Texan furniture and impressive pre-Columbian, Egyptian, Oceanic, Asian, and Islamic art. *(200 W. Jones Ave. ☎978-8100; www.samuseum.org. Open early Sept. to mid-June Su noon-5pm, Tu 10am-9pm, W-Sa 10am-5pm; mid-June to early Sept. Su noon-6pm, Tu and Th 10am-8pm, W, F, Sa 10am-5pm. $6, seniors $5, students $4, ages 4-11 $1.75; Tu 4-8pm free. Free parking.)*

OUTSIDE CITY CENTER

BRACKENRIDGE PARK. To escape the commercialism of downtown San Antonio, amble up to Brackenridge Park. The 343-acre show ground includes a miniature train, extensive bike trails, and a driving range. The main attraction of the park is a lush Japanese tea garden with pathways weaving in and out of a pagoda and around a goldfish pond. *(3910 N. Saint Mary's St., 5 mi. north of the Alamo. Take bus #8. ☎207-3022. Open 24hr. Train runs daily 9:30am-6:30pm. $2.50, children $2.)* Directly across the street, the **San Antonio Zoo** exhibits 3500 creatures, utilizing the area's varied clime to aid create natural seeming habitats for the animals. The zoo also engages in numerous wildlife preservation, field conservation, and education programs. *(3903 N. Saint Mary's St. ☎734-7184; www.sazoo-aq.org. Open daily Memorial Day through Labor Day 9am-6pm; Labor Day through Memorial Day 9am-5pm. $8, seniors and ages 3-11 $6.)*

ENTERTAINMENT & NIGHTLIFE

In late April, the 10-day **Fiesta San Antonio** (☎227-5191) ushers in spring with concerts, carnivals, and plenty of Tex-Mex celebrations to commemorate Texas' heroes as well as the state's diverse cultural landscape. The first Friday of every month is a fiesta in San Antonio: the art galleries along S. Alamo St. put on **Artswalk** (☎207-6748), with free food and drink. For excitement after dark any time, any season, stroll down the Riverwalk. The **Theatre District,** just north of the Riverwalk downtown, puts on concerts, opera, and theater in three restored 1950s movie houses. *The Friday Express* or weekly *Current* (available at the tourist office and many businesses in town) are guides to concerts and entertainment.

Sam's Burger Joint, 330 E. Grayson St. (☎223-2830), hosts the **Puro Poetry Slam** every Tuesday night at 10pm ($2). Sam's also features live music and the "Big Monster Burger," a pound of beef for $7. For authentic **Tejano music**—the bizarre, beautiful, and vaguely polka-sounding child of Mexican and country music traditions—head to the **Cadillac Bar,** 212 S. Flores St., where every weeknight a different band whips the huge crowd (anywhere from 500-1000 people) into a cheering and dancing frenzy. (☎223-5533. 21+. Open M-Sa 11am-2am.) Right around the corner from the Alamo, San Antonio's biggest gay dance club, the **Bonham Exchange,** 411 Bonham St., plays high-energy music with house and techno on the side. Strut your stuff on the sunken dance floor, boogie to top 40 in the video bar, or hustle over to the retro pumping gameroom. A younger, more mixed crowd files in on Wednesdays for college night. (☎271-3811. Three dancefloors, seven bars. Cover up to $5. Open W-Sa 4pm-3am, Su 8pm-3am.) Some of the best traditional jazz anywhere goes down at **Jim Cullum's Landing,** 123 Losoya St., in the Hyatt downtown, including the legendary Cullum and his jazz band and the improv jazz quintet Small World. (☎223-7266. Small World performs al fresco Su nights. Stop by for a cold one after a day on the riverwalk. All ages. Cover $5; Su no cover. Open M-F 4pm-midnight, Sa-Su noon-1am; Cullum band performs M-Th 8pm-midnight, F-Sa 8pm-1am.) **Cowboys Far West,** 3030 Rte. 410 NE, plays two types of music—country and Western. With a mechanical bull and two dance floors, you best bring your ten-gallon hat to enjoy the fun. Can't two-step? Don't worry—every Thursday the evening begins with dance lessons. (☎646-9378. 18+. Cover $3-6. Open Th 7pm-2am, F-8pm-2am, Sa 8pm-3am.) **Sunset Station,** 1174 E. Commerce St. (☎222-9481), across from the Amtrak Station, houses concerts and clubs in a restored train depot.

AUSTIN ☎512

Austin attempts to put the final nails in the coffin of the stereotype of rough-and-tumble cattle ranchers riding horses across the plains. Exhibiting the trendiness of Soho and the funk of Seattle, Austin is a cultural microcosm buried deep in the heart of the Lone Star State. Proud of its panache, Austinites sport a bumper sticker campaign to "Keep Austin Weir." As the "Live Music Capital of the World," and home to 50,000 University of Texas college students, Austin's vibrance radiates from its diverse offerings. From food co-ops to boundless supplies of live music, Austin is a liberal, alternative oasis in a traditional state. Leave your spurs at the city limits and get ready to groove.

TRANSPORTATION

Airport: Austin Bergstrom International, 3600 Presidential Blvd. (☎530-2242; www.ci.austin.tx.us/austinairport). Head east on Cesar Chavez, which terminates at Hwy. 183, 8 mi. from downtown. Take bus #100 (the Airport Flyer) or #350. Taxi to downtown $20-25.

Trains: Amtrak, 250 N. Lamar Blvd. (☎476-5684 or 800-872-7245); take bus #38. Office open daily 7am-9:30pm. To: **Dallas** (8hr., 1 per day, $25-57); **El Paso** (20 hr., 3 per week, $65-151); **San Antonio** (3hr., 1 per day, $10-21)

Buses: Greyhound, 916 E. Koenig Ln. (☎458-4463 or 800-231-2222), several miles north of downtown off I-35. Easily accessible by public transportation; bus #7 and 15 stop across the street and run downtown. Schedules and prices vary. Station open 24hr. To: **Dallas** (3hr., 15 per day, $28); **Houston** (3½hr., 5 per day, $27); and **San Antonio** (2hr., 18 per day, $14.)

Public Transit: Capitol Metro, 323 Congress. (☎474-1200 or 800-474-1201; call M-F 6am-10pm). Office has maps and schedules. Buses run 4am-midnight; most start later and end earlier. Office open M-F 7:30am-5:30pm. $0.50; students $0.25; seniors, chil-

TEXAS HILL COUNTRY DRIVE

TIME: 2hr.

DISTANCE: 70 mi.

SEASON: Apr.-Nov.

Parts of the **Texas Hill Country** are as country as they come. Longhorns graze in rolling expanses of scraggly brush interrupted by jagged hills, while rusty pickup trucks driven by big men in big hats dominate the roads. But the Texas Hill Country is more than ranches and cattle: the limestone-rich soil is well-suited for wine-making and peach-growing. There is a noticeable German influence in the area, dating back to 1846 and the founding of **Fredericksburg**—stop off at a biergarten to sample some German cuisine. Finally, a series of well-maintained parks links San Antonio and Austin while offering campers and day visitors alike the chance to experience the natural beauty of Texas firsthand. Although not the most direct route between these two cities, unique diversions and beautiful scenery make up for the few extra miles.

1 NEW BRAUNFELS. The entire economy of New Braunfels, TX, depends on the inner tube. Almost 2 million visitors per year come to this town hoping to spend a day floating along the spring-fed Comal River. **Rockin' "R" River Rides** will send you off with a life jacket and tube before picking you up downstream 2½hr. later. (193 S. Liberty. ☎830-620-6262. Open May-Sept. daily 9am-7pm. Tube rentals and bottomless floats $10. Car keys, proper ID, or $25 deposit required for rental.) If the Comal doesn't float your boat, head for the chlorinated waters of **Schlitterbahn,** a 65-acre waterpark extravaganza with 17 waterslides, nine tube chutes, and three miles of tubing. The park is home to the planet's only uphill watercoaster, the Master Blaster. A less official, but more universally enjoyed, attraction is running barefoot across the parking lot, burning the soles of your feet. For both attractions, take I-35 to Exit 189, turn left, and follow the signs for Schlitterbahn. (400 N. Liberty. ☎830-625-2351. Call for hours; generally around 10am-8pm. Open May-Sept. Full-day passes $28.50, ages 3-11 $24. Mid-day pass $20) From New Braunfels, take Rte. 46 west for 6½ mi., then turn left on Herbelin Rd. Here you'll find **Dry Comal Creek Vineyards,** 1741 Herbelin Rd., beckoning with free tastings and tours of the small vineyard. (☎830-885-4121. Open W-Su noon-5pm.) Yes, Texas makes wine—in fact, the state is currently fifth in the nation in wine production.

2 GUADALUPE RIVER STATE PARK. Twenty-five miles west of Dry Comal Creek along Rte. 46 you can swim in the cliff-lined river or camp on the nearby sites of **Guadalupe River State Park ❶.** (☎830-438-2656, for reservations 512-389-8900. Open M-F 8am-8pm, Sa 8am-10pm. Day entrance $4 per person, under 12 free; $17 for water and electricity, $13 for water only. Additional charge of $4 per person, under 12 free.)

3 BOERNE. Farther down Rte. 46 is Boerne (pronounced BUR-nee), a jewelery lover's paradise where a string of converted barns and old farmhouses sell a wide array of odds and ends.

4 BANDERA. After 12 mi. of twists through a series of low hills along the way to Bandera, Rte. 46 intersects with Rte. 16; take Rte. 16 north. Bandera's central street passes through a row of ramshackle buildings that look like backdrops to old cowboy movies. Consistent with the image, Bandera is home to the **Frontier Times Museum,** 510 13th St., a haven for cowboy memorabilia , odd knick-knacks, and relics of the old west. (☎830-796-3864. Open M-Sa 10am-4:30pm, Su 1-4:30pm. $2, ages 6-18 25¢.)

5 MEDINA. Continuing down 15 mi. of zig-zag roads through dramatic countryside, Rte. 16 N then brings you to the town of Medina, the "apple capital of Texas." Stop off at **Love Creek Orchards** (☎800-449-0882), on Rte. 16 in, fittingly enough, the heart of town, to buy a 15lb apple pie (16, $2.50 per slice) for the trip. Leaving Medina on Rte. 16 N, the next 35 miles wind through some of the most breathtaking Texas country. *Be especially cautious driving this leg of the trip; hairpin turns and steep inclines can be treacherous.* Safety aside, the real reason to proceed slowly is to enjoy the scenery.

6 KERRVILLE. The **Cowboy Artists of America Museum,** 1550 Bandera Hwy., take Rte. 173 S from Rte. 16 N, showcases action-packed scenes of the Wild West that demonstrate the creative side of America's gun-toting heroes. (☎830-896-2553. Open June-Aug. M-Sa 9am-5pm, Su 1-5pm; Sept.-May Tu-Sa 9am-5pm, Su 1-5pm. $5, ages 6-18 $1, seniors $3.50.)

7 FREDERICKSBURG. Twenty-two miles along Rte. 16 from Kerrville sits historic Fredericks-

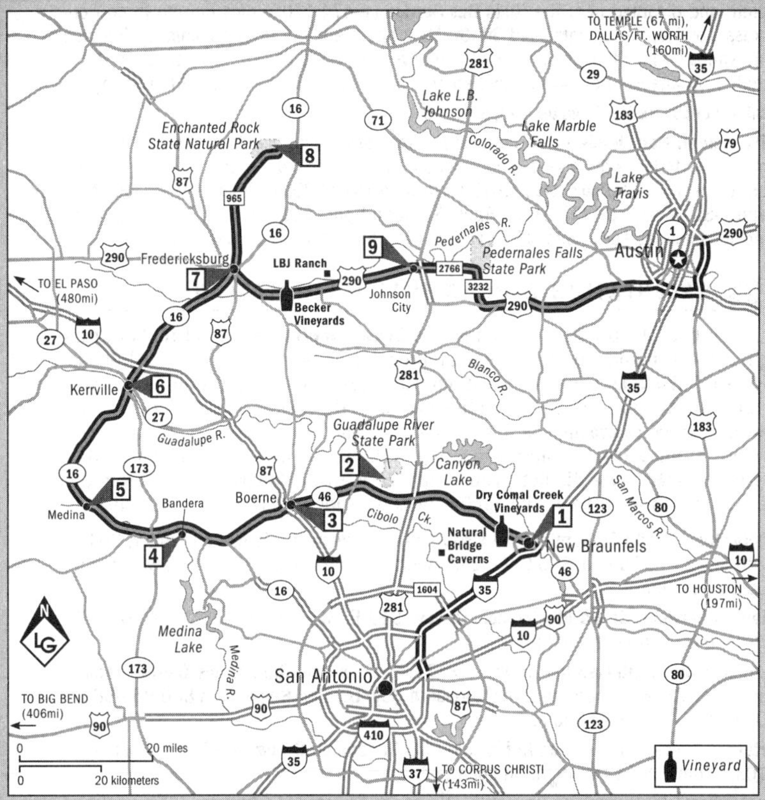

burg, a German-rooted town of biergartens, wineries, and sausage, and the heart of the Hill Country. **The Fredericksburg Convention and Visitors Bureau,** 106 N. Adams (☎888-997-3600), has maps and information. (Open M-F 9am-5pm.) Fredericksburg's **Admiral Nimitz Museum,** 340 E. Main St., contains an excellent exhibit on the Pacific theater of World War II. (☎830-997-4379. Open daily 10am-5pm. $5, students $3.)

8 ENCHANTED ROCK STATE NATURAL PARK. With the double allure of being both a natural wonder (a tree-less, 440 ft. dome of pink granite) as well as a place to pitch a tent, **Enchanted Rock State Natural Park ❶,** 18 miles north of Fredericksburg on Rte. 965, offers hiking—a relatively easy scramble to the top—and rock-climbing for the experienced. (☎800-792-1112. Open daily 8am-5pm. Entrance fee $5, under 12 free. 46 regular tent sites available with shower, water, and grill $10; 60 primitive sites $8. No RVs or trailers permitted. Reservations strongly recommended.)

9 JOHNSON CITY. Ten miles east of Fredericksburg on U.S. 290, **Becker Vineyards,** on Jenschke Ln., offers tastings as well as free tours of the winery. (☎830-644-2681. Open daily 10am-5pm.) Farther down U.S. 290, is Johnson City, the **birthplace of 36th President Lyndon Baines Johnson.** Nine miles east of Johnson City off Rte. 2766 is **Pedernales Falls State Park ❶.** Waterfalls, extensive hiking trails, tent sites, and swimming/tubing areas make the park a favorite getaway from Austin. (☎800-792-1112. Park open daily 8am-10pm; office open M-Th 8am-7pm, F 8am-10pm, Sa-Su 8am-8pm. Entrance fee $4 per person, under 12 free. Sites with water and electricity $16, primitive sites $7.)

dren, and disabled free. The **'Dillo Bus Service** (☎474-1200) runs downtown on Congress, Lavaca, San Jacinto, and 6th St. Most operate M-F every 10-15min. during rush hr.; varies during off-peak times. Red and Silver service daily. The 'Dillos, which look like trollies on wheels, are always free. Park free in the lot at Bouldin and Barton Springs.

Taxi: American Yellow Checker Cab, ☎452-9999.

Bike Rental: Completely yellow bicycles are free rides–compliments of the city. If used, make sure to leave the bike in a conspicuous spot for the next person. Most buses have bicycle racks. **Waterloo Cycles,** 2815 Fruth St. (☎472-9253), offers rentals. Open M-W and F-Sa 10am-7pm, Th 10am-8pm, Su noon-5pm. $15 per day, Sa-Su $20; fee includes helmet. Lock rental $5 ($1.50 each additional day). Delivery available.

ORIENTATION & PRACTICAL INFORMATION

The majority of Austin lies between **Mopac Expressway/Route 1** and **I-35,** both running north-south and parallel to one another. UT students inhabit central **Guadalupe Street ("The Drag"),** where plentiful music stores and cheap restaurants thrive. The state capitol governs the area a few blocks to the southeast. South of the capitol dome, **Congress Avenue** has upscale eateries and classy shops. The many bars and clubs of **6th Street** hop and clop at night, though some nightlife has moved to the growing **Warehouse District,** around 4th St., west of Congress. Away from the urban gridiron, **Town Lake** is a haven for the town's joggers, rowers, and cyclists.

Visitor Info: Austin Convention and Visitors Bureau/Visitors Information Center, 201 E. 2nd St. (☎478-0098 or 800-926-2282; www.austintexas.org). Open M-F 8:30am-5pm, Sa-Su 9am-5pm.

Medical Services: St. David's Medical Center, 919 E. 32nd St. (☎476-7111). Off I-35, close to downtown. Open 24hr.

Hotlines: Crisis Intervention Hotline, ☎472-4357. **Austin Rape Crisis Center Hotline,** ☎440-7273. Both operate 24hr. **Outyouth Gay/Lesbian Helpline,** ☎800-969-6884. Open W, F, Su 5:30-9:30pm.

Internet Access: Austin Public Library, 800 Guadalupe St. (☎947-7400). Open M-Th 10am-9pm, F-Sa 10am-6pm, Su noon-6pm.

Post Office: 510 Guadalupe (☎494-2210), at 6th St. Open M-F 8:30am-6:30pm. **Postal Code:** 78701. **Area Code:** 512.

ACCOMMODATIONS

Chain motels lie along **I-35,** running north and south of Austin. This funkified city, however, is a great place to find cheap accommodations with character. In town, **co-ops** run by college houses at UT peddle rooms and meals to hostelers. Guests have access to all co-op facilities, including fully stocked kitchens. (☎476-5678, though it may be difficult to reach someone over the phone. Reservations recommended. Open May-Aug.) For ,those interested in camping, a 10-20min. drive separates Austin and the nearest campgrounds.

Hostelling International-Austin (HI-AYH), 2200 S. Lakeshore Blvd. (☎444-2294 or 800-725-2331), about 3 mi. from downtown. From the Greyhound station, take bus #7 "Duval" to Burton, then walk 3 blocks north. From I-35, exit at Riverside, head east, and turn left at Lakeshore Blvd. A beautifully situated, well kept, and quiet hostel with a 24hr. common room overlooking Town Lake. Features live music by local acts M-Sa. 40 dorm-style beds, single-sex rooms. Rents bikes, kayaks, and canoes ($10 each). Linen provided; no sleeping bags. No curfew. No alcohol. Reception 8-11am and 5-10pm; arrivals after 10pm must call ahead to check in. $16, nonmembers $19. ❶

TEXAS

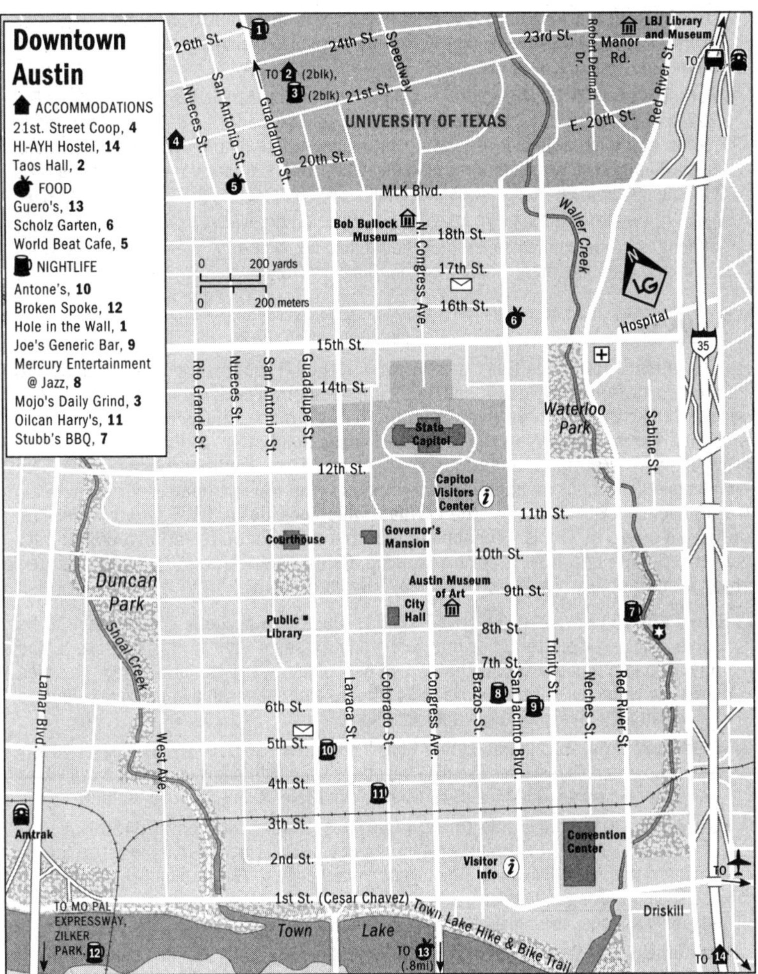

Taos Hall, 2612 Guadalupe St. (☎476-5678), at 27th St. The UT co-op where you're most likely to get a private room. Those staying a week or more are drafted into the chore corps. Office open M-F 10am-6pm. Open June-Aug. 3 meals and a bed $20. ❶

21st St. Co-op, 707 W. 21st St. (☎476-5678). Take bus #39 on Airport Blvd. to Koenig and Burnet, transfer to the #3 S, and ride to Nueces St.; walk 2 blocks west. Treehouse-style building arrangement and hanging plants have residents calling the co-op the "Ewok Village." A bit grungy, but only from all the fun. Suites with A/C, and common room on each floor. Office open M-F 10am-6pm. $20 per person includes 3 meals and kitchen access. ❶

McKinney Falls State Park, 5808 McKinney Falls Pkwy. (☎243-1643, reservations ☎389-8900), southeast of the city. Turn right on Burleson off Rte. 71 E, then right on McKinney Falls Pkwy. Caters to RV and tent campers. Swimming permitted in the stream; 7 mi. of hiking trails. Open Su-Th 8am-5pm, F 8am-8pm, Sa 8am-7pm. Primitive sites (accessible only by foot) $10; with water and electricity $14. Day-use fee $2 per person, under 13 free. ❶

Austin Lonestar RV Resort (☎444-6322 or 800-284-0206), 6 mi. south of the city; Exit 227 off I-35 and continue on the northbound service road. Offers a pool, clean bathrooms, game room, laundry facilities, convenience store, and playground. Open 8am-9pm. RV and tent sites with water and electricity $35, full hook-up with telephone $47; third night free if a weekday. 4-person cabins $48; 6-person $59. 10% off with AAA. ❷

Motel 6, (☎339-6161), 9420 I-35; just north of downtown; Exit 241. This exemplary offering from the omnipresent motel chain offers very well-kept, clean rooms with HBO, pool, and complimentary morning coffee. Singles $30; doubles $36. ❷

FOOD

Scores of fast-food joints line the west side of the UT campus on **Guadalupe Street.** Patrons can often enjoy drink specials and free hors d'oeuvres around **6th Street,** south of the capitol, where the battle for Happy Hour business rages with unique intensity. Farther down the road, **Barton Springs Road** offers a diverse selection of inexpensive restaurants, including Mexican and Texas-style barbecue joints. The **Warehouse District** has swankier, more expensive options. Prepare your own meals from groceries purchased at the **Wheatsville Food Co-op,** 3101 Guadalupe. The only food co-op in Texas, Wheatsville features organic foods and is a community gathering place and information resource. Grab a smoothie ($3) in the deli and enjoy it on the patio. (☎478-2667. Open daily 9am-11pm.)

Ruby's BBQ, 512 W. 29th St. (☎477-1651). Ruby's barbecue is good enough to be served on silver platters, but that just wouldn't seem right in this cow-skulls and butcher-paper establishment. The owners only order meat from farm-raised, grass-fed cows. Scrumptious brisket sandwich $4.25 and amazing rosemary, mozzarella-infused homefries $3. Open daily 11am-midnight. ❶

World Beat Cafe, 600 Martin Luther King Jr. Blvd. (☎236-0197). This eclectic eatery dishes up African specialties like okra vegetable soup ($5) and yam fu fu with egusi, as well as terrific burger and fries ($4). Open M-Sa 11am-10pm, Su noon- 8pm. ❶

Threadgill's, 301 W. Riverside Dr. (☎472-9304); another location at 6416 N. Lamar Blvd. (☎451-5440). A legend in Austin since 1933, Threadgill's serves up terrific Southern soul food, including the obligatory fried chicken ($8), among creaky wooden floors, slow-moving ceiling fans, and antique beer signs. Large variety of vegetarian and non-dairy options. Live music Th 7pm. Open M-Sa 11am-10pm, Su 11am-9pm. ❷

The Kerbey Lane Cafe, 3704 Kerbey Ln. (☎451-1436), is an Austin institution. Locations throughout town, including 2700 Lamar, 2606 Guadalupe, 12602 Research Blvd. For dinner, try their fajitas ($10); for breakfast, order their *migas*, a corn tortilla soufflé ($6). Open 24 hr. ❷

Magnolia Cafe, 1920 S. Congress Ave. (☎445-0000); another location at 2304 Lake Austin Blvd. (☎478-8645). A colorful, lively place with a variety of healthy, tasty dishes. Try the Magnolia enchiladas stuffed with avocado and black olives ($7). Open 24hr. ❷

Guero's, 1412 S. Congress Ave. (☎447-7688), across the river from downtown. This wholesome Mexican restaurant is very popular with locals and is the locus of South Congress activity. Lunch specials $6-8. Combo plates $8-12. Open M-F 11am-11pm, Sa-Su 8am-11pm. ❸

Trudy's Texas Star, 409 W. 30th St. (☎477-2935), 8800 Burnet Rd. (☎454-1474), and 4141 Capital of Texas Hwy. S. (☎326-9899). Tex-Mex dinner entrees ($7-9) and fantastic margaritas. Famous *migas* ($6). Happy Hour all-day M. W. 30th St. open M-F 7am-2am, Sa 8am-2am, Su 8am-midnight; bar open M-Th 2pm-2am, F-Su noon-2am. ❷

Scholz Garten, 1607 San Jacinto Blvd. (☎474-1958), near the capitol. UT students and state politicians alike gather at this Austin landmark, recognized by the legislature for "epitomizing the finest traditions of the German heritage of our state." Popular chicken-fried steak dinners ($8), sausage and bratwurst po' boys ($6), and Reuben ($6). Open M-W 11am-10pm, Th-Sa 11am-11pm. ❷

SIGHTS

GOVERNMENT. Not to be outdone, Texans built their **state capitol** 7 ft. higher than the national one. *(At Congress Ave. and 11th St. ☎463-0063. Open M-F 8:30am-4:30pm, Sa 9:30am-3:30pm, Su noon-3:30pm. 45min. tours every 15min. Free.)* The **Capitol Visitors Center** is located in the southeast corner of the capitol grounds. *(112 E. 11th St. ☎305-8400. Open daily 9am-5pm. Parking: 12th and San Jacinto St. 2hr. garage.)* Near the capitol, the **Governor's Mansion** is open for tours. *(1010 Colorado St. ☎463-5516. Free tours M-Th every 20min. 10-11:40am.)* The **Austin Convention and Visitors Bureau** sponsors free walking tours of the area from March to November. *(☎454-1545. Tours Th-F 9am and Sa-Su 9, 11am, 2pm. Tour starts at the capitol steps.)*

MUSEUMS. The first floor of the **Lyndon B. Johnson Library and Museum** focuses on Texas-native LBJ and the history of the American presidency, while the eighth floor features a model of the Oval Office. *(2313 Red River St. Take bus #20. ☎916-5136; www.lbjlib.utexas.edu. Open daily 9am-5pm. Free.)* If you've ever wondered about "The Story of Texas," the **Bob Bullock Texas State History Museum** is waiting to tell it to you in three floors of exhibits and two IMAX theaters. The museum traces the history of the state from its Native American legacy and Spanish colonization to statehood and the 20th-century oil boom. *(1800 N. Congress Ave. ☎936-8746; www.thestoryoftexas.com. Open M-Sa 9am-6pm, Su noon-6pm. Exhibits $6, seniors $5 , under 18 free; IMAX $6.50, seniors $5.50, under 19 $4.50; cheaper combination tickets available.)*

The downtown **Austin Museum of Art** features American and European masters and an Asian collection. *(At the corner of Congress Ave. and 9th St. ☎495-9224; www.amoa.org. Grounds open Tu-Sa 10am-5pm, Su noon-5pm. $5, seniors and students $4, ages 12 and under $3.)* A second branch, at 3809 W. 35th St., is housed in a Mediterranean-style villa in a beautiful country setting with an exquisite sculpture garden. The **Mexic-Arte Museum** features a permanent collection of Mexican masks and photos. *(419 S. Congress Ave. ☎480-9373; www.mexic-artemuseum.org. Open M-Sa 10am-6pm.)*

WHERE HAVE ALL THE HIPPIES GONE? 15 mi. northeast of downtown Austin lies Hippie Hollow. Free spirits go *au naturel* in the waters of the lovely Lake Travis, Texas' only public nude swimming and sunbathing haven. Take Mopac (Rte. 1) north to the exit for F.M. 2222. Follow 2222 west and turn left at I-620; Comanche Rd. will be on your right. *(7000 Comanche Tr. ☎473-9437. 18+. Open daily 8am-9pm, no entry after 8:30pm. $5 per car, pedestrians $2.)*

PARKS. **Mount Bonnell Park** offers a sweeping view of Lake Austin and Westlake Hills from the highest point in the city. *(3800 Mt. Bonnell Rd., off W. 35th St.)* On hot afternoons, Austinites come in droves to riverside **Zilker Park,** just south of the Colorado River. Rejuvenate in the Zilker Botanical Gardens. *(2201 Barton Springs Rd. Take bus #30. ☎477-7273. Open daily 5am-10pm. Free.)* Flanked by walnut and pecan trees, **Barton Springs Pool,** a spring-fed swimming hole in the park, stretches 1000 ft. long and 200 ft. wide. The pool's temperature hovers around 68°F. (*☎974-6700. Pool open M-W and F-Su 5am-10pm, Th 5-9am and 7-10pm. M-F $2.50, Sa-Su $2.75; ages 12-17 $1, under 12 $0.50. Free daily 5-8am and 9-10pm.)* The **Barton Springs Greenbelt** offers challenging hiking and biking trails.

OTHER SIGHTS. The **University of Texas at Austin (UT)** is both the wealthiest public university in the country, with an annual budget of almost a billion dollars, and America's largest, with over 50,000 students. UT forms the backbone of city cultural life. Just before dusk, head underneath the south side of the **Congress Avenue Bridge,** near the Austin American-Statesman parking lot, and watch the massive swarm of **Mexican free-tail bats** emerge from their roosts to feed on the night's mosquitoes. When the bridge was reconstructed in 1980, the engineers unintentionally created crevices which formed ideal homes for the migrating bat colony. The city began exterminating the night-flying creatures until **Bat Conservation International** moved to Austin to educate people about the bats' harmless behavior and the benefits of their presence—the bats eat up to 3000 lb. of insects each night. Today, the bats are among the biggest tourist attractions in Austin. The colony, seen from mid-March to November, peaks in August, when a fresh crop of pups increases the population to around 1.5 million. *(For flight times, call the bat hotline ☎416-5700, ext. 3636; Commissioner Gordon mans the bat signal, ext. POW!)*

ENTERTAINMENT & NIGHTLIFE

Beverly Sheffield Zilker Hillside Theater (☎397-1463 for events schedule), across from the Barton Springs pool, hosts free outdoor bands, ballets, plays, musicals, and symphony concerts most weekends from May to October. In mid-March, the **South by Southwest Music, Media, and Film Festival** draws entertainment industry giants and thousands of eager fans (☎467-7979; www.sxsw.com). In early April, The Austin Fine Arts Guild sponsors **The Fine Arts Festival,** attracting 200 national artists, local eateries, live music, and art activities. Austin's smaller events calendar is a mixed bag. Each spring, **Spamarama** (www.spamarama.com) gathers Spam fans from all walks of life to pay homage to the often misunderstood meat. A cookoff, samplings, sports, and live music at the **Spam Jam,** are all in store.

Austin has replaced Seattle as the nation's underground music hot spot, so keep an eye out for rising indie stars, as well as old blues, folk, country, and rock favorites. On weekends, nighttime collegiate revelers and swingers seek out dancing on **6th Street,** an area bespeckled with warehouse nightclubs and theme bars. More mellow, gentrified night owls gather at the cocktail-lounge infested **4th Street Warehouse District.** Still another area for nightlife in Austin is along **Red River Street,** with a series of bars and clubs that have all of the grit of 6th St., but less of the glamour. If you aren't in the mood to face club crowds, try Austin's regionally unparalleled coffeehouse scene. The weekly *Austin Chronicle* and *XL-ent* provide details on current music performances, shows, and movies. The *Gay Yellow Pages* is free at stands along Guadalupe St.

Mojo's Daily Grind, 2714 Guadalupe St. (☎477-6656), is simply "the hub of subculture in Austin," replacing coffee with beer in the evenings. DJs spin the first M of every month, and poets wax eloquent on the first F. Open 24hr.

Antone's, 213 W. 5th St. (☎ 320-8424; www.antones.net). This legendary blues paradise has attracted the likes of B.B. King and Muddy Waters and was the starting point for Stevie Ray Vaughn. Now offering a variety of music to all ages. Shows at 10pm. Cover $5-25. Open daily 9pm-2am. Visit web site for specific daily times and covers.

Mercury Entertainment @ Jazz, 214 E. 6th St. (☎478-6372; www.myplanetmercury-.com). Hip 20-somethings looking for the latest in jazz, funk, and hip-hop will revel in this scene, which represents the new side of Austin that has moved away from the usual country music and classic rock. Cavernous and lantern-lit, Mercury hosts 2 bars and a pool table. Mood depends on the musical act of the evening–check the web site to see whether you need to bring your dancin' shoes or your smoking jacket. Cover ages 18-20 from $9, 21+ from $6. Open W-Sa 9:30pm-2am.

Spider House, 2908 Fruth St. (☎480-9562), just off Guadalupe St. This coffee shop and vegetarian cafe with large booths in a dark interior and patio seating whips up a popular cafe mocha ($3.25). Open daily 8am-2am.

Stubb's BBQ, 801 Red River St. (☎480-8341). Don't miss Stubb's fabulous (but pricey) Sunday gospel brunch–all-you-can-eat buffet plus live gospel for $15 (reservations recommended, sittings at 11am and 1pm). Otherwise, the 18+ club downstairs hosts nightly acts. Swing by earlier for some scrumptious, inexpensive grub like the chopped beef sandwich, served with Stubb's famous sauce (available for purchase) and one side for $4.25. All ages welcome for amphitheater shows. Cover $5-25. Shows at 10:30pm. Open Tu-W 11am-10pm, Th-Sa 11am-11pm, Su 11am-9pm; nightclub open Tu-Sa 11am-2am.

Hole in the Wall, 2538 Guadalupe St. (☎477-4747), at 26th St. Its self-effacing name belies the popularity of this renowned music spot, which features a mix of "Austin music"–punk/alternative and country-western bands. Music most nights. 21+. No nightly cover; however, expect to pay on nights with headliners. Open M-F 11am-2am, Sa-Su noon-2am.

Joe's Generic Bar, 315 E. 6th St. (☎480-0171). Enter through the door marked with Joe's generic barcode on any night and you'll be greeted with good-humored, raunchy Texas-style blues that are anything but generic. 21+. No cover. Open daily 7pm-2am.

Broken Spoke, 3201 S. Lamar Blvd. (☎442-6189; www.brokenspokeaustintx.com). Pull up your bolo and slap on the fringe. One of the top honky-tonks in the land, the Broken Spoke is real country, with wagon wheel decor and Southern hospitality. The restaurant serves the world's best chicken-fried steak dinner for $8.25. All ages. Cover $5-8. Music starts nightly at 9pm, closing time varies. Open Su-Th 11am-10:30pm, F-Sa 11am-11:30pm. To check music listings visit site.

Oilcan Harry's, 211 W. 4th St. (☎320-8823). One of the biggest and best gay bars in Austin. Strip shows bare-all on Th and Sa 10:30pm and midnight. 21+. No cover. Open daily 2pm-2am.

DALLAS ☎214

Denim and diamonds define the Dallas decor, skyline, and attitude. Rugged western virility coupled with cosmopolitan offerings create the city's truly Texan aura. Big Tex welcomes visitors to one of the country's finest collections of Asian art and a slew of restaurants—more per capita than any other US city. The city's mix of oil and conservative politics composes part of the intrigue surrounding the assasination of President Kennedy, whose death haunts the city to this day. But behind this darker shroud lies a shiny Texan star waiting to be discovered.

TRANSPORTATION

Airport: Dallas-Fort Worth International (☎972-574-8888; www.dfwairport.com), 17 mi. northwest of downtown; take bus #202 ($2). For door-to-gate service, take the **Super Shuttle,** 3010 N. Airfield Dr. (☎800-258-3826). 24hr. service. First passenger $27; each additional passenger $8. No reservation needed. Taxi to downtown $38.

Trains: Amtrak, 400 S. Houston St. (☎653-1101), in Union Station. Open daily 9am-6:30pm. To: **Los Angeles** ($43 hr., 3 per week, $110.); **Austin** (6½hr., 1 per day, $21); **Little Rock** (7½hr., 1 per day, $45).

Buses: Greyhound, 205 S. Lamar St. (☎655-7727), 3 blocks east of Union Station. Open 24hr. To: **New Orleans** ($12, 12 per day, $81); **Houston** (4hr., 13 per day, $33); **Austin** (3hr., 19 per day, $28).

Public Transit: Dallas Area Rapid Transit (DART), 1401 Pacific Ave. (☎979-1111). Open M-F 5am-10pm, Sa-Su 8am-6pm. Buses dispatch from 2 downtown transfer centers, East and West, and serve most suburbs. Darts daily 5:30am-9:30pm, to suburbs 5:30am-8pm. All day pass $2.50, suburban park-and-ride stops; transfers free. Maps at Elm and Ervay St. office (open M-F 7am-6pm). **DART Light Rail** runs north-south through downtown. Operates daily 5:30am-12:30am.

Taxi: Yellow Cab Co., ☎426-6262.

ORIENTATION & PRACTICAL INFORMATION

Most of Dallas lies within the **I-635** loop, which is bisected north-south by **I-35 E (Stemmons Freeway)** and **U.S. 75 (Central Expressway)** and east-west by **I-30.** The suburbs stretch along the northern reaches of Central Expwy. and the **Dallas North Toll Road,** northwest of downtown. Many of downtown Dallas' shops and restaurants lie underground in a maze of tunnels accessible from any major office building. Driving and parking in Dallas can be tricky. Beware of ravenous downtown parking meters which demand feeding until 10pm. Check out Ross Ave. for cheap daily parking rates, which tend to go down after 5pm.

Visitor Info: Dallas Convention and Visitors Bureau, 100 S. Houston St. (☎571-1000, 24hr. events hotline ☎571-1301; www.dallascvb.com), at Main St., in the Old Red Courthouse. Open M-F 8am-5pm, Sa-Su 9am-5pm.

Hotlines: Contact Counseling Crisis Contact Center, ☎972-233-2233, for general counseling. **Dallas Gay and Lesbian Community Center:** 2701 Reagan St. (☎528-9254). Both operate 24hr.

Internet Access: Dallas Public Library, 1515 Young St. at Ervay St. (☎670-1400). Open M-Th 9am-9pm, F-Sa 9am-5pm, Su 1-5pm. *Be careful around this area at night.*

Post Office: 401 Dallas-Ft. Worth Tpk. (☎760-4545). Take Sylvan exit. Open daily 24hr. **Downtown branch** is located in the Federal Building on Main St. Open M-F 9am-5pm. **General Delivery** is at 1500 Dragon St. Go north on Lamar St., which turns into Continental; take the first right after I-35. Open M-F 9am-noon. **Postal Code:** 75201; for General Delivery 75221. **Area Codes:** 214, 817, and 972. In text, 214 unless otherwise noted.

ACCOMMODATIONS

Cheap lodging in Dallas is nearly impossible to come by; big events such as the Cotton Bowl (Jan. 1) and the state fair in October exacerbate the problem. Look within 10 mi. of downtown along three of the major roads for inexpensive motels: north of downtown on **U.S. 75,** north along **I-35,** and east on **I-30.**

Bed and Breakfast Texas Style, (☎800-899-4538), a statewide service that places travelers in a home, usually near town, with hospitable residents full of Texan hospitality. Call a few days ahead. Open M-F 8:30am-4:30pm. Singles from $55; doubles from $65. ❸

Classic Inn, 3629 U.S. 80 E (☎972-613-9989), lies 15min. from downtown; after bearing right onto U.S. 80 from I-30, exit at Town East Blvd. Rooms with HBO, pool. Singles $35; doubles $40. ❶

The Hotel Lawrence, 302 S. Houston St. (☎761-9090), downtown near Dealey Plaza and the West End, stands 2½ blocks from the Light Rail and CBD West transfer center and is your cheapest bet in the city center. Singles $69; doubles $79. ❸

Cedar Hill State Park (☎972-291-3900, for reservations ☎972-291-6641), near Lake Joe Pool 20-30min. southwest of the city, provides 355 tent and RV sites. Take I-35 E to Rte. 67 and turn right onto FM 1382; the park is on the left. Swimming area, marina,

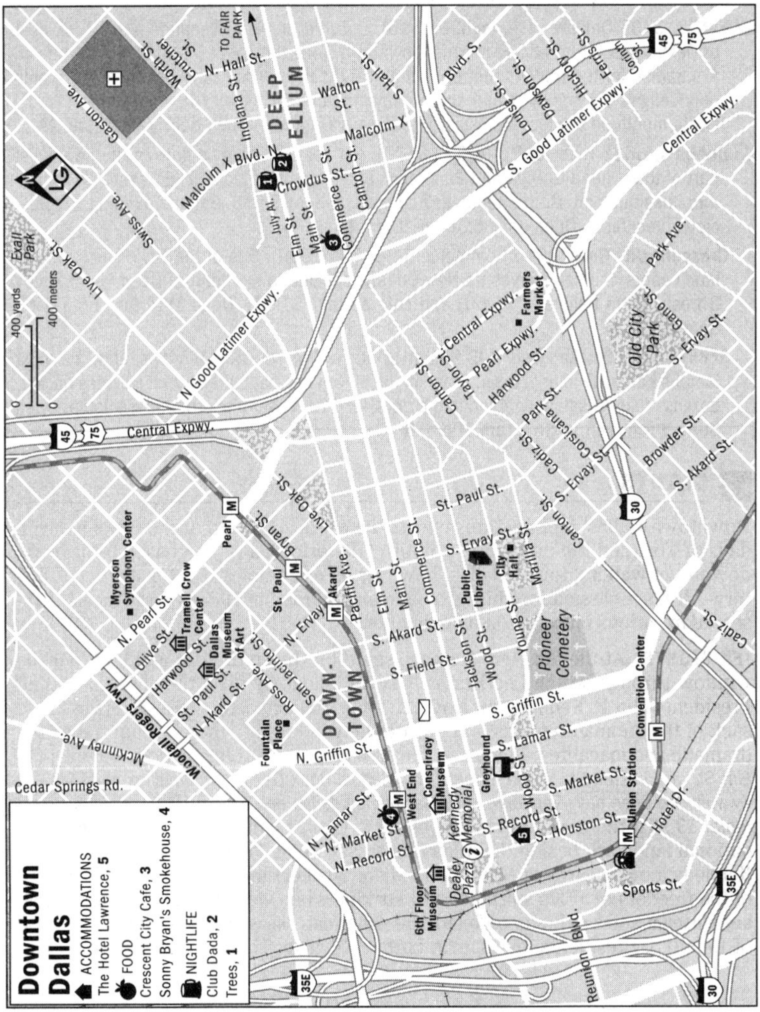

Downtown Dallas

ACCOMMODATIONS
The Hotel Lawrence, **5**

FOOD
Crescent City Cafe, **3**
Sonny Bryan's Smokehouse, **4**

NIGHTLIFE
Club Dada, **2**
Trees, **1**

0 400 yards
0 400 meters

Cedar Springs Rd.
McKinney Ave.
Woodall Rogers Fwy.
N. Pearl St.
Olive St.
Harwood St.
St. Paul St.
N Akard St.
Myerson Symphony Center
Tramell Crow Center
Dallas Museum of Art
Pearl
Fountain Place
Ross Ave.
San Jacinto St.
N. Ervay
St. Paul
Bryan St.
Live Oak St.
Akard
Pacific Ave.
DOWN-TOWN
N. Griffin St.
N. Lamar St.
N. Market St.
N. Record St.
West End
6th Floor Museum
Conspiracy Museum
Dealey Plaza
Kennedy Memorial
Elm St.
Main St.
Commerce St.
S. Akard St.
S. Field St.
Jackson St.
Wood St.
Public Library
S. Ervay St.
St. Paul St.
City Hall
Young St.
Marilla St.
Greyhound
S. Record St.
S. Lamar St.
S. Griffin St.
Pioneer Cemetery
S. Houston St.
S. Market St.
Reunion Blvd.
Union Station
Convention Center
Sports St.
Hotel Dr.
Cadiz St.
Central Expwy.
N Good Latimer Expwy.
Exall Park
Swiss Ave.
Gaston Ave.
Worth St.
Crutcher St.
Malcolm X Blvd. N
N. Hall St.
Indiana St.
TO FAIR PARK
July Al.
Crowdus St.
DEEP ELLUM
Elm St.
Main St.
Commerce St.
Canton St.
Malcolm X
Walton St.
S Hall St.
Canton St.
Taylor St.
Central Expwy.
Pearl Expwy.
Harwood St.
Farmers Market
Blvd. S.
Louise St.
Dawson St.
Hickory St.
Ferris St.
Corinth St.
S. Good Latimer Expwy.
Canton St.
S. Ervay St.
Cadiz St.
Corsicana St.
Park St.
Old City Park
Gano St.
Park Ave.
Browder St.
S. Akard St.
S. Ervay St.
Central Expwy.
30
35E
45
75

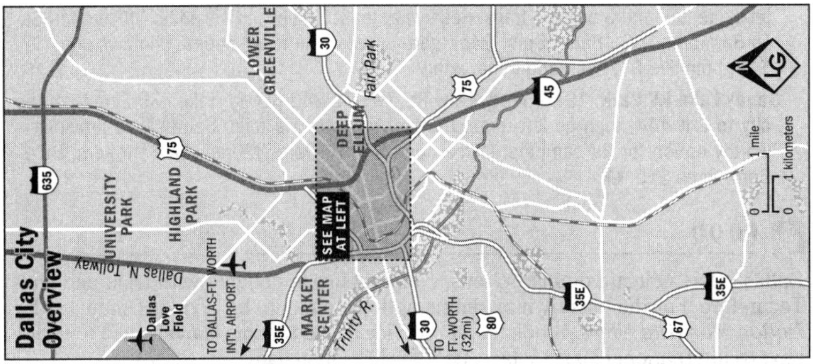

Dallas City Overview

635
UNIVERSITY PARK
HIGHLAND PARK
Dallas N. Tollway
Dallas Love Field
75
TO DALLAS-FT. WORTH INT'L AIRPORT
LOWER GREENVILLE
35E
MARKET CENTER
SEE MAP AT LEFT
DEEP ELLUM
30
Trinity R.
Fair Park
TO FT. WORTH (32mi)
80
75
45
35E
67
35E
0 1 mile
0 1 kilometers

jet-ski rental, and 3 walking trails. Reserve at least 2 weeks in advance. Office open Su-Th 8am-5pm, F-Sa 8am-10pm. 24hr. gate access with reservations. Primitive sites $7, $18, primitive $7; each additional adult $5. ❶

Sandy Lake RV Park, 1915 Sandy Lake Rd. (☎972-242-6808). Take I-35 E north of the city to Exit 444, then go left under the highway about a mile. Sandy Lake provides a worthy option for RV campers. Office open M-F 7:30am-7:30pm, Sa 8am-7pm, Su 1-6pm. Sites $25. ❶

FOOD

Dallas offers eclectic dining options, coupling urban delights with tried and true Texan fare. For the lowdown on dining options, pick up the "Friday Guide" of the *Dallas Morning News.* Stock up on produce at the **Farmers Market,** 1010 S. Pearl, next to International Marketplace. (☎939-2808. Open daily 7am-6pm.)

EatZi's, 3403 Oaklawn Ave. (☎526-1515), in Turtle Creek, at Lemmon Ave., 1 mi. east of Oaklawn exit from I-35 E, north of downtown. Take the #2 or 51 bus from downtown. A paradise for the frugal gourmet, this grocery, cafe, kitchen, and bakery forms a culinary delight. Sounds of Vivaldi accompany fabulous focaccia ($4), sandwiches ($4-9), and a multitude of other delicacies. Free sample platters. Open daily 7am-10pm. ❶

Bubba's, 6617 Hillcrest Dr. (☎373-6527). For the best no-frills grub in the swankiest part of town, head to Highland Park for Bubba's famous fried chicken. Primarily a drive thru/take-out joint. Grab 5 tenders, 2 veggies, and roll for $8. Banana pudding $2. Delicious breakfasts. Open daily 6:30am-10pm. ❷

Crescent City Cafe, 2615 Commerce St. (☎745-1900). One of the city's most popular lunch spots, the cafe serves up New Orleans cooking in the heart of Deep Ellum. Enjoy 3 fresh, warm beignets ($1.50) and cafe au lait ($1.35). Open M-Th 8am-3pm, F-Sa 8am-10pm. ❶

Sonny Bryan's Smokehouse, 302 N. Market St. (☎744-1610), in the West End. The most famous barbecue joint in town. Feast on the all-you-can-eat buffet, which includes brisket, dozens of sides, salad, cobbler, and a drink for $12. Vegetarian options available. Open Su-Th 11am-9pm, F-Sa 11am-10pm. ❸

SIGHTS

Downtown Dallas' architecture reflects the art-deco period of the city's halcyon days of Tor (and the initial burst of oil). "Historic Dallas" can easily be seen via downtown walking tours. Dallas, however, is more notorious for its recent history—JFK's assassination during a campaign parade in 1963 is permanently preserved in various museums and landmarks.

JFK SIGHTS. At the **6th Floor Museum,** stand on the sixth floor and look out the window through which Lee Harvey Oswald allegedly fired the shot that killed President John F. Kennedy on Nov. 22, 1963. Immaculately preserved (the lunch sack of the gunman remains underneath the windowsill), the museum traces the dramatic and macabre moments of the assassination through various media. *(411 Elm St., at Houston St., in the former Texas School Book Depository building. ☎747-6660; www.jfk.org. Open daily 9am-6pm. $10; seniors, students, and ages 6-18 $9. Audio cassette rental $3.)* To the south of the depository, Elm St. runs through **Dealy Plaza,** a national landmark beside the infamous grassy knoll. **Philip Johnson's Memorial** to Kennedy looms nearby at Market and Main. The cenotaph (open tomb), a symbol of the freedom of JFK's spirit, is most striking when viewed at night. The **Conspiracy Museum** hosts exhibits on historical American assassinations, including those of four U.S. Presidents and Martin Luther King, Jr. Their conspiracy collection includes the Zapruder film that captured JFK's killing—available for purchase, creepily enough, in the museum store. *(110 Market St., across the street from the Memorial. ☎741-3040. Open daily 10am-6pm. $10, students and seniors $6, children $3.)*

ART & ARCHITECTURE. The architecture of the **Dallas Museum of Art** is as graceful and beautiful as its impressive collections of Egyptian, African, Early American, Impressionist, modern, and decorative art. *(1717 N. Harwood St. ☎922-1200; www.dm-art.org. Open Tu-Su 11am-5pm, Th 11am-9pm. $6, seniors $4, children under 12 and students with ID free. Special exhibit admission varies.)* Directly across Harwood St., the **Trammell Crow Center** has a must-see collection of Asian art, and its beautiful sculpture garden displays works by Rodin, Maillol, and Bourdelle alongside famous American pieces. *(2010 Flora St., at Hardwood and Olive St. ☎979-6430. Open Tu-Su 10am-5pm, Th 10am-9pm. Free. Sculpture garden always open.)* The ubiquitous **I.M. Pei** designed many downtown Dallas buildings. Pei's **Fountain Place** at the Wells Fargo Bldg., on Ross St. just past Field St., creates an indelible mark on the city's skyline, and cools weary travelers with a two-acre water garden. The **Morton H. Meyerson Symphony Center,** 2301 Flora St., a few blocks east, and the imposing **Dallas City Hall** were also designed by Pei. Free tours of the Symphony Center are sometimes available. *(100 Marilla St., off Young St. ☎670-3600. Tours on selected M, W, F-Sa 1pm.)*

ATTRACTIONS. The multilevel rainforest, giant river otters, and Japanese fighting crabs at the **Dallas World Aquarium** make this spot worth a plunge. *(1801 N. Griffin St., northeast of the West End, 1 block north of Ross Ave. ☎720-2224; www.dwazoo.com. Open daily 10am-5pm. $11.85, seniors and children $6.50.)* In bloom year-round, the 66-acre **Dallas Arboretum,** on the southeast shore of White Rock Lake, provides a haven for pedestrian horticulture fans. *(8617 Garland Rd. Take bus #19 from downtown. ☎327-8263. Open 10am-9pm. $7, seniors $6, ages 6-12 $4. Parking $4.)*

FAIR PARK. Home to the state fair since 1886, **Fair Park** has earned national landmark status for its Art Deco architecture. During the fair, **Big Tex**—a 52 ft. smiling cowboy float—towers over the land, and only the **Texas Star,** a huge ferris wheel, looms taller. The 277-acre park also hosts the **Cotton Bowl** on January 1. In association with the Smithsonian Institute, **The Women's Museum: An Institute for the Future** features a timeline of US women's history from 1500 to the present along with exhibits on famous American women. *(3800 Parry Ave. ☎915-0860; www.thewomensmuseum.org. Open Tu 10am-9pm, W-Sa 10am-5pm, Su noon-5pm. $5, seniors and children $4. Tu after 5pm free.)*

HISTORIC DALLAS. The city's oldest park, aptly named **Old City Park,** hosts 35 renovated and restored 19th-century edifices. Locals enjoy luncheoning al fresco in the antiqued ambience. *(1717 Gano St., 9 blocks south of City Hall at Ervay St. ☎421-5141. Open daily 9am-6pm. Exhibit buildings open Tu-Sa 10am-4pm, Su noon-4pm. $7, seniors $5, children $3.)* The **West End Historic District and Marketplace,** full of broad sidewalks, shops, and restaurants, lies north of Union Station. *(Most stores open M-Sa 11am-10pm, Su noon-6pm.)* Dallas' **mansions** are in the **Swiss Avenue Historic District** and along the ritzy, boutique-lined streets of **Highland Park,** between Preston Rd. and Hillcrest Ave. south of Mockingbird Ln.

ENTERTAINMENT

The Observer, a free weekly found in stands across the city, has unrivaled entertainment coverage. For the scoop on Dallas' **gay scene,** pick up copies of the *Dallas Voice* and *Texas Triangle* in **Oak Lawn** shops and restaurants.

Prospero works his magic at the **Shakespeare in the Park** festival, in Samuel-Grand Park just northeast of Fair Park. During June and July (no performances the last week of June), two free plays run six nights per week. (☎559-2778. Performances

Tu-Su 8:15pm. Gates open 7:30; arrive early. $7 optional donation.) At Fair Park, the **Music Hall** hosts Broadway national tours in the **Dallas Summer Musicals** series. (☎691-7200 or 373-8000 for tickets; shows run June-Oct. $10-70.) The **Dallas Symphony Orchestra** plays in the Symphony Center, at Pearl and Flora St. in the arts district. (☎692-0203; www.dallassymphony.com. Aug.-May. Box office open M-Sa 10am-6pm. $12-100.) In the summer, free outdoor jazz concerts are held every Thursday night at 9pm in front of the Museum of Art.

If you come to Dallas looking for cowboys, the **Mesquite Championship Rodeo,** 1818 Rodeo Dr., is the place to find them. Take I-30 east to I-635 S to Exit 4 and stay on the service road. Nationally televised, the rodeo is one of the most competitive in the country. (☎972-285-8777 or 800-833-9339; www.mesquiterodeo.com. Shows Apr. to early Oct. F-Sa 8pm. Gates open 6:30pm. $10, seniors $5, children 3-12 $5. Barbecue dinner $9.50, children $6.50. Pony rides $3. Parking $3.)

Six Flags Over Texas, 20 mi. from downtown off I-30 at Rte. 360 in Arlington, between Dallas and Fort Worth, boasts 38 rides, including the speedy, looping roller coasters "Batman: The Ride" and "Mr. Freeze." (☎817-640-8900. Open June-early Aug. daily from 10am; late Aug.-Dec. and Mar.-May Sa-Su from 10am. Park sometimes opens at 11am and closing times vary from 7-10pm. $40, over 55 or under 4 ft. $25. Parking $9.) Across the highway lies the 47-acre waterpark, **Hurricane Harbor.** Shoot down superspeed water flumes or experience simulated seasickness in the million gallon wave pool. (☎817-265-3356. Open late May to mid-Aug. daily 10:30am-8pm. $28, over 55 and under 4 ft. $18. Parking $7.) Find coupons for both parks on soda cans and at Dallas or Ft. Worth tourist information offices.

In Dallas, the moral order is God, country, and the **Cowboys.** See "The Boys" in action at **Cowboys Stadium** at the junction of Rte. 12 and 183, west of Dallas in Irving. (☎972-785-5000. Sept.-Jan. Ticket office open M-F 9am-5pm. From $36.) **The Ballpark in Arlington,** 1000 Ballpark Way, plays host to the **Texas Rangers.** (☎817-273-5100. Apr.-Sept. Ticket office open M-F 9am-6pm, Sa 10am-4pm, Su noon-4pm. $5-55.) Experience the mystique of the game with a 1 hr. tour of the locker room, dugout, and the press box on the **ballpark tour.** (☎817-273-5600. Non-game days tours M-Sa 9am-4pm, Su-11am-4pm every hr.; hours vary for game days. $10, students and seniors $8, ages 4-18 $6.)

 NIGHTLIFE

For nightlife, head to **Deep Ellum,** east of downtown. In the 1920s, the area was a blues haven for legends Blind Lemon Jefferson, Lightnin' Hopkins, and Robert Johnson; in the 1980s, Bohemians revitalized the area. The first Friday of every month is **Deep Friday,** when a $7 wrist band gets you into 9 Deep Ellum clubs featuring local rock acts. Other nightlife epicenters include **Lower Greenville Avenue; Yale Boulevard,** near Southern Methodist University's fraternity row; and **Dallas Alley** (☎720-0170; $3-6), an amalgam of seven differently themed clubs located in the touristy **West End.** Many gay clubs rock a bit north of downtown in **Oak Lawn.**

Trees, 2709 Elm St. (☎748-5009), rated the best live music venue in the city by the *Dallas Morning News*, occupies a converted warehouse with a loft full of pool tables and tree trunks in the middle of the club. Bands tend to play alternative rock music. 17+. Cover $2-10. Open W-Th 8:30pm-1am, F-Sa 9pm-2am.

Club Dada, 2720 Elm St. (☎744-3232). A former haunt of Edie Brickell and the New Bohemians, this hoppin' club boasts eclectic clientele and decor. Live local acts and outdoor patio add to the fun. 21+. Cover W-Sa $3-5. Open W-Th 7pm-2am, F-Sa 5pm-2am, Su 8pm-2am.

Poor David's Pub, 1924 Greenville Ave. (☎821-9891), stages live music ranging from Irish folk tunes to reggae. Tickets available after 6pm at the door. Cover up to $30. Open Tu-Sa 7pm-2am; closed nights when no performance is scheduled.

The Beagle, 1806 Lower Greenville Ave. (☎824-8767). Dallas' college crowd hot spot. Enjoy the view from the third story rooftop deck, shoot pool, or boogie down to a wide variety of musical options—everything from old country to top 40. Open daily 5pm-2am.

Roundup, 3912 Cedar Springs Rd. (☎522-9611), at Throckmorton St. A huge, cover-free country-western bar that packs a large, mixed crowd on weekends. Free dance lessons Th 8:30pm. Open daily 3pm-2am.

FORT WORTH ☎817

If Dallas is the last Eastern city, Fort Worth is undoubtedly the first Western one. Less than 40min. west on I-30, Fort Worth boasts raw Texan flair with cultural refinement. Fort Worth is divided into three districts, each marked by red brick streets: the **Stockyards Historic District, Sundance Square,** and the **Cultural District.**

The Stockyards Historic District, located along East Exchange Ave., 10min. north of downtown on Main St., remains the stompin' ground for area cowboys as well as western wannabes. Exchange Ave., the main drag, provides a window into the Wild West, offering a slew of saloons, restaurants, shows, and gambling parlors. Catch the **cattle drive** down Exchange Ave. daily at 11:30am and 4pm. With live country music every night, brass footrails, and a prodigious collection of cowboy hats, the **White Elephant Saloon,** 106 Exchange Ave., is a local favorite. (☎624-1887. Cover F-Sa $8. Open Su-Th noon-midnight, F-Sa noon-2am.) For more Stockyards info visit www.fortworthstockyards.org.

Fort Worth's newest museum pays homage to the glitz, glamour, and guts of America's cowgirls. **The National Cowgirl Museum and Hall of Fame**, 1720 Gendy St., displays rhinestone-encrusted saddles, cowgirl apparel, and Andy Warhol's rendition of Annie Oakley. (☎336-4475; www.cowgirl.net. Open Tu 10am-8pm, W-Sa 10am-5pm, Su noon-5pm. $6, seniors $5, children under 18 $4. W half-price.)

Just down the road at 121 Exchange Ave., the **Cowtown Coliseum** (☎625-1025 or 888-269-8696; www.cowtowncoliseum.com) hosts two weekly events: **rodeos** (F and Sa 8pm; $9, seniors $7.50, children $5.50) and **Pawnee Bill's Wild West Show.** Yelp and yowl at the fearless trick ropers, riders, shooters, and bullwhip act every Saturday and Sunday at 2:30 and 4:30pm. ($8, seniors $6.50, ages 3-12 $4.50.) To uncover the mystery of cattle raising, visit the **Cattle Raisers Museum,** 1301 7th St., between the Stockyards and Cultural Districts. (☎332-8551; www.cattleraisersmuseum.org. Open M-Sa 10am-5pm, $3, seniors and ages 13-18 $2, ages 4-12 $1.)

The world's largest honky-tonk, **Billy Bob's Texas,** 2520 Rodeo Plaza, ropes in the crowds for some clubbing with big names in country music. The 100,000 sq. ft. of floor space includes restaurant, pool tables, and 42 bar stations. (☎624-7117. Free dance lessons Th 7pm. Professional bull-riding F-Sa 9 and 10pm. Cover before 6pm $1; after 6pm Su-M $3, Tu-Th $4, F-Sa $6.50-11, depending on performers. Under 18 must be accompanied by parent. Open M-Sa 11am-2am, Su noon-2am.)

Downtown, Sundance Square, a pedestrian-friendly area, offers quality shops, museums, and restaurants. Parking is free in lots and garages on weekends and after 5pm on weekdays. In the square, the **Sid Richardson Collection,** 309 Main St., displays 60 paintings primarily by Western artists Remington and Russell. (☎332-6554. Open Tu-W 10am-5pm, Th-F 10am-8pm, Sa 11am-8pm, Su 1-5pm. Free.)

A few minutes west of downtown along 7th St., the Cultural District offers an array of intimate collections and exhibitions. The **Kimbell Art Museum,** 3333 Camp Bowie Blvd., touted as "America's best small museum," displays masterpieces from Caravaggio to Cézanne. (☎332-8451; www.kimbellart.org. Open Tu-Th and Sa 10am-5pm, F noon-8pm, Su noon-5pm. Free; special exhibits $10, students and seniors $8, ages 3-18 $6.) Across the street on 3200 Darnell, the **Modern A Museum,** 1309 Montgomery St., is hard to miss, so don't. (☎738-9 www.mamfw.org. Open Tu-F 10am-5pm, Sa 11am-5pm, Su noon-5pm. Fre **Worth Convention and Visitors Bureau:** 415 Throckmorton St., in Sundance S

TEXAS

8791 or 800-433-5747; www.fortworth.com. Open M-F 8:30am-5pm, Sa 10am-4pm.) **Post Office:** 251 W. Lancaster Ave. (☎870-8104. Open M-F 8:30am-6pm.) **Postal Code:** 76102. **Area Code:** 817.

HOUSTON

☎713

Though often overshadowed by its more famous counterparts, Houston has quietly become America's fourth-largest city. Coupling classy cosmopolitan amenities with a distinctively Texan attitude, Houston is home to an $88-million-dollar performing arts center as well as two new sports arenas. Once a city fueled by maritime commerce, Houston's economy is now reliant upon oil; the headquarters of energy conglomerates dominate the city's skyline. Yet beyond the glass-and-steel skyscrapers culture abounds with an impressive array of world-class restaurants, museums, and cultural organizations that call Houston home. With her many resources (both natural and achieved), Houston is waiting to be discovered as America's next great city.

TRANSPORTATION

Flights: George Bush Intercontinental Airport (☎281-230-3000), 25 mi. north of downtown. Get to city center via **Express Shuttle** (☎523-8888); buses daily from Astrodome, Downtown, Galleria, Greenway Plaza, and Westside area hotels every 30min.-1 hr., depending on the destination. Runs 5:30am-6pm. $19-20, ages 5-12 $6, under 5 free. From downtown, allow 1hr. to get to the airport. **William P. Hobby Airport,** 7800 Airport Blvd. (☎640-3000; www.houstonairportsystem.org), lies about 10 mi. south of downtown and specializes in regional travel.

Trains: Amtrak, 902 Washington Ave. (☎224-1577). From downtown, during the day, catch a bus west on Washington Ave. to Houston Ave.; at night, call a cab. To **San Antonio** (5hr., 3 per week, $26-59) and **New Orleans** (9hr., 3 per week, $40-93). Open M-F 9am-midnight, 9am-4:30 Su. *Be careful entering and exiting station; the surrounding area can be unsafe, especially at night.*

Buses: Greyhound, 2121 Main St. (☎759-6509). *At night call a cab–this is an unsafe area.* Open 24hr. To: **Dallas** (4-6hr., 10 per day, $30); **San Antonio** (3½hr., 12 per day, $22); **Santa Fe** (24hr., 7 per day, $115).

Public Transit: Metropolitan Transit Authority (☎635-4000; www.ridemetro.org). Offers reliable service anywhere between NASA (15 mi. southeast of town) and Katy (25 mi. west of town). Operates M-F 6am-9pm, less frequently Sa-Su 8am-8pm. $1, seniors $0.40, ages 5-11 $0.25; day pass $2. The METRO operates a free trolley throughout downtown. Free maps available at the **Houston Public Library** (see **Internet Access,** below) or at Metro stores. (720 Main or 1001 Travis. Open M-F 7:30am-5:30pm.)

Taxi: United Cab, ☎699-0000.

ORIENTATION & PRACTICAL INFORMATION

Though the flat Texan terrain supports several mini-downtowns, the true down- quarish grid of interlocking one-way streets, borders the **Buffalo** section of I-10 and I-45. **The Loop (I-610)** encircles the city center mi. Anything inside the Loop is easily accessible by car or bus. *ne areas of south and east Houston, as they may be unsafe.* nain drag for the ritzy "Uptown" district can be found west of urants and shops line the nearby mansion infested **Kirby Drive** and but look out for detours, as these up and coming areas are per- nstruction.

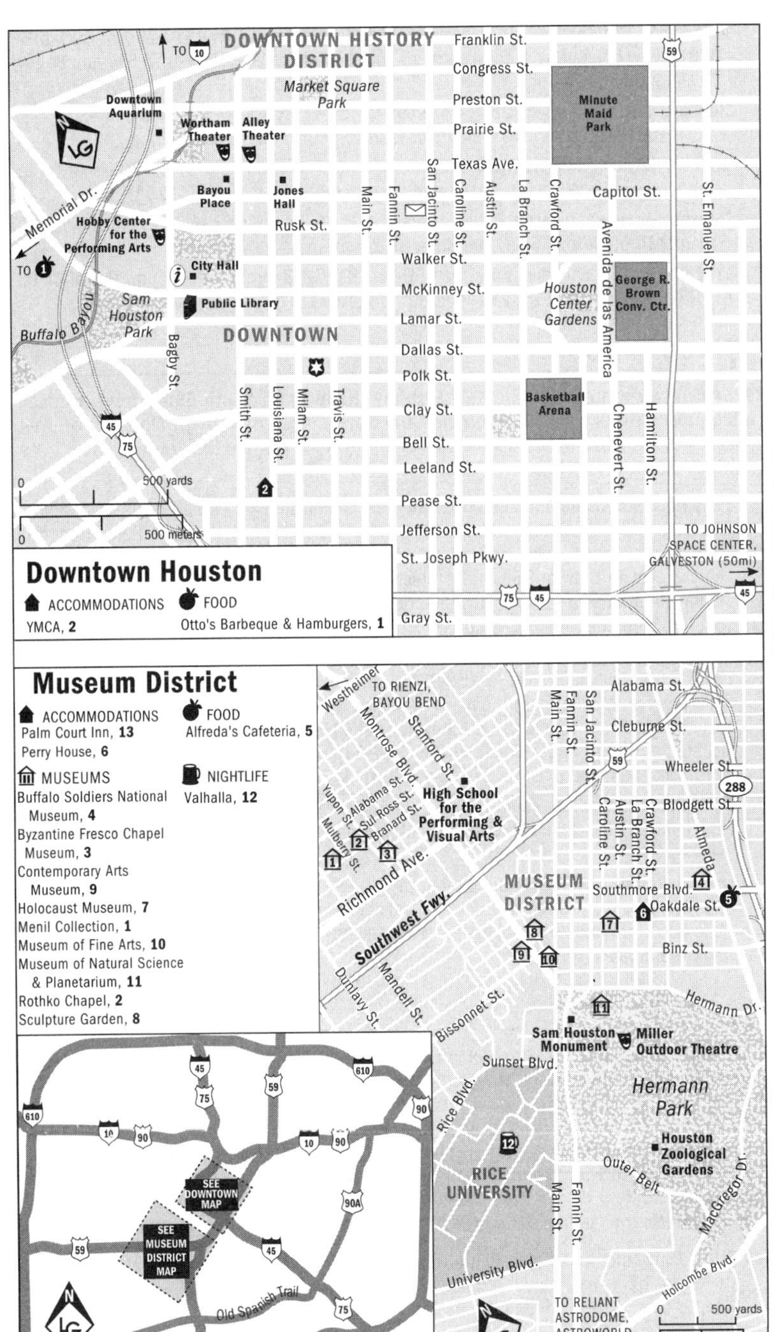
Downtown Houston
ACCOMMODATIONS
YMCA, 2
FOOD
Otto's Barbeque & Hamburgers, 1
DOWNTOWN HISTORY DISTRICT
Market Square Park
Downtown Aquarium
Wortham Theater
Alley Theater
Bayou Place
Jones Hall
Hobby Center for the Performing Arts
City Hall
Public Library
Sam Houston Park
Buffalo Bayou
Memorial Dr.
DOWNTOWN
Minute Maid Park
George R. Brown Conv. Ctr.
Houston Center Gardens
Basketball Arena
Franklin St.
Congress St.
Preston St.
Prairie St.
Texas Ave.
Capitol St.
Rusk St.
Walker St.
McKinney St.
Lamar St.
Dallas St.
Polk St.
Clay St.
Bell St.
Leeland St.
Pease St.
Jefferson St.
St. Joseph Pkwy.
Gray St.
Bagby St.
Smith St.
Louisiana St.
Milam St.
Travis St.
Main St.
Fannin St.
San Jacinto St.
Caroline St.
Austin St.
La Branch St.
Crawford St.
Avenida de las America
Chenevert St.
Hamilton St.
St. Emanuel St.
TO JOHNSON SPACE CENTER, GALVESTON (50mi)
500 yards
500 meters
Museum District
ACCOMMODATIONS
Palm Court Inn, 13
Perry House, 6
FOOD
Alfreda's Cafeteria, 5
MUSEUMS
Buffalo Soldiers National Museum, 4
Byzantine Fresco Chapel Museum, 3
Contemporary Arts Museum, 9
Holocaust Museum, 7
Menil Collection, 1
Museum of Fine Arts, 10
Museum of Natural Science & Planetarium, 11
Rothko Chapel, 2
Sculpture Garden, 8
NIGHTLIFE
Valhalla, 12
TO RIENZI, BAYOU BEND
Westheimer
Montrose Blvd.
Stanford St.
High School for the Performing & Visual Arts
Yupon St.
Alabama St.
Sul Ross St.
Branard St.
Mulberry St.
Richmond Ave.
Southwest Fwy.
Dunlavy St.
Mandell St.
Bissonnet St.
MUSEUM DISTRICT
Alabama St.
Cleburne St.
Wheeler St.
Blodgett St.
Almeda
Southmore Blvd.
Oakdale St.
Binz St.
Hermann Dr.
Sam Houston Monument
Miller Outdoor Theatre
Hermann Park
Houston Zoological Gardens
Outer Belt
MacGregor Dr.
Holcombe Blvd.
Sunset Blvd.
Rice Blvd.
RICE UNIVERSITY
University Blvd.
TO RELIANT ASTRODOME, ASTROWORLD, 13, 610 LOOP
SEE DOWNTOWN MAP
SEE MUSEUM DISTRICT MAP
Old Spanish Trail

TEXAS

Visitor Info: Greater Houston Convention and Visitors Bureau (☎437-5200 or 800-446-8786; www.houston-spacecityusa.com), in City Hall, at the corner of Walker and Bagby St. Open daily 9am-4pm.

Hotlines: Crisis Center, ☎228-1505. **Rape Crisis,** ☎528-7273. **Women's Center,** ☎528-2121. **Gay and Lesbian Switchboard of Houston,** ☎529-9615. All operate 24hr.

Medical Services: Bellaire Medical Center, 5314 Dashwood (☎512-1200), has a 24hr. emergency room. **Woman's Hospital of Texas,** 7600 Fannin (☎790-1234).

Internet Access: Houston Public Library, 500 McKinney (☎236-1313), at Bagby St. Open M-Th 9am-9pm, F-Sa 9am-6pm, Su 2-6pm.

Post Office: 701 San Jacinto St. (☎800-275-8777). Open M-F 8am-5pm. **Postal Code:** 77052. **Area Codes:** 713, 281, and 832; in text 713, unless indicated.

ACCOMMODATIONS

A few cheap motels dot the **Katy Freeway (I-10W)** and **South 59th Street.** Budget accommodations along **South Main Street** are more convenient (located on bus route #8), but *not all are safe.* Most campgrounds in the Houston area lie a considerable distance from the city center.

Perry House, Houston International Hostel, 5302 Crawford St. (☎523-1009; resv@houstonhostel.com) at Oakdale St., in the museum district near Hermann Park. From the Greyhound station, take bus #8, #15, #2, or #65 south to Southmore St., walk 6 blocks east to Crawford St. and 1 block south to Oakdale St. 33 beds in 7 well-kept rooms. Internet ($5 per hr.), kitchen, and 24hr. common area. Office open 8-10am and 5-11pm. Although there is no dorm access between these hours, the house common area remains open all day. Dorms $13; non-members $15. ❶

YMCA, 1600 Louisiana Ave. (☎758-9250), between Pease and Bell St. Downtown location features small, bright rooms—all singles with daily maid service. Some have private baths. Towel deposit $2.50. Key deposit $10. Singles $25-38. **Another branch** is located at 7903 South Loop East (☎643-2804), off the Broadway exit from I-610, near I-45. Take bus #50 to Broadway. Key deposit $15. Singles $28. ❶

Palm Court Inn, 8200 South Main St. (☎668-8000 or 800-255-8904; www.palmcourtinn.com). Plain, clean rooms. HBO, outdoor pool and spa, and continental breakfast. Singles $41; doubles $49. ❸

Traders Village, 7979 N. Eldridge Rd. (☎281-890-5500). Off I-10, take Eldridge Pkwy. exit, head north. This RV park not only provides shower, pool, and laundry facilities, but also hosts an area-wide flea-market on weekends. Sites $20-26; RVs $24-26. Hookup included in rates. ❶

FOOD

As a city by the sea, Houston has harbored many immigrants, and as such their cultures are well represented in the city's eclectic, ethnic cuisine. Mexican, Greek, Cajun, and Asian fare next to with barbecue and southern soul food supply travelers with many options. Bust your belt, not your budget, below ground in the **tunnels** connecting downtown's skyscrapers, or along the **chain-laden streets** of Westheimer and Richmond Avenue. While cheap Mexican food can be found in just about anywhere, the **East End** is peppered with authentic fare. Check out Chinatown, **DiHo,** on Bellaire, or **Little Vietnam** on S. Main for tasty, inexpensive eats.

Otto's Barbeque and Hamburgers, 5502 Memorial Dr. (☎864-2573). A Houston institution for 52 years, the unassuming Otto's, located in the corner of an old strip shopping center, dishes up great barbecue and all the fixins. The Bush Plate (sliced beef, links, ribs, potato salad, and beans; $9.50) is a favorite among both customers and a certain former President (who has been known to drop by for a bite). Open M-F 11am-7pm, Sa 11am-6pm. ❸

One's A Meal: The Greek Village Restaurant, 607 W. Gray St. (☎523-0425), at Stanford St. This family-owned, Greek-American establishment serves everything from chili 'n' eggs ($6) to a gyro with fries ($6). Try the 4 varieties of Greek pizza (6 in. $6) or the crowd pleasing *dolmades* (stuffed grape leaves) which are, yes, $6. Open 24hr. ❶

Ragin' Cajun, 4302 Richmond Ave. (☎623-6321). A local favorite for Cajun-style seafood. Indoor picnic tables, creole music, and a casual atmosphere. Po' boys $6-9. Gumbo $4. Longneck beers $2.75. Open M-Th 11am-10pm, F-Sa 11am-11pm. ❷

Alfreda's Cafeteria, 5101 Almeda Rd. (☎523-6462), close to Perry House. Alfreda's serves up soul food for cheap; the special of the day includes meat, 2 vegetables, and bread for only $4.50. Open daily 7am-7pm. ❶

House of Pies, 6142 Westheimer Blvd. (☎782-1290). This quaint diner serves breakfast all day ($5-6.50), but as their name suggests, they are popular for their pastry. $2.40 fruit pies. $4 strawberry cheesecake. Open 24hr. ❶

SIGHTS

TEXAS

JOHNSON SPACE CENTER. The city's most popular attraction, **Space Center Houston,** is located outside Houston city limits in Clear Lake, TX. Admission includes tours of the center's historic mission control and educational films in Texas' largest Giant Screen theater. The complex also houses models of Gemini, Apollo, and Mercury crafts. Take the new Level Nine Tour, a 4hr. behind-the-scenes excursion that includes stops at the neutral bouyancy laboratory—an astronaut preparatory facility—and access to high security areas like the new and active mission control center. *(1601 NASA Rd. 1. Take I-45 south to NASA Rd. exit, then head east 3 mi.; or take bus #246. ☎281-244-2100 or 800-972-0369; www.jsc.nasa.gov. Open June-Aug. daily 9am-7pm; Sept.-May M-F 10am-5pm, Sa-Su 10am-7pm. $17, seniors $16, ages 4-11 $13. Parking $3.)*

THE SAN JACINTO BATTLEGROUND STATE HISTORICAL PARK. This 570ft. monument built in honor of those who fought for Texas independence is the world's largest memorial tower. Riding to the top provides a stunning view of the battleground upon which Sam Houston's outnumbered Texan Army defeated Santa Anna's Mexican troops, forever sealing Texas' independence from Mexico. The base of the monument houses a museum celebrating Texas history with remnants like the Battleship Texas—not only the last surviving Dreadnought, but also the only surviving battleship to have served in both World Wars. *(Take loop 610 to Hwy. 225 E. Take the Battleground Road (Hwy. 134) exit, head north, and exit onto Juan Seguin Blvd. ☎281-479-2421. Open daily 9am-6pm. $3, seniors $2.50, under 11 $2. Museum: ☎281-479-2431. Open daily 9am-6pm. Free. 40min. projector, multimedia slide show daily every hr. 10am-5pm. $3.50/3/2.50. Combo tickets with elevator ride $6/5/4. Battleship: ☎281-479-2431. Open daily 10am-5pm. $5, seniors $4, ages 6-18 $3, under 6 free.)*

HERMANN PARK. Consisting of 445 acres of carefully preserved urban green space and located near Rice University, the Texas Medical Center, and Miller Outdoor Theater (see **Entertainment,** below), **Hermann Park** is home to a children's zoo, golf course, sports facilities, kiddie train, and Japanese garden. Near the northern entrance of the park, the **Houston Museum of Natural Science** includes a planetarium, IMAX theater, six-story glass butterfly center, and a hands-on learning gallery. Be sure to walk through the new Weiss Energy Hall, an installment funded by Houston's biggest oil companies, illustrating through sleeve guns and interactive computer stations how an urban cowboy can strike it rich. At the southern end of the park lies the **Houston Zoological Gardens,** entertaining crowds with 3500 exotic animals representing over 700 species. *(Museum of Natural Science: 1 Hermann Circle Dr. ☎ 639-4629; www.hmns.org. Exhibits open M-Sa 9am-6pm, Su 11am-6pm. Museum $6, seniors and under 12 $3.50; IMAX $7/4.50; planetarium $5/3.50; butterfly center $5/3.50. Japanese tea garden: Open daily 10am-6pm. Free. Zoo: 1513 N. MacGregor. ☎ 533-6500; www.houstonzoo.org. Open daily 10am-6pm. $7, seniors $5, ages 3-12 $3.)*

DOWNTOWN AQUARIUM. Located on the western border of downtown, this underwater adventure isn't your average fishtank. With valet parking and upscale drinking and dining, the **Downtown Aquarium** caters to a varied clientele. Kids enjoy the intricately choreographed dancing fountains and ferris wheel, while grown-ups flock to the Dive Lounge for after dinner drinks. *(410 Bagby St. ☎ 223-3473. Aquarium exhibits open Su-Th 10am-10pm, F-Sa 10am-11pm. $7.50 adults, $6.50 seniors, ages 2-12 $5.30. Restaurants and lounge operate on different hours—call to check.)*

ART ATTRACTIONS. At Houston's **Museum of Fine Arts,** the Caroline Wiess Law building showcases contemporary and modern collections, while the Audrey Jones Beck building displays everything from ancient European art to Impressionist pieces. Be sure to see the Glassell Collection of African Gold, considered one of the best of its kind in the world. *(1001 Bissonet. ☎ 639-7300; www.mfah.org. Open Tu-W 10am-5pm, Th 10am-9pm, F-Sa 10am-7pm, Su 12:15-7pm. $5, students and seniors $2.50, Th free. Garden: 5101 Montrose Blvd. Open daily 9am-10pm. Free.)* Across the street, the **Contemporary Arts Museum** frequently rotates exhibits. *(5216 Montrose St. ☎ 284-8250; www.camh.org. Open Tu-W and F-Sa 10am-5pm, Th 10am-9pm, Su noon-5pm.)*

The **Menil Foundation** consists of four buildings grouped within a block of each other. Housing Surrealist paintings and sculptures, Byzantine and medieval artifacts, and European, American, and African art, the **Menil Collection** also provides temporary residence to touring installments. *(1515 Sul Ross. ☎ 525-9400; www.menil.org. Open W-Su 11am-7pm. Free.)* A block away, the **Rothko Chapel** houses 14 of Mark Rothko's famous monochromatic paintings in a non-denominational sanctuary. The Broken Obelisk sculpture out front provides a backdrop for area religious festivals staged on the chapel's grounds. *(3900 Yupon. Open daily 10am-6pm. Free.)* The **Byzantine Fresco Chapel Museum** displays the carefully restored ornate dome and apse from a 13th-century Byzantine chapel in Cyprus that was rescued in 1983 from antiquity thieves before its pieces were sold on the black market. *(4011 Yupon. ☎ 521-3990. Open F-Su 11am-6pm. Free.)*

OTHER MUSEUMS. Between the end of the Civil War in 1866 and the integration of the armed forces in 1944, the US Army had several all-black units. During the Indian Wars of the late 1800s, the Cheyenne soldiers nicknamed these troops "Buffalo Soldiers," both because of their naturally curly hair and as a sign of respect for their fighting spirit. Learn the history of the Buffalo Soldiers and African-Americans in the military from the Revolutionary War to the present at the **Buffalo Soldiers National Museum.** *(1834 Southmore. ☎ 942-8920; www.buffalosoldiermuseum.com. Open M-F 10am-5pm, Sa 10am-4pm. Free.)* The **Holocaust Museum** features a chilling architectural style that recalls that of the Nazis' concentration camps. The museum also has a rotating art gallery and two films about the Holocaust. *(5401 Caroline St. ☎ 942-8000; www.hmh.org. Open M-F 9am-5pm, Sa-Su noon-5pm. Free.)*

BAYOU BEND. The Hogg collection of American decorative art found in the **Bayou Bend Collection and Gardens** in **Memorial Park** is an antique-lover's dream. This mecca of Americana includes John Singleton Copley portraits and Paul Revere silver pieces, all preserved in the Hogg mansion. *(1 Westcott St. ☎ 639-7750, ext. 7750; www.bayoubend.uh.edu. Collection open Tu-Sa 10am-5pm, Su 1-5pm. $10, seniors and students $8.50, ages 10-18 $5, under 10 not admitted. Gardens open Tu-Sa 10am-5pm, Su 1-5pm. 1½hr.*

garden tours by reservation. $3, under 10 free.) For the European counterpart to Bayou Bend, visit Rienzi, located along the same ravine. Formerly the residence of Houstonian Harris Masterson III, the **Rienzi Mansion** exhibits Georgian English decorative art including gilded footstools made for Spencer House, once the London home of Princess Diana. *(1406 Kirby Dr. ☎ 639-7800. M and Th-Sa 10am-4pm, Su 1-5pm. $4. Viewing of the house is only available via tour, so call ahead to reserve your spot.)*

ENTERTAINMENT

From March to October, symphony, opera, ballet companies, and various professional theaters stage free performances at the **Miller Outdoor Theatre** (☎284-8352), in Hermann Park. The annual **Shakespeare Festival** struts and frets upon the stage in August. The downtown **Alley Theatre,** 615 Texas Ave., puts on Broadway-caliber productions at moderate prices. (☎228-8421; www.alleytheatre.org. Tickets $37-54; Su-Th $12 student rush tickets 1hr. before the show.) For downtown entertainment, **Bayou Place,** 500 Texas Ave., holds several restaurants, and live music venues. The **Angelika Film Center and Café,** 510 Texas Ave., plays foreign, independent, and classic American films. (☎225-5232. $8, students $6.) The new **Hobby Center for the Performing Arts,** 800 Bagby St. (☎227-2001; www.thehobbycenter.org), features a dome ceiling with a fiberoptic display of the Texas night sky and hosts **Theatre Under the Stars** as well as the **Broadway in Houston Series. Jones Hall,** 615 Louisiana Blvd. (☎227-3974), stages more of Houston's highbrow entertainment. The **Houston Symphony Orchestra** performs in Jones September-May. (☎227-2787. $25-70.) Between October and May, the **Houston Grand Opera** (www.houstongrandopera.org) produces six operas in the nearby **Wortham Center,** 500 Texas Ave. (☎546-0200. $30-275; student rush available day of show $10-25, call ahead to reserve.) The **Houston Astros** play ball at Minute Maid Park (☎295-8000), located at the intersections of Texas, Crawford, and Congress St. near Union Station downtown. From February to mid-March, there's plenty of space in both the Reliant Center and Reliant Arena to house the **Houston Livestock Show and Rodeo** (☎832-667-1000; www.hlsr.com). Its nothin' but net in the new downtown Basketball Arena, at Polk and Crawford St., home of the **Houston Rockets,** while the **Houston Texans** pass the pigskin at **Reliant Stadium,** 8400 Kirby Dr. (☎336-7700).

NIGHTLIFE

As Houston's downtown evolves in preparation for the 2004 Super Bowl and its new light rail system, the bars and clubs in the skyscraper district are multiplying. Most of Houston's nightlife, however, happens west of downtown around Richmond and Westheimer Ave. Montrose is home to several gay bars and clubs, while enormous, warehouse-style dance halls line the upper reaches of Richmond. For a evening drowning in swank head farther west to the uptown (Galleria) district.

City Streets, 5078 Richmond Ave. (☎840-8555) gives you the opportunity to booty-shake or boot-scoot in its 5 different clubs. W no cover; Th ladies free, men $5; F-Sa $5. Open W-F 5pm-2am, Sa 7pm-2am.

Valhalla, Keck Hall, Rice University, (☎348-3258). For "gods, heroes, mythical beings, and cheap beer," descend to the depths of Keck Hall located in the center of the Rice campus. Beers on tap from $0.85. Open M-F 4pm-2am, Su 7pm-2am. Lunch ($3-4) served weekdays 11:30am-1pm.

J.R.'s, 808 Pacific St. (☎521-2519.) This upbeat gay nightclub serves moderately priced drinks ($3-5) to the tune of techno and dance. No cover. Open daily noon-2am.

NO WORK, ALL PLAY

WHAT IN THE DICKENS?

Every first full weekend in December, sunny Galveston's historic Strand District is transformed into a bustling Victorian town, replete with over 3000 costumed street vendors, strolling carolers, and street musicians. **Dickens on the Strand,** hosted by the Galveston Historical Society, began 30 years ago as a fundraiser to finance the preservation of historic downtown Galveston. The festival not only prevented the destruction of the Strand District, but was also largely responsible for the District's induction as a National Historic Landmark. Today the festival attracts over 50,000 visitors each year.

The weekend includes two parades heralded by "Queen Victoria" herself, as well as a costume contest in which competitors dressed as their favorite Dickens character vie for a coveted spot in the Pickwick Lanternlight Parade. For those of a less competitive ilk, dressing in traditional Victorian garb will get you in the festival free of charge. "Dickens on the Strand" goes so far as to forecast "snow" for the festivities, using over 30,000 pounds of ice. But get there early, as the tropical clime prevents any polar precipitation from lasting too long.

Tickets: $12 at the gate; $10 when purchased before Dec. 6. $16 2-day pass. For more info, visit www.dickensonthestrand.org.

DAY TRIP FROM HOUSTON

GALVESTON ISLAND

When cotton was King, Galveston was "Queen of the Gulf." However, the glamourous port that played a large role in the expansion of Western trade was dethroned on September 8, 1900, when a devastating hurricane ripped through the city and claimed 6000 lives. Yet with over 32 mi. of sand and a wealth of history, it's no wonder today's tides perpetually bring in scores of visitors. A popular spring break destination for Texan co-eds, the southern end of the island, **Seawall Boulevard,** is full of cheap eats and rentals, while the northern end, the historic **Strand District,** attracts antique collectors and history buffs. Found along Strand St. between 20th and 25th St., the Strand District is a national landmark restored with authentic gas lights and brick-paved walkways, along with many Victorian buildings, cafes and shops. The elegant **Moody Mansion,** 2618 Broadway, features hand-carved wood and stunning stained glass. (☎762-7668. Open M-Sa 10am-4pm, Su noon-4pm. $6, seniors $5, ages 6-18 $3.) On the west side of the island lies an amusement park by the same name. The Moody Gardens consists of three glass pyramids housing interactive space exhibits, an IMAX 3-D theater, a tropical rainforest, over 25 acres of garden, and an artificial white sand beach complete with lagoons and palm trees. (1 Hope Blvd. From Seawall Blvd., take a right on 81st St. ☎683-4200 or 800-582-4673; www.moodygardens.com. Open summer daily 10am-9pm; winter 9am-6pm. Aquarium $14, seniors $10, ages 4-12 $7. Rainforest $9/7/6. IMAX $9/7/6. Ridefilm $8/7/6. Day pass to all attractions $30. Adult admission discounted after 6pm.)

The only beach in Galveston which permits alcoholic beverages is **R.A. Apffel Park,** on the far eastern edge of the island (known as East Beach). On the west end of the island, east of Pirates Beach, **#3 Beach Pocket Park** has bathrooms, showers, playgrounds, and a concession stand. (Open daily 10am-6pm; some open later. Car entry for beaches generally $7.) At Ferry Rd. (off the far eastern end of Seawall, across from the Sandpiper Motel), catch a ferry to **Bolivar Island,** fondly dubbed "The Zoo" by spring breakers. The oldest restaurant on the island, **The Original Mexican Cafe ❷,** 1401 Market St., dishes up tasty enchilada plates starting at $4.50. (☎762-6001. Open M-Th 11am-9pm, F 11am-10pm, Sa 8am-10pm, Su 8am-9pm.)

CORPUS CHRISTI ☎361

Corpus Christi's shoreside locale makes it a multi-faceted money-maker. The warm gulf waters produce Corpus' copious amounts of tourists and crude oil. Summer vacationers are replaced in the cooler months by "winter Texans," a breed of northern mobile-home owners who head south to enjoy coastal warmth. Defined by its pricey knick-knacks, natural stretches of sand, and the encroaching waste that floats in from the Gulf, Corpus Christi is a unique Texas stopover.

TRANSPORTATION **Greyhound,** 702 N. Chaparral (☎882-9206; open daily 7am-2am) runs to: Austin (6hr., 3 per day, $27.50); Dallas (10-11hr., 6 per day, $45); Houston (5hr., 7 per day, $24). **Regional Transit Authority** (☎289-2600), also known as the "B," buses within Corpus Christi. Pick up maps and schedules at the Visitors Center or at **The B Headquarters,** 1806 S. Alameda (☎883-2287; open M-F 8am-5pm). City Hall, Port Ayers, Six Points, and the Staples St. stations serve as central transfer points. (Runs M-Sa 5:30am-9:30pm, Su 11am-6:30pm. Fare $0.50; students, seniors, and children $0.25; Sa $0.25; transfers free.) The **Harbor Ferry** follows the shoreline and stops at the aquarium (runs daily 10:30am-6:30pm; each way $3 day pass). On the north side of Harbor Bridge, the free **Beach Shuttle** also travels to the beach, the Aquarium, and other attractions (runs May-Sept. 10:30am-6:30pm). **Taxi: Yellow Cab,** ☎884-3211.

PRACTICAL INFORMATION. Corpus Christi's tourist district follows **Shoreline Drive,** which borders the Gulf Coast, 1 mi. east of the downtown business district. **Convention and Visitors Bureau,** 1823 Chaparral, 6 blocks north of I-37 and 1 block from the water. (☎561-2000 or 800-766-2322; www.corpuschristi-tx-cvb.org. Open daily 9am-5pm.) **Medical Services: Spohn Hospital Shoreline,** 600 Elizabeth St. (☎881-3000). **Hotlines: Hope Line** (☎855-4673) and **Battered Women and Rape Victims Shelter** (☎884-2900); both operate 24hr. **Internet Access: Corpus Christi Public Library,** 805 Comanche. (☎880-7000. Open M-Th 9am-9pm, F-Sa 9am-6pm, Su 2-6pm.) **Post Office:** 809 Nueces Bay Blvd. (☎800-275-8777. Open M-F 7:30am-5:30pm, Sa 8am-1pm.) **Postal Code:** 78469. **Area Code:** 361.

ACCOMMODATIONS. Cheap accommodations are scarce downtown, and posh hotels and motels take up much of the shoreline. The best motel bargains lie several miles south on Leopard St. (take bus #27) or at the Port Ave. exit off I-37. One of the cheapest bets in town, the **Howard Johnson ❸,** 722 N. Port Ave., provides clean, comfortable rooms with microfridges. (☎883-7400. M-F singles $60; doubles $65.) Campers should head to **Padre Island National Seashore** (p. 710). Nueces River **City Park ❶** (☎241-1464), off I-37 N from Exit 16 and approximately 18 mi. from downtown Corpus, has free tent sites but only pit toilets and no showers. Camping permits available from the tourist info center at 14333 IH-37 S.

FOOD & NIGHTLIFE. Corpus Christi manages to bring a bit of the Gulf Coast into its otherwise chain-laden cuisine, with several inexpensive seafood shacks found along the shore. Try **Pier 99 ❷,** 2822 N. Shoreline Dr., which specializes in fried fresh fish, including shrimp or oyster baskets ($7). (☎887-0764. Open daily 11am-10pm.) **Blackbeard's ❷,** 3117 N. Surfside Blvd., serves true Texan cuisine—both Mexican platters and country fried goodness. The lunch specials are inexpensive and great after a morning on beach. Try either the enchiladas or the chicken fried steak both $5. Full bar. (☎884-1030. Open daily 11am-10pm.) Get your groove on boot-scooting to top 40 country at **Dead Eye Dick's,** then bump and grind to top 40 dance at **Stinger's,** both located at 301 N. Chaparral St. (☎882-2192. Cover $3-8. Open W-Sa 11pm-2am.)

SIGHTS. Although obstructed by monolithic seaside motels and overrun by ravenous gulls, Corpus Christi's endless shoreline provides quite a sight. The best beach is **Port Aransas,** reachable by ferry (on Rte. 361). To find beaches that allow swimming (some lie along Ocean Dr. and north of Harbor Bridge), just follow the signs. On the north side of Harbor Bridge, the **Texas State Aquarium,** 2710 N. Shoreline Blvd., showcases sharks and rays roaming, in true Texas fashion, beneath an oil platform (☎881-1200 or 800-477-4853; www.texasstateaquarium.org. Open June-Aug. M-Sa 9am-6pm, Su 10am-6pm; early Sept.-late May M-Sa 9am-5pm, Su 10am-5pm. $12, seniors $10, ages 4-12 $7.) Just offshore floats the aircraft carrier **USS Lexington,** a WW II relic now open to the public. Today's Lexington has an on-deck flight simulator. (☎888-4873 or 800-523-9539. Open daily June-Aug. 9am-6pm; early Sept.-late May 9am-5pm. $10, seniors $8, ages 4-12 $5.) Pick up $1-off coupons to the aquarium and ship at the Visitors Center.

PADRE ISLAND ☎361

With over 80 mi. of painstakingly preserved beaches, dunes, and wildlife refuge land, the **Padre Island National Seashore (PINS)** is a priceless (though debris-flawed) gem sandwiched between the prolific condos of North Padre Island and the scandalous spring-break hordes of South Padre Island. The seashore provides excellent opportunities for windsurfing, swimming, or surf fishing. Driving is permitted at most places on the beach, though four-wheel drive is recommended. Padre Island is divided into several areas; gain entrance to each area through the access roads. Access 1A is at the far northern tip of the island near Port Aransas, while Access 6 is closest to PINS. Motorists enter the PINS via the JFK Causeway, from the Flour Bluff area of Corpus Christi. PINS can only be reached by car. For up-to-date info on prices and activities, as well as maps and exhibits about the island, call or visit the **Malaquite Visitors Center.** (☎949-8068; www.nps.gov/pais. Open daily summer 8:30am-6pm; winter 8:30am-4:30pm.) Garbage from nearby ships frequently litters the sands, but a lucky few may spot one of the endangered Kemp's Ridley sea turtles nurtured by PINS. A yearly pass into PINS costs $20 for cars, or buy a weekly pass ($10). Windsurfing or boat-launching from the Bird Basin costs a $10 for a yearly pass or $5 for a day. Many avoid these fees by going to **North Beach. Bob Hall Pier,** Access 4, is the main fishing pier. (☎949-0999. Open 24hr. $1.)

Five miles south of the entrance station, **Malaquite Beach** provides all the amenities for a comfy day on the beach. In summer, a rental station is set up on the beachfront (inner tubes $2 per hr., chairs $2 per hr., body boards $2.50 per hr.) Loose sands prevent most vehicles from venturing far onto the beach. Visitors with four-wheel drive and a taste for solitude should make the 60 mi. trek to the **Mansfield Cut,** the most remote and untraveled area of the seashore. Call the **Malaquite Ranger Station** (☎949-8173), 3½ mi. south of the park entrance, for emergency assistance. No wheels? Hike the **Grasslands Nature Trail,** a ¾ mi. paved loop through sand dunes and grasslands. Guide pamphlets are available at the trailhead. The **PINS Campground ❶,** 1 mi. north of the Visitors Center, consists of an asphalt area for RVs, restrooms, and cold-rinse showers. (Sites $8.) Outside of this area—with the exception of the 5 mi. pedestrian-only beach—camping is free. **Area Code:** 361.

WEST TEXAS

AMARILLO ☎806

Named for the yellow clay of nearby Lake Meredith (*amarillo* is Spanish for "yellow"), Amarillo began as a railroad construction camp in 1887 and ultimately evolved into a Texas-size truck stop. After years of cattle and oil, Amarillo is now the prime overnight stop for motorists en route from Dallas, Houston, or Oklahoma City to Denver and other Western destinations. For travelers, it's little more than a one-day city—but what a grand, shiny truck stop it is.

The largest history museum in the state of Texas, the **Panhandle-Plains Historical Museum,** 2401 4th Ave., I-27 S to Rte. 87 in nearby Canyon, displays an impressive collection of "cowboy" art as well as a replicated, life-size pioneer town and working oil derrick. (☎651-2244. Open summer M-Sa 9am-6pm, Su 1-6pm; low-season M-Sa 9am-5pm, Su 1-6pm. $4, seniors $3, ages 4-13 $1.) The **American Quarter Horse Heritage Center and Museum,** 2601 I-40 E, at Exit 72B, presents the heroic story of "America's horse." Try your hand at a galloping steed on the museum's mechanical horse ride. (☎376-5181 or 888-209-8322; www.panhandleplains.org. Open M-Sa 9am-5pm, Su noon-5pm. $4, seniors $3.50, ages 6-18 $2.50.) At **Cadillac Ranch,** Stanley Marsh III planted 10 Cadillacs—model years 1948 to 1963—at the same angle as the Great Pyramids, and as one local notes, "they didn't take root, neither." Get off I-40 at the Hope Rd. Exit, 9 mi. west of Amarillo, cross to the south side of I-40, turn right at the end of the bridge, and drive ½ mi. down the highway access road.

Amarillo provides over 4000 beds for travelers to leave their boots under. Budget motels proliferate along the entire stretch of I-40, I-27, and U.S. 287/87 near town. Prices rise near downtown. One of the most popular options is the **Big Texan Motel ❸,** 7701 I-40 E, adjacent to the Big Texan Steak Ranch, which promises a free 72 oz. steak dinner, if you can eat the cut in under an hour. (☎372-5000. Restaurant and swimming pool. Singles $45; doubles $65.) **KOA Kampground ❶,** 1100 Folsom Rd., has a pool in summer. Take I-40 to Exit 75, head north to Rte. 60, then east 1 mi. (☎335-1792. Laundry and coffee. Reception daily June-Aug. 8am-10pm; Sept.-May 8am-8pm. Sites $20; with water and power $27; full hookup $28.)

At **Dyer's BBQ ❷,** I-40 at Georgia, heaping portions and a friendly vibe make this a local favorite. The rib plate includes three ribs, potato salad, cole slaw, baked beans, apricots, and onion rings for $8—sharing is advised. (☎358-7104. Open M-Sa 11am-10pm, Su 11am-9pm.) For a taste of West Texas Mexican eats, head to the most popular joint in town, **Tacos Garcia ❷**, 1100 S. Ross. Try the Laredo platter (3 roast beef flautas with rice, beans, and guac; $7), and satisfy your sweet tooth with flaky, fresh *sopapillas*—a pastry covered in sugar and honey; three for $3. (☎371-0411. Open M 10:30am-9:30pm, Tu-Sa 10:30am-10pm, Su 10:30am-3:30pm.)

Amarillo sprawls at the intersection of I-27, I-40, and U.S. 287/87. To explore, you need a car. Rte. 335 (the Loop) encircles the city. Amarillo Blvd. (historic Rte. 66) runs east-west, parallel to I-40. **Greyhound,** 700 S. Tyler (☎374-5371; open 24hr.), buses to Dallas (8hr., 4 per day, $60-66) and Santa Fe (10hr., 3 per day, $58-64). **Amarillo City Transit,** 801 SE 23rd, operates eight bus routes departing from 5th and Pierce St. Maps are at the office. (☎378-3095. Buses run every 15-30min. M-Sa 6:30am-6:30pm. $0.75.) The **Texas Travel Info Center,** 9700 I-40E, at Exit 76, has state info. (☎335-1441. Open daily 8am-6pm.) The **Amarillo Convention and Visitors Bureau,** 401 S. Buchanan St. Suite 101, dishes the local scoop. (☎374-8474 or 800-692-1338; www.amarillo-cvb.org. Open M-F 8am-5pm.) **Internet Access: Public Library,** 413 E. 4th Ave., at Buchanan and Pierce across from the CivicCenter. (Open M-Th 9am-9pm, Sa 9am-6pm, Su 2-6pm.) **Post Office:** 505 E. 9th Ave., at Buchanan St. (☎468-2148. Open M-F 7:30am-5pm.) **Postal Code:** 79105. **Area Code:** 806.

NEAR AMARILLO: PALO DURO CANYON STATE PARK

Twenty-three miles south of Amarillo, Palo Duro Canyon, known as the "Grand Canyon of Texas," covers 20,000 acres of breathtaking beauty. Take I-27 to Exit 106 and head east on Rte. 217. The 16 mi. **scenic drive** through the park begins at the headquarters. Rangers allow backcountry **hiking,** but the majority of visitors stick to the interconnected marked trails. Most hikers can manage the **Sunflower Trail** (3 mi.), the **Juniper Trail** (2 mi.), or the **Paseo del Río Trail** (2 mi.), but only experienced hikers should consider the rugged **Running Trail** (9 mi.). Avid bikers enjoy the **Capitol Peak Mountain Bike Trail** (4 mi.). The **Lighthouse Trail** (5 mi.) leads to magnificent geological formations. (Park open summer daily 7am-10pm; winter 8am-10pm. $3, under 12 free.) Temperatures in the canyon frequently climb to 100°F; bring at least 2 quarts of water. The park headquarters, just inside the park, has maps of hiking trails and info on park activities. (☎488-2227. Open daily summer 7am-10pm; winter 8am-5pm.) The official play of Texas, the musical **Texas Legacies,** performed in Pioneer Amphitheater, 1514 5th Ave., is not to be missed. With the canyon as its back drop, the epic drama includes a tree splitting lightning bolt and is heralded by a fearless horseback rider who greets the audience galloping along the canyon's rim. (☎655-2181. Summer M-Tu and Th-Su 8:30pm. $11-26, under 12 $5-23.)**Old West Stables,** ¼ mi. farther along, rents horses and saddles. (☎488-2180. Rides offered Apr.-Oct. 10am, noon, 2, 4pm; June-Aug. 10am, noon, 2, 4, 6pm. $20 per hr., wagon rides for groups of 10 or more. $5, children $3. Reservations recommended.) A ½ mi. past the HQ, the **Visitors Center** displays exhibits on the canyon's history. (Open M-Sa 9am-5pm, Su 1-5pm.)

GUADALUPE MOUNTAINS NATIONAL PARK ☎915

Rising austerely above the parched west Texas desert, these peaks form the highest and most remote of the west Texas ranges. Mescalero Apaches hunted and camped on these lands, until they were driven out by the US army. Today, Guadalupe Mountains National Park encompasses 86,000 acres of desert, caves, canyons, and highlands. Drivers can glimpse the park's most dramatic sights from U.S. 62/180: **El Capitán,** a 2000 ft. limestone cliff, and **Guadalupe Peak,** the highest point in Texas (8749 ft.). The mountains promise over 80 mi. of challenging desert trails to those willing to explore the area. Entrance to the park is $3 per person.

The major park trailhead is at Pine Springs Campground, near the Main Visitors Center (see below). From this starting point, a difficult but rewarding full-day hike scales imposing **Guadalupe Peak** (5-7hr., 8½ mi.). A shorter trek (3-4hr., 4¼ mi.) traces the sheltered streambed of **Devil's Hall.** Accessible from a trailhead at its eponymous Visitors Center, **McKittrick Canyon** attracts people from hundreds of miles away in late October-early November with brilliant foliage (2¼-11mi. one-way). The **Smith Spring Trail** (1-2hr., 2¼ mi.) leads from the **Frijole Ranch,** about 1 mi. north of the Visitors Center, to a mountain spring frequented by wildlife.

The park's lack of development is attractive to backpackers, but it creates some inconveniences. The nearest gas and food spot is the **Nickel Creek Cafe ❶,** 5 mi. north of Pine Springs. (☎828-3295. Burgers $4. Open M-Sa 7am-2pm and 6-9pm. Cash only.) The park's two campgrounds, **Pine Springs ❶,** just past park headquarters, and **Dog Canyon ❶,** south of the New Mexico border at the north end of the park, have water and restrooms but no hookups or showers. (☎828-3251. No wood or charcoal fires. Reservations for groups only. Sites $8.) Dog Canyon is accessible only via Rte. 137 from Carlsbad, NM (72 mi.), or by a full-day hike from the **Main Visitors Center** at Pine Springs, off U.S. 62/180. (☎828-3251. Open daily June-Aug. 8am-6pm, Sept.-May 8am-4:30pm. After hours, info is posted on the outside bulletin board.) Free **backcountry camping** permits are available at the Visitors Center.

Carlsbad, NM (see p. 871), 55 mi. northeast, and **El Paso** (see p. 713), 110 mi. west, both make good bases for visiting the park. **TNM&O Coaches** (☎505-887-1108) runs along U.S. 62/180 between them and will stop at the Pine Springs Visitors Center if you call ahead (from Carlsbad 2½hr., $26). For additional info, check the web site (www.nps.gov/gumo), call the Visitors Center, or write to **Guadalupe Mountains National Park,** HC 60, Box 400, Salt Flat, TX 79847. **Area code:** 915.

EL PASO ☎915

The largest of the US border towns, El Paso boomed in the 17th century as a stopover on an important east-west wagon route that followed the Río Grande through "the pass" (*el paso*) between the Rocky Mountains and the Sierra Madre. Today, the El Paso-Ciudad Juárez metropolitan area has nearly three million inhabitants, a number that keeps growing due to an increase in the cross-border enterprises fueled by NAFTA. Nearly everyone in El Paso speaks Spanish, and the majority are of Mexican descent. After dark, activity leaves the center of town, migrating toward the suburbs and south of the border to raucous Ciudad Juárez.

ORIENTATION & PRACTICAL INFORMATION. San Jacinto Plaza, at the corner of Main and Oregon, is the heart of El Paso. **I-10** runs east-west and **U.S. 54** north-south from the city. El Paso is divided east-west by **Santa Fe Street** and north-south by **San Antonio Avenue.** *Tourists should be wary of the streets between San Antonio and the border late at night.* **El Paso International Airport** (☎780-4749; take Sun Metro bus #33 to the city center) has major airline service. **Amtrak** runs trains from **Union Train Depot,** 700 San Francisco St., to **Tucson** (6hr., 3 per week, $43-145) and **San Antonio** (12½hr., 3 per week, $116-225). **Greyhound,** 200 W. San Antonio, (☎532-2365) near the Civic Center, has daily service to: **Albuquerque** (5½hr., 3 per day, $38); **Tucson** (6hr., 12 per day, $37); **Dallas** (12hr., 11 per day, $54). **El Paso-LA Bus Lines,** 720 Oregon St. (☎532-4061), on the corner of 6th Ave., is significantly cheaper than Greyhound and offers service to major destinations in the Southwest. **Visitor Info: Visitors Center,** 1 Civic Center Plaza, at Santa Fe and San Francisco. (☎544-0062; www.visitelpaso.com. Open daily 8am-5pm.) **Post Office:** 219 E. Mills, between Mesa and Stanton. (☎532-8824. Open M-F 8:30am-5pm, Sa 8:30am-noon.) **Postal Code:** 79901. **Area Code:** 915.

ACCOMMODATIONS & FOOD. El Paso offers safer, more appealing places to stay than Ciudad Juárez. The town center, near Main St. and San Jacinto Sq. hosts several good budget hotels. The best place in town is the **El Paso International Hostel ❶,** 311 E. Franklin, between Stanton and Kansas in the Gardner Hotel, where great pride is taken in customer care. From the airport, take bus #33 to San Jacinto Park, walk two blocks north to Franklin, turn right, and head east 1½ blocks. (☎532-3661. Sheets $2, towels $0.50. Dorms $15.) **Gardner Hotel ❷,** 311 E. Franklin, is the oldest continually operating hotel in El Paso. John Dillinger stayed here in 1934. All rooms have A/C and cable TV. (☎532-3661;www.gardnerhotel.com. Singles with shared bath $20; doubles with shared bath $30, private baths from $40.) Camp at **Hueco Tanks State Historical Park ❶** (see below), 32 mi. east of town. (☎849-6684. Water and showers. Entrance fee $4, sites $10.)

The Tap Bar and Restaurant ❶, 408 E. San Antonio, is dimly lit but has excellent Mexican food. Don't mind the mirrored walls or the waitresses' skimpy dresses—just enjoy the tasty burritos ($1.75-4), enchiladas ($4.25), and grilled shrimp in garlic for $9. (☎532-1848 Open M-Sa 7-2am, Su noon-2am.) **Manolo's Cafe ❶,** 122 S. Mesa, between Overland and San Antonio, serves $2 *menudo* and $1 burritos. (☎532-7661. Open M-Sa 7am-5pm, Su 7:30am-3pm.)

SIGHTS. Historic **San Jacinto Plaza** swarms with activity and affords many a shaded bench. For a view of the Río Grande Valley, head northwest of downtown along Stanton and make a right turn on Rim Rd. (which becomes Scenic Dr.) to reach **Murchison Park,** at the base of the ridge. The Park offers a commanding vista of El Paso, Ciudad Juárez, and the Sierra Madre Mountains that is particularly impressive at night. The **El Paso Museum of Art,** 1 Arts Festival Plaza, is one of the largest art museums in the Southwest, with over 5000 works. Particularly exten-

sive are the holdings of 19th- to 20th-century Southwestern art and 18th- to 19th-century Mexican colonial art. (☎532-1707. Open Tu-Sa 9am-5pm, Su noon-5pm. Free.) **Hueco Tanks State Historical Park,** 32 mi. east of town off U.S. 62, has a national reputation for rock climbing and bouldering. Call ahead: only 70 people are allowed in the park at one time. (☎849-6684. Call ☎512-389-8900 in advance to reserve a spot. Park open Oct.-Apr. daily 8am-6pm; May-Sept. M-Th 8am-6pm, F-Su 7am-7pm. Park admission $4, children free.)

NIGHTLIFE. **Club 101,** 500 San Francisco, is El Paso's oldest club, drawing a vibrant crowd with its three dance floors and widely varying scene. (☎544-2101. W-F 18+, Sa 21+. Cover $5. Open W-Sa 9pm-3am.) **Xcape D'club,** 209 S. El Paso St., sits downtown in a beautifully restored theater and caters to a chic Latin crowd. (☎542-3800. Open F-Sa 9pm-2am.)

BIG BEND ☎915

Roadrunners, coyotes, wild pigs, mountain lions, and a few black bears make their home in Big Bend National Park, an 800,000-acre tract (about the size of Rhode Island) cradled by the mighty Río Grande. Spectacular canyons, vast stretches of the Chihuahua Desert, and the airy Chisos Mountains occupy this "far-out" spot.

TRANSPORTATION. There is no transportation service into or around the park. **Amtrak** offers trains to Alpine, 103 mi. north of the park entrance. **Car rentals** are also available there. Three roads lead south from U.S. 90 into the park: from Marfa, U.S. 67 to Rte. 170; from Alpine, Rte. 118; from Marathon, U.S. 385 (the fastest route). There are two **gas stations** within the park, one at **Panther Junction** (☎477-2294; open daily Sept.-Mar. 7am-7pm; Apr.-Aug. 8am-6pm; 24hr. credit card service), next to the park headquarters, and one at **Río Grande Village** (☎477-2293; open daily Mar.-May 9am-8pm; June-Feb. 9am-6pm). On Rte. 118, about 1 mi. from the western park entrance, the **Study Butte Store** also sells gas. (Open 24hr. Credit cards only.)

ORIENTATION & PRACTICAL INFORMATION. Park headquarters is at **Panther Junction,** 26 mi. south of the northern park boundary. (☎477-2251; www.nps.gov/bibe. Open daily 8am-6pm; vehicle pass $15 per week, pedestrians and bikers $5.) **Visitor Centers** are located at Río Grande Village (☎477-2271; usually closed June-Oct.), Persimmon Gap (☎477-2393; open daily 8am-5pm), and Chisos Basin (open daily 9am-4:30pm). The Río Grande Village Store has **showers** ($0.75). **Post Office:** Main office in Panther Junction, next to Park Headquarters. (☎477-2238. Open M-F 8am-4pm.) Chisos Basin office is inside the grocery store. (Open M-Sa 9am-5pm.) Post Office accepts general delivery mail addressed to visitor's name, Big Bend National Park, TX. **Postal Code:** 79834. **Area Code:** 915.

TEXAS

ACCOMMODATIONS & FOOD. The expensive **Chisos Mountains Lodge ❹,** in the Chisos Basin, 10 mi. from park headquarters, offers the only motel-style shelter within the park. Reservations are a must for high season; the lodge is often booked a year in advance. (☎477-2291. Singles $73; doubles $78. Additional person $10.) The lodge contains the only **restaurant ❷** in the park, serving three square meals a day. (Open daily 7-10am, 11:30am-4pm, and 5:30-8pm. Breakfast buffet $6.75. Lunch sandwiches $4-8. Dinner entrees $6-15.) The closest budget motel to the park, the **Chisos Mining Company Motel ❷,** on Rte. 170, ¾ mi. west of the junction with Rte. 118, provides clean rooms with A/C and an offbeat atmosphere. Life at this gateway to Big Bend is welcoming enough to skip staying in the Basin. (☎371-2254. Singles $37; doubles $45-55; 5-6 person cabins with kitchenettes $60.)

The three developed campsites within the park do not take reservations and are run on a first come, first served basis. During Thanksgiving, Christmas, March, and April the campgrounds fill early; call park headquarters (☎477-2251) to inquire about availability. The **Chisos Basin Campground ❶,** at 5400 ft., has 65 sites with running water and flush toilets and stays cooler than the other campgrounds in the summer. (Sites $10.) The **Río Grande Village Campground ❶,** at 1850 ft., has 100 sites near the only showers in the park. Flush toilets and water are also available. (Sites $10.) The **RV park ❶** at Río Grande Village has 25 full hookups. (Sites $18.50 for up to 2 people; $1 per additional person.) **Backcountry camping ❶** in the park is free but requires a permit from one of the Visitors Centers.

Restaurants are scarce in the Big Bend area, though there are some options near Terlingua and Lajitas. **Ms. Tracy's Cafe ❶,** on Rte. 118 just south of the intersection with Rte. 170, has outdoor seating and decorative cacti. Ms. Tracy serves eggs, hamburgers, and burritos as well as vegetarian entrees. (☎371-2888. Open daily Oct.-May 7am-9:30pm; June 7am-2pm; July-Sept. 7am-5pm.) Off Rte. 170 in Terlingua, 7 mi. from the park entrance, the lively **Starlight Theater Bar and Grill ❸** has healthy portions of Tex-Mex ($7-16) and live music on weekends. (☎371-2326. Open daily 5:30-10pm; bar open Su-F 5pm-midnight, Sa 5pm-1am. Indoor pool.)

OUTDOOR ACTIVITIES. Big Bend encompasses several hundred miles of hiking trails, ranging from 30min. nature walks to multi-day backpacking trips. *Always carry at least one gallon of water per person per day in the desert.* For those short on time, the best sight-seeing is along the **Ross Maxwell Scenic Drive,** a 30 mi. paved route from the western edge of the Chisos Mountains leading down to the Río Grande and Santa Eleña Canyon. Call ahead for road conditions.

Park rangers at the Visitors Centers are happy to suggest hikes and sights. Pick up the *Hiker's Guide to Big Bend* pamphlet ($2), available at Panther Junction. The **Window Trail** (2-3hr., 5¼ mi. round-trip) departs the Chisos Basin parking lot and leads to the u-shaped Window rock formation, passing a variety of other formations and flora along the way. The **Lost Mine Trail** (3-4hr., 4¾ mi. round-trip) leads to an amazing view of the desert and the Sierra de Carmen in Mexico. Also in the Chisos, the **Emory Peak Trail** (5-8hr., 4½ mi. one-way) requires an intense hike. An easier walk (1¾ mi., 1½hr.) ambles through the **Santa Eleña Canyon** along the Río Grande. Canyon walls rise as high as 1000 ft. over the riverbank.

Though upstream damming has markedly decreased the river's flow, rafting on the Río Grande is still highly enjoyable. Free permits and info are available at the Visitors Center. Several companies rent kayaks and offer **river trips** down the 118 mi. of designated Río Grande Wild and Scenic River within park boundaries. **Far-Flung Adventures,** next door to the Starlight Theater Bar and Grill in Terlingua, organizes 1- to 7-day trips. (☎371-2633 or 800-839-7238; www.farflung.com/tx.) In Terlingua off Hwy. 170, **Big Bend River Tours** (☎371-3033 or 800-545-4240; www.bigbendrivertours.com) rents canoes ($45 per day) and inflatable kayaks ($35 per day). Guided trips available. (Half-day $62, full day $130.) Both offer **shuttle services** to pick people up downriver.

ROCKY MOUNTAINS

Created by immense tectonic forces some 65 million years ago, the Rockies mark a vast wrinkle in the North American continent. Sculpted by wind, water, and glaciers over eons, their weathered peaks extend 3000 miles from northern Alberta to New Mexico and soar to altitudes exceeding two vertical miles. Cars overheat and humans gulp thin alpine air as they ascend into grizzly bear country. Dominated by rock and ice, the highest peaks of the Rockies are accessible only to veteran mountain climbers and wildlife adapted for survival in scant air and deep snow.

Although the whole of the Rocky Mountain area supports less than 5% of the US population, each year millions flock to its spectacular national parks, forests, and ski resorts, while hikers follow the Continental Divide along the spine of the Rockies. Nestled in valleys or appearing out of nowhere on the surrounding plains, the region's mountain villages and cowboy towns welcome travelers year-round.

HIGHLIGHTS OF THE ROCKY MOUNTAINS

HIKING. Memorable trails include the Gunnison Rte. in the Black Canyon, CO (p. 741); lake, geyser and canyon trails in Yellowstone National park (p. 774); and just about anything in the Grand Tetons (p. 783).

SKIING. The Rockies are filled with hot spots, but try Sawtooth, ID (p. 754); Vail, CO (p. 734); or Jackson Hole, WY (p. 788).

SCENIC DRIVES. Going-to-the-Sun Rd. in Glacier National Park (p. 767) is unforgettable, as is phenomenally high San Juan Skyway in Colorado (p. 745). The Chief Joseph Scenic Hwy. (p. 782) explores the rugged Wyoming wilderness.

ALPINE TOWNS. Aspen, CO (p. 736), and Stanley, ID (p. 754): two of the loveliest.

COLORADO

In the high, thin air of Colorado, golf balls fly farther, eggs take longer to cook, and visitors tend to lose their breath just getting out of bed. Hikers, skiers, and climbers worship Colorado for its peaks and mountain enclaves. Denver—the country's highest capital—has long since shed its cow-town image and matured into the cultural center of the Rocky Mountains. Colorado's extraordinary heights are matched by its equally spectacular depths. Over millions of years, the Gunnison and Colorado Rivers have etched the natural wonders of the Black Canyon and the Colorado National Monument. Silver and gold attracted early settlers to Colorado, but it is Mother Nature that has continued to appeal to travelers.

PRACTICAL INFORMATION

Capital: Denver.

Visitor Info: Colorado Travel and Tourism Authority, CTTA, 1620 Broadway, Ste. 1700 Denver 80202 (☎303-893-3885, vacation guide 800-COLARAD/265-6723; www.colorado.com). **US Forest Service,** Rocky Mountain Region, 740 Sims St., Golden, 80401 or P.O. Box

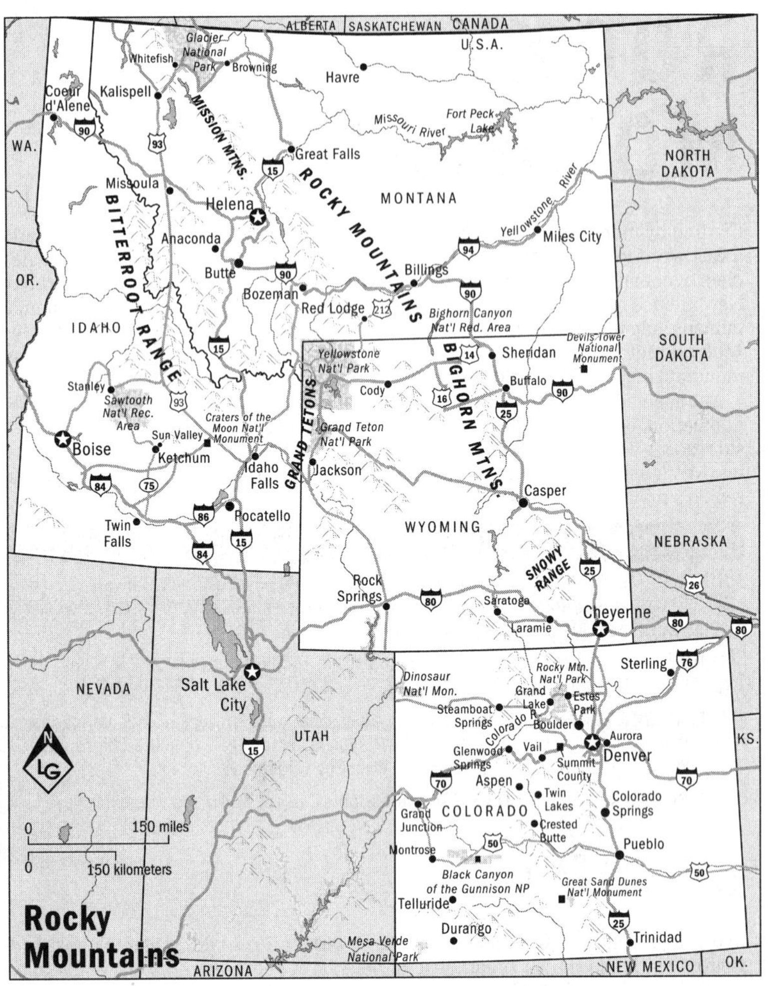

25127, Lakewood 80225 (☎303-275-5350). Open M-F 7:30am-4:30pm. **Ski Country USA,** 1507 Blake St., Denver 80202 provides info on all Colorado ski resorts. (☎303-837-0793.) Open M-F 9am-5pm. **Colorado State Parks,** 1313 Sherman St., #618, Denver 80203 (☎303-866-3437; state park reservations ☎800-678-2267). Open M-F 7am-4:45pm. $8 reservation fee; make reservations at least 3 days in advance.

Postal Abbreviation: CO. **Sales Tax:** 7.4%.

DENVER ☎303

In 1858, the discovery of gold in the Rocky Mountains brought a rush of eager miners to northern Colorado. After an excruciating trek through the plains, the desperados set up camp before heading west into "them thar hills." Overnight, Denver became a flourishing frontier town. Recently named the number one sports town in America, Denver also boasts the nation's largest city park system, brews the most beer of any metropolitan area, and has the highest number of high school and college graduates per capita. However, the city's greatest characteristic is its atmosphere—a unique combination of urban sophistication and Western grit.

TRANSPORTATION

Airport: Denver International (☎342-2000; www.flydenver.com), 23 mi. northeast of downtown off I-70. Shuttles run from the airport to downtown and ski resorts. The **RTD Sky Ride** (☎299-6000) runs buses every hr. from the Market St. station to the airport. Office hours M-F 6am-8pm, Sa-Su 9am-6pm. Buses operate daily 5am-10:30pm. $8, seniors and disabled $4, under 15 free. From the main terminal, **Supershuttle** (☎370-1300 or 800-525-3177) runs to downtown hotels (1hr., $19). Taxi downtown $50.

Trains: Amtrak, Union Station, 1701 Wynkoop St. (☎534-2812 for arrivals/departures, ☎825-2583 or 800-872-7245 for ticket office), at 17th St. Office open daily 6am-9pm. To: **Chicago** (20hr., 1 per day, from $196); **Salt Lake City** (15hr., 1 per day, from $131); **San Francisco** (35hr., 1 per day, from $194). **Río Grande Ski Train** (☎296-4754), in the same building, chugs 2¼hr. through the Rockies, stopping in **Winter Park.** Free ground transport to town. Reservations required. Runs Jan. Sa-Su; Feb. to late Mar. F-Su; mid-June to mid-Aug. Sa. Round-trip $45, over 61 $35, under 14 $25.

Buses: Greyhound, 1055 19th St. (☎293-6555). Office open daily 6am-midnight. To: **Chicago** (20-22hr., 6 per day, $95); **Colorado Springs** (1½hr., 7 per day, $14); **Salt Lake City** (10-13hr., 5 per day, $56); **Santa Fe** (7½-9hr., 4 per day, $61).

Public Transit: Regional Transportation District (RTD), 1600 Blake St. (☎299-6000 or 800-366-7433). Serves Denver, Longmont, Evergreen, Golden, and suburbs. Route hours vary; many lines shut down by 9pm. $0.75, seniors and disabled $0.25; peak hours $1.25. Exact change required. Regional routes run to Boulder and outlying areas for $3. Major terminals are at Market and 16th St. and at Colfax and Broadway. The free 16th St. **mall shuttle** covers 14 blocks downtown. Runs daily 5:45am-1am.

Taxi: Yellow Cab, ☎777-7777. **Zone Cab,** ☎444-8888.

Car Rental: Enterprise, 7720 Calawaba Ct. (☎800-720-7222), at the airport. Open daily 7am-10pm. Prices fluctuate but usually start around $50 per day; extra $15 per day for ages 21-24. Security deposit of $250 or a major credit card required.

ORIENTATION & PRACTICAL INFORMATION

Running north-south, **Broadway** slices Denver in half. East of Broadway, **Colorado Boulevard** is also a major north-south thoroughfare. **Colfax Avenue,** running east-west, is the main north-south dividing line. Both named and numbered streets run diagonally in the downtown area. In the rest of the city, numbered avenues run east-west and increase as you head north. Named streets run north-south. Many of the avenues on the eastern side of the city become numbered streets downtown. The **16th Street Mall** is the hub of Denver's downtown and could easily be called the social, dining, and entertainment center of the city. *At night, avoid the west end (Colfax between Speer Blvd. and Kipling St., Federal Blvd., and S. Santa Fe Blvd. beyond Alameda), the Capitol Hill area (on the east side of town beyond the Capitol), and 25th-34th St. on the west side of the* **Barrio.**

Visitor Info: Denver Visitors Bureau, 918 16th St. (☎892-1505: www.denver.org), in the 16th St. Mall. Open June-Aug. M-F 9am-5pm, Sa 9am-1pm; Sept.-May M-F 9am-5pm.

Hotlines: Rape Crisis Hotline, ☎322-7273.

Bi-Gay-Lesbian Organization: The Gay, Lesbian, and Bisexual Community Services Center of Colorado, ☎733-7743. Open M-F 9am-5pm.

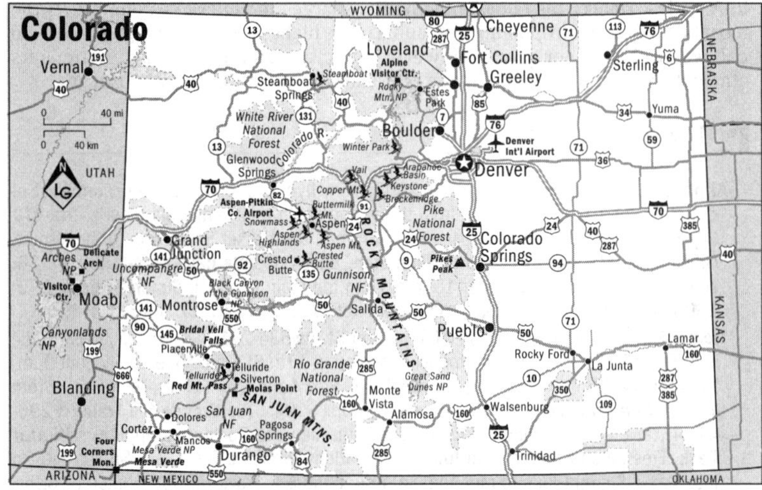

Internet Access: Public Library, 10 W. 14th Ave. (☎865-1363). Open M-W 10am-9pm, Th-Sa 10am-5:30pm, Su 1-5pm.

Post Office: 951 20th St. (☎296-4692). Open M-F 7am-10:30pm, Sa 8:30am-10:30pm.

Postal Code: 80202. **Area Code:** 303. 10-digit dialing required.

ACCOMMODATIONS

Inexpensive hotels line E. Colfax Ave., as well as Broadway and Colorado Blvd. Denver hotels tend to be less vacation and more commerce oriented, thus not showing as much price variation year-round. As commercial hotels, however, they do tend to give much better rates on weekends than during the week, which is a bonus for those looking for a weekend getaway.

Hostel of the Rocky Mountains (HI-AYH), 1530 Downing St. (☎861-7777), just off E. Colfax Ave. The hostel is the best value in Denver. Laundry facilities, library, kitchens. Internet access $1 per 10min. Free pickup from the Greyhound depot or Union Station. Airport drops $17. Breakfast free. Linen $2. Key deposit $5. Reception daily 7am-11:30pm. Reservations recommended. Dorms $19; private rooms $40. ❶ The affiliated **B&B of the Rocky Mountains,** next door to the hostel, shares the same address and phone number. Classier and decidedly quieter than the hostel, the rooms here are clean and spacious with shared baths. Guests can enjoy free breakfast next door at the hostel or use the kitchen facilities to fend for themselves. Rooms $40-55. ❷

Broadway Plaza Motel, 1111 Broadway (☎893-0303), 3 blocks south of the Capitol building. Spacious, clean rooms within walking distance of downtown Denver. Free HBO. Singles $45-55; doubles $55-65. ❸

Budget Host Inn, 2747 Wyandot St. (☎458-5454), has clean, comfortable rooms conveniently located near Six Flags Elitch Gardens. $15 discounts on Six Flags tickets. Singles from $46; doubles from $56. ❸

Cherry Creek State Park, 4201 S. Parker Rd., in Aurora (☎699-3860), is conveniently located in an urban area anchored around Cherry Creek Lake. Take I-25 to Exit 200, then head north for about 3 mi. on I-225 and take the Parker Rd. Exit. Pine trees provide limited shade. Boating, fishing, swimming, hiking, and horseback riding available. Arrive early. Open May-Dec. Sites $12; with electricity $18. Additional day-use fee $7. ❶

FOOD

Downtown Denver offers a full range of cuisines, from Russian to traditional Southwestern. Al fresco dining in warm weather and people-watching are available along the **16th Street Mall.** Gourmet eateries are located southwest of the Mall on Larimer St., in **Larimer Square.** Sports bars and trendy restaurants occupy **LoDo,** (lower downtown) the neighborhood extending from Wynkoop St. to Larimer Sq., between Speer Blvd. and 20th St. Outside of downtown, **Colorado Boulevard** and **6th Avenue** also have their share of posh restaurants. **East Colfax Avenue** offers a number of reasonably priced ethnic restaurants, including Greek and Ethiopian cuisine. You may wonder what sort of delicacies **"Rocky Mountain oysters"** are, especially given Denver's distance from the ocean. Fear not; these salty-sweet bison testicles, sold at the **Buckhorn Exchange,** 1000 Osage St. (☎534-9505), do not hail from the sea.

Mercury Cafe, 2199 California St. (☎294-9281), at 22nd St. Decorated with a new-age flair, the Merc specializes in home-baked wheat bread and a slew of reasonably priced soups ($2-3), salads ($6-9), enchiladas ($5.50-7), and vegetarian specials. Live bands provide jazz, salsa, and reggae music in the dining room, while the upstairs dance area hosts free swing and tango lessons Su and Th. Open Tu-F 5:30-11pm, Sa-Su 9am-3pm and 5:30-11pm; dancing F-Sa until 2am, Tu-Th and Su 1am. Cash only. ❷

Spicy Pickle Sub Shop, 745 Colorado Blvd. (☎321-8353) and 10th and Lincoln (☎860-0730), serves up fresh grilled focaccia sandwiches ($6) with—what else—a spicy pickle. Open daily 10:30am-8pm. ❷

Benny's Restaurant and Cantina, 301 E. 7th (☎894-0788), remains a local favorite for cheap, tasty Mexican food, including their trademark breakfast burritos ($4.25) and fish tacos ($7). Open M-F 8am-10pm, Sa-Su 9am-11pm. ❷

Wazee Lounge & Supper Club, 1600 15th St. (☎623-9518), in LoDo. The black-and-white tile floor, depression-era wood paneling and a mahogany bar create a unique bohemian ambiance at this laidback diner. Wazee's award winning pizza ($6-8) and strombolis ($8) are popular favorites year after year. Happy Hour M-F 4-6pm. Kitchen open M-Sa 11am-1am, Su noon-11pm. Bar open M-Sa until 2am, Su until midnight. ❷

Wynkoop Brewery, 1634 18th St. (☎297-2700), at Wynkoop St. across from Union Station in LoDo. Colorado's first brewpub serves beer (20 oz. $4) and homemade root beer, along with full lunch and dinner menus including "big mouth" burgers and "two-fisted" sandwiches ($7-8). 20 pool tables, dart lanes, and shuffleboard. An independent improv comedy troupe performs downstairs Th-Sa (☎297-2111). Pints $2. Happy Hour M-F 3-6pm. Free brewery tour Sa 1-5pm. Kitchen open M-Th 11am-11pm, F-Sa 11am-midnight, Su 11am-10pm. Bar open M-Sa until 2am, Su until midnight. ❷

Swing Thai, 845 Colorado Blvd. (☎302-8210) and 301 S. Pennsylvania (☎765-1061), is an understandably popular restaurant with a wide assortment of high-quality food at cheap prices. Indulge in the hot jungle curry ($6.50), pad thai noodles ($6), or pineapple fried rice ($5.50). Huge wok specials from $6.50. Open daily 11am-10pm. ❷

SIGHTS

CULTURAL CONNECTION TROLLEY. One of the best tour deals around, the trolley visits over 20 of the city's main attractions. The easiest place to begin a tour is along the 16th St. Mall, near the Mall Ride stops, but the tour can be joined at many local attractions; look for the trolley symbol sign. *(☎289-2841. Runs daily June-Aug. Buses depart every hr. 8:30am-4:30pm. $16, under 13 $8.)*

COLORADO STATE CAPITOL. Many of the best sights in Denver center around downtown, which makes touring on foot easy. The **Capitol Building** is a sensible place to start a visit to the Mile High City—marked by a small engraving, the 15th step leading to the building's entrance sits exactly 1 mi. above sea level. *(☎866-2604. 30min. tours M-F 9am-3:30pm every 45min. Open M-F 7am-5:30pm.)*

DENVER ART MUSEUM. Near the Capitol stands the Denver Art Museum (DAM), a unique seven-story "vertical" museum. The DAM houses a world-class collection of Native American art and pre-Colombian artifacts. *(100 W. 14th Ave. Pkwy. ☎720-865-5000; www.denverartmuseum.org. Open Tu and Th-Sa 10am-5pm, W 10am-9pm, Su noon-5pm. Daily tours of special exhibits; call for times. $6; students, ages 13-18, and over 65 $4.50.)*

SIX FLAGS. Make a splash at the Island Kingdom water park at Six Flags Elitch Gardens, across the freeway from Mile High Stadium. The Boomerang, Mind Eraser, and the new Flying Coaster keep thrill seekers screaming. *(At Elitch Circle and Speer Blvd. ☎595-4386. Open June-Aug. daily 10am-10pm; spring and early fall Sa-Su, call for hrs. $36, seniors and under 4 ft. $21. Look for coupons in the Elitch Gardens brochures.)*

OCEAN JOURNEY. Denver's brand new aquarium guides visitors through two spectacular underwater exhibitions: the Colorado River Journey, descending from the Continental divide to the Sea of Cortez in Mexico, and the Indonesian River Journey, emptying from the volcanic Barisan Mountains in Sumatra into the South China Sea. The aquarium also houses over 15,000 exotic marine creatures, including several species of sharks, sea otters, and the magnificent Napoleon wrasse. *(700 Water St. ☎561-4450 or 888-561-4450; www.oceanjourney.org. Open daily June-Aug. 10am-6pm; Sept.-May 10am-5pm. $15, over 65 and ages 13-17 $13, ages 4-12 $7.)*

DENVER MUSEUM OF NATURE AND SCIENCE. This gigantic museum hosts a variety of interesting exhibits, including the Hall of Life and the Prehistoric Journey room. Ride the skies in the museum's digital **Gates Planetarium,** one of the first of its kind in the country. *(2001 Colorado Blvd., at Colorado and Montview St. ☎322-7009 or 800-925-2250; www.dmns.org. Open daily 9am-5pm. $9; students, seniors over 60, and ages 3-18 $6. IMAX and museum $13/9, Planetarium and museum $13/9. Call for show times.)*

COORS BREWERY. Located in nearby Golden, this is the world's largest one-site brewery. Interestingly, the brewery also has one of the nicest wellness centers in the corporate world. All 42,000 workers are allowed two free beers after every shift, and can work them off in the company workout center. Free tours take visitors through the Coors brewing process from start to finish. Coors samples available after tour. *(Take I-70 W to Exit 264; head west on 32nd Ave. for 4½ mi., then turn left on East St. and follow the signs. A shuttle bus runs from the parking lot to the brewery, but not before a very short historical tour of Golden. ☎277-2337. 1½hr. tours every 30min. M-Sa 10am-4pm.)*

ENTERTAINMENT & OUTDOOR ACTIVITIES

Life in Denver is never boring for sports fans. Denver's baseball team, the **Colorado Rockies,** plays at **Coors Field,** 20th and Blake St. (☎762-5437 or 800-388-7625. Tickets $4-41. $4 "Rockpile" bleacher tickets available day of game.) Football's **Denver Broncos** have moved to **Mile High Stadium (Sometime referred to as Invesco Mile High Stadium, but rarely by locals, and not at all by us),** 2755 W. 17th Ave. (☎720-258-3333), which is used by soccer's **Colorado Rapids** (☎299-1599) during the spring and summer. The NBA **Denver Nuggets** and the NHL **Colorado Avalanche** share the state-of-the-art **Pepsi Center,** 1000 Chopper Cir. (☎405-1100 for info on both teams).

Denver has more public parks per square mile than any other city, providing prime space for bicycling, walking, or lolling. **Cheesman Park,** 8th Ave. and Humboldt St., offers picnic areas, manicured flower gardens and a view of snow-

ROCKY MOUNTAINS

capped peaks. **Confluence Park,** at Cherry Creek and the South Platte River, lures bikers and hikers with paved riverside paths. Free diverse live music is the name of the game at **Confluence Concerts,** along the banks of the South Platte. (☎455-7192. July-early Aug. Th 6:30-8pm.) One of the best parks for sporting events, **Washington Park,** at Louisiana Ave. and Downing St., hosts impromptu volleyball and soccer games most every summer weekend. Wide paths for biking, jogging, and in-line skating encircle the park, and the two lakes in the middle are popular fishing spots. **City Park** (☎697-4545) houses the **Museum of Nature and Science** and the **Denver Zoo** on its east end parks and a golf course on the west end. **Colorado State Parks** has the lowdown on nearby state parks. (☎866-3437. Open M-F 8am-5pm.) At **Roxborough State Park,** (☎973-3959) visitors can hike and ski among rock formations in the **Dakota Hogback** ridge. Take U.S. 85 S, turn right on Titan Rd., and follow it 3½ mi. (Open dawn-dusk.) The mammoth **Red Rocks Amphitheater and Park** (Ticketmaster ☎830-8497), 12 mi. southwest of Denver, on I-70 at the Morrison Exit, is carved into sandstone. Performers like R.E.M. and the Denver Symphony Orchestra compete with the view. The actual Red Rocks Park contains more than 600 acres. Forty miles west of Denver, the road to the top of **Mount Evans** (14,264 ft.) is the highest paved road in North America. Take I-70 W to Rte. 103 in Idaho Springs. (☎567-2901. Open late May-early Sept. Daily vehicle fee $10.)

The **Denver Performing Arts Complex (DPAC),** at Speer Blvd. and Arapahoe St., is the largest arts complex in the nation. DPAC is home to the Denver Center for the Performing Arts, Colorado Symphony, Colorado Ballet, and Opera Colorado. (☎893-4100 or 800-641-1222 for tickets M-Sa 10am-6pm.) The **Denver Center Theater Company** offers one free performance per play, a Saturday matinee. (☎893-4000. Tickets distributed day of performance; call for schedule.)

Small theaters in the metro area put on fantastic productions at bargain prices. In the intimate **Geminal Stage Denver,** 2450 W. 44th Ave., every seat is a good one. Their repertoire ranges from traditional to more experimental plays. (☎455-7108. Shows F-Su $14-18.) **The Bluebird Theater,** 3317 E. Colfax Ave., is an old theater-turned-music venue that hosts local and national acts. (☎322-2308. W-Sa Live music including rock, blues, folk, reggae, Latin, and jazz. Su movie nights.)

FESTIVALS

Every January, Denver hosts the nation's largest livestock show and one of the biggest rodeos, the **National Western Stock Show & Rodeo,** 4655 Humboldt St. Cowboys compete for prize money while over 10,000 head of cattle, horses, sheep, and rabbits compete for "Best of Breed." Between big events, all sorts of oddball fun take place, including western battle re-creations, monkey sheep herders, and rodeo clowns. (☎295-1660; www.nationalwestern.com. Tickets $10-20.)

The whole area vibrates during the **Denver March Pow-Wow,** at the Denver Coliseum, 4600 Humboldt St., when over 1000 Native Americans from tribes all over North America dance simultaneously in full costume to the beat of the drums. (☎934-8045; www.denvermarchpowwow.org. March 19-21, 2004. $6 for a 1-day pass, $12 for a 3-day pass, under 6 and over 60 free.) **Cinco de Mayo** (☎534-8342, ext. 106), held at Civic Center Park between Colfax Ave. and 14th St., attracts 250,000 visitors per year in celebration of Mexico's victory over the French in 1862.

Held in the same location a month later during the first full week of June, the **Capitol Hill People's Fair** (☎830-1651; www.peoplesfair.com), is one of the largest arts and crafts festivals in Colorado. Along with over 500 exhibitors, this large outdoor celebration includes food, dance, and local bands. Originally named to celebrate Denver's dual personalities as the Queen City of the Plains and the Monarch Metropolis of the Mountains, **The Festival of Mountain and Plain: A Taste of Colorado** (☎295-6330; www.atasteofcolorado.com) packs Civic Center Park on Labor Day weekend. Food, crafts, entertainment, and carnival rides are all part of the fun.

 NIGHTLIFE

Downtown Denver, in and around the 16th St. Mall, is an attraction in itself. With ample shopping, dining, and people-watching opportunities, there's something for everyone. A copy of the weekly *Westword* gives the lowdown on LoDo, where much of the action lies after dark.

El Chapultepec, 1962 Market St. (☎295-9126), at 20th St., is a be-boppin' jazz hold-over from Denver's Beat era of the 50s. Live music nightly starting at 9pm. No cover. 1-drink min. per set. Open daily 8am-2am. Food until 1am. No credit cards.

The Church, 1160 Lincoln St. (☎832-3528). In a remodeled chapel complete with stained glass windows and an elevated altar area, the Church offers 4 full bars, a cigar lounge, and a weekend sushi bar. On weekends, the congregation swells with 3 floors of dancing to a variety of music styles. Th 18+, F-Su 21+. Cover after 10pm $5-15. Open Th and Su 9pm-2am, F-Sa 8pm-2am.

Fado Irish Pub, 1735 19th St. (☎297-0066). Built in Ireland and brought to Denver piece by piece, Fado's is as authentic an Irish pub as you'll find. With a perfect pint of Guinness in hand, relax in one of the cozy nooks or make your way around the crowds at the bar. Live traditional Irish music W, Sa, Su, M. Open M-F 11:30am-2am, Sa-Su 10am-2am. Food until midnight.

Foxhole Lounge, 2936 Fox St. (☎298-7378). A popular gay club, this is the place to be on Su nights, so get there early or expect to wait. Open Th-F 8am-2am, Sa-Su 2pm-2am.

Charlie's, 900 E. Colfax Ave. (☎839-8890), at Emerson, is a well-known gay bar with a big dance floor and a Western-style atmosphere. Open daily 11am-2am.

ROCKY MOUNTAINS

MOUNTAIN RESORTS ON I-70 ☎970

WINTER PARK & THE FRASER VALLEY

Hwy. 40 connects Winter Park with Fraser just 2 mi. north, and together the towns thrive as a unique mountain community with genuine small-town charm. Nestled among mountain pines in the upper Fraser River Valley, the popular **Winter Park Resort** is the closest ski and summer resort to Denver, a mere 67 mi. from downtown. Named after a local lady of pleasure, **Winter Park Mary Jane Ski Area** (☎726-5514 or 800-453-2525) is home to the first man-made ski trail in the western US, laid on land Mary Jane had received for providing favors to the local railroad workers and miners. The ski area boasts a 3060 ft. vertical drop, 22 lifts, and the most snow in Colorado. Though affiliated, Winter Park caters to families, while Mary Jane serves the expert crowd. (Single-day lift ticket $61, multiday tickets $47-49.) **Fraser Tubing Hill,** half a mile off Hwy. 40 in Fraser, offers another popular winter escapade as some forgo the skis for a day and just head down on tube. (☎726-5954. $12 per hr., ages 12 and under $10 per hr.) Also on the vanguard of summer sports, Winter Park boasts over 600 mi. of biking trails and is known as the "Mountain Bike Capital USA." Biking and hiking trails climb the mountains of the Continental Divide, and the **Zephyr Express** chairlift blows to the summit of Winter Park Mountain, allowing bikers and hikers to start at the top and then make their way down. (☎726-1564. Open mid-June to early Sept. daily 10am-5pm. Full-day chair pass $22, includes bike haul. Mountain bike rentals from $14 per hr., $33 per day. 2hr. clinic $35.)

Winter Park Resort also hosts a variety of summer activities including the scenic chairlift, a human maze, climbing walls, bungee jumps, and a zip-line. (Open mid-June to early Sept. daily 10am-5:30pm. Park pass $38 half day, $47 full day.) **Viking Ski Shop,** on Hwy. 40, under the Viking Lodge, rents ski packages in winter and bikes in summer. (☎800-421-4013. Open daily June-Sept. 8am-6pm; Sept.-June

8am-9pm. Ski packages from $13 per day; kids rent skis free with adult rental. Bikes from $18 per day.) **Mad Adventures,** is a popular **whitewater rafting** company. (☎726-5290 or 800-451-4844. Half-day $38, full-day $56; ages 4-11 $33/46.) The **High Country Stampede Rodeo** bucks at the John Work Arena, west of Fraser on County Rd. 73, with competitions in calf roping, ladies barrel racing, and bareback bronc and bull riding. (☎726-4118 or 800-903-7275. Open July-Aug. Western barbecue 5pm $8, ages 6-13 $4. Rodeo 7:30pm. $10, ages 62 and over $8, ages 6-13 $6.)

MUDSLIDE. During mud season–typically May, October, and November–many places close or shorten their hours, and lodging prices are generally lower. For those traveling during mud season, be sure to call ahead.

The Rocky Mountain Inn & Hostel ❶, on Hwy. 40, 2 mi north of Winter Park in Fraser, offers immaculate, newly renovated rooms with a Julia Childs caliber kitchen, hot tub, and outdoor patio and grill. The hostel offers DVDs, discounts for lift tickets, ski and mountain bike rentals, raft trips, and horseback rides. (☎726-8256 or 866-467-8351. Reception 8am-10pm. Internet access $3 per hr. Linen $3. Dorms $19-22; private rooms from $53.) The **Viking Lodge ❷,** on Hwy. 40 in Winter Park, next to the shuttle stop for the lifts, offers tiny rooms with phones and TVs. Lodgings include access to the hot tub, sauna, and game room, and a 10% discount on rentals at the adjacent store. (☎726-8885 or 800-421-4013. Reception 8am-9pm. Singles $35; doubles $40. Winter singles $45-70; doubles $50-75.) The Fraser River Valley Lions Club offers campgrounds in the surrounding Arapaho National Forest from mid-May to early Sept. The closest site to town, **Idlewild ❶,** just 1½ mi. south of Winter Park on Hwy. 40, offers 24 sites right along the Fraser River. (No hook-ups. Max. stay 14 days. Sites with water $12.)

Deliciously healthy breakfasts and lunches ($5-8) are served on the patio at **Carver's Bakery Cafe ❷,** at the end of the Cooper Creek Mall off U.S. 40. (☎726-8202. Massive cinnamon rolls $2.25. Open daily summer 7am-2pm; winter 7am-3pm.) Located right off Hwy. 40 in downtown Fraser, **Crooked Creek Saloon & Eatery ❷,** 401 Zerex Ave., is a local landmark with wise advice: "Enjoy a few laughs, eat 'til it hurts, and drink 'til it feels better." (☎726-9250. Breakfast from $3, burgers, pasta, and Mexican fare $5-8. Open daily 7am-10pm, bar open until 1am.)

The Lift Resort Shuttle provides free bus service between Winter Park and Fraser, July-Sept. and late Nov. to mid-Apr. (☎726-4163.) To reach Winter Park from Denver, take I-70 W to Hwy. 40. The Chamber of Commerce (see below) also serves as the **Greyhound** depot with service to Denver (1¾hr., 1 per day, $15-16). **Home James Transportation Services** runs door-to-door shuttles to and from Fraser, Winter Park and the Denver airport. (☎726-5060 or 800-359-7536. Office open daily 8am-6pm. Reservations required. $42.) The **Río Grande Ski Train** (☎303-296-4754; Dec.-Mar. Sa-Su; mid-June to Aug. Sa) leaves Denver's Union Station for Winter Park (see p. 719). **Visitor Info: Winter Park-Fraser Valley Chamber of Commerce,** 78841 Hwy. 40. (☎726-4118 or 800-903-7275; www.winterpark-info.com. Open daily 8am-5pm.) **Internet Access: Fraser Valley Library,** 421 Norgren Rd. (☎726-5689. Open M-W 10am-6pm, Th noon-8pm, F 10am-6pm, Sa 10am-4pm.) **Post Office:** 520 Hwy. 40 (☎726-5578. Open M-F 8am-5pm, Sa 10am-noon.) **Snow conditions:** ☎303-572-7669 or 800-729-5813. **Postal Code:** 80442. **Area Code:** 970.

BRECKENRIDGE

Fashionable Breckenridge lies east of Vail on I-70, 9 mi. south of Frisco on Rte 9. The most popular ski resort in the country, **Breckenridge** (☎453-5000 or 800-789-7669; snow conditions ☎453-6118), has a 3398 ft. vertical drop, 139 trails, the best halfpipe in North America, and 2043 acres of skiable terrain made accessible by 25 lifts. Most of the summer action takes place at the **Breckenridge Peak and Fun Park** on **Peak 8,** 3 mi. west on Ski Hill Rd., including a scenic **chairlift** ride (single ride $8, seniors 65-69 and ages 7-12 $4), a superslide ($10/8), Colorado's largest human maze ($5, ages 5-12 $4), and a climbing wall ($6 per climb). The **Breckenridge Mountain Bike Park** at the same location offers a variety of biking trails. (Chairlift including bike haul $10, ages 7-12 $8.) Along with the majestic mountains, beautiful music surrounds Breckenridge in the summer. From late May to late Sept., the **Breckenridge Music Festival** provides a wide selection of musical acts from jazz and pop to Broadway and blues, including performances from the Breckenridge Music Institute Orchestra and the National Repertory Orchestra. (☎547-3100; www.breckenridgemusicfestival.com. Box office open Tu-Su 10am-5pm. Many shows free, for classical concerts $17-27, ages 18 and under $7.)

Despite the many expensive restaurants and stores in town, you can still find reasonably priced, smoke-free accommodations at the **Fireside Inn (HI-AYH) ❷,** 114 N. French St., two blocks east of Main St. on the corner of Wellington Rd. The indoor hot tub is great for après-ski and the "Afternoon Tea" offers a taste of charming British hospitality. (☎453-6456. Breakfast $3-6. Office open daily 8am-9:30pm. Dorms in summer $25; winter $35. Private rooms $65/105.) A few miles north of town on Hwy. 9, right next to the Breckenridge Golf Course, **Wayside Inn ❸,** 165 Tiger Rd., offers tidy rooms along with a nice soak in the hot tub, a warm fire in the lounge, and a price that's pretty hot. (☎453-5540 or 800-927-7669. Mid-Apr. to late Nov. singles $45, doubles $55; Dec. $65/75; Jan. to mid-Apr. $88/98.)

Taste the difference of high altitude slow-roasted coffee beans at **Clint's Bakery and Coffeehouse ❶,** 131 S. Main St., where you'll also find breakfast croissant sandwiches ($3.50), homemade quiche ($2.50), pastries, and soups made daily from scratch. The hot portobello mushroom and turkey pepperjack sandwiches ($5) are local lunch favorites. (☎453-2990. Open daily 7am-8pm, sandwiches made til 3pm.) Spiced up in Caribbean style with colorful murals and a straw-covered bar, **Rasta Pasta ❷,** 411 S. Main St., serves creative pasta entrees with Jamaican flare, like the Chicken Montego Bay. All entrees come with garlic bread and salad. Outside dining available alongside the creek. (☎453-7467. Lunch entrees $4-7, dinner $8-11. Open daily 11am-9pm.) With a name like **Fatty's ❷,** 106 S. Ridge St., you know the burgers are gonna be big ($5-6). Decked out with 10 TVs and $1.75 drafts during Happy Hour (daily 4-7pm), Fatty's knows how to keep the locals satisfied. (☎453-9802. Open daily 11am-10pm. Bar open until 12:30am.)

Free Ride Breckenridge shuttles skiers and bikers around town and to the mountains for free. (☎547-3140. Operates daily 6:30am-midnight.) **Summit Stage** provides free shuttle service from Breckenridge to surrounding areas in Summit County. (☎668-0999. Operates daily 6:30am-1:30am.) **Breckenridge Activities Center:** 137 S. Main St., at Washington St. (☎453-5579. Open daily 9am-5pm.) **Ski Conditions and Weather:** ☎453-6118. **Internet Access: Summit County Library,** 504 Airport Rd. (☎453-6098. Open M-Th 9am-7pm, F-Sa 9am-5pm, Su 1-5pm.) **Post Office:** 305 S. Ridge Rd. (☎453-5467. Open M-F 8am-5pm, Sa 10am-1pm.) **Postal Code:** 80424. **Area Code:** 970.

BOULDER ☎303

The 1960s have been slow to fade in Boulder. A liberal haven in an otherwise conservative region, the city brims with fashionable coffeeshops, teahouses, and organic juice bars. Boulder is home to both the central branch of the University of Colorado (CU) and Naropa University, the only accredited Buddhist university in the US. Seek spiritual enlightenment through meditation and healing workshops at Naropa, or pursue a physical awakening through Boulder's incredible local outdoor activities, including biking, hiking, and rafting along Boulder Creek.

ORIENTATION & PRACTICAL INFORMATION. Boulder is a small, manageable city, easily accessible from Estes Park and Denver by Rte. 36. The most developed area lies between **Broadway (Route 7/Route 93)** and **28th Street (Route 36),** two busy north-south streets. Broadway, 28th St., **Arapahoe Avenue** and **Baseline Road** border the **University of Colorado (CU)** campus. The area around the school is known as **the Hill.** The pedestrian-only **Pearl Street Mall,** between 9th and 15th St., is lined with cafes, restaurants, and posh shops. **Greyhound,** at 30th St. and Diagonal Hwy. (☎800-231-2222; open 24hr.), rolls to: Denver (1hr., 2 per day, $5); Glenwood Springs (6-7hr., 2 per day, $40); Vail (5-5½hr., 2 per day, $33). Boulder's extensive but confusing **public transit** system is run by **RTD,** at 14th and Walnut St., in the center of town. (☎299-6000 or 800-366-7433. Open M-F 6am-8pm, Sa-Su 9am-6pm. Call for schedules and fares.) **Taxi: Boulder Yellow Cab,** ☎442-2277. **Bike Rental: University Bicycles,** 839 Pearl St., downtown, rents mountain bikes with helmet and lock. (☎444-4196. Open M-F 10am-7pm, Sa 10am-6pm, Su 10am-5pm. $25 per 24hr., snowshoes $10 per 24hr.) **Visitor Info: Boulder Chamber of Commerce/Visitors Service,** 2440 Pearl St., has info and free **Internet access.** (☎442-1044; www.boulderchamber.com. Open M-Th 8:30am-5pm, F 8:30am-4pm.) **University of Colorado Information,** second floor of the University Memorial Center (UMC) student union, has both **Internet Access** and free local calls. (☎492-6161. Open summer M-F 7am-10pm, Sa 9am-11pm, Su noon-10pm; term-time M-F 7am-11pm, Sa 9am-midnight, Su 12pm-11pm.) **Post Office:** 1905 15th St., at Walnut St. (☎938-3704. Open M-F 7:30am-5:30pm, Sa 10am-2pm.) **Postal Code:** 80302. **Area Code:** 303. 10-digit dialing required.

ACCOMMODATIONS. With a great location right on the Hill next to the CU campus, **Boulder International Hostel ❶,** 1107 12th St., at College Ave., is the best deal in town. Youthful travelers fill the spacious downstairs lobby to watch cable TV and surf the Internet ($2 per 30min.). The front door is locked after 11pm, but guests are given a code to enter after hours. (☎442-0522. Kitchen, laundry. Linen $5. Key deposit $10. 3-day max. stay in dorms during the summer. Reception 8am-11pm. Lockout 10am-5pm. Dorms $17; singles July-Sept. $49 first night, $39 each additional night. Prices lower in winter.) Located 2 mi. west of Boulder off Canyon Blvd./Hwy. 119, **Boulder Mountain Lodge ❸,** 91 Four Mile Canyon Dr., is in the mountains, yet just 5min. from downtown. Guests are treated to clean rooms at great rates, as well as a hot tub by the stream. (☎444-0882 or 800-458-0882. Summer singles $68; doubles $88. Winter $53/68.) **Chautauqua Association ❸,** off Baseline Rd. at the foot of the Flatirons, has lodge rooms as well as private cottages. To get there, turn at the Chautauqua Park sign and take Kinnikinic to Morning Glory Dr. or take RTD bus #203. (☎442-3282, ext. 11. Office open June to early Sept. M-F 8:30am-7pm, Sa-Su 9am-5pm; Sept.-May M-F 8:30am-5pm, Sa-Su 9am-3pm. Reserve months in advance. Small additional charge for stay fewer than 4 nights. In summer lodge rooms $57-102; 1-bedroom suites $84-114; 2-bedroom cottages $119-139; 3-bedroom cottages $144-159. In winter, limited number of cottages $94-139.)

Camping info for **Arapahoe/Roosevelt National Forest ❶** is available from the **Boulder Ranger District,** 2140 Yarmouth Ave., just off of Rte. 36 to the north of town. (☎541-2500, reservations 877-444-6777. Open mid-May to early Sept. M-Th 8am-4:30pm, F 8am-5:30pm, Sa 9am-3pm; Sept. to mid-May M-F 8am-5pm. Campsites open mid-May to Oct. $13 per night unless otherwise noted. Most sites have water, none have electric hookups.) **Kelly Dahl**, 17 mi. west on Hwy. 119, is the closest campground to Boulder. Their 46 sites lie among pine trees and picnic tables with open views of the Continental Divide. For a more primitive and quieter camping experience, **Rainbow Lakes** lies 6½ mi. north of Nederland off Hwy. 72; turn at the Mountain Research Station (CR 116) and follow the dirt road for 5 mi. The 16 sites are first come, first served. (No water. $7 per night.)

FOOD & NIGHTLIFE. The streets on **the Hill,** along the **Pearl Street Mall,** burst with eateries, natural food markets, and colorful bars. Boulder nearly has more options for vegetarians than meat-eaters. A standout among all the other sandwich shops, **Half Fast Subs ❶,** 1215 13th St., makes over 90 oven-baked subs. 7 in. cheesesteak, meat specialty, stuffed and vegetarian subs galore ride at ridiculously inexpensive prices ($3.50-5). All 7 in. subs are $3.75 during Happy Hour, M-F 5-7pm. (☎449-0404. Open Su-W 11am-10pm, Th-Sa 11am-1:30am.) **Illegal Pete's ❶,** 1320 College Ave., on the Hill, and 1447 Pearl St., on the Mall, creates scrumptious burritos for $4.85. (☎444-3055. Open daily Sept.-May 11am-8pm; June-Aug. 11am-3:30pm.) At **Moshi Moshi Bowl ❶,** 1628 Pearl St., fill up on tasty noodle and rice bowls, salads, and sushi, all for under $5. (☎720-565-9787. Open M-Th 11am-8pm, F 11am-9pm, Sa noon-8pm.) Right next to the **Boulder Co-op Market** (open daily 8am-9pm), 1904 Pearl St., **Cafe Prasad ❶** serves a full menu of vegan and organic sandwiches and baked goods, along with their all-organic juice and smoothies. Live music Friday 7-8:30pm. (☎447-2667. Open daily 11am-8pm.)

Boulder overflows with nightlife hot spots, each with its own unique spin. For bluegrass, funk, and the best brews in Boulder (try the "kind crippler"), head to **Mountain Sun Pub and Brewery,** 1535 Pearl St. (☎546-0886. Acoustic performances Su 10pm-1am. $2 pints during Happy Hour, daily 4-6pm and 10pm-1am. Open M-Sa 11:30am-1am, Su noon-1am.) A Boulder classic, **The Sink,** 1165 13th St., still awaits the return of its one-time janitor, Robert Redford, who quit his job and headed to California in the late 1950s. The Sink serves surprisingly upscale new cuisine and great pizzas amid wild graffiti, low ceilings, and pipes. Students fill the place for late-night drinking. (☎444-7465. Burgers $6-8. Open M-Sa 11am-2am, Su noon-2am; food served until 10pm.) **The West End Tavern,** 926 Pearl St., has a rooftop bar with quite the view of downtown. (☎444-3535. Draft beers $3-4. Kitchen open M-Sa 11am-11pm, Su 11:30am-11pm; bar open until 1:30am.) **The Library Pub,** 1718 Broadway, boasts the largest outdoor patio in Boulder, right along the creek. Punk, hardrock, and reggae fans flood the floors for live music Th-Sa. (☎443-2330. Happy Hour daily 4-6pm, 9-11pm. Open daily noon-2am.)

SIGHTS & OUTDOOR ACTIVITIES. Due to its proximity to the mountains, Boulder's location supports many outdoor activities. Starting at **Scott Carpenter Park,** hiking and biking trails follow **Boulder Creek** to the foot of the mountains. **Chautauqua Park** has many trails varying in length and difficulty that climb up and around the **Flatirons.** Starting at the auditorium, the **Enchanted Mesa/McClintock Trail** is an easy 2 mi. loop through meadows and ponderosa pine forests. For a more challenging hike, **Greg Canyon Trail** starts at the Baird Park parking lot and rises through the pines above Saddle Rock, winding back down the mountain past Amphitheater Rocks. Before heading into the wilderness, grab a trail map at the entrance to Chautauqua Park. *Beware of mountain lions.* The **Dushanbe Teahouse ❸,** 1770 13th St., was built by artists in Tajikistan, and then was piece-mailed from Boulder's sister city of Dushanbe. The building is owned by the city and leased to a private restauranteur, who lays out a scrumptious spread from cultures spanning the globe. (☎442-4993. Tea $2-4. Lunch $7-9. Dinner $9-12. Open M-F 8am-3pm. Tea time 3-5pm. Dinner Su-Th 5-9pm, F-Sa 5-10pm.) The intimate **Leanin' Tree Museum,** 6055 Longbow Dr., presents an acclaimed collection of over 200 paintings and 80 bronze sculptures depicting Western themes. (☎530-1442, ext. 299; www.leanintreemuseum.com. Open M-F 8am-4:30pm, Sa-Su 10am-4pm. Free.) Minutes away, **The Celestial Seasonings Tea Company,** 4600 Sleepytime Dr., lures visitors with tea samples and free tours of the factory, including the infamous Peppermint Room. (☎581-1202. Open M-Sa 9am-4pm, Su 11am-4pm. Tours M-Su every hr.)

ENTERTAINMENT. An exciting street scene pounds through both the Mall and the Hill; the university's kiosks have the lowdown on downtown happenings. From June to August, find live music and street performances on Pearl St. Mall Tu, Th, and F during lunch, noon-1:30pm. The **University Memorial Center,** 1609 Euclid St. (16th St. becomes Euclid St. on campus), hosts many events. (☎492-6161.) On the third floor, the **Cultural Events Board** (☎492-3221) has the latest word on all CU-sponsored activities. From late June to early Aug., the **Colorado Shakespeare Festival** draws over 50,000 people, making it the third-largest festival of its kind. (☎492-0554; www.coloradoshakes.org. Tickets $10-50, previews $5-25. $5 student and senior discount.) The **Colorado Music Festival** performs July through August. (☎449-2413; www.coloradomusicfest.org. Lawn seats $5; other prices vary.) The local indie music scene is on display at the popular Fox Theater and Cafe, 1135 13th St. (☎447-0095; www.foxtheater.com.) Twice a week from April through October, Boulder shuts down 13th St. between Canyon and Arapahoe for a **Farmers Market.** (Open Apr.-Oct. W 5-8pm, Sa 8am-2pm.)

ROCKY MOUNTAIN NATIONAL PARK ☎970

Of all the US national parks, Rocky Mountain National Park is closest to heaven, with over 60 peaks exceeding 12,000 ft. A third of the park lies above the treeline, and Longs Peak tops off at 14,255 ft. Here among the clouds, the alpine tundra ecosystem supports bighorn sheep, dwarf wildflowers, and arctic shrubs interspersed among granite boulders and crystal lakes. The city of **Estes Park,** immediately east of the park, hosts the vast majority of would-be mountaineers and alpinists who crowd the area in the summer. To the west of the park, the town of **Grand Lake,** on the edges of two glacial lakes, is a more tranquil base from which to explore Rocky Mountain National Park's less traversed but equally stunning western side.

ORIENTATION & PRACTICAL INFORMATION

You can reach the national park from Boulder via U.S. 36 or scenic Rte. 7. From the northeast, the park can be accessed up the Big Thompson Canyon via Rte. 34, but beware of flash floods. **Trail Ridge Road (Route 34)** runs 48 mi. through the park.

Visitor Info: Park Headquarters and Visitors Center (☎586-1206), 2½ mi. west of Estes Park on Rte. 36, at the Beaver Meadows entrance to the park. Open daily mid-June to late Aug. 8am-9pm; Sept. to mid-June 8am-5pm. Evening programs in summer daily 7:30pm; year-round Sa 7pm.

Kawuneeche Visitors Center (☎627-3471), just outside the park's western entrance, 1¼ mi. north of Grand Lake, offers similar info. Open daily mid-May to late Aug. 8am-6pm; Sept. 8am-5pm; Oct. to mid-May 8am-4:30pm. Evening programs in summer Sa 7pm; call for winter program.

Alpine Visitors Center, at the crest of Trail Ridge Rd., has a great view of the tundra. Open daily mid-June to late Aug. 9am-5pm; late May to mid-June and late Aug. to mid-Oct. 10am-4:30pm.

Lily Lake Visitors Center, 6 mi. south of Headquarters on Rte. 7. Open June-Oct. daily 9am-4:30pm.

Fall River Visitor Center, 5 mi west of downtown Estes Park on Rte. 34 at the northern entrance to the park, is the newest center. Open May-Oct. daily 8:30am-6pm.

Park entrance fee: $15 per car, $5 per motorbike, cyclist, or pedestrian; valid for 7 days.

Weather: Park Weather and Road Conditions, ☎586-1333.

Medical Services: Estes Park Medical Center, ☎586-2317. **Park Emergency,** ☎586-1399.

Internet Access: Estes Park Public Library, 335 E. Elkhorn (☎586-8116). Open summer M-Th 9am-9pm, F-Sa 9am-5pm, Su 1-5pm; winter M-Th 10am-9pm, F-Sa 10am-5pm, Su 1-5pm.

Post Offices: Grand Lake, 520 Center Dr. (☎627-3340). Open M-F 8:30am-5pm. **Estes Park,** 215 W. Riverside Dr. (☎586-0170). Open M-F 9am-5pm, Sa 10am-2:30pm. **Postal Codes:** 80447 and 80517. **Area Code:** 970.

ACCOMMODATIONS

ESTES PARK

Although Estes Park has an abundance of expensive lodges and motels, there are a few good deals on indoor beds near the national park, especially in winter, when temperatures drop and tourists leave.

The Colorado Mountain School, 341 Moraine Ave. (☎586-5758). Tidy, dorm-style accommodations are open to travelers unless booked by mountain-climbing students. Wood bunks with mattresses, linen, and showers. 16 beds. Reservations recommended in advance. Office open June-Sept. daily 8am-5pm. Winter hours vary. $25 per person. ❶

Saddle & Surrey Motel, 1341 S. Saint Vrain (Hwy. 7) (☎586-3326 or 800-204-6226), offers clean and comfy rooms, each decorated in a unique style. Heated outdoor pool and spa on site. Microwave, fridge, and cable TV. Singles $45-70; doubles $50-99.) ❸

YMCA of the Rockies, 2515 Tunnel Rd. (☎586-3341, ext. 1010), 2 mi. from the park entrance. Follow Rte. 36 to Rte. 66. Guests have access to extensive facilities on the 860-acre complex, including mini-golf, gym, and a pool, as well as horseback rides, fly fishing, and daily hikes. Call ahead; reservations for summer accepted starting May 1st. 4-person lodge $41; 4-person cabin with kitchen and bath from $74; 5-person cabins $133; 7-person cabins $179. 1-day "guest membership" required: $3; families $5. ❹

GRAND LAKE

Grand Lake is the "snowmobile capital of Colorado" and offers spectacular cross-country routes. Boating and fishing are popular summertime activities.

Shadowcliff Hostel (HI-AYH), 405 Summerland Park Rd. (☎627-9220). From the western entrance, go left to Grand Lake, then take the left fork into town on W. Portal Rd. The hand-built pine lodge perches on a cliff. Kitchen, showers, wood burning stove. Internet $3 per day. Linen $2. Open June-Sept. Dorms $14, non-members $18. Private singles or doubles with shared bath $45; additional person $10. 6-8 person cabins $100. 6-day min. stay for cabins. Make cabin reservations as far as 1 year in advance. ❶

Sunset Motel, 505 Grand Ave. (☎627-3318), stands out against the mountains with its yellow front and baby-blue trim. Friendly owners, cozy rooms, and the only heated indoor pool in Grand Lake. Summer singles $60; doubles $90. Winter $40/60. ❸

Bluebird Motel, 30 River Dr. (☎627-9314), on Rte. 34 west of Grand Lake, overlooks Shadow Mountain Lake and the snowcapped Continental Divide. Some rooms have couches, many have fridges, and others have kitchenettes. Access to the indoor swimming pool at Sunset Motel in Grand Lake. Singles $30-55; doubles $50-75. ❷

CAMPING

Visitors can camp a total of 7 days anywhere within the park. In the backcountry, the maximum stay increases to 14 days during the winter from Oct. to May. All five **national park campgrounds** ❶ are $18 in the summer, while winter sites are $12 unless otherwise noted. A backcountry camping **permit** ($10 for a 3-day pass, $15 for a 7-day pass, $30 annual pass) is required in summer. On eastern slopes, permits are available from the **Backcountry Permits and Trip Planning Building,** 2min. from the park headquarters. (☎586-1242. Open daily mid-May to late Oct. 7am-7pm; Nov. to mid-May 8am-5pm.) In the west, go to the **Kawuneeche Visitors Center.**

GRAND LAKE

The only national park campground on the western side of the park is **Timber Creek,** 10 mi. north of Grand Lake. Open year-round, it offers 100 wooded sites on a first come, first served basis. Campsites can also be found in the surrounding **Arapaho National Forest.** (☎887-4100.) **Stillwater Campground,** west of Grand Lake on the shores of Lake Granby, has 127 tranquil sites. (Open year-round. Sites $16; with water $19; with hookup $21.) **Green Ridge Campground,** on the south end of Shadow Mountain Lake, is also a good bet with 78 sites. (Open mid-May to mid-Nov. Sites $13.) For both sites, reservations, which should be made at least 5 days in advance, are available at ☎877-444-6777 or www.reserveusa.com.

EAST SIDE OF THE PARK

Moraine Park, 3 mi. west of Beaver Meadows Park Headquarters on Bear Lake Rd., is open year-round and has 247 open, sunny sites as well as nightly campfires and evening programs from mid-June to mid Aug. Open only in summer, **Glacier Basin,** 9 mi. from Estes, south of Moraine Park, provides 150 secluded sites. Both Moraine Park and Glacier Basin require summer reservations. (☎800-365-2267; http://reservations.nps.gov.) **Longs Peak Campground** has 26 year-round sites—in a prime location to climb Longs Peak—but also has a 3-night maximum stay.

FOOD

ESTES PARK

The Notchtop Bakery & Cafe, 459 E. Wonderview, #44 (☎586-0272), in the upper Stanley Village Shopping Plaza, east of downtown off Rte. 34. Locals flock here for homemade "natural foods and brews." Breads, pastries, and pies baked fresh every morning. Soups $4. Salads $5-8. Sandwiches and wraps $6-7. Open daily 7am-5pm. ❷

Local's Grill, 153 E. Elkhorn Ave. (☎586-6900), in the heart of downtown, is a self-proclaimed "world-famous gathering place." Customers crowd the front patio for gourmet sandwiches ($5-8) and pizza ($5-11). Open M-Th 11am-9pm, F-Su 11am-10pm. ❷

Sweet Basilico Cafe, 401 E. Elkhorn Ave. (☎586-3899). The intimate seating area overflows with patrons seeking a taste of authentic Italian cuisine including focaccia bread sandwiches ($6) and freshly made pastas of every kind ($7-10). Open June-Sept. M-F 11am-10pm, Sa-Su 11:30am-10pm; Oct.-May Tu-Su 11am-2:30pm and 4:30-9pm. ❷

GRAND LAKE

Chuck Hole Cafe, 1119 Grand Ave. (☎627-3509). A popular breakfast and lunch spot, this Grand Lake tradition has been boasting of its homemade cinnamon rolls and famous reuben sandwiches ($6-8) for over 65 years. Open daily 7am-2pm. ❷

Pancho and Lefty's, 1120 Grand Ave. (☎627-8773). With an outdoor patio overlooking Grand Lake and a bar large enough to fit most of its residents, Pancho and Lefty's is an understandably popular hangout. Try the *rellenos fritos* ($11) or crunchy *chimichangas* ($10.25), and wash it all down with a margarita ($4.50). Live music W 8pm, Sa 9pm. Open daily June-Sept. 11am-9pm, bar until 11pm; Sept.-June 11am-8pm. ❷

Mountain Inn, 612 Grand Ave. (☎627-3385). Serving up the best dinner deals in town, including mouth-watering chicken fried steak ($10-11). Live blues and rock during the summer Sa 12:30-4pm. Open M-F 5-10pm, Sa-Su 11:30am-2:30pm and 5-10pm. ❸

OUTDOOR ACTIVITIES

SCENIC DRIVES

The star of the park is **Trail Ridge Road** (U.S. 34), a 48 mi. stretch that rises 12,183 ft. above sea level into frigid tundra. The round-trip drive takes roughly 3hr. by car. *Beware of slow-moving tour buses and people stopping to ogle wild-*

life. The road is sometimes closed or inaccessible—especially from October to May—for weather reasons. Many sights within the park are accessible from Trail Ridge Rd. Heading west, steal an open view of the park from the boardwalk along the highway at **Many Parks Curve. Rainbow Curve** and the **Forest Canyon Overlook** offer impressive views of the vast tree-carpeted landscape. The 30min. **Tundra Communities Trail** provides a once-in-a-lifetime-look at the fragile alpine tundra. Signposts along the paved trail explain local geology and wildlife. The **Lava Cliffs** attract crowds, but are worth the hassle. After peaking at **Gore Range,** a mighty 12,183 ft above sea level, Trail Ridge Rd. runs north to the **Alpine Visitors Center.** Entering the west side of the park past the Alpine Visitors Center, congestion becomes noticeably less.

A wilder alternative to Trail Ridge Rd. is **Old Fall River Road.** Entering Rocky Mountain National Park from the east side on Rte. 34, you'll pass **Sheep Lakes,** a popular crossing for bighorn sheep. After Sheep Lakes, veer right toward the **Alluvial Fan** and Old Fall River Rd. Starting at **Endovalley** picnic area, Old Fall River Rd. is a 9 mi. unpaved, one-way uphill road open only in the summer that features spectacular mountain views. Drivers will notice the destruction caused by flooding. The road intersects Trail Ridge Rd. behind the Alpine Visitors Center.

Bear Lake Road, south of Trail Ridge Rd., leads to the most popular hiking trails within the park. **Moraine Park Museum,** off of Bear Lake Rd. 1½ mi. from the Beaver Meadows entrance, has exhibits on the park's geology and ecosystem, as well as comfortable rocking chairs with a view of the mountains. (☎586-1206. Open summer daily 9am-5pm.) From May 1 to Oct. 31, 2004, Bear Lake Rd. will be closed between Bear Lake and Sprague Lake due to a reconstruction project. Free **Shuttle Buses** will run every 30min. 5am-10pm.

SCENIC HIKES

Numerous trailheads lie in the western half of the park, including the Continental Divide and its accompanying hiking trail. Trail Ridge Rd. ends in **Grand Lake,** a small town with ample outdoor opportunities. An overnight trek from Grand Lake into the scenic and remote **North** or **East Inlets** leaves the crowds behind.

Lake Nanita (11 mi., 5½hr.), one of the most photogenic destinations in the park, possibly enhanced because you need to work to get there. Starts at North Inlet trailhead just north of Grand Lake. Don't let the easy and well-shaded first 6½ mi. fool you. After reaching **Cascade Falls,** the last half of the trail is a steep grade that ascends 2240 ft. through pristine wilderness to a fantastic view of the lake.

Lake Verna (7 mi., 3½hr.), starts at East Inlet trailhead at the far east end of Grand Lake. This moderate hike gains a total of 1800 ft. in elevation as it passes **Adams Falls** and **Lone Pine Lake** and rewards hikers with open views of **Mount Craig** before reentering the forest. The culmination of the hike is an overlook of the fjord-like lake.

Mill Creek (1½ mi., 40min.), beginning at Hollowell Park off Bear Lake Rd. This easy and pleasant trail crosses an open meadow and then empties out into a serene field of aspen, providing a look at the significant beaver activity along the creek and the soaring hawks in the sky.

Bear Lake Hikes. The park's most popular trails are all accessible from the Bear Lake Trailhead at the south end of Bear Lake Rd. Bear Lake serves as the hub for snowshoeing and cross-country skiing. Due to construction on the south end of Bear Lake Rd. during the summer, take the free shuttle to **Bear Lake Trailhead** (see above).

Flattop Mountain (4½ mi., 3hr.), the most challenging and picturesque of the Bear Lake hikes, climbs 2800 ft. to a vantage point along the Continental Divide.

Nymph (½ mi., 15min.); **Dream** (1 mi., 30min.); and **Emerald Lakes** (1¾ mi., 1hr.) are a series of 3 glacial pools offering inspiring glimpses of the surrounding peaks. Although the first 2 legs of the hike are relatively easy, the Emerald Lake portion is steep and rocky at points.

Lake Haiyaha (2¼ mi., 1¼hr.), forking left from the trail, is more intimate, with switchbacks through dense sub-alpine forests and superb views of the mountains. A scramble over the rocks at the end of the trail earns you a peek at the hidden (and sometimes difficult to find) Lake Haiyaha, arguably the most astounding of the 4 lakes.

VAIL

☎970

The largest one-mountain ski resort in all of North America, Vail has its fair share of ritzy hotels, swank saloons, and sexy boutiques, but it's the mountain that wows skiers with its prime snow and back bowls. Discovered by Lord Gore in 1854, Vail and its surrounding valley were invaded by miners during the Rockies gold rush of the 1870s. According to local folklore, the Ute Indians adored the area's rich supply of game, but they became so upset with the white settlers that they set fire to the forest, creating the resort's open terrain.

PRACTICAL INFORMATION. The communities of Vail consist of **East Vail, Vail Village, Lionshead Village, Cascade Village,** and **West Vail.** Vail Village and Lionshead Village, which are the main centers of action, are pedestrian only; visitors must park in garages off **South Frontage Road,** but parking is free during the summer. Free **Vail Buses** take you within and between each of the villages all year round. (☎477-3456 for schedule info.) **EcoTransit** runs bus routes between Vail and its surrounding areas, including Eagle, Edwards, and Beaver Creek. (☎328-3520 for schedule info. Office open daily 6:30am-10pm. $2-3.) **Greyhound,** in the Transportation Building next to the main Visitors Center, (☎476-5137; ticket office open daily 7:30am-6:30pm) buses eager skiers to: Denver (2hr., 5 per day, $21); Glenwood Springs (1½hr., 4 per day, $16); Grand Junction (3½hr., 4 per day, $16). Vail's two **Visitors Centers** are both on S. Frontage Rd. The larger one is in Vail Village at the **Vail Transportation Center** (☎479-1394 or 800-525-3875; open daily summer 8am-7pm; winter 8am-6pm), and the smaller is at the parking structure in **Lionshead Village** (☎800-525-3875; open daily summer 8:30am-7pm; winter 8am-5pm). **Weather: Road report,** ☎476-2226. **Snow report,** ☎476-8888. **Internet Access: Vail Public Library,** 292 W. Meadow Dr. (☎479-2184. Open M-Th 10am-8pm, F 10am-6pm, Sa-Su 11am-6pm.) **Post Office:** 1300 N. Frontage Rd. W. (☎476-5217. Open M-F 8:30am-5pm, Sa 8:30am-noon.) **Postal Code:** 81657. **Area Code:** 970.

ACCOMMODATIONS. The phrase "cheap lodging" is not part of Vail's vocabulary. Rooms in the resort town rarely dip below $175 per night in winter, and summer lodging is often equally pricey. Call the Visitors Centers for info on special rates; hotels and lodges often offer big discounts during the summer and slower seasons. The **Roost Lodge ❹,** 1783 N. Frontage Rd., in West Vail, provides affordable lodging right on the free bus route. The small rooms are impressively clean and come with cable TV, fridge, microwave, and access to a jacuzzi, sauna, and heated indoor pool. (☎476-5451 or 800-873-3065. Continental breakfast in winter. Singles summer from $49; winter from $89.) Located in Eagle, about 30 mi. west of Vail, **The Prairie Moon ❸,** 738 Grand Ave., offers some of the cheapest lodging near the resort. EcoTransit shuttles visitors daily between Eagle and Vail (see **Practical Information,** above). The large, clean rooms have fridges and microwaves. (☎328-6680. Singles $30-55; doubles $45-65.) **Lionshead Inn ❸,** 705 W. Lionshead Cir., has great deals on luxury accommodations. With an exercise room, game room, hot tub, fireplace lounge, free Internet access, and alpine breakfast included, the inn also offers plush robes and down comforters on every bed. Call for walk-in rates and book online for 50% off rooms during the summer. (☎476-2050 or 800-283-8245; www.lionsheadinn.com. Singles from $69.) The **Holy Cross Ranger District,** right off I-70 at Exit 171 (follow signs), provides info on the six summer campgrounds near Vail. (☎827-5715. Open M-F 8am-5pm.) With 25 sites, **Gore Creek ❶** is the closest and most popular campground. Well-situated among birch trees, wild flowers, and mountains just outside East Vail, Gore Creek is within hiking distance of the free East Vail Express bus route. (Max. stay 10 days. Sites with water $12.)

FOOD & NIGHTLIFE. You'll never need to cook breakfast in Vail as long as the griddle is hot at **DJ's Classic Diner ❶,** 616 W. Lionshead Plaza, on the west end of Lionshead Village. During the winter, locals ski in 'round the clock to warm up to DJ's crepes ($4-5), omelettes ($4), and pasta frittatas from $7.50. (☎476-2336. Open summer M-Th and Sa-Su 7am-1pm, F 10pm-3am; winter M 7am-1pm, Tu 7am-Su 1pm continuously.) With Alabama-style barbecue, **Moe's Original BBQ ❷,** 675 W. Lionshead Cir., proves to be "A Southern Soulfood Revival." Their box lunches ($8-9) with pulled pork or smoked chicken along with two choices of sides (baked beans and homemade banana puddin' are favorites) might be the best deal in town. (☎479-7888. Open M-Sa 11am-sellout.) Stuffing burritos and chiles chock-full, **La Cantina ❶,** in Vail Transportation Center, serves up a fine selection of Mexican food ($3-6) for an even finer price. (☎476-7661. Open daily 11:30am-10pm.)

With two clubs, three floors, four bars, and seven decks, **The Tap Room & Sanctuary,** 333 Bridge St. in Vail Village, attracts all types of crowds. While the Tap Room caters to those looking for good rowdy fun, the Sanctuary upstairs is for those in search of a more sleek and classier nightclub. (☎479-0500. $0.50 Coors F 5-8pm. Tap Room open daily 10am-2am, Sanctuary open Tu-Sa 8pm-2am). **Garfinkel's,** 536 E. Lionshead Cir., a hidden hangout accessible by foot in Vail's Lionshead Village (directly across from the gondola) calls out "Ski hard, party harder." Enjoy your meal on a slope-side porch. (☎476-3789. Meals $8-10. Restaurant open June-Sept. and Nov.-Apr. daily 11am-10pm; bar open until 2am.)

SIGHTS. The **Ski Hall of Fame** is housed in the **Colorado Ski Museum,** in the Vail Transportation Center, and captures both the history of the sport and of Vail. (☎476-1876 or 800-950-7410. Open June-Sept. and Nov.-Apr. Tu-Su 10am-5pm. $1, under 12 free.) In the summer, the **Gerald R. Ford Amphitheater,** right at the east edge of Vail Village, presents a number of outdoor concerts, dance festivals, and theater productions on its grounds. (☎476-2918. Box office open M-Sa noon-6pm. Lawn seats $15-40; Tu free.) Next door in the lovely **Betty Ford Alpine Gardens,** view the peaceful meditation and rock gardens. (☎476-0103. Guided tours offered M, Th, Sa 10:30am. Open May-Sept dawn-dusk. Free.) The **Vilar Center for the Arts,** in Beaver Creek, hosts world-renowned performers and shows from Shakespeare to Broadway. (☎845-8497 or 888-920-2787. Box office open M-Sa 11am-5pm.)

OUTDOOR ACTIVITIES. Before slaloming, the unequipped visit **Ski Base,** 610 W. Lionshead Cir., for equipment. (☎476-5799. Open winter daily 8am-7pm. Skis, poles, and boots from $14 per day. Snowboard and boots from $20 per day.) The store transforms into the **Wheel Base Bike Shop** in the summer. (Open summer daily 9am-6pm. Path bikes $15 per 8hr.; mountain bikes from $27 per 8hr.) Vail caters to sun worshippers in the summer, when the ski runs turn into hiking and biking trails. The **Eagle Bahn Gondola** in Lionshead and the **Vista Bahn Chairlift,** part of the Vail Resort, whisk hikers, bikers, and sightseers to the top of the mountains for breathtaking views. (☎476-9090. Office open daily 8:30am-4:30pm. Eagle Bahn open summer Su-W 10am-4pm, Th-Sa 10am-9pm; winter F-Su 10am-4pm. All-day pass on either Bahn $17, ages 65-69 and 5-12 $10, 70 and over $5; $29 for bike haul. Vista Bahn open mid-July to early Sept. F-Su 10am-4pm.) During the summer months, enjoy the **Eagle Bahn Gondola Twilight Ride.** (Th-Sa 5-9pm. Free.) The Holy Cross Ranger District (see above) provides maps and information on the many snowmobile, cross-country skiing, and hiking routes near Vail Pass. The **Gore Creek Fly Fisherman,** 183-7 Gore Creek Dr., reels in the daily catch and has river info. (☎476-3296. Rod rentals $15 per half-day, with boots and waders $30.)

ASPEN

☎970

Aspen was founded in 1879 as a silver mining camp, but the silver ran out quickly and by 1940 the town was almost gone. Wealthy visionaries took one look at the location of the floundering village and transformed it into a winter playground. Today, Aspen's skiing, scenery, and festivals are matched only by the prices in the exclusive boutiques downtown. To catch Aspen on the semi-cheap, stay in Glenwood Springs, 40 mi. north on Rte. 82.

PRACTICAL INFORMATION. **Aspen Shuttles** provide year-round free service all around town (☎925-8484). **Visitors Centers:** 320 E. Hyman Ave., in the Wheeler Opera House (☎920-7148; open daily 10am-6pm); 425 Rio Grand Pl. (☎925-1940 or 888-290-1324; open M-F 8am-5pm). **The Aspen Ranger District,** 806 W. Hallam, provides info on hikes and camping within 15 mi. of Aspen. (☎925-3445. Open June-Aug. M-Sa 8am-5pm; Sept.-May M-F 8am-4:30pm. Topographic maps $4.) **Roads and Weather:** ☎877-315-7623. **Snow Report:** ☎925-1221 or 888-277-3676. **Internet Access: Pitkin County Library,** 120 N. Mill St. (☎925-4025. Open M-Th 10am-9pm, F-Sa 10am-6pm, Su noon-6pm) **Post Office:** 235 Puppy Smith Rd. (☎925-7523. Open M-F 8:30am-5pm, Sa 9am-noon.) **Postal Code:** 81611. **Area Code:** 970.

ACCOMMODATIONS. Staying in Aspen means biting the bullet and reaching deep into your pockets. The last sound deal in town, **St. Moritz Lodge ❷,** 344 W. Hyman Ave., charms ski bums with continental breakfast, a pool, steam room, and hot tub. (☎925-3220 or 800-817-2069. Reception hours 8am-6pm. Dorm beds $26-44, depending on season. Hotel rooms $55-159.) All the pampering of an Aspen resort, without the heavy price tag, **Limelite Lodge ❹,** 228 E. Cooper St., is outfitted with two outdoor pools, two jacuzzis, and a fireplace lounge. (☎925-3025 or 800-433-0832. Singles May-June and Sept.-Oct. $59-109; July-Aug. $89-129; mid- Nov. to mid-Dec. $77-139; Jan. $167-239; Feb.-Mar. $207-257.) Unless more than 6 ft. of snow covers the ground, **camping ❶** is available in one of the nine National Forest campgrounds that lie within 10 mi. of Aspen. **Silver Bar, Silver Bell, and Silver Queen** campgrounds lie 5 mi. southwest of town on Maroon Creek Rd. and fill quickly. Five miles southeast on Rte. 82, **Difficult** campground usually has more openings. (☎877-444-6777. 5-day max. stay throughout the district. Water, but no hookups. Open June to mid-Sept. Reservations recommended. Sites $12-15 per night.)

FOOD. Fast, cheap, and easy, **The Big Wrap ❷,** 520 E. Durant Ave., rolls up gourmet wraps ($6), like the tasty "To Thai For." (☎544-1700. Fresh salads $5. Smoothies $4. Open M-Sa 10am-6pm.) Always packed, the **Hickory House ❸,** 730 W. Main St., smokes up award-winning barbecue favorites. (☎925-2313. Lunch specials $7-10. Dinner $10-20. Open for breakfast M-F 6-11:30am, Sa-Su 6am-2:30pm; for lunch M-F 11:30am-2:30pm, Sa-Su noon-2:30pm; dinner daily 5-10pm.) Try the famed beef stew at **Little Annie's Eating House ❸,** 517 E. Hyman Ave., a longtime Aspen staple for booze and burgers. Everyday, all day long, put back a beer and a shot for $2.75. (☎925-1098. Burgers $8.25. Veggie lasagna $10. Open daily 11:30am-10pm; bar until 2am.) With an espresso bar and freshly squeezed juices, **Main Street Bakery ❷,** 201 E. Main St., also serves up gourmet soups ($5) and vegetarian sandwiches ($7). Their patio offers al fresco dining and a prime people-watching spot. (☎925-6446. Open daily 7am-9:30pm.) With jukeboxes and TVs blaring, the **Cooper Street Pier ❷,** 508 E. Cooper St., is the local hot spot and one of the best deals in town, especially the hamburger special (burger with fries and a soda or beer; $6.50). (☎925-7758. Open daily 11am-10pm; bar open until 2am. Cash only.)

ENTERTAINMENT. Entering its 54th year, the internationally acclaimed **Aspen Music Festival** features jazz, opera, and classical music late June through August. A variety of shows are held every night in many venues around town. A free Music

Shuttle bus transports listeners from Rubey Park to the music tent every 30min. prior to the concert. (☎925-9042; www.aspenmusicfestival.com. Many concerts free.) Take the Silver Queen Gondola (see Outdoor Activities) up to Aspen Mountain for open-air free **Saturday Classic Music Concerts** (late June to mid-Aug., Sa 1pm) and **Bluegrass Sundays** (mid-June to late Aug., Su noon-3pm). **Aspen Theatre in the Park** presents a variety of shows each night from mid-June to late August. (☎925-9313, box office ☎920-5770; www.aspentip.org. $25-30.)

SKIING. Skiing is the main attraction in Aspen. The surrounding hills contain four ski areas: Aspen Mountain, Aspen Highlands, Buttermilk Mountain, and Snowmass, known collectively as **Aspen/Snowmass.** A free **Skier Shuttle Service** runs between the four mountains 8am-4:30pm. Interchangeable lift tickets enable the four areas to operate as a single extended resort; for the best deal, buy multiday passes at least 2 weeks in advance. (☎925-1220 or 800-525-6200. Day passes from $68, ages 65-69 $63, ages 13-17 $53, college students 24 and under $49, ages 7-12 $43, over 70 and under 7 free; prices vary by season.) **Incline Ski Shop,** on the corner of Durant and Hunter St., one of the oldest and most experienced retailers around, rents boots and skis. (☎925-7748.) Each of the mountains offers unique skiing opportunities of varying difficulty. **Buttermilk's** gentle slopes are perfect for beginners interested in lessons (and snowplowing down the mountain). The **Highlands** now includes the steep cliffs of Highland Bowl and offers a diverse selection for advanced and expert skiers. **Aspen Mountain,** though smaller than the Highlands, also caters to experts; there are no easy trails. The granddaddy of the Aspen ski areas, **Snowmass,** with its 20 lifts and countless runs, remains the most family-friendly of the mountains. All but the most timid will find something to enjoy here. Snowmass, with half-pipes and terrain parks, is popular among snowboarders.

OUTDOOR ACTIVITIES. The **Silver Queen Gondola** heads to the 11,212 ft. summit of Aspen Mountain, providing an unparalleled panorama. (☎920-0719 or 800-525-6200. Open daily mid-June to early Sept. 10am-4pm, late Nov. to mid-April 9am-4pm. $17 per day, ages 4-12 $10, $30/20 per week.) At Snowmass Mountain, you can take a chairlift to the top and ride your mountain bike down. (Open summer daily 9:30am-4pm. $8.) **Rick's Adventure Cafe,** at the corner of Durant and Hunter St., offers great deals on mountain bike rentals. (☎925-8200. Open late-May-Oct 8am-5pm. Full suspension bikes half day (4hr.) $35, full day (8hr.) $45.) Hikers can explore the **Maroon Bells** on the unforgettable 1¾ mi. trek to Crater Lake. Maroon Creek Rd. is closed to traffic 8:30am-5pm daily in an effort to preserve the wilderness. RFTA tour buses to the Bells operate during these times and depart from Aspen Highlands Village every 20min. ($5.50 per person.) If you're planning a hike outside these times, there is a $10 per car fee to drive into the area. The steep but short (2½ mi.) **Ute Trail** departs from Ute Ave. and weaves its way to the top of Aspen Mountain, a spectacular sunset-watching spot. The gentler **Hunter Trail** wanders through town and is popular for jogging and biking.

COLORADO SPRINGS ☎719

Once a resort town frequented only by America's elite, Colorado Springs has grown to be the second most visited city in Colorado. When early Colorado gold seekers found bizarre red rock formations here, they named the region Garden of the Gods, partly because of a Ute legend that the rocks were petrified bodies of enemies hurled down by the gods. Today the US Olympic Team continues the quest for gold at Colorado Springs' modern training facility, while jets from the US Air Force Academy roar overhead.

ORIENTATION & PRACTICAL INFORMATION. Colorado Springs is laid out in a grid of broad thoroughfares. **Nevada Avenue** is the main north-south strip, just east of **I-25.** Starting at **Nevada Avenue,** numbered streets ascend moving westward. I-25 from Denver bisects downtown, separating Old Colorado City from the eastern sector of the town, which remains largely residential. **Colorado Avenue** and **Pikes Peak Avenue** run east-west across the city. Just west of Old Colorado City lies Manitou Springs and the Pikes Peak Area. Colorado Ave. becomes **Manitou Avenue** as it extends into Manitou Springs and serves as the main street through town. **Greyhound,** 120 S. Weber St. (☎635-1505; tickets sold daily 5:15am-10pm), runs buses to: Albuquerque (8hr., 4 per day, $61); Denver (1½-2hr., 6 per day, $14); Pueblo (1hr., 6 per day, $10). **City Bus Service,** 127 E. Kiowa St. (☎385-7423), at Nevada Ave., serves the local area as well as surrounding Garden of the Gods, Manitou Springs, and Widefield. Pick up a schedule at the Kiowa bus terminal. ($1.25, seniors and ages 6-11 $0.60, under 6 free; to Ft. Carson, Widefield, Fountain, Manitou Springs, and Peterson AFB $0.95 extra.) **Pikes Peak Tours,** 3704 W. Colorado Ave. (☎633-1181 or 800-345-8197; open daily 8am-5pm), offers whitewater rafting trips on the Arkansas River (7hr.; $75, under 12 $40; includes lunch), as well as a combo tour of the US Air Force Academy and the Garden of the Gods (4hr.; $30, under 12 $15). **Taxi: Yellow Cab,** ☎634-5000. **Visitor Info: Visitors Bureau,** 515 S. Cascade Ave. (☎635-7506 or 800-888-4748; www.coloradosprings-travel.com. Open M-F 8:30am-5pm, Sa-Su 9am-5pm.) **Internet Access: Penrose Public Library,** 20 N. Cascade Ave. (☎531-6333. Open M-Th 10am-9pm, F-Sa 10am-6pm, Su 1-5pm.) **Post Office:** 201 E. Pikes Peak Ave., at Nevada Ave. (☎570-5336. Open M-F 7:30am-5:30pm, Sa 8am-1pm.) **Postal Code:** 80903. **Area Code:** 719.

ROCKY MOUNTAINS

ACCOMMODATIONS. Motels can be found all along Nevada Ave. near downtown, although the best options can be found farther west in and around Manitou Springs. Located at the south entrance of the Garden of the Gods, **Beckers Lane Lodge ❸,** 115 Beckers Ln., supplies clean rooms with microwave, fridge, and cable TV, along with an outdoor swimming pool and barbecue area. (☎685-1866. Rooms $40-50.)**Ute Pass Motel ❸,** 1123 Manitou Ave., is more expensive, but makes up for that nicely with an indoor hot tub or settle on the hammock in the upper deck, as well as barbecue and picnic on the lower deck next to Fountain Creek. Rooms with kitchens available. Laundry facilities on site. (☎685-5171. In summer, singles $55; doubles $75-90. In winter singles $35; doubles $50.) The **Apache Court Motel ❷,** 3401 W. Pikes Peak Ave., at 34th St., has pink adobe rooms with A/C, cable TV, microwave, refrigerator, and a common hot tub. (☎471-9440. Rooms $37-59.) Located conveniently on the main bus line, the **Maverick Motel ❷,** 3620 W. Colorado Ave., is an explosion of pastels. Rooms come fully equipped with cable TV, fridge, and microwave. (☎634-2852 or 800-214-0264. Singles $40; 2-room unit $45-55, call to reserve.)

Several **Pike National Forest Campgrounds ❶** lie in the mountains flanking Pikes Peak, about 30min. from Colorado Springs. No local transportation serves this area. Campgrounds clutter Rte. 67, 5-10 mi. north of **Woodland Park,** 18 mi. northwest of the Springs on U.S. 24. **Colorado, Painted Rocks,** and **South Meadows** are near Manitou Park; others border U.S. 24 near the town of Lake George, 50 mi. west of the Springs. (Generally open May-Sept. Sites $12-14.) Farther afield, visitors may camp by Lake George Reservoir, at the **Eleven Mile State Recreation Area ❶,** off County Rd. 90 from U.S. 24. (☎748-3401, for reservations ☎800-678-2267. Reservations M-F 7:30am-4:30pm. Pay showers and laundry. Sites $12, with electricity $16; vehicle fee $5.) Unless otherwise posted, you can camp on national forest property for free if you are at least 500 ft. from a road or stream. The **Pikes Peak Ranger District Office,** 601 S. Weber St., has maps. (☎636-1602. Open M-F 8am-4:30pm.)

FOOD & NIGHTLIFE. Students and the young-at-heart perch among outdoor tables in front of the cafes and restaurants lining **Tejon Avenue. Old Colorado City** is home to a number of fine eateries. During the summer months, there are several **Farmers Markets** scattered throughout the city. **Poor Richard's Restaurant ❷,** 324½ N. Tejon Ave., is a popular local hangout with great New York-style pizza (cheese slices $3.25; pies $12), sandwiches ($6), and salads ($5-6). (☎632-7721. W live bluegrass, Th Celtic. Open Su-Tu 11am-9pm, W-Sa 11am-10pm.) Vegans and carnivores alike find heaven at **Organic Earth Cafe ❷,** 1124 Manitou Ave. The extensive menu aims and succeeds at pleasing every appetite. An amazing list of smoothies and plant shakes ($4-5) sets apart this establishment, consisting of a 1904 Victorian Tea Room, the Future Earth Room, and Fairy Tale Rose Gardens bordering Fountain Creek. (☎685-0986. Su 8pm-2am open mic, M 8-10pm drum circle, Tu and Th guest speakers and films, W 8pm-midnight spoken word, F 8pm-2am live funk/jazz. Open M-Th 9am-midnight, F-Su 9am-2am.) The oldest Mexican restaurant in town, **Henri's ❷,** 2427 W. Colorado Ave., has served up chimichangas ($7.50) and a wide variety of cerveza on the cheap for over 50 years. *Tacos al carbone* ($8.50) is also a popular house favorite. Drop in for a margarita during Happy Hours (M-Th 4-8pm, F 3-8pm) or check out the strolling Mariachi singers Friday and Saturday nights. (☎634-9031. Open Su-Th 11am-9pm, F-Sa 11am-10pm.) **Meadow Muffins ❷,** 2432 W. Colorado Ave., is a virtual museum of old movie props. The two buckboard wagons hanging from the ceiling were used in the filming of *Gone With The Wind*, and the windmill-style fan installed above the bar was originally cast in *Casablanca*. (☎633-0583. Drafts $3.50. Burgers $6-7. Tu-Sa live music; Tu all day Happy Hour; W karaoke; Sa ladies night. 21+ after 8pm every night. Open daily 11am-2am.) If an unbeatable breakfast is what you're looking for, **The Olive Branch ❷,** 23 S. Tejon Ave, is famous for their omelettes ($6) and country style skillets ($7) and is outfitted with a full smoothie, juice, and espresso bar ($2-4). Lunch and dinner menus also feature the hearty pot pie ($8). (☎475-1199. Open daily 6:30am-9pm.) Recently expanded, **Rum Bay Bourbon Street,** 20 N. Tejon St., is a multi-level bar and club complex with six clubs included under one cover charge ($5). Besides the main Rum Bay club, the crowds swell into Masquerade (a disco club), Copy Cats (a karaoke bar), Fat City (a martini lounge with live blues), and Sam's (the world's smallest bar as noted in the *Guinness Book of World Records*). (☎634-3522. Specialty rum drinks $6-7. Th ladies night. 21+ after 8pm. Rum Bay open Tu-Sa 11am-2am. All other clubs open Th-Sa 6pm-2am.)

SIGHTS. Olympic hopefuls train with some of the world's most high-tech sports equipment at the **US Olympic Complex,** 1750 E. Boulder St., on the corner of Union St. The complex has free 1hr. tours. The best times to get a glimpse of athletes in training are 10-11am and 3-4pm. (☎578-4792 or 888-659-8687. Open M-Sa 9am-5pm, Su 10am-5pm. Tours M-Sa every ½hr.) Earlier quests for gold are recorded at the **Pioneers' Museum,** 215 S. Tejon Ave., which recounts the settling of Colorado Springs. (☎385-5990. Open summer Tu-Sa 10am-5pm, Su 1-5pm; winter closed Su. Free.) The **World Figure Skating Museum and Hall of Fame,** 20 1st St., just north of Lake St., traces the history, art, and science of skating through film and photos and boasts an extensive collection of rare medals and skating outfits. The only institution of its kind in the world, the museum pays homage to the great American and international skaters that have etched their mark on ice. (☎635-5200; www.worldskatingmuseum.org. $3, ages 6-12 $2, over 59 $2. Open M-F 10am-4pm, Nov.-Apr. Sa 10am-4pm; May-Oct. 10am-5pm.) Adding life to earth with only fire and water for over 100 years, potters at **Van Briggle Pottery,** Hwy. 24 and 21st St., display their skill and passion during free tours through the studio and historic showroom. Patrons can witness the spinning, casting, and etching process that has produced pieces displayed in the world's most famous museums. (☎800-847-6341. Open M-Sa 8:30am-5pm, Su 1-5pm. Free tours M-Sa.) Among the old vehicles, saddles, and riding accessories found at **El Pomar Foundation Carriage Museum,** 16 Lake Cir., travelers can take a closer look at two presidential inaugural coaches and a Conestoga wagon, the colors of which supposedly inspired the design of the American flag. (☎634-7711. Open M-Sa 10am-5pm, Su 1-5pm. Free.)

OUTDOOR ACTIVITIES. Between Rte. 24 (Colorado Ave.) and 30th St. in northwest Colorado Springs, the red rock towers and spires of the **Garden of the Gods Park** rise strikingly against a mountainous backdrop. (Open daily May-Oct. 5am-11pm; Nov.-Apr. 5am-9pm.) **Climbers** are lured by the large red faces and over 400 permanent routes. Climbers must register at the Visitors Center; $500 fines await those who climb without permit or proper gear. A number of exciting **mountain biking** trails cross the Garden as well. The park's hiking trails, many of which are paved wheelchair-accessible routes, have great views of the rock formations and can easily be completed in one day. A map is available from the park's **Visitors Center,** 1805 N. 30th St., at Gateway Rd. (☎634-6666; http://gardenofgods.com. Open daily June-Aug. 8am-8pm; Sept.-June 9am-5pm. Daily walking tours depart in summer 10, 11am, 1, 2pm; winter 10am, 2pm.)

From any part of town, one can't help but notice the 14,110 ft. summit of **Pikes Peak** on the horizon. Ambitious climbers can ascend the peak along the strenuous, well-maintained **Barr Trail.** (26 mi. round-trip, 7400 ft. altitude gain, approx. 16hr. round-trip. Overnight shelter is available at Barr Camp (7 mi. from the trailhead) and the Timberline Shelter (8½ mi.) The trailhead is in Manitou Springs by the "Manitou Incline" sign on Ruxton Ave. Just down the street from the trailhead, visitors can hop on the **Pikes Peak Cog Railway,** 515 Ruxton Ave., operating since 1891, which takes visitors to the summit every 80min. From the summit, the Sangre de Cristo Mountains, the Continental Divide, and the state of Kansas unfold in a lofty view that inspired Kathy Lee Bates to write "America the Beautiful." (☎685-5401; www.cograilway.com. Open mid-Apr. to late Dec.; about 6-8 trips a day, call for hours. Round-trip $25.50, ages 3-11 $14. Reservations recommended.) Avoid crowded parking lots at both the Railway and Barr Trailhead by using the free Manitou Springs Trolley ("SMART" Shuttle) which runs along Manitou and Ruxton Ave. Memorial Day-Labor Day. You can pay to drive up the gorgeous 10mi. Pikes Peak Hwy. (☎385-7325 or 800-318-9505. Open mid-Sept. to Apr. daily 9am-3pm; May to mid-Sept. 7am-7pm. $10, $5 ages 6-15; max. $35 per vehicle.)

For adventurous hiking through subterranean passages, head to the contorted caverns of the **Cave of the Winds,** on Rte. 24, 6 mi. west of Exit 141 off I-25. Discovery and lantern tours go into the more untamed areas of the cave. (☎685-5444; www.caveofthewinds.com. Guided tours daily late May-Aug. every 15min. 9am-9pm; Sept, late May 10am-5pm. 45min. Discovery tour $15, ages 6-15 $8. 1-1½hr. Lantern Tour $18/9. Laser light show in summer daily 9pm $10/5.) Just above Manitou Springs on Rte. 24, the **Cliff Dwellings Museum** contains replicas of ancestral Puebloan dwellings dating from AD 1100-1300 and actual ruins which serve as backdrop for Indian dancers in colorful traditional dress performing from June to August. (☎685-5242 or 800-354-9971; www.cliffdwellingsmuseum.com. Open daily June-Aug. 9am-8pm; Sept.-May 10am-5pm. $8, seniors $7, ages 7-11 $6.) The only waterfall in Colorado to make it on *National Geographic's* list of international waterfalls, **Seven Falls,** 10min. west of downtown on Cheyenne Blvd., cascades 181 ft. in seven distinct steps down Pikes Peak and is lit up on summer nights. (☎632-0765; http://sevenfalls.com. Open June-Aug. 8:30am-10:30pm. Before 5pm $8.25, ages 6-15 $5.25; after 5pm $9.75/6.25.)

SAN JUAN MOUNTAINS

Ask Coloradoans about their favorite mountain retreats, and they'll most likely name a peak, lake, stream, or town in the San Juan Range of southwestern Colorado. Four **national forests**—the **Uncompahgre** (un-cum-PAH-gray), the **Gunnison,** the **San Juan,** and the **Río Grande**—encircle this sprawling range. **Durango** is an ideal base camp for forays into these mountains. Northeast of Durango, the **Weminuche Wilderness** tempts the hardy backpacker with a vast expanse of rugged terrain. Get maps and hiking info from the **USFS headquarters** at 15 Burnett Ct., Durango. (☎247-4874. Open Apr. to mid-Dec. M-F 8am-5pm; mid-Dec. to Mar. 8am-4:30pm.)

The San Juan Mountains are easily accessible via U.S. 50, which is traveled by hundreds of thousands of tourists each summer. **Greyhound** serves the area, but very poorly; traveling by car is the best option in this region. On a happier note, the San Juans are loaded with HI-AYH hostels and campgrounds, making them one of the most economical places to visit in Colorado.

BLACK CANYON OF THE GUNNISON NATIONAL PARK ☎970

Native American parents used to tell their children that the light-colored strands of rock streaking through the walls of the Black Canyon were the hair of a blonde woman—and that if they got too close to the edge they would get tangled in it and fall. The edge of **Black Canyon of the Gunnison National Park** is a staggering place, literally—watch for those trembling knees. The Gunnison River slowly gouged out the 53 mi. long canyon, crafting a steep 2500 ft. gorge that is, in some places, deeper than it is wide. The Empire State Building, if placed at the bottom of the river, would reach barely halfway up the canyon walls.

The Black Canyon lies 15 mi. east of the town of **Montrose.** The **South Rim** is easily accessible via a 6 mi. drive off U.S. 50 ($7 per car, $4 walk-in or motorcycle); the wilder **North Rim** can only be reached by an 80 mi. detour around the canyon followed by a gravel road from Crawford off Rte. 92. The road is closed in winter. The spectacular 8 mi. South Rim Drive traces the edge of the canyon, and boasts jaw-dropping vistas including the spectacular **Chasm View,** where you can peer 2300 ft. down the highest cliff in Colorado at the Gunnison River and the "painted" wall. *Don't throw stones;* you might kill a defenseless hiker in the canyon. On the South Rim, the moderate 2 mi. round-trip **Oak Flat Loop Trail** gives a good sense of the terrain below, while the North Rim's 7 mi. round-trip **North Vista Trail** provides a spectacular view. From the South Rim, you can scramble down the **Gunnison Route,** which drops 1800 ft. over a 1 mi. span, or tackle the more difficult **Tomichi** or **Warner Routes,** which make good overnight hikes. Not surprisingly, the sheer walls of the Black Canyon are climbers' paradise; register at the South Rim Visitors Center. Between the **Painted Wall** and **Cedar Point Overlooks,** a well-worn path leads to **Marmot Rocks,** which offer great bouldering for those not ready for the big walls.

At the canyon, the **South Rim Campground ❶** has 102 well-designed sites with pit toilets, charcoal grills, water, and some with wheelchair access ($10, full hookup $15). The **North Rim Campground ❶** offers 13 sites, rarely fills, and is popular with climbers (water and toilets; $10). In Montrose, inexpensive motels line Main St./U.S. 50 east of downtown, including the **Western Motel ❷,** 1200 E. Main St. (☎249-3481 or 800-445-7301; singles summer from $50, winter from $35), and **Canyon Trails Inn ❷,** 1225 E. Main St. (☎249-3426. Hot tub, continental breakfast. Singles $32-45.)

Nav-Mex Tacos ❶, 475 W. Main St., serves up the best Mexican cuisine around. (Tacos $1.25; tostadas $3. Open M-F 11am-9pm, Sa-Su 9am-9pm.) For tasty sandwiches ($5) and omelettes ($6), head for the **Daily Bread Bakery and Cafe ❶,** 346 Main St. (☎249-8444. Open M-Sa 6am-3pm.)

Greyhound (☎249-6673; tickets sold Su-Tu 7:30am-8:30am, 7-8pm, W-Sa 7:30am-12:30pm, 7-8pm) shuttles once a day between Montrose and the **Gunnison County Airport,** 711 Rio Grande (☎641-0060), and will drop you off on U.S. 50, 6 mi. from the canyon ($15). A **Visitors Center** sits on the South Rim. (☎249-1914, ext. 423; www.nps.gov/blca. Open daily May-Oct. 8am-6pm; Nov.-Apr. 8:30am-4pm.) **Post Office**: 321 S. 1st St. (☎249-6654. Open M-F 8am-5pm, Sa 10am-noon.) **Postal Code**: 81401. **Area Code:** 970.

CRESTED BUTTE ☎970

Crested Butte, 27 mi. north of Gunnison on Rte. 135, was first settled by miners in the 1870s. The coal was exhausted in the 1950s, but a few years later the steep powder fields on the Butte began attracting skiers. Thanks to strict zoning rules, the historic downtown is a throwback to those early mining days. Three miles north of town, **Crested Butte Mountain Resort,** 12 Snowmass Rd., takes skiers to "the extreme limits" and offers over 800 acres of bowl skiing. Many of the other 85 runs are less spine-tingling, but the panoramic views are equally inspiring. (☎800-544-8448. Open mid-Dec. to mid-Apr. Prices vary. Day passes around $50; ages 65-74 half-price; over 75 free; children 5-12 pay the numerical value of their age.)

Come summertime, Crested Butte becomes the mountain biking capital of Colorado. During the last week of June, the town hosts the **Fat Tire Bike Festival** (www.ftbw.com), 4 days of mountain biking, racing, and fraternizing. In 1976, a group of cyclists rode from Crested Butte to Aspen, starting the oldest mountain biking event in the world. Every September, experienced bikers repeat the trek over the 12,705 ft. pass to Aspen and back during the **Pearl Pass Tour,** organized by the **Mountain Biking Hall of Fame,** 331 Elk Ave. (☎349-1880.) Biking trail maps are available at bike shops and **The Alpineer,** 419 6th St. (☎349-5210. Open June to mid-Sept. and Dec. to mid-Apr. 9am-6pm; otherwise 10am-5pm.) Trails begin at the base of Mt. Crested Butte and extend into the exquisite Gothic area. **Trail 401** is a demanding and famous 24 mi. round-trip loop with an excellent view. The beautiful trek to **Green Lake** (3 mi.) is also a favorite.

Finding budget accommodations in the winter is about as easy as striking a vein of gold, but there are a few possibilities. **Crested Butte International Hostel and Lodge (HI-AYH) ❶,** 615 Teocalli Ave., two blocks north of the four-way stop, treats travelers to a tidy stay in gorgeous modern facilities. Its huge kitchen and bright common area make it an ideal base for exploring the area. (☎349-0588 or 888-389-0588; www.crestedbuttehostel.com. Showers for non-guests $5. No curfew or lockout. Coin-op laundry. Roomy 4-6 bed dorms $20, non-members $20; doubles $55-85. Spacious 3rd-floor apartment sleeps up to 6; $125-200. Rates vary depending on season, call in advance for prices and reservations. Group discounts available.) **Campsites ❶** can be found just south of town off Rte. 135 on Cement Creek Rd. and Taylor Canyon Rd. Find more info on area campgrounds at **Gunnison National Forest Office,** 216 N. Colorado, 30 mi. south in Gunnison. (☎641-0471. Open M-F 7:30am-4:30pm.)

Pitas in Paradise ❶, 214 Elk Ave., a self-proclaimed "Mediterranean Cafe with Soul," wows diners with its delicious $5 gyros, $3-5 salads, and $3 smoothies. Watch your meal being made at the counter or sit down to wait for it in the backyard. (☎349-0897. Open daily 11am-10pm.) **The Secret Stash ❷,** 21 Elk Ave., at the west end of town, operates one of the highest altitude coffee roasters in the world. With a menu ranging from eclectic pizzas ($8-17) to salads and wraps ($3.50-8) to grilled wings (10 for $7), this hip joint aims to please. Sip a soy latte in the side garden or on the vast second floor, where one might mistake the cushy couches, mood lighting, and acoustic guitar for a hippie's living room. (☎349-6245. Open M-Sa 5-10pm with additional lunch hours during summer and winter seasons.)

The **Crested Butte Chamber of Commerce:** 601 Elk Ave. (☎800-545-4505; www.crestedbuttechamber.com. Open daily 9am-5pm.) A free **shuttle** to the mountain leaves from the chamber. (☎349-5616. Every 40min. 7:20-10:20am and 8pm-midnight, every 20min. 10:20am-8pm.) **Internet Access: The Old Rock Community Library,** 507 Maroon Ave. (☎349-6535. Open M,W, F 10am-6pm, Tu and Th 10am-7pm, Sa 10am-2pm.) **Post Office:** 215 Elk Ave. (☎349-5568. Open M-F 7:30am-4:30pm.) **Postal Code:** 81224. **Area Code:** 970.

TELLURIDE ☎970

Site of the first bank Butch Cassidy ever robbed (the San Miguel), Telluride was very much a town of the Old West. Locals believe that their city's name derives from a contraction of "to hell you ride," a likely warning given to travelers to the once hell-bent city. Things have quieted down a bit in the last few years; outlaws have been replaced with film celebrities, and six-shooters with cinnamon buns. Skiers, hikers, and vacationers come to Telluride to pump gold and silver *into* the mountains, and the town also claims the most festivals per capita of any postal code in the US. Still, a small-town feeling prevails—rocking chairs sit outside brightly painted houses, and dogs lounge on storefront porches.

PRACTICAL INFORMATION. Telluride sits on a short spur of Rte. 145, 125 mi. northwest of Durango in the heart of the San Juan Mountains. Most action lies on Colorado Ave./Rte. 145. The public bus line, **Galloping Goose,** runs the length of town on a regular basis. (☎728-5700. Runs M-F May-Nov. every 20min. 7:30am-6pm; Dec.-Apr. every 10min. 7am-midnight. Town loop free, outlying towns $1-2.) A free gondola, which runs continuously between downtown and Mountain Village, provides a spectacular view of the surrounding San Juans. The station is at the corner of Oak St. and San Juan Ave. (☎728-8888. 15 min. each way. Runs late May-early Apr. daily 7am-midnight.) **Taxi** service from **Mountain Limo** serves the western slope. (☎728-9606 or 888-546-6894. Airport fare $8.) The **Visitors Center** is at the corner of Davis St. and W. Colorado Ave. near the entrance to town. (☎800-525-3455; http://telluridemm.com. Open summer M-Sa 9am-7pm, Su noon-5pm.) **Police:** ☎728-3818. **Rape Crisis Hotlines:** ☎728-5660. **Telluride Medical Center,** 500 W. Pacific (☎728-3848). **Internet Access: Wilkinson Public Library,** 100 W. Pacific St. (☎728-4519. Open M-Th 10am-8pm, F-Sa 10am-6pm, Su noon-5pm.) **Post Office:** 150 S. Willow St. (☎728-3900. Open M-F 9am-5pm, Sa 10am-noon.) **Postal Code:** 81435. **Area Code:** 970.

ACCOMMODATIONS. If you're visiting Telluride during a festival, bring a sleeping bag; the cost of a bed is outrageous. The **Oak Street Inn ❸,** 134 N. Oak St., offers cozy rooms at the cheapest price in town. (☎728-3383. Singles with shared bath $42, with private bath $60; doubles $58/72; rooms around $20 more during festivals.) William Jennings Bryan delivered his "Cross of Gold" speech from the front balcony of the **New Sheridan Hotel ❹,** 231 W. Colorado Ave., and if you can afford it, the luxurious rooms, full breakfast, and free Internet access make it worth your while. (☎728-4351 or 800-200-1891. Rooms with shared bath from $90.) The **Telluride Town Park Campground ❶,** east of downtown, offers particularly nice sites along the San Miguel River. (☎728-2173. Water, full bathrooms, no hookups. 7-night max. stay. Open Mid-May to mid-Oct. $12 per vehicle; primitive sites $10. Office open M-W 8am-5pm, Th-F 8am-7pm, Sa-Su 8am-4:30pm.) During festival times, if you have a ticket to the festival in town park, you can crash anywhere in the campground; hot showers ($2) are available at the high school.

ROCKY MOUNTAINS

FROM THE ROAD

EAST MEETS WEST

There exist a multitude of sparkling stars in the big skies of Montana, an excess of champagne powder ski slopes throughout Colorado, a handful of stomping rodeos in Wyoming, and about one or two Chinese women in the entire Rockies region—including myself. As a young Asian woman traveling alone, I was an unusual breed around these parts, to say the least. Strange reactions guaranteed continuous sources of amusement as I traveled.

Relaxing in a Telluride coffee shop early one morning, I noticed a woman looking over my shoulder. As she sipped her tea, she smiled at me and asked, "So how long have you been in the country studying English?" In Cody, a waitress graciously informed me that any item could be cooked or grilled with soy sauce.

Being Chinese sometimes elevated me to celebrity status. The owner of a hot dog stand in Vail stopped me in front of his store, thinking I was an actress he had seen on TV. Despite my protests, he was certain he had seen me before, and offered me a dog as thanks for the spices "my people" supplied to America. Being the only woman in a Cheyenne bar during Happy Hour one afternoon, the bartender renamed the drink special "Miss Korea" in my honor; I didn't bother to correct him.

-Jennie Wei, 2003

FOOD. La Cocina de Luz ❷, "the kitchen of light," 123 E. Colorado Ave, serves authentic and affordable taqueria-style Mexican cuisine. Featuring hand-made fresh tortillas and fire-roasted chiles, La Cocina's cooking methods add flavor to their quesadillas and tamales ($5-9). Large selection of vegetarian options available. (☎728-9355. Open daily 9am-9pm.)The wooden benches and long tables at **Fat Alley Barbeque ❸,** 122 S. Oak St., are reminiscent of the sawdust saloons of yore, but Telluride's miners never ate barbecue ($5-17) like this. (☎728-3985. Open daily 11am-10pm.) **Baked in Telluride ❷,** 127 S. Fir St., has enough rich coffee, delicious pastries, pizza, sandwiches, and $0.69 bagels to get you through a festival weekend. The apple fritters ($2) and enormous calzones ($6-9) are justifiably famous. (☎728-4775. Open daily 5:30am-10pm.) The subterranean locale makes **Deli Downstairs ❶,** 217 W. Colorado St., feel more like a food stand at a Grateful Dead show than a sedentary establishment, and the sandwiches ($5-6) will keep you boogying for hours. Finish off with a scoop of ice cream ($1-2); they have the largest selection in town. (☎728-4004. Open daily 10am-midnight. Cash only.)

FESTIVALS & NIGHTLIFE. Given that only 1900 people live in Telluride, the sheer number of festivals in the town seems staggering. For general festival info, contact the **Telluride Visitors Center** (☎800-525-3455). Gala events occur throughout the summer and fall, from the quirky **Mushroom Festival** (late Aug.; www.shroomfestival.com), to the multi-sport challenge of the **360° Adventure** (early July; www.telluride360.org), to the renowned **Bluegrass Festival.** (☎800-624-2422; www.planetbluegrass.com. 3rd weekend in June. $55 per day, 4-day pass $155.) One weekend in July is actually designated "Nothing Festival" to give locals a break from the onslaught of visitors and special events. The **Telluride International Film Festival** premiers some of the hippest independent flicks; *The Crying Game* and *The Piano* were both unveiled here. (☎728-4640; www.telluridefilmfestival.com. 1st weekend in Sept.) Telluride also hosts a **Jazz Celebration** during the first weekend of August (☎728-7009; www.telluridejazz.com) and a **Blues & Brews Festival** (☎728-8037; www.telluride-blues.com) during the third weekend in September. For most festivals (including the more expensive Bluegrass Fest and Jazz Celebration), volunteering to usher or perform other tasks can result in free admission. Call the contact number of the specific event for more info. Throughout the year a number of concerts and performances go on at the **Sheridan Opera House,** 110 N. Oak St. (☎728-6363.)

Telluride may have a new-age air by day, but its bars still rollick with old-fashioned fun by night. Telluride's freshest musical talent jives at **Fly Me to the Moon Saloon,** 136 E. Colorado Ave., which thrills groovers with its spring-loaded dance floor. (☎728-6666. $2-5 cover. Open daily 7pm-2am. Cash only.) The lively **Last Dollar Saloon,** 100 E. Colorado Ave., affectionately referred to as "the buck," is a favorite among locals. With the juke box blaring and darts flying, it's easy to see why. (☎728-4800. Open daily 11:30am-2am. Beer $3-4.50. Cash only.) The historic **New Sheridan Bar,** 231 W. Colorado Ave., inspires hubbub around town. With $3.50 drinks during Happy Hour (daily 5-7pm), New Sheridan also features Tuesday pool tournaments and Wednesday open poker nights. (☎728-9100. 21+ after 8pm. Open daily 3pm-2am.) The **Roma Bar & Cafe,** 133 E. Colorado Ave., is great for ending the evening. (☎728-3669. M 2-for-1 pizza. Open daily 11:30am- 2:30pm and 5:30pm-2am; dinner until 10pm.)

OUTDOOR ACTIVITIES. Biking, hiking, and backpacking opportunities are endless; ghost towns and lakes are tucked behind almost every mountain crag. The tourist office has a list of suggestions for hikes in the area. The most popular trek (about 2hr.) is up the jeep road to **Bridal Veil Falls,** the waterfall visible from almost anywhere in Telluride. The trailhead is at the end of Rte. 145. Continuing another 2½ mi. from the top of the falls will lead to **Silver Lake,** a steep but rewarding climb. Starting from the north end of Aspen St., the **Jud Wiebe Trail** takes you on a 2¾ mi. loop with panoramas of the entire valley. For more Rocky Mountain highs, ride the free gondola to St. Sophia station at the top of the mountain, where a number of hiking and biking trails run.

In winter, even avowed atheists can be spied praying before hitting the "Spiral Stairs" and the "Plunge," two of the Rockies' most gut-wrenching ski runs. For more info, contact the Telluride Ski Resort, P.O. Box 11155, Telluride 81435. (☎728-3856. Regular season lift tickets: full-day $65, half-day $58; children $36/28.) Paragon Ski and Sport, 213 W. Colorado Ave., rents bikes in summer and skis in winter. (☎728-4525. Open daily in ski season 8:30am-9pm; 9am-7pmin summer. Bikes from $18 per half-day, $35 per day; skis and boots $28 per day.)

SCENIC DRIVE: SAN JUAN SKYWAY

More a runway to the mountains and clouds than a terrestial highway, the San Juan Skyway soars across the rooftop of the Rockies. Winding its way through San Juan and Uncompahgre National Forests, Old West mountain towns, and Native American ruins, the byway passes a remarkably wide range of southwestern Colorado's splendors. Reaching altitudes up to 11,000 feet, with breathtaking views of snowy peaks and verdant valleys, the San Juan Skyway is widely considered one of America's most beautiful drives. Travelers in this area inevitably drive at least parts of it as they head to destinations like Telluride, Durango, and Mesa Verde. Call the San Juan (☎970-247-4874) or Uncompahgre (☎970-874-6600) National Forests to check road conditions or to inquire about driving the skyway.

A loop road, piggy-backing on Rte. 550, 62, 145, and 160, the skyway voyage can be started from anywhere along the loop. Beginning in Durango, the skyway heads north along **Route 550 N (Million Dollar Highway),** climbing into the San Juan Mountains, and paralleling the Animas River. 27 mi. north of Durango, the road passes **Durango Mountain Resort** as it ascends. (☎800-979-9742. Annual snowfall 260 in. Open late Nov. to early Apr. 9am-4pm. Full day lift ticket $55, under 12 $29.) At Mi. 64 on Rte. 550, the road reaches Molas Point, a whopping 10,910 ft. above sea level. Less than 1 mi. further north, **Molas Lake Public Park Campground** ❶ offers visitors an oasis with tent and RV sites ($15) right near the lake. (☎759-5557. Potable water available, no hookups.) Descending to a mere 9000 ft., the skyway arrives in easy-going Silverton. A mining town until the early 1990s, **Silverton** is a subdued mountain village that boasts some of Colorado's best ice climbing. The **Visitors Center** sits close to the entrance to town on Rte. 550. (☎387-5654 or 800-752-4494; www.silverton.org. Open daily June-Sept. 9am-6pm; Oct.-May 10am-4pm.) Hiking, mountain biking, and skiing at **Kendall Mountain** ($6 lift tickets) await those who can still catch their breath. From Silverton, the San Juan Skyway climbs higher until it reaches 11,018 ft. at Mi. 80 on Rte. 550. Known as **Red Mountain Pass,** this scenic point has some hiking and more than a few Kodak moments. Continuing north, the drive from Silverton to Ouray showcases stellar 14,000 ft. mountain peaks and defunct mines. In 1991, the Reclamation Act shut down most of the mines, leaving only remnants of the past. The skyway next arrives in **Ouray.** Find the **Visitors Center** at the north end of town on Rte. 550. (☎325-4746; www.ouraycolorado.com. Open M-F 9am-5pm, Sa 10am-4pm, Su noon-4pm.) With fabulous mountain views and hedonistic hot springs, this heavily Swiss-influenced town known as "America's Switzerland" is a relaxing stop for the weary. Beyond Ouray, the skyway returns to Earth. Traversing mesas, Rte. 550 junctions with Rte. 62 in Ridgeway. Rte. 62 assumes the reigns of the skyway and leads travelers to Placerville, where the skyway connects with Rte. 145.

Telluride next awaits travelers along Rte. 145. Past the Mountain Village, the dubiously named **Lizard's Pass** offers a tranquil 6 mi. hike reaching over 12,000 ft. From the pass, the skyway glides down along the Taylor Mesa through the quiet towns of Rico, Stoner, and Dolores. Rte. 145 connects with Rte. 160 just east of Cortez and west of **Mesa Verde National Park.** Moving east along Rte. 160, the skyway cuts through **Mancos** and finally returns to Durango.

ROCKY MOUNTAINS

DURANGO ☎970

In its heyday, Durango was one of the main railroad junctions in the Southwest. Walking down the town's main thoroughfare today, it is easy to see that Durango remains a crossroads. Dreadlocked, hemp-clad youths share the sidewalks with weathered ranchers in ten-gallon hats and stiff Wranglers; toned, brazen mountain bikers rub shoulders in the bars with camera-toting tourists. These folks are brought together by their experiences in the great expanses of wilderness that engulf the town: enjoying the flora, roping dogies at the rodeo, biking the San Juans, or riding the narrow gauge railroad.

PRACTICAL INFORMATION. Durango is at the intersection of U.S. 160 and 550. Streets run east-west and avenues run north-south, but everyone calls Main Ave., the principal road through town, "Main St." **Greyhound,** 275 E. 8th Ave. (☎259-2755; open M-F 7:30am-noon and 3:30-5pm, Sa 6:30am-noon, Su and holidays 6:30-10am), runs once per day to: Grand Junction (5hr., $33-35); Denver (11½hr., $64-68); Albuquerque (5hr., $43-48). The **Durango Lift** provides trolley service in and around town. (☎259-5438. Runs Memorial Day-Labor Day M-F 6:30am-7:30 pm, Sa 9:30am-7:30 pm. $1, seniors $0.50.) **Taxi: Durango Transportation,** ☎259-4818. The **Durango Area Chamber Resort Association,** 111 S. Camino del Río, on the southeast side of town, offers info on sights and hiking. (☎247-0312 or 800-525-8855; www.durango.org. Open M-Sa 8am-5:30pm, Su 10am-4pm.) **Road Conditions:** ☎264-5555. **Police:** 990 E. 2nd Ave. (☎385-2900). **Internet Access: Durango Public Library,** 1188 E. 2nd Ave. (☎385-2970. Open M-W 9am-9pm, Th-Su 9am-5:30pm, closed Su in the summer.) **Post Office:** 222 W. 8th St. (☎247-3434. Open M-F 8am-5:30pm; Sa 9am-1pm.) **Postal Code:** 81301. **Area Code:** 970.

ACCOMMODATIONS & FOOD. One of the best places to stay in Durango for a reasonable price, **Budget Inn ❷,** 3077 Main Ave., offers clean rooms with on-site hot tub, outdoor pool, and laundry facility. (☎247-5222. Cable TV, telephone, some with microwave and fridge. June-Aug. singles $40, doubles $60; Sept.-May $27/47.) If you don't mind staying 20 mi. north of Durango, you'll be pampered at **Silverpick Lodge ❸**, 48475 U.S. 550, with luxurious rooms, on-site hot tub, huge game room, laundromat, and library. Call within 48hr. of check-in for their "Last Second Special" and get any available room for only $48, about ½ the price of what they usually run for. (☎259-6600. "Last Second Special" available year-round.) Find great camping at **Junction Creek Campground ❶**, on Forest Rd. 171. From Main Ave., turn west on 25th St., which becomes Forest Rd. 171 after 4 mi.; the turn-off is 1 mi. past the national forest entrance. (☎247-4874. 14-night max. stay. $12 per vehicle, each additional person $6.) Back in Durango, "dill-icious" pickles and subs abound at **Johnny McGuire's Deli ❶**, 601 E. 2nd Ave., where pictures and postcards have accumulated over the years and filled its walls. Choose from more than 25 sandwiches ($5.50) with names like the Free Iron Willy and the 4:20 Vegan. (☎259-8816. Open daily 7am-9pm. Cash only.) Decked out with Texas and local paraphernalia, **Serious Texas BBQ ❶**, 3535 N. Main Ave., doles out generous ½ lb. portions of smoked meat ($6.50), Texas tacos ($3.50) and "cheezy potatoes" ($1.25). (☎946-1149. Open daily 11am-9pm.) Locals eat at **Carver's Bakery and Brewpub ❷**, 1022 Main Ave., where breakfast specials ($3-5) and pitchers of home-brewed beer ($8.75) are favorites that can be enjoyed on the outdoor patio. (☎259-2545. Open M-F 6:30am-10pm, Su 6:30am-1pm.) **Skinny's Grill ❷**, 1017 Main Ave., offers great Southwestern food, as well as vegetarian options, in a low-key atmosphere. Thai chicken tacos ($8) and fajitas ($10) are local favorites. (☎382-2500. Open Su-Th 11:30am-9pm, F-Sa 11:30am-10pm.) Right at the south end of town, **Kachina Kitchen ❶**, in Centennial Center at the junction of Hwy. 550 and 160, serves up huge burrito and tamale platters ($5). Check out the over-stuffed sopapillas ($5.15) and piping hot Indian fried bread. (☎247-3536. Open M-Sa 10am-8pm.) The ski-lodge atmosphere and frequent live music at **The Summit**, 600 Main Ave., near the train station, attracts the college crowd for good, rowdy fun. Happy Hour M-F 4-7pm with $1.75 drafts and free pool. (☎247-2324. Open M-F 4pm-2am, Sa 8pm-2am.)

SIGHTS & ENTERTAINMENT. More of a tourist attraction than a means of transportation, the **Durango and Silverton Narrow Gauge Train**, 479 Main St., runs up the Animas River Valley to the historic mining town of Silverton. Old-fashioned, 100% coal-fed locomotives wheeze through the San Juans, making a 2hr. stop in Silverton before returning to Durango. It may be cheaper and more comfortable to drive the route yourself, but you'll miss out on a piece of living history in continuous operation since 1881. The train also offers access to the Weminuche Wilderness, dropping off and picking up backpackers at various scenic points; call for more info on this service. While waiting for the train, step into some of the first iron horses to operate for a glimpse into the glory days of the industry at the **Railroad Museum** across the tracks. (☎247-2733; www.durangotrain.com. Office open daily June to mid-Aug. 6am-8pm; mid-Aug. to Oct. 7am-7pm; Nov.-Apr. 8am-5pm; May 7am-7pm. Morning trains from Durango and afternoon trains from Silverton; 9hr. including stop, layover day optional. Mid-June to mid-Aug. $60; Sept. to late Oct. $55. Ages 5-11 $30. Trains to Cascade Canyon from Sept. to early Oct. $60, late Nov. to early May $45. Ages 5-11 $30/22.) The **Durango Pro Rodeo Series**, at the LaPlata County Fairgrounds at 25th St. and Main Ave., moseys into town in summer. Saddling up on Friday and Saturday nights and sometimes Tuesday and Wednesday, the action starts at 7:30pm with a barbecue at 6pm. (☎946-2790; www.durangoprorodeo.com. $12, under 12 $6; barbecue $7. Open mid-June to Aug.) On U.S. 550, 7 mi. north of Durango, **Trimble Hot Springs** allow visitors to soak in two hot pools and one regular one with a great view of Missionary Ridge. During the summer on Su afternoons 1-

4pm, lie out on their huge lawn and picnic area and enjoy live jazz music. (☎247-0111; www.trimblehotsprings.com. Open summer daily 8am-11pm; winter Su-Th 9am-10pm, F-Sa 9am-11pm. $9, ages 3-12 $6.50.)

OUTDOOR ACTIVITIES. Unlike most Colorado towns that thrive on tourism, Durango's busiest season is summer, though winter is no stranger to strangers. **Durango Mountain Resort,** 27 mi. north on U.S. 550, hosts skiers of all levels (see p. 745). Bikes are available at **Hassle Free Sports,** 2615 Main St. (☎259-3874 or 800-835-3800. Open summer M-Sa 8:30am-6pm, Su 9am-5pm; winter daily 7:30am-7pm; spring and fall M-Sa 8:30am-6pm. Half-day (4hr.) $16, full-day $25. Full suspension $24/35. Ski rental packages $16-27 per day.) **Southwest Adventures,** 1205 Camino del Río, offers mountain bikes, climbing gear, and backpacking gear. (☎259-0370. Open daily 8am-6pm.) The Durango area is engulfed by the **San Juan National Forest.** Call the Forest Headquarters for info on hiking and camping, especially if you're planning a trip into the massive **Weminuche Wilderness,** northeast of Durango. (☎247-4874. Open daily Apr. to mid-Dec. 8am-5pm; mid-Dec. to Mar. 8am-4:30pm.) The **Animas River** offers rapids from placid Class II splashes to intense Class V battles. The largest area outfitter is **Mild to Wild Rafting,** 701 Main Ave. (☎247-4789 or 800-567-6745. Open daily Apr.-Sept. 9am-9pm. Half-day mild trips $41, full-day mild trips $65; children $32/55. Full-day intense trips $105. Reservations recommended.)

PAGOSA SPRINGS ☎970

The Ute people—the first to discover the waters of Pagosa—believed that the springs were a gift of the Great Spirit, and the Chamber of Commerce would be hard-pressed not to think so, too. From the Ute Indian word "Pag-Osah," meaning "healing waters," Pagosa contains some of the world's hottest and largest springs, which bubble from the San Juan Mountains 60 mi. east of Durango on Rte. 160 and draw visitors from around the globe. Follow the sulfur smell to **The Springs,** 165 Hot Springs Blvd., where 17 naturally hot, therapeutic mineral baths ranging from 84° to 114°F are available "to relax the body and refresh the spirit." (☎264-2284 or 800-225-0934. Open daily 7am-1am. $12 per person, seniors $11, age 2-7 $4.) **Chimney Rock Archaeological Area,** 17 mi. west of Pagosa Springs on U.S. 160 and Rte. 151 S, is a National Historical Site containing the ruins of a high-mesa ancestral Puebloan village, where over 200 undisturbed structures have been found in a 6 sq. mi. area. (☎883-5359 or 264-2268; www.chimneyrockco.org. Open mid-May to late Sept. daily 9am-4:30pm. 2½hr. tours leave at 9:30, 10:30am, 1, 2pm. $6, ages 5-11 $2.) **Wolf Creek Ski Area,** 20 mi. east of Pagosa, claims to have the most snow in Colorado, and offers access to many glades and bowls. Six lifts service over 1500 acres and 1600 ft. of vertical drop. (☎264-5639 or 800-754-9653; www.wolfcreekski.com. Open mid Nov. to early Apr. Adult full day lift ticket $43, rental $13.)

The **Mountain Express** bus line provides transportation in and around town. (☎264-2250. M-F about every 1½hr. 6am-8pm, $0.50.) The **Pagosa Springs Chamber of Commerce,** 402 San Juan St., offers info on accommodations, food, and sights. (☎264-2360 or 800-252-2204; www.pagosaspringschamber.com. Open May-Oct. M-F 8am-5pm, Sa-Su 9am-5pm; Nov.-Apr. Sa-Su 10am-2pm.) **Pinewood Inn ❸,** 157 Pagosa St. (Hwy. 160), downtown, rents 25 wood-paneled rooms with cable TV and phones, several with kitchens. (☎264-5715 or 888-655-7463. Reception 7:30am-11pm. Check-in 2pm. Check-out 11am. Singles $38-55; doubles $48-85.) **East Fork Campground ❶,** on East Fork Rd., 11 mi. east of Pagosa Springs, offers many shaded, rarely crowded sites. (☎264-2268. 14-night max. stay. Open May-Sept. $8 per vehicle.) **Bear Creek Saloon & Grill ❷,** 473 Lewis, right off Hwy. 160, is the best place for burgers in town. You'll barely get your mouth around their Jalapeno cream cheese or Pagosa bacon green chili burgers ($5-7). Along with pool tables, arcades, and a big screen TV, Bear Creek Saloon features live classic rock and blues F-Sa nights and karaoke W. (☎264-5611. Drafts $3.50. Bar open daily 11am-2am. Food served summer M-Sa 11am-10pm, Su 11am-9pm; winter M-Sa 11am-9pm, Su 11am-7am.) **Daylight Donuts & Cafe ❶,** 2151 W Hwy. 160, dishes out big portions of classic breakfast and lunch fare for just $2.50-5. (☎731-4050. Open for breakfast daily 6am-1pm, lunch M-F 11am-1:30pm.) **Harmony Works ❶,** 145 Hot Springs Blvd., sells organic food and a large selection of vegetarian and vegan options ($3-5), including veggie wraps, breakfast burritos, and smoothies. (☎264-6633. Open May-Sept. M-Th 8am-9pm, F-Sa 8am-10pm, Su 8am-8pm; Oct.-Apr. M-Th 8am-8pm, F-Sa 8am-9pm, Su 8am-7pm.) **Area Code:** 970.

IDAHO

Idaho is a land of tremendous geographic diversity. The Rocky Mountains divide the state into three distinct regions, each with its own natural aesthetic. Northern Idaho possesses the greatest concentration of lakes in the western US, interspersed by lush green valleys and rugged mountain peaks. In Central Idaho, plentiful ski slopes, hiking trails, and hot springs span across the semi-arid landscape. To the southeast, world-famous potatoes are cultivated in valleys rich with volcanic sediment. With miles of untouched National Forest and wilderness, has seen little change since 1805, when Lewis and Clark first laid eyes on the state.

PRACTICAL INFORMATION

Capital: Boise.

Visitor Info: Idaho Department of Commerce, 700 W. State St., P.O. Box 83720, Boise 83720 (☎208-334-2470 or 800-842-5858; www.visitid.org.) **State Parks and Recreation Dept.,** 5657 Warm Springs Ave., Boise 83712 (☎334-4199). **Idaho Outfitters and Guide Association,** P.O. Box 95, Boise 83702 (☎800-494-3246; www.ioga.org). Open summer M-F 6am-5pm.

Postal Abbreviation: ID. **Sales Tax:** 6%. **Area Code:** 208.

ROCKY MOUNTAINS

BOISE ☎208

Built along the banks of the Boise River, Idaho's surprisingly cosmopolitan capital straddles the boundary between desert and mountains. A network of parks protects the natural landscape of the river banks, creating a greenbelt perfect for walking, biking, or skating. Most of the city's sights cluster in the ten-block area between the Capitol and the River, making Boise supremely navigable. A revitalized downtown offers a vast array of ethnic cuisine as well as a thriving nightlife.

PRACTICAL INFORMATION. The pedestrian-friendly Grove is Boise's Town Plaza and sits right in the heart of downtown. Its brick walkway extends along 8th St. between Main and Front St. **Greyhound,** 1212 W. Bannock (☎343-3681; station open 5:30am-9pm and 11pm-2:30am), a few blocks west of downtown, runs to: Portland (11hr., 4 per day, $48); Salt Lake City (7hr., 4 per day, $47); Seattle (14hr., 5 per day, $47). **Boise Urban Stages** (the **BUS**) has several routes throughout the city. (☎336-1010. Maps available at the Visitors Center. Buses operate M-F 5:15am-7:40pm, Sa 7:45am-6:10pm. M-F $0.75, ages 6-18 $0.50, over 59 $0.35; Sa all fares $0.35.) **McU's Sports,** 822 W. Jefferson St., rents outdoor gear and offers hiking tips. (☎342-7734. M-Th 9:30am-6pm, F 9:30am-7pm, Sa 9:30am-6pm, Su 11am-5pm. In-line skates $10 for 3hr., $15 for 8hr. Mountain bikes $15 per half-day, $25 per day.) McU's also has a **ski shop** at 2314 Bogus Basin Rd. (☎336-2300. Ski equipment $16 per day, children $13.) **Visitors Center:** 245 8th St., at Boise Centre on the Grove. (☎344-5338. Open M-F 10am-4pm, Sa 10am-2pm.) **Internet Access: Boise Public Library,** 715 S. Capitol Blvd. (☎384-4076. Open M-Th 10am-9pm, F 10am-6pm, Sa 10am-5pm, June-Sept. also open Su noon-5pm.) **Post Office:** 750 W. Bannock St. (☎331-0037. Open M-F 8:30am-5pm.) **Postal Code:** 83702. **Area Code:** 208.

ACCOMMODATIONS. A recent addition to the town of Nampa, **Hostel Boise (HI-AYH) ❶,** 17322 Can-Ada Rd., is 15-20min. from downtown Boise. Take Exit 38 off I-84 W and turn right onto Garrity Blvd., which turns into Can-Ada Rd. This country-style home has mountain views and evening campfires. (☎467-6858. Internet access $1 per 15min. Check-in 5-10:30pm. Linens $1.50. 3-night max. stay. Dorm-style beds $17, HI members $14; private room $31.) Inexpensive motels bunch around Exit 53 of I-84, near the airport. For all the comforts of home at an unbeatable price, **Bond Street Motel Apartments ❷,** 1680 N. Phillippi St. right off Fairview Ave., rents out beautiful, fully furnished studio and one-bedroom apartments with full size kitchens. Pots, pans, dishes—just about everything is included here, even the kitchen sink. (☎322-4407 or 800-545-5345. Office open M-F 8am-5pm. Reservations recommended. Studio $44; 1 bedroom $50.) The newly renovated **University Inn ❸,** 2360 University Dr., next to Boise State University, has cable TV, continental breakfast, and a free shuttle to the airport. The lovely courtyard also holds an outdoor pool and jacuzzi. (☎345-7170 or 800-345-7170. Singles $50-58; doubles $55-65.) With some of the best rates in town, **Budget Inn ❷,** 2600 Fairview Ave., has modern rooms with cable TV, free local calls, fridges, and microwaves. (☎344-8617. Singles $35; doubles $45.) The **Boise National Forest Office/Bureau of Land Management,** 1387 S. Vinnell Way, provides info about Boise's RV-oriented campgrounds. (☎373-4007. Open M-F 7:45am-4:30pm.) It's always a party at **Fiesta RV Park ❶,** 11101 Fairview Ave, with an outdoor pool and game room. (☎375-8207. Laundry facilities on site. Reception Oct.-May daily 8am-6pm; June-Sept. 8am-9pm. Sites $23; partial hookup $25; full hookup $28.)

FOOD & NIGHTLIFE. Boise offers much more than spuds for hungry budget travelers. Besides its fine selection of potato wedges, it is also home to 80 restaurants of varying cuisines. The downtown area, centered around **8th** and **Main Street,** bustles with lunchtime delis, coffeeshops, ethnic cuisine, and several stylish bistros. For amazingly fresh and creative vegetarian food, try **Kulture Klatsch ❷,** 409 S. 8th. This hip and multicultural eatery has an extensive veggie menu, including numerous vegan options, and a full juice and smoothie bar. Live music T-Th 8-10pm, F-Sa 9-11pm, Su 11am-1pm including jazz, classical guitar, folk, and rock. (☎345-0452. Breakfasts $4-7. Lunch specials $5-6. Dinners $7-9. Open M 7am-3pm, Tu-Th 7am-10pm, F 7am-11pm, Sa 8am-11pm, Su 8am-3pm.) For breakfast, head to **Moon's Kitchen ❶,** 815 W. Bannock St., a vintage diner that has blended malts since 1955. (☎385-0472. Shakes $4. Breakfast $4.50-7. Burgers $6-8. Open M-F 7am-3pm, Sa 7am-3:30pm, Su 9am-2pm) **Zeppole Baking Company ❶,** 217 N. 8th St., puts together gourmet sandwiches ($2-3) on their famous freshly baked bread. Soup, salad, and sandwich combos ($4-5). (☎345-2149. Open M-Sa 7am-5pm, Su 7am-4pm.) The casual yet trendy **Bittercreek Alehouse ❷,** 246 N. 8th St., in downtown Boise, has burgers and pita sandwiches for $6-9. (☎345-1813. 21+ after 10pm. Kitchen open daily 11am-10pm. Bar open until 1 or 2am.)

Musicians regularly perform on Main St., while vendors from nearby restaurants hawk food and beer. Cheap drinks and live music draw the locals to **Blues Bouquet,** 1010 Main St. Free swing lessons Monday at 8pm. (☎345-6605. 21+. $1-2 drink specials every night. Cover F-Sa nights $5. Open M-F 1pm-2am, Sa-Su 8pm-2am.)

Upstairs at **The Balcony,** 150 N. 8th St., #226, one block from the Grove, DJs spin nightly with 10 TVs surrounding the dance floor. All kinds of people gather at this gay-friendly bar to dance, relax on the outdoor terrace, and play pool. (☎336-1313. Happy Hour daily 2-7pm. 21+. Cover F-Sa $3. Open daily 2pm-2am.)

SIGHTS. The logical starting point for exploring Boise is the beautiful **Julia Davis Park** at Myrtle and Capitol Blvd. (☎384-4240.) With paddleboating on the pond, a bandshell featuring free summer entertainment, and sweet smelling rose gardens, the park is also home to several of Boise's most popular museums and attractions. The **Boise Tour Train** begins and ends in the parking lot at Julia Davis Park and covers approximately 75 city sights in 1¼hr. (☎342-4796. Tours Apr-May Sa-Su 1, 2:30pm; June-early Sept. M-Sa 10am-3pm, Su noon-3:45pm; fall W-Su noon-3pm. $7, seniors over 61 $6, ages 4-12 $4.50.) To learn about Idaho and the Old West at your own pace, stroll through the **Idaho Historical Museum,** 610 Julia Davis Dr. in the park, which showcases a replica 19th-century bar complete with a display of a two-headed calf. Other notable exhibits include Native American artifacts and sitting tall saddles. (☎334-2120. Open summer Tu-Sa 9am-5pm, Su 1-5pm. Nov.-Apr. closed Su. $2, ages 6-18 $1.)

Also in Julia Davis Park, the **Boise Art Museum,** 670 Julia Davis Dr., displays an impressive selection of contemporary international and local works while offering educational programs, lectures, and tours. (☎345-8330. Open June-Aug. M-W and F-Sa 10am-5pm, Th 10am-8pm, Su noon-5pm. Sept.-May closed M. $5, college students and seniors over 61 $3, ages 6-18 $1. Free the first Th of every month.) Raptors perch and dive at the **World Center for Birds of Prey,** 566 W. Flying Hawk Ln. From I-84, take Exit 50 and go south on S. Cole; turn right onto W. Flying Hawk Ln. Tiptoe through their actual breeding chambers and observe the rare and striking birds up close. (☎362-8687. Open daily Mar.-Oct. 9am-5pm; Nov.-Feb. 10am-4pm. $4, over 61 $3, ages 4-16 $2, under 4 free.) Basque culture is preserved at the **Basque Museum and Cultural Center,** 611 Grove St. at the corner of Grove St. and Capital Blvd. This fascinating museum includes a gallery of Basque art and a replica of a Basque herder's house. (☎343-2671. Open Tu-F 10am-4pm, Sa 11am-3pm. Free, donations accepted.) In the **Alive for Five** series, live music infuses The Grove every Wednesday 5-7:30pm from May-Sept. (☎336-2631.) The **Capitol City Market** takes over 8th St. between Main and Bannock St. every Saturday morning in the summer. Stroll through for a look at local produce and innovative crafts.

The **Boise River Greenbelt** provides over 20 mi. of biking and skating paths that extend along the Boise River. Fishing and tubing along the Greenbelt are popular summer pursuits. The ever-growing **Boise Shakespeare Festival** (☎336-9221; tickets $18-26) hits town from June to September. Every year in late June, Boise hosts a **River Festival,** featuring hot-air balloons, a carnival, live music, fireworks, and sporting events, all free to the public (☎338-8887). Upcoming events are showcased in Thursday's *The Boise Weekly.*

KETCHUM & SUN VALLEY ☎208

In 1935, Union Pacific chairman Averill Harriman sent Austrian Count Felix Schaffgotsch to scour the western US for a site to develop into a ski resort that would rival Europe's best. After traveling for months, the Count stumbled onto the small mining and sheep-herding town of Ketchum in Idaho's Wood River Valley and was awestruck. Harriman immediately purchased the land and built the world's first chairlift. Sun Valley was quickly recognized as a world-class ski resort, fulfilling Harriman's dream. The permanent population is only 5300; traffic extends for miles in each direction during peak months. Skiing reigns supreme in winter, while in summer the days are long and the nights are even longer, as those who come for the biking, hiking, and fishing sample the vibrant nightlife.

PRACTICAL INFORMATION. The best time for fun in the Sun is winter and summer. The town does its best to shut down in "slack" times (Oct.-Nov., May-early June), but during these periods accommodations offer lower rates and the natural beauty stays the same. Most of the food and nightlife centers around Main St. (Rte. 75) in Ketchum while Sun Valley, just 3 mi. northeast on Sun Valley Road, governs the ski slopes. **Sun Valley Express** picks up door-to-door in the Sun Valley/Ketchum area and runs daily to the Boise airport. (☎877-622-8267. 3hr. Leaves Sun Valley 8:30am, leaves Boise 2:45pm. 2 additional buses from Dec.-Mar. leave Sun Valley 6:30am, 12:30pm, and leave Boise 12:45, 5:45pm. Closed late Oct.-late Nov. Standard rates $59, under 12 $49. Peak season (Aug., Dec.-Mar.) $69/59. Reservations recommended.) **KART,** Ketchum's bus service, tours the city and its surrounding areas including Sun Valley, Warm Springs, and Elkhorn. (☎726-7576. Runs daily 7:20am-midnight. Free.) **Chamber of Commerce/Visitors Center:** 4th and Main St. in Ketchum. (☎726-3423 or 800-634-3347; www.visitsunvalley.com. Open Nov.-Apr. and July-Sept. daily 9am-6pm; May-June and Oct. M-Sa 9am-5:30pm.) **Internet Access: Community Library,** 415 Spruce Ave. (☎726-3493. Open M and Sa 9am-6pm, Tu and Th noon-9pm, W 9am-9pm, F 1-6pm. Free.) **Post Office:** 151 W. 4th St. (☎726-5161. Open M-F 8:30am-5:30pm, Sa 11am-2pm.) **Postal Code:** 83340. **Area Code:** 208.

ACCOMMODATIONS. From early June to mid-October, camping is the best option for cheap sleep in the Sun Valley area. Check with the **Ketchum Ranger Station,** 206 Sun Valley Rd., just outside of Ketchum on the way to Sun Valley. (☎622-5371. Open M-F 8:30am-5pm.) **Boundary Campground ❶,** 3 mi. northeast of town on Trail Creek Rd. past the Sun Valley resort, is closest to town and has eight wooded sites near a creek. (Restrooms, picnic area. No water. 7-night max stay. Sites $11.) **Federal Gulch and Sawmill Campground ❶,** both 15 mi. southeast of Ketchum on East Fork Rd. off Hwy. 75, each have 3 free sites with water, restrooms, grills and picnic areas with a 3-day max stay. Up Rte. 75 into the SNRA lie several scenic camping spots; the cheapest are **Murdock ❶** (11 sites with water, $10) and **Caribou ❶** (7 sites, no water; $8). They are, respectively, 2 and 3 mi. up the unpaved North Fork Rd., which begins as a paved road to the right of the Visitors Center. The **North Fork ❶** (29 sites; $11) and **Wood River** (30 sites; $11) are 8 mi. north of Ketchum, along Rte. 75, and are popular fishing spots along Big Wood River. For North Fork, take the first campground road north of SNRA headquarters; Wood River is 2 mi. north. Those looking for a more civilized sleeping experience will enjoy comfortable rooms, great views from the outdoor jacuzzi, and continental breakfast at the **Lift Tower Lodge ❸,** 703 S. Main St. (☎726-5163 or 800-462-8646. Rooms $69-90.) **Bald Mountain Lodge ❸,** 151 S. Main St., rents out basic rooms with cable TV for prices about as low as can be found in Ketchum. (☎726-9963. Rooms $65-70.)

FOOD & NIGHTLIFE. Ketchum's small confines bulge with over 80 restaurants catering to the gourmet tastes of resort visitors, but relatively cheap eats can still be found. Build your own burrito at the colorful **KB's Ketchum Burritos ❷,** on the corner of 6th and Washington, or choose from their selection of favorites "just like mom used to never make" ($6). Locals also rave about their fish tacos and quesadillas ($3-5). (☎726-2232. Open daily 11:30am-9pm.) Beer cans of all shapes and sizes grace the walls of **Grumpy's ❶,** 860 Warm Springs Rd., a flavorful hangout. (Burger specials $3-5. PBR cans $1. 32 oz. goblet of beer $3.25. Open daily 11am-10pm.) Head downstairs to the **Cellar Pub,** 400 Sun Valley Rd. near Leadville Ave., for a young crowd, excellent burgers ($8-9) and bangers, and inventive pints like the "straight jacket." (☎622-3832. Open daily 5pm-2am. Food served until 10pm.) Chase back some stiff drinks for $1 on Sunday and Tuesday at **Whiskey Jacques,** 251 N. Main St. (☎726-5297. Live music most nights 9:30pm-2am. Happy Hour daily 4-7pm. 21+ after 9pm. Cover $5. Open daily 4pm-2am. Food served until 9pm.)

OUTDOOR ACTIVITIES. The **Wood River and Sun Valley trail system** consists of over 20 mi. of paved trails for bikers, skiers, skaters, joggers, and horseback riders. The trail begins in Bellevue and parallels Hwy. 75 north through Ketchum and Sun Valley, passing by ski slopes and historic sites along the way. The *Wood River Trails* pamphlet, available at the Visitors Center, has more info. Visible for miles, **Bald Mountain,** or "Baldy," is a beacon for serious skiers. Two plazas serve Baldy—River Run on the north side of town and Warm Springs on the south side. Whereas mostly advanced skiers are on Bald Mountain, the gentle slopes of **Dollar Mountain** are perfect for beginners. (☎622-6136, ski conditions ☎800-635-4150. Full-day lift ticket $66, under 13 $37.)

The Sawtooth area is nationally renowned for its stunning mountain bike trails, which traverse the gorgeous canyons and mountain passes of the SNRA. *Beware: trails might be snowbound or flooded well into July.* Take a high-speed quad to the top of Bald Mountain and ride down on a mountain bike during summer months. (☎622-2231. Open summer daily 9am-3:45pm. $15 per ride, $20 per day; ages 3-12 $7/10.) Inquire about trail conditions and rent gear at **Formula Sports,** 460 N. Main St. (☎726-3194. Bikes from $14 per 4hr., $18 per day; full suspension $25/35; tandems $25/35. Skis $18-40.) **The Elephant's Perch,** 280 East Ave., at Sun Valley Rd., has a complete stock of outdoor gear. (☎726-3497. Open daily 9am-6pm. Bikes $15 per 4hr., $20 per day. Backpack $15 per day, sleeping bag $25 per day, tents $20 per day. Nordic and telemark ski packages $15-25 per day.) Inquire about biking trails at the Chamber of Commerce or the SNRA Headquarters.

THE SUN VALLEY ALSO RISES Ernest Hemingway's love affair with both rugged outdoor sports and wealthy celebrities fits Ketchum's dualistic spirit. After spending many vacations hunting and fishing in the Sawtooth Range, the author built a cabin in Sun Valley where he died from a self-inflicted gun-shot wound on July 2, 1961. While Hemingway's house is off-limits, there are a number of sites in town that commemorate the author. His grave is located in the Ketchum Cemetery, just north of town on Rte. 75. The **Ketchum-Sun Valley Heritage and Ski Museum** houses exhibits on Hemingway's life. (180 1st St. E, at Washington Ave. ☎726-8118. Open M-F 11am-5pm, Sa 1-4pm. Times vary in winter.) A bust of Hemingway is tucked away in a shady spot along the river at the **Hemingway Memorial,** about 1 mi. outside of Sun Valley on the way to Boundary Campground (see **Accommodations,** above). Each year on Hemingway's birthday, July 21, the community library hosts a lecture. (☎726-3493.)

A more civilized take on the outdoors is offered by the **Sun Valley Summer Symphony,** behind the Sun Valley Lodge in Sun Valley. Expect a free open-air classical concert series running from late July to early Aug. featuring chamber music and full orchestra. (☎622-5607 for exact dates. Concerts 6:30-7:30pm.) Local and invited bands of all styles including rock, latin, and bluegrass gather at the public park on 1st St. and Washington Ave. every Wednesday from June to August to put on a free show starting at 7:30pm.

After a hard day of biking or hiking, Ketchum locals soak their weary legs in one of several hot springs. Hidden in the hills and canyons of Ketchum, the hot springs are no longer a well-kept secret. Melting snow and rain can bury the springs underwater, rendering them inaccessible in spring and early summer. The springs are safe for swimming once the current subsides in July. The Chamber of Commerce has suggestions on which pools are safe and accessible. One of the more accessible, non-commercial springs is **Warfield Hot Springs,** on Warm Springs Rd., 11 mi. west of Ketchum, which lingers right around 100°F. Just west, **Worswick Hot Springs** bubbles and soothes at a steamy 150°F. An alternative to these pools is the more commercial **Easley Hot Springs,** 12 mi. north of Ketchum on Rte. 75. (☎726-7522. Open summer Tu and Th-Sa 11am-7pm, W 11am-5pm, Su noon-5pm; winter Sa 11am-5pm, Su noon-5pm. $6, under 15 $5, seniors $4.50.) For the best info on **fishing,** including equipment rentals, stop by **Silver Creek Outfitters,** 500 N. Main St. (☎726-5282 or 800 732-5687. Open M-Sa 9am-6pm, Su noon-5pm; hours vary in peak season. Fly rods, waders, and boots $15 per day.)

SAWTOOTH NATIONAL RECREATION AREA (SNRA) ☎208

Established by Congress in 1972, the **Sawtooth National Recreation Area (SNRA)** sprawls over 756,000 acres of National Forest, including 217,000 acres of untouched wilderness. The park is home to four mountain ranges with more than 40 peaks over 10,000 ft. The Sawtooth and White Cloud Mountains tower above the surrounding landscape in the north, while the Smokey and Boulder Mountains dominate the southern horizon. Over 300 mountain lakes and the headwaters of four of Idaho's major rivers are interspersed throughout the park's dense forest.

PRACTICAL INFORMATION. The tiny (pop. 100), frontier-style town of **Stanley,** located 60 mi. north of Ketchum at the intersection of Rte. 21 and 75, serves as a northern base for exploring Sawtooth. The small business district is located one block south of Rte. 21, along Ace of Diamonds St. **Lower Stanley** is a small continuation of the business region and lies on Hwy. 75 just 1 mi. north of Stanley. The **Stanley Ranger Station,** 3 mi. south of Stanley on Rte. 75, offers maps, SNRA passes, and sage outdoor advice. (☎774-3000. Open summer M-F 8:30am-5pm; winter M-F 8:30am-4:30pm.) The **Redfish Lake Visitors Center** provides additional info, including educational programs about wildlife and geology. The center also has a small museum with exhibits detailing the diversity of flora and fauna in the Redfish Lake area. (☎774-3376. Open mid-June to early Sept. daily 9am-5pm; late May to mid-June Sa-Su 9am-5pm.) **Sawtooth National Recreation Area (SNRA) Headquarters,** 9 mi. north of Ketchum off Rte. 75, stocks detailed info on the hot springs and area forests and trails. SNRA maps are $6-7 and local hiker Margaret Fuller's excellent trail guides are $15. (☎727-5013 or 800-260-5970. Open daily summer 8:30am-5pm; winter 9am-3:30pm.) **Chamber of Commerce:** Located on Rte. 75 between Stanley and Lower Stanley. (☎774-3411 or 800-878-7950. Open summer 9am-5pm; shortened hours in winter.) **Post Office:** Ace of Diamonds St., Stanley. (☎774-2230. Open M-F 8-11am and noon-5pm.) **Postal Code:** 83278. **Area Code:** 208.

ACCOMMODATIONS. The SNRA boasts 33 campgrounds scattered throughout the park; consult a ranger for help in selecting (and locating) a campsite. **Alturas Lake ❶,** 21 mi. south of Stanley on Rte. 75 (the Alturas Lake Rd. turn-off is marked about 10 mi. north of Galena Pass), has three first come, first served campgrounds with fishing and swimming. (Vault toilets and water. 55 sites. $10.) The area around **Redfish Lake ❶,** 5 mi. south of Stanley off Rte. 75, is a scenic but sometimes overcrowded spot. The eight campgrounds in the area are conveniently close to Stanley and many trailheads. (☎877-444-6777 for reservations for **Glacier View, Outlet,** and **Point.** Sites $13 with 6 to 10-day max. stay.) East on Rte. 75, past the town of Stanley, numerous campgrounds are available alongside the wild and scenic **Salmon River ❶.** (Water available; no hookup. First come, first served. 10-day max. stay. Sites $11.) Among these, one of the best campgrounds is **Mormon Bend,** 8 mi. east of Stanley on Rte. 75, with 15 sites close to whitewater rafting. Other scenic and inviting spots right along the Salmon River are **Casino Creek,** 6 mi east of Stanley on Rte. 75; the **Salmon River Campground,** 5 mi east of Stanley on Rte. 75; and **Upper and Lower O'Brien,** 2 mi. past Sunbeam Dam. Showers available for $3 at the Laundromat on Ace of Diamonds St. in Stanley.

For a real bed, Stanley provides more scenic and reasonable lodging than Ketchum. At **Danner's Log Cabin Motel ❸,** on Rte. 21, ex-mayor and Stanley history buff Bunny Danner rents historic cabins built by gold miners in 1939. The office, built in 1906, is the oldest building in town and originally served as the ranger station. (☎774-3539. Cabins summer $55-75; spring and fall $45-60.) **Redwood Cabins,** on Hwy. 75 at the east end of lower Stanley, has cottages along the Salmon River with cable TV. (☎774-3531. Open May-Sept. Singles $56; doubles $62.)

FOOD & NIGHTLIFE. Dining options are rather limited in Stanley. Before exploring the SNRA, stock up on food and gas, as well as fishing licenses, at **Jerry's Country Store and Motel,** on Rte. 75 in Lower Stanley. (☎774-3566 or 800-972-4627. Open May-Sept. M-Sa 9am-8:30pm, Su 9am-8pm; winter hours vary.) Locals rave about the $5 deli sandwiches at **Papa Brunee's ❶,** Ace of Diamonds St., downtown. (☎774-2536. Individual pizzas $4. Open daily 11am-10pm.) The local watering hole is the **Rod and Gun Club Bar,** on Ace of Diamonds St. This authentic western bar has pool tables, a dance floor, and live music on the weekends. (☎774-9920. 21+. Open daily 6pm-1:30am.)

OUTDOOR ACTIVITIES. The rugged backcountry of the SNRA is perfect for hiking, boating, fishing, and mountain biking. Parking at most trailheads in the park requires a **trailhead pass** ($5 for 3 days, $15 annual pass), obtained at the SNRA headquarters or Stanley Ranger Station (see **Practical Information** above). Pick up a free map of the area and inquire about trail conditions at SNRA headquarters before heading into the park, particularly in early summer, when trails may be flooded. Much of the backcountry stays buried in snow well into the warm weather. Watch out for black bears; ranger stations have information about necessary precautions. The Sawtooth Scenic Byway (Rte. 75) spans 60 mi. of National Forest land between Ketchum and Stanley, crossing the Galena Pass at 8701 ft. Pause at the **Galena Overlook,** 31 mi. north of Ketchum, for a spectacular view of the Sawtooth Range and headwaters of the Salmon River.

Redfish Lake is the source of many trails. Some popular, leisurely hikes include those to **Fishhook Creek** (excellent for children), **Bench Lakes,** and the **Hell Roaring trail.** The long, gentle loop around **Yellow Belly, Toxaway,** and **Petit Lakes** is a moderate overnight trip suitable for novices. Starting at the Inlet Trailhead on the southern end of Redfish Lake, the challenging 5½ mi. hike to **Alpine Lake** rewards with stunning views and exposure to the diverse land that the Sawtooths have to offer. (Redfish Lake Lodge operates ferries to and from the south end of the lake to access the trailhead. One way $5). Two miles northwest of Stanley on Rte. 21, the 3 mi. Iron Creek Rd. leads to the trailhead of the 5½ mi. **Sawtooth Lake Hike.** Bionic hikers can try the steep 5 mi. hike to **Casino Lakes,** which begins at the Broadway Creek trailhead southeast of Stanley.

The Sawtooths have miles of mountain biking, but check a map first; biking is allowed in National Forest areas but prohibited in the Sawtooth Wilderness. **Riverwear,** on Rte. 21 in Stanley, rents bikes. (☎774-3592. Open daily 7am-10pm. Front suspension $17 per day, full suspension $25.) The 18 mi. **Fischer/Williams Creek Loop,** starting at the Williams Creek trailhead 10 mi. south of Stanley, is the most popular biking trail, ascending to an elevation of 8280 ft. Beginners will enjoy riding the dirt road that accesses the North Fork campgrounds from SNRA headquarters. This gorgeous passage parallels the North Fork of the Wood River for 5 mi. before branching off into other narrower and steeper trails for more advanced riders. These trails can be combined into loops; consult the trail map or the ranger station. The steep **Boulder Basin Road,** 5 mi. from SNRA headquarters, leads to pristine Boulder Lake and an old mining camp.

Topographical maps ($6) and various trail books ($5-10) are available at **McCoy's Tackle and Gift Shop,** on Ace of Diamonds St. McCoy's also sells sporting goods, fishing tackle, and licenses ($10.50 first day, $4 each additional day). (☎774-3377. Open June-Sept. daily 8am-8pm; low-season hours vary.) **Sawtooth Adventure Company,** on Rte. 75 in Lower Stanley, rents kayaks and rafts and leads guided kayak and fly fishing trips along the Salmon River. (☎866-774-4644. Open May-Sept. Kayaks $25-50 for 24hr. Rafts $75 for 8 people. Kayak trips $30-65 for half day. Fly fishing trips $200 for full day.) For boat tours of the lake, head for **Redfish Lake Lodge Marina.** (☎774-3536. Open summer daily 7am-8:30pm. 1hr. tours $8, ages 6-12 $5; $32 minimum. Paddleboats $5 per 30min. Canoes $10 per hr., $32 per half-day, $50 per day. Kayaks $7/20/35. Outboards $15/50/80.) The most inexpensive way to enjoy the SNRA waters is to visit the **hot springs** just east of Stanley. **Sunbeam Hot Springs,** 10 mi. northeast of Stanley on Rte. 75, triumphs over the rest, though high water can wash out the hot springs temporarily. The natural rock pools of **Kem Hot Springs**, 6 mi. northeast of Stanley on Rte. 75, in the Salmon River, are less discovered but also hot soaking spots. Both free to the public and open 24hr.

CRATERS OF THE MOON ☎208

The otherworldly landscape at **Craters of the Moon National Monument** first drew national attention in the 1920s. An early visitor to the landscape claimed it was "the strangest 75 square miles on the North American continent." The same geological hot spot responsible for the thermal activity in Yellowstone National Park created the Monument's twisted lava formations. Located 70 mi. southeast of Sun Valley at the junction of Rte. 20 and 26/93 between Arco and Carey, the park's unusual craters and rock formations make for an interesting visit. ($5 per car, $3 per person, $3 per bike.)

There are 51 **sites** ❶ scattered throughout the monument's single campground, located just past the entrance station. (Water and restrooms. No hookups. $10.) Wood fires are prohibited, but charcoal fires are permitted in the grills. Camping at unmarked sites in the dry lava wilderness of the park is permitted with a free **backcountry permit,** available at the **Visitors Center,** right before the entrance to the monument. (☎527-3257. Open daily summer 8am-6pm; low-season 8am-4:30pm.) **Echo Crater,** a short and easy 4 mi. hike from the Tree Molds parking lot, is one of the most popular backcountry campsites.

The Visitors Center has videos, displays, and printed guides outlining the area's geological past. A 7 mi. drive winds through much of the monument, guiding tourists to the major sights. Several short trails lead to more unusual rock formations and a variety of caves; bring a flashlight. The 2 mi. **Broken Top Loop,** starting at Tree Molds parking lot, goes through Buffalo Caves and is a quick but comprehensive survey of the surrounding land. Don't forget sturdy shoes, water, sunscreen, and hats; the black rocks absorb heat and there are no trees for miles.

The town of **Arco,** 18 mi. east of the Craters of the Moon on Rte. 20, claims to be the "first city in the world lighted by atomic energy." Arco is also the closest source of services and lodgings for travelers visiting the monument. Comfy, modern rooms with telephones and cable TV are available at the **D-K Motel** ❷, 316 S. Front St. Laundry facilities are on site. (☎527-8282 or 800-231-0134. Singles $32;

doubles $40-47.) The reasonably priced **Arco Inn ❷,** 540 W. Grand Ave., is also a great value for a clean room. Rooms have cable TV, some with microwave and fridge. (☎527-3100. Singles $38-46; doubles $42-54.) With a big green rocking chair in front, **Pickle's Place ❶,** 440 S. Front St., is an easy diner to identify. Home of the atomic burger ($4-5), Pickle's also dishes out plentiful portions of classic breakfast ($4-5). (☎527-9944. Open daily June-Aug. 6am-11pm, Sept.-May 6am-10pm.) barbecue chicken and ribs are grilling in the backyard at **Grandpa's Southern Bar-B-Q ❷,** 434 W. Grand Ave. Grab a seat on the front porch for a killer pork sandwich ($5) and some small-town hospitality. (☎527-3362. Full dinners $7-13. Open summer daily 11am-8pm; winter Th-Sa 11am-8pm.) The **Arco Deli Sandwich Shop ❷,** on Rte. 20/26/93, at Grand Ave. and Idaho St., serves fresh deli sandwiches. (☎527-3757. 6 in. sandwiches $4, ft.-long $7. Open M-F 8am-8pm, Sa 8am-7pm.) The **Chamber of Commerce** (☎527-8977; open M-F 8am-5pm), 159 N. Idaho St., has info on local attractions. If traveling from Arco to Sun Valley (see p. 754), you can also pick up a free cassette tour of the Central Idaho Rockies.

MONTANA

If any part of the scenery dominates the Montana landscape more than the pristine mountain peaks and shimmering glacial lakes, it's the sky—welcome to Big Sky country. With 25 million acres of national forest and public lands, Montana's grizzly bears, mountain lions, and pronghorn antelope outnumber the people. Small towns, set against unadulterated mountain vistas, offer a true taste of the Old West. Copious fishing lakes, 500 species of wildlife (not including millions of insect species), and beautiful rivers combine with hot springs and thousands of ski trails to make Montana an American paradise.

PRACTICAL INFORMATION

Capital: Helena.

Visitor Info: Travel Montana, P.O. Box 200533, Helena 59620-0533 (☎800-847-4868; www.visitmt.com). **National Forest Information,** Northern Region, Federal Bldg., 200 E. Broadway, Box 7669, Missoula 59807 (☎406-329-3511).

Postal Abbreviation: MT. **Sales Tax:** Varies.

BILLINGS ☎406

Situated along the Yellowstone River and surrounded by six mountain ranges, including the distinctive sandstone rimrock cliffs to the north, Billings is the largest city in Montana. The area was first marked when William Clark carved his name on Pompey's Pillar in 1806, the only permanent physical evidence of Lewis and Clark's expedition. Soon after its humble beginnings as a railhead for the Northern Pacific, the city earned the nickname "Magic" due to its instantaneous and phenomenal growth in the 1880s. Today, Billings is the undisputed hub of commerce and trade in the region, but the modern metropolitan flavor doesn't take away from its rich history ready to be rediscovered.

PRACTICAL INFORMATION. Billings lies on I-90 just west of the I-90/94 junction. Downtown centers around the intersection of N. 27th St and Montana/Minnesota Ave. Flights flow in through **Billings Logan International Airport,** 1901 Terminal Circle, 5 mi. north of downtown (☎238-3420; www.flybillings.com). **Greyhound,**

2502 1st Ave. N. (☎245-5116; open 24hr.) makes trips to: Bozeman (3hr., 3 per day, $25); Butte (5hr., 3 per day, $37); Helena (7hr., 2 per day, $37). The **MET Transit System** city buses get you around town. (☎657-8218. Buses run M-F 6am-7pm, Sa-Su 8am-5pm. $0.75, seniors $0.25, under 6 free.) **Taxi: City Cab,** ☎252-8700. **Visitors Info: Billings Area Chamber of Commerce Convention and Visitors Council,** 815 S. 27th St. (☎252-4016 or 800-735-2635; http://billingscvb.visitmt.com. Open June-Sept. M-Sa 8:30am-6pm, Su 10am-4pm; Oct.-May M-F 8:30am-5pm.) **Internet Access: Parmly Billings Library,** 510 N. Broadway (28th St.). (☎657-8257. Open M-Th 10am-9pm, F 10am-6pm, Sa 10am-5pm, Su 1-5pm; June-Aug. closed Su.) **Post Office:** 841 S. 26th St. (☎657-5700. Open M-F 8am-5:30pm.) **Postal Code:** 59101. **Area Code:** 406.

ACCOMMODATIONS. Reasonable rates on rooms line 1st Ave. N and N. 27th St. **Big 5 Motel ❷,** 2601 4th Ave N, has clean modern rooms with cable TV and some of the lowest rates in town. (☎245-6646 or 888-544-9358. Singles $33; doubles $44.) For a little taste of luxury at an unbeatable price, **The Cherry Tree Inn ❷,** 823 N. Broadway, provides a free continental breakfast and an exercise room and sauna. (☎252-5603 or 800-237-5882. Reservations recommended. Singles $40-45; doubles $50-60.) Escape the city for a night at the **Sanderson Inn Bed & Breakfast ❷,** 2038 S. 56th W, 15min. west of downtown on King Ave. W. The wonderfully young Margaret Sanderson, who has been living here for over 80 years, maintains a charming country home and cooks up homemade breakfast with fresh fruit. (☎656-3388. 1-2 person rooms $40-50. Cash or check only.) The commercial campgrounds and RV parks in Billings are almost as expensive as the indoor lodgings. For a more natural and cheaper camping experience, **Riverside Park ❶,** in Laurel, 13 mi. west on I-90 at Exit 434, lies along the Yellowstone River and has grills, picnic areas, showers, and flush toilets. (Open June-Sept. Sites $10; full RV hookup $15.)

FOOD. An abundance of budget eateries lie along N. 27th St. and west of downtown on Kings Ave W. Wake up to the freshly baked breads, cakes, and muffins at **Stella's Kitchen & Bakery ❷,** 110 N. 29th St. Their breakfast combos ($5-6), corn beef hash ($6), and warm cinnamon rolls ($1.50) have been saying a bright good morning to Billings for years. (☎248-3060. Open M-F 5:30am-5:30pm, Sa 5:30am-4pm.) Authentic Irish cuisine is the order of the day at the friendly **Pug Mahon's ❷,** 3011 1st Ave N., where people travel for miles to taste their famous $8 pork chop sandwich and ribbon fries. (☎259-4190. Open M-Th 11am-10pm, F-Sa 11am-10:30pm, Su 8am-2pm. Bar open M-Sa until 2am.) The **Pickle Barrel ❶,** 1503 13th St. W, piles up hefty 9 in. sandwiches ($5) with, of course, a free pickle from the barrel. (☎248-3222. Open M-Sa 7am-10pm, Su 8am-9pm.) The chic **McCormick Cafe ❷,** 2419 Montana Ave., is always bustling with lunchtime chatter. Along with a sizable selection of heart-healthy salads and sandwiches ($5-6), McCormick prepares delectable Parisian crêpes ($2) and works a full espresso and juice bar. (☎255-9555. Open M-F 7am-4pm, Sa 8am-3pm.)

SIGHTS & NIGHTLIFE. The largest event in the state, **MontanaFair,** at MetraPark just east of downtown, is a full-fledge 1-week western state fair experience. Country western's top music performers grace the stage, along with buckin' bull rodeos and the Wissota Challenge motorsport races. (☎256-2400; www.montanafair.com. Second full week of Aug. Concert tickets $20-30. Rodeo $14. Wissota Challenge $25-35.) **Little Bighorn Days and Custer's Last Stand Reenactment,** in downtown Hardin, 45 mi. east of Billings on I-90, honors the anniversary of the historic Battle of Little Bighorn with western-style street dancing, period costume balls, carnivals, and chuckwagon feeds. (☎665-1672; www.custerslaststand.org. During the weekend closest to the June 25th anniversary.) The history of the untamed Yellowstone River Valley is preserved at the **Western Heritage Center,** 2822 Montana

Ave. Interactive exhibits and over 17,000 artifacts and photos retell the story. (☎256-6809; www.ywhc.org. Open June-Aug. Tu-Sa 10am-5pm, Su 1-5pm; Sept.-May Tu-Sa 10am-5pm. Free.) Once the living quarters of prehistoric hunters, **Pictograph Cave State Park,** east of Billings at Exit 452 on I-90, then 6 mi. south on Coburn Rd., explores some of the relics, pictographs, and stories they left behind. Bring binoculars for the best views along the ½ mi. trail. (☎247-2940. Open dawn-dusk. $5 per vehicle.) On Coburn Rd. along the way to Pictograph Cave, notice **Sacrifice Cliff,** the site of an old Crow Indian village. When a war party returned to find the village here decimated by smallpox, warriors blindfolded their horses and rode them over the cliff to appease the gods and halt the epidemic.

Vintage record albums cover every inch of the walls at the award winning **Casey's Golden Pheasant,** 222 N. 28th St. (N. Broadway), where the stage rocks six nights a week with live blues, jazz, rock, and reggae. Free pool during Happy Hour M-F 5-7pm. (☎256-5200. Drafts $2-3. Cover $5-20 for weekend bands.) **Scoops Tavern,** 2329 River Woods Dr. along Sunshine River, was originally built in 1903 in honor of the six Kjev sisters who nurtured injured railroad workers back to health. In keeping with tradition, there are six $1 drink specials every night, always drawing a rowdy crowd. (☎355-8826. Open daily 2pm-2am.)

HELENA ☎406

As Montana's capital city, Helena has successfully modernized while still retaining the historical feel of the Old West. A product of the 1864 Gold Rush at Last Chance Gulch, Helena has transformed itself from a humble mining camp into a sophisticated city equipped with a symphony, several theaters, and an outdoor walking mall downtown. Halfway between Glacier and Yellowstone National Parks, Helena provides a pleasant stopover for travelers tackling the two, but is an outdoors destination in its own right with hiking, boating, and fishing opportunities.

PRACTICAL INFORMATION. **I-15, U.S. 12,** and **U.S. 287** intersect in Helena. Last Chance Gulch (Main St.) and Park Ave. (Benton Ave. north of downtown) are the main north-south roads through the city. Euclid Ave. extends east-west. **Rimrock Trailways,** 3100 U.S. 12 E (☎442-5860), behind the High Country Travel Plaza Truck stop, departs daily at 8:15am and sends separate buses to: Billings (6½hr., $37); Bozeman (3½hr., $18); Missoula (5½hr., $21). **Greyhound** connects in all three cities to further points. **Helena Area Chamber of Commerce,** 225 Cruse Ave., has visitor information. (☎442-4120; www.helenachamber.com. Open M-F 8am-5pm.) **Internet Access: Lewis & Clark Library,** 120 S. Last Chance Gulch. (☎447-1690. Open M-Th 10am-8pm, F-Sa 10am-5pm.) **Post Office:** 2300 N. Harris. (☎443-3304. Open M-F 8am-6pm, Sa 9am-noon.) **Postal Code:** 59601. **Area Code:** 406.

ACCOMMODATIONS. There aren't that many cheap places in Helena to hang your hat, but **Budget Inn Express ❷,** 524 N. Last Chance Gulch, has an attractive downtown location and large, tidy rooms. (☎442-0600 or 800-862-1334. Laundry, cable TV, and kitchenettes. Summer singles $37; doubles $47. Winter $34/44.) The best deal in town for women, **Helena YWCA ❶,** 501 N. Park Ave., rents private singles with shared bath and use of the full kitchen and laundry facilities. (☎442-8774. Women only. Free Internet access. $12 key deposit. Singles $18.) The **Helena Campground and RV Park ❶,** 5820 N. Montana Ave., north of Helena just west of I-15, has grassy, shaded tent sites and an outdoor pool and recreation room. (☎458-4714. Laundry and showers. Sites $23; full hookup $26; cabins $39.) Fifteen miles east of Helena, 13 public campgrounds line **Canyon Ferry Reservoir ❶,** popular for both fishing and boating; take either Canyon Ferry Rd. or Rte. 284 from U.S. 12. (7 campgrounds $8 per site. 6 campgrounds free.) The free **Fish Hawk Campground ❶**, on West Shore Dr., has tent sites and toilets, but no drinking water. The **BOR Canyon Ferry Office,** 7661 Canyon Ferry Rd., has more info. (☎475-3310 or 475-3921.)

FOOD & NIGHTLIFE. The extensive gallery of local paintings and the forest of records dangling from a graffiti ceiling compete with the clubfoot sandwich as the most creative work of art at the **Staggering Ox ❷**, 400 Euclid Ave. in the Lundy Center. Their patented bread is baked in a soup can and constructed into sandwiches with names like "Yo' Momma Osama" and "Headbanger Hoagie." The very popular bread guts are sold with such sauces as "Camel Spit." (☎443-1729. Open M-F 9am-8pm, Sa 10am-8pm, Su 11am-7pm.) All the meats, grains, and produce are organic and locally-grown at **No Sweat Cafe ❶**, 427 N. Last Chance Gulch, where whole wheat pancakes ($4) and delightful egg dishes ($5-6) are their specialties. (☎442-6954. Open Tu-F 7am-2pm, Sa-Su 8am-2pm.) For a taste of regional sesame flavor, head over to **Bert & Ernie's ❷**, 361 N. Last Chance Gulch, and sink your teeth into a juicy ½ lb. burger ($7-8). Sandwiches ($7) and heart-healthy entrees satisfy burger-phobes. (☎443-5680. Open M-Sa 11am-9pm.)

Miller's Crossing, 52 S. Park Ave., has pool tables, a large dance floor, and all kinds of live music two to three times a week, including rock, funk, and blues. Special $2.50 brew always on tap. (☎442-3290. Cover $2-5. Open daily 11am-2am.) Drinking starts early at **O'Tooles,** 330 N. Last Chance Gulch, and with $1 drafts all day everyday, it's no wonder why. (☎443-9759. Open daily 8am-2am.)

SIGHTS & OUTDOOR ACTIVITIES. A strategic point from which to begin an exploration of Helena, the **Montana Historical Society Museum,** 225 N. Roberts St., runs several tours of the city. (☎444-2694; www.his.st.mt.us. Open June-Aug. M-W and F-Sa 9am-5pm, Th 9am-8pm; Sept.-May M-F 8am-5pm, Sa 9am-5pm. $3, ages 5-18 $1.) Among the historical society's tours is the popular 1hr. **Last Chance Tour Train.** (☎442-1023. Tours M-Sa. May and Sept. 3 per day; June 5 per day; July-Aug. 7 per day. $5.50, seniors $5, ages 4-12 $4.50.) The **State Capitol** building, 1301 6th Ave. at Montana Ave., has several pieces of notable artwork, including a statue of Jeannette Rankin, the first woman elected to Congress. (☎444-4789. Self-guided tours M-F 8am-6pm, Su noon-6pm; guided tours every hr. M-Sa 10am-1pm. Free.) The towering spires of the **Cathedral of Saint Helena,** at Lawrence and Warren St., are visible throughout downtown. The marble furnishings and stained glass windows of this neo-Gothic structure have many admirers. (☎442-5825. Open M-Sa June-Aug. 7am-9pm; Sept.-May 7am-7pm. Guided tours Tu-Th 1pm.) The gold vanished from **Last Chance Gulch** long ago, but today this mall offers restaurants, shops, and public artwork. Housed in the old jail, the **Myrna Loy Center,** 15 N. Ewing St., presents foreign films, dance, music, and performance art. (☎443-0287.)

Take in all of Helena and the surrounding area from the top of **Mount Helena** (5460 ft.); the trail begins from the Adams St. Trailhead, just west of Reeders Alley. Observe the Missouri River just as Lewis and Clark did by taking a 2hr. boat tour of the **Gates of the Mountains,** 18 mi. north of Helena, off I-15. The boat stops near Mann Gulch, where a 1949 forest fire killed 13 smokejumpers. (☎458-5241. Tours June-Sept., 2-4 per day. Call for times. $9.50, seniors $8.50, ages 4-17 $6.)

LITTLE BIG HORN

Little Big Horn National Monument, 60 mi. southeast of Billings, off I-90 on the Crow Reservation, marks the site of one of the most dramatic episodes in the conflict between Native Americans and the US government. Here, on June 25, 1876, Sioux and Cheyenne warriors, led by Sioux chiefs Sitting Bull and Crazy Horse, retaliated against years of genocide by annihilating five companies of the US Seventh Cavalry under the command of Lt. Colonel George Armstrong Custer. White stone graves mark where the US soldiers fell. The exact Native American casualties are not known, since their families and fellow warriors removed the bodies from the battlefield almost immediately. The renaming of the monument, formerly known as the Custer Battlefield Monument, signifies the government's admission that Custer's brutal acts against Native Americans merit no glorification. Congress also prescribed that a memorial be built in honor of the Native Americans killed at the battle. This memorial, which the Cheyenne had been working toward since 1925, was finally completed in September 2002.

The **Visitors Center** has a small movie theater and an electronic map of the battlefield. (☎638-3224; www.nps.gov/libi. Monument and visitors center both open daily June-Aug. 8am-9pm; Sept. 8am-6pm; Oct.-May 8am-4:30pm. Entrance $10 per car, $5 per pedestrian.) Rangers here offer thorough explanatory talks daily during the summer (every hr. 9am-6pm). Visitors can also ride through the monument guided by an audio tour ($15) that narrates the battle's progression. A one-hour bus tour leaves from the Visitors Center in the summer months. (Daily June-Aug. 9, 10:30am, noon, 2, 3:30pm. $10, seniors $8, under 12 $5.)

BOZEMAN ☎406

Surrounded by world-class hiking, skiing, and fishing, Bozeman has recently become a magnet for outdoor enthusiasts. To Montanans, however, Bozeman remains "that boisterous college town." Cowboy hats and pickup trucks are still popular among students at Montana State University (MSU), but the increasing diversity of the student body reflects the cultural vigor of this thriving community.

PRACTICAL INFORMATION. Greyhound and **RimRock Stages,** 1205 E. Main St. (☎587-3110; open M-F 7:30am-5:30pm and 7pm-midnight; Sa-Su 7:30am-noon, 3:30-5:30pm, and 7pm-midnight), both send buses to: Billings (3hr., 3 per day, $25); Butte (2hr., 3 per day, $18); Helena (4hr., 2 per day, $18); Missoula (5hr., 3 per day, $34). **Car Rental: Budget,** at the airport. (☎388-4091. Open daily 7:30am-11pm, or until last flight. Rental $75 per day, unlimited mileage. Ages 21-24 $15 per day surcharge. Credit card required.) **Visitor Info: Bozeman Area Chamber of Commerce,** 2000 Commerce Way, at the corner of 19th Ave. and Baxter Ln. (☎586-5421 or 800-228-4224; www.bozemanchamber.com. Open M 9am-5pm, Tu-F 8am-5pm.) **Summer Visitors Center,** 1003 N. 7th Ave. (Open June-Sept. daily 9am-6pm.) **Internet Access: Bozeman Public Library,** 220 E. Lamme St. (☎582-2400. Open winter M-Th 10am-8pm, F-Sa 10am-5pm, Su 1-5pm; summer closed Su.) **Post Office:** 32 E. Babcock St. (☎586-2373. Open M-F 9am-5pm.) **Postal Code:** 59715. **Area Code:** 406.

ACCOMMODATIONS. Budget motels line Main St. and 7th Ave. north of Main. **Bozeman Backpacker's Hostel ❶,** 405 W. Olive St., has a kitchen, living room, three dogs, and the cheapest bed in town. Shower and linens included, and laundry facilities on site. Rooms are co-ed. (☎586-4659. Dorm beds $14; private room with shared bath $32.) The **Blue Sky Motel ❸,** 1010 E. Main St., offers comfortable rooms with microwave, fridge, and cable TV. (☎587-2311 or 800-845-9032. Continental breakfast included. Singles $49; doubles $58.) The **Bear Canyon Campground ❶,** 4 mi. east of Bozeman at Exit 313 off I-90, has great views of the surrounding countryside. (☎587-1575 or 800-438-1575. Laundry, showers, and pool. Open May to mid-Oct. Sites $16; with water and electricity $21; full hookup $26. Each additional person $2.) **Spire Rock Campground ❶,** 26 mi. south of Bozeman on U.S. 191, is one of several national forest campgrounds that line the highway. (☎522-2520. Open mid-May to mid-Sept. $8 per night.) The **Bozeman Ranger Station,** 3710 Fallon, Ste. C, has more info on camping in the Gallatin National Forest. (☎522-2520.)

FOOD & NIGHTLIFE. Thrifty eateries aimed at the college crowd line W. College near the university. Now a popular chain throughout Montana, the original **Pickle Barrel ❶** resides at 809 W. College. Enormous sandwiches with fresh ingredients and free pickles have drawn MSU students for years. (☎587-2411. Hefty 9 in. sandwiches $5. Open summer 10:30am-10pm; winter 11am-10:30pm.) **The Cateye Cafe ❷,** 23 N. Tracy Ave., is a downtown diner with a colorful new paint job and a menu with a sense of humor. Banana bread french toast ($5) and sandwiches on "fogatcha" bread ($6-7) feed any craving. (☎587-8844. Open M and W-F 7am-2:30pm, Sa-Su 7am-2pm.) **La Parrilla ❷,** 1533 W. Babcock, wraps up just about everything in their giant 1 ft. tortillas ($5-6), including homemade barbecue, fiery jambalaya, and fresh seafood. (☎582-9511. Open daily 11am-9pm.) **Sweet Pea Bakery and Cafe ❷,** 19 S. Wilson St., cooks up a gourmet lunch and brunch, with dishes like mango chicken salad, for around $8. (☎586-8200. Open Su-Tu 7am-3pm, W-Sa 7am-10pm.) **Montana Harvest,** 31 S. Wilson, has a supply of granola, soy nuts, and other natural and organic foods. (☎585-3777. Open M-Sa 8am-8pm, Su 10am-6pm.)

Get the lowdown on music and nightlife from the weekly *Tributary* or *The BoZone.* Locals and travelers thirsty for good beer and great live music head over to the **Zebra Cocktail Lounge,** in the basement at Rouse Ave. and Main St. The large selection of beers and the hipster atmosphere always draw a young, cool crowd. (☎585-8851. W-Sa DJ or bands. Open daily 8pm-2am.) One of only two non-smoking bars in Bozeman, the **Rocking R Bar,** 211 E. Main St., lives up to its name with hot drink specials every night and free food W-F 5-9pm. (☎587-9355. Live music W and Sa. Karaoke Th. Open daily 11am-2am.) Sample some of Montana's best brews with over 40 on tap at **Montana Ale Works,** 601 E. Main St. This former storage facility for the Northern Pacific Railway Co. now houses six pool tables for serious sharks. (☎587-7700. Open Su-Th 4pm-midnight. F-Sa 4pm-1am.)

SIGHTS & OUTDOOR ACTIVITIES. Get up close and personal with dinosaurs and other artifacts of Rocky Mountain history at the **Museum of the Rockies,** 600 West Kagy Blvd., near the university. Dr. Jack Horner (the basis for *Jurassic Park's* Alan Grant) and other paleontologists make this their base for excavating prehistoric remains throughout the West. (☎994-3466; www.montana.edu/www-mor. Open daily summer 8am-8pm; low-season M-Sa 9am-5pm, Su 12:30-5pm. $8, ages 5-18 $4.) Standing on the site of the old county jail, **The Pioneer Museum,** 317 W. Main St., offers a look at the gallows and actual jail cells. (☎522-8122; www.pioneermuseum.org. Open mid-May to mid-Sept. M-Sa 10am-4:30pm; mid-Sept. to mid-May Tu-F 11am-4pm, Sa 1-4pm. Free.)

Surrounded by three renowned trout fishing rivers—Yellowstone, Madison, and Gardiner—the small town of **Livingston,** about 25 mi. east of Bozeman off I-90, is an angler's heaven; the film *A River Runs Through It* was shot here and in Bozeman. Livingston's Main St. features a strip of early 20th-century buildings, including bars (with gambling), restaurants, fishing outfitters, and a few modern businesses. If fishing's your thing, **Dan Bailey's,** 209 W. Park St., sells licenses and rents gear. (☎222-1673 or 800-356-4052. Open summer M-Sa 8am-7pm; winter M-Sa 8am-6pm. Fishing license 2-day $22, season $67. Rod and reel $10; waders and boots $10.)

Bozeman provides its share of downhill thrills. The world-class ski area, **Big Sky,** 45 mi. south of town on U.S. 191, has over 150 trails and short lift lines. The Lone Peak trams reach an altitude of 11,166 ft. for extreme skiing options. (☎995-5000 or 800-548-4486. Open mid-Nov. to mid-Apr. Full-day ticket $59, college students and ages 11-17 $47, seniors $30. Ski rentals $27-39, juniors $19. Snowboards $33.) More intimate and less expensive than Big Sky, **Bridger Bowl Ski Area,** 15795 Bridger Canyon Rd., 16 mi. northeast of town on Hwy. 86, has trails for a variety of abilities. (☎586-1518 or 800-223-9609. Open early Dec.-early Apr. Full-day ticket $35, seniors $29, ages 6-12 $13. Ski rentals $20, juniors $10. Snowboards $30.) In summer, scenic **lift rides** soar up Big Sky. (Open June-early Oct. daily 9:45am-5pm. $14, seniors $9, under 10 free.) Full suspension mountain bike rentals also available up top. ($23 per hr., $46 per 8hr.)

Equestrian types gallop at nearby **Big Sky Stables,** on the spur road off U.S. 191, about 2 mi. before Big Sky's entrance. (☎995-2972. Open mid-May to early Oct. $32 per hr., $52 per 2hr. 1-day notice required.) The warm and shallow **Madison River** makes floating a popular, relaxing, and cheap way to pass the long summer days. Rent inner tubes ($3 per day) at **Big Boys Toys,** 28670 Norris Rd., west on Main St. 7 mi. from downtown. (☎587-4747. Open daily 8am-6pm. Canoes $25 per day; windgliders $25 per day.) **Yellowstone Raft Co.** shoots the rapids of the Gallatin River, 7 mi. north of the Big Sky area on U.S. 191. Trips meet at the office, between mileposts 55 and 56 on U.S. 191. (☎995-4613 or 800-348-4376. Half-day $39, children $30; full-day $79/63.)

MISSOULA ☎406

A liberal haven in a largely conservative state, Missoula attracts new residents every day with its revitalized downtown and bountiful outdoors opportunities. Home to the University of Montana, downtown Missoula is lined with bars and coffeehouses spawned by the large student population. Four different mountain ranges and five major rivers surround Missoula, supporting skiing during the winter and fly fishing, hiking, and biking during the summer.

PRACTICAL INFORMATION. Flights stream into the **Missoula International Airport,** 5225 Hwy. 10 W (☎728-4381; www.msoairport.org), 6 mi. west of town. Follow Broadway, which turns into Hwy. 10/200. **Greyhound,** 1660 W. Broadway (☎549-2339; ticket office M-F 6:15am-4pm and 8pm-midnight, Sa noon-4pm and 9-10pm, Su 1-4pm and 9-10pm), has buses to Bozeman (4½-5½hr., 4 per day, $34) and Spokane (4hr., 3 per day, $37). From the same terminal, **Rimrock Stages** serves Whitefish via St. Ignatius and Kalispell (3½hr., 1 per day, $25) and Helena (4 hr., 2 per

THE LOCAL LEGEND

CASHING OUT

Cattle rancher Grover Chestnut from Bozeman, MT might have come up with the best way to ensure visitors visit his grave. Before his death in 2002, Chestnut supposedly had an ATM installed at his tombstone. He gave debit cards to his 10 heirs and told them that they were allowed to withdraw $300 from the grave every week. Joel Jenkins, who helped create the ATM tombstone, states that the system seems to be working, as Chestnut's relatives are setting up camp in Bozeman to be as close as possible to the Gravy Train.

Casting some doubt on this story is the fact that there is no record of a Grover Chestnut in the Bozeman obituaries, nor do any cemeteries in Bozeman have electrical outlets to keep the ATM working. Joel Jenkins does claim to own an ATM company, but when asked the whereabouts of the cash-spitting tomb, Jenkins conveniently cites security reasons for his refusal to reveal such information.

The story made it a long way out of Bozeman before being successfully debunked–the *San Francisco Chronicle's* online edition ran the story as fact before printing a terse retraction. Grover Chestnut and his posthumous ATM may have never existed, but you can bet it will be a long time before either are forgotten.

day, $21). Catch a ride on **Mountain Line City Buses** from the Transfer Center, at Ryman and Pine St., or at a curbside around town. (☎721-3333. Buses operate M-F 6:45am-8:15pm, Sa 9:45am-5:15pm. $0.85, seniors $0.35, under 18 $0.25.) **Taxi: Yellow Cab,** ☎543-6644. **Rent-A-Wreck,** 1905 W. Broadway, provides free transportation to and from the airport and great rental prices. (☎721-3838 or 800-552-1138. 21+. $29-45 per day; 150 free mi., $0.25 each additional mi.) **Visitor Info: Missoula Chamber of Commerce,** 825 E. Front St. at Van Buren. (☎543-6623; www.missoulachamber.com. Open M-F 8am-5pm.) **Internet Access: Missoula Public Library,** 301 E. Main St. (☎721-2665. Open M-Th 10am-9pm, F-Sa 10am-6pm.) **Post Office:** 200 E. Broadway St. (☎329-2222. Open M-F 8am-5:30pm.) **Postal Code:** 59801. **Area Code:** 406.

ACCOMMODATIONS. There are no hostels in Missoula, but there are plenty of inexpensive, if not super cheap, alternatives along **Broadway.** In a quiet setting, but still right in the hub of downtown, the **Royal Motel ❷,** 338 Washington, supplies clean rooms with cable TV, fridges, and microwaves. (☎542-2184. June-Sept. singles $40; doubles $42-46. Oct.-May $32/36.) Rooms at the **City Center Motel ❷,** 338 E. Broadway, also have cable TV, fridges, and microwaves. (☎543-3193. May-Sept. singles $45; doubles $48-52. Sept.-Dec. $35/42.) The **Missoula/El-Mar KOA Kampground ❶,** 3450 Tina Ave., just south of Broadway off Reserve St., one of the best KOAs around, has shaded tent sites apart from RVs. (☎549-0881 or 800-562-5366. Pool, hot tub, mini-golf courses, and laundry facilities. Sites for 2 $21; with water and electricity $23; full hookup $31; cabins $38-46. Each additional person $3.)

FOOD & NIGHTLIFE. Missoula, the culinary capital of Montana, boasts a number of innovative, delicious, and thrifty eateries. Head downtown, north of the Clark Fork River along Higgins Ave., and check out the array of restaurants and coffeehouses that line the road. **Worden's ❶,** 451 N. Higgins Ave., is a popular local deli, serving a variety of world-class sandwiches in 3 sizes: 4 in. roll ($4), 7 in. ($6), and 14 in. ($11). You can also pick up groceries while munching. (☎549-1293. Open summer M-Th 8am-10pm, F-Sa 8am-11pm, Su 9am-10pm; winter M-Th 8am-9pm, F-Sa 8am-10pm, Su 9am-10pm.) **Tipu's ❷,** 115½ S. 4th St. W in the alley, functions as one of the only all-veggie establishments and the lone Indian restaurant in Montana. (☎542-0622. All-you-can-eat lunch buffet $7. Open daily 11:30am-9:30pm.) For authentic Creole and Cajun cooking, look for the **Dinosaur Cafe ❶,** 428 N. Higgins, hidden behind Charlie B's bar. New Orleans-style po' boys heat you up for under $5. (☎549-2940. Open M-F 11am-midnight, Sa noon-midnight.) Boasting fine espresso and billiards, the hip **Raven Cafe ❷,** 130 E. Broadway, handles heavenly slices of quiche ($3) and black bird pizza pies (10 in. $7-8). With free Internet access, a fresh jukebox, and plenty of books, magazines, and decadent desserts with which to cozy up, the cafe keeps people sipping coffee for hours. (☎829-8188. Open M-Sa 8am-11pm, Su 8am-3pm.) At **Tacos del Sol ❶,** 422 N. Higgins Ave., get $2 fish tacos and a Mission Burrito for under $4. (☎327-8929. Open M-F 11am-7pm.)

College students swarm the downtown bar area around Front St. and Higgins Ave. during the school year. Bars have a more relaxed atmosphere in summer. **Charlie B's,** 420 N. Higgins Ave., draws an eclectic clientele of bikers, farmers, students, and hippies. Framed photos of longtime regulars blot out the walls. (☎549-3589. Drafts $1.75. Wells $2-3. Open daily 8am-2am.) The popular **Iron Horse Brew Pub,** 501 N. Higgins Ave., always packs a crowd; the large patios fill up during the summer months. (☎728-8866. $2 Drafts. Open daily 11am-2am.) Follow the advice of the "beer coaches" at **The Kettle House Brewing Co.,** 602 Myrtle, one block west of Higgins between 4th and 5th, and "support your local brewery." The Kettle House serves a delectable assortment of beers, including their hemp beer—Bongwater Stout. (☎728-1660. Open M-Th 3-9pm, F-Sa noon-9pm; no beer served after 8pm. 2 free samples; then $3-3.25 per pint.) The *Independent* and *Lively Times*, available at newsstands and cafes, offer the low-down on the Missoula music scene, while the *Entertainer*, in the Friday *Missoulian*, has movie and event schedules.

SIGHTS. Missoula's hottest sight is the **Smokejumper Center,** 5765 W. Broadway, just past the airport, 7 mi. west of town. It's the nation's largest training base for smokejumpers—aerial firefighters who parachute into remote forests and serve as an initial attack against wildfires. (☎329-4934. Open daily May-Sept. 8:30am-5pm. Tours every hr. 10-11am and 2-4pm. Free.) The **Carousel,** in Caras Riverfront Park, is one of the oldest hand-carved carousels in America. (☎549-8382. Open daily June-Aug. 11am-7pm; Sept.-May 11am-5:30pm. $1, seniors and under 19 $0.50.) **Out to Lunch,** also in Caras Riverfront Park, offers free performances in the summer along with plenty of food vendors; call the Missoula Downtown Association for more info. (☎543-4238. June-Aug. W 11am-1:30pm.) If you miss "Out to Lunch," the food vendors return Thursday nights for **Downtown Tonight,** which features live music, food, and a beer garden. (☎543-4238. July-Sept. Th 5-8pm.) The **Western Montana Fair and Rodeo,** held the beginning of August, has live music, a carnival, fireworks, and concession booths. (☎721-3247; www.westernmontanafair.com. Open 10am-10pm.)

Soak your weary feet at the **Lolo Hot Springs,** 35 mi. southwest of Missoula on Hwy 12. The 103-105°F springs served as an ancient meeting place for local Native Americans and were frequented by Lewis and Clark in 1806. (☎273-2290 or 800-273-2290. Open daily June-Sept. 10am-10pm; Oct.-May 10am-8pm. $6, under 13 $4.) Farther along Rte. 12 into Idaho are two free natural **hot springs,** Jerry Johnson and Weir, which are well worth the extra miles.

OUTDOOR ACTIVITIES. Nearby parks, recreation areas, and surrounding wilderness areas make Missoula an outdoor enthusiast's dream. The bicycle-friendly city is located along both the Trans-America and Great Parks bicycle routes, and all major streets have designated bike lanes. **Open Road Bicycles and Nordic Equipment,** 517 S. Orange St., has bike rentals. (☎549-2453. Open M-F 9am-6pm, Sa 10am-5pm, Su 11am-3pm. Front suspension $3.50 per hr., $17.50 per day; full suspension $7.50/35.) **Adventure Cycling,** 150 E. Pine St., is the place to go for info about Trans-America and Great Parks routes. (☎721-1776 or 800-755-2453. Open M-F 8am-5pm.) The **Rattlesnake Wilderness National Recreation Area,** 11 mi. northeast of town off Exit 104 on I-90, and the **Pattee Canyon Recreation Area,** 3½ mi. east of Higgins on Pattee Canyon Dr., are highly recommended for their biking trails. For more info on local trails, contact the **Missoula Ranger District,** Building 24-A at Fort Missoula. (☎329-3814. Open M-F 7:30am-4:30pm.) **Missoulians on Bicycle,** P.O. Box 8903, Missoula 59807 (www.missoulabike.org), is a local organization that hosts rides and events for cyclists .

Alpine and Nordic **skiing** keep Missoulians busy during winter. **Pattee Canyon** has groomed trails that are conveniently close to town, and **Marshall Mountain** is a great place to learn how to downhill ski, with night skiing and free shuttles from downtown. (☎258-6000. $24 per day, ages 6-12 $19.) Experienced skiers should check out the extreme **Montana Snowbowl,** 12 mi. northwest of Missoula, with a vertical drop of 2600 ft. and over 35 trails. (☎549-9777 or 800-728-2695. Open Nov.-Apr. daily 10am-4:30pm. Full-day $31, seniors and students $18, ages 6-12 $14.)

Floating on rafts and tubes is a favorite activity for locals on weekends. The Blackfoot River, along Rte. 200 east of Bonner, makes a good afternoon float. Call the **Montana State Regional Parks and Wildlife Office,** 3201 Spurgin Rd., for information about rafting locations. (☎542-5500. Open M-F 8am-5pm.) Rent tubes or rafts from the **Army and Navy Economy Store,** 322 N. Higgins. (☎721-1315. Open M-F 9am-7:30pm, Sa 9am-5:30pm, Su 10am-5:30pm. Tubes $4 per day. Rafts $40 per day, credit card required; $20 deposit.)

Hiking opportunities also abound in the Missoula area. The relatively easy 30min. hike to the "M" (for the U of M, not Missoula) on Mount Sentinel, has a tremendous view of Missoula and the surrounding mountains. The **Rattlesnake Wilderness National Recreation Area,** named after the shape of the river (there are no rattlers for miles), makes for a great day of hiking. Other popular areas include **Pattee Canyon** and **Blue Mountain,** located south of town. Maps ($6) and information on longer hikes in the Bitterroot and Bob Marshall areas are at the **US Forest Service Information Office,** 200 E. Broadway; the entrance is at 200 Pine St. (☎329-3511. Open M-F 7am-4pm.) For equipment rentals, stop by **Trailhead,** 110 E. Pine St., at Higgins St. (☎543-6966. Open M-F 9:30am-8pm, Sa 9am-6pm, Su 11am-6pm. Tents $10-14 per day; backpacks $9; sleeping bags $5.)

Western Montana is **fly fishing** country, and Missoula is at the heart of it all. Fishing licenses are required and can be purchased from the **Department of Fish, Wildlife, and Parks,** 3201 Spurgin Rd. (☎542-5500), or from local sporting goods stores. **Kingfisher,** 926 E. Broadway, offers licenses (2-day $22, 10-day $50, season $67) and pricey guided fishing trips. (☎721-6141 or 888-542-4911. Open June-Aug. daily 6am-8pm; Sept.-May 9am-5pm.)

ROCKY MOUNTAINS

FROM MISSOULA TO GLACIER

St. Ignatius Campground and Hostel ❶, off U.S. 93 at Airport Rd. in **Saint Ignatius** (look for the camping sign), offers lodging in its recently renovated "earthship"—an eco-friendly structure built into a hillside and made from recycled tires and aluminum cans. Faux cave paintings decorate the plaster walls. The hostel rents skiing equipment and new mountain bikes ($10 per day) and is a convenient blasting-off point for exploring the backcountry. (☎745-3959. Showers, laundry, and kitchenette. Rooms are co-ed. Campsites for 1 $10; for 2 $12. Cots under a teepee $10. Beds $14.) **RimRock Stages** (☎745-3501) makes a stop ½ mi. away in St. Ignatius, at the Malt Shop on Blaine St.

The **National Bison Range** was established in 1908 in an effort to save the dwindling number of bison from extinction. At one time 30-70 million roamed the plains, but after years of over-hunting the population dropped to less than 1000. The Range is home to 350-500 buffalo as well as deer, pronghorn, elk, bighorn sheep, and mountain goats. The 2hr. Red Sleep Mountain self-guided tour is a 19 mi. drive on steep gravel roads and offers a spectacular view of the Flathead Valley and the best chance for wildlife observation. To access the range, travel 40 mi. north of Missoula on U.S. 93, then 5 mi. west on Rte. 200, and 5 mi. north on Rte. 212. (☎644-2211. Visitors Center open mid-May to Oct. M-F 8am-7pm, Sa-Su 9am-6pm; Nov. to mid-May M-F 8am-4:30pm. Red Sleep Mountain drive open mid-May to mid-Oct. daily 7am-7pm. $4 per vehicle.) With large displays of old posters, uniforms, vintage cars, motorcycles, and weapons, the **Miracle of America Museum,** 58176 U.S. 93, at the southern end of Polson, houses one of the country's greatest collections of Americana. A general store, saddlery shop, barber shop, soda fountain, and gas station sit among the classic memorabilia. The museum celebrates Live History Day the third weekend in July. (☎883-6804. Open June-Sept. daily 8am-8pm; Oct.-May M-Sa 8am-5pm,

Su 2-6pm. $3, ages 3-12 $1.) Fresh fruit stands line **Flathead Lake,** the largest natural lake west of the Mississippi. Renowned for fresh cherries and fresher fish, the lake is on U.S. 93 between Polson and Kalispell.

WATERTON-GLACIER PEACE PARK

Waterton-Glacier transcends international boundaries to encompass one of the most strikingly beautiful portions of the Rockies. Both established in 1932, the two parks are connected by a natural unity of landscape and wildlife. The massive Rocky Mountain peaks span both parks, providing sanctuary for many endangered bears, bighorn sheep, moose, mountain goats, and gray wolves. Perched high in the Northern Rockies, Glacier is sometimes called the "Crown of the Continent," and the high alpine lakes and glaciers shine like jewels.

PRACTICAL INFORMATION

Technically one park, Waterton-Glacier is actually two distinct areas: the small **Waterton Lakes National Park** in Alberta, and the enormous **Glacier National Park** in Montana. There are several **border crossings** nearby: **Piegan/Carway,** at U.S. 89 (open daily 7am-11pm); **Roosville,** on U.S. 93 (open 24hr.); and **Chief Mountain,** at Rte. 17 (open daily mid- to late May and Sept. 9am-6pm; June-Aug. 7am-10pm). The fastest way to Waterton is to head north along the east side of Glacier, entering Canada through Chief Mountain. Since snow can be unpredictable, the parks are usually in full operation only from late May to early September—check conditions in advance. The *Waterton Glacier Guide*, provided at any park entrance, has dates and times of trail, campground, and border crossing openings. To find out which park areas, hotels, and campsites will be open when you visit, contact the **Park Headquarters,** Waterton Lakes National Park, Waterton Park, AB T0K 2M0 (☎403-859-2224), or **Glacier National Park,** West Glacier, MT 59936 (☎406-888-7800). Mace and firewood are not allowed into Canada.

GLACIER NATIONAL PARK ☎406

TRANSPORTATION

Amtrak (☎226-4452) traces a dramatic route along the southern edge of the park. The station in West Glacier is staffed mid-May to September, but the train still stops at the station in the winter. Trains chug daily to: East Glacier (1½hr., $14); Seattle (14hr., $790-117); Spokane (6hr., $46-59); Whitefish (30min., $7-8). Amtrak also runs from East Glacier to Chicago (32hr., $152-198). **Rimrock Stages** (☎800-255-7655), the only bus line that nears the park, stops in Kalispell at the Kalispell Bus Terminal, 3794 U.S. 2 E, and goes to Missoula (3 hr., 1 per day, $21-23) and Billings (14 hr., 1 per day, $70-75). As in most of the Rockies, a car is the most convenient mode of transport, particularly within the park. **Glacier Park, Inc.'s** famous red jammer buses run tours on Going-to-the-Sun Rd. (4hr. tours $25, 6hr. $32; children half-price.) **Sun Tours** offers additional tours, leaving from East Glacier and St. Mary. (☎226-9220 or 800-786-9220. All-day tour from East Glacier $55, from St. Mary $40.) Shuttles for hikers ($8 per person per segment, under 12 $4) roam the length of Going-to-the-Sun Rd. from early July to early September; schedules are available at Visitors Centers (see **Practical Information,** below) or at www.nps.gov/glac/shuttles.htm.

ORIENTATION

There are few roads in Glacier, and the locals like it that way. Glacier's main thoroughfare is the **Going-to-the-Sun Road,** which connects the two primary points of entry, West Glacier and St. Mary. **U.S. 2** skirts the southern border of the park and is the fastest route from Browning and East Glacier to West Glacier. At the "Goat Lick," about halfway between East and West Glacier, mountain goats traverse steep cliffs to lap up the natural salt deposits. **Route 89** heads north along the eastern edge of the park past St. Mary. Anyone interested in visiting the northwestern section of the park can either take the unpaved **Outside North Fork Road** and enter the park through Polebridge or brave the pothole-ridden **Inside North Fork Road,** which takes an hour longer and is a rougher gravel path to tackle. While most of Glacier is primitive backcountry, a number of villages provide lodging, gas, and food: St. Mary, Many Glacier, and East Glacier in the east, and West Glacier, Apgar, and Polebridge in the west.

PRACTICAL INFORMATION

Before entering the park, visitors must pay **admission:** $10 per week per car, $5 for pedestrians and cyclists; yearly passes $20. The accessible and knowledgeable rangers at each of the three **Visitors Centers** give the inside scoop on campsites, day hikes, weather, flora, and fauna. **Saint Mary** guards the east entrance of the park. (☎732-7750. Open daily May and Sept. to mid-Oct. 8am-5pm; June 8am-6pm; July-Aug. 8am-9pm.) **Apgar** is located at the west entrance. (☎888-7939. Open daily May-June and Sept.-Oct. 8am-5pm; late June-Aug. 8am-8pm.) A third Visitors Center graces **Logan Pass,** on the Going-to-the-Sun Rd. (Open daily June 10am-4:30pm; July-Aug. 9am-7pm; Sept.to mid-Oct. 10am-4:30pm.) The **Many Glacier** ranger station can also help answer important questions. (Open daily May-June and Sept. 8am-4:30pm; July-Aug. 8am-6pm.)

Visitors planning overnight backpacking trips must obtain the necessary **backcountry permits.** With the exception of the **Nyack/Coal Creek** camping zone, all backcountry camping must be done at designated campsites equipped with pit toilets, tent sites, food preparation areas, and food hanging devices. (June-Sept. overnight camping fee $4 per person per night, ages 9-16 $2; Oct.-May no fees. For an additional $20, reservations are accepted beginning in mid-Apr. for trips between June 15 and Oct. 31.) Reservations can be made in person at the Apgar Permit Center, St. Mary Visitors Center, Many Glacier Ranger Station, and Polebridge, or by writing to Backcountry Reservation Office, Glacier National Park, West Glacier, MT 59936. Pick up a free and indispensable *Backcountry Camping Guide* from Visitors Centers or the **Backcountry Permit Center,** next to the Visitors Center in Apgar, which also has valuable info for those seeking to explore Glacier's less-traveled areas. (Open daily May-June and mid-Sept.-Oct. 8am-4pm; July to mid-Sept. 7am-4pm.) **Medical Services: Kalispell Regional Medical Center,** 310 Sunny View Ln. (☎752-5111), north of Kalispell off Rte. 93. **Post Office:** 110 Going-to-the-Sun Rd., in West Glacier. (☎888-5591. Open M-F 8:30am-12:30pm and 1:30-4:45pm.) **Postal Code:** 59936. **Area Code:** 406.

ACCOMMODATIONS

Staying indoors within Glacier is expensive, but several affordable options lie just outside the park boundaries. On the west side of the park, the small, electricity-less town of **Polebridge** provides access to Glacier's remote and pristine northwest corner. From Apgar, take Camas Rd. north, and take a right onto the poorly-marked gravel Outside North Fork Rd., just past a bridge over the North Fork of the Flathead River. (Avoid Inside North Fork Rd.—your shocks will thank you.) From Columbia Falls, take Rte. 486 north. To the east, inexpensive lodging is just across the park border in **East Glacier.** The distant offices of **Glacier Park, Inc.** (☎756-2444; www.glacierparkinc.com) handle reservations for all in-park lodging.

Brownies Grocery (HI-AYH), 1020 Rte. 49 (☎226-4426), in East Glacier Park. Check in at the grocery counter and head upstairs to the spacious hostel on the second floor. Travelers can refuel with a thick huckleberry shake ($4) or a vegan sandwich ($5). Kitchen, showers, linens, laundry, and a stunning view of the Rockies from the porch. Key deposit $5. Check-in by 9pm; call ahead for late arrivals. Check-out 10am. Reservations recommended; credit card required. Open May-Sept., weather permitting. Internet access $1.75 per 15min. Dorms $13, nonmembers $16. Private singles $18/21; doubles $26/29; family room for 4-6 $38/41. Tent sites $10. Extra bed $5. ❶

North Fork Hostel, 80 Beaver Dr. (☎888-5241), in Polebridge; follow the signs through town. The wooden walls and kerosene lamps are reminiscent of a deep woods hunting retreat. Showers and beautiful fully-equipped kitchen, but no flush toilets. During the winter, old-fashioned wood stoves warm frozen fingers and toes after skiing or snowshoeing. Internet access $2 per 20min. Call ahead for a pickup from the West Glacier Amtrak station ($30-35). Canoe rentals $20 per day; mountain bikes $15; snowshoes $5; nordic ski equipment $5. Showers $4 for non-lodgers. Linen $2. Check-in by 10pm. Check-out noon. Call ahead, especially in winter. Dorms $15, $12 after 2 nights; teepees $10 per person; cabins $30; log homes $65. ❶

Backpacker's Inn Hostel, 29 Dawson Ave. (☎226-9392), just east of the East Glacier Amtrak station and behind Serrano's Mexican Restaurant, has 14 clean beds in co-ed rooms. Hot showers. Sleeping bags $1. Open May-Sept. Rooms $10; private room with queen-sized bed and full linen $20 for 1 person, $30 for 2. ❶

Swiftcurrent Motor Inn (☎732-5531), in Many Glacier Valley, is one of the few budget motels in the area. Open early June-early Sept. All cabins are shared bath. 1-bedroom cabins $43, 2-bedroom $53. ❷

FOOD

Polebridge Mercantile Store (☎888-5105), on Polebridge Loop Rd. ¼ mi. east of N. Fork Rd., has homemade pastries ($1-3) that are as splendid as the surrounding peaks. Gas, gifts, and pay phones are also available. Open daily June-Sept. 8am-9pm; Oct.-May 8am-6pm. ❶

Northern Lights Saloon (☎888-5669), right next to the Polebridge Mercantile, serves fabulous cheeseburgers burgers ($5-6) and all-Montana-brewed cold pints ($3) in a 1-room log cabin with slices of tree trunk for bar stools. Kitchen open June-Sept. M-Sa 4-9pm, Su 9am-noon and 4-9pm; bar open until midnight. ❶

Whistle Stop Restaurant (☎226-9292), in East Glacier next to Brownies Grocery. Sample homemade Montanan delicacies at this restaurant best known for its huckleberry french toast and omelettes ($6-7). Open mid-May to mid-Sept. daily 7am-9pm. ❷

Park Cafe (☎732-4482), in St. Mary on Rte. 89, just north of the park entrance, provides sustenance to those who dare to cross the Going-to-the-Sun Rd. Incredible homemade pies $2.75 per slice. "Hungry Hiker" special (2 eggs with hash browns and toast) $4.25. Vegetarian Caribbean burrito $5.25. Open daily May-Sept. 7am-10pm. ❶

THE LOCAL STORY

FIRE IN THE SKY

While most people run from wildfires, Mark Wright is part of the elite group of aerial firefighters who jump right on in.

LG: How did you start jumping?
MW: I started working for the Helena National Forest as a summer job. Among other things like cleaning picnic tables, cutting brush, and patrolling, one of the things they train you to do is put out fires. So I started out as a young firefighter putting my way through college. The "problem" is that it gets in your blood and you become addicted to it. After 4 years of firefighting through college, I got a teaching degree and ended up continuing to fight fires in my summers off. I've been doing it for the past 27 years.

LG: What does smokejumper training involve?
MW: To be a smokejumper, you need recommendations and a minimum of 2 years firefighting experience. Many people apply and only a limited number get selected to go through rookie training, which is over a month long. I would compare it to boot camp. They start their morning with calisthenics, go through daily training, and have to pass physical fitness tests. People wash out at any time, and they need to make a minimum of 15 jumps before they're even allowed in a fire.

HIKING

Most of Glacier's spectacular scenery lies off the main roads and is accessible only by foot. An extensive trail system has something for everyone, from short, easy day hikes to rigorous backcountry expeditions. Stop by one of the Visitors Centers for maps with day hikes. *Beware of bears and mountain lions. Familiarize yourself with the precautions necessary to avoid an encounter, and ask the rangers about wildlife activity in the area in which you plan to hike.*

Avalanche Lake (4 mi. round-trip, 3hr.) is a breathtaking trail and by far the most popular day hike in the park. Starting north of Lake McDonald on the Going-to-the-Sun Rd., this moderate hike climbs 500 ft. to picture-perfect panoramas.

Trail of the Cedars (¾ mi. loop, 20min.) begins at the same trailhead as Avalanche Lake and is an easy nature walk that also has a shorter, wheelchair-accessible hike.

Numa Ridge Lookout (12 mi. round-trip, 9hr.) starts from the Bowman Lake Campground, northeast of Polebridge. After climbing 2930 ft., this challenging hike ends with sweeping vistas of Glacier's rugged northwest corner.

Grinnell Glacier Trail (11 mi. round-trip, 7hr.) passes within close proximity of several glaciers and follows along Grinnell Point and Mt. Grinnell, gaining a steady and moderate 1600 ft. Trailhead at the Many Glacier Picnic Area.

Hidden Lake Nature Trail (3 mi. round-trip, 2hr.), beginning at the Logan Pass Visitor Center, is a short and modest 460 ft. climb to a lookout of Hidden Lake and a chance to stretch your legs while winding along the Going-to-the-Sun Rd.

OUTDOOR ACTIVITIES

BIKING & HORSEBACK RIDING

Opportunities for bicycling are limited and confined to roadways and designated bike paths; cycling on trails is strictly prohibited. Although the Going-to-the-Sun Rd. is a popular **bike route,** only experienced cyclists with appropriate gear and legs of titanium should attempt this grueling ride; the sometimes nonexistent shoulder of the road can create hazardous situations. From mid-June to August, bike traffic is prohibited 11am-4pm from the Apgar campground to Sprague Creek and eastbound (uphill) from Logan Creek to Logan Pass. The Inside North Fork Rd., which runs from Kintla Lake to Fish Creek on the west side of the park, is good for **mountain biking,** as are the old logging roads in the Flathead National Forest. Ask at a Visitors Center for more details. **Equestrian** explorers should check to make sure trails are open; there are steep fines for riding on closed trails. **Trail rides** from **Mule Shoe Outfitters** (May-early Sept. 2hr. guided rides leave every 2hr. 8:30am-3:30pm; $45) are available at Many Glacier (☎732-4203) and Lake McDonald (☎888-5121).

BOATING

The **Glacier Park Boat Co.** (☎257-2426) provides **boat tours** that explore all of Glacier's large lakes and surrounding peaks. Tours leave from **Lake McDonald** (☎888-5727; 1hr., 4 per day, $10); **Two Medicine** (☎226-4467; 45min., 5 per day, $9.50); **Rising Sun,** at St. Mary Lake (☎732-4430; 1½hr., 5 per day, $11); and **Many Glacier** (☎732-4480; 1¼hr., $12). Children ages 4-12 ride for half price. The tours from Two Medicine, Rising Sun, and Many Glacier provide access to Glacier's backcountry, and there are sunset cruises from Rising Sun and Lake McDonald. **Glacier Raft Co.,** in West Glacier, leads trips down the middle fork of the Flathead River. (☎888-5454 or 800-235-6781. Half-day $40, under 13 $30; full-day trip with lunch $65/48.) You can rent **rowboats** ($10 per hr.) at Lake McDonald, Many Glacier, Two Medicine, and Apgar; **canoes** ($10 per hr.) at Many Glacier, Two Medicine, and Apgar; **kayaks** ($10 per hr.) at Apgar and Many Glacier; and **outboards** ($17 per hr.) at Lake McDonald and Two Medicine. Call Glacier Boat Co. for more details.

FISHING

No permit is needed to **fish** in the park, and limits are generally high. Some areas, however, are restricted, and certain species may be catch-and-release. Pick up *Fishing Regulations*, available at Visitors Centers for info. Lake Ellen Wilson, Gunsight Lake, and Lake Elizabeth are good places to sink a line. Outside the park, on Blackfoot land, a special permit is needed, and everywhere else in Montana a state permit is required.

NEAR GLACIER

BROWNING

The center of the **Blackfeet Indian Reservation,** Browning, 12 mi. east of East Glacier, provides a glimpse into the past and present of Native American life. The **Museum of the Plains Indian,** at the junction of U.S. 2 and 89, displays traditional clothing, artifacts, and crafts. (☎338-2230. Open June-Sept.

LG: What happens in a typical fire?
MW: Smokejumpers are initial attack, so we get calls right when the fire is detected and still fairly small. One of the great advantages smokejumpers have is that we are on an airplane above the fire with the door off. We take a good look at the terrain and see what the fire behavior is. People coming from the ground can only see smoke and don't know what they're getting into. Before we even jump out of the plane, we check for safety zones to see which ways we can approach the fire, pinpoint safe jump spots that are close to the fire but not endangering ourselves, and look for routes out of the fire. After we land in parachutes, we pack it up to put in a safe spot. The plane flies over and drops our cargo, which contains chainsaws, tools, water, freeze dried food, everything we'll need to fight the fire and camp overnight.

LG: What is one of your most memorable smokejumping experiences?
MW: This was about 21 years ago. I had just jumped a fire and we had it pretty well whipped. Smoke was coming off the last dying embers and the sun was coming up. As I was wiping the soot off my face, the dispatcher came on the radio and asked, "Is there a smokejumper there named Mark Wright?" I knew immediately what he was going to tell me. I started hooting and hollering as he announced, "Congratulations. You have a healthy baby girl."

daily 9am-4:45pm; Oct.-May M-F 10am-4:30pm. $4, ages 6-12 $1; Oct.-May free.) During **North American Indian Days** (the second weekend in July), Native Americans from the surrounding Blackfoot Reservation and elsewhere gather for a celebration that includes tribal dancing, a rodeo, and a parade. Call **Blackfeet Planning** (☎338-7406) for details.

WATERTON LAKES NATIONAL PARK, ALBERTA ☎403

Only a fraction of the size of its Montana neighbor, Waterton Lakes National Park offers spectacular scenery and activities without the crowds that plague Glacier during July and August. The town of Waterton is a genuine alpine town, complete with a Swiss-style chalet. Bighorn sheep and mule deer frequently wander down the surrounding slopes into town, causing unexpected traffic delays.

PRACTICAL INFORMATION. Admission to the park in summer is CDN$5 per day, seniors CDN$4, ages 6-12 CDN$2.50, groups of two to seven people CDN$12.50; in winter free. The only road from Waterton's park entrance leads 8.5km south to **Waterton Park.** En route, stop at the **Waterton Visitors Center,** 8km inside the park on Rte. 5, for a schedule of events and hikes. (☎859-5133. Open daily mid-June to Aug. 8am-7pm; mid-May to mid-June and Sept.-Oct. 9am-6pm. Hours may vary with weather.) In winter, pick up info at **Park Administration,** 215 Mt. View Rd. (☎859-2224. Open M-F 8am-4pm.) Although all businesses in the park accept US dollars, each has its own currency exchange rate. To get the most Canadian for the US dollar, exchange money at the **Tamarack Village Square** on Mt. View Rd, which always has the best rate. (☎859-2378. Open July-Aug. daily 8am-8pm; May-June and Sept.-Oct. usually 10am-5pm.)

Pat's Gas and Cycle Rental, Mt. View Rd., Waterton, rents bikes. (☎859-2266. Path bikes CDN$6 per hr., CDN$30 per day; full suspension mountain bikes CDN$10/40.) **Medical Services: Ambulance,** ☎859-2636. **Post Office:** In Waterton on Fountain at Windflower Ave. (Open M, W, F 8:30am-4:30pm, Tu and Th 8:30am-4pm.) **Postal Code:** T0K 2M0. **Area Code:** 403.

ACCOMMODATIONS & FOOD. The park's three campgrounds are very affordable. **Belly River ❶,** is outside the park entrance on Chief Mountain Hwy. 3 mi. north of the border and has scenic, uncrowded primitive sites with pit toilets and water. (☎859-2224. Open mid-May to mid-Sept. Sites CDN$12.) **Crandell ❶,** on the road to Red Rock Canyon, is situated in a forest area and has flush toilets and running water but no showers. (Open mid-May to late Sept. Sites CDN$14.) Camp with 200 of your best RV pals at **Townsite ❶** in Waterton Park, which has showers and a lakeside vista, but no privacy. The walk-in sites are satisfactory and are generally the last to fill. (Open mid-Apr. to late Oct. Walk-in sites CDN$16; sites CDN$18; full hookup CDN$24.) **Backcountry camping** requires a permit from the Visitors Center. Campsites are rarely full, and several, including **Crandell Lake ❶,** are less than one hour's hike from the trailhead. (☎859-5133. Permit CDN$8 per person per night. Reserve up to 90 days in advance for an additional CDN$12.) Travelers preferring to stay indoors should reserve one of the 21 comfy beds with thick mattresses at the **Waterton International Hostel (HI-AYH) ❶,** in the Waterton Lakes Lodge. (☎859-2151, ext. 2016. Discounted rate to fitness room and pool next door. Laundry and kitchen. CDN$31, nonmembers CDN$35.)

The thick 9 in. subs at **The Big Scoop ❶,** on Waterton Ave., are only CDN$5 and definitely a steal. (☎859-2346. Open May-Oct. M-Sa 10am-10pm, Su 1:30-10pm.) **Peace Park Pitas ❷,** on the corner of Cameron Falls Dr. and Windflower Ave., rolls up sandwiches ($7) and bakes pizzas ($7) on pitas. (☎859-2259. Internet access $0.50 per min. Open daily 9am-10pm. Cash only.)

OUTDOOR ACTIVITIES. Waterton Lakes include 120 mi. of trails of varying difficulty. In addition to exploring the snow-capped peaks, many of these trails link up with the trail network of Glacier National Park. **Waterton-Glacier International Peace Park Hike,** a free all day (8hr.) guided hike, takes off from the Bertha Trailhead, just south of the Waterton townsite, and crosses the border into the US. (Hikes late June-late Aug. Sa 10am. Only US citizens can cross the border into the US.) After 8½ mi. of moderately easy hiking, participants can take a boat back from the station ($15, ages 13-17 $8, ages 4-12 $6). The **Hiker Shuttle** runs from Tamarack Village Sq., in town, to many trailheads. (☎859-2378. Reservations strongly recommended. CDN$9.) The popular **Crypt Lake Trail** trickles past waterfalls in a narrow canyon, through a 20m natural tunnel, and, after 6km, arrives at icy, green Crypt Lake, straddling the international border. (10½ mi. round-trip, 2297 ft. elevation gain, 5-6hr.) To get to the Crypt trailhead, take the **water taxi** run by **Waterton Inter-Nation Shoreline Cruises,** in Waterton Park. The marina also runs a 2hr. boat tour of Upper Waterton Lake. (☎859-2362. Open mid-May to mid-Sept. Crypt Lake water taxi: departs Waterton 9, 10am; returns from Crypt Landing 4, 5:30pm. round-trip CDN$13, ages 4-12 CDN$6.50. Tour: CDN$25, ages 13-17 CDN$13, ages 4-12 CDN$9.) Gear is available at **Waterton Outdoor Adventures,** in the Tamarack Village Sq., which also sponsors guided hiking tours. (☎859-2378. Open daily July-Aug. 8am-8pm; May-June and Sept.-Oct. usually 10am-5pm.) Horses are allowed on many trails. **Alpine Stables,** 1km north of the townsite, conducts trail rides. (☎859-2462. Open May-Sept. 1hr. rides leave on the hour 9am-4pm, CDN$20; 4hr. ride leaves 1:30pm, CDN$65.)

Fishing in Waterton requires a **license** good at any of the national parks in Canada and available from the park offices, campgrounds, warden stations, and service stations in the area (CDN$7 per day, CDN$20 per season). Lake trout cruise the depths of **Cameron** and **Waterton Lakes,** while pike prowl the weedy channels of **Maskinonge Lake.** Most of the backcountry lakes and creeks support rainbow and brook trout. There are many fish in the creeks that spill from Cameron Lake, about 200m to the east of the parking lot, and Crandell Lake, a 1.5km hike. Rent **rowboats, paddleboats, kayaks,** or **canoes** at Cameron Lake. (CDN$20 first hr. for 2 people, CDN$17 each additional hr.; CDN$25/20 for 4.)

WYOMING

The ninth-largest state in the Union, Wyoming is also the least populated. This is a place where men don cowboy hats and boots, and livestock outnumbers citizens. It is also a land of unique firsts: it was the first state to grant women the right to vote without later repealing it, and was the first to have a national monument (Devils Tower) and national park (Yellowstone) within its borders. Those expecting true Western flavor will not be disappointed; Wyoming boasts the "Rodeo Capital of the World" in Cody, replete with dazzling cowboys and girls.

PRACTICAL INFORMATION

Capital: Cheyenne.

Visitor Info: Wyoming Business Council Tourism Office, I-25 at College Dr., Cheyenne 82002 (☎307-777-7777 or 800-225-5996; www.wyomingtourism.org). Info center open daily 8am-5pm. **Dept. of Commerce, State Parks, and Historic Sites Division,** 122

W. 25th St., Herschler Bldg., 1st fl. E., Cheyenne 82002 (☎307-777-6323; http://wyoparks.state.wy.us). Open M-F 8am-5pm. **Game and Fish Dept.,** 5400 Bishop Blvd., Cheyenne 82006 (☎307-777-4600; http://gf.state.wy.us). Open M-F 8am-5pm.

Postal Abbreviation: WY. **Sales Tax:** 4%.

YELLOWSTONE NATIONAL PARK ☎307

Yellowstone National Park holds the distinctions of being the largest park in the contiguous US and the first national park in the world. Yellowstone also happens to be one of the largest active volcanoes in the world, with over 300 geysers and thousands of thermal fissures spewing steam and boiling water from beneath the earth's crust. The park's hot springs are popular among local wildlife; bison and elk gather around the thermal basins for warmth during the winter months.

Today, Yellowstone is still recovering from devastating forest fires that burned over a third of the park in 1988. The destruction is especially evident in the western half of the park, where charred tree stumps line the roads. Despite the fires, Yellowstone has retained its rugged beauty, and the park's roads are clogged with RVs and tourists eagerly snapping photos of geysers and wildlife. With the reintroduction of wolves in 1995, all of the animals that lived in the Yellowstone area before the arrival of Europeans still roam the landscape, with the exception of the black-footed ferret.

AT A GLANCE

AREA: 2,219,791 acres.

VISITORS: Almost 3 million annually.

HIGHLIGHTS: Be astonished by the 140 feet eruptions of Old Faithful, visit Yellowstone's very own Grand Canyon and frolic with bighorn sheep, and relax alongside North America's largest high altitude lake.

CLIMATE: Extremely varied.

"ROUGHING" IT: Embrace the corporate behemoth Xanterra's borg-like camping options ($17), or get there early for the Park Service's first come, first served sites.

FEES: $20 per car entrance fee, $10 per pedestrian. Backcountry permit free.

TRANSPORTATION

The bulk of Yellowstone National Park lies in the northwest corner of Wyoming with slivers in Montana and Idaho. There are five entrances to the park. **West Yellowstone, MT,** and **Gardiner, MT** are the most developed entrance points. **Cooke City, MT,** the northeast entrance to the park, is a small rustic town nestled in the mountains. East of Cooke City, you can pick up the **Beartooth Highway (U.S. 212),** which is open only in summer, and ascend the surrounding slopes for a breathtaking view of eastern Yellowstone. **Cody** lies 53 mi. east of the East Entrance to the park along Rte. 14/16/20. The southern entrance to the park is bordered by **Grand Teton National Park** (see p. 783). The only road within the park open year-round is the northern strip between the North Entrance and Cooke City. All other roads are only open from May through October. Payment of the park's **entrance fee** is good for 1 week at both Yellowstone and Grand Teton. (Cars $20, pedestrians $10, motorcycles $15.)

Car Rental: Big Sky Car Rental, 415 Yellowstone Ave. (☎406-646-9564 or 800-426-7669), West Yellowstone, MT. Open daily May to mid-Oct. 8am-5pm. $49 per day, 10% discount for 7 days or more, unlimited mi. 21+ with a credit card.

Bike Rental: Yellowstone Bicycle and Video, 132 Madison Ave. (☎406-646-7815), West Yellowstone, MT. Open May-Oct. daily 8:30am-9pm; Nov.-Apr. 11am-7pm. Mountain bikes with helmet and water $3.50 per hr., $12.50 per 5hr., $19.50 per day.

ORIENTATION

Yellowstone is huge; both Rhode Island and Delaware could fit within its boundaries. Yellowstone's roads are designed in a figure-eight configuration, with side roads leading to park entrances and some of the lesser-known attractions. The natural wonders that make the park famous (e.g. Old Faithful) are scattered along the Upper and Lower Loops. Construction and renovation of roads is continually ongoing; call ahead (☎344-7381; www.nps.gov/yell) or consult the extremely helpful *Yellowstone Today*, available at the entrance, to find out which sections will be closed during your visit. Travel through the park can be arduously slow regardless of construction. The speed limit is 45 mph, and steep grades, tight curves, and frequent animal crossings increase driving delays.

Yellowstone can be a dangerous place. While roadside wildlife may look tame, these large beasts are unpredictable and easily startled. Stay at least 75 ft. from any animal, 300 ft. from bears. Both black bears and grizzly bears inhabit Yellowstone; consult a ranger about proper precautions before entering the backcountry. If you should encounter a bear, inform a ranger for the safety of others. Bison, regarded by many as mere overgrown cows, can actually travel at speeds of up to 30 mph; visitors are gored every year. Finally, watch for "widow makers"—dead trees that can fall over at any time, especially during high winds.

PRACTICAL INFORMATION

The park's high season extends roughly from mid-June to mid-September. If you visit during this period, expect large crowds, clogged roads, and filled-to-capacity motels and campsites. Most of the park shuts down from November to mid-April, then gradually reopens as the snow melts.

Over 95% of Yellowstone—almost 2 million acres—is backcountry. To venture overnight into the wilds of Yellowstone requires a **backcountry permit.** The permit is free if you reserve in person at any ranger station or Visitors Center no earlier than 48hr. in advance of the trip. There is almost always space available in the backcountry, although the more popular areas fill up in July and August. For a $20 fee, you can reserve a permit ahead of time by writing to the **Central Backcountry Office,** P.O. Box 168, Yellowstone National Park 82190, and receive a **trip planning worksheet.** (☎344-2160. Open daily 8am-5pm.) Before heading into the backcountry, visitors must watch a short film outlining safety regulations. No firearms, pets, or mountain bikes are permitted in the backcountry. In many backcountry areas campfires are not permitted; plan on bringing a stove and related cooking gear. Consult a ranger before embarking on a trail; they can offer tips on how to avoid bears, ice, and other natural hindrances.

Fishing and **boating** are both allowed within the park, provided visitors follow a number of regulations. Permits, available at any ranger station or Visitors Center, are required for fishing, and some areas may be closed due to feeding patterns of bears. The park's three native species are catch-and-release only. (Permits $10 for 10-day pass, $20 for season; ages 12-15 require a non-fee permit.) In addition to Yellowstone Lake, popular fishing spots include the Madison and Firehole rivers; the Firehole is available for fly fishing only. To go boating or even floating on the lake, you'll need a **boating permit,** available at backcountry offices (check *Yellowstone Today*), Bridge Bay marina, and the South, West, and Northeast entrances to the park. (Motorized vessels $10 for 10-day pass, $20 for season; motor-free boats $5 for 10-day pass, $10 for season.) **Xanterra** rents row boats, outboards, and dockslips at Bridge Bay Marina. (☎344-7311. Mid-

June to early Sept. Rowboats $7.50 per hr., $34 per 8hr.; outboards $33 per hr.; dockslips $14-19 per night.) Parts of Yellowstone Lake and some other lakes are limited to non-motorized boating; inquire at the Lake Village or Grant Village ranger stations for more advice.

Visitor Info: Most regions of the park have their own central station. All centers offer general info and backcountry permits, but each has distinct hiking and camping regulations and features special **regional exhibits.** All stations are usually open late May-early Sept. daily 8am-7pm. Albright and Old Faithful are open year-round.

Albright Visitors Center (☎344-2263), at Mammoth Hot Springs: History of Yellowstone Park and the Beginnings of the National Park Idea. Open daily late May-early Sept. 8am-7pm; early Sept. to May 9am-5pm.

Grant Village (☎242-2650): Wilderness and the 1988 Fire. Open daily late May to Aug. 8am-7pm, Sept. 9am-6pm.

Fishing Bridge (☎242-2450): Wildlife and Yellowstone Lake. Open late May-Aug. 8am-7pm; Sept. 9am-6pm.

Canyon (☎242-2550): Bison, open late May-Aug. daily 8am-7pm; **Old Faithful** (☎545-2750): Geysers, open daily late May-early Sept. 8am-7pm; early Sept.-May 9am-5pm.; **Norris** (☎344-2812): Geothermic Features of the Park, open late May to mid-Oct. daily 10am-5pm.

Madison (☎344-2821): Bookstore, open daily late May-Aug. 9am-6pm, Sept. 9am-5pm; and **West Thumb** (☎242-2652): Bookstore, on the southern edge of the Lake, open late May-late Sept. 9am-5pm.

West Yellowstone Chamber of Commerce, 30 Yellowstone Ave. (☎406-646-7701; www.westyellowstonechamber.com), West Yellowstone, MT, 2 blocks west of the park entrance. Open daily late May to early Sept. 8am-8pm; early Sept. to early Nov. and mid-April to late May M-F 8am-4pm.

General Park Information: ☎344-7381. **Weather:** ☎344-2113. **Radio Information:** 1610AM.

Medical Services: Lake Clinic, Pharmacy, and Hospital (☎242-7241), across the road from the Lake Yellowstone Hotel. Clinic open late May to mid-Sept. daily 8:30am-8:30pm. Emergency room open May-Sept. 24hr. **Old Faithful Clinic** (☎545-7325), near the Old Faithful Inn. Open early May to mid-Oct. daily 7am-noon and 1-7pm. **Mammoth Hot Springs Clinic** (☎344-7965). Open summer Su-Tu and Th-Sa 8:30am-1pm and 2-5pm, W 8:30am-1pm; winter M-Tu and Th-F 8:30am-1pm and 2-5pm, W 8:30am-1pm. **Clinic at West Yellowstone,** 236 Yellowstone Ave. (☎406-646-0200), in West Yellowstone. Open late May-early Sept. M-F 8am-noon and 1-5pm, Sa 10am-2pm; early Sept. to late May hours vary.

Disabled Services: All entrances, Visitors Centers, and ranger stations offer the *Visitor Guide to Accessible Features.* Fishing Bridge RV Park, Madison, Bridge Bay, Canyon, and Grant campgrounds have accessible sites and restrooms; Lewis Lake and Slough Creek have accessible sites. Write the **Park Accessibility Coordinator,** P.O. Box 168, Yellowstone National Park, WY, 82190. For more info visit www.nps.gov/yell.

Internet Access: West Yellowstone Public Library, 220 Yellowstone Ave. (☎406-646-9017). Open Tu and Th 10am-6pm, W 10am-8pm, F 10am-5pm, Sa 10am-3pm. Free.

Post Office: There are 5 post offices in the park at **Lake, Old Faithful, Canyon, Grant,** and **Mammoth Hot Springs** (☎344-7764). All open M-F 8:30am-5pm. Specify which station at Yellowstone National Park when addressing mail. **Postal Code:** 82190. In **West Yellowstone, MT:** 209 Grizzly Ave. (☎406-646-7704). Open M-F 8:30am-5pm, Sa 8-10am. **Postal Code:** 59758.

Area Codes: 307 (in the park), 406 (in West Yellowstone, Cooke City, and Gardiner, MT). In text, 307 unless noted otherwise.

ACCOMMODATIONS

Camping is cheap, but affordable indoor lodging can be found with advanced preparation. Lodging within the park can be hard to come by on short notice but is sometimes a better deal than the motels along the outskirts of the park. During peak months, the cost of a motel room can skyrocket to $100, while in-park lodging remains relatively inexpensive.

IN THE PARK

Xanterra (☎344-7311; www.travelyellowstone.com) controls all accommodations within the park, employing a unique code to distinguish between cabins: "Roughrider" means no bath, no facilities; "Budget" offers a sink; "Pioneer" offers a shower, toilet, and sink; "Frontier" is bigger, more plush; and "Western" is the biggest and swankiest. Facilities are located close to cabins without private bath. Rates are based on two adults; $10 for each additional adult; under 12 free. Reserve cabins well in advance of the June to September tourist season.

Roosevelt Lodge, in the northeast portion of the upper loop, 19 mi. north of Canyon. A favorite of Teddy Roosevelt, who seems to have frequented every motel and saloon west of the Mississippi. Provides cheap and scenic accommodations, located in a relatively isolated section of the park. Open June to early Sept. Roughrider cabins with wood-burning stoves $52. Frontier cabins with full bath $88. ❸

Mammoth Hot Springs, on the northwest portion of the upper loop near the north entrance, makes a good base for early-morning wildlife sighting excursions. Open early May to early Oct. Lattice-sided Budget cabins without bath $61; frontier cabins (some with porches) from $88; hotel room without bath $71. ❸

Canyon Lodge and Cabins, in Canyon Village at the middle of the figure-eight, overlooks the "Grand Canyon" of Yellowstone. Less authentic than Roosevelt's cabins, but centrally located and more popular among tourists. Open late May to mid-Sept. Budget cabins with bath $40. Pioneer cabins $58. Frontier cabins $80. Western cabins $115. ❸

Old Faithful Inn and Lodge, 30 mi. southwest of the west Yellowstone entrance, is awash with ice cream-toting tourists and RVs, but is conveniently located. Open mid-May to mid-Sept. Pleasant Budget cabins $53; frontier cabins $75; well-appointed hotel rooms without bath from $75, with private bath $96-131. ❷

Lake Lodge Cabins, 4 mi. south of Fishing Bridge, is a cluster of cabins from the 1920s and 50s, all just a stone's throw from Yellowstone Lake.Open mid-June to late Sept. Pioneer cabins $56; Larger Western cabins $115. Next door, **Lake Yellowstone Hotel and Cabins** has yellow Frontier cabins with no lake view for $84. ❸

WEST YELLOWSTONE, MT

Guarding the west entrance of the park, West Yellowstone capitalizes on the hordes of tourists who pass through en route to the park. The closest of the border towns to popular park attractions, West Yellowstone has numerous budget motels, with more reasonable prices than Gardiner.

West Yellowstone International Hostel, 139 Yellowstone Ave. (☎406-7745 or 800-838-7745), at the **Madison Hotel,** provides the best indoor budget accommodations around the park. The friendly staff and welcoming lobby make travelers feel at home. Kitchen only has microwave and hot water. Internet access $5 per hr. Open late May to mid-Oct. Dorms $23, with hostel membership $20; private singles and doubles with shared bath $29-39. ❶

Lazy G Motel, 123 Hayden St. (☎406-646-7586), has an affable staff and spacious 1970s-style rooms featuring queen-sized beds, refrigerators, and cable TV. Open May-Mar. Singles $32-48; doubles $40-59, with kitchenette $42-68. ❷

THE GREAT OUTDOORS

WOLVES ARE BITEY

For many years, the only wolves in Yellowstone were the pair stuffed and on display in the Albright Visitors Center. These two, along with all the other wolves in Yellowstone, were killed in 1922 when these predators were considered a menace to Yellowstone's other wildlife.

When gray wolves were declared endangered in 1973, talk of bringing back the wolf population started up. After more than 20 years of public debate, 14 wolves from Canada were released into the park in 1995. Today, over 270 wolves roam the area. Although every effort has been made to reduce the concerns of opponents, the reintroduction of wolves has undoubtedly meant that some livestock and domestic animals have become prey. A wolf compensation trust, brainchild of the Bailey Wildlife Fund, has been established to pay ranchers for losses due to wolves, and this shift in the economic responsibility from ranchers to wolf supporters has created broader acceptance. Wolves seem to be a hit with the ecosystem as well as other animals and scavengers have benefited from the food remaining after wolf kills, and studies indicate that biodiversity in the ecosystem will increase now that wolves have returned.

For more on the Bailey Wildlife fund, check out http://www.defenders.orgo

GARDINER, MT

The Town Cafe and Motel (☎406-848-7322), on Park St. across from the park's northern entrance. The wood-paneled, carpeted rooms are among the best deals in town. Cable TV but no phones. Singles June-Sept. $45; Doubles $55. Oct.-May $25/30-35. ❷

Hillcrest Cottages (☎406-848-7353 or 800-970-7353), on U.S. 89 across from the Exxon, rents out deluxe cabins with kitchenettes. Open May to early Sept. Singles $64; doubles $76; $6 per additional adult, $2 per additional child under 18. ❸

COOKE CITY, MT

Cooke City is located 3 mi. east of the northeast entrance to the park. The Nez Percé slipped right by the US cavalry here, Lewis and Clark deemed the area impassable, and few people visit this rugged little town. Nonetheless, Cooke City is a great location for exploring the remote backcountry of Yellowstone and is conveniently situated between the park and the junction of two scenic drives: the **Chief Joseph Scenic Highway (Route 296)** and the **Beartooth Highway (Route 212).**

Range Rider's Lodge (☎406-838-2359), in Silver Gate on Rte. 212, 1 mi. east of the park on the way to Cooke City. As the second largest all-wood structure in the US, this lodge was originally a brothel commissioned by Teddy Roosevelt to keep the miners in good spirits. Remnants of the previous business still exist, as the wooden tags on the room doors are still carved with Lucy, Mae, Sweet Sue, and 20 other girls' names. Clean, comfortable rooms with shared bath. Open June-Sept. Singles $40; doubles $52. Cash or check only. ❸

Antler's Lodge (☎406-838-2432). Built in 1936, each cabin has its own personality and a great mountain view. Ernest Hemingway spent several nights editing *For Whom the Bell Tolls* here. 2-person cabins $60. ❸

CAMPING

Campsites fill quickly during the summer months; be prepared to make alternate arrangements. Call **Park Headquarters** (☎344-7381) for info on campsite vacancies. **Xanterra,** P.O. Box 165, Yellowstone National Park 82190, runs five of the 12 developed campgrounds within the park: **Canyon, Grant Village, Madison, Bridge Bay** ❶ (all $17), and **Fishing Bridge RV** ❷ ($31; RVs only). All five sites have flush toilets, water, and dump stations. Canyon, Grant Village, and Fishing Bridge RV also have showers ($3) and coin laundry facilities (open 7am-9pm). Campgrounds are usually open mid-May to mid-September Xanterra accepts advance (☎344-7311) and same-day reservations (☎344-7901). Reservations are accepted up to 2 years in advance. During peak summer months (especially on weekends and holidays) all available sites may be reserved beforehand. The two largest Xanterra campgrounds, Grant Village (425 sites) and Bridge Bay (431 sites), are the best bet for last-minute reservations.

The seven **National Park Service campgrounds** ❶ do not accept advance reservations. During the summer, these smaller campgrounds generally fill by 10am, and finding a site can be frustrating. Check-out time is 10am, and the best window for claiming a campsite is 8-10am. Two of the most beautiful campgrounds are **Slough Creek Campground,** 10 mi. northeast of Tower Jct. (29 sites; vault toilets; open June-Sept.; $10) and **Pebble Creek Campground** (32 sites; vault toilets; no RVs; open mid-June to late Sept.; $10). Both are located in the northeast corner of the park, between Tower Falls and the Northeast Entrance (generally the least congested area), and offer relatively isolated sites and good fishing. Travelers can also try **Lewis Lake** (85 sites; vault toilets; open late June-early Nov.; $10), halfway between West Thumb and the South Entrance, or **Tower Falls** (32 sites; vault toilets; open mid-May to late Sept.; $10), between the Northeast entrance and Mammoth Hot Springs. **Norris** (116 sites; water and flush toilets; open late May-late Sept.; $12); **Indian Creek,** between the Norris Geyser Basin and Mammoth Hot Springs (75 sites; vault toilets; open mid-June to mid-Sept.; $10); and **Mammoth** (85 sites; water and flush toilets; $12) are less scenic but still great places to camp. The lodges at Mammoth and Old Faithful have showers for $3 (towels and shampoo included), but no laundry facilities.

FOOD

Buying food at the restaurants, snack bars, and cafeterias in the park can be expensive; stick to the **general stores** at each lodging location. The stores at Fishing Bridge, Lake, Grant Village, and Canyon sell lunch-counter style food. (Open daily 7:30am-9pm, but times may vary.) Stockpile provisions at the **Food Round-Up Grocery Store,** 107 Dunraven St., in West Yellowstone. (☎406-646-7501. Open daily in summer 7am-10pm; winter 7am-9pm.) Marking the original entrance to the park, Gardiner is smaller and less touristy than West Yellowstone; it is also significantly pricier. **Food Farm,** on U.S. 89 in Gardiner across from the Super 8, has cheap food. (☎406-848-7524. Open M-Sa 7am-9pm, Su 8am-8pm.)

Running Bear Pancake House, 538 Madison Ave. (☎406-646-7703), at Hayden in West Yellowstone, has inexpensive breakfasts and sandwiches. Meals $5-6. Open daily 7am-2pm. ❶

The Gusher Pizza & Sandwich Shoppe (☎406-646-9050), at the corner of Madison and Dunraven in West Yellowstone, carries an extensive menu of red, white, or pesto sauce pizzas (10 in. $7-8, 15 in. $11-13), ½ lb. burgers, and hot sandwiches ($6-7). Food is only half their specialty—partake of the full video game room, pool tables, and casino. Open daily 11:30am-10:30pm. ❷

Timberline Cafe, 135 Yellowstone Ave. (☎406-646-9349), in West Yellowstone, prepares travelers for a day at the park with a large salad-and-potato bar and homemade pies. Burgers, sandwiches, and omelettes $6-7. Open daily 6:30am-10pm. ❷

Helen's Corral Drive-In (☎406-848-7627), a few blocks west on U.S. 89 in Gardiner, rounds up killer ½ lb. buffalo burgers and pork chop sandwiches ($4-7). Open summer daily 11am-10pm. ❷

Grizzly Pad Grill and Cabins (☎406-838-2161), on Rte. 212 on the eastern side of Cooke City, serves the Grizzly Pad Special—a milkshake, fries, and large cheeseburger ($7). Open June to mid-Oct. daily 7am-9pm; Jan. to mid-Apr. hours vary. ❷

The Miner's Saloon (☎406-838-2214), on Rte. 212 in downtown Cooke City, serves up tasty burgers and fish tacos ($6-7) and is the best place to go for a frosty Moose Drool beer. Open daily noon-10pm, bar until 2am. ❷

SIGHTS

Xanterra (☎344-7311) organizes tours, horseback rides, and chuckwagon dinners. However, these outdoor activities are expensive, and, given enough time, Yellowstone is best explored on foot. Visitors Centers give out informative self-guiding tour pamphlets with maps for each of the park's main attractions ($0.50 including Old Faithful, Mammoth Hot Springs, and Canyon). Trails to these sights are accessible from the road via walkways, usually extending ¼-1½ mi. into the various natural environments.

Yellowstone is set apart from other National Parks and Forests in the Rockies by its **geothermal features**—the park protects the largest geothermic area in the world. The bulk of these geothermal wonders can be found on the western side of the park between Mammoth Hot Springs in the north and Old Faithful in the south. The most dramatic thermal fissures are the **geysers.** Hot liquid magma close to the surface of the earth superheats water until it boils and bubbles, eventually builds up enough pressure to burst through the cracks with steamy force. The extremely volatile nature of this area means that attractions may change, appear, or disappear due to forces beyond human control.

While bison-jams and bear-gridlock may make wildlife seem more of a nuisance than an attraction, they afford a unique opportunity to see a number of native species co-existing in their natural environment. The best times for viewing are early morning and just before dark, as most animals nap in the shade during the hot midday. The road between Tower-Roosevelt and the northeast entrance, in the Lamar Valley, is one of the best places to see wolves and grizzlies (among other species). Consult a ranger for more specific advice.

ROCKY MOUNTAINS

Beware: the crust around many of Yellowstone's thermal basins, geysers, and hot springs is thin, and boiling, acidic water lies just beneath the surface. Stay on the marked paths and boardwalks at all times. In the backcountry, keep a good distance from hot springs and fumaroles.

OLD FAITHFUL AREA

Yellowstone's trademark attraction, **Old Faithful,** is the most predictable of the large geysers and has consistently pleased audiences since its discovery in 1870. Eruptions usually shooting 120-140 ft. in height typically occur every 45min. to 2hr. (average 90min.) and last about 1½-5 min. Predictions for the next eruption, usually accurate to within 10min., are posted at the Old Faithful Visitors Center. Old Faithful lies in the **Upper Geyser Basin,** 16 mi. south of the Madison area and 20 mi. west of Grant Village. This area is the largest concentration of geysers in the world and boardwalks connect them all. The spectacular **Morning Glory Pool** is an easy 1½ mi. from Old Faithful, and provides up-close-and-personal views of hundreds of hydrothermal features along the way, including the tallest predictable geyser in the world, **Grand Geyser,** and the graceful **Riverside Geyser,** right along the banks of the Firehole River.

Between Old Faithful and Madison, along the Firehole River, lie the **Midway Geyser Basin** and the **Lower Geyser Basin.** Many of these geysers are visible from the side of the road, although stopping for a closer look is highly recommended. The **Excelsior Geyser Crater,** a large, steaming lake created by a powerful geyser blast, and the **Grand Prismatic Spring,** the largest hot spring in the park, are located in the

Midway Geyser Basin, and sit about 5 mi. north of Old Faithful and are well worth the trip. Continuing north from here 2 mi. is the less touristy but just as thrilling **Firehole Lake Drive,** a 2 mi. side loop through hot lakes, springs, and dome geysers. Eight miles north of Old Faithful gurgles the **Fountain Paint Pot,** a bubbling pool of hot milky mud. Four types of geothermal activity present in Yellowstone (geysers, mudpots, hot springs, and fumaroles) are found along the trails of the Firehole River. There is a strong temptation to wash off the grime of camping in the hot water, but swimming in the hot springs is prohibited. You can swim in the **Firehole River,** near Firehole Canyon Dr., just south of Madison Jct., but prepare for a chill; the name of the river is quite deceiving. Call park info (☎344-7381) to make sure the river is open.

NORRIS GEYSER BASIN

Fourteen miles north of Madison and 21 mi. south of Mammoth, the colorful **Norris Geyser Basin** is both the oldest and the hottest active thermal zone in the park. The geyser has been erupting hot water at temperatures of up to 459°F for over 115,000 years. The area has a ½ mi. northern **Porcelain Basin** loop and a 1½ mi. southern **Back Basin** loop. **Echinus,** in the Back Basin, is the largest known acid-water geyser, erupting 40-60 ft. every 1-4hr. Its neighbor, **Steamboat,** is the tallest active geyser in the world, erupting over 300 ft. for anywhere from 3-40min. Steamboat's eruptions, however, are entirely unpredictable; the last eruption occurred April 26, 2002 after 2 years of inactivity.

MAMMOTH HOT SPRINGS

Shifting water sources, malleable limestone deposits, and temperature-sensitive, multicolored bacterial growth create the most rapidly changing natural structure in the park. The hot spring terraces resemble huge wedding cakes at **Mammoth Hot Springs,** 21 mi. to the north of the Norris Basin and 19 mi. west of Tower. The **Upper Terrace Drive,** 2 mi. south of Mammoth Visitor Center, winds for 1½ mi. through colorful springs and rugged limestone ridges and terraces. When visiting, ask a local ranger where to find the most active springs. Also ask about area trails that provide some of the park's best wildlife viewing. Xanterra offers **horse rides** just south of the Hot Springs. (☎344-7311; call at least 1 day ahead. Open late May to early Sept. 5-7 trail rides per day. $28 per hr., $42 per 2hr.) **Swimming** is permitted in the **Boiling River,** 2½ mi. north. Check with a ranger to make sure that this area is open.

GRAND CANYON

The east side's featured attraction, the **Grand Canyon of the Yellowstone,** wears rusty red and orange hues created by hot water acting on the rock. The canyon is 800-1200 ft. deep and 1500-4000 ft. wide. For a close-up view of the mighty **Lower Falls** (308 ft.), hike down the short, steep **Uncle Tom's Trail** (over 300 steps). **Artist Point,** on the southern rim, and **Lookout Point,** on the northern rim, offer broader canyon vistas and are accessible from the road between Canyon and Fishing Bridge. Keep an eye out for bighorn sheep along the canyon's rim. Xanterra also runs **horse rides** at Canyon, as well as in the Tower-Roosevelt area 19 mi. north. (☎344-7311; reservations needed. Open June-Aug. $28 per hr., $42 per 2hr.) **Stagecoach rides** ($7.75, ages 2-11 $6.50) are available early June to late Aug. at Roosevelt Lodge.

YELLOWSTONE LAKE AREA

Situated in the southeast corner of the park, **Yellowstone Lake** is the largest high-altitude lake in North America and serves as a protective area for the cutthroat trout. While the surface of the lake may appear calm, geologists have found evidence of geothermal features at the bottom. **AmFac** offers lake cruises that leave from the marina at Bridge Bay. (☎344-7311. 5-7 per day early June to mid-Sept.

$9.75, ages 2-11 $5.) Geysers and hot springs in **West Thumb** dump an average of 3100 gallons of water into the lake per day. Notwithstanding this thermal boost, the temperature of the lake remains quite cold, averaging 45°F during the summer. Visitors to the park once cooked freshly-caught trout in the boiling water of the **Fishing Cone** in the West Thumb central basin, but this is no longer permitted. Along this same loop on the west side of the lake, check out the **Thumb Paint Pots,** a field of puffing miniature mud volcanoes and chimneys. On the northern edge of the lake is **Fishing Bridge,** where fishing is now prohibited due to efforts to help the endangered trout population. The sulphurous odors of **Mud Volcano,** 6 mi. north of Fishing Bridge, can be distinguished from miles away, but these unique turbulent mudpots are worth the assault on your nose. The unusual geothermal features with their rhythmic belching, acidic waters, and cavernous openings have appropriate names such as **Dragon's Mouth, Sour Lake,** and **Black Dragon's Cauldron.**

OFF THE (EXTREMELY WELL) BEATEN PATH

Most visitors to Yellowstone never get out of their cars, and therefore miss out on over 1200 miles of trails in the park. Options for exploring Yellowstone's more pristine areas range from short day hikes to long backcountry trips. When planning a hike, pick up a topographical trail map ($9-10) at any Visitors Center and ask a ranger to describe the network of trails. Some trails are poorly marked; allow extra time (at least 1hr.) in case you get lost. The 1988 fires scarred over a third of the park; hikers should consult rangers and maps on which areas are burned. Burned areas have less shade, so hikers should pack hats, extra water, and sunscreen.

In addition to the self-guiding trails at major attractions, many worthwhile sights are only a few mi. off the main road. The **Fairy Falls Trail,** 3 mi. north of Old Faithful, provides a unique perspective on the Midway Geyser Basin. The 5¼ mi. round-trip trail begins in the parking lot marked Fairy Falls just south of Midway Geyser Basin. The trail to the top of **Mount Washburn** is enhanced by an enclosed observation area with sweeping views of the park. This trail begins at Chittenden Rd. parking area, 10 mi. north of Canyon Village, or Dunraven Pass, 6 mi. north of Canyon Village, and totals about 6 mi. round-trip with a steady 1500 ft. elevation gain. The free *Backcountry Trip Planner* and rangers can help plan more extended trips.

SCENIC DRIVE: NORTH FORK DRIVE

Linking Yellowstone National Park with Cody, WY, the **Buffalo Bill Cody Scenic Byway (U.S. 14/16/20)** bridges the majestic peaks of the Absaroka Mountains (ab-SOR-ka) with the sagebrush lands of the Wyoming plains. This 52 mi. drive winds through the canyon created by the North Fork of the Shoshone River and is a spectacular departure from Yellowstone. The high granite walls and sedimentary formations of the **Shoshone Canyon** are noticeable from the road, as is the smell of sulfur from the DeMaris springs in the Shoshone River. Once the world's tallest dam, the **Buffalo Bill Dam Visitors Center and Reservoir,** 6 mi. west of Cody, celebrates man's ability to control the flow of water to fit human needs. Built between 1904 and 1910, the Buffalo Bill Dam measures 350 ft. in height. (☎527-6076. Visitors Center open June-Aug. 8am-8pm; May and Sept. daily 8am-6pm.) West of the dam, **strange rock formations,** created millions of years ago by volcanic eruptions in the Absarokas, dot the dusty hillsides. Continuing west to Yellowstone, sagebrush and small juniper trees gradually lead into the thick pine cover of the **Shoshone National Forest,** the country's first national forest. This area, known as the **Wapiti Valley,** is home to over 18 dude ranches. The **East Entrance** to Yellowstone National Park guards the west end of the scenic byway and is closed in winter.

The **Chief Joseph Scenic Highway (Route 296)** connects Cooke City, MT, to Cody, WY, and passes through rugged, sagebrush-covered mountains across the summit of **Dead Indian Hill.** This scenic byway traces the route traveled by the Nez Percé Indians as they skillfully evaded the US army in the summer of 1877. From Cody, follow the Buffalo Bill Cody Scenic Byway back into eastern Yellowstone, completing a spectacular drive through the western half of Wyoming.

GRAND TETON NATIONAL PARK ☎307

The Grand Tetons are the youngest mountains in the entire Rocky Mountain system, their jagged peaks (12 over 12,000 feet) sculpted by glaciers more than 3000 feet thick. When French trappers first observed the three most prominent peaks—South Teton, Grand Teton, and Mt. Teewinot—they dubbed the mountains *"Les trois tetons,"* meaning "the three breasts." Later discovering that these were surrounded by numerous smaller peaks, the erstwhile Frenchmen renamed the range *"Les grands tetons."* Grand Teton National Park, officially established in 1929, continues to delight hikers with miles of strenuous trails and steep rock cliffs along the range's eastern face.

ORIENTATION & PRACTICAL INFORMATION

Grand Teton's roads consist of a main loop through the park with side roads coming from Jackson in the south, Dubois in the east, and Yellowstone in the north. There are two entrances to the park, at Moose and Moran Jct. The east side of the main loop, **Route 89,** does not pass through either entrance and offers excellent, free views of the Tetons. All roads in the park are open year-round. Those who elect to enter the park pay an **entrance fee.** ($20 per car, $15 per motorcycle, $10 per pedestrian or bicycle. Pass good for 7 days in Tetons and Yellowstone.)

Permits are required for all **backcountry camping** and are free if reserved in person within 24hr. of the trip. Reservations made more than 24hr. in advance require a $15 service fee. Advance reservations are recommended for backcountry spaces in a mountain canyon or on the shores of a lake, which fill up early in the summer. Requests are accepted by mail from January 1 to May 15; write to Grand Teton National Park, Permits Office, P.O. Drawer 170, Moose, WY 83012. (For more info, contact the **Moose Visitor Center,** ☎739-3309.) After May 15, two-thirds of all backcountry spots are available first come, first served; the staff can help plan routes and find campsites. Wood fires are only permitted within existing fire grates, so check with rangers before singing around the campfire. At high elevations, snow often remains into July, and the weather can become severe or even deadly any time of the year. Severe weather gear is strongly advised.

Public Transit: Grand Teton Lodge Co. (☎800-628-9988) runs in summer from Colter Bay to Jackson Lake Lodge. (7 per day, round trip $7). Shuttles also run to the **Jackson Hole** airport (by reservation only, $30) and **Jackson** (3 per day, $40).

Visitor Info: Visitors Centers and campgrounds have free copies of the *Teewinot,* thc park's newspaper containing info on special programs, hiking, camping, and news. For general info and a visitor's packet, or to make backcountry camping reservations, contact **Park Headquarters** (☎739-3600) or write the **Superintendent,** Grand Teton National Park, P.O. Drawer 170, Moose WY 83012.

Moose Visitors Center and Park Headquarters (☎739-3399), Teton Park Rd., at the southern tip of the park, ½ mi. west of Moose Jct. Open daily early June-early Sept. 8am-7pm; early Sept. to mid-May 8am-5pm.

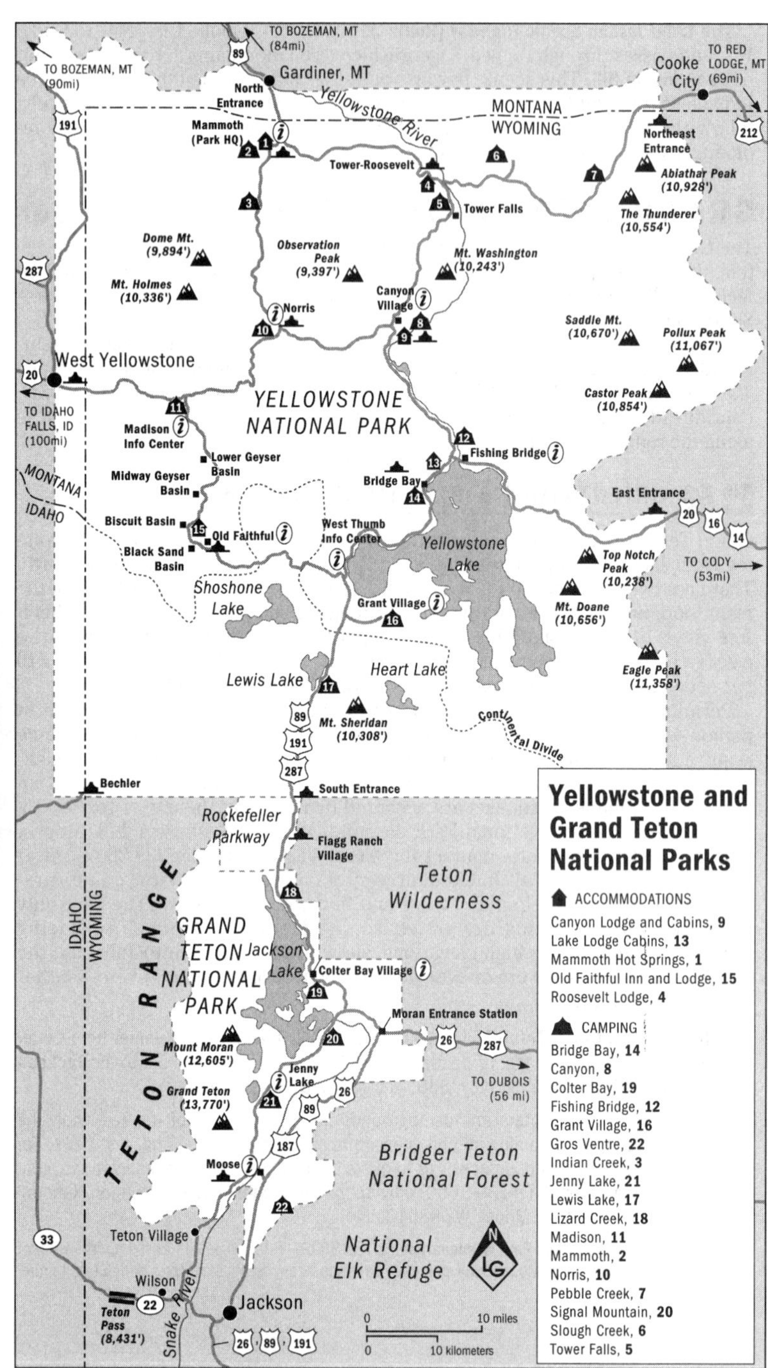
Yellowstone and Grand Teton National Parks
ACCOMMODATIONS
Canyon Lodge and Cabins, 9
Lake Lodge Cabins, 13
Mammoth Hot Springs, 1
Old Faithful Inn and Lodge, 15
Roosevelt Lodge, 4
CAMPING
Bridge Bay, 14
Canyon, 8
Colter Bay, 19
Fishing Bridge, 12
Grant Village, 16
Gros Ventre, 22
Indian Creek, 3
Jenny Lake, 21
Lewis Lake, 17
Lizard Creek, 18
Madison, 11
Mammoth, 2
Norris, 10
Pebble Creek, 7
Signal Mountain, 20
Slough Creek, 6
Tower Falls, 5
TO BOZEMAN, MT (84mi)
TO BOZEMAN, MT (90mi)
TO RED LODGE, MT (69mi)
Cooke City
Gardiner, MT
North Entrance
Yellowstone River
MONTANA
WYOMING
Mammoth (Park HQ)
Northeast Entrance
Tower-Roosevelt
Abiathar Peak (10,928')
Tower Falls
The Thunderer (10,554')
Dome Mt. (9,894')
Observation Peak (9,397')
Mt. Washington (10,243')
Mt. Holmes (10,336')
Canyon Village
Norris
Saddle Mt. (10,670')
Pollux Peak (11,067')
West Yellowstone
Castor Peak (10,854')
TO IDAHO FALLS, ID (100mi)
YELLOWSTONE NATIONAL PARK
Madison Info Center
Fishing Bridge
Lower Geyser Basin
Midway Geyser Basin
Bridge Bay
MONTANA
IDAHO
East Entrance
Biscuit Basin
West Thumb Info Center
Old Faithful
Yellowstone Lake
Black Sand Basin
Top Notch Peak (10,238')
TO CODY (53mi)
Shoshone Lake
Grant Village
Mt. Doane (10,656')
Heart Lake
Lewis Lake
Eagle Peak (11,358')
Mt. Sheridan (10,308')
Continental Divide
Bechler
South Entrance
Rockefeller Parkway
Flagg Ranch Village
Teton Wilderness
TETON RANGE
IDAHO
WYOMING
GRAND TETON NATIONAL PARK
Jackson Lake
Colter Bay Village
Moran Entrance Station
Mount Moran (12,605')
Jenny Lake
TO DUBOIS (56 mi)
Grand Teton (13,770')
Bridger Teton National Forest
Moose
Teton Village
National Elk Refuge
Wilson
Teton Pass (8,431')
Snake River
Jackson
0 10 miles
0 10 kilometers
LG

Jenny Lake Visitors Center (☎739-3392), next to the Jenny Lake Campground in South Jenny Lake. Open daily early June-early Sept. 8am-7pm; Sept. 8am-5pm.

Colter Bay Visitors Center (☎739-3594), on Jackson Lake in the northern part of the park. Houses the Indian Arts Museum. Open daily June-early Sept. 8am-8pm; May and Sept. 8am-5pm.

Info Lines: Weather, ☎739-3611. **Wyoming Highway Info Center,** ☎733-1731. **Wyoming Department of Transportation,** ☎888-996-7623. **Road Report,** ☎739-3614.

Emergency: Sheriff's Office, ☎733-2331. **Park Dispatch,** ☎739-3300.

Medical Services: Grand Teton Medical Clinic, Jackson Lake Lodge (☎543-2514, after hours ☎733-8002). Open daily late May to mid-Oct. 10am-6pm. **St. John's Hospital,** 625 E. Broadway (☎733-3636), in Jackson.

Post Office: In Moose (☎733-3336), across from the Park HQ. Open M-F 9am-1pm and 1:30-5pm, Sa 10:30-11:30am. **Postal code:** 83012 **Area code:** 307.

ACCOMMODATIONS & FOOD

The Grand Teton Lodge Company runs all indoor accommodations in the park. (Reservations ☎800-628-9988; or write **Reservations Manager,** Grand Teton Lodge Co., P.O. Box 240, Moran 83013. Deposits are required.) Most lodges are pricey, but there are two options for affordable, rustic cabins at Colter Bay. **Colter Bay Village Cabins** ❷ maintains 208 quaint log cabins near Jackson Lake. The cabins with shared baths are probably the best deal in the entire Jackson Hole area; book early. Ask the staff about hikes and excursions. (☎543-2828. Open late May-late Sept. Office open 24hr. 2-person cabins with shared bath from $35, 1-room with private bath $70-109; 2-rooms with private bath $115-134.) **Colter Bay Tent Cabins** ❷ provide less shelter from the elements. The cabins are charming but primitive log and canvas shelters with dusty floors, tables, wood-burning stoves, and bunks. Sleeping bags, cots, and blankets are available for rent. (☎800-628-9988. Open early June-early Sept. Restrooms and $3 showers. Tent cabins for 2 $36; each additional person $5.)

The best way to eat in the Tetons is to bring your own food. Non-perishables are available at the **Trading Post Grocery,** in the Dornan's complex in Moose. Their deli also stacks up thick subs for $5-6. (☎733-2415. Open daily May-Sept. 8am-8pm, deli open 8am-7pm; Oct.-Apr. 8am-6pm, deli open 8am-5pm.) Jackson has an **Albertson's** supermarket, 105 Buffalo Way, at the intersection of W. Broadway and Rte. 22. (☎733-5950. Open daily 6am-midnight.) Gather 'round pots of ribs, stew, and mashed potatoes at **Dornan's Chuckwagon** ❷, across from the Trading Post Grocery in Moose, for an authentic old West chuckwagon dinner. (☎733-2415 ext 203. Breakfast $5-7. Lunch $6-9. Chuckwagon dinner $14, ages 6-11 $7. Open mid-June to mid-Sept. daily 7am-9pm.) **John Colter Cafe Court** ❷, in Colter Bay, bakes pizza ($7) and grills burgers and sandwiches. (☎543-2811. Open daily 11am-10pm.)

CAMPING

To stay in the Tetons without emptying your wallet, find a tent and pitch it. The park service maintains five campgrounds, all first come, first served. (☎739-3603 for info. Sites generally open mid-May to late Sept.) All sites have restrooms, cold water, fire rings, dump stations, and picnic tables. The maximum length of stay is 14 days, except for Jenny Lake sites, where it is 7 days. There is a maximum of six people and one vehicle per site; Colter Bay and Gros Ventre accept larger groups.

Jenny Lake has 51 sites that are among the most beautifully developed in the US. Mt. Teewinot towers 6000 ft. above tents pitched at the edge of the lake. Sites usually fill before 8am; get there early. No RVs. Open mid-May to late Sept. Vehicle sites $12, bicycle sites $3 per person. ❶

Lizard Creek, closer to Yellowstone than the Tetons, has 60 spacious, secluded sites along the northern shore of Jackson Lake. The campsites fill up by about 2pm. Open June to early Sept. Vehicle sites $12, bicycle sites $3 per person. ❶

Colter Bay is not exactly a wilderness experience–with its 350 crowded sites, grocery store, laundromat, and two restaurants, it's more accurately described as a suburb. Sites usually fill by 2pm. Open late May to late Sept. Showers $3. Vehicle sites $12; full hookup $31. ❷

Signal Mountain, along the southern shore of Jackson Lake. The 86 sites are roomier and more secluded than at Colter Bay. The campground is usually full by 10am. Open early May to late Oct. Sites $12. ❶

Gros Ventre (☎739-3516; Jan.-May ☎739-3473), along the edge of the Gros Ventre River, close to Jackson, is the biggest campground with 360 sites and 5 group sites. The Tetons, however, are hidden from view by Blacktail Butte. The campsite rarely fills and is the best bet for late arrivals. Open early May to mid-Oct. Sites $12. ❶

OUTDOOR ACTIVITIES

While Yellowstone wows visitors with geysers and mudpots, the Grand Tetons boast some of the most scenic mountains in the US, if not the world. Only 2-3 million years old, the Tetons range between 10,000-13,770 ft. in elevation. The absence of foothills creates spectacular mountain vistas that accentuate the range's steep rock faces. These dramatic rocks draw scores of climbers, but less seasoned hikers can still experience the beauty of the Teton's backcountry.

HIKING

All Visitors Centers provide pamphlets about day hikes and sell numerous guides and maps ($3-10). Rangers also lead informative hikes; check the *Teewinot* or the Visitors Centers for more info. Before hitting the trail or planning extended hikes, be sure to check in at the ranger station; trails at higher elevations may still be snow-covered. During years with heavy snowfall, prime hiking season does not begin until well into July.

The Cascade Canyon Trail (14 mi. round-trip with boat ride, 18 mi. without boat ride; 6-8hr.) begins on the far side of tranquil Jenny Lake and follows Cascade Creek through U-shaped valleys carved by glaciers. The **Hidden Falls Waterfall** is located ½ mi. up; views of Teewinot, Mt. Owen, and Grand Teton are to the south. Hikers with more stamina can continue another ½ mi. upwards towards **Inspiration Point,** but only the lonely can trek 6¾ mi. further to **Lake Solitude** (9035 ft.). Ranger-led trips to Inspiration Point depart from Jenny Lake Visitor Center every morning June-Aug. 8:30am. Hikers can reach the Cascade Canyon Trial by following part of the 6½ mi. trail around Jenny Lake or by taking one of the shuttles offered by **Jenny Lake Boating.** (☎733-2703. Boats leave Jenny Lake Visitors Center every 20min. daily 8am-6pm. $5, ages 7-12 $4; round-trip $7/5.) Trail begins easy to moderate, but becomes more difficult as you progress.

Taggert Lake (3¼ mi. round-trip, 2hr.) passes through the 1000-acre remains of the 1985 Beaver Creek fire, which opportunely removed most of the tree cover for an open view of the Tetons and Taggert lakeshore. This moderate trail also winds through the broad spectrum of plant and wildlife that has developed since the fire.

Hermitage Point (8¾ mi. round-trip, 4hr.), beginning at Colter Bay, is an easy hike along gently rolling meadows and streams. The trail is a unique perspective on Jackson Lake and a prime spot for observing wildlife.

The Amphitheater Lake Trail (9¾ mi. round-trip, 8hr.), originating just south of Jenny Lake at the Lupine Meadows parking lot, is a strenuous trek with 3000 ft. elevation change and a number of switchbacks up to a couple of the park's glacial lakes: **Surprise Lake** and **Amphitheater Lake.** Lupines, the purple flowers visible all along the roads in the park, bloom from June-July along the trail.

Static Peak Divide (15½ mi. round-trip, 10hr.), one of the most challenging trails in the park, is a loop trail up 4020 ft. from the Death Canyon trailhead, 4½ mi. south of Moose Visitors Center. With some of the best vistas in the park, the Death Canyon area is prime for longer 2- to 3-day hikes. Be prepared for ice in this area, even well into July.

The Cunningham Cabin Trail (¾ mi. round-trip, 1hr.) relives the history of cattle ranching in the valley. Trailhead lies 6 mi. south of Moran Jct.

CLIMBING

Two climbing guide companies offer more extreme backcountry adventures, including 4-day packages that let beginners work their way up to the famed Grand Teton. **Jackson Hole Mountain Guides and Climbing School,** 165 N. Glenwood St., in Jackson, has a 1-day beginner course for $90 and a 1-day guided climbing course, $125; more advanced (and more expensive) programs are also available. (☎733-4979 or 800-239-7642. Reservations necessary.) **Exum Mountain Guides** offer similar classes and rates. (☎733-2297. 1-day beginner rock-climbing course $105. Guided 1- to 2-day climbs $110-385. Reservations necessary.)

BOATING, FISHING, & BIKING

Non-motorized **boating** and hand-powered crafts are permitted on a number of lakes; motorboats are allowed only on Jackson, Jenny, and Phelps Lakes. Permits for boating can be obtained at the Moose or Colter Bay Visitors Centers and are good in Yellowstone National Park as well. (Motorized boats $10 per 7 days, $20 annual; non-motorized craft $5/10.) **Grand Tetons Lodge Company** rents boats at Colter Bay and Jenny Lake and has scenic cruises of Jackson Lake, leaving from Colter Bay. (Colter Bay Marina ☎543-2811; Jenny Lake ☎733-2703. 1½hr. cruises $16, ages 3-11 $8. Canoes $10 per hr., motor boats $22 per hr.; 2hr. min. Rentals available daily May-Aug. 8am-4pm.)

Fishing is permitted within the park with a Wyoming license, available at Moose Village Store, Signal Mountain Lodge, Colter Bay Marina, and Flagg Ranch Village. ($10 Wyoming Conservation stamp required with all annual fishing licenses. WY residents $3 per day; $15 per season, ages 14-18 $3 per season. Non-residents $10 per day; $65/15 per season.) The Grand Teton Lodge Company offers float trips on the Snake River. (☎800-628-9988. $40, ages 6-11 $20.) **Mountain biking** is a popular activity on roads in the park, but is strictly forbidden on hiking trails.

Outdoor equipment rentals are all found next to each other in the Dornan's complex. **Adventure Sports,** rents bikes and provides advice on the best trails. (☎733-3307. Open May-Oct. daily 8am-8pm. Front suspension $8 per hr., $25 per day; full suspension $9/28; kayaks and canoes $40 per 24hr. Credit card or deposit required.) **Snake River Angler** has fishing advice and rents rods. (☎733-3699. Open Apr-Oct. daily 8am-8pm. Rods $15-25 per day.) **Moosely Seconds** rents a variety of outdoor equipment. (☎733-7176. Open summer daily 8am-8pm. Climbing shoes $5 per day, $25 per week; crampons $10/50; ice axes $6/30; trekking poles $4/20.)

WINTER ACTIVITIES

In the winter, all hiking trails and the unploughed sections of Teton Park Rd. are open to **cross-country skiers.** Pick up winter info at Moose Visitors Center. Guides lead free **snowshoe hikes** from the Moose Visitors Center. (☎739-3399. Jan.-Mar. Tu-Th 1pm.) **Snowmobiling** is only allowed on the Continental Divide Snowmobile Trail; pick up a $15 permit at Moose Visitors Center and a map and guide at the Jackson Chamber of Commerce. **Grand Teton Park Snowmobile Rental,** near Moran Jct., rents snowmobiles. (☎733-1980 or 800-563-6469. $79 per ½ day, $119 per day; includes clothing, helmet, and boots.) The Colter Bay and Moose parking lots are available for parking in the winter. All **campgrounds** close in winter, but **backcountry snow camping** (only for those who know what they're doing) is allowed with a permit obtained from the Moose Visitors Center (see **backcountry camping** above).

Before making plans, consider that temperatures regularly drop below -25°F. Be sure to carry extreme weather clothing and check with a ranger station for current weather conditions and avalanche danger.

SCENIC DRIVE: CENTENNIAL SCENIC DRIVE

Passing through some of the most beautiful country on earth, this all-day drive is like a vacation unto itself. For 162 mi., the Centennial Scenic Byway passes by the high peaks, roaring whitewater rivers, and broad windswept plains of western Wyoming. The drive is open year-round but may occasionally close due to snow.

The drive begins in the small frontier town of **Dubois,** home of the **National Bighorn Sheep Interpretive Center,** 907 W. Ramshorn St., a fascinating and bizarre museum that educates visitors about the furry creatures. (☎455-3429 or 888-209-2795. Open summer 9am-8pm; winter 8am-5pm. $2, under 12 $0.75; families $5.) Leaving town on Rte. 26, the crumbly breccia of the volcanic Absaroka mountains becomes visible to the north; the 11,920 ft. high towering mountain is **Ramshorn Peak.** Gently rising through a conifer forest, the road eventually reaches **Togwotee Pass,** elevation 9544 ft., 30 mi. west of Dubois.

As the road begins to descend, the famed panorama of the Teton mountain range becomes visible. The highest peak is the Grand Teton (13,770 ft.); the exhibit at the Teton Range Overlook labels each visible peak in the skyline. After entering **Grand Teton National Park** (see p. 783), the road winds through the flat plain of the **Buffalo Fork River,** a striking contrast to the high peaks and mountain forests. This floodplain is the beginning of the wide, long valley known as Jackson Hole (early trappers referred to any high mountain valley as a hole).

Once in the park, the road follows the legendary **Snake River,** renowned for its whitewater rafting and kayaking. Nearing Jackson (see p. 788), the **National Elk Refuge** is visible to the east and is the winter home of 6000-7000 elk. To bypass Jackson, take U.S. 189/191 south. As the route turns east at Hoback Jct., one of the West's most popular whitewater rafting segments, the **Grand Canyon of the Snake,** is just downstream. The road winds through the deep and narrow Hoback Canyon with the boiling Hoback River cutting through. As the Tetons fade out of sight, the **Wind River Range** appears on the horizon, and soon the highest peak in Wyoming, **Gannet Peak** (13,804 ft.), appears against the horizon. The drive ends in the tiny, authentically Western town of **Pinedale.** In Pinedale, the **Museum of the Mountain Man** chronicles the history of the Plains Indians, the fur trade, and the white settlement of western Wyoming. (☎877-686-6266. Open early May-late Sept. daily 10am-5pm; Oct. M-F 10am-noon and 1-3pm. $4, seniors $3, children $2.)

JACKSON ☎307

Jackson Hole, the valley that separates the Teton and Gros Ventre mountain ranges, is renowned for its world-class skiing, but that is not the area's only attraction. In recent years, the small town of Jackson (pop. 5000) has exploded into a cosmopolitan epicenter. Downtown is lined with chic restaurants, faux-Western bars, and expensive lodgings. The area's true beauty, however, can only be appreciated by exploring the nearby Tetons or navigating the winding Snake River.

ORIENTATION & PRACTICAL INFORMATION. Downtown Jackson is centered around the intersection of Broadway and Cache St. and marked by the **Town Square Park.** The majority of shops and restaurants are within a four-block radius of this intersection. South of town, at the intersection with Rte. 22, W. Broadway becomes U.S. 191/89/26. To get to **Teton Village,** take Rte. 22 to Rte. 390 (Teton Village Rd.) just before the town of Wilson. Winding backroads, unpaved at times, connect Teton Village to Moose and the southern entrance of the National Park. North of Jackson, Cache St. turns into Rte. 89, leading directly into the park.

Jackson Hole Express (☎733-1719 or 800-652-9510) runs to the Salt Lake City airport (5½hr., 2 per day, $56) and the Idaho Falls airport (2hr., 2 per day, $35). Reservations are required. **Jackson START** runs buses all around town and between Jackson and Teton Village. (☎733-4521. Daily Mid-May to late-Sept. 6am-10:30pm, free; early Dec. to early Apr. 6am-11pm. In town free, on village roads $1, to Teton Village $2; under 9 free.) **Leisure Sports,** 1075 Rte. 89, has boating and fishing equipment and the best deals on camping and backpacking rentals. (☎733-3040. Open daily summer and winter daily 8am-6pm, in fall and spring 8am-5pm. Tents for 2 $7.50, for 6 $25, sleeping bags $5-8, backpacks $3.50-7.50. Canoes and kayaks $35-45 per day, rafts $65-110 per day.) **Visitor Info: Jackson Hole and Greater Yellowstone Information Center,** 532 N. Cache St. (Open early June to early Sept. daily 8am-7pm; early Sept. -early June M-F 8am-5pm.) **Internet Access: Jackson Library,** 125 Virginian Ln. (☎733-2164. Open M-Th 10am-9pm, F 10am-5:30pm, Sa 10am-5pm, Su 1-5pm.) **Post Office:** 1070 Maple Way, at Powderhorn Ln. (☎733-3650. Open M-F 8:30am-5pm, Sa 10am-1pm.) **Postal Code:** 83002. **Area Code:** 307.

ACCOMMODATIONS. Jackson draws hordes of visitors year-round, making rooms outrageously expensive and hard to find without reservations. **The Hostel X (HI-AYH) ❸,** 12 mi. northwest of Jackson in Teton Village, lets skiers and others stay close to the slopes for cheap. Along with free Internet, the hostel has a lounge with TVs, pool and ping-pong tables, and shelves of puzzles and games. Perks also include laundry facilities, a ski-waxing room, and a convenient location just a close stumble from the Mangy Moose (see **Nightlife,** below). All rooms are private with either four twin beds or one king-size bed. Private bath and maid service are included. (☎733-3415. Open summer and winter. 1-2 people $52; 3-4 $65.) Just one block from Town Square is Jackson's own hostel, **The Bunkhouse ❶,** 215 N. Cache St., in the basement of the Anvil Motel. Besides the most affordable beds in town, the bunkhouse also offers a lounge with HBO and a kitchen with fridge and microwave. (☎733-3668. Showers, coin laundry, and ski storage. Beds $22.) One of the few lodgings in Jackson with rooms under $100 during peak season, **Alpine Motel ❹,** 70 S. Jean, provides clean basic rooms with cable TV, free local calls, and an outdoor pool. (☎739-3200. June-Sept. singles $68; doubles $80. Oct.-May $56/64.)

For those willing to rough it, the primitive campgrounds in Grand Teton National Park and the **Bridger-Teton National Forest** are the cheapest accommodations in the area. **Gros Ventre** campground (see p. 786) is only a 15min. drive north of Jackson on Rte. 89. There are 45 **developed campgrounds ❶** in the Bridger-Teton National Forest, including several along U.S. 26 west of Jackson. (☎739-5500. Most have water, no showers. Sites $5-15.) The publication *The Bridge* is available at the Visitors Center in Jackson; the National Forest offices have additional info. Dispersed **camping ❶** is free within the National Forest; campers must stay at least 200 ft. from water and 100 ft. from roads or trails. Consult with a ranger beforehand, as some areas may be restricted. Showers including towels are available at the Anvil Motel, 215 N. Cache St., for $5.

FOOD. Jackson has dozens of restaurants, but few are suited to the budget traveler. **The Bunnery ❷,** 130 N. Cache St., attracts both locals and tourists for their delicious breakfasts and baked goods, including classic and southwest omelettes and the special O.S.M. (oats, sunflower, and millet) bread. (☎733-5474 or 800-349-0492. Breakfast $3-6. Omelettes $7.50. Sandwiches $6-8. Open daily in summer 7am-9pm; winter 7am-2pm.) Locals flock to **Betty Rock Cafe ❷,** 325 W. Pearl Ave., for lunch, where they grill fresh paninis on homemade focaccia bread ($6-7) and stuff pot pies chock full with goodies ($8). (☎733-0747. Open M-Sa 10am-5pm; June-Aug. M-Sa 5-10pm.) For a homeopathic remedy, or just a healthy bite to eat, the **Harvest Bakery and Cafe ❷,** 130 W. Broadway, is a New Age jack-of-all-trades. (☎733-5418. Smoothies $3-4.50. Fresh pastries $2. Soup and salad $6. Breakfast $5-

6. Open M-Sa 7:30am-7:30pm, Su 9am-4pm; winter M-Sa 8:30am-6pm, Su 9am-4pm.) A popular family restaurant, **Bubba's Bar-B-Que ❸,** 515 W. Broadway, serves generous portions of ribs and sides. (☎733-2288. Lunch specials $6. Spare ribs $9.50. Open daily summer 7am-10pm; winter 7am-9pm.) At **Mountain High Pizza Pie ❸,** 120 W. Broadway, build your own pizza or choose from a large selection of pies. (☎733-3646. Pizza 10 in. $7, 15 in. $13. Subs $6-7. Open daily summer 11am-midnight; winter 11am-10pm.)

FESTIVALS & NIGHTLIFE. When the sun goes down on a long day of skiing, hiking, or rafting, Jackson has bars, concerts, and festivals to suit all tastes. Frontier justice is served at the **Town Square Shootout.** Live reenactments M-Sa at 6:15pm during the summer months in Jackson's Town Square. (☎733-3316. Free.) Catch cowboy fever at the **JH Rodeo,** held at the fairgrounds, at Snow King Ave. and Flat Creek Dr. (☎733-2805. June to early Sept. W and Sa 8pm. $10, ages 4-12 $8; reserved tickets $13; families $32.) Over Memorial Day weekend, the town's population explodes as tourists, locals, and nearby Native American tribes pour in for the free dances and parades of **Old West Days;** for info call the Chamber of Commerce (☎733-3316; www.jacksonholechamber.com). World-class musicians roll into Teton Village each summer for the **Grand Teton Music Festival.** (☎733-3050, ticket office ☎733-1128; www.gtmf.org. Early July-late Aug. Festival orchestra concerts F-Sa 8pm. $35. Spotlight concerts Th 8pm. $26. Chamber music concerts Tu-W 8pm. $16. All student (ages 6-18) tickets $5. Adult half-price seats Th and F nights.) In mid-September, the **Jackson Hole Fall Arts Festival** (☎733-3316) showcases artists, musicians, and dancers in a week-long party.

Head straight from the slopes to **The Mangy Moose,** in Teton Village at the base of Jackson Hole Ski Resort, a quintessential après-ski bar. The atmosphere is more sedate during the summer, but in winter, this is the place to be. The entertainment lineup has headlined everyone from Blues Traveler to Dr. Timothy Leary. (☎733-4913, entertainment hotline ☎733-9779. Cover $7-15, big names $20-25. Kitchen open daily 5:30-10pm; bar open 11:30am-2am.) Slither on down to the **Snake River Brewery,** 265 S. Millward St., for the award-winning "Zonkers Stout." Pub favorite burgers and brats $6-9. (☎739-2337 or SEX-BEER. Pints $3.50, pitchers $11. Open daily noon-1am; food served until 11pm.) Live music and good beer make the **Stagecoach Bar,** 7 mi. west of Jackson on Rte. 22 in Wilson, a popular nightspot, especially on Thursday Disco Night. (☎733-4407. Live music Su-M. Bar open M-Sa 11am-2am, Su 11am-1am.)

OUTDOOR ACTIVITIES. Jackson puts on a good show, but the feature presentation is the quality of outdoor adventure. World-class skiing and climbing lie within minutes of Jackson, and **whitewater rafting** on the legendary Snake River is an adrenaline rush. **Barker-Ewing,** 45 W. Broadway, provides tours of varying lengths and difficulty levels. (☎733-1000 or 800-448-4202. 8 mi. tour $41-46, ages 6-12 $33-38; 16 mi. tour $72/55; overnight 16 mi. adventure $130/100; 13 mi. scenic trip $35/25.) **Mad River,** 1255 S. Rte. 89, 2 mi. south of Town Sq., offers similar trips with a promise of "small boats, big action." (☎733-6203 or 800-458-7238. 8 mi. trip $41, under 13 $31.)

During winter months, skiing enthusiasts flock to Jackson to experience pure Wyoming powder. **Jackson Hole Mountain Resort,** 12 mi. north of Jackson in Teton Village, has some of the best runs in the US, including the jaw-droppingly steep Corbet's Couloir. (☎733-2292. Open early Dec. - Apr. Lift tickets $62, ages 15-21 $48, seniors and under 14 $31.) Even after the snow melts, the **aerial tram** whisks tourists to the top of Rendezvous Mountain (elevation 10,450 ft.) for a view of the valley. (☎739-2753. Open late May - late Sept. daily 9am-5pm. $17, seniors over 65 $14, ages 6-12

$6.) Mountain bike rentals also available atop Rendezvous. (☎739-2753. Front suspension $19 per half day, $29 per day. Full suspension $25/39. Located in the town of Jackson, **Snow King** presents less expensive and more relaxed skiing. (☎733-5200. Lift tickets: half-day $25, full-day $35, night $15; under 15 and over 60 $15/25/10. $17 for 2hr.) Snow King also has summer rides to the summit for views of the Tetons. ($8 round-trip.) Jackson Hole is a prime locale for **cross-country skiing. Skinny Skis,** 65 W. Delorney, in downtown Jackson, points nordics in the right direction. (☎733-6094. Open 9am-8pm. Rentals with skis, boots, and poles half-day $10; full-day $15.)

CHEYENNE ☎307

"Cheyenne," the name of the Native American tribe that originally inhabited the region, was considered a prime candidate for the name of the whole Wyoming Territory. The moniker was struck down by notoriously priggish Senator Sherman, who pointed out that the pronunciation of Cheyenne closely resembled that of the French word *chienne*, meaning "bitch." Once one of the fastest-growing frontier towns, Cheyenne may have slowed down a bit, but its historical downtown area still exhibits traditional Western charm, complete with simulated gunfights.

PRACTICAL INFORMATION. Greyhound, 222 Deming Dr. (☎634-7744; open 24hr.), off I-80, makes trips to: Chicago (19hr., 3 per day, $135); Denver (3-5hr., 5 per day, $19); Laramie (1hr., 3 per day, $13); Rock Springs (5hr., 3 per day, $55); Salt Lake City (8hr., 3 per day, $74). **Powder River Transportation** (☎634-7744), in the Greyhound terminal, honors Greyhound passes and sends buses daily to: Billings (11½hr., 2 per day, $79); Casper (4hr., 2 per day, $37); Rapid City (10hr., 1 per day, $74). For local travel, flag down one of the shuttle buses provided by the **Cheyenne Transit Program.** (☎637-6253. Buses run M-F 6am-7pm. $1, Students $0.75, 4-6pm $0.50.) **Visitors Info: Cheyenne Area Convention and Visitors Bureau,** 15th and Capitol Ave. in the Cheyenne Depot. (☎778-3133 or 800-426-5009; www.cheyenne.org. Open May-Sept. M-F 8am-6pm, Sa 9am-5pm, Su 11am-5pm; Oct.-Apr. M-F 8am-5pm.) **Hotlines: Domestic Violence and Sexual Assault Line,** ☎637-7233. 24hr. **Internet Access: Laramie County Public Library,** 2800 Central Ave., has 30min. first come, first served slots available. (☎634-3561. Open mid-May to mid-Sept. M-Th 10am-9pm, F-Sa 10am-6pm, mid-Sept. to mid-May also Su 1-5pm.) **Post Office:** 4800 Converse Ave. (☎800-275-8777. Open M-F 7:30am-5:30pm, Sa 7am-1pm.) **Postal Code:** 82009. **Area Code:** 307.

ACCOMMODATIONS. As long as your visit doesn't coincide with **Frontier Days,** the last full week of July during which rates skyrocket and vacancies disappear, it's easy to land a cheap room here among the plains and pioneers. Budget motels line Lincolnway (16th St./U.S. 30). The **Ranger Motel ❷,** 909 W. 16th St., has comfortable modern rooms each with cable TV, microwave, and fridge. (☎634-7995. Singles from $30.) Sleep among the bison, horses, and singing cowboys in the original bunkhouses at the **Terry Bison Ranch ❷,** 51 I-25 Service Rd. E, 5 mi. south of Cheyenne. A fishing lake and Wyoming's first cellar are also on site. The ranch offers bison tours, horseback riding, and even stables to board your own horse. (☎634-4171. Private rooms with shared bath $38; cabins $79.) Located right in the middle of downtown, the aging **Pioneer Hotel ❶,** 208 W. 17th St., provides the cheapest lodgings in town. (☎634-3010. Cable TV. Singles with shared bath $18.) **Curt Gowdy State Park ❶,** 1319 Hynds Lodge Rd., 24 mi. west of Cheyenne on Happy Jack Rd. (Rte. 210) provides year-round camping centered around two lakes with excellent fishing, and also offers horseback riding (bring your own horse) and archery. (☎632-7946. Sites $12.)

FOOD. Cheyenne has only a smattering of non-chain restaurants with reasonably priced cuisine. The walls at the popular **Sanford's Grub and Pub ❷,** 115 E. 17th St., are littered with every type of kitschy decor imaginable. The extensive menu includes everything from burgers ($5-7) and pasta ($8-10) to gizzards ($5) and crawfish jambalaya ($13). Fifty-five beers on tap, 99 bottles of beer on the wall, and 132 different liquors. While waiting for food, check out the game room downstairs. (☎634-3381. Open M-Sa 11am-midnight, Su 11am-10pm.) Psychedelic mobiles hang from the ceiling and glitter glue quotes mark the pastel walls at **Zen's Bistro ❷,** 2606 E. Lincolnway, where you'll find a healthy selection of salads (with names like the Zeppelin and Joplin) and sandwiches ($6) as well as a full espresso and smoothie bar. Sip your tea in the garden room, or take it to the back where live music, poetry readings, and local art exhibits are staged. (☎635-1889. Open M-F 7am-10pm, Sa 8am-10pm, Su noon-5pm.) **Luxury Diner ❶,** 1401A W. Lincolnway, has a fairly inconspicuous sign, but a far more obvious railroad motif. Shaped like a red caboose, Luxury serves up hearty classic breakfast platters ($3-5) all day with names like the "Engineer" and "Boxcar." (☎638-8971. Open daily 6am-4pm.) For a dirt-cheap breakfast or lunch, the **Driftwood Cafe ❶,** 200 E. 18th St. at Warren St., has a mom-and-pop atmosphere that complements the homestyle cooking. (☎634-5304. Burgers $3-6. Cinnamon rolls $1.45. Slice of pie $2. Open M-F 7am-3pm.)

SIGHTS & NIGHTLIFE. During the last week of July, make every effort to attend the one-of-a-kind **Cheyenne Frontier Days,** a 10-day festival of non-stop Western hoopla appropriately dubbed the "Daddy of 'Em All." The town doubles in size to see the world's largest outdoor rodeo competition and partake of the free pancake breakfasts, parades, big-name country music concerts, and square dancing. (☎778-7222 or 800-227-6336. July 23-Aug.1, 2004. Rodeo $10-22.) During June and July, a "gunfight is always possible," as the entertaining **Cheyenne Gunslingers,** W. 16th and Carey, shoot each other in a not altogether convincing display of undead rancor. (☎653-1028. M-F 6pm, Sa high noon.) Take a free **S & V Carriage Ride** through historic downtown Cheyenne. Boarding at 16th and Capitol Ave. (☎634-0167. Rides M, Tu, F-Su noon-6pm.) The **Wyoming State Capitol Building,** at the base of Capitol Ave. on 24th St., has beautiful stained glass windows and a gorgeous rotunda under the gold-leaf dome; self-guide brochures are available. (☎777-7220. Open M-F 8:30am-4:30pm. Free.) The **Old West Museum,** 4610 N. Carey Ave., in Frontier Park, houses a collection of Western memorabilia, including the third largest carriage collection in the nation. Their most recent addition is a tribute to the legendary Cheyenne Frontier Days. (☎778-7290. Open summer M-F 8:30am-5:30pm, Sa-Su 9am-5pm; winter M-F 9am-5pm, Sa-Su 10am-5pm. $5, under 12 free.) **Vedauwoo Recreation Area,** 28 mi. west of Cheyenne on Happy Jack Rd. (Rte. 210), consists of a collection of oddly jumbled rocks eroded into seemingly impossible shapes by wind and weather. From the Arapaho word meaning "earthborn spirits," Vedauwoo was once considered a sacred place where men went on vision quests; today, rock climbers worship the towering granite formations. Vedauwoo also provides an excellent backdrop for hiking, picnics, and biking. (☎745-2300.)

At **The Outlaw Saloon,** 3839 E. Lincolnway, live country music pours out onto the dance floor inside and leaks out to the patio, where there's always a good game of sand volleyball to be played. Free dance lessons Tu and Th 7:30-8:30pm. Happy Hour with free food M-F 5-7pm. (☎635-7552. Live music M-Sa 8:30pm-1:45am. Open M-Sa 2pm-2am; Su noon-10pm.) Twang with the locals at the popular **Cowboy Restaurant and Bar,** 312 S. Greeley Hwy., and test your skill as a cowboy on the mechanical bull ($5 per ride). The live music and large dance floor always draw a crowd. (☎637-3800. Live music Tu-Sa 9pm-1:30am. Open M-Sa 11am-2am, Su noon-

2am.) Shoot pool upstairs with DJ "Tonto" spinning weeknights at the **Crown Bar,** or descend below for techno alternative dance at the **Crown Underground,** 222 W. 16th St. at the corner of Carey St. (☎778-9202. Bar open M-Sa 11am-2am, Su 11am-10pm. Food until 1am. Dancing Th-Sa 9pm-2am.)

THE SNOWY RANGE ☎307

Local residents call the forested granite mountains to the east of the Platte Valley the Snowy Mountain Range because snow falls nearly year-round on the higher peaks. Even when the snow melts, quartz outcroppings reflect the sun, creating the illusion of a snowy peak. The Snowy Range is part of the **Medicine Bow National Forest,** spread over much of southeastern Wyoming. Cross-country skiing is popular in the winter; campsites and hiking trails usually don't open until May or June. On the west side of the Snowy Range along Rte. 130, chase the cold away with the geothermal stylings of **Saratoga's hot springs,** at the end of E. Walnut St., behind the public pool. Running between 104° and 120°F, the Hobo Pool's soothing waters are especially popular during the early morning and evening hours. (Free. Open 24hr.) A few feet from the springs, the **North Platte River** offers excellent fishing. Fishing permits ($10) are available at the **Country Store Gas Station** (☎326-5638) on Rte. 130. **Hack's Tackle Outfitters,** 407 N. 1st St., also sells hunting and fishing licenses. The store's knowledgeable owner offers both fishing advice and guided trips. (☎326-9823. Scenic tours $40 per half-day, $90 per day. Fishing trips for 2 $235 per half-day, $350 per day. Canoes $35 per day, rafts $95 per day; $100 per boat deposit required.) At **Snowy Range Ski and Recreation Area,** enjoy 25 downhill trails, cross-country trails, and a snowboard halfpipe. Take Exit 311 off I-80 to Rte. 130 W. (☎745-5750 or 800-462-7669. Open mid-Dec. to Easter. Lift ticket full day $32, half day $25; ages 6-12 and over 60 $18/14.)

From late May to November, the **Snowy Range Scenic Byway (Route 130)** is cleared of snow, and cars can drive 27 mi. through seas of pine trees and around treeless mountains and picture-perfect crystal lakes to elevations of two vertical miles. Early along the byway, the Barber Lake Rd. branches off along noisy Libby Creek and bypasses the entrance to the Snowy Range Ski Area before returning to Rte. 130. At the summit of the byway, the **Libby Flats Observation Point** features a very short wildflower nature walk and an awe-inspiring view of the surrounding land. Before the road begins to descend in earnest, don't miss the pullout for Silver Lake, a gorgeous view of the waters and surrounding area. The challenging 4½ mi. **Medicine Bow Trail** has trailheads at both **Lake Marie** and **Lewis Lake** and climbs through open rocky alpine terrain to **Medicine Bow Peak** (12,013 ft.), the highest point in the forest. All 16 of the park's developed **campgrounds** ❶ are only open summer and have toilets and water, but no hookups or showers. Reservations for some campgrounds are available through the National Recreation Reservation Service. (☎877-444-6777; www.reserveusa.com. Sites $10. Reservation fee $9.) The most popular campgrounds, **Sugarloaf** ❶ and **Brooklyn Lake** ❶, open in July and are reservable. West of the Centennial entrance, **Nash Fork** ❶ is a serene and untrammeled campground with 27 well-shaded sites. A drive up **Kennaday Peak** (10,810 ft.), Rte. 130 to Rte. 100 and 215, at the end of Rte. 215, leads to an impressive view.

Mountain biking is generally prohibited on high country trails. However, biking and driving are permitted on designated trails in the high country and on trails below 10,000 ft. The 7 mi. **Corner Mountain Loop,** just west of Centennial Visitors Center, is an exhilarating roller coaster ride through forests and small meadows. During winter, the mountain biking and hiking trails are used for cross-country skiing and snowmobiling. **Brush Creek Visitors Center** is located at the west entrance. (☎326-5562. Open daily mid-May to Oct. 8am-5pm.) **Centennial Visitors**

Center, 1 mi. west of Centennial, guards the east entrance. (☎742-6023. Open daily 9am-4pm.) Rent cross-country equipment at the **Cross Country Connection,** 222 S. 2nd St., in Laramie. (☎721-2851. Open M-F 10am-6pm, Sa 9am-5pm, Su noon-4pm. $10 per day.) Downhill ski and snowboard rentals can be found at **The Fine Edge,** 1660E N. 4th St. (☎745-4499. Open winter M-Th 8am-6pm, F-Sa 7am-6:30pm, Su 7:30am-5pm; summer M-Th 8am-6pm, F-Sa 8am-6:30pm, Su 10am-5pm. Skis $16 per full-day, children $12. Snowboards $22/17; boots $9. $300 credit card or check deposit required boards.) **Area Code:** 307.

THE SOUTHWEST

The Ancestral Puebloans of the 10th and 11th centuries were the first to discover that the Southwest's arid lands could support an advanced agrarian civilization. Years later, in 1803, the US claimed parts of the Southwest with the Louisiana Purchase. The idealistic hope for a Western "empire of liberty," where Americans could live the virtuous farm life, motivated further expansion and inspired the region's individualist mentality. Today, the Southwest's vastness—from the dramatically colored canvas of Arizona's red rock, scrub brush, and pale sky, to the breathtaking vistas of Utah's mountains—invites contemplation and awe. The area's potential for outdoor adventures is as unparalleled as its kaleidoscopic mix of cultures. True to the land's eccentric spirit, cowboys, New Age spiritualists, Native Americans, Mexican-Americans, government scientists, conservatives, outdoor junkies, and droves of tourists have all called the Southwest home. For more on the region, check out *Let's Go Adventure Guide: Southwest USA 2004*

HIGHLIGHTS OF THE SOUTHWEST

NATIONAL PARKS. Experiencing Utah's "Fab Five" (p. 813) and Arizona's Grand Canyon (p. 821) is nothing short of a spiritual revelation.

SKIING. In a region famous for its blistering sun, the sublime slopes (p. 807) near Salt Lake City, UT boast some of the plushest powder in the world.

LAS VEGAS. Drop some slots and throw the bones: Lady Luck is waiting for you, dice in hand, in Sin City (p. 795).

MEXICAN FOOD. You can't get away from it, and in the colorful eateries of New Mexico's Albuquerque (p. 861) and Santa Fe (p. 852), you won't want to.

NEVADA

The deserts of Nevada's Great Basin stretch for hundreds of miles across land that rejects all but the most hardy forms of life. At the few outposts of human habitation, prostitution and gambling mark the state as a purveyor of loose, Wild West morality. Beyond patches of shimmering lights, sin, and showtunes, Nevada is barren and dusty, but this hasn't kept it from becoming the US's fastest growing state. Nevada exemplifies America at its most excessive and contradictory.

PRACTICAL INFORMATION

Capital: Carson City.

Visitor Info: Nevada Commission on Tourism, Capitol Complex, Carson City 89701 (☎800-638-2328; line staffed 24hr.). **Nevada Division of State Parks,** 1300 S. Curry St., Carson City 89703-5202 (☎702-687-4384). Open M-F 8am-5pm.

Postal Abbreviation: NV. **Sales Tax:** 6.75-7%; 9% room tax in some counties.

LAS VEGAS ☎702

Las Vegas is a shimmering tribute to excess, an oasis of vice and greed, and one very, very good time. Nowhere else in America do so many shed inhibitions and indulge otherwise dormant appetites. The mega-casinos that dominate Vegas are

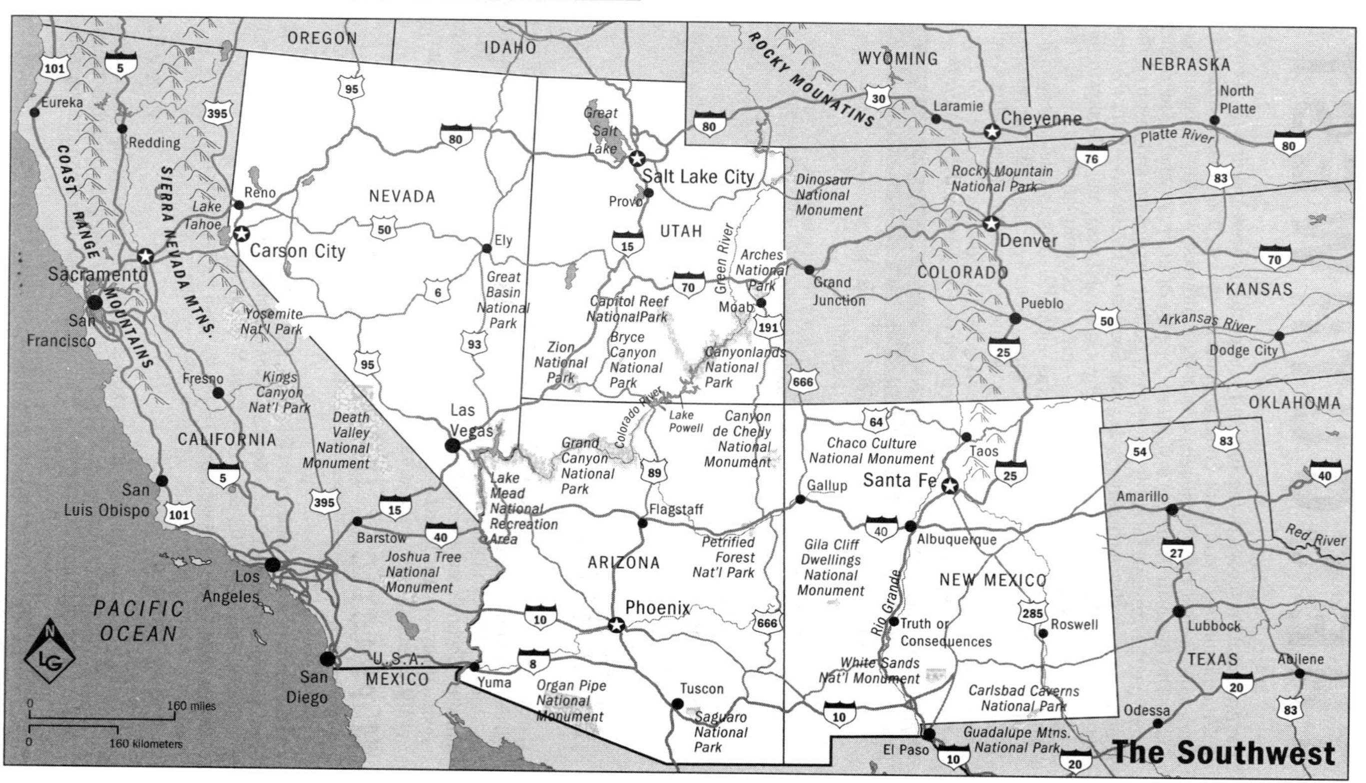
The Southwest
OREGON
IDAHO
WYOMING
NEBRASKA
ROCKY MOUNATINS
North Platte
Platte River
Laramie
Cheyenne
Rocky Mountain National Park
Denver
COLORADO
Pueblo
Grand Junction
Dinosaur National Monument
KANSAS
Arkansas River
Dodge City
OKLAHOMA
Red River
Amarillo
Lubbock
TEXAS
Abilene
Odessa
Eureka
Redding
COAST RANGE MOUNTAINS
SIERRA NEVADA MTNS.
Sacramento
San Francisco
Lake Tahoe
Reno
Carson City
NEVADA
Ely
Great Basin National Park
Yosemite Nat'l Park
Fresno
Kings Canyon Nat'l Park
Death Valley National Monument
Las Vegas
CALIFORNIA
San Luis Obispo
Barstow
Joshua Tree National Monument
Los Angeles
PACIFIC OCEAN
San Diego
U.S.A.
MEXICO
Yuma
Organ Pipe National Monument
Great Salt Lake
Salt Lake City
Provo
UTAH
Green River
Arches National Park
Moab
Capitol Reef NationalPark
Bryce Canyon National Park
Zion National Park
Canyonlands National Park
Colorado River
Lake Powell
Canyon de Chelly National Monument
Grand Canyon National Park
Lake Mead National Recreation Area
Flagstaff
ARIZONA
Petrified Forest Nat'l Park
Phoenix
Tuscon
Saguaro National Park
Chaco Culture National Monument
Taos
Santa Fe
Gallup
Albuquerque
Gila Cliff Dwellings National Monument
NEW MEXICO
Rio Grande
Truth or Consequences
Roswell
White Sands Nat'l Monument
Carlsbad Caverns National Park
Guadalupe Mtns. National Park
El Paso
101
5
395
95
80
30
76
83
50
15
70
6
93
191
25
666
64
54
40
89
27
10
8
285
20
N
LG
0
160 miles
0
160 kilometers

stupendously successful at snatching dollars, but the entertainment is outstanding and cheap deals are everywhere. Just remember that for every winner, there's always a loser—a broken heart and a busted wallet for every light in Vegas.

TRANSPORTATION

Airport: McCarran International (☎261-5743), at the southwestern end of the Strip. Main terminal on Paradise Rd. Shuttles to the Strip (one-way $4-5) and downtown (one-way $5.50); taxi $13-14.

Buses: Greyhound, 200 S. Main St. (☎384-9561 or 800-231-2222), downtown. To **L.A.** (5-7hr., 22 per day, $38) and **San Francisco** (13-16hr., 6 per day, $65).

Public Transportation: Citizens Area Transit (CAT; ☎228-7433). Bus #301 serves downtown and the Strip 24hr.; buses #108 and 109 serve the airport. All buses wheelchair-accessible. Buses run daily 5:30-1:30am (24hr. on the Strip). Routes on the Strip $2, residential routes $1.25, seniors and ages 6-17 $0.60. For schedules and maps, try the tourist office or the **Downtown Transportation Center,** 300 N. Casino Center Blvd. (☎228-7433). **Las Vegas Strip Trolleys** (☎382-1404) are not strip joints; they cruise the Strip daily 9:30am-1:30am. Trolley fare $1.65 in exact change.

Taxi: Yellow, Checker, Star (☎873-2000).

Car Rental: Sav-Mor Rent-A-Car, 5101 Rent-A-Car Rd. (☎736-1234 or 800-634-6779).

ORIENTATION & PRACTICAL INFORMATION

Driving to Vegas from L.A. is a straight, 300 mi. shot on I-15 N (4½hr.). From Arizona, take I-40 W to Kingman and then U.S. 93 N. Las Vegas has two major casino areas. The **downtown** area, around 2nd and Fremont St., has been converted into a pedestrian promenade. The **Strip,** a collection of mammoth hotel-casinos, lies along **Las Vegas Boulevard.** Parallel to the east side of the Strip and in its shadow is **Paradise Road,** also strewn with casinos. *Some areas of Las Vegas are unsafe. The neighborhoods just north of Stewart St. and west of Main St. in the downtown vicinity merit particular caution.* Despite, or perhaps as a result of, its reputation for debauchery, Las Vegas has a **curfew.** Those under 18 are not allowed unaccompanied in most public places Sunday through Thursday 10pm-5am and Friday through Saturday midnight-5am. On the Strip no one under 18 is allowed unless accompanied by an adult Monday to Friday 9pm-5am and weekends 6pm-5am. The drinking and gambling age is 21.

Visitor Info: Las Vegas Convention and Visitor Authority, 3150 Paradise Rd. (☎892-0711), 4 blocks from the Strip in the big pink convention center by the Hilton. Info on headliners, conventions, shows, hotels, and buffets. Open M-F 8am-5pm.

Marriage: Marriage License Bureau, 200 S. 3rd St. (☎455-4416), in the courthouse. 18+ or 16+ with parental consent. Licenses $55; cash only. No waiting period or blood test required. Open Su-Th 8am-midnight, F-Sa 24hr.

Divorce: Must be a Nevada resident for at least 6 weeks. $150 service fee. Permits available at the courthouse M-F 8am-5pm.

24hr. Crisis Lines: Compulsive Gamblers Hotline, ☎800-567-8238. **Gamblers Anonymous,** ☎385-7732. **Rape Crisis Center Hotline,** ☎366-1640. **Suicide Prevention** ☎731-2990 or 800-885-4673.

Post Office: 4975 Swenson St. (☎736-7649), near the Strip. Open M-F 8:30am-5pm. **Postal Code:** 89119. **Area Code:** 702.

ACCOMMODATIONS

Even though Vegas has over 100,000 rooms, many hotels are fully booked on weekends. Rates fluctuate greatly; a $30 room during a slow period can cost hundreds during a convention weekend. Use the prices below as a general guide. Check free, readily available publications like *What's On In Las Vegas*, *Today in Las Vegas*, and *24/7* for discounts, info, and schedules of events. If you get stuck, call the **Room Reservations Hotline** (☎800-332-5333) or go to a tourist office.

Strip hotels are at the center of the action, but their inexpensive rooms sell out quickly. More hotels cluster around Sahara Rd. and S. Las Vegas Blvd. Motels line **Fremont Street,** though this area is a little rougher; it is best to stay in one of the casinos in the **Fremont Street Experience.** Inexpensive motels are also along the southern stretch of the Strip, across from the ritzy **Mandalay Bay.** The 9% state hotel tax is not included in the room rates listed below.

San Remo, 115 E. Tropicana Ave. (☎800-522-7366). Just off the Strip, this is a smaller, friendlier version of the major casinos, without the gimmicks, crowds, and high prices. Live entertainment every night, featuring the "Showgirls of Magic" ($39). Rooms may dip to $32 during slow periods, but are usually Su-Th $42, F-Sa $70. ❸

Silverton, 3333 Blue Diamond Rd. (800-588-7711; www.silverton-casino.com). Cheaper because it's off the Strip (4 mi. south on I-15), this mining town-themed gambling den offers clean and updated accommodations, a relief from the tired and worn budget hotels in the area. Free Las Vegas Blvd. shuttle until 10pm. Singles Su-Th $35, F-Sa $69. Beyond 2 adults, additional person $10. RV hook-ups $24-28. ❸

Whiskey Pete's (☎800-367-7383), in Primm Valley, NV, 45min. south of Vegas on I-15, just before the California stateline. Whiskey Pete's is the cheapest of 3 Western-themed casinos right in the middle of the desert. Cheap as fool's gold and across the street from Desperado, the wildest roller-coaster in Nevada ($6). Beware young guns; you must be 21 to rent a room. Su-Th $19, F-Sa $50; prices vary with availability. ❷

USAHostels Las Vegas, 1322 Fremont St. (☎800-550-8958 or 385-1150; www.usahostels.com). A funky, fun place to stay with friendly staff, but far from the Strip and in an unattractive neighborhood. Rooms are sparse but clean. Pool, jacuzzi, laundry, kitchen, and billiard room. Shared bathrooms. Offers free pickup from Greyhound station 10am-10pm. Dorms Su-Th $14-19, F-Sa $17-23; suites $40-42/49-51. Must have international passport, proof of international travel, or student ID. ❷

Goldstrike, 1 Main St. (☎800-634-1359), in Jean, NV, 20min. from the Strip on I-15, exit 12. A genuine Vegas experience at cut-rate prices. Inexpensive restaurants (prime rib $7, dinner buffet $7.50), loose slots, and low-limit tables. Making a reservation may net cheaper prices. Rooms Su-Th $20-30, F $40, Sa $50. Additional person $3. ❸

FOOD

Sloshed and insatiable gamblers gorge themselves day and night at Vegas' gigantic buffets; for the bottomless appetite, it's hard to name a better value. Beyond the buffets, Vegas has some of the best (most expensive) restaurants in the world.

Le Village Buffet, 3655 Las Vegas Blvd. (☎946-7000). French cooking without the French portions. Set in a recreated French Alps village, the Le Village buffet, crammed with crab legs, salmon, prime rib, veal, and crepes, is more than worth its higher price. Restrain yourself during the main course; the dessert will be worth it. Breakfast $13, lunch $17, dinner $22. Open daily 7am-10pm. Su brunch 11:30am-4:30pm. ❸

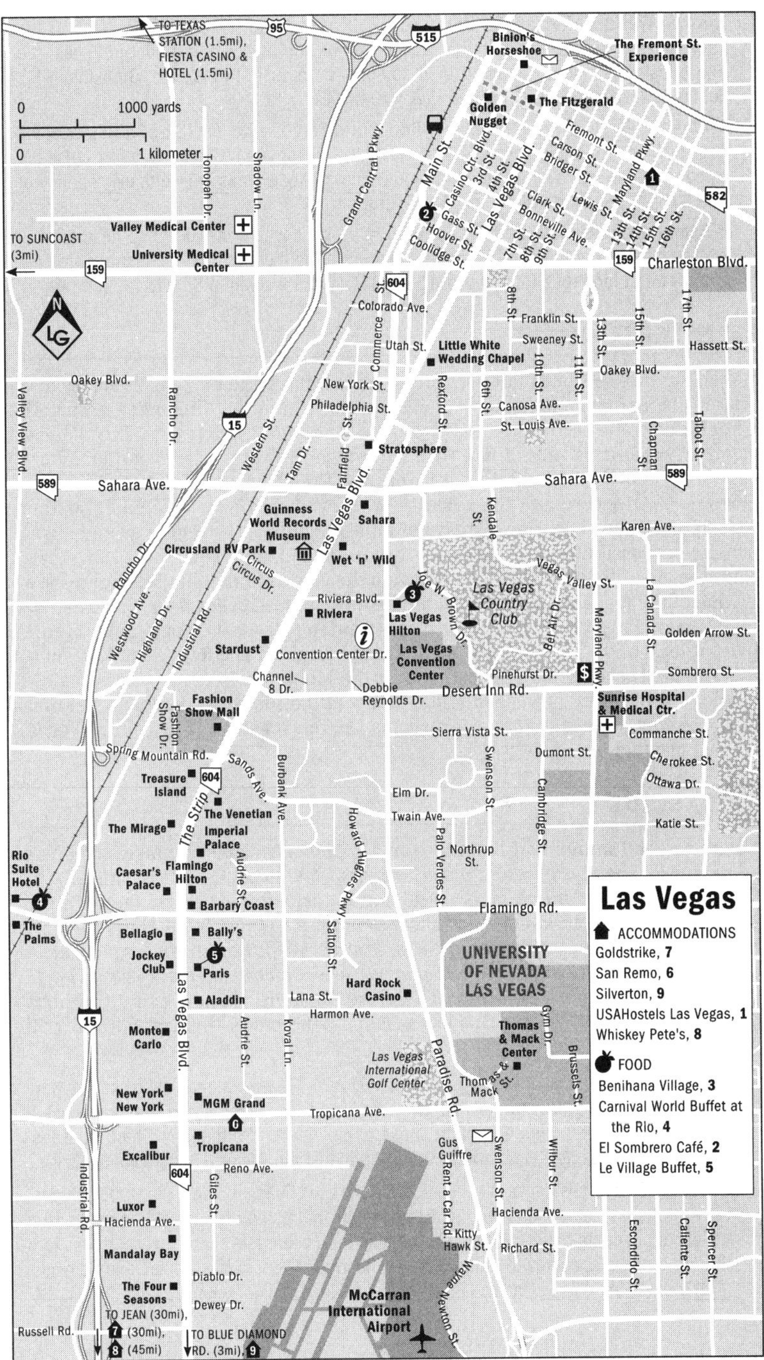
Las Vegas
ACCOMMODATIONS
Goldstrike, 7
San Remo, 6
Silverton, 9
USAHostels Las Vegas, 1
Whiskey Pete's, 8
FOOD
Benihana Village, 3
Carnival World Buffet at the Rio, 4
El Sombrero Café, 2
Le Village Buffet, 5
0 1000 yards
0 1 kilometer
TO TEXAS STATION (1.5mi), FIESTA CASINO & HOTEL (1.5mi)
TO SUNCOAST (3mi)
TO JEAN (30mi), 7 (30mi), 8 (45mi)
TO BLUE DIAMOND RD. (3mi), 9
95
515
582
159
604
15
589
Binion's Horseshoe
The Fremont St. Experience
Golden Nugget
The Fitzgerald
Fremont St.
Carson St.
Bridger St.
Lewis St.
Clark St.
Bonneville Ave.
Maryland Pkwy.
13th St.
14th St.
15th St.
16th St.
Main St.
Casino Ctr. Blvd.
3rd St.
4th St.
Las Vegas Blvd.
Gass St.
Hoover St.
Coolidge St.
7th St.
8th St.
9th St.
Charleston Blvd.
Grand Central Pkwy.
Shadow Ln.
Tonopah Dr.
Valley Medical Center
University Medical Center
Colorado Ave.
Commerce St.
Utah St.
Little White Wedding Chapel
Franklin St.
Sweeney St.
10th St.
11th St.
13th St.
15th St.
17th St.
Hassett St.
Oakey Blvd.
Valley View Blvd.
Rancho Dr.
New York St.
Philadelphia St.
Rexford St.
6th St.
Canosa Ave.
St. Louis Ave.
Chapman St.
Talbot St.
Western St.
Tam Dr.
Fairfield St.
Stratosphere
Sahara Ave.
Guinness World Records Museum
Sahara
Kendale St.
Karen Ave.
Circusland RV Park
Wet 'n' Wild
Circus Circus Dr.
Vegas Valley St.
La Canada St.
Riviera Blvd.
Riviera
Joe W. Brown Dr.
Las Vegas Country Club
Las Vegas Hilton
Bel Air Dr.
Maryland Pkwy.
Golden Arrow St.
Westwood Ave.
Highland Dr.
Industrial Rd.
Stardust
Convention Center Dr.
Las Vegas Convention Center
Pinehurst Dr.
Sombrero St.
Channel 8 Dr.
Debbie Reynolds Dr.
Desert Inn Rd.
Sunrise Hospital & Medical Ctr.
Fashion Show Mall
Fashion Show Dr.
Sierra Vista St.
Commanche St.
Spring Mountain Rd.
Sands Ave.
Burbank Ave.
Swenson St.
Dumont St.
Cherokee St.
Treasure Island
Ottawa Dr.
Elm Dr.
Cambridge St.
The Venetian
Twain Ave.
Katie St.
The Mirage
The Strip
Imperial Palace
Howard Hughes Pkwy.
Palo Verdes St.
Northrup St.
Rio Suite Hotel
Caesar's Palace
Flamingo Hilton
Audrie St.
Barbary Coast
Flamingo Rd.
The Palms
Bellagio
Bally's
Salton St.
UNIVERSITY OF NEVADA LAS VEGAS
Jockey Club
Paris
Hard Rock Casino
Aladdin
Lana St.
Harmon Ave.
Gym Dr.
Monte Carlo
Audrie St.
Koval Ln.
Thomas & Mack Center
Brussels St.
Las Vegas International Golf Center
Paradise Rd.
Thomas & Mack St.
New York New York
MGM Grand
Tropicana Ave.
Excalibur
Tropicana
Gus Guiffre
Swenson St.
Wilbur St.
Reno Ave.
Industrial Rd.
Giles St.
Rent a Car Rd.
Luxor
Hacienda Ave.
Escondido St.
Caliente St.
Spencer St.
Mandalay Bay
Kitty Hawk St.
Richard St.
Wayne Newton St.
Diablo Dr.
The Four Seasons
Dewey Dr.
McCarran International Airport
Russell Rd.

Carnival World Buffet at the Rio, 3700 W. Flamingo Rd. (☎252-7777). One of the great Vegas feasts. Perhaps the most well-known and highly-rated buffet in Vegas, the Rio boasts 12 uniquely themed food stations, from sushi to Mexican. Breakfast $10, lunch $12, dinner $17. Open daily 7am-10pm. ❸

Benihana Village at the Las Vegas Hilton, 3000 Paradise Rd. (☎732-5755). Indoor village with koi pond, rain, bonzais, and multi-level dining area. Charismatic hibachi chefs slice and sear your 5-course meal as you watch. Filling entrees are worth every penny of the $16-30 price tag. Open daily 5:30-10:30pm. ❹

El Sombrero Cafe, 807 S. Main St. (☎382-9234), is where the locals go for authentic Mexican food. The portions are huge and the staff is friendly. Their combination plates offer a lot of food for a little money ($8-11). Lunch $7. Open M-Sa 11am-10pm. ❷

ENTERTAINMENT

A made-in-the-USA phenomenon, the **Vegas spectacular** features marvels such as waterfalls, explosions, fireworks, and casts of hundreds (including animals). Check out some of the free show guides—*Showbiz, Today in Las Vegas, What's On*—for listings. Some "production shows" are topless and many are tasteless, but there are a few exceptions: the **Cirque de Soleil's** creative shows—*O*, *Mystere* and the brand-new, racy *Zumanity*—are bank-busting ($88-150) yet awe-inspiring displays of human agility and strength channeled as artistic expression at the Bellagio, Treasure Island, and New York, New York. "Limited view" tickets are discounted, and the view isn't that limited. For a show by one of the musical stars who haunt the city, such as **Celine Dion** (Caesar's Palace), **Gladys Knight** (Flamingo), or **Wayne Newton** (Stardust), you'll have to fork over at least $50. "Magicians of the Century" **Siegfried and Roy** go for $105.50 at the Mirage. **Lance Burton's** (a mainstay at the Monte Carlo) tricks are good, old magic ($55-60), while **Penn and Teller's** show at the Río is far darker. With some of everything, former street performer **The Amazing Jonathan** stages one of Vegas' edgiest productions ($47-58).

CA$INOS

Casinos spend millions of dollars to fulfill guests' escapist fantasies of being somewhere, anywhere, else. "Exact" images of Venice, New York, Rio, Paris, Cairo (complete with Pyramids), and Monte Carlo already thrive on the Strip. Look for casino "funbooks" that allow gamblers to buy $50 in chips for only $15. *Never bring more money than you're prepared to lose cheerfully. Keep your wallet in your front pocket, and beware of thieves trying to nab winnings from jubilants.* There are far more casinos and attractions than can be listed here; use this list as a compendium of the best. Virtually all casinos are open 24hr.

Mandalay Bay, 3950 S. Las Vegas Blvd. (☎632-7777; www.mandalaybay.com). Mandalay Bay does its best to convince New York and L.A. fashionistas they haven't left home. Swank restaurants and clubs make gambling an afterthought. Shark Reef features 15 shark species. Open daily 10am-11pm; last admission 10pm. $15, 5-12 $10.

Bellagio, 3600 S. Las Vegas Blvd. (☎693-7444; www.bellagio.com). The world's largest 5-star hotel houses a gallery of fine art, carefully maintained botanical gardens, and a variety of big-name haute-couture. On the lakefront, water jets shoot several stories into the air during a spectacular aquatic ballet. Shows M-F 3-8pm every30min. and 8pm-midnight every 15min., Sa-Su and holidays noon-8pm every 30min. Free.

Venetian, 3355 S. Las Vegas Blvd. (☎414-1000; www.venetian.com). Singing gondoliers push tourists down the chlorinated "canal" inside this palatial casino, which features the upscale Grand Canal Shoppes. (☎414-4500). Shoppes open Su-Th 10am-11pm, F-Sa 10am-midnight. The **Guggenheim Hermitage Museum** (☎866-484-4849) embodies the "new Vegas," with artwork from Russian and Austrian collections, as well as from the Guggenheim Foundation. Guggenheim open daily 9:30am-8:30pm. $15, students $11, children 6-12 $7.

Caesar's Palace, 3570 S. Las Vegas Blvd. (☎731-7110; www.caesars.com). Busts abound at this Strip trendsetter: some are plaster, others barely concealed by cocktail waitress' low-cut get-ups. The pricey **Forum Shops** (☎893-4800) began the high-end shopping craze, offering fine eateries and animatronic shows. Shops open M-F 10am-11pm, Sa-Su 10am-midnight.

Paris, 3655 S. Las Vegas Blvd. (☎946-7000; www.parislasvegas.com). The Paris has enough "real" Parisian attractions, including an Eiffel Tower with a view of the Strip and near-scale Arc de Triomphe, to please any French post-modernist.

NEAR LAS VEGAS

HOOVER DAM

On Hwy. 93, 30 mi. from Las Vegas, the Hoover Dam, built to subdue the Colorado River and provide water and energy to the Southwest, took 5000 men 5 years of 7-day weeks to construct. When their sweat dried, over 6.6 million tons of concrete had been crafted into a 726 ft. colossus that now shelters precious agricultural land, pumps big voltage to Vegas and L.A., and furnishes jet-skiers with azure waters to churn. The excellent tours and interpretive center explore the dam's history. This is a prize artifact from America's "think-big" era of ambitious landscaping and culture-transforming public works projects. The **Visitors Center** leads **tours** to the generators at the structure's bottom. (☎294-3510. Open daily 9am-5pm. Self-guided tours with short presentation $10, seniors $8, ages 6-16 $4.)

LAKE MEAD

Take Lake Mead Blvd./Hwy. 147 off I-15 east 16 mi. to Northshore Rd. When the Colorado River met the Hoover Dam, Lake Mead was formed. This 100 mi. long behemoth is the largest reservoir in the US and the country's first national recreation area. First-time visitors to the lake will benefit from a trip to the **Alan Bible Visitors Center,** 4 mi. east of Boulder City, for its helpful staff and informative brochures and maps. (☎293-8990; www.nps.gov/lame. Open daily 8:30am-4:30pm. $5 fee to enter the recreation area.) For maps and abundant information about area services, pick up *Desert Lake View* at one of the several ranger stations dotting Lake Mead's shores. For the unprepared, various conessionaires rent boats and more along the shores. Popular **Boulder Beach,** the departure point for many water-based activities, is accessible from Lakeshore Dr. at the south end of the lake.

RENO ☎775

Reno, with its decadent casinos cradled by snowcapped mountains, captures both the natural splendor and capitalist frenzy of the West. Acting as the hub of northern Nevada's tourist cluster, including nearby Lake Tahoe and Pyramid Lake, the self-proclaimed "biggest little city in the world" does a decent job of compressing Las Vegas-style gambling, entertainment, and dining into a few city blocks.

PRACTICAL INFORMATION. Amtrak is at 135 E. Commercial Row. (☎800-872-7245. Open daily 8:30am-4:45pm.) **Greyhound,** 155 Stevenson St. (☎800-231-2222), rolls to: Las Vegas (1 per day, $72); Salt Lake City (4 per day, $57-61); and San Francisco (17 per day, $30-33). **Reno-Sparks Convention and Visitors Authority,** 1 E. 1st St., is on the second floor of the Cal-Neva Building. (☎800-367-7366; www.renolaketahoe.com. Open M-F 8am-5pm.) **Post Office:** 50 S. Virginia St., at Mill St. (Open M-F 8:30am-5pm.) **Postal Code:** 89501. **Area Code:** 775.

ACCOMMODATIONS. While weekend prices at casinos are usually high, gambler's specials, weekday rates, and winter discounts mean great deals. Prices fluctuate, so call ahead. **Eldorado ❸,** 345 N. Virginia St. (☎800-648-5966 or 786-5700), and **Silver Legacy ❸,** 407 N. Virginia St. (☎800-687-7733 or 325-7401), offer good deals, including central locations and massive facilities. (Rates can get as low as $32, but generally hover around $60 for a single.) Be advised—heterosexual prostitution is legal in most of Nevada (though not in Reno itself), and certain motels are therefore cheap but lacking in wholesomeness. Southwestern downtown has the cheapest lodging. *Add a 12% hotel tax to all prices listed.*

Harrah's Reno ❸, 219 N. Center St., leaves little to be desired, boasting a central location, seven restaurants, pool, health club, and a 65,000 sq. ft. casino. (☎800-247-7247. Singles/doubles M-Th from $49, F-Su $89.) Off Hwy. 395 at the Glendale Exit, the **Reno Hilton ❸,** 2500 E. 2nd St., has over 2000 elegant rooms, a 9000-seat outdoor amphitheater, a driving range, 50-lane bowling center, a health club, and a shopping mall. If Harrah's isn't big enough, the Hilton's casino is 115,000 sq. ft. (☎800-648-5080. Rooms $35-149.) For some of the lowest rates in town, the **Sundowner ❷** is a working man's casino. No frills here, but the rooms are clean and come with everything you'd expect, such as A/C, telephones, and a pool and jacuzzi. (☎800-648-5490. Rooms Su-Th from $26, F $50, Sa $70.)

FOOD. The cost of eating in Reno is low, but the food quality doesn't have to be. In order to entice gamblers and prevent them from wandering in search of food, casinos offer a wide range of buffets and $0.99 breakfasts. Buffet fare, admittedly, can be greasy and overcooked, and Reno's other inexpensive eateries offer better food. The large Basque population cooks up spicy, hearty cuisine. **The Pneumatic Diner ❷,** 501 W. 1st St. in the Truckee River Lodge, is a funky, subversive melting pot at odds with Reno's homogenous wall o' casinos. (☎786-8888, ext. 106. Open M-F 11am-11pm, Sa 9am-11pm, Su 7am-11pm.) Those who seek refuge from the seemingly inescapable steak and burritos will enjoy the Thai flavors of **Bangkok Cuisine ❷,** 55 Mt. Rose St. (☎322-0299. Open M-Sa 11am-11pm.) In the Eldorado Hotel at 345 N. Virginia St., **La Strada ❷** has won numerous accolades for its dazzling northern Italian cuisine. (☎348-9297. Open daily 5-10pm.)

ENTERTAINMENT. Almost all casinos offer live nighttime entertainment, but many shows are not worth their sky-high admission prices. **Harrah's,** however, is an exception, carrying on a dying tradition with its **Night on the Town** in Sammy's Showroom. Starting at $39, Harrah's offers dinner and a performance by one of its cadre of critically acclaimed entertainers. At **Circus Circus,** 500 N. Sierra (☎329-0711), a small circus performs "big top" shows above the casino every 30min. For more entertainment listings and casino info, check out the free *This Week* or *Best Bets* magazines. *The Reno News & Review*, published every Thursday, provides an alternative look at weekly happenings and events off the casino path.

NEAR RENO: PYRAMID LAKE

Thirty miles north of Reno on Rte. 445, on the Paiute Indian Reservation, lies emerald green Pyramid Lake, one of the most heart-achingly beautiful bodies of water in the US. The pristine tides of Pyramid Lake are set against the backdrop of a barren desert, making it a soothing respite from Reno's neon, and a fantastic spot for fishing and boating. **Camping ❶** is allowed anywhere on the lake shore, but only designated areas have toilet facilities. Permits are required for day-use ($6), camping ($9), and fishing ($7) and are available at the **Ranger Station,** 2500 Sutcliffe Dr. (☎476-1155), on the western side of the lake. **Boat rental** (☎476-1156) is available daily at the marina near the Ranger Station; call for reservations.

UTAH

In 1848, persecuted members of the Church of Jesus Christ of Latter-Day Saints (colloquially called Mormons) settled on the land that is now Utah, intending to establish and govern their own theocratic state. President James Buchanan struggled to quash their efforts in 1858, as many others had tried before. The Mormons eventually gave up their dreams of theocracy and their rights to polygamy, and statehood was finally granted on January 4, 1896. Today the state's population is 70% Mormon—a religious presence that creates a haven for family values. Utah's citizens dwell primarily in the 100-mile corridor along I-15, from Ogden to Provo. Outside this area, Utah's natural beauty dominates, intoxicating visitors in a way that Utah's watered-down 3.2% beer cannot. Just east of Salt Lake City, the Wasatch range beckons skiers and bikers. Southern Utah is like no other place on Earth; red canyons, river gorges, and sculpted cliffs attest to nature's creativity.

PRACTICAL INFORMATION

Capital: Salt Lake City.

Visitor Info: Utah Travel Council, 300 N. State St., Salt Lake City 84114 (☎801-538-1030 or 800-200-1160; www.utah.com), across from the capitol building. Distributes the *Utah Vacation Planner's* lists of motels, national parks, and campgrounds, as well as brochures on statewide biking, rafting, and skiing. **Utah Parks and Recreation,** 1594 W. North Temple, Salt Lake City 84116 (☎801-538-7220). Open M-F 8am-5pm.

Controlled Substances: Mormons abstain from "strong drinks" (coffee and tea), nicotine, alcohol, and, of course, illegal drugs. While you probably won't have trouble getting cigarettes or coffee, alcohol is another matter. State liquor stores are sprinkled sparsely about the state. Grocery and convenience stores only sell beer. While most upscale restaurants serve wine, licensing laws can split a room, and drinkers may have to move to the bar for a mixed drink. Law requires that waiters not offer drink menus; diners must request one. Establishments that sell hard alcohol are required to be "members only;" tourists can find a "sponsor"–i.e., an entering patron–or get a short-term membership.

Postal Abbreviation: UT. **Sales Tax:** 5.75-7.75%.

SALT LAKE CITY ☎801

Tired from five gruelling months of travel, Brigham Young looked out across the Great Salt Lake and proclaimed: "This is the place." He believed that in this desolate valley his band of Mormon pioneers had finally found a haven where they could practice their religion freely, away from the persecution they had faced in the East. To this day, Salt Lake City remains dominated by Mormon influence. The Church of Jesus Christ of Latter-Day Saints (LDS) owns the tallest office building downtown and welcomes visitors to Temple Square, the spiritual epicenter of the Mormon religion. Despite its commitment to preserving tradition, Salt Lake is rapidly attracting high-tech firms and droves of outdoor enthusiasts. The city, for all its homogeneity, supports a surprisingly diverse set of communities.

TRANSPORTATION

Airport: Salt Lake City International, 776 N. Terminal Dr. (☎575-2400), 6 mi. west of Temple Sq. UTA buses #50 and 150 run between the terminal and downtown ($1.25). Buses leave hourly M-Sa 7am-11pm, Su 7am-6pm. Taxi to Temple Sq. costs about $15.

Trains: Amtrak, 340 S. 600 W (☎322-3510). *Be advised: the area around the station can be dangerous at night.* To **Denver** (15hr., 1 per day, $75-112) and **San Francisco** (19hr., 1 per day, $77-115). Station open daily 10:30pm-6am.

Buses: Greyhound, 160 W. South Temple (☎355-9579), near Temple Sq. To Denver (7-10hr., 5 per day, $54) and Las Vegas (12-13hr., 2 per day, $49). Open summer 6:30am-2:30am; winter 6:30am-11:30pm, ticket window until 10:30pm.

Public Transit: Utah Transit Authority (UTA; ☎743-3882). Frequent service to University of Utah campus; buses to suburbs, airport, mountain canyons, and the #11 express runs to Provo ($2.25). New TRAX light rail follows Main St. from downtown to Sandy and to the University of Utah. Buses every 20min.-1hr. M-Sa 6am-11pm. Fare $1-2, senior discounts, under 5 free. Maps available at libraries and the Visitors Center. UTA Buses and TRAX trains traveling downtown near the major sites are free.

Taxi: Ute Cab, ☎359-7788. **Yellow Cab,** ☎521-2100. **City Cab,** ☎363-5550.

ORIENTATION & PRACTICAL INFORMATION

Salt Lake City's grid system may seem confusing, but once you get the hang of it, it makes navigation easy. Brigham Young designated **Temple Square** as the heart of downtown. Street names increase in increments of 100 and indicate how many blocks east, west, north, or south they lie from Temple Sq.; the "0" points are **Main Street** (north-south) and **South Temple** (east-west). State St., West Temple, and North Temple are 100 level streets. Occasionally, streets are referred to as 13th S or 17th N, which are the same as 1300 S or 1700 N. Local address listings often include two cross streets. For example, a building on 13th S (1300 S) might be listed as 825 E 1300 S, meaning the cross street is 800 E (8th E). Smaller streets and those that do not fit the grid pattern sometimes have non-numeric names.

Visitor Info: Salt Palace Convention Center and Salt Lake City Visitors Bureau, 90 S. West Temple (☎534-4902). Located in Salt Palace Convention Center. Open daily 9am-5pm.

Hotlines: Rape Crisis, ☎467-7273. **Suicide Prevention,** ☎483-5444. Both 24hr.

Gay/Lesbian Information: The **Little Lavender Book** (☎323-0727; www.lavenderbook.com), a directory of gay-friendly Salt Lake City services. Distributed twice yearly.

Internet Access: Salt Lake Public Library, 209 E. 500 S (☎524-8200). Open M-Th 9am-9pm, F-Sa 9am-6pm, Su 1-5pm.

Post Office: 230 W. 200 S, 1 block south and 1 block west of Visitors Center. Open M-F 8am-5pm, Sa 9am-2pm. **Postal Code:** 84101. **Area Code:** 801

ACCOMMODATIONS

Affordable chain motels cluster at the southern end of downtown, around 200 W and 600 S, and on North Temple.

Base Camp Park City, 268 Historic Main St. (☎655-7244, 888-980-7244; www.parkcitybasecamp.com), 30 mi. east of Salt Lake City on I-80 and south on Rte. 224. This dazzling, state-of-the-art hostel offers 70 affordable beds in the heart of expensive Park City. Free Internet, free parking, discounts on selected Main St. restaurants, spectacular

movie/DVD theater, and free transportation to Deer Valley, The Canyons, and Park City ski areas. Taxis/shuttles from Salt Lake City airport available. Dorms summer $25, winter $35. Private room (sleeps up to 4) $80/120. Make reservations by phone or on-line far in advance during ski season. ❷

City Creek Inn, 230 W. North Temple (☎533-9100; citycreekinn.com), a stone's throw from Temple Sq. Offers 33 immaculate ranch-style rooms for the cheapest rates downtown. Two wheelchair-accessible rooms. Singles $53; doubles $64. AAA discount. ❸

Ute Hostel (AAIH/Rucksackers), 21 E. Kelsey Ave. (☎595-1645 or 888-255-1192), near the intersection of 1300 S and Main. Young international crowd. Free pickup can be arranged from airport, Amtrak, Greyhound, or the Visitors Center. Kitchen, free tea and coffee, parking, linen. Check-in 24hr. Reservations accepted in advance only with pre-payment, recommended from July-Sept. and Jan.-Mar. Dorms $15; singles $25; doubles $35. Cash only. ❶

The Avenues Hostel (HI-AYH), 107 F St. (☎359-3855). 15min. walk from Temple Sq. in a residential area. Features free parking, a new entertainment system, 2 kitchens, and mountain bike rentals ($10 per day, $100 deposit). Reception 7:30am-noon, 4-10:30pm. Reservations recommended July-Aug. and Jan.-Mar. Dorms $17 (non-members), doubles $36 (non-members), $5 key deposit. ❶

MORAL FIBER

Good, cheap restaurants are sprinkled around the city and its suburbs. Despite its white bread reputation, Salt Lake hosts a number of ethnic cuisines. If you're in a hurry downtown, **ZCMI Mall** and **Crossroads Mall,** both across from Temple Sq., have standard food courts.

Sage's Cafe, 473 E. 300 S (☎322-3790). This organic, vegan cafe is a hotbed of culinary innovation. Describing themselves as "culinary astronauts," talented chefs produce a variety of delectable dishes. Try the basil and macadamia nut pesto pasta dish for $13. Sugar- and oil-free meals available. Weekday lunch buffet $6.75. Open W-Th 5pm-9:30pm, F 5pm-10pm, Sa 9am-10pm, Su 9am-9pm. ❷

Ruth's Diner, 2100 Emigration Canyon Rd. (☎582-5807; www.ruthsdiner.com). Vending the best breakfasts in Salt Lake City and a full bar with live music at night. Originally run out of a trolley car, Ruth's is the second-oldest restaurant in Utah and has been a Salt Lake City landmark for 70 years. Huge portions, delicious omelettes like the "Rutherino" ($6-7), and brownie sundaes ($6) help it outlast rivals. Open daily 8am-10pm. ❶

SIGHTS

LATTER-DAY SIGHTS. The majority of Salt Lake City's sights are sacred to the Church of Jesus Christ of Latter-Day Saints, and free. The seat of the highest Mormon authority and the central temple, **Temple Square** is the symbolic center of the Mormon religion. The square has two **Visitors Centers,** north and south. Visitors can wander around the flowery 10-acre square, but the sacred temple is off-limits to non-Mormons. An automated visitor info line *(☎800-537-9703)* provides up-to-date hours and tour info. Forty-five-minute tours leave from the flagpole every 10min., showing the highlights of Temple Sq. *The Testaments*, a film detailing the coming of Jesus Christ to the Americas (as related by the Book of Mormon), is screened at the **Joseph Smith Memorial Building.** *(☎240-4383 for films, 240-1266 for tours. Open M-Sa 9am-9pm. Free.)*

Temple Sq. is also home to the **Mormon Tabernacle** and its famed choir. Weekly rehearsals and performances are free. *(Organ recitals M-Sa noon-12:30pm, Su 2-2:30pm; in summer also M-Sa 2-2:30pm. Choir rehearsals Th 8-9:30pm; choir broadcasts Su 9:30-10am, must be seated by 9:15am.)* In the summer, there are frequent free concerts at **Assembly Hall** next door. *(☎800-537-9703.)*

The **Church of Jesus Christ of Latter Day Saints Office Building** is the tallest skyscraper in town. The elevator to the 26th floor grants a view of the Great Salt Lake in the west opposite the Wasatch Range. *(40 E. North Temple. ☎240-3789. Observation deck open M-F 9am-4:30pm.)* The LDS church's collection of genealogical materials is accessible and free at the **Family Search Center,** 15 E. South Temple St., in the Joseph Smith Memorial Building. The Center has computers and staff to aid in your search. The actual collection is housed in the **Family History Library.** *(35 N. West Temple. ☎240-2331. Center open M-Sa 9am-9pm. Library open M 7:30am-5pm, Tu-Sa 7:30am-10pm.)*

CAPITOL HILL. At the northernmost end of State St., Utah's **State Capitol** features beautiful grounds, including a garden that changes daily. *(☎538-3000. Open M-F 8am-5pm. Tours M-F 9am-4pm.)* Down State St., the **Hansen Planetarium** has free exhibits and laser shows set to music. *(15 S. State St. ☎531-4925. Open M-Th 9am-9pm, F-Sa 9:30am-midnight, Su 1-5pm. Laser show $6; planetarium science show $4.50.)*

MUSEUMS. Visiting exhibits and a permanent collection of world art wow enthusiasts at the newly expanded **Utah Museum of Fine Arts,** on the University of Utah campus. *(☎581-7332. Open M-F 10am-5pm, Sa-Su noon-5pm. Free.)* Also on campus, the

Museum of Natural History focuses its display space on the history of the Wasatch Front. *(☎581-6927. M-Sa 9:30am-5:30pm, Su noon-5pm. $4, ages 3-12 $2.50, under 3 free.)* The **Salt Lake Art Center** displays an impressive array of contemporary art and documentary films. *(20 S. West Temple. ☎328-4201. Open Tu-Th and Sa 10am-5pm, F 10am-9pm, Su 1-5pm. Suggested donation $2.)*

THE GREAT SALT LAKE. The Great Salt Lake, administered by Great Salt Lake State Marina, is a remnant of primordial Lake Bonneville and is so salty that only blue-green algae and brine shrimp can survive in it. The salt content varies from 5-27%, providing the unusual buoyancy credited with keeping the lake free of drownings. Decaying organic material on the lake shore gives the lake its pungent odor, which locals prefer not to discuss. **Antelope Island State Park**, in the middle of the lake, is a favorite for visitors. *(Bus #37, Magna, will take you within 4 mi., but no closer. To get to the south shore of the lake, take I-80 17 mi. west of Salt Lake City to Exit 104. To get to the island, take Exit 335 from I-15 and follow signs to the causeway. ☎625-1630. Open daily 7am-10pm; winter dawn to dusk. Day use: vehicles $8, bicycles and pedestrians $4.*

ENTERTAINMENT & NIGHTLIFE

Salt Lake City's sweltering summer months are jammed with frequent evening concerts. Every Tuesday and Friday at 7:30pm, the **Temple Square Concert Series** presents a free outdoor concert in Brigham Young Historic Park, with music ranging from string quartet to unplugged guitar (☎240-2534; call for a schedule). The **Utah Symphony Orchestra** performs in **Abravanel Hall,** 123 W. South Temple. (☎533-6683. Office open M-F 10am-6pm. Tickets Sept.-early May $15-40. Limited summer season; call 1 week in advance.) The University of Utah's **Red Butte Garden,** 300 Wakara Way (☎587-9939; www.redbuttegarden.org), offers an outdoor summer concert series with reputable national acts.

The free *City Weekly* lists events and is available at bars, clubs, and restaurants. Famous for teetotaling, the early Mormon theocrats instated laws making it illegal to serve alcohol in a public place. Hence, all liquor-serving institutions fall under the "private club" designation, serving only members and their "sponsored" guests. In order to get around this cumbersome law, most bars and clubs charge a "temporary membership fee"—essentially a cover charge. Despite the Mormons' contempt for the bottle, Salt Lake City has an active nightlife scene, centering on S. West Temple and the run-down blocks near the railroad tracks. **Bricks,** 200 S. 600 W, is the city's oldest and largest dance club, with arguably its best sound system. (☎238-0255. Separate 18+ and 21+ areas. Cover $5-7. Open nightly 9:30pm-2am.) SLC's version of a pretentious super-club, **Club Axis,** 100 S. 500 W, features VIP lounges, a jungle-themed bar, and multiple dance floors. (☎519-2947; www.clubaxis.com. F gay/alt. lifestyle night, W and Sa dress to impress. Separate 18+ and 21+ areas. Cover $5-7. Open W-Sa 10pm-2am). At six stories, **DV8,** 115 S. West Temple, is the city's second largest club and features live acts M-Th for all ages. (☎539-8400. F-Sa club nights 9pm-2am, 21+. Cover $5-7.) A diverse mix of Salt Lake City's gay and lesbian crowd flocks to the classy **Zipperz,** 155 W. 200 S, to sip martinis ($4.75) in wingchairs and groove on the dancefloor. (☎521-8300. 21+. Cover $5-6. Open nightly Su-Th 2pm-2am, F-Sa 5pm-2am.)

PARK CITY & SKI RESORTS

Utah sells itself to tourists with pictures of intrepid skiers on pristine powder, hailed by many as "the greatest snow on earth." Seven major ski areas lie within 45min. of downtown Salt Lake, making Utah's capital a good, inexpensive base camp for the winter vacation paradise of the Wasatch Mountains. Nearby **Park City**

THE BIG SPLURGE

OLYMPIAN FOR A DAY

With a range of camps that take place at the same facilities that hosted the 2002 Winter Olympics, summer at **Olympic Park** has its own highs for the adrenaline junky. Ski jumper wannabes can take a literal crash course in freestyle aerial thanks to the park's **Flight School and aerial jumping arena,** which includes multiple bungee jumping stations and a 750,000 gal. splash pool. The steepest ramp launches wetsuit-clad skiers and snow boarders some 60 ft. into the thin mountain air before they cannon-ball into the water below. 1988 Olympian Chris "Hatch" Haslock is on hand to teach you the tricks that qualify you as totally fearless and just shy of insane. *(Jun.-Sept. Tu-Su beginning at 12:30pm. $40 per session.)*

If soaring and flipping aren't your thing, the Comet awaits on solid ground. One of only two **Olympic bobsled** courses in the US, this ride can hurtle you in summer months through 15 curves over 0.8 mi. at a screaming 70 mph top speed. Special rolling bobsleds and professional pilots let passengers experience up to 4 Gs of force. Paying $200 in the wintertime may seem too pricey, but making a $65 advance reservation during the summer is well worth it. (☎435-658-4206; www.olyparks.com. Late May-late Aug. Tu-Sa 1-4pm.)

is the quintessential ski town with the excellent but lonely **Base Camp Park City** (see p. 804) as its only budget option. Call, or check ski area web sites for deals before purchasing lift tickets. Besides being a good source of fun, the Utah ski hills are also an excellent source of employment. If you are interested in working while you ski, check the employment section on each hill's web site or call Snowbird's job hotline (☎947-8240). Most slopes are open in the summer for hiking, mountain biking and horseback riding. Note: the area code for some resorts is ☎435. Unless otherwise noted, all other numbers share the ☎801 area code of Salt Lake City.

Alta (☎359-1078; www.alta.com), 25 mi. southeast of Salt Lake City in Little Cottonwood Canyon. Cheap tickets; magnificent skiing. No-frills resort continues to eschew opulence and reject snowboarders. 500 in. of champagne powder annually. Open mid-Nov. to mid-Apr. daily 9:15am-4:30pm. Lift tickets: full-day $38, half-day $29; day pass for beginner lifts $22; joint ticket with nearby Snowbird $68.

Solitude (☎800-748-4754; www.skisolitude.com), in Big Cottonwood Canyon 30min. south of Salt Lake. Uncrowded slopes and 20km of nordic trails at Silver Lake (8700 ft.) promise tranquility. Open Nov.-late Apr. daily 9am-4pm. Lift tickets: full-day $44, half-day $37; seniors (60-69) $37, children $24, over 70 $10. Nordic Center full-day $10, half-day $7. Rentals: adult ski package $24 per day, snowboards $28, high performance ski package $38.

Brighton (☎800-873-5512; www.skibrighton.com), south of Salt Lake in Big Cottonwood Canyon. Bargain skiing and snowboarding in a down-to-earth atmosphere. Especially family- and beginner-friendly. Open early Nov. to late Apr. M-Sa 9am-9pm, Su 9am-4pm. Lift tickets: full-day $39, half-day $34, night $24, children under 10 free. Rentals: ski/board packages $26-32 per day, child $18.

The Canyons (☎435-649-5400; www.thecanyons.com), in Park City. Lodges, shops, and restaurants styled in Southwestern motifs, and an abundance of territory. Open Nov.-Apr. M-F 9am-4pm, Sa-Su 8:30am-4pm. Lift tickets: full-day $62, half-day $45; children and seniors $31/24. Rentals: adult ski/board package $34-40 per day, child ski package $24, child board package $27. Free season pass in exchange for 1 day of work at the resort per week.

Deer Valley (☎435-649-1000; www.deervalley.com), in Park City. Host of several Winter Olympics events in 2002 and a world-class ski area, if expensive. No snowboards. Open Dec.-Apr. daily 9am-4:15pm. Lift tickets: full-day $67, half-day $46; seniors $46/30; children $36/28. Ski rentals: adult package $39-49 per day, child package $28.

DAYTRIP FROM SALT LAKE CITY: TIMPANOGOS CAVE

Legend has it that a set of mountain lion tracks first led Martin Hansen to the mouth of the cave that today bears his name. **Hansen's Cave** forms but one-third of the cave system of American Fork Canyon, collectively called Timpanogos Cave. Situated in a rich alpine environment, Timpanogos is a true gem for speleologists (cave nuts) and tourists alike. Though early miners shipped boxcar loads of stalactites and other mineral wonders back east to sell to universities and museums, enough remain to bedazzle guests along the 1hr. walk through the depths. Today, the cave is open to visitors only through ranger-led tours.

Timpanogos Cave National Monument is solely accessible via Rte. 92 (20 mi. south of Salt Lake City off I-15, exit 287; Rte. 92 also connects with Rte. 189 northeast of Provo). The **Visitors Center** dispenses tour tickets and info on the caves. Reservations for busy summer weekends should be made as early as 30 days in advance; during less busy times they are available up to the day before the tour. Bring water and warm layers: the rigorous hike to the cave climbs 1065 ft. over 1½ mi., but the temperature remains a constant 45°F inside. (☎756-5238. Open mid-May to late Oct. daily 7am-5:30pm. 3hr. hikes depart daily 7am-4:30pm every 15min. $6, ages 6-15 $5, Golden Age Passport and ages 3-5 $3, age 2 and under free.)

The National Monument is dwarfed by the surrounding **Uinta National Forest,** which blankets the mountains of the Wasatch Range. The **Alpine Scenic Drive (Route 92)** provides excellent views of Mt. Timpanogos and other snowcapped peaks. The 20 mi. trip takes almost 1hr. in one direction. The Forest Service charges $2 for recreation along the road. The **Timpooneke Trail** (16¼ mi.) leads to the sheer summit of **Mt. Timpanogos** (11,749 ft.), beginning at the Aspen Grove Trailhead (6860 ft.) and meeting the summit trail at Emerald Lake.

The **Pleasant Grove Ranger District** has info on the **campgrounds** ❶ in the area (☎800-280-2267 for reservations. Sites $11-13.) **Backcountry camping** ❶ throughout the forest requires no permit or fee as long as you respect minimum-impact guidelines. While the National Park Service forbids camping within the national monument itself, **Little Mill Campground** ❶, on Rte. 92 past the monument provides an excellent jumping-off point from which to beat the Timpanogos Cave crowds. (Open early May-late Sept. Sites $11.)

DINOSAUR NATIONAL MONUMENT AND VERNAL ☎435

Dinosaur National Monument was created in 1915, 7 years after paleontologist Earl Douglass happened upon an array of fossilized dinosaur bones here. The rugged landscape that today includes the beautiful Green and Yampa rivers was once home to legions of dinosaurs that eventually left their remains for tourists to ogle. The monument's main attraction is the dinosaur quarry, but adventurous types may find more distractions in the less-explored parts of the area. The town of Vernal, west of Dinosaur on U.S. 40, is a popular base for exploring the monument, Flaming Gorge, and the Uinta Mountains.

ORIENTATION & PRACTICAL INFORMATION. The national monument collects an entrance fee of $10 per car, and $5 per cyclist, pedestrian, or tour-bus passenger. The national monument's western entrance lies 20 mi. east of Vernal on Rte. 149, which splits from U.S. 40 southwest of the park in Jenson, UT. Once inside the park, pay a visit to the **Dinosaur Quarry Visitors Center,** a remarkable Bauhaus building that houses exhibits, a bookstore, and an exposed river bank brimming with dinosaur bones. During summer, a **shuttle** whisks passengers ½ mi. to the Visitors Center; between Labor Day and Memorial Day cars can drive directly to the Center. (☎781-7700. Open June-Aug. daily 8am-7pm, Sept.-May M-F 8am-4:30pm.) **Monument Headquarters** is 45 mi. along

Rte. 40 from the Rte. 149 turnoff in Dinosaur, CO. (☎970-374-3000. Open June-Aug. daily 8am-4:30pm, Sept.-May M-F 8am-4:30pm.) **Gas** is available in Vernal, Jenson, and Dinosaur, CO.

Greyhound runs buses to **Denver** (8hr., 2 per day, $56) and **Salt Lake City** (4½hr., 2 per day, $35) from Frontier Travel, 72 S. 100 W. (☎789-0404. Open M-F 8:30am-5:30pm.) Jensen is a flag stop, as is Monument Headquarters, 2 mi. west of Dinosaur, CO. **The Northeast Utah Visitors Center,** 235 E. Main St., provides info on regional recreational activities. (☎789-7894. Open daily 8am-7pm.) The **Ashley National Forest Service Office,** 355 N. Vernal Ave., has info about hiking, biking, and camping in the Ashley and Uinta National Forests. Mail kitschy dino postcards from the **Post Office,** 67 N. 800 W. **Postal Code:** 84078. **Area Code:** 435.

ACCOMMODATIONS & FOOD. The most easily accessible camping site during summer months, **Green River ❶,** lies along Cub Creek Rd. about 5 mi. from the entrance fee station. (88 sites. Flush toilets and water. Sites $12.) Nearby **Split Mountain** hosts only groups during summer but is free and open to all during winter. **Echo Park ❶,** 13 mi. along Echo Park Rd. from Harper's Corner Drive (four-wheel-drive road and impassable when wet), provides the perfect location for an evening under the stars. (9 sites. Pit toilets and water in summer. Sites $6, free in winter.) Free **backcountry camping ❶** permits are available from Monument Headquarters or the Quarry Visitors Center.

For those less inclined to rough it, **Vernal** is civilization's beacon. The comfortable **Sage Motel ❸,** 54 W. Main St., has standard rooms, A/C, satellite TV, and free local calls. (☎789-1442 or 800-760-1442. Singles in winter $45; in summer $50. Doubles $55/60.) On the outskirts of town toward the National Monument, **Split Mountain Motel ❷,** 1015 E. U.S. 40, has clean rooms with A/C, microwave, and minifridge. (☎789-9020. Singles in summer $45; winter $40. Doubles $50/55.)

Betty's Cafe ❶, 416 W. Main in Vernal, piles breakfast favorites ($5-7) and cinnamon rolls ($1.50) on your plate. (☎781-2728. Open M-Sa 6am-4pm, Su 6am-noon. Cash only.) Imported to the Weston Inn from nearby LaPointe, **Stockman's ❶,** 1684 W. U.S. 40, lures hungry Vernalites for an exciting menu of Southwest cuisine. Burgers ($5-7), all you can eat sirloin steak ($11), and gargantuan desserts ($5-6) are highlights. (☎781-3030. Open Tu-F 10am-11pm, Sa 11:30am-11pm.)

SIGHTS. Some 350 million tons of dinosaur remains have been carted away from this Jurassic cemetery, but over 1600 fossils remain exposed in the **Quarry Visitors Center** (see **Practical Information,** above). Scenic drives and hikes are good ways to appreciate the unique beauty and history of the area. Stop by the Visitors Center in Vernal to pick up free guides to auto tours in the area. These pamphlets direct motorists to historical sights and beautiful vistas. **Harper's Corner,** at the confluence of the Green and Yampa Rivers (take the Harper's Corner Rd. from the monument headquarters) has one of the best views around. At the end of the road, an easy 2 mi. round-trip hike leads to the view.

Perhaps the best way to see Dinosaur National Monument is as the early explorers did: by boat. **Don Hatch River Expeditions,** 221 N. 400 E. in Vernal, is descended from one of the nation's earliest commercial rafting enterprises. Well-respected Hatch Expeditions floats through the monument and the nearby Flaming Gorge. Be sure to request a paddle trip if you're interested in helping steer the raft. (☎789-4316 or 800-342-8243; www.hatchriver.com. Open M-F 9am-5pm. 1-day trip $66, age 6-12 $56; seniors 10% off. Advance reservations recommended.)

FLAMING GORGE NATIONAL RECREATION AREA ☎435

Seen at sunset, the contrast between the red canyons and the aquamarine water of the Green River makes the landscape appear to glow. Apparently not everyone was satisfied with this natural beauty; legislation was passed in 1963 to dam the

Green River. The resulting body of water is now home to the Flaming Gorge National Recreation Area. Boating and fishing enthusiasts descend into the gorge every summer to take advantage of the water.

The Green River below the dam teems with trout, allowing for top-notch **fishing.** To fish, obtain a **permit,** available at Flaming Gorge Lodge and Dutch John Recreation Services. For more info, call the **Utah Division of Wildlife Resources,** 1594 W. North Temple, in Salt Lake City. (☎800-538-4700. Open M-F 7:30am-6pm.) Several establishments rent the required gear for reservoir recreation. **Cedar Springs Marina,** 2 mi. before the dam, rents boats and offers guided fishing trips. (☎889-3795. Open daily 8am-6pm. 10-person pontoon boats from $120 for 3hr., $200 per day. 6-person fishing boats $50/90.) Nearby, **Flaming Gorge Lodge** rents fishing rods. (☎889-3773; www.fglodge.com. Open daily 6:30am-8pm. $10 per day.)

Hikers and bikers will delight in the area's trails, some of which snake along dangerous cliff edges. All trails allow bikes. The **Canyon Rim Trail** (5 mi. one-way) has access points at Red Canyon Visitors Center and several campgrounds. Another popular hike begins at **Dowd Mountain** (3hr., 5 mi.), off Rte. 44 west of Manila, and travels up Hideout Canyon. The strenuous **Elk Park Loop** (20 mi.) departs Rte. 44 at Deep Creek Rd., follows it to Forest Rd. 221 and Forest Rd. 105, skirts Browne Lake, and runs singletrack along **Old Carter and South Elk Park Trails.**

Camping in the area is scenic and accessible. With over 30 campgrounds spread around the lake, the **Visitors Center** offers sound advice for reserving sites. (☎888-444-6777; call 5 days ahead.) The 19 secluded sites at **Dripping Springs ❶,** just past Dutch John on Rte. 191, mark a prime fishing location. Sites $14. Reservations accepted.) **Canyon Rim ❶,** on the road to the Red Canyon Visitors Center, offers a feeling of high-country camping with nearby views of the red-walled gorge. (Sites $14; late Oct.-late Apr. free.) For a roof and four walls, the **Red Canyon Lodge ❸,** 2 mi. south of the Visitors Center on Rte. 44, offers a great location, views, and activities in line with a luxury resort, but at budget prices. (☎889-3759. Private lake, restaurant. 2-person cabins with restrooms $95; 4-person $105; each additional adult $6, under 12 $2; rollaway beds $6 per night.) In **Manila,** the **Steinnaker Motel ❷,** at Rte. 43 and 44, offers cramped but clean rooms. (☎784-3104. Check-in at the Chevron station. Singles $36; doubles $44; tax included.)

From Vernal, follow U.S. 191 north to the recreation area. The reservoir extends as far north as Green River, WY, and is also accessible from I-80. A recreation pass ($2 per day, $5 per 16 days) can be obtained at the **Flaming Gorge Visitors Center,** on U.S. 191 atop the Flaming Gorge Dam, or at most stores surrounding the Gorge. The Visitors Center also offers free tours of the dam. (☎885-3135. Open daily 8am-6pm; low-season 10am-4pm.) A few miles off U.S. 191 and 3 mi. off Rte. 44 to Manila, the **Red Canyon Visitors Center** hangs 1360 ft. above the reservoir, offering staggering views into the canyon. (☎889-3713. Open late May-Aug. daily 10am-5pm.) **Post Office:** 4 South Blvd., in Dutch John. (☎885-3351. Open M-F 7:30am-3:30pm, Sa 8:30am-11am and 1:45-3:15pm.) **Postal Code:** 84023. **Area Code:** 435.

MOAB ☎435

Moab first flourished in the 1950s, when uranium miners rushed to the area and transformed the town from a quiet hamlet into a gritty desert outpost. Today, the mountain bike has replaced the Geiger counter, as tourists rush into the town eager to bike the red slickrock, raft whitewater rapids, and explore the surrounding Arches and Canyonlands National Parks. The town itself has changed to fit the new visitors and athletes; microbreweries and t-shirt shops now fill the rooms of the old uranium mine headquarters on Main St.

ORIENTATION & PRACTICAL INFORMATION. Moab sits 30 mi. south of I-70 on U.S. 191, just south of the junction with Rte. 128. The town center lies 5 mi. south of the entrance to Arches National Park and 38 mi. north of the turnoff to the Needles section of Canyonlands National Park. U.S. 191 becomes Main for 5 mi. through downtown. The closest **Amtrak** (☎800-872-7245) and **Greyhound** (☎800-454-2487) stations are in Green River, 52 mi. northwest of town. Some hotels and hostels will pick guests up from the train or bus for a fee. In addition, **Bighorn Express** (☎888-655-7433) makes a daily trip to and from the Salt Lake City airport, with stops in Green River and Price along the way. Shuttles leave from the Ramada Inn, 182 S. Main. (Departs Salt Lake City airport at 2pm, departs Moab at 7:30am. 4½hr. trip, $56. Reservations recommended.) **Roadrunner Shuttle** (☎259-9402) and **Coyote Shuttle** (☎259-8656) take you where you want to go on- or off-road in the Moab area. **Moab Information Center,** 3 Center St., at the intersection of Center and Main. (☎259-8825 or 800-635-6622.) This umbrella organization for the **Chamber of Commerce,** the **National Park Service,** the **US Forest Service,** and the **BLM,** doles out copious information on the city and the surrounding outdoors. (Open daily Jan.-Feb. 9am-5pm; Mar. 8am-7pm; Apr.-May and Oct.-Nov. 8am-8pm; June-Sept. 8am-9pm; Nov.-Dec. 9am-5pm.) **Post Office:** 50 E. 100 N. (☎259-7427. Open M-F 8:30am-5:30pm, Sa 9am-1pm.) **Postal Code:** 84532. **Area Code:** 435.

ACCOMMODATIONS. Chain motels clutter Main, but Moab is not cheap and fills up fast from April to October, especially on weekends. **Lazy Lizard International Hostel ❶,** 1213 S. U.S. 191, is 1 mi. south of Moab on U.S. 191. The owners of this well-maintained hostel will give you the lowdown on the area, while the kitchen, VCR, laundry, and hot tub draw a mix of college students, backpackers, and aging hippies. (☎259-6057. Reception 8am-11pm, but late arrivals can be arranged. Check-out 11am. Reservations recommended for weekends in the spring and fall. Tent sites $6, dorms $9; private rooms for 1 or 2 from $22; cabins sleeping up to 6 $27-47;) At **Hotel Off Center ❶,** 96 E. Center St., a block off Main, the gracious owners offer eclectically lavish rooms accented by such items as a miner's hat, a Victrola, and fishing nets. (☎259-4244. Open Mar.-Nov. Dorms $12; singles $39; doubles $49.)

One thousand campsites blanket the Moab area, so finding a place to sleep under the stars shouldn't be a problem. **Goose Island, Hal Canyon, Oak Grove, Negro Bill,** and **Big Bend Campgrounds ❶,** all on Rte. 128, sit on the banks of the Colorado River three to nine mi. northeast of downtown Moab. Many of the sites are shaded, and the locations couldn't be better. (☎259-2100. Fire pits but no hookups or showers. Water is available at Negro Bill at the intersection of U.S. 191 and Rte. 128. Sites $10.) The shaded, secluded **Up the Creek Campground ❶,** 210 E. 300 S, is just a walk away from downtown and caters solely to tent camping. (☎259-6995. 20 sites. Showers. Open Mar.-Oct. $10 per person.)

FOOD. Retro booths at the **Moab Diner and Ice Cream Shoppe ❷,** 189 S. Main, might take you back to the 1950s, but with veggie specials and tasty green chili ($4-10), the food won't. (☎259-4006. Open Su-Th 6am-10pm, F-Sa 6am-10:30pm.) **EklectiCafe ❶,** 352 N. Main St., dishes out a wide array of delicious pastries, coffee drinks (all made with organic, fair trade beans), breakfasts ($3-7), and lunch options ($4-8). Locals perform music on Sunday mornings to an audience crunchier than the brunch food. (☎259-6896. Open M-Sa 7:30am-2:30pm, Su 7:30am-1pm.) The **Peace Tree Juice Cafe ❶,** 20 S. Main, will cool you off with a smoothie or fresh juice ($2.50-5), the perfect antidote to a hot day in the desert. (☎259-6333. Open Su-Th 9am-5pm, F-Sa 9am-9pm.) Adding a little Fifth Ave. flare to an otherwise Western town, Breakfast at **Tiffany's ❶,** 90 E. Center St., defies the bacon-and-eggs breakfast standard. The almond French toast and catfish and eggs are favorites. (☎259-2553. Open M-F 7am-2pm, Sa-Su 7am-7:30pm. Open for appetizers M and F-Su 7pm-closing. Cash only.)

OUTDOOR ACTIVITIES. **Mountain biking** and **rafting,** along with nearby national parks, are the big draws in Moab. The well-known **Slickrock Trail** (10 mi.) rolls up and down the slickrock outside of Moab. The trail has no big vertical gain, but is technically difficult and temperatures often reach 100°F. **Rim Cyclery,** 94 W. 100 N., rents bikes and distributes info about the trails. (☎259-5333. Open Su-Th 9am-6pm, F-Sa 8am-6pm. $32-50 per day; includes helmet.)

Countless raft companies are based in Moab. **OARS/North American River Expeditions,** 543 N. Main St., offers the best guides on the river. (☎259-5865 or 800-342-5938. Half-day $36, ages 5-17 $27; includes snacks and a natural history lesson.) **Western River Expeditions** offers good deals as well. (☎259-7019 or 800-453-7450. Half-day $37, full-day $49; children $29/37; includes lunch.) Various outfitters arrange horseback, motorboat, canoe, jeep, and helicopter rides.

UTAH'S NATURAL WONDERS

Arches, Canyonlands, Bryce Canyon, Zion, and Capitol Reef National Parks sit in a line running northeast to southwest through the southern portion of Utah, connected by a well-traveled series of scenic highways. These popular parks are geographically dwarfed by Grand Staircase-Escalante National Monument, the new kid on the block, sprawling south and east of Bryce Canyon and west of Capitol Reef. The spectacular arches, canyons, amphitheaters, plateaus, and vibrant redrock of these public lands make them perhaps the densest collection of geological and panoramic brilliance the nation has to offer.

From Moab in the northeast, take U.S. 191 N 5 mi. to **Arches.** Continue 60 mi. north on U.S. 191 to Rte. 313 S and the Islands in the Sky area of **Canyonlands.** Or, take U.S. 191 south from Moab to Rte. 211 W to reach the Needles area of Canyonlands (87 mi.). To reach **Capitol Reef,** continue driving north on U.S. 191 and then west on I-70; leave I-70 at Exit 147, and follow Rte. 24 S to Hanksville; then west to the park (81 mi. from I-70). Rte. 24 W runs to Torrey, where scenic Rte. 12 branches south and west through the Dixie National Forest to **Bryce Canyon.** For **Zion,** stay on Rte. 12 W to U.S. 89 S through Mt. Carmel Jct., and pick up Rte. 9 W. The 122mi. stretch of **Route 95** between Blanding and Hanksville, known as the Bicentennial Highway because it was built in 1976, is one of the most scenic in the lower 48 states and highlights a diverse cross-section of southern Utah.

The two national forests in Southern Utah are divided into districts, some of which lie near the national parks and serve as excellent places to stay on a cross-country jaunt. **Manti-La Sal National Forest** has two sections near Arches and the Needles area of Canyonlands. **Dixie National Forest** stretches from Capitol Reef through Bryce all the way to the western side of Zion NP.

ARCHES ☎435

Wrote Edward Abbey of Arches National Park, "This is the most beautiful place on earth." Thousands of sandstone arches, spires, pinnacles, and fins tower above the desert in overwhelming grandeur. Some arches are so perfect in form that early explorers believed they were constructed by a lost civilization. Deep red sandstone, green piñon pines and juniper bushes, and a strikingly blue sky combine in an unforgettable palette of colors.

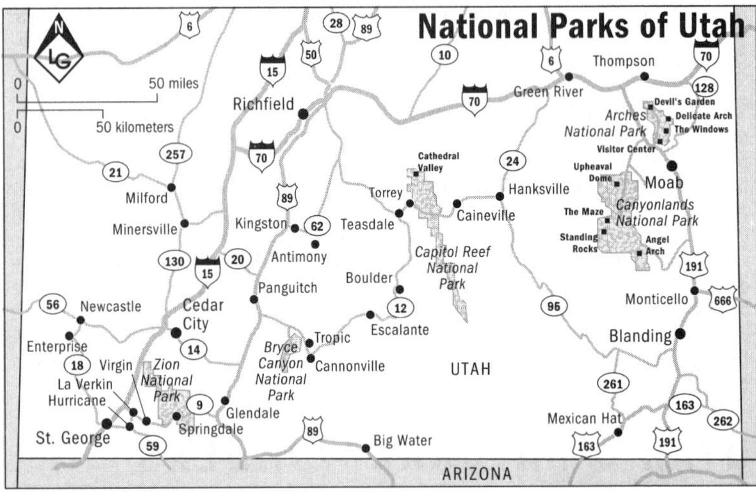

ORIENTATION & PRACTICAL INFORMATION. The park entrance is on U.S. 191, 5 mi. north of Moab. Although no public transportation serves the park, shuttle bus companies travel to both the national park and Moab from surrounding towns and cities. While most visitors come in the summer, 100°F temperatures make hiking difficult; bring at least one gallon of water per person per day. The weather is best in the spring and fall when temperate days and nights combine to make a comfortable stay. In the winter, white snow provides a brilliant contrast to the red arches. The **Visitors Center,** to the right of the entrance station, distributes free park service maps. (☎719-2299. Open daily 8am-4:30pm; extended hours Mar.-Sept.) An **entrance pass** ($10 per carload, $5 per pedestrian or biker) covers admission for a week. Write the Superintendent, Arches National Park, P.O. Box 907, Moab 84532, or check the web site (www.nps.gov/arch).

CAMPING. The park's only campground, **Devil's Garden ❶,** has 52 excellent campsites nestled amid piñons and giant red sandstone formations. The campsite is within walking distance of the Devil's Garden and Broken Arch trailheads; however, it is a long 18 mi. from the Visitors Center. Sites go quickly, but at the time of publication Devil's Garden was considering a reservation system. (☎719-2299. Bathrooms, water, no wood-gathering. 1-week max. stay. Sites $10.)

If the heat becomes unbearable at Arches, the aspen forests of the **Manti-La Sal National Forest** offer a respite. Take Rte. 128 along the Colorado River and turn right at Castle Valley, or go south from Moab on U.S. 191 and turn to the left at the Shell Station. There are a number of campgrounds here including **Warner Lake ❶,** where beautiful sites sit 4000 ft. above the national park and are invariably several degrees cooler. (Sites $10; Oowah Lake sites free.) **Oowah Lake,** a 3 mi. hike from the Geyser Pass Rd., is a rainbow trout haven. Fishing permits are available at stores in Moab and at the Forest Service Office, 62 E. 100 N, for $5 per day. Contact the Manti-La Sal National Forest (☎259-7155).

HIKING. While the striking red slickrock around Arches may seem like attraction enough, the real points of interest here lie off the paved road. Load up on water and sunscreen and seek out the park's thousands of natural arches, each one pinpointed on the free map and guide passed out at the fee collection booth.

For more detailed maps and info on hiking, especially desert precautions, stop at the Visitors Center. Hiking in the park is unparalleled, especially in the cool days of spring and fall. Stay on trails; the land may look barren, but the soil actually contains cryptobiotic life forms that are easily destroyed by footsteps. The most popular hike in the park leads to the oft-photographed **Delicate Arch.** The trail (2½hr., 3 mi.) leaves from the Wolfe Ranch parking area and climbs 480 ft.; be sure to bring lots of water. To view the spectacular Delicate Arch without the 3 mi. hike, take the **Delicate Arch Viewpoint "Trail"** which begins in the Viewpoint parking area. This 300 ft. trail takes around 15min. and is wheelchair-accessible. The loop through **Devil's Garden** (3-5hr., 7¼ mi.) requires some scrambling over rocks, but hearty travelers will be rewarded by the eight arches visible from this trail. The trek is not recommended in wet or snowy conditions. **Tower Arch** (2-3hr., 3½ mi.) can be accessed from the trailhead at the Klondike Bluffs parking area via Salt Valley Rd. This moderate hike explores one of the remote regions of the park, and is a good way to escape crowds. The trail ascends a steep, short rock wall before meandering through sandstone fins and sand dunes. Salt Valley Rd. is often washed out—check at the Visitors Center before departing.

CAPITOL REEF ☎435

What do you get when you cross rock formations that strangely resemble the capitol dome of the State House in Washington with precipitous rock cliffs? A strangely inappropriate name for Utah's stunning, youngest national park. The hundred-mile Waterpocket Fold is a geologist's fantasy and the park's feature attraction. With its rocky peaks and pinnacles, the fold bisects Capitol Reef's 378 square miles, presenting visitors with millions of years of stratified natural history.

ORIENTATION & PRACTICAL INFORMATION. The middle link in the Fab Five chain, east of Zion and Bryce Canyon and west of Arches and Canyonlands, Capitol Reef is unreachable by major bus lines. The closest **Greyhound** and **Amtrak** stops are in Green River. For a fee, **Wild Hare Expeditions** (see **Sights and Outdoor Activities,** below) will provide shuttle service between Richfield and the park. **Entrance** to the park is free except for the scenic drive, which costs $5 per vehicle. The **Visitors Center,** on Rte. 24, supplies travelers with waterproof topographical maps, regular maps, free brochures on trails, and info on daily activities. (☎425-3791. Open daily June-Aug. 8am-6pm; Sept.-May 8am-4:30pm.) The free park newspaper, *The Cliffline*, lists a schedule of park activities. *When hiking, keep in mind that summer temperatures average 95°F. After rain, beware of flash floods.* Contact the Superintendent, Capitol Reef National Park, HC 70 Box 15, Torrey 84775 (☎425-3791; www.nps.gov/care). **Post Office:** 222 E. Main St., in Fruita. (☎425-3488. Open M-F 7:30am-1:30pm, Sa 7:30-11:30am.) **Postal Code:** 84775. **Area Code:** 435.

ACCOMMODATIONS & FOOD. The park's campgrounds offer sites on a first come, first served basis. The main campground, **Fruita ❶,** 1¼ mi. south of the Visitors Center off Rte. 24, contains 71 sites with water and toilets but no showers. The campground nestles between orchards, and visitors can eat all the fruit (usually apricots and cherries) they want. (Sites $10.) **Cedar Mesa Campground ❶,** on the Notom-Bullfrog Rd. and **Cathedral Valley ❶,** in the north (accessible by four-wheel-drive vehicle or on foot), have only five sites each; neither has water, but they're free. Both areas and all backcountry camping require a free **backcountry permit,** available at the Visitors Center.

Torrey, a sleepy town 11 mi. west of the Visitors Center on Rte. 24, is home to the nearest lodging and restaurants to Capitol Reef. The friendly **Sandcreek Hostel ❶,** 54 Rte. 24, features an espresso and smoothie bar, organic produce, local

THE SOUTHWEST

crafts, and remarkably inexpensive accommodations. A single dorm room houses eight comfy beds, a minifridge, and a microwave. There are also 12 tent sites, 12 hookups, and two rustic cabins that sleep up to four people. (☎425-3577. Showers for non-guests $4. Linens $2. Reception 7:30am-8pm. Check-out 11am. Open Apr. to mid-Oct. Dorms $10; tent sites $11; hookups $16-18; cabins $28-34.) Down the road, the **Capitol Reef Inn ❷**, 360 W. Main St., puts up guests with flair in Southwestern themed rooms with handmade furniture, plus access to a jacuzzi. (☎425-3271. Reception 7am-10pm. Check-out 11am. Open Apr.-Oct. Rooms $40; each additional person $4.)

The **Capitol Reef Cafe ❷**, in the Capitol Reef Inn, dishes up local rainbow trout (smoked or grilled) and other fresh, natural specialties in a dining room that looks out on the russet hills. Don't miss the grilled trout sandwich served on a bagel with cream cheese ($7.75) or one of their $8-11 lush salads. (Open Apr.-Oct. daily 7am-10pm.) Greasier offerings await at **Brink's Burgers ❶**, 163 E. Main St. (☎425-3710. Take-out available. Entrees $2-5. Open daily 11am-9pm. Cash only.)

SIGHTS & OUTDOOR ACTIVITIES. The Reef's haunting landforms can be explored from the seat of your car on the 25 mi. **scenic drive,** a 1hr. round-trip jaunt next to the cliffs along paved and improved dirt roads. Along Rte. 24, you can ponder the bathroom-sized **Fruita Schoolhouse** built by Mormon settlers, 1000-year-old **petroglyphs** etched on the stone walls, and **Panorama Point. Chimney Rock** and the **Castle** are two striking sandstone formations along the route.

Wild Hare Expeditions, 2600 E. Rte. 24, in the Best Western Capitol Reef Resort, embarks on a variety of backpacking and hiking tours. (☎425-3999 or 888-304-4273. Hours vary. $40-50 per half-day, children $35; full-day $60-75/50.) If you want to strike out on your own, the easy Capitol Gorge Trail (2 mi. round-trip, 2-3hr.) runs off the scenic drive and makes a good warm-up for longer treks. The **Rim Overlook and Navajo Knobs Trail** (9 mi. round-trip, 4-8hr.), one of the more challenging routes in the park, departs from the Hickman Bridge parking area and climbs to the canyon rim above the river. Vistas from Rim Overlook (2¼ mi.) and Navajo Knobs (4½ mi.) are breathtaking.

For a change of scenery check out the **orchards,** which lie within the park in the Fruita region. Eat as much fruit as you like while in the orchards, but you must pay to take some home. In the northern and southern sections of the park, all hikes are considered backcountry travel. Be sure to get a **free backcountry permit** for all overnight trips. More reasonable and plebeian day hikes depart from trailheads along Rte. 24. Check at the Visitors Center for more info on hikes.

BRYCE CANYON ☎435

If Nature enjoys painting with a big brush in the Southwest, she discarded her usual coarse tools when creating Bryce Canyon. The canyon brims with slender, fantastically shaped rock spires called hoodoos. What it lacks in Grand Canyonesque magnitude, Bryce makes up for in intricate beauty. Early in the morning or late in the evening the sun's rays bring the hoodoos to life, transforming them into color-changing stone chameleons. The first sight of the canyon can be breathtaking: as Ebenezer Bryce, a Mormon carpenter with a gift for understatement, put it, the canyon is "one hell of a place to lose a cow."

ORIENTATION & PRACTICAL INFORMATION. Approaching from the west, Bryce Canyon lies 1½hr. east of Cedar City; take Rte. 14 or Rte. 20 to U.S. 89. From the east, take I-70 to U.S. 89, turn east on Rte. 12 at Bryce Jct. (7 mi. south of Panguitch), and drive 14 mi. to the Rte. 63 junction; head south 4 mi. to the park entrance. There is no public transportation to Bryce Canyon. The park's entrance fee is $20 per car, $15 if parking outside the park, and $10 per pedestrian. The **Visitors Center** is just inside the park. (☎834-5322. Open June-Aug. 8am-8pm; Apr.-May and Sept.-Oct. 8am-6pm; Nov.-Mar. 8am-4:30pm.) To assuage the park's traffic problem, the Park Service has implemented a **shuttle system,** serving all destinations via three routes. Private vehicles can travel park roads, but the Park Service offers a $5 admission discount to those who park at the junction of Rte. 12 and 63 and ride the shuttle into the park. **Post Office:** In Ruby's Inn Store (☎834-8088), just north of the park entrance. Window open M-F 8:30am-noon and 12:30-4:30pm. No credit cards accepted. **Postal Code:** 84717. **Area Code:** 435.

ACCOMMODATIONS & FOOD. **North** and **Sunset Campgrounds ❶,** both within 3 mi. of the Visitors Center, offer toilets, picnic tables, potable water, and 216 sites on a first come, first served basis. (Sites $10; arrive early to claim the best spots.) Two campgrounds lie just west of Bryce on scenic Rte. 12, in Dixie National Forest. The **King Creek Campground ❶,** 11 mi. from Bryce on Forest Service Road 087 off Rte. 12 (look for signs to Tropic Reservoir), features lakeside sites. (☎800-280-2267. Sites $10.) At 7400 ft., the **Red Canyon Campground ❶** has 36 sites on a first come, first served basis amid the glory of the red rocks. (Sites $11.) Obtain **backcountry camping permits** ($5) from the ranger at the Visitors Center.

Sleeping inside the park requires either a tent and sleeping bag or a fat wallet. Away from the park, rates drop; better deals line Rte. 12 in Tropic, and Panguitch, 23 mi. west of the park on U.S. 89, has more than 15 inexpensive, independent motels. Winter rates are much, much lower, and in slow summers, bargain walk-in rates abound. **Bybee's Steppingstone Motel ❷,** 21 S. Main St., in Tropic, offers clean, spacious and cheap rooms minutes from the park entrance, but far away from the tourist bustle. (☎679-8998. Singles summer $40; doubles $45.) In Panguitch, the **Marianna Inn ❷,** 699 N. Main St., boasts large, newly remodeled rooms and amenities such as a large outdoor porch for relaxing on hot summer days and a hot tub for warming up on chilly fall afternoons. (☎676-8844. Singles summer $45, winter $30; doubles $60.)

Inside and immediately surrounding the national park, food options are scarce. A quick slice of pizza or a microwaved burrito await at the **Bryce Canyon General Store.** For a sit-down lunch inside the park, try the $5-6 burgers and sandwiches at **Bryce Canyon Lodge Dining Room ❷.** With a little driving, more affordable and varied alternatives multiply. Thick, golden brown pancakes ($2) await starving passersby at the **Hungry Coyote ❶,** on N. Main St. in Tropic. (☎679-8811. Open Apr.-Oct. daily 6:30-10:30am and 5-10pm.) Several miles west of the park on Rte. 12, the **Bryce Pines Restaurant ❸** serves delicious home-cooked meals. (☎834-5441. Sandwiches $5-8; dinner entrees $13-19. Open summer daily 6:30am-9:30pm.)

SIGHTS & OUTDOOR ACTIVITIES. Bryce's 18 mi. main road winds past spectacular lookouts such as **Sunrise Point, Sunset Point, Inspiration Point,** and **Rainbow Point,** but a range of hiking trails makes it a crime not to leave your car. A word to the wise: the air is thin—if you start to feel giddy or short of breath, take a rest. Very sturdy shoes or hiking boots are a must for hiking into the canyon. One oft-missed viewpoint is **Fairlyland Point,** at the north end of the park, 1 mi. off the main road, with some of the best sights in the canyons. From overlooks on the **Rim Trail** (4-6hr., 11 mi.) hikers can see over 100 mi. The loop of the **Navajo** and **Queen's Garden Trails** (2-3hr., 3 mi.) leads into the canyon past some natural bridges. More challenging options include **Peek-A-Boo Loop** (3-4hr., 3½ mi.), winding in and out through hoodoos, and the **Trail to the Hat Shop** (4 mi.), an extremely steep trail (tough both ways). **Canyon Trail Rides** arranges guided horseback rides. (☎679-8665. 2hr. rides $30, half-day $45.)

GRAND STAIRCASE-ESCALANTE NAT'L MONUMENT ☎435

The last corner of American wilderness to be captured by a cartographer's pen, Grand Staircase-Escalante National Monument remains remote, rugged, pristine, and beautiful. The 1.9 million acre expanse of painted sandstone, high alpine plateau, treacherous canyons, and raging rivers shelters diverse areas of geological, biological, and historical interest. Travelers just passing through the Escalante area en route to national parks east and west have a variety of options for getting a brief glimpse of the Monument's wild beauty. Scenic **Route 12,** tracing picturesque slickrock hills 28 mi. between Boulder and Escalante, is arguably one of the Southwest's most spectacular stretches of highway. Just before descending into the farming community of Boulder, the highway threads a narrow flat between dramatic drops, the vehicular equivalent to a titillating summit-ridge hike.

A **free backcountry permit** is required for all multi-day trips into the monument. The most popular destination for backpacking trips are the **Canyons of Escalante,** in the eastern portion of the monument. Cutting through the slickrock towards Lake Powell, the Escalante and its feeder drainages create a series of canyons ripe for exploration. Many routes require technical canyoneering skills. Primary access to the canyons of Escalante comes via the **Hole-in-the-Rock Road,** heading south from Rte. 12 east of Escalante. One of the most challenging routes in the area, this 30 mi. trek through Death Hollow Wilderness, which earns its ominous name with lethal flash floods, navigates narrow slot canyons north of town. The hike involves technical climbing and long stretches of swimming with a heavy pack through pools. Two campgrounds reside in the Escalante area. The 13 shaded sites at **Calf Creek Campground ❶,** 15 mi. east of Escalante, offer access to the Calf Creek Trail. (Toilets and water. Sites $7.) Six miles north of Boulder on Rte. 12, there are seven primitive sites at **Deer Creek ❶.** (Toilets. No water. Sites $4.)

Nearly two million acres is a lot of space, probably more than an entire lifetime's worth of walking could cover. Being so large, several communities serve as gateways to different portions of the monument. In the south, **Route 89** between Kanab and **Lake Powell** cuts into the monument and provides access to the popular **Cottonwood Canyon Road.** At the far eastern limit of the monument, many Glen Canyon recreationalists park their boats for day hikes in the lower canyons of the Escalante drainage. Visitor information is available at the **Escalante Interagency Visitors Center,** 755 W. Main (☎826-5499), in Escalante. The official **monument headquarters** is at **Kanab Field Office,** 745 Rte. 89E, in Kanab. (☎644-4680. Open late Mar. to mid-Nov. daily 7:30am-5:30pm.)

ZION NATIONAL PARK ☎435

Russet sandstone mountains loom over the puny cars and hikers that flock to Zion National Park in search of the promised land, and rarely does Zion disappoint. In the 1860s, Mormon settlers came to the area and enthusiastically proclaimed that they had found Zion, the promised land. Brigham Young disagreed, however, and declared that the place was awfully nice, but "not Zion." The name "not Zion" stuck for years until a new wave of explorers dropped the "not," giving the park its present name. The park might very well be the fulfillment of Biblical prophecy for outdoor recreationalists. With unparalleled hiking trails and challenging and mysterious slot canyons set against a tableau of sublime sandstone, visiting Zion is a spiritual event.

ORIENTATION & PRACTICAL INFORMATION. The main entrance to Zion is in **Springdale,** on Rte. 9, which borders the park to the south along the Virgin River. Approaching Zion from the west, take Rte. 9 from I-15 at Hurricane. In the east, pick up Rte. 9 from U.S. 89 at Mt. Carmel Jct. **Greyhound** (☎800-231-2222), has service as far as Hurricane, while Zion Canyon Transportation (☎877-635-5993) has 24hr. shuttle service from St. George to Zion (round-trip $27.) The brand new, ecologically harmonious **Zion Canyon Visitors Center,** just inside the south entrance, houses an info center, bookstore, and backcountry permit station. (☎772-3256; www.nps.gov/zion. Open daily Memorial Day to Labor Day 8am-7pm; mid-Apr. through Memorial Day and Labor Day to Sept. 8am-6pm; Oct. through mid-Apr. 8am-5pm.) At the northwest entrance to the park, the **Kolob Canyons Visitors Center** offers info on the Kolob Canyon Scenic Drive and the surrounding trail system, as well as books and maps. (☎586-9548. Open daily Memorial Day-Labor Day 7am-7pm; mid-Apr. through Memorial Day 7am-6pm; Labor Day-Sept. 7am-6pm; and Oct. through mid-Apr. 8am-4:30pm.) The park's entrance fee is $20 per car, $10 per pedestrian. **Emergency:** ☎911 or ☎772-3322. **Post Office:** Inside the Zion Canyon Lodge. (☎772-3213. Open M-F 8am-4:30pm, Sa 8am-noon.) **Postal Code:** 84767. **Area Code:** 435.

ACCOMMODATIONS & CAMPING. The closest hostel is the **Dixie Hostel (HI-AYH) ❶,** 73 S. Main St., 20 mi. west of Zion in Hurricane. Bright, airy, and immaculate, the hostel is a comfortable stay and only 2hr. from Las Vegas, the North Rim, and Bryce Canyon. (☎635-8202. Linen, laundry, kitchen, and continental breakfast. Internet access $1 per hr. Dorms $15; singles $35.) The family-owned **El Río Lodge ❸,** 995 Zion Park Blvd., welcomes guests with clean rooms, friendly service, and dazzling views of the Watchman Face. (☎772-3205 or 888-772-3205. Singles $47; doubles $52. Winter rates dip to around $35.) Across the street, the **Terrace Brook Lodge ❸,** 990 Zion Park Blvd., offers clean and reasonably inexpensive rooms. (☎800-342-6779. Singles $49-55; doubles $65-71. $10 less in winter. AAA discounts.) More than 300 sites are available at the **South** and **Watchman Campgrounds ❶,** near the brand new Visitors Center. Campgrounds fill quickly in summer; arrive before noon to ensure a spot. **Watchman Campground** takes reservations, but **South** is first come, first served. (☎800-365-2267 for Watchman reservations. Water, toilets, and sanitary disposal station. Both $14.)

FOOD. The Zion Canyon lodge houses the only in-park concessions: **Castle Dome Cafe ❶** (burgers, salads, and subs $3-7; open daily Apr.-Oct. 10am-7pm.) and the **Red Rock Grill ❷** (☎772-3213; open daily 6-10am, 11:30am-2:30pm, and 4:30-10pm.) **Sol Foods ❶,** 95 Zion Park Blvd. (connected with the Visitors Center by a footbridge), has big breakfasts, crafted sandwiches, and juicy burgers, all for $4-6. (☎772-0277. Open daily mid-Feb. to Dec. 7am-9pm, Jan. to mid-Feb. 8am-8pm.) The funky **Oscar's Cafe ❷**, 948 Zion Park Blvd., also has burgers and breakfasts ($4-8), along with innovative Mexican entrees for $10-13. (☎772-3232. Open daily Mar.-Oct. 6:30am-10:30pm, Nov.-Feb. 7:30am-10pm.)

OUTDOOR ACTIVITIES. Zion seems to have been made for hiking; unlike the foreboding canyons that surround it, most of the trails won't have you praying for a stray mule to show up. However, a number of trails spiral around cliffs with narrow ledges and long drop-offs. Hiking boots are recommended on trails like Angel's Landing or Hidden Canyons. The trails are serviced by a prompt shuttle bus system that delivers bright-eyed hikers to and from trailheads (runs 6:30am-11:15pm). Shuttle maps are available at the Visitors Center.

The **Riverside Walk** (1-2hr., 2 mi.), paved and wheelchair-accessible with assistance, begins at the Temple of Sinawava at the north end of Zion Canyon Dr. Running alongside the Virgin River and some beautiful wildflower displays, Riverside is Zion's most popular and easiest trail. The **Emerald Pools Trail** (1-3hr., 1-

3.1 mi.) has wheelchair access along its lower loop, but the middle and upper loops are steep and narrow. Swimming is not allowed in any of the pools. The challenging **Angel's Landing Trail** (4hr., 5 mi.) begins in the Grotto picnic area, and rises 1488 ft. above the canyon; the last terrifying stretch climbs a narrow ridge with guide chains blasted into the rock. A shorter, but equally harrowing trail is **Hidden Canyon Trail** (2-3hr., 2 mi.), rewarding hikers with impressive valley views. The difficult **Observation Point Trail** (5hr., 8 mi.) leads through **Echo Canyon,** a spectacular kaleidoscope of sandstone, where steep switchbacks explore the unusually gouged canyon. Overnight hikers can spend days on the 13 mi. course of the **West Rim Trail.**

One of the best ways to take in Zion's splendor is to ride the shuttle bus loop. Called the **Zion Canyon Scenic Loop,** this 1½ hr. narrated ride gives great views of the rocks from below. Another motorized way to take in the scenery is the 10 mi. **Zion-Mt. Carmel Highway,** connecting the east and south entrances. Spiraling around the Canyon, the highway gives excellent views of the valley, as well as a fun trip through an 80 year-old mountain tunnel.

When visiting the **Kolob Canyons,** check out **Zion Canyon.** The 7 mi. dead-end road on the canyon floor rambles past the giant **Sentinel, Mountain of the Sun,** and the symbol of Zion, the **Great White Throne.** A shuttle from the Lodge runs this route every hour on the hour. (During summer daily 9am-5pm. $3.)

Despite being overshadowed by the boastful Moab, the Zion area has a loyal **mountain biking** following and trails to compete with the big boy to the north. **Gooseberry Mesa,** about 15 mi. from Springdale, has some great singletrack and novice trails. **Springdale Cycles,** 1458 Zion Park Blvd., offers high-quality bike rentals, single and multi-day tours, and trail advice. (☎772-0575 or 800-776-2099; www.springdalecycles.com. Open M-Sa 9am-7pm. Front suspension half day $25, full day $35; full suspension $35/45; kids $7/10.)

NEAR ZION: CEDAR BREAKS NATIONAL MONUMENT ☎435

Shaped like a gigantic amphitheater, the semicircle of canyons that makes up Cedar Breaks National Monument measures more than 3 mi. in diameter and 2000 ft. in depth. A gallery of sandstone spires decorate the red, orange, and yellow surface of the bowl. To reach this marvel of geology, take Rte. 14 east from Cedar City and turn north on Rte. 148. A 28-site **campground** ❶ perched at 10,200 ft. (open June to mid-Sept.; water, flush toilets; sites $12) and the **Visitors Center** (☎586-0787; open June to mid-Sept.; open 8-6pm) await at **Point Supreme.** There are no services inside the monument; the nearest gas, food, and lodging are found either in Cedar City or Brian Head. (☎586-9451. $3; under 17 free.)

Tourists travel to the Monument nearly exclusively for the view, most easily reached by parking at the Visitors Center and walking to Point Supreme, or by stopping at one of several vistas along the 5 mi. stretch of scenic Rte. 143. The Monument has two established trails that provide for a more extended visit. Originating at the **Chessman Ridge Overlook** (10,467 ft., roughly 2 mi. north of the Visitors Center), the popular 2 mi. round-trip **Alpine Pond Trail** follows the rim to a spring-fed alpine lake whose waters trickle into the breaks, winding toward slow evaporation in the Great Basin. The hike takes 1-2hr. and is accompanied by an instructive trail guide available at the Visitors Center or trailhead ($1). The 4 mi. round-trip **Ramparts Trail** departs from the Visitors Center at 10,300 ft. and traces the edge of the amphitheater through a Bristlecone grove to a 9950 ft. point, providing spectacular views of the terrain below. Though reaching the monument during the winter proves difficult on snowy roads, cross-country skiers cherish the rolling meadows and serene winter scenery.

ARIZONA

Home to the Grand Canyon, the majority of the Navajo Reservation, seven national forests, and two large cities, Arizona constantly defies its image as a land of endless desert highway. The dry scrub of the Sonoran desert, spotted with cacti and the occasional dusty, pit-stop town, makes for a starkly beautiful landscape, while Arizona's cities, temperate sky-island forests, and northern mountain biking country provide enough variety for hours, days, or weeks of captivating exploration.

Populated primarily by Native Americans until the end of the 19th century, Arizona has been hit in the past hundred years by waves of settlers—from the speculators and miners of the late 1800s, to the soldiers who trained here during World War II and returned after the war, to the more recent immigrants from Mexico. Traces of lost Native American civilization remain at Canyon de Chelly, Navajo National Monument, and Wupatki and Walnut Canyons, while deserted ghost towns are scattered throughout the state. The descendents of area tribes now occupy reservations on one-half of the state's land, making up one-seventh of the US Native American population, while urban Phoenix sprawls wider and wider.

PRACTICAL INFORMATION

Capital: Phoenix.

Visitor Info: Arizona Tourism, 2702 N. 3rd St., #4015, Phoenix 85004 (☎602-230-7733 or 888-520-3434; www.arizonaguide.com). Open M-F 8am-5pm. **Arizona State Parks,** 1300 W. Washington St., Phoenix 85007 (☎602-542-4174 or 800-285-3703). Open M-F 8am-5pm.

Postal Abbreviation: AZ. **Sales Tax:** variable 5%.

Time Zone: Mountain Standard Time. *With the exception of the Navajo reservation, Arizona does not observe Daylight Savings Time.*

GRAND CANYON

Long before its designation as a national park in 1919, the Grand Canyon captured the imagination of each person who strolled to its edge and beheld it. Every summer, millions of visitors travel from across the globe to witness this natural wonder which, in one panorama, captures the themes that make the Southwest so captivating. First, there's the space: 277 miles long and over one mile deep, the Canyon overwhelms the human capacity for perception. Then, there's the color: a panoply of hues demarcate billions of years of geologic history. Finally, there's the river: the chaotically creative force behind most of the Southwest's beautiful landforms is on full display.

The Grand Canyon extends from Lee's Ferry, AZ to Lake Mead, NV. In the north, the Glen Canyon Dam backs up the Colorado into mammoth Lake Powell. To the west, the Hoover Dam traps the remaining outflow from Glen Canyon to form Lake Mead. Grand Canyon National Park is divided into three sections: the most popular South Rim; the more serene North Rim; and the canyon gorge itself. Traveling between rims takes approximately 5hr., either via a 13-mile hike or a long drive to the bridge in Lee's Ferry. Sandwiched between the national park and Lake Mead, the Hualapai and Havasupai Reservations abut the river.

SOUTH RIM ☎928

During the summer, everything on two legs or four wheels converges on this side of the Grand Canyon. If you plan to visit at this time, make reservations well in advance for lodging, campsites, and/or mules, and prepare to battle the crowds. A friendly Park Service staff, well-run facilities, and beautiful scenery help ease crowd-anxiety. Fewer tourists brave the canyon's winter weather; many hotels and facilities close during the off season. Leading up to the Park entrance, Rte. 64 is surrounded by Kaibab National Forest and encompasses the North Rim.

TRANSPORTATION

There are two park entrances: the main **south entrance** is about 6 mi. from the Visitors Center, while the eastern **Desert View** entrance is 27 mi. away. Both are accessed via Rte. 64. From Las Vegas, the fastest route to the South Rim is U.S. 93 S to I-40 E, and then Rte. 64 N. From Flagstaff, head north on U.S. 180 to Rte. 64.

Trains: The **Grand Canyon Railway** (☎800-843-8724) runs an authentically restored train from Williams, AZ to the Grand Canyon (2¼hr.; leaves 10am, returns 3:30pm; $68, children $27). Guided tours of the rim area run $25-35.

Buses: North Arizona Shuttle and Tours (☎866-870-8687) departs its Flagstaff depot, 1300 S. Milton St., for the Grand Canyon daily (2hr.; leaves 7:30am and 2:30pm, returns to Flagstaff 10am and 4:30pm; $20 each way). Fares don't include $6 entrance fee. Shuttles also head to Sedona twice a day ($25).

Public Transit: Free shuttle buses run the West Rim Loop (daily 1hr. before sunrise to sunset) and the Village Loop (daily 1hr. before sunrise to 11pm) every 10-30min. A free **hiker's shuttle** runs every 30min. between the info center and the South Kaibab Trailhead, on the East Rim near Yaki Point. Early buses run at 4, 5, and 6am.

Taxi: ☎638-2822.

ORIENTATION & PRACTICAL INFORMATION

Posted maps and signs in the park make it easy to orient oneself. Lodges and services concentrate in **Grand Canyon Village,** at the end of Park Entrance Rd. The east half of the village contains the Visitors Center and the general store, while most of the lodges and the challenging **Bright Angel Trail** lie in the west section. The shorter but more difficult **South Kaibab Trail** is off East Rim Dr., east of the village. Free shuttle buses to eight rim overlooks run along **West Rim Dr.** (closed to private vehicles during the summer). Avoid walking on the drive; the rim trails are safer and more scenic. The **entrance pass** is $20 per car and $10 for travelers using other modes of transportation, including bus passengers. The pass lasts for one week. For most services in the Park, call the main switchboard number at ☎638-2631.

Visitor Info: The new **Canyon View Information Plaza,** across from Mather Point just after the entrance to the park, is the one-stop center for Grand Canyon info. The Visitors Center stocks copies of *The Guide* (an essential), and assorted other pamphlets. To get there, park at Mather Pt., then get out and hoof it for ½ mi. to the info plaza. The Park Service, through the Grand Canyon Association, sells a variety of informational books and packets (☎800-858-2808; www.grandcanyon.com, or check out www.nps.gov/grca). The **transportation info desks** in **Bright Angel Lodge** and **Maswik Lodge** (☎638-2631) handle reservations for mule rides, bus tours, plane tours, Phantom Ranch, taxis, and more. Open daily 6am-8pm.

Equipment Rental: In the General Store. Comfy hiking boots, socks included ($8 first day, $5 per additional day); sleeping bags ($9/5); tents (2 person $15/9, 4 person $16/9); day packs ($6 large, $4 small); and other camping gear (stoves $5). Deposits required; major credit cards accepted. Open daily 7am-8:30pm.

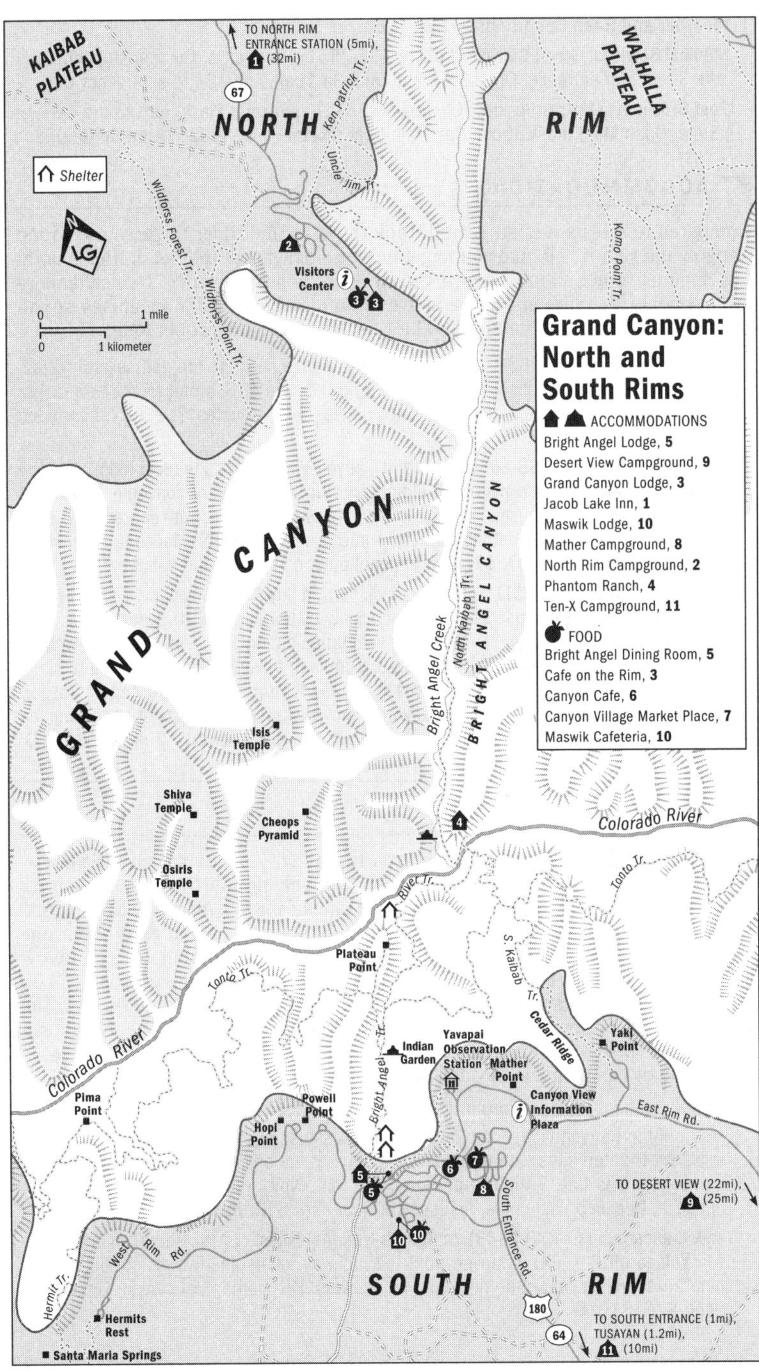
Grand Canyon: North and South Rims
ACCOMMODATIONS
Bright Angel Lodge, 5
Desert View Campground, 9
Grand Canyon Lodge, 3
Jacob Lake Inn, 1
Maswik Lodge, 10
Mather Campground, 8
North Rim Campground, 2
Phantom Ranch, 4
Ten-X Campground, 11
FOOD
Bright Angel Dining Room, 5
Cafe on the Rim, 3
Canyon Cafe, 6
Canyon Village Market Place, 7
Maswik Cafeteria, 10
Shelter
KAIBAB PLATEAU
WALHALLA PLATEAU
NORTH RIM
GRAND CANYON
SOUTH RIM
BRIGHT ANGEL CANYON
TO NORTH RIM ENTRANCE STATION (5mi), (32mi)
67
Ken Patrick Tr.
Uncle Jim Tr.
Widforss Forest Tr.
Widforss Point Tr.
Komo Point Tr.
Visitors Center
0 1 mile
0 1 kilometer
North Kaibab Tr.
Bright Angel Creek
Isis Temple
Shiva Temple
Cheops Pyramid
Osiris Temple
Colorado River
Tonto Tr.
River Tr.
Plateau Point
S. Kaibab Tr.
Cedar Ridge
Yaki Point
Indian Garden
Bright Angel Tr.
Yavapai Observation Station
Mather Point
Canyon View Information Plaza
East Rim Rd.
Pima Point
Powell Point
Hopi Point
TO DESERT VIEW (22mi), (25mi)
West Rim Rd.
Hermit Tr.
South Entrance Rd.
180
64
Hermits Rest
Santa Maria Springs
TO SOUTH ENTRANCE (1mi), TUSAYAN (1.2mi), (10mi)

THE SOUTHWEST

Weather and Road Conditions: ☎638-7888.

Medical Services: Grand Canyon Clinic (☎638-2551). Turn left at the first stoplight after the South Rim entrance. Open M-F 7am-7pm, Sa 10am-4pm. 24hr. emergency aid.

Post Office: 100 Mather Business Ctr. (☎638-2512), in Market Plaza, next to the General Store. Open M-F 9am-4:30pm, Sa 10am-5pm. **Postal Code:** 86023. **Area Code:** 928.

ACCOMMODATIONS

Compared to the six million years it took the Colorado River to carve the Grand Canyon, the year it will take you to get indoor lodging near the South Rim is nothing. Summer rooms should be reserved eleven months in advance. That said, there are frequent cancellations; if you arrive unprepared, check for vacancies or call the operator (☎638-2631) and ask to be connected with the proper lodge.

Maswik Lodge (☎638-2631), in Grand Canyon Village near the rim and several restaurants. Small, clean cabins with showers but no heat are $66. Motel rooms with queen beds and ceiling fans are also available. Singles $79; doubles $121. $7-9 for each additional person. ❹

Bright Angel Lodge (☎638-2631), in Grand Canyon Village. The cheapest indoor lodging in the park, located in a historic building right on the rim. Very convenient to Bright Angel Trail and shuttle buses. "Rustic" lodge singles and doubles with shared bath $53, with private bath $71. "Historic" cabins, some of which have fireplaces, are available for 1 or 2 people $84-107. $7 per additional person in rooms and cabins. ❸

Phantom Ranch (☎638-2631), on the canyon floor, a day's hike down the Kaibab Trail or Bright Angel Trail. Breakfast $17; box lunch $8.50; stew dinner $20; steak dinner $29, prepared the same way for over 50 years; vegetarian option $20. Don't show up without reservations, which can be made up to 23 months in advance. If you're dying to sleep on the canyon floor but don't have a reservation, show up at the Bright Angel transportation desk at 6am on the day prior to your planned stay and take a shot on the waiting list. Male and female dorms $28; seldom-available cabins for 1 or 2 people $71.50; $10.50 per additional person. ❷

CAMPING

The campsites listed here usually fill up early in the day. In the **Kaibab National Forest,** along the south border of the park, you can pull off a dirt road and camp for free. No camping is allowed within a quarter-mile of U.S. 64. **Dispersed camping** sits conveniently along the oft-traveled N. Long Jim Loop Rd.—turn right about one mile south of the south entrance station. For quieter and more remote sites, follow signs for the Arizona Trail into the national forest between miles 252 and 253 on U.S. 64. Sleeping in cars is not permitted within the park, but it is allowed in the Kaibab Forest. For more info, contact the **Tusayan Ranger Station,** Kaibab National Forest, P.O. Box 3088, Tusayan, AZ 86023 (☎638-2443). Reservations for some campgrounds can be made through **SPHERICS** (☎800-365-2267).

Mather Campground (call SPHERICS, ☎800-365-2267) in Grand Canyon Village, 1 mi. south of the Canyon Village Marketplace; follow signs from Yavapai Lodge. 320 shady, relatively isolated sites with no hookups. Check at the office even if the sign says the campground is full. 7-night max. stay. For Mar.-Nov., reserve up to 3 months in advance; Dec.-Feb. first come, first served. Sept.-May $12; June-Aug. $15. ❶

Ten-X Campground (☎638-2443), in Kaibab National Forest, 10 mi. south of Grand Canyon Village off Rte. 64. Removed from the highway, offers shady sites surrounded by pine trees. Toilets, water, no hookups, no showers. First come, first served. Open May-Sept. Sites $10. ❶

Desert View Campground (☎638-7888), 25 mi. east of Grand Canyon Village. Short on shade and far from the hub of the South Rim, but a perfect place to avoid the crowd. 50 sites with phone and restroom access, but no hookups or campfires. Open mid-May to Oct. No reservations; usually full by early afternoon. Sites $10. ❶

 FOOD

Fast food has yet to sink its greasy talons into the South Rim (the closest McDonald's is 7 mi. south in Tusayan), but you can find meals at fast-food prices and get a slightly better return for your money. The **Canyon Village Market Place ❶,** at the Market Plaza 1 mi. west of Mather Point on the main road, has a deli counter with the cheapest eats in the park, a wide selection of groceries, camping supplies, and enough Grand Canyon apparel to clothe each member of your extended family. (☎638-2262. Sandwiches $2-4. Open daily summer 7am-8:30pm; deli open 7am-6pm.) The well-stocked **Canyon Cafe ❶,** across from the General Store inside the Yavapai Lodge, offers a wider variety of food than the deli. (Hamburgers $3, pizza $3.50-5, dinners $5-7. Open daily 6:30am-9pm.) **Maswik Cafeteria ❶,** in Maswik Lodge, serves a variety of grilled food, country favorites, and Mexican specialties in a wood-paneled cafeteria atmosphere. (Hot entrees $6-7. Sandwiches $3-5. Open daily 6am-10pm.) **Bright Angel Dining Room ❷,** in Bright Angel Lodge, serves hot sandwiches ($7-9) and breakfasts ($6-7), while pricey dinner entrees range $10-15. (☎638-2631. Open daily 6:30am-10pm.) Just outside the dining room, the **Soda Fountain ❶** at Bright Angel Lodge chills eight flavors of ice cream and stocks a variety of snack-bar sandwiches. (Open daily 8am-8pm. 1 scoop $2.)

HIKING

Hikes in and around the Grand Canyon can be broken down into two categories: day hikes and overnight hikes. Confusing an overnight hike for a day hike can lead to disaster, and permanent residency in the canyon. Hiking to the Colorado River is reserved for overnight trips. All overnight trips require permits obtained through the Backcountry Office. In determining what is an appropriate day hike, remember that the Canyon does not have any loop hikes. Be prepared to retrace every single footstep uphill on the way back. Begin before 7am for day hikes, and consult a ranger before heading out. Park Service rangers also present a variety of free, informative talks and guided hikes; times and details are listed in *The Guide.*

The **Rim, Bright Angel, South Kaibab,** and **River** trails are the only South Rim trails regularly maintained and patrolled by the park service. There are a number of other trails and paths into and around the Canyon, such as **South Bass, Grandview,** and **Tonto.** These trails are only for the experienced hiker, and may contain steep chutes and technical terrain. Consult a ranger and *The Guide* before heading out.

Rim Trail (4-6hr., 12 mi. one way). With only a mild elevation change (about 200 ft.) and the constant security of the nearby shuttle, the Rim Trail is excellent for hikers seeking a tame way to see the Canyon. The handicap accessible trail follows the shuttle bus routes along Hermit Rd. past the Grand Canyon Village to Mather Point. The Rim Trail covers both paved and unpaved ground, with 8 viewpoints along Hermit Rd. and 3 east of it. Near the Grand Canyon Village, the Rim Trail resembles a crowded city street that runs behind the lodges, but toward the eastern and western ends, hikers have a bit more elbow room. Hopi Point is a great place to watch the sun set with its panoramic canyon views—*The Guide* lists times for sunsets and sunrises, and the "Choose your view" kiosk at the Visitors Center allows photographers to preview typical scenery at different locations and times of day. Bring lots of water, as little is available along the trail.

Bright Angel Trail (1-2 days, up to 18 mi. round-trip). Bright Angel's frequent switchbacks and refreshing water stations make it the into-the-canyon choice of moderate hikers. Depending on distance, the trail can make either a day or overnight hike. The trail departs from the Rim Trail near the western edge of the Grand Canyon Village, and the first 1-2 mi. of the trail generally attract droves of day hikers eager to try just a taste of canyon descent. Rest houses are strategically stationed 1½ and 3 mi. from the rim, each with water from May to Sept. **Indian Gardens,** 4½ mi. down, offers restrooms, picnic tables, 15 backcountry campsites open year-round, and blessed shade. From rim to river, the trail drops 4420 ft. Although spread over 9 mi., the round-trip is too strenuous for a day hike. With the compulsory permit, overnighters can camp at Indian Gardens or on the canyon floor at Bright Angel Campground, while day hikers are advised to go no farther than Plateau Point (12¼ mi. round-trip) or Indian Gardens (9¼ mi. round-trip). Yield and wave bitterly to tourists descending by mule train. The **River Trail** (1¾ mi.) runs along the river, linking the Bright Angel with South Kaibab.

South Kaibab Trail (4-5hr. descent, 7 mi. one way to Phantom Ranch). Those seeking a more challenging hike down might consider this route. Beginning at Yaki Pt. (7260 ft.), Kaibab is trickier, steeper, and lacks shade or water, but it rewards the intrepid with a better view of the canyon. Unlike most canyon-descending trails, the South Kaibab avoids the safety and obstructed views of a side-canyon route and instead winds directly down the ridge, offering panoramic views across the expanse of the canyon. Day hikes to Cedar Ridge (3 mi. round-trip; toilet facilities available) and Skeleton Point (6 mi. round-trip) are reasonable only for experienced, well-conditioned hikers due to the trail's steep grade. For overnight hikes, Kaibab meets up with Bright Angel at the Colorado River. Fewer switchbacks and a more rapid descent make the South Kaibab Trail 1¾ mi. shorter than the Bright Angel to this point. Guests staying at the Phantom Ranch or Bright Angel Campground (the only permitted camping area on the trail) use either the Bright Angel or South Kaibab to reach the ranch. Many hikers believe that the best route is to descend the South Kaibab Trail (4-5hr.) and come back up the Bright Angel (7-8hr.) the following day, though this is very strenuous. 4880 ft. elevation change.

OUTDOOR ACTIVITIES

Beyond using your feet, there are other ways to conquer the canyon. **Mule trips** from the South Rim are expensive and booked up to one year in advance, although some do cancel. (☎303-297-2757. Daytrip to Plateau Point 6 mi. down the Bright Angel Trail $127, overnight including lodging at Phantom Ranch and all meals at $343 per person.) Mule trips from the North Rim (☎435-679-8665) are cheaper and more readily available, such as the 8hr. day trip to Roaring Springs waterfall ($95). Looking up at the Grand Canyon from a **whitewater raft** is also both popular and pricey. Trips into the Grand Canyon proper vary in length from a week to 18 days and are booked far in advance. The *Trip Planner* (available by request at the info center) lists several commercial guides licensed to offer trips in the canyon; check the park web site for info in advance of your visit. If the views from the rim fail to dazzle and astound you, try the higher vantages provided by one of the park's many **flightseeing** companies, all located at the Grand Canyon Airport outside of Tuyasan. **Grand Canyon Airlines** flies 45min. canyon tours hourly during the summer. (☎866-235-9422. $75, children $45. Reservations recommended, but walk-ins generally available. Discount for lunchtime tours, 11am-2pm.) For a list of flight companies in the park, write the Grand Canyon Chamber of Commerce, Box 3007, Grand Canyon, AZ 86023.

NORTH RIM ☎928

If you're coming from Utah or Nevada, or want to avoid the crowds at the South Rim, the park's North Rim is more rugged and more serene, with a view almost as spectacular as that from the South Rim. Unfortunately, it's hard to reach by public

From your first glimpse of the canyon, you may feel a compelling desire to see it from the inside, an enterprise that is harder than it looks. Even the young at heart and body should remember that an easy downhill hike can become a nightmarish 50° incline on the return journey. Also, keep in mind that the lower you go, the hotter it gets; when it's 85°F on the rim, it's around 100°F at Indian Gardens and around 110°F at Phantom Ranch. Heat stroke, the greatest threat to any hiker, is marked by a monstrous headache and red, sweatless skin. *For a day hike, you must take at least a gallon of water per person; drink at least a quart per hour hiking upwards under the hot sun.* Footwear with excellent tread is also necessary—the trails are steep, and every year several careless hikers take what locals morbidly call "the 12-second tour." Safety tips can be found in *The Guide,* but speak with a ranger before embarking on a hike. Parents should think twice about bringing children more than 1 mi. down any trail.

transportation, and by car it's a long drive. From October 15 to December 1, the North Rim is open for day use only; from December 1 to May 15, it is closed entirely. Any visit to the North Rim centers on the North Rim Lodge, an elegant structure overlooking the canyon.

ORIENTATION & PRACTICAL INFORMATION

To reach the North Rim from the South Rim, take Rte. 64 E to U.S. 89 N, which runs into Alt. 89; from Alt. 89, follow Rte. 67 S to the edge. Altogether, the beautiful drive is over 220 mi. From Utah, take Alt. 89 S from Fredonia. From Page, take U.S. 89 S to Alt. 89 to Rte. 67 S. Snow closes Rte. 67 from early December to mid-May and park facilities (including the lodge) close between mid-October and mid-May. The visitor **parking** lot lies near the end of Rte. 67, strategically close to both the Visitors Center and lodge, about 13 mi. south of the park entrance. Trailhead parking is also available at North Kaibab and Widforss Trails and at scenic points along the road to Cape Royal.

Visitor Info: North Rim Visitors Center (☎638-7864), on Rte. 67 just before the Lodge. Open daily 8am-6pm. **Kaibab Plateau Visitors Center** (☎643-7298), at Jacob Lake, next to the Inn. Interpretive displays provide details on the creation of the canyon and its ecosystem, and backcountry permits are issued here. Open daily 8am-5pm.

Buses: Transcanyon, P.O. Box 348, Grand Canyon 86023 (☎638-2820). Buses run to the South Rim (5hr.; late May-Oct. leaving 7am from North Rim Lodge, 1:30pm from Bright Angel Lodge at the South Rim; $65, round-trip $110). Reservations required.

Public Transit: A **hikers' shuttle** runs from the Lodge to the North Kaibab Trailhead (late May-Oct. 5:20am, 7:20am; $5, $2 per additional person). Tickets must be purchased in advance at the Lodge.

Weather Conditions: (☎638-7888). Updated 7am daily.

Post Office: Grand Canyon Lodge (☎638-2611). Open M-F 8-11am and 11:30am-4pm, Sa 8am-1pm. **Postal Code:** 86052.

ACCOMMODATIONS

The North Rim has one campground, creatively named "North Rim Campground," and it generally fills entirely by reservation during the summer. **SPHERICS** (☎800-365-2267) handles reservations. If you can't get in-park lodgings, head for the **Kaibab National Forest,** which runs from north of Jacob Lake to the park entrance. You can camp for free, as long as you're ¼ mi. from the road, water, or official campgrounds, and 1 mi. from any commercial facility. Less expensive accommodations may be found in **Kanab, UT,** 80 mi. north.

Grand Canyon Lodge (☎638-2611; reservations ☎1-888-29-PARKS), on the edge of the rim. This swank rustic lodge is the only indoor rim lodging in the park. Reserve as early as 6 months in advance, or 2 years in advance for 1 of the 4 rim-view cabins. Check out the overlook near the reception area, providing comfy seats and a truly stunning look at the chasm. No TVs. Reception 24hr. Open mid-May to Oct. Singles or doubles in frontier cabins and hotel rooms $91. 4-person pioneer cabins $91-116. ❺

Jacob Lake Inn (☎643-7232), 32 mi. north of the North Rim entrance at Jacob Lake. Charming lodge, gift shop, cafe (see below), and bakery. Reception daily 6am-9pm. Furnished cabins for 2 $72-83; triples $86-88; quads $90-92; motel units $91-106. ❸

North Rim Campground (call SPHERICS ☎800-365-2267), on Rte. 67 near the rim, the only park campground on this side of the chasm. Well-spaced pine- and aspen-shaded sites. Groceries, laundry, and showers nearby. 83 sites; no hookups. Open mid-May to mid-Oct. 7-night max. stay. Sites $15; 4 "premier sites" with canyon views $20. ❶

FOOD

Grand Canyon Lodge (☎638-2612, ext. 160) monopolizes in-park eating options, which tend toward the pricey side. The lodge's dining room, treating guests to sweeping canyon views and *haute cuisine,* serves breakfast for $5-8, lunch for $6.50-8.50, and dinner for $13 and up. Open daily 6:30-10am, 11:30am-2:30pm, and 5-9:30pm. Reservations required for dinner. ❸

Cafe on the Rim dishes out standard salads from $4-6, and cheese pizza by the slice goes for $2.50. Breakfasts range $3-5. Open daily 7am-9pm. ❷

Jacob Lake Inn is a superb alternative to the North Rim establishments. The intimate diner counter, a fine-dining restaurant, and amiably staffed bakery combine to offer a variety of options. Pick up a gravity-defying milkshake ($3) to make the remaining miles a bit more enjoyable. Sandwiches $6. Breakfasts $5-6. Dinners $12-15. ❸

OUTDOORS

Hiking in the leafy North Rim seems like a trip to the mountains—the mountain just happens to be upside-down. All precautions for hiking at the South Rim are even more important at the North Rim, where the elevations are higher and the air is thinner. In-depth info on trails can be found in the North Rim's version of *The Guide.* Day hikes of variable lengths beckon the active North Rim visitor. Pick up the indispensable *Official Guide to Hiking the Grand Canyon*, available in all Visitors Centers and gift shops. Overnight hikers must get permits from the **Backcountry Office** in the ranger station. (Open daily 8am-noon and 1-5pm.)

Park Rangers run nature walks, lectures, and evening programs at the North Rim Campground and Lodge. Check the info desk or campground bulletin boards for schedules. One-hour ($20), half-day ($45), and full-day ($9) **mule trips** through **Canyon Trail Rides** circle the rim or descend into the canyon. (☎435-679-8665. Open daily 7am-5pm. No credit cards.) Reservations are recommended but walk-ins can be accommodated more frequently than on the South Rim.

HAVASUPAI RESERVATION ☎928

To the west of the hustle and bustle of the South Rim lies the tranquility of the Havasupai Reservation. Meaning "people of the blue-green water," the Havasupai live in a protected enclave, bordered by the national park. Ringed by dramatic sandstone faces, their village, Supai, rests on the shores of the Havasu River. Just beyond town, a rushing wonder of crystal-clear water cascades over a series of spectacular falls. Such beauty attracts thousands yearly, but a grueling 10 mi. hike separates the falls from any vehicle-accessible surface and prevents over-exposure of the reservation. For most, blistered feet or a saddle-sore rump make bathing in the cool waters even sweeter.

Supai and the campground can only be reached by a trail originating on the rim at the Hualapai Hilltop. To reach the trailhead, take I-40 E until Rte. 66 at Seligman; follow Rte. 66 for 30 mi. until it meets with Indian Rd. 18, which ends at the Hilltop after 60 mi. No roads lead to Supai, although mules and helicopters can be hired to carry bags or people. For mule reservations, contact **Havasupai Tourist Enterprise.** (☎448-2141. One-way $75, half of which is required as a deposit. Includes 4 pieces of luggage not exceeding 130 lb. total. Groups leave at 10am) **Skydance Helicopter** flies between the hilltop and village four days per week. (☎800-882-1651. Flights every 15-20min. on M, Th-F, and Su 9am-3pm. One-way $70; first come, first served.)The hike is not to be underestimated. The well-marked trail is a grueling, exposed 8 mi. to Supai and then an additional 2 mi. to the campground. *Do not hike down without a reservation*—you may have to turn around and walk right back to the trailhead.

Reservations for the campground, lodge, and mules can be made by calling the **Havasupai Tourist Enterprise.** Visitors must first check-in at the **Tourist Office** in Supai before heading onto the campground. In the village, there's a Post Office, a general store, and cafe. Prices are high, because everything must be brought in by mule or helicopter. Bringing your own food to the campground is advised. All trash must be packed-out. No **gas** or **water** is available past Rte. 66; stock up beforehand.

The Havasupai tribe operates two accommodations: the **Havasupai Campground** and the Havasupai Lodge, both on the canyon floor. The friendly campground, 2 mi. beyond Supai, lies between Havasu and Mooney Falls, bordering the blue-green water of the Havasu River and near swimmer-friendly lagoons. The Tribe charges a one-time entry fee ($20 per visitor and $10 per night) at the campground. There are no showers, and the non-flush toilets tend to smell up the sites. A spring provides fresh water, and the falls are a quick jaunt away. The **Havasupai Lodge ❹**, in Supai, offers basic accommodations ($75-95 for up to 6 people, plus the entrance fee). The trail from Supai to the campground extends to **Mooney Falls** (1 mi. from campground), **Beaver Falls** (4 mi.), and the **Colorado** (7 mi.). The steep hike down to Mooney Falls may turn your stomach. Extreme caution should be exercised—shoes with good tread are a must. Swimming and frolicking are both permitted and encouraged in the lush lagoons at the bottom of the falls.

FLAGSTAFF ☎928

Born on the 4th of July, Flagstaff began as a rest stop along the transcontinental railroad; its mountain springs provided precious refreshment along the long haul to the Pacific. These days, Flagstaff is still a major rest stop on the way to Southwestern must-sees. Trains plow through town 72 times a day, while travelers pass through on their way to the Grand Canyon, Sedona, and the Petrified Forest—all within day-trip distance. The energetic citizens welcome travelers to their rock formations by day and their breweries by night; many have wandered into town with camera in hand and ended up settling down. Retired cowboys, earthy Volvo owners, New Agers, and serious rock climbers comprise much of the population.

TRANSPORTATION

Flagstaff sits 138 mi. north of Phoenix (take I-17), 26 mi. north of Sedona (take U.S. 89A), and 81 mi. south of the Grand Canyon's south rim (take U.S. 180).

Trains: Amtrak, 1 E. Rte. 66 (☎774-8679). Two trains leave daily. Eastbound train leaves at 5:28am for: **Kansas City** and **Chicago** via **Winslow** (1hr., $14-23); **Gallup, NM** (2½hr., $35-61); and **Albuquerque** (5hr., $63-110). Westbound train leaves at 9:23pm for **Los Angeles** (12hr., $68-119). Station open daily 4:45pm-7:30am.

Buses: Two bus lines provide service to regional destinations. Check at the Grand Canyon and Debau International Hostels for their Grand Canyon and Sedona shuttles.

Greyhound: 399 S. Malpais Ln. (☎774-4573), across from Northern Arizona University (NAU) campus, 3 blocks southwest of the train station on U.S. 89A. Turn off 89A by Dairy Queen. To: **Albuquerque** (6½hr., 5 per day, $41); **Las Vegas** (5-6hr., 3 per day, $47); **Los Angeles** (10-12hr., 8 per day, $49); **Phoenix,** including airport (3hr., 5 per day, $22). Terminal open 24hr.

Sedona Shuttle Service: Coconino/Yavapai Shuttle Service (☎775-8929 or 888-440-8929) offers daily trips from Flagstaff to **Sedona.** The 1hr. trip leaves from Flagstaff M-F 8am, 4pm and returns from Sedona at 2:30pm. On Sa, the Flagstaff-Sedona leg leaves 10am with no return trip. One-way $18.

Public Transit: Mountain Line (☎779-6624). Routes cover most of town. Buses run once per hr.; route map and schedule available at Visitors Center in Amtrak station. One-way $0.75,children $0.60, seniors and disabled $0.35. Book of 20 passes $13.

Taxi: Friendly Cab ☎774-4444.

Car Rental: Enterprise Rent-A-Car (☎526-1377), 3420 E. Rte. 66. Starting at $39 per day. 21+. Must have license and credit card. Open M-F 7:30am-6pm, Sa 9am-noon.

ORIENTATION & PRACTICAL INFORMATION

The downtown area revolves around the intersection of **Leroux Street** and **Route 66** (formerly Santa Fe Ave.). The Visitors Center, bus station, both hostels, and a number of inexpensive restaurants lie within a half mile of this spot. **South San Francisco Street,** a block east of Leroux St., hosts many outdoors shops. Split by Rte. 66, the northern area of Flagstaff is more touristed and upscale while the area south of the tracks is down to earth, housing hostels and vegetarian eateries.

Visitor Info: Flagstaff Visitors Center, 1 E. Rte. 66 (☎774-9541 or 800-842-7293), in Amtrak station. Open daily Memorial Day-Labor Day 7am-7pm; rest of year 8am-5pm.

Equipment Rental and Outfitting: Peace Surplus, 14 W. Rte. 66 (☎779-4521), 1 block from Grand Canyon Hostel. Rents tents ($7-9 per day), packs ($5-6 per day), sleeping bags ($6 per day), and stoves ($3 per day), as well as alpine, nordic, and snowshoe packages in winter. 3-day min. rental; hefty $100-200 credit card or cash deposits are required. Open M-F 8am-9pm, Sa 8am-8pm, Su 8am-6pm. **Summit Divers and Watersports,** 103 S. Milton (the western part of Rte. 66 in town) rents kayaks for $35 per day, $45 for 2 days, and $65 for a weekend. (☎556-8780. Open M-Sa 10am-5pm.) **Four Season Outfitters and Guides,** 107 W. Phoenix Ave. (☎226-8798; www.fsoutfitters.com), offers guided backcountry hikes and canyoneering in Escalante or the Grand Canyon. Reflecting Flagstaff's love affair with its natural surroundings, **Goshawk Ecotours** (☎773-1198) guides nature trips of all kinds for $18 per hr. ($50 minimum).

Emergency: ☎911. **Police:** Sawmill Rd. (general info ☎556-2316, non-emergencies ☎774-1414).

Medical Services: Flagstaff Medical Center, 1200 North Beaver St. (☎779-3366), provides medical services in the area, including 24hr. emergency service.

Internet Access: Free access at NAU's **Cline Library** (☎523-2171). Take Riordan Rd. east from Rte. 66. Open M-Th 7:30am-10pm, F 7:30am-6pm, Sa 10:30am-5pm, Su noon-10pm. $3 per ½hr., $5 per hr. at the **Flagstaff Public Library,** 300 W. Aspen Ave. (☎779-7670). Open M-Th 10am-9pm, F 10am-7pm, Sa 10am-6pm.

Post Office: 2400 N. Postal Blvd. (☎714-9302), on Rte. 66, for general delivery. Open M-F 9am-5pm, Sa 9am-noon. **Postal Code:** 86004. **Downtown,** 104 N. Agassiz St. (☎779-3559). Open M-F 9am-5pm, Sa 9am-1pm. **Postal Code:** 86001.

ACCOMMODATIONS

The Weatherford Hotel, 23 N. Leroux St. (☎779-1919). The oldest hotel in Flagstaff, dating to 1898, the Weatherford has 8 spacious rooms with amazing balconies and bay windows. Equipped with elegant furnishings and located in the middle of downtown, but lacks TV and in-room phones. Reservations recommended. Rooms $55. ❸

Hotel Monte Vista, 100 N. San Francisco St. (☎779-6971 or 800-545-3068; www.hotelmontevista.com), downtown. Feels like a classy hotel, with quirky decor and a faux peeling-brick lounge that was used in the filming of *Casablanca*. Chock-full of colorful history; staff swears the hotel is chock-full of ghosts too. Private rooms named after the movie stars they once slept start at $60 on weekdays. ❹

CAMPING

Free backcountry camping is available around Flagstaff in designated wilderness areas. Pick up a map from the **Peaks Ranger Station,** 5075 N. 89A (☎526-0866), to find out where. All backcountry campsites must be located at least 200 ft. away from trails, waterways, wet meadows, and lakes. There is a 14-night limit for stays in the Coconino National Forest. For info on camping, call the **Coconino National Forest Line.** (☎527-3600. Open M-F 7:30am-4:30pm)

Lakeview Campground, on the east side of Upper Lake Mary, 11½ mi. south on Lake Mary Road (off I-17 south of Flagstaff), is surrounded by a pine forest that supports an alpine ecosystem. Drinking water, pit toilets, no reservations. Open May-Oct. $10 per vehicle per night. ❶

Pinegrove Campground (☎877-444-6777; reservations www.reserveamerica.com), sits 5 mi. south of Lakeview at the other end of Upper Lake Mary. Set in a similarly charming locale, offers drinking water and flush toilets. $12 per vehicle. ❶

Ashurst/Forked Pine Campground, flanks both sides of Ashurst lake (a smaller, secluded lake on Forest Rd. 82E). Turn left off Lake Mary Rd., across from Pine Grove Campground. Water and flush toilets are on-site, and the fishing is stupendous. 64 sites are available on a first come, first served basis. $10 per vehicle. ❶

FOOD

Macy's European Coffee House and Bakery, 14 S. Beaver St. (☎774-2243), behind Motel Du Beau. A cheery and earthy hangout serving only vegetarian food and

THE HIDDEN DEAL

FLAGSTAFF TWIN HOSTELS

Grand Canyon International Hostel, 19 S. San Francisco St. (☎779-9421, 888-442-2696; www.grandcanyonhostel.com), near the train station. Sunny, clean, and classy, and friendly despite its size (32 beds). Free parking, showers, linen, tea, and coffee. Access to kitchens, TV room with cable, Internet ($2 per 30min.), free breakfast (7-10am), and laundry facilities ($1 wash, $0.25 per dry). Free pick-up from Greyhound station. Offers tours to the Grand Canyon ($50) and to Sedona ($25). Reception 7am-midnight. No curfew. Sometimes travelers work for lodging–inquire with the manager. Reservations with credit card. 4-bed dorms Oct.-May $15, June-Sep. $17; private rooms without bath Oct.-May $30/33 week/weekend and June-Sept. $34/37. ❶

Du Beau International Hostel, 19 W. Phoenix St. (☎774-6731, 800-398-7112; www.dubeau.com), also just behind the train station. The Du Beau lives up to its ritzy name with recently renovated dorm rooms (most with 8 beds), private bathrooms, and a lively, well-equipped common room. Reception 7am-midnight. Under the same ownership as the Grand Canyon Hostel, Du Beau offers all the same services. 8-bed dorms Oct.-May $15, June-Aug. $17. Private rooms with bath Oct.-May $32/35 and June-Sep. $36/39. ❶ excellent vegan selections. $4-7 specials change daily. Get there early and start the day with a bowl of granola ($4) and one of their fresh-roasted coffees ($1-3.50). Open Su-Th 6am-8pm, F-Sa 6am-10pm. Food served until 1hr. before close. No credit cards. ❶

Mountain Oasis Global Cuisine and Juice Bar, 11 E. Aspen St. (☎214-9270), offers a pleasant, softly lit eating area with live classical guitar on F during the summer. A wide variety of food from around the world, including vegetarian, vegan, and organic options. Open Su-Th 11am-9pm, F-Sa 11am-10pm, but may close early if business is slow. ❷

Alpine Pizza Company, 7 Leroux St. (☎779-4109). Comfortably worn-in wood panelling sets the mountain-town tone of this eatery. Pool tables, foosball, and neon beer ads are standard; newspapers with scrawled public commentary as wallpaper in the men's room are anything but. Small single-topping pizza $8. Happy Hour Tu-Th 4-8pm. Open daily 11am-10pm. ❷

SIGHTS

In 1894, Percival Lowell chose Flagstaff as the site for an astronomical observatory, and then spent the rest of his life here, devoting himself to the study of heavenly bodies, and culling data to support his theory that life exists on Mars. The **Lowell Observatory,** 1400 W. Mars Hill Rd., 1 mi. west of downtown off Rte. 66, where he discovered the "planet" Pluto, doubles as both a general tribute to his genius and as a high-powered research center sporting five mammoth telescopes. During the daytime, admission includes tours of the telescopes, as well as a museum with hands-on astronomy exhibits. If you have stars in your eyes, come back at night for an excellent program about the night sky and the constellations. (☎774-3358; www.lowell.edu. Open daily Nov.-Mar. noon-5pm; Apr.-Oct. 9am-5pm. Evening programs Nov.-Mar. F-Sa 7:30pm; Apr.-May and Sept.-Oct. W, F, Sa 7:30pm; June-Aug. M-Sa 8pm. $4; students, seniors, and AAA $3.50; ages 5-17 $2.)

ENTERTAINMENT & NIGHTLIFE

North of town near the museum, the **Coconino Center for the Arts** houses exhibits, festivals, performers, and even a children's museum (☎779-2300). In the second weekend of June, the annual **Flagstaff Rodeo** comes to town with competitions, barn dances, a carnival, and a cocktail waitress race. Competitions and events go on from Friday to Sunday at the Coconino County Fair Grounds. (On Hwy. 89A just south of town, ask at the Flagstaff Visitors Center for details.) On the 4th of July, the town celebrates its birthday with street fairs, live music, outdoor barbecues, a parade, and, of course, fireworks. At the tail-end of the summer (Labor Day), the **Coconino County Fair** digs its heels into Flagstaff with rides, animal competitions, and carnival games. **Theatrikos,** a local theater group, stages plays year-round. (11 W. Cherry Ave. ☎774-1662; www.theatrikos.com.)

Charly's, 23 N. Leroux St., plays live jazz and blues in one of the classiest buildings in town. (☎779-1919. Happy hour 5-7pm. Open daily 11am-10pm; bar open daily 11am-1am.) Joe's Place, on the corner of San Francisco and Rte. 66, hosts indie bands weekend nights. (☎774-6281. Happy hour 4-7pm. Open 11am-1am.) The Alley plays to a similar crowd as Joe's, and sees many out-of-towners. (☎774-7929. Happy hour M-Sa 3-7pm, Su free nacho bar. Open daily 3pm-1am.) If country is your thang, the Museum Club, 3404 E. Rte. 66, a.k.a. the Zoo, is the premier spot for honky-tonk action. (☎526-9434. Cover $3-5. Open daily 11am-3am.)

OUTDOOR ACTIVITIES

With the northern **San Francisco Peaks** and the surrounding **Coconino National Forest,** Flagstaff offers numerous options for the rugged outdoorsman or those simply interested in walking off last night's fun. Nature's playground provides skiing, hiking, biking, and general awe-struckedness. Due to the 7000 ft. plus altitudes, bring plenty of water, regardless of the season or activity. In late spring and summer, National and State Park Rangers may close trails if the potential for fire gets too high. The mountains occupy national forest land, so **backcountry camping ❶** is free.

SKIING

The **Arizona Snow Bowl,** operates four chairlifts (and a tow rope) and maintains 32 trails. The majestic **Humphrey's Peak** (12,633 ft.) is the backdrop for the Snowbowl, though the skiing takes place from 11,500 ft. off of **Agassiz Peak.** With an average snowfall of 260 in. and 2300 ft. of vertical drop, the Snow Bowl rivals the big time ski resorts of the Rockies and easily outclasses its Arizona competition. To reach the Snow Bowl, take U.S. 180 about 7 mi. north to the Fairfield Snow Bowl turnoff.

The Snow Bowl caters to a wide range of skiers and snowboarders and is evenly divided between beginner, intermediate, and advanced runs. (☎779-1951; www.arizonasnowbowl.com. Open daily 9am-4pm. Lift tickets adult weekend half-day $32, full-day $40; midweek $40/25; ages 8-12 $22/17.) **Equipment rental** is available on the mountain. (Half-day ski package $15, full-day $20; extreme performance package $30/20; snowboards $27/20.)

HIKING

In the summer, these peaks attract hikers and bikers aplenty. The Coconino National Forest has many trails for hikers of all abilities. Consult the **Peaks Ranger Station,** 5075 N. 89A (☎526-0866), for trail descriptions and possible closures. For the more energetic hiker, the **Elden Lookout Trail** is ideal for jaw-dropping mountain-top views. Only 6 mi. in length (round-trip), the trail climbs 2400 ft.; it is demanding, but worth the view. The trail begins at the Peaks Ranger station. The most popular trail in the area is the hike to **Humphrey's Peak,** Arizona's highest mountain. This 9 mi. round-trip begins in the first parking lot at the Snow Bowl ski area. For a longer hike, the moderate to strenuous 17½ mi. round-trip **Weatherford Trail** offers excellent opportunities for bird- and animal-spotting. The trailhead can be found next to Schultz Tank, about 7 mi. from Flagstaff.

MOUNTAIN BIKING

Flagstaff promises excellent mountain biking. The **Schultz Creek Trail** leads bikers into an extensive network of trails in the San Francisco Mountains. Take 180 north to Schultz Pass Rd. (Forest Service Rd. 420) and park in the dirt lot just as the road becomes unpaved. The trail climbs north along the bottom of a ravine and after almost 4 mi. splits into **Sunset Trail** heading south and **Little Elden Trail** heading east. Sunset Trail climbs through the woods before cresting and descending along **Brookbank Trail** down glorious singletrack dropoffs and switchbacks. This 4 mi. stretch spits out riders bearing sloppy grins of satisfaction onto Forest Service Road 557. This road can either be used to ride safely 4 mi. back to the trailhead or to access locally renowned and more technical **Rocky Ridge Trail,** which leads to the same trailhead.

DAYTRIPS FROM FLAGSTAFF

WALNUT CANYON NATIONAL MONUMENT

The remnants of more than 300 rooms in 13th-century Sinaguan dwellings make up Walnut Canyon National Monument. A glassed-in observation deck in the **Visitors Center,** 10 mi. east of Flagstaff, at Exit 204 off I-40, overlooks the whole canyon. (☎526-3367. Open daily 8am-6pm; low-season 8am-5pm. $3, under 17 free.) The steep, self-guided **Island Trail** snakes down from the Visitors Center past 25 cliff dwellings. The **Rim Trail** (¾ mi.) offers views of the canyon and passes rim-top sites. Every Saturday morning from 10am-1pm, rangers lead groups of five on 2 mi. hikes into Walnut Canyon to the original Ranger Cabin and more remote cliff dwellings. Reservations are required for these challenging 2½hr. hikes. There's also a trailhead for the Mexico-to-Utah portion of the Arizona trail.

SUNSET CRATER VOLCANO NATIONAL MONUMENT

The crater encompassed by Sunset Crater Volcano National Monument appeared in AD 1065. Over the next 200 years, a 1000 ft. high cinder cone took shape as a result of periodic eruptions. The self-guided **Lava Flow Nature Trail** wanders 1 mi. through the surreal landscape surrounding the cone, 1½ mi. east of the Visitors Center, where gnarled trees lie uprooted amid the rocky black terrain. Hiking up Sunset Crater itself is not permitted. The **Visitors Center,** 12 mi. north of Flagstaff on U.S. 89, supplies additional info. (☎526-0502. Open daily 8am-6pm; low-season 8am-5pm. $5, under 16 free; includes admission to Wupatki.)

WUPATKI NATIONAL MONUMENT

Wupatki possesses some of the Southwest's most scenic Pueblo sites, situated 18 mi. northeast of Sunset Crater, along a stunning road with views of the Painted Desert. The Sinagua moved here in the 11th century, after the Sunset Crater eruption forced them to evacuate the land to the south. Archeologists speculate that in less than 200 years, droughts, disease, and over-farming led the Sinagua to abandon these stone houses. Five empty pueblos face the 14 mi. road from U.S. 89 to the Visitors Center. Another road to the ruins begins on U.S. 89, 30 mi. north of Flagstaff. The largest and most accessible, **Wupatki,** located on a ½ mi. round-trip loop trail from the Visitors Center, rises three stories. The spectacular **Doney Mountain Trail** rises ½ mi. from the picnic area to the summit. Get info and trail guide brochures at the **Visitors Center.** Backcountry hiking is not permitted. (☎679-2365. Monument and Visitors Center open daily 8am-5pm.)

SEDONA ☎928

One wonders if the Martians said to make frequent visits to Sedona are simply mistaking its deep red-rock towers for home. The scores of tourists who descend upon the town year-round (Sedona rivals the Grand Canyon for tourist mass) certainly aren't; they come for sights that put others in the area to shame, and Newton's theories into doubt. Dramatic copper-toned behemoths dotted with pines tower over Sedona, rising from the earth with such flair and crowd appeal that they seem like manufactured tourist attractions—they aren't. Though the downtown is overrun with overpriced shops, the rocks are worth a visit.

ORIENTATION & PRACTICAL INFORMATION. Sedona lies 120 mi. north of Phoenix (take I-17 north to Rte. 179) and 30 mi. south of Flagstaff (take I-17 south to Rte. 179). The **Sedona-Phoenix Shuttle** (☎282-2066) runs six trips daily ($40). The **Sedona Chamber of Commerce,** at Forest Rd. and U.S. 89A, provides info on accommodations and local attractions. (☎282-7722. Open M-Sa 8:30am-5pm, Su 9am-3pm.) **Post Office:** 190 W. U.S. 89A. (☎282-3511. Open M-F 8:45am-5pm.) **Postal Code:** 86336. **Area Code:** 928.

ACCOMMODATIONS. Lodging in town is a bit pricey, but a few deals can be had. Just the same, it's not a bad idea to make Sedona a daytrip from Flagstaff or Cottonwood. **White House Inn ❸,** 2986 W. U.S. 89A (☎282-6680), is the second cheapest option, with singles and doubles, some with kitchenettes, from $47. A popular alternative to commercial lodging is renting a room in a private residence. Check the local papers or bulletin boards at New Age shops for opportunities. In addition, cheaper options can be found in Cottonwood, 15 mi. away, where a number of budget motels line U.S. 89. **Hostel Sedona ❶,** 5 E. Soldier Wash Dr., is the cheapest place to stay in town and possibly the only establishment without a trace of pretension. (☎282-2772. Check-in 7-10am and 5-10pm. Linen and towels $5. Dorms $15; singles $30; doubles $35. Weekly discounts available.)

Most of the campsites in the area are clustered around U.S. 89A as it heads north along Oak Creek Canyon on its way to Flagstaff. There are private campgrounds aplenty, but most cater to the RV crowd rather than to backpackers. The **US Forest Service campsites ❶** along 89A provide the best, cheapest option for tent-toters. North of Sedona, between nine and 20 mi. from the town, four separate campgrounds—**Manzanita, Bootlegger, Cave Springs, and Pine Flat (east and west)**—maintain over 150 campsites. They all have similar facilities, with picnic tables, toilets, drinking water (except at Bootlegger). (☎527-3600 for local info; ☎877-444-6777 national reservation service number. 7-night max. stay. Tent sites $12.)

FOOD. **Casa Rincon ❷,** 2620 U.S. 89A, attracts patrons with a daily Happy Hour (3-6pm; $3 margaritas), mouth-watering combination platters ($10-13), and almost daily live entertainment (☎282-4849. Open daily 11:30am-9pm.) **The Coffee Pot Restaurant ❶,** 2050 W. U.S. 89A, a local favorite, serves 101 varieties of omelettes ($5-8) and 3 kinds of tacos for $4. (☎282-6626. Open daily 6am-2:30pm.) **The Red Planet Diner ❷,** 1665 W. U.S. 89A, beams patrons in with a flying saucer and extraterrestrial allure. Martian milkshakes ($4) and Universal noodle bowls ($6-13) are "totally tubular." (☎282-6070. Open daily 11am-11pm.)

SIGHTS. The incredible formations at **Red Rock State Park** (☎282-6907) invite strolling or just contemplation. Located 15 mi. southwest of Sedona, the Park entrance can be found along the Red Rock Loop Road off U.S. 89A. Rangers lead occasional nature hikes into the nearby rock formations and are happy to give trail recommendations. The **Chapel of the Holy Cross,** on Chapel Rd., lies just outside a 1000 ft. rock wall in the middle of red sandstone. The view from the parking lot is a religious experience itself. (☎282-4069. Open M-Sa 9am-5pm, Su 10am-5pm.)

Montezuma Castle National Monument, 10 mi. south of Sedona on I-17, is a 20-room cliff dwelling built by the Sinagua tribe in the 12th century. Unfortunately, you can't get very close to the ruins, but the view from the paved path below is excellent and wheelchair-accessible. (☎567-3322. Open daily 8am-7pm; low-season 8am-5pm. $3, under 17 free.) A beautiful lake formed by the collapse of an underground cavern, **Montezuma Well,** off I-17 11 mi. north of the castle, once served as a source of water for the Sinagua who lived here. (Open daily 8am-7pm. Free.) Take U.S. 89A to Rte. 279 and continue through Cottonwood to reach **Tuzigoot National Monument,** 20mi. southwest of Sedona, a Sinaguan ruin by the Verde Valley. (☎634-5564. Open daily 8am-7pm; low-season 8am-5pm. $3, under 17 free.)

OUTDOOR ACTIVITIES. In terms of hiking, it's nearly impossible to go wrong with any of the well-maintained and well-marked trails in and around Sedona. Most trailheads are located on the forest service roads that snake from the highways into the hills and canyons around Sedona. Highlights include the **Wilson Mountain Loop** (4½ mi.), ascending Wilson Mountain, and the **Huckaby Trail** (5¼ mi. round-trip), traversing fantastic red rocks. Biking offers similar wonders. Considered a rival to Moab, UT by those in the mountain-biking know, Sedona has some of the best tracks in the world. Tamer trails can be found along the **Bell Rock Pathway,** which lies south of town. Bike rentals (starting at $25 per day) and good trail information can be found at **Mountain Bike Heaven,** 1695 W U.S. 89A. They also lead occasional free bike trips (call for dates and times) and do repairs for devilish spills. (☎282-1312. Open M-F 9am-6pm, Sa 8am-5pm, Su 9am-5pm.)

Scenic driving is nearly as plentiful as the red rocks. The Chamber of Commerce is very helpful in suggesting routes. The **Red Rock Loop** (20 mi., 1hr.) provides a little dirt road adventure and views of mind-blowing rock formations. Dry Creek and Airport Rd. are also good drives. For those hoping to see Sedona's wild off-road side, jeep tours are available from a number of companies. Generally, trips are $35-75 and 2-4hr. in length. **Canyon Outfitters,** 2701 W. U.S. 89A, provides climbing gear. (☎282-5294. Open M-F 9am-6pm, Sa 9am-5pm, Su 11am-4pm.)

NAVAJO RESERVATION

Although anthropologists believe the Navajo are descended from groups of Athabascan people who migrated to the Southwest from Northern Canada in the 14th and 15th centuries, the Navajo themselves view their existence as the culmination of a journey through three other worlds to this life, the "Glittering World." Four sacred mountains bound Navajoland—Mt. Blanca to the east, Mt. Taylor to the south, San Francisco Peak to the west, and Mt. Hesperus to the north.

During the second half of the 19th century, Indian reservations evolved out of the US government's *ad hoc* attempts to prevent fighting between Native Americans and Anglos while facilitating white settlement on native lands. Initially, the reservation system imposed a kind of wardship over the Native Americans, which lasted for over a century, until a series of Supreme Court decisions beginning in the 1960s reasserted the tribes' standing as semi-sovereign nations. Today, the **Navajo Nation** is the largest reservation in America and covers more than 27,000 sq. mi. of northeastern Arizona, southeastern Utah, and northwestern New Mexico.

For visitors to the reservation, cultural sensitivity takes on a new importance; despite the many state and interstate roads that traverse the reservation, the land is legally and culturally distinct. Superficially, much of the Navajo Nation and other reservations resemble the rest of the US. In reality, deep rifts exist between Native American and "Anglo" culture–the term used to refer to the non-reservation US society. The reservation has its own police force and laws. Driving or hiking off designated trails and established routes is considered trespassing unless accompanied by a guide. Possession and consumption of alcohol are prohibited on the reservation. General photography is allowed unless otherwise stated, but photographing the Navajo people requires their permission (a gratuity is usually expected). Tourist photography is not permitted among the Hopi. As always, the best remedy for cultural friction is simple respect.

Lively reservation politics are written up in the local *Navajo Times.* For a taste of the Navajo language and Native American ritual songs, tune your **radio** to 660AM, "The Voice of the Navajo." Remember to advance your watch 1hr. during the summer; the Navajo Nation runs on **Mountain Daylight Time,** while the rest of Arizona, including the Hopi Reservation, does not observe daylight savings, and thus operates on Pacific Time during the warmer months and Mountain Standard Time during the cooler months. The **area code** for the reservation is ☎928 in Arizona, 505 in New Mexico, 435 in Utah.

Monument Valley, Canyon de Chelly, Navajo National Monument, Rainbow Bridge, Antelope Canyon, and the roads and trails that access these sights all lie on Navajo land. Those planning to hike through Navajo territory should head to one of the many **parks and recreation departments** for a backcountry permit, or mail a request along with a money order or certified check to P.O. Box 9000, Window Rock, AZ 86515 ($5 per person). The "border towns" of **Gallup, NM** (see p. 865) and **Flagstaff, AZ** (see p. 829) are good gateways to the reservations, with car rental agencies, inexpensive accommodations, and frequent Greyhound service on I-40. Budget travelers can camp at the National Monuments or Navajo campgrounds, or stay in one of the student-run motels in high schools around the reservation.

MONUMENT VALLEY ☎435

The red sandstone towers of Monument Valley are one of the southwest's most otherworldly sights. Perversely, they're also one of the most familiar, since countless Westerns have used the butte-laden plain as their backdrop. Long before the days of John Wayne, ancestral Puebloans managed to sustain small communities here despite the arid climate. The park's looping 17 mi. **Valley Drive** winds around 11 of the most spectacular formations, including the famous pair of **Mittens** and the slender **Totem Pole.** However, the gaping ditches, large rocks, and mudholes on this road can be jarring to both you and your car—drive at your own risk and observe the 15 mph speed limit. The drive takes at least 1½hr. Other, less-touristed parts of the valley can be reached only by four-wheel-drive vehicle, horse, or foot. The Visitors Center parking lot is crowded with booths selling jeep, horseback, and hiking tours. (1½hr. jeep tour about $25 per person, full-day $100; horseback tours $30/120.) In winter, snow laces the rocky towers. Call the Visitors Center for road conditions.

The park entrance lies on U.S. 163 just across the Utah border, 24 mi. north of **Kayenta,** at the intersection of U.S. 163 and U.S. 160. The **Visitors Center** has info. (☎727-3353. Park and Visitors Center open May-Sept. $3, under 7 free.) There are few accommodations in the area. **Mitten View Campground,** ¼ mi. southwest of the Visitors Center, has showers but no hookups. (Sites $10; winter $5. Register at the Visitors Center.) Cheap motels can be found in **Mexican Hat, UT** and **Bluff, UT.**

NAVAJO NATIONAL MONUMENT ☎520

Until the late 1200s, a small population of the ancestors of the modern Hopi inhabited the region, though hard times left the villages vacant by 1300. Today, the site contains three cliff dwellings. **Inscription House** has been closed to visitors since the 1960s due to its fragile condition; the other two admit a very limited number of visitors. The stunning **Keet Seel** (open late May-early Sept.) can be reached only via a challenging 17 mi. round-trip hike. Hikers can stay overnight in a free campground nearby (no facilities or drinking water). Reservations for permits to visit Keet Seel must be made up to two months in advance through the Visitors Center (see below). Ranger-led tours to **Betatakin,** a 135-room complex, are limited to 25 people. (Open May-late Sept. 8:15am; first come, first served.) If you're not up for the trek to the ruins, the paved, 1 mi. round-trip **Sandal Trail** lets you gaze down on Betatakin from the top of the canyon. The **Aspen Forest Overlook Trail,** another 1 mi. hike, overlooks canyons and aspens, but no ruins. To get to the monument, take Rte. 564 from U.S. 160, 20 mi. southwest of Kayent. The **Visitors Center** lies 9 mi. along this road. (☎672-2700. Open daily 8am-5pm.) The free **Navajo Campground** ❶ next to the Visitors Center is a forested refuge and relief in the summer from the heat of the flatlands, has 30 sites.

HOPI RESERVATION ☎520

An island of coal-rich ore amid a sea of Navajo Nation grassland, Black Mesa and its three constitutive spurs, First Mesa, Second Mesa, and Third Mesa, have harbored the Hopi people and its traditions for over a millennium. The villages on **First Mesa** are the only places in the reservation really geared toward visitors. The **Ponsi Hall Community Center** serves as a general info center and a starting point for **guided tours.** (☎737-2262. Open daily June-Aug. 9am-6pm; Sept.-May 9:30am-5pm. Tours $5.) The villages on the **Second** and **Third Mesas** are less developed for tourism. However, on Second Mesa, the **Hopi Cultural Center,** 5 mi. west of the intersection of Rte. 264 and 87, serves as a Visitors Center and contains the reservation's only museum, displaying Hopi baskets, jewelry, pottery, and info about the tribe's history. (☎734-6650. Open M-F 8am-5pm, Sa-Su 9am-3pm. $3, under 14 $1.) **Free camping** is allowed at ten primitive sites next to the Cultural Center.

Visitors are welcome to attend a few Hopi **village dances** throughout the year. Often announced only a few days in advance, these religious ceremonies usually occur on weekends and last from sunrise to sundown. The dances are formal occasions; do not wear shorts, tank tops, or other casual wear. Photos, recordings, and sketches are strictly forbidden. Often several villages will hold dances on the same day, giving tourists the opportunity to village-hop. The **Harvest Dance,** in mid-September at the Second Mesa Village, is a spectacular ceremony with tribes from all over the US. Inquire at the cultural center, or the **Hopi Cultural Preservation Office** (☎734-2214), Box 123, Kykotsmovi 86039, for the dates and sites of all dances.

PETRIFIED FOREST NATIONAL PARK ☎520

Spreading over 60,000 acres, the Petrified Forest National Park looks like the aftermath of some prehistoric Grateful Dead concert—an enormous tie-dye littered with rainbow-colored trees. Some 225 million years ago, when Arizona's desert was a swampland, volcanic ash covered the logs, slowing their decay. When silica-rich water seeped through the wood, the silica crystallized into quartz, producing rainbow hues. Layers of colorful sediment were also laid down in this floodplain, creating the stunning colors that stripe its rock formations.

ORIENTATION & PRACTICAL INFORMATION. Roughly speaking, the park can be divided into two parts: the northern Painted Desert and the southern Petrified Forest. An entrance station and Visitors Center welcomes guests at each end and a 28 mi. road connects the two sections. With lookout points and trails strategically located along the road, driving from one end of the park to the other is a good way to take in the full spectrum of colors and landscapes.

You can enter the park either from the north or the south. (Open June-Aug. daily 7am-7pm; call for low-season hours. Entrance fee $10 per vehicle, $5 per pedestrian; $5 motorcycle.) There is no public transportation to either part of the park. To access the southern section of the park, from St. Johns take U.S. 180 36 mi. west or from Holbrook 19 mi. east. The **Rainbow Forest Museum** provides a look at petrified logs up close and serves as a **Visitors Center.** (☎524-6822. Open June-Aug. daily 7am-7pm. Free.) To reach the northern Painted Desert section of the park, take I-40 to Exit 311, 107 mi. east of Flagstaff and 65 mi. west of Gallup, NM. The **Painted Desert Visitors Center** is less than 1 mi. from the exit. (☎524-6228. Open summer daily 7am-7pm; call for low-season hours.) **Water** is available at both Visitors Centers and the Painted Desert Inn. There is also **gas** at the Painted Desert Visitors Center. In case of **emergency,** call the ranger dispatch (☎524-9726).

There are no established campgrounds in the park, but **backcountry camping ❶** is allowed in the fantastical Painted Desert Wilderness with a free permit. Backpackers must park their cars at Kachina Point and enter the wilderness via the 1 mi. access trail. No fires are allowed. Budget accommodations and roadside diners abound on Rte. 66. To get a real taste of the road, stay at the **Wigwam Motel ❸,** 811 W. Hopi Dr., where 15 concrete tepees await travelers. (☎524-3048; clewis97@apartrails.com. Reception 4-9pm. Check-out 11am. Singles $42; doubles $48.) **Gallup** and **Flagstaff** offer more lodging and eating options.

SIGHTS. Most travelers opt to drive the 27 mi. park road from north to south. From the north, the first stop is **Tiponi Point.** From the next stop at **Tawa Point,** the **Painted Desert Rim Trail** (½ mi. one-way) skirts the mesa edge above the Lithodendron Wash and the Black Forest before ending at **Kachina Point.** The panoramas from Kachina Point are among the best in the park, and the point provides access for travel into the **Painted Desert Wilderness,** the park's designated region for backcountry hiking and camping. As the road crosses I-40, it enters the Petrified Forest portion of the park. The next stop is the 100-room **Puerco Pueblo.** A short trail through the pueblo offers viewpoints of nearby petroglyphs. Many more petroglyphs may be seen at **Newspaper Rock,** but at a a distance. The road then wanders through the eerie moonscape of **The Tepees,** before arriving at the 3 mi. **Blue Mesa** vehicle loop. The **Long Logs** and **Giant Logs Trails,** near the southern Visitors Center, are littered with fragments of petrified wood. Both trails are less than 1 mi. and fairly flat but travel through the densest concentration of petrified wood in the world. Picking up fragments of the wood is illegal and traditionally unlucky.

PHOENIX ☎602

The name Phoenix was chosen for a small farming community in the Sonoran desert by Anglo settlers who believed that their oasis had risen from the ashes of ancient Native American settlements like the legendary phoenix of Greek mythology. The 20th century has seen this unlikely metropolis live up to its name; the expansion of water resources, the proliferation of railroad transportation, and the introduction of air-conditioning have fueled Phoenix's ascent to its standing as one of America's leading cities.

Phoenix's explosive expansion has caused it to outgrow its original 602 area code. The city is split into three area codes, with 602 limited to Phoenix proper, 623 for western greater Phoenix, and 480 for the East Valley (including Scottsdale, Tempe and Mesa). As a consequence, even calls made within the city require an area code. *Unless otherwise noted, all listings here are within the 602 area code.*

THE SOUTHWEST

TRANSPORTATION

Airport: Sky Harbor International (☎273-3300; www.phxskyharbor.com), just southeast of downtown. Take the Valley Metro Red Line bus into the city (3:15am-11:45pm, $1.25). The largest city in the Southwest, Phoenix is a major airline hub and tends to be an affordable and convenient destination.

Buses: Greyhound, 2115 E. Buckeye Rd. (☎389-4200). To: **El Paso** (8hr., 14 per day, $37); **Los Angeles** (7hr., 14 per day, $37); **San Diego** (8hr.; 4 per day; M-Th $52, F-Su $56); and **Tucson** (2hr., 11 per day, $16). Open 24hr. There is no direct rail service to Phoenix, but

Amtrak (☎800-USA-RAIL, www.amtrak.com) operates connector buses to and from rail stations in Tucson and Flagstaff for those interested in train travel. The Greyhound bus station is their busiest connecting Thruway motorcoach service location.

Public Transit, Downtown Phoenix: Valley Metro (☎253-5000). Most lines run to and from Central Station, at Central and Van Buren St. Routes tend to operate M-F 5am-8pm with reduced service on Sa. $1.25; disabled, seniors, and children $0.60. All-day pass $3.60, 10-ride pass $12. Bus passes and system maps at the Terminal. In Tempe, the **City of Tempe Transit Store,** 502 S. College Ave., Ste. 101, serves as public transit headquarters. The red line runs to and from Phoenix, and the last few stops of the yellow line are also in Tempe. The red line also extends beyond Tempe to service Mesa. Bus passes and system maps at the Terminal. Loloma Station, just south of Indian School and Scottsdale Rd., is Scottsdale's main hub for local traffic. The green line runs along Thomas St. to Phoenix.

Taxi: Yellow Cab, ☎252-5252. **Discount Taxi,** ☎254-1999.

Car Rental: Enterprise Rent-A-Car, 1402 N. Central St. (☎257-4177; www.enterprise.com), with other offices throughout the city. Compact cars at around $45 per day, with lower weekly and monthly rates. Surcharge for drivers under 21. A valid credit card and driver's license are required. N. Central St. office open M-F 7:30am-6pm, Sa 9am-noon; other offices' hours vary.

ORIENTATION & PRACTICAL INFORMATION

The intersection of **Central Avenue** and **Washington Street** marks the heart of downtown. Central Ave. runs north-south, Washington St. east-west. One of Phoenix's peculiarities is that numbered avenues and streets both run north-south; avenues are numbered sequentially west from Central, while streets are numbered east. Greater Phoenix includes a number of smaller municipalities. **Tempe,** east of Phoenix, is dominated by students from Arizona State University. **Mesa,** east of Tempe, handles much of Tempe's overflow. **Scottsdale,** north of Tempe, is a swank district brimming with adobe palaces, shopping centers, and interesting sights.

Visitor Info: Phoenix and Valley of the Sun Convention and Visitors Center (☎254-6500 or 877-225-5749, recorded info and events calendar ☎252-5588; www.phoenixcvb.com). Downtown location: 2nd and Adams St. Open M-F 8am-5pm. Free **Internet** (5min. limit). Biltmore Fashion Park location: 24th St. and East Camelback. Open daily 8am-5pm. Camping and outdoors information available at the **Bureau of Land Management Office,** 222 N. Central (☎417-9200).

Hotlines: Crisis Hotline ☎800-631-1314. 24hr. **Gay Hotline** ☎234-2752. Daily 10am-10pm. **Sexual Assault Hotline** ☎254-9000. **Suicide Prevention** ☎480-784-1500.

Internet Access: Burton Barr Central Library, 1221 N. Central Ave. (☎262-4636). Open M-Th 10am-9pm, F-Sa 9am-6pm, Su noon-6pm.

Post Office: 522 N. Central Ave. (☎800-275-8777). Open M-F 8:30am-5pm. General delivery: 1441 E. Buckeye Rd. Open M-F 8:30am-5pm. **Postal Code:** 85034.

ACCOMMODATIONS

Budget travelers should consider visiting Phoenix during July and August when motels slash their prices by as much as 70%. In the winter, when temperatures drop and vacancies are few, prices go up; make reservations if possible. The reservationless should cruise the rows of motels on **Van Buren Street** east of downtown, toward the airport. Parts of this area can be unsafe; *guests should examine a motel thoroughly before checking in.* Although they are more distant, the areas around Papago Fwy. and Black Canyon Hwy. are loaded with motels and may present some safer options. **Mi Casa Su Casa/Old Pueblo Homestays Bed and Break-**

Phoenix

ACCOMMODATIONS
Metcalf Hostel, **5**
YMCA, **6**

FOOD
Los Dos Molinos, **7**

NIGHTLIFE
Ain't Nobody's Bizness, **1**
Boom, **3**
Char's Has the Blues, **2**
Willow House, **4**

W. Cypress St.
TO 2 (2mi)
Heard Museum
TO 1
E. Monte Vista Rd.
Monte Vista Rd.
N. 3rd St.
E. Palm Ln.
1st St.
E. Coronado Rd.
Phoenix Art Museum
TO 3 (1mi)
E. McDowell Rd.
N. 3rd Ave.
N. Central Ave.
E. Brill St.
E. Willetta St.
W. Willetta St.
Burton Barr Central Library
N. 7th Ave.
N. 5th Ave.
W. Culver St.
10
Papago Fwy.
10
TO PAPAGO PARK (5mi), TEMPE (5mi)
1st St.
E. Portland St.
Portland St.
Roosevelt St.
Roosevelt St.
7th Ave.
5th Ave.
3rd Ave.
1st Ave.
Central Ave.
Garfield St.
McKinley St.
McKinley St.
3rd St.
5th St.
7th St.
N. 9th St.
Pierce St.
Fillmore St.
Fillmore St.
Taylor St.
Taylor St.
Arizona Center
Phoenix Union Municipal Center
Polk St.
Central Bus Station
TO (1.5mi)
Van Buren St.
Van Buren St.
Herberger Theater Center
Monroe St.
Museum of History
HERITAGE SQUARE
S. 9th St.
Phoenix Civic Plaza
Adams St.
Orpheum Theater
Renaissance Square
Visitor Information
Central Ave.
Arizona Science Center
Washington St.
Symphony Hall
E. Washington St.
CESAR CHAVEZ PLAZA
PATRIOTS SQUARE
Jefferson St.
Jefferson St.
Jefferson St.
TO SKY HARBOR INTERNATIONAL AIRPORT (3mi)
6th Ave.
5th Ave.
4th Ave.
Madison St.
America West Arena
7th Ave.
3rd Ave.
2nd Ave.
1st Ave.
1st St.
Jackson St.
3rd St.
Bank One Ballpark
7th St.
E. Jackson St.
Union Station Amtrak
TO GREYHOUND (3mi)
TO 7 (5mi), THE MYSTERY CASTLE (7mi)
Buchanan St.
N
LG
0 600 yards
0 600 meters

THE SOUTHWEST

fast, P.O. Box 950, Tempe 85280, arranges stays in B&Bs throughout Arizona, New Mexico, southern Utah, southern Nevada, and southern California. (☎800-456-0682. Open M-F 9am-5pm, Sa 9am-noon. $45 and up.)

Metcalf Hostel (HI-AYH), 1026 N. 9th St. between Roosevelt and Portland (☎258-9830, phxhostel@earthlink.net), a few blocks northeast of downtown. Look for the house with lots of foliage out front. The ebullient owner fosters a lively community in this renovated house. Kitchen, common room. Bikes for rent, and discounts to some city sights included in the price. Check-in 7-10am and 5-10pm. Light cleaning or other chores required. Dorms $15. ❶

Super 8 Motel, 4021 N. 27th Ave. (☎248-8880; www.super8.com), west on Indian School Rd. from the 17 Fwy. just north of downtown. Straightforward service, safe and well lit, and close enough to a freeway and downtown to serve as a base for the Phoenix area. High season (winter) $49; low-season $39. ❸

YMCA Downtown Phoenix, 350 N. 1st Ave. (☎253-6181). Another option in the downtown area, the YMCA provides small, single-occupancy rooms and shared bathrooms. Various athletic facilities. A small supply of women's rooms available. Ask at the desk about storing valuables. Open daily 9am-10pm. 18+. Daily $30; weekly $119. ❷

FOOD

Downtowners feed mainly at small coffeehouses, most of which close on weekends. **McDowell** and **Camelback Road** offer a (small) variety of Asian restaurants. The **Arizona Center,** an open-air shopping gallery at 3rd St. and Van Buren, boasts food venues, fountains, and palm trees. Sports bars and grilles hover around the America West Arena and Bank One Ballpark.

Dos Gringos Trailer Park, 216 E. University (☎480-968-7879). The best atmosphere in Tempe, bar-none. Dos, as it's affectionately known, draws people of all walks of life with its open, laidback feel and its inexpensive yet tasty Mexican food. Contribute to the tally that makes Dos the #1 national consumer of Coronas, and chase your drinks with one of countless meals for under $6. Open M-Sa 10am-1am, Su 11-1am. ❶

Los Dos Molinos, 8646 S. Central Ave. (☎243-9113). From downtown, head south on Central Ave. Once you leave the *barrio*, it comes up suddenly on your right, between South Mountain and Euclid. Lively, colorful, and fun, Los Dos Molinos is worth the trip. Locals throng here on weekends, filling the restaurant and the colorful courtyard and spilling onto the street. Come early, as they don't take reservations, or try its sister establishment on 260 S. Alma School Dr. in Mesa. Enchiladas $3.50, burritos $3-7. Open Tu-F 11am-2:30pm and 5-9pm, Sa 11am-9pm. ❶

5 & Diner, 5220 N. 16th St. (☎264-5220), with branches in the greater metro area. 24hr. service and all the sock-hop music that one can stand. Vinyl booths, pleasant service, and innumerable juke boxes convey a 50s feel. Burgers go for $6-7.50 and sandwiches are $5-8. Best milkshakes in town run only $4. Afternoon blue-plate specials (M-F 11am-7pm, $3-6) change daily but are always worth the money. Open 24hr. ❷

SIGHTS

DOWNTOWN. Downtown Phoenix offers a few museums and mounting evidence of America's growing consumer culture. The price of most downtown attractions hovers around $7; fortunately, the majority are worth it. The **Heard Museum** is renowned for its presentation of ancient Native American art, and features exhibits focusing on contemporary Native Americans. *(2301 N. Central Ave., 4 blocks north of McDowell Rd. ☎252-8840, recorded info ☎252-8848. Open daily 9:30am-5pm. Free tours at noon, 1:30, 3pm. $7, seniors $6, ages 4-12 $3, Native Americans with status cards free.)* Three blocks south, the **Phoenix Art Museum** exhibits art of the American West, including paintings from the Taos and Santa Fe art colonies. There are also impressive collections of 19th-century European and American works. *(1625 N. Central Ave., at McDowell Rd. ☎257-1880. Open Su, Tu-Sa 10am-5pm, Th 10am-9pm. $7, students and seniors $5, ages 6-17 $2. Free after 4:15pm and on Th.)*

PAPAGO PARK AND FARTHER EAST. The **Desert Botanical Garden,** in Papago Park, 5 mi. east of downtown, grows a colorful collection of cacti and other desert plants. The park's trails make a pleasant stroll, and many of the desert flowers are hard to find in the wild. *(1201 N. Galvin Pkwy. ☎941-1225, recorded info ☎481-8134. Open daily May-Sept. 7am-8pm; Oct.-Apr. 8am-8pm. $7.50, seniors $6.50, students with ID $4, ages 5-12 $3.50.)* Take bus #3 east to **Papago Park,** on the eastern outskirts of the city. The park has spectacular views of the desert along its hiking, biking, and driving trails. If you spot an orangutan strolling around the cacti, it's either a mirage or you're in the **Phoenix Zoo,** located within the park and boasting a formidable collection of South American, African, and Southwestern critters. *(455 N. Galvin Pkwy. ☎273-1341. Open Sept.-May daily 9am-5pm. $12, seniors $9, children $5. June-Aug. 7am-9pm. $9, seniors $7, children $5.)* Still farther east of the city, in Mesa, flows the **Salt River,** one of the last remaining desert rivers in the US. **Salt River Recreation** arranges tubing trips. *(☎984-3305. Open May-Sept. daily 9am-4pm. Tube rental $9.)*

SCOTTSDALE SIGHTS. **Taliesin West** was originally built as the winter camp of Frank Lloyd Wright's Taliesin architectural collective; in his later years he lived there full-time. It now serves as a campus for an architectural college run by his foundation. *(12621 Frank Lloyd Wright Blvd. Head east on the Cactus St. Exit from the 101. ☎480-860-2700. Open Sept.-June daily 9am-4pm, closed Tu-W during July-Aug. 1hr. or 1½hr. guided tours required. See www.franklloydwright.org for specific tour info. $12.50-16, students and seniors $10-14, ages 4-12 $4.50.)* Wright also designed the **Arizona Biltmore** hotel. *(24th St. and Missouri. ☎955-6600.)* One of the last buildings designed by Wright, the **Gammage Memorial Auditorium** wears the pink-and-beige earth tones of the surrounding environment. *(Mill Ave. and Apache Blvd., on the Arizona State University campus in Tempe. Take bus #60, or #22 on weekends. ☎965-3434. 20min. tours daily in winter.)* One of Wright's students liked Scottsdale so much he decided to stay. **Cosanti** is a working studio and bell foundry designed by the architect and sculptor Paolo Soleri. The buildings here fuse with the natural landscape even more strikingly than those at Taliesin West. *(6433 Doubletree Rd., in Scottsdale. With I-10 behind you turn right off of Scottsdale Rd. ☎480-948-6145. Open M-Sa 9am-5pm, Su 11am-5pm, $1 donation suggested.)*

ENTERTAINMENT & NIGHTLIFE

Phoenix offers many options for the sports lover. NBA basketball action rises with the **Phoenix Suns** (☎379-7867) at the **America West Arena,** while the **Arizona Cardinals** (☎379-0101) provide American football excitement. The 2002 World Series Champions **Arizona Diamondbacks** (☎514-8400) play at the state-of-the-art **Bank One Ballpark,** complete with a retractable roof, an outfield swimming pool, and "beer gardens." (☎462-6799. Tickets start at $6. Special $1 tickets available 2hr. before games, first come, first served. Tours of the stadium; proceeds go to charity.)

Char's Has the Blues, 4631 N. 7th Ave., houses local jazz acts. On Friday night, come early for the Barbecue. (☎230-0205. For shows, doors open 7pm. Cover F-Sa $7. Hours vary.) **Bandersnatch Brew Pub,** 125 E. 5th St. in Tempe (☎480-966-4438). One of the last real taverns in the greater metro area, Bandersnatch has a huge patio and a dimly lit, but amusing, inside. (Happy Hour M-F 3pm-7pm. 21+ after 9pm. Open M-Sa 11am-1am, Su noon-1am.) **The Willow House,** 149 W. McDowell Rd., is a self-proclaimed "artist's cove," combining a chic coffee house, a New York deli, and a quirky musicians' hangout. (☎252-0272. No alcohol. 2-for-1 coffee

THE INSIDER'S CITY

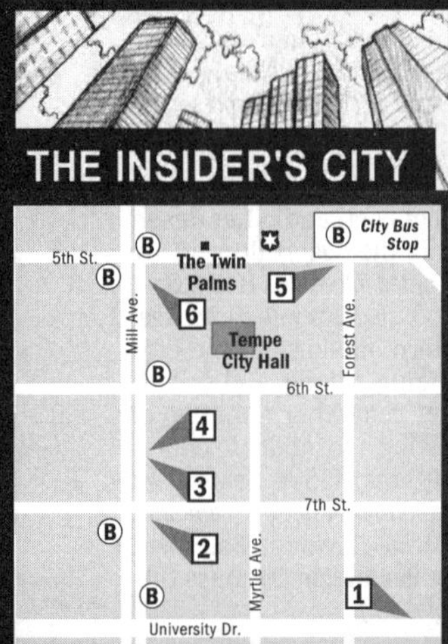

TEMPE PUB CRAWL

Near Phoenix, and home of Arizona State University, Tempe has more watering holes than you can shake a dead armadillo at. Catch a green line bus when your liver gives up.

1. Start at **Dos Gringos Trailer Park,** munching tasty Mexican food as you sip on a seemingly bottomless $4 margarita.
2. Dig into some of Arizona's finest chicken wings at **Long Wong's.** Try the "suicide" variety–if you dare.
3. Rack 'em up at the **Mill Cue Club** and prepare to get schooled by the ASU kids.
4. Nurse your bruised ego back to health on sweet, sweet microbrews at the **Mill Ave. Beer Co.**
5. Stagger down to the last real tavern in Tempe, the **Bandersnatch Brew Pub.** If you love beer, try it topically and join the "Beer in your Face Club."
6. Stumble onto one of the broken couches at Library's Bar & Grill to end the night with live music and gyrating bartenders.

Happy Hour M-F 4-7pm. Live music Sa starting at 8pm. Open M-Th 7am-midnight, F 7am-1am, Sa 8am-1am, Su 8am-midnight.) A large lesbian bar, **Ain't Nobody's Bizness,** 3031 E. Indian School Rd. #7, has more space devoted to pool tables than to the dance floor. (☎224-9977. No regular cover, but occasional guest vocalists and charges. Open M-F 4pm-1am, Sa-Su 2pm-1am.) **Boom,** 1724 E. McDowell Rd., *the* place for young gay men in Phoenix to see and be seen, is popular with throngs of gyrating Adonis-featured youth who like to party until the wee hours. (☎254-0231. 18+ after 10pm. Open Th-F 4pm-1am, Sa 4pm-4am.) The free *New Times Weekly*, available on local magazine racks, lists club schedules for Phoenix's after-hours scene. The *Cultural Calendar of Events* covers area entertainment in three-month intervals. *The Western Front*, found in bars and clubs, covers gay and lesbian nightlife.

SCENIC DRIVE: APACHE TRAIL

Steep, gray, and haunting, the **Superstition Mountains** derive their name from Pima Native American legends. Although the Native Americans were kicked out by the Anglo gold prospectors who settled the region, the curse stayed. In the 1840s, a Mexican explorer found gold in these hills, but was killed before he could reveal the location of the mine. More famous is the case of Jacob Waltz, known as "Dutchman" despite having come from Germany. During the 1880s, he brought out about $250,000 worth of high-quality gold ore from somewhere in the mountains. Upon his death in 1891, he left only a few clues to the whereabouts of the mine. Strangely, many who have come looking for it have died violent deaths—one prospector burned to death in his own campfire, while another was found decapitated in an *arroyo*. Needless to say, the mine has never been found.

Rte. 88, a.k.a. **Apache Trail,** winds from **Apache Junction,** a small mining town 40 mi. east of Phoenix, through the mountains. Although the road is only about 50 mi. long one-way, trips require at least 3hr. behind the wheel because it's only partially paved. The car-less can leave the driving to **Apache Trail Tours,** which offers on- and off-road Jeep tours. (☎480-982-7661. 2-4hr. tours $60 per person. Reserve at least 1 day in advance.) For more info, head to the **Apache Junction Chamber of Commerce,** 112 E. 2nd Ave. (☎480-982-3141. Open M-F 8am-5pm.)

The scenery is the Trail's greatest attraction; the dramatic views of the arid landscape make it one of the most beautiful driving routes in the nation. The deep blue waters of the manmade **Lake Canyon, Lake**

Apache, and **Lake Roosevelt** contrast sharply with the red and beige-hued rock formations surrounding them. **Goldfield Ghost Town Mine Tours,** 5 mi. north of the U.S. 60 junction on Rte. 88, offers tours of the nearby mines and gold-panning in a resurrected ghost town. (☎480-983-0333. Open daily 10am-5pm. Mine tours $5, ages 6-12 $3; gold-panning $4.) "Where the hell am I?" said Jacob Waltz when he came upon **Lost Dutchman State Park ❶**, 1 mi. farther north on Rte. 88. At the base of the Superstitions, the park offers nature trails, picnic sites, and campsites with showers but no hookups. (☎480-982-4485. Entrance $5 per vehicle. First come, first served sites $10.) Grab a saddle for a bar-stool at **Tortilla Flat,** another refurbished ghost town 18 mi. farther on Rte. 88. The town keeps its spirits up and tourists nourished with a restaurant, ice cream shop, and saloon. (☎480-984-1776. Restaurant open M-F 9am-6pm, Sa-Su 8am-7pm.) **Tonto National Monument,** 5 mi. east of Lake Roosevelt on Rte. 88, preserves 800-year-old masonry and Pueblo ruins. (Open daily 8am-4pm. $4 per car.) **Tonto National Forest ❶** offers nearby camping. (☎602-225-5200. Sites $4-11.) The trail ends at the **Theodore Roosevelt Dam** (completed in 1911), the last dam constructed by hand in the US. For those who complete the Trail, Rte. 60 is a scenic trip back to Phoenix; the increased moisture and decreased temperatures of the higher elevations give rise to lush greenery (by Arizona standards).

TUCSON ☎520

A little bit country, a little bit rock 'n' roll, Tucson is a city that carries its own tune and a bundle of contradictions. Mexican property until the Gadsden Purchase, the city retains many of its south-of-the-border influences and shares its Mexican heritage with such disparate elements as the University of Arizona, the Davis-Monthan Airforce Base, and McDonald's. Boasting mountainous flora beside desert cacti and art museums next to the war machines of the Pima Air and Space museum, the city nearly defies categorization.

TRANSPORTATION

Airport: Tucson International Airport (☎573-8000; www.tucsonairport.org), on Valencia Rd., south of downtown. Bus #6 goes downtown from the terminal drop-off area. **Arizona Stagecoach** (☎889-1000) goes downtown for around $14 per person; $3 each additional person. 24hr. Reservations recommended.

Trains: Amtrak, 400 E. Toole Ave. (☎623-4442) on 5th Ave., 1 block north of the Greyhound station. To: **Albuquerque** via El Paso (4 per week, $99); **Las Vegas** via LA (3 per week, $124); **Los Angeles** (3 per week, $72); **San Francisco** via LA (3 per week, $130). Book 2 weeks ahead or rates are substantially higher. Open M and Sa-Su 6:15am-1:45pm and 4:15-11:30pm, Tu-W 6:15am-1:45pm, Th-F 4:15-11:30pm.

Buses: Greyhound, 2 S. 4th Ave. (☎792-3475), between Congress St. and Broadway. To: **Albuquerque** (12-14hr., 7 per day, $90); **El Paso** (6hr., 9 per day, $37); **Los Angeles** (9-10hr., 7 per day, $48); **Phoenix** (2hr., 7 per day, $16). Open 24hr.

Public Transit: Sun-Tran, (☎792-9222). Buses run from the Ronstadt terminal downtown at Congress and 6th St. Fares $1.00, seniors, disabled, and students $0.40, day pass $2. Service roughly M-F 5:30am-10pm, Sa-Su 8am-7pm; times vary by route.

Taxi: Yellow Cab, ☎624-6611.

Bike Rental: Fairwheels Bicycles, 1110 E. 6th St. (☎884-9018), at Fremont. $20 first day, $10 each additional day. Credit card deposit required. Open M-F 9am-6pm, Sa 9am-5:30pm, Su noon-4pm.

ORIENTATION & PRACTICAL INFORMATION

Just east of I-10, Tucson's downtown area surrounds the intersection of **Broadway Boulevard** and **Stone Avenue,** two blocks from the train and bus terminals. The **University of Arizona** lies 1 mi. northeast of downtown at the intersection of **Park** and **Speedway Boulevard.** Avenues run north-south, streets east-west; because some of each are numbered, intersections such as "6th and 6th" are possible. Speedway, Broadway, and **Grant Road** are the quickest east-west routes through town. To go north-south, follow **Oracle Road** through the heart of the city, **Campbell Avenue** east of downtown, or **Swan Road** farther east. The hip, young crowd swings on **4th Avenue, University Boulevard,** and **Congress Street,** all with small shops, quirky restaurants, and a slew of bars.

Visitor Info: Tucson Convention and Visitors Bureau, 130 S. Scott Ave. (☎624-1817 or 800-638-8350), near Broadway. Open M-F 8am-5pm, Sa-Su 9am-4pm.

Bi-Gay-Lesbian Organization: Gay, Lesbian, and Bisexual Community Center, 300 E. 6th St. (☎624-1779). Open M-F 10am-7pm, Sa 10am-5pm.

Hotlines: Rape Crisis, ☎624-7273. **Suicide Prevention,** ☎323-9373. Both 24hr.

Medical Services: University Medical Center, 1501 N. Campbell Ave. (☎694-0111).

Internet Access: Free at the **University of Arizona main library,** 1510 E. University Blvd. Open Sept.-May M-Th 7:30am-1am, F 7:30am-9pm, Sa 10am-9pm, Su 11am-1am; June-Aug. M-Th 7:30am-11pm, F 7:30am-6pm, Sa 9am-6pm, Su 11am-11pm.

Post Office: 1501 S. Cherry Bell (☎388-5129). Open M-F 8:30am-8pm, Sa 9am-1pm. **Postal Code:** 85726.

ACCOMMODATIONS

There's a direct correlation between the temperature in Tucson and the warmth of its lodging industry to budget travelers: expect the best deals in summer, when rain-cooled evenings and summer bargains are consolation for the midday scorch. **The Tucson Gem and Mineral Show,** the largest of its kind in North America, is an added hazard for budget travelers. The mammoth show fills up most of the city's accommodations, and drives prices up considerably during its 2-week run at the end of January and the beginning of February.

Hotel Congress and Hostel, 311 E. Congress (☎800-722-8848 or 622-8848). Conveniently located across from the bus and train stations, this hostel offers superb lodging to night-owl hostelers. The cafe downstairs serves great salads and omelettes. Private rooms come with bath, phone, vintage radio, and ceiling fans. Dorms $18, nonmembers $24. Singles start at $40 and doubles can run up to $90, depending on the season. 10% discount for students, military, and local artists. ❶

Loews Ventana Canyon Resort, 7000 N. Resort Dr. (☎299-2020). A quintessential 5-star hotel 5 mi. north of downtown off Oracle Rd. At the base of an 80 ft. waterfall, the incredible Ventana delivers on every level—from its relaxing spa to its championship golf course to the beautiful surrounding Catalina Mountain foothills. Singles start at $80. ❹

The Flamingo Hotel, 1300 N. Stone Ave. (☎800-300-3533 or 770-1910). Houses not only guests but Arizona's largest collection of Western movie posters. There are dozens of rooms available, from the Kevin Costner room to the Burt Lancaster suite (both with A/C, cable TV, telephones, and pool access). Laundry facilities are on-site; breakfast, pool. AAA and AARP discounts. Singles and doubles May-Aug. $29; Sept.-Nov. all rooms $49; Dec.-Apr. up to $85. ❹

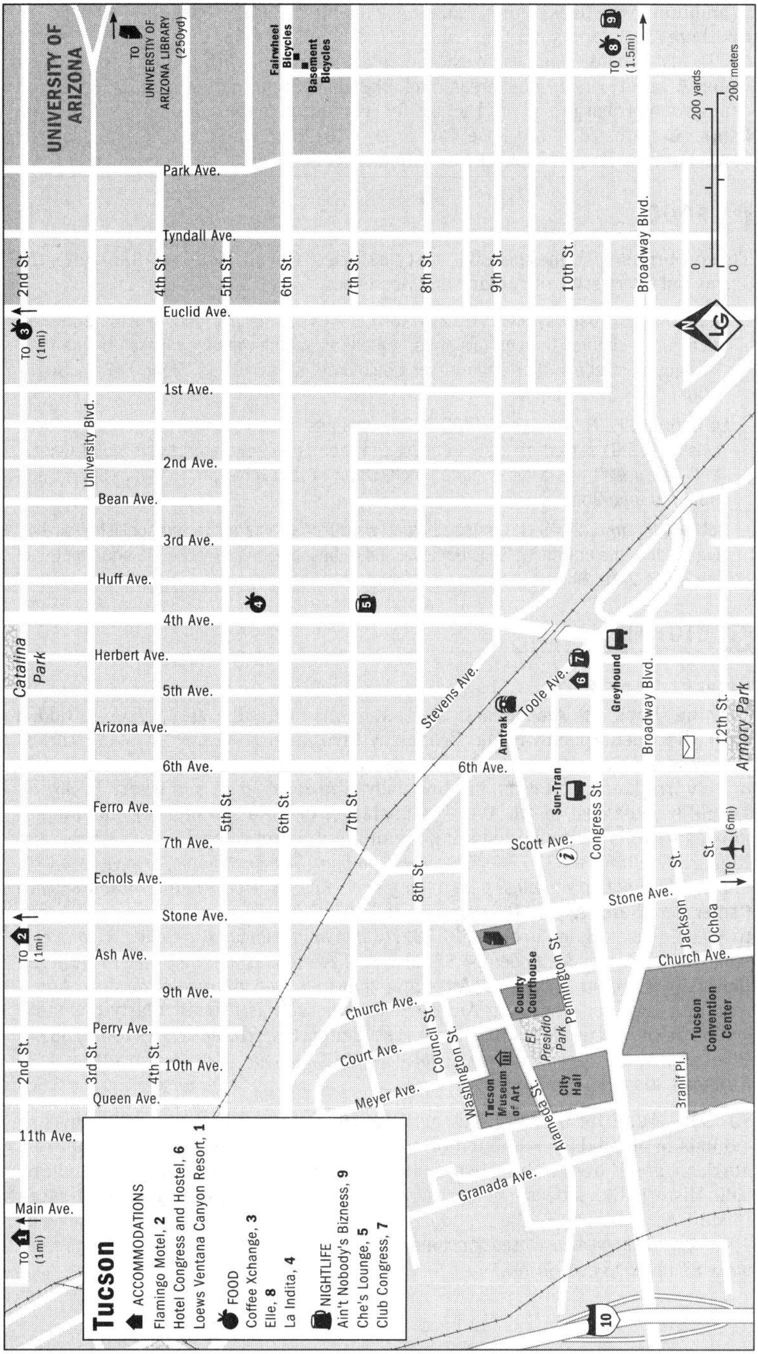

Tucson

ACCOMMODATIONS
Flamingo Motel, **2**
Hotel Congress and Hostel, **6**
Loews Ventana Canyon Resort, **1**

FOOD
Coffee Xchange, **3**
Elle, **8**
La Indita, **4**

NIGHTLIFE
Ain't Nobody's Bizness, **9**
Che's Lounge, **5**
Club Congress, **7**

University of Arizona
To University of Arizona Library (250yd)
Fairwheel Bicycles
Basement Bicycles
To 8, 9 (1.5mi)
To 3 (1mi)
To 2 (1mi)
To 1 (1mi)
To (6mi)
Catalina Park
Armory Park
Amtrak
Greyhound
Sun-Tran
County Courthouse
El Presidio Park
Tucson Museum of Art
City Hall
Tucson Convention Center

Park Ave.
Tyndall Ave.
Euclid Ave.
1st Ave.
University Blvd.
2nd Ave.
Bean Ave.
3rd Ave.
Huff Ave.
4th Ave.
Herbert Ave.
5th Ave.
Arizona Ave.
6th Ave.
Ferro Ave.
7th Ave.
Echols Ave.
Stone Ave.
Ash Ave.
9th Ave.
Perry Ave.
10th Ave.
Queen Ave.
11th Ave.
Main Ave.
2nd St.
3rd St.
4th St.
5th St.
6th St.
7th St.
8th St.
9th St.
10th St.
Broadway Blvd.
12th St.
Stevens Ave.
Toole Ave.
Congress St.
Scott Ave.
Church Ave.
Court Ave.
Meyer Ave.
Council St.
Washington St.
Alameda St.
Pennington St.
Jackson St.
Ochoa St.
Granada Ave.
Cushing St.
10

200 yards
200 meters

THE SOUTHWEST

In addition to the backcountry camping available in **Saguaro Park** and **Coronado Forest,** there are a variety of other camping options. **Gilbert Ray Campground** ❶ (☎883-4200), just outside Saguaro West, offers $7 campsites with toilets and drinking water. A variety of camping areas flank **Sky Island Scenic Byway** at Mt. Lemmon. All campgrounds charge a $5 road access fee in addition to the camping costs. **Spencer Canyon** ❶ (sites $12) and **Rose Canyon** ❶ ($15) have water and toilets. Call the Santa Catalina Ranger District for more info (☎749-8700).

FOOD

Tucson brims with inexpensive, tasty eateries. Cheap Mexican dominates the scene, but every style of cooking is represented.

elle, 3048 E. Broadway Blvd. (☎327-0500), brings out the gastronome in all. Cool classical jazz resonates through this stylish eatery, as mouth-watering chicken penne ($12 is enjoyed in elle's *über*-elegant, yet welcoming, surroundings. Open M-F 11:30am-10pm, Sa 4:30-10pm. ❸

La Indita, 622 N. 4th Ave. (☎792-0523), delights customers with traditional Mexican cuisine ($3-9) served on tasty tortillas. The food is still prepared by *la indita* herself, and as a result has a bit of added kick. Open M-Th 11am-9pm, F 11am-6pm, Sa 6-9pm, Su 9am-9pm. ❶

Coffee Xchange, 2443 N. Campbell Ave. (☎409-9433), caters to the bookish crowd living north of the university. Sells bagels, sandwiches, and salads ($2-6) in addition to hot joe. Open 24hr. ❶

SIGHTS

UNIVERSITY OF ARIZONA. Lined with cafes, restaurants, galleries, and vintage clothing shops, **4th Avenue** is an alternative magnet and a great place to take a stroll. Between Speedway and Broadway Blvd., the street becomes a historical shopping district with increasingly touristy shops. Lovely for its varied and elaborately irrigated vegetation, the **University of Arizona's** mall sits where E. 3rd St. should be, just east of 4th Ave. The **Center for Creative Photography,** on campus, houses various changing exhibits, including the archives of Ansel Adams and Richard Avedon. *(☎621-7968. Open M-F 9am-5pm, Sa-Su noon-5pm. Archives available to the public, but only through print-viewing appointments. Free.)* The **Flandrau Science Center,** on Cherry Ave. at the campus mall, dazzles visitors with a public observatory and a laser light show. *(☎621-7827. Open M-Tu 9am-5pm, W-Sa 9am-5pm and 7-9pm, Su noon-5pm. $3, under 14 $2. Shows $5/4, seniors and students $4.50.)* The **University of Arizona Museum of Art** offers visitors a free glimpse of modern American and 18th-century Latin American art, as well as the singularly muscular sculpture of Jacques Lipchitz. The best student art is exhibited here too. *(1031 N. Olive. ☎621-7567. Open mid-Sept. to mid-May M-F 9am-5pm, Su noon-4pm; otherwise M-F 10am-3:30pm, Su noon-4pm.)*

TUCSON MUSEUM OF ART. This major attraction presents impressive traveling exhibits in all media, in addition to its permanent collection of varied American, Mexican, and European art. Historic houses in the surrounding and affiliated Presidio Historic Block boast an impressive collection of Pre-Columbian and Mexican folk art, as well as art of the American West. *(140 N. Main Ave. ☎624-2333. Open M-Sa 10am-4pm, Su noon-4pm. Closed M between Memorial Day and Labor Day. $5, seniors $4, students $3, under 13 free. Su free.)*

SIGHTS ON WEST SPEEDWAY. As Speedway Blvd. winds its way west from Tucson's city center, it passes by a variety of sights. The left fork leads to **Old Tucson Studios,** an elaborate Old West-style town constructed for the 1938 movie *Arizona* and used as a backdrop for Westerns ever since, including many John Wayne films and the 1999 Will Smith vehicle *Wild Wild West.* It's open year-round to tourists, who can stroll around in the Old West mock up and view gun fight reenactments and other tourist shows,. *(☎883-0100. Open daily 10am-6pm, sometimes closed on M in winter. Call ahead as occasionally Old Tucson is closed for group functions. $15, seniors $13.45, ages 4-11 $9.45.)* Those opting to take the right fork will eschew the Wild Wild West for the merely wild West; less than 2 mi. from the fork lies the **Arizona-Sonora Desert Museum,** a first-rate zoo and nature preserve. The living museum recreates a range of desert habitats and features over 300 kinds of animals. A visit requires at least 2hr., preferably in the morning before the animals take their afternoon siestas. *(2021 N. Kinney Rd. ☎883-2702. Follow Speedway Blvd. west of the city as it becomes Gates Pass Rd., then Kinney Rd. Open Mar.-Sept. daily 7:30am-5pm; Oct.-Feb. daily 8:30am-5pm, June-Sept. Sa 7:30am-10pm. $9, Oct.-May. $12; ages 6-12 $2.)*

CAVES. Caves are all the rage in Tucson. The recently opened **Kartchner Caverns State Park** is enormously popular, filled with magnificent rock formations and home to over 1000 bats. This is a "living" cave, which contains water and is still experiencing the growth of its formations; the damp conditions cause the formations to shine and glisten in the light. Taking a tour is the only way to enter the cave. *(Located 8 mi. off I-10 at Exit 302. ☎586-4100. Open daily 7:30am-6pm. 1hr. tours run every 30min. 8:30am-4:30pm. Entrance fee $10 per vehicle, tour $14, ages 7-13 $6. Reservations strongly recommended.)* Near **Saguaro National Park East** (see p. 850), **Colossal Cave** is one of the only dormant (no water or new formations) caves in the US. A variety of tours are offered; in addition to 1hr. walking tours that occur throughout the day, a special ladder tour through otherwise sealed-off tunnels, crawlspaces, and corridors can be arranged. *(☎647-7275. Open mid-Mar. to mid-Sept. M-Sa 8am-6pm, Su 8am-7pm; mid-Sept. to mid-Mar. M-Sa 9am-5pm, Su 9am-6pm. $7.50, ages 6-12 $4. Ladder tour: Sept.-Mar. Sa 5:30-8pm, Mar.-Sept. Sa 6:30-9pm; $35, includes meal and equipment rental, reservations required.)*

PIMA AIR AND SPACE MUSEUM. This impressive museum follows aviation history from the days of the Wright brothers to its modern military incarnations. While exhibits on female and African-American aviators are interesting, the main draw is a fleet of decommissioned warplanes. *(☎574-0462. Open M-F 7am-3pm, Sa-Su 7am-5pm; in summer daily 9am-5pm. $7.50, seniors $6.50.)* Tours of the **Davis-Monthan Air Force Base** are also offered. *(M-F 5 tours per day. $5, ages 6-12 $3.)*

ENTERTAINMENT & NIGHTLIFE

The free *Tucson Weekly* is the local authority on nightlife, while the weekend sections of the *Star* or the *Citizen* also provide good coverage. UA students rock 'n' roll on **Speedway Boulevard,** while others do the two-step along **North Oracle.** Young locals hang out on **4th Avenue,** where most bars have live music and low cover.

Club Congress, 311 E. Congress St. (☎622-8848), has DJs during the week and live bands on weekends. The friendly hotel staff and a cast of regulars make it an especially good time. Congress is the venue for most of the indie music coming through town. M is 80s night with $0.80 vodkas. Cover $3-5. Open daily 9pm-1am.

Che's Lounge, 350 4th Ave. (☎623-2088), has lines early in the night on weekends and crowds during the week. Live music Sa. Open daily 4pm-1am.

Ain't Nobody's Bizness, 2900 E. Broadway Blvd. (☎318-4838), in a shopping plaza, is the little sister of its namesake and the big mama of the Tucson lesbian scene. With a large bar, themed contests, and pool tournaments, "Biz" attracts crowds of all backgrounds and has some of the best dancing in Tucson. Open daily 2pm-1am.

OUTDOOR ACTIVITIES

SAGUARO NATIONAL PARK

The western half of Saguaro National Park (Tucson Mountain District) has hiking trails and an auto loop. The **Bajada Loop Drive** runs less than 9 mi., but passes through some of the most striking desert scenery the park has to offer. The paved nature walk near the **Visitors Center** passes some of the best specimens of Saguaro cactus in the Tucson area. (☎733-5158. Park open 24hr.; Visitors Center daily 8:30am-5pm; auto loop 7am-sunset. Free.)

There are a variety of hiking trails through Saguaro West; **Sendero Esperanza Trail,** beginning at the Ez-kim-in-zin picnic area, is the mildest approach to the summit of **Wasson Peak,** the highest in the Tucson Mountain Range (4687 ft.). The **Hugh Norris Trail** is a slightly longer, more strenuous climb to the top of Wasson Peak.

Mountain biking is permitted only around the **Cactus Forest Loop Drive** and **Cactus Forest Trail,** at the western end of the park near the Visitors Center. The trails in Saguaro East are much longer than those in the western segment of the park. One of the only trails that can easily be completed in a single day is the Cactus Forest.

DAYTRIPS FROM TUCSON

BIOSPHERE 2. Ninety-one feet high, with an area of more than three acres, Biosphere 2 is sealed off from Earth—"Biosphere 1"—by 500 tons of stainless steel. In 1991, eight research scientists locked themselves inside this giant greenhouse to cultivate their own food and knit their own socks as they monitored the behavior of five man-made ecosystems: savanna, rainforest, marsh, ocean, and desert. After two years, they began having oxygen problems and difficulty with food production. No one lives in Biosphere 2 now, but it's still used as a research facility. *(Biosphere is 30min. north of Tucson; take I-10 west to the "Miracle Mile" exit, follow the miracles to Oracle Rd., then travel north until it becomes Rte. 77 N. From Phoenix, take I-10 to exit 185, follow Rte. 387 to Rte. 79 (Florence Hwy.), and proceed to Oracle Junction and Rte. 77. ☎800-838-2462. Call for daily tour info. Open daily 8:30am-5:30pm, last admission at 5pm. $13, seniors and students $11.50, ages 13-17 $9, ages 6-12 $6.)*

MISSION SAN XAVIER DE BAC. Built by the Franciscan brothers in the late 1700s, the "white dove of the desert" is the northernmost Spanish Baroque church in the Americas, and the only such church in the US. *(South of Tucson off of I-19 to Nogales, take the San Xavier exit and follow the signs. ☎294-2624. Open for viewing 7am-5pm; masses held daily. Free, but donations are appreciated.)*

TOMBSTONE ☎520

Long past the glory days when it was the largest city between the Pacific and the Mississippi, Tombstone is now a veritable Cowboy Disneyland. By inviting visitors to view the barnyard where Wyatt Earp and his brothers kicked some serious butt, Tombstone has turned the **Shootout at the O.K. Corral,** on Allen St. next to City Park, into a year-round tourist industry. The voice of Vincent Price narrates the town's history next door to the O.K. Corral in the **Tombstone Historama,** while a plastic mountain revolves onstage and a dramatization of the gunfight is shown on a movie screen. (☎457-3456. Shootout open daily 9am-5pm, arrive before 2pm re-enactment. Historama shows daily 9am-4pm, every hr. $7.50 for admission to both attractions.) Site of the longest poker game in Western history (8 years, 5 months, and 3 days), the **Bird Cage Theater,** at 6th and Allen, was named for the suspended cages that once housed prostitutes. (☎457-3421. Open daily 8am-6pm. Self-guided tour. $6, $5.50 seniors.) The **tombstones** of Tombstone, largely the result of all that gunplay, stand in Boothill Cemetery on Rte. 80 just north of town. (☎457-3421 or 800-457-3423. Open daily 7:30am-6pm. Free.)

A good idea is to stay in Benson and commute out for a day in Tombstone. If you want to stay in town, the **Larian Motel ❷,** on the corner of Fremont and 5th, is clean, nicely furnished, roomy, and within easy walking distance of all sights. (☎457-2272. Singles $40-45, doubles $45-59.) **Nellie Cashman's Restaurant ❶,** named after the "angel of the mining camps" who devoted her life to clean living and public service, is a little less Old West and a bit more down-home. Delicious ½ lb. hamburgers start at $5.50. (☎457-2212. Open daily 7:30am-9pm.) For a bit of moonshine and country music, smell your way to **Big Nose Kate's Saloon,** on Allen St., named for "the girl who loved Doc Holliday and everyone else too." (☎457-3107. Live music. Open daily 10am-midnight.)

To get to Tombstone, head to the Benson Exit off I-10, then go south on Rte. 80. The nearest **Greyhound** station is in **Benson.** The **Douglas Shuttle** (☎364-3761) has service to: Tucson ($10); Bisbee ($5); Benson ($5). The **Tombstone Visitors Center,** a large, white building on 4th St. and Allen, provides brochures and maps, although Tombstone is so small that nothing takes long to find. (☎457-3929. Open M-F 9am-4pm, Sa-Su 10am-4pm.) The Tombstone **Marshal's office** (☎457-2244) is just behind City Hall. **Internet access** is available at **Gitt Wired**, 5th and Fremont. (☎457-3250. Open 7am-5pm. $0.15 per min.) The **Post Office** is at 100 N. Haskell Ave. **Postal Code:** 85638.

BISBEE ☎520

One hundred miles southeast of Tucson and 20 mi. south of Tombstone, mellow Bisbee, a former mining town, is known throughout the Southwest as a laidback artists' colony. Visitors revel in the town's proximity to Mexico, picture-perfect weather, and excellent, relatively inexpensive accommodations.

Queen Mines, on the Rte. 80 interchange entering Old Bisbee, ceased mining in 1943 but continues to give educational 1¼hr. tours. (☎432-2071. Tours at 9, 10:30am, noon, 2, 3:30pm. $12, ages 4-15 $5.) The Smithsonian-affiliated **Mining and Historical Museum,** 5 Copper Queen, highlights the discovery of Bisbee's copper surplus and the lives of the fortune-seekers who extracted it. (☎432-7071. Open daily 10am-4pm. $4, seniors $3.50, under 3 free.) For a less earthly and more heavenly experience, visit the **Chihuahua Hill Shrines.** A 25min. hike over rocky ground leads to a Buddhist, and then a Mexican-Catholic, shrine.

About 18 mi. west of Bisbee along Rte. 92, along the Mexican border, **Coronado National Memorial** marks the place where Francisco Coronado and his expedition first entered American territory. **Coronado Cave,** a small, relatively dry cave, is ¾ mi. from the Visitors Center along a short, steep path. A free permit is required to explore the cave, and can be picked up at the Visitors Center as long as each spelunker has a flashlight. (☎366-5515. Park open daily dawn to dusk. Visitors Center open daily 8am-5pm.) **Ramsey Canyon Preserve,** 5 mi. farther down the road, attracts nearly as many bird-watchers as birds. In the middle of migratory routes for many North American birds, thousands of hummingbirds throng here in the late summer. (Open daily 8am-5pm. $5, under 16 free. First Sa of every month free.)

About a 10min. walk from downtown, the **Jonquil Inn ❷,** 317 Tombstone Canyon, offers clean and smoke-free rooms. (☎432-7371. Singles $40-45; doubles $55-65. Winter about $10 more.) On Tombstone Canyon Rd., at the south end of town, the **School House Inn ❸** houses guests in a remodeled 1918 school house. Rooms are all themed and vary in size; the Principal's Office is palatial, while the numbered classrooms have a cozier sort of charm. (☎432-2966 or 800-537-4333. All rooms have private bath. Full breakfast included, TV in common room. Ironically, no children under 14. Single bed $60; double/queen/king $75-85; 2-bed suite $95.) **Old Tymers ❷** serve steak ($11) and hamburger ($5) any way you like, from bleeding to burnt. (☎432-7364. Open M-Th 11am-9pm, F-Sa 11am-10pm, Su 11am-8pm.)

The **Chamber of Commerce,** 31 Subway St., provides maps that will help you navigate the labyrinthine streets of Bisbee. (☎432-5421. Open M-F 9am-5pm, Sa-Su 10am-4pm.) The **Post Office,** on Main St., is one block south of the highway exit. (☎432-2052. Open M-F 8:30am-4:30pm.) **Postal Code:** 85603. **Area Code:** 520.

NEW MEXICO

Sometimes overshadowed by its more extreme neighbors, New Mexico is nevertheless a dreamscape of varied terrains and peoples. Going back to the days when Spaniards arrived with delusions of golden riches, this expansive land of high deserts, mountain vistas, and roadrunners has always been a place where people come to fulfill their fantasies. Today, most explorers arrive in search of natural beauty, adobe architecture, and cultural treasures rather than gold. It makes sense that New Mexico is a haven for hikers, backpackers, cyclists, mountain-climbers, and skiers. And with its mix of Spanish, Mexican, Native American, and Anglo heritage, the state is as culturally varied as it is geographically diverse.

PRACTICAL INFORMATION

Capital: Santa Fe.

Visitor Info: New Mexico Dept. of Tourism, 491 Old Santa Fe Trail, Santa Fe 87501 (☎800-545-2040; www.newmexico.org). Open M-F 8am-5pm. **Park and Recreation Division,** 2040 S. Pacheco, Santa Fe 87505 (☎505-827-7173). Open M-F 8am-5pm. **US Forest Service,** 517 Gold Ave. SW, Albuquerque 87102 (☎505-842-3292). Open M-F 8am-4:30pm.

Postal Abbreviation: NM. **Sales Tax:** 6.25%.

SANTA FE ☎505

You're much more likely to encounter khaki-clad tourists than conquistadors in Santa Fe today; nonetheless, it is still possible to find places with character and authenticity in the cracks. Founded by the Spanish in 1608, Santa Fe is the second-oldest city in the US and the only state capital to serve under the administrations of three countries. These days, art is the trade of choice, with Native Americans, native New Mexicans, and exiled New Yorkers all hawking their wares on the streets and in the galleries surrounding the Central Plaza. In recent years, Santa Fe's popularity has skyrocketed, leading to an influx of gated communities, ritzy restaurants, and Californian millionaires. The city can be expensive, but the fabulous art museums, churches, and mountain trails make it a worthwhile stop.

TRANSPORTATION

Trains: Amtrak's nearest station is in Lamy (☎466-4511 or 800-USARAIL), 18 mi. south on U.S. 285. 1 train daily to: **Albuquerque** (1hr., $18-27); **Flagstaff** (7hr., $64-118); **Kansas City** (17hr., $83-198); **Los Angeles** (18½hr., $56-132). Call ☎982-8829 in advance for a shuttle to Santa Fe ($16). Open daily 8am-5pm.

Buses: Greyhound, 858 St. Michael's Dr. (☎471-0008), goes to: **Albuquerque** (1½hr., 4 per day, $10.50); **Denver** (8-10hr., 4 per day, $59); **Taos** (1½hr., 2 per day, $14). Open M-F 7am-5:30pm and 7:30-9:45pm, Sa-Su 7-9am, 12:30-1:30pm, 3:30-5pm, and 7:30-9:30pm.

Public Transit: Santa Fe Trails, 2931 Rufina St. (☎955-2001). Schedules available at the Visitors Center or the public transit office. Runs 9 downtown bus routes M-F 6am-11pm, Sa 8am-8pm, Su (routes 1, 2, 4, and M only) 10am-7pm. Most bus routes start at the downtown Sheridan Transit Center, 1 block from the plaza between Marcy St. and Palace Ave. Buses #21 and 24 go down Cerrillos Rd., the M goes to the museums on Camino Lejo, and #5 passes the Greyhound station on its route between St. Vincent Hospital and the W. Alameda Commons. $0.75, ages 6-12 $0.50; day pass $1. **Sandía Shuttle Express** (☎474-5696 or 888-775-5696) runs from downtown hotels to the Albuquerque airport every hr. on the hr. 5am-5pm, and from Albuquerque to Santa Fe hourly 8:45am-10:45pm (one-way $23, round-trip $40). Reserve at least 4 days in advance. Open M-F 6am-6pm, Sa-Su 6am-5pm.

Car Rental: Enterprise Rent-a-Car, 2641 Cerrillos Rd. (☎473-3600). Must be 21+ with driver's license and major credit card. Open M-F 8am-6pm, Sa 9am-noon.

Taxi: Capital City Taxi, ☎438-0000.

ORIENTATION

Abutting the **Sangre de Cristo Mountains,** Sante Fe stands at an elevation of 7000 ft., 58 mi. northeast of Albuquerque on I-25. The streets of downtown Santa Fe seem to wind without rhyme or reason; it's helpful to think of the city as a wagon wheel, with the Plaza in the center and roads leading outwards like spokes. **Paseo de Peralta** forms a loop around the downtown area, and the main roads leading out towards I-25 are **Cerrillos Road, Saint Francis Drive,** and **Old Santa Fe Trail.** Except for the museums southeast of the city center, most upscale restaurants and sights in Santa Fe cluster within a few blocks of the **downtown plaza** and inside the loop formed by the **Paseo de Peralta.** Narrow streets make driving troublesome; park your car and pound the pavement. You'll find several public **parking lots** within walking distance of the plaza. Most convenient is the municipal parking lot, one block south of the plaza on Water St. between Don Gaspar Ave. and Shelby St.

PRACTICAL INFORMATION

Visitor Info: Visitors Information Center, 491 Old Santa Fe Trail (☎875-7400 or 800-545-2040). Open daily 8am-6:30pm; low-season 8am-5pm. **Santa Fe Convention and Visitors Bureau,** 201 W. Marcy St. (☎800-777-2489 or 955-6200). Open M-F 8am-5pm. **Info booth,** at the northwest corner of the plaza, next to the First National Bank. Open mid-May to Aug. daily 9:30am-4:30pm.

Hotlines: Rape Abuse, ☎986-9111. 24hr. **Gay and Lesbian Information Line,** ☎891-3647.

Medical Services: St. Vincent Hospital, 455 St. Michael's Dr. (☎983-3361).

Internet Access: Santa Fe Public Library, 145 Washington Ave. (☎955-6781), 1 block northeast of the Plaza. Open M-Th 10am-9pm, F-Sa 10am-6pm, Su 1-5pm.

Post Office: 120 S. Federal Pl. (☎988-6351), next to the courthouse. Open M-F 7:30am-5:45pm, Sa 9am-1pm. **Postal Code:** 87501.

ACCOMMODATIONS

Hotels in Santa Fe tend toward the expensive side. As early as May they become swamped with requests for rooms during **Indian Market** and **Fiesta de Santa Fe.** Make reservations early or plan to sleep in your car. In general, the motels along **Cerrillos Road** have the best prices, but even these places run $40-60 per night. For budget travelers, nearby camping is pleasant during the summer and is much easier on the wallet. Two popular sites for free primitive camping are **Big Tesuque** ❶ and **Ski Basin Campgrounds** ❶ on national forest land. These campgrounds are both off Rte. 475 toward the Ski Basin and have pit toilets.

Thunderbird Inn, 1821 Cerrillos Rd. (☎983-4397). Slightly closer to town than the motel, and an excellent value (for Santa Fe, anyway). Large rooms with A/C and cable TV, some with fridges and microwaves. Reception 24hr. Summer singles $50-55; doubles $55-60. Winter $39-44/44-49. ❸

Silver Saddle Motel, 2810 Cerrillos Rd. (☎471-7663). Beautiful adobe rooms decorated with cowboy paraphernalia have A/C and cable TV. Reception 7am-11:30pm. Summer singles $67; doubles $72. Winter $45/50. ❹

Hyde State Park Campground (☎983-7175), 8 mi. from Santa Fe on Rte. 475. Over 50 sites in the forest with water, pit toilets, and shelters. Sites $10, hookups $14. ❶

FOOD

The **Santa Fe Farmers Market** (☎983-4098), near the intersection of Guadalupe St. and Paseo de Peralta, has fresh fruits and vegetables. (Open late Apr.-early Nov. Tu, Sa 7am-noon. Call to inquire about indoor winter location and hours.)

Tia Sophia's, 210 W. San Francisco St. (☎983-9880). It looks and feels like a diner, but—as the long waits will testify—the food is exceptional. The most popular item is the Atrisco plate ($6)—chile stew, cheese enchilada, beans, *posole,* and a *sopapilla.* Open M-Sa 7am-2pm. ❷

Cafe Oasis, 526 Galisteo St. (☎983-9599), at Paseo de Peralta. Take a break from the bustle of the city at this laidback restaurant where all the food is organic and artistic expression is a way of being. Creative dishes range from veggie enchiladas ($10.75) to *Samari* stir-fry ($13.50). Breakfast served all the time. Live music nightly. Open M-W 10am-midnight, Th-F 10am-2am, Sa 9am-2am, Su 9am-midnight. ❸

The Shed, 113½ E. Palace Ave. (☎982-9030), up the street from the plaza. Feels like a garden, even in the enclosed section. Lots of vegetarian dishes, like quesadillas ($6) and excellent blue corn burritos ($8.75). Meat-eaters will enjoy the amazing chicken enchilada verde ($10.75). Open M-Sa 11am-2:30pm and 5:30-9pm. ❷

SIGHTS & ENTERTAINMENT

The grassy **Plaza de Santa Fe** is a good starting point for exploring the museums, sanctuaries, and galleries of the city. Since 1609, the plaza has been the site of religious ceremonies, military gatherings, markets, cockfights, and public punishments—now it shelters ritzy shops and packs of loitering tourists. Historic **walking tours** leave from the blue doors of the Palace of the Governors on Lincoln St. (May-Oct. M-Sa 10:15am. $10.)

MNM MUSEUMS. Sante Fe is home to six imaginative, world-class museums. Four are run by **The Museum of New Mexico.** They all keep the same hours and charge the same admission. A worthwhile 4-day pass *($15)* includes admission to all four museums and can be purchased at any of them. *(☎827-6463; www.museumofnewmexico.org. Open Tu-Su 10am-5pm. $7, under 16 free. The 2 downtown museums—Fine Arts and Palace of the Governors—are both free F 5-8pm.)* Inhabiting a large adobe building on the northwest corner of the plaza, the **Museum of Fine Arts** dazzles visitors with the works of major Southwestern artists, as well as contemporary exhibits of controversial American art. *(107 W. Palace Ave. ☎476-5072. Open daily 10am-5pm.)* The **Palace of the Governors,** on the north side of the plaza, is the oldest public building in the US and was the seat of seven successive governments after its construction in 1610. The *haciendas* palace is now a museum with exhibits on Native American, Southwestern, and New Mexican history and an interesting exhibit on Jewish Pioneers. *(☎476-5100.)* The most distinctive museums in town are 2½ mi. south of the Plaza on Old Santa Fe Trail. The fascinating **Museum of International Folk Art** houses the Girard Collection, which includes over 10,000 handmade dolls, doll houses, and other toys from around the world. Other galleries display changing ethnographic exhibits. *(706 Camino Lejo. ☎476-1200.)* Next door, the **Museum of Indian Arts and Culture Laboratory of Anthropology** displays Native American photos and artifacts. *(710 Camino Lejo. ☎476-1250.)*

OTHER PLAZA MUSEUMS. The popular **Georgia O'Keeffe Museum** attracts the masses with O'Keeffe's famous flower paintings, as well as some of her more abstract works. The collection spans her entire life and demonstrates the artist's versatility. *(217 Johnson St. ☎946-1017. Open daily 10am-5pm. $8, under 17 and students with ID free. F 5-8pm free. Audio tour $5.)* Downtown's **Institute of American Indian Arts Museum** houses an extensive collection of contemporary Indian art with an intense political edge. *(108 Cathedral Place. ☎983-8900. Open M-Sa 9am-5pm, Su noon-5pm. $4, students and seniors $2, under 16 free.)* The New Mexico State Capitol was built in 1966 in the form of the Zia sun symbol. The House and Senate galleries are open to the public, and the building also contains an impressive art collection. *(☎986-4589. 5 blocks south of the Plaza on Old Santa Fe Rd. Open M-F 7am-7pm; June-Aug. Sa 8am-5pm. Free tours M-F 10am and 2pm.)*

CHURCHES. Santa Fe's Catholic roots are evident in the Romanesque **St. Francis Cathedral,** built from 1869 to 1886 under the direction of Archbishop Lamy (the central figure of Willa Cather's *Death Comes to the Archbishop*) to help convert westerners to Catholicism. The cathedral's architecture is especially striking against the New Mexican desert. *(213 Cathedral Pl. ☎982-5619. 1 block east of the Plaza on San Francisco St. Open daily 7:30am-5:30pm.)* The **Loretto Chapel** was the first Gothic building west of the Mississippi River. The church is famous for its "miraculous" spiral staircase. *(207 Old Santa Fe Trail. ☎982-0092. 2 blocks south of the Cathedral. Open M-Sa 9am-5pm, Su 10:30am-5pm. $2.50, seniors and children $2.)* About five blocks southeast of the plaza lies the **San Miguel Mission,** at DeVargas St. and the Old Santa Fe Trail. Built in 1610 by the Tlaxcalan Indians, the mission is the oldest functioning church in the US. Also in the church is the San Jose Bell, made in Spain in 1356 and the oldest bell in the US. *(☎988-9504. Open M-Sa 9am–5pm, Su 10am-4pm; may close earlier in winter, 5pm mass Su only. $1.)*

GALLERIES. Santa Fe's most successful artists live and sell their work along Canyon Rd. To reach their galleries, depart the Plaza on San Francisco Dr., take a left on Alameda St., a right on Paseo de Peralta, and a left on Canyon Rd. For about 1 mi., the road supports galleries displaying all types of art and many indoor/outdoor cafes. Most galleries are open from 10am until 5pm. The **Hahn Ross Gallery's** work is hip, enjoyable, and expensive. *(409 Canyon Rd. ☎984-8434. Open daily 10am-5pm.)*

A BIT OF CLASS. Old verse and distinguished acting invade the city each summer when **Shakespeare in Sante Fe** raises its curtain. The festival shows plays in an open-air theater on the St. John's College campus from late June to late August. *(Shows run F-Su 7:30pm. Number of shows per week varies; call to check the schedule. Reserved seating tickets $15-32; lawn seating is free, but a $5 donation is requested. Tickets available at show or call ☎982-2910.)* The **Santa Fe Opera,** on Opera Dr., performs outdoors against a mountain backdrop. Nights are cool; bring a blanket. *(7 mi. north of Santa Fe on Rte. 84/285. ☎800-280-4654, 877-999-7499; www.santafeopera.org. July W and F-Sa; Aug. M-Sa. Performances begin 8-9pm. Tickets $20-130, rush standing-room tickets $8-15; 50% student discount on same-day reserved seats. The box office is at the opera house; call or drop by the day of the show for prices and availability.)* The **Santa Fe Chamber Music Festival** celebrates the works of Baroque, Classical, Romantic, and 20th-century composers in the **St. Francis Auditorium of the Museum of Fine Arts** and the **Lensic Theater.** *(☎983-2075, tickets 982-1890; www.sfcmf.org. Mid-July to mid-Aug. Tickets $16-40, students $10.)*

FESTIVALS. Santa Fe is home to two of the US' largest festivals. In the third week of August, the nation's largest and most impressive **Indian Market** floods the plaza. The **Southwestern Association for Indian Arts** (☎983-5220) has more info. Don Diego de Vargas' peaceful reconquest of New Mexico in 1692 marked the end of the 12-year Pueblo Rebellion, now celebrated in the 3-day **Fiesta de Santa Fe** (☎988-7575). Held in mid-September, festivities begin with the burning of the *Zozobra* (a 50 ft. marionette) and include street dancing, processions, and political satires. The *New Mexican* publishes a guide and a schedule of the fiesta's events.

NIGHTLIFE

Only in Santa Fe can you walk into a bar and sit between a Wall Street investment banker and a world-famous sculptor. Here, nightlife tends to be more mellow than in Albuquerque. The **Cowgirl Hall of Fame,** 319 S. Guadalupe St., has live music hoe-downs that range from bluegrass to country. Barbecue, Mexican food, and burgers are served up all evening, with midnight food specials and 12 microbrews on tap. (☎982-2565. Sa-Su ranch breakfast. Happy hour 3-6pm and midnight-1am; Cowgirl Margaritas $3.50. 21+ after midnight. Cover varies but is never more than $3. Open M-F 11am-2am, Sa 8:30am-2am, Su 8:30am-midnight.) **Paramount,** 331 Sandoval St., is the only dance club in Santa Fe. Everyone in town shows up for trash disco Wednesdays. (☎982-8999. Live music Tu, Th, Su. Sa dance. 21+. Cover $5-7, Sa $5-20. Open M-Sa 9pm-2am, Su 9pm-midnight.) **Bar B** has a futuristic setting and live music. (☎982-8999. Cover $2-7. Open M-Sa 5pm-2am, Su 5pm-midnight.)

OUTDOOR ACTIVITIES

The nearby **Sangre de Cristo Mountains** reach heights of over 12,000 ft. and offer countless opportunities for hikers, bikers, skiers, and snowboarders. The **Pecos** and **Río Grande** rivers make great playgrounds for kayakers, rafters, and canoers. Before heading into the wilderness, stop by the **Public Lands Information Center,** 1474 Rodeo Rd., near the intersection of St. Francis Rd. and I-25, to pick up maps, guides, and friendly advice. (☎438-7542, 877-276-9404; www.publiclands.org. Open M-F 8am-5pm; winter 8am-4:30pm.) The Sierra Club Guide to *Day Hikes in the Santa Fe Area* and the Falcon Guide to *Best Easy Day Hikes in Santa Fe* are good purchases for those planning to spend a few days hiking in the area.

The closest **hiking** trails to downtown Santa Fe are along Rte. 475 on the way to the Santa Fe Ski Area. On this road, 10 mi. northeast of town, the **Tesuque Creek Trail** (2hr., 4 mi.) leads through the forest to a flowing stream. Near the end of Rte. 475 and the Santa Fe Ski Area, trailheads venture into the 223,000 acre **Pecos Wilderness.** A variety of extended backpacking trips can be had throughout this swath of pristine alpine forests. For a rewarding day hike 14 mi. northeast of Santa Fe on Rte. 475, the strenuous full-day climb to the top of 12,622 ft. **Santa Fe Baldy** (8-9hr., 14 mi.) affords an amazing vista of the Pecos Wilderness to the north and east.

The best skiing is 16 mi. northeast of downtown, at **Ski Santa Fe.** Located in the towering Sangre De Cristo Mountains on Rte. 475, the ski area operates six lifts, including four chairs and two surface lifts, servicing 43 trails (20% beginner, 40% intermediate, 40% advanced) on 600 acres of terrain with a 1650 ft. vertical drop. *(☎982-4429. Annual snowfall 225 in. Open late Nov.-early Apr. 9am-4pm. Lift tickets: full day $45, teens $37, children and seniors $33, half-day $33. Rental packages start at $18.)*

DAYTRIPS FROM SANTA FE

BANDELIER NATIONAL MONUMENT

Bandelier, 40 mi. northwest of Santa Fe (take U.S. 285 to 502 W, then follow the signs), features some amazing pueblos and cliff dwellings, as well as 50 sq. mi. of mesas, ancient ruins, and spectacular canyon views. The **Visitors Center,** 3 mi. into the park at the bottom of Frijoles Canyon, has an archaeological museum and shows a short video. (☎672-3861, ext. 517. Open June-Aug. daily 8am-6pm; Sept. to late Oct. daily 9am-5:30pm; late Oct.-late Mar. 8am-4:30pm; late Mar.-May 9am-5:30pm.) All visitors to the park should start by hiking the 1½ mi. **Main Loop Trail** to see the cliff dwellings and the ruins of the Tyuonyi Pueblo. Those with more time should continue ½ mi. further to the Ceremonial Cave, a *kiva* carved into a natural alcove, high above the canyon floor. **The Frijoles Falls Trail** (3hr., 5 mi.), begins at the Visitors Center parking lot and follows the Frijoles Creek downstream 2½ mi. to the Río Grande. Upper Frijoles Falls, dropping 80 ft., is 1½ mi. from the trailhead. A strenuous 2-day, 22 mi. hike leads from the Visitors Center to Painted Cave, decorated with over 50 Ancestral Puebloan pictographs. Free permits are required for backcountry hiking and camping; topographical maps ($10) are sold at the Visitors Center. Just past the main entrance, **Juniper Campground** ❶ offers the only developed camping in the park, with water and toilets (sites $10). The park entrance fee is $10 per vehicle and $5 per pedestrian; National Park passes are accepted.

LOS ALAMOS

Known only as the mysterious P.O. Box 1663 during the heyday of the Manhattan Project, Los Alamos is no longer the nation's biggest secret. The birthplace of the atomic bomb, Los Alamos now attracts visitors with its natural beauty and outdoor activities. Overlooking the Río Grande Valley, Los Alamos hovers above the Pueblo and Bayo Canyons on thin finger-like mesas, 35 mi. to the northeast of Sante Fe. In town, the **Bradbury Science Museum,** at 15th St. and Central, explains the history of the Los Alamos National Laboratory and its endeavors with videos and hands-on exhibits. (☎667-4444. Open Tu-F 9am-5pm, Sa-M 1-5pm. Free.) Not to be missed in Los Alamos is the **Black Hole,** 4015 Arkansas St., a store that sells all the junk the laboratory doesn't want anymore, including 50-year-old calculators, fiber-optic cables, flow gauges, time-mark generators, optical comparators, and other technological flotsam. Leave with your very own $2 atomic bomb detonator cable. (☎662-5053. Open M-Sa 10am-5pm.) Outdoors, the town brims with great activities. The **Sante Fe National Forest** provides countless trails for hiking and biking in and along the town's many canyons. The **Valles Caldera,** an expansive and lush volcanic crater, has recently become a National Preserve. It's 15 mi. to the east on Rte. 4. **Los Alamos Visitors Center** is on Central Ave. just west of 15th St. (☎662-8105. Open M-F 9am-5pm, Sa 9am-4pm, Su 10am-3pm.)

TAOS ☎505

Before 1955, Taos was a remote artist colony in the Sangre de Cristo Mountains. When the ski valley opened and the thrill-seekers trickled in, they soon realized that the area also boasted the best whitewater rafting in New Mexico, as well as some excellent hiking, mountain biking, and rock climbing. By the 1970s, Taos had become a paradise for New-Age hippies, struggling artists, and extreme athletes. Tourists weren't far behind. Today, Taos has managed to balance a ski resort culture with a Bohemian pace and lifestyle without losing any of its sunflower charm.

ORIENTATION & PRACTICAL INFORMATION. Taos is located 79 mi. north of Santa Fe (see p. 852), between the dramatic Río Grande Gorge and the mighty Wheeler Peak. **Paseo del Pueblo** (Rte. 68) is the main north-south thoroughfare in town, dubbed **"Paseo del Pueblo Norte"** north of Kit Carson Rd. and **"Paseo del Pueblo Sur"** to the south. Be aware that traffic on Paseo del Pueblo tends to move in inches during the summer and the ski season—use Rte. 240 and Upper Ranchitos Rd. as a bypass if possible. Drivers should park on **Camino de la Placita,** a block west of the plaza, or at meters on side streets. Visitor info is available at the **Chamber of Commerce,** 1139 Paseo del Pueblo Sur, 2 mi. south of town at the junction of Rte. 68 and Paseo del Cañon. (☎758-3873 or 800-732-8267. Open daily 9am-5pm.) The **Carson National Forest Office,** 208 Cruz Alta Rd., has free info on camping and hiking. (☎758-6200. Open M-F 8am-4:30pm.) Services include: **Pinch Penny Wash-O-Mat,** 823 Paseo del Pueblo Norte (☎758-1265; open M-Sa 7am-8pm, Su 7am-5pm); **police,** 107 Civic Plaza Dr. (☎758-2216); **emergency;** ☎911; **Holy Cross Hospital,** 1397 Weimer Rd. (☎758-8883); **Internet Access** ($1 per 30min.) at the **public library,** 402 Camino de la Placita (☎758-3063; open M noon-6pm, Tu-Th 10am-7pm, F 10am-6pm, Sa 10am-5pm); **Post Office,** 318 Paseo Del Pueblo Norte. (☎758-2081. Open M-F 8:30am-5pm.) **Postal Code:** 87571.

ACCOMMODATIONS. The **Abominable Snowmansion Hostel (HI-AYH) ❶**, 9 mi. north of Taos in the village of Arroyo Seco, is a snowbird's delight with spacious dorm rooms and a pool table adorning the common room. A hostel by summer, ski lodge by winter, the Snowmansion is only 9 mi. west of the ski valley. Teepees and camping are available in the warmer months, but it is accessible by public transportation only during the ski season. (☎776-8298. Reception 8am-noon and 4-10pm. Reservations recommended. Mid-Apr. to mid-Nov. dorms $15, non-members $17, weekly $95; dorm tepees $15/17; private doubles $38-42; tent sites $12. Mid-Nov. to mid-Apr. dorms (breakfast included) $22, weekly $120; private rooms $40-52.) The **Budget Host Motel ❷,** 1798 Paseo del Pueblo Sur, 3¼ mi. south of the Plaza, is the least expensive motel in Taos, with spacious rooms. (☎758-2524 or 800-323-6009. Singles $39-54; doubles $49-61. 10% AAA discount.)

Camping around Taos is easy with a car, and considering the price of lodging, sleeping under the stars is a particularly appealing option. The **Orilla Verde Recreation Area ❶,** 15 mi. south of Taos on Rte. 68, has 5 campgrounds in the scenic **Río Grande Gorge ❶.** (☎751-4899 or 758-8851. Water and toilets available. Sites $7.) The **Carson National Forest ❶** has four campgrounds to the east of Taos on Rte. 64. Tent sites sit adjacent to a stream and are surrounded by tall pines on one side and piñon forest on the other. The closest two, **El Nogal** and **Las Petacas,** are 2 and 4 mi. east of Taos and have vault toilets but no drinking water. For more info about these campgrounds, contact the **Carson National Forest Office** in Taos (☎758-6200; sites $12.50). Campgrounds on the road to Taos Ski Valley are free, but have no facilities. **Backcountry camping** doesn't require a permit. Dispersed camping is popular along Rte. 518 south of Taos and Forest Rd. 437. Park on the side of the road and pitch your tent a few hundred feet inside the forest.

FOOD. Restaurants cluster around Taos Plaza and Bent St. but cheaper options can be found north of town along Paseo Del Pueblo. **Island Coffees and Hawaiian Grill ❷,** 1032 Paseo del Pueblo Sur, just might get you lei-ed at a reasonable price, in a grass hut to boot. Popular Polynesian and southeast Asian dishes include mango coconut chicken ($6) and *lomi lomi* vegetables ($8). Many of the dishes are vegetarian. (☎758-7777. Open M-Sa 10am-9pm.) **Abe's Cantina y Cocina ❷,** 6 mi. north of Taos on the road to Taos Ski Valley in the village of Arroyo Seco and a block up from the Abominable Snowmansion Hostel, is the place to go for cheap, delicious, homestyle New Mexican food. The breakfast burrito ($3.25) will keep you going all day, or try the tamales ($3.50) to cast off your hunger later on. (☎776-8516. Open M-F 7am-6:30pm, Sa 7am-2pm, bar open until around 10pm.)

SIGHTS. For a small town, Taos has a surprising number of high-quality art museums. The **Harwood Museum,** 238 Ledoux St., houses works by early and mid-20th-century local artists, including a gallery of minimalist painter Agnes Martin, as well as a large collection of Hispanic Art including a striking *Día de los Muertos* piece. (☎758-9826. Open Tu-Sa 10am-5pm, Su noon-5pm. $5.) The **Millicent Rogers Museum,** 4 mi. north of the Plaza on Rte. 64, turn left at the sign, has an extravagant collection of Indian jewelry, textiles, pottery, and Apache baskets once belonging to Millicent Rogers, a glamour queen and socialite. (☎758-2462. Open Apr.-Oct. daily 10am-6pm; Nov.-Mar. Tu-Su 10am-6pm. $6, students and seniors $5, under 16 $2.)

The **Martinez Hacienda,** 2 mi. southwest of the plaza on Ranchitos Rd., is one of the few surviving Spanish Colonial mansions in the United States. Built in 1804, this fortress-like structure was home to the prosperous Martinez family and the headquarters of a large farming and ranching operation. The restored 21-room hacienda features exhibits on life in the northern reaches of the Spanish Empire. (☎758-1000. Open daily Apr.-Oct. 9am-5pm; Nov.-Mar. 10am-4pm. $5, children $3.)

Taos ranks second only to Santa Fe as a center of Southwestern art. Galleries clustered around the Plaza and Kit Carson Rd. include the **Lumina Gallery and Sculpture Garden,** which is more captivating than any art museum in town. Set in a stunning adobe home with five acres of rolling grassy lawn, gardens, and fountains, the cutting-edge contemporary paintings and sculptures here are captivating.

The five-story adobe homes of the **Taos Pueblo** are between 700 and 1000 years old, making it the oldest continuously inhabited settlement in the US. Taos Pueblo was named a UNESCO world heritage site in 1992, and is the only pueblo in Northern New Mexico where the inhabitants still live traditionally. Guided tours are offered daily May through September, and visitors can take self-guided tours all day. The Pueblo includes the **San Geronimo Church,** the ruins of the old church and cemetery, the adobe houses, and the *kivas.* (☎758-1028. Open May-Sept. M-Sa 8am-4:30pm, Su 8:30am-4:30pm; Oct.-Apr. M-Sa 8am-4pm, Su 8:30am-4pm. $10, seniors $8, students $3, 12 and under free. Camera permit $10, video cameras $20.)

OUTDOOR ACTIVITIES. Hailed as one of the best ski resorts in the country, **Taos Ski Valley,** about 15 mi. northeast of town on Rte. 150, has 72 trails and 12 lifts. Ski Valley boasts over 2500 ft. of vertical drop and over 300 in. of annual snowfall. (☎776-2291, lodging info 800-992-7669, ski conditions 776-2916. Lift tickets $31-51.) Reserve a room well in advance if you plan to come during the winter holiday season. There are also two smaller, more family-oriented ski areas near Taos: **Angel Fire** (☎377-6401; lift tickets $43, teenagers $35) and **Red River** (☎800-494-9117; lift tickets $43). Money-saving multi-day passes are available for use at all three resorts (from $36 per day). In summer, the nearly deserted ski valley and the nearby **Wheeler Peak Wilderness** become a hiker's paradise (most trails begin off Rte. 150). Due to the town's prime location near the state's wildest stretch of the Río Grande, **river rafting** is very popular in Taos. **Los Ríos River Runners** (☎776-8854 or 800-544-1181), **Far Flung Adventures** (☎758-2628 or 800-359-2627), and **Native Sons Adventures** (☎758-9342 or 800-753-7559) all offer a range of guided half-day ($40-50) and full-day ($80-110) rafting trips. For bike rentals, visit **Gearing Up,** 129 Paseo del Pueblo Sur. (☎751-0365. Open daily 9:30am-6pm. Bikes $35 per day, $90 per 5 days.)

ALBUQUERQUE ☎505

Albuquerque is a place full of history and culture, with many ethnic restaurants, offbeat cafes, and raging nightclubs. Most residents still refer to Central Ave. as Route 66, and visitors can feel the energy flowing from this mythic highway. The University of New Mexico is responsible for the town's young demographic, while the Hispanic, Native American, and gay and lesbian communities chip in cultural vibrancy and diversity. From historic Old Town to modern museums, ancient petroglyphs to towering mountains, travelers will be surprised at how much there is to see and do in New Mexico's largest city.

TRANSPORTATION

Flights: Albuquerque International, 2200 Sunport Blvd. SE (☎244-7700), south of downtown. Take bus #50 from 5th St. and Central Ave., or pick it up along Yale Blvd. **Airport Shuttle** (☎765-1234) shuttles to the city ($12, second person $5). Open 24hr.

Trains: Amtrak, 214 1st St. SW (☎842-9650). 1 train per day to: **Flagstaff** (5hr., $71-106); **Kansas City** (17hr., $98-207); **Los Angeles** (16hr., $58-120); **Santa Fe** (1hr. to Lamy, 20min. shuttle to Santa Fe; $34). Reservations required. Open daily 10am-6pm.

Buses: Greyhound (☎243-4435) and **TNM&O Coaches,** 300 2nd St. Both run buses from 3 blocks south of Central Ave. to: **Denver** (10hr., 4 per day, $64); **Los Angeles** (18hr., 4 per day, $75); **Santa Fe** (1½hr., 4 per day, $10). Station open 24hr.

Public Transit: Sun-Tran Transit, 601 Yale Blvd. SE (☎843-9200). Open M-F 8am-6pm, Sa 8am-noon. Maps at Visitors Centers, the transit office, or the main library. Most buses run M-Sa 6:30am-8:30pm and leave from Central Ave. and 5th St. Bus #66 runs down Central Ave. $1, seniors and ages 5-18 $0.25. Request free transfers from driver.

Taxi: Albuquerque Cab, ☎883-4888.

ORIENTATION & PRACTICAL INFORMATION

Central Avenue (Route 66), is still the main thoroughfare of Albuquerque, running through all the city's major neighborhoods. Central Ave. (east-west) and **I-25** (north-south) divide Albuquerque into four quadrants. All downtown addresses come with a quadrant designation: NE, NW, SE, or SW. The adobe campus of the **University of New Mexico (UNM)** spreads along Central Ave. from University Ave. to Carlisle St. **Nob Hill,** the area of Central Ave. around Carlisle St., features coffee shops, bookstores, used-CD stores, and art galleries. The revitalized **downtown** lies on Central Ave. between 10th St. and Broadway. Historic **Old Town Plaza** sits between San Felipe, North Plaza, South Plaza, and Romero, off Central Ave.

Visitor Info: Albuquerque Visitors Center, 401 2nd St. NW (☎842-9918 or 800-284-2282), 3 blocks north of Central Ave. in the Convention Center. Open M-F 9am-5pm. Recorded info 24hr. **Old Town Visitors Center,** 303 Romano St. NW (☎243-3215), in the shopping plaza west of the church. Open daily Apr.-Oct. 9am-5pm; Nov.-Mar. 9:30am-4:30pm. Airport **info booth** open Su-F 9:30am-8pm, Sa 9:30am-4:30pm.

Hotlines: Rape Crisis Center, 1025 Hermosa SE (☎266-7711). Center open M-F 8am-noon and 1-5pm, hotline 24hr. **Gay and Lesbian Information Line,** ☎891-3647. 24hr.

Medical Services: Presbyterian Hospital, 1100 Central Ave. SE (☎841-1234).

Post Office: 1135 Broadway NE, at Mountain St. (☎346-8044). Open M-F 7:30am-6pm. **Postal Code:** 87101.

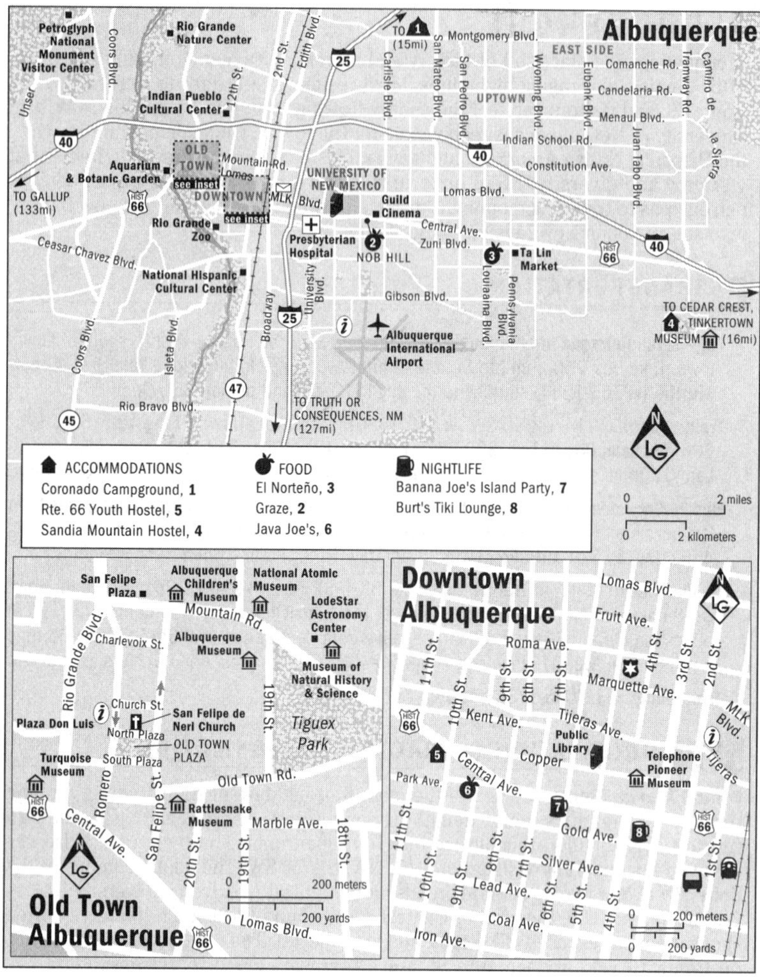

ACCOMMODATIONS

Cheap motels line **Central Avenue,** even near downtown. Though many of them are worth their price, be sure to evaluate the quality before paying. During the October **balloon festival,** rooms are scarce; call ahead for reservations.

Sandía Mountain Hostel, 12234 Rte. 14 N (☎281-4117). In nearby Cedar Crest. Take I-40 E to Exit 175 and go 4 mi. north on Rte. 14. Call ahead and the owners will pick you up in Albuquerque. Only 10 mi. from the Sandía Ski Area, this large wooden building makes a great ski chateau. Living room with fireplace and kitchen, plus a family of donkeys out back. Hiking and biking trails are across the street. Linen $1. Coin-op laundry. Wheelchair-accessible. Camping $8. Dorms $14; private cabin $32. ❶

Route 66 Youth Hostel, 1012 Central Ave. SW (☎247-1813), at 10th St. Get your kicks at this friendly hostel located between downtown and Old Town. Dorm and private rooms are simple but clean. Key deposit $5. Reception daily 7:30-10:30am and 4-11pm. Check-out 10:30am. 10 easy chores required. Dorms $14; singles with shared bath $20; doubles $25; twin bed doubles with private bath $30. ❶

Coronado Campground (☎980-8256). About 15 mi. north of Albuquerque. Take I-25 to Exit 242 and follow the signs. A pleasant campground on the banks of the Río Grande. Adobe shelters offer a respite from the heat. Toilets, showers, and water available. Open M and W-Su 8:30am-5pm, self-service pay station after hours. Tent sites $8, with shelters and picnic tables $18; full hookup $18-20. ❶

FOOD

A diverse ethnic community, a lot of hungry interstate travelers, and one big load of green chiles render Albuquerque surprisingly tasty. The area around **UNM** is the best bet for inexpensive eateries. A bit farther east, the hip neighborhood of **Nob Hill** is a haven for yuppie fare—you can't throw a dead rat without hitting an avocado sandwich or an iced cappuccino.

Java Joe's, 906 Park Ave. SW (☎765-1514), 1 block south of Central Ave. and 2 blocks from the Rte. 66 Hostel. This lively restaurant with a casual atmosphere has hearty wraps ($5), sandwiches ($5.50), salads ($4-5), and great breakfast burritos ($3). Lots of vegetarian dishes and occasional live music. Open daily 6:30am-3:30pm. ❶

El Norteño, 6416 Zuni (☎256-1431), at California. A family-run joint renowned as the most authentic and varied Mexican in town. The shrimp roasted with garlic is a treat, and their vast repertoire runs from chicken *mole* ($8) to *caldo de res* (a beef stew) to beef tongue ($7-9). Lunch buffet M-F 11am-2pm, $6. Open daily 8:30am-9pm. ❷

Graze, 3128 Central Ave. SE (☎268-4729). Patrons are encouraged to graze over the eclectic menu and eat what they like without the limits of conventional courses. The menu is highly seasonal but has a stuffed poblano pepper with a goat cheese and truffle sauce ($9). Chic but friendly; smallish servings. Open Tu-Sa 11am-11pm. ❷

SIGHTS

OLD TOWN. When the railroad cut through Albuquerque in the 19th century, it missed Old Town by almost 2 mi. As downtown grew around the railroad, Old Town remained untouched until the 1950s, when the city realized that it had a tourist magnet right under its nose. Just north of Central Ave. and east of Río Grande Blvd., the adobe plaza today looks much like it did over 100 years ago, save for ubiquitous restaurants, gift shops, and jewelry vendors. Although a tourist trap, Old Town is an architectural marvel, and a stroll through it is worthwhile. **Walking tours** of Old Town meet at the Albuquerque Museum. *(1hr. Tu-Su 11am. Free with admission.)* On the north side of the plaza, the quaint **San Felipe de Neri Church,** dating back to 1706, has stood the test of time. *(Open daily 9am-5pm, accompanying museum open M-Sa 10am-4pm; Su mass in English 7, 10:15am, in Spanish 8:30am.)* A posse of museums and attractions surrounds the plaza. To the northeast, the **Albuquerque Museum** showcases New Mexican art and history. The comprehensive exhibit on the Conquistadors and Spanish colonial rule is a must-see for anyone interested in history. Tours of the Sculpture Garden are available Tu-F at 10am and free with admission. *(2000 Mountain Rd. NW. ☎243-7255. Open Tu-Su 9am-5pm. $3, seniors and children $1. Wheelchair-accessible.)* No visit to Old Town would be complete without seeing the **Rattlesnake Museum,** which lies just south of the plaza. With over 30 species ranging from the deadly Mojave to the tiny Pygmy, this is the largest collection of live rattlesnakes in the world. *(202 San Felipe NW. ☎242-6569. Open M-Sa 10am-6pm, Su 1-5pm. $2.50, seniors $2, under 18 $1.50.)* One more museum lies just outside the main Old Town area but remains within easy walking distance. Spike and Alberta, two statuesque dinosaurs, greet tourists outside the kid-friendly **New Mexico Museum of Natural History and Science.** Inside, interactive exhibits take visitors through the history of life on earth. The museum features a five-story dynatheater, planetarium, and simulated ride through the world of the dinosaurs. *(1801 Mountain Rd. NW. ☎841-2802. Open daily 9am-5pm, closed M in Sept. $5, seniors $4, children $2; admission and Dynamax theater ticket $10/8/4.)*

UNIVERSITY MUSEUMS. The University of New Mexico has a couple of museums on campus that are worth a quick visit. The **University Art Museum** features changing exhibits that focus on 20th-century New Mexican paintings and photography. *(☎277-4001. Near the corner of Central Ave. and Cornel St. Open Tu-F 9am-4pm. Free.)* **The Maxwell Museum of Anthropology** has excellent exhibits on the culture and ancient history of Native American settlement in the Southwest. *(☎277-5963. On University Blvd., just north of MLK Blvd. Open Tu-F 9am-4pm, Sa 10am-4pm. Free.)*

CULTURAL ATTRACTIONS. The **Indian Pueblo Cultural Center** has a commercial edge but still provides a good introduction to the history and culture of the 19 Indian Pueblos of New Mexico. The center includes a museum, store, and restaurant. *(2401 12th St. NW. ☎843-7270. Take bus #36 from downtown. Museum open daily 9am-4:30pm. Art demonstrations Sa-Su 11am-2pm, Native American dances Sa-Su 11am, 2pm. $4, students $1, seniors $3.)* The **National Hispanic Cultural Center** has an excellent art museum with exhibits that explore folk-art and surreal representations of Hispanic social and cultural life in America. *(1701 4th St. SW, on the corner of Bridge St. Open Tu-Su 10am-5pm. $3, seniors $2, under 16 free.)*

NIGHTLIFE & FESTIVALS

If you're looking for a change from honky-tonk, Albuquerque is an oasis of interesting bars, jamming nightclubs, art film houses, and a large university. Check flyers posted around the university area for live music shows or pick up a copy of *Alibi*, the free local weekly. During the first week of October, hundreds of aeronauts take flight in colorful hot-air balloons during the **balloon festival.** Even the most grounded of souls will enjoy the week's barbecues, musical events, and the surreal experience of a sky full of hot air.

Most nightlife huddles on and near Central Ave., downtown and near the university; Nob Hill establishments tend to be the most gay-friendly. The offbeat **Guild Cinema,** 3405 Central Ave. NE, runs independent and foreign films. (☎255-1848. Open M-Th at 4:30, 7pm, F-Su at 2, 4:30, 9:15pm. $7. Students, seniors, and all shows before 5pm $5.)

Burt's Tiki Bar, 313 Gold St. SW (☎247-2878). Situated a block south of the Central Ave. strip of clubs, the difference shows in its friendlier, more laidback atmosphere. Surf and tiki paraphernalia line the walls and ceiling, while anything from funk to punk to live hip-hop takes the stage. Live music Tu-Sa and occasionally Su-M. No cover. Normally open Tu-Sa 9pm-2am.

Banana Joe's Island Party, 610 Central Ave. SW (☎244-0024), is the largest club in Albuquerque. With 6 bars, a tropical outdoor patio, a concert hall, and 1 big dance floor, Banana Joe's brings nightlife to the masses. Nightly live music ranges from reggae to flamenco. DJ downstairs Th-Sa. Happy Hour daily 5-8pm. 21+. Cover Th-Sa $5. Open Tu-Su 5pm-2am.

OUTDOOR ACTIVITIES

Rising a mile above Albuquerque to the northeast, the sunset-pink crest of the **Sandía Mountains** gives the mountains their name—"watermelon" in Spanish. The crest beacons to New Mexicans, drawing thousands to hike and explore. One of the most popular trails in New Mexico, **La Luz Trail** (7½ mi. one-way) climbs the Sandía Crest, beginning at the Juan Tabo Picnic Area. From Exit 167 on I-40, drive north on Tramway Blvd. 9.8 mi. to Forest Rd. 333. Follow Trail 137 for 7 mi. and take 84 to the top. To eliminate one leg of the journey, hikers can drive or take the tram. The Sandía Mountains have excellent mountain biking trails. Warm up on the moderately easy **Foothills Trail** (7 mi.), which skirts along the bottom of the mountains, just east of the city. The trail starts at the Elena Gallegos Picnic Area, off Tramway Blvd. The most popular place for biking is at the **Sandía Peak Ski Area,** 6 mi. up Rte. 536 on the way to Sandía Crest. Bikers can take their bikes up the chairlift and then ride down on 35 mi. of mountain trails and rollers, covering all skill levels. (☎242-9133. Chairlifts run June-Aug. Sa-Su 10am-4pm. Full-day lift ticket $14, single ride $8. Bike rentals at the summit $38 per day. Helmets required.)

Sandía Peak Ski Area, only 30min. from downtown, is a serviceable ski area for those who can't escape north to Taos or south to Ruidoso. Six lifts service 25 short trails (35% beginner; 55% intermediate; 10% advanced) on 200 skiable acres. The summit (10,378 ft.) tops a vertical drop of 1700 ft. (☎242-9133. Snowboards allowed. Annual snowfall 125 in. Open mid-Dec. to mid-Mar. daily 9am-4pm. Full-day $38, half-day $29;, ages 13-20 $32, under 13 and seniors $29.) There are also excellent cross-country skiing trails in the **Cibola National Forest.** The North Crest and 10-K trails are popular with skiers.

DAYTRIPS FROM ALBUQUERQUE

PETROGLYPH NATIONAL MONUMENT

Located on Albuquerque's west side, this national monument features more than 20,000 images etched into lava rocks between 1300 and 1680 by Pueblo Indians and Spanish settlers. The park encompasses much of the 17 mi. West Mesa, a ridge of black basalt boulders that formed as a result of volcanic activity 130,000 years ago. The most easily accessible petroglyphs can be found via three short trails at **Boca Negra Canyon,** 2 mi. north of the Visitors Center. The **Rinconada Canyon Trail,** 1 mi. south of the Visitors Center, has more intricate rock art and is an easy 2½ mi. desert hike along the base of the West Mesa. To see the nearby volcanoes, take Exit 149 off I-40 and follow Paseo del Volcán to a dirt road. The volcanoes are 4¼ mi. north of the exit. To reach the park itself, take I-40 to Unser Blvd. (Exit 154) and follow signs for the park. (☎899-0205. Park open daily 8am-5pm. Admission to Boca Negra Canyon M-F $1, Sa-Su $2; National Parks passes accepted.)

GALLUP ☎505

Gallup's proximity to the Petrified Forest National Park (see p. 838), Navajo Reservation (see p. 836), Chaco Culture National Historic Park (see p. 866), and El Morro National Monument (see p. 867) makes it a good base for exploring the region.

Old Route 66, which runs parallel to I-40 through downtown, is lined with dirt-cheap motels (often with emphasis on the dirt), while the chains cluster on the western edge of town. The best place to stay in town, hands down, is **El Rancho Hotel and Motel ❸,** 1000 E. Rte. 66. You'll find a step up in price from most other options, but a leap up in quality. The who's-who of the silver screen all stayed here (John Wayne, Jack Benny, Kirk Douglas) and had rooms named after them. (☎863-9311. Singles $47; doubles $55.) One of the best spots for those watching their bottom line is the **Blue Spruce Lodge ❷,** 119 E. Rte. 66, with clean, well-maintained rooms. (☎863-5211. Singles $24; doubles $26.) You can pitch a tent in the shadow of red sandstone cliffs at **Red Rock State Park Campground ❶,** Rte. 566, which offers access to hiking 5 mi. east of town off Rte. 66. During the warmer months Red Rock is often the site of concerts, rodeos, and motorcycle races—call ahead to make sure the park is open for regular camping. (☎863-1329. 142 sites with showers and hookups. Tent sites $10; hookups $14.) In addition to the usual fast-food suspects, a number of diners and cafes line both sides of I-40. **Oasis Mediterranean Restaurant ❷,** 100 E Rte. 66, has Mediterranean fare with a slight Southwestern kick. (Open M-Sa 10am-9pm.) **The Ranch Kitchen ❷,** 3001 W. Rte. 66, has filling breakfasts, sandwiches and burgers ($5-7), and steaks. (Open daily summer 7am-10pm; winter 7am-9pm.)

You can visit the **Gallup Visitors Center,** 701 Montoya Blvd. (☎863-4909 or 800-242-4282; www.gallupnm.org), just off Rte. 66, for info on all of New Mexico. (Open daily 8am-5pm; June-Aug. 8am-6pm.) **Greyhound,** 201 E. Rte. 66 (☎863-3761), runs buses to **Albuquerque** (2½hr., 4 per day, $21) and **Flagstaff** (4hr., 4 per day, $37).For mail, check out the **Post Office:** 950 W. Aztec. (☎722-5265. Open M-F 8:30am-5pm, Sa 10am-1:30pm.) **Postal Code:** 87301.

CHACO CULTURE NATIONAL HISTORICAL PARK ☎505

Sun-scorched Chaco Canyon served as the first great settlement of the Ancestral Puebloans. The ruins here, which date from the 9th century, are among the most well-preserved in the Southwest. Evidence of inhabitance thousands of years older than even the oldest Ancestral Pueblo dwellings enriches the landscape, though the societies that flourished during the turn of the first millennium make the site truly remarkable. The Chaco societies demonstrated superior scientific knowledge and designed their buildings in accordance to solar patterns. One such structure, **Pueblo Bonito,** is the canyon's largest pueblo; it was once four stories high and housed more than 600 rooms. Nearby **Chetro Ketl** houses one of the Southwest's largest *kivas.* The largest pueblos are accessible from the main road, but **backcountry hiking trails** lead to many others; snag a free **backcountry permit** from the Visitors Center before heading off.

Chaco Canyon lies 92 mi. northeast of Gallup. From the north, take Rte. 44/550 to County Rd. 7900 (3 mi. east of **Nageezi** and 50 mi. west of **Cuba**), and follow the road for 21 mi., 16 of which are unpaved. From the south, take Rte. 9 from **Crownpoint** (home of the nearest ATM and grocery stores to the park) 36 mi. east to the marked park turn-off in Pueblo Pintado; turn north onto unpaved Rte. 46 for 10 mi.; turn left on County Rd. 7900 for 7 mi.; turn left onto unpaved County Rd. 7950 and follow it 16 mi. to the park entrance. *There is no gas in the park, and gas stations en route are few and far between.* Call the park in advance (☎988-6727) to inquire about road conditions, which may deteriorate in bad weather.

The **Visitors Center,** at the east end of the park, has an excellent museum exhibiting Ancestral Puebloan art and architecture and includes an enlightening film. All the ruins have interpretive brochures at their sites that can be purchased for $0.50-$0.75. (☎786-7014. Open June-Aug. daily 8am-5pm; Sept.-May 8am-5pm. $8 per vehicle.) Offering a closer look at the ruins, the **Wijiji Trail** (1½hr., 3 mi.) starts at the Wijiji parking area 1 mi. east of the Visitors Center and explores Wijiji, a great house built around AD 1100.

No food is available at the park. **The Gallo Campground ❶**, a little more than 1 mi. from the Visitors Center, offers serene desert camping for $10 per site; register at the campground. The 48 sites have access to tables, fireplaces, and central toilets. An accessible inexpensive option is the **Circle A Hostel ❶,** just northwest of Cuba, promising friendly, cheap lodging. A worthwhile retreat in itself, Circle A is a converted ranch house and a stopover for hikers seeking a rest from trails that pass right next to the property. The ranch sits 5 mi. east of U.S. 550 on Los Piños road; follow the signs along Los Piños. (Dorm $18, private rooms $38-48; tent $15, includes use of facilities. Group use available. Reservations recommended.)

EL MORRO NATIONAL MONUMENT ☎505

With signatures dating back to 1605, **Inscription Rock** has been the center piece of El Morro National Monument since its founding in 1906. The monument offers two hiking options. The ½ mi. wheelchair-accessible **Inscription Trail** winds past the rock and large pool of rainwater that attracted visitors in centuries past, providing excellent views of the signatures and neighboring petroglyphs. The 2 mi. **Mesa Top Trail** climbs 200 ft. to the top of the rock before skirting the edge of an ancient pueblo. The trail is well-marked and affords impressive panoramas of the region. Trails close 1hr. before the Visitors Center. The monument is located west of the Continental Divide on Rte. 53, 42 mi. west of Grants and 56 mi. southeast of Gallup. The **Visitors Center** includes a small museum and warnings against emulating the graffiti of old. (☎783-4226. Open daily 9am-5pm, occasionally later June-Aug. $3, under 17 free.) The small, tranquil **El Morro Campground ❶** has running water, primitive toilets, and is rarely full. (9 sites, 1 wheelchair-accessible. Sites $5.)

TRUTH OR CONSEQUENCES ☎505

In 1950, the popular radio game show *Truth or Consequences* celebrated its 10th anniversary by renaming a small town, formerly Hot Springs, NM, in its honor. As its maiden name suggests, T or C was a tourist attraction prior to the publicity stunt. The mineral baths infuse the town with fountain-of-youth effects and a funky down-home spirit. Maybe there's something in the water.

ORIENTATION & PRACTICAL INFORMATION. T or C sits about 150 mi. south of Albuquerque on I-25. The **Chamber of Commerce,** 400 W 4th St., has free maps and brochures about area accommodations and attractions. (☎894-3536. Open M-F 9am-5:30pm, Sa 9am-1pm.) The **Post Office,** 300 Main St., is in the middle of town (open M-F 9am-3pm), or 1507 N. Date St. (open M-F 8:30am-5pm). **Postal Code:** 87901. **Area Code:** 505.

ACCOMMODATIONS. Riverbend Hot Springs Hostel (HI-AYH) ❶, 100 Austin St. (☎894-6183; www.nmhotsprings.com), can be reached from I-25. Take Exit 79, turn right, and continue 1½ mi. to a traffic light. Turn left at the light, then immediately turn right onto Cedar St. and follow it down to the river and the blue building at the road's bend. Use of on-site mineral baths and a meditation cove are free for guests. (Kitchen and laundry. Reception open 8am-10pm, call ahead for late-night arrivals. Tent site $10, non-members $12. Teepees or dorms $14/16; private rooms $30-48.) The **Charles Motel and Spa ❷,** 601 Broadway, offers simple and clean accommodations. The large rooms have kitchenettes, A/C, and cable TV. There are also mineral baths on the premises. (☎894-7154 or 800-317-4518; www.charlesspa.com. Singles $39; doubles $45.) **Campsites** at the nearby **Elephant Butte Lake**

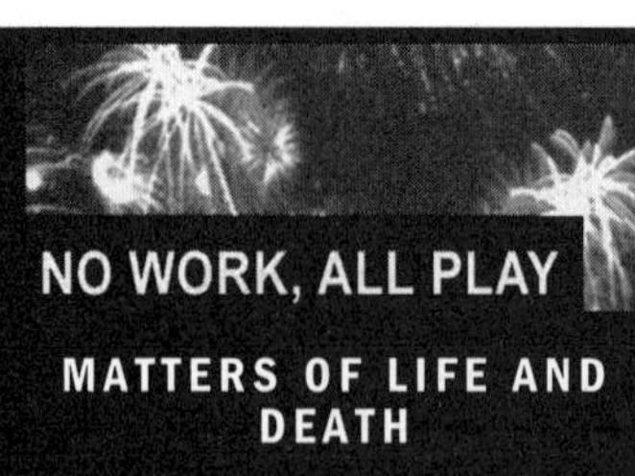

NO WORK, ALL PLAY

MATTERS OF LIFE AND DEATH

November 1's **Día de los Muertos (Day of the Dead)** is a Southwestern holiday of colorful traditions. Visitors in Mexico are likely to see a raucous festival of mariachis and drunken revelry, and in urban areas the influence of the US's Halloween is visible in the witch and vampire costumes that children wear. North of the border, however, Mexican-Americans observe *Día de los Muertos* as a way of celebrating and preserving their heritage. Families construct altars in their homes and decorate them with candles, *papel picado* (colorful tissue paper cut into intricate designs influenced by Aztec traditions), pictures of deceased relatives, flowers, and offerings of food. *Calaveras*, humorous skeleton figurines made of sugar or chick peas, are placed on the altar or given to children.

The goal of *Día de los Muertos* is primarily to honor and remember the dead, but the *Calaveras* and sometimes festive atmosphere serve another purpose: they aid in the acceptance of death as a part of life and confirm that to fear death is to deny an inevitable aspect of living.

If you're in southern New Mexico on November 1, the celebration at historic Mesilla near Las Cruces is worth attending. In the north there are usually several *Día de los Muertos* gallery events in artsy Santa Fe.

State Park ❶ have access to restrooms and cold showers. (Primitive sites $8; developed sites with showers $10, electricity $14.)

FOOD. Nearly all of T or C's restaurants are as easy on the wallet as the baths are on the body. For groceries, try **Bullock's,** at the corner of Broadway and Post. (☎894-6622. Open M-Sa 7:30am-8pm, Su 8am-7pm.) **La Hacienda ❷,** 1615 S. Broadway, is well worth the short drive out of the center of town. *Arroz con pollo* (rice with chicken; $7), and breakfast *chorizo con huevos* (sausage with eggs, $5) make this the best Mexican food around (open Tu-Su 11am-9pm). The popular **La Cocina ❷,** 1 Lake Way Dr. (look for the "Hot Stuff" sign above N. Date St.), pleases with huge portions of Mexican and New Mexican food, including *chimichangas* ($7). A Carrizozo cherry cider ($1.50) will surely slake your thirst. (☎894-6499. Open daily 10:30am-10pm.) **Hot Springs Bakery Cafe ❷,** 313 Broadway, located in a turquoise stucco building, has an outdoor patio and cactus garden. Pizzas go for $7-14. (☎894-5555. Open Tu-Sa 8am-3pm.) **Bar-B-Que on Broadway ❷,** 308 Broadway, serves plentiful breakfast specials that start at $2.50 and hearty lunch entrees running $5-8, as well as local gossip. (☎894-7047. Open M-Sa 7am-4pm.)

SIGHTS & OUTDOOR ACTIVITIES. Mineral baths are the town's main attraction; locals claim that the baths heal virtually everything. The only outdoor tubs are located at the **Riverbend Hostel,** where four co-ed tubs abut the Río Grande. Access to the baths is $6 per hr. for the public (10am-7pm), but complementary for hostel guests (7-10am and 7-10pm).

Five miles north of T or C, **Elephant Butte Lake State Park** features New Mexico's largest lake (take Date St. north to a sign for Elephant Butte; turn right onto 181 and follow the signs). A public works project dammed up the Río Grande in 1916 after the resolution of a major water rights dispute between the US and Mexico. The resulting lake is named after the elephantine rock formation at its southern end. The park has sandy beaches for swimming and a marina for boating. (Cars $4, bikes and pedestrians free.) **Sports Adventure,** on the lake at the end of Long Point Rd., north of the town of Elephant Butte, rents jet skis. (☎744-5557 or 888-736-8420. Rentals start at $35 per 30min.) **Marina del Sur** rents motorized boats of all kinds. (☎744-5567. Must be 18+ and have a valid driver's license to rent. Jet skis $35 per hr., pontoon boats $30 per hr., ski boats $45 per hr., 3hr. min. and deposit on all rentals.) There is a **Visitors Center** at the entrance to the park with a small museum on the natural history of the area. (☎877-664-7787. Open M-F 7:30am-4pm, Sa-Su 7:30am-10pm.) An easy 1½ mi. nature trail begins in the parking lot just past the Visitors Center.

GILA CLIFF DWELLINGS & NATIONAL MONUMENT ☎505

The mysterious Gila Cliff Dwellings National Monument preserves over 40 stone and timber rooms carved into the cliff's natural caves by the Mogollon tribe during the late 1200s. Around a dozen families lived here for about 20 years, farming on the mesa top and along the river. During the early 1300s, however, the Mogollon abandoned their homes for reasons unknown, leaving the ruins as their only trace.

From Silver City, the Cliff Dwellings are 44 mi. down **Forest Road 15** through Piños Altos. From San Lorenzo, **Route 35** leads 26 mi. and ends 19 mi. south of the monument at an intersection with Forest Rd. 15. Though both roads are narrow and winding, Forest Rd. 15 is somewhat steeper and more difficult. Both require 2hr. for safe passage. Road conditions can be impassable in winter; pay close attention to the weather and the road surface.

The **Visitors Center,** at the end of Rte. 15, shows an informative film and sells various maps of the Gila National Forest. (☎536-9461. Open daily 8am-6pm; low-season 8am-4:30pm.) The picturesque 1 mi. round-trip **hike** to the dwellings begins past the Upper Scorpion Campground, and rangers occasionally give short interpretive tours through the cliffs. A trail guide ($0.50) can be purchased at the trailhead or Visitors Center. (Dwellings open daily 8am-6pm; low-season 9am-4pm. Entrance fee $3, under 12 free.)

The nearest accommodations can be found at the comfy **Grey Feathers Lodge ❸,** 20 mi. south at the intersection of Forest Rd. 15 and Rte. 35. Drawing as many as 4000 hummingbirds on some summer weekends, the lodge is a perfect place to relax and bird-watch. (☎536-3206. Singles $40-45; doubles $45-50; suites $65-75.) The adjoining **cafe ❶** offers sandwiches ($3-7) and ice cream ($1.25 per scoop).

WHITE SANDS NAT'L MONUMENT ☎505

Situated in the Tularosa Basin between the Sacramento and San Andres Mountains, the world's largest dunes formed as rainwater flushed gypsum from the nearby peaks and into Lake Lucero. As desert heat evaporated the lake, the gypsum crystals were left behind and now form the blindingly white sand dunes. These drifts of fine sand create the look of arctic tundra, but don't be fooled: the midday sun assaults the shadeless with a light and heat that can be unbearable—be prepared with protective clothing and eyewear, heavy-duty sunscreen, and plenty of water. Trekking or rolling through the dunes can provide hours of mindless fun or mindful soul-searching; the sand is particularly awe-inspiring at sunset.

ORIENTATION & PRACTICAL INFORMATION. White Sands lies on Rte. 70, 15 mi. southwest of Alamogordo and 52 mi. northeast of Las Cruces. Rte. 70 is prone to closures due to missile testing at the nearby military base. Delays can run up to 1hr.; call the park **Visitors Center** to check the status of Rte. 70 closures. The center itself has a small museum with an introductory video and a gift shop. (☎479-6124. Park open daily June-Aug. 7am-10pm, last entrance 9pm; Sept.-May 7am-sunset. Visitors Center open daily June-Aug. 8am-7pm; Sept.-May 8am-5pm. Park admission $3, under 16 free.) The nearest **grocery store, ATM, Post Office, hospital,** and **Internet Access** are in Alamogordo. In an **emergency,** call ☎911. For more info visit the park web site (www.nps.gov/whsa).

CAMPING. The only way to spend the night inside the park is to camp at one of the **backcountry campsites ❶.** Ten daily permits for the sites ($3 per person in addition to the park entry fee) are available on a first-come, first-served basis. The sites have no water or toilet facilities and are not accessible by road, requiring up to a 2 mi. hike through the sand dunes. Campers must register in person at the Visitors Center and be in their sites before dark. Campfires are prohibited, but stoves are allowed. Sleeping amid the white dunes can be an extraordinary experience, but plan ahead because sites fill up early on full-moon nights. Occasionally, the sites are closed due to missile range launches.

SIGHTS & OUTDOOR ACTIVITIES. The 8 mi. **Dunes Drive** is a good way to begin a visit to White Sands. However, really experiencing the uniqueness of the monument means getting out of your car and taking a walk across the dunes. Off-trail hiking is permitted anywhere in the eastern section of the park. Anyone considering a backcountry hike should bring a compass and map, as it is easy to get lost in the vast sea of seemingly uniform gypsum dunes.

The only wheelchair-accessible trail in the park is the **Interdune Boardwalk,** an easy ¼ mi. walk above the sand. The best hike in the park is the **Alkali Flat Trail,** a moderately strenuous 4½ mi. loop through the heart of the dunes to the parched, salty lakebed of Lake Otero. The trail is marked by white posts with orange reflective tape. Do not hike the trail in strong winds, when blowing sand reduces visibility and makes it very easy to lose the trail. Bring lots of water and protect yourself from the intense sunlight.

There is a free, guided **sunset stroll** every evening (call ahead), and on summer nights, a park ranger gives an **evening talk** on various topics (June-Aug. 8:30pm). On **full-moon nights** in the summer, the park stays open late (until 11pm, last entrance 10pm), and a guest speaker or performer takes the stage at 8:30pm. A **star talk** takes place most Fridays during the summer at 8:30pm. During the **Perseid Meteor Shower** (around second week of Aug.), the park stays open until midnight.

ROSWELL ☎505

With giant inflatable Martians advertising used cars, streetlights donning painted-on pointy eyes, and flying saucers adorning fast-food signs, one thing is certain: aliens *have* invaded Roswell. The fascination began in July 1947, when an alien spacecraft reportedly plummeted to the earth near the dusty town. The official press release reported that the military had recovered pieces of a "flying saucer," but a retraction arrived the next day—the wreckage, the government claimed, was actually a harmless weather balloon. Many people weren't convinced.

Both believers and skeptics will find the alien side of Roswell entertaining, if not enlightening. During the first week of July, the **UFO Festival** commemorates the anniversary of the alleged encounter, drawing thousands for live music, an alien costume contest, and a 5km "Alien Chase" race. With a plastic flying saucer above its storefront, the popular **International UFO Museum and Research Center,** 114 N. Main St., recounts what happened near Roswell in 1947. Exhibits feature testimonials and newspaper clippings about the incident, as well as features on alien sightings worldwide. (☎625-9495. Open daily 9am-5pm. Free. Audio tour $1.)

Fast-food restaurants are as prevalent in Roswell as allusions to alien life, and they are concentrated along N. Main St. and W. 2nd St. Side streets are home to less commercial budget eateries. **Albertson's Supermarket** is at 1110 S. Main St. (☎623-9300. Open daily 6am-midnight.) Just around the corner from the UFO Museum, the **Crash Down Diner ❶,** 106 W. 1st St., is an out-of-this-world-themed restaurant, albeit with standard fare. Try a Starchild burrito creation ($5.75), a "hungry alien" sub ($3-5), or an "unidentified" burger ($4). A giant alien mural covers the wall, and even the salt and pepper shakers are shaped like aliens. (☎627-5533. Open M-Sa 8am-6pm, Su 8am-6pm.) **Tia Juana's ❸,** 3601 N. Main St., is the kind of funky Tex-Mex restaurant that the big chains try to imitate. Try the chili rubbed ribeye for $15, or refresh yourself with something from the huge margarita menu for $5-8. (☎624-6113. Dining room open M-Th 11am-9:30pm, F-Sa 11am-10pm, Su 11am-9pm; bar open daily 11am-10pm.) **Peppers Bar and Grill ❷,** 500 N. Main St., serves American and Mexican food indoors and on a mist-cooled outdoor patio. (☎623-1700. Apr.-Oct. F-Sa live music; DJ spinning on the patio W. Dining room open M-Sa 11am-10pm, bar open 11am-midnight.)

Aside from its extraterrestrial peculiarities, Roswell is a fairly normal town. The intersection of **2nd Street** (Rte. 70/380) and **Main Street** (Rte. 285) is the sun around which the Roswell solar system orbits. To reach Roswell from Albuquerque, head 89 mi. south on I-25 to San Antonio, then 153 mi. east on U.S. 380. **Greyhound,** 1100 N. Virginia Ave. (☎622-2510), in conjunction with TNM&O, runs buses to **Albuquerque** (4hr.; 2 per day Tu-Sa, 1 on Su; M-Th $36, F-Su $38) and **El Paso** (4½hr.; 3 per day; M-Th $41, F-Su $44). **Pecos Trails Transit,** 515 N. Main St., runs buses all over town. (☎624-6766. M-F 6am-10:30pm, Sa 7:10am-10pm, Su 10:30am-7pm. $0.75, students $0.50, seniors $0.35.) The cheery and helpful **Visitors Center** is at 426 N. Main St. (☎624-0889 or 623-5695. Open M-F 8:30am-5:30pm, Sa-Su 10am-3pm.) The **Post Office** occupies 415 N. Pennsylvania Ave. (☎623-7232. Open M-F 7:30am-5:30pm, Sa 8am-noon.) **Postal Code:** 88202. **Area Code:** 505.

CARLSBAD CAVERNS ☎505

Imagine the surprise of European wanderers in southeastern New Mexico at the turn of the century when 250,000 bats appeared at dusk, seemingly out of nowhere. This swarm led to the discovery of the Carlsbad Caverns. By 1923, colonies of tourists clung to the walls of this desolate attraction. Carlsbad Caverns National Park marks one of the world's largest and oldest cave systems; even the most jaded spelunker will be struck by its unusual geological formations. (Natural entrance open daily June to mid-Aug. 8:30am-3:30pm; mid-Aug. to May 8:30am-2pm. Big room open daily June to mid-Aug. 8:30am-5pm; mid-Aug. to May 8:30am-3:30pm. $6, age 6-15 $3. Audio tour $3.) The **King's Palace Tour,** guided by a ranger, passes through four of the cave's lowest rooms and some of its most awesome anomalies. (1½hr. tours every hr. 9-11am and 1-3pm. $8, Golden Age Passport holders and ages 6-15 $4. Advance reservations required.) Other guided tours in the Big Room include a lantern tour though the **Left Hand Tunnel** (daily; $7) and a climbing tour of the **Lower Cave** (M-F; $20). Plan your visit for late afternoon to catch the magnificent **bat flight.** The ritual, during which hungry bats storm out of the cave at a rate of 6000 per min., is preceded by a ranger talk. (May-Oct. daily just before sunset.) **Backcountry hiking** is permitted above ground, but a permit, a map, and massive quantities of water are required.

Tours of the undeveloped **Slaughter Canyon Cave** offer a more rugged spelunking experience. A reliable car is required to get there; there's no public transportation, and the parking lot is 23 mi. down Rte. 418, an unpaved road, several miles south of the main entrance to the park on U.S. 62/180. The cave entrance is a steep, strenuous ½ mi. from the lot. Ranger-led tours (bring a flashlight) traverse difficult and slippery terrain; there are no paved trails or handrails. (2hr. tours; June-Aug. 2 per day, Sept.-May Sa-Su only. $15, Golden Age Passport holders and ages 6-15 $7.50. Call the Visitors Center as least 2 days ahead to reserve.) Tours of **Hall of the White Giant** and **Spider Cave** require crawling and climbing through tight passages. (☎800-967-2283. Tours 4hr. 1 per week. $20. Call at least a month in advance to reserve.)

A slew of budget motels line U.S. 62/180 south of downtown. The **Stage Coach Inn ❷,** 1819 S. Canal St. (☎887-1148), is the nicest of the lot with an outdoor pool, indoor jacuzzi, and laundry. Comfortable, clean rooms have A/C, cable, and refrigerators. (Singles $34-40; doubles $36-47. 15% AAA and AARP discount.) The **Carlsbad RV Park and Campground ❶,** 4301 National Parks Hwy. (☎888-885-6333), 4 mi. south of town, has two wooden camping cabins with a full-size bed, two bunk beds, and A/C ($30; linen not provided). Low-privacy tent camping ($14.50) is also available. All guests have access to showers and a swimming pool.

The closest town to the park is **White's City,** on U.S. 62/180, 20 mi. southwest of the much larger **Carlsbad** and 6 mi. from the park Visitors Center. Flash floods occasionally close the roads; call the park for road conditions. **El Paso, TX** (p. 713) is the nearest big city, 150 mi. west past **Guadalupe Mountains National Park** (p. 712). **Greyhound,** in cooperation with **TNM&O Coaches** (☎887-1108), runs four buses per day between El Paso and Carlsbad ($37) and will make a flag stop at White's City. **Caverns Visitors Center** has trail maps and tour info. (☎785-2232. Open daily 8am-7pm; late Aug.-May 8am-5:30pm. Entrance fee $6.) Make reservations by phone through the **Guided Tour Reservation Hotline** (☎800-967-2283) or on the web (http://reservations.nps.gov). **Post Office,** 23 Carlsbad Caverns Hwy., resides next to the Best Western gift shop. (☎785-2220. Open M-F 8am-noon and 12:30-4:30pm, Sa 8am-noon.) **Postal Code:** 88268. **Area Code:** 505.

CALIFORNIA

California is a place to freak out—to redefine boundaries, identities, and attitudes. It is a land that destroys the past to experiment with the new and unexplored, anticipating changes in mass culture and channeling them into the trends of the future. Glaring movie spotlights, clanging San Francisco trolleys, *barrio* bustle, vanilla-scented Jeffrey pines, alpine lakes, and ghostly, shimmering desert landscapes all thrive in California. It is the edge of the West, the testing ground of extremes, the drawing board for the American dream. There's so much going on you'd need a whole book (like *Let's Go: California 2004*) to describe it.

HIGHLIGHTS OF CALIFORNIA

LOS ANGELES. Follow your star to the place where media legends carouse, Ice Age fossils calcify, and boardwalk freaks commune (p. 873).

SAN FRANCISCO. Drive through the Golden Gate Bridge to the City by the Bay, where bluesmen, iconoclasts, students, and old hippies all congregate (p. 924).

SCENIC DRIVES. Along the coast, Rte. 1 and U.S. 101 breeze past earthy beach towns and along soaring cliffs, passing Santa Barbara (p. 916), Hearst Castle (p. 921), and Redwood National Park (p. 959).

NATIONAL PARKS. Hike among the granite peaks of Yosemite (p. 964), or climb a boulder and view the sunset at Joshua Tree (p. 913).

PRACTICAL INFORMATION

Capital: Sacramento.

Visitor Info: California Office of Tourism, 801 K St., #1600, Sacramento 95814. (☎800-862-2543; www.visitcalifornia.com). **California State Parks Department,** P.O. Box 942896, Sacramento 94296. ☎800-777-0369.

Postal Abbreviation: CA. **Sales Tax:** 7-8%, depending on county.

LOS ANGELES

In a city where nothing seems to be more than 30 years old, the latest trends demand more respect than the venerable. Many come to this historical vacuum to make (or re-make) themselves. And what better place? Without the tiresome duty of bowing to the gods of an established high culture, Angelenos are free to indulge in a culture of their own. Some savor L.A.'s image-bound culture, while others may be appalled by its narcissism and excess. Either way, it's one hell of a show.

INTERCITY TRANSPORTATION

Despite L.A.'s reputation for existing in a permanent celluloid vacation from reality, five major freeways connect California's vainest city to the rest of the state. I-5 (Golden State Freeway), which travels the length of California, bisects L.A. on a north-south axis; it heads north to Sacramento and south to San Diego. U.S. 101 and the Pacific Coast Highway (PCH) link L.A. to other coastal cities, heading west out of L.A. before turning north towards San Francisco and paralleling I-5. I-10 and I-15 come in from the east, providing access from Las Vegas and Arizona.

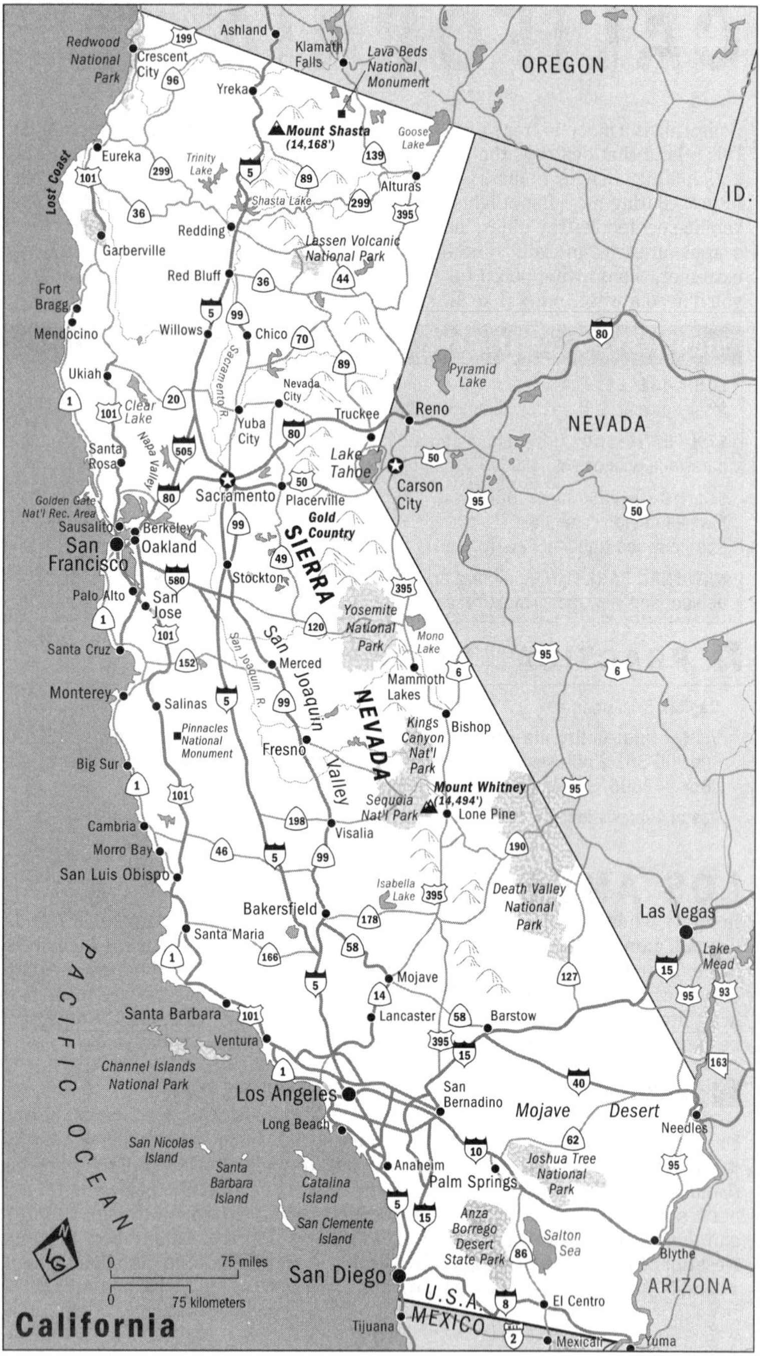

California

OREGON
NEVADA
ID.
ARIZONA
MEXICO
U.S.A.
PACIFIC OCEAN
SIERRA NEVADA
San Joaquin Valley
Mojave Desert

Redwood National Park
Crescent City
Ashland
Klamath Falls
Lava Beds National Monument
Yreka
Mount Shasta (14,168')
Goose Lake
Eureka
Lost Coast
Trinity Lake
Alturas
Shasta Lake
Redding
Lassen Volcanic National Park
Garberville
Red Bluff
Fort Bragg
Mendocino
Willows
Chico
Sacramento R.
Pyramid Lake
Ukiah
Nevada City
Clear Lake
Yuba City
Truckee
Reno
Napa Valley
Santa Rosa
Lake Tahoe
Carson City
Sacramento
Placerville
Golden Gate Nat'l Rec. Area
Sausalito
Berkeley
Gold Country
San Francisco
Oakland
Stockton
Palo Alto
San Jose
Yosemite National Park
Mono Lake
Santa Cruz
San Joaquin R.
Merced
Mammoth Lakes
Monterey
Salinas
Kings Canyon Nat'l Park
Bishop
Pinnacles National Monument
Fresno
Big Sur
Mount Whitney (14,494')
Sequoia Nat'l Park
Lone Pine
Cambria
Visalia
Morro Bay
San Luis Obispo
Isabella Lake
Death Valley National Park
Bakersfield
Las Vegas
Santa Maria
Lake Mead
Mojave
Santa Barbara
Lancaster
Barstow
Ventura
Channel Islands National Park
San Bernadino
Los Angeles
Long Beach
Needles
San Nicolas Island
Anaheim
Joshua Tree National Park
Santa Barbara Island
Catalina Island
Palm Springs
San Clemente Island
Anza Borrego Desert State Park
Salton Sea
Blythe
San Diego
El Centro
Tijuana
Mexicali
Yuma

0 75 miles
0 75 kilometers

199 96 5 89 139 299 101 36 395 44 99 70 20 1 80 505 50 95 49 580 120 152 6 198 46 190 178 58 166 127 14 15 93 163 40 62 10 86 8 2

CALIFORNIA

By Plane: Los Angeles International Airport (LAX) is in Westchester, about 15 mi. southwest of Downtown. LAX information (☎310-646-5252) will help Spanish and English speakers. Airport police (☎310-646-7911) are there 24hr. a day. **Traveler's Aid,** a service for airport info, transportation, accommodation, and major transit emergencies, in all terminals. (☎310-646-2270. Open M-F 8:30am-noon and 1-5pm.)

By Train: Amtrak rolls into Union Station, 800 N. Alameda St. (☎213-683-6729 or 800-USA-RAIL/872-7245), at the northeastern edge of Downtown.

By Bus: Greyhound (☎800-231-2222 or 213-629-8401), consider bypassing its Downtown station, 1716 E. 7th St. at Alameda St. (☎213-629-8536), which is in an extremely rough neighborhood. If you must get off in Downtown, *be very careful near 7th and Alameda St.,* one block southwest of the station, where you can catch MTA bus #60 traveling north to Union Station. The new terminal in Hollywood, 1715 N. Cahuenga Blvd. (☎323-466-1249), is at a great location close to many hotels, restaurants, and sights. From Union Station, buses leave to **Greyhound Routes: San Francisco** (17 per day; $42, round-trip $82); **Las Vegas** (17 per day; $38, round-trip $71); **Tijuana** (4hr.; $17, round-trip $27). Route maps $3.

THE LAY OF THE L.A.ND

I-5 (Santa Ana Freeway, Golden State Freeway, and San Diego Freeway), I-405 (San Diego Freeway), I-110 (Harbor Freeway), U.S. 101 (Hollywood Freeway), and **Pacific Coast Highway (PCH or Highway 1)** all run north-south. **I-10 (Santa Monica Freeway)** is the most popular freeway for east-west drivers. I-5 intersects I-10 just east of Downtown and serves as one of the two major north-south thruways. I-405, which goes from **Orange County** in the south all the way through L.A., parallels I-5 on a route closer to the coast, and separates **Santa Monica** and **Malibu** from the L.A. **Westside.**

DOWNTOWN. A legitimate **Downtown L.A.** exists, but few go there except to work. The heart of Downtown is relatively safe on weekdays, but *avoid walking there after dark and on weekends.* The predominantly Latino section of the city is found east of Downtown in **Boyle Heights, East L.A.,** and **Montebello. Monterey Park** is one of the few cities in the U.S. with a predominantly Asian-American population. The **University of Southern California (USC), Exposition Park,** and the mostly African-American districts of **Inglewood, Watts,** and **Compton** stretch south of Downtown. **South Central,** the name of this area, suffered the brunt of the 1992 riots, is known for rampant crime and holds few attractions for tourists.

HOLLYWOOD & WESTSIDE. Nowhere is the myth/reality divide more dramatic in Los Angeles than in the sharp contrast between the movieland glamour associated with **Hollywood** and its unromantic modern existence. **Sunset Boulevard** presents a cross-section of virtually everything L.A. has to offer. The **Sunset Strip,** hot seat of L.A.'s best nightlife, is the West Hollywood section of Sunset Blvd. closest to Beverly Hills.The region known as **The Westside** encompasses prestigious **West Hollywood, Westwood, Century City, Bel Air, Brentwood,** and **Beverly Hills, Pacific Palisades, Santa Monica,** and **Venice.** A good portion of the city's gay community resides in West Hollywood, while Beverly Hills and Bel Air are home to some of the highest concentrations of wealth and celebrity in the state. Westside's attractions include the **University of California at Los Angeles (UCLA)** in Westwood and the trendy **Melrose Avenue. West L.A.** is a municipal distinction that refers to Westwood and the no-man's land including Century City. The area west of Downtown and south of West Hollywood is known as the **Wilshire District.**

OUTSIDE L.A. Eighty miles of beaches line L.A.'s **coastal region. Zuma Beach** is northernmost, followed by **Malibu, Santa Monica,** and **Venice.** South across the Palos Verdes Peninsula is **Long Beach.** The **San Fernando Valley** sprawls north of the Hollywood Hills and the Santa Monica Mountains.

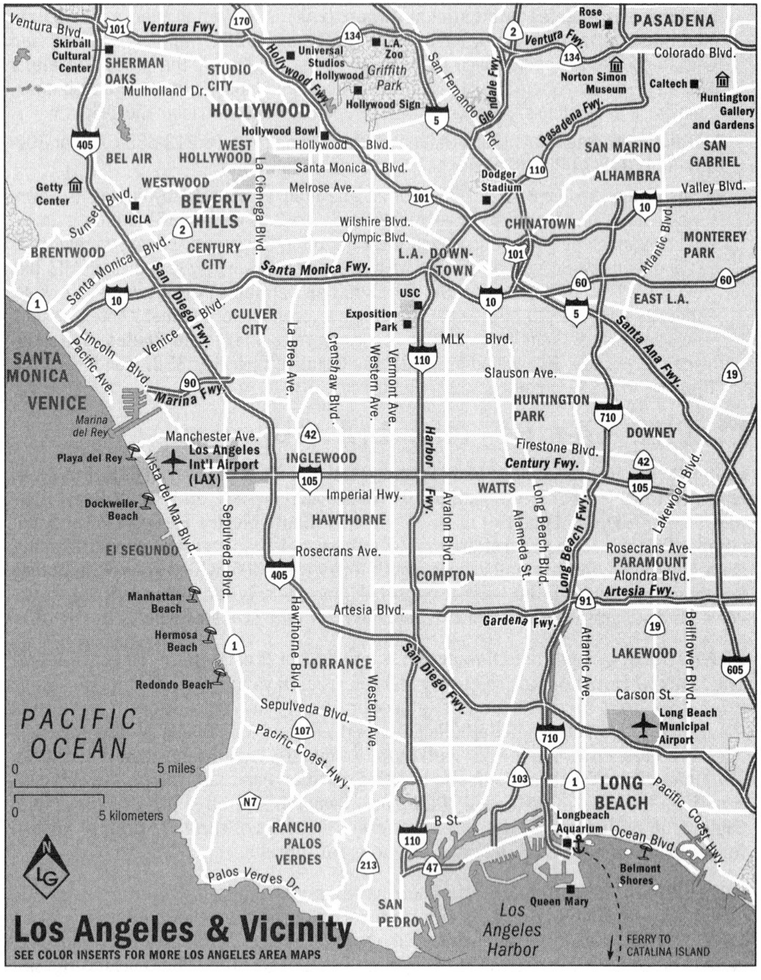

Los Angeles & Vicinity

SEE COLOR INSERTS FOR MORE LOS ANGELES AREA MAPS

LOCAL TRANSPORTATION

Nowhere is the Automobile God more revered than in L.A.; the freeway is perhaps the most enduring image of L.A. Sometimes it seems like all 16 million residents are flooding I-405 and I-101 all at once, transforming the City of Angels into Transportation Hell. A quick reminder: no matter how jammed the freeways are, they are almost always quicker and safer than surface streets. Heavy traffic moves toward Downtown from 7 to 10am on weekdays and streams outbound from 4 to 7pm. Though renting a car is expensive, especially if you are under 25, driving is the best way to get around. If you must forego the rental, use the subway and the bus, although these public transportation systems are limited and inconvenient.

Walking or biking around the city is simply not feasible—distances are just too great. Worse–it's uncool. Admittedly, some colorful areas such as Melrose, Third Street Promenade in Santa Monica, Venice Beach, Hollywood, and Old Town Pasadena are best explored by foot. At night, those on **foot,** especially outside the Westside, should exercise caution. *If you hitchhike, you will probably die.* It is exceptionally dangerous, not to mention illegal. Don't even consider it.

By Bus: 6 **Metropolitan Transit Authority (MTA) Metro Customer Centers** are available to point mass transit users in the right direction. **Downtown:** Arco Plaza, 515 S. Flower St., Level "C" (open M-F 7:30am-3:30pm); Gateway Transit Center, Union Station E. Portal (open M-F 6am-6:30pm). **East L.A.:** 4501-B Whittier Blvd. (open Tu-Sa 10am-6pm). **San Fernando Valley:** 14435 Sherman Way, Van Nuys (open M-F 10am-6pm). Centers are also located in Baldwin Hills and Wilshire. MTA's basic fare is $1.35 (transfer $0.25), seniors and disabled $0.45 (transfer $0.10); exact change is required. Weekly passes ($11) are available at customer service centers and grocery stores. Transfers can be made between MTA lines or to other transit authorities. Unless otherwise noted, all route numbers are MTA; BBBus stands for **Big Blue Bus** and indicates Santa Monica buses. (☎800-COMMUTE/266-6883; www.mta.net. Open M-F 6am-8:30pm, Sa-Su 8am-6pm.) The local **DASH shuttle** ($0.25), designed for short distance neighborhood hops, serves major tourist destinations in many communities. (☎213-808-2273; www.ladottransit.com. Open M-F 9am-5pm, Sa 10am-2pm.)

By Train and Subway: The Blue Line runs from Downtown to the southern L.A. communities and Long Beach. The Green Line goes along I-105 from Norwalk to Redondo Beach, with shuttle service to L.A.X at Aviation/I-105. The Red Line runs from Downtown through Hollywood to the San Fernando Valley; other lines go west to Wilshire and east to Union Station. A one-way trip costs $1.35, with bus and rail transfers $1.60; seniors and disabled are $0.45, with transfers $0.55. All lines run daily 5am-11pm (☎800-266-6883/COMMUTE; www.mta.net). The new Beige Line runs from Union Station to Pasadena. Metrolink trains (☎800-371-5465) run out of the city from Union Station to Ventura and Orange Counties (M-F), and to Riverside via San Bernardino, Santa Clarita, and Antelope Valley (M-Sa). One-way fares are $4.25-10.75, depending on the destination. You can only buy them from machines in the station within 3hr. of your departure time. Discounts are available if traveling Sa or off-peak hours (8:30am-3:30pm and after 7pm). Beware—trains come and go up to 5min. ahead of schedule.

By Taxi: **Independent** (☎213-385-8294 or 800-521-8294)**, L.A. Taxi/Yellow Cab Co.** (☎800-711-8294 or 800-200-1085), or **Bell Cab** (☎888-235-5222). Fare is about $2 per mi. in the city and approximately $30-35 from LAX to Downtown.

Car Rental: Avon, 7080 Santa Monica Blvd. (☎323-850-0826; www.avonrents.com), at La Brea Blvd. Cars $29 per day with 150 mi. free, $179 per week with 750 mi. free, or $550-600 per month with 3325 mi. free. Collision Damage Waiver $9 per day. No under-25 surcharge. Open M-F 6am-7pm, Sa-Su 7am-5pm. The **Automobile Club of Southern California (AAA),** 2601 S. Figueroa St., at Adams Blvd., has additional driving info and maps. Club privileges are free for AAA members and cost $2-3 for non-members. (☎213-741-3686, emergency assistance 800-400-4222. Open M-F 9am-5pm. Other offices in greater L.A.)

PRACTICAL INFORMATION

Visitor Info: L.A. Convention and Visitor Bureau, 685 S. Figueroa St. (☎213-689-8822; www.visitlanow.com), between Wilshire Blvd. and 7th St. in the Financial District. Multilingual staff. Detailed bus map of L.A. available. California road map $3. Distributes *L.A. Now,* a free booklet with tourist and lodging info. Open M-F 8am-5:30pm.

Rape Crisis: ☎310-392-8381.

Medical Services: Cedars-Sinai Medical Center, 8700 Beverly Blvd. (☎310-423-3277, emergency 423-8644). **Good Samaritan Hospital,** 616 S. Witmer St. (☎213-977-2121, emergency 977-2420). **UCLA Medical Center,** 10833 Le Conte Ave. (☎310-825-9111, emergency 825-2111).

Post Office: Central branch at 7101 S. Central Ave. (☎800-275-8777). Open M-F 7am-7pm, Sa 7am-3pm. **Postal Code:** 90001.

AREA CODES. L.A. is big. Real big. 213 covers Downtown L.A. 323 covers Hollywood, Huntington Park, Montebello, and West Hollywood. Prestigious 310 covers Beverly Hills, Santa Monica, and the Westside. 562 covers Long Beach and the South Bay. 626 covers Pasadena. 818 covers Burbank, Glendale, San Fernando Valley. 909 covers San Bernardino and Riverside.

ACCOMMODATIONS

In choosing where to stay, the first consideration should be location. Decide which element of L.A. appeals to you the most, especially if you're going it without a car. Those looking for a tan should choose lodgings in Venice, Santa Monica or the South Bay. Sightseers will be better off in Hollywood or the more expensive (but nicer) Westside. One campground fairly close to L.A. is **Leo Carrillo State Beach** ❶ (☎805-488-5223), on PCH 20 mi. north of Malibu. It has 135 sites with flush toilets and showers ($13). Listed prices do not include L.A.'s 14% hotel tax.

HOLLYWOOD

Hollywood Bungalows International Youth Hostel, 2775 W. Cahuenga Blvd. (☎888-259-9990; www.hollywoodbungalows.com), just north of the Hollywood Bowl in the Hollywood Hills. This newly renovated hostel cultivates a wacky summer camp atmosphere. Spacious rooms and nightly jam sessions. Outdoor pool, billiards, weight room, big screen TV, and mini-diner. Cable in some rooms. Breakfast $3.50, dinner $10. Lockers $0.25. Linen and parking included. Laundry $1.25 wash; $0.75 dry. On-site Universal Rent-a-Car (see p. 877). Check-in 24hr. Internet access $2 per 10min. 6- to 10-bed co-ed dorms $15-19; private doubles $59. ❷

USA Hostels Hollywood, 1624 Schrader Blvd. (☎323-462-3777 or 800-524-6783; www.usahostels.com), south of Hollywood Blvd., west of Cahuenga Blvd. Crawling with young travelers, this lime-green and blue-dotted chain hostel is filled with energy and organized fun. Special events nightly. Stay for 5+ days and get free pick-up from airport, bus, and train stations (3+ nights, half-price pick-up). Free beach shuttles run Su, T, and Th. To use lockers, bring your own lock or buy one for $0.50. Linen and all-you-can-eat pancakes included. Free street parking or parking lot $4.50 per day. Dinner $4. Dorms (6-8 beds) with private bath $15-21; private rooms for 2-4 people $39-52. Prices $1-2 less in winter. Passport or proof of travel required. ❷

Flamingo Hotel, 1921 N. Highland Ave. (☎323-876-6544), just north of Hollywood Blvd. An 8-story maze of rooms offering peace, quiet, and quick access to sights. Private rooms well-furnished and large. Use a common kitchen or ask for a room with its own kitchen. Lounge with free billiards, TV, and video games. Internet access $1 per 10min. Laundry $1 wash; $0.75 dry. 4-bed dorms $15-19; private rooms $40-80. ❸

SANTA MONICA, VENICE, & THE SOUTH BAY

Los Angeles/Santa Monica (HI-AYH), 1436 2nd St. (☎310-393-9913; http://hostel-web.com/losangeles), Santa Monica. 1 block from the Promenade and 2 blocks from the beach, this popular hostel regularly organizes discounted tours, outings, comedy shows, open mic, and movie nights. Dining room, newly renovated kitchen, game room, TV room, pool table, Internet access, linens, and library. No-alcohol policy and strict 10pm-8am quiet hours. Breakfast 7:30-10:30am ($2-4). Safe deposits and lockers. Laundry $1 wash; $0.75 dry. 24hr. security and check-in. 10-day max. stay. In summer, reserve by phone or online. 4- to 10-bed dorms $28, non-members $31; private doubles $70/75. Group packages available for 8 or more. ❷

Los Angeles Surf City Hostel, 26 Pier Ave. (☎798-2323), in Hermosa Beach's Pier Plaza. Free airport pick-up 8am-8pm, $10 drop-off. Young, mostly international clientele enjoying the nightlife. Downstairs is the Beach Club, a popular bar and nightclub. Discount car rentals, showers, Internet access, kitchen, TV lounge, and downstairs bar. Includes boogie boards, breakfast, and linen. Laundry. Key deposit $10. 28-night max. stay; 3-day max. stay for U.S. citizens. No parking. Reservations recommended. Passport or driver's license required for all guests. 4-bunk dorms May-Nov. $19; Dec.-Apr. $15.50. Private rooms $48. ❷

Venice Beach Hostel, 1515 Pacific Ave. (☎310-452-3052; www.caprica.com/venice-beach-hostel), just north of Windward Ave in Venice. Its central location, friendly staff, and lively atmosphere make this a popular hostel for backpackers. A full kitchen, 2 enormous lounges, and 10 super-comfy couches encourage mingling. Lockers, storage rooms, and linen included. Laundry $1 wash, $0.75 dry. $25-100 security deposit at check-in. Internet access $1 per 10min. 4- to 10-bed dorms $19-22; private rooms for 1 or 2 people $55. Weekly discounts available. ❷

THE WESTSIDE: BEVERLY HILLS & WESTWOOD

Orbit Hotel and Hostel, 7950 Melrose Ave. (☎323-655-1510 or 877-672-4887; www.orbithotel.com), a block west of Fairfax Ave. in West Hollywood. Opened by 2 young L.A. locals 3 years ago, Orbit is setting new standards for swank budget living. Fashion-conscious furniture, spacious retro kitchen, big-screen TV lounge, small courtyard, and late-night party room. Breakfast and lockers included. Free TV show tickets. Car rental $20 per day. Internet access. 6-bed dorms $20; private rooms for up to 4 from $55. Dorms only accept international students with passport. ❷

Hotel Claremont, 1044 Tiverton Ave. (☎310-208-5957 or 800-266-5957), in Westwood Village near UCLA. Pleasant and inexpensive. Still owned by the same family that built it 60 years ago. Clean rooms, ceiling fans, and private baths. Fridge and microwave next to a pleasant Victorian-style TV lounge. Reservations recommended, especially in June. Singles $50; doubles $56; 2 beds for up to 4 $65. ❸

Beverly Hills Reeves Hotel, 120 S. Reeves Dr. (☎310-271-3006). Cheap stays are hard to come by in Beverly Hills, but this recently renovated mansion near Rodeo Dr. offers both budget and beauty. Rooms with A/C, TV, microwave, and fridge. Continental breakfast included. Parking $6. Rooms with shared bathrooms $50 per night, private bathroom $69, $250/349 per week. ❹

FOOD

Thin figures and fat wallets are a powerful combination—L.A. luxuriates in the most heavenly and healthy recipes. At the same time, L.A. elevates chain restaurants to heights unknown. For the supreme burger-and-fries experience, try the beloved **In-N-Out Burger.** The current craze is lard- and cholesterol-free "healthy Mexican"—**Baja Fresh** leads the pack. If you're looking to cook, **Trader Joe's** specializes in budget gourmet food. (☎800-SHOP-TJS/746-7857 for locations. Most open daily 9am-9pm.) **Farmer's Market,** 6333 W. 3rd St. at Fairfax Ave., attracts about 3 million people every year and has over 160 produce stalls, as well as international food booths, handicraft shops, and a phenomenal juice bar. A cheaper and less touristy source of produce is the **Grand Central Public Market,** 317 S. Broadway, between 3rd and 4th St. in Downtown. Entrances are on both Broadway and Hill St. between 3rd and 4th St. (☎213-624-2378. Open daily 9am-6pm.)

HOLLYWOOD

The Griddle Cafe, 7916 Sunset Blvd. (☎323-874-0377), in West Hollywood. One of the most popular brunch spots on the strip, the Griddle prides itself on its breakfast food creativity. Especially popular are the "Apple Cobbler French Toast" ($7) and "Black Magic" (Oreo crumb-filled flapjacks; $7). Consider sharing the enormous portions. A 45min. wait is not uncommon on weekends. Open M-F 7am-3pm, Sa-Su 8am-3pm. ❷

Duke's Coffee Shop, 8909 Sunset Blvd. (☎310-652-3100), in West Hollywood. Legendary Duke's is the best place to see hungry, hungover rockers slumped over in the communal, canteen-style tables. The walls are plastered with autographed album covers. Try "Sandy's Favorite" (green peppers, potatoes, and scrambled eggs) for $7.25. Entrees $5-11. Attendant parking $1. Open M-F 7:30am-8:30pm, Sa-Su 8am-3:30pm. ❷

Roscoe's House of Chicken and Waffles, 1514 Gower St. (☎323-466-7453), at the corner of Gower and Sunset Blvd. The down-home feel and all-day menu make this a popular spot for regular folk and celebs alike. Try "1 succulent chicken breast and 1 delicious waffle" ($7). Be prepared to wait (30min.-1hr.) on weekends. Open Su-Th 8:30am-midnight, F-Sa 8:30am-4am. Other location at 5006 W. Pico Blvd, L.A. ❷

Pink's Hot Dog Stand, 709 N. La Brea Ave. (☎323-931-4223; www.pinkshollywood.com), at Melrose. An institution since 1939, Pink's serves up chili-slathered happiness in a bun. The aroma of meaty chili and freshly-cooked dogs draws crowds far into the night. Try the special "Ozzy Osbourne Spicy Dog" for $5. Chili dogs $2.40; chili fries $2.20. Open Su-Th 9:30am-2am, F-Sa 9:30am-3am. Cash only. ❶

SANTA MONICA & MALIBU

Fritto Misto, 601 Colorado Ave. (☎310-458-2829), at 6th St. "Neighborhood Italian Cafe" with cheery waitstaff lets you create your own pasta ($6+). Vegetarian entrees $8-12. Daily hot pasta specials $8. Weekend lunch special of all-you-can-eat calamari and salad $12. Omelettes Su 11:30am-4pm ($7-8). Open M-Th 11:30am-10pm, F-Sa 11:30am-10:30pm, Su 11:30am-9:30pm. ❷

Mariasol, 401 Santa Monica Pier (☎310-917-5050). Prime sunset views from the westward tip of the Santa Monica Pier accompany your meal in the glass-enclosed dining room. Locals recommend the "campechana," a combination of shrimp, octopus calamari, and ceviche ($12). Appetizers $6-10. Entrees $9-15. Open Su-Th 10am-10pm, F-Sa 10am-11pm. Reservations recommended for second floor dining room. ❸

Reel Inn, 1220 Third St. Promenade (☎310-395-5538). Right on the popular tourist strip, the Inn reels in fresh fish from all over the world. Long, communal tables and outdoor seating. Tasmanian salmon and Chilean swordfish are specialties ($10-14). Beer $3-4. Open Su-Th 11:30am-9:30pm, F-Sa 11:30am-10:30pm. ❸

Bread & Porridge, 2315 Wilshire Blvd. (☎310-453-4941). This all-day breakfast and lunch (after 11am) spot prides itself on exceptional service and pancakes (banana, strawberry, chocolate chip, blueberry, and pecan; $5.55-6.55). Omelettes $9. Sandwiches and entrees $7-12. Oatmeal $4.55. Open M-F 7am-2pm, Sa-Su 7am-3pm. ❷

VENICE & THE SOUTH BAY

Rose Cafe and Market, 220 Rose Ave. (☎310-399-0711), at Main St. Gigantic walls painted with roses, local art, industrial architecture, and a gift shop might make you think this is a museum, but the colorful cuisine is the main display. Healthy deli specials, including sandwiches ($6-8) and salads ($6-8) available from 11:30am. Limited menu after 3pm. Open M-F 7am-5:30pm, Sa 8am-6pm, Su 8am-5pm. ❷

Where the famous stars boozed, binged, and blacked out.

Bogart. Sinatra. Hepburn. Gable. Monroe. The greatest livers of a generation were destroyed here. Those who say L.A. has no sense of history need look no further than the bottom of their cocktail glass at these venerable (and still standing) Old Hollywood bars. Here's looking at you, kid!

Barney's Beanery, 8447 Santa Monica Blvd. (☎323-654-2287), in West Hollywood. Some like it hot—especially Marilyn Monroe. While filming the picture of the same name, she'd drop in for chili. Odd, because this rough-and-tumble Rte. 66 roadhouse is more suited to Janis Joplin, who partied here the night she died. Expect an excellent jukebox, 50¢ pool, and several hundred kinds of beer. Happy hour M-F 4-7pm. Open daily 11am-2am.

Chez Jay, 1657 Ocean Ave. (☎310-395-1741), in Santa Monica. A tiny, crusty beachside dive festooned with Christmas lights, red check tablecloths, and pictures of Sinatra. Why not? Ol' Blue Eyes dented the red vinyl here regularly in his day. Now, slip into the crowd of Westside types too "real" to go to a martini bar and order up some Jack Daniels—the Chairman's favorite. Open M-F 6pm-2am, Sa-Su 5:30pm-2am.

Coach & Horses Pub, 7617 W. Sunset Blvd. (☎323-876-6900), in Hollywood. A dark, tiny ye olde hole-in-the-wall where Richard Burton used to start his benders. If you feel like following suit, start early on a weekday. F-Sa the hipsters invade, armed with apple martinis and leather pants. Open M-Sa 11am-2am, Su 5pm-2am.

The Gallery Bar at the Biltmore Hotel, 506 S. Grand Ave. (☎213-612-1532), in Downtown L.A. Glide into wood-paneled elegance, sip a martini, and wonder what really happened to the Black Dahlia. This was, after all, the last place aspiring starlet Beth Short (nicknamed for her pin-up quality black dresses) was seen alive. Back in 1947, a doorman tipped his cap to her, and five days later her severed body made her the most famous victim of an unsolved murder case in city history. Open daily 4:30pm-1:45am.

Formosa Cafe, 7156 Santa Monica Blvd. (☎323-850-9050), in Hollywood. The more than 250 star headshots plastering the walls are rumored to have been dropped off in person. Cozy up in a booth like Lana Turner used to (*L.A. Confidential* wasn't kidding—she really did hang out here) and drink all you want, but avoid the greasy "Chinese" food at all costs. Open M-F 4pm-2am, Sa-Su 6pm-2am.

Musso & Frank Grill, 6667 Hollywood Blvd. (☎323-467-7788), in Hollywood. Where Bogie boozed, Sinatra swilled, and Bukowski blew his cash. The drinks ain't cheap, but oh, what ambience! Honeyed light, high-backed booths, and curmudgeonly red-jacketed waiters. The martini is the city's best, but if you want something different, try a gimlet. Bar denizen Raymond Chandler immortalized Musso's gin and lime juice concoctions in "The Long Goodbye." Open Tu-Sa 11am-10:45pm.

The Polo Lounge at the Beverly Hills Hotel, 9641 Sunset Blvd. (☎310-276-2251), in Beverly Hills. Where the loudest thing is the pink paint on the walls. Ask to be seated in the patio section, order up a Singapore Sling, and dream about the days when Kate Hepburn and Marlene Dietrich held court here. Come F mornings and see why this place coined the term "power breakfast"—tables on the outer edge of the terrace are a classic place for movie deals to be struck. Open daily 7am-1am.

Trader Vic's at the Beverly Hilton Hotel, 9876 Wilshire Blvd. (☎310-274-7777), in Beverly Hills. A dim, linen tablecloth tiki bar that George Hamilton allegedly singled out as a great place for celebrity affairs owing to its two entrances, or rather, two exits. The $10 price tags of the house cocktails are more than made up for in presentation—the pina colada is served in a whole pineapple; a floating gardenia graces the gin-laced scorpion bowl. Open Su-Th 5pm-2am, F-Sa 5pm-1am.

Stephanie L. Smith was a Researcher-Writer for Let's Go: California 1997 and New Zealand 1998. She worked as a freelancer for CitySearch Los Angeles, reviewing restaurants, bars, and attractions, and is now working in Hollywood as the features editor/writer for the online division of Channel One News.

Aunt Kizzy's Back Porch, 4325 Glencoe Ave. (☎310-578-1005), in a huge strip mall at Glencoe Ave. and Mindanao Way in Marina Del Rey. A little slice of Southern heaven, offering specialties like Cousin Willie Mae's smothered pork chops with cornbread and veggies. Save room for sweet potato pie ($3). Dinner $12-13. All-you-can-eat brunch buffet $13 (Su 11am-3pm). Open Su-Th 11am-9pm, F-Sa 11am-11pm. ❸

Wahoo's Fish Tacos, 1129 Manhattan Ave. (☎796-1044), in Manhattan Beach. A small but quality chain, each funky Wahoo's shack pays homage to surfing with a non-stop surfing video, decal stickers, and surfing posters plastered over its counters and plywood walls. Famous for cheap, flavorful Mexican grub. 2 tacos or enchiladas (fish, chicken, steak, or vegetarian) with a large plate of beans and rice for only $5. Many swear by the teriyaki steak Maui Bowl ($7). Mug of Ono Ale for $2. 25 SoCal locations. Open M-Sa 11am-10pm, Su 11am-9pm. ❷

Hennessy's Tavern, 8 Pier Ave, (☎372-5759), in Hermosa Beach. Located just where the concrete meets the sand, this restaurant and bar offers the best sunset views in South Bay, especially from the second floor deck. 3 full bars all day. Sandwiches $6-9, entrees $10-18. Fantastic and unique specials include 2-for-1 Tuesdays and Luck of the Irish on W (flip an Irish coin; if you call it correctly, any Irish meal is free). Sa after 5pm, dinner comes with a free martini. Happy Hour M-F 4-7pm with $3 beers. Open daily 7am-2am; kitchen closes at 12:30am. ❸

BEVERLY HILLS

TOURING THE BURGER KINGDOM Los Angeles has spawned many tasteless trends, but few realize that it's also the birthplace of perhaps the world's farthest-sweeping trend, one guaranteed to leave a curious taste in your mouth: good ol' American fast food. Unlikely as it sounds, this obsessively health-conscious city spawned some of the nation's greasiest, most cholesterol-packed grub. An international synonym for fast food, **McDonald's** was founded by Angeleno brothers Richard and Maurice McDonald in 1937 (serving, incidentally, hot dogs only). The oldest standing golden arches still glow proudly at 10807 Lakewood Blvd. in Downey, with walk-up rather than drive-thru service. A small museum pays tribute to the oldest operating franchise in the world. (The brothers granted Ray Kroc exclusive U.S. franchising rights.) Home to the original double-decker hamburger, the oldest **Bob's Big Boy,** 4211 Riverside Dr. (☎818-843-9334), in Burbank, still looks as sleek and streamlined as the day it opened in 1949. Check out the car-hop service (Sa-Su 5-10pm). **Carl's Jr.** started off as a Downtown hot dog stand at Florence and Central Ave. in 1941. **Denny's** and doughnut joint **Winchell's** also got their start in the fast-food fertile L.A. Basin.

Al Gelato, 806 S. Robertson Blvd. (☎310-659-8069), between Wilshire and Olympic St. Popular among the theater crowd, this homemade gelato spot also does large portions of pasta with a delicious basil tomato sauce. Giant meatball ($4.75) and rigatoni ($11). For dessert, stick to the famous gelato ($3.75-5.75) and made-to-order cannoli ($4.50). Open Su, Tu, Th 10am-midnight, F-Sa 10am-1am. No credit cards. ❶

Nate 'n Al Delicatessen, 414 N. Beverly Dr. (☎310-274-0101; www.natenal.com), near Little Santa Monica Blvd. For 55 years, this delicatessen has been serving up hand-pressed latkes ($8.75), blintzes ($9), and Reubens ($11.50). Open daily 7am-9pm. ❸

Mulberry Street Pizzeria, 240 S. Beverly Dr. (☎310-247-8100) and 347 N. Canon Dr. in Beverly Hills. Great pizza by the slice is hard to come by in L.A., which makes this pizzeria all the more exceptional; the wide, flat pizza is among the best anywhere. Everything from veggie to tomato and eggplant. Slice $2.50-4, whole pies $15-26. Open Su-W 11am-11pm, Th-Sa 11am-midnight. ❶

WESTWOOD & THE WILSHIRE DISTRICT

Sandbag's Gourmet Sandwiches, 1134 Westwood Blvd. (☎310-208-1133), in Westwood. Other locations at 11640 San Vicente Blvd. (☎310-207-4888), in Brentwood, and 9497 Santa Monica Blvd. (☎310-786-7878), in Beverly Hills. A healthy, cheap lunch comes with a complimentary chocolate cookie. Try the "Sundowner" (turkey, herb stuffing, lettuce, and cranberries). Sandwiches $5.75. Open daily 9am-4pm. ❷

Gypsy Cafe, 940 Broxton Ave. (☎310-824-2119), next to Diddie Riese. Modeled after a sister spot in Paris, this cafe's fare is more Italian than French (penne cacciatore $8.25), and its mood is more Turkish than Italian (hookahs for rent, $10 per hr.). The buffet is bountiful, but the hookah smoke might not appeal to some. Mediterranean kabobs $9. The tomato soup ($5) is famous throughout Westwood. Beer $3.50-4.50, wine $4.50. Open Su-Th 7am-2am, F-Sa 7am-3am. ❷

Nyala Ethiopian Cuisine, 1076 S. Fairfax Ave. (☎323-936-5918), two blocks south of Olympic Blvd. Large plates of spongy crepe *(injera)* topped with stews (lunch $7.50, dinner $10.50). The vegetarian lunch buffet (M-F 11:30am-3pm) is a steal at $5.35. Open M-Th 11:30am-11pm, F 11:30am-2am, Sa noon-2am, Su noon-midnight. ❷

DOWNTOWN

Philippe, The Original, 1001 N. Alameda St. (☎213-628-3781; www.philippes.com), 2 blocks north of Union Station. A long-time fixture of Downtown, Philippe's is one of the most popular lunch eateries. Choose from pork, beef, ham, turkey ($4.40), or lamb ($4.70). Top it off with pie ($2.65) and coffee ($0.09—no, that's not a typo). Free parking. Open daily 6am-10pm. ❶

The Pantry, 877 S. Figueroa St. (☎213-972-9279). Since 1924, it hasn't closed once—not for the earthquakes, not for the '92 riots (when it served as a National Guard outpost), and not even when a taxicab punched through the front wall. There aren't even locks on the doors. Owned by former L.A. mayor Richard Riordan. Diner-like atmosphere. Known for its large portions, free cole slaw, and fresh sourdough bread. Giant breakfast specials $6. Lunch sandwiches $8. Open 24hr. No credit cards. ❷

La Luz Del Dia, 1 W. Olvera St. (☎213-628-7495), tucked inside El Pueblo Historic Park along the circular walking path, this family-run Mexican restaurant provides an authentic eating experience. The park's trees and performance artists are a nice complement to the great food. Though most customers are Spanish-speaking, the owners are bilingual. Specialties are the homemade tortillas, tacos, and rice and beans ($5-6). Open Tu-Th 11am-9pm, F 11am-10pm, Sa 10am-10pm, Su 8:30am-10pm. ❷

SAN FERNANDO VALLEY & PASADENA

Fair Oaks Pharmacy and Soda Fountain, 1516 Mission St. (☎626-799-1414), at Fair Oaks Ave. in South Pasadena. From Colorado Blvd., go south 1 mi. on Fair Oaks Ave. to Mission St. This old-fashioned drug store, with soda fountain and lunch counter, has been serving travelers on Rte. 66 since 1915; now, a bit of Pasadena's upscale boutique flavor has crept in. Hand-dipped shakes and malts $4.25. Deli sandwiches $5.50. Patty melts $6. Soda fountain open M-F 9am-9pm, Sa 9am-10pm, Su 11am-8pm; lunch counter open M-F 11am-9pm, Sa 11am-10pm, Su 11am-8pm. ❷

Miceli's, 3655 W. Cahuenga Blvd. (☎323-851-3344), in Universal City, and 1646 N. Las Palmas in Hollywood (☎323-466-3438). From Hollywood Blvd., go north on Highland Ave., which turns into Cahuenga. Would-be actors serenade dinner guests. Pizza or lasagna $8-15. Open M-Th 11:30am-11pm, F-Sa 11:30am-midnight, Su 3-11pm. Lunch served M-Sa 11:30am-3pm. ❸

Holly Street Bar & Grill, 175 E. Holly St. (☎626-440-1421), between Marengo St. and Arroyo Pkwy. From Colorado Blvd., go 2 blocks north on Marengo. Contemporary eatery with choice of seating in the peaceful garden or leopard-printed indoors. Live jazz com-

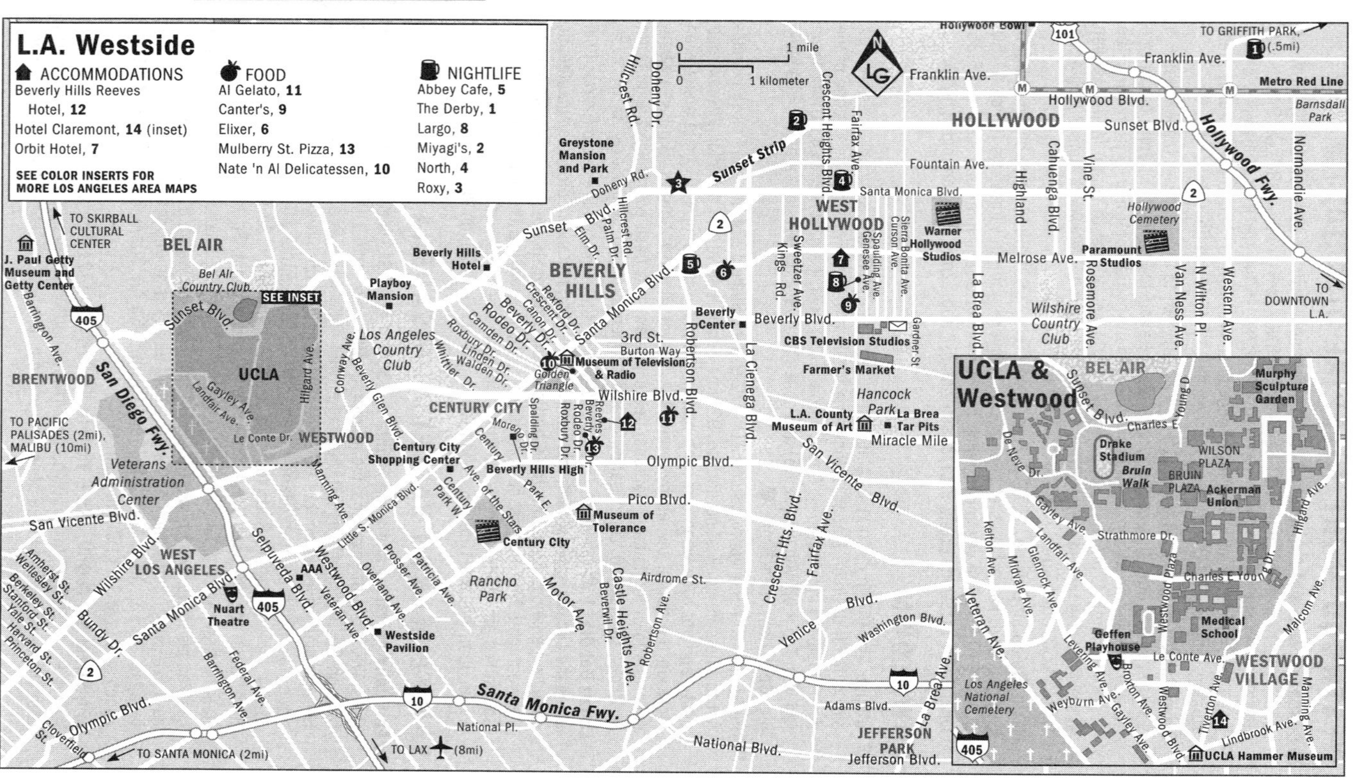
L.A. Westside
ACCOMMODATIONS
Beverly Hills Reeves Hotel, 12
Hotel Claremont, 14 (inset)
Orbit Hotel, 7
SEE COLOR INSERTS FOR MORE LOS ANGELES AREA MAPS
FOOD
Al Gelato, 11
Canter's, 9
Elixer, 6
Mulberry St. Pizza, 13
Nate 'n Al Delicatessen, 10
NIGHTLIFE
Abbey Cafe, 5
The Derby, 1
Largo, 8
Miyagi's, 2
North, 4
Roxy, 3
UCLA & Westwood
HOLLYWOOD
WEST HOLLYWOOD
BEVERLY HILLS
CENTURY CITY
BEL AIR
WESTWOOD
BRENTWOOD
WEST LOS ANGELES
JEFFERSON PARK
WESTWOOD VILLAGE
Hollywood Fwy.
San Diego Fwy.
Santa Monica Fwy.
Sunset Strip
Sunset Blvd.
Santa Monica Blvd.
Wilshire Blvd.
Olympic Blvd.
Pico Blvd.
Venice Blvd.
La Cienega Blvd.
La Brea Blvd.
Fairfax Ave.
Robertson Blvd.
Beverly Blvd.
Melrose Ave.
Paramount Studios
Warner Hollywood Studios
CBS Television Studios
Farmer's Market
L.A. County Museum of Art
La Brea Tar Pits
Miracle Mile
Museum of Television & Radio
Museum of Tolerance
Century City Shopping Center
Beverly Hills Hotel
Beverly Hills High
Playboy Mansion
Greystone Mansion and Park
Westside Pavilion
Nuart Theatre
J. Paul Getty Museum and Getty Center
Veterans Administration Center
UCLA
Drake Stadium
Murphy Sculpture Garden
Ackerman Union
Medical School
Geffen Playhouse
UCLA Hammer Museum
Los Angeles National Cemetery
TO GRIFFITH PARK
TO DOWNTOWN L.A.
TO LAX (8mi)
TO SANTA MONICA (2mi)
TO PACIFIC PALISADES (2mi), MALIBU (10mi)
TO SKIRBALL CULTURAL CENTER

plements the elegant dining experience on F and Sa nights (7pm), and live classical guitar at Su brunch (10:30am). Salads $9. Entrees $8-22. Full bar. Beer $3.50-4, cocktails $6. Open M 11am-2pm, Tu-Th 11am-2pm and 4:30-9:30pm, F-Sa 11am-2pm and 4:30-10pm, Su 10am-2:30pm and 4:30-9pm. Bar may stay open later. ❹

SIGHTS

HOLLYWOOD

Exploring the Hollywood area takes a pair of sunglasses, a camera, cash, and a whole lot of attitude. Running east-west at the foot of the Hollywood Hills, **Hollywood Boulevard** is the center of L.A.'s tourist madness, home to the Walk of Fame, famous theaters, souvenir shops, and museums.

HOLLYWOOD SIGN. Those 50 ft. high, 30 ft. wide, slightly erratic letters perched on Mt. Lee in Griffith Park stand as a universally recognized symbol of the city. The original 1923 sign read HOLLYWOODLAND and was an advertisement for a new subdivision in the Hollywood Hills. The sign has been a target of many college pranks, which have made it read everything from "Hollyweird" to "Ollywood" (after the infamous Lt. Col. Oliver North). A fence keeps you at a distance of 40 ft. *(To get as close to the sign as possible requires a strenuous 2½ mi. hike. Take the Bronson Canyon entrance to Griffith Park and follow Canyon Dr. to its end, where parking is free. The Brush Canyon Trail starts where Canyon Dr. becomes unpaved. At the top of the hill, follow the road to your left; gaze at Hollywood on one side and the Valley on the other; the sign looms just below. For those satisfied with driving, go north on Vine St., take a right on Franklin Ave. and a left on Beachwood, and drive up until you are forced to drive down.)*

GRAUMAN'S CHINESE THEATRE. Formerly Mann's Chinese Theatre, this 75-year-old theater is back to its original name because of local efforts to establish historical culture. Loosely modeled on a Chinese temple, the theater is a hot spot for movie premieres. The exterior columns—known as "Heaven Dogs"—were imported from China, where they once supported a Ming Dynasty temple and were believed to ward off evil spirits. In front of the theater are the footprints of more than 200 celebrities, encased in cement. Whoopi Goldberg's dreadlocks and R2D2's wheels are also here. *(6925 Hollywood Blvd., between Highland and Orange St. ☎323-461-3331. Tours 4-5 times a day; call ahead. $7.50, under 6 free.)*

WALK OF FAME. Pedestrian traffic along Hollywood Blvd. mimics L.A. freeways as tourists stop midstride to gawk at the sidewalk's over 2000 bronze-inlaid stars, which are inscribed with the names of the famous, the infamous, and the downright obscure. Stars are awarded for achievements in one of five categories—movies, radio, TV, recording, and live performance; only Gene Autry has all five stars. The stars have no particular order, so don't try to find a method to the madness. The celebs to receive their stars in 2004 include Halle Berry and Kevin Costner. To catch today's (or yesterday's) stars in person, call the Chamber of Commerce for info on star-unveiling ceremonies. *(☎323-469-8311; www.hollywoodchamber.net. Free.)*

OTHER SIGHTS. The hillside **Hollywood Bowl** is synonymous with picnic dining and classy summer entertainment. All are welcome to listen to the L.A. Philharmonic at rehearsals on Mondays, Tuesdays, Thursdays, and Fridays. *(2301 N. Highland Ave. ☎323-850-2058, concert line 850-2000; www.hollywoodbowl.org. Open July-Sept. Tu-Sa 10am-8pm; Sept.-June Tu-Sa 10am-4:30pm. Free.)* The sizable complex of the **Hollywood & Highland Mall** is centered around two monstrous elephant sculptures, and contains ritzy brand name stores, restaurants, and the $94 million **Kodak Theater,** built specifically to be the home of the Academy Awards. *(6801 Hollywood Blvd. Box office ☎323-308-6363. Open non-show days 10am-6pm, show days 10am-9pm. Tours every 30min.,*

THE LOCAL STORY

BATMAN BY DAY, CLOONEY BY NIGHT

Max was spotted in costume as Batman outside of Grauman's Chinese Theatre on Hollywood Blvd.

LG: So Batman, how long have you been working outside Mann's Chinese theatre?

M: About a year now. I'm actually George Clooney's stand in, I'll show you a script from the movie we are doing (pulls out script). It's called Celaris, you gotta see this, you like psychological thrillers?

LG: I love them. How did you land that job?

M: Well, 'cause I look exactly like him.

LG: You obviously have the experience as Batman

M: Obviously [laughs]. Technically speaking, I have actually fought crime. I've caught two purse snatchers and had five fights in this suit.

LG: WOW!

M: I have been on the news and everything else. I'm about as close to Batman as you can get.

LG: Do you have aspirations for leaving the Bat wings and getting into acting full time?

M: Well it's kind of hard. I'm having a real hard time due to the fact that I look so much like Clooney, it's hard to get an agent to take me seriously. So I double for him.

daily 10:30am-2:30pm. $15, seniors and children under 12 $10.) **Capitol Records Tower** was designed to look like a stack of records with a needle on top, which blinks H-O-L-L-Y-W-O-O-D in Morse code. *(1750 Vine St., just north of Hollywood Blvd.)*

SANTA MONICA

Given the cleaner waters and better waves at Malibu or South Bay beaches, Santa Monica is known more for its shoreside scene than its shore. Indeed, locals head away from the Pier for swim and surf, since sewage runoff inevitably fouls the water. Much of Santa Monica is best seen by foot or bike, so plan on parking in one of the main lots near Third St. Promenade before hitting the turf.

THIRD STREET PROMENADE. Angelenos always claim that nobody walks in L.A., but the rules change on this ultra-popular three-block stretch of mosaic art tiles, fashionable stores, movie theaters, and lively restaurants. The Promenade truly heats up when the sun sets. The trendy shopping runs from overpriced bikini stores to great book and art stores left over from the Promenade's more bohemian days. On Wednesday and Saturday mornings, the area transforms into a popular **farmer's market** selling fresh California-grown flowers and produce, with Saturdays featuring exclusively organic products. *(Between Broadway and Wilshire in downtown Santa Monica. Exit off 4th St. from I-10.)*

SANTA MONICA PIER & PACIFIC PARK. The famed pier is the heart of Santa Monica Beach and home to the roller coasters, arcades, and ferris wheels of the carnivalesque family funspot, Pacific Park. Along the pier look for free TV show tickets (the variety and late-night kinds) near the north entrance. *(Off PCH on the way to Venice Beach from Santa Monica Beach. ☎310-458-8900; http://santamonicapier.org. Pier open 24hr. Park open summer Su, M-Th 11am-11pm, F-Su 11am-12:30am; winter hours vary, so call ahead. Ticket window closes 30min. before the park closes. Tickets $2 each, most rides 2-3 tickets; day passes $20, children under 42 in. $11. Parking off PCH $5-8 per day.)*

MALIBU, VENICE & THE SOUTH BAY

North of Santa Monica along PCH, the cityscape gives way to appealing stretches of sandy, sewage-free shoreline. **Malibu's** beaches are clean and relatively uncrowded, easily the best in L.A. County for surfers, sunbathers, and swimmers alike. You can jet through the wave tubes at **Surfrider Beach,** a section of Malibu Lagoon State Beach north of the pier at

23000 PCH. Walk there via the Zonker Harris Access Way (named after the beach-obsessed Doonesbury character) at 22700 PCH. Along the 30000 block of PCH, 30min. west of Santa Monica, stretches **Zuma Beach,** L.A. County's northernmost, largest, most popular, and happiest sandbox.

Ocean Front Walk, Venice's main beachfront drag, is a seaside three-ring circus of fringe culture. Street people converge on shaded clusters of benches, evangelists drown out off-color comedians, and bodybuilders pump iron in spandex outfits at **Muscle Beach,** 1800 Ocean Front Walk, closest to 18th St. and Pacific Ave. Fire-juggling cyclists, master sand sculptors, bards in Birkenstocks, and **"skateboard grandmas"** define the bohemian spirit of this playground population. Vendors of jewelry, henna body art, fatty snacks, and beach paraphernalia overwhelm the boardwalk.

About 20 mi. southwest of downtown L.A., PCH swings the core beach scenes at **Manhattan Beach, Hermosa Beach,** and **Redondo Beach.** Manhattan Beach is favored for surfing; Hermosa Beach, the most popular urban beach in L.A. County, is also one of the cleanest. Both beaches host elite beach volleyball and surf competitions (☎426-8000; www.avp.com or www.surffestival.org). Most visit Redondo Beach for its harbor, pier, and seafood-rich boardwalk. **The Strand** is a concrete bike path crowded with tanned bikers and inline skaters that runs right on the beach from Santa Monica (where it's called Ocean Front Walk) to Hermosa Beach.

BEVERLY HILLS

Conspicuous displays of wealth border on the vulgar in this storied center of extravagance. Residential ritz reaches its peak along the mansions of Beverly Dr.

RODEO DRIVE. The heart of the city, known for its clothing boutiques and jewelry shops, is in the **Golden Triangle,** a wedge formed by Beverly Dr., Wilshire Blvd., and Santa Monica Blvd. Built like an old English manor house, Polo Ralph Lauren *(444 N. Rodeo Dr.)* stands out from the white marble of the other stores. The divine triple-whammy of Cartier *(370 N. Rodeo Dr.),* Gucci *(347 N. Rodeo Dr.),* and Chanel *(400 N. Rodeo Dr.)* sits on some prime real estate, where rents approach $40,000 per month. At the south end of Rodeo Dr. (the end closest to Wilshire Blvd.) is the all-pedestrian shopping of **2 Rodeo Drive,** a.k.a. **Via Rodeo,** which contains Dior, Tiffany, and numerous salons frequented by the stars. Across the way is the venerable **Beverly Wilshire Hotel,** 9500 Wilshire Blvd. (☎310-275-5200), where Julia Roberts went from Hollywood hooker to Richard Gere's queen in *Pretty Woman.*

OTHER SIGHTS. Complete with a radio broadcast studio and two theaters, the **Museum of Television & Radio's** biggest highlight is its library, which holds 117,000 television, radio, and commercial programs. You can request your favorite tube hits, and 5min. later the library staff will have the full-length episodes ready and waiting for your viewing pleasure at your own private screening station. *(465 N. Beverly Dr., corner of Santa Monica Blvd. and Beverly Dr. ☎310-786-1000. Open Su and W-Sa noon-5pm. Suggested donation $10, students and seniors $8, under 14 $5. 2hr. free parking in the museum's lot off Little Santa Monica Blvd.)* A pink, palm-treed array of 182 rooms and suites and 21 bungalows, hidden among 12 acres of tropical gardens and pools, the ludicrously extravagant **Beverly Hills Hotel** is as famous as the stars who romanced here. Marilyn Monroe reportedly had trysts with both JFK and RFK in the bunga lows. Rooms run from $380-5000. *(9641 Sunset Blvd. ☎310-276-2251.)*

THE WESTSIDE CELEBRITY TOUR

The reason why all the maps to stars' homes in **Beverly Hills** only seem to show dead stars is that while the A-list may still *shop* here, most no longer *live* here. The area still houses plenty of multi-millionaires, but the real fame and money has moved away from the hype to areas that afford privacy, namely **Bel Air, Brentwood,** and **Pacific Palisades.** The best way to see their compounds is to pick up a star map, available at the Santa Monica Pier, local newsstands, or from vendors along Sunset Blvd., but it's doubtful you'll see them taking out the trash.

WEST HOLLYWOOD

Bring your walking shoes and spend a day on the 3 mi. strip of **Melrose Avenue** from Highland Ave. west to the intersection of Doheny Dr. and Santa Monica Blvd. This strip began to develop its funky flair in the late 1980s when art galleries, designer stores, lounge-like coffee shops, used clothing and music stores, and restaurants began to take over. Now it is home to the hip, with the choicest stretch lying between La Brea and Fairfax Ave. While much sold here is used ("vintage"), none of it is really cheap (see **Shopping,** p. 895). Rest your feet after a long march at **Elixer** (p. 896), as you rejuvenate in its peaceful Zen gardens with a herbal tonic. North of the **Beverly Center** is the **Pacific Design Center,** 8687 Melrose Ave. (☎310-657-0800; www.pacificdesigncenter.com), a sea-green glass complex nicknamed the Blue Whale and constructed in the shape of a rippin' wave.

DOWNTOWN

The **DASH Shuttle** runs six lines Downtown that cover most of the major tourist destinations. ($0.25, see p. 876. References to DASH shuttles in the listings below are for M-F travel.) If driving, park in a secure lot, rather than on the street. Due to expensive short-term lot parking ($3 per 20min.) and exorbitant meter prices ($0.25 per 10min.), it's best to park in a public lot ($5-10 per day) and hit the pavement on foot. The **L.A. Visitors Center,** 685 S. Figueroa St., should have answers to your travel queries. (Open M-F 8am-4pm, Sa 8:30am-5pm. See p. 877.)

EL PUEBLO HISTORIC PARK. The historic birthplace of L.A. is now known as **El Pueblo de Los Angeles Historical Monument,** bordered by Cesar Chavez Ave., Alameda St., Hollywood Fwy., and Spring St. (DASH B). In 1781, 44 settlers established a pueblo and farming community here; today, 27 buildings from the eras of Spanish and Mexican rule are preserved. Established in 1825, the **Plaza** is the center of El Pueblo, and hosts several festivals including the Mexican Independence celebration (Sept. 16), *Dia de los Muertos* celebrations (Nov. 1-2), and *Cinco de Mayo* (May 5). Treat yourself to the cheapest churros around (2 for $1). Walk down one of L.A.'s historic streets, **Olvera Street,** which resembles a colorful Mexican marketplace, and bargain at *puestos* (vendor stalls) selling everything from Mexican handicrafts and food to personalized t-shirts. The **Avila Adobe** (circa 1818), 10 E. Olvera St., is the "oldest" house in the city *(open daily 9am-3pm).*

MUSIC CENTER. The Music Center is an enormous, beautiful complex that includes **The Dorothy Chandler Pavilion,** home of the L.A. Opera *(☎213-972-8001; www.laopera.org)*, former site of the Academy Awards. Across the street rise the radical silver slices of the Frank Gehry-designed **Walt Disney Concert Hall.** This gleaming 2265-seat structure is the brand-new home of the L.A. Phil and the L.A. Master Chorale. *(151 S. Grand Ave. ☎213-972-7211; www.disneyhall.org.)* Also part of the Music Center are the **Mark Taper Forum** and the **Ahmanson Theatre,** known for their world-class shows. *(☎213-628-2772; www.taperahmanson.com. Tours of the 3-theater complex offered weekdays at 11:30am, 12:30, and 1:30pm as performance schedules permit. Go to the outdoor information booth in the large outdoor courtyard between the theaters.)*

OTHER SIGHTS. One of the best-known buildings in the Southland, **City Hall,** 200 N. Spring St., "has starred in more movies than most actors." Bargain hounds can haggle to their hearts' delight in the **Fashion District,** which is bordered by 6th and 9th St. along Los Angeles St. The **Library Tower,** 633 W. 5th St., has a distinctive glass crown and is the tallest building between Chicago and Hong Kong at 1017 ft. The

Westin Bonaventure Hotel, 404 S. Figueroa St., is composed of five squat but somehow sleek cylinders sheathed in black glass, and has appeared in *Rain Man, In the Line of Fire,* and *Heat.* The historic **Biltmore Hotel,** 506 S. Grand Ave., is a $10 million, 683-room hotel designed by Schultze and Weaver (best known for New York's Waldorf-Astoria). **The Japanese American Cultural and Community Center** in Little Tokyo is the largest Asian-American cultural center in the country. Make sure to visit the serene **James Irvine Garden,** better known as *Seiryu-en* or "Garden of the Pure Stream." *(244 S. San Pedro St. ☎213-628-2725. www.jaccc.org. Gallery open Tu-F noon-5pm, Sa-Su 11am-4pm. Small donation may be requested.)*

NEAR DOWNTOWN

UNIVERSITY OF SOUTHERN CALIFORNIA (USC). North of Exposition Park, USC's 30,000 students bring a youthful character to the streets of Downtown. The alma mater of celebrities such as astronaut Neil Armstrong, the school has had a gold-medal winning athlete in every summer Olympics since 1912. L.A. sports fans salivate when the burnished USC Trojans clash with the blue-and-gold UCLA Bruins in annual football and basketball classics. *(University Park Campus. From downtown, take Figueroa St. south and turn right into campus on 35th street, or exit I-110 on Exposition Blvd. ☎213-740-2311; www.usc.edu. Campus tours offered M-F on the hr. 10am-3pm.)*

GRIFFITH PARK & GLENDALE. For a breath of fresh air and a respite from city life, take to the rugged, dry slopes of Griffith Park, the nation's largest municipal park, nestled in the hills between U.S. 101, I-5, and Rte. 134. A stark contrast to the concrete heights of Downtown and the star-studded streets of Hollywood, the park is a refuge from the city and the site of many outdoor diversions. Fifty-two miles of hiking and horseback trails, three golf courses, a planetarium, an enormous zoo, several museums, and the 6000-person Greek Theatre are contained within its rolling 4107 acres. *(Nestled in the hills above L.A. 101, I-5, and Rte. 134. The Visitors Center and Ranger Headquarters doles out trail info at 4730 Crystal Spring Dr. ☎323-913-4688, emergency 323-913-7390. Park open daily 5am-10pm.)* The park has numerous equestrian trails and places to saddle up, such as **J.P. Stables.** No experience is necessary, and guides are provided. *(1914 Maripose St., Burbank. First come, first served. ☎818-843-9890. Open daily 8am-6pm. $18 for 1hr., $12 each additional hr. Cash only.)*

PLANETARIUM & OBSERVATORY. The world-famous white stucco and copper domes of the castle-like mountaintop Griffith Park Observatory would be visible from nearly anywhere in the L.A. basin, were it not for the smog. The parking lot affords a terrific view of the Hollywood sign and L.A. You may remember the planetarium from the James Dean film *Rebel Without A Cause.* The observatory and planetarium are closed for renovations until 2005. The grounds remain open. *(Drive to the top of Mt. Hollywood on Vermont Ave. or Hillhurst St. from Los Feliz Blvd., or take MTA #180 or 181 from Hollywood Blvd. ☎323-664-1181, recording 323-664-1191; www.griffithobs.org. Grounds open summer daily 12:30-10pm; winter Tu-F 2-10pm, Sa-Su 12:30-10pm.)*

L.A. ZOO. The recently added Komodo dragon and Red Ape Rain Forest exhibits, along with the elephants and the chimps, are among the most popular spots in the zoo's well-kept 113 acres. The Children's Zoo offers a petting zoo, an interactive adventure theater, and a storytime area. Watch the sea lion training in the Aqatics Section, 11:30am and 2:30pm daily. Be on the lookout for the completion of a new, spectacular home for the sea lions near the zoo's entrance, slated to finish in the summer of 2004. *(5333 Zoo Dr. From Los Feliz Blvd., take Crystal Springs Dr. into the park; the Zoo will be on your left. ☎323-644-4200; www.lazoo.org. Open daily Sept.-June 10am-5pm; July-Aug. 10am-6pm. $8.25, seniors $5.25, ages 2-12 $3.25.)*

FOREST LAWN CEMETERY. A rather twisted sense of celebrity sightseeing may lead some travelers to Glendale, where they can gaze upon stars who can't run away when asked for an autograph. Among the illustrious dead are Clark Gable, George Burns, and Jimmy Stewart. The cemetery has a 30 ft. by 15 ft. reproduction of Leonardo da Vinci's *The Last Supper (every 30min. 9:30am-4pm)*. If you're still obsessed with oversized art, swing by the Forest Lawn in Hollywood Hills (only a 10min. drive) to see "Birth of Liberty," America's largest historical mosaic composed of 10 million pieces of Venetian glass. *(1712 S. Glendale Ave. ☎800-204-3131. Open daily 8am-6pm. Mausoleum open daily 9am-4:30pm.)*

SAN FERNANDO VALLEY

TV and movie studios redeem the Valley (somewhat) from its bland warehouses, blonde Valley Girls, and faceless strip malls. Passing Burbank on Rte. 134, you might catch glimpses of the Valley's most lucrative trademark studios: **Universal, Warner Bros., NBC,** and **Disney.** To best experience the industry, attend a **free TV show taping** or take one of the tours offered by most studios.

UNIVERSAL STUDIOS. A movie and television studio that happens to have the world's first and largest movie-themed amusement park attached, Universal Studios Hollywood is the most popular tourist spot in Tinseltown. Located north of Hollywood in its own municipality of Universal City (complete with police and fire station), the park began as a public tour of the studios in 1964. The signature Studio Tour tram brings riders face-to-face with King Kong and Jaws, rattles through a massive earthquake, and wanders past blockbuster sets from America's movie tradition, including *Apollo 13*, *Jurassic Park*, and the infamous Bates Motel from *Psycho*. The movie itself may have bombed, but the live stunts and pyrotechnics at the *Waterworld* spectacular are impressive. Careen through time on Doc Brown's Delorean in **Back to the Future: The Ride,** take a magical bike trip with **E.T.** across the galaxies, or brave the blazing inferno in **Backdraft.** Don't miss **Animal Planet Live!** and the **Special Effects Stages.** *(Take U.S. 101 to the Universal Center Dr. or Landershim Blvd. Exits. By MTA rail: exit North Hollywood Red Line at Universal Station. ☎800-UNIVERSAL; www.universalstudios.com. Open July-Aug. M-F 9am-8pm, Sa-Su 9am-9pm; Sept.-June M-F 10am-6pm, Sa-Su 10am-7pm. Last tram leaves M-F 5:15pm, Sa-Su 6:15pm; low-season 4:15pm. Tours in Spanish daily. $47, under 48 inches $37, under 3 free. Parking $8.)*

UNIVERSAL CITY WALK. This neon-heavy, open-air strip of shopping, dining, movie theaters, and nightlife is the Valley's more colorful but less charming answer to Santa Monica's Third St. Promenade. The mammoth green guitar outside the Hard Rock Cafe, a lurid King Kong sign, and the towering IMAX screen at the Cineplex Odeon cinemas set the tone for the vivid, larger-than-life complex. *(☎818-622-4455; www.citywalkhollywood.com. City Walk parking $8. Full parking refund with purchase of 2 movie tickets before 6pm, $2 refund after 6pm.)*

MISSION SAN FERNANDO REY DE ESPAÑA. Founded in 1797, the **San Fernando Mission** is rich with history and is the largest adobe structure in California. The grounds, with museum and gift shop, are beautifully kept and definitely worth a visit. *(15101 San Fernando Mission Blvd. ☎818-361-0186. Mass M-Tu and Th-Sa 7:25am, Su 9 and 10:30am. Open daily 9am-4:30pm. $4, seniors and ages 7-15 $3, under 7 free.)*

SIX FLAGS THEME PARKS. At the opposite end of the Valley, 40min. north of L.A. in Valencia, is thrill-ride heaven **Magic Mountain,** boasting the most roller coasters in the world. Its newest addition, **Scream!,** is Southern California's first floorless mega-coaster where your feet dangle in the air as you scream through 4000 ft. of twists, plunges, and loops. **X** spins riders 360 degrees, creating a sensation of flying. **Goliath** hits 85 mph and hurtles through an underground tunnel. Other highlights of the park include **Revolution,** one of the earliest coasters to do a full loop and **Viper,** the world's largest looping roller coaster. Temperatures here frequently soar above 100°F in the summer, so come prepared. Next door, Six Flags' waterpark **Hurricane Harbor** features the world's tallest enclosed speed slide. *(Take U.S. 101 N to Rte. 170 N to I-5 N to Magic Mountain Pkwy. ☎661-255-4100. Open daily Apr.-Sept. 6; hours vary. Sept.-Mar. open weekends and holidays. $45, seniors and under 48 inches tall $30, under 2 free. Parking $7. Hurricane Harbor: ☎661-255-4527. Open May-Sept.; hours vary. $22, seniors and under 48 inches tall $15, under 2 free. Combo admission to both parks that can be used on the same day, consecutive days, or for a return visit $55.)*

PASADENA & AROUND

With its world-class museums, graceful architecture, and classy, vibrant shopping and dining mecca of **Old Town Pasadena,** Pasadena is a welcome change from its more hectic Southland neighbors such as Hollywood or Santa Monica. The splendid **Convention and Visitors Bureau,** 171 S. Los Robles Ave., is a useful first stop. (☎626-795-9311; www.pasadenacal.com. Open M-F 8am-5pm, Sa 10am-4pm.)

TOURNAMENT OF ROSES PARADE AND ROSE BOWL. New Year's Day, January 1, is always a perfect, sunny day in Southern California. Some of the wildest New Year's Eve parties happen along Colorado Blvd., the parade route. If you miss the parade, which runs from 8-10am, you can still see the floats on display that afternoon and on January 2 on Sierra Madre Blvd. between Washington Blvd. and Sierra Madre Villa Ave. *(☎626-449-7673. Parade free; float viewing $6.)* In the gorge that forms the city's western boundary stands Pasadena's most famous landmark, the sand-colored, 90,000-seat **Rose Bowl.** *(1001 Rose Bowl Dr. ☎626-577-3100.)* The bowl hosts an enormous monthly flea market that attracts upwards of 2000 vendors, selling nearly one million items. *(☎323-560-7469. Held the second Su of each month 9am-4:30pm. Admission 5-7am $20, 7-8am $15, 8-9am $10, 9am-3pm $7.)*

ARTS AND SCIENCES. The **Pasadena Playhouse** nurtured the careers of William Holden, Dustin Hoffman, and Gene Hackman, among others. Founded in 1917 and restored in 1986, it now offers some of L.A.'s finest theater. *(39 S. El Molino Ave., between Colorado Blvd. and Green St. ☎626-356-7529. For more info, see* *theater, p.894.)* Some of the world's greatest scientific minds do their work at the **California Institute of Technology (Caltech).** Founded in 1891, Caltech has amassed a faculty that includes several Nobel laureates and a student body that prides itself both on its staggering collective intellect and its loony practical jokes, which range from unscrewing all the chairs in a lecture hall and bolting them in backwards to a nationally televised message added to the Rose Bowl scoreboard during the January 1 game. *(1201 E. California Blvd., about 2½ mi. southeast of Old Town. ☎626-395-6327. Tours M-F 2pm.)* **NASA's Jet Propulsion Laboratory,** about 5 mi. north of Old Town, executed the journey of the Mars Pathfinder. Ask to see pictures of the face of Mars. *(4800 Oak Grove Dr. ☎818-354-9314. Free tours by appointment.)*

HUNTINGTON LIBRARY, ART GALLERY, AND BOTANICAL GARDENS. Opened to the public in 1928, the 150 stunning acres of gardens are broken into thematic areas including the Rose, Shakespeare, and Japanese Gardens. (Picnicking and sunbathing among the greens is strictly forbidden.) The library holds one of the world's most important collections of rare books, including a Gutenberg Bible, Benjamin Franklin's handwritten autobiography, a 1410 manuscript of Chaucer's *Canterbury Tales*, and a number of Shakespeare's first folios. The art galleries are known for their Renaissance, 18th- and 19th-century British paintings, as well as a strong collection of American art. *(1151 Oxford Rd., between Huntington Dr. and California Blvd. in San Marino, south of Pasadena, about 2 mi. south of the I-210 Allen Ave. Exit. From Downtown L.A., take MTA bus #79 and 379 out of Union Station to San Marino Ave. and walk 1½ mi. (45min. trip). ☎626-405-2100; www.huntington.org. Open Memorial Day-Labor Day Tu-Su 10:30am-4:30pm; winter Tu-F noon-4:30pm, Sa-Su 10:30am-4:30pm. $12.50, seniors $10, students $8.50, ages 5-11 $5, under 5 free. First Th of each month free.)*

DESCANSO GARDENS. The 165-acre garden includes one of the world's largest camellia forests, a historic rose collection, and manmade waterfalls. Blooming peaks in early spring. *(1418 Descanso Dr., by the intersection of Rte. 2 and 210. ☎818-949-4290. Open daily 9am-5pm. $6, students and seniors $4, ages 5-12 $1.50.)*

MUSEUMS

J. Paul Getty Center & Museum, 1200 Getty Center Dr. (☎310-440-7300; www.getty.edu), Exit I-405 (San Diego Fwy.) at the Getty Center Dr. Exit. Above Bel Air and Brentwood in the Santa Monica Mountains shines a modern Coliseum, "The Getty." Wedding classical materials to modern designs, renowned architect Richard Meier designed the stunning $1 billion complex, which opened to the public in 1997. The museum consists of five pavilions overlooking the Robert Irwin-designed Central Garden, a living work of art that changes with the seasons. The pavilions contain the impressive permanent Getty collection of Impressionist paintings. Headset audio guides $3. Open Su and Tu-Th 10am-6pm, F-Sa 10am-9pm. Parking reservations required Tu-F before 4pm ($5 per car); no reservations needed for college students or Sa-Su. Free.

Los Angeles County Museum of Art (LACMA), 5905 Wilshire Blvd. (☎323-857-6000; www.lacma.org). Opened in 1965, the renowned L.A.CMA is the largest museum on the West Coast. The Steve Martin Gallery, in the Anderson Building, holds the famed comedian's collection of Dada and Surrealist works. (This explains how Steve was able to roller skate through LACMA's halls in the film *L.A. Story*.) Open M-Tu and Th noon-8pm, F noon-9pm, Sa-Su 11am-8pm. $9, students and seniors $5, under 18 free; free 2nd Tu of each month. Free jazz F 5:30-8:30pm, chamber music Su 6-7pm. Film tickets $8, seniors and students $6. Parking $5, after 7pm free.

Norton Simon Museum of Art, 411 W. Colorado Blvd. (☎626-449-6840; www.nortonsimon.org). Rivaling the much larger Getty Museum in quality, this world-class private collection chronicles Western art from Italian Gothic to 20th-century abstract. Paintings by Raphael, Van Gogh, Monet, and Picasso are featured, as well as rare print etchings by Rembrandt and Goya. The Impressionist and Post-Impressionist hall, the Southeast Asian sculptures, and the 79,000 sq. ft. sculpture garden, by California landscape artist Nancy Goslee Power, are particularly impressive. Open M, W-Th, Sa-Su noon-6pm, F noon-9pm. $6, seniors $3, students with ID and children under 18 free. Free parking.

UCLA Hammer Museum of Art, 10899 Wilshire Blvd. (☎310-443-7000; www.hammer.ucla.edu). The UCLA Hammer Museum houses the world's largest collection of works by 19th-century French satirist Honoré Daumier, with works by Rembrandt, Monet, and Pissarro. The museum's gem is Vincent Van Gogh's *Hospital at Saint Rémy.* Open Su, Tu, Sa noon-7pm, W-F noon-9pm. Summer jazz concerts F 6:30-8pm. $5, seniors $3, under 17 free. Th free. Free tours of permanent collection Su 2pm, of traveling exhibits Th 6pm, Sa-Su 1pm. 3hr. parking $2.75, $1.50 each additional 20min.

Autry Museum of Western Heritage, 4700 Western Heritage Way (☎323-667-2000), in Griffith Park. City slickers and lone rangers may discover that the American West is not what they thought—the museum insists that the real should not be confused with the reel, drawing the line between Old West fact and fiction. Open Tu-W and F-Su 10am-5pm, Th 10am-8pm. $7.50, students and seniors $5, ages 2-12 $3. Th after 4pm free.

Petersen Automotive Museum (PAM), 6060 Wilshire Blvd. (☎323-930-2277; www.petersen.org), at Fairfax. This slice of Americana showcases one of L.A.'s enduring symbols—the automobile. PAM is the world's largest car museum, showcasing over 150 classic cars, hot rods, motorcycles, and movie and celebrity cars, not to mention the 1920s service station, 50s body shop, and 60s suburban garage. Call to set up a guided tour. Open Su and Tu-Sa 10am-6pm; Discovery Center closes 5pm. $7, students and seniors $5, ages 5-12 $3, under 5 free. Full-day parking $6.

George C. Page Museum of La Brea Discoveries, 5801 Wilshire Blvd. (☎323-934-7243). The smelly **La Brea Tar Pits** fill the area with an acrid petroleum stench and provides bones for this natural history museum. Thirsty prehistoric mammals became stuck and perished in these oozing tar pools; their bones are arranged in interesting displays and depicted in murals of primeval L.A. A viewing station exists at Pit 91 where archaeologists continue to dig. Open M-F 9:30am-5pm, Sa-Su 10am-5pm. Tours of grounds Su and Tu-Sa 1pm, museum tours Su and Tu-Sa 2:15pm. $7, students and seniors $4.50, ages 5-12 $2. First Tu of each month free. Parking $6 with validation.

Museum of Contemporary Art (MOCA), 50 S. Grand Ave. (☎213-626-6222; www.moca.org). Architect Arata Isozaki found inspiration for the facade's celebrated-curve in L.A.'s favorite daughter, Marilyn Monroe; inside is a compelling collection of Western modern visual art. Open Su, Tu-W, and F-Sa 11am-5pm, Th 11am-8pm. The Frank Gehry-renovated **MOCA at The Geffen Contemporary,** 152 N. Central Ave. (☎213-626-6222; www.moca.org), was once the garage for the LAPD fleet. The "Temporary Contemporary" and its highly-acclaimed installation art exhibitions eventually became permanent to the delight of its adoring public. Open Tu-W and F-Su 11am-5pm, Th 11am-9pm. $8, students and seniors $5, under 12 free, Th 5-8pm free. Admission good for both MOCA locations. Shuttle transportation between the 2 locations offered.

ENTERTAINMENT

There are many ways to get a taste of the silver screen glitz created and peddled by the entertainment capital of the world. **Shopping** (see p. 895) is a major pastime in the L.A. area, crafted by its devotees into performance art. For after-hours fun, L.A. features some of the trendiest, celeb-frenzied **nightlife** (see p. 896) imaginable. For amusement parks, check out giants like **Disneyland** (see p. 900), **Knott's Berry Farm** (see p. 901), **Magic Mountain** (see p. 890), and **Universal Studios** (see p. 890).

TELEVISION STUDIOS

A visit to the world's entertainment capital isn't complete without some exposure to the actual business of making a movie or TV show. Fortunately, most production companies oblige. **Paramount** (☎323-956-5000), **NBC** (☎818-840-3537), and **Warner Bros.** (☎818-954-1744) offer 2hr. guided tours that take you onto sets and through backlots. Tickets to a taping are free but studios tend to overbook, so holding a ticket does not always guarantee you'll get in. Show up early. **NBC,** 3000 W. Alameda Ave., at W. Olive Ave. in Burbank, is your best bet. Show up at the ticket office on a weekday at 8am for passes to Jay Leno's **Tonight Show,** filmed at 5pm the same evening (2 tickets per person, must be 16+). Studio tours run on the hour. (☎818-840-3537. M-F 9am-3pm. $7.50, ages 5-12 $4.) Many of NBC's other shows are taped at **Warner Bros.,** 4000 Warner Blvd. (☎818-954-6000), in Burbank.

A **CBS box office,** 7800 Beverly Blvd. (☎323-575-2458; open M-F 9am-5pm), next to the Farmer's Market in West Hollywood, hands out free tickets to Bob Barker's *The Price is Right* (taped M-Th) up to 1 week in advance. Audience members must be over 18. You can request up to 10 tickets on a specific date by sending a self-addressed, stamped envelope to *The Price is Right* Tickets, 7800 Beverly Blvd., Los Angeles, CA 90036, about 4- to 6-weeks in advance. If all else fails, **Audiences Unlimited, Inc.,** 100 Universal City Plaza, Building 4250, Universal City, CA 91608 (☎818-506-0067; www.tvtickets.com), is a great resource. To find out which shows are available during your visit, check the web site.

MOVIES

L.A.'s movie palaces show films the way they were meant to be seen: on a big screen, in plush seats, and with top-quality sound and air-conditioning. It would be a cinematic crime not to partake of the city's incredible moviegoing experiences.

The gargantuan theaters at **Universal City,** as well as those in **Westwood Village** near UCLA, are incredibly popular. In **Santa Monica,** there are 22 screens within the three blocks of Third Street Promenade. To ogle the stars as they walk the red car-

SO, YOU WANNA BE IN PICTURES? Honey! Baby! Sweetheart! You don't have to be beautiful and proportionally perfect to grace celluloid—just look at Tom Arnold or Lili Tomlin. The quickest way to get noticed is to land yourself a job as an extra—no experience necessary. One day's work will land $40-130 in your pocket and two meals in your tummy. Step One is to stop calling yourself an extra—you're an "atmosphere actor" (it's better for both your ego and your resume). Step Two is to contact a reputable casting service. **Cenex Central Casting,** 220 S. Flower St., Burbank 91506 (☎818-562-2755), is the biggest, and a good place to start. You must be at least 18 and a U.S. citizen or have a Resident Alien/ Employment Authorization card. Step Three is to show up on time; you'll need the clout of DeNiro before you can waltz in after call. Don't forget to bring $20 in cash to cover the "photo fee." Step Four is to dress the part: don't wear red or white, which bleed on film and render you unusable. Finally, after you collect three **SAG** (**Screen Actors Guild;** 5757 Wilshire Blvd., Los Angeles, CA 90036; ☎323-937-3441) vouchers, you'll be eligible to pay the $1272 to join showbiz society. See you in the movies!

pet into the theater for a **premiere,** drop in on the four premiere hounds: **Grauman's Chinese** (about 2 per month); **El Capitan** (Disney films only); **Mann's Village** and **Bruin,** in Westwood. For info on what's playing in L.A., call ☎323-777-3456 or read the daily Calendar section of the *L.A. Times.* Devotees of second-run, foreign-language, and experimental films can get their fix at the eight **Laemmle Theaters** in Beverly Hills (☎310-274-6869), West Hollywood (☎323-848-3500), Santa Monica (☎310-394-9741), and Pasadena (☎626-844-6500).

Arclight Cinerama Dome, 6360 Sunset Blvd. (☎323-466-3401), in **Hollywood,** near Vine St. The ultimate cineplex for the serious moviegoer. 14 movie screens surround a gigantic dome that seats 820 people and displays a screen that expands from 80 to 180 ft. A spectacular, rumbling sound system. Recent movies only. Don't be late—doors close 7min. after movies begin. Tickets range from $7.75-14.

Grauman's Chinese Theatre, 6925 Hollywood Blvd. (☎323-464-8111), between Highland and La Brea Ave. in **Hollywood.** Hype to the hilt. For details, see **Hollywood Sights,** p. 885. Tickets $10, ages 3-12 and over 65 $7; first show of the day $7.50.

Nuart Theatre, 11272 Santa Monica Blvd. (☎310-478-6379), in **West L.A.,** just west of I-405 (the San Diego Fwy.), at Sawtelle Ave. Perhaps the best-known revival house. The playbill changes nightly. Classics, documentaries, animation festivals, and foreign and modern films. *The Rocky Horror Picture Show* screens Sa night at midnight with a live cast. Tickets $9.25, seniors and under 12 $6. Discount card (5 movie tickets) $34.

Mann's Village Theatre, 961 Broxton Ave. (☎310-208-0018), in **Westwood.** One huge auditorium, one big screen, one great THX sound system, a balcony, and Art Deco design. Watch the back rows and balcony for late-arriving celebrities. Tickets $10, students $7.50, seniors $7, under 12 $6.50. Weekday shows before 6pm $7.

LIVE THEATER & MUSIC

L.A.'s live theater scene does not hold the weight of New York's Broadway, but its 115 "equity waiver theaters" (under 100 seats) offer dizzying, eclectic choices for theatergoers, who can also view small productions in art galleries, universities, parks, and even garages. Browse listings in the *L.A. Weekly* to find out what's hot. L.A.'s music venues range from small clubs to massive amphitheaters. The **Wiltern**

Theater (☎213-380-5005) shows alterna-rock/folk acts. The **Hollywood Palladium** (☎323-962-7600) is of comparable size with 3500 seats. Mid-sized acts head for the **Universal Amphitheater** (☎818-777-3931). Huge indoor sports arenas, such as the **Great Western Forum** (☎310-330-7300) and the newer **Staples Center** (☎213-742-7100), double as concert halls for big acts. Few dare to play at the 100,000-seat **Los Angeles Memorial Coliseum and Sports Arena;** only U2, Depeche Mode, Guns 'n' Roses, and the Warped Tour have filled the stands in recent years. Call Ticketmaster (☎213-480-3232) to purchase tickets for any of these venues.

Hollywood Bowl, 2301 N. Highland Ave. (☎323-850-2000), in **Hollywood.** The premier outdoor music venue in L.A. Although sitting in the back of this outdoor, 18,000-seat amphitheater makes the L.A. Philharmonic sound like it's on a transistor radio, bargain tickets and a panoramic view of the Hollywood Hills make it worthwhile. Free open house rehearsals by the Philharmonic and visiting performers usually Tu and Th at 10:30am. Parking at the Bowl is limited and pricey at $11. It's better to park at one of the lots away from the Bowl and take a shuttle (parking $5, shuttle $2.50; departs every 10-20min. starting 1½hr. before showtime). Lots at 10601 and 10801 Ventura Blvd., near Universal City; at the Kodak Theatre at 6801 Hollywood Blvd.

Geffen Playhouse, 10886 LeConte Ave. (☎310-208-5454), in **Westwood.** Off-Broadway and Tony award-winning shows. Tickets $34-46; student rush ($10) 1hr. before shows.

Pasadena Playhouse, 39 S. El Molino Ave. (☎626-356-7529 or 800-233-3123; www.pasadenaplayhouse.org), in **Pasadena.** California's premier theater and historical landmark has spawned Broadway careers and productions. Tickets $35-60. Call for rush tickets. Shows Su 2, 7pm, Tu-F 8pm, Sa 5, 9pm.

SPORTS

Exposition Park and the often dangerous city of **Inglewood,** southwest of the park, are home to many sports teams. The **USC Trojans** play football at the **L.A. Memorial Coliseum,** 3911 S. Figueroa St. (tickets ☎213-740-4672), which seats over 100,000 spectators. It is the only stadium in the world to have the honor of hosting the Olympic Games twice. Basketball's doormat, the **L.A. Clippers** (☎213-742-7500), and the dazzling 2000-02 NBA Champion **L.A. Lakers** (☎310-426-6000) play at the new **Staples Center,** 1111 S. Figueroa St. (☎213-742-7100; box office 213-742-7340), along with the **L.A. Kings** hockey team (☎888-546-4752) and the city's women's basketball team, the **L.A. Sparks** (☎310-330-3939). Lakers tickets start at $23, Kings at $24.50, and Sparks at $7.50. Call Ticketmaster (☎213-480-3232) for tickets. **Elysian Park,** about 3 mi. northeast of Downtown, curves around the northern portion of Chavez Ravine, home of **Dodger Stadium** and the popular **L.A. Dodgers** baseball team. Single-game tickets ($6-21) are a hot commodity during the April-October season, especially if the Dodgers are playing well. Call ☎323-224-1448.

SHOPPING

In L.A., shopping isn't just a practical necessity; it's a way of life. Many Southland shopping complexes are open-air, which makes for a nice stroll down a sunny tree-lined walkway. The hub of the shop-'til-you-drop spots is the Westside, with the Santa Monica's Third Street Promenade, Pasadena's Old Town, the Westside Pavilion (10800 W. Pico Blvd.; ☎310-474-6255), the Beverly Center, 8500 Beverly Blvd. (☎310-854-0070; www.beverlycenter.com), and the Century City Shopping Complex (10250 Santa Monica Blvd.; ☎310-277-3898) topping the list.

Book Soup, 8818 Sunset Blvd., in West Hollywood, has a maze of new books in every category imaginable, with especially strong film, architecture, poetry, and travel sections. The Addendum next door is a gem for bargain-shopping book lovers, featuring discounts of up to 50%. (☎310-659-3110; www.booksoup.com. Main store open daily 9am-11pm. Addendum open daily noon-8pm.) **Samuel French Bookshop,** 7623 Sunset Blvd., in Hollywood, can prep you for your audition at this haven for entertainment industry wisdom: acting directories, TV and film reference books, trade papers, and a vast selection of plays and screenplays. (☎323-876-0570. Open M-F 10am-6pm, Sa 10am-5pm.) Huge independent records store **Amoeba Music,** 6400 Sunset Blvd. in Hollywood, carries all genres and titles, including a lot of underground music. Take advantage of the daily $1 clearance sales. (☎323-245-6400; www.amoebamusic.com. Open M-Sa 10:30am-11pm, Su 11am-9pm.) For novelties, **Dudley Doo-Right Emporium,** 8200 Sunset Blvd., in West Hollywood, is cluttered with Rocky and Bullwinkle and George of the Jungle memorabilia. (☎323-656-6550. Open Tu, Th, Sa 11am-5pm. No credit cards.)

NIGHTLIFE

LATE-NIGHT RESTAURANTS

Given the extremely short shelf-life and unpredictability of the L.A. club scene, late-night restaurants have become reliable hangouts.

Canter's, 419 N. Fairfax Ave. (☎323-651-2030), in **Fairfax,** north of Beverly Blvd. An L.A. institution and the heart and soul of historically Jewish Fairfax since 1931. Grapefruit-sized matzoh ball in chicken broth $4.50. Giant sandwiches $8-9. Visit the Kibbitz Room for nightly free rock, blues, jazz, and a chance to spot Lenny Kravitz in the audience. Cheap beer ($2.50). Open 24hr.

Fred 62, 1850 N. Vermont Ave. (☎323-667-0062), in **Los Feliz.** "Eat now, dine later." Look for a booth with headrests. Hip, edgy East L.A. crowd's jukebox selections rock the house. The apple waffles ($4.62–all prices end in .62 and .97) are divine. Open 24hr.

The Rainbow Bar and Grill, 9015 Sunset Blvd. (☎310-278-4232; http://rainbowbarandgrill.com), in **West Hollywood,** next to the Roxy. Dark red vinyl booths, dim lighting, loud music, and colorful characters set the scene. Marilyn Monroe met Joe DiMaggio on a blind (and apparently, rather silent) date here. Brooklyn-quality pizza $6. Calamari $8. Grandma's chicken soup $3.50. Open M-F 11am-2am, Sa-Su 5pm-2am.

Jerry's Famous Deli has multiple locations, including 8701 Beverly Blvd. (☎310-289-1811), corner of San Vicente Ave. in **West Hollywood,** 10925 Weyburn Ave. (☎310-208-3354), in **Westwood,** and 12655 Ventura Blvd. (☎818-980-4245), in **Studio City.** An L.A. deli with sleek red leather and sky-high prices. Note the menu's height—Jerry reportedly wanted "the longest menu possible while still maintaining structural integrity." Something here is bound to satisfy your 4am craving ($13-15). Open 24hr.

COFFEEHOUSES

In a city where no one eats very much for fear of rounding out that mannequin figure, espresso, coffee, and air are vital dining options.

Elixer, 8612 Melrose Ave. (☎310-657-9300), just east of San Vicente Blvd. in **Hollywood.** Drink your herbal tonic or tea in the outdoor garden that imitates a tranquil tropical paradise or sit among the trees. An enormous collection of tonics ($4-5) based on Chinese herbal traditions and teas from all over the world. Licensed herbalists are on duty daily 11am-6pm for spontaneous consultations (call ahead for a one-on-one session). Open M-Sa 9am-10pm, Su 10am-8pm; summer hours M-F 9am-11pm.

UnUrban Coffeehouse, 3301 Pico Blvd. (☎310-315-0056), in **Santa Monica.** 3 separate rooms of funky old furniture, campy voodoo candles, Mexican wrestling masks, musty books, and leopard-print couches. Iced mocha blends $3.50; Italian sodas $2. Open mic poetry W 8pm; open mic comedy Th 7:30pm; open mic songwriters F 8pm; music showcase Sa 7pm. Sign up for open mic 30min. before the show. No cover. Open M-Th 7am-midnight, F 7am-1am, Sa 8am-1am, Su 8am-7pm.

COMEDY CLUBS

The talent may be imported from New York, but it doesn't change the fact that L.A.'s comedy clubs are the best in the world.

L.A. Improv, 8162 Melrose Ave. (☎323-651-2583), in **West Hollywood.** L.A.'s best, including Robin Williams and Jerry Seinfeld, have fished for laughs here. Drew Carey and Ryan Stiles often join the show. Dinner at the restaurant (entrees $6-14) includes priority seating for the show. 18+. Cover $10-15. 2-drink min. Shows Su-Th 8pm, F-Sa 8:30, 10:30pm. Bar open daily until 1:30am. Reservations recommended.

Groundling Theater, 7307 Melrose Ave. (☎323-934-4747; www.groundlings.com), in **Hollywood.** One of the most popular improv and comedy clubs in town. The Groundling's alums include Pee Wee Herman and Lisa Kudrow, and *Saturday Night Live* regulars like Will Farrell and Julia Sweeney. *SNL* producer Lorne Michaels might be sitting in back. Polished skits. Cover $7-18.50. Shows Su 7:30pm, W-Th 8pm, F-Sa 8 and 10pm.

BARS

The 1996 film *Swingers* has had a homogenizing effect on L.A.'s hipsters. Grab your retro-70s polyester shirts, sunglasses, goatees, and throwback Cadillac convertibles, 'cause if you can't beat them, you have to swing with them, daddy-o. Unless otherwise specified, bars in California are 21+.

North, 8029 Sunset Blvd. (☎323-654-1313), between Laurel Ave. and Crescent Heights Ave. in **West Hollywood.** A classic L.A. undercover bar where the entrance is hard to find and you need to be "in the know" to know about it. Small, upscale bar where good-looking people buy good-looking drinks and dance until the morning. Drinks $6. DJ spins hip-hop and house Th-Sa nights. Open daily 6pm-1am.

Miyagi's, 8225 Sunset Blvd. (☎323-650-3524), on **Sunset Strip.** With 3 levels, 7 sushi bars ($5-7), 6 liquor bars, and indoor waterfalls and streams, this Japanese-themed restaurant, bar, lounge, and hip-hop dance club is a Strip hot spot. "*Sake* bomb, *sake* bomb, *sake* bomb" $4.50. Open daily 5:30pm-2am.

3 of Clubs, 1123 N. Vine St. (☎323-462-6441), at the corner of Santa Monica Blvd. in **Hollywood.** In a small strip mall beneath a "Bargain Clown Mart" sign, this simple bar is famous for appearing in *Swingers.* Live bands Th, DJ F-Sa. Open daily 7pm-2am.

Beauty Bar, 1638 Cahuenga Blvd. (☎323-464-7676), in **Hollywood.** Where else can you get a manicure and henna tattoo while sipping a cocktail and schmoozing? It's like getting ready for the prom again, except that the drinking starts before rather than after. Drinks like "Perm" are $8. DJ nightly 10pm. Open Su-W 9pm-2am, Th-Sa 6pm-2am.

CLUBS

With the highest number of bands per capita in the world and more streaming in every day, L.A. is famous for its club scene. The distinction between music and dance clubs is murky in L.A.—and given L.A.'s fickleness, club venues may host completely different crowds on different nights. L.A. clubs are often expensive but many are still feasible for budgeteers. Coupons in *L.A. Weekly* (see **Publications,** p. 878) and those handed out by the bushel inside the clubs can save you a bundle. To enter the club scene, it's best to be at least 21 (and/or beautiful) to avoid a hefty cover charge for a less desirable venue. All clubs are 21+ unless otherwise noted.

The Derby, 4500 Los Feliz Blvd. (☎323-663-8979; www.the-derby.com), corner of Hillhurst Ave. in **Los Feliz.** Still jumpin' and jivin' with the kings of swing. Ladies, grab your snoods; many dress the 40s part. Choice Italian fare from Louise's Trattoria next door. Full bar. Free swing lessons Sa 8, 9pm. Cover $5-12. Open daily 7:30-2am.

Largo, 432 N. Fairfax Ave. (☎323-852-1073), between Melrose Ave. and Beverly Blvd. in **West Hollywood.** Intimate sit-down (or, if you get there late, lean-back) club. Original rock, pop, and folk, and comedy acts. Cover $2-12. Open M-Sa 8:30pm-2am.

Roxy, 9009 Sunset Blvd. (☎310-278-9457), on **Sunset Strip.** Known as the "Sizzling Showcase," it's one of the best-known Sunset Strip clubs. Bruce Springsteen got his start here. Live rock, blues, alternative, and occasional hip-hop. Many big tour acts. All ages. Cover varies. Opens 8pm.

Whisky A Go-Go, 8901 Sunset Blvd. (☎310-652-4205), in **West Hollywood.** Historically, this is the great prophet of L.A.'s music scene. It hosted progressive bands in the late 70s and early 80s and was big in the punk explosion. The Doors, Janis Joplin, and Led Zeppelin played here. All ages welcome. Cover M-Th $10, F-Su $13. Shows begin 8pm.

GAY & LESBIAN NIGHTLIFE

While the Sunset Strip features all the nightlife any Jack and Jill could desire, gay men and lesbians may find life more interesting a short tumble down the hill on **Santa Monica Boulevard.** Still, many ostensibly straight clubs have gay nights; check *L.A. Weekly* or contact the Gay and Lesbian Community Services Center. Free weekly magazine *fab!* lists happenings in the gay and lesbian community. **Motherload,** 8499 Santa Monica Blvd. (☎310-659-9700), and **Trunks,** 8809 Santa Monica Blvd. (☎310-652-1015), are two of the friendliest and most popular bars. Neither has a cover and both are open until 2am. All clubs are 21+ unless otherwise noted.

Abbey Cafe, 692 N. Robertson Blvd. (☎310-289-8410), at Santa Monica Blvd. in **West Hollywood.** 6 candlelit rooms, 2 huge bars, a large outdoor patio, and a hall of private booths make this beautiful lounge and dance club the best place around. The comfy couches cry out for some lovin'. Open daily 8am-2am.

Micky's, 8857 Santa Monica Blvd. (☎310-657-1176), in **West Hollywood.** Huge dance floor filled with delectable men. On a weekend night when other bars close, head to Micky's for another 2hr. of grooving. Music is mostly electronic dance. M night drag shows. Happy Hour M-F 5-9pm. Cover $3-5. Open Su-Th noon-2am, F-Sa noon-4am.

The Palms, 8572 Santa Monica Blvd. (☎310-652-6188), in **West Hollywood.** Pool room and full bar with lots of drink specials like Tu $3 frozen drinks. DJ Th-Sa; music ranges from house to disco to salsa. Men are welcome but may feel very alone. Don't hesitate to hop in the 2-person dance cage. W 9pm-midnight $1 drinks. Su Beer Bust $0.50 drafts and free buffet. Open daily 4pm-2am.

ORANGE COUNTY

Directly south of L.A. County lies Orange County (pop. 2.9 million). Composed of 34 cities, it is a microcosm of Southern California: dazzling sandy shoreline, bronzed beach bums, oversized shopping malls, homogenized suburban neighborhoods, and frustrating traffic snarls. One of California's staunchest Republican enclaves, Orange County supports big business, and its economy (along with its multi-million-dollar hillside mansions oozing luxury cars and disaffected teens) shows it. Disneyland, stronghold of the late Walt Disney's ever-expanding cultural empire, is the premier inland attraction. The coast runs the gamut from the surf burg of Huntington Beach to the opulent excess of Newport Beach and the artistic vibe of Laguna. A little farther south lies the quiet mission of San Juan Capistrano, amid hills that spill onto the laidback beaches of Dana Point and San Clemente.

TRANSPORTATION

Airport: John Wayne Airport, 18601 Airport Way (☎949-252-5006), Santa Ana, 20min. from Anaheim. Newer and easier to get around than LAX; domestic flights only.

Trains: Amtrak (☎800-USA-RAIL/872-7245; www.amtrakcalifornia.com) stations, from north to south: **Fullerton,** 120 E. Santa Fe Ave. (☎714-992-0530); **Santa Ana,** 1000 E. Santa Ana Blvd. (☎714-547-8389); **Irvine,** 15215 Barranca Pkwy. (☎949-753-9713); **San Juan Capistrano,** 26701 Verdugo St. (☎949-240-2972).

Buses: Greyhound (☎800-231-2222) has 3 stations: **Anaheim,** 100 W. Winston Rd., 3 blocks south of Disneyland (☎714-999-1256; open daily 6:30am-9:15pm); **Santa Ana,** 1000 E. Santa Ana Blvd. (☎714-542-2215; open daily 6:15am-8:30pm); and **San Clemente,** 2421 S. El Camino Real (☎949-366-2646; open daily 7am-9pm.)

Public Transit: Orange County Transportation Authority (OCTA), 550 S. Main St., Orange County. Thorough service is useful for getting from Santa Ana and Fullerton Amtrak stations to Disneyland and for beach-hopping along the coast. Bus #1 travels the coast from Long Beach to San Clemente (every hr. until 8pm). Buses #25, 33, and 35 travel from Fullerton to Huntington Beach; #91 goes from Laguna Hills to Dana Point. (☎714-636-7433; www.octa.net. Fare $1, day pass $2.50.) **Info center** open M-F 6am-8pm, Sa-Su 8am-5pm. **MTA Info** (☎800-266-6883; open daily 5am-10:45pm) for MTA buses running from L.A. to Disneyland and Knott's Berry Farm.

Visitor Information: Anaheim Area Visitors and Convention Bureau, 800 W. Katella Ave. (☎714-765-8888; www.anaheimoc.org), in Anaheim Convention Ctr. Lodging and dining guides. Open M-F 8am-5pm. **Newport Visitors Bureau,** 3300 West Coast Hwy. (☎949-722-1611 or 800-942-6278), in Newport Beach. Eager-to-help staff, maps, and events brochures. Open M-F 8am-5pm. **Laguna Beach Visitors Bureau,** 252 Broadway (949-497-9229). Open M-F 9am-5pm, Sa 10am-4pm, Su noon-4pm.

Police: Anaheim, 425 S. Harbor Blvd. (☎714-765-1900). **Huntington Beach,** 2000 Main St. (☎714-960-8811).

Crisis Lines: Sexual Assault Hotline, ☎714-957-2737. **Orange County Referral Hotline,** ☎714-894-4242.

Medical Services: St. Jude Medical Center, 101 E. Valencia Mesa Dr. (☎714-871-3280), Fullerton. **Lestonnac Free Clinic,** 1215 E. Chapman Ave. (☎714-633-4600). Hours vary; call for an appointment.

Post Office: 701 N. Loara St. (☎714-520-2639 or 800-275-8777), 1 block north of Anaheim Plaza, Anaheim. Open M-F 8:30am-5pm, Sa 9am-3pm. **Postal Code:** 92803. **Area Codes:** 714 (Anaheim, Santa Ana, Orange, Garden Grove), 949 (Newport, Laguna, Irvine, Mission Viejo, San Juan Capistrano).

ACCOMMODATIONS

The Magic Kingdom is the sun around which the Anaheim solar system revolves; countless budget chain motels and garden-variety "clean, comfortable rooms" flank it on all sides. Keep watch for posted family and group rates, and seek out establishments offering the 3-for-2 passport (3 days of Disney for the price of 2).

Huntington Beach Colonial Inn Youth Hostel, 421 8th St. (☎714-536-3315), in Huntington Beach, 4 blocks inland at Pecan Ave. This house was once a brothel. Things have quieted down since then (quiet hours after 10pm). Common bath, large kitchen, reading/TV room, coin-op laundry, Internet access, deck, and shed with outdoor equipment. Linen and breakfast included. Key deposit $5. Check-in 8am-10pm. No lockout. Reserve 2 days in advance for summer Sa-Su. Dorms $18; doubles $48. ❷

Fullerton Hostel (HI-AYH), 1700 N. Harbor Blvd. (☎738-3721), in Fullerton, 10min. north of Disneyland. Shuttle from L.A. Airport $21. In the woods and away from the thematic craziness of nearby Anaheim with an international feel. Enthusiastic, resourceful staff invites questions but forbids drinking. Offers services like ISICs. Kitchen, relaxing living room, communal bathrooms. Linen $2. Laundry wash and dry $0.75. 7-night max. stay. Check-in 8-11am and 2-11pm. Reservations encouraged. Open June 1-Sept. 30. Single-sex and co-ed dorms $17.50, non-members $20.50 (including taxes). ❷

Balboa Inn, 105 Main St. (☎949-675-3412; www.balboainn.com), on the sand at Newport. From PCH, follow signs to Balboa Peninsula and turn onto Main St. This recently renovated historical landmark offers rooms with ocean or bay views and is close to area attractions. Relax in the pool or jacuzzi. Continental breakfast and room service offered. Fans, cable TV, and fridge. Overnight parking $7. Room rates start at $119. ❺

FOOD

Orange County's restaurants offer California Cuisine of the light and seafood-oriented variety.

Rutabegorz, 211 N. Pomona Blvd. (☎738-9339; www.rutabegorz.com), in Fullerton. Other locations at 264 N. Glassell St. (☎633-3260) in Orange and 158 W. Main St. (☎731-9807) in Tustin. With a name derived from the unloved rutabaga, this hippie/hipster joint supplies a 20-page menu (on recycled newsprint, of course). Mexican casserole $7. Open M-Th 11am-10pm, F-Sa 11am-11pm, Su 4-9pm. ❷

Laguna Village Market and Cafe, 577 S. Coast Hwy. (☎949-494-6344), 5 blocks south of Broadway in **Laguna Beach.** Located on top of a cliff, the restaurant is housed in an open-air gazebo selling art and jewelry by local artists and designers. Its ocean-front terrace is the main draw. Lap up the view, along with some seafood or the house specialty, Village Huevos ($9.50). Calamari plate $9. Open daily 8:30am-dark. ❷

Ruby's (☎714-969-7829), at the end of the **Huntington Beach** Pier. A 5-7min. trek down the pier. Enclosed by windows on all walls, this flashy white and neon red 50s-style diner has great burgers ($6) and a fabulous ocean view. ❷

The Dutch Bakery, 32341 Camino Capistrano (☎949-489-2180), in **San Juan Capistrano.** In the Vons Center plaza down the street from the Mission, this bakery provides excellent sandwiches, all on fresh-baked ciabatta bread. Wash them down with a strawberry banana smoothie ($3). Open Tu-F 6am-4pm, Sa 7am-3pm. ❷

SIGHTS & BEACHES

DISNEYLAND. Disneyland calls itself the "Happiest Place on Earth," and a part of everyone agrees. After a full day there, your precious wallet, of course, may not. Weekday and low-season visitors will undoubtedly be the happiest, but the clever can wait for parades to distract children from the epic lines or utilize the line-busting FastPass program. Just recently, Disneyland introduced its new kid brother, "California Adventure," (with separate admission) to the Southern California theme park family. The park features ambitious attractions divided into four districts. **Sunshine Plaza,** the gateway to the park, is anchored by a 50-foot-tall sun enlivened by a wealth of red, orange, and yellow lights at night. Built as a shrine to the greatest state of them all, **Golden State** offers an eight-acre mini-wilderness, a citrus grove, a winery, and even a replica of San Francisco. **Paradise Pier** is dedicated to the so-called "Golden Age" of amusement parks—with rides such as **California Screamin'** and **Mulholland Madness,** which, sadly, is not based on the David Lynch movie. Finally, the **Hollywood Pictures Backlot** realizes your aspirations to stardom without demanding talent or effort. (*Main entrance on Harbor Blvd., and a smaller one on Katella Ave. Parking $8. ☎781-4565; www.disneyland.com. Disneyland open Su-Th 8am-11pm, F-Sa 8am-midnight; hours may vary, so call ahead. California Adventure open Su-Th 9am-10pm, F-Sa 9am-10:30pm. Disneyland passes $43, ages 3-9 $33, under 3 free; allows* *repeated single-day entrance. 2- and 3-day passes also available. California Adventure passes $43, ages 3-9 $33, under 3 free. Combination tickets available. Lockers are located west of the ticket booths and at the lost and found facility on Main Street, USA.)*

(K)NOT(T) DISNEYL.A.ND. Knott's is a local favorite and holds the title for first theme park in America, and aims at being "the friendliest place in the West"—it has long since given up on being the happiest place on Earth. The park's highlights include roller coasters like **Boomerang** and **Ghostrider.** The latest addition is **Xcelerator,** bringing you from 0 to 80 mph in three seconds. *(8039 Beach Blvd. at La Palma Ave., 5 mi. northeast of Disneyland. From downtown L.A., take MTA bus #460 from 4th and Flower St.; 1¼hr. If driving from L.A., take I-5 south to Beach Blvd., turn right at the end of the exit ramp and proceed south 2 mi. Recorded info ☎220-5200. Open Su-Th 9am-10pm, F-Sa 9am-midnight; hours may vary, so call ahead. $43, seniors and ages 3-11 $33, under 3 free; after 4pm all tickets half price. Summer discounts available. Parking under 3hr. free, each additional hr. $2.)* **Soak City USA** marks Knott's 13-acre effort to make a splash in the already drenched waterpark scene. *(Next to Knott's Berry Farm. ☎220-5200. Open Su-Th 10am-6pm, F-Sa 10am-8pm; hours may vary, so call ahead. $24, ages 3-11 $17, under 3 free.)*

SPORTS. For more evidence of Disney's world domination, catch a game by one of the teams they own: the major league **Anaheim Angels** play baseball from early April to October at **Edison Field.** *(☎940-2000 or 800-626-4357. General tickets $6-25.)* To check out some NHL action, catch a **Mighty Ducks** hockey game at **Arrowhead Pond.**

ORANGE COUNTY BEACH COMMUNITIES. Orange County's various beach communities have cleaner sand, better surf, and less madness than their L.A. County counterparts; it is here that L.A. residents seek refuge.

Huntington Beach is the prototypical Surf City, USA, the epicenter of the surfing craze that swept over California beaches in the early 1900s. This town has surf lore galore, and the proof is on the **Surfing Walk of Fame** (the sidewalk along PCH at Main St.) and in the **International Surfing Museum,** 411 Olive St. (☎714-960-3483. Open daily noon-5pm; call for details. $2, students $1.) Multi-million dollar summer homes, the world's largest leisure-craft harbor, and **Balboa Peninsula** are all packed closely enough on ritzy **Newport Beach's** oceanfront to make even New Yorkers feel claustrophobic. Surfing and beach volleyball are popular, as is strolling on residential Balboa Peninsula. Punctuated by rocky cliffs, coves, and lush hillside vegetation, lovely but traffic-ridden **Laguna Beach** cultivates a decidedly Mediterranean and artsy character. **Ocean Avenue,** at PCH, and **Main Beach** are the prime parading areas. The latest incarnation of the original 1914 Laguna Beach art association is the **Laguna Art Museum,** 307 Cliff Dr. The collection showcases local and state art, including some excellent early 20th-century Impressionist works. (☎494-8971; www.lagunaartmuseum.org. Open daily 11am-5pm. Tours daily 2pm. $7, students and seniors $5, children under 12 free. free first Th of each month.) The evocative **Mission San Juan Capistrano,** 30min. south of Anaheim on I-5, was established by Father Junípero Serra and is considered the "jewel of the missions."

BIG BEAR ☎909

Big Bear Lake draws hordes with its fluffy downhill and cross-country skiing in winter, and stellar fishing, sailing, and watersports in the summer. The nearby mountains and forest offer enjoyable hikes and campgrounds.

Hiking the trails in the surrounding mountains is a superb way of exploring the San Bernardino wilderness. Maps, trail descriptions, and the *Visitor's Guide to the San Bernardino National Forest* are available at the **Big Bear Discovery Center (BBDC).** The 3½ mi. **Alpine Pedal Path** runs its gentle, paved course from the Stanfield Cutoff on the lake's north shore to the BBDC. Moderately difficult 2½ mi. **Castle Rock Trail,** starting one mi. east of the dam on Hwy. 18, is a steep haul to stupendous views of Big Bear Lake. In summer, **mountain biking** takes over the Big Bear slopes. Grab a *Ride and Trail Guide* at the BBDC or at **Snow Summit,** 1 mi. west of Big Bear Lake, which runs lifts in summer so armored adrenaline monsters can grind serious downhill terrain. (☎866-4621. $10 per ride, day pass $20; ages 7-12 $5/10. Helmet required. Open M-F 9am-4pm, Sa 8am-5pm, Su 9am-4pm.) **Team Big Bear,** 476 Concklin Rd., operating out of the Mountain Bike Shop at the base of Snow Summit, rents bikes and sponsors organized bike races each summer. (☎866-4565. $9 per hr., $27 for 4hr., $50 per day; helmet included.) Big Bear Lake is well-stocked with rainbow trout and catfish. State **fishing** licenses are available at sporting goods stores (day $10, season $28). Boats can be rented at **Holloway's Marina,** 398 Edgemor Rd., on the south shore. (☎800-448-5335; www.bigbearboating.com. Full day $50-175.) **Big Bear Parasail,** 439 Pine Knot Landing, straps you into your vessel of choice and tows you behind high-speed watercraft. (☎866-IFLY/4359. Parasailing $45 per hr., tandem $80; waterskiing and tubing $95 per hr.; 2-person Wave Runner $75 per hr., 3-person $95 per hr.)

When snow conditions are favorable, ski areas quickly run out of lift tickets, which may be purchased through Ticketmaster (☎714-740-2000). **Big Bear Mountain Resorts** (www.bigbearmountainresorts.com) splits 55 runs between two ski resorts. The huge vertical drops and adventure skiing terrain at **Bear Mountain,** 43101 Goldmine Dr., is geared toward freestyle skiing and snowboarding. (☎585-2519; www.bearmtn.com.) **Snow Summit,** 880 Summit Blvd., welcomes families with beginner runs, snowmaking, and night skiing capacities. (☎866-5766; www.snowsummit.com. Lift tickets are interchangeable, and a shuttle runs between the 2 parks. $43, ages 13-19 $35, ages 7-12 $14; holidays $50/50/21. Skis $25, snowboards $30; deposit required.) **Renting** ski and snowboard equipment from the ski stores along Big Bear Blvd. can save you up to half the price of renting at the mountains. **Snow Valley,** 35100 Highway 18 near Running Springs, is the most family-oriented resort in Big Bear. (☎867-2751. Lift ticket $37, ages 6-13 $23. Ski rental $17, snowboard $30.) **Cross-country skiing** is very popular in Big Bear. The Rim Nordic Ski Area, across the highway from Snow Valley, is a network of cross-country ski trails. An Adventure Pass ($5) is required (see p. 900).

In the winter, budget accommodations are next to impossible to find; even in summer, rooms below $50 a night often only exist in San Bernardino, down the mountain. Big Bear Blvd. is lined with accommodations. **Robinhood Inn ❹,** 40797 Lakeview Dr., has a courtyard complete with spa and barbecue, and fireplaces and kitchenettes in many rooms. (☎800-990-9956. Singles and doubles begin at $64 in summer and $79 in winter; suites accommodating up to 6 under $100.) The 48 secluded and cool **campsites** at **Pineknot ❷,** 7000 ft., on Summit Blvd. are popular with mountain bikers. (Flush toilets and water. Wheelchair-accessible. Sites $18.) Food can get pricey, so those with kitchens should forage at **Stater Bros.,** 42171 Big Bear Blvd. (☎866-5211. Open daily 7am-11pm.) Many cutesy village eateries offer all-you-can-eat specials. The motley but tasty menu at **Virginia Lee's ❶,** 41003 Big Bear Blvd. overflows with hot dogs, tamales, fancy hot chocolate, and potato and pasta salads. Everything $2-4. (☎866-3151. Open W-Su 10am-4pm.)

To reach Big Bear, take **I-10** to **Route 30** in San Bernardino. Take Rte. 30 north to **Route 330** (Mountain Rd.),which turns into **Route 18,** a winding 30-45min. ascent. Rte. 18 hits the west end of Big Bear Lake and forks into a continuing Rte. 18 branch along the south shore, where it is called Big Bear Blvd., and Rte. 38 along the north shore. Driving time from L.A. is about 2½hr., barring serious weekend traffic or road closures. Driving to Big Bear should not be attempted during the winter without checking road conditions with **CalTrans.** (☎427-7623; www.dot.ca.gov.) **Mountain Area Regional Transit Authority (MARTA)** runs two **buses** per day from the Greyhound station in San Bernardino to Big Bear. (☎584-1111. $5, seniors and disabled $3.75.) The **Big Bear Chamber of Commerce,** 630 Bartlett Rd., in Big Bear Village, is helpful. (☎866-4608, fax 866-5412; www.bigbearchamber.com.

Open M-F 8am-5pm, Sa-Su 9am-5pm.) Other services include: the ranger station (☎383-5651); **Internet Access, Big Bear Public Library,** 41930 Garstin Dr. (☎866-5571. Open M-Tu noon-8pm, W-F 10am-6pm, Sa 9am-5pm); and the **post office,** 472 Pine Knot Blvd. (☎866-7481. Open M-F 8:30am-5pm, Sa 10am-noon.) **Postal Code:** 92315.

SAN DIEGO ☎619

San Diegans are fond of referring to their near-perfect seaside hometown as "America's Finest City." The claim is difficult to dispute—San Diego (pop. 1,130,000) has all the virtues of other California cities without the frequently cited drawbacks. No smog fills this city's air, and no sewage spoils its shores. Its zoo is the nation's best, and the temperate year-round climate is unbeatable.

TRANSPORTATION

San Diego rests in the extreme southwest corner of California, 127 mi. south of Los Angeles and 15 mi. north of the Mexican border. **I-5** skirts the eastern edge of downtown on its way to the Mexican border; **I-15** runs northeast through the desert to Las Vegas; and **I-8** runs east-west along downtown's northern boundary, connecting the desert with Ocean Beach. The downtown core is laid out in a grid.

Airport: San Diego International (Lindbergh Field), at the northwest edge of downtown. Bus #2 goes downtown ($2), as do cabs ($8).

Trains: Amtrak, 1050 Kettner Blvd. (☎800-872-7245), just north of Broadway in the Santa Fe Depot. To **L.A.** (11 trains daily 6am-8:30pm; $25, summer $28). Station has info on buses, trolleys, cars, and boats. Ticket office open daily 5:15am-10pm.

Buses: Greyhound, 120 W. Broadway (☎239-8082 or 800-231-2222), at 1st St. To **L.A.** (30 per day 5am-11:35pm; $15, round-trip $25) and **Tijuana** (16 per day 5am-11:35pm; $5, round-trip $8). Ticket office open 24hr.

Public Transit: San Diego Metropolitan Transit System (MTS). MTS's automated 24hr. information line, **Info Express** (☎685-4900), has info on San Diego's buses, trains, and trolleys. The **Transit Store** at 1st Ave. and Broadway has info. Get a 1- to 4-day **Day Trippers Pass** if you plan to use public transit of any kind more than once. (Open M-F 8:30am-5:30pm, Sa-Su noon-4pm. 1-day pass $5, 2-day $9, 3-day $12, 4-day $15.)

Car Rental: Bargain Auto, 3860 Rosecrans St. (☎299-0009). Used cars available to renters 18+. Cars from $19 per day with 150 mi. free, $105 per week with 500 mi. free. Ages 18-25 pay $6 per day surcharge, $35 per week. $39 per day for insurance if driving to Mexico. Credit card required. Open M-F 8am-6pm, Sa-Su 8am-4pm.

Bike Rental: Action Sports, 4000 Coronado Bay Rd. (☎424-4466), at the Marina Dock of the Loews Coronado Bay Resort on **Coronado Island.** Beach cruisers and mountain bikes $10 per hr., $30 per 4hr. Open M-F 9am-6pm, Sa-Su 8:30am-6:30pm.

ORIENTATION & PRACTICAL INFORMATION

The epicenter of San Diego tourism is historic **Balboa Park.** Northwest of the park is stylish **Hillcrest,** the city's gay enclave with great shopping and restaurants. The reinvigorated **Gaslamp Quarter** sits in the southern section of downtown between 4th and 6th St. and contains signature theaters and nightclubs, as well as fine restaurants. Just north of downtown in the southeast corner of the I-5 and I-8 junction lies a little slice of old Mexico known as **Old Town.** Discriminating travelers may find Old Town's touristy kitsch a bit contrived, but the fantastic Mexican food and lively scene make this place worth a visit. San Diego has two major bays: **San Diego Bay,** formed by **Coronado Island,** south of downtown, and **Mission Bay,** to the northwest. A jaunt up the coast leads to the swanky tourist haven of **La Jolla.** Farther up the coast are the laidback and sun-soaked beach communities of the **North County.**

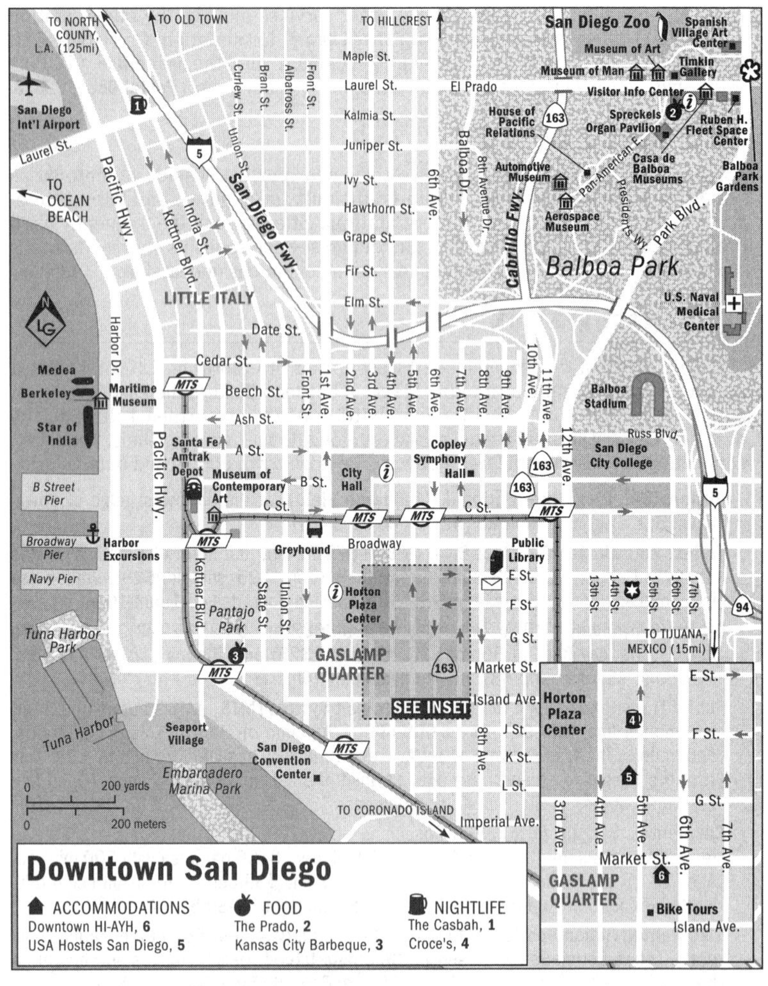

Visitor Info: San Diego Convention and Visitors Bureau, 401 B St., #1400, Dept. 700, San Diego 92101 (☎236-1212; www.sandiego.org), provides info. **Just Call** (☎615-6111) is an information line operated by the city of San Diego.

Library: San Diego Public Library, 820 E St. (☎236-5800), offers **Internet access,** foreign newspapers, borrowing privileges for visitors, and more. Open M-Th 10am-9pm, F-Sa 9:30am-5:30pm, Su 1-5pm.

Police: ☎531-2000.

Medical Services: Kaiser Foundation, 4647 Zion Ave. (☎528-5000).

Hotlines: BGLT Crisis Line, ☎800-479-3339. **Rape Hotline,** ☎233-3088. Both 24hr.

Post Office: 2535 Midway Dr. (☎800-275-8777. Open M 7am-5pm, Tu-F 8am-5pm, Sa 8am-4pm.) **Postal Code:** 92186. Another post office is located at 2150 Comstock St. (Open M-F 8am-5pm, Sa 8am-4:30pm.) **Postal Code:** 92111. **Area Code:** Most of San

Diego, including downtown, Coronado, and Ocean Beach: **619.** N area codes (including Del Mar, La Jolla, parts of North County, an and **760.** Unless otherwise specified, the area code for the San Die

ACCOMMODATIONS

Rates predictably rise on weekends and in summer. Reserve ahead. Be hostel and residential hotel scene, San Diego is littered with generic chain generally clean and safe. There is a popular cluster known as **Hotel Circle** (2- east of I-5 along I-8), where summer prices begin at $60 for a single and $70 fo double during the week ($70 and $80, respectively, on weekends). Several beaches in North County, as well as one on Coronado, are state parks and allow camping.

USA Hostels San Diego, 726 5th Ave. (☎232-3100 or 800-GET-TO-CA/438-8622; www.usahostels.com), between F and G St. in the Gaslamp. This colorful Euro-style fun house fits in well with the rocking atmosphere of the Gaslamp district. Hosts frequent parties and organizes Tijuana tours ($10.50) and Gaslamp pub crawls ($4). Pancake breakfast included. Dinner $4. Linen, lockers, and coin-op laundry. International passport or student ID required. Dorms $19-21; 3 private rooms $46-50. ❷

San Diego Downtown Hostel (HI-AYH), 521 Market St. (☎525-1531 or 800-909-4776, ext. 156; www.sandiegohostels.org), at 5th Ave., in the heart of Gaslamp. This hostel is well-suited to the traveler seeking calm. Airy common room, kitchen, and communal bathrooms. Smoking and drinking not allowed. Pancake breakfast, lockers (bring your own lock), and laundry. No curfew. Reception 7am-midnight. Groups welcome. 4- to 6-bed dorms $18-25, non-members add $3; doubles $45-60. ❷

International House at the 2nd Floor, 4502 Cass St. (☎858-274-4325) in Pacific Beach, and 3204 Mission Bay Dr. (☎858-539-0043) in Mission Beach. These 2 hostels offer clean rooms, comfortable beds, Internet access, breakfast, free surf and boogie board use, and great beach locations. 28-day max. stay. Out-of-state ID or international passport required. Dorm rooms $20, students $18; $110 per week. ❷

Old Town Inn, 4444 Pacific Hwy. (☎260-8024 or 800-643-3025; www.oldtowninn.com), near I-5 and I-8. Clean rooms with standard amenities are a 10min. walk from Old Town. Some rooms have kitchenettes. Pool. Large continental breakfast included. Rooms can go as low as $60, but prices vary depending on the season. ❹

FOOD

With its large Hispanic population and proximity to Mexico, San Diego is renowned for its exemplary Mexican cuisine. **Old Town** serves some of the best authentic Mexican food in the state. Beyond this, San Diego also offers a spectacular assortment of ethnic and more traditional eateries, highly concentrated in both the **Hillcrest** neighborhood and the historic **Gaslamp Quarter.**

Casa de Bandini, 2754 Calhoun St. (☎297-8211). An Old Town institution, repeatedly voted best Mexican restaurant in San Diego. In a Spanish-style architectural landmark built in 1829. Dishes out superb food and boisterous music. The colossal combo plates ($5-8) are fantastic, but it's the heavyweight margarita ($4-7) that's responsible for Bandini's legendary status. Indoor tables and outdoor tables on a beautiful tiled patio with fountain. Open M-Th 11am-9:30pm, F-Sa 11am-10pm, Su 10am-9:30pm. ❷

The Corvette Diner, 3946 5th Ave. (☎542-1001), in Hillcrest. The ultimate flashback to the days of nickel milkshakes, this 50s-style diner has more chrome than Detroit and more neon than Las Vegas. Serves extraordinary greasy-spoon classics and a number of unique creations like the house favorite, the Rory Burger (peanut butter and bacon burger, $7). A live DJ spins oldies every night (6-9pm) while costumed waitresses give as much lip as service. Open Su-Th 11am-10pm, F-Sa 11am-midnight. ❷

Kono's Surf Club, 704 Garnet Ave. (☎483-1669), across from the Crystal Pier in Pacific Beach. Identifiable by the line stretching for a block out the door, Kono's is a surfer's shrine. Breakfast served all day ($3-4). Try the huge Egg Burrito #3, which includes bacon, cheese, potatoes, and sauce ($4). Open M-F 7am-3pm, Sa-Su 7am-4pm. ❶

Kansas City Barbecue, 610 W. Market St. (☎231-9680), near Seaport Village. The location of *Top Gun*'s Great Balls of Fire bar scene. While the wooden piano remains, all that's left of Goose and Maverick is an abundance of autographed posters and neon signs. Vegetarians will find themselves in the Danger Zone in this barbecue-slathered meatfest. Entrees $9-16. Open daily 11am-2am; kitchen closes 1am. ❷

Berta's, 3928 Twiggs St. (☎295-2343). You may have to buy a copy of *Let's Go: Central America* to make your way through this menu. Dozens of Guatemalan, Honduran, and Costa Rican specialities $9-14. Open Su and Tu-Sa 11am-10pm. ❸

The Prado, 1549 El Prado (☎557-9441), in the heart of Balboa Park. Since this Latin-Italian fusion restaurant opened 3 years ago, it's had nothing but rave reviews. The patio seating is beautiful year-round, and the calamari appetizer is big enough to be a meal ($10). Dinner entrees from $19. Open M-Sa 11am-9:30pm, Su 11am-8pm. ❺

SIGHTS

San Diego's world-famous attractions are extremely varied, enough to keep any traveler engaged. Pick the free weekly *Reader* for local event listings. The **San Diego 3-for-1 Pass** offers unlimited admission for five consecutive days at discounted rates to three of the city's premier sights—Sea World, the San Diego Zoo, and the San Diego Wild Animal Park (visitwww.sandiegozoo.org or the web sites of the other two parks for information and online ticketing; $89, children 3-9 $63).

DOWNTOWN. San Diego's downtown attractions are concentrated in the corridor that includes its business, Gaslamp, and waterfront districts—all testaments to San Diego's continuing renaissance. The steel-and-glass structure of the **San Diego Museum of Contemporary Art** encases 20th-century works of art from the museum's permanent collection as well as visiting exhibits. Works include those of Andy Warhol and a wall that looks as though it breathes, which is as weird as it sounds. This is a smaller, but worthy, branch of the museum in La Jolla. *(1001 Kettner Blvd. ☎234-1001. Open Su-Tu and Th-Sa 11am-5pm. Free.)* The **Gaslamp Quarter** houses antique shops, Victorian buildings, trendy restaurants, and nightclubs. (see **Nightlife,** p. 909). By day, the area's charm lies in its fading history. The **Gaslamp Quarter Foundation** offers guided walking tours as well as a museum. *(William Heath Davis House, 410 Island Ave. ☎233-4692; www.gaslampquarter.org. Museum open Su and Tu-Sa 11am-3pm. $3 donation suggested. 2hr. guided walking tours Sa 11am. $8; students, seniors, and military $6; under 12 free. Self-guided tour maps are available for $2.)* The **Horton Grand Hotel,** like most old buildings in San Diego, is supposedly haunted. Believers may catch a glimpse of Wild West lawman Wyatt Earp. *(311 Island Ave. ☎544-1886. Tours W at 3pm. Free.)* Spanish for "dock," the **Embarcadero** has boardwalk shops and museums that face moored windjammers, cruise ships, and the occasional naval destroyer. *(Most afternoon tours of naval craft free.)* The jewel of San Diego's redevelopment efforts is **Horton Plaza,** at Broadway and 4th, a pastel, open-air, multi-level shopping center.

SAN DIEGO ZOO. With over 100 acres of exquisite habitats, this zoo well deserves its reputation as one of the finest in the world. Its unique "bioclimatic" exhibits group animals and plants together by habitat. The legendary **panda** exhibit is the most timeless feature of the park, and the zoo invests over one million dollars a year on panda habitat preservation in China. The educational 40min. **double-decker bus tour** covers about 75% of the zoo. Although the popular choice (bringing lines twice as long) is for seats on the upper deck, the trees can obstruct views and the seats are in the sun; the lower deck is a better choice. A non-narrated express bus will take you to stops throughout the park during the day. *($8.50, ages 3-11 $6.50.)* The **Skyfari Aerial Tramway** rises 170 ft. above the park and lasts about two minutes but can save on walking time; don't expect to see anything but the tops of trees. *(One-way $2.)* If the bus and tramway appeal to you, purchase your tickets when you buy zoo admission. *(2920 Zoo Dr., Balboa Park. ☎234-3153, Giant Panda viewing info 888-MY-PANDA/697-2632; www.sandiegozoo.org. Open daily late June-early Sept. 9am-10pm; early Sept.-late June 9am-dusk. $19.50 ($32 with 35min. bus tour and 2 tickets for the aerial tramway), ages 3-11 $11.75 ($19.75 with 35min. bus tour and aerial tramway; free in Oct.). Military in uniform free. Group rates available. Free on Founder's Day, the first M in Oct.)*

BALBOA PARK & THE EL PRADO MUSEUMS. It would take several days to see all of Balboa Park's museums. Most reside within the resplendent Spanish colonial-style buildings that line **El Prado Street** south of the zoo. These ornate structures, many of which were designed for exhibits in 1916 or 1936, were originally intended to last 2 years. Since many of the buildings are now going on 80, they are being renovated. You can reach the park by bus #7, and parking is free. Most museums offer free admission at least one Tuesday a month. The **Visitors Center** is in the House of Hospitality on El Prado St. at the Plaza de Panama. It sells park maps *($0.50)* and the Passport to Balboa Park *($30)*, which allows admission into 13 of the park's museums, and cold beverages, which are scarce within Balboa Park. *(1549 El Prado. ☎239-0512; www.balboapark.org. Open daily summer 9am-4:30pm; winter 9am-4pm.)* Creationists beware: the **Museum of Man** dedicates an entire floor to the 98.4% of DNA we share with chimpanzees. The real treat, however, is on the outside: the gleaming Spanish mosaic tiles of the museum's much-photographed tower and dome. *(On the west end of the park. ☎239-2001; www.museumofman.org. Open daily 10am-4:30pm. $6, seniors $5, ages 6-17 $3; free 3rd Tu of each month.)* The **Aerospace Museum** displays 24 full-scale replicas and 44 original planes, as well as exhibits on aviation history and the International Space Station project. *(2001 Pan American Plaza. ☎234-8291; www.aerospacemuseum.org. Open daily 10am-4:30pm; extended summer hours. $8, seniors $6, ages 6-17 $3, under 6 and military in uniform free. Free fourth Tu of each month.)* The **Reuben H. Fleet Space Theater and Science Center** houses interactive exhibits and the world's first hemispheric Omnimax theater. *(1875 El Prado Way. ☎238-1233; www.rhfleet.org. Open daily 9:30am-8pm. Exhibit entrance $6.75, with one Omnimax show $11.50; seniors over 65 $6/8.50; children ages 3-12 $5.50/9.50. Exhibit entrance free first Tu of each month.)* The small, ultra-modern **Museum of Photographic Arts (MOPA)** features contemporary photography in 8 to 10 exhibits per year. Its film program ranges from cult classic film festivals to technical and thematic examination of more serious cinematic works. *(☎238-7559; www.mopa.org. Open M-W and F-Su 10am-5pm, Th 10am-9pm. $6, students $4. Free 2nd Tu of each month. Theater admission $5, students $4.50.)* The **San Diego Museum of Art** has a collection ranging from ancient Asian to contemporary Californian works. At the adjoining outdoor **Sculpture Garden Court,** there's a sensuous Henry Moore piece. *(Museum ☎232-7931; www.sdmart.org. Open Su and Tu-Sa 10am-6pm, Th 10am-9pm. $8, seniors and college students $6, ages 6-17 $3; special exhibits $2-20 more.)* The fragrant **Botanical Building** looks like a giant, wooden birdcage. The orchid collection is particularly striking among the murmuring fountains. The **Desert Garden** is in full bloom from January to March, while the roses are best admired between April and December. *(2200 Park Blvd. ☎235-1100, tour info 235-1121. Botanical Building open M-W and F-Su 10am-4pm. Free.)* Constructed in 1937, the **Old Globe Theater** is the oldest professional theater in California. *(☎239-2255; www.theoldglobe.org. Call for listings, show times, and ticket prices.)*

OLD TOWN. In 1769, Father Serra, supported by a brigade of Spanish infantry, established the first of 21 missions that would eventually line the California coast in the area now known as Old Town. The remnants of this early settlement and its Mexican restaurants have become one of San Diego's tourist mainstays. The most popular of the area's attractions, the **State Park's** early 19th-century buildings contain museums, shops, and restaurants. **Seely Stable** houses a huge museum of 19th-century transportation, namely of the horse and carriage. *(☎220-5427; open daily 10am-5pm. Tours every hr. 11am-2pm.)* The **Whaley House** stands on the site of San Diego's first gallows and is one of two **official haunted houses** recognized by the State of California. *(2482 San Diego Ave. ☎298-2482, tours 293-0117; open daily 10am-4:30pm; entrance closes 4pm. $5, seniors $4, ages 3-12 $2.)* The stout adobe walls of the **Serra Museum** were raised at the site of the original fort and mission in 1929. *(In Presidio Park. ☎279-3258. Open summer Su and Tu-Sa 10am-4:30pm; Sept.-May Su and F-Sa 10am-4:30pm. $5; seniors, students, and military $4, ages 6-17 $2.)*

CORONADO ISLAND. While cultural and business centers downtown make San Diego a world-class city, it is the sandy coast that brings the city near perfection. A slender 7 mi. strip of hauled sand known as the "Silver Strand" tethers the lovely peninsula of **Coronado Island** to the mainland down near Imperial Beach. Famous for its elegant colonial Hotel Del Coronado, the island is perfect for strolling, blading, or biking over 7 mi. of paved trails, browsing through the quaint downtown area, or watching the water babies enjoy frothy waves that break along the southern shore. The birthplace of American naval aviation, the **North Island Naval Air Station,** comprises the northern chunk of the island. Also among the island's many military enterprises is the training area of the elite **Navy SEAL (sea, air, and land)** special forces teams. Coronado's most famed sight is its Victorian-style **Hotel Del Coronado,** one of America's largest wooden buildings. The long white verandas and the vermilion spires of the "Del" were built in 1888. It has since become one of the world's great hotels (rooms start at $270 per night), hosting 10 presidents and one blonde bombshell—Marilyn Monroe's 1959 *Some Like it Hot* was filmed here. *(1500 Orange Ave. ☎435-6611. Tours depart from the lobby of the Glorietta Bay Inn, 1630 Glorietta Bay Blvd. ☎435-5993. Tours Tu, Th, Sa 11am. $8.)* Built in 1969, the graceful **Coronado Bridge** guides cars to Coronado along I-5. Bus #901 follows the same route, carrying passengers from the Hotel Del Coronado to San Diego and back *($2.25).*

OCEAN, MISSION & PACIFIC BEACHES. Much of San Diego's younger population is drawn to these communities by the surf and hopping nightlife; noisy bars and grills crowd these shores (see **Food,** p. 905, and **Nightlife,** p. 909). It is said that home-grown and earthy **Ocean Beach (O.B.)** is what the world would be like if the hippies had lasted past the 70s. Anglers can cast from the Western Hemisphere's longest fishing pier. Farther north, **Mission Beach,** at the corner of W. Mission Bay Dr. and Mission Blvd., is a people-watcher's paradise. **Belmont Park,** a combination amusement park and shopping center, draws a youthful crowd. **Pacific Beach** and its boisterous Garnet Ave. is home to the best nightlife. **Ocean Front Walk** is packed with joggers, walkers, cyclists, and the usual beachfront shops.

SEA WORLD. Take Disneyland, subtract most of the rides, add a whole lot of fish and marine life, and you've got Sea World. Though critics have long condemned the practice of training highly intelligent marine mammals, the goofy shows are surprisingly charming. The A-list poster-whale is the killer whale **Shamu,** whose signature move is a cannonball splash that soaks anyone in the first 20 rows. The best show in the park, however, is **Fools with Tools,** a takeoff with seals and sea otters on Tool Time from the TV show *Home Improvement.* There are also impressive habitats for sharks, penguins, and the endangered manatee. Even the most popular events occur only a few times daily, so take a quick look at the schedule. *(☎226-3900; www.seaworld.com. Open daily summer 9am-11pm. The park opens at 10am in winter, but closing hours vary. $45, ages 3-9 $35. Parking $7, RVs $9.)*

NIGHTLIFE & ENTERTAINMENT

Nightlife in San Diego isn't centered around any one strip, but scattered in several distinct pockets of action. Upscale locals and party-seeking tourists flock to the **Gaslamp Quarter.** The **Hillcrest** area, next to Balboa Park, draws a young, largely gay crowd to its clubs and dining spots. Away from downtown, the **beach areas** (especially Garnet Ave. in Pacific Beach) are loaded with clubs, bars, and cheap eateries that attract college-age revelers. The city's definitive source of entertainment info is the free *Reader*, found in shops, coffeehouses, and visitors centers. Listings can also be found in the *San Diego Union-Tribune's* Thursday "Night and Day" section. If cruisin' and boozin' isn't your idea of nightlife, you can spend a more sedate evening at one of San Diego's excellent theaters, such as the **Balboa Theatre,** 225 Broadway Ave. (☎544-1000), and the **Horton Grand Theatre,** 444 4th Ave. (☎234-9583), both downtown. The **La Jolla Playhouse,** 2910 La Jolla Village Dr., presents shows on the UCSD campus. (☎858-550-1010; www.lajollaplayhouse.com.)

CLUBS & BARS

Croce's Top Hat Bar and Grille and **Croce's Jazz Bar,** 802 5th Ave. (☎233-4355), at F St. in the Gaslamp. Ingrid Croce, widow of singer Jim Croce, created this rock/blues bar and classy jazz bar side-by-side on the first floor of the historic Keating building. Live music nightly. Cover $5-10, includes 2 live shows. Top Hat open F-Sa 7pm-1:30am. Jazz bar open daily 5:30pm-12:30am with shows starting at 8:30pm.

Pacific Beach Bar and Grill and **Club Tremors,** 860 Garnet Ave. (☎858-483-9227), one of the only dance clubs in Pacific Beach. Live DJ packs the 2-level dance floor with a young and oh-so-hip crowd. The Bar and Grill has respectable food, more than 20 beers on tap, and live music on Sundays. Cover $5 if you enter through Club Tremors, but the same club is accessible through the Grill for free, so start there. Club open Tu-Sa 9pm-1:30am; bar open 11am-1:30am; kitchen closes midnight.

Canes Bar and Grill, 3105 Oceanfront Walk (☎858-488-1780 or 858-488-9690), in **Mission Beach.** One of the best live music venues in the city, this beachside bar has unbeatable sunset views from the second story terrace, and a DJ and dancing every night until 2am. Directly on the water. Canes features standard Mexican fare, and the Tacos Supremas ($9-10) are a favorite. Open daily 11am-2am.

The Casbah, 2501 Kettner Blvd. (☎232-4355). Eddie Vedder of the alternative rock legend Pearl Jam owns this intimate nightspot, one of the best live music venues in the city. Cover varies, but it is always 21+. Call ahead for a schedule, as sometimes tickets sell out. Hours vary, usually 5pm-2am.

The Comedy Store, 916 Pearl St. (☎858-454-9176), in La Jolla. Sister to the landmark Hollywood club. Go for your big break on open mic Su nights. 21+. 2-drink min. Drinks $3. Shows W-Sa 8 and 10:30pm. W-Th $5-10, F $15, Sa $20.

The Flame, 3780 Park Blvd. (☎295-4163), in Hillcrest. One of the most popular lesbian dance clubs in the nation. 21+. Open daily 5pm-2am.

Bourbon Street, 4612 Park Blvd. (☎291-0173), in **University Heights.** A perennially popular piano bar with a gay following. Open M-F 2pm-2am, Sa-Su 11am-2pm.

CALIFORNIA

DAYTRIPS FROM SAN DIEGO

LA JOLLA. Pronounced *la-HOY-a*, this affluent seaside locality houses few budget options, but offers some of the finest public beaches in the San Diego area. *(Take the Ardath Exit west from I-5 or bus #30 or 34 from downtown.)* The **La Jolla Cove** is popular with scuba divers, snorkelers, and brilliantly colored Garibaldi goldfish. Wander south along the cliffs to a striking semi-circular inlet known as **The Children's Pool,** whose inhabitants are a famously thriving community of sea lions. Some of the best breaks in the county can be found in La Jolla at **Tourmaline Beach** and **Wind 'n Sea Beach.** However, these are notoriously territorial spots, so outsiders might be advised to surf elsewhere. **La Jolla Shores** has gentle swells ideal for new surfers, boogie boarders, and swimmers.

Next to La Jolla Shores, the **Birch Aquarium at the Scripps Institute of Oceanography** has great educational exhibits including a tank of oozing jellyfish, a large collection of seahorses, and a 70,000-gallon kelp and shark tank. *(2300 Expedition Way. ☎858-534-3474; http://aquarium.ucsd.edu. Open daily 9am-5pm. $9.50, students with ID $6.50, seniors $8, ages 3-17 $6. Parking $3.)* The **San Diego Museum of Contemporary Art** shares its rotating collection of pop, minimalist, and conceptualist art from the 1950s with the downtown branch. With high ceilings, ocean views, and light-filled spaces, the museum is as visually stunning as its art. *(700 Prospect St. ☎858-454-3541. Open M-Tu and F-Su 11am-5pm, Th 11am-7pm. $6; students, seniors, military, and ages 12-18 $2. Free third Tu and first Su of every month.)* Be sure to check out the terraces and buttresses of **Geisel Library** at the **University of California San Diego (UCSD),** a space-age structure endowed by La Jolla resident Theodore Geisel, better known by his middle name as the late and beloved children's books author, Dr. Seuss. *(☎858-534-2208. Open M-F 7am-9pm, Sa-Su 7am-5:30pm.)*

ESCONDIDO. A look at the free-roaming endangered species of the 2100-acre **San Diego Wild Animal Park** is an essential part of any trip to San Diego. While some of the exhibits are similar to any other zoo, the highlight of the park is the large enclosures where many species roam freely. Rhinos, giraffes, gazelles, and tigers can be found on the park plains. The open-air **Wgasa Bush Line Railway,** a 1hr. monorail safari included in park admission, travels through four created habitat areas. The park has typical shops, restaurants, and animal shows, but for adventure, try the 1 mi. Heart of Africa hike. For those willing to shell out more money, the open-air **Photo Caravan** and the **Roar and Snore** overnight camping safari offer up-close and personal views of many animals. *(From I-15, take the Via Rancho Pkwy. Exit ☎747-8702; www.wildanimalpark.org. Rail tours June-Aug. 9:30am-9pm; Sept.-May 9:30am-4pm; sit on the right if possible. Parking $6. Park open daily 9am, closing times vary with the season. $26.50, ages 3-11 $19.50. Discounts are often available at tourist bureaus and hotels.)*

Escondido (pop. 125,000) lies 30 mi. north of San Diego, amid rolling, semi-arid hills that blossom with wildflowers in the spring. The **San Diego North Convention and Visitors Bureau,** 360 N. Escondido Blvd., gives info on Escondido, the surrounding countryside, and the beach cities to the west. (☎745-4741, 24hr. hotline 800-848-3336. Open M-F 8:30am-5pm.) **Greyhound** (☎745-6522) stops at 700 W. Valley Pkwy. and sends seven buses per day to San Diego ($9) and 12 to L.A. ($13).

TIJUANA ☎664

In the shadow of sulfur-spewing factories and the fences of the U.S.-Mexican border lies the most notorious specimen of border subculture: Tijuana (pop. 2 million; often referred to as "TJ"). The city's cheap booze, haggling vendors, and kitschy hedonism attract 30 million U.S. visitors each year. *Revolución,* the city's main strip, reverberates with *mariachi* bands, thumping nightclubs, and eager tourists unloading cash. The city has recently made a conscious effort to clean up, virtually eliminating sex shops and prostitution from the town center. This is not to say Tijuana has lost its sleazy edge; TJ is one of the largest ports of entry for illegal drugs and undocumented migrants into the U.S. As an introduction to Mexican culture, TJ is about as unrepresentative and unrepentant as they come.

ORIENTATION & PRACTICAL INFORMATION. For the vast majority of visitors, Tijuana simply *is* **Avenida Revolución,** in the middle of **Zona Centro,** the tourist hot spot. *Calles* run east-west and are named and numbered; *avenidas* run parallel to Revolución and perpendicular to the *calles.* The **Tourist Office** is located in the small free-standing booth on the corner of Revolución and Calle 3. English-speaking staff offer good maps and advice. (☎685 2210; open M-Th 10am-4pm, F-Su 10am-7pm. Other branches at the Mexicoach station and at the border crossing.) The **Customs Office** is at the border on the Mexican side after crossing the San Ysidro bridge. (☎683 1390; open 24hr.) **Consulates: Canada,** Gérman Gedovius 10411-101 (☎684 0461, after hours emergency 800 706 2900), in the Zona Río. Open M-F 9am-1pm. **UK,** Salinas 1500 (☎681 8402, after-hours emergency 681 5320), in Col. Aviación, La Mesa. Open M-F 9am-5pm. **US,** Tapachula Sur 96 (☎622 7400 or 681 8016), in Col. Hipódromo, adjacent to the racetrack southeast of town. In an **emergency,** call the San Diego office at ☎619-692-2154 and leave a message; an officer will respond. Open M-F 8am-4pm. Banks along Constitución **exchange money.** Banamex, Constitución at Calle 4, has shorter lines (☎688 0021; open M-F 8:30am-4:30pm) than the more central **Bital,** Revolución 129 at Calle 2. (☎688 1914. Open M-F 8am-7pm, Sa 8am-3pm.) Both have 24hr. **ATMs.** *Casas de cambio* offer better rates but may charge commission and refuse to exchange travelers' checks. In general, the exchange rate between pesos and U.S. dollars hovers around 10 to 1. **Emergency:** dial ☎060. **Police:** (☎685 6557, specialized tourist assistance 688 0555), Constitución at Calle 8. English spoken. **Hospital General,** Centenario 10851 (☎684 0237 or 684 0922), in the Zona Río. **Post Office:** on Negrete at Calle 1. (☎684 7950. Open M-F 8am-5pm, Sa 9am-1pm.) **Postal Code:** 22000. **Area Code:** 664.

ACCOMMODATIONS & FOOD. As a general rule, hotels in Tijuana become less reputable the farther north you go. Avoid any in the area downhill from Calle 1 (the Zona Norte). Rooms at some motels may not fit the standards of cleanliness expected by U.S. travelers. **Hotel Colonial ❷,** Calle 6a 1812, between Constitución and Niños Héroes, has large, very clean rooms with A/C and private baths in a quieter, residential neighborhood. Singles and doubles 260 pesos. **Hotel Perla de Occidente ❶,** at Mutualismo 758, between Calles 1a and 2a, four blocks from Revolución, also has private baths. (☎685 1358. Singles 150 pesos; doubles 300 pesos.) For those too squeamish for Tijuana's truly budget offerings, **Hotel La Villa de Zaragoza ❸,** Madero 1120, between Calles 7a and 8a, has semi-affordable luxury in the form of spacious rooms, TV, phone, king-sized beds, and many clean towels. Laundry, room service, and 24hr. security keep you and your car very safe. (☎685 1832. Singles from 393 pesos; doubles 474 pesos. Reservations accepted.)

As with most things in Tijuana, loud, in-your-face promoters try to herd tourists into the overpriced restaurants lining **Revolución.** For ultra-cheap food, **taco stands ❶** all over the *centro* sell several tacos or a *torta* for 10 pesos. The supermarket **Calimax** is at Calle 2 at Constitución. (☎633 7988. Open 6am-midnight.) **La Cantina de los Remedios ❷,** Diego Rivera 19, in the Zona Río, has competing *mariachis,* lots of tequilas, and a big crowd. Authentic Mexican cuisine starts at 75 pesos and extends well beyond the usual options. (☎634 3065. Open M-Th 1pm-midnight, F-Sa 1pm-2am, Su 1-10pm.) **Restaurante Ricardo's Tortas ❶,** at Madero and Calle 7, serves the best *tortas* in town (25-40 pesos). Try the *super especial,* with ham, *carne asada,* cheese, avocado, tomato, and mayo. (☎685 4031. Open 24hr.)

SIGHTS & FIGHTS. Many of the most entertaining sights in town are right on Revolución. While the so-called "attractions" of the main tourist drag tend toward mind-numbing predictability, Tijuana's cultural assets and parks counter its one-dimensional image. Explore these areas and go home with a less impressive collection of straw hats but a more balanced sense of the city's life. The huge sphere and plaza of Tijuana's cultural center, **Centro Cultural Tijuana (CECUT),** is the most visually striking feature of Paseo de los Héroes. The superb **Museo de las Californias** traces the history of the peninsula from its earliest inhabitants through the Spanish conquest to the Mexican-American war and the 20th century. (☎687 9633. Museum open daily 10am-7pm. 20 pesos, students and children 12 pesos.) Pleasant walks, rides, an open-air theater, and a small zoo await at the sprawling state-run park of **Parque Morelos,** Blvd. de los Insurgentes 26000. (Take an orange and grey communal cab for 5 pesos on Calle 4 and Madero. ☎625 2470. Open Tu-Su 9am-5pm. Adults 5 pesos, children 2 pesos; parking 10 pesos.) If you're in town on the right Sunday, you can watch the graceful and savage battle of *toreador* versus bull in one of Tijuana's two bullrings. **El Toreo de Tijuana,** southeast of town just off Agua Caliente, hosts the first round of fights. (Catch a bus on Calle 2a west of Revolución. Alternate Su, May-July.) The seaside **Plaza Monumental** hosts the second round (Aug.-Oct.). Mexicoach sends buses (round-trip U.S.$4) to Plaza Monumental on fight days. Or take the blue-and-white local buses (5 pesos) on Calle 3a at Constitución all the way down Calle 2a. Tickets to both rings go on sale at the gate (☎685 1510 or 685 1219) or at the Mexicoach office (☎685 1470) on Revolución between Calles 6A and 7a the Wednesday before a fight (tickets 95-400 pesos).

NIGHTLIFE. In the 1920s, Prohibition drove U.S. citizens south of the border to revel in the forbidden nectars of cacti, grapes, and hops. The flow of North Americans thirsty for booze remains unquenched, with many taking advantage of Mexico's drinking age (18) to circumvent U.S. prohibitions. Stroll down Revolución after dusk and you'll be bombarded with thumping music, neon lights, and abrasive club promoters. Gay and lesbian clubs cluster in the southern part of the *centro* around Calle 6a and 7a or down the hill to the north of Calle 1a. **Animale,** Revolución at Calle 4a, is the biggest, glitziest, and loudest hedonistic haven in Tijuana. Watch out—the similarly named Animale Continental next door is an altogether more "adult" experience. (Open daily 10am-4am.) A sublimely wacky, tacky world of life-sized plaster clowns and an authentic yellow school bus can be found at **Iguanas-Ranas,** Revolución at Calle 3a. (☎685 1422. Open M-Th 10am-2am, F-Su 10am-5am.) At **People's,** Revolución and Calle 2a, fluorescent constellations and crudely painted sportsmen decorate the terrace, and revelers guzzle 10 beers for U.S.$15. (☎688 2706. Open M-Th 10am-2am, F-Su 10am-4am.)

THE CALIFORNIA DESERT

California's desert can be one of the most beautiful places in the world; it can also be the loneliest. Roads cut through endless expanses of barren earth and landscapes that seem untouched by human existence. Exploration turns up elusive treasures: diverse flora and fauna, staggering topographical variation, and scattered relics of the American frontier. Throughout the year, the desert transforms from a pleasantly warm refuge to an unbearable wasteland, and back again.

PALM SPRINGS ☎760

From the Cahuilla Indians to today's geriatric fun-lovers, the oasis of Palm Springs (pop. 43,520) has always attracted many. With warm winters, celebrity residents, and more pink than *Miami Vice,* this city is a sunny break from everyday life.

Mt. San Jacinto State Park, Palm Springs' primary landmark, offers outdoor recreation like hiking and cross-country skiing. If the 10,804 ft. peak seems too strenuous, the world-famous **Palm Springs Aerial Tramway** can whisk you to the top in 10min. (☎325-1449 or 888-515-8726. Trams run at least every 30min. M-F 10am-8pm, Sa-Su 8am-8pm. Round-trip $21, seniors $19, ages 3-12 $14, 2 and under free.)

Palm Springs' namesake, the **Desert Hot Springs Spa,** 10805 Palm Dr., features eight naturally heated mineral pools, saunas, massages, and body wraps. (☎800-808-7727; open daily 8am-10pm. M and W $5; Tu $3; Th women $5, men $3; F men $5, women $3; Sa-Su $6. After 3pm weekdays $3, weekends $4, holidays $7.) Prep for nearby Joshua Tree at **Uprising Rockclimbing Center,** 1500 Gene Autry Trail, a gigantic outdoor structure, the only one of its kind in the U.S. (☎888-254-6266. Open Sept.-June M-F 10am-8pm, Sa-Su 10am-6pm; July-Aug. Tu-F 4-8pm, Sa-Su 10am-6pm. Day pass $15, equipment rental $7, lessons $45+ per day.)

Like most famous resort communities, Palm Springs caters to those seeking a tax shelter, not a night's shelter. Nonetheless, affordable lodgings are fairly abundant, especially in summer. **Orchid Tree Inn ❺,** 251 S. Belardo Rd., has large rooms with tasteful Spanish ambience overlooking a lush courtyard. (☎325-2791. 1- or 2-person rooms from July-Aug. $79; winter $110-175. Weekend rates $15-20 more. Studios, suites, and bungalows also available.) Palm Springs offers a variety of great food, from classic greasy-spoons to ultra-trendy fusions. Authentic and inexpensive Thai cuisine is served at **Thai Smile ❷,** 651 N. Palm Canyon Dr. Don't miss the $5 lunch specials. (☎320-5503; open daily 11:30am-10pm.) The promise of delicious Italian foods draws crowds to **Banducci's Bit of Italy ❸,** 1260 S. Palm Canyon Dr. For a treat, try the rich fettucine alfredo ($13) that comes with antipasto, minestrone soup, and buttery garlic bread. (☎325-2537. Entrees $8-15. Open daily 5-10pm.) To experience Palm Springs' heralded nightlife, head to **Village Pub,** 266 S. Palm Canyon Dr., to relive your college glory days by swilling beer and grooving to folksy live rock. (☎323-3265; open daily 11am-2am.)

Greyhound, 311 N. Indian Canyon Dr. (☎325-2053), runs buses to: L.A. (7 per day, one-way $19.50-21); San Diego (7 per day, $23.50); Las Vegas (6 per day, weekdays $53-59). **SunBus** covers Coachella Valley cities (☎343-3451. $0.75). **Visitor Info: Chamber of Commerce,** 190 W. Amado Rd. (☎325-1577. Open M-F 8:30am-4:30pm.) **Post Office:** 333 E. Amado Rd. (☎322-4111. Open M-F 9am-5pm, Sa 9am-1pm.) **Postal Code:** 92262; General Delivery 92263. **Area Code:** 760.

JOSHUA TREE NATIONAL PARK ☎760

When devout Mormon pioneers crossed this faith-testing desert in the 19th century, they named the enigmatic tree they encountered after the Biblical prophet Joshua. The tree's crooked limbs resembled the Hebrew general, and seemed to beckon these Latter-Day pioneers to the Promised Land. Joshua Tree National Park inspires reverence in those who happen upon it. Piles of wind-sculpted boulders, guarded by eerie Joshua Trees, are offset by five lushly Edenic oases.

ORIENTATION & PRACTICAL INFORMATION. The park is ringed by three highways: **Interstate 10** to the south, **Route 62 (Twentynine Palms Highway)** to the west and north, and **Route 177** to the east. The north entrances to the park are off Rte. 62 at the towns **Joshua Tree** and **Twentynine Palms.** The south entrance is at **Cottonwood Spring,** off I-10 at Rte. 195, southeast of Palm Springs. The **park entrance fee,** valid for a week, is $5 per person, $10 per car. **Visitor Info: Headquarters and Oasis Visitor Center,** 74485 National Park Dr. (☎367-5500; www.nps.gov/jotr. Open daily 8am-5pm.) **Post Office:** 73839 Gorgonio Dr. (☎367-1161), in Twentynine Palms. Open M-F 8:30am-5pm, Sa 9am-noon. **Postal Code:** 92277. **Area Code:** 760.

ACCOMMODATIONS & CAMPING. Most campgrounds in the park operate on a first-come, first-camp basis. Group reservations can be made at Cottonwood, Sheep Pass, Indian Cove, and Black Rock Canyon online at www.nps.gov/jotr. All established sites have tables, firepits, and pit toilets, but no hookups. **Indian Cove ❶,** 3200 ft., on the north edge of Wonderland of Rocks, is a popular spot for climbers. (Sites $10; group sites $20-35.) **Jumbo Rocks ❶,** 4400 ft., near

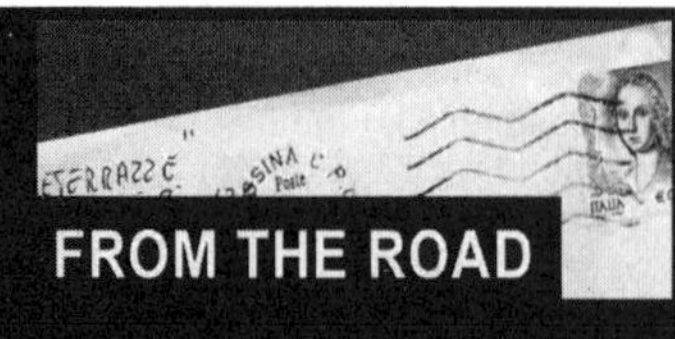

FROM THE ROAD

THE LONE CAMPER

When I approached Borrego Springs at night, the only life in sight was the ghostly desert underbrush silhouetted by the full moon. I compared myself (in my trusty red Cherokee) to the Lone Ranger, riding Trigger under the stars, but as darkness settled in, camping alone in the sand seemed somehow less appealing. I drove to the first motel I could find, but the cheapest room was $60. I did the math–that was 55 Slurpees, 12 GI Joes, or 240 chances at a Vegas quarter slot–and headed back to my car. After finding the nearest campground in Anza Borrego, I circled a site in my car for 20 min. When I finally decided the site was secure, without apparent wild animal or tarantula infestations, I moved in for the kill, setting up my tent 12 ft. from a well-lit shower station.

As it turned out, the night was perfect for desert camping. A full moon hung overhead among stars and a desert breeze kept the temperature around 80°F, which felt like a cold front. I drifted off at around 2am to the sounds of a soft breeze and the howl of a distant coyote. Hours later I woke up groggy and sweating bullets. By 7am, the sun was blazing and the desert heat was unbearable. Here I learned the most important lesson of desert camping: enjoy the cool dark while you can by shutting your fool eyes and going to sleep.

- Jay Gierak, 2004

Skull Rock Trail on the eastern edge of Queen Valley, is the highest and coolest campground. (Free.) Experienced campers can register for a **backcountry permit** at the Visitors Center or at self-service boards throughout the park. Those who can't stomach desert campgrounds will find inexpensive motels in Twentynine Palms. The **29 Palms Inn ❹,** 73950 Inn Dr., is an attraction in its own right, with 19 rooms facing the Mara Oasis. Robert Plant composed "29 Palms" here. (☎367-3505; www.29palmsinn.com. Reservations required Feb.-Apr. Doubles June-Sept. Su-Th $50-75, F-Sa $75-115; Oct.-May $10-20 extra. Cottages for 4-8 available.)

OUTDOOR ACTIVITIES. Over 80% of Joshua Tree is designated wilderness, safeguarding it against development and paved roads. Hikers eager to enter this primitive territory should pack plenty of water and keep alert for flash floods and changing weather conditions.

A **driving tour** is an easy way to explore the park and linger until **sunset.** All roads are well marked, and signs labeled "Exhibit Ahead" point the way to unique floral and geological formations. One of these tours, a 34 mi. stretch winding through the park from Twentynine Palms to the town of Joshua Tree, provides access to the park's most outstanding sights and hikes. An especially spectacular leg of the road is **Keys View** (5185 ft.), 6 mi. off the park road and just west of Ryan Campground. On a clear day, you can see to Palm Springs and the Salton Sea; the sunrise from here is amazing. The **Cholla Cactus Garden** lies just off the road. Those with 4WD have even more options, including the 18 mi. **Geology Tour Road,** which climbs through striking rock formations and ends in Little San Bernardino Mountains.

Hiking is perhaps the best way to experience Joshua Tree. On foot, visitors can tread through sand, scramble over boulders, and walk among the park's namesakes. Anticipate slow progress even on short walks; the oppressive heat and scarce shade exact a toll. Although the 1 mi. **Barker Dam Trail,** next to Hidden Valley, is often packed with tourists, its (sadly vandalized) petroglyphs and eerie tranquility make it a worthwhile stroll, especially at twilight. From the top of **Ryan Mountain** (3 mi. round-trip), the boulders in the valley look like enormous beasts of burden toiling toward a distant destination. Bring lots of water for the strenuous, unshaded climb to the summit. The Visitors Center has info on the park's other hikes, which range from a 15min. stroll to **Oasis of Mara** to a 3-day trek along the 35 mi. **California Riding and Hiking Trail.** The ranger-led **Desert Queen Ranch Walking Tour** covers a restored ranch ($5; call for reservations).

The crack-split granite of Joshua provides some of the best rock climbing and bouldering on the planet for experts and novices alike. The world-renowned boulders at **Wonderland of Rocks** and **Hidden Valley** are always swarming with hard-bodied climbers, making Joshua Tree the most climbed area in America. Adventurous novices will find thrills at **Skull Rock Interpretive Walk,** which runs between Jumbo Rocks and Skull Rock. The walk has info on local plants and animals in addition to exciting yet non-technical scrambles to the tops of monstrous boulders.

You have made it through our entire Joshua Tree coverage without being subjected to a U2 joke. You're welcome.

DEATH VALLEY NATIONAL PARK ☎760

The devil owns a lot of real estate in Death Valley. Not only does he grow crops (at Devil's Cornfield) and hit the links (at Devil's Golf Course), but the park is also home to Hell's Gate itself. The area's extreme heat and surreal landscape support just about anyone's idea of the Inferno. Winter temperatures dip well below freezing in the mountains and summer readings in the Valley average 115°F. The second-highest temperature ever recorded in the world (134°F in shade) was measured at the Valley's Furnace Creek Ranch on July 10, 1913.

TRANSPORTATION. Cars are virtually the only way to get to and around Death Valley, but conditions are notoriously hard on vehicles. **Radiator water** (*not* for drinking) is available at critical points on Rte. 178 and 190 and Nevada Rte. 374. There are only four **gas stations** in the park, and though prices are hefty, be sure to keep the tank at least half full at all times. Always travel with 2 gallons of water per person per day. In the case of a breakdown, stay in the shade of your vehicle. Of the seven **park entrances,** most visitors choose Rte. 190 from the east. Although this is the steepest entrance, the road is well-maintained and the visitors center is relatively close. But since most of the sights adjoin the north-south road, the day-tripper can see more by entering from the southeast (Rte. 178 W from Rte. 127 at Shoshone) or the north (direct to Scotty's Castle via Nevada Rte. 267). Unskilled mountain drivers in passenger cars should not attempt to enter on the smaller Titus Canyon or Emigrant Canyon Dr. No regular public transportation runs in the Valley. *It goes without saying that attempting to hitchhike through Death Valley is suicide. Don't try to hitchhike through Death Valley. It's suicide.*

PRACTICAL INFORMATION. Visitor Info: Furnace Creek Visitors Center, on Rte. 190 in the Valley's east-central section. (☎786-3244; www.nps.gov/deva. Open daily 8am-6pm.) Ranger stations are at **Grapevine** (☎786-2313), at Rte. 190 and 267 near Scotty's Castle, **Stovepipe Wells** (☎786-2342), on Rte. 190, and **Shoshone** (☎832-4308), at Rte. 127 and 178 outside the Valley's southeast border. Fill up outside Death Valley at Lone Pine, Olancha, Shoshine, or Beatty, NV. **Post Office: Furnace Creek Ranch** (☎786-2223. Open Oct.-mid-May M-F 8:30am-5pm; mid-May-Sept. M, W, F 8:30am-3pm, Tu and Th 8:30am-5pm.) **Postal Code:** 92328. **Area Code:** 760.

ACCOMMODATIONS. Motel rooms in surrounding towns are cheaper than those in Death Valley, but are far from top sights. Never assume rooms will be available, but chances (and prices) will be better in summer. In winter, camping with a stock of groceries saves money and driving time. In summer, camping can get quite uncomfortable. **Stovepipe Wells Village** ❸ is right in Death Valley. (☎786-2387. RV sites available, full hookups $22. Rooms for up to 2 people $50-92; each additional person $11.) The National Park Service maintains nine **campgrounds** in

Death Valley. All have toilets but no showers, and limit stays to 30 days (except Furnace Creek with its 14-day limit). **Backcountry camping ❶** is free and legal, provided you check in at the Visitors Center and camp 2 mi. from your car and any road and a ¼ mi. from any backcountry water source.

HIKING. Death Valley has hiking to occupy the gentlest wanderer and hardiest adventurer. Camera-toters should keep in mind that the best photo opportunities are at sunrise and sunset. Astronomy buffs should speak to the rangers, who often set up telescopes at **Zabriskie Point** to capitalize on the Valley's clear skies. Perhaps the most spectacular sight in the park is the light-hued vista at **Dante's View,** reached by a 13 mi. paved road from Rte. 190. **Badwater,** a briny pool four times saltier than the ocean, is in the lowest point (282 ft. below sea level) in the western hemisphere. The boardwalk provides a closer look at the strange orange floor. **Artist's Drive,** 10 mi. south of the Visitors Center, is a one-way loop that contorts its way through brightly colored rock formations. The loop's early ochres and burnt siennas give way at **Artist's Palette** to vivid green, yellow, periwinkle, and pink mineral deposits in the hillside. About 5 mi. south is **Devil's Golf Course,** a vast expanse of gnarled salt pillars formed by flooding and evaporation where Death Valley is at its most surreal; jagged crystalline deposits, some quite delicate and beautiful, stretch as far as the eye can see.

THE CENTRAL COAST

The 400 mi. stretch of coastline between L.A. and San Francisco embodies all that is purely Californian: rolling surf, a seaside highway built for cruising, dramatic bluffs topped by weathered pines, self-actualizing New Age adherents, and always a hint of the offbeat. This is the solitary magnificence that inspired John Steinbeck's novels and Jack Kerouac's musings. Among the smog-free skies, sweeping shorelines, and dense forests, inland farming communities and old seafaring towns beckon enticingly. The landmarks along the way—Hearst Castle, the Monterey Bay Aquarium, Carmel, Santa Cruz's boardwalk, the historic missions—are well worth visiting, but the real point of the Central Coast is the journey itself.

SANTA BARBARA ☎805

Santa Barbara (pop. 92,500) epitomizes worry-free living. The town is an enclave of wealth and privilege, but in a significantly less aggressive and flashy way than its SoCal counterparts. Spanish Revival architecture decorates the hills that rise over a lively pedestrian district. Santa Barbara's golden beaches, museums, historic missions, and scenic drives make it a frequent weekend escape for the rich and famous, surfers, artists, and backpackers alike.

TRANSPORTATION

Driving in Santa Barbara can be bewildering, as dead-ends, one-way streets, and congested traffic abound. Beware of intersections on State St. that surprise motorists with quick red lights. Many downtown lots and streets offer 1¼hr. of **free parking,** including two underground lots at Pasco Nuevo, accessible by the 700 block of Chapala St. All parking is free on Sundays. **Biking** is a nice alternative; most streets have special lanes. The **Cabrillo Bikeway** runs east-west along the beach from the Bird Refuge to the City College campus. MTD buses run throughout the city.

Flights: Santa Barbara Municipal Airport (☎683-4011; www.flysba.com), in Goleta. Offers intrastate and limited national service.

Trains: Amtrak, 209 State St. (☎963-1015 schedule and fares 800-USA-RAIL/872-7245). *Be careful around the station after dark.* To **L.A.** (5-6hr., 2 per day, $20-25) and **San Francisco** (7hr., 3 per day, $48-68). Reserve in advance. Open daily 6:30am-9pm. Tickets sold until 8pm.

Buses: Greyhound, 34 W. Carrillo St. (☎965-7551), at Chapala St. To **L.A.** (2-3hr., 9 per day, $12) and **San Francisco** (9-10hr., 7 per day, $34). Open M-Sa 5:30am-8pm and 11pm-midnight, Su 7am-8pm and 11pm-midnight. **Santa Barbara Metropolitan Transit District (MTD),** 1020 Chapala St. (☎683-3702), at Cabrillo Blvd. behind the Greyhound station, provides schedules and serves as a transfer point. Open M-F 6am-7pm, Sa 8am-6pm, Su 9am-6pm. $1, seniors and disabled $0.50, under 5 free. The MTD runs a purple electric **crosstown shuttle** from Franklin Center on Montecito St. to Mountain and Valerio, running on Chapala St. Runs M-F 7am-6:30pm. $1. The **downtown-waterfront shuttle** along State St. and Cabrillo Blvd. runs every 10min. Su-Th 10:15am-6pm, F-Sa 10:15am-8pm. Stops marked by blue signs. $0.25.

ORIENTATION & PRACTICAL INFORMATION

Santa Barbara is 92 mi. northwest of L.A. and 27 mi. from Ventura on **U.S. 101** (Ventura Fwy.). Since the town is built along an east-west traverse of shoreline, its street grid is slightly skewed. The beach lies at the south end of the city, and **State Street,** the main drag, runs northwest from the waterfront. The major east-west arteries are U.S. 101 and **Cabrillo Boulevard;** U.S. 101, normally north-south, runs east-west between Castillo St. and Hot Springs Rd.

Visitor Info: Tourist Office, 1 Garden St. (☎965-3021), at Cabrillo Blvd. across from the beach. Hordes of folks clamor for maps and brochures. First 15min. free parking in summer and on weekends, then $1.50 per hr. Open July-Aug. M-Sa 9am-6pm, Su 10am-6pm; Sept.-Nov. and Feb.-June M-Sa 9am-5pm, Su 10am-5pm; Dec.-Jan. M-Sa 9am-4pm, Su 10am-4pm. Outdoor 24hr. computer kiosk. **Hotspots,** 36 State St. (☎564-1637 or 800-793-7666), is an espresso bar with free tourist info, hotel reservation service, and an **ATM.** Cafe open 24hr.; tourist info M-Sa 9am-9pm, Su 9am-4pm.

Police: 215 E. Figueroa St. (☎897-2300).

Medical Services: St. Francis Medical Center, 601 E. Micheltorena St. (☎962-7661), 6 blocks east of State St.

Post Office: 836 Anacapa St. (☎800-275-8777), 1 block east of State St. Open M-F 8am-6pm, Sa 9am-5pm. **Postal Code:** 93102. **Area Code:** 805.

THE LOCAL STORY

FROM BADWATER TO WORSE

In 1977, Al Arnold inaugurated one of the world's most painful endurance races when he ran from Badwater, the lowest point in the western hemisphere, to the top of Mt. Whitney, the highest peak in the contiguous US. It took him 84 hours and he shed 17 pounds. Now this brutal run is the Badwater Ultramarathon.

Each year 70-80 runners embark on this grueling 135 mi.run, enduring scorching temperatures that reach 130°F, 13,000 feet in cumulative elevation change, and 4700 feet of joint-rattling descents. IVs are prohibited and there are no official aid stations. Two-time finisher Greg Minter told the Associated Press "I saw a dinosaur around mile 108." Runners get a belt buckle if they finish.

Pam Reed, a 42-year-old mother from Arizona, has won the past two years, finishing in just under 28 hours. She sustainedherself on an all-liquid diet, including eight Red Bull energy drinks and her support crew raced to spray her down every quarter-mile.

"People I meet there don't brag about it, they just do it," Al Arnold, now 75, told the *Contra-Costa Times.* He addresses the runners every year. When he's done, he shouts "BANG!" at 6am sharp, and they're off.

ACCOMMODATIONS

A 10min. drive north or south on U.S. 101 will reward you with cheaper lodging than that in Santa Barbara proper. **Motel 6** ❹ is always an option—this chain of budget-friendly motels originated in Santa Barbara. **Campsites** can be reserved through Reserve America (☎800-444-7275) up to seven months in advance.

Hotel State Street, 121 State St. (☎966-6586), on the main strip one block from the beach and next to the train station. Welcoming, comfortable, and meticulously clean European-style inn. Common bathrooms are pristine. Rooms have sinks and cable TV; a few have skylights. Reserve ahead. Rooms $50-70; $5-10 higher July-Aug. ❹

Santa Barbara International Tourist Hostel, 134 Chapala St. (☎963-0154; reservations sbres@bananabungalow.com). Great location near the train station, beach, and bustling State St. Bike and surfboard rentals. Laundry. Internet $1 per 20min. Ask about 2- to 3-day camping trips to surrounding areas. Dorm rooms sleep 6-8 people; private rooms have 1 double bed. Dorms $18-20; private rooms $45-55. Under construction at press time; call ahead to ensure you're not sleeping in a pile of plaster. ❷

Traveler's Motel, 3222 State St. (☎687-6009). Take bus #6 or 11 from downtown. Although it's a bit far from the downtown spread, this motel is clean and spacious, and has pastel floral bedspreads to soften the atmosphere and sweeten your stay in the gosh-darn prettiest place on State St. Cable TV, A/C, direct-dial phones, microwaves, and fridges. Complimentary fruit and coffee 7:30-10am. Singles June-Sept. Su-Th $55-70, F-Sa $129-149; Oct.-May Su-Th $40, F-Sa $69-99. Palatial rooms with full kitchenettes $10-$15 more; each additional person (up to 4) $5. ❺

FOOD

Santa Barbara may have more restaurants per capita than anywhere else in the U.S.; finding a place to eat is easy, especially on State and Milpas St. (State St. is hipper while Milpas St. is cheaper.) Ice cream lovers flock to award-winning **McConnel's** ❶, 201 W. Mission St. (☎569-2323. Scoops $2.50. Open daily 10am-midnight.)

Palazzio, 1026 State St. (☎564-1985). Their reproduction of the Sistine Chapel ceiling is nearly as impressive as the enormous pasta dishes ($17-18, $12-14 for half-portion), amazing garlic rolls, and the serve-yourself wine bar. Open Su-Th 11:30am-3pm and 5:30-11pm, F-Sa 11:30am-3pm and 5:30pm-midnight. ❸

Pacific Crepes, 705 Anacapa St. (☎882-1123). This comfortable, classy French cafe is not only filled with the delicious smells of crepe creations, but is *authentique*—owned and run by a French couple who speak French only. Luckily, non-Francophiles can rely on the English menu. The heavenly "Brittany" is topped with fresh strawberries and blueberries, fruit sauce, and ice cream—the perfect dessert ($6.25). Lunch and dinner special $15. Beer, wine, and champagne available. Open Su-Tu and Th-Sa 9am-9pm. ❷

The Taj Cafe, 905 State St. (☎564-8280). Enjoy traditional village-style Indian cooking with all natural ingredients. Taj has tasty items like tandoori chicken in a sweet, tangy mango sauce ($10). Lunch specials $5.50-7.50. Vegetarian entrees galore ($6.50-8). Open M-Th 11:30am-3pm and 5-10pm, F-Sa 11:30am-3pm and 5-11pm. ❷

SIGHTS

Santa Barbara is best explored in three sections—the beach and coast, swingin' State St., and the Missionary Mountains. Essential to discovering local events is the *Independent*, published every Thursday and available at city newsstands. The downtown-waterfront **shuttle** ($0.25) runs from the beach up State St.

SANTA BARBARA ZOO. The delightfully leafy habitat has such an open feel that the animals seem kept in captivity by lethargy alone. A mini-train provides a park tour. There's also a miniaturized African plain where giraffes stroll lazily, silhouetted against the Pacific. *(500 Niños Dr., off Cabrillo Blvd. from U.S. 101. Take bus #14 or the downtown-waterfront shuttle. ☎962-533; open daily 10am-5pm. $8, seniors and ages 2-12 $6, under 2 free. Train $1.50, children $1. Parking $2.)*

BEACHES & ACTIVITIES. Santa Barbara's beaches are breathtaking, lined on one side by flourishing palm trees and on the other by countless sailboats around the local harbor. **East** and **Leadbetter Beaches** flank the wharf on either side. **Skater's Point Park,** along the waterfront on Cabrillo Blvd., south of Stearns Wharf, is a free park for skateboarders. **Beach Rentals** will rent beachgoers a **retro surrey:** a covered, Flintstone-esque bicycle. You and up to eight friends can cruise the beach paths in this stylish buggy. *(22 State St. ☎966-6733. Open daily 8am-8pm. Surreys $15-28 per 2hr., depending on number of riders.)* **Beach House,** 10 State St., rents surfboards and body boards plus all the necessary equipment. *(☎963-1281. Surfboards $7-35; body boards $4-16; wet suits $3-16. Credit card required.)*

BEST SUNSET. For the best sunset view around, have a drink (soda $3.75-4.50, beer and wine $5.50-12) at the bar of the **Four Seasons Biltmore Hotel.** Appetizers run $9-100 (Beluga caviar is $100). This five-star hotel is off-limits to most budgets, but the view of the Pacific is priceless. *(Take Hwy. 101 S to Channel Dr. Exit. 1260 Channel Dr., Montecito. ☎969-2261. Park across the street; valet parking runs to $50 including tip.)*

STATE STREET. State St., Santa Barbara's monument to city planning, runs a straight, tree-lined two miles through the center of the city. Among the countless shops and restaurants are cultural and historical landmarks. Everything that doesn't move has been slathered in Spanish tile. The **Santa Barbara Museum of Art** owns an impressive collection of classical Greek, Asian, and European works, mostly donated by wealthy local residents. *(1130 State St. ☎963-4364. Open Su noon-5pm, Tu-Th and Sa 11am-5pm, F 11am-9pm. Tours Tu-Su noon, 2pm. $7, seniors $5, students ages 6-17 $4, under 6 free. Free Th and first Su of each month.)*

MISSION SANTA BARBARA. Praised as the "Queen of Missions" when built in 1786, the mission was restored after the 1812 earthquake and assumed its present incarnation in 1820. Towers with Moorish windows stand around a Greco-Roman temple and facade and a Moorish fountain bubbles outside. *(At the end of Las Olivas St. Take bus #22. ☎682-4149. Open daily 9am-5pm. Self-guided museum tour starts at the gift shop. $4, under 12 free. Mass M-F 7:30am, Sa 4pm, Su 7:30, 9, 10:30am, noon.)*

SANTA BARBARA BOTANICAL GARDEN. Far from town but close to Mission Santa Barbara, the garden offers an amazing array of flora along meandering paths. Five miles of trails wind through 65 acres of native trees, wildflowers, and cacti. The garden's water system was built by the Chumash and is now one of the last vestiges of the region's native heritage. *(1212 Mission Canyon Rd. ☎682-4726. Open Mar.-Oct. M-F 9am-5pm, Sa-Su 9am-6pm; Nov.-Feb. M-F 9am-4pm, Sa-Su 9am-5pm. Tours M-Th 10:30am, 2pm, Sa 2pm, Su 10:30am; special demonstrations Su and F 2pm, Sa 10:30am. $5; students, seniors, and ages 13-19 $3; ages 5-12 $1; under 5 free.)*

HIKING. Very popular **Inspiration Point** is a 3½ mi. round-trip hike and climbs 800 ft. Half of the hike is an easy walk on a paved road. The other half is a series of mountainside switchbacks. The reward on a clear day is an extensive view of the city, the ocean, and the Channel Islands. Following the creek upstream will lead to **Seven Falls.** *(From Santa Barbara Mission, drive toward the mountains and turn right onto Foothill Rd. Turn left onto Mission Canyon Rd. and continue 1 mi. Bear left onto Tunnel Rd. and drive 1¼ mi. to its end.)* **Rattlesnake Canyon Trail** is a moderate 3½ mi. round-trip hike to Tunnel Trail junction with a 1000 ft. gain. It passes many waterfalls, pools, and secluded spots, but is a highly popular trail—expect company. *(From Santa Barbara Mission, drive toward the mountains and turn right onto Foothill Rd. Turn left onto Mission Canyon Rd. and continue for ½ mi. Make a sharp right onto Las Conas Rd. and travel 1¼ mi. Look for a large sign on the left side of the road.)*

UNIVERSITY OF CALIFORNIA AT SANTA BARBARA (UCSB). This beautiful outpost of the UC system is stuck in Goleta, a shapeless mass of suburbs, gas stations, and coffee shops, but the beachside dorms and gorgeous student body more than make up for the town. The excellent **art museum** is worth visiting. It houses the Sedgwick Collection of 15th- to 17th-century European paintings. *(Museum off U.S. 101. Take bus #11. ☎893-2951. Open Su 1-5pm, Tu-Sa 10am-4pm. Free.)*

SEASONAL EVENTS

One of the most special events in Santa Barbara is not organized by humans. Starting in October, and assembling most densely from November to February, hordes of **monarch butterflies** cling to the eucalyptus trees in Ellwood Grove, just west of UCSB, and at the end of Coronado St. off Hollister Ave.; take the Glen Annie/Storke Rd. Exit off U.S. 101. Other events include: **Santa Barbara International Film Festival** (☎963-0023; www.sbfilmfestival.com), late February to early March, **I Madonnari Italian Street Painting Festival** (☎569-3873), on Memorial Day weekend, and the Pre-Bacchanalian **Summer Solstice Parade and Fair** (☎965-3396), on June 21, 2004, when words, vehicles, religious symbols, and animals are not allowed.

ENTERTAINMENT & NIGHTLIFE

Every night of the week, the clubs on **State Street,** mostly between Haley St. and Canon Perdido St., are packed. This town is full of those who love to eat, drink, and be drunk. Consult the *Independent* to see who's playing on any given night. Bars on State St. charge $4 for beer almost without exception; search for specials.

The Hourglass, 213 W. Cota Street (☎963-1436). Soak in an indoor bath or watch the stars from a private outdoor tub. Towels $1. 2 people $25 per hr.; each extra person $7. $2 student discount, children free with parent. Open Th-Su 5pm-midnight.

Q's Sushi A-Go-Go, 409 State St. (☎966-9177). A tri-level bar, 8 pool tables, and dancing. Chew on some sushi ($3.50-13.50) and accompany with *sake* for $3.50. Happy Hour M-Sa 4-7pm includes 20% off sushi plates and half-priced drinks and appetizers. M Brazilian night. W karaoke. Cover F-Sa after 9pm $5. Open daily 4pm-2am.

Club 634, 634 State St. (☎564-1069). Cocktails, dancing, and 2 large patios. Live bands and DJs. Su and W karaoke, Th Red Bull and vodkas $3, F 5-8pm select beers $1.50. Occasional cover. Open M-F 2pm-2am, Sa-Su noon-2am.

O'Mally's, 525 State St. (☎564-8904). An Irish pub and sports bar. DJs and dancing. Cover charged only 5 times a year during major local events. Open daily 1pm-1:30am.

MONTEREY ☎831

Although luxury hotels and tourist shops abound in Monterey (pop. 33,000) and the *Cannery Row* of Steinbeck fame has all but vanished, many sites retain the city's colorful past. This preservation is, at least in part, due to Monterey's abundant wealth; multi-million-dollar homes and golf courses line the shore and droves of luxury cars cruise the streets, cutting a sharp contrast with Monterey's gritty industrial past.

ROSEBUD. Newspaper magnate and multi-millionaire owner William Randolph Hearst casually referred to it as "the ranch," or in his more romantic moments, "La Cuesta Encantada" (Spanish for the Enchanted Hill). The hilltop estate is an indescribably decadent dreamland of limestone castle, shaded cottages, exquisite pools, fragrant gardens, and Mediterranean *esprit.* The castle rests high on grassy hills sloping down to the Pacific. Officially referred to as the Hearst San Simeon State Historic Monument, it stands as a monument to Hearst's unfathomable wealth and Julia Morgan's architectural genius. While countless memorable cast parties were held on these grounds, the only things ever filmed here were 30 seconds of *Spartacus* and the end of a Kodak Funsaver commercial. Hearst Castle is also famous for what was not filmed here—Orson Welles' *Citizen Kane,* which bears more than a passing resemblance to Hearst's life. Stop by the **Visitors Center** at the base of the hill, which features a surprisingly frank portrait of Hearst's failed days at Harvard University, his central role in yellow journalism, and the scandals of his life. The banisters or staircases are the only things you may touch in the castle, but there's plenty to occupy your eyes. *(☎927-2020, reserve through DESTINET 800-444-4445. Tours from $7)*

PRACTICAL INFORMATION. Monterey-Salinas Transit (MST), 1 Ryan Ranch Rd., runs buses. (☎899-2555. Call M-F 7:45am-5:15pm, Sa 10am-2:30pm.) The free *Rider's Guide,* available on buses, at motels, and at the visitors center, has route info. **Monterey Peninsula Visitor and Convention Bureau:** 150 Olivier St. (☎657-6400 or 888-221-1010; www.montereyinfo.org). **Post Office:** 565 Hartnell St. (☎372-4003. Open M-F 8:30am-5:00pm, Sa 10am-2pm.) **Postal Code:** 93940. **Area Code:** 831.

ACCOMMODATIONS & FOOD. Inexpensive hotels line **Lighthouse Avenue** in Pacific Grove (bus #2, partly covered by #1) and the 2000 block of **Fremont Street** in Monterey (bus #9 or 10). Others cluster along **Munras Avenue** between downtown Monterey and Hwy. 1. The cheapest hotels in the area are in the less appealing towns of Seaside and Marina, just north of Monterey. The **Monterey Carpenter's Hall Hostel (HI-AYH) ❷,** 778 Hawthorne St., one block west of Lighthouse Ave., is a clean, modern, 45-bed hostel. (☎649-0375. Towels $0.50. Linens provided. Free parking lot. Lockout 11am-5pm. Curfew 11pm. Small chore. Reservations essential June-Sept. Dorms $22, non-members $25, ages 7-17 $17, under 6 $13; private rooms for up to 4 start at $60 for 2.) **Del Monte Beach Inn ❹,** 1110 Del Monte Blvd., near downtown and across from the beach, is a Victorian-style inn with pleasant rooms. (☎649-4410. Check-in 2-8pm. Reserve ahead. Rooms with shared bath Su-Th $55-66, F-Sa from $77; rooms with private bath and one with kitchenette $88-99.) Call the **Monterey Parks** line (☎755-4895 or 888-588-2267) for camping info.

Once a hot spot for the canned sardine industry, Monterey Bay now yields crab, red snapper, and salmon. Seafood is bountiful but expensive—early-bird specials (usually 4-6:30pm) are easier on the wallet. **Fisherman's Wharf** has smoked salmon sandwiches ($7) and free chowder samples. Get free samples of fruit, cheese, and seafood at the **Old Monterey Market Place,** on Alvarado St. (☎655-2607. Open Tu 4-8pm.) **Thai Bistro II ❷,** 159 Central Ave., in Pacific Grove, offers quality Thai cuisine in a flower-encircled patio. (☎372-8700. Lunch combos $6. Open daily 11:30am-3pm and 5-9:30pm.) At the vegetarian mecca of **Tillie Gort's ❷,** 111 Central Ave., large portions will please even the most devout carnivore. (☎373-0335. Open daily 8am-10pm; Nov.-May M-F 11am-10pm.)

SIGHTS. The extraordinary **Monterey Bay Aquarium,** 886 Cannery Row, has the **world's largest window;** gaze at an enormous marine habitat with sea turtles, giant sunfish, large sharks, and yellow- and blue-fin tuna. There's a new, provocative exhibit connecting the shape, movement, and beauty of jellyfish to various art forms. Watch the **sea otters** at feeding time. The lines are unbelievable; pick up tickets the day before and save 20-40min. (☎648-4888 or 800-756-3737; www.montereybayaquarium.org. Open daily June-early Sept. and holidays 9:30am-6pm; early Sept.-late May 10am-6pm. $18; students, seniors, and ages 13-17 $16 with ID; disabled and ages 3-12 $9.) Along the waterfront south of the aquarium, **Cannery Row** was once a dilapidated street of languishing sardine-packing plants. Take a peek at the **Great Cannery Row Mural;** local artists have covered 400 ft. of a construction-site barrier on the 700 block with depictions of 1930s Monterey. The second floor "Taste of Monterey" **Wine and Visitors Center,** 700 Cannery Row, offers a taste of the county's booming wine industry with well-priced bottles, winery maps, and a great bay view. (☎888-646-5446. 6 tastings $5. Open daily 11am-6pm.) Catch a glimpse of otters in the wild from **Otter Point,** in Pacific Grove. (Touching an otter is illegal; "harassing" one in Monterey Bay may lead to a $10,000 fine.) In mid-September, the **Monterey Jazz Festival** (☎373-3366), the longest-running in the world, brightens the town. Several companies on Fisherman's Wharf offer critter-spotting boat trips around Monterey Bay. The best time to go is during **gray whale migration season** (Nov.-Mar.), but the trips are hit-or-miss year-round. The lucky spot dolphins frolicking in the currents. Everybody else sees a lot of water. **Chris' Fishing Trips,** 48 Fisherman's Wharf, offers tours and charters. (☎375-5951. Open daily 4am-5pm. 2-3hr. tours May-Nov. 11am and 2pm. $25, under 13 $20. 2hr. gray whale migration tours Dec.-Apr. $18, under 13 $12.)

In nearby Carmel, the amazing 550-acre, state-run wildlife sanctuary of **Point Lobos Reserve** is popular with skindivers and day hikers. From the cliffs, watch otters, sea lions, seals, brown pelicans, and gulls. There are also tidepools, scuba access, and marvelous vantage points for watching the winter whale migration. (☎624-4909. Open daily Apr.-Oct. 9am-7pm; Nov.-Mar. 9am-5pm. $4 per car, seniors $3, free for campers registered with one of the state parks. Divers must call ☎624-8413 or email ptlobos@mbay.net for reservations. Dive fee $7.)

SANTA CRUZ ☎831

One of the few places where the 1960s catchphrase "do your own thing" still applies, Santa Cruz (pop. 56,000) simultaneously embraces sculpted surfers, aging hippies, free-thinking students, and same-sex couples. This small city has both Northern California cool and Southern California fun, whether you find it sipping wheatgrass at poetry readings or gobbling cotton candy on the boardwalk.

ORIENTATION & PRACTICAL INFORMATION. Santa Cruz is on the north tip of Monterey Bay, 65 mi. south of San Francisco. Through west Santa Cruz, Hwy. 1 becomes **Mission Street.** The **University of California at Santa Cruz (UCSC)** blankets the hills inland from Mission St. Southeast of Mission St. lies the waterfront and downtown. By the ocean, **Beach Street** runs roughly east-west. **Greyhound,** 425 Front St. (☎423-1800 or 800-231-2222; open daily 8:30-11:30am and 1-6:45pm and for late arrivals and departures), runs to: **L.A.** (6 per day, one-way $42); San Francisco (5 per day, $11); San Jose (5 per day M-Th, $6). **Santa Cruz Metropolitan Transit District (SCMTD),** 920 Pacific Ave. (☎425-8600; www.scmtd.com; open M-F 8am-4pm), handles local transportation. (Buses run daily 6am-11pm. $1, seniors and disabled $0.40, under 46 in. free; day pass $3/1.10/free.) The **Santa Cruz County Conference and Visitor Council,** 1211 Ocean St. (☎425-1234 or 800-833-3494; www.santacruzca.org), publishes the free *Santa Cruz County Traveler's Guide.* (Open M-Sa 9am-5pm, Su 10am-4pm.) **Post Office:** 850 Front St. (☎426-8184. Open M-F 8:30am-5pm, Sa 9am-4pm.) **Postal Code:** 95060. **Area Code:** 831.

ACCOMMODATIONS & CAMPING. Santa Cruz gets jam-packed in summer, especially on weekends; room rates skyrocket and availability plummets. Nicer motels tend to have more reasonable summer weekend rates, but more expensive rates at other times. Always make reservations. Camping may be the best budget option. **Carmelita Cottage Santa Cruz Hostel (HI-AYH) ❷,** 321 Main St., is a 40-bed Victorian hostel. (☎423-8304. Chores requested. Linen provided. Towels $0.50. Overnight parking free, day permits $1.25. July-Aug. 3-night max. stay. Reception 8-10am and 5-10pm. Lockout 10am-5pm. Strict curfew 11pm. Call for reservations. Dorms $20, members $17, ages 12-17 $15, ages 4-11 $10, ages 3 and under free.) The **Harbor Inn ❺,** 645 7th Ave., is a beautiful 19-room hotel well off the main drag. Summer weekend rates are likely to be lower than others'. In late June, pick plums from the trees out back. (☎479-9731. Check-in 2-7pm; call to arrange late check-in. Check-out 11am. Rooms Su-Th from $75-115, F-Sa from $75-175; low-season $65-105/75-115.) Sleeping on the beach is strictly forbidden. **Big Basin Redwoods State Park ❶,** offers great camping and breezy trails.

FOOD. Santa Cruz offers an astounding number of budget eateries. Fresh local produce sells at the **farmer's market** (W 2:30-6:30pm) at Lincoln and Cedar St. downtown. **Zoccoli's ❷,** 1534 Pacific Ave., is a phenomenal deli that uses only the freshest ingredients. (☎423-1711. Open M-Sa 10am-6pm, Su 11am-5pm.) Healthy, vegetarian Sri Lankan cuisine and incredible flatbread by candlelight can be found at **Malabar ❷,** 1116 Soquel Ave. (☎423-7906. Open M-Th 11am-2:30pm and 5:30-9pm, F 11am-2:30pm and 5:30-10pm, Sa 5:30-10pm. No credit cards.)

SIGHTS. Santa Cruz has a great beach, but the water is frigid. Many casual beachgoers catch their thrills on the **Boardwalk,** a three-block strip of over 25 amusement park rides, guess-your-weight booths, shooting galleries, and corn-dog vendors. It's a gloriously tacky throwback to 50s-era beach culture. Highly recommended is the **Giant Dipper,** the 1924 wooden roller coaster where Dirty Harry met his enemy in 1983's *Sudden Impact.* (Boardwalk open daily May 31-Sept. 6, plus many low-season weekends and holidays. $30 per 60 tickets, with most rides 4 or 5 tickets; all-day pass $25 per person. Mini golf $4.) The **Santa Cruz Wharf** off Beach St. is the longest car-accessible pier on the West Coast. Seafood restaurants and souvenir shops will try to distract you from expansive views of the ocean. Munch on candy from local favorite **Marini's** (☎423-7258) while watching sea lions hang out on rafters beneath the end of the pier.

BEACHES & ACTIVITIES. The **Santa Cruz Beach** (officially named Cowell Beach) is broad, reasonably clean, and packed with volleyball players. Beach access points line Hwy. 1. The best vantage points for **watching surfers** are along W. Cliff Dr. To learn more about surfing, stop at **Steamer's Lane,** the deep water where Hawaiian "Duke" Kahanamoku kick-started California's surf culture 100 years ago. For surfing lessons, contact the **Richard Schmidt Surf School,** 236 San Jose Ave., or ask around for him at the beach. (☎423-0928; www.richardschmidt.com. 1hr. private lesson $65, 2hr. group lesson $70. Lessons include equipment.)

Around the point at the end of W. Cliff Dr. is **Natural Bridges State Beach.** Only one natural bridge remains standing, but the park offers a pristine beach, awe-inspiring tidepools, and tours during **monarch butterfly** season (Oct.-Mar.). In November and December, thousands of the stunning *lepidoptera* swarm along the beach and cover the nearby groves with their orange hues. (☎423-4609. Open daily 8am-dusk. Parking $3, seniors $2, disabled $1.) Parasailing and other pricey pastimes are popular on the wharf. **Kayak Connection,** 413 Lake Ave., offers tours ($40-45), and rents ocean-going **kayaks** at decent rates. (☎479-1121. Open-deck single $33 per day, closed-deck single $37. Paddle, life jacket, brief instruction, and wetsuit included. Open M-F 10am-5pm, Sa-Su 9am-6pm.)

NIGHTLIFE. There are comprehensive events listings in the free *Good Times* and *Metro Santa Cruz*, and in *Spotlight* in Friday's *Sentinel.* The Boardwalk bandstand offers free summertime Friday concerts around 6:30 and 8:30pm. **Caffe Pergolesi,** 418A Cedar St., is a chill coffeehouse/bar with small rooms and a spacious patio for reading, writing, or socializing. (☎426-1775. Open M-Th 6:30am-11:30pm, F-Sa 7:30am-midnight, Su 7:30am-11:30pm.) At modest but lively **99 Bottles Restaurant and Pub,** 110 Walnut Ave., in the heart of downtown, there are really 99 different types of beer. (Happy Hour M and F 4-6pm, Tu-W 4-6pm and 10pm-1:30am, "Thirsty Thursdays" 4pm-1:30am. Open M-Th 11:30am-1:30am, F-Sa 11:30am-2am, Su 11:30am-midnight; kitchen closes 10pm.) Innovative programs are at **Kuumbwa Jazz Center,** 320 Cedar St. (☎427-2227; www.kuumbwajazz.org). The mega-popular gay-straight club **Blue Lagoon,** 923 Pacific Ave., has won many awards including "best place you can't take your parents." (Happy Hour with $3 drinks daily 6-9pm. Su Bloody Marys $3. Cover $2-5. Open daily 4pm-1:30am.) The town's primary music/dance venue is **The Catalyst,** 1011 Pacific Ave. (☎423-1338. Shows W-Sa. Open M-Sa 9am-2am, Su 9am-5pm. Food served Su-Tu 9am-3pm, W-Sa 9am-10pm.)

SAN FRANCISCO ☎415

If California is a state of mind, then San Francisco is euphoria. Welcome to the city that will take you to new highs, leaving your mind spinning, your tastebuds tingling, and your calves aching. Though it's smaller than most "big" cities, the City by the Bay more than compensates for its size with personality. The dazzling views, daunting hills, one-of-a-kind neighborhoods, and laidback, friendly people fascinate visitors and residents. The city manages to pack an incredible amount of vitality into its 47 square miles, from its thriving art communities and bustling shops to the pulsing beats in some of the country's hippest nightclubs and bars.

By California standards, San Francisco is steeped in history. The lineage of free spirits and troublemakers started in the 19th century, with smugglers, pirates, and Gold Rush '49ers. In the 1950s came the brilliant, angry, young Beats, and the late 60s ushered in the most famous of SF rabble rousers—hippies and flower children, who turned one generation on and freaked out another by making love, not war. The queer community became undeniably visible in the 70s as one of the city's most vocal groups. Anti-establishment rallies and movements continue to fill the streets and newspapers. In addition, Mexican, Central American, and Asian immigrants have made SF one of the most racially diverse cities in the United States. For more coverage of the City by the Bay, see *Let's Go: San Francisco 2004*.

INTERCITY TRANSPORTATION

San Francisco is 403 mi. north of Los Angeles and 390 mi. south of the Oregon border. The city lies at the northern tip of the peninsula separating the San Francisco Bay from the Pacific Ocean. San Francisco radiates outward from its docks, which lie on the northeast edge of the 30 mi. peninsula, just inside the lip of the Bay.

The city is 6hr. from L.A. via I-5, 8hr. via U.S. 101, or 9½hr. via Rte. 1. U.S. 101 compromises between velocity and vistas, but the stunning coastal scenery along Rte. 1 makes getting there fun. From inland California, **I-5** approaches the city from the north and south via **I-580** and **I-80,** which runs across the **Bay Bridge** (westbound toll $2). From the north, U.S. 101 and Rte. 1 come over the **Golden Gate Bridge** (southbound toll $3).

Airport: San Francisco International (☎650-821-8211; ground transportation info 650-821-2735; www.flysfo.com), 15 mi. south of downtown via U.S. 101. **San Mateo County Transit (SamTrans;** ☎650-817-1717) runs 2 buses to downtown. Express bus KX (35min.) runs to the Transbay Terminal. $3, seniors at off-peak times and under 17 $1.25. Bus #292 (1hr.) stops frequently along Mission St. $2.20/0.50/1.50.

Trains: Amtrak (☎800-872-7245). Connects from both Oakland and Emeryville to downtown SF ($3.50-7). To **Los Angeles** (8-12hr., 5 per day, $50). **Caltrain** (☎800-660-4287; www.caltrain.org), at 4th and King St. in SoMa (operates M-F 5am-midnight, Sa-Su unreliable due to construction), is a regional commuter train that runs south to Palo Alto ($4.50, seniors and under 12 $2.25) and San Jose ($5.25/2.50), making many stops along the way.

Buses: Greyhound runs buses from the **Transbay Terminal,** 425 Mission St. (☎495-1575), between Fremont and 1st St. downtown. To **Los Angeles** (8-12hr., 25 per day, $45) and **Portland** (14-20hr., 8 per day, $66). **Golden Gate Transit** (Marin County, ☎923-2000; www.goldengate.org), **AC Transit** (East Bay, ☎510-817-1717), and **SamTrans** (San Mateo County) also stop at the terminal.

ORIENTATION

NEIGHBORHOODS

This orientation, like the listings that follow, will move roughly from the tourist-laden western section of downtown San Francisco to the neighborhoods in the south, then over to the residential parts in the west. Neighborhood boundaries get a bit confusing; a good map is a must.

You'll have to visit touristy **Fisherman's Wharf** at least once, and from there, move on to the posh stucco of the **Marina** and cool culture in **Fort Mason.** Just south of the Wharf, **North Beach,** a historically Italian area, overflows with restaurants and cafes in the northeastern corner of the peninsula. Food is the cornerstone of **Chinatown,** the largest Chinese community outside of Asia. To round out the northwest corner of the city, old money presides on ritzy **Nob Hill,** newer money walks its dogs on **Russian Hill,** and retail-heavy **Union Square** is just north of Market St.

The majestic **Golden Gate Bridge** stretches over the Bay from the **Presidio** in the city's northwest corner. Just south of the Presidio, **Lincoln Park** reaches westward to the ocean, while vast **Golden Gate Park** dominates the western half of the peninsula. On the opposite side of the city, the skyscrapers of the **Financial District** crowd down to the **Embarcadero.** City Hall, the Public Library, and Symphony Hall crown a small but impressive cluster of municipal buildings in the **Civic Center,** which lines Market St. and is bounded on the west by wide Van Ness Ave. On the other side of Van Ness Ave., newly hip **Hayes Valley** draws gallery-goers and shoppers. To the west, Union Sq. gives way to the **Tenderloin,** where—despite attempts at urban renewal—drugs, crime, and homelessness prevail. South of Market St. to the east, the **South of Market Area (SoMa)** holds large, glassy attractions near 3rd St. and thumping clubs scattered among industrial buildings down to 14th St.

Fillmore St. leads north to the Victorians of **Pacific Heights.** Further south, the few *udon*-filled blocks of **Japantown** offer Asian fare and shopping opportunities. West of SoMa and Hayes Valley, near Golden Gate Park, sits the former hippie haven of **Haight-Ashbury.** The diners and cafes of the **Castro,** legendary as a "gay mecca," dazzle on Castro and Market St. northwest of the Mission. To the south of the Castro, **Noe Valley** rises up into the spectacular views of **Twin Peaks.**

The very trendy **Mission,** largely populated by Latino residents during the day and super-hip barhoppers by night, takes over south of 14th St., and **Bernal Heights** is on the rise south of the Mission. **Potrero Hill,** often forgotten because of Hwy. 101, offers wonderful eats and a quaint feel. Some interesting strips of activity run among the residential neighborhoods west of Masonic Ave., including the residential **Richmond** and **Sunset Districts.** Just east of the Sunset, **Ocean Beach** runs into the cliffs at **Fort Funston** and the shores of **Lake Merced.** And, of course, if you want to get away from land, you can head to **Alcatraz** and **Angel Island** in the bay.

LOCAL TRANSPORTATION

San Francisco Municipal Railway (**MUNI;** ☎673-6864; www.sfmuni.com) is a system of buses, cable cars, subways, and streetcars and is the most efficient way to get around the city. Runs daily 6am-1am. $1.25, seniors and ages 5-17 $0.35. **MUNI passports** are valid on all MUNI vehicles (1-day $9, 3-day $15, 7-day $20). Weekly Pass ($9) is valid for a single work week and requires an additional $1 to ride the cable cars. **Owl Service** runs limited routes daily 1-5am. Wheelchair access varies among routes; all below-ground stations, but not all above-ground sites, are accessible.

Cable cars: Noisy, slow, and usually crammed full, but charming relics. To avoid mobs, ride in the early morning. The **Powell-Mason (PM)** line, which runs to the wharf, is the most popular. The **California (C)** line, from the Financial District up through Nob Hill, is usually the least crowded, but the **Powell-Hyde (PH)** line, with the steepest hills and the sharpest turns, may be the most fun. $3, seniors and disabled $2, under 6 free; before 7am and after 9pm $1. No transfers.

Bay Area Rapid Transit (**BART;** ☎989-2278; www.bart.org) operates trains along 4 lines connecting San Francisco with the **East Bay,** including Oakland, Berkeley, Concord, and Fremont. All stations provide maps and schedules. There are 8 BART stops in San Francisco proper, but BART is not a local transportation system. Runs M-F 4am-midnight, Sa 6am-midnight, Su 8am-midnight. $1.15-4.90. Wheelchair-accessible.

Car Rental: City, 1748 Folsom St. (☎877-861-1312), between Duboce and 14th St. Compacts from $29-35 per day, $160-170 per week. Small fee for unlimited mileage. 21+; under 25 $8 per day surcharge. Open M-F 7:30am-6pm, Sa 9am-4pm. Additional location: 1433 Bush St. (☎866-359-1331), between Van Ness Ave. and Polk St.

Taxi: Luxor Cab, ☎282-4141. **National Cab,** ☎648-4444.

PRACTICAL INFORMATION

Visitor Info: California Welcome Center (☎956-3493), Pier 39 at the Great San Francisco Adventure. Open Su-Th 9am-9pm, F-Sa 9am-10pm.

Hotlines: Rape Crisis Center, ☎647-7273. **AIDS Hotline,** ☎800-342-2437. **Drug Crisis Line,** ☎362-3400. **Suicide Prevention,** ☎781-0500.

Internet Access: For complete listings in SF, check www.surfandsip.com. The California Welcome Center also hosts an Internet cafe.

Post Office: Union Square Station, 170 O'Farrell St. (☎956-0131), at Stockton St., in the basement of Macy's. Open M-Sa 10am-5:30pm, Su 11am-5pm. **Postal Code:** 94108. **Area Code:** 415, unless otherwise noted. 10-digit dialing required.

ACCOMMODATIONS

Beware that some of the cheapest budget hotels may be located in areas requiring extra caution at night. Reservations are always recommended if possible.

HOSTELS

Adelaide Inn, 5 Isadora Duncan (☎359-1915 or 800-359-1915; www.adelaidehostel.com), at the end of a little alley off Taylor St. between Geary and Post St. in Union Sq. Those needing wheelchair accessibility can arrange for nearby hotel accommodations at Adelaide's rates. Small shared hallway bathrooms. No curfew. Hostel offers shuttle to SFO airport each morning ($8). Reception 24hr. Check-out noon. Reservations recommended. Dorms $24; singles and doubles from $65. ❶

Green Tortoise Hostel, 494 Broadway (☎834-1000; www.greentortoise.com), off Columbus Ave. at Kearny St. in North Beach. Breakfast and kitchen access. Storage lockers $1 (small lockers free), coin laundry, free sauna, and free Internet access. Key deposit $20. Check-in noon. Check-out 11am. 10-day max. stay. Dorms $19-22; private rooms $48-56. No credit cards. ❶

Fort Mason Hostel (HI-AYH), Bldg. #240 (☎771-7277), at the corner of Bay and Franklin St. in Fort Mason. No smoking or alcohol. Movies, walking tours, kitchen, bike storage. Usually booked weeks in advance, but a few beds are reserved for walk-ins. Minor chores expected. Lockers, laundry, parking. Check-in 2:30pm. Check-out 11am. No curfew, but lights-out at midnight. Dorms $24.50. ❶

Hostel at Union Square (HI-AYH), 312 Mason St. (☎788-5604; www.norcalhostels.org), between Geary and O'Farrell St. in Union Square. $5 deposit for locker, iron, board game, or key. 3-week max. stay. Reception 24hr. Quiet hours midnight-7am. Internet $1 per 10min. Tidy and unadorned dorm-style triples and quads $22, non-members $25; private rooms $60/66. Under 13 half-price with parent. ❶

Easy Goin' Travel and California Dreamin' Guesthouse, 3145-47 Mission St. (☎552-8452), at Precita Ave. in the Mission. Additional location at Harrison and 7th, but check-in and booking is here, and a shuttle to Harrison and 7th St. is provided. In-room TVs, kitchen, laundry, Internet access, bike rental, and travel services. 2-night min. stay. Check-in noon. Check-out 11am. $20 security and key deposit. Reservations recommended. Dorm beds $18-19; private rooms $40-43. ❶

San Francisco Hostel-City Center (HI-AYH), 685 Ellis St. (☎474-5721; www.norcalhostels.org). Rooms are spare, but come with perks like cheap Internet access, nightly movie, and listings of walking tours and pub crawls. Check-in 3pm. Check-out noon. Reservations recommended. Dorms $22, nonmembers $25; doubles $66/69. ❶

NO WORK, ALL PLAY

GOT CRABS TOO?

SF is known for its subversive art and cultural festivals; the month of February, though, is reserved for the Dungeness Crab. The month-long **San Francisco Crab Festival** (www.sfvisitor.org/crab) sprawls from Fisherman's Wharf to Union Square during the peak of the crab season. Each year, over two million pounds of crabmeat are imported from the Central California Fishery.

The festivities include the Wine & Spirits Focus, a weekend in which chefs from elite spots such as Hawthorne Lane, Rubicon, and Greens host tastings of their crab delicacies and choice wines. The Crab & Wine Marketplace offers tastings, demonstrations, and activities for crustacean connoisseurs. Throughout February, local businesses on the Wharf offer great crab deals and specials. **Volunteers** are often welcomed for setup, maintenance, and information staffing. Contact the San Francisco Convention & Visitors Bureau (☎283-0106) for more information. In 2004, San Francisco will again **salute the crab** for the month of February, this time with a classic car show in a supporting role.

The Wine & Spirits Focus and the classic car show will take place Feb. 13-6 at Pier 45 from 9am-6pm. The Crab & Wine Marketplace will take place Feb. 28-29 at Fort Mason from 11am-6pm.

Interclub Globe Hostel, 10 Hallam Pl. (☎431-0540), off Folsom St. between 7th and 8th St. in SoMa. MUNI bus #12 to 7th and Howard St. Happening common room has pool table, TV, microwave, and fridge. All rooms have private bath. Key deposit $10. **Passport required**. Internet access. Dorms $19; 3 nights $45; private single or double $50. Low-season rates reduced. No credit cards. ❶

SoMa Inn, 1082 Folsom St. (☎863-7522), between 6th and 7th St. Clean, no-frills rooms on an industrial block of Folsom St. Shared hall bath. Kitchen and Internet access. Reception 24hr. Refundable key deposit $5. Dorms $17; singles $28; doubles $36; triples $66; quads $88. Weekly $100/160/180/330/440. ❶

Downtown San Francisco

ACCOMMODATIONS
Adelaide Inn, **32**
Ansonia Abby Hotel, **30**
Fort Mason Hostel, **1**
Green Tortoise Hostel, **13**
Hotel Triton, **29**
Interclub Globe Hostel, **51**
San Francisco Hostel-City Center (HI-AYH), **39**
San Remo Hotel, **4**
SoMa, **53**

FOOD
Ananda Fuara, **48**
Basil, **50**
The California Culinary Academy, **41**
Chef Jia, **18**
Dottie's True Blue Café, **31**
Golden Gate Bakery, **16**
House of Nanking, **17**
L'Osteria del Forno, **12**
Mario's Bohemian Cigar Store Café, **11**
Patisserie Café, **52**
Pat's Café, **3**
Rico's, **7**
Sushigroove, **8**
Tommy's Joynt, **26**
Zarzuela, **8**

ENTERTAINMENT/NIGHTLIFE
111 Minna, **38**
The Bigfoot Lodge, **19**
Café Royale, **27**
Curran Theatre, **35**
The EndUp, **54**
Geary Theater, **36**
Golden Gate Theater, **44**
Hotel Utah Saloon, **55**
Lefty O'Doul's, **37**
Louise M. Davies Symphony Hall, **46**
The Orpheum, **49**
Velvet Lounge, **14**
Yerba Buena Center for the Performing Arts, **42**

SIGHTS
509 Cultural Center/Luggage Store, **43**
Cable Car Powerhouse and Museum, **20**
City Hall, **47**
City Lights Bookstore, **15**
Coit Tower, **9**
"Crookedest Street in the World", **5**
Giardelli Square, **2**
Grace Cathedral, **25**
Hang, **28**
Justin Herman Plaza, **24**
Maiden Lane, **34**
Martin Lawrence Gallery, **33**
Ross Alley, **21**
San Francisco Art Institute, **6**
San Francisco Museum of Modern Art, **40**
Transamerica Pyramid, **23**
Washington Square, **10**
Waverly Place, **22**
ZEUM, **45**

SEE COLOR INSERTS FOR MORE SAN FRANCISCO MAPS

GUEST HOUSES

Ansonia Abby Hotel, 711 Post St. (☎673-2670 or 800-221-6470), between Jones and Leavenworth St. in Union Square. Free breakfast daily, dinner M-Sa, overnight storage and safety deposit, TV and fridge in every room. Laundry. Check-out 11am. DSL access. Singles $56-66; doubles $66, with bath $79; weekly rates for summer students. ❸

The San Remo Hotel, 2237 Mason St. (☎776-8688; www.sanremohotel.com). Built in 1906, this non-smoking hotel has rooms that are small but elegantly furnished with antique armoires, bedposts, lamps, and complimentary (if random) backscratchers. Friendly staff will book tours, bikes, cars, and airport shuttles and recommend restaurants. Free modem connections. Laundry. Check-in 2pm. Check-out 11am. Reservations required. Singles $55-85; doubles $65-95; triples $95. ❸

The Queen Anne Hotel, 1590 Sutter St. (☎441-2828 or 800-227-3970; www.queenanne.com), at Octavia St. Each room in this beautiful mansion is elaborately decorated with period furnishings. Breakfast, afternoon tea, and sherry served daily. Fireplaces, jacuzzis, and wheelchair-accessible rooms available. All rooms include spacious private bath and TV. "Moderate" rooms from $139; deluxe from $159; suites from $179. ❺

The Parker House, 520 Church St. (☎621-3222 or 888-520-7275; www.parkerguesthouse.com), near 17th St. in the Castro. Regularly voted best BGL B&B in the city. Cable TV and modem ports in every room. Heavenly down comforters. Spa and steam rooms. Breakfast included in a sunny porch overlooking rose gardens. 2-night min. stay on weekends. Check-in 3pm. Check-out noon. Reservations recommended. Rooms with shared bath from $119, with private bath from $139. ❺

The Willows, 710 14th St. (☎431-4770; www.willowssf.com), near Church St. Handmade willow-branch furnishings, window gardens, and kimono bathrobes make for a little glen of queer happiness. Cable TV, VCR. Expanded continental breakfast, evening cocktails, pantry with microwave and fridge, sparkling hall baths, and washbasins in all 12 rooms. Reception 8am-8pm. Singles $100-140; doubles $120-160. ❺

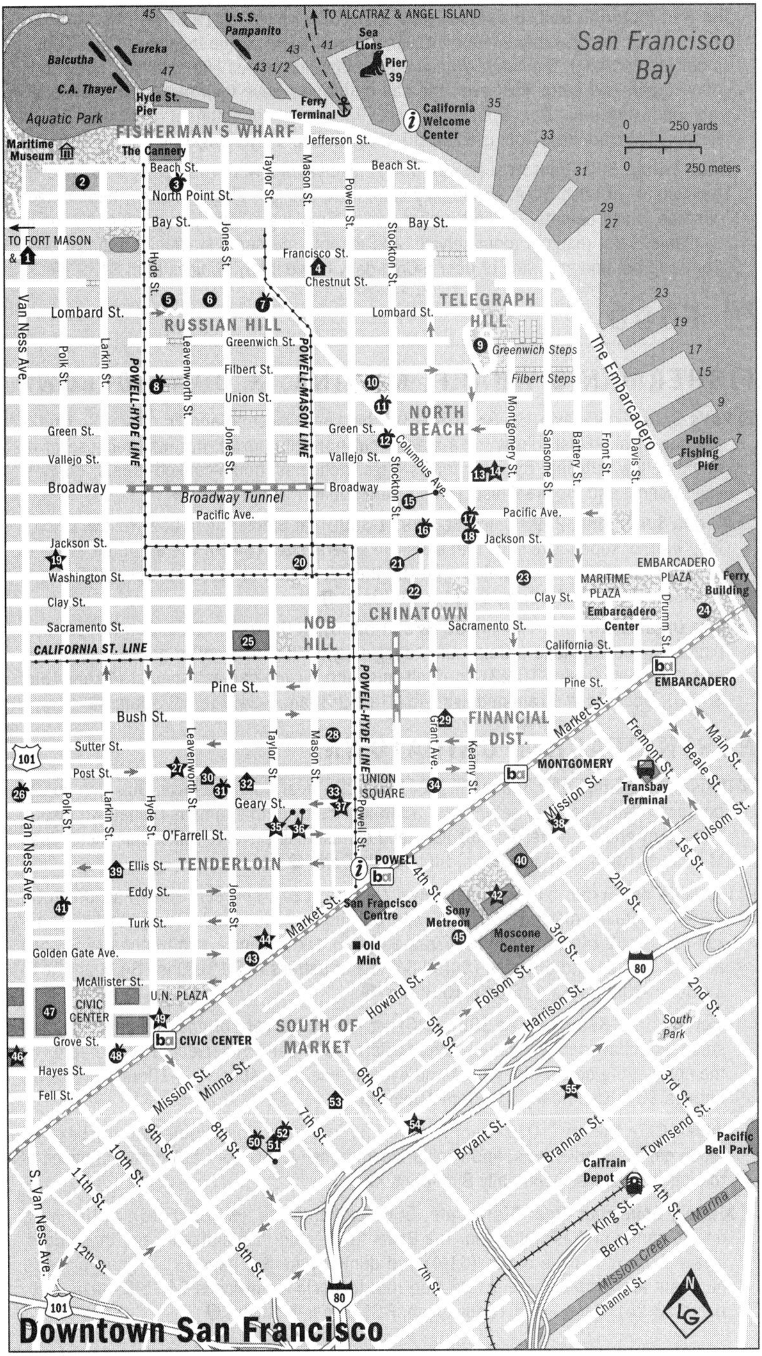
TO ALCATRAZ & ANGEL ISLAND
U.S.S. Pampanito
Sea Lions
Pier 39
San Francisco Bay
Balcutha
Eureka
C.A. Thayer
Hyde St. Pier
Aquatic Park
Ferry Terminal
California Welcome Center
0 250 yards
0 250 meters
FISHERMAN'S WHARF
Maritime Museum
The Cannery
Jefferson St.
Beach St.
North Point St.
Bay St.
TO FORT MASON & 1
Francisco St.
Chestnut St.
Lombard St.
RUSSIAN HILL
TELEGRAPH HILL
Greenwich St.
Greenwich Steps
Filbert St.
Filbert Steps
Union St.
Green St.
Vallejo St.
Broadway
Broadway Tunnel
Pacific Ave.
Jackson St.
Washington St.
Clay St.
Sacramento St.
California St.
CALIFORNIA ST. LINE
POWELL-HYDE LINE
POWELL-MASON LINE
NORTH BEACH
CHINATOWN
NOB HILL
FINANCIAL DIST.
The Embarcadero
Public Fishing Pier
EMBARCADERO PLAZA
MARITIME PLAZA
Embarcadero Center
Ferry Building
EMBARCADERO
MONTGOMERY
Transbay Terminal
Van Ness Ave.
Polk St.
Larkin St.
Hyde St.
Leavenworth St.
Jones St.
Taylor St.
Mason St.
Powell St.
Stockton St.
Columbus Ave.
Grant Ave.
Kearny St.
Montgomery St.
Sansome St.
Battery St.
Front St.
Davis St.
Drumm St.
Pine St.
Bush St.
Sutter St.
Post St.
Geary St.
O'Farrell St.
Ellis St.
Eddy St.
Turk St.
Golden Gate Ave.
McAllister St.
Grove St.
Hayes St.
Fell St.
UNION SQUARE
TENDERLOIN
POWELL
Market St.
Mission St.
Minna St.
Howard St.
Folsom St.
Harrison St.
Bryant St.
Brannan St.
Townsend St.
King St.
Berry St.
Channel St.
Fremont St.
Beale St.
Main St.
1st St.
2nd St.
3rd St.
4th St.
5th St.
6th St.
7th St.
8th St.
9th St.
10th St.
11th St.
12th St.
S. Van Ness Ave.
San Francisco Centre
Sony Metreon
Moscone Center
Old Mint
U.N. PLAZA
CIVIC CENTER
SOUTH OF MARKET
South Park
CalTrain Depot
Mission Creek
Marina
Pacific Bell Park
101
80
Downtown San Francisco

The Red Victorian Bed, Breakfast, and Art, 1665 Haight St. (☎864-1978; www.redvic.com). Striving to create peace through tourism, guests come together at breakfast to meditate and chat. Individually decorated rooms in themes like sunshine, redwoods, playground, and butterflies; even the hall bathrooms have their own motifs. Breakfast included. Reception 9am-9pm. Check-in 3-9pm or by appointment. Check-out 11am. Reservations required. Rooms $79-200, discounts for stays longer than 3 days. ❹

Hotel Triton, 342 Grant Ave. (☎394-0500, reservations 800-433-6611; www.hotel-tritonsf.com), at Bush St. A wonderfully surreal experience. Elegant rooms, bead-fringed curtains, plush carpets, TV, and rubber ducks. Smoking, wired, and pet-friendly rooms available. Tarot reading, room service, and in-room massage. Mezzanine fitness room. Cookies 3pm and free wine or beer 5-6pm daily in the lobby. Singles from $139. ❺

FOOD

FISHERMAN'S WHARF, MARINA, & COW HOLLOW

Pat's Café, 2330 Taylor St. (☎776-8735), between Chestnut and Francisco St. One of a string of breakfast joints, Pat's stands out from the crowd, not just because of its bright yellow building, but also for its huge, delicious, home-cooked meals. Burgers, sandwiches, and big breakfasts ($4-7). Open daily 7:30am-2pm. ❷

Marina Submarine, 2299 Union St. (☎921-3990), at Steiner St. in Cow Hollow. Often a long wait for superlative subs that satisfy in several sizes ($4-8). The art of the avocado is perfected at this unassuming spot (try the avocado and sprouts). Open M-F 10am-6:30pm, Sa 11am-4:30pm, Su 11am-3:30pm. ❶

Pizza Orgasmica, 3157 Fillmore St. (☎931-5300), at Greenwich St. in Cow Hollow. With pizzas named "ménage à trois" and "doggie style," it's hard not to get excited. Prices can get steep (pies $10-23) so don't miss the all-you-can-eat special (11am-4pm; $5.50). Open Su-W 11am-midnight, Th 11am-2:30am, F-Sa 11am-2:30am. ❷

NORTH BEACH & CHINATOWN

House of Nanking, 919 Kearny St. (☎421-1429), near Columbus Ave. Big, high-quality portions offset a low-key setting and a low-key check in this famous Chinatown institution. Many entrees under $8. Regulars tend to trust their server to select their meal. Open M-F 11am-10pm, Sa noon-10pm, Su noon-9:30pm. ❷

L'Osteria del Forno, 519 Columbus Ave. (☎982-1124), between Green and Union St. Acclaimed Italian roasted and cold foods, plus homemade breads. Terrific thin-crust pizzas (slices $2.50-3.75, whole pizzas $10-17) and focaccia sandwiches ($5-6.50) abound. Salads and antipasti ($4.50-8.50) and entrees ($7-15). Open Su-M and W-Th 11:30am-10pm, F-Sa 11:30am-10:30pm. ❸

Chef Jia, 925 Kearny St. (☎398-1626), at Pacific St. Lots of good, cheap food in a small, informal space. Yummy lunch specials (all under $5) served 11:30am-4pm (try the spicy string beans with yams) and evening rice plate specials 4-10pm (all $4.80). Entrees $6-7. Open daily 11:30am-10pm. ❷

Golden Gate Bakery, 1029 Grant Ave. (☎781-2627), in Chinatown. This tiny bakery's moon cakes, noodle puffs, and vanilla cream buns (all $0.75-1.50) draw long lines of tourists and locals. Open daily 8am-8pm. ❶

Mario's Bohemian Cigar Store Café, 566 Columbus Ave. (☎362-0536), at Union St. on the corner of Washington Sq. The Beats frequented this laidback cafe; these days, locals drop by to have coffee ($1-4) and drinks (wine $4, beer $3). A great place to hang out and grab some first-rate grub (hot focaccia sandwiches $4.25-8; pizza $7-9; pasta $8.25). Open Su-Th 10am-11pm, F-Sa 10am-midnight. ❷

NOB HILL & RUSSIAN HILL

Rico's, 943 Columbus Ave. (☎928-5404), between Taylor and Lombard St. An unpretentious, cafeteria-style restaurant. Choose from over a dozen enormous specialty burritos ($3.50-6), sandwiches ($5.50), and quesadillas ($7). Open daily 10am-10pm. ❶

Zarzuela, 2000 Hyde St. (☎346-0800), at Union St. in Russian Hill. Spanish homestyle cooking and a festively upscale setting make *chorizo al vino* ($4-7) the highlight of the evening. Entrees $8-14. Open Tu-Th 5:30-10pm, F-Sa 5:30-10:30pm. ❸

Sushigroove, 1916 Hyde St. (☎440-1905), between Union and Green St. Without a full kitchen, this chic, inexpensive sushi-*sake* joint (most sushi and *maki* $3-7) serves up a lot of rolls (many vegetarian) but nothing that has seen the inside of an oven. Open Su-Th 6-10pm, F-Sa 6-10:30pm. ❷

UNION SQUARE & THE TENDERLOIN

Dottie's True Blue Café, 522 Jones St. (☎885-2767), between Geary and O'Farrell St. Despite tiny portions, quirky variations like chicken-apple sausage and grilled eggplant with goat-cheese sandwich ($6) keep a line waiting. Open M and Th-Su 7:30am-3pm. ❷

The California Culinary Academy, 625 Polk St. (☎292-8229 or 800-229-2433), at Turk St. Watch and eat as Academy students prepare expert confit and sweetbreads behind the glass kitchen windows, which look into the elegant dining room. Tu-W features 3-course dinners ($24); Th French Buffet ($30); F Grande Buffet ($36). Open Tu-F 11:30am-1pm and 6-8pm. ❺

Tommy's Joynt, 1101 Geary Blvd. (☎775-4216; www.tommysjoynt.com), at Van Ness Ave. A delicious hybrid of a saloon, school cafeteria, and slaughterhouse. Guzzle monster meat sandwiches ($4.45) or carnivorous daily specials ($4.25-6.65). Domestic and imported beers ($2 glass, $8 pitcher). Open daily 11am-2am. ❷

CIVIC CENTER & HAYES VALLEY

It's Tops Coffee Shop, 1801 Market St. (☎715-6868), at Octavia St. With a soda fountain, an old-school counter, orange booths, and a doo-wop sound track, this 1952 establishment has been around since this nostalgic decor was cool. Breakfast $4.50-9. Burgers $6-8. Fountain drinks $2.50-5. Open M and W-F 8am-3pm and 8pm-3am, Tu 8am-3pm, Sa 8am-3am, Su 8am-11pm. ❷

Ananda Fuara, 1298 Market St. (☎621-1994), at Larkin St. If you can handle the sky blue interior, this vegetarian cafe with vegan tendencies offers creative combinations of super-fresh ingredients. The most popular dish and house specialty is the "neatloaf" (topped with mashed potatoes and gravy; $10.25). Open M-Tu and Th-Sa 8am-8pm, W 8am-3pm; occasional Su brunch, call for dates. ❷

Moishe's Pippic, 425-A Hayes St. (☎431-2440), between Gough and Octavia St. A good old kosher-style Jewish deli, with corned beef, pastrami, chopped liver, and, of course, matzoh ball soup. Sandwiches $6-8. Open M-F 8am-4pm, Sa 9am-4pm. ❷

SOUTH OF MARKET AREA (SOMA)

Patisserie Café, 1155 Folsom St. (☎703-0557; for cooking classes write chefmohamed@yahoo.com; www.patisseriecafe.com), between 7th and 8th St. A place where you can get a cheap breakfast (coffee and croissant $3), a reasonable lunch (fancy sandwich and dessert $9), or a decadent dinner (appetizers around $6, entrees $9-12) and ponder the experimental decor. Open M-F 8am-5pm. ❸

Basil, 1175 Folsom St. (☎552-8999; www.basilthai.com), near 8th St. Somberly sophisticated ambience sets the mood for delectably classy Thai. Curries and entrees "from the grill" or "from the wok" (all $9-12) include "drunken tofu" and piquant "mussels inferno." Open M-F 11:30am-2:45pm and 5-10pm, Sa-Su 5-10:30pm. ❸

HAIGHT-ASHBURY

Squat and Gobble, 1428 Haight St. (☎864-8484; www.squatandgobble.com), between Ashbury St. and Masonic Ave. In addition to the best name ever, this popular, light-filled cafe offers enormous omelettes ($5-7) and equally colossal crepes ($4-7). Lots of salads, sandwiches, and vegetarian options. Additional locations: 237 Fillmore St. in the **Lower Haight** and 3600 16th St. in the **Castro.** Open daily 8am-10pm. ❷

Blue Front Café, 1430 Haight St. (☎252-5917), between Ashbury St. and Masonic Ave. This Genie-marked joint is a great place to fill up on starchy goodness. Large portions, flowing conversation, and general wackiness. Down a beer or ginseng chai (both around $2.50), to go with your sizable wrap ($6) or Middle Eastern meal ($5-8.50). 10% student discount. Open Su-Th 7:30am-10pm, F-Sa 7:30am-11pm. ❷

Kate's Kitchen, 471 Haight St. (☎626-3984), near Fillmore St. Start your day off right with one of the best breakfasts in the neighborhood (served all day). It's often packed, so sign up on a waiting list outside. Try the "French Toast Orgy," with fruit, yogurt, granola, and honey ($5.25) or anything else on the extraordinarily economical menu ($4-8). Open M 9am-2:45pm, Tu-F 8am-2:45pm, Sa-Su 8:30am-3:45pm. ❷

MISSION & THE CASTRO

Home, 2100 Market St. (☎503-0333), at 14th and Church St. Inventively Californian take on meat and veggie dishes varies seasonally according to the chef's preferences. Sausalito watercress salad with jicama, peaches, and citrus vinaigrette $6. Entrees $8-13. Open M-W 5:30-10pm; Th-Sa 5:30-11pm; Su brunch 10:30am-3pm ($11), "Flip-Flop" cocktail party 2-6pm, and dinner 5:30-10pm. ❸

Taquería El Farolito, 2779 Mission St. (☎824-7877), at 24th St. The spot for cheap and authentic Mexican food—chow down as Latin beats blast through this fast-food joint. After any kind of evening activity in the Mission, El Farolito is a great late-night fix. Tacos $1.75. Open Su-Th 10am-3am, F-Sa 10am-4am. ❶

Nirvana, 544 Castro St. (☎861-2226), between 18th and 19th St. Heavenly Thai entrees ($7-12), a plethora of vegetarian options, and specialty drinks like the nirvana colada ($7-8) all help you reach apotheosis in a simple, swanky setting. Open M-Th 4:30-10pm, F 2-10:30pm, Sa 11:30am-10:30pm, Su noon-10pm. ❸

Mitchell's Ice Cream, 688 San Jose Ave. (☎648-2300), at 29th St. Mitchell's litany of awards is almost as long as its list of flavors. No seating, so take your cantaloupe, *buko* (baby coconut), *ube* (yam), or avocado ice cream outside. Open daily 11am-11pm. ❶

RICHMOND

Le Soleil, 133 Clement St. (☎668-4848), between 2nd and 3rd Ave. Serves Vietnamese food at prices so low they rival Chinatown's best. Huge vegetarian selection, and nothing on the menu cracks $8. Open Su-Th 11am-10pm, F-Sa 11am-10:30pm. ❷

Lee Hou Restaurant, 332 Clement St. (☎668-8070), at 5th Ave. Some of the best dim sum New Chinatown has to offer. Service is basic, but come for the food. 13 pieces of dim sum $8. Lunch $4-10. Open Su-Th 8am-1am, F-Sa 8am-2am. ❷

SIGHTS

FISHERMAN'S WHARF & THE BAY

Piers 39 through 45 provide access to San Francisco's most famous and touristy attractions. Easily visible from boats and the waterfront is Alcatraz Island.

ALCATRAZ. In its 29 years as a maximum-security federal penitentiary, **Alcatraz** harbored a menacing cast of characters, including Al "Scarface" Capone, George "Machine Gun" Kelly, and Robert "The Birdman" Stroud. There were 14 separate escape attempts—some desperate, defiant bolts for freedom, others carefully calculated and innovative. Only one man is known to have survived crossing the Bay; he was recaptured. On the rock, the cell-house audio tour takes you back to the infamous days of Alcatraz. A **Park Ranger guided tour** can take you around the island and through its 200 years of occupation, from a hunting and fishing ground for Native Americans to a civil war outpost to a military prison, a federal prison, and finally a birthplace of the Native American civil rights movement. Now part of the **Golden Gate National Recreation Area,** Alcatraz is home to diverse plants and birdlife. *(To get to the island, take the Blue and Gold Fleet from Pier 41. ☎ 773-1188, tickets 705-5555. Ferries 9:30am and every 30min. 10:15am-4:15pm; arrive 20min. early. $9.25, seniors $7.50, ages 5-11 $6. Reservations recommended 1 day in advance, preferably 1 week. On sold-out days, the ticket counter in the basement of the DFS Galleria in Union Square offers a limited number of "extra" tickets for $2.25 extra. Audio tours daily $4, ages 5-11 $2. Park Ranger tours free. "Alcatraz After Dark" $20.75, seniors and ages 12-17 $18, ages 5-11 $11.50; call for times and availability. Other boating companies run shorter boats around the island for about $10.)*

GHIRARDELLI SQUARE. A chocolate-lover's heaven, Ghirardelli Square is a mall in what used to be a chocolate factory. No golden ticket is required to gawk at the **Ghirardelli Chocolate Manufactory's** vast selection of chocolatey goodies, or the **Ghirardelli Chocolate Shop and Caffe,** with drinks, frozen yogurt, and a smaller selection of chocolates. Both hand out **free samples** of chocolate, but the Caffe is usually less crowded. *(Mall: 900 North Point St. ☎ 775-5500. Stores open M-Sa 10am-9pm, Su 10am-6pm. Ghirardelli Chocolate Manufactory: ☎ 771-4903. Open Su-Th 10am-11pm, F-Sa 10am-midnight. Soda fountain: Open Su-Th 10am-11pm, F-Sa 10am-midnight. Chocolate Shop and Caffe: ☎ 474-1414. Open M-Th 8:30am-9pm, F 8:30am-10pm, Sa 9am-10pm, Su 9am-9pm.)*

MARINA & FORT MASON

PALACE OF FINE ARTS. With its open-air domed structure and curving colonnades, the **Palace of Fine Arts** is one of the best picnic spots in the city. It was originally built to commemorate the opening of the Panama Canal and testify to San Francisco's recovery from the 1906 earthquake. Shakespearean plays are often performed here during the summer. *(On Baker St., between Jefferson and Bay St. next to the Exploratorium. Open daily 6am-9pm. Free.)* The **Palace of Fine Arts Theater,** located directly behind the rotunda, also hosts various dance and theater performances and film festivals. *(☎ 563-6504; www.palaceoffinearts.com. Call for shows, times, and ticket prices.)*

FORT MASON. Fort Mason Center is home to some of the most innovative and impressive cultural museums and resources in San Francisco. The array of outstanding attractions seem to remain unknown to most travelers and locals alike, making it a quiet waterfront counterpart to the tourist blitz of nearby Fisherman's Wharf. On the first Wednesday of every month all museums are free and open until 7pm. The grounds are also the headquarters of the **Golden Gate National Recreation Area (GGNRA).** *(The park is at the eastern portion of Fort Mason, near Gashouse Cove. ☎ 441-3400, ext. 3; www.fortmason.org.)*

NORTH BEACH

WASHINGTON SQUARE. Washington Sq., bordered by Union, Filbert, Stockton, and Powell St., is North Beach's *piazza*, a pretty, not-quite-square, tree-lined lawn. The wedding site of Marilyn Monroe and Joe DiMaggio, the park fills every morning with practitioners of *tai chi*. By noon, sunbathers, picnickers, and bocce-ball players take over. **St. Peter and St. Paul Catholic Church,** 666 Filbert St., beckons sightseers to take refuge in its dark nave. Turn-of-the-century San Francisco philanthropist and party-girl Lillie Hitchcock Coit donated the **Volunteer Firemen Memorial** in the middle of the square after being rescued from a fire as a young girl.

COIT TOWER. Also built by Lillie Hitchcock Coit, the **Coit Tower** stands 210 ft. high and commands a spectacular view of the city and the Bay. The view from the base of the tower is by no means shabby, and paying for the elevator is not necessarily worth it. During the Great Depression, the government's Works Progress Administration employed artists to paint the colorful and surprisingly subversive murals in the lobby. *(MUNI bus #39, or climb up the Filbert Steps from the Embarcadero. ☎362-0808. Open daily 10am-7pm. Elevator $3.75, seniors $2.50, ages 6-12 $1.50, under 6 free.)*

CITY LIGHTS BOOKSTORE. Drawn by low rents and cheap bars, the Beat writers came to national attention when Lawrence Ferlinghetti's **City Lights Bookstore**—opened in 1953—published Allen Ginsberg's *Howl.* First banned, then subjected to a long trial in which a judge found the poem "not obscene," the book vaulted the Beats into literary infamy. City Lights has expanded since its Beat days and now stocks fiction and poetry but remains committed to publishing young poets and writers under its own imprint. Index card boxes in the back stairwell hold postings for jobs, housing, and rides, and writers without permanent addresses can have their mail held in the store. *(2261 Columbus Ave. ☎362-8193. Open daily 10am-midnight.)*

CHINATOWN

WAVERLY PLACE. Find this little alley (between Sacramento and Washington St. and between Stockton St. and Grant Ave.) and you'll want to spend all day gazing at the incredible architecture. The fire escapes are painted in pinks and greens and held together by railings cast in intricate Chinese patterns. Tourists can also visit **Tien Hou Temple,** 125 Waverly Pl., the oldest Chinese temple in the U.S.

ROSS ALLEY. Ross Alley was once lined with brothels and opium dens; today, it has the cramped look of old Chinatown. The narrow street has stood in for the Orient in such films as *Big Trouble in Little China*, *Karate Kid II*, and *Indiana Jones and the Temple of Doom.* Squeeze into a tiny doorway to watch fortune cookies being shaped by hand at the **Golden Gate Cookie Company.** *(56 Ross Alley. ☎781-3956. Bag of cookies $3; with "funny," "sexy," or "lucky" fortunes $5. Open daily 10am-8pm.)*

NOB HILL & RUSSIAN HILL

THE CROOKEDEST STREET IN THE WORLD. The famous curves of **Lombard Street**—installed in the 1920s so that horse-drawn carriages could negotiate the extremely steep hill—serve as an icon of SF. From the top, both pedestrians and passengers enjoy the view of city and harbor. The view north along Hyde St. isn't too shabby either. *(Between Hyde and Leavenworth St. at the top of Russian Hill.)*

GRACE CATHEDRAL & HUNTINGTON PARK. The largest Gothic edifice west of the Mississippi, **Grace Cathedral** is Nob Hill's stained-glass studded crown. The castings of its portals are such exact imitations of the Baptistery in Florence that they were used to restore the originals. Inside, modern murals mix San Franciscan and national historical events with saintly scenes. The altar of the AIDS Interfaith Memorial Chapel celebrates the church's "inclusive community of love." *(1100 California St., between Jones and Taylor St. ☎749-6300; www.gracecathedral.org. Open Su-F 7am-6pm, Sa 8am-6pm. Services: Su 7:30, 8:15, 11am, 3, 6pm, M-F 7:30, 9am, 12:10, 5:15pm, Sa 9, 11am, 3pm. Tour guides available M-F 1-3pm, Sa 11:30am-1:30pm, Su 1:30-2pm. Suggested donation $3.)* Outside, the building looks onto the neatly manicured turf and trees of **Huntington Park,** equipped with a park and playground.

UNION SQUARE & THE TENDERLOIN

MAIDEN LANE. When the Barbary Coast (now the Financial District) was down and dirty, Union Sq.'s **Morton Alley** was dirtier. Around 1900, murders on the Alley averaged one per week and prostitutes waved to their favorite customers from second-story windows. After the 1906 earthquake and fires destroyed most of the brothels, merchants moved in and renamed the area **Maiden Lane** in hopes of changing the street's image. It worked. Today, the pedestrian-only street that extends two blocks from Union Square's eastern side is as virtuous as they come and makes a pleasant place to stroll or sip espresso wearing newly purchased Gucci shades.

GOLDEN GATE BRIDGE & THE PRESIDIO

GOLDEN GATE BRIDGE. When Captain John Fremont coined the term "Golden Gate" in 1846, he meant to name the harbor entrance to the San Francisco Bay after the mythical Golden Horn port of Constantinople. In 1937, however, the colorful name became permanently associated with Joseph Strauss' copper-hued engineering masterpiece—the **Golden Gate Bridge.** Built for only $35 million, the bridge stretches across 1¼ mi. of ocean, its towers looming 65 stories above the Bay. It can sway up to 27 ft. in each direction during high winds. On sunny days, hundreds of people take the 30min. walk across. The views from the bridge are amazing, especially from the Vista Point in Marin County just after the bridge. To see the bridge itself, it's best to get a bit farther away: Fort Point and Fort Baker in the Presidio, Land's End in Lincoln Park, and Mt. Livermore on Angel Island all offer spectacular views of the Golden Gate on clear days.

PRESIDIO. When Spanish settlers forged their way up the San Francisco peninsula from Baja California in 1769, they established *presidios*, or military outposts, as they went. San Francisco's **Presidio,** the northernmost point of Spanish territory in North America, was dedicated in 1776. The settlement stayed in Spanish hands for 45 years, then was given to Mexico when it won independence, then was passed to the U.S. as part of the 1848 Treaty of Guadalupe Hidalgo. The outpost expanded during the Gold Rush and is part of the Golden Gate National Recreation Area (GGNRA), run by the National Park Service and the Presidio Trust.

THE LOCAL STORY

ULTIMATE SURROUND SOUND

On any given day, a trip to the waterfront will provide a view of the crashing waves and a few solitary joggers. But just past the Marina Green, near the Golden Gate Yacht club, stands one of San Francisco's strangest and most natural musical instruments.

What most people don't realize is that one of San Francisco's best hidden treasures, the **Wave Organ**, rests among the rocks. A magnificent interplay between art and nature, the wave organ is an acoustic environmental sculpture consisting of 25 pipes jutting out of the ocean. Each pipe creates a different musical sound as waves crash against it.

Conceived by Peter Richards, the project was completed in 1986. George Gonzalez, a sculptor and stone mason, designed the seating area around the pipes using granite and marble pieces from an old decimated cemetery. Far from morbid though, the effect is rather meditatively intriguing. A series of carvings can be discerned if you look closely enough at the structure.

The music itself is quite subtle, like listening to a sea shell, and is best heard at high tide. If you take the time to sit for a while, tones from the organ will begin to harmonize with the clinking boat masts, fog horns, and sea gulls, synthesizing into a sublime oceanic symphony.

LINCOLN PARK & OCEAN BEACH

TRAILS. The **Coastal Trail** loops around the interior of Lincoln Park for a scenic and sometimes hardcore coastal hike. The entrance to the trail is not particularly well marked, so be careful not to mistakenly tackle a much more difficult cliffside jaunt. The path leads first into **Fort Miley,** a former army post. Near the picnic tables rests the **USS San Francisco Memorial.** The USS *SF* sustained 45 direct hits (which started 25 fires) in the battle of Guadalcanal on November 12-13, 1942. Nearly 100 men died in the clash, but the ship went on to fight in 10 more battles. *(Trail begins at Pt. Lobos and 48th Ave. Free.)* The Coastal Trail continues for a 3 mi. hike into **Land's End,** famous for its views of both the Golden Gate Bridge and the "sunken ships" that signal treacherous waters below. Dense pine and cypress trees, colorful flowers, and a wide array of cheerful fauna line the rocky coastline. Except for the occasionally harsh winds, the trail is a few talking animals short of a Disney film paradise. Biking is permitted on the trail, although parts contain stairs and bumpy terrain better suited to mountain bikes. From Land's End, onlookers have the option to hike an extra 6 mi. into the Presidio and on to the arches of Golden Gate Bridge. For hikers and bikers who aren't so inclined, the brisker (and flatter) walk along **El Camino Del Mar** originates close to the Coastal Trail but runs farther in from the shore. Enjoy the forested views and a stop at the **Palace of the Legion of Honor** before finishing "The Path of the Sea" at **China Beach.** In all, this makes for a pleasant 1½ mi. afternoon stroll through the best of Lincoln Park. *(Begins at Pt. Lobos and Sea Rock Dr.)*

BEACHES. Swimming is permitted but dangerous at scenic **China Beach** at the end of Seacliff Ave. on the eastern edge of Lincoln Park. Adolph Sutro's 1896 **bathhouse** lies in ruins on the cliffs. Cooled by ocean water, the baths were capable of packing in 25,000 occupants at a time, but after an enthusiastic initial opening, they rarely had to. **Ocean Beach,** the largest and most popular of San Francisco's beaches, begins south of Point Lobos and extends down the northwestern edge of the city's coastline. The strong undertow along the point is very dangerous, but die-hard surfers brave the treacherous currents and the ice-cold water anyway.

GOLDEN GATE PARK

Take your time to enjoy this park. Intriguing museums (see p. 940) and cultural events pick up where the lush flora and fauna leave off, and athletic opportunities abound. The park has a municipal golf course, equestrian center, sports fields, tennis courts, and stadium. On Sundays, traffic is banned from park roads, and bicycles and in-line skates come out in full force. The **Visitors Center** is located in the Beach Chalet on the western edge of the park. *(☎751-2766. Open daily 9am-7pm.)* **Surrey Bikes and Blades in Golden Gate Park** rents equipment. *(50 Stow Lake Dr. ☎668-6699. Open daily 10am-dusk. Bikes from $6 per hr., $21 per day. Skates $7/20.)*

GARDENS. The soil of Golden Gate Park is rich enough to support a wealth of flowers. The **Garden of Fragrance** is designed especially for the visually impaired; all labels are in Braille and the plants are chosen specifically for their textures and scents. Near the Music Concourse off South Dr., the **Shakespeare Garden** contains almost every flower and plant ever mentioned by the Bard. Plaques with the relevant quotations are displayed, and maps help you find your favorite hyacinths and rue. *(Open summer daily dawn-dusk; winter Tu-Su dawn-dusk. Free.)* The **Japanese Cherry Orchard,** at Lincoln Way and South Dr., blooms intoxicatingly the first week in April. Created for the 1894 Mid-Winter Exposition, the elegant **Japanese Tea Garden** is a serene collection of wooden buildings, small pools, graceful footbridges, carefully pruned trees, and lush plants. *(☎752-4227. Open daily summer 8:30am-6pm; winter 8:30am-5pm. Adults $3.50, seniors and ages 6-12 $1.25. Free summer 8:30-9:30am and 5-6pm; winter 8:30-9:30am and 4-5pm.)*

FINANCIAL DISTRICT

TRANSAMERICA PYRAMID. The leading lady of the city's skyline, this distinctive office building was designed to allow as much light as possible to shine on the streets below. Unless you're an employee, tight security means there is no chance of a top-floor view. The lobby is currently undergoing renovation to modernize a "virtual viewing lounge" in the Washington St. entrance so you can peer down on the masses from ground-level. Now a pillar of commerce, the location was once a site of revolutionary disgruntlement; Sun Yat-Sen scripted a dynastic overthrow in one of its second-floor offices. *(600 Montgomery St., between Clay and Washington St.)*

JUSTIN HERMAN PLAZA. When not overrun by skateboarders, the Plaza is home to bands and rallyists who sometimes provide lunch-hour entertainment. U2 rock star Bono was arrested here after a concert in 1987 for spray painting "Stop the Traffic—Rock and Roll" on the fountain. Recently, the plaza has been the starting point for Critical Mass, a pro-bicyclist ride that takes place after 5pm on the last Friday of every month. If you happen to be around on a rare hot day, walk through the inviting mist of the Vaillancourt Fountain to cool off.

JAPANTOWN & PACIFIC HEIGHTS

SAINT DOMINIC'S ROMAN CATHOLIC CHURCH. Churchgoers and architecture buffs alike will appreciate **Saint Dominic's** towering altar, carved in the shape of Jesus and the 12 apostles. With its imposing gray stone and gothic feel, St. Dominic's is a must see, especially its renowned shrine of **Saint Jude,** skirted by candles and intricately carved oak. *(2390 Bush St., at Steiner St. Open M-Sa 6:30am-5:30pm, Su 7:30am-9pm. Mass M-F 6:30, 8am, 5:30pm, Sa 8am, 5:30pm, Su 7:30, 9:30, 11:30am, 1:30, 5:30, 9pm candlelight service.)*

FUJI SHIATSU & KABUKI SPRINGS. After a rigorous day hiking the city's hills, reward your weary muscles with an authentic massage at **Fuji Shiatsu.** *(1721 Buchanan Mall., between Post and Sutter St. ☎346-4484. Morning $41, afternoon $44.)* Alternatively, head to the bathhouse at **Kabuki Hot Springs** to relax in the sauna and steamroom, or enjoy the *Reiki* treatment to heal, rejuvenate and restore energy balance. *(1750 Geary Blvd. ☎922-6000; www.kabukisprings.com. M-F before 5pm $15, after 5pm and Sa-Su $18. Open 10am-10pm; men only M, Th, Sa; women only Su, W, F; co-ed Tu.)*

CIVIC CENTER

CIVIC CENTER. Referred to as "The Crown Jewel" of American Classical architecture, **City Hall** reigns supreme over the Civic Center, with a dome to rival St. Paul's cathedral and an area of over 500,000 sq. ft. *(1 Dr. Carlton B. Goodlett Pl., at Van Ness Ave. ☎554-4000. Open M-F 8am-8pm, Sa-Su noon-4pm.)* The seating in the $33 million glass-and-brass **Louise M. Davies Symphony Hall** was designed to give audience members a close-up view of performers. Visually, the building is a smashing success. Its **San Francisco Symphony** is equally esteemed. *(201 Van Ness Ave. ☎552-8000; tickets ☎431-5400. Open M-F 10am-6pm, Sa noon-6pm.)* The recently renovated **War Memorial Opera House** hosts the well-regarded **San Francisco Opera Company** and the **San Francisco Ballet.** *(301 Van Ness Ave., between Grove and McAllister St. Box office at 199 Grove St. ☎864-3330. Open M-Sa 10am-6pm and in Opera House 2hr. before each show.)*

MISSION

MISSION DOLORES. Founded in 1776 in the old heart of San Francisco, the **Mission Dolores** is thought to be the city's oldest building. Due to its proximity to the Laguna de Nuestra Señora de los Dolores (Lagoon of Our Lady of Sorrows), the mission became universally known as *Misión de los Dolores.* Bougainvillea, pop-

ACID TEST In 1938, in Basel, Switzerland, Albert Hoffman synthesized a compound called lysergic acid diethylamide (LSD). The new wonder drug was said to cure psychosis and alcoholism. In the early 1950s, the CIA adopted LSD as part of Operation MK-ULTRA, a series of Cold War mind control experiments. By the end of the 60s, the drug had been tested on some 1500 military personnel in a series of shady operations. Writers Ken Kesey, Allen Ginsberg, and the Grateful Dead's Robert Hunter were first exposed to acid as subjects in these government experiments. The CIA soon abandoned the unpredictable hallucinogen, but it had been discovered by Bohemian proto-hippies in Haight-Ashbury. Amateur chemists began producing the compound, and prominent intellectuals like Timothy Leary and Aldous Huxley advocated its use as a means of expanding consciousness. In October 1966, the drug was banned in California, and Kesey's Merry Pranksters hosted their first public Acid Test. Once a secret weapon of the military-industrial complex, acid became an ingredient of the counterculture, juicing up anti-war rallies and love-ins across the Bay Area and the nation.

pies, and birds-of-paradise bloom in its cemetery, which was featured in Alfred Hitchcock's 1958 film *Vertigo. (3321 16th St., at Dolores St. ☎621-8203. Open May-Oct. daily 9am-4:30pm; Nov.-Apr. 9am-4pm. Adults $3, ages 5-12 $2. Mass: in English M-F 7:30, 9am; Sa 7:30, 9am, 5pm; Su 8, 10am. In Spanish Su noon.)*

MISSION MURALS. A walk east or west along 24th St., weaving in and out of the side streets, reveals the Mission's **magnificent murals.** Continuing the Mexican mural tradition made famous by Diego Rivera and Jose Orozco, the murals have been a source of pride for Chicano artists and community members since the 1980s. Standouts include the more political murals of **Balmy Alley,** off 24th St. between Harrison and Folsom St., a three-building tribute to guitar god **Carlos Santana** at 22nd St. and Van Ness Ave., the face of **St. Peter's Church** at 24th and Florida St., and the **urban living center** on 19th St. between Valencia and Guerrero St.

CASTRO & NEARBY

THE CASTRO. Stores throughout the area cater to gay-mecca pilgrims, with everything from rainbow flags and pride-wear to the latest in BGLT books, dance music, and trinkets of the more unmentionable variety. Many local shops, especially on the wildly colorful **Castro Street,** also double as novelty galleries. Discover just how anatomically correct Gay Billy is at **Does Your Father Know?,** a one-stop kitsch-and-camp overdose. To read up on gay history and culture, enlighten yourself at **A Different Light Bookstore.** End your day shopping for vintage pizzazz at **Getups.**

WALKING TOURS. For a guided tour of the Castro that includes sights other than biceps and abs, check out **Cruisin' the Castro.** Trevor Hailey, a resident since 1972, is consistently recognized as one of SF's top tour leaders. Her 4hr. walking tours cover Castro life and history from the Gold Rush to the present. *(☎550-8110; www.webcastro.com/castrotour. Tours Tu-Sa 10am. $40; lunch included. Reservations required.)*

HAIGHT-ASHBURY

FORMER CRIBS. The former homes of several counterculture legends still attract visitors. From the corner of Haight and Ashbury St., walk just south of Waller St. to check out the house occupied by the **Grateful Dead** when they were still the Warlocks. *(710 Ashbury St.)* Look across the street for the **Hell's Angels** house. If you walk back to Haight St., go right three blocks, and make a left on Lyon St., you can check out **Janis Joplin's** old abode. *(122 Lyon St., between Page and Oak St.)* Cross the Panhandle, continue three blocks to Fulton St., turn right, and wander seven blocks toward the park to see where the Manson "family" planned murder and mayhem at the **Charles Manson** mansion. *(2400 Fulton St., at Willard St.)*

SAN FRANCISCO ZEN CENTER. Appropriately removed from the havoc of the Haight, the **San Francisco Zen Center** offers a peaceful retreat. Call for information on any of the multitude of classes they offer here. The temple is called Beginner's Mind Temple, so don't worry if you don't even know where to begin looking for your *chi*. The best option for most beginners is the Saturday morning program, which includes a mediation lecture at 8:45am followed by other activities and lunch ($6). Or just visit the bookstore and the library. *(300 Page St., at Laguna St. ☎863-3136. Office open M-F 9:30am-12:30pm and 1:30-5pm, Sa 9am-noon. Bookstore open M-Th 1:30-5:30pm and 6:30-7:30pm, F 1:30-5:30pm, Sa 11am-1pm. Library open Tu-F 1:30-5pm.)*

MUSEUMS & GALLERIES

MARINA

Exploratorium, 3601 Lyon St. (☎563-7337 or 561-0360; www.exploratorium.edu). The Exploratorium can hold over 4000 people, and when admission is free, it usually does. Over 650 interactive displays—including miniature tornadoes, computer planet-managing, and giant bubble-makers—explain the wonders of the world. The **Tactile Dome**—a dark maze of tunnels, slides, nooks, and crannies—refines your sense of touch. On the second W of each month Nov.-Mar., the Exploratorium hosts avant-garde **art cocktail nights** that feature Bay area artists, a DJ, and bar. Open June-Aug. daily 10am-6pm; Sept.-May Tu-Su 10am-5pm. $12; students, seniors, disabled, and ages 9-17 $9.50; ages 4-8 $8, under 3 free. Free first W of each month. Tactile Dome $15, reservations recommended.

FORT MASON

Museum of Craft and Folk Art, Bldg. A., first fl. (☎775-0990; www.mocfa.org). The MOCFA brings together a fascinating collection of crafts and functional art (vessels, clothing, furniture, and jewelry) from past and present, near and far, showcasing everything from 19th-century Chinese children's hats to war-time commentary made through lightbulbs. Open Su and Tu-F 11am-5pm, Sa 10am-5pm. $4, students and seniors $3, under 18 free. Free Sa 10am-noon and first W of each month 11am-7pm.

African-American Historical and Cultural Society Museum, Bldg. C, #165 (☎441-0640). Displays historic artifacts and artwork, modern works, and a permanent collection by local artists. Open W-Su noon-5pm. $3, seniors and children over 12 $1, under 12 free. First W of each month free.

SF Museum of Modern Artists Gallery, Bldg. A., first fl. (☎441-4777). Over 1200 Bay Area artists show, rent, and sell their work here. Monthly curated exhibits are on display downstairs, while most other pieces are sold upstairs, with proceeds split between the artist and the museum. Rentals from $35 per month for 2-3 months. Every May, the gallery hosts a benefit sale—all works half-price. Open Tu-Sa 11:30am-5:30pm. Free.

NOB HILL & RUSSIAN HILL

San Francisco Art Institute, 800 Chestnut St. (☎771-7020 or 800-345-7324; www.sfai.edu). The oldest art school west of the Mississippi, the Institute is lodged in a converted mission and has produced a number of American greats including Mark Rothko, Ansel Adams, Imogen Cunningham, Dorothea Lange, and James Weeks. To the left as you enter is the **Diego Rivera Gallery,** 1 wall of which is covered by a huge 1931 Rivera mural. The gallery hosts weekly student exhibits with receptions every other Thursday. Open daily June-Aug. 9am-8pm; Sept.-May 9am-9pm. Professional exhibits are housed in the **Walter and McBean Galleries.** Open Tu-Sa 11am-6pm but call ahead.

Cable Car Powerhouse and Museum, 1201 Mason St. (☎474-1887). After the steep journey up Nob Hill, you'll understand what inspired the development of the vehicles celebrated here. More an educational breather than a destination in its own right, the modest building is the working center of San Fran's cable car system. Look down on 57,300 ft. of cable whizzing by or view displays about the cars, some of which date back to 1873. Open daily Apr.-Oct. 10am-6pm; Nov.-Mar. 10am-5pm. Free.

UNION SQUARE

Martin Lawrence Gallery, 366 Geary St. (☎956-0345). A 2-story space that displays works by pop artists like Warhol and Haring, as well as studies by Picasso and America's largest collection of Marc Chagall. Haring once distributed his work for free to New York commuters in the form of graffiti; it now commands upwards of $13,000 in print form. Open M-Th 9am-8pm, F-Sa 9am-10pm, Su 10am-7pm. Free.

Hang, 556 Sutter St. (☎434-4264; www.hangart.com). Sleek, urban gallery housed in a cozy chrome warehouse in which the works hang from the exposed beams in the ceiling. An annex recently opened directly across the street on the second floor of 567 Sutter. Hang specializes in the rental of paintings and sculpture "by emerging artists for emerging collectors." Open M-Sa 10am-6pm, Su noon-5pm. Free.

TENDERLOIN

509 Cultural Center/Luggage Store, 1007 Market St. (☎255-5971) and 1172 Market St. (☎865-0198). Started by a group of artists and residents in the late 80s, the centers draw on the neighborhood's diversity to foster community. Performing arts events, exhibitions, and arts education initiatives are presented at its 2 venues. With its pyromaniac nipple-clamp photographs and religious-themed BDSM paintings, the often graphic art exhibits probably won't be grandma's favorites. Regular events include comedy open mic (Tu 8pm), improvisational music concerts, and the annual "In the Street" theater festival in June. (Th 8pm. $6-10 suggested donation for each.) Next door to 509 Cultural Center, the **Cohen Alley** houses a third venue for the area's creative talent; the once-abandoned alley is leased to the Luggage Store, whose vibrant murals and ornately sculpted gate have transformed the alley into an artistic showcase.

LINCOLN PARK

California Palace of the Legion of Honor (☎863-3330; www.legionofhonor.org), in the middle of Lincoln Park. A copy of Rodin's *Thinker* beckons visitors into the grand courtyard, where a little glass pyramid recalls another Paris treasure, the Louvre. A thorough catalogue of great masters, from the medieval to the modern, hangs inside. Other draws include a pneumatically operated 4500-pipe organ, played in free recitals weekly (Sa-Su 4pm). Just outside the Palace, a **Holocaust memorial** depicts the Holocaust through a mass of emaciated victims with a single, hopeful survivor looking out through a barbed-wire fence to the beauty of the Pacific. Open Tu-Su 9:30am-5pm. Adults $8, seniors $6, under 17 $5, under 12 free. $2 discount with MUNI transfer; Tu free.

GOLDEN GATE PARK

California Academy of Sciences, 55 Concourse Dr. (☎750-7145; www.calacademy.org), on the east side of the park at 9th Ave. Houses several museums specializing in different fields of science. The **Steinhart Aquarium,** home to over 600 aquatic species, is livelier than the natural history exhibits. Shark feedings M-W and F-Su 10:30am, 12:30, 2:30, 4:30pm. Open ocean fish feedings daily 1:30pm. Penguin feeding daily 11:30am, 4pm. At the **Natural History Museum,** the Earthquake Theater shakes visitors, while the Far Side of Science Gallery pays tribute to Gary Larson. Open June-Aug. daily 9am-6pm; Sept.-May 10am-5pm. Combined admission $8.50; seniors, students, and ages 12-17 $5.50; ages 4-11 $2. Free first W each month (open until 8:45pm). The **Morrison Planetarium** re-creates the heavens with impressive sky shows M-F 2pm, with additional summer showings. $2.50; students, seniors, and ages 6-17 $1.25.

SOMA

San Francisco Museum of Modern Art (SFMOMA), 151 3rd St. (☎357-4000; www.sfmoma.org), between Mission and Howard St. This black-and-gray marble-trimmed museum houses 5 spacious floors of art, with an emphasis on design. It houses the largest selection of 20th-century American and European art this side of New York. Free gallery tours: 4 per day. Open Sept. 3-May 24 M-Tu and F-Su 11am-5:45pm, Th 11am-8:45pm; May 25-Sept. 2 M-Tu and F-Su 10am-6pm, Th 10am-9pm. $10, seniors $7, students $6, under 13 free. Th 6-9pm half-price. First Tu of each month free.

Yerba Buena Center for the Arts, 701 Mission St. (☎978-2787; www.yerbabuenaarts.org). The center runs an excellent theater and gallery space, with programs emphasizing performance, film, viewer involvement, and local multicultural work. It is surrounded by the **Yerba Buena Rooftop Gardens,** a vast expanse of concrete, fountains, and foliage. Open Tu-Su 11am-6pm. $6, students and seniors $3. Th free.

ZEUM, 221 4th St. (☎777-2800; www.zeum.org), at Howard St. Within the Yerba Buena gardens, this recently opened "art and technology center" is aimed at children and teenagers. The best draw may be the reopened carousel, created in 1906. Open summer Tu-Su 11am-5pm; low-season W-Su 11am-5pm. $7, seniors and students $6, ages 5-18 $5. Carousel open daily 11am-6pm. $2 for 2 rides.

ENTERTAINMENT

MUSIC

The distinction between bars, clubs, and live music venues is hazy in San Francisco. Almost all bars will occasionally have bands, and small venues have rock and hip-hop shows. Look for the latest live music listings in *S.F. Weekly* and *The Guardian*. Hard-core audiophiles might snag a copy of *Bay Area Music (BAM)*.

Café du Nord, 2170 Market St. (☎861-5016), between Church and Sanchez St. in the Castro. Excellent live music nightly—from pop and groove to garage rock. Local favorites include vintage jazz, blues, and R&B. Special weekly events include the popular M Night Hoot, a showcase of local singing and songwriting talent. Happy Hour daily 6-7:30pm; martinis and cosmos $2.50. 21+. Cover after 8:30pm $5-10. Open Su-Tu 6pm-2am, W-Sa 4pm-2am.

Justice League, 628 Divisadero St. (☎440-0409), at Hayes St. in the Lower Haight. Live hip-hop is hard to find in San Francisco, but the Justice League fights ever onward for a good beat. Excellent variety of artists. M reggae and dub. W soul night. 21+. Tickets at www.ticketweb.com. Cover $5-25. Usually open daily 9pm-2am.

Bottom of the Hill, 1233 17th St. (☎626-4455; www.bottomofthehill.com), between Missouri and Texas St. in Potrero Hill. Intimate rock club with tiny stage is the last best place to see up-and-comers before they move to bigger venues. Most Su afternoons feature local bands and all-you-can-eat barbecue. 21+. Cover $5-10. Open M-Th 8:30pm-2am, F 3pm-2am, Sa 8:30pm-2am, Su hours vary.

The Fillmore, 1805 Geary Blvd. (☎346-6000; www.thefillmore.com), at Fillmore St. in Japantown. Bands that pack stadiums are often eager to play at the legendary Fillmore, the foundation of San Francisco's 1960s music scene. Grand, brightly lit, and filled with anecdotal and nostalgic wall-hangings. All ages. Tickets $15-40. Call for hours.

THEATER

Downtown, **Mason Street** and **Geary Street** constitute **"Theater Row,"** the city's prime place for theatrical entertainment. **TIX Bay Area,** located in a kiosk in Union Sq. on the corner of Geary and Powell St., is a Ticketmaster outlet with tickets for almost all shows and concerts in the city. Buy a seat in advance, or try for cash-only, half-price tickets on the day of the show. (☎433-7827; www.theaterbayarea.org. Open Tu-Th 11am-6pm, F-Sa 11am-7pm, Su 11am-3pm.)

Magic Theatre, Bldg. D, 3rd fl. (☎441-8822; www.magictheatre.org) in Fort Mason Center. The theater stages both international and American premieres. Shows start 8 or 8:30pm; previews and Su matinees 2 or 2:30pm. W-Th $22-32, F-Su $27-37, previews and Su matinees $15. Student and senior rush tickets available 30min. before the show; $10. Call for exact times. Box office open Tu-Sa noon-5pm.

The Orpheum, 1192 Market St., at Hyde St. near the Civic Center. Box office at 6th and Market St. (☎512-7770). This famous San Francisco landmark hosts big Broadway shows. 2 sister theaters in the area host smaller shows: **Golden Gate Theatre,** 1 Taylor St., and **Curran Theatre,** 445 Geary St. Individual show times and ticket prices vary.

Geary Theater, 415 Geary St. (☎749-2228; www.act-sfbay.org), at Mason St. in Union Square. Home to the renowned American Conservatory Theater, the jewel in SF's theatrical crown. The elegant theater is a show-stealer in its own right. Tickets $11-61 (cheaper for previews and on weekdays). Half-price student, teacher, and senior tickets available 2hr. before showtime. Box office open Tu-Su noon-6pm.

Theatre Rhinoceros, 2926 16th St. (☎861-5079; www.therhino.org), at South Van Ness Ave. in the Mission. The oldest queer theater in the world and innovator in the arts community since 1977. The Rhino emphasizes playwriting by and for the gay, lesbian, bisexual, transgender community. Tickets $10-30. Discounts for students, seniors, disabled, and groups of 10+. Box office open Tu-Su 1-6pm. Not wheelchair-accessible.

MOVIES

Castro Theatre, 429 Castro St. (☎621-6350; www.thecastrotheatre.com), near Market St. in the Castro. Eclectic films, festivals, and double features, and live organ music before evening shows. Far from silent—a bawdy, hilarious crowd turns many a movie into *The Rocky Horror Picture Show.* Highlights include the sing-along *Sound of Music,* for those who believe Julie Andrews would be much better with chest hair. $8, seniors and under 12 $5. Matinees W and Sa-Su $5. Box office opens 1hr. before first show.

DANCE

Alonzo King's Lines Contemporary Ballet (☎863-3360; www.linesballet.org), in Hayes Valley. Dancers combine elegant classical moves with athletic flair to the music of great living jazz and world music composers. Springtime shows are performed at the Yerba Buena Center for the Arts (p. 941). Tickets $15-25.

Oberlin Dance Company, 3153 17th St. (☎863-9834; www.odctheater.org), between South Van Ness and Folsom St. in the Mission. Mainly dance, but occasional theater space with gallery attached. Tickets $10-20 dollars, but occasional 2-for-1 and "pay what you can" nights. Box office open W-Sa 2-5pm.

California Contemporary Dancers, 530 Moraga St. (☎753-6066; www.ccdancers.org), in the Sunset. The all-woman modern dance company brings together the best of widely diverse dance and musical traditions to create exciting, innovative performances. They play at venues throughout the city; check web site for ticket and show information.

SPORTS

Home to the five-time Super Bowl champion **49ers** (☎468-2249; tickets 656-4900; www.sf49ers.com), 3COM Park, also known as **Candlestick Park,** sits right on the ocean, resulting in trademark gusts that led to one of the lowest homerun averages in baseball back when the Giants played there. If you're driving, take U.S. 101 8 miles south to the Candlestick Park exit. MUNI buses #9X, 28X, and 47X "Ballpark Express Line" also service the stadium. The **Giants** now play at the newly built **Pacific Bell Park,** 24 Willie Mays Plaza (☎972-2000; tickets 510-2255 or 888-464-2468; www.sfgiants.com), in SoMa near the ocean off Townsend St. Take Hyde St. to 8th St., turn left on Bryant St. and right on 4th St. Via public transportation, take the Metro Ballpark Service beginning either at the Balboa Park (via M-Ocean View route) or West Portal Station.

FESTIVALS

If you can't find a festival going on in San Francisco, well, you just aren't trying hard enough. Cultural, ethnic, and queer special events take place year-round. For two consecutive weekends in April, the Japanese **Cherry Blossom Festival** (☎563-2313) lights up the streets of Japantown with hundreds of performers. The oldest film festival in North America, the **San Francisco International Film Festival** shows more than 100 international films of all genres over two weeks. (☎561-5022; www.sffs.org. Kabuki and Castro Theaters. Most $9.) If film's your thing, you may also want to check out the **San Francisco International Gay and Lesbian Film Festival** (☎703-8650; www.frameline.org; June 26-27, 2004), California's second-largest film festival and the world's largest gay and lesbian media event. The $6-15 tickets go fast. It takes place at the Roxie (at 16th and Valencia St.) and Castro Theatre (see p. 942) during the 11 days leading up to **Pride Day.** The High Holy Day of the queer calendar, Pride Day celebrates with a parade and events downtown starting at 10:30am. (☎864-3733; www.sfpride.org; June 27, 2004.)

For a bit of high culture, consider the free **San Francisco Shakespeare Festival,** every Saturday and Sunday in September in Golden Gate Park. (☎865-4434. Shows 1:30pm, but arrive at noon for a seat.) You'll find guilt-free chocolate heaven at the **Ghirardelli Square Chocolate Festival** (☎775-5500; www.ghirardellisq.com) in early September, when proceeds from sampling all the chocolate goodies go to Project Open Hand. The oldest in America, **San Francisco Blues Festival** attracts some of the biggest names in the business. (☎979-5588; 3rd weekend in Sept. in Fort Mason.) Finally, the leather-and-chains gang lets it all hang out at the **Folsom Street Fair,** Pride Day's ruder, raunchier, rowdier little brother. (☎861-3247; www.folsomstreetfair.com; Sept. 26, 2004, on Folsom St. between 7th and 11th St.)

NIGHTLIFE

Nightlife in San Francisco is as varied as the city's personal ads. Everyone from the "shy first-timer" to the "bearded strap daddy" can find places to go on a Saturday (or Tuesday) night. The spots listed below are divided into bars and clubs, but the lines get pretty blurred in SF after dark, and even cafes hop at night. For additional information, check out the nightlife listings in the *S.F. Weekly*, *S.F. Bay Guardian*, and *Metropolitan*. **All clubs listed are 21+ only.** San Francisco is not a particularly friendly city to underagers.

Politics aside, nightlife alone is enough to earn San Francisco the title of "gay mecca." Generally, the boys hang in the **Castro** neighborhood, while the girls gravitate to the **Mission** (on and off Valencia St.); all frolic along **Polk Street** (several blocks north of Geary Blvd.), and in **SoMa.** *Polk St. can seem seedy and SoMa can appear barren, so keep a watchful eye, especially late at night.* Most clubs and bars listed below are gay-friendly. *The Sentinel* offers information on gay community events, and the free *Odyssey* and *Oblivion* are excellent guides.

BARS & PUBS

Hotel Utah Saloon, 500 4th St. (☎546-6300) in SoMa. More than average bar food, including veggie options and burgers (from $7). Stage hosts live rock or country music nightly and one of the best open mics in the city on M (shows begin 8:30-9pm). Beer $3.75. Show cover $3-7. Open M-F 11:30am-2am, Sa-Su 6pm-2am.

The Bar on Castro, 456 Castro St. (☎626-7220), between Market and 18th St. A refreshingly urbane Castro bar with plush couches perfect for eyeing the stylish young crowd, scoping the techno-raging dance floor, or watching *Queer as Folk* on Su. Happy Hour M-F 3-8pm (beer $2.25). Su beer $1.75. Open M-F 4pm-2am, Sa-Su noon-2am.

Café Royale, 800 Post St. (☎441-4099). "Creamsicle" *sake* cocktails and fresh sandwiches ($7.50) make this the right place for relaxing. DJs sometimes spin for a mixed crowd. Happy Hour M-F 3-7pm. Brunch Su 11am-5pm with omelettes and chicken-apple sausage ($5-7). Open Su 11am-midnight, M-Th 4pm-midnight, F-Sa 4pm-2am.

111 Minna, 111 Minna St. (☎974-1719; www.111minnagallery.com), at 2nd St. "Art and Leisure" at this funky up-and-comer's art gallery by day, hipster groove-spot by night. Cocktails and beer $3-10. Cover $5-15 for bands and progressive house DJs. Open M-Tu noon-10pm, W noon-11pm, Th-F noon-2am, Sa 10pm-2am, Su 9pm-2am.

Lefty O'Doul's, 333 Geary St. (☎982-8900), between Mason and Powell St. Named after iconic baseball hero Frank "Lefty" O'Doul, this colossal Irish tavern is like 3 smaller bars in one: a piano lounge, a vast bar and buffet (entrees $7, sandwiches $5) with booths and sit-down tables, and a sports bar in the back. Come for the drinks (most $4) and the nightly piano sing-along. Open daily 7am–2am; kitchen closes at midnight.

The Bigfoot Lodge, 1750 Polk St. (☎440-2355), between Clay and Washington St. in Nob Hill. Campy bear heads and bartenders uniformed as scouts keep up more of an image than does the easy-going crowd in this log cabin retreat. Beer $3.50-4.50, cocktails around $5. Happy Hour daily until 8pm. Open M-F 3pm-2am, Sa-Su noon-2am.

CLUBS

SF Badlands, 4121 18th St. (☎626-9320), near Castro St. Strutting past the sea of boys at the bar, the Castro's prettiest faces and bodies cruise a futuristic blue-and-chrome dance floor, where Madonna, George Michael, and Destiny's Child are transmitted in enthralling teleprojection. Cover F-Sa $2. Open daily 2pm-2am.

Velvet Lounge, 443 Broadway (☎788-0228), between Kearny and Montgomery St., in North Beach. Decked-out 20- and 30-somethings pack this club and thump along to top 40, hip-hop, and house. F occasional live cover bands. No sneakers or athletic wear. Cover usually $10. Open W-Sa 9pm-2am.

Liquid, 2925 16th St. (☎431-8889), at South Van Ness Ave., in the Mission. Nightly mix usually includes trip-hop and hip-hop, but mainly house. Young but mellow crowd fills the small space. Meet a cutie and practice those long-forgotten back seat skills; all of Liquid's couches are car seats. Cover $4-5. Open daily 9pm-3am.

The Endup, 401 6th St. (☎357-0827; www.theendup.com), at Harrison St. A San Francisco institution—complete with outdoor garden and patio—where everyone eventually ends up. DJs spin progressive house for the mostly straight KitKat Th, the pretty-boy Fag F, and the hetero-homo mix during popular all-day Sa-Su parties. Sa morning "Otherwhirled" party 4am. Infamous Su "T" Dance (27 years strong) 6pm-4am. Cover $5-15. Open Th 10:30pm-4am, F 10pm-4am, Sa 6am-noon and 10pm-4am, Su 6am-4am.

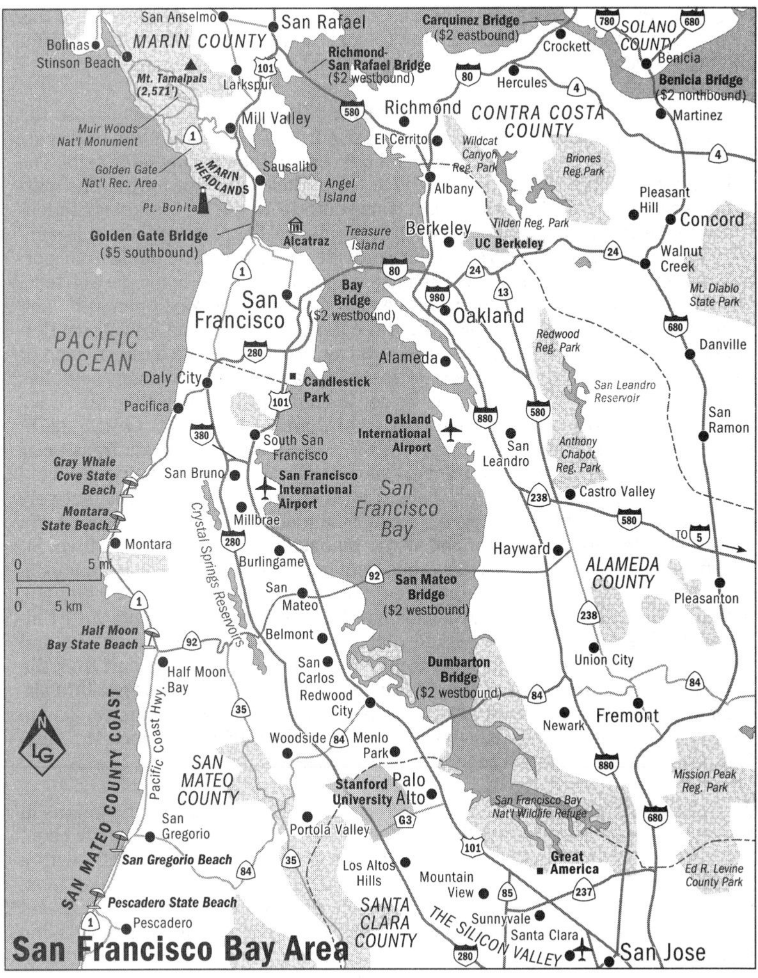

THE BAY AREA

BERKELEY ☎510

Famous as an intellectual center and a haven for iconoclasts, Berkeley continues to live up to its reputation. Although the peak of its political activism occurred in the 1960s and 70s—when students attended more protests than classes—**UC Berkeley** continues to cultivate consciousness and an intellectual atmosphere. The vitality of the population infuses the streets, which are strewn with hip cafes and top-notch bookstores, with a slightly psychotic vigor. **Telegraph Avenue,** with its street-corner soothsayers, hirsute hippies, and itinerant musicians, remains one of this town's main draws. Travelers looking to soak up all that Berkeley has to offer should also venture to the north and south of the UC Berkeley campus.

ORIENTATION & PRACTICAL INFORMATION. Berkeley lies across the Bay Bridge northeast of San Francisco, just north of Oakland. If you're driving from SF, cross the Bay Bridge on **I-80** and take one of the four Berkeley exits. The **University Avenue Exit** leads most directly to UC Berkeley and downtown. The magnetic heart of town, **Telegraph Avenue,** runs south from the UC Berkeley Student Union, while the **Gourmet Ghetto,** just north of campus, has some of California's finest dining. **Berkeley TRiP,** 2033 Center St., provides information on public transportation and biking, and sells extended-use transit passes and maps. (☎644-7665. Open Tu-F noon-5:30pm. Satellite office at 2543 Channing Way; open M-F 9am-2pm.) **Bay Area Rapid Transit (BART)** has three Berkeley stops. The Downtown Berkeley station, 2160 Shattuck Ave., at Center St., is close to the western edge of campus, while the North Berkeley station, at Delaware and Sacramento St., lies four blocks north of University Ave. To get to Southern Berkeley, take the BART to the Ashby stop at the corner of Ashby and Adeline St. (☎465-2278; www.bart.gov. 20-30min. to downtown SF, $2.65.) **Alameda County Transit** city buses #15, 43, and 51 run from the Berkeley BART station to downtown Oakland on Martin Luther King, Jr. Way, Telegraph Ave., and Broadway, respectively ($1.50; seniors, disabled, and ages 5-12 $0.75; under 5 free; 1hr. transfers $0.25). **Visitor Info: Berkeley Convention and Visitor Bureau,** 2015 Center St., at Milvia St. Helpful area maps, friendly service, up-to-date practical information, accommodation resources, the latest happenings, and tons of brochures. (☎549-7040; www.visitberkeley.com. Open M-F 9am-5pm.) **UC Berkeley Visitors Center,** 101 University Hall (☎642-5215; www.berkeley.edu), at the corner of University Ave. and Oxford St. Detailed maps and campus info. Guided campus tours depart from the center M-Sa 10am, Su 1pm. Open M-F 8:30am-4:30pm. **Internet Access: UC Computer,** 2569 Telegraph Ave. (☎649-6089. Open M-Sa 10am-6pm. 15min. $3, 30min. $5, 1hr. $7) **Post Office:** 2000 Allston Way, at Milvia St. (☎649-3155. Open M-F 9am-5pm, Sa 10am-2pm.) **Postal Code:** 94704. **Area Code:** 510.

ACCOMMODATIONS. There are surprisingly few cheap accommodations in Berkeley. The **Berkeley-Oakland Bed and Breakfast Network** (☎547-6380; www.bbonline.com/ca/berkeley-oakland) coordinates some great East Bay B&Bs with a range of rates (singles $50-150; doubles $60-150; twins $85-150). Although most motels are technically within walking distance of downtown Berkeley, UCB, and other attractions, they are much more accessible with a car. No-frills motels line University Ave. between Shattuck and Sacramento St.; ritzier joints are downtown, especially on Durant Ave. **UC Berkeley Summer Visitor Housing ❸** has simple college dorms, great location, shared baths, and free Internet access. (☎642-4108. Parking $6 per day. Open June to mid-Aug. Singles $53; doubles $68; seventh night free. Availability limited due to construction.) The **YMCA ❷,** 2001 Allston Way, has a communal kitchen, shared bath, computer room, and TV lounge. Use of pool and fitness facilities included. (☎848-6800. 10-night max. stay; special application for longer stays. Reception daily 8am-9:30pm. 18+. Singles $39; doubles $49; triples $59.) **Capri Motel ❹,** 1512 University Ave., at Sacramento St., has clean, tasteful rooms with cable TV, A/C, and fridge. (☎845-7090. 18+. Rooms from $85.)

FOOD. Berkeley's **Gourmet Ghetto,** at Shattuck Ave. and Cedar St., is the famous birthplace of California Cuisine. The north end of **Telegraph Avenue** caters to student appetites and wallets, with late-night offerings of all varieties along **Durant Avenue.** If you'd rather talk to a cow than eat one, you're in luck; Berkeley does greens like nowhere else. A growing number of international establishments are helping to diversify the area. **Solano Avenue** to the north is great for Asian cuisine while **4th Street** is home to some more upscale (but cheaper than Gourmet Ghetto) eats. **Café Intermezzo ❶,** 2442 Telegraph Ave., is a veritable veggie-lover's paradise, serving heaping salads with homemade dressing ($3.50-7), huge sandwiches on freshly baked bread ($5), and tasty soups, all at delicious prices. (☎849-4592. Open daily 10am-10pm.) North of Cedar St., **César ❷,** 1515 Shattuck Ave., is a great place for savory tapas ($3-12), *bocadillos* (a small sandwich on french bread, $5-7), desserts ($4-5), and an impressive list of spirits. (☎883-0222. Open daily noon-midnight; kitchen closes Su-Th 11pm, F-Sa 11:30pm.) An icon of Berkeley gastronomic life, **Yogurt Park ❶,** 2433 Durant Ave., just west of Telegraph Ave., serves huge portions of yogurt made daily ($1.75-2.20; additional toppings $0.65). (☎549-2198; 549-0570 for daily list of flavors. Open daily 10am-midnight.) For quality Ethiopian cuisine, try **The Blue Nile ❸,** 2525 Telegraph Ave. Eat *injera* bread with your fingers while sipping *mes* (honey wine; $2). (☎540-6777. Open Tu-Su 5-10pm. Reservations recommended.)

SIGHTS. In 1868, the private College of California and the public Agricultural, Mining, and Mechanical Arts College united as the **University of California.** The 178-acre university in Berkeley was the first of nine University of California campuses, so by seniority it has sole right to the nickname "Cal." Campus is bounded on the south by Bancroft Way, on the west by Oxford St., on the north by Hearst Ave., and on the east by Tilden Park. Enter through **Sather Gate** into **Sproul Plaza,** both sites of celebrated student sit-ins and bloody confrontations with police. Tours leave from **Sather Tower,** the tallest building on campus; you can ride to its observation level for a great view. (Open M-F 10am-4pm, $2; tip-top is not wheelchair-accessible.) **Berkeley Art Museum,** 2626 Bancroft Way, is most respected for its collection of 20th-century American and Asian art. BAM is also associated with the **Pacific Film Archive.** (☎642-0808; www.bampfa.berkeley.edu. Open W-Su 11am-7pm. Adults $8; students, seniors, disabled, and ages 12-17 $5. First Th of each month free.) You haven't really visited Berkeley until you've been on **Telegraph Avenue,** lined with a motley assortment of cafes, bookstores, and used clothing and record stores. For some off-campus fun, check out the **Takara Sake USA Inc.,** 708 Addison St. Take bus #51 to 4th St. and walk down to Addison St. Learn the history and science of sake making and sample 15 different types of Japan's merciless fire-water. (☎540-8250; www.takarasake.com. Open daily noon-6pm. Free.)

THE BIG SPLURGE

OAKLAND'S AVANT GARDE

Tucked away under the veneer of suburbia is an underground and emerging culture of cutting edge, experimental, performance, installation, and avant garde art. Here are a couple of places in Oakland to check out, if you're into that sort of thing.

The Black Box houses a technologically equipped theater space and art gallery and is getting increasing support from the cityfor its commitment to "the spirit of experimentation, multicultural collaboration, and community building through the celebration of life, art, and the cosmos." Check the web site for listings. *(1928 Telegraph Ave., just south of 20th St. ☎451-1932; www.blackboxoakland.com.)*

The Oakland Metro was spawned by the Oakland Opera Theater with the vision of creating an affordable, intimate performance space. *(201 Broadway, near Jack London Sq. ☎763-1146; www.oaklandmetro.org.)*

The Expressions Art Gallery offers incredible displays with a focus on installation art. *(815 Washington St., at 8th St. ☎451-6646. Open daily noon-8pm.)*

The Vulcan Lofts leads the underground revolution with Barbara's Cocktail Hour—an Internet radio show turned public party—at its Studio 56. Live broadcasts F 9pm-midnight. *(At High St. and San Leonardo Blvd. in East Oakland.)*

When you're ready to get out of town, Berkeley is happy to oblige. In the pine and eucalyptus forests east of the city lies the beautiful anchor of the East Bay park system—**Tilden Regional Park.** By car or bike, take Spruce St. to Grizzly Peak Blvd. to Canon Ave. Hiking, biking, running, and riding trails criss-cross the park and provide impressive views of the Bay Area. For those looking to frolic without getting sweaty, a 19th-century carousel inside the park is a fun option. (☎635-0135. Open daily dawn-dusk.) Also inside the park, the small, sandy beach at **Lake Anza** is a popular swimming spot during the hottest summer days. (☎843-2137. Open summer 11am-6pm. $3, seniors and children $2.)

ENTERTAINMENT & NIGHTLIFE **Jupiter,** 2181 Shattuck Ave., near the BART station, houses a huge beer garden and offers live music and terrific pizza for $8. (☎843-8277. Open M-Th 11:30am-1am, F 11:30am-2am, Sa noon-2am, Su noon-midnight.) **Caffè Strada,** 2300 College Ave., at Bancroft Way, is a glittering jewel of the caffeine-fueled intellectual scene. (☎843-5282. Open daily 6:30am-midnight.) **924 Gilman,** 924 Gilman St., is a legendary all-ages club and a staple of California punk. (☎524-8180. Cover $5 with $2 membership card, good for 1 year.) The boisterous and friendly **Triple Rock Brewery,** 1920 Shattuck Ave., north of Berkeley Way, was the first (and to many remains the best) of Berkeley's many brewpubs. Award-winning Red Rock Ale $3.25. (☎843-2739. Open Su-W 11:30am-midnight, Th-Sa 11:30am-1am. Rooftop garden closes 9pm, kitchen closes Su-W 10:30pm, Th-Sa midnight.)

MARIN COUNTY ☎415

Just across the Golden Gate Bridge, the jacuzzi of the bay—Marin (muh-RIN) County—bubbles over with enthusiastic (some might say dogmatic) residents who help the area strike a balance between upscale chic and counterculture nostalgia. Marin's pleasure spots lend themselves nicely to roadtrippers, and a web of trails combs the string of state and national parks that welcome mountain bikers and hikers. On the eastern side of the county, Sausalito, Mill Valley, and San Rafael line U.S. 101, and San Anselmo, Fairfax, and San Jose are easily accessible as well.

TRANSPORTATION

Buses: Golden Gate Transit (☎455-2000, in SF ☎923-2000; www.goldengate.org), provides bus service between San Francisco and Marin County via the Golden Gate Bridge, as well as local service in Marin. $2-5. **West Marin Stagecoach** (☎526-3239; www.marin-stagecoach.org) provides weekday service connecting West Marin communities to the rest of the county. Stops include: Muir Beach, Pt. Reyes Station, Samuel P. Taylor Park, and Stinson Beach. Call for schedules and routes. $1.50.

Ferries: Golden Gate Ferry (☎455-2000) runs from San Francisco to the Sausalito terminal at the end of Market St. ($5.60, under 18 $4.20, seniors and disabled $2.80), and to the Larkspur terminal (M-F $3.10/2.35/1.55; Sa-Su $5.30/4/2.65). **Blue and Gold Fleet** (☎773-1188) runs ferries from Pier 41 at Fisherman's Wharf to Sausalito and Tiburon ($6.75, under 5 free). Offices open M-F 6am-8pm, Sa-Su 7am-8pm.

Taxi: Belaire Cab Co., ☎388-1234.

Bike Rental: Cycle Analysis (☎663-9164; www.cyclepointreyes.com), out of a hitch-up in the empty, grassy lot at 4th and Main St. (Hwy. 1 in Point Reyes Station), rents unsuspended bikes ($30), front-suspension mountain bikes ($35), and child trailers ($25-30). Helmets included. Open F-Su 10am-5pm; weekdays by appointment.

ORIENTATION & PRACTICAL INFORMATION

The Marin peninsula lies at the northern end of the San Francisco Bay and is connected to the city by **U.S. 101** via the **Golden Gate Bridge.** U.S. 101 extends north inland to Santa Rosa and Sonoma County, while **Route 1** winds north along the Pacific coast. The **Richmond-San Rafael Bridge** connects Marin to the East Bay via **I-580.** Gas is scarce and expensive in West Marin, so fill up in town before you head out for the coast. Drivers should exercise caution in West Marin, where roads are narrow, sinuous, and perched on the edges of cliffs.

Visitor Info: Marin County Visitors Bureau, 1013 Larkspur Landing Cir. (☎499-5000; www.visitmarin.org), off Sir Francis Drake Blvd. Exit from U.S. 101, near the ferry terminal. Open M-F 9am-5pm.

Park Visitor Info: Marin Headlands Visitors Center, Bldg. 948, Fort Barry (☎331-1540), at Bunker and Field Rd., has info about hiking and biking in the park, permits for free campsites, maps, and trail advice. The center is also a museum with artifacts and exhibits on the history of the Headlands. Open daily 9:30am-4:30pm. Rangers at **Point Reyes National Seashore Headquarters,** known as **Bear Valley Visitor Center** (☎464-5100; www.nps.gov/pore), on Bear Valley Rd. ½ mi. west of Olema, give out camping permits, maps, and advice on trails, tides, and weather conditions, and lead guided hikes. Open M-F 9am-5pm, Sa-Su 8am-5pm. **Pan Toll Ranger's Station,** 801 Panoramic Hwy. (☎388-2070), in Mt. Tamalpais State Park, about 2½ mi. inland from Stinson Beach (bus #63), operates Mt. Tam's campgrounds and trails. **Muir Woods National Monument Visitors Center** (☎388-2596; www.nps.gov/muwo), near the entrance to Muir Woods. Muir Woods trail map $1. Great selection of hiking, biking, and driving maps of Marin and Mt. Tam. Open daily 9am-6pm.

Medical Services: Marin General Hospital and Community Clinic, 250 Bon Air Rd. (☎925-7000), in Greenbrae off the U.S. 101 San Anselmo exit. 24hr. emergency care.

Post Office: 15 Calle Del Mar (☎868-1504), at Shoreline Hwy. in Stinson Beach. Open M-F 8:30am-5pm. **Postal Code:** 94970. **Area Code:** 415.

ACCOMMODATIONS

West Point Inn (☎388-9955, reservations 646-0702), on Mt. Tamalpais, 2 mi. up Stage Rd. Park at the Pan Toll Ranger Station ($4) and hike or bike up. Not the lap of luxury, but one hell of an experience. Propane-generated heat, light, and refrigeration. No other electricity around. 35-person capacity. 7 private rooms. 5 private cabins. Well-equipped, shared kitchen. $30, under 18 $15, under 5 free. Bring your own linens, sleeping bags, food, and flashlight, but not your pets. Reservations required. Sa vacancies are rare. Closed Su and M nights. Call for wheelchair-accessibility. ❶

Marin Headlands Hostel (HI-AYH), Bldg. 941 on Rosenstock (☎331-2777 or 800-909-4776; www.headlandshostel.homestead.com), up the hill from the Visitors Center. 2 spacious and immaculate Victorian houses with 100 beds, game room, kitchens, and common rooms. Linen $1; towels $0.50. Laundry $1.50. Key deposit $10. Check-in 3:30-10:30pm. Check-out 10am. Lockout 10am-3:30pm. Internet access $0.10 per min. Reservations recommended for private rooms and weekends. Dorms $18, under 17 with parent $8; private doubles $54. ❶

The Headlands (☎331-1540; www.nps.gov/goga/camping), offers 3 small walk-in campgrounds with 11 primitive campsites for individual backpackers and small groups. Bring your own water and camp stove. No fires or pets allowed. Showers and kitchen

($2 each) at Headlands Hostel. Free outdoor cold showers at Rodeo Beach. 3-day max. stay. Reserve up to 90 days in advance. For all campgrounds, individual sites are free with a permit that can be obtained at the Marin Headlands Visitors Center (p. 949). ❶

FOOD

Marinites take their fruit juices, tofu, and double-shot cappuccinos very seriously; restauranteurs know this, and raise both alfalfa sprouts and prices.

Avatar's Punjabi Burrito, 15 Madrona St. (☎381-8293), in Mill Valley. Take chickpeas, chutney, yogurt, and spice. Add tofu and other things nice. Wrap in yummy Indian bread, and you have a delicious meal for $5.50-8.50. Open M-Sa 11am-8pm. ❷

Bubba's Diner, 566 San Anselmo Ave. (☎459-6862), in San Anselmo. A local favorite that serves all the essentials with daily specials. Bubba's famous oyster sandwich $13. Open M and W-F 9am-2pm and 5:30-9pm, Sa-Su 8am-2:30pm and 5:30-9:30pm. ❸

Venice Gourmet Delicatessen, 625 Bridgeway (☎332-3544), in Sausalito. Serves sharable sandwiches ($6) and side dishes ($3-5) in a Mediterranean-style marketplace with water-side seating. Open daily summer 9am-7pm; winter 9am-6pm. ❷

Sushi Ran, 107 Caledonia St. (☎332-3620) in Sausalito, is a local favorite. It offers upscale Asian fare, including *sake* bar and vegetarian *maki*. California roll $6.50. Open for lunch M-F 11:30am-2:30pm, dinner M-Sa 5:30-11pm, Su 5:30-10:30pm. ❷

SIGHTS

Marin's proximity to San Francisco makes it a popular daytrip destination. Virtually everything worth seeing or doing in Marin is outdoors. An efficient visitor can hop from park to park and enjoy several short hikes along the coast and through the redwood forests in the same day, topping it off with a pleasant dinner in one of the small cities. Those without cars, however, may find it easier to use one of the two well-situated hostels as a base for hiking or biking explorations.

MOUNT TAMALPAIS & MUIR WOODS

Beautiful **Mount Tamalpais State Park** (tam-ull-PIE-us) rests between the upscale towns of East Marin and the rocky bluffs of West Marin. The 6300-acre park, one of the oldest and most popular in the California State Park System, has miles of hilly, challenging trails on and around 2571 ft. high **Mount Tam,** the highest peak in the county. The **Mountain Theater** is known throughout the area for its Mountain Play, staged every summer since 1913. The natural 3750-seat amphitheater houses many special events as well. Mt. Tam also offers an annual **Astronomy Program,** a series of free lectures held in the Mountain Theater followed by telescope observation in the Rock Spring Parking Area. On a clear day, you can gaze from Mt. Tam across all of the San Francisco shoreline. *(Take Hwy. 1 to the Panoramic Hwy. Continue for 5¼ mi. to reach the Ranger Station and Pan Toll Rd. ☎388-2070. Open summer 8am-9pm; winter 9am-8pm. Free. Astronomy Program: ☎455-5370.)*

TRAILS. Mt. Tam has over 50 mi. of trails, suitable for a variety of fitness levels. The bubbling waterfall on **Cataract Trail** and the **Gardner Lookout** on Mt. Tam's east peak are worthy destinations. The **Bootjack Trail** up to the Mountain Theater offers breathtaking views. The **Steep Ravine Trail** heads to the beach, and the **Matt Davis Trail** winds itself up towards the peak (connect with **Fern Creek Trail** to make it all the way to the top). The **Pan Toll Ranger Station** (see p. 949) sells maps and can offer suggestions for loops of various length and difficulty.

MUIR & STINSON BEACHES. Sheltered Muir Beach is scenic and popular with families. The crowds thin out significantly after a 5min. climb on the shore rocks to the left. Six miles to the north, Stinson Beach attracts a younger, rowdier, good-looking surfer crowd, although cold and windy conditions often leave them high and dry. The Bard joins the Stinson Beach crowds from July to October during Shakespeare at Stinson. Between Muir Beach and Stinson Beach lies the nudist **Red Rocks Beach,** a secluded spot reached by a steep hike down from a parking area 1 mi. south of Stinson Beach. *(☎868-1115; www.shakespeareatstinson.org. Muir Beach open daily dawn-9pm. Stinson Beach open daily dawn-dusk. Bus #63 runs from Sausalito to Stinson Beach on weekends and holidays.)*

MARIN HEADLANDS

Fog-shrouded hills just west of the Golden Gate Bridge constitute the Marin Headlands. These windswept ridges, precipitous cliffs, and hidden sandy beaches offer superb hiking and biking within minutes of downtown SF. For instant gratification, drive up to any of the several look-out spots and pose for your own postcard-perfect shot of the Golden Gate Bridge and the city skyline.

POINT BONITA. The well-preserved little lighthouse at the end of **Point Bonita** really doesn't seem up to the job of guarding the whole San Francisco Bay, but it has done so valiantly with the same glass lens since 1855. The lens was actually lowered in 1877 in order to duck below the Bay's relentless fog. The lighthouse is accessible via a short tunnel through the rock and a miniature suspension bridge. Strong winds make Point Bonita a chilly spot; bring a jacket. *(Lighthouse: 1 mi. from Visitors Center, ½ mi. from nearest parking. Open Sa-M 12:30-3:30pm. Guided walks Sa-M 12:30pm. Free. No dogs or bikes in tunnel.)*

PALO ALTO ☎650

Called "the World's Largest Taco Bell" by Berkeley students, **Stanford University** is the product of an academic-architectural collaboration between Jane and Leland Stanford (who wanted to build a university to honor their dead son) and Frederick Law Olmsted (who designed Manhattan's Central Park). Completed in 1885, the co-educational, secular university is built around the colonnaded **Main Quadrangle,** which is also the sight of most undergraduate activity. An **Information Booth** is across from Hoover Tower, (☎723-2053; open daily 8am-5pm), in Memorial Auditorium. Free student-led tours depart daily 11:15am and 3:15pm; times vary on holidays and during exam periods.

Hidden Villa Ranch Hostel (HI-AYH) ❶, 26870 Moody Rd., is about 10 mi. southwest of Palo Alto in Los Altos Hills. Dorm, family, and private are rooms available. (☎949-8648. Reception 8am-noon and 4-9:30pm. Reservations required for weekends and groups. Open Sept.-May. Dorms $15, nonmembers $18; children $7.50. Private cabins $30-42.) **Café Borrone ❷,** 1010 El Camino Real, offers great salads and entrees. (☎327-0830. Open M-Th 8am-11pm, F-Sa 8am-midnight, Su 8am-5pm.) Every day is a fiesta at **Nola ❸,** 535 Ramona St., thanks to the late-night menu and cocktails. (☎328-2722. Open daily 5:30pm-2am.)

Palo Alto is 35 mi. southeast of San Francisco; from the north, take **U.S. 101 South** to the University Ave. Exit, or the Embarcadero Rd. Exit directly to the Stanford campus. Alternatively, motorists from San Francisco can split off onto **Interstate 280 (Junípero Serra Highway)** for a slightly longer but more scenic route. From I-280, exit at Sand Hill Rd. and follow it to the northwest corner of Stanford University. The **Palo Alto Transit Center,** on University Ave., serves local and regional buses and trains. (☎323-6105. Open daily 5am-12:30am.) The transit center connects to points north via **San Mateo County buses** and to Stanford via the free **Marguerite Shuttle.**

WINE COUNTRY

NAPA VALLEY ☎707

Napa catapulted American wine into the big leagues in 1976, when a bottle of red from Napa's Stag's Leap Vineyards beat a bottle of critically acclaimed (and unfailingly French) Château Lafitte-Rothschild in a blind taste test in Paris. While not the oldest, and not necessarily the best, Napa Valley is certainly the best-known of America's wine-growing regions. Its golden hills, natural hot springs, and sunlight inspired Gold Rush millionaires to build luxury spas for vacationers in the 1850s. Indeed, it wasn't until the 1960s, when the now big-name wineries like Mondavi first opened, that the region was able to assert itself not as a spa retreat, but as Wine Country. Now firmly established as such, Napa draws a mostly older, well-to-do crowd, but in the midst of the tasting carnival there are plenty of young, budget-minded folks looking forward to their fill of chardonnay and their share of class.

ORIENTATION & PRACTICAL INFORMATION

Scenic **Route 29 (Saint Helena Highway)** runs north from **Napa** through Napa Valley and the well-groomed villages of **Yountville** and **Saint Helena** (where it's called Main St.) to **Calistoga's** soothing spas. The relatively short distances between wineries can take unpleasantly long to cover on weekends when the roads crawl with visitors. The **Silverado Trail,** parallel to Rte. 29, is less crowded, but watch out for cyclists. Napa is 14 mi. east of Sonoma on **Route 12.** If you're planning a weekend trip from San Francisco, avoid Saturday mornings and Sunday afternoons; the roads are packed with like-minded people. Although harvest season in early September is the most exciting time to visit, winter weekdays are less packed and offer more personal attention. From San Francisco, take U.S. 101 over the Golden Gate Bridge, then follow Rte. 37 east to catch Rte. 29, which runs north to Napa.

Public Transportation: Napa City Bus, or **Valley Intercity Neighborhood Express (VINE),** 1151 Pearl St. (☎800-696-6443 or 255-7631), covers Vallejo (M-F 5:20am-8pm, Sa 6:15am-5:30pm, Su 11am-6pm; $1.50, students $1.10, seniors and disabled $0.75) and Calistoga (M-F 5:20am-8pm, Sa 6am-6:40pm, Su 9:30am-4:30pm; $2, students $1.45, seniors and disabled $1). A Greyhound station, 1500 Lemon St. (☎643-7661 or 800-231-2222), is in Vallejo. A bus runs to Napa and Calistoga, but it's slow—almost 3hr. from Vallejo to Calistoga—and doesn't stop near wineries.

Airport Service: Evans Airport Transport, 4075 Solano Ave. (☎255-1559 or 944-2025), in Napa, runs daily shuttles from the **San Francisco** and **Oakland** airports via Vallejo to downtown Napa. Reservations required. To **Napa** (one-way $29, children 12 and under $15) and **Vallejo** (one-way $24, children 12 and under $15).

Visitor Info:

Napa Conference & Visitors Bureau, 1310 Town Ctr. (☎226-7459; www.napavalley.com/nvcvb.html). Very friendly staff. Free maps and info. Also sells the *Napa Valley Guidebook* ($6) with more comprehensive listings and fold-out maps. Ask about any specials during your visit (they come in daily) and pick up coupons from local businesses. Open daily 9am-5pm.

St. Helena Chamber of Commerce, 1010A Main St. (☎963-4456), across from Taylor's Refresher (see p. 953). Eager to help. Open M-F 10am-5pm.

Calistoga Chamber of Commerce, 1458 Lincoln Ave. (☎942-6333; www.calistogafun.com). Open M-F 10am-5pm, Sa 10am-4pm, Su 11am-3pm.

Winery Tours: Napa Valley Holidays (☎255-1050; www.napavalleyholidays.com). Afternoon tours $75 per person, $85 with round-trip transportation from San Francisco.

Car Rental: Budget, 407 Soscol Ave. (☎224-7846), in Napa. Cars $40 per day; under 25 surcharge $20 per day. Unlimited mileage. Must be at least 21 with credit card. Promotional specials often available; call Budget Reservation Center at ☎800-537-0700.

Bike Rental: **St. Helena Cyclery,** 1156 Main St. (☎963-7736). Hybrid bikes $7 per hr., $30 per day; road bikes $15/50; tandem bikes $20/70. All bikes come with maps, helmet, lock, and picnic bag. Reservations recommended for road and tandem bikes. Open M-Sa 9:30am-5:30pm, Su 10am-5pm.

Police: In **Napa,** 1539 1st St. (☎253-4451). In **Calistoga,** 1235 Washington St. (☎942-2810).

Hospital: Queen of the Valley, 1000 Trancas St. (☎252-4411), in Napa.

Post Office: 1627 Trancas St. (☎255-0360), in Napa. Open M-F 8:30am-5pm. **Postal Code:** 94558. **Area Code:** 707.

ACCOMMODATIONS & CAMPING

Rooms in Napa Valley can go quickly despite high prices; reserving ahead is best. Though Napa is close to the Bay Area and has the advantages of a city, smaller towns will prove more wallet-friendly. Calistoga is a good first choice; the quaint town is a short drive from many wineries and is close to Old Faithful Geyser, the Petrified Forest, and Bothe-Napa State Park. It is also home to natural hot-spring spas. The least expensive alternative, as always, is camping, but be prepared for the intense heat which might drive you back to the air-conditioned civilization.

Golden Haven Hot Springs Spa and Resort, 1713 Lake St. (☎942-6793; www.goldenhaven.com), a few blocks from Lincoln Ave. in Calistoga. More of a nice motel than a resort. Large, well-decorated standard-issue rooms with TVs and phones. Rooms with king beds, kitchenettes, jacuzzis, and saunas also available. Mineral swimming pool and hot tub access. No children under 16. Weekends 2-night min. stay, holiday weekends 3-night min. stay. Queen $79, with private sauna $145; king $95, with kitchenette $135, with private jacuzzi $185. Nov.-Mar. M-Th $69/115/75/109/145. ❺

Calistoga Inn and Brewery, 1250 Lincoln Ave. (☎942-4101; www.calistogainn.com), at the corner of Rte. 29 in Calistoga. 18 clean, simple, country inn double- and queen-sized rooms. Microbrewery and restaurant downstairs; the walk home from the pub is just a short stumble upstairs. Shared bathrooms. Restaurant and bar open 11:30am-11pm. Rooms Su-Th $75, F-Sa and holidays $100. ❹

Bothe-Napa Valley State Park, 3801 Rte. 29 (☎942-4575, reservations 800-444-7275), north of St. Helena. The 50 quiet sites near Ritchey Creek Canyon are fairly rustic, though there are toilets, fire pits, and picnic tables. Pool $2, under 17 free. Check-in 2pm. Picnic area day-use $4. Hot showers $0.25 per 4min. $16, seniors $10. ❶

FOOD

Eating in Wine Country ain't cheap, but the food is worth it. Picnics are an inexpensive and romantic option—supplies can be bought at the numerous delis. Many wineries have shaded picnic grounds, often with excellent views, but most require patronage to use. The **Napa farmer's market,** at Pearl and West St., offers a sampling of the valley's non-alcoholic produce. (☎252-7142. Open daily 7:30am-noon.)

Taylor's Refresher, 933 Main St. (☎963-3486), on Rte. 29 across from Merryvale Winery in St. Helena. Roadside stand dishes up big burgers ($4.50-7) and phenomenal milkshakes ($4.60). Outdoor seating. Beer and wine served. Open daily 11am-9pm. ❷

First Squeeze Cafe & Juice Bar, 1126 First St. (☎224-6762), in Napa, offers sandwiches, soups, salads, and smoothies. Try their most popular plate, huevos rancheros ($8), or grab a fresh fruit smoothie ($4). Also serves beer and wine. Breakfast every day until 2pm. Free downtown delivery. Open M-F 7am-3pm, Sa-Su 8am-3pm. ❷

Calistoga Natural Foods and Juice Bar, 1426 Lincoln St. (☎942-5822), in Calistoga. One of a few natural foods stores in the area. Organic juices ($3-5), smoothies ($4.50), sandwiches ($4-6.25), and vegetarian specialties like the Cherry Wrapture ($6.50) and Yummus Hummus wrap ($6.50). Organic groceries also sold. Open M-Sa 9am-6pm. ❷

WINERIES

There are more than 250 wineries in Napa County, nearly two-thirds of which line Rte. 29 and the Silverado Trail in Napa Valley, home of Wine Country's heavy-weights. Some wineries have free tastings and some have free tours; all have large selections of bottled wine available for purchase at prices cheaper than in stores. A good way to begin your Napa Valley experience is with a tour such as the ones offered at **Domaine Carneros,** or a free tastings class, like the one on Saturday mornings at **Goosecross Cellars,** 1119 State Ln. (☎944-1986; open daily 11am-4pm), in Yountville. Go to wine school and become a well-educated lush.

Kirkland Ranch, 1 Kirkland Ranch Rd. (☎254-9100), south of Napa off Rte. 29. Reminiscent of a ranch house, this family-operated winery has windows overlooking the production facilities. True to its Country Western style, the winery's walls are adorned with family pictures of cattle-herding cowboys. Tours by appointment. Tastings $5. U.S. military personnel and veterans receive 30% off wine purchases.

Domaine Carneros, 1240 Duhig Rd. (☎257-0101), off Rte. 121 between Napa and Sonoma. Picturesque estate with an elegant terrace modeled after a French *château.* "Be prepared to feel like royalty" is their slogan. Owned by Champagne Taittinger and known for its sparkling wines. The free tour and film (daily every hr. 10:15am-4pm) is a great way to kick off a day of wine tasting. No tastings here, but wines by the glass $5-10 with complimentary *hors d'oeuvres.* Open daily 10am-5:30pm.

Clos Du Val Wine Company, Ltd., 5330 Silverado Trail (☎259-2225; www.closduval.com), north of Oak Knoll Rd., in Yountville. Small, stylish grounds attract lots of tourists. Tastings $5; price applicable towards wine purchase. Free tours by appointment. Open daily 10am-4:30pm.

Domaine Chandon, 1 California Dr. (☎944-2280 or 800-934-3975; www.chandon.com), in Yountville. Owned by Moët Chandon (the French makers of Dom Perignon), the winery produces 4-5 million bottles of sparkling wine annually. The sleek Visitors Center and manicured gardens evoke a Zen-like meditative spirit. French restaurant on site. 3 tastes for $9, by the glass $4.50-12. Open daily 10am-6pm.

Niebaum-Coppola Estate Winery, 1991 St. Helena Hwy. (☎968-1100). Famed film director Francis Ford Coppola and his wife bought the historic 1880 Inglenook Chateau and Niebaum vineyards in 1975. Restoring the estate to production capacity, Coppola also added a family history museum upstairs; it includes memorabilia from his films such as the desk from *The Godfather* and his Oscar and Golden Globe statues (free access). $8.50 fee includes 4 tastes and commemorative glass. Regular tours ($20) daily 10:30am, 12:30, 2:30pm; vineyard tours ($20) 11am daily; Rubicon tours ($45) by reservation Su, Th, and Sa at 1pm. Open daily 10am-5pm.

SIGHTS & OUTDOOR ACTIVITIES

Napa's gentle terrain makes for an excellent bike tour. The area is fairly flat, although small bike lanes, speeding cars, and blistering heat can make routes more challenging, especially after a few samples of wine. The 26 mi. **Silverado Trail** has a wider bike path than Rte. 29. **St. Helena Cyclery,** 1156 Main St., rents bikes (see **Practical Information,** p. 953).

CALISTOGA. Calistoga is known as the "Hot Springs of the West." Its luxuriant mud baths, massages, and mineral showers will feel welcome after a hard day of wine-tasting, but be sure to hydrate; alcohol-thinned blood and intense heat do not mix. A basic package consisting of mud bath, mineral bath, eucalyptus steam, blanket wrap, and massage costs around $80. The **Calistoga Village Inn & Spa** gives friendly service. *(☎942-0991. Mud bath treatment $45; 25min. massage $45; 25min. facial*

$49; ultimate 3hr. package of mud bath treatment, salt scrub, 55min. massage, and mini facial $185.) For a less pretentious spa, try **Golden Haven.** *(☎942-6793. Mud bath treatment $65, 30min. massage $45, 30min. facial $45.)*Cooler water is at **Lake Berryessa** *(☎966-2111)*, 20 mi. north of Napa off Hwy. 128, where swimming, sailing, and sunbathing are popular along its 169 mi. shoreline.

OLD FAITHFUL GEYSER OF CALIFORNIA. The geyser, not to be confused with its more famous namesake, regularly jets boiling water 60 ft. into the air. The ticket vendor will tell you the estimated time of the next spurt. *(1299 Tubbs Ln. off Hwy. 128., 2 mi. outside Calistoga. ☎942-6463. Open daily 9am-6pm; winter 9am-5pm. $6, seniors $5, ages 6-12 $2, disabled free.)*

MARINE WORLD. This 160-acre Vallejo attraction is an enormous zoo-oceanarium-theme park. It has animal shows and special attractions like the Lorikeet Aviary, the Butterfly Walk, and the Shark Experience. The park was recently purchased by Six Flags. *(Off Rte. 37, 10 mi. south of Napa. ☎643-6722. Vallejo is accessible from San Francisco by BART (☎510-465-2278) and the Blue and Gold fleet (☎415-705-5444). Open Mar.-Aug. Su-Th 10am-8pm, F-Sa 10am-9pm; Sept.-Oct. F-Su 10am-6pm. $34, seniors $25, ages 4-12 or under 48 in. $17. Parking $6.)*

OTHER SIGHTS. **The Petrified Forest,** 4100 Petrified Forest Rd., west of Calistoga, was formed over three million years ago when molten lava from a volcano eruption 7 mi. northeast of Mt. St. Helens covered a forested valley and preserved the trees. The quarter-mile trail is wheelchair-accessible. *(☎942-6667. Open daily 10am-6pm; winter 10am-5pm. Free.)* Experience an authentic Venetian gondola ride on Napa River with **Gondola Servizio Napa,** 540 Main St., inside Hatt Market. *(☎257-8495. 30min. private ride $55 per couple; $10 each additional person.)* **Napa Valley Wine Train,** 1275 McKinstry St., offers dining and drinking on board in the style of the early 1900s, traveling from Napa to St. Helena and back. *(☎253-2111 or 800-427-4124; www.winetrain.com. Train ride 3hr. M-F 11am and 6pm; Sa-Su 8:30am, 12:10, 5:30pm. Ticket and meal plans $35-90. Advance reservations and payments required.)*

SONOMA VALLEY ☎707

Sprawling Sonoma Valley is a quieter alternative to Napa, but home to bigger wineries than the Russian River Valley. Many wineries are on winding side roads rather than a freeway strip, creating a more intimate wine-tasting experience. Sonoma Plaza is surrounded by art galleries, novelty shops, clothing stores, and Italian restaurants. Petaluma, west of the Sonoma Valley, has more budget-friendly lodgings than the expensive wine country.

TRANSPORTATION

From San Francisco, take **U.S. 101 North** over the Golden Gate Bridge, then follow Rte. 37 E to Rte. 116 N, which turns into Rte. 121 N and crosses Rte. 12 N to Sonoma. Alternatively, follow U.S. 101 N to Petaluma and cross over to Sonoma by Rte. 116. Driving time from San Francisco is 1-1½hr. **Route 12** traverses the length of Sonoma Valley, from **Sonoma** through **Glen Ellen** to **Kenwood** in the north. The center of downtown is **Sonoma Plaza. Broadway** dead ends at Napa St. in front of City Hall. Numbered streets run north-south. **Petaluma** lies to the west and is connected to Sonoma by **Route 116,** which becomes **Lakeville Street** in Petaluma.

Buses: Sonoma County Transit (☎576-7433 or 800-345-7433; www.sctransit.com) serves the entire county. Bus #30 runs from **Sonoma** to **Santa Rosa** (daily every 1½hr. 6am-4pm; $2.05, students $1.70, seniors and disabled $1, under 6 free); buses #44 and #48 go to **Petaluma** (M-F; $1.75, students $1.45, seniors and disabled $0.85). **County buses** stop when flagged down at bus stops (M-Su 8am-4:25pm; $0.95, students $0.75, seniors and disabled $0.45). **Golden Gate Transit** (☎541-2000 from Sonoma County or 415-923-2000 from San Francisco) runs buses frequently between **San Francisco** and **Santa Rosa.** **Volunteer Wheels** (☎800-992-1006) offers door-to-door service for people with disabilities. Call for reservations. Open daily 8am-5pm.

Bike Rental: Sonoma Valley Cyclery, 20093 Broadway (☎935-3377), in Sonoma. Bikes $6 per hr., $25 per day; includes helmet. Open M-Sa 10am-6pm, Su 10am-4pm.

PRACTICAL INFORMATION

Visitor Info: Sonoma Valley Visitors Bureau, 453 E. 1st St. (☎996-1090; www.sonomavalley.com), in Sonoma Plaza. Maps $2. Open daily June-Oct. 9am-7pm; Nov.-May 9am-5pm. **Petaluma Visitors Program,** 800 Baywood Dr. (☎769-0429), at Lakeville St. Open May-Oct. M-F 9am-5:30pm, Sa-Su 10am-6pm; shorter weekend hours in the low-season. The free visitor's guide has listings of restaurants and activities.

Police: ☎778-4372 in Petaluma, ☎996-3602 in Sonoma.

Medical Services: Petaluma Valley, 400 N. McDowell Blvd. (☎781-1111).

Post Office: Sonoma, 617 Broadway (☎996-9311), at Patten St. Open M-F 8:30am-5pm. **Postal Code:** 95476. **Petaluma,** 120 4th St. (☎769-5352). Open M-F 8:30am-5pm, Sa 10am-2pm. **Postal Code:** 94952. **Area Code:** 707.

ACCOMMODATIONS

Pickings are pretty slim for lodging; rooms are scarce even on weekdays and generally start at $85. Less expensive motels cluster along **U.S. 101** in Santa Rosa and Petaluma. Campers with cars should try the **Russian River Valley.**

Redwood Inn, 1670 Santa Rosa Ave. (☎545-0474), in Santa Rosa. A decent drive from Sonoma. Clean, comfortable rooms and suites with kitchenettes, cable TV, phones, and bath. Singles $55; doubles $65. $5 less in winter. AARP and AAA discounts. ❹

Sonoma Creek Inn, 239 Boyes Blvd. (☎939-9463 or 888-712-1289), west off Hwy. 12, in Sonoma. Just 10min. from the Sonoma Plaza, restaurants, and wineries. Colorful rooms with kitchenette, cable TV, phone, and full bath. Rooms $89-159. ❺

Sugarloaf Ridge State Park, 2605 Adobe Canyon Rd. (☎833-5712), off Rte. 12, north of Kenwood in the Mayacamas mountains. Around a meadow with flush toilets and running water (but no showers) are 49 sites with tables and fire rings. In summer and fall, take advantage of the sky-watching at Ferguson Observatory. Reserve sites through ReserveAmerica (☎800-444-7275; www.reserveamerica.com). Sites $15, seniors $10; day-use $4. No credit cards at the park, but ReserveAmerica accepts MC/V. ❶

San Francisco North/Petaluma KOA, 20 Rainsville Rd. (☎763-1492 or 800-992-2267; www.petalumakoa.com), in Petaluma off the Penngrove Exit. Suburban camp with 300 sites plus a recreation hall with activities, petting zoo, pool, store, laundry facilities, and jacuzzi. Many families. Hot showers. Check-in 1pm. Check-out 11am. 1-week max. tent stay. Reservations recommended. 2-person tent sites $31-35; each additional adult $5, child $3. RVs $38-41. Cabins (sleep 4; no linens) $55-60. ❸

FOOD

Fresh produce is seasonally available directly from area farms and roadside stands. Those in the area toward the end of the summer should ask about the ambrosial **crane melon,** a tasty hybrid of fruits grown only on the Crane Farm north of Petaluma. The **Sonoma Market,** 520 W. Napa St., in the Sonoma Valley Center, is an old-fashioned grocery store with deli sandwiches ($5-7) and very fresh produce. (☎996-0563; open daily 6am-9pm.) The **Fruit Basket,** 18474 Sonoma Hwy., sells inexpensive fruit. (☎996-7433. Open daily 7am-7pm. No credit cards.)

Sonoma Cheese Factory, 2 Spain St. (☎996-1931 or 800-535-2855; www.sonomajack.com), in Sonoma. Forget the wine for now—take a toothpick and skewer the free cheese samples. You can even watch the cheese-making process in the back room. Sandwiches ($4.50-5.50). Open daily 8:30am-5:30pm. ❷

Maya, 101 E. Napa St. (☎935-3500), at the corner of 1st St. E in Sonoma's Historic Town Square. Brings Yucatan spirit to Sonoma. The festive decor, mouth-watering food, and extensive wine and tequila menu are truly impressive. Entrees $10-20. Occasional live music in summer. Open daily 11am-11pm. ❸

Basque Boulangerie Cafe, 460 First St. E. (☎935-7687), in Sonoma Plaza. Below the wall of freshly baked French breads is a counter filled with tarts, mini-gateaus, and pastries ($2-20). Delicious sandwiches $5.50 for lunch. With 24hr. advance notice they'll even arrange a box lunch ($10.50) for vineyard picnicking. Open daily 7am-6pm. ❸

Murphy's Irish Pub, 464 First St. E. (☎935-0660; www.sonomapub.com), tucked in an alleyway off Sonoma Plaza. A sign here reads, "God created whiskey to keep the Irish from ruling the world." Ponder the geopolitical ramifications over a grilled chicken sandwich ($7.50), fish 'n' chips ($6.25), or other popular pub grub. Extensive beer list. Live music on the outdoor patio almost every night (8pm). Open daily 11am-11pm. ❷

WINERIES

Sonoma Valley's wineries, near Sonoma and Kenwood, are less touristy but just as elegant as Napa's. As an added bonus, there are more complimentary tastings of current vintages.

Gundlach-Bundschu, 2000 Denmark St. (☎938-5277; www.gunbun.com), off 8th St. E. Established in 1858, this is the second oldest winery in Sonoma and the oldest family-owned, family-run winery in the country. Fragrant wines and a setting of pronounced loveliness. In the summer it hosts outdoor events like the Mozart series. Free wine storage cave tours Sa-Su noon, 1, 2, 3pm. Free tastings daily 11am-4:30pm.

Benziger, 1833 London Ranch Rd. (☎935-4046 or 888-490-2379; www.benziger.com). This winery is known for its big, buttery, accessible wines. Tourists flock here for the acclaimed 45min. tram ride tour ($10, under 21 $5) through the vineyards, which runs in the summer M-F every hour 11:30am-3:30pm and Sa-Su every half-hour 11:30am-3:30pm. Self-guided tours lead from the parking lot through the vineyards and peacock aviary. Tastings of current vintage free, limited $5, reserves $10. With tram tour, free reserve tasting and 20% discount on purchases. Open daily 10am-5pm.

Buena Vista, 18000 Old Winery Rd. (☎938-1266; www.buenavistawinery.com). Take E. Napa St. from Sonoma Plaza and turn left on Old Winery Rd. The oldest premium winery in the valley. Famous stone buildings are preserved just as Mr. Haraszthy built them in 1857 when he founded the California wine industry. Theater shows July-Sept. Guided tour daily at 2pm. Tastings ($5, including glass) daily 10am-5pm.

Ravenswood, 18701 Gehricke Rd. (☎938-1960 or 888-669-4679; www.ravenswood-wine.com), north of Sonoma. "Unwimpy" wines from a surprisingly light-hearted group that says "wine should also be fun." Price of tastings ($4) applicable to wine purchase and well worth it. Tours by appointment daily at 10:30am. Open daily 10am-4:30pm.

SIGHTS

SONOMA STATE HISTORIC PARK. Within the park, an adobe church stands on the site of the **Mission San Francisco-Solano,** the northernmost and last of the 21 Franciscan missions. It marks the end of the El Camino Real, or the "Royal Road." Built in 1826 by Padre Jose Altimira, the mission has a fragment of the original California Republic flag, the rest of which was burned in the 1906 post-San Francisco earthquake fires. *(E. Spain and 1st St., in the northeast corner of town. ☎938-1519; open daily 10am-5pm. $2, children under 17 free. Includes admission to Vallejo's Home, Sonoma Barracks, Petaluma Adobe, Bale Grist Mill, and Benicia Capital Historic State Park.)*

GENERAL VALLEJO'S HOME. The site is often referred to by its Latin name, *Lachryma Montis*, meaning "Tears of the Mountain." This "Yankee" home of the famed Mexican leader, who also was mayor of Sonoma and a California senator, is open for tours of the museum, pond, pavilions, and gardens. *(Located on W. Spain St. at Third St. ☎938-1519. Open daily 10am-5pm. $2, under 17 free.)*

JACK LONDON STATE PARK. Around the turn of the 20th century, hard-drinking and hard-living Jack London, author of *The Call of the Wild* and *White Fang*, bought 1400 acres here, determined to create his dream home. London's hopes were frustrated when the estate's main building, the Wolf House, was destroyed by arsonists in 1913. London died 3 years after the fire and is buried in the park, his grave marked by a volcanic boulder intended for the construction of his house. The nearby **House of Happy Walls,** built by London's widow in fond remembrance of him, is now a two-story museum devoted to the writer. Scenic trails in this area abound. *(Take Hwy. 12 4 mi. north from Sonoma to Arnold Ln. and follow signs. ☎938-5216. Park open daily 9:30am-7pm; winter 9:30am-5pm. Museum open daily 10am-5pm.)*

THE NORTH COAST

Wrapped in fog and larger than life, the remote North Coast is a hidden jewel of California's natural wonders. The North Coast begins in the San Francisco Bay Area and continues north to the Oregon border. Roadtrips on the North Coast can follow one of two scenic highways. The famous **Highway 1** (the Pacific Coast Highway, or PCH) snakes along cliffs between pounding surf and humbling redwoods. An hour north of Fort Bragg, Hwy. 1 merges with **U.S. 101,** which meanders through California's wine country (see p. 952) on its way to the North Coast.

MENDOCINO ☎707

Teetering on bluffs over the ocean, isolated Mendocino (pop. 1107) is a charming coastal community of art galleries, craft shops, bakeries, and B&Bs. The town's greatest feature lies 900 ft. to its west, where the earth falls into the Pacific at the impressive **Mendocino Headlands.** The windy quarter-mile meadow of tall grass and wildflowers separates the town from the rocky shore. Poor drainage, thin soil, and ocean winds have all contributed to the creation of an unusual bonsai garden 3 mi. south of town at the **Pygmy Forest** in **Van Damme State Park ❶.** (Camping $16; day-use $4; free for hikers. Off Hwy. 1 past the park.) Stress is chased away at sauna, steam room, and gardens of the clothing-optional resort **Orr Hot Springs,** 13201 Orr Springs Rd., just east of Mendocino, off Comptche Ukiah Rd. (☎462-6277. Day-use $20. 18+. Open daily 10am-10pm.)

Tiny Mendocino sits on **Highway 1,** right on the Pacific Coast, 30 mi. west of U.S. 101 and 12 mi. south of Fort Bragg. Like all northern coast areas, Mendocino can be very chilly, even in summer. Travelers should prepare for 40-70°F temperatures. The nearest **bus** station is 2hr. away in Ukiah. **Greyhound** runs two buses per day to Ft. Bragg. **Mendocino Stage** provides a shuttle service along the north Mendocino coast and runs buses between Ft. Bragg and Ukiah. (☎964-0167. 2 per day, $10.) **Visitor Info: Fort Bragg-Mendocino Coast Chamber of Commerce,** 332 N. Main St., in Fort Bragg. (☎961-6300 or 800-726-2780. Open daily 9am-5pm.) **Park Info:** ☎937-5804 or the **MacKerricher State Park Visitors Center,** 2½ mi. north of Fort Bragg. (☎964-8898. Open summer daily 11am-3pm; winter Sa-Su 11am-3pm.) Other services include: **Internet access** at the **Regional Branch Library of Mendocino,** 499 Laurel St., in Fort Bragg (open Tu-W 11am-7:45pm, Th-F 11am-5:45pm, Sa 10am-4:45pm); the **police** (☎961-0200), stationed in Fort Bragg; **Mendocino Coast District Hospital:** 700 River Dr. (☎961-1234), Ft. Bragg; and the **Post Office:** 10500 Ford St. (☎937-5282; open M-F 7:30am-4:30pm). **Postal Code:** 95460.

Jug Handle Creek Farm ❶, 5 mi. north of Mendocino off Hwy. 1, across the street from the Jug Handle State Reserve, is a beautiful 133-year-old house sitting on 40 acres of gardens, campsites, and small rustic cabins. One hour of chores (or $5) is required per night. (☎964-4630. 30 beds. No linen. Reservations recommended in summer. Dorms $20, students $14, children $9; sites $9; cabins $28 per person.) **MacKerricher State Park campground ❶,** 2½ mi. north of Fort Bragg, has excellent views of tidepool life, passing seals, sea lions, and migratory whales, as well as 9mi. of beaches and a murky lake for trout fishing. (☎937-5804. Showers, bathrooms, and drinking water. Reservations necessary in summer. Sites $16; day use free.) Picnicking on the Mendocino Headlands should be preceded by a trip to **Mendosa's Market,** 10501 Lansing St. Like most things in Mendocino, it's pricey, but most items are fresh and delicious. (☎937-5879. Open daily 8am-9pm.) Restaurants in Mendocino often close unusually early. **Tote Fête ❶,** 10450 Lansing St., has delicious tote-out food. An asiago, pesto, and artichoke heart sandwich ($4.75) hits the spot. (☎937-3383. Open M-Sa 10:30am-7pm, Su 10:30am-4pm. Bakery open daily 7:30am-4pm.)

AVENUE OF THE GIANTS ☎707

About 10 mi. north of Garberville off U.S. 101 in the **Humboldt Redwoods State Park,** the Avenue of the Giants winds its way through 31 mi. inhabited by the world's largest living organisms. The knowledgeable staff at **Humboldt Redwoods State Park Visitors Center** can highlight the Avenue's groves, facilities, great trails, and bike routes. (☎946-2263. Open Apr.-Oct. daily 9am-5pm; Oct.-Apr. Th-Su 10am-3pm.) The plentiful campsites in the park offer coin showers, flush toilets, and fire rings. (☎946-2409. Sites $15.) At **Founder's Grove,** the ½ mi. loop features the 1300 to 1500-year-old **Founder's Tree,** and the fallen 350 ft. **Dyerville Giant,** whose massive, three-story rootball looks like a mythic evil entanglement. Uncrowded trails wind through **Rockefeller Forest** in the park's northern section, which contains the largest grove of continuous old-growth redwoods in the world.

REDWOOD NATIONAL & STATE PARKS ☎707

The redwoods in Redwood National and State Parks are the last remaining stretch of the old growth forest that used to blanket two million acres of Northern California and Oregon. Wildlife runs free here, with black bears and mountain lions roaming the backwoods and Roosevelt elk grazing in the meadows.

PRACTICAL INFORMATION

Redwood National and State Parks is an umbrella term for four contiguous parks. From south to north, they are: **Redwood National Park, Prairie Creek Redwoods State Park, Del Norte Coast Redwoods State Park,** and **Jedediah Smith Redwoods State Park.**

Entrance Fees: Charges are particular to each park, and often differ depending on whether you are camping, parking, or just hiking. Usually there is no charge to enter, and $2 per car for day-use of parking and picnic areas.

Buses: Greyhound, 500 E. Harding St., Crescent City (☎464-2807). Greyhound runs two buses daily, one in the morning and one in the evening, to **San Francisco** and **Portland.** Bus fare approximately $60. Call for exact rates and departure times.

Auto Repairs: AAA Emergency Road Service (☎800-222-4357). 24hr.

Visitor Info: Redwood National Park Headquarters and Information Center, 1111 2nd St. (☎464-6101, ext. 5064), Crescent City. Headquarters of the entire national park. Ranger stations are just as well-informed. Open daily 9am-5pm. Closed Su winter.

Medical Services: Sutter Coast Hospital, 800 E. Washington Blvd. (☎464-8511), Crescent City.

Internet Access: Humboldt County Library, Arcata Branch, 500 7th St., Arcata (☎822-5954), has free Internet access. Open Tu 2-5pm, W 1-8pm, Th-Sa 10am-5pm.

Post Office: Crescent City: 751 2nd St. (☎464-2151). Open M-F 8:30am-5pm, Sa noon-2pm. **Postal Code:** 95531

ACCOMMODATIONS

Ravenwood Motel, 151 Klamath Blvd. (☎866-520-9875), off U.S. 101. Clean rooms with a modern decor. Conveniently located next to a market, cafe, and laundromat. Doubles $58; family units with full kitchen $100. ❸

Historic Requa Inn, 451 Requa Rd. (☎482-1425 or 866-800-8777), west off U.S. 101. B&B with lace-curtained windows, Victorian-styled parlor, and glorious views overlooking the Klamath River. Reservations recommended June-Sept. Rooms $79-120. ❺

Redwood Youth Hostel (HI-AYH), 14480 U.S. 101 (☎482-8265), at Wilson Creek Rd. 7 mi. north of Klamath. Chores and rules (no shoes inside) keep the 30-bed hostel immaculate. Kitchen and 2 ocean-view sundecks. No sleeping bags allowed, so bring your own sleepsack or rent linen ($1). Check-in 5-9pm. Check-out 10am. Lockout 11am-5pm; day storage available. Curfew 11pm. Reservations recommended in summer. Dorms $16, under 17 $7. Pay in advance. ❶

Jedediah Smith Redwoods State Park, north of Crescent City on U.S. 199. Picnic tables, water, restrooms, and showers. Campfire programs and nature walks offered during the summer. Sites $12, day's use $4, hikers/bikers without vehicles $1. ❶

FOOD

There are more picnic tables than restaurants in the area, so the best option for food is probably the supermarket. In Crescent City, head to the 24hr. **Safeway,** 475 M St. (☎465-3353), on U.S. 101 between 2nd and 5th St. The **Palm Cafe ❷,** on U.S. 101 in Orick, bakes delicious fruit, coconut, and chocolate pies. (☎488-3381. Pie slices $2.25. Open daily 5am-8pm.) The dedicated regulars at **Glen's Bakery and Restaurant ❶,** at 3rd and G St., love the huge pancakes ($4) and sandwiches ($4-6.50). Breakfast served all day. (☎464-2914. Open Tu-Sa 5am-6:30pm.)

SIGHTS & HIKING

In the parks, all plants and animals are protected—even bird feathers are off-limits. **California fishing licenses** are required for fishing off any natural formation, but fishing is free from any man-made structure. Call the Fish and Game Department (☎445-6493) for permits (one-day $30) and weight and catch restrictions.

The **Orick Area** covers the southernmost section of Redwood National and State Parks. The **Visitors Center** lies on U.S. 101, just 1 mi. south of Orick and half a mile south of the Shoreline Deli (the Greyhound bus stop). A popular sight is the **Tall Trees Grove,** accessible by car to those with permits (free from the Visitors Center) when the road is open. Allow at least 3 to 4hr. for the trip.

The criss-crossing 70 mi. of trials in the **Prairie Creek Area** can be confusing; be sure to pick up a trail map ($1). The **James Irvine Trail** (4½ mi. one-way) snakes through old-growth redwoods and small waterfalls to Gold Bluffs Beach. The less ambitious can cruise part of the **Foothill Trail** (¾ mi. one-way) to a 1500-year-old behemoth, the 306 ft. high **Big Tree.** The **Elk Prairie Trail** (1½ mi. one-way), built for the visually impaired, skirts the prairie and loops around to join the nature trail.

The **Klamath Area** to the north connects Prairie Creek with Del Norte State Park; the main attraction here is the spectacular coastline. The **Klamath Overlook,** where Requa Rd. meets the steep **Coastal Trail** (8 mi.), is an excellent **whale-watching** site.

An outstanding location from which to explore the parks, **Crescent City** calls itself the city "where the redwoods meet the sea." The **Battery Point Lighthouse** is on a causeway jutting out from Front St. and houses a museum open only during low tide. (☎464-3089. Open Apr.-Sept. W-Su 10am-4pm, tide permitting. $2, children $0.50.) From June through August, **tidepool walks** leave from Enderts Beach. (Turn-off 4 mi. south of Crescent City; call ☎464-6101, ext. 5064 for schedules.)

THE SIERRA NEVADA

The Sierra Nevada is California's backbone, marking the 450 mi. line where two gigantic tectonic plates, the Pacific and North American, collided four hundred million years ago. Stretching from stifling Death Valley to just below the Oregon border, the range is a product of Mt. Lassen's volcanic activity hundreds of millions of years ago and granite-smoothing glaciation. It also nurtures some of the most breathtaking scenery in the country, including Lake Tahoe's crystalline waters, Mono Lake's giant tufa formations, Sequoia National Park's redwoods, and the roiling rivers of Yosemite, but the entire range is worthy of homage and scrutiny, and millions of visitors eagerly undertake the pilgrimage every year.

LAKE TAHOE ☎530/775

Outdoor fanatics from across the globe are attracted to Tahoe's blue waters, tall pines, and high-rise casinos silhouetted by the setting sun. A town without a low season, Tahoe has miles of biking, hiking, and skiing trails, long stretches of golden beaches, lakes stocked with fish, and any watersport imaginable.

TRANSPORTATION

Trains: Amtrak (☎800-872-7245) runs trains between Chicago and San Francisco that stop at the Truckee Depot. 1 train daily to: **Sacramento** (4½hr., $22-40); **Oakland/San Francisco** (6½hr., $45-93); **Reno** (1hr., $10-21).

Buses: Greyhound (☎800-231-2222). At the Truckee Depot, get buses to: **Sacramento** (3hr.); **San Francisco** (5½hr., 5 per day, $37-39); **Reno** (1hr., 3 per day, $10-12).

Public Transit:

Tahoe Casino Express (☎775-785-2424, 800-446-6128). Shuttle service between Reno Airport and South Shore casinos. (Daily 6:15am-12:30am; $19, round-trip $34, children under 12 free.)

Tahoe Area Regional Transport or **TART** (☎550-1212 or 800-736-6365). Connects the west and north shores from Incline Village through Tahoe City to Meeks Bay. Stops daily every hr. or 30min. 6:30am-6pm. Runs to Truckee and Squaw Valley. $1.25, day pass $3. Exact fare required.

South Tahoe Area Ground Express or **STAGE** (☎542-6077). Operates in both NV and CA on the South Shore. (6:40am-12:40pm. $1.25, day pass $2, 10-ride pass $10.) Casinos operate complimentary shuttle services along Hwy. 50 to California ski resorts and motels.

Bus Plus (☎542-6077) runs door-to-door service within city limits (24hr., $3) and within El Dorado County (7am-7pm, $5). Summer buses connect STAGE and North Shore's TART at Emerald Bay.

ORIENTATION

In the northern Sierra on the California-Nevada border, Lake Tahoe is a 3hr. drive from San Francisco. The lake rests 100 mi. northeast of Sacramento (via **Highway 50**) and 35 mi. southwest of Reno (via **Highway 395** and **431**). **Highway 395** runs 20 mi. east. Lake Tahoe is divided into two main regions, **North Shore** and **South Shore.** The North Shore includes **Tahoe City** in California and Incline Village in Nevada; the South Shore includes **South Lake Tahoe** in California and Stateline in Nevada.

PRACTICAL INFORMATION

Visitor Info: North Lake Tahoe North Visitors Bureau, 380 North Lake Blvd. (☎583-3494; www.mytahoevacation.com). A helpful office with tons of info on the area. Open M-F 9am-5pm, Sa-Su 9am-4pm. Taylor Creek Visitors Center (USFS; ☎543-2674; www.fs.fed.us/r5/ltbmu), 3 mi. north of South Lake Tahoe on Hwy. 89. Permits for Desolation Wilderness. Camping fee $5 per person per night, $10 per person for 2 or more nights, $20 for yearly pass. Under 12 free. Reservations (☎644-6048, $5) are available for overnight permits mid-June to Sept. 6. Open daily May 31 to mid-June and Oct. 8am-4pm; mid-June through Sept. 8am-5:30pm.

Medical Services: Incline Village Community Hospital, 880 Alder Ave. (☎775-833-4100), off Hwy. 28 in Incline Village. **Barton Memorial Hospital,** 2170 South Ave. (☎541-3420), at 3rd St. and South Ave. off Lake Tahoe Blvd.

Post Office: Tahoe City, 950 North Lake Blvd. (☎800-275-8777). Open M-F 8:30am-5pm. **Postal Code:** 96145. **South Lake Tahoe,** 1046 Al Tahoe Blvd. (☎800-275-8777). Open M-F 8:30am-5pm, Sa noon-2pm. **Postal Code:** 96151. **Area Code:** 530 in CA, 775 in NV; in text, 530 unless otherwise noted.

ACCOMMODATIONS

On the South Shore, the blocks along Hwy. 50 on the California side of the border support the bulk of the area's motels. The North Shore offers more polished and refined accommodations along Hwy. 28, but the rates are relatively high. Campgrounds ring the entire lake, but **Route 89** is inundated with sites between Tahoe City and South Lake Tahoe. Backcountry camping is allowed in designated wilderness areas with a permit from the Forest Service.

Firelite Lodge, 7035 North Lake Blvd. (☎800-934-7222 or 546-7222), in Tahoe Vista 8 mi. east of Tahoe City. Sleek, modern quarters with pool and spa. Open daily 8am-11pm. Singles summer and winter from $59; spring and fall from $49. ❸

Tahoe Valley Lodge, 2214 Lake Tahoe Blvd. (☎800-669-7544 or 541-0353), in South Lake. These immaculate, luxurious rooms have rough-hewn logs and mile-high comforters. All rooms have queen-sized beds and cable TV; many have microwaves, refrigerators, and in-room spas. Reception 24hr. Singles $95; doubles $125. ❺

Royal Inn, 3520 Lake Tahoe Blvd. (☎544-1177), in South Lake. Clean rooms and cable TV. Heated pool and laundry facilities. Singles Su-Th $28-35; doubles $39-49. Rates inflate greatly on weekends and holidays. Mention *Let's Go* for a possible discount. ❷

Doug's Mellow Mountain Retreat, 3787 Forest Ave. (☎544-8065). Turn onto Wildwood Rd. west of downtown Stateline, then left on Forest Ave. Woodsy and residential. Kitchen, barbecue, and fireplace. No curfew. Flexible check-in and check-out. Internet access $5 per hr. Dorms $15; private rooms $25. Discounts for stays over a week. ❶

William Kent (☎583-3642), on Hwy. 89, 2 mi. south of Tahoe City, with 95 shady sites, is one of the most popular campgrounds on the west shore. Beach access, clean flush toilets, and water. Open June-Sept. 6. Sites $16; $5 per additional vehicle. ❶

FOOD

Casinos offer low-priced buffets, but grilles and burger joints also dot the shores.

Jakes on the Lake (☎583-0188), in Boatworks Shopping Mall, Tahoe City. Hawaii-inspired dishes dominate the menu beside options like New Rack of Lamb ($22). Open M-F 11:30am-2:30pm and 5:30-9:30pm, Sa-Su 11:30am-2:30pm and 5-9:30pm. ❹

Sprouts Natural Foods Cafe, 3123 Harrison Ave. (☎541-6969), at the intersection of Lake Tahoe Blvd. and Alameda Ave. in South Lake. Satisfying natural foods in unnaturally large portions. Try the breakfast burrito with avocados ($5), a tasty smoothie ($3-3.75), or a shot of wheat grass ($2). Open daily 8am-10pm. ❶

The Red Hut Cafe, 2723 Lake Tahoe Blvd. (☎541-9024), in South Lake. Another location at 22 Kingsbury Grade (☎588-7488). A Tahoe original since 1959, the friendly staff dishes out homestyle cooking like waffles piled with fruit and whipped cream ($5.75) and avocado burgers ($6.50). Open daily 6am-2pm. No credit cards. ❶

Syd's, 550 North Lake Blvd. (☎583-2666), in the center of Tahoe City. Serves coffee ($2-3), smoothies ($3.75), and sandwiches like Hummus Humongous ($4.50) and The Gobbler ($5). Open daily 6:30am-5pm; July-Aug. 6am-7pm. ❶

OUTDOOR ACTIVITIES

BEACHES

Many beaches dot Lake Tahoe, providing the perfect setting for sunning and people-watching. Parking generally costs $3-7; bargain hunters should leave cars in turn-outs on the main road and walk. On North Shore, **Sand Harbor Beach,** 2 mi. south of Incline Village on Hwy. 28, has gorgeous granite boulders and clear waters that attract swimmers, snorkelers, and boaters to its marina. **Tahoe City Commons Beach,** in the heart of Tahoe City, has a playground, sandy beach, and pristine lake waters. **Baldwin Beach,** on South Shore, and neighboring **Pope Beach,** near the southernmost point of the lake off Hwy. 89, are popular, shaded expanses of shoreline. Quiet spots on both can be found on the edges. **Nevada Beach,** on the east shore, 3 mi. north of South Lake Tahoe off Hwy. 50, is close to casinos but offers sanctuary from jangling slot machines. Recently renovated **Zephyr Cove Beach,** 5 mi. north of South Lake Tahoe, hosts a youthful crowd keen on beer and bikinis. The West Shore offers **Meeks Bay,** 10 mi. south of Tahoe City, a family-oriented beach with picnic tables and volleyball courts. **D.L. Bliss State Park,** 17 mi. south of Tahoe City on Hwy. 89, is home to **Lester** and **Calawee Cove Beaches** on striking Rubicon Bay and is the trailhead for the Rubicon Trail.

HIKING

After decades of work, the 165 mi. **Tahoe Rim Trail** has been completed. The route encircles the lake, following the ridge tops of the Basin, and welcomes hikers, equestrians, and, in most areas, **mountain bikers.** On the western shore, the route is part of the Pacific Crest Trail. In the north, **Mount Rose,** at 10,778 ft., is one of the tallest mountains in the region as well as one of the best climbs. The panoramic view from the summit includes views of the lake, Reno, and the surrounding Sierras. Take Hwy. 431 N from Incline Village to the trailhead. The **Granite Chief Wilderness,** west of Squaw Valley, is a spectacular destination; its rugged trails and mountain streams wind through secluded forests in 5000 ft. valleys up to the summits of 9000 ft. peaks. The **Alpine Meadows Trailhead,** at the end of Alpine Meadows Rd. off Hwy. 89 between Truckee and Tahoe City, and the **Pacific Crest Trailhead,** at the end of Barker Pass Rd. (Blackwood Canyon Rd.), provide convenient access into the wilderness. The picturesque **Emerald Bay,** on Hwy. 89 between South Lake Tahoe and Tahoe City, is best explored on foot. This crystal-clear lake area embraces Tahoe's only island, Fannette. Dramatic waterfalls make the area a mini-paradise. **Emerald Bay State Park,** which abuts Desolation Wilderness, offers hiking and biking trails of varying difficulty. One of the best hikes in Tahoe is **Rubicon Trail,** which wraps 6 mi. around the beach and granite cliffs.

ROCK CLIMBING

Alpenglow Sports, 415 North Lake Blvd., in Tahoe City, provides rock and ice climbing literature and lots of know-how. (☎583-6917. Open M-F 10am-6pm, Sa-Su 9am-6pm. Shoe rental $8 per day.) Safety precautions and equipment are a must. The inexperienced can try bouldering in **D.L. Bliss State Park.** Popular climbing spots dot the South Shore, including the celebrated **Ninety-Foot Wall** at Emerald Bay and **Twin Crags** at Tahoe City. **Lover's Leap,** in South Lake Tahoe, is an incredible, albeit crowded, route spanning two giant cliffs. East of South Lake Tahoe off Hwy. 50, **Phantom Spires** has amazing views, while **Pie Shop** offers serious exposure.

SKIING

With world-class alpine slopes, 15 resorts, knee-deep powder, and California sun, Tahoe is a skier's mecca. Skiing conditions range from bikini to frostbite, and snow covers the slopes into early summer. Rates listed are for peak season. **Squaw Valley,** 5 mi. north of Tahoe City off Hwy., site of the 1960 Winter Olympics, has 4000 acres of terrain across six Sierra peaks. The 33 ski lifts, including the 110-passenger cable car and high speed gondola, access high-elevation runs for all levels. (☎583-6985 or 888-766-9321. Open late Nov.-May. Full-day lift ticket $58; half-day $42, seniors and ages 13-15 $29, under 12 $15, over 76 free. Night skiing mid-Dec. to mid-Apr. daily 4-9pm; $20.) The largest and most popular resort is **Heavenly,** on Ski Run Blvd. off South Lake Tahoe Blvd., with over 4800 acres, 29 lifts, and 84 trails. Its vertical drop is 3500 ft., Tahoe's biggest. (☎775-586-7000. Full-day lift ticket $57, ages 13-18 $47, seniors and ages 6-12 $29.)

One of the best ways to enjoy the solitude of Tahoe's pristine snow-covered forests is to **cross-country ski** across the thick braid of trails around the lake. **Spooner Lake,** at the junction of Hwy. 50 and 28, offers 57 mi. of machine-groomed trails and incredible views. (☎775-749-5349. $19, children $3.) **Tahoe X-C,** 2 mi. northeast of Tahoe City on Dollar Hill off Hwy. 28, maintains 40 mi. of trails for all abilities. (☎583-5475. $18, mid-week $13; children $6.) Snowshoeing is easier to pick up. Follow hiking or cross-country trails, or trudge off into the woods. Equipment rentals are available at sporting goods stores for about $15 per day.

YOSEMITE NATIONAL PARK ☎209

In 1868, a young Scotsman named John Muir arrived by boat in San Francisco and asked for directions to "any place that is wild." Anxious to run the crazy youngster out, Bay Area folk directed him east to the lands of Yosemite. The wonders that Muir beheld there sated his lust for wandering and spawned a lifetime dedicated to conservationism. His efforts won Yosemite its national park status in 1890.

Yosemite and its more than four million yearly visitors have given rise to a small city in the middle of one of America's wildest regions. With only 6% of the park (roughly the size of Rhode Island) developed and paved for visitors, most of Yosemite remains undisturbed and untamed. Despite the endless rows of tents, RVs, and SUVs that clog the paved 6%, Yosemite Valley, at the bustling, awe-inspiring heart of the park, still lives up to its old name: "The Incomparable Valley."

AT A GLANCE

AREA: 1189 sq. mi.

CLIMATE: Temperate forest.

FEATURES: Tuolumne (tah-WALL-um-ee) Meadows, Mariposa Grove, Hetch Hetchy Reservoir, Yosemite Valley.

HIGHLIGHTS: Hike to Glacier Point, photograph Bridalveil Falls, whitewater raft on the Merced River.

GATEWAYS: Mariposa, Sonora, Mammoth Lakes (p. 969), and Merced.

CAMPING: Reservations necessary to get a spot. 7-night max. stay in the Valley and Wawona, 14-night max. stay elsewhere. Permits needed for camping in the high country within the Park.

FEES & RESERVATIONS: Necessary-pass $10 per hiker, biker, or bus ride; $20 per car. Good for one week. Annual pass $40. National park passes also accepted here.

TRANSPORTATION. Yosemite runs public **buses** that connect the park with Fresno, Merced, and Mariposa. **Yosemite VIA** runs buses from the Merced bus station at 16th and N St. to Yosemite. (☎384-1315 or 800-VIA-LINE/842-5463. 4 trips per day; one-way $10.) VIA meets Amtrak trains at the Merced train station. Tickets can be purchased from the driver. (☎384-1315. Buses run M-F 8am-5pm. Fares include Yosemite entry.) **Yosemite Gray Line (YGL)** runs buses to and from **Fresno Yosemite International Airport (FYI),** Fresno hotels, and Yosemite Valley ($20). **YARTS** (☎877-989-2787 or 388-9589) provides four daily trips to Yosemite from Merced, making stops along the way, and sends one bus a day along Rte. 120 and 395, hitting Mammoth and June Lakes, Lee Vining, and Tuolumne Meadows. (Buses depart Merced 7, 8:45, 10:30am, 5:25pm. Round-trip $20. Fares include Yosemite entry.) **Amtrak** runs a **bus** from Merced to Yosemite (4 per day, $22) and **trains** (☎800-USA-RAIL/872-7245) from **San Francisco** (3½hr., 5 per day, $22-29) and **L.A.** (5½hr, 4 per day, $28-51) to Merced. Despite traffic and congestion, the best way to see Yosemite is by **car.** Be sure to fill the tank before heading out, as there is no gas in Yosemite Valley except for emergency gas at the Village Garage ($15 for 5 gallons). There are overpriced 24hr. gas stations at Crane Flat, Tuolumne Meadows, and Wawona. Within the Valley, there is no reason to drive since the shuttle system is free and very convenient.

ORIENTATION & PRACTICAL INFORMATION. Yosemite covers 1189 sq. mi., most of it rugged and wild with small areas of intense development. The center of activity, **Yosemite Valley** hosts the most enduring monuments, including **El Capitan, Half Dome,** and **Yosemite Falls. Yosemite Village,** the Valley's service and info center, feels more like Disneyland. Facing the sheer southern wall of the valley and incomparable 360-degree views, **Glacier Point** brims all summer with tourists. **Tuolumne Meadows,** in the northeast, is a rock-strewn alpine meadow surrounded by streams and snow-capped peaks. **Mariposa Grove** is a forest of giant sequoia trees in the south. **Wawona,** just north of Mariposa, is a historic, upscale development that features museums and a golf course. The vast majority of the park, however, is wild. (7-day pass $10 per hiker, biker, or bus rider; $20 per car. Annual pass $40. National park passes accepted.)

General Park Information (☎372-0200; www.yosemite.org). **Yosemite Valley Visitors Center** (☎372-0299), in Yosemite Village. Open daily 8am-6pm; winter 9am-5pm. **Wilderness Center** (☎372-0745; www.nps.gov/yose/wilderness), in Yosemite Village. Wilderness permit reservations up to 24 weeks in advance (☎372-0740; $5 per person per reservation; M-F 8:30am-4:30pm), or first come, first served (free). 40% of backcountry quota is held for first come, first camp. Open daily 7:30am-6pm; winter 8am-5pm. **Tuolumne Meadows Visitors Center** (☎372-0263). The high-country headquarters. Open daily summer 9am-7pm; spring and fall 9am-5pm; closed in winter.

Auto Repairs: Village Garage (☎372-8320). Open daily 8am-noon and 1-5pm. Cars towed 24hr. Emergency gasoline available. AAA and National Auto Club accepted.

Bike Rental: Yosemite Lodge (☎372-1208) and **Curry Village** (☎372-8319) for $5.50 per hr., $21 per day. Driver's license or credit card required as security deposit. Both open daily 9am-6pm, weather permitting; open on a limited basis after Sept. 6.

Equipment Rental: Yosemite Mountaineering School (☎372-8344 or 372-8436), in Tuolumne Meadows. Sleeping bags $10.50 per day, backpacks $8.50; third day half-price. Climbing shoes rented to YMS students only. Driver's license or credit card required for deposit. Rock climbing classes daily. Open daily 8:30am-noon and 1-5pm.

Weather and Road Conditions: ☎372-0200. 24hr.

Medical Services: Yosemite Medical Clinic (☎372-4637). 24hr. emergency room. Walk-in urgent care and appointments M-Sa 8am-5pm.

Post Office: Yosemite Village, next to the Visitors Center. Open M-F 8:30am-5pm, Sa 10am-noon. Lobby open 24hr. **Postal Code:** 95389. **Area Code:** 209.

ACCOMMODATIONS. When Ralph Waldo Emerson visited Yosemite in 1884, he was awakened in the morning by the clucking of a hen climbing over his bed. These days, Yosemite's accommodations have become much more comfortable. Reservations are necessary and can be made up to 1 year in advance at ☎559-252-4848. All park lodgings provide access to dining, laundry, showers, and supplies. **Curry Village ❹,** 2 mi. southeast of Yosemite Village, has a pool, nightly amphitheater shows, snack stands, cafeteria, and ice rink (Nov.-Feb.). (☎252-4848. Canvas tent cabin $60; cabin $77, with bath $92; standard motel room $112.) The Army barracks-style **Housekeeping Camp ❶,** feels slightly less developed. "Camping shelters" for up to four include two bunk beds, a double bed, a picnic table, and a fire-pit for $64. (☎372-8338. Showers, laundry, equipment rental.) **Tuolumne Meadows Lodge ❹,** on Tioga Pass Rd., in the park's northeastern corner, has rustic tranquil cabins. (☎372-8413. Canvas-sided cabins, wood stoves, no electricity. Cabins $67; additional adult $9, child $4.) Outside of the park, the **Yosemite Bug Hostel ❷** on Rte. 140 in Midpines, 25 mi. west of Yosemite, is a woodsy, spirited spot where backpackers lounge in hammocks. (☎966-6666; www.yosemitebug.com. Swimming hole with waterfall. Live music. Internet access $1 per 10min. Dorms $16; tent sites $17; family and private rooms with shared bath $40-70, with bath $55-115.) One mile before the park entrance, the **Evergreen Lodge ❹,** 33160 Evergreen Rd. (☎379-2606; www.evergreenlodge.com), 7 mi. off Rte. 120, is near the quieter Hetch Hetchy region and is secluded and cozy. Cabins have porches, patio and grill, and on-site restaurant, bar, deli, and market. (Standard cabins $79; family cabins $99; large family cabins $104. $10 extra when busy.)

CALIFORNIA

CAMPING. One of the first views of Yosemite a visitor gets during the summer may be of the endless "tent cities" in the Valley. Make reservations as far in advance as possible, especially in summer. (☎800-436-7275; http://reservations.nps.gov. Reserve by phone or online daily 7am-7pm.) All Valley campgrounds fill completely every summer night. Natural stream water must be boiled,

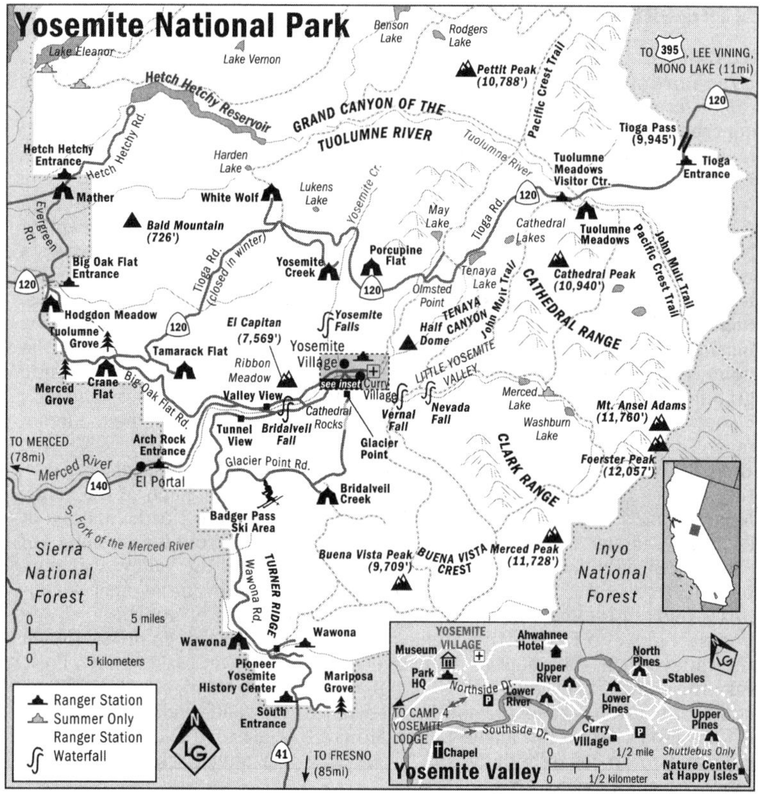

filtered, or treated. **Backcountry camping** is prohibited in the Valley but encouraged outside it. Warm enough for winter camping, **Hodgdon Meadow** 2, 4900 ft., on Rte. 120 near Big Oak Flat Entrance, 25 mi. from the Valley, has 105 wooded, secluded sites. (Water, toilets, and tables. Sites May-Sept. $18; Oct.-Apr. $12 and first-come, first-camp.) Catering to seasoned climbers, **Camp 4 ❶**, 4000 ft., at the western end of the Valley, past Yosemite Lodge, has 35 walk-in sites that fill up before 9am. Meet new friends; every site is filled with 6 random people. (Water, flush toilets, and tables. First-come, first-camp. Limited parking. $5 per person.) Drive in or escape the RVs in the 25 sites saved for walk-in hikers at **Tuolumne Meadows ❶**, 8600 ft., on Rte. 120, 55 mi. east of the Valley. (152 sites require advance reservations, 152 saved for same-day reservations. Open July-Sept., depending on snow. Drive-in sites $18; backpacker sites $3 per person.)

FOOD. The **Village Store** (open daily June-Sept. 8am-10pm; Oct.-May 8am-9pm) is your best bet for groceries, with only moderately inflated prices. Outstanding views of Yosemite Falls from nearly every seat in **Mountain Room Restaurant ❺**, in Yosemite Lodge, make this ideal for a post-hike meal. (☎372-9033. Hearty American fare $17-28. Open daily 5:30-9pm.) **Degnan's Delicatessen ❷**, in Yosemite Village, is inside a convenience store and adjacent to an ice cream parlor and pizza place, and doubles as a cafe. (☎372-8454. Sandwiches $5.75. Open daily 7am-7pm.)

THE GREAT OUTDOORS

BY CAR. Although the view is better if you get out of the **car,** you can see a large portion of Yosemite from the bucket seat. The **Yosemite Road Guide** ($3.50; at every visitors center) is keyed to roadside markers and outlines a superb tour of the park; you might as well have a ranger riding shotgun. Spectacular panoramas and beautiful glades are omnipresent along **Route 120 (Tioga Pass Road)** from Crane Flat to Tuolumne Meadows. This stretch of road is the highest highway strip in the country; as it winds down from Tioga Pass through the park's eastern exit, it plunges a mile down to reach the lunar landscape of Mono Lake. The drive west from the pass brings you past **Tuolumne Meadows** with its colorful grasses and rippling creeks to shimmering Tenaya Lake. No less incredible are the views afforded by the southern approach to Yosemite, **Route 41.** Most recognizable is the Wawona Tunnel turnout (also known as **Inspiration Point**), the subject of many Ansel Adams photographs. From the point, **Yosemite Valley** unfurls its famed, humbling beauty. **El Capitan,** a gigantic granite monolith (7569 ft.), looms over awestruck crowds. If you stop and look closely, you will see what appear to be specks of dust moving on the mountain face. They are actually world-class climbers inching toward fame. Nearby, **Three Brothers** (three adjacent granite peaks) and misty **Bridalveil Falls** are captured by hundreds of snapshots every day. A drive into the heart of the Valley leads to the staggering **Yosemite Falls** (the highest falls in North America at 2425 ft.), **Sentinel Rock,** and mighty **Half Dome.** The view from **Glacier Point,** off Glacier Point Rd. from Rte. 41, conveys the epic scale of the Valley. This gripping overlook, 3214 ft. above the valley floor, can stun even the most wilderness-weary traveler. When the moon is full, this is an extraordinary (and popular) place to visit. Arrive at sunset and watch the fiery colors fade over the valley as the stars appear. To marvel at the Sierra Nevada's famous flora, take the short hiking trail through the giant sequoias of **Mariposa Grove,** 35 mi. south of the Valley near the southern entrance. This self-guided walk begins off Mariposa Grove Rd. at the Fallen Monarch, a massive trunk lying on its side, and continues to both the 209-ft.-tall, 2700-year-old Grizzly Giant and the fallen Wawona Tunnel Tree.

DAY HIKING IN THE VALLEY. For the full Yosemite experience, visitors must travel the outer trails on foot. World-class hiking abounds for anyone willing to lace up a **pair of boots.** Daytrip trails are well populated—at nearly any point in the day, you may find yourself stuck behind groups of other tourists on trails. Hiking just after sunrise is the best and sometimes the only way to beat the crowds; even then, though, trails like Half Dome are already busy. A colorful trail map of short day hikes from the Valley with difficulty ratings and average hiking times is available at the Visitors Center ($0.50; see **Yosemite Valley Visitors Center,** p. 966). The **Mirror Lake Loop** is a level 3 mi. walk past Mirror Lake (half a mile), up Tenaya Creek, and back. **Bridalveil Falls** is an easy ¼ mi. stroll from the nearby shuttle stop, and its cool spray is as close to a shower as many Yosemite campers will get. The **Lower Yosemite Falls Trail** is a favorite of all ages and starts just opposite the Yosemite Lodge. On moonlit nights, mysterious moon-bows (the moon's answer to the rainbow) can sometimes be spotted off the water. Both the Lower Yosemite and Bridalveil Falls trails are wheelchair-accessible. **Upper Yosemite Falls Trail,** a back-breaking 3½ mi. trek to the windy summit, climbs 2700 ft. but rewards the intrepid hiker with an overview of the 2425 ft. drop. Those with energy to spare can trudge on to **Yosemite Point** or **Eagle Peak,** where views of the valley below rival those from heralded Glacier Point. The trail begins with an extremely steep, unshaded ascent. A sign warns, "If you go over the waterfall, you will die."

From the Happy Isles trailhead at the eastern end of the Upper Pines campground, the **John Muir Trail** leads 211 mi. to Mt. Whitney, but most visitors prefer to take the slightly less strenuous 1½ mi. **Mist Trail** along the Merced River and past the base of **Vernal Falls** to the top of **Nevada Falls.** This is perhaps the most popular day-use trail in the park, and with good reason—views of the falls from the trails are outstanding, and the cool drops from the nearby water-pounded rocks are quite welcome. From Nevada Falls, the trail continues to the base of **Half Dome,** Yosemite's most recognizable monument. The hike is 17 mi. round-trip, rises 4800 vertical ft., and takes a full day to complete (6-12hr), and is well worth it.

Although you'll have to share your achievement with the multitudes who opt to drive, the steep 5 mi. hike to **Glacier Point** will earn you the satisfaction of knowing you've worked for the staggering views. The 3200 ft. ascent is grueling, making the presence of a snack bar at the top welcome as well as absurd. You can find the trailhead on Southside Dr., 1 mi. southwest of the village. The wildflower-laden **Pohono Trail** starts from Glacier Point, crosses Sentinel Creek (spectacular **Sentinel Falls,** the park's second-largest cascade, lies to the north), and parallels the south rim of the Valley on its way to **Taft Point, Dewey Point,** and other secluded lookouts.

WINTERTIME IN YOSEMITE. In Yosemite's quietest season, the cold dramatically transforms the landscape as the waterfalls freeze over and snow masks the meadows. Unlike much of the mountain range, Yosemite Valley remains accessible year-round. **Route 140** from Merced, a designated all-weather entrance, is usually open and clear. Although Tioga Pass and Glacier Point Rd. invariably close at the first sign of snowfall, **Route 41** from the south and **Route 120** from the west typically remain traversable. Verify road conditions before traveling (☎372-0200) and carry tire chains. Although Yosemite may lose some of its celebrity appeal in the winter, the crowds clear out and the experience is more personal and serene.

Several well-marked trails for **cross-country skiing** and **snowshoeing** cut into the backcountry of the Valley's South Rim at Badger Pass and Crane Flat. Rangers host several snowshoe walks from mid-December through March, but the winter forests are perhaps best explored without guidance. Snowshoes and cross-country skis can be rented from the **Yosemite Mountaineering School** (see p. 966). **Badger Pass Rental Shop** (see below) also rents winter equipment and downhill skis. Guided cross-country skiing trips (☎327-8444) with meals and accommodations at the huts are available. The state's oldest ski resort, **Badger Pass Ski Area,** on Glacier Point Rd. south of Yosemite Valley, is the only downhill ski area in the park. The family-fun atmosphere fosters learning.

Ice skating at Curry Village is a beautiful (if cold) experience, with Half Dome towering above a groomed outdoor rink encircled by snow-covered pines. (☎372-8319. Open in winter M-F noon-9:30pm, Sa-Su 8:30am-9:30pm. $5; skate rental $2.) **Sledding** and **tobogganing** are permitted at Crane Flat off Rte. 120.

MAMMOTH LAKES ☎760

Home to one of the most popular ski resorts in the U.S., the town of Mammoth Lakes (pop. 5305) is a giant year-round playground. The snowfall averages over 350 in. a year, creating 3500 acres of skiable terrain. When the snow melts, mountain bikers invade to take on Mammoth Mountain, skateboarders come to test their skills in competitions, and fisherfolk come to the magma-warmed creeks. A **free shuttle bus (MAS)** transports skiers between lifts, town, and the main lodge.

As with most ski resorts, lodging is much more expensive in winter. Condo rentals are a good choice for groups of three or more and start at $100 per night. **Mammoth Reservation Bureau** (☎800-462-5571; www.mammothvacations.com) can make rental arrangements. For lone travelers, dorm-style motels are cheapest. Reservations are highly recommended. **Davison St. Guest House** ❷, 19 Davison Rd., off Main

St., is a homey lodge and one of the best values in town. (☎924-2188. Dorms $25; private rooms $60-75.) There are nearly 20 Inyo Forest public **campgrounds ❶** (sites $13-16) in the area, sprinkled around Mammoth Lakes, Mammoth Village, Convict Lake, Red's Meadow, Agnew Meadow, and June Lake. All sites have piped water and most are near fishing and hiking. Contact the **Mammoth Ranger District** (☎924-5500) for info. Reservations for some can be made at nearby Sherwin Creek (☎877-444-6777; www.reserveusa.com). **Schat's Bakery and Cafe ❶,** 3305 Main St., is the best in town. (☎934-6055. Open Su-Th 5:30am-6pm, F-Sa 5:30am-8pm.)

Devil's Postpile National Monument is a sheer basalt wall 60 ft. high, made of eerily uniform hexagonal columns that formed less than 100,000 years ago when the basalt lava that oozed through Mammoth Pass cooled and contracted. A pleasant 2 mi. walk from the Devil's Postpile Monument is **Rainbow Falls.** The **Inyo Craters** are huge conical volcanic blast holes in the ground filled with bright green water. The ¼ mi. jaunt to the craters can be reached from Mammoth Scenic Loop Rd. The stately climbing wall at **Mammoth Mountain High Adventure** beckons both the inexperienced and the professional. (☎924-5683; open daily 10am-6pm. $6 per climb, $13 per hr., $22 per day; discount for groups of 3 or more.) The **Map and Compass Course** has more of an outdoor sleuth/guerrilla warfare approach to freedom. ($15 round-trip for 2hr. course; includes compass rental, map, and intro lesson.) Visitors can ride the **Mammoth Mountain Gondola** for a spectacular view miles above the rest. (☎934-2571; open daily 8am-4pm. Round-trip $16, children $8; day pass for gondola and trail use $25. Chair ride round-trip $10, children $5.) Exit the gondola at the top for a mountain biking extravaganza of more than 80 mi. of twisted trails in **Mammoth Mountain Bike Park,** where the ride starts at 11,053 ft. and heads straight down on rocky ski trails. (☎934-0706. Helmets required. Open 9am-6pm. Day pass $29, children $15. Unlimited day pass and bike rental $62/31.)

HAWAII

The most remote island group in the world, the Hawaiian islands are separated from the mainland US by over 2000 miles. Hawaii is composed of eight major islands— "The Big Island" (officially named Hawaii), Maui, Molokai, Lanai, Oahu, Kauai, and Ni'ihau—and over 120 other small islands and atolls. Due to the islands' location, the so-called "crossroads of the Pacific" has developed into a unique environment of tropical enticements and a melting pot of cultures. The awe-inspiring landscape is alive, in every sense of the word, with the forces of creation. This allure has enticed voyagers from Polynesia, Europe, Asia, and beyond; today Hawaii is the most ethnically diverse state in the US. The culture is an amalgamation of Hawaiian tradition, laidback surfer lifestyle, the influence of an on-going military presence, waves of tourists, and more, all united by the *aloha* spirit.

HIGHLIGHTS OF HAWAII

WAIKIKI. Miles of sand and world-class resorts create a playground for the world's jet-setters (p. 975).

VOLCANOES NATIONAL PARK. Take a sunset hike and watch lava flows illuminate the night sky (p. 983).

KAUAI. Get back to the basics on one of Hawaii's most pristine islands (p. 980).

PRACTICAL INFORMATION

Capital: Honolulu.

Visitor Info: Hawaii Tourism Authority (☎808-973-2255; www.hawaii.gov/tourism), Hawaii Convention Center, 1801 Kalakaua Ave., Honolulu 96815.

Postal Abbreviation: HI. **Sales Tax:** 4%. **Accommodations Tax:** 11.42%.

Area Code: ☎808.

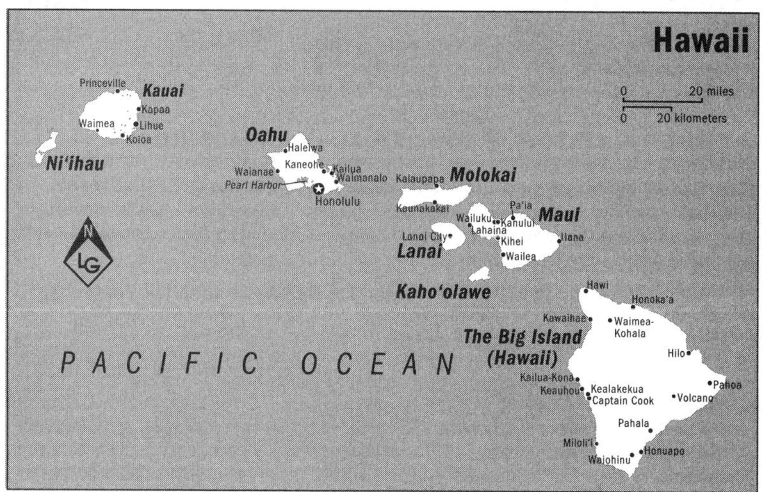

INTERISLAND TRANSPORTATION

Oahu is the major hub for transportation to all the Hawaiian islands, as international flights, flights between Hawaii and the mainland, and interisland flights depart from **Honolulu International Airport** in Honolulu (see p. 972). See each island's **Transportation** sections for local transportation.

OAHU

Oahu is known as "the gathering place" for good reason—it is the seat of the state government, Hawaii's financial and business center, and home to nearly three-quarters of the state's total population. Over half of these residents are concentrated in Honolulu. Waikiki, the southeastern quarter of the city, is one of the most famous tourist destinations in the world, a magical mile of beachfront hotels, shops, restaurants, and endless entertainment. Oahu isn't all souvenir shops and guided tours, however. Consider this your crash course in Hawaiian appreciation.

HONOLULU & WAIKIKI TRANSPORTATION

Airport: Honolulu International Airport (☎836-6413; www.honoluluairport.com) is off the Airport Exit from H-1, 9 mi. west of Waikiki. It hosts most incoming domestic and international flights, with carriers like **Aloha Airlines** (☎800-367-5250; www.alohaair.com) and **Continental Airlines** (☎800-214-1469; www.continental.com).

Bus: TheBus (☎848-4500, Waikiki ☎296-1818; www.thebus.org), Oahu's public transit system, was voted "America's Best Transit System," in 2000, and still offers safe, reliable service. One-way fare $1.75; seniors, the disabled, and students under 19 $0.75; children under 6 free. Free transfers for 2hr., available by request from driver.

Car: Driving is the easiest way to get around Oahu, despite traffic congestion and limited parking. The major **national car rental** chains have branches by the airport. Waikiki has some excellent smaller car and moped rental companies.

HONOLULU ☎804

As Hawaii's commanding capital and largest city, Honolulu is the point of entry for most visits to the islands. The city alternates as a beach resort, urban center, commercial hub, international port, and living landmark of Hawaiian history.

ORIENTATION & PRACTICAL INFORMATION

Depending on who you ask, Honolulu can include the urban and suburban sprawl that stretches along the south shore of Oahu, from Koko Head to the airport, or only the comparatively small downtown area surrounded by **Chinatown, Ala Moana, Waikiki, Kaimuki,** and **Manoa.**

Tourist Office: Hawaii Visitors & Convention Bureau Information Center, 2250 Kalakaua Ave., Ste. 502 (☎924-0266; www.gohawaii.com), at Waikiki Shopping Plaza. Open M-F 8am-4:30pm, Sa-Su 8am-noon.

Police: 801 S. Beretania St. (☎529-3111). Downtown/Chinatown substation (☎527-6990). Airport sheriff (☎836-6606).

Hospital: Queen's Medical Center, 1301 Punchbowl St. (☎538-9011). An **Emergency Services Department** (☎547-4311) provides pre-hospital emergency medical care and ambulance services. Their referral line (☎537-7117) can help visitors find a doctor.

Internet Access: etopia, 1363 S. Beretania St. (☎593-2050; www.theetopia.com), on the corner of Beretania and Keeaumoku St. Members ($10 per month) get a better rate ($2.50 per hr.). Under 18 not allowed during school hours. Open 24hr.

Post Offices: Airport branch, 3600 Aolele (☎423-6029). Offers the only general delivery services on the island. Open M-F 7:30am-8pm, Sa 8am-4pm. Postal Code: 96819. Downtown Honolulu branch, 335 Merchant St. (☎532-1987), west of Ali'Iolani Hale in the civic center. Open M-F 8am-4:30pm. Postal Code: 96813. Area Code: 804.

ACCOMMODATIONS

Manoa Valley Inn, 2001 Vancouver Dr. (☎947-6019; manoavalleyinn@aloha.net). Take Kapiolani Blvd. or H-1 to University Ave. *mauka* (toward the mountains) and turn left onto Vancouver Dr. 2 miles from rainforest hiking and Waikiki, this cozy mansion-turned-inn is a perfect hideaway from hectic Honolulu. Check-in 3pm. Check-out 11am. Doubles with shared bath $99, private bath $140. ❸

Hostelling International Honolulu, 2323A Seaview Ave. (☎946-0591; www.hiayh.org). Opposite the University of Hawaii 4 blocks north of H-1. Best-kept hostel in Honolulu in a residential neighborhood within walking distance of nightlife. Free lockers. $2 linen deposit. Shared bath, full kitchen, lounge. Reception 8am-noon and 4pm-midnight. 1-week max. stay. Single-sex 6-bed dorms $14, non-members $17. ❶

Ala Moana Hotel, 410 Atkinson Dr. (☎800-367-6025 or 955-4811; www.alamoanahotel.com), 2 blocks from Kapiolani Blvd. on Atkinson Dr. A perfect location, within walking distance of the Ala Moana Shopping Center, TheBus routes, Ala Moana Beach Park, and Waikiki. Fitness room, pool, and sundeck, as well as **Aaron's** fine continental dining and **Rumours** nightclub. Check-in 3pm. Check-out noon. Doubles $125-215. ❹

Aston at the Executive Centre Hotel, 1088 Bishop St. (☎800-949-3932 or 539-3000; www.astonexecutive.com). From H-1 east, take Exit 21A and turn right onto Pali Hwy., which becomes Bishop St. Rooms come with full amenities, fitness center, sauna, outdoor whirlpool, and sundeck with a 20m lap pool. Breakfast included. Check-in 3pm. Check-out noon. Business suite $190. Ask about weekend discounts. ❺

FOOD

Palomino, 66 Queen St. (☎528-2400), on the third fl. in Harbor Court. Plush interior with glass chandeliers. Thin crust pizzas ($9-13.50), desserts ($6-7), and specials like lobster *paella* ($29). First seating (5-6pm) offers a 3-course dinner for under $20. Reservations recommended before 8:30pm. The bar serves the full menu during restaurant hours. Open for lunch M-F 11:15am-2:30pm; dinner daily 5-10pm. ❹

Auntie Pasto's, 1099 S. Beretania St. (☎523-8855), on the corner of Beretania and Pensacola St. Pasta dishes ($7-9) big enough to fill a hungry *braddah* (brother) and authentic enough to satisfy any Italian. Open M-Th 10:30am-10:30pm, F 10:30am-11pm, Sa 4-11pm, Su 4-10:30pm. ❷

Legends Seafood Restaurant, 100 N. Beretania St. #108 (☎532-1868), in the Chinatown Cultural Plaza. Legends serves true dim sum, with succulent dishes to share family-style in small ($2.15), medium ($3), and large ($3.75). Open M-F 10:30am-2pm and 5:30-10pm, Sa-Su 8am-2pm. ❷

Volcano Joe's Island Bistro, 1810 University Ave. (☎941-8449), across the street from the UH campus. This new restaurant serves up an affordable, informal gourmet menu to the university crowd. Salads ($5.25-7), 9 in. pizzas with 3 toppings ($6), and vegetarian/vegan options. Open Su-Th 11am-9pm, F-Sa 11am-10pm. ❶

SIGHTS

PEARL HARBOR. Just before 8am, December 7, 1941, a wave of 350 Japanese fighter planes wrenched the US out of its steadfast neutrality and into the thick of WWII. Pearl Harbor, about 40min. outside of Honolulu, held the whole of the US Pacific Fleet and was the target of Japan's swift surprise attack. During the 2hr. onslaught, over 2400 military personnel and civilians were killed, 188 planes were demolished, and eight battleships were either damaged or destroyed. Solemn and graceful, the **USS Arizona Memorial** is a fitting tribute to the 1177 crewmen who died aboard the ship. The memorial spans the partially sunken battleship, affording visitors a close, poignant view of the ship that still entombs 1100 men. The **Visitors Center** has a historical museum and leads free tours. Each visitor must pick up a ticket in person, wait times can reach 2hr., and on busy summer days most are gone by 1pm.*(From Honolulu, take H-1 West to the Arizona Memorial/Stadium Exit to Kamehameha Hwy. and follow the signs, turning left after half a mile. TheBus #20, 42 or CityExpress A will also get you there. ☎422-0561. Open daily 7:30am-5pm. 1¼hr. tours every 15min., 7:45am-3pm. Free.)*

IOLANI PALACE. Hawaii's latter monarchs resided in the Florentine-style Iolani Palace, situated on lovely coral-fenced grounds. The palace was originally built in 1883 as a show of the strength and independence of the Hawaiian Kingdom and was the official residence of King Kalakaua and Queen Liliuokalani until American businessmen led a coup d'état and abolished the monarchy in 1893. After falling into disrepair while serving as the capitol of the subsequent Republic, Territorial, and State governments, the palace has been restored and maintained by the Friends of Iolani Palace. The **Royal Hawaiian Band** plays a free concert Fridays at noon. *(364 King St. ☎538-1471; call ☎522-0832 for tour reservations. Purchase admission to the palace interior at the ticket office inside the Iolani Barracks, the white structure on the Richards St. side of the grounds. Open Tu-Sa 9am-2:15pm. 1hr. grand tour $20, military $15 (no children under 5). Self-guided gallery tour $10, children 5-17 $5, under 5 free. Gallery open 9am-4pm, last ticket sold at 3:30pm.)*

BISHOP MUSEUM. Designated the Hawaii State Museum on National and Cultural History in 1988, the Bishop Museum is the best place for tourists and scholars to learn about indigenous Hawaiian land and practices. The pricey admission is justified by the spectacular collection of nearly 25 million works of art and artifacts, including historical artifacts and millions of species of plant and animal life, many of which are extinct. Tours run every 30min. from 10am to 3:30pm. *(1525 Bernice St. From Kuhio Ave., heading away from Diamond Head, take the #2 School St./Middle St. bus to School St. and Kapalama Ave. Walk toward the ocean on Kapalama Ave. to Bernice St. ☎847-3511; fax 842-4703. $15, seniors and children ages 4-12 $12.)*

FOSTER BOTANICAL GARDENS. These amazing gardens are home to 26 of Oahu's "exceptional trees," so designated for their outstanding rarity, age, size, aesthetic quality, location, endemic status, or historical and cultural significance. Meeting nearly all of these criteria is the garden's great *Bo* tree, which Hindus consider sacred as the abode of Bhavani, and Buddhists honor as the tree under which Buddha attained enlightenment. *(50 N. Vineyard Blvd. Take H-1 West or Ward Ave. north from Ala Moana Blvd. to Vineyard Blvd. Turn right into the parking lot after the Kuan Yin Temple. Otherwise, take TheBus #4 from University to Nu'uanu Ave. and Vineyard Blvd. and walk up the block past Zippy's, towards the river. ☎522-7066. Free guided tours M-F 1pm or by phone request. $5, ages 6-12 $1, under 5 free. Open daily 9am-4pm.)*

NIGHTLIFE

Compadres Bar and Grill, 1200 Ala Moana Blvd. (☎591-8307), on the 2nd floor of the Ward Center. Compadres is normally a calm cantina for enjoying a $2 draft beer or Mai Tai but it gets crowded for the $1 beef or chicken tacos Tu 4-7pm. *Aloha* F also draws a crowd with $1 oysters and live Hawaiian music. Open M-Th 11am-midnight, F-Sa 11am-midnight, Su 11am-10pm.

Anna Banana's, 2440 S. Beretania St. (☎946-5190). A Manoa and UH institution, this dim, love-worn bar has been rocking live music for 33 years. Outstanding Happy Hour daily 3-6pm (beer $2). Live music 4 nights a week. 21+. Cover only for special events $5. Open daily 3pm-2am.

Kapono's, 1 Aloha Tower Dr. (☎536-2161), in the Aloha Tower Marketplace. Named after Hawaiian music legend Henry Kapono (who plays regularly W 5:30-8:30pm and F 6-9:30pm), Kapono's has excellent live, contemporary Hawaiian music every night in its outdoor amphitheater. On *Pau Hana* F Kapono's rocks with pre-partiers in search of its multiple Happy Hours: from 11am on ($2 drafts), from 4-8pm (add 25% off wells and *pupus* $4-8, or *poke* for $10), and from 8pm-midnight. No cover. Open daily 11am-2am, kitchen open M-Sa 3-10pm, bands start around 5:30-7pm.

WAIKIKI

PRACTICAL INFORMATION

Tourist Office: Hawaii Visitors and Convention Bureau Information Office, 2250 Kalakaua Ave., Ste. 502 (☎800-GoHawaii or 924-0266; www.gohawaii.com), at Waikiki Shopping Plaza. Open M-F 8am-4:30pm, Sa-Su 8am-noon.

Banks and ATMS: Bank of Hawaii, 2228 Kalakaua Ave. (☎800-643-3888). Open M-Th 8:30am-4pm, F 8:30am-6pm.

Police: Substation at **Duke Paoa Kahanamoku Building,** 2425 Kalakaua Ave. (☎529-3801), on Waikiki beach opposite the Hyatt Regency. Open 24hr. **Emergency:** ☎911.

Medical Services: Urgent Care Clinic of Waikiki, 2155 Kalakaua Ave. (☎432-2700), at Beachwalk above the Planet Hollywood. Open daily 8am-8pm. **Straub Doctors on Call Waikiki** (☎971-6000).

Internet Access: Caffe G, 1888 Kalakaua Ave. C106 (☎979-2299; fax 979-7889). A hip sandwich joint. Fast Internet $1 per 10min., $1 minimum. Open daily 8am-11pm.

Post Office: Waikiki Station, 330 Saratoga Rd. (☎973-7515). Open M-F 8am-4:30pm, Sa 9am-1pm. **Postal Code:** 96815.

ACCOMMODATIONS

Waikiki Grand Hotel, 134 Kapahulu Ave. (☎923-1814 or 888-336-4368; www.queens-surf.com). Queen's Surf Vacation Rentals lets out these privately-owned rooms, which offer more thoughtful amenities than chain hotels. Hosts Hula's gay bar on the 2nd floor. Doubles $85, with ocean view $105; studio with kitchenette $150. $20 discount Apr.-June and Sept.-Dec. 22 on the Internet. Call to ask about discount rates. ❸

Aqua Bamboo, 2425 Kuhio Ave. (☎922-7777; www.aquabamboo.com). Trendy beige and black decor is dominated by a bamboo-and-Buddha motif. The small pool is surrounded by a beautiful garden area, spa and sauna. Complimentary cocktail reception W at 5pm. Doubles $145; studio with kitchenette $165. ❹

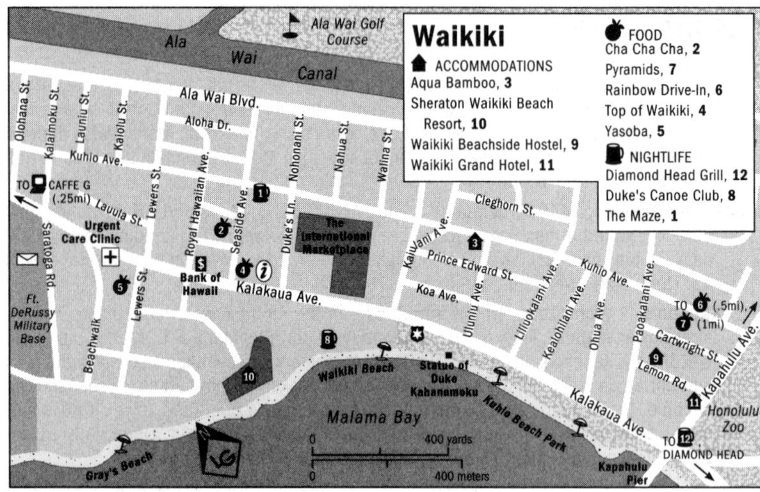

Sheraton Waikiki Beach Resort, 2255 Kalakaua Ave. (☎922-4422; www.starwood.com/hawaii). 80% of the rooms in the unique layout have fabulous ocean views and 95% have private lanais. 2 pools. 24hr. room service. City view $290, mountain view $360, partial ocean view $410, ocean front $495. ❺

Waikiki Beachside Hostel, 2556 Lemon Rd. (☎923-9566; www.hokondo.com). Young international travelers populate this hostel. All rooms have full kitchens and cable TV, and some have A/C. Breakfast and Circle Island tour included. Internet access $1 per 10min. 2 week advance reservations recommended in summer. 8-bed dorms $18 per person per night, $108 per week. Private rooms $90/458.❶

FOOD

Cha Cha Cha, 342 Seaside Ave. (☎923-7797). Caribbean-Mexican cuisine (grilled Jamaican jerk chicken $12, mahi mahi fish tacos $9.75) and 2 Happy Hours (4-6pm and 9-11pm; lime margaritas $2.50). Open daily 11:30am-11pm. ❷

Pyramids, 758 Kapahulu Ave. (☎737-2900). Authentic high-quality Egyptian food. *Shwarma* with beef, lamb, chicken and rice $16. Belly dancer M-Sa 7:30 and 8:30pm, Su 7 and 8pm. Open M-Sa 11am-2pm and 5:30-10pm, Su 5-9pm. ❸

Rainbow Drive-In, 3308 Kanaina Ave. (☎737-0177). The Rainbow's walk-up window is the gateway to one of Hawaii's tastiest local dishes, plate lunch ($4-6). Or try the Mix Plate ($6), with steak, mahi mahi, and chicken. Open daily 7:30am-9pm. ❶

Yasoba, 255 Beachwalk (☎926-5303), next to Arancino. Don't be alarmed when the entire staff turns and addresses you with *"irasshai"* (welcome). The *Tenmori Gozen* ($15) features both of the restaurant's specialties, assorted tempura and handmade soba noodles, as well as rice and dessert. Open daily 11:30am-2:30pm and 5:30-9:30pm. ❸

Top of Waikiki, 2250 Kalakaua Ave. (☎923-3877), on the 21st fl. of the Waikiki Business Plaza Building. With a 360° view of Waikiki, upscale food (Hawaiian-style mahi mahi $20), and a romantic atmosphere, the Top of Waikiki is a favorite among tourists. Go during the Sunset Special (5-6pm, steak and lobster $20) for the view. Reservations recommended F-Su. Open daily 5-9:30pm. ❺

VARIOUS & SUNDRY TROPICALIA

WAIKIKI BEACH. Waikiki Beach is the general name that refers to any and all of the beaches on the south shore of Oahu, beginning on the Waikiki side of the Hilton Lagoon in the west, and stretching all the way to the fringes of Diamond Head Crater. During the day, the Waikiki beaches are awash in aquatic activities as surfers paddle between catamarans, canoes paddle around snorkelers, and swimmers jostle into each other. Quieter, romantic moments occur at dawn and sunset when the crowds have dispersed and the plumeria breeze soothes burned skin.

DIAMOND HEAD. The 350-acre Diamond Head Crater was created about 300,000 years ago during a single, brief eruption that spewed ash and fine particles into the air. These particles eventually cemented together into a rock called **tuff;** geologists consider Diamond Head one of the world's best examples of a tuff cone. The 30min. hike to the 560 ft. summit is strenuous enough to give hikers of all ages a feeling of accomplishment once they've reached the top. *(Take the #22 or #58 bus from Waikiki (15min., every 30min.). It will let you off across from the entrance rd., which leads through a tunnel to the park. By car from Waikiki, take Monsarrat Ave. to Diamond Head Rd. Watch for the sign to the park on the right. Open 6am-6pm. Last hike 4:30pm. Entrance fee $1 per person, private vehicle $5.)*

HULA SHOWS. In Waikiki, watching beautiful island girls shake their hips and surf-chiseled local men flex and posture is not only completely civilized, it's also free. The **Kuhio Beach Torch Lighting and Hula Show** has Hawaiian music and performance at the Kuhio Beach Hula Mound, near the Duke Kahanamoku statue at Uluniu and Kalakaua Ave. *(☎843-8002. Hula show nightly 6:30-7:30pm. Waikiki style show with hula lesson M-Th. Hawaiian music and hula pageant by celebrated* halau *(hula troupes) F-Su. Free.)* The **Pleasant Hawaiian Hula Show** has been enticing tourists with the sounds and sights of traditional Hawaiian music and dance performances since 1937. *(Blaisdell Center in Kapiolani Park. Tu-Th 10-11am. Free.)* For more information on free Waikiki events, see www.co.honolulu.hi.us/events.

NIGHTLIFE

The Maze, 2255 Kuhio Ave. (☎921-5800), on the second floor of the Waikiki Trade Center. Three cavernous rooms: the Maze Arena, spinning house, hard house, and trance; Red Room dropping hip-hop and crowd-pleasing Top 40; and Paradox Lounge with live instrumental, funk, disco, and house. Dress "absolutely fabulous," especially on F. 18+. Cover M-Th $5, under 21 $10; F-Su $10, under 21 $15. Open nightly 10pm-4am.

Diamond Head Grill, 2885 Kalakaua Ave. (☎922-3734), in the W Honolulu Hotel. The poshest place in town to see and be seen, the Diamond Head Grill offers 2 rooms—1 dance, 1 hip-hop—for the socially suave of Honolulu. Club open F and Sa nights only, though F is by far the more popular night to go. Domestic beer $4, mixed drinks $5.50. Dress to impress. Cover $10, $20 on special event nights. Open F-Sa 9pm-2am.

Duke's Canoe Club, 2355 Kalakaua Ave. (☎922-2268), inside the Outrigger Waikiki, on the beach. A Waikiki institution, Duke's is a casual bar that mixes drinks with live contemporary Hawaiian music (F-Su 4-6pm nightly 10pm-midnight, on the lower lanai). Beachside seating is perfect for that sunset Mai Tai ($5). Duke's is also a thriving restaurant. Lunch buffet $10.50. Open daily 7am-midnight, bar open until 1am.

MAUI

Not nearly as developed as Oahu, Maui makes a solid claim for the motto that locals hold to be true: *Maui no ka 'oi!* (Maui is the best!). Visiting families delight in the activities available on the buzzing beaches of Ka'anapali and Kihei and honeymooning couples discover romance on secluded coasts and waterfall hikes. On the dry, leeward side of the island, the resorts have turned *kiawe* deserts into golf courses. The less developed windward side of the West Maui mountains has acres of dense rainforest, while the high altitudes of Haleakala Crater has forests of towering pines, redwoods, and eucalyptus.

TRANSPORTATION & PRACTICAL INFORMATION

Flights to Maui from the neighboring islands start at around $100 round-trip. Maui's major airport is **Kahului International Airport (OGG).** The best way to get around Maui is by **car.** National car rental chains operate out of Kahului airport.

Tourist Office: Maui Visitors Bureau, 1727 Wili Pa Loop (☎244-3530; www.visitmaui.com), in Wailuku. Open M-F 8am-4:30pm. The **Maui Information and Visitors Center** (☎874-4919) in Kihei will make reservations free of charge. **Lahaina's** tourist office is at 648 Wharf St. (☎667-9193; www.visitlahaina.com)

Banks: Bank of Hawaii at 2105 W. Main St. (☎871-8200), in Wailuku. **First Hawaiian Bank** at 215 Papalaua St. (☎661-3655) in Lahaina. **American Savings Bank,** 1215 S. Kihei Rd. (☎879-1977), in the Kihei Town Center

Internet Access: Free with the purchase of a $10 visitor card, valid for 3 mo., at **Kahului Public Library,** 90 School St. (☎873-3097), **Wailuku Public Library,** 251 High St. (☎243-5766), **Kihei Public Library,** 35 Waimahaihai St. (☎875-6833), **Lahaina Public Library,** 680 Wharf St. (☎662-3950)

Medical Services: Maui Memorial Hospital, 221 Mahalani St. (☎244-9056), Wailuku, has 24hr. emergency service.

Post Office: 138 S. Pu'unene Ave., Kahului (open M-F 8:30am-5pm, Sa 9am-noon) or 250 Imi Kala St., Wailuku, off Mill St. (open M-F 8am-4:30pm, Sa 9am-noon). **Kahului Postal Code:** 96732.

ACCOMMODATIONS

Camping on Maui is possible with **permits.** There are a few **cabins** in state and national parks, but they book months in advance. Each type of park issues its own permits; call or check web sites for details: **County parks** (☎270-7389; www.co.maui.hi.us) and **State parks** (☎984-8109), with **Haleakala National Park** issuing its own permits at the Park Headquarters.

Banana Bungalow, 310 N. Market St. (☎800-846-7835; www.mauihostel.com), Wailuku. Dorms are cozy and clean, and extensive tours are free. Stay a week, and you'll feel like family. Linens, storage, and safe available. Free Internet. Communal kitchen and TV lounge with foosball table. Reception 8am-11pm. Quiet time after 10pm. Check-out 10am. Reservations recommended. 4- and 6-bed dorms $20; singles $38; doubles $52; triples $64. ❶

Kai's Bed & Breakfast/Vacation Rentals, 80 E. Welakahao Rd. (☎800-905-8424, ext. 24 or 874-6431; www.mauibb.com), Kihei. Each themed room has stone floors, TV, microwave, and fridge. Continental breakfast with fruit from the garden served in a basket on your porch. Beach towels, coolers, boogie boards, snorkels, bicycles, jacuzzi, and washer/dryer available for guest use. Check-in 2pm. Check-out 10am. Reserve with 50% deposit at least 2 months ahead in low season (Apr. 15-Dec. 15), earlier for high season (Dec. 16-Apr. 14); balance due 30 days prior to arrival. $50-95 per night, $400-650 per week; slightly less in low season. ❸

Rainbow's End Surf Hostel, 221 Baldwin Ave.(☎579-9057; www.mauigateway.com/~riki/), Pa'ia. Clean and friendly, this hostel is within walking distance of both Pa'ia and the beach. Free Internet, a safe for valuables, board and bike storage, coin-op laundry, and parking. Linens included. Common living room with TV/VCR. No curfew; quiet time after 10pm. Reserve in advance with $50 deposit. Dorms $110 per week, $335 per month; doubles $200 per week, $675 per mo. Shorter stays also available. ❶

Star Lookout, 622 Thompson Rd. (☎907-346-8028; www.starlookout.com), Kula. The perfect setting for a peaceful retreat, the cottage has a full kitchen and sleeps 4-8. Landscaped gardens, a bonfire pit, gas barbecue, celestial telescope, wrap-around deck, cable, VCR, and a wood-burning stove. Laundry available. 2-night min. stay. Reserve 6 months to 1 year in advance. $150 per night for 4 people, each additional person $15. ❺

FOOD

Mañana Garage, 33 Lono St.(☎873-0220), Kahului. The namesake metal garage door in the back creates an inviting atmosphere that complements the Latin American cuisine. The entrees are pricey (*paella* $25; guava tamarind salmon $18.50), but on *La Familia* Su and *Aloha* M they come at half-price. Tempting desserts (chocolate *dulce de leche* cake $5), martinis ($5-7), and margaritas ($22 per pitcher). Live music Tu-Sa. Dancing after dinner Sa. Happy Hour M-F 3-6pm. Open M-Tu 11am-9pm, W-F 11am-10:30pm, Sa 5-10:30pm, Su 5-9pm. ❷

Cafe O'Lei Lahaina, 839 Front St. (☎661-9491), Lahaina. The ocean breeze and sunset view from the restaurant's 2-tiered dining room are delightful; nightly live music on the upper deck puts the dining experience over the top. The food emphasizes fresh local ingredients, (*taro* salad with Okinawan sweet potatoes $9; sauteed mahi mahi with ginger butter and papaya salsa $16), and all entrees come with a dinner salad. Lunch menu features salads and foccacia sandwiches ($7-8). Reservations recommended. Open daily 10:30am-9pm. ❸

Cafe des Amis, 42 Baldwin Ave. (☎579-6323), Pa'ia. The crepes at this intimate and funky cafe are just as popular with the morning latte crowd as with the evening diners toting their own Merlot. Savory crêpes ($6-9), sweet crêpes ($2-4), curries, and huge salads ($8). Take-out available. BYOB. Open daily 8:30am-8:30pm. ❷

Pa'ia Fishmarket, 100 Hana Hwy. (☎579-8030), Pa'ia. A Pa'ia landmark, filled with long wooden tables. Mahi mahi burgers ($6.50), fries, fish tacos, salads, seafood entrees ($12-17), and sushi. Counter service. Open daily 11am-9:30pm. ❷

VARIOUS & SUNDRY TROPICALIA

HALEAKALA NATIONAL PARK. The gradually sloping shield volcano of Haleakala ("house of the sun") dominates the island of Maui. Haleakala National Park preserves the unique and fragile ecosystems of the Haleakala summit.

There are three **Visitor Centers** in the park. **Park Headquarters** at 7000 ft. issues **camping** ❶ and **cabin** ❶ permits and has information on the park. (Open daily 8am-4pm.) The **Haleakala Visitor Center** at 9740 ft. has restrooms, geological and environmental displays, a glassed-in overlook of the crater, and a helpful, knowledgeable staff. (Open daily summer 6am-3pm, winter 6:30am-3pm.) **Kipahulu** also has a Visitor Center and public phones. (Open daily 9am-5pm.) *Pregnant women, young children, and those with respiratory and heart conditions should consult with a doctor before traveling to high altitudes.*

To see the **sunrise;** check times and weather conditions by calling ☎877-5111, and remember that the first light hits about 30min. before the actual sunrise. Weather conditions at the summit are extreme and can change rapidly. Be prepared for cold (30-50°F). Talks on natural and cultural history are held at the Summit building daily at 9:30, 10:30, 11:30am. Park rangers lead two guided hikes. Dozens of independent companies offer activities in the park, including biking down the volcano and horseback-riding in the crater. *(P.O. Box 369, Makawao, 96768. ☎572-4400; www.nps.gov/hale. Park open 24hr. Entrance fee $10 per vehicle, good for 7 days.)*

THE ROAD TO HANA. The 52 mi. trip from Kahului to Hana is one of the world's most impressive coastal drives, with over 600 curves, more than 50 single-lane bridges, and incredible views of rainforests and waterfalls. While it takes about 2hr. to drive the route, the experience is much more rewarding if you stop along the way. Fill up on gas in Pa'ia (there are no gas stations along the way), pack a cooler with snacks, and go! Stop along the way at Ho'okipa Lookout, Twin Falls (go early—like 7am early), the Waikamoi Ridge Nature Walk, Puahokamoa Falls, the freshwater pools of Pua'a Ka'a, and the small fishing village of Nahiku.

ONELOA BEACH. North of Kapalua Beach, Oneloa is a gem of a beach located below the Ritz Carlton. Usually nearly empty, it's perfect for secluded sunbathing and body boarding—the sand gives way to reef, and the waves are rather large. To reach public parking and beach access, take Office Rd. and turn left at the end, then right on Ironwood Ln.

WHALE-WATCHING. From December to April, anywhere you can see the ocean in South Maui, you can see whales. The **Ocean Center** in Ma'alaea, the **Whale Observatory** near Kaleolepo Park off S. Kihei Rd., and any of the hotels in Wailea are terrific whale-watching perches. To learn more about these magnificent sea mammals, stop by the **Hawaiian Islands Humpback Whale National Marine Sanctuary,** 726 S. Kihei Rd. (☎800-831-4888; www.hihwnms.nos.noaa.gov). Open M-F 10am-3pm.

KAUAI

Hawaiian spirit flourishes among the island's 58,000 residents, and locals are fiercely proud of both their heritage and Kauai's relative lack of commercial development. Aptly nicknamed "The Garden Isle," Kauai's rainforest jungle is best described as primordial (*Jurassic Park* was filmed here, after all), but markers of the island's 6 million weathered years are apparent in its impressive geological features. Kauai's miles of sandy shoreline contrast the cliffs of the Na Pali Coast, the island's deep valleys, and the jagged Waimea Canyon. Kauai's peaceful solitude and untamed landscape once attracted a healthy hippie culture, and still draws a more rugged, individualistic type of traveler than Maui or Oahu. Whatever your draw, Kauai is a paradise within Paradise.

TRANSPORTATION AND PRACTICAL INFORMATION

All commercial flights fly into **Lihue Airport (LIH).** Direct flights to Kauai from the mainland are rare; most passengers connect in Honolulu. Flights from other islands begin at around $100 round-trip.

The Kauai Bus runs six routes around the island, but the easiest and most convenient way to get around Kauai is by car.

Tourist Office: Kauai Visitor's Bureau, 4334 Rice St. #101 (☎245-3971; www.kauaivisitorsbureau.com), in Lihue. Open M-F 8am-4:30pm.

Banks: Bank of Hawaii, 4455 Rice St. (☎245-6761), Lihue, in Kapa'a at 1407 Kuhio Hwy. (☎822-3471), in Princeville next to the post office (☎826-6511), and at 2360 Kiahuna Plantation Dr. in Po'ipu (☎742-6800).

Internet Access: Internet access is free with the purchase of a $10 visitor card, valid for 3 months, at 4344 Hardy St. (☎241-3222) in Lihue, 1464 Kuhio Hwy. (☎821-4422), in Kapa'a, and 4343 Emmalani Dr. (☎826-4310), in Princeville.

Police: 3060 Umi St. (☎241-1711), Lihue.

Hospital: Wilcox Memorial Hospital, 3420 Kuhio Hwy. (☎245-1100), Lihue.

Post Office: 4441 Rice St.(☎800-275-8777), Lihue. Open M-F 8am-4pm, Sa 9am-1pm.

Lihue Postal Code: 96766.

ACCOMMODATIONS

The state and county parks on the island allow **camping** with a permit, though campers must have tents. Some state parks also have **cabins** available for rent. Each type of park issues its own **permits;** check web sites or call for details: **county parks** (☎241-6660; www.kauaigov.org/parks.htm); **state parks** (☎274-3444; www.state.hi.us/dlnr/dsp/dsp.html); and **forest reserves** (☎274-3433).

The Kauai Inn, 2430 Hulemalu Rd.(☎245-9000, www.kauai-inn.com), Lihue, just past Nawiliwili Harbor on the left. It may lack the extravagance of the larger resorts on the island, but is nicely located off the beaten path, and offers beautifully landscaped grounds, tropical flowers, lush palm trees, and deluxe rooms–arguably Lihue's best deal. Continental breakfast served on the outdoor patio. Coin laundry. Reception 8am-9pm. Basic room $69, with A/C $79, suite $109. ❸

Kapa'a Beach House, 1552 Kuhio Hwy. (☎822-3313). A relaxed, family-run hostel, the Beach House has a shared outdoor kitchen, patio-style common area with TV, VCR, stereo, and comfy couches, laundry, and a fantastic view of the Pacific from the signature rooftop shower. Spacious dorms with extra-long full bunks open up to oceanfront patios. Linens provided. Single bunks $23, doubles $35. Private rooms, with 4 beds and shared bath $50 for 2 people; each additional person $5. Cash only. ❶

Koloa Landing Cottages, 2704B Ho'onani Rd., Koloa (☎800-779-8773; www.koloa-landing.com). Four airy, clean cottages, from studios to a 2-bedroom house, all boast full kitchens and lanais. Friendly owners can negotiate discounts. Units $85-200. ❹

FOOD

Deli and Bread Connection (☎245-7115), Lihue, in Kukui Grove Shopping Center. A deli, bakery, and kitchenware store rolled into one, the Connection is a popular lunch-time stop for those who want to stay or take their meal to go. Vegetarian selections (Veggie Burger served hot $5.50) and fresh daily soups compliment the menu of standard (B.L.T. $4.25) and unique ("crimp," or crab and shrimp $5) sandwiches. Open M-Th and Sa 9:30am-7pm, F 9:30am-9pm, Su 10am-6pm. ❶

Lighthouse Bistro (☎828-0480), located in Kong Lung Center, in Kilauea. This open-air restaurant serves gourmet food. Dinner entrees include fresh fish ($20) and mango cherry chicken, with an extensive list of wines and mixed drinks (Mai Tai $7). Lunch M-F 11am-2pm, Sa noon-2pm. Dinner daily 5:30-9pm. ❹

Beach House Restaurant, 5022 Lawai Rd. (☎742-1424; www.the-beach-house.com), Po'ipu. Endless views and the best location on the South Shore keep this casually elegant beachfront restaurant packed. The menu blends international flavors with local seafood and vegetables. Try the fish nachos with refried black Thai rice, roasted Hawaiian corn and chili salsa, and mango *chipotle* sauce ($10), or the crusted Macadamia nut mahi mahi ($28). Reservations recommended. Lounge open daily 5-10pm. Dinner Oct.-Apr. 5:30-10pm; May-Sept. 6-10pm. ❺

Puka Dog (☎635-6354; www.pukadog.com), in Po'ipu Shopping Village. A puka dog (sausage or veggie $6), is a Hawaiian-style hot dog. One solid choice is the Kekaha special, with mango relish and garlic lemon sauce. Open M-Sa 11am-6pm. ❶

VARIOUS & SUNDRY TROPICALIA

SECRET BEACH. Officially Kauapea Beach, near Kilauea, this hidden spot has outgrown its mysterious nickname. Despite its discovery, it is still a gem. A vast expanse of superfine golden sand sprinkled with lava rocks, the beach features big surfing waves (especially in winter) and beautiful views. *(From Hwy. 56 northbound, turn right on the first Kalihiwai Rd., just before the 24 mi. marker, and then right again at the first dirt road. Park with all the other cars and follow a well-marked trail to the beach.)*

LUMAHAI BEACH. Considered by many to be Kauai's most beautiful beach, a picture of Lumahai can be found on almost every rack of postcards on the island. Devastating surf and powerful currents make swimming here **unsafe** year-round. The eastern half of Lumahai, also known as **Kahalahala Beach,** is even more picturesque than its western counterpart. *(In Haena. To access the western end of the beach, an opening in the trees leads to a dirt parking lot three-quarters of a mile after the 5 mi. marker. The eastern end is accessible via a short (100 yd.) trail that leads from a highway turnout down to the beach. Leaving Hanalei, the highway takes a U-curve toward the sea before the 5 mi. marker. Long turnouts lined with parked cars hug the base of the curve, and a short marked trail leads down to the beach from the second turnout.)*

TUNNELS BEACH. Also in Haena, a wide horseshoe reef encloses the fine sand of the North Shore's premier **snorkel** and **shore dive** locale. Despite its fame for complex underwater topography, the beach's name actually describes its characteristic curving winter surf break. Trees back the long sandy beach, providing much-appreciated shade, and limited parking translates into plenty of space for snorkelers. A lifeguard sits at the western end, which also has fabulous views of the surrounding mountains. *(Access is via 2 unmarked dirt roads. The first is half a mile west of the 8 mi. marker, just before a "Weight Limit 10 Tons" sign, and the second is a quarter mile further. The 2nd road is slightly longer and offers more parking spaces.)*

NA PALI COAST. Comprised of 15 rugged miles of jagged cliffs and pristine coastline, the Na Pali Coast stretches from Ke'e Beach in the north to Polihale State Park in the south. There is no way to drive through this part of Kauai; visitors can journey either by foot or by boat. Those who do gain access to the coast's hidden treasures will encounter steep lava rock walls, lush green valleys, secluded sandy beaches, and cascading waterfalls. Today, adventurers from around the globe come to travel 11 mi. along the **Kalalau Trail,** alternating between exposed ocean-side cliffs and ridges with outstanding views of the coastline, and sheltered, quiet stretches through valleys with shade and streams. Some hikers cover the entire 22 mi. round trip in 2 days, but most people allow up to 5 days to enjoy the stunning vistas and pristine beaches.

PO'IPU BEACH PARK. Extensive facilities attract a diverse crowd to Po'ipu's most popular beach. At low tide, sunbathers can walk all the way out to the point. Swimming is safe on both sides of the point, but snorkelers prefer the shallow area to the west. Po'ipu Beach is also home to one of the South Shore's better surf breaks, especially in the summer, and it's a cinch to rent a board across the street at **Nukumoi Surf Shop.** Sand space is at a premium; don't be late! *(Access at Hoowili Rd. From eastbound Po'ipu Rd., turn right at the "Po'ipu Beach" sign a few blocks past Po'ipu Shopping Village. 2 parking lots lie at the end of the road.)*

KOKE'E STATE PARK. Continuing up the road, past the 14 mi. marker, Waimea Canyon State Park gives way to the cool forests of Koke'e State Park, with temperatures often 10-15°F cooler than at sea level. For trail information, maps, and advice, head to the **Koke'e Natural History Museum** (☎335-9975; www.aloha.net/~kokee), on the left after the 15 mi. marker. (Open daily 10am-4pm. Free, but donations appreciated.) The main attraction of Koke'e State Park is its network of over 40 mi. of trails, from short forest walks through groves of Methley plums to heart-pounding, narrow, rocky ridges. The trails cover four types of terrain: the Na Pali Coast, Waimea Canyon, the forests of Koke'e, and Alaka'i Swamp. Our favorites are the moderate **Canyon Trail** and the hard-core **Nu'alolo-Nu'alolo Cliff-Awa'awa'puhi Loop.**

THE BIG ISLAND

The spirit of Hawaiian pioneers is still strong in Hawaii (nicknamed "The Big Island"), the birthplace of the islands' greatest king, Kamehameha I. Geologically the youngest of all her sisters, The Big Island is nonetheless the largest—and growing, thanks to Kilauea's constant eruptions. Within the island's borders 11 out of 13 climate ecosystems are represented, from the subarctic summits of Mauna Loa and Mauna Kea to the rainforests of the Hamakua Coast to the lava fields of the Ka'u desert.

INTERISLAND TRANSPORTATION

Flights between the Big Island and neighboring islands start at around $90 each way. **Keahole-Kona International Airport,** Keahole Airport Rd. (☎329-2484), 7 mi. north of downtown **Kailua-Kona** off Rte. 19, is closest to South Kohala's crescent of resorts and sees the majority of international traffic. It is also served by interisland carriers **Aloha Airlines** (☎800-367-5250 or 935-5771; www.alohaairlines.com) and **Hawaiian Airlines** (☎800-882-8810; www.hawaiianair.com).

One half-mile south of the intersection of Rte. 11 and Rte. 19, **Hilo International Airport,** Airport Access Rd. (☎934-5801), sees mostly interisland flights from **Aloha Airlines** and **Hawaiian Airlines,** but is also served by **United Airlines** (☎800-241-6522). An $8-10 **taxi** ride is the only available transport from the airport to Hilo.

LOCAL TRANSPORTATION

Based in Hilo, the **Hele-On Bus** (☎961-8744; www.co.hawaii.hi.us) is the Big Island's only island-wide system of public transport. Catching a bus from anywhere other than downtown Hilo can be a challenge, though. Renting a **car** is the best and most convenient way to see the Big Island. Many beaches, volcanoes, and waterfalls are otherwise inaccessible, and some remain so without 4WD. Strangely, 4WD vehicles are hard to come by—only Alamo, Dollar, and Harpers guarantee 4WD upon reservation.

HAWAII VOLCANOES NATIONAL PARK

Home to the world's most active oceanic hot spot and the only two active volcanoes on the Hawaiian Islands (Mauna Loa and Kilauea), Volcanoes National Park is never the same place twice. Along the park's southeastern coast, 2000°F lava flows boil into the Pacific Ocean, constantly redefining the boundaries of the island. At press, the current eruption from the Pu'u O'o vent along Kilauea's east rift zone had added 544 acres of new land since 1983, and that number grows daily. Both Mauna Loa and Kilauea are shield volcanoes with gentle slopes that rise gradually over many miles. Every day, visitors witness lava flows oozing and dripping from the east rift zone near the end of Chain of Craters Road. One of the most unforgettable experiences in the park is the hike that many visitors take after sunset to watch lava flows light up the night sky.

AT A GLANCE: HAWAII VOLCANOES NATIONAL PARK

AREA: 218,000 acres.

CAMPING: Camping available free of charge and without reservations at designated campsites (p. 985). Stays limited to 7 days per mo. and no more than 30 days per yr. Registration required for backcountry camping.

FEES & RESERVATIONS: $10 per vehicle; $5 per pedestrian, bicyclist or motorcyclist.

HIGHLIGHTS: Hiking over *a'a* and *pahoehoe* lava rocks, steam vents, cinder cones, pit craters, ancient petroglyphs, and (if lucky) active lava flows.

ORIENTATION

The entrance to the park is from Rte. 11 (Hawaii Belt Road), 30 mi. southwest of Hilo and 96 mi. southeast of Kona. Within the park there are two main roads: the 11 mi. Crater Rim Drive circles Kilauea Caldera, and the 20 mi. Chain of Craters Road descends the eastern flank of Kilauea toward the coast and abruptly ends where the road meets a bank of lava from an ongoing flow. Hilina Pali Road accesses the more remote western portion of the park, while Mauna Loa Road ascends the mountain and ends at the trailhead of a route to the summit.

TRANSPORTATION

Volcano (p. 983) is the nearest gateway town, and can satisfy visitors' basic needs. A car is the best way to see the park (and parking is easy), but the **Hele-On bus** runs between the park's Visitor Center and Mooheau Bus Terminal in Hilo. (☎961-8744. M-F leaves Volcanoes National Park 8:10am, arrives Hilo 9:20am; leaves Hilo 2:40pm, arrives Volcanoes National Park 3:45pm. $2.25 or three Hele tickets.)

PRACTICAL INFORMATION

Volcanoes National Park is hospitable at any time of year, but visitors should come prepared for extremes of hot, cold, wet, and dry, often within the same day.

Information: Hawaii Volcanoes National Park, P.O. Box 52, Hawaii National Park, 96718-0052. ☎985-6017. www.nps.gov/havo.

Hours: Open 24hr.

Fees, Permits, and Regulations: $10 per car or $5 per pedestrian, bicyclist, or motorcyclist; good for 7 days. Year-long Hawaii Volcanoes Pass $20.

Gas: Volcano Store (☎967-7210), next to the Volcano post office, is open daily 5:30am-7pm. Aloha gas station, 19-3972 Old Volcano Rd. (☎967-7555), is at the Kilauea General Store. Open daily 6:30am-7:15pm.

Weather: For weather conditions, call ☎961-5532 or 935-8555. **Eruption Information** is available at ☎985-6000. The park also broadcasts a radio bulletin on AM 530.

Emergency: ☎911. **Hilo Medical Center** is at 1190 Waianuenue Ave. (☎974-4700).

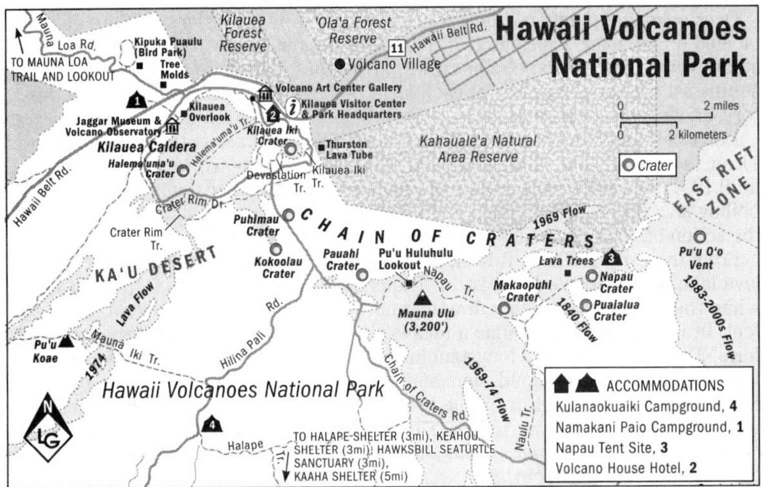

Facilities: Kilauea Visitor Center (☎985-6017; www.nps.gov/havo) and **Park Headquarters** (☎985-6000), a couple hundred yards beyond the entrance station along the northern arc of Crater Rim Dr. should be everyone's first stop in the park for maps and eruption updates. Office open daily 7:45am-5pm.

Guided hikes and events: The Visitor Center shows a 25min. introductory film about the park daily 9am-4pm on the hr. The ranger-led **lectures** and **walks** schedule varies.

Banks and ATMs: There is a 24hr. **ATM** in the Volcano House Hotel, across the street from the Visitor Center. The nearest banks are in Hilo: **Bank of Hawaii,** 120 Pauahi St. (☎935-9701), and **First Hawaiian Bank,** 1205 Kilauea Ave. (☎969-2211).

IN THE PARK

Backcountry camping ❶ is allowed at designated cabins, shelters, and campgrounds by permit only. Permits are free and can be easily obtained at the Visitor Center on a first come, first served basis no sooner than one day before you begin your trek. Tent sites, a small shelter, pit toilets, and water are available on the coast at **Ka'aha, Halape,** and **Keauhou Shelters. Apua Point** on the coast has tent sites, but no shelter or water. The **Pepeiao Cabin** in the Ka'u desert has three bunks and water. **Napau Crater** only has tent sites and pit toilets. There are two cabins en route to the summit of Mauna Loa, one at Red Hill (7½ mi. from the trailhead) and the second at the summit caldera (11½ mi. from Red Hill). Stays are limited to three nights per site and to groups of no more than 12. Water at all of these sites must be treated before drinking. No fires are allowed. **Volcano House Hotel ❸** (☎967-7321), along Crater Rim Dr., across from the Visitor Center, was built in 1877. Clean, simple rooms are comfortable, but a bit pricey. The restaurant serves buffet-style breakfast, lunch, and a la carte dinners ranging from $9.50-22. *(Reception 24hr. Check-in 3pm. Check-out noon. Reservations required. Singles and doubles $85-185; each additional person (up to 2) $15. Park entrance fees apply.)*

Many of the park's major attractions can be accessed by car along **Crater Rim Drive, Chain of Craters Road,** and **Mauna Loa Road.** All three roads are biker-friendly. Beginning at the Visitor Center, **Crater Rim Drive** is an 11 mi. loop that circles the Kilauea Caldera, passing through a cross-section of recent and historic lava landscapes. Consider walking at least part of the 11 mi. **Crater Rim Trail.**

Overlooks and points of interest are all marked by road signs and are clearly labeled on the maps distributed at the Visitor Center. You will pass sulfur banks, steam vents, crater pits, cinder cones, lava tubes, and deep fissures along the southwest rift zone. Placards at each sight offer information on the geology, history, and legends of each sight.

Don't be fooled; the barren summit crater of **Kilauea Caldera** that you circle for 11 mi. is currently one of the most active volcanoes in the world. From the 1800s until 1954, the caldera was the site of Kilauea's most dramatic eruptions, including boiling lava lakes and fountains up to 2000 ft. high. However, since 1955, most of the action has shifted to Kilauea's southwest and east rift zones.

From the early 1800s until 1924, **Halema'uma'u Crater** was the site of a dramatic lava lake that captivated the world. The crater visible today was formed in 1924 when the lava lake suddenly drained and the ground dropped several hundred feet. In Hawaiian, Halema'uma'u means "house surrounded by the *ama'uma'u* fern." The reference is to a longstanding battle between volcano goddess Pele and Kamapua'a, the god of cloud, rain, and forest, over a personal insult. Eventually, Kamapua'a saved himself from the last bit of Pele's rage by surrounding Kilauea with the rugged *ama'uma'u* fern. *Take caution: due to strong sulfur fumes, children, pregnant women, and those with heart and/or respiratory problems should avoid the crater.*

The drive along **Chain of Craters Road** is about 40 mi. round-trip, and there is neither gas nor water available below the Visitor Center. It is also the road most likely to be closed due to lava flow or fires; check with the Visitor Center for conditions.

Mauna Loa is the world's most massive mountain. Rising 18,000 ft. from the ocean floor below the surface of the Pacific, and climbing another 13,677 ft. above sea level, Mauna Loa towers over Mt. Everest. The scenic drive of **Mauna Kea Road** starts about 2 mi. west of the park entrance off of Rte. 11. The road climbs 3000 ft. through rainforest to the **Mauna Loa Lookout** (13½ mi. from Rte. 11), a secluded spot great for a quiet moment of reflection. Near the start of the road there is a turn-off to see the lava trees. These phantoms of the old forest were formed when *pahohoe* lava flows engulfed an especially moist tree (usually *'ohi'a*) and hardened around it before the tree burned away. Just over 1 mi. on Mauna Loa Rd. after the turnoff from Hwy. 11, is **Kipuka Puaulu,** an enclave of native forest that has managed to avoid the torrents of lava that have ravaged Mauna Loa over the centuries. An easy 1¼ mi. trail offers a good view of this treasure.

There are over 150 mi. of trail to choose from in Volcanoes National Park. There is a list of suggested hikes at the Visitor Center that includes routes for all skill levels. Trails over lava flows are loosely designated by piles of neatly arranged rocks known as *ahu* (cairns). If you only have time for one hike in the park, hit the **Kilauea Iki Trail.** Just over 40 years ago, the surface of Kilauea Iki Crater was a boiling lake of molten lava. Today, hikers revel in the experience of walking on what could be termed hell frozen over. The hike descends 400 ft. through *'ohi'a* and *hamu'u* rainforest, to the barren moonscape inside the crater. The hike provides an opportunity to see the first stages of volcanic succession following an eruption. *(4 mi., 2-3hr. round-trip. Trailhead: Lava Tube parking lot along Crater Rim Dr. Level: moderate.)*

The challenging **Napau Trail** is the only trail in the park that brings you face to face with the breathing heart of the current eruption at the Pu'u O'o vent. It is also the only dayhike in the park that requires hikers to register at the Visitors Center. Bring lots of water; the trail is hot and there is only a pit toilet and tent sites. *(14 mi., 6-9hr. return. Trailhead: Mauna Ulu parking lot along Chain of Craters Rd.)*

PACIFIC NORTHWEST

The Pacific Northwest became the center of national attention when gold rushes and the Oregon Trail ushered masses into the region, jump-starting the political machine that had already taken over the eastern US. In the 1840s, Senator Stephen Douglas argued, sensibly, that the Cascade Range would make the perfect natural border between Oregon and Washington. Sense has little to do with politics, and the Columbia River, running perpendicular to the Cascades, became the border instead. Yet even today, the range and not the river is the region's most important cultural divide: west of the rain-trapping Cascades lies the microchip, mocha, and music meccas of Portland and Seattle; to the east sprawls farmland and an arid plateau. For more, see *Let's Go: Pacific Northwest*.

HIGHLIGHTS OF THE PACIFIC NORTHWEST

SEATTLE. The offbeat neighborhoods, fine museums, ample green space, and pioneering cafes of this thriving city are not to be missed (p. 988).

NATIONAL PARKS. Oregon's Crater Lake National Park (p. 1020) puts a volcanic past on display. In Washington, Olympic National Park (p. 1004) has mossy grandeur and deserted beaches, and life beautifully blankets the dormant Mt. Rainier (p. 1010).

SCENIC DRIVES. Rte. 20 (p. 1006) winds through the emerald North Cascades, while U.S. 101 takes visitors on a ride through the Oregon Coast (p. 1018).

WASHINGTON

On Washington's western shores, Pacific storms feed one of the world's only temperate rainforests in Olympic National Park. To the east, low clouds linger over Seattle, hiding the Emerald City. Visitors to Puget Sound, Washington's deep, ecologically staggering inlet, can experience everything from isolation in the San Juan Islands to cosmopolitan entertainment on the mainland. Moving west over the Cascades, the state's eastern half spreads out into fertile farmlands and grassy plains as inland fruit bowls run over.

PRACTICAL INFORMATION

Capital: Olympia.

Visitor info: Washington State Tourism, Dept. of Community, Trade, and Economic Development, P.O. Box 42500, Olympia, WA 98504 (☎800-544-1800; www.experiencewashington.com). **Washington State Parks and Recreation Commission,** P.O. Box 42650, Olympia, WA 98504 (☎360-902-8844 or 888-226-7688 for reservations; www.parks.wa.gov).

Postal Abbreviation: WA. **Sales Tax:** 7-9.1%, depending on the county.

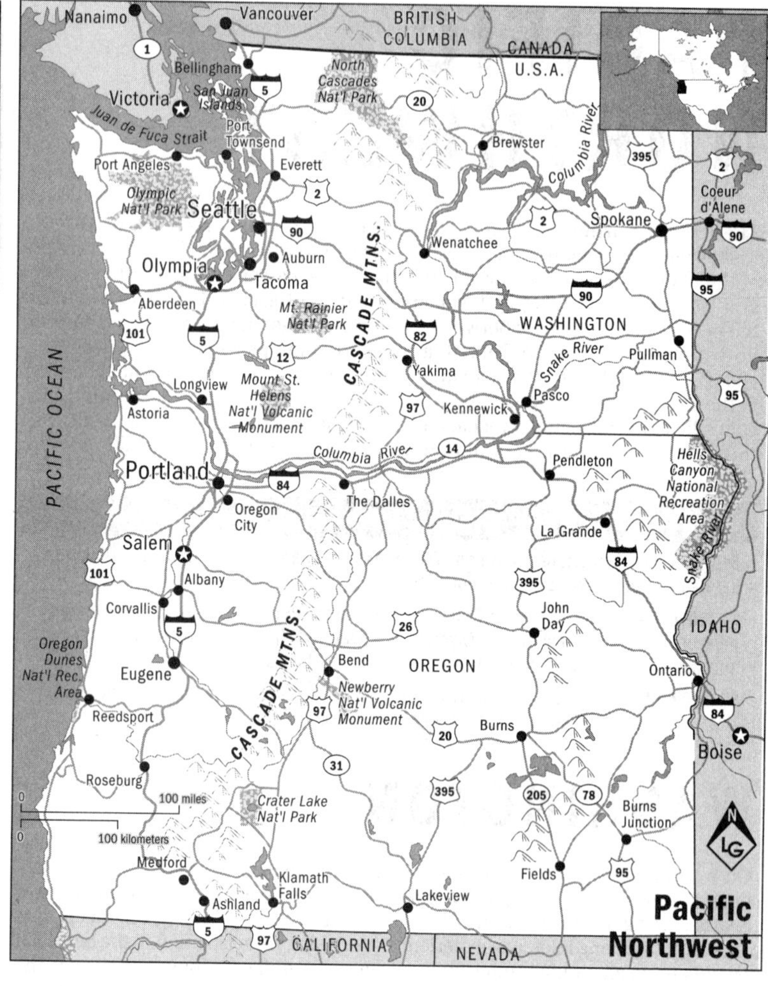

SEATTLE

☎206

Seattle's mix of mountain views, clean streets, espresso stands, and rainy weather proved to be the magic formula of the 90s, attracting transplants from across the US. The droves of newcomers provide an interesting contrast to the older residents who remember Seattle as a city-town, not a thriving metropolis bubbling over with young millionaires. Computer and coffee money have helped drive rents sky-high in some areas, but the grungy, punk-loving street culture still prevails in others. In the end, there is a nook or cranny for almost anyone in Seattle. Every hilltop offers an impressive view of Mt. Olympus, Mt. Baker, and Mt. Rainier. The city is shrouded in cloud cover 200 days a year, but when the skies clear, Seattle-ites rejoice that "the mountain is out" and head for the country.

INTERCITY TRANSPORTATION

Airports: Seattle-Tacoma International or **Sea-Tac** (☎431-4444), on Federal Way, 15 mi. south of Seattle, right off I-5. Bus #194 departs the underground tunnel at University St. and 3rd Ave.

Trains: Amtrak (☎382-4125 or 800-872-7245 for reservations), King St. Station, at 3rd and Jackson St., 1 block east of Pioneer Sq. next to the stadiums. Ticket office and station open daily 6:15am-10:30pm. To: **Portland** (4 per day, $26-37); **Tacoma** (4 per day, $9-15); **Vancouver** (1 per day, $23-36).

Buses: Greyhound (☎628-5526 or 800-231-2222), at 8th Ave. and Stewart St. *Try to avoid night buses, since the station can get seedy after dark.* Ticket office open daily 6:30am-2:30am. To: **Portland** (11 per day, $22.50); **Spokane** (3 per day, $28); **Tacoma** (8 per day, $5); **Vancouver** (8 per day, $23.50). **Quick Shuttle** (☎604-940-4428 or 800-665-2122; www.quickcoach.com) makes cross-border trips daily (8 in summer, 5 in winter) from Seattle (Travelodge hotel at 8th and Bell St.) and the Sea-Tac airport to the Vancouver airport and the Holiday Inn on Howe St. in downtown Vancouver (4-4½hr.; $33 from downtown, $41 from Sea-Tac). Call or check their web site for service to other hotels. Discounted fares for students, seniors, military, and children.

Ferries: Washington State Ferries (☎464-6400 or 888-808-7977; www.wsdot.wa.gov/ferries) has 2 terminals in Seattle. The main terminal is downtown, at Colman Dock, Pier 52. From here, service departs to: **Bainbridge Island** (35min.; $5.40, with car $10-12); **Bremerton** on the Kitsap Peninsula (1hr., passenger-only boat 40min.; $5.40, with car $10-12); and **Vashon Island** (25min., passenger-only boat $7.40). The other terminal is in Fauntleroy, West Seattle; to reach the terminal, drive south on I-5 and take Exit 163A (West Seattle) down Fauntleroy Way. Sailings from Fauntleroy to **Southworth** on the Kitsap Peninsula (35min.; $4, with car $8-10) and **Vashon Island** (15min.; $3.50, with car $12-16). Discounted fares available.

ORIENTATION

Seattle stretches from north to south on an isthmus between **Puget Sound** to the west and **Lake Washington** to the east. The city is easily accessible by car via **I-5,** which runs north-south through the city, and **I-90** from the east, which ends at I-5 southeast of downtown. Get to **downtown** (including **Pioneer Square, Pike Place Market,** and the **waterfront**) from I-5 by taking any of the exits from James St. to Stewart St. For the **Seattle Center,** take the Mercer St./Fairview Ave. Exit; follow signs from there. The Denny Way Exit leads to **Capitol Hill,** and, farther north, the 45th St. Exit heads toward the **University District (U District).** The less crowded **Route 99** (also called **Aurora Avenue** and Aurora Hwy.) runs parallel to I-5 and skirts the western side of downtown, with great views from the Alaskan Way Viaduct. Rte. 99 is often the better choice when driving downtown or to **Queen Anne, Fremont, Green Lake,** and the northwestern part of the city. For more detailed directions to these and other districts, see the individualized neighborhood listings under **Food** (p. 993), **Nightlife** (p. 998), and **Sights** (p. 995).

The **Metro ride free zone** includes most of downtown Seattle. Metro buses cover King County east to North Bend and Carnation, south to Enumclaw, and north to Snohomish County, where bus #6 hooks up with **Community Transit.** This line runs to Everett, Stanwood, and into the Cascades. Bus #174 connects to Tacoma's Pierce County System at Federal Way. All buses have free, easy-to-use bike racks. Between 6am and 7pm, bikes may only be loaded or unloaded at stops outside the ride free zone. Check out Metro's *Bike & Ride*, available at the Visitors Center. **City of Seattle Bicycle Program** (☎684-7583) has city bike maps.

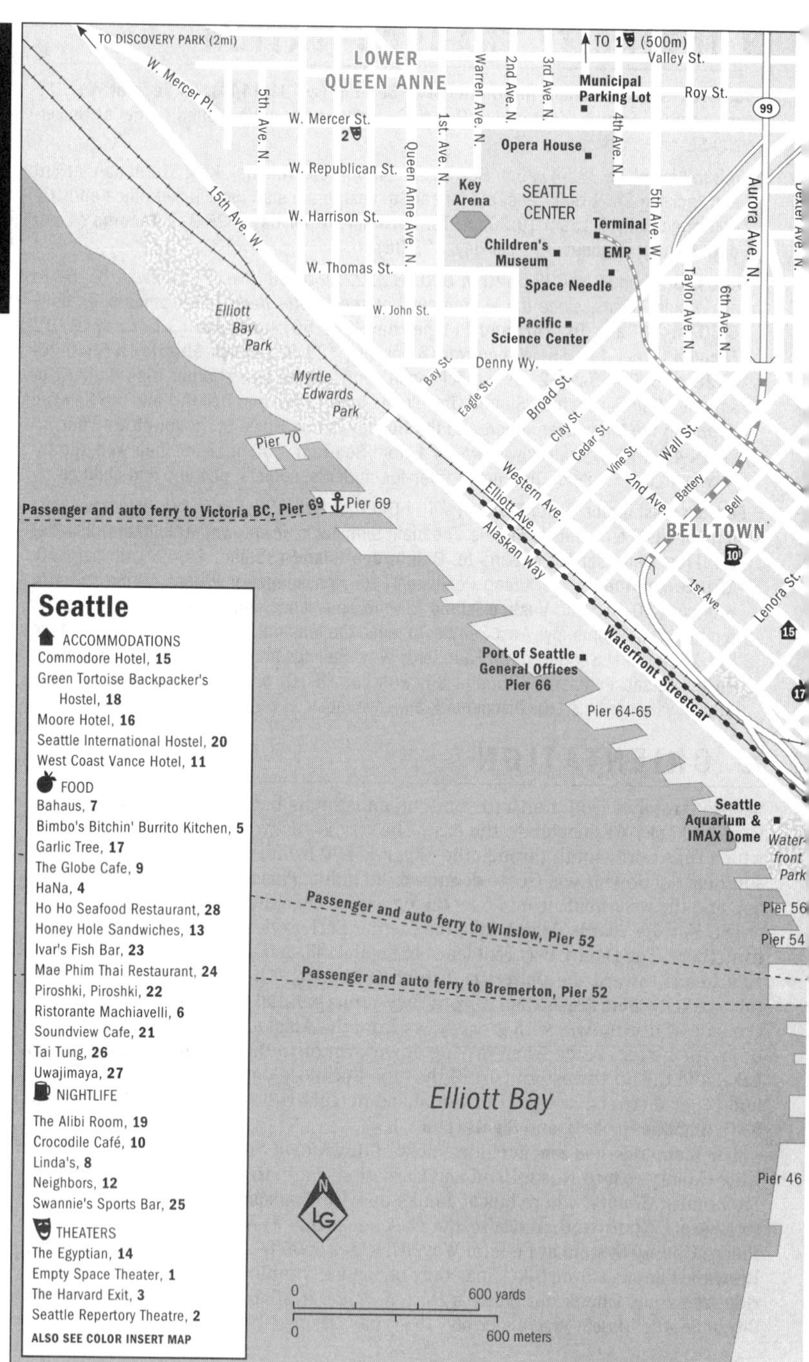

Seattle

ACCOMMODATIONS
Commodore Hotel, **15**
Green Tortoise Backpacker's Hostel, **18**
Moore Hotel, **16**
Seattle International Hostel, **20**
West Coast Vance Hotel, **11**

FOOD
Bahaus, **7**
Bimbo's Bitchin' Burrito Kitchen, **5**
Garlic Tree, **17**
The Globe Cafe, **9**
HaNa, **4**
Ho Ho Seafood Restaurant, **28**
Honey Hole Sandwiches, **13**
Ivar's Fish Bar, **23**
Mae Phim Thai Restaurant, **24**
Piroshki, Piroshki, **22**
Ristorante Machiavelli, **6**
Soundview Cafe, **21**
Tai Tung, **26**
Uwajimaya, **27**

NIGHTLIFE
The Alibi Room, **19**
Crocodile Café, **10**
Linda's, **8**
Neighbors, **12**
Swannie's Sports Bar, **25**

THEATERS
The Egyptian, **14**
Empty Space Theater, **1**
The Harvard Exit, **3**
Seattle Repertory Theatre, **2**

ALSO SEE COLOR INSERT MAP

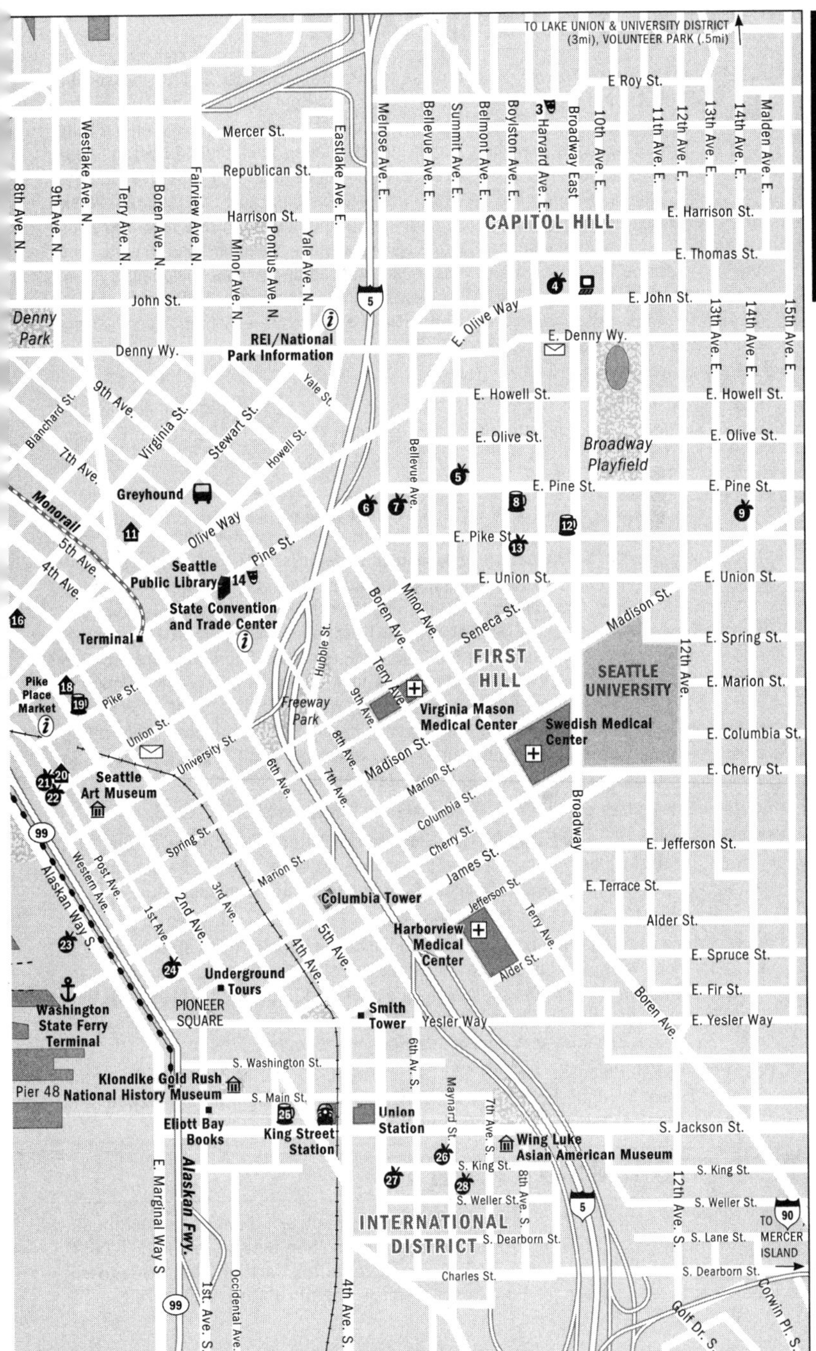

TO LAKE UNION & UNIVERSITY DISTRICT (3mi), VOLUNTEER PARK (.5mi)
E Roy St.
Mercer St.
Republican St.
Harrison St.
John St.
Denny Wy.
Denny Park
CAPITOL HILL
E. Harrison St.
E. Thomas St.
E. John St.
E. Olive Way
E. Denny Wy.
REI/National Park Information
E. Howell St.
E. Olive St.
E. Pine St.
E. Pike St.
E. Union St.
Broadway Playfield
Greyhound
Monorail
Olive Way
Pine St.
Seattle Public Library
State Convention and Trade Center
Terminal
Pike Place Market
Pike St.
Union St.
University St.
Freeway Park
FIRST HILL
SEATTLE UNIVERSITY
Virginia Mason Medical Center
Swedish Medical Center
Madison St.
Seneca St.
E. Spring St.
E. Marion St.
E. Columbia St.
E. Cherry St.
Seattle Art Museum
Spring St.
Marion St.
Columbia St.
Cherry St.
James St.
Jefferson St.
E. Jefferson St.
E. Terrace St.
Alder St.
E. Spruce St.
E. Fir St.
E. Yesler Way
Columbia Tower
Harborview Medical Center
Underground Tours
Washington State Ferry Terminal
PIONEER SQUARE
Smith Tower
Yesler Way
S. Washington St.
Pier 48
Klondike Gold Rush National History Museum
S. Main St.
Eliott Bay Books
King Street Station
Union Station
Wing Luke Asian American Museum
S. Jackson St.
S. King St.
S. Weller St.
S. Lane St.
S. Dearborn St.
Charles St.
INTERNATIONAL DISTRICT
TO MERCER ISLAND
Golf Dr. S.
Corwin Pl. S.
Alaskan Way S.
Alaskan Fwy.
E. Marginal Way S
1st. Ave. S.
Occidental Ave.
4th Ave. S.

LOCAL TRANSPORTATION

Public Transit: Metro Transit, Pass Sales and Information Office, 201 S. Jackson St. (☎553-3000, 24hr. ☎800-542-7876). Open M-F 9am-5pm. The bus tunnel under Pine St. and 3rd Ave. is the heart of the downtown bus system. Fares are based on a 2-zone system. **Zone 1** includes everything within the city limits (peak hours $1.50, off-peak $1.25). **Zone 2** includes everything else (peak $2, off-peak $1.25). Ages 5-17 always $0.50. Peak hours in both zones are M-F 6-9am and 3-6pm. Exact fare required. Weekend day passes $2.50. Ride free daily 6am-7pm in the downtown **ride free area,** bordered by S. Jackson on the south, 6th and I-5 on the east, Blanchard on the north, and the waterfront on the west. Free **transfers** can be used on any bus, including a return trip on the same bus within 2hr. Most buses are wheelchair-accessible (info ☎684-2046). The **Monorail** runs from the Space Needle to Westlake Center. (Every 10min. daily 7:30am-11pm. $1.50, seniors $0.75, ages 5-12 $0.50.)

Taxi: Farwest Taxi, ☎622-1717.

Bike Rental: The Bicycle Center, 4529 Sand Point Way (☎523-8300), near the Children's Hospital. $5 per hr., 2hr. min.; $25 per day. Open M-Th 10am-8pm, F 10am-7pm, Sa 10am-6pm, Su 10am-5pm. Credit card required.

PRACTICAL INFORMATION

Visitor Info: Seattle's Convention and Visitors Bureau (☎461-5840; www.seeseattle.org), at 8th and Pike St., on the first fl. of the Convention Center. Helpful staff doles out maps, brochures, newspapers, and Metro and ferry schedules. Open M-F 9am-4pm. **Seattle Parks and Recreation Department,** 100 Dexter Ave. N (☎684-4075), has info and pamphlets on city parks. Open M-F 8am-5pm. **Outdoor Recreation Information Center,** 222 Yale Ave. (☎470-4060), in REI. A joint operation between the Park and Forest services, this station is able to answer any questions that might arise as you browse REI's huge collection of maps and guides. Unfortunately, the desk is not set up to sell permits. Free brochures on hiking trails. Open M-F and Su 10:30am-7pm, Sa 10am-7pm. The center is closed M late Sept.-late spring.

Hotlines: Crisis Line, ☎461-3222. **Sexual Assault Center,** ☎800-825-7273.

Medical Services: International District Emergency Center, 720 8th Ave. S, Ste. 100 (☎461-3235). Medics with multilingual assistance available. Clinic M-F 9am-6pm, Sa 9am-5pm; phone 24hr. **Swedish Medical Center, Providence Campus,** 500 17th Ave. (☎320-2111), for urgent care and cardiac. 24hr.

Internet Access: Seattle Public Library, 800 Pike St. (☎386-4636), is stashed away in a temporary building near the convention center until spring 2004. After renovations are complete, the library will return to its original site at 1000 4th Ave. (at Madison). One-time visitors can use Internet for free with photo ID. Open M-W 10am-8pm, Th-Sa 10am-6pm, Su 1-5pm. Schedule may change; call for current hours.

Post Office: 301 Union St. (☎748-5417 or 800-275-8777), at 3rd Ave. downtown. Open M-F 8am-5:30pm, Sa 8am-noon. General delivery window M-F 9-11:20am and noon-3pm. **Postal Code:** 98101. **Area Code:** 206.

ACCOMMODATIONS

Seattle's hostel scene is not amazing, but there are plenty of choices and establishments to fit all types of personalities. **Pacific Reservation Service** (☎800-684-2932) arranges B&B singles for $50-65. For inexpensive motels farther from downtown, drive north on Aurora Ave. or take bus #26 to the neighborhood of Fremont.

Seattle International Hostel (HI), 84 Union St. (☎622-5443 or 888-622-5443), at Western Ave., by the waterfront. Take Union St. from downtown; follow signs down the stairs under the "Pike Pub & Brewery." Great location, laundry, and Internet access. 7 night max. stay in summer. Reception 24hr. No curfew. Reservations recommended. 199 beds. $22, nonmembers $25; Private rooms for 2-4 $54/60. ❶

Green Tortoise Backpacker's Hostel, 1525 2nd Ave. (☎340-1222), between Pike and Pine St. on the #174 or 194 bus route. A young party hostel downtown. M, W, F free dinner. Laundry, kitchen, Internet access. Key deposit $20 cash. Blanket $1. Free breakfast 7-9:30am. Reception 24hr. No curfew. Beds $18-20. ❶

Moore Hotel, 1926 2nd Ave. (☎448-4851 or 800-421-5508), at Virginia St. 1 block from Pike Place Market. Open lobby, cavernous halls, and attentive service. Singles $39, with bath $59 (double occupancy $10 extra). Doubles $49/68. ❸

Commodore Hotel, 2013 2nd Ave. (☎448-8868), at Virginia St. Pleasant decor only a few blocks from the waterfront. Front desk open 24hr., no visitors past 8pm. Singles $59, with bath $69; double with bath $79. ❸

West Coast Vance Hotel, 620 Steward St. (☎441-4200). Built in 1926, the West Coast Vance has charming rooms from $95. The hotel is located within walking distance from Pike Place Market and the 5th Ave. shopping district. ❺

FOOD

Although Seattleites appear to subsist solely on espresso and steamed milk, they do occasionally eat. When they do, they seek out healthy cuisine, especially seafood. **Puget Sound Consumer Coops (PCCs)** are local health food markets at 7504 Aurora Ave. N (☎525-3586), in Green Lake, and 6514 40th St. NE (☎526-7661), in the Ravenna District north of the university. Capitol Hill, the U District, and Fremont close main thoroughfares on summer Saturdays for **Farmers Markets.**

PIKE PLACE MARKET & DOWNTOWN

In 1907, angry citizens demanded the elimination of the middle-man and local farmers began selling produce by the waterfront, creating the Pike Place Market. Business thrived until an enormous fire burned the building in 1941. Today thousands of tourists mob the market daily to watch flying fish. (Open M-Sa 9am-6pm, Su 11am-5pm. Produce and fish open earlier; restaurants and lounges close later.) In the **Main Arcade,** on the west side of Pike St., fishmongers compete for audiences as they hurl fish from shelves to scales.

Piroshki, Piroshki, 1908 Pike Pl. (☎441-6068). The Russian *piroshki* is a croissant-like dough baked around sausages, mushrooms, cheeses, salmon, or apples doused in cinnamon ($3-4). Watch the *piroshki* process in progress. Open daily 8am-7pm. ❶

Soundview Cafe (☎623-5700), on the mezzanine in the Pike Place Main Arcade. The sandwich-and-salad bar is a good place to brown-bag a moment of solace. Breakfast and lunch $3-6. Open M-F 8am-5pm, Sa 8am-5:30pm, Su 8am-5pm. ❶

Garlic Tree, 94 Stewart St. (☎441-5681), 1 block up from Pike Place Market. This smell will drag you in. Loads of fabulous veggie, chicken, and seafood stir-fries ($7-9). Open M-Sa 11am-8pm. ❷

THE WATERFRONT

Budget eaters, steer clear of Pioneer Sq. Instead, take a picnic to **Waterfall Garden,** on the corner of S. Main St. and 2nd Ave. S. The garden sports tables and chairs and a man-made waterfall that masks traffic outside. (Open daily dawn to dusk.)

Mae Phim Thai Restaurant, 94 Columbia St. (☎624-2979), a few blocks north of Pioneer Sq. between 1st Ave. and Alaskan Way. Slews of pad thai junkies crowd in for cheap, delicious Thai cuisine. All dishes $6. Open M-Sa 11am-7pm. ❷

Ivar's Fish Bar, Pier 54 (☎467-8063), north of the square. A fast-food window that serves the definitive Seattle clam chowder ($2). Clam and chips $5. Open M-Th and Su 10am-midnight, F-Sa 10am-2am. ❶

INTERNATIONAL DISTRICT

Along King and Jackson St., between 5th and 8th Ave. east of the Kingdome, Seattle's International District is packed with great eateries.

Uwajimaya, 600 5th Ave. S (☎624-6248). The Uwajimaya Center–the largest Japanese department store in the Northwest–is a full city block of groceries, gifts, videos, and CDs. There is even a food court, plying Korean BBQ and Taiwanese-style baked goods. Pork dumpling $7. Open M-Sa 9am-11pm, Su 9am-10pm. ❷

Tai Tung, 655 S. King St. (☎622-7372). Select authentic Mandarin cuisine from a comprehensive menu. Entrees $5-12. Open Su-Th 10am-11pm, F-Sa 10am-1:30am. ❷

Ho Ho Seafood Restaurant, 653 S. Weller St. (☎382-9671). Generous portions of tank-fresh seafood. Stuffed fish hang from the ceilings. Lunch $5-7. Dinner $7-12. Open Su-Th 11am-1am, F-Sa 11am-3am. ❷

CAPITOL HILL

With bronze dance-steps on the sidewalks and neon storefronts, **Broadway Avenue** is a land of espresso houses, imaginative shops, elegant clubs, and good eats.

Bimbo's Bitchin' Burrito Kitchen, 506 E. Pine St. (☎329-9978). The name explains it, and the decorations (fake palm trees and lots of plastic) prove it. Walk right on through the door to the **Cha Cha,** a similarly-decorated bar (tequila shots $3.50). Spicy Bimbo's burrito $4.25. Dining room open M-Th noon-10pm, F-Sa noon-1am, Su 2-9pm. ❶

Ristorante Machiavelli, 1215 Pine St. (☎621-7941), across the street from Bauhaus. A small Italian place that locals fiercely love. Pasta $8-10. Open M-Sa 5-11pm. ❸

HaNa, 219 Broadway Ave. E (☎328-1187). Packed quarters testify to the popularity of the sushi here. Lunch sushi combo platter with rice and soup $7.25. Dinner $9-10. Open M-Sa 11am-10pm, Su 4-10pm. ❷

Honey Hole Sandwiches, 703 E. Pike St. (☎709-1399). The primary colors and veggie-filled sandwiches make you feel healthy and happy. The hummus-loaded "Daytripper" is a treat ($5.50). Lunch menu available until 5pm. Open daily 10am-2am. ❷

UNIVERSITY DISTRICT

The neighborhood around the immense **University of Washington** ("U-Dub"), north of downtown between Union and Portage Bay, supports funky shops, international restaurants, and coffeehouses. The best of each lies within a few blocks of University Way, known as "the Ave."

Flowers, 4247 University Way NE (☎633-1903). This 1920s landmark was a flower shop; now, the mirrored ceiling tastefully reflects an all-you-can-eat vegetarian buffet ($7.50). Great daily drink specials: W $2 tequila shots; Th $3 well sours; Sa $3 margaritas. Open M-Sa 11am-2am, Su 11am-midnight. ❷

Neelam's, 4735 University Way NE (☎523-5275), serves up the best authentic Indian cuisine in the University District, and the price is right. Lunch buffet $6. Brunch $7. Open daily 11:30am-3pm and 5-10pm. ❷

Araya's Vegan Thai Cuisine, 4732 University Way NE (☎524-4332). Consistently among the top vegan restaurants in Seattle, Araya's will satisfy any meatless desire. Lunch buffet $6.55. Open M-Th 11:30am-9pm, F-Sa 11:30am-9:30pm, Su 5-9pm. ❷

CAFES

The coffee bean is Seattle's first love; you can't walk a single block without passing an institution of caffeination. The city's obsession with Italian-style espresso drinks even has gas stations pumping out thick, dark, soupy java.

Bauhaus, 301 E. Pine St. (☎625-1600), in Capitol HIll. The Reading Goddess, looming above the towering bookshelves, protects patrons and oversees the service of drip coffee ($1) and Kool-Aid ($1). Open M-F 6am-1am, Sa 7am-1am, Su 8am-1am.

The Globe Cafe, 1531 14th Ave. (☎324-8815), in Capitol Hill. Seattle's next literary renaissance is brewing as quotes overheard at the Globe are plastered on the tables. Fabulous all-vegan menu. Stir-fry tofu $5.50. Open Tu-Su 7am-3pm.

Espresso Roma, 4201 University Way NE (☎632-6001). Pleasant patio and former warehouse interior result in spacious tables with an open air feel. The Ave.'s cheapest coffee (mocha $2). Open M-F 7am-10pm, Sa-Su 8am-10pm.

Ugly Mug, 1309 43rd St. (☎547-3219), off University Way. Off-beat in a Belle and Sebastian-thrift store sort of way—eclectic chair collection is quite comfortable. Wide sandwich selection (turkey foccaccia $4). Open daily 7:30am-6pm.

Gingko Tea, 4343 University Way NE (☎632-7298). If you dig tea, you'll find a niche at Gingko's. Classical music and wood furniture along with 5 types of chai ($2.55). Bubble tea $2.45. Open M-Th 10:30am-11pm, F-Sa 10:30am-midnight, Su 11am-10pm.

SIGHTS

It takes only three frenetic days to get a decent look at most of the city's major sights, since most are within walking distance of one another or within the Metro's ride free zone (see p. 989). Seattle taxpayers spend more per capita on the arts than any other Americans, and the investment pays off in unparalleled public art installations throughout the city (self-guided tours begin at the Visitors Center) and plentiful galleries. The investments of Seattle-based millionaires have brought startlingly new and bold architecture in the Experience Music Project and International Fountain. Outside cosmopolitan downtown, Seattle boasts over 300 areas of well-watered greenery (see **Outdoors,** p. 999).

DOWNTOWN & THE WATERFRONT

The **Pike Place Hillclimb** descends from the south end of Pike Place Market past chic shops and ethnic restaurants to the Alaskan Way and waterfront. You will not be lonely in the harbor; the waterfront is lined with vendors.

SEATTLE ART MUSEUM. Housed in a grandiose building designed by Philadelphia architect and father of postmodernism Robert Venturi, the **Seattle Art Museum (SAM)** balances special exhibits with the region's largest collection of African, Native American, and Asian art and an eclectic bunch of contemporary western painting and sculpture. Call for info on special musical shows, films, and lectures. Admission is also good for the Seattle Asian Art Museum (see p. 996) for a week. *(100 University St., near 1st Ave. ☎654-3100. Open Tu-W and F-Su 10am-5pm, Th 10am-9pm. $7, students and seniors $5, under 12 free. First Th of the month free.)*

THE SEATTLE AQUARIUM. The star attraction of the **Seattle Aquarium** is a huge underwater dome, and the harbor seals, fur seals, otters, and plenty of fish won't disappoint. Touch tanks and costumes delight kids, while a million-dollar salmon exhibit and ladder teaches about the state's favorite fish. Feedings occur throughout the day. Next door, the **IMAX Dome** cranks out films, many focusing on natural events or habitats. *(Pier 59, near Union St. ☎386-4320, TDD ☎386-4322. Open daily summer 9:30am-8pm; fall/winter 10am-6pm; spring 9:30am-6pm; last admission 1hr. before closing. $11, ages 6-12 $7, ages 3-5 $5. IMAX: Dome ☎622-1868. Films daily 10am-10pm. $7, ages 6-12 $6. Aquarium and IMAX Dome combo ticket $16.50, ages 6-12 $11.75, ages 3-5 $5.)*

THE SEATTLE CENTER

The 1962 World's Fair demanded a Seattle Center to herald the city of the future. Now the Center houses everything from carnival rides to ballet. The center is bordered by Denny Way, W. Mercer St., 1st Ave., and 5th Ave. and has eight gates, each with a model of the Center and a map of its facilities. It is accessible via a **monorail** which departs from the third floor of the Westlake Center. The anchor point is the **Center House,** which holds a food court, stage, and **Info Desk.** *(For info ☎684-8582. Monorail every 15min. M-F 7:30am-11pm, Sa-Su 9am-11pm. $1.50, seniors and "juniors" $0.75. Info Desk open daily 11am-6pm.)*

EXPERIENCE MUSIC PROJECT (EMP). Undoubtedly the biggest and best attraction at the Seattle Center is the new, futuristic, abstract, and technologically brilliant **Experience Music Project.** The museum is the brainchild of Seattle billionaire Paul Allen, who originally wanted to create a shrine to worship his music idol Jimi Hendrix. Splash together the technological sophistication and foresight of Microsoft, dozens of ethnomusicologists and multimedia specialists, a collection of musical artifacts topping 80,000, the world-renowned architect Frank Gehry, and enough money to make the national debt appear small (fine, it was only $350 million), and you have the rock 'n' roll museum of the future. The building alone—consisting of sheet metal molded into abstract curves and then acid-dyed gold, silver, purple, light-blue, and red—is enough to make the average person gasp for breath. Walk in and strap on a personal computer guide (MEG) that allows you to interact with the exhibits. Hear clips from Hendrix's famous "Star Spangled Banner" while looking at the remnants of the guitar he smashed on a London stage. Move into the **Sound Lab** and test your own skills on guitars, drums, and keyboards linked to computer teaching devices and cushioned in state-of-the art sound rooms. When you are ready, step over to **On Stage,** a first-class karaoke-gone-haywire, and blast your tunes in front of a virtual audience. *(325 Fifth St., at Seattle Center. From I-5, take Exit 167 and follow signs to Seattle Center. Bus #3, 4, or 15. ☎367-5483 or 877-367-5483. Open summer Su-Th 9am-6pm, F-Sa 9am-9pm; fall Su-Th 10am-5pm, F-Sa 10am-9pm. $20, seniors, military, and ages 13-17 $16, children 7-12 $15, under 7 free. Free live music Tu-Sa in the lounge; national acts perform F-Sa in the Sky Church.)*

SPACE NEEDLE. Until the EMP came to town, the **Space Needle** appeared to be something from another time—now it matches quite well with its futuristic neighbor. On a clear day, the Needle provides a great view and an invaluable landmark for the disoriented. The elevator ride itself is a show, and operators are hired for their unique talents. The Needle houses an observation tower and a high-end 360° rotating restaurant. *(☎905-2100. $12.50, seniors $11, ages 4-10 $5.)*

THE INTERNATIONAL DISTRICT/CHINATOWN

SEATTLE ASIAN ART MUSEUM. What do you do when you have too much good art to exhibit all at once? Open a second museum; this is just what SAM did, creating a wonderful stand-on-its-own attraction. The **Seattle Asian Art Museum** collection is particularly strong in Chinese art. *(In Volunteer Park just beyond the water tower. ☎654-3100. Open Tu-Su 10am-5pm, Th 10am-9pm. Suggested donation $3, under 12 free. Free with SAM ticket from the previous 7 days; SAAM ticket good for $3 discount at SAM.)*

ARBORETUM. The **University of Washington Arboretum** nurtures over 4000 species of trees, shrubs, and flowers, and maintains superb trails. Tours depart the **Graham Visitor Center,** at the southern end of the arboretum. *(10 blocks east of Volunteer Park. Visitors Center on Arboretum Dr. E, off Lake Washington Blvd. Bus #11, 43, 48. ☎543-8800. Open daily sunrise to sunset; Visitors Center 10am-4pm. Free tours 1st Su of the month.)*

JAPANESE TEA GARDEN. The tranquil 3½ acre park is a retreat of sculpted gardens, fruit trees, a reflecting pool, and a traditional tea house. *(At the south end of the UW Arboretum, entrance on Lake Washington Blvd. ☎684-4725. Open Mar.-Nov. daily 10am-dusk. $3; students, seniors, disabled, and ages 6-18 $2; under 6 free.)*

ENTERTAINMENT

Seattle has one of the world's most notorious underground music scenes and the third-largest theater community in the US. The city supports performances in all sorts of venues, from bars to bakeries. In summer the free **Out to Lunch** series (☎623-0340) brings everything from reggae to folk dancing into parks, squares, and office buildings. Check cheeky free weekly *The Stranger* for event listings.

MUSIC

The **Seattle Opera** performs favorites from August to May. In October 2003, the Opera House will reopen after renovations. Until then all Opera House performances will be in the **Mercer Arts Arena.** Buffs should reserve well in advance, although rush tickets are sometimes available. (☎389-7676; www.seattleopera.com. Open M-F 9am-5pm. Tickets from $35. Students and seniors can get half-price tickets 1½hr. before the performance.) From September to June, the **Seattle Symphony** performs in the new Benaroya Hall, 200 University St. at 3rd Ave. (☎215-4747; www.seattlesymphony.org. Ticket office open M-F 10am-6pm, Sa 1-6pm. Tickets from $15-39; seniors half-price; students day of show $10.)

THEATER & CINEMA

The city hosts an exciting array of first-run plays and alternative works, particularly by many talented amateur groups. Rush tickets are often available at nearly half-price on the day of the show from **Ticket/Ticket.** (☎324-2744. Cash only.) **The Empty Space Theatre,** 3509 Fremont Ave. N, one and a half blocks north of the Fremont Bridge, presents comedies from October to early July. (☎547-7500. Tickets $10-40. Half-price tickets 30min. before curtain.) **Seattle Repertory Theater,** 155 Mercer St., at the wonderful Bagley Wright Theater in the Seattle Center, presents contemporary and classic winter productions. (☎443-2222; www.seattlerep.org. $15-45, seniors $32, under 25 $10. Rush tickets 30min. before curtain.)

Seattle is a cinephiles paradise. Most of the theaters that screen non-Hollywood films are on Capitol Hill and in the University District. On summer Saturdays, outdoor cinema in Fremont begins at dusk at 670 N. 34th St., in the U-Park lot by the bridge, behind the Red Door Alehouse. (☎781-4230. Entrance 7pm; live music 8pm. $5.) TCI Outdoor Cinema shows everything from classics to cartoons at the Gasworks Park. (Live music 7pm to dusk. Free.) Unless otherwise specified, the theaters below charge $5.50 for matinees and $8.50 for features. **The Egyptian,** 801 E. Pine St. (☎323-4978), at Harvard Ave. on Capitol Hill, is an Art Deco art house best known for hosting the **Seattle International Film Festival** in the last week of May and first week of June. **The Harvard Exit,** 807 E. Roy St. (☎323-8986), on Capitol Hill near the north end of the Broadway business district, has its own ghost, an enormous antique projector, and offers quality classic and foreign films. ($9, seniors and under 12 $6.) **Grand Illusion Cinema,** 1403 50th St. NE, in the U District at University Way, is one of the last independent theaters in Seattle and often shows old classics and hard-to-find films. (☎523-3935. $7, seniors and children $5.)

SPORTS

The Mariners, or "M's" are now playing baseball in the half-billion dollar, hangar-like **Safeco Field,** at First Ave. S and Royal Brougham Way S, under an enormous retractable roof. (☎622-4487. From $10.) Seattle's football team, the **Seahawks,** are stuck playing in UW's Husky Stadium until construction on their new stadium is finished. (☎628-0888. From $10.) On the other side of town, the sleek **Key Arena,** in the Seattle Center, hosts Seattle's NBA basketball team, the **Supersonics.** (☎628-0888. From $9.) The **University of Washington Huskies** football team has contended in the PAC-10 for years and doesn't plan to let up. Call the Athletic Ticket Office (☎543-2200) for schedules and prices.

FESTIVALS

Pick up a copy of the Visitors Center's *Calendar of Events*, published every season, for event coupons and an exact listing of area happenings. The first Thursday evening of each month, the art community sponsors **First Thursday,** a free and popular gallery walk. Watch for street fairs in the University District mid- to late May, at Pike Place Market over Memorial Day weekend, and in Fremont in mid-June. The International District holds its annual 2-day bash in mid-July, featuring arts and crafts booths, East Asian and Pacific food booths, and presentations by, among others, the Radical Women/Freedom Socialist Party to the Girl Scouts. For more info, call Chinatown Discovery (☎(425) 885-3085).

Puget Sound's yachting season begins in May. **Maritime Week,** during the third week of May, and the **Shilshole Boats Afloat Show** (☎634-0911), in August, give area boaters a chance to show off their crafts. Over the 4th of July weekend, the Center for Wooden Boats sponsors the **Wooden Boat Show,** on Lake Union. Size up the entrants (over 100 wooden boats), then watch a demonstration of boat-building skills. (☎382-2628. Suggested donation $8 per person, families $15.) The **Quick and Daring Boatbuilding Contest,** features hopefuls try to build and sail wooden boats of their own design, using a limited kit of tools and materials. Plenty of music, food, and alcohol make the sailing smooth.

NIGHTLIFE

DOWNTOWN

The Alibi Room, 85 Pike St. (☎623-3180), across from the Market Cinema in the Post Alley in Pike Place. A remarkably friendly local indie filmmaker hangout. Bar with music. Downstairs dance floor F-Sa. Brunch Sa-Su. No cover. Open daily 11am-3pm and 5pm-2am.

Crocodile Cafe, 2200 2nd Ave. (☎448-2114), at Blanchard St. in Belltown. Cooks from scratch by day, and features live music by night (Tu-Sa). Shows usually start 9pm; some require advance ticket purchase. 21+ after 9pm. Cover $6-22. Open Tu-F 11am-11pm, Sa 8am-11pm, Su 9am-3pm.

PIONEER SQUARE

Most bars participate in a joint cover (Su-Th $5, F-Sa $10) that will let you wander from bar to bar to sample the bands. The larger venues are listed below. Two smaller venues, **Larry's,** 209 1st Ave. S (☎624-7665), and **New Orleans,** 114 1st Ave. S (☎622-2563), feature great blues and jazz nightly. Most clubs close at 2am weekends and midnight weekdays.

Bohemian Cafe, 111 Yesler Way (☎447-1514). Reggae pumps every night through 3 sections—a cafe, bar, and stage—all adorned with art from Jamaica. Live shows, often national acts on weekends. Happy Hour 4-7pm. Th, F, Sa joint cover. Open M-Th and Sa 4pm-2am, F 3pm-2am.

Central Tavern, 207 1st Ave. S (☎622-0209). One of the early venues for grunge has now become a favorite for bikers. Live rock M and W-Su 9:30pm. Tu open mic. Part of the joint cover. Open daily 11:30am-2am; kitchen closes 8pm.

Last Supper Club, 124 S. Washington St. (☎748-9975), at Occidental. 2 dance floors, DJed with everything from 70s disco to funky house, drum & bass, and trance (Su). Cover varies. Open W-Su 5pm-2am.

Swannie's Sports Bar, 222 S. Main St. (☎622-9353). Share drink specials with pro ballplayers who stop by post-game. Any Seattle sports junkie will swear this is the place to be. Drink specials change daily. Open daily 11:30am-2am.

CAPITOL HILL

East off Broadway, find your atmosphere and acclimatize in a cool lounge on Pine St. West off Broadway, Pike St. has the clubs that push the limits (gay, punk, industrial, fetish, dance) and break the sound barrier.

Linda's Tavern, 707 Pine St. E (☎325-1220). A very chill post-gig scene for Seattle rockers. On Tu night a live DJ plays jazz and old rock. Expanded menu, liquor, and breakfast on weekends. W movie night. No cover. Open daily 4pm-2am.

Neighbors, 1509 Broadway Ave. (☎324-5358). Enter from the alley on Pike St. A gay dance club for 20 years, Neighbors prides itself on techno slickness. Open 7 nights a week with drag nights and special events.

DROP THE PACK After a few months backpacking, it's no surprise that your shoulders start bruising like unrefrigerated steaks. Fortunately, there is a cure: sea kayaks. Kayaking is the perfect way to explore the nooks of Washington's labyrinthine Puget Sound, and rental boats are readily available. A truly unique resource is the **Cascadia Marine Trail,** a network of seaside campsites and launching spots maintained specifically for paddlers and sailors. The trail stretches from the San Juans south to Olympia and has over 40 places to pitch a tent along the way. Routes in the south of the Sound tend to be shorter and more protected, perfect for beginner to intermediate boaters. For information on planning a trip contact the **Washington Water Trails Association.** (4649 Sunnyside Ave. N, #305. ☎545-9161; www.wwta.org.)

OUTDOOR ACTIVITIES

BIKING

Over 1000 cyclists compete in the 190 mi. **Seattle to Portland Race** in mid-July. Call the bike hotline (☎522-2453) for info. On five **Bicycle Sundays** from May to September, Lake Washington Blvd. is open exclusively to cyclists from 10am to 6pm. Call the **Citywide Sports Office** (☎684-7092) for info. The **Burke-Gilman Trail** makes for a longer ride from the University District along Montlake Blvd., then along Lake Union St. and all the way west to Chittenden Locks and Discovery Park.

WHITEWATER RAFTING

Although the rapids are hours away by car, over 50 **whitewater rafting** outfitters are based in Seattle and willing to undercut one another with merciless abandon. **Washington State Outfitters and Guides Association** (☎877-275-4964) provides advice; although their office is closed in summer, they do return phone calls and send out info. The **Northwest Outdoor Center,** 2100 Westlake Ave., on Lake Union, gives instruction in whitewater and sea kayaking. (☎281-9694. Kayak rentals $10-15 per hr. M-F third and fourth hours free. Instructional programs $50-70. Make reservations.)

HIKING

The 4167 ft. **Mt. Si** is the most climbed mountain in the state of Washington. Just an hour from downtown Seattle, hikers can in just a few hours reach a **lookout** (1 mi. one-way) that showcases Mt. Rainier, the Olympic Mountains, and Seattle. A 4hr. hike (4 mi. one-way) brings you to **Haystack Basin,** the false summit. Don't try climbing higher unless you have rock-climbing gear. To get to Mt. Si, take I-90 E to SE Mt. Si Rd., 2 mi. from Middle Fork, and cross the Snoqualmie River Bridge to the trailhead parking lot. **Tiger Mountain** is another great day-hike near Seattle. A 4hr. hike (5½ mi. round-trip) leads to the summit of West Tiger Mountain (2522 ft.). Take I-90 to Tiger Mountain State Forest. From the Tradition Plateau trailhead, walk to Bus Road-Trail and then to West Tiger Trail. If you parked outside the gated lot, stay for sunset. For additional information, check out *55 Hikes Around Snoqualmie Pass*, by Harvey Manning. The mothership of camping supply stores, **REI,** 222 Yale Ave., near Capitol Hill., rents everything you might need, from camping gear to technical mountaineering equipment. (☎223-1944. Open M-F 10am-9pm, Sa-Su 10am-7pm.)

NEAR SEATTLE: VASHON ISLAND

Only a 25min. ferry ride from Seattle, Vashon Island has remained inexplicably invisible to most Seattleites. With its forested hills and expansive sea views, this artists' colony feels like the San Juan Islands without the tourists, and budget travelers will feel well cared for in the island's hostel. Most of the island is covered in Douglas fir, rolling cherry orchards, wildflowers, and strawberry fields, and all roads lead to rocky beaches. **Point Robinson Park** is a gorgeous spot for a picnic, and free tours (☎217-6123) of the 1885 **Coast Guard lighthouse** are available. **Vashon Island Kayak Co.,** at Burton Acres Park, Jensen Point Boat Launch, runs guided tours and rents sea kayaks. (☎463-9257. Open F-Su 10am-5pm. Singles $15 per hr., $55 per day; doubles $25/80.) More than 500 acres of woods in the middle of the island are interlaced with mildly difficult hiking trails. The **Vashon Park District** can tell you more. (☎463-9602. Open daily 8am-4pm.)

The **Vashon Island AYH Ranch Hostel (HI-AYH) ❶,** at 12119 S.W. Cove Rd., west of Vashon Hwy., is sometimes called the "Seattle B." Resembling an old Western town, the hostel offers bunks, open-air teepees, and covered wagons. (☎463-2592. Free pancake breakfast and one-speed bikes. Sleeping bag $2. Open May-Oct. $13, nonmembers $16; bicyclists $11.) The hostel runs **The Lavender Duck B&B ❸** down the road (rooms $70).

Vashon Island stretches between Seattle and Tacoma on its east side and between Southworth and Gig Harbor on its west side. **Washington State Ferries** (☎464-6400 or 800-843-3779) runs ferries to Vashon Island from Seattle (see **Transportation,** p. 989). The local **Thriftway,** 9740 S.W. Bank Rd. (☎463-2100), provides maps, as does the Vashon-Maury **Chamber of Commerce** (☎463-6217), 17633 S.W. Vashon Hwy.

OLYMPIA ☎360

Inside Olympia's seemingly interminable network of suburbs, there lies a festive downtown area known for its art, antiques, liberalism, and irresistible microbrews. Evergreen State College lies a few miles from the city center, and its highly pierced tree-hugging student body spills into town in a kind of chemistry experiment that only gets weirder when Olympia politicians join in. The product of this grouping resists definition, but it is worth experiencing for yourself.

PRACTICAL INFORMATION. Olympia is at the junction of I-5 and U.S. 101. **Amtrak,** 6600 Yelm Hwy. (☎923-4602; open daily 8:15-11:45am, 1:30-3:30pm, and 5:30-8:10pm), runs to Portland (2½hr., 4 per day, $22-27) and Seattle (1¾hr., 4 per day, $13-18). **Greyhound,** 107 7th Ave. SE (☎357-5541), at Capitol Way, goes to Seattle (1¾hr., 4-6 per day, $7.50) and Portland (2¾hr., 6-7 per day, $22.50). **Intercity Transit (IT)** provides service almost anywhere in Thurston County and has bicycle racks. (☎786-1881 or 800-287-6348. $0.75; day passes $1.50.) **Washington State Capitol Visitors Center** is on Capitol Way at 14th Ave., next to the State Capitol; follow the signs on I-5. (☎586-3460. Open M-F 8am-5pm, summers also Sa-Su 10am-3pm.) The **Olympic National Forest Headquarters,** 1835 Black Lake Blvd. SW, provides info on land inside and outside the park. (☎956-2400. Open M-F 8am-4:30pm.) **Post Office:** 900 Jefferson SE (☎357-2289. Open M-F 7:30am-6pm, Sa 9am-4pm.) **Postal Code:** 98501. **Area Code:** 360.

ACCOMMODATIONS & FOOD. Motels in Olympia cater to policy-makers ($60-80), but chains in nearby Tumwater are more affordable. **Millersylvania State Park ❶,** 12245 Tilly Rd. S, 10 mi. south of Olympia, has 168 sites. Take Exit 95 off I-5 S or Exit 95 off I-5 N, then take Rte. 121 N, and follow signs to 6 mi. of trails and Deep Lake. (☎753-1519 or 800-452-5687. Showers $0.25 per 6min. Wheelchair-accessible. Sites $15; with hookup $21.) Diners, veggie eateries, and Asian quick-stops line bohemian 4th Ave. east of Columbia. The **Olympia Farmer's Market,** 700 N. Capital Way, proffers produce and fantastic fare. (☎352-9096. Open Apr.-Oct. Th-Su 10am-3pm; Nov.-Dec. Sa-Su 10am-3pm.) **The Spar Cafe & Bar ❷,** 114 E. 4th Ave., is an ancient logger haunt that moonlights as a pipe and cigar shop. (☎357-6444. Restaurant open M-Th 6am-9pm, F-Sa 6am-11pm, Su 6am-9pm. Bar open Su-Th 11am-midnight, F-Sa 11am-2am.)

SIGHTS. Olympia's crowning glory is **State Capitol Campus,** a complex of state government buildings, fabulous fountains, manicured gardens, and veterans' monuments. Tours depart from just inside the front steps, at 4th and Capitol. (☎586-3460. Tours daily on the hr. 10am-3pm. Building open M-F 8am-5pm, Sa-Su 10am-4pm.) **Wolf Haven International,** 3111 Offut Lake Rd., 10 mi. south of the capitol, provides a permanent home for captive-born gray wolves reclaimed from zoos or illegal owners. (☎264-4695 or 800-448-9653. Open May-Sept. M and W-Su 10am-5pm; Oct.-Apr. M and W-Su 10am-4pm; Nov.-Jan. and Mar. Sa-Su 10am-4pm. 45min. tours on the hr.; last tour leaves 1hr. before closing. $6, seniors $5, ages 3-12 $4.)

NIGHTLIFE. Olympia's ferocious nightlife seems to have outgrown its daylife. *The Rocket* and the daily *Olympian* list live music. At **Eastside Club and Tavern,** 410 E. 4th St., old men play pool, college students slam micro pints, and local bands play often. (☎357-9985. Open M-F noon-2am, Sa-Su 3pm-2am.) The **4th Ave. Alehouse & Eatery,** 210 E. 4th St., serves "slabs" of pizza ($3.75), 26 micropints, and live tunes from blues to reggae. (☎786-1444. Music Th-Sa 9pm. Open M-F 11:30am-2am, F-Sa noon-2am.)

SAN JUAN ISLANDS ☎360

With hundreds of tiny islands and endless parks and coastline, the San Juan Islands are an explorer's dream. The Islands are filled with great horned owls, puffins, sea lions, and pods of orcas (killer whales) patrolling the waters. Over 1½ million visitors come ashore each year during the peak of summer. To avoid the rush and enjoy good weather, visit in late spring or early fall.

PRACTICAL INFORMATION

Washington State Ferries (☎206-464-6400 or 800-843-3779), in Anacortes, serves Lopez (40min.), Shaw (1hr.), Orcas (1½hr.), and San Juan Island (2hr.); check the schedule at the Visitors Centers in Puget Sound. To save on fares, travel to the westernmost island on your itinerary, then return: eastbound traffic travels for free. In summer, arrive 1hr. prior to departure. (For peak/non-peak travel $9/11; vehicle $26/35; bike $2/4. Cash only.) To reach Anacortes, take I-5 N from Seattle to Mt. Vernon, then Rte. 20 west to town; follow signs. The **Bellingham Airporter** (☎380-8800 or 866-235-5247) shuttles between Sea-Tac and Anacortes (10 per day; $31, round-trip $56). Short hops and good roads make the islands great for biking. **Area Code:** 360.

SAN JUAN ISLAND

The biggest and most popular of the islands, San Juan is the easiest to explore, with ferry docks right in town, flat roads, and a shuttle bus running throughout the island. Seattle weekenders flood the island in summer. A drive around the 35 mi. perimeter of the island takes about 2hr., and the route is good for a day's cycle. The **West Side Road** traverses gorgeous scenery and provides the best chance for sighting orcas offshore. Mullis Rd. merges with Cattle Point Rd. and goes straight into **American Camp,** on the south side of the island. Volunteers in period dress re-enact daily life from the time of the Pig War, a mid-19th-century squabble between the US and Britain over control of the Islands. (☎378-2240. Visitors Center open 8:30am-5pm. Camp open dawn-11pm June-Aug. daily; Sept.-May Th-Su dawn-11pm. Guided walks Sa 11:30am. Reenactments summer Sa 12:30-3:30pm.) **English Camp,** the second half of the **San Juan National Historical Park,** lies on West Valley Rd. in the sheltered **Garrison Bay.** (Buildings open late May-early Sept. daily 9:30am-6pm.) **Lime Kiln Point State Park,** along West Side Rd., is renowned as the best whale-watching spot in the area. The **San Juan Island Jazz Festival** swings in late July.

San Juan County Park ❶, 380 Westside Rd., 10 mi. west of Friday Harbor on Smallpox and Andrews Bays, offers the chance to catch views of whales and a great sunset. (☎378-1842. Water and flush toilets; no showers or RV hookups. Park open daily 7am-10pm. Reservations recommended. Vehicle sites $23; walk-ins $6.) **Thai Kitchen ❸,** 42 1st St., next to the Whale Museum, is a popular dinner spot with a beautiful patio for flower-sniffing or star-gazing. (☎378-1917. Entrees $8-12. Dinner daily 5-9pm; lunch Tu-Sa 11:30am-2:30pm.)

San Juan Transit (☎378-8887 or 800-887-8387) circles the island every 35-55min. and will stop on request. (Fares also good on Orcas Island. Point-to-point $4; day pass $10; 2-day pass $17.) If you plan to only see San Juan Island, it may be cheaper to leave your car in Anacortes and use the shuttles. **Island Bicycles,** 380 Argyle St., up Spring St., rents bikes. (☎378-4941. Open daily 9am-6pm. $6 per hr., $30 per day.) The **Chamber of Commerce** (☎378-5240 or 888-468-3701) is a booth on East St. up from Cannery Landing.

ORCAS ISLAND

Retirees, artists, and farmers dwell on Orcas Island in understated homes surrounded by green shrubs and the red bark of madrona trees. The trail to **Obstruction Pass Beach** is the best way to clamber down to the rocky shores. **Moran State Park** is unquestionably Orcas' star outdoor attraction. Over 30 mi. of hiking trails range from a one-hour jaunt around **Mountain Lake** to a day-long trek up the south face of **Mt. Constitution** (2407 ft.), the highest peak on the islands. Part-way down, **Cascade Falls** is spectacular in the spring and early summer. The **Orcas Tortas** makes a slow drive on a green bus from Eastsound to the peak. **Shearwater Adventures** runs an intense sea kayak tour of north Puget Sound and is a great resource for experienced paddlers. (☎376-4699. 3hr. tour with 30min. of dry land training $49.) **Crescent Beach Kayak,** on the highway 1 mi. east of Eastsound, rents kayaks. (☎376-2464. $18 per hr., $50 per half-day. Open daily 9am-6pm.)

Doe Bay Resort ❶, on Star Rte. 86, off Horseshoe Hwy. on Pt. Lawrence Rd., 5 mi. out of Moran State Park, includes kitchen, health food store and cafe, a treehouse, guided kayak trips, a steam sauna (bathing suits optional; coed), and a mineral bath. (☎376-2291. Reception 8am-10pm. Sauna free for campers; bathing suits optional; coed. Reservations recommended. Dorms $35; 1 double $55; campsites $35.) **Moran State Park ❶,** on Star Rte. 22 in Eastsound, follow Horseshoe Hwy., has 12 sites and restrooms year-round. (☎888-226-7688. Boats $12 per hr., $38 per day. Reservations recommended May-early Sept. Car sites $25, hiker/biker sites $10.) In Eastsound Sq. on N. Beach Rd., **Cafe Jama ❷** serves up a Northwest breakfast (specialty coffees and homemade muffins) and a variety of tasty lunch options. (☎376-4949. Soups, salads, and sandwiches $6-8.)

The ferry lands on the southwest tip of Orcas, and the main town of **Eastsound** is 9 mi. northeast. **Olga** and **Doe Bay** are an additional 8 and 11 mi. respectively down the eastern side of the horseshoe. **San Juan Transit** (☎378-8887) runs ferries to most of the island. Wildlife Cycle, at A St. and North Beach Rd. in Eastsound, rents bikes. (☎376-4708. Open M-Sa 10am-5pm, Su noon-3pm. $7.50 per hr., $30 per day.)

LOPEZ ISLAND

Smaller than either Orcas or San Juan, "Slow-pez" lacks some of the tourist facilities of the larger islands. The small **Shark Reef** and **Agate Beach County Parks,** on the southwest end of the island, have tranquil and well-maintained hiking trails, and Agate's beaches are calm and deserted. Roads on the island are ideal for biking. **Lopez Village** is 4½ mi. from the ferry dock off Fisherman Bay Rd. To rent a bike or kayak, head to **Lopez Bicycle Works,** south of the village. (☎468-2847. Open July-Aug. daily 9am-9pm; Apr.-June and Sept.-Oct. 10am-5pm. Bikes $5 per hr., $25 per day. Kayaks from $12-25 per hr.) **Spencer Spit State Park ❶,** on the northeast corner of the island 3½ mi. from the ferry terminal, has primitive sites on the beach and the hill. (☎468-2251. Toilets. Open Feb.-Oct. daily until 10pm. Reservation fee $6. Sites $15; hiker/biker $6.) Ferry transport means price inflation, so it may be wise to bring a lunch. Those without lunches should munch on fresh pastries at **Holly B's ❶,** Lopez Village plaza. (☎468-2133. Open M and W-Su 7am-5pm, Su 7am-4pm.)

OLYMPIC PENINSULA

Due west of Seattle and its busy Puget Sound neighbors, the Olympic Peninsula is a remote backpacking paradise. Olympic National Park dominates much of the peninsula, and it prevents the area's ferocious timber industry from threatening the glacier-capped mountains and temperate rainforests. To the west, the Pacific Ocean stretches to a distant horizon; to the north, the Strait of Juan de Fuca separates the Olympic Peninsula from Vancouver Island; and to the east, Hood Canal and the Kitsap Peninsula isolate this sparsely inhabited wilderness from the ever-spreading sprawl of Seattle.

PORT TOWNSEND ☎360

Unlike the salmon industry, Port Townsend's Victorian splendor has survived the progression of time and weather. Countless cafes, galleries, and bookstores line somewhat drippy streets, cheering the urbanites who move here. The **Ann Starret Mansion,** 744 Clay St., has nationally renowned Victorian architecture, frescoed ceilings, and a three-tiered spiral staircase. (☎385-3205 or 800-321-0644. Tours daily noon-3pm. $2.)

Two hostels crouch in old military haunts. The **Olympic Hostel (HI-AYH) ❶,** in Fort Worden State Park, 1½ mi. from town, has bright dorms and private rooms. (☎385-0655. Check-in 5-10pm. Dorms $14.) To reach **Fort Flagler Hostel (HI-AYH) ❶,** in Fort Flagler State Park on gorgeous Marrowstone Island, 20 mi. from Port Townsend, go south on Rte. 19, which connects to Rte. 116 E and leads directly into the park. (☎385-1288. Check-in 5-10pm. Lockout 10am-5pm. Book ahead. Dorms $14, non-members $17.) You can camp on the beach at the 116-site **Fort Flagler State Park ❶.** (☎385-1259. Book ahead. Tents $15; RVs $21; hiker/biker $10.)

Port Townsend sits at the terminus of Rte. 20 on the northeastern corner of the Olympic Peninsula. It can be reached by U.S. 101 on the peninsula or from the Kitsap Peninsula across the Hood Canal Bridge. **Washington State Ferries** (☎206-464-6400 or 800-843-3779) runs from Seattle to Winslow on Bainbridge Island, where a **Kitsap County Transit** bus runs to Poulsbo. From Poulsbo, **Jefferson County Transit** runs to Port Townsend. A free shuttle goes into downtown from the Park 'N' Ride lot. (☎385-4777. Most buses M-Sa, some Su. $0.50.) **Visitor Info: Chamber of Commerce,** 2437 E. Sims Way, 10 blocks southwest of town on Rte. 20. (☎385-2722 or 888-365-6987. Open M-F 9am-5pm, Sa 10am-4pm, Su 11am-4pm.) **P.T. Cyclery,** 232 Tyler St., rents mountain bikes. (☎385-6470. Open M-Sa 9am-6pm. $7 per hr., $25 per day.) Kayak P.T., 435 Water St., rents kayaks. (☎800-853-2252. Singles $25 per 4hr.; doubles $40 per 4hr. Over 84 free.) **Post Office:** 1322 Washington St. (☎379-2996. Open M-F 9am-5pm.) **Postal Code:** 98368. **Area Code:** 360.

OLYMPIC NATIONAL PARK ☎360

With glacier-encrusted peaks, river valley rainforests, and jagged shores along the Pacific coast, Olympic National Park has something for everyone. Roads lead to many corners of Olympic National Park, but they only hint at the depths of its wilderness. A dive into the backcountry leaves summer tourists behind and reveals the richness and diversity of the park's many faces.

ORIENTATION & PRACTICAL INFORMATION

Only a few hours from Seattle, Portland, and Victoria, the wilderness of Olympic National Park is most easily and safely reached by car. U.S. 101 encircles the park in the shape of an upside-down U with Port Angeles at the top. The park's vista-filled **eastern rim** runs up to Port Angeles, from which the much-visited **northern rim** extends westward. The tiny town of **Neah Bay** and stunning **Cape Flattery** perch at the northwest tip of the peninsula. Farther south on U.S. 101, the slightly less tiny town of **Forks** is a gateway to the park's rainforested **western rim.** Separate from the rest of the park, much of the Pacific coastline comprises a gorgeous **coastal zone.** The **entrance fee,** good for 7 days' access to the park, is charged during the day at ranger stations and developed entrances such as Hoh, Heart o' the Hills, Sol Duc, Staircase, and Elwha. ($10 per car; $5 per hiker/biker; backcountry users $2 extra per night. Parking $1.)

Olympic National Park Visitors Center, 3002 Mt. Angeles Rd., is off Race St. in Port Angeles. (☎565-3130. Open daily summer daily 9am-5:30pm; winter 9am-4pm.) Staff at the **Olympic National Park Wilderness Information Center** (☎565-3100), just behind the Visitors Center, helps design trips within the park.

ACCOMMODATIONS

The closest budget accommodations are at the **Rainforest Hostel ❶,** 169312 U.S. 101, 20 mi. south of Forks. Follow the signs from U.S. 101. Two family rooms, a men's dorm (5 double bunks in summer), and rooms for couples require deposits. A morning chore is required. (☎374-2270. Internet and laundry. Dorms $12.) Olympic National Park maintains many **campgrounds ❶,** some of which can be reserved (☎800-280-2267). Quota limits apply to popular spots. Most drive-up camping is first come, first served. Olympic National Forest requires a trailhead pass to park at sites located off a main trail. The Washington Department of Natural Resources allows free **backcountry camping ❶** 300 ft. off any state road on DNR land, mostly near the western shore along the Hoh and Clearwater Rivers. From July to September, most spaces are taken by 2pm. Popular sites, such as those at Hoh River, fill by noon.

OUTDOOR ACTIVITIES

EASTERN RIM

What ONP's western regions have in ocean and rainforest, the eastern rim matches with canals and grandiose views. Canyon walls rise treacherously, their jagged edges leading to mountaintops that offer glimpses of the entire peninsula and Puget Sound. Steep trails lead up **Mt. Ellinor,** 5 mi. past Staircase on Rte. 119. Once on the mountain, hikers can choose the 3 mi. path or an equally steep but shorter journey to the summit; look for signs to the Upper Trailhead along Forest Road #2419-04. Adventure-seekers who hit the mountain before late July should bring snow clothes to "mach" (as in Mach 1) down a ¼ mi. snow chute.

A 3¼ mi. hike ascends to **Lena Lake,** 14 mi. north of Hoodsport off U.S. 101; follow Forest Service Rd. 25 off U.S. 101 for 8 mi. to the trailhead. The Park Service charges a $3 trailhead pass. The **West Forks Dosewallip Trail,** a 10½ mi. trek to **Mt. Anderson Glacier,** is the shortest route to any glacier in the park. The road to **Mt. Walker Viewpoint,** 5 mi. south of Quilcene on U.S. 101, is steep, has sheer dropoffs, and should not be attempted in foul weather or a temperamental car. Yet another view of Hood Canal, Puget Sound, Mt. Rainier, and Seattle awaits intrepid travelers on top. Inquire about base camps and trails at **Hood Canal Ranger Station,** southeast of reserve lands on U.S. 101 in Hoodsport. (☎877-5254. Open summer daily 8am-4:30pm; winter M-F 8am-4:30pm.)

NORTHERN RIM

The most developed section of Olympic National Park lies along its northern rim, near Port Angeles, where glaciers, rainforests, and sunsets over the Pacific are only a drive away. Farthest east off U.S. 101 lies **Deer Park,** where trails tend to be uncrowded. Past Deer Park, the **Royal Basin Trail** meanders 6¼ mi. to the **Royal Basin Waterfall.** The road up **Hurricane Ridge** is an easy but curvy drive. Before July, walking on the ridge usually involves a bit of snow-stepping. Clear days provide splendid views of Mt. Olympus and Vancouver Island set against a foreground of snow and indigo lupine. From here, the uphill **High Ridge Trail** is a short walk from Sunset Point. On weekends from late December to late March, the Park Service organizes free guided snowshoe walks atop the ridge.

Farther west on U.S. 101, 13 mi. of paved road penetrates to the popular **Sol Duc Hot Springs Resort,** where retirees de-wrinkle in the springs and eat in the lodge. (☎327-3583. Open late May-Sept. daily 9am-9pm; spring and fall 9am-7pm. $10, ages 4-12 $7.50; last 2hr. twilight $7. Suit, locker, and towel rental available.) The **Sol Duc trailhead** is a starting point for those heading up; crowds thin dramatically above **Sol Duc Falls.** The **Eagle Ranger Station** has info and permits. (☎327-3534. Open summer daily 8am-4:30pm.)

NEAH BAY & CAPE FLATTERY

At the westernmost point on the Juan de Fuca Strait and north of the park's western rim lies **Neah Bay.** The only town in the **Makah Reservation,** Neah Bay is renowned as the "Pompeii of the Pacific" and is a remarkably preserved 500-year-old village that was buried in a landslide at Cape Alava. You can reach Neah Bay and Cape Flattery by a 1hr. detour from U.S. 101. From Port Angeles, Rte. 112 leads west to Neah Bay; Rte. 113 runs north from Sappho to Rte. 112. The Makah Nation, whose recorded history goes back 2000 years, still lives, fishes, and produces artwork on this land. Just inside the reservation, the **Makah Cultural and Research Center,** in Neah Bay on Rte. 112, presents artifacts from the archaeological site. (☎645-2711. Open June-Aug. daily 10am-5pm; Sept.-May W-Su 10am-5pm. Free tours W-Su 11am. $4, students and seniors $3.) During **Makah Days,** on the last weekend of August, Native Americans from the region come for canoe races, dances, and bone games. Visitors are welcome; call the center for details. **Clallam Transit System** runs bus #14 from Oak St. in Port Angeles to Sappho, then #16 to Neah Bay. (☎452-4511. $1, seniors $0.50, ages 6-19 $0.85. All-day pass $2.)

Cape Flattery, the most northwestern point in the contiguous US, is drop-dead gorgeous. Get directions at the Makah Center or just take the road through town until it turns to dirt, past the "Marine Viewing Area" sign 4 mi. to a parking area where a trailhead leads toward the cape. To the south, the reservation's **beaches** are solitary and peaceful; respectful visitors are welcome.

WESTERN RIM

In the temperate rainforests of ONP's western rim, ferns, mosses, and gigantic old growth trees blanket the earth in a sea of green. The drive along the **Hoh River Valley,** actively logged land, is alternately overgrown and barren. **Hoh Rainforest Visitors Center** sits a good 45min. drive from U.S. 101 on the park's western rim. (☎374-6925. Open daily mid-June to early Sept. 9am-5pm; early Sept. to mid-June 9am-4pm.) From the Visitors Center, take the quick ¾ mi. **Hall of Mosses Trail** for a whirlwind tour of the rainforest. With a smattering of educational panels explaining bizarre natural quirks, the slightly longer **Spruce Nature Trail** leads 1¼ mi. through lush forest and along the banks of the Hoh River. The **Hoh Rainforest Trail** is the most heavily traveled path in the area, beginning at the Visitors Center and paralleling the Hoh River for 18 mi. to **Blue Glacier** on the shoulder of Mt. Olympus.

Several other trailheads from U.S. 101 offer less crowded opportunities for exploration of the rainforest amid surrounding ridges and mountains. The **Queets River Trail** hugs its namesake east for 14 mi. from the free **Queets Campground ❶;** the road is unpaved and unsuitable for RVs or large trailers. High river waters early in the summer can thwart a trek. Hiking is best in August, but there's still a risk that water will cut off trail access. A shorter 3 mi. loop passes a broad range of rainforest, lowland river ecosystems, and the park's largest Douglas fir.

The 4 mi. **Quinault Lake Loop** or the ½ mi. **Maple Glade Trail** leave from the **Quinault Ranger Station,** 353 S. Shore Rd. (☎288-2525. Open summer M-F 8am-4:30pm, Sa-Su 9am-4pm; winter M-F 9am-4:30pm.) Snow-seekers flock to **Three Lakes Point,** an exquisite summit covered with powder until July. **Quinault Lake** lures anglers, rowers, and canoers. The **Lake Quinault Lodge,** next to the ranger station, rents canoes and rowboats. (☎288-2900 or 800-562-6672. Rentals from $10 per hr.)

COASTAL ZONE

Pristine coastline traces the park's slim far western region for 57 mi., separated from the rest of ONP by U.S. 101 and non-park timber land. Eerie fields of driftwood, sculptured arches, and dripping caves frame flamboyant sunsets, while the waves are punctuated by rugged sea stacks. Between the Quinault and Hoh Reservations, U.S. 101 hugs the coast for 15 mi., with parking lots just a short walk from the sand. North of where the highway meets the coast, **Beach #4** has abundant tidepools, plastered with sea stars. **Beach #6,** 3 mi. north at Mi. 160, is a favorite whale-watching spot. Near Mi. 165, sea otters and eagles hang out amid tide pools and sea stacks at **Ruby Beach.** Beach camping is only permitted north of the Hoh Reservation between **Oil City** and **Third Beach** and north of the Quileute Reservation between **Hole-in-the-Wall** and **Shi-Shi Beach.** Day hikers and backpackers adore the 9 mi. loop that begins at **Ozette Lake.** The trail is a triangle with two 3 mi. legs leading along boardwalks through the rainforest. One heads toward sea stacks at **Cape Alava,** and the other goes to a sublime beach at **Sand Point.** A 3 mi. hike down the coast links the two legs, passing ancient petroglyphs. More info is available at the **Ozette Ranger Station.** (☎963-2725. Open intermittently.) Overnighters must make permit reservations (☎565-3100) in advance; spaces fill quickly in summer.

CASCADE RANGE

Intercepting the moist Pacific air, the Cascades divide Washington into the lush, wet green of the west and the low, dry plains of the east. The Cascades are most accessible in July, August, and September. Many high mountain passes are snowed in during the rest of the year. Mt. Baker, Vernon, Glacier, Rainier, Adams, and St. Helens are accessible by four major roads. The North Cascades Hwy. (Rte. 20) is the most breathtaking and provides access to North Cascades National Park.

Scenic U.S. 2 leaves Everett for Stevens Pass and descends along the Wenatchee River. Rte. 20 and U.S. 2 can be traveled in sequence as the Cascade Loop. U.S. 12 approaches Mt. Rainier through White Pass and passes north of Mt. St. Helens. I-90 sends four lanes from Seattle past the ski resorts of Snoqualmie Pass.

MOUNT ST. HELENS ☎360

In a single cataclysmic blast on May 18, 1980, the summit of Mt. St. Helens erupted, transforming what had been a perfect cone into a crater. The force of the ash-filled blast robbed the mountain of 1300 feet and razed entire forests, strewing trees like charred matchsticks. Ash from the crater rocketed 17 mi. upward, blackening the sky for days. The explosion was 27,000 times the force of the atomic bomb dropped on Hiroshima. Today, Mt. St. Helens is made up of the middle third of the **Gifford Pinchot National Forest** and the **Mount St. Helens National Volcanic Monument.** The monument is part national park, part laboratory, and encompasses most of the area affected by the explosion.

ORIENTATION Vigorous winter rains often spoil access roads; check at a ranger station for road closures before heading out. From the west, take Exit 49 off **I-5** and use the **Spirit Lake Memorial Highway (Route 504).** For most, this is the quickest and easiest daytrip to the mountain, and the main Visitors Centers line the way to the volcano. **Route 503** skirts the south side of the volcano until it connects with **Forest Service Road 90.** Though views from this side don't highlight recent destruction, green glens and remnants of age-old explosions make this the best side for hiking and camping. From the north, the towns of **Mossyrock, Morton,** and **Randle** line **U.S. 12** and offer the closest major services to the monument.

PRACTICAL INFORMATION The monument charges an entrance fee at almost every Visitors Center, viewpoint, and cave. (1-day all access $6, ages 5-15 $2. Individual monument fees $3/1.) With displays and interactive exhibits, **Mt. St. Helens Visitors Center,** across from Seaquest State Park on Rte. 504, is most visitors' first stop. (☎274-2100. Open daily 9am-6pm.) **Coldwater Ridge Visitors Center,** 38 mi. farther on Rte. 504, has an emphasis on the area's recolonization by living things through exhibits, a short film, and a ¼ mi. trail. (☎274-2131. Open daily 10am-6pm.) Overlooking the crater, **Johnston Ridge Observatory,** at the end of Rte. 504, focuses on geological exhibits and offers the best roadside view of the steaming dome and crater. (☎274-2140. Open May-Sept. daily 10am-6pm.)

Woods Creek Information Station, 6 mi. south of Randle on Rd. 25 from U.S. 12, is a drive-through info center. (Open June-Aug. daily 9am-4pm.) **Pine Creek Information Station,** 17 mi. east of Cougar on Rd. 90, shows an interpretive film of the eruption. (Open June-Sept. daily 9am-6pm.) **Apes Headquarters,** at Ape Cave on Rd. 8303 on the south side of the volcano, answers all of your lava tube questions. (Open June-Sept. daily 10am-5:30pm.) From mid-May through October, the Forest Service allows 100 people per day to hike to the crater rim (applications accepted from Feb. 1; $15). Procrastinators should head for **Jack's Restaurant and Country Store,** 13411 Louis River Rd., 5 mi. west of Cougar (I-5 Exit 21) on Rte. 503, where a lottery is held at 6pm each day to distribute the next day's 50 unreserved permits. (☎231-4276. Open daily 6am-8:30pm.)

CAMPING. Although the monument itself contains no campgrounds, a number are scattered throughout the surrounding national forest. Free dispersed camping is allowed within the monument, but finding a site takes luck. **Iron Creek Campground ❶,** just south of the Woods Creek Information Station on Rd. 25, near its junction with Rd. 76, is the closest campsite to Mt. St. Helens, with good hiking and striking views of the crater and blast zone. (☎877-444-6777. Sites $14-28.) Spacious **Swift Campground ❶** is on Rd. 90, just west of the Pine Creek Info Station.

NORTH CASCADES HIGHWAY

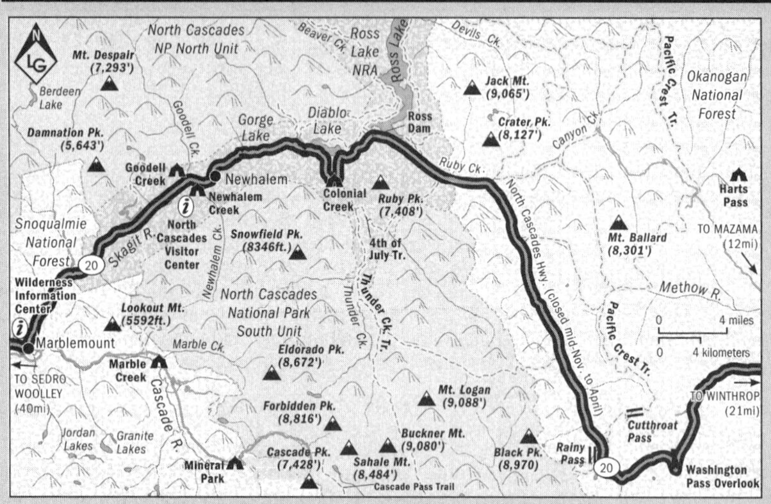

Weaving its way through the craggy peaks and lush valleys of Washington's North Cascades Range, Rte. 20 is nothing short of a blissful driving experience—the road seems to have been designed for view-hungry drivers. Spectacular vistas await visitors at every turn, and a string of small towns scattered along the road provides services. Rte. 20 runs east-west through northern Washington, traversing the astounding scenery of Mt. Baker Snoqualmie National Forest, North Cascades National Park, and Okanogan National Forest.

TIME: 2hr.

DISTANCE: 70 mi.

SEASON: Apr.-Nov.

WEST OF NORTH CASCADES NATIONAL PARK

The westernmost town of note on Rte. 20 is **Sedro Woolley,** a logging town nestled in the rich farmland of the lower Skagit Valley. Sedro Woolley is home to **North Cascades National Park** and **Mt. Baker-Snoqualmie National Forest Headquarters,** at 810 State Rte. 20, near the intersection with Rte. 9. The helpful rangers and information on activities in the park can help you move out of Sedro, which should be done as quickly as possible, considering the spectacular landscape farther west. (☎856-5700. Open daily summer 8am-4:30pm; winter M-F 8am-4:30pm.)

Marblemount Wilderness Information Center, 1 mi. north of West Marblemount on a well-marked road, is the main attraction of **Marblemount,** a town 40 mi. west of Sedro Valley. The Information Center is the best resource for backcountry trip-planning in the North Cascades. It is best to explore the park on a multi-day hiking trip. The Center is also the only place to pick up backcountry **permits;** they also have updates on trails and weather. Permits must be picked up in person no earlier than the day before a trip date. (☎873-4500. Open July-Aug. Su-Th 7am-6pm, F-Sa 7am-8pm; low-season call ahead.) Once you leave Marblemount, there are **no major service stations** for more than 69 mi. west—you are entering the wild land of the National Park.

NORTH CASCADES NATIONAL PARK

East from Marblemount and across the Skagit River, Rte. 20 enters the wildest, most rugged park in Washington. The North Cascades National Park is unlike any other—as amazing as the views seem from the car, you can't experience this park's flavor from a vehicle. Hop out and explore; the area is rife with hiking trails.

The dramatic pinnacles rising abruptly from the park's deep glacial valleys make for the most complex and challenging mountaineering in the continental US—the region is commonly referred to as "the Alps of North America" Those determined to penetrate the park should allot a hardy pair of boots and several days. As with every national park in Washington, North Cascades is surrounded by ample national forest. Know which forest you are headed into, as different agencies, permits, and rules apply. Another source for hiking is the **North Cascades Visitors Center and Ranger Station.** (☎386-4495. Open daily summer daily 8:30am-6pm; winter 9am-5pm.) The National Park is divided into four sections. The **North Unit** reaches up to the Canadian border and is the most remote area of the park. The few trails that do cross it mainly begin near **Mt. Baker** or **Hozemon,** a small camp accessible from British Columbia. The **Ross Lake National Recreation Area** runs along Rte. 20 and north along Ross Lake. This is the most highly used area of the park, and the one in which most confine their stay. **South Unit** is pocked by glaciers and accessible from trails leaving Rte. 20 along its north and east sides. Finally, at the park's southernmost tip, the **Lake Chelan National Recreation Area** protects the beautiful wilderness around Stehekin and the northern tip of Lake Chelan.

The park's **Goodell Creek Campground ❶,** at Mi. 119 just west of Newhalem, is a gorgeous confined area with 21 leafy sites suitable for tents and small trailers and a launch site for whitewater rafting on Skagit River. Water is shut off after October, when sites are free. (Pit toilets. Sites $10.) **Newhalem Creek Campground ❶,** at Mi. 120, shares a turn-off with the Visitors Center. It is a larger facility with 111 sites ($12) geared toward RV folk.

The amazing **Cascade Pass Trail** (moderate to difficult) begins 22 mi. south of Diablo Lake, and continues to Stehekin Valley Rd. The 3hr. hike gains 1700 ft. of elevation in 3½ mi. **Thunder Creek Trail** (easy) is among the most popular hikes in the area. The 1½ mi. meander through old-growth cedar and fir begins at Colonial Creek Campground, at Mi. 130 of Rte. 20. A more challenging variation is the 3¼ mi. **Fourth of July Pass Trail** (moderate to difficult). It begins 2 mi. into the Thunder Creek trail and climbs 3500 ft. toward stupendous views of glacier-draped Colonial and Snowfield peaks.

EAST OF NORTH CASCADES NATIONAL PARK

The stretch of road from **Ross Lake,** near the Eastern border of North Cascades National Park, to **Winthrop,** in the Okanogan National Forest, is the most breathtaking section of Rte. 20. The frozen creases of a mountain face stand before you—snow and granite rise on one side of the road, while sheer cliffs plummet on the other. Leaving the basin of Ross Lake, the road begins to climb, revealing the craggy peaks of the North Cascades.

The **Pacific Crest Trail** crosses Rte. 20 at **Rainy Pass** (Mi. 157) on one of the most scenic and difficult legs of its 2500 mi. course from Mexico to Canada. Near Rainy Pass, short scenic trails can be hiked in sneakers, provided the snow has melted, usually around mid-July. Just off Rte. 20, an overlook at **Washington Pass** (Mi. 162) rewards visitors with one of the state's most dramatic panoramas, an astonishing view of the red rocks exposed by **Early Winters Creek** in **Copper Basin.** The area has many well-marked trailheads off Rte. 20 that lead into the desolate wilderness. The popular 2½ mi. walk to **Blue Lake** begins half a mile east of Washington Pass—it's usually snow-free by July and provides a gentle ascent through meadows. An easier 2 mi. hike to Cutthroat Lake departs from an access road 4½ mi. east of Washington Pass. From the lake, the trail continues 4 mi. farther and almost 2000 ft. higher to **Cutthroat Pass** (6820 ft.), treating determined hikers to a view of towering, rugged peaks.

About 5 mi. east of Winthrop, the **North Cascades Smokejumper Base** is staffed by courageously insane smoke jumpers who give thorough and personal tours of the base, explaining the procedures and equipment they use to help them parachute into forest fires and put them out. To get there, drive east through Winthrop. At the bridge, instead of turning right to follow Hwy. 20, go straight and follow the curves of the main road; after about 5 mi., the base will be on your right. (☎997-2031. Open summer and early fall. Daily tours 10am-5pm.)

(☎503-813-6666. Sites $12.) Along Yale Lake are **Cougar Campground ❶** and **Beaver Bay ❶**, 2 and 4 mi. east of Cougar respectively. Cougar Lake has 60 sites that are more spread out and private than Beaver Bay's 78 sites ($12-26).

OUTDOOR ACTIVITIES. Along each approach, short interpretive trails loop into the landscape. The 1hr. drive from the Mt. St. Helens Visitors Center to Johnston Ridge offers spectacular views of the crater and its resurgence of life. Another 10 mi. east, the hike along **Johnston Ridge** approaches incredibly close to the crater where geologist David Johnston died studying the eruption. On the way west along Rd. 99, **Bear Meadow** provides the first interpretive stop, an excellent view of Mt. St. Helens, and the last restrooms before Rd. 99 ends at **Windy Ridge.** The monument begins just west of Bear Meadow, where Rd. 26 and 99 meet. Rangers lead ½ mi. walks around emerald **Meta Lake;** meet at Miner's Car at the junction of Rd. 26 and 99. (Late June-Sept. daily 12:45, 3pm.) Farther west on Rd. 99, **Independence Pass Trail #227** is a difficult 3½ mi. hike with overlooks of Spirit Lake and superb views of the crater and dome. For a serious hike, continue along this trail to its intersection with the spectacular **Norway Pass Trail,** which runs 8 mi. through the blast zone to the newly reopened **Mt. Margaret peak.** Farther west, the 2 mi. **Harmony Trail #224** provides access to Spirit Lake. From spectacular **Windy Ridge,** at the end of Rd. 99, a steep ash hill grants a magnificent view of the crater from 3½ mi. away. The **Truman Trail** leaves from Windy Ridge and meanders 7 mi. through the **Pumice Plain,** where hot flows sterilized the land.

Spelunkers should head to **Ape Cave,** 5 mi. east of Cougar just off Rd. 83. The cave is a broken 2½ mi. lava tube formed by an ancient eruption. When exploring the cave, wear a jacket and sturdy shoes, and take at least two flashlights or lanterns. Rangers lead 10 free 30min. guided cave explorations per day.

MOUNT RAINIER NATIONAL PARK ☎360

At 14,411 ft., Mt. Rainier presides regally over the Cascade Range. The Klickitat native people called it Tahoma, "Mountain of God," but Rainier is simply "the Mountain" to most Washington residents. Perpetually snowcapped, this dormant volcano draws thousands of visitors from around the globe. Clouds mask the mountain 200 days each year, frustrating visitors who come solely to see its distinctive summit. Over 305 mi. of trails weave peacefully through old-growth forests, alpine meadows, rivers, and bubbling hot springs.

ORIENTATION. To reach Mt. Rainier from the west, take **I-5** to Tacoma, then go east on **Route 512,** south on **Route 7,** and east on **Route 706.** Rte. 706 meanders through the town of Ashford and into the park by the **Nisqually** entrance, leading to the Visitors Centers of **Paradise** and **Longmire.** Snow usually closes all other park roads from November to May. **Stevens Canyon Road** connects the southeast corner of the national park with Paradise, Longmire, and the Nisqually entrance, unfolding superb vistas of Rainier and the Tatoosh Range along the way.

PRACTICAL INFORMATION. **Gray Line Bus Service,** 4500 W. Marginal Way SW, runs buses from the Convention Center, at 8th and Pike in Seattle, to Mt. Rainier (depart 8am, return 6pm), allowing about 3½hr. at the mountain. (☎206-624-5208 or 800-426-7532. Runs May to mid-Sept. daily. 1-day round-trip $54, under 12 $27.) **Rainier Shuttle** (☎569-2331) runs daily between: Sea-Tac; Ashford (2hr., 2 per day, $37); Paradise (3hr., 1 per day, $46).

The best place to plan a backcountry trip is at the **Longmire Wilderness Information Center** (☎569-4453; open May 23-Oct. 5 daily 7:30am-4pm), east of the Nisqually entrance; or the **White River Wilderness Information Center** (☎663-2273; open May 23-Sept. Su-W 7:30am-4:30pm, Th 7:30am-7pm, F 7am-7pm, and Sa 7am-

5pm), off Rte. 410 on the park's east side. Both distribute **backcountry permits.** Permits are good for 7 days; an **entrance fee** is required. ($10 per car, $5 per hiker. Gates open 24hr.) **Rainier Mountaineering, Inc. (RMI),** in Paradise (☎253-627-6242 or 888-892-5462), rents climbing gear, and expert guides lead summit climbs. (Open May-Sept. daily 7am-8pm; Oct.-Apr. M-F 9am-5pm.) **Post Office:** National Park Inn, Longmire. (Open M-F 8:30am-noon and 1-5pm.) Paradise Inn, Paradise. (Open M-F 9am-noon and 12:30-5pm, Sa 8:30am-noon.) **Postal Code:** 98397 (Longmire), 98398 (Paradise). **Area Code:** 360.

ACCOMMODATIONS & FOOD. **Hotel Packwood ❷,** 104 Main St., in Packwood, is a charming reminder of the Old West with a sprawled-out grizzly gracing the parlor. (☎494-5431. Shared or private bath; singles and doubles $39-49.) **Whittaker's Bunkhouse ❶,** 6 mi. west of the Nisqually entrance, offers spiffy rooms with firm mattresses and sparkling clean showers, as well as a homey espresso bar, but no kitchen. Bring your own sleeping bag. (☎569-2439. Reservations strongly recommended. Bunks $30; private rooms $75-100.)

Camping ❶ in the park is first come, first served from mid-June to late September. (Low-season reservations ☎800-365-2267. Prices range from free up to $15.) National park campgrounds all have facilities for the handicapped, but no hookups or showers. Coin-operated showers are available at Jackson Memorial Visitors Center, in Paradise. **Sunshine Point** (18 sites), near the Nisqually entrance, and **Cougar Rock** (200 sites), 2¼ mi. north of Longmire, are in the southwest. The serene high canopy of **Ohanapecosh** (205 sites) is 11 mi. north of Packwood on Rte. 123, in the southeast. **White River** (112 sites) is 5 mi. west of White River on the way to Sunrise, in the northeast. **Backcountry camping** requires a **permit,** free from ranger stations and Visitors Centers. Inquire about trail closures before setting off. Hikers with a valid permit can camp at well-established trailside, alpine, and snowfield sites (most with toilets and water source). Fires are prohibited in backcountry.

Blanton's Market, 13040 U.S. 12 in Packwood, is the closest decent supermarket and has an ATM. (☎494-6101. Open daily summer 7am-9pm; winter 7am-8pm.) **Highlander ❷,** in Ashford, serves standard pub fare in a single dimly-lit room with a pool table. (☎569-2953. Burgers $6-7. Open daily 7am-9pm; bar hours vary.)

OUTDOOR ACTIVITIES. Ranger-led interpretive hikes delve into everything from area history to local wildflowers. Each Visitors Center conducts hikes on its own schedule and most of the campgrounds have evening talks and campfire programs. Mt. Adams and Mt. St. Helens aren't visible from the road, but can be seen from mountain trails like **Paradise** (1½mi.), **Pinnacle Peak** (2½ mi.), **Eagle Peak** (7 mi.), and **Van Trump Park** (5½ mi.). One of the oldest stands of trees in Washington, the **Grove of Patriarchs** grows near the Ohanapecosh Visitors Center. An easy 1½ mi. walk leads to these 500- to 1000-year-old Douglas firs, cedars, and hemlocks. The **Summerland** and **Indian Bar Trails** are excellent for serious backpacking—this is where rangers go on their days off. **Carbon River Valley,** in the northwest corner of the park, is one of the only inland rainforests in the US and has access to the Wonderland Trail. Winter storms keep the road beyond the Carbon River entrance in constant disrepair. The most popular staging ground for a summit attempt, **Camp Muir** (9 mi. round-trip) is also a challenging day hike. It begins on Skyline Trail, another popular day hiking option, and heads north on Pebble Creek Trail. The latter half of the hike is covered in snow for most of the year. A segment of the **Pacific Crest Trail,** which runs from Mexico to the Canadian border, dodges in and out of the park's southeast corner. A trip to the summit of Mt. Rainier requires substantial preparation and expense. The ascent involves a vertical rise of more than 9000 ft. over a distance of 9 or more mi., usually taking two days and an overnight stay at Camp Muir on the south side (10,000 ft.) or **Camp Schurman** on the east side (9500 ft.). Permits for summit climbs cost $30 per person.

OREGON

Over a century ago, families liquidated their possessions, sank their life savings into covered wagons, corn meal, and oxen, and high-tailed it to Oregon in search of prosperity and a new way of life. Today, Oregon remains a popular destination for backpackers, cyclists, anglers, beachcrawlers, and families. The caves and cliffs of the coastline are still a siren call to tourists. Inland attractions include Crater Lake National Park and Ashland's Shakespeare Festival. From microbrews to snowcapped peaks, Oregon is worth crossing the Continental Divide.

PRACTICAL INFORMATION

Capital: Salem.

Visitor info: Oregon Tourism Commission, 775 Summer St. NE, Salem 97310 (☎800-547-7842; www.traveloregon.com). **Oregon State Parks and Recreation Dept.,** 1115 Commercial St. NE, Salem, OR 97301 (☎503-378-6305; www.prd.state.or.us).

Postal Abbreviation: OR. **Sales Tax:** 0%.

PORTLAND ☎503

With over 200 parks, the pristine Willamette River, and snowcapped Mt. Hood in the background, Portland is an oasis of natural beauty. An award-winning transit system and pedestrian-friendly streets make it feel more like a pleasantly overgrown town than a traffic-jammed, dirty metropolis. In the rainy season, Portlanders flood pubs and clubs, where musicians often strum, sing, or spin for free. Improvisational theaters are in constant production, and the brave can chime in at open-mic nights all over town. And throughout it all, America's best beer pours from the taps in the microbrewery capital of the US.

TRANSPORTATION

Airport: Portland International Airport (☎877-739-4636) is served by almost every major airline. The airport is connected to the city center by the **MAX Red Line** (38min., every 15min. daily 5am-11:30pm, $1.55), an efficient light rail system. Taxis are also available, with flat rates to downtown.

Trains: Amtrak, 800 NW 6th Ave. (☎273-4866; reservations ☎800-872-7245), at Hoyt St. Open daily 7:45am-9pm. To **Eugene** (2½hr., 5 per day; $17-29) and **Seattle** (4hr., 4 per day, $30-37).

Buses: Greyhound, 550 NW 6th Ave. (☎243-2310 or 800-229-9424), at N.W. Glisan St. by Union Station. Ticket counter open daily 5am-1am. To: **Eugene** (2½-4hr., 9 per day, $16); **Seattle** (3-4½hr., 8 per day, $22.50); **Spokane** (7½-11hr., 4 per day, $41.50).

Public Transit: Tri-Met, 701 SW 6th Ave. (☎238-7433), in Pioneer Courthouse Sq. Open M-F 8:30am-5:30pm. **Call-A-Bus** info system (☎231-3199). Buses generally run 5am-midnight with reduced hours on weekends. $1.25-1.55, ages 7-18 $0.95, over 65 or disabled persons $0.60; all-day pass $4; 10 fares $10.50. All buses and bus stops are marked with one of 7 symbols and have bike racks. Anywhere north and east of 405, west of the river and south of Hoyt St.–the **No-Fare Zone**–all of the city's public transportation is free. **MAX** (☎228-7246), based at the Customer Service Center, is Tri-Met's light rail train running between downtown, Hillsboro in the west, and Gresham in the east. A new line serves the airport from the main line's "Gateway" stop. Transfers from buses can be used to ride MAX. Runs M-F about 4:30am-1:30am, Sa 5am-12:30am, Su 5am-11:30pm.

Taxi: Radio Cab, ☎227-1212. **Broadway Cab,** ☎227-1234.

Car Rental: Crown Auto Rental, 1315 N.E. Sandy Blvd. (☎230-1103). Although it has a limited selection, Crown is by far the cheapest option for anyone under 25. Ages 18-25 must have credit card and proof of insurance. Transport from airport available upon request. Open M-Sa 9am-5pm or by appointment. From $20 per day, $137 per week.

ORIENTATION & PRACTICAL INFORMATION

Portland lies in the northwest corner of Oregon, where the Willamette River flows into the Columbia River. **I-5** connects Portland with San Francisco and Seattle, while **I-84** follows the route of the Oregon Trail through the Columbia River Gorge, heading along the Oregon-Washington border toward Boise, ID. West of Portland, **U.S. 30** follows the Columbia downstream to Astoria, but **U.S. 26** is the fastest path to the coast. **I-405** runs just west of downtown linking I-5 with U.S. 30 and 26.

Every street name in Portland carries one of five prefixes: **N, NE, NW, SE,** or **SW,** indicating where in the city the address is to be found. **Burnside Street** divides the city into north and south, while east and west are separated by the **Willamette River.** SW Portland is known as **downtown** but also includes the southern end of Old Town and a slice of the wealthier **West Hills. Old Town,** in NW Portland, encompasses most of the city's historic sector. *Some areas in the NW and SW around W. Burnside St. are best not walked alone at night.* To the north, **Nob Hill** and **Pearl District** hold recently revitalized homes and many of the chic-est shops in the city. **Southeast** Portland contains parks, factories, local businesses, and residential areas of all income brackets. A rich array of cafes, theaters, and restaurants lines **Hawthorne Boulevard. Williams Avenue** frames "the North." **North** and **Northeast** Portland are chiefly residential, punctuated by a few parks and the **University of Portland.**

Visitor Info: Visitors Association (POVA), 701 SW Morrison St. (☎275-9750), in Pioneer Courthouse Sq. Walk between the fountains to enter. Free *Portland Book* has maps and info on local attractions. Open M-F 8:30am-5:30pm, Sa 10am-4pm, Su 10am-2pm.

Internet Access: Portland Architecture Library, 722 SW 2nd Ave. (☎725-8742), has free 1hr. access. Summer open M-Th 10am-3pm. Call for current hours.

Hotlines: Women's Crisis Line, ☎235-5333. 24hr.

Post Office: 2425 NE 50th Ave. (☎282-4761). Open M-F 8:30am-5pm. **Postal Code:** 97208.

ACCOMMODATIONS

Although Marriott-esque hotels dominate downtown and smaller motels are steadily raising their prices, Portland still welcomes the budget traveler. Prices tend to drop as you leave the city center, and inexpensive motels can be found on SE Powell Blvd. and the southern end of SW 4th Ave. All accommodations in Portland fill up during the summer months, especially during the Rose Festival, so make your reservations early.

Portland International Hostel (HI), 3031 SE Hawthorne Blvd. (☎236-3380), at 31st Ave. across from Artichoke Music. Take bus #14 to SE 30th Ave. Lively common space and a huge porch define this laidback hostel. Recently-installed wireless Internet access is free; "conventional" Internet is $1 per 10min. Kitchen and laundry. All-you-can-eat pancakes $1. Reception daily 8am-10pm. Check-out 11am. Fills early in summer. Dorms $16, nonmembers $18; private rooms $36-42. ❶

Northwest Portland International Hostel (HI), 1818 NW Glisan St. (☎241-2783), at 18th Ave. between Nob Hill and the Pearl District. Take bus #17 down Glisan to corner of 19th Ave. This snug Victorian building has a kitchen, lockers, laundry, and a small espresso bar. 34 dorm beds (co-ed available). Reception daily 8am-11pm. Dorms $16-18; 2 private doubles $40-50. ❶

McMenamins Edgefield, 2126 SW Halsey St. (☎669-8610 or 800-669-8610), in Troutdale. Take MAX east to the Gateway Station, then Tri-Met bus #24 (Halsey) east to the main entrance. This beautiful 38-acre former farm is a posh escape that keeps two hostel rooms. On-site brewery, vineyards, 18-hole golf course, and several restaurants and pubs. 2-day rafting trips $140. Lockers included. Reception 24hr. Call ahead in summer; no reservations for the hostel. Single-sex dorm-style rooms $20 plus tax; singles $50-90; doubles $95-120. ❶

The Clyde Hotel, 1022 SW Stark St. (☎224-8000), west of 10th Ave. Take MAX to SW 10th Ave. and walk towards Burnside St. Built in 1912, the charming and historic Clyde has kept all its furniture in the original style, from Victorian tubs to bureau-sized radios. Continental breakfast included. Reception daily 10am-9pm; front desk open 24hr. Reservations recommended. Rooms (double or queen) $60-190; low-season $10 less. ❸

FOOD

Portland ranks high nationwide in restaurants per capita, and dining experiences are seldom dull. Downtown tends to be expensive, but restaurants and quirky cafes in the NW and SE quadrants offer great food at reasonable prices.

Western Culinary Institute (☎223-2245) would leave the Frugal Gourmet speechless. WCI has 4 eateries, each catering to a different budget niche, all of them reasonable. The Institute is planning a new restaurant, to start construction in Oct. 2003, due to which all locations are subject to change. Call for current addresses. **Chef's Diner** ❶ opens mornings to let cheerful students serve, taste, and discuss sandwiches, the breakfast special, or the occasional all-you-can-eat buffet ($5). Open Tu-F 7am-noon. **Chef's Corner Deli** ❶ is good for a quick meal on-the-go. Enormous sandwiches $1.25. Open Tu-F 8am-6:30pm. Moving up the price scale, the elegant **Restaurant** ❹ serves a classy 5-course lunch ($10) rivaled only by its superb 6-course dinner (Tu-W and F; $20). Open Tu-F 11:30am-1pm and 6-8pm. Reservations recommended. **International Bistro** ❸ serves cuisine from a different region of the world every week, at prices that range just below those at Restaurant.

The Roxy, 1121 SW Stark St. (☎223-9160). Giant crucified Jesus with neon halo, pierced wait staff, and quirky menu. Slash (from Guns N' Roses) and other celebs have been known to stop by. Visiting the Dysha Starr Imperial Toilet seems like an important thing to do, if only because of its name. An ideal post-movie or after-bar stop. Quentin Tarantuna Melt $6.25. Coffees and chai about $1-3. Open Tu-Su 24hr. ❷

Muu-Muu's Big World Diner, 612 NW 21st Ave. (☎223-8169), at Hoyt St.; bus #17. Where high and low culture smash together. Artful goofiness—the name of the restaurant was drawn from a hat—amidst red velvet curtains and gold upholstery. Brutus salad, "the one that kills a caesar" $6. 'Shroom-wich $7.50. Open M-F 11:30am-1am, Sa-Su 10am-1am. ❷

Nicholas's Restaurant, 318 SE Grand Ave. (☎235-5123), between Oak and Pine St. opposite Miller Paint; bus #6 to the Andy and Bax stop. Phenomenal Mediterranean food and atmosphere. Sandwiches $5-6. Open M-Sa 11am-9pm, Su noon-9pm. ❷

Delta Cafe, 4607 SE Woodstock Blvd. (☎771-3101). Pastoral paintings in 1 room, voodoo dolls and a lone, framed Chewbacca (the wookie) portrait in the other. 40 oz. Pabst Blue Ribbon comes in champagne bucket $3. Po' Boy Samwiches $4-7. Open M-F 5-10pm, Sa-Su noon-10pm. ❶

Pied Cow Coffeehouse, 3244 SE Belmont St. (☎230-4866). Bus #15. Sink into velvety cushions in this off-beat and friendly Victorian parlor or puff a hookah in the garden. Espresso drinks $1-3. Cakes about $4. Open M-Th 4pm-midnight, F 4pm-1am, Sa 10am-1am. ❶

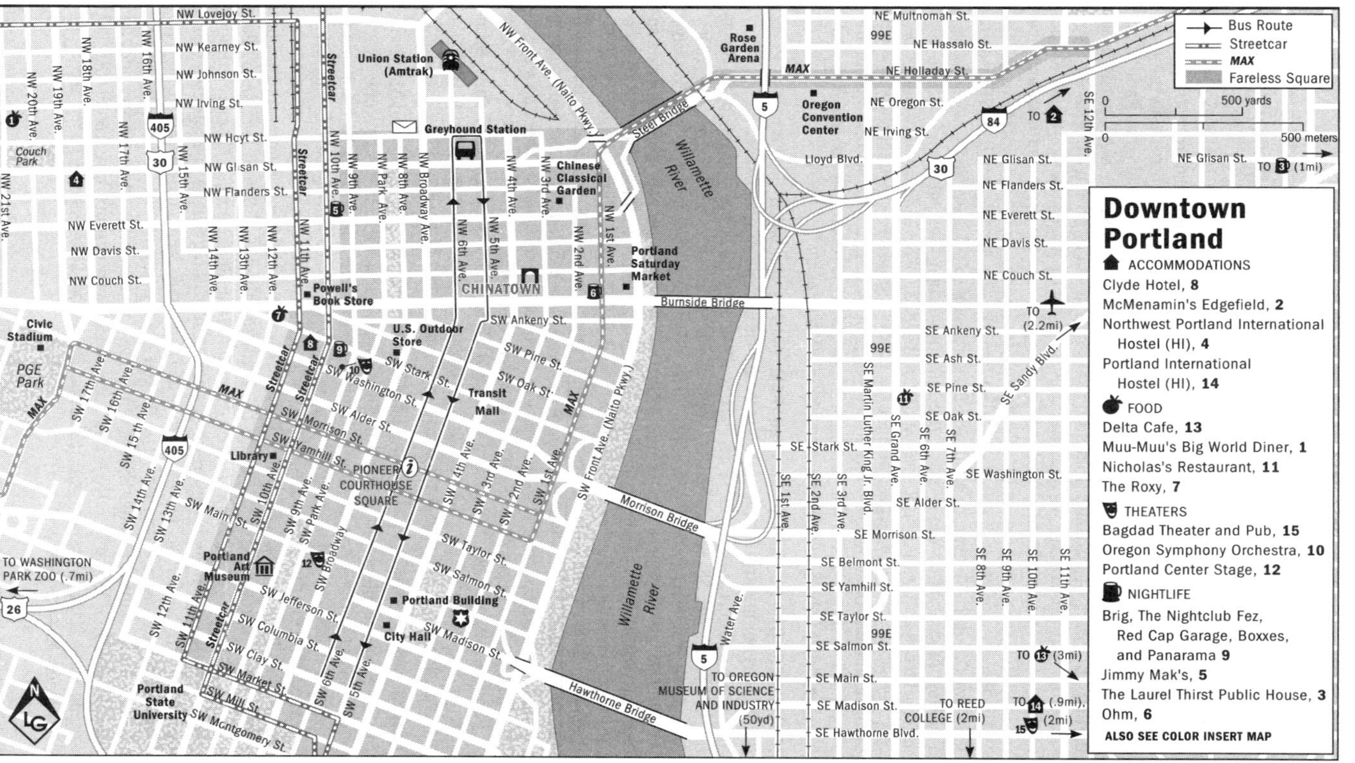
Downtown Portland
ACCOMMODATIONS
Clyde Hotel, 8
McMenamin's Edgefield, 2
Northwest Portland International Hostel (HI), 4
Portland International Hostel (HI), 14
FOOD
Delta Cafe, 13
Muu-Muu's Big World Diner, 1
Nicholas's Restaurant, 11
The Roxy, 7
THEATERS
Bagdad Theater and Pub, 15
Oregon Symphony Orchestra, 10
Portland Center Stage, 12
NIGHTLIFE
Brig, The Nightclub Fez, Red Cap Garage, Boxxes, and Panarama 9
Jimmy Mak's, 5
The Laurel Thirst Public House, 3
Ohm, 6
ALSO SEE COLOR INSERT MAP
Bus Route
Streetcar
MAX
Fareless Square
0
500 yards
0
500 meters
TO 3 (1mi)
TO 2
TO (2.2mi)
TO 13 (3mi)
TO 14 (.9mi), 15 (2mi)
TO REED COLLEGE (2mi)
TO OREGON MUSEUM OF SCIENCE AND INDUSTRY (50yd)
TO WASHINGTON PARK ZOO (.7mi)
Willamette River
Steel Bridge
Burnside Bridge
Morrison Bridge
Hawthorne Bridge
Rose Garden Arena
Oregon Convention Center
Portland Saturday Market
Chinese Classical Garden
CHINATOWN
Greyhound Station
Union Station (Amtrak)
U.S. Outdoor Store
Powell's Book Store
Transit Mall
PIONEER COURTHOUSE SQUARE
Portland Building
City Hall
Library
Portland Art Museum
Portland State University
Civic Stadium
PGE Park
Couch Park
Streetcar
NE Multnomah St.
NE Hassalo St.
NE Holladay St.
NE Oregon St.
NE Irving St.
NE Glisan St.
NE Flanders St.
NE Everett St.
NE Davis St.
NE Couch St.
Lloyd Blvd.
SE 12th Ave.
SE 11th Ave.
SE 10th Ave.
SE 9th Ave.
SE 8th Ave.
SE 7th Ave.
SE 6th Ave.
SE Grand Ave.
SE Martin Luther King Jr. Blvd.
SE 3rd Ave.
SE 2nd Ave.
SE 1st Ave.
SE Sandy Blvd.
SE Ankeny St.
SE Ash St.
SE Pine St.
SE Oak St.
SE Washington St.
SE Stark St.
SE Alder St.
SE Morrison St.
SE Belmont St.
SE Yamhill St.
SE Taylor St.
SE Salmon St.
SE Main St.
SE Madison St.
SE Hawthorne Blvd.
Water Ave.
NW Front Ave. (Naito Pkwy.)
SW Front Ave. (Naito Pkwy.)
NW 1st Ave.
NW 2nd Ave.
NW 3rd Ave.
NW 4th Ave.
NW 5th Ave.
NW 6th Ave.
NW Broadway Ave.
NW 8th Ave.
NW Park Ave.
NW 9th Ave.
NW 10th Ave.
NW 11th Ave.
NW 12th Ave.
NW 13th Ave.
NW 14th Ave.
NW 15th Ave.
NW 16th Ave.
NW 17th Ave.
NW 18th Ave.
NW 19th Ave.
NW 20th Ave.
NW 21st Ave.
NW Lovejoy St.
NW Kearney St.
NW Johnson St.
NW Irving St.
NW Hoyt St.
NW Glisan St.
NW Flanders St.
NW Everett St.
NW Davis St.
NW Couch St.
SW Ankeny St.
SW Pine St.
SW Oak St.
SW Stark St.
SW Washington St.
SW Alder St.
SW Morrison St.
SW Yamhill St.
SW Main St.
SW Taylor St.
SW Salmon St.
SW Madison St.
SW Jefferson St.
SW Columbia St.
SW Clay St.
SW Market St.
SW Mill St.
SW Montgomery St.
SW 1st Ave.
SW 2nd Ave.
SW 3rd Ave.
SW 4th Ave.
SW 5th Ave.
SW 6th Ave.
SW Broadway
SW Park Ave.
SW 9th Ave.
SW 10th Ave.
SW 11th Ave.
SW 12th Ave.
SW 13th Ave.
SW 14th Ave.
SW 15 th Ave.
SW 16th Ave.
SW 17th Ave.
99E
5
84
30
405
26
LG

SIGHTS

PARKS & GARDENS. Portland has more park acreage than any other American city, thanks in good measure to **Forest Park,** a 5000-acre tract of wilderness in Northwest Portland. Washington Park provides easy access by car or foot to this sprawling sea of green, where a web of trails leads through lush forests, scenic overviews, and idyllic picnic areas. Less than 2 mi. west of downtown, in the middle of the posh neighborhoods of **West Hills,** is mammoth **Washington Park,** with miles of beautiful trails and serene gardens. From there, take the MAX to the **Rose Garden,** the pride of Portland. In summer months, a sea of blooms arrests the eye, showing visitors exactly why Portland is the City of Roses. *(400 SW Kingston St. ☎823-3636.)* Across from the Rose Garden, the scenic **Japanese Gardens** are reputed to be the most authentic this side of the Pacific. *(611 SW Kingston Ave. ☎223-1321. Open Apr.-Sept. M noon-7pm, Tu-Su 10am-7pm; Oct.-Mar. M noon-4pm, Tu-Su 10am-4pm. Tours Apr.-Oct. daily 10:45am, 2:30pm. $6.50, seniors over 62 $5, students $4, under 6 free.)* The **Hoyt Arboretum,** at the crest of the hill above the other gardens, features 200 acres of trees and trails. *(4000 Fairview Blvd. ☎228-8733 or 823-8733. Visitors Center open daily 9am-4pm. Free)* The largest Ming-style gardens outside of China, the **Classical Chinese Gardens** occupy a city block. The large pond and ornate decorations invite a meditative stay. *(NW 3rd Ave. and Everett St. ☎228-8131. Open daily Apr.-Oct. 9am-6pm; Nov.-Mar. 10am-5pm. $7, seniors $6, students $5.50, children under 5 free.)*

MUSEUMS. The **Portland Art Museum (PAM)** sets itself apart from the rest of Portland's burgeoning arts scene on the strength of its collections, especially in Asian and Native American art. *(1219 SW Park St. At Jefferson St. on the west side of the South Block Park. Bus #6, 58, 63. ☎226-2811. Open summer Tu-W and Sa 10am-5pm, Th-F 10am-8pm, Su noon-5pm; winter Tu-Sa 10am-5pm, Su noon-5pm. $10, students and over 55 $9, under 19 $6, under 5 free; special exhibits may be more.)* The **Oregon Museum of Science and Industry (OMSI)** keeps visitors mesmerized with exhibits, including an earthquake simulator chamber, an Omnimax theater, and the Murdock Planetarium. *(1945 SE Water Ave., 2 blocks south of Hawthorne Blvd. next to the river. Bus #63. ☎797-4000. Open mid-June to Aug. daily 9:30am-7pm; Sept. to mid-June Tu-Sa 9:30am-5:30pm. Museum and Omnimax admission each $8.50, ages 3-13 and seniors $6.50. Omnimax: ☎797-4640. Shows daily on the hr. 11am-4pm and 7-9pm. Th 2-for-1 tickets after 2pm. Planetarium: ☎797-4610. Matinees daily $5; laser shows Th-Sa evenings (subject to change) $7.50. U.S.S. Blueback ☎797-4624. Open summer daily 10am-5:40pm. 40min. tour $5. Combo admission to the museum, an Omnimax film and either the planetarium or sub $18, seniors and children $14.)*

OTHER SIGHTS. The still-operational **Pioneer Courthouse,** at 5th Ave. and Morrison St., is the centerpiece of the **Square.** Since opening in 1983, it has become "Portland's Living Room." Tourists and urbanites of every ilk hang out in the brick quadrangle. *(715 SW Morrison St. along the Vintage Trolley line and the MAX light-rail. Events hotline ☎525-3738.)* Downtown on the edge of the Northwest district is the gargantuan **Powell's City of Books,** a cavernous establishment with almost a million new and used volumes, more than any other bookstore in the US. *(1005 W. Burnside St. Bus #20. ☎228-4651 or 866-201-7601. Open daily 9am-11pm.)* **The Grotto,** a 62-acre Catholic sanctuary, houses magnificent religious sculptures and gardens just minutes from downtown. *(U.S. 30 at NE 85th Ave. ☎254-7371. Open daily May-Oct. 9am-7:30pm; Nov.-Apr. 9am-5:30pm; closing times can vary.)* The **Oregon Zoo** has gained fame for its successful efforts at elephant breeding. Exhibits include a goat habitat and a marine pool as part of the zoo's "Great Northwest: A Crest to Coast Adventure" program. *(4001 SW Canyon Rd. ☎226-1561. Hours vary by season. $8, seniors $6.50, ages 3-11 $5. Second Tu every month free after 1pm.)*

ENTERTAINMENT

Portland's major daily newspaper, the *Oregonian*, lists upcoming events in its Friday edition, and the city's favorite free cultural reader, the Wednesday *Willamette Week*, is a reliable guide to local music, plays, and art. **Oregon Symphony Orchestra,** 923 SW Washington St., plays classics from September to June. On Sundays and Mondays, students can buy $5 tickets one week before showtime. (☎228-1353 or 800-228-7343. Box office open M-F 9am-5pm; in Symphony Season Sa 9am-5pm, as well. $17-76; "Symphony Sunday" afternoon concerts $20, students $14.) **High Noon Tunes,** at Pioneer Courthouse Sq., presents a potpourri of rock, jazz, folk, and world music. (☎223-1613. July-Aug. Tu and Th at noon, subject to change.)

Portland Center Stage, in the Newmark Theater at SW Broadway and SW Main St., stages classics, modern adaptations, and world premiers. (☎248-6309. Late Sept.-Apr. Tu-Th and Su $25-41, F-Sa $28-46; ages 25 and under $16.) The **Bagdad Theater and Pub,** 3702 SE Hawthorne Blvd., puts out second-run films and has an excellent beer menu. (☎288-3286. 21+.) Basketball fans can watch the **Portland Trailblazers** at the **Rose Garden Arena,** 1 Center Ct. (☎321-3211).

Northwest Film Center, 1219 SW Park Ave., hosts the **Portland International Film Festival** in the last two weeks of February, with 100 films from 30 nations. (☎221-1156. Box office opens 30min. before each show. $7, students and seniors $6.) Portland's premier summer event is the **Rose Festival** (☎227-2681) during the first 3 weeks of June. In early July, the outrageously good three-day **Waterfront Blues Festival** draws some of the world's finest blues artists. (☎800-973-3378. Suggested donation $3-5 and 2 cans of food to benefit the Oregon Food Bank.) The **Oregon Brewers Festival,** on the last full weekend in July, is the continent's largest gathering of independent brewers, making for one incredible party at Waterfront Park. (☎778-5917. Mug $3; beer tokens $1 each. Under 21 must be accompanied by parent.)

NIGHTLIFE

Once an uncouth and rowdy frontier town, always an uncouth and rowdy frontier town. Portland's nightclubs cater to everyone from the clove-smoking college aesthete to the nipple-pierced neo-goth aesthete.

Ohm and January's Grill, 31 NW 1st Ave. (☎223-9919), at Couch St. under the Burnside Bridge. Restaurant and club dedicated to electronic music and unclassifiable beats. Achieve oneness dancing in the cool brick interior or mingle outside. Weekends often bring big-name live DJs. Th the band Dahlia, W spoken-word with live band, Su drum 'n' bass. Cover $5. Music starts at 9pm. Open M-Th 10am-2pm, starting F open 24hr. until 2am Su.

The Laurel Thirst Public House, 2958 NE Glisan St. (☎232-1504), at 30th Ave. Bus #19. Local talent makes a name for itself in 2 intimate rooms of groovin', boozin', and schmoozin'. Burgers and sandwiches $5-8. Free pool all day Tu. Free Happy Hour show 6-8pm daily. Cover after 8pm $2-5. Open daily 9am-2am.

Jimmy Mak's, 300 NW 10th Ave. (☎295-6542), 3 blocks from Powell's Books at Flanders St. Jam to Portland's renowned jazz artists. Shows 9:30pm. Cover $3-6. Vegetarian-friendly Greek and Middle Eastern dinners $8-17. Open M 11am-3pm, Tu-W 11am-1am, Th-F 11am-2am, Sa 6pm-2am.

Brig, The Nightclub Fez, Red Cap Garage, Panorama, and Boxxes, 1035 SW Stark St. (☎221-7262), form a network of clubs along Stark St. between 10th and 11th. On weekdays the clubs are connected, but on weekends they are often sealed off—check at the door to see what is happening where. The 23-screen video and karaoke bar is where magic happens. Cover $2-5. Open daily 9pm-2:30am; Panorama later F-Sa.

PACIFIC NORTHWEST

INLAND OREGON

EUGENE ☎541

Epicenter of the organic foods movement and a haven for hippies, Eugene has a well-deserved liberal reputation. As home to the University of Oregon, the city is packed with college students during the school year before mellowing out considerably during summer. The town's Saturday market, nearby outdoor activities, and sunny disposition make Oregon's second-largest city one of its most attractive.

ORIENTATION & PRACTICAL INFORMATION. Eugene is 111 mi. south of Portland on I-5. The main north-south arteries are, from west to east, **Willamette Street, Oak Street,** and **Pearl Street. High Street Highway 99** also runs east-west and splits in town—**6th Avenue** runs west, and **7th Avenue** goes east. The **pedestrian mall** is downtown, on Broadway between Charnelton and Oak St. The numbered avenues run east-west and increase toward the south. Eugene's main student drag, **13th Avenue,** leads to the **University of Oregon (U of O)** in the southeast of town. Walking the city is very time-consuming—the most convenient way to get around is by bike. Every street has at least one bike lane, and the city is quite flat. *The Whittaker area, around Blair Blvd. near 6th Ave., can be unsafe at night.* **Amtrak,** 433 Willamette St., at 4th Ave. (☎687-1383; open daily 5:15am-9pm and 11pm-midnight), treks to Seattle (6-8hr., 2 per day, $35-60) and Portland (2½-3hr., 2 per day, $17-29). **Greyhound,** 987 Pearl St. (☎344-6265; open daily 6:15am-9:35pm), at 10th Ave., runs to Seattle (6-9hr., 7 per day, $34) and Portland (2-4hr., 10 per day, $16). **Lane Transit District (LTD)** handles public transportation. Map and timetables at the LTD Service Center, at 11th Ave. and Willamette St. (☎687-5555. Runs M-F 6am-11:40pm, Sa 7:30am-11:40pm, Su 8:30am-8:30pm. $1.25, seniors and under 18 $0.50. Wheelchair-accessible.) **Taxi: Yellow Cab,** ☎746-1234. **Visitor Info:** 115 W. 8th Ave., #190, door on Olive St. (☎484-5307 or 800-547-5445. Courtesy phone. Free maps. Open May-Aug. M-F 8:30am-5pm, Sa-Su 10am-4pm; Sept.-Apr. M-Sa 8:30am-5pm.) **University of Oregon Switchboard,** 1244 Walnut St., in the Rainier Bldg., is a referral service for everything from rides to housing. (☎346-3111. Open M-F 7am-6pm.) **Outdoors Info: Ranger Station,** about 60 mi. east of Eugene on Rte. 126. Sells maps and $5-per-day parking passes for the National Forest. (☎822-3381. Open daily 8am-4:30pm summer; closed weekends in winter.) There's **free Internet access** at **Oregon Public Networking,** 43 W. Broadway. (☎484-9637. Open M 10am-6pm, Tu 10am-4pm, W-F 10am-6pm, Sa noon-4pm.) **Post Office:** 520 Willamette St., at 5th Ave. (☎800-275-8777. Open M-F 8:30am-5:30pm, Sa 10am-2pm.) **Postal Code:** 97401. **Area Code:** 541.

ACCOMMODATIONS & FOOD. The cheapest motels are on E. Broadway and W. 7th Ave. and tend toward seediness. Make reservations early; motels are packed on big football weekends. **Hummingbird Eugene International Hostel ❶,** 2352 Willamette St., is a graceful neighborhood home and a wonderful escape from the city, offering a back porch, book-lined living room, (vegetarian) kitchen, and mellow atmosphere. Take bus #24 or 25 south from downtown to 24th Ave. and Willamette, or park in back on Portland St. (☎349-0589. Check-in 5-10pm. Lockout 11am-5pm. Dorms $16, nonmembers $19; private rooms from $30. Cash or traveler's check only.) Tenters have been known to camp by the river, especially in the wild and woolly northeastern side near Springfield. Farther east on Rte. 58 and 126, the immense **Willamette National Forest ❶** is full of campsites ($6-16).

Eugene's downtown area specializes in gourmet food; the university hangout zone at 13th Ave. and Kincaid St. has more grab-and-go options, and natural food stores are everywhere. Everything, *everything* is organic. **Keystone Cafe ❶,** 395

W. 5th St., serves creative dinners with entirely organic ingredients and many vegetarian options. Famous pancakes for $3.25. (☎342-2075. Open daily 7am-5pm.) **The Glenwood ❶**, 1340 Alder St., on 13th Ave., has delicious, cheaper-than-usual sandwiches and a sunny deck—just expect to compete with crowds of students during the school year. (☎687-0355. Open daily 7am-10pm.) **Bene Gourmet Pizza ❸**, 225 W. Broadway, serves just that. (☎284-2700. Pies $12-19. Open M-F 11am-9pm.)

SIGHTS. Every Saturday the area around 8th Ave. and Willamette St. fills up for the **Saturday Market,** featuring live music and stalls hawking everything from hemp shopping bags to tarot readings. The food stalls serve up delicious, and cheap, local fare. Right next to the shopping stalls is the **farmer's market,** where you can buy (you guessed it) organic, locally-grown produce. (Sa 10am-5pm, rain or shine.) Take time to pay homage to the ivy-covered halls that set the scene for *National Lampoon's Animal House* at Eugene's centerpiece, the **University of Oregon.** The visitor parking and info booth is just left of the main entrance on Franklin Blvd. A few blocks away, the **Museum of Natural History,** 1680 E. 15th Ave., at Agate St., shows a collection of relics from native cultures, including the world's oldest pair of shoes. (☎346-3024; http://natural-history.uoregon.edu. Open W-Su noon-5pm. Suggested donation $2.)

The **Eugene Emeralds** are the local Triple-A minor league baseball team; they play in **Civic Stadium,** at 20th Ave. and Pearl St., throughout the summer. (For tickets call ☎342-5376. The season lasts from mid-June to mid-Sept. Adults $5-8, children $4-7.) The *Eugene Weekly* has a list of concerts and local events, as well as features on the greater Eugene community. From June 25 to July 11, 2004, during the **Oregon Bach Festival,** Baroque authority Helmut Rilling conducts performances of Bach's concerti. (☎346-5666 or 800-457-1486; http://bachfest.uoregon.edu. Concert and lecture series $13; main events $20-45.) The vast **Oregon Country Fair,** the most exciting event of the summer, actually takes place in **Veneta,** 13 mi. west of town on Rte. 126. During the festival, 50,000 people, many still living in Haight-Ashbury happiness, drop everything to enjoy ten stages' worth of shows and 300 booths of art, clothing, crafts, herbal remedies, furniture, food, and free hugs. (☎343-4298; www.oregoncountryfair.org. Every year on the weekend after the Fourth of July. Tickets F and Su $10, Sa $15.)

OUTDOOR ACTIVITIES. Within an 1½hr. drive from Eugene, the McKenzie River has several stretches of class II-III whitewater. It is best enjoyed in June, when warm weather and high water conspire for a thrilling but comfortable ride. The Upper McKenzie is continuous for 14 mi. and can easily be paddled within 2-2½hr. **High Country Expeditions** (☎888-461-7233), on Belknap Springs Road about 5 mi. east of McKenzie Bridge, is one of the few rafting companies that floats the Upper McKenzie. (Half-day, 14 mi. trips $50; full-day, 18-19 mi. trips $75. Student and senior discounts.)

The large and popular Cougar Lake features the Terwilliger Hot Springs, known by all as **Cougar Hot Springs.** Drive through the town of Blue River, 60 mi. east of Eugene on Rte. 126, and then turn right onto Aufderheide Dr. (Forest Service Rd. 19), and follow the road 7¼ mi. as it winds on the right side of Cougar Reservoir. (Open dawn until dusk. $3 per person. Clothing optional.)

East from Eugene, Rte. 126 runs adjacent to the beautiful McKenzie River, and on a clear day, the mighty snowcapped Three Sisters of the Cascades are visible. Just east of the town of McKenzie Bridge, about 70 mi. east of Eugene, the road splits into a scenic byway loop; Rte. 242 climbs east to the vast lava fields of McKenzie Pass, while Rte. 126 turns north over Santiam Pass and meets back with Rte. 242 in Sisters. Often blocked by snow until the end of June, Rte. 242 is an exquisite drive, tunneling its narrow, tortuous way between **Mount Washington** and the **Three Sisters Wilderness** before rising to the high plateau of McKenzie Pass.

The 26 mi. **McKenzie River Trail** starts 1½ mi. west of the ranger station (trail map $1). Parallel to Rte. 126, the trail winds through mossy forests, and leads to two of Oregon's most spectacular waterfalls—**Koosah Falls** and **Sahalie Falls.** They flank Clear Lake, a volcanic crater now filled with crystal clear waters. The entire trail is also open to mountain bikers and considered fairly difficult because of the volcanic rocks. A number of Forest Service campgrounds cluster along this stretch of Rte. 126. More ambitious hikers can sign up for overnight permits at the ranger station and head for the high country, where the hiking opportunities are endless.

NIGHTLIFE. Come nightfall, bearded hippies mingle with pierced anarchists and muscle-bound frat boys in Eugene's eclectic nightlife scene. In the *Animal House* tradition, the row by the university along 13th Ave. is often dominated by fraternity-style beer bashes. **Sam Bond's Garage,** 407 Blair Blvd., is a laidback gem in the Whittaker neighborhood. Live entertainment every night complements an always-evolving selection of local microbrews ($3 per pint). Take bus #50 or 52 or a cab at night. (☎431-6603. Open daily 3pm-1am.) **The Downtown Lounge/Diablo's,** 959 Pearl St., offers a casual scene with pool tables upstairs and Eugene's most beautiful people shaking their thangs amid flame-covered walls downstairs. (☎343-2346. Cover $2-3. Open W-Sa 9pm-2:30am.) **John Henry's,** 77 W. Broadway, is Eugene's prime site for punk, reggae, and virtually any other kind of live music you'd like to hear. Call or check the web site for schedule and covers. (☎342-3358; www.johnhenrysclub.com. Open daily 5pm-2:30am.) Across from 5th St. Market, **Jo Federigo's Jazz Club and Restaurant,** 259 E. 5th Ave., swings with jazz nightly. (☎343-8488. Shows start 9:30pm. Open M-F 11:30am-2pm and 5-10pm, Sa-Su 5-10pm. Jazz club daily 8:30pm-1am.)

CRATER LAKE ☎541

The deepest lake in the US, the seventh deepest in the world, and one of the most beautiful anywhere, Crater Lake is well worth a visit. Formed 7700 years ago in a cataclysmic eruption of Mt. Mazama, it began as a deep caldera and gradually filled itself with centuries worth of melted snow. The circular lake plunges from its shores to a depth of 1936 ft.

From the Visitors Center at the rim to the **Sinnott Memorial Overlook** it is an easy 300 ft. walk to the park's most panoramic and accessible view. High above the lake, **Rim Drive,** which does not open entirely until mid-July, is a 33 mi. loop around the rim of the caldera. Trails to **Watchman Peak** (¾ mi. one-way, 1hr.), on the west side of the lake, are the most spectacular. The strenuous 2½ mi. hike up **Mount Scott,** the park's highest peak (almost 9000 ft.), begins from near the lake's eastern edge. The steep **Cleetwood Cove Trail** (2¼ mi. round-trip, 2hr.) leaves from the north edge of the lake and is the only route down to the water. All trails provide spectacular views of **Wizard Island,** a cinder cone rising 760 ft. from the lake, and **Phantom Ship Rock,** a rock formation. In addition to trails around the lake, the park contains over 140 mi. of wilderness trails for hiking and cross-country skiing. Picnics, fishing (with artificial lures only), and swimming are allowed, but surface temperatures reach a maximum of only 50°F. Park rangers lead free tours daily in the summer and periodically in the winter (on snowshoes).

A convenient base for forays to Crater Lake, **Klamath Falls** has several affordable hotels. The **Townhouse Motel ❷,** 5323 6th St., 3 mi. south of Main St., offers clean, comfy rooms. (☎882-0924. Cable TV, A/C, no phones. Singles $30; doubles $35.) Campgrounds abound near the lake. The best is **Williamson River Campground ❶,** run by the National Forest Service, 30 mi. north of Klamath

Falls on U.S. 97N. Situated on the winding river, it offers secluded sites with one toilet and water. (Tents only, $6.) The massive **Mazama Campground ❶,** near the park's south entrance off Rte. 62, is swarmed by tenters and RVs from mid-June until October. (☎594-2255, ext. 3703. Showers $0.75 per 4min. Wheelchair-accessible. No reservations. Sites $16; RVs $21.) Where's **Waldo's Mongolian Grill and Tavern ❸?** It's at 610 Main St. and ready to grill your choice of veggies and meats. (☎884-6863. Medium bowl $8.50. All-you-can-eat $10. Open M-Th 11am-11:30pm, F-Sa 11am-1am.)

Crater Lake averages over 44 ft. of snow per year, and snowbound roads can keep the northern entrance closed as late as July. Before July, enter the park from the south. The park entrance fee is $10 for cars, $5 for hikers and cyclists. **Amtrak** (☎884-2822; open daily 7:30-11am and 8:30-10:15pm) and **Greyhound** are both in Klamath Falls; from Main St., turn right onto Spring St. and immediately left onto Oak St. One train per day runs to Redding, CA (4½hr., $26), while one bus per day rolls to Eugene (4½hr., $19) and then on to Portland ($42-48). **Visitor Info:** Chamber of Commerce, 507 Main St. (☎884-0666 or 800-445-6728; www.klamath.org. Open M-F 8am-5pm.) The **William G. Steel Center** issues free backcountry camping permits. (☎594-2211, ext. 402; www.nps.gov/crla. Open daily 9am-5pm.) **Post Office:** 317 S. 7th St. in Klamath. (☎800-275-8777. Open M-F 7:30am-5:30pm, Sa 9am-noon.) **Postal Code:** 97604. **Area Code:** 541.

ASHLAND ☎541

Set near the California border, Ashland mixes hip youth and British literary history, setting an unlikely but intriguing stage for the world-famous **Oregon Shakespeare Festival,** P.O. Box 158, Ashland 97520 (☎482-4331; www.osfashland.org). From mid-February to October, drama devotees can choose among 11 Shakespearean and newer works performed in Ashland's three elegant theaters: the outdoor **Elizabethan Stage,** the **Angus Bowmer Theater,** and the intimate **Black Swan.** The 2004 schedule includes *The Comedy of Errors*, *King Lear*, and all three *Henry VI* plays, as well as Suzan-Lori Parks' *Topdog/Underdog*. Ticket purchases are recommended 6 months in advance. (In spring and fall $22-39; summer $29-52. $5 fee per order for phone, fax, or mail orders.) At 9:30am, the **box office,** 15 S. Pioneer St., releases any unsold tickets for the day's performances and sells 20 standing room tickets for sold-out shows on the Elizabethan Stage ($11). Half-price rush tickets are sometimes available 1hr. before performances. **Backstage tours** provide a wonderful glimpse of the festival from behind the curtain. (Tu-Sa 10am. $10, ages 6-17 $7.50, under 6 not admitted.)

In winter, Ashland is a budget paradise; in summer, hotel and B&B rates double, while the hostel bulges. Only rogues and peasant slaves arrive without reservations. **Ashland Hostel ❶,** 150 N. Main St., is well-kept and cheery with an air of elegance. (☎482-9217. Laundry and kitchen. Check-in 5-10pm. Lockout 10am-5pm. Dorms $20; private rooms $50. Cash or traveler's checks only.) Campers should check out the **Mount Ashland Campground ❶,** 20 mi. south of Ashland off I-5 at Exit 6. Follow signs for Mt. Ashland Ski Area through the parking lot. (7 sites with pit toilets and no drinking water. Suggested donation $3.)

The incredible food selection on N. and E. Main St. has earned the plaza a culinary reputation independent of the festival, though the food tends to be pricey. **The Ashland Food Cooperative,** 237 1st St., stocks cheap and mostly organic groceries in bulk. (M-Sa 8am-9pm, Su 9am-9pm.) If you're hungry and sick of the Man keeping you down, fight back at **Evo's Java House and Revolutionary Cafe ❶,** 376 E. Main St., where the politics are as radical as the vegetarian burritos and sandwiches ($3.50-$5) are tasty. (☎774-6980. Open M-Sa 7am-

5pm, Su 7am-2pm.) **Morning Glory ❸**, 1149 Siskiyou Blvd., deserves a medal for "most pleasant dining environment," earned either inside by the fireplace and bookcases or outside by the rose-covered porticos. (☎488-8636. Sandwiches around $9. Open daily 7am-2pm.) Ashland's renowned nightlife is concentrated around N. and E. Main St. Try the excellent microbrews at **Siskiyou Brew Pub,** 31 Water St., just off N. Main St. by the hostel. (☎482-7718. Occasional live music. Open daily until around 11pm.)

Ashland is in the foothills of the Siskiyou and Cascade Ranges, 285 mi. south of Portland and 15 mi. north of the California border, near the junction of **I-5** and **Rte. 66. Greyhound** (☎482-8803) runs from Mr. C's Market, where I-5 meets Rte. 99 north of town, and sends three buses per day each to Portland (8hr., $45); Eugene (6hr., $25); Sacramento (7hr., $46); San Francisco (11hr., $53). **Visitor Info: Chamber of Commerce,** 110 E. Main St. (☎482-3486; www.ashlandchamber.com. Open M-Sa 10am-6pm, Su 10am-5pm.) **Ashland District Ranger Station,** 645 Washington St., off Rte. 66 by Exit 14 on I-5, provides info on hiking, biking, and the Pacific Crest Trail. (☎482-3333. Open M-F 8am-4:30pm.) **Post Office:** 120 N. 1st St., at Lithia Way. (Open M-F 9am-5pm.) **Postal Code:** 97520. **Area Code:** 541.

BEND ☎541

Surrounded by a dramatic landscape, with volcanic features to the south, the Cascades to the west, and the Deschutes River running through its heart, Bend attracts outdoor enthusiasts from all over the Pacific Northwest. Its proximity to wilderness areas makes Bend an unbeatable base for hiking, rafting, and skiing, while the charming downtown is packed with restaurants, pubs, and shops.

The **Three Sisters Wilderness Area,** north and west of the Cascade Lakes Hwy., is one of Oregon's largest and most popular wilderness areas. Pick up a parking permit at a ranger station or the Visitors Center ($5). Within the wilderness, the **South Sister** is the most accessible peak, making for a simple hike in late summer that threads between glaciers. Mountain-biking is forbidden in the wilderness area, but Benders have plenty of other places to spin their wheels. Try **Deschutes River Trail** (6 mi.) for a fairly flat, forested trail ending at the **Deschutes River.** To reach the trailhead, go 7½ mi. west of Bend on S. Century Dr. (Cascade Lakes Hwy.) until Forest Service Rd. 41, then turn left and follow signs to Lava Island Falls. You can rent bikes and get outfitted at **Sunnyside Sports,** 930 NW Newport Ave. (☎382-8018. Open Sa-Th 9am-7pm, F 9am-8pm. Mountain bikes $20-40 per day.) A few miles south of Bend, the **High Desert Museum,** 59800 Rte. 97 S, is one of the premier natural and cultural history museums in the Pacific Northwest. Life-size dioramas recreate rickety cabins, cramped immigrant workshops, and Pauite tipis. An indoor desertarium offers a peek at shy desert creatures. (☎382-4754; www.highdesert.org. Open daily 9am-5pm. $7.75, seniors and ages 13-18 $6.75, ages 5-12 $4.)

Most of the cheapest motels line 3rd St. just outside of town, and rates are surprisingly low. **Deschutes National Forest ❶** maintains a huge number of lakeside campgrounds along the **Cascade Lakes Highway,** west of town; all have toilets. (tents $12-18; RVs $15-21.) The closest campsite is at **Tumalo State Park,** 4 mi. north of Bend off U.S. 20 W, though it's crowded and expensive. (☎382-3586. Showers $2. Tents $17; RVs $21; hikers and bikers $4.) **Taqueria Los Jalapeños ❶**, 601 NE Greenwood Ave., fills a simple space with locals hungry for good, cheap food, like $1.75 burritos. (☎382-1402. Open summer M-Sa 11am-8pm, in winter 11am-7pm.) For coffee and pastries, try **Tuffy's Coffee & Tea ❶,** 961 NW Brooks St., right off the intersection of Wall St. and Greenwood Ave. (☎389-6464. Open daily 7am-7pm.)

Bend is 160 mi. southeast of Portland. **U.S. 97 (3rd Street)** bisects the town. Downtown lies to the west along the Deschutes River; **Wall and Bond Street** are the two main arteries. **Greyhound,** 63076 U.S. 97 N, in the Highway 97 gas station (☎382-2151; open M-F 8am-1:30pm and 2:30-5pm, Sa 8:30am-3pm, Su 8:30am-2pm), runs twice a day to Eugene (2½hr., $23) and once to Portland (4½hr., $25-27). **Bend Chamber and Visitors Bureau,** 63085 U.S. 97 N, stocks free maps, provides coffee, and has **Internet** Access. (☎382-3221; www.visitbend.org. Open M-Sa 9am-5pm.) **Deschutes National Forest Headquarters,** 1645 U.S. 20 E, has forest and wilderness info. (☎383-5300. Open M-F 7:45am-4:30pm.) **Post Office:** 777 NW Wall St. (Open M-F 8:30am-5:30pm, Sa 10am-1pm.) **Postal Code:** 97701. **Area Code:** 541.

WESTERN CANADA

All prices in this chapter are listed in Canadian dollars unless otherwise noted.

For every urban metropolis like Vancouver in Western Canada, there's a stunning national park or outdoor area, like Banff, Jasper, and Pacific Rim. Hikers, mountaineers, and ice climbers find a recreational paradise in the Canadian Rockies; the parks represent Western Canada's most consistent draw, and with good reason. They pack enough scenic punch, exhilarating thrills, and luxurious hostels to knock travelers of all ages flat. The region boasts thousands of prime fishing holes, internationally renowned fossil fields, and centers of indigenous Canadian culture.

HIGHLIGHTS OF WESTERN CANADA

THE YUKON. Flightseeing in **Kluane National Park** (p. 1047) is unusual and memorable.

NATIONAL PARKS. **Banff** (p. 1042) and **Jasper** (p. 1044) in Alberta reign as two of the region's most beautiful. Pacific Rim National Park, BC contains the **West Coast Trail** (p. 1033) with its isolated beaches and old growth rainforest.

BRITISH COLUMBIA

With stunning parks and vibrant cities, British Columbia (BC) is home to the third largest movie production center in the world and a huge tourism industry. Don't worry, though; this Canadian province has room for all. At over 900,000 sq. km, BC is more than twice as large as California and borders four US states (Washington, Idaho, Montana, and Alaska) two territories (the Yukon and Northwest) and a province (Alberta).

PRACTICAL INFORMATION

Capital: Victoria.

Visitor Info: Tourism British Columbia, P.O. Box 9830, Stn. Prov. Govt., 1803 Douglas St., 3rd Fl., Victoria V8W 9W5 (☎800-435-5622; www.hellobc.com). **British Columbia Parks Headquarters,** www.bcparks.ca.

Drinking Age: 19. **Postal Abbreviation:** BC. **Sales Tax:** 7% PST, plus 7% GST.

VANCOUVER ☎604

Like any self-respecting city on the west coast of North America, Vancouver boasts a thriving multicultural populace; the Cantonese influence is so strong that it is often referred to by its nickname, "Hongcouver." With the third largest China-

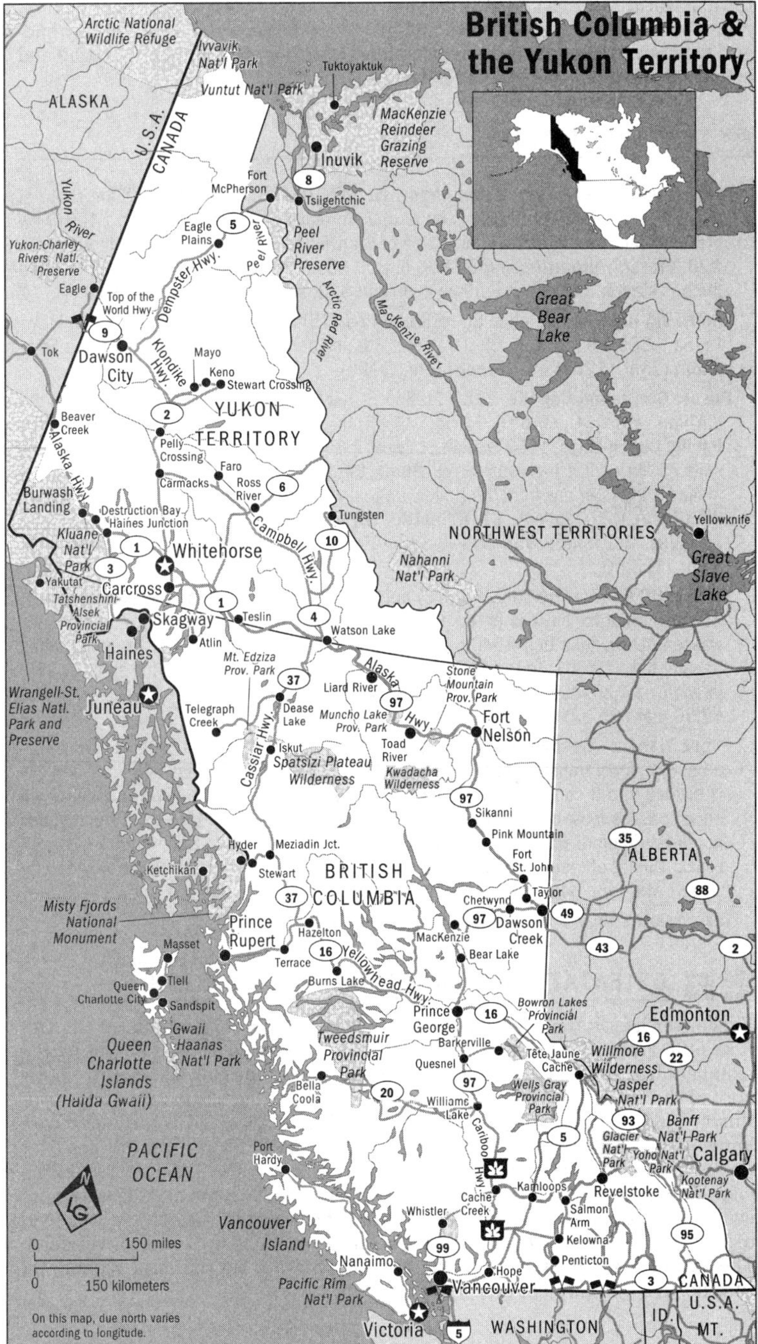
British Columbia & the Yukon Territory
Arctic National Wildlife Refuge
Ivvavik Nat'l Park
Tuktoyaktuk
Vuntut Nat'l Park
ALASKA
U.S.A.
CANADA
MacKenzie Reindeer Grazing Reserve
Inuvik
Fort McPherson
Tsiigehtchic
Yukon River
Eagle Plains
Peel River
Peel River Preserve
Yukon-Charley Rivers Natl. Preserve
Eagle
Top of the World Hwy.
Dempster Hwy.
Arctic Red River
MacKenzie River
Great Bear Lake
Tok
Dawson City
Klondike Hwy.
Mayo
Keno
Stewart Crossing
YUKON TERRITORY
Beaver Creek
Pelly Crossing
Alaska Hwy.
Faro
Carmacks
Ross River
Burwash Landing
Destruction Bay
Haines Junction
Tungsten
Yellowknife
Kluane Nat'l Park
Whitehorse
Campbell Hwy.
NORTHWEST TERRITORIES
Nahanni Nat'l Park
Great Slave Lake
Yakutat
Carcross
Tatshenshini-Alsek Provincial Park
Skagway
Teslin
Watson Lake
Haines
Atlin
Mt. Edziza Prov. Park
Alaska Hwy.
Stone Mountain Prov. Park
Liard River
Wrangell-St. Elias Natl. Park and Preserve
Juneau
Telegraph Creek
Dease Lake
Muncho Lake Prov. Park
Fort Nelson
Toad River
Cassiar Hwy.
Iskut
Spatsizi Plateau Wilderness
Kwadacha Wilderness
Sikanni
Pink Mountain
Hyder
Meziadin Jct.
ALBERTA
Fort St. John
Ketchikan
Stewart
BRITISH COLUMBIA
Taylor
Misty Fjords National Monument
Chetwynd
Dawson Creek
Prince Rupert
Hazelton
MacKenzie
Masset
Terrace
Yellowhead Hwy.
Bear Lake
Tlell
Burns Lake
Queen Charlotte City
Sandspit
Prince George
Bowron Lakes Provincial Park
Edmonton
Gwaii Haanas Nat'l Park
Tweedsmuir Provincial Park
Barkerville
Queen Charlotte Islands (Haida Gwaii)
Quesnel
Tête Jaune Cache
Willmore Wilderness
Bella Coola
Jasper Nat'l Park
Williams Lake
Wells Gray Provincial Park
Banff Nat'l Park
Cariboo Hwy.
PACIFIC OCEAN
Port Hardy
Glacier Nat'l Park
Yoho Nat'l Park
Calgary
Kamloops
Revelstoke
Kootenay Nat'l Park
Cache Creek
Whistler
Salmon Arm
Vancouver Island
Kelowna
0
150 miles
0
150 kilometers
Nanaimo
Penticton
Hope
Pacific Rim Nat'l Park
Vancouver
CANADA
U.S.A.
Victoria
WASHINGTON
ID.
MT.
On this map, due north varies according to longitude.
8
5
9
2
6
10
1
3
1
4
37
97
97
35
37
88
97
49
16
43
2
16
16
22
97
20
93
5
99
95
3
5

town in North America and a strong showing by almost every other major culture, visitors are never hard-pressed to find exotic food or entertainment for any budget. Vancouver matches its cultural splendor with a lush, gorgeous setting and quick and easy access to outdoor adventure.

TRANSPORTATION

Airport: Vancouver International Airport (☎207-7077), on Sea Island, 23km south of the city center. **Visitors Center** is on level 2. To reach downtown, take bus #100 "New Westminster Station" to the intersection of Granville and 70th Ave. Transfer there to bus #20 "Fraser." **Airporter** (☎946-8866 or 800-668-3141) runs to downtown hotels and the bus station. (4 per hr.; 6:30am-midnight; $12, seniors $9, ages 5-12 $5.)

Trains: VIA Rail, 1150 Station St. (☎888-842-7245) runs eastbound trains. Open M, W-Th, Sa 9:30am-6pm; Tu, F, Su 9am-7pm. 3 trains per week to eastern Canada via **Edmonton** (23hr., $263) and **Jasper** (17hr., $196).

Buses: Greyhound Canada, 1150 Station St. (☎683-8133 or 800-661-8747), in the VIA Rail station. Open daily 7:15am-11:45pm. To **Calgary** (15hr., 4per day, $129). **Pacific Coach Lines,** 1150 Station St. (☎662-8074), runs to **Victoria** every time a ferry sails (3½hr., $29; includes ferry). **Quick Shuttle** (☎940-4428 or 800-665-2122) makes 8 trips per day from the Holiday Inn on Howe St. via the airport to: **Bellingham, WA** (2½hr., $22, students $17); **Seattle, WA** (4hr., $33/22); **Sea-Tac airport** (4½hr., $41/29). **Greyhound USA** (☎402-330-8552 or 800-229-9424) goes to **Seattle** (3-4½hr., $23.50).

Ferries: BC Ferries (☎888-223-3779) arrive and leave from the **Tsawwassen Terminal,** 25km south of the city center (take Hwy. 99 to Hwy. 17). To reach downtown from Tsawwassen (1hr.), take bus #640, or take #404 "Airport" to the Ladner Exchange, then transfer to bus #601. To the **Gulf Islands, Nanaimo** (2hr.; 4-8 per day; in summer $10, in winter $8.25; cars $25-34), and **Victoria** (1½hr.; 8-16 per day; $8.25-10; bikes $2.50, car $25-34).

Public Transit: Coast Mountain Buslink (☎953-3333) covers most of the city and suburbs, with direct transport or easy connections to airport and the ferry terminals. The city is divided into 3 concentric zones for fare purposes. Riding in the **central zone,** which encompasses most of Vancouver, costs $2, seniors and ages 5-13 $1.50. During peak hours (M-F before 6:30pm), it costs $3/2 to travel between 2 zones and $4/3 for 3 zones. During off-peak hours, all zones are $2/1.50. Ask for a **free transfer** (good for 1½hr.) when you board buses. Day passes $8/6.

Taxi: Yellow Cab, ☎800-898-8294. **Vancouver Taxi,** ☎871-1111.

ORIENTATION & PRACTICAL INFORMATION

Vancouver lies in the southwestern corner of mainland BC. South of the city flows the **Fraser River,** and to the west lies the **Georgia Strait,** separating the mainland from Vancouver Island. **Downtown** juts into the Burrard Inlet from the core of the city, and **Stanley Park** goes farther north. The **Lions Gate Bridge** over Burrard Inlet links Stanley Park with North Vancouver and West Vancouver, known as **West Van.** The two are known as the **North Shore.** The bridges over False Creek south of downtown link it with **Kitsilano ("Kits")** and the rest of the city. West of Burrard St. is the **West Side** or **West End. Gastown** and **Chinatown** are east of downtown. The **University of British Columbia (UBC)** lies on the west end of Kits on Point Grey, while the **airport** is on Sea Island in the Fraser River delta. The **Trans-Canada Highway (Highway 1)** enters town from the east; **Highway 99** runs north-south through the city.

Visitor Info: 200 Burrard St., plaza level (☎683-2000), near Canada Pl. BC-wide info on accommodations, tours, and activities. Open daily 8:30am-6pm.

Bi-Gay-Lesbian Resources: The Centre, 1170 Bute St. (☎684-5307), offers counseling and info. *Xtra West* is the city's gay and lesbian biweekly, available at the Centre and around Davie St. in the West End. Open M-F 9:30am-5pm.

Hotlines: Crisis Center, ☎872-3311. **Rape Crisis Center,** ☎255-6344. Both 24hr.

Medical Services: Vancouver General Hospital, 895 W. 12th Ave. (☎875-4111). **UBC Hospital,** 2211 Westbrook Mall (☎822-7121), on the UBC campus.

Internet Access: Public Library, 350 W. Georgia St. (☎331-3600) and at 20 other branches. Open M-Th 10am-8pm, F-Sa 10am-5pm, Su 1-5pm. Free.

Post Office: 349 W Georgia St. (☎662-5725). Open M-F 8am-5:30pm. **Postal Code:** V6B 3P7. **Area Code:** 604.

ACCOMMODATIONS

Vancouver Hostel Downtown (HI-C), 1114 Burnaby St. (☎684-4565 or 888-203-4302), in the West End. Sleek and clean 225-bed facility between downtown, the beach, and Stanley Park. Library, kitchen, rooftop patio. Pub crawls W and F; frequent tours of Granville Island. Reservations strongly recommended in summer, when prices may increase slightly. $20, nonmembers $24; private doubles $55/64. ❶

Global Village Backpackers, 1018 Granville St. (☎682-8226 or 888-844-7875), at Nelson St. Ask the hostel for a refund of your taxi fare. Funky technicolor hangout in an area with great nightlife. Internet access, pool, laundry. Dorms for HI, ISIC, other hosteling members $21.50, nonmembers $25; doubles $57/60, with bath $62/65. ❶

Vancouver Hostel Jericho Beach (HI), 1515 Discovery St. (☎224-3208 or 888-203-4303), in Jericho Beach Park. Follow 4th Ave. west past Alma and bear right at the fork. Bus #4 from Granville St. downtown. Peaceful location with a great view across English Bay. Free linen, kitchen, TV room, laundry, and cafe (breakfasts around $6, dinner $7-8). Open May-Sept. $18.50, nonmembers $22.50; family rooms $51-61. ❶

C&N Backpackers Hostel, 927 Main St. (☎682-2441 or 888-434-6060), 300m north on Main St. from the train station. Cheap meal deals with the **Ivanhoe Pub** ($2.50 breakfast all day) make this recently renovated hostel a bargain. Kitchen, laundry, bikes ($10 per day). May-Sept. dorms $16; single, double, or family room $40. Weekly rates available, monthly rates available in winter. ❶

Cambie International Hostel, 300 Cambie St. (☎684-6466 or 877-395-5335). Free airport pickup 10am-8pm. Easy access to the busy sights and sounds of Gastown. Common room, laundry. No kitchen, but free hot breakfast. Pool tables in the pub. June-Sept. dorms $20; doubles $45. Oct.-May $17.50/20. ❶

FOOD

The Naam, 2724 W. 4th Ave. (☎738-7151), at MacDonald St. Bus #4 or 7 from Granville Mall. Diverse vegetarian menu with great prices. Crying Tiger Thai stir fry $9, *tofulati* ice cream $3.50. Live music nightly 7-10pm. Open 24hr. ❷

Subeez Cafe, 891 Homer St. (☎687-6107), at Smithe, downtown. Serves hipster kids in a cavernous setting. Eclectic menu, from vegetarian gyoza ($7) to organic beef burgers ($9), complements a lengthy wine list and home-spun beats (DJs W and F-Sa 9pm-midnight). Entrees $7-15. Open M-F 11:30am-1am, Sa 11am-1am, Su 11am-midnight. ❷

Mongolian Teriyaki, 1918 Commercial Dr. (☎253-5607). Diners fill a bowl with meats, veggies, sauces, and noodles, and the chefs fry everything and serve it with miso soup, rice, and salad for $5 (large bowl $6). Take-out menu. Open daily 11am-9:30pm. ❶

Benny's Bagels, 2505 W. Broadway (☎731-9730). Every college student's dream. Serves the requisite beer ($3 per glass), bagels ($0.75, $2.25 with cream cheese), and sandwiches and melts ($5.50-7.50). Open Su-Th 7am-1am, F-Sa 24hr. ❶

Downtown Vancouver

ACCOMMODATIONS
C&N Backpackers Hostel, **11**
Cambie International Hostel, **2**
Global Village Backpackers, **7**

FOOD
Benny's Bagels, **17**
Mongolian Teriyaki, **14**
The Naam, **16**
Subeez Café, **8**
Hon's Wun-Tun House, **9**

THEATRES
Arts Club Theatre, **13**
Orpheum Theatre, **5**

NIGHTLIFE
Atlantis, **12**
The Irish Heather, **3**
Sonar, **1**
Sugar Refinery, **10**

SIGHTS
Dr. Sun Yat-Sen Classical Chinese Garden, **6**
Granville Island Brewing Co., **15**
World's Skinniest Building, **4**

ALSO SEE COLOR INSERT MAP

Hon's Wun-Tun House, 268 Keefer St. (☎688-0871). This award-winning Cantonese noodle-house is the place to go (bowls $3.50-6). Over 300 options make the menu as long as dinner. Open daily 8:30am-10pm; summer F-Su until 11pm. Cash only. ❶

SIGHTS

DOWNTOWN

VANCOUVER ART GALLERY. The Vancouver Art Gallery has excellent temporary exhibitions and is home to a varied collection of contemporary art. *(750 Hornby St., in Robson Sq. ☎662-4700. Open M-W and F-Su 10am-5:30pm, Th 10am-9pm; call for winter hours. $12.50, students $7, seniors $9. Th 5-9pm pay-what-you-can.)*

GARDENS

The city's temperate climate, which also includes ample rain most months of the year, allows floral growth to flourish. Locals take great pride in their private gardens, and public parks and green spaces showcase displays of plant life.

VANDUSEN BOTANICAL GARDEN. Some 55 acres of former golf course have been converted into the immense **VanDusen Botanical Garden,** showcasing 7500 taxa from six continents. An international **sculpture** collection is interspersed among the plants, while more than 60 species of birds can be seen in areas like the Fragrance Garden, Bonsai House, Chinese Medicinal Garden, or Elizabethan Maze, which is planted with 3000 pyramidal cedars. The **Flower & Garden Show** is the first weekend of June. *(5251 Oak St., at W 37th. Take #17 Oak bus to W. 37th and Oak. ☎878-9274. Free parking. Mostly wheelchair-accessible. Open daily June-Aug. 10am-9pm; mid-Aug. to Sept. 10am-8pm; Oct.-Mar. 10am-4pm;. Apr. 10am-6pm; May 10am-8pm. $5 in winter, $7 in summer; for seniors and ages 13-18 $3.50/5.50; ages 6-12 $2/3.75.)*

BLOEDEL FLORAL & BIRD CONSERVATORY. Journey from tropics to desert in 100 paces inside this 43m diameter triodetic geodesic dome, constructed of plexiglass and aluminum tubing. The conservatory, maintained at a constant 18°C (65°F), is home to 500 varieties of plants and 150 birds. Its elevation affords great views of downtown Vancouver. *(Center of Queen Elizabeth Park on Cambie and 37th Ave., a few blocks east of VanDusen. ☎257-8584. Open Apr.-Sept. M-F 9am-8pm, Sa-Su 10am-9pm; Oct.-Mar. daily 10am-5pm. $4, over 65 $2.80, ages 13-18 $3, ages 6-12 $2, under 5 free.)*

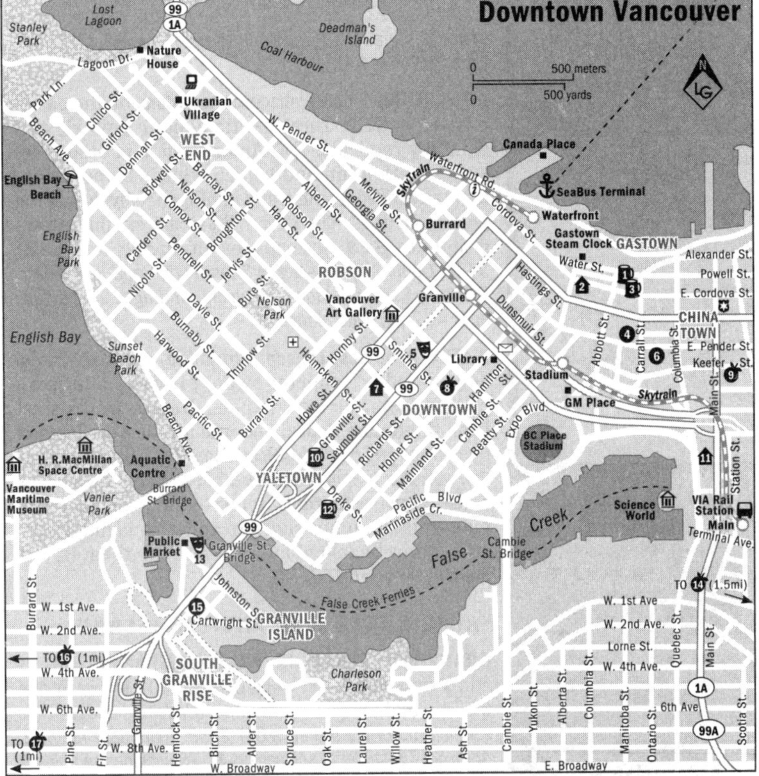

UNIVERSITY OF BRITISH COLUMBIA (UBC)

The high point of a visit to UBC is the breathtaking **Museum of Anthropology.** The high-ceilinged glass and concrete building houses totems and other massive carvings, highlighted by Bill Reid's depiction of Raven discovering the first human beings in a giant clam shell. *(6393 NW Marine Dr. Bus #4 or 10 from Granville St. Museum. ☎822-5087. Open May-Sept. Tu 10am-9pm, M and W-Su 10am-5pm; Oct.-May Tu 11am-9pm, M and W-Su 11am-5pm. $9, students and seniors $7, under 6 free; Tu after 5pm free.)* Across the street, caretakers tend to **Nitobe Memorial Garden,** the finest classical Shinto garden outside of Japan. *(☎822-6038. Open daily mid-Mar. to mid-May 10am-5pm; mid-May through Aug. 10am-6pm; Sept.-Oct. 10am-5pm. $3, seniors $2, students $1.50, under 6 free.)* The **Botanical Gardens** encompass eight gardens in the central campus, including the largest collection of rhododendrons in North America. *(6804 SW Marine Dr. ☎822-9666. Same hours as Nitobe Garden. $5, seniors $3, students $2, under 6 free. Discounted admission for both Nitobe and the Botanical Gardens.)*

STANLEY PARK

Established in 1889 at the tip of the downtown peninsula, the 1000-acre **Stanley Park** is a testament to the foresight of Vancouver's urban planners. The thickly wooded park is laced with cycling and hiking trails and surrounded by a popu-

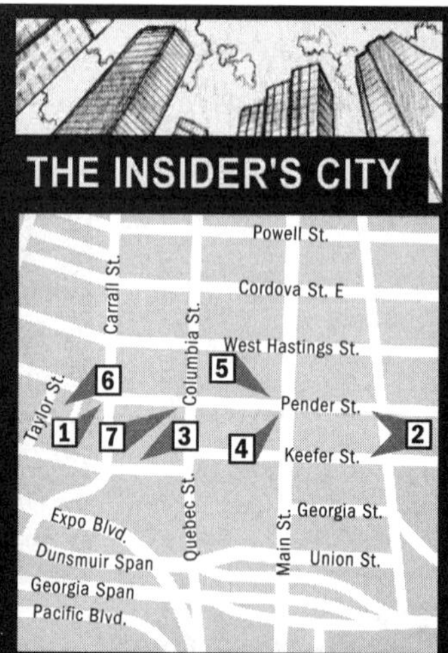

CHINATOWN HIGHLIGHTS

Savy tourists should take a break from downtown's slick hot spots and experience Chinatown, Vancouver at its most energized.

1. Gawk at the impossibly narrow **Sam Kee Building,** said to be the narrowest in the world.
2. Haggle at the **Chinatown Night Market.** Open June-Sept. F-Su 6:30-11:00pm.
3. Let the tranquil **Dr. Sun Yat-Sen Classical Chinese Garden** (☎682-4008) ease your stress.
4. Enjoy great Chinese food on the cheap at **Kam's Garden Restaurant** (☎669-5488).
5. Recognize the trials and successes of Chinese Canadians at the Winds of Change Mural.
6. Choose your meal from hundreds at **Hon's Wun-Tun House** (☎688-0871).
6. Visit the huge **Western Han Dynasty Bell.**
7. Explore the permanent and changing exhibitions at the **Chinese Cultural Centre** (☎687-0282).

lar 10km **seawall** promenade. *(To get to the park, take bus #23, 123, 35, or 135. A free shuttle runs between major destinations throughout the park June-Sept. 10am-6pm. ☎257-8400.)*

AQUARIUM. The **Vancouver Aquarium,** on the park's eastern side, features exotic aquatic animals and skillfully replicates BC, Amazonian, and other ecosystems. Dolphin and beluga whales demonstrate their advanced training and intelligence by drenching gleeful visitors. The new Wild Coast exhibit allows visitors to get a close-up view of marine life. *(☎659-3474. Open daily July-Aug. 9:30am-7pm; Sept.-June 10am-5:30pm. $15.75; students, seniors, and ages 13-18 $12; ages 4-12 $9; under 4 free.)*

WATER. The **Lost Lagoon,** brimming with fish, birds, and the odd trumpeter swan, provides a utopian escape from the skyscrapers. Nature walks start from the **Nature House,** underneath the Lost Lagoon bus loop. *(☎257-8544. Open June-Aug. F-Su 11am-7pm. 2hr. walks Su 1, 3pm. $5, under 12 free.)* The park's edges boast a few restaurants, tennis courts, a cinder running track with hot showers and a changing room, swimming beaches, and an outdoor theater, the **Malkin Bowl** *(☎687-0174).*

FALSE CREEK & GRANVILLE ISLAND

GRANVILLE ISLAND BREWING COMPANY. Canada's first micro-brewery offers daily tours of the facility, including free samples. *(Under the bridge at the southern tip of the island. ☎687-2739. Tours daily noon, 2, 4pm. $9.75, students and seniors $7.75, includes samples of 4 brews and a souvenir glass. Call for store hours.)*

H.R. MACMILLAN SPACE CENTRE. Housed in the same circular building as the **Vancouver Museum,** the space center runs a motion-simulator ride, planetarium, and exhibit gallery, as well as frequent laser-light rock shows. *(1100 Chestnut St. Bus #22 south on Burrard St. ☎738-7827. Open July-Aug. daily 10am-5pm; Sept.-June closed M. $13.50, students and seniors $10.50; laser-light show $9.35. Vancouver Museum ☎736-4431. $10, seniors $8, under 19 $6. Combined admission to both museums available.)*

ENTERTAINMENT & NIGHTLIFE

The **Vancouver Symphony Orchestra** (☎876-3434) plays September to May in the **Orpheum Theatre,** at the corner of Smithe and Seymour. In summer, tours of the theater are given. (☎665-3050. $5.) The VSO often joins forces with other groups such as the **Vancouver**

Bach Choir (☎921-8012). The **Vancouver Playhouse Theatre Co.** (☎873-3311), on Dunsmuir and Georgia St., and the **Arts Club Theatre** (☎604-687-1644), on Granville Island, stage low-key shows, often including local work. The **Ridge Theatre,** 3131 Arbutus, shows arthouse, European, and vintage film double features. (☎738-6311. $5, seniors and children $3.)

Sugar Refinery, 1115 Granville St. (☎331-1184). Where Vancouver's arts scene goes to relax. An ever-changing program of events, music, and spoken word entertains while the tasty vegetarian meals please the stomach. Entrees $7.50-9. Big sandwiches $5-7.50. Tap beers served in mason jars $4.25-5.75. Open daily 5pm-2am.

Sonar, 66 Water St. (☎683-6695). A popular beat factory. W hip-hop and reggae, F turntablist, and Sa House. Pints $3.75-5. Open daily 8pm-2am.

The Irish Heather, 217 Carrall St. (☎688-9779). The 2nd-highest seller of Guinness in BC, this true Irish pub and bistro serves up 20oz. draughts ($5.20), mixed beer drinks ($5.60), and a helping of bangers and mash ($14) to keep those eyes smiling. Lots of veggie dishes, too. Live music Tu-Th. Open daily noon-midnight.

Atlantis, 1320 Richards St. (☎662-7707). Candlelit dining booths and a weekend dress code. Wields one of the most advanced stereo and light systems in Vancouver. M, F-Sa hip-hop. Open M 9pm-2am, F-Sa 9am-4.

The King's Head, 1618 Yew St. (☎738-6966), at 1st St., in Kitsilano. Cheap drinks, cheap food, relaxing atmosphere, and a great location near the beach. Bands play acoustic sets on a tiny stage. Daily drink specials. $3 pints. Open daily 8am-midnight.

WESTERN CANADA

NEAR VANCOUVER: WHISTLER ☎604

Thirty-three lifts (15 of them high-speed), three glaciers, over 200 marked trails, a mile (1609m) of vertical drop, and unreal scenery make **Whistler/Blackcomb** a top destination for skiers and boarders. Whistler Creekside offers the shortest lines to park and the closest access for those coming from Vancouver. (☎800-766-0449. Lift tickets $42-69 per day. Better deals for longer trips.) A **Fresh Tracks** upgrade ($15), available daily at 7am, provides a basic breakfast in the mountaintop lodge on Blackcomb and the opportunity to begin skiing as soon as the ski patrol has finished avalanche control. Most **snowboarders** prefer the younger Blackcomb for its windlips, natural quarter-pipes, and 16-acre terrain park. Endless **backcountry skiing** is accessible from resort lifts and in Garibaldi Park's **Diamond Head** area. Equipment rentals are widely available.

The gorgeous lakeside **Whistler Hostel (HI-C) ❶,** 5678 Alta Lake Rd., lies 5km south of Whistler Village on Hwy. 99. BC Rail stops here on request. (☎932-5492. $19.50; nonmembers $23.50.) The **Fireside Lodge ❶,** 2117 Nordic Dr., 3km south of the village, offers spacious cabins with mammoth kitchens, lounge, sauna, and a game room. (☎932-4545. Dorms $20; private rooms from $60.)

Greyhound (☎932-5031 or 800-661-8747) runs to Vancouver from the Village Bus Loop (2½hr., 7 per day, $22.50). **Activity and information center:** in the heart of the Village. (☎932-2394. Open daily 8:30am-5pm.) **Post Office:** in the Market Place Mall. (☎800-267-1177. Open M-F 8am-5pm.) **Postal Code:** V0N 1B0. **Area Code:** 604.

VICTORIA ☎250

Clean, polite, and tourist-friendly, today's Victoria is a homier alternative to cosmopolitan Vancouver. Although many tourist operations would have you believe that Victoria fell off Great Britain in a neat little chunk, its High Tea tradition began in the 1950s to draw American tourists. Double-decker buses motor past native art galleries, new-age bookstores, and countless English pubs.

PRACTICAL INFORMATION. Victoria surrounds the **Inner Harbour;** the main north-south thoroughfares downtown are **Government Street** and **Douglas Street.** To the north, Douglas St. becomes Hwy. 1, which runs north to Nanaimo. **Blanshard Street,** one block to the east, becomes Hwy. 17. The **E&N Railway,** 450 Pandora St. (☎888-842-0744), near the Inner Harbour at the Johnson St. Bridge, runs daily to Nanaimo (2½hr.; $23, students with ISIC $15). **Gray Line of Victoria,** 700 Douglas St. (☎800-318-0818), at Belleville St., and its affiliates, **Pacific** and **Island Coach Lines,** run buses to: Nanaimo (2½hr., 6 per day, $17.50); Port Hardy (9hr., 1-2 per day, $93); Vancouver (3½hr., 8-14 per day, $29). **BC Ferries** (☎888-223-3779) depart Swartz Bay to Vancouver's Tsawwassen ferry terminal (1½hr.; 8-16 per day; $8.25-10, bikes $2.50, car and driver $25-35), and to the Gulf Islands. **Victoria Clipper** (☎382-8100 or 800-888-2535) passenger ferries travel to Seattle (2-3hr.; 2-4 per day May-Sept., 1 per day Oct.-Apr.; US$62-77). **Victoria Taxi,** ☎383-7111. **Visitor Info: Tourism Victoria,** 812 Wharf St., at Government St. (☎953-2033. Open summer daily 8:30am-6:30pm; winter 9am-5pm.) **Post Office:** 706 Yates St. (☎800-267-1177. Open M-F 8am-5pm.) **Postal Code:** V8W 2L9. **Area Code:** 250.

ACCOMMODATIONS. The colorful **Ocean Island Backpackers Inn ❶,** 791 Pandora St., downtown, boasts a better lounge than most clubs, tastier food than most restaurants, and accommodations comparable to most hotels. Undoubtedly one of the finest urban hostels in North America. (☎385-1788 or 888-888-4180. 140 beds in small rooms. Free linen and towels, laundry, Internet access. Parking $5. Depending on the time of year, dorms $18-23, students and HI members $18-20; doubles $22-55.) To reach the **The Cat's Meow ❶,** 1316 Grant St., take bus #22 to Gernwood and Grant St. A mini-hostel with 12 quiet beds three blocks from downtown, it offers free parking, discounts on kayaking and whale watching, and complimentary breakfast. (☎595-8878. $18.50; private rooms $40-45.) **Goldstream Provincial Park ❶,** 2930 Trans-Canada Hwy., 20km northwest of Victoria, offers a forested riverside area with great hiking trails and swimming. (☎391-2300 or 800-689-9025. Flush toilets and firewood. $22.)

FOOD & NIGHTLIFE. Diverse food options exist in Victoria, if you know where to go; ask locals, or wander through downtown. **Chinatown** extends from Fisgard and Government St. to the northwest. Cook St. Village, between McKenzie and Park St., offers an eclectic mix of creative restaurants. **John's Place ❷,** 723 Pandora St., is a hopping joint serving wholesome Canadian fare with a Thai twist and Mediterranean flair. (☎389-0711. Entrees $5-11. Open M-F 7am-9pm, Sa-Su 8am-9pm.) A trip to Victoria is just not done without a spot of tea. The Sunday High Tea ($10.25) at the **James Bay Tea Room & Restaurant ❷,** 332 Menzies St., behind the Parliament Buildings, is lower-key and significantly less expensive than the famous High Tea at the Empress Hotel. (☎382-8282. Open M-Sa 7am-5pm, Su 8am-5pm.) The free weekly *Monday Magazine*, lists venues and performers. At night, **Steamers Public House,** 570 Yates St., attracts a young dancing crowd. (☎381-4340. Open stage M, jazz night Tu. Open M-Tu 11:30am-1am, W-Su 11:30am-2am.)

SIGHTS & OUTDOOR ACTIVITIES. The **Royal British Columbia Museum,** 675 Belleville St., presents excellent exhibits on the biological, geological, and cultural history of the province. A new IMAX theater shows films that are larger than life. (☎356-7226. Open daily 9am-5pm. Museum and current exhibit $13; students, seniors, and youth $10; under 6 free. IMAX double features $15, seniors and youth $12.75, children $7.) Unwind with an educational and alcoholic tour of the **Vancouver Island Brewery,** 2330 Government St. (☎361-0007. 1hr. tours F-Sa 3pm. $6 for four 4 oz. samples and souvenir pint glass. 19+ to sample.)

The elaborate landscaping of the **Butchart Gardens** includes a rose garden, Japanese and Italian gardens, fountains, and wheelchair-accessible paths. (Bus #75 "Central Saanich" runs from downtown. 1hr. ☎652-4422. Open mid-June through Aug. daily 9am-10:30pm. $20, ages 13-17 $10, ages 5-12 $2, under 5 free. The Gray Line (☎800-440-3885) runs a package from downtown including round-trip transportation and admission to gardens. $42, youth $32, children $13.) Mountain bikers can tackle the **Galloping Goose,** a 100km trail beginning downtown and continuing to the west coast of the Island through towns, rainforests, and canyons. **Ocean River Sports** offers kayak rentals, tours, and lessons. (☎381-4233 or 800-909-4233. Open M-Th and Sa 9am-5:30pm, F 9:30am-8pm, Su 11am-5pm. Single kayak $42 per day, double $50; canoe $42.) Many whale-watching outfits give discounts for hostel guests. **Ocean Explorations,** 532 Broughton St., runs 3hr. tours. (☎383-6722. Apr.-Oct. $70, students $60, children $50; less during low season.)

PACIFIC RIM NATIONAL PARK ☎250

The Pacific Rim National Park stretches along a 150km sliver of Vancouver Island's remote Pacific coast. The region's frequent downpours create a lush landscape rich in both marine and terrestrial life. Hard-core hikers trek through enormous red cedar trees while long beaches on the open ocean draw beachcombers, bathers, kayakers, and surfers.

A winding, 1½hr. drive up Hwy. 14 from Hwy. 1 near Victoria lands you in **Port Renfrew.** Spread out in the trees along a peaceful ocean inlet, this isolated coastal community of 400 people is the southern gateway to the world-famous **West Coast Trail.** The other end of the trail lies 75km north, in Bamfield. The route weaves through primeval forests of giant red cedars and spruce, waterfalls, rocky slopes, and rugged beach. Exciting challenges lie at every bend, but wet weather and slippery terrain can make the trail dangerous. Hikers pay about $120 per person for access to the trail (reservation fee $25, backcountry camping $90 in summer, ferry-crossings (2) $14 each). If you only want to spend an afternoon roughing it, visit the gorgeous **Botanical Beach Provincial Park,** but be sure to go at low tide or you won't see much (Visitors Centers will have tide charts).

Whalers on the Point Guesthouse (HI-C) ❶, 81 West St., voted the best hostel in Canada by HI, has a free sauna, billiards, linen, and harborside views. Internet access $1 per 10min. (☎725-3443. Check-in 7am-2pm and 4-11pm. $22, nonmembers $24.) Near Port Renfrew and adjacent to the West Coast Trail registration office lies the **Pacheedaht Campground ❶.** (☎647-0090. Sites are first come, first served: tents $10; RV sites $15.) The **Lighthouse Pub & Restaurant ❷** (☎647-5505), on Parkinson Rd., serves up tasty fish and chips.

Seek out maps, information on the area, and registration info at one of the two **Trail Information Centers,** one in **Port Renfrew** (☎647-5434), at the first right off Parkinson Rd. (Hwy. 14) once in "town"; and one at **Pachena Bay** (☎728-3234), 5km south of Bamfield. Both open daily May-Sept. 9am-5pm. **West Coast Trail Express** (☎888-999-2288) runs daily from Victoria to Port Renfrew via the Juan de Fuca trailhead (May-Sept., 2¼hr., $35); from Nanaimo to Bamfield (3½hr., $55); from Bamfield to Port Renfrew (3¼hr., $50); and from Port Renfrew or Bamfield to Nitinat (2hr., $35). Reservations are recommended, and can be made for beaches and trailheads from Victoria to Port Renfrew. The **Juan de Fuca Express** operates a water taxi between Port Renfrew and Bamfield. (☎888-755-6578. 3½hr., $85.)

ALBERTA

With its gaping prairie, oil-fired economy, and conservativism, Alberta is the Texas of Canada. Petrol dollars have given birth to gleaming cities on the plains, while the natural landscape swings from the Canadian Rockies down to beautifully desolate badlands. Alberta is a year-round playground for outdoor adventurers.

PRACTICAL INFORMATION

Capital: Edmonton.

Visitor Info: Travel Alberta, P.O. Box 2500, Edmonton T5J 2Z4 (☎780-427-4321 or 800-661-8888; www.travelalberta.com). **Parks Canada,** 220 4th Ave. SE, Rm. 550, Calgary T2G 4X3 (☎888-773-8888).

Drinking Age: 18. **Postal Abbreviation:** AB. **Sales Tax:** 7% GST.

EDMONTON ☎780

This popular destination hosts the Canadian Finals Rodeo and is home to the world's largest shopping mall. A plethora of museums attracts children and art lovers, while the Saskatchewan River valley draws hikers and bikers. A perpetual stream of music, art, and performers brings summer crowds to the self-proclaimed "City of Festivals." A happening strip on Whyte Avenue transforms Edmonton into an urban oasis near the overpowering splendor of the neighboring Rockies.

TRANSPORTATION & ORIENTATION

The city lies 294km north of Calgary, an easy but tedious 3hr. drive on the **Calgary Trail (Highway 2).** Jasper is 362km to the west, a 4hr. drive on Hwy. 16. Edmonton's streets run north-south, and avenues run east-west. Street numbers increase to the west, and avenues increase to the north. The first three digits of an address indicate the nearest cross street: 10141 88 Ave. is on 88 Ave. near 101 St. The **city center** is quite off-center at 105 St. and 101 Ave.

Airport: Edmonton International Airport (☎890-8382) sits 29km south of town, a $35 cab fare away. The **Sky Shuttle Airport Service** (☎465-8515 or 888-438-2342) shuttles downtown, to the university, or to the mall for $13 ($20 round-trip).

Trains: VIA Rail, 12360 121 St. (800-842-7245) is a 10min. drive NW of downtown in the CN tower. 3 per week to **Jasper** (5hr.; $141, students $92) and **Vancouver, BC** (24hr.; $263, students $171). No train service to Calgary.

Buses: Greyhound, 10324 103 St. (☎420-2400). Open M-F 5:30am-1:30am, S 5:30am-midnight, Su and holidays 10am-6pm. To: **Calgary** (11 per day, $43); **Jasper** (5hr., 4 per day, $55); **Vancouver, BC** (16-21hr., 6per day, $148); **Yellowknife, NWT** (22-28hr.; 2 per day M-F, winter 3 per week; $203). Locker storage $2 per day. **Red Arrow,** 10010 104 St. (☎800-232-1958), at the Holiday Inn. Open M-F 7:30am-9pm, Sa 8am-9pm. 10% discount with hosteling card. To **Calgary** (4-7 per day, $51).

Public Transportation: Edmonton Transit (schedules ☎496-1611, info 496-1600; www.gov.edmonton.ab.ca). Buses and **Light Rail Transit (LRT)** run frequently. LRT is **free downtown** between Grandin Station at 110 St. and 98 Ave. and Churchill Station at 99

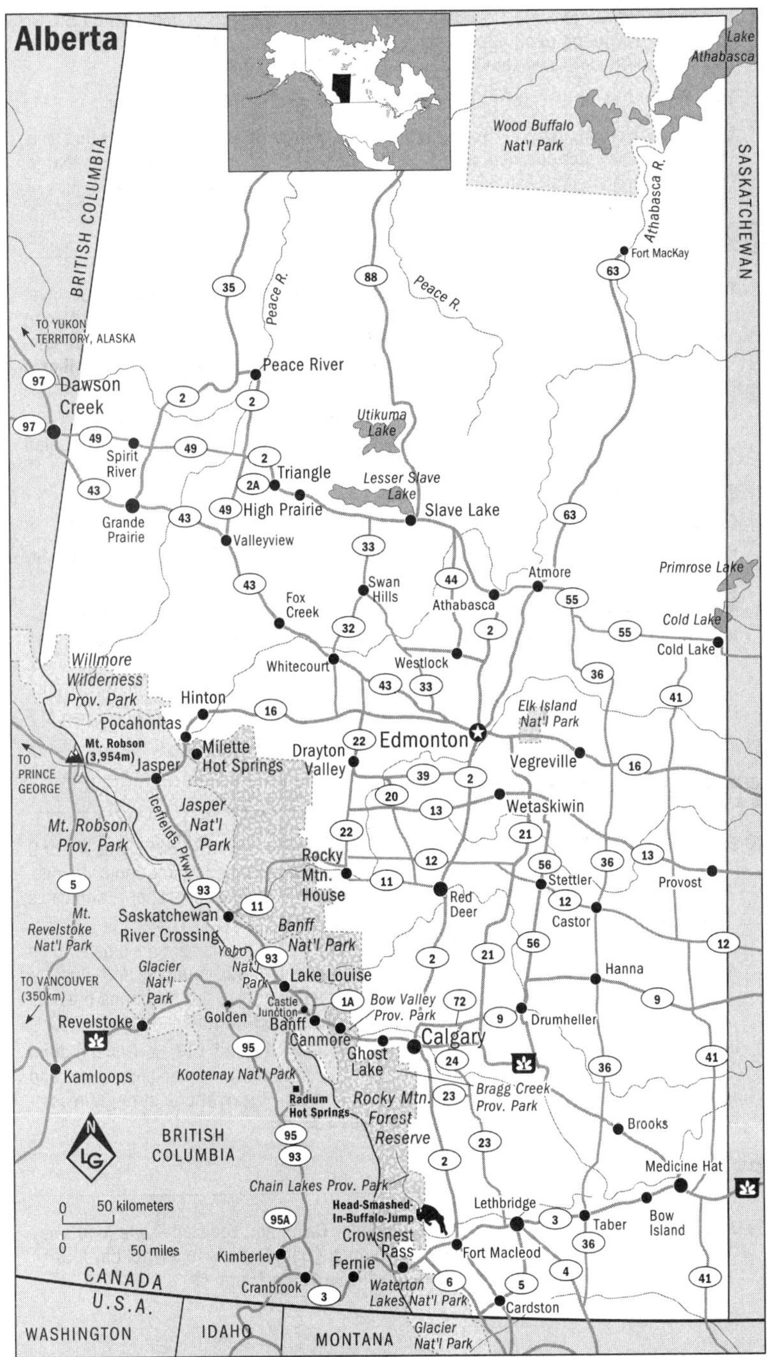
Alberta
Wood Buffalo Nat'l Park
Lake Athabasca
Athabasca R.
SASKATCHEWAN
BRITISH COLUMBIA
Fort MacKay
Peace R.
Peace R.
TO YUKON TERRITORY, ALASKA
Peace River
Dawson Creek
Spirit River
Grande Prairie
Utikuma Lake
Lesser Slave Lake
Triangle
High Prairie
Slave Lake
Valleyview
Atmore
Primrose Lake
Fox Creek
Swan Hills
Athabasca
Cold Lake
Cold Lake
Whitecourt
Westlock
Willmore Wilderness Prov. Park
Hinton
Pocahontas
Mt. Robson (3,954m)
TO PRINCE GEORGE
Jasper
Milette Hot Springs
Edmonton
Elk Island Nat'l Park
Drayton Valley
Vegreville
Wetaskiwin
Icefields Pkwy.
Jasper Nat'l Park
Mt. Robson Prov. Park
Rocky Mtn. House
Red Deer
Stettler
Provost
Castor
Mt. Revelstoke Nat'l Park
Saskatchewan River Crossing
Banff Nat'l Park
Yoho Nat'l Park
Glacier Nat'l Park
TO VANCOUVER (350km)
Lake Louise
Hanna
Castle Junction
Bow Valley Prov. Park
Revelstoke
Golden
Banff
Canmore
Drumheller
Calgary
Ghost Lake
Kamloops
Kootenay Nat'l Park
Bragg Creek Prov. Park
Radium Hot Springs
Rocky Mtn. Forest Reserve
Brooks
BRITISH COLUMBIA
Chain Lakes Prov. Park
Medicine Hat
0 50 kilometers
0 50 miles
Head-Smashed-In-Buffalo-Jump
Lethbridge
Taber
Bow Island
Crowsnest Pass
Fort Macleod
Kimberley
Fernie
CANADA
U.S.A.
Cranbrook
Waterton Lakes Nat'l Park
Cardston
WASHINGTON
IDAHO
MONTANA
Glacier Nat'l Park
WESTERN CANADA

St. and 102 Ave. Runs M-F 9am-3pm, Sa 9am-6pm. $2, over 65 or under 15 $1.50. No bikes on LRT during peak hours traveling in peak direction (M-F 7:30-8:30am and 4-5pm); no bikes on buses. Info booth open M-F 8:30am-4:30pm.

Taxi: Yellow Cab (☎462-3456). **Alberta Co-op Taxi** (☎425-0954). Both 24hr.

Car Rental: Budget, 10016 106 St. (☎448-2000 or 800-661-7027); call for other locations. From $46 per day, with unlimited km. 21+. Ages 21-24 $15 per day surcharge. Must have major credit card. Open M-F 7:30am-6pm, Sa 9am-3pm, Su 9am-2pm.

PRACTICAL INFORMATION

Tourist Information: Edmonton Tourism, Shaw Conference Centre, 9797 Jasper Ave. (☎496-8400 or 800-463-4667), on Pedway Level. Open M-F 8:30am-4:30pm. Also at **Gateway Park** (☎496-8400 or 800-463-4667), on Hwy. 2 south of town. Open summer daily 8am-8pm; winter M-F 8:30am-4:30pm, Sa-Su 9am-5pm. **Travel Alberta** (☎427-4321 or 800-252-3782) is open M-F 7am-7pm, Sa-Su 8:30am-5:30pm.

Gay and Lesbian Services: Gay/Lesbian Community Centre, Ste. 45, 9912 106 St. (☎488-3234). Open M-F 7-10pm. **Womonspace** (☎482-1794) is Edmonton's lesbian group. Call for a recording of local events.

Emergency: ☎911.

Crisis Line: ☎482-4357. **Sexual Assault Centre** ☎423-4121. Both 24hr.

Pharmacy: Shoppers Drug Mart, 11408 Jasper Ave. (☎482-1011), or 8210 109 St. (☎433-2424) by Whyte Ave. Open 24hr.

Medical Services: Royal Alexandra Hospital, 10240 Kingsway Ave. (☎477-4111).

Internet Access: Dow Computer Lab, 11211 142 St. (☎451-3344), at the Odyssium (see **Sights,** below); free with admission. Free at the **library,** 7 Sir Winston Churchill Sq. (☎496-7000); 1hr. per day for a week. Open M-F 9am-9pm, Sa 9am-6pm, Su 1-5pm.

Post Office: 9808 103A Ave. (☎800-267-1177), adjacent to the CN Tower. Open M-F 8am-5:45pm. **Postal Code:** T5J 2G8.

ACCOMMODATIONS

Edmonton International Youth Hostel (HI), 10647 81 Ave. (☎988-6836). Bus #7 or 9 from the 101 St. station to 82 Ave. Facilities include a kitchen, game room, lounge, laundry, and a small backyard. Just around the corner from the clubs, shops, and cafes of Whyte Ave. $20, nonmembers $25; semi-private rooms $22, $27. ❶

St. Joseph's College, 89 Ave. at 114 St. (☎492-7681). The rooms here are smaller than those at the university. Library, huge lounges, rec room, and laundry, and close to sports facilities. Reception open M-F 8:30am-4pm. Call ahead; the 60 dorms often fill up quickly. Rooms available early May-late Aug. Singles $33, with full board $43. ❷

University of Alberta, 87 Ave. (☎492-4281), between 116 and 117 St. Generic dorm rooms. Dry cleaning, kitchen, Internet access ($1 for 10min.), convenience store, and buffet-style cafeteria downstairs. Check-in after 4pm. Reservations strongly recommended. Rooms available late May-Aug. Singles $33. ❷

FOOD

Dadeo's, 10548 Whyte Ave. (☎433-0930). Spicy Cajun and Louisiana-style food away from the bayou at this funky 50s diner. Su brunch 10am-2pm. M-Tu $7 po' boys. Open M-Th 11:30am-11pm, F-Sa 11:30am-midnight, Su 10am-10pm. ❷

The Silk Hat, 10251 Jasper Ave. (☎425-1920). The oldest restaurant in Edmonton maintains enough character and sass to outlive the competition. This diner in the heart of downtown serves a huge array of food, from seafood to veggie-burgers ($6.25) to breakfast all day. Open M-F 7am-8pm, Sa 10am-8pm. ❶

The Pita Pit, 8109 104 St. (☎435-3200), near Whyte Ave. Surprisingly delicious pitas, fast-food style. Souvlaki $5.25. Students don't pay sales tax. Open Su noon-3am, M-W 11am-3am, Th-Sa 11am-4am. ❶

Kids in the Hall Bistro, 1 Sir Winston Churchill Sq. (☎413-8060), in City Hall. This lunchroom is truly one-of-a-kind. Every employee, from waiter to chef, is a young person hired as part of a cooperative community service project. Various entrees ($5-10) and sandwiches ($5-7). Takeout available. Open M-F 8am-4pm. ❷

SIGHTS

WEST EDMONTON MALL. Yet another blow against Mother Nature in the battle for tourists, the $1.3 billion **the world's biggest mall** engulfs the general area between 170 St. and 87 Ave., water slides, the world's largest indoor wave pool, an amusement park, miniature golf, dozens of exotic animals, over 800 stores, an ice-skating rink, 110 eateries, a full-scale replica of Columbus' *Santa Maria*, an indoor bungee jumping facility, a casino, a luxury hotel, a dolphin show, swarms of teenagers, and twice as many submarines as the navy. Just remember where you park. *(Bus# 1, 2, 100, or 111. ☎444-5200 or 800-661-8890; www.westedmall.com. Open M-F 10am-9pm, Sa 10am-6pm, Su noon-6pm. Amusement park open later.)*

FORT EDMONTON PARK. At the park's far end sits the fort proper: a 19th-century office building for Alberta's first capitalists, the fur traders of the Hudson Bay Company. Between the fort and the park entrance are three streets—1885, 1905, and 1920 St.—bedecked with period buildings from apothecaries to blacksmith shops, all decorated to match the streets' respective eras. *(Park: On Whitemud Dr. at Fox Dr. Buses #2, 4, 30, 31, 35, 106, and 315 stop near the park. ☎496-8787; www.gov.edmonton.ab.ca/fort. Open mid-May to late June M-F 10am-4pm, Sa-Su 10am-6pm; late June to early Sept. daily 10am-6pm; rest of Sept. wagon tours only from M-Sa 11am-3pm, Su 10am-6pm. $8.25, seniors and ages 13-17 $6.25, ages 2-12 $4.50, families $26.)*

ODYSSIUM. The reincarnated Space and Science Centre still appeals to the curiosities of all ages with exhibits on the human body and the environment, including a **Gallery of the Gross** and a hands-on **Crime Lab.** Housed in a building shaped like an alien spacecraft, the largest **planetarium dome** in Canada uses a booming 23,000 watts of audio during its laser light shows. The **IMAX theater** makes the planetarium seem like a child's toy. *(11211 142 St. ☎451-3344; www.odyssium.com. Open summer daily 10am-9pm; winter Su-Th 10am-5pm, F-Sa 10am-9pm. Day pass includes planetarium shows and exhibits: $10, students and seniors $8, ages 3-12 $7; families $39. General admission and IMAX show $16, students and seniors $13, ages 3-12 $11; families $60.)*

RIVER VALLEY. The best part of Edmonton would have to be the longest stretch of urban parkland in Canada. Edmonton's **River Valley** boasts over 50km of easy to moderate paved multi-use trails and 69km of granular and chip trails for hiking and cycling. Any route down the river leads to the linked trail system; pick up a map at the Ranger Station. *(12130 River Valley Rd. ☎496-2950. Open daily 7am-1am.)*

FESTIVALS & ENTERTAINMENT

"Canada's Festival City" (www.festivalcity.com) is hosting some kind of celebration year-round. The **Jazz City International Music Festival** packs 10 days with club dates and free performances by top international and Canadian jazz musicians. (☎432-7166. June 25-July 4, 2004.) Around the same time is a visual arts celebration called **The Works.** (☎426-2122. June 25-July 7, 2004.) In August, the **Folk Music Festival,** considered one of the best in North America, takes over Gallagher Park. (☎429-1899. Aug. 5-8, 2004.) All the world's a stage for the **Fringe Theater Festival,** when top alternative music and theater pours from parks, stages, and streets. This is the high point of Edmonton's festival schedule, and 500,000 travelers come to the city just to find the Fringe. (☎448-9000. Mid-Aug.)

The **Edmonton Oilers,** the local NHL franchise, remain in an extended rebuilding period following their glorious Wayne Gretzky-led Stanley Cup runs of the 1980s. But this is Canada, and it is hockey. The Oilers play at 11230 110th St. (☎451-8000; www.edmontonoilers.com. Season runs Oct.-April.)

NIGHTLIFE

Squire's, 10505 82 Ave. (☎439-8594), lower level by Chianti. Popular with the college crowd. Nightly drink specials. Open M-Tu 7pm-3am, W-Su 5pm-3am.

The Armory, 10310 85 Ave. (☎432-7300). This well-known dance club shows Edmonton's younger crowd how to party. M is Ladies Night, with $1 highballs until 11pm. Th is "Lowball" Night, with $2.50 highballs. Open M and Th-Sa 9pm-2am.

Blues on Whyte, 10329 82 Ave. (☎439-5058). If blues is what you want, blues is what you'll get. Live blues and R&B from top-notch performers every night; Sa afternoon jam starts at 3pm. This joint may deserve its reputation as a biker bar; these blues are anything but sedate. 8 oz. glasses of beer for just $1. Open daily 10am-3am.

CALGARY ☎403

Mounties founded Calgary in the 1870s to control Canada's flow of illegal whisky, but oil made the city what it is today. Petroleum fuels Calgary's economy and explains why the city hosts the most corporate headquarters in Canada outside of Toronto. As the host of the 1988 Winter Olympics, Calgary's dot on the map grew larger; already Alberta's largest city, this thriving young metropolis is the second fastest-growing in all of Canada.

TRANSPORTATION

Flights: The **airport** (☎735-1200) is 17km northeast of the city center. Take Bus #57.

Buses: Greyhound, 877 Greyhound Way SW (☎260-0877 or 800-661-8747). To: **Banff** (1¾hr., 4 per day, $23); **Drumheller** (2hr., 3 per day, $25); **Edmonton** (3½-5hr., 10-11 per day, $44), with lower student rates. Free shuttle from Calgary Transit C-Train at 7th Ave. and 10th St. to bus depot (every hr. near the ½hr. 6:30am-7:30pm). **Red Arrow,** 205 9th Ave. SE (☎531-0350), goes to **Edmonton** (4-7 per day, $51) and points north. 10% HI discount; student and senior rates. **Brewster Tours** (☎221-8242), from the airport to **Banff** (2hr., 2 per day, $42) and **Jasper** (8hr., 1 per day, $80). 10% HI discount.

Public Transportation: Calgary Transit, 240 7th Ave. SW (☎262-1000). Open M-F 8:30am-5pm. C-Trains free in downtown zone on 7th Ave. S from 3rd St. E to 10th St W. Buses and C-Trains outside downtown $2, ages 6-14 $1.25, under 6 free. Day pass $5.60, ages 6-14 $3.60. Book of 10 tickets $17.50, ages 6-14 $10. Runs M-F 6am-midnight, Sa-Su 6am-9:30pm. Tickets at stops, the transit office, or Safeway stores.

Taxi: Checker Cab ☎299-9999. **Yellow Cab** ☎974-1111.

Car Rental: Rent-A-Wreck, 113 42nd Ave. SW (☎287-1444). From $40 per day. $0.12 per km over 250km. 21+. Need credit card. Open M-F 8am-6pm, Sa-Su 9am-5pm.

PRACTICAL INFORMATION

Tourist Information: ☎800-661-1678; www.tourismcalgary.com. A booth at the airport is open daily.

American Express: Boulevard Travel, 1322 15th Ave. SW (☎237-6233). Open M-F 8am-5:30pm.

Equipment Rental: Outdoor Program Centre, 2500 University Dr. (☎220-5038), at U of Calgary, rents tents (from $10), canoes ($18), and downhill skis ($21). Open daily 8am-8pm. **Mountain Equipment Co-op,** 830 10th Ave. (☎269-2420) rents watercraft ($15-55 per day, including all safety equipment and paddles), camping gear ($4-21), rock- and ice-climbing gear ($4-22), and snow sports equipment ($8-35). Both companies have weekend specials. Be prepared to shell out a large deposit.

Gay and Lesbian Services: Events and clubs ☎234-9752. Counseling ☎234-8973.

Weather: ☎299-7878.

Emergency: ☎911.

Pharmacy: Shopper's Drug Mart, 6455 Macleod Trail S (☎253-2424). Open 24hr.

Medical Services: Peter Lougheed Centre, 3500 26th Ave. NE (☎943-4555).

Internet Access: At the **library,** 616 Macleod Trail SE (☎260-2600). $2 per hr. Open M-Th 10am-9pm, F-Sa 10am-5pm; mid-Sept. to mid-May also Su 1:30-5pm.

Post Office: 207 9th Ave. SW (☎974-2078). Open M-F 8am-5:45pm. **Postal Code:** T2P 2G8.

ACCOMMODATIONS

Calgary International Hostel (HI), 520 7th Ave. SE (☎269-8239), near downtown. Walk east along 7th Ave. from the 3rd St. SE C-Train station; the hostel is on the left just past 4th St. SE. Busy and sometimes impersonal, this urban hostel has some nice accessories; the clean kitchen, lounge areas, laundry, and backyard with barbecue are pluses. Information desk, occasional guest activities. Wheelchair-accessible. 120 beds. $22, nonmembers $26; Oct. 16-May 1: $17, $21. Private rooms $75, nonmembers $83. ❶

University of Calgary, the ex-Olympic Village in the NW quadrant, far from downtown if you're walking. Accessible by bus #9 or a 12min. walk from the University C-Train stop. Popular with conventioneers and often booked solid. Coordinated through **Cascade Hall,** 3456 24th Ave. NW (☎220-3203). Rooms available May-Aug. only. Shared rooms $25 per person; singles $34-100. Rates subject to change; call ahead. ❶

YWCA, 320 5th Ave. SE (☎232-1599). Walk 2 blocks north of the 3rd St. SE C-Train station. 2 newly renovated residential floors. **Women only.** 150 beds available. Singles from $40; doubles from $50; triples $130; quads $140. Seniors 10% discount. ❸

FOOD

Thi-Thi Submarine, 209 1st St. SE (☎265-5452). Some people have closets larger than Thi-Thi, but this place manages to pack in 2 plastic seats, a bank of toaster ovens, and the finest Vietnamese submarines in Calgary. Most meaty subs are sub-$5; the veggie sub is an unreal $2.25. Open M-F 10am-7pm, Sa-Su 10:30am-5pm. ❶

Peter's Drive In, 219 16th Ave. NE (☎277-2747). Peachy keen! A generational anomaly and worthy destination, Peter's is one of the city's last remaining drive-ins. Hordes of chummy patrons attest to the swell quality. Drive-in or walk to the service window. Famous milkshakes under $3 and burgers under $4. Open daily 9am-midnight. ❶

Take 10 Cafe, 304 10th St. NW (☎270-7010). Take 10 became a local favorite by offering dirt-cheap, high-quality food. All burgers are under $5.75, and the menu also sports some sizzling Chinese food (under $8). Open M-F 9am-4pm, Sa-Su 8:30am-3pm. ❷

Wicked Wedge, 618 17th Ave. SW (☎228-1024). Serves large, topping-heavy slices of pizza ($3.75) to Calgary's post-party scene. 3 varieties of pie dished out nightly. Open M-Th 11am-midnight, F-Sa 11am-3am, Su 11am-midnight. ❷

SIGHTS

OLYMPIC LEFTOVERS. For two glorious weeks in 1988, the world's eyes were on Calgary for the Winter Olympics. Almost fifteen years later, the world has moved on, but the city still has some very exciting facilities, and relentlessly clings to its two weeks of Olympic stardom. Visit the **Canada Olympic Park** and its looming ski jumps and twisted bobsled and luge tracks. The **Olympic Hall of Fame,** also at Olympic Park, honors Olympic achievements with displays, films, and a **bobsled simulator.** In summer, the park opens its hills and a lift to **mountain bikers.** *(A 10min. drive northwest of downtown on Hwy. 1. ☎247-5452. Open summer daily 8am-9pm; winter M-F 9am-9pm, Sa-Su 9am-5pm. $10 ticket includes chair-lift and entrance to ski-jump buildings, Hall of Fame, and icehouse. Tour $15; families $45. Mountain biking open May-Oct. daily 9am-9pm. Roadway pass $9 for cyclists. Front-suspension bike rental $12 per hr., $31 per day.)* Keep an eye out for ski-jumpers, who practice at the facility year-round. The miniature mountain (113m vertical) also opens up for recreational **downhill skiing** in winter. *(Snow report ☎289-3700. $21.)* The **Olympic Oval,** an enormous indoor speed-skating track on the University of Calgary campus, remains a major international training facility. Speedskaters work out in the early morning and late afternoon; sit in the bleachers and observe the action for free. *(☎220-7890; www.oval.ucalgary.ca. Public skating hours vary, so call ahead. $4.75, children and seniors $2.75; families $10.50, under 6 free. Skate rental under $5.)*

PARKS AND MUSEUMS. Footbridges stretch from either side of the Bow River to **Prince's Island Park,** a natural refuge only blocks from the city center. In July and August, Mount Royal College performs **Shakespeare in the Park.** *(☎240-6908. Various matinees and evening shows; call for shows and times.)* Calgary's other island park, **St. George's Island,** is accessible by the river walkway to the east or by driving. It houses the **Calgary Zoo,** including a botanical garden and children's zoo. For those who missed the wildlife in Banff and Jasper, the **Canadian Wilds** exhibit has recreated animal habitats. For those who missed the Cretaceous Period, life-sized plastic dinosaurs are also on exhibit. *(Parking is off Memorial Dr. on the north side of the river. ☎232-9300. Open daily 9am-5pm. $15, seniors $13, ages 13-17 $9, ages 3-12 $6.50.)*

STAMPEDE. The more cosmopolitan Calgary becomes, the more tenaciously it clings to its frontier roots. The **Stampede** draws one million cowboys and tourists each summer, in the first couple weeks of July, when the grounds are packed for world-class steer wrestling, bareback and bull-riding, pig and chuck wagon races. Check out the livestock shows, cruise the midway and casino, ride the roller coaster, or hear live country music and marching bands. The festival spills into the streets from first thing in the morning (free pancake breakfasts all around) through the night. Depending on your attitude, the Stampede will either be an impressive spectacle rekindling the Western spirit or an overpriced, slick carnival where humans assert their hegemony over lesser animals. *(Stampede Park is just southeast of downtown, bordering the east side of Macleod Trail between 14th Ave. SE and the Elbow River. The C-Train features a Stampede stop. Tickets ☎269-9822 or 800-661-1767; www.calgarystampede.com. $11, ages 65+ and 7-12 $6, under 7 free. Rodeo and evening shows $22-63, rush tickets on sale at the grandstand 1½hr. before showtime.)*

NIGHTLIFE

Nightgallery Cabaret, 1209B 1st St. SW (☎264-4484, www.nightgallerycabaret.com). A large dance floor and a diverse program attract clubbers. House at "Sunday Skool." Reggae-Dub on M draws a slightly older crowd. Call for info. Open daily 8pm-3am.

Vicious Circle, 1011 1st St. SW (☎269-3951). A very relaxing bar, "The Vish" offers a solid menu, colored mood lights, and a disco ball, plus pool tables, couches, eclectic local art, and TV. All kinds of coffee, a full bar, and 140 different martinis. Summer patio seating. Happy Hour all night Su, live music W. Open M-Th 11:30am-1am, F 11:30am-2am, Sa-Su noon-2am.

Eau Claire Market IMAX, 132 200 Barclay Parade SW (☎974-4629). Pit your imagination against a large-screen feature that claims to be bigger. Box office open M-F 11:30am-10pm, Sa-Su 10:30am-10pm. IMAX films $10.50, ages 65 and up $8.50, under 13 $7.50, night double feature $15. Also at Eau Claire, Cineplex Odeon shows regular films; call for times (☎263-3166).

DAYTRIP FROM CALGARY: ALBERTA BADLANDS

Once the fertile shallows of a huge ocean, the Badlands are now one of the richest dinosaur fossil sites in the world. After the sea dried up, wind, water, and ice molded twisting canyons into sandstone and shale bedrock, creating the desolate splendor of the Alberta Badlands. The **Royal Tyrrell Museum of Paleontology** (TEER-ull), with its remarkable array of dinosaur exhibits and hands-on paleontological opportunities, is the region's main attraction. **Greyhound** runs from Calgary to **Drumheller** (1¾hr., 2 per day, $24), which is 6km southeast of the museum.

ROYAL TYRRELL MUSEUM OF PALEONTOLOGY. The world's largest display of dinosaur specimens is a forceful reminder that *Homo sapiens* missed out on the first 2½ billion years of life on earth. From the Big Bang to the present, the museum celebrates evolution's grand parade with quality displays, videos, computer activities, and towering skeletons, including one of only 12 reconstructed

Tyrannosaurus rex skeletons in existence. You cannot miss the Predator Room, which features cunning dinosaurs and creepy background lighting. It does not, at any point in earth's evolution, ever get cooler than this. *(6km northwest of Drumheller, which itself lies 138km northeast of Calgary. Get there by driving east on Hwy. 1 from Calgary, then northeast on Hwy. 9. ☎403-823-7707 or 888-440-4240; www.tyrrellmuseum.com. Open Victoria Day-Labour Day daily 9am-9pm; Labour Day-Thanksgiving daily 10am-5pm; Thanksgiving to Victoria Day Tu-Su 10am-5pm. $10, seniors $8, ages 7-17 $6, under 7 free, families $30.)*

DIGS. The museum's hugely popular 12-person **Day Digs** include instruction in paleontology and excavation techniques, and a chance to dig in a fossil quarry. The fee includes lunch and transportation; participants must also agree that all finds go to the museum. *(July-Aug. daily; June Sa-Su. Digs depart 8:30am, returning 4pm. $90, ages 10-15 $60. Reservations required; call the museum.)*

DINOSAUR PROVINCIAL PARK AND BADLANDS BUS TOUR. The Badlands, a UNESCO World Heritage Site, are the source of many finds on display at the Tyrrell Museum; more fossil species—over 300, including 35 species of dinosaurs—were discovered here than anywhere else in the world. The museum's **Field Station,** 48km east of the town of **Brooks** in **Dinosaur Provincial Park,** contains a small museum, but the main attraction is the **Badlands Bus Tour.** The bus chauffeurs visitors into a restricted hot spot of dinosaur finds. Many fossils still lie within the eroding rock. The park's **campground** ❶ is shaded from summer heat, and grassy plots cushion most sites. Although it stays open year-round, the campground only has power and running water in summer. *(To reach the Field Station from Drumheller, follow Hwy. 56 south for 65km, then take Hwy. 1 about 70km to Brooks. Once in Brooks, go north along Hwy. 873 and east along Hwy. 544. Field Station ☎378-4342. Field Station Visitor Centre exhibits $3, seniors $2.50, ages 7-17 $2. Open mid-Oct. to mid-May M-F 9am-4pm; mid-May through Aug. daily 8:30am-9pm; Sept. to mid-Oct. daily 9am-5pm. Tours $6.50, ages 7-17 $4.25. Reservations ☎378-4344. Sites $15; with power $18.)*

THE ROCKIES

Every year, some five million visitors make it within sight of the Rockies' majestic peaks and stunning glacial lakes. Thankfully, much of this traffic is confined to highwayside gawkers, and only a tiny fraction of these visitors make it far into the forest. Of the big two national parks—Banff and Jasper—Jasper feels a little farther removed from the crowds and offers great wildlife viewing from the road. Without a car, guided bus rides may be the easiest way to see some of the park's main attractions. **Brewster Tours** has an express bus from Banff to Jasper and offers tours at an additional cost. (☎403-762-6767. 9½hr.; $57.) **Bigfoot Tours** does the trip in two days. (☎888-244-6673 or 604-278-8224. $95.)

BANFF NATIONAL PARK & LAKE LOUISE ☎403

Banff is Canada's best-loved and best-known natural park, with 6641 square kilometers of peaks, forests, glaciers, and alpine valleys. Itinerant twenty-somethings arrive with mountain bikes, climbing gear, and skis, but a trusty pair of hiking boots remains the park's most popular outdoor equipment.

ORIENTATION & PRACTICAL INFORMATION. The park hugs Alberta's border with BC, 129km west of Calgary. Civilization in the park centers around the towns of **Banff** and **Lake Louise,** 58km apart on Hwy. 1. All of the following info applies to Banff Townsite, unless otherwise specified. **Greyhound,** 100 Gopher St. (☎800-661-8747; depot open daily 7:45am-9pm), runs to Calgary (1½hr., 5 per day, $23) and Vancouver, BC (12½-15hr., 4 per day, $118). **Brewster Transportation,** 100 Gopher St. (☎762-6767), runs buses to: Calgary (2hr., $42); Jasper (5hr., $57); and Lake Louise (1hr., $13.50). The **Banff Visitor Centre,** 224 Banff Ave., includes the **Banff/Lake Louise Tourism Bureau** and the **Canadian Parks Service.** (Tourism Bureau: ☎762-8421. Parks Service: ☎762-1550. Open daily June-Sept. 8am-8pm; Oct.-May 9am-5pm.) **Lake Louise Visitor Centre,** at Samson Mall in Lake Louise, shares a building with a museum. (☎522-3833. Open daily June-Sept. 9am-7pm; Oct.-May 9am-4pm.) **Post Office:** 204 Buffalo St. (☎762-2586. Open M-W 8:30am-5:30pm, Th-F until 7pm, Sa until 5pm.) **Postal Code:** T0L 0C0. **Area Code:** 403.

ACCOMMODATIONS & FOOD. HI runs a **shuttle service** connecting all the Rocky Mountain hostels and Calgary ($8-90). Beds on the wait-list become available at 6pm, and the larger hostels save some standby beds. **Lake Louise Alpine Centre (HI-C) ❶,** 500m west of the Visitors Center in Lake Louise Townsite, on Village Rd., is more like a hotel with a reference library, common rooms with open, beamed ceilings, a stone fireplace, two full kitchens, ski/bike workshops, and a cafe. (☎670-7580. Dorms $24-34, nonmembers $28-38. Private rooms also. Wheelchair-accessible.) **Castle Mountain Hostel (HI-C) ❶,** on Hwy. 1A, 1.5km east of the junction of Hwy. 1 and Hwy. 93, between Banff and Lake Louise. A quieter alternative, with running water, electricity, a general store, a library, and a fireplace. (☎670-7580 or 866-762-4122. Linen $1. Dorms $19, nonmembers $23). Three rustic hostels—**Hilda Creek ❶, Rampart Creek ❶,** and **Mosquito Creek ❶**—can be booked by calling Banff International Hostel. At any of Banff's park **campgrounds,** sites are first come, first served ($10-24). On Hwy. 1A between Banff Townsite and Lake Louise, **Johnston Canyon ❶** is close to hiking. The only winter campsite is Village 2 of **Tunnel Mountain Village ❶,** 4km from Banff Townsite, on Tunnel Mountain Rd.

FLOUR POWER Many lakes and streams in the Rockies have an unusual color. Noticing the swimming-pool's glowing blue color, you might wonder if this is a gimmick staged by park wardens attract tourists. In reality, the cause of the color is **rock flour.** This fine dust is created by the pressure exerted by the glacier upon rocks trapped within the ice; the resulting ground-up rock is washed into streams and lakes in the glacial meltwater. Suspended particles trap all colors of the spectrum except for the blues and greens that are reflected back for your visual pleasure.

The Banff and Lake Louise Hostels serve affordable meals ($3-8), but **Laggan's Deli ❶** (☎522-2017), in Samson Mall in Lake Louise, is the best thing going. A thick sandwich on whole wheat costs $4-5; a fresh-baked loaf to save for later runs $3. **Aardvark's ❸,** 304A Caribou St., does big business after the bars close. The place is skinny on seating but serves thick slices of pizza. (☎762-5500. Slices $3; small pizza $6-9, large $13-21. Open daily 11am-4am.)

OUTDOOR ACTIVITIES. Near Banff Townsite, **Fenland Trail** (2km, 1hr.) zooms through an area shared by beaver, muskrat, and waterfowl, but is closed for elk calving in late spring and early summer. Follow Mt. Norquay Rd. out of town and look for signs across the tracks on the road's left side. The summit of **Tunnel Mountain** (2.3km, 2hr.) provides a dramatic view of the **Bow Valley** and **Mt. Rundle.** Follow Wolf St. east from Banff Ave. and turn right on St. Julien Rd. to reach the head of the steep trail. At 2949m, Mt. Rundle offers a more demanding day hike (5.5km; 7-8hr.; 1600m elevation gain). **Johnston Canyon,** about 25km from Banff toward Lake Louise along the Bow Valley Pkwy. (Hwy. 1A), is a popular half-day hike that runs past waterfalls to blue-green cold-water springs known as the **Inkpots.**

The park might not exist if not for the **Cave and Basin Hot Springs,** southwest of town on Cave Ave., once rumored to have miraculous healing properties. The **Cave and Basin National Historic Site,** a resort built circa 1914, is now a museum. (☎762-1566. Open daily summer 9am-6pm; winter 9:30am-5pm. Tours 11am, daily summer, weekends-only in winter. $4, seniors $3.50, ages 6-18 $3.) For a dip in the hot springs, follow the sulphuric smell to the 40°C (104°F) pools.

The highest community in Canada, at 1530m (5018 ft.), Lake Louise and its surrounding glaciers have often passed for Swiss scenery in movies. Once at the lake, the hardest task is escaping fellow gawkers at the posh **Château Lake Louise.** Several hiking trails begin at the water; the 3.6km **Lake Agnes Trail** and the 5.5km **Plain of Six Glaciers Trail** both end at teahouses.

Fishing is legal in most of the park's bodies of water during specific seasons, but live bait and lead weights are not. Permits ($6) are available at the Visitors Center. Winter activities range from world-class ice climbing to ice fishing. Those 1600km of hiking trails make for exceptional **cross-country skiing,** and three allied resorts offer a range of **skiing** and **snowboarding** opportunities from early November to mid-May. **Sunshine Mountain** has the largest snowfall (reservations and snowfall ☎762-6500 or 760-7669; lift tickets $59); **Mt. Norquay** is smaller, closer to town, and less busy (☎762-4421; $49); but **Lake Louise,** the second-biggest ski area in Canada, has the most expert terrain (☎522-3555, snow report 762-4766; $58).

SCENIC DRIVE: ICEFIELDS PARKWAY

The 230km Icefields Parkway is one of the most beautiful routes in North America, heading north from Lake Louise to Jasper Townsite. Free maps of the Parkway are available at Visitors Centers in Jasper and Banff, or at the **Icefield Centre,** at the boundary between the two parks, 132km north of Lake Louise and 103km south of Jasper Townsite. (☎780-852-6288. Open May to mid-Oct. daily 9am-5pm.) Although the center is closed in winter, the parkway is only closed for plowing after heavy snowfalls. An extensive campground and hostel network along the Parkway makes longer trips convenient and affordable. **Cycling** the highway is also a popular option; bikes can be rented in Banff or Jasper for a one-way trip.

However you travel the Parkway, set aside time for hikes and magnificent vistas. At **Bow Summit,** the Parkway's highest point (2135m), a 10min. walk leads to a view of fluorescent aqua **Peyto Lake,** especially vivid toward the end of June. The **Athabasca Glacier,** a great white whale of an ice flow, spreads from the 325 sq. km **Columbia Icefield,** the largest accumulation of ice and snow between the Arctic and Antarctic Circles. **Columbia Icefield Snocoach Tours** carries visitors right onto the glacier in bizarre monster buses for an 1¼hr. trip. (☎877-423-7433. Open Apr.-Oct. daily 9am-5pm. $28, ages 6-15 $14.)

JASPER NATIONAL PARK ☎780

Northward expansion of the Canadian railway system led to the exploration of the Canadian Rockies and the creation of Jasper National Park in 1907. The largest of the four national parks in the region, Jasper encompasses herculean peaks and plummeting valleys that dwarf the battalion of motorhomes and charter buses parading through the region. In the winter, the crowds melt away, a blanket of snow descends, and a ski resort welcomes visitors to a slower, more relaxed town.

PRACTICAL INFORMATION. All of the addresses below are in **Jasper Townsite,** near the center of the park. **VIA Rail** (☎888-842-7245), on Connaught Dr., sends three trains per week to Edmonton (5hr., $151) and Vancouver (17hr., $210). **Greyhound** (☎852-3926), in the train station, runs to Edmonton (4½hr., 3 per day, $55) and Vancouver (11-12hr., 3 per day, $109). **Brewster Transportation Tours** (☎852-3332), in the station, runs daily to Calgary (7½hr., $80) via Banff (5½hr., $57). The **Park Information Centre,** 500 Connaught Dr., has trail maps. (☎852-6176. Open daily mid-June to early Sept. 8am-7pm; early Sept.-late Oct. and late Dec. to mid-June 9am-5pm.) In an **emergency,** call ☎911 or 852-4421. **Post Office:** 502 Patricia St. (☎852-3041. Open M-F 9am-5pm.) **Postal Code:** T0E 1E0. **Area Code:** 780.

ACCOMMODATIONS. HI runs a shuttle service connecting all the Rocky Mountain hostels and Calgary; call the Jasper Hostel for reservations. The modern **Jasper International Hostel (HI-C) ❶,** 3km up Whistlers Rd. from Hwy. 93, also known as **Whistlers Hostel,** anchors the chain of HI hostels stretching from Jasper to Calgary. Jasper International attracts gregarious backpackers and cyclists, but a "leave-your-hiking-boots-outside" rule keeps the hardwood floors and dorm rooms clean. (☎852-3215 or 877-852-0781 for all HI hostels. Curfew 2am. Dorms $18-20, nonmembers $23-25.) **Maligne Canyon Hostel (HI-C) ❶,** 11km east of town on Hwy. 16, has small cabins on the bank of the Maligne River. (Check-in 5-11pm. Oct.-Apr. $13, nonmembers $18.) **Mt. Edith Cavell Hostel (HI-C) ❶,** 12km up Edith Cavell Rd., off Hwy. 93, offers cozy quarters with wood-burning stoves. In winter, the road is closed, but pick up keys at Jasper International Hostel and ski there. (Propane, pump water, solar shower, firepit. Dorms $13, nonmembers $18.)

Most of Jasper's campgrounds have primitive sites with few facilities ($13-22). They are first come, first served, and none are open in winter. Call the park Visitors Center (☎852-6176) for details. A 781-site behemoth, **Whistlers ❶,** on Whistlers Rd., off Hwy. 93, is closest to the townsite. (Open early May to mid-Oct. $13, full hookup $30.) The highlight of the Icefields Pkwy. campgrounds is **Columbia Icefield ❶,** 109km south of the townsite, which lies close enough to the Athabasca Glacier to intercept an icy breeze and even a rare summer night's snowfall. **Mountain Foods and Cafe ❷,** 606 Connaught Dr., offers a wide selection of sandwiches, salads, home-cooked goodies, and take-out lunches for the trail. Turkey focaccia sandwich and assorted wraps are $7.50, and a fantastic breakfast special is $5.50. (☎852-4050. Open daily 8am-8pm.)

OUTDOOR ACTIVITIES. The Visitors Center distributes *Day Hikes in Jasper National Park.* **Cavell Meadows Loop,** featuring views of the glacier-laden peak of **Mt. Edith Cavell,** is a rewarding half-day hike. The trailhead is 30km south of the townsite; take Hwy. 93 to 93A to the end of the bumpy 15km Mt. Edith Cavell Rd. (Open June-Oct.) Or tackle the **Sulpher Skyline Trail,** a challenging 4-6hr. hike with views of the limestone Miette Range and Ashlar Ridge (9.6km round-trip, 700m elevation gain). The trail leaves from the **Miette Hot Springs,** 42km north of the townsite on Hwy. 16. (☎866-3939. Open daily mid-June to Oct. 8:30am-10:30pm; early Oct. and May to mid-June 10:30am-9pm. $6.25; swimsuit $1.50.)

The spectacular, if overcrowded, **Maligne Canyon** is 11km east of the townsite on Maligne Lake Rd. From the trailhead, a 4km path follows the Maligne River as it plunges through the narrow limestone gorge, across footbridges, and eventually into Medicine Lake. Brilliant turquoise **Maligne Lake,** the longest

(22km) and deepest lake in the park, sprawls at the end of Maligne Lake Rd. The **Opal Hills Trail** (8.2km loop) winds through subalpine meadows and ascends 460m to views of the lake. **Maligne Tours,** 627 Patricia St., rents kayaks and leads fishing, canoeing, rabbiting, horseback riding, hiking, and whitewater rafting tours. (☎852-3370. Kayaks $85 per day.) **Rocky Mountain Unlimited** serves as a central reservation service for many local outdoor businesses. They provide prices and recommendations for rafting, fishing, horseback riding, and wildlife safaris. (☎852-4056. Open daily 9am-9pm; winter 8am-6pm.) **Fishing permits** are available at fishing shops and the Parks Canada Visitors Center ($7 per day, $20 per year).

The **Jasper Tramway,** 4km up Whistlers Rd., climbs 1200m up Whistlers Mt., leading to a panoramic view of the park and, on a clear day, very far beyond. (☎852-3093. Open daily Apr.-May. 9:30am-4:30pm; June 9:30am-6:30pm; July 8:30am-10pm; Aug. 9am-9pm; Sept. 9:30am-6pm. $20, 5-14 $10, under 5 free.) The demanding 9km **Whistlers Trail** covers the same ground.

THE YUKON TERRITORY

If you want to be alone with the land, then go to the Yukon, where vistas cross glaciated, sawtooth mountains and ease down into lakes, tundra, verdant forests, and plateaus. And best of all for adventure travelers and solitude-seekers, most of it is virtually unpopulated. The human footprint on the land vanishes meters away from asphalt, and the highway system is but a tiny skeleton laid over a huge area. It's an intimidating wilderness territory, but one that demands exploration

WHITEHORSE ☎867

Whitehorse was born during the Klondike Gold Rush, when gold-hungry prospectors used it as a layover on their journey north. As the territorial capital, Whitehorse is home to 23,000 folks—70% of the territory's residents. The town itself is clogged with acres of RVs during the summer, and an adventure traveler's best bet is to mine Whitehorse for provisions and head out into the surrounding wilds—the drone of urban life disappears just a kilometer or two outside city limits.

TRANSPORTATION & PRACTICAL INFORMATION. Whitehorse is 1471km northwest of Dawson Creek, BC, along the Alaska Highway, and 536km south of Dawson City. The Whitehorse Airport (☎888-247-2262) is off the Alaska Hwy., southwest of downtown, serviced mainly by Air Canada. Alaska Direct, 509 Main St. (☎668-4833 or 800-770-6652), runs 3 buses per week to Anchorage, AK ($165) and Fairbanks, AK ($140); and Skagway, AK (M at 12pm, $50). Greyhound, 2191 2nd Ave., services Dawson Creek ($187) and Vancouver, BC ($340). (☎667-2223) Whitehorse Transit has limited service to downtown, the airport, Robert Service Campground, and Yukon College. (☎668-7433. M-Th 6:15am-7:30pm, F 6:15am-10:30pm, Sa 8am-7pm. $1.50.) Yellow Cab (☎668-4811) has 24hr. service. Norcan Leasing, 213 Range Rd., rents only to those 21+ with a credit card. (☎668-2137; www.norcan.yk.ca. Compacts from $50 per day. Winter prices lower.)

The **Tourism Centre,** 100 Hanson St., provides multilingual help. (☎667-3084. Open daily mid-May to mid-Sept. 8am-8pm; winter M-F 9am-5pm.) The **Yukon Conservation Society,** 302 Hawkins St., has advice on paddles and hikes, and publishes the *Whitehorse Area Hikes and Bikes.* (☎668-5678; www.yukonconservation.org.) The **Post Office,** 211 Main St., is in the basement of **Shopper's Drug Mart.** (☎667-2485. Open M-F 9am-6pm, Sa 11am-4pm.) **General delivery** is at 300 Range Rd. (☎667-2412. Open daily 10am-1:40pm and 2:15-4:45pm.) **Postal Code:** for last names beginning with A-L: Y1A 3S7; for M-Z: Y1A 3S8. **Area Code:** 867.

ACCOMMODATIONS & FOOD. Stay in the continent-themed room of your choice and pick your endangered species-labeled bed in Hide on Jeckell Guesthouse ❶, 410 Jeckell, between 4th Ave. and 5th Ave. (☎633-4933. Free kitchen, bikes, Internet, linens, lockers, and outdoor grill. No curfew. 6 dormitory-style rooms, 2 family rooms. $20 per person.) Clean and friendly, Beez Kneez Bakpakers Hostel ❷, 408 Hoge St., off 4th Ave., is equipped with Internet and a barbecue deck. (☎456-2333. 8 bunks $20 each; private rooms $50.) The Cranberry Bistro ❷, 302 Wood St., draws from cuisines around the world for an inventive gourmet experience. (☎456-4898. Open daily 8am-4pm.) Festooned with local and First Nations art, the Talisman Cafe ❸, 2112 2nd Ave., dishes out heaps of fresh food from Mexican to Middle Eastern (☎667-2736. Open M-F 9am-8pm; Sa 10am-4pm.)

SIGHTS & ENTERTAINMENT. Folks with a powerful thirst can be sated along Main St. Most have nightly live music. The scene ranges from pop at **Lizard Lounge,** 401 Main St. (☎668-7644), to classic rock at the **Roadhouse Saloon,** 2163 2nd Ave. (☎667-2594), to Canadian rock at **Capitol Hotel,** 103 Main St. (☎667-2565). At the **Yukon Beringia Interpretive Centre,** on the Alaska Hwy., 2km northwest of the Robert Service Way junction, mastodonic woolly mammoths, slavering saber-toothed tigers, and other reconstructed Ice Age critters make you realize how rough the first settlers had it. (☎667-8855. Open mid-May to June and Sept. daily 9am-6pm; July-Aug. daily 8:30am-7pm; winter Su 1-5pm. $6, seniors $5, students $4.)

OUTDOOR ACTIVITIES. Paralleling the Yukon River, the **Miles Canyon Trail Network** is a favorite for hiking and biking, and cross-country skiing in the winter. Take Lewes Blvd. to Nisutlin Dr. and turn right; just before the fish ladder, turn left onto Chadbum Lake Rd. and continue 4km up to the parking area. The 8km round-trip **Fish Lake Trail** traces the lake and ascends to a ridge, where hikers can catch some fine views of the Bonneville Lakes before turning back. From Whitehorse, drive 2km north on the Alaska Hwy.; a left on Fish Lake Rd. leads to the lake after 15km. **Up North Adventures,** 103 Strickland St., outfits and provides logistical support for self-guided river trips on the Yukon's many wild and scenic rivers. (☎667-7035; www.upnorth.yk.ca. Daytrip $40. Multiday $200-560.) **Kanoe People,** at Strickland and 1st Ave., rents mountain bikes, canoes, and kayaks. (☎668-4899. Open daily 9am-6pm.) **Tatshenshini Expediting,** 1602 Alder St., leads full-day whitewater rafting trips on the Tatshenshini River. (☎633-2742. $107 per person.)

KLUANE NATIONAL PARK ☎867

Home to dizzyingly massive glaciers, ice-fed lakes and rivers, and raw boreal forest, Kluane doesn't shy from natural grandeur. The soaring titans of the Icefield Range, including Canada's highest peak, Mt. Logan (5959m), are a haven for experienced mountaineers, but their remoteness renders two-thirds of the park inaccessible except by plane. Fortunately, the northeastern section of the park (by the Alaska Hwy.) offers splendid accessible backpacking, biking, fishing, and hiking.

PRACTICAL INFORMATION. Kluane is bounded by the **Alaska Highway** to the north, and the **Haines Highway (Highway 3)** to the east. **Haines Junction,** 158km west of Whitehorse on the Alaska Hwy., at the park's eastern boundary, is the gateway to the park. Travelers can also access trails in the north of the park from the mindbogglingly beautiful **Sheep Mountain** area, spanning the south end of Kluane Lake, 72km northeast of Haines Junction on the Alaska Hwy. The **Kluane National Park Visitor Reception Centre,** on Logan St. in Haines Junction (on the Alaska Hwy. Km 1635), should be the first stop. Rangers distribute the free Recreation Guide and Map, trail and weather info, and permits. (☎634-7207. Open May-Sept. daily 9am-7pm; Oct.-Apr. M-F 10am-noon and 1-5pm.) **Sheep Mountain Ranger Station,** Alaska Hwy. Km 1707, provides the same services as the park visitor center in Haines Junction. Several excellent hiking trails start here. (Open May-Labour Day daily 9am-5pm.) The **Post Office** is in **Madley's Store.** (☎634-3802. Open M-F 8:15am-noon and 1-5pm.) **Postal Code:** Y0B 1L0. **Area Code:** 867.

ACCOMMODATIONS & FOOD. On National Park land near the King's Throne and Cottonwood trailheads, Kathleen Lake Campground ❶, off Haines Rd. 27km south of Haines Junction, sits on a hilltop with views of the lake and the steep mountains tracing its shores. (Toilets, fire pits. Firewood $4. Boil water. Open mid-May-mid-Sept. 39 sites, $10.) The popular Pine Lake ❶, 7km east of town on the Alaska Hwy., features a sandy beach with a swim float, a pit for bonfires, and a trail along the river. (Water, pit toilets. Firewood, $4. $12.) Most Haines Junction restaurants offer standard highway cuisine. But the Village Bakery ❶ bucks the trend, offering fresh veggie dishes, beefy sandwiches, and tray upon tray of sweets. (☎634-2867. Open May-Sept. daily 7am-9pm.)

OUTDOOR ACTIVITIES. While much of Kluane consists of wild backcountry, the handful of trails that do venture into the park are varied and very accessible. The visitor centers are great sources for advice and lead guided hikes. The free *Recreation Guide and Map* is indispensable for solo hikers. Routes, as opposed to trails, are not maintained, do not have marked paths, are more physically demanding, and require backcountry navigation skills and topo maps. Overnight backcountry travelers must register at one of the visitors centers, and use bear-resistant food canisters, which the park rents for $5 per night (with $150 cash or credit refundable deposit). Beware of the bears.

The rewarding but difficult 10km round-trip **King's Throne Trail and Route** begins at the Kathleen Lake day-use area and rises to an alpine basin with a gorgeous panoramic view. More experienced hikers can continue up the steep left-handed ridge for the King's Throne Route (10km round-trip). **Backcountry hiking** can quickly become a dangerous and challenging enterprise in the glaciated Kluane interior. Be confident in your route-finding, buy the proper topographic maps, and consult rangers before you head out. Don't underestimate the bears, either. The **Slims River** East and West routes to the foot of the **Kaskawulsh Glacier** (3-4 days) and the equally remote **Cottonwood Trail** (4-6 days) reveal the wild Kluane.

Anglers can readily put the park's reputation for plentiful fishing to the test at **Kathleen Lake,** home to lake trout, grayling, and rare freshwater Kokanee salmon (usually in season mid-May to early June). Kluane waters require a **National Parks fishing permit,** available at the visitors center in Haines Junction.

If you've got the cash, guides are invaluable. In addition to guiding services, **PaddleWheel Adventures,** directly down the road from the Village Bakery, arranges flightseeing with **Sifton Air** (☎634-2916), hike-out helicopter rides to the **Kluane Plateau,** and full-day rafting trips on the **Blanchard** and **Tatshenshini Rivers** with Tatshenshini Expeditions (see Whitehorse, p. 1047). They also rent the gear you'll need to explore the park on your own, including tents, packs, and bear spray. (☎634-2683.)

ALASKA

Home to North America's highest mountains and broadest flatlands, windswept tundra, vast rainforests, and 15 incredible national parks, Alaska just doesn't quit. Disillusioned with the region's dwindling fur trade, Russia sold the region to the US for a piddling 2 cents per acre in 1867. Critics mocked "Seward's Folly," named after the Secretary of State who negotiated the deal, but just 15 years after the purchase, huge deposits of gold were unearthed in the Gastineau Channel.

Many say the Klondike gold rush of 1898 was only the first in a string, from the "black gold" of the oil pipeline boom to the "ocean gold" pulled up in the form of king crab pots in the Bering Sea. Boom and bust has always been the state's reality, but travelers looking for adventure never fail to find it here. From the 850 sq. mi. Malaspina Glacier to the 2000 mi. Yukon River to the 20,320 ft. Denali, Alaska is a land where everything is bigger, tougher, and more exciting. For more on Alaska and its wonders, check out *Let's Go: Alaska Adventure Guide 2004*.

HIGHLIGHTS OF ALASKA & THE YUKON

NATURAL WONDERS. Denali National Park (p. 1054) is the state's crown jewel, while Glacier Bay National Park (p. 1061) basks in a symphony of sea and ice.

WILDLIFE. Cruises in the Kenai Fjords National Park (p. 1053) are stuffed with opportunities to view sea critters. Grizzlies and black bears amble all over the state. Beware.

RECREATION. One of Alaska's best escapes is kayaking in Misty Fjords Monument (p. 1060).

PRACTICAL INFORMATION

Capital: Juneau. **Biggest City:** Anchorage. **Biggest Party City:** Ketchikan.

Visitor Info: Alaska Division of Tourism, P.O. Box 110804, Juneau 99811 (☎907-465-2017; www.dced.state.ak.us/tourism). **Alaska Department of Fish & Game,** P.O. Box 25526, Juneau 99802 (☎907-465-4100; www.state.ak.us/adfg/adfghome.htm).

Postal Abbreviation: AK. **Sales Tax:** 0%.

TRANSPORTATION

The **Alaska Marine Highway** (☎800-642-0066) remains the most practical and enjoyable way to explore much of the Panhandle, Prince William Sound, and the Kenai Peninsula. The **Alaska Railroad** (☎800-544-0552) covers 470 mi. from Seward to Fairbanks, with stops in Anchorage and Whittier. Most of the state's major **highways** are known by their name as often as their number (e.g., George Parks Hwy. is the same as Rte. 3, which is the same as The Parks). Highways reward drivers with stunning views, but they barely scratch the surface of the massive state. For Alaska's most remote destinations, **air travel** is an expensive necessity. The state's major airline, **Alaska Airlines** (☎800-252-7522) links up major cities and towns in the state and connects Alaska with destinations all over the US and worldwide.

ANCHORAGE ☎907

Anchorage, Alaska's foremost urban center, is home to 270,000 citizens—two-fifths of the state's population. As far north as Helsinki and almost as far west as Honolulu, the city achieved its large size (2000 sq. mi.) by hosting three major eco-

nomic projects: the Alaska Railroad, WWII military developments, and the Trans-Alaska Pipeline. Anchorage serves as a good place to get oriented and stock up on supplies before journeying into the breathtaking wilderness outside.

TRANSPORTATION. Most Alaskan airstrips can be reached from **Anchorage International Airport** (☎266-2525). **Alaska Railroad,** 411 W. 1st Ave., runs to: Denali (8½hr., $125); Fairbanks (12hr., $175); Seward (4hr., summer only, $59). Flagstops are anywhere along the route; wave the train down with a white cloth. (☎265-2494 or 800-544-0552; ticket window open M-F 5:30am-5pm, Sa-Su 5:30am-1pm.) Though the **Alaska Marine Highway** does not service Anchorage, their office on 605 W. 4th Ave. sells tickets and makes reservations. (☎800-642-0066. Open summer daily 9am-5pm; winter M-F 10am-5pm.) **People Mover Bus,** in the Transit Center on 6th Ave. between G and H St., does public transportation. (☎343-6543. M-F 6am-11pm, Sa 8am-8pm, restricted service Su 9:30am-6:30pm. $1.25; day passes $2.50.) **Affordable Car Rental,** 4707 Spenard Rd., charges $39 per day, with unlimited mileage. (☎243-3370. Open M-F 8am-8pm, Sa-Su 9am-6pm. Must be 22+; under 25 surcharge $5 per day.) **Taxi: Yellow Cab,** ☎272-2422.

ORIENTATION & PRACTICAL INFORMATION. The **Log Cabin Visitor Information Center,** on W. 4th Ave. at F St., sells a $4 bike guide. (☎274-3531. Open daily June-Aug. 7:30am-7pm; May and Sept. 8am-6pm; Oct.-Apr. 9am-4pm.) The **Alaska**

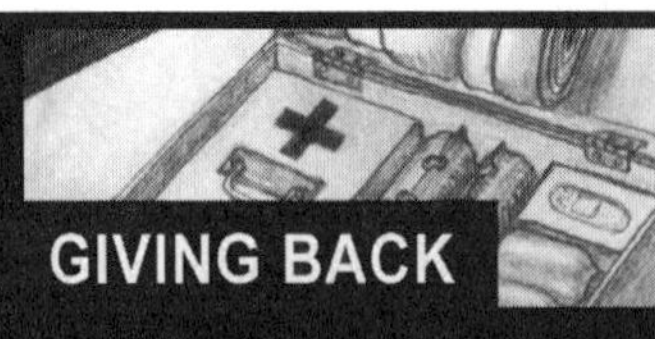

GIVING BACK

ALASKA NATIVE HERITAGE CENTER

At first sight, the Alaska Native Heritage Center in Anchorage appears to be like any old museum, with exhibits, guided tours, and an educational purpose. But more than that, it aims to provide a living home where contemporary Native arts and culture can flourish. Founded as a communal center for all Alaskan Natives, the Center brings together the traditions of the 11 indigenous tribes of Alaska. Oral tradition, dance performances, workshops, and art studios and demonstrations all preserve and perpetuate Native culture as it has been passed down from the ancestral past as well as recreated in the present. Special programs for schools, youth, and adults complete the educational experience. The center is a nonprofit organization and is funded by admissions, gift shop sales, and donations. Consequently, it relies very much on its volunteers, who help organize and run major events and fundraisers, serve on committees, and carry out other important tasks. Not only that, but they also get a chance to interact with Native arts and cultures on an in-depth scale for an extended period of time. Additionally, the center has a few seasonal job openings. For an application, visit their website, or call. *(☎907-330-8000; www.alaskanative.net. 8800 Heritage Center Dr., Anchorage, AK 99506.)*

Public Lands Information Center, Old Federal Building, 605 W. 4th Ave., between F and G St., combines the NPS, USFS, State Parks, and Fish and Wildlife under one roof. (☎271-2737. Open summer daily 9am-5:30pm; winter M-F 10am-5pm.) **Internet Access: Loussac Library,** on 36th Ave. and Denali St., a real architectural oddity. Buses #2, 36, and 60 stop out front; bus #75 stops at C St. and 36th is within half a block. (☎343-2975. Open M-Th 10am-8pm, F-Sa 10am-6pm; winter also Su noon-6pm. 1hr. free.) **Post Office:** W 4th Ave. and C St. (☎800-275-8777. Open M-F 10am-5:30pm.) **Postal Code:** 99510. **Area Code:** 907.

ACCOMMODATIONS. Visitors can call **Alaska Private Lodgings** (☎888-235-2148; open M-Sa 9am-6pm) for lodgings or the **Anchorage Reservation Service** (☎272-5909) for out-of-town B&Bs (from $80). Grab a copy of *Camping in the Anchorage Bowl* (free) at the Visitors Center for crowded in-town camping, or head to nearby **Chugach State Park** (☎354-5014). Guests take pride in the elegant kitchen and common area at the **Anchorage Guesthouse ❶,** 2001 Hillcrest Dr., and gladly earn their keep with a chore. Take bus #3, 4, 6, 36, or 60 from downtown; get off at West High School, and go west on Hillcrest. Bikes $2.50 per hr., $20 per day. $5 key deposit. (☎274-0408. Bunks $28; private rooms $74.) Originally a commune, the **Spenard Hostel ❶,** 2845 W. 42nd Pl., still retains its original character without sacrificing cleanliness. On Spenard, turn west on Turnagain Blvd., then left onto 42nd Pl., or take bus #7. (☎248-5036. Reception 9am-1pm and 7-11pm. Chore requested; free stay for 3hr. work. $16.) The clean and modern **Puffin Inn ❺,** 4400 Spenard Ave., has a range of rooms, continental breakfast, laundry services, and a 24hr. airport shuttle. (☎243-4044. Economy rooms $99, moderate $139, deluxe rooms $159. $10 AAA discount.)

FOOD & NIGHTLIFE. Moose's Tooth ❷, 3300 Old Seward, bus #2 or 36, serves pizza and brews as hearty as the climbers who tackle the nearby peak. Try the chicken ranch pizza. (☎258-2537. Open mic M 9-11pm. Open M-Th 11am-midnight, F-Sa noon-1am, Su noon-midnight.) **Sweet Basil Cafe ❶,** 335 E. St., turns out a whole array of fresh baked treats, juices and smoothies, and sandwiches on homemade bread. (☎274-0070. Open M-F 8am-3pm, Sa 9am-4pm.) Art-bedecked **Snow City Cafe ❷,** 1034 W. 4th St., at L St., is famous for the best breakfast in town and its reindeer sausage. (☎272-2489. Live acoustic music W and Su. Open daily 7am-4pm, W and Su also 7-11pm.) The Historic Alaska Art Tile Building, 817 W. 6th Ave., houses solid sandwiches

($5-9), salads ($9-10), and veggie options ($5-8) at **Muffin Man ❷.** Muffins and scones ($2) baked daily. (☎279-6836. Open summer M-F 6am-3pm, Sa-Su 7am-2pm; winter M-F 7am-3pm.)

The brewpub revolution has hit Anchorage, and microbrews gush from taps like oil through the pipeline. Catch a flick with brew in hand at the **Bear Tooth Grill,** 1230 W. 27th St. (☎276-4200. Pints $3.75. Cover for movie $3.) The young and retro at **Bernie's Bungalow Lounge,** 626 D St., relax in one of many wingback chairs as they sip a $5 lemon drop martini. (☎276-8808. Open summer noon-2am; winter 3pm-2am.) **Chilkoot Charlie's,** 2435 Spenard Rd. bus #7, has cavernous dance floors and 10 differently themed bars. (☎272-1010. $1 drink specials until 10pm. Cover $3-6. Open Su-Th 10:30am-2:30am, F-Sa 11am-2:30am.)

SIGHTS & OUTDOOR ACTIVITIES. **Cyrano's Off Center Playhouse,** 413 D St., between 4th and 5th, contains a cafe, bookshop, the **Eccentric Theatre Company,** and a cinema screening foreign and art films. (☎274-2599. Theater summer M-Tu and F-Su 7pm; winter Su, Th-Sa 7pm. Tickets $15, students $10.) With a tremendous collection of Native and national and international artwork and a fascinating gallery on Alaska's rough history, **Anchorage Museum of History and Art,** 121 W. 7th Ave., tops all the others in the state. (☎343-4326. Open May 15-Sept. 15 Su-W, F-Sa 9am-6pm, Th 9am-9pm; Sept. 16-May 14 Su 1-5pm, Tu-Sa 10am-6pm. $6.50, seniors and military $6, under 18 $2.) The **Alaska Native Heritage Center,** 8800 Heritage Ctr. Dr., brings exhibits to life with cultural shows, storytelling, and dancing from Alaska's eleven Native American traditions. (☎330-8000. First right off the North Muldoon Exit from the Glenn Hwy. Bus #4 from the Transit Center. Open daily 9am-6pm. $21, ages 7-16 $16, under 7 free.) At **Resolution Point,** take in sweeping views of Cook Inlet, Mt. Sustina, beluga whales, and Denali. Near town off Northern Lights Blvd., **Earthquake Park** recalls the 1964 Good Friday quake, the biggest ever recorded in North America, registering 9.2 on the Richter scale.

In town, hikers and bikers crowd the 13 mi. **Tony Knowles Coastal Trail,** one of the best urban bike paths in the country; in the winter, it's groomed for cross-country skiing. The serene **Chugach State Park,** surrounding the city to the north, east, and south, has 25 established day hiking trails, including **Flattop Mountain** (4500 ft.), the most frequently climbed mountain in Alaska. A bit further from Anchorage along the Seward Hwy., the bohemian ski town of Girdwood and the **Alyeska Ski Resort** offers world-class terrain. **Nancy Lake State Recreation Area,** just west of the Parks Hwy. (Rte. 3) near Mile 67¼, contains the **Lynx Lake Loop,** at the Tanaina Lake Canoe Trailhead, Mile 4½ of the Nancy Lake Pkwy. Canoeing the entire loop takes 1-2 days and weaves through 8 mi. of lakes and portages with designated campsites along the way. For **canoe rental,** call **Tippecanoe.** (☎495-6688; www.paddlealaska.com. Open mid-May to mid-Sept. M-F call for hours, Sa-Su 8:30am-5:30pm.) **Lifetime Adventures** leads guided float and whitewater trips down **Eagle River,** 10 min. from Anchorage in the Chugach State Park. (☎746-4644; www.lifetimeadventures.net. Class III trip $25, float and wildlife trip $55.)

SEWARD & KENAI FJORDS ☎907

Seward serves as a gateway to the hulking tidewater glaciers and yawning ice fields of **Kenai Fjords National Park** and the alpine trails of **Chugach National Forest. Exit Glacier,** the only road-accessible glacier in the park, lies 9 mi. west of Mile 3¾ of the Seward Hwy. (Rte. 9). **Kenai Fjords Tours** leads a variety of informative boat tours to different locations in the park. (☎224-8068 or 800-478-8068. 3-9½hr. $56-149, children $28-74.) **Major Marine Tours** brings along a ranger to narrate natural history. (☎224-8030 or 800-764-7300. 3-6hr. $54-109, children $27-54.) **Sunny Cove Sea Kayaking** offers a joint trip with Kenai Fjords

Tours, including the wildlife cruise, a salmon bake, kayaking instruction, and a 2½hr. wilderness paddle. (☎224-8810. 8hr. Joint trips $149-169, daytrips $59-129.) Although pricey, **Scenic Mountain Air's** flight tours provide the best appreciation of the **Harding Ice Field's** vastness. (☎288-3646. 45min. tours from $99, 1hr. tours from $129 per person.)

The rustic **Snow River Hostel ❷,** Seward Hwy. Mile 16, lures travelers with a peaceful atmosphere under the eaves of the surrounding Chugach National Forest. (☎440-1907. Dorms $15. Cozy cabin for two, $40. Office open daily 6-10pm.) Ogle the peaks across the bay as you fish from the front deck of the **Alaska Saltwater Lodge ❹,** 3 mi. south of town on Beach Rd. (☎224-5271. Rooms with full bath and continental breakfast $85; suites with kitchen $159.) **Exit Glacier Campground ❶,** at the end of the road to Exit Glacier, creates the idyllic illusion of roughing it alone on the glacier outwash, complete with food storage, pit toilets, and a cooking shelter. (Max. stay 14 days. Walk-in, tents-only. Free.) Rejoice in Seward's fresh fish at the **Railway Cantina ❷,** 1401 4th St., where the halibut burritos ($8) arrive with chips, Mexican slaw, and a choice of salsas. (☎224-8226. Open Jan.-Oct. daily 11am-8pm.) Mountainous portions of reindeer sausage and salmon and a thoroughly Alaskan feel grace the **Exit Glacier Salmon Bake ❹,** Mile ¼ Exit Glacier Rd. (☎224-2204. M-F 3-10pm, Sa-Su noon-10pm.)

Seward is 127 mi. south of Anchorage on the scenic **Seward Highway (Route 9).** Most services and outdoor outfits cluster in the small boat harbor on Resurrection Bay. The **Alaska Marine Highway** (☎800-642-0066) docks at 4th Ave. and Railway St., with connections to: Homer (25hr., $118); Kodiak (12hr., $64); Valdez (12hr., $68). At the **Alaska Railroad** depot, trains leave for Anchorage in summer at 6pm. (round-trip $98, ages 2-11 $49.) **Park Connection** (☎800-266-8625) has two buses daily to Anchorage at 11am and 6:30pm. (3hr., one-way $49.) The **Kenai Fjords National Park Visitors Center** is at the small boat harbor. (☎224-3175. Open summer daily 8am-7pm; winter M-F 8am-5pm.) **Post Office:** 5th Ave. and Madison St. (☎224-3001. Open M-F 9:30am-4:30pm, Sa 10am-2pm.) **Postal Code:** 99664.

DENALI NATIONAL PARK & PRESERVE ☎907

Only a solitary ribbon of gravel less than 100 mi. long dares to interrupt Denali's six million acres of snowcapped peaks, braided streams, and glacier-carved valleys. Visitors to the park are guests of the countless grizzly bears, moose, caribou, wolves, and Dall sheep that thrive here. With 18,000 of its 20,320 ft. towering over the surrounding lands, the park's centerpiece, Denali (Mt. McKinley), is the world's tallest mountain from base to peak. August is an excellent time to visit—fall colors peak, mosquito season has virtually ended, and September's snows have not yet arrived. Be sure to check out the park's newspaper, *Alpenglow*.

TRANSPORTATION. The **George Parks Highway (Route 3)** makes for smooth and easy traveling to the park 237 mi. north from Anchorage or 120 mi. south from Fairbanks. The rough dirt **Denali Highway (Route 8)** meets the Parks Hwy. 27 mi. south of the park entrance at Cantwell and extends 136 mi. east to Paxson, but is closed in winter. The **Alaska Railroad** (☎265-2494 or 800-544-0552; open daily 10am-5pm) stops at Denali Station, 1½ mi. from the park entrance, and runs to Anchorage (8hr., $125) and Fairbanks (4½hr., $50). **Parks Highway Express** (☎888-600-6001) runs here daily from Anchorage (5hr., $109 round-trip) and Fairbanks (3½hr., $69).

Only the first 14 mi. of the park road are accessible by private vehicle; the remaining 75 mi. of dirt road can be reached only by shuttle bus, camper bus, or bicycle. **Shuttle buses** leave from the Visitors Center daily 5am-6pm, pause at the sighting of any major mammal, and turn back at various points along the park road. Most buses are wheelchair-accessible. **Camper buses** transport only those visitors with campground or backcountry permits, and move faster than the shuttle buses. (5 buses daily, 6:40am-6:45pm. $22.50, ages 13-16 half-price.) Advance reservations for campsites and shuttle buses will spare you long lines upon arrival.

PRACTICAL INFORMATION. All travelers must stop at the **Denali Visitors Center,** half a mile from the Parks Hwy. (Rte. 3), for orientation. Most park privileges are first come, first served; conduct business at the Visitors Center as early as possible. (☎683-1266. Open daily Memorial Day-Labor Day 7am-8pm; late Apr. to Memorial Day and Labor Day-late Sept. 10am-4pm. Entrance fee $5, good for 7 days.) **Denali Outdoor Center,** at Parks Hwy. Mile 238.5, north of the park entrance, rents bikes. (☎683-1925. Half-day $25, full-day $40.) **Medical Services: Healy Clinic,** 13 mi. north of the park entrance. (☎683-2211. On call 24hr.) **Post Office:** a quarter mile from the park entrance. (☎683-2291. Open May-Sept. M-F 8:30am-5pm, Sa 10am-1pm; Oct.-Apr. M-Sa 10am-1pm.) **Postal Code:** 99755. **Area Code:** 907.

ALASKA

ACCOMMODATIONS & FOOD. The rustic **Denali Mountain Morning Hostel ➊,** 13 mi. south of the park entrance, has showers, Internet, groceries, $3 park shuttles, helpful advice, and outdoor gear rental. (☎683-7503. Backpacker kit $30 first day, $7 each additional day. Bunks $23, ages 5-13 $17. Semi-private and private rooms start at $50. Tent sites $15. Reservations recommended.) **Campers** must obtain a permit from the Visitors Center and may stay for up to 14 nights in the five **campgrounds ➊** lining the park road. (☎272-7275 or 800-622-7275 for advance reservations. First come, first served sites are distributed rapidly at the Visitors Center.) Unless otherwise noted, all campgrounds are open May-Sept. and have running water and flush toilets. All except Sanctuary River are wheelchair-accessible. Backcountry campers must obtain a free backcountry permit.

Riley Creek Mercantile provides groceries from its convenient location next to Riley Creek Campground. (☎683-9246. Open daily 5am-11pm.) Once you board that park bus, there is no food available anywhere. At **Black Bear Coffee House ➊,** 1 mi. north of the park entrance, the coffee is hot and strong, the muffins are fresh, and the staff is all smiles. (☎683-1656. Half-sandwich with chips $6. Internet access. Open May-Sept. daily 6:30am-10pm.)

FLIGHTSEEING. Oddly, the best services for flightseeing around Denali are actually in Talkeetna, 60 mi. to the south, where the same flights come at cheaper prices. If the weather cooperates, these flights are worth every penny and will leave you itching for more. Flights come in two standard flavors: a 1hr. flight approaching the mountain from the south ($115-135 per person), and a 1½hr. tour that circumnavigates the peak ($180-195). The 15-30min. glacier stop-off costs an extra $50-55 per person but is definitely worthwhile. All flights are weather-dependent, with most companies flying over the rugged Talkeetna Mountains to the south if Denali weather is uncooperative. Discounts to groups of four or five may be available. **K2 Aviation** (☎733-2291 or 800-764-2291), **McKinley Air Service** (☎733-1765 or 800-564-1765), **Doug Geeting Aviation** (☎733-2366 or 800-770-2366), and **Talkeetna Air Taxi** (☎733-2218 or 800-533-2219) offer standard services, plus a variety of other specialized trips. All flight services suspend glacier landings in mid-July due to unpredictable snow conditions. In Denali itself, try **Denali Air** (☎683-2261) or **ERA Helicopters Flightseeing Tours** (☎683-2574; www.eraaviation.com).

OUTDOOR ACTIVITIES. The best way to experience Denali is to get off the bus and explore the land. Beyond Mile 14 (the point which only shuttle and camper buses can cross), there are no trails. As long as you don't plan on staying overnight, no permits are required, although you will need a shuttle ticket. You can begin day hiking from anywhere along the park road by riding the shuttle bus to a suitable starting point and asking the driver to let you off. It's rare to wait more than 30min. to flag a ride back. **Primrose Ridge,** beginning at Mile 16, is bespangled with wildflowers and has spectacular views of the Alaska Range and the carpeted emerald valley below. A walk north from Mile 14 along the **Savage River** provides a colorful, scenic stroll through this valley. **Polychrome Overlook** at Mile 47 offers a spectacular 360° view of the park and grants easy ridge access. The more challenging **Mt. Healy Overlook Trail** affords the best views, climbing from the hotel parking lot to an impressive 3400 ft. view. (5 mi. round-trip; 1700 ft. elevation gain; 3-4hr.) **Discovery hikes** are guided 3-5hr. hikes departing on special buses from the Visitors Center. The hikes are free but require reservations and a bus ticket.

There are **no trails** in the backcountry. The park's backcountry philosophy rests on the idea that independent wandering creates more rewards and less impact than would a network of trails or routes. Only 2-12 backpackers can camp at a time in each of the park's 43 units. Overnight stays in the backcountry require a **free permit,** available no earlier or later than one day in advance at the backcountry desk in the Visitors Center. Hikers line up outside as early as 6:30am to grab permits for popular units. Talk to rangers and research your choices with the handy *Backcountry Description Guides* and *Denali Backcountry Companion*, available at the Visitors Center, which also sells essential topo maps ($4). Most zones in Denali require that food be carried in **bear-resistant food containers,** available for free at the backcountry desk. With the park's cool, drizzly weather and many rivers and streams, your feet will get wet. **Hypothermia** can set in quickly and quietly; talk with rangers about prevention and warning signs. **Mosquito repellent** is a must.

FAIRBANKS ☎907

Fairbanks stands unchallenged as North American civilization's northernmost hub. Things have changed since the free-wheeling, gold-mining days, which lasted here well into the 1960s. But even so, Fairbanks remains a sprawling frontier town, where men outnumber women, four-wheel-drive pickups choke the streets, and the beer flows more freely than the Chena River's muddy waters. From here, adventurers can drive, float, or fly to experience the true Arctic wilderness.

PRACTICAL INFORMATION. Most tourist destinations lie within the square of Airport Way, College Rd., Cushman Blvd., and University Way. Fairbanks is a bicycle-friendly city, with wide shoulders, multi-use paths, and sidewalks. The **airport** is 5 mi. from downtown on Airport Way. **Alaska Railroad,** 280 N. Cushman St. (☎458-6025 or 800-544-0552; open daily 6:30am-3pm and for evening arrivals), runs one train per day to Anchorage ($175) via Denali ($50); service is reduced during the winter. **Parks Highway Express** (☎479-3065 or 888-600-6001) runs daily to Denali ($39 one-way) and Anchorage ($79). **Municipal Area Commuter Service (MACS)** runs through downtown. (☎459-1011. $1.50; students, seniors, and disabled $0.75; day pass $3. Service M-F 7am-8pm; limited on Sa.) **King Diamond Taxi,** ☎455-7777. **Visitor Info:** 550 1st Ave. (☎456-5774 or 800-327-5774. Open summer daily 8am-7pm; winter M-F 9am-5pm.) The **Alaska Public Lands Info Center,** 250 Cushman St., #1A, is in the basement of the Federal Building, at 3rd. Ave. (☎456-0527. Open daily 9am-6pm; winter Tu-Sa 10am-6pm.) **Post Office:** 315 Barnette St. (☎452-3223. Open M-F 9am-6pm, Sa 10am-2pm.) **General Delivery:** 99701. **Postal Code:** 990709.

ACCOMMODATIONS & FOOD. **Boyle's Hostel ❶,** 310 18th Ave., has TVs in every room and two full kitchens. (☎456-4944. Showers and laundry. Dorms $17; private doubles $30; outside cabins $15 per person. Monthly rates available.) **Billie's Backpackers Hostel ❶,** 2895 Mack Rd., is a somewhat cluttered but welcoming place to meet outdoorsy international travelers. Choose from 10 bunks in coed rooms. (☎479-2034. Sites $15, beds $22, sites $15, private double with jacuzzi $50.) **Chena River State Campground ❶,** off Airport Way on University Ave., has a boat launch and camping on a quiet stretch of the river. (56 sites. $15, walk-in $10.) The **Fairbanks Hotel ❸,** 517 Third Ave., has spacious Art Deco rooms, all with cable TV and a slough of services. Complimentary airport/train shuttle and bike rental. (☎456-6411. Singles with shared bath $55, with private $89; doubles $65/110.)

An artery-blocking good time fills Airport Way and College Rd. **Bun on the Run ❶,** located in a trailer in the parking lot between Beaver Sports and the Marlin on College Rd., whips up scrumptious pastries. (Open M-F 7am-6pm, Sa 9am-4pm.) **Second Story Cafe ❷,** 3525 College Rd., above Gulliver's, has the best and freshest wraps in town, plus salads, sandwiches, and veggie-friendly soups. All wraps and sandwiches $6.50. (☎474-9574. Open M-F 9am-9pm, Sa 9am-7pm, Su 10am-6pm.) A chic addition to the Fairbanks culinary scene, **Cafe Alex,** 310 1st Ave., serves up contemporary fusion cuisine. (☎452-2539. Entrees $7-11.25.)

ALASKA

SIGHTS & SKIING. The **University of Alaska Museum,** a 10min. walk up Yukon Dr. from the Wood Center, features a thorough look at the Aleut/Japanese evacuation during WWII, Native culture, and Blue Babe, a 36,000-year-old steppe bison recovered from the permafrost. (☎474-7505. Open June-Aug. daily 9am-7pm; May and Sept. 9am-5pm; Oct.-Apr. M-F 9am-5pm. $5, seniors $4.50, ages 7-17 $3.) Stand upwind of the **Large Animal Research Station,** which offers a rare chance to see baby musk oxen and other arctic animals up close. Take Farmer's Loop to Ballaine Rd. and turn left on Yankovich; the farm is 1 mi. up on the right. (☎474-7207. Tours June-Aug. daily at 11am; Sept. Sa at 1:30pm. $5, seniors $4, students $2.)

Moose Mountain, 20min. northeast of Fairbanks, grooms over 30 ski trails. Take the Parks Hwy. until the Sheep Creek Rd. Exit. (☎479-4732. Open Su, Th-Sa 10am-5pm, or dusk. Lift tickets $23, ages 7-12 $18. Rentals $20, under 12 $15.) Another option, **Mt. Aurora Ski Land,** 2315 Skiland Rd., holds over 20 trails. Take a right onto Fairbanks Creek Rd. off the Steese Hwy. (Rte. 6) at Mile 20½ and then turn left. (☎389-2314. Open Nov.-Apr. on weekends, holidays, and spring break 10am-6pm or dusk. Lift tickets $28, students $24, ages 13-17 and seniors $20. Rentals $20.)

ENTERTAINMENT & NIGHTLIFE. **The Marlin,** 3412 College Rd., is a refreshingly mellow outlet amidst the rowdy sea of Fairbanks bars, with frequent live music and a youthful, local clientele. (☎479-4646. Pints $3.50. Open till 2am.) The **Blue Loon Saloon,** 2999 Parks Hwy., screens a range of movies most nights ($5); music some nights with higher covers. The grille serves a bar menu ranging from $2.50-15.75. (☎457-5666. Hours vary.) In mid-July, Fairbanks citizens don old-time duds and whoop it up for **Golden Days,** a celebration of Felix Pedro's 1902 discovery that sparked the Fairbanks gold rush. A true sports spectacular, the **World Eskimo-Indian Olympics,** in mid- to late July, gathers Native Alaskans from all over the state in traditional tests of strength and survival. Witness the ear pull, but be warned: ears have been pulled off in this event. (☎452-6646. Daily pass $6, season pass $20.)

BARROW ☎907

Barrow (pop. 4000) holds a distinctive position as the northernmost point of the US. Polar bears prowl the pack ice on the edges of this town of mostly Inupiat (Eskimo) descent. With no roads leading out of town, lonely Barrow must fly in all of its supplies, and most visitors arrive on one- or two-day **"A Day At The Top"** package tours. But don't be fazed by the remoteness or the frosty temperatures—Barrow offers a challenging exploration of the Arctic at its wildest and most desolate.

The **Inupiat Heritage Center,** on Ahkovak St. and North Star St., has exhibits on the indigenous people, natural history, native whaling, and more. Performances, games, art shows, and the annual spring whale hunt blend the border between archaic relics and living culture. (Open M-F 8:30am-5pm. $5, students $2, ages 7-14 $1, under 6 and seniors free.) A **hike** above the Arctic Circle to **Point Barrow,** the northernmost tip of the US, is reward enough for those who come for the latitude. Take Stevenson St. north out of town, past the **Naval Arctic Research Laboratory (NARL)** to a beachy area. The road ends in front of a sign warning of polar bears, and a strenuous walk along a sandy spit leads to Pt. Barrow. **Alaskan Arctic Adventures** runs polar bear tours and trips to Pt. Barrow. (☎852-3800; www.arctic-adventures.com. 2hr. polar bear tours $60; dog mushing $85.)

Out of town in the NARL complex, **NARL Hotel ❸,** on Stevenson St., caters mainly to visiting scientists with warm and comfortable rooms. (☎852-7800. Shared bath. $75. Cash only.) With immaculate pine furnishings, **King Eider Inn ❺,** 1752 Ahkovak St., has become the lodging of choice for those in Barrow with money to spend. (☎852-4700. $170; winter $130.) **Arctic Pizza ❷,** 125 Apayuak St., cranks out the best pizzas north of the Arctic Circle ($11), Mexican dishes and—go figure—Indian food. (☎852-4222. Open daily 11am-11pm.)

Barrow can only be reached via air. The **airport** is on Ahkovak St., on the south edge of town. The bus system ($1) runs two routes in town and one to the NARL complex. (☎852-2611, ext. 689.) The **Visitors Shack,** 1772 Ahkovak St., is next to the Alaska Airlines terminal. (☎852-4117. Open only in the summer, M-F 2-4pm.) The police (☎852-6111) will provide emergency beacons for hikers. Failing that, there's the **North Slop Borough Search and Rescue** (☎852-2822). The **Post Office** sits at Eben Hopson St. and Tahak St. (☎852-6800. Open M-F 9am-5pm, Sa 10am-2pm.) **Postal Code:** 99723. **Area Code:** 907.

THE PANHANDLE

Southeast Alaska, sometimes called "the Panhandle," spans 500 miles from the Misty Fjords National Monument to Skagway and the foot of the Chilkoot Trail. Countless straits weaving through the Panhandle, collectively known as the **Inside Passage,** divide up thousands of islands, inlets, and fjords. The absence of roads in the steep coastal mountains has helped most Panhandle towns maintain their small size and hospitable personalities.

KETCHIKAN ☎907

Ketchikan may be Alaska's fourth-largest city (population 14,000), but its island location enlaces the town's fringes with dense wilderness, stunting sprawl and attracting an array of eclectic residents. Surrounded by the Tongass National Forest and Misty Fjords National Monument, Ketchikan provides a vital base for some of the most outstanding hiking, kayaking, fishing, and flightseeing opportunities in Southeast Alaska.

PRACTICAL INFORMATION. Ketchikan clings to Revillagigedo Island (ruh-VIL-ya-GIG-a-doe). Renting a bike may be the most economic way to see the sights out of town. The **airport** is across from Ketchikan on Gravina Island, connected to town by a small **ferry.** (Every 30min. $6 one-way and round-trip if same day.) **Alaska**

Marine Highway (☎800-642-0066) docks at the far end of town on N. Tongass Hwy. and goes to Juneau ($87); Sitka ($64); Wrangell ($27). The bus route loops between the airport parking lot near the ferry terminal, the dock, and Saxman Village. (M-Sa every 30min. 5:30am-11pm, Su every hr. 9am-3pm. $1.50-$2.25. Seniors, and children free.) **Taxi: Sourdough Cab,** ☎225-5544. **Ketchikan Visitors Bureau:** 131 Front St., on the cruise ship docks downtown. (☎225-6166 or 800-770-3300. Open daily 8am-5pm.) **Southeast Alaska Discovery Center (SEADC),** 50 Main St., helps plan outdoor adventures in the Tongass. (☎228-6220. Open May-Sept. M-Sa 8am-5pm, Su 8am-4pm; Oct.-Apr. Tu-Sa 10am-4:30pm.) **Post Office:** 3609 Tongass Ave. (☎225-9601. Open M-F 8:30am-5pm.) **Postal Code:** 99901. **Area Code:** 907.

ACCOMMODATIONS & FOOD. The **Ketchikan Reservation Service** specializes in B&Bs. (☎800-987-5337. Singles from $69.) The **Ketchikan Youth Hostel (HI-AYH) ❶,** at Main and Grant St. in the First Methodist Church, has clean and functional dorm rooms. (☎225-3319. Common area, kitchen. Linens $1.25. 4-night max. stay. Lockout 9am-6pm. Curfew 11pm. Call ahead if arriving on a late ferry. Open June-Aug. $12, nonmembers $15. No credit cards.) Rooms and furnishings are elegant and individual at the **New York Hotel ❹,** 207 Stedman St. (☎225-0246. Singles $94. Less for multiple nights. Prices drop by as much as 60% in the winter.)

Campgrounds are a refuge from expensive beds. **Signal Creek ❶** sits on Ward Lake Rd. in the temperate rainforest. Drive 5 mi. north of the ferry terminal on Tongass Hwy. and turn right at the sign for Ward Lake. Bring your fishing gear. (Open May-Sept. Water, pit toilets. $10.) Anyone can **camp ❶** for free up to 30 days in **Tongass National Forest,** but may not return for six months after that time.

The freshest seafood swims in **Ketchikan Creek;** in summer, anglers frequently hook king salmon from the docks by Stedman St. Come to the **New York Cafe ❷,** 207 Stedman St., for soup, healthful lunch specials (around $8), and veggie options. (☎225-1800. Open Su-Th 7am-5pm, F-Sa 7am-10pm.) **Ocean View Restaurante ❷,** 1831 Tongass Ave., serves up enchiladas and pizza with equal gusto. The fried ice cream is a winner for dessert. (☎225-7566. Open daily 11am-11pm.)

SIGHTS & NIGHTLIFE. Saxman Totem Park, south of town on the Tongass Hwy, has brightly colored carvings up to 150 years old—the state's largest collection of totems. The **Totem Heritage Center,** 601 Deermount St., up Park St., houses 33 19th-century totem poles from Tlingit, Haida, and Tsimshian villages in their raw, unrestored state. (☎225-5900. Open May-Sept. daily 8am-5pm; Oct.-Apr. Tu-F 1-5pm. $5.) A $11 combination ticket also provides admission to the **Deer Mountain Fish Hatchery and Raptor Center,** across the creek. (☎225-6760. Open May-Sept. daily 8am-4:30pm. $8.) **First City Saloon,** ¼ mi. north of the tunnel on Water St., is the most spacious hangout in town and liberally distributes Guinness and a variety of microbrews. (☎225-1494. Live local music Su, Th-Sa. Open M-Sa noon-2am, Su 4pm-2am.) **Arctic Bar,** 509 Water St., is a hop, skip, and stagger north of the downtown tunnel. Distinguished by their copulating bears logo, this popular bar sports a deck with harbor view. (☎225-4709. Open daily until 2am.)

OUTDOOR ACTIVITIES. A hike up the 3001 ft. **Deer Mountain** provides inexpensive access into the wilderness. Walk up the hill past the city park on Fair St.; at the crossroads, follow the signs, and veer left to the trailhead. A steep climb yields sparkling views of the sea and surrounding islands. While most hikers stop at the peak after 2½ mi., the trail continues for another 8 mi., passing Blue Lake and over John Mountain to the Beaver Falls Fish Hatchery. This portion of the trail is poorly marked, and snow and ice are common on the peaks into summer;

ALASKA

arrange transportation at the far trailhead, bring raingear, and inform someone in town of your planned return date. Ketchikan offers sumptuous **kayaking** in nearby Tongass Narrows, Naha Bay, George Inlet, and the Tatoosh Islands. Only experienced kayakers should tackle the waters alone; beginning paddlers can join **Southeast Sea Kayaks** for their small group guided tours with personal attention. (☎225-1258. 2½hr. Tongass Narrows $76; 4hr. Orca Cove $139.) They also rent kayaks. (Singles $40 per day; doubles $60.)

NEAR KETCHIKAN: MISTY FJORDS NATIONAL MONUMENT

The sawtooth peaks, ravine abysses, and dripping vegetation of **Misty Fjords National Monument,** 20 mi. east of Ketchikan, make biologists dream and outdoors enthusiasts drool. Only accessible by kayak, boat, or float plane, the 2.3 million-acre park offers superlative camping, kayaking, hiking, and wildlife-viewing. **Camping** ❶ is permitted throughout the park, and is best on the sandy beaches. The Forest Service maintains first come, first served **shelters** (free) and 14 **cabins** ($25). Contact the **Misty Fjords Ranger Station,** 3031 Tongass Ave. (☎225-2148), Ketchikan, or ask the SEADC (see p. 1059) for advice. Misty Fjords is one of North America's best sea kayaking destinations. **Southeast Sea Kayaks** charges $150-300 for drop-off and pick-up at the entrance to the fjords. For independent trip planning, contact SEADC for helpful advice. **Flightseeing** remains one of the best ways to see the park, with most flights based out of Ketchikan. Check out **Taquan Air** (☎225-8800) and **Island Wings** (☎225-2444), who both run a similar 1½hr. trip for $189. The cheapest way is to hop on the mail plane. Taquan will let you go with the mail for around $129. Call to reserve; availability is dependent upon the weight of the mail.

ALASKA

JUNEAU ☎907

Springing up during the gold rush, Juneau went from hard-rock mining capital to Alaska's state capital. Built upon the fortunes of its mines, the city now has the most diverse economy, cultural sights, and population of any city in Southeast Alaska. Accessible only by water and air, Juneau is still swamped by hordes of travelers heading for the Mendenhall Glacier, numerous hiking trails, and access to Glacier Bay, so be prepared to share the beauty.

PRACTICAL INFORMATION. **Franklin Street** is the main drag downtown. **Glacier Highway (Egan Drive)** connects downtown, the airport, the Mendenhall Valley, and the ferry terminal. **Juneau International Airport** is 9 mi. north on Glacier Hwy. **Alaska Marine Highway** (☎465-3941) docks at the Auke Bay terminal, 14 mi. from the city on the Glacier Hwy., and runs to: Ketchikan (18-36hr., $83); Sitka (9hr., $30); Haines (4½hr., $26). **Capital Transit** runs buses from downtown to the Mendenhall Glacier every 30min., with express service to the airport every hour. (☎789-6901. Runs M-Sa 7am-11:30pm, Su 9am-6:30pm; express bus M-F 8:10am-5pm. $1.50.) **Taku Cab** (☎586-2121) runs to the airport ($30). The **Visitors Center** is at 101 Egan Dr. in Centennial Hall. (☎586-2201 or 888-581-2201. Open June-Sept. M-F 8:30am-5pm, Sa-Su 9am-5pm; Oct.-May M-F 9am-4pm.) The **Forest Service** has a desk here. (Closes 3pm. Weekdays only.) **Trail Hotline,** ☎856-5330. **Post Office:** 709 W. 9th St. (☎586-7987. Open M-F 9am-4pm.) **Postal Code:** 99801. **Area Code:** 907.

ACCOMMODATIONS & FOOD. On a steep hill, the spacious **Juneau International Hostel (HI-AYH)** ❶, 614 Harris St. at 6th St., exudes a relaxed atmosphere. (☎586-9559. Free Internet, coffee, linens. 4-night max. stay if full. Lockout 9am-5pm. Curfew midnight. Reservations available by phone. Beds $10.) **Alaskan Hotel**

❸, 167 Franklin St., downtown, has been restored to its original 1913 decor. (☎586-1000. Kitchenettes, laundry. Rooms $67.50-$85; weekly rates $225-$325.) **Mendenhall Lake Campground** ❶ has stunning views of the glacier and trail access. Take Glacier Hwy. north 10 mi. to Mendenhall Loop Rd. and turn left on Montana Creek Rd. (Open June-Sept. Firepits, water, toilets, showers, and firewood. 14-night max. stay. No reservations. Sites $10; RVs $24-26.) **Silverbow Bagels ❶,** 120 2nd. St., is known statewide for bagels and quality sandwiches. (☎586-9866. Open May-Sept. M-Sa 7am-6pm, Su 8am-4pm; Oct.-Apr. M-F 7am-6pm, Sa 8am-4pm, Su 9am-3pm. **Back Room** ❸ restaurant open for dinner.) Local favorite **Fiddlehead Restaurant ❸,** 429 Willoughby Ave., has the best gourmet vegetarian options in town. (Open June-Aug. daily 7am-10pm; Sept.-May M-F 7am-9pm, Sa-Su 8am-9pm.)

OUTDOOR ACTIVITIES. The steep **Mt. Roberts Trail** winds five miles through old-growth forest and alpine meadows, past gorgeous views to the summit of Mt. Roberts. The trail begins at the end of 6th St., up a stairway. The **West Glacier Trail** begins off Montana Creek Rd., by the Mendenhall Lake Campground. The 3½ mi. walk yields stunning views of **Mendenhall Glacier** from the first step in the western hemlock forest to the final outlook at the peak of 4226 ft. **Mt. McGinnis.** At the end of Basin Rd., the easy 3 mi. **Perseverance Trail** leads to the ruins of the Silverbowl Basin Mine and booming waterfalls. **Tracy Arm,** a mini-fjord near Juneau, is known as "the poor man's Glacier Bay," for it offers the same spectacular beauty as the national park at under half the cost. The Native-run **Auk Nu Tours,** 76 Egan Dr., has a naturalist on board for its iceberg-studded cruise through Tracy Arm. (☎800-820-2628. 8hr. tour $111, under 18 $72; includes lunch, snacks, and binoculars.) **Above and Beyond Alaska** (☎364-2333) offers customized kayak trips from Juneau, as well as **glacier treks,** including overnight trips and ice climbing.

GLACIER BAY NATIONAL PARK ☎907

Explorer Jean François de Galaup de la Perouse called Glacier Bay "perhaps the most extraordinary place in the world." Crystal monoliths, broken off from glaciers, float peacefully in fjords, while wildlife maneuver through the maze of the icy blue depths. The landscape of this roadless, trailless park changes daily as about a dozen of its glaciers advance and retreat at geologically rapid speeds, opening up new land for colonization by plants and wildlife. A mere two centuries ago, the **Grand Pacific Glacier** covered the entire region under a sheet of ancient ice. Charter flights, tours, and cruise ships all probe Glacier Bay, providing close encounters with glaciers, rookeries, whales, and seals. The bay is divided into two major arms: the **West Arm** reaches north to the termini of the Grand Pacific and Margerie Glaciers, which advances 6 ft. every year, while the **East Arm,** closed to most motorized boat traffic, is a solitude-filled haven for kayakers. **Mt. Fairweather,** part of the highest coastal range in the world, reigns over it all.

Getting to **Bartlett Cove,** the principle access point to the bay, is relatively easy. A plane takes visitors to **Gustavus,** and from there a taxi or shuttle (about $10) goes to **Glacier Bay Lodge** and the **Visitor Information Station** (☎697-2230; open mid-May to mid-Sept. daily 7am-9pm), both close to the campground in the immediate Bartlett Cove area. The ferry from Juneau docks directly at Bartlett Cove. Wilderness camping and hiking are permitted throughout the park, though there are no trails except the two near the lodge. Backcountry hiking and kayaking are possible in the Dry Bay area, as is **rafting** down the Alsek River. For info, contact the **Yakutat District Office** of the National Park Service (☎784-3295). The Glacier Bay Lodge operates a daily **Glacier Cruise** popular with both sightseers and paddlers optimizing their time in the upper bay. The boat delivers (and picks up) kayakers, hikers and their gear at rotating locations within the Bay. (☎697-2225 or 800-451-5952. $95, round-trip $190, tour alone $160.)

THE END. Congratulations! You've made it across the North American continent, conceivably from Key West (p. 519) to Barrow (p. 1057), meaning you've earned your stripes. Take a deep breath, go get your film developed, and get some sleep. Thanks for taking us along for the ride.

DISTANCES (MI.) AND TRAVEL TIMES (BY BUS)

	Atlanta	Boston	Chic.	Dallas	D.C.	Denver	L.A.	Miami	N. Orl.	NYC	Phila.	Phnx.	St. Lou.	Sa. Fran.	Seattle	Trnto.	Vanc.	Mont.
Atlanta		1108	717	783	632	1406	2366	653	474	886	778	1863	560	2492	2699	959	2825	1240
Boston	22hr.		996	1794	442	1990	3017	1533	1542	194	333	2697	1190	3111	3105	555	3242	326
Chicago	14hr.	20hr.		937	715	1023	2047	1237	928	807	767	1791	302	2145	2108	537	2245	537
Dallas	15hr.	35hr.	18hr.		1326	794	1450	1322	507	1576	1459	906	629	1740	2112	1457	2255	1763
D.C.	12hr.	8hr.	14hr.	24hr.		1700	2689	1043	1085	2375	139	2350	845	2840	2788	526	3292	665
Denver	27hr.	38hr.	20hr.	15hr.	29hr.		1026	2046	1341	1785	1759	790	860	1267	1313	1508	1458	1864
L.A.	45hr.	57hr.	39hr.	28hr.	55hr.	20hr.		2780	2005	2787	2723	371	1837	384	1141	2404	1285	2888
Miami	13hr.	30hr.	24hr.	26hr.	20hr.	39hr.	53hr.		856	1346	1214	2368	1197	3086	3368	1564	3505	1676
New O.	9hr.	31hr.	18hr.	10hr.	21hr.	26hr.	38hr.	17hr.		1332	1247	1535	677	2331	2639	1320	2561	1654
NYC	18hr.	4hr.	16hr.	31hr.	5hr.	35hr.	53hr.	26hr.	27hr.		104	2592	999	2923	2912	496	3085	386
Phila.	18hr.	6hr.	16hr.	19hr.	3hr.	33hr.	50hr.	23hr.	23hr.	2hr.		2511	904	2883	2872	503	3009	465
Phoenix	40hr.	49hr.	39hr.	19hr.	43hr.	17hr.	8hr.	47hr.	30hr.	45hr.	44hr.		1503	753	1510	2069	1654	2638
St. Louis	11hr.	23hr.	6hr.	13hr.	15hr.	17hr.	35hr.	23hr.	13hr.	19hr.	16hr.	32hr.		2113	2139	810	2276	1128
San Fran.	47hr.	60hr.	41hr.	47hr.	60hr.	33hr.	7hr.	59hr.	43hr.	56hr.	54hr.	15hr.	45hr.		807	2630	951	2985
Seattle	52hr.	59hr.	40hr.	40hr.	54hr.	25hr.	22hr.	65hr.	50hr.	55hr.	54hr.	28hr.	36hr.	16hr.		2623	146	2964
Toronto	21hr.	11hr.	10hr.	26hr.	11hr.	26hr.	48hr.	29hr.	13hr.	11hr.	13hr.	48hr.	14hr.	49hr.	48hr.		4563	655
Vancvr.	54hr.	61hr.	42hr.	43hr.	60hr.	27hr.	24hr.	67hr.	54hr.	57hr.	56hr.	30hr.	38hr.	18hr.	2hr.	53hr.		4861
Montreal	23hr.	6hr.	17hr.	28hr.	12hr.	39hr.	53hr.	32hr.	31hr.	7hr.	9hr.	53hr.	23hr.	56hr.	55hr.	7hr.	55hr.	

INDEX

A

B

I

J

K

L

M

INDEX

N

O

T

Y

Z

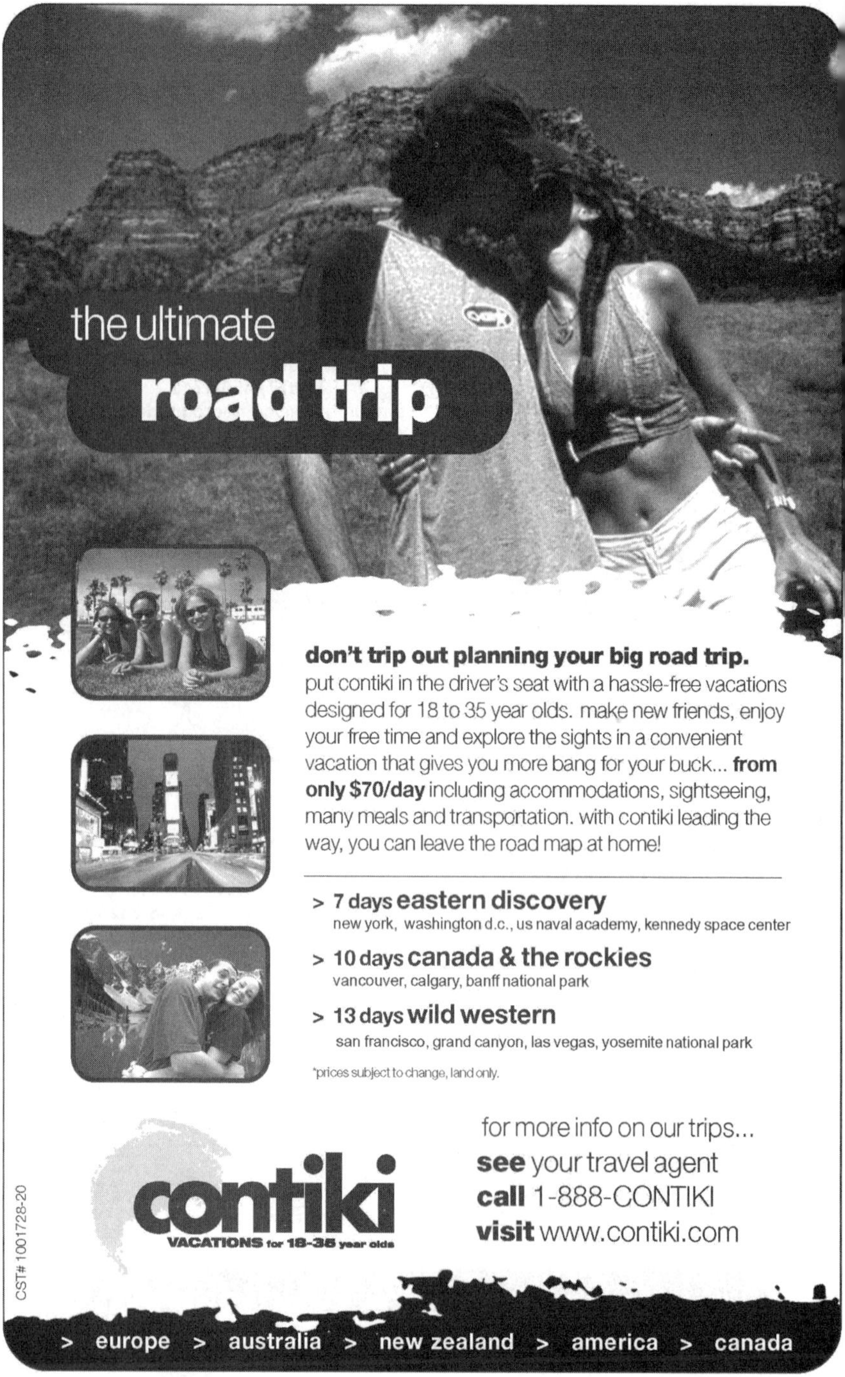
the ultimate
road trip
don't trip out planning your big road trip.
put contiki in the driver's seat with a hassle-free vacations designed for 18 to 35 year olds. make new friends, enjoy your free time and explore the sights in a convenient vacation that gives you more bang for your buck... from only $70/day including accommodations, sightseeing, many meals and transportation. with contiki leading the way, you can leave the road map at home!
> 7 days eastern discovery
new york, washington d.c., us naval academy, kennedy space center
> 10 days canada & the rockies
vancouver, calgary, banff national park
> 13 days wild western
san francisco, grand canyon, las vegas, yosemite national park
*prices subject to change, land only.
contiki
VACATIONS for 18-35 year olds
for more info on our trips...
see your travel agent
call 1-888-CONTIKI
visit www.contiki.com
CST# 1001728-20
> europe > australia > new zealand > america > canada

MAP INDEX

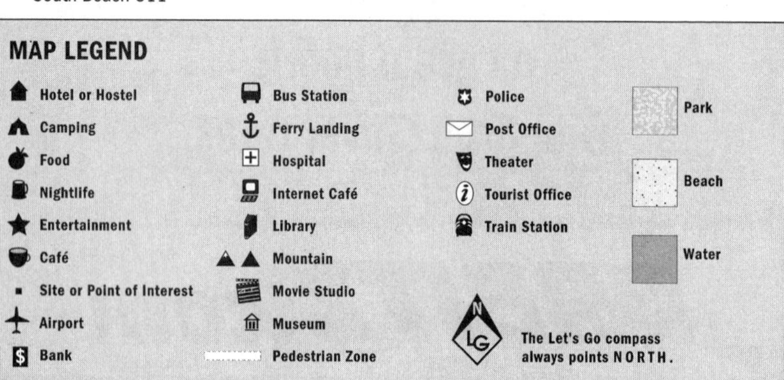

MAP LEGEND
Hotel or Hostel
Camping
Food
Nightlife
Entertainment
Café
Site or Point of Interest
Airport
Bank
Bus Station
Ferry Landing
Hospital
Internet Café
Library
Mountain
Movie Studio
Museum
Pedestrian Zone
Police
Post Office
Theater
Tourist Office
Train Station
Park
Beach
Water
N
LG
The Let's Go compass always points NORTH.